REVISED
MEDIEVAL LATIN
WORD-LIST

Oxford University Press, Walton Street, Oxford OX2 6DP

London Glasgow New York Toronto
Delhi Bombay Calcutta Madras Karachi
Kuala Lumpur Singapore Hong Kong Tokyo
Nairobi Dar es Salaam Cape Town
Melbourne Auckland
and associates in
Beirut Berlin Ibadan Mexico City Nicosia

Oxford is a trade mark of Oxford University Press

Published in the United States by Oxford University Press, New York

New material in this edition
© The British Academy, 1965

ISBN 0 19 725891 3

First published 1965
Reprinted 1973, 1980, 1983

Printed in Great Britain
at the University Press, Oxford
by Eric Buckley
Printer to the University

REVISED
MEDIEVAL LATIN
WORD-LIST

FROM BRITISH AND
IRISH SOURCES

PREPARED BY

R. E. LATHAM, M.A.

UNDER THE DIRECTION OF
A COMMITTEE APPOINTED BY
THE BRITISH ACADEMY

LONDON: *Published for* THE BRITISH ACADEMY
by THE OXFORD UNIVERSITY PRESS

MEMBERS OF THE DICTIONARY COMMITTEE

Sir Frank Stenton, F.B.A. (*Chairman*)

Rev. Prof. J. H. Baxter (*Vice-Chairman*)
The Very Rev. David Callus, O.P.
Sir David Evans, O.B.E.,
Prof. V. H. Galbraith, F.B.A.
R. W. Hunt, F.B.A.

H. C. Johnson, C.B.E. (*Secretary*)
Prof. Sir Roger Mynors, F.B.A.
F. J. E. Raby, C.B., F.B.A.
E. Ashworth Underwood

Sir Mortimer Wheeler, C.I.E., F.B.A. (*Secretary of the British Academy*)

Former Members

Prof. H. E. Butler
G. C. Coulton, F.B.A.
Sir Cyril Flower, C.B., F.B.A.
Sir Stephen Gaselee, K.C.M.G., C.B.E.
J. P. Gilson
Sir Israel Gollancz, F.B.A.
M. R. James, O.M., F.B.A.
Rev. Prof. C. Jenkins
Sir Hilary Jenkinson, C.B.E.
C. Johnson, C.B.E., F.B.A. (*Secretary* 1924–1934)
Sir F. G. Kenyon, G.B.E., F.B.A.
Prof. R. Klibansky
Prof. M. L. W. Laistner
Prof. W. M. Lindsay, F.B.A.
Prof. A. G. Little, F.B.A.

Prof. E. A. Lowe
Sir Henry Maxwell-Lyte, K.C.B., F.B.A. (*Chairman to* 1941)
C. T. Onions, C.B.E., F.B.A.
W. Page
Rev. C. Plummer, F.B.A.
Prof. Sir Maurice Powicke, F.B.A.
Prof. C. Singer
A. E. Stamp, C.B.
Prof. A. Hamilton Thompson, F.B.A.
Prof. T. F. Tout, F.B.A.
Prof. Sir Paul Vinogradoff, F.B.A.
Rev. Prof. E. W. Watson
C. C. J. Webb, F.B.A.
Rev. Dom A. Wilmart, O.S.B.

The following have served on the Scottish Committee

J. T. T. Brown
Rev. Prof. J. H. Baxter
W. R. Cunningham (*Secretary*)
J. Edwards
Prof. C. J. Fordyce

Prof. V. H. Galbraith, F.B.A.
Prof. J. D. Mackie
David Murray (*Chairman*)
Prof. J. S. Phillimore
D. Baird Smith, C.B.E.

The following have served on the Irish Committee

E. Alton, M.R.I.A.
Prof. L. Bieler (*Secretary*)
Rev. Prof. T. Corcoran, S.J., M.R.I.A.
Rev. Prof. J. D'Alton
Rev. J. Fahey

Rev. A. Gwynn, S.J., M.R.I.A. (*Secretary*)
Prof. R. M. Henry, M.R.I.A.
Prof. J. Hogan, M.R.I.A.
Prof. E. MacNeill, M.R.I.A. (*Chairman*)
Prof. L. C. Purser, F.B.A., M.R.I.A.

The following have served on the American Committee

Prof. C. A. Beeson (*Secretary*)
Rev. Prof. F. S. Betten, S.J.
Prof. H. Caplan
Prof. G. R. Coffman
Prof. R. J. Deferrari
Prof. G. H. Gerould
L. R. Lind (*Secretary*)
Prof. W. E. Lunt

Prof. M. R. P. McGuire
Prof. W. A. Morris
Prof. N. Neilson
Prof. J. S. P. Tatlock
Prof. J. F. Willard (*Chairman and Acting Secretary*)
Prof. G. E. Woodbine

PREFACE

The *Medieval Latin Word-List from British and Irish Sources* edited by the Rev. Professor J. H. Baxter and Mr. Charles Johnson under the direction of a committee appointed by the British Academy was published in 1934, and reissued five times (last in 1962). Its declared object was to stimulate interest in the project of a dictionary of Medieval Latin and to attract volunteers for the collection of new material. The committee, which in 1931 united two committees appointed in 1924, the one to collect material for an international dictionary of Medieval Latin up to the eleventh century, the other to do the same for a dictionary of later Latin used in the British Isles, envisaged a full-scale dictionary, national or international and covering the whole period to 1500, as its ultimate goal. Its genesis and early history and the relation of its work to the more comprehensive scheme sponsored by the International Union of Academies are summarized in the Preface to the 1934 publication.

Since then, in spite of setbacks due to the war and its aftermath, considerable progress has been made with the preparation of an international *Novum Glossarium Mediae Latinitatis* under the direction of the Union. With the financial support of UNESCO a preliminary fascicule covering the letter L was published in 1957 and has since been followed by a series of fascicules for M, under the editorship of Professor Franz Blatt and including material supplied by the British committee. The *Glossarium*, however, deals only with the period from A.D. 800 to 1200. There is at present no project for an international dictionary to cover the far more extensive sources available for later centuries. Work is accordingly proceeding in a number of countries on a series of separate dictionaries on a national or regional basis with a wider chronological scope; and material is continuing to be collected for a dictionary of this sort to deal with the British Isles.

As a further step towards such a dictionary, the present *Revised Word-List* has been prepared with the same primary purpose as its predecessor and on the same general plan. The later (post-Conquest) material, considerably enlarged in scope and quantity since 1934, has been revised and edited by Mr. R. E. Latham, with valuable assistance, until his death in 1961, from Mr. Charles Johnson, who edited this material in the original *Word-List*. No systematic revision has been made for the pre-Conquest period, but additional material has been supplied by Professor Baxter, who had editorial responsibility for it in the earlier volume. Mr. Latham, who has been responsible for the arrangement of the entries and has written the Introduction, has seen the whole work through the press.

The new book, like its predecessor, has been made possible by the continued support of the British Academy and the hospitality of the Public Record Office, which *inter alia* has provided house-room for the slips. It is also no less indebted to the often arduous labours of volunteer readers, who have contributed slips from a wide range of sources hitherto untapped. It would be impracticable to mention all these contributors by name and invidious to single out a few. An exception must, however, be made of the late Mr. B. W. Swithinbank, whose contributions, extending over some thirty years, far outnumber those of any other contributor. There is still much work of this nature to be done, and helpers are welcome. Those who are interested should see the *Rules* for their guidance printed below (pp. xii–xiv). For illustrative samples of the sort of slips required and an indication of the use it is hoped to make of them, they may consult an article by Mr. Latham in *Archivum Latinitatis Medii Aevi (Bulletin Du Cange)*, xxvii (1957), pp. 189–229.

Finally, acknowledgement must be made of the Committee's indebtedness to its former members and the former members of its associated national committees who have not lived to see the completion of this stage in their labours; but above all to Mr. Charles Johnson, to whose sustained and practical enthusiasm, as a principal initiator and guide, as contributor, propagandist, editor, and, for many years, secretary of the Committee, the project mainly owes its continued vitality and hope of realization.

FRANK M. STENTON

30 May 1963   *Chairman*

PREFACE TO THE 1980 REPRINT
WITH SUPPLEMENT

The *Revised Medieval Latin Word-List* has been widely used since its publication in 1965, and both the British Academy and the Committee for the *Dictionary of Medieval Latin from British Sources* have been concerned to keep it in print through the propitious years ahead, when the *Dictionary* itself will be published fascicule by fascicule. Once again we have been very grateful to Mr. Ronald E. Latham, who has generously provided, from the material which he and his colleagues have collected over the years, some corrigenda and addenda at the end of this reprint. We take the opportunity of paying our warm tribute to Mr. Latham, recently retired but still extremely active in the cause, and to our former Chairmen, Mr. Harold Johnson, who was active for over forty years in the work of the *Dictionary* before his death in 1973, and Dr. Richard Hunt, whose recent death has sadly deprived us of a wise and generous adviser.

CHRISTOPHER N. L. BROOKE

26 November 1979   *Acting Chairman*

INTRODUCTION

THE *Revised Word-List* includes in principle all words collected to date from British and Irish sources, in so far as they are non-Classical either in form or in meaning. The interpretation of the term 'non-Classical' has been left to the discretion of the editor. The diligence of readers has now provided nearly half a million slips, drawn from about a thousand sources. The abundance of fresh material has not only supplied a great many new words, forms, and meanings[1] and extended the range of most of those already recorded, but has also shed much new light on material included in the former edition and made possible a more synoptic view of the whole field. The opportunity has accordingly been taken to effect a comprehensive revision, involving some rearrangement of the entries on a somewhat different principle, less rigidly alphabetic and with more regard to etymology. More space has been allotted to official titles and institutions of historic interest (see **clericus, custos, curia,** &c.) and to the classification of natural products and artefacts (**piscis, pirum, panis, pannus, pons,** &c.). A few proper names have been admitted, including national appellatives (**Angligena, Dacus,** &c.); but material has not been collected for a thorough treatment of these. A selection of words from vocabularies (indicated by a double dagger ‡) is now included, in so far as these are not merely obvious perversions of Classical words.

The process of excerpting texts has now reached a point at which the more accessible printed sources have been fairly well covered, though there are probably few that would not yield fresh material if re-read in the light of fuller knowledge of the requirements. Nevertheless, the collection still falls short of providing the raw material for a lexicon as authoritative or definitive as any standard dictionary of a Classical or modern language, even if it were more intensively scrutinized than it has been possible to do in preparing this edition. As the reasons for this deficiency may not be fully appreciated by all users of this *Word-List*, a brief explanation may be helpful.

The body of writings to which this volume is intended to serve as a guide is at once immensely greater in bulk than the whole extant corpus of Classical Latin and incomparably less investigated and digested. While the basic vocabulary throughout remained that of Classical or Biblical Latin and the same rules of accidence and even of syntax were observed in

---

[1] A rough estimate, based on sample pages, suggests that the first edition of the *Word-List* dealt with about 20,000 words, of which some 8,000 were recorded once only, besides about 3,000 word-groups or phrases (**homo ad arma, per furcam et flagellum,** &c.). For the *Revised Word-List* the corresponding figures are approximately 40,000, 13,000 and 7,000. The above figures take no account of variant spellings, gender-forms, &c., or of the various meanings assigned to particular words.

principle, if not always in practice, the Latin language in the British Isles, as elsewhere in Western Europe, continued for over a thousand years to enrich its means of expression in order to meet the varying needs of an ever-changing society. During the Saxon period, apart from a certain taste for Hellenisms, British writers of Latin departed relatively little from their Classical or Patristic models. They seldom, if ever, latinized vernacular words—a practice already common on the Continent, where the distinction between Latin and vernacular was blurred by the prevalence of Romance dialects. After the Conquest, however, when Latin ousted Anglo-Saxon for both literary and official purposes, a distinctive Anglo-Latin was quick to appear. Already in the Conqueror's charters and in Domesday Book we find numerous words derived not only from Romance and Continental Germanic but direct from English (**hida, soca, thanus,** &c.). The Latin versions of Anglo-Saxon laws (c 1115) teem with words of English origin, some of which became well established while others are not known to have been used again. Later these drafts on the vernacular were extended to Welsh (**amobragium, gogeretta, havotria, ringildus**) and to Irish and Scottish Gaelic (**betagius, kernus, cateranus, marta**). From the twelfth to the fifteenth century, while scholars wrote for an international public in a Latin that scarcely betrays their British background and diplomats corresponded in a language almost equally international, though admitting many words of Romance origin, the practitioners of the common law developed a host of *vocabula artis* that can have meant nothing to a Continental lawyer, and the clerks who drew up manorial accounts and court rolls did not scruple to latinize terms employed by local peasants, fishermen, and craftsmen that were quite possibly unintelligible in the next parish. In the late fifteenth century British scholars and diplomats, following the fashion started in Italy, began to remodel their Latin on the humanistic pattern, stiffening their syntax and drastically pruning their vocabulary (though at the same time resuscitating such archaisms as **cala, fala, falarica, numella**). Less learned scribes had already decided that, if you did not know or could not decline the word *sinapi*, it was even easier to write *pro gryndynge de le mustarde* than *pro molitura mustardi*. It was not long before they abandoned all pretence of writing the common language of Christendom, though some of them struggled bravely on into the seventeenth century and even tried to cope with the new demands of the humanists. The common lawyers, apart from a brief interlude during the Commonwealth (1651–60), stuck to their **murdrum, burglaria,** and **felo de se** down to the year 1733; entries in the Receipt Books of the Exchequer continued to be made in Latin till 1834; and the ancient universities have not yet hauled down the last flag.[1]

Lexicographically this immense and varied terrain is almost uncharted. The first task is to delimit it. In dealing with British and Irish sources the

[1] This subject is more fully dealt with by the present editor in an article on *The Banishment of Latin from the Public Records* published in 1960 (*Archives*, iv, pp. 158–69).

initial date presents no problem, since those that might be ruled out as pre-Medieval are negligible. If examples of Classical Latin usage are excluded, the *terminus ad quem* practically fixes itself with the advent of humanism. While originality of language as well as of thought is still to be found in a few latinists of the seventeenth century such as Bacon and Newton, and some novelties continue to appear in legal and administrative records of this period, the development of Latin as in some sense a living language virtually ends in this country in the sixteenth century. This exclusion of Classical or would-be Classical forms, however regrettable from the standpoint of linguistic history, is inevitable in a preliminary survey. To interpret it too literally, however, would be to omit some very rare Classical words and usages whose general adoption or sporadic appearance in Medieval writings may be a fact of historic interest and which, to judge by the number of slips for them submitted by readers, are generally regarded by potential users of the *Word-List* as candidates for inclusion. In any event, at least in tracing the growth of specialized meanings, the boundary of Classical Latin can never be sharply drawn.

If it is hard to decide how much of Medieval Latin is really Medieval, it is no less hard to decide how much is Latin. The principle laid down in the Committee's *Rules for the Guidance of Readers* (see below, p. xiii) of admitting only words 'with Latin inflexions or with marks of suspension suggesting inflexion' has dictated the omission of many words included by Du Cange and even of a few that crept into the first edition of this *Word-List*. But this too is an elastic principle, leaving a wide discretion to readers and editor. Even the expression 'British and Irish' sources is not wholly rigid, and it has here been extended to include the works of such immigrants as Anselm and Titus Livius, letters from foreign correspondents printed in Rymer's *Foedera*, &c., and records of English administration on the Continent, such as the *Gascon Rolls*, besides some works of doubtful provenance.

But this is only the beginning of the problem. A high proportion of Medieval Latin literature, and by far the greater part of the documentary material in which Britain is so rich, exists only in manuscript. Of the sources available in print, few have been edited with anything like the care normally expended on Classical or even Middle English texts. Some texts abound in verbal monstrosities or conundrums, either left without comment or annotated with an erudite ingenuity that evokes admiration rather than confidence. The more aberrant forms, even when they can be confirmed by reference to the manuscript, are a temptation to the lexicographer to trespass into the field of textual criticism. Some words appear in a Protean guise not wholly due to the vagaries of editors (see **approvamentum, aurifragium, cherchettum, tuallia, wainagium**); and there are some quite common words whose standard Medieval form cannot be regarded as certain. The confusion between *n* and *v*, which sometimes worries editors even of Classical Dictionaries (*internecinus*, Lewis and Short;

internecivus, Forcellini), is much in evidence. In view of the common variant **vertewella,** and the English derivative *varvel*, we must certainly read **vertevella** rather than **vertenella. Mastinus** (like French *mâtin*) seems preferable to **mastivus** (like English *mastiff*). **Poliva** (ultimately from πολίδιον) is attested by English forms *polyffe*, &c.; but there seems to have been some confusion with *poulain*, 'brewer's ladder' (from *pullanus*). **Mesuagium** may have originated in a misreading of **mesnagium** (French *ménage*, from *mansionaticum*); but **meswagium** is apparently recorded as early as the thirteenth century. Early scribes certainly wrote **pannagium** (from *pastinaticum*); but the sixteenth-century clerk who wrote **pawnagium** must have read **paunagium.** And in rarer words the difficulty of interpreting a row of minims is an admissible plea for the editor who prints **bunulus** or **coniva, juvamin** or **sungina.** As to the equally common confusion of **per-** (or **par-**), **pre-,** and **pro-** (see PERJACT, PREPED, PREPOSIT, PROFECT, PROGNOSTIC), it is impossible to say how far this is due to actual usage or scribal error, how far to misreading of contractions. Certainly many seeming variants spring from such misreading or from injudicious expansion of suspended forms. If a noun is recorded only with the ending suspended or in an oblique case, the form to be assigned to the nominative singular may be a matter of pure conjecture. Even the gender of the Romance original, if there is one, may be a faulty guide. The infinitive **manere,** for instance, gives rise not only to a neuter **manerium** but to a masculine **manerius** and a feminine **maneria.** Beside Fr. *manteau* we find **mantella** as well as **mantellus** and **mantellum.** In words of Germanic origin also, forms of all three genders (e.g. **crofta, croftus, croftum**) may be equally common. Most newly coined verbs are assigned to the first conjugation; but variants (e.g. **cambire** beside **cambiare**) are not unknown. The uncertainty may extend to the form of a whole phrase: **redditus assisus** is probably earlier than **redditus assise**, but this could not safely be inferred from printed texts, which may well represent conjectural extensions of **redditus assis'.**

Much more important, and much harder to deal with, are uncertainties of meaning. The development of a new vocabulary in international Latin cannot be satisfactorily studied from British sources alone. Latinized reflexions of vernacular words cannot be adequately elucidated till much more is known of the dialectal and technical resources of Middle English and Anglo-Norman. Words whose approximate meaning is shown by the context may bear either a more general or a more specific sense than can be inferred with confidence. The words **ledon** (or **liduna**) and **malina,** for instance, when they first appear in Marcellus Empiricus, are related in some way to the phases of the moon; British writers apply them to spring and neap tide, but in some passages they appear to confuse these with high and low tide or with the rise and fall of tidal waves. Names of fishes, birds, and plants in the writings of the learned are not necessarily used with conscious reference to any actual species. In more practical documents

they must have had a definite significance; but from the various inter-
pretations that appear in glossaries it is clear that different clerks were
liable to use them in different senses. The **lentisci** that were felled in Dela-
mere Forest in 1386 for making scaffold-poles may have been beeches or
birches—both meanings are given in fifteenth-century glossaries. They
may represent an attempt to find a Latin equivalent for the English *linden*.
But it is botanically certain that they were not (as rendered by the editor)
'mastich trees'. Technical terms of agriculture or architecture, local
administration or scholastic philosophy, may often have had a very precise
connotation; but even when this can be ascertained it may not be definable
without reference to a framework of highly specialized knowledge. In such
cases the most that a word-list on the present scale can hope to do is to
set the reader on the right track. A few words that baffle the editor completely have been included here in the hope that some reader may be able to
throw light on them (e.g. **abete, almericum, attria, bifultum, casta**).

The problem of dating entries, at least approximately, is not usually
a major one; but there are some sources about which editors are undecided,
some to which early editors allotted mistaken dates that may have found their
way on to our slips, and in certain cases (e.g. a supposedly pre-Conquest
charter found in a fourteenth-century manuscript) any dating is liable to
mislead. In this edition approximate dates have been assigned on a more
conservative principle, so as to avoid antedating in doubtful cases, and
some words repeated in copies or derivative chronicles have been noted
only on their first occurrence.

Finally, though no one is more conscious than the present editor of the
vast amount of conscientious work put in by readers for the Dictionary
Committee, it is too much to expect that their slips should always reproduce
the exact reading of the text before them, with an adequate context, full
reference to editorial emendation and annotation, and the soundest possible
dating. But with the limited man-power available it has not been possible
to check their errors and omissions (not to speak of those contributed by the
present editor himself) with the thoroughness we should all desire.

This explanation is offered not by way of criticism or apology, but simply
in order that those who use the *Word-List* may do so with a full awareness
of its limitations, whether as a key to the form and meaning of particular
words or as a general extent and perambulation of this neglected portion of
our linguistic heritage. It is directed in particular to those who are them-
selves engaged in the exacting labour of editing Medieval texts, or who may
be able and willing in other ways to help forward the co-operative task to
which this latest edition of the *Word-List*, itself the product of many hands
and minds, is a transitory contribution. Anyone who has laboured in this
thorny field may justly feel that he has earned the commendation bestowed
on Abbot Samson by Jocelin of Brakelond: *Plura assartavit et in agri-
culturam reduxit, in omnibus utilitati prospiciens.*

R. E. L.

RULES FOR THE GUIDANCE OF THOSE READING TEXTS FOR THE DICTIONARY

1. Write invariably on a slip of paper 6 in. wide by 3¾ in. high, using a separate slip for each quotation. Slips of the right size will be supplied on application.

2. The material to be given on the slips comprises:
   (i) the *Word* or *Phrase*, written boldly and legibly in the left-hand top corner;
   (ii) the *Meaning* (if certain) in the right-hand top corner;
   (iii) the *Date*;
   (iv) the *Source*; and
   (v) the *Quotation*.

   Any notes, emendations, or conjectures should be written below the quotation, at the foot of the slip or, if necessary, on the back.

3. The *Word*, if a noun, should be in the nom. sing.; if an adjective, in the positive degree and masc. gender; if a verb, in the 1st pers. sing. pres. indic. (unless impersonal or defective).

4. The *Date* of the book or document quoted may be approximate (e.g. 13th c[entury] or c[irca], a[nte], or p[ost] 1250), but should in any case be that of the particular passage quoted, not of a collection as a whole.

5. The description of the *Source* should comprise—(i) (CAPS.) *author's name* (if known); (ii) (*itals.*) *title* or description of work, which may be in a shortened form agreed with the Secretary; (iii) *exact reference* (so far as possible) to volume, book, chapter, and page or column, and in poetry to stanza and line, with special indication of any extract taken from a passage cited by the author or compiler from an earlier source, e.g.:

   1166 *Charter of Hen. II* ap. HOVEDEN III, p. 216.

   12c. Customs of Newcastle-on-Tyne ap. STUBBS *Sel. Chart.* (3rd Ed. p. 211).

   If preferred, a space may be left blank for *date*, *author*, and *title* (or for author and title if the date is variable), and these can then be supplied by stamp in the Secretary's office; in this case great care must be taken to ensure that slips from different sources are kept separate.

6. The following is a sample of a completed slip:

GUNNA   gun

c 1370 KNIGHTON, *Chron.* II, p. 107.

dominus Thomas de Morreus percussus est medio de una
gunna

7. In general a slip should be made for (i) any word obviously non-
Classical and (ii) any Classical word used in a non-Classical manner
(e.g. *servitium* in a feudal sense, or *forma* in a scholastic one). Words
and usages given in a standard dictionary of Classical Latin (e.g. Lewis
and Short) should normally be disregarded. So should words marked
with an asterisk in the *Revised Word-List*, unless the new example
is a particularly good one or is of earlier or later date than there
shown. Slips should include *phrases* used in a specialized sense (e.g.
breve clausum, serviens ad arma, fieri facias, super judicium, capio ad).
Vernacular words (English, French, Welsh, Gaelic) found in Latin
texts will not be included in the Dictionary unless they appear in a
latinized form (i.e. with Latin inflexions or with marks of suspension
suggesting inflexion), but in cases of special interest notes of such
words may be useful for the guidance of the editor; they will eventually
be passed to the compilers of a Middle English or other appropriate
dictionary. Loan-words from Greek, Hebrew, Arabic, &c., should be
included even if not latinized. Slips may also be made for passages
that define a Classical word in an interesting way or suggest an odd
etymology for it, e.g. *nox dicitur a nocendo, eo quod nocet oculis.*

8. Where it seems desirable to record peculiarities of grammatical usage,
unless they can be assigned to a particular word (e.g. *quia* in the sense
of 'that' to introduce indirect statement, *habeo* with inf.), they should
be noted on slips headed 'Grammar' and collected at the end of the
alphabet.

9. The following types of proper name may be included: (i) deformations of Classical names, e.g. '*Hypocras*' for 'Hippocrates'; (ii) sobriquets such as '*Magister Sententiarum*' or '*Doctor Subtilis*'; (iii) translations of geographical and family names, e.g. '*Castrum Puellarum*' for Edinburgh, '*Nigra Nox*' for Neirnuit; (iv) Christian names with an unusual vernacular equivalent, e.g. *Eugenius* for Owen, *Ivo* for Hugh; (v) national and territorial appellatives, e.g., *Scotus*, *Gallus*, *Americus*, *Dextralis* (of Deheubarth), and names of languages, e.g. *Cornubicum*, *Cornubice*; (vi) titles of books, not purely descriptive, e.g. *Analytica*, *Almagesti*; (vii) parties, sects, &c., named after persons (e.g. *Gibellinus*, *Calvinianus*).

10. Extracts quoted should always be such as to make connected sense and show the meaning and use of the word. Irrelevant words may be omitted, but their omission should be indicated by dots (. . .). Preference should be given to self-explanatory extracts, particularly definitions, distinctions drawn between words of similar form or meaning, and indications of the vernacular equivalent. It is also helpful to have quotations that show the precise *form* of the word (e.g. whether a noun of the second declension is masculine or neuter). Common usages need not be illustrated more than once in each author or century; but it is helpful to indicate whether a particular usage is of frequent or exceptional occurrence. If there is reason to think that a usage may represent a local peculiarity (*cf.* 1 **hopa**), the locality should be indicated.

11. Any note suggesting that the passage quoted is derived from an earlier source should be included, with a precise reference if possible.

12. Retain the spelling of the text or give reasons for departing from it.

13. Remember to examine *Errata* and (in critical editions) the *Apparatus*, so as to note important variants, before completing the slips. Full use should be made of glossaries and subject indexes where available, but it cannot be assumed that they will include all words of lexicographic interest.

14. Sort slips in alphabetical order. It will be helpful if readers will, so far as convenient, follow the usage of the *Word-List*, e.g. arranging words beginning with the diphthongs *ae-* and *oe-* under '*e-*', forms such as *fiala* under '*ph-*', &c.

15. Add a slip with the *full title* of the book read, specifying the edition used and the abbreviations (if any) adopted, and giving your own name and address, and send the slips to THE SECRETARY, THE MEDIEVAL LATIN DICTIONARY COMMITTEE, PUBLIC RECORD OFFICE, CHANCERY LANE, LONDON, W.C. 2.

ARRANGEMENT OF ENTRIES

THIS arrangement is designed primarily to give maximum information in minimum space. As explained, it sounds highly complicated; but it is hoped that in practice it will be found easy to grasp and unambiguous.

The words to be explained are printed in **bold face,** other foreign words and grammatical indications in *italics*, meanings and explanations in roman. The words are grouped in ENTRIES under key-words, usually nouns, followed by derivative or cognate words, with verbs normally at the end. Entries are in strict alphabetical order; but the arrangement of words within an entry is dictated in part by logical sequence or practical convenience. The initial letters of the key-word, or of another word in the entry, may be marked off by an oblique line, and repetition indicated by a hyphen (**abat/atio,** annulment; **-o,** to annul). If two or more words within a single entry are divided in this way (**anteced/entia, antecess/or;** *cf.* **maeremium, trithingum**), an initial hyphen indicates the repetition of the first part of *the last preceding word* so divided.

Entries are divided by semicolons into SECTIONS. Each section comprises: *either* (*a*) Latin word+English equivalent+date (or extreme dates) of occurrence;[1] *or* (*b*) various forms of the Latin word, or various cognate and approximately synonymous Latin words, each followed by date or dates, with a single English equivalent at the end; *or* (*c*) an additional English equivalent of the Latin word *at the beginning of the preceding section*, followed by the date or dates; *or* (*d*) additional date or dates, similarly referring to the Latin word at the beginning of the preceding section, followed as in (*b*) by Latin variants or synonyms with their dates and with the English equivalent at the end.

Thus in the entry under **advoc/amen**[2] the first two sections, based on pre-Conquest sources only, are quite straightforward. The third section begins with the dates 'c 1160, 1583', referring to **advocatio,** the first word of the second section, which is accordingly to be understood as the first word of this section also. Next we have the probably spurious form †**adductatio** and two cognate words, **advocantia** and **advocatia,** each followed by its earliest and latest date of occurrence. The section concludes with the English equivalent 'advowson', applying to all four words and further elucidated by the qualification '(eccl.)', i.e. 'ecclesiastical' (see List of Abbreviations on p. xix). The fourth section also begins with two dates, still referring to **advocatio** (as the first word of the second section and notionally also of the third section) and recording its earliest and latest appearance with the 'legal' meaning 'avowry'. The asterisks indicate that in both senses the form **advocatio** is of regular occurrence between the

---

[1] Where a word is recorded for both the pre-Conquest and the post-Conquest period, the dates are shown separately with a full-stop between the two (e.g. **ablutio,** cleansing c 730, 1060. c 1090, 1461). Occasionally, when the professed date of the document in which a word occurs is much earlier than that of the manuscript source, the date of the latter is added in round brackets thus: **dirocheum,** (?) *for* **dittocheum,** twofold nurture (?) 981 (c 1300).

[2] The variant (**avoc-**) indicates that in this entry the forms with an initial hyphen may begin with either **advoc-** or **avoc-**.

dates specified, while the letter (G.) shows that certain variants are peculiar to Gascony (in a wide sense). The fifth section shows that **advocatio** is recorded in the fourteenth century with a specialized meaning, peculiar to Wales and the Welsh Marches, usually expressed by **advocaria,** of which **avowaria** (misread or misprinted **anowaria**) is a variant. Similarly under ACEPHAL the third and fourth sections refer to the form **acephalus,** as first word of the first section and notionally also of the second section, *not* to the other variants noted in the first two sections.

When an entire word is due to be repeated later in the entry as part of a phrase, it is commonly represented by its initial letter only. If this occurs within a single section, it normally refers back to the first word of that section (e.g. under DECAN, **d. ecclesie** stands for **decanus ecclesie,** without reference to the rare variant **decennus**). Similarly, when it follows a section containing more than one Latin word, it refers back to the first word of that section (e.g. **plastrum, predecessor**). But variant spellings of a single word (e.g. **feodum, garnestura, sucrum, warderoba**) are not always distinguished in the list of phrases illustrating its special uses, so that **f. talliatum** may stand equally well for **feodum talliatum, feudum talliatum,** &c. The treatment of such quasi-compounds may be exemplified by the entry under **mola**: this includes **molendinum ad ventum** but not **molendinum ventriticum,** which as involving a non-Classical derivative of **ventus** appears under VENT. Cross-references have been added to both entries to offset the difficulty which users as well as editor are likely to experience in applying a consistent principle to such cases. Cross-references from an adjective (e.g. **albus, altus**) are meant to indicate substantives with which it is used in a highly specialized sense. In some instances, instead of cross-reference a phrase has been entered under both the key-words involved.

Variant forms are cross-referred to the key-word of the entry in which they occur, or to its initial letter-group; where this latter is marked off by an oblique stroke and clearly distinguishable from any other entry with the same initial letters, it is referred to in small capitals. Thus '**ante-,** *see also* **anti-**' may refer to several different entries; '**ansporto,** *see* ASPORT' can refer to one only. The words '*see also*' refer the reader to another entry containing a word or words of the same form or with the same initial letters; '*cf.*' is used when the relation is one of origin or meaning rather than strictly alphabetical.

Words of identical form but presumably diverse origin have been put in separate entries with serial numbers for use in cross-reference (see **palus, pela, pila, polus, inoperatio, interminatio,** &c.). In a few cases, however, words of diverse origin that had become practically indistinguishable in Medieval usage (e.g. CONCIL and CONSIL, or certain compounds with **de-** and **dis-** or O.F. **des-**) have been grouped together. In dealing with words of common origin, including those remotely or indirectly connected (e.g. derivatives of **caput** and **chef, cuppa, cupa,** and **cuva,** δέκα and **decem, impedire, impetere,** and *empêcher,* **ligare** and *liege,* **mare** and *mere,* **vallum** and *wall*), it has not been found practicable to adhere to any fixed rule. In some cases, in order to obviate very cumbrous and complicated entries, it has been found convenient to make separate entries for particular sets of derivatives (e.g. of **caput, teneo, quatuor, unus**) or for groups of words of the same ultimate origin but of widely different sense (see **discus, habitus, linea, tallia**). In other cases (e.g. **domus, tabula**) the different meanings have not been thought to warrant separate entries but have been arranged in separate paragraphs. Some other lengthy entries, including those for the common prepositions, have also been broken up into paragraphs. Certain entries have been grouped for convenience under 'Classical' key-words for which no reference-dates are shown: these entries are distinguished by the use of a colon (*cf.* **chytropus, pharetra, psittacus**). Etymology is not normally indicated except implicitly, by the grouping in entries or by the English equivalent given; but in special cases, where derivation is not self-evident, it has seemed worth while to note a presumed cognate in some other language (Anglo-Saxon, Old French, Greek, &c.). Vowel-quantities, since they played little part in Medieval usage, have generally been disregarded; but words containing long and short vowels according to Classical usage have normally been grouped in separate entries (**lāb-, lăb-; sēd-, sĕd-; dīc-, dĭc-; vōc-, vŏc-; dūc-, dŭc-**), and this distinction is occasionally indicated in the text (see **deliberatio, redditus,** &c.). Indications of national or local (county) provenance have been given when they appear to be of special significance.

Explanations have been kept as short as possible, and no systematic attempt has been made to indicate innovations in grammar or idiom. The distinction between active and deponent forms of verbs, however, and that between transitive and intransitive usage have been noted when they are clearly recognizable in the sources. It has not been found practicable to distinguish between adjectival and substantival use of certain words (e.g. **Anglicus, Cisterciensis**). Idiomatic uses of some familiar words (e.g. the common prepositions and such verbs as **capio, facio, pono**)[1] have been illustrated, but by no means exhaustively.

[1] The help of readers is particularly invited to increase the supply of source material for such words.

SPELLING

N.B. The information given under this heading is important to all users of the *Revised Word-List*, as it may be necessary to look under several spellings before finding a particular word.

The spelling of words of purely Latin or Greek origin has been standardized, as shown below, by disregarding certain variants commonly found in Medieval texts, which may or may not correspond to variants in the manuscripts. In dealing with other words it has proved harder to apply a consistent rule, and variant spellings (e.g. **t** and **th** representing A.S. þ or ð) have been more frequently included.

The following variants have normally been disregarded:

e, ae, oe, all shown as **e**; ae and oe appear only where they represent Classical disyllables (**aër, coëvus**) or are employed in Medieval MSS. significantly (**aenecia, poenacium**) or abnormally (**praecium, loetum**).

e, i, before vowels (**linia** for **linea, coreum** for **corium**).

i and **u** always represent vowels; where they are presumed to have consonantal value they are printed **j** and **v**.

i, y, (**phthysicus; phisicus**).

c, k (**karus; calendarium**).

ci, ti, medially before vowels (**pocius; sotius**).

ct, tt (**waretta; bilecta**).

f for **ph** (**fiala**); but **ph** for **f** (**pheudum, tophtum**) is noted.

h omitted or intrusive (**onor, corus; honus, charus**).

Double consonants for single or *vice versa* (**ommitto, comitto; carretta, caruca**).

The following variants have normally been noted, but in some cases without detailed indication of their distribution:

ar, er
ex, exs, es, x, s
mpn, mn, nn
mpt, mt, nt

gn, ngn
g, j, hi (hy)
g, gu, gw, w, v
s, c, sc, before **e, i, y**

Other variants have been disregarded in specific instances and are noted accordingly in the text: e.g. '**supp-**, *see also* **subp-**', or such entries as that beginning '**subprior (supp-)**', in which any word printed in truncated form may be deemed to occur with alternative spellings (**subprioratus** or **supprioratus**, &c.).

ABBREVIATIONS AND SIGNS

a = *ante*
A.S. = Anglo-Saxon
abl. = ablative
ac. = academic
acc. = accusative
act. = active
adj. = adjective
adv. = adverb
alch. = alchemical, chemical
Ar. = Arabic
arch. = architectural
astr. = astrological, astronomical
bibl. = biblical (see note below)
bot. = botanical
c (before a figure) = *circa*
c. (after a figure) = century
C.I. = Channel Islands
cf. = *confer* (compare)
Cl. = Classical
coll. = collective
conj. = conjugation
dat. = dative
decl. = declension, declinable
dep. = deponent
eccl. = ecclesiastical (see note below)
Eng. = English
esp. = especially
f. = feminine
f.l. = *falsa lectio*
falc. = used in falconry
fig. = figurative
Fr. = French
G. = Gascon (including neighbouring
   territories)
gen. = genitive
geom. = geometrical
Gk. = Greek
gram. = grammatical
Heb. = Hebrew
her. = heraldic
imp. = imperative

impers. = impersonal
ind. = indirect
indecl. = indeclinable
inf. = infinitive
interj. = interjection
intr. = intransitive
Ir. = Irish
It. = Italian
leg. = legal
log. = logical
m. = masculine
M.E. = Middle English
man. = manorial
math. = mathematical
med. = medical
met. grat. = *metri gratia*
mon. = monastic
mus. = musical
n. = neuter
naut. = nautical
Norm. = Norman
O.F. = Old French
p = *post*
p.p. = past participle
pass. = passive
phil. = philosophical
phys. = physical
pl. = plural
Port. = Portuguese
ppl. = participle
prep. = preposition
s. = singular
Sc. = Scots
Sp. = Spanish
subj. = subjunctive
subst. = substantive
theol. = theological
trans. = transitive
v. = verb
v.l. = *varia lectio*
W. = Welsh

N.B. The qualification (bibl.) or (eccl.) *without indication of date* denotes a word occurring in the Vulgate or the Fathers and in regular Medieval use.

The names of English counties appear in a somewhat abbreviated form (Beds. = Bedfordshire, Norf. = Norfolk); the initials N.S.E.W. denote North, South, East, and West.

A query (?) indicates doubt as to the meaning or date assigned to a word, or the justifiability of its inclusion in a particular group.

An obelisk (†) indicates a suspicion (sometimes amounting to certainty) that the form of a particular word is due to a misprint, a misreading, or a scribal error.

An asterisk (*) indicates that a word is of regular occurrence in the sense noted and between the dates specified. Further examples of words thus marked are not required for the Dictionary unless they represent an extension of date or afford a particularly good illustration of meaning or usage.

A double dagger (‡) before a word indicates that in the sense noted it has been found only in a glossary. Where it immediately precedes a date (e.g. **sinoglossi-torium** ‡c 1440, 1539), it signifies that the occurrence of the word at that particular date is attested by glossarial evidence only.

Double quotes (" ") indicate that the word or phrase enclosed is given in the original text or glossary, not necessarily with the same spelling, as the equivalent of the Latin word under reference. Single quotes (' ') indicate an obsolete or otherwise unusual English word or one used in an unusual sense.

The word '*or*' in italics indicates that the possible meanings suggested are alternatives that cannot, generally speaking, both be applicable—at any rate not in any specific context; where 'or' is in roman type, the meanings are not so sharply contrasted. Thus the entry '**parcarius**, parker, *or* (?) pinder' implies that some of the men described by this title may be pinders (pound-keepers) rather than park-keepers; '**parmentarius**, parmenter, robe-trimmer, or furrier' implies that both the trimming of robes and the sale of furs might come within the parmenter's province.

SELECT CLASSIFIED BIBLIOGRAPHY OF AUTHORS AND COLLECTIONS USED FOR THE *REVISED WORD-LIST*

THIS includes only a small minority of the works that have been read, in whole or in part, since an exhaustive list would run to a length out of all proportion to its utility. This select bibliography, confined to certain works that have made a substantial contribution to this *Word-List*, should enable any who are interested to recognize the source of a large number of the words quoted. Thus a legal term recorded for c 1115, c 1185, c 1258, c 1290, c 1443 or 1684 can be assigned with fair confidence to the source in Section F bearing a corresponding date; if it bears a precise date other than these, it is probably derived from a Plea Roll or some other record mentioned in general terms under F or G.

The inclusion of an author in this bibliography does not necessarily imply that all his published works have been read for the *Word-List*. The dates shown are those assigned in the *Word-List* to the work named, or the principal work of the author named; where there are two dates, they are those assigned to the author's earliest and latest major works. The numbers prefixed to the names refer to the *Index of British and Irish Writers* published in vol. vii of the *Bulletin Du Cange*.

A. HISTORY AND GENERAL LITERATURE

2 Patrick (5c.)
3 Gildas (6c.)
4 *Lorica* (6c.)
5 *Hisperica Famina* (c 550)
9 Columbanus (a 615)
17 *De Alfabeto* (7c.)
16 *De XII Abusivis Seculi* (7c.)
19 Aldhelm (c 690)
18 Adamnan (c 700)
20 Bede (c 730)
27 Egbert (c 760)
42 Alcuin (c 790)
64 Frithegode (c 950)
61 Dunstan (10c.)
63 Ethelwold (c 980)
56 Aelfric (c 1000)
102 *Encomium Emmae* (c 1041)

82 Goscelin of Canterbury (c 1090)
146 Florence of Worcester (c 1118)
139 Eadmer (a 1125)
237 William of Malmesbury (c 1125)
151 Geoffrey of Monmouth (c 1136)
191 Orderic Vitalis (a 1142)
164 Henry of Huntingdon (c 1155)

Daniel of Beccles: *Urbanus Magnus* (c 1180)
166 Herbert of Bosham (c 1185)
369 Ralph de Diceto (c 1188, c 1200)
326 Giraldus Cambrensis (c 1188, c 1220)
188 Walter Map (c 1190)
243 Nigel Wireker (c 1190)
322 Gervase of Canterbury (c 1200, c 1210)
324 Gervase of Tilbury (c 1212)
361 Matthew of Paris (c 1250)
583 Richard of Bury (c 1345)
557 Henry Knighton (c 1370)
517 John Fordun (Sc.) (a 1385)
747 John Gower (a 1408)
736 Thomas Elmham (c 1414)
810 Thomas Walsingham (a 1422)
762 Titus Livius (c 1437)
714 (840) *Liber Pluscardensis* (Sc.) (1461)
890 Thomas More (1518)
888 John Major (Sc.) (1521)
897 Polydore Vergil (1555)
William Camden (1586)
Monastic and minor chronicles (various)
Lives of Saints, &c.

B. THEOLOGY, PHILOSOPHY, AND LOGIC

50 John Scotus (c 850)

124 Anselm (c 1080)
180 John of Salisbury (c 1160)
114 Adam Scot (c 1180)
328 Robert Grosseteste (a 1233)
    Pseudo-Grosseteste (c 1270)
302 Roger Bacon (13c., 1267)
348 Robert Kilwardby (c 1270)

374 Richard of Middleton (c 1270)
362 John Peckham (1280)
511 Duns Scotus (c 1300, p 1300)
634 William of Ockham (c 1343)
494 Thomas Bradwardine (1344)
630 John Wyclyffe (c 1360, 1378)
771 Thomas Netter (c 1427)
    Lancelot Andrewes (c 1610)
    Francis Bacon (c 1620)

C. MATHEMATICS AND NATURAL SCIENCE

(ALCHEMY, ASTRONOMY, MEDICINE, BOTANY, ZOOLOGY)

46 Dicuil (astr.) (c 810)

115 Adelard of Bath (math., astr., falc.)
    (c 1115, a 1150)
210 Robertus Anglicus (math., astr.) (1144,
    a 1150)
189 A Ocreatus (math.) (c 1150)
122 Alfredus Anglicus (med., bot.) (a 1200)
137 Daniel of Morley (astr.) (a 1200)
354 Alexander Neckam (encyclopedic)
    (a 1200, c 1200)
389 Michael Scot (astr., &c.) (c 1215,
    a 1235)

334 John of Holywood (math.) (c 1230)
303 Bartholomaeus Anglicus (encyclo-
    pedic) (a 1250)
325 Gilbertus Anglicus (med.) (a 1250)
376 Richard of Wendover (med., alch.)
    (c 1210, a 1252)
508 John Dastin (alch.) (c 1320)
    William Turner (bot., ornithological)
    (1538, 1544)
    Thomas Johnson (bot.) (1629, 1641)
    Isaac Newton (math., astr.) (1686)

D. MUSIC

624 Walter of Evesham (c 1320)
619 Simon Tunstede (c 1350)

749 John Hanboys (c 1470)

E. HERALDRY

    John of Guildford (p 1394)
808 Nicholas Upton (a 1446)

Henry Spelman (c 1595)
Edward Bysshe (1654)

F. LAW

267–73 *Leges Henrici I*, &c. (c 1115)
159 Ranulf Glanvill (c 1185)
407 William of Drogheda (canonist)
    (c 1245)
308 Henry Bracton (c 1258)
456 *Fleta* (c 1290)
742 John Fortescue (c 1443)
    Francis Clarke: *Praxis in Curiis
    Ecclesiasticis* (1596; *ed.* 1684)

H. M. Bigelow: *Placita Anglo-
    Normannica* (c 1066–c 1135)
Curia Regis Rolls (1194–1232)
Bracton's Note-Book (1217–40)
Registrum Brevium (15c.)
Leges Wallicae (a 1250, a 1300)
Regiam Majestatem (Sc.) (13c.)
Selden Society publications
Plea Rolls, &c. (MSS.)

G. ADMINISTRATION (CIVIL AND ECCLESIASTICAL) DOCUMENTARY SOURCES

W. de G. Birch: *Cartularium Saxonicum*

J. M. Kemble: *Codex Diplomaticus*

Regesta Regum Anglo-Normannorum I & II (1066–1135)

Domesday Book (1086)

Pipe Rolls (1130–1210)

144 *Dialogus de Scaccario* (c 1178)

Book of Fees (1198–c 1250)

Charter Rolls (1199–1516)

Patent Rolls (1201–1566)

Close Rolls (1204–1509)

Liberate Rolls (1226–1272)

Hundred Rolls (1255, 1275–6)

Placita de Quo Warranto (c 1280–c 1330)

Feudal Aids (1284–1431)

Parliament Rolls (1290–1552)

Record of Caernarvon (1284–1568)

Rotuli Scotiae (1291–1516)

Rotuli Scaccarii (Sc.) (1291–1469)

Registrum Magni Sigilli (Sc.) (1424–1513)

Acts of Parliament of Scotland (1424–1707)

Statutes etc. of the Parliament of Ireland (1216–1460)

Norman Pipe Rolls (1180–1203)

Norman Rolls (1201–5, 1417–18)

Gascon Rolls (1254–1317)

William Stubbs: *Select Charters* (1066–1307)

Thomas Rymer: *Foedera* (1101–1654)

Thomas Madox: *Formulare Anglicanum* and *History of Exchequer*

Thomas Rastell: *Collection of Entries, &c.* (a 1564)

William Dugdale: *Monasticon Anglicanum*

David Wilkins: *Concilia Magnae Britanniae et Hiberniae*

English Historical Review (Latin texts)

Archaeological Journal (Latin texts)

Exchequer Accounts (mainly MSS.)

Manorial Accounts, Custumals, &c.

Monastic Accounts, Cartularies, &c.

Bishops' Registers

Municipal Archives

University and College Archives

Publications of local Record Societies. &c.

H. GLOSSARIES, COLLECTIONS OF SYNONYMS, ETC.

354 Alexander Neckham (c 1200)

339 John of Garland (c 1250)

573 John Mirfield (bot.) (14c.)

682 *Alphita* (bot.) (15c.)

745 *Promptorium Parvulorum* (c 1440)

855 *Catholicon Anglicum* (1483)

T. Wright & R. P. Wülcker: *Old English Vocabularies* (15c.)

898 Robert Whittington (c 1520)

Peter Levins: *Manipulus Vocabulorum* (1570)

William Thompson: *Lexicon Chymicum* (1652)

A

A, musical note 1351.
a, ab, than 12c., c 1180;
(of space or distinction) a cruce, across 1575; a directo, straight (from) a 1350; a facie, in the presence of a 1250; a foris (afforis), outside a 1100, c 1400; a longe, see LONG; a retro, on the back a 1275; behind c 1430, 15c.; ab extra, from without 1347, 1511; ab hinc, hence c 1191, 1508; ab inde, thence c 1115, 1545; ab intus c 1197, a 1408, ab intra 1309, from within; *ab invicem, mutually 7c. c 1170, 1543;
(of time) a diu c 1337, c 1470, a diu est c 1309, c 1415, a jam diu 1321, 1433, for a long time past; a modo, from now on (eccl.); a repente, suddenly c 1400; ab ante, formerly 1397, 1464; ab antiquo, from of old c 1230, 1508; ab hucusque, hitherto c 1250; ab inde, from that time 1143, c 1470; ab olim, long since 1278, c 1465;
(of origin or relation) a fortiori c 1337, c 1343, a majori 1413, à plus forte raison; a majori, a minori, see locus; a posteriori, inductively c 1300, 1380; a priori, deductively c 1300; a probabili 1412, a verisimili c 1400, probably; a proposito, purposely 1336; a retro, *in arrears 1199, c 1534; heretofore 1231; a simili, likewise c 1197, 1393; a toto, entirely 1240;
(of office or function) ‡a batis, one who measures grain, 'avener' c 1219, 1483 (cf. 2 batus); ‡a caliculis c 1440, ‡a cellariis 1483, butler; a consili/is, -o, counsellor 1516; ab intimis consiliis 1570; ‡a responsis, lawyer 15c., 1483; a secretis, confidential adviser, secretary, treasurer c 1125, 1550.
aaron, see aron.
abactio, taking away 12c.; repulsion c 1612.
abac/ula, "cupboard cloth" 1551; -ista, calculator c 1125, c 1400.
†abalternatim (v.l. subalternatim), alternatively c 1340.
†aband/atio (? abaud-), incitement 1352; -o, to train (dogs) 1237, 1238; cf. 1 baldus.
abandono, to abandon, surrender c 1258.
‡abarath, white lead 14c.
abarno, to detect or bring to judgement c 1115.
abastardo, to bastardize 1199, 1202.
abat/atio, annulment 1413; -o, to annul 1513.
abat/iamentum, abatement, wrongful entry 14c., 1365; -o, to abate, enter wrongfully on freehold (leg.) 1539.
abatis, see a batis.
abatudus, debased (of money) (Fr.) 1209.
abaud-, see ABAND; OBAUD
abay/a 1235, -um 1283, mill-dam; cf. baia.
abba, father (bibl.); *abbas (eccl.), abia c 550, abbat/erius c 740, abbot; a. niger, Benedictine abbot c 1400; a. de Marham 1521, a. de Marall 1547, a. de Mayvole 1542, abbot of misrule (on May-day); -atus

c 1125, -iatus c 1400, -ia 9c., office of abbot; -ia, higher clergy 747; *1086, 1565, -ica c 1308, -icia 1205, -us c 1243, 15c., abbey; *-ialis, of or for an abbot 8c., 9c. 1349, 1549; *-issa 6c., c 1000. c 1080, 1517, abbissa 1588, abbess; -issalis, of or for an abbess 1525; abbathania 1310, abthania 1291, 1358, 'abthainry', abbey estate (Sc.); -io c 1200, -izo a 1100, c 1395, to be abbot.
abberg/ageria, -uata, see herbergagium.
‡abbita, kind of fish 15c.
abblandior (adb-), to flatter c 1180, 1648.
abbreg/eo, to shorten, expedite 1276; -io, to lessen a 1309.
abbrevi/atio a 1090, c 1470, -amentum 1581, cutting short, diminution; *c 1125, 1461, -amentum c 1500, -arium 1378, epitome; -amentum, note-book 1391; -atus, brief account 1171; -ator, epitomist c 1188; official of Papal Chancery 1406, c 1444; -ate, in short a 1350; -o, *to shorten 7c., 8c. c 1125, a 1564; 1214, p 1330, adbrevio 13c., to note, record.
abc-, see also absc-
abcari/atio, carrying away 1471, 1566; -o 1491, a 1564, acario 1215, 1331, to carry, carry away.
abdellum, see BDELL
abdic/atio 9c., -amentum c 1000, negation; -abilis, able to be renounced c 1376; -ativus, renunciatory c 1283.
abdico, to take away by decree 8c.; to deprive c 1549.
abditorium, box, receptacle ‡1200, 1519.
abdom-, see HEBDOM
abduct/or, abductor, remover c 1290, 1464; -ivus, misleading 12c.
abecedarium 7c, 760. c 1125, ABCdarium a 1000, alphabet; abgatoria 7c., abgetorium 7c. 13c., abecedary.
abellana, filbert: avellana a 1150, 1467, avalana 1416.
abellus, abele, white poplar 1279.
abeo viam meam, to die c 1115.
abequo, to make unequal a 1180.
aberratio, aberration, mistake 1620; (math.) 1686.
abertivum, see ABOR
aberunco, see AVERRUNC
‡abesamum, see alchazanon.
abesse (subst.), absence c 1170, c 1180; absit (interj.), God forbid! (bibl.).
abete, an item in inventory of jewels, etc. 1255.
*abett/um 1247, 15c., -amentum 1309, a 1540, -atio a 1564, 1587, instigation, abetment; -ator 1285, 1575, -or c 1285, abettor; -o, to abet c 1290, 1587.
abexcommunicatus, excommunicated 1397.
abfugo, see AUFUG
abg/atoria, -etorium, see abecedarium.
abhinc, see ab hinc.
abia, see abba.
abi/etinus c 1200, 1315, †-genus for -egnus

950, made of fir; †**abjectivus,** wood-tar
c 550; *see also* **gluten; ebes,** fir-tree 1478.
abigeus, (*adj.*) cattle-stealing c 1258; (*subst.*)
7c., **abigevus** c 1258, †**ambiguus** c 1290,
cattle-thief; *see also* **Albigensis.**
abil-, *see* HABIL
abinde, abintus, abinvicem, *see* ab.
abinterpono, to impose 1397.
abject/io, something thrown away c 1180;
abasement, humiliation c 730. c 1090,
1378; contempt 7c.; **a. verborum,** un-
distinguished style c 1172; **-or,** rejecter
c 1190; **-ivus,** abasing c 1376; *see also*
abietinus.
abjudic/atio, deprivation by judicial sentence
c 1258, 1500; denial 7c.; **-o,** (with *inf.*) to
deny c 1170.
abjur/atio, recantation on oath c 1344, c 1489;
a. regni (*etc.*), abjuration of the realm 1201,
1500; †**objuratio libertatis,** abjuration of
a liberty (by felon) 15c.; **-ator,** one who dis-
claims or renounces by oath 1306; **a. regni**
c 1290; *-o c 1115, 1560,*†**objuro** 12c., 15c.,
to abjure, disclaim or renounce by oath.
ablact/atio c 1070, a 1452, †**-io** 1299, weaning; **-aneus,** weaned c 1397; **-o** 7c., 8c.
c 1125, c 1430, **-rio** 1345, **ablecto** 6c., 8c.
c 1290, to wean; **-o,** to suckle 14c.
ablambo, to lick off 1461.
ablat/io, *taking away c 730, 1062. a 1090,
1652; subtraction (math.) 1686; stolen goods
c 1130; **-arius,** person deprived c 1378;
-icius, subtracted (math.) 1686; **-ive,** by
robbery 1461; in the ablative case p 1300,
c 1332; **-ivus,** of or for taking away c 1220,
16c.; **-ivus consequentiae,** ablative absolute 1524; **-or,** usurper 1199, 1308.
ablecto, *see* ABLACT
ablienigena, *see* ALIEN
ablongo, to 'eloign', entice away 1352.
ablu/tio, *cleansing c 730, 1060. c 1090,
1461; water in which something has been
washed c 1072, c 1330; ‡**a. chymica,** purification 1652; **-tor,** cleanser c 800; **-ibilis,**
that can be washed off a 1361.
abminiculum, *see* adminiculum.
abneg/atio, right to clear oneself by oath 790.
c 1115; **-ativus,** denying 790; negative
(gram.) 790; **-o,** to deny guilt, clear oneself
by oath c 1115.
abolitanus, ancient 9c. c 1125; *cf.* **ab olim.**
*abomin/atio (abhomin-),** abomination,
detestable thing (bibl.); *-abilis,** abomin-
able (bibl.); **-abiliter,** abominably 8c., 9c.
c 1233; **-ator,** hater 794; *-o,** to abominate
(eccl.).
abor/sus, abortion: **oborsus** 1232; **-tive,** by
abortion c 1470; **-tivum** (**abertivum,
aburtivum**) c 1445, **parchamenum a.**
1265, 'abortive', uterine vellum; **-tior** (*dep.*),
to bring forth prematurely 8c. a 1250.
‡**abra,** handmaid c 1440, 1483.
abradico 1308, 1419, **aradico** 1271, to tear out.
abra/sio, shaving off 14c.; erasure c 1180,
c 1258; **-sor,** extortioner c 1250; **-do,** to erase
c 1178, 1427.
abremissio, remission c 550; **arremissa**
(*pl.*), payments remitted 1378.
abrenunti/atio (eccl.), †**-o** c 1125, renunciation.

abrepticius, *see* ARREPT
abric, *see* alkibric.
abroc/atio 1300, **-agium** 1291, 1419, **-amen-
tum** 1306, 1333, **abroggamentum** 1355,
brokerage; **-arius** 1419, **-ator** 1255, 1419,
†**-tator** 14c., **abroketor** 1291, broker; *cf.*
2 broca.
Abrodita, Norwegian c 1250.
abrogabilis, revocable 1427, a 1452.
abrupt/um, steep descent: **abrutum** 1302;
ex -o c 1330, 15c., **ex arrupto** 1297, 1461,
suddenly.
†**abrutio** (? *for* obruitio), (right of) demolition
1509.
abscessio, departure: **absessio** 12c., **abces-
sus** c 1200, 1297; **abcedo** 12c., c 1255,
absedo 12c., *for* **abscedo.**
abscisio c 1188, 1467, **abscissio** c 1125,
1620, †**abscitio** 1326, †**absesio** 1386,
cutting, mutilation; **abcisio bursarum**
1291; **abscissa** (geom.) 1686; **assisus,** cut
1199; **abscido** 1291, **abcido** 1267, c 1340,
to cut; **a. (absido) bursam** 1299, 1583.
abscon/ditio a 1564, *-sio** 8c., 9c. c 1239,
c 1439, **-ditum** 1461, (place of) concealment; **-dite** c 1258, **-se** (eccl.), **in -so**
c 1330, **sub -so** c 1190, **sub -dito** c 1408,
secretly; †**absonditus** c 1200, **ascunditus**
c 1150, *for* **-ditus; -sa** c 1072, c 1330, **sconsa**
c 1220, c 1510, sconce, screened light;
†**sconsorum,** (?) lamp-stand 1402.
absecundus, *see* OBSECUND
absent/atio, secession, staying away c 1337,
1415; **-ialiter,** in absence c 826; **-o** c 1218,
c 1415, *-o me** c 1140, 1684, to absent
oneself.
abses, *see* obses.
abs/ida, -is, *see* apsis.
absinth/um c 1257, **abscinthium** a 1250,
c 1298, **azinbia** a 1250, *for* **-ium,** wormwood; **absincium,** drug, potion c 826;
-iose, bitterly c 1470.
absit, *see* abesse.
†**absolesco,** *for* obsolesco, c 950.
absol/utio, delivery 8c.; quittance c 1178,
c 1260; discharge from office c 1250,
c 1330; *absolution** (eccl.) 1006. a 1090,
1543; absoluteness c 1250, c 1300; **dies
Jovis -utionis** 1207, **d. J. -uti** 12c., 14c.,
Maundy Thursday; **-utivus,** final (gram.)
1524; **-utoria,** declaration of absolution
1546; **-utorius,** conferring absolution 13c.,
c 1357; **-utum,** the absolute (log.) c 1332;
-vo, to dismiss c 1258, c 1330; to interpret,
proclaim c 1090; *to absolve** (eccl.) a 1090,
1543; **a. defunctos,** to recite collect for the
dead c 1148, c 1200.
absonditus, *see* ABSCON
absonio, to eschew c 1115.
abson/us, soundless 1267; ‡**-o,** to "discord"
1483.
absor/ptio, swallowing c 1255; 9c., **-bitio**
c 820, concealment; **-tus,** *for* **-ptus,** overwhelmed c 730, 784. 12c., c 1280; **-tus**
(*subst.*) **maris,** engulfing c 1397.
absque, minus (math.) 1145; 1262, **a. pluri**
c 1440, without more ado; **a. eo quod**
c 1380, 1505, **a. hoc quod** c 1285, 1583,
a. quod 1426, on such terms that . . . not;
†**a. quaque,** *for* usquequaque, 1318.

abster/tio, wiping 13c.; **-sivus,** cleansing a 1250, c 1270; **-sorium,** napkin (eccl.) 1295; **-sorius,** of or for a napkin 1295.

abstinentia, fast (eccl.); c 1300, 1409, **a. guerrarum** 1385, armistice.

absto, to cease to exist a 1408.

abstract/io 1509, **-us** a 1300, extraction; *****abstraction** (log.) a 1250, c 1360; **-ibilis** c 1270, **abstrahibilis** c 1250, a 1347, susceptible of abstraction (log.); **-e** 1292, **-ive** c 1286, 15c., abstractly, in the abstract; **-um,** abstract, summary c 1500; the abstract (log.) 1301; **-us** a 1250, 1564, **-ivus** 13c., c 1363, abstract (log.); **-a vita,** secluded life 16c.; **abstraho,** to subtract (math.) 1145; to retire 13c.; to abstract, summarize c 1290; *****to abstract** (log.) c 1160, c 1301.

abstralogia, *see* ASTRO

†**abstringo,** to clarify, cleanse a 1250, 1276; (?) *for* **obstringo,** to bind c 1223.

abstructio, abstruo, *see* OBSTRUCT

abstuppo, *see* obstuppo.

absumptor, consumer, waster 12c.

absurd/is, *for* **-us,** absurd c 1192.

abt-, *see also* APT; **obt-**

abthania, *see* abbathania.

abuco, (?) to accept c 550.

abumbro, *see* OBUMBR

1 abunda 1407, **habundantia** 12c., 1461, abundance; *see also* **ex.**

2 abunda (hab-), *for* **bunda,** 1210, 1317.

aburneus, *see* **alba.**

aburtivum, *see* ABOR

abuschi/amentum, ambush 1283; **-o,** to ambush 1223.

abus/io, vice c 650; *****c 1125, c 1520, *****-us** c 1200, 1562, **-a** 1573, †**-ium** c 1540, ‡**-itas** 1483, abuse, misuse; **-us,** disuse 1419; **-ivus,** faulty, perverse c 650, 1060. c 1332, 1461; insulting c 1250; **-ive,** improperly (gram.) c 700. c 1350; **-or,** one who abuses, misuser c 1240, a 1408; **-itatus,** ignorant 7c.; †**-oto,** *for* **-ito,** to deceive c 1204; ‡**abutisso,** to misuse 1483; **abutor,** to become useless c 1000.

abutt/atio, partition 1535; **-ale,** abutment, terminal boundary 13c, **-amentum,** (?) embankment c 1290; buttress 1251; **-o** 1415, 1450, **-o me** 1270, 1278, **-isso** c 1200, a 1224, **-izo** a 1200, 1316, †**ambutto** c 1270, **a.** a c 1219, **a. ad** 1299, c 1443, **a. contra** p 1200, **a. cum** 15c., **a. in** 15c., *****a. super** 12c., c 1452, **a. versus** c 1270, 1502, to abut (on).

*****abyss/us** (bibl.), **-a** c 1450, abyss, bottomless pit; depth c 781; **-alis,** of the abyss c 1241.

ac si, *see* **acsi.**

‡**acacia ferrea,** iron spoon (alch.) 1652.

academi/a, university c 1511, 1655; **-ca,** letter c 800; **-cus,** member of university c 1578, 1620.

acalant/is, -ida, nightingale 7c.; *cf.* **agalancia.**

acap-, *see* ACCAP

acario, *see* ABCARI

†**acaristum,** sort of drug a 1250.

acatalepsia, scepticism 1620.

†**acator,** (?) *for* **arcator,** c 550.

*****acatum,** 'achate', acquisition, property purchased or acquired 1130, 1507; **achator,** caterer 1362; *cf.* **accaptum.**

acca marina, kind of fish, (?) hake 1213.

accabli/amentum, knocking down (C.I.) 1309, 1324; **-o,** to knock down (C.I.) 1300, 1309; *cf.* CABLI

accapito 1226, c 1290, **achevio** 1220, 1244, **achevo** 1206, †**acheo** c 1300, †**achesunor** 1291, to acknowledge feudal liability to; **a. super,** to abut on 13c.; **achevio,** to conclude (a plea) 1258.

accap/tum (acap-) 1289, **-tagium** 1283, 1313, **-tamentum** (†**acceptamentum**) 1289, **achata** 1242, payment on change of lord (G.); *cf.* **acatum; captagium.**

accasatus, resident tenant, *chasé* (G.) 1289.

accausatio, molestation c 1240; **adcauso,** to accuse c 1115.

acced/entia, approach, advance c 1620; **-ere** (*subst.*), right of entry (leg.) 1199; **-entius,** with added force a 1200; **-as ad curiam,** name of a writ 15c.; **-o pro,** to apply for 1271; **accido,** *for* **-o,** to approach 1461; *cf.* ACCESS

acceler/atio c 1200, 1426, **accelaratio** c 1480, haste; **-ate** c 1187, **-atim** 12c., swiftly; **-atior,** swifter c 1250; **-atrix,** accelerative (*f.*) 1686; **-o** c 730. c 1125, 15c., **adcelero** c 730, to hasten (with *inf.*).

accens-, *see also* ACENS

accens/io, kindling a 1250, 1620; **a. lune,** New Moon 1120, 1267; **-ibilis,** inflammable a 1250; **-or,** one who rouses c 1125; **-orius,** rousing, urging a 1155, c 1436; **accendo ad,** to desire passionately c 1185.

*****accent/uo** 12c., 1472, **-o** c 1266, c 1330, **accino** c 1182, 1267, to accent.

accept-, *see also* ACCAP; ACET

accept/atio *****1220, 1448, **exceptatio** 1290, accepting, acceptance; c 1263, **-io** c 1187, c 1363, acceptation, meaning; **a. personarum** (bibl.), **a. in persona** c 1430, **-io in p.** 1426, regarding of persons, obsequiousness; **-abilis** (bibl.), **-ibilis** c 1300, p 1300, **-iosus** c 1465, acceptable; **-abiliter,** acceptably 870. 1419; **-ivus,** apt to receive 13c., 1374; **-or** (bibl.), **-rix** (*f.*) c 804, one who accepts; *see also* **accipiter; -orium** 685, †**-urium** c 1000, book of extracts for reading at meals; ‡**-ifero,** to quitclaim c 1180; **-o,** to welcome, accept as satisfactory c 1239, 1551; **a. personam, accipio** p. 1268; **accipio graviter, a. moleste** c 1130, **a. pro malo** c 1334, to take amiss; **a. radicem,** to extract root (math.) 1145.

accerrus, sting a 1350.

accer/sio 1200, **-cio** c 1325, 1421 **accierso** c 1125, *for* **-so,** to send for.

access/io, fitment, gear (naut.) 1602, 1606; **a. temporum,** process of time c 1115; **-or,** helper, accomplice c 1362, 1503; *****-orius** c 1160, 1620, **-arius** c 1218, 1511, accessory, subordinate (*adj.*); **-orie,** as an accessory 1252, c 1444; **-orium, -arium,** act of being accessory to a crime c 1400, 1573; **-orium,** subordinate matter c 1191, c 1444; **-o,** to enter on a position c 1220; *cf.* ACCED

acchiricus, *see* ARTHRIT

accid/ens, chance, occurrence c 1190, 1408; *****accident** (log.) c 850. a 1100, 15c.; **per -ens,** accidentally (log.) c 1200, 1345; **-entia,** (*n. pl.*) extraordinary services 1200, c 1233; casual profits 1393; inflexions, accidence (gram.) 1271, 17c.; (*f. s.*) book of accidence 1519; accidency (log.) c 1365; **-entalis**, occurring by chance c 1160, c 1400; accessory c 1290; concerned with accidents (log.) 9c. a 1090, c 1460; **domus a.**, ruling house (astr.) 1387; **-entalitas,** accidentality c 1290, c 1363; **-entaliter,** accidentally, by chance c 870. c 1200, a 1446; in relation to accidents (log.) c 1250, c 1444; **-ento**, to affect in relation to accidents (log.) c 1365, 1427; **-o,** *to accrue, fall to the share of c 1267, 1417; to arise accidentally (log.) a 1250; **ascido,** *for* **-o,** to happen 1321; *see also* ACCED, **acedia.**

accierso, *see* **accersio.**

accin/ctus 1260, **ascingtus** 1262, circuit, compass; readiness, preparation c 1070, c 1185; **-cta,** curtain wall 1252; **-go,** to surround c 1170, c 1400; to bind (corn) c 1300; **a. gladio,** to knight c 1200.

accino, *see* ACCENT

accinus, *see* **assassinus.**

accipio, *see* ACCEPT

accipit/er, hawk (esp. sparrow-hawk): **arcipiter** 1155, **ancipiter** (? **aucipiter**) c 1150, 1573, **anceps** (*gen.* **ancipitis**) 1212, 1388, **anticiper** a 1200, c 1280, **antiscipiter, anticepeter** 1370, **acceptor** 748; **a. Hibernensis,** peregrine falcon c 1178; **a. Hispanensis,** saker c 1178; **a. Norrensis** c 1178, **a. Norrescus** 1086, **a. Norriscus** 1130, 1156, gerfalcon; **a. ruber,** sore hawk 1388; **-rarius** 893. 1086, c 1400, **ancipitrarius** 1086, **anceps** (*gen.* **ancipitis**) 1153, 1287, falconer; *cf.* 1 **falco.**

accito, to hasten 1200.

acclam/atio, love 870; **-atrix,** informer (*f.*) c 1115; **-eum,** claim 1509; **-o,** to proclaim c 1190, c 1408; to claim 12c., 1569; *see also* QUIET

‡**acclaudicatus,** "accloyed", pricked by nail c 1440; *cf.* **inclavo.**

acclausum, enclosure 1274; **adclaudo,** to enclose c 1140; **accludo,** to shut to (of a door) 14c.

acclino (adc-), to incline c 730.

†**accli/vis** (? **-nis**), obedient c 1436.

accoillo (frigore), to overtake, overcome c 1218.

accol/a (bibl.), **accula** c 550, inhabitant; **-atus,** act of dwelling in c 1125.

*accommod/atio, lending, loan 1086, a 1564; **-arius,** enjoying usufruct c 1366; **-ator,** lender 1260; †**-otarius,** borrower c 1377; **-atorie,** by way of loan c 1377; **ex -ato,** on loan c 1335; ***-o,** to lend 1086, 1561; to borrow 1287.

accomplementum, accomplishment, fulfilment 1545, 1624.

accomputo, to account 1661.

acconcordo, to assent 13c.

accopa (? *for* **apocha**) c 1300, c 1380, †**ancopa** c 1380, receipt, tally; *cf.* **anticopa.**

accop/io, -o, accoupo, *see* ACCUP

accord/um, agreement 1299; **-o,** to bring into agreement, harmonize c 1305, 1461.

accosto (acosto), to adjoin c 1200.

accostomo, *see* ACCUST

*accred/o 1166, 1285, **-ito** a 1135, to lend; **adcredulito,** to clear oneself by oath c 1115.

accre/mentum 1136, 1588, †**acramentum** c 1170, c 1300, **-censia** a 1190, **-tum** c 1220, †**-scum** c 1310, increase, addition; **-tus,** having accrued 1583; **-sco,** to add, augment 1086, c 1356; ***to accrue** c 1185, a 1564; **a. etatem,** to attain age 1583; **jus -scendi,** right of joint tenant in survivorship 1502, 1601; **accresso,** *for* **-sco,** to increase 1213, c 1322.

accresto, to fit (a wall) with cresting 1265.

accroch/iamentum, accroachment 1401, 1580; **-o** c 1387, ***-io** 1401, 1583, to accroach.

accrocito, to rejoice at c 1115.

accubator, stone-layer 1242.

accubit/as (acubit-), drooping, heaviness (of eyelids) a 1250; **-alis,** for reclining on a 1142.

accula, *see* **accola.**

accumulat/io, amassing c 1376; **-ior,** more numerous 12c.; **-ive,** cumulatively c 1444.

accup/amentum 1255, c 1290, **aucupamentum** 1276, charge, accusation; **acculpo** 1256, 1307, **accopo** 1293, **accopio** 1270, **accoupo** 1257, p 1341, **-o** 1247, 1306, **aucupo** 1275, to charge, accuse.

‡**accur/ator,** proctor 1483; **-atus,** (?) careworn, impoverished 1508; **-o, acuro,** (?) to finish off, put to death 1214.

accurro, to flow in c 1362.

accurto c 1210, 1241, **akorto** 1286, to shorten, abridge.

accus/amentum, accusation 1388; acknowledgement, receipt 1378; **-atiuncula,** insinuated accusation 1662; **-o,** to betray 1265.

accust/omabilis 1564, **-omatus** 1550, **-umatus** c 1502, customary; **-umaliter,** as a prostitute 1541; **accostomo,** to levy custom on (G.) 1254.

acdenna, oak-dene (Kent) a 1170.

acedia 8c. a 1180, 1271, ***accidi/a** 7c. 12c., c 1433, 'accidy', spiritual sloth (ἀκηδία) **-ose,** slothfully c 1238, c 1376; **-osus,** slothful 980. 12c., a 1408; **-or,** to rest slothfully 1240, c 1454; **accedio,** to weary, bore 1349.

aced/o, sourness c 1270, 1620 (*cf.* **acredo**); **-ula** a 1250, ‡1483, (?) **axsedula** 1414, sourdock (bot.); crowfoot a 1519.

acelg/a 12c., **-as** a 1250, beet (Ar. *selg*).

acella, *see* 2 **axella; sella.**

acemo, *see* ASSEM

acens/a (**accens-, ascens-, assens-**) 1255, 1357, **-arium** 1298, **-amentum** 1259, lease, farm (G.); **-amentum,** property (G.) 1207; **-atio,** farming out (G.) 1253, 1289; **-ator,** lessor (G.) 1289, 1357; **-o** (G.) 1253, 1311, **adcensa** 1086, to lease, farm out.

acensorius, *see* ASCEN

acephal/us a 1090, a 1408, **azephalus** c 1310, headless; ***c 1250, c 1546, **asephalus** 1461, **azephalus** 1260, c 1362, leaderless; without feudal lord c 1115; acephalic (of verse) c 700. c 1125; **-o** 1252, **azephalo** c 1322, to behead.

*acer/ 1282, c 1420, **ascer** 1173, 1364, **asser** 1308, 1367, **-ium** c 1160, ***-um** 1232, 1362, **assera** 1271, **asserum** 1284, **azerum** 1304, steel; **-atio** 1354, 1412, **asceratio** 1333,

1367, steeling (of iron tools, by welding steel to cutting edge); **-o** 1223, c 1384, **ascero** 1224, 1325, **assero** 1280, c 1378, **asselo** 1412, to steel (tools); *see also* **vinum**.

acertum, *see* EXSART

aceta, *see* **acidula**.

acet/ositas, sourness 12c., 1427; **-osus** c 1180, 1403, **-us** c 870, sour; ‡**herba -osa**, sorrel 14c.; **acceptabulum**, *for* **-abulum**, saucer c 1180, c 1306; **-abulum**, cymbal 1267; **assetum**, *for* **-um**, vinegar 1313.

achacio, to drive (cattle) 1252.

†**achalus**, without Chalus Castle c 1190.

achar/is c 1344, ‡c 1440, **-us** 1344 thankless, graceless.

achat-, *see also* **acatum**; **accaptum**

achates, a herb c 1212; c 1212, ‡1652, **agathes** c 1362, agate (gem).

achellarium, achillarium, *see* **asshelarium**.

Acheron/ c 550, **-ticum** c 940, **Cheron** 1149, the Christian Hell.

achersetus, measure of grain, *etc.* a 1128.

acheta, *see* **excidamentum**.

ache/vio, -vo, -o, -sunor, *see* **accapito**.

Achilles, conclusive argument 1267, p 1300.

achor/, scab: **-a** a 1250.

‡**acicu/larium** 1570, **-raria theca** a 1519, pin-case; ‡**-larius**, pinner 1520.

acidula c 1180, **aceta** c 1200, kind of bird, (?) woodcock; *cf.* **acredula**.

acies, scaling-ladder c 1280.

†**acirma**, wheelbarrow 1573; *cf.* **civera**.

acmasticus, occurring at the crisis (of fever): **augm/asticus** c 1200, a 1250; **etas -atica**, maturity a 1250.

*acolyt/us 980. c 1164, c 1546, **-es** 1215, **acoluthus** 1229, acolyte (eccl.); **-atus** 1200, 1552, **occolitatus** 1258, order or status of acolyte.

‡**acon**, shad (fish) 1570.

‡**acortinus**, lupin (bot.) 1652.

acosus, *see* **aqua**.

acot/o, -imus, *see* **aketo**.

acoustica (*f. s.*), acoustics 1620.

acquestus, *see* **acquisitio**.

acquiesco (with *inf.*), to agree 12c., c 1400.

*acquiet/atio (**adquiet-, aquiet-**) a 1135, a 1452, †**adequietatio** c 1293, **acquitatio** 1385, **-antia* c 1160, 1533, **acquitantia* 1278, c 1450, quittance, discharge; **-antialis** 1340, a 1564, **-antiarius** c 1445, **-antius** c 1334, **acquitatorius** 13c., **acquitorius** 1362, of or for quittance; **-o* (**acquito**), to bring to rest, settle c 1290, 14c.; **to acquit, free* (land, *etc.*) of a claim or charge 1086, 1564; **to acquit, discharge* (person) c 1115, 1540; **to discharge, pay* (debt, *etc.*) 1192, 1464; **to pay for, purchase* 1242, 1419; to pay off (ships) 1242; (*intr.*) to be quit, exempt c 1185; **a. me**, to clear oneself 1086, 1415; **a. fidem**, to fulfil an engagement c 1122; **a. foris**, to redeem (from pawn) 1482.

acquisi/tio (**adq-**) c 630, 9c. a 1090, 1474, **-tum** 1225, 1324, **acquestus** c 1250, **aquesta** (G.) 1283, purchase, property purchased or acquired; procurement, inducement 1194; **a. carbonum**, winning coal 1533; **a. lapidum (petrarum)**, quarrying 1434, 1519; **a. talparum**, mole-

catching 1479; **-bilis** 13c., c 1444, **acquiribilis** c 1362, able to be acquired; **-tivus**, concerned with acquisition c 1340, 1350; **-tor** 12c., a 1350, **-trix** (*f.*) c 1180, acquirer, collector; **acquiro** 1086, 1459, †**adquireto** c 1250, to acquire, procure, purchase.

*acr/a 1086, 1567, **-um** c 1220, **-us** 1086, c 1107, **acerra** a 1135, **aecra** 11c., **ager** 1086, 13c., **agra** c 1200, acre, acre-strip; *champ clos*, duel (Sc. Marches) 1237; **a. capitalis**, strip lying in a head-land 1234, 1346; **a. carruce** c 1115; **a. regalis** 1295; **a. baronum** c 1278; **a. per (secundum) perticam** 12c., 1449; **a. (terre) Cornubiensis**, virgate (or larger unit) 1337, 16c.; **a. Flandrensis** 1211; **a. legalis** (W.) a 1300; **a. precum**, boon-acre c 1115; **a. prima**, (?) customary acre c 1240, 1586; **akrehevedum**, head-land c 1300; **-emannus** 1251, 1336, **aecremannus** c 1115, **akermannus** 1222, 1336, **akirmannus** 1297, 'acre-man', customary tenant; **-emanelanda**, land held by acre-man 13c.; **hakeresweda**, (?) 'acre-swathe', meadow appurtenant to acre-strip 13c.

acredo, bitterness, harshness c 730. a 1100, c 1330; *see also* **vinum**; *cf.* **acedo**.

‡**acredula**, "goldfinch" 1483; ‡**agre/dula**, "titmouse" 15c.; 13c, ‡**-cula** 1483, frog; *cf.* **acidula**.

acr/ementum, -amentum, *see* ACCRE

acreo, to discreate c 1408.

acribologia, exactitude c 1608.

acrieto, *see* **aries**.

acrifolium, thorn-tree 1411.

acrimonia, *see* **agrimonia**.

acrisia a 1205, 1427, †**acroisia** 1189, lack of discernment, blindness; *cf.* **aorasia**.

acrocornis, wart containing blood (med.) a 1250.

acr/oma, *for* **-oama**, pleasant sound c 1125, c 1370.

‡**acromell/um (agromell-)**, "grout", wort 1483; ‡**-arium**, wort-vat 1483; *cf.* **ciromellum**.

acrumina (*n. pl.*) c 1200, c 1315, **acumina** a 1250, pungent foods.

†**acrusticus**, morbid (med.) a 1250.

*acsi, used as **quasi**, 7c., 9c. c 1090, c 1470.

act-, *see also* **att-**

actinus, *see* **hactinus**.

act/io, treatise c 870; mystery play c 1225; thanks (*cf.* **gratia**) 1244; sitting of a court (leg.) c 1115; **a. injurialis**, action for redress of wrong (leg.) c 1290; **a. pacis**, enforcement of peace c 1115; **-ionarius**, official, agent 747. 14c., c 1500; **-arius**, notary, scribe 790 (*cf.* **actuarius** *below*); **-or**, proctor, advocate (leg.) 1219, 1445; disputant (ac.) 1267; **-rix**, agent (*f.*) a 1408; *see also* **pars**; **-ivus** c 1220, 16c., **-ualis** 7c., 790, **-uosus** c 1270, active, practical; active (gram.) 790. a 1304; **-ive**, actively c 1180, c 1444; **-ivitas**, activity a 1235, 1630;

-us, (bringing of) legal action 1324, 1546; act of Parliament 1456, 1548; act, statute (ac.) c 1322, 1510; actuality (log.) a 1100, 1471; **a. purus**, actuality unmixed with potentiality c 1250, 1620; **-us** (*pl.*), Acts of

the Apostles c 1006. 1267, c 1444; ***-ualis,**
actual c 730. a 1090, 1563; *see also* **pecca-**
tum; **-ualiter,** actually 8c., 9c. a 1200,
1485; forthwith, at the present time (*cf.* Fr.
actuellement) c 1300, c 1520; ***-ualitas,**
actuality, actualization a 1233, c 1457;
-uabilis, able to be actualized c 1300, 1344;
-uarius, busy person 790; clerk, registrar
(of convocation) c 1533; **-uatio,** actualization c 1367; **-uativus,** able to actualize
c 1300; **-iono** 1362, †**-anno** c 1290, to sue,
implead; **-ito,** to transact c 1125, c 1440;
to deliberate, discuss c 1178, c 1188; to
enact (Sc.) c 1500, 1539; **-o,** to drive c 1188;
-ivo c 1250, **-uo** 1620, 1622, to energize,
activate; **-uo,** to actualize, bring into actuality
c 1300, 1564; *cf.* **agentia.**
acto/, -na, *see* **aketo.**
†**actolicus,** (?) *for* (**nuntius**) **apostolicus**
1465.
acub, *see* **alcubd.**
acubitas, *see* **accubitas.**
acuro, *see* ACCUR
acurtino, to decorate with hangings 1274; *cf.*
curtino.
1 **acus** (*gen.* **acuris**), husk c 1170.
2 **acu/s,** point a 1408; pen c 1330; compass
needle c 1200, 1620; **a. nautica,** mariner's
compass 1620; **a. capitis,** hair-pin 1461;
a. ad pallium, pall-pin c 1294, c 1328;
‡**-arium,** needle-case 15c., 1483;
-atio 1316, 1564, **-itio** 1327, 1433, **-tatio**
1409, sharpening; **-itas,** lengthening or
accentuation (of syllable) 1267; alkalinity
1292; **-lea,** (?) barb a 700; **-leosus,** piercing
c 1430; **-leus,** tick, or tick-bite a 1150;
eculeus, sting c 1400; **-men,** needle
c 1060; **-mina,** *see* **acrumina; -minatus,**
ridged c 1180, 1518; **-perium,** whetstone
1393,‡15c.;**-pictor,**embroiderer ‡15c.,1710;
-variatus, embroidered c 1436; **-atus,**
made pungent a 1250; **-ta,** acute fever, ague
a 1204, c 1260; **-tarius,** for whetting 1279;
aguzorium, sharpener 1235; ‡**-tella,** rest-
harrow (bot.) 14c.; **-ties,** sharpness, acute-
ness 1267, 1431; **-tus,** prolonged or accented
1267; treble (mus.) 1351; alkaline a 1292;
-leo, to peck at c 550; **-o,** to lengthen, accent
870. 1267; to make pungent (med.) a 1250.
ad, *to (*ind. object* after **dico,** *etc.*) (bibl.);
(of place) at, in 1086, 1448; **ad manum**
c 1130, c 1265, **ad manus** 1327, 1412, at
hand; **ad manum habens,** red-handed
c 1115; **ad herbam,** at grass 1234, 1327;
ad fenum 1327; **ad propria,** (to) home
1132, 1432;
(of time) **ad modicum,** a little, for a short
time c 1188, c 1411; **ad punctum,** punctually 1425; **ad remanens,** for the future
1164, c 1250; **ad terminum,** name of a
writ 1259;
(of purpose) for 1086, 1507; *see also*
capio, facio, juro; ad effectum c 1335,
c 1458, **ad finem** 1343, 1406, to the end
(that); **ad hoc,** for the purpose c 1265,
1545; ***ad opus,** for the use or benefit (of)
1086, c 1538; **ad quod damnum,** name of a
writ 1385;
in return for (**cibum, potum,** *etc.*) a 1128,
c 1400;

(of number or measure) at the rate of
1225, 1559; **ad plus,** at a higher (or the
highest). rate 1207, c 1283; **ad obolum,**
see **auca; ad numerum,** (reckoning) by
tale 1086, 1130; **ad pondus,** by weight
1086, 1258; *cf.* PENS;
(expressing various relations) **ad creden-**
tiam 1216, 1376; **ad fidem** 1217, 1237;
*ad firmam 1086, 1486; **ad litteram,**
literally c 1260, c 1363; **ad oculum,** by sight
c 1430; **ad opus,** by labour service c 1120,
p 1160; **ad periculum proprium,** at
one's own risk 1432; **ad valens** 1130,
*ad valentiam 1142, 1588, **ad valitudinem**
c 1180, c 1400, **ad valorem** 1274, c 1587,
to the value (of); *see also* **beneplacitum,**
guerra, libitum, placitum, rectum,
roba, velle; ad voluntatem, *see* **teneo;**
(of appointment or proof) as, (so as) to be
c 1219, c 1383;
*(in attributive phrases) at, of, with, for,
see **ballista, canis,** 1 **equus, homo,**
molendinum, pannus, serviens, *etc.*;
(with *adj.*) (**blodius**) **ad album,** (?)whitish
1388; **ad cassum,** in vain c 1450; **ad**
condignum, worthily c 1365, 1441; **ad**
†**facilem,** easily c 1212; **ad integrum,**
entirely c 1250; ***ad largum,** at large 1375,
1575; **ad longum,** at length c 1444, 1461;
ad oppositum, opposite c 1325, c 1470;
*ad plenum, fully a 1125, 1686; **ad**
purum, purely, thoroughly c 600, 8c.
c 1343; **ad transversum,** across 1255; **ad**
verum, truly 13c.;
(with *adj.* or *adv., comparative* equivalent to
superlative) **ad altius** c 1200, **ad carius**
12c., at the dearest; **ad cautius et dili-**
gentius, ad prudentius 1265; **ad citius,**
at soonest 1239, 1461; **ad magis** c 1362,
1389, **ad** (**omne**) **majus** 1505, **ad plus**
c 1218, 1419, at most; **ad melius,** on the
best terms 1227, c 1324; ***ad minus,** at
least 1086, c 1545; **ad omne minus** a 1570;
ad tardius, at latest 1254, 1368;
(with *adj., superlative*) **ad minimum,** at
least c 1550; **ad ultimum,** at last, at latest
c 730, a 910. 1086, c 1434;
(with *adv.* or *prep.*) **ad a retro,** again
1420; **ad circa,** round a 1490; **ad extra,**
outside 1280, 1534; **ad infra** c 1452, c 1470;
ad intra 1416, 1432, inside; **ad intus et**
extra, more or less (Sc.) 1454, 1551; **ad**
insimul, at the same time 1213; **ad in-**
vicem, *mutually c 1090, c 1542; together
1300, c 1470; **ad prope,** near c 1400; **ad**
semper, for ever c 1343; **ad sero,** late 1194;
*ad statim, immediately 1418, 1686; ***ad**
tunc, then c 1390, 1581; **ad ultra,** beyond
1514.
ada, *see* **atha.**
‡**adagonista,** lawyer 15c., 1483.
adaliqualitas, relativity (to something) c 1300.
adam/as, lodestone, magnet a 1233, c 1360;
-antius, adamantine 1271; **lapis -anticus**
9c.; *cf.* **amans.**
adapertio, opening, revealing c 790.
adapt/atio, adaptation c 1230; application,
comparison c 1250, 1267; training (falc.)
1259; **-o,** to insert c 1090; to adapt, apply
c 1194, 1537; to 'blood' (hounds) 1256.

adaqu/atio, (right of) watering cattle 1239, c 1290; **-arium**, ewer 1398; **-o**, to water (cattle) 1236, 1331; to dissolve, liquefy (alch.) c 1320.

adar/ca, efflorescence on sedge: **-cis, -sis** a 1250.

adaugma, increase c 1310, ‡1483.

adauratus, woven with gold c 1380, 1591.

adb-, *see* **abb-**

adc-, *see also* **acc-**

†**adcantarium**, measure of weight, quintal c 1298.

adcenso, *see* ACENS

addea, *see* **ardea.**

addico, to promise, assign c 1150, c 1595.

addic/o, to decree c 1115; c 1365, **-to** c 1370, to accuse, indict; **-to**, to condemn 1291.

addigito, to point at c 1180.

addis/citio, further knowledge c 1210; **-so**, *for* **-co**, to learn in addition 1370.

addisro, *see* **adiro.**

add/itio, thing added c 1283, c 1470; title or description (appended to name) 1494; **-ibilis**, able to be added 1344; **-itionalis**, additional 1684; **-o**, to go on to (with *inf.*) c 730, 798. 13c.

addubbo, to stud (with gems) 1245.

adductatio, *see* ADVOC

adduc/tio, conveying, bringing in 1204, c 1444; **-tivus**, productive c 1370; **-o**, to adduce a 1290, c 1444.

adelingus a 1142, 1315, **edelingus** c 1140, atheling, prince; *cf.* **ethleta.**

adelphus, brother c 550, c 980. 1079.

adempt/orius, -ivus, taking away 1344.

adeps frumenti, (?) white flour 1362.

adeptio, getting: †**adoptio** 1530; **adipisc/o**, *for* **-or**, to arrive at, gain 8c. c 1290, c 1362; *see also* ADOPT

adequ/atio, balancing, levelling a 1250, 1255; *correspondence c 1227, c 1367; **-abilitas**, potential correspondence c 1270; **-ate**, adequately, correspondingly a 1350, 1686; **-atus**, adequate, corresponding c 1332, 1378.

adequietatio, *see* **acquietatio.**

adequo, to harness 1345.

ades, lizard a 1150.

adespotus, anonymous 1534.

adessens, present 1427.

adf-, *see* **aff-**

adg-, *see also* **agg-**

adgeniculatio, kneeling, prostration 9c.

adgest-, adgist-, *see* 1 AGIST

adhabeo, *see* **adhibitio.**

adherbo, to graze, put out to grass c 1115.

adhesia, *see* **azeisa.**

adhe/sio, an appurtenance 13c.; sexual connexion c 1342; c 1300, 1425, **-sitio** a 1361, *-rentia 12c., 1461, adherence, support, confederacy; **-rentia**, adhesion, clinging a 1233, a 1250; **-sivus**, expressive of adherence or assent 1344; **-rens**, (*subst.*) adherent 1296, 1584.

adhibitio, employment (of persons) c 1343, a 1446; **adhabeo**, to receive in addition 1296.

adhorreo, to shudder, be horrified c 1319.

adiaphorus, undifferentiated c 1612, 1620.

‡**adiascordion**, agrimony (bot.) 14c.

adimbrevio, to record, note c 1290.

adimmensus, immense 1303.

*adimple/tio**, fulfilment 7c., 8c. c 1100, 1440; *-o**, to fulfil, complete 6c., 9c. a 1090, c 1466.

adinduco, to induce, exhort 1350.

adinebrio, to inspire c 730.

adinjungo, to add an injunction 1433.

adinquiro, to acquire c 1460.

adinsto, to be present 15c.

adintelligo, to understand c 1363.

adinven/tio, invention, new thing or theory 6c., 7c. c 1130, 1505; †**-tatio**, invasion 14c.; **-tarium**, inventory 1310; **-tor**, deviser of new things 6c., 7c. 12c., a 1446; *-io**, to invent, devise c 1165, 1537.

†**adinventulo**, to discuss a 1540.

adinvicem, *see* **ad invicem.**

adipisco, *see* **adeptio.**

adiro 1221, c 1258, **addisro** c 1290, to 'eloign', remove.

adjac/entia, nearness, neighbourhood 13c., 1427; appurtenance 1086, c 1414; state of being an attribute c 1362; **-enter**, attributively c 1160, a 1233; **-ens**, attribute c 1361; **-entior**, to be adjacent c 1289; *-eo**, to appertain 676, 957. 1086, c 1324; to be an attribute c 1376; *cf.* **adnascentia.**

adject/io, throwing c 1200; assigning 1236; additional clause 12c., 1191; c 1343, **-ivum** c 1405, epithet; **-ivus**, added, positive (math.) 1145; adjectival (gram.) c 790. 1267; **-um**, adjective 1520; **-ive**, adjectivally p 1300; **-ivatio**, qualification (gram.) 1427; **-us**, devoted, attached to p 1377; **-ivo**, to qualify (gram.) 1427.

adjest-, *see* **agistamentum.**

adjocor, to joke with 1200.

adjorn/atio c 1290, 1545, *-amentum c 1290, a 1564, **ajornamentum** 1292, adjournment; *-o** c 1258, 1545, **ajorno** 1262, c 1305, **adjourno** c 1284, 1336, **adjurno** c 1271, to adjourn.

adjudic/atio, judicial decision c 1400, 1499; **-ator**, doomster (Sc.) 1539, a 1609; **-atorius**, judicial 1684; †**adjudex**, additional judge c 1236; **-o**, *to condemn a 1090, 1687; to decree 1229, 1468; **a. legem** 1194, 1221.

adjun/ctio (†**admictio**) a 1300, 1416, **-ctura** a 1300, c 1380, drafting (of farm animals) into next age-group; **-ctivus**, conjunctive (gram.) 790; **-ctum**, repetition (gram.) c 1258; accident (log.) 1610; **-go**, to draft (animals) into age-group 1209, 1416; **a. super**, to adjoin 1588.

adjur/atio, exorcism a 1120, ‡1483; **-ator**, one who has taken an oath c 1000; exorcist c 1182, 1517; **-ative**, in earnest. entreaty a 1090; **-atorius**, supplicatory c 1340; **frater -atus**, fellow monk 12c.; **-o**, to adjure, bind by oath c 1067, c 1437; to assign by oath 1199, c 1204.

adju/vatio a 1564, **-vamen** 7c. a 1175, c 1470, **-vamentum** a 1250, aid, help; **-torium**, feudal aid 1111, 1330; **a. liberum** a 1250; **a. regis** c 1160; **-vativus**, helpful a 1250; **sic me Deus -vet** 1269.

adl-, *see also* **all-**

adleta, *see* **athleta.**

admallaratus, *see* **admiralius.**

admallo, to bring before a moot (*cf.* **mallum**) c 1115.

admallum, *see* **esmallum.**

admannio (†**admoneo**), to claim or collect (A.S. *amanian*) c 1115; **a. ad,** to hand over to c 1115.

admenso, to put on the table c 1180.

admensur-, *see* AMENSUR

admercandizo, to trade 1354.

admictio, *see* **adjunctio.**

admillus, *see* **admiralius.**

adminicul/um (**amm-**), adminicle, corroborative evidence (leg.) c 1180, a 1446; **abminiculum** 7c., *for* **-um, -atio** c 1000, **-atus** 8c., help, support; **-arius,** helper a 1142.

administr/atio (**amm-**), supply c 980, c 1000. c 1115; administration of property (of deceased) 12c., c 1520; Franciscan province c 1250; **a. sacramentorum** 1549; **-ativus,** affording a supply c 1115; inclined to control c 1270; **-ator,** administrator of property, executor c 1345, 1543; administrator (eccl.) c 1261, 1549; **a. generalis** (eccl.) c 1337, 1535; **-atorie,** by way of administration c 1376; **-atorius,** (*adj.*) of or for administration of property 739. 1587; (*subst.*) minister, official c 1150; **-atrix,** administratrix (of property) 1356, 1573; **-o** 15c., c 1452, **-o de** 1261, to administer (property).

admir/abundus, overawed 1537; **-ande,** admirably 1267; **-ativus,** admiring, wondering p 1348; ‡**-ificus,** wonderful 1483; **ammir/abilis,** admirable 7c. 12c.; **-o,** to marvel 5c.

admir/alius, a 1142, c 1362, †**admillus** c 1436, **-abilis** a 1142, c 1255, **-alis** c 1192, **-ellus** c 1436, **-aldus** 12c., c 1436, **-audus** c 1190, **-atus** c 1125, c 1300, **amiralius** a 1155, c 1400, **amiraldus** c 1220, 15c., **amyraudus** c 1300, **amiras** 12c., c 1188, *emir,* governor (Ar.); **-atus,** *podestà* (It.) c 1250; **amiravisius,** *emir-vizir* a 1142, c 1265; ***-allus** 1295, 1608, **-alius** c 1320, 1608, **-abilis** 1342, **-aldus** c 1553, †**-antus** (?-**autus**) 1295, **-atus** 1177 (Sicily), 1296, **amerallus** 1300, c 1360, **amarallus** c 1470, **amirallus** 1274 (Fr.), c 1540, **ammirallius** 1421, **ammiraldus** 1521, **amiratus** 1315, admiral; **-alia,** flag-ship 1461; **-alatus** 1357, 1438, **admarallatus** (Sc.) 1460, **-alitas** 1339, 1606, **-abilitas** 1587, **-atus** 1344, 1379, admiralty, office of admiral; **Curia -alitatis** 1383, 1587; †**admallaratus** (Sc.) (*for* **admarallatus**), prize dues 1459.

admiss/io, induction (eccl.) 1229, c 1520; perpetration 14c.; **-ibilis** c 1444, 1549, **admittibilis** a 1361, a 1564, **-ivus** 1485, admissible; **-orius,** for permission to receive ordination c 1467; for admission to a monastery c 1470; **amissum,** misdeed c 760. c 1330; **admitto,** to induct (eccl.) c 1200, c 1529; to acknowledge c 1090, 1419; (? *for* **omitto**), to omit 1201, 1450; **a. diem,** to accept a day (appointed) 1327, 1333.

admixtio: amixtio carnis, copulation 597, c 730.

admoneo, *see* **admannio.**

admonit/io (**amm-**), admonition (eccl.) 604.

c 1115, 1537; **-iuncula,** mild rebuke 546; **-orius,** admonitory 796. c 1250.

admoror, to stay, be engaged 1289.

admullono, to stack 1375.

†**admustrisona,** (?) muster (*cf.* O.F. *amostrer*) 1223.

adn-, *see also* **ann-**

†**adnascentia** (? *for* **adjacentia**), contiguity of unlike bodies c 1361.

adnecia, *see* **esnecia.**

adolat/io, -or, *see* **adulatio.**

adoleo, adolesc-, *see* **adultio.**

adolio, to put in casks 1180.

adomenon, song (ᾀδόμενον) c 970.

adoperatio, working c 1607; application 1620.

adopt/io, adoption (bibl.); †**adeptio,** *for* **-io,** c 1290; **-io,** choice c 1275, c 1367; **-ive,** by adoption c 804. c 1218; **-ivus,** adopted (child) c 730, 870. 1268; *see also* **adeptio.**

ador/atio horarum, sequence of genuflexions imposed as penance c 700; **-amentum** c 1378, **-atus** c 1430, worship; ***-ator,** adorer, worshipper (bibl.); **-atrix,** suppliant (*f.*) 1435; **Crux -ata,** Good Friday 1309; *see also* ODOR

adordino, to set in order c 1360.

adorna/tio 680. a 1452, c 1488, **-tus** 12c., adornment; **-tivus,** ornamental c 1255.

adorti, *see* **aorta.**

adp-, *see also* **app-**

adplacito, to claim 13c.

adprim/as 1267, **-o** 1537, first of all, especially.

adq-, *see* **acq-**

adr-, *see also* **arr-**

adregnio, to tether (O.F. *aresner*) c 1115.

adress/o 13c, **adrescio** c 1185, c 1270, **adrecio** 1198, 1223, to redress, restore (leg.); **-o,** to apply, put on (mortar) 1320.

adrianum, adrion', sort of drug a 1250.

adrio, (?) to array, trim (a hedge) 1297.

adrop, lead (alch.) 1144, ‡1652.

adrudo, to grunt assent 1523.

adsc-, *see* **asc-**

adsil/eo *or* **-esco,** to keep silence c 730.

adsisa, inrush of a wave of the tide c 550; *see also* ASSESS

adst-, *see* **ast-**

adstatim, adtunc, *see* **ad.**

adt-, *see* **att-**

adu, of Hades (ᾍδου) c 550.

aduber, copious c 1255.

adul, (?) plane-tree (Ar. *ad-dulb*) 12c.

adul/atio, flattery: **adolatio** c 800; **-ativus** a 1564, **-osus** 1349, **-atrix** (*f.*) c 1180, 1207, flattering; **adolator,** *for* **-ator,** c 800; **-atorie,** flatteringly c 1341, 1461.

adulter/ 1189, c 1196, **-inus** 1180, 1274, unauthorized; **-ator,** adulterer 1207; forger c 1204; **-ium,** fine for adultery 1086; (?) an adulterous pair c 1200; **-or** (*dep.*), to commit adultery c 1160, c 1448.

adultio, growing up 1344; **adolescentul/a,** young girl 12c., c 1325; **-us,** young boy c 1190, 1571; **-atio,** childish prank 15c.; **adoleo,** to grow 1376.

adumbror (*dep.*), to take umbrage, be angry c 1395.

adun/atio (†**adimatio**), union, reconciliation c 800, c 870. c 1125, c 1354; assemblage, throng 14c.; 1252, 1449, **-iatio** c 1315 gathering in (of hay); **-ate** c 870, **-atim** c 1293, singly, unitedly; **-ativus**, unitive c 1320; **-ator**, unifier c 1200; **-atrix**, uniting (*f.*) c 870; **-io** 8c., c 870. 1276, c 1488, ***-o** 8c., c 870. c 1125, 1461, to bring together, unite, reconcile; **-io** 1284, 1314, **-o (fenum)** 1251, 1302, **-o (pratum**, *etc.*) c 1257, c 1345, to gather in (hay, *etc.*).

adunc/ino c 1125, c 1250, **-o** c 1190, c 1325, to catch with a hook.

†**adurna**, (?) *f.l.* for **advena**, a 1300.

adust/io, branding 1458; firing (a lime-kiln) 1420; **-atio**, burning 14c.; **-ibilis**, combustible a 1252, 15c.; **-ivus** (†**-inus**), incendiary 1415; **-or laterum**, brick-burner c 1400; **vinum -um**, brandy 1674; **-o**, to reclaim (land) by beat-burning 1475.

advan-, *see* AVAN

advect/io, conveyance c 760; **-ivus** 1550, **-rix** (*f.*) c 1180, bringing; **-o**, to bring 1136.

advenagium, gift from the king when visiting a city 1513; *cf.* AVEN

adventagium, *see* avantagium.

adventale, *see* aventallum.

adven/tio a 1574, **-tatio** c 1306, c 1412, coming; 1379, **-tus** 1285, 15c, suit of court; ***-tus (Domini)**, Advent (eccl.) c 760. 1074, 1583; **a. vicecomitis**, sheriff's appearance at Exchequer 1225, 1332; **-tatus**, having arrived c 1250; **-tivus**, new-comer 14c.; *see also* dos; **-tura (aventura)**, knightly adventure, jousting 1233, 1419; 1353, **a. mortis** 1377, accidental death; trading venture c 1253, 1489; **a. maris** goods washed up by sea 1254, 1309; **-turarius**, *see* mercator; **-turo** 1471, **a. me** 1461, to venture; **-ienter**, by messenger a 1130; **-io**, to approach (*trans.*) c 1473; **-io ad**, to come by, get 1318, 1382.

adverb/um, *for* **-ium**, adverb 1520; **-ialis**, adverbial 790. 1271, 1381; **-ialiter**, adverbially 9c. c 1265, p 1347; **-io**, to use as adverb 1524.

advers/io, transgression 1102; disposition 1255; **-abilis**, able to be opposed 1378; **-antia**, adversity c 1325; opposition c 1380; **-ative**, in opposition c 1140; **-ativus**, opposed (to) c 1200; expressing opposition c 1344; **-ator**, opponent c 1220, c 1437; ***-itates** (*pl.*), adversities 7c. c 1250, c 1470; **-a parte**, on the other hand c 1250.

advertentia, attention c 1283, 1620.

advesper/at, *for* **-ascit**, 1041.

adviatio, approach a 1180.

advideo, to notice, observe c 1200.

advincula, *see* VINCUL

advisagium, *see* AVES

advis/atio (avis-) 1401, 1492, ***-amentum** 1295, 1686, **avizamentum** 1313, c 1458, **avisiamentum** 1321, 1461, **avisitamentum** 1461, **-us** 1324, advice, consideration; **-ator**, adviser 1422; **avisatus** (†**amsatus**), (?) aiming (of springald) 1313; **-o** 1306, 1560, **-io** 1365, 1406, **avizo** c 1305, a 1452, to advise, inspire with the intention; **-o me**, to seek advice 1305, 1505.

advoc/amen (avoc-), intercession 9c.; **-atio**, 'call', death c 796; ***c** 1160, 1583, †**adductatio** 1177, **-antia** c 1400, 1437, **-atia** c 1223, 1422, advowson (eccl.); ***c** 1115,

15c., **advoatio (G.)** c 1285, **avoatio (G.)** 1289, **avoamentum (G.)** 1293, **avoamentum (G.)** 1313, **-are** 1351, a 1400, **-aria** 1238, a 1564, **avoeria** 1181, **awoaria** 13c., **-atia** c 1110, c 1324, 'avowry', (payment for) warranty or protection (leg.); 14c., ***-aria** c 1218, 1537, **avowaria** (†**anowaria**) c 1370, 'advowry', (rent paid for) protection of new settlers on lord's demesne (W. & Marches); **-arius**, tenant in advowry (W., *etc.*) 1218, 1366; bailiff of advowry (W.) 1335;

-ata c 1170, 1272, **-atrix** c 1450, patroness (eccl.); 13c., 1434, **-atrix** c 1160, 1458, patron saint (*f.*); **-atrix**, intercessor, pleader (*f.*) c 1620; **-atus** *1160, 15c., **-ator** 1288, patron of benefice; patron of religious house c 1170, 1279; patron saint 12c., c 1245; warrantor 1086, c 1115; advocate (eccl. law) a 1245, 1684; advocate (Sc. law) 1461; **a. communis** 1301; **a. curie de Arcubus** c 1452, 1573; **a. generalis** (eccl.) 1686; **a. itinerans**, vagrant advocate 1243; **-atus** (*4th decl.*), protection c 1170, c 1194; **-atorie**, as an advocate c 1430; **-o** c 1115, 1419, **aoco** c 1138, **advoo (G.)** c 1281, c 1285, **avoo (G.)** 1283, 1289, to avouch, avow, claim, acknowledge; to vouch to warranty 1086, 1194; to appeal against (leg.) c 1115; to act as advocate (leg.) a 1245, 1684; **a. me (per)**, to avow myself (by), claim (as warranty) c 1185, c 1353; **a. a** 1166, **a. de** 1164, **a. me** (with *dat.*) (G.) 1280, to claim to hold from.

advolatio, flight, recourse 1620.

advoveo, to vow, dedicate 1461.

advunculus, *see* AVUNCUL

adzurius, *see* AZUR

ae-, *see also under* e-

ae-, *for* e-: **ae** c 834; **aecclesia** c 757, 1049. 1086, 12c.; **aecclesiasticus** 736; **aecclesiola** 1086; **aeditus** c 730; **aegregius** 939, 956; **aelemosyna** 838; **aemendo** c 850, c 868; **aepiscopus** 967, c 1000; **aepulae** 802; **aequitatus** c 730; **aequus** 822, 11c.; **aesca** c 870; **aet** 875, 11c.; **aetiam** 9c.; **aevangelicus** 11c., 12c.; **aexamen** 858.

aecr/a, **-emannus**, *see* acra.

aeisamentum, *see* AIS

aellio, a bird of prey a 1446.

aenecia, **aenescia**, *see* esnecia.

†**aen/um**, round brazen vessel (alch.) 1652; ‡**kettle** 1570; **enum**, pail c 1200; c 550, **eneus** 7c., cauldron; †**euneus** 1331, 1467, †**cenneus** 1478, brazen; **-arius**, brasier, brass-worker 1561.

aer/, (?) ceiling 1283, 1314; ‡**a. chymicus**, mixture of all the elements 1652; **-a** c 1400, a 1408, **er** c 1400, **aier** c 1380, 1415, *for* **aer**, air, weather; **-eus**, sky-blue c 1255, c 1412; *see also* **ignis, rota**; **-imantia**, divination by air c 1160, c 1260; **-eitas** a 1250, **-itas** a 1250, p 1394, **aieritas** a 1446, airiness, quality of air; **aria**, air, song c 1370.

aera, fixed number c 870.

aer/ia 1215, c 1320, **-a** c 1200, **-ium** 1212, c 1300, **ayeria** 13c., **ayerium** 1370, **aeira** 1086, **aira** 1086, 13c., **airea** 1086, 1336, **eyria** 1199, 1243, **eyra** 1219, 1305, **area**

B

1086, **aria** 1232, **eria** 1219, 1325, **erius** 1272, **heyrius** 1272, eyrie *or* brood; **-ium,** room at top of tower c 1300; **-arius** (*adj.*) 1308, 1422, **errarius** 1276, 1391, **aierarius** 1380, **-eus, -ius** 1301, 1351, nesting, breeding (of swans, *etc.*); **eyrerius** (*subst.*), nesting bird 1245; **-io** 1235, 1351, **-o** 1322, **eyero** 1381, to nest.

Aeriani (Heriani), followers of the heretic Aërius 12c.

aes-, *see also* AIS; **esnecia.**

aesnus (**†etsnus**), unfree, poor, helpless (A.S. *esne*) c 1115.

afait-, afeit-, afeys-, *see* AFFECT

affabulatio, moral attached to fable 1610.

†affalco, (?) to trespass in mowing 1280.

affaleisio, to execute by hurling over cliff (*cf.* infalisio) 1234.

affa/men 967, 1041, **-tus** 7c., 1062, address; **-tus** (*pl.*) epistolares, correspondence 1297; **-tim,** eloquently 1267; **-ta** (*pl.*), matters discussed c 1365; **-tus** (*p.p.*), narrated, aforesaid 8c. 1281.

affarium 1255, 1312, **auffarium** 1289, estate, tenement (G.).

affeagium, affedatio, *see* 1 **affidatio.**

affect/io, affection: **effectio** 1587; **-abilis,** lovable c 1250; **-ativus** p 1300, **-ivus** c 1270, 1328, **-ualis** c 1250, c 1270, **-ionalis** c 1205, a 1250, concerned with affection or volition; **-ionatus,** attached, devoted c 1350, 1684; **-anter** c 1220, **-e** c 1290, c 1410, **-u** 1414, **-ualiter** c 1283, 1555, **-ive** 796. c 1397, **†-iose** c 1254, ***-uose** c 600, c 730. a 1100, 1421, **effectuose** 1229, 1434, affectionately, passionately, earnestly; ***-uosus,** affectionate, emotional 797. c 1109, a 1452; **-uositas,** emotionality c 1109; **-ator,** pretender c 1290; **-ata malitia** malice aforethought 15c.; **-us,** pretence 546; (?) **afeitus** (**†aseitus**), 'afaite', wrought 1281; **affaitatio, afeitatio,** 'entering' (of hawks) 1243; **-o** (G.) 1243, **afaito** 1204, 1243, **afaitio** 1222, **afeitio** 1221, 1239, **afeiteio** 1235, **afieto** a 1190, **affetio** 1228, **affeto** 1250, **affatto** 1222, **afeyso** 1275, to 'enter', train (hawks or hounds); **afficior, *to** be devoted (to) c 1300, c 1453; (with *inf.*) to be disposed c 1415; **efficio,** *for* **afficio,** c 1270.

affeffamentum, feoffment c 1260.

†affenicum, "*anima*" (alch.) 1652.

affer/antum 1251, 1275, **-entum** 1254, **-amentum** 1252, 1275, sum due; **-entia** 1443, 1485, **afforamentum** c 1270, **affuramentum** 1324, **affratio** 1366, affeerment, assessment; **-ator** 1353, 1663, **affirator** 1604, **afforiator** 14c., **affurator** 1433, 1533, **affrator** 1364, affeerer, assessor of fines; **-ua,** share (O.F. *aferue*) a 1250; **-o** 1178, a 1564, **affiro** 1408, 1604, ***afforo** 1176, a 1564, **afforio** 1387, **affuro** 1319, 1451, to affeer (leg.); **afforo** 1258, 1419, **affuro** 1287, 1291, to appraise, bargain, fix prices.

affertor, importer 1492; *cf.* ALLAT

afferus, *see* 2 **averium.**

affet-, *see* AFFECT

affeuatus, feudal vassal (G.) 1289, 1433.

affibulo, to fasten c 1180, a 1275.

afficior, *see* AFFECT

1 **affid/atio** p 1245, **affedatio** 1378, lease, feu

(Sc.); **-agium** 1253, **affeagium** 1236, a feudal due (Óléron, G.).

2 **affid/atio,** (declaring on) oath c 1185, 1428; betrothal c 1375, a 1564; **-atus,** man bound by oath 1208, 1211; **†-us,** *for* **-atus,** pledged c 1160; **-o *c** 1100, c 1414, **a. me** c 1400, **a. in manum (manu)** 1136, 1467, to pledge faith, declare on oath; 1224, c 1540, **†affito** 1461, to betroth, affiance; **a. corporaliter,** to take corporal oath c 1238; **a. super,** to trust in c 1400.

affigo, *see* AFFIX

affil/acium, file (of records) 1376; ***-o,** to file (records) 1327, 1541.

affinantia, ransom 1358.

affin/atio a 1235, 1323, **-itio** c 1470, refining (of metal), refinery; **†-a,** "workhouse" 15c.; **-ator,** refiner c 1295, 1325; ***-o,** to refine (metal) a 1235, 1323.

affinitas, marching of borders c 1130; neighbourhood c 1090; **-es** (*pl.*), (?) *for* **fines,** 960.

affir-, *see also* AFFER

affirm/atio, fastening 1400; **-ativa,** affirmation c 1332, 1620; **-ative** affirmatively c 1125, c 1570; **-ativus** a 1250, 1573, **-atorius** 15c., affirmative; positive (math.) 1686; **-atura,** (?) affirmation on oath (G.) 1305; **-o,** to fasten c 1253, 1445; to establish 1461; **a. in manum,** to undertake c 1150.

affirmo 1185, c 1530, **adfirmo** c 1414, to farm out; to take at farm 1348.

affix/io, fixing on 760; c 1592, **-tio** c 1582, posting up; **†-malium** (? *for* **firmaculum**), brooch a 1200; **-o,** to fix in place c 1330; **affigo,** to propound (an opinion) 1515.

affl/ator, inspirer 10c.; **-o spiritum,** to give up the ghost c 1296.

afflict/io (bibl.), **afflixio** 13c., c 1325, pain, torment; bodily injury, mutilation c 1160, c 1200; **-us,** conflict p 1341; **-ivus,** distressing c 1334, 15c.; **affligo penam,** to inflict a penalty 14c.

affluent/er, copiously (bibl.); **-issime** c 1000; **-ius** 1090; **-issimus** 795. c 1250.

affodillus, *see* **asphodelus.**

affolia, 'offal' (of trees) 1496.

affonitrum, *see* APHRO

affor/amentum, -iator, -o, -io, *see* AFFER

afforest/atio, afforestation, putting (land) in forest status c 1310; ***-o,** to afforest c 1150, 1586.

afforis, *see* **a foris.**

afforti/amentum, strengthening, fortification c 1258, 1357; afforcement of court (leg.) 1231, 1293; **-atus** 1257, 14c., **afforsatus** c 1280, reinforced, stiffened (of cloth); **-o,** to strengthen, fortify, reinforce c 1185, 1449; to strengthen (beer) c 1296; to season (vegetables) c 1514; to compel c 1390, 1419; to violate (a woman) 1375; to afforce (a court) c 1218, c 1290; *cf.* EFFORT

affr-, *see also* 2 **averium.**

affra, *see* **astrum.**

affrai/a c 1232, 1583, **-amentum** 1388, c 1500, affray; **effraium,** scaring 1293; **effraihura,** uproar 1375; **e. ignis,** outbreak of fire 1366; **-ator (pacis)** 1371, **affreiator** 1375, brawler; **-o,** to scare, intimidate 1308, 1446; to make an affray 1539; **exfredio** (**†diffrodio**), to disturb c 1115.

affrat/io, -or, see AFFER

†**affrenatus,** draught animal 1283; (?) *cf.*
2 averium.

affrett/atio (affrect-) 1277, 1394, **-amentum**
1434, 1470, **affreightamentum** 1447,
freight, freightage; **-o,** to freight, load
(ships) 1264, 1549.

affrodillus, see **asphodelus.**

affronto, to delimit (G.) 1289.

affug/io, to run away c 1266, 1309; **-o,** to
drive away 1274, 1461; *see also* **aufugo.**

affundro, to founder (of horses) 1281.

1 affurator, borer (mine-worker) 1299.

2 affur/ator, -amentum, -o, see AFFER

afieto, see AFFECT

‡**afingea,** bacon fat 14 c.

‡**afoho,** mercury 14c.

aforis, see **a foris.**

†**africana,** (?) *f.l.* 1277; *cf.* **2 averium.**

afroniosus, see **aphroniosus.**

agaitus, see **awaita.**

‡**agal/ancia, -auda,** "plover" 15c.; *cf.*
acalantis, alanus.

‡**agallium,** rest-harrow (bot.) 1652.

agalma, statue, image c 950. 12c., c 1220;
‡1483, **algalma** 15c., **algamma** c 1230,
'high place'.

agap/e, Eucharist 6c., 7c.; love-feast a 1142,
c 1150; alms c 1302; **a. pauperum** 760;
-eta, (?) host or guest at love-feast c 1160;
lapis -is, a medicament a 1250.

agard-, see AWARD

agarecto, to hamstring 1255; *cf.* **esgarato.**

agarenno, to put (land, *etc.*) in status of
warren 1312; *cf.* WARENN

Agar/enus c 800. a 1143, a 1350, †**-tenus** 13c.,
child of Hagar, Saracen.

agaseus, "gaze-hound" 1576.

agatus, good (ἀγαθός) 1344.

agausea, magpie 12c.

agello, see **aggelo.**

agell/ulus, little field 670, c 974. c 1188;
‡**-arius,** "husbandman" 1483; ‡c 1440, 15c.,
agillarius 1397, 1519, (?) **agularius** c 1200,
hayward.

agenfri/ga (†-ca, -da), owner (A.S.) c 1115.

ag/entia 1344, c 1377, **-ere** (*subst.*) c 850,
action, activity; **-ibilis,** practicable c 1300,
c 1362; *-ibilia* (*pl.*) 1328, 1476, †**-ilia**
c 1377, *-enda* (*pl.*) 12c., 15c., business;
-enda (*pl.*) 1200, c 1400, (*f.s.*) c 730. c 1212,
c 1400, mass for the dead; **-enda** (*pl.*), legal
processes c 1115; **a. pacis,** terms of peace
c 1115; **-ens** (*subst.*), active power, agent
870. a 1250, 1542; **-o in extremis,** to be
at the point of death c 1188, c 1400; **a.**
(diem) in humanis 1361, c 1504, **a. in**
rebus humanis c 1325, to be alive; **a. vices,**
to take the place of 8c. 12c., c 1250; *cf.* ACT

ager Dominicus, the Lord's field (scrip-
tural) c 1327, 1559; *see also* **acra; agr/aria**
c 1332, **-eria** (G.) 1289, 1366, land tax or
chief rent; **-icolatus,** agriculture c 1125;
-iculosus, arable 1604; **-ister,** agricultural
1414.

agerarius, see AGGREG

agest-, see **1 agistamentum.**

ageus, see **hagios.**

aggelo (agello), to freeze a 1205.

aggelus, see ANGEL

aggener/ativus (adg-) a 1250, **-atrix** (*f.*)
a 1233, productive; **-o,** to produce 13c.

agger/, 'rig' (of land) (Sc.) 1487; **-atim,** in
heaps c 950.

aggisto, see **2 agistamentum.**

aggracilio, to thin, shrink c 1210.

aggratul/atio, pleasure, delight 9c.; congratulation, thanksgiving 12c., 1232; **-or,**
to be grateful c 1188, c 1250.

aggrav/atio, aggravating, increase, overburdening c 730, c 1000. c 1236, a 1452;
aggravation of excommunication 1342, 1545;
-amen, grievance, oppression 1275, a 1452;
-ativus a 1250, c 1257; **-atorius** 1423,
weighty, increasing weight; **-o,** to aggravate
sentence of excommunication c 1258, c 1520.

aggreg/atio, gathering together, aggregation
a 1120, 1459; ‡**-arius** (†**agerarius**), sheep-
dog 15c., 1483; **-ative,** collectively c 1362,
1378; **-ativus,** aggregative, cumulative
a 1250, p 1394; **-atum,** group of words
c 1444; **-o,** to gather together, aggregate
c 1090, 1573.

aggress/io, undertaking, tackling c 1250,
c 1336; c 1250, 1461 **-us** c 1250, 1461,
attack; **aggred/ior,** (*pass.*) to be attacked,
urged 1298, p 1446; **-io,** *for* **-ior,** c 760.

aggrunnio (adg-), to grunt assent 1523.

agia, see **athia.**

agialus, beach, shore (αἰγιαλός) c 550.

agiamentum, see AIS

agibil/is, -ia, †**agilia,** see **agentia.**

agillarius, see AGELL

agil/limus, *superl.* of **-is,** 1521.

1 *agist/amentum 1181, a 1564, **adgista-**
mentum 1321, **-iamentum** 1201, 1542,
adgistiamentum 1293, **agestiamentum**
1373, 1529, **adjestiamentum** 1604, **-atio**
1220, c 1300, **egestura** 1572, agistment of
pasturage; **-atio,** rating (of men for arms)
c 1360; **-ator** a 1190, 1329, **agestator**
c 1283, **-or** 1224, **agitor** 1224, agister, forest
official; **-o** 1184, a 1564, **adgisto** c 1293,
1335, **agesto** 1334, **adgesto** 1233, **agito**
a 1564, to agist (cattle or pasturage); **-o,** to
annex (land) 1234; to assess for taxation
c 1298, 1311; **a. (ad arma),** to rate (men)
for arms 1355, c 1360; *cf.* **gistamentum.**

2 agist/amentum, lists (for jousting) 1397;
-iamentum, raising water-level (of mill)
c 1250, 1316; **-a,** joist 1271; **-o** 1316, **-io**
c 1270, to raise level of (mill-water); to
protect (land) with dikes 1296; **-o (aggisto)**
1324, 1375, **adjesto** 1359, to build up (mill-
dam); to provide with joists 1237, 1249;
cf. **gista.**

agitat/io, driving (of cattle) 1438, 1469; **-orius,**
potent (of drug) 1634; *see also* **1 agistamen-**
tum.

ag/ius, -iographus, see **hagios.**

agn/ellus (angn-) c 1200, 15c., **-ellulus**
c 1470, **-icillus** c 1250, **-icula** 790, **-iculus**
790. c 1212, a 1275, lambkin; **-ellus** 1388,
1416, **-us,** 1200, 1257, lamb's wool; †**-ellus**
(*adj.*), of a lamb 1415; **-ellinus** 1206, c 1335,
-inus 1188, 1329, of lamb's wool; **-ellatio**
1234, 1417, **-ilatio** 1284, 1306, **-atio** 1364,
lambing; **-inus,** lamb-like 1435; **-a auri,**
agnel d'or (coin) 1341 (*see also* **florenus**);
-us Dei, hymn c 1067, 15c.; **a. Paschalis**

1368, **anulus** 1293, (wax image of) Agnus Dei; **-elo**, to lamb 1297; **-izo**, to act like a lamb 1220.

agnicium (†aguicium), tag for appending seal (O.F. *agnice*) 1268, 1290; *see also* **alnus.**

agnom/entum, surname c 1500; **-ino**, to surname c 1150, 1344.

agnosc/ibilis, recognizable 790; **-ibiliter**, recognizably c 1090; **agnitivus**, concerned with recognition c 1270; †**-o**, (?) *for* **ignosco**, to forgive c 1500.

agnus castus (bot.) c 1212, a 1350.

ago, *see* **agentia.**

agon/ c 730, 804. a 1142, c 1430, **-ia** 1345, **-ium** 960, **-izatio** 1378, ‡1483, struggle, battle; lawsuit a 1408; c 1150, c 1450, **-ia** c 1072, c 1430, agony, suffering (esp. of martyrs); (?) worship 1150; **-ista** c 1000. 1090, 1570, **-itheta** c 550. a 1100, **-ithetes** 7c. c 1250, **-otheta** 690. 12c., c 1546, spiritual athlete, leader of martyrs; **-istica**, art of combat c 1180, c 1324; **-izo** c 1090, c 1434, **-izor** c 1310, to struggle, fight; **-izo** c 730, c 900. c 1125, c 1450, **-izor** c 1075, c 1330, to suffer (martyrdom).

agr-, *see also* **ager.**

agrammat/us 8c. c 1200, ‡15c., ‡**-icus** 1483, illiterate.

*****agre/amentum** 1425, 1573, **-mentum** 1472, agreement; **-abilis**, agreeable 1457; **-o** 1411, 1573, **agrio** 1587, **-o me** 1374, 1472, to agree.

agre/dula, -cula, *see* **acredula.**

agresta, verjuice 1315, 1622.

agresticus, rustic 13c.

†**agriacus**, a shade of green a 1250.

agrimonia, acrimonia, agrimony (bot.) a 1250.

‡**agrimulatum**, tare or corncockle (bot.) 14c.

agrio, *see* **agreamentum.**

agripenna, *see* ARPEN

Agrippa, sort of unguent a 1250, 1414.

agritudo, *see* EGR

aguicium, *see* **agnicium.**

agularius, *see* AGELL

aguzorium, *see* ACU

agyrta, conjuror, mountebank 1609, 1620.

‡**ahoho**, skimmed milk 14c.

†**aicla**, (?) *f.l.* for **citula**, bucket 1317.

aier, aieritas, *see* **aer.**

aimall-, aimell-, *see* **esmallum.**

aina, eye c 550.

air/a, -ea, aierarius, *see* **aeria.**

air/ale, -iale, *see* **area.**

ais/ia (ays-) a 1120, 1208, **aesia** a 1185, 1224, **esia** 13c., *****-iamentum** 1136, 1583, **-amentum** 15c., 1583, **ayciamentum** 1272, **asiamentum** c 1187, 1567, †**agiamentum** 1301, **asyementum** 14c., **asayamentum, assaysamentum** 13c., **aiesiamentum, aiesamentum** 1573, **aeisamentum** c 1200, **aesiamentum** 1190, 1588, **eisiamentum** (eys-) 1155, 1296, **esiamentum** (hes-) c 1155, 1587, **essaiamentum** c 1270, **easiamentum** c 1556, 1582, **easimentum** 1466, easement (leg.); **-iamentum prisonum**, fee paid by prisoners (*cf.* **sueta**) 1353; **eisio**, to ease, accommodate 1277, 1300.

aisnecia, *see* **esnecia.**

aissella, *see* **2 axella.**

---

aius, *see* **hagios.**

ajorn-, *see* ADJORN

aker-, akir-, akre-, *see* **acra.**

aket/o (haket-) 1297, c 1350, **-ona, -onus** 13c., 1333, **-unus** 1271, **akedonus** c 1300, **aquito** 1322, **acoto** 1223, **acotunus** (†acotimus) 1215, **acto** c 1315, c 1322, **actona** 1327, **auketonus, auketunus** 1213, **alcato** c 1250, **alcoto** 1209, **alketonum** 1226, 'haketon', padded tunic.

akorto, *see* **accurto.**

al-, *see also* **au-**

ala *****12c., 1430, **ela** 1431, c 1450, aisle of church; aisle of barn, *etc.* c 1155, 1313; fin a 1087; **a. molendini**, sail of windmill 1287; **aletta, ailette**, shoulder-plate 1303; **alifer**, bearing (a representation of) wings c 1595; **alor**, to have wings c 1200; *see also* **ulna.**

alabastarius, *see* ARBAL

alabast/um 1369, **alabaustrum** c 1315, 1420, **alebastrum** 1442, **albestus** 12c., *for* **-rum**, alabaster; **-ricus** c 1553, **-rinus** 1365, of alabaster; ‡**-ratum** 1483, **-riculus** 1629, casket.

‡**alabr/um** 1483, 1570, **allibrum** 12c., reel, spindle; ‡**-izo**, to reel c 1440.

†**Alaceb**, title of book by Albumazar a 1233.

alacriter, with alacrity c 730. 12c., 1439.

‡**alahehi**, ceterach (bot.) 14c.

alalagma, loud noise 13c.

alamandina 1245, 1295, **alemandina** 1220, *for* **alabandina**, a gem.

alambicus, *see* **alembicus.**

alanius, forest officer, (?) derived from proper name Alan c 1178.

†**alanus**, (?) *for* **alauda**, lark 1392.

alap/a, accolade 1654; **-atio**, slap on the face 1427.

‡**alapsa**, oak-apple 14c.

alara, *see* **avalaria.**

alario, 'alerion', kind of eagle 12c., c 1160.

alaso, *see* **allecho.**

alastogia, parallel series 1344.

alathia, truth (ἀλήθεια) c 1310.

‡**alator**, "wanlassor", beater 15c.

ala/torium, -tura, *see* **alura.**

alaud/a fera, meadow pipit 1544; ‡**-arius**, hobby (bird) c 1440, 1570; *cf.* **alanus.**

alaudium, *see* **allodium.**

alausa, shad: **alosa**, kind of fish c 1200, c 1270; ‡loach or bream 15c.; *cf.* **usula.**

†**alaz**, bramble (Ar. '*olliq*) 12c.

*****alb/a** 760, 980. c 1125, 1518, **-um** c 1170, **-ula** c 1524, **auba** c 1467, c 1510, alb, vestment (eccl.); **-e** (*pl.*) c 1195, c 1265, Dominica in **-is** c 1300, 1463, Low Sunday; **-um**, dairy produce 1243, 1331; 1267, 1435, **pars -a** 1372, 15c., front of membrane; **-um varii**, white vair (fur) 1188, c 1432; **-us**, (*subst.*) small coin 1409; white bread 760. p 1147; (*adj.*) blank (of document) 1257, 15c.; of ungilt silver 1208, 1448; blanched (of money) 1086, 1297; *see also* **allec, auxilium, canonicus, corium, ferrum, 2 firma, fumus, 2 mina, monachus, monialis, ordo, panis, Pascha, plumbum, pulvis, redditus, religio, sal, scissor, spina, 2 stagnum, vinum;**

†-amentum, fair complexion c 730; -anellus, a bird of prey c 1160; ‡-aras, *morfea alba* (med.) 14c.; ‡arsenic 1652; -ardeola, spoonbill (bird) 1544; -atio c 1365, -efactio 1520, whitening; c 1392, c 1470, -ificatio 1465, whitewashing; tawing c 1300; -ator coriorum, whittawyer c 1290; -atus, dressed in baptismal garments c 730, 790. a 1155, 1414; -edo *c 1000. c 1200, c 1480, -itudo c 1180, -or c 550. a 1350, whiteness; whitening c 1400; dairy produce 1325; white of egg c 1450; ‡white of eye 15 c.; -ugo, cataract (med.) c 1280, ‡14c.; a. ovi, white of egg a 1250, a 1446; -ugineus, *see* humor; -eus c 550, -ifluus 804, white; ‡-or, urine, -anum, *sal urine*, 1652; †-ula (? *for* hastula) regia, woodruff (bot.) a 1150; -urnus, shining 685; -urnum 1237, 1244, auburnum 1236, 1239, aubournum 1319, kind of wood (Fr. *aubour*); -urneus c 1191, auburneus 1297, 1300, aburneus, eburneus 1327, made of *aubour*; -ifico, to taw (leather) 1284, 1313; c 1215, c 1470, -efacio a 1270, c 1320, to make silver (alch.); 13c, a 1446, -o 690, to whiten; -o, to blanch, pay in blanched silver 1227, 1275.
albal-, *see* ARBAL
alb/anus c 1130, -inus 1333, (?) -anarius 1307, outsider, alien; -ania 1376, -anaria 1384, *aubaine*, payment by alien serf for right to reside on manor.
Alban/us a 1155, c 1360, -icus c 1210, Scot; -ice, in Gaelic 14c.
albareda, *see* ARBOR
‡**alb/ederagi**, columbine (or other plant) 14c.; ‡-atorium, southernwood 15c.
†**albeolus, alveolus**, atheling a 1142.
alberg/ades, -agia, -amentum, -ata, -o, *see* herbergagium.
alberg/ellus, -etum, -us, *see* HAUBER
‡**alberus**, *staphis agria* (bot.) 1652.
‡**albe/sardi** 14c., **-tud** 1652, *galbanum* (bot.).
albesterium, *see* arbalista.
‡**albest/os** 1652, **-us** c 1200, **-on** 1220, a 1250, **-is** c 1315, asbestos; *cf.* ALABAST
albetum, *see* alpha.
Albi/gensis c 1212, c 1250, **-ensis** c 1212, **-us** (*met. grat.*) 1252, **Abigeus** 13c., **Ambigensis** 1274, Albigensian heretic.
albilaki, dragagantum, sort of vitriol 13c.
albinus, *see* albanus.
Albio, Briton a 1275.
albion, sort of planisphere (astr.) 1326, c 1395.
albisterium, name of a building in Rome c 1315.
‡**albo/tim, -tai** 1652, ‡-cyn 14c., (?) **albutium** a 1250, (?) **botam** 12c., terebinth (Ar. *al-botham*).
albubit, alcabrick, *see* alkibric.
albus, *see* ALB
alcald/us 1311, 1331, **-is** 1388, **alcadus** c 1322, c 1394, **escaldus** (†escabinus) 1309, constable, *alcalde* (Sp.).
alcalisatus, alchaloim, *see* alkali.
alcanna, henna c 1250, 1538; guayacum 1652.
alcassinum, coarse silk a 1100.
alcato, *see* aketo.
‡**alchazanon**, ‡**abesamum**, "*lutum rotae fabrorum*" 1652.

alchim/ia 1144, 1620, **alkimia** a 1200, c 1270, **alkemonia** 1329, **alkomia** c 1395, alchemy; -ista c 1320, 1620, **alkimista** 13c., c 1270, **alkemista** a 1235, **alchemista** a 1252, 1564, **alkimicus** c 1270, 1378, alchemist; **alkimicus** c 1270, **alzimicus** a 1250, †**alkumitus** c 1501, -isticus a 1350, **alkimisticus** 1267, 1550, alchemical; -istice, alchemically c 1260.
alchimilla, lady's mantle (bot.) 1632; ‡sanicle 1652.
alchiticus, *see* ASCIT
alchitram, *see* kitran.
alchorismus, *see* algorismus.
alcinoe, *see* Alcyonite.
1 ‡**alcohol** 14c., 1652, **alcofol** a 1250, kohl, antimony, stibium; ‡**alcol/**, fine powder 1652; ‡-ismus, pulverization 1652.
2 ‡**alcohol (vini), alcol**, alcohol, tartar 1652.
‡**alcon**, cuckoo-pint (or other plant) 14c.
Alcoran/ c 1144, **-um** c 1270, 1528, **Alchoram** 12c., **Alkeron'** 1443, Koran.
alcotar c 1215, ‡**alcore** 1652, sort of stone (alch.).
alcoto, *see* aketo.
†**alcubd** 1652, †**acub** 14c., butter (Ar.).
alcufar, *see* CAPPAR
Alc/yonite dies (*pl.*), halcyon days c 1160; -inoe, *for* -yon, kingfisher c 1200; ‡halcyonium, "*spuma maris concreta*" 1652.
aldea, village (Sp.) 1282.
aldermann/us (?) c 1000. c 1115, 13c., **ealdormannus** c 1170, ealdorman, nobleman; head of guild 1130, 1541; official of hundred or county c 1115, 1275; *a 1123, c 1553, **aldremannus** c 1170, 1382, **alremannus** 1428, **aldirmannus** (Sc.) 1329, 1399, **aldormannus** c 1170, alderman, borough official; **a. hospitalis** 1447; **a. regis** c 1115; -atus 1274, -ia 1217, c 1397, -eria 1198, p 1330, -ria c 1193, 1423, **aldemaneria** c 1265, **aldremaneria** 1281, **aldremanria** 1382, **alremaria** 1283, office of (or ward governed by) borough alderman.
aldio, semi-servile vassal (Lombard) a 1446.
alea, *see* aleya; allium.
ale/alis, of dice c 1170; -atrix, dice-player (*f.*) c 1170; ‡-ola, small die 1483.
alebastrum, *see* ALABAST
alebrot, *see* alembrottus.
alect/or (allect-), cock 8c.; -ricius, -rius, *for* -orius, kind of gem a 1250.
alemanda, *see* AMYGD
alemandina, *see* alamandina.
Aleman/icus 12c., 1456, **-us** 9c. 12c., c 1265, **Almannus** 1336, Almain, German.
alembic/us, -um c 1215, 1620, **alambicus** a 1250, alembic.
alembrottus a 1235, **sal alebrot** c 1215, ‡**alembroth, allabrot** 1652, chloride of mercury and ammonium (alch.).
†**alenaceraris**, (?) *f.l.* for veltrarius, c 1300.
alenat/ius, -icus, *see* anelacius.
alenzco, *see* allecho.
aleph, Hebrew letter a 1200.
aleria, *see* ALIER
alesta, *see* aresta.
aletafur, a resinous tree (Ar.) 12c.
aletta, *see* ala.
alevoso, traitor (Sp.) 1177.

‡alexand/er 14c., -rum 15c., alexanders (bot.). ‡lignum -rinum, brasil wood c 1440; see also burdis.

alexanthi, see alos.

‡Alexinus, panis, biscuit 15c.

alexir, see elixir.

ale/ya (-ia) 1238, 1440, -ium 1404, -a 1237, 1574, alley, passage.

alf-, see also ALPH

†alfagi, agnus castus (bot.) 14c.

alfarsungi, see asparagus.

alfebordum, see halva.

‡alfefe, disease of tongue 14c.

‡alfefur, (?) white bryony (bot.) 14c.

alferezia, office of standard-bearer (Sp.) 1254.

alfetum, ordeal kettle c 1115.

alf/inus (alph-) c 1280, ‡1483, -ilus c 1280, -icus a 1200, 15c., 'alfin', bishop (in chess).

alga, see alveus.

algalma, algamma, see agalma.

algare, (?) hollow, cave (cf. Sp. algar) (G.) 1289.

algasullus, alguazil (Sp.) c 1394.

‡algebra, restorative 14c., 1483.

alge/ma c 1000, †-va 974 (12c.), pain (ἄλγημα); ‡-nia, "cold ache" 15c.

alge/us, -a, see alveus.

algoris/mus c 1225, c 1409, augorismus 1274, alchorismus a 1150, opus -ticum 1267, 'augrim', Arabic notation (math.).

Alhigera c 1150, Alligera 1184, c 1270, Hegira, Hijra.

alias, otherwise called c 1306, 1531; to another lord 1086; name of a writ a 1452.

alice, see alyce.

alicitor, see haliaëtus.

alicotus, see ALIQU

alictarius, see ALUT

alie/nitas c 1290, c 1362, *-tas a 1233, 1499, otherness; -nator, one who alienates (property), grantor c 1290, c 1315; †-gina 1241, 1483, †aligenigena 1041, †ablienigena c 1290, for -nigena, alien; -niloquium, allegory c 1182; -no, to alienate (person from property) 13c.; a. (de pena), to exempt c 1285; a. loquelam, to vary plea (leg.) 1220.

alier/a, -us 1225, 1263, aleria 1263, (?) hawthorn (cf. Fr. alisier, O.F. alier, service-tree).

alietus, see haliaëtus.

alifer, see ala.

alimanda, see AMYGD

aliment/atio, nourishment, sustenance 1457, 1622; -abilis, susceptible of nourishment 1622; alimonia, alimony (allowed to wife) 1684; a. ecclesie 1126; -o 1620, 1684, †aliemento 1513, to nourish; cf. alumnus.

alimino, see ILLUMIN

alipta, (?) ointment a 1250.

aliqu/itas, 'somethingness', essence (log.) p 1300, 1427; *-alis a 1230, 1686, -imodus 1485, of some or any sort; -aliscumque, of whatever sort c 1370; -aliter, in some or any way a 1250, 1494; -antillulum, a very little c 1470; -antillulus, very little c 1470; -antisper, to some extent c 1180; -ilibet, some, any c 1250; -is quam, anyone other than c 1341; uno -o die, once upon a time c 1212; -osculos (acc. pl.), a few c 1370; -orsum, in some direction c 1125, c 1225;

-ota (alicota) pars, aliquot part (math.) a 1233, c 1430; -ota, a certain amount c 1470; -otiens, at any time c 1170.

alisma, primrose or cowslip 1634.

alitilia, see altile.

ali/us, *for alter, the other (of two) 1086, 1464; -us a, different from 11c. c 1516; -ubi, to another master 1086; alubi, elsewhere 1461; -unde, for another reason 1200; otherwise, about other things c 1218, c 1400.

aliva, see alura.

aliwerus, see HAUBER

alkakengi, alkekengi, winter cherry (bot.) 1538.

alkal/i (sal a.) c 1215, ‡1652, -e 1418, alchaloim, alzali a 1250, alkali; ‡chali, lye 14c.; ‡amnis alcalisatus, river flowing through limestone 1652.

‡alkel, juniper fruit 14c.; cf. arceuthis.

Alkeron', see Alcoran.

alketonum, see aketo.

‡alkibric, alcabrick, abric, etc. 1652, alzebric 1144, †albubit a 1250, sulphur (Ar. al-kibrit); cf. Gabricus.

alkien, a secret potency (alch.) c 1320.

‡alkiffil, ‡alpin, rosemary (bot.) 14c.

alkim-, see also ALCHIM

allacrimor, to weep over c 1190.

allacto, see ALLECT

allai/a, -um c 1280, 1534, eslaium 1280, aluvia 1245, alloy; -atio, alloying p 1280; -ator, alloyer p 1280; -o, to alloy p 1280, 1295; cf. 3 lega.

allambo, to wash or lap against (of a lake or river) c 1170.

allapo, see ALLOP

allaqueo, to snare 14c.

allater/alis, companion c 1188; -o, to be beside c 1130, c 1400; -or, to support, approve p 1127.

allat/io, conveying, bringing 12c., 1267; -ivus, for bringing a 1452; -or, bringer c 1250; contributor c 1365.

allea, see allium.

alleaster, (?) for oleaster, kind of tree 1292.

*allec/ (halec-) 1086, 1587, allic 1298, *-ia, -ium 1086, 1419, -a (G.) 1242, herring; a. album, herring prepared in stock 1309, 1550; a. rubeum 1284, 1490, a. rufum 1230, 1250, a. sorum 1297, 1534, red herring; a. poudrum, salt herring 1390; a. siccum, dried herring a 1100, 1334; a. viride, fresh herring 1288; a. plenum 1394, 1550, a. vacuum 1463, 1550, herring with or without roe; ‡-ula 1570, halicula 1565, pilchard.

allecho (C.I.) 1331, alaso 1268, alenzco 1241, allencella 1263, cog of a wheel.

allect-, see also ALECT

allect/io c 1109, c 1340, -orium c 1204, c 1220, allicientia a 1349, enticement, inducement; -icius 1348, -ivus a 1100, c 1450, enticing; allacto, to entice 1461.

‡allefias, fleabane (bot.) 14c.

allegantia, see ALLIG

1 *alleg/atio, allegation, charge c 1100, 1684; -abilis, adducible a 1300, 1610; -ans c 1341, 1684, -ator c 1341, one who alleges or adduces proof; -atrix, urging (f.) c 1125;

-ative, by way of proof c 1343; **adlego,** to depute as helper c 730; **-o,** to bequeath 1414; **a. forum,** to allege the court (leg.) c 1200.

2 **alleg/atio, -iatio (adleg-),** oath of clearance c 1115; **-io,** to admit as accuser c 1115; to clear by oath or ordeal c 1115.

allegiantia, allegiance 1630; *cf.* **alligantia.**

allegor/ia, allegory c 870. a 1090, c 1500; **-icus,** allegorical c 730. a 1090, p 1380; **-ice,** allegorically 780. a 1090, c 1343; **-izo,** to speak in allegories 1144, 1427.

allelui/a (hal-), versicle in the mass 12c.; wood sorrel (bot.) ‡14c., 1629; **a. clausum,** Septuagesima Sunday c 1290; **-aticus,** of Alleluias, triumphal 8c. c 1125, 1345.

allencella, *see* **allecho.**

allenetum, *see* ALN

alleo/sis 1552, **-theta** (? *for* **-tica)** c 1363, alteration (figure of speech).

allerectum, *see* **holus.**

allerium, *see* **alura.**

alleum, alletum, *see* **allium; 2 aula.**

alleur/atio, allurement (falc.) 1333; **-o,** to allure (falc.) 1333.

allev/iatio c 1103, 1508, **-atio** 1511, 1549, **-iamen** c 1450, **-amen** a 1130, **-iatorium** 1375, lifting, lightening, relief; **a. prisone** 1358; **-iamentum,** relief, pardon c 1125; lighterage, unloading due (naut.) 1205; **-abilis,** leviable 1479; **-ativus,** tending to lift or lighten a 1250; **-io,** to lighten (bibl.); to unload c 1289; to lift hay from 1279; to levy (troops) 1346; **-o,** to levy (fine, *etc.*) 1230, 1425; to set up (a commune) 1234.

alliatus, *see* **allium.**

allibrum, *see* **alabrum.**

allic, *see* **allec.**

allicientia, *see* ALLECT

allidada (hall-), alidade, sighting-rod (astr.) 1326, a 1350.

allig/atio, braid, twist of hair 793; c 1105, 12c., **-antia** 1356, compact, bond; c 1360, p 1377, **-antia** 1337, 1441, alliance; c 1321, 1419, **-antia** 1345, 1377, **allegantia** 1357, 1588, conspiracy, maintenance; 1331, **-antia** 1325, 1430, marriage tie; †**allingantia,** faction, followers (*coll.*) 1215; **-amentum** bond 690; c 1212, **-atura** c 1180, ligature, tying on (as amulet); **-anter,** in alliance 1405; **-atus,** confederate, ally c 1300, 1508; **-o,** to ally c 1320, c 1362; to moor, make fast (*intr.*) c 1337; to impose (a burden) c 1250; *cf.* ALLEG, **allegiantia.**

Alligera, *see* **Alhigera.**

alliotinus, *see* **gluta.**

allipias, *see* **alypias.**

allis/io, dashing down, stroke 9c. a 1100, 14c.; **-us,** unleavened (O.F. *alis*) (G.) 1312.

‡**allistrigium,** mease of herring 1483.

†**allito,** (?) *for* **alligo,** to land or moor c 1125.

all/ium, garlic: **-eum** 1224, c 1423, **-ea (alea)** c 1100, c 1358; **-iaria,** garlic mustard (bot.) 1538; ‡**-earius,** garlic-seller 1483; **-iata,** food seasoned with garlic c 1200, a 1250; **-iatus,** garlic-seasoned 1620.

alloc/atio, hiring 1294, 1424; *1221, 1565, **allogatio** c 1449, **-antia** 1290, 1576, **allowantia** 1400, **-amentum** 1225, c 1285, **-atum** 1425, allowance (in accounts); **-abilis,** allowable c 1290, 1502; **-abilitas,**

allowability c 1376; **-abiliter,** allowably c 1450; **-ate,** name of a writ 1257, 1296; **-atorius,** of allowance 1435; **-atus,** lieutenant, deputy (C.I.) 1274; **-o,** to stow 1234, 1243; to let or hire 1253, 1427; *1196, c 1546, **allogo** c 1449, to allow (in accounts); to credit (with personal *obj.*) 1338, 1523; to allow, uphold (leg.) 1202, 1583.

allocutus, questioned 1309, c 1400; impleaded, accused 1292, 15c.

*allod/ium c 1080, 1362, -ia 1086, alaudium 1608, a. francum (G.) c 1305, 'allod', freehold, (land held by) allodial tenure; **-ialis,** allodial 1608; **-iarius** 1086, 1414, **-arius** 1086, 15c., **aloarius** 1086, **-is** 1608, freeholder; *see also* **lodium.**

allog-, *see also* ALLOC

allogi/amentum, (right of) lodging 1511; **-atus,** encamped 14c.

allogium, (?) *for* **elogium,** compliment 14c.

allop/iamentum, abduction 1277; **-o** c 1218, 1365, **-io** 1301, 1384, **allapo** 1380, †**allocpo** 14c., to entice away, abduct, seduce; *cf.* **elopo.**

alloppo, to lop (branches) 1539.

†**allotay,** sal ammoniac a 1250.

allotto, to allot c 1443, a 1564.

allouo, to please, satisfy 1214.

alloveria, wallet, pouch (O.F. *aloiere*) c 1290.

allowantia, *see* ALLOC

all/ox 690, **-ux** 1267, ‡1483, *for* **-ex** *or* **-us,** thumb *or* big toe.

allu/sio, ‡dalliance 1570; allusion, hint 8c.; sport c 1125; **-do,** to cover (of animals) c 1115; to allude, refer c 1341, 1424.

allut-, *see* ALUT

alluvio, an increase 12c.

alma, *see* **alva.**

†**almachor (†almothec), †amach/es, -el** sea-eagle a 1250; *cf.* **haliaëtus.**

Alm/agesti a 1200, 1439, **-ajesti** c 1150, **-ogesta** c 1565, Ptolemy's *Almagest.*

almagre, red ochre *or* brass (alch.) 1144, ‡1652.

almagrip, almeri, points of the astrolabe c 1110; **almuri,** 'almury', indicator of instrument (astr.) a 1350.

‡**alma/har** 14c., ‡**almarchaz** 1652, litharge.

almal, *see* **animal.**

alman/ach 1267, **-ac** c 1553, almanac.

almar-, *see* ARMARI; ELEEMOSYN

almatica, *see* **dalmatica.**

almeri, *see* **almagrip.**

†**almericum,** (?) some article associated with siege engines 14c.

almici/a, -um, *see* ALMUCI

almi/tas, benignity (title) 793. c 1125; **-fer** c 1090, **-ficus** c 1000. c 1090, 1418, **-fluus** 970. c 1090, c 1423, **-volus** 7c., c 800, gracious, beneficent; **-para,** gracious mother c 1250; **-pater,** gracious Father c 800; **-phonus** c 1258, c 1414, **-sonus** c 750, gracious-sounding; **-potens,** gracious in might 7c., c 800.

‡**almi/zadar, amizadar,** sal ammoniac 1652; **-zadir,** (?) sal ammoniac 1144; ‡**verdigris** 1652.

almon-, almor-, *see* ARMARI; ELEEMOSYN

almucabola, algebra, equation (Ar. = 'off-setting') 1145.

almuchantarath, almicanterath, almu-
cantar, celestial latitude (astr.) 1326.
almuci/a, -um c 1230, 1453, almici/a, -um
1277, 1523, almusia 1406, aumucia 1331,
amucia c 1230, c 1336, amusium 1400,
amicia c 1360, amisia 1397, 1517, almuce,
fur hood; see also amictus.
almuri, see almagrip.
almustakim, equinoctial circle a 1200.
almuthemen, desired quantity (math.) (Ar.
al-muthamman) 1145.
almuzarar, unit of measurement (math.)
(Ar. al-musa-'ir) 1145.
aln/a, -o, see ulna.
alnacius, see anelacius.
†alner/ia, -ium (? alver-) 1332, -um 1300,
(?) surcoat or tabard.
aln/us nigra, buckthorn 1634; -etum 1086,
1587, -eta 1279, allenetum 1278, aunetum
c 1135, c 1400, augnetum 1250, agnicium
a 1222, alder grove; -etum, alder timber
1317, 1377; -eta 1307, -ea 1287, alder tree;
aniceus, of alder c 1393.
aloarius, see ALLOD
alo/e, aloe (bot.): -a a 1250, -xis 12c.; -e
Cicotrinum, Socotra aloe 1307; a. citrinum 1414.
alog/a (pl.), irregularities a 1200; -icus,
illogical c 1620.
aloigna, wormwood (O.F. aloigne) c 1290.
†alon/azontes, †-axdi (pl.), monks (? for
μονάζοντες, μόναχοι) a 1142.
alop/icia (all-) c 1248, 1468, -edes c 1200,
-ides a 1250, for -ecia, disease of hair,
sporadic (partial) baldness; -ecurinus,
-ecuroides, fox-tail grass 1634.
alor, see ala.
‡alos/, alo, salt (ἅλς) (alch.) 14c., 1652;
†-anthos (alexanthi), flos salis 1652.
alosa, see alausa.
alotatus, see ALUT
aloxis, see aloe.
alpha/, letter alpha 8c.; -betum (eccl.),
-beticus 1555, †albetum c 730, alphabet; instruction c 1436; -betarius, alphabetic 1564.
alphachinus, alfaqui, expounder of Islamic
law c 1190.
alpheus, see alveus.
alphita, barley meal a 1250, ‡c 1440.
alph/us (alf-), morphew, skin disease a 1250,
‡14c.; -icus, (?) leper (fig.) c 1250; -isca-
biosus, afflicted with white scab a 1250;
‡-oleucas, white morphew 14c.; †-ueme-
las, black morphew 14c.; see also ALF
‡alpin, see alkiffil.
alre/mannus, -maria, see aldermannus.
alszarar, price per unit (math.) (Ar. al-si'r)
1145.
alta nutrix, see assassinus.
altaraxacon, see taraxacon.
*alt/are (eccl.), *-arium (eccl.), -ar c 950,
-aria 1537, altar; a. annuale, (?) altar used
for anniversary masses 1409; a. authenticum c 1330, 1556, *a. magnum c 1190,
1537, a. majus c 1330, 15c., a summum
13c., c 1530, high altar; a. matutinale, morning altar (for ferial celebrations) c 1433;
*a. portatile, portable altar c 1308, 1518;
-ariolum, little altar c 1250, c 1440; -are
c 1185, -aria (n. pl.) 1289, *-aragium

c 1190, 1532, *-eragium c 1230, 1575,
-eriagium 1228, -alagium 1217, 1279,
-elagium p 1200, 1300, autelagium 13c.,
-ilagium 1285, 1311, 'altarage', altar-dues;
-arista, acolyte, attendant at altar c 1250,
c 1520.
alter/, for uter, either 1240, c 1310; a. gradus,
'other ranks' 15c.; a. melior, second-best
1279; -itas, otherness, difference 870.
a 1200, 1344; c 1180, c 1200, *-atio c 1160,
1622, alteration; -abilis, alterable c 1200,
1622; -abiliter, so as to be alterable 1344;
-ativus, alterative, producing change a 1250,
1622; -ative, by way of alteration c 1367;
-iusmodi 1266, altrimodus c 1160, of
another kind; -utrum, mutually (bibl.);
*-o a 1100, 1620, -utro c 1170, to alter,
change; -utro, to interchange c 1200.
altercamen, dispute c 550.
altern/atio: sub -atione, *alternatively (of
attorneys, etc.) 1253, a 1452; 1296, *-atim
1226, c 1500, interchangeably (of seals
appended to indentures); -atim, *alternately, by turns 760, c 1000. c 1125, 1584;
mutually c 1115, c 1390; -alis, of one from
another c 1115; -ativa, alternative, choice
1527.
althemen, amount to be expended (math.)
(Ar. al-thaman) 1145.
altil/e, fatling, capon (bibl.); -is, cock c 1200;
alitilia (pl.), poultry c 1443.
alt/itudo, exalted rank 1093; altitude (astr.)
1267; -itudines (pl.), lofty themes 1285;
-itudinalis, of altitude c 1360; -iduplex
(festum), solemn c 1330; -iger, high-
placed 7c.; -iloquus, grandiloquent c 1250,
c 1540; -imetria, measurement of height
12c.; -ipetax, soaring 9c.; -ipotentia,
exalted power 1327, 1461; -ithronus 8c.,
935. c 1414, a 1520, -itonans c 1180, 1262,
divine epithets; -ivagus, high-moving
c 1015;
-us, high (of price) 1086, 15c.; see also
2 caminus, curia, dies, filum, jurisdictio, justitia, manus, missa, patria,
proditio, ripa, socagium, strata, via,
vicus; -e, in -o, aloud c 1072; -e et basse
1256, 1454, -o et basso 1293, 1315, ad -um
et bassum c 1306, de -o et (de) basso
1266, c 1450, in -o et (in) basso c 1377,
a 1564, in basso et in -o 1490, totally; ad
-ius, at the highest (dearest) c 1200; -issi-
mus, the Most High a 1180, 1545; -isono,
to sound loudly c 1180; -itono, to fulminate
c 1180, 1427; -o, to exalt c 1125, 1331; -ioro,
to heighten 1184.
alubi, see alius.
‡alucium, drain c 1200, 1483.
aluctor, see haliaëtus.
aludellum c 1345, ‡alutel 1652, 'aludel'
sort of vessel (alch.).
‡alumbis, a water-bird (? κολυμβίς) c 1200.
alum/en, alum: -a c 1226, 1304, -inum 1303,
†-pinum 1267; a. Jammenum c 1215,
‡1652, ‡a. janem' 14c.; a. de pluma
c 1215, ‡14c., a. de plume 1317, ‡a.
plumosum 1652, plume alum; a. de rocco
c 1215, ‡a. roccum 1652, roche alum;
a. rotundum c 1270, ‡1652; a. rubeum
c 1215, a. rubrum a 1235; a. scissibile

c 1270, **a. scissum** a 1250, ‡14c.; **a. zucharinum** c 1215, ‡14c., **a. zuccherinum** a 1235, ‡**a. zacharinum** 1652; **aqua -inosa** a 1250; **-pniosus,** clayey c 1200.

alum/inator, -pnatio, *see* ILLUMIN

alumn/us (alumpn-), ward, foster-child c 1285, c 1481; foster-father, patron 1428, c 1470; **-a,** foster-mother c 1250, c 1470; †**-ia,** female ward c 1290; **-atio,** rearing, breed c 1470; ‡**-aria,** nursery 1483; **-ia,** sustenance (of poor) 1221; **-ulus,** little disciple c 1000. c 1184; *cf.* ALIMENT

*****alur/a** 1188, c 1488, †**aliva** 1266, **alatura** 1320, **alatorium** (Norm.) 1091, **allerium** 1241, 'alure', rampart-walk; **-atio,** making an alure 1343.

alut/a (allut-) 1252, 1419, **-um** 1225, 1309, tawed leather; **-um album, a. nigrum** 1365; *****-arius** c 1220, 1506, †**-a** 1274, †**alictarius** c 1294, c 1400, †**ablutarius** 1294, leather-dresser, tawyer; **-oria,** tawyers' quarter 1354; **-us** 1304, (?) **alotatus** c 1180, tawed.

aluvia, *see* allaia.

alva 1191, 1213, †**alma** 1220, saddle-flap; *see also* **alveus.**

alver-, *see* ALNER

alv/eus (-ius), trough: **alpheus** 1324, **-ea** 1297, **alwea** 1270, **algea** 1295, c 1450, **augea** 1280, **alga** c 1160, 1345, **auga** c 1240, 1266; **-eus,** fuller's trough 1337; **a. vini** 1233; **-us** 1209, **-a** 1312, **algeus** 1209, 1324, **algea** 1312, 1323, **augea** 1237, 1443, trough of water-mill; **-eus** c 1232, 1325, **auga** 13c., boat, barge; **-eolus,** shield (her.) 1654; **a. apum** c 1110, **-eare apum** 1304, bee-hive; *see also* **albeolus.**

alyc/e (alice) 13c., c 1250, **-is** a 1250, tossing about, distress (ἀλύκη, ἄλυσις).

alypias (allipias), anodyne, (?) spurge laurel (bot.) a 1250, ‡14c.

alzali, *see* alkali.

alzebric, *see* alkibric.

alzimicus, *see* ALCHIM

amach/es, -el, *see* almachor.

amalgam/a c 1345, c 1470, **amalagma** 1622, ‡**asmaga** 1652, amalgam (alch.); ‡**-atio,** calcination by means of mercury 1652.

amal/um, -ium, -lo, *see* esmallum.

am/amen, affection c 1200; ‡love-gift c 1440; **-abo** (*interj.*), please! c 1219; **-asia** c 1212, 1570, **-azia** 1411, sweetheart, mistress; **-ativus,** of or for loving, affectionate 1267, 1412; **-ativitas** (? **-ativitas**), capacity for love 1344; **-or,** compromise (leg.) c 1115; *see also* **dies, pro; -orosus,** amorous p 1327, a 1446.

amanda, *see* AMYGD

aman/s, diamond, lodestone c 1250, 1272; ‡**-divus,** gem of varied colour 1652; *cf.* ADAM, alamandina.

amarallus, *see* admiralius.

amar/auda, -illus, *see* smaragdo.

amarco, *see* amurcalis.

amarellus, kind of water-fowl 15c.

amar/itudines (*pl.*), bitter herbs 8c.; **-icatio** 9c. 12c., c 1320, †**-iscatio** a 1250, **-icatus** (†**-itatus**) 1284, **-ulentia** 1517, embitterment, bitterness; **-efactus,** embittered c 1250; **-esco,** to grow bitter c 1340, c 1362; *****-ico** (†**-ito**), to embitter (bibl.).

amartus, *see* hamartus.

amar/usca 1296, ‡14c., **-oca** 1315, **-ocus** 1306, (?) *for* **-acus,** may-weed (bot.).

amasso, (?) to incorporate c 1215.

amatis, *see* amiantus.

amatista, *see* amethystus.

amaubragium, *see* AMOBR

†**amazus,** (?) *f.l.* for **amarus,** c 1422.

amba, part of a mill 1232.

ambades (*pl.*), some animal used as food (? *for* **anates**) c 1286.

ambages (*pl.*), recesses c 1390.

ambanum 1276, 1315, **enbannum** 1289, **inbannum** 1284, market-stall *or* (?) barrier (G.) (*cf.* O.F. *embanie*).

ambarata, suburbs, environs (G.) 1254.

ambass/ata 1340, 1408, **-ada** (†**-anda**) 1461, **ambaciata** 1406, **-iata** 1388, 1476, **ambascata** 1395, **ambaxiata** (Sc.) 1400, 1485, **-iatum** 1491, **-iatus** 1345, 1477, **ambascia** c 1422, **-iatio** c 1250, **-iatria** 1399, 15c., embassy; **-ator** 1297, 1461, *****-iator** 1333, 1487, **ambaciator** 1406, 1467, **ambasciator** 1408, **ambaxator** c 1430, **ambaxiator** 1370, 1485, **embassator** 1318, **embassiator** (en-) c 1450, c 1494, **bassator** p 1341, ambassador; **-atorius** p 1341, **imbassatorius** a 1470, **inbasciatrix** (*f.*) 15c., ambassadorial; **-io,** to send on an embassy 1413.

ambelerius, *see* AMBUL

ambi/dexter, ambidextrous 790. a 1164, 1395; taking fees from both sides (leg.) c 1258, a 1564; **-dextria,** taking of fees from both sides 1357, 1460; **-dextraliter,** equivocally 1427; **-levus** a 1164, **-sinister** c 1197, c 1430, doubly left-handed; **-gena,** hybrid 1164; †**-gua** (? *for* **-gena**), ewe bearing two lambs 15c.; **-go,** to speak ambiguously c 1300, c 1444; *see also* **abigeus.**

Ambigensis, *see* Albigensis.

ambilatio, (?) wearing of an amulet 13c.

ambi/tiones (*pl.*), pomps, displays 7c.; **-tiositas,** ambition, ostentation 1472; **-tatio,** courting, coveting c 1283; **-o,** to commit (a sin) c 1120; to concede (a right) c 1115.

ambo, pulpit or lectern c 1006. a 1142, c 1550.

1 **ambra** (†**manbra**), 'amber', measure (of salt or ale) 832. 1086, 1285.

2 **ambr/a** c 1200, ‡14c., **a. grisia** 1622, **-egrisea** 1620, 1626, ambergris, spermaceti; **-a** c 1250, 1313, **-um** 1415, 1504, **aumbrum** c 1411, **lambra** 1349, ‡14c., (?) **lambrum** 1295, amber; **a. orientalis,** (?) ambergris or liquidambar 1307; *see also* **pomum.**

ambra/chion 12c., **-thion** 13c., shrub.

ambro/, spendthrift, glutton 6c., 8c. c 1147, c 1250; ‡**-ninus,** gluttonous, lecherous c 1440, c 1483.

ambrogium, *see* amobragium.

ambrosciatim, on ambrosia, luxuriously c 990.

Ambrosianum, hymn-book c 1330.

ambul/acrum 1530, 1539, **-atura** 1531, **-atorium** 1241, 1535, covered walk, ambulatory; **-abiles** (*pl.*), walking animals a 1200; **-ans** c 1264, 1428, **ambolans** 1378, **-aris** 1425, **ambelerius** 1401, ambling (of horses); **-ata** (*n. pl.*), beaten bounds 1320; **-atio,** beating the bounds c 1258, 1300; **-ator**

nocturnus, 'night-walker', prowler 1389;
-atorius, variable, adjustable (of tithes)
1264; †-us, (?) for ambitus, circuit, compass 1209.
amb/urbala (n. pl.), (?) for -urbium or
-arvalia, expiatory procession 12c.
†amb/us (ex -a parte), for uterque, c 1115.
ambutto, see ABUTT
amelior/atio, amelioration c 1250; -o, to
ameliorate c 1342.
amell-, see esmallum.
amend-, see EMEND
amenerium, see ELEEMOSYN
amensur/atio (adm-), *measuring, assessing
1227, 1378; (?) assessed rent 1356; a. dotis
1196, 15c., -amentum dotis 1203, assessment of dower; a. pasture 1238, c 1400;
-ator, assessor, affeerer 1230; *-o, to
measure, assess a 1100, 1419; a. dotem
1201, 1287; a. pasturam 15c.
ament/u, strap, thong c 550; -alis, hurled
from a sling c 1290.
‡amentum, alumen scissum 1652; a. dulce,
ingredient of ointment a 1250.
ameos, an umbelliferous plant (bot.) a 1250,
‡14c.
amerald-, ameraud-, see smaragdo.
amerallus, see admiralius.
*amerci/amentum (adm-) 1168, 1583,
asmerciamentum 1285, emerciamentum 1275, -atio c 1375, 1539, amercement,
fine; -abilis, liable to amercement c 1290,
1334; -ator, assessor of amercement c 1258;
-atus, person amerced 1230; *-io 1188,
c 1448, amersio 16c., to amerce, fine; cf.
mercia, immercio.
Americus, American 1564.
ames, see hama.
amessio, to let slip (dogs) 13c.
ameta, see amictus.
amethystus, amethyst: amatista 1245, 1300.
amfract-, see anfractus.
amiantus, amianth, asbestos: amatis a 1250;
cf. amyton.
amiclius, see Amycleus.
*amic/tus (decl. 4) 1200, c 1520, (decl. 2)
c 1160, c 1315, -ta 1217, c 1503, *amita
1251, 1448, amitum c 1200, 1251, ameta
1436, 16c., (?) amisia c 1455, c 1511, amice
(eccl.); see also almucia; -io monachum,
to put on monkish habit c 1188.
amic/us, kinsman c 1150; a. propinquior
1285, a. propinquus 1507, next friend (leg.);
*-abilis 10c. c 1188, 1489, -alis c 730, 838,
a 1275, -itialis c 1250, friendly, benign;
*-abiliter, in a friendly manner c 1000,
1086, 1461; -abilitas, friendliness, benignity a 1250, 1461; -itia, amiability (title)
c 1242, c 1322; compromise (leg.) c 1115;
-itior, more friendly, closer friend c 1250,
c 1459; -o, to make friendly 1220, 14c.;
a 1529, -or c 1437, c 1470, to be friendly.
amidola, see AMYGD
amidum, see amylum.
amilaso, see esmallum.
aminito, see AMUNT
amir-, see admiralius.
amisia, see almucia; amictus.
amiss/or, loser c 1290; -um, loss, c 1226;
amitto, to leave, depart from 5c.; to sur-

render, hand over c 1115, c 1290; a. ludum
(chess) a 1200; see also ADMISS
amisticus, see nux.
amit/a, aunt: †habita c 1000; see also
amictus.
amixtio, see admixtio.
amizadir, see almizadar.
amm-, see also adm-
ammaylo, see esmallum.
ammoniacus, see sal.
ammoriolum, see ARMAR
ammot-, ammov-, see amovitio.
ammutatio, changing (of money) 1329.
amnestia, peace 7c.
1 amn/is, stream: ampnis c 1325, 1516,
ampnus c 1530; -ifluus, of a flowing stream
c 1115; -ilis, found in a stream 10c.
2 †amnis, hive c 1290.
amobilis, see amovitio.
amobr/agium 1284, 1501, -ium 1334,
amaubragium 1301, †ambrogium 1378,
(?) hamoverium (Cheshire) 1219, payment
for bondwoman's marriage or incontinence,
amobyr (W.); -arius, collector of amobyr 1334.
amodo, see a modo.
amogdalum, see AMYGD
amonto, see AMUNT
amor/, -osus, see amamen.
amoretum, see 3 morus.
*amort/izatio (adm-) c 1412, 1529, -uatio
a 1564, -izamentum c 1386, 1426, alienation in mortmain; *-izo c 1350, a 1564, -icio
1386, -ifico 1283, 1421, -uo 1348, to grant
in mortmain.
amo/vitio (ammo-), for -tio, removal c 1375;
-tibilis c 1258, 1337, -bilis 1376, 1416,
-vibilis 1419, 1534, -tivus 1395, a 1564,
removable; -veas manus, name of a writ
a 1564.
ampar-, see EMPAR
amph/emerinus, daily (med.): -imerinus
a 1250; -imera, daily fever a 1250.
amphi/balum, (?) for -mallum, garment,
cloak 6c., 7c. ‡c 1440, ‡1483.
amphi/bius, amphibious c 870; ‡-via, seal or
porpoise c 1200, 1483.
amphibo/logia c 1130, 1413, †amphilogia
c 1250, ambiguity; -licus 1378, -logicus
c 1250, c 1434, ambiguous; -logice, ambiguously c 1250, c 1444.
amphi/curvus, curved over c 550; -kyrtos,
moon almost at the full c 1212; -scius,
throwing a shadow both ways 1267.
amphi/sebena c 1200, -vema 12c., ‡-bim,
apaphsibena 15c., amphisbaena (fabulous
serpent); †-silena, Satan a 1142.
Amphitrites, ocean girdling earth longitu-
dinally a 1233; anfritri/dis, -tis, sea c 550.
amphora, iron-bound vessel of wood or
leather 1448, 1496; anfora, dry measure
1144; a. vini 8c.; †ansera, (?) for anfora,
bucket 1286.
amphorismus, see aphorismus.
amplastr-, see EMPLAST
amplex/io 1378, -atio c 1236, embrace;
-abilis, to be embraced, approved 12c.;
-o c 950, amplect/o c 730, 797. c 1188,
c 1325, to embrace; -or, to put on c 550.
ampli/atio, *increase, enlargement c 1198,
c 1515; extension (log.) a 1292, c 1362;

-amentum, stock (of cattle) 1286; **-ator,** increaser, benefactor 1439; **-atrix,** causing increase (*f.*) 1519; **-ativus** a 1304, c 1363, **-cativus** a 1361, ampliative, extending (log.); **-cative,** by way of extension (log.) c 1363; **-ficatio,** better maintenance 1350; **amplus,** broad-headed (of arrow) 1456; **in amplo,** in width, extent c 1393; **-o** a 1249, **-co** a 1361, to extend (a term) (log.); **-o,** to throw open, leave room c 1115; †**applio,** to extend 1276.

amplustr/e, -um, *see* **aplustre.**
ampn-, *see* 1 **amnis.**
amponenth, *see* **emponenth.**
ampsoca, *see* **hamfara.**
ampull/a, cruet for consecrated oil c 760, c 1000. 13c., 1433; surge, swelling 1267; bubble a 1250; **-e** (*pl.*), abusive words c 1000; **-atio,** blistering a 1250; **-osus,** bottle-shaped c 1250; bubbly a 1250; *bombastic 1136, 1440; **-ose,** bombastically c 1255, c 1453; **-ula,** small flask c 1125; **-o,** to bubble a 1250.
amput/abilis, able to cut off c 1250; **-o bursam,** to cut a purse 1291.
amsatus, *see* **ADVIS**
‡**amseges** (†**aviseges**), "headland" 1483; ‡**amsages,** "butt of land" 15c.
†**amua,** wine-jar 1383.
amucia, amusium, *see* **almucia.**
†**amulinga,** (?) path or fence 1146.
amulo, *see* **esmallum.**
amunt/ia, amount 1262; **-antia,** extent 1279; **-o** (†**aminito**) 1199, 1293, **amonto** 1253, 1333, to amount (to).
amurc/a, oil lees: ‡**murca** 14c.; †**amarco,** (?) olive-tree c 550; **-alis,** of or for oil lees 690. c 1125.
amusus, illiterate (ἄμουσος) 1515.
Amycleus (**amiclius**), watch-dog c 550.
amygd/ola, -olum 1252, 1395, **amidola** 1358, **amogdalum** 1265, **amydena** 1349, **amanda** 1157, **alemanda** 1205, 1220, **alimanda** 1424, *for* **-alum,** almond; ‡**-ale** (*pl.*), superfluous flesh at root of tongue 1652; **-alatum,** almond-milk a 1250, ‡15c.; **-aloides,** almond-like 1629.
amylum, starch: **amidum** a 1250, 13c.
†**amyton,** (?) *for* **amiantus,** wood purified by burning c 1180.
ana, at the rate of (ἀνά) 1235, c 1345; equal quantity or number c 1215, c 1400.
Anabaptista, Anabaptist 1538, 1561.
anabata, scarf (eccl.) 1425.
anaba/trum ‡c 1440, 1516, ‡**-strum** 13c., dosser, hanging.
‡**anabol/adium,** neckerchief 1483; ‡**-andium,** rochet 15c.
anabulla, spurge (bot.) a 1250, ‡c 1440.
anacard/us, cashew-nut a 1250, ‡14c.; **-inum,** confection of cashew a 1250.
anacephaleosis, recapitulation 7c. c 1182.
anachor/eta (eccl.), *-ita 10c. c 1125, c 1440, **-ista** c 1272, **anchorita** c 730, **anchorista** 1321, **ankerettus** 1428, anchorite, hermit; **-ita** (*f.*) c 1340, c 1480, ‡**-issa** c 1483, anchoress; **-esis,** eremitic life c 690. 12c., c 1200; **-eticus** c 730. c 1090, 1517, **-iticus** c 1191, c 1414, **anchoreticus** c 1414, **anchoriticus** 15c., †**anocariticus** 1418,

-itanus c 1250, **anchoritalis** 12c., eremitic, of an anchorite; **-itice,** as an anchorite c 1135, c 1436.
anacrotulus, *see* **onocrotulus.**
anadochus, secure 9c.
‡**anagallicum,** comfrey (bot.) 14c.
anager, *see* **onager.**
ana/glyphum, *for* **-glyphum,** carved work c 1125, 1267; ‡**-gliptes,** carver 1520; **-glafarius,** ‡for embroidery c 1200; ‡**em**broiderer 1483; **-glafatus,** embroidered 1433.
‡**anagodan,** sumach (bot.) 14c.
anagog/e, ‡vomiting 14c.; lifting up of the soul 9c.; 8c., 9c. c 1182, 1245, **-ea** 9c., **-ia** c 1180, 1378, (?) **angilogia** c 950, symbolism, mystical interpretation; **-ice,** allegorically, mystically c 1182, 1267; **-icus,** allegorical, mystical 9c. c 1180, c 1343; *see also* **analogium.**
anagramma, anagram c 1620.
‡**ana/lepsia** 14c., **-lempsia** c 1180, a 1250, analepsy, gastric epilepsy; **-lenticus,** analeptic a 1250.
analet/ichi, -izo, *see* **analysis.**
analis, kermes oak c 1212.
analog/ia c 1365, 1620, **annologia** 13c., analogy, relation; **-ice** c 1238, 1610, **annologice** 13c., **analoyce** c 1362, by analogy; **-us** 13c., **anologus** 1380, **annologicus** 13c., analogical, figurative; **-a** (*pl.*), regularities a 1200; **-um,** analogue 1344, c 1362; **-ico** c 1367, **-izo** 1378, to analogize.
analogium c 790. a 1090, c 1517, **anologium** c 1395, c 1400, †**anagogium** 16c., reading desk, lectern.
analy/sis 1564, 1686, **-tica** (*f. s.*) c 1620, analysis; **-tica** (*n. pl.*) c 1160, c 1549, **analetichi** c 1180, Aristotle's *Analytics*; **-tice,** analytically 1686; **-ticus,** analytical 1686; **analetizo,** to analyse c 1160.
†**anamag,** (?) fennel (bot.) c 1257.
ana/mello, -millo, *see* **ENAM**
anancia, *see* **avencia.**
anaphus, cup, beaker c 1000.
anaranti/us, -cus, tawny c 1595; *cf.* **AURANT**
anarchia, anarchy 1523, 1620.
anaroxia, (?) recovery (med.) (ἀνάρρωσις) a 1250.
anas errarius, nesting duck 1351 (*cf.* **aeria**); **anetinus,** *for* **anatinus,** of a duck a 1250.
anasarca, dropsy a 1250, 1634.
anastasis, resurrection c 870.
†**ana/stomasis,** †**-stamosis,** anastomosis (med.) a 1250.
anastrophe, anastrophe (gram.) c 790; ‡**anostropha,** gastric spasm 14c.
anathema/ maranatha (bibl.); **-tismus** 797, **-tizatio** 8c. a 1090, c 1450, anathematizing; **-tizo,** to anathematize (eccl.).
Anathole, East (ἀνατολή) c 1180.
anatileon, *see* **aneta.**
anatomizo, to deprive by anatomy a 1250.
anatron, *see* **nitrum.**
anatropa, (gastric) upheaval a 1250.
anax, king, ruler (ἄναξ) c 870.
‡**anca,** "ankle" 15c.; *cf.* **hancha, auca.**
anceps, *see* **accipiter.**
ancer/, -ilus, -olus, -ulus, *see* **anser.**
ancera, *see* **auncella.**

ancess/eria, -or, *see* ANTECED

anchor-, *see also* ANACHOR

anchor/a a 1118, 1417, **ancra** 1294, **ancrium** 1242, **ankura** c 1390, anchor; ***-agium** 1286, 1587, **ancaragium** 1439, 1525, **ankeragium** 1417, 1545, anchorage, anchor-dues; **-arius,** anchor-master 1565; **-io** 1370, ***-o** 1276, 1427, to anchor.

anchreta, chain c 550.

anchusa, alkanet (bot.): **encusa** a 1250.

anciani, *see* antiani.

ancila, *see* auca.

ancill/a, handmaiden (eccl.); **a. Christi** 1060. c 1240, **a. Dei** 786, nun; **a. -arum Dei,** abbess c 700; **-atio,** enslavement, subservience c 1250, c 1456; **-atus,** service c 950; **-o,** to enslave 1166, 15c.; †**-or** (*dep.*), to get possession of c 1125.

ancionarius, *see* AUCTION

ancipiter, *see* accipiter.

ancistrum, fish-hook (ἄγκιστρον) 12c.

anclatio, *see* ANHEL

†**anclidia,** ordeal-kettle c 1115.

ancopa, *see* accopa.

ancora, sanicle (bot.) a 1250.

ancr-, *see* ANCHOR

andanicus, *see* 2 andena.

andaria, *see* 3 andena.

andatus, (?) street c 1200.

andefeldum, *see* anfeldum.

Andegavensis (libra) 1156, 1214, **Angevinus** c 1200, coin of Anjou.

andegravius, *see* LAND

1 **and/ena** a 1200, c 1256, **-oena** (†**audoena**) 1500, **-o** a 1290, c 1340, **-ela** a 1245, measure of meadow-land, swathe (O.F. *andeyne*); *cf.* **dayna, handayna.**

2 **and/ena** 1267, ‡1652, **ferrum -anicum** c 1227, ondanique, high-grade, (?) Indian (*Hundwāniy*), steel.

3 ***and/ena** 1390, 1450, **-eona** 1409, ‡**-ela** 1570, **-era** c 1290, c 1396, **-eria** 1283, 1286, **-aria** 1307, **aunderia** 1303, **-ernum** 1388, andiron; *cf.* **handerium.**

Andreanus, *see* crux.

andricon, an electuary 13c.

andr/ochia c 1290, c 1395, ‡**-ogia** c 1200, 15c., dairy-maid; ‡**-ochius,** dairy-man 1483; **-ochiarium** c 1290, ‡1483, †**-ochianum** c 1440, **-ochiatorium** 15c., †**-eseya** 1255, dairy.

andrum, *see* antrum.

andulla, sausage (Fr. *andouille*) 1245.

anealo, *see* esmallum.

anecius, *see* esnecia.

anel-, *see also* ANHEL; ANUL; **esmallum.**

anelacius c 1250, c 1320, **anlaci/us** 1276, **-a** 1268, **alenatius** 1234, **alenaticus** 1253, **alnacius** 1267, c 1270, 'anlace', dagger.

anella, old woman 1275.

anelo, to anneal (tiles) c 1370; **anulatio,** annealing (of tiles) 1458.

anem/alo, -ello, *see* ENAM

anepigraphus, without title or superscription 8c.

anesis, relaxation (ἄνεσις) c 1200, ‡14c.

ane/ta, dill (bot.) 1303; **anisum** 1538, **anisium** 1265, ‡14c., anise; **-thinus,** of dill a 1250, 13c.; **-tileon** a 1250, ‡**anatileon** c 1200, oil of dill or anise (ἀνηθέλαιον).

anetinus, *see* anas.

anetius, causeless (ἀναίτιος) p 1300.

anfeldum 1449, **andefeldum** 1504, anvil.

anfora, *see* amphora.

anfractus, a winding: **amfract/us** c 1250, 1463; **-uosus,** tortuous c 1250, a 1446.

anfritri/dis, -tis, *see* Amphitrites.

angar/ia (bibl.), **-iagia** (G.) 1498, forced service; toll c 1070; ***tribulation** c 1130, 15c.; fasting 1200, 15c.; **-onia,** rough usage c 1300; **-ialis,** grievous c 1253; **-iarius,** concerned with forced service 1608; ‡**-ius,** "catchpoll" c 1440; **-io** (bibl.), **-izo** 8c., to compel; to tax, extort money from a 1100, c 1250; †**angurio,** *for* **-o,** to afflict 1485.

angel/us, angel (coin) c 1510, c 1533; **-otus** 1588, 1608, **-ettus** 1532, (?) **-atus** 1535, angelet, half angel; **aggelus,** *for* **-us,** angel c 870; **-icus,** angelic (bibl.); **-ica,** (?) spurge laurel (bot.) a 1250, ‡14c.; angelica (bot.) 1620, 1629.

Angevinus, *see* Andegavensis.

angildum, simple weregeld c 1115.

angilogia, *see* anagoge.

angiportus, alley: **anguiportus** c 1434.

*Angl/us a 710, a 1000. c 1067, 1543, ***-icus** a 1087, c 1450, **-icanus** c 1200, 1431, **-iacus** c 1595, ***-igena (-igenus)** c 1000, 1020. c 1068, c 1562, **-ensis** c 1150, English, Englishman; **ecclesia -icana** 12c., c 1600; **-i Orientales,** East Angles c 730, a 910; **-icum** 1236, c 1443, **-ica** (*pl.*) 1415, c 1529, English language; **-ice,** in English 9c., c 1000. c 1070, c 1440; **-icatio,** translation into English 1413, 15c.; **-icatus,** Anglicized, Anglophile 1297, 1461; **-ia,** silver or gold (alch.) 1267; **-echeria** c 1268, **-escheria** 1186, c 1290, **-ischeria** 1205, **Engl/echeria** 1266, 1292, ***-escheria** 1185, 1313, **-eseria** 1198, **-esaria** 14c., **-isheria** 1188, 1285, **-ashiria** 1285, **-egeria** 1229, Englishry (leg.); **Anglo/-Hibernus** 1584; **-Normannicus** c 1595; **-Saxo** 1586, c 1595, **Angul-saxo** a 910. c 1100; **-ico,** to translate into English 1413.

angn-, *see* AGN

angoreus, painful c 1000.

anguill/a rubea, salted eel 1240; **angwilla** 1247, c 1376, †**angulla** c 1410, *for* **-a,** eel; **anguiculus,** small eel c 730; **-aris,** of or for eels c 730. c 1212; *see also* **argentum; -osus,** abounding in eels c 1170; ‡**-arium,** eel-bed 1483; **-ula,** little worm c 1200.

anguina, halliard c 1180, c 1255.

anguiportus, *see* angiportus.

angulator (piscium), angler 1508.

angul/us, canton (her.) 1654; crookedness, dishonesty 1378; stratagem c 1325; **a. caprinus,** *see* CAPR; **a. contactūs** (geom.) 1686, **a. contingentie** (geom.) a 1200, c 1360; **a. incidentalis,** angle of incidence 1378; **a. terre** a 1184, c 1311, **a. prati** 1086, corner, nook; **-are,** (?) corner-plate 1245; **-aris,** of or for a corner c 730; ***situated at a corner** 1236, c 1438; (?) out-of-the-way c 1070, c 1500; **-aricus,** angular c 1361; **-ariter,** at an angle a 1250, c 1280; **-atus,** gyronny (her.) p 1394; **-osus,** crafty 12c.; **-ositas,** many-corneredness 1649; **-o,** to bring to an angle

a 1250; to corner, drive into a corner 1320;
see also ANUL

angurio, *see* ANGAR

*angust/ia (bibl.), -atio 1268, distress; -iatio,
contraction, narrowing 1620, 1622; -ifolius,
narrow-leaved 1634; -iosus, anguished, dis-
tressed a 1250, 1422; -iose, in anguish
a 1250; *-io, to distress (bibl.).

anhel/itus (hanel-) 1210, a 1349, -atio
(†anclatio) 1350, eager pursuit or desire;
-a, breath 6c., 9c.; -anter, eagerly c 1218;
-us, ambitious c 1250; -osus, gasping,
asthmatic a 1250; -o (ad) *796. c 1160, 1494,
aneleo 1332, to strive after; -o, to breathe,
be alive 957.

aniceus, *see* alnus.

anigerulus, *see* avis.

anim/a, *soul (eccl.); person c 1130; essence
(alch.) 13c., ‡1652; schedule containing gist
of message 1259, c 1353; (*coll.*) 898, -e (*pl.*)
1358, 1503, masses for the soul of deceased;
see also cura, forum, JUR, salus; -a mundi
a 1232; a. rationalis a 1250, 1267; *-e (pl.)
1194, 1343, Omnes -e 1347, *-arum dies
12c., 1555, -arum commemoratio 1239,
16c., All Souls' Day (2 Nov.); -abilis, full
of soul c 1200; -atus, animate, living a 1250,
c 1343; -atio, soul c 870; 7c., -ositas (bibl.),
wrath, enmity; -o, to support (proposals)
1421.

animal/ 1086, 1573, almal c 1200, farm
animal, head of cattle; a. ad carrucam,
plough-beast c 1280; -culum, lowly animal
1518, 1662; -is, concerned or endowed with
animal (not spiritual) life c 1160, 1620;
bestial 1241; *see also* spiritus; -itas, animal
nature or form 8c., 950. 1267, c 1367.

aniosus, *see* annus.

anisium, anisum, *see* aneta.

anitas, 'whetherness', existence c 1270.

ank/eragium, -ura, *see* anchora.

ankerettus, *see* ANACHOR

anlepi/mannus, annelepemennus 1272,
-mennus 1270, (?) bondsman without
tenement (Norf.).

ann/ale, -ata, *etc.*, *see* annus.

annello, *see* esmallum.

annellus, *see* anulus.

annex/atio 1240, 1448, adnexio 1288, an-
nectio c 1465, annexing, annexation; -itas,
constipation c 1220; -o, to annex, attach
1279, 1588.

annihil/atio (adnichil-) 1267, c 1670, -antia
c 1367, annihilation; -abilis, annihilable
c 1270, 1427; -ativus c 1367, 1427, -atrix
(*f.*) c 1180, annihilating; *-o, to annihilate
a 1090, c 1514.

annisus (adn-), effort 601, c 730. c 1125,
c 1250.

anniv-, *see* annus.

annolog-, *see* ANALOG

annomin/atio, paronomasia c 1210; -o, to
nominate c 1120, 1252; to assign c 1178.

annon/a, food, diet 7c., 9c. 1200; grain-rent
1086; monastic allowance of food c 1296,
c 1330; earnest money 14c., c 1450; a. sicca,
a. viridis 1106; -o, to seize as earnest 14c.

annotatio, chronicle 12c.

annotinus, *see* Pascha.

annua-, *see* annus.

annul-, *see also* ANUL

annull/atio (adn-) c 1173, 1511, -itas 1377,
destruction, annulment; -abilis, liable to
annulment 1374; -ativus, annulling c 1420;
-atorie, by way of annulment c 1357; *-o,
to annul 790. a 1100, 1543.

annunti/atio (adn-), announcement 620, 793.
c 1150, 1341; *(feast of) Annunciation (25
March) c 730, 870. a 1090, c 1550; -abilis,
able to be proclaimed a 1228.

ann/us, year's rent 1203, 1513; year's study
(ac.) c 1450; *see also* de; *a. domini 12c.,
c 1594, a. Christi 15c., a. dominicalis
a 1100, c 1188, *a. incarnationis dominice
c 1070, 1565, a. ab incarnatione (Christi,
domini, dominica) 1086, 1437, a. carnis
dominice a 1100, a. verbi incarnati
c 1125, 1177, a. a dominico natalitio
1476, *a. gratie 12c., c 1467, a. reparatio-
nis humane 1570, a. salutis (restaurate)
1537, 1570, a. secundum Evangelium
c 1210, year of the Christian era; a.
Arabum a 1233, a. Arabicorum c 1138,
year of the Hegira; a. Egyptius, solar year
1344; a. emergens, Jewish year reckoned
from Exodus c 1212; a. legitimus, Jewish
lunar year c 1212; a. requietionis, jubilee
year c 1265; a. magnus a 1200, a. mundia-
lis c 1265, great year (astr.); ‡a. philosophicus, month 1652; -i collecti, collected
years (planetary table) c 1138, c 1265; -i
expansi, expanse years (planetary table)
c 1265; -i discretionis, years of discretion
c 1220, c 1420; -i minores, nonage 1346;
-is communibus, in normal years 1261,
c 1400; *-us, dies et vastum, year, day and
waste, royal right to felon's property 1241,
c 1448; -i donum, New Year's gift c 1432;
-ale 1206, 1559, -uale c 1216, c 1450,
-iversale (missarum) 13c., 1339, -iver-
saria 1306, c 1395, *-iversarium 1168,
1567, (dues paid for) annals (eccl.), anniversary (mass); -ale, -alis, yearling beast 1233,
1398; -uale, year's income c 1250, 13c.;
-alis, (*subst.*) year-roll c 1178 (*see also*
rotulus); (*adj.*) 1195, a 1564, -atus c 1290,
1316, -ularis 1269, 1350, one-year-old;
*-ualis 6c., c 870. c 1125, a 1564, -iculus
1232, 1412, -uarius 1262, 15c., -uatus 1440,
c 1517, annual, yearly; *see also* altare; -aliter
a 1100, -atim c 1200, *-uatim c 730, 797.
c 1125, 1686, annually; -ata (*n. pl.*), an-
nates, first-fruits paid to Pope 1441, c 1620;
-iversaria (*pl.*), book of obits 980; -iversa-
rius (*adj.*) 730. c 1220, c 1504, -uarius 1405,
of or for an anniversary (eccl.); (*subst.*) 1239,
c 1395, -ivellarius 1337, 1430, -uellarius
1416, 1430, -uvellarius 1310, -ualarius
1411, 1444, priest in charge of anniversaries;
†-iosus, (?) *for* -osus, aged, continued, or
annual c 550; -otinus, daily 980; -otinus,
-uus, *see* Pascha; -uatio, esnecy, right of
eldest sister 1201; -uitas, annuity, annual
payment c 1350, 1547; -uo, to accrue after
a year 1542.

anocariticus, *see* ANACHOR

anodyno, to soothe, allay pain a 1250.

anolog-, *see* analogia; analogium.

anomalus 790. c 1204, c 1258, *anormalus
c 1200, c 1430, anomalous, abnormal.

anomeomereus, heterogeneous c 1300.
anomia, sin c 550.
anonium, dead-nettle (bot.) 1538.
‡anorexia 14c., †avarexia a 1250, loss of appetite.
ans/a, stalk c 550; plough-stilt c 1280; ‡chair-arm c 1200; ‡curtain-ring 1483; anca, (?) for a., handle c 1500; -ata, dart c 670; -ula, cord for fastening dress 1308, c 1380.
anser/ Bassanus, gannet 1544; ancer (†aucer), for a., gander 1296, 1403; -ulus c 1250, 1296, -culus 1544, ancerulus 1454, ancerolus 1283, ancerilus 1513, gosling.
ansera, see amphora.
ansis, demigod 6c.
‡ansorium, cobbler's shaping-knife c 1440, 1483.
ansporto, see ASPORT
†antabata, (?) adversary 1527.
antanimo, to animate c 1220.
†antapo/te, for -che, counter tally c 1180; cf. anticopa.
antarcticus, antarctic: entarticus c 1250.
ante, in the presence of c 1072, c 1130; c 1218, 1253, a. quod 5c., for a. quam; a. et retro, fore and aft (the mast) 1290, 1325 (see also facio); a. bordam navis, at the ship's side 13c., 14c.; a. malum 1260, a. mastum 1327, before the mast; a. manum, beforehand a 1408; a. diu, before long 1507; a. modo, before now 14c.; a. sero, before it is too late 1345.
ante-, see also anti-
antealtare, altar frontal 15c.
anteca, see antela.
antecamera, antechamber 1620.
antecastellum c 1138, anticastellum c 1140, besiegers' entrenchment.
anteced/entia, antecedence (log.) c 1290, 1344; -ens c 1332, c 1357, antecessivus c 1270, antecedent (log.); -enter, previously, antecedently c 1290, a 1452; -ens 1461, ancessor 1200, ancestor c 1200, anticessor 1243, *antecess/or c 730, 933. c 1067, c 1520, ancestor or predecessor; see also mors; -or, officer attending on a dean or chapter 1324; -atrix 1225, -rix 1230, -istris 1231, ancestress or predecessor (f.); ancesseria, ancestry 1200;-io (equinoctii), precession 1267; -us, excess c 1255.
antecommissus, committed previously c 870.
antedecessor, predecessor 8c.
antedenuntiatus, previously denounced 1169.
*antedictus, aforesaid 12c., c 1439.
antefac/ta (pl.), past deeds c 1115; -io, to make before 1226.
antefatus, aforesaid c 1200, c 1470.
antefenestra, (?) space or ledge in front of window (G.) 1276, 1315.
antefissus, (?) for antefixus, fastened in front c 1330.
antefossatum, moat lying in front c 1280.
ante/garda, -guarda, see antewarda.
antegenit/or, ancestor p 1330; -us, previously begotten 1236.
antehabitus, preceding c 1185.
antejuramentum, preliminary oath of an accuser (leg.) 9c. c 1115.

antel/a c 1000. c 1200, anteca 1229, front peak of saddle; -a 1395, ‡15c., ‡-o a 1519, ‡ antilena 1570, poitrell.
antelatio, preference c 1444, 1473.
antelectus, read of before c 1325.
‡antelucan/a, lark 15c.; (pl.) matins and lauds 14c.; ‡-o, to rise before dawn 1483.
ant/elupus c 1450, -ilupus c 1422, -ilopus 1413, 1472, -lappus c 1509, antelope.
antema, see ANTIPHON
antememoratus, aforementioned 679, c 890. c 1500.
antemissus, put as preface 1424.
antem/pna, derrick 1450; ‡-ne (pl.), "em-battlements" 1570.
antemuralis, before the walls c 1150.
antenat/io, (right of) primogeniture 1198; -us, first-born, eldest c 1198, 1287; older (of document) 1237; a. quam 1230; cf. esnecia.
anteped/ale, cobbler's vamp 15c.; antipedia (pl.), uppers of shoes c 1330; antipedites, toe-caps (of stirrups) 1246; -o, to buck (of a horse) c 1200.
antependium, altar frontal (Sc.) 13c.; curtain before table of sacrament-house (Sc.) 16c.
antepenultimus, antepenultimate (gram.) 790. 1267; (in dating) c 1408, c 1529.
antepestilentialis, dating from before the pestilence c 1412.
antepetitus, previously sought c 1250.
‡antephalarica, "portcullis" c 1440.
anteplasmatus, fashioned beforehand c 550.
antepositio, (right of) first placing a 1280.
antepredicamenta, a section of Aristotle's Logic p 1300.
antepremissa (f. s.), chapter before last 1326.
anteprisa, 'forfeng', fine for taking prise before the king 13c.
anterior/, *lying in front a 1090, 1559; former c 1172, 1452; future c 1204; eastern 7c. a 1186; a. flator, foreblower (at iron foundry) c 1333; see also glacialis; anterius, in front a 1090, 1440; -atio, placing before 1344, 1427; -itas, antecedence a 1270 c 1365; -o, to place before (in time) 1344, c 1370.
antescriptus, afore-written c 1283, c 1489.
‡antesellum, front peak of saddle 15c.
antesigna/tus, for -nus, guardian of standard 1245.
antesituatus, situated in front 1405, 1446.
antespecificatus, before-specified 1526.
antest/es, -o, see antistes.
antesubstitutus, substituted before c 870.
anteverto, to outdo 1537.
antevigilia, eve of the eve c 1300.
antevolo, to outstrip c 1090.
ante/warda, -guarda c 1212, -garda 1239, 1274, vanguard.
anthema, see ANTIPHON
anthleta, see athleta.
anth/os (ant-), rosemary 13c., ‡14c.; -ismos, literary adornment c 1000.
anthr/ax (†autrax) c 1200, 1319, -aca c 1180, carbuncle (med.).
anthrop/os c 1170, c 1198, antropus c 550, 8c., man; ‡-ocedus, man-slayer c 1200; -ologice, anthropomorphically c 1361; -omorphite a 1090, c 1250, -omorphosite 8c., -omorphi p 1381, †autophormoite

13c., anthropomorphite heretics; **-omoros**, *for* **-omorphos**, mandrake a 1250; **-opathos** c 1370, **-ospathos** c 1220, c 1367, rhetorical figure, anthropopathy.

anti-, *see also* **ante-**

antia, forelock c 670.

antiani, anciani, noblemen (It.) 1288, 1484; **aunciatus**, ancient c 1437.

anticardinalis, cardinal adherent to antipope 1406, 1421.

Antichrist/us 6c., 8c. c 1343, 1378, **-ianus** 1412, c 1620, **-inus** 1378, 1427, anti-Christian, of or for Antichrist; **-ine**, in an anti-Christian manner c 1380.

anticidum, *see* **antidotum**.

anticip/atio, hysteron proteron (gram.) c 870; (reward for) recovery of stolen property a 1130; advance payment 1416; **-ativus**, anticipatory c 1250; **-ator fori**, forestaller of the market 13c.; **-o**, to foresee 8c.; to arrest c 1115.

anticipter, *see* **accipiter**.

ant/icopa c 1380, ‡c 1440, **-ocopa** c 1300, (?) *for* **-apocha**, counter-tally; *cf.* **accopa**, **antapote**, **apocha**.

anticrux, rival cross c 1190.

anti/dotum 1347, **-dodum** 1437, 1442, **-dorum** c 1213, c 1303, **-donum** c 1180, †**-cidum** c 1350, recompense, guerdon; **-todum**, *for* **-dotum**, antidote c 870. a 1408; **-dotarium**, book on antidotes a 1250, c 1450.

antiepiscopus, rival bishop a 1205.

antifolium, *see* **antophalum**.

antigenus, belonging to opposite kinds c 1160.

antigraph/us, scribe c 1150; c 1549, **-arius** 1570, controller.

antilena, *see* **antela**.

‡**antillium**, shield c 1200; (?) *cf.* **attillium**.

antilogia (play on **apologia**), adverse discourse 1610.

†**antilopum**, (?) lump of metal 1420.

anti/lopus, -lupus, *see* **antelupus**.

†**antilum**, (?) goblet 9c.

antimoni/um a 1250, ‡14c., **-a** c 1200, antimony (sulphide).

antinotator, controller 1508.

Antipap/a, antipope c 1192, 1461; **-ista**, adherent of antipope 1406.

antiparies, breastwork 1304.

†**antipasis**, (?) prophylactic (med.) a 1250.

antipatres (*pl.*), opponents of the Fathers (eccl.) a 1205.

antipedia, *see* **ANTEPED**

‡**antipera**, screen 15c., 1483.

anti/peristasis 1344, 1620, **-paristasis** 1521, interchange, reciprocal replacement.

antipharmacum, antidote a 1250.

*antiphon/a** 8c., 9c. 11c., 1536, **antema** 1458, **anthema** 1483, antiphon, anthem; †**-ium** c 1316, **-ale** 1420, **-are** 1329, c 1506, *-arium**, **-arius** 980, 1006. c 1080, c 1450, †**antiphenarium** 1388, antiphoner, book of antiphons; **-arius** (*adj.*), antiphonal 12c., c 1250; **-atim**, antiphonally 790, 9c. c 1125, c 1385; **-o**, to chant antiphons c 1364.

*antiphras/is**, use of word in contrary sense 9c. c 1125, a 1408; **-ius**, opposite of what it says 790; **-tice**, by antiphrasis 1189, c 1260.

Antipontifex, antipope c 1546.

anti/ptosis, substitution of one case for another (gram.): **-tosis** c 1218, c 1258.

antiqu/us, senior (of persons of the same name) c 1094, 1429; ancient, pre-conquest c 1103; *see also* **ab, ex**; **-i** (*pl.*), logicians writing before the discovery of Aristotle's *Analytics* and *Topics* c 1160; **-ior**, (*adj.*) senior (in service) 13c.; (*subst.*) an elder 13c., 1420; **-arius**, scribe a 1142, c 1355; **-itas**, anciently, length of tenure 1311; **-itus** (? *adj.*), former 1300; **-atus**, old c 1190, 1518; **-or**, to grow old (bibl.).

anti/sima, *for* **-sigma**, letter X c 1200.

antismos, *see* **ANTH**

*anti/stes** 7c., 9c. c 1070, c 1553, **-stis** c 790, **antestes** 796, bishop; **-stitium**, bishopric c 1125, 1518; **-sto** 10c., **antesto** c 1390, to stand before.

Antisthenicus, Cynic c 1300.

antistroph/e, transition (in mutually opposite directions) 1620; **-us**, converse c 1607, 1622.

antithe/sis 1610, †**architesis** a 1408, contrast; **-tarius**, counter-accuser c 1115.

antitodum, *see* **antidotum**.

antitosis, *see* **antiptosis**.

antityp/ia, resistance, impenetrability c 1612, 1620, **-um**, antitype 1562.

antlappus, *see* **antelupus**.

antlerans, (?) antlered beast c 1500.

antlo, *like* **exantlo**, to exhaust, weary c 1190.

antonom/asia (†**autonom-**), excellence 1267; *-astice** c 1200, c 1367, †**-aice** 1258, **-asice** c 1160, 15c., *-atice** c 1180, 1427, **-ice** 1291, 1378, †**automatice** 1570, antonomastically, *par excellence*; **-asticus**, antonomastic 13c.

‡**anto/phalum**, gillyflower, pink (bot.) 14c.; **-folium**, antifolium, kind of herb (med.) a 1250; *cf.* **anthos**.

ant/orsum 12c., **-rorsum** c 1227, ‡1570, forwards.

antropus, *see* **ANTHROP**

antrum, ditch 1311; pitfall c 1112; **andrum**, cave c 550.

anul/us (**annul-**), pig-ring 1366; door-handle, knocker c 1200, 1418; ring for tilting at 1508; p 1394, a 1446, **annellus** c 1595, annulet (her.); **a. gemellus**, gimbal ring 1224, 1241; **a. medicinalis**, cramp ring 1369, 1413; *see also* **per**; **-aris** 1267, 1686, **-osus** c 1210, 1267, annular, ring-shaped; **-osus**, marked with rings a 1275; **animal -osum**, insect or worm a 1250; **-atio**, ringing (of pigs) 1445; **-atus**, ringed (of pigs) c 1327, 1511; **capistrum -atum** 1388; **-ator porcorum** 1731; **-o**, to put a ring or hoop on 1320, 1388; 1287, 1573, **angulo** 1632, to ring (pigs); *see also* **anelo**.

anx/agia, -ungia, *see* **I axella**.

anxi/amen, distress c 1250; **-o**, *to make anxious (bibl.); to straiten 8c. c 1110.

anxima, *see* **axioma**.

Anza, *see* **hansa**.

aoco, *see* **ADVOC**

aolagium, *see* **oleagium**.

aorasia, blindness; †**aur/ata** a 1250, **-isia** c 1250; *cf.* **acrisia**.

aorta (med.): **adorti** c 1210.

apelioticus, *see* **aphelion**.

apellatus, *see* **apparatio.**

aper/ liber, liberty of boar (man.) c 1280; **-culus** a 1408, **apriolus** 1388, 1441, little boar; **-iatio,** service of providing boars 1295; **-na caro,** pork 14c.; †**apriola,** (?) wild sow (or *f.l.* for **capriola**) c 1362; †**apris,** (?)*f.l.* for **affris,** 1308.

aper/itio c 1340, a 1564, **-itura** c 1340, opening; **-tio,** outcome 8c.; **-itivus** c 1115, a 1250, **-tivus** 14c., concerned with opening; **-itivus** a 1250, 13c., **-iens** a 1250, aperient (med.); **-tilis,** capable of opening 1518; **-te littere,** letters patent c 1285, 1436; **-ta rapina,** open, unconcealed, robbery c 1110; *see also* **tempus; -io,** to release (a substance) from the limitations of its own nature (alch.) a 1252; **a. hepar et splenem** (med.) 1424.

apex, chief, head 797, c 950. c 1400; letter of alphabet, **apic/es** (*pl.*) letter, epistle (eccl.); point (Hebrew gram.) 1564; **a. scutaria,** chief (her.) 1654; **-ellus,** little letter c 1000; **-ulus,** breathing (Greek gram.) 1515.

aphaltus, *see* **asphaltus.**

aphelion, aphelion (astr.) 1686; **apelioticus,** east wind c 870.

aphonia, discord a 1180.

aphorism/us (af-) 960. c 1075, 1620, **amphorismus** a 1250, ‡14c., **-a** c 1200, **aporismum** 1241, aphorism; *cf.* APOR

aphrodisia (aff-) (*f. s.*), sexuality, puberty a 1250.

aphro/niosus (af-), foaming c 550; †**affonitrum,** †**affrenitum,** *for* **-nitrum,** a 1250.

†**aphum,** faggot 1310.

apicularius, bee-taker (Norm.) 1180.

apistus, infidel 1427, ‡1570.

apium ravinum, (?) *for* **a. risus,** ranunculus a 1250.

aplan/os, firmament, sphere of fixed stars c 1115, 1252; **-es** 811. c 1250, **-eticus** c 1115, a 1200, fixed (astr.); †**aplasmus,** (?) fixed position (astr.) c 815.

aplustre c 1172, ‡**amplustr/e, -um** 15c., rudder.

apocalyp/sis, Book of Revelation (eccl.); **-ticus,** mentioned in the Apocalypse c 1620; ‡**-so,** to reveal 1483.

apo/cha c 1305, 1608, **-ccia** 1381, †**-te** c 1180, †**-cope** 1516, receipt (ἀποχή); *cf.* **accopa, anticopa, apodixa.**

apoco, to put, place c 550.

apocop/a, -e, 790. c 1200, a 1452, **apocape** a 1408, **-atio** c 1200, **apocapatio** c 1430, apocope (gram.), cutting short; **-o** c 1170, 1427, **apocapo** a 1408, **apocupo** c 1460, to cut short.

apocri/siarius c 1100, 1438 **-sarius** 991, †**-farius (apocrypharius)** c 1362, ‡1483, apocrisiary, Papal official.

apocrusticus, 'apocrustic', repellent (med.) a 1250.

apocryph/us (apocrif-), apocryphal 1068, c 1363; cryptic, mystical 1378; †**-e,** (?) Apocalypse 12c.; †**apocrisa,** the Apocrypha c 1396; **-o,** to declare apocryphal c 1376; *see also* APOCRI

apo/dixa 1237, **-dissa** 1454, receipt (? ἀποδοχή).

Apo/dixis, Aristotle's *Posterior Analytics* c 1180; **-dicticus,** demonstrative, indicative a 950.

apogeum, apogee (astr.) c 1616, 1686; *see also* **hypogea.**

apollogiticus, *for* **apologeticus,** c 790.

‡**apomel,** hydromel, mead 14c.

apopempeus, averter of evil (ἀποπομπαῖος) c 950.

apo/phaticus (-faticus), negative c 850.

apo/phlegmatisma, riddance of phlegm a 1250; ‡**-phleumaticus,** apophlegmatic (med.) 14c.

apophore/sis, draining off (med.) a 1250; **-ticus,** (?) epigrammatic c 1212.

apophthegma, apophthegm 1570.

apoplexia (med.): **appoplesia** a 1250.

apor/ia (bibl.), **-iamen** a 1300, difficulty hardship; **-iatio** c 1308, 15c., **-atio** c 1412, †**-iatus** c 1540, impoverishment; **-iator,** impoverisher c 1250; **-isma** (*for* **-ema**) contradictory argument c 1160, c 1180; *see also* **aphorismus; -io,** to impoverish a 1090, 1421; to forgo a 1125, c 1125; †(?) to disfigure c 1172.

aposta/sia (eccl.), **-sis** c 730, **-tatus** c 1250, apostasy; c 1125, c 1540, **-sis** 13c., **-tatio** c 1395, **aposteria** 1511, breach of vows (mon.); *see also* **apostema; *-ta** (eccl.), **-ticus** 799, apostate; renegade monk c 1223, 1549; **-ticus** (*adj.*), apostatizing c 1180, 15c.; **-tice,** as a renegade c 1250, a 1452; ***-to** (bibl.), **-tizo** c 1375, to apostatize, to turn heretic or pagan; **-to** 12c., c 1451, **aposto** 1332, to break vows (mon.); **-to legem,** to break a law c 1115.

apostem/a a 1200, 1370, ‡**postema** c 1440, **postuma** a 1514, imposthume, abscess; **-atio** (†**aposchematio**) 1345, **apostasis** a 1250, suppuration, formation of abscess; **-osus,** festering a 1250; **-or,** to fester, suppurate a 1250, c 1260.

apostill/a (*n. pl.*), notes 1432; **-o,** to add to the end of a document c 1465; *see also* APOSTOL, POSTILL

aposto, *see* **apostasia.**

apostol/atus *c 730, 1062. c 1125, c 1436, **-icatus** c 1192, 1421, papacy; episcopacy 12c.; **-a,** female apostle c 1325; **-i** (*pl.*) 1245, 1549, †**apostilli** 13c., letters dimissory, letters of appeal (eccl.); **a. refutatorii,** letters disallowing appeal 1684, 1686; **-ice,** apostolically c 1227, c 1325; **-icon, -icum,** a sort of drug or plaster a 1250, 1322; **-icus,** (*adj.*) apostolic (eccl.); *papal 803. c 1070, 1586; episcopal c 1000; (*subst.*) *Pope 790. c 1115, c 1400.

apostroph/a, musical accent 1326; **-atio,** apostrophe (figure of speech) c 1210, 13c.; **-o,** to address, speak to a 1185, c 1220; ‡**-or,** to turn to evil courses, backslide 1483.

apotacticus, irregular, violating order 1609.

apothec/a 13c., 1398, apothecary's shop; **-aria,** apothecaries' quarter c 1330, 1388; **-aria** (*n. pl.*), store-rooms c 1315, c 1362; ‡**apoticaria,** "spicer wife" 15c.; **-arius,** treasurer c 1198; *a 1270, 1573, **apoticarius** 1340, 1462, **hypothecarius,** 1299, 1492, **potecarius** 1392, **poticarius** 1524, 1534, **bothecarius** a 1241, apothecary, dealer in spices and drugs.

apozema, decoction (med.): **-zima** a 1250.

appal/tator (†-cator), agent, contractor (It.) 1506.
appalus, see hapalus.
apparantia, see apparitio.
appar/atio 12c., c 1266, -itio c 1330, -amentum c 1295, 1466, -atum 1250, -itus 1305, equipment, furnishing; -atus 1204, 1422; -ella 1444, 'parrel', rigging (naut.); 1234, 1445, -itura 1423, c 1517, apparel (eccl.); commentary 1270, c 1470; a. altaris, decoration of altar for mass c 1330, 1424; a. misse, commentary on the mass 1434; -atura 1432, -ellum 1414, bedding; -ator 1292, 1376, -ilator 1333, 1351, -iliator 1325, overseer of building works; †apellatus, (?) for -ellatus, fitted c 1510; -o c 1331, -ito c 1290, c 1350, to elucidate, provide with commentary; a. fenum, to make hay a 1128.
apparco, to impark, enclose 1428.
appar/es (pl.), letters couched in similar terms 12c., c 1250.
appar/itio, apparition 7c., 8c. a 1090, a 1520; Epiphany (6 Jan.) 1182, 1461; retinue, convoy c 1100; p 1240, 15c., †-atio c 1258, -entia c 1272, a 1564, -antia c 1290, appearance (in court); curia -entie (Lancs.) 1505, 1521; -entia, evidentness 1516; -ibilis, visible c 1260; -itor, royal official 845; (?) hundred bailiff c 1115; 12c., 1684, -ator 1327, 1400, apparitor (eccl.); -enter, apparently, seemingly a 1252, 1686; -ens, apparent, seeming 1475; conspicuous, outstanding 1238; clear, certain c 1343; see also heres, lex; -eo, to appear in court (leg.) c 1210, 1288.
appat/iciamentum 1444, -issamentum 1433, fixed charge, tribute (G.).
appell/atio, summons by bell (mon.) c 1296, (?) 1457; voucher to warranty c 1115; *appeal (to higher court) c 1196, 1686; a 1120, 15c., -amentum 1292, -atus 1201, c 1315, *-um 1150, c 1400, 'appeal', accusation (leg.); *a. tuitoria, appeal for protection 1299, a 1452; -amen, name c 960; -ans, appellant (leg.) c 1334, 1684; 1208, 1381, *-ator c 1185, 15c., -atrix (f.) 1284, 1312, appellor, accuser (leg.); -antes, Lords Appellant 1388; -ator, approver (leg.) 1259, 15c.; -atus, adversary of appellant 1684; appellee, accused person 1265, 1309; -ativum, appellative (gram.) c 1160, c 1258; -ativus, vocative (gram.) 790; naming by name 690, 946; so-called 793. 1283; -atorie (pl.) 1167, -atorium 1548, 1549, letter of appeal (eccl.); -atorius, appellatory (eccl.) 12c., 1446; -o, to 'appeal', accuse 1130, 1583; to appeal (to higher court) against 1684; to vouch to warranty c 1115.
appello, for aspello, to drive away 12c.
appen/sio, *affixing (of seal), sealing 1231, 1606; hanging (of bells) 1414; weight a 1125; pension 1189; -dicium, pendant, fringe a 1100, ‡15c.; hanging, curtain c 1459; c 1070, 1493, -ticium c 1095, c 1160, -tisium a 1150, -dentia c 1115, a 1564, appendage, appurtenance; 1141, -dicia 1212, -ticium 1175, 1431, -ticia 1288, -cium 1237, pentice, pent-house; Curia -ticii, Pentice Court (Chester) 1403, a 1550; -dicius c 1125, c 1220, -diticius c 1265,

-dulus 1181, c 1250, appurtenant; -diculum, appendage (? plumb-line) for adjusting beam of balance 1267; †-dium, yarnwinder, reel 15c.; -deo, to be affixed 1217; *-deo (-do), to appertain 1070, a 1574; -do, to adorn, fringe c 1400; *-do sigillum 1225, 1564; -dor, to be exchanged for, be worth 7c.
appersono, to appoint as parson c 1255; cf. impersono.
appertineo, to appertain c 1000. 1086, 1270.
appet/ibilitas, desirability c 1270, p 1300; -ibilis, *desirable 690, 870. 12c., c 1444; c 1190, c 1470, -itivus c 1160, c 1443; †-ivus c 1260, desirous, relating to desire; †-itudo, appetite 1344; -itor, wooer c 1090; -itrix, desirer (f.) p 1327; -o post, to crave for c 1430.
appietantia, pittance 1362, 1489; cf. pietantia.
applan/atio, levelling 1622; -o, to level, smooth a 1250, a 1275.
*applau/sus c 1070, c 1536, †-sitio, †-sio c 1200, applause, welcome; -denter, with applause 1286, 1380.
applectatus, folding (adj.) 1553.
applegi/amentum, surety (G.) 1282; -o, to become pledge or surety for c 1185, 1309.
applic/atio, (payment for) mooring, access to shore c 1108, 1327; 'application' (astr.) 1184; application (of rule, etc.) 1267, c 1457; -abilis, able to apply itself c 1218, a 1347; -ata, applicate (geom.) 1686; -atus, landing (of cargo) 1324; -o, to bring (cargo) to land 1388; (with dat.) to attribute to 7c.
applio, see AMPLI
applumb/atio c 1290, -atura c 1258, soldering with lead.
†applutus, (?) enriched c 1150.
appod/iamentum c 1200, c 1375, -ium c 1250, prop, buttress; ‡-encium, lever and counterpoise for drawing water 1483; -io, -ior a 1100, c 1362, -io me a 1250, to lean on, be supported by.
appois/ono 1258, -iono 1324, to poison.
appon-, see appositio; sponsagium.
apport/ionatio 1297, 1342, †-iatio 1315, portion, allotment; -iono, to apportion 1315, 1416.
apport/um, -us c 1235, c 1502, -atum, -atus c 1100, 1296, revenue, profit; -um, cargo, merchandise 1337; -o, to derive (profit) c 1350; to contribute 1195, 1298.
appos/itio (bibl.), †-io 1120, placing, affixing; application (med.) c 730. 1333; apposition (gram.) 1271; *a. sigilli, affixing a seal c 1160, 1437; -itivus, appositional (gram.) 13c.; concerned with application, attentive c 1277; -itor, apposer (Exchequer official) 1327 (cf. oppositor); a. luti, worker in wattle and daub c 1324; appon/ibilis, capable of addition c 1250; -o, to add c 1086, c 1275; to contrive c 1185, c 1293; to pledge, give as pledge 12c., 1436; to lay a charge (leg.) 1203, 1223; to put up for trial 1309; 1263, a. custum 1204, 1447, *a. expensas c 1267, c 1352, to expend; a. clamium, to lay a claim (of third party) (leg.) c 1218, c 1328; *a. manum (manus), to set hand to c 1218, c 1340; *a. sigillum,

to affix a seal c 1192, c 1450; **a. signum crucis,** to make one's mark 933.

appoto, to give to drink c 760.

appras-, *see* APPRETI

apprebend/atio, granting (of church) as prebend 1268, 1269; **-o,** to grant as prebend 1220, 1332.

apprehen/sio, arrest a 1188, 1438; **a. colli,** portion of weregeld c 1115; **-sibilitas,** apprehensibility c 1270; **-sibiliter,** apprehensibly 1345; **-siva,** faculty of apprehending a 1250; **-sivus,** concerned with apprehension a 1250, 1374; **-sor,** one who seizes c 1200; possessor c 1443; apprehender, perceiver c 1367; **-sus,** perception 1271; **†-tia,** a customary service a 1300; **aprisa** 1280, 1301, **aprisia** c 1281, 1313, **aprizia** 1309, report; **-do,** to apprise 1274; **apprendo,** to gain 8c.

***apprentici/us** 1293, c 1530, **apprentizius** 1661, **apprinticius** c 1392, apprentice; c 1290, **a. ad barras** c 1285, barrister; **a. de banco** p 1341, 1345; **a. juris, a. in jure** 15c.; **a. legis** 1305, 1456, **a. ad legem** 1348, **a. in lege** 1468; **prenticius de jure canonico** 15c.; **-a,** a female apprentice 1384; *cf.* PEREMPT; **-atus** 1378, 1419, **-agium** 1412, **-alitas** 1419, **-etas** c 1450, c 1500, apprenticeship.

apprest/atio, paying, payment 1345; 14c., **-um** 1377, loan; **-o,** to lend 14c.

***appreti/atio** 1199, 1562, **†-o,** 15c., **appresciatio** 1257, **-amentum** 1567, **apprisiamentum** 1610, appraisal, valuing; **-abilis,** appreciable c 1376; **-ator** 1240, c 1470, **apprisator** 1493, appraiser, valuer; **-o,** to purchase (bibl); ***-o** (eccl.), **-or** (*dep.*) c 1130, c 1461, **adpretio** c 1115, **appressio** a 1300, c 1397, **†appras/o** 1294, **-io** 1302, to appraise, value.

apprido, to take in mortgage (W.) 1416.

appris-, *see also* APPREHEN; APPRETI

apprisono, to emprison (G.) 1315.

approb/atio testamenti, probate of testament (leg.) 1341, 1684; **-abilis** 14c., c 1407, **adprobabilis** 597, worthy of approval; **-ative,** approvingly c 1343, 1378; **-ativus,** affirming, proving c 870; c 1290, a 1350, **-atorius** 1423, 1488, approving; **-atior,** most respected 1299; **-o testamentum** (leg.) c 1450; *see also* **approvatio.**

approp/iatio (**†-riatio**), approach c 1325; **-iabilis,** liable to approach c 1362; **-io *7c.,** c 730. a 1100, a 1452, **-rio** c 730. 1149, 1415, to approach; **-io** 1220, **-inquo** c 1260, to bring near; *see also* **approvatio.**

appropri/atio, appropriation, making one's own c 1295, c 1332; assignment, adaptation c 1200, c 1270; application 1380; ***c** 1220, 1484, **†appropatio** 1504, appropriation (eccl.); **-abilis,** adaptable, assignable c 1270, p 1300; **-ate,** by adaptation or assignment p 1300, c 1365; appropriately, properly 13c., 1427; **-atius,** more properly c 1270; **-atus,** appropriate, peculiar, proper 1202, a 1452; **-ator** 1303, 15c., **-etarius** 1537, appropriator (eccl.); **-atorius,** of appropriation (eccl.) 1313; **-o, *to** appropriate, make one's own c 1170, 1505; to assign, grant c 1190, c 1450; ***to** appropriate

(eccl.) c 1220, 1583; *see also* APPROP, **approvatio.**

appro/vatio 1392, **appruatio** 1334, **-vamentum** c 1250, 1537, **-viamentum** 1290, 15c., **-wamentum** c 1180, c 1300, **-wiamentum** 1301, 1364, **-fiamentum** a 1420, **-pviamentum** c 1400, **-priamentum** 1262, 1317, **-iamentum** 1259, 1306, **appruamentum** 1261, 15c., **appruiamentum** (**†apprivamentum**) 1252, c 1295, **appruviamentum** c 1200, 'approvement', 'improvement', enclosure or exploitation (of land), profit therefrom; **-ator** c 1465, **-eator** 1267, **-etator** 1272, **-iator** c 1284, **-viator** 1261, 1327, **-wiator** 1301, **-priator** c 1266, p 1330, ***appruator** 1262, 1542 (**comitatus** **regis**), 'improver' (royal official); **a. ulnagii** 1465; **-bo** 1253, 1260, **-vo** 1256, 1349, **-wo** 1402, **-o** c 1279, **‡**1483, **-bio** 1254, **-pio** c 1304, **-prio** 1317, **-io** 1256, 1279, **-vio** c 1273, 1331, **-wio** 1280, 1302, **approuvio** (G.) 1312, ***appruo** c 1245, 1523, **appruio** c 1265, c 1295, **appruvo** 1338, **-bo** (**-vo,** **-vio, -pwio, †-co, *appruo, †apprivo,** **apperuio,** *etc.*) me de (*or* in) c 1200, 15c., to 'improve', exploit (land, *etc.*); *cf.* **impruiamentum.**

approxim/atio, nearness, approach c 1236, 1620; **-abilis,** approaching c 1200; **-atus** (**inter**), (?) intermediate 12c.; **-o,** to approach, come near c 870. c 1212, c 1540; to bring near 1263, c 1361.

appru-, *see also* **approvatio.**

apprunto, to borrow c 1193, c 1220.

appulsio, driving (to) 1287; landing c 1125, c 1400.

***appunct/uatio** 1426, 1482, **-atio** 15c., ***-uamentum** 1426, 1498, **-amentum** 1414, 1468, agreement, settlement; **-uo, *to** agree, settle 1429, 1583; 1380, 1562, **-o** 1454, 1562, to appoint, prescribe.

appur/amentum 1276, **-us** c 1500, liquidation of debt; **-o,** to liquidate (debt) 1274, 1284.

apric/us, dry c 550; mild-tempered c 1350, c 1365; **-o,** to dry up c 550.

apriol/a, -us, *see* aper.

apris-, *see* APPREHEN

†aproximeron, sexual impotence a 1250.

apsi/s, absis, lozenge, mascle (her.) c 1595; apsis (math.) 1686; **absida,** apse c 685; **-dalis,** lozenge-shaped c 1565.

apso, to lay waste (G.) c 1250.

apt/atio c 1115, 1431, **-ificatio** a 1250, **-atura** 15c., **-ura** 1431, 1462, fitting together, adaptation; **-abilis** c 1218, **abtabilis** 7c., apt, fit; **-amen,** book-cover c 1080; **-anter,** suitably 15c.; **‡-atorium,** shaping-board 1483; **-atrix,** adaptive, combinative (*f.*) c 1270; ***-itudo,** aptitude, faculty, special quality or occasion c 1190, c 1542; **-itudinalis,** concerned with aptitude c 1290, 1427; **-itudinaliter,** by way of aptitude c 1300; **-ifico,** to fit, adapt a 1250; **‡-ito,** to shape 1483; **-o,** to train, form (falc.) a 1150, 1313.

†apterium, (?) *for* **apodyterium,** vestry c 1200.

apud, to, towards (motion) 1274, 1461; **a. acta,** in, by, the acts of court (leg.) c 1250, 1684; **aput,** *for* apud, a 1130, 1277.

Apulia, gold of fine quality (alch.) 1267.

aqu-, *see also* acqu-

aqu/a, ordeal by water 1134, c 1219 (*cf.* lex); ‡learning 15c., 1483; ‡people 15c., 1483; ‡sorrow 15c.; a. acuta, a. alkali, alkaline water a 1292; ‡a. amoris, philtre made of human blood 1652; a. ardens, spirit ‡14c., 1390; corrosive fluid c 1470; a. bassa, low tide 1445; a. benedicta a 1125, 1464, a. exorcizata a 690, a. sanctificata (?) c 1000, holy water; a. celestina, *see* a. philosophorum; ‡a. celestis, rectified wine 1652; a. cinerum, water containing potash c 1390; a. fetida, *aqua Mercurii* 1144, ‡1652; a. fortis c 1345, 1620, ‡a. nitri 1652, nitric acid; a. Gregoriana, water blest by Gregorian rite c 1514; ‡a. lilii, orpiment 1652; a. limonis, lime-water 1380; a. maritima, tidal river 1400, 1403; a. metallorum, solvent fluid (alch.) c 1227; a. permanens c 1320, ‡1652, ‡a. philosophica 1652, a. philosophorum a 1252, ‡a. celestina 1652, ‘philosophers’ mercury’ (alch.); a. recens, fresh (unsalted) water 1290, 1546; a. regis, mixture of nitric and hydrochloric acids 1620; ‡a. rosacea 14c., a. rosalia 1421, a. rosarum 1418, a. rosata c 1190, 1307, rose-water; ‡a. rubicunda, a. Megi, a. segi, *“aqua vitrioli”* 1652; a. ‡salmantina a 1250, ‡a. salmatina 1652, “water made from salt”; a. saponis, lye 13c.; a. solis 13c., ‡a. elsabon, holsobon 1652, potable gold; a. viscosa a 1250, c 1345, a. vite c 1320, ‡1652, a. viva c 1320, mercury (vapour); a. vite, ardent spirit, whisky 1267, 1677;

-aductile 1348, ‡15c., -aductus c 1300, ‡15c.,-eductile ‡15c.,1509,-educta c 1511, -eductum c 1375, c 1471, -eductus c 1174, 1501, -eductulus 1476, lade, conduit (*cf.* avidotus); -agium, (payment for) supply of water to mill 1209, (?) 1223; (payment for) carriage of goods by water (Norm.) 15c.; c 1266, 1453, †-agangium 1361, -alicium ‡1483, 1514, -alicola 1628, water-course, gutter; ‡-alium, top of head 1483; -amanile, *for* -emanalis, washbasin for hands c 760. a 1090; -aria, (office of) ewery 1399, 1574; -arius, ewerer, officer of royal or noble household c 1136, 1391; -aria 1330, 1431, *-arium 7c. c 1250, a 1452, -arius 1328, ewer (especially for holy water); -arium, (?) watering-place 1308, 1445; 1326, -erium 1326, (?) drain; ‡-ariolum, “sink” a 1519; -arius, -aticus, *see also* caretta, frenum, molendinum, porta, rete, rota, sapphirus, via; -aticum trussing’, portable ewer 1421; -aticus, Moses c 1000; locus -aticus, watering-place (for cattle) 1384; vir -aticus, water-man c 1411; ‡-aster, hallucination 1652; -atio, watering (of cattle) 1365;

-ebajulatrix, water-carrier (*f.*) 1357; -ebajulus 1334, 1535, -ebagilus 1397, 1518, ‡-ebachelus 15c., -arius 1348, ‡1483, holy-water clerk (*cf.* BAJUL); -ebajulatus, office of holy-water clerk c 1427, c 1530; -eballivus, water-bailiff 1475, 1507 (*cf.* baillivus); -eitas a 1250, c 1270, -ositas c 1115, 1620, wateriness; -eus, watery,

aqueous c 1212, c 1470; acosus, well watered 1353; -ifluus c 550, -efluus (?) c 873, flowing with water; -ifolia, holly 1544; -ivomus, spouting water 1634; -atico, (?) to irrigate 1321; to ret (flax) 1340; -o, to wet 1299, 1437; to water (cattle) c 1257, 1327.

aquesta, *see* acquisitio.

aquil/a c 1300, auquilata (G.) 1268, -etta 1297, ‘eagle’, base coin; mercury vapour (alch.) c 1320, ‡1652; petra -e, eagle-stone (gem) 1383; -aris, eagle-like 14c.; -ianus, Imperial 1347; -us, with an aquiline nose c 1200.

‡aquile/gia 14c., -ia a 1250, (?) avigilia a 1150, columbine (bot.); *“genista”* 1652; -na, *“consolida regalis”* 1652.

aquilon, *see* diaquilon *s.v.* dia-.

*aquil/onalis c 630, c 870. a 1125, 1461, †-o (*adj.*) 1206, -ensis, -encis 12c., -onarius 1540, -onicus a 1408, aquinalis c 730, *for* -onaris, northern.

†aquiror, (?) *for* acqueror, to complain 13c.

aquito, *see* ACQUIET; aketo.

1 ara, *for* hara, pig-sty c 1150, 1510.

2 ara, (?) oar 1342.

Arabicum, Arabic language 1271.

*arab/ilis 1215, 1315, †-ies 1232, -blis 1232, -bulus 1252, aralus c 1200, maple (Fr. *érable*); *see also* aratrum.

arachnos c 870, arena c 1495, (?) †armaria a 1250, *for* aranea, spider; *cf.* 3 tela.

aradico, *see* abradico.

araenum, *see* opus.

aragiatus, mad (O.F. *aragie*) 1205.

aragium, *see* arreragium; 2 averium.

arantium, *see* AURANT

‡arapag/ator, miner 1483; ‡-o, to shovel, mine c 1440, 1483.

ar/atrum 738, 858. 1414, -atum 1196, -atura 1086, -alia (*n. pl.*) 1086, terra -atri 697, c 831. a 1142, c 1414, ploughland; *-abilis, arable 1086, 1559; *see also* bos; -atiuncula (†-acuincula, -euncula), furrow, channel c 1160, c 1180; -atorius c 1220, -tralis 11c., of or for a plough or ploughing; *-atura c 1115, 14c., *-ura 1193, c 1400, -urum c 1250, c 1300, ploughing, plough-service; a. gabuli, ‘gavel-erthe’ 1363; -ans homo, ploughman (086, -o, to write (*cf.* exaro) c 1212.

arbal/ista a 1347, -esta, arbelesta 1190, -asta 1194, -astis 1276, arbelasta 1212, albelasta 1293, arblasta 1275, 1335, arblastus 1380, arblast, crossbow; -istrum ad viz’, crossbow worked by winch 1297; -istaria 1198, -isteria 1190, 1212, -asteria 1199, alblastaria 1212, alblasteria c 1227, crossbow service; *-istarius 1086, c 1293, -ister 1086, -estarius 1086, 1157, -astarius 1184, arbelastarius 1160, 1212, arbelesta-rius c 1180, arblastarius 1291, alabasta-rius c 1130, c 1200, ‡alblastarius c 1440, albrastarius 1212, crossbowman; telum albalaste, crossbow-bolt c 1540; arbela-stata, crossbow-shot (distance) 1204; arbla-steria 1251, -astareia 1203, albesterium c 1219, arrow-slit; *cf.* arcubalista.

arbitr/atio 15c., a 1452, -amentum 1430, 1608, decision, arbitration; -alis c 1291,

1448, **-amentalis** 1461, of or for arbitration; **-arie**, in accordance with decision 1284; **-ativus**, optional or arbitrary c 1258; ***-ator**, arbiter c 1279, c 1518; **-a** c 1341, **-ix** 1254, arbitress; **-or** (*dep.*), to expect 790.

arbor/, Jesse 1303; wooden saddle-base 1368, 1396; ‡**a. maris**, coral 1652; **a. molendini** 1271, 1331 **-a m.** 1232, mill-shaft; ‡**a. Sancte Marie**, feverfew (or other plant) 14c.; ‡**-es**(*pl.*), skin disease, morphew 1652; **-arius**, (?) stock-maker c 1120, 1159; **-atus**, embroidered with figures of trees 1245; **albareda**, plantation (G.) 1289, 1315; **-eus**, wooden, wooded c 550; **-iferus**, borne on trees c 1362; **-osus**, arboreal 14c.

‡**arb/utus** 15c., **-itus** 1467, ‡1483, "crab-tree"; **-itum** 1481, ‡1483, crab-apple.

arc/a (arch-), Noah's ark (bibl.); 'trunk', illegal weir for fishing 1297, 1454; **a. cyrographorum**, chest containing Jewish bonds 1244, 1274; **a. libraria**, book-case 690; **a. pectoris, a. sinus**, chest, breast c 1170; **a. sancta**, reliquary c 1090; **-agium**, (?) (payment for) use of chests (mon.) (Norm.) c 1075; **-arium**, treasure-chest c 1306; **-arius**, treasurer 796. c 1135, 1575; **-ator**, (?) satchel-bearer, *i.e.* student c 550;‡ **-ella**, little chest, "forcer" '15c.; *see also* **arcus**.

arcagium, *see* **arca**; **arcus**.

arcan/e, secretly 1441; *see also* **archangelus**.

arc/arius, -ellus, *see* **arcus**.

‡**arcecosus**, (?) *for* **acetosus**, 15c.

arcenocum, *see* **arsenicum**.

arceo (ad), to compel 1246, 1298; *cf.* **arcto**.

arceticus, archerica, *see* **arthritica**.

‡**arceuthis**, juniper 14c.; *cf.* **alkel**.

arceutum (†**arcentum**), procuration, forced hospitality (Béarne) 1190.

arch-, *see also* **arcus**.

†**archades** (*pl.*), (?) rulers c 950.

‡**archaltes**, pillar supporting the earth 1652.

archangel/us (bibl.), **archagelus** c 870, (?) **archanus** c 950, archangel; **-icus**, archangelic 1124, 1413; ‡**-ica**, white deadnettle (bot.) 14c.

archbuttans, *see* **archibuteraceus**.

archemacherus, *see* **archimagirus**.

archeus (Paracelsi), vital spirit or principle 1620, ‡1652.

archi/abbas, chief abbot c 1188, c 1300; **-adversarius**, chief adversary c 1220.

archiat/er, physician a 1142; **-ros animarum** c 1000.

archibutera/ceus, -sius 1320, †**archbuttans** 1385, flying buttress.

archi/cancellarius, high chancellor c 1188, 1570; **-cantator** c 730. c 1150, **-cantor** c 730. c 1118, c 1414, head singer or precentor; †**-clocus**, (?) *for* **clopus**, robber 7c.; **-cocus** 1461, ‡1483, **-quoquus** 1588, chef; **-dapifer**, chief steward 1450; †**-decanus**, chief dean c 1298; **-diabolus**, arch-fiend 1169.

archidiaco/ c 1102, ***-nus** (eccl.), archdeacon; **-nus major** (G.) 1289; **-nalia** (*pl.*), rights or dues of archdeacon 1249, 1361; **-nalis**, archidiaconal 1222, 1469; ***-natus** 8c., 9c. c 1125, 1684, **archideaconatus** 1229, archdeaconry.

archi/didascalus 1560, c 1620, **-didascolus** 1541, headmaster; **-doctus**, highly trained c 1437; **-dominus**, abbot 1299; **-ductor**, chief leader c 960; **-dux**, archduke 1487, 1558; **-ducissa**, archduchess 1513.

*archiepiscop/us (eccl.), **erchiepiscopus** 1225, archbishop; **-alia** (*pl.*), duties of archbishop c 1130; ***-alis**, archiepiscopal 797, c 900. a 1125, 1535; (*subst.*) adherent of archbishop c 1193; ***-atus** c 730, 1006. 1086, 1535, **-ium** c 1325, c 1436, office or province of archbishop, archbishopric; **-ium**, archbishop's palace c 1125; **-or**, to be made archbishop 1164.

archierarchus, archbishop c 950.

archi/factor, -fector, -fer, *see* **arcus**.

archifenium, *see* **arcifinium**.

archi/flamen, high-priest 1136, 1535; arch-bishop c 1210, 1521; **-forestarius**, head forester c 1450; **-grammateus**, Lord Chancellor 1570; **-hereticus**, arch-heretic 1378; **-justitiarius**, chief justice c 1180; **-keraunus** (†**arigikeminus**), epithet of Jupiter 1344; **-latro**, arch-robber 1413; **-levita**, archdeacon 1151, a 1452; **-leviticus**, archidiaconal c 1218; †**-lius**, *for* **-chilius**, chiliarch c 950; **-lollardus**, arch-Lollard 1413; **-magirus** (**archemacherus**), chief cook 1443; **-magus**, magical c 1112; **-mandrita**, archimandrite, abbot (eccl.) c 705, 960. c 1125, 1417; **-marescallus**, chief marshal 1140; **-minister**, governor c 1150.

archimium, *see* **ARCHIV**

†**archi/monasterium**, (?) cathedral 12c.; **-pastor**, archbishop c 974; archdeacon 1438; **-pater**, chief priest 797, c 950; **-philosophus, -sophus**, the arch-philosopher (Aristotle) 1345; **-pirata**, admiral 971; **-polites**, prince c 950; **-polus**, celestial pole c 840. c 1100.

archiponti/fex, archbishop 9c. 11c., 15c.; **-ficalis**, archiepiscopal 1442, 15c.; **-ficatus**, archbishopric 745, 803.

archi/predo, arch-robber c 1377; **-prefectus**, governor 1498.

archipresbyter/, chief priest, president of collegiate church, rural dean c 1182, 1500; Roman Catholic archpriest in England 1621; **a. cardinalis** c 1220; **-atus**, rural deanery 1243, 1547; **archiprisbitralis**, ruridecanal 1440.

*archipresul/, archbishop 956, 1060. a 1090, 1570; **-aris**, archiepiscopal 1253; ***-atus**, archbishopric c 1188, c 1553.

archi/princeps, prince elector 16c.; **-prior**, head prior 12c.; †**-ptes**, archbishop c 1000; **-sacerdos**, archbishop 798, 813. c 1150; **-schismaticus**, leader of schism c 1188; **-schola**, head of school 1091, p 1408; **-senior Hibernie** c 1112; **-sigillarius**, keeper of Great Seal c 1193; **-sophus**, *see* **archiphilosophus**; **-speculator**, chief scout 801; archbishop (?) 986; **-strategus** 7c., **-strateias** c 950, commander-in-chief.

archist/erium, -eum, *see* **aristerium**.

archisynagog/a, chief synagogue c 870; c 1362, c 1546, **-us** a 1250, chief ruler (of synagogue).

architect/atio, planning c 1200; **-or** c 1170,

c 1595, **-onicus** c 1246, 1345, architect, founder; **-or,** thatcher 1375, ‡1483; **-onicus,** fundamental 1610; **-orius,** architectural c 1250.

architenens, one who holds chief place 8c.; ‡captain, chieftain 1483; *see also* **arcus.**

archit/es, -icus, *see* ASCIT

architesis, *see* **antithesis; arcus.**

archi/thalassus, ·Lord High Admiral 1586, c 1595; **-thronatus,** archbishop c 1381; **-triclinus,** master of a feast 8c. c 1090, 1271; *(adj.)* suitable for master of feast 1432; **a. regius,** marshal 1528; **-triclineum,** parlour 1551; **-tyrannus,** arch-tyrant 1461.

*archiv/a *(n. pl.),* archives c 1080, 1535; **-us,** secretary 15c.; †**archimium,** chest c 550.

archon/, ruler c 550, c 1000; archbishop 948. c 1090; **-ticon** 13c., †**arcoticon** (†**artoricon**) a 1250, an electuary.

archticus, *see* ARTHRIT

‡**arcifinium** (†**artifinium**), "headland" 1483; ‡**archifenium,** "croft" 15c.; **ortiphinium,** (?) headland 15c.

arcillum, *see* ARGILL

arcion/us, -arius, *see* **2 arco.**

arcipiter, *see* **accipiter.**

arcist/erium 955. 12c., c 1170, **-eum** a 975, monastery (? *for* asceterium); *cf.* **ergasterium.**

‡**arcistria,** lectern 1483.

arcitula, arcistes, *see* **arcus.**

1 †**arco,** (?) bracket for altar curtains c 1080.

2 arc/o 1217, **arso** c 1285, **arzo** 1237, **-ionus** 1232, **-unus** 1233, saddle-bow; **-ionarius,** for a saddle-bow 1213; **-onerius** 13c., **arzonarius** c 1230, maker of saddle-bows; *cf.* **arcus selle;** †**artuuerum.**

arcon/ius c 1380, 16c., †**-omalus,** †**-omolus** 1239, stack, rick; **-iatio,** stacking (Sc.) 1466, 1467; ‡**-istus** (? **-istes**), stacker 15c.; **-izo** 1229, ‡c 1440, ‡**-io** 15c., to stack.

arcoticon, *see* ARCHON

arct/atio (**art-**) c 1250, 15c., **-itudo** 1336, c 1450, restraint, constraint, straitness; **-amen,** fitting, adaptation c 550; **-anter,** urgently 1385; **-ate,** strictly 1288; **-ator,** gaoler 1314; **-um,** difficult position c 1192, c 1367; **-ura,** part of mill, (?) sluice 1328; **-us,** narrow, confined c 1090, c 1420; **-o,** to fit, adapt c 550; to contract, limit c 550; to restrain, constrain c 1157, c 1556; to make a compact 1267.

arct/uri *(pl.),* north c 870; **articus,** *for* **-icus,** extremity, (?) region c 550; †**arotus,** (?) star c 550.

arcubalist/a c 1185, c 1400, **archibalista** c 1180, 1212, arblast, crossbow; c 1125, 1370, **-arius** c 1250, c 1400, **-erius** c 1400, **archibalistarius** 1084, 12c., **archibalestarius** 1086, crossbowman; *cf.* **arbalista.**

arcudium, *see* **armicudium.**

arc/us, bow: **-ūs spatium,** bow-shot 1478; **-us** 1270, 1299, **a. boum** 1248, 1454, **a. ad carrucam** 1270, **-ulus** 1350, **arquilla, arquillus** a 1300, 1338, ox-bow; 12c., 1420, **-a, archa** c 1140, a 1490, **archea** 1233, 1340, **archiola** c 1325, arch, vault; *see also* **consistorium, curia,** DEAMBUL, **decanus;** **-us anguli,** arc subtending angle 1326; **a. balistus** (*cf.* **arcubalista**) 1328, **a. crucia-**

tus 1532, **a. crucifer** 1513, crossbow; **a. busius,** *see* **harcabusarius; a. latus** 1390; **a. manualis,** hand-bow 1306; **a. de petra,** stone-bow 1419; **a. pravus,** evil course 1167, 1409; **a. selle** 1324, **a. ad sellam** 1226, **-ellus** 1225, ‡**-ulus** c 1200, 1483, saddle-bow (*cf.* **2 arco**); **-agium,** payment to masons on completion of arch 1326, 1333; **-arius** 1086, c 1470, **-uarius** 1086, 1473, **archiarius** 1156, 1575, **archerius** 1198, 1347, †**archius** c 1347, **archerus** 1191, 1288, **archerarius** a 1142, †**arques** c 1180, **archifer** 1453, **arcister** 690, **arcistes** 8c., **architenens** c 970. c 1137, c 1540, **-ubajulus** c 1255, ‡**-ubilus** 15c., **-uatus** (? **-uator**) c 1465, archer, bow-bearer; **archeria,** archer-service 1198, 1244; archery 13c.; 1260, **arquerium** (G.) 1304, arrow-slit; **archifactor** 1369, **archifector** 1466, 1578, bowyer; ‡**architesis,** bow-case 1483; ‡**-itula** 15c., **corda** †**-ua** 1419, bow-string; **-ulus,** fiddle-bow 1483; **arkillus,** bow of a crossbow 1205, 1228; †**archallus,** (?) arch, vault c 1300; **baculus -ualis,** bow-stave 1420; **-ualis** 1267, 1461, **-uosus** c 1361, **-uatus** c 1200, **archeatus** 1292, curved, arched; **-ualiter,** in a curve c 1315, c 1362; **-uatio,** arching, vaulting c 1150; closing of the hand c 1200; **a. superciliorum** a 1250; **-uositas,** curvature c 1375; **-uo,** (?) to inflict with a bow a 1225; to encircle 1376; †**-utio,** to shoot at with a bow 1284; **archerio,** to practice archery 1290.

ard/ea, heron: ‡**-ua** 15c., **addea** a 1300; **-earius** 1242, 1257, **-uarius** 1253, 1290, for hunting herons; **-uum,** (?) heronry 1451; *cf.* **tardearius.**

ard/elia, bigotry c 1620; ‡**-uliosus,** sly c 1440.

ard/entia, ardour c 1250; **-or,** smelter 1213, 1290; **-ator calcis,** lime-burner 1351; **-ens,** (?) bright-coloured 1213; *see also* **aqua;** **-eo,** *to burn, set fire to c 1188, c 1451; to burn (lime) 1396; to smelt (ore) 1196, c 1315; to blanch (silver) 1086, 1275; to lose weight when blanched c 1178, 1238; *see also* **arsio.**

ardicus, *hardi* (coin of Guienne) 1409, 1410.

ardu/itas, difficulty c 1218, 1424; eminence (title) 1220; **-e,** with difficulty c 1250; **-us,** (?) important (of documents) 1376; *see also* **ardea.**

are/a, (?) fire-place 1273, 1469; church-yard c 1280; floor, story c 1255, c 1444; deck (naut.) c 1250; 1086, 1334, **a. salinaria** 1307, salt-floor, enclosure for salt-making; area (math.) 1145; **a. tentoriorum,** tenter-yard 1385; **-iata,** measure of straw from threshing-floor (C.I.) 1247, 1248; **-ola,** field (her.) 1654; small area (math.) 1686; †**-ra** 1254, **airale** 1279, 1291, **airiale** 1289, open space (G.); *see also* **aeria.**

arefac/tio, drying, parching a 1250, c 1530; **-io** c 550, **arifacio** 1459, to dry (*trans.*).

aren/, *for* **-a,** sand c 1185; **-a,** sand-stone c 950.

arena, tin (alch.) 1144; *see also* **arachnos.**

arend-, arent-, *see* ARREN

arenga, *see* **aurantia; haranga.**

areno, *see* ARRAIN

are/ola, -ra, *see* **area.**

Areopagita 12c., **Areiopagita** c 1470, Areopagite.

‡**Ares,** second natural principle, subordinate to *Archeus* (alch.) 1652.

aresta 1223, **arista** c 1250, *****pannus de a.** 1215, 1295, **p. de arista** 1245, **p. de aristo** 1300, **p. de lareste** 1310, **p. de alesta** 1244, a rich oriental fabric; *see also* **arista.**

arestatio, remainder 1282; *see also* ARREST

aret/e, virtue (ἀρετή) 1267; ‡**-icus,** virtuous 14c.; *see also* **arthritica.**

aretro, *see* **a retro.**

arga, cuckold a 1446; *see also* **erga.**

‡**argelzarus,** verdigris 14c.

argent/um, cash 1301, 1393; name of a comet c 1270; **a. anguillare,** eel-silver (customary payment) 1596; **a. de decenna,** tithing silver 1268; **a. Dei,** God's penny, earnest money 1275, 1360; **a. fractum,** money less than 1d. 1446; **a. vinee,** 'vineyard silver' (paid at Ramsey) 1307; **a. vivum extinctum,** (?) a mercuric salt a 1250; **-arius,** *see* **miles; -eus,** silver coin c 1090, c 1444; **-eius** 1537, **argens** c 1423, *for* **-eus,** silvern; **-osus,** containing silver 1325; silvered (of ermine) c 1595; ‡**-ifilum,** silver wire 14c.; **-ifrisum,** silver embroidery or fringe c 1080; **-illa** a 1250, ‡14c., **-ina** 1626, silverweed (bot.).

*****argill/um** 1293, c 1471, **-a** c 1182, **-ium** 1388, **arzillum** 1239, 1349, **arcillum, arisillum** 1279, **arsillum** 1283, 1288, **arsilium** 1306, 'argil', clay; **a. figulatorum,** potters' clay 1501; ‡**-arium,** "clay-pit" 1483; **arzilosus,** clayey 1258.

argisterium, *see* **ergasterium.**

argu/ella c 1250, 1340, **-illa** 1281, **arzilium** 1260, archil, violet dye.

argu/itio, argument 1362, 1427; 1378, **-tio** c 1239, 1427, reproof; **-tio** c 1250, **-ties** 1457, subtlety; **-tiuncula,** quibble 1344; **-itive** p 1300, c 1430, **-tive** 1427, **-mentative** p 1394, a 1446, inferentially, by way of proof; **-mentativus,** inferential, logical c 1290; **-mentose,** convincingly, plausibly c 1160, c 1293; **-mentosus,** plausible, ingenious 870. c 1170, 1518; **-mentum,** argument (ac.) 1462; 'argument', quantity from which another is inferred (math.) 1686; **-mentor,** to calculate c 815.

argyritus, silvered (of ermine) c 1595.

aria, *see* **aer; aeria.**

ariagium, *see* **2 averium.**

†**aricto,** (?) to place c 550.

arid/itas, dryness of spirit c 730; ‡**-ura,** wasting away, consumption (med.) 1652; **-us,** dried (of fish) 1429, 1479; **-a,** dry land c 1180; **-atus,** dried, withered a 1564.

arierefeodum, *see* **retrofeodum.**

arie/s, sort of quintain 1233, 1414; builders' ram 1286; **-ta,** ewe 1575; ‡**-tulus,** young ram 1483; **-tatio,** battering with a ram 1620; †**acrieto,** to butt c 550.

arifacio, *see* AREFAC

arigikeminus, *see* **archikeraunus.**

arill/us, -a, grape-stone a 1250, ‡14c.

ari/meticus, -smeticus, *see* ARITHMET

aripendus, *see* **arpenna.**

arist/a, ear of corn: **aresta** c 1290, ‡**-ella** 1483; **-a** c 1180, c 1255, **aresta** 1260, ridge,

'hip' or 'herring-bone' strip (arch.); ridge (of cloth) c 1370; ‡**-ator,** gleaner 1483; ‡**-o,** to glean 1483; *see also* **aresta,** ARREST

aristocrati/a, aristocracy c 1341, c 1434; **-ce,** aristocratically c 1343; **-cus,** aristocratic c 1341, c 1376.

aristo/lochia, birthwort (bot.): **-logia** c 1200, 13c.

Aristotelicus, Aristotelian a 1200, c 1348.

arithmet/rica c 730, **arismetica** c 1180, c 1300, **arismetrica** a 1235, c 1400, **arsmetica** c 1180, **arsmetrica** 1326, 1432, *for* **-ica,** arithmetic; **-icus** 797, **arismeticus** 1267, **arismetricus** 1374 arithmetician; **arimeticus** c 1150, **arismeticus** c 1178, **arismetricus** c 1365, arithmetical.

†**arkastella,** (?) *for* **arbalista,** 1516.

arkillus, *see* **arcus.**

arkmannus, *see* **2 averium.**

arlecho, *see* HARN

arm/a (*f. s.*), arm, weapon 1295, 1514; (*n. pl.*), *****arms** (her.) c 1250, 1517; **causa -orum,** plea of arms (her.) 1395; **jus -orum,** military law 1347; **-a defensiva** c 1217, 1571; **a. invasiva** c 1340, 1571; **a. offensiva** c 1217, 1569; **a. Domini,** (?) instruments of the Passion (eccl.) 1448; **a. duplicata,** double arms (her.) p 1394; **a. emolita** 1251, c 1290, **a. moluta** 1243, c 1290, edged weapons; **a. libera** c 1115, c 1210, **a. militaria** a 1142, 15c., arms of free man or knight; **a. servitutis,** arms of unfree man c 1115; **-amentum** (*coll.*), arms c 550; **-aria** 1436, **-ania, -andia** 1608, armoury; **-arius** 1475, 1479, **-ararius** 1355, ‡1520, **-orarius** 1606, **-ourerius** 1390, **-urarius** 1333, 1426, **-ator** 1292, 1549, **-ifaber** c 1393, armourer; **-urarius lineus (leneus)** 1380, 1461, **a. linearum armaturarum** 1327, maker of linen armour; **-ata,** army c 1400, 1461; armada, fleet 1360, 1472; **-atio,** arming, wearing armour 13c., 1327; **-atrix,** protective (*f.*) a 1446; **-atura,** *****armour, armament, weapon 1166, 1496; manufacture of arms 13c.; armoury 1439, 1440; armed force 1468, 1583; arms (her.) 1311; **a. (latronis),** fetters 1230; **a. (navigii),** equipment c 1125; **a. ferrea** c 1243, 1324; **a. linea** 1213, 1549; **-ura,** armour 1306, 1418; **-icudium** 1448, 1516, **-iscudium** c 1448, **-acudium** 1554, 1573, †**arcudium** 1549, ‡**-iturium** 15c., dagger; **-iductor** (†**-doctor**), commander (Sc.) 1461, c 1540;
-iger, *****squire (armour-bearer, man-at-arms or attendant) a 1123, 1586; *****esquire (title) 1430, 1687; armigerous person (her.) c 1595; **a. pro corpore,** esquire of the body c 1484, 1501; **-istitium,** armistice 1335; **-o duellum,** to arm for a judicial combat c 1218, 13c.; **-o rotam molendini** 1324, 1334; *see also* 1 **equus, frater, gens, homo, serviens, tunica, vir.**

†**armagium,** (?) *f.l.* for **arrivagium,** (Fr.) 1361.

armaria, *see* **arma, arachnos.**

*****armari/um** c 1000. c 1160, c 1480, **almaria** 1386, c 1456, *****almarium** 12c., 1432, **almare** c 1330, **almerium** c 1180, 1419, **almererium** 1212, **almoria** 1359, 1423, aumbria 1520, *-olum 12c., 1601, **almariola** c 1250, 1354, **almariolum** c 1330, 1435, **almarialum** a 1452, **armoriola** 1461, **almoriolum** 1434, **ammoriolum** 1458, **-culum** c 1409, aumbry, cupboard, chest, book-case, study; **-us**, librarian c 1266, c 1330; cf. ELEEMOSYN

armebolta, manacle, handcuff 1486.

armelinus, armilium, see **ermina**.

Armenicus, see **bolus**.

armi-, see also **arma**.

armifraudita, see **hermaphrodita**.

*arm/ilausa 1386, a 1560, -ilousa 1419, -ellosa c 550, †-igaisum, †-ilcaisia c 1397, ‡-iclausa 15c., cloak; ‡-iclausum, "clasp" 15c.

1 †**arm/illa**, (?) arm-pit c 1280; †**-ister**, for **-us**, shoulder a 1250.

2 **armilla**, armillary sphere (astr.) 1267, 1326; **a. suspensoria**, ring for hanging up 1326.

armoniacus, see **sal**.

Arn/aldensis 1281, 1282, **Ernaldensis** 1289, **-audensis** 1285, 1290, **-oldensis** 1281, 1289, **-aldinus** 1283, a local coinage (G.).

arnaldia, a disease, (?) Syrian fever c 1192.

arn/amentum, -ementum, see **atramentum**.

arnoglossa, plantain (bot.) a 1250, ‡14c.

aro, see **aratrum**.

arogon, kind of unguent a 1250.

*aroma/, spice (bibl.); -tarius 1516, 1542, ‡-topola 1520, 1570, spicer, apothecary; -ticitas, fragrance a 1200, 13c.; cella -tica, drug-store 793; -tizo, to perfume 1378; ‡to anoint 1483.

aron, arum (bot.): **aaron** a 1250; cf. **barba, iarus**.

arotus, see **arcturi**.

arp/a, -o, see **harpa; harpo**.

arpen/na 1086, 1238, **-nus** 1086, 1246, **-num** c 1200, **-dus** 1086, **-ta** c 1080, **-tum** 1086, 1289, **aripendus** 1086, **agripenna** a 1142, measure of land (esp. vineyard), **arpent**.

arq-, see also **arcus**.

arquinetta, alkanet (bot.) 1380.

arr-, see also ARRH

arracio, to pull up 1234.

Arracium, see **Atrebaticus**.

arrai/a (array-), outfit, trappings 1455; **-amentum** 1335, **-atio** 1394, fitting out, equipment; drawing up (of panel of jurors) 1387, 1513; 1312, 1337, **-atio** 1337, 1434, drawing up, drafting (of document); **-atio**, *array, mustering (of troops) 1327, 1442; **-atus**, array, procession 1425; **-ator**, arrayer (of troops) 1322, 1536; commissioner of array (eccl.) 1359; **a. equorum** 1326; **a. pacis**, keeper of the peace 1326; **a. venationum**, master of the hunt 1443; **-o**, *1322, 1511, **arreo** 1324, **arrio** 1403, c 1457, to array (troops); **-o**, to fit out (ship) c 1377, 1419; to draw up (document) 1327, c 1456; **a. panellum** 1387, 1419; †**a. assisam**, to summon an assize 1327, 14c.; *see also* ARRAM

arrain/amentum 1385, **arenamentum** 1327, arraignment, accusation; **-o, -io** 1320, 1334, **arreino (arrenio)** 1331, 15c., **areno** 1292, 15c., **reno** 1309, †**arroinano** (C.I.) 13c., **arrationo** 1274, 1300, to arraign, accuse, interrogate; *see also* ARRAM

arraizus, naval officer, *arraez* (Port.) 1386.

arral-, see ARRH

arramenta, see **erramenta**.

*arram/o, -io (†arrain-) assisam, to 'arraign' (summon, hold) an assize (leg.) 1199, c 1448; a. custodiam 1380; a. duellum 1292; a. juratam 1201; a. recognitionem 1203; a. sectam 1277; †arraindo assisam 1319; †-atio assise 1342, a 1564; cf. ramio.

arranto, see **arrenda**.

arrastrium, hearth (at ironworks) 1351.

†**arratellus**, *f.l.* for **martellus**, 1298.

arratiomo, see ARRAIN

arreagium, see 2 **averium**.

arremissa, see **abremissio**.

arren/da (aren-) a 1452, 1546, **-damentum** 1289, 1440, **-tamentum** 1262, 1265, **-datio** 1289, 1559, *-tatio 1266, 15c., **-taria** 1250, 1297, rent, renting, commutation; **-dator** 1308, 1435, **-datorius** 1479, renter; **-tator serjantiarum** c 1271; **-do** c 1280, 1567, †**arredo** 1328, **-to** 1257, 1550, **arranto** 1334, to let for a rent, farm out; **-to**, to rate, assess 1251, c 1290; to commute (customary service or serjeanty) 1260, 1504; *see also* **donum, serjantia**.

arrenio, see ARRAIN

arrept/io, seizing a 1250; **a. (febris)**, seizure, bout (med.) a 1250; *a. itineris, starting on a journey 1163, 1424; **-icius** c 1190, 1265, **abrepticius, -ivus** 7c., possessed, mad; *arripio iter c 1180, c 1534, a. viam a 1180, c 1407, a. viagium 1411, a. gressus c 1390, to start on a journey; a. fugam, to take flight c 1188, 1426.

arr/eragium, rear (of building) 1270, 1287; *1197, 1536, †-erarium c 1290, -aragium 1246, 1308, **-earagium** 1289, c 1452, **-iragium** 1279, **-etragium** (G.) 1253, **-agium** 1224, 1308, arrears (of payment, etc); cf. **reragium**.

arrest/a c 1217, 1486, **-um** c 1298, 1537, **-ia** 1505, **-amentum** c 1290, 1535, *-atio 1201, 1587, **adrestatio** (G.) 1285, **aristatio** c 1500, **-atus** (G.) 1315, arrest, seizure; **-um**, judgement, *arrêt* (Fr.) 1312, c 1620; **-abilis**, liable to arrest 1292; *-o c 1185, 1687, **aristo** 1225, to arrest, seize; to hobble, confine 1315, 1317; *see also* **arestatio**.

arresurgo, to rise up again c 730.

arretragium, see **arreragium**.

arrett/amentum, charge, action (leg.) 1295, c 1443; **-o**, to charge, accuse c 1268, 1476; cf. RETT

arrh/a (arr-), earnest money: **erra** 1184; **-alis**, taking the form of a pledge or earnest c 1366; **-aliter**, by way of pledge c 1370; **-o**, to pledge c 1090, 14c.; to pay earnest money for 1269, ‡1483.

arridentia, prosperity c 1470; **adrideo** (with *inf.*), to rejoice 784.

arrio, see **arraio**.

arripio, see ARREPT; ARRIV

arriragium, see **arreragium**.

arriv/agium, payment for landing or mooring 1279, c 1370; **-o** a 1135, 1468, †**arripio** 1461, to come to land, arrive.

Arroacensis 1251, **Arusiensis** 1519, Aroasian (mon.).

arroinano, see ARRAIN

arrolius, roll or 'piece' of cloth (Sp.) 1470.

arrova, liquid measure, 'rove'(Sp. *arroba*)16c.

arruptum, *see* ABRUPT

ars, craft-guild c 1380, c 1491; kind, sort 1392; **a. nec pars**, 'art nor part' 1221, 1295; **art/es** (*pl.*), compendia c 1160; arts, branch of study (ac.) a 1180, c 1560; **-ista**, student in arts (ac.) c 1250, 1451; †**-iste**, ingeniously c 1150; ‡**-itus**, educated 1483.

ars/enicum c 1215, c 1270, **arcenocum** 1415, ‡**-aneck**, **-ag**, **-ar**, **artanec** 1652, arsenic; **-anoquita**, sodomite (ἀρσενοκοίτης) 790.

arsietura, *see* 1 hercia.

arsilium, *see* argillum.

ars/io 1278, **-ura** 1409, smelting; c 1400, **-o** 1274, **-ona** 13c., **-ina** (G.) 1283, **-ura** 1192, 1384, arson; **arcio**, burning 13c., c 1366; **-io**,**-ura**, blanching, assaying (of silver) 1086; **-ura**, fire, blaze c 870, 10c.; (?) fever heat (med.) a 1250; sweepings of goldsmith's workshop c 1100; **a. calcis**, lime-burning 1333; *see also* ardentia.

arsmet/ica, **-rica**, *see* ARITHMET

arso, to make a rattling noise like a stork 7c.; *see also* 2 arco, arsio.

art-, *see also* ARCT

†**artaratus**, (?) ornamented 1419.

artav/us 546. c 1180, 14c., **-ulus** c 1172, knife, dagger.

artel-, *see* ARTILL

artem/esia, *for* **-isia**, mugwort (bot.) a 1250, ‡14c.; †**-isia**, (?) for Ar. *ad-dimashquia* (damson) or *al-damasit* (laurel) 12c.

artemo, top-mast c 950.

arteri/acus, bronchial a 1250; †**-ca** (? **-aca**) bronchitis a 1250; **sanguis -alis**, arterial blood a 1250; **-osus**, well supplied with arteries a 1250; **artherea** (**pectorea**), (?) recesses c 550.

arthrit/ica, primrose 1538; 1345, **artetica** c 1180, a 1250, **archetica**, †**archerica** a 1250, ‡**arthesis** 1483, gout; **arteticus** (†**arceticus**, †**areticus**) c 1170, c 1470, †**archticus**, †**acchiricus** a 1250, *for* **-icus**, gouty; ‡**artetiscus**, physically defective 1652.

articul/us *8c., 9c. c 1160, 1559, **-um** 794. c 1185, c 1400, article, clause; **-us**, time-division (mus.) c 1160; number greater than digit (math.) c 1150, 15c.; **a. corone** 1283, 1409, **a. itineris** 1313 (*cf.* **capitulum**); **a. fidei** c 1250, c 1580; **a. mortis**, point of death c 730, 790. c 1150, c 1446; **a. necessitatis**, emergency c 1250, 1559; **-aris** a 1250, **-atus** 790, articulate (of sounds); **-ariter** c 1365, **-ate** 1552, **-atim** c 1250, 1684, clause by clause; **-arius**, more precisely 15c.; **-atio**, articulation, analysis c 1608; *-o 1317, 1684, **-or** (*dep.*) 1425, to draw up in articles or clauses.

artifex 1086, 1514, **artific/iarius** 1333, 1424, †**-ialis** 15c., **-alis** c 870, skilled craftsman, artificer; **a. manuum**, handicraftsman 15c.; **-ialis**, skilled, requiring craftsmanship c 1266, c 1330; artificial, produced by art a 1250, c 1270; **dies a.**, working day, period of daylight c 1212, 1461; **-e** 690, **-ialiter** 9c. c 1250, 1402, **-iabiliter** 1419, by art, artistically; **-ialius**, more precisely 1378;

-iolum, trade, craft 760. c 1160, 1378; **-ium**, work done by a craftsman c 1205; body of craftsmen, craft-guild c 1370, c 1490; **-io** 1267, c 1362, **-o** c 800, to design, create, make.

artifinium, *see* arcifinium.

artig/a 1288, **-ale** 1291, newly reclaimed land, assart (G.).

artill/aria 1384, 1469, **-arium** 1548, **-eria** 1430, 1466, **-iaria** 1460, 1461, **-yeria** 1486, **-yearia** 1474, **artellaria** 1377, 1397, **arteleria** 1381, artillery, (weapons for) shooting; **-aria**, furniture 1435; **-arius** 1382, 1454, **-ator** c 1307, maker or supervisor of artillery; **-um**, gear, equipment (arch.) 1292; *cf.* ATTILL

art/ista, **-itus**, *see* ars.

artius, even (of numbers) (ἄρτιος) 13c.

arto/caseus, cheesecake 13c., ‡c 1440; **-copus** c 1180, ‡c 1440, **panis -copi** 1293, c 1324, fine bread, simnel; **-copa**, **-crias**, torteau, roundel (her.) p 1394.

artoricon, *see* ARCHON

†**artuuerum**, (?) an article of apparel or (*possibly*) for **arcunerum**, saddle-bow 1208.

†**arucus**, (?) *for* **aruncus**, goat's-beard (bot.) c 550.

aruginosus, *see* auriginosus.

arur/a, **-um**, *see* aratrum.

Arusiensis, *see* Arroacensis.

‡**arvambulus**, "land-leaper" 15c.

arvin/a 1173, a stain (fig.) c 1125; ‡**-osus**, fat 1483.

arx Palatina 1267, **a.** †**cartata** 1267, Tower of London; *see also* COEDIFIC, CONFECT, conditio, CONSTRUCT, **cooperatio**, EDIFIC, 2 funda, INSTRUCT, JUV, 1 munimen, RECUPER, RENOV, RESTAUR, RESTRUCT, STRUCT

arzilium, *see* arguella.

arzillum, *see* argillum.

arzo/, **-narius**, *see* 2 arco.

asabon, *see* sapo.

asafetida, asafetida a 1250, ‡14c.

asaldus, 'assaut', rutting 1330; *cf.* ASSAL

‡**asaphatus**, impetigo (med.) 14c., 1652.

asara baccara a 1250, ‡14c., **azarabaccara** 1538, (?) **azarum** 1414, hazelwort (bot.).

asarcha, Lent (ἀσαρκία) 1517.

asarus, blessed c 550.

asayamentum, *see* aisia; exagium.

ascaeta, *see* excidamentum.

ascaldo, *see* SCALD

ascambium, *see* EXCAMB

ascapura, *see* ESCAP

ascar/is, threadworm c 1180, a 1250; ‡**-ida**, sheep-louse, tick 15c.

ascarletum, *see* SCARL

asce-, *see also* ace-

‡**ascella**, agrimony (bot.) 14c.; *see also* 2 axella, astula.

ascen/sio 815. a 1233, 1326, **-sus** a 1250, ascension (astr.); (?) graduation (ac.) 1461; ambition c 1197, c 1430; *6c., 9c. c 1090, 1461, **-cio** 1254, c 1279, **Assencio** 1202, c 1549, **Assensio** 1354, *dies -sionis 1086, 1461, *A. Domini 1107, c 1400, A. Dominica 1006. c 1250, 1416, **-sus Domini** c 1268, Ascension (day); **-sus maris**, high tide c 1250; **-sive**, on a rising scale c 1397; **-sor celi** (theol.) 760; **-sorium**, stirrup c 1090, c 1325; mounting-block c 1125,

1462; 1006. 12c., 13c., **assensorium** 1412, staircase; †**assensorium**, (?) step 1498; **scala -soria**, ascending scale c 1607, 1620; ‡**-sorius** c 1200, ‡**acensorius** 15c., hobby (bird); **-sus** (**equum, equo**), having mounted c 1150, a 1400; **-dens** (*subst.*), ascendant (astr.) 1267, 1387; **-do**, to be in the ascendant (astr.) 1344; to pass to heir of earlier generation or prior birth c 1185, 1206; 1461, **assendo gradum** c 1350, to take a degree (ac.); **assendo**, *for* **-do**, to rise 1266, 1458; **-do ad**, to amount to c 1250, c 1457; **a. ex adverso**, to contradict c 1100, c 1321.

ascer-, *see* **acer**.

asceticus, ascetic 1153; *cf.* **arcisterium**.

asci-, *see also* **acci-**

asci/a, (?) lancet (med.) a 1250; **-atus**, large knife 13c.; ‡**-ola, -culus**, hatchet, mason's axe 1483; **hascia** 1201, †**aza** 1291, (?) adze or axe; **assiatio**, chopping c 1450; ‡**-o**, to sharpen 15c.; *cf.* **axa, hachia**.

asciciput, tonsured man 7c.

ascido, *see* ACCID

ascit/es (†**archites**), ascites, abdominal dropsy a 1250; **-icus** (†**alchiticus**, †**architicus**), ascitic a 1250.

asciticius, adventitious c 1546, 1620.

asco, boat 7c.

ascripticius c 1178, 13c., **a. glebe** c 1258, (one) bound to the soil, villein.

ascult-, *see* AUSCULT

ascunditus, *see* ABSCON

aseitus, *see* AFFECT

‡**asep** 14c., 1652, **assos** 1144, alum.

asephalus, *see* **acephalus**.

asiamentum, *see* **aisia**.

asidus, *see* ASSIDU

asilium, *see* **asylum**.

asilus, gadfly: **azilus** 1521.

asin/itas, asinine nature 13c., c 1270; **-arium**, ass-load 15c.; **-inus**, a precious stone(?) 14c.; **-o**, to ride an ass c 1070, c 1451; **-or** (*dep.*) c 1177, **-ino** 1267, 1271, to behave like an ass.

asm/a, -aticus, *see* **asthma**.

asmaga, *see* **amalgama**.

asmal/, -lum, *see* **esmallum**.

asmerciamentum, *see* AMERCI

asnaso, to stab (A.S. *asnæsan*) c 1115.

asnecia, *see* **esnecia**.

asori/um, -us, *see* AZUR

asparagus (bot.): **sparagus** a 1250, 1538, ‡**alfarsungi** (Ar.) 14c.

aspatilis, *see* **aspratilis**.

aspect/io a 1250, **-us** a 1233, 1344, 'aspect', angular distance between planets (astr.); **-us sextilis** 13c.; **in -u**, in wait (ambush) 1397; **aspicio**, to be in aspect (astr.) a 1233.

asper, Greek coin, half bezant (ἄσπρος) 1292.

asper/ativus, concerned with roughening or prickling a 1250, c 1270; †**-sus**, rough c 1204.

‡**aspergo**, sea-mew, cormorant c 1440, 15c.; *see also* **aspersio**.

aspergula, goosegrass (bot.) 1538; *cf.* **spergula**.

asperi/olus, -alus, *see* **scurellus**.

asper/sio, outpouring (of light) c 730; c 730. c 1188, 1558, **-sura** 14c., sprinkling (with

holy water) or baptism; ***-sorium** c 1080, 1537, **-gillum** 1609, holy water sprinkler; **clericus -sorius**, holy water clerk c 1362; **-go**, to sprinkle (eccl.) c 730; *cf.* **sparsio**.

aspervarius, *see* **spervarius**.

asphaltus, asphalt: **aphaltus, aspaltus** a 1250.

asphodelus 1538, **affodillus** c 1215, ‡14c., **affrodillus** a 1250, daffodil.

aspicio, *see* ASPECT

aspilogia, heraldry c 1595.

aspinetum, *see* **spina**.

aspiratio, aspiration, desire c 1305, c 1430; inspiration a 1180, c 1250.

‡**aspi/s**, "ask", "eft" 1570; **-dalis**, of an asp c 1250.

asporta, *see* SPOR

asport/ator, remover, transporter c 1290, 1525; **-ata** (*n. pl.*), goods removed 1337; **-atus**, removal c 1195; **-o toloneum**, to avoid paying toll 1194, 14c.; **ansporto**, to carry off c 550.

asp/ratilis, kind of fish: **-atilis**, (?) stickleback a 1250, ‡15c.

ass/a, -abilis, *see* **assatio**.

assahilo, *see* **assaltus**.

assai-, assag-, *see* **alxo exagium**.

assaia, *see* **sagum**.

assaisi/eno, -ono, *see* **asseisona**.

assaisio, to seize 1168.

assal/tus 1130, 1461, **assultatio** a 1450, assault; **assultus**, fine (for assault) c 1138; **-io** 1086, 1410, **assailio** 1091, c 1115, **assahilo** 1413, **-to** 1235, 1265, to assail, assault; **-to**, to mount (of stallion) 1330; *cf.* **asaldus**; *see also* **assatio**.

assart-, *see* EXSART

assarum, *see* **asser**.

assassin/us 1269, 1609, **assessinus** c 1250, c 1272, **assisinus** c 1250, c 1436, **hassacinus** c 1362, **haccasinus** a 1450, **hausassisus** c 1200, †**accinus** c 1192, **Arsacida** 1535, †**alta nutrix** c 1436, follower of Sheikh of the Mountains, assassin; **-ium**, assassination 1609.

ass/atio c 1250, c 1456, **-atus** 1467, roasting; 1449, **-a** c 1200, a roast, joint; **-abilis** c 1270, 1450, †**-atilis** 1570, roastable; **ovum -ativum** a 1250; **-ator**, roaster 1443; **-atura renum**, part of the ribs c 1110; **-aturis** (G.) 1283, ‡**-atorium** 1483, gridiron or toast-fork; **-uratio**, roast meat c 1540; †**-altus**, (?) for **-atus**, 15c.; †**assugia**, meat c 1190; *-**o**, to roast, broil (bibl.).

assaysamentum, *see* **aisia**.

asse-, *see also* **ace-, asce-**

assec/la, steward, *dystein* (W.) a 1300; **-ula**, attendant c 1362.

assecur/atio 1152, 1434, **asseuratio** 14c., **-antia** 1383, 1461, assurance, security, surety; **-itas**, security, safety c 1362; **assurantia**, conveyance (of land) a 1564; **assuranter**, firmly 1405; **-o**, to assure, make sure, give safe-conduct to 1101, c 1540; to insure, cover by insurance 1565; 1142, **assuro** a 1564 to convey (land); **a. me**, to venture, make bold 1293; **assiro**, to fasten, make fast 1338.

assecut/io, pursuit c 1200, 1459; **-ivus, assequentior**, subsequent (log.) 12c.

*assed/atio, renting, leasing (Sc.) 1329, 1608; **-atarius**, tenant (Sc.) 1566, 1608; ***-o**, to rent, lease (Sc.) 1294, 1564.

assed/eo, -itor, assegio, *see* ASSESS

assei-, *see also* ASSESS; **exagium**.

asseisona, (?) season 1290; †**assaisi/eno**, to sow, cultivate 1282; **-ono**, to dry, mature (hay) 1230.

assel-, *see also* **acer**; 2 **axella**.

assell/atio, privy c 1109; evacuation of bowels a 1250, 13c.; **-ator**, one who evacuates the bowels c 1180; **-o**, to evacuate the bowels a 1250, 13c.

assem/atio 1284, 1290, **assummatio** 1290, †**acemo** 1286, 'enseaming'; **-o** 1290, **-io** 1287, **essaimo** 1241, **essaimio** 1219, **esseymo** 1219, 1254, **exsiaimio** 1220, †**semio** (? **adsemio**) 1222, to 'enseam', cleanse of fat (falc.).

assembl/atio 1573, 1593, **-ea** 1397, **-eia** 1338, **-ia** 1501, assembling, assembly; **-o** 1569, 1573, **-io** 1389, **assimulo** c 1115, 15c., to assemble.

assens-, *see* **acensa**; **ascensio**.

assent/aneus, partisan c 1150; **-ator**, assenter (to charter) c 1150; **-ivus**, assenting c 1360; **-us**, assent (G.) 1253; **-o**, to assent c 1000. 1571.

assequentior, *see* ASSECUT

*asser c 1180, c 1530, **assarum** 1506, lath, slab, board; *****board for book-binding c 1250, 16c.; lattice c 1125; **a. ad pacem**, pax (eccl.) 1287, c 1400; *see also* **acer**.

assergeanticus, *see* SERJ

*assert/io c 730, 790. a 1100, c 1534, **assersio** c 1396, **-orium** c 1290, **-um** 1425, assertion; **-ibilis**, capable of assertion c 1367; ***-ive**, positively 12c., 1419; **-ivus** 12c., p 1381, **-orius** c 1290, c 1414, assertive, confirmatory; *see also* EXSART

asservo, to reserve 1517.

assessinus, *see* **assassinus**.

assess/io 1229, a 1564, **-atio** 1467, assessment; **-ibilis**, liable to assessment a 1564; ***-or** c 1218, c 1400, †**assor** 1280, **assisor** 1225, c 1445, **assisar** (Sc.) 1509, **assisarius** (Sc.) 1609, assessor; rider c 1125, c 1362; pupil c 1188; table-companion c 1250; **a. ferculorum**, table-layer c 1290; **asseditor**, stone-layer 13c., 1253;

   -a 1359, ***assisa** a 1120, 1330, **assizia** (G.) 1310, assessment, charge, tax; **assisa** *****1166, 1462, **assisia** c 1298, **sisa** c 1240, 1270, **assisum** c 1200, 1202, 'assize', standard, regulation (esp. as to price or quality of commodities); ration c 1296; 1296, 1587, **sisa** a 1540, (standard) size; shaped block of stone 1253, 1293 (*cf.* **azeisia**, [EXCIS]; *****1168, 1586, **assisia** (G. & C.I.) 1283, 1313, **asseisa** 1289, †**asseisina** c 1250, c 1290, **assessium, assissium** (Sc.) 1521, (body of persons constituting) assize (leg.); action or claim (leg.) 1229, 1443; limit of action (leg.) c 1185, 13c.; entrance-money to guild, guild-meeting 1210, c 1250; **a. antiqua**, (?) form of chess c 1197; **a. aque**, regulation of water (for mill) 1440; **a. foreste** 1393; **a. magna**, grand assize (leg.) 1184, 1456; **a. mortis antecessoris, a. nove disseisine,**

a. ultime presentationis, possessory assizes 1196, 15c.; **a. nocumenti**, assize of nuisance 1397; ***a. panis et cervisie**, assize (regulation of quality, *etc.*) of bread and ale a 1190, 1452; **a. pannorum** 1221; **a. (vini)** c 1200; **a. prima**, first session (of eyre) c 1290; **a. Scaccarii** c 1225, 1238; **a. rusticorum**, land not in demesne a 1158; **a. waide**, measure of woad 1367; *see also* **bursa, pes, redditus, res, vinum**; **assisagium, assisatum** 1316, **assisiatus** 1308, 1316, a form of jurisdiction (G.);

   assidella, table dormant or side-board 1446, ‡1483, **assidentia**, fixing in position 1266; **assidens**, sejant (her.) 1654; **assideo** (**assedeo, assido**), *****to set in place, fix a 1210, 1419; *****to assign, appoint c 1155, 1461; to have a seat (at Exchequer) c 1178, 1238; 1221, 1271, **assegio** 1279, to besiege; to settle (land) c 1115, c 1290; *****1218, 1559, **-o** 1446, 1573, **assiso** 1270, 1318, **sesso** 1480, to assess, fix; **a. ad arma**, to equip or array (troops) 1333, 1511; **a. ad billas** (leg.) 1336.

assetum, *see* ACET

asseuratio, *see* ASSECUR

assev-, asseu-, assew-, *see* **exaquia**.

asshelarium 1318, **achellarium** 1420, **achillarium** c 1400, ashlar.

assiatio, *see* **ascia**.

assiator, *see* **exagium**.

assid-, *see also* ASSESS

assidio, to waylay 1195.

assidu/atio, practice 13c.; **-aliter**, assiduously 1415; **asidus**, assiduous c 550; **-o**, to be busy 13c., c 1257.

assieta, assignment of dowry (Fr.) 1473; state, condition (C.I.) 1368.

assign/atio (assignn-) *****1269, 1583, **-amentum** 1391, a 1539, assignment of interest; attribution 1267; direction, appointment c 1290, 1513; appointment to special duties (mon.) c 1250, 14c.; assignation, tryst 1419; **-abilis**, attributable c 1300; **-anter**, especially, specifically 1483; **-ator**, director c 1150; **-ata**, grant, promise 14c.; †1285, ***-atus** c 1200, 1565, assign, assignee; **frater -atus**, friar assigned as lector to convent c 1250; **-o**, to assign (interest, *etc.*) c 1217, 1539.

assilis, round c 550.

assilum, *see* **asylum**.

assimil/atio, model, likeness 980; assimilation, making like a 1250, a 1290; **a. alimenti** c 1361; **-abilis**, assimilable c 1277, p 1300; **-ativus**, that can be likened to, that makes like to 9c.; promoting assimilation (of food) a 1250, c 1361; **-o** c 1130, c 1443, **-io** c 1270, to assimilate.

assimulo, *see* ASSEMBL

assiro, *see* ASSECUR

assis-, *see also* ASSESS

assisinus, *see* **assassinus**.

*assist/entia, presence, assistance c 1250, 1610; **-ens** c 1150, 1545, **-ator** 1538, **-rix** (*f.*) 1248, c 1450, †**-ria** (*f.*) c 1180, assistant, companion; **-o**, to assist (*trans.*) c 1180, c 1280; to place, cause to stand c 1266, p 1377.

assisus, *see* abscisio; ASSESS
asso, *see* assatio.
associ/atio c 1115, c 1450, -etatio 1466, associating, joining.
asson-, assun-, *see* ESSONI
assos, *see* asep.
assub, nostoc, "star-slime" 1345, ‡c 1440; (?) *cf.* alcubd.
assubvolvo, to revolve in addition (astr.) c 1270.
assuefactio, habituation a 1228, c 1444.
assu/eo, -o, *see* exaquia.
assugia, *see* assatio.
assult-, *see* ASSAL
assumentum, clout, patch 1440, ‡1483.
assummatio, *see* ASSEM; *cf.* ASSUMPT
assummo, to add up c 1255, c 1296.
assumpt/io (abs-), taking up, consummation 9c.; beginning c 1160; coronation (of Pope) 1417; agreement 1382, a 1564; 760. *a 1090, a 1530, assumatio c 1400, (feast of the) Assumption (15 Aug.); a Salvatoris, Ascension day c 1343, c 1536; -ibilis, able to be assumed, taken up c 1290, c 1376; -or, one who takes up 1333, c 1362; -us (*pl.*), costs 1334; assumo (her.), to assume (arms) a 1446; a. cameram, to be brought to childbed a 1470; a. crucem, to become a crusader 1254; a. radicem, to extract root (math.) 1145.
assur/anter, -antia, -o, *see* ASSECUR
assuratio, *see* assatio.
assur/rectio, showing honour to 13c.; -rexio, rising up c 1414.
assurus, *see* AZUR
Assyrius, Saracen 1252.
astagium, *see* stagium.
astall/agium, -amentum, -o, *see* STALL
ast/allaria, -elaria, -illaria, *see* hasta; hastellaria.
astantivus, *see* STANT
ast/ella, -illa, *see* astula.
astenta, *see* EXTEN
aster, *see* astrum; auster.
aster/iscus, asterisk (gram.) 790. 12c., 15c.; -ismus, constellation 1620.
ast/es, in the same rank 1610; -o, to cause to stand c 550.
asthma (med.): asm/a c 1210, c 1540; -aticus c 1200, ‡14c.
†astinctus, (?) distinct a 1520.
astipul/atio (adst-), agreement 6c., c 974; confirmation a 1105; éator, adherent 8c., c. 1000; -o, to agree (with *dat.*) 799.
asto, *see* astes.
astoppo, *see* ASTUPP
astovarium, *see* estoverium.
astr/a, -arius, *see* astrum.
astraco, to 'strake', sound hunting-horn 1271.
astracta, *see* EXTRACT
astraura, *see* straia.
astrepo, *see* STREPP
astrict/io c 1190, 1493, -us 14c.(?), restriction, obligation; astringency c 1620; -ivus, astringent c 1620; -e, zealously 1230.
astr/ifer c 550, c 950, †-igenus (? *for* -iger) c 1000, -eus c 870, starry; -ifugus, putting the stars to flight c 1184; -ivagus, wandering among the stars c 1180; ‡-alis, -osus, lunatic 1483.
*astro/labium c 1110, c 1400, -lapsus c 1110,

astrolabe; -labicus, pertaining to astrolabe c 1145; -linus, starred with gems 1157; abstralogia, *for* -logia, 13c.; -logia practica, astrology 1267; a. speculativa, astronomy 1267; -logice, astrologically 1267, c 1410; -logicus, astrological or astronomical c 1125, c 1457; -nomice, astronomically 1267.
astruct/io, demonstration a 1142; -or, originator 826; astruo (adstr-), *to assert or prove c 730, 9c. c 1080, c 1450; to instruct 1324, 1438.
*astr/um 1221, 1465, -ium 1221, 1353, -a 1297, aster c 1436, austrum 16c., hearth, home; a. antiquum 1463, a. vetus c 1290, 1347, ancestral home; in -o c 1258, 1279, in †affra 14c., in the parental home; a. picche, (?) measure of pitch 1338; -arius (frater a., heres a.), heir who receives inheritance during donor's lifetime 1239, 1291; *see also* auster.
ast/ula (hast-) c 1188, c 1390, -ella c 700, -illa 1275, splinter, chip; -ella (†ascella), piece of firewood 1233, 1361; *see also* hasta.
ast/um, accusation (Lombard) a 1446; -o animo, maliciously (Lombard) a 1446.
astupp/o 1266, -io 1275, astoppo p 1124, 1275, to stop up; *cf.* STUP, OBSTUP
asturco, steed: †sturco 1508; *see also* AUSTUR
astutia, guile: estuctia 1201.
asur-, asuurius, *see* AZUR
asylum, sanctuary, refuge: assilum 10c., asilium 15c., azilum c 1430.
asymbolus, non-armorial (her.) c 1595.
asymmeter, asymmetric c 1160, a 1250.
asymptotos, asymptote (math.) 1686.
aszeisia, *see* azeisa.
ata, *see* hachia.
atav/a, *for* -ia, great-great-grandmother 1432, ‡15c.; grandmother c 1000; -unculus, brother of *atavus* c 1258.
aten-, *see* attinentia.
atha (?) 944. c 1125, ada a 1137, oath of compurgation.
Athalaticus, *see* ATLANT
ath/aleta, -eleta, *see* ATHLET
athana/sia 1241, a 1250, atonasia 13c., electuary for prolonging life; ‡14c., 1538, tanacetum a 1250, 1634, ‡tanesetum 13c., ‡tansetum 15c., a 1520, tansy (bot.); ‡tanacetum agreste, t. album, silverweed 14c.; -tos, immortal 1271, 1345.
atharafa, tamarisk (Ar. *tharfa*) 12c.
†athath (†achat), kind of eagle (? ἀετός) a 1250.
atheis/mus, atheism 1620, 1713; -ta, atheist 1620; -ticus, atheistical 1662; atheologus, untheological c 1620.
†atheria, (?) loin of pork (Fr.) c 1130; *cf.* hasta.
*athia (atia, hatia) 1191, c 1324, †agia 1275, hatred, malice (leg.).
athlet/a c 1100, 1461, -us 1461, atheleta 1461, athaleta 1525, champion; anthleta, athlete 6c.; a. Christi 6c., c 1000, adleta Dei 9c., martyr, saint; *cf.* ethleta.
athronizo, to enthrone (eccl.) c 1385.
atill-, *see* ATTILL
atincar, *see* tincar.
atir-, *see* ATTIR; AZUR
atlant/es (*pl.*), pillars c 950; †Athalaticus, (?) *for* -icus, 1274.

atmatertera, sister of an *atavia* c 1258.

atmosphera, atmosphere 1686.

atom/us (temporis), instant c 1170; 1/376 of a minute c 1265; **-alis**, atomic 1427; **-osus**, tiny c 1250.

atonasia, *see* athanasia.

atpatruus, brother of an *atavus* 1258.

atque, also c 1296.

atrament/um 8c., **-arium** 1192, 15c., **-orium** c 1534, ink-pot; **-um** 1248, 1344, **arnamentum** 1284, **arnementum** 1334, 'arnement', salve for animals; colouring matter (alch.) c 1215, ‡14c.; ‡a. **sutorium**, copperas 1652; **-osus**, inky c 1270, ‡1520.

Atrebaticus operator 1710, **textor Attrabat/ensis** 1478, t. **Atripotens** 1475, 1479, arras-weaver; **pannulus -ensis** c 1550, **pannus de -o** 1436, c 1550, p. **Arrace** 1432, p. **de Arracio** 1461, arras; *cf.* **opus**.

atrichio, *see* ATTACH

†**atri/cus**, †**-tus**, black haemorrhoid (? *for* anthrax) a 1250; *see also* **atrum**.

atrium, home, father's house 1224, 1234; porch, narthex or churchyard (eccl.) c 1100, c 1468.

atro/phia (med.): **-fia** (†**-sia**) a 1250.

atrox, (?) sour (of milk) 1284.

atr/um, the dark 1241; **-itus**, dark c 550.

attabern/ator, tavern-keeper (C.I.) 1324; ‡**-io**, **-alis**, "tavern ganger" 1483; **-o**, to expose for sale in a tavern (C.I.) 1324.

attach/ia, fastening, cord c 1170, 1309; **-iamentum**, appurtenance c 1254; *c 1250, 1497, **-amentum** 1358, 1507, abutment (of mill or fish-pond); *1195, c 1456, **-ementum** 1270, c 1448, **-iatio** c 1258, 1376, **attaccatio** 1185, attachment, arrest (leg.); object seized as exhibit 1253, 1331; (meeting of a) court of attachments (minor forest court) 1316, 1347; a. **de foresta** 1217, a. **foreste** 1295, a. **forestariorum** 1445; a. **forinsecum**, foreign attachment (leg.) 1419, a 1564; a. **de spinis** 1230, 1266, a. **bosci** 1388, right of using thorn-bushes or brushwood; **-iabilis**, liable to attachment (leg.) c 1290, 1314; **-iator**, officer making attachments (leg.) c 1258, 14c.; **-io** 1228, 1364, **-o** c 1306, **attagio** 1235, to attach, fasten; to stud, set (with gems) 1245; 13c., 1342, †**atrichio** c 1250, to make as an abutment (of mill-pond); *1188, p 1464, **attaco** c 1200, **attagio** 1195, 1318, to attach, seize (leg.); *cf.* **tachia**.

attagines (*pl.*), heathcocks c 870.

attaglio, to tallage c 1352.

attaintus, *see* ATTINCT

1 **attamino**, to taint, defile 8c., 9c. c 1188, 1326; to dung, manure 1376.

2 **attam/ino** 1290, **-io** 1291, 1367, **-eo** 1305, to broach, unload; ‡to bolt (flour) c 1440; **-io**, to broach (a matter) 1360, 1368.

†**attasho**, (?) *for* attraho, to drag c 1180.

†**attastator**, taster (of ale) 1401.

atted/iatio 1452, **-ium** 1437, wearying, weariness; **-io**, to weary 1325.

atteincta, *see* ATTINCT

attela, part of plough harness (Fr. *attelle*) 1350; *cf.* ATTILL

attemper/atio, cooling 1622; **-amentum**, sign of moderation p 1394; **-o**, to adjust c 1182.

attempt/atio (attent-) 1233, 1463, **-amentum** 1402, **-atum** 1237, 1684, attempt, attack; **-ator**, one who attempts or ventures 1284, 1438; **-o**, to dispute 1238.

*attend/entia**, attendance 1431, a 1564; **-o**, to aim at c 804; to wait for, expect c 1204, c 1305; to tend (med.) a 1250; 1379, a. **super** 1471, 1583, to attend on, look after; a. **penes**, to measure by c 1340; *cf.* **tenditor**.

attenero, to make tender a 1250.

attenuativus, tending to thin a 1250.

attermin/atio, adjournment (leg.) 1331, 15c.; attermination (of debt), fixing terms for payment 1302, 1352; **adtermino**, to appoint a day (leg.) c 1115; **-o**, *to adjourn (leg.) 1221, 15c.; *to attermine (debt or debtor) 1238, 1339; *cf.* **termino**.

atterno, *see* ATTORN

atteuiriamentum, *see* ATTIR

*attill/ium (atill-)** 1213, 1378, **-um** 1213, 1277, †**-e** c 1385, **-io** 1336, **-amentum** c 1290, **-iamentum** 1212, **-ura** 1242, equipment, gear, apparatus; **-ator** c 1254, 1300, **-iator** 1246, 1349, **tilliator** 1304, 1325, **-iaris** c 1272, maker or supervisor of artillery; **tillaria**, arsenal 1339; **-o**, to rig, equip (galley) 1215, 1233; to fit out (crossbow) 1242, 1255; *cf.* ARTILL, **attela**, ATTIR

*attinct/a** 1222, a 1564, **atteincta** c 1265, **-io** 1400, 1517, **-us** 1260, **-ura** 1540, 1569, attaint, attainder (leg.); *-us** 1227, 1593, **-atus** 1569, **attaintus** (Sc.) a 1330, c 1395, **atteyntatus** 15c., attainted; **atting/ibilis**, attainable c 1270, 1427; **-o**, to decide, give a verdict 1204, 1275; to attaint 1205, 1583; a. **ad** 1285, c 1452, a. **me ad** c 1461, c 1530, to amount to; a. **affinitate**, to be related to 1212, c 1290; a. **pacem regis**, to maintain the peace 1283.

attinentia, close relationship 1325; retinue 1405; appurtenance 1475; **aten/tus**, extension, augmentation a 1171; **-eo**, to extend, continue a 1135, c 1192.

attinus, *see* hactinus.

attir/um (atir-), attire, suit (of armour) 1295; **-amentum**, fittings 1324, 1325; †**atteuiriamentum**, gear, equipment (of ship) 1208; **-iator**, maker of artillery 1257; **-o**, to attire, dress, fit 1301, 1310; *cf.* ARTILL, ATTILL

attitulo, to assign c 1070, 1276; to ordain (eccl.) c 1100.

attonsus, (*adj.*) tonsured 810. 12c., c 1395; (*subst.*) tonsured monk c 804.

attorn/amentum, acknowledgement (by tenant) of new lord 1333, c 1459; 1443, **-atio** 1449, attornment of property, delivery as symbol of seisin; c 1288, *-atio** c 1166, c 1453, **atturnatio** 1168, **-atus** (*4th decl.*) c 1325, 1497, attorneyship, procuration; **-atio**, refitting, adaptation 1214; **littere -atorie** 1330, 1684, l. **-ati** 1450, letters of attorney; **tornatorius**, of attorney 1467; *-atus** 1200, 1564, **-iatus** c 1250, 1312, **atturnatus** c 1260, 1309, **atturniatus** c 1255, **turnatus** 1203, **-ator** c 1300, 15c., †**-us** c 1288, **-ata** (*f.*) 1203, 1300, attorney, proxy; a. **feoffatus**, tenant holding by doing suit of court for landlord 1279; a. **generalis**, attorney for all suits c 1290, 15c.; a. **regis**

1281, 1507, **a. generalis regis** 1535, 1686; **a. specialis**, attorney for a specified plea 1298; **a. in communi banco** 1336; **-o *c** 1185, c 1530, **atturno** 12c., 1200, to depute, appoint as attorney; 1221, c 1285, **atturno** c 1285, to turn (tenant) over to new lord; 1333, a 1564, **a. me** 1232, c 1323, to acknowledge (as tenant) a new lord; to divert (water-course) c 1175; 1168, 1275, †**atterno** 1421, **atturno** 1163, 1168, **atturnio** 13c., to attorn (property); *1202, c 1345, **atturno** 1274, 1276, to treat, dress, fit out; to train (falcon) 1237, 1252; **a. in defalta**, to count as default 1207.

attract/io 1267, 1686, **-us** c 1340, attraction; usurping jurisdiction c 1358; **-us**, admission, introduction 14c., c 1377; *(service or means of) haulage 1171, 1256; **-abilis** (*v.l.* **attrectabilis**), attractive c 937. c 1125; **attrectabilis**, tangible c 1090, 1170; **-iva**, attractive power c 1212; **-ivus**, attractive c 1200, 1686; **attrectator**, despoiler 1222; **-o**, to draw in c 1320; **attraho**, to lead in (harvest) c 1182; **a. petras** a 1128; **-o** a 1100, 1415, **-o mihi** 1353, to appropriate, usurp.

†**attria**, some chemical substance c 1270.

attriator, trier (of juries) a 1564; *cf.* **triator**.

attribo, to beat (earth) 1365.

attribu/tio, imputation, charge 9c.; attribution, reference 13c., p 1300; **-talis**, of the nature of an attribute p 1300, 1344; **-tor**, bestower 760.

attrit/io, chastisement 1301; **-or**, oppressor 12c.

attrunco, to cut short 1267.

atturn-, *see* ATTORN; **tornus**.

†**atuus**, vessel for distilling (? *f.l.* for **catinus**) 13c.

aub-, *see* ALB; HAUBER

*__auc/a__ (†**anc-**) c 1000. c 1090, 1566, (?) **oga** c 1325, goose; **a. erraria**, nesting goose 1277; **a. mariola**, unmated goose 1282, 1398; **a. ad obulum** 1307, **a. obulata** 1417, halfpenny goose; **a. rosata** 1339, **a. rosetta** 1326, **a. rosaria** a 1191, **a. rosera** 1247, 1324, (?) sheldrake; **a. silvestris**, wild goose a 1200; **a.** †**stubulata**, stubble goose 1408; †**-arius**, gooseherd 15c., 1483; **-ella** 1321, c 1380, **-ila** (†**ancila**) 1296, **-ula** c 1200, 1403, gosling; **caro-ina**, goose-flesh c 1180, 15c.; **-o**, gander 1312.

auceparia, *see* AUCUP

aucipiter, *see* **accipiter**.

aucer, *see* **anser**.

aucment-, *see* AUGMENT

auctentic-, *see* AUTHENTIC

‡**auction/ator, -atrix**, "hucker and huckster" 15c.; **-arius** (†**ancionarius**), (?) agent, hireling 15c.; **auxionarius** 1268, 1419, **oxionator** 1371, retailer; ‡**-aria** 1483, **auxionatrix** 1290, ‡c 1440, **auxiatrix** 1395, huckster.

auctius, nourishing 870.

auctor/izatio (author-) 1344, 1441, **-isatio** c 1362, authorization; **-abilis** 13c., 1345, **-alis** a 1186, **-itativus** c 1376, c 1430, **-izabilis** 1378, ‡1483, authoritative; **-itative**, authoritatively p 1300, 1427; **auctrix**, **autrix**, authoress c 1180, c 1414; **-iso**

c 1175, 1442, *-**izo** 971. c 1125, 1577, to authorize.

auctuario, corn-bunting (bird) 1544.

auctumn-, *see* AUTUMN

aucula, *see* **auca**.

aucup/amentum, -o, *see* ACCUP

*__aucup/atio__ 785. c 1212, 1582, **-atus** c 1362, **-itium** c 1200, a 1446, fowling, hawking; †**auceparia**, fowling-place 1388; **aves -es** (*pl.*), birds of prey 1529; **-arius** 1279, **-ator** 1378, ‡**-iscus** 1483, fowler; **-ator**, seeker c 1170, c 1204; **-ativus**, used in hawking a 1446; desirous, covetous c 1204; ‡**aucubaculatus**, "bat-fowling" (catching birds after dark) c 1440.

aud/acitas, audacity c 680, c 1000. c 1194, c 1362; **-eo**, *perfect* **audi**, 15c.

audi/entia, assembly (mon.) c 1100, c 1400; lecture (ac.) c 1350; hearing of appeal, *etc.*, jurisdiction, court (eccl. and civil law) c 1188, c 1456; (equitable or prerogative) 1426, 1461; c 1344, 1416, **curia -entie** 1586, 1684, Court of Audience (Canterbury); **in -entia**, publicly, loudly 1556; **-entia** 1327, **-tio** c 1333, 1549, **-tus** 1448, c 1533, audit (of account); **-tio** c 1311, c 1409, **-tura** c 1453, study (ac.); **-bilis**, audible 1267, 1503; **-tivus**, concerned with hearing c 1290, c 1361; **-tus**, ear 1284, c 1285 (*see also* **avidotus**); **-torium**, parlour (mon.) a 970, c 1006. c 1148, 1512; episcopal court 12c., 1427; **-tor**, *auditor (of account) 1277, 1567; *ecclesiastical judge 1255, 1684; **a. contradictorum**, judge of appeals 1256, 1467; **a. petitionum (in parliamento)** c 1322; **a. querelarum (apud Westmonasterium)** c 1290; **-toriatus (curie causarum)**, auditorship 1417; **-trix**, pupil (*f.*) c 1180, c 1362; **-ta querela**, name of a writ 15c.; **-o**, *to audit (account) c 1216, c 1517; *to study, attend lectures in (ac.) c 1180, 17c.; **a. cursorie** c 1275, **a. cursus** c 1350, c 1409 (ac.); **a. ordinarie** c 1231, **a. ordinaria** c 1453 (ac.); **a. dici** 1201, 1223, **a. loqui** 1309, to hear tell; **a. dure**, to be hard of hearing c 1255; *__a. missam__ (eccl.) 1199, 1535; **a. et termino**, *oyer & terminer* (leg.) 1252, 1587; **a. et t. compotum** 1238.

auferibilitas, removability 1610.

auffarium, *see* **affarium**.

‡**aufug/ium**, escape 1570; **-o** a 1155, c 1436, **abfugo** a 1564, to drive away; *see also* AFFUG

aug/a, -ea, *see* **alveus**.

augibilis, capable of increase c 1290.

augis, *see* **aux**.

augm/asticus, -aticus, *see* **acmasticus**.

*__augment/atio__ c 730, 870. 1216, 1564, **aucmentatio** c 1400, **aumentatio** 1212, c 1283, *__-um__ (bibl.), **aucmentum** 12c., **aumentum** c 1160, p 1300, increase; *see also* **Curia**; **-abilis**, liable to increase a 1233, c 1361; **-ativus** a 1250, c 1361, **-ivus** c 1301, causing increase; **-ator**, augmenter c 1212, 1461; *__-o__ c 730. a 1090, c 1556, †**augmo** c 1297, **aumento** 1204, 1383, to augment, increase.

augnetum, *see* ALN

augorismus, *see* **algorismus**.

august/alis c 1125, c 1212, **-eus** c 1414, imperial; imperial coin 1254; ‡**-eum**,

marble 1483; **-ie** (*pl.*), honours c 1190; **-us,** title of the king of the Romans 1274, 1341.
Augustanus, of Augsburg, Lutheran 1672.
August/inensis p 1381, 1429, **frater A.** 1356, 1523, †**f.** -iensis 1380, f. -iniensis 1358, **f. -inencis** 1429, 1437, (f.) **-inianus** 1284, 1349, **f. (ordinis) S. -ini (de S. -ino)** 1255, 1290, **f. heremitarum ordinis S. -i** (*sic*) 1249, Austin friar.
auket/onus, -unus, *see* aketo.
1 aul/a, **hall, room 1086, 1537; court baron (man.) c 1130, 1292; *house 1086, 1430; ***hall, college** (ac.) c 1313, 1636; (?) 'inland', demesne 1086; guild, guild-hall 1367, 1373 (*see also* **gilda**); **a. ecclesie,** nave 12c., 1358; **a. ad elemosinam** c 1224, **a. elemosinaria** 1254; **a. placitorum,** guildhall 1272, 1320; **a. regis,** king's court (leg.) 1419; **a. Sartoria,** Cloth Hall 1508; **a. Alemannorum** 1331, **a. Teutonicorum** c 1320, steelyard; **ab -a recedo,** (?) to be out of favour a 1250; **-e,** court-yard 960; **-aris** c 1470, **-arius** c 1150, of the court; of a college c 1412, c 1514; (*subst.*) college-mate c 1556; **-ensis,** of or for a hall 797; **-eus,** of the royal mint c 1336; **-icus,** (*adj.*) courteous, courtly 12c., 1241; (*subst.*) courtier a 1100, c 1324.
2 aul/a c 1315, 1430, **-ale** 1458, **-are** 1434, 1435, **-arium** 1431, **alleum** c 1450, **alletum** c 1500, halling, hanging, arras; ‡**textor -earius,** "arras-maker" 1520.
aul/o, strait (αὐλών) c 1212; **-omenon,** flute-music 970.
auloagium, *see* oleagium.
aulodium, *see* lodium.
aumbr-, *see* 2 ambra; armarium.
aumell-, aumoll-, *see* esmallum.
aument-, *see* AUGMENT; omentum.
aumonera, *see* ELEEMOSYN
aumucia, *see* almucia.
aun/cella 1357, **ancera** 1371, **-cer** 1308, **-ser** 1303, 'auncel', balance; *cf.* lanx.
auncerum, *see* haucera.
aunciatus, *see* antiani.
aunderia, *see* 3 andena.
aunetum, *see* ALN
auquilata, *see* aquila.
aura, weather 980; *see also* 2 averium.
‡**auran/cum, -tum,** egg-shell 1652.
aurant/ia 1609, 1626, **arantium** 1622, (?) **arenga** a 1250, orange; **-ius,** orange-coloured, tawny c 1595.
aurarius, patron c 870.
aurat/io, gilding 1391; **-us,** *see* eques.
aure/a, name of a comet c 1270; **a. Alexandrina, a. Tyria,** drugs a 1250; **-ola,** golden crown or circlet 1285, p 1330; *celestial crown, aureole a 1100, c 1340; **-olus** c 1150, a 1250, **oriolus** a 1446, (*probably*) oriole (bird); **-us,** gold coin (esp. bezant) c 1162, 1274; *see also* numerus, oriolum.
‡**aurealis,** earwig c 1440, 15c.
aurica, orphrey 1339.
auricalc-, *see* orichalceus.
auricudor, *see* aurimalliator.
auricul/a, ear-shaped appendage, lug a 1350, 1388; staple 1345; 1307, 1347, **-us** 1319, 1359, plough-ear; auricle (of heart) c 1210, a 1250; **a. muris,** chickweed 1538; ‡mouse-

ear hawkweed, pennyroyal or other herb 14c.; **-are** a 1100, c 1360, **-arium** 1348, **orriale** c 1323, pillow, cushion; **-aris,** (?) ear 12c.; *for* **-arius,** confidant a 1142, c 1225; little finger c 1178, ‡15c.; *see also* **1 digitus, confessio, herba; -ariter,** by way of auricular confession c 1381; **-atio,** whispering 1400; **-ator,** whisperer, confidant c 1470; **-atus,** having ears c 550; **-o,** to cut off ear 1250; **-o, -or,** to whisper 1323, c 1420.
****auri/faber,** goldsmith 1086, 1552; **-fabria** 1259, c 1290, **-fabrica** 1235, goldsmiths' shop or quarter; 1239, 1300, **opus -fabrile** c 1255, c 1400, **orbateria** 1275, goldsmith's work; **-factorius,** worked in gold thread c 1090, 14c.; **-ficium,** heaping up riches 1196 (*see also* **aurifragium**); **-filum,** gold thread 1235, ‡15c.; **-flamba** c 1595, **oriflamma** a 1347, **oloflamma** a 1260, **oloflammea** (*pl.*) 1252, oriflamme, banner; **-fluus,** golden c 1000; **-formis,** gold-like 9c.; **-folium,** gold-leaf (as drug) a 1250;
****-fragium** c 1200, c 1396, **-fregium** 1289, ****-frigium** c 1109, 15c., **-frasium** a 1140, 1368, ****-frisium** 1086, c 1400, **-frisum** 13c., c 1400, **-fisium** c 1160, 13c., **-fraxum** 1251, **-frixium** 1180, **-frixum** 1155, 1302, **-fixum** a 1100, **-fricium** 1521, **-ficium** 13c., 1445, **-fratum** 1240, **-frigenum** c 1315, **-frigerium** c 1500, c 1510, **orfresium** 1164, **orphragium** 1493, **orfrarium** c 1360, 1424, **orfarium (orphareum)** 1398, 1426, **orpharum** 1404, **orfereum** 1432, **orfra, orfrum** 1371, 1477, **orfreum** 1345, 1498, †**offrum** 1451, **aurum friscum** 1204, **-frigiatura** c 1500, orphrey, gold fringe; **-frigiaria** (f.) c 1250, **-frixaria** (f.) 1183, **-frigerius** 1377, **-fraser** 1234, †**-fusarius** c 1350, †**-frixa** 1286, **-frixarius** 1292, **-fixarius** 1335, **-fixorius** 1355, orphreyer, worker in gold fringe; **-fragiatus** c 1321, 1388, ****-frigiatus** c 1200, c 1500, **-frigeratus** 15c., **-friatus** c 1452, **-fricatus** 1373, **-frisiatus** 1402, **-friziatus** c 1365, ornamented with orphrey; **orfero,** to ornament with orphrey 1419;
-genus 955, **-ger** 810, golden; **-legium,** gold-finding c 1200; **-malliator** 1311, 1396, **-cudor** 14c., gold-beater; **-nus (pannus),** of gold c 1315, c 1340; **-pellis,** brass foil (Fr. *oripeau*) c 1250, 1494; **-pictus,** gold-embroidered 1402; **-pigmentum** c 1227, ‡14c., **orpimentum** 1284, 1291, orpiment; †**-stragulatum,** gold stripe c 1395; **-textura,** gold weaving a 1275; **-vittis,** goldfinch 1544; **-vomus,** showering gold c 798. 1528.
aurifrisius, *for* ossifragus, osprey (bird) a 1200, ‡15c.
auriginosus (†**aruginosus**), jaundiced a 1250.
aurigo, to guide, drive (fig.) c 1090.
aur/is, plough-ear c 1280; **-es habeo,** to be obedient c 1193; ‡**-ifodium, -ifricium,** ear-pick 1483.
aurisia, *see* aorasia.
aurkemonnus, *see* 2 averium.
auronum, 'averoyne', southernwood (bot.) 1538.
aur/um, gold coin 1422; **a. novum,** reduced coinage of Edward IV 1464; **a. benevolum,**

sort of gold, used for decoration 1366; **a. Cypri** a 1452, **a. de Cipro** 1369, **a. de Cypre** 1333, 1449, cloth of gold (*see also* **pannus**); **a. de Luke** (= Lucca) 1435, 1450; **a. de muscia**, *see* **musca**; **a. de Venicia** 1412, **a. de Veneciis** 1449, **a. Venesie** 1421; **a. de pondere, a. de pretio** 1242; **a. in folio**, gold leaf 1253 (*see also* **folium, malleus**); ‡**a. fulminans**, precipitate of gold dust dissolved in *aqua regia* 1652; ‡**a. philosophorum**, lead (alch.) 1652; *****a. regine**, queen's gold (queen's shares of fines, *etc.*, paid to king) 1086, 1419; **a. sophisticum**, faked gold a 1252; ‡**a. vivum**, mercury (alch.) 1652; **-oclavus, -oclavatus**, gold-striped c 1595; **-otextus**, woven with gold thread 1415, c 1450; *see also* AURAT, AURE, AURI

auscult/atio, collating copies of documents 1440, 1479; **ascultator**, scout 1297, 1461; ‡**ascultus**, audience c 1410; **-o**, to collate 1319; *****asculto**, to listen c 550. c 1245, c 1408.

ausilium, *see* **auxilium**.

Ausonic/e, in Latin c 1000; **-us**, Latin c 550.

ausor, *see* **haucera**.

‡**auspica/cissime** (? **-tissime**), most auspiciously 1537.

austagium, a customary payment, (?) August money (Dorset) 1258.

aust/er, the south (bibl.): **aster** c 1253; **ex -ro, per -rum** 957, **-raliter** 1423, 1587, southwards, on the south; **-raliter erga occidentem** c 1697; **Mare -rale**, Pacific Ocean 1586; **-ralis**, of the southern nation (Oxford) c 1265, c 1425; **-raris**, *for* **-ralis**, southern 1372; **-ralissimus**, southernmost c 1270; ‡**-romantia**, divination by winds 1652; *see also* **astrum**.

auster-, *see also* AUSTUR

auster/itas, violence 893; **-us**, powerful c 1102; steady a 1408.

austo, to oust (leg.) 1284.

Austr/arius 13c., **-asiensis** c 1200, **-icus** 1252, **-ius** c 1200, Austrian.

Austrogothus, Ostrogoth c 1315.

*****austur/cus** 1159, 1346, **-cius** 1334, **-ius** 1212, 1250, **-us** 1225, 1250, **-co** a 1200, c 1279, **-kinus** 1320, **austrurcus** 1224, **auxturcus** 1222, **auxturus** 1223, **auxurus** 1224, **austercus** 1228, 1259, **austerius** 1205, **asturcus** c 1200, 15c., **asturcius** 1258, **asturco** 1086, 1528, **osturcus** 1210, 1242, **osturcius** 1244, c 1275, **osturus** 1200, 1242, **osturius** c 1150, 1219, **ostor** 1274, **ostorius** 1208, 1333, **osterius** 1402, **esturus** 1232, **outorius** 1231, **hasturus** 1217, **haustorus** 1292, **hostricus** 1425, goshawk (falc.); **-caria** 1212, 1234, **-ciaria** 1208, **austriceria** 1212, **ostriciaria** 1207, **ostreceria, hostriceria** 1198, **hosteracaria** 1240, **-cia** 13c., **ostrucia** 13c., service of supplying or keeping goshawks; **-cia**, hawking 1243; *****-carius** 1160, 1296, **-ciarius** 1239, **asturcarius** 1159, 1300, **osturcarius** c 1150, **austriciarius** 1161, **ostricarius** c 1187, 1213, **ostriciarius** 1185, 1195, **ostricerius** 1212, 'ostringer', falconer.

*****ausus**, (deed of) daring c 1160, c 1520.

aut, otherwise (= *sin minus*) 1254, a 1410.

autelagium, *see* **altare**.

autem . . . autem, on the one hand . . . on the other hand c 1390; **autum**, *for* **autem**, c 730.

*****authentic/um (auctentic-)** 1194, 1427, **-a** 1314, c 1501, original document; **-a** (*n. pl.*), section of Digest 1196, 14c.; **-e**, formally, legally c 1250, 1549; *****-us**, authentic, authoritative 760. c 1125, 1684; *see also* **altare**; ‡**authentus protus**, first tone in plain-song c 1200; **-atio** c 1250, 1435, **authentificatio** c 1376, authentication; *****-o**, to authenticate, confirm c 1210, 1421.

author-, autrix, *see* AUCTOR

authypostatus, self-substantial, requiring no external proof 1620.

autonom-, autom-, *see* ANTONOM

autrax, *see* **anthrax**.

autum, *see* **autem**.

autum/eo, -eto, to abandon c 550.

autumn/us (auctumn-, autumpn-) 1295, c 1356, **-alia** (*n. pl.*) c 1270, harvest, harvest-work; **autompnus** c 1376, **auptumnus** 1209, **auptumpnus** c 1220, autumn; ‡**-arius** 1483, **-ans** 1298, harvester; **-o**, to do harvest work c 1230, 1295.

auvus, *see* **avus**.

aux a 1233, 1686, **augis** c 1200, apogee (astr.).

auxesis, heightening c 1200.

auxili/um *****1103, 1430, **ausilium** c 1235, 1327, feudal aid; *****1201, 1330, **a. curie** c 1219, 1352, legal aid; (*probably*) first-fruits 12c.; entourage 1327; **in -um** 1202, **in -o** 1221, giving help; **a. album**, a rent (man.) 14c.; **a. burgi** 1167, c 1178; **a. civitatis** 1130, 1168; **a. commune** 1184, 1430; **a. domus**, house-bote 1194, 1242; **a. hundredi** c 1250, **a. hundredarii** 1240; **a. militare**, scutage c 1250; **a. novum**, customs duty (of 1266) 1269; **a. (abbatis)** S. Edmundi c 1200; **a. secundum**, a customary payment (eccl.) c 1160; **a. vicecomitis**, sheriff's aid a 1135, 1311; **-abilis**, helpful a 1250; **-arius** (bibl.), **-atrix** (*f.*) 797. c 1194, 1570, ‡**auxiculatrix** 1430, ‡**auxiatrix** 8c., helper, helpful; **-anter**, helpfully c 1250; **-or** (*dep.*), to grant a feudal aid c 1202, 1221.

auxion-, auxiatrix, *see* AUCTION

auxungia, auxatio, *see* 1 **axella**.

aval/agium 1174, c 1271, **avelagium** 1225, 1242, toll on goods going down river (Thames); **a. vinorum**, wine toll (G.) c 1224, 1267; **-atio** 1323, ‡**avagium** 1504, carrying down, lowering; *****-atio** c 1160, 1308, **ebalatio** 1231, ‡**averagium** 1655, migration of eels downstream; **-o**, to let down 1198, 1297; to take down (from gallows) 1318; *cf.* **vallis**.

avalana, *see* **abellana**.

avalaria 1213, **avellaria** 1214, **alara** 1213, breeching (of harness).

avancia, *see* **avencia**.

avan/tagium a 1216, a 1564, **vantagium** a 1185, **advantagium** 1299, 1588, **avauntagium** c 1479, 1488, **aventagium** 1299, **adventagium** 1348, profit, gain; difference between heaped and razed measure 1297, 1327; **advanciamentum**, betterment 1587.

avar/agium, -ium, *see* 2 **averium**.

avarexia, see anorexia.

avaria, see AVEN

ave c 1340, c 1365, a. Maria 15c., 1496, prayer; bead 1357.

avel-, see also AVAL

avellana, see abellana.

avell/um, battle c 550; -osus, of or for battle c 550.

aven/a, oats: advena 1270, a 1300, awena 1302; a. cursalis 1372; a. grossa 1286; a. minuta c 1280, 1286; a. nigra 1329; -agium, feudal payment of oats (Norm.) 1180; ‡-aceum 1570, -agium 1180, -atum a 1250, oat gruel, porridge; -alis c 1365, -aticus 1266, 1556, -icius 1215, -osus 1269, of oats; -aria 1290, 1492, -eria 1443, avaria 1460, averia 1461, 1496, office of avener; -arius 1188, 1529, avynarius 1379, -ator 1209, 1325, avener, provider of oats (for fodder).

†avenacius, (?) f.l. for a[d]venticius, c 1350.

avenagium, see avena, ulnagium; cf. advenagium, havenagium.

avenama, see offnama.

avenantum, instalment of debt or rent (O.F. avenant) 1166, 13c.

‡avencia 13c., 15c., avancia (†anancia) a 1250, avens (bot.).

avendo ad firmam, to farm c 1457.

avenicius, see AVEN

avent-, see also ADVEN

avent/allum 1382, -alium 1313, -ailum 1386, adventale 1343, aventail; cf. ventaculum; -um, vent-pipe 1388.

averagium, see 1 and 2 averium; AVAL

avergo, to verge a 1164.

1 aver/ium 1274, 1419, -e c 1192, goods, merchandise; a. de pondere 1286, 1316, a. ponderis 1267, 15c., a. ponderatum 1305, averipondus c 1314, avoirdupois, goods sold by weight; ‡-agium, loss due to damage at sea 1664.

2 *aver/ium 1185, 1583, avarium c 1200, 1276, -ius c 1255, -us 1185, 1449, avrus 1130, 1232, awrus 1227, afferus 1247, c 1300, *affrus 1086, 1487, affrum c 1300, -ia c 1185, a 1300, avra (aura) c 1120, 13c., affra 1234, 1284, draught animal; a. grossum a 1300, 1370; a. otiosum, animal out of work 1237, c 1290; a. trahens 1382; corium affrinum, hide of draught animal 1344; *-agium c 1185, 1547, avaragium 13c., 1371, avragium c 1220, affragium c 1253, 1279, ariagium (arre-, hare-, aragium) (Sc.) 1553, 1593, -arium c 1236, c 1300, -ata 1086, a c 1310, carrying-service, arriage; -agium pedile, carrying service on foot 1251; -arius, stockman 16c.; -arius c 1236, -ius c 1300, of or for carrying-service; -landum c 1300, -clandus c 1182, 1299, land liable to carrying-service; -mannus c 1250, c 1277, -menus c 1182, †arkmannus 1299, aurkemonnus 13c., tenant liable to carrying-service; *-o c 1185, c 1422, -or (dep.) c 1283, -io c 1115, 1279, evero c 1310, afro c 1250, to perform carrying-service.

averocus, see haverocus.

averrunc/us, see crux; -o, to abolish c 950; aberunco, to banish c 1435.

avers/io, loss, ruin 1277; -or, thief 799; avertibilis, avertible 1344.

aves/agium 1336, 1535, avisagium 1400, 1587, advisagium 1587, (payment for) pasturage or pannage (A.S. æfesne); a. vaccarum 1485; -o, to pay for pannage of (pigs) 1279, 1336.

avi/captio, -cida, -cipula, -cula, see avis.

avicino, to approach c 900.

avido/tus 1301, a 1307, -dus 1301, 1323, auditus 1459, adit, gallery or drainage tunnel of mine.

avigilia, see aquilegia.

avincula, see VINCUL

†avionia, (?) reef or shore c 550.

avir/o 1225, 1462, -onus c 1225, -onatus 1279, -unatus 1146, oar; cf. viro.

avis 1168, 1199, a. generosa a 1200, a. regalis 1309, a. regia c 1178, falcon; a. campi a 1250; a. Ganymedis, puffin p 1327; a. Hercynia, a bird found in Germany 12c.; a. paradisi, a bird of the Nile a 1446; a. Petri, petrel a 1446; a. prede a 1250, 1307, a. de preda 1361, a. rapax a 1200, bird of prey; a. Sancti Colemanni, teal c 1315; a. Sancti Cuthberti, eider duck 1399; a. Socratis, hoopoe 13c.; aves incipiunt cantare (12 Feb.) 12c., 14c.; avi/captio, (?) fowling-glade c 1328; ‡-cipula, pitfall 15c., 1483; -cida, bird-slayer c 1200; -cula, little bird 690. c 1090, c 1430; ‡-cularius, fowler 1483; -gerulus (†anigerulus), poulterer c 1393, ‡1483; -ticus c 550, -tius 1524, avian.

avis-, see ADVIS; AVES

aviseges, see amseges.

avo-, see also ADVOC

avolat/io 8c. 12c., 1552, -us 12c., c 1250, ascension or flying away.

avolta, see VOLU

avr-, see 2 averium.

avulsorius, tending to pull away c 1620.

avuncul/a, aunt c 1267; -us magnus, great-uncle 1445; avonculus 1223, advunculus c 1200, 1294, *awnculus a 1190, c 1265, awunculus c 1266, adwunculus 1263, for -us, uncle.

avus, grandfather: auvus 1199.

avynarius, see AVEN

aw-, see also av-

awaita maris, coast watch 1203; agaitus, ambush 1203, 1414; cf. WAIT

award/um 1258, c 1372, -a 1491, agarda 1491, evardum 1279, esgard/um 1251, 1315, -ia a 1190, esguardum (G.) 1275, 1315, award, legal decision; agardo, to award 1556.

ax/a c 1429, -ia 1301, axe; cf. ASCI, hachia.

1 ax/ella 1351, -us 1486, exa 1344, exus 1281, for -is, axle; -is, optic axis a 1361; a. campane c 1400; a. molendini 1276; -itona, wheel or axle 9c.; -sa, post 1316; -atio 1316, 1425, auxatio 1391, -io 1276, fitting with axles; †-urgia 1347, anxungia, auxungia a 1250, 1378, exungia 1376, †anxagia 1531, for axungia, axle-grease; *-o 1233, 1381, -io 1316, 1325, yaxo 1280, exo 1324, axilio 1300, exulo 1211, to fit with axles.

2 axella 1427, 1528, ascella 7c., 8c. c 1100

c 1325, **acella** c 1197, a 1446, **aissella** 1280, **assella** c 1210, c 1250, **assellia** c 1250, arm-pit; **vena assellaris,** axillary vein a 1250.

axiom/a 1610, 1620, †**anxima** c 1150, axiom, proposition; **-aticus,** concerned with propositions 1610.

axsedula, see ACED

ay, aya, an exclamation c 1250, 1271.

ayeri/a, -um, see aeria.

aymeraldus, see smaragdo.

ays-, see AIS

aza, see ascia.

azabar, gem and herb potent against scorpions c 1270.

azarabaccara, azarum, see asara baccara.

azeis/a 1175, **aszeisia** 1172, **azesia** 1172, 1187, **azezia** 1179, **-ia** (coll.) 1205, **adhesia** 1203, flat stone for roofing; cf. ASSESS, EXCIS

azephalus, see acephalus.

azerum, see acer.

†**Azige,** book by Ptolemy a 1150.

azil-, see asilus.

azimuth, azimuth, celestial longitude (astr.) 1326.

azinbia, see ABSINTH

azoara c 1143, c 1395, **azophara** 1378, sura, verse of Koran.

azot (†**azoc**), mercury 1144.

azur/a c 1200, **-ium** 1267, ‡14c., **-um** c 1227, 1346, **azorium** 1245, 15c., **asura** 1289, ‡c 1440, **asurum** 1342, **asorium** c 1400, †**azorantum** 1444, †**atirum** c 1180, azure, lapis lazuli; 1389, **color azoreus (asorius)** p 1394, azure (her.); **-eus** c 1215, 1528, **adzurius** a 1250, **asureus** 1314, **asuurius** 1208, **assurus** c 1321, azure (adj.); cf. LAZUL

azym/a, feast of unleavened bread (bibl.); **-us,** unleavened bread (bibl.); **-ita,** Latin Christian, as using unleavened bread in eucharist c 1100; a 1142, **-atus** c 1118, (?) eastern heretic.

B

(See also V)

B, musical note 1351; **B durum, B quadrata,** B natural 1351; **B molle** c 1200, 1351, **bemolle** c 1200, c 1436, **B rotunda** 1351, B flat.

‡**babatum,** horse-shoe c 1440.

bab/ewinus (†**habewinus**) 1295, 1388, **-winus** 1314, 1388, **-o** c 1405, **-onus** c 1443, †**bobinus** (?) 12c., 'baboon', grotesque figure.

‡**bab/iger,** fool, foolish c 1440, 1483; **-illo,** babbler c 1434; ‡**-urra,** folly c 1440, 1483; **-ico,** to slobber c 1200; cf. bava.

babti-, see BAPT

babtuta, see balducta.

bacca caprarum, (?) ivy 12c.; **b. Turcica,** coffee 1701.

bacc/alarius c 1350, c 1422, **bachelarius** 1200, 1293, **bachelerius** 1202, **bachilarius** 1263, 1400, **bakelarius** 1385, **bacularis** a 1142, lad, young retainer (esp. aspirant for knighthood); see also **miles; bachelarius** 1263, **bacularis** a 1100, riotous lad; junior craftsman (? apprentice or journeyman) 13c.; c 1231, c 1320, ***-alarius** c 1314, 1587; ***bachilarius** c 1264, c 1477, **-ularius** 1267, 1506, **-alaureus** 1382, a 1564, bachelor (ac.); **bacularius,** (?) senior pupil in grammar school 1315, 1388; **bachelaria, bacheleria,** young retainers (coll.) 1259; **-alariatus** 14c., c 1518, **bachelariatus** 1311, **bachilariatus** c 1592, **-ulariatus** c 1410, 1507, **-alaureatus** c 1522, c 1549, **bacchilaureatus** c 1592, degree of bachelor (ac.).

baccaria, see 1 bercaria.

baccaulus, bier 10c.

‡**bacch/anal,** wine-press 1483; **-analius,** graduate of Bacchus (pun on **baccalarius**) 1523; ‡**-arium,** wine-pot 1483; †**-eriosus,** (?) terrible a 700; **-iferus,** wine-bearing c 800; **-inus,** frenzied 7c.; **-ilatria,** worship of Bacchus c 1200, c 1430.

bac/cile, -ellum, -enettus, see bacinus.

bacellus, see BACUL

bacerellus, see 3 batellum.

†**bacha,** boat, barque c 800; cf. 1 batellum; see also 1 bechium.

bachel-, bachil-, see baccalarius; BACUL

bachia, see besca.

bachinator, overseer (of castles) (G.) 14c.

baci/a, -um 1248, 1381, **bazum** 1267, 1273, **baseum** 1299, **bassum** 1282, 1486, †**vassum** 1298, **baso** 1245, **baco** 1265, 'base' saddle-pad or (?) pack-saddle.

bacillus (bach-), see bacinus, BACUL

*bacin/us 1130, 1414, **-a** a 1273, **-um** c 1300, **-ia, -ium** a 1100, 12c., **bascinus** 13c., 1259, **bassina** c 1450, **bassinus** 1391, c 1450, **bacilla** 13c., **bacillus** 13c., **bacillum** c 1321, **bacellum** (†**batellum**) c 1266, ***bacile (baccile)** c 1087, 15c., **bacena** 1212, basin; **-us** a 1241, c 1423, **bascinus** c 1330, basin-shaped lamp; **-us** 1275, c 1350, **-ius** 1289, ***-ettus** 1292, 1381, **basinettus** 1318, 1390, **bacenettus** 1312, **bassenettus** 1380, 1416, †**borcinettus** (f.l.) 1326, 'basnet', light helmet.

*bac/o c 1115, c 1400, **-onus** 1205, 1392, 'bacon', salt carcass of hog or part of it; **-ono,** to salt bacon 1214; see also **bacia.**

bacuatus, see bateria.

bacul-, see also baccalarius.

bacul/us, fork-handle 1278; stave of barrel 1282; ingot 1245; gun-stock 1385; plough-beam 1236, 1355; pole of cart 1248, 1318; beam of weigh-beam 1352; a 1449, **bacillus sinister** 1654, baton sinister (her.); staff of portable cross (eccl.) 1448; ***a** 1100, 1414, **b. choralis** 1235, c 1255, ***b. pastoralis** c 1125, 1499, crozier; **b. arcualis,** bowstave 1420; **-a ad ballistam,** (?) crosspiece 1247; **-us cibi,** staff of life 1136; **b. peregrinationis,** pilgrim staff c 1160;

C

b. festivalis, Christmas staff 1388; **b. stultorum,** crozier of 'bishop' in Feast of Fools 1245; **b. vigilie,** 'wake-staff' (Sc.) c 1270; *see also* **per; frango -um,** to deprive of office c 1155, c 1258; **bachillus** 1240, **bacellus** 14c., (?) **basillus** c 1180, stick, staff; **pila -aris,** game ('staff-ball' or hurley) 1363, 1447; **funda -ina** 1302, **f. ad. -os** 1298, sort of sling; **-osus,** having a crozier 12c.; **-ator,** cudgeller 1220; **-o,** to cudgel 1220, c 1470; to fit (cart) with poles 1290.

bacus, ferry-boat (Fr. *bac*) (Norm.) 1198; *cf.* **bacha, 1 batellum.**

badellus, *see* **bedellus.**

badia, *see* **baia.**

badius, *see* **baius.**

badivola, *see* BAJUL

bag/a (bagg-) 1277, 1523, **-us** 1326, 1417, **-ea** 1300, bag; **b. de secretis,** bag containing certain King's Bench indictments 1357, 1414; **B. Parva** 1389, **-ia Parva** 1586, Petty Bag (department of Chancery); **-agium** 1422, 1461, **-acium** 1461, baggage; **-epipa,** bag-pipe c 1287.

bagi/a c 1421, 1542, **-um** a 1446, badge (of overlord).

bahardum, *see* **baiardum.**

bahud/a, -um, *see* **barhudum.**

bai/a *1175, c 1333, **-um** 1213, c 1266, **badia** 1359, **beum** 1212, **beda** c 1160, 1548, **bedum** 1260, 1538, **beodum** 1337, †**benium** c 1215, bay of pond, mill-dam; 1236, 1518, **-us** 1474, bay of building; †**-agium,** customary payment (? *f.l.* for **kaiagium**) 1359.

***baiard/um** 1279, 1371, **bahardum** 1279, **-eum** 1198, 'bayard', hand-barrow; **-arius** 1320, **-or** c 1280, 1333, barrow-man; *see also* **baius.**

baicha, *see* **barca.**

baidius, *see* **baius.**

1 baill/ium 1142, 14c., **-um** 1215, **-ia** 1203, 1216, ***ball/ium** 1156, 1446, **-ia** 1172, 1331, †**baluum** 1204, **-iva** 1274, 1313, **-ivia** c 1306, castle bailey; **b. exterius** 1304, 1336, **b. forinsecum** 1203, 1331, **-ia extrinseca** 1216, outer bailey; **b. interius** 1304, 1336, **b. intrinsecum** 1234, **balliva intima** 1313, inner bailey; **b. superius,** upper bailey 1257; **b. medium** 1251, **ballia media** 1327, middle bailey; **balliva inferior,** lower bailey 1313.

2 baill/ium 1223, 1274, **-ia** 1241, ***ballium** 1238, 1513, bail, security; 1213, 1240, **-ia** c 1218, ***ballium** 1224, c 1268, **ballia** 1196, 1221, bailment, grant; **ballium,** wardship of minors 1199, c 1289; ***-ia** a 1135, 1370, **-a** c 1414, ***ballia** c 1072, 1476, **-iva** 12c., a 1300, **-ivia** c 1305, ***balliva** c 1180, 1419, **ballivia** 1213, c 1331, **ballivium** 1200, **ballivata** 1276, 1587, **ballivatus** 1281, 1559, **balliviatus** c 1422, a 1430, ‡**balliatus** c 1440, **-agium** (Fr.) 1378, **-iagium** 1408, 1462, **balliagium** 1406, 1486, **ballagium** 1487, †**ballivicus** 1314, (area of) jurisdiction, office of bailiff, bailiwick; **ballia** 1237, 1293, **balliva** 1242, 1256, 'ward', division of county (N. Engl.); **balliva marine,** office of water-bailiff 1329; ***-ivus** c 1185, 1376, ***ballivus** c 1192, 1583, **-ius** 1105,

1224, **ballius** c 1155, 1332, bailiff, official (esp. subordinate of sheriff); **b. aque** 1454, 1485, **b. aque maritime** 1398, 1400, **b. de marina** 1325, water-bailiff (*cf.* **aqua**); **b. capitalis** 13c., 1297, **b. superior** 1300, 1496; **b. hundredi** 1200, 14c.; **b. itinerans** 1304, 1505, **b. errans** 1307, bailiff errant (not attached to a hundred); **b. marisci** (Romney) 1258, 1298; **b. parvus** 1275, 1313; *cf.* **bajulus.**

baissa, lip c 1200.

bai/us c 1200, c 1290, **-ardus** 1284, 1427, ***badius** 1297, 1588, **baidius** 1444, **basius** c 1452, bay (horse); *see also* **baia.**

bajul/us, (*adj.*) bearing c 1112, c 1170; portable, carried c 1188, 1392; (*subst.*) bailiff, official (Fr. *baile*) c 1070, 1438; ***bearer** of letter 12c., c 1458; **b. crucis** 12c., 1279, **-ator crucis** c 1200, c 1250, crusader; **b. sigilli** c 1250, c 1412, **-ator sigilli** 1252, keeper of the seal; **-ator** 1347, 1434, **-a** (*f.*) 12c., 1252, bearer; **-a aque,** holy water stoup 1415 (*cf.* **aqua**); †**badivola,** litter a 1142; **-atio,** giving of bail 1355; bailment 1374; **b. crucis,** bearing a cross 1278, 1467; **-atus,** bearing of burden a 1100, 1284; office, bailiwick 1284; **-ia,** commandery (of Hospitallers) 1313, 1375; ***-o** (bibl.), **bajolo** a 1250, to carry.

bakaveragium, (?) carrying-service on back of beast 1302.

bakelarius, *see* **baccalarius.**

***bal/a** c 1242, 1387, **-um, -us** 1303, 1449, **-ea** 1523, †**-esium** 1397, (?) **balna** 1413, bale; **-eta** 1461, **-etum** 1443, small bale.

balan-, *see also* **bilanx.**

balangera, *see* **balena.**

balanites, a precious stone: †**balamites** 1338.

bal/asius 1205, 1424, **-assus** 1424, c 1486, ***-esius** 1215, 1425, **-eisius** 1420, **-agius** a 1446, 1508, **-istus** 1409, balass (precious stone).

balast-, *see* **ballista.**

balatio, bleating c 1000.

balatola, ballot (It.) 1370.

balatr/o, glutton c 1219; **baratro,** buffoon c 1180; †**-o,** to bawl c 1470; *see also* **blaserius.**

balbushardus, 'bald-buzzard', osprey 1544.

balb/uties 1345, ‡1483, **-utıs** 826, stammering; **-utive,** stammeringly 1427, **-esco,** to stammer a 1446, ‡1483; **-utio,** to ring false c 1270.

balcan/us, -ifer, *see* **bauzanus.**

balchus, *see* **balteus.**

balc/us *c 1150, 1452, **-a** c 13c0, (?) **baucus** (†**bancus**) 1246, (?) **bulcus** (?) 12c., baulk, strip of land; baulk, beam 1141, 1335; **-o,** balcony 10c. c 1100.

bald/ekinus 1218, 15c., **-achinum** 1494, **-equinus** 1392, **balkenus** 1245, ***baud/e-kinus, -ekinum** 1218, 15c., **-equinus** c 1305, **-ekenus** 1336, baldachin, brocade; *see also* **baudkinus.**

‡**baldemonia,** baldmoney (bot.) 14c.

baldr/edum 1205, **baudrea** 1203, baldric, ornamental belt; 1287, 1326, **-eus** 1221, **baud/erea** (†**band-**) 1263, **-rea** 1289, 1301, **-ra** 1270, **-rellus** c 1290, 1301, **-ricus** c 1253, c 1282, **-ero** 1282, (?) †**bausterium**

c 1350, belt for bending cross-bow; *cf.* **balteus.**

‡**bal/ducta** c 1440, 1483, ‡**bedulta** 15c., †**babtuta** c 1000, posset; **-thuta,** butter-milk 546.

1 baldus, (?) spirited (of dogs) 1210, 1214; (?) bold 1315.

2 bal/dus 1311, **-lidus** 1390, **-idinus** 1236, 'bald', pie-bald (of horses); *cf.* **bauzanus.**

bale/a, broom, besom (Fr. *balai*) 1335; **mensura -ata,** razed measure 1335; **-o,** to sweep 1261; *see also* **bala.**

Balearicus (fig.), epithet of Satan's weapons c 950.

bal/ena, whale-bone 1284, 1322; **-eina** 1199, 1265, **-erium** 1490, ‡**-eria** 1652, **-nea** c 1258, **-neta** 1331, **-ignus** 1296, *for* **-ena,** whale, whale-meat; **-enatus,** small whale (G.) 1281; **-enaria** 1403, **-ingaria** c 1420, **-angera** c 1374, *** -ingera** 1379, 1495, whale-boat, 'balinger'.

balesium, balet/a, -um, *see* **bala.**

bal/esius, -eisius, -istus, *see* **balasius.**

balesta, *see* **ballista.**

balidinus, ballidus, *see* **2 baldus.**

baling/aria, -era, *see* **balena.**

‡**balitistera,** "*terra rubea*" (alch.) 1652.

balkenus, *see* **baldekinus.**

ball-, *see also* BAILL

ballada, form of composition (mus.) 1326.

ballardus, *see* **2 baslardus.**

ballast/um 1462, **-rum** 15c., ballast; **-agium,** ballast due 1606.

ballebeta, *ballibetagh,* area of 960 acres (Ir.) c 1606.

†**ballenrum,** (?) *for* **balzenum,** white patch c 1258; *cf.* **bauzanus.**

ballenum, *see* **balneum.**

balleuca, *see* **banleuca.**

***ballist/a** 12c., 1535, **balesta** 1429, **balissa** c 1224, crossbow; **b. ad cornu** 1261, **b. de cornu** 1213, 1306; **b. de fusto** 1228; **b. de ifo** 1306; **b. de omello** 1306; **b. lignea** 1246; **b. cum bauderone, cum baudrica** c 1282; **b. sine telariis** 1246; **b. ad pedes** 1300, **ad duos pedes** 1205, 1280, **duorum pedum** 1307; **b. ad unum pedem** 1205, 1300, **de uno pede** c 1335, **unius pedis** 1307; **b. pedalis** 1297; **b. ad stritum,** crossbow with stirrup 1213; **b. ad (de) troil' (truill')** 1222, 1264, **b. de trullio** 1266, **b. ad turnas (turnum)** 1205, 1300, **b. de torno** 1307, **b. ad viceas** 1282, **b. de vicio (viscio, vice, vyz)** 1297, c 1335, crossbow worked by winch; **b. Turonica** 1253; **-aria** 1219, 1235, **balisteria** 13c., **balastaria** 1203, crossbow service; *** -arius** 1086, 1490, **balestarius** 1086, c 1220, **balastarius** 1086, 1235, **-er** 1608, crossbowman; **b. eques** 1214, 1327; **b. pedes** 1212, 1263; **-o,** to shoot with crossbow 14c.

ballo, to shoot 1413; to sweep c 1290 (*cf.* **balea**); ‡"to quake" 1483.

ballum, clapper c 1150.

balna, *see* **bala.**

balne/a, -ta, *see* **balena.**

balne/um, bath: **ballenum** c 1000; **-um,** bath of knighthood a 1446, 1586; **b. Marie,** *bain Marie* c 1345, 1620; **-arium** c 1266, c 1400, **-ria** c 1483, **-atorium** c 1330,

c 1397, bath, bath-house; **baynum,** bath (for falcons) 1275; **-atio,** bathing 13 c.; *** -o** a 1100, c 1457, †**banneo** (? **bauneo**) 12c., 1377, to bathe, conduct to the bath; **-o** a 1150, 1634, **b. me** c 1192, c 1400, **-or** c 1072, c 1293, to take a bath.

balsam/us, balsam tree c 1212, ‡14c.; **-ita,** horse-mint a 1250, ‡14c.; **-iticus** c 1400, †**-itus** (? **-icus**) c 1125, 15c., ‡**-ensis** 1483, balmy; **-o,** to perfume 1220; to embalm 14c.

balt/eus, fess (her.) c 1595; †**balchus,** belt for bending crossbow 1257; **-eus militaris,** belt of knighthood c 1200, c 1595; **-icus,** fesswise c 1595; **-inus,** (?) belonging to a belt or baldric c 1385; *cf.* **baldredum, belta.**

balthuta, *see* **balducta.**

bal/um, -us, *see* **bala.**

baluum, *see* 1 **baillium.**

bambillus, horse-clog 1498.

bambulo, *see* **fambulo.**

bamum, banum, that which is above, a height c 550.

ban/a, -um, bane, cause of death 1195, c 1320.

banar-, *see* BANER

ban/astrum a 1307, 1325, **-iastrum** a 1307, basket (for charcoal) (O.F. *banastre*); **-esteria,** basket-bearer (*f.*) c 1172.

bancinus, *see* **bauzanus.**

banc/us c 1200, 1378, **-a** 1247, 1375, bank, hill, mound (*cf.* **balcus**); **b. maris,** dune 1274; *** -us** 1086, c 1437, **-a** c 1340, bench, stall; c 1450, 1535, **-atus** 1497, bank (for money); bench, court of law (esp. at Westminster, as distinct from eyre) c 1185, c 1448; **coram -o** 1259, 1274; **infra (inter) iiij bancos,** in court (county or hundred) 12c., 1269; *** -us communis** 1327, 1586, **b. magnus** 1282, Court of Common Pleas; **b. regis** 1245, 1419, **b. regius** 1331, 1586, **b. regalis** 15c., King's Bench; **B. Superior,** Upper Bench (Commonwealth) 1651; **b. francus** 1217, 1419, **b. liber** 1246, 1357, **bangius l.** 1260, free-bench, widow's dower (leg.); **-um** (†**brancum**) tornatile, revolving seat 12c.; **-agium,** rent for dunes (C.I.) 1331; stall-due (G.) 1254; **-ale** a 1090, 1466, **-alium** c 1170, **-arium** c 1300, c 1443, **banquarium** 1285, **banquerium** c 1290, **bankerium** c 1331, c 1443, **bankerius** 1328, **bankerus** 1290, **baunkerum** 1365, **-orium** 1329, †**boncarium** 1205, **banchetum** c 1093, c 1112, 'banker', bench-cover; **-arius,** banker, money-changer 1436.

band-, *see* **baldredum;** BANER; BANN; BEND

baner/a 1198, 1497, **-ia, -ium** c 1200, 1386, **banarium** 1212, **banderium, bandum** c 1595, banner; **bandophorus** c 1595, **ban-nifer** c 1360, standard-bearer; **-ettum,** bannerette 1466; **-ettus** 1264, 1586, **bana-rettus** 1370, **-itus** 1608, **banarista** c 1385, banneret; **miles b.** 1400, **m. -icius** 1260, **m.** †**-icus** 1283, knight banneret; *cf.* **baronettus.**

ban/esteria, -iastrum, *see* **banastrum.**

bangius, *see* **bancus.**

ban/leuca 1171, 1441, **balleuca** 1255, 1321, **-eleuga** 1233, **-leuga** c 1190, **-lega** 1219, **-lucum** 1293, **-cleuca** 14c., **batleuca**

1236, 1313, **batleuga** 1316, **benleuca** 1203, -**na leuca** c 1220, -**num leuge** 12c., **leuga bannalis** c 1185, banlieu, area of jurisdiction (esp. Fr.); *cf.* **bannum.**
banneo, *see* BALNE
bannifer, *see* BANER
bannita, syllable 7c.
bannoka, bannock (Sc.) 1521.
bannonium, open season for grazing (C.I.) (O.F. *banon*) 1300.
bann/um *c 1115, 1326, -**ium** c 1230, 1275, -**us** 1275, *proclamation, edict, penalty; *12c., 1598, -**a** c 1477, -**us** c 1290, marriage-bann; -**um** 1273, 1415, -**ium** 1309, -**iamentum** (G.) 1289, -**imentum** (Fr.) 1279, 1309, -**iatio** 1327, -**itio** 1289, 1438, banishment; **(exercitus)** -**itus,** (?) unlawful 1262; -**io,** to proclaim 1223, 1233; to sequestrate c 1252, c 1285; *c 1188, 1450, -**o** 1274, 1684, -**ero** 13c., -**ezo** (It.) 1247, -**izo** 13c., **bandio** 1303, to banish; *see also* **banleuca.**
banqu-, *see* BANC
banum, *see* bamum, bana.
banus, provincial governor (Hungary) a 1446.
baphus, *see* paphus.
bapt/isma, *-**ismus** (bibl.), **babtisma** c 791, **babtismus** 7c., **bautismus** 7c., -**izatio** c 1400, 1559, baptism; -**ismalis** c 1194, c 1500, -**izalis** c 1220, baptismal; -**ismaliter,** in virtue of baptism 1427; -**isecula,** cornflower 1632; *-**ista** (eccl.), †-**iza** c 1400, **batista** c 1268, the Baptist; 1414, -**izator** (eccl.), baptizer; (?) hermit of St. John a 1270; -**isterium** 8c. 1362, **liber -ismi** 9c., baptismal service-book; c 1130, 1345, -**izarium** 1353, baptismal rights or dues; *c 1000. c 1190, 15c., -**istarium** c 1250, -**izarium** 1242, -**izaterium** 731. c 1250, -**ismatorium** 1446, baptistery, font; *-**izo** (-**iso**) (eccl.), **babtidzo** 7c., to baptize.
baralipton, a logical mood 13c.
bar/atator, impostor c 1250, 1334; -**ator** 13c., -**ettor** 1541, -**ettator** 1516, 1588, -**ritator** c 1620, -**atrius** 1608, barrator (fomenter of lawsuits), disturber; -**ettum,** barter 1437; -**atria,** barratry (Sc.) 1608.
barathr/um, Hell c 870, c 980. 12c., 1336; **voratrum** c 1255, **vorotrum** c 550, abyss; -**alis,** infernal c 1250, 1252.
baratro, *see* balatro.
‡**barb/a** Aaron, arum (bot.) 14c.; ‡**b. Anglica,** deadnettle 14c.; **b. capri,** meadowsweet 1634; ‡**b. elexis,** burdock 14c.; **b. filicana,** ribwort plantain a 1250; ‡**b. hircina,** hypocistis 14c.; -**arius** 1292, -**erius** c 1177, 1460, -**irius** 1292, *-**ator** a 1205, 1340, -**etor** 1475, -**etonsor** 1447, 1535, *-**itonsor** 1272, 1505, barber; -**atura,** barber's craft c 1300; -**aria** 1303, -**etonsio** 1474, barbering, beard-trimming; ‡-**itondium** c 1440, 1483, -**itonsorium** 1454, barber's shop; -**ifer,** bearded friar a 1270; -**osus** c 1050. c 1370, (?) **berbatus** 1458, bearded; -**esco,** to grow a beard a 1250; -**o,** to 'barb', clip (wool) 1441, 1532; *cf.* BARD; *see also* **barbilla.**
barbac-, barbec-, barb/aria, -ataria, *see* **barbicana.**
barbara, a logical mood 13c.

barbaratus, *see* **barbilla.**
barbarea, winter-cress (bot.) 1632.
barbar/ius (*adj.*), barbarian c 1298, c 1346; -**ice,** savagely 13c.; -**izatio,** translation into vernacular 1427; -**izo,** to speak barbarously c 1190, 1419; ‡to behave barbarously 1483.
barbarum, *see* berberis.
barbascus, *see* verbascum.
barbatus, *see* barbilla; barbita.
barb/ellus 1234, a 1450, -**ulus** c 1200, -**atilus** a 1519, -**o** 1570, †**burbux** a 1275, barbel (fish); ‡**burbarus,** "carp" 1570.
barbetta, 'barbette', platform in fortification 1359.
barb/icana 1250, -**icanum** 1323, c 1380, -**acana** 1180, c 1255, -**acanum, -akanus** 1255, 1275, -**akena, -ekena** 1175, -**ecana** 1225, 1230, -**ecanum** 1260, -**ukana** 1274, †-**aria** c 1425, †-**ataria** 1243, barbican; -**icanagium** 1336, 1415, †-**icagium** 1463, toll or due for building a barbican.
barb/illa, barb, tip (for arrow) 1542; -**illatus** c 1245, -**alatus** 1247, -**aratus** 1224, -**ellatus** 1204, 1250, -**eletus** 1286, -**ulatus** 1224, 1271, -**atus** 1209, 1437, -**etus** 1204, 1247, -**elius** 1243, barbed (of arrows, *etc.*); -**o,** to set (a fence) with spikes c 1300, 1384; *see also* **barba, burbilia.**
barb/ita, organ 7c.; -**iton** c 1125, †-**atus** c 1400, wind-chest of organ.
barb/o, -osus, *see* barba, barbellus.
barbota, armoured boat c 1250.
barc-, *see also* BERC
barc/a c 800. 12c., 1484, †**baicha** 1317, **barqua** 1497, -**ellus** (G.) 1242, barque; ‡-**arius,** "ship-maker" 1483; *cf.* 1 **bargia.**
barcius, *see* barsa.
barco, *see* BARR
bard/a, measure of cloth 1307, 1340; -**o** 1441, 1504, **berdo** 1441, 1503, **bordo** 1460, to 'bard', clip (cloth); **berdo,** to set (a fence) with spikes 1374; *cf.* **barba, barbilla.**
bardana, burdock (bot.) a 1250, 1632.
bardisa, *see* 1 **bargia.**
barecto, *see* WARECT
barefell-, barfell-, *see* BEREFELL
*bar/ellus** 1184, 1556, †**varellus** c 1485, -**ella** 1390, 1566, -**ellum** 1368, c 1429, -**lellus** 1388, *-**illus** 1170, c 1336, -**ele** 1480, -**ile** 1428, 1460, **berillum** a 1250, †-**ettus** 1310, barrel, cask; 1305, 1388, -**illus** 1274, barrel or roller for burnishing armour; **b. verne,** part of windlass 1333; -**elula** 1480, -**isellus** a 1250, small barrel, costrel; -**illatum,** barrelful, liquid measure c 1290; -**elborda,** stave 1325; -**ello,** to pack in a barrel 1225, 1449; *see also* **beryllus.**
†**barelus** (? *f.l.* for **karelus**), study in cloister 1294; *cf.* **carola.**
barett-, *see* baratator; barellus.
barg/a, -agia, *see* 1 **bargia.**
barg/anea 1383, a 1564, -**anium** 1315, 1428, -**ennia** 1417, -**anizatio** 1392, c 1539, **burganizatio** 1522, bargain, bargaining; -**anizator controversiarum,** fomenter of disputes 1347; -**anizo** 1400, 1543, -**annio** c 1115, 1353, -**anno** c 1150, 1315, -**enio** 1206, -**ino** 1282, to bargain.

1 *barg/ia, -ea 1217 c 1540, -a c 1200, 1427, -agia 1335, -etta 1403, †bardisa c 1404, barge, boat; -iata, barge-load 1302; -emannus 1362, bergemannus 1377, barge-man; *cf.* barca.

2 barg/ia 1213, 1316, -a 1280, 1336, -ium 1306, barica 1208, saddle-bag, saddle-pad *or* (?) collar-pad (of harness).

†barginus, (?) foreign 695.

†Bargoma, *for* Barjona, 595.

*barhudum 1172, 1330, bahud/a, -um 1225, 1332, barhutum 1160, 1186, barhuzium 1176, barrutum 1204, 1214, barruzum 1180, baridum 1205, 1342, barura 1314, 1334, 'barehide', cart-cover (*cf.* Fr. *bahut*); *cf.* palludum.

bariam, bad omen a 1235.

barica, *see* 2 bargia; *cf.* barrica.

†baricus, fabulous Indian monster a 1250.

baril-, barisellus, *see* barellus.

barinettus, *see* baro.

barko, *see* 2 bercaria.

†barleka, kind of barley (Sc.) 1330.

barmannus, *see* beremannus.

‡barna, glazed vessel (alch.) 1652.

barn/ax, -eca, *see* bernaca.

baro, slave 735; *a 1070, 1609, boro 1275, baron, magnate, tenant-in-chief of the crown; tenant-in-chief of earl, *etc.* 1109, p 1128; *citizen, burgess (of London, Cinque Ports, *etc.*) a 1158, 1419; official appointed to hear market pleas (Ir.) 13c.; c 1178, 1535, b. scaccarii a 1120, c 1220, *b. de scaccario a 1127, 1583, baron (assessor) of the Exchequer; assessor at monastic exchequer (Canterbury) 1456, 1473; boro, husband (O.F. *baron*) 13c.; baro capitalis, tenant-in-chief c 1185; b. capitalis (scaccarii, de scaccario), Chief Baron 1317, 1440; b. ecclesie (Ramsey) c 1110, c 1170; b. errans, justice in eyre a 1200; b. Hibernie 1200, 1213; b. regni 1100; b. regis 1086, 1256; *see also* curia; baron/ettus p 1327, 1587, barinettus c 1400, -ulus 1513, ‡barunculus 15c., lesser baron, banneret (*cf.* banerettus); baronet 1611; -alis, adherent of barons c 1300; -agium c 1250, 1586, barnagium 1233, 1461, bernagium c 1400, -ia c 1370, body or order of barons; 1269, 15c., *-ia 1142, 1560, -atus 1212, barony, land held by baronial tenure; -ia 1185, c 1350, barunia 1212, 1225, baronial tenure; temporal estate of bishop 1232; tenement held by burgess 1286, c 1300; -icus, baronial 1586; -icius, 'obedient servant' (in letter) (It.) 1266; -issa c 1258, a 1347, -essa 1496, baroness.

baroco, a logical mood 13c.

barometrum, barometer 1686.

barqua, *see* barca.

barr/a *c 1160, 1444, *-era 1238, c 1470, -eria 1291, 1365, -ura 1336, 15c., bar, rail, barrier; *1282, 1495, -era 1333, c 1470, -ura 1442, bar of law-court; 'bar' (for strengthening barrel) 1196, 1198; 1238, c 1533, -us 1331, (iron) bar (of window); stripe, band 1245, 1414; fess (her.) p 1394, a 1446; bar, exclusion (leg.) 1384, 1587; b. laci, (?) sluice (Lincs.) 1234, 15c.; -a

Novi Templi 1315, 1587, -i (*pl.*) Novi Templi 1512, -us suburbii 1419, Temple Bar; -agium, toll paid on passing barrier (G.) 1314; -atim, wedging, pinning (of barrels) 1221, 1230; -atim, fess-wise (her.) p 1394; -atus, in fess p 1394, a 1446; -atus invectus, vairy (her.) a 1446; -atio, exclusion, barring out (leg.) 1417; -ator 1237, -istarius 1213, (?) bar-maker (for barrels); -ador, worker in iron bars (G.) 1254; -erarius 1292, 1341, -erus 1455, -iarius 1369, 1506, -estarius 1626, bar-keeper (leg.), barrister (*cf.* apprenticius); -ium, suburb, extra-mural quarter (G.) 1289, 1317; -ula, barrulet (her.) p 1394, a 1446; -o, to bar (door or window) c 1218, 1280; 1205, c 1335, -eo 1226, †barco 1225, to wedge, brace or pin (barrel); to stripe, hoop (a belt with metal) 1215, 1297; to bar, exclude (leg.) 1236, 1504; -eo, to proscribe, put under a ban (G.) 1254.

barrarius, (?) pall-bearer 1386.

barras, *see* variola.

barri/ca 1445, -qua 1606, breaker, cask.

barrid/itas, haughtiness 620; -us, haughty oppressive c 950. c 1370, 1440.

barritator, *see* baratator.

barritum, cry, noise c 550, 690.

barritus (pecten), (?) toothed c 1200.

barru/tum, -zum, *see* barhudum.

bar/sa 1266, 1294, -cius 1267, c 1324, bass, sea-fish.

bart/atio, -agium, *see* batatio.

bartona, *see* bertona.

barun/ia, -culus, *see* baro.

barura, *see* barhudum.

baryton/us, ill-sounding c 1419; ‡-o, to accent gravely 15c.; ‡to shorten 1483.

basa, *see* vasa.

basalardus, *see* 1 baslardus.

basan/a 1277, 1304, -um 1272, -tum 1272, basayna 1307, basena 1419, bascenum 1329, baszenum 1265, bazannum 1275, 1278, bazeyna c 1324, bazenum 1296, 'basan', sheep's leather; -arius, worker in basan 1272; basianus, made of basan c 1255.

bascatum, *see* baskettum.

bascin-, *see* BACIN

basculus, (?) *for* vasculum, measure of grain 1259, 1311.

Basc/ulus 1283, 1314, -lensis c 1188, Basque.

baselard-, basilard-, *see* 1 baslardus.

baseum, *see* bacia.

basia, *see* vas.

basileris, *see* 2 baslardus.

basil/eus (-eos) c 930, c 970. 1069, 15c., -io c 550, king; -ea, queen 1068; -ides, atheling c 1120; -eros, kind of palm-tree c 1160; -ica, *church, cathedral 6c., a 940. c 1090, 1480; monastery a 725. c 1189, 1212; basilic vein (med.) a 1250; part of turquet (astr.) a 1350; hepatica (bot.) c 1210; ‡14c., 1570, -ico a 1270, basil (bot.); b. matrix, parish church 6c., 9c. 1200; -eius c 950, -icius 990, royal.

Basilidianus, Basilidian heretic 12c.

basillus, *see* BACUL

basin-, *see* BACIN

bas/is, foot c 550, 6c.; face, surface (geom.) 1344; base, foundation 1308, 1445; -or, to be based 1417.

basius, *see* baius.

baskettum 1274, c 1515, bascatum 1388, basket.

1 bas/lardus 1379, c 1500, -larda c 1438, -alardus 1416, 1450, -elardus 1373, 1419, -ilardus c 1370, 15c., -ilarda 1431, -lerdus (†-terdus) 15c., †batilardus (? bac-) 1380, 'baslard', dagger.

2 bas/lardus c 1400, -elard' c 1250, †-ileris 13c., ballardus 1301, 14c., bellardus 1309, base coin.

baso, bassum, *see* bacia.

bass/atio, lowering 1348; -itudo, depth c 1361; -e, in a low position c 1340, c 1470; in a low voice c 1320; *-us, low 1205, 1534; -a tenura, base tenure c 1300, 1495; b. justitia (G.) 1279, 1285, b. jurisdictio (G.) 1313; in -o, in a lower room 1406; *see also* altus; missa.

bassator, *see* AMBASS

bassenettus, bassin/a, -us, *see* BACIN

bassinates (*pl.*), (?) porpoises (Sc.) 1528.

bastard/us (*adj.*), *bastard 12c., 1533; spurious, impure 1256, 1333; planta -a, bastard slip a 1250; (vinum) -um, 'bastard' (sweet) wine 1265, 1443; gladius -us, 'bastard sword' 1410; pannus -us 1410; -us (*subst.*) c 1115, c 1540, -a (*f.*) 1203, c 1330, bastard; -ia, bastardy 1199, 1608; -io, to declare bastard 1253.

†bastare, (?) cart-saddle 1299.

bastaso, porter (It. *bastaggio*) c 1434.

basterna, carriage 690.

bast/ida 1274, 1351, -ita c 1305, settlement (usually fortified), *bastide* (G.), -ile c 1370, -illia 1461, -illa (†batilla) c 1400, -illus 15c., -ellum c 1470, tower, fortification, *bastille* (Fr.); -illiatus, fortified (Fr.) 1461.

bast/o, stick, staff, pole c 1200, 1312; bezel (of ring) 1303; 'baston', licence to leave gaol 1504; -onarius, cudgel-bearer 1290; -onatus, attached to a pole 1368; -ono, to fit (cart) with poles 1266; *see also* bastum, PAST, per.

†bastula, (?) dormouse's nest a 1100.

bast/um 1212, 1350, -lum 1297, -o 1292, bast.

‡basura, seed 1652.

baszenum, *see* BASAN

batagium, *see* batatio; 1 batellum.

bat/ailliamentum, -allo, *see* 2 batellum.

bat/atio 1454, bartatio 1444, -agium (*v.l.* bartagium) c 1472, †-eringa 1342, baiting (of horses).

bateicius, plaited, wattled 1213, 1225; *see also* baticium.

*batell/e, -i 1348, 1636, batalli c 1395, batilli 1557, 'batells', allowance for board, *etc.* (ac.); -arius, receiving batells c 1488, 1507; -o, to receive batells c 1410, 1508.

1 batell/um 1220, 1364, *-us 1156, 1461, *-a 1276, 1495, -ballum 1285, c 1370, batillus 1309, c 1341, batilla 1467, batilda 1479, bettella 1505, batulus (†baculus) 11c., batus 11c., 1417, †batha 1270, boat; *cf.* bacha; -us incense boat c 1315; -ula 1041, -ulus 1286, little boat; -a 1443, -ata 1225, 1296, -ia a 1204, boat-load; -agium c 1311, 1512, *batillagium 1282, 1418, (?) botillagium 1358, batagium 1325, 1454, botagium a 1172, 1547, -aria 1299,

boat-hire; *-arius 1289, 1419, batillarius 1286, 1332, †-us c 1180, boatman; -o, to carry by boat 1401.

2 batell/um 1325, -aria, -iaria 1286, batailliamentum 1355, -amentum 1317, 1318, batillamentum 1313, 1492, batilmentum 1512, battlement, parapet; -o 1325, 1491, batillo 1317, batallo 1433, to fortify, battlement; batillo, to provide (ships) with turrets 1213, 1234; *see also* bateria.

3 bat/ellum c 1340, ‡-illus c 1440, -erellus 1237, clapper (of mill); -illus 1420, 1523, -ellulus 1325, -erellus 1243, 1268, -erellum 1247, clapper (of bell); -erellus, "wash-beetle" 1305; -erellus (†bacerell'), part of horse's harness 1214, 1230.

4 batellum, *see* bacinus.

bat/eria *1258, c 1397, -ura 1256, 1419, battery, assault; 1232, 1297, bettaria 1257, threshing; 1222, 1248, -eressa, -erissa 1155, threshing barn or floor; 1250, 1471, †buteria 1286, kitchen-ware, coppersmith's work; -itura, metal filing a 1250, ‡14c.; -ura, crushing (of spices) 1286; -uatus (†bacuatus) 1215, (?) -ellatus 1385, (?) -illatus 1440, c 1500, of beaten metal; -eratio, 'battering' (of iron tools) 1332, 1401; trimming, dressing (of slates) 1401; -rarius, stone-dresser 1317, 1450; -ero, to 'batter', rework (iron tools) 1325, 1335; -ro 1317, 1354, batiro 1316, to dress, trim (stone); battuo, to beat up 7c.

batha, *see* 1 batellum.

bathm/us (†patmum) c 550, -a 6c., foot or (?) thigh.

*bat/icium 1236, 1356, -isceum 1286, boteicium (beteicium, †bocercium, †becercium) 1277, 1280, -icia 1321, -icinium 14c., newly reclaimed land or reclamation of waste land by 'beat-burning' (S.W. Engl. and Berks.); -icio, to reclaim, 'beat' 1347; *cf.* 2 butta.

batil-, *see* 1 baslardus; bastida; batell-

‡batis, skate (fish) 1570.

batleu/ca, -ga, *see* banleuca.

batrachium, ranunculus (bot.): †vastracium a 1250.

batrachum, *see* borax.

bat/rarius, -ro, -tuo, -ura, *see* bateria.

batrax, toad; botrax 12c., a 1446.

battolog/ia, vain repetition 1535, 1610; -us, utterer of vain repetitions c 1620.

battum, 'bat', wad (of wool) 1351.

1 bat/us, -ulus, *see* 1 batellum.

2 bat/us c 1200, 1553, ‡-ulus, -illus 1483, measure of grain, *bath* (Heb.); *cf.* a batis.

bau-, *see also* bal-

baubellum, jewel 1199, c 1296.

bauc/eus, -eanus, -inus, *see* bauzanus.

baucia, parsnip a 1250, ‡c 1440.

baudkinus, a copper coin p 1280; *see also* baldekinus.

baunkerum, *see* BANC

baurach, *see* borax.

bausterium, *see* baldredum.

†bautaura, (?) *bahádur*, title of honour (Ar.) c 1298.

bautismus, *see* BAPT

bau/zanus 1207, 1317, -canus 1207, -ceanus 1313, balcanus 1265, -cennus c 1200,

-sannus 1311, 1325, -szandus 1316, -standus 1313, (?) bucstanus 1242, 'bausond', piebald (horse); †-ceus, 'bauson', badger 1321; -cinus (†bancinus), of a badger 1355; -sanum c 1450, balcanum a 1260, *beauséant*, black and white standard of Templars; balcanifer, Templars' standard-bearer c 1250; *see also* 2 baldus, ballenrum.

bav/a, saliva (Fr. *bave*) 12c.; -osus, drivelling, stupid c 1190; *cf.* babiger.

bay-, *see also* bai-

‡bayda, a still (alch.) 1652.

baynum, *see* balneum.

bayrum, *see* varietas.

baz/annum, -enum, -eyna, *see* BASAN

bazantius, *see* BYZANT

bazum, *see* bacia.

‡bdell/erum, leech (βδέλλα) 1652; ‡abdellum, for -ium, gum c 1200.

beatific/atio, beatification c 1270, p 1380; -abilis, capable of beatitude c 1270, c 1381; -abilitas, capacity for beatitude c 1367; -ator, author of beatitude c 1283, 1344; -ativus c 1340, c 1375, -us (eccl.), beatific; -us, blessed 1414; -e, beatifically 1344; *-o, to bless (eccl.).

beat/itudo, happiness, blessedness 6c., 676. c 1080, 1559; one of the gospel beatitudes 1267, c 1400; (papal) title 793. c 1080, c 1457; -ivus, beatific c 1185; -im, with a blessing c 1190; -ulus, a favourite c 1160; *-us, blessed (eccl.) 9c. c 1090, 1587.

becca, tail c 550.

beccabunga, brooklime (bot.) 1632.

beccum, beak c 1250.

becercium, *see* baticium.

bech/a, -ia, becka, becco, *see* besca; beta.

1 bechium c 1230, (?) bacha 1606, beach.

2 ‡bechium, coltsfoot (bot.) 1652.

bechlatha, beech-lath 1333.

becnus, kind of fish c 1324.

†beconagium, beacon 1547.

bed/a, bead 1380, 1386; prayer 1421; -emannus 1275, 1423, -mannus 1505, -mennus 1379, bedesman; *see also* baia.

beddum, 'bed', lower framework (of cart) 1276.

bedegar, bedeguar, rose-gall a 1250, ‡14c.

bedell/us *1086, 1583, badellus 1273, bidellus 1300, 1535, budellus 1270, 1425, pedellus (Sc.) (?) 13c., 1649, beadle, bailiff (or under-bailiff); 1338, c 1590, bidellus 1442, c 1522, -anus (Sc.) 1444, bedell (ac.); 1509, bidellus 1467, 1497, beadle of church; b. inferior 1442, c 1556, b. superior c 1337, c 1598 (ac.); b. parvus, under-beadle 1276; -aria 1238, 1588, -eria 1222, 1298, bedelria 1280, 1329, bidellaria 1418, budelaria 1348, -inga 1234, office (or area of jurisdiction) of beadle; -atus, office of bedell (ac.) 1456.

bed/emannus, -mannus, -mennus, *see* beda.

bederna, 'bedern', canons' close or hall (A.S. *bed-ærn*) (Yorks.) a 1230, 1549.

bedewerus (? *for* berowerus), bandit (Fr.) 1258.

Bed/ewinus 1188, -uinus c 1190, -uwinus c 1227, Bedouin; lapis b., a precious stone 1215.

bed/repa 1268, 1279, -repium 1225, -eripa c 1185, 1392, -eripia 1388, -eripium 1408, -erippus 1307, 1324, -ripa a 1185, 1437, -ripus 1234, 1299, bidripa 1196, bydrippus 1299, boon-reaping, harvest-service (man.); -hurtha, boon-ploughing 1260.

bedulta, *see* balducta.

bed/um, *see* baia.

Beelzebutinus, diabolic c 1000.

been, behen-nut (bot.) a 1250.

beera, *see* 2 bera.

begardus, 'beghard', vagrant friar 1344.

beg/uinus c 1250, -uina c 1250, 1385, -ina c 1250, 1332, biguina c 1250, †bigrina 13c., *béguine*, member of religious order; -ina, head-dress 1329, 1373; -inum c 1337, pannus -inus 1310, sort of cloth.

beja, (?) silver (alch.) c 1320, ‡1652.

belago, a form of law (Gothic) 8c.; *cf.* birelagium.

belbericus, *see* bellericus.

belbicinus, *see* belualis.

belecta, weasel (Fr. *belette*) 1322.

belenum 1267, 1271, ‡bengi 14c., henbane (bot.).

bel/freidum, -efreidum, *see* berefredum.

†belidens, closing naturally (of wounds) (A.S. *behlidend*) c 1115.

bella, *see* bolla.

bellardus, *see* 2 baslardus.

bel/lericus (†-bericus) 13c., -liricus a 1250, ‡14c., ‡-leregus 1652, belleric (bot.).

belliator, *see* belmannus.

‡bellium, thornback (fish) 1570.

bellula, (?) daisy (bot.) a 1250.

bell/um, *battle 1086, 1461; judicial combat 1086, 1419; military service a 1120; line of battle 1217, c. 1415; b. primum, vanguard 1366; b. secundum 1461, b. posterius c 1415; b. campale, b. campestre, *see* CAMP; -atim 1461, -icose p 1377, c 1400, in battle; †-icicsus c 550, -ificus c 1280, -igerosus c 1408, warlike; -icamen, war c 550; -iger 1461, -igerans 12c., soldier; -igeratio, waging of war 690; -ico 12c., 1238, ‡-ifico 1483, to fight; -igero, to defeat c 550.

belmannus, bell-man, bell-ringer 1405, 1462; belliator, 'bell-yetter', bell-founder 1475.

belong/um: de -o, aslant 1246.

belota, acorn (Ar. *belluth*) 12c.

belta, belt for a bell 1341; *cf.* balteus.

bel/ualis c 1296, c 1470, -uinus (eccl.), bestial; -uicinus, -bicinus, of or for a monster c 550.

bema, platform (βῆμα) c 870.

bemolle, *see* B.

bemum, plough-beam 1276.

ben/a, boon-work (man.) c 1182, 1342; -eroda, boon-rood c 1252; -hirda c 1182, -eria a 1250, boon-ploughing; -ripa, boon-reaping 13c., 1299; *cf.* bedrepa.

bend/a *1216, 1339, banda, bandum 1329, 1443, bonda c 1300, band, strip (of metal); b. pedalis, 'foot-bend' (of plough) 1307; (?) barellus de magna bonda 1357; -a, band, stripe 1245; 1389, a 1446, banda p 1394, bend (her.); -arius, bandarius p 1394, -atus 1322, a 1446, bendy (her.);

-**atim,** per bend (her.) p 1394; **-ula,** bend-let (her.) p 1394, a 1446; **-o,** to border 1216, 1252.

bene: in b. et in pace a 1550; **de b. esse,** provisionally (with moral rather than legal validity) 1272, 1419.

Benedictinus, Benedictine (monk) 1518, 1586.

*__benedic/tio__ (eccl.), †-**atio** c 1334, **benedixio** c 1340, blessing; consecrating, consecration c 1106, c 1534; gift, alms c 1080, 1380; **-ibilis,** worthy of blessing 1200; *__-tionale__ 1200, 1336, **liber -tionalis** c 1093, 1388, **-tionarius** c 1200, c 1330, **liber b.** c 1266, benedictionary (eccl.); **-torius,** conferring a blessing c 1197; **-ta,** holy water c 1362 (cf. **aqua**); (?) valerian (bot.) 13c., ‡14c. (cf. **herba**); c 1340, **-tus** c 1080, 1245, anti-phons; **-tus,** salutary 1620; cursed 1526; see also **panis; -tus Deus** (interj.), God be praised! c 1236, c 1336; **-amus,** a liturgical greeting 1245; *__-o,__ to bless (eccl.).

bene/dilectus, well-beloved 1438, 1461; **-dispositus,** well-disposed 1439.

benefac/ientia, good luck c 870; **-tor,** bene-factor (eccl.); **-trix,** benefactress 1298, 1570; **-tivus,** beneficent a 1529; **-tum,** benefit (eccl.).

benefic/ium, benefit, profit c 1148, c 1336; miracle 10c.; *__ecclesiastical benefice 1086, 1585; fief, feudal estate 1058. c 1125, 1309; loan-land 858; **b. clericale** 1364, **b. trium literarum** 1535, benefit of clergy; **b. ecclesie,** goodwill of the church c 1130; **b. curatum,** benefice with cure of souls c 1357, c 1450; **b. simplex,** benefice with-out cure 1242, c 1260; **-ialis,** concerning a benefice c 1444, 1684; **-ialia** (pl.), matters concerning benefices 1549; **-ialiter,** gener-ously 1486, a 1564; **-iarius,** beneficiary c 1299, c 1328; vassal 1535, 1608; **-iator,** benefactor 14c.; **-ientia,** beneficence c 1115, c 1343; **-iosus,** beneficent 793, c 1000; **-iatus,** beneficed clerk (eccl.) c 1220, c 1520; **-io** 1200, 1537, **-o** c 1218, to present to an ecclesiastical benefice; to prosper 1303; **-o,** to benefit, bless 7c.

benemer/ita (pl.), benefits, merits 1558, 1559; **-itus** 1426, 1537, **-ens** 1452, meri-torious.

beneol/ax 9c., **-ens** c 870, fragrant.

*__beneplac/itum__ (bibl.), **-entia** 15c., pleasure, will; **ad -itum** c 1188, 1547, **de -ito** c 1330, 15c., **pro -ito** c 1192, c 1300, at pleasure, at will; *__-itus,__ well-pleasing (bibl.).

ben/eria, -eroda, see **bena.**

ben/eta, -tha c 1220, **-etum** 1326, bent, coarse grass; **-tea,** "heath" 1635.

benevalentia, health c 1380.

beneven/io, to welcome 1398; **-eor,** to be welcome c 1362.

benevol/entia (benivol-), 'benevolence', forced loan 1475, 1549; (n. pl.) acts of kind-ness 8c.; **-e,** voluntarily c 1420; **-us** (subst.), well-wisher c 1250, 1480.

bengi, see **belenum.**

ben/hirda, -ripa, see **bena.**

benign/itas, benevolence (title) 7c. c 1125, 1440; **-ivolus,** benevolent c 950; **-or,** to be happy, content (eccl.).

benium, see **baia.**

benleuca, see **banleuca.**

ben/tea, -tha, see **beneta.**

ben/zoinum 1626, **-jovin** 1622, **-jovis** c 1615, benzoin.

beodum, see **baia.**

1 bera, bier 1268.

2 ber/a, 'bere' (kind of barley) 1271; 1397, 1496, **-ea** 1581, **-ia** 1634, **beera** 1397, 1413, **biera** 1421, **-isia** 1480, **birra** 1438, 1454, **birrum** 1460, 1463, **birria** 1500, 1584, beer; **b. duplex,** beer of double strength 1480, 1554; **-ebarellus,** beer-barrel 1417; **-ezisum** 1282, **-sisa** c 1185, 1261, **-ziza** 1280, **-zillum** 1277, barley malt, wort.

berallus, see **BERYLL**

berbatus, see **barba.**

berbena, see **verbena.**

berberis a 1250, 1538, **barbarum** 1587, bar-berry (bot.).

berbi-, berbragium, see **verveculus.**

berbrettus, see **berebretus.**

berca, see **brecca.**

1 ber/caria c 1180, c 1400, †-**ca** c 1306, **-cia** 1276, **-ciaria** 1144, **-cheria** c 1200, 1307, **-keria** 1209, p 1290, **barcaria** 1182, 1553, †**baccaria** c 1290, †-**icheria** 1319, **-geria** 1191, 1199, **-queria** c 1240, sheep-fold; **-caria** 1222, 1230, **-cheria** c 1090, sheep-run; *__-carius__ a 1128, 1504, **-quarius** 1086, **barcarius** 14c., **brebicarius** 1284, (?) **burgarius** 1274, **-cator** 1275, 1316, shepherd; **barco,** to fold sheep 1426.

2 berc/aria, tannery 1486; **-arius,** tanner 1486; **-o** 1478, 1486, **barco** 1478, **barko** 1335, to tan.

bercel-, see **BERS**

bercenarius, see **BERTON**

berci/a, cradle 1268, 1309; **-o,** to rock in the cradle 1212; see also **1 bercaria, BERS**

berdo, see **barda.**

berea, see **2 bera.**

bere/bretus c 1115, 14c., **-breitus** 13c., **-brittus** 1314, **berbrettus** 1214, **-bruttus** 1260, 1377, †-**beuttus** 1401, †-**bruttarius** 1297, granger, official in charge of granges.

berefell/arius 1305, 1398, **berfellarius** 1315, **clericus de -o** (barefell', barfellis, **berfella,** etc.) 1290, 1422, clerk (? wearing bear-skin collar), later minor canon (of Beverley).

ber/efredum c 1200, **-fredum** a 1142, **-efri-dum** (G.) 1253, 1293, **-eferris** 1224, **-frarium** 1300, movable siege-tower; **-efre-dum** 1234, **-fredum** 1284, **-efrida** 1253, **-efridum** c 1200, 1371, **-frarium** 1259, **bel-freidum** c 1310, **belefreidum** 14c., belfry; **berfreta,** the Belfry (a gaol at Berwick) 1331.

ber/emannus 1225, c 1300, **-mannus** 1226, 1290, **barmannus** 1224, 1299, 'berman', wine-porter; **-mannus,** tenant charged with carrying-service (Sussex) c 1285; **-man-nagium** 1290, 1315, **bermenagium** 1304, 1367, **brimmannagium, brummanna-gium** 1313, (payment for) wine-porterage.

ber/emotum, -motum a 1307, **-manne-motum** 1243, 'berg-moot', 'barmoot', miners' court.

berevagium, see **beveragium.**

ber/ewica 1086, c 1165, -ewicus 1078, c 1170, -uwica c 1080, -wica 1086, 12c., -wicus c 1080, 1134, -vica 1285, †-ia c 1120, c 1174, 'berewick', outlying portion of manor.
berezisum, *see* 2 bera.
berfell-, *see* BEREFELL
ber/fredum, -freta, -frarium, *see* berefredum.
berga, barrow, mound c 1200, c 1250.
bergander, merganser (bird) 1544.
bergelettus, *see* BERS
bergemannus, *see* 1 bargia.
ber/geria, -keria, *see* 1 bercaria.
†bergueta, sort of candle (G.) 1312.
beria, *see* 2 bera; berewica.
berill/us, -um, *see* barellus; beryllus.
berisia, *see* 2 bera.
berlagius, *see* birelagium.
†berlugum, (?) pole 1285.
ber/mannemotum, -motum, *see* beremotum.
bermann/us, -agium, bermenagium, *see* beremannus.
bern-, *see also* vernaculum; vernica.
bern/aca c 1200, -eca 12c., barneca c 1212, -ax 1208, c 1362, barnax c 1437, -acula 1584, -icla 1544, barnacle-goose.
bernagium, *see* baro; bernarius.
Bernardinus, (monk) of the order of St. Bernard 1526.
bern/arius c 1136, 1399, -erius 1213, -ator 1271, berner, keeper of dogs, kennel-man; b. daemericius, b. haericius 1312; -agium, feudal payment for feeding dogs (O.F. *brenage*) (Norm.) a 1100, 1203.
berqu/arius, -eria, *see* 1 bercaria.
bers/a, fence, enclosure for game 1205, 1255; -aria 1212, -eria 1207, poaching; -ator, poacher 1209, 1330; -elettus c 1271, 1287, bercelettus 1253, 1312, -eretius 1213, -erettus 1215, 1242, canis b. 1213, †bergelettus 1287, 'bercelet', hunting dog, lyam-hound; bercellus, dog similar to bercelet 14c.; bercelettarius 1229, 1312, †percenettarius 1314, man in charge of bercelets; -orium, place for shooting 1280; -o 12c., 1340, bercio 1237, to drive, hunt, or shoot.
bersisa, *see* 2 bera.
bertachia, *see* bretescha.
bertha, city ward or ward-moot (Canterbury) c 1200, c 1250.
*berton/a 1217, 15c., -um 14c., bertouna c 1358, bartona 1219, 1449, barton, demesne farm; -arius 1238, 1467, †bercenarius 1376, bartoner, steward or farmer of a barton.
†bertro, (?) to plaster 1376; *cf.* PERJACT
berugabulum, *see* 2 brueria.
ber/wica, -wicus, -uwica, -vica, *see* berewica.
beryll/us (berill-) 1383, 1503, -a 1503, birellus 15c., barellus c 1305, glass reliquary; ‡-us, gazing crystal 1652; berallus, beryl 1404; birillus 1419, oculus berellinus c 1300, magnifying glass, spectacles; -inus, of beryl a 1275, 1564; ‡-istica, crystal-gazing 1652; -isticus, crystal-gazer 1564.

berz/iza, -illum, *see* 2 bera.
bes/aca, -acium, -agium, *see* bisaccia.
1 †besanda, (?) pannier, wallet 1328.
2 †besanda, (?) sort of sweetmeat 1328.
besant-, besent-, *see* BYZANT
‡besasa, rue, violet, *or* other plant (bot.) 14c.
besc/a *c 1160, 1325, -ia 1194, 1238, -illa 1171, bechia c 1184, 1286, becka 14c., bachia 1265, spade (esp. for peat); c 1193, 14c., -ia 14c., -ata (†boscata) 1193, 1208, area of land (in turbary) that can be dug in a year; -ata, spit, spade's depth c 1250; becco, to dig (Norm.) 1198.
bes/ilamentum, mutilation (of documents) 1397; -ello, to mutilate or falsify (a document) 1276; *cf.* imbesillatio.
besti/a, farm animal 1086, 1583; *beast of chase 1086, 1365; skin, fur 1403; -a (*n. pl.*), beasts 1274; b. aratoria 1220, b. carruce 1325, b. carrucataria 1326, plough-beast; *b. grossa, beast of chase 1283, 1419; -alis, bestial (eccl.); -alissimus, fiercest c 870; -aliter, bestially 8c. c 1200, c 1450; -alitas, bestiality c 1367, c 1370; -arium, herd of animals c 1289; ‡dairy 1483; bestiary, book on beasts c 1396, c 1432; -ola c 700, -uncula c 1150, insect.
†bet/a, (?), beetle, beating instrument 1337; c 1250, †becha 1279, -ella 1265, 'beat', bundle of flax.
*bet/agius c 1200, 1404, -achius 1283, -acus 1212, -asius a 1242, bitagius 14c., petagius 1290, -aldus 1252, -axus 1260, unfree tenant, *betagh* (Ir.); -agium, *betagh*-tenure 1365.
beteicium, *see* baticium.
betemayum, bank, mound (Norfolk) 1313.
Bethlehemita, frater B., Bethlehemite 1257.
betonica, *see* vettonica.
bettaria, *see* bateria.
bettella, *see* 1 batellum.
beum, *see* baia.
beutificatio, beautification 1582.
bever/ c 1191, ‡15c., -ius 1303, -us 1444, beaver; -inus, of a beaver 1138, 1444.
*bev/eragium 1199, 1391, †berevagium 1284, drink-money; -ragium, (?) drink, beverage (Norm.) 1421; *cf.* BIB
beveria, *see* bos.
bez, Hebrew letter *beth* c 1200.
bezacium, *see* bisaccia.
bezoar/ 1622, ‡-ticum, bezaar, bezar 1652, bezoar stone.
†bezonis, sort of electuary a 1250.
biannum (Fr.) 1192, wianum (G.) 1289, (biannual) labour-service, *corvée*; servitium †brianneum (?) 13c.
bib/itio c 1332, -atio c 1220, drinking; -ale 1539, 16 c., -acium 1509, -arium 1420, -erium c 1470, 1509, -era 1394, drink, drink-money; -eres (*pl.*), 'bevers', drink c 1148; -era c 700, -ero 1300, glass, beaker; domus -itoria, "guild-house" c 1190; *cf.* BEV
‡bibleo, to bubble 1570.
bibl/us 790, c 950. c 1337, *-ia 7c. 1245, 1565, *-iotheca c 800. 1200, 1489, Bible; b. celestis 735; -iothica, coffin 7c.; -ice, textually, with exposition (ac.) 1311, c 1350; -iographus, "scrivener" 1520;

-iothecarius (*adj.*), of libraries 1588; -iotista, librarian c 1465.

bibona, *see* 3 bubo.

bic/a (byk-), -um a 1250, 1277, biga 1397, 'bike', nest or swarm of bees (N.W. Engl.); -arius 1277, bigrus (Norm.) a 1200, beetaker (*cf.* Fr. *bigre*); *see also* bika.

bicamer/a, double chamber 14c.; -atus, tworoomed 8c., 805. c 1212.

‡biceps, "twibill" c 1440; bicipitium, twoheadedness c 1595.

bicirculus, double circle 1388.

bickaria, *see* BIK

bidell-, *see* bedellus.

*biden/s, sheep, ewe 1221, 1487; -tinus, of a sheep c 1000; -tatus, having two teeth c 1362, c 1436; †-tile, pitchfork 14c.

bidictionalitas, composition of two words 13c.

bidripa, *see* bedrepa.

bidu/ana, two days' fast 7c. c 1160, 13c.; -anus c 730. 12c., 1274, -alis c 1090, lasting two days.

biennis, pertaining to two years 720, 790.

biera, *see* 2 bera.

bi/facius 1245, -fax c 550, two-faced.

bifar/ius, twofold c 800, c 974. c 1125, c 1385; -ie, in two parts, doubly 893. c 1172, 1433.

bifidus, two-faced, insincere 1620.

†bifinium, boundary stone *or* headland 1483.

biflis, *see* BUBAL

bifoliatus, two-leaved c 1443.

bifores (*pl.*), double doors c 1200, 1516.

†bifultum, something adjoining a mill (Heref.) 1232.

bifurc/atus, *fourché* (her.) p 1394; -atus (canonicus), wearing a two-peaked bonnet 1396, 1421; ligna -ata, gallows c 1307; scriptum -atum, deed in duplicate 1259, 1268; -o, to bifurcate, divide c 1200, 1423.

big/a, cart c 1184, 1510; -ata 1212, 1499, -atus 1495, c 1507, -atura c 1527, cartload; -arius c 1190, 1537, -ator 1395, c 1505, carter; -o, to drive a cart c 1451; *see also* bica.

bigam/ia, marrying twice, second marriage 12c., 1513; -us, twice married a 1090, a 1564; married to widow c 1300, 1368.

‡bi/gera c 1440, (?) -girdellus 1360, doublet.

‡bigermen, maslin 1483.

bigrus, *see* bica.

big/uina, †-rina, *see* BEG

†bigulus, (?) *f.l.* for angulus, c 1400.

‡bijug/es (*pl.*), crocks of a house 1570; -uus, double yoke c 550.

bik/a c 1250, a 1383, -aria, bickaria (G.) 1243, beaker, liquid measure (? βῖκος); *see also* bica.

bilan/x 13c., 1620, -cia 1440, c 1500, balan/x 1340, c 1397, *-cia 1196, 1509, †-ca 1204, †-cum 1300, -dum 1404, balance, scales; -cia, 'weight', measure of yarn 1212.

bilegium, bilex, *see* birelagium.

bilett-, *see* billa (1 & 2).

bil/ho, -ium, *see* 2 bullio.

bilitter/alitas, composition of two letters 13c.; -arius, -atus, using two letters (of a cipher) 1620.

1 bill/a *c 1290, 1587, -ata 1428, 1514, *-eta,

-etum 1285, 15c., -etus 1419, -neta 1417, -ula c 1452, bill, schedule; *c 1290, 1583, *-eta, -ettum 1290, 1356, bill (of complaint), notice, precept (leg.); b. excambii, bill of exchange 1595; b. fracta, (?) bill with seal broken 1318; b. originalis, originating bill (leg.) 1319; -atus, labelled 1326; -o, to enter on a schedule 1300; -ico, (?) to embody in a bill 1275.

2 bill/a *1209, 1383, -us 1272, 1314, bill or pick for dressing mill-stones; 1438, 1521, -us 1413, 1588, -arium 1521, bill (tool or weapon); -us c 1115, -etum 1290, 1455, log, rod, billet; -eta, billet of standard size for measuring meshes 1300; -ettum, 'billet', swingle-bar of plough 1311, 1340; -us, game, (?) single-stick or tipcat 1326; -o, to trim with a bill 1343; 1305, bilo 1302, (?) to chop (apples) (*cf.* pilatio).

billingis, sort of loaf c 1250.

1 bill/io, -onus, bilo, *see* bullio (2 & 3).

2 billio, metal rod or the like kept in ampulla of holy oil for infusion 14c.

biloquium, duologue 760.

bima, *see* binna.

bimaritimus, lying between two seas c 730.

bimembris, twofold c 1300, 1515.

bimenstris, space of two months 795.

bin/arius, the number two 804. c 1160, c 1414; pair of opposites c 1270, 1378; (*adj.*), divisible by two a 1350; -alis, two 690; -itas, duality 1610; -us, twofold c 1250, c 1456; -i et -i, two and two 1398, c 1400; -o, to double c 1180, ‡1483; to replough c 1220, c 1413.

bind/a c 1080, 1303, -um 1275, †lunda c 1290, 'bind', measure of eels, skins, *etc.*; tie (for thatching) 1361.

binhaia 13c., bingaia 14c., 'binghay', arable enclosure (Devon & Cornw.).

binn/a c 1220, 1313, -um 1307, †bima 1297, bin.

binomi/um, double name c 1296, c 1362; -us, having two names c 730, c 870. 12c., c 1390.

biothanatus, violent death 685; (?) one who deserves a violent death a 1142.

bipart/itio (bipert-), division into two c 870; -ijocus, †-eocus, †-iloquus, -io, -itum, jeopardy (leg.) 14c. (*cf.* jocus); -itor, *métayer* 1215; -itus, party (her.) 1370; c 1315, 1393, -us c 1550, party (of colour).

bipedalis, two-footed c 800. 1345.

bipenn/ula, small axe 9c.; -ella, great burnet (bot.) ‡1570, 1629.

bipunctalis, of two points c 1361.

birelag/ium (Lancs.) 1257, 1660, birelegium (Lancs.) 1412, bilegium (Suff.) 1577, bilex (Middx.) 1671, burlawa (Sc.) a 1500, 'bylaw', village regulation about harvest, pasturage, *etc.*; -ius 1501, 1598, birelegus 1569, burelegius 1508, burlegius 1536, berlagius 1577, 'burleyman', enforcer of 'by-laws' (Lancs.); *cf.* belago, builares, plebiscitum, statutum.

birillus, birellus, *see* beryllus.

biriscus, *see* bitriscus.

biro, barley and bran loaf (Wilts.) 1340.

birr/a, -ia, -um, *see* 2 bera.

*birr/etum 1298, 1549, †birottum 1523, burretum 1417, piretum c 1306, pirottum

1291, ‡-us 1570, cap; *see also* per; -etarius, capper 1427, †1520.

birr/us, cloak c 950. c 1090; rag c 1180, c 1200; 1200, c 1350, -a 1346, pleat; -atus 1281, 15c., buratus 1281, 1300, pleated; byrritrica, pleating c 1200; *cf.* burra.

†birwa, barrow-load 1275.

‡bisacci/a (*for* -um) 1440, besaca 1221, besacium 1228, besagium 1372, bezacium 1229, saddle-bag; †visatie (*pl.*), (?) luggage 7c.

bisacut/a, -um, two-edged axe, twibill c 1180, 1404; -us, two-edged c 1150, 15c.

bisant-, *see* BYZANT

biscinus, *see* bissa.

biscoccus, doubly scarlet c 800.

biscoctus, twice-cooked (of bread), biscuit c 1200, c 1540.

bisec/tio, bisection (math.) 1686; -o, to bisect 1686.

bisettum, *see* bissus.

bisext/us, intercalary day, month, or year 790, 815. 12c., c 1400; ill luck a 1142; -ilis, intercalary 797, 815. 1252, 1419.

†bisia *or* †grisia (? trisia), bird, (?) grey goose c 1200.

bismalva, mallow or hollyhock (Fr. *guimauve*) a 1250, 1538.

bisocula (*pl.*), spectacles 1620.

*biss/a 1130, 1387, -ia 1221, hind, female red deer (Fr. *biche*); †-us, (?) *f.l.* for -a, 1293, 1362; -illa, young hind 1261; -a, -us 1189, 1425, -ea 1214, †byum 1331, 'byse', (?) hind-skin (also applied to squirrel); -inus 1247, biscinus 1313, of byse; *see also* BYSS

bisse (*pl.*), two-thirds of an hour 795.

bissus a 1128, 1419, bixus 1259, brown (of bread) (Fr. *bis*); †bisettum, (?) brown loaf (or *f.l.* for biscoctum) 13c.

bistinctus, double-dyed 1307.

bistorta, (?) bistort (bot.) a 1250, 1634; "tormentil" 1538.

bitagius, *see* betagius.

bitellus, *see* buccula.

†biterni, (?) *for* bis terni, twice three c 550.

bithalassum, *for* dithalassus, place where waters meet 12c., c 1200.

bitirum, *see* butyrum.

bitriscus, kind of bird, (?) wren a 1150, c 1160; ‡biriscus, briscus, "fieldfare" 15c.

bituleus, *see* bulus.

bitum/en c 1375, buttumen 1350, tar used as sheep-salve; butumen 1326, (?) bytonum 1288, tar, pitch; -ino 798. c 1340, c 1362, †-o 1357, to cover with pitch; *cf.* butimen.

bixus, *see* bissus.

bizant-, *see* BYZANT

blada, (?) 'blad', lump (of wax) 1272.

blad/um *c 1150, 1522, -ium 1279, 1346, -us (C.I.) 1331, bleium c 1080, corn, grain (esp. wheat); -o c 1180, c 1450, -ium c 1353, blatum 1086, standing corn, crop; -ium, measure of corn, sheaf (C.I.) c 1190; -um ad semen, seed corn 1236; b. durum 1222, 1276; b. molle 1222; b. tolneti, toll-corn 1288; b. totum, b. integrum, *see* panis; -arius, corn-dealer 1303, 1434; -arius c 1270, -alis c 1330, 1574, -ifer 1368, 1584, -onicus 1319, †blatarius (†blacarius) c 1220, blaereticus 1337,

1418, blaericius 1237, for (grinding) corn (of mills); -ifer, for carrying corn 1282, 1449; -atura c 1300, 1340, -ura 1246, -imentum 1215, sowing with corn, corncrop; blaeria, (?) corn-market (Norm.) 1200; -o, to sow with corn a 1564.

blan/cus, white 1286, 1442; *1086, 1324, -ceus 1199, 'blanched', tested by assay; -cum, blanched money 1167, 1242; *see also* punctum, vinum; -chiatura, blanching of money 1236, 1324; -chetum c 1180, c 1330, -ketum, -ketus 1207, 1399, blanket cloth; -cheta, blaunchetta 1235, -ketum, -ketus 1254, 1417, blaunketum 1303, woollen garment or blanket; -o, to white-taw (leather) 1309.

blandi/torius, flattering c 1283; -enter, flatteringly c 1250.

blas/erius (†balatro), an incendiary c 1115; -ius, wind c 1250; blessagha, forge (Norm.) 1172.

*blasphem/ia, -e, -us, -ator, -o (eccl.); -abilis, censurable c 1341; -ialis, blasphemous c 1255.

blast-, *see* BLEST; PLAST

blat-, *see also* BLAD

‡blata, bat (animal) 13c., 1483.

blateola, *see* blettro.

blatro, *see* blettro.

blatta (†blacca) Byzantia, sort of drug a 1250.

blauhornum, hunting-horn (A.S.) c 1115.

blaunc-, blaunk-, *see* BLAN

blaund/rellus 1393, -ellus 1390, -urellus 1315, 'blaundrel', kind of apple.

blav-, blefum, bleodum, *see* BLU

blebo, to see (βλέπω) c 550.

blecchio, to bleach 1365.

blectero, *see* blettro.

bledstodia, *see* blodstodia.

bleium, *see* bladum.

blemio, to blemish, bruise (C.I.) 1324.

blese, lispingly c 1340.

blessagha, *see* BLAS

blest/a c 1250, 1416, -ia c 1250, bleta 1307, peat, turf; bleta mora, peat-moss 13c.; -aria c 1150, 13c., blastarium c 1250, -era 1476, blethera 1324, -atura 1281, -ura 13c., 1389, -iatus 1250, turbary, peatcutting; blastratio, (?) clearing of turf (Kent) 1370; -o, to cut peats (in) (*cf.* O.F. *blester*) 1281, 1348; blastro, (?) to clear (land) of turf (Sussex) 1321; -io hordeum (Sussex) 1321.

blet/a, -is, *see* blesta; blita.

*blettro 1215, 1373, blectero 1233, blestro 13c., blatro 1377, bretto 1353, sapling, esp. young oak (O.F. *bleteron*).

blev-, blew-, *see* BLU

bliauta, tunic (O.F. *bliaut*) 1204.

blid/a 1244, 1302, -ehum 1244, catapult.

blit/a, -is a 1250, blet/a, -is a 1250, 13c., spinach.

blocc/a, wooden block (used as fuel in smelting lead) a 1307; -arius 1302, -ator c 1295, -walterius 1300, stoker (of smelting furnace); blokbordum, rough, unpolished board 1324; -o, to stoke (furnace) 1302.

blodium, pudding 1519; *see also* BLU

†blodstodia, †bledstodia, (?)*ff.ll.* for bastardus, c 1115.

blod/wita a 1105, 1415, **-ewita** 1086, **-weta** 1250, **bludewita** (Sc.) 1431, 1555, 'blood-wite', fine for bloodshed.

blom/a 1086, 1351, **-us** 1330, **plumba** 1086, 'bloom', mass of iron; **fabrica -eria** 1314, **-forgium** 1357, bloomery.

blotto, to blot (with ink) 1433.

*****blu/etum**, **-etus** 1203, 1404, **-vetum** 1253, **blavetum** 1267, **blevetum** 1278, 1292, **blewetum** 1295, **blovetum** c 1250, **-um** 1236, **-tum** 1239, **-dum** 1242, 1249, **-dium** 1242, 1316, **blodium** c 1365, c 1452, **bleodum** 1286, **blavium** 1245, **blevium** 1231, **blefum** 1207, 'bluet', blue cloth; **blodium de Lyra** 1391 (cf. **pannus**); **blaveum**, blue dye 690; **blavium**, corn-flower 1538; **-etus** 1269, 1404, **-wetus** 1371, *****blodius** 1390, 1504, **blavius** 735, a 1250, c 1540, **blavus** a 1250, **blovius** 16c., blue; **blodius**, azure (her.) c 1450; *see also* **petra**; **b. celestinus**, sky-blue 1432.

blumb-, *see* **plumbum**.

blund/us, fair, blond c 1200; **-a firma**, blanch farm 1238.

boa, serpent: **boas** 12c.

boaria, *see* **bos**.

boat/us 790, 960. 12c., c 1462, ‡**-io** 1570, bellow, shout; **-icus**, bellowing (*adj.*) c 1470.

bobino, to shout abuse c 1470.

bobinus, *see* **babewinus**.

bobulus, *see* **bos**.

boca, *see* **bucca**.

bocardo, a logical mood 13c.; a prison c 1318, ‡15c.; a privy (Cambridge) 1495, 1504.

bocaseum, bocasine (cotton fabric) 1436.

bocattum, *see* BUKETT

bocca, *see* **boeta**; **bocium**.

bocca marina, sea bass (fish) c 1200.

boccus, *see* BOSC

bocercium, *see* **baticium**.

bocetum 690. ‡1483, **buchettum, bugittum** 1381, cattle-shed, byre; cf. **bos, bostar.**

bochelanda, 'book-land' (granted by charter) 1086.

boch/eria, **-eius**, *see* **bucheria**.

bochus, *see* BOSC

boc/ium a 1250, ‡**botium** 1652, swelling (impostume) in throat; 1241, 1419, **bosa** 1289, †**bosca** 1477, boss, knob; **-ia, -ea** (†**bocca**), (?) bastion (arch.) 1291; ‡**bothor**, pustules 14c., 1652; ‡**butiga**, swelling of face 1652.

boclearium, bocul-, *see* BUCCUL

bocramum, *see* **bukaramum**.

boda, bodagium, *see* **botha**.

bodellus, budellus, bowel, gut a 1150; bundle *or* file (? strung on gut) 1233; **bouellarius**, sausage-seller 1333.

boe, boge, *see* **boie**.

boeria, *see* **bos**.

boeta 1287, 15c., †**bocca** 1229, lantern.

Boetes, *see* **Boötes**.

boffettum, *see* **buffettum**.

1 †**boga**, dry measure, 'bodge', peck c 1300, 1307.

2 bog/a 1285, **-ia** 1303, 1305, **bugium** 1426, **-etum** 1314, 1338, **bugetum** 13c., 1348, **budgetum, bujettum** 1327, 'budge', high-grade lamb-skin, (?) originally from Bougie in Algeria.

3 bog/a, -ea, -etta, *see* **bulga**.

bogum 1185, 1309, **bug/um** 1235, 1277, **-lum** 1235, ox-bow.

bohalla, *see* **bova**.

boie c 1090, 1324, **boge** 1302, **boe** 1309, fetters (Fr. *buies*); **boii anuli** (*pl.*), ring chains 1202.

boill-, *see* 1 **bullio**.

boiria, *see* **bos**.

boiscagium, *see* BOSC

boisio (*or* **bosio**), to rebel, break fealty (Fr. *boiser*) 1103.

boissellus, *see* **bussellus**.

bokel-, *see* BUCCUL

bok/eranda, -orammum, *see* **bukaramum**.

bokerellum, (?) windlass *or* 'hawk' (cf. **hauka, 2 falco**) 1325; *see also* BUCCUL

bokett-, *see* BUKETT

bokkestallo, *see* **buckstalla**.

bol/a, 'bole', furnace with natural draught for smelting c 1295, 1508; **-ata**, amount of ore smelted in one 'bole' 1302; **-arius** 1300, 1325, **-iarius** 1370, 1371, **fusor -arius** 1323, smelter.

bolcagium, *see* BULC

bole, *see* **bula**.

bolendinus, token, counter 1465.

bolengari/us 1155, 1332, **-a** (*f.*) c 1320, **bulengarius** 1156, 1170, **bulingarius** 1185, baker (Fr. *boulanger*); **b. panis, b. cervisie** (C.I.) 1332; **bolongeria**, bakery 1426.

bolet-, *see* 1 **bulla**; BULT; **bulus**.

bolga, *see* **bulga**.

bolhagium, (?) quay 1252; cf. BULC

‡**bol/is** c 1440, 1483, ‡**-ideum** 15c., plummet (βολίς).

bolism-, *see* **bulimus**.

boll/a, -us (?) c 1000. 1316, c 1423, **bella** 1420, c 1485, bowl; liquid measure, bowlful a 1140, 1322; dry measure, boll 1202, 1562; measure of tin 1451, 1587; **-etta**, small bowl c 1266.

bollagium, *see* BULC

bollardus, nickname for Benedictine, (?) trickster (cf. O.F. *boleor*) 1291.

bolletum, bolnetum, *see* **bulus**.

bollio, *see* 1 **bullio**.

bolone, dolphin (cf. βελόνη) 1508.

bolongeria, *see* **bolengarius**.

bolst/era, bolster 1393; **-rum** c 1295, 1304, **-urum** 1388, metal 'bolster' of machine; cf. **pulvinar.**

bolt/a, -um, bolt (for door, *etc.*) 1306, c 1478; bolt, arrow 1363; 1329, **-us** 1393, 'bolt', measure of cloth.

bolt/arius, -erium, *see* BULT

†**boltera**, (?) 'boulter' (line with hooks attached) 1352.

1 bolus, mouthful (βῶλος) c 1180, c 1250; large pill c 1260; ‡purified essence (alch.) 1652; **b. Armenicus**, earth containing iron oxide a 1250, ‡14c.; *see also* **lana**.

2 bolus, *see* **bulus**.

bombac-, *see* **bombyx**.

*****bombard/a, -us** 1413, c 1608, **-ula** 1561, **bumbarda, bumbardus** 1436, 1553, **bumblastum** 1460, **machina -ica** 1461, bombard, cannon, cannon-ball; **-us duplex, b. simplex** 1568; **pulvis -iaricus**, gunpowder 1567; **-arius** 1481, **bumbardarius**

1479, -iator 1547, **bombator** 1456, bombardeer, gunner.
bomb/um c 1370, ‡**bumbum** 15c., 1483, **bunbum** 1235, **bumbulum** 1250, "fart"; **-arius**, noisy, jabbering c 1361; **-osus**, loud, booming c 550, a 710; **-ilo** 1520, **-ino** c 1370, **-izo** a 1408, ‡1483, to buzz.
bomb/yx 7c., **-ex** 1220, ‡**bumbax** 15c., silkworm; **-ax**, silk or cotton 1208, 1342; **-icinium** 1364, 1390, **-acinium** 1275, **-acium** 1336, ⅃-**acilium** 15c., **bumbacinium** c 1300, **bumbix** 1517, 'haketon', jack, doublet; ‡**lombesina**, "paltock" 15c.; **-ycifer**, downy 1629; **textrix -icinaria**, "silk-woman" 1520.
bona, see BUNDA.
1 †**bonagium** (or **bovagium**), (?) toll on goods or cattle 1282, 1298.
2 **bonagium**, tribute, bonaght (Ir.) 1525, 1557.
boncarium, see BANC
†**boncha**, bunch 1421.
bond/a, head of household c 1115; *****-a, -us** 1086, 1482, **bundus** a 1290, 1380, **-agius** 1279, 1409, **-arius** (v.l. **bordarius**) 1183, **-emannus** 1324, **bundemannus** 1236, 'bond', bondage tenant; **-us custumarius** 1322; *****-agium** c 1227, 1528, **bundagium** 1330, bondage (tenure or status); *****-agium**, bondage (tenement) a 1221, c 1357; **-acra**, acre held by bondage-tenure c 1300; see also **benda**, **bunda**.
bondellus, see **bundellus**.
bondono, see **bundono**.
bonettus, 'bonnet', extra piece of canvas at foot of sail 1352, 1437.
bon/itas, bounty, gratuity c 1325, 1415; **-us**, good (of debts) 1273; **B. Homo** 13c., 1586, **B. Vir** 1283, Bon Homme, member of religious order; Albigensian heretic c 1200; **b. Henricus**, good king Henry (bot.) 1632; **de -o et malo**, (leg.) c 1220, 1352; *****pro -o pacis**, for the sake of concord c 1220, c 1423; see also **forum**; **-ificatio** c 1380, †**-ifacatio** 1378, creation of good; **-ifactivus** c 1370, **-ificus** 1497, creative of good; **-ifico**, to make good c 1362, 1374; see also **melior**, OPTIM
bono, see BUND
bootaurus, see **butaurus**.
Bootes (astr.): **Boetes** (pl.), polar stars c 550.
borach/a, -ia, see **burrochius**.
‡**borades**, (metal) filing 1652.
borago, borage (bot.) c 1200, 1622.
bor/ax c 1215, a 1250, **baurach** a 1250, 13c., ‡**batrachum** 1652, **-teza** 1144, borax.
borcellum, 'bossell', 'print' of a mazer (O.F. boursel) 1458.
borcinettus, see **bacinus**.
*****bord/a, -um** 1167, 1573, **burda** 1506, board; **b. mensalis**, board of (trestle) table 1359; *****b. navis**, side of ship c 1242, 14c.; **b. shope** 15c.; see also **Estrensis**, **fenestra**, **infra**, THAC; **-arius**, (?) keeper of tables c 1136; fitter of boards (naut.) 1294; see also **bordagium**; **-cula**, keel 1267; **-nalum**, board-nail 1510; **-tolla**, moorage due c 1400; **-ula**, little board 1487; **-ura**, boarding 1240, 1250; **-io** 1240, *****-o** 1235, 1402, **burdo** 1406, to board up.

bord/agium, bordage (tenure or tenement) (C.I.) 1274, 1331; *****-arius** 1086, c 1324, **-aria** (f.) c 1120, **-aius** (C.I.) 1274, **-ilerius** (G.) 1347, bordar, bordage-tenant; **-arius capitalis** (C.I.) 1361; **b. dimidius** 1086; **-ellum, -ellus** a 1128, 1251, **-ile** (G.) 1292, 1347, cottage; 1485, **b. commune** 1442, **burdellus communis** 1397, brothel; **-landa** (Sc.) 1464.
bordeo, see **burda**.
bord/era 1433, 1484, *****-ura** 1236, 1481, **-eura** 1238, **burdura** 14c., border; **-ura**, bordure (her.) p 1394, a 1446; see also **crux**; **-ero** 1436, 1489, **-uro** 1245, 1388, **-o** 1245, c 1250, to border; see also **barda**.
bordonus, see 1 **burdo**.
bor/ealis 793, **-iens** 1417, north; *****-ealis** (**-ialis**) 12c., a 1564, **eboralis** 1244, **-ientalis** 1251, 1522, **-iens** 1387, northern; **-ialis**, northerner c 1300; student of northern 'nation' (ac.) c 1268, c 1425; **-ialiter** 1423, 1587, **-ientaliter** 1587, northerly; ‡**-ias**, "south" 1483; **-eo**, to utter in windy language c 1180.
borellus, see **burellus**.
borg-, see also **burgus**.
*****borg/a** (**borgh-**) 1230, c 1397, **-us** 1177, c 1236, **burga** 1318, 1535, **borwa** 1315, †**broga** c 1250, tithing (Kent & Sussex); **-us** 1462, **-asaldrus** 1284, **-esalder**, **-esaldrus** c 1236, 1339, **-saldrus** 1313, **boresaldrus** 1348, **borusaldrus** 1326, **burghesaldrus** 1361, **burgitentor** 1258, 'borsholder', headborough (Kent & Sussex); **bortrem/inga** 1275, †**-ium** 14c., borghtriming, view of frank-pledge (Suff.); cf. **tremura**.
†**boriarium**, borer 1390.
†**bor/ica** a 1150, ‡**-ith** (**-ich**) 14c., **-iza** 13c., borith or borage (bot.); cf. **borago**.
borittus, **borrokus**, see **burrochius**.
†**borla**, (?) candle-wick 1306; cf. BURELL
boro, see **baro**.
borreum, see **butyrum**.
borsa, see **bursa**.
bortrem-, **borwa**, see **borga**.
borus, see **burgus**.
bos arabilis c 1185, 1232, **b. arans** 1086, **b. arator** c 1290, **b. carruce** 1260, 1313, **b. ad carrucam** 1086, **b. in carruca** 1086, plough-ox; *****bov/arius** 1086, c 1345, **-erius** 1260, **-ettarius** 1269, 1277, oxherd; *****-aria** 1155, 1419, **-arium** 1200, 1404, **boaria** 1314, *****-eria** 1152, a 1564, **-erium** 1325, ‡15c., †**-orea** c 1310, **boeria** 1245, †**beveria** 1329, **-ellum** c 550, cattle-shed, byre; **-aria** (Norm.) 1415, (?) **boiria** (G.) 1308, *****-ata** 1086, 1583, **-eta** c 1109, 1331, **-atus** 12c., 1242, **-atis** c 1200, **bouvatus** 1230, **buvetum** (Norm.) 1422, **-inus** 13c., measure of arable land, oxgang, bovate (⅛ carrucate); **-ata magna**, double bovate c 1185; **-eta minor** a 1172; **-ata prati**, meadow appurtenant to a bovate of arable 1184; **-ettarius**, 'bovater', tenant of bovate 1375; **-encus**, ox c 550; **-ella** 1379, **-etta** 1253, 1414, **-icula** 1222, 1434, heifer; **-ellus** 1363, *****-ettus** 1202, a 1564, *****-iculus** 1220, c 1540, **-eculus** 1304, †**-iolus** 1416, *****-icillus** 1227, **bownculus** 1280, **bobulus**

1208, bullock, steer (**-ettus** commonly in third or fourth year, **-iculus** in second or third); **-ettus taurellus** 1339; **-iculus bisse** 1366, **-iculus cervi** 1353, 1366, fawn; **-igenus,** progeny of an ox (βουγενής) c 1250; ‡**-illa,** beef c 1440, 1570; **-inus,** ox-like c 1180; **bowinus,** of an ox 1214.

bosa, *see* **bocium.**

bos/agium 13c., 1388, (?) **-cagium** 1296, 1436, **busagium** c 1250, 15c., a customary payment, (?) 'bosing' (E. Anglia) (? *cf.* **bousa,** or M.E. *bose* = stall).

1 bosca, small duck (βοσκάς) 1544.

2 bosc/a 1250, c 1310, **-us** 1182, 1419, *****busca** 1185, 1573, **buschia** c 1180, p 1290, †**bucca** 1208, **buscus** 1256, 1313, wood (material), firewood; *****-us** c 1070, 1583, **-um** 1199, 1583, †**boccus** c 1260, †**bochus** a 1130, †**bossus** 1352, 1388, *****-agium** c 1160, 1421, **-alium** 1421, **-ura** 1555, wood, woodland; **-us clarus,** wood cleared of undergrowth (G.) 1243; **b. grossus,** big timber c 1219, c 1306; *****b. mortuus** 1108, 1334, **busca mortua** 1234, **busca sicca** 1225, dry wood; **-us viridis,** green (fresh) wood 1281, 1382; **busso,** bush 1209; **-ellus** c 1160, 1310, **-ellum** 1220, **-iculus** 1280, **-ulus** 1143, 1571, little wood; **buscagium** 1325, **boiscagium** 1275, due paid by householders (Lincoln); *cf.* **bosagium;** **-alis,** of wood c 1308; 1571, 1587, **-atus** c 1575, **bossatus** 1567, wooded; †**-ata,** *see* **besca; buscarius,** *see* **bucheria; boskeronius,** wood-cutter (Norm.) 1198; **-o,** to cut firewood 1260.

3 bosca, *see* **bocium.**

boscaria, *see* **bucheria.**

bosio, *see* **boisio.**

bos/o, -onus, -unus, *see* **1 buzo.**

bosretum, birch-rod (Fr. *bourrée*) c 1164.

bossellus, *see* **bussellus.**

bossetum, *see* **buffettum.**

‡**bossor,** "beef flesh" c 1440.

*****bostar/** c 1180, 1502, **-ia** 1345, **-ium** c 1140, c 1350, (?) **bustallum** 1385, cattle-shed, byre; *cf.* **bocetum, bos.**

‡**bostio,** plough-boy c 1440, 1483.

bot-, *see also* **but-**

1 bota, 'hay-boot', fencing material 1255.

2 *****bot/a c 1170, 1534, **-um** 1298, 1368, (?) **-ellum** 1360, boot (footwear).

3 bota, *see* **butta** (1 & 2).

botagium, *see* **1 batellum; 1 butta.**

botam, *see* **albotim.**

bot/anatus, -enarium, *see* **buto.**

botan/icus, botanical 1634; botanist 1641; ‡**-um,** lead oxide 1652.

boteicium, *see* **baticium.**

botell-, *see also* **2 bota; buticularia.**

botellus, botel of hay 1419; sheaf of darts c 1335.

bot/eracia, -erassis, -eracus, -erasus, -ericius, *see* **butteracia.**

*****both/a** 1183, 1587, **-um** c 1200, (?) **boda** 1240, booth, stall; tolbooth 1244, c 1348; **-agium** or **bodagium,** payment for erecting booths 1232; **-etarius,** (?) stall-holder c 1200; *but cf.* APOTHEC

bothecarius, *see* APOTHEC

bothena, lordship (Sc.) c 1190, 14c.

bothor, *see* **bocium.**

boticium, *see* **2 butta.**

botillagium, *see* **1 batellum.**

botium, *see* **bocium.**

botizella, *see* **butisellus.**

bot/o, -onus, -onatus, *see* **buto.**

botor/, -us, *see* **butaurus.**

botr/aria, -ia, *see* **buticularia.**

botrax, *see* **batrax.**

*****botr/us,** *for* **-ys,** cluster of grapes c 730. c 1125, 1439.

botsata, right of abode granted to aliens (London) c 1324.

botta, bottus, *see* **butta** (1 & 2).

bottum, *see* **buttorium.**

botum, *see* **2 bota.**

botunus, *see* **buto.**

‡**botus barbatus,** form of crucible (alch.) 1652.

bou-, *see also* **bu-, bul-**

bouellarius, *see* **bodellus.**

boul/a, -us, *see* **bulus.**

boulletus, *see* **1 bulla.**

boulum, builum, buielum, 'boul', 'bulle', curved handle (of plough) (Yorks.) 1264.

bound-, *see* **bund-**

bourdenagium, collectorship of a toll (G.) 1424.

bousa 1334, **busacia** 12c., dung (Fr. *bouse*); *cf.* **bosagium.**

boutellus, boss (of fan-vaulting) 1291.

boutirum, *see* **butyrum.**

bov-, bouv-, *see also* **bos.**

bova, vault or crypt 1198, 1296; cess-pit 1270; **bohalla,** (?) vaulted hall 13c.

bovagium, *see* **1 bonagium.**

bowga, *see* **bulga.**

bowinus, bownculus, *see* **bos.**

box-, *see* BUX

boy/o, -zo, to fit (barge) with extra strakes (naut.) 1327.

bozonus, *see* **1 buzo.**

Brab/antinus c 1420, **-anus** c 1360, **-acenus, Braibacenus** c 1200, **Brebantio** 1179, **Bribantio** c 1198, **Brebantius** c 1250, **Brebeazo** c 1190, Brabanter, routier; coin of Brabant c 1190; **-anicus,** of Brabant c 1302.

bra/beum (bibl.), **-dium** c 550, 7c., *****-vium** 6c., 8c. c 1080, 1458, prize, reward; **-vialis,** earning a prize c 1470; **-vio,** to gamble 1433.

braca, *see* **brecca.**

bracato, *see* BRAS

bracatus, *see* **brachettus.**

bracc/ale 1213, 1330, **-alis** a 1250, **-ile** c 1180, c 1330, **braellum** 1207, 1419, **braiellum** c 1325, (?) **braierium** 1292, ‡**-itectum** 15c., breech-girdle, belt; **braellum,** belt for bending cross-bow 1299; **-arii** (*pl.*) c 1230, **-ie** 1310, breeches.

bracch/ium 1332, 15c., **bracia** (G.) 1253, 1254, **-iata** c 1283, 1329, **brassata** (G.) 1283, **braceria** (G.) 1253, measure of length, fathom; reliquary shaped to hold arm c 1255, c 1510; arm of balance 1307, c 1340; c 1150, **-ia** 1331, pier, mole; part of windlass 1296, 1325; 1255, 1374, **brasum** 1235, 1286, part of mill; brace (timber) 1233, 1327; arm of river c 1102;

arm of sea 1189, 1416; arm of cross 1295; side (of chapel) 1498; (?) handle (of box) 1186; **bracia, bracius** 1223, 1325, **bracea** 1215, **bracera** 1303, 1327, brace, strap; **-ium fortitudinis** (bibl.), the strong arm, force c 1470; b. **longum** (fig.) a 1142; **B. Sancti Georgii,** Hellespont 1267, c 1320; b. **seculare,** secular arm c 1250, c 1450; **-ius (branchius),** arm 1234; ‡**-iale,** sleeve c 1440, a 1520; **garba -ialis,** sheaf that can be held under one arm 1234.

brace-, see BRACCH; BRAS

bracha, see brachettus.

brachanum, carpet c 1190.

brach/e c 550, **bratthea** (f.) 960, short; **-ilexium,** brief utterance c 950.

*****brach/ettus** c 1157, c 1437, **bracatus** c 1150, 1336, **braschettus** c 1192, brachet (hound); **-a** 1278, **-ia** 1279, **-eta** c 1350, 1393, brachet bitch; **braconarius,** man in charge of hounds c 1136, 1300; **braconeria,** mastership of hounds 1331.

brachinellum, measure of wine c 1266, c 1450.

‡**brachium,** copper (alch.) 1652.

braci-, see also BRACCH; BRAS

bracon/arius, -eria, see brachettus.

†**bractea,** cyclamen (bot.) a 1250.

bract/eus, gold-plated c 1188; **brateus,** in sheets or plates 685; **-ea ferrea,** iron plate 1373; †**brittea,** plate c 1200; †**blateola,** gold leaf 781.

brada, 'brade', broad field (Beds.) a 1205.

bradium, see brabeum.

braellum, see BRACC

braes-, see BRAS

bragator, see 2 briga.

bragma, see bregma.

1 **Bragmannus,** Brahmin c 1190, 1267.

2 **bragmannus,** routier, mercenary soldier (cf. Provençal braiman) c 1200, c 1220.

bragm/aticus, chief (W.) a 1100; **-inatio,** chieftainship, primacy (W.) a 1100.

brai/a, infant's cry (Sc.) 1608; **-o, brago,** to cry (of an infant) (Sc.) c 1270.

Braibacenus, see BRAB

brai/ellum, -erium, see BRACC

brais-, see BRAS

brakia, see 2 broca.

brama, see brema.

bramum, well, pit c 1100.

branca ursina a 1250, 1629, ‡**francursina** 15c., bear's-foot (bot.).

branch/ia 1205, c 1275, **-a** c 1253, **-ium** 13c., branch; b. **crucis** 14c.; **brauncha,** (?) design of branches 1489; **-iatura** 1242, **-ura** 1222, 1331, branches (coll.); **-io,** to lop 1324.

branchos, hoarseness: **brancus** a 1250, 13c.; †**broncus,** (?) brusque c 1200; **brongidus,** hoarse c 700.

brandatus, see BROUD

Brandones, first Sunday in Lent 1262, 1268.

branga, see pronga.

branis, see 1 brao.

brannum, see brennum.

brannus, see brema.

branta 1544, **anser brendinus** 1570, brant goose.

1*** bra/o** 1225, 1338, **-onus** 1225, brawn,

fatted boar; **-nis** 1284, **braunus** 1320, brawn, muscle of arm.

2 **brao,** to bray, caulk 1237, 1316.

‡**braricia,** glass 1652.

braschettus, see brachettus.

brasill/um a 1204, 1303, **-a** 1284, **-ium** a 1250, 1419, **bresilium** 1303, **lignum -icum** 1625, brasil, red dye; **-arius,** (?) dyer 12c.

brasinus, (?) brazen 16c.

*****bras/ium (-eum)** 1086, 1530, **bracium** c 1300, 1454, **braxium** 1521, **-seium** 1537, **braesium** 1212, c 1330, **braesia** 1251, **breesium** 1224, **bresium** 1266, c 1284, **bresia** c 1255, **braisium** 1086, c 1160, **braysia** c 1250, **braisis** c 1080, 1086, **braces** 7c., †**-erium** 14c., **-iatorium** c 1300, malt; b. **avene** 1266, 1457; b. **hordei** 1266, 1533, b. **hordeaceum** 1284, 1329, b. **hordeiceum** 1223; b. **mixtum** 1329; b. **capitale,** first-grade malt c 1297, c 1376; b. **commune** 1258, b. **cursale** 1297, c 1375, b. **cursarium** 1235, second-grade malt; b. **fusum** c 1441, b. **infusum** c 1444, wort; **molendinum -arium** 1297, m. **braissanum** (Norm.) 1113, malt-mill; **-agium** (C.I.) 1309, 1331, **-inagium** 1407, **bracenagium** 1271, c 1380, **bracenagium** c 1270, (payment for) right to brew; *****-ina, -inum** 13c., 1555, **-ena** 1398, **-cina, -cinum** 1230, 1254, **bracina, bracinum** a 1128, c 1500, **bracinium** c 1160, 1265, **-aria** c 1453, **-eria** c 1250, c 1302, **braxaria** 1349, †**brixeria** (?) 14c., **breseria** c 1284, **-ura** 1560, ‡**-iarium, -orium** 13c., **-iatorium** 1466, **-itorium** 1675, **braceatorium** c 1258, brew-house; **braciatricius** 1303, **-ineus** 1451, 1576, **bracineus** c 1300, 1435, for brewing; **-ina** p 1330, **-cina** 1230, **bracina, bracinum** 1221, 1390, **braciatum** 1251, a brew; **braciamentum** 1326, **-iatio** c 1448, 1531, †**-io** 1457, **braciatura** 1228, 1430, **braciniatura** 1265, brewing; **-iator** c 1255, 1534, **braciator (braceator)** c 1160, 1430, **-sator** c 1539, **braxiator** c 1325, **braziator** 1583, ‡**-iarius** 15c., **bracerius** 1230, **bracharius** a 1128, **bracista** 12c., brewer; **-iatrix** 1275, 1495, **braciatrix** 1191, 1419, †**bractatrix** 1281, **braxatrix** c 1291, **bracerissa** 1276, c 1300, brewster, ale-wife; ‡**-ipurgium,** draff 1483; **panis braciatus,** (?) malted bread 1294; **-io** 1236, 1511, **-cio** 1221, 1538, **bracio** c 1150, 1419, **braxo** 1495, **brazio** 1086, †**bracato** 1281, **bracinio** 1265, to brew; **braceo tabernam** c 1300.

brassata, brasum, see bracchium.

‡**brassa/tella, -della,** snake's tongue (bot.) 1652.

brassilis, see brusca.

†**brat/a,** (?) brattice or screen 1336; **-eschia,** see bretescha.

brateus, see BRACT

bratthea, brache.

braud-, see BROUD

brauncha, see branchia.

braunus, see 1 brao.

bravitor, see 1 brevis.

bravi/um, -alis, -o, see brabeum.

brax-, braz-, see brasium.
braya, 'braye', embankment 1342.
braydatus, see BROUD
breb-, see BRAB; 1 bercaria; verveculus.
brecc/a 1203, c 1433, -um 13c., brechia
1233, 1236, berca 1314, breach, gap;
brechia c 1220, c 1300, †brecis a 1100,
1234, (?) brekka 1275, braca c 1150,
'breach', assart.
bredna, breisna, see brema.
breesium, see brasium.
bregma, top of head (Gk.): ‡bragma 15c.
brehonius, law-giver, brehon (Ir.) 1584.
breido (breydo) 1367, 1478, brudo 1401,
c 1477, to wattle.
brejudico, see PREJUDIC
‡brella, starch 15c.
brem/a 1205, 1535, -na (brennia) 12c., 1237,
-ia (brenna) c 1180, 1265, brama 1260,
brannus c 1324, brenha c 1180, braemia
1256, 1261, breyma 1273, bredna 1231,
breisna 12c., bresma (bresnia) 1171,
c 1290, bresmia 1231, bretnia 1228, -enta
1415, bream (fish); -etta 1306, ‡-etica 15c.,
‡brimellus 15c., young bream.
brendatus, see BROUD
brendinus, see branta.
brenn/um (†bremium) a 1190, c 1300, -ium
1204, c 1298, -a 1297, ‡-o 15c., brannum
1239, 1329, bran.
bres-, see also bras-; brema.
brest/clutum 1299, 14c., -eclutum, -clou-
tum 14c., clout for breast-board of plough.
bresura, see presura.
bret/escha, -eschum 1156, 1242, -eschia
1174, c 1219, -ascha 1173, 1241, -aschia
1174, 1242, -achia, -achium 1241, 1331,
-agium 1297, 1386, bertachia 1245,
brateschia 1241, britasca c 1218, brita-
schia c 1218, c 1266, briteschia 1241,
britachia c 1267, britachium c 1300,
britagium 1245, c 1300, brutescha 1226,
brutaschia c 1135, brutachia (G.) 1255,
brutagium 1331, 1360, brutascaria 1271,
-issementum c 1400, brattice (palisade or
(?) wooden tower); -agium, service of
making brattices 1336; -aschio 1271, -agio
1338, britaschio 1214, to brattice; cf. brata.
bretnia, see brema.
bretta, harness (G.) 1254.
bretto, see blettro.
Brettonicus, see BRIT
breud-, see BROUD
breugabulum, see 2 brueria.
1 brev/is 1080, 1305, *-e 1086, 1573, writ;
-e, letter a 1090, c 1470; amulet c 1180,
c 1200; list of duties (eccl.) c 1160; c 1290,
b. defunctorum c 1296, b. mortuorum
c 1148, -is c 1123, -is pro defunctis c 1072,
mortuary roll (soliciting masses for deceased monk); b. ad quod damnum 1385,
c 1395; b. clausum 1190, 1419; b. commune c 1219; b. cursorium c 1290, b. de
cursu 1199, 1436, writ of course; b. de
allocate 1257, 1296; b. de computate
1242, b. de computabitur 1256, 1266; b.
de errore 1419; b. de exitu c 1178; b. de
firmis, rotulus exactorius c 1178; b. de
gratia, writ issuing as of grace 1313; b.
de Griffone, writ under Griffon seal 1343;

b. individuale 15c., 1595; b. de ingressu
1236, 1269; b. de introitu 1274; b.
judiciale c 1258, 1595; b. de liberate
1230, 15c.; b. magistrale c 1258, c 1290;
b. originale, original writ (not copy) c 1178;
1200, 1595, b. capitale 1200, 1205, originating writ; b. de pace habenda, writ of
protection 1236; b. Pape, papal brief 1201,
1515; b. parvum 1279; b. patens 1220,
1380; b. placitabile 1282, 15c.; b. posses-
sorium 1308; b. de precepto 1274; b.
recti a 1157, c 1250; b. de recto c 1158,
1586; b. remediale c 1290; b. retor-
nabile 1293, 1454; b. irretornabile 1301,
1327; b. vicecomitale 15c.; -ettum,
'brief' for collection of alms (eccl.) 1324;
†-itellus, (?) for -icellus, strip of parchment a 1250; -iculum, little letter or writ
a 1125, c 1190; c 1266, c 1330, -icula
c 1435, little mortuary roll; -arius, clerk
acting as steward (Norm.) a 1100; -icu-
larius c 1266, c 1330, -iger 1493, -igerulus
c 1266, 1488, -iator 1244, 1450, -itator
c 1447, -itor c 1296, c 1433, bravitor
c 1483, bearer of mortuary roll (eccl.);
-iator, collector of alms, 'limiter' 1335;
-ifactor, (?) letter-writer, scribe c 1150;
-itor, (?) beggar 1291; -itor compotorum,
account-writer 1492; -io, to commit to
writing, reduce to writs c 1180, 1354; to
summon by writ 1211.
2 brev/is, early (of future date) 1260; see also
in, infra, post; short note, breve (mus.)
1326, c 1470; b. erecta 1326, c 1470, b.
recta c 1470, erect breve; b. altera 1326,
c 1470, b. alterata 1326, double breve; b.
plicata, breve with neume 1326, c 1470;
-iarium, abridged edition c 1300, 1362;
*c 1200, 1455, -iarius c 1093, -iare 1250,
-iariolum 12c., breviary (eccl.); -iloquium,
brief speech 1282, 1453; -iloquus, laconic
c 1188, c 1521; sub -itate, in condensed
form 946; -iusculus, shortish c 550. 15c.,
1526.
brewgabulum, see 2 brueria.
breydo, see breido.
breyserius, brazier (official of the Mint) 1359.
bria, measure (esp. of wine) (cf. It. bria)
c 1194, c 1470.
brianneus, see biannum.
briba, bribe 1376.
Bribantio, see Brabantinus.
†bricius, kind of trout c 1200.
†brico, ornament or precious stone 14c.
brid/a 1213, 1320, (?) briga c 1250, 1405,
bridle; -ilbittum, bridle-bit 1439, 1510.
bridguma, bridegroom c 1115.
1 briga, 'bridge', gang-plank (naut.) 1201;
see also brida.
2 *brig/a, brawl, dispute 1289, 1473; -ator
(†bragator), brawler 14c., 1504; -ans
1418, -antinus 15c., brigand; *-osus,
contentious c 1378, 1475; -o, to brawl
c 1360, 1458.
brigan/da 1460, -dina 1462, -dinum 1459,
brigantine (naut.).
brig/andera 1451, -andina 1466, -antina
1418, brigandine, body-armour; -andinarius
1486, -andarius 1526, 1606, -endarius
1537, 1549, armourer.

brigbota (†brugbota), 'brigbote', repair of
  bridges c 1115.
Brigitt/inus 15c., -ensis 1570, Brigidianus
  1586, Brigittine (mon.).
brika, brick 1340.
brimellus, see brema.
brimma (brymma), surface-sheet (of lead)
  1369.
brimmagium, see primagium.
brimmannagium, see beremannus.
‡brisa, privy 1483.
‡brisca, honeycomb 1483.
briscus, see bitriscus.
brisia, watercress (Ir.) a 980.
bris/o, -ura, see brusura.
brit-, see also bretescha.
Brit/annice a 910. 1136, c 1250, -onice 1324,
  in Welsh; Brettonicus, British c 730;
  -annigena c 1325, Brittus 1149, Briton;
  lingua -annica, English 1544; falco
  -annicus, peregrine a 1446; -onizo, to
  speak Welsh 1521; see also vettonica.
britno c 1360, brutno 1355, to 'britten', trim
  (timber).
brittea, see bracteus.
briucca, see 1 broca.
briwera, see 1 brueria.
brixeria, see BRAS
briza, trade-wind 1622.
1 broc/a 1086, 1298, -us a 1220, 1594,
  †briucca 1292, 'brook', marsh or water-
  meadow; -ella, (?) little marsh c 1140;
  -alis c 1270, 1325, brucosus 690, marshy.
2 broc/a (brocc-, broch-, brokk-) 1185,
  1301, -ia 1233, 1383, -ium 1250, -etum
  1303, 1309, 'broach', pin, skewer, spit;
  b. (†brakia) anguillarum, stick of eels
  c 1150, 1200; b. auri, brooch 1207; b.
  ferrea ad herciam, spike for harrow 1293;
  vinum ad -am vendo, to sell wine 'on the
  broach' (i.e. retail) c 1200, 1289; -agium
  c 1299, 1419, -uragium 1443, 1462, bro-
  gagium c 1390, -aria 1300, brokerage;
  -arius 1284, 1444, -ator 1315, 1575,
  -urator 1313, broggator 1355, 1395,
  broker (cf. ABROC); -ulatrix, tapstress 1256;
  brochio, to stretch (cloth) on a tenter-
  frame 1255, 1262; to stake 1257; see also
  brusca.
brocardicum, canon of Burkhard a 1245;
  brogardicum, rule, formula a 1361.
broccatus, brocaded 1494.
1 broccus, brock, badger 1279.
2 broccus, (?) pannier (G.) 1252, 1288.
broch-, see 2 broca; brusca.
broddum, brad-nail 1276, 1407.
brod/eraria, -atus, see BROUD
1 *brodi/um a 1235, 1482, †broidum c 1250,
  ‡-ellum c 1440, bruettum c 1266, broth.
2 brod/ium 1395, -us 1377, brood, fry (of
  fish).
broeillus, see BRUILL
broga, see borga.
brog/agium, -gator, see 2 broca.
brogardicum, see brocardicum.
broid-, see 1 brodium; BROUD
broiheria, see 1 brueria.
broill-, broll-, see BRUILL
brokettus, 'brocket', young stag 1223, 1278.
brom, marine worm (It. bruma) c 1200.

†bromius, (?) wastrel 12c.
bromus, broom, besom 1313.
bron-, see branchos.
brosca, see brusca.
broud/eria 1397, c 1420, brauderia 1398,
  broderaria 1494, -atura 1305, c 1420,
  -ura 1253, 1423, breudura 1245, broidura
  1251, embroidery; -erarius 1395, 1452,
  brauderarius 1462, -ator c 1378, -eator
  1367, 1397, brauderator 1461, braudiator
  1401, †brusiator 1514, embroiderer; ars
  brudataria, a. brudatoria c 1467; -atus
  c 1243, 1432, brodatus 1222, c 1411, brau-
  datus (†brand-) 1338, 1409, breudatus
  (†brend-) 1240, 1345, *brudatus 1240,
  c 1500, -eratus 1402, browderatus 1468,
  broidatus 1303, broideratus 1393, braydatus 1332, brusdatus c 1080, 1282,
  (?) bustratus c 1180, bruslatus c 1300,
  c 1350, brullatus 1267, c 1330, embroidered;
  breudo, to embroider 1245.
broun-, see BRUN
bruc-, see 1 broca; brusca.
bruchus, locust or caterpillar (bibl.).
brud-, see breido; BROUD
bruellus, see bruillus.
1 *bru/eria, -erium 1107, 1555, *-era,
  -erum p 1212, 1582, -aria, -arium 1086,
  1435, broiheria c 1175, -iera c 1160, 1205,
  briwera 1294, heath (plant or land).
2 bru/eria 1390, 1608, -arium 1580, brewery;
  -gabulum c 1110, 12c., burgabulum 1141,
  c 1399, breugabulum 1223, 1297, brewgabulum 1300, †berugabulum c 1155,
  brew-gavel, payment for licence to brew.
bruettum, see 1 brodium.
brugbota, see brigbota.
*bruill/us c 1154, 1327, -ius c 1223, 1229,
  *brullius 1220, 1328, brullus 1218, 1228,
  bruellus c 1220, 1275, brollus 1179,
  brollius 1157, 1230, broillus 1165, 1256,
  broillius 1261, broeillus 1273, brulletus
  1200, 1235, thicket, covert (O.F. breuil, etc.).
brukestus, 'brisket', breast 1244.
brullatus, see BROUD
brum/a, hoar-frost c 550; -alius 590, -osus
  c 550, wintry; -alis, northern c 1000; -esco,
  to grow foggy c 1200; to blow cold c 1362;
  to wither c 1184; -o, (?) to cause pain c 1180.
brumesta, unproductive vine c 1212.
brummannagium, see beremannus.
brumo, to 'bream', clean (naut.) 1303; see also
  bruma.
‡bruncus (†gruncus, †grinicus), dodder
  (bot.) 14c.
brunellus, see burnellus.
1 *brun/us c 1115, 1427, -ius 1465, burnetus
  (of cloth) 1244, c 1443, brown; b. badius
  1300, 1316, brounbadius 1325, brown-
  bay; -aticus, brownish 1275; -um 1432,
  -ettum 1374, 1342, *burnet/a, -um 1188,
  1414, burnet, brown cloth; -eta a 1250,
  ‡burneta 13c., 14c., burnet (bot.); bur-
  neta, (?) hedge-sparrow 12c., 14c.
2 ‡brunus, erysipelas 1652.
*brus/ca, -cus a 1160, c 1350, -cia 1204,
  1317, -sa 1222, 1238, brucia, brucium
  a 1190, c 1318, brosca 1190, brochia
  c 1185, 1297, -ula c 1180, -kettum 1302,
  brucetum 13c., -setum 1203, 1292,

-satum 1328, †bursimus c 1250, †brassilis 1345, brushwood, scrub, thicket; 1423, brussa 1352, bristle, brush; †bursela, (?) quick-set hedge (Lincs.) 1624; -cosus, scrubby a 1160; †-tura, browsing 13c.; -co 1237, brucio 1233, to browse (on trees, *etc.*).

bruscus, butcher's broom (bot.) a 1250, 1634; *cf.* uruscus.

brus/datus, -latus, -iator, *see* BROUD

Bruselensis, coin of Brussels a 1275.

bruss-, *see* brusca.

brus/ura 1198, c 1258, brisura 1572, bruise; b. domorum, house-breaking 1212, 1303; b. forcelli, forcing a strong-box 1277; -o, to bruise 1198, 1221; 1212, -io 1303, briso 1204, to break into; *see also* BURS

brut-, *see also* bretescha.

brutno, *see* britno.

*brut/um, brute c 1197, c 1343; *-alis c 1180, p 1394, -eus c 1190, brutal, brutish; -alitas, brutishness 15c.; -aliter, brutishly a 1452.

Brutus, Brute, book of British history 13c., 15c.

bubal/arius, (?) ox-herd 1172; -inus a 1142, a 1250, ‡-iceus 1570, of a wild ox or buffalo; †biflis, buffle, ox-skin c 1200; *see also* bubulcus.

1 bubo, rascally camp-follower c 1370.

2 bubo, (?) bittern a 1300.

3 bub/o a 1250, -um c 595, swelling (med.); -onocele, inguinal rupture c 1620; bibona, (?) boss (on basin) 1370.

bub/ulcus a 1128, 1243, -ulus 13c., -alus 1275, oxherd or ploughman.

†bucacion, kind of herb a 1250.

bucc/a, (?) bit 1351; boca, river mouth 15c.; -ata, mouthful c 1160, 1232; -ellatim, by mouthfuls 12c., a 1446; -ellatio, assimilation, 'feeding' (alch.) 13c.; -io, a babbler c 1200; -o, to blow a 1529; *see also* BOSC, buscia.

buccellus, *see* bussellus; buticularia.

buccul/a 1204, 1255, bucla c 1254, 1439, bokela 1335, †bitellus 1295, bugula c 1270, bokeletta 1292, buckle; boculus, (?) ringlet c. 1340; buchelerum 1417, bukelarium 1298, 1324, bokelarium 1314, 1351, boclearium 1298, 1314, bokerellus 1320, buckler, small shield; bokelaria, bocularia c 1340, c 1350, -arium 1300, shield-play, fencing.

bucea, *see* buscia.

bucher/ia 1201, 1275, bocheria 1255, 1455, (?) boscaria 1275, shambles, butchers' quarter; -us 1201, †bocheius 1180, (?) buscarius 1311, 1350, butcher *or* (?) wood-monger.

buchetum, *see* bocetum.

bucinator, trumpeter: busynator 1209.

buckstall/a 1279, -us 1336, bukestalla 1199, 1240, buck-stall, hunting net; bokkestallo, to fit (palisade) with buck-stalls 1379.

†bucliamen, (?) midriff 6c.

bucor, *see* buttorium.

bucstanus, *see* bauzanus.

†budellum, (?) bowl (alch.) 14c.; (?) *cf.* aludellum.

budel/lus, -aria, *see* bedellus; bodellus.

budgetum, *see* 2 boga.

buff/a, trifle, jest (*cf.* It. *buffa*) 1299; -o, to puff 12c.; *see also* buscia.

buffettum, 'buffet', stool 1141; bellows (O.F. *buffet*) 1294; boffettum (†bossetum), chest 1328, 1412.

†bufficius, (?) leather curtain a 1100.

buf/o, residue after sublimation (alch.) c 1320; ‡-onitis, 'toad-stone' 1652.

Bug/arus, -erus, -garia, *see* BULGAR

bugeramus, *see* bukaramum.

bugerescha (†lugereschia), (?) 'budge', wallet 1213, 1214; *cf.* bulga.

bug/etum, -ium, *see* 2 boga.

bugia, lie, falsehood c 1323; *see also* bulga.

bugittum, *see* bocetum.

bug/la a 1250, -ula ‡14c., 1634, bugle (bot.); *see also* buccula.

buglossa (bot.): bugulossa a 1250.

bug/lum, -um, *see* bogum.

bugo, log 1236.

buguli cornu, bugle-horn 1212, 1289.

buhurdicium, *see* burda.

†builares (*pl.*), (?) joint meetings (between manors) c 1340; *cf.* birelagium.

buill-, *see* 1 bullio.

builum, buielum, *see* boulum.

buinardus, fool (O.F. *buisnard*) 1169.

buisellus, *see* bussellus.

buistarius, *see* BUX

bujettum, *see* 2 boga.

bukaramum 1238, bocramum 1292, bok/-erammum c 1315, -orammum c 1400, -eranda 1225, bugeramus 1235, (piece of) 'buckram', fine cotton or linen fabric.

bukelarium, *see* BUCCUL

bukestalla, *see* buckstalla.

*bukett/a, -um, -us 1236, c 1345, *bokett/a, -um, -us 1223, c 1389, bucatta 1211, bocattum 1276, 1279, bukellus 1239, bucket; -us, bokettus (quarellorum), tre-buchet 1265.

bukinus, of a goat (G.) 1243.

bukkum, 'plough-buck' (end of beam) 1352.

bula c 1219, bole c 550, counsel, resolution (βουλή).

bulbus caninus, small onion, 'chibol' a 1250.

bulc/um, cargo (Kent) 1347; -agium 1343, 1506, bolcagium 15c., (?) bollagium 1451, payment for discharging cargo.

bulcus, *see* balcus.

bul/engarius, -ingarius, *see* bolengarius.

bulet-, *see* BULT

bulfinca, bullfinch 1544.

bulg/a 690. 1188, 1301, -ia c 1125, 1477, -ium 1304, a 1307, bolga 1180, boga 1455, *bogea 1422, 1495, bougea 1041, bugia 1213, bowga a 1446, -etta 1515, bogetta 1484, 1499, bougetta 1515, 'bouge', 'budge', budget, (leather) bag, saddle-bag; -a, bouget (her.) c 1595; -ee (*pl.*), bellows 1325.

Bulgar/us, -is, Bug/arus, -aris, Bulgarian (*or* Albigensian) heretic c 1250; bugerus, usurer (Fr.) c 1255, c 1308; buggaria, sodomy 1660.

bulimus, voracious (unnatural) appetite: bolism/us c 1193, a 1250; -alis 15c., -aticus a 1250, voracious.

1 bull/a, *(papal) seal 12c., c 1450; *papal bull c 1130, 1562; document c 1204, 1411;

b. dimidia, half-bull 1294; **-aria,** office for sealing bulls a 1452, c 1488; **-aris,** conveyed by a bull c 1376; **-ariter,** in a bull c 1383; †**-arius** a 1452, **-ator** c 1250, c 1350, official sealing papal bull; **-ata,** (?) blank form sealed with a bull 1248, 1294; **-etta,** (payment for) customs certificate 1485; **-etarius** 1471, **boletarius** 1484, official granting customs certificates; **boulletus,** cannon-ball 1550; ***-o,** to seal with a (papal) bull c 950. c 1125, c 1465.

2 ‡**bull/a** 14c., **-io** a 1250, (?) mullein (bot.).

bullaccus, bullock 1252.

bull/ainus, -inus, measure of skins 1204.

1 bull/io 1086, 1290, **-o** 1216, 1319, **-itio** 1086, boiling, measure of salt; **-io,** measure of alum 1291; 1234, 1256, **buillo** 1224, 1306, **buillonus** 1242, **bollio** 1258, **boillo** 1237, 1307, measure of almonds; **-aria** 1441, 1584, **-arium** 1549, 1575, **-eria** 1348, 1376, **-earium** 14c., **-era** 1500, **boilleria** 1298, 1397, salt-vat, boilery; **-iator,** salt-boiler 1316; **-iatio,** (?) melting down (of lead) 1508; 1387, **-itio** 1325, **-itus** c 1115, boiling; **-itio,** frothing c 1462; **-ens,** (?) *for* **-iens,** boiling 1478; ***-io,** to boil 1086, 1363; **-io, -or,** to turn sour (of wine) 1305; *see also* **2 bulla; corium.**

2 bull/io 1465, 1472, **-iona, -onia** 1506, **bilo** 1282, 1367, **billio** 1369, 1380, **billona** 1496, **billonus** a 1300, **bilho** (G.) 1289, **bilium** (G.) 1254, bullion, ingot; **bilho,** billon, base coin p 1280; **-iona,** (?) melting-house, mint 1397.

3 bullio 1484, **bilo** 1475, bullion (boss or stud).

bulluga, kind of apple 6c.

‡**bulmago,** rest-harrow (bot.) 14c.

bulso, *see* **1 buzo.**

*bult/ellum, -ellus 1256, 1390, **buletellum** c 1250, 1304, **boletellum** 1265, (?) †**volitellum** c 1200, **-arium** 1292, **buletarium** c 1335, **-erum** 1320, **bolterium** 1310, **buretellum** c 1250, †**buneterum** a 1190, ‡**boletus** 15c., **-clathum** 1395, bolting-cloth, sieve; **-ellum,** fineness (of flour) c 1290, 1419; **-ator** 1338, **buletor** c 1268, **boletarius** 1322, (?) **boltarius** c 1215, c 1220, bolter, sifter; **-atio** 1348, **buletatio** 1243, **boletura** 1290, bolting, sifting; **-ura,** (?) bran 1259; **-ello** 1327, 1344, **-io** 1333, 1335, **-o** 1308, 1348, **buleto** c 1072, c 1330, **boleto** 1288, 1328, to bolt, sift (flour); *cf.* BURELL

bulus *1215, 1326, **boula** 1292, **boulus** 1289, 1305, †**buulus** p 1212, **bolus** 1327, birch-tree (Fr. *bouleau*); **bulus** 13c., **bituleus** c 550, of birch; **bolnetum** 1251, **bolletum,** **boletum** 1261, 1280, birch-wood.

bulwarka, bulwark 1573.

bumb-, *see* **bomb-**

bund-, *see also* BOND

bund/a *c 1135, 1671, **-us** 1275, 1369, **bonda** (Sc.) c 1200, 1580, **bounda** c 1300, bound, boundary; measure of width (of cloth) 1346; target (for archery) 1282; †**bona,** baulk (of land) 13c.; **-atio** c 1400, 1599, **bondura** 1282, fixing of boundary; **-ator,** 'bounder', tenant of claim (in stannary) 1508, 1613; **-atus** c 1250, 1278, **bondatus** 1565, 1586, **boundatus** 1512, bounded;

bondatus, bordered, fringed 1205; **-o** 1275, 1599, **-io** p 1290, **bono** (Ponthieu) 1281, to fix bounds, delimit; *cf.* **2 abunda;** *see also* **bonda.**

bundellus 1340, c 1530, **bondellus** 1421, bundle.

bundono 1228, **bondono** 1237, to bung (a barrel).

buneterum, *see* BULT

bungellus, bundle c 1397.

bunnum, stump 1452; cask 1470.

buntinga, corn-bunting (bird) 1544.

†**bunulus,** *f.l.* for **bimulus,** c 1200.

‡**buphagon,** appetizer 14c.

buprestis, beetle: **burestis** a 1250, 14c.

bur/arium, -atum, *see* **butyrum.**

buratus, *see* **birrus.**

burbarus, *see* **barbellus.**

‡**burb/ilia, -ia, -atia, -ula, -uria** 15c., **barbilla** 1494, umbles (of deer).

burbium, *see* SUBURB

burbux, *see* **barbellus.**

burc-, *see* BURS

burd-, *see also* BORD

burd/a c 1364, **-atio** c 1376, jest; **-eicia** 1306, **buhurdicium** 1226, 1234, joust, tourney; **-o,** to jest 14c., c 1450; 1252, **-io** 1242, 1419, **bordeo** 1299, to joust; *see also* HURD

Burdegalensis (libra), coin of Bordeaux (? ⅓ or ⅙ of sterling) 1242, 1317.

burd/egalium 1426, **-iwa** 1253, estate, vineyard (G.).

burdina, (?) burden, measure of fish or moss 1472, 1536.

burdis Alexandri c 1450, †**bourdealisamide** 1444, **alexander** 1521, bord-alexander (silken material).

1 burdo 1136, c 1400, **bordonus** 1351, pointed staff, wand of office.

2 burdo, drone (wind-instrument) c 1255; drone (insect) c 1112, 14c.

*burell/us 1172, 1377, **borellus** 13c., **burallus** 1311, **burillus** c 1226, †**burlus** 1257, **pannus -atus** 1245, **p. burillatus** c 1226, 'burel', coarse woollen material; **bureale,** (?) cloak of burel c 1330; **-arius** 1250, 1419, **burillarius** c 1295, †**burlarius** 1305, **-ator** c 1324, maker of burel; **burlura,** burling (of cloth) 1465, 1587; *cf.* **borla,** BULT

burerum, *see* **butyrum.**

burestis, *see* **buprestis.**

bureta, 'burette', cruet 1435.

buretellum, *see* BULT

burga, *see* BORG; **burgus.**

burgabulum, *see* **2 brueria.**

burganizatio, *see* **barganea.**

*burg/aria 1191, 1419, **-eria** 1201, 1297, **-laria** 1285, **-ularia** 1544, 1583, **-atio** 1211, **-atura** 1309, burglary; **b. gaole** 1331, **b. prisone** 1347, gaol-breaking; **-ator** 1201, c 1320, **-lator** c 1250, **-ulator** 1530, **-isor** 1292, burglar; **-ulariter** 1505, 1583, †**virgulariter** 1551, burglariously; **-o** 1202, 1381, **-io** 1309, to burgle; *see also* **1 bercaria.**

*burg/us 1086, 1608, **-a** c 1362, c 1450, **-um** c 1125, 1587, **borgus** c 1236, (?) †**borus** 1274, fortified town, borough; **tenementum in -o Anglico** (Nottingham), land held in borough English 1336; **b. liber** c 1150, 1395; **b. mercatorius** 1398; **-ellus,**

township (C.I.) 1178; **-agium** a 1135, 1314, **-agia** c 1400, borough-right, burgage-tenure; *a 1150, a 1564, **borgagium** 1242, 1284, **-aticum** 1226, 13c., †**-esaticum** (Sicily) 1239, **-asium** 1261, **-aria** c 1150, **-arium** 1487, burgage, house or land held by burgage-tenure; *b. **liberum** c 1125, 1573, b. **liberale** 12c.; **-ageria** 1230, 1496, †**-aregia** c 1294, **-aria** 1282, area of bur-gage-tenure (Ir.); **-agius** 1396, 1552, **-alis** c 1125, 1539, of or for burgage-tenure; **-bota, burhbota** c 1115, **-i claustura** c 1150, 13c., **-i refectio** c 1115, burhbote; **-ensis** (*adj.*), of a town 14c.; *-ensis 1086, 1539, **-encis** 1293, 1316, **-agensis** (Ir.) c 1365, **burhmannus** c 1115, burgess; b. **adventicius** 1307; b. **bastide** (G.) 1315; b. **curie** 12c., b. **de curia** 14c.; b. **liber** 1156, 1461; b. **magnas, b. magnus** c 1256; b. **manens** 1086; b. **minutus** 1086, b. **minor** 1086, c 1256; b. **parliamenti** 1419, 1503; b. **regis** 12c.; b. **de vento** 1280, 1304, b. **de v. et vico** 1275, rent-paying tenant in borough (W.); **-encia**, house or land held by a burgess (Norm.) a 1135; **-ensia** 1383, 1484, **-esia** (G.) 1314, burgess-right; **-ensialis** 1407, **-encialis** 1263, 1297, of a burgess; **-herita**, 'borough-right' 12c.; **-imotus** c 1115, 1247, **-emotus** 1212, 1480, **-esmotus** c 1310, **-motus** 1313, c 1437, **burmotus** c 1250, borough-moot; *-ima-gister 1315, 1586, **-omagister** 1392, 1395, burgomaster; **burgravius**, burgrave (Germ.) 1441.

burl-, burill-, *see also* BURELL

bur/lawa, -legius, *see* birelagium.

burna, burn, stream c 1135, 1430.

‡**burnea**, pitch 1652.

burnellus c 1250, 1344, **brunellus** p 1300, name of an ass.

burnet-, *see* 1 brunus.

burn/itio, burnishing 1277; **-io (-eo)** 1233, 1303, **-iso** 1315, to burnish.

burprestora, *see* purprestura.

burr/a 1208, 1316, **-um** 1206, c 1335, stuffing for horse-collars, *etc.*; *cf.* **birrus**.

burretum, *see* birretum.

burric/us 1221, **-a** (*f.*) 1221, ass.

burr/ochius a 1200, 1269, **-occus** 1263, 1281, **-ochia** 1234, **-oca** c 1225, **-usca** 1231, **borrokus** 1282, **boracha** 1281, **borachia** 1257, 1326, †**borittus** (? **boracus**) 1253, 'burrock', fish-trap.

burs/a *a 1128, 1583, **pursa** 1206, **borsa** 1313, **-ula** c 1224, ‡1483, **-ila** a 1250, bag, purse, treasury; scrotum (med.) a 1250; (?) pig's scrotum *or* ear 1302; exchange, *bourse* a 1130; weekly statement of expenses 13c.; scholarship, allowance (ac.) c 1292, c 1379; fee (ac.) 1469; b. **braccalis**, purse worn on arm 1275; b. **cissa** 1221, **-um cissum** 1419, b. **assisa** 1199, **-arum abscisio** 1291, purse-cutting; b. **pastoris**, shepherd's purse (bot.) ‡13c., 1629; **pre-benda -alis**, prebend carrying a stipend 1321, 1523 (Exeter); **-arius**, taker of bribes c 1190; 1327, 1451, **-ista** c 1393, purse-maker; *1167, c 1578, **burcerius** 1230, bursar, treasurer; 1485, 1560, **burcerius** 1475, **-or** 15c., **-emagister** 1385, 1412,

ship's purser; **-arius**, holder of bur-sary (ac.) 1521; **-aria**, treasuress 1397, 1441; c 1290, 15c., **-ariatus** 1446, †**-uria** 1330, office of bursar or treasurer; **-icissor** 1275, ‡**burcida** c 1440, **-arum scissor** 1275, c 1290, **burci sector** 1304, cutpurse; **-o** 1291, 1378, **bruso** 1291, 1296, to pack; †**-o** (†**vurso**), to fit (wheels) with boxes (*cf.* BUX) 1318.

burs/ela, -imus, *see* brusca.

†**burthum**, measure of steel (30 gads) 1326.

burus, free peasant 1086, 1130; *cf.* geburus.

busa, stream (? Flemish) c 1070.

busacia, *see* bousa.

busagium, *see* bosagium.

busardus 12c., 14c., **busharda** 1544, (?) **buso** 1528, buzzard.

busc-, *see also* BOSC; BUCHER

†**busca**, measure of barley 1317; *cf.* bussellus.

buscellus, *see* bussellus; buticularia.

busc/ia c 1192, c 1436, **-a** 13c., **-ium** 1242, **bucea** (†**bucca**, †**butea**) c 1193, c 1436, **bussa, bussha** 1417, †**buffa** c 1433, **buza** c 1200, c 1255, **-ardus** 1230, **bussardus** 1234, 1309, **buzardus** 1214, 1230, 'buss', transport ship; **butsecarla, buzsecarla** c 1118, c 1200, **buzecarla** 1086, 'buscarl', boatman or coastguard.

busia, wisp of hay c 1180.

bussa 1242, **busza** 1184, **buza** 1185, **buscis** 1245, (?) wine-skin; *cf.* 1 butta.

*****bussell/us** 1186, c 1533, **-um** 1212, 1335, **-a** 1258, 1409 **busseilla** c 1200, **buccellus** 1409, **buscellus** 1331, **buschellum** 1468, **bushellus** 1300, 15c., †**bussollus** 1247, **buisellus** a 1128, **boissellus** (Norm. & C.I.) c 1160, 1331, **bossellus** p 1200, c 1248, **-ata** 1234, dry measure, bushel; b. **fili** 1255; b. London', de **Londoniis** 1297, 15c., b. **standardus** c 1356; **-us** 1373, 1419, **buscellus** 1390, bushel measure, pot.

busso, buszo, *see* 2 bosca; buzo.

bussulus, busta, *see* BUX

bustallum, *see* bostar.

bustardus, bustard 1480.

bustianum, 'bustian', a coarse cloth c 1412, c 1467.

bustratus, *see* BROUD

busynator, *see* bucinator.

butaurus, bootaurus c 1200, **butor/** 1241, 1309, **-us** 1241, **-ius** a 1446, **butt/ora, -ourus** 1544, **botor** 1318, **botorus** 1342, bittern.

butea, *see* buscia.

buteirum, *see* butyrum.

buter/acius, -iceus, -ettus, *see* butteracia.

buteria, *see* bateria.

buticium, *see* 2 butta.

but/icularia 1262, 1282, **-eillaria** c 1160, **-eilleria** 1204, 1230, *-ellaria 1204, 1462, **-ellarium** 1242, 1390, *botellaria c 1135, 1466, **-elleria** c 1136, 15c., **botel-leria** c 1265, c 1334, **-elria** c 1331, 1360, **-illaria** 1219, c 1270, **-illeria** 1234, 1495, †**botularia** p 1348, **-laria** 1410, **botlaria** 1450, **botraria** 1419, **-ellia** c 1400, **-eria** 1297, 1390, **-iria** 1432, **-ria** 1376, **boteria** 1415, c 1470, **botria** 1437, buttery, butler's office or room; **-iclarus** c 800, **-icularius** c 1177, 1284, **boticularius** (Fr.) c 1300,

-ellarius c 1270, 1459, **botellarius** 1303, 1378, botelerius c 1333, botelerus 1352, -illarius 1290, 1364, **botillarius** 1405, -ilerus 1309, ‡-ularius 15c., butler; botellarius, (?) bottle-maker c 1419; **botteleragium** 1519, -leragium 1530, butlerage, wine custom; -ellus (bucellus) 1114, 1294, **buscellus** 1171, 1294, (?) **butallus** 1296, botellus 1391, 1416, (?) -illa 1215, botella 1534, small butt, wine-skin, bottle; cf. bussa, 1 butta.

butiga, see bocium.

but/imen, swamp 1254; -innosus, swampy 1334; cf. bitumen.

butineus, see luter.

butinum, booty (Norm.) 1429.

butio, butitorium, see buttorium.

butir-, see butyrum.

butisellus 1234, 1236, botizella 1258, bunch of ginger.

but/o 1235, 1261, ‡-unus 13c., bot/o 1242, 1303, -inus 1298, -onus 1290, 1352, **botunus** 1272, -onettus 1417, button, stud; botenarium, knob 1344; -anatus 1423, -enatus c 1365, -onatus 1344, 1351, buttoned.

butor, see butaurus; buttorium.

butrac-, see butteracia.

butrista, see 1 butta.

butrum, road, bothar (Ir.) c 1200.

butsecarla, see buscia.

1 butt/a (?) c 840. 1164, a 1564, -us (†buccus) c 1160, botta (bota) c 1220, 1460, bottus 1417, †butrista c 790, (?) buzca 1238, (?) buzius 1205, butt, cask; -etta, small cask 1237; -arius, cooper c 1136, (?) 1230; botagium c 1163, 1189, boutagium c 1163, duty on butts; cf. bussa, buticularia.

2 butt/a *1167, 1514, -is c 1182, 1325, -us 1199, 1306, botta 14c., bottus 13c., -icium 1316, boticium 1276, 1358, -era 1207, -eria 1315, butt of land; buticium (boticium) sepis (man.) 1245; -um, salt-pan 1191; -a, butt-hinge 1423; *-o (super), to abut 12c., 1472; see also buttorium; (?) cf. baticium.

butteracia c 1447, but/eracius 1320, c 1337, -erettus 1275, -ericeus 1249, -racius, -racus c 1340, bot/eracia, -eracium 1298, c 1412, -racus 1301, -rasia 1368, -erassis

c 1450, -rasus 1424, †-ria 1472, buttress; columpna botericia 1271; pilerius -ericius 1249.

butt/orium (†butitorium), (?) casting-net a 1330; 1241, butor (†bucor) 1310, bottum 1326, rammer; -o, to hit, whack 13c.; †butio, (?) to push c 1150.

butt/ourus, -ora, see butaurus.

buttumen, see bitumen.

*but/yrum (-irum) 1086, c 1540, -yrium 1313, -ira c 1305, -eirum 1282, -ur c 800, -urum 1573, -urium 1290, bitirum 1303, boutirum 1308, butter; ‡b. antimonii, mercuriale, saturni (alch.) 1652; -irarium (G.) 1254, (?) burarium c 1300, burerum 1292, (?) †borreum 1302, (?) buratum 1200, butter-dish or keg of butter; -yrositas, butteriness a 1250; -irosus, buttery a 1250, a 1275; ‡-yro, to butter 1570.

buulus, see bulus.

buvetum, see bos.

bux/is a 1100, -a 1265, boxa 1517, 16c., busta 1220, 1390, bussulus a 1235, box, casket; buistarius, box-maker 1220; -eria, (?) box-grove (Norm.) c 1160; boxo, to fit with axle-boxes 1299, 1378; cf. BUSSELL, PYX

buz/a, -ardus, see buscia, bussa.

buzca, buzius, see 1 butta.

buz/ecarla, -secarla, see buscia.

1 buz/o c 1218, 1294, -onus 1294, bulso 1209, buszo 1212, buzennus 1236, boso 1271, bozonus 1274, bosonus 13c., bosunus 1348, bird-bolt, arrow; boso 1313, busonus 1318, bolt (fastening).

2 buzo, decisive member of bench of judges 1212, c 1258.

bya, 'bee' (ring) 1385.

byrritrica, see birrus.

byss/us (biss-), cotton (bibl.); piece of paper c 612; satin ‡1483, a 1564; -inus, of satin 1455, 1459; see also BISS

bytonum, see bitumen.

byum, see bissa.

*byzant/ius (bizant-, bisant-), -ia, -ium a 1142, c 1595, -inus c 1125, c 1595, bizans 1331, bes/antius 1295, -antus c 1324, bazantius 1173, 1175, bezant, gold coin; -anto 1295, -ento 1328, 1345, to decorate with bezants.

C

(See also K, T, QU)

C, a musical note 1351.

caabla, see cabula.

caabulum, see cablicium.

caagium, see CAI

Caan, see Chanus.

cabal-, see also cablicium; cabula.

Cabal/a 1564, 1662, kabala 1609, Cabbala, secret tradition; -ista, initiate of the Cabbala 1564; -istice, according to the Cabbala 1564; -isticus, Cabbalistic, esoteric 1564, ‡1652.

1 cabal/lus, horse: cavallus a 1250, 1275, cabellus c 1280; -cata 1199, cavalcata

(G.) 1259, 1377, cavalgata (G.) 1238, cavalcatus 1287, 1353, calvacatia c 1265, †caulvatus c 1298, chevalchea 1200, chivalcia 1166, military expedition or escort duty on horseback; -larius 7c., c 730. c 1125, c 1437, -linus c 1115, 1274, drawn or carried by a horse; (subst.) knight (in chess) a 1150; -larus 7c., chivalerus 1438, knight; chevelria, chivalry, gentry 15c.; panis -linus, horse-bread 1326.

2 ‡cabal/lus, -is, spirit of one prematurely dead, living out his span in astral body 1652.

caban/a (G.) 1253, 1289, capana 13c., ‡15c.,

†**capaneya** c 1180, cabin, hut; **-a, -us,** cabin (naut.) 1392; **capana,** cupboard c 1200.

cabanum c 1190, **gabanium** 1499, sleeveléss coat (Fr. *caban*).

cabardius, *see* **cobardus.**

cabatellus, *see* **cabotellus.**

cabdellus, *see* **capital.**

cabeatus, *see* **cagia.**

cabel-, *see* 1 **caballus; cablicium; cabula; cavillatio; sabelus.**

caberus, caber, pole (Sc.) 1464.

cabli/amentum, knocking down (C.I.) 1309; **-o,** to knock down (C.I.) 1300; *cf.* ACCABLI

***cab/licium** 1204, 1334, ***-leicium** 1222, 1269, **-lecium** 1235, **-alicium** 1239, **-elicium** 1263, **-ilicium** 1222, **-ulicium** 1224, ***caplicium** 1224, 1315, **capleicium** 1236, c 1269, **capelicium** 1237, **capulicium** 1224, **gablicium** 1337, 1383, **gableicium** 1235, **scablicium** 1268, †**stabiliceum** c 1290, **cabulum** 1188, 1330, **caabulum** 1179, 1188, cablish, windfallen wood; *see also* **cabula.**

‡**cabo,** stallion 15c., 1483.

***cab/otellus** 1240, 15c., **-atellus** 1274, **-otella** 1331, dry measure (⅛ quarter) or liquid (20 quarts), *caboteau* (C.I.); **-ote frumenti** (Devon) 1277.

cab/ula 1253, 1312, **-ulus, -ulum** 1198, 1382, †**scabulus** 1302, ***-la, -lus** 1173, 1417, **-lia** c 1224, **-lium** 1239, 15c., **-licium** 1394, **caabla** 1173, **kaabulus** 1181, **-ella** 1433, **-ellus** 1446, **-illus** 1338, ‡**-allus** 15c., **gabula** 1461, **gabella** c 1377, cable; *see also* 2 **gabella.**

cac/a (cacha) ferri, iron slag a 1250; **-abunda,** privy 13c., ‡1483.

cacabre (kakabre, karabe, carabre), gum, (?) amber a 1250, ‡14c.

cacabum, dry wood 7c.

cacab/us, brain-pan 1277; ‡**c. Veneris,** water-lily 14c.; **-a** 1405, **-o** 1423, **cacubus** 1311, ‡c 1440, *for* **-us,** cooking-pot; †**citabus,** (?) bucket 1506 (*cf.* situla); **-arius,** tinker 1561; **-atus,** sooty, black c 685; **-osus,** pot-bellied c 1250.

cacademon, *see* **cacodemon.**

cacangelista, evil gospeller 1523.

†**cacella,** (?) *for* **vascella,** vessel, vat c 1325.

cacellus, *see* **cancellus.**

cacemphaton c 700, **cachephaton** c 1200, a 1452, verbal cacophony.

1 **cacha,** ketch (naut.) 1359.

2 †**cacha,** catch (for a window) 1418.

3 **Cacha,** *see* **caca.**

cachepoll/us, catchpoll, bailiff c 1115, 1414; **-eria** 1383, **-ria** 1360, office of catchpoll.

cacher/ellus (†**cather-**) 1275, c 1285, **-illus** 1309, 'cacherel', under-bailiff.

cachexia (med.): †**catheciza** a 1250.

cachinnatio, guffaw; †**cacihinnatio** 7c.

‡**cacia,** small colander 14c.; ‡**c. ferrea,** iron spoon 1652; *see also* 1 **chacea.**

‡**caco/chyla** 1652, ‡**-chymia** 14c., 1652, (?) **-chia** a 1250, evil bodily humour (med.); ‡**-chismaticus,** full of evil humours 14c.

cac/odemon 8c., c 960. 1150, 1552, **-ademon** 16c., evil spirit; **kakia,** malice 10c.

cacor, *see* 1 **chacea.**

caco/zygia, *for* **-zelia,** affectation a 1180.

cacubus, *see* **cacabus.**

cadapultra, *see* **catapulta.**

cadaver/ator, inspector of carcasses (man.) 1343, 1370; **-inus,** of or for a corpse c 700. a 1250.

cad/entia, inflexion, accidence (gram.) c 1250; **-itio,** fall, collapse 1398; felling c 1352; **-ix terre,** 'fall', measure of forest-land 1583; **casus,** fallen 1250, 1290; **-o,** to fall due 1086, 1359; to fail (in ordeal) c 1110; **c. in,** to incur 1202, 1330; **c. super,** to fall upon, attack 1338; *cf.* **casus.**

cadetra, *see* **cathedra.**

cadium, *see* **caia.**

cadius (†**cadmis**), *cadi*, judge (Ar.) c 1250.

cadivus, *see* **gutta.**

cadmeus, *see* **camahutus.**

cad/mia (†**-ima,** †**-imia,** †**-ivia**) c 1200, 13c., †**cidima** 13c., **cathimia** a 1250, ‡1652, spume of gold or silver; **-meauri** 1307; ‡**catma,** gold filing 1652.

cadmis, *see* **cadius.**

cado, *see* **cadentia.**

caduc/a (*n. pl.*), transitory things, this world 7c., 939. 12c.; **-alis** 12c., **-is** 939. 14c., transitory; **-itas,** transience 14c.; **-us,** *see* **gutta.**

cadurc/a, cuirass c 1520; ‡**-um** 1483, †**caduldum** c 1219, booth, hut.

1 ***cad/us** 1172, 1530, **-ulus** c 1540, 16c., **cauda** 1431, 'cade'; cask.

2 **cadus,** wave c 550.

cae-, *see* **ce-**

caetria, *see* **cateria.**

cafa, *see* **camphora.**

cafta, nut-shell (Ar.) 12c.

cageta, 'cageat', basket or box (Sc.) c 1450.

cag/ia (-ea) 1238, c 1340, **gabia** 1212, cage; **cabeatus,** encaged 11c.

cai/a (kay-) 1245, c 1456, ***-um** 1180, 1588, **-us** c 1219, 1324, **keya** 1401, **keyum** 13c., **cadium** 1287, **gayum** c 1289, quay, wharf; ***-agium** c 1170, 1485, **caagium** 13c., 1415, quay-dues, wharfage.

caicio (caycio), wooden fortification, (?) caisson 1304.

Cainite, *see* **Caymite.**

cainsil-, *see* **camisia.**

cal-, *see also* **cau-**

cala, (?) faggot 1580; *cf.* **calum.**

calab-, *see also* CHALYB

cal/abre 1364, 1435, **-abrum** 1378, **-ebrum** 15c., 'calaber', squirrel-fur (originally from Calabria); **-ebrius,** of calaber 1441.

caladrius, *see* **charadrius.**

†**caladum,** (?) gullet c 550.

calafactorium, *see* CALEFAC

calage, *see* **caliga.**

calam/are, -arium, -atio, *see* **calamus.**

calamentum, calaminth (bot.) a 1250, ‡14c.; *see also* **calamina, colamentum.**

calameon, *see* **chameleo.**

calam/ina a 1250, 1267, **lapis -inaris** a 1250, ‡15c., **-entum** 15c., calamine, zinc ore.

calamis, *see* CHLAMY

1 **calamita,** lodestone c 1227, ‡1440.

2 **calamita,** gum, storax c 1200, a 1250.

calamito, to harass 1415, ‡1483.

†**calamitum,** (?) muzzle c 1218; *cf.* **camus.**
calam/us, water-pipe, conduit c 1180, 1298; eucharistic reed 1079, 1295; 1443, **calmus** (†**calinus**) 14c., a lead for glazing; quill (for playing spinet) 1620; **c. Indicus,** (?) sugar-cane 1626; ‡**caulamaula,** shepherd's pipe 15c.; **-are** 1412, **-arium** 1450, ‡1483, pen-case (*cf.* **oculamarium**); **caumus** 1238, 1281, **cauma** 1234, **caumia** 1239, stubble; **-atio,** cutting stubble after reaping 1364; **-istra,** weaver's reed c 1190; **-istro,** to curl the hair c 1160; **-izo,** to pipe, sing, exult 7c. c 1170, c 1370; ‡**-o,** to gather handfuls 1483; **calemo** 1340, **calmo** 1324, 1361, **caumo, caumio** 1325, to cut stubble (of wheat or rye) after reaping; *see also* **latomus.**
calapodium, *see* **calopodium.**
calastreus, pebbly, shingly (? Celtic) c 550.
calath/us, cocoon a 1200; wicker container for oil-flask 1356; **-arius,** "pedlar" 1519.
calc-, *see also* CHALC
calc/aneum, -aneus, heel (bibl.); end of life 7c.; **-abilis,** capable of being trodden c 550, 9c. c 1200; **-ar,** ram (of ship) c 1200; cog (of wheel) 1285; **-aria** 1201, 1333, **-arium** 1212, 13c., †**-ular** 1448, spur; **-arius,** spurrier 1419; **-aratus,** fitted with spurs c 1250; **-atio,** wearing spurs 13c.; caulking 1437; treading (of grapes) 1620; ‡**-atorium,** wine-press 1483; **-atius,** more pointedly, emphatically 796. c 1160, a 1180; **-ator,** treader down, abaser c 1215; caulker 15c. (*cf.* **calfator**); **calx,** foot (of document) 1541; **-etenus,** from top to toe, completely 12c., 14c.; **-atrappa** 1207, ‡**-atrepa** 15c., caltrop; **-itratio,** kicking a 1450; **-ario,** to put spurs on 15c.; **-o (querelam),** to quash 1198; to tread out (grain) 1277; to pack, stack (hay) c 1220, 1299.
1 **calc/ea,** *for* **-eus,** shoe a 1216; **chauco** 1306, **chauso** c 1282, sock (Fr. *chausson*); **-o,** part of plough, (?) share *or* shoe 1222; ***-eamentum (-iamentum)** 980. 1086, c 1382, ***-eatura (-iatura)** c 1115, c 1418, **-itura** c 1450, **calsiatura** c 1335, footwear, shoe-money; **terra -iatoria,** (?) land subject to shoe-money a 1275; **-earius** 1221, 1661, †**calecarius** 1185, **-eolarius** 1558, **-eator** 1376, **-ifactor** 1598, **-ifex** 1521, shoemaker; ‡**-eatorium,** shoe-horn 1483; **-io calcaria,** to buckle on spurs c 1250, c 1436.
2 ***calc/ea** c 1156, 1331, **-eum** 1199, **-ia** c 1174, 1214, **-eia** c 1120, c 1230, †**calsa** 1487, **caucea** 1212, 1297, **cauceum** 1275, **causea** c 1370, 1425, ***-eta** c 1180, 1476, ***-etum** c 1190, 1587, **calseta, calsetum** 1375, **caucetum** 12c., 1433, **-eda** 1130, c 1250, **-atum** c 1200, 13c., **-iata** c 1160, **causetum** 16 c., †**collectum** 1441, **cauceria** c 1260, causey, causeway.
3 **calc/ea** c 1324, **-etum** 1373, 1419, (?) **causia** c 1280, *for* **calx,** lime, chalk; **calx** a 1235, ‡**c. chymica** 1652, fine, dry powder, calx (alch.); **c. lune,** silver, **c. Saturni,** lead, **c. solis,** gold, **c. Veneris,** copper (alch.) 1267; **-eta,** (?) lime-kiln 1164; **-eratura,** branding 1461; **-ina ustrina** 1443, **-eustorium** 1539, **-ifornium, chauffornium** 1278, 1284, lime-kiln;

-eria, lime-house 1372; **-iarius** 1313, **calxiarius** 1320, **calfonarius, calfonaria** (*f.*) 1260, **califurnarius** 1313, **calfurnator, calfurniator** 1279, lime-burner; ***-inatio** (†**-antio**), calcination c 1215, c 1320; ***-ino,** to calcine c 1215, c 1615.
calcite/os a 1250, ‡**-a** 1652, tragacanth.
calco, *see* **calcaneum; 1 calcea.**
‡**calcula,** (?) *for* **a caliculis,** "page, scullion" 1483.
calcul/us, number c 550; decision, issue c 1160, 1220; fortune, lot, position c 1160, 1421; scruple, nicety c 1190; **c. denuntiatus,** (?) marked pawn c 1160; **-atio,** calculation, arithmetic 796, 815. c 1125, c 1362; **-ator** c 730, 798, **-atrix** (*f.*) c 730, arithmetician; **-atorius,** of or for calculation 1200, 1444; **-o,** to reckon, calculate c 730, 796, c 1160, c 1574; *see also* **calcaneum.**
*cald/aria (chald-), -arium c 1000. c 1150, 1570, **calidarium** 13c., **-erium** 1213, 1450, **-era** 1260, **cauderia** (†**cand-, chaud-**) 1243, 1495, **caudera** c 1227, 1246, ‡**-ria** 1483, †**-ea** c 1283, †**caudia** 1205, **cawdrena** 1537, cauldron, kettle; **-aria,** ordeal kettle c 1100, ‡**-arium** 1483, **kaldellum** 12c., caudle; **-ronium** (? **-ronum**) 1303, **-rum** 1327, 1336, **chaldrium** 1504, ***ceudra (cheldra), celdrum** 1174, 1602, **ceudra** 13c., †**eccheudrum** 1237, **sceldra** 1303, **seldra** 1429, **seudra** 1290, **celera** 1460, chalder, chaldron (dry measure).
caldo, chawdron, entrails 1419.
calea, *see* **2 galea.**
caleb-, *see* **calabre; chalybs.**
calecarius, *see* 1 **calcea** (but *cf.* **caliga**).
calecha, *see* **galocha.**
calefac/torium, heated room (mon.) c 1148, 1537; foment, application of hot water (med.) a 1250; bath 1328; 1255, 1498, **calafactorium** 1395, **calfarium** 1388, **chaffor** 1291, c 1482, chafing-dish; 1358, **califactorium** c 1510, **pila -toria** 1388, hand-warmer, 'pome'; **-tibilis,** heatable a 1200, c 1300; ***-tivus,** calorific c 1180, 1620; **-tor cere,** chafe-wax (Chancery official) 1300, c 1500; **calefagium** (Norm.) a 1200, **calfagium** (Norm.) a 1128, **caufagium** (G.) c 1284, (right of gathering) fuel; **-tura** c 1290, **calificatio** c 870, heating; **-tus,** 'heated', rotted (of grain) 1335; **-io,** to be heated c 730. c 1115, c 1178; **califico,** to heat c 550, 10c. c 1270.
calefurcia (*pl.*) 1316, 1367, ‡**calofurca** 1483, gallows.
calefurina mulier, woman of the streets (*cf.* Fr. *carrefour*) c 1380.
calege, *see* **caliga.**
calegeri, *see* **calogeri.**
calemo, *see* **calamus.**
calend-, *see also* KALEND
calend/ris a 1446, **kalandra** a 1250, bird resembling lark (κάλανδρος); †**-ula** (**canendula**), "plover" 15c.; ‡**talendiola,** "holste" 15c.
calendula, marigold (bot.) a 1250, 1622.
caleng-, *see* CALUMN
cale/podium, -pos, *see* **calopodium.**
caleptr/um, -a, *see* **calyptrum.**
calepungnus c 1315, **calpunus** c 1245

chaufepeynum 1255, 'pome', hand-warmer.
calepus, see **calupus**.
caleriga, "spiced cake" (? hot cross bun) 1581, 1606.
cales, with good things (καλαῖς) c 550.
cal/ewarus 1251, **-warus** 1367, **-ewerus** 1240, **escawardus** 1233, ‡**calvarium** a 800, ‡**calviale**, ‡**calmaria** a 1000, ‡**galmaria** c 700, a 1000, ‡**galmilla** a 800, ‡**galbalacrum** c 700, **gabalacrum** a 800, a 1000, 'calver' (of salmon).
calfacium, see **scaffaldum**.
calf/agium, **-arium**, see CALEFAC
calf/atio 1437, **-atura** 1393, **-ettatio** 1337, caulking; **-ator** (†**calsator**), caulker 1401, 1427; **-ato**, to caulk 1346; cf. **calcator**.
calfon-, **calfurn-**, **califurn-**, see 3 **calcea**.
calib-, see CHALYB
calic-, see **calix**.
Calicutianus, **pannus**, calico 1701.
calid/itas c 870. c 1227, 1652, **-um** 1424, heat; **-atus**, heated c 900; see also CALD, **herba**.
califac-, **calific-**, see CALEFAC
calig/a, mesh 1269, 1279; *-e (pl.) 980. a 1090, 1588, **calage** 1402, **calege** 1407, **galige** 1407, c 1430, hose, stockings (cf. **galocha**); 1201, 1549, **-e de ferro** 1213, c 1220, *-e **ferree** 1184, 1289, **-ines ferree** 1213, greaves; **-a**, **-ata**, hoseful 1252; **-aria**, hosiers' quarter 1290; **-arius** 1286, 1388, **sutor -arius**, c 1520, **-ator** (†**taligator**) 1275, hosier; **-atura**, hosiery c 1370; **-o**, to make hose c 1220.
calig/atio, darkness, cloud 790; **-ino**, to be dark, blind 799; **-o**, to blind, dazzle 1439.
†**caligo** (**furnum**), to heat 1365.
calingo, see CALUMN
calinus, see **calamus**.
Caliph/es c 1200, **-a**, **-us** a 1142, c 1250, **Galdiffa** 1344, Caliph.
calistrigium, see **collum**.
caliv-, see CHALYB
cal/ix 7c., 9c. 12c., 1532, †**culix** 1266, chalice (eccl.); **-iculatus**, cup-shaped 1629; ‡**-igna**, bowl 1570; ‡**-ico**, to drink 1483.
calla, see **caula**.
callangia, see CALUMN
callarium, see **collarium**.
calliacus, a green gem c 1362.
†**callida**, hedge 1287.
1 **callis**, road c 730. 1086, c 1400; **c. regis** 1086.
2 **call/is**, callosity c 1362, c 1400; ‡**caro -ata**, brawn 1570.
callitrichos (bot.): **gallitricus** a 1250, 1538.
calm-, see **calamus**; **calewarus**.
calnetum, see **jampnum**.
calodemon, good spirit c 1212, 1267.
caloferus, see **caloreus**.
calofurca, see **calefurcia**.
cal/ogeri (†**-egeri**) (pl.), veteran monks (Gk.) 1438.
calompnia, see **calumnia**.
calon, called (καλῶν) c 950.
‡**cal/opodium** 1483, 1570, **colopedium** 1424, **-apodium** 1472, **-epodium** 1424, ‡c 1440, **-epos** c 1452, clog, patten, or stilt; ‡**-opifex**, maker of stilts or pattens 1530; cf. **galocha**.

cal/oreus, hot c 550; †**-oferus** (? **-oriferus**), calorific c 1250.
calpunus, see **calepungnus**.
cals-, see **calcea** (1 & 2); CALF
†**calum**, measure of steel, (?) sheaf c 1300; cf. **cala**.
column/ia (**calumpn-**), c 730. c 1110, 1535, **calompnia** 1375, charge, accusation; *1086, 1554, **-a** (G.) 1313, **calengium** 1086, 12c., **callangia** c 1180, **-iatio** c 1290, c 1320, claim, dispute, challenge; †**-ia** (n. pl.), calumnies 12c.; **-iabilis**, challengeable, disputable c 1270, 1344; **-ians** c 1200, **-iator** a 1130, c 1200, accuser; a 1120, a 1135, **-iator** c 1130, c 1170, †**-itator** 1155, claimant, challenger; **-ifer**, false 1004; **-iose**, calumniously, vexatiously a 1300, a 1564; **-iosus**, calumnious, vexatious a 1090, p 1377; subject to challenge or dispute 1086, c 1342; **-io** 838. 1086, 1419, **-ior** (dep.) c 1125, c 1443, to accuse; **-io** 1086, 1513, **-ior** c 1080, 1461, **-izo** 1382, **chalengo** 1313, **calengio** 1287, **calingo** 1211, **calengizo** c 1200, to claim, challenge.
cal/upus 1243, **-epus** 1298, **galupa** 1289, sloop (G.).
‡**calusa**, crystal 1652.
calvacatia, see 1 **caballus**.
calvari/a, place of execution c 1390; **-um**, bone, body 810; see also **calewarus**.
calv/atio, shaving the head 1382; **-us**, bishop (in chess) a 1150.
Calvinianus, Calvinistic 1558.
calwarus, see **calewarus**.
†**calx**, (?) f.l. for **clates**, hurdle c 1290; see also **calcaneum**, 3 **calcea**.
calyptrum 1466, **caleptr/um**, **-a** 1439, 1492, "hat", "cap", "bonnet"; ‡ **-a**, "horse's mane" 1483.
cam/aca 1345, 15c., **kameka** 1338, **-ica** c 1365, **-oca** 1331, c 1395, **-boca** c 1315, a fine material, (probably) silk; cf. **cameraka**.
cam/ahutus 1251, 1303, **-au** 1239, **-acu** 1245, **-ehu**, **-eu** (†**kamen**) c 1220, a 1250, **-eus** c 1255, †**-ahitta** 1311, **-aetus** 1245, **cadmeus** c 1255, **catmaheu** 1239, **kathmatha** 1205, ‡**gamatheus**, **gamahe** 1652, cameo.
camal-, see **camelettum**, **chameleo**.
camara, **camararius**, see **camera**.
‡**camaroca**, goose-grass (bot.) c 1440.
camaum, see **commotum**.
camb-, see also CAMER
camba, see **cannabus**, **gamba**.
cambagium, payment for right to malt (C.I.) 1180.
cambi/dextria, (?) confusion of **-partia** and **ambidextria**, 1403.
camb/io, see **cambium**; **cambrus**.
cambi/pars 1338, 15c., *-partia (-pertia) 1357, 1588, **-partus** c 1452, **campipars** 1293, **campipartia** c 1422, **champertia** 15c., champerty, collusion by third party (leg.); **-particeps**, one guilty of champerty 1360.
camb/ium, change 1378; transformable matter (med.) a 1250; 1309, c 1533, **changia** c 1200, **-itio** c 1080, 1335, **-iatio** c 1367, **campsio** 12c. **cansio** 1240, **-itus** 1368

exchange; **-ium,** (rate of, or allowance for) exchange of money 1252, 1432; *1198, 1556, **cangium** 1159, †-io 13c., **-eria** 1218, (place of) exchange of money, mint; **-itio,** object acquired by exchange c 1115; **littere -ii** 1423, 1491, l. **-itorie** 1368, 15c., bill of exchange; **-iator** c 1090, 1419, **-itor** 1086, a 1275, **campsor** c 1218, 1514, **camsor** c 1283, c 1430, money-changer, assayer; coiner 13c.; **-io** 1086, 1550, **-o** c 1540, ‡**campso** c 1440, to exchange, barter; **-io,** to change or coin (money) 1100, c 1324.

camboca, see **camaca.**

cambra, see **camera.**

Cambr/ensis, -icus, -igena, see KAMBR

cambrium, see CANNAB

camb/rus, (?) curved 1244; **-io,** to bend 1329, 1332.

camb/uca c 1130, 1303, **-utta** 760, 1006, **sambuca** c 1397, crozier, pastoral staff; game of hockey 1363; ‡**ulcer,** impostume, in groin 1652; †**-urta,** crutch c 1100.

camelarius, camel-driver 1392.

cameleo/ 8c., **-pardus, -pardalis** a 1250, camelopard; cf. **chameleo.**

camel/ettum 1252, 15c., **camaletum** 1493, **-otum** 1235, 1505, **chamletum** c 1553, camlet (cloth); **-inum, -inus** 1236, 15c., **-ina** 1244, **camolinum** 1303, cameline (cloth).

camer/a *798, 1041. 1086, 1501, **cammara** 1459, **crabra** c 894. 12c., **-ale** 13c., room, chamber; **camara,** vault c 690; **-a,** residence, suite 1334, 1433; 1289, 1415, **-alia** (pl.) 1458, †**-aria** (pl.) 1432, furniture, hangings; chamber (of gun) 1455, 1568; law-court 1274, 1574; small estate (of Hospitallers) 1328, 1338; treasury c 1136, 1450; treasurership 1206; **-am assumo,** to be brought to childbed a 1470; **-e** (pl.), chambering, fornication c 1220; **cambra,** trap for deer 1292; **-a ad stagium** 1229, 1257, **c. ad estagium** c 1245, upper room; **c. bassa,** lower room 1458, 1534; **c. per terram,** (?) parterre 1274; **c. communis** 1309, **c. necessaria** 1254, 1419, **c. privata** 1155, 1275, privy; **c. fausa,** (?) compartment 1323; **c. feni,** hay-loft 1348; **c. apostolica,** Papal Chamber 1463, c 1520; **c. consilii,** council chamber 1375; **c. curie** 1130, 1190, **c. regis** 1190, c 1397, king's privy purse; **c. maritima regis,** territorial waters 1605; **c. regine** 13c., 1350; **c. Scaccarii** 1423, 1565, **c. juxta Scaccarium** 1382, 1569, (court of) Exchequer Chamber; **c. Stellata** 1376, 1619, **c. Stellarum** 1421, **c. cum stellis depicta** 1375, (court of) Star Chamber; **c. tripudiantium,** dancing chamber 1388; **-alis,** secret a 1260; **lectus c.,** bed in (royal) bedchamber a 1470; **-aliter,** secretly c 1376, c 1420; **chamberandum, chamerandum,** chamberand (arch.) 1253; **-aria** *1142, c 1483, †-**ia** c 1220, **-ariatus** 1330, 1539, **camberaria** c 1350, **chamberlengaria** 1198, 1215, **chamberlangeria** 1227, **chaumberlenggaria** 1230, **skamberlengeria** c 1324, **chamberlanceria** 1225, **chamberlaneria** 1230, **cam-**

berlania 1230, **chamberlaria** c 1222, office or service of chamberlain; **-aria magistra,** office of Great Chamberlain 1133; **-aria,** chambress c 1125, 1520; chamber-maid 1423; *-**arius** c 1000. 1066, 1566, **camararius** 1212, **camberarius** c 1140, **-ator** 15c., *camberlanus 1185, 15c., **cambellanus** (Sc.) 1464, 1474, **camerlanus** c 1232, **chamberlencus** 12c., 1176, **chamberlengus** 12c., 1199, chamberlain; **c. de curru regine** 1285; **c. Londoniarum** 1204, 1419; **c. Scaccarii (de Scaccario)** 1200, 1552; **c. Magnus** c 1439, c 1549, **c. Major** 15c., Lord Great Chamberlain; **c. regine** 1212, 1238; **c. regis** 1086, 1451;
‡**-ella** 1483, **-ula** 1283, 1345, little room, compartment; **-atio,** vaulting c 1212; **-atus,** vaulted c 1150, c 1436; **-o,** to round off (utterance) 1427.

cameraka, (?) cambric 1415; cf. **camaca.**

†**cameram,** f.l. for **causam;** see **traho.**

camesia, see **camisia.**

cam/eu, -eus, see **camahutus.**

camica, see **camaca.**

caminum, see **pergamenum.**

1 *camin/us 1171, 1532, **-um** a 1250, 1386, **-a** 1377, **-ea** c 1190, **cheminus** 1238, **cheminata** 1160, **cheminea** 1223, chimenea 1257, **chimeneya** 1275, 1286, **chiminea** 1237, **chimineus** 1237, **chimineius** 1218, stove, fire-place, chimney; **c. ignis,** chimney-corner 1371; **c. lapideus** 1343, 1472; **-ator,** lover of the fireside a 805; **-o,** to flare up (of slander) c 1180.

2 **caminus** 1220, 1310, **chemin/us (kemin-)** c 1130, c 1300, **-a** 1290, **-um** 1222, 1349, **-ium** c 1250, *chimin/us 1142, 1436, **-um** 1187, 1349, road, highway; **c. altus** a 1216; **c. liber** 1230; **c. regalis** 1275, **c. regis** 1130, 1220; **cheminum viride** c 1221; **chiminium** 1227, 15c., *cheminagium 1185, 1330, *chiminagium 1217, 1436, †chiminihagium, **chiminachium** 1236, †chimnachium c 1260, †chimiagium 1330, 1629, †chimeagium 1549, (payment for) right of way, cart-toll (esp. in forest); **cheminagium liberum** 1231, 1279.

cam/isia (eccl.), **-isa** 1391, **-esia** 12c., 16c., **chemisia** 1206, **-silis** (? **cainsilis**) c 1050, **-issale** 803, **chansia** 1204, underwear, shirt, vest, "smock"; **c. ad equum** 1200; **cainsilum,** fine linen (O.F. chainsil) 1130.

camletum, see **camelettum.**

cammarus, lobster: **gamarus, gamalus** 12c., ‡**gorra** 15c.; ‡**gomerus,** "stickleback" 15c.

camoca, see **camaca.**

camolinum, see **camelettum.**

camomilla, see **chamemelon.**

camoria, a disease of horses c 1109.

camoyseatus, see **camusius.**

camp-, see also **campus.**

campages, see COMPAG

campan/a *6c., 980. c 1135, 1583, **compana** c 1415, bell; bell as appurtenance of commune a 1150, (G.) 1315; clock 1371, 1464; **de -a,** o'clock 1419; **c. manualis,** handbell 1280, 1502; **c. sacramentalis,** sacring bell 1460; **-ella** 1245, c 1520, **-iola** c 1397,

-iculum 1425, -ile c 1330, -ula 1295, 1620, little bell; *-arium 1238, c 1400, *-ile c 1180, c 1608, -ilis 1573, 1577, belfry, bell-tower; -arius 1202, 1508, campenarius 1217, -istarius 1284, 1313, bell-founder; 1229, 1437, -erius 1451, -itor c 1400, bell-ringer; 1502, (?) 1509, †campagerius 1478, -ator (communis) 1435, -ista 1252, bellman, crier.

campestres, a logical mood 13c.

camphor/a c 1215, 1344, caphura c 1605, 1622, ‡cafa 1652, camphor; oleum -atum, sapo -atus (med.) a 1250; see also CANNAB

campipar/s, -tia, see cambipars; campus.

†campologica, f.l. for campo logica, a 1180.

camps-, cams-, see cambium, camisia.

camp/us, *open field (man.) 1086, 1587; field (in mining) 1288, 1322; blank space (in MS.) c 1500; 1235, 1432, (?) -edo 1358, field (in pattern or material); field (her.) c 1400, c 1488; 1313 (G.), c. artus a 1150, c. clausus 1461, champclos, lists; c. remansit cum, victory rested with a 1347; c. apertus, pitched battle a 1142; c. belli, battlefield 1441; c. communis, common field 1553, 1671; c. domini, demesne 1368; c. †Martii, general assembly 12c.; chaumpbluetum, (?) cloth with a blue ground c 1325; -ane, (?) in the country c 1540; -aneus, rural c 550; -ania, 'champion', unenclosed land c 1120, 13c.; -ana (pl.), fields, plains c 1200; -anus, flat, level c 1200; inula -ana, see inula; -ulus, small field, plot c 700, 930; -ernolla 1347, †compernola 1385, †-eriolis (-ernolis) 1385, (?) mushroom or mushroom-shaped ornament; -ester, peasant c 1370, 1461; ‡fieldfare (bird) 15c., 1483; bellum -ale, land war c 1115; 1199, b. -estre 12c., 1461, certamen -estre c 1250, prelium -estre 1136, 1406, open war, pitched battle; terra -estris c 1215, t. -estralis 1378, open (unenclosed) land; see also 1 capella, ecclesia, lectus, porcus, villa; -estriter, in the country 1318; opus -estrinum, field-work, (agricultural) 1365; -idoctor Peripatetice discipline, Aristotle a 1180; -iductor, commander a 1180, 1421; -igena 1225- -io c 1192, 15c., champion; -io regis 1104; *-ipars 1257, 1331, -ipartitio, -iportio c 1240, -ipartura 1270, -ipartus, -ipartum 1247, 1331, -artus (-ertus) a 1142, 1309, -artia, -artaria 1274, †-artagium c 1050, champart, portion of crop, métayage (esp. C.I.); -ipartiens c 1240, -ipartor 1309, métayer (C.I.); -anio, to camp c 1400; -io, to fight as a champion c 1187; †-erto (? -ertito), to exact champart (C.I.) 1324.

camur, see crux.

camus (chamus), muzzle or halter (eccl.).

cam/usius, chamois c 1212; -oyseatus, of chamois leather 1285.

*can/a, -um c 1140, 1608, (?) †conum, †cunum 1396, -agium (†cavagium) 1302, 1357, 'cain', rent in kind (Sc.); see also canna.

can/aba, hut 690; -ava, (?) wine-cellar or kiln 790; cf. cabana; see also CANNAB

†canagium, (?) right to make a fish-trap (Norm.) c 1180; see also cana.

can/ale 1213, 1533, -alis 1267, -ellum, -ellus 1197, 1419, chenella 1279, c 1400, †-eulla 1290, tube, water-pipe, gutter; eucharistic reed 1405; 1461, -ella 1415, c 1422, gun; c. pulmonis, windpipe (med.) a 1250; -aliter, like a water-course c 937; -ill' tegula, drainage tile 1388; -ellatus, refined in a pipe c 1215, ‡15c.; cf. 2 canna.

canalis, see canale, canola.

canamella, see 2 canna.

canap-, canav-, see CANNAB; conopeum.

canardus, big ship (Norw.) a 1142, (Norm.) 1195.

Canaria avis, canary 1544.

†canarthum, "cornu cervinum" (bot.) a 1250.

canathus, see caryota.

canav-, see canaba, CANNAB

cancell/us *c 1172, 1552, *-a c 1264, 1583, -um c 1250, c 1300, cancilla 1289, cansella 13c., ‡15c., -aria 1461, †cacellus 1241, -atura c 1500, chancel; -us, niche 13c.; enclosed space in barn 1352; lattice c 1170, c 1445; ‡oriel of a window 15c.; chink, loop-hole (fig.) 1268; fret (her.) c 1595; per -um, crosswise 1241; -ulus, small cross-beam c 1325; -aria *a 1142, 1421, -ariatus 13c., 1608, chancellorship; *c 1178, 1591, -eria 1224, -i (pl.) c 1125, c 1196, chancery; chancellor in female guise c 1192; -arius* 1062, 1069, 1535, -ator (metri gratia) a 1410, chancellor (royal); *chancellor (eccl.) 1169, 15c.; *chancellor (ac.) c 1214, c 1503; c. de Scaccario 1248, 1526, c. in Scaccario 1265, 1526, c. Scaccarii 1271, 1604; -atim, fretty (her.) 1654; -atio 1205, 1223, -atura c 1258, cancellation; -atio, making the sign of the cross 13c., c 1430; -o, *to cancel, strike out c 1178, 1543; to abolish c 1192, 15c.; to intersect (geom.) c 1361; *to cross (the hands) c 1180, c 1500; to stagger, totter (Fr. chanceler) 13c., a 1446; see also CANTELL

cancer, (?) beam or pillar c 700; 'crab' (for hoisting weights) (?) 14c.

canc/erosus c 1160, c 1385, †cauterosus 1300, -rosus a 1250, cancerous, cankered, gangrenous; -ro, to canker, ulcerate a 1250.

candarides, see cantharides.

candel/a, allowance of candles 12c., 1359; 1252, dies -arum 1090, festum -arum c 1115, -aria 1132, 1508, Candlemas (2 Feb.); c. de assisa 14c.; c. dispensabilis, spensabilis c 1330, c. expensabilis c 1400, c. de cursu 1346, candle in ordinary use; c. nympharum, St. Elmo's fire c 1150; c. Parisiaca 1316, c. Parisiensis 1314, c 1472; c. regia, mullein (bot.) 1634; c. de cepo (for sebo), tallow candle 1288, c 1550; candalabrum for candelabrum, candlestick c 1300, 15c.; -aria 1265, 1399, chandria (Sc.) 1444, 1475, schandria (Sc.) 1495, chandlery; ‡-arium, candlestick 15c.; -arius, (royal) candle-bearer (W.) a 1250; *1270, c 1498, -erius 1330, chaundelarius 1467, -ator 1476, -ifex 1561, chandler, candle-maker.

candescentia, brilliance c 1410.

candi, candy a 1250, 1253; see also sucrum.

candid/atio, whiteness a 1100, 1200; ‡-aria, laundress 1483; ‡-arius, launderer 15c.; parchmenter 1483; -atrix, prostitute c 1200; -atus, novice (eccl.) c 1160, 1537; ‡c. artium, bachelor of arts 1570; c. crucis, crusader c 1595; -us, blanched (of money) 1086; -ulus, white c 950; -ifico c 1090, candifico c 800, to whiten.

candred-, see CANTRED
canell-, see also canale; canis; canola.
*canella, cinnamon 1157, 1593.
canellus, one's own c 550.
canendula, see calendris.
canes, see cano.
canestell/us 1185, 1212, -um c 1266, c 1450, wafer (O.F. chanestel).
canetellum, see CANTRED
caneulla, see canale.
caneus, see caro.
canev-, canib-, see CANNAB
cangium, sort of cloth 1285; see also cambium.
canibar, kind of caper (bot.) a 1250.
canicul-, canillum, see canis; cuniculus.
canill-, see canale; canis; cavilla.
Canini, see Catini.
canipis, see CANNAB
canipulus, see cnipulus.
can/is ad leporem 1199, c. ad ursum 1086, c. ad vulpem 1199, 1203; c. pro cervis 1393; c. currens, coursing hound 1205, 1332; c. marinus, (?) seal 1303; c. pastoralis, sheep-dog a 1300; ‡c. ponticus, "beaver" 15c.; c. pro ripa, retriever (for fowling) 1332; -is, (?) dog-fish c 1200; inter -em et lupum, see inter; -ettus 1290, kenettus 1334, ‡-iculus 15c., 1570, pup, whelp; ‡-icularium 1483, ‡-ile 1570, -illum 1183, -ella c 1380, kenillum 1271, kenilia, kenelina 1283, kenelium 1274, kennel; -icularius, keeper of dogs 893. 12c.; -icularius (adj.) 799, -inalis c 1250, -inus 13c., of or for the dog-days; -icularis a 1250, ‡-iculata 14c., henbane (bot.); -iformis, dog-like c 615; †-inum (? cannum), (?) dog's mercury (bot.) a 1150; -itas (play on caritas), snappishness c 1200; -ino, to snarl c 1180.
canistrum, casket, coffin c 950; c. apum, bee-skep 1170.
canmol/a 1530, firma de cannemol 1322, ale custom (Leicester); curia -ata 1558.
1 canna, can 1229, c 1409.
2 cann/a (can-), arrow c 1200; measure of length, (?) yard (?) 8c. 1265, 1494; ‡c. mellis 14c., -amella c 1125, sugar-cane; c. pulmonis, windpipe a 1250 (cf. canale); -arius, reed-cutter c 1200; -eus, made of a reed c 1200.
*cannab/us, -um 1186, 1461, -ium 1266, 1515, †channum 1283, (?) kanna 1228, can/ibis 1587, -iba (†camba) 1421, -ibum c 1327, -obis, -obum 1213, 1376, -obium 1315, 1328, -ubium 1266, 1460, cambrium 1329, *-apis 1300, 1502, -apus 1331, -ipis c 1298, -opis 1527, (?) †camphora 1297, for -nabis, hemp (or canvas); -aba, -apa, (?) canvas sling (for lifting boat) 9c.; -avazium 1236, -avasium 1523, -avetum c 1312, *-evacium 1207, 1419, †-evacca

1341, -evasium 1312, 1523, -evecium 1219, (?) †-arium c 1300, (piece of) canvas; -nabaria, (?) wild hemp (bot.) a 1250, ‡14c.; -nabeus 1433, 1516, -ubius 1461, c 1500, -ubinus 1438, for -nabinus, hempen, of canvas; -evinum, (?) awning, tilt 1213, 1215; -evacius, canvas-coloured (of a young hawk) 1222; -abizo, to cover with canvas 1323; see also conopeum.
cannocus, see crannocus.
can/o, to recite (of charters, etc.) c 1325, 1417; to be consonant 1483; -es, name of a particular step in a church c 1330; cf. CANT
can/ola 1267, c 1315, -ellum 1263, os -ale 1442, collar-bone.
1 *canon/ (? cano) 1382, 1453, -us a 1396, cannon, gun; 1485, -ator 1388, 1461, cannoneer.
2 canon/ (? cano) c 716, c 860. a 1090, c 1520, -e c 950, -icum 1294, canon, rule, standard (eccl.), canon law; c 1197, 1252, c. misse c 1188, 1523, canon of the mass; canon (astr.) 1267; payment, pension (eccl.) 8c. 1157, 13c.; 1201, c 1452, *-icus 1086, 1565, canon, member of chapter; see also jus, justitia; -icus albus, Premonstratensian c 1220, c 1400; c. claustralis c 1530; c. collegiatus a 1452; c. major 1283, 1441; c. minor 1283, 1558, c. parvus 1320, petty canon; c. niger, Austin canon c 1220; c. prebendarius 12c.; *c. regularis, canon regular (bound by monastic rule) 1199, 1549; c. secularis, canon secular c 1180, 1461; c. residentiarius 1356, 1536, c. stadiarius 1330, c. stagiarius a 1400, canon residentiary; -ia c 1125, 1483, -ica c 1160, 1421, *-icatus (†-itatus) 1109, 1547, canonry, body or house of canons, collegiate church; -ica, canonical book 7c. c 1340, c 1363; *-icalis a 1100, 1546, *-icus c 730, c 900. a 1100, c 1543, canonical; a 1142, *-icus c 1180, c 1310, of or for canons (members of chapter); see also panis; -ice, canonically 670, 765. a 1090, 1583; -issa, canoness (regular) 1310, c 1320; *-ista, canonlawyer 1312, 1608; *-izatio (-is-), canonization (of saint) c 1250, 1487; -ico, to invest with canonical habit or appoint to prebend c 1180, 1215; -ico 1378, -izo c 1310, c 1362, to include in the canon of Scriptures; -izo, to reduce to rules 1622; to authorize by Papal sanction 1200, c 1444; *to canonize (a saint) c 1175, 1461.
canop-, see CANNAB; conopeum.
cans-, see cambium; CANCELL
‡cantacon, garden crocus 1652.
†cantagium, (?) auctioneer's dues (Sc.) c 1250.
cantaredus, see CANTRED
canta/ria, etc., see cantus.
*cantell/us c 1135, c 1356, -um (†cancellum) 1274, -a 14c., cantle, (heaped) measure of grain, etc.; -o, to measure by cantle (G.) 1297.
canter/a, -um 1229, 1390, caunterium 1290, †catellus 1241, †captrenum 1266, ganterium 1312, gantry (for barrels); -a, (?) staithe 1293; ganterium, (?) cart-shaft 1311; -agium, provision of gantries 1328.

cantharides (med.): candarides a 1250.
canther/ius, chevron (her.) 1654; -inus, horse c 1000.
canthus (cantus), rim of wheel, felloe c 1200, 1329; cauntus, (?) rim (of vessel) 14c.; cf. gantus.
canti/culum, etc., see cantus.
cantillagium, chontilagium c 1300, †chensillagium c 1170, payment for right to sell wine, chantelage (Fr.).
canto, canton (her.) 1650; see also cantus.
*cantred/us, -um 1186, c 1437, -a 1200, c 1362, candred/us, -um, -a 1214, 1284, cantaredus c 1190, c 1204, contredus 1205, †canetellum c 1310, division of land, cantred (W. & Ir.).
cant/us curiosus c 1500, c. divisus 1519, c. fractus 1483, 1526, -ifractus 1326, a 1490, c. precatus 1504, prick-song; c. directus 820; c. Gregorianus a 1142, c 1400; c. organicus, (?) song with organ accompaniment 1326, 1467; c. in parte, part-song 1515; c. planus 1434, 1502, c. simplex 1526, plain-song; see also schola;
*-aria c 1192, 1583, -eria 1291, -uaria 1272, 1583, -oria c 1450, chantry; c. magna c 1330; c. parva c 1330, 15c.; c. perpetua 12c., c 1450; -aria 1091, 1440, -oria 1255, c 1444, precentorship; sacerdos -arialis 1498, *-arista 1415, 1588, -ista c 1452, chantry priest; -arista (f.) 1511, 1530, -orissa c 1320, -rix 1279, 1530, precentress; -arius c 1276, -ator c 730, 1245, 1526, -or c 980. a 1090, c 1553, cantor, precentor; -ate, fourth Sunday after Easter c 1300; -atorius, tuneful 1648; †-orius, engaged in singing c 1266; -eloquium, (?) mass-singing, mummery c 1450; ‡-es (pl.), organ pipes c 1440, 1483;
-icum a 1090, 1537, -ata 1377, -ilena 796. a 1100, chant, canticle (eccl.); divine service 12c., 1345; byword c 1240; c. graduum 12c., 15c., c. graduale 12c.; psalm of degrees; -icularium c 1280, -ulare c 1397, book of canticles; -ilena, vernacular song 12c., 1549; -io, method of singing c 730; -o, to chant (eccl.) 841. 1086, 1549; cf. cano; see also canthus.
canub-, see CANNAB
canum, see cana.
Caorcinus, of Cahors, (hence) usurious c 1293; Caursinus, usurer c 1250.
†caorracorum, (?) f.l. for celdr' carbonum, 1345.
cap/a (capp-), *cape, cloak (with hood) 690, 826. c 1160, c 1533; 9c., c 1000. 11c., 1686; copa 1553, *cope (eccl.); c. choralis c 1250, c 1255, c. chori 1260, c 1340, c. de choro c 1203, 1288, cope worn in choir; c. clausa (eccl.) c 1220, c 1325; *c. pluvialis a 1170, 1416, c. ad pluviam, c. pluviarum 1216, c. pluvie a 1300, rain-cloak; c. professionalis c 1363, 1444, c. professionis c 1315, cope given to archbishop by bishop, etc., at his profession; c. puerilis, cope for boy bishop 1398; ‡-ula, little cape 1483; -atio, wearing a cloak 13c.; -atus, cloaked c 1180, c 1330; see also CAPP, dies.
capan-, see cabana.

cap/aro c 1250, -ero 1388, †scapero 1421, (?) -arium 1303, hood.
capasa, see capsa.
capd-, see capital, capitolium.
cape, see capio.
cap/edo, (?) receptacle, sink 1241; ‡c 1440, -ido 7c., space.
capelicium, see cablicium.
1 capell/a, *chapel 796. 1086, 1583; *portable equipment of chapel 1188, 15c.; chancery (esp. Sc.) a 1123, 1366; see also forma, littera; c. ad levamen, chapel of ease 1620; c. campestris, chapel without cemetery c 1115; c. libera 1259, 1550; -ana, female chaplain (mon.) 1299, 1530; *-ania c 1135, 1567, †-ana 1200, -anatus c 1395, 1506, -aria 1138, chaplaincy; -anaria c 1300, -aria 1155, 1315, chapelry; *-anus 803, 893. a 1086, 1583, capillanus 1286, capulanus c 1415, chaplain; (?) fully ordained priest a 1210, 1327; c. cantarie 1430, c. cantarista 1415; c. honoris 1389; c. de Judaismo 1219; c. perpetuus 1454; c. secularis 1235; frater c. (mon.) 1294; -ula, little chapel 13c., c 1540; -ulatus, possessed of a little chapel c 1470.
2 ‡capella, bittern 1570.
3 capell/a *1272, 1417, *-us, -um 1185, c 1450, capilla 1443, hood, hat, cap; -us ferreus 1173, 1321, c. de ferro 1247, 1318, -etum ferreum 1207, 1214; -a c 1275, 1293, -um 1213, 1286, chapelettum 1397, 1401, chaplet, wreath; -a, (?) chimney-hood c 1331; (?) pent-house 1401; -atio, (?) coping (arch.) 1405; -arius 1239, 1419, (?) -ator 1222, hatter, capper; see also chapa.
†cap/ellum, (?) for -itulum, chapter c 1276; domus †-ellaris, (?) chapter-house 15c.
cap/eracius 1208, 1243, -racium 1244, -erettum 1207, 1214, chapericium 1222, sort of cloth; cf. caparo, 2 caputium.
capernum (cipernum), (?) form of sulphur (alch.) c 1215.
caperol/us, -inus, see CAPR
cap/esco, for -esso, to seize 1274, c 1434.
capestrum, see capister.
†capeta, f.l. for tapeta, 1353.
capetium, see 2 caputium.
†capha, (?) for casa or castrum, 1362.
caphe, coffee 1622.
caphicesium, see capitegium.
caphnius, see coffinus.
caphura, see camphora.
capias, see capio.
capicer/ia, treasury 1159; -ius 1086, 1234, -us 1376, treasurer, sacristan (Fr. chevecier).
capicoperinum, (?) kerchief 1242.
capido, see capedo.
capil-, see also CAPELL
†capilla, piece of land, (?) headland 1557.
capill/ositas, hairy appearance (of urine) a 1250; -osus, hairy c 700; ‡-are, hair-net 1570; vena -aris a 1250, c 1361, venula -aris 1210, capillary vein; see also herba.
capilupus, wolf-catcher c 1620.
capio, *to receive, exact (payments) 1086, 1439; *to seize, arrest 1086, c 1441; to take, hunt (beasts of chase) 1086, 1374; to take (chessman) c 1280, c 1346; to take as prise, for use of king 1230, 1267; *to hold (court

or inquiry) 1217, 1583; to cause a 1250; to take, understand (in a particular sense) a 1413, c 1444; to hold good c 1178; to strike root, become established c 1180; ***c. ad** 1208, c 1330, **c. me ad** 1201, c 1324, **c. contra** c 1373, to proceed against; **c. me ad,** to have recourse to c 1258; **c. ad cor,** to take to heart c 1396; **c. ad partem,** to practise champerty 1293; **c. aerem,** to take the air c 1343, c 1365; **c. arma,** to receive the order of knighthood 1277; **c. campum,** to take the field (in war) 1413; **c. crucem,** see **crux; c. curam de,** to take care of 1217, 1254; **c. cursum,** to be current (of money) 1355; **c. diem,** to fix a date 1242, 1256; **c. dilationem,** to suffer delay 1230, 1275; **c. finem,** to come to an end c 1298, 1301; **c. fugam,** to take flight 1290; **c. gradus,** to take a degree (ac.) c 1396; **c. hominem,** to take as vassal c 1400; **c. in manum** c 1185, 1334, **c. ad manum** c 1279, c 1307, to take (land, *etc.*) into the lord's possession; **c. in manu** 1142, c 1210, **c. in manum** 1200, 1225, to undertake; **c. justiciam,** to administer justice 1086; **c. licentiam,** to take leave, bid farewell 1266, p 1330; **c. mensuram, c. quantitatem,** to measure 1476; **c. navim,** to take ship 1471; **c. ordinem,** to give an order 1556; **c. per scapulas,** to seize by the scruff 1554, 1567; **c. pro malo,** to take amiss c 1391; **c. sacramentum,** to take an oath c 1390; **c. sanctuarium,** to take sanctuary a 1564; **c. super,** to capture or seize from 1219, c 1400; **c. supra me,** to undertake 1233; ***c. treugas,** to arrange a truce 1217, 15c.; **c. vindictam (super),** to take vengeance 1228, c 1362; **c. virum,** to take as husband 1221, 1296; **cape,** name of a writ 1202, 1419; **c. magnum, c. parvum** 1202, c 1290; **capias,** name of a writ 1367, 1469; *cf.* **captio.**

capist/er 1205, 1311, **-ra** 1356, †**-re** 1415, **capestrum** a 1300, 1467, **capustrum** 1250, 1381, **chevestrum** 1264, **capiterum** 1360, *for* **-rum,** halter; **-rum,** wood supporting floor-board (Fr. *chevêtre*) 1313; ‡**c. auri,** borax (alch.) 1652; **-ralis,** serving as a halter c 1115; ‡**-rius,** maker of halters 15.; **-ro,** to halter, *or* break in 1306, 1315; to adapt for use as halter c 1193.

‡**capita,** dace (fish) 15c.

capitagi/um 1219, 1353, **chevagium** 1251, 1286, head-penny, chevage, paid by suitors at view of frankpledge or law-hundred; 1378, 1460, **chevagium** c 1258, 1426, **chivagium** 1401, **chyvachium** 1399, payment by villein for leave to reside outside manor; 1236, 1247, **chevagium** 1254, 1300, **chivagium** c 1335, 1349, royal offering at shrine; **chevagium** 1199, c 1290, **chewagium** a 1128, customary payment of uncertain nature; poll-tax paid by Jews 1277, 1280; payment to Hospitallers for confraternity 1275; **c. garcionum** 1270, 1353, **c. (-um) anlepimannorum (de hanelepimen)** 1270, 1306, **-um liberum** 1340, customary payments (man.); **-arius** 1309, 1342, **chevagiarius** 1350, tenant paying chevage.

capital/, -e, pillow (?) c 1080, c 1330, 1417;

‡headstall 1570; headland (in field) 1182; head (of garlic) a 1300; mortal sin 12c.; *see also* **capitellum, catallum; -is,** (*adj.*) of the head c 1250; at the end or top c 1266, 1348; **terra -is** 1240, **t. captalis** 1355, headland; *see also* **acra, brasium, corda, curia, debitor, denarius, dominus, littera, manerium, messuagium, placitum, redditus, selio, signum; -is,** (*subst.*) headborough c 1130; capital letter c 1503; c 1290, 1313, **capdellus** c 1242, 1278, **cabdellus** 1243, chief judge, *chaptal* (G.); **c. feodi,** tenant-in-chief c 1225; **-iter,** principally c 1376, c 1380.

capitan/eus, (*adj.*) principal 1271, p 1327; (*subst.*) *a 1142, 1608, **-us** 1311, captain, leader; governor 1308, 15c.; captain (naut.) 1444, 1484; chieftain (Ir.) 1350, c 1376; ***c. castri** (Sc.) 1432, c 1540; **c. civitatis** (Ital.) 1288; **c. generalis** c 1250; **c. itineris,** chief of the eyre c 1321; **c. Kancie,** Jack Cade 1451; **c. ville** (Norm.) 1374, 1417; **-ea** 1449, c 1450, **-eatus** 1558, captaincy; **-ee,** as a captain 1378.

capit/atio, fitting (arrows, *etc.*) with heads 1377, 1387; fitting (plough) with a head 1323, 1350; **-atus,** fitted with a head 1399; having a chief (her.) a 1449; **-o** 1267, 1361, **caputo** 1269, to fit (plough) with a head; to head, serve as a head to c 1380; to behead 1225, c 1370; (?) to be imported 1392; to extend c 1353, 1460; **c. ad** c 1230, 1325, **c. super** 13c., 1359, **c. versus** c 1380, to abut on.

capi/tegium c 1266, c 1451, †**-tergium** 1351, †**caphicesium** c 1200, night-cap.

capit/ellum (bibl.), **-ale** 12c., c 1430, **chapitrallum** 1293, **chepitrum** 1253, capital of a column; hood 1393; flower-head 1342, ‡14c.; lye a 1250, 13c.; *see also* **capitolium, capitulum.**

cap/itennium, -tennium, payment for royal protection (G. *captenh*) 1312.

†**capitense,** *f.l.* for **caput,** 1295.

capi/terra 1321, **-terum** 1315, headland (in field); *see also* **capister.**

capitium, *see* **caputium** (1 & 2).

capito, *see* **capitatio.**

cap/itolium, -dolium, fort, castle (G.) 1289; guild-hall c 1500; †**-itellum,** capitol, citadel c 1188, 15c.; *see also* **capitulum.**

capitos/itas, headstrong character, obstinacy 13c., 15c.; ***-us,** headstrong, arbitrary 1252, a 1566; **-e,** rashly, arbitrarily 1384, 1461.

capitul/um, *chapter, article (in document or inquiry) 6c., c 870. a 1090, c 1470; *6c., 7c. a 1090, 1565, **capitolium** 1147, c 1160, chapter, chapter meeting, chapter-house (eccl.); right of confraternity (mon.) c 1266, c 1330; **c. (placitorum) corone** 1194, c 1320, **c. itineris** 1324, article of royal eyre or inquiry; **c. culparum** c 1451, **c. servientium** c 1266, chapter meeting for correction of faults; **c. generale,** chapter general 1219, c 1341; **c. provinciale** c 1250, 1506; **c. rurale** 1279; **-ar(e)** 786. c 1300, 1425, **-arium** 1245, 15c., **capitellarium** 1236, capitulary, chapter-book; **-aris,** (*adj.*) capitular, of or for a chapter (eccl.) c 1192, 1559; *see also* **domus,**

littera; (*subst.*) member of a chapter 1276;
-ariter, in chapter (eccl.) 1396, 1565; in
accordance with the rules of a chapter 1310,
1559; 1380, -atim 790. 12c., a 1519, by
chapter and verse; -atio, capitulation,
agreement 1482; -o, to capitulate, agree
1480; to be a member of a chapter 1382.
cap/licium, -leicium, *see* cablicium.
cap/o, capon: -ona 1389, caupo 13c., 1459;
‡-unculus, "caponet" 1570.
Capotensis, *see* Chipotensis.
capp/a (cap-) (?) 1390, c 1400, -us 1381,
1419, cap; 1397, 1477, c. honoris 1470,
1586, cap of honour (of duke or marquis);
c. ferrea 1451; -a 1219, ‡1483, ‡-ilegium
15c., cap (band) of flail; cap, head (of bird-
bolt) 1348; iron cap of plough-harness 1307,
1414; c. ad herciam 1310; c. fontium,
font-cover 1297, ‡-o, to cap 1483; *see also*
capa; *cf.* 3 capella.
cappar/us, *for* -is, caper-bush c 1070; ‡alcu-
far, caper (Ar.) 14c.
capr/a, harlot ‡13c., (?) 1290; 1265, c.
marina 1267, 1305, goat-fish; †-ata 1419,
-is c 1275, she-goat; ‡-icornus, "unicorn"
1483; -ifolium, honeysuckle a 1250, 1538;
-inus, of goat's milk c 1067; angulus
-inus, corner of eye a 1250 (*cf.* 2 hircus);
-illus (G.) 1289, -iolus a 1245, 1334,
(?) cheverillus 1231, kid; -eola (-iola)
c 1090, 1354, cheverella 1293, doe;
*-eolus (-iolus) 1086, 1378, †caperolus
c 1230, -eus 12c., cheverellus c 1200,
1298, chiverallus 1281, cheverillus 1334,
chevro 1209, roe-buck; cheverellus, kid-
skin 1472; -eolus, chevron (her.) 1654 (*cf.*
capro); canis -eolarius, roe-hound 1213;
caro -eolina c 1180, a 1250, c. †caperolina
15c., roe flesh; nasus -izans, flattened nose
13c.; -iso, to behave like a goat c 1177.
capracium, *see* caperacius.
†capricium, (?) *for* caputium, 1244; *cf. also*
caperacius.
capro 1245, *chever/o 1203, 1336, -onus
1245, 1294, -ennus 1291, -ingus 1208,
kevero 1205, 1233, cheviro 1462, chivero
1276, chiverellus 1286, bent piece of wood,
rafter; -o, (?) sapling 1243; -nus, chevron
(her.) 1586.
caps/a 790. c 1090, 1528, -is c 1255, c 1325,
-ella 12c., 1493, -ula 1200, c 1528, reliquary; -ella 690, 10c., -ellula 690, -ile
c 1255, small box, casket; †capasa 1309,
capcia 1406, †scapsa 1295, *for* -a, case,
box; -ulator, cabinet-maker 1703, 1710;
cf. 1 cassa.
capsaces, wallet (*cf.* καμψάκης) c 950.
†capsilide (*pl.*), persons of defective eye-
sight 1180.
capsoldium, fee paid to money-changer (G.)
1289.
capstenagium, hoisting dues 1606.
capsula, *see* capsa; 1 casula.
captagium, payment on change of lord (G.)
1312; *cf.* ACCAP
captale, *see* catallum.
captalis, *see* capital.
capt/atio, taking heed or advantage 1378;
-anter, greedily c 1293; -atrix, winner (*f.*)
1345.

captennium, *see* capitennium.
capt/io, *capture, seizure, arrest 1086, p 1464;
prisoners (*coll.*) 1220; taking, catching (of
game, *etc.*) c 1192, 1281; removal, transport
1269, c 1530; distraint c 1115; payment
received 1391; taking on lease, renting 1366,
1378; (right of) exaction c 1219, c 1448; 'cap-
tion', prise, right to buy at special price
c 1235, 1266; mainprise, bail 1274; holding
(of court or inquiry) 1219, c 1508; c. in
manum 1284, 1335, c. in manu 1348,
taking (of land, *etc.*) into lord's possession;
c. treugarum, conclusion of truce 1234,
c 1325; *-ivatio, capture, arrest c 1250,
c 1470; -ivitas, the Babylonian captivity
12c.; persons or things seized (*coll.*) 12c.,
1446; -ive, in captivity 1343; -ivus, poor
wretch (*cf.* Fr. *chétif*) c 1250; -or a 1090,
c 1520, -ivator c 1180, a 1400, captor;
exactor (of dues) 1248, c 1448; 'taker' (of
wine *etc.*, as royal prise) 1246, 1268; c.
cervisie, "ale-taker" c 1472; c. operariorum 1354; -ura, capture, arrest 5c. 1159,
c 1470; c. piscium 7c., 740. 12c.; -urarius,
keeper of fisheries 7c.; *-ivo a 1090, c 1540,
†-ito 1421, to capture, arrest; *cf.* capio.
captrenum, *see* cantera.
capud, *see* caput.
capudicium, capuc-, *see* caputium (1 & 2).
capul-, *see also* cablicium; capa; 1 capella;
scapula.
capul/atio, mutilation 1171; -o, to mutilate,
cut off c 1204; ‡to poll (a tree) c 1440; *cf.*
scapulatio.
capunculus, *see* capo.
‡capus, musket (hawk) c 1180, 1483.
capustrum, *see* CAPIST
cap/ut c 1184, c 1492, †caapa a 1185, headland (in field); headland, cape c 1436; part
of cannon 1384; headpiece (of armour)
1368; hood 1223, 1413; measure of cloth
1230, 1284; measure of figs 1447; ‡cabbage
15c.; zenith (astr.) c 1200; upper half of
shield, chief (her.) p 1394, a 1446; *-ud *for*
-ut a 1183, 1417; ad -ut, at the end (of a
period of time) (O.F. *a chef*) (G.) c 1220;
a -ite usque ad caudam 1570, a c. ad
pedes 1537, universally, thoroughly ; ex
(proprio) -ite, of one's own accord or
invention 1342, 1455; ex hoc -ite, on this
account c 1450; in -ite, *in chief (of
tenure) a 1120, 1572; chiefly c 1305; -ut
abbatie 1086, *c. baronie c 1188, c 1290,
c. honoris 1086, c 1224 (with reference to
manor); c. curie a 1183, 1189; c. anguli,
corner-stone (fig.) c 1320, c 1470; c. anni,
new year 12c., c 1283; c. aqueductus 1433;
c. carruce, 'plough-head', share-beam
c 1315; c. collegii, head of college (ac.)
c 1412, 1623; c. dolii, top of cask 1335;
c. domicelle, 'maidenhead', ornament
of the Virgin's head 1393; c. draconis,
ascending node of moon's orbit with
ecliptic 1120, c 1200; c. ecclesie c 1185,
1431, c. capelle c 1502, apse; c. jejunii
c 1150, c 1565, c. Quadragesime c 1200,
c 1450, Ash Wednesday; ‡c. leonis (bot.)
14c.; c. lupinum, *see* 1 lupus; c. manerii,
capital messuage 1086; c. molendini
1325, 1473, c. stagni 1269, 1497, c.

vivarii c 1268, c 1400, mill-dam, weir, sluice; **c. monachi**, dandelion ‡14c., 1629; ‡**c. mortuum**, *"terra mortua"* (alch.) 1652; **c. placiti**, beginning of plea c 1115; **c. porci**, hogshead, cask 1407, 1417; **c.** (†-itense, †-tense) **ad quarellum** 1295; **c. spatule** (med.) a 1250; **c. thethinge**, headborough 1221; **c. Veneris aut Saturni**, (?) brazen head used in divination 1344; **c. ville**, town's end 1221, 1287; *see also* capit-

1 **cap/utium** c 1230, 1284, **-uca** 1276, **-itium** 1230, 1284, **-udicium** 13c., **kevescium** c 1200, *****chev/icium** 1287, 1315, **-iscium** c 1290, **-isium** 1359, **-ecium** c 1280, 14c., (?) †**thenecium** 1305, **-escium** c 1200, 1316, **-esium** 1279, **-essa** 13c., 1291, **-etta** a 1200, 1372, **-eseia** 13c., **-acia** 14c., †**chavesea** 12c., **kevescia** a 1192, **-agium** 1372, headland (in open field).

2 **cap/utium** *****a 1090, 1533, **-itium** 802. a 1090, c 1565, **-etium** 1364, c 1400, †-**itum** 1343, 1346, **-uscium** c 1299, **-ucinum** c 1353, hood, cowl; "collar" 1393; **-itium** 1354, **-uta** 1279, hood (falc.); **-itium ecclesie**, chevet, apse c 1213; **-utiorum secta**, *Caputiati* (sect founded in Auvergne) c 1200; **-utiatus**, Lollard c 1400, 15c.; hooded 1402, 15c.; **-utio**, to hood c 1350.

caputpurgium a 1250, **catapurgium** 14c., medicine for clearing the head.

caraba, *see* CAROB

carabia, *see* **caracta**.

carabre, *see* **cacabre**.

carabus, coracle 8c. c 1100, c 1385.

carac/a, **-ata**, *see* **carraca**.

caracalla, vestment, cope (eccl.) c 730, 8c. c 1250, 15c.

car/acta, **-actum** 1438, 1608, **-ata** 1344, c 1350, **-ectes** 1267, **-abia** 13c., carat, weight of gold.

caracter, *see* **cataracta**; **character**.

car/agium, **-aio**, **-ator**, *see* 1 **carra**.

caragius, diviner, geomancer 8c.

caravan-, *see* **carvanna**.

caravella, *see* **carvella**.

carax-, *see* CHARAX

carba, *see* **garba**.

carbana, *see* **corbana**.

car/basa, sails: **-bosa** 15c.; **-pasitus**, made of linen 1415.

carb/o, coal (*not* charcoal) 1278, 1534; **scarbo**, *for* **-o**, charcoal 8c.; **-ones** (*pl.*), coal-cellar 1351; coal-pit 1376; **-o adustus** 1498, **c. de busca** 1279, **c. ligneus** 1334, 1504, **c. silvester** 1398, 1545, **c. de sicco** 1315, charcoal; **c. more**, peat charcoal a 1307; **c. fossilis** 1586, ‡**c. lapideus** 1652, **c. maris** 1236, 1317, **c. marinus** 1266, 1399, **c. maritimus** 1300, 1573, **c. subterraneus** c 1357, **c. subterrenus** 1499, **c. de terra** 1240, **c. terre** 1305, **c. terrestris** c 1340, 1496, **c. terreus** 1306, sea-coal, pit-coal; **-onaria**, **-onarium** (?) a 1200, 1555, **-onera** (subterranea) 1301, **-ocidium** 1487, 1504, **-ifodinum** 1305, **-ofodina** 1506, 1528, **-onifodina** 1608, **puteus -onalis** 1417, coal-mine; **-onaria**, (?) charcoal pit 1261; **-onagium**, right to burn charcoal 1203;

-onarius, coal-miner 1376, 1534; **-unarius** 1172, **-onator** 1234, c 1250, *for* **-onarius**, charcoal-burner; ‡**-onella**, "collop", fried rasher 15c.; **-onificus**, charcoal-making c 1325; **-unculus**, escarbuncle (her.) c 1595; **-onizatio** (**humorum**) blackening (med.) a 1250; **-ono**, to make charcoal (of) a 1250, 1305.

carbona, *see* **corbana**.

carbosa, *see* **carbasa**.

‡**carbuta**, laden ship 1483.

carc/a 1198, 1486, **-um** 1417, **carqua** 1434, **chargia** 1219, 13c., load, cargo; **chargea**, measure of salt 1317; **cargia** 1201, **karkia** 1207, toll; **-um forinsecum**, foreign charge (man.) 1306; **c. vicecomitis**, sheriff's charge 1292; **-agium** (†**carta-gium**), (payment for) loading 1221, 1353; *see also* **carcasium**, **carrucagium**; †**-an-nicum** (? **-amentum**), charge (of debt) 1360; **-atio**, loading 1212, 1418; *****-o** (†**carto**) 1166, 1444, **chargio** c 1190, 1355, **charchio** 1222, 1355, to load (on cart or ship); **-o me**, to take on a load 1312; **-o**, to charge, debit 1232, 1334; to inculpate 1292; to charge, instruct (jury) c 1240, 1366; **c. sacramentum**, to administer oath c 1240; *see also* **careca**, 1 **carra**.

carcan/a 1245, **-um** c 1115, **-eum** 1254, c 1290, iron collar, pillory.

carc/asium, **-asius** 1284, 1386, **-agium** (Sc.) 1266, 1462, **skarcasium** 1350, *****-osium** 1199, c 1380, †**cascoseum** 1403, **-osia** 1390, †**-osus** 1275, **-osum** c 1291, c 1380, **-oisus** 1241, c 1397, **corcosium** 1268, carcass; *cf.* 2 **cassa**.

carcellus, *see* **cercella**.

carcer/ (*f.*), prison 8 c.; **c. liber**, (?) free custody 1258; **-ia publica**, common gaol (G.) 1315; **stridor -alis** (*coll.*), fetters 14c.; **tenebre -ales** 760; **-aliter**, in prison 1382; **-atio**, imprisonment c 1325, 15c.; **-ator**, gaoler 1317; **-o**, to imprison c 1218, 1535.

carcin/ea, *for* **-oma**, cancer c 1160.

carcuca, *see* 2 **carruca**.

carculo, *see* **sarculatio**.

carculum, *see* **cartallum**.

1 **card/a** 1293, 1378, **-um** 1252, **-eum** 1292, sort of muslin; Franciscan robe 1245; (?) curtain 1275; **c. campane**, (?) bell-cover c 1295; *see also* 1 **carta**.

2 **carda** 1275, **garda** 1291, a 1564, impurity in wool, (?) piece of teasel, *etc.*, used for carding; *cf.* 1 **cardo**.

cardeborda, *see* 1 **carta**.

cardetum, *see* 1 **cardo**.

cardi/a c 1180, ‡**-a** 15c., ‡**-aca** c 1440, "cardiacle", heartburn; †**-tus**, *for* **-acus**, cardiac c 1290; **-an** (*n.*), heart c 990.

*****cardinal/is** c 1125, 1570, **cardineus** (*metri gratia*) c 1562, a cardinal (eccl.); *see also* **archipresbyter**, **diaconus**, **episcopus**, **presbyter**; 1534, **c. chori** 1254, 16c., canon in charge of choir; *****-atus** 1278, 1528, **-itas** c 1388, office of cardinal; **-eus** 1525, 1535, **-icius** 1546, 16c., of a cardinal.

cardiolus, snipe (bird) c 1220.

cardi/um, **-narius**, *see* GARDIN

1 **card/o** c 1190, 1419, **-us** c 1210, teasel,

thistle; **c. benedictus** a 1250, **-uus bene-dictus** ‡14c., 1622, **-uncellus** a 1250, 1634, groundsel (bot.); ‡**-inarius**, teaseler 15c.; **-etum**, thistle-patch 1252.

2 cardo, "threshold" 1482.

care-, *see also* **1 carra.**

†**careca,** (?) *for* **carca**, load a 1131.

carect-, *see* **caracta; caretta.**

carellus, *see* **quarellus.**

‡**carena,** one-twentieth of a drop 1652.

carent/ena, -ela, *see* **quadragena** (1 & 2).

*****carentia,** lack, want a 1180, 1461.

carentivill/a 1265, 1431, **-um** c 1200, c 1451, canvas.

carenum, sweet wine 685, c 1000.

carenutus, *see* **carifotus.**

carera, *see* **2 carruca.**

carestia, *see* **caristia.**

*****carett/a** (**carect-, charett-**) c 1150, 1457, **-us** 1346, †**caroca** a 1221, **charietta, chariota** 1388, **chariettum** c 1412, 1431, **chariota** 1367, **chariotum** c 1360, (small) cart; **c. aquatica,** water-cart p 1340; **c. curta** 1311, 1330; **c. longa** c 1243, 1388; **c. manualis,** hand-cart 1364; **c. ferrata** 1209, 1221, **c. ferro ligata** 1378, cart with iron tires; **c. nuda,** cart with unbound wheels 1388, 1486; *****-a** 1086, c 1533, *****-ata** c 1155, 1583, **-atum** 1303, 1504, **-edis** 1086, **carritata** c 1266, †**carrucata** c 1323, c 1450, cart-load; **-ata plumbi** 1172, 1180; ‡**-area,** cart-house 1483; ‡**-areus,** cart-wright 1483; *****-arius** c 1136, c 1483, **chariettarius** 1359, **-ator** 1191, **-or** 1242, 1515, †**-us** 1396, carter; **-arius** 1155, 1299, **equus -arius** 1155, 1421, **e. caractarius** c 1340, **e. -erius** 13c., **e. -ivus** 1410, c 1485, cart-horse; **opus -arium,** cartage service (man.) 1297; **via -aria** 1269, **v. -ata** 1467, cart-road; **domus -iva,** cart-house c 1300; *see also* **sella; -eia** c 1300, **-ea** 1212, cartage service; **-illa, -illum** 1215, 1369, †**kietillum** (? **kerietillum**) 1214, **cartillum** 1294, 1345, cart-body; *see also* **1 carra, 2 carta, garita.**

†**car/etus,** (?) *for* **-ex,** sedge 943; **-ictum,** sedge-bed a 1250.

carg-, *see* **carca.**

cari-, *see also* CARR

†**caricum,** (?) *f.l.* for **cericum** (*i.e.* **sericum**), c 1397.

‡**car/ifotus,** †**-enutus,** "cockney", milksop c 1440.

carinula, little boat c 1170, 1334.

cariola, *see* **caryota.**

cariscea, *see* **carsea.**

*****car/istia** 1234, 16c., **-estia** 1461, **-isties, -ities** c 1293, **-itudo** 1234, c 1365, dearth or dearness; **ad -ius,** at the dearest 12c.; **-istio, -isto** 1419, **-io** 1287, **-ioro** 1287, to enhance prices.

carit/as (**charit-**), *****charity (Christian virtue) c 793. c 1090, 1549; grace (title) c 730, c 800. c 1140, c 1462; *****allowance, measure of food or drink (mon.) 980. a 1090, 1344; name of a religious order 1305; **c. S. Petri,** customary payment (Peterborough) a 1128; **de -ate,** as a favour 1086, c 1130; **in -ate,** in grace (theol.) c 1343; **opera** (*pl.*) **-atis** 12c., 1361; **-arie** 1526, **-ative** 9c., c 1000.

a 1100, 1549, out of charity, charitably; **-ans** 1587, *****-ativus** 8c., 9c. c 1070, c 1530, †**charativus** 1539, charitable, affectionate.

carium, *see* **carui.**

carlanda, *see* **garlanda.**

carlina, ground thistle 1632.

car/linus, *see* **carolinus.**

*****Carmel/ita** 1283, 1586, **-anus** c 1250, **-inus** a 1309, **-itanus** 1358, 1461, **-itis** 1358, †**-us** 1303, **Carmalita** 1468, 1488, **Carmilita** 1490, Carmelite (*subst.* or *adj.*); **frater de -o** 1256, c 1366, **f. de Monte -o** 1255, **f. (ordinis B. Marie) de M. -i** 1245, c 1330.

carmellus (**k-**), hornbeam (Fr. *charme*) 1268.

carm/en, charter 867; **-iger,** versifier 790; **-inale,** song, singing c 690; **-inatio,** enchantment 13c., 1344; **-ino,** to set forth in verse 685; to enchant c 1180, 1344.

‡**carmentum,** fluff 1570.

†**carmerum,** (?) *for* **calamarium,** reed-bed c 1300.

carm/osinus, -usinum, *see* CRIM

carn-, *see also* **caro.**

1 carnell/us 1242, c 1414, **quarnellus** 1288, *****kernellus** 1227, 1414, **kernillus** 1356, **kirnellus** 1297, 1299, **cornelus** 1336, **curnellus** 1312, **carnalis** 1445, **cranellus** (G.) 1304, crenel, battlement; **-atio,** *****-o** 1205, 1491, *****kernello** 1193, 1460, **karnalo** 1271, **karnollo** c 1244, **kirnello** 1398, 1422, to crenellate.

2 carnellus (**karn-**) 1246, **kernellus** 1221, slice, gobbet (of whale meat).

†**carnillus,** (?) *for* **camillus,** attendant 13c.

carnoc-, *see* **crannocus.**

caro, flesh, mortality (eccl.); **c. (Christi),** Eucharist 1245, 13c.; *see also* **annus, dies; in carn/e** c 1250, c 1400; **in c. et osse** 1287; **secundum -em** c 1250, c 1444; **-is debitum solvo** c 1342, **c. d. exsolvo** 1338, **c. tributum solvo** c 1300, c 1327, to die; *see also* **via; in -e, versus -em,** on the side of the parchment next to the flesh 1235; **-acus,** fleshly, bodily c 550; **-alis,** consisting of flesh c 550; in the flesh 890. c 1125, c 1536; *****worldly, given to carnal pleasures 7c., 8c. c 1125, 1461; *see also* **1 carnellus; -alitas,** worldliness, fleshly lust 1223, 1570; **-aliter,** after the flesh 7c., 760. c 1180, 1430; in a worldly manner a 1090, 1324; **-aria** 1409, **-arium** c 1300, 1455, **charnellaria** 1398, **charnellum** 1458, 1471, charnel-house, charnel-chapel; **-ator** 1351, 1413, **caronator** 1356, **corona-tor** 1342, 1572, inspector of carcasses (*cf.* CRON); *****-eus** (†**caneus**), of the flesh c 550, 793. c 1197, c 1536; **-ifer,** having flesh upon it c 550; **-ifex** c 550. 12c., c 1450, **-ificus** 1437, butcher; **-ificus,** homicidal 800; **-ificium,** butchery c 1160; meat market, shambles c 1190, c 1506; **-ilevaria** Shrove Tuesday c 1190; *****-iprivium** c 1198, 1532, †**-ipricium** 1321, *****-isprivium** c 1182, 1476, ‡**-ibrevium** 15c., **-isbrevium** 1461, beginning of Lent (sometimes applied to Septuagesima or Sexagesima Sunday); *cf.* **privicarnium; -ivorax,** carnivorous 1515; **-ositas,** fleshiness, fleshy part a 1250, 1620.

carob/la c 1260, ‡**-ia** 14c., (?) **caraba** a 1250, carob (bot.).

carocata, *see* 2 carruca.
carogium, *see* 1 carruca.
carol/a, ring, circle 1295, c 1331; assembly (at Bruges) c 1300; *c 1266, c 1509, -us 1424, 1524, carula 1327, c 1330, 'carol', study in cloisters (*cf.* barelus); carulum, (?) ring-fence 1271; -o, to dance in a ring c 1200, p 1330.
car/olinus (florenus) 1555, -linus c 1321, carlin (Sicilian coin).
caronator, *see* caro.
carpa, *see* carpitura; carpine.
carpasitus, *see* carbasa.
carpella, saddle-bow c 1225.
carp/entaria *1158, 1532, -enteria 1295, -entria 1246, 1446, -intaria, -intria 1332, -entura 1419, -entatio 1227, 1317, carpentry; -entaria, office of carpenter 1219; carpenter's yard 1336; -enteria, service of carpenter 1212; opus -entarinum c 1456; ars -entaria 16c., c 1553, a. -entoria 13c.; *-entarius 1080, 1528, -enterius 1196, 1396, -intarius 1332, c 1455, -untarius 1199, 1221, -entator c 1250, 16c., -entor 1266, 1459, -untor 1296, carpenter; -ento 1232, 1400, †-o c 1390, to shape (wood).
carpet/a c 1524, -um c 1521, -us 1456, carpet.
carpi/a, ‡tinder 14c.; a 1250, -ta 1328 (piece of) lint.
carp/ine (*pl.*) 1515, 1516, -e 1483, game, (?) dice.
carpio, carp (fish) 1622.
carp/itura (lane), teasing, carding 1285; -inatio lini a 1250; ‡-onarius 1483, ‡-trix 15c., 1483, carder; -a 1390, ‡-tarium 1483, card(wool-comb); ‡-tarius, card-maker 15c., 1483; -ino a 1250, ‡-to 15c., *for* -o, to card.
carpo/balsamum, fruit of balsam tree c 1212, ‡14c.; -careos, (?) caraway seed a 1250, ‡14c.; ‡-scissus, *for* -cissus, ivy berry 14c.
carpunt-, *see* carpentaria.
carqua, *see* carca.
1 *carr/a (car-, kar-, charr-) 785, 9c. 1185, 1504, -is 1363, -ea 1293, -aba c 1000, *for* -us, cart; -us manualis, hand-cart 1289, 1291; -a, (?) dinner wagon, trolley (mon.) c 1330; via -aria, cart road c 1216; -eria 1276, 1315, quareria 1316, street (G.); -eriola, lane (G.) 1289; -earius, carter c 1283; -ata, -atum, -atus 790, 805. c 1155, c 1533, -atis 1185, -iata, -eata c 1185, c 1350, -iatis c 1247, †carcata 1331, 1336, †-uca c 1272, -ea 1182, c 1300, †kaira 1334, cart-load; c. ad duos boves c 1180; -a 1321, *-ata 1220, 1336, -eata a 1128, 1222, -ea 1213, 1259, -eia 1181, 1290, -us c 1290, a 1307, carr' aquatica 1323, measure (cart-load) of lead;
-eium c 1160, 1334, -ieta, -ietum 1222, -etum c 1180, -opera (*pl.*) 1660, -agium c 1170, 1555, *-iagium c 1160, 1608, carrying-service or toll on carts; -agium 1177, 1333, *-iagium, -eagium 1180, c 1494, †-igiagium 1178, carriage, transport; -iagium, cart, means of transport 1240, 1419; capacity, burthen (naut.) 1325; (?) baggage 1397; -iagius c 1540, -igiamannus c 1365, -iator a 1271, 1378,

carator a 1128, carter, carrier; *-iatio, carriage, carrying a 1200, a 1452; *-io 1086, 1583, -aio 1200, -ico 1086, 1166, -uco a 1128, 1205, -ego (G.) 1254, -igo c 1185, to carry, convey; -ico 8c. 1234, 1470, -io 1287, 1324, to load; *see also* carca, caretta, carraca, 2 carruca, 2 carta.
2 carra c 1200, 1272, -um a 1185, c 1240, kerra c 1190, 1419, keira 1301, 'carr', swamp (N.Eng.).
carr/aca 1416, c 1460, †-a 15c., -ica 1421, †-uca c 1450, -acata 1547, carrack (ship); *cf.* tarita.
carrelis, *see* quarellus.
carrera, *see* tarrera.
1 carr/uca 1236, -ochium c 1250, carogium 1229, (car bearing) imperial standard.
2 *carr/uca (car-) 1086, p 1478, -ua 1250, †-us c 1260, †carcuca 1249, (?) -era 1348, quadruga c 1150, plough or plough-team; plough or team as unit for tax assessment 1086, c 1350; c. boum 1208, 1242, -ucata boum 1182, 1242; c. dimidia, half the service of a plough 1086, 1225; c. estivalis, summer plough 1302, 1344; c. hiemalis, winter plough 1325; c. juncta 1242, 1261, -ucata juncta 1243, plough with team; c. iens, working plough 1415; c. consuetudinaria, plough of customary tenant c 1255; c. dominica, demesne plough 1086, 1224; c. pedalis, foot-plough 1352; c. rotabilis, wheeled plough 1352; -ucagium 1198, 1331, -uagium 1199, c 1308, -ugagium 1200, 1237, -uaticum (G.) 1291, kariagium 1224, †carcagium 1228, carrucage, tax on ploughland; -ucarius, (*adj.*) 1244, 1411, -alis 14c., of or for a plough; *(subst.*) 1209, c 1386, -ucator 1234, (?) 1363, ploughman; equus -ucator, plough-horse 13c.; *-ucata 1086, p 1478, -ugata c 1175, 1212, -ocata c 1235, -uata (C.I.) 1331, -uecta (C.I.) c 1309, quarrucata c 1100, quadrugata a 1150, c 1200, quadrigata c 1155, measure of land, carrucate, ploughgate (usually from 80 to 120 acres; *cf.* 2 hida); c. parva 12c.; -ucatarius, tenant bound to plough-service c 1306; bestia -ucataria, plough-beast 1326; -ucatus, ploughing 1438; *see also* CARETT, 1 carra, carraca.
carr/um, -us, *see* carra (1 & 2).
car/sea 1428, charesea 1547, charisea 1554, -iscea 1555, -setum 1517, pannus cersegus (†tersegus) 1262, kersey.
carsum, *see* crassum.
1 cart/a (chart-, kart-), *charter, deed, document (?) 675, 993. 1086, 1591; paper 1518; chart, map c 1550, c 1553; 1518, c. lusoria 1499, c. picta 1576, carda 1541, playing card; c. alba, blank charter, *carte blanche* 1347, c 1400; c. divisa 1297, c. indentata 1348, 1506, indenture; c. frettagii 1333, c. de fretto 1354, bill of lading; c. ingenuitatis, letters of manumission c 1115; C. Magna 1218, 1341; c. partita, charter party 1424, 1525; c. Wintonie, Domesday Book 1127; cardeborda, card-board 1421; -icula 842, -ula c 675, 956. c 1106, 1414, little charter, deed or document; -ula chirographi, chirograph c 900;

D

-aceus 1366, 1518, -aneus 12c., 13c., made of paper; -alis, made by deed c 1376; -ualiter, on paper c 1397; -alarius (G.) 1289, -ilarius (G.) 1276, -olarius (G.) 13c., 1254, -ularius (G.) 1275, -igraphus 960, notary; -olaria, office of notary (G.) 1281; ‡-ifilago, cudweed (bot.) 1570; -aphylacium 1358, -ophylacium c 1145, 1586, chest or register of documents; -aria (pl.), notes 1560; -aria c 1380, -raria 13c., muniment room; -uaria 1339, c 1450, -uarium c 1380, 1472, -ularium 13c., 1442, cartulary, register; -o, to register, record 1272; cf. **1 carda.**

2 †cart/a, -um, cart c 1293, 1424; †-a, (?) cart-way 1314; †-agium, cartage 1333, c 1335 (or (?) for carcagium); -arius, carter 12c., c 1317; -clutum 1283, 1371, -eclutum 1270, c 1330, -cloutum 1371, cart-clout; -nailum, cart-nail 1351; -rapum, cart-rope 1400; -o, see carca; cf. CARETT, **1 carra.**

3 cart/a, see quarta.

†cartabellum, (?) spell, enchantment a 1250.

cartago, see sartago.

cartall/um, -us (bibl.) 1200, ‡c 1440, †carculum a 1250, basket, creel; †"creek" a 1564; cf. scarkella.

cartatus, see arx.

cartellus, see quartelettus.

carteria, see quartarium.

carthamus, bastard saffron (bot.) a 1250, ‡15c.

cartillum, see CARETT

carto, see carca; **1 carta;** quarta.

*Cartu/siensis 1200, 1573, †-ariensis c 1160, -asiensis 1441, -asensis 1454, -sianus 1586, Carthusian (adj. or subst.).

caru/a, -agium, caruc-, see **2 carruca.**

carubdis, see charybdis.

car/ui a 1250, ‡14c., (?) -ium 1357, caraway (bot.).

carul/a, -um, see carola.

carus, see caristia.

car/vanna c 1192, c 1437, cavarna c 1192, -varna c 1216, -avana, karavenna c 1250, caravan; -avanarius, caravan attendant c 1250; karavannus 1297, -vannus, karvannus 1290, 1313, baggage train; equus karvannarius 1300, e. carvannus 1332, horse used for transport.

car/vella 1468, 1497, -avella 1470, 1622, kervellum 1454, carvel (ship).

caryophyllum, see gariofilum.

caryota, kind of date: cariola 1257, † canathus a 1250.

cas/a (cass-), house 859; village c 1200; 12c., -ata 701, 955. 13c., -atus 670, c 1000. c 1125, 1397, -atura 1021. 13c., measure of land (appurtenant to household), 'hide'; c. ex virgis compacta, mew (falc.) a 1200; -ale a 1142, 1550, -allum 836, -ella a 950. c 1200, c 1320 -ulus 11c., cottage or cotland; -ale, village 13c., 1267; -allus, villager 836; †-etallagium, house-rent 1269; -amentum, tenement (Norm.) c 1075, c 1254; -atus, resident tenant 1086, c 1088; -o me, to reside (G.) 1255; see also **1 cassa.**

cas/accum, cassock c 1595; cf. casicka.

casalephistula, see cassia.

cascia, see **1 chacea.**

cascoseum, see carcasium.

†cascus, (?) f.l. for caseus, 1207.

case/us, cheese: c. durus, c. friscus 1297; c. estivalis, summer cheese 1258, 1306; c. hiemalis 1232, 1306, c. de relucro 1277, 1345, c. de rewayno 1232, 1310, winter or rowen cheese; c. de Brie 1367; -olus, little cheese 1325, 15c.; -alis, cheese-shaped 1267; coagulative a 1250; -arium, cheese-vat, mould 1283, ‡1483; -arius 1286, 1376, -ator 1348, 1389, -atrix (f.) c 1290, cheese-maker; -atus, cheesy, made of cheese a 1250, 13c.; -itas, cheesiness a 1250.

casicka, (?) f.l. for casula, 1337; cf. casaccum.

casimentum, see cassa.

†casita, part of thurible 1245; cf. cassula.

caskettum (k-), casket 1441, 1480.

†caslamus, (?) basket (Sc.) 1326.

†caspella, (?) brier (cf. It. caspo) 1223.

1 cass/a (cas-) c 1200, 1434, -us, -um, 1295 1407, -ia c 1368, 1513, chassia 1213, (?) -is 1328, (?) -o 1222, case, box; -a 1255, 1296, -um 1325, -imentum 1439, casement (of window); -ella 1388, -ula c 1135, 1390, casket, cover (of shrine); -ula, little case, covering a 1250; c. fenestre, casement or moulding 1329; c. plumbea, coffin 1461; see also casa; cf. capsa, caskettum.

2 cass/a, -um, carcass 1274, 1421; cf. carcasium.

cassamus, cyclamen (bot.) a 1250, ‡14c.

cassat/a, -us, -ura, see casa.

cass/atio, quashing, nullification 1220, a 1452; -abilis 1396, a 1564, quassabilis 15c., liable to be quashed; ‡-atum, diseased blood 1652; -o a 1100, c 1530, -io c 1242, *quasso 1155, 1553, to quash, annul; -o, to cashier, dismiss 1215, c 1540; to deprive 14c., c 1400; see also QUASS

‡cassator, mower 15c.

cassi/a fistula a 1200, 1480, -ofistula c 1357, casalephistula 1414, purging cassia (bot.); c. lignea, cassia (wild cinnamon) bark a 1250.

cassiatus, hooded 760, 10c.

cassibula, see **1 casula.**

cassilago, henbane (bot.) a 1250, 1267.

cassinus, Islamic preacher c 1190.

cass/um, -ula, see cassa (**1 & 2**).

cassura, see casura.

cass/ytha, -utha, see cuscuta.

1 †casta, part of a deer, (?) for costa, 1265.

2 †casta, (?) article of apparel (Sc.) 1332.

castal-, see also CASTELL

castald/us 9c. c 1180, c 1220, gastaldus c 1137, a 1142, gastoldus c 1100, -io 1157, provost, prefect; proctor, chamberlain 1608; -ia, proxy 1608.

castan/a c 1258, -us c 1200, castenea 1278, -arius 1255, -earius 1282, castenarius 1229, chestnut tree; casteneum, chestnut 1315; -ea major a 1250; -eola, nux vomica a 1250, ‡14c.; -earia, chestnut grove (Norm.) 1180.

castell/um, castle (of ship) 1294, c 1390; c. posterius, after castle (naut.) 1357; c. forinsecum, outer bailey 13c.; c. portatile, siege-tower 1370; -o, for -um,

castle 1385; **-um** 12c., **-warda** 1381, **-guardia** 1608, castle-ward; **opus -i** 1097, c 1176, **operatio -i** a 1100, 1190, burhbote; **-ettum** 1216, 1222, **-ulum** 1086, c 1362, **-ula** c 1364, small castle; ***-ania** c 1188, 1290, ***-aria, -arium** 1085, c 1333, **-eria** 1166, 1199, **castelria** 1194, **castallaria** c 1166, 1213, **-atio** 1086, **-atus** 1086, **-ionatus** (G.) 1314, office, service or jurisdiction of castellan, lowy; **-anus** 1176, 1290, **-anarius** p 1229, **-arius** 1222, castellan, governor of castle; occupant of castle a 1142, 1461; **-anus** (*adj.*) c 1140, 1584, **-ensis** 12c., **-inus** c 1138, c 1140, of a castle; **-are** 1289, **castillum** 1253, castle, fortalice (G.); **-atio**, fortification c 1115; **-mannus**, tenant performing castle-ward 1183; **-o**, to fortify 1214, c 1395.
casten/arius, -eum, *see* **castana.**
caster, *see* **castrum.**
castia, a disease of horses 1319.
castig/atio, correction of a text 1516, 1526; **-ator,** corrector of a text 1516; **-ativus,** of chastisement c 1377; **-atorium,** whipping-post 1267, 1305; **-o,** to deter from evil ways c 1115; to train (dogs) 1290, 1490; to purify (blood) 1390; to skim c 1200.
cast/itas, purity of doctrine c 730; **-imonialis,** nun c 1120; **-ifico,** to purify (eccl.).
*cast/o 1205, 15c., **-onus** 1238, 'chaston', collet (of ring).
cast/or c 1290, **-ritius** 1235, c 1350, **-ritus** c 1160, 1242, (?) **-rix** c 1250, wether; **-ratum,** castration c 1258; **caro -rativa,** flesh of a castrated animal c 1260.
castoreleon, castor oil a 1250.
castrimarg-, *see* GASTRIMARG
castrisius, *see* **contricius.**
castr/um, hamlet 771; castle (of ship) 1296, 1346; ‡"pavise" (shield) 1483; **c. amorosum** (in revel) 1313; **c. capitale,** topcastle (naut.) 1296; **c. claustrale** 1274, **caster sanctus** c 1000, monastery; **chestra,** Roman camp c 1160; **caustrum,** castle 1478; **operatio -i** 1415, **restructio -orum** (?) 1066, c 1160, burhbote; **-ametatio** c 1470, **-amitatio** 15c., pitching a camp; (Roman) camp 1586; **-ensis,** occupant of castle c 1140, 13c.; **-iwarda,** castle ward (Sc.) 1359, 1459; **-unculum,** fort 1408; ***-ametor,** to pitch camp c 1118, 16c.
castum, *see* **encaustum.**
casual/e, case-ending (*gram.*) 1271; **-ia** (*pl.*), accidental occurrences 1267; casual profits 1300, 1600; ***-is,** casual, accidental c 1160, c 1520; **-itas,** accident, chance 1330, 1539; **-iter,** casually, accidentally a 1100, c 1540.
casu/arium, -arius, -ate, -ista, *see* **casus.**
1 ***casul/a** 797, c 1000. a 1090, 1537, **-are** 15c., **capsula** c 1486, **cassibula** 1225, 1337, **chesibla** 1350, chasuble (eccl.); **-arius,** chasuble-maker c 980.
2 **†casula,** clause 1328; *cf.* 1 **clausa.**
3 **casula,** *see* 1 **cassa.**
casulla, *see* 1 **cavilla.**
casulus, *see* **casa.**
cas/um, -us, *see* 1 **cassa.**
casura (**cass-**), fall 760; decline, decay 12c.; loss (of coinage) through melting down 1199, 1225; part of tunic c 1350.

cas/us, Fall (theol.) c 1225, c 1362; wreck c 1353; deficiency, loss (in assay) a 1275; ***case,** cause, suit (leg.) c 1250, a 1564; hypothesis (log.) c 1350, c 1370; **a casu** c 1260, c 1422, **ex c.** c 1341, by chance; **in c.,** in a special case c 1341, c 1357; **in eo c.,** in that case 1564; **-u quia** c 1430, **-u quo** 1559, c 1593, **in c. quo** c 1338, 1461, **in c. quod** c 1400, c 1470, **in c. si** a 1228, c 1343, in case, if; **pono in -u,** to risk 1197; **super -um,** on the case (leg.) 1538, a 1564; **-us de facto,** case (question) of fact 13c.; **c. legis** c 1400; **c. reservatus,** case reserved for special absolution c 1451, c 1476; **c. statuti,** circumstances necessary for application of statute 1315; **c. virge,** measure of land, 'rod-fall' c 1270; **-uarium, -uarius,** case-book (leg.) c 1430, 15c.; **-uate,** casually, accidentally c 1450; **-uista,** casuist 1646; *cf.* **cadentia,** CASUAL
caszorius, *see* 1 **chacea.**
1 **cata,** according to (κατά) c 800.
2 **cata,** *see* **cateria.**
3 **cata,** *see* **catus.**
Catabaptista, Catabaptist, abuser of baptism 1526.
†catabulum, pigsty c 1440.
cataclys/ma 966, **-mus** c 797. 12c., 1380, **-is** 1344, cataclysm, deluge.
†catacrines (*pl.*), (?) haunches 6c.
cata/crisis, *for* **-chresis,** misuse of word c 1250.
cata/cumba c 1188, c 1250, **-comba** c 1362, catacomb; ‡privy 15c.
†cataduppa, underground gutter, conduit c 1440.
catagor-, *see* CATEGOR
Catalaunense, *see* **chalo.**
cata/lepsia (med.): **-lempsia** c 1180, a 1250; **†-lepsius,** (?) *for* cachexia, bad physical condition 13c.
cat/allum *1086, 1684, **-ellum** a 1190, 1331, **capitale, captale** c 1115, chattel, cattle, movable goods; c 1200, **capitale** c 1115, (compensation for) value of stolen goods; capital, principal of debt a 1190, 1298; **captale,** price of slave c 1115; **c. primum,** homestead c 1115; **c. vivens, c. vivum,** livestock c 1115; **-allum liberum,** free chattel (of land) 1204; **c. immobile** 1231; **c. mobile** 1231, 13c.; **-alla** (*pl.*) **guerrina,** military stores 1243; **-allagium,** (?) poll-tax 1275; **-allarius,** a class of tenant (Glos.) 1348, (Ir.) 1427, 1451; *cf.* **capital.**
cata/logus (eccl.), **-lagus** c 1372, **cathologus** c 1250, 1461, **catholigus** 1499, list.
‡catantrum, trendle 15c.
catapanus, *podestà* (Sicily) c 1165.
cataphaticus, affirmative 850.
cataplasm/a, poultice 7c., c 1000. 1285; **-o,** to poultice a 1250, 1345.
cataplus, arrival of ships (κατάπλους) 7c.
catapolicus, urban (play on **catholicus**) 1609.
catapucia, spurge (bot.) a 1250 ‡c 1440.
catapulta a 1142, 1394, **cadapultra** 1471, arrow or crossbow bolt; **c. †parcuum,** (?) broad arrow a 1654.
catapurgium, *see* **caputpurgium.**
cat/aracta c 1414, ‡c 1440, **-eractis** c 1200,

drain, conduit; c 950, **-eracta** 1361, ‡15c., **-haratha** 1508, grated window; **-aracta,** cataract of the eye a 1250, 1620; **c. gutturis** (med.) a 1250; **-aracte** (*pl.*) **celi** (bibl.), **-eracte** c 1470, ‡15c., **-aracteres** c 1200, **caracteres** a 1250, c 1400, floodgates of heaven.

cataria, *see* **cateria.**

catarra, holy water stoup 1537.

catascopus (legis Dei), bishop 961. 12c.

catassa, 'caddis', cotton-wool or fabric 1380.

cat/asta, bird-cage a 1408, a 1446; St. Lawrence's gridiron c 1170; **-esta** c 1410, **-atista** 1535, scaffold.

catasyllogismus, counter-proof c 1160.

catator, *see* **catus.**

†**cata/tropha** (? *for* **-stropha** *or* **-tropa**), kind of upheaval (med.) a 1250.

catavolatilia, *see* **catumvolatile.**

catax, paralytic, limping 695.

cat/echismus c 1341, c 1579, **-hacismus** 1279, catechism; **-echetice,** categorically 1374; **-echizatio** 12c., 1374, **-hezizatio** c 1197, **-icuminatio** 14c., catechizing; **-echista** c 1579, **-hezeta** 1200, ‡**-hezizista, -herizista** 1483, catechist; **-echumenus** (eccl.), **-echuminus** 795. 12c., 1271, **-icumenus** c 803, **-icuminus** a 690, catechumen; **-acuminium, -icuminium,** status of catechumen c 730; **-echizo** c 730. c 1125, c 1414, **-ezizo** c 730, 706. c 1200, c 1325, ‡**-erizo** 1483, to catechize.

categor/ia (eccl.), ‡**catagoria** 1483, category; **-ie** (*pl.*), Aristotle's *Categories* 11c., 1345; **-ema** 13c., 1610, **-euma** a 1249, a 1347, predicate; **-ematice** c 1250, 1378, **-eumatice** c 1290, **-ice** a 1361, categorically, as a predicate; **-ematicus** p 1300, **-ewmaticus** a 1360, **-icus** a 1249, c 1343, categorical, predicative; **-izo,** to predicate a 1249, c 1390; c 1380, **-o** c 950, to preach; **-izo celebrationem,** to say mass 14c.

catellum, *see* **catallum.**

catellus, *see* **cantera; catus.**

caten/a, chain for book 1384; (?) skein 1346; **c. gule** (med.) a 1250; **cheyna, cheynia** 1282, **cheynus** 1390, chain; **-ula,** little chain 790, c 970. c 1196, 1528; **-alis** a 1446, **-atus** p 1394, in the form of chains (her.); **-atio,** joint (med.) c 1210; chaining (of books) c 1470; **-atus,** adorned with chains 1562; **-o,** to enchain 9c. c 1177, 15c.; to chain (books) 1368, 1456; to add, link on 1427.

cateracta, *see* **cataracta.**

cateran/us (katheran-) 1383, 1521, **ketheranus** 1415, **kethranus, vir kethranicus** 1389, **cateran** (Sc.); **-atus,** state of a cateran 1383.

cat/eria 1453, **-aria** 1468, **caetria** 1444, catery, acatry (department of royal household); **-or,** caterer 1439, 1537; †**-a,** (?) purchase c 1160; *cf.* **acatum.**

catervula, small company c 1060.

catez-, cathac-, *see* **catechismus.**

Cathaius, Kataius, Cathayan, Chinese 1267.

catharatha, *see* **cataracta.**

Cathar/us, Albigensian heretic c 1192, c 1200; c 1610, **-ista** c 1643, Puritan; **-izatio,** (ritual) purification 1267; **-ma,** refuse, sweepings 1562; **-ticum imperiale,** pur-

gative containing rhubarb or scammony a 1250.

catheciz-, *see* **cachexia; catechismus.**

cathedr/a, *bishop's throne or office 676, 10c. c 1090, c 1546; c 1516, **c. magistralis** 1314, 1345, chair (ac.); **c. plicabilis,** 1345, 1421, **c. applectata** 1553, folding chair; **c. clausa,** "close chair" 1553; **c. stercoris,** cucking stool 1086; *c. S. Petri 1200, 1409, **festum -e S. (B.) Petri** c 1250, 1314, **f. S. Petri in -a** c 1253, c 1334, feast of St. Peter's Chair (22 Feb.); **cadetra,** seat c 550; **-alis,** (*adj.*) of or for a cathedral c 1196, 1549; episcopal 1241, c 1400; professorial (ac.) c 1340; (*subst.*) cathedral c 1217; **-aliter,** from the pulpit, *ex cathedra* c 1204, c 1250; in the style of a cathedral c 1213; **-aticum** 12c., 1473, †**-acum** 1417, synodal, due paid by clergy to bishop; **-atio,** enthronement 15c.; **-atus,** enthroned 1320; **-o,** to enthrone (bishop) c 1265, c 1470; to sit on bishop's throne 12c.; **-izo,** to appoint to chair (ac.) a 1385.

catherellus, *see* **cacherellus.**

catheriz-, cathez-, *see* **catechismus.**

cathet/us a 1150, 1267, **-icus** c 1375, perpendicular line.

cathimia, *see* **cadmia.**

catholic/us, universal c 1160, 1620; *catholic, orthodox c 790. c 1125, 1565; (*subst.*) Catholic, orthodox Christian 787, 11c. c 1100, 1549; bishop c 1395; **C. Romanus,** Roman Catholic 17c.; *see also* **herba; -e,** in a catholic, orthodox, manner 799. c 1090, 1456; **-ismus,** Catholicism 1609; **-on,** primatial see 12c.; dictionary c 1390, c 1450; **-atio,** making or declaring catholic, orthodox c 1382; **-o,** to make or declare catholic, orthodox 1378, a 1484.

cathologus, catholigus, *see* **catalogus.**

catia, *see* **1 chacea.**

catic-, *see* **catechismus.**

†**catietatia,** (?) *f.l.* for **advocacia,** c 1200.

†**catillatus,** (?) *for* **cavillatus,** contradicted c 950; *see also* **catus.**

‡**catillia,** weight of nine ounces 1652.

Catini, (†Canini) (*pl.*), an heretical sect, Städinger c 1250.

catinus, *see* **catus.**

†**cationabilis,** (?) *f.l.* for **rationabilis,** 12c.

catma, *see* **cadmia.**

catmaheu, *see* **camahutus.**

Cato, distichs of Cato 14c., 1364; **C. moralizatus** 1439; *see also* **catus.**

cator, *see* **cateria.**

catorthoma, judgement c 950.

catul/us, (?) whelp (naut.), projection on windlass 1359, 1372; **c. currens,** hound pup 1284; **-aster,** cur c 1000; *see also* **catus.**

cat/umvolatile, -ovolatile c 1180, **-avolatilia** 12c., fine linen.

cat/us (catt-) *9c. c 1125, a 1408, **-o** 1510, **-a** (*f.*) c 1212, a 1250, cat, wild cat; kind of trout c 1200; siege-engine c 1200, 1300; **c. ignius,** domestic cat c 1100, 1303; **c. muntesius** 1172, **c. savagius** c 1250, **c. silvagius** 1303, **c. silvester** 1190, wild cat; **-arius** 12c., **-ator** c 1136, (?) cat-hunter (*or* (?) hunter; *cf.* **1 chacea); mentha -aria,** catmint (bot.) 1634; **-inus** c 1100, c 1436,

-icus a 1250, c 1361, (?) **-ulinus** 1387, feline; ‡**-ulus, -ellus**, kitten 15c. (*see also* CATUL); **-o**, to see a 1250, a 1446; ‡**-ello** 15c., ‡**-illo** c 1440, to mew.

catz-, *see* 1 **chacea**.

cauc-, *see also* 2 **calcea**.

caucidonius, *see* **chalcedon**.

caucus, drinking vessel c 730. a 1155, c 1400.

caud/a, back, rear (of building or plot of land) c 1200, 1440; rear (of army) c 1370, 1461; rear end (of gun) 1460; tail, train (of garment) 1554; *tag, thong for attaching a seal c 1255, 1530; tail, stem (of musical note) 1351, c 1470; end (of verse), coda 14c.; end, last clause (of document) 1543; **facio -am**, to turn tail c 1293; **-a carruce**, plough-tail c 1185, 1283; **c. draconis**, descending node of moon's orbit with ecliptic c 1133, c 1200; ‡**c. caballina** 14c., ‡**c. equi** 14c., **c. equina** 1538, 1634, ‡**c. pulli** 14c., horse-tail (bot.); ‡**c. pecorina, c. porcina**, gromwell (bot.) 14c.; **c. lete**, latter end of court leet 1521; ‡**c. vulpis rubicunde**, red lead 1652; ‡**-ile** 14c., **-arium** 1245, **-irium** 1248, **-erium** 1271, crupper-strap; **-atus**, having a tail (of the English) c 1193, 1461; having a tail (of tunic) c 1197; tagged (of writ) 13c.; 'tailed' (of verse) 14c.; **-o**, to furnish with a tail (of the English) 15c.; (of a musical note) 1351; *see also* 1 **cadus, caldaria**.

caufagium, *see* CALEFAC

†**caufara**, (?) for **caldaria**, ordeal-kettle c 1115.

caul/a *c 1150, 1549, **-aris** 1455, **calla** c 1185, **cawla** 1549, sheep-fold, pigsty, or hurdle; flock c 950; (fig.) cell (mon.) c 1000; (*pl.*) fold of the church c 550, 9c.

caulamaula, *see* **calamus**.

caulandrius, *see* **charadrius**.

caul/eria, cauliflower 1392; **cholettus** 1248, **scholettus** 1271, small cabbage (O.F. *cholet*); ‡**-iculus agrestis**, wild cabbage 14c.; ‡**c. aquaticus**, water lily 14c.; ‡**-is Sancti Cuthberti**, mallow 14c.; **-icularis**, belonging to the stem 1620.

caulvatus, *see* 1 **caballus**.

1 cauma, heat (bibl.); **c. eternum**, Hell-fire c 950; **c. mysticum**, inspiration a 975.

2 caum/a, -ia, -io, -us, -o, *see* **calamus**.

caumolata, *see* CANMOL

caunterium, *see* **cantera**.

cauntus, *see* **canthus**.

caupallus, boat 690; *cf.* **cobella**.

caup/o 1486, **taberna -onaria** 1608, inn; *see also* **capo**.

Caursinus, *see* **Caorcinus**.

Caurus, north-west wind: **Chorus** 760.

caus/a, thing (Fr. *chose*) 1086, c 1200; the *trimoda necessitas* c 799, 11c. 12c., 14c.; **c. armorum**, plea of arms (her.) 1389, 1395; **c. efficiens** (log.) c 1200, a 1233; **c. finalis** a 1200, c 1444; **c. formalis** a 1200, c 1370; **c. materialis** a 1200, a 1233; **c. movens** 1350; *c. rationabilis** a 1090, c 1520; **c. sanguinis** (leg.) 1218, 13c.; **-ā quia**, because 1380; *see also* **sigillum**; **-abilis**, able to be caused, assignable to a cause 1344, a 1361; †**-alis**, casual, accidental 870. (?) c 1290; causal c 1170, a 1361;

***-alitas**, causality c 1225, 1381; **-aliter**, causally, with reference to a cause 870. c 1188, c 1363; **-antia**, jurisdiction 1348; 1374, **-atio** c 1290, 1378, causation; **-atio**, plea or objection (leg.) c 1187, 1620; **-ative**, by way of causation 870. c 1258, c 1444; **-ativus**, causative 870. 1267, 15c.; **-ativitas**, causativity c 1361; **-ator**, plaintiff, pleader c 1115, 1220; instigator c 1450; pretender c 1608; **-atrix**, complainant (*f.*) c 1180; *-atum**, effect c 1250, c 1290; **-o** c 1450, **-or** 7c. a 1100, to complain, object; **-or**, to challenge, attack 1130, 1494; *-o** c 1200, 1661, **-or** c 1170, 1409, to cause.

cause/a, -tum, causia, *see* **calcea** (2 & 3).

causiarius, hat-maker 1563.

†**causilis**, (?) *for* **clausilis**, closable 7c.

causon/, fever a 1142, 1622; **c. synochides, synochus -ides**, fevers due to excess of choler and blood a 1250.

caustrum, *see* **castrum**.

caut/ela, trick, device c 1115, 1461; **ad -elam** 1244, c 1330, **per c.** c 1551, provisionally; *-elose**, prudently, craftily 1295, c 1412; **-elosus** 1315, 15c., †**-elis** c 1220, †**-elus** 15c., ‡**-icus** 1483, prudent, crafty; **-illeria**, a tax (Span.) 1282; **-io**, schedule of debts c 1178; **c. litterarum**, written warranty 1190; **-ionarius**, guarantor, bail 1593; (*adj.*) cautionary c 1337; *cf.* **cavitio**.

cauter/ium, brand, stigma 7c. c 1180, 1421; **cawterium**, branding iron 1517; **-iatissimus**, deeply branded or seared c 1218; **-iatio** 14c., **-isatio** (**-izatio**) a 1250, 1380, searing; *-io** a 1100, a 1452, **-iso** (**-izo**) a 1250, 1500, to cauterize, brand, sear.

cauterosus, *see* **cancerosus**.

†**cautes** (*pl.*), (?) *for* **cantharides**, maggots 1445.

cautica, causeway 893; *cf.* 2 **calcea**.

cauvillus, *see* 2 **cavilla**.

cavagium, *see* **cana**.

caval-, *see* 1 **caballus**.

cav/amen c 670, **-atura** 690. c 1180, 1267, **-itas** c 690. c 1300, 1686, hollowness, cavity; **-ana**, (?) cistern 8c.; **-arius**, (?) sapper 1435, 1436; **-erne** (*pl.*), pits, hollows (of the body) c 550; **-ernula**, small cave 1172, p 1394; **-atio**, engraving 1506.

†**cavannus**, owl 685.

cavarna, *see* **carvanna**.

cavelatus, cachalot, sperm whale (G.) 1281.

cavella (Sc.) c 1240, **covilla** (†**conilla**) 1212, **kuvulia** (†**ruvulia**) 1201, 'cavel', lot.

cavellatio, *see* **cavillatio**.

caveo, *see* **cavitio**.

cavile, 'toil', snare (for deer) 1548, 1560.

1 cav/illa c 1180, a 1250, **-ela** c 1260, **-icula** 12c., †**casulla** 1423, **kivillum** 1243, ankle.

2 cavilla (†**canilla**) *c 1200, 1517, **cauvillus** 1206, †**kanevillus** 1214, **kevellus** 1368, **kevillus** 1284, c 1310, †**kevildus** 1222, **chevile** 1343, **kivellus** 1251, **kivillus** 1254, 1321, **chivillus** 1241, **cuvilla** 1276, 1282, 'kevel', wedge, peg, pin, or hammer; 1324, 1486 **kevilla** 1321, **kivilla** 1318, tooth of a harrow; **-a**, part of a gun 1340; clapper of a bell c 1182; (?) magnifying glass c 1200; **cavillo**, to fit (harrow) with teeth 1300; ‡to pin 1483.

cavill/atio 933. c 1160, 1482, **cavellatio** 1235, c 1369, **cabellatio** 7c., **-amentum** 1552, cavil, quibbling, objection; **-antissimus**, most captious 12c.; **-ator**, caviller c 1250, p 1330; **-atorie** c 1150, **-ose** c 1250, c 1343, captiously; **-atorius** a 1180, c 1430, **-osus** c 1250, c 1343, cavilling, railing, captious; †**-ium**, mockery, insult 1521; **-o**, *to cavil, quibble, bring frivolous suits c 1270, c 1332; to devise tricks c 790.

cavitas, see **cavamen**.

cav/itio, avoidance 1378; **-eo** (with *acc.* and *inf.*), to guard against 793; *cf.* CAUT

cawagium, royal pew (Westminster Abbey) 1388.

cawdrena, see **caldaria**.

cawla, see **caula**.

cawterium, see **cauterium**.

cay-, see also CAI

Caymit/e (*pl.*) 1427, **Cainite** 1344, Cainites; **-icus**, fratricidal c 1191, 1427.

cayrellus, see **quarellus**.

caz/a, -orius, see 1 **chacea**.

ce-, see also **se-**

ceapgildum, see CHEP

†**cebar** (†**lebar**), *alias* †**kini**, kind of eagle a 1250.

‡**cebus**, monkey (κῆβος) 1570.

cec/atio, blinding a 1250, 1378; †**-ator**, (?) blind man 13c.; ‡**-ula**, blindworm 15c., 1483; **-e**, blindly 1377; **secus**, *for* **-us**, blind 1541; **ictus -us**, blow not causing bloodshed c 1115; **fons -us**, hidden spring *or* (?) *for* siccus (Sc.) 1256.

cecias, north wind (καικίας) c 700.

‡**cecidos**, ‡**scicidon** 14c., (?) **secida**, **siccida** a 1250, gall or (?) gall-bearing oak (κηκίς) (bot.); *cf.* **sicyos**.

ceco, see **seca**.

cect/abilis, -ator, see 1 **secta**.

ceda, cedela, see SCHED; 1 **seta**.

cedes, slaughter: **sedes** 15c.

cedo, see 1 **cessus**; **sedes**.

cedrinus, cedar-like 1433; see also **pomum**.

cedul-, see SCHED; SCIND

cedu/us: **-i** (*pl.*) 1573, **boscus -us** 1358, **silva -a** 1287, 1425, **s. sedua** 1345, coppice-wood.

celabrum, see **cerebrum**.

cel/amentum, concealment, secret 1278; **-anda** (*pl.*), privy parts 12c., c 1400; **-ate**, secretly c 1250; see also 2 **celum**.

cel/antes, -arent, logical moods 14c.

celarium, see **salarium**.

cela/torium, -tura, see 2 **celum**.

celc-, see CELS

celda, see **selda**.

cel/dra, -drum, see CALD

celea, see **celia**.

celeb/ratio 798, 993. c 1188, 1545, **-ritas** a 1090, c 1450; **-ia** (*pl.*) 1416, celebration of mass or divine service; **c. judicii**, pronouncing judgement c 1115; **c. ordinum**, ordination (eccl.) 1294; **-rabilis**, memorable 1090; **-ratrix**, performer (*f.*) c 1180; **-er**, loud c 1330; **-ria** (*pl.*), rites c 1000; **-rior**, more celebrated c 730; **-riter**, solemnly, ceremonially 12c., 15c.; **-ro**, to insist c 1115; *to celebrate mass or divine service 630, 798. c 1090,

1583; ***c. concilium**, to hold a council (eccl.) 1131, 1562; **c. divortium (inter)** 1340; **c. judicium**, to pronounce judgement c 1115; **c. ordinationes** c 804, ***c. ordines** c 1236, c 1350, to ordain (eccl.); **c. parliamentum** 1427; **c. synodum** 12c., 1220.

celebs, unmarried (of a woman) c 1125; see also CHALYB

cel/eitas, see 1 **celum**.

‡**celena**, hemlock (bot.) 14c.

celer, speedy: **sceler** 1244.

celer-, see CALD; **scelus**.

celest-, see also 1 **celum**.

Celestinus, Celestine (mon.) 15c.

celeuma, command 6c., c 800.

celi-, see also 1 **celum**.

cel/ia acerba, bitter beer, bitters c 550, 797; **-ea**, *for* **-ia**, ale, beer c 1000. 1459, 1461; ‡**-ioforum**, "ale-pot" 15c.

celiamentum, see 2 **celum**.

cell/a a 1090, 1549, **-ula** 7c., 9c. c 1190, 1620, monk's cell; *1236, 1583, **-ula** 1216, 1284, 'cell', daughter-house (mon.); (?) case for banner 1384; c 1200, c 1270, **-ula** a 1200, c 1270, chamber (of brain); **-ula**, chapel c 690, c 790; square on abacus 15c.; ovary c 1210; cell (biological) 1620; **c. memorialis** c 1200, 1424, **c. memorie** a 1250, seat of memory; **c. fantastica, c. rationis**, seats of imagination and reason (in brain) a 1250; **-ulatus**, contained in cells (biological) 1620, 1622; **-atus**, cloistered c 1193; **-icola** 1200, **-ista** c 1450, monk; see also SELL

cell/arium *c 730. a 1090, 1586, **-erium** 1300, 1376, **sellarium** 1281, 1538, storeroom, cellar; treasure-chamber 8c.; thesaurus (of writings) 797; ‡**a -ariis**, butler 1483; **-aragium** 1387, **-eragium** 1291, 1392, cellarage, (payment for) storage in cellar; **-eraria** c 1204, 1498, **-aria** c 1220, office of cellarer; **-eraria** c 1180, 1441, **-erarissa, -erissa** c 1415, cellaress (mon.); ***-erarius** c 790. a 1090, c 1553, **-ararius** c 1125, c 1138, **-arius** 10c. c 1185, 1567, **scelerarius** c 1220 (play on **scelus**), c 1378, **sellerarius** 1290, 1455, **salerarius** 1379, cellarer; **c. exterior, c. forinsecus**, (opposed to **c. interior, c. intrinsecus**) c 1266; see also **salarium**.

†**cellis**, (?) *for* **collis**, c 550.

†**celmostinus**, (?) *for* τεκνοποιητικός, procreative c 1343.

cel/o, -orium, -orum, see 2 **celum**.

celsa, food-rent (W. *cylch*) 1378.

cels/itudo, *height c 1090, c 1580; highness (title) 660, c 985. a 1090, 1583; **c. regia** 1263, 1536; **c. imperialis** c 1242, c 1422; ‡**-a, -us**, mulberry tree a 1200, 14c.; **-ithronus** c 730, 810. a 1408, **celcithronus** 12c., **-itonans** 12c., a 1408, epithets of God.

celta, see **teldum**.

celtica, spikenard (bot.) a 1250, ‡15c.

celt/is a 1180, c 1362, **-a** a 1452, **sceltis** c 1190, celt, chisel.

1 **cel/um, -i** (*pl.*), heaven (eccl.); **c. empyreum** c 1212, c 1225; **c. primum** a 1233; **-i** (*pl.*), spiritual men c 1180; **-itus**, from heaven (eccl.); **-eitas**, celestiality c 1270; **-estialis** c 1227, **-icalis** c 1283, **-icus**

(eccl.), †-itus c 550. 14c., heavenly; -estis
c 1217, -estinus c 1320, 1432, -icus 1528,
sky-blue; -ice, celestially c 1250; -icida,
slayer of Heaven c 1250; -icola, Culdee
c 1188; -igena, heavenly being 1439;
-imantia, divination by heavenly bodies
c 1260.

2 cel/um c 1285, c 1290, selum 1328,
-amentum 1415, -iamentum 1370, -atura
c 550. c 1255, 1518, sellatura 1505, -ura
c 1267, 1415, selura 1415, 1481, ciluratio
1444, silluratio 1440, -atorium 15c.,
-orium c 1510, -orum 1421, cilurum
1380, selare c 1450, sylarium 1384, sylor
1446, 1464, ceiling, canopy, panelling,
carving; -ura dimidia, half canopy (of
bed) 1388; -atorius, of or for a carver 794.
14c.; -atum, engraved vessel a 1250;
†-atus, (?) engraved c 550; scelatus,
(?) shaped, designed a 1200; -o 1173, c 1412,
selo 1373, 1411, seluro c 1412, to ceil or
panel.

cema, see schema.

*cement/um c 900. 1136, 1578, sementum
c 1300, 1461, ‡cimentum 1483, simentum 1318, cement, mortar; chimentum,
chip c 550; -aria 1219, 1389, -ria 1360,
cymentria 1296, mason's service, masonry;
-arius, (adj.) c 1220, 1415, sementarius
1382, of or for a mason; *(subst.) c 1000.
1077, c 1533, sementarius 1347, 1416,
*cimentarius 1218, 1419, cimetarius
(?) c 910, cemetarius 1242, cimiterius
1230, mason; c. liber 1438, c. libere petre
1341, freestone worker, free-mason; -o, to
cement c 1200, 1333.

*cemeterium a 1090, 1508, cemiterium
c 1125, 1552, cim/eterium 1131, c 1520,
*-iterium c 730. 1086, 1569, -itorium
c 1470, semiterium 1361, semitorium
1549, simeterium 1403, simiterium
c 1310, cemetery, churchyard; -eterialis,
of a cemetery c 1250.

cemzebrata, see zinziber.

cena, Lord's supper (eccl.); sena, for -a,
1294; *c. Domini a 1060. c 1135, c 1530,
c. Dominica a 1090, c 1400, dies cene
12c., 1523, d. c. ad mandatum c 1300,
Maundy Thursday.

cenagium, see SYNOD

cenap/e, -ium, see sinapium.

cenceo, see census.

cend/allum 1216, 1380, -ale 1230, cin-
dalium c 1200, c 1255, scendallum 1227,
1257, scindallum 1245, 1254, scindellum
1260, sendallum 1225, 1392, sendale
c 1365, sendellum 1391, sendillum 15c.,
sandalum 1303, sandallium 1305, 15c.,
sandellum 1388, -iapilum 1288, -atum
1222, 1295, cindatum 1303, 1328, senda-
tum 1245, 1351, sandatum 1245, sindatum 1327, cendal, sort of silk; cf. sindo.

cendre, ceneres, see cinis.

cendula, see scindula.

cenegildum, see cynegildum.

cen/evectorium c 1200, 1449, -ovectorium
c 1180, 1291, scenevectorium c 1480, sce-
nefactorium c 1460, ‡senvectorium 15c.,
†semevectorium 1405, †cemivecto-
rium c 1445, sennevectoria, †semi-

vectoria c 1460, †fenoveciorium c 1450,
senevectorium 1388, 1467, senefectorium
1474, zenefactorium c 1460, cinefactorium 1468, sinefecturum 1453, dung-cart,
barrow; c. manuale, hand-barrow c 1300,
‡15c.; c. rotatum, wheel-barrow c 1445,
‡15c.; via †semivectoria, barrow-way
(for coal) 1460.

cenibita, see CENOB

cenit, see chenix.

cenith, see zenith.

cenl/a, -atus, see scindula.

cenneus, see AEN

cenninga, 'team', voucher to warranty
(A.S.) c 1115.

ceno, see cenulentus.

cenob/ium (eccl.), cenubia c 800, cinobium
1313, monastery; -iolum, small monastery
c 1100, 1538; *-ialis 676, 1062. 1090,
c 1470, -italis 6c., -itaris c 1280, monastic;
cenubialiter, monastically 12c.; -iarcha,
head of monastery 1528, 1608; -ita (eccl.),
cenibita 10c., cynubita 5c., -icus c 1470,
cenobite, monk.

cenodochi-, see XENO

cenodox/ia 590, c 860. c 1160, 1271, senodoxia 12c., xenodoxia c 1180, vainglory;
-us, vainglorious c 870.

cenofarus, see CYNO

Cenomannensis (libra), coin of Maine
1156, 13c.

cenomyia, fly (bibl.): cynomia 1267,
a 1408; (?) flea-bane (bot.) 8c.

cenon, carmen, common song c 700.

cenosus, see cenulentus.

cenovectorium, see cenevectorium.

cens/ura 1459, sensura 1375, censer; see also
census; francum -um, frankincense 1573;
cf. INCEN

*cens/us 940, 11c. c 1070, 1559, sensus
c 1095, -a c 1185, 1277, †tensa (G.) 1284,
-iva, -ivum (G.) 1289, rent, customary
payment; redditus sensivus, a parish rent
(C.I.) 1394; -us, amount 13c.; coinage
a 1130, c 1370; opera posita ad -um,
services commuted for rent 1252; -us
anticipationis, 'forfang', reward for return
of stolen goods a 1130; c. capitalis,
compensation for stolen goods a 1130; c. burgi
1086, 1281; c. domorum 1086; c. ecclesie
a 1130, 1310, c. ecclesiasticus 12c.,
church-scot; c. foreste 1167, c. nemorum
c 1178; c. morthidis 11c., 12c., c. mor-
thedis c 1156, c. †mortbildis c 1160,
murder fine or mortuary due; c. regis 1086;
c. statutus 1167; c. villanorum 1086;
-aria 1298, c 1370, sensaria 1337, -eria
c 1283, 1301, cenceria c 1283, -ura 1337,
1378, chenseria 1313, 1349, †chensa
1485, chensura 1483, 1547, †ghenseria
(W.) 1348, a burgage rent, (?) paid by non-
burgesses (Devon, Cornw., Ir., W.); a rent-
paying area, 'farm' (in Savernake Forest)
1276, 1491; -arius, (adj.) c 1115, -alis (G.)
1289, -ualis c 1163, c 1457, subject to rent,
tributary; (subst.) 1086, c 1120, -or, -orius
1086, -uarius 1222, 1479, -ualis 1181,
13c., rent-paying tenant (? unfree); tenant at
farm (Savernake) 1276; c 1220, 1346, sensarius 1307, 1337, -erius 1297, chensarius

(W.) 1275, 1304, **chencer, chencerius** (W.) c 1300, non-burgess resident in borough (*cf.* TENS); **-or**, tax-collector 14c.; ***-ura** c 1090, 1545, **sensura** c 1303, censure, condemnation; creed, cult 770; **c. Christianitatis**, Christian creed 12c.; **c. regia**, royal dignity c 1115; **-eo**, to assign, appoint c 550; (?) *for* **sentio**, to feel c 1430; **cenceo**, to consider c 1356, c 1476; **senseo**, to tax, assess (Sc.) 1464; **-o**, to pay rent 13c.; *cf.* **2 cessus**, TENS; *see also* SENS

*cent/ena a 1204, a 1564, **-enum** 1136, c 1362, **-enarium** (**-enarius**) c 1178, c 1488, **-um** 1230, c 1324, **†-a** (G.) 1254, **†-urium** 839, hundredweight or set of one hundred; **-ena** 1331, 1387, **-enarium** (**-enarius**) c 1155, 1476, **-inarium** 1460, 1474, **-um** 1252, c 1290, **-ena major** c 1296, **-enarius major** a 1199, ***-um majus** 1160, 1342, **-um per vj^{xx}** 1286, long hundred; **-ena minor** 1284, **-um minus** 1294, 1388, **-um per v^{xx}** 1286, short hundred; **-enarium** c 1102, c 1400, **-uria** 1086, 1586, **-uriata** c 1178, **-uriatus** (?) 11 c., hundred (division of county); **-enarius** c 1115, c 1150, **-urio** c 1150, **‡1570**, hundredman, hundred-bailiff; **-urio**, rook (at chess) a 1620; **-enarius**, commander of one hundred men 1297, 1355; (*adj.*) hundredfold c 1380, c 1410; c 1250, c 1341, **-enus** 8c. c 1180, **-ennis** 6c. c 1190, one hundred years old, centenarian; **-enarius annorum**, century c 1414, 1552; **-enus**, having weregeld of 100 shillings c 1115; hundredth c 1190, c 1450; of hundredths c 870; **-igamus**, a hundred times married c 1184; **-ilogium**, book attributed to Ptolemy 1267, 1344; **-inervia** a 1250, **‡14c.**, **-umnervia** a 1250, ribwort plantain (bot.); **-inodia** a 1250, 1634, **-inodium** 13c., **‡14c.**, knotgrass *or* vetch (bot.); **‡-um capita**, asphodel (bot.) 14c.; **-opolis**, ἑκατόμπολις, hundred-citied c 1212; **-upliciter** c 730. 11c., **-uplum** (bibl.), a hundredfold; **-uplo**, to multiply by a hundred c 1270.

cent/o, patchwork quilt c 1467; **‡-osus**, ragged 1570; **-onizo**, to arrange for singing 13c.

centonica, *see* **santonicum**.

‡centrix, (?) mayweed (bot.) 15c.

centr/um galli, cock's-spur, clary (bot.) a 1250, 1538; **-aliter**, at the centre a 1250, 1378; **-ie** *or* **-ii** (*pl.*), mid-parts c 1212; **-ifugus**, centrifugal 1686; **-ipetentia**, centripetal tendency 1686; **-ipetus**, centripetal 1686.

cenub-, *see* CENOB

cen/ulentus c 1125, c 1325, **scenulentus** 1360, **-ulens** 12c., foul, muddy; **-osus**, sinful c 950; **-o**, to befoul c 1180; *cf.* **cenevectorium**.

ceola, *see* **kela**.

ceorlus, cirl/us, **-iscus homo**, churl c 1115.

cep-, *see also* SEB; SCEPTR; **sep-**

cep/a, onion: **-e** c 1200, ***sepa, sepum** 1282, 1469, **†geba** a 1408, (?) **†thepa** 1448; **c. canina** a 1250, **‡c. marina, -ula marina** 14c., **‡c. maris** c 1440, squill; **c. silvestris** 1535; **-ula** a 1250, **‡sepula, sipula**,

†sinollus 15c., **‡cibolus** c 1440, "chibol", small onion; *cf.* **civeta**; **‡separium**, "pickle-sauce" c 1440; **‡sepulator**, "sewer at meat" 15c.; **‡sepulo**, to "sew", serve 15c.

ceparius, horticultural (*cf.* κηπουρός) c 870.

†cepeatus, (?) sepia-coloured 1245.

cephal/ 690, 8c., **†-e** 6c., **-on** 8c., **cephas** c 1080, 1327, head; **-ea** c 1200, a 1250, **-argia, -oponia** a 1250, **-ica** c 1180, **‡14c.**, **†cephatica infirmitas** a 1250, headache, migraine; **-argicus**, of headache c 900. a 1100, a 1250; **vena -ica bracchii** a 1250; **-icus**, in chief (her.) c 1595; **-us**, chief (her.) c 1595; **†-us**, *for* **acephalus**, stupid 13c.

cephus, cepus, *see* **scyphus**.

cepicio, *see* COLP

cepp-, *see* CIPP

cepsito, *see* CESP

cer-, *see also* ser-

cer/a, wax: part of a falcon a 1150; **in -a**, with seal unbroken 1398; **sine -a**, unsealed 1292; **c. falsa**, (?) forgery of seal 1172; **c. Paschalis**, wax for Easter candle 1202; **c. virginea**, virgin wax a 1250, 1331; ***c. viridis**, estreat sealed with green wax 1275, 1431; **sera** c 1500, **†cora** 1248, 1286, *for* **-a**; **-e minister**, chafe-wax (Chancery official) 1586 (*cf.* CALEF); **-aculum**, wax tablet 7c. 12c.; **-agium** 1194, 1340, **ciragium** c 1210, 1289, **siragium** (**†gyragium**) 1275, 1290, wax-scot; **panis ciragii**, (?) cake of wax, *or* bread in lieu of wax-scot 1274, 1340; **-arius** c 1172, c 1393, **-efactor** 1476, 1519, **-ofactor** c 1330, chandler; (?) **-arius** 1205, **-ofer** 1278, ***-oferarius** 760. c 1250, 1517, **-eoferarius** c 790, **-eferarius** 1524, candle-bearer, acolyte; **-oferarius** c 1350, 1423, **-eferarius** 1422, 1524, candle-stick; **-eolus** c 1136, p 1341, **-ulus** 1194, small candle; **-eus**, (?) sealed 1274; **-ea** c 1444, **caereus** c 870, **sereus** 1388, 1461, **serius** c 1500, **sergia** c 1466, *for* **-eus**, 'cerge', candle; ***-eus Paschalis** 12c., 1555, **c. Pasche** 1245; **c. processionalis** 15c.; **c. sacramentalis** 1376, 1423, **-eostrata** c 790, **-ostata** (*pl.*) c 760, candelabra; **-icus**, (?) waxen 1461; **cirona**, shoe-polish (O.F. *ciroine*) 1307; **-atio**, (?) waxing (of hides) 1368; melting together (alch.) c 1215, **‡1652**; **-aton** c 1215, **-otum** c 1215, a 1250, wax plaster (alch.); **cyratus**, waxed 1345; *see also* **2 pannus**; **-o**, to melt together (alch.) c 1215, **‡1652**.

ceragra, *see* **chiragra**.

ceramus, *see* **ceraunius**.

cer/astes, (?) horn (material) 13c.; **-estes**, *for* **-astes**, horned serpent, i.e. the Devil 10c.

cer/asum, cherry: **-atium** 1243, **-esum** c 1330, 1390, **-iacum** 1296, **-icum** 1390, 1415, **-isum** c 1266, **ciricum** 1297, **cirisum** c 1400, **seresum** 1390; **serusum** 'cherry', roundel (her.) p 1394; **-icus** 1275, **-isarius** c 1290, **-osarius** 1239, cherry tree.

cer/aunius, kind of gem: **-oneum** c 1215, **‡14c.**, **†-amus** a 1250, **†-omina** c 1362.

*cercell/a c 1192, c 1436, **-us** (?) c 1200, c 1300, **sarcella** 1412, **carcellus** 1290, 'sarcelle', teal; **-arius** 1203, 1223, **†cereeolarius** 1200, **sercellarius** c 1155, for hunting teals.

cercellum, see CIRCUL

cerchi/a 1221, p 1360, **-um** c 1303, **serchia** 1234, search (esp. for strayed beasts or stolen chattels); cf. †**coumecherchia; c. vicecomitis,** aid to sheriff in recovering chattels 1234; **serchator,** searcher (guild official) c 1378; **-o** 1209, 1299, **cherchio** 1299, **serciero** 1495, to search; cf. **2 circa.**

cercl-, cercul-, see CIRCUL; **sarculatio.**

‡**cere/brum arietis, c. bovis,** tartarum combustum (alch.) 1652; **celabrum,** brain 13c.; **-bellaris,** ephemeral fever a 1250; **-vellarium,** (?) brain-cover, skull-cap 1303.

cerecum, see 1 **sericum.**

ceremon-, see CERIMON

Cerena, see **Siren.**

cerestes, see **cerastes.**

ceresum, see **cerasum.**

cereteca, ceriteca, see **chirotheca.**

cereum, see **cherogryllus.**

cere/us, -olus, -ostrata, see **cera.**

cerevellarium, see **cerebrum.**

cerevisia, see **cervisia.**

ceric-, see **cerasum;** CHERCH; 1 **sericum.**

cerimon/ialiter (ceremon-), with fitting solemnity 8c.; **-ico,** to give ceremonially c 550.

ceris-, see **cerasum.**

cerjantia, see **serjantia.**

†**cerna** c 1200, †**charna** 1359, measure of flax.

cernellatus, see **cornelinus.**

‡**cernid/a** (†**cervid-**), "tap-tree", spigot 1483; ‡**-o,** "to tap" 1483.

cern/itio, beholding, sight 9c.; **-ibilis,** discernible 930.

cernuus, low, downcast (of voice) 760.

cero, see **cera; seroitas.**

cero-, see also **cera; chiro-**

ceroma carnis, earthly battleground c 950.

cero/neum, -mina, see **ceraunius.**

cerophea, see **girophea.**

cerritus, insane: **ciritus** c 1220.

cersegus, see **carsea.**

cersina, see **sarcina.**

certa, see **certitudo.**

certago, see **sartago.**

cert/amen, ordeal (leg.) c 550, c 1115; see also CAMP; **-ator Christi** c 1000; **-atus,** contest (eccl.); **-atrix,** competitive (f.) c 1160; **-o** (with acc.) to fight with c 550.

*****certific/atio** c 1109, 1549, **-atoria** 1283, **-atorium** c 1305, 1684, **-arium** c 1476, 1526, assurance, certification, certificate; discussion of an hypothesis (log.) 1344, c 1370; **-atorius** a 1245, a 1564, **-ativus** c 1270, certifying; **-atorie** (sc. littere) a 1452; **-abilis,** ascertainable 1267; **-e,** certainly 1427; **-o,** to make known, demonstrate 1267, c 1363; *****to inform, assure, certify 799. c 1090, 1684; **c. me** 1200, 1231; see also **creta.**

*****cert/itudo,** certainty 735, 796. c 1251, 1620; **c. lete** 1535, 1647, **-um** 1274, 1649, tithing-penny, 'head-silver' (payment in lieu of reading roll of suitors at view of frankpledge); *****-itudinaliter** a 1240, 1511, **-issime** c 790. c 1250, **-issimo** c 1245, **per -itudinem** c 1341, c 1343, **pro -o** 11c., c 1250, certainly, with certainty; **-o -ius** a 1200; †**-um,** boun-

dary-mark c 1130; fixed allowance or wage 1299, c 1397; fixed quota of labour service c 1320; 1324, **-a** 1413, **redditus -us** 1462, 1535, fixed rent; see also **visus; sertus,** for **-us,** 947, (12c.); **-ioratio,** information, notification a 1452, c 1470; **-iorari,** name of a writ 1500; *****-ioro** c 1160, 1583, †**-o** 1279, to inform, notify.

†**certsura,** chasing, engraving 1420.

cerucha, see **cerycium.**

ceruchus, sail-yard: **cheruc/a** c 1200; **-a,** weather-cock c 1200, ‡15c.

cerul/a 865, **-um** c 1000, wave (of the blue sea).

cerulus, see **cera.**

cerura, see **sera.**

cerus/ium rubeum, red lead 1549; **gersa,** for **-sa,** a 1250, ‡14c.

cerv- see also **cervulus;** SERV

†**cervica,** (?) f.l. for **cernue,** c 1200.

cervic/es (pl.), brains 1285, 1288; ‡**-arium** 15c., **servical** 1345, a 1564, †**cervale** 13c., for **-al,** pillow, cushion; **-aria,** Canterbury bell (bot.) 1634; **-ose,** stubbornly c 1220, c 1250; *****-ositas,** stubbornness 9c. c 1125, 1456; **-osus,** stubborn, stiff-necked c 1180, 1409; ‡**-o,** to pry 1483.

cervid-, see CERNID

cervis/ia *****1086, c 1500, **cervicia** 1368, 15c., **-a** c 590, c 1000. 1086, 1213, *****cerevisia** 12c., 1608, **cervoisia** c 1230, 1474, **servisia** c 1230, 1474, **servisium** c 1270, *****servicia** c 1266, 1547, **serevisia** 1120, c 1355, ‡**-era** 1483, ale; **-ia,** ale-feast 1198, 1254; boon-work with allowance of ale 13c.; **c. beate Marie** 1255, **c. sancti Cudberti** 1327, customary payments; **c. conventualis** 13c., 1474, **c. monachalis** 1322; **c. duplex,** strong ale 13c.; **c. mediocris** c 1135, **c. parva** 1275, **c. tenua** 1511, small ale; **c. prepositi,** compulsory brewing for reeve c 1255; **c. secunda** 1254, 1322; **c. tertia** 13c., 1254; **-ialis,** fond of ale c 1200; **vasculum -arium,** ale-mug a 1150; **-iaria** 1552, **taberna -iaria** 1516, ‡1520, **domus -iana** c 1542, ale-house; **-arius,** tenant paying ale-rent 1086; **-iarius,** brewer (mon.) 1086; ‡"tippler", alehouse-keeper 1520; ‡**-iator** 1520, **coctor -iarius** 1561, brewer; **-io,** to turn (water) into ale c 1200.

cerv/ulus, fawn 709. ‡15c.; ‡**-aria, -i ocellus,** elaphoboscon, wild parsnip (bot.) 14c.; **-erettarius** 1322, **(canis) -erettus** 1234, 1290, **c. -ereticus** 1284, **c. -ericius** 1225, 1290, **brachettus -ericius** 1280, stag-hound; †**-ica,** (?) for **-a,** doe 1368; **-icida,** deer-slayer c 1196, c 1300; **pellis -ilis,** deer-skin 1369; see also **herba.**

cer/ycium, staff of office: **ciriceus** 760; **-ucha,** herald c 1200.

1 Cesar/, the king c 1115; **-eus** 802. 1380, 1427, **-inus** 13c., 1378, imperial; **jus -eum,** civil law 1508.

2 ces/ar, -era, see **sicera.**

cesare, a logical mood 13c.

cesionalis, see **seiso.**

cesor, hewer (bibl.).

cesp/es, earth c 550; stock of descent 1199 (cf. **cippus**); (fig.) cover, cloak c 1470; **sespes,** for **-es,** turf 1277; **-itatio,** stumbling c 1255; *-ito c 1200, c 1540, cepsito c 1400, †seppito 1338, to stumble, fall.

1 cess/us, departure, retirement, decline 13c., a 1564; gait 1461; -atio, ceasing 1324, 1589; end of term (ac.) c 1395, c 1502; withdrawal, leave of absence c 1335; retirement or dismissal from office c 1407, 1419; -atus, delay c 1254; -avit, name of a writ 1419, 1445; -ibilis, yielding 1427; -im, (?) the past c 950; *-io c 1223, c 1593, sessio 1348, retirement, resignation; sessio, yield, payment 1532; -ionaria (f.) 1546, -ionarius 1397, 1608, cessioner (leg.); -or, successor 9c.; -o, to cease, stop (trans.) c 1290, c 1407; cedo, to count, be valid 1327; c 1362, c. in fata 1240, 14c., to die; c. ad 13c., c 1373, c. in c 1219, 1380, to tend to, result in.

2 cess/us, rent 781; property 1086; -o, to tax, assess 1485; cf. CENS, SESS

cest-, see SEXT

cet/e, whale c 1200, c 1343; coetia (pl.), sea monsters c 550; †-oima, (?) whale-oil 1334; see also sperma.

ceter/, other c 1433; -i (pl.), some c 550; -is paribus c 1311, c 1357.

cet/erach c 1212, -erac a 1250, ‡-rac 14c., citerac 1538, ceterach (bot.).

cetewallum, see zedoaria.

cetha, see theca.

cetula, see situla.

cetus (coetus) cardinalium, college of cardinals 1258, 1293.

ceu, like: seu c 1130, c 1470.

ceudra, see CALD

†ceutrum, (?) throat 6c.

cevera, see civera.

ceverunda, see severunda.

cha-, see also ca-

Chaan, see Chanus.

chabilo, see chalo.

1 *chac/ea, -ia 1183, c 1470, chascia (cascia) 1200, c 1308, chasea p 1290, 1587, caza c 1120, 1183, scachia 12c., 1275, chase, (land for or right of) hunting, private forest; c. libera 1236, 1582; *-ea 1239, c 1400, chasea 1285, chazcia 1241, †clasia 1293, (?) catia c 1200, katia 1250, jacia 1236, (?) schasea 1293, drove-way, (right of) driving cattle; pursuit 1468; c. (chatia) zabuli, driving, heaping up, of sand 1230; -iabilis, fit for hunting 1237; -eator 14c., caciator 1299, caszorius (†coszorius) 13c., driver; -ur 1166, 1205, cacor c 1200, chasurus 1242, chazurus 1198, catzurus 1205, cazorius a 1190, chascurus 1205, 1214, †chascunus 1210, hunter (horse); cf. catus; *-eo 1184, 1355, -io 1228, 1278, chasio 1428, †chasco 1214, chazcio 1238, chazio 1274, to chase, hunt; -eo a 1160, 1285, -io 1238, 15c., cacio c 1155, c 1195, scacio (schacio, †stacio) 12c., 1276, to drive (cattle); -io carrucam a 1300.

2 chac/ea, chasing, engraved work 1338; -eatus 1441, 1468, chaseatus 1468, chased, engraved.

3 chac/ea, -ia, see scacia.

chaffor, see CALEFAC

Chaganus, see Chanus.

chalc/anthum (calc-) a 1233, 1577, †-ata 13c., †-adis c 1215, blue vitriol; -ucecumenon a 1250, -ecumenon 13c., -ecuminon 1267, ‡-os cecaumenos 14c., smelted copper; *-ographus, printer 1515, c 1553.

chalcedon/ c 1200, caucidonius 1267, for -ius, chalcedony.

Chald/eum, Aramaic language 1271; -aice, in Aramaic 1271.

chaldrium, see caldaria.

chalendra c 1250, kalandra 13c., chelindra c 1200, c 1260, 'chaland', flat-bottomed boat.

chalengo, see calumnia.

chali, see alkali.

*chalo/ 1201, 1419, schalo 1274, Catalaunense c 1180, pannus -nicus c 1220, p. Katalonicus 1245, p. de chabilone 1206, 'shalloon', blanket or coverlet; -narius, blanket-maker 1240.

chalyb/s (calib-), steel: calabs 1314, 1573, ‡calebs c 1440, †celebs c 1270, †calaba c 1489, calive (abl.) c 1250; Curia -is, Steelyard (London) 1394; -atus c 1200, c 1220, -einus 1265, -eus 1264, 1686, made of steel; firm as steel c 1218, c 1220; -eatus, impregnated with iron, chalybeate 1622; calaberium, (?) smithy 1539; Caliburnus, Excalibur 1136, a 1446.

Cham, see Chanus.

chamber-, chames-, see CAMER

chameleo, chameleon: camaleon c 1301, calameon 1271; ‡camalion, Gabriel hound 1483; cf. cameleo.

chamemelon, camomile (bot.): camomilla c 1200, 1622.

Chamicus, of Ham (son of Noah) 1427.

champertia, see cambipars.

chamus, see camus.

chandria, see candela.

chanferitus, chamfered, fluted (arch.) 1252.

changia, see cambium.

channum, see CANNAB

chansia, see camisia.

Chanus 1609, Caan c 1250, Chaan (†Thaan) 1271, Cham 1302, Chaganus 12c., Khan.

‡chaomantia, divination by air 1652.

chap/a 1284, 1369, -ia c 1448, 'chape', metal ornament; capelleta, (?) 'chapelet', spur-buckle 1357; see also 3 capella.

chapericium, see caperacius.

chapitrallum, see capitellum.

chapmanneshala, see CHEP

Chapotensis, see Chipotensis.

chapul-, see SCAPUL

chapusatus, trimmed, carpentered (O.F. chapuisie) 1282.

char/acter (car-, kar-), written letter of alphabet 932. 1164, 1427; 1281, 1344, -acta 1331, magical sign; printer's type 1520; character, distinctive quality c 1300; c. clericalis, tonsure 1262, 1375; c. crucis 1017, 1042. 1254, 15c., -ecter crucis c 1266, 1383, c. domini c 1196, c. dominicus c 1400, sign of the cross; -acteristicus, characteristic p 1300; bearing the mark (of the Beast) 1610; -acterizo, to take the shape of 870; to characterize p 1300, 1344; to tonsure c 1190; see also cataracta.

charadrius, kind of bird (bibl.): **caladrius** a 1250, a 1446, **caulandrius** c 1200.

charativus, *see* **caritas**.

charax/atio (**carax-**), scarification (med.) a 1250; **-atura** 960, 974, ‡**-is** 15c., writing; **-o** 767, 1031. a 1100, 15c., **-so** 685, 875, **craxo** c 700, c 950, **karexo** 1336, to write.

char/esea, -isea, *see* **carsea**.

charg/erium 1385, c 1450, **-erum** 14c., **-erus** 1386, 1423, **-ourus** 1324, **-eatorium** 1357, 'charger', dish.

charg/ia, -io, charchio, *see* **carca**.

chari/ettum, -otum, charett-, *see* **caretta**.

char/is (**car-**), grace c 950; **-isma**, *grace, spiritual gift 6c., 10c. a 1090, 1487; Holy Spirit 10c.; Whit-Sunday 15c.; **icarisma**, free gift 14c.; **-ientismus**, courtesy 1609.

charn-, *see* **caro; cerna; 2 garnetta**.

charopos, karopos (†**katapos**), a bluish colour c 1200, a 1250.

charr-, *see* 1 **carra**.

chart-, *see* 1 **carta**.

charybdis, whirlpool: **carubdis** 9c.

chas-, chasc-, chaz-, chatia, *see* **chacea**.

chasator, (?) wedge, bar (arch.) 1313.

chasonus, lopping (of vine), pruned spray 1274.

chauco, *see* 1 **calcea**.

chaud-, *see* CALD

chaufepeynum, *see* **calepungnus**.

chauffornium, *see* 3 **calcea**.

chaumagium 1304, **cheumagium, chumagium** 1282, **chimagium** 1312, (payment for) enforced idleness (of mint).

chaumb-, *see* CAMER

chaump-, *see* **campus**.

chaundelarius, *see* **candela**.

chauso, *see* 1 **calcea**.

chavesea, *see* 1 **caputium**.

chaz-, *see* 1 **chacea**.

Chazarus, Khazar c 1250.

chebena, *see* **cheveyna**.

cheker-, chekmat, *see* SCACC

cheldra, *see* CALD

cheldum, *see* **geldum**.

‡**chelidon/ia minor,** (?) lesser celandine (bot.) 14c.; **-ium minus,** (?) figwort 1538.

chelindr/a, -us, *see* **chalendra; cylindrus**.

chelydrus, the Serpent, Satan 13c.; **helydrus** 8c., **ilider** (?) 12c., serpent.

chemia, *see* CHYM

chemin-, *see* **caminus** (1 & 2).

chemisia, *see* **camisia**.

chenc-, chens-, *see* CENS

chenella, *see* **canale**.

chenitewilda, *see* **cnichtengilda**.

chenix, dry measure (χοῖνιξ): †**cenit** a 1250.

chennetum, oak sapling (Fr. *chênaie*) 1233.

chensillagium, *see* **cantillagium**.

cheo, chio, to pour (χέω) 8c.

chep-, *see also* CHIPP; SKEPP

chep/ingabulum, market-gavel c 1300; **-ingbotha**, market-hall (Bristol) 14c.; **-manessela** 1159, 1167, **-emanesela** 1130, chapmanneshala 1189, chapmen's hall (Winchester); **ceapgildum**, compensation c 1115.

chepitrum, *see* **capitellum**.

‡**cheras**, tumour, scrofula 1652.

cherch/ambrum, church-amber, payment of corn c 1170; **chyricbota**, church-bote, service of repairing church c 1115; **chericsceattum, ciricsceattum, curicsceattum** c 1115, **cherechsectum** c 1300, **cherichettum** 1307, **cherisettum** 1209, 1234, **cherisatum** 1234, **-ettum** 1276, 1397, **chersettum** 1284, 1388, **chiricsettum** 12c., **chirechetum** 1294, **chirichetum** c 1280, **chirisetum** 1234, **chirsetum** 1234, 1296, **chirssheta** 1337, **chisetum** 1464, **churchesectum** 1269, **churicsettum** 1277, **churichetum** c 1280, **churscettum** 1260, c 1375, **chursettum** 1234, 1308, **circietus** 1086, **shirichetum** c 1280, church-scot; **ciricsocna**, sanctuary c 1115.

cherchio, *see* **cerchia**.

cheries, 'cheer', countenance a 1142.

‡**cheri/o**, "occult accidental virtue of external elements" (alch.) 1652; ‡**-onium**, "that in which nature cannot be altered" (alch.) 1652.

chern/a, -um 1279, 1311, **churna** 1278, churn.

cherogryllus 1267, **chirogryllus** 13c., coney (bibl.) (χοιρόγρυλλος); **cirogrillus** a 1250, 1300, **sirogrillus** 1475, ‡1483, †**sigrillus** 1521, squirrel; ‡**kyrius** c 1440, ‡**kirrius** 1483, "swine"; †**cereum**, (?) pig-sty (χοιρεών) 12c.

Cheron, *see* **Acheron**.

chersettum, *see* CHERCH

cherubicus, cherubic 1345; **scherumbinus** 1240, **hirubin** 1079, cherub, cherubim.

cheruca, *see* **ceruchus**.

cheseclathum, cheese-cloth 1348; **chusevattum**, cheese-vat 1276.

chesibla, *see* 1 **casula**.

chesta, *see* **cista**.

chestra, *see* CASTR

cheterlingus, *see* **chitus**.

chetum, *see* **scheta**.

cheumagium, *see* **chaumagium**.

chevacia, *see* 1 **caputium**.

chevag-, *see* **capitagium**; 1 **caputium**.

chev/alchea, -elria, *see* 1 **caballus**.

chev/antia 1342, 1419, **-ansia** 1426, **-isantia** 1254, 1588, 'chevisance', loan or contract; **-io** 1346, 1365, **-iso** 1419, to borrow, agree to borrow.

chev/ecium, -esium, -etta, *etc.*, *see* 1 **caputium**.

chever-, *see* **capra; capro**.

chevestrum, *see* **capister**.

cheveyna 1415, **chebena** a 1564, ‡**clepa** a 1520, chevin, chub (fish).

chev/ezailla 1220, **-icellum** 1316, 'chevesaile', collar.

chev/icium, -iscium, -isium, *see* 1 **caputium**.

chevile, *see* 2 **cavilla**.

cheviro, *see* **capro**.

chev/isantia, -io, -iso, *see* **chevantia**.

chewagium, *see* **capitagium**.

cheyn/a, -ia, -us, *see* **catena**.

chiatum, *see* **cyathus**.

chifra, *see* **cifra**.

chihera, 'chare', lane (co. Durham) 13c.

child/wita a 1160, **-ewita** 1260, 'child-wite', payment by villein on birth of bastard.

chim-, *see also* **caminus** (1 & 2).
chima, chime 1521.
chimagium, *see* **chaumagium**.
chimentum, *see* CEMENT
chimer/a, harlot 13c.; riding-cloak c 1350, c 1430; sort of boat 12c.; chimera, fantasy c 1177; **-icus** c 1620, **-inus** 1521, chimerical, nugatory; **-or**, to be debauched c 1200.
chimia, *see* **chymia**.
†**chiminilis**, staff 15c.
china, china root c 1615.
chincia, *see* **cincia**.
chio, *see* **cheo**.
chiphus, *see* **scyphus**.
Chipotensis (libra, moneta) 1289, 1317, Capotensis 1297, Chapotensis 1313, Shipotensis 1305, coin of Bigorre (usually ⅛ of sterling).
chipp/us 1248, 1284, **-a** 1364, **cheppus** 1276, 1362, **cippus** 1248, **sheppus** 1345, 'chip' or 'chep', share-beam (of plough); **chipclutum** 1294, **chepclutum** 1351, **chupclutum** 1325, **kipclutum** 1270, 1291, 'chip-clout'; **kyplynea**, 'chip-line' 1297; **-atio**, fitting (plough) with a chip 1368, 1387; ***-o** 1267, 1451, **-io** 1284, 1410, **cheppo** 1336, **chuppo** 1330, **schippo** 1314, 1372, †**schirpio** 1333, to fit (plough) with a chip; *cf.* CIPP
chira (**chyra**), hand (χείρ) c 1000; *see also* **schira**.
chiragra, gout; **ceragra** 1267, **cyragra**, †**tyragra** a 1250.
chirapia, *see* **chytropus**.
chiricsettum, *etc.*, *see* CHERCH
chiriinomus, *see* **kyrius**.
*chirograph/um (cir-, cyr-) 749, 1044. 1085, c 1643, **cherographum** 1522, **sirographum** 1419, c 1430, **serographum** 1329, **-atum** c 1320, deed, chirograph; **c. mortis** (theol.) c 1190; **-alis** 13c., ***-atus** c 1162, 1430, made in the form of a chirograph; **-arius** 1215, a 1564, **-erus** 1469, writer of chirographs; **-aria** 1262, 1333, **-ia** 1388, 1421, office of chirographer; **-aria**, (?) stencilling 1434; **-izatio**, confirmation by chirograph (or charter) a 1100; **-izo** to grant or confirm by chirograph a 1100; **-o**, to make a chirograph 1275.
chirogryllus, *see* **cherogryllus**.
chiromant/ia, chiromancy, palmistry 1378, 1517; **-icus**, palmist c 1160, c 1320.
chiro/phus, **-pus**, *see* **chytropus**.
chirothec/a (cir-, cyr-) ***a** 1090, 1552, ***ceroteca** c 1250, c 1450, **cereteca** c 1485, **ceriteca** c 1397, **cerotica** 1506, **girotheca** 1436, **siroteca** c 1300, 1390, **seroteca** 1349, 1507, **seriteca** 1472, **serotica** 1425, **scirotega** c 1220, †**citherica** 1552, glove; a 1150, a 1250, **c. ad austurcum** a 1213, **c. ad erodium** c 1260, falconer's glove; **c. ferrea** 1335, **c. de guerra** 1318, **c. de plate** 1318, c 1415, mailed glove; **c. pontificalis** 1317, 1328; **c. distincta per digitos** c 1330; **c. duplex**, lined glove 1434 (opposed to **c. simplex**); ‡**c. vulpis**, foxglove (bot.) 14c.; ***-arius** c 1220, c 1450, ‡**sutor c.** c 1520, **cerotecarius** 1265, c 1384, **-ator** 1240, glover; **-atus** c 1160, c 1422, **cerotecatus** c 1330, **cerotegatus** c 1266, wearing gloves.

chirsetum, *see* CHERCH
chirurg/us (cir-, cyr-) 1267, a 1564, **sirurgus** 1345, **-ius** 1287, 15c., (?) †**cynigus** a 1235, ***-icus** c 1210, c 1540, **sirurgicus** 1242, a 1447, **sururgicus** 1243, 1429, **cirugicus** c 1254, 1277, †**circurgicus** 1260, **cyrogicus** c 1267, **cirigecus** 1495, **surrigicus** 1258, 1339, **surugicus** 1251, **surgicus** (G.) 1305, **surgecus** 1498, **surrogus** 1587, surgeon; **-icus**, surgical 1200, c 1422; **-ia** c 900. c 1210, c 1550, **cirorgia** 1420, **sirurgia** c 1290, c 1400, **sururgia** 1315, **surgeria** c 1430, surgery.
chisellus, *see* **cisellus**.
chisetum, *see* CHERCH
chitrapus, *see* **chytropus**.
chitus (porcorum) 1235, **cheterlingus** c 1335, chitterling.
Chi/us: stelle **-e**, pole-stars 815.
chivagium, *see* **capitagium**.
chival-, *see* 1 **caballus**.
chivereum, *see* **civera**.
chiver/o, **-ellus**, **-allus**, *see* **capra**, **capro**.
chivewarda, *see* CLIV
chivillus, *see* 2 **cavilla**.
chlamy/s (clami-), cloak (fig.), disguise c 1295; **calamis**, cloak c 550; †**clamine**, (?) *for* **-de**, 12c.; **-dalis**, in the nature of a cloak c 1180; **-dula**, short cloak 1508; **-do**, to cloak, disguise c 1180; **-dor**, to wear a cloak 1266.
choca, *see* 1 **cogga**.
choi/sellus (choy-), reservoir (O.F. *choisel*) 1245.
chol/era (col-), bile a 1150, 15c.; choleric humour, anger c 1200, 1622; **c. adusta** c 1200; **c. citrina**, **c. erugi[n]osa** a 1250; **c. nigra** c 1180, 15c.; ‡**c. prasina** 14c.; **c. rubea** a 1150, 15c.; **c. vitellina** a 1250; **-ericus**, choleric, bilious c 900. a 1200, 1424; **-agogum**, medicine to draw off bile a 1250, ‡14c.; **decoctio -agogica** a 1250; **-inum**, gall c 1298.
cholettus, *see* **cauleria**.
chondritum, grain 9c.
chop/inum 1331, **copina** 1459, **schopina** c 1320, **-eta** 15c., liquid measure, *chopine*.
chopio, *see* **coopertio**.
choppa, *see* **shopa**.
choragia (*pl.*), (?) rites (*cf.* χορηγία) c 950.
chord-, *see* CORD
chor/episcopus, archdeacon 760. c 1100, c 1220; **tabula -ographica**, map 1586.
chorita, clerk intruded into benefice by lay authority c 1218.
1 **chor/us** (cor-), ***choir of singers** (eccl.) c 980. c 1100, 1586; ***a** 1090, 1570, **quorum** 1331, choir (part of church); **c. primarius**, chancel 1528; **c. sinister** 13c.; **c. monasticus** c 1000; ***-alis** c 1217, 1498, **-istalis** p 1408, **-arius** 1470, of or for a choir (eccl.); *see also* **capa**, **sacerdos**, **vicarius**; **-arius** 1434, **-aula** 1374, ‡15c., choir-leader, precentor; **-aula**, soloist c 1204, c 1220; **-ea**, dance tune 1326; circuit, precinct 1414; **C. gigantum**, Stonehenge 1136, c 1385; **-icus**, song-writer c 1250; †**-inus**, dancer 15c.; ***-ista** 1267, c 1452, ‡**-icista** 15c., **-usta** 1430, ‡15c., **querista** 1283, **-istarius** 1535, 1546, **querestarius** c 1440, chorister

(eccl.); **-eo**, to dance c 1190; **-izo**, to sing in a choir c 1090, c 1100.

2 chor/us (cor-), 'crowd', fiddle c 1200, ‡c 1483; ‡**-icista**, "crowder" 15c.; *cf.* **crudarius**.

3 chorus, *see* **Caurus**.

4 chorus, *see* **corus**.

choysellus, *see* **choisellus**.

***chrism/a**, chrism (eccl.) 760, c 1000. c 1080, c 1514; **cremagium**, due paid for chrism 1285, 1414; **-alis** c 950. c 1170, c 1500, **-aticus** c 1250, **-atorius** c 1250, 1535, chrismal; **-al** 685, **-ale** 10c. a 1100, 14c., **-atica** c 1190, **-arium** a 1125, c 1125, **-atorium** c 1125, 1517, chrism-cloth or chrismatory; **-arium**, reliquary 8c.; **-atio**, anointment, confirmation 1385, 1400; **cremium**, cream 1265; ***-o** 5c. 1245, c 1450, †**crusino** c 1200, to anoint, confirm.

‡**christ/ofora** 14c., **-ophoriana** 1641, herb Christopher (bot.).

Christ/us, anointed one 793. c 1341, c 1470; **C. Dei** c 1070; ***C. Domini** c 1125, c 1540; **C. vincit**, an anthem 12c., 14c.; **-eleison** a 1130, c 1266; **-eitas**, Christhood 1427; **-iana**, Christian woman 1279; **-ianicida**, Christian-slayer c 1172; **-ianissime**, in a very Christian manner c 1125, c 1450; **rex (princeps) -ianissimus**, title of English king c 1180, c 1544; **-ianismus**, Christianity c 730. c 1125, c 1546; c 1190, a 1452, **-ianitas** c 1188, c 1540, †**-ianitata** 679, Christendom; **-ianitas**, oath as a Christian c 1178; title of Pope -a 1130; spiritual jurisdiction, ecclesiastical law 1073, 1559; ecclesiastical court 1181; *see also* **curia, decanus, herba**; **-ianitas** 8c., 10c. c 1125, **-ianizatio** c 1500, conversion to Christianity; ***-icola** (eccl.), **-icolus** (*adj.*) 9c., **-ifidelis** (*subst.*) 1139, 1545, Christian; **-iformis**, Christ-like 865. 1345, 1427; †**-iformiter**, (?) as Christ's representative 865; **-igenus**, belonging to Christ's family c 870; **-otoca**, the Virgin c 950; **-ianizo**, to make Christian c 1150; **-ianor**, to become Christian 12c., c 1293; **-ifico**, to make like Christ 1271.

chroko, *see* **THROCC**

chromatic/a, chromatic melody 1252; **-um genus (musice)** c 1000. a 1200.

***chron/ica** (*f. s.*) c 1100, 1461, **-icalia** (*pl.*) 15c., **-icon** 16c., **-icula** 1361, **-iculi** (*pl.*) 1399, **-ographia** a 1186, 1413, **liber -icalis** c 1400, chronicle, annals; **papirus -icularis** 1458; **-icans** c 1400, **-icarius** 1521, **-icator** 14c., 1414, **-igraphus** 14c., 1461, **-ologus** 1608, chronicler; ‡**-ia**, chronic disease 14c.; **-ice**, for a long time c 1408; chronically (*astr.*) c 1233; **-icus**, chronical (*astr.*) c 1233; long-continued c 1250, 1377; **modo -ico**, in chronicle form c 1362; **-ico** 1345, 1378, **-izo** 15c., to chronicle.

chrys/ochalcheos (cris-), of gold and copper c 1620; **-oclavus**, gold-striped c 1595; †**-ocana** (†**-otania**), (?) chrysoprase a 1250; **-osplenium**, golden saxifrage (bot.) 1634; **-eus**, golden c 1200, ‡14c.

chuchator, *see* **cucherius**.

chumagium, *see* **chaumagium**.

chupa, lady's dressing-gown (? *cf.* It. *cioppa*) 1235.

chupp-, *see* **CHIPP**

church-, churic-, churs-, *see* **CHERCH**

churna, *see* **CHERN**

chusevattum, *see* **cheseclathum**.

chyl/us, chyle (med.) c 1320, ‡14c.; **-osus**, chylous a 1250; ‡**-atricum**, columbine (bot.) 14c.

chym/ia (chim-) c 1260, ‡1652, ‡**chemia** 1652, alchemy; **-icus**, alchemic, chemical c 1320, 1620; **-ista** alchemist, chemist c 1320, 1622.

chyr-, *see also* **chir-**

chyric-, *see* **CHERCH**

chytropus, chafing-dish or trivet (bibl.): **chiropus** 1267, **chirophus** 1551, **chitrapus** 1560, **chirapia** 1553.

ci-, *see also* **si-**; **sci-**

ciasis, *see* **ischia**.

ciatus, *see* **cyathus**.

cibitas, *see* **civis**.

cibolus, *see* **cepa**.

ciboneus, *see* **gibonifer**.

cib/orium, 'severy', bay or compartment of vaulted ceiling c 1188; 1436, **-urium** c 1220, 'baldacchino'.

cib/us quadragesimalis, lenten fare 12c., 1351; **ad -um domini**, with food provided by the lord a 1128, 1449; **-alis** 655. c 1115, 1427, **-abilis** 12c., a 1250, alimentary; **-agium**, fodder c 1360; **-amen**, food c 550; **-arius**, victualler (naut.) 1598; ‡**-atio**, incorporation (alch.) 1652; **-icida**, carver (at table) 1616.

cic/a, -ario, *see* **2 sica**.

cicadatio, idle chatter a 1180.

cicator, *see* **seca**.

cicatri/zatio, scarring a 1250; **-zor**, *for* **-cor**, to form a scar a 1250.

‡**cicer/ erraticus**, thyme (bot.) 14c.; ‡**-bita**, sow-thistle 1570; **jus -um**, pea-soup 13c.

cicera, *see* **sicera**.

ciceserum, *see* **SCISS**

cic/indela, glow-worm *or* firefly: **-indile** 709, **-endula** 1622, **cincendula** c 1188; **cincenella**, (?) mosquito or sand-fly c 1200; ‡**-endulum**, lamp-wick c 1440, 1483; ‡**-endium**, censer 1483.

cicl-, *see* **cyclus**; **siclus**.

cicn-, cicinus, *see* **CYGN**

‡**ciconi/a**, "curlew" 1570; **cigonia** c 1200, **sigonia** 15c., *for* **-a**, stork; **-us**, cock stork c 1212; **unguentum -atum**, ointment made of a stork boiled in various oils a 1250.

Cicotrinus, *see* **aloe**.

‡**cicut/aria**, geranium (bot.) 14c.; ‡**secuta**, *for* **-a**, 15c.; ‡**secuticen**, piper 15c.

cidaris, turban (bibl.).

cidile, *see* **sedile**.

cidima, *see* **cadmia**.

cidon, hauberk (? χιτών) c 550.

cidula, *see* **scindula**.

ciens, singing c 550.

cif-, *see also* **scyphus**.

cifr/a (chifr-, cyphr-) c 1300, 1609, **-e** a 1150, c 1150, cipher, zero (math.); **-a** 1412, c 1620, **-um** c 1200, mere cipher, thing of no account; **ziphera**, cipher, code 1499.

cign-, *see also* **CYGN**; **SIGN**

cignus, liquid measure (6 *cochlearia*) c 1100; *cf.* **mystron.**
cigonia, *see* **ciconia.**
ciko, *see* **seca.**
cilex, *see* **silex.**
‡**ciliacus,** gastric (κοιλιακός) 14c.
cilic/ium *a 1090, c 1540, -inum c 1530, hair shirt; horse-cloth 1307; *1291, 1434, -ia 1324, silicium 1314, strainer, sieve (of hair-cloth); -inus, made of hair-cloth c 1180, 1493; -iatus, wearing a hair-shirt c 1255, c 1414.
cilicivus, *see* **salicia.**
ciligo, *see* **siligo.**
ciliquum, *see* I **sericum.**
cili/um (montis), brow of hill c 1200, 1401; -o, to hood (falc.) a 1250.
cilur-, *see* 2 **celum.**
cilvella, *see* SILV
cim-, *see also* CYM
cima, *see* **cuva.**
cimb-, *see* **cymba;** SYMBOL
cimea, *see* **simia.**
ciment-, cimiterius, *see* CEMENT
cim/eterium, -iterium, -itorium, *see* **cemeterium.**
cimilium, treasure (κειμήλιον) c 1160.
cimin-, *see* CYMIN
cin-, *see also* scin; sin-; syn-; zin-
cinaria, *see* CIVER
cincathegorema, *see* **syncategorema.**
cincen/dula, -ella, *see* **cicindela.**
cincia 1276, **chincia** 1267, **scinchia** 1423, 1534, **sinchia** 1414, 1533, little bag for coins or gems; ‡**sincio,** "to poke" (? put in a bag) 1483.
·**cinciber,** *see* **zinziber.**
cinct/io, girding 7c., c 730; -or 1382, **cintorium** 1206, girdle; -orius, encircling c 1325; -um 1256, -erium c 1390, precinct; Christianus de -ura, Copt 1392; ‡**calige** -urales, "hose to the knee" a 1520; -erarius 1227, -urarius 1332, ‡-uarius 1520, girdler; -us, armament c 1595; **cingo,** to knight a 1142, c 1365; c. in **comitem** 1654; *see also* **miles.**
cind-, *see* CEND; **cinis;** SCIND; **sundra.**
cinefactorium, *see* **cenevectorium.**
ciner-, *see* **cinis;** **civera.**
cinglocetorium 1540, **sinoglossitorium** ‡c 1440, 1539, sluice-gate.
cingnus, *see* **cygnus.**
cingul/um, curtain-wall (arch.) 1186; -a c 1200, 1343, **singulum** 1268, 1587, **scingulum** 1259, *for* -um, belt, girdle, girth; -um canonicum 1686; c. **militare** 12c., 1461, c. **militie** a 1142, c 1450, belt of knighthood; c. **nocturnale** (mon.) c 1330; -us signorum, ecliptic (astr.) a 1233; *see also* **scindula;** *cf.* CINCT
cinifes, *see* **cinyphes.**
cinis, potash 1228, 1504; c. **plumbi,** lead ash 1254, 1420; **cendre** (*pl.*), ashes 1131; *Ciner/es (*pl.*) 1199, 15c., **Ceneres** 1203, *dies -um 1208, c 1447, dies -is c 1218, c 1565, festum -um 1331, c 1589, Ash Wednesday; ‡**cinefactio,** incineration, calcination (alch.) 1652; ‡**cinificatus,** calcined 1652; †-arius, (?) worker in lead ash 1300 (*cf.* **civerarius**); 1185, **cinderarius**

c 1214, -ator a 1235, charcoal-burner; -ata, cupel c 1280; **aqua** -ata (med.) a 1250; ‡-icium, (?) *aqua regia* 1652; -icius c 1400, 1586, -osus 14c., ashen-coloured; **panis** -icius 13c., **p.** -icus 14c., bread mixed with ashes; -esco, to wither 793. c 1170; -o, to turn to ashes (*trans.*) 12c., c 1180; to cover with ashes c 1250.
cin/nabrium c 1215, c 1320, (?) -obrium, †-abatim, **sinobrium** a 1250, cinnabar; *cf.* **sinopis.**
cinnam/omum (†-onium), cinnamon: -a-mum 1258, **cynamonum** 1310, **sinamo-mum** (†**sinamonium**) 1440, **sinomomum** 1438, ‡**sym/omum,** †-amum c 1530.
†**cinniligium** (? *for* **cingillum**), girdle 1499.
cinob-, *see* CENOB; **cinnabrium.**
cinoprum, *see* **sinopis.**
cinoroceros, *see* **rhinoceros.**
cinterna, scinterna, (?) plasterer's 'hawk' c 1300.
cintorium, *see* CINCT
cintr/a (cyntr-) c 1180, 1335, -ia 1282, -us 1227, 1264, †**cinta** 1280, †**cytrus** 1295, **synctor** 1413, -ela 1325, -illus 1291, centering, vault rib (arch.).
cin/us, -um, *see* **cygnus;** **schinus.**
cin/yphes, -ifes (eccl.), **scynifes** c 720, **sciniphes** c 1090, stinging-fly, gnat.
ciphus, cipus, cippa, *see* **scyphus.**
cipp/us 1251, 1338, -ius c 1290, **ceppus** c 1200, 1256, tree-stump; *c 1100, c 1397, -es (*pl.*) 1387, -e (*pl.*) 1535, 1573, **sippe** (*pl.*) 1389, **ceppus** 1201, 1576, **seppi** c 1337, stocks, imprisonment (*cf.* **stipes**); -us, horse-clog 1392; **ceppus,** stock of descent 1227 (*cf.* **cespes**); -agium 1330, 1391, **ceppagium** 13c., c 1290, (right to take) tree-stumps; *see also* CHIPP
cipra, *see* **cypra.**
ciragium, *see* **cera.**
†**ciratio,** (?) *f.l.* for **creatio,** c 1344.
I **circa,** *towards, with regard to c 730, 9c. c 1160, 1534; upon 7c., 865.
2 **circ/a (†cirta),** circle, circuit a 1090, c 1296; c 1072, c 1330, -ator c 1148, c 1250, -atrix (*f.*) c 1250, inspector, obedientiary who goes the rounds (mon.); -aria, round of visita-tions (mon.) 1267; -ata (-ada), payment to bishop or archdeacon during round of inspection 1080, c 1164; *cf.* **cerchia.**
circamundanus, *see* **circummundanus.**
circaregio, *see* **circumregio.**
circellus, *see* CIRCUL
circ/ialis c 1385, -ianus 680, -ionalis c 1315, north-western.
circietus, *see* CHERCH
circ/inus, circle c 1185, c 1375; ‡-inatorium, "circinatory" 15c.; -ius c 550, -io 6c., circle, company; †-innium, (?) round of inspection c 1115; -ino, to mark out, *or* arrange in, a circle †c 1290, 14c.
circiter, thereabouts (of numbers) 1258, c 1340.
circuilineus, including an arc (geom.) a 1200.
circuit/us, circle c 730; round, circuit c 1280; neighbourhood 6c., 946. a 1100, c 1188; c. **generalis,** general eyre (leg.) 1269; -u, thereabouts (of numbers) 1347; **per -um,** round c 1190, 1415; -io, round (mus.)

c 1000; eyre 1537; **-ium**, circumlocution 6 c.; **-or** c 1266, c 1330, **circumitor** c 1072, **circitor** c 1190, inspector (mon.); **-orius**, going the rounds c 1266; **circueo**, to enclose (= circumdo) c 1321; **circuo**, to surround 1239, c 1370; **circumeo cum**, to keep company with c 1115.

circul/us *1196, 1396, **circuellus** 1324, barrel hoop; hoop for cart-wheel, millwheel, *etc.* 1267, 1351; (?) bow of crossbow 1370, 1455; ring, edge (of coin) c 1192; turn, succession c 1283; argument in a circle c 1300; 1418, **c. aureus** 1386, coronet; ‡1570, **c. nullus** a 1150, cipher, zero sign; **c. crucis**, circlet containing crucifix c 1400; **c. annorum**, period a 1175; **c. brevis, c. promovens**, epicycle (astr.) a 1200; **c. equator**, equator 1516; **c. ferreus**, item of armour 1277; **c. lune** a 1200, c 1362, **c. lunarius** 1234, lunar cycle; **c. magnus**, great circle (astr.) 1326; **c. meridianus, c. meridiei**, meridian c 1233; **c. obliquus**, zodiac c 1233; **c. Paschalis**, Easter cycle c 1250; **c. pudicus, c. pudibundus**, anus a 1250; **quirculus (argenteus)**, (?) hoop (on a mazer) c 1509; **circellus**, small circle (geom.) 1686; **cercellum**, small ring, doorknocker 7c.; **sarcellus**, (?) ring-fence c 1275; **cercleia**, circular hut (for defence) c 1210; **-agium**, (payment for) hooping barrels 1304, 1320; **-amen**, roundness 13c.; **-aris**, *circular 870. c 1192, 1362; a 1250, c 1400, **-osus** c 793, roundabout, indirect; cyclic, revolving (of tune) 14c.; cyclic (of a disease) a 1250; moving in circles (of an argument) c 1300; (?) told by strolling minstrels 1528; **numerus -aris**, square number a 1250, 1344; **opus -are**, embroidery in rings c 1315; **-aritas**, roundness c 1270, 1378; **-ariter**, in a circle, round about 870. c 1172, 1620; cyclically (med.) a 1250; **-arium**, collar c 1200; **-atio**, circular movement c 1200, c 1361; cycle, vicious circle a 1250; ‡circulation (of fluid) 1652; hooping (of barrels) 1287; **-ator** 1283, 1560, **cerclator** 1237, hooper, cooper; ‡**-atorium**, 'pelican', vessel for circulation of fluid (alch.) 1652; **-atus**, curled 793; (?) crowned c 1315; **-o**, to encircle c 1172, 13c.; *1230, 1392, **cerclo** 1224, **serclo** 1226, 1245, to hoop (barrels); *see also* **sarculatio**.

circ/um, *for* **-a**, concerning c 1265.

†**circuma**, (?) *f.l.* for **communa**, a common c 1250.

circumadjacens, surrounding 1243.

circumadsto, *see* **circumassisto**.

circumagro, to journey round 760.

circumallo, to circulate 1464.

circumambitus, surrounded a 1186.

circumamictus, enveloped c 1150, c 1488.

circumamplecto, to encompass 8c.

circumanfractus, a winding round c 1192.

circumassideo, to sit round c 1200.

circum/assisto c 1125, **-asto (-adsto)** 8c. c 1198, c 1400, to stand round.

circumatramento, to ink round 12c.

circumcalc/atio, treading round c 870; **-o**, to tread round c 1212.

circum/captus, -ceptus, *see* **circumseptio**.

circumcingo, to gird about c 730. c 1250, c 1362; to bind (a book) c 1365.

circum/cisio, clipping (of coins) c 1250, c 1293; *circumcision a 1090, 1457; **C. Dominica** c 1125, c 1192, **C. Domini** 1200, 1446 (1 Jan.); **-cisus**, circumcised person 12c.; **-cissus**, clipped, rounded 1286; **-cido**, to clip (coin) c 1180; to cut off, separate 1350; to circumcise c 730, 793. 12c., c 1400.

circumcollatus, having the neck encircled c 1450.

circumcoloro, to paint over, veneer 870.

circumconfero, to carry round c 1250.

circumcurs/atio, running around c 1607; **-ator**, explorer 1622; **-us**, encircling stream 1274; **-ito**, to keep running about 1609.

circum/datio, surrounding (bibl.); **-do**, to encircle, envelop c 1090, c 1362; to gather round 15c.

circumdego, to dwell near c 1250.

circumdico, to speak about 12c.

circumduc/tio, perimeter (math.) 1145; **-o**, to surround c 1300, 1430; to carry about c 1250; to overwhelm 1289.

circumeo, *see* **circuitus**.

circumexisto, to be round c 1293.

circumfer/entia, canopy 1436; bordure (her.) c 1450; **c. sigilli** 1293; **-entialiter** c 1270, c 1360, **-enter** c 1270, at the circumference; **-entialis**, lying at the circumference c 1270, c 1360.

circumfingo, to imagine, devise 865.

circumfinitus, limited 865.

circumflexus, circumflex accent 1267.

circumflu/xus, circumfluence 1649; **-entia**, superabundance 6c.

‡**circumforarius**, "micher", "market-runner" 15c., 1483.

circumformo, to surround 870.

circumfosso, to surround with a ditch c 1155, c 1300.

circumfoveo, to foster 870.

circum/fulsus, (?) *for* **-fusus**, spread around 870; **-fulcio**, to support round about 1311, 1508.

circumfuro, to rage around c 1180.

circum/gacens, *for* **-jacens**, bordering, surrounding 867.

circumgestatio, carrying round 1562, 1610.

circumglobo, to wrap round c 850.

circum/gyro (-giro), to surround, encircle 725, 948. c 1125, 1649.

circumhabito, to dwell round c 793. c 1125, c 1250.

circumin/cessio c 1290, p 1300, **-sessio** 1427, interpenetration, mutual indwelling (theol.).

circumitor, *see* **circuitus**.

circumjovialis, encircling Jupiter (astr.) 1686.

circumlabor, to glide round c 870.

circumlatio, carrying round 870.

circumligo, to hoop 1315, 1375.

circumlocut/ivus, descriptive c 1300; **-orius**, circumlocutory c 1180.

circumlustro, to encircle, roam around 815. c 1266, c 1330.

circummaneo, to dwell round 12c., a 1300.
circummeabilis, going round 870.
circummordeo, to engulf c 1184.
circummundanus 870, circamundanus 1344, extending round the world.
circumorno, to surround with ornament c 1250, 1388.
circumpalpito, to flutter round 1380.
circumplasmo, to form or mould round 870.
circumplect/ivus, embracing p 1300; -or, to embrace (a way of life) c 800.
circumpondero, to weigh carefully 870.
‡circumporto, to carry round 7c.
circumposit/io, environment, circumstances 870; -i (pl.) neighbours 11c.; -us, set (with gems) c 1420.
circumprehendo, to circumscribe 870.
‡circumpres, "prayer of a word" 15c.
circumpressus, pressed round about 870.
circumpugnabilis, striven for (περιμάχητος) 1344.
circumquaque, *on every side c 986. a 1100, c 1540; all over (prep.) 1322.
circumradio, to shine round c 1240.
circ/umregio (-aregio), environment c 1400.
circumroboro, to strengthen round about 12c., 13c.
circumrotatio, rotation a 1233.
circumsaturnius, encircling Saturn (astr.) 1686.
circumscript/io, legend of seal 1261, 1365; counter-signature 1321; -ibilis, susceptible of limitation c 1200, 1267; -ionalis, spatial c 1109; -ive, by way of spatial limitation c 1270, 1610; -ivus, circumscribing, limiting c 1270, c 1290; -ura, surrounding inscription (on coin) 1338; circumscribo, to inscribe all round c 1400.
circum/septio, encirclement 12c.; -ceptus c 1400, 1461, †-captus 12c., encircled.
circumsequor, to follow round 870. 1271.
circumsolaris, encircling the sun (astr.) 1686.
circumspect/io vestra, title (eccl.) c 1242, 1301; -e agatis, name of a writ (of 1286) 1307, 1419; -issime, very carefully c 1190; -ive, circumspectly a 1100; -ivus, circumspect 1411; -us de, informed about 1385.
circumspicuus, conspicuous c 1365.
circumspiro, to breathe all over, surround with an atmosphere 870.
*circumstant/ia, circumstance, condition, accident c 1200, c 1593; -ionabilis, subject to the effect of circumstances p 1300; -ionatus, affected by circumstances, conditioned p 1300, 1378; -iono, to condition, affect c 1362.
circumsubjectus, an inferior 870.
circumtego, to shield on all sides c 793. c 1180.
circumtergo, to wipe round c 1180.
circumtero, to stir c 1190.
circumtondeo, to shave all round c 1250, c 1330.
circumtubicino, to sound the trumpet round 870.
circumvag/or, to fly about c 1120; -o, to wander about c 1362.
circumvall/atio, encirclement c 1470; -o, to go round 760; to stand round 12c.; to fortify (fig.) c 1250.

circumvectio, getting round, tricking 1440.
circumvel/amen, covering 870; -o, to veil, cover 870.
circumven/ientia, trickery c 1404; -io, to compass the death of 11c.; (?) to give heed to c 1400.
circumvicinus, neighbouring, surrounding c 1260, c 1540.
circumvolativus, mobile a 1250.
circumvol/utio 9c. c 1212, 1649, -utatio 12c., rolling round, revolution; -ubilis, revolving c 1200.
circunicula, see sarcina.
circuo, see circuitus.
cirefalco, see girfalco.
ciri-, see also cerasum; cerycium; CHERCH; CHIRURG; I sericum.
cirileison, see kyrius.
‡ciriogon, gromwell (bot.) 14c.
ciripis, see syrupus.
ciritus, see cerritus.
cirl-, see ceorlus.
cirmanagium, cismanagium 1255, scir/-mengium 1254, rent payable on house-site (Béarn); -mentum, house-site (Béarn) 1254.
ciro c 1200, siro c 1200, a 1250, ciron, itch-mite; see also 2 tiro.
ciro-, see also chero-, chiro-
ciromelum 1390, ‡15c., ‡siromellum 15c., wort, grout (for ale-making).
†ciromerus, human being c 550.
cirona, see cera.
cirp-, see scirpus.
cirr/itus, for -atus, curly-headed a 1142, c 1220; crested a 1200.
cirta, see 2 circa; cyrta.
Cisalpin/us, north of Alps a 1142; -o, to cross the Alps northwards c 1250.
cis/ara, -era, see sicera.
ciscilia, see QUISQU.
†cise (pl.), (?) scissors 1222.
cisellus 1229, chisellus 1289, 1291, scisel-lus c 1188, c 1210, (?) schesellus 1298, chisel.
Cishumbranus, south of the Humber c 1400.
cisim/us c 1188, c 1250, scisimus c 1200, ‡c 1440, "vair", a fur or fur-bearing animal, (?) squirrel; -inus, of vair a 1260.
cism-, see also SCHISM
cismanagium, see cirmanagium.
*cismarinus, on this side of the sea c 1188, c 1420.
cisor-, see sicera.
ciss-, see SCISS
cist/a, coffin, cist 1370, 1512; 1274, c. an-guillarum 1365, c. stagni 1350, (?) stew-pond or fish-trap; *sista, chest, box 1287, 1526; c. communis, common chest 1302, c 1530; chesta ad carrucam, axle-box 1308; -arius, box-maker 1272; 1434, 1474, -ator 1442, 1474, cofferer, treasurer; see also cystis.
cistar/cia, -ida, see sitarchia.
*Cister/ciensis c 1138, 1549, Sisterciensis 1428, -nensis a 1160, Cistercian (adj. or subst.).
cisterium, see SEXT
cisternalis aqua, tank water a 1250.
cistis, see cystis.

cist/ula, -olator, *see* citola.
cit-, *see also* sit-
citabus, *see* cacabus.
citacus, *see* psittacus.
cit/atio *1164, c 1474, sitatio c 1310, -atorie
(*pl.*) c 1195, 1200, -atorium c 1289, c 1448,
-atus 1272, citation, summons (leg.);
‡-ator 15c., 1483, ‡sitarius 15c., summoner
(leg.); -ator austurcariorum regis (falc.)
1284; citer, quoter 1609; -atorius c 1196,
1686, †-orius 1413, -atorialis 1518, cita-
tory, summoning; -anter p 1348, -ius
c 796. c 1250, c 1362, scitius 13c., soon,
quickly; -ius, rather 1302, a 1408; soonest
c 1300, 1400; quam c. c 1250; ad c.
1239, 1461; c. quo, as soon as c 1283, 1415;
-eritas 1374, -itas c 1362, -oitas c 1361,
soonness; -ivolus c 870, -uvolus c 1200,
swift-flying; scito, *for* -o, to summon
c 1310.
citera, *see* citra.
citerac, *see* ceterach.
‡citeranum, cyclamen (bot.) 14c.
citerium, *see* 1 seta.
citern-, *see* citria.
cithar/a 1136, 1336, -era 1395, harp (or other
stringed instrument); -eda 1370, -edus
1172, c 1335, citheredus 1458, 1480,
citherator c 1290, c 1520, -isator c 1350,
-ista 1136, 1461, sitharista 1360, ‡15c.,
cithyarista 1203, citherista c 1447, 1471,
cithirista 1464, harper, minstrel; -isatio
1344, c 1376, citherizatio c 1200, 1497,
harping; -izo c 1000. c 1194, 1267, ‡-edo
15c., -o 1334, to harp; *cf.* citola.
citherica, *see* chirotheca.
cit/itas, -ius, -ivolus, *see* citatio.
‡citol/a 15c., ‡citella c 1440, cistula,
situla c 1393, 'citole' (mus.); ‡-ator 15c.,
(?) cistolator 1266, 'citoler', minstrel; *cf.*
cithara.
citonia, *see* cydonomeli.
cito/valens, -walla, -aldum, *see* zedoaria.
citra (*prep.*), since 1373, 1388; extunc c.,
thereafter 1356; c. hec, hereafter 1352;
c. quam, before 1239; sitra, *for* c., 1320;
citera, *f.* of citer, near, early 6c.
citramarinus, south of Forth p 1327; north
of English Channel 1420.
citramontanus, north of Alps c 1125; south
of Alps 1460.
citr/ia, lemon 1622; -ulus, -ullus, 'citrul',
water melon a 1250; -angulum a 1250,
‡14c., ‡-omelum 14c., orange; sitrenada,
citronade 1421; -inatio, turning yellow
a 1252, ‡1652; -initas 1144, a 1292, †citer-
nitas a 1250, yellowness; c. aurium, discharge of yellow wax (med.) c 1200; -inus
1144, 1622, †citernus a 1250, yellow; (*subst.*)
kind of myrobalan 13c., c 1257; *see also* sapphirus; -inesco, to become yellow a 1250,
c 1320; -ino, to make yellow c 1250, c 1320.
citta, abnormal appetite (κίττα) 1518.
citu-, *see also* situs.
citula, *see* situla.
cituvolus, *see* citatio.
ciula, *see* kela.
*civer/a (†ciner-) 1209, 1429, -ia c 1172,
1466, cevera 1421, sivera 1297, severa
1417, 1419, severia c 1422, †cinaria 1463,

†chinaria c 1182, chivereum 1198, barrow,
bier, stretcher; c. manualis 1297; c. (s.)
cum rota 1209, c 1320, c. rotabilis 1388,
c. rotalis 1349, c 1430, c. rotatilis c 1172,
c. rotaria 1257, 1264, c. rotata c 1345,
1466, wheelbarrow; c. virgea, wicker
hand-barrow 1257; †-arius, (?) barrow-
man 1300 (*see also* cinerarius); -ata,
barrow-load 1225.
civ/eta c 1180, (?) -us c 1150, chive; *cf.* cepa.
civ/is, inhabitant 6c. 13c.; -ilis, civil (as
distinct from ecclesiastical) c 1260, 1562,
liber -ilis, book of civil law 1414, 1421;
-ilis 1344, -ilista c 1376, c 1443, civil
lawyer; -ilitas, statesmanship c 1160, 1377;
citizenship c 1405; civilization 1624; -iliter,
according to civil law c 1185, c 1290;
*-itas, cathedral city 805, 963. 1086, 1586;
cibitas, city 867; -itatis emendatio,
burhbote c 1110; -itatensis, citizen c 1190,
1346; -iter, like a citizen 13c.
cizer, *see* sicera.
claa, clada, clades, claga, clai-, *see* clata.
clacc/um (clakk-), 'clack' lump of tar, *etc.*
(in wool) 1276, 1338; -o, to 'clack' (wool)
1442, 1503.
clacendix, (?) conch: claxendix (†clanxen-
dix), trumpet c 950.
†cladum, (?) neck 6c.
†clalissum, abyss 8c.
clami-, *see also* CHLAMY
*clam/ium, -eum (†claimum) c 1185,
1583, -ia 15c., -um c 1180, 1230, †-erum
15c., -atio 1219, 15c., †-atium a 1327,
-entia 1258, -itatio a 1452, *-or a 1086,
c 1395, claim; -eum, cry (of hue and cry)
1361, 1375; -atio, utterance, proclamation 956. 14c., 15c.; c 1148, 1294, -or a 1090,
c 1266, accusation in chapter (mon.); -or,
*complaint, outcry c 1090, 1595; *cry (of
hue and cry) c 1115, 15c.; c. communis,
common talk c 1290; -abilis, open to
accusation c 1243; -ans c 1266, -ator
c 1072, c 1330, accuser, complainant (mon.);
-ator, crier (of a court) a 1275, a 1553;
town crier 1469; c. Parliamenti c 1320;
-atoria, office of (Parliamentary) crier
c 1320; -atus, accused party (mon.) 1234;
†-ivus, plaintiff 1243; -oreus, noisy c 550;
-eo 1298, -io 1297, -ito 13c., a 1452, *-o
1086, 1459, to claim; *-o (with *inf.*), to
claim (the right) to 1252, a 1452; -o, to
summon c 730; to accuse in chapter (mon.)
c 1148, c 1330; c. ad warant 1086, c.
warantum 1167, to vouch to warranty;
c. havok, to cry havoc c 1420; c. liberum
c 1150, *c. quietum c 1070, 1451, to quit-
claim; *see also* QUIET.
clampa, clamp (for repairing wheel) 1279.
clan/culus, secret c 793. c 1120; -gulo
c 1250, -destinam a 1230, *-destine c 1250,
1473, †clamstine 1347, secretly; -culo,
to hide 7c.
claneta, *see* glena.
clang/orium, belfry c 1245; †-ator, *see*
CLAR; ‡-ito, "to clack" 1570.
claper/a, -um, bell-clapper 1323, 1469; 1441,
-ia 1288, 1305, 'clapper', hutch or enclosure
(for rabbits).
claps/a 1388, -um 1448, 1489, claspum

c 1482, 1521, **-ula** 1413, c 1432, **-ura** 1414, clasp (of a book); **-a** 1325, **clospa** 1418, clasp (for fastening door, *etc.*); **claspum campane** 1533; **-atus**, fitted with clasps c 1448.

clar/itas, glory (theol.) c 1343; **-e** 1446, **de -o** 1256, c 1472, **in -o** 1397, net; **-um**, forest clearing 1251 (*cf.* **2 bosca**); ***-us***, net, clear (of accounts) 12c., c 1480; **historia -a**, clerestory 1482; **-us badius**, light bay (of horse) 1308, 1325; **vinum -um** c 1135, 1497, **v. -etum** 1536, 1622, ***-etum** c 1200, 1537, spiced wine, clary; **pulvis -eti**, a kind of spice 1313; ‡**-eta**, white of egg 1652; **-ifer**, glorious c 550; **-ificus**, light-giving c 865; 1497, **-ificativus** 1421, enlightening; **-ificatio**, becoming clear, clarification c 1241, 1620; clearing up (of liability) 14c., c 1470; title to fame c 1100; glorification, Transfiguration (theol.) 8c. c 1090, c 1125; **-igator** (†**clangator**), bugler c 1200, 15c.; **-imonia**, fame 1426; **-io**, clarion 1346; **clerenarius**, (?) clarion-player 1303; **-ioritas**, greater clarity 1427; **-ifico**, to clear, cleanse, illumine c 1266, 1412; to clarify (a liquid) a 1250, 13c.; to explain c 1250, c 1340; to clear (of liability) c 1470; ***to glorify (theol.) 6c., 8c. c 1090, c 1546; **-efio**, to become plain c 1365.

†**clasma**, (?) *for* **phasma**, apparition c 685.

claspum, *see* CLAPS

classa, an ingredient of gunpowder 1335; *cf.* **clyssus**.

class/is, class (ac.) 1541, 1549; c 1140, 1425, **-icum** c 1080, 1486, **clasculum** 13c., **glascum** 1300, peal of bells; ‡**-icum**, peal of guns 1570; **-ica**, fleet c 1362; **-icus**, sounding a summons 933; ‡**-atorium**, "steeple" *or* "clapper" 15c.

clas/tura-, -ura, *see* 2 **clausa**.

***clat/a** 1209, 1486, **-es** c 1280, 1411, **clada** 1286, 1397, **clades** c 1305, 1390, **cleta** c 1115, 13c., **cleda** 1521, **claa** 1205, 1419, ***claia (claya)** 1086, 1419, **claius** 1312, **clea** c 1226, 1307, ***cleia (cleya, †clera)** 1171, 1419, **claga** 1295, †**glaga** c 1290, 'claye', hurdle; **-a**, (?) pillory a 1408; **c. ad carettam**, hurdle to increase loading capacity of cart 1330; **cleagium**, (?) service of providing hurdles 1212; **cleio**, to provide with hurdles 1215; *cf.* **crata**.

clatr/um, grating, lattice c 1365; **-us**, "door-bar" 15c.; (fig.) seal c 1370.

clat/um, -eus, *see* SCLAT

claucicomans, *see* GLAUC

claudi/cus, lame c 1177; ‡**-pes**, cripple 1570.

claudo, *see* 2 **clausa**.

claumenta, key 7c.

1 claus/a 13c., a 1564, ***-ula** c 1188, 1588, †**clasula** 1317, **-ura** c 1254, a 1452, clause; **-ulatim**, clause by clause 1281.

2 claus/a c 1400, c 1450, ***-um** c 1183, 1543, **-us** 1270, c 1353, **-ula** 1200, ***-ura** 1203, c 1540, **clusura** (?) 704, **-tura** c 1115, c 1342, **clostura** a 1128, close, enclosed place (*see also* **exclusa**); **-ula**, hermit's cell a 1118, c 1293; **-ulatio**, (?) fastening 1505; **-um** cathedral close 1341, c 1643; **-ura**, precincts (mon.) 1182, 1461; **-tura**, cloister c 1432 (*cf.* CLAUSTR); **-ura**, mountain pass

c 1076, 1267; prohibition, suspension 1200, 1338; shutting c 1450; ***shutter**, lock, fastening 1378, 1501; a 1190, 1419, **-tura** 1286, right of (*or* payment for) enclosing; ***820, 1031. 1086, a 1564, **clasura** 1434, ***-tura** c 1220, 1419, **clastura** 1215, **clo-stura** c 1160, 1231, **glostura** c 1330, enclosing, fencing, fence, barrier; 1281, **closura** a 1128, **-tura** c 1195, 1315, **cla-stura** c 1270, 1306, **clostura** a 1157, 1306, wood for fencing; **-tura burgi**, burhbote c 1150, 13c.; **c. pontium**, brigbote 1331; **-io**, confinement 1267; **c. pororum** (med.) a 1250; **c. ville**, fortification 1230; **-ibilis**, closable 7c. c 1350; **-icurrus**, closed carriage 1584; **clusilla**, barrier c 1225; **-iva**, conclusion (of lesson) c 1266; **-um**, close, end c 793; **c. vite** 1467; **c. Alleluia**, eve of Septuagesima 1199; ***c. Pascha** c 1188, 1289, ***c. Pasche** 5c. 1194, c 1456, **clusum Pasche** 1224, **c. Paschatis** 1280, Close of Easter, Sunday after Easter; **c. Pentecostes**, Trinity Sunday 1155; **-us**, close, fastened (of cloak) 13c.; webbed (of feet) a 1250, a 1146; obscure c 1343; **cathedra -a, scabellum -um**, "close chair", "close stool" 1553; *see also* **breve, campus, capa, littera, sigillum**; **-o** 13c., **-uro** 1450, 1483, **clau/do** 1232, 1356, **-do circa** 1307, 1325, to fence, enclose; **-do**, to enter a monastery c 1050; **-do Alleluiam**, to say Hallelujah for the last time 11c.; **-do contra**, to fence on the side of a 1120; ***-do diem (extremum)**, to die c 1135, c 1359.

claustr/um 1180, c 1234, **-a** 1306, partition in house; †**-a**, closing of fingers c 1115; lock c 1250; **-um**, enclosed plot 1363; virginal membrane, hymen c 1385; ***7c., 980. a 1090, 1570, **clausterium** c 1365, **-alia** (*pl.*) c 1440, cloister, monastery; **c. pendens**, cloister with pentice roof 1252; **-alia**, monastic matters c 1365; **-alis**, (*adj.*) enclosing c 1325; ***claustral** c 1125, 1526; (*subst.*) inmate of cloister, monk (esp. one who is not an obedientiary) c 1160, c 1450; *see also* **prior; -aliter**, according to monastic rule 1380, a 1452; **-arius**, beadle (mon.) c 1532, †1570; **-ensis** c 1146, **-icola** 12c., monk; **clustellum**, confined space, prison c 570, c 685; ‡**-inus**, "pinner" 1570; **-atus**, enshrined 1433.

1 clava 1355, **clauua** 1315, **clauwa** c 1270, 1301, **clawa** 1233, 1301, **clowa** 1293, 1457, small plot of land, (?) close.

2 clav/a 1378, 1587, **-us** 15c., mace; **c. ad arma**, mace ornamented with (royal) arms 1437; **clova**, *for* c., club 1262; (?) **-arius** 1306, 1311, **-iator** 1321, **-iger** 1286, 1468, mace-bearer; **pila -aria**, (?) golf (Sc.) 17c.; *see also* **clavis, clavus, serviens**.

clavellatus cinis, 'clavellated ashes', dyers' potash a 1250.

claverus, (?) cleaver (tool) 1290; **cloverus**, (?) cleaver (workman) 1388; *cf.* **cloera**.

clavica, *see* **cloaca**.

clavinium, *see* **sclavina**.

clav/is, key: (of crossbow) 1226, 1284; (of gun) 1577; stop-cock, plug 1355; key-stone *or* boss of vaulting (arch.) c 1188, 1359; a 1180, 1326, **-us** 12c., key, clef (mus.); 1298, c 1402, **-a** 1603, quay; symbol of office a 1164, 1494; **c. artis** (alch.) a 1292; **c. ecclesie**, power of the keys c 1220, 1461; **c. penitentie** 1220; **c. scientie** (theol.) c 1343; **c. Rogationum** c 1422; **c. termini**, formula for finding feast-days 13c.; **-es** (*pl.*), **c. legum**, House of Keys (Isle of Man) 1418; **-eus** 1312, **-us** 1510, key; **-icularius** 8c., ***-iger** 1177, 1414, **-igerius** 13c., c 1533, **-igeratus** c 1450, **-es-gerens** 1454, keeper of the keys, treasurer or cellarer; **-icularius** (**celestis**) c 570, c 793. 12c., c 1450, **-iger** (**celestis**) c 668, c 957. c 1100, c 1450, St. Peter; **-iger**, ruler c 950; **-icymbalum**, harpsichord c 1430; "virginals" 1622.

clav/us *1232, 1463, **-is** 1211, 1326, 'clove', weight of wool; weight of other products 1290, c 1345; **c. medius**, weight of gold 1274; †**-inus**, weight of flour (Sc.) 12c.; ***c. gariofili** (**c. de gylofre**, *etc.*) 1257, 1538, **-a** 1303, **-is** 1279, **clouha** 1253, clove; ***-is** c 1200, c 1494, †**clevis** 1297, *for* **-us**, nail; **-us ligneus** 1234, c 1400, **-is lignea** 1296, trenail; ‡**-arium** 15c., **cloera** c 1250, **cloeria** 1213, 1215, **clovarium** 1313, box or bag for nails (Fr. *clouvière*); **cloera** 1212, **cluarium** c 1180, forge; ‡**-atorium**, "nail-tool" 1483; **cloviator** (†**clomator**) lignorum, (?) nailer 1446; **-iculus**, tacket 1316, ‡1483; ‡**-illus**, boss (on book-binding) 1483; **-atio** 1416, **-atura** 1312, 1322, nailing; **-osus**, full of nails 1343; **-atus**, striped c 1197; **-ello** c 1250, **-o** c 1254, 1440, **clouo** 1343, to nail, rivet; *see also* **2 clava**.

clawa, *see* 1 **clava**.

claxendix, *see* **clacendix**.

claya, clea, cleagium, cleda, cleia, *see* **clata**.

claysica, *see* **cloysica**.

clebanus, *see* **clibanus**.

cledris, *see* **clethera**.

clef-, *see* CLIV

clementia, clemency (title) 1356.

Clement/ine (*pl.*) 1380, c 1443, **constitutio -ina** c 1360, 15c., section of canon law (vol. 6 of Decretals).

clench/ator 1294, **-arius** 1325, clincher; **-o** 1325, **clynso** 1339, to clinch (nails).

clenodium, *see* **clinodium**.

cleos, glory (κλέος) c 1200.

clepa, *see* **cheveyna**.

cleps/edra c 1140, a 1260, **clysedra** c 1204, †**clipsadrum** 1260, *for* **-ydra**, spigot, tap; water-clock 13c.

clept/es c 850, c 1000. c 1100, c 1370, **-or** c 1118, c 1236, thief; **-o**, to steal 810.

clera, (?) aperture 1272; *see also* **clata**.

clerenarius, *see* CLAR

*cleric/us, clerk c 597, 870. 1086, 1613; **c. capituli**, chapter clerk 1338; **c. chori** c 1450; **c. closette regis** c 1472; **c. communis**, recorder 1376, 1402; **c. consilii regis** 1391, 1409; **c. coquine**, kitchen clerk c 1290, c 1390; **c. corone**, clerk of the crown c 1390, 1586; **c. curie**, clerk of the court 1269, 1458; **c. de cursu**, cursitor 15c.; **c. Inferni**, 'Clerk of Hell' (official of the Common Pleas) c 1530; **c. justiciarie**, justice clerk (Sc.) 1456, 1569; ***c. mercati**,

clerk of the market 1358, c 1556; **c. navium regis** 1394; **c. officiorum**, clerk of the offices (in royal household) 1437; **c. operationum** 1320, c 1458, **c. operum** 1365, clerk of the works; **c. pacis**, clerk of the peace c 1420, c 1470; **c. panni viridis** c 1472; **c. parochialis**, parish clerk 1288, 17c.; **c. pedes**, cursitor c 1290; **c. pipe**, clerk of the Pipe (Exchequer) 1586; **c. ad robas**, first-class chancery clerk 1389, c 1420; **c. ad rotulos** c 1286, **c. rotulorum** 1265; **c. regularis**, clerk in religion 1193, 1382; **c. secularis** 13c., 1382; **c. de sigillo** c 1125, **c. secreti sigilli** 1385, **c. de signeto** 1385; **c. de statuto** (Cornw.) 1388; **c. summonitionum** (in Scaccario) 1324, 1586; **c. ville**, town clerk 1348; **-i Cancellarie Sex**, Six Clerks 1586; **-a**, (?) wife or widow of clerk 1185; **-alis** (eccl.), **-ilis** c 730, clerical; **-aliter**, as a clerk a 1142, c 1520; **-atus**, clerical office (eccl.); scholarship, learning c 1200; clerical staff 760; c 1150, c 1109, **clerimonia** c 1250, 1426, **clerus** (eccl.), clergy; **-ellus** a 1100, 14c., **-olus** 1086, ***-ulus** c 1180, 1427, **clerigaster** c 1255, young *or* inferior clerk; **-idium**, murder of clergy 1324, 15c.; **cleroborus**, devourer of clergy c 1590; **-o**, to make into a clerk 14c.

cleronomus, heir c 950, c 1038. 12c.

cleta, cleya, *see* **clata**.

clethera 1609, **cledris** 1383, post or rail of mill (W. *cledr*).

cletum, cleat (naut.) 1299.

clevis, *see* **clavus**.

clewa, *see* **cluva**.

†**cliaulia** (†**diaulia**) (*pl.*), (?) illustrious halls 950.

cliban/us, (eccl.), **clebanus** c 1496, oven or furnace; **panis -arius**, oven-bread a 1250.

clien/s, companion c 550· household monk a 1130; 1379, 1450, **c. communis** 1405, serjeant-at-mace; **-tela**, flock (eccl.) c 950; †**-tefaris** (? **-telaris**), feudal c 1200; **-tellus** c 793, **-tulus** 990, c 1000, insignificant dependant; **-tulus, -tula** (*f.*), devotee (of the Devil) c 1212; **-to**, to be in attendance c 1180.

clif-, *see* CLIV

clikettum 1275, 1388, ‡**clit/ella** 15c., 1468, ‡**-orium** 15c., clicket, door-latch.

*clim/a, region of the world c 550, 991. c 1100, c 1445; part (of building) c 1000; **-ectra**, part of the heavens c 550.

climax Hermetis, compound of 60 simples (med.) a 1250.

clinicus c 950. 12c., c 1200, †**clunicus** 1415, bed-ridden, palsied.

clinodium 1449, 1463, **clenodium** 1241, 1443, jewel.

cliothedrum, seat of fame c 950.

clipe/us, shield of arms, scutcheon (her.) p 1394, c 1595; noble family 13c.; **c. apri**, brawn, boar's flesh wrapped in the hide 1409; **sub -o**, secretly c 1300; **-olus**, small shield c 1595; ‡**-ola**, shield-shaped ring 15c.; **-ocentrum**, device at centre of shield (her.) c 1595; **-alis**, of a shield 15c.; ‡**-arius**, shield-maker 1483.

clipp/a, -um 1285, 1392, **cluppum** 1317,

1393, -ellum 1306, clupellum 1267, 1311, (?) metal plate or shield (for cart-wheel).

clipsadrum, see clepsedra.

clipsis, see ECLIP

clissus, see clyssus.

clit/ella, -orium, see clikettum.

clitell/e (pl.), baggage 12c., c 1250; -arius, pack-animal c 1191, c 1250.

clit/o (?) 938, c 1000. c 1100, a 1142, -on 10c. 12c., -unculus c 1118, prince, atheling.

clitt/a, -um, -rum, see 1 clutum.

†cliutis, ascent, climbing 7c.

cliv/a, cliff 1336; -is, baulk in open field 13c.; -ewarda a 1135, †chivewarda 1208, -ewardus 1383, clifwarda a 1200, 1291, clefwarda 1307, (due paid for) service of cliff-ward.

†clivippa, (?) a musical instrument 934.

cloac/a, privy 1282, c 1497; cloca c 1250, 1390, coacla 1381, clavica 1158, 1216, for -a, drain, sewer; -arius, drain-cleaner c 1503; mons clocarius, dung-hill 1463; -o, to purge oneself 1319; see also 2 cloca.

1 cloc/a, -arius see cloaca.

2 cloc/a 1229, c 1450, -um 1320, clochia 1265, 1351, cloaca 1336, cloga 1395, cloak; c. duplicata, doublet 1371; clokettum, small cloak 1364.

3 cloc/a c 550, c 1000. 1274, 1610, gloccum c 760, bell; de -a, o'clock c 1450; -a 1381, -arium a 1120, c 1520, clocherium 1225, c 1400, clocherum c 1300, clogerium c 1310, clocebarium 1207, belfry, bell-tower; -ula c 793. c 1325, cloketta 1235, little bell.

clochbulgie (pl.), bagpipes c 1540.

clocito, see closso.

cloer/a, -ia, see clavus.

cloga, (?) wooden block (naut.) 1295; clogga, clog (footwear) a 1389; see also 2 cloca.

clohus, clough, ravine (Lancs.) c 1200.

cloiph/a, -us, see coifa.

clokett-, see cloca (2 & 3).

clomator, see clavus.

clos-, see also CLAPS; CLAUS

‡closera, alexanders (bot.) 13c.

closett/um 1388, 1489, -a 1411, closet; -a regis c 1472.

closso, to limp (Fr. clocher) 1242; clocito, to be rickety 1342.

clotes olei, clots of oil 1365.

clotto, (?) to measure 1279.

clouha, clouo, see clavus.

clout-, see 1 clutum.

clova, see 2 clava.

clov/arium, -iator, see clavus.

cloverus, see claverus.

clowa, see 1 clava.

Cloynensis, see Cluniacensis.

cloysica, claysica, 'claw-sick', sheep-scab 1297.

clua, see cluva.

cluarium, see clavus.

cluentia, fame 7c.

Cluniacensis (adj. or subst.) 1077, c 1500, Cloynensis 1227, Cluniac.

clunicus, see clinicus.

cluo, to cover, protect c 550.

clupellum, cluppum, see clippa.

clus-, see CLAUS; CLAUSTR; EXCLUS

1 *clut/um 1232, 1486, -us 1279, -eum a 1300, 1387, cloutum 1387, 1415, †clittum 1286, †clitta 1343, †clittrum 1313, clout, cart-clout (iron patch to protect woodwork); c. pedale (for plough) 1278, 1299; cloutnailum, clout-nail 1352; clouta-tio, clouting, 1377; -o 1294, 1324, clouto 1387, to clout, fit (cart or plough) with clouts; to clout, patch (a sarplier) 1338.

2 clut/um 1300, 1303, -ettum (†-ellum) 1301, bag, case.

clu/va 1344, †-a 1324, clewa 1347, clue, ball of twine.

†clymeterium, (?) oratory c 730.

clynso, see CLENCH

clysedra, see clepsedra.

‡clyssus (clissus), occult virtue or compound of antimony, sulphur, and nitre (alch.) 1652; cf. classa.

clyster/ (med.): glister' 1307; -izatio, use of clyster a 1250.

cnichten/gilda c 1144, -egilda c 1150, cnicthenegilda a 1100, a 1125, chenite-wilda a 1135, knyttegilda c 1300, knights' guild (London).

*cnipulus (knypulus) c 1178, c 1330, cnu-pulus 1301, canipulus a 1197, 1275, cuni-bulus p 1153, nipulus c 1266, knivettus 1282, 1300, knife.

*coabbas c 1160, 1435, conabbas 6c., fellow abbot.

coaccido, to coincide c 1250, 1267.

coacervat/io, accumulation 9c. 15c.; -or, one who accumulates a 1186; coadservo, to heap up 1279.

coacla, see cloaca.

1 *coact/io 9c., 940. c 1115, 1461, cogentia c 1250, c 1367, compulsion, cogency; -ura, (?) piecing together (of garment) 1289; -ile, "kirtle" 1502; -icius, -ius c 730, *-ivus c 870. c 1340, 1647, compulsory; littere -ive a 1205; -ive, by force c 1332, c 1376; -um, duty 1241; ‡15c., ‡quactum c 1200, 15c., quattum 9c., cream; cogens, cogent c 1250, c 1334; cogentius, more cogently c 1250; -o, to bind together c 730.

2 coact/io 1344, coagentia c 1370, co-activity; -ivus, acting jointly 1344; coagens party to suit (leg.) c 1115; joint agent a 1233; coag/o, to act together, co-operate 870. p. 1300, p 1470; -ito, (?) for coadjuto, to work with, help 1346.

coad, see QUOAD

coadhereo, to stick together c 870. c 1250.

coadjacens, adjacent c 1376, 1558.

coadjun/ctio, assembly, conventicle c 1530; -go, to join together, set next to c 1300.

coadju/vatio 1513, -vamentum a 1250, -torium c 1190, assistance; *-tor c 1204, 1549, coagitor 1412, -trix (f.) c 1185, 15c., assistant, helper; -toria, assistantship 1461; -torius, assisting 12c.; *-vo c 1115, c 1400, quoadjuvo 1307, to help; cf. 2 coactio.

coadministra/tio, joint administration c 1326; -tor 1293, a 1564, -trix (f.) 15c., joint administrator (of goods of deceased).

coadservo, see COACERVAT

coadumbro, to represent together 870.

coadun/atio, uniting a 1250, ‡1652; as-sembly c 1200, 1588; †-ator (?coadjutor) uniter c 1100; **-o** c 1125, c 1242, **coduno** 1086, to join together, heap up; to stack (hay) a 1200, 1237; *to assemble, muster (persons) c 1000. c 1090, c 1450.

coadversitas, common adversity 1300.

coadvocatus, fellow advocate 1507.

coaffirmo, to affirm jointly 1344.

coafflictus, fellow sufferer a 1250.

coag-, *see also* 2 **coactio**, COADJU

coaggeratio, heaping together c 1250.

coagistator, fellow agister 1243.

coagmen, synod c 950.

coagul/atio (*coll.*), beestings 1459; **-abilis**, able to be curdled a 1250, p 1300; **-ativus**, curdling a 1250, c 1270; ‡**-atorium**, churn 15c.; **-atrix**, dairy-maid 1284; **-um**, mass, amalgam c 1212, c 1400; **-atissimus** a 1250; **-o**, to bind together c 870. c 1197.

coales, fellow-bird c 1325.

coaltare, joint altar c 1254.

coaltern/itas, mutual alternation a 1250; **-ativus**, **-ans** a 1250, **-us** c 1361, mutually alternating.

coal/tio, joint nourishment c 1500; **-umnus**, fellow pupil c 1170, c 1250; **-esco**, to increase together 13c.; **c. in**, (?) to grow into 1324.

coam/bassiator 1441, **-baxator** 1316, fellow ambassador.

coambio, to surround, include 870. 1344.

coam/or, mutual love 1497; **-ator**, one who loves in return 9c.; **-icus**, mutual friend c 1470.

coancilla, fellow maid-servant c 1325.

coangust/ia, joint exaction 12c.; **-us**, confining 8c.; **-o**, to blockade 1041; 1246, c 1430, **-io** c 1367, to constrain, oppress.

coanhelo, to pant with desire 1345.

coannexa (*pl.*), appurtenances 1538.

coaperio, *see* **coopertio**.

coapostolus, fellow apostle 720, 1006. 12c., c 1400.

coappello, to address together c 793.

coapt/atio, fitting together c 1250, c 1450; ‡**cooptatio**, fixation (alch.) 1652; **-io**, assembly 760; *-o, to fit together 8c., 870. a 1090, 15c.; ‡**coopto**, *for* **-o**, to adapt c 1204.

coar/atio, joint ploughing a 1300; **-ator**, joint plougher a 1250; **-o**, to plough together c 1160.

coarbiter, fellow arbiter 1225, 13c.

coarceo, *see* COERC

coart/atio, constraint c 1241, 1406; restriction (leg.) c 1258; **-abilis**, confinable 13c.

coascendo, to ascend together 9c. c 1236.

‡**coassator**, joiner 1520.

coassess/io, sitting together c 1250; **-or**, assessor 1228, c 1400; **coassedeo**, to sit with (leg.) c 1400.

coassigno, to appoint with c 1357.

coassist/entia, coexistence, compresence p 1300; **-o**, to exist or be present together c 1238, 1521.

coassumo, to co-opt c 1250, c 1488; to assume simultaneously 13c., 1344.

coasto, to stand by together c 1400.

coathleta, fellow champion a 1250.

coaudi/tor, fellow auditor c 1280, a 1452; **-o**, to hear together c 1125.

coaugeo, to increase 870. ‡15c.

coaugustus, colleague in empire 12c.

coaul/aris, member of the same college (ac.) c 1432, c 1448; **-icus**, fellow courtier c 1190.

coauxilio, to assist 1320.

coax, croak (κοάξ) a 1408, ‡1483.

‡**cobaltum**, *cadmia nativa*, cobalt 1652.

cobardus 1322, 1398, **cabardius** 1377, 'cobbard', cob-iron.

cobba, cob-loaf 1281, c 1310.

cobbus marinus, "sea cob", gull (bird) 1544.

cobell/a, **-um** 1228, 1319, ‡**gobellum** 13c., coble (boat); *cf.* **caupallus**.

‡**coborarius**, an obedientiary (mon.) 1239.

coburgensis, *see* **comburgensis**.

cocativus, *see* 3 **coketus**.

cocc/ineus, gules (her.) c 1595; **cochenellis** 1572, **cochinilla** 1701, **cuchinela** 1607, cochineal; **-onidium**, *for* **-um** Gnidium, a 1250.

coccinum, **coccymelum**, *see* **cottanum**.

cocco, *see* 1 **cogga**.

‡**coccula**, Irish cloak a 1300.

coccy/smus, cuckoo-cry 1609; **-zo**, to cry cuckoo 1609.

cocellus, *see* 2 **cota**.

cocha, *see* 1 **cogga**.

cocherius, *see* **cucherius**.

‡**cochia pillula**, sort of pill (med.) a 1250.

cochle/a (**cocle-**, **cocli-**), spiral staircase 8c. c 1070, 1537; ‡round-tower, topcastle 15c.; part of an organ, (?) slide or shutter c 1170; screw-thread 1686; bath c 1212; **cockla**, cockle (shellfish) 1311; **-ellus**, (?) shell-shaped vase 1359; **cokilla** 1267, 1303, **cokillus** 1357, (?) shell, mother of pearl; *-ar a 1090, 1537, **-arium** 1251, 1323, **cocular** 1461, c 1496, **coquilar** c 1302, ‡**coklium** c 1502, spoon; **c. ad ova**, egg-spoon c 1331; **-aria**, scurvy-grass (bot.) 1622; **-atus** 1295, **-aratus** 1215, 1245, **-ariatus** 1290, scalloped.

‡**cocilio**, weight of 12 oz. 1652.

cocius, *see* COQU

cocodo, *see* **cokedonius**.

cocodrillus, *see* **crocodilus**.

‡**coconellus**, **cucunellus**, "cockney", milk-sop c 1440.

coconsularis, fellow consul c 1405.

cocquetto, *see* 3 **cokettus**.

cocreo, *see* OCRE

coct-, *see* COQU; **cottanum**; **cottum**.

cocular, *see* COCHLE

cocuma, *see* **cucuma**.

Cocytus, Hell (theol.) c 550. 12c., 1362.

1 coddus, 'cod', metal bolster (of mill) 1322, 1422.

2 coddus, measure of grain, (?) bag 1158, 1388.

*cod/ex, code, law-book 1281, c 1511; **c. Justinianeus** 12c.; **c. divinus**, scripture a 1090; **-icellus** 11c., 14c., **-icella** c 1397, document; c 980, 1041. c 1172, c 1414, **-iculus** 815, small book, section of book; 1451, **-icillus** c 1285, 1430, codicil (to will).

‡**codium** 14c., ‡**comodio** a 1250, poppy (κώδεια).

cod/lingus c 1340, 1525, **-elyngus** c 1350, codling.

codo, 'code', cobbler's wax 1301.

‡**codr/us** c 1440, **-inus** c 1250, wretched, needy; *see also* **cudermus.**

codsellus, *see* 2 **cota.**

coduno, *see* COADUN

coedific/atio, building up, construction 957; **c. arcis,** burhbote 940. 12c., 15c.; **c. pontis,** brigbote 940. 12c., 15c.; **-o,** to build jointly 1082.

coeffect/ivus, producing simultaneously 13c.; **-or,** co-operator 1344; **coeffici/entia,** co-operation 1344, a 1361; **-ens,** a coefficient (math.) 1686; **-o,** to co-operate 1344, c 1361.

coeffodio, to dig out 1345.

coegenus, partner in want c 1170, 1200.

coe/lectus, elected jointly c 1250, 1469; **-ligens,** co-elector 13c.; **-ligo** 13c., **-lego** 1414, to share in electing.

coelementatio, co-ordination 1344.

coempt/io, forced sale, requisition 1189; **-or,** joint purchaser c 1470.

coen-, *see also* **cen-**

coenumero, to enumerate together c 1250.

coepecia, *see* COLP

*coepiscopus c 596, c 1000. a 1100, 1536, **conepiscopus** 6c., fellow bishop.

coepulator, table-companion c 1213.

coequ/atio, equalization, correspondence c 1150, c 1290; compensation 1307; equation (math.) 1145; **-alis** 11c. c 1414, **-us** c 1172, c 1450, coequal; **-alitas,** coequality c 670. c 1180, a 1250; **-evus** a 1233, 1344, †**-aneus** 13c., coeval; **-iparo** c 1160, c 1260, **quoequo** c 1300, to equalize.

coequ/es, fellow rider or knight c 1190, c 1225; **-ito,** to ride with c 1115, p 1341.

coerchivium, *see* **covrechiefum.**

coerc/io (**coertio**), *for* **-itio,** coercion c 1190, a 1564; **c. regia,** impressment (naut.) 1732; **-itrix, -trix,** coercive (*f.*) 1519; **coarceo,** to coerce 13c.

coerus, *see* **sorus.**

coescaetor 1247, 1261, **coexcaet/ator** 1247, **-or** c 1253, fellow escheator.

coessen/s, being with, accompanying c 900. c 1090, c 1310; **-tialis,** jointly essential c 870. c 1470, c 1620; **-tialitas,** joint essentiality c 1612; **-tialiter,** so as to be of one essence c 793.

coetern/itas, co-eternity 7c. 12c., a 1233; **-aliter,** co-eternally c 1270; **-us,** co-eternal 781, 1006. c 1090, 1344.

coev/itas, equality in age c 1180, p 1300; **-e,** coevally 1344; **-us,** of the same age c 550. c 1170; **coeval,* contemporary c 1150, 1536.

coexcito, to raise up together 7c.

coexecut/or, joint enforcer c 1210; 1226, 1471, **quoexecutor** c 1283, co-executor (of will); **-rix,** co-executrix 1327, 1425.

coexempl/aris, jointly exemplary 1374; **-o,** to afford a joint example c 1366.

coexeo, to proceed along with 13c.

coexercitatio, common exercise 1610.

coexig/entia, simultaneous requirement p 1300, 1344; **-o,** to require simultaneously p 1300, c 1357.

*coexist/entia, co-existence c 1270, c 1363; **-o,** to coexist a 1233, 1344.

coexpectatio, common expectation c 1330.

coexten/sio, coextension, commensuration a 1323, a 1361; **-do,** to coextend, coincide c 1270, 1412.

coexul/ c 1130, 15c., **-ans** c 1200, fellow exile.

cofata, *see* **cuva.**

cofeoffatus 1423, 1485, **confeoffatus** 1451, co-feoffee.

coffa, *see* **coifa.**

coffatus, *see* COSS

coff/inus (**coph-**), basket ‡15c., 1506; **c* 1166, 1461, †**caphnius** 12c., **-ina** 1290, 1416, †**-ia** 1251, **covinus** 15c., **-era** 1262, 1463, †**confera** 1415, **-erum, -erus** c 1190, 1279, **-ra** 1186, 1468, **-rum, -rus** 1160, 1381, **-orum** 1262, 1429, **-reum** 1172, **-retum** 1328, chest, coffer; ‡**-inarius,** basket-maker 1483; **-raria,** office of cofferer 1288; **-erarius* c 1290, 1505, **-rarius* 1256, 1327, cofferer, keeper of (royal) coffer; **-rarius,** coffer-maker 1367; **-ro,** to fit with axle-boxes 1360.

cofrater, *see* **confrater.**

cog/allus c 1230, †**-anus** 1266, †**tonegalla** (? **couegalla**) 1290, measure of cheese (Sc.).

cog/entia, -ens, *see* 1 **coactio.**

1 **cogg/a** (**cog-**) c 1200, p 1330, **-um** 1374, **-o** c 1234, 1421, **cocha** (**choca**) 1317, 1371, **coka** c 1303, **coqua** 1311, 1404, **cocco** 13c., **kockus** c 1330, **goga** 1213, **cokettus** 1346, 1437, 'cog', cock-boat; **cokettus,** (?) part of rigging (naut.) 1313; **-arius** 1192, **-orius** 1191, (?) master of 'cog'.

2 **cogg/a, -us** 1280, 1325, **goggus** 1280, cog (of wheel) or cog-wheel; **rota -alis,** cog-wheel 1406; **-o,** to fit (wheel) with cogs 1354.

cogit/amen 7c., **-atus* 7c. c 1250, c 1412, thought, intention; **-ativus,** cogitative, thoughtful c 1220, c 1350.

cogn/agium, -io, *see* **cuneus.**

cognat/io, compensation for death of kinsman c 1115; **-ionalis,** kindred c 704; **-us* c 1070, 1476, **congnatus** 1269, kinsman, cousin; **-a,** kinswoman, cousin 1185, 14c.; **cognitus,** *for* **-us,** 868.

cognistabilis, *see* CONSTAB

cognit/io, home (A.S. *cyððe*) c 1115; confession, acknowledgement c 1218, 15c.; cognizance, arms (her.) a 1142, 1384; 1228, c 1430, **cognotio** c 1329, cognizance (leg.); **c. realis et feodalis** (G.) 1314; **litere -ionales,** letters of cognizance (leg.) 1239; **-or,** juror (leg.) 1196 (*cf.* **recognitor**); **C. absconditorum** c 1180, **C. occultorum** c 1100, 13c., **C. omnium** c 1218, **C. secretorum** 1219, 1404, divine epithets; **-ivitas,** faculty of cognition c 1367; **-ive** 13c., 1374, **cognoscitive** a 1360, by way of cognition; **-ivus** 870. c 1260, 1378, **cognosc/ivus** 13c., c 1365, **-itivus** 13c., 1344, concerned with knowing, cognitive; **-ibilis,* knowable, recognizable c 1212, a 1361; **-ibilitas,** intelligibility c 1290, c 1361; †**-ulum,** (?) inkling a 1361; **-o** (**congnosco**), recognize c 730. 1221, 1287; to confess, acknowledge, admit c 1130, c 1450; to acknowledge a right to a 1090, c 1219; **c. ab,** to distinguish from c 1343; **c. de,** to take cognizance of (leg.) c 1185, 1684; **c. qualiter** (with *indic.*), to learn (that) c 740.

cognominatio, name c 870.

cognotator regius, controller of the king's household 1508.

cohabeo, to have simultaneously 1276.

cohabit/atio, *dwelling together 7c. c 1125, 1415; near presence c 790; joint abode c 1180; cohabitation 1301, 1684; **-atrix,** dwelling with (*f.*) 7c. c 1325; **-o,** *to dwell together c 730, 1060. c 1070, 1549; to cohabit c 1115, 1553.

‡**cohardus,** coward 1570.

coheredit/as, coheirship c 870; **-o,** to be coheir a 1100.

coheremita, fellow hermit 1328.

cohibit/ivus c 1283, **-orius** 1427, restraining.

cohortatorius, hortatory c 1125.

‡**cohos,** total content of human body (alch.) 1652.

†**cohuagium,** (?) payment of fees to minor courts (Norm.) 1323.

cohumilio, conhumilio, to reduce to the same humble level a 1205.

coidar/ius, cudarus, forester (W.) 1334; **-ia,** forestership 1334.

coif/a 1214, 1385, **-ia** 1220, 1263, †**cloiph/a,** †**cloiphus** 1268, **cufa** 13c., 1310, **cuphia** c 800, **coffa** 1256, **cucupha** c 1350, coif, head-dress; **-a ferrea** c 1200, 1305, **c. ferri** 1196; **c. Turkasia** c 1217, **Turkeisia** 1220, **c. de Torkeys** 1287; **-eria,** coif-makers' quarter 1455; **cufator,** (?) coif-maker 1415.

coign-, *see* **cuneus.**

coimpetro, to gain a joint request c 1255.

coinanimo, to become the dwelling-place of the Spirit c 865.

coincid/entia, coincidence c 1250, 1267; **-o,** to coincide, agree 1267, 1686.

coinclino (*trans.*), to incline, bend 870.

coincola, fellow inhabitant 1305.

coincorporo, to embody 870.

coinditus, jointly implanted c 1270.

coinfinitas, co-infinity c 1612.

coin/o, -io, *see* **cuneus.**

coinquinatio, pollution (bibl.).

coint/eisia, -isa, *see* **queintisa.**

cointell/ectus c 1290, **-igentia** 870, implication, understanding along with; **-ectualis,** of like intellect, sharing the mind of 9c.; **-igo,** to imply, understand along with 9c. a 1290, 1374.

cointro, to enter together c 1255.

cointroduco, to help to originate 870.

coinus, *see* **cuneus.**

coitiner/ans fellow traveller 1497; **-o,** to walk with c 1250.

coit/ivus, unitive c 1612, 1620; †**-or,** (?) companion c 1408.

cojurisdictio, joint jurisdiction c 1340.

coka, *see* **1 cogga.**

cokebertus, a malapert c 1218.

coked/onius 1300, 1303, **-enus** 1303, **cocodo** 15c., debased French coin; *cf.* **crocardus.**

cok/erellus 1278, **-rellus** a 1300, cockerel.

1 coketus (cokettus), *see* **1 cogga.**

2 coket/us 1256, c 1300, **quachetus** (Sc.) (?) 14c., **panis c.** c 1324, **p. de -o** c 1355, cocket-loaf.

3 coket/us, -a, -um 1281, 1559, **coquettus** 1475, 1483, *cocket, customs-house seal; sealed customs-certificate 1306, 1398; †**co-**

cativus, (?) requiring a cocket c 1500; **-atio,** sealing with a cocket 1397; **-o** 1320, 15c., **cocquetto** 1242, to seal with a cocket.

cokeya, 'cockey', drain (Norfolk) 1288.

cok/illa, -la, -lium, *see* **cochlea.**

cokinus c 1252, 1307, (?) **culqwanus** 1329, courier, messenger.

cokrellus, *see* **cokerellus.**

cokrio, *see* OCRE

cola, *see* **colla; collacus.**

colagium, *see* **colacium.**

colagog-, *see* **cholera.**

col/amentum c 1200, 1385, †**calamentum** a 1250, filtrate; **-atio** 13c., **-atura** a 1250, a 1446, straining, filtration, filtrate; **-atura Patriarche,** an emetic a 1250; **-atorium** 870. c 1197, 13c., (?) **-idor** 1326, **-ura** 1306, **-endrum** 1553, **cularium** 1267, strainer, colander; **-ix,** (?) 'cullis', broth 13c.; **culo,** to strain 1267.

colanum, *see* **coulanum.**

colaph/us, buffet, blow: **colpus** c 1115, **culpus** c 1306; **colofizatio,** buffeting 15c.; **-izo** c 730. c 1180, c 1430, **colophizo** 1287, to buffet; to dub (a knight) c 1370; *cf.* COLP

colarius, *see* **collarium.**

colatro (coll-), fellow robber 7c., c 730. 1167.

colbutatio, overturning (Fr. *culbuter*) 1266.

colcotar, colcothar, iron peroxide c 1215, a 1252.

colehicius, *see* **pons.**

*****col/endissimus,** most reverend 1452, c 1520; **-ito,** to worship 8c., 10c.

coler-, *see* **cholera; collarium; color.**

colficum, *see* **colon.**

coliarius, (?) collier, charcoal-burner c 1390.

coliatus 1306, 1329, **cullus** 1283, culled, weeded out (of sheep).

colibertus 8c. 1086, 1336, **quolibertus** 1086, freed serf; ‡"churl" 15c.; (?) member of 'free company' c 1370; **culvertagium,** reduction to status of freed serf 1211, c 1250; **colliberalis,** fellow freeman 13c.

colic-, *see also* **colon; solum.**

colicia, *see* **culacium.**

Colideus c 1188, c 1220, **Culdeus** 1528, **Keledeus** p 1100, 1249, **Killedeus** c 1385, Culdee (Sc.).

colidor, *see* **colamentum.**

colimbrum, *see* **cozymbrum.**

colina, *see* **culina.**

colingaria, *see* CUNI

colinum, *see* CHOL

colito, *see* **colendissimus.**

colius, green woodpecker (κολιός) 1544.

colix, *see* **colamentum.**

coll/a (cola), glue, size (κόλλα) 1275, 1351; spider's thread 13c.; **-ema,** fragrant gum (fig.) c 950; **-o,** to unite 1324; *see also* **collarium.**

collabor/atio, property acquired jointly by man and wife c 1115; **-o,** to work together a 1090, 1433.

collacus c 1289, (?) **cola** 1337, shad (fish).

collanguesco (conl-), to languish together c 1200.

collapsus, collapse c 1400; river junction c 1362; **collabor,** to be weakened 1296.

collaqueatus, roofed over c 1200; laced up c 1180.

collardus, see **cuillardus.**

collargior, to bestow c 1196, c 1436.

collarium 1213, 1451, **collarum** 1277, **coler**/ 1388, 1485, **-ium** 1179, 1419, **-a**, **-um** c 1215, c 1450, **-ettus** 1304, horse-collar; dog-collar c 1120, 1435; 1252, **colarius** 1275, **-ettus** 1295, c 1350, **colrettus** c 1290, c 1320, gorget (armour); a 1446, **-ium** 1416, †**colla** 1412, collar of livery; **-ium** 1393, 1436, **-ia** 1391, **-a, -um** 1240, 1491, **coloreum** 1415, †**colla** 1472, †**callarium** 1251, **-ettus** 1300, collar, necklace; **-um,** collar of mill-shaft 1273; **-ium axis (molendini)** 1384; **colorium,** collar of windlass 1333; **collarius,** (*adj.*) worn round neck c 1080; (*subst.*) pedlar, packman c 1190, a 1260; collar-maker 1561; *cf.* **collum.**

collatarius, see **collatio.**

collater/alis (conl-), *by the side of, helping, associated with 9c. c 1148, a 1564; adjoining (of winds) c 1270, c 1430; (of teeth) a 1250; collateral (of descent) 1339, 1461; *see also* **color;** (*subst.*) helper, associate, confidential official c 1090, c 1470; 1069, **-ana** 972, 1045. 12c., c 1400, consort, wife; ‡15c., **-ile** 1301, costrel; *-aliter,** by the side of, laterally, contiguously 9c. c 1130, 1464; **-o,** to set by one's side, associate c 1193, 1241; to accompany c 1200; to adjoin 1302.

collat/io (conl-), *conference, talk c 793, 948. a 1180, c 1450; *reading at meals, sermon (mon.) a 1090, 1439; collation, repast 1200, c 1406; celebration of a sacrament c 1197, c 1363; bestowal, grant c 1217, 1380; *collation to benefice (eccl.) 1131, 1549; **-iuncula,** brief summary c 1283; **-ivus,** connective, comparative c 1270, p 1300; **-arius,** one collated to a benefice 1341, 1421; **-or,** one who collates to a benefice (eccl.) c 1230, 1483; supervisor of disputations (ac.) c 1346, c 1477; 760, **-rix** (*f.*) 13c., bestower; **-iono,** to collate, compare 1423, 1496; *cf.* **conferentia.**

collatro, see **colatro.**

collavo, to join in cleansing 1344.

collect/io, group, society 9c. 1343; *collection of taxes, *etc.*, tribute a 1090, 1559; sweepings, pickings 1322, 1449; collection (of books, *etc.*) 1329, 15c.; synthesis c 850. c 1160; sum (math.) 1145; collectivity (log.) 13c.; collections (ac.) c 1561; **c. bidentium,** a rent (W.) 1326; **c. lane, -a lane,** wool gathered from the fields 1276; **-a,** crowd, assembly 9c., 1006; (?) levy, muster (of armed men) 14c.; *levy, collection of taxes or tithes or sum collected c 1150, 15c.; collector's district 1406, 1487; (?) collation, repast c 1266, c 1330; 980, c 1000. a 1090, 1521, **-us** 760. 1437, collect, prayer (eccl.); **c. generalis** 1509; **c. specialis** c 1340, c 1509; **c. magistra** 13c.; **-a** c 1250, **-aneum** c 1072, c 1396, **-aneus** 15c., **-are** c 1330, c 1385; **-arium** c 1182, 1432, book of collects; **-aneum,** compilation 12c., 1537; **-im** 870, c 950. c 1361, **-ive** 8c., 870. a 1250, 1378, unitedly, collectively; *-or** a 1123, c 1546, **-arius** 1467, collector (of taxes, tithes, *etc.*); **-oria,** collectorship c 1354, 1443; **-orium,**

(?) collecting-book 1538; **-orius,** of a collector c 1586; **-rix,** collecting (*f.*) a 1452; †**-um,** *see* **2 calcea; -ura,** collection c 550; **-us,** close-fisted, stingy c 793; *see also* **annus; collig/ibilis,** derivable 1495; **-o,** to rescue, pick up 893. c 1180; to collect corn from (fields) 1321; 1267, c 1333, **collecto** c 1450, to tax, collect fees from; **c. signa,** to join battle c 1400; **-or cum patribus meis,** to die 1461.

collegatio, see **COLLIG**

colleg/ium c 550, 1024. c 1125, 1620, **-a** c 1150, **colligium** c 550, gathering, company, community; *college of canons 1237, 1583; college of cardinals 1277, 1377; *college (ac.) 1379, 1636; **c. mercatorum,** guild-merchant 1597; **c. militare de garterio** 1419; **sum in -io,** to be in company, *or* on a journey c 1115; **-ialis** 1300, 17c., *-iatus** 1225, 1684, collegiate (eccl.); **-ialiter,** in a collegiate manner 1344, 1458; **-iasticus** 1499, **-iatus** c 1433, c 1579, **-ista** 1524, ‡**-ionista** 1570, member of college.

collema, see **colla.**

colleprosus, fellow leper c 1180.

colletor c 700, 8c. c 1125, c 1307, to rejoice with or in.

collevator, one who shares in easing c 1125.

collevita (conl-), fellow Levite a 1100.

colli-, *see also* **collum.**

colliberalis, see **colibertus.**

collibro, to weigh one against another c 1470.

colliculus, hillock 760. c 1250, c 1385; **c. formicarius,** ant-hill c 1470.

collig-, *see also* **COLLECT; COLLEG**

collig/atio 1261, **-antia** a 1250, c 1377, **-amentum** c 1220, 1414, connexion, bond; league, confederacy 1255, c 1408; **collegatio,** compact 1309; **-ar,** bandage 1250; **-ator,** book-binder 1345; c 1408, **-atus** c 1350, 1406, confederate, ally; **-o (pacem),** to cement c 1362; **-ulo,** to attach with latchets c 1365.

collimo, *for* **collineo,** to shoot 1584; to appraise rightly c 1562.

collinio, to smear over c 1361, 1380.

colliqu/atio, liquefaction 1620, ‡1652; **-o,** to liquefy ‡1483, 1620.

coll/isio, contraction (gram.) 790; c 1150, c 1540, **-usio** c 1298, c 1385, shock, blow; *see also* **collusio.**

collistrigium, see **collum.**

collitigans, fellow litigant 1549.

collo, see **colla.**

collobium, see **COLOB**

colloc/atio, grant, bestowal 1251, 1421; **-abilis,** stationary, fixed c 870. 1344; **-o,** to settle (*intr.*) 14c.; to build c 700; **collogo,** to place c 550.

collocutor/ium, parlour (mon.) c 1283; **-ius,** keeper of parlour (mon.) 1206; **colloquium matutinale** 1476, 1543, ‡**c. crastinum** c 1440, 'morn-speech', guild meeting.

collubescens, pleased, agreeable 969.

collucror (dep.), to purchase 11c.

colluctamen, struggle 14c.

colludium, see **collusio.**

coll/um fusilli, neck ('halse') of mill-spindle 1327, 1374; **c. oculi, c. vesice** (med.)

a 1250; **c. pedis,** ankle c 1191; **-ulum,** little neck c 1200, 1622; **-icipium,** one-tenth of weregeld (A.S. *halsfang*) c 1120; †**-ifi-cium,** (?) mutilation c 1115; ***-istrigium** 1279, 1436, **-ostrigium** 1471, **-istridum** 1275, c 1420, **-istruxum** 1336, †**cullistri-gium** 1364, **-istringium** 1298, †**calistri-gium** 1381, pillory; **pena -istrigialis** c 1250; *see also* **collarium.**

collumen, companion-light 8c.

colluseus, *see* **porta.**

coll/usio, collusion: **-utio** 1318, **-isio** 1381; **colludium,** deception c 570. c 1192, 1268; *see also* **collisio.**

collustrum, *see* **colostrum.**

collybista, money-changer: **colobysta** c 730.

collyri/um, bribe, *douceur* c 1218; **-atus,** mixed into a salve a 1250.

colo, *see* **colonus.**

colobalsamum, *see* XYLO

colober, *see* **coluber.**

colob/us a 1360, †**-on** c 1367, mutilated, defective (κολοβός); ***-ium,** tabard, shirt, sleeveless tunic *or* cloak 790, c 1000. c 1130, 1517.

colobysta, *see* **collybista.**

colo/cynthis (bot.): **-quintida** a 1250, 1427.

colof-, coloph-, *see* COLAPH

‡**colomen,** *assara baccara* (bot.) 14c.

†**colomus,** *for* **calamus** *or* **culmus,** straw 1295.

col/on, colon (punctuation-mark) 1267; **-ica, dolor -icus,** (?) **-ficum,** colic (med.) a 1250.

colonellus, colonel, officer 1587, 1666.

Colon/ensis, coin of Cologne a 1275; **marca -iensis** c 1185.

col/onus, villein c 1115; **c. fiscalinus,** king's under-tenant c 1115; **-o,** husbandman c 1190, a 1408; **-ono,** to cultivate (fig.) 1430.

colopedium, *see* **calopodium.**

colophon/ia a 1235, ‡c 1440, **-a** a 1250, colophony, Greek tar; ‡**-iso,** to tar c 1440.

coloquintida, *see* **colocynthis.**

color/, timbre (mus.) c 1470; *see also* **2 pannus; -es principales,** sable and argent (her.) p 1394, a 1446; **c. medii,** azure, gules, and *or* p 1394, a 1446; secondary colours a 1200; **c. submedii,** vert, *etc.* p 1394; **c. collaterales,** colours other than principal a 1446; **-alis,** specious, plausible c 1390; **-abiliter,** speciously c 1390, a 1452; **-atius,** more speciously 1378, 1380; **-atio,** production of colour a 1250, 1267; blushing c 1290; argument that lends colour to a proposition c 1300, p 1300; 1328, 1435, **coleratio** 1517, tinting, dyeing; **-ativus,** producing colour a 1250; **-ator,** dyer a 1446; **-eitas,** colouredness c 1300: **-o,** to tint (wine) 1337; *see also* **collarium.**

colostrum, collustrum, beestings c 1180.

colp/atio c 1245, 1350, **culpatio** c 1200, **-atura** c 1293, **culpatura** c 1200, †**coe-pecia** 1237, **coupagium** 1327, cutting of wood; **coupagium** 1355, 15c., **-erones** (*pl.*) 1330, ***coperones** a 1220, 1334, **coprones** 13c., 1370, **coperoni** 1224, **coporones** 1234, 1270, **couperones** 1244, 1301, **couparones** 1263, **couprones** 1306, **co-operones** 1232, 1255, †**coopertiones**

c 1250, **copices** (*pl.*) 1327, **copicia** (*pl.*) 1303, **couplicia** (*pl.*) 1330, **colspicium** 1269, crop and lop of trees; ***copicia,** **copicium** 1299, 1587, **copecia** 1538, **coupeicia** 1260, **coopicium** 1356, c 1498, **copia** 1539, **copius** 1527, coppice; **-ator** c 1250, **coupiator** 1282, 1315, wood-cutter; **-o** c 1200, c 1400, **-unus** c 1330, †**-inus** c 1245, **culpo** c 1400, **culponus** 13c., candle-stump, lump of wax; **cul-pinatus,** (?) 'culponed', ornamented with material of a different colour 1358; **-o** 1296, 1409, **culpo** 1298, **copo** c 1200, 1276, **coupo** 1335, to cut, chop; **-o,** to strike, ring (a bell) c 1245; **coupo (terram),** to clear (land) of trees, reclaim 1234; †**cepicio,** to crop (trees) 1335; *cf.* COLAPH, CULP

colpinda, 'colpindach', heifer (Sc.) c 1450.

colpus, gulf: **culpus** c 700, **gulf/us** c 1192, c 1436, †**-rus** c 1200.

colton/a, an office or establishment (? of charcoal-burners) at Canterbury 1213; **-arius,** servant in charge of the above 1322, 1335.

colub/er, serpent: **colober** c 685; **-rina librilla** 1466, **culverinus** 1474, culverin, hand-gun.

columb/a, dove-shaped pyx (eccl.) 1222; **c. ramata** 1255, **c. ramera** 1249, wood-pigeon; ***-ella, -ellus,** young dove, pigeon 1212, 1535; †**-a** 1242, **-ar** c 1200, aperture; ***-ar, -are** c 1270, 1559, **-arium** 1205, 1583, **culumbarium** c 1376, dove-cot; pillory c 1200; horse-collar ‡c 1440, 1461; dog-collar 1461, 1469; **-aria** ‡14c., 1632, ‡**-ina** 14c., 1483, columbine, *etc.* (bot.); **-aris,** dove-like a 1275; **-ina,** floral design 1409; **-ine,** with the innocence of a dove c 1190.

columellaris, paly (her.) c 1595.

column/a (columpn-) c 1225, c 1450, **-ella** 1267, column of page; wand of office c 1584; book-stand 1400; **c. boteraz** 1256, **-ula** 1345, buttress; **-ula,** columnar particle 1662; **-o,** to prop, support with columns 1220, 1244.

†**columpnus,** area, (?) commote (W.) 1304.

colura, *see* **colamentum.**

***colurus,** colure (astr.) c 1200, 14c.

colus, distaff as symbol of inheritance in female line c 1145; *see also* **jus.**

colymbus, (?) sort of arrow c 1200.

1 com/a, tail of comet a 1233, c 1320; **c. equina,** horse-hair 1409; **-am amitto,** to be tonsured 820; **-ata** c 1408, **stella -ata** 1267, 1468, **s. -eta** c 1400, **s. -etis** c 1132, c 1188, comet; **-eticus,** cometary c 1270; *see also* **comma.**

2 coma, comb 1395.

comba, part of mill-wheel 1303; *see also* **1 cumba.**

comballivus (conb-), fellow bailiff 1322.

combaro (conb-), fellow baron 1217, c 1397.

combell/ator, fellow warrior 14c.; **-o,** to fight 1378.

combin/atio, combination, union 1267, c 1550; **-ati** (*pl.*), two by two c 1188, c 1250; **-o,** to compile c 1440.

combl-, *see* **cumulus.**

Combrito (Conb-), fellow Briton 1136.

combrus, weir (O.F. *combre*) (Fr.) a 1200.

combu/ratio, baking (of tiles) 1535; 1369, c 1380, **-risio** 1488, **-stio** 1337, 1479, burning (of lime); **-stio,** branding (of animals) 1376; smelting 13c., 1409; blanching, assay (of silver) 1086, 1229; *c 1090, a 1564, **-stura** c 1120, arson; **locus -stionis,** focus a 1233; **-rator sepium** 1295, **-ratrix** (f.) **cepium** 1293, one who uses fencing for firewood; **-stor** 1200, 1559, **-ssor** c 1290, one who commits arson; **-stialis** c 1325, **-stilis** c 1345, c 1400, **-stibilis** a 1233, 1620, **-ssibilis** c 1540, combustible; **-stivus,** torrid a 1233; **-ro,** to burn (feloness) 1220, 1416; to bake (tiles) 1355, c 1390; to burn (lime) 1268, 1356; to smelt c 1266, 1292; to blanch, assay (silver) c 1178, 1226; to reclaim (land) by 'beat-burning' 1246.
*‌**comburgens/is** (conb-) c 1287, c 1540, **coburgensis** 1399, †**combursis** 1331, fellow burgess; **-ia,** status of fellow burgess 1463.
comc-, *see* **conc-**
comedia (pl.), songs sung at banquets c 790.
comedium 1279, *‌**comest/io** (commest-) 9c., 10c. a 1090, c 1470, **-us** c 1290, c 1353, meal, feast, feasting; **-ibilia,** victuals c 1540; *‌**-ibilis,** eatable c 1266, c 1362; **commistibilis,** fit for grazing 1267; **-ibilitas,** eatability 13c.; **-or,** glutton 12c., 1461; **comedo,** to dine, feed c 1160, 1458.
comelingus, *see* **cumelingus.**
comes, official, magnate c 691, 956. c 1103, 15c.; *‌count, earl a 1070, 1586; **c. civitatis,** port-reeve 1419; **c. Marescallus,** earl marshal 1230, 1569; **c. Palatinus** c 1135, 1586, **c. Palatii** 12c.; **c. stabulariorum,** *see* CONSTAB; **c. de tertio denario** 1155, **c. tertii denarii** c 1437, earl receiving third penny of county; ‡**comes** 1570, **cometissa** c 1150, 12c., *‌**comit/issa** 6c. 1085, c 1540, **-essa** 16c., lady, countess; **-issa Mareschallie** 1377; **-alis,** of an earl a 1120, 1418; **-aneus,** (?) companion a 1228; **-anter,** concomitantly 1344, 1380; **-antia,** accompaniment c 1250, 1524; 14c., **-as** 1248, 1345, **-ativa** 1255, *‌**-iva** 1188, c 1483, †**-ura** c 1540, company, escort; **commetiva,** (entertainment of) company c 1390, 1521; **-as,** gentry 1356, c 1362; **-atenses** (pl.), retinue c 1370; **-atrix,** companion (f.) c 1180;
-atus *‌1086, 1586, **-iva** c 1325, **-ium** c 1194, county or earldom; *‌county court or suit thereat (attendance or fine for non-attendance) c 1072, 1442; countship 1461; **c. palatinus** 1297, 1542, **c. pallatii** 1310, county palatine; **c. plenus** 1203, c 1290, **c. magnus** 1279, regular meeting of county court; **-ia** (pl.), law-court c 1115; Parliament p 1327, c 1550; **-ia** (f. s.), meeting c 1070, c 1414, **cometia** c 1417, c 1428, meeting for audit.
comessatio, *see* **comissatio.**
comestabulus, *see* CONSTAB
comet-, *see* 1 **coma; comes; commetrus.**
comf-, *see* **conf-**
Comicus, Terence 12c.
comin/ata, -um, *see* CYMIN
comissatio, feasting: *‌**com(m)essatio** c 730, c 793. 11c., 1526; *cf.* COMMENS

Comista, heretic from Como, Waldensian 12c., 1461.
comm/a (coma), (?) poetry, numbers c 793; minute interval (mus.) c 1160; (?) interpretation 1241; **-aticus,** short saying c 793.
commacto, to sacrifice together a 1275.
commagister, fellow master (ac.) c 1317, 1350.
commalignans, fellow criminal 1169.
commanipularis, fellow soldier c 1100, c 1150.
comman/sio, companionship c 1212; **-eo,** to dwell (together), stay with c 1090, 1422.
commansuesco, to grow tame c 1250.
commar/cio, boundary c 1115; **-chio,** fellow marcher 1233, c 1300.
commartyr/, fellow martyr c 1400; **-isor,** to be martyred 14c.
commasso, to incorporate in a mass 8c.; to stuff 12c.; to heap together 1412.
†**commastitio,** chewing 13c.
*‌**commater,** godmother 1102, 1552.
commaticus, *see* **comma.**
comme/atio, intercourse, communication c 1200, c 1302; **-abilis,** ready to be crossed c 1190, c 1250.
commembris, fellow member c 704.
commemorat/io Animarum, All Souls' Day (2 Nov.) 1239, 16c.; **c. Sanctorum** a 1090, c 1190, **c. de Omnibus Sanctis** c 1266, (1 Nov.), 15c.; **-ivus** 1610, **-orius** c 730. c 1220, 15c.; **-ivus** 1610, **-orius** c 730. c 1370, c 1400, reminding, commemoratory.
commend/atio 1086, 1517, **-atus** 1086, c 1325, commendation, entrusting; commendatory office for the dead 980. c 1130, 1467; **-atiuncula,** brief commendation c 1450; **-a,** commendation, entrusting (eccl.) 1280, 1549; **de -a,** provisionally 1260; **in -am** 1253, 1537, **in -as** 1549, in commendation (eccl.); **-abilis,** recommendatory c 1337; **-abilitas,** praiseworthiness c 1283; **-abiliter,** commendably c 1140, c 1396; *‌**-atarius** (Sc.) 1441, 1567, **-atorius** 16c., commendator (eccl.); **-ativus,** eulogistic 1439; **-ator,** officer in religious order of knighthood c 1407, 1451; abbot *in commendam* 1573; **-atorie,** by way of commendation c 1334; **-atorie** (pl.) 1287, **littere -atorie** c 1125, c 1467, **l.** †**-arie** 13c., letters of commendation; **-atus, -ata** (f.), commended person, tenant 1086; **-esia,** payment for commendation 1190; **-isa,** commendation 1215, 1219; **-o,** to commend, grant 1086, c 1430.
commens/alis, (adj.) commensal (eccl.) 1281, 1425; (subst.) c 1204, a 1564, **commessalis** 1234, **commessarius** 12c., member of same household, mess-mate; †**-atio,** feasting 1472 (*cf.* **comissatio**); **-o,** to dine with 1498.
commensur/atio a 1205, c 1444, **-itio** 870, measurement, commensuration; **-abilis,** commensurable c 1192, 1267; **-abilitas,** commensurability 1344; **-ative,** commensurately p 1300; **-ativus,** commensurate 1526; **-atior,** more commensurate a 1233; **-o me** c 1250, 1267, *‌**-or** c 1170, c 1430, to measure oneself with.

comment/io falsitatis, fraud, falsehood 852, c 862; -atrix, liar, deceiver (f.) a 1200.

comment/um, commentary, treatise 870. 11c., c 1460; -ariensis, reeve a 700; secretary c 1160, 1310; -ator, Averroes a 1233, c 1460.

commercator, merchant c 1340.

commere/o, for -or, to earn c 793.

commess-, see comissatio; COMMENS

commest-, commist-, see comedium.

commetrus (cometrus), commensurate c 1361.

commigratio ex seculo, passing c 1182.

commil/es, fellow knight 1277; -ito, fellow worker or monk 770, 790; -itaneus 8c., cummilito p 1330, for -ito, fellow soldier.

commin/atorium, threat c 1188, c 1430; -atorie c 1290, 1378, -anter c 1308, threateningly; -atorius, threatening c 1200, p 1377; -atorie (pl.) 1169, littere -atorie 1287, c 1540, threatening letter.

comminist/er 956. c 1414, c 1546, -ra (f.) 1090, fellow servant; -ratorius, of a fellow servant c 1377; -ro, to minister jointly 12c.

commin/utio, fragmentation a 1250, c 1605; -ubilis, †-uabilis c 1270, -utivus a 1250, friable, crumbly.

commisero (with dat.), to pity 9c.

*commiss/io 1177, c 1580, †-a 1366, commission; -a, fine, penalty 1336; -ariatus, office of commissary (eccl.) c 1352, 1427; 1438, 1542, †-ioratus 1470, commissariat (Sc.); -arie, as a commissary c 1376; -arius c 1334, -ionarius 1435, -ivus c 1377, of a commissary, agent, or of commission; *-arius 1236, 1684, -ionarius 1316, 1559, -ionator 1508, commissary, commissioner; -arius burgi, commissar, Parliamentary representative of burgh (Sc.) 1450, 1451; c. ecclesie 1467; c. generalis 1329, 1560; -or, one who entrusts c 1290; littere -orie 1204, 1540, l. -ionales 1508, 1684, letters of commission; -um, (?) parish or diocese c 793; -iono, to commission 1330, c 1353; committo, to commit to prison or for trial a 1185, 1415; c. penam, to incur a penalty c 1243, 1293.

commix/tio (commis-) 870. c 1150, a 1452, -io c 1258, commingling; combination of the two natures in Christ 8c., 870; adulteration c 1266, c 1330; temperament 1267; a 1090, 14c., c. carnalis 1231, c 1258, c. carnis c 1170, sexual union; -tibilis, miscible c 1320; -tim, in combination a 1250; -ticius, mingled, united 7c.

commod/atio, loan 1219; -arius, benefactor c 1395; *-itas, easement, profit, produce c 1185, 1583; *-ifer 1319, c 1440, -osus c 1448, c 1470, profitable, advantageous; -ifere 1359, -ose c 1430, advantageously; -ista, assistant (unbeneficed) priest c 1200; -ifico, to adapt c 1070, see also commotum.

commoderatio, measurement with 870.

*commonach/us c 1090, 1512, -alis a 1452, fellow monk.

commoneto, to coin c 1200.

commonialis, fellow nun 1281, 1481.

commonit/io, warning: communitio a 1250, c 1353, -orium 1006; -orie (pl.), letter of instruction 1169, c 1194; -ive, by reminder 12c.

commor/abilis, (?) durable c 1310; -o, for -or, to remain 1315, c 1400.

commortha, customary payment, cwmhorth (W.) 1316, 1609.

commot/io castrorum, moving camp a 1180; -atio, disturbance c 700; see also COMMUT

commot/um, -us 1225, 1583, -a 1259, kemmotum c 1190, kimotha 1200, comodum 1202, †camaum 1199, commokum 1212, commote, cymwd (W.).

commultiplico, to multiply together c 1361.

*commun/a 1130, c 1350, -ia c 1193, 14c., -e 1147, 1370, -is c 1265, 1274, -io c 1160, 1535, -iatio (Fr.) c 1322, -itas 1086, 1684, -itatus 1281, commune, association, corporation, community, commonalty; see also curia; -e armate, armed forces, garrisons c 1210; *-a c 1240, c 1318, -ia 1199, 1540, -itas 1391, common, common land; *-a c 1170, 15c., -ia c 1160, c 1473, -ia (pl.) 1241, 1372, -is c 1180, 1405, -itas c 1127, c 1350, rights of common; *-a 1183, 1327, -ia c 1197, c 1275, -e a 1190, c 1340, common property or fund (eccl.); -a 12c., 15c., *-e (pl.) c 1340, 1535, -um c 1452, -ia c 1190, -ia (pl.) c 1437, c 1520, -ie (pl.) 1371, commons, allowance of food (eccl. & ac.); -ium, banquet 1353; -a (Fr.) 1261, -e (Fr.) 1200, -itas 1253, common tax, payment; -a 1200, 1233, -ia (pl.) 1586, converse, intercourse; -ia (pl.), general principles 1267; 1218, c 1440, c. memoranda 1199, common matters, day-to-day business (of Exchequer); -e sanctorum, service for saints' days c 1250, c 1300; -es (pl.) 1347, 1513, -ienses (Sc.) 1327, -itas (coll.) 1248, c 1492, commons (estate of the realm); -is, common, habitual (in derogatory sense) 1375, c 1448; ordinary, of frequent occurrence a 1200, 1684; united under one lord 1246; see also in, annus, bancus, camera, campus, domus, forma, jus, justitia, lex, locus, pastura, placea, placitum, secta, sensus, terminus, terra; -ius 1221, 1613, -us 1126, c 1400, for -is; -ior, more general 1245, a 1400; -issimus, most universal 1378, c 1444; -iter, as a whole 1209, c 1250; commonly, usually c 1283, 1351; publicly 1239, 1432; in a general sense c 1332; -issime, in the most general sense c 1334; -itim, in common 1583;

-alis, common, communal 1191, c 1457; -aria 1339, -eria 1324, office of 'commoner' (mon.); -arius, commoner, one enjoying rights of common 1318, 1331; common council man 1419; 1321, 1419, -iarius 1313, 1419, commoner, member of commune or commonalty; 1191, 1456, -iarius 1318, 1534, -ator 1366, 'commoner' (mon. & ac.); -iloquium, general introduction c 1283;

-io, common assent a 1210, 1230; anthem c 1000. c 1188, 1326; *980. c 1125, c 1520, c. corporis et sanguinis Christi 814, c. c. et s. Domini c 1436, c. c. Dominici c 1238, c. sacra c 1185, c 1362, c. sancta c 1090, 1508, c. sacrosancta c 1550, c. sacramenti 1461, Holy Communion, Eucharist; c. aque, access to water 1260; **c. ecclesie** a 1090, 1461; **c. sanctorum,** communion of saints p 1381, c 1457; **-itas,** community, generality (log.) c 1110, 1380; **-ioritas,** greater generality (log.) c 1367; **-io** 1280, ‡1483, *-o 1274, 1380, to have rights of common.

communic/atio, Holy Communion 980. c 1115, a 1452; converse, intercourse 1461; 'participation' (of individual in species) c 1380; **c. idiomatum,** interchange of properties (between the two natures of Christ) p 1300; **-abilis,** affable c 1200; communicable, able to be imparted c 1270, 1620; fit for Holy Communion c 1520; **-abilitas,** communicability c 1290, c 1360; **-arius,** member of commonalty 1408; **-ative,** by participation 1378, 1412; **-ativus,** communicative, apt to impart a 1250, 1620; **-ator,** accomplice a 1075; one who imparts 14c.; **-o,** to have a share in c 1115, 1419; to participate (log.) c 1380, c 1444; to agree, have something in common 1267; to conspire c 793; to associate, have intercourse with a 1090, c 1520; to converse 1519; to communicate, correspond (by letter) c 1324, 1342; *to have rights of common c 1225, 1433; to administer the sacraments to 705, 1006. c 1150, c 1400; to participate in the sacraments 8c., 9c. c 1125, 1575.

communi/men, barricade a 1452; **-tus,** armoured, barded 1370; **-o,** to corroborate a 1140, 1684; *see also* COMMONIT

commun/itas, -o, *etc., see* **communa.**

commut/atio c 802, 940. 1086, 1461, **commotatio** 930, **-atus** 1380, exchange; **-abilitas,** changefulness, difference c 793, c 870; **-abiliter,** changeably 9c.; **-ativus,** retributive 1344; **-uo,** *for* **-o,** to exchange 765.

comod-, *see* **codium; commotum.**

comorbanus, *see* **coverbus.**

compact/io c 1230, 1530, **-atum** 1437, compact, agreement; composition, consistency (of matter) a 1250; **-ura,** constriction (med.) a 1250; **-or librorum,** book-binder 1561; **-o** p 1440, **compango** c 1366, to put together, join.

compadium, *see* **companagium.**

compag/inatio, agreement 14c.; **c. colorum,** picture c 793; †**campages,** bond 1509; **-ator,** one who holds together c 1125; **-inator,** companion in covenant 943; **c. lignorum,** joiner c 1170; †**-iatus,** composed, compact c 1283; **-ino,** to compile c 1204, c 1250.

compagus, fellow countryman a 1000.

compana, *see* **campana.**

*****compan/agium** c 1115, c 1400, **-aticum** 1212, †**compadium** 12c., **cumpanagium** 1186, c 1240, **componagium** c 1238, **compernagium** 13c., c 1370, **cumpernagium** 1307, relish, something eaten with bread.

compango, *see* COMPACT

compar/ a 1142, c 1353, **cumpar** (G.) 1313, compeer; fellow burgess (Winchester) 1412; **-iter,** in like manner c 1431; **-abiliter,** comparably c 1265; **-abilitas,** comparability c 1300; **-ativa,** comparison, analogy 1620; **-ative,** comparatively c 1470,

1686; by way of similitude c 1204; **-io** (*met. grat.*), *for* **-o,** to compare 13c.

compar/abilis, obtainable, purchasable c 1300; **-eo,** *for* **-o,** to procure c 704.

*****compar/itio (comper-)** 1267, 1549, **-atio** 1416, 1560, **-entia** 1447, 1620, appearance, presence; **-itio personalis,** appearance in person 1286, a 1452; *-eo c 1188, a 1564, -o c 1270, 1290, -io c 1537, -ior c 532, to appear (in court), 'compear' (leg.); **-eo,** to produce in court 1460.

comparochianus, fellow parishioner 1266, c 1414.

comparti/ceps 12c., c 1458, **coparticeps** c 1443, **-onarius** 1274, c 1308, **comportionarius** c 1308, 1451, coparcener, sharer; **coparcenaria,** coparcenary, joint inheritance a 1564; **-cipo** c 1250, c 1375, **-cipo me** 12c., to share.

compascualis terra, common pasture c 1115.

1 *compass/io (conp-), compassion, sympathy c 793. c 1090, c 1470; **-ibilis** 870. c 1200, 1372, **compatibilis** 1384, 1451, **competabilis** 1515, compatible, able to be held simultaneously (eccl.); **compatibiliter,** compatibly (of benefices) 1451; **-ibilitas,** compatibility 870; **-ibilior,** more compassionate a 1205; **-ionabilis,** pitiable 1308; **-ionabiliter** 1308, **-ionaliter** 1301, **compatienter** c 1344, compassionately; **-iosus** 14c., **-ivus** c 1150, 1421, compassionate; **compatientissimus,** most compassionate 1200, 1327; **compatior,** to suffer with (eccl.); 8c. c 1250, c 1470, **-ionor** c 1465, to be compassionate, sympathize; c 870. c 1258, c 1344, **c. me** a 1233, a 1361, **c. mecum** c 1270, c 1363, to be compatible with.

2 compass/io, -atio 1567, **-amentum** 1397, compassing, contrivance; **-um,** compass (geom.) c 1320; mariner's compass 1586; **-o** 1451, 1573, **compatior** 1451, **cumpatior** 1571, to compass, contrive.

compasto, *see* COMPOST

compat-, *see also* **compassio (1 & 2).**

compat/er, joint father (of the faithful) c 793; fellow priest 1610; 11c., 1551, **-rinus** 15c., godfather; gossip, companion c 1190, 1518; **-ra** c 1110, **-rix** 1467, godmother; **-ernitas,** common paternity c 1197; sponsorship, spiritual relationship c 1200, 1435.

*****compatriot/a** a 1100, c 1540, **-us** c 1070, compatriot, fellow countryman, neighbour; **-alis,** of a compatriot c 1255.

compauperatus, sharing poverty a 1205.

compauso, to rest together a 1452, c 1470.

comped/ium, shackles *or* stocks 1308; **-ito,** to shackle c 1290.

compedo, to break wind c 1220.

compell/atio, 'appeal', accusation c 1115, a 1446; **-ans, -ator,** appellor, accuser c 1115; **-atus,** appellee, accused person c 1115; **-o,** to appeal, accuse c 1115.

†**compellum (pili),** (?) halter 1488.

compend/ium, dependency, appurtenance 8c.; c 1160, c 1501, **-iloquium** c 1283, epitome; Exchequer roll containing estreats still leviable c 1325; *sub -io,** briefly c 1250, c 1470; **-arium,** short cut c 1362; **-iolum,** trifling profit c 1250; **-ior,** shorter c 1362; **-iositas,** brevity, compactness,

summariness a 1250, c 1375; *see also* COM-
PENS
compenetratio, compenetration (phil.) 1344.
compens/atio c 1204, 1461, **-a** 1456, compensation; **-abilitas,** possibility of compensation c 1343; **-ativus,** compensatory
1338, p 1377; **-ator,** one who recompenses
c 1410; **-o** c 1280, c 1356, **compendo** 15c.,
to pay, contribute.
comper-, *see also* **comparitio.**
compercutio, to join in stabbing 1573.
comperegrinor, to join in pilgrimage c 1180.
comperfectus, complete, absolute 870.
compernagium, *see* **companagium.**
compernola, *see* CAMP
compert/io, finding c 1300, 1410; **-issime,**
quite certainly 9c.; **-orium,** inquiry, inquest 1425; **-um,** fact found at visitation
c 1327, c 1473; **-um est,** it is found (by the
court) (leg.) 1255, 1358.
compesco (ad), to constrain 1313; *see also*
COMPOST
compet-, *see also* 1 **compassio; compita;**
COMPUT
compet/entia, circumstance, opportunity
12c., 13c.; suitability, sufficiency, com-
petence c 1250, 1684; ***-ens,** suitable,
adequate 692, 1030. a 1090, 1543; ***-enter,**
suitably a 1090, 15c.
compigrescens, fellow sluggard a 1180.
*compil/atio, crowd, press c 1070; compilation c 1200, c 1520; **-atiuncula,** small compilation 15c.; **-ator,** compiler c 700, 933.
c 1122, c 1450; **-o,** to compile c 1188, c 1540.
compilo, to pull out hairs c 1219.
compistor, fellow baker 1419.
com/pita (*f. s.*), cross-roads 12c.; **-petum,**
limit, boundary c 550.
complac/atio, conciliation c 1200, a 1452;
*-o, to conciliate c 1125, c 1453.
complac/entia c 1240, c 1540, **complicentia** 1458, **†-ia** 1417, satisfaction, goodwill,
pleasure; **-enter,** pleasingly 14c., c 1360;
-ibilis, pleasing, favourable 1403; **-itior,**
more favourable 12c., 15c.; **-itius,** more
pleasingly 11c.; **-itum,** pleasure a 1253,
14c.; **ex -ito,** by common consent c 865;
-eo, to satisfy (with alms) 1301.
complan/atio, explanation, gloss 1529; **-a**
(*pl.*), plains c 1235.
complan/ta, complaint 1353; **-go,** to lament
(together) c 1200, c 1213.
complasmo, to create 1552.
complausus, united applause c 1470.
complect-, *see* **complementum;** COMPLEX
complegius, fellow pledge 13c.
comple/mentum *c 740. c 1188, 1539, ***-tio**
c 730, c 1000. a 1090, c 1532, **-tudo** 1344,
fulfilment, completion; full actuality (log.)
a 1233, a 1346; complement (math.) 1686;
c. juris 1254, ***c. justitie** 1253, c 1430;
-mentum 1413, **complendum** 1200, **-tio**
c 1245, ***-torium (complectorium)** 793.
a 1090, 1537, compline, evening service
(eccl.); **-bilis, -tibilis,** capable of completion 13c.; ***-te,** completely c 1250, 1559;
-tive, by way of completion 13c., a 1347;
*-tivus, complementary, completing 8c.,
9c. c 1080, c 1290; fulfilled c 1115; **-torius,**
of or for compline p 800.

*complex/, accomplice, confederate, adherent
c 730, 969. a 1100, a 1564; **complective,**
comprehensively c 870; **-e,** complexly
1344, c 1363; **-us,** complex 1267, c 1363;
*-io (complectio), circumference 12c.;
constitution, temperament c 1180, 1503;
-ibilis c 1270, **-ionalis** c 1115, 1427, constitutional, temperamental; **-ionabiliter,**
in constitution 1267; **-ionatus,** constituted,
tempered 1200, 1378; **-ionor,** to constitute
a 1200, c 1257; **complecto** 870, **-o** 1006,
to embrace; to involve 1461; **complector,**
to consider c 1115.
complic/atio, synthesis c 850; involvement
p 1381; **-abilis,** susceptible of complication
c 1270; **-iamentum,** folding up 1488; **-atus,**
surrounded c 1170; *see also* **denarius; -itus,**
involved p 1381; (*subst.*) accomplice 1311.
complicentia, *see* **complacentia.**
complo/sio manuum, wringing of hands
c 1200; **-sis manibus,** with hands tightly
clasped c 1330; **-do,** to compress *or* collide
c 1115.
complurimi (*pl.*), very many c 1438.
†complustrum, cluster of nuts 15c., 1483.
complu/tor, rain-giver 9c.; **-tus,** rained upon
c 1150, c 1340.
compon-, *see also* COMPOSIT
componagium, *see* **companagium.**
compondero, to weigh together 870. c 1210.
comport/ator, †-or, fellow carrier 12c.
comportionarius, *see* COMPARTI
compos, enjoying possession: **compus voti**
943.
composit/io, composition, synthesis (log.)
13c., c 1344; compound word 1167; composition, (settlement by) payment c 1115,
1559; **c. mortis,** weregeld c 1115; **c.
personalis** (leg.) 1226, 1247; **c. realis**
(leg.) 1226, a 1452; **c. secunda,** process
productive of metals (alch.) c 1227; **-ive,**
in combination 13c., c 1362; **-ivus,** synthetic 1241, c 1365; **-or,** author 1282,
a 1408; ***reconciler,** peacemaker 1270, 1461;
-ura, (literary) composition 14c.; **-um,**
compound (drug) 1252; compound (of
matter and form) 1267, c 1287; **-us,** refined (alch.) 12c.; manured c 1350; **com-
pon/ibilis,** capable of being compounded
c 1270, c 1381; **-ibilitas,** capability of being
compounded c 1290, c 1365; **-entia** (*pl.*),
components c 1200; **-o,** to compound (by
payment), make fine 11c., c 1546; to till
(land) 15c.
compossessor, joint possessor c 1488.
*compossibilis, simultaneously possible,
compatible a 1228, 1378.
compost/atio 1260, 1302, **-ura** 1282, c 1388,
manuring; **-um,** manure 1221, a 1564; ***-o**
c 1265, 15c., **†compasto** c 1290, **†com-
pesco** 15c., **-io** c 1284, to manure; *see also*
COMPUT
compot-, *see also* COMPUT
compot/atio, scot-ale a 1220; **-atrix,** "drunken gossip" 1520.
comprandeo, to sup with 1168.
comprecator, fellow suppliant a 1620.
compredic/ativus, completing the sense
a 1249; **-o,** to preach together with 9c.
comprehen/sio furis, infangthief 12c.; **-tio,**

for -**sio**, perception 13c.; **-sibilitas**, power of comprehending c 1270; **-sim**, with perception, *or* at one stroke c 865; **-sivus**, comprehensive, capable of comprehending c 1115, p 1300; **-sor**, catcher 1177; one who attains c 1197, c 1362; associate c 1237; **-sus**, grasp c 1108.

comprelior, to fight on the same side c 1194, c 1240.

compresen/s, present at the same time 1233; **-tatio**, joint presentation (to benefice) c 1190; **-to**, to present jointly c 1190.

compresid/ens, fellow president c 1310, 1423; **-eo**, to preside together with 1429.

compress/ura, pressing together 870; **-ivus**, compressive c 1250.

comprim/us, associated in primacy 12c.; †**-ote** (*pl.*), men of the first rank 14c.

comprinceps, fellow prince *or* noble 1165, c 1400.

comprob/atio, proof, test c 850, a 975; ***-o**, to prove c 1125, c 1534.

comprocurator, fellow proctor 1261, 1399.

comproditor, fellow traitor 1322, 1327.

comproduc/tio, simultaneous production 1344; **-o**, to produce simultaneously 1374.

comprofessus, fellow monk 14c.

comproficio, to share success c 1160.

comproficiscor, to set out together c 1200.

compromiss/io c 1180, 1426, **-um** 1302, compromise, submission to arbitration; 1221, c 1400, **-um** 1261, 1484, **-aria** (*n. pl.*) 1336, election by delegates (eccl.); **-arius**, arbitrator 1366, 1528; *c 1200, 1484, **-orius** c 1340, delegate appointed to elect bishop, *etc.*; **compromitto**, to promise 9c. 1138, c 1415; to elect by delegates, appoint delegates for electing c 1290, c 1400.

comproportio/l, mutual proportion, correlation c 1344; **-nabiliter** c 1205, **-naliter** c 1200, c 1205, correlatively; **-nalis** c 1205, c 1260, **-natus** a 1250, 1344, correlative.

comprovideo, to provide for simultaneously 1425.

comprovincialis, belonging to same province 8c., c 1060. c 1125, 15c.; (*subst.*) inhabitant of same province a 1100, c 1400; bishop of same province a 1180, 1284.

compsallo, to join in singing (eccl.) 6c., 7c. 1398.

comptator, *see* **computus**.

comptrarotulator, *see* CONTRAROTUL

compt/us, adornment a 1408; **-im**, elegantly 810.

compug/il, sparring partner c 1340; **-io**, fellow champion a 1100; **-nantia**, conflict c 1250, 1437.

compuls/atio, chiming of bells c 1182, c 1460; **-ativus** c 870, **-ivus** c 1258, **-orialis** 1465, 1516, **-orius** 1324, 1465, compulsive; **testis -ivus**, witness produced under compulsion 1347; **-orium**, order directing witnesses to appear in court 1684; **-o**, to join in supplicating 1429.

compunct/io, compunction, remorse (eccl.); **-us**, remorseful (eccl.); **compungens**, causing remorse c 1250.

compunio, to punish c 1470.

compurg/ator, compurgator (leg.) c 1223, 1684; **-o**, to clear, purge (leg.) 1312, c 1365.

compus, *see* **compos**.

comput/resco, to rot: †**-esco** c 1430, **-ruo** c 1197.

comput/us (**compot-**), calculation, reckoning (math. & astr.) c 730. c 1125, c 1370 (*see also* **tabula**); *1086, 1573, **-um** c 1210, 1583, †**compostus** 1415, **compotuus** 1268, 1294, †**competus** c 1475, **-atio** 1239, 1526, account, financial statement; **ad -um**, by tale 1086, 1194; **sine -o**, beyond reckoning c 1125; **super -um**, *see* **onus**, VEND; **teneo -um de**, to have regard for 1461;

-abilis, accountable, answerable 1377, 1584; relevant c 1375; **-ative**, on the account only, notionally c 1300; **-abitur** 1256, 1268, **-ate** 1242, names of writs; **littere de -etur** (G.) 1242; ***-ans** 1343, c 1546, **-arius** c 1290, accountant, one who renders account; **comptator**, official of mint (G.) 1253; **-ator**, (?) compurgator (leg.) 1182, 1194; auditor 1277; teller (Exchequer official) c 1178, 1447; 1249, 1408, **-arium** 1249, 1319, **-orium** 1274, 1417, **-atorium** 1314, c 1472, **contourus** 1465, **cuntreum** 1201, counter (dummy used for coin) *or* counting-board or table; **mensa -alis** 1371; **-arium** a 1564, **-atorium** 1388, a 1564, Compter (sheriffs' prison); **-atorium** 1383, 1456, **comtaria** 1279, counting-house; **-atorius** (**solidus** 1311, **pannus** 1344, **cubiculum** c 1365) used for counting; **-ista**, calculator, mathematician 12c., 1521; **sterlingus -atus**, penny with allowance for deficiency 1274; **-o**, to reckon (as) a 700; *to render an account, account for c 1178, 1584; to credit 1141, c 1283; **-or** (*pass.*), to account (for), be assessed at 1086; †**conpeto**, to count c 1290.

comurbanus, *see* **coverbus**.

comus, *see* **cuneus**.

cona, eye c 550, 6c.; *see also* **cuneus**.

conabbas, *see* **coabbas**.

conabula, *see* **cuna**.

conagium, *see* **cuneus**.

1 con/atus, force (phys.) a 1670; **quonamen**, attempt 15c.; **-abundus**, striving, trying c 790; **-o**, *for* **-or**, to try 13c.

2 con/atus, **-alis**, **-arium**, **-atim**, *see* **conus**.

conb-, *see also* **comb-**

conberto, *see* CONVER

conc/a, **-agium**, **-ata**, *see* CONCH

concabata, *see* CONCAV

concal/eo, to be very hot: †**-oro** c 1370.

***concambi/um**, exchange c 1160, c 1480; **-o**, to exchange c 1200.

***concanonicus**, fellow canon (eccl.) c 1160, 1549.

concanto, to sing together c 1125, a 1452.

†**concanus**, (?) *f.l.* for **concinnus**, 1431.

concapellanus, fellow chaplain 1289, 1430.

concapitaneus, joint captain 15c.

†**concapt/io**, (?) ransom c 1362 (*v.l.* **compactio**); **-us** (**desiderio**), seized c 1362.

concardinalis, fellow cardinal 1280, 1421.

concaus/a, contributory or joint cause c 1250, c 1616; **-atio**, contributory causation 13c., a 1361; **-o**, *to cause jointly 13c., c 1458; †to litigate c 1115.

concavillatio, pinning (arch.) 1478.

concav/itas, hollowness 1167, a 1233; *c 1125, c 1540, -um c 730. c 1260, c 1362, hollow, cavity; c. navis, hold 1438, c 1480; -um, (?) cauldron 14c.; c. nervi communis, retina 1267; -oconvexus (geom.) 1686; -atio, hollowing, digging out c 1200, 1419; -ativus, concerned with making space c 1270; via -ata (†concabata), sunken road 1436, 1492; -o, to hollow out 1237.

concedo, see CONCESS

*concel/atio 1177, 1375, *-amentum 1198, 1593, conselamentum 1334, 1445, †consolomercum c 1300, -um 1275, 1278, consellum 1331, -ium 1199, 1263, conceilum 1330, 1354, (fine for) concealment; -ator, concealer 1356, 1425; *-o 1168, 1583, conscelo 1470, conselo 1384, to conceal.

conceno, to sup together 870. c 1180.

concenobitalis, fellow monk 12c.

concens-, concentio, see CONSEN

concentr/icitas, concentricity 1267; -icus c 1200, 1686, -is c 1184, concentric; (subst.) concentric circle 1267, 1326; -ice, concentrically 1686.

concept/io, syllable c 1200, 1271; *c 850. a 1180, a 1564, *-us c 1250, 1570, -ura c 1458, conception, concept; horoscope (astr.) 1344; *c. B. (S.) Marie c 1030. 1129, 1446, c. B. Virginis c 1314, Feast of the Conception (8 Dec.); -ibilis, conceivable 1267, c 1340; -ualiter, as a mental concept a 1345; -or, originator c 1290; concipio, to capture with others c 1405.

conceraria, see consergeria.

concerno 1230, 1594, conserno 1324, to concern, have regard to; to consider, perceive 1329, 1408.

†concerro, (?) f.l. for contero, to rub down 1275.

concertator, antagonist 1274.

concess/io, concession, grant: consessio c 1443, -iva 1338, -ura c 1324, -us 1086, c 1175; -or, grantor 8c. 1200, 15c.; -atus, granted 1368; -ibilis, easily conceded, allowable a 1233, 1620; -e, in a conciliatory manner 1285; -ive, by way of concession 870; -o quod, granted that c 1332; ex -o, admittedly 1252; -o, to grant 1388; concedo (with inf.), to undertake, promise 1238, c 1540; c. in fata, to die c 1188, 1421; quietum c., to quit-claim a 1100.

conch/a (conc-), basin of fountain a 1200; egg-shell c 1180; (?) lid (of censer) c 1500; 1254, 1289, cunka 1242, †corica 1254, -ata 1283, -atus 1255, measure of grain (G.); c. marina, oyster c 1115; c. nucis, nut-shell c 1180; -us, for -a, shell 980; conquata 1275, 1315, (?) conkagium 1313, land for a concha of seed (? c. 5–6 acres) (G.); -ula, liquid measure (3 cochlearia) c 1100; -ile c 1270, 1530, †-irum 1339, conquilium c 685, -elinus piscis 1385, shell-fish; -iliatus, purpure (her.) 1654; -osus, having a shell c 1200.

conchoralis, belonging to the same choir 1475.

†concides (pl.), barriers of felled trees a 1200.

concientia, see CONSCIENTI

concil-, see CONSIL

concin/enter, in harmony 655; -no, for -o, to agree c 700.

concinero, to sprinkle with ashes c 1180.

concinn/atio, arrangement c 798; -o, to illumine (of altar lamps) a 1220, 1414; see also CONCIN

concipio, see CONCEPT

concistorium, see consistorium.

concitharista, fellow harper 7c.

concit/us, quick c 550; -e 8c., c 1000. c 1090, 1200, -o c 1180, 1461, quickly; -ativus, provocative 14c.

*concivis 1124, 1552, conscivis c 1172, consivis 1348, fellow citizen.

conclamor, concerted shout 1252.

conclango, to make an uproar c 1302.

conclarifico, to be glorified together with 9c.

conclaustralis, fellow monk 12c.

conclav/e c 1380, 1610, -is c 1400, papal conclave; -is, (?) key-hole 1384; †-a, (?) vein or artery c 550; -ium, (?) shoulder c 1000; -iger, chamberlain c 1385.

conclavo, to nail (together), rivet c 1250, 1438.

concliens, fellow client c 550.

conclivus, slope c 1320.

conclus/io, prison, imprisonment 8c.; decision, resolve 1336, 1461; a 1233, c 1450, -a 1425, doctrine, thesis; -ura, enclosure 14c.; -ionaliter c 1366, c 1470, -ionabiliter 1409, -ionarie 1433, -ive c 1470, concludenter 1684, finally, conclusively; -ivus, conclusive 1421, c 1470; -or januarum, janitor c 1150; -a (pl.), convex sides c 730; †-us, recluse 13c.; concludo (a), to exclude c 1290; *to establish, determine, decide 10c. c 1250, 1521; to be conclusive c 1332, 1418; c. in ore gladii, to put to the sword 1461.

concoequo, to level, raze c 1450.

concomit/atio, accompaniment c 1367; -antia, concomitance, co-existence 1267, 1610; company 1381; -iva, community 1378; -anter, concomitantly p 1300, 1391; -o, for -or, to accompany c 1177, c 1488.

concommissarius, fellow commissary 1399, 1426.

concommunic/atio, joint discussion 1433; -or, to impart 1378.

concompromissarius, fellow delegate (in election) c 1290, 1347.

conconatus, with cones meeting in centre, gyronny (her.) c 1595.

conconomus, see ECONOM

concord/ia 1086, 1408, *-antia c 793. c 1197, c 1400, -atio c 1130, 1558, -atus 1567, reconciliation, agreement, compromise; *-ia finalis, fine c 1132 16c.; -antia c 1200, c 1500, liber -ans 1432, concordance of the Bible; -ator, reconciler c 1320; -atissimus, most harmonious c 1250; -anter, in agreement 1344, a 1564; -antisse c 1578, *-iter c 1190, c 1450, unanimously; concors (with gen.), in agreement with c 793; -o, to reconcile (persons) 1130, c 1458; to reconcile, harmonize (things, ideas) 1241, c 1433; to harmonize, adapt (mus.) c 1362; *to come to an agreement c 1154, c 1534;

*to fix by agreement c 1282, 1461; to be suitable, becoming 7c.; to agree, correspond (of things) c 1220, c 1362; **-o me**, to adapt oneself 1098; to agree c 1090, 1199; **-or**, to compromise (leg.) 1196, 1450.

concorpor/atio, union in one body 9c. 1378, 1427; **-eus**, sharing one body c 1595.

concorrumpo, to spoil utterly 870.

concraticulatus, wattled c 1250.

concre/atio, simultaneous creation 13c.; **-atrix**, jointly creative (*f.*) c 1360, c 1367; **-o**, to create simultaneously a 1250, c 1332.

concredo, to answer for c 930; to believe c 1340, 1406.

concrematio, conflagration 826. 12c.

concrepo, to call together 11c.

concret/io, connexion with a substance, concreteness (log.) 13c., p 1300; **-ive**, in a concrete manner or sense 1267, 15c.; **-ivus**, concerned with the concrete c 1160, c 1270; **-us**, concrete a 1180, 1564.

concrucifixus, crucified together with 870.

concub/a c 1112, ‡1483, **-inaria** c 1180, concubine; **-icularius**, room mate 12c., 1517; ‡**-iculum**, ‡**-ile**, "*lectus concubinarum*" 15c.; **-ile**, lair (of animals) 9c.; **-inarius**, (*adj.*) having a concubine 12c., c 1436; born of a concubine 1549; (*subst.*) concubinary priest c 1250, 1549; **-inatus**, tainted with concubinage c 1220; **-inium**, common abode 1200; **-o**, to sleep together c 1194.

concudo, to draw up (a document), compose jointly c 1200.

conculc/atio, trampling down, oppression 1167, c 1343; **c. pannorum**, 'walking', fulling 1408; **-ator**, treader down, oppressor c 1250, c 1470; **-abiliter**, as a victim of oppression c 1250.

concumbo (*trans.*), to violate 1340.

concumulo, to heap up 870. 1441, c 1470.

concupisc/entia, concupiscence, lust a 1090, 1472; **-entialis**, provoked by lust 1344; c 1250, **-itivus** 1344, provoking lust; **-ibilis**, lustful, appetitive 8c., 9c. a 1233, p 1300; desirable, tempting c 937. c 1150, 15c.; **-ibilitas**, ability to desire a 1200, c 1270; **-ibiliter**, lustfully p 1300.

concurialis, fellow official 1159.

concurr/entia c 1250, 1620, **concursus** c 1361, 1559, concurrence; **concursus**, reciprocity 7c.; †**-e**, equally 1296; **-ens**, (*subst.*) concurrent number corresponding to a year-letter 1045. 1115, c 1265; concurrent day 1101, c 1255; **-enter** c 1407, 1474, †**concussorie** 1430, concurrently; **-o**, to agree, concur c 793. c 1125, 15c.

concuss/io, excitement 7c.; **-ivus**, disturbing 1282; **concutio (silvam)**, to 'beat' (for game) c 1090; *see also* CONCURR

concust/os, fellow keeper 1292, c 1300; **-odio**, to guard carefully c 1185.

concustumarius, fellow customary tenant 1364.

condam, *see* **quondam**.

condebitor, fellow debtor 6c.

condecanto, to sing together c 1380.

condecent/ia 1280, c 1504, **condescentia** c 1277, 1348, fitness, suitability; **-er**, in a seemly fashion c 793. c 1338, 1466.

condeclaro, to declare solemnly 13c.

condeclino, to incline, consent a 1200.

†**condecurio**, (?) fellow clerk c 1250.

condedico, to join in dedicating c 1290.

condego, to live together c 1160.

condeleo, to destroy c 1250.

condemn/atio (condempn-), penalty, fine 1289, 1593; damnation (theol.) c 1090, c 1250; **-abiliter**, with condemnation c 1250; **-ativus** c 1200, **-atorius** c 1300, 1684, condemnatory; **-o**, to damn (theol.) c 1334.

condemptio, purchase 1339.

condenominatio, joint denomination (math.) a 1150.

condens/atio a 1250, a 1367, **condempsatio** c 1250, condensation; **-abilis** a 1233, **-ibilis** c 1267, capable of condensation; **-ativus**, causing condensation a 1250; **-itas**, density, thickness c 1125, c 1267; **-o**, (?) to rivet together c 700; **condempso**, *for* **-o**, to condense c 1250.

condeputatus, fellow deputy 1360.

condescen/sio, descent from heaven 8c. 9c.; c 1125, c 1534, **-sus** 1232, c 1250, condescension; †**-dentia**, (?) complacency 1237; **-sive**, in a spirit of compromise 1408; **-sivus**, condescending c 1283; **-do**, to have recourse to 7c.; ***to** condescend, acquiesce c 1070, 1564; *see also* CONDECENT

condetum, *see* CONDIC

condiaconus, fellow deacon c 793.

condicio/ (conditio), status (free or servile) 1275, 1293; **-nalis**, conditional (gram.) c 793; conditional (esp. leg.) 793. 1152, 15c.; (*subst.*) conditional proposition a 1233, c 1363; **-naliter quod** c 1480, **c. ut** 13c., on condition that; **-nate** c 1270, 1516, **-nabiliter** c 1343, a 1564, conditionally; ***-natus**, conditional, conditioned a 1250, 1508; **-no**, to limit by conditions 1427, c 1450; *see also* **conditio**.

condic/tum, promise c 730; ***c** 730. c 1090, c 1450, **-tus** c 1150, 1298, †**condetum** a 1190, agreement, decision; **-o**, to agree c 1188, 1315; **-to**, to dictate together with 1378.

†**condigena**, (?) *for* **coindigena**, fellow resident a 1260.

condign/itas, equal dignity 870; worthiness c 1365, c 1367; condignity, merit (theol.) c 1620; **ad -um**, worthily c 1365, 1441.

condilectio, mutual love c 1430; **-us**, beloved a 1452, c 1470.

‡**cond/imum**, **-uum**, warden pear 15c.; ‡**-imus**, **-uus**, warden pear-tree 15c.

cond/io, to season: **-o** 7c.; *see also* **conditio**.

condirus, dreadful c 1302.

condispertitus, divided off with, limited by 870.

condistinctus, distinct c 1363, 1427.

condisum, black hellebore (bot.) a 1250, ‡14c.

cond/itio, founding, foundation 7c., 8c. 12c., c 1400; gift, grant 812. 11c., 15c.; interment 12c.; **c. arcis**, burhbote 12c.; **-itivus**, able to establish c 1260; **-itor**, the Creator c 730. 12c., c 1504; **-io**, *for* **-o**, to inter 11c.; ***-o testamentum**, to make a will c 1228, 1517; *see also* **condicio**.

condivido, to divide (exhaustively) a 1233, 1647.

condo, *see* **condio**; **conditio**.

condoctor, fellow doctor 1427.
condol/entia, condolence 1497; -eo, to pity
6c., 9c. c 1090, 1440.
condolomaticus, see condylomaticus.
condomin/us, joint lord (G.) 1293, 1313;
-ium, fief in joint lordship (G.) 1289.
*condon/atio 1187, 1562, -amentum 1199,
pardon; -abilis 1344, -alis a 1450, pardon-
able; -o (with *inf.*), to pardon for c 793; to
demarcate 1279, 1430.
condormio, to sleep with 1506.
con/dorsum c 1180, c 1300, -dosum c 1180,
c 1220, -dosium 1227, (?) **kondesium**
c 1300, slope (O.F. *condos*).
conduct/io, 9c., -us c 1060, guidance; 10c.,
-us 1421, meeting; c 1000, -us 9c., transport; -us *c 1125, 15c., *c. salvus a 1150,
p 1504, c. securus 1216, 1409, -um c 1188,
c 1375, company, escort, safe-conduct;
c 1265, littere -rices 1353, letter of safe-
conduct; passage-money 1164; harmonized
song 1326; 1422, 1437, -um 14c., -ura
1450, hire; customary payment 1440; 1176,
c 1502, c. aque 1086, 15c., c. aquarum
c 1533, cundutus 1271, -arium c 1250,
water-pipe, conduit; c. thesauri, service
of escorting treasure c 1200; -arius 1234,
c 1266, -orius c 1330, maker or supervisor
of conduits; -icius 1367, -ivus 1452, of or
for safe-conduct; *-icius 12c., c 1526,
-ivus 13c., stipendiary (eccl.); -ivus, hired
c 1250, c 1400; 12c., -ibilis c 1434, profitable; -or, one who conducts or escorts
1229, 1419; -us, hired priest 15c.; conduco,
*to conduct, escort c 1150, 1419; to take
to wife c 1194, c 1362; c. aquam, to lead
water (by means of conduits) 1234.
condu/um, -us, see condimum.
‡condylomat/icus, "knotty" 1483; -us
(†condolomatus), swollen with disease
c 950.
†conea, (?) something provided for altar-
slab 1346.
coneger/a, -ia, see cuniculus.
conepiscopus, see coepiscopus.
conestab-, conestaulus, see CONSTAB
conevetum, see convetum.
confac/tus, made 1263; -io, to help to make
1622.
confalonerius, see gunfanum.
confamiliaritas, family group 780.
con/fautor, supporter c 1265; -faveo, to
favour 12c., c 1400.
*confect/io a 1100, 1509, -a, -um c 1290,
1501, confita a 1250, 1305, confitura
1622, confection, mixed drug *or* comfit;
c. corporis Christi c 1272, 1342; c. (con-
fextio) arcis 14c., c. munitionis 12c.,
burhbote; c. pontis, brigbote 12c., 14c.;
†-atio, making 1321; -ionaria c 1472,
-ionarium 1504, office of (royal) confectioner; -ionarius, confectioner 1403, 1405;
conficio, to consecrate (bread *or* wine)
12c., 1382.
confeder/atio c 1188, 1608, -atia 1384,
confederation, league, conspiracy; -ator,
conspirator c 1408; 1298, -atus (*subst.*)
c 1137, 1599, ally; -o, to confederate, join
in a league c 900. c 1125, c 1470; (*trans.*) to
plot 1451.

confedo, to dirty c 1180.
confello, to wipe out c 1298.
confeodatus, joined together by fief c 1200.
confeoffatus, see cofeoffatus.
confera, see coffinus.
confer/entia, bestowal c 1000; conference
1207; constituent 13c.; -o, to collate (eccl.)
c 1125, c 1290; to conduce, suit c 1340,
a 1408; to wear (clothes) c 1350; *cf.* collatio.
confer/t, -nova, -vetus, types of omen a 1235.
conferva, comfrey (bot.): confirma c 1000.
confess/io, homage, oath of fidelity a 1142;
place where relics are kept 760. c 1200;
*8c. c 1080, 1526, -us 1378, 1528, con-
fession (eccl.); -io auricularis c 1380,
1562; pater -ionum, father confessor
c 1118; audio -ionem 1221, c 1520;
-ionale, privilege or payment in respect of
hearing confessions 1426, c 1472; -ionalis,
confessional 1334, 15c.; ‡-ionista, "con-
fessionist" 1570; -ivus, affirmative, assertive 9c.; *-or, confessor (eccl.) c 850, c 938.
c 1100, 1537; c. Christi 1250, c 1365;
actio -oria, action claiming property for
plaintiff (leg.) c 1258; *-o, to confess 1275,
c 1400; *confiteor, to confess (to a priest)
c 1080, c 1470; to say the *confiteor* 1245;
(*subst.*) *confiteor* c 1340; c. fidem, to profess the faith c 1343.
confesto, (?) to make trouble c 1334.
confext-, see CONFECT
confibulo, to fasten with a clasp, "to button"
c 1218, ‡1483.
conficio, see CONFECT
conficte, by feigned pretexts 1255; †con-
fingo, (?) to agree, speak with one voice
a 700.
confid/entia, trust (leg.) 1456, c 1457; littere
de -entia, credentials c 1255; -ucia, trust,
confidence 1216; -entialis, audacious
c 1318; -ens 1279, 1415, confisus 1456,
1483, confidential, trusted; -o de c 1216,
1587, -o in (with *acc.* or *abl.*) 8c. c 1250,
1424, -o me in a 700, to trust in.
configuratio, configuration, conformity to
pattern 1267, 1620.
confili/a, god-daughter 1502, 1533; -us,
godson 1502, 1533; -olitas, fellow sonship
870.
confilo, to file (documents) 1505.
confingo, see conficte.
confin/ia (*for* -ium) 759, -itas 1043, 11c.,
boundary, border; -ia vite c 950; -alis,
similar a 1564; †-itimus, adjoining 1480.
confirma, see conferva.
confirmarius, fellow farmer 1327.
*confirm/atio 760. c 1194, 1549, -atus 11c.,
confirmation (eccl.); confirmation in grace
(theol.) c 1150; -amentum, confirmation
(of grant) 1227; ‡"astral body" 1652;
-ative, confirmatively c 745; -ator, con-
firmer (of election) c 1341, c 1451; -ato-
rium, corroboration c 1326; -atorius,
confirmatory 13c. 1620; -o, (*intr.*) to regain
health 5c.; (*trans.*) *to confirm (eccl.) 838.
c 1100, c 1514; to confirm in grace (theol.)
c 1150; †-or (*dep.*), (?) to bear witness to
738.
confisc/atio, confiscation p 1327, 1608;

E

-abilis, liable to confiscation 1378; **-ator,** confiscator c 1125, c 1370; 1431, ‡1483, ‡**-arius** 1483, escheator; †**-us,** confiscated 15c.

confisus, see CONFID

confita, see CONFECT

confiteor, see CONFESS

confixio (dominica) clavi, crucifixion c 1325.

conflat/io, smelting 1267, p 1300; c 1204, **-us** c 1320, conspiracy, plot; **-ilis** c 1255, **-orius** c 793, concerned with smelting; **-or** 1304, 1325, **-rix** (*f.*) 1325, blower (of bellows); **c. typorum,** type-founder 1688; **-orium,** smithy, foundry a 1180, 1416; **conflo,** to blow 1461; to puff out c 1197.

conflector, to incline towards 12c.

conflict/us (*2nd decl.*) 6c. c 1400, **conflectus** 1289, fight; (*4th decl.*) dispute 8c. c 1390; **c. Gallicus,** tournament c 1200; **-atiuncula,** little conflict 1520.

confluct/uatio c 1500, **-us** c 1450, **confluentia** 1235, c 1478, **conflux/io** 13c., **-us** 870. a 1250, 13c., conflux, gathering; **-o** c 1390, **confluito** 810, to flow together.

*****conform/itas,** similarity, conformity 9c. c 1160, 1503; **-abilis,** conformable p 1300; ‡**-ale,** "counterfeit" c 1440; **-aliter** c 1363, *****-iter** 12c., 1620, similarly, conformably; **-ativus,** conforming, adapting p 1300; *****-o,** to conform, adapt c 1200, c 1380.

*****confort/atio (comfort-)** c 793. 1240, 1622, **-atus** 7c., **-amen** c 1336, 1461, **-amentum** c 1400, 1504, comfort, strengthening, encouragement; **-abilis,** comfortable a 1349, 15c.; **-ativus** c 1172, 1622, **-ivus** a 1150, 1378, **-atorius** 1468, c 1470, comforting, strengthening; **-ator** a 1130, ‡1483, **-atrix** (*f.*) 1267, comforter; **-o,** to establish, corroborate c 730, 971. c 1400; to cure c 793; (with *inf.*) to enable c 793. c 1412.

confoss/io, piercing c 1330; **-or (fovearum)** (play on **confessor**) 1281.

confotio, cherishing 1236.

confract/io, break-up, downfall c 1300; confraction (of the host) 790, 14c.; commingling 13c.; **-us,** blow 1308; **confrag/a** (*pl.*), felled trees c 1250; **-ia** (*pl.*), wilderness p 1394; **confrango,** to break up 1507; **confringo breve,** to break open a writ 1262; **c. litteras** c 1200; **c. corde,** to break the heart 1415.

confraganeus, colleague, confederate c 1150, c 1190.

*****confra/ter** c 793. a 1090, 1570, **cofrater** c 1331, colleague, fellow, brother; **-ternitas,** confraternity (eccl.) 1224, 1487; title (eccl.) 1440, c 1444; 1286, 1517, **-tria** c 1200, 1243, **-ria** 1230, **-eria** 1309, fraternity, brotherhood, association; **-tria** c 1250, **-ria** 1338, 15c., payment for confraternity.

confrenatrix, restrictive (*f.*) a 1520.

confrequent/ia, conversation c 1250; **-o,** to assemble c 1380.

confric/atio, rubbing c 1180, c 1540; **-o,** to tread down 7c.; **-o me (ad),** to excite oneself 1267.

confringo, see CONFRACT

confrixorium, grilling, torment 1307.

confront/atio 1308, **confruntatio** 1289, boundary (G.); **-o,** to march, be contiguous (G.) 1289, 1291.

confruor, to enjoy together c 1242.

confug/a, seeking refuge c 1340; **-iator,** fugitive 1317, 1320; **-ium pacis,** (right of) sanctuary c 1115.

confultus, packed 1426.

confuro, to rage together c 1160.

confus/io, ruin, undoing 1086, c 1343; shame, embarrassment a 1142, c 1340; perplexity 1461; **-ibilis** 9c. c 1204, c 1450, **-ivus** 1378, shameful, confusing; **-ibiliter,** shamefully 1284, c 1405; **in -o,** confusedly, generally c 1343, c 1443; **confund/ator,** confounder, despoiler c 1300; **-ans,** shocking, embarrassing c 1340; **-or,** to be ashamed (of) 1267.

confut/atio, confutation c 1180, 1208; †**-o,** to drive back c 1400.

congarrio, to babble a 1260.

congaud/ium, shared rejoicing 1274, 1497; **-enter,** joyfully 1409; **-eo,** *to rejoice together c 1090, c 1534; c 1289, a 1564, **conguaudeo** (G.) 1369, to enjoy (together).

congel/amen, gathering together c 550; **-o,** to gather together c 550.

congel/atio, solidification (alch.) a 1235, c 1320; **-abilis,** able to be congealed a 1250; **-o,** to solidify (alch.) a 1252, c 1320; **-asco** 9c. c 1180, 1200, **-esco** 14c., to freeze.

‡**congelima,** stook (of corn) 15c., 1483.

congemisco, to join in bewailing 8c., 9c.

congeneratio, unity or likeness of birth 870.

†**congenus,** (?) *f.l.* for **congruus,** suitable 1418.

cong/er, conger-eel: **-erus** 1265, **-reus** 1266, **-rus** c 1200, **-ruus** c 1200, 1364, **cunger** 1236, 1337, **cungruus** 1243.

†**congermino** (?) *f.l.* for **congemino,** to heap together, to double 870.

congestio, mound c 700; assembly 10c.; **conjeries,** *for* **congeries,** c 1320.

congild/a, -o c 1115, **-anus** 1443, guild-brother.

conglaciatio, congelation 1620.

conglut/inatio, structure c 1000; **-inum,** bond c 1200; **-inaliter,** firmly, assiduously 9c.; **-inate,** accurately 13c.; **-inativus,** adhesive a 1250; **-ino,** to collect, accumulate a 700; †**-io,** *for* **-ino,** to stick together a 1275.

conglutio, to swallow c 1250.

congiuvies, body, mass c 1390.

congn-, see **cogn-**

congratul/atio, rejoicing c 1125, a 1452; **-atorius** c 1196, **-arius** 1443, congratulatory; **-anter,** in a spirit of congratulation a 1452; **-or,** to give thanks c 793. c 1316, c 1470; to fawn on c 1150.

congremiales, brethren 1509.

congreus, see **conger.**

congrex, of the same congregation c 950; **congreg/atio,** body of men c 730. 13c., 15c.; monastic community 799, 993. 1086, 15c.; convocation (eccl.) c 1197, c 1332; congregation (ac.) 1257, c 1584; congregation, addition (math.) 815. a 1233; **c. feni,** hay-making 13c.; **-arius,** common soldier c 1192; **-atim,** all together 815; **-ativus,**

copulative (gram.) 790; **-atrix**, assembler (*f.*) 1344; **-atus**, added together 11c.; **-o**, to add (math.) 815; **-o fenum**, to gather hay 1086, 13c.

congru/itas, agreement, congruity c 1250, c 1608; **-entius** c 730, **-entissime** c 730. c 1343, c 1444 (*adv.*); *see also* **conger.**

conguaudeo, *see* CONGAUD

con/hibentia, -ibentia, *see* **coniventia.**

conhumilio, *see* **cohumilio.**

coni-, *see also* **cuneus; cuniculus.**

conica, conifer, *see* **conus.**

conilla, *see* **cavella.**

conisma, *see* **icon.**

coniva, *see* **covina.**

coni/ventia, connivance: **-ventio** 7c.; **-bentia** 7c., **conhibentia** c 900, support.

conjaceo, to be adjacent c 1300, 1507.

conject/amentum, conjecture 1388; **-ivus**, conjectural 1344; **-ura** 1369, c 1397, **-uratio** c 1250, plot or misrepresentation; **-uratio**, indication, prognostication c 1470; **-orie**, by way of conjecture c 1430; **-orium**, book of interpretation of dreams c 1160; **-o** 1371, c 1400, **-uro** 1385, to plot, plan; *-**uro**, to conjecture, infer c 1150, 1461.

conjeries, *see* **congestio.**

conjubilo, to rejoice together (with) c 1125, a 1452.

conju/cundor (conjo-), to rejoice with (bibl.).

conjudex, fellow judge c 1188, 1401.

conjug/atio, complicity in crime c 1290; religious community 1291; marriage 1041; **-ium liberum**, frank-marriage c 1175; **-atus** c 1188, 1684, **-uatus** (G.) 1315, married; (*subst.*) married man 6c. 1200, 1419; **-ata**, married woman c 1188, c 1250; **argumentum a -atis** 1535, **locus a -atis** a 1233 (log.).

conjunct/io, *conjunction (astr.) c 1150, 1686; a musical figure 1326; **-ibilis**, combinable 13c.; **cunjunctim**, jointly c 1272; **-iva** (*sc.* **tunica**), optical membrane c 1210, a 1250; **-ivus**, conjunctive (gram.) 760; **-ivus**, compound (alch.) 1267; **-or**, joiner 1581; **-um**, combination (of body and soul) a 1250; **-us**, (*subst.*) partner 1381; (*adj.*) conjoined with matter, embodied p 1300; **mensa -a, cathedra -a** 1553; *see also* **2 feria; ex -o**, jointly 1222; **conjung/ens**, compatible 1267; **-or**, to be in conjunction (astr.) a 1233.

conjur/atio, conventicle c 793; commune c 1193; invocation, incantation c 850, a 975. 1267, 1510; **-ator** c 1250, c 1408, **-atrix** (*f.*) c 1306, conspirator; c 1258, c 1290, **-atus** c 1235, p 1254, fellow juror; **frater -atus**, fellow monk 12c., c 1210; **-o**, to swear 12c., 1461; to conjure, invoke 793, ‡1483.

conjustitiarius, fellow justice 15c.

conl-, *see* **coll-**

†**conletum**, (?) *for* **covertum** *or* **coriletum**, thicket c 1362.

†**connativus**, (?) natural c 1397.

connatur/a, joint nature c 1270; **-alis**, innate, native 870. c 1240, 1609; of like nature, akin c 870. c 1267, 1622; **-alitas**, natural likeness, affinity 870. c 1612, 1620; **-aliter**, congenitally 870; conformably to human nature c 870.

connavigo, to sail with a 1250.

connebulatio, heaping up of clouds, thickening of the air 870.

connecessitatio, contributory causation 1344.

connervo, to bind together c 1180.

connesciens, companion in ignorance 1345.

connestab/ilarius, -ularius, *see* CONSTAB

connex/io, (?) combination, compound a 700; **-itas**, affinity, intimacy c 1300, 1423; **-im**, word for word 870; **-ivus**, binding together 1495.

conniteo, to shine c 1324.

connodo, to twist, bind together c 1180, p 1330.

connomin/atio, joint nomination, election c 1500; **-o**, to name with 870.

connotarius, fellow notary 1608.

connot/atio, connotation (log.) c 1200, 1378; additional signification a 1361; **-ative**, by way of connotation 1378; **-ativus**, connotative a 1323, a 1347; *-**o**, to connote c 1182, c 1444.

connubialis, connubial: **quonubialis** 15c.

connumer/atio, enumeration c 850. a 1250; **-o**, *to enumerate, mention c 1170, 1518; to reckon among c 1160, c 1556; (?) to imply, connote c 1267.

connuntius, fellow messenger c 1317.

connutri/tio, joint nourishment c 1500, **-tura**, growing up together 870; **-cia**, foster-sister c 1150; **-cius**, foster-brother c 1397.

cono, *see* 1 **conatus; cuneus.**

conon, *see* **conus.**

conopeum 7c., **can/opeum** c 1200, c 1422, ‡**-opus** 1570, **-apeum** 1408, 1530, **-apum** 1345, **-ipa** 1432, **-abeum** 1516, **-abum** 1245, 1326, canopy; **-opum** c 1250, **-apium** 1518, **-apa** 1364, 1442, veil for pyx (eccl.); *cf.* CANNAB

conp-, *see* **comp-**

conphilosophus, fellow student of philosophy c 1125.

conquadro, to correspond c 1170; to be equal to 1421.

conquassator, wrecker c 1404.

conquata, *see* CONCH

1 **conquest/io**, bill of complaint (leg.) 1549; **-ivus**, plaintive c 1184; **conquesitor**, complainer c 1000; **conquer/ens**, plaintiff (leg.) 1199, 1419; **-o** 8c. 1371, **conquiror** 1267, c 1358, *for* **-or**, to complain.

2 **conquest/io** c 1450, c 1540, **-a** 1468, *-**us** c 1200, 1543, **conquisitio** c 1178, c 1320, conquest; **-us**, the Norman Conquest 1198, c 1450; 1184, c 1540, **-a** c 1276, **conquesitio** c 1380, **conquisitus** 13c., property acquired (not inherited), acquisition, purchase; **-or** 1199, c 1540, **-ator** 1292, **conquisitor** c 1320, the Conqueror; **-or**, a conqueror 13c., 1461; **conquisitor**, acquirer 1518; **-o** 1354, 1482, **conquero** c 1293, 1461, **conqueror** c 1400, 15c., **conquiro** 1086, 1461, to conquer.

conquiesco, to agree, acquiesce 14c.

conquilium, *see* CONCH

conr-, *see* **corr-**

con-Romanus, fellow Roman 1239.

consac/erdos, fellow priest c 1125, c 1362; **-ramentalis**, compurgator (leg.) c 1115.

consanctus, equally holy 870.

consanguin/eitas, consanguinity c 1343; **-itas,** kindness 1460; kinsfolk (coll.) c 730.

consarcinator, packer 1710.

consc-, see also **conc-**

conscabinus, fellow échevin (Flanders) 1298.

consceleratus, fellow criminal c 730.

conschismaticus, fellow schismatic 12c.

***conschol/aris** c 1163, c 1350, **-asticus** c 1170, c 1180, fellow student.

conscienti/a, conscience: **concientia** 1268; **-am facio,** to make (something) a point of conscience 1426; see also **forum; -atus** (? **-osus**), conscientious p 1300; **consciosus,** conscious of guilt p 1330.

conscissio, cutting c 1178.

conscopo, to sweep away c 1100.

conscript/io c 1250, 14c., **-um** 12c., written grant, charter; **conscribo,** to grant by charter 811, 11c., 13c.; (intr.) to be enrolled, assigned 8c., 9c.

conscruta/tor 1456, **-trix** (f.) 1415, fellow scrutineer.

consecr/atio, *consecration (of bishop, etc.) 1138, 1684; (of sovereign) c 1125, 1461; (of altar or building) c 1130, c 1480; (of the elements) c 1080, c 1520; **-abilis,** ready for consecration 1535; **-ator,** consecrator 10c. c 1265, 15c.; **-atorius,** consecratory c 1212, c 1620; **-o,** *to consecrate (bishop, etc.) c 1080, c 1444; (sovereign) 1068, 1461; (altar or building) c 1080, 15c.; (the elements) c 1357, 1545.

consecret/alis, confidential a 1100; a 1142, **-arius** 9c. c 1170, confidential friend.

consec/utio, pursuit of criminals c 1115; **-tatus,** act of following c 730; **consequutor,** fellow suitor (at hundred court) 1437; **-utivus,** consequent c 1160, 1443; **-utive** 12c., a 1361, **consequ/enter** 8c., 870, **-entialiter** c 1363, *per **-ens** 1232, c 1470, **ex -enti** c 1340, consequently, in consequence; **-enter,** conformably, consecutively 7c., 8c. 11c., 1345; subsequently c 1196, 1461; **fallacia -entis** 13c., c 1334, **f. secundum -ens** a 1200, fallacy of the consequent (log.); **-entia,** chain of reasoning, argument 8c. 11c., a 1304; precedent (leg.) c 1188, 1419; **-entialis,** consequential 1344, a 1360.

consed/eo, -o, see CONSESS

consedilis, "pew-fellow" 1613.

consedulitas, zeal 9c.

consel-, see CONCEL

consempiternus, co-eternal 8c.

consenescallus, fellow steward c 1263.

†**consensus,** (?) for **consonus,** c 1268.

consen/taneus, confederate, ally c 1150, 1415; **-tor,** accomplice 1275; **-tibilis,** in agreement c 1180; **-teria** 1194, **-tia** c 1220, **concensio** 1276, abetment, collusion; **-tio** (with acc.), to obey, agree to c 793; **-sio** c 755, a 1188, **concentio** 1284, 1382, **concensio** 1427, **-to** 1461, for **-tio,** to agree.

consequ-, see CONSEC

consereno, to exhilarate 1433.

consergeria (Fr.) 1278, (?) **conceraria** (mon.) 1262, conciergerie.

consermocinor, to talk together a 1519.

conserno, see **concerno.**

consero, to lock up c 1180, a 1447.

conserv/atio constabularie, 'constable ward' (Chester) (?) 14c.; **c. pacis,** keeping the peace 1242; **-a,** conserve, sweetmeat 1501; **-antia** c 1266, c 1412, **-atia** 1324, 1417, preservation, maintenance; **-ative,** in relation to preservation 1292; *-ativus,** preservative c 1200, 1620; **-ator,** judge delegate to protect against manifest wrong (eccl.) c 1298, c 1547; official of Hospitallers 1275, 1338; (bishop appointed as) conservator of Franciscan privileges 1245, 1420; **c. consilii,** bishop empowered to enforce decrees of synod (Sc.) 13c., c 1390; **c. aque,** water-keeper 1419; **c. cervisie,** ale-warden 1366; **-atoria,** office of conservator (eccl.) c 1357; **-atorium,** writ of protection 1250; conservatory 1622; strong-box 1537, c 1550; **-atorius,** of or for a protector or conservator (eccl.) c 1290, c 1414.

conservitium, joint service c 1290.

consess/io, sitting down c 1190; sitting down together (of Jesus in heaven, or of believers at his side) 8c., 9c. c 1250; assembly c 1000; **-or,** neighbour c 1000. a 1300, 14c.; **-or in celis** 1345; **-orium,** common sitting-room (mon.) a 1100; **-us regius,** King's Bench a 1536; **consed/eo,** to sit down together with 6c., 9c. a 1100, 1296; **-o** c 550, **consideo** c 1072, 1518, to sit down.

†**conseta,** stiff, rough hair 1287.

1 consideratio, conjunction (astr.) 1344.

2 consider/atio, purpose c 1192, c 1229; deliberation, decision (leg.) 1130, c 1520; consideration for a contract c 1215, 1588; regard, consideration c 1200, c 1533; **habeo -ationem** 1313, 1569; **in -atione quod** c 1567; **-abilis,** considerable 1290, c 1300; **-ativus,** reflective c 1283; **-osus,** considerate 1281; **-o,** to give judgement (leg.) 1201, 1575; to award damages (leg.) 1318.

consigill/atio, sealing together a 1200, 1488; **-o,** to join in sealing 12c., 14c.

consign/atio, sealing 1205, c 1363; signing c 1470; branding 1334; (?) conspiracy 1408; **c. mentis,** perception 1610; **c. sacramenti,** signing the host (eccl.) c 1500; **-aculum,** sacrament c 1500; **c. Christi,** sign of the cross 12c.; **-ator,** one who signs with the cross 12c.; **-um,** sign of the cross 957; word significant only in context a 1304; **-o,** to consign, grant c 793. c 1090, 1423; to sign with the cross 943, 1017. c 1185, c 1220.

consignific/atio, additional or associated signification a 1180, 1344; **-ativus,** significant only in composition a 1250; having a kindred significance p 1300; **-o,** to be significant only in composition a 1250; to convey an additional meaning c 1270, 1524.

consil/ium (concil-), flock c 550; counsel, advice c 550, 692. c 1115, c 1542; counsel, legal adviser 1200, c 1395; medical attention a 1235; time given to accused to prepare his defence 1419; church council c 802, 993. c 1188, 1461; **c. Anglie** 1109; **c. civitatis** 1314, **c. ville** 1301 (G.); **c. commune** 1131, 15c., **c. magnum** 1379, Great Council; **c. generale** (eccl.) 12c., 1461; **c. provinciale** 13c., 1549; **c. Parliamentale** 1426; **c. privatum** 1324,

1555, **c. regale** 1415, 1458, ***c. regis** 1218, 1442, **c. secretum regis** 1367, **c. regium** 1586, Privy Council; **c. universale,** oecumenical council c 1125, 15c.; **a -iis, a -io,** counsellor 1516; **ab intimis -iis,** Privy Councillor 1570; **dominus -ii,** judge of the Supreme Court (Sc.) 1566; **-iabilis,** capable of deliberation (βουλευτικός) 1344; **-iabulum,** council, deliberation c 802. 11c., 15c.; **-ialis,** belonging to a council c 700; **-iamen,** counsel, advice c 1470; **-iariter,** with the authority of a council 1609; ***-iarius** c 1290, c 1549, **-iaris** (*met. grat.*) c 1402, a 1408, †**-iorius** 1524, **-iatus** 11c., counsellor; **dominus c.,** counsel (leg.) 14c.; **c. barram Cancellarie frequentans** c 1420; **c. legis,** counsellor at law 1480; **c. majoris** 1374, 1392, **c. majoratus** 1394, municipal official; **c. regis** 1237, 1570, **c. specialis** c 1250, **c. privati consilii** 1555, **-iator regalis** c 1250, Privy Councillor; **c. regis,** king's counsel 1505, 1550; **c. statūs** 1586; **-iatio,** decree c 1110, c 1343; **-iativus** (concil-), conciliatory 1609; **-iativus** (consil-), deliberative c 1300, c 1376; **-iatorius,** advisory c 1365; **-iose,** prudently c 1125; **-io,** to take counsel for c 793; to give judgement (leg.) c 1324; c 1188, 1350, **-o** c 1390, c 1408, to advise; *cf.* **consul.**
consimilitudo, similarity 12c., c 1267; like situation (astr.) 1344.
†**consinuatio,** insinuation 1451.
consist/entia, presence in a place 12c.; consistency (phys.), soundness a 1250, 1620; **tempus -endi,** prime of life 13c.
consistor, (?) constable (Yorks.) 1125, c 1160.
*consistori/um 1102, a 1564, **concistorium** 1274, c 1520, †**constarium** 1376, consistory, ecclesiastical court or assembly, **c. de Arcubus,** court of Arches 1293, c 1323; **-alis,** consistorial 1399, 1589; **-aliter,** in a consistory 1470.
consitus, tenant (G.) 1285.
consivis, *see* **concivis.**
consoci/us *c 1060. 1198, c 1470, **-alis** c 1160, comrade, associate; fellow (ac.) 1299, c 1538; **-etas,** association, fellowship 760. 12c., 1456.
consodalis, comrade, fellow 7c. c 1172, 1475.
consol-, *see also* **consul.**
consol/amen (eccl.), **-atorium** a 1275, consolation; **-atiuncula,** slight consolation 7c.; **-abiliter,** consolably 1421; ‡**-abundus,** comforting 1570; **-ator,** Comforter, Holy Ghost (bibl.); **-atrix,** comforter (*f.*) 8c. c 1100, 13c.
consolida, 'consound' (daisy, primrose, comfrey, *etc.*) c 1000. a 1150, 1315.
consolid/atio, strengthening, establishment c 1250, a 1539; uniting c 1160, c 1448; soldering 1486; 1267, **-ativa** 1267, sclerotic of eye; **consoldatio,** repair 1354; **-ativus,** confirmatory a 1250; **-o,** to unite c 1188, a 1539; to solder together 1277, 1381.
consolomercum, *see* **CONCEL**
conson/antia, harmony (of sound) 6c. 12c., c 1470; agreement 7c. c 1315, 1414; **c. campanarum,** peal of bells 14c.; **c. rhythmica,** rhyme 1516; **c. Leonina** 1241; **-is,** of like sound 870.

*con/soror 12c., 1530, †**-sonor** 1060, fellow nun.
consor/s, queen consort c 1250, c 1504; opponent c 1150; fellow (ac.) 1438; **-tialis,** of or for church expenses 1290, c 1298; **-tio,** fellowship c 950; **-tior,** more akin 13c.
conspectivus 870, **conspicandus** 8c., conspicuous; optical c 1283.
conspersio (consparsio), baptism 980; complexion, temperament 7c., c 793. 12c., c 1200.
‡**conspic/a,** ear of corn 15c., 1483; ‡**-atio,** gleaning 15c.; ‡**-ator,** gleaner 1483; **-o** c 1400, 1405, **-or** c 1219, to glean; **-o,** to pierce c 1060.
conspir/amen, consent, agreement 12c.; **-amentum,** conspiracy c 1470; **-atia,** champerty (leg.) 1306, 1338; **-ativus** 1423, **-atorius** c 1385, 15c., conspiratorial; **-ator,** *conspirator c 1190, c 1556; champertor (leg.) 1306, 1346; **-o,** to conspire to get, aim at c 1200, 1461.
constabilitio, establishing c 570.
constab/ularius *1086, 1581, **-ilarius** c 1217, 1295, **connestabularius** c 1140, 1453, **connestabilarius** 16c., **cunestabularius** c 1160, 13c., **custabilarius** 1275, **constapularius** 11c., **constubularius** 1321, **-ulus** 1169, 1413, **conestabulus** 1136, c 1400, **conestablus** c 1080, a 1087, **conestablius** 17c., **conestaulus** 1537, **-ulo** a 1140, c 1170, **cunestabla** 1086, **conestabulis** 1521, **conestabilis** 1415, 1586, **cunestabilis** 1266, **cognistabilis** 1085, **comestabulus** 12c., **comes stabulariorum** a 1142, constable (commander, warden of castle, *etc.*); **-ularius,** constable of manor, parish, *etc.*, 1252, 1581; **c. Anglie** 1282, c 1370; **c. Francie** c 1320, 1461; **c. Scotie** 1449, 1461; **c. exercitus** 1346; **c. capitalis,** high constable (of hundred) 1242, 1361; **c. navis** 1299, 1353; **c. pacis** 1313, c 1395; **c. stapule** 1428, a 1564; **c. superior** (of county) 1349; **c. Turris** 1205, 1494; **-ularius** (*adj.*) a 1190, **connestabularis** 1346, **-ularis** 13c., of or for a constable; **-ularia,** troop of horse c 1257, 1324; 1285, **-lia** 1255, constable's room; ward (division of town) 1510 (*cf.* CONSERV); 1169, 1460, **-ilaria** c 1398, 1476, **-ilia** c 1220, **conestablia** c 1254, **-leria** 1286, **-ulariatus** (Sc.) 1461, 1528, **-ulatus** c 1140, 15c., **-ulatio** c 1140, office or jurisdiction of constable; 1203, **cunestabularia** 1203, female (*or* wife of) constable; ‡**-ulum,** company 13c.
1 const/amen, steadfastness c 1125; **-antia,** constancy (title) c 1390; **pro -anti** c 1300, c 1430, **pro -antissimo** c 1365, for certain; **-o,** to be c 1410; to belong 1388; (with *acc.*) to continue c 793; **c. esse,** to be agreed to be (*personal*) 8c.; to make clear, establish c 1520; **c. lectum,** to found a bed (in a hospital) 1241.
2 const/amen (coust-) (?) c 1100, **-amentum** a 1142, c 1185, **costamentum** c 1140, 1285, **custamentum** 1155, 1197, **custumentum** 1389, **-antia** 1141, 1152, **custantia** 1086, **-agium** 1377, ***costagium** 1228, 1578, **custagium** c 1290, 1573,

coste (*pl.*) c 1400, **costi** (*pl.*) 1274, 1375, **costus** (*pl.*) 1556, ***custus** c 1185, 1477, **custum** 1203, 1252, cost, expense; **-o** c 1190, c 1405, **costo** c 1222, **custo** c 1243, c 1350, to cost; **custo**, to spend 1282.

constapularius, *see* CONSTAB

constarium, *see* **consistorium**.

constellatio, constellation 9c. 1267, c 1470.

constimulo, to spur on 1252.

constip/atio, (?) accumulation 1272; constipation (med.) a 1250, c 1260; **-ativus**, costive a 1250; **-ator**, personal attendant c 1118; **-atus**, constipated (med.) c 1172, 13c.; **-or** (*dep.*), to attend, surround 893.

constipul/atus crucis, sign of the cross 11c.; **-ator**, one who stipulates, desires jointly 955, c 1038; **-o**, to stipulate, bargain 14c.

constitu/tio, building, constructing 1391, 1423; appointment (of proxy) 1420, 1426; papal decree c 1125, 1334; **c. apostolica** c 1300, **c. papalis** c 1430; **c. generalis** c 1430; **c. legatina** c 1430, 1433; **c. declaratoria**, **c. revocatoria** c 1430; **c. mundi**, the Creation 1461; *see also* Clementine, Extravagans; **-tive**, by its constitution c 1270; **-tivus**, constitutive, constructive 1144, 1662; **-tus**, being (*ppl.*) c 1268, c 1435; **-ens**, (*subst.*) constituent, principal (appointing proxy or attorney) 1420, c 1475.

consto, *see* **constamen** (1 & 2).

constrepito, to resound c 1216.

constrict/io, knitting together 9c.; tightness 9c.; binding force (alch.) 1115, a 1292; **-ivus**, binding, compressive a 1250, c 1270; **-orium**, constrictive drug a 1250; **constring/o**, to constipate 15c.; to distrain 1106; (with *inf.*) to compel c 1327, c 1414; **c. ad** 1339; **-or in**, to be bound to pay c 1400.

†**constricto**, (?) *f.l.* for **contristo**, c 1250.

construct/io arcis 943. 12c., 13c., **c. ville** (?) 836, burhbote; **c. pontis**, brigbote 858, 943; **-ibilis**, to be construed 13c.; capable of construction (gram.) p 1300; **-ivus**, constructive (log.) 13c.; **-or**, builder c 730. c 1125, c 1400; **-orius**, constructive a 1180; **-ura**, process of building 1453, 16c.; **construo**, to construe c 1250, a 1408; (?) to observe, respect a 700.

constubularius, *see* CONSTAB

constud/ens, fellow student c 1325, 1433; **-eo**, to study together 1497.

consubjectus, fellow subject c 570.

consublevo, to raise up together 870.

consubstanti/alitas, consubstantiality c 1286, 1552; **-alis**, consubstantial c 1150, c 1620; **-ator**, believer in consubstantiation (theol.) 1552; **-o**, to make of one substance, identify a 1205.

consubstituo, to place together c 870.

consuetud/o, *customary service or due 1042. c 1070, 1611; *custom, duty (on goods) a 1130, 1560; decree, decision c 1270; **c. Anglie** 1199, 1203, **c. regni** 1198, 1276, common law; **c. maritima** 1127; **c. Apostolica**, Rome-scot c 1400; **c. libera** c 1105, 1215; **c. servilis** 1198; **c. villana** 1228, c 1258; **-inalis**, customary

c 1000. c 1190, 1429; **-inaliter** 1086, 15c., **-inarie** 655. 1204, 1429, in accordance with custom; **-inarium**, **-inarius**, (*subst.*) customal, customary (eccl.) c 1200, 1472; book of customs (payable on goods) 1423; **-inarius**, (*adj.*) subject to customary services 1086, 1234; c 1448, **consuetus** 1270, common, habitual (in derogatory sense); *see also* **lex, jus**; **-inarius** (*subst.*), hardened sinner 1351; 1086, c 1434, **consuetus** 1274, customary tenant; **consue/te**, usually, habitually c 730, c 1000. 1318; in the usual manner c 730, 980. c 1344; **-tum**, customary number, quota 7c.; custom 1236; **-o**, *for* **-sco**, c 700, 10c.

consufflo, to breathe upon c 1180.

consuffraganeus, fellow suffragan 1279, 1293.

consu/itio 1332, 1533, **-ictio** 1507, **-etio** 1329, 1332, **cusatio** 1335, **-etura** 1392, **-tura** c 1185, 1445, **custura** 1265, 1292, stitching together, seam; **-ticius** 1223, 1351, **-tilis** c 1200, stitched together; **-trix** 1350, **custrix** 1269, **custuraria** 1196, 1214, seamstress; †**cosevarius** 1454, (?) **custarius** 1208, **custurarius** 1285, stitcher; **-o**, to pierce, riddle 12c.; **-to**, to stitch on 1375; **cuso**, to sew 1336, 1362.

consul/, count or earl 1086, c 1450; municipal officer, counsellor, councillor 1202, 1553; sheriff 1588; consul, head of body of foreign merchants c 1320, c 1404; **c. artis**, president of guild (It.) p 1341; **C. Palatinus**, Count Palatine a 1142; **c. Parliamenti** 1461; **-aris** p 1348, **-ator** c 1192, c 1437, **consolarius** c 793, counsellor; **-atoria**, letter of advice 1301; **-atorius**, consultative c 1260; **consolatum**, advice c 550; **-atus**, county or earldom 1086, c 1400; city magistracy (Fr.) 1219, c 1283; office of emir 1272; county court 1086, 1166; **c. Palatinus** c 1265; **-tamen** c 1430, **-tio** c 1367, **-tus** 823, 1041. c 1070, 15c., advice; **-tatio**, modification of writ of prohibition (leg.) 1376, 15c.; **-tim**, in consultation c 1500; **-tivus**, directive, giving guidance c 1367, 1378; **-torie**, by way of advice c 1341; **-torius**, purposeful 870; **-tum**, piece of advice c 550; **pro nunc -tus**, as at present advised c 1390; **-o**, to provide for vacant benefice (eccl.) 1164, 15c.; *cf.* CONSIL

consumm/atio, end, destruction, death c 1362, c 1509; ***c. seculi** c 1125, c 1546; **consumpnatio**, *for* **-atio**, completion 1295; **-abilis**, perfect, complete c 1200, c 1213; **-atius**, more completely c 1236; **-ative**, completely c 870; **-ativus** 870. c 1250, 1378, **-atorius** 1344, completing, crowning; **-o**, to dispatch, make an end of c 1190; **c. matrimonium** 1297, c 1520; *see also* CONSUMPT

consumpt/io, waste, destruction c 1250, 1472; wasting disease ‡14c., c 1470; **-ibilis**, exhaustible a 1250, c 1332; ***-ivus**, destructive, wasteful 1188, 1421; **-uose**, wastefully, wantonly 1317; **consum/mo**, *for* **-o**, to consume c 1227, 1461.

consupernus, jointly supreme c 1380.

consut-, *see* **consuitio**.

consymbolus, of like quality 1427.

contabesco, to become foul c 730.

contactus, dispute 1201; *cf.* CONTING

†**conta/ginatio,** (?) *for* **-minatio,** contamination 1292.

***contagiosus,** contagious c 1204, a 1452.

contaminabilis, contaminating a 1275.

contectalis, dwelling under same roof 9c.; (*subst.*) house-mate c 1400.

contemn-, contempno, *see* CONTEMPT

contemper/atio, submission 870; **-amentum** p 1300, 1502, **-antia** 870. c 1290, harmony, harmonious blend; **-ativus,** harmonizing 870; **-o,** to temper c 1080, c 1180; to conciliate c 1160, c 1318; to submit c 1250, 1381.

contempl/ativa, contemplative life 1345; **-abilis,** able to be contemplated c 1270; spectacular c 1090; **-abiliter** 14c., **-ative** 7c. 1485, in, according to, the contemplative life; **-antior,** more thoughtful 870.

***contempor/aneus** 9c. c 1125, c 1540, **-alis** c 1185, contemporary (*adj.*); **-aneus** c 1188, 1345, **-arius** c 1450, contemporary (*subst.*).

contempt/us curie, contempt of court (leg.) c 1185, 1684; **-ibilis,** *contemptible 7c., 1062. c 1080, c 1400; c 1344, 1357, **-uosus** 9c. c 1380, 1427, contemptuous; ***-ibiliter** c 1200, c 1545, **-uose** 1296, 1344, **contemnabiliter** c 1265, contemptuously, despitefully; ***contemno, contempno** (with *inf.*), to refuse c 1090, 1502.

conten/ementum c 1185, 1366, **continementum** 1229, 1253, **continentia** c 1204, c 1390, 'contenement', maintenance of status; **-tibilis,** capable of being contained c 1225; **-tive,** with reference to the container c 1380; **-tivus** c 1180, 15c., †**continentivus** c 1225, **-tativus** a 1250, containing, embracing; **-tum** a 1250, 1686, **-tus** (*4th decl.*) c 1330, content; **-ta** (*n. pl.*), contents c 1250, c 1509; **-tus,** contained 1257, 1549; **contin/ens** c 1190, a 1250, **-entia** 13c., container; **-ens,** (?) site, block (of land) 13c.; **numerus -ens,** divisible (not prime) number a 1250; †**-enter,** forthwith, incontinently c 1204; **-entia,** containing c 1260, c 1366; disposition 1203; content 1261; **sub -entia infrascripta,** as follows 1302, 1393; **-eo me,** to behave oneself 6c. c 1150; **conteneo,** *for* **-eo,** to contain 1220.

contenens, fellow tenant 1279.

content/atio, satisfying, paying c 1280, a 1564; ***-o,** to satisfy, pay 1296, a 1564.

conten/tio, dispute: †**-tia** 1478; **-tiuncula,** minor dispute c 1250; **-tiositas,** rivalry c 1070; **-tiosus,** contending, opposing 7c.; *c 1185, c 1444, **-tionalis** c 1250, disputed, disputable; **-sus,** eager c 1354, c 1550.

conterebro, to pierce 820.

contergeo, *see* **contersio.**

contermin/itas, borderland c 1248; **-alis** c 1170, c 1300, †**conterinus** (*for* **-us**) c 1200, contiguous, neighbouring.

conteror, *see* **contritio.**

conterraneus, fellow-countryman 1520, 1557.

conter/sio, wiping c 1180; **-geo,** to wipe c 1180, 15c.

contest/atio litis, joining of issue (leg.) c 1218, c 1300; **-anter,** in united witness

1344; **lis -atoria,** action for calling witness c 1414; **-ator,** witness 9c.; **-is,** fellow witness p 1361, 1610; **-ificatio,** simultaneous attestation 1065; **-ifico,** to attest at the same time c 1020. c 1070; **-or** (*dep.*), to assert strongly c 730. c 1125, c 1337; to adjure, command c 793. c 1072, c 1220.

contex/tio, structure, composition 9c., 1041; combination (of premisses) a 1109; literary composition a 1142; **-io,** *for* **-tio,** web c 1150.

conthesauraria, cothesauraria, fellow-treasuress (mon.) 1441.

conthoralis, *see* **contoralis.**

conticinium noctis, silent hours 8c. c 1150, 15c.

†**contidalis,** (?) *for* **conicalis,** heart-shaped c 1200.

contig/uitas 1245, c 1361, **-uum** c 1115, c 1125, †**-uatio** (? *recte* **-natio**) 1267, 1427, (point of) contact, contiguity; **-uor** (*dep.*), to adjoin c 1237, c 1478.

contin-, *see also* **contenementum.**

conting/entia, contingency 1219, c 1470; *see also* **angulus;** **-ibilis,** realisable 1521; **-enter,** contingently, conditionally a 1250, c 1363; **-entissime** 1378; ***-ens,** contingent, conditional c 1160, c 1433; ***-o,** to appertain to a 1180, 1360; **c. familiaritate,** to be akin 1242; **-it** †**humaniter de** 1253, **c. humanitus de** 1217, 1426, death befalls.

continu/atio, adjournment 1320, c 1470; extent (in space) c 1380; c 1360, **-antia** c 1412, ***-itas** a 1250, c 1460, continuance; **-abilis,** capable of continuity c 1380; **-alis,** continual c 1460; **-atim** 704. c 1192, **-ate** 815, forthwith; continually 870. c 1150; continuously 1200; **-ativus,** linking up 870. 13c.; persistent c 1270; continuative, inceptive (gram.) 1524; **-atissimus,** most permanent 870; **-ator,** continuer 13c., 16c.; **-um,** continuum a 1233, c 1330; **in -o,** continually c 1343; **-o,** to adjourn 1268, c 1427.

†**continus** (Alexandrie), title of Sultan (?) 1457; *cf.* **comes.**

contion/atio c 1443, 1560, **cunctio** 8c., discourse, sermon; **-abulum,** meeting-place c 1385, †c 1440; **-atim,** in a group 1432; **-ator,** preacher c 740. c1160, c 1595; **c. verbi Dei** 1575, 1587; **-atrix,** speaker (*f.*) 12c.; **-or,** to preach c 1550, c 1580.

contitulo, to entitle c 1400.

contoralis (**conthoralis**), spouse c 1300, 1452; (?) *f.l. for* **centralis,** c 1376.

contorno, to turn round a 1125.

contor/sio, hurling c 1250; **-queo,** to extort 1274; to force c 1200.

contourus, *see* COMPUT

contra, towards (of feeling) 893; *against (of time), in preparation for 1157, c 1400; against, in exchange for 1086, c 1400; as distinct from c 1300, c 1343; **c. invicem,** mutually c 730. c 1210; **c. vallem aque,** upstream 1268.

contrabello, to oppose c 1310.

contrabraseum, second-grade malt 1235, 1297.

contrabreve c 1178, 1268, **controbreve** 1208, counterpart of writ.

contracalumpnia, counter-claim c 1102.

contracausator, opposing party (leg.) c 1115.

contracerto, to strive against 870.

contracingula 1213, 1316, **cuntracingula** 1316, **cowntersigla** 1391, overgirth (for horse).

contraclavis, 'counter-key' (of treasury) 1278.

contraconatus, gyronny (her.) a 1446.

†**contracriminatio,** countercharge (leg.) c 1115.

contract/atio, contract, agreement 1358, 1482; **-io** c 1365, **-us** 1378, restriction, limitation; c 1200, **-us** c 1188, 1263, marriage; **-io (debitorum),** incurring c 1250; **-e** c 1362, c 1365, **-ive** c 1362, in a restricted sense; **-ibilis,** subject to contraction a 1360; **-ilis,** tightened 1518; **-ivus,** causing contraction 1620; **-us,** narrowing (of channel) c 1285; **c. aureus,** money contract c 1308; **-us** 1086, c 1400, ‡**contrait/us, -a** 15c., cripple; **syllogismus c.,** syllogism in the third figure 1610; **contrah/ibilis,** capable of contraction c 1290, p 1300; **-entes,** contracting parties (leg.) 1229, 1336; **-o** c 1193, c 1448, **c. matrimonium** c 1250, 1684, **c. matrimonialiter** 1254, **c. maritagium** 1224, **c. sponsalia** 1315, 1420, to marry; **c. debitum,** to incur a debt c 1250, c 1289; **c. in usum,** to make into a precedent 1268; **c. moram** 1262, **contracto m.** 1314, to abide; *cf.* CONTRECT

contracuniculus, countermine 1415.

contrada, *see* **contrata.**

contradic/tio, opposition c 1000; withdrawal of service 1272; dilemma c 1332, c 1343; **c. (placiti),** postponement c 1320; **c. formalis,** self-contradictory statement c 1314; **libertas -tionis,** freedom of choice between opposites c 1344, a 1361; **-ta** 1302, c 1363, **-tum** 12c., **-toria** c 1397, **contraditio** 13c., objection; **a -toribus,** on opposite sides c 1324; **-torie,** in opposition, in relation to opposites c 870. a 1228, a 1400; **-torius,** contradictory c 850. c 1218, c 1470; **-entia** (*n. pl.*), diametrical opposites 1610; **-o,** to refuse c 1194, 1461.

***contrado,** to hand over, deliver c 965. c 1080, c 1517; **c. oblivioni** c 1200.

contraduco, to adduce in opposition 1086.

contraeo, to oppose (with *dat.*) 1070, c 1450; (with *acc.*) 1204, 1427.

contrafac/tio, p 1280, 15c., †**contrafractio** 1298, **controfactio** 1318, 1382, **-tura** 1551, **controfactura** 1606, counterfeiting; **-tor,** impostor c 1293; 1415, **controfactor** 1415, 1437, counterfeiter, forger; **-io,** to act against 9c. 1220, c 1556; *1245, 1588, **counterfacio** 1444, 1588, to counterfeit, forge.

contrafalsitas, counterfeiting 1569.

contrafero, to bring against 13c.

contrafides, heresy c 1343.

contrafolium, counterfoil 1367.

contrafossata, counter-dike c 1400.

contrafrontale, counter-frontal (eccl.) 1397, 1427.

contrah-, contraitus, *see* CONTRACT

contraindentura, counterpart of indenture 1327.

contralig/atio, counter-obligation c 1258; **-o,** to bind, oblige, in return (leg.) c 1258.

contraloquor, to refuse 1276.

contraluctor (*dep.*), to strive against c 870.

contramagister 1503, **contromagister** 1424, 1501, contre-master, "quarter-master" (naut.); *cf.* **quartenarius.**

contramand/atio, countermanding c 1115; **-o,** to countermand c 1115; to command, instruct, in response c 1220.

contramar/qua 1446, 1496, **-ca** 1505, **contromar/qua** 1413, 1480, **-che** (*pl.*) 1410, **contremarqua** 15c., reprisals against letters of marque (naut.).

contramemoranda (*pl.*), counterparts of (Exchequer) memoranda 1220.

contramur/ale 15c., **-us** 1387, bulwark.

contranitor, to struggle against c 730. c 1125, c 1200.

contransitorius, transitory c 1212.

contrapassum, reciprocation c 1250, c 1362.

contraplacit/um, counter-plea (leg.) a 1564; **-o,** to counter-plead 1292, 15c.

contraplegi/um 1214, 1270, **-amentum** c 1280, bail, security; **-us,** (person acting as) pledge on the other side a 1170.

contrapondus, counterpoise 1244, 1284.

contrapositio, counter-plea (leg.) c 1115; oppositeness c 1211; contraposition (log.) 13c., p 1347.

contrapris/a (*f. s.*) 1371, **-ia** (*n. pl.*) 1318, reprisals.

***contrari/etas** 870. 1080, c 1534, **-tas** 1441, **-ositas** c 1448, 1552, opposition; **c. temporis,** stress of weather 1294; **-o** 1344, c 1470, **e -o** 11c., on the other hand; **e -o,** inversely c 1330; **-anus,** opponent 1336; **-antes,** rebels against Edward II 1322, 1327; **-o** 14c., c 1390, ***-or** (*dep.*) c 1250, 1610, to oppose.

contra/riveator (†**-rimator**), hawker *or* beater 1363, 1367; **-ripo,** to hawk (falc.) 1306.

contrarivetto, to counter-rivet 1311.

contrarotul/us, counter-roll 1242, 1419; **-amentum,** entry on a counter-roll 1333, 1526; 1325, 1480, **controrotulamentum** 1440, controlment; **-atio,** entering on a counter-roll 1380, 1606; **-aria** 1289, 1312, **-atura** (G.) 1309, 1313, comptrollership; **-arius** c 1268, ***-ator** c 1290, c 1550, **controrotulator** 1583, **controlator** 1570, **comptrarotulator** c 1274, 1587, **-atorius** c 1280, keeper of a counter-roll, comptroller; **-o,** to enter on (or check by) a counter-roll 1298, 1504.

contrascaccarium, controllership of Exchequer (Caernarvon) 1383.

contra/scriptum, counterpart (of document) c 1127, c 1224; **-scribo,** to countersign 1223, c 1414.

contrasig/illum 1289, 1311, **-num** c 1225, counterseal; **-no,** to counterseal 1219.

contrastatio, opposition, attack c 1110.

contra/ta 1275, 1380, **-da** c 1250, country.

contratabula, index 1388.

contra/tallia 1222, c 1508, **-talea** c 1178, **-taillia** 1238, **controtallia** 1370, countertally; **-talliator** 1155, c 1300, **-taillator** 1190, counter-tallier.

contratendo, to resist 1344.
contrateneo, to withhold c 1115.
contravadium, counter-pledge 1235.
contravaleo, to be equivalent to c 1115, 1308.
contraven/tio, transgression c 1377, c 1556; -io, to contravene, disobey 1220, c 1540.
contravers/ia 940. 13c., 1536, -io 12c., c 1192, *for* controversia; -or, to dispute 7c.; controverto, to controvert 1610.
contrect/ator, handler c 1212; negotiator c 1130; -o de, to treat of, discuss c 1130, c 1250; *cf.* CONTRACT
contrelus, *see* cantredus.
contremarqua, *see* contramarqua.
contrem/efactus, frightened c 1170; -esco, *for* -isco, to fear c 730; -ulo me, to tremble a 1125.
contribilis, *see* contritio.
contribul/atio, contrition c 793. c 1250; tribulation 12c.; -atus, contrite c 793. c 1125, 14c.
contribu/lis 9c., 10c. c 1115, 1233, -lius 7c., -lus c 685, -nalis 760. c 1150, fellow tribesman, supporter, associate; -lus, friendly c 1125.
*contribu/tio c 1250, 1543, -tus c 1450, contribution, payment; -tarius 1377, -tor 1493, contributor; -torius, contributory 1378, 1419; -o, to contribute, supply c 1250, 1461.
†contricius (*v.l.* castrisius), a Greek official 1274.
contrico, to plait c 1220.
contristabilis, distressing 13c.
contri/tio, contrition (bibl.); crushing, wearing down 6c., 9c. 13c., a 1292; -bilis, easily pounded c 1345; -tor, oppressor c 1315, c 1362; *-tus, contrite 6c., 8c. 12c., c 1540; conteror, to repent c 1266, 1428; *cf.* concerro.
contrivo a 1564, †contruvo 1351, to contrive.
contro-, *see also* contra-
contropazio, controversy 7c.
contror, to search, poke about c 1370.
contubern/ium, squad c 793; c 740, -alitas 9c., fraternity; -a, a companion (*f.*) 770.
contu/itio 9c., -entia c 1470, vision, gaze; contemplation c 1250, 1267; -itus (*pass.*), seen c 950.
contulus, measure of length, pole 6c.
‡contum/acitas, "pride" 1483; -aciose, arrogantly c 1434; -ax capitis, (?) hard part of head a 1250.
†contumatio, (?) *f.l.* for continuatio, 1292, 1463.
cobtumelio, to revile c 1115, 1368.
contumeo, to swell 1252.
contumulo, to bury together c 1170, 15c.
contumultuor (*dep.*), to raise a tumult c 1288.
conturbinosus, tempestuous c 1375.
conturnix, *see* coturnix.
‡contut/ator, "hider" 15c.; -o, to hide c 781; -or, to protect a 1150, 15c.
cuonlarius, *see* cuniculus.
conum, *see* cana.
con/us, corner (her.) p 1394, 1595; a 1270, c 1450, cunus 1432, corner, point, nook; -on, *for* -us, cone a 1250; -alis, of the apex c 1360; of the corner (her.) p 1394; -arium, pineal gland 1649; -atim, point to point, cone-wise (her.) a 1446; -atus,

cone-shaped (her.) a 1446; -ifer, forming cones c 1595; -iferatus, formed from meeting cones, gyronny (her.) c 1595; -ica (*pl.*), conics (math.) 1686; -iformis, conical 1686; *cf.* contidalis, cuneus.
convadeo, to wager 15c.
conval/entia c 1180, c 1380, *-escentia 1166, a 1564, convalescence, cure; -eo, to convalesce c 793. 1204, 1461; to be able a 1175; to prevail 1461.
convallatio, curve c 1200.
convasator, extortioner, misappropriator 1515.
conve/antia 1575, -iantia a 1564, 1587, conveyance (leg.); -o, to convey, transport 1492; -io, to convey (leg.) 1587, 1588; *cf.* conviatio.
convecto me, to have recourse 1507.
convena, flock c 1280.
conven/ientia, conjunction (astr.) 1120; permission c 793; compromise c 793; convenience, easement a 1115, c 1154; †-tia, concurrence 13c., 1271; -ticula 760. 1274, 1480, -ticulus c 1192, *for* -ticulum, conventicle, assembly; cunventio 1086, coventio 11c., *for* -tio, agreement; -tio, fine, oblation c 1178; agreed salary 1431; 1297, 1437, -tionaria 1337, 1439, conventionary tenure (Cornwall); -tionabilis, (?) appropriate, acceptable c 1258; scriptum -tionale, deed of covenant 1260, 15c.; littere -tionales 1303; -tionarie, by conventionary tenure (Cornw.) 1332; -tionarius, (*adj.*) conventionary (Cornw.) 1332, 1534; (*subst.*) covenanter, witness to contract c 1190, 1282; outsider with trading rights c 1300; conventionary tenant (Cornw., *etc.*) c 1080, 1535; c. liber 1297, 1355; c. nativus 1297, 1355; -us, conformable c 1170; -tus, defendant (leg.) 1684; -io, *to convene, summon, sue c 1178, 1458; to consult c 1180, 1252; (with *inf.*) to agree 1237; *-tiono 1130, c 1436, †-tino c 1230, -tuo 1504, 1573, to agree, covenant.
convent/us, *convent, religious house 11c., 1586; district assigned to a city 1518; -ualis, (*adj.*) *conventual (eccl.) c 1192, 1526; *see also* panis; (*subst.*) conventual friar c 1250, 1549; -tualiter, as a convent c 1450, c 1500.
conveo, *see* conveantia.
conver/satio, *'conversation', manner of living, behaviour 7c., c 1000. 1090, 1549; -sio, conversion (log.) a 1250, p 1300; reduction (of equation, math.) 1145; version, translation 1516; monastic life, profession of monastic vows 7c. c 1125, c 1400; *conversion to Christianity c 793. c 1090, c 1536; *c. S. Pauli c 1188, 1399, -satio S. Pauli c 1217, 1385, (25 Jan.); ‡c. stomachi, digestion 14c.; -sim 815, c 850. a 1100, c 1410, e -so 11c., 1522, conversely; -sive, (?) convertibly p 1381; -sivus; causing conversion or change a 1250, 1427; -siva (*sc.* virtus), transformatory power a 1250; -tentia 13c., c 1362, -tibilitas 13c., c 1361, convertibility; -tibile, a convertible a 1323, c 1361; -tibilis, convertible, changeable, involving change a 1150, 1610; digestible a 1250; -tibiliter, interchangeably c 1260,

1610; **-sum**, (?) coffer (G.) 1312; **-sa**, lay sister (mon.) 1238, 1520; (Jewish) convert (*f.*) 1290; **-sus** *1080, 1537, ***frater -sus**. 12c., 1570, lay brother (mon.); *convert to Christianity 1227, 1586; ***-to** (**ad**), to convert (to Christianity) 8c. c 1080, c 1414; **-to**, to convert (log.) c 1160, c 1340; to convert (leg.), appropriate 1261; to admit to monastic life c 1160, c 1202; **conberto**, *for* **-to**, c 853, 873.

convescor, to feed together c 760. c 1125, c 1340.

convestitus, costume 1427.

con/vetum 1221, **-evetum** c 1200, allowance of food, *conveth* (Sc.).

convi/atio, escorting a 1361, c 1540; **-ator**, escort, fellow traveller 760. c 1200, c 1250; **o-**, to escort c 1070, c 1540; *cf.* **conveantia**.

convican/eus, (*adj.*) of the same town or village a 1142, c 1150; *(*subst.*) c 1150, c 1430, **-ea** (*f.*) c 1204, fellow villager.

convicin/ium, neighbourhood 1288; **-us**, (*adj.*) *neighbouring 1234, c 1430; (*subst.*) 1345, c 1470, **-a** (*f.*) 1446, neighbour; **-ior**, nearer 1339; **-or**, to adjoin a 1250.

convici/osus c 1280, 1684, **-atorius** 1299, abusive; **-antissimus**, most abusive 1523; **-atrix**, scold, shrew 1378.

convict/io, attaint (leg.) 1222, 1559; **-or**, fellow victor c 1250; attainter (leg.) c 1258; **-us**, attainted person 1221; **convinc/ibilis**, demonstrable 1378; **-o**, to conquer p 1330, c 1362; to attaint (a jury) c 1185, 1228; to find (of a jury) 1203, 1323; **c. gaiolae**, to condemn to prison c 1290.

convict/us, battels (ac.) c 1503, c 1549; **vacca -ualis**, cow used for food (A.S. *metecu*) c 1115.

convilesco, to become worthless 12c.

convill/anus, fellow villein 1279, c 1320; **-ata**, township, vill 1379.

convinc-, *see also* CONVICT

convinc/io, to fetter c 1180; **-ulo**, to bind together, join c 1040.

convio, *see* **conviatio**.

convisceratio, feasting *or* public distribution of meat c 1160, a 1180.

convisitator, joint visitor 1570.

convito, to invite c 1437.

conviv/atio, banquet c 1350, c 1432; **-arius**, boarder 1395; **-ans** c 1280, **-ens** c 1432, banqueter; **-ium**, food due (W.) 1283; **-iolum**, little party 1372; **-o** c 1294, c 1470, †**-io** 1408, to entertain, feast.

convoc/atio, convocation (eccl.) c 1276, 1586; convocation (ac.) c 1412, c 1584; funeral party, wake 1360; **c. voluntatis**, (?) concentration c 1270; **littere -atorie** 1303, 1312; **-o**, to summon (an individual) a 1245, 1317; to implore with united voice c 793.

convol/atus, flying together 14c.; **c. ocellorum**, rolling of eyes 930; **-o ad**, to resort, have recourse to c 1188, 1684; **c. ad celestia** c 1250.

convolut/io, turning or bending back 870; **-e**, so as to be fastened together or interwoven 870.

convuls/io, plucking 12c.; **-or**, destroyer c 1060, c 1077.

conyera, *see* **cuniculus**.

‡**conyza**, hemlock 14c. (κόνυζα confused with κώνειον).

coofficialis, fellow official c 1440.

coomnipotens, co-omnipotent c 1223, c 1310.

coop-, *see also* COLP

cooper/atio, co-operation c 1223, 1440 (*see also* **coopertio**); **c. arcis**, burhbote 14c.; **c. pontis**, brigbote 14c.; **-arius**, partner 1609; **-ative**, co-operatively c 1444; **-ativus** a 1228, 1267, **-atorius** 1276, co-operative; **-atrix**, fellow labourer (*f.*) 8c., 9c. 1137, 12c.

cooper/tio 1239, a 1400, **-atio** 1238, 1534, **coperatio** 1316, **-atura** 1373, *-**tura** 1190, 1540, †**cooptura** 1395, **coveragium** 1352, covering, roofing; **c. librorum** 1519; **coveragium** 1403, 1587, **cuveragium** 1280, 1341, **keveragium** 1341, 'coverage', (payment for) putting goods under cover; **-arius** c 1310, **-ator** 1198, 1335, *-**tor** 1185, 1413, **copertor** c 1215, †**cooptor** c 1300, **-torius** 1279, 1316, **-tarius** c 1220, c 1260, roofer; **coperculum** c 550. 1282, 1320, **cooparculum** 1419, **coverculum** 1257, 1388, **cufferclia** 1251, **cupperum** 1237, *for* -**culum**, cover; **-cula** c 1180, **-lectula** 1388, **coperlectile** c 1330, **coperlectum** 1322, **coverlectum** (**coverletum**) 1328, 1454, **coverlittum** 1359, †**coverellum** 1430, coverlet; **coverettum**, container (for butter) 1248; **-imentum**, roof, roofing 1259, 1322; lid c 1508; **c. librorum** (**libri**) 1460, **-torium** 1. c 1135, **-tura** 1. c 1386, 1473, book-cover;

-torium c 793. a 1128, 1432, **-turium** 1292, **-tura** a 1128, 1419, **copertura** c 1430, roof, roofing material; 1219, a 1452, **-ticulum** 1280, corporal, altar-cloth; a 1360, c 1460, **cooportorium** 1409, 1450, lid; *c 1135, c 1488, †**cooptorium** 1267, **cooportorium** 1402, 1520, **-tura** c 1115, 1427, coverlet; 1224, 1288, **-toria** 1241, **-tura** 1196, 1224, armour; 1188, 1461, **-tura** 1253, 1387, caparison; c 1421, **-tura** 1418, awning (of boat); a 1200, 1412, *-**tum** c 1135, 1378, **-atum** 1217, **copertum** 1224, **covertum** 1189, 1221, covert (of woods); **-ta**, deck (naut.) 1344; **res -torie**, covering materials 1217; **quopertura**, cover, pretext 1299; **-tura**, coverture (of wife) 1418;

-ta (*adj.*), covert (of wife) 1363, 1513; **miles -tus**, armed knight 1224; **equus -tus**, barded horse 12c., 1419; **coveratus**, brindled (of dog) 1246; †**-io**, (?) *for* **discooperio**, to discover 1274; *-**io** c 1140, c 1533, **-o** c 1265, 1360, **coaperio** 1478, **coperio** 1322, **quoopero** a 1300, (?)†**chopio** 1261, †**corperio** 1349, **covero** 1352, to roof (with tile or thatch); 1378, 1399, **-o** 1268, to cover (a book); to clothe 1314, 1386; **c. equum** 1295.

cooppidanus, fellow townsman (Dutch) 1442.

coopt-, *see* COAPT; **coopertio**.

coordin/atio, co-ordination (log.) c 1277, c 1361; **-ator**, joint ordainer 1258; **-atus**, co-ordinate (log.) c 1290; **-o**, to set in equal authority c 865; to set in order 1345.

cooro, to join in prayer c 730.

coosculum, joint kiss c 1500.

‡**coostrum**, intermediate part of diaphragm 1652.
cop-, *see also* COLP; **coopertio**; **cup-**
copa, *see* **capa**; **cupp-**.
copart-, *see* COMPARTI
copatio, coping (arch.) c 1377; †**cowpecia**, (?) coping-piece 1357; ‡**coppio**, to cope (a wall) or (?) *f.l.* for **cooperio** 1425; *cf.* COLP
Coperniceus, Copernican 1686.
coperos-, *see* **cuprum**.
coph-, *see* COFF
1 ***cop/ia**, copy 1219, 1535; 15c., **c. curie** 1432, 1540, **c. rotuli curie** 1573, 1585, 'copy of court roll' (leg.); **-iositas**, abundance, multitude 7c. 1336, 1513; **-ista**, copyist 1466; **-io**, to enrich c 1200; ***to copy** c 1330, c 1540.
2 **cop/ia**, **-ius**, **-icia**, *etc.*, *see* COLP
copina, *see* CHOP
copio, to toil (κοπιάω) 961; *see also* 1 **copia**, CULP, **cuparius**.
copla, *see* **copula**.
1 **coppa**, hen a 1408.
2 **copp/a**, 'cop', shock of hay, corn, or vetch c 1253, a 1540; †**-um (marisci)**, (?) cutting of hay or reeds c 1300 (*cf.* COLP); **-o**, to stook, put in cops c 1283, 1425.
coppio, *see* **copatio**.
copr-, *see* **cuprum**.
copsclutum, clout on 'cops' (of plough-harness) 1297; *cf.* **cospellum**.
copul/a c 1218, 1535, **copla** c 1395, couple, pair, brace; coupling for dogs 12c., 1334; plough-harness 1289; *1171, 1504, **copla** c 1250, 1456, **cupla** 1354, 1359, tie-beam, pair of tie-beams (arch.); bay in a building (distance between beams) 1241, 1446; (?) *for* **cupula**, small cask 1393; *1304, c 1413, **coupla** 1315, measure of dried fruits (? 2 frails); measure of grain (? produce of 1 acre sown) (Ir.) 1457 (*cf.* 2 **coppa**); **copula** (gram.) a 1250, c 1343; choral harmony over pedal-bass 1326; c 1188, 1370, **c. carnalis** c 1125, c 1520, sexual union; spouse c 1414; **c. mali** (naut.) 1304; **-atim**, as a copula (between terms) c 1361; **-atio**, coupling (gram.) a 1250, c 1334; coupling, joining rafters 1379; **-ativa**, copula (gram. & log.) c 1334, c 1363; **-ative**, as a copula (gram. & log.) 13c., c 1366; **-ativus**, copulative (gram.) 790. a 1250; **-o**, (?) to group together, arrange 1279.
coqua, *see* 1 **cogga**.
coquilar, *see* **cochlea**.
coqu/ina, (allowance for) provisions c 1250, 1380; cooked food 1263; kitchen furniture 1415; cookshop 1280, c 1324; †**-itra** c 1550, **quoquina** 1212, 1446, **quaquina** 1446, *for* **-ina**, kitchen; **-inagium**, cooking *or* kitchen service 1336; **-inaria**, kitchen-dues 1294; office of kitchener (mon.) 1255; **c. salis**, salt-pan 863; **-inaria**, kitchener (of nunnery) 1441; **-inarius** a 1197, c 1485, **quoquinarius** 1280, **quisinarius** 1242, kitchener (mon.); **cueria**, office of cook 1262; cooks' quarter (Norwich) 1283; †**cocius** 1288, **quoquus** 1575, *for* **-us** (**cocus**), cook; **-ino** c 1190, **quoquo** c 550, to cook; **-o**, to poultice a 1150, 1284; (?) to

brand 1308; **c. (aurum)**, to refine c 1115; **c. sal** 732; **cocto**, to malt 1316.
‡**coquinella**, damson c 1440; (?) *cf.* **cottanum**.
cor, centre c 1130, c 1362; ‡gold *or* fire (alch.) 1652; ‡**c. abietis**, agaric (fungus) 14c.; **c. comitatus** (contrasted with liberties) 1255; ***cord/etenus**, by heart 990, c 1038. c 1115, 1405; **-intime** 1437, 1438, ***-iter** c 1190, 1462, †**-itus** c 1177, ***-ialiter** c 1302, c 1470, cordially, sincerely; **-atius**, more profoundly c 1000; **-iale**, a cordial, stimulant a 1564, 1622; **-ialis**, cardiac c 1210, c 1540; hearty, cordial c 1320, 1571; **-ulum**, little heart c 1200; **corasium**, sweetheart c 1434; **corculum**, heart c 950.
cora, *see* **cera**.
coraagium, *see* **cornu**.
†**coragium**, a form of impost (Ir.) 1429; *cf.* **choragia**.
†**coralis**, (?) *f.l.* for **toralis**, kiln 1287.
corall/um c 1362, **-us** a 1250, c 1432, **-ius** c 1200, **corrella** c 1450, **curallus** 1303, 1415, coral; **-ina**, coralline (bot.) 1634; *see also* **curallum**.
corailus 1253, 1325, **curallus** 1254, 1280, sort of light warship (G.).
coram (with *acc.*), before, to the presence of 9c. 1274, c 1341; *(with *abl.*) in front of a 1190, c 1480; **C. Banco**, in the Bench (at Westminster) 1259, 1274; **C. Rege**, in the king's court *or* King's Bench 1167, 17c.; **in C. Rege** 1205.
coran/tum 1275, **curantum** 1292, (?) **-dum** c 1300, (?) grooved side-piece holding louver-boards (arch.).
corarius, *see* **corium**.
corasium, *see* **cor**.
coraustus, upper line of figure (geom.) a 1150.
†**corba**, (?) *for* **sorbum**, berry c 1362.
corb/ana c 1197, 1629, **-onum** 1541, **carbona** c 1430, **curbana** c 1000, **carbana** c 1450, treasure-chest (Heb.); *see also* 2 **corbellus**.
‡**corbatum**, copper (alch.) 1652.
1 **corb/ellus** 1232, 1419, **-allus** 1286, 1292, **-aillus** 1295, **corbayila** 1372, **-alis** 1249, **courblus** 1336, (?) **corvellus** 1293, corbel (arch.).
2 **corb/ellus**, **-ella** c 1160, 1345, †**coribella** 1297, **-ellia** c 1180, **-ellis** 1253, **-allus** 1279, 1292, **-illa** 12c., **-illum** c 1300, **-illo** 1237, 1310, **-ulus** 1316, **-anum** 1223, basket; **-ellus**, **-ella**, weel, fish-trap c 1210, 1322; **-ellagium**, (?) payment for having fish-trap (man.) 1316; **-is**, coracle c 1200; ‡**-io**, basket-maker 15c., 1483.
corbita, *see* **cucurbita**.
‡**corciscus**, nut-hatch (bird) 1483.
corcosium, *see* **carcasium**.
corculum, **cord-**, *see* **cor**.
cord/a (**chord-**) *1183, 1469, (?) **cortum** 1290, cord, string, rope; 1190, 1393, **c. arcus** 1363, **c.** †**arcua** 1419, bow-string; friar's cord p 1348; tendon c 1210; (?) measure of length (of dike) 1271; 'cord', measure of wood 1250, 1587; (?) bale (of hay) (G.) 1294; book-mark c 1296; chord (math.) a 1250, 1686; **c. ad puteum**, well-rope 1162, 1255; **c. capitalis**, shroud

(naut.) 1296; **c. falsa,** false cord (of cross-bow) 1327; **-agium,** cordage 13c., 1309; **-ella** c 1172, 1455, **-icula** 1272, **-ula** c 1200, c 1520, little cord, string; **-ula,** bowstring 1399, 1420; lace 1587; string of musical instrument a 1446; wick c 1485; **-eria,** Ropery (London) 1301, 1419; **-arius** 1254, 1364, **-erius** 1324, **-elarius** 1265, ‡**-ator** 1483, ‡**-ex** 15c., 1483, †**-ifer** a 1556 (? *for* **-ifex**), roper, rope-maker; **-atus** 1255, **-elatus,** **-ilatus** 15c., Cordelier, Franciscan; **-atus** 1221, 1461, **-ellatus** 1303, **-ulatus** c 1450, corded, roped up; *see also* **crux.**

cor/dubanum c 1200, 1213, **-dubalum** c 1300, **-dovanum** 1199, **-duanum** a 1190, 1290, **-duwanum** c 1397, ***-dewanum** 1189, c 1324, **-dewana** 1331, **corveic[i]um** 1329, Cordovan leather, cordwain **-duanaria** 1260, **-dueneria** 1455, **-dewanaria** c 1192, c 1260, **-dywanria** 1280, **-veisoria** 1246, †**-vasia** c 1270, **-veseria** 1212, 1324, cordwainers’ quarter; **-veseria,** cord-wainers’ craft 1443;

-dubanarius 1155, c 1418, **-duanarius** c 1175, 1257, **-duenarius** c 1200, **-duenerius** 1206, ***-dewanarius** 1188, c 1324; **-dewenarius** c 1320, **-diwanarius** c 1270, 1330, **-dwanarius** a 1300, c 1424, **-dwanerus** 1414, †**-denerius** 1448, **-dwonarius** 1301, **-donarius** 1450, **-duanator** 12c., (?) †**cortuarius** c 1325, **-vesarius** a 1128, c 1515, **-veisarius** 1155, c 1321, **-vesiarius** 1157, **-veisiarius** 1163, **-visarius** 1212, 1257, **-viserius** c 1185, **-vaiserus** 1230, **-veisor** c 1367, cordwainer; **-duanus** c 1130, **-dewaninus** a 1200, made of cordwain.

core-, *see also* **corium.**
Corebus, a fool (deaf to admonition) 1523.
coreddo, *see* **sursum.**
†**coredula,** kind of predatory bird 1411.
corell-, *see* COROLL
corelus, *see* **corylus.**
coremannus (†**cornemannus**), member of the *Keure* (criminal court) at Calais 1376.
corenelina, (?) squirrel fur 1208; *cf.* **scurellus.**
cores, *see* **gurges.**
coresonantia, *see* **corresonantia.**
coretarius, *see* **corretarius.**
†**corf/ecina** 1359, †**-icina** 1385, (?) retailing (W.).
coribella, *see* 2 **corbellus.**
corica, *see* CONCH
corigalis, *see* CORRECT
corimbrum, *see* **cozymbrum.**
†**corinphus,** (?) sort of head-dress 1214.
Coriscus, a nobody c 1160; **C. coopertus,** ‘pig in a poke’ c 1172, c 1195.
cori/sona, -zona, *see* CURR
cori/um (**core-**) **album,** white-tawed leather c 1148, c 1450; **c. nigrum** 1252, 1409; **c. rubeum** c 1148, 1404; **c. bullitum,** *cuir bouilli* 1303, 1344; **c. recens,** untanned hide 1221, 1407; **-a** 1294, p 1341, **-us** 1219, 1279, **coreia** 1285, **coreium** 1403, *for* **-um;** **-alis** c 550, c 1200, **-us** c 1470, 1493, leathern; **-atio,** (?) covering with leather 1404; **-ata** (*n. pl.*), *curée,* quarry (flesh laid on hides) 1205; **quirea** 1234, c 1340,

curacia 1453, leather jerkin, cuirass; 1177, 1316, **quireta** 1316, (?) leather cover (for cart); **-arius** c 1150, 1504, †**corarius** 1180, †**corerarius** 1272, †**courearius** 1300, currier, leather-dresser; *see also* **correatio.**
corluvus, *see* **curlius.**
‡**cormiranda,** cormorant 1483.
corn/agium, -arium, -era, *etc., see* **cornu.**
corn/elinus 1245, c 1315, ‡**-elius** 1652, **-eolus** c 1200, ‡1652, **-olus** 1204, (?) **cer-nellatus** 1268, cornelian (gem).
cornelus, *see* 1 **carnellus.**
cornemannus, *see* **coremannus.**
corn/ix 1222, **-aila** (? **corvaila**) 1278, crow-bar; **c. aquatica,** dipper (bird) 1544; **c. Hibernica,** hooded crow 1544; **-ailla,** rook 1290, 1291; (**falco**) **-elarius,** used for rook-hunting 1290; **-iceus,** belonging to a rook p 1394; **-iculus,** cornice (arch.) 1461; **-iliata,** ‘corvy’, grappling-iron 1293; *cf.* CORV
corn/u, hunting-horn 1342, 1368; drinking-horn c 1130, c 1325; 12c., 1395, **c. atramentarium** 1520, ink-horn; horn of dilemma c 1115; horn of mitre c 1220, 15c.; horn of lady’s head-dress 1413; corner (her.) p 1394; corner, projection 12c., c 1266; **ad -u,** put to the horn (of outlawry) (Sc.) 1383, 1608; **-u sub -u,** ‘horn under horn’ (i.e. sharing pasture equally) c 1150; **-ua do,** to en-courage, give a fillip c 1251; **-ua figo,** to cuckold c 1177; **-u altaris,** horn of the altar (bibl.); **c. capitis** (med.) a 1250; **c. cervi,** swine’s cress (bot.) 1634; **c. cervinum,** buck’s-horn plantain (bot.) 1634; **c. com-mune,** (summons by) town horn 1264, c 1397; **c. regis,** royal summons 1471; **c. crucis** c 1400, 15c.; **c. matricis** (med.) c 1210; **-a** 11c., **-um** 1276, †**-uum** c 1325, 14c., *for* **-u;**

*-agium 1130, 1398, **coronagium** 1278, 1482, **corunagium** 1278, †**coraagium** c 1258, ‘cornage’, horngeld, rent paid for grazing rights (Cumb., Northumb.); ‡**-amu-sa,** bagpipe (Fr. *cornemuse*) c 1440; **-arius,** worker in horn 1419; c 1136, c 1358, ‡**-icarius** 15c., **-ator** 1157, **-itor** 1160, horner, horn-blower; **-uarius,** official pro-claiming outlawries 1532; **-atio** 1378, **-icatio** c 1190, ‡**-iculatum** 15c., **-icinium** c 1000. c 1200, blowing the horn; ‡**-ici-nium,** bugle 1570; **c. gallorum,** cock-crow a 1100; **-ea,** cornea of eye 1267; **-ale** (G.) 1291, **-arium** c 1150, 1422, ***-erium** c 1180, 1529, **-eria** a 1200, 1321, **-erum** 1271, 1587, ***-era** 1227, 1449, **-etum** 13 c., 1422, corner; **-arium,** corner-tile 1370, 1374; **-erius** 1418, 1434, **-ereius** 1275, **-eirius** 1217, situated at a corner; **-etum,** peak of hood 15c., 1463; †**-icalia** (*pl.*), (?) covering for altar-horns c 1396; **-iculum,** ink-horn c 704; ‡**cornet** 15c.; **-ifer** 1426, **-iger** 1245, horned; **-ipes,** steed 1060. c 1137; **-uacopia,** *for* **-ucopia,** c 1450; ‡**-ubium,** “hornpipe” 15c.; ‡**-utamentum,** tip of bolt 1483; †**-utaurus,** symbolic animal c 1250 (*f.l.* for **cornu taurus** c 1150);

-utus, bound with horn a 1446; trumpet-toned p 1330; horned (of a lady’s head-dress) c 1300; mitred c 1160, c 1395; (*subst.*) mitred bishop c 1330, 15c.; **crux -uta**

a 1275; (**superbia**) **-uta**, (?) exalted 15c.;
-ico c 1197, c 1400, **-iculo** c 1000, c 1250,
‡**-ucino** 1570, **-io** 14c., **-o** 1217, 1378, **-uo**
(?) c 1200, to blow the horn; **-o hutesium**
1214, 1218; **c. post** 1293, **-uto pro** 1366, to
summon by horn; **-uto**, to butt a 1408; ‡to
tip (with horn) 1483; to cuckold a 1446.

Corn/ubice 1507, **-wallice** 1586, in Cornish;
-ubiensis c 1125, 1518, **-ubius** 1252,
-ubicus 1355, 1437, **-ualensis** 1222, **-wal-
lensis** 1586, Cornish.

‡**corocrum**, leaven 1652.

†**corolata**, dry measure, (?) chalder (Sc.) 1292.

corollari/um 1267, 1457, **corellarium** 1292,
1380, **correlaria** c 1396, corollary (log.);
-e p 1300, c 1360, **corellarie** 1378, 1380,
by way of corollary.

coron/a, *(power or prerogative of) the
crown 1130, 1551 (*cf.* **placitum**); crown of
martyrdom 7c., 8c.; crown of glory 8c.
c 1250; circular apse c 1125, 1537; altar of
the Crown (Canterbury) c 1330, c 1510;
circular chandelier c 1210, c 1330; crown
of head c 730. c 1190, 1319; iris of eye
a 1250; 7c. c 1080, 1549, **c. rasa** 1251,
c. rasilis c 1192, c 1430, **c. uncta** a 1408,
c. unctionis 12c., clerical tonsure; **c.
benedicta**, first tonsure 1303, 1376; **-a**
1424, 1534, **c. auri** 1341, **c. de duplici
rosa, c. de sole** 1532, **c. Francana** c 1530,
c. Gallica 1595, **-atus** 1335, c 1620,
crown (coin); ‡**c. celica**, extract of wine
1652; **c. vite** c 1343; **vendo sub -a**, to
sell into slavery c 710; **-ale** 1332, ‡15c.,
-ella 1297, 1461, **-ula** 1307, 1345, coronal,
coronet; **-ella ducatus** 1461; **-amentum**
1170, 1323, *-atio 1170, 1535, coronation,
crown-wearing; **-atio**, tonsuring 1219;
c. B. Marie c 1328, c 1511; **c. spinea**,
crowning with thorns c 1340; **-ativus**,
crowning, completing 1344;
-ator, one who crowns c 1090, c 1340;
see also **caro**; **-ator** 1202, 1583, **-arius**
1203, c 1474, coroner; **c. hospicii regis**
1330, 1403, **c. marescalcie regis** 1334;
c. coram rege 1397, **c. in Banco Regis**
1399, **c. Banci Regis** 1503; **-aria** 1221,
1260, **-atoria** 1333, coronership; **-motum**,
crown-moot (Chester) 1492; **-atus**, tonsured
priest 1128, c 1140; **clavus -atus**, sort of
nail 1164; **-ello**, to crown with coronet 1461;
-o, to crown (as king) a 1087, 1461; to
tonsure 893. 1128, 1325; to crown with
glory c 1230, c 1340; ‡to 'dub' (a cock),
remove the wattles 1570.

coronagium, *see* **cornu**.

coronis, conclusion, peroration (κορωνίς) 1552,
1646; **c. scutaria**, chief (her.) 1654.

corperio, *see* **coopertio**.

corp/us, bodily service in time of war 1302;
c. pro corpore (formula of mainprise)
1271, 1322; **per c. suum** (formula of
judicial combat) 1130, 1219; **c. cum causa**,
name of a writ 1383, 1419; *see also* **habitus**; **in -ore**, in a bodily sense c 793; **-ore-
tenus** in the flesh 1200; **c. ecclesie**, body of
the church, nave c 740. 12c., 1540; **c. aule**
c 1270; **c. capelle** 1241; **c. carecte** 1300,
1486, **c. carectivum** 1419, cart-frame,
chassis; **c. castri**, castle alone, as distinct

from external appurtenances 1255, 1326;
c. celeste, the heavens c 1300; **c. cistarum**,
nest of chests 1569; *c. Christi, 679. c 1148,
c 1520, **c. Domini** c 1110, c 1400, **c. Dominicum** c 1090, p 1480, consecrated
wafer; **festum (dies) -oris Christi** (Thursday after Trinity) 1278, c 1514; **c. comitatus**, territory of county 1416; sum of rents
and profits accounted for by sheriff c 1178,
15c.; **c. corporatum**, body corporate
c 1465, 1587; **c. ferie**, area of a fair 1300;
c. fictum, effigy 1375; **c. Hibernicum**,
gold (alch.) 1267; **c. immundum**, lead
(alch.) 1144; **c. mundum**, tin (alch.)
1144; ‡**c. invisibile**, "soul" (alch.) 1652;
c. manerii, (?) demesne 1189, c 1258;
c. prebende c 1380, 1535; **c. navis**, hull
1253, 15c.; **c. peregrinum**, foreign body
c 1270; **c. quercus**, oak trunk 1256; **c.
veli**, 'course' (naut.), sail as distinct from
bonnets 1411, 1437;
*-orale 760, 790. c 1197, c 1550, **pannus
-oralis** 1388, corporal cloth (eccl.);
(?) waistcoat 1622; †**-oralia** (*pl.*) **prioratus**,
(?) *for* **temporalia**, 1271; **-oralis**, *corporal**, physical c 740. c 1125, c 1500;
solid, three-dimensional 1267; corporal (of
oaths) 1218, 1520; **-oralitas** 1267, p 1380,
-eitas a 1250, c 1366, **-ulentia** a 1200,
1267, corporeality, existence in bodily form;
-oraliter 8c., 1006. c 1080, c 1468, **-ulente**
9c., corporeally, bodily; *by a corporal
oath c 1190, 1549; **-oratio**, corporation
a 1564, 1587; **c. civitatis** 1442; **-ulen-
tus**, corporeal, material a 1200, p 1210;
-usculum, frail body c 790, 9c.; small
volume 12c.; **gilda -orata** a 1564; **villa c.**
1472; **-oro**, to fit (plough) with framework
1402; to incorporate in a volume c 1400;
-oror, to receive bodily form, be created 10c.

corrad-, *see also* **correatio**; **corredium**.

corradico, to root firmly c 865.

corraghtum, curragh (Ir.) 1299.

corration/abilis (**conr-**) c 870, **-alis** 9c., of
like mind, analogous.

corre/atio (**conre-**, †**coure-**) 13c., **-agium**
1378, curing (of herrings); **-atura**, currying
(of leather) a 1307; **-ator**, currier, leather-
dresser 1279, c 1300; **-o** a 1190, 1328,
curreo (**cunreo**, †**cuvreo**) 1213, 1336,
corradio 1300, **corredio** 1221, **corrodio**
1332, ‡c 1440, **corrodo** 1381, to curry, dress
(leather); **cunreo** (†**cuureo**) 1205, **corredio** (**corradio**, **corrodio**) c 1115, to
cure (meat); **-o**, to cure (fish) 1239, 1253; to
curry, comb (a horse) 1284; *cf.* **corium**,
corredium.

correcreo (**conr-**), to entertain jointly c 1250.

correctarius, *see* **corretarius**.

correct/io, repair c 1336, 1549; fine 1275,
1388; **cum -ione**, under correction 1461;
-ivus c 1204, **-orius** 12c., a 1155, **-rix** (*f.*)
870. 1269, 1318, corrective; *-or, corrector,
reformer (esp. eccl.) c 1000. 1227, 1416;
boatswain (naut.) 1565; **c. generalis**,
diocesan official 1310; **-orie** (*pl.*), letters of
correction 1166; **-orium** (used as book-
title) a 1252, 14c.; ‡**vinum -um**, alcohol
1652; †**corigalis**, (?) error needing correction c 1200; **corrig/ibilis**, corrigible c 1197,

c 1344; **-ibiliter**, contritely c 1200; **-ibili-**
tas, corrigibility c 1343; **-o**, to mend,
repair 1285, 1356; *cf.* **corrigia.**
***corre/dium (conre-)** 1086, c 1397, **-dia**
c 1266, **-gium** 1084, **-dum** 1136, c 1300,
cunredium 1212, 1245, **cunredum** 1199,
corridium c 1135, **corradium** 1249, 1300,
conradium 1245, c 1255, ***corrod/ium**
1183, 1608, **conrodium** 1237, possessions,
supplies, (allowance of) food, maintenance,
corrody (esp. mon.); **-arius** 1324, 1346,
-iarius 1304, a 1447, **corrostus** 1213,
recipient of corrody; *cf.* **correatio.**
corregia, *see* **corrigia.**
corregn/atio (conr-), ruling together (of
Christ with the Father) 9c.; fellowship of
kings 1307; ***-o**, to reign together c 1090,
1461.
correlat/io, mutual relation c 1240, a 1250;
-ive, correlatively, mutually 13c., c 1306;
-ivum, a correlative 1292, c 1300; **-ivus**
c 1240, 15c., **-us** 13c., correlative.
correlegatus (conr-), fellow exile c 1400.
corrella, *see* **corallum.**
corrept/io, touch 7c., 8c.; *chastisement,
reproof 8c. c 1070, 15c.; **-ibilitas,** liability
to reproof c 1377; **-ive,** by way of reproof
1298; **-or,** reprover c 1125, c 1250; **-orius,**
reproachful 1298; **-orium,** rod (for punishment) *or* (?) conductor's baton (mus.)
c 1164; **corripio,** to cause to sin, bring to
ruin 12c.; to chastise, rebuke 8c. 1300,
c 1470.
correpugno, to be mutually repugnant 1374.
correrius, *see* CURR
cor/resonantia (co-), consonance 1497.
correspon/dentia, mutual agreement, correspondence c 1240, c 1608; **-dentalis**
c 1361, **-sivus** c 1430, c 1470, corresponding; **-denter,** correspondingly c 1343, 1427;
-deo, *to correspond, harmonize c 1236,
c 1470; to repay c 1503; to reciprocate
(*trans.*) c 1300; **c. de,** to answer, account,
for c 1290.
corresurgo (conr-), to rise again with (bibl.).
corretarius 1287, 1324, **correctarius** 1350,
1419, **curet/arius (†curaterius)** 1307,
1374, broker (Fr. *couratier*); **-agium** 1343,
-aria 1344, brokerage.
correus, accomplice c 1304, c 1510.
corridium, *see* **corredium.**
†corri/frigium (-srigium, -sigium), incontinence, fornication 1310.
corrig-, *see also* CORRECT
corrig/ia c 1080, 1421, **corregia** c 550, strap,
thong; purse-string, purse c 1180, c 1220;
thong (of standard length) for binding
sheaves 1234, c 1283; **‡-iarius** 15c., 1483,
-iator 1349, girdler; **-iatus,** tied with a
strap c 1255, c 1346; **-iola,** small strap
c 1180, c 1200; honeysuckle a 1250, **‡**c 1440;
theca -ialis, (?) container for straps (*or*
made of leather) c 1200.
corripio, *see* CORREPT
corrix/atio (conr-), squabble c 1200; **-or,** to
squabble c 1173.
corrobor/, strength c 1225; **-amentum** 1335,
-atio 7c., 9c. c 1080, 1514, corroboration,
confirmation; **‡-ativus** 14c., **-atorius** 1684,
corroborative; **-ator,** supporter a 1130.

corrod-, *see* **correatio; corredium.**
corrog/atio, comparison c 1300, 15c.; **-ator,**
beggar 1153.
corros/io, gnawing c 1180, c 1478; pain
c 1280; **-itas,** ruinous state 1273; **-ivus,**
corrosive c 1200, 1622; **-us,** ruined 1273;
worn 15c.
corrostus, *see* **corredium.**
corroto (conr-), to roll over and over a 1408.
corruca, *see* 1 **curuca.**
corrugatio, wrinkling 9c. 1267, 17c.
corrupt/us c 1340, **curruptila (***for* **-ela)** 13c.,
corruption; **-ivus,** perishable a 1100, a 1250;
a 1180, c 1376, **-ifer** 12c., corruptive;
-icola, a heretic c 1164; **-atus,** decayed
1443; **corrumpo,** to infect 1260.
corrusio, (?) *for* **corrosio,** slander 12c.
***corsett/us, -um,** corset, bodice, tunic 1265,
1346; **c. ferreus** 1322; **c. de maille** 1325.
cort-, *see also* CURT
†corta (word said to be derived from Greek)
1271.
†cortas, (?) *f.l.* for **communitas,** 1397.
cort/ex, strip between lines (geom.) c 1360;
(?) parchment c 950; (?) tally 1279; superficial meaning 1342, 1344; *see also* 2 **deli-**
beratio; ‡c. eris, copper filing 14c., 1652;
-icalis, like bark 1267; superficial, external
c 1375; **-icula,** cell 7c.
cortin-, *see* **curtina.**
cortuarius, *see* **cordubanum.**
cortum, *see* **corda;** 2 **curtana.**
corul/us, -inus, *see* **corylus.**
corunagium, *see* **cornu.**
corus (chorus), measure of grain (Heb. *kor*),
(?) quarter 870. c 1200, 1617.
corusc/atio, 770, 9c. c 1160, 15c., **-um** c 550.
c 1400, **-us** c 730, brilliance, flash; polishing
1554; **-abilis** c 1160, 15c., **-ativus** 15c.,
brilliant, flashing; **-o,** to become illustrious
c 730. 1382; to produce a literary master-
piece 8c.
corv-, *see also* **cordubanum.**
†corvagium, (?) exaction, *corvée* 1180.
corvellus, *see* 1 **corbellus.**
corv/iculus (? corniculus), small crow or
rook 14c., 1379; **-i caput,** form of discoloration (alch.) c 1320; **-a aquatica,** kind of
water-fowl a 1275; **capucium -inum,**
(?) hood for raven 1369; *cf.* **cornix.**
cor/ylus, hazel: **-elus** 1272, **quorulus** 1331;
-ulus, tally 1234; **tallia -ulina** c 1370;
coudr/a, hazel-wood (Fr. *coudre*) 1274;
-eium hazel-grove 1249; **-us Sancti**
Philiberti, filbert 1275; *cf.* **querulus.**
cos, touch-stone c 1270; **cot/icula** 8c., **-um**
c 1296, whetstone.
coscet-, *see* 2 **cota.**
coscina, *see* **custuma.**
cosevarius, *see* **consuitio.**
cosinus, cosine (math.) 1686; *see also* QUISSIN
cosm/us, universe 990. c 1100, a 1275;
-etica, science of beautifying the body
1620; **-icus,** worldly c 950; **ortus -icus**
(astr.) c 1233, c 1252; **-imetra,** astronomer
c 1233; **-imetria, -ometria,** celestial measurement 12c.; **-egraphia** 1520, **-ographia**
c 1396, c 1549, cosmography; **-ographicus,**
cosmographic 1620; **-ographus,** geographer
9c. c 1125, 1518; **-opoeia,** the Creation

c 700, c 793; **-opoliticus**, concerned with universal polity 1564.

cospellum, 'cosp', 'copsole' (cross-piece) 1245; *cf.* **copsclutum**.

coss/a, pod (Fr. *cosse*) 1265; **-atus** (†**coffatus**), in the pod 1267; *cf.* 1 **cota**.

cossetlum, *see* 2 **cota**.

cossus, bent c 950.

cost-, *see also* 2 CONST; **custos**.

cost/a, rib: **-is** 1294, **-er** 1332; **-a**, side (of building, *etc.*) 1377, 1384; **in -a**, beside c 1320; **-a**, incommensurate part of diameter (geom.) c 1200, 1344; stub of wood 1282 (*cf.* **coxa**); ‡baker's "ribber" 15c.; *1225, 1311, **-um** 1302, **-erum** 1302, bow of an arblast; c 1310, 1315, **c. maris** c 1154, 1331, ***-era (maris)** c 1193, 1468, **-eria (maris)** 1317, 1331, **-erium** c 1298, **-erius** 1299, **coustera maris** 1326, **-ela** 1279, shore, coast; **-era** 1225, 1380, **-eria** 12c., **-ra** 1316, **-ura** 12c., side; ***-era (-erum, -erus)** 1384, 1464, **-rum** 1429, **-ura** 1419, 1440, 'coster', side-curtain of bed; **-era navis**, gunwale 1325; **-ula**, rib 1528; rib, vein (of leaf) c 1180; ‡clove of garlic c 1440, 1483; hoop (of barrel) 1282; **-illagium**, rent for coastal pastures (C.I.) 1309, 1331; **-atus** 1303, 1388, **-ilatus** 1295, ribbed, fluted; ‡**-o**, to rib (flax) 1483; **-o versus**, to skirt 1276; **-io**, to adjoin c 1200, c 1260.

costallus, sack (Sp. *costal*) 1311.

costardum 13c., 15c., **pomum c.** 1316, costard.

costellus, (?) sort of pillory (G.) 1289.

†**costentus**, (?) proper name (Constantine) 1246.

costinus (†**-ivus**), made of *costum* (bot.) a 1250, 13c.

costoreria, *see* **custor**.

cost/rum, keg 1500; **-rallum** 1388, **-rella** 1422, **-rellus** 1236, 1434, **-rellum** 1275, 1393, **-erellum** 1244, 1303, **-rillum** a 1250, **-ellus** 1296, **-rettus, -rettum** 1298, 1388, costrel, small keg slung at waist.

costum-, *see* **custuma**.

cosum, *see* **coessens**.

cot-, *see also* **quot-**

1 **cot/a**, **-um** c 1128, 1343, (?) **scota** 1359, **-arium** 1331, **-uca** c 1308, c 1422, (sleeveless) coat, tunic; **-earmera**, (?) surcoat worn over armour 1250; **-ela**, bean-pod (G.) 1242 (*cf.* **cossa**); **-ella**, sugar-bag 1307.

2 **cot/a**, **kota** c 1150, **kota** 1285, **-um** 1234, 1289, ***-agium** 1200, 1686, **-ella** (†**-elda**) 13c., **-ellum** a 1310, †**-ara** 1231, **-aria, -arium** c 1220, 1304, ***-eria, -erium** 1197, c 1300, **-erellum** 1277, **-landa, -landum** a 1135, c 1350, **-landia** c 1250, 1279, **-londa** c 1182, 1279, **-londia** 12c., 1279, **-unlonda** c 1300, **-setla, -setlum** c 1115, 1297, **cossetlum** 1275, **-setlia** 12c., **codsellus** 12c., **-settum** c 1200, **-selda** 1274, **-sthelanda** c 1120, **-sethelanda** c 1130, **-setlanda** c 1165, 1246, **-setlondia** 12c., cote, cottage, cot-land; **-ellata terre** 1448; **-agium**, cottar's tenure 1270; **c. pro canibus**, kennel 1542; **-aria** 1086, **-eria** c 1283, female cottar; ***-arius** 1086, 1511, **quotarius** 1086,

-erius 1296, 1330, **-erus** 1086, **-orus** 1185, **-iarius** 1307, **-ieris** (G.) c 1288, †**-ivus** c 1250, **-erellus** 1086, 1542, **-rellus** 1326, **-orallus** 1253, **-eldus** 13c., **-agius** 13c., 1388, **-agiarius** 1279, 1390, **-landarius** 1252, **-mannus** 1086, 1537, **-emannus** 1240, 1307, **-setlus** c 1200, 1234, **-ecellus**, **coscetulus** c 1500, **cocellus** 1275, **-setus** c 1115, a 1128, **cocetus** 11c., 1086, **coscetus**, **quoscetus** 1086, cottar, cottager, tenant of cot-land; **-mannus dimidius** 1183, **-erellus d.** 1351, tenant of half a cot-land.

cot/ela, -ella, *see* 1 **cota**.

cotellarius, *see* **culter**.

coterellus, mercenary soldier (Fr.) 1159, c 1200; *see also* 2 **cota**.

cothurno, to praise in exalted style 12c.

coticula, *see* **cos**.

cotidi/ana (quotidi-) (*pl.*), daily payments 1414; **-anarius**, sufferer from quotidian ague a 1250; **-anus**, happening by day 893; **in die -e**, each day c 793.

cot/o 1213, c 1350, **-ona** 1285, 1304, **-onus** 1214, **-unus** 1215, **cutunus** 1208, cotton; **-uno**, (?) to felt 1260.

cottanum, Syrian fig, confused with **cotoneum**, quince (*cf.* **cydonomeli**): **coctan/-um** c 1109, c 1250, **cactanum** 1213, (?) **cotonum** 1316, ‡**coctonum** c 1440, ‡**coccinum**, ‡**coccymelum** 15c., fig *or* quince; **-us** c 1200, ‡15c., ‡**coccinus** 15c., fig *or* quince tree.

cottum (coctum), 'cot', matted wool in fleece 1280, 1303.

cotuca, *see* 1 **cota**.

cotula, camomile (bot.) a 1250, 1632.

cotum, *see* **cos**; **cota (1 & 2)**.

cotun-, *see* **coto**.

cotura, *see* **cultura**.

coturnix, quail: **conturnix** 1386.

cotus, bedspread, quilt c 1250; *cf.* 1 **cota**.

cotyl/us, -iscus, cup 1654; **cotillido**, *for* **-edon**, part of uterine membrane a 1200; ‡navelwort (bot.) 14c.

couchatio, (?) flattening (of stockfish) 1387; *cf.* **cucherius**.

coudr-, *see* **corylus**.

couegalla, *see* **cogallus**.

coulanum 1333, **colanum** 1297, Irish headdress, *culan*.

†**coumecherchiam**, (?) *f.l.* for **communem cherchiam** a 1170; *cf.* **cerchia**.

coun/io c 1180, c 1335, **-o** c 1350, a 1408, to unite.

counter-, *see* **contra-**

coup-, *see* COLP; COPUL; **cup-**

cour-, *see also* **cor-, cur-**

†**coure-(conre-)**, *see* **correatio; corredium**.

courtceldra, (?) short chaldron (*or* chaldron by court standard) c 1420.

cous, vault of heaven c 550.

coust-, *see* 2 CONST; **costa; cust-**

couta 1544, ‡**cuta** 1483, coot (bird).

coutor, to associate with 12c., c 1250; **c. habitu**, to wear a dress 1376.

coutra, *see* **culcitra**.

couva, *see* **cuva**.

couvina, *see* **covina**.

1 **cova**, pantry (Durham) 1355, 1451: *see also* **cuva**.

2 †cova, lath' de, (?) sap-lath 1366.
covata, covey (of swans) 1246.
coventio, *see* CONVEN
cover-, *see also* coopertio.
coverbus c 1182, comorbanus 1427, 1672, comurbanus 1428, 1438, *coarb*, successor to abbot (Ir.).
†coveria, (?) *for* torveria, turbary (Ir.) 1281.
covilla, *see* cavella.
*covin/a (†coniva) 1290, 1542, couvina 1408, (?) cuvina (†tunina) 1270, covin, illegal compact or association; -osus, covinous, fraudulent a 1564.
covinus, *see* coffinus.
covrechiefum 1243, coerchivium 1298, keverchevium 1249, woman's kerchief.
cowntersigla, *see* contracingula.
cowpa, *see* cuppa.
cowparius, *see* cuparius.
cowpecia, *see* copatio.
coxa, metal joint 1326; 1282, cucca 1442, stub or limb of a tree; *cf.* costa, quissa.
coylardus, *see* cuillardus.
coyn-, *see* cuneus.
cozymbrum, corimbrum, kind of incense a 1250, ‡14c.; ‡corimbrum, "basil" c 1200; ‡colimbrum, marjoram 14c.
craanto, *see* GRANT
1 crabba 1290, scrabo (Sc.) c 1269, crab.
2 crabba, part of mill 1325; *cf.* gropa.
crab/ro, hornet: -o 12c., ‡scrabo 15c.; *cf.* scarabo.
cracch/a 1280, 1504, -ia 1284, -us 1279, (?) †trachia 1431, crecha 1299, crechia 1306, crechius 1272, †crethum 1316, 'cratch', crib.
cracetum, *see* CRASS
cradillum, mason's cradle 1385; credellum, cradle for carrying glass 1539.
craftum, craft, status of craftsman 1260.
cragga, crag (Sc.) 12c.
craiera (crayera) 1347, 1606, creiera 1341, 1399, 'crayer', small boat.
crakenellus, cracknel 1366.
crakeria, offence committed by Jew, (?) spitting 1277.
‡crama matris, herb wine 15c.
cram/acenum, -asetum, -osium, *see* CRIM
crampa, cramp, spasm a 1250, ‡14c.
cramp/o 1295, 1388, -onus 1307, 1327, craumpounus 1326, -us 1291, 1458, craumpus 1325, crombus 1323, iron cramp (arch.).
1 crana, crane (bird) (?) 1216, c 1472.
2 cran/a 1348, 1462, -um 1431, 1438, -arium a 1564, crane (for hoisting); part of rudder 1296; -agium 1376, 1587, -atio a 1564, (payment for) hoisting, 'cranage'; -o, to hoist a 1564.
3 crana, *see* 1 grava.
†cranca, (?) *f.l.* for carruca, c 1365.
cranellus, *see* 1 carnellus.
cran/ium c 1190, p 1330, -eum c 1115, 1309, skull (κρανίον).
*crannoc/us (†cannoc-), -a, -um 1184, 1334, carnocus 1470, †carnocata 1474, crannucus 1334, crennocus c 1182, 1352, cronnocus 1182, 1339, cronna 13c., cronnus 13c., 14c., crannock, dry measure (esp. W. & Ir.).

cranto, *see* GRANT
crapaudinus 1261, crapodin/us 1315, a 1446, -a 1272, 1298, †orapondina a 1250, toadstone.
1 crappa, finial (? in form of grapes) 1241.
2 crappa c 1290, scrappa (Sussex) 1292, †crodinum (? *for* crapinum) c 1115, 'crap', chaff.
crapul/a, surfeit, gluttony c 1178, 1497; -atio, banquet c 1211; ‡-o, -or, to surfeit 15c., 1570.
cras/alis, -icus, *see* crassum.
crasis, temperament (κρᾶσις) a 1250, 1620.
crasp/esius a 1160, 1189, graspesius 1390, graspecia 1589, †grapia 15c., -iscis c 1100, *crassus piscis 1107, 1268, grassus p. a 1130, c 1288, grasci (*gen.*) p. 1230, 15c., 'grampus', whale *or* large fish.
crass/atio, fattening 1355; greasing c 1273; -atum c 1330, -etum c 1266, c 1397, -etus c 1245, c 1330, cracetum 1290, cressetum 1290, 1332, cresseta 1375, greaselamp, cresset; cressetarius 1286, 1337, (?) -ator 1294, 1295, custodian of cressets (mon.); -imembris, of solid or earthly limbs 9c.; -itudo, hardening c 730; 1284, 1443, gressia 1234, 1290, grescia 1290, gressum 1370, season of grease (of deer); grassitudo, thickness 1234; -iusculus, thickish 1620; -um a 1087, grassa 1309, gressa 1250, gracetum 1290, fat, grease; -ula a 1150, 1634, (?) -ura c 1200, stonecrop (bot.); ‡c. major, orpine 14c., 1483; ‡-ulentus 1483, grassus 1204, c 1300, fat, large; -atus, crass, stubborn c 1470; ‡-eo, to be fat 1483; to be dense, stupid 1303; -o a 1408, 1542, grasso 1329, to fatten; *cf.* GROSS
crassipulum, *see* crucibulum.
crassor, *see* GRASS
†cras/sum (†carsum), (?) back, belly *or* breast 6c.; -alis, -icus, pectoral (*adj.*) c 550.
crasta, *see* CRIST
crastin/um, morrow, day after: in -um c 1130, 1414, in -o c 1080, c 1452; *cf.* incrastinum; -o, to procrastinate, postpone c 1172, a 1452.
crat/a 1232, 1361, -ea 1350, -icula c 1150, hurdle; measure of straw 1383; 1331, -icla 1290, 1335, -ile 1378, -is 1149, 1537, -ula 1446, gridiron; c. tenebrarum, candleframe (*cf.* 2 hercia) c 1340; -e (hostium), serried ranks a 1142; -icula, grating, lattice 8c. c 1197; vas -icularium, grate, brasier c 1180; -iculatus, latticed c 1255; ‡-io, to wattle (a house) 1570; -o c 1278, grato 1286, to harrow.
cratena, *see* cretio.
crater/a, catch-basin (for sewage) 1403; c. plana, "flat-piece" (of plate) 1471; -us, *for* -a, bowl 1362, 1450.
†crathifer, (? *for* craterifer *or* cyathifer) cup-bearer 1534.
crator, *see* creantia.
cratus, flour of the second grinding 1300.
crava, *see* 1 grava.
crav/atio (grav-), craving, claim (leg.) c 1115; -o, to crave c 1115.
crawa, crow-bar 1245.
craxo, *see* charaxatio.

craya, *see* **creta.**

crayera, *see* **craiera.**

†**creagium,** sort of game (? *for* **treagium,** 'trey ace') 1300.

cre/antia, creation 1344, 1374; **-atio,** (?) edification 1262; **-abilis,** able to be created 12c., c 1314; **-ativus,** creative p 1300, c 1340; **-ans** 1021, **crator** 11c., creator; **-atum,** creature c 1225; *see also* CRED

creanto, *see* GRANT

†**creba,** (?) 'crab' (trivet) *or* crib 1387.

creb/rum, -larius, *see* CRIB

crec/a (crek-) 1242, 1550, **-um** 1541, **crica** 1359, 1463, creek, subordinate port.

crecea, *see* **crocea.**

crech/a, -ia, -ius, *see* **craccha.**

credellum, *see* **cradillum.**

cred/entia, *belief, faith 1289, 1461; 'credence', table for sacramental vessels (eccl.) 1494; *c 1240, a 1564, creantia 1220, 1461, (establishment of) credit, credentials; **creantia,** (craving for) quarter (in duel) 1271; *cf.* GRANT; **ad -entiam,** on credit 1216, 1376; **littere -entie,** l. **de -entia** a 1205, 15c., l. **-entiales** 1215, 1437, l. **de -ulitate** 1234, letter of credit; **-entialiter,** in trust 1438; **-ibilitas,** credence, belief 1252; ‡**-itarius,** chamberlain 1483; **audientia -itiva,** believing ear 1437; **fides c.,** credence 1297, 1440; **-itor,** tutor (ac.) c 1190, 1479; **-itorie,** on credit 1313; **-ulitas,** credit, belief c 1250, a 1564; (?) homage 1365; (Christian) faith 7c., 10c. c 1125, 1378; **-ulus,** trustworthy c 1330; **-ens,** (*subst.*) adherent 1311; believer, Christian c 1090, c 1343; **-e mihi,** a guide-book 1275; **-o,** (*subst.*) creed 8c., 10c. 12c., c 1365; **-o,** to be a believer c 730; to believe in c 793, c 930. c 1200, c 1343; to intend 1242, c 1437; **c. male,** *see* **malecredo; c. melius** 1209, 13c.

†**credus, panis,** (?) *for* **cretus,** cribble-bread a 1205; *cf.* CRIB

creia, *see* **creta.**

creiera, *see* **craiera.**

creka, *see* **creca.**

crela, creel, basket 1506.

†**crema,** (?) bauble a 1529.

cremagium, *see* CHRISM

crement/um, *growth, increase 12c., 1442; *1086, 1333, **cressimentum** a 1200, **creissementum** c 1200, increment, increased profit or rent; **c. burgi** 1198, 1203; **c. comitatus** 1167, 1233; **c. terre** c 1109, 1306; **c. ville** 1198, 1230; ‡**-o,** to increase, overflow 1483; *cf.* CRESC

crem/ium a 1300, 14c., **gremium** c 1000, tinder; **-abilia** (*pl.*), combustibles 13c., a 1350; **-abilis,** combustible c 1220, c 1270; **-ator cinerum,** burner of ashes (for smelting) 1326; **-o,** to burn (*intr.*) c 1362, 1380; *see also* CHRISM

cremosus, *see* CRIM

‡**cren/a, -ale,** notch, score 1570; ‡**-o,** to score 1570.

crenin-, *see* CRON

crennocus, *see* **crannocus.**

creparata, opinion c 550.

crepera, tree-creeper (bird) 1544.

crep/erum, (?) **-itaculum,** darkness c 950.

crepido, *see* **crepita** (1 & 3).

‡**crepin/us,** *morbus Gallicus,* pox 1652; ‡**-um introversum,** *tartarum correctum* 1652.

1 crep/ita c 1130, c 1308, **-ido** c 700, *for* **-ida,** sandal; **c. estivalis** 1296.

2 crep/ita, tapping sound c 1180; ‡**-itaculum,** mill-clack 1580 (*see also* **creperum**); ‡**-ulum,** shower of rain c 1440; ‡**-undia** (*pl.*) 1570, ‡**-odium** 15c., ‡**-edium** 1483, cradle; **-undia** (*pl.*), cradle songs 1220; (?) pains of labour c 1250; ‡**-undarius,** "rocker" 15c.; ‡**-undaria,** "rockster" 15c.; ‡**-undio,** to rock 1483; **-itundo,** †**cripitundo,** to support, applaud c 550.

3 ‡**crep/ita** "den" 1483 (*cf.* **crypta**); **-ido,** vault 13c.

†**crepitum,** (?) margin, rim c 550.

cresc/entia, growth, production 1309, 1461; a 1315, **-ens** 1300, 15c., **cressans** 1417, **cressantus** 1416, c 1443, crescent; **-itivus,** promoting growth a 1250; †**cresse,** a form of copyhold tenure 17c.; **cresso,** *for* **-o,** 1293; **-o,** to increase (*trans.*) 1086, c 1250; *cf.* CREMENT

cresmannus, *see* GRAS

crespa, *see* CRISP

cress-, *see also* CRESC

cresset-, *see* CRASS

cressimentum, *see* CREMENT

cress/o a 1250, ‡**c. ovis** 14c., **-o aquaticus** a 1150, **crisso** a 1250, watercress; ‡**-io,** groundsel 14c.; ‡**-ula,** madder 15c.; **kers/enaria** 13c., **-unera** (†**-imera**) a 1200, watercress-bed.

crest-, *see* CRIST

cret/a adusta, burnt lime c 1502; ‡**c. nigra,** *sulphur nigrum* 1652; **creia** 1245, **craya** 1317, (?) *for* **-a,** chalk; **-aceus,** composed of chalk 1632; **-efodina,** chalk-pit 1608; ‡**-arium,** "marl-pit" 1483; ‡**-ifico** (†**certifico**), to marl 15c.

crethmos, samphire (bot.): †**cretanus marinus** a 1250, **crithmum** 1634.

crethum, *see* **craccha.**

cretic-, *see* CRIST

cret/io maris 1379, **-ena aque** 1378, p 1394, **-enum aque** 1397, **-ennium aque** c 1390, †**-enimum** (? **-einnium**) **aque** 1396, **-ina (aque)** 1180, 1418, **-inum aque** 1304, 1383, **-inium** a 1564, **cratena** 1425, flood, flooding.

Cretiso, to lie like a Cretan c 1562.

‡**cretonia,** oil lees 14c.

1 crev/icia 1325, **-acia** c 1255, crevice, crack.

2 crevicia, crayfish (O.F. *crevice*) 1265, 1290.

crex, corncrake (κρέξ) 1544.

creya, *see* **creta.**

crib/rum 13c., **-ra** a 1290, **-era** 1230, **-la** c 1282, 1319, **-latus** 1299, **-rata** c 1268, 1334, **-rarium** 1334, 'sieve', sieveful (measure of grain); **crebrum** 1277, 1351, †**-ulum** 1325, *for* **-rum,** sieve; **-rum crinale,** hair-sieve 1277; **-ellus,** small sieve c 685; **-elatus** 14c., **panis -atus** 14c., 1543, p. **-rarius** c 1197, c 1400, cribble-bread (*cf.* **credus**); ‡**-rarius** 15c., **-larius** 1255, **creblarius** 13c., sieve-maker; **-ratio,** sifting c 1320, c 1430; **-o** c 1195, (?) **scribro** a 1250, *for* **-ro,** to sift; ‡"to examine" 1483; **-ro,** to rack, afflict c 1250.

crica, *see* creca.
cricor, cry of a bird a 1150.
crida, proclamation 1385; office of crier (G.) 1279, 1293.
crimin/ale, crime c 1188, c 1197; peccata -alia, deadly sins 1237; -abilis, culpable 1427; -ositas, guilt c 1212; -osus, (*adj.*) guilty, criminous c 730, c 870. c 1160, c 1514; (*subst.*) criminal 1289, 1494.
crim/isinus (†-ismus) 1432, a 1452, -esinus 1441, carmosinus 1622, cremosus 1436, crimson; carmusinum 1494, cram/acenum 1432, -asetum 1493, -osium c 1550, crimson cloth, cramoisy.
crin/ale, head-band c 1200, 1220; cribrum c., hair-sieve 1277; ‡-etum, tuft of hair 1570; -iculum, cord 6c.; curl a 1142; -iger, fleecy 760; long-haired a 1142; -um, mane (O.F. *crine*) 1308; ‡-eo, -esco, to grow hair 1483.
criniosus, flaming c 704.
crinn/um, sediment (med.) a 1250; -oydes, sedimentary (κριμνώδης) a 1250.
1 †crippa, "furze" 1525.
2 †crippa, (?) apparel a 1150.
cris-, *see also* CHRYS
crisiatus, *see* crux.
crisis, crisis (med.) a 1252, 13c.; critus, choice, excellent c 550; criticus c 1193, 1267, cretic/us c 1190, 13c., critical (med.); -abilis, subject to crisis (med.) a 1250; -atio, coming to a crisis a 1250; -o, to come to a crisis a 1250.
crisp/a c 1200, crespa c 1317, ‡-acium, -atura 15c., -ella, -ula a 1250, roll of pastry, *crêpe*; ‡-ula, mugwort (bot.) 15c.; -ans (?) rippling c 1170; -atio, ruffling (of water) 1622; a 1233, 1622, -itudo 13c., curliness; -ina, crepine, hair-net 1289; -is, (?) lock of hair 1297; -osus, curly c 550; made of crape 1400; -um, crape (cloth) 1389, 1397; -us, curly-fleeced 1194, 1211; *see also* crista.
‡crispio, to cluck c 1440.
crissaria, witch (? of Crisa) c 1193.
crisso, *see* cresso.
crissum, (?) 'cristegray', sort of inferior squirrel-fur 1207.
crist/a 1239, †crispa 1276, cresta 1224, 1438, crasta 1292, 1425, (?) crusta 1276, crest, ridge, embankment; c 1200, 15c., cresta 1163, c 1412, roof, canopy; cresta *1280, 1504, crestra 1275, ridge-tile; crest (of helmet) 1300; crest (her.) 1394; braid (on vestment) 1256; 'crest' (of broadcloth) c 1429, 1587; c. mortuorum, pall-frame c 1245; -ilia, small crest c 704; crestatio 1292, c 1470, crestatura 1302, crestura 1250, 1356, (fixing of) ridge-pieces; -o c 1380, *cresto 1224, c 1412, crestello 1281, 1404, crestilo 1271, to fit (wall or roof) with ridge-pieces.
crithmum, *see* crethmos.
crit/icus, -us, *see* crisis.
croa, *see* croia.
crocardus, crocard (base coin) 1299, 1419; *cf.* cokedonius.
crocca, crock, pot c 1115.
croce-, *see also* 1 crocus.
croc/ea 1250, †-a c 1245, -ium c 1245,

crossa (G.) 1285, crosier (eccl.); *-ea (-ia) a 1190, 1372 (Ir.), 1253, 1254 (G.), †crecea 1255 (G.), dignitas crocee 1241 (W.), crochia 1560 (Ir.), liberties appurtenant to crosier, cross-lands; -iarius, crosier-bearer 1290.
crocitatio, croaking, chattering c 1200, c 1400.
crocodilus: cocodrillus, crocodile c 1200, 1392; ‡cockatrice 1483.
1 croc/us, saffron: c. ferri a 1235, -ium a 1235, c. Martis 1620, iron peroxide (alch.); -ealis, yellowish 1245; †-eruleus, (?) blue and yellow c 1250; -eitas, yellow colour a 1270; ‡-otyrium, "bun" 1570; -esco, to turn yellow a 1250.
2 croc/us (crok-) 1174, 1443, cruka 1341, 1373, -ulus c 1370, crokellus 1302, crokettus 1275, 1332, crochettus 1224, 1392, crook, hook; -us, curl 1237; crocheta, crotchet (mus.) c 1470; -atus, hooked 1309.
crodinum, *see* crappa.
†croeria, bird, (?) shrike c 1200.
*croft/a 1086, 1552, *-um (†crostum) c 1180, 1588, crophtum c 1180, -us 1199, c 1452, crufta (†crusta) a 1200, 15c., cruftum 1319, crouftum c 1160, c. terre 1485, 1559, croft, plot, small holding; -a pasture 1364; -um, church-yard (Yorks.) 1553; -ula, small croft 13c.; -agium, croft-rent 1511; -erium, land allotted to crofters c 1250; -arius c 1250, 1279, -mannus c 1252, 1280, crofmannus 1238, crofter.
*croia c 1315, 1496, croea 1482, croa 13c., 1489, crovus c 1300, p 1305, crowus c 1300, 'cruive', fish-trap (Sc.).
crok-, *see* 2 crocus.
cron/ardus, crone, old sheep a 1377, 1378; -atus, old, worn out (of sheep) 1287, 1388; (?) withered (of oak saplings) 1293; -agium, -ura 1350, †cromium 1297, †crenina 1279, weeding out of old animals; -ator, weeder out of old animals 1354, 1491 (*cf.* caro); -o 1410, †crenino 1350, to weed out old animals.
cronn-, *see* crannocus.
†crontochium, (?) *for* gerontocomium, infirmary (mon.) a 1142.
crop/a, croup, crupper (of horse) 1468; 1461, -arium 1242, 1285, -erium 1318, 1342, crup/arium 1265, 1316, -erium 1282, 1316, crupper, crupper-strap; crupo, to squat, crouch c 1180.
cropp/a a 1200, 1567, *-us 1181, 1460, crupa 13c., cruppus 1286, crop, harvest; -us, crop and lop of trees 1143, 1443; -atio, cropping, cutting back (of hedge) 1357; terra -ata, land with a growing crop c 1350; -o, to crop (trees) 1355, 1539.
crosbarra, crossbar 1336.
croseria, crossadus, *see* crux.
crossa, *see* crocea.
crossitudo, *see* GROSS
crota, splash of dirt (Fr. *crotte*) 1241; *see also* crypta.
crot/on, knock (κρότος) c 1160; -alistria, stork c 1200; -olo, to make a rattling noise like a stork c 1180, ‡1483.
croudewaynum, *see* crudwaynum.
crouftum, crostum, *see* CROFT

crovus, crowus, *see* croia.
crua, 'crew', reinforcement (of troops) 1457.
crubbus, 'crub' (crook) of pack-saddle 1276.
crubitum, *see* crypta.
cruc-, *see also* crux.
cruci/aculum c 1390, -amen 1062. c 1170, c 1250, -um c 1200, torture; -aliter, under torture c 1390; -ativus, torturing 1344; -atrix, tormentress c 1200.
cruci/bulum, crucible c 1215, 1622; c 1290, 1429, -bolum c 1245, c 1418, crusibolum c 1325, ‡crassipulum 15c., lamp, cresset; *cf.* CRASS
crucifix/io, crucifixion c 1250, c 1454; c. carnis, mortification of the flesh 1283; -us, *Christ crucified 8c. c 1188, c 1464; *crucifix c 1080, 1605; prerogativa -a, promotion to benefices 1438; -or, crucifier c 1180, c 1343; crucifig/aliter, in a state of crucifixion 16c.; *-o, to crucify 8c., 9c. c 1080, 1559.
crudarius, 'crowder', harpist (W.) 1313; *cf.* 2 chorus.
crud/us, crude (of metal) 1279, c 1290; unfinished, undyed (of cloth) 1221, 1432; †-elus, for -elis, 1549; -eliter, irreconcilably (of discrepancy) 1267; -ivorus, eating raw flesh c 1595; -efacio, to make raw, bruise c 1412.
crud/waynum 1313, -weynum 1283, croudewaynum 1388, 'crowd-wain', handcart; -waynor, -weynerius, handcart-man 1283.
cruento, (*intr.*) to bleed 1384.
cruett/a, -um, cruet (eccl.) 1360, 1424.
cruft-, *see* CROFT
cruis/iatus, -itus, *see* crux.
cruka, *see* 2 crocus.
crumenarius, purse-maker 1563.
cruorifer, blood-stained 9c.
crupa, cruppus, *see* croppa.
crup/arium, -erium, -o, *see* cropa.
crus, 'leg' (geom.) 1686; crusculum, leg c 950; ‡crur/ale, leg-armour, cuisse 15c.; -alia (*pl.*), garment worn by woman 1265; ‡-atus 1483, -itus 1654, long-legged.
crus-, *see also* crucibulum, crux.
crusa, (?) cruse 1467.
crusino, *see* CHRISM
crusma, single note on lyre (κροῦσμα) 960.
crusta, *see* crista; CROFT
crust/ella c 550. c 1180, ‡-ellum 15c., 1483 cake; -aceus 1609, ‡-ulentus 1570, baked, crusty; -ata c 1362, -ilum c 1250, -is p 1330, lump or coating of ice; ‡-ator, tinker 15c.; -ula, mosaic-work c 793; -ulatus, crusted 1662; -um, (?) silver-embossed vessel a 1260; -us, adorned, equipped c 550; grustifico, to crust over c 1327; ‡-o, to "tinker" c 1440, 15c.
cruta, *see* crypta; curtis.
crux, mark of the cross (on documents) c 1090, 1426; sign of a crusader 12c., 1377 (crucem accipio a 1142, 1188, c. assumo 1254, c. capio 1274, c 1374, c. recipio a 1200, c. suscipio 1586); crusade 1203, 1271 (crucem facio c 1190, c. levo 1377); ecclesiastical rights or property 8c. 1194, c 1337; c 1200, crucesignatus 1254, crossadus c 1500, cross (coin), *crusado*; transept c 1070, c 1545; cross-piece (holding

sailyards of windmill) 1285; optical commissure 1267; crux (log.) 1620; a cruce, across 1575; c. adorata, Good Friday 1309; c. alta 1361; c. (Sancti) Andree 1425, 1430, c. Andreana c 1595; c. averunca, camura, molaris, runcata c 1595, c. inversa, c. molendinaris p 1394, a 1446, cross moline (her.); c. bordurata, fimbriata, bordered cross a 1446; c. cordata p 1394, c. intorta c 1595, cross wreathed like a cord (her.); c. cruciata p 1394, a 1446, c. crucigera c 1595, cross crosslet; c. decussata, saltire c 1595; c. dupla partita p 1394, a 1446; c. ereminalis, eremetica, cross with ermine spots p 1394, a 1446; c. figitiva p 1394, c. gestatoria, cuspidata c 1595, cross fitchy; c. florida, cross flory p 1394, a 1446; c. furcata, cross fourché p 1394, a 1446; c. imbricata c 1595, c. ingradata p 1394, a 1446, cross engrailed; c. inequalis, cross formy a 1446; c. invecta, cross vairy p 1394, a 1446; c. masculata, cross of mascles or lozenges p 1394, a 1446; c. nodulata, cross trefly p 1394, a 1446; c. patens, cross pattée p 1394, 1486; c. perforata, cross pierced with a hole p 1394; c. petasata, pointed cross c 1595; c. portabilis 1448, c. portatilis 1268, c 1315, c. processionalis 13 c., 15c., c. processionaria 13c., processional cross; c. stans, fixed cross 1448; c. talentata, cross bezanty p 1394, a 1446; c. transmarina c 1400; c. truncata, tau cross p 1394, a 1446; c. undosa, cross barry wavy p 1394, a 1446; c. vestita, bound rood 1384; C. Sancta, *see* exaltatio, inventio; cruc/es nigre, Gregorian litany c 1595; frater (de ordine) S. -is 1249, 1419, f. -esignatus 1421, Crutched Friar; -esignatio 1250, c 1462, -issignatio 1220, c 1250, †-io 1201, -iamentum 1192, *-iata c 1370, c 1500, -iatus c 1395, crusata 1383, croseria c 1395, taking the cross, crusade; -esignatus (-sign-) 1191, 1517, -isignatus 13c., 1461, -iatus c 1293, -itus 1203, crusiatus, crisiatus 1198, cruisiatus 1191, cruisitus 1204, crusader; -icola, Christian c 700; -icula, mark of the cross (as signature) 12c.; crosslet (her.) 1654; -ifer, cross-bearing 1090; arcus c., crossbow 1513; -ifer a 1142, c 1283, miles c. 1608, crusader; 1244, 1508, -iferarius 1511, Crutched Friar; cross-bearer (in Eastern church) 1438; 1309, a 1450, -iferarius 1296, c 1445, bishop's cross-bearer; -iformiter, in the shape of a cross p 1381; -iger, cross-bearing c 1595; -igerum, cross-staff 1550; -ilecta 1388, -ula 1654, crosslet; -ula, crutch 1252 (*cf.* 2 crocus);
-iosus, inclined towards a crusade c 1370; -iatus, crossed, set crosswise 1329, a 1446; arcus -iatus, crossbow 1532; ‡herba -iata, crosswort 14c.; -io c 1184, -ior 1203, crusior 1201, -izor c 1200, -izo me c 1265, -esignor c 1190, 1461, to take the cross, become a crusader, *see also* cruciaculum, crucifixio.
*cryp/ta c 1080, 1562, cruta 1221, crota c 1212, crubitum c 1306, crypt, grot (*cf.* 3

crepita); -sis, insinuation 1609, 1610; -ticus, employing insinuation 1610.

crystall/um, gazing crystal 1467; -inus, see humor.

†cuallia, piece of land, (?) 'quillet' 1224.

cuba, (?) palm or elbow 6c.; see also cubus.

cub/eba a 1270, c 1357, †-ela a 1250, 15c., †-ele 13c., cucube 13c., -iba 1310, quibiba 1285, 1330, †quinba 1424, ‡quiper/um c 1440, ‡-ium 15c., cubeb (pepper) (Ar.); quibebatus, spiced with cubeb 1244.

cub/icularius, *chamberlain 1086, 1517; -icularia, chambress 1535; hora -icularis, bed time c 1344; -iculum computatorium, counting-house 15c.; -itus, (4th decl. for 2nd) c 793; -itus, fathom c 700; †c. de plum', see culcitra; †-ularium, (?) bedroom 1555; -atio, laying (of lead on roof) 1461; -ator 1295, c 1440, -itor c 1253, 1317, stone-layer; -ans, cumbens, see levans; *-o 1269, 1383, -ito 1274, to lay (stones, etc.); to layer (a hedge) 1305; to incubate a 1446; cumbo, to lie down c 1220; to occupy, lie hid in 8c.

cub/us, cubical p 1300; -a, cheese-die 1449; -ice, cubically 1267, p 1341; -ocubus, sixth power (math.) 1686.

cucca, see coxa.

cucher/ius, cocherius 1290, -us 1280, -ettus 1214, setter (dog); chuchator, stone-layer 1238.

cuchestola, cucking-stool 14c.

cuchinela, see coccineus.

cucina, see QUISSIN

cuc/lus, -ulus, see cyclus.

cucneus, see cuneus.

cucube, see cubeba.

*cucull/a 9c., c 1000. c 1080, 1506, -us c 1160, c 1180, ‡culla, cullula 1483, cowl (mon.); c. equestralis, riding-hood 1476; -atus c 1080, 15c., ‡cullatus 1483, wearing a cowl; (subst.) monk a 1100, c 1255; -o, to make a monk of c 1255, c 1436.

cucul/us, cuckold c 1433, a 1517; -a, hen cuckoo 12c., c 1362; †-atum majus, aqua vitae (alch.) 1652; -inus, cuckoo-like 1427.

cucuma, cooking-pot: cocuma c 685.

cucumis asininus, wild cucumber a 1250, †14c.

cucunellus, see coconellus.

cucupha, see coifa.

cucurbit/a, ‡gourd-shaped vessel (alch.) 1652; cuckold 1608; curcurbita, gourd c 1260; ‡corbita, curbita, adultery (Lombard) 1608; -o, to cuckold a 1446, 1608.

cudarus, see coidarius.

†cud/ermus 1147, †-rinus, codrinus c 1164, †-rus 14c., †codrus 1326, weight of cheese (Sc.) (cf. Gaelic cudthrom).

cud/itio, -ium, -us, see cussio.

cuellum, see tuellus.

cueria, see coquina.

cuf-, see also coifa; cuva.

cufalda, cow-fold 1251.

cufferclia, see coopertio.

†cufmelum, (?) some form of waste product 1485.

cugn-, cuin-, see cuneus.

cuillardus 1234, 1280, cullardus, collardus 1234, coylardus 1376, ram.

cuilta, see culcitra.

†cuisoria (pl.), (?) cooked food 1325.

cuissaria, see QUISS

cujus gratia, see quid.

cul/acium 1141, 1244, colagium 1325, curicia 1291, cullis roof, lean-to, compartment (arch.); -icatus, having a cullis roof 1292; colicia, groove of a portcullis 1304; see also fenestra, pons, porta.

cul/agium, -iagium, see kela.

cularium 1214, 1248, (?) cula 1312, crupperstrap; see also colamentum.

culc/itra 1155, 1570, -edra 1441, †cultrix 1382, -itrum 1434, quilcitra c 1337, cuilta 1225, quilta 1303, quilt, mattress, bolster; c. hebdomadaria 1257; c. de plumis 1276, c. plumalis c 1200, 1496, -itura plumalis 1438, †culatra plum' 1323, †cubitus de plum' 1300, feather-bed; c. perpuncta 1178, c. punctata c 1200, 1496, culta puncta 1208, coutra puncta 1198, counterpane; ars -itaria, art of quilting c 1185; -itrarius 1238, 1295, -itor 1290, quilter.

Culdeus, see Colideus.

culic-, see also culacium.

culicilega, wagtail, (κνιπολόγος) 1544.

culina, kitchen: colina c 1000.

†culium, (?) f.l. for culmen, c 1200.

culix, see calix.

cull-, see coliatus; collum; cuculla; cuillardus; kela.

1 culm/en, highness (title) c 1250, c 1390; c. regale, royalty c 730; -us, roof-ridge 1236 (cf. cumulus); (?) ridge-tile 1505; -inator, (?) ridge-tiler 1504; -ino, to make ridged or gabled c 700.

2 culm/en, for -us, straw 14c.

culmus, 'culm', coal-dust 1348; see also culmen.

culo, see colamentum.

culp-, see also colaphus, colpatio, colpus.

culp/a mortalis, mortal sin c 1357; -abilitas 1378, -atio a 1361, guilt, blame; -ator, blamer c 1180; -atus, culprit 7c.; copio, to blame, accuse 1271.

culqwanus, see cokinus.

cult/a, -rix, see culcitra.

cult/er 1135, 1389, -rum c 1458, -ura 1388, 1406, coulter; -ellus 1069, c 1458, †-elius 1359, -ella 1507, -ellulus c 1330, cutellus 1256, 1361, †custellus 1461, -ellina 13c., †-inus 1359, knife; -ellus (fig.), hawk's wing c 1150; c. ad mensam, table knife 1236; c. plicatus (oblation in token of seisin) c 1180, 1258; cutellus, slice 1107; -ellaria 1305, cutelleria 1305, cutillarium 1379, cutlery; -arius a 1223, 1313, -ellarius 1241, 1582, cutellarius c 1220, cutillarius 1275, 1332, cotellarius 1312, cutler; -ellarius, sheath 1406; -ellifer, Assassin a 1260; -ello ventum, to cleave the air c 1150.

cultilagium, see curtis.

‡cultotum, "calcinatum" (alch.) 1652.

cult/ura, cult, religious doctrine or practice c 730, c 1000. c 1125, c 1542; *1086, c 1436, †custura 1202, cotura 13c., strip of ploughland in open field, furlong; c. hiemalis, winter ploughing 13c.; terra

-ibilis 12c., **t. -ilis** (C.I.) 1309, plough-land; **-or divinus** c 1137, **c. ecclesie** c 1040, priest; **-o**, to cultivate 9c.; *see also* **culter.**

culumbarium, *see* COLUMB

culverinus, *see* COLUB

culvertagium, *see* **colibertus.**

cum, by, with (*instrumental*) c 1150, 1588; (in surnames) **c. Baculo** 1430; **c. Barba** c 1290; **c. Dentibus** 12c.; **c. Uno Oculo** 1260.

cum quotiens, whenever 1269.

1 **cumba** c 1112, 1291, **comba** c 1180, combe, valley.

2 ***cumb/a** 1155, 1418, **-us** 1224, 14c., 'coomb', dry measure, (?) half quarter; **†tumbatio,** (?) *for* **-atio,** packing (of salt) in coombs 1311.

cum/berlachus, -erba, (?) runaway serf of monastery (Sc.) a 1200.

cumbl-, *see* CUMUL

cumbo, *see* **cubicularius.**

cum/elina, -elinus, -ila, *see* KIM

cume/lingus, -lingum 1258, 1323, **-lynus, comelingus** 1279, **†cunnelinga** 1284, **kimelingus** 13c., 'comeling', stray beast.

cumerba, *see* **cumberlachus.**

cuminata, *see* CYMIN

Cum/inenses 1327, **-ynnenses** 1461, partisans of the Comyns (Sc.).

cumma, climbing, ascent 7c.

cummilito, *see* COMMIL

cump-, *see* comp-

cumul/us (**†cumil-**) *1180, 1315, **cumblus** 1238, **comblus** 1284, **cumbla** 1299, **cumblea** 1320, **comblea** 1313, 1320, roof, ridge, vault; end of a document 759. 15c.; c 1140, 1401, **-um** 1548, **comblus** 1298, measure of grain, cheese, or plaster (*cf.* **monticellus**); heaped measure 1356, c 1389; c 1508, 1522, **-atio** 1424, c 1578, 'culet', payment of fees (ac.); **-atio,** heaping up 870. c 1200, 1533; **‡-arius,** stacker 15c.; **-ativus,** extraneous 1620; **-o,** to amount to 815; to stack (hay) 13c.; to pay fees (ac.) c 1310, c 1598; 1234, 1255, **cumlo** 1293, **cumblo** c 1270, to give or reckon in heaped measure (*see also* **mensura**); *see also* KIM

cun/a c 1362, **-abila** (*pl.*) c 1318, 1461, **conabula** (*pl.*) c 1000, cradle; **natura -abilis,** infancy c 1290; **‡-abulator** 15c., **-abularia** (*f.*) 1386, 1399, **-abilaria** 1385, cradle-rocker, nurse; **-alis,** cradled c 1180; *see also* **cuneus, cuva.**

†cunagium, a form of emolument (eccl., Ir.) 1453; *see also* **cuneus.**

cunct/amen c 950. c 1250, 1414, **‡-a** 1483, delay, doubt; **‡-atim,** doubtfully 1483; **cuntor,** to delay c 1434.

cuncti/creans 10c., **-creator** c 1200, Creator of the universe; **-gena,** of all kinds 11c., 12c.; from all parts (of a country) 957. 14c., 15c.; **-potens,** Almighty 855, 950. 11c., 1461; **-potentia,** omnipotence 1265; **-tenens,** all-embracing 966; **-tonans,** all-thundering 9c., c 1038; **cuntus** 12c., c 1434, **gnunctus** c 550, *for* **cunctus,** all.

cunctio, *see* CONTION

cundutus, *see* CONDUCT

cunera, *see* CUNI

cunestab-, *see* CONSTAB

cun/eus, -ius, crowd, troop 7c., 933. c 1130, 1378; (?) ingot 1253, 1254; 1086, 1588, **-ea** 1338, 1579, **-a** 1404, a 1564, **conius, quonius** c 1248, **conus** c 1115, **cona** (Sc.) 1434, 1487, **cucneus** c 1217, **cugnus** 1289, **-agium** 1333, 1508, **conagium** 1534, **cognagium** 1227, **coignagium** 1298, 1410, **coynagium** 1297, coinage, mint, die *or* stamp, (payment for) coining *or* stamp; **†cuinus** (? **cunius**) 1225, **coynus** c 1280, **†coyneya** 1253, *for* **-eus,** wedge; **†comus** (? **coinus**), ridge-tile 1393; **-eo** 1220, 1551, **-io** 1292, 1482, **-o** 1291, 1486, **cono** c 1200, **cugno** 15c., **cognio** c 1220, 1312, **coignio** 1305, **coinio** 1340, **coino** 1301, to coin *or* stamp.

cung/er, -ruus, *see* **conger.**

cunibulus, *see* **cnipulus.**

cuni/culus, (?) drain 1090; ant-hill a 1446; *1176, 1484, **coniculus** 1208, 1291, **†caniculus** a 1204, **†cunulus** 1213, **-nus** 1189, 1235, **coninus** 1194, **cunningus** 1219, **coningus** c 1324, rabbit, rabbit-skin; locum tenens **-culorum** (at Clarendon) 1553; **-cularia** 1284, c 1290, **-clarium** c 1290, **-cularium** 1297, 1555, **-culare** 1386, 1431, **†-culicuria** 1252, **coniculairium** 1388, **†conularius** 1307, **-gara** 1284, **-garia** 1204 (Ir.), 13c., **cunegaria** 1302, **-gera** 1275, **-ngera** 1241, c 1400, **-ngeria** 1260, **gunyngera, guningeria** (**†gimingeria**) 1288, **conegera** 1290, **conigera** 1251, **coneghería** c 1350, **conengaria** c 1268, **coningaria** 1254, 1270, **colingaria** 1260, **coningera** c 1250, 1293, **conyera** 1255, **†cunera** 1242, rabbit warren; **‡-culinus,** of a rabbit 1483; **-culatus,** undermined 15c.; *see also* **cuva.**

cunjunctim, *see* CONJUNCT

cunka, *see* CONCH

cunnelinga, *see* **cumelingus.**

cunred-, *see* **corredium.**

cunreo, *see* **correatio.**

cunstabilarius, *see* CONSTAB

cunt-, *see also* CUNCT; CUNCTI

cuntracingula, *see* **contracingula.**

cuntreum, *see* COMPUT

cunum, *see* **cana.**

cunus, *see* **conus.**

cupa, 'coop', fish-trap 1278; *see also* **cuppa.**

***cup/arius** 1208, 1450, **-erius** 1266, **‡15c., couparius** 1338, **cowparius** 1458, **-ator** 1300, 1450, cooper; **-eragium** 1328, **couperagium** 1367, 1392, (?) **coperagium** 1507, cooperage; **-o** 1300, **copio** 1276, to hoop; *cf.* **cuva.**

cupero, to seize a 1408.

cuphia, cupha, *see* **coifa.**

cup/idinarius c 1293, **‡c** 1440, **-edinarius** c 1150, **-idineus, -idiosus** c 1100, covetous.

cupla, *see* **copula.**

cup/pa, -a *c 803, 11c. 1086, 1424, **coupa** 1297, 1461, **cowpa** 1461, **copa** 1295, (?) 1337, **-anum** c 1000, cup, bowl (usually bigger than **scyphus**); chalice (for eucharist) 1242, 1496; socket (of banner-staff) 1412; **-ula glandis,** acorn-cup a 1250; **-atorium** c 1300, **-ebondum** 1419, brace for stringing cups on; **-bordum,** cupboard 1414; **coppe-housa,** cup-house 1329; *cf.* **cuva.**

cupperum, *see* **coopertio.**

***cup/rum** 1178, 1566, **coprum** 1345, copper; copper vessel 1313; **-reus (-rius),** of copper c 1170, c 1503; **-ratus,** fitted with copper 1388; **-rifodina,** copper-mine 1262; **-rosa** a 1250, **-erosum** c 1215, ‡**-orosum** 1652, **-erosa** a 1250, ‡14c., **coperosa** 1297, 15c., **coperosium** 1307, **coprosa** 1421, copperas, iron sulphate.

cur, because a 461, c 780; that (in *ind. request*) c 1115.

cur/a, obedientiary (mon.) c 1118; *1248, c 1520, **-atus** 1435, **-a animarum** c 1163, 1575, *cure of souls (eccl.); **c. expeditionum,** military service 14c.; **-abilitas,** curability (med.) a 1250; **-abilior,** more curable a 1250; **-abiliter,** remedially 1343; **-agulus,** guardian, ruler 935, p 960; **-amen,** cure (med.) c 1310; **-ativus,** curative, remedial c 1200, c 1240; **-ator,** curer, healer c 1125, a 1275; tutor (ac.) 1321; prior superior (Carthusian) c 1328; c 1275, 1595, **c. animarum** 1216, *-atus 1300, 1591, priest having cure of souls; **-atrix,** guardian (*f.*) c 1258; **ecclesia -ata,** church with cure of souls c 1317, 1335; **beneficium -atum** c 1357, c 1450; **-o,** to have cure of souls a 1408; *see also* ESCUR

curacia, *see* **corium.**

cural/is, -itas, *see* CURI

***cur/allum** 1230, 1504, **-aillum** 1205, 1209, **-alium** 1276, **-ale** 1242, **corallum** 1230, 1419, †**coraltum** a 1564, **scurallum** 1275, **escurellum** 1284, (?) **squirrallum** 1350, dross-corn *or* chaff (O.F. *curail*); *see also* **corallum, corallus.**

curantum, *see* **corantum.**

curaterius, *see* **corretarius.**

curb/a 1228, 1312, **courba** 1362, curved piece of wood (for mill, plough-harness, or boat); c 1311, **-ia** 1238, curb of well or wall; 13c., 1286, **courba** 1257, dam or river-bank; **-o,** to fit (cart) with curved wood 1226; *cf.* CURV

curbana, *see* **corbana.**

curcerius, curcista, *see* CURS

curculio, weevil; ‡**gurgulio** 1483.

curcurbita, curbita, *see* **cucurbita.**

curda, *see* **gurda.**

curet/arius, -agium, *see* **corretarius.**

curi/a, *courtyard *or* house c 1080, 15c.; court (of king) 1086, 1586; *law-court, persons constituting a court, right of jurisdiction c 1043. c 1090, 1686; *see also* **camera, de, falso, finis, peto, rotulus, traho, verbum;** Papal Curia c 1327, 1461; **-am exerceo,** to practise the legal profession 1432; **-am facio,** to pay court c 1125; **-a Admiralitatis** 1383, 1587; **c. alta,** prior's court (Canterbury) c 1440; **c. Apparentie** (Penwortham, Lancs.) 1505, 1521; **c. de Arcubus,** court of Arches 1289, 1686; **c. Audientie** (Canterbury) 1586, 1684; **c. Augmentationum** (Exchequer) 1537, 1550; **c. de Banco,** Common Pleas c 1229; **c. baronie** 1230, 1462, **c. baronum** 1091, 1645, court baron; **C. Calibis,** Steelyard (London) 1394; **c. capitalis** (man.) 1193, 1470; **c. Celestis,**

court of Heaven c 1250, 1545; **c. Christianitatis,** court-Christian 1183, 1545; **c. commoti** (W.) 1388; **c. communitatis,** folkmoot (London) 1324; **c. consistorialis** 1465, 1589; **c. domini** 1115, 15c., **c. dominica** a 1135, hall-moot, court baron; **c. Facultatum** 1586, **c. ad Facultates** 1684 (Canterbury); **c. franciplegii** 1269, **c. visus f.** 1392; **c. Gardianitatis,** Warden court (Sc. Marches) 1471; *c. legalis** 1299, 1514, **c. leta** c 1393, c 1544, court leet; **c. legalis hundredi,** law-hundred, sheriff's tourn 1451; **c. magna** (in various senses) 1198, 1292; **c. Marescalcie** c 1470; **c. marina** 1383, **c. maritima** (†**maratima**) 1391, 1462; **c. militaris** 1385, 1637, **c. militie** 1389, court of chivalry; **c. militis** 1325, **c. militum** 1274, 1286, a local (man.) court; **c. mercatoria** 1417; **c. nundinarum** 1441; **c. pedis pulveris,** *etc., see* **pes; c. pacis,** town (A.S. *friðbyrig*) c 1115; **c. plena,** open court 1252, c 1290; **c. Peculiarium** 1586, **c. Prerogativa** 1586, 1684 (Canterbury); **c. de recordo** 1574, 1587; *c. regis** 1086, 1461; **c. Requestarum** 1586, **c. Requestuum** 1550; *c. Romana** c 1100, c 1487; **c. secularis** a 1347; **c. simplex,** court of limited jurisdiction 1269; **c. Wardorum (et Liberationum)** 1572, 1620;

-alis, courteous c 1080, 1385; forensic c 1125, c 1400; **littera c.,** court-hand 1419, 1560; **-alis** (*subst.*) a 1100, c 1470, **curalis** 960, courtier or court official; guild official 1368; **-alista,** courtier 1521; **-alitas,** courtesy, courtliness 12c., 1461; 1204, 1477, †**curalitas** 13c., **-aliagium** 1326, gratuity, gift; form of usury 1290; **c. Anglie** 1305, 1339, **c. Scotie** c 1385, 1608, 'curtesy' (leg.); **-aliter,** courteously 12c., c 1436; by way of gratuity 1255, c 1400; in forensic matters c 1130, c 1200; **-ensis,** member of Papal Curia c 1444.

curicia, *see* **culacium.**

curicsceattum, *see* CHERCH

†**curile,** *"tribunal"* (eccl.) (? *for* **curulis**) c 1200.

curios/itas, oddity, refinement, elaboration 1246, c 1450; curious inquiry, subtle point c 1197, 1378; anxiety, care c 793; **-us,** obedientiary (mon.) c 1220; (?) courtier (*cf.* **curialis**) a 1142; **cantus c.,** prick-song c 1500.

curisona, *see* CURR

curlius 1241, **corluvus** c 1324, curlew.

curlus, curl 1453.

curnellus, *see* I **carnellus.**

curo, *see* **cura.**

curopalata, master of the imperial household 12c.

‡**currago** 15c., ‡**guriaga** 14c., persicaria (bot.) (*cf.* O.F. *culrage*).

curr/amentum ville, parading through town (as penalty) (G.) 1315; **-arius** 1392, **-erius** 1298, 1332, **correrius** 1294, **-ator** 1302, †**-utarius** (? **carectarius**) 1265, courier; **-iculum,** curriculum (ac.) 1633; **-icula** 11c., **-iculum annorum** c 1150, c 1400, **c. temporum** c 1110, 1461, **-uculum annorum** c 1458, course, period, of time; **-ilis contentio,** chariot-race 7c.;

-iso 1323, **-isona** 1300, 1445, **corisona** 1328, **-izona, corizona** 1367, **cursona** 1300, **-usona** 1319, leakage (from cask); **-us**, cart-load 1086; **-ulus**, little chariot 1523; **-izo**, to ride in a carriage c 1320; **-ens**, flowing stream, current 847. 1383, c 1616; **-enti calamo** 1177; **-ens sermo** 1153; *see also* **canis, cyclus, porta; misse -entes**, ordinary masses 1439, 1475; **-o**, to hunt 1205, 1313; to be on the run (in a rebellion) 1265; to run (of machinery) 1306, 1376; to run, be imposed (of tax, *etc.*) a 1135, 1430; *to be current (of money) 1182, 1608; to be valid (of command, prohibition, *etc.*) c 1218, 1433; to accrue (of usury) c 1242, c 1298; to be entered (in an account) c 1418, 1439; to run (of memory) 1340; to run, be of effect (of time) c 1258, c 1400; to exercise (a horse) 1303; **c. ad baculos**, to play staff-ball c 1330; **c. cum pilis ad manus**, to play hand-ball c 1330; **c. in demanda**, to be outstanding (in debit account) 1377, 1404; **c. in vanum**, to come to nothing c 1325; **c. super**, to attack 1364; to prosecute c 1227; **c. super rotas** 1427; **c. villam**, to be paraded through town (G.) 1315; **c. vitam**, to lead life 15c.

curreo, *see* **correatio**.
curruptila, *see* CORRUPT
curso, *see* CURS; **curzo**.
curs/us, hunt 1262; 1269, 1419, **c. aque** c 1135, 1472, watercourse; row (in cornfield) 1286; row (of cogs) 1325; course, level (in tile-kiln) 1356; course, measure of height of fence c 1250; *course (of meal) c 1266, 1424; course of lectures (ac.) c 1340; turn, round, spell of work 1279, 1461; 790, **c. canonicus** 980, canonical round of duties; currency (of money) 1355, 1468; currency (of writ) 1434; **c. brevium**, right to issue writs 1291; common form of writs 1279; **breve de -u**, writ of course 1199, 1436; **clericus de -u**, cursitor 15c.; **extra -um**, out of the regular course 1286; **-us anguillarum**, eel fishery 1238; **c. artis**, course of instruction in a craft 1554; **c. Cancellarie** 1508; **c. curie**, course of procedure (leg.) c 1185, 1389; **c. ecclesie Anglicane**, method of reckoning time c 1290, c 1465; **c. falde** 1325, 1573, **c. ovium** 1583, sheep-walk (with right of foldage); **c. maritimus**, inlet 1427; **c. misse**, routine celebration of mass 1298; **c. petre**, course, layer of stones (arch.) 1237; **c. tauri**, use of bull (man.) 1361; **c. ventris**, flux, purging c 1180, ‡14c.; **c. ultimus vite**, term of life 947. 15c.;

-alis 1297, c 1375, **-abilis** 1286, **-arius** 1235, **-orius** c 1290, c 1398, regular, ordinary; 1218, 1237, **-ibilis** c 1305, **-ilis** c 1300, **-ualis** 1331, **-orius** c 1178, current; 1242, **-arius** c 1200, **-orius** c 1188, 14c., **-atilis** c 1150, **-ilis** 870, swift, running; **-aria**, swift ship c 1192; ‡**cyrserum**, carrick 1570; **-arius**, corsair, pirate 1234; 1290, 1429, **-erus, -erius** 1390, **-orius** 1313, **-or** 12c., 1416, courser (horse); **curcerius**, courser, quail (bird) a 1446; **-arius** c 1290, 1468, **-ester** 1575, **-ista** 1389, 1586,

curcista 1587, **-istarius** 1621, **-istor** c 1420, cursitor (Chancery clerk); **-atim** c 1308, **-im** c 1400, **-orie** c 1250, 1503, in order, in due course; **-ivus**, fluent (of a pen) c 1450; **-or**, courant (her.) 1654; cursory lecturer (ac.) c 1270; merchant not owning stall 1199; **-itor** a 1142, **-orius** 1326, *for* **-or**, courier; **-or de brevibus impetrandis in Cancellaria** 1314; **-oria**, aptitude for running 13c.; **breve -orium**, writ of course c 1290; **-ualiter**, by running, swiftly c 1412, c 1470; **-o**, to hunt c 1370.
curt/a, -aria, -arius, *see* **curtis**.
curtallus, (?) small pig, runt 1166.
1 curtana, sword of mercy 1236, 1377.
2 curt/ana 1270, 1310, **-ena** 1300, c 1350, **corta** 1270, **cortum** 1286, short cart (*cf.* **caretta**); ‡**-ator** 1377, **-inarius** (?) 1164, 1377, **corterius** 1336, carter.
curtell-, *see* **curtis**; **kirtella**.
curtena, *see* **2 curtana**; **curtina**.
curt/epia 1263, c 1330, **-epium** 1311, **-ebyum** 1369, **cortepia** 1316, **courtepetum** 1317, 1387, ‘courtepie’, short jacket.
curticus, sort of cloth 1345; **corticium**, sort of garment 1397.
*curt/ina** c 685. 1236, a 1564, **-inum** 15c., **-ena** 1433, c 1503, *cortina** c 1000. a 1100, 1588, ‡**-inula** 1483, **courtina** 1331, ‡**-issima** c 1450, curtain, hanging; **cortinarius**, curtain-maker c 1136; **-ino** 1274, **cortino** 1090, 1274, to decorate with hangings.
curtinarius, *see* **2 curtana**.
*curt/is** 6c., c 834. c 1100, 1608, **cortis** c 1200, 1414, **-a, -us** 11c., (?) ‡**cruta** 12c., **-icula** 1065. c 1160, **-illum** c 1115, 1330, **cortillium** 1234, **-ellum** 1228, **-elagium** c 1080, 1611, *-illagium** c 1120, 1588, **cortillagium** c 1117, 1200, **-ulagium** c 1330, 14c., **-ilegium** 1261, **-ulagium** c 1545, **cultilagium** 1363, ‡**cortinum** (Sc.) c 1400, ‘curtilage’, yard, courtyard; **-is**, hamlet 9c.; **-us regius**, king’s court 893; ‡**-ulum**, (?) cloister c 793; **-arium**, (?) kennel 1281; **-aria**, office of curtarian (mon.) c 1335; **-arius** 1239, c 1485, **-illarius** a 1128, curtarian, obedientiary in charge of secular buildings (mon.); **-isanus**, courtier 1441, c 1450; c 1444, 1450, **-esanus** 14c., **-ezanus** 1428, papal official or adherent; **-esia**, courtesy (leg.) 1608.
curt/itudo, shortness a 1250; **-is**, quickly c 793; **cortus**, *for* **-us**, short 1504.
‡**cur/tuma, -suma**, lesser celandine (bot.) 1652.
Curtus, Kurd a 1142.
‡**curuana**, headgear, (?) bonnet or hood c 550.
1 curuc/a, “titling” 1544; ‡hedgesparrow c 1440, c 1570; ‡cuckoo c 1483; ‡**corruca**, bunting 15c.; ‡**-o**, to cuckold c 1483.
2 curuc/a, -us, ship 6c., 7c.
curv/atio c 1250, c 1360, **-edo** c 1360, **-itas** c 1180, c 1470, curvature, curvedness; c 1330, **-itas** 1388, c 1450, crook of a crosier; **-abilis**, flexible c 1360, 1374; **-alis**, curved c 1250; **-iceps**, curved-headed 5c.; **-ilineus**, curvilinear 1686.
curzo c 1200, **curso** 1336, ridge of land.
cus, *see* CUSS

cus/atio, -o, *see* consuitio.
cuscuta a 1250, 1634, cass/ytha 1634, -utha 1538, ‡1570, gasitha a 1250, dodder (bot.).
cuspidatus, fitchy (her.) c 1595.
cussin-, *see* QUISSIN
cuss/io 1346, 1446, cuditio p 1280, striking (of coins); -or, striker c 1250; lancea -oria 1462; cudium (? *or* ferricudium), striker (of clock) 1504; cudus 810, cus 15c., *for* incus, anvil.
cust-, *see also* 2 CONST; Ostmannus.
custarius, custrix, *see* consuitio.
custellus, *see* culter.
custim-, custom-, *see* CUSTUM
custor, church servant, (?) sacristan (*cf.* O.F. coustre) (Exeter) 1337, 1385; costoreria (capelle), (?) office of sacristan (Norm.) 1203.
custos, *keeper (of land, castle, *etc.*) 1184, 1415; guardian (of minor) a 1120, 1324; *custodian (Franciscan official) c 1240, c 1400; warden (of hospital) c 1188, 1352; warden (ac.) 1335, 1499; monitor (in school) 1560; side-curtain 1388; 'guard', cover (of book) 1473, 1485; c. Anglie c 1340, 1415; c. apium, bee-keeper 1086, 1183; c. aquarum (Thames) 13c.; c. aucarum, goose-herd 1297; c. autumpni 1294, 1311, c. de statutis autumpnalibus 1289, c. ad campum custodiendum 1273, harvest warden; c. bonorum ecclesie 1417, 1432, c. ecclesie 1478, churchwarden; c. cambii, warden of the mint 1223, 1333; c. casei (man.) 1230; c. clavorum, municipal official (Norf.) 1345, 1347; c. comitatus 1274, 1322; c. escaetarum 1201; c. forgee, ironmaster 1409; c. Marchie 1309, c. Marchiarum 1461; c. mensurarum 1202; c. munditiarum (mon., Canterbury) 1322, 1422; *c. ordinis, sub-prior or third prior (mon.) 1214, c 1400; c. pacis 1265, c 1510; c. placitorum corone, coroner 1194, c 1324; c. p. mercati 1256; c. †plebicitatis, 'burleyman' (Yorks.) 1573; c. Portuum 12c., 15c., c. Quinque Portuum 1236, c 1330, warden of Cinque Ports; c. regni a 1120, 1461; c. Rotulorum 1269, 1509, c. R. et Recordorum 1466, 1516, Master of the Rolls; c. Sigilli (Magni) regis a 1123, 1426; c. S. Privati c 1290, 1586; custodes libertatis Anglie 1651;
  custod/ia, keeping, tenure (of land, *etc.*) 1086, 15c.; *wardship of minors 1155, 1482; administration of church property 1200, 1485; service of watch and ward 1086, 1285; ward (division) of castle 1324, 1461; ward (division) of town (Cambridge, Stamford) 1086, (London) 1213, 1535; battle-line c 1300; 'custody', division of a Franciscan province c 1240, 15c.; group of manors (Canterbury) 1252, c 1330; office of sacristan (mon.) 1236, 1341; wardenship (ac.) c 1335; guard, cover, case (of book, *etc.*) 1245, 1450; costodia *for* -ia c 1187; *-ia carceralis, imprisonment c 1160, c 1450; c. castelli, (service of) castle-ward 1167, c 1180; c. maris, coast-guard 1338; c. pacis 1242, 1415; c. salva, safe-keeping 1231, c 1314; c. sigilli regis 13c.; -ialis, belonging to a (Franciscan) custody c 1450; -iarium, store-house 1223;

-itio, keepership (of park) 1567; preservation (of laws) c 1283; -itivus, preservative, protective c 870. c 1290; -io, to be keeper of (land, *etc.*) 1086, 1430; to preserve (eggs) 1390; to 'guard', cover (a book) 1393; to keep, observe (law, rules, *etc.*) c 1220, 1416; to take care, make sure 815; c. me, to keep, remain sound (of food) 1322; c. duellum 1169; c. mare 1086, 1420; c. mercatum, to maintain the market price 1391; c. pacem 12c., 1295.
custum/a, customary right (?) c 1130, 12c.; *1272, 1583, cutuma 1324, costuma c 1095, 1342, coustuma 1331, 1385, customa 1219, 1300, customia 1289, †custima c 1255, 1383, †coscina 1200, -agium 1507, costomagium (Ir.) 1510, customary payment, customs duty; c. antiqua 1326, 1404, c. vetus p 1330, c. lanarum c 1290, 1357, c. magna 1573, c. nova 1289, wool custom (of 1275); c. nova 1303, 1325, c. parva 1304, 1606, petty custom (of 1303); c. magna (Sc.) c 1320, 1539; c. minuta (Sc.) 1479, c. parva (Sc.) 1344, 1467; c. mercati 1304; c. pannorum, cloth custom (of 1347) 1349; c. reya, royal custom (G.) 1267; c. ville (Southampton) 1342;
-abilis 1341, 1430, -alis 1483, 1538, -erus c 1303, liable to pay customs; -abilis 1279, -arius c 1290, 1690, customarius a 1564, costumarius c 1283, customary (of tenure); -abiliter, customarily, usually a 1564; -ale, list of customs rates 15c.; -arium, custumal, book of customs c 1300, 1487; -arie, by customary tenure c 1320, c 1345; *-arius c 1230, 1449, costomarius 1239, 1308, †custimarius a 1300, 1301, customary tenant; inferior member of guild 1302, 1318; c. (ad), habitual (of criminals) 1300; *-arius 1325, 1573, -ator (Sc.) c 1325, customs-collector; -atio, levying of customs 1315, 1397; -marta (Sc.), customary mart (beast) 1461, 1496; -o, to assess for customs, impose custom on 1228, 1460; c 1285, 1419, coustumo (G.) 1315, to pay custom on; customo, to pay custom 15c.
custur-, *see* consuitio; cultura.
cuta, *see* couta.
cutell-, cutill-, *see* culter.
Cuthbert/us: volucres Sancti -i, eider-duck 1381.
cut/ineus 717, -eus c 1220, made of hide.
cuttus, 'cut', lot, measure of lead 12c.
cutum, (?) (keepership of) strong-room (*cf.* O.F. cute) (G.) 1317.
cutuma, *see* custuma.
cutunus, *see* coto.
cuureo, *see* correatio.
cuv/a (†cun-, †cim-) 1086, c 1500, cova 1460, cufa (cupha) c 1285, 1412, tub, vat, bowl (Fr. cuve); holy water vat c 1500; cufa, cupping-glass (med.) a 1250; -ella, small vat c 1300, 15c.; -a. balnei 1355, c. de balniando 1324, couva pro intus balniendo 1304, bath-tub; c. butiri, measure of butter (W.) 1294, 1351; -arius, cooper 1213, 1498; -ata 1211, 1212, cofata 1232, measure of ale; -icula (†cunicula), salt-vat 1374; *cf.* cuparius, cuppa.

cuveragium, *see* coopertio.
cuvilla, *see* 2 cavilla.
cuvina, *see* covina.
cyan/us (*subst.*), -eus (*adj.*), azure (her.)
c 1595; **kianos**, blue a 1250; -eus, corn-
flower (bot.) 1620; -enus, lapis lazuli 1528.
cyathus (ciatus), wine-ladle: **chiatum** 11c.
‡cycima, litharge 1652.
cycl/us (cicl-), **cuclus** 15c., **cuculus** 1382,
cycle (of time); c. **currens** 1237, c. **lunaris**
1267, lunar cycle; c. **Dionysii** c 1125,
c 1250; c. **magnus** 1086, 14c.; c. **Paschalis** a 1294, c. **Pasche** 12c., c 1400; c.
solaris c 1080; *see also* **decennovenalis**;
-as a 710. c 1180, p 1350, **siclas** a 1380,
c 1437, cyclas, sort of robe; 1256, c 1300,
sicladon a 1450, 'ciclatoun', rich fabric;
-ois, cycloid (math.) 1686; -oidalis,
cycloidal (math.) 1686; -opedia, encyclopedia 1517, 1622.
cyco, *see* seca.
‡cydonomeli 15c., **citonia** c 1200, a 1250,
quince; *cf.* **cottanum**.
cygminus, *see* oinonetta.
cygn/us (cign-), swan: **cingnus** 1204, 1291,
scignus 1349, **signus** c 1307, 1532, sin-
gnus c 1300, **cinus** 1289, 1378; c. **campester**, wild swan c 1337; -eus c 1125,
cicneus, cicnius, †**cicinus** c 550, white
as a swan; -eolus c 1400, -iculus 1372,
1410, **signiculus** 1448, 1561, -ettus 1407,
synettus 1499, -ottus 1388, cygnet.
cylindr/us (chyl-), part of balance or
(?) weight c 950; **chelindrus**, roller a 1200;
-icus, cylindrical 1686.
cym/a (cim-) 1403, ‡15c., **sima** a 1250,
sprout, shoot; -atio (**arborum**), lopping
a 1510; †-ator, (?) wood-cutter, pruner
1279, 1292; -itas, summit (of belfry) 1345;
-eria, crest (of helmet) (Fr. *cimier*) 1348.
cymachum, *see* sumach.
cymba (cimba), chime, bell (mon.) 1277,
1460; ‡**churn** 1483; **symba (simba)**,
(?) reliquary (eccl.) 1439, 1462.
*cymbal/um (cimbal-) c 1072, c 1396,
cembellum 1091, **simbalum** 1398, bell
(mon.); ‡-a (*pl.*), virginals 1570; -aria,
navelwort (bot.) a 1250, ‡15c.; -itis, bell-
shaped (her.) 1654.
cymbolum, *see* symbolum.
cyment-, *see* CEMENT

*cymin/um (cimin-) c 1133, 1536, -ium
c 1240, **siminum** (†**sinimum**) 1294, 1380,
ziminum 1213, **sciminum** 1212, seminum 1319, ‡15c., **comminum** 1277, *for*
cuminum, cumin; ‡c. **dulce**, anise 14c.;
c. **Ethiopicum**, gith (nigella) a 1250, ‡14c.;
‡-ella, ammi (bishopweed) 14c.; -ata
a 1250, 1265, **cuminata** 1253, **cominata**
1252, (?) cumin water.
cynanch/e, quinsy: **synanchia** (sinancia)
c 1180, a 1250, ‡**sinantis**, **quinancia** 14c.,
squinancia 12c., a 1452, ‡**squacia** 15c.;
-icus 1634, **sinanticus, squinanticus**
a 1250, **quinciacus** c 1130, of or for
quinsy; **squinantium**, squinancy-wort
(bot.) a 1250.
cynegildum (cenegildum), compensation
for king (A.S.) c 1115.
cynice, cynically 1620.
cynigus, *see* CHIRURG
‡cynnia, **cymia**, vessel resembling urinal
(alch.) 1652.
cyno/glossa, hound's-tongue (bot.) c 1200,
‡14c.; ‡"horehound" a 1520; (?) -phagus
(†**cenofarus**), dog-eater 1243; ‡*-rodoxa,
(?) *for* -rexia, canine hunger, bulimy 15c.
cynomia, *see* cenomyia.
Cynthia, moon: †**Sinchialis**, lunar 1220.
cyntr-, *see* CINTR
cynubita, *see* CENOB
cynus, *see* schinus.
cyph-, *see* cifra, scyphus.
cypr/a (cipra), *for* -us, henna 13c.
cyr-, *see also* chir-
cyra, *see* schira.
‡cyramia, "*faex olei*" 1652.
cyratus, *see* cera.
cyrbes (*pl.*), tables of the law (κύρβεις) 1344.
‡cyrnea, goblet (? *cf.* κέρνος) 1570.
cyrpus, *see* scirpus.
cyrserum, *see* CURS
cyrta (cirta), hump (*cf.* κυρτός) c 1210.
cysta, *see* gista.
cysteria, *see* sitarchia.
cyst/is (cist-) c 1210, 1622, **scistis** a 1200,
bladder; **cista fellis** a 1250; ‡-eolythos,
sponge-stone 1652.
cytowalla, *see* zedoaria.
cytrus, *see* cintra.
cyul/a, -us, *see* kela.
Czechus, Czech 1586.

D

dab-, *see also* DEALB
‡dabes/sis, -tis, tortoise 1652.
dabilis, *see* 2 data.
dabitis, a logical mood 13c.
dabsilis, *see* DAPSIL
daca, *see* Dacus.
dacheum, *see* drasca.
*dacr/a a 1204, 1460, -um c 1224, 1359, -is
c 1216, 1323, **dakera** 1216, †**darkera** 14c.,
dikera 1275, **dagera** 1379, †**tacris** 1242,
†**tarqua**, †**tracta** (G.) 1409, 1413, 'dicker',
measure of 10 hides; measure of (? 20)

horse-shoes 1195; measure of knives 1472;
dicra, measure of iron 1086.
1 dact/ylus, finger: -ulus, talon c 550.
2 dact/ylus, date (fruit): -alus 13c., c 1450,
-ilis 1234, 1390, -ulus 15c., 1532, **dat/a,
-um** 1239, 15c.; -ilicius, of or for dates
c 793.
Dac/us, Dane, Danish 1086, 1461; -a 1276,
‡15c., **hachia -en[sis]** 1200, Danish axe,
pole-axe; *cf.* **Danus**.
daemericius, daimerettus, *see* damus.
daeria, *see* DAY

daga c 1322, †diga 1554, dagg/ardum 1389, p 1478, -arium, -arius 1399, 1514, -arum c 1500, -erum 1389, 1492, -erius c 1390, c 1397, (?) -ma c 990, dagger; -arium longum 1440; see also dacra.
dai-, see also day-
dail/a, -us, daiela, see dalus.
dakera, see dacra.
dakerhenna, daker-hen, corncrake 1544.
dal/a, -is, see dalus.
dalb-, see DEALB
‡dalitaria, "common slaughter" 1483.
*dalmat/ica c 760, 980. c 1080, 1537, †-a 1246, -icula 1327, dealmatica 1238, 1313, almatica 1240, 1344, tunica d. 1268, dalmatic (vestment); see also 2 pannus.
dalph-, see DELPHIN
daltinus, camp-follower, skirmisher, dailtean (Ir.) 1584.
dal/us 1084, 1270, -a 12c., 1248, -is 1370, dola c 1260, 1364, dolus c 1330, daila 12c., c 1315, dailus 1451, deila 12c., 1262, daiela 1413, delea c 1250, dole, portion of meadow; cf. della.
dalvata, see davaca.
damagium, see damnum.
dam/ala, -aricius, -arium, see damus.
1 †damascus, (?) for domesticus, 1251.
2 damasc/us 1388, 1509, sericum de -o 1462, pannus de -o 1447, p. -enus 1445, damasenus 1493, damask; see also rosa.
damer-, see damus.
dami/cella, -sella, see domicella.
damm/a 13c., -um 1281, 1282, dampa 1479, dam; -o, to dam c 1370.
*damn/um (dampn-) 1086, c 1470, -abilitas 1373, -atio c 740. c 1438, damagium 1555, loss, damage, injury; ad quod d., name of a writ 1385, c 1395; in -o esse, to be a loser c 1253; see also lucrum; -a (pl.), damages, compensation 1274, 1558; d. clericorum, 'damages cleer' (leg.) 1280, 1336; *-abilis, damnable, reprehensible c 1080, 1440; -abiliter, culpably, with risk of damnation c 1190, c 1520; -aliter, ruinously c 1450; -aticius, person condemned to death 1200; -atio, damnation (theol.) c 730, 11c. c 1080, c 1476; -ativus, damning c 1325; -ificabilis c 1367, -ificus c 1160, a 1400, injurious; -ificatio, injury 1309, 15c.; curse 1378; -ificator, damager 1426; -ifico, to injure c 1160, 1587; to damn (theol.) 1377; to deprive 1228; -o, to injure c 1250; *to damn (theol.) 679. c 1080, 1549; (?) to fine c 1290; to cancel, annul 1225, 1462; to block up c 1125 (? cf. dammo); see also DOMIN
dampa, see damma.
dampn-, see DAMN; DAPHN
*dam/us 1188, 1387, -a (m.) 1490, -a masculus 1446, buck (fallow deer); -arium, deerpark c 1500, 1544; -ula c 1192, 1480, -ala 1361, -ila c 1500, for -a, (fallow) doe; ‡-unculus, "pricket" 1570; -icula 1274, †-incula 1354, fawn; -illus a 1532, -inus c 1180, 15c., of venison; canis -aricius 1230, 1366, c. -erecius 1227, c. -ericius 1223, 1237, c. -erettus 1290, c. deimericius, c. demericius 1225, c. daemericius 1312, c. daimerettus 1229, brachettus

deymeretus 13c., buck-hound; bernarius -ericius, keeper of buckhounds 1312.
dan-, see also Danus.
‡dan/ati, -ic, weight of six barleycorns 1652.
danatio, see donum.
danbera, see denna.
dan/dum, -tia, dans, see 2 data.
danerellus, see 1 denarius.
danger-, see domigerium.
dangio, see dunjo.
Dani/elitas, essence of Daniel (log.) c 1310; -heliticus, of Daniel a 1100.
*Dan/us a 910, a 1000. 1086, 15c., -aus c 730, -icus c 1118, 12c., Dane, Danish; *-egeldum c 1070, c 1400, -egeldus c 1178, -ageldum 1324, -egaldum 1324, -egildum c 1130, 1234, Denegeldum c 1130, 1324, Denegaldum 1209, Denegildum c 1115, 13c., Denagildum c 1115, Dengeldum 1214, Danegeld; -elaga c 1325, c 1370, Denelaga c 1115, c 1437, Denalaga c 1115, Danelaw (district or law); see also hachia, securis; cf. Dacus.
daphn/is, laurel a 1250, ‡14c.; ‡-eleum (†dampnelicon) 14c., -ileon a 1250, oil of laurel; -ococcus (†dampnococcus), laurel berry a 1250, ‡14c.
*dapi/fer 1069, 1461, -cida 1437, 1443, -scida, -scidus 1437, 1462, -cidarius 1468, -ficus 13c., sewer, steward or seneschal; -feratus a 1100, c 1320, -feria 13c., stewardship; -fera, stewardess (eccl.) 12c.; provider (f.) a 1275; ‡-cus, profuse 1483; daps, abundance c 1218; dapsifer, festive a 1425.
dapsil/itas, bounty, generosity c 730, 1001. c 1125, c 1436; -is 956, c 1000. c 1130, c 1470, dabsilis c 550, bountiful, generous; gluttonous c 1190; -iter, bountifully c 1000, c 1038. c 1125; -ito, to bestow bountifully 930.
dar/apti, -ii, logical moods 13c.
‡dar/chem 1652, ‡-sen 14c., choice cinnamon.
Dardanus, see 1 pugna.
darkera, see dacra.
darmatio, see DEARM
dar/sus c 1180, 1253, -us 1257, 1338, dace (fish).
dartus, dart 1293, c 1335.
1 dat/a, -ilis, etc., see 2 dactylus.
2 *dat/a a 1100, 1545, c 1520, -us a 1564, date, dating clause; d. regis, regnal year 1390; portans -am, bearing date 1419, 1432; dabilis, admissible c 1360, 1427; dantia, giving c 1376; -arius, official of papal chancery (responsible for dating letters, etc.) c 1444, 1562; -io ad firmam, grant at farm c 1234; d. fidei, pledging faith c 1220, c 1364; d. manus, intromission of hands (eccl.) 1119; †dotio, gift 867; -ium 1418, 1485, -ia 1490, octroi, toll; -ivus, prone to give c 1180, 16 c.; to be given 1416; removable (of monastic obedientiaries) c 1317, 1418; -orius a 1452, †dotarius c 1376, recipient, donee; -rix, giver (f.) a 1275, 1374; dare, giving (subst.) 1241; pro suo dando 1250, 1384, pro suo dante 13c., de suo dando c 1320, (?) on his own authority, arbitrarily or in so

far as donor has the right to give; **dans,** celebrant (eccl.) 1229; **-o quod,** granted that 1295, 1415; **dedimus potestatem,** name of a writ 1462, 1508; **do,** to give in marriage 1100, c 1400; **do ad censum** 1086, **do ad firmam** 1086, 1266, to farm out; **do computum,** to render account 1468; **do diem,** to appoint a day (leg.) 1218, c 1400; **do faciem,** to confront c 1300; **do fidem,** to pledge faith c 1192, c 1564; **do foras,** to alienate (land) 930; **do in commissionem** c 1520, *do in mandatis** c 1180, c 1457, **do in preceptis** 1264, c 1400, to appoint, direct; **do in inferias,** to lay under a curse c 1125; **do in manu,** to pledge c 1115; **do intelligere** c 1192, c 1470, *do intelligi** 1220, c 1458, **do intelligentem** (*met. grat.*) 13c., to give to understand; **do viam,** to make way c 1434; *see also* **terra.**

datalicium, *see* **dos.**

datisi, a logical mood 13c.

daub-, dawb- *see* DEALB

daungerium, *see* **domigerium.**

daur-, *see* DEAUR

*davac/a** (†**davat-**) c 1220, 1455, **-us** c 1200, **-ata** c 1220, **dalvata** 1468, **dawata** 1484, measure of land, *davach* (Sc.).

Davi/dicus a 710. a 1142, 1555, **-ticus** c 1190, c 1370, of David.

1 **day/a** (**dai-**) 1086, 1398, **deia** 1234, a 1300, 'dey', dairymaid *or* dairyman; **-aria** 1253, 1461, *-eria** 1242, 1425, **-era** 1364, c 1442, **-ria** a 1300, 1480, *daeria** c 1160, 1411, **deiria** 1337, a 1441, **deira** 1446, **diaria** 1587, dairy.

2 **daya** (**daia**), 'day', division of mullioned window 1384.

dayn/a (**daia**), day's work or allowance 1189, 1234; 1307, 14c., **-ia** c 1340, measure of land (Somerset, S. Wales); *cf.* 1 **andena.**

daytida, tide flowing in day-time 15c.

daywerc/a 1204, 1461, **-ata** 1356, 1412, **daywarca** 1310, 1381, **dayworca** 1342, **daywrca** 1274, **deiwerca** 1225, 1360, **deyuerca** 13c., **deiworca** 1214, 1247, **diwerca** 13c., 'day-work', measure of labour or land (Kent, Essex).

de, *of, from (with place-names, used to form surnames) c 1067, 1537; *of (belonging to, consisting of, *etc.*) 1086, 1458; *in respect of (*various usages*) 1201, 15c.; (with *gerundive,* equivalent to *inf.*) 1212, c 1250; (with *inf.*) 1277; with, by (*instrumental*) 1086, c 1362; by (*agent*) 1195, c 1434; by reason of, on the ground of (*causal*) c 1200, 15c.; in the (pound, *etc.*; *distributive*) c 1322, 1462; by (denoting degree of difference) 1230, 1265; than (after **minus**) a 1300;

(with *noun*) **de assensu,** in agreement c 1290; **de auditu,** by hearsay 13c.; **de avo et proavo,** ancestrally 14c.; **de bene esse,** *see* **bene; de consensu,** with the consent (of) 1221, 15c.; **de gracia,** as an act of grace c 1254, c 1350; **de jurisdictione,** subject to the jurisdiction (of) c 1300, c 1343; **de manu in gulam,** from hand to mouth c 1204; **de pretio,** valuable 1226, 1230;

de ann/o in -um from year to year 1199,

c 1306; **de bienni/o in -um** c 1534; **de curi/a in -am,** at successive courts 1324; **de reg/e in -em,** in successive reigns c 1220; **de die in diem** 1188, c 1503; **de octo in octo diebus** (G.) 1315; **de mens/e in -em** 1294; **de punct/o in -um,** punctiliously 1446; **de temp/ore in (ad) -us** 13c., c 1503; **de iij septiman/is in iij -as,** every three weeks c 1283, c 1324; **de uno in unum,** one by one 1245; **de verb/o in (ad) -um,** word for word 1198, 1549;

(with *pronoun*) **de eadem,** of the same place (denoting surname) 1238; **de eodem,** of that ilk (Sc.) c 1370, c 1520; **de eo quod** 1226, c 1340, **de hoc quod** c 1105, c 1290, because, on the ground that; **de ipso,** personally c 1135, c 1172; **de se,** in itself, essentially c 1334, 1684; **de tanto,** to such a degree c 1380, c 1383; **de quanto ... de tanto** c 1444;

(with *adj.*) **de cetero** c 1125, c 1493, †**decetere** 1262, **de futuro** c 1255, c 1520, **de reliquo** 14c., henceforth, in the future; **de diverso,** (?) forwards 1147; **de difficili,** with difficulty 1382, c 1470; *de facili** c 1180, 1461, *de levi** 1217, 1461, easily; **de integro,** in full payment 1315; **de lato,** in width 1283; **de miro,** wonderfully c 1390; **de novo,** *newly, anew, as a novelty or innovation 1209, 1484; recently 1233, c 1362; **de pari,** on equal terms c 1204; **de plano,** summarily c 1155, 1558; **de pleno,** fully 1266, 1289; **de postfacto,** afterwards a 1408; **de presenti,** at present c 1344, c 1520; **de propri/o,** spontaneously 1265; **de -is** (*sc.* expensis) 1460; **de proximo,** in the near future c 1180, c 1470; **de puro,** net 1397; **de raro,** seldom c 1470; **de sero (cero),** late, in the evening c 1450, 1461; **de toto,** wholly 1268; **de vago,** astray 1393; **de verisimili,** probably c 1432, 1546;

(with *adv.* or *prep.*) **de a retro,** in arrears 1346; **de ante,** formerly 13c.; **de contra,** opposite c 1180; **de extra,** from outside 1406; **de foris, de foras,** *see* **deforis; de ibidem,** thence c 1273, c 1444; **de int/er, -us,** *see* **deinter; de invicem,** about each other c 1180; **de juxta,** *see* **dejuxta; de longe,** from afar c 1090, 1461; **de noctu,** at night c 1160; **de post,** behind 1415, 1455; afterwards c 1447, c 1470; **de prope,** *see* **deprope; de sicut,** *see* **desicut; de sub, desub; de subtus,** *see* **desub; de super, de supra,** *see* **desuper; de superplus,** surplus 1086, c 1235; **de sursum,** *see* **desursum; de trans mare** c 1200, c 1400, **de ultra m.** c 1200, 1428, from overseas; **de ultra,** beyond 1322, c 1470; **de versus,** towards a 1184, 1253.

dea-, *see also* **dia-; diaconus.**

deabilito, to injure 1378; *cf.* **dishabilito.**

deaccept/atio, refusal, objection 1378; **-us,** unacceptable c 1380; **-o,** to refuse 1378, a 1452.

deacervatio, unheaping, spreading out 1622.

deacus, *see* **deicus.**

deadvoc/atio, disavowal c 1258, a 1564; **-o,** to disavow, deny 1180, a 1564; to sue, implead c 1115; *cf.* DEVOC, **disadvoco.**

deafforest/atio, 'deforestation', removal of land from forest status (leg.) 1204, c 1306; -o 1204, 15c., diaforesto 1275, to 'deforest' (leg.) 1203, 15c.; cf. DEFOREST, DISAFFOREST

deagito (causam), to deal with 1266.

dealb/atio c 1236, 1560, daubatio 1305, 1366, dobatio 1423, daubatura 1305, 1461, daubitura 1483, dabatura c 1445, dabitura 1580, dalbura 1306, 1533, daubura 1237, 1400, dabura 1458, doubura 1454, whitewashing, plastering daubing; whitening a 1250; bleaching (linen) 1302, 1395; dressing, white-tawing (leather) 1276, 1533; blanching (money) a 1260, 1297; transmutation into silver (alch.) a 1235, c 1320; wearing white clothes (mon.) c 1330, a 1452; -ativus, whitening, cleansing 1344; -ator 1212, c 1324, daubator 1305, c 1503, daubiator 1336, dawbator 1415, dabator 1274, dobator c 1449, daubor 1286, daberus 1498, dauberius 1326, doberius c 1397, plasterer, dauber; -ator, whitewasher (of character) c 1160; d. coriorum, whittawyer 1184; ordo -atus, Cistercian order c 1188; *-o 1195, c 1400, -io 1255, daubo 1280, c 1460, daubio 1336, dawbo 1478, dobo 1373, c 1395, dobio 1370, to whitewash, plaster, daub; -o, to bleach (linen) 1292, 1363; to dress, curry (leather or parchment) 1198, 1338; to blanch (money) c 1178, 1280; to cover with, or transmute into, silver (alch.) c 1227; to dress in white (mon.) c 1266, a 1400.

deal/itas, godhead 793; -is, representing the Deity 1432; dialis, divine c 704.

dealloco, to disallow (leg.) 1327, 1456; cf. DISALLOC

dealmatica, see dalmatica.

deambul/atio, beating the bounds, perambulation 1219, a 1300; sheep-walk 1588; c 1200, *-atorium 12c., 1537, arcus -atorius c 1130, 'deambulatory' (promenade, arcade, gallery); -ans 13c., -ator 1219, 1606, surveyor, beater of the bounds; -ator poli c 1000; -ativus, mobile a 1250, c 1257; justitiarius (judex) -atorius, justice in eyre c 1178; -o, to walk through or over (trans.) c 1250, c 1362; to perambulate, beat the bounds 1133, a 1260.

deamelatus, enamelled 1329.

deangustatio, narrowing a 1250.

deappello, to call away c 1127.

deappetitus, disinclination, distaste a 1361.

deapto, to disable a 1250.

dearcto (viam), to widen, restore to proper width 15c.

*deargent/atus c 1170, c 1450, -oratus 1427, -eus c 1315, 1388, silver-plated.

dearm/atus, disarmed 1220; †darmatio, disarming c 1422; -o, to disarm 1413.

dearrest/atio, release from arrest 1295, 1335; -o, to release from arrest 1279, 1419.

dearticulate, under separate heads c 1444.

deasp-, see DIASP

deastupo, to stop up, block 1223.

deauctorizo, to disavow, deny c 1308.

deaur/atio, *gilding a 1200, 1531; (?) removal of gilt 1136; -ata 1248, daurata a 1250, †doracus (? doratus) c 1324, doreta 1265, dorea c 1188, c 1324, fish, (?) dory; *-atus

c 1160, 1537, -eus 1406, gilded, gilt; -atus duplex, double gilt 1313; -o, to gild 1155, 15c.

deawarenno, to remove from status of warren 1227, 1419; cf. dewarenno.

debacch/atio c 1197, c 1470, -antia c 1190, fury; -atior, more furious c 1310; -o, to rage c 1343, 1399.

debaelo, to carry down, carry away c 550.

debat/a, -um, debate, dispute 1313, a 1564; -abilis 1446, 1506, †-ablis 1492, debatable, disputable; -arius 1374, -or (Norm.) 1417, disputant, brawler; -o 1458, †debuto 1213, 1309, to dispute.

debaudatus, see debroudatus.

debell/atio, conquest 9c.; warfare, attack c 1150, 1587; †-io, rebellion 1339; -o, to fight judicial combat against (Sc.) 1230.

deb/erium (G.) 1297, -ere (G.) 1254, -endum (G.) 1282, -etum 1224, -itus 12c., -itorium 1220, for -itum, debt (cf. deverium); -entura, debenture 1660; billa de -entura, bill of indebtedness 1427; -ite 8c. 1221, c 1520, -iter 1540, ex -ito 1086, 1301, duly; -itatus, indebted 1415; -itor sum (with inf.), to be bound to c 793. c 1180, c 1343; -itor capitalis (distinguished from plegius) 1233; d. principalis 1264; -etum vini, wine due (G.) 1254, 1289; in -ito, in debt 1227, 1380; sub -ito (fidelitatis, etc.), in virtue of 1220, 1528; -itum clarum 12c., 1419 (?) d. merum 1306, clear or net debt; d. malum, bad debt 1408; d. principale, principal sum of a debt c 1275, 1290; -ita (pl.) itineris, debts wholly outstanding from eyre (as distinct from partialia) 1211, 1229; d. plura, debts collected in lump sums by intermediaries 1297; -endus, due 5c.; -ens, debtor (G.) 1289; -et (impers.), it is necessary 1200, 1324; -eo, to be intended to 740; to own c 1350; *to be charged, suspected, reputed 1086, c 1340; to be about to (auxiliary) c 1188, c 1520.

debil/itas, deficiency in weight (of money) 1282; diminution of potency (astr.) a 1233; -is, worn out c 1393, 1464; weak, low-grade (of wine or ale) a 1250, c 1448; poor (of grain or malt) c 1304, c 1327; waste, barren (of land) c 1254, 1329; debased, deficient (of money) a 1222, 1425; -itamentum p 1377, -itatio p 1300, a 1361, weakening; -io, for -ito, to weaken, enfeeble c 1362.

†deblandifico, to flatter 1483.

debotus, see DEVOT

debrio 8c. c 1130, c 1540, deebrio 1344, to inebriate; *to intoxicate (fig.), inspire, inflame 1091, c 1450; to be intoxicated (fig.) 1200; to inundate, impregnate c 1220, c 1433.

debroudatus 1382, †debaudatus c 1294, debrauditus c 1396, embroidered.

deburgo 1275, 1376, †defurgo 1298, to burgle, break into.

debuto, see DEBAT

decaballatus, unhorsed 1346.

deca/da, number ten 1426; -chordus, tenstringed instrument 1267, ‡1483, -gonus, decagonal c 1300; -logus, *decalogue 8c. 12c., 1549; c 1362, -lagus 1387, list; †d.

sterlingorum, a sum of money c 1323; **-schemus,** of ten syllables c 685; of ten forms c 1125.

de/cado, -caisatus, *see* **decasus.**

deca/gesimus, tenth c 793; **-nonus,** nineteenth c 1190; **-quartus,** fourteenth 1413; †**-tertius,** thirteenth 15c.

decagium, *see* **diketta.**

decalc/eatus (-iatus), barefoot c 1258, 1274; **-io,** to take off shoes 1461; *cf.* DISCALC

decalco, to knock down a 1260; to dirty, befoul 1275, ‡1483; to defile (a woman) 1324.

decalv/atio, (?) decapitation 12c.; **-o,** to shave 12c.; to strip bare 1414; (?) to behead 12c., c 1180.

decantatio, singing, chanting 8c., c 1000. c 1070, 1517.

decan/us *11c., 1543, **decennus** 1276, **d. ecclesie** c 1250, 1440, **d. episcopi** c 1150, c 1310, dean (eccl.); (?) *doyen,* senior (of bishops) 1261; chief c 1000; dean (ac.) 1382, c 1549; dean of guild 1389, 1559; third of a sign of the zodiac (astr.) a 1233, c 1270; **d. de Arcubus** c 1267, 1684, **d. Archiarum** a 1564, dean of Arches; **d. capelle** 1413, 1437; ***d. Christianitatis** 1239, 1559, **d. loci** 1181, **d. patrie** 1206, **d. plebanus** c 1213, **d. ruralis** c 1220, 1559, rural dean; **d. major** 1242, c 1270; *see also* **pars;** **-alis,** decanal 1261, c 1438; **-atim,** deanery by deanery 12c.; **-atus** c 1150, 1546, **-ia** c 1125, c 1436, deanery; **d. de Arcubus** 1295, 1684; **d. capelle** c 1217, **d. Christianitatis** 1403, **d. ruralis** 1303; *see also* DECENN

decapill/atio, removal of hair c 1340; **-atus,** gaol-cropped 1290; **-o,** (?) to scalp c 1115.

decapit/atio, beheading a 1100, 1419; felling (of trees) 1143; **-o,** *to behead c 685. c 1125, c 1540; **d. quercum** 1432.

decap/utiatus c 1375, **-itiatus** 1365, unhooded, bare-headed.

decar/co 1225, **-io** 1258, to unload; **-io,** (?) to carry away c 1395; *cf.* DISCAR

†**decardianus,** cited as word of Greek origin 1271.

decarius, *see* DECENN

decaschemus, *see* **decada.**

decas/us, decay, collapse, diminution, depreciation 1259, 1620; 1280, †**decensus** a 1275, loss in assay; **d. compoti** 1524; **d. firme** c 1400; **d. redditus** c 1270, 1354; **-us** (*p.p.*) 1250, c 1550, **-atus** 1587, **decaisatus** 1308, 1588, decayed, ruined; **decado,** to be deducted, subtracted 1248; *cf.* DECID, **discaetus.**

decaudo, to dock, curtail 1143, a 1408.

decedo, *see* **decessus.**

decendium, period of 10 days 1249, 1344.

decendo, *see* DESCEN

decenn/a, set of ten 1312; measure of charcoal 1333; weight (of iron) 1313; **dizena,** (weekly) payment of a tenth c 1300; *-a 1191, 1444, **-ia** 1305, c 1345, **-ium** 1421, **desena** 1392, **desainum** 1276, **dezenna** 1292, **dicena** 1274, 1360, **discena** 1276, 1368, **dycenum** 1277, 1392, **dysenum** a 1300, †**docinna** 13c., **-aria** 1282, 1302, **decania** c 1115, tithing, frankpledge group *or*

division of the hundred (*cf.* **decima; tethinga**); (?) **-a** 1274, **-arius** 1183, c 1540, **dezennarius** 1286, **dissenarius** 1278, **-ator** 1266, 1300, **dussinator** 1415, **decanus** c 1043. c 1150, tithingman, headborough; **-arius,** captain of ten (G.) c 1295; c 1285, **-alis** c 1130, of a tithing; c 1188, **numerus -arius** p 1394, c 1440, n. †**decarius** c 1102, n. **-alis** 1527, group of ten.

decenno/venalis, cyclus, 8c., 825. 12c., p 1341, c. †**-valis** (? **-nalis**) c 1200, 14c., c. **-velis** 11c., cycle of 19 years.

decenseo, to assign 9c.

decensus, *see* **decasus;** DESCEN

decenti, *see* DUCENT

dec/entia, fitness: **-ensia** 13c.; **-ibilis,** meet, fitting c 1000; **-eo** (with *inf.*), to be fit or meet to 8c.

decentus, *see* **discantus.**

decept/itas, state of being deceived a 1361; **disceptio,** *for* **-io,** deceit 11c.; **-iuncula,** little deception 1497, **-abilis** 8c. c 1400, c 1414, **-ibilis** c 1298, **-atorius** 1461, **-ivus** c 1080, 1588, **-uosus** 14c., deceptive, deceitful; **-ibilis,** fallible 1344; **-ive** 1289, 1332, **-orie** 1080, 1428, **-uose** 1324, deceitfully; **-o,** to act or conduct deceitfully 1309, c 1390; *see also* DISCEPT

decerno, *see* DISCRET

decert/atio, dispute (leg.) a 1135, c 1150; **-ator,** disputant 1236.

decess/us, deduction 1271; **d. civilis,** entry into religion 1247; **-or,** predecessor c 1000; **decedo** 1275, c 1483, **d. ab hac luce** a 1525, **d. in fata** c 1220, c 1470, to die; *cf.* **discessus.**

deceter/o, -e, *see* **de cetero.**

decibilis, *see* **decentia.**

decico, *see* **dedico.**

decid/entia 1342, 1462, **-ium** 1422, diminution, loss; **-uus** 6c., **desiduus** c 1130, transitory; feeble, decadent 950. c 1250; **-o,** to fall short, be deducted or unpaid 1086, 1460; *cf.* DECAS, DECIS

decies tantum, name of a writ 1393, 1445.

decim/a, tithing, division of the hundred c 1108, 14c. (*cf.* **decenna**); *(tax of) a tenth 1285, 1461; *1070, 1565, **dessima** c 1250, (?) **disana** 13c., **-ale** 1355, ‡**-ula** 1483, tithe (eccl.); **d. alba,** "white tithe" (?) of milk, *etc.* 1570; **d. constituta** 1167, 1169; **d. garbalis** 1320, 1549, **d. garbarum** c 1254, 1537; **d. grossa** 1245, a 1564, **d. major** c 1262, 1439, great tithe; **d. minuta** c 1200, 1570, **d. minor** c 1280, 1439, **d. privata** 1535, 1580, **d. vicaria** 1608, small, privy or vicarial tithe; **d. separata** tithe paid to others than the holder of the living 13c., 1255; **d. personalis** 1315, 1535; **d. predialis** 1378, 1588; **d. realis** 1323, 15c.; **d. Terre Sancte,** papal tenth in aid of crusade 1287; **-abilis,** tithable c 1236, 1482; *-alis, of or for tithes 11c., a 1533; **-alis** (†-us) c 1115, **-arius** 1226, **-ationarius** c 1102, tithingman; **-aria,** "dimery" 1554; **-atio,** tithing, division of the hundred c 1102; (payment or exaction of) tenth c 1190, 1461; *(payment or exaction of) tithe 8c., c 1010. c 1110, 1475; tithe area 1313; **d. minuta** c 1214;

-ator, taker of tithe 1385; tither, tithe-payer 1461, 1462; **-o,** tenthly 1279, c 1343; **-onono, -ooctavo, -oseptimo, -osexto** c 1343; **-o,** to assess for tithe, take tithe of c 1150, a 1564; to pay tithe (on) c 1115, 15c.

†**decimale,** (?) *for* **medicinale,** medicine a 1564.

decinct/or, oppressor, detractor 12c.; **-us,** ungirt c 1258; **decingo,** to ungird c 1330.

decindo, *see* **discissio.**

decino, to sing to a close c 1160.

deciphr/atio, decipherment 1620; **-o,** to decipher 1620.

decis/io, cutting down c 1252; diminution c 1204, c 1357; 1188, 1292, **discisio** 1188, c 1202, **descicio** c 1200, **desicio** 1223, retailing (of cloth); **d. (desisio) seminis,** 'decision', separating of seed (in procreation) 13c., 1267; **d. vultus,** tearing of cheeks c 1184; **discisio,** *for* **-io,** decision c 1300; **-ibilis,** to be decided 1378; **-ivus** 1291, 1303, **-orius** 1311, 1620, decisive; **-or,** slayer c 1462; decider, arbiter 1342, c 1470; **-us,** 'cut', slashed or tagged (of cloth) 1188; (of shoes) c 1350; **decid/o** 1267, p 1300, †**descindo** a 1250, 13c., to separate (of seed in procreation); **descindo** c 1236, 14c., **discido** c 1434, **discindo** c 1092, *for* **-o,** to decide.

decius, dice a 1185, 1344; **deiciatus,** dice-shaped 1355.

declam/atio, proclamation c 1258; crying down, depreciation (of money) 1486; **-atorium,** brawling-place c 1140; **-o,** to proclaim 1207, c 1236; to disclaim 1293; to cry down (money) 1484.

declar/atio, exposition, explanation 1281, 1559; clearing (of reputation) 1381, 1433; blazon (her.) a 1446; **d. compoti,** declaration of account 1526; **-abilis,** expressible c 1270, p 1300; **-ator,** expositor 1461; arbiter (G.) 1242; **-atoria,** judgement 1608; **-ativus** a 1300, 1350, **-atorius** 1301, 1684, **-atrix** (*f.*) c 1400, explanatory, expository; **-o,** to clear (reputation) 1460, c 1470; to blazon (her.) a 1446; to 'declare', verify (an account) 1670.

declausus, unenclosed 1250; **decludo,** to disenclose 1275.

declin/atio, declination (astr.) c 1233, 1686; decline (of fever) a 1250; visit c 1333; evening lecture (at Chartres) c 1160; **-antia,** deviation c 1376; **-ativus,** prone to decline c 1184; **exceptio -atoria** (leg.) 1309; **-atorie,** by way of declinatory exception 1389; **-ax,** prone, inclined c 1370; **-o,** to draw to an end c 730. c 1125; to pass near, meet, or visit c 1130, 1439; to retire 1304; to abate, die down 1406; to lay low c 1250; to draw off (med.) a 1250; **-or in somnum,** to fall asleep 1241; *see also* DECLIV

decliv/ium c 550, 685. a 1100, 15c., **-um** 1306, 1415, declivity, slope; **-um anni,** waning of the year c 1250; **-is,** humble, unassuming c 1125; **-us** c 1267, **-osus** (†**declinosus**) a 1250, sloping, hilly.

decludo, *see* **declausus.**

†**declutio,** (?) *for* **deglutio,** to swallow c 1280.

decoc/tio, melting down (of metal) 1279, ‡14c.; baking (of bread) c 1330; mellowing

c 1160; digestion a 1250, c 1260; **decoquo,** to smelt (alch.) c 1200; 1286, **-uo** 1289, to bake; to digest c 1260; to ruminate, ponder c 1125, c 1343; **dequoquo,** to squander c 1180.

decoll/atio, beheading c 900. c 1200, 15c.; **d. latronum,** *"hevedstoke"* 1280; **d. S. Johannis Baptiste* c 1080, 1540, **dies -ationis S. J. B.** 1204, 1338, **festum -ationis S. J. B.** 1246, 1415, decollation of St. John (29 Aug.); **sotulares -ati,** 'cut shoes' c 1350.

†**decolorus,** disgraceful c 1125.

decolpo, to fell 1228.

decomatio, scalping or shaving the head c 1115.

deconsto, to clear (of debt) 1390; **decosto,** to cost 1317.

decopulo, to uncouple (dogs) 13c., 1255; *cf.* **discopulo.**

decoquo, *see* **decoctio.**

decor/atio, adornment c 1238, 1418; **militia -ata,** belted chivalry 1461; **-eus,** handsome, doughty c 550; **-ositas,** elegance c 870, 11c.; **decuso,** to adorn, honour, c 950, c 960. 12c., ‡15c.

decorio, to plunder, strip c 1125, c 1192.

decoron/atio, scalping *or* beheading 12c.; **-o,** to scalp *or* behead 12c.; to discrown c 1190.

decorrosivus, caustic c 1184.

decorruo, to decline 1465.

†**decorto,** *for* **decortico** *or* **decurto,** 771.

decosto, *see* **deconsto.**

decredo, to disbelieve c 1170, 1427; *cf.* DISCRED

decre/mentum c 1250, 1538, **-scentia** c 1423, **-scum** 1302, decrease; loss, damage c 1458, 1450; **-sco** (†**-co**), to diminish (*trans.*) c 550; to be lost, incurred 1240; **-ssit,** *for* **-scit,** c 1266.

decrepi/tas 1227, †**decurpitas** c 1255, **-tatio** c 1290, decrepitude; **-dus,** *for* **-tus,** a 1428.

decret/um, decree (in Chancery) 1507; **-a** (*n. pl.*), decretals 11c., 1537; **-ale* c 1188, c 1450, **-alis* a 1245, c 1540, **epistola d.** c 1125, 1461, †**-abile** 1335, decretal; **-alis,** of or for a decretal c 1204, 1455; **-ista* a 1228, 1435, †**decrestista** c 1325, student of the decretals, canonist; **-o** 1278, c 1470, **discerno** (*for* **decerno**) 12c., c 1430, to decree; *cf.* DISCRET

decrudesco, to mellow 1178.

decrust/atus (panis), stripped of the crust 14c.; **-o,** to break up, melt down 12c., 1385.

decub/atio, lying ill 15c.; **-ie** (*pl.*), childbed 1347, ‡c 1440; **-itus,** repose, inertia 1620, 1622; **-o** to lie down (esp. sick or in childbed) c 1177, 1425; to guard c 1200.

†**decultus,** hidden a 1100.

decupedalis, ten-foot c 1404.

decupl/icatio, multiplication by ten c 1150; **-us,** tenfold a 1100, c 1150; **in -o* c 1180, c 1400, **in -um** c 1302; **-o-sextuplo,** sixteenfold c 1615; **-atus,** multiplied by ten c 730.

decuratus, uncared for c 1302.

decuri/a, tithing, division of the hundred c 1293, 14c. (*cf.* **decenna**); **-o,** tax-collector or fiscal officer c 1115; **-o,** to try (leg.) 973; ‡to dub (a knight) 1570.

‡**decurio,** to put out of court 1483.
decurpitas, *see* **decrepitas.**
decur/sio (†**decussio**), lapse c 1200; **-rentia,** running down, failing 1344; **-satorius** c 870, †**-sibilis** (*v.l.* **-ribilis**) (?) 934, transient; **-sus aque,** watercourse c 1070, 1407; **d. annorum,** lapse of years c 1407; **-sus** (*p.p.*), elapsed c 1330, c 1400.
decurt/atio, shortening 1267; **-ator,** clipper of coins c 1178.
decus, boundary (Provençal *dec*) (G.) 1283, 1308.
decuso, *see* DECOR
decussio, *see* **decursio.**
decuss/is, crux **-ata,** saltire (her.) c 1595; **-atorius,** intersecting 1649.
dedalinus, daedal c 1400.
dedampnifico, to indemnify 1288, 1426.
dedbanna, perpetrator or instigator of murder (A.S. *dǣdbana*) c 1115.
dedda, *see* **dodda.**
dedec/entia c 1250, 1283, **-or** a 1349, **dedicus** 1461, *for* **-us,** disgrace; ‡**-oro,** "to unbeautify" 1570.
dedicat/io, (celebration of) anniversary of dedication (eccl.) 1523; **-or** (eccl.); **-issimus,** wholly dedicated c 1460.
dedico *1219, c 1465, †**dedisco** c 1250, †**decico** 1309, to deny, refuse; to contradict, give the lie to 1307, a 1408; to repudiate 1290.
dedign/atio, taking offence c 1350; **-anter,** disdainfully c 1190, c 1365; shamefully 1267; **-abundus** 1506, a 1519, **-osus** a 1408, disdainful; **-itor** c 1165, **-o** (with *inf.*) c 793, *for* **-or,** to disdain, refuse.
dedil/ectio, estrangement a 1452; **-igo,** to cease to love 1177, c 1320.
dedimus potestatem, *see* **2 data.**
dediscalus, *see* **didascalus.**
dedisco, *see* **dedico.**
dedoctus, unlearned c 1180.
deduc/tio, (?) bringing in, gathering a 700; transport 1453; guidance 1620; conduct (of lawsuit) 1549; deduction (log.) c 1300, c 1546; 1252, *-tus 1215, 1575, game, hunting; **-tus cygnorum** 1472; **d. aque,** watercourse a 1290; **-ibilis,** deducible (log.) a 1361, c 1382; **-tive,** by deduction (log.) c 1325, c 1357; **-tivus,** conducive a 1250; **-tor ferarum,** game-keeper 1549; **-torius,** affording guidance 1620; **-o,** to levy c 1266; to subtract, deduct 1302, c 1593; *to bring to trial c 1115, 1391; to deal with 1201, c 1448; to pass, spend (life) c 1250, c 1400; to deduce (log.) c 1332, c 1363; to relate c 1378, a 1405; **d. de,** to invest with, put in possession of 1198, 1206; **d. super,** to extend over (space) c 1330; **d. breve,** to bring a writ (into court) c 1260; **d. lecto,** to marry c 1362; **d. mercatum,** to exercise a trade c 1160; **d. ad notitiam** 1295, c 1451, **d. in n.** c 1330, **d. notitie** c 1427, to bring to notice.
deebrio, *see* **debrio.**
deedifico, to demolish 1537.
deeligo, to fail to choose 1380.
deessentia, want, lack c 1377.
deexalt/atio, lowering 1358; **-o,** to lower 1334, 1347.

deexisto, to be lacking, non-existent a 1360.
def-, *see also* **diff-**
defacio, to deface (a seal) 1290, a 1564; to undo 1262; *cf.* DEFECT, DIFFAC
defalc/atio, mowing 1455; deduction, scaling down c 1258, 1540; **-atorius,** tending to impair c 1470; **-o,** to mow c 1212, 1684; to cut down, diminish, impair 1286, c 1470; *to deduct, scale down 1299, 1538.
defal/ta, lack 1237; *1198, 1419, **-tus, -tum** c 1290, 1597, **defaulta** 1312, 1690, **defauta** 1199, 1292, **diffalta** 1223, **-limentum** (G.) p 1250, default (leg.); absence from work 1301; **-ta recti** c 1258.
defam-, *see* DIFFAM
defatigabilis, subject to weariness 1620.
defatuo, to cure of folly c 1180.
defaulta, defauta, *see* **defalta.**
defect/us, loss c 793; defect, deduction c 1188, 1547; default (leg.) 1185, 1451; **d. sanguinis,** want of an heir 1333; **-um habeo,** to have need 1238; **in -u,** in need (of) 1417; *-ibilis, liable to defect, imperfect c 1270, c 1370; **-ibilitas,** imperfection c 1270, p 1300; **-ibiliter,** imperfectly p 1300; **-ivitas,** defectiveness a 1290; **-ivus,** defective (gram.) 790; **-uosus,** faulty c 1343, 1549; **deficilis,** in default 1411; **deficiens,** deficit c 1350; **-o,** to impair a 1250; **deficio,** to 'defeat', annul (leg.) 1227, 1587; **deficior,** to be wanting, to default 1204, c 1230; **difficio,** to fail a 700. c 1180; *cf.* **defacio, defesantia.**
defedatio, defilement a 1250.
defedero, *see* **diffedero.**
defeneratus, obsessed c 1125.
defen/sio 1086, 1301, **-cio** 1282, **-sa** c 1247, c 1470, *-sum 1086, 1419, **-sus** 1086, 'defence', enclosure, fencing off; ‡"defiance" 1570; forfeiture c 1165; c 1080, 1419, **-sum** 1212, 1234, prohibition; 1086, c 1125, **-sa** 1181, (area of) assessment; area of protection c 1113; **-cio** (**salmonum**), close season c 1395; **-sa** a 1446, **-sum** c 1187, p 1330, **-saculum** a 1250, ‡1483, **-samen** 1438, **-satio** 9c. 1425, **-cio** c 1296, c 1536, **diffencio** c 1333, *for* **-sio,** defence, protection; **locus -sationis,** asylum 9c.; **-saculum,** shield c 685. c 1100; **-sabilis,** fenced off 1267; fortified 1086; c 1193, 1511, **-salis** 1316, 15c., **-sibilis** 1205, 1587, 'fencible', capable of defending; **-sibile,** defensive weapon 1472, a 1539; **-sibiliter** 1587, **-sive** c 1457, defensively; **-siva,** fence 1585; **-sive** (*pl.*), militia c 1200; **-sivus,** defensive c 1217, 1620; **-sorium,** protection, cover c 1090, 1508; jack (armour) 1443, c 1450 **-sor,** warrantor 1086; advocate (leg.) c 1115; **d. regis** (G.) 1313; **d. fidei,** royal title 1521, 17c.; **-sor** c 1070, c 1115, **-dens** 1269, c 1450, defendant (leg.); *-do, to enclose, fence 1225, c 1260; to 'defend', deny (leg.) 1166, 1406; to forbid c 1070, 1436; to uphold a thesis (ac.) c 1556; 1086, 1387, **d. pro** c 1250, to maintain, hold (land); **d. me,** to be assessed (of land) 1086, 1238; **diffendo,** to defend, guard 1461.
‡**defercio,** to empty 1483.
defer/ens, deferent (astr.) c 1233, 1326; **-o,** to dismantle c 1180; *676, 1082, 1549,

differo 13c., c 1343, *to defer to, have regard for; to wear 1222, c 1520; **d. arma,** to bear arms 1268, c 1340; **d. teloneum,** to misappropriate toll a 1215; *cf.* **delatio;** *see also* DIFFER

deferratus, unshod (of horses) c 1250, 1275.

defesantia, defeasance, undoing 1365; c 1352, 1504, **diffesantia** c 1400, (?) **defessio** c 1432, defeasance, (condition for) annulment (of bond, *etc.*); **defessio justicie,** defect of justice 1193.

defeteor (*dep.*), to acknowledge 1200.

deff-, *see* **diff-**

defic-, *see* DEFECT

defido, *see* DIFFID

defidus, separated c 550.

defigur/atus, deformed 1335; **-atissime,** most unattractively c 1190; *see also* DIFFIGUR

defin/itio (**diffin-**), ending c 1000; c 730, 939. c 1115, 1587, **-itiva** c 1357, 1549, determination, decision, decree; **-itiuncula,** limitation 9c.; **-ibilis,** definable c 1270, c 1365; ***-itive,** definitely, definitively 1205, 1610; **-itivus** c 850. c 1192, 1587, **-itorius** c 1357, definite, definitive; **-itor,** definitor (eccl.) c 1235, 1454; definer 1610; ***-io,** to define, determine, decide c 760, c 865. 1086, 1531; to come to an end 1320.

deflenter, mournfully 1417.

deflor/atio, selection, anthology c 1436, c 1553; **-atiuncula,** small selection c 793; **-o,** to pick out, select from c 685. c 1125, c 1436; to blight c 1170; **diffloro,** to ravish c 1382.

deflux/io, ebb c 1160; **-us** c 1366, **defluentia** 14c., ebbing away (fig.); estuary 1537.

defodio, *see* DEFOSS

deforest/atio 1204, c 1306, **difforestatio** 1224, **disforestatio** 1307, 'deforestation', removal of land from forest status (leg.); **-o** 1205, 1279, **difforesto** 1583, to 'deforest' (leg.); *cf.* DEAFFOREST, DISAFFOREST

deforis, from without c 1115, 1344; **de foras,** abroad 1346.

deform/aliter, non-formally 1380; †-atorius (?) *for* **defam-,** defamatory 1686; **difformo,** *for* **-o,** to disfigure 1344.

defort/iatio (**deforc-**) 1247, **diffortiatio** c 1115, 1279, **disfortiatio** 1188, **-iamentum** 1198, 1468, **diffortiamentum** c 1115, 1359, **disfortiamentum** 1191, deforcement (leg.); **-iamentum (mulierum),** violation 1289; **-ians** 1220, 1424, **-ens** 1587, **-iator** 1205, 1539, **-itor** 1199, deforciant, deforcer (leg.); **-io** *c 1115, 1595, **diffortio** c 1115, a 1242, **disfortio** c 1115, c 1225, to deforce (leg.), withhold, eject, or hinder by force; to violate, ravish (C.I.) 1309.

defoss/io, digging c 1250; burial 1620; **-atus,** dug c 1430; **defodio** c 1086, **diffodio** c 1115, to dig up, disinter.

†**defranmo** (? **defrainno**), (?) to break up (Norm.) 1195.

defraud/atio, defrauding c 1250, 1348; **defrado,** *for* **-o,** to defraud 11c.

defrond/atio, stripping of leaves c 1406; ‡-ator, stripper of leaves 1483; **-o,** to strip of leaves 1410, ‡1483.

defrust/is, torn c 1250; **-ro,** *for* **-o,** to break in pieces c 1180.

defuco, to feign c 1200; to paint 1337.

defullo, to knock down, trample on (O.F. *defoler*) 1244.

defunct/io, death c 1170, c 1464; mortuary due 1155; **pars -i,** deceased's share (Sc. law) 13c.; **diffunctus,** *for* **-us,** deceased c 1490.

defurgo, *see* **deburgo.**

‡**defurno,** to take from the oven 1483.

degagio, *see* DIVAD

degarnelo, *see* **dekarnelo.**

degelo, to thaw ‡15c., 1496.

degener/atio, degeneration, decline c 1250, a 1452; **-ositas,** degradation 14c.

degero, *see* **dejero;** DIGEST

degest/io, settling down, lying down 1461; **-o,** to disparage, decry c 1310.

degetus, *see* 1 **digitus.**

deglad/iatus, deprived of a sword c 1180; *see also* DIGLADI

deglob/io 12c., **-o** c 685, *for* **deglubo,** to flay.

degrad/us, stairway 1288, 1332; **-atio,** staircase 1272; *c 1070, 1686, **-atus** c 1258, degradation; **degressio,** descent c 865; **-o,** *to degrade c 1100, 1461; †-o, to rush down 1461.

degrano, to grind corn 1331.

deguajo, deguadio, *see* DIVAD

degust/atio, taste, tasting 14c., c 1357; **-ator,** taster c 1325.

degutto, to drip down, sprinkle, baste 1153, c 1400.

deher/editatio, disherison, dispossessing 1200; **-edatus,** disinherited c 1150; **-edito** (†-ito), to disinherit c 1150; *cf.* DISHERED

dehonor/atio c 700. c 1290, 1385, **-estas** 1376, dishonour.

dehortativus, dissuasive (gram.) c 790.

dehospit/o c 1250, 1381, **-or** (*dep.*) c 1170, c 1252, to dislodge, dispossess.

deia, *see* 1 **daya.**

deiciatus, *see* **decius.**

deicio, *see* DEJECT

deicius, *see* 1 **discus.**

dei/cus c 1150, c 1375, **-ticus** c 1200, †**deacus** c 1250, divine; **-cola,** Christian 8c., c 1000. 1088, c 1450; **-datorius,** almoner 1558; **-fer,** God-possessed 793. c 1100.

deific/atio, apotheosis c 870. c 1250, c 1255; **-ativus,** making for godliness c 870; **-e,** in divine nature, divinely 793, 11c.; **-us,** divine c 1000, 1006. 1066, 1432; **-o,** to deify, make divine (eccl.); to offer to God c 740.

deiform/itas, likeness to God c 870. c 1238, c 1500; **-is,** Godlike c 870. 1166, c 1500; **-iter,** in a Godlike manner c 870. 1344, c 1375.

deigerus, uplifting God c 870.

deila, *see* **dalus.**

deiloquus, divinely inspired 793.

deimer/icius, -etus, *see* **damus.**

deincumbro (ecclesiam), to vacate (by cancelling a presentation) 1278.

deinotes, cleverness (δεινότης) 1344.

deinstauro, to unstock 13c.

deint/er (*prep.*), between 1121, c 1204; (*adv.*) 1300, **-ro** c 1172, c 1197, ***-us** c 1115, p 1377, (from) within.

deinvadio, to redeem from pledge (Norm.) 1203.

Deipara, mother of God c 1520, 1549.
deir/a, -ia, *see* **1 daya.**
deisius, *see* **1 discus.**
deitero, to continue a 1150.
deiticus, *see* **deicus.**
deividus, one who sees God c 865. c 1200;
(*adj.*) bringing a vision of God c 1090.
dei/werc-, -worc-, *see* DAYWERC
deject/io, dejection, detriment (astr.) a 1200;
-or, evictor c 1258; **deicio me,** to abase
oneself c 1180.
dejejuno me, to break fast c 1266, c 1330.
dejer/o, (?) to commit perjury 1303, 1310;
degero, *for* **-o,** to swear c 1200.
dejudic-, *see* DIJUDIC
dejuxta, approximately c 1200; near by 1260.
dekarnelo, degarnelo, to strip of battlements 1250.
delacero, *see* **dilaceratio.**
delanguidus, enfeebled c 1184.
delanio, delamo, *see* **dilanio.**
delapid-, *see* DILAPID
delaqueo, to disentangle 1220.
delassatio, weariness 1537.
delat/io, carrying, bearing a 1190, 1622; **d.**
armorum 1289, c 1340, **dilatio** a. c 1340;
-ivus, transmissive c 1270; **-or,** bearer
p 1330, 15c.; **-rix,** informer (*f.*) c 1160,
13c.; **-ura,** (reward for) laying information
c 1115; **-o,** to take away, steal 1361; **dilato,**
to delate, inform against 1509; *cf.* DEFER; *see*
also dilat-
delatro, to snarl, rage 1444.
delayum, delay 1383.
delea, *see* **dalus.**
delebiliter, delectio, *see* **deletio.**
delect/amen 1043, **-abilitas** c 1250, **-antia**
c 1366, delight; **-ativus,** delightful 13c.;
-ator, delighter c 1343; **dilectabilis,** *for*
-abilis, 838; **dilecto,** *for* **-o,** c 1335.
delectus, *see* DELICT; DILECT
deleg/atio, delegation c 1170, 1364; safe-
keeping 1296; **-atia,** dispute referred to
delegate 1303; **-ativus,** delegative a 1250,
1427; **-atorie,** as or for a delegate c 1397;
-atorius, acting as delegate c 1397; **-atus,**
delegate 1200, a 1564; **judex -atus,** ecclesiastical judge c 1210, 1684.
delegiatus (†diligiatus), outlaw or person
not law-worthy c 1115.
delenio, to soothe, flatter: **delin/io** 12c.,
1518, **dilinio** c 1362; **-itio,** soothing a 1250,
‡1483.
del/etio a 1228, a 1428, **delectio** 14c., dele-
tion, destruction; **-ebiliter,** delibly 1326.
1 deliber/atio, *deliverance c 1140, 1461;
delivery, handing over, feoffment 1086,
1543; disposal c 1150; **d. gaole,** gaol
delivery 1285, a 1564; **diliberatio,** *for* **d.,**
deliberation c 1300, 1425; **moneta -abilis,**
money fit for issue p 1280; **-ate,** deliberately
c 1250, 1417; **-ator,** counsellor 12c.; one
who hands over c 1290; **-atorius,** concerned
with deliberation 12c., 1684; **indutie**
-atorie (†-atorii), interval for deliberation c 1196, c 1400; *cf.* vacatio; **-o**
*c 1155, 1461, **dilibero** c 1400, to deliver,
liberate; *1086, c 1553, **delivero** 1448,
1518, to deliver, hand over; to quit (a
place) 1291; (with *inf.*) to decide c 1100,

c 1212; **d. gaolam,** to deliver gaol (by
trying prisoners) 1220, c 1470; **d. me de,**
to get rid of 1271; **-or de,** to be delivered
of (a child) 1361.
2 deliberatio (corticis), stripping off of bark
1330.
delibutio, anointing c 1000. c 1193, c 1200.
delic/atio c 1283, **-acia** 1434, **-iositas** c 1283,
‡15c., delicacy, luxury; **-ie,** dainties, provisions c 1000; **dilicie** 7c., **dilicium** c 1336,
for **-ie, -ium;** **-abilis** a 1275, **diliciatus**
c 550, delightful; **-aciter,** delicately c 1190;
dilicatus, *for* **-atus,** c 1410; **-atulus,**
effeminate 1588, 1608; **-iose,** luxuriously,
ornately c 1188, 15c.; moderately (without
undue effort) 1242; **-iosus,** luxurious c 793.
c 1180, 1528; **†-ior,** more luxurious c 1450;
-ior, to delight in c 1200, 1562.
delic/ie: flos -iarum 1388, c 1443, **folicia**
-iarum c 1503, flower-de-luce (fleur-de-lis).
delict/um, sin of omission, transgression:
†-a c 1197, **delectus** c 1200, **dilictum** 1278,
1313, **deliquium** 11c.; **-us,** abandoned
c 1242, 1290; **delinqu/ens,** delinquent 7c.,
8c. c 1250; **-o** (with *dat.*), to sin against
8c. c 1380; *see also* DILECT
deligo, *see* **disligo.**
delilio, to rob of whiteness or purity c 1184,
c 1250.
delin/itus, (?) *for* **-eatus,** marked, depicted
1298; *see also* **delenio.**
1 delir/us, crazy: **diliramentum,** *for*
-amentum, delirium 15c.
2 ‡delirus (*i.e.* delyrus), out of tune c 1219,
1483.
delit/escentia, concealment 1552; **-eo** a 1155,
c 1376, **dilitesco** c 1470, to lie hidden;
-eo me, to hide c 1450.
delivero, *see* DELIBER
†della, (?) dell, *or* dole (Sussex) c 1285; *cf.*
dalus.
delphi/anus (delf-), of or for dolphins c 550;
dolphinus, dolphin (G.) c 1305.
Delphin/us 1535, **Dalphinus** c 1422, **Dol-**
phinus 1414, 16c., Dauphin; **-a, Dal-**
phinella, Dauphiness 1461; **-atus** 1535,
Dolphinatus a 1446, status of Dauphin;
-ensis, member of the Dauphin's forces
1421; **-ianus,** of the Dauphin 1535.
delta, book c 870.
deluc-, *see also* DILUC
†delucior, (?) *for* **dilutior,** paler c 1500.
delugeo, to deplore c 1500.
delus/io, delusion c 870. 1169, c 1343; **-or,**
scoffer, deceiver 7c., c 793. c 1185, c 1437;
-orius, delusive a 1205, 1609; **-orie,** in
mockery 1344.
delv/a a 1540, **-um** 12c., pit; **†-o,** (?) to
delve, cut 1269.
delyrus, *see* **2 delirus.**
dema, body (δέμας) 10c.
demagogus, *see* **democratia.**
demain-, deman-, *see* DOMIN
***demand/a** a 1170, 1564, **-um** c 1456, 1494,
demaunda 1587, **-atio** 1467, 1684, demand, claim; **in -a,** in dispute 1258;
-abilis, liable to be claimed a 1452; **-ans,**
claimant (leg.) c 1280; **-o,** to demand,
claim, summon 8c., 811. c 1115, a 1564; to
give notice, tell 8c. c 1130, 1305; **d. effectui**

F

1347, **d. executioni** c 1273, 1684, to put into effect.

demanicatus, sleeveless c 1184.

demartyrizo, to martyr c 1325.

dematur/esco, to lose maturity c 1184; **-o,** to make haste c 1414.

demedio, to put out of the way, kill c 1115.

demembr/atio, dismembering, mutilation (of person) c 1200, c 1220; (of empire) c 1188; **-atus,** crippled 1389; **-o,** *to dismember, mutilate (person or image) 12c., 1461; (estate, etc.) c 1200, 1536; cf. **dismembro.**

dememini, to forget c 1184.

demen-, see also DOMIN

demensus, having elapsed 1299; **demeti/o,** for **-or,** to measure c 1362; see also DIMENS

dementatio, madness 9c. 1344; leading astray 8c.

dementior (dep.) 1300, **dimentior** 1339, to give the lie to.

†demer/go, (?) for **-eo,** to earn 9c.

demericius, see **damus.**

***demer/itum,** demerit, fault a 1228, 1588; **-itorie,** faultily c 1180, p 1300; **-itorius,** undeserving, blameworthy p 1300, c 1444; **-eo** c 1160, p 1348, **-eor** (dep.) c 1160, c 1340, to deserve ill, to forfeit.

demersio, immersion, drowning c 793. 15c.; **dimergor,** to be sunk c 700. c 1150, c 1370.

demetio, see **demensus.**

demico, see **dimico.**

demigratio, decease 14c.

demin-, see DIMIN; DOMIN

demiss-, demitt-, see DIMISS

demivirgat/a, half-yardland 1381; **-arius,** tenant of half-yardland 1381; cf. **semivirgata.**

dem/ocratia, democracy c 1343, c 1434; **-ocraticus,** democratic c 1608; **-agogus,** demagogue c 1343; **-iurgus,** speaker (of Parliament) 1555; **-us,** policeman (δῆμιος) c 1433.

demol/itio, destruction: **-utio** 1480; **-itor,** destroyer c 1432; **-io,** to demolish, destroy c 865. c 1100, c 1476.

***demon/, -ium,** evil spirit, pagan god (eccl.); **-iacus** c 793, 10c. 1124, 15c., **-ialis** 12c., c 1250, of demons; **-iosus,** (adj.) possessed by demons c 730; (subst.) demoniac c 730. a 1186, c 1400; **-iaca,** demoniac possession 13c.

demonach/us, a non-monk 1472; **-or,** to make unsuitable for a monk c 1170.

demonstr/atio, muster (of troops) 1373; statement of claim (leg.) a 1564; **d. foreste,** view, regard c 1185; **d. quia,** proof of existence (log.) p 1300; **d. potissima,** conclusive proof p 1300; **-abilis,** demonstrable 12c., a 1361; **-abilitas,** demonstrability c 1361; **-ative,** by way of demonstration c 700. c 1173, c 1363; **-ator,** demonstrator (log.) 13c., a 1280; **-o,** (?) to claim a 1100.

demor/atio, delay c 1090, c 1434; **-o,** to remain, delay 1294, 1558; **-or** (dep.), to dwell c 730. c 1130, 1439.

demordeo, to slander c 1200.

‡demotinus lapsus, sudden death 1652.

dempsus, see DENS

demptio, removal 990.

demulgo, see DIVULG

demultiplic/atio, decrease in space c 1360; **-o,** to decrease in space c 1360.

demulto, to despoil c 1376.

demundo, to cleanse 1312.

demus, see **democratia.**

demutatio, translation (of saint) a 1125.

denachia, Danish axe 1250; see also **hachia.**

Dena/gildum, -laga, etc., see **Danus.**

denarium, see **deverium.**

1 **denar/ius** *c 831, c 1027. c 1070, c 1502, **denerius** c 1236, penny; *1166, 1373, (?) **†-ium** (G.) 1253, 1316 (cf. **deverium**), money, cash; c 1100, 1324, **d. ponderis** 1425, pennyweight; **non d.** c 1256, 1390, **nunquam aliqui d.** 1365, **d. nullus** 1460, not a penny (i.e. nothing); **ad -ios,** at the expense c 1225, 1264; **-ius argenti** 1372; **d. aureus** 1275, 1487, **d. auri** 1270; **d. animarum,** 'soul-penny' (contributed by guild brethren for masses) 1389; **d. Sancti Benedicti** (mon.) c 1397, c 1423; **d. Calesie,** payment for exporting wool elsewhere than to the Calais staple 1382; **d. capitalis,** head-penny, chevage 1279, 1296; **d. complicatus** a 1270, c 1280, **d. plicatus** 1275, 1290, penny paid as oblation (eccl.); **d. coronatus** c 1400; **d. crucis,** tithe-money in aid of crusades 1254; **d. Dei,** God's penny, earnest-money c 1240, c 1335; **d. de duobus,** twopenny piece 1517; **d. fumalis,** reek-penny 1356; **d. missalis,** mass-penny c 1218, 1433; **d. molendini,** treth melen (W.) 1505; **d. de Murcia, de musce,** see **musca; d. papalis** c 1310, **d. Beati Petri** c 1155, c 1501, ***d. Sancti Petri** c 1080, 1531, **d. Rome** 13c., Peter's pence, Rome-scot; ***d. tertius,** third penny of county 1086, c 1437; **-ii** (pl.) **sicci,** hard cash 1269, 1295; ***-iata** a 1135, 1555, **-ata** 1217, 1448, ***-iatus** 1233, a 1564, **-atus** 1291, 1348, **deneriata** c 1185, pennyworth, penny-rent; **-iata** (n. pl.) 1461, **-ata** 1290, goods sold retail (Fr. denrées); **gallus -iatus,** penny-cock 1408; **-iatim,** at a penny each 1432, 1438; **-ata** 1247, **-iata** 1248, **denerellus** 1331, **danerellus** 1309, **denerel,** 1/6 (or 2/11) bushel (C.I.).

2 **denarius,** decalogue c 1180, c 1450.

denascor, to be born of c 1400.

denaturo, to behave degenerately a 1408.

denbera, see **denna.**

‡dendrolibanum, rosemary 14c., 1483.

deneg/atio, denial, refusal c 730. 11c., c 1564; **denico,** for **-o,** to deny 1290, 1310; **denio,** to throw out an indictment (leg.) c 1290.

Denescha, see **hachia.**

†denichilo, to annul 1461.

denig/ratio, blackening, dyeing black a 1250, a 1446; ***denigration,** defamation c 1204, c 1482; **†-er,** black 1214; **-resco,** to grow black a 1270, 1370; **-ro,** to blacken, dye black a 1250, 1477; to darken, sadden 1436, 1461; *c 1160, a 1564, **dinigro** 1370, to defame, disgrace.

denio, see DENEG; **dennagium.**

denique, for **autem,** c 1000.

deniz/atio, denization 1608, 1682; **-o,** to denizate, naturalize 1608.

***den/na,** dene, denn (Kent) 1086, 1535;

-bera (?) 8c. 12c., **danbera** (?) 12c., swine-pasture; *see also* **duna.**
***den/nagium,** dunnage (naut.) 1298, 1377; **-no** 1300, **-io** 1351, to stow.
‡**denod/atio,** solution (alch.) 1652; **-o,** to untie c 1250, c 1370; to solve, elucidate c 1180, 13c.; *cf.* **disnodo.**
***denomin/atio,** naming, nomination a 1110, c 1416; **-abilis** c 1270, a 1323, **-alis** c 1270, distinguishable by name; **-anter** c'1362, **-ative** c 865. a 1110, a 1250, by derivation; **-ativus,** denominative, derivative a 1110, c 1362; **-ator,** denominator (math.) 15c., 1686; **-atus,** above-mentioned a 1125; **-o,** to name, nominate, appoint 1086, 1438.
denosco, *see* DINO
denot/atio, expression, profession 1173; †note of proceedings (leg.) 1205; †**-e,** by way of description or definition c 1363.
dens, tooth, tine (of harrow) 1364; ‡**d. caballinus,** henbane (bot.) 15c.; **d. leonis** ‡14c., 1629, (?) **dent/alio** a 1250, dandelion; **-es** (*pl.*), grating 1344; **invitis -ibus** 1282, 1320, **malegratis -ibus** 1278, reluctantly, against one's will; ‡**-aria,** "tooth iron" 1483; ‡pyrethrum (bot.) 14c.; **-atio,** blazon dancetty (her.) c 1595; **-iculatio,** indenting (her.) c 1595; **-atus,** dancetty c 1595; **-iculatus,** indented (her.) c 1595; ‡**-ile,** *for* **-ale,** share-beam c 1200; **-iloquus, -ilocus,** *for* **-ilegus,** spitting out teeth c 1437; ‡**-o,** "great-toothed" 1570; **-osus,** biting 1167; toothed c 1362, ‡1483; **-rix,** tooth-pick 1450; **-ura** 1470, **cyrograffum -atum** c 1290, indenture; **-o,** to fit with a point 1279, 1297.
dens/itas silve, thicket 940, 955. 12c., 15c.; **-ilitas,** thick growth a 1350; †**-io,** thickness a 1275; **-anter,** frequently c 1150; **-atim** c 1188, **-im** c 1190, in masses; **dempsus,** *for* **-us,** c 1250, 1421; **-esco,** to grow thick, condense c 685. c 1212; (fig.) c 1200.
dentr/ix, pike *or* (?) dog-fish 1399, a 1564; **-iculus,** pickerel ‡c 1440, 1466; *see also* **dens.**
denud/atio, stripping, exposing 13c., 15c.; clearing (of quarry) 1371; revelation c 1188; **-o,** to strip off 1461; to reveal, declare 7c.
denumer/ator, counter, teller 1398; **-o,** to enumerate c 1100, 14c.
denunti/atio, publishing marriage-banns c 1223, 1236; **-ativus** c 1248, a 1270, **-atorius** c 1545, 1684, declaratory; **-ator** denouncer, informer 1289, 1382; **-o,** to renounce c 1279; *see also* **calculus.**
denuo, to reject, contradict c 1270.
denus, tenth, the tenth c 1190, c 1470.
denutrio, to deprive of nourishment 13c.
Deo-, *see also* **Deus.**
deoblig/atio, release p 1381; **-o,** to release from obligation c 1357, 1378.
deobstru/ctio, removal of obstruction c 1340, 1620; **-o,** to free from obstruction 1279, 1425.
deobstup/atio, freeing from obstruction 1375, c 1400; **-o,** to free from obstruction 1368, 1387; (?) to block up 1313; *cf.* **deastupo.**
deoculo, to blind c 1450.
deoner/atio, discharge (of debit) 1482; c 1376, **deonustatio** c 1377, disburdening; **-o,** to discharge (on account) a 1300, c 1400.
deopinor, to change one's mind about a 1205.

deoppil/atio, freeing from obstruction 13c.; **-ativus,** deobstruent (med.) a 1250; **-o,** to free from obstruction a 1250, 13c.; *see also* DEPIL
***deordin/atio,** disorder, disobedience, deviation 1267, 1457; **-ate,** in disorder c 1450; **-o,** to disorder, derange c 1270, p 1300; to lead astray c 1290; to disordain, deprive of rank or holy orders c 1250, c 1425.
deornatus, adorned c 1330.
deorsum (*prep.*), below a 1525; **d. pono,** to take down c 1330; *cf.* **jusum.**
deoscul/atio, kiss c 1193; **-atorium,** pax (eccl.) 1368, 1498; **-o,** *for* **-or,** to kiss 10c. c 1250, c 1362.
depallio, to reveal c 1250.
‡**depanno,** to unclothe 1483.
deparco, to rescue (cattle) from pound 1276.
‡**deparieto,** "to cast down walls" 1483.
depart/itio, dissolution (of Parliament) c 1320; **-itus,** particoloured 1421; **-io,** to depart, withdraw 15c.; to disperse c 1360; c 1308, **-ior** c 1125, to distribute; (of Parliament) c 1320.
depas/tio 1239, **-centia** 1378, **-tus** 15c., grazing down, depasturing; **-tor,** consumer c 1400; **-tus,** emaciated a 1300; **-catus,** *for* **-tus,** fattened by grazing 1488, a 1564; **-co,** to feed, nourish 1299; **-sor** (*1st conj.*) 1364, *for* **-cor,** to feed on; **-turo,** to depasture c 1437, 1567.
depatrio, to leave home c 1452.
depatrisso, to be unlike one's father a 1205, c 1456.
***depauper/atio,** impoverishment c 1250, 1559; **-ator,** impoverisher c 1295; ***-o,** to impoverish a 1185, c 1540.
depeculatio, plundering c 1546.
depejoro, to worsen, damage a 1228.
depend/entia, dependence (log.) c 1270, c 1300; balance of debt (Sc.) 1461, 1539; dependency (mon.) 1495, 1528; 1399, a 1452, **-ens** 1495, **-icium** c 1400, c 1440, dependency, appurtenance; **-entia** (litis), pendency (leg.) 1336; (?) 1410, **-entium** 1444, hanging, pendent altar-frontal; **-enter,** dependently 1238, c 1361; **-eo,** to be dependent (mon.) c 1336, c 1458; 1261, c 1470, **-o** 1236, to be pending.
depennatus, plucked, stripped of plumage a 1408.
deperd/itio c 1240, 1628, **-itura** 1573, 1617, **-itum** 1195, 1577, loss, destruction; **-ibilis,** liable to loss p 1300, a 1361; **-itivus,** destructive a 1350; **-ens,** loser 1230.
depersono, to degrade a 1260; to slander 1240; *cf.* **dispersono.**
depessulo, to unbolt 13c., 14c.
depicatus, coated with pitch c 1000.
depict/io 1397, 1490, **-ura** 1242, 1308, painting; **d. agie crucis,** sign of the cross 971; **-o,** to paint 1354; **depingo,** to sign, make the sign of the cross 949, 960. 12c.; to put in writing 15c.; to decorate with painting a 1210, c 1500.
‡**depignero,** to redeem a pledge 1483.
depil/atio c 1190, a 1250, †**deoppilatio** a 1250, loss of hair; spoliation 1385, c 1443; **d. ovium** 1300; **-atorium,** depilatory a 1250, 14c.; **-atius,** more baldly (fig.) a 1295.

deplacito, to establish a claim to c 1077, 1086.
deplaco, to calm 9c.
deplico, to unfold 1295; to fold back c 1370.
deplois, *see* **diplois.**
deplor/atrix, deploring (*f.*) c 1196, c 1300; **-abiliter,** deplorably 1541.
deplumo, to strip of plumage, pluck, despoil 1143, c 1470; to plume (falc.) a 1150.
depon-, *see* DEPOSIT
deport/um, common-room (mon.) 1298, 1506 (*cf.* DISPORT); favour 1275; **-atio,** leading (chosen candidate) to altar (eccl.) 13c.; **-ator,** bringer c 1332; **-o,** to wear 1222; to bear (a fiscal due) c 1110; to endure 1422; to favour 1274; †**d. classica,** (?) to toll c 1280.
deposit/io, depositing (of valuables) 1219, c 1260; taking down, dismantling 1447, 1470; putting off, discarding c 1125, 15c.; lowering of pitch (mus.) c 1296; (commemoration of) burial (of saint or benefactor) 760. c 1100, c 1505; deposition from office 1102, c 1370; *deposition, testimony (leg.) a 1300, c 1475; deposition, masters' testimony to fitness of doctorand (ac.) a 1350, c 1516; refutation (log.) p 1347, a 1350; **d. carnalis,** laying aside earthly life c 900; **-icius,** given in deposit 1516; **-or,** sewer, waiter at table 1489, 1504; c 1387, **-orius** c 1382, 1533, official in charge of funerals (mon.); **-arium** 1301, **-orium** 13c., storeroom, safe; **-a,** anchoress c 1223; **-um,** mortal remains 14c.; temporary preserve for live fish 1254; deposit, thing deposited for safe keeping 1218, c 1317; **in -o** 1233, c 1556, **in -o salvo** 1291, c 1320, in safe keeping; **depon/ibilis,** deposable 1521; **-ens,** deponent (leg.) 1310; **-o,** to deposit for safe keeping c 1232, 1492; to bury c 730; to do away with, kill a 1115; *to depose from office c 1080, 1549; to give up (an opinion) c 1343; to depose in evidence (leg.) c 1218, c 1597; to depose (ac.) a 1350, 15c.; to oppose, refute (log.) c 1370; **d. actionem** c 1257, **d. querelas** 1262, 1301, **d. querimonias** c 1325, to lodge complaints (leg.).
depossum, to be able 1325; †to prevail in, win c 1180.
depost, *see* **de.**
depotesto, to deprive of power c 1193.
deprav/atio, slander 1378; **-ator,** slanderer c 1172, 1380; **-o,** to slander 1378, c 1450.
deprec/atio c 793. a 1125, 1461, **-atus** c 1250, 13c., prayer, entreaty; boonwork a 1128; **-abilis,** open to entreaty a 1230, c 1337; **-atoria,** written request c 1250, 1301; **-atorie,** by way of entreaty 1200, c 1363; *-atorius, deprecatory, intercessory 793. c 1180, c 1408; **-atoria** (*pl.*) 1350, ‡**-ule** c 1440, beads; **-o,** *for* **-or,** to pray for, beseech c 1000. c 1189, c 1323.
*deprED/atio, plundering c 900. c 1070, c 1470; **-ate,** in a plundered condition c 1070; *-ator, plunderer c 1230, 1461; **-atorius** a 1205, c 1250, **-ativus** c 1250, **-atrix** (*f.*) 1620, predatory, rapacious; †**-itus,** plundered 1339; *-o, to plunder, despoil 760, c 793. c 1150, a 1564.
depredico, to preach against, cry down c 1165.

deprehensor, captor c 1102, c 1250; **deprenso,** to capture 13c.
depress/io, *oppression, injury c 730. c 1150, 15c.; depression (astr.) 1267; **-ivus** c 1250, deprimens c 1340, burdensome, oppressive; **-or,** oppressor 6c. c 1365; **deprimo,** to oppress 12c., c 1380.
depretio, to lessen the value of, cheapen 8c. c 1125, c 1170.
depriv/atio, deprivation, deposition (eccl.) c 1520, 1686; **-ativus,** privative a 1360; **-o,** to deprive, depose (eccl.) 1267, c 1520.
depromo, to disclose, declare c 550. c 1190, 15c.
deprope, near 1290, a 1452.
depublico, to publish, advertise 12c.
depulver/o c 1212, **-iso** 1421, to brush, rub down (a horse).
depur/atio, purification, refining a 1200, 1620; **-ativus** c 1215, a 1250, **-atorius** a 1250, purifying; **-o,** to purify, refine c 1200, 1622; to clear, discharge (of debt) 1284.
†**depurpuratus,** (?) dyed purple 10c.
*deput/atio, assignment, appointment c 1332, c 1478; body of delegates (*coll.*) 1433; **-atia,** †**-atus,** deputyship (Calais) 1533, 1552; **-atorie** (*sc.* **littere**), letters of appointment 1312; *-atus, deputy c 793. 1369, c 1550; **dominus D.** (Ir.) 1556; *-o, to depute, appoint c 1090, 1586.
dequadro, to change from square shape 13c.
dequoquo, *see* **decoctio.**
deratio-, deraino, dereino, deresno, *see* DIRATIO
deraubo, *see* DEROB
†**dereddo,** to give up c 1198.
derego, *see* DEROG
deregulo, to disorder c 1200.
derelicta, relict, widow c 1118.
dereptio, *see* **direptio.**
derevestio, to take off vestments c 1330.
derevoco, to revoke, cancel c 1306.
derige, *see* DIRECT
deris/ibilis, ridiculous 1267, c 1340; *-orie a 1155, c 1540, **dirisorie** c 1400, derisively; **-orius,** derisive c 1250, c 1444; **-ui habeo,** to deride 8c.
deriv/atio, overflowing 1268; **-ativus** 15c., **dirivativus** 939, derived, effluent (of streams); **causa -ativa** c 1250; **dirivo,** *for* **-o,** to derive, draw off c 793. c 1125, 1518.
derob/ator, robber a 1350; **d. viarum,** highwayman 1453; **-oratio,** *for* **-atio,** robbery 1465; **-o** c 1310, 1392, **deraubo** 1313, to rob; *cf.* DISROB
derog/atio a 1090, 1462, **-amen** 1367, **-atoria** 1462, 1519, detraction, detriment; **-ativus** c 1378, c 1412, **-atorius** c 1306, c 1470, **dirogatorius** 1543, derogatory; **-atorie,** in derogation 1502; **-o** a 1090, 1549, †**derego** 1317, to derogate, detract; to obtain, win a 1408.
†**deronicum,** (?) *for* **doronicum** *or* **veronica** (bot.), a 1250.
derta, impetigo (med.) a 1250, ‡15c.
derudo, to decry 12c.
deruo, *see* DIRU
des-, *see also* **dis-**
desainum, *see* **decenna.**

desampar/atio, surrender of possession (G.) 1289; **-o, dezampero,** to surrender, resign (Fr. *désemparer*) (G.) 1289.

desca, *see* 1 discus.

descandalizo, to cause to stumble c 570.

descen/sio 815. a 1233, **-sus** a 1250, descension (astr.); ‡dreg 1652; **-sus** c 1236, 1430, **decensus** 1213, 1279, **-dere** (*subst.*) a 1564, descent, inheritance; **d. nasi,** bridge of nose c 1330; **discensus,** *for* **-sus,** descent c 1250, 1461; **-sive,** by (hereditary) descent 1313; ‡**-sorium,** furnace in which distilled fluid descends 1652; **-dens,** descendant 15c.; **-do** c 1185, 1430, **decendo** 1205, 1292, **discendo** 1461, 1583, to descend (of rights, property); to come to moorings (naut.) c 1320; to bring down 1257; †to die (? *for* discedo) a 1250; to change the subject, advert to c 1343, c 1411; (?) to draw an inference c 1357; **d. in genera,** to pass from absolute to categories c 1300.

descepto, *see* disceptatio.

descerno, *see* DISCRET

descicio, descindo, *see* DECIS; **discissio.**

descio, to unlearn c 1200, a 1205.

descript/io, tax, levy c 1150, c 1173; census c 1362; definition c 1343; description (geom.) 1686; **d. Anglie,** Domesday survey 1087; **discriptio,** *for* **-io,** description 1444; **discriptiuncula,** drawing c 700; **-ibilis,** describable (geom.) 1267, c 1360; **-ive,** by definition c 1283, 1378; **discriptor,** delineator 6c.; **-rix** (*f.*), describing (geom.) 1686; **describo,** to blazon (her.) p 1394; **discribo,** to describe, draw c 700.

descus, descum, *see* 1 discus.

desecro, to unfrock (eccl.) 1517.

desen-, *see* decenna; dissensio.

desepelio 1231, †**disspellio** 1314, to disinter.

deser/tio, abandonment 1285, 1392; **d. appellationis,** dropping an appeal (leg.) 1684; **-tatio,** devastation c 1300; **-tiva,** woman separated from her husband c 1102; **-tive,** into the desert 1378; **-tum,** hermitage (Ir.) a 615; **d. regis,** king's waste, *diffeith brenhin* (W.) a 1300; **-o** (with *inf.*), to fail c 1250, c 1343; **d. appellationem,** to drop an appeal c 1593, 1684; **d. jus** 1315, **dissero jus** 1335, to deny justice; **d. placitum,** to abandon a plea 1086; **dissero,** *for* **-o,** to desert c 1316; *see also* DISERT

deser/vitio, religious observance, service 7c.; officiating (eccl.) c 1545; **-tum,** desert, merit 1220; **-viens,** servant 1379, 1429; **-vio,** to give feudal service 1086, 1166; to officiate (eccl.) a 1128, c 1470; to serve out (food) 1326, 1363; c 1115, 1581, †**-vo** 12c., to deserve, earn; **-vio de,** to provide, pay (Sc.) 1329, 1389; **d. pro,** to serve for, be used for c 1427; **d. terram,** to hold land by service 1086, 12c.

desevero, to remove, dismiss 1425.

desevio, to plunder 6c.

deseysio, *see* DISSAIS

†**desiando,** (?) *f.l.* for **defraudo,** c 1322.

desicc/atio, drying up c 1115, c 1362; drainage 1277; **-abilis,** liable to be dried up p 1300; **-ativus,** drying a 1250, 1307; ‡**-atrix,** "kiln wife" 15c.; **-o,** to drain 1279, 1329.

desicio, *see* decisio.

*desicut, as, as if, whereas, inasmuch as 1137, 15c.

desider/ium, (?) loving-cup c 1334; **-abilis** 8c. a 1350, **desirabilis** c 1223, 1347, **-andus** 8c., desirable, lovable; 8c. c 1458, **-iosus** c 1180, desirous, eager, loving; **-abiliter,** desirably, lovably 8c. c 1250; 1312, c 1380, **desirabiliter** c 1407, ***-anter** 8c. a 1100, 1438, **-iose** c 1250, c 1397, eagerly; **-antissime** 1169, †**-atissime** 1328, most eagerly; **-antissimus,** most eager c 1070; **-andissimus,** most desirable 1439; **-ativus,** concerned with desire 8c. a 1250, 1344; **-ator,** desirer, seeker after 1079, 14c.; **desiro** c 1300, **disidero** 1545, *for* **-o,** to desire; **-o *** (with *inf.*) 8c. c 1130, c 1465, **d. quod** c 1470, **d. ut** c 1320, to desire; **d. ad, in,** to yearn for 9c.

desidium, *see* discidium.

desiduus, *see* DECID

desigillo, to unseal 1290; *cf.* dissigillo.

design/atio, design 1537; **-abilis,** definable c 1270; **-ativus,** significant a 1090, 1292; **-o,** to promise or indicate beforehand c 793.

desilio (a proposito), to withdraw 1268.

†**desilo,** to unhorse, unsaddle 1221.

desin/itio c 1363, **desitio** c 1250, c 1465, **-entia** c 1360, cessation; **-ibilis,** finite 1378.

desipisco, to go mad a 1250.

desir-, *see* DESIDER

desisio, *see* decisio.

desist/entia, cessation c 1256, 1299; **descisto,** *for* **-o,** 1327.

desitio, *see* DESIN

desius, *see* 1 discus.

desligo, *see* disligo.

desma, power to bind (δέσμα) c 950.

*desol/atio 8c. c 1170, 1461, **-amen** c 1440, **-atus** p 1348, desolation, devastation; vacancy (eccl.) 1281; **-abilis,** desolate 1291; **-atius,** more hopelessly c 1190; **-atorie,** devastatingly 1432; **-atorius,** desolate, desert c 1250; **-o,** to devastate c 1343, c 1470.

desolut-, *see* DISSOLU

desonus, *see* DISSON

despect/us * a 1090, 1461, **dispectus** c 730. 1274, 1280, **dispectio** 1294, contempt; a fine c 1102, c 1110; **d. curie,** contempt of court c 1220, 1281; **-abilis** c 1220, **-ibilis** c 793, c 1220, **dispectibilis** c 793, lowly, contemptible; **-issimus,** most despised c 730; **-ive** c 1130, 1347, **-uose** c 1337, 1461, **despicienter** c 1190, contemptuously; **-ivus** c 1380, **-uosus** c 1362, contemptuous; **dispector,** despiser a 1564; **despic/abiliter,** despicably c 1172; †**-ate,** (?) with a feeling of shame 826; **-io** (with *inf.*) 8c. c 1180, 1281, **dispicio** (with *inf.*) c 793, to disdain, decline to.

despens-, *see* DISPENS

desper/atio, despair: **disperatio** c 793; **-abilior,** more desperate c 570; **-abiliter,** desperately c 730. c 1190, c 1400; **-abundus,** despairing 1564; **-ativus,** leading to despair 1344; **-atus** c 1197, 1461, **disperatus** 14c., desperate, hopeless; **dispero** (disparo), *for* **-o,** to despair c 794. 1588.

despic-, *see also* DESPECT

despicor, to glean c 1220, ‡1483.

despina, *see* DESPOT

despoliatio, spoliation: **dispoli/atio** 1447, a 1564; **-o**, to despoil 1274, 1415.

*****despons/atio** 1188, 1543, **disponsatio** c 1353, 1442, **-io** c 1125, c 1250, **-alia** (*pl.*) 1229, 1450, **disponsalia** (*pl.*) 14c., 1452, **-alicia** (*pl.*) 1200, espousals (betrothal or marriage); 'espousal' of a church to a monastery c 1150; *****-o** c 1102, c 1514, **disponso** 1243, c 1540, to espouse, give in marriage 13c.

despot/es c 1340, c 1434, **dispotus** 1438, despot; **despina**, despot's wife (δέσποινα) c 1434; **-ia**, despotism c 1343; **-ice**, despotically c 1340; **-icus** c 1340, c 1434, **dispoticus** p 1300, despotic.

despum-, *see* DISPUM

desquis, *see* 1 discus.

dessero, *see* DISERT

dessima, *see* decima.

destabiliter, *see* DETEST

destemnatus, *see* distainiatus.

destillatio, *see* distillatio.

destina, prop, pillar 8c.; cell c 1090.

destin/atio, sending, delivery c 1185, 1507; **-ator**, providence c 1260, 1344; *****-o** a 1100, c 1450, **distino** c 1267, to send, dispatch.

destinctus, deceased 1204; *see also* DISTINCT

*****destitu/tio** c 1150, 1423, **distitutio** a 1452, destitution, deprivation (eccl.); **-o**, to destitute (eccl.) c 1125, 1427; **distituo**, to deprive 1259; *see also* natura.

destomachatio, angry outburst 1609.

dest/rarius, -erarius, *see* dextrarius.

destrescia, destrict-, destring-, *see* DISTRICT

destribuo, *see* DISTRIB

destruct/io, destruction: **destruxcio** c 1300, **distructio** 811. c 1265, 1498, **-us** 14c.; **-orium**, refutation c 1160; destructive force c 1535; **-ibilis**, destructible 1344; **-ivus**, destructive c 1260, 1378; **destru/o**, to refute c 1110, c 1160; **distruo**, *for* **-o**, to destroy c 1266, 1497.

desturb-, *see* DISTURB

desuadeo, *see* DISSUAS

*****desub/** 12c., 1436, **-tus** c 1180, c 1470, under, from under.

desubit/atio c 1200, **disubitatio** c 1115, sudden action or attack; **-us**, taken by surprise c 1220; **-o**, to attack suddenly, take by surprise c 1115, c 1190.

desubstantiatio, destruction of substance 1610.

desult/orie, irregularly 1620; **-o**, to gallop through (fig.) c 1457.

desuper, (*adv.*) moreover c 793; thereon (on that site) c 1130, 1409; thereanent 1453, 1504; (*prep.* with *acc.*) above c 1180, c 1450; (?) below 1355; (with *abl.*) (?) in accordance with c 1115; **de supra**, over and above c 1440.

desursum, (*adv.*) from above c 1180, 1474; (*prep.*) above c 1260; **d. aqua**, upstream c 1400.

desuto, to caulk 1336.

deswarenno, *see* diswarenno.

detaillum, **vendo per**, a 1190, **v. per detalli/am** 1324, **v. ad -um** 1421, to retail.

detect/io, detection, revelation c 1100, 1684; **-or**, informer 14c.

detego, to conceal 9c.; to cover c 1362.

detegul/atio, untiling, unroofing 1472; **-o**, to untile 1362.

*****deten/tio**, detention, detinue (leg.) c 1115, 1546; **-tatio**, occupation, possession 1295, a 1433; **detinentia**, detainment c 1250; *****-tor** c 1185, c 1520, **-tator** 12c., c 1340, detainer, withholder; **-eo**, *for* **detineo**, to detain c 1218; **detineo**, to ebb 1416.

deterior/atio 1227, 1419, †**-iatio** 1380, †**deteriatio** c 1320, **-amentum** 1207, deterioration, damage; **-o**, to damage *8c. a 1185, c 1452; to deteriorate, suffer damage 1231, c 1332.

determin/atio, completion c 1000; limitation, qualification c 1190, a 1347; determinateness c 1300; direction (math.) 1686; decision c 1080, c 1542; opinion, thesis, 'determination' (ac.) c 1300, c 1534; **-abilis**, determinable, definable c 1205, a 1564; **-abilitas**, determinability p 1300; **-ans** 1414, 16c., **-ator** c 1268, 15c., determining bachelor (ac.); **-ator**, determiner, decider c 1334, c 1566; **-ate** c 1160, c 1443, **-ative** c 1275, 1427, determinately, definitely, finally; **-ativus**, determining 13c., p 1300; **-atus**, definite a 1361; **-o**, to come to an end c 1330; to determine, settle, decide c 1178, 1419; to assert, maintain a thesis 12c., c 1580; to 'determine', graduate (ac.) 1267, 1421; **d. actu** c 1509, **d. actualiter** c 1350 (ac.); **d. compotum**, to settle an account 1533.

†**deterreo**, (?) *for* detero, to crush c 1102.

detest/abilitas, execration 1286; **-abiliter** c 1250, 1478, †**destabiliter** 1386, execrably; **-ator**, swearer c 1180; **-or** (with *inf.*), to hate, be reluctant c 730. c 1250, c 1450.

detestatio, making a will c 1102.

detesticulo, to geld 1330.

detexo, to unweave, fray 13c.

detin-, *see* DETEN

detitulo, to dishonour c 1180.

detogo, to divest c 1185.

detonatio, detonation, report 13c.

deton/sor, coin-clipper c 1178; **-deo**, to tonsure (mon.) 1537.

detorchiatus, plastered 1212.

detorno, to make a return 1608.

detorsio, declension (gram.) c 1210.

detract/io, drawing (of criminals) 1274, c 1293; retractation c 1362; *a 1090, 1494, **-atio** c 1250, c 1434, **detrectatio** 1434, **-us** c 1460, detraction, slander; **detraxio**, *for* **-io**, withdrawal c 1436; **-abilis**, disreputable 1427; **-ivus** c 1340, *****-orius** c 1178, 1387, disparaging, slanderous; **-orie**, slanderously c 1340; **-o** c 1290, 1292, **detrecto** 1279, **detraho** 1221, 1318, to draw (criminals); **-o**, to tear off c 1400; to slander c 1327; **detraho in placitum**, to implead (leg.) c 1236.

†**detrado** (? **detrudo**) **in carcerem**, to imprison 1282.

detrencho, to dig a trench from 1330.

detrimen/tum, harm c 1000; diminution (astr.) c 793; **d. lune** a 1250; †**-dum** c 1025, **detrementum** c 1266, *for* **-tum**, detriment, loss.

detrunc/atio, beheading c 1190, 1267; **-atus**, raguly (her.) c 1595.

detru/sio, banishment, seclusion 1223; **d. in monasterium** 1219; **-do**, to get rid of c 1180; *see also* **detrado.**

‡detuber/atio, "burling" 1483; ‡**-ator, -atrix** (*f.*), "burler" 1483.

detum/eo, to subside 1252; **-esco**, to be humbled c 1185.

†detumulo (*v.l.* **tumulo**), to bury c 1293.

detunico, to reveal c 1250.

deturp/atio, disfigurement a 1200, 1344; **-abilis,** capable of disfigurement 1344; **-ativus,** disfiguring 1344.

deultra, *see* **de ultra.**

Deus Optimus Maximus 1564; **novit D.** 1339, 1340; **dei** (*pl.*), (?) judges c 1115; *see also* **argentum, denarius; pro Deo,** gratis (leg.) 1382; **deuspater,** godfather c 1500; **Deo/amabilis,** dear to God 7c.; ***-danda, -dandum,** deodand 1199, a 1564; **-data** (*pl.*), gifts to God 1406; **deunculus,** minor deity c 800.

deusitatus, deprived by disuse c 1258; **deutor,** to cease to use, disuse c 1258.

deuter/us, second a 1100; ‡**-ogamia,** second marriage 1483; **-onomium** c 1180, 1345, **-onomius** c 1396, **deutronomium** 14c., c 1470, Deuteronomy; **-onomicus,** of Deuteronomy c 1546; **-osis,** repetition c 730.

dev-, *see also* **div-**

†devalo, (?) *for* **divello** *or* **detraho,** p 1330.

devapulo, to be soundly flogged a 1100.

devarium, *see* **deverium.**

devast/atio, devastation 12c., c 1470; **-atrix,** devastating (*f.*) 14c.; **divasto,** *for* **-o,** c 1562.

devectio, carrying away 12c.

deven/tio (ad manum), coming 1586; becoming (a vassal) c 1450; **-io,** to come round, occur 1379; to come into (state or ownership), to belong 1208, 1461; ***to become** (a vassal) c 1115, c 1450; a 615. 1086, 1379, **-ior** 1255, 1583, to become; **d. ad,** to come by, acquire 1295; **d. ad (in) manum** (**manus**), to come into the possession c 1266, 1430.

devenusto, to disfigure c 1160, 15c.

deverium 1259, 1482, (?) **devarium** (†**denarium**) 1316, **diverium** 1315, **devori/a, -um** 1398, 1569, **divorium** 1539, 1562, duty, service due (G. & Sc.); *cf.* DEB

deversus, *see* **de versus;** *cf.* DIVER

devestio, *see* **divestio.**

deveto, *see* DEVIT

devi/atio c 1182, 1620, **-um** 1342, deviation, straying, transgression; †abandonment 13c.; **-ativus,** deviating 15c.; **-o,** to lead astray 1041. c 1125, a 1408.

devid-, *see* DIVID

devigilo, to awake c 1395, ‡1483.

devill/atio, leaving town, 'going down' (ac.) 1424; **-o,** to leave town 1320, 1553; to absent oneself from monastery c 1330, c 1400.

deviolo, to violate a 1408.

1 deviro, to unman 13c.

2 deviro, to strip of verdure c 1435.

devis-, *see* DIVIS

devit/atio, avoidance c 1277; ‡**-abilis,** avoidable 1570; **-o,** to neglect, leave unfulfilled c 1025. c 1102; **deveto** (with *inf.*), (?) *for* **-o,** to refuse 1275.

‡devitio, to defile 1483.

devoc/ator, challenger 8c.; **-o,** to call a 1361; to sue, implead c 1115, c 1404; to disavow, deny c 740. c 1178, 1203; *cf.* DEADVOC, **disadvoco.**

devolatio, flying down 1552.

devol/utio, devolution, transference c 1290, 1549; **d. annorum,** lapse of years a 1564; ‡**-utorium,** yarn-reel 1483; **-vendus,** liable to devolve 1303; **-vo me (de),** to get rid of c 1290, 1389; ***-vor (ad** *or* **in)** c 1200, 1583, **divolvor** 1414, to devolve upon; **divolvo** (**venditioni**), to set apart for c 1290.

devoratio, engulfing c 550, c 1400.

devori/a, -um, *see* **deverium.**

devort-, *see* DIVORT

devot/io, devotion (title) c 1200, c 1350; **-atio,** zeal c 1125, 1245; **-ionalis,** devotional c 1423; **-ivus,** devoted 15c.; ***-e,** devoutly, zealously 760. c 1090, c 1555; **-ius** 12c., c 1450; **-issime** 980. c 1090, c 1432; **-us,** holy (of places) c 1304, 1432; *c 730. c 1090, 1461, **debotus** c 1000, devout; **-ior** 1219, c 1250; **-issimus** c 1250, c 1430; **devoveo,** to renounce c 1190; (with *inf.*) to set oneself to c 793; to refuse c 1250.

devulgo, *see* DIVULG

dewarenno, to remove from status of warren 1227, c 1370; *cf.* **deawarenno, diswarenno.**

dew/legga, -illegga, *see* **douella.**

dexia, (?) success c 950.

dext/er c 700, **-eralis** c 900, **-ralis** c 700. c 1190, 14c., southern (esp. of South Wales, *Deheubarth*); **-eralis** c 550, **-ralis** c 700. c 1360, c 1430, to the right; **-re** 12c., c 1180, **-raliter** c 1430, on the right; **-imus,** rightmost c 950; **-reolum,** *for* **-rale,** bracelet 13c.; **do-ram,** to pay homage 14c.; **-ro,** to turn to the right c 1192; to accompany on the right 1177, c. 1270.

*dext/rarius c 1150, 1453, **-erarius** c 1150, 1224, **destrarius** 1176, p 1341, **desterarius** 1217, **distrarius** c 1346, destrier, warhorse.

dextraura, *see* **straia.**

deyeria, (?) dye-house 1455; **dio,** to dye 1434; *cf.* DAY

dezampero, *see* DESAMPAR

dezenn-, *see* DECENN

dia-, confections (esp. electuaries) of various ingredients: **-aloes,** aloes a 1250; **-ambra** 1322, **diambra** a 1250, ambergris; **-basilicon,** basil a 1250; **-borraginum,** borage a 1250; **-butirum,** butter a 1250; **-calamentum,** calamint a 1250; **-cameron** (?) a 1250, 1322; **-cappare,** capers a 1250; **-castoreum,** (?) castor oil a 1250; **-ceraseos,** cherries a 1250; **-cicoreatum,** chicory a 1250; **-citoniton** a 1250, 1253, **-citoiniton** 1322, quince; **-codion,** poppies, **-costum,** nard, **-cubebe,** cubebs, †**-cucurma** (?), **-cusi,** (?) ivy (κισσός), a 1250; **-culon, -quilotum** 1322, **-kilon** a 1250, **-quilon** 13c., **de aquilon** 1307, *diachylon* (lead plaster containing various plant juices); **-cyminum,** cumin 1241, 1322; **-disnia** (?), a 1250; **-dragagantum** a 1250, **-dragantum** 1253,

1322, tragacanth; **-galanga,** galingale a 1250, 1322; **-gariofilatum,** cloves a 1250; **-gredium,** *for* **-grydium,** scammony a 1250; **-hermis** (?), **-hyssopus,** hyssop, a 1250; **-iris,** iris a 1250; **-lacca,** gum lac a 1250; **dialthea,** marsh mallow a 1250; **-malvatum,** mallow a 1250; **-maratrum,** (?) *for* **-marathum,** fennel a 1250; **-margariton** a 1250, 1322, **deamargariton** 1296, dissolved pearls; **diambra,** *see* **-ambra** *above;* **-micon,** poppy (μήκων) a 1250, 1322; **-milon,** (?) melon a 1250; **-moron,** mulberry a 1250; **diampnis** (?) a 1250 (*see also* DIAMPN); **-musco,** musk 1322; **-nardinum,** nard a 1250; **-nenufaratum,** water-lily a 1250; **dianisum,** anise a 1250; **dianthos,** rosemary a 1250, 13c.; **-olibanum,** frankincense, **-orob[on],** bitter vetch, a 1250; **-papaveris,** poppy a 1250, ‡14c.; **-palma, -phenicon** 1414, †**-patma** 1622, palm oil; **-penidion,** 'pennet' (sugar) 1241, 1322; **-pente,** five ingredients a 1250; †**-pigamum,** (?) *for* **-peganum,** rue a 1250; **-prasium, -prasin'** horehound 13c., ‡14c.; **-prunis,** plums 1241, a 1250; **-pyrethrum,** pyrethrum a 1250; **-reubarb',** rhubarb a 1250; **diaromaticon,** aromatics a 1250; **diarris,** orris-root a 1250, 13c.; **-rrodon,** roses a 1250, ‡15c.; **d. abbatis,** including sandalwood, *etc.* 1265; **-satyrion,** aphrodisiac 12c., ‡1652; **-sene,** senna, **-spermaton,** seeds, a 1250; **-stomaticon,** medicines for mouth 1322; ‡**-strobilion,** (?) pine-cones 15c.; **-tarascos** 1322, **-trascos** 1307, (?) taraxacum; **-tessaron,** four ingredients a 1250; **-trion pipereon,** three kinds of pepper a 1250; **-viola,** violet a 1250; **-zinziberis** a 1250, 1253, **-zingiberos** 1265, ginger.

diabet/es, diabetes (med.) a 1250, ‡14c.; **-icus,** diabetic a 1250, ‡14c.; *cf.* DIAMPN

*****diabol/us** (bibl.), **diabulus** 11c., **zabulus** (eccl.), ‡**zabulon** 1483, the Devil; devil (as term of abuse) c 1193, c 1434; **-ice,** diabolically 1412; **-icus** (bibl.), **diobolicus** 1573, **zabolicus** 6c., **zabulicus** 1019. 14c., **zabuleus** 10c., diabolic.

diaboresis, corrosion (διάβρωσις) a 1250.

diaconios, waxing moon c 1212.

*****diacon/us** 1086, c 1500, **diaco** c 1200, c 1362, **deaconus** 1569, deacon (eccl.); *****d. cardinalis** c 1142, c 1345; **-issa** 760, **-a** c 1250, deaconess; **-alia** (*pl.*), deacon's vestments 1080; **-alis,** diaconal c 1250, c 1400; **-atus** c 1080, c 1450, **-ia** 1610, diaconate, deaconry.

diacrisis, imagery, vivid representation a 1180.

diadem/a, crown, royal power 12c., c 1580; **-a** (*f.*), diadem c 1000; **-atizo** a 1100, c 1150, **-o** c 1180, 1654, to crown.

diaforesto, *see* DEAFFOREST

†**diagnatus,** near relative (nephew) 12c.

diagnosticus, discerning c 865.

diagonius, bend (her.) c 1595.

diale, dial (of clock) 1325, c 1412.

dia/lecticus c 850. a 1110, **-leticus** a 1250, c 1430, logician; **dioleticus,** dialectical c 1365; **-logice,** in dialogue 1461; **-logizo,** to carry on a dialogue 1344.

dialis, *see* DEAL

diam/as 1205, 1622, ‡**-ans** 1483, **-antus** 1310, 1401, **-andus** 1300, 1442, diamond.

diamet/er a 1233, c 1400, **-rum** a 1150, diameter (geom.); **-ralis** c 1270, c 1362, **-rabilis** 1326, **-ricalis** c 1265, **-rus** c 1250, diametrical; **-raliter** c 1233, c 1345, **ex -ro** 1535, 1570, diametrically; **ex -ro,** on the contrary c 950; **-rus,** remnant c 865; ‡"double metre" 15c.; **-ro,** to pierce through the centre a 1270, a 1350.

†**diamicus,** close friend 12c.

diampn/es, -is, a form of diabetes a 1250, c 1470; ‡**-eticus,** diabetic 14c.; *see also* **diano/ia,** reason or significance 1610; **-eticus,** inferential 1610.

diaphan/eitas c 1260, 1620, **-itas** a 1250, †**diaphinitas** c 1500, **-ia** c 1200, **-um** a 1233, ‡1652, †**diafonum** c 1260, transparency; **-us,** transparent a 1250, 1662.

diaphon/ia a 1250, 1326, **-us** 1267, diaphony, (?) two-part harmony.

diaphor/esis, opening of pores a 1250; **-eticus,** sudorific a 1250.

diaphragma, diaphragm, midriff c 1200, c 1370.

diapr-, *see* DIASP

diapsalma, section of a book c 1115.

diarcha, diarch, co-regent c 1090, c 1325.

diaria, *see* 1 **daya.**

dias, *see* **dyas.**

diasima, diaschisma (mus.) c 1200.

diasp/era 1250, **-ra** 1260, **-erum** c 1220, 1345, **-rum** 1204, 1303, **deasperum** 1245, diaper; **-eratus** 1295, 15c., **deasperatus** c 1400, **diapratus** 1358, **diapretus** 1418, a 1447, **diaprus** 1553, diapered.

diaspinetus, *see* **spina.**

‡**diastasis,** disagreement 1483.

diastema, diastem, interval (mus.) a 1250.

diasynthe/sis 1345, (?) **-tica** 1271, (?) †**diasyrtica** c 1160, syntax.

‡**dia/tessadelton** (**-celtatesson**), mercury precipitate 1652.

dia/tessaron c 1180, c 1470, †**-tapsalon** 1248, fourth (musical interval); *see also* **diatetragrammaton,** a plane figure (geom.) a 1250.

‡**diathesis,** disposition 1652.

†**diatigi,** (?) *for* διάταξις, 1344.

*****diatim** a 1100, c 1448, **dietim** c 1193, 1557, daily.

diatonicus, diatonic (mus.) c 1000. a 1200, 1267.

diaulia, *see* **cliaulia.**

dic-, *see also* **disc-**

dica, tally, receipt c 1115, c 1300; (?) gratuity, tip 1301.

dicaciter, *see* **dicentia.**

dic/agium, -delvum, *see* **diketta.**

dic/atio, dedication 7c. c 1620; religious service c 1212; preaching c 1450; ‡**-ator,** preacher 1483; **-ata,** nun c 1362.

dicena, *see* **decenna.**

dic/entia, speech, utterance c 1366; **-aciter,** sarcastically c 1194, 1562; **-ibilis,** expressible 1267, 1516; ‡pleadable 1570; **-tamen,** *****literary style c 550, 1041. c 1100, 16c.; *****a literary composition c 1125, c 1414; motto c 1378, 1423; *****dictate,** precept c 1177, c 1534; 1275, 1276, **-tamentum** 1243, 1276, indictment; **-tativus,** dictating p 1300; authoritative a 1347; **-tator,** scribe, secretary c 1190, c 1327; 12c., 1262, **d. treuge** c 1242, 1260, arbitrator; stylist, composer c 1258, c 1390; **d. canonum** 14c.; **d. carminum** c 1320; **d. rotulorum** 1468; **-tatrix,** dictatress c 550; **-tatus,** dictating c 793; a literary work c 1140; **-tatorius,** stylistic c 1380; **-tio,** declaration, decree c 1115; word c 1200, a 1400; **-tionalis,** concerned with words a 1180, 1344; **-tionaliter,** so far as concerns words 13c.; **-tionalitas,** literary polish c 950; **-tionarius** a 1250, 1610, **dixionarius** c 1500, dictionary; **-titivus,** sophistic a 1180; **-trix,** speaking, vocal (*f.*) c 685. c 1125, c 1553; **-tum,** plea (leg.) 1130; decision, award (leg.) 1199, 1419; **-tum est quia,** it is said that 838; **-to citius,** immediately c 1390; ***-tus,** aforesaid 1150, c 1470; **-ere** (*subst.*), speech 1382; ***-o,** to command, enjoin 1226, 1405; to recite, chant (eccl.) 1293, 1556; **d. warantum,** to vouch to warranty 1292; **-tito,** to dictate c 1000, 11c. 12c., 14c.; **-to,** to compose (in verse or literary prose) 1245, c 1432; **d. judicium,** to pronounce judgement c 1115; **d. privilegium,** to draw up a charter a 1070.

dichotom/ia, dichotomy 1610, 1620; **-us,** halved a 1200, c 1265.

dicidium, *see* **discidium.**

dicra, *see* **dacra.**

dictamnus, dittany (bot.): **diptanus** c 1180, 13c.

dicum, *see* **diketta.**

didasc/alus c 1170, 1317, **-olus** c 1325, 1440, **-ulus** 11c. 1284, ‡15c., **dediscalus** c 1000, teacher; **-alicon** c 1396, **-alion** c 1396, **-ulum** c 1510, name of a book; **-alicus,** instructive c 700; **-ulatus,** office of teacher c 798; ‡**-ulo,** to teach 1483.

didisco, *see* **discentia.**

didragma, didrachm 1381, c 1536.

diduco (causam), (?) to decide c 1200; *cf.* DEDUC

didymus, twin 1620; ‡"doubting" (as epithet of Thomas?) 1483; *cf.* **dindymus.**

diegesis, explanation 1608.

‡**diennium,** biennium 1483.

diereticus, divisive c 870. 1620.

dies, (*s. & pl.*) *epoch, time, lifetime 798, 11c. 1086, c 1460; day of death 1232, 1324; day for appearance in court (leg.) 1196, 1419; day's allowance (of food, *etc.*) 1086; 'day', 'light', pane (of window) 1367; **de die in diem** 1218, c 1503; **Dierum libri,** Books of Chronicles c 1180, c 1546; **liber dierum meorum** (fig.) c 1346; **d. abstinentie,** fast-day c 1472; **d. alta** c 1412, 1486, **d. clara** 1442, **d. magna** 1233, full day, broad daylight; **d. amoris** a 1230, c 1395, **d. concordie** c 1220, **d. concordandi** 1260, **d. pacis reformande** 1219, love-day (leg.); **d. artificialis,** 12 hours or period of daylight a 1200, 1461; **d. baronum,** baronial parliament to decide disputes of vassals (Fr.) 1290; **d. brevis,** early date 1268; **d. caparum,** day when copes are worn (mon.) a 1273; **d. carnalis** 1268,

c 1384, **d. carnis** 1257, c 1283, **d. carnium** c 1266, day when flesh is eaten; **d. Egyptiacus** 12c., a 1250, **d. Pharius** 1252, day of ill omen; **d. extremus** c 1170, **d. generalis** c 870, **d. judicii** 671. c 1090, 1549, **d. Judicis** 1252, **d. magnus** 815, Judgement Day; day of death a 1135; **diem clausit extremum,** name of a writ (issued in 1255) 1301, 1573; **d. fori** (G.) 1283, 1315, **d. mercatus** 1419, **d. mercatorius** a 1564, market day; **d. de gratia,** day of grace c 1290; **d. de la hok',** *see* **hockdies; d. inutilis,** day lost to litigant (leg.) c 1185; **d. legalis,** law-day, sheriff's tourn 1375; **d. legibilis,** lecture day (ac.) c 1350, c 1593; **d. major duplex,** day of major festival (eccl.) c 1412; **d. marchie,** 'march-day', law-day (W.) 1291, 1423; **d. mensis (obitus)** 1412, 1420, **d. mentionarius** c 1452, month's mind (eccl.); ***d. naturalis** solar day (24 hours) a 1200, 1453; **d. operis,** day's work 1185; **d. parliamenti,** 'march-day' (W.) 1248, 1291; **d. piscalis** 1661, **d. piscinus** 1268, **d. piscis, piscium** 1257, 1493, fast-day; **d. saltatus,** leap-day 1307; **d. utilis,** day available for pleading (leg.) c 1185; **d. venialis,** day's indulgence (eccl.) c 1250;

***d. Dominic/a, -us** 1086, a 1564, **d. -alis** 15c., **d. Solis** a 1200, 1585, Sunday; ***d. Lune,** Monday c 1115, 1583; 'Monday-land' 1299 (*cf.* **luna**); ***d. Martis,** Tuesday c 1135, c 1545; ***d. Mercurii** c 1115 c 1590, **d. Marcurii** a 1525, **d. Wodenis** a 1142, Wednesday; ***d. Jovis** c 1115 c 1556, Thursday; **d. J. Sanctus,** Ascension day c 1115; ***d. Veneris,** Friday 1086, c 1590; **d. V. bonus** p 1330, **d. V. sancta** c 1250, 15c., Good Friday; ***d. Sabbati** 1086, 1491, **d. Sabbatinus** c 1370, 1434, **d. Saturni** c 1584, Saturday;

diesco, *to dawn, gleam forth c 1180, a 1452; to spend the day c 1200.

diesis, quarter-tone (mus.) a 1250; (?) (astr.) c 1200.

diet/a, *diet, régime a 1166, c 1325; physical constitution 1378; starvation diet (for refusal to plead) c 1290, 1384; *day's allowance (of food or money) c 1220, 1583; 1464, 1495, **liber -arum** 1450, account of daily expenditure; (space of) a day 12c., 15c.; *day's journey c 1112, 1464; *day's work 1214, 1442; day's output of coin (at mint) p 1280; 'day-work' (measure of land) 1233, 1358; daily office (eccl.) c 1182; diet, assembly c 1232, 1487; **zeta,** dwelling-place, chamber c 685. c 1200, ‡1483; watch-tower or sentry-box a 1142; **-e computate,** journeys accounts (leg.) a 1564; **-arium,** dietary, rule of living c 1283, 1424; **-o,** to diet 1171, 1424; to sojourn c 1325.

dietim, *see* **diatim.**

diff-, *see also* **def-**

diffac/tio (†**diffractio**), mutilation c 1115; **-io** c 1115, 13c., **disfacio** c 1115, 1167, to mutilate; *cf.* **defacio.**

diffam/atio (**defam-**), defamation c 1250, a 1553; ‡**-abilis,** "defamable" 1570; **-ator** 13c., 15c., **-ans** 1684, **-atrix** (*f.*) 1519, defamer; **-atorie,** defamatorily c 1334;

-atorius, defamatory c 1320, 1684; **-atus,** party defamed 1684; **-o,** to defame, accuse, c 1250, a 1553; to spread abroad, rumour c 730. c 1250, c 1362; to celebrate, glorify c 1270, 1438.

diffatigo, to tire out c 1125.

diffedero c 1200, **disfedero** c 1220, **defedero** c 1180, to disunite.

differ/entia, disagreement, contention c 1458; mode of the antiphon c 1230; section of a document 1344; position in decimal notation (math.) a 1150; 1387, a 1446, **defferentia** 1532, 'difference' (her.); **ad -entiam,** in contradistinction a 1200, 1461; **sine -entia,** indiscriminately 1490; **-entialis,** differential (log.) c 1365; **versus -entiales,** verses distinguishing between homonyms c 1296; **-entius,** more excellent c 1080; differently c 1200, 1345; **-entio,** to differentiate c 1360; **-o** (with *gerund* or *inf.*) c 730, **defero** c 1140, 1461, to delay; to distinguish, draw distinctions c 1400, 15c.; to attack or ill-treat c 1115; to carry c 1214, 1431; **d. ab,** to refrain from 1388; *cf.* **dilatio;** *see also* DEFER

diffibulo, to loosen, scatter c 1180, c 1400.

diffic/ultas, burden, tax 836, 867. c 1080; obstruction, troublesomeness 1216, 1265; a difficulty c 1300; **-ilitas,** difficulty 1349, a 1452; **-ulto,** to make difficult, raise objections to a 1361, 1427; *cf.* DEFECT

***diffid/atio** c 1250, 15c., **-entia** p 1330, c 1450, **-uciatio** c 1200, 14c., **deffiamentum** 1360, 'defiance', renunciation of allegiance; **-uciator,** one who declares war c 1200; ***-o** a 1142, c 1450, **defido** c 1150, 1360, **-ucio** c 1180, 15c., to defy (renounce, *or* release from, allegiance).

diffigium, *see* DIFFUG

diffigur/atio, dressing up, disguise 1397; **-atus,** disguised c 1250, 1421; **disfiguro** c 1400, **defiguro** c 1250, to disguise; *cf.* DEFIGUR

diffilo, to unwind 6c.

diffin-, *see* DEFIN

diffluo, to give away (in alms) a 1228; *cf.* DEFLUX

difforest-, *see* DEFOREST

***difform/itas,** dissimilarity, aberration c 1250, c 1362; ***-is,** dissimilar 1267, c 1390; **motus uniformiter -is,** uniform acceleration c 1340; ***-iter,** dissimilarly 1267, 1378; **-o,** to differ, vary c 1344, a 1361; *see also* DEFORM

diffort- (difforc-), *see* DEFORT

diffortunium (? *for* dys-), ill-fortune c 1250.

diffractio (†defractio, †diffactio), fracture (of limb) c 1115.

diffranchiso, to disfranchise (a burgess) 1434.

diffrodio, *see* AFFRAI

diffug/ium, refuge 1041; ***1188, 1423, diffigium** 1275, subterfuge, evasion; **d. more,** delay 1425; ***-io,** to avoid, evade c 1130, c 1400; to refute 1344.

diffulcio, (?) to prop at the ends c 1180.

diffunctus, *see* defunctio.

diffus/io, diffusion, extension 655, 870. c 1125, c 1330; **-ivus,** diffusive, apt to spread c 1250, 1620; **-culus,** somewhat protracted

1267; **-us,** protracted, long delayed c 1210, c 1450.

diga, *see* **daga.**

digam/ia, bigamy 1523; **-us,** twice married c 1562.

digest/io, decoction (alch.) a 1252, c 1345; maturing (of wine) 13c.; **-ivus,** digestive a 1200, 1378; **-us,** digestion c 865. c 1180; **-um,** Justinian's *Digest* c 1258, c 1362; **D. Novum** 1231, c 1450; **D. Vetus** c 1250, 1438; **D. Infortiatum** c 1350, 1414, **D. Fortiatum** 1438; **digero,** to decoct (alch.) c 1345; to mature (of wine) 13c.; **degero,** to digest, think over c 1435, 1461.

1 **digit/us,** finger: **degetus** 1439; **-us,** digit (math.) c 1150, c 1445; (?) (metal) spray 1281; **d. auricularis,** little finger c 1172, 1411; **d. index,** forefinger 1266; **d. medicus,** third finger 1266, 1488; **-ale** 1328, ‡1483, **-orium** 1558, finger-stall *or* thimble; **-alis,** foxglove (bot.) 1634; **-aliter,** with the finger 1363; **-ata** 1247, **-atus** 1246, finger's breadth; **-atio,** pointing (with the finger of scorn) a 1452; **-o,** to point at, indicate c 1180, 1252; to finger c 1180, a 1408.

2 **digitus,** dais, high table 13c., 14c.

digladi/abilis c 1125, c 1400, **-alis** c 1265, ferocious; **-o,** to slash a 1275; **degladio,** to cut, pierce 1252.

dign/arium, -erium, -are, *see* **dinarium.**

dign/itas (dingn-), privilege, 'liberty' 1088, 12c.; ***1242, 1380, †-itale** 1377, †-**itatus** c 1298, high office (eccl.); dignity of a planet (astr.) 1184, 1344; axiom c 1250, c 1300; power (math.) 1686; (?) decision, decree c 1150; c 740. c 1210, **-atio** c 1080, 1470, honour (title); **-atio,** condescension 9c. c 1125, a 1250; grace (theol.) c 1170, 1452; **-anter,** with condescension c 793. c 1090, c 1400; **-ificantia** 1374, **-ificatio** 1344, c 1366, dignifying; **-iter,** worthily c 1125, c 1188; **-um,** high table c 1390, c 1410; **-us,** worthy, qualified (leg.) c 1090, c 1115; (with *dat.*) worthy c 1235; **d. legum,** law-worthy 1324; **-efacio** c 870, **-ifico** c 1240, c 1444, to dignify, deem worthy, exalt.

dignosc-, *see* DINO

digress/ive, by way of digression c 1210, 1276; **-o,** to distract, divert c 1200; **disgredior,** to digress c 1343, c 1376.

dijudic/atio c 1080, c 1310, **dejudicatio** c 1270, judgement; **-ativus,** discriminatory a 1250; **-ator,** arbiter a 1140; **-o,** to judge, adjudge 1086, 1461; c 793. c 1200, **dejudico** 11c., 1331, to set at nought, condemn; *cf.* DIVIDIC

dikera, *see* **dacra.**

diketta 1241, (?) **dicum** (C.I.) 1154, **dic/delvum** 1209, dike, ditch; **-agium** 1462, **decagium** 1482, duty on wool (?) stored on dike (Boston).

dilaceratio, gnawing, devouring 6c.; plundering 6c. 14c.; **dilaseratrix,** one who tears up (*f.*) 1436; **delacero,** to tear 1368, 1378.

dilanio 1385, **delanio (†delamo)** c 1200, butcher; **dislaniator,** slaughterer c 1457; **delanio,** to mangle 1220.

dilapid/atio, dilapidation, disrepair 1440, 1684; *c 1250, 15c., **delapidatio** c 1326, 1340, squandering, waste; **-ator** 7c. c 1192, 1593, **-atrix** (*f.*) c 1250, squanderer; **-o,** to stone to death 1220; 1170, 1552, **delapido** 1162, c 1328, to squander.

dilargus, extravagant 7c.

dilat-, *see also* DELAT

dilat/atio, enlargement c 730. 1236, c 1410; c 1250, 15c., **†-io** p 1330, spreading, propagation; **-abilis,** expansible c 1270; **delatatius,** more at large 1497; **-ator,** spreader 1090, 1377; **delato** 1245, (?) **†tylato** 1336, *for* **-o,** to spread, extend; **-o,** to exalt c 1250; **-esco,** to be widespread 1435.

*****dilat/io** 1219, c 1511, **†-atio** 1348, **†dilitatio** 1389, **†dilectatio** c 1225, delay; **delativus,** delaying 1408; **-orie,** dilatorily, tardily c 1430, 1461; by way of dilatory exception (leg.) c 1258, a 1300; **-oria** 1281, **-orie** (*pl.*) 1310, 1549, **-orium** c 1400, dilatory exception (leg.); *****-orius,** dilatory (leg.) c 1196, 1461; **-o,** to delay c 1290, 1588; *cf.* DIFFER

dilect-, *see also* DELECT; **dilatio.**

*****dilect/io** (bibl.), **dilexio** 1463, love; *****beloved,** amiability (address or title) 6c., 8c. c 1125, c 1400; favour 1270; **-or** 7c. 1107, 1345, **-rix** (*f.*) a 1100, c 1480, lover; **delectus** c 1520, **delictus** 1289, **dilictus** 1289, *for* **-us,** beloved; **dilig/iblis,** lovable c 1290, c 1444; **-ibilitas,** lovableness c 1290, p 1300; **-o** (with *inf.*), to desire c 730. c 1180, 13c.

diliber-, *see* DELIBER

dilic-, dilict-, *see* DELIC; DELICT; DILECT

dilig-, *see* delegiatus; DILECT; **disligo.**

dilinio, *see* delenio.

diliramentum, *see* DELIR

dilit-, *see* DELIT; **dilatio.**

diluc/idatio c 1250, 1425, **delucidatio** 1431, explanation; **†-itas,** lucidity 1524; **-idus,** sane 1286, 1422; *****-ido** c 730, 980. c 1115, c 1456, **delucido** c 1380, 1427, to elucidate, explain; **deluceo,** to shine 1420.

diluvi/um, the Flood 12c., 1461; **-us,** a flood a 1300.

dimco, *see* 1 dimico.

dimed-, *see* **dimidietas.**

dimembro, *see* dismembro.

dimens/io 12c., 1686, **demensio** 7c. 12c., 1267, **-us** 1620, dimension; **-ionalis** c 1270, 1381, **-ivus** a 1290, c 1340, dimensional; **-ionaliter** c 1250, 1381, **demencionaliter** 1412, **-ive** c 1225, 1381, dimensionally; **-or,** measurer, surveyor c 1315, c 1362; **-itas,** extension in space c 1270; **-iono,** to extend in space c 1250, 1427; *cf.* **demensus.**

dimentior, *see* **dementior.**

dimergor, *see* **demersio.**

dimettum, dimity (δίμιτος) 1300.

dimi, *see* **dynamis.**

1 dimic/o (with *acc.*), to fight against c 550. c 1250, p 1330; **†dimco** 14c., **demico** c 550, *for* **-o.**

2 †dimico, to chop up p 1330.

*****dimidietas** c 865. 1199, 1505, **dimed/ietas** (Sc.) c 1350, 1526, **-ies** 1031, **-ium** 11c., 1460, half, moiety; **-ius** (Sc.) 13c., 1492, **demedius** 812, half (*adj.*); **dimidiator,**

half-sharer c 1180; **dimidio** (**†dividio**), to halve (eccl.).

diminium, *see* DOMIN

dimin/utio (demin-) c 760. c 1090, c 1414, **†-iculum** 15c., diminution; subtraction (math.) 1145; c 1330, **d. sanguinis** c 1235, 1510, blood-letting; **d. membrorum,** mutilation c 1204, c 1230; **-uibilis,** capable of decrease c 1290, p 1300; **-ute,** in a lessened degree, inadequately 1256, 1344; **-utius,** in more detail c 1500; **-utive,** in a depreciative sense c 700. 13c.; **-utivus,** diminutive c 700, c 800. 1267, a 1446; subtracted, minus (math.) 1145; **-utellum** 13c., **†-utium** (? **-utivum**) p 1394, a diminutive; **-utor,** diminisher c 1087, c 1450; **-utum,** deficit 1345; **de -uto,** in abatement (leg.) 1423; **numerus -utus,** fraction 1145; number exceeding the sum of its aliquot parts a 1200, a 1250; *****-uo,** to diminish, lessen c 1070, c 1470; to subtract (math.) 1145.

*****dimiss/io** c 1150, 1540, **demissio** 1225, **demissus** c 1300, handing over, surrender, demise; **d. belli,** fyrdwite c 1110; **-e,** *for* **demisse,** negligently c 1258; **-ibilis** a 1384, a 1564, **dimittabilis** 1557, able to be demised (leg.); **-or,** demiser, lessor 1279, 1419; **-orie** (*pl.*), letters dimissory 1303; **-orius** 1221, c 1467, **-orialis** c 1408, 1529, dimissory (eccl.); **demitto,** to lessen 749; **dimitto** *****1086, 1540, **demitto** c 1290, 1375, to hand over, demise; to leave behind 8c. c 1090, c 1436; (with *inf.*) to leave off, forgo c 793. c 1072, c 1343; 9c. 1167, c 1362, **demitto** 836, to permit; **demitto me,** to withdraw (from claim) 1220; **dismitto,** to dismiss c 1125.

dimotio, mutual separation 1649.

dimpnia, *see* dyspnia.

dimulg-, *see* DIVULG

dimultiplico, to multiply c 1500.

dinaldis, *see* **dynamis.**

din/arium 1212, c 1250, **-erium** 1213, 14c., **-nierium** 1214, **-gnerium** 1212, **dignare** 13c., **dignarium** 1207, c 1350, **dignarius** c 1260, **dignerium** c 1180, 1257, **dis- nerium** 1206, dinner.

dindym/a (*pl.*), mysteries, *sancta* c 950, c 1000; **‡-us,** "seat of angels" 1483; **‡genital** duct (? *for* didymus) 14c., 1483.

dingia, *see* dungia.

dingn-, *see* DIGN

dingus, *see* thanus.

dinigro, *see* DENIG

dino/tio, perception c 1100; **dignoscibiliter,** so as to recognize 1200; *****-sco** c 730, c 1038. c 1125, 1549, **denosco** 1276, c 1450, to know, recognize.

dintellus, *see* ductio.

dio, *see* deyeria.

diobolicus, *see* DIABOL

*****dioces/is** (diosces-) c 700, c 804. 1094, 1565, **-a** 1237, c 1380, **dioecesa** 1438, diocese (eccl.); province (eccl.) 1274; *****-anus** c 1142, c 1321, **-eus** a 1100, **-ianus** a 1100, diocesan (*adj.*); 1181, 1549, **diocisanus** c 1300, **-anius** 1274, **-ianus** a 1100, c 1180, **-enarius** 1354, diocesan bishop; 1248, 1549, **-eus** 12c., member of a diocese.

dioleticus, *see* **dialecticus.**
diomedit/a, -is, heron a 1446.
Dionola, (?) harlot c 1200.
†**dionysia,** sunflower c 1200; chicory 15c.
dioptr/ica (*pl.*), science of refraction 1648; ‡**-a,** perforated board *etc.* for looking into furnace (alch.) 1652.
diorisma, definition c 950.
‡**diota (dy-),** diota, two-eared vessel (alch.) 1652.
diphthera, fur (her.) 1654; ‡**diptericus,** (?) black hellebore (bot.) 14c.
diphthong/os c 800, **-us** c 1200, c 1270, diphthong.
diplo/is c 1180, 1549, **-ida** 1508, **-dea** 1506, †**-ega** 1507, **deplois** 1440, 1554, **displois** 1293, **duplois** 1427, 1571, **duploida** 1569, 1573, **duplommis** 1375, doublet (garment); **d. defensivus** 1426, 1451.
diplom/a c 950. 1512, 1565, **duploma** 1163, c 1200, (papal) letter of appointment; **utor -ate,** to travel post-haste c 1180, p 1348; **duploma,** (?) peace treaty (fig.) c 1200.
dipsas, kind of snake: **gyps/as** a 710, **-a** c 1060.
diptanus, *see* **dictamnus.**
diptotus, having two cases (gram.) 8c.
diradio, to irradiate c 1500.
diratio/ (disratio/) c 1120, c 1443, **-cinamentum** a 1125, **-cinatio** c 1115, c 1258, **-cinium** c 1125, c 1397, **-namentum** c 1110, c 1414, **-natio** 1160, 1208, †**disreinium** 1280, deraignment, proof (leg.); **disrationator,** deraigner c 1395; **-cino** c 1077, c 1234, †**disratiocinio** 1234, **deratiocino** 1086, *-no c 1080, c 1450, **disraisno** 1086, †**disrenio** c 1192, †**disreinio** 1282, **derationo** 1086, a 1275, **deraino** a 1200, **dereino** 1211, **deresno** c 1180, to deraign, prove, establish a title to (leg.); **-no** c 1145, c 1414, **derayno** 13c., to decide, adjudge c 1200; **-no me,** to clear oneself (leg.) c 1115, 1331.
direct/io c 740. 1173, 1520, **-ura** 1219, directing, controlling, rule, order; west-to-east movement in epicycle (astr.) c 1233; **punctum -aneum,** chant on one note (mus.) c 1330; **-ivum,** guiding principle c 1414, c 1457; **-ivus,** directing, controlling 1267, c 1620; **-or** c 1000. c 1253, 1549, **-rix** (*f.*) 1461, director, controller; **-orie,** (?) under guidance c 1450; **-orium,** dresser, serving-board 1301; guidance c 1381; directory, guide-book 1497, 1555; **dreitura,** jurisdiction (G.) 1250; **dra...turia,** a customary render (G.) 1255; **-a** (*pl.*), instructions 1236; **-um,** obverse 1286; **a -o** a 1350, **e -o** 1470, **in -o** 1267, c 1470, **in -um** c 980. c 1080, c 1306, **in dirigium** 12c., straight, directly, in a line; **-us,** travelling, bound 1319; direct, immediate (of feudal lords) c 1362, 1461; **dirigibilis,** subject to guidance p 1300, c 1457; *dirige c 1190, c 1503, **derige** 1471, dirge, antiphon at matins in the office for the dead; **-ivo,** to regulate c 1376; **dirigo,** to appoint c 1090, c 1194; to legalize c 1115; to put right, redress c 1185, 1294; to 'dress' (a ploughshare) 1356; *(with *dat.* or **ad**) to direct, address (documents, *etc.*) c 793. c 1130, c 1520; (*intr.*) to make one's way c 1362.

diremo, *for* **dirimo,** to renounce 1461.
direptio, plundering: **dereptio** c 1322.
dirictus, *see* **dirutio.**
dirig/eo c 1433, **-esco** c 1125, 1200, *for* **derig-,** to become stiff.
dirisorie, *see* DERIS
diriv-, *see* DERIV
dirnum 1408, **durnellum** 1227, 'durn', door-post; **dornedies,** "durne-day", (court held on) day when burgage-rents were payable under pain of sealing tenant's door (Bridgwater) 1388.
†**dirocheum,** (?) *for* **dittocheum,** twofold nurture (?) 981 (c 1300).
dirogatorius, *see* DEROG
dirritio, *see* 2 **duratio.**
diruptio, breaking forth 12c.; breaking down 1380, 1461.
diru/tio, destruction, ruin c 1260, c 1400; †**dirictus,** (?) *for* **-tus,** 1279, 1297; **deruo,** *for* **-o,** c 730.
disaccordo, to disagree c 1258.
disadvoco a 1275, 1334, **disavoco** 1411, **desawoo** 1263, to disavow; *cf.* DEADVOC, DEVOC
disafforest/atio, 'disafforestation', removal of land from forest status (leg.) a 1300, 1307; **-o** 1201, 1304, **desafforesto** c 1214, 1292, to 'disafforest' (leg.); *cf.* DEAFFOREST, DEFOREST
disagreo, to disagree a 1540.
disalloc/atio, disallowance (of item in account) 1398, 1449; **-abilis,** liable to be disallowed (leg.) a 1275; **-o** 1362, 1445, **disloco** 1380, to disallow (expenditure, *etc.*); **-o,** to disallow (a petition) 1456; *cf.* DEALLOC, DISLOC
disamis, a logical mood 13c.
disana, *see* **decima.**
disannexus, detached 1587.
disappropri/atio, cancellation of an appropriation (eccl.) 1380, 16c.; **-o,** to disappropriate (eccl.) 1576.
disarresto, to release from arrest 1294, 1327.
disauthentic/atio, invalidation 1400; **-o,** to invalidate 1400.
disban/iamentum, release from sequestration (G.) 1289; **-nio,** to release from ban or sequestration (G.) 1285.
disbrigo, to clear of debt (Sc.) 1391.
disc-, *see also* **diss-, dys-**
disca, *see* 2 **discus.**
discaetus, decayed 1297, 1315; *cf.* DECAS
discalc/eo (-io), take off shoes 8c., 980. 1101, c 1450; **d. me** c 1000. c 1080, 1243; **d. vineam,** to clear roots, hoe (Fr. *déchausser*) c 1235, 1274; **scalciatus,** bare c 1130; *cf.* DECALC
discaligatus, bare-legged 15c.
discant/us 1326, 1606, **descantus** c 1504, **decentus** c 1250, descant (mus.); **-o,** to sing a contrary song, refute c 1218.
†**discapum,** (?) *for* **waterscapum,** watercourse (Norm.) (?) a 875 (c 1413).
discar/catio 1212, 1387, **-cagium** 1242, 1387, †**-iagium** 1272, †**-ragium** 1298, (payment for) unloading; **dischargia, dischargium,** discharge (of debts) 1514; *-co (†-to) c 1115, a 1564, **-go** c 1300, **-gio** c 1220, c 1300, **-io** 1215, 1324, to unload, discharge; to dismantle 1239; *cf.* DECAR

disc/arius, -atorius, *see* 2 discus.
disced-, *see* discessus; DISSID
discena, *see* decenna.
discen/do, -sus, *see* DESCEN
discensio, *see* dissensio.
disc/entia, learning c 1365; -ens, learner
c 1180; -ibilis, able to be learnt c 1361;
-ibilitas, ability to be learnt c 1361; -o
12c., †didisco c 1350, to teach.
discept/atio, dispute: deceptatio c 1250,
p 1478; decepto c 1250, (?) 1378, descepto
c 1443, *for* -o, to dispute; *see also* DECEPT
discern-, *see* DECRET; DISCRET
discerp/tus, erased (her.) c 1595; dicerpo,
for -o, 13c.
discess/us, decease 9c. 1168, c 1538; -or,
departer c 704; discedo 1229, c 1503, d.
ab hac luce 12c., d. in fata 1220, 1331,
to die; *cf.* decessus.
discharg/ia, -ium, *see* DISCAR
discid-, *see also* DECIS; DISSID
discidium, strife, disagreement, divorce:
*dissidium c 1140, 1562, dicidium c 1180,
desidium c 1318.
disci/fer, -formis, *see* 2 discus.
disciliabulum, misguided or divided council
(play on conciliabulum) 1164.
discindo, *see* DECIS; DISCISS
disciplin/a 7c. c 1148, 1461, -atio c 1430,
c 1546, 'discipline' (eccl.), penance, scourg-
ing; d. regularis (mon.) 12c., 1526; -abilis,
able to profit by discipline, teachable 7c.,
8c. a 1250, c 1430; -abilitas, teachability
c 1283; -ale, book of discipline (eccl.) 14c.;
-alis 1132, 1344, -aris c 1115, concerned
with instruction; virga -alis, rod of
penance c 1192, c 1400; -arius, Puritanical
1647; -aliter c 870. c 1160, 14c., -ariter
c 1200, a 1452, -ate 8c. c 1220, 1610, by
way of, *or* in accordance with, discipline;
-atus, education, study c 1180, c 1443;
(*ppl.*) pupil receiving instruction a 615; -o,
to discipline, train c 1125, c 1540; to scourge
c 1148, c 1447.
discipul/atus, band of disciples c 730; dis-
cipleship 8c. c 1125, 1382; noviciate c 1000;
1060. 1231, -atio c 1430, teaching, training;
-ariter, like disciples 1378, c 1430; ‡-o,
to teach 1483.
discisio, *see* decisio.
disciss/io, dispute c 1120; -o c 1400, decindo
c 1200, descindo 1229, c 1422, *for* discindo, to tear apart; *cf.* DECIS
disclam/atio a 1564, 1608, †-ium 1330, dis-
claimer, disavowal; -o, to disclaim, disavow
1309, 1608; (with *inf.*) to disclaim the right
c 1320.
disclaudo, to disenclose, leave unfenced
c 1115; to unlock 1195; discludo, to
unwall, dismantle 1328.
disclavo, to unnail a 1275.
disco, *see* discentia; 2 discus.
discoagul/atio, uncurdling a 1250; -o, to
uncurdle a 1250.
discoher/entia, incoherence, disunity c 1160,
1284; -eo, to disagree 1344.
discol-, *see also* DYSCOL
discolor/itas, difference in colour c 1200;
-atio, discoloration a 1250; -ativus, dis-
colouring a 1250; -o, to turn pale, dis-

colour a 1250, c 1500; to mark as distinct
c 1108.
dis/computo 1270, -cumputo c 1327, to
discount, deduct (C.I.).
disconcordia, disagreement 1489.
discon/fitura (discom-) 1223, p 1377, -fectura
c 1300, discumfitura 1230, c 1400, dis-
comfiture, defeat; -fictus 1252, †-flictus
c 1408, discomfited.
‡disconform/itas, disagreement 1483; -is,
not conforming 1351, a 1452.
disconforto, to discourage 15c.; (?) to dis-
comfit 1403.
disconsulo, to dissuade c 1250.
discontiguitas, discontinuity 1608.
discontinu/atio a 1233, 1620, -itas a 1233,
1620, discontinuity, breach of succession;
-ativus, breaking continuity a 1250; -us,
discontinuous c 1250, 1455; -o, to discon-
tinue, interrupt c 1267, 1684.
disconvenientia, disharmony 1217, 1399.
discooper/tio 1273, -tura 1315, 1470, unroofing; -tura, disclosure, information 1395;
-tor 1372, -ator 1339, spy; -tum, open land
(as distinct from covert) 1238, 1448; d.
faciei, the open face c 1200; -tus (equus),
unbarded 1288, 1300; -io, to uncover, lay
bare, remove a covering 9c. c 1080, 1533;
*1086, 1480, discoperio 1237, 1274, to
unroof; to explore 1501; c 1218, 15c., -o
1550, discupero 1352, to disclose, betray.
discophorus, *see* 2 discus.
discopulo c 1150, c 1325, discupulo 1293,
to uncouple (dogs); to dismantle 1322; *cf.*
decopulo.
discoragium, discouragement (C.I.) 1454.
discord/antia 13c., ‡1483, -atio c 1376, disagreement, rupture; c 1400, -ia 1326, discord (mus.); -iter, out of tune c 1266,
c 1330; p 1300, 1423, ‡-anter 1483, in a
spirit of discord; †-eo, *for* -o, to disagree
c 1358; -o, to cause dissension 1412.
discorio, to lay bare 11c.
discoronatus, discrowned 15c.
discorporo, to disembody, kill a 1450.
discred/entia, unbelief 1378, ‡15c.; -ibilis,
incredible c 1220; -o, *to disbelieve c 730.
c 1070, 15c.; to discredit a 1564; *cf.* decredo.
discrep/antia, dissimilarity c 1080, c 1250;
-atio, dispute c 1130.
discret/io, discrimination, distinction (bibl.);
c 793. c 1080, 1549, discrescio c 1283,
c 1480, discressio 1325, discernment,
prudence; *see also* annus; *discretion (title)
12c., c 1448; decision 1419; blazon (her.)
p 1394, a 1446; -alis, discrete, separate
9c.; -ive, by way of distinction c 1115,
c 1365; -ivus, separative (gram.) c 793;
a 1100, c 1430, discressivus c 1367, distinctive, discriminative; -or, sorter 1481;
-e, discretely, separately c 1080, 1610; dis-
creetly, prudently c 1192, c 1520; in due
proportion c 1125; -us, discrete, separate
c 1160, c 1470; prime (of numbers) a 1250;
*c 730. c 1070, 1549, decretus 1307, dis-
creet, prudent; discrescior, more discreet
1215, 1293; discern/iculum, difference
(her.) c 1595; -ere (*subst.*), understanding
c 1212; -o, to blazon (her.) p 1394, a 1446;

decerno 1497, **decerno** 1271, *for* -o, to distinguish; *cf.* DECRET

discribo, discript-, *see* DESCRIPT

discrimen, disaster c 550; a 1250, **discrimin/ale** a 1250, (?) top of head; c 1595, **-ale** c 1595, 'difference' (her.); **-ale,** hairpin 790; **vene -ales,** (?) veins at top of head a 1250; **-atim,** separately c 1500; **-atio,** decision 1196; **-ose,** dangerously 1339; **-osus,** dangerous c 550. c 1250, c 1450; **-o,** to difference (her.) c 1595.

discumbens, couchant (her.) c 1595.

discumfitura, *see* disconfitura.

discupero, *see* DISCOOPER

discupulo, *see* discupulo.

discurs/us, argument a 1304, c 1363; **d. temporis,** passage of time c 1321; **-io,** passage through life, lifetime c 700; **-itatio,** gadding about c 1283; **-ivus,** dysenteric c 1270; discursive c 1290, 1620; **-or,** monk who rides abroad c 1220, c 1330; raider 1250; **-orius,** syllogistic 14c.; **discurr/imen,** going backwards and forwards c 550; **-o,** to be current, circulate 1218, c 1298; to discourse, treat of 1229, 1610.

1 **discus,** high table (in refectory) c 1204, c 1330; 13c., c 1458, **desca, descus** 1250, 1416, **desquis** 1405, desk, lectern; **descum pendens, d. versatile** 1405; **discus** c 1330, **descus** 1251, a 1452, **desius** 1237, **deicius** 1244, **deisius** 1236, 1243 daïs; **descus summus** c 1300.

2 **disc/us,** disk (astr.) 1686; ***-us** (bibl.), **-a** 1265, c 1300, dish; measure of grain c 1182, c 1375; measure of salt 13c., c 1270; (unauthorized) measure of ale 1361, 1375; measure of ore 1243, 1451; fire-pan 1563; **-um-portans,** barmaster (in lead mine) 1517; **-arius** 1265, 1285, **-atorius** c 1335, servant in charge of dishes; **-ifer** c 685. 1238, 14c., **-ophorus** 1345, ‡1483, steward; **-iformis,** disk-shaped c 870; ‡**-o,** to make dishes 15c.

†**discusitus,** (?) unstitched a 1235.

discuss/io, right to try pleas (leg.) c 1077, c 1300; affray c 1362; **discuscio** 1378, **discutio** 1253, 1336, *for* -io, discussion, investigation; **-ivus,** rebutting 1277; **-or,** disperser 1497; investigator, examiner c 1266, 1456; **discutio** *8c., 9c. a 1100, 1549, †**duscio** 13c., to discuss, investigate, determine; to arrange 8c.

disert/itudo (dissert-), fluency, eloquence (bibl.); †**-io,** knowledge c 730; **-or,** speaker c 1434; **desertus,** eloquent 1293; **dessero (linguam),** to make eloquent c 1260.

disf-, *see* DIFF

disgarnitus, unarmed 1313.

‡**disgerbigator,** "tedder" 15c.

disglobo, to dissolve, thin out a 1250.

disgredior, *see* DIGRESS

disgreg/atio, separation, interpenetration 1050. a 1250, c 1608; **-ativus,** penetrative a 1180, a 1446; **-ator,** disperser c 1218; **-o,** to separate, disperse 12c., p 1377; to interpenetrate 12c., a 1446.

dishabil/itatio, disqualification 1477; **-is,** disabled, disqualified a 1564; **-ito,** to disqualify 1477; *cf.* deabilito.

†**disherbigatus,** uninhabited 1331.

dishered/itatio (-atio), disherison, dispossession a 1564, 1571; †**desherito,** to disinherit 1201; *cf.* DEHER

dishon/eratio, dishonour 1468; **-oro,** to dishonour, degrade p 1394, c 1470.

disidero, *see* DESIDER

disjectio, demolition c 1608.

disjugata, unmarried woman c 1500.

disjunct/io, alternative c 1318; **-ura,** disjointing (med.) a 1250; **-a** c 1343, **-iva** p 1300, c 1430, disjunctive proposition (log.); **-ive,** separately 13c., c 1400; **-ivus** (gram. or log.) 790. 1312, 1357; **disjungo,** to dismantle 1316; to subtract (math.) 815; (with *acc.* and *dat.*) to separate 6c.

diskippagium, disembarkation 1290, 1393.

dislaniator, *see* dilanio.

disligo 1345, 1365, **diligo** 1357, **deligo** 1271, **desligo** 1403, to unbind.

disloc/atio, breaking up c 1361; dislocation (of bone) a 1250, ‡15c.; **-o,** to displace c 1362; to dislocate a 1250, ‡1483; to cancel a lease 1426; *see also* DISALLOC

dismembro 1250, 1404, **dimembro** c 1540, to dismember, mutilate (a man); 1308, 1491, **dimembro** 1478, to dismember, detach (an estate, *etc.*); *cf.* DEMEMBR

dismitto, *see* DIMISS

disnerium, *see* dinarium.

disnodo, to disentangle c 1125; *cf.* DENOD

disno/ia, -icus, *see* dyspnia.

disobedi/entia, disobedience c 1478, 1498; **-o,** to disobey c 1448, 15c.

disobstruo, to free from obstruction 1290.

disobstupo, to free from obstruction 1387.

disoner/atio (desoner-), discharge 1433; **-o,** to discharge from debt 1292, 1495; to disfranchise 1434, 1492.

disordin/atio, disarrangement c 1605; **-atus,** inordinate c 1266, p 1327.

dispacco, to unpack 1399.

dispalatim, dispersedly 1528.

dispar/agatio (disper-) 1215, 1500, **-gatio** 1309, 1575, **-agium** a 1566, 1608, disparagement in marriage; **-agio** 1194, 1243, **-ago** 1200, a 1566, to disparage in marriage.

dispar/atio c 1270, c 1300, **-antia** c 1360, disparateness, difference; **-atus,** disparate, different c 1270, 1610; **-or,** to be distant 1090; to be disparate 1610.

disparco (disperco), to dispark, remove from status of park 1550, 1586.

dispar/itas c 730. c 1204, 1649, disparity, difference, inequality; **-iter,** in a different way or degree, for a different reason c 1250, 1457.

dispar/itio, disappearance c 1612; ***-eo,** to disappear c 730, c 793. c 1090, c 1450.

disparo, to strip of ornaments c 1072; *see also* DESPER, **disparatio.**

dispect-, *see* DESPECT

dispend/ium, injury, wrong c 1000. c 1090, 1520; **d. et mora** 14c., ***d. more** c 1230, c 1400, **mora -ialis** 14c., delay; **-iose,** injuriously c 1160, 1435; **-iosus,** ***injurious, prejudicial c 1178, 1473; dilatory, prolix c 1190, c 1400; *see also* DISPENS

dispens/a *c 1102, c 1400, **despensa** 1395, **-aria** 1214, ‡**-orium** 15c., **-atoria** 1435, **-atorium** c 1200, 1380, 'spense', store-room, pantry; **-a**, expense a 1185, p 1341; **-abilis**, susceptible of dispensation (eccl.) c 1200, c 1444; capable of distribution c 1620; belonging to the store-room a 1190; 1205, c 1363, **despensabilis** c 1330, ordinary, in everyday use (of bread, wine, or candles); **-anter**, economically c 1190; **-aria** 1185, 1219, **-eria** 1198, stewardship, service of store-keeper; **-arius**, recipient of dispensation (eccl.) c 1376; *c 1130, c 1365, *-ator c 1000. 1086, 1535, steward, bursar; **-ator**, purser (naut.) 1560; grantor of dispensation 1385; **-atio**, ordering, ordinance c 730. c 1170, 15c.; doling out 1549; behaviour, bearing 1200; *dispensation, pardon 1153, 1586; suspension from office 1274; **d. divina**, Providence c 730; *-ative, by way of dispensation 1167, 1334; **-ativus** c 1197, c 1443, **-atorius** c 1180, c 1357, dispensatory; (?) optional c 1180; **-atorie**, by divine dispensation c 730; prudently 7c. c 1180, c 1200; as a deputy c 1172; **-atorium**, pharmacopoeia c 1608; †**-io**, *for* **-atio**, management 1338; (?) hanging c 1250; **-o**, to allow 1107, 1425; a 1170, 1535, *d. **cum** c 1220, 1518, **d. circa** c 1343, **d. contra** c 1340, c 1350, to grant dispensation, exempt; **d. sacramenta** p 1300, dispendo s. c 1343, **dispendo sacra** c 1370, to dispense the sacraments; **dispendo**, to squander c 1230; *cf.* SPEN

disper-, *see also* DESPER; **dispar-**
disperc-, *see* DISPARC; DISPER
disperd/itio, perdition, ruin 16c.; **-o**, (?) to neglect c 1115.
dispergatio, *see* **disparagatio**.
disperquiro, to seek hither and thither, explore c 1410, 15c.
disper/sio feni, hay-making 1439; **-cio**, *for* **-sio**, scattering 1493, 1532; **-sabilior**, more widespread c 1385; **-sor**, squanderer, waster 12c., 13c.; **-sus**, rayed (her.) 1595; **-go pratum**, to make hay 1234.
disperson/atio, insult, slander 1424, a 1566; **-ator**, slanderer 1424; **-o** c 1250, 1424, **disperciono** c 1327, c 1330, to insult, slander; *cf.* **depersono**.
†**dispic/uus**, (?) visible c 550; *see also* DESPECT
†**dispissitudo**, thickness a 1250.
displic/entia, displeasure a 1250, 1437; **-enter**, with displeasure 1322, 1440; **-ibilis**, displeasing p 1300, 1343; **-ibiliter**, displeasingly p 1341.
displico 1266, 1571, **desplico** 1265, to unfold, unfurl.
displois, *see* **diplois**.
displosio, explosion c 1608, c 1643.
dispoli-, *see* **despoliatio**.
dispon-, *see also* DISPOSIT
dispondius, *for* **dupondius**, 13c.
dispons-, *see* DESPONS
disport/us 1275, **-a** 1406, **-atio** c 1400, 1412, remission, exemption; enjoyment, sport 1415, 1450; **-um**, recreation, *or* (?) recreation room (mon.) 1330 (*cf.* DEPORT); **-a** (*pl.*), (?) grounds, gardens 1351; **sportum**, (?) courtyard c 1420; **-o** 1336, **desporto** 1276, to exempt.
disposit/io, *ordering, regulation c 1080, 1549; congregation c 870; disposal, grant

1426, 1559; testamentary disposition 1290, 1429; disposition, inclination c 1343, c 1458; (?) dispossession 1382; **d. divina**, Providence c 1090, c 1340; **despositio**, arrangement 1279; **-ive** c 1277, c 1444, **-orie** c 1376, by way of disposition or disposal; **-ivus**, disposing c 1277, 1415; **nomina -iva**, names signifying the same thing in different ways 1344; **-or** c 7c., 760. c 1125, 1451, **-rix** (*f.*) c 1150, disposer, regulator; ruler (astr.) a 1233; administrator (of goods of deceased) 1415; patron of benefice (eccl.) 1426; **-orium**, disposal, command c 1376; **bono -o**, with a good will c 1362; **-ior**, more inclined 1378, 1380; **-issimus**, most favourably disposed a 1180; **-us**, disposed, inclined c 1324, c 1470; well disposed, in good order p 1300; **bene d.** c 1250; **male d.** c 1455; **dispon/ibilis**, capable of being disposed c 1367; **causa -ens** a 1250; **-o**, *to order, decree 8c. c 1253, 1545; to spend 1425, c 1502; to bequeath 1425; *(with *inf.*) to intend, prepare 8c., 9c. c 1080, 1461; (with *dat.*) to provide for 12c., c 1200; *d. **de**, to dispose of c 1188, c 1495; **d. pro**, to provide for c 1290, c 1434.
dispot-, *see* DESPOT
disproprio, to reject a 1408.
dispum/arium 1553, ‡**-atorium** 1483, skimmer; **-o** a 1250, **despumo** c 1215, a 1446, to skim; **despumo**, to froth out c 950.
dispun/ctuo, to settle accounts 1485; **-ctuor**, (?) to disagree 1503; **-go**, (?) to strike out, dismiss c 950.
disput/atio, disputation (ac.) c 1346, 1636; **dies -abilis**, day for disputation (ac.) c 1350, c 1425; **-ans** c 1407, c 1433, **-ator** c 1549, disputant (ac.); **-ative**, by way of disputation c 1343, c 1363; **-atorius**, of a disputation c 865. c 1583; **-aturio**, to be disputatious 1646; **-o**, to dispute (ac.) c 1282, c 1550.
disquieto, to disturb a 1452.
disquipar/antia, disquiparance (relation between heteronymous correlates) p 1300; **-ativus**, involving disquiparancy c 1360; **-o**, to reduce to disquiparancy c 1360.
disqui/sitor, scrutineer c 1450; **-ro**, to ascertain (leg.) c 1185.
disr-, *see also* **dir-**
disratio-, disrein-, *etc.*, *see* **diratio**.
disrevestio, to unfrock c 1296.
disripatio, displacement of river bank c 1300.
disrob/atio, robbery 1444; **-o**, to rob 1419; *cf.* DEROB
†**disrupio**, to pull down 1336.
dissacaria, pillaging 1301.
*dissais/ina** 1165, a 1290, **dessaisina** c 1185, 1211, **dissasina** (Sc.) 13c., c 1320, †**dissasisa** (Sc.) 1319, *disseisina** 1196, c 1516, **dissesina** 1275, c 1400, **-iatio** c 1115, **-itio** 1122, disseisin, dispossession (leg.); *d. **nova** c 1185, c 1448, †**disseisio nova** 1200, novel disseisin; **-iator** 1199, c 1218, **disseisator** c 1285, **disseisiator** c 1218, 1236, **-itor** c 1218, 1325, **dissasitor** (Sc.) c 1320, *disseisitor** c 1236, 15c., **-itrix** (*f.*) c 1290, disseisor; **-itus**, person disseised 1236; *-io** c 1115, 1319, **dessaisio** 1086, 1233, **dissasio** c 1130, c 1320, *disseisio** a 1087, 1440, **dissesio** 1280, c 1400, **disseiso** 12c.,

deseysio 1285, **-isco** (Norm.) 1080, to disseise.

dissectio, dismemberment c 1293; dissection 1620.

disseisono 1261, **disseyono, dysseono** 1302, to sow (land) out of turn.

dissemin/atus, unsown c 1400; **-o,** to fill by scattering broadcast c 1343.

dissenarius, *see* DECENN

dissen/sio, disagreement: ***-tio** (-cio) c 1250, 1461, **desensio** c 1411, **discensio** 1327, †**distensio** c 1408, †**distentio** c 1455; **desensator,** dissentient, schismatic a 700.

dissenteria, *see* **dysenteria.**

disserenatio, clearing (of sky) 1622.

dissero, *see* **desero.**

dissertus, *for* **dissitus,** distinct c 1362; *see also* DISERT

dissid/entia c 1150, c 1362, **dissessio** c 1266, disagreement; **discideo** c 1320, c 1340, **discedeo** c 1321, *for* **-eo,** to disagree.

dissidium, *see* **discidium.**

dissig/illo c 1300, c 1397, **-no** 12c., to unseal.

dissimilar/itas, dissimilarity 1620; **-is,** dissimilar 1620.

dissim/ulatio, dissimulation: †**-ilatio** c 1470; **-ulativus,** dissembling 1385; †**-ilative,** dissemblingly 1461; **-ulatrix,** dissembler (*f.*) 12c., c 1200; **-ultas,** dissimilarity, dissension 705; †**-ilo,** *for* **-ulo,** to dissemble 1461; **-ulo,** to neglect, disregard c 793. c 1200, a 1273; to pass over, concede c 1258; (with *inf.*) to forbear c 1115, c 1400.

dissinter/ia, -icus, *see* **dysenteria.**

dissip/atio, dismantling c 1180; **-antia,** whittling away 1378; **-ativus,** dissipative c 1376; ***-ator** c 710, 9c. c 1125, c 1549, **-atrix** (*f.*) c 1180, waster; **-o,** to dismantle 1086, c 1180.

dissipi/entia, folly c 1250; **-ens,** foolish c 793.

‡**dissoleo,** to be unaccustomed 1483.

dissologia, equivocation c 950.

dissolu/tio, opening (of a pack) 12c.; elucidation c 1534; dissolution (of monasteries) 1538, 1553; **desolutio,** dissoluteness 1234; **-bilis,** soluble (of a problem) c 1100; **-tivus** a 1250, 14c., **-torius** c 1115, solvent; **desolutus,** *for* **-tus,** 15c.; **dissolv/o,** to let slip (hounds) 1150; to dismantle (a house) 1432; to dissolve (a monastery *etc.*) 1538; to release (prisoners) c 1362; **d. obsidionem,** to raise a siege c 1330; **d. concilium** 1312, 1549, **d. Parliamentum** 1399, 15c.; **d. trussellum,** to open a pack 1086; **-or in risum,** to burst into laughter 12c.

disson/antia, discrepancy, disagreement 8c., 9c. c 1125, c 1385; **-e,** differently, in disagreement c 865; **desonus,** *for* **-us,** c 685.

disspellio, *see* **desepelio.**

dissuas/orius, dissuasive 9c.; **-ibilis,** inadvisable c 1334; **desuadeo,** to advise against, discourage c 1250.

dissue/tudo, desuetude, disuse c 1180, 1419; **-tus,** unaccustomed, obsolete c 1295, 1595; **-sco,** to become unaccustomed c 1180.

dissultus, leaping apart, severance 12c.

†**dissumptio,** melting c 1408.

dissu/te, in broken order c 1250; **-o,** to tear apart, separate 12c., 1537.

†**dissutus,** (?) *for* **dissolutus,** melted c 1115.

dissyllabus, *see* **disyllabus.**

distainiatus (†**distannatus**) 1389, **desteinnatus** (†**destemnatus**) c 1412, embroidered or woven in various colours; *cf.* **stainiatus.**

distant/ia, marked superiority 9c.; quarrel, dissension c 1180, c 1400; **-er,** at a distance 1267, c 1363.

distemper/antia, disproportion, disorder c 1115, c 1375; disease c 1197, c 1470; anger c 1470; c 1115, **d. aeris** c 1173, c 1262, intemperate climate; **-atio,** excess c 1173; **-o,** to blend, steep c 1172, 14c.; to distemper, disorder c 1160, c 1404.

disten/sio, extension, expansion c 1160, 1360; stretching a 1250, 15c.; **-sivus,** extensive, tending to spread a 1270; tending to stretch a 1250; *see also* **dissensio.**

distich/on 815, **-ium** a 1180, distich.

distigno, to fix (bars) at intervals c 1200.

distill/atio, *for* **destillatio,** dripping down c 1350; 1267, 1620, **destillatio** c 1360, distillation; **-abilis,** distillable c 1360; **-atorium,** alembic 14c.; **-o,** to drip down c 1150, 1370; to distill 1267, a 1564.

distinct/io, *section, division (of book, *etc.*) c 1090, c 1470; division of Carmelite province 1324, 1446; c 1245, 1452, †**distrinctio** 1241, compartment, partition; distinction (log.) c 1260; 'difference' (her.) 1654; (with *de*) distinction from c 730; **-iuncula,** slight distinction 1609, c 1670; **-e** c 870. c 1250, **-im** c 1212, separately; **-im,** by way of distinction or decoration c 793; **-ive,** distinctively 1236, c 1360; **-ivus,** distinctive 9c. a 1250, c 1360; **-us,** separate position c 793; **distinguibilis,** distinguishable 13c., c 1300; **destinguo,** *for* **dis-,** c 1343.

distino, *see* DESTIN

distitium, opposed or separate position c 1180.

distitu/tio, -o, *see* DESTITU

distonatio, discord a 1452.

distoppo, to block (access to) 1279.

distorno, to divert, turn aside 13c.

distorte, distortedly 13c.

distract/io c 1250, p 1382, †**districtio** 1415, drawing (of criminals); squandering, waste c 1218, c 1380; **d. bonorum,** distraint (G.) 1311 (*cf.* DISTRICT); **-a,** estreat 1267 (*cf.* EXTRACT); **-or** 1143, c 1265, **-rix** (*f.*) 1261, squanderer; †**-us,** oblique c 1115; **distrah/enter,** by division 1378; **-o,** to draw (criminals) c 1250, 1415; to sell, dispose of c 1188, c 1400; to distinguish, analyse a 1250; to squander, waste 1185, 1346; to injure, harm c 1115; to distrain c 1178, c 1549.

distrarius, *see* **dextrarius.**

distribu/tio, distribution (log.) 13c., c 1343; **d. pauperum,** largesse 1340; **-ibilis,** capable of distribution (log.) p 1347, a 1360; **-tim,** severally c 1357; **-tive,** in a distributive sense 13c., a 1304, **-tivus,** distributive c 1258; ***-tor,** distributor 760. c 1160, c 1477; **-tissimus,** most widely distributed (log.) c 1340; **-o,** to 'distribute', apply universally (log.) 1276; **destribuo,** *for* **-o,** 1461.

district/io c 1200, **-us** c 1192, **-a** c 1192, c 1436, strait; 16c., ***-us** c 1242, 1502, **-a**

c 1270, (area of) jurisdiction, district; extent c 1145; bond 9c.; *rigour, compulsion, strictness 7c., c 1050. c 1100, 15c.; punishment 7c., 8c. c 1220, 15c.; *c 1190, 1485, **distrinctio** 1230, 1299, **destrictio** 1375, **destrescia** 1194, -**us** 1268, **distrinctus** 1382, (goods taken in) distress, distraint (*see also* **distinctio, distractio**); **d. magna,** grand distress c 1196, 1359; -**e** c 1080, 1553, **distrincte** 1204, strictly; -**ius,** more strictly a 1200, c 1470; -**or,** distrainer c 1290, c 1414; †(?) *for* **discretor** c 1180; -**ualis,** neighbour 1393, 1478; -**uales** (*pl.*), *distrettuali* (Genoa) 1370; -**um,** tight place c 1255; thing taken in distraint 1558; -**us,** narrow 1261; *strict c 1080, 1419; -**um examen** c 1178, -**um judicium** c 1340, 1419, Last Judgement; **distring/ibilis** a 1242, 1516, **destringibilis** 1444, liable to distraint; -**as,** name of a writ c 1400; *-**o** 1183, 1558, **destringo** 1228, c 1306, to distrain, compel by distraint; (?) to delimit (G.) 1289.
distroppo, to unstrap 1333.
distructio, distruo, *see* DESTRUCT
distrusso, (?) to steal 1275.
†**distrusus,** expulsion 13c.
distundo, to burst asunder 1649.
*disturb/atio a 1100, a 1564, **desturbatio** 1330, 1423, -**amentum** a 1195, -**ium** 1284, c 1540, **desturbium** 1416, disturbance, interference; -**ativus,** disruptive 1408; -**ator,** disturber 1222, 1433; -**o** 1091, c 1218, **desturbo** 13c., 1331, to disturb, interfere; -**o,** to parry (a blow) a 1266; **desturbo,** to block (a road) 1279.
disubitatio, *see* DESUBIT
dis/vad-, -vagimonio, -wagio, *see* DIVAD
disvestio, *see* **divestio.**
diswarenno 1289, 1331, **deswarenno** 1275, to remove (land) from status of warren; *cf.* **dewarenno.**
disyllabus (diss-), disyllabic 12c., c 1194.
dit/atio, enrichment 1200, c 1460; -**abilis,** concerned with riches c 1376; -**ator,** enricher c 1196, c 1458; -**esco,** to enrich a 1408.
†**ditativus,** (?) *f.l.* for **litativus,** litigious a 1180.
diton/us, major third (mus.) 1351; a 1452, -**icus** c 1200, double-toned; -**ica,** diatonic melody 1252; -**ice,** in two tones 1252.
diu/, (?) late 1271; **d. est** c 1250, 1438, **jam d. est** c 1269, 1310, long ago (*see also* **a diu, ex diu**); **non est d.,** not long ago c 1289, c 1341; -**scule** c 1196, †-**tiuscule** c 1380, -**tile** (*for* -**tule**) c 1125, c 1188, for not very long; -**sculus,** longish 1266; **dutior,** more prolonged 1257.
diurn/itas, lapse of time 930. 12c., c 1390; 1531, 1537, -**us** c 1250, 1380, **jornantia** 1414, **jorneta** 1200, day's work; **jornata,** day's journey c 1290; -**a** a 1302, **jornale** (Fr.) 1280, **jornata** (G.) 1289, **jornea** (Fr.) 1331, **jornetum** (Ir.) 13c., measure of land, day-work; -**ale** c 1330, 1519, **jurnale** 1384, 1482, †**jurinale** 1466, service-book containing the daytime hours; **jornale,** journal, day-book (of accounts) 1354; 1371, **jurnale** 1460, **jurnellum** 1477, (?) candle

to burn for a day (eccl.); -**alia** (*pl.*), daytime footwear c 1072; -**alis** c 980. c 1080, c 1414, **jornalis** 1462, -**ius** c 1362, 1423, of or for daytime; -**o,** by day c 1250; **diuturno,** to spend the day c 1310.
diusius, *see* **dusius.**
diva, *see* **duva.**
divad/iatio (†**dividiatio**), distraint c 1115; recovery, redemption from pledge (Norm.) 1195; **devadiator legis,** one who wages law c 1290; -**io** 1086, 1309, **devadio** 1187, 1304, **degagio** 1274, to distrain, attach, compel by taking security; **devadio** 1086, **deguajo** c 1130, c 1200, **disvadio** (†**disvado**) 1086, c 1414, **diswagio, disvagimonio** c 1130, to redeem, recover (land, *etc.,* held as security); ‡**deguadio,** "to break custom" 1483; **devadio duellum,** to quash wager of battle 1212, c 1258.
divagatio c 1327, **devagatio** c 1300, going astray.
‡**divaporatio,** exhalation (alch.) 1652.
divaric/atio, straddling c 1190; powdering (her.) c 1595; -**atus,** divided (of clothes) 13c.; -**o,** to vary a 1408.
divasto, *see* DEVAST
diverbero, to thrash out, debate 1291.
divergo, to go astray c 1400.
diverium, *see* **deverium.**
divers/arium, -atorium, *see* **diversio.**
diversiclinium, spreading in different directions 1200; cross-road c 1150, ‡1483.
diversific/atio, diversification, variation a 1250, c 1380; *-**o,** to diversify, differentiate c 1150, c 1470.
diversigenus, of many kinds c 870.
*diversimod/us 1232, 15c., **deversimodus** 1266, of various kinds; *-**e** a 1240, 1478, *-**o** c 1290, 1461, in various ways.
diver/sio, diversion, turning aside c 1222, a 1564; †division, part 9c.; -**sorium** c 1450, -**satorium** 1136, by-way; c 1180, c 1321, -**sarium** c 1266, private compartment, niche (mon.); partition 1300, c 1324; light (of a window) 1348; (*for* **deversorium**), lodging-house, inn 1542, 1587; -**sitor** (*for* **de**-), stranger c 1620; ‡-**talium, -tallum,** generation out of elements (alch.) 1652; -**ticulum** (*for* **de**-), by-way c 793, 11c. c 1172, 1292; (?) cross-roads c 1325; winding, digression c 1125, 1528; refuge, lurking-place a 1100, c 1434; evasion, loop-hole c 1115, 1609; -**sa** (*n. pl.*), sundries c 1494; **de** -**so,** (?) forwards 1147; -**so,** to divert c 1125; to differentiate, distinguish a 1250, 1526; -**sor** (*for* **de**-), to be engaged, employed c 1125, c 1450; -**to,** to divert, turn aside 1199, 1493; to alienate (land) 1086; to remove (a plea) c 1275; to misappropriate a 1446; (*intr.*) to turn round (of mill-wheel) 1473; 8c. c 1090, 1536, -**tio** (G.) c 1243, to resort, turn aside (to); **d. in,** to turn into c 730; -**tor** (*dep.*), to turn in c 730.
diversivocus, heteronymous c 1160.
divestio c 1130, 1560, **disvestio** c 1072, a 1450, **devestio** c 1072, c 1195, to undress, disrobe; c 1130, **devestio** c 1250, 1438, to divest, deprive.
divexatio, molestation 1497, 1537.
divia, *see* **duva.**

divid/entia 1482, 1587, **devidentia** 1535, **-endus** a 1150, dividend, sum to be divided; **-enda**, indenture 1297, 1327; **tallia -enda,** tally covering a number of payments 1284; **-ens**, divisor (math.) a 1150; **cantus divisus**, prick-song 1519; **-o**, to cast lots c 1160; **d. contra**, to distinguish from c 1332; **devido**, *for* **-o**, to divide 1281; *see also* DIVIS

dividiatio, *see* **dimidictas.**

†**dividic/atio** (? dijudic-), separation c 870; **-ativus**, separating c 865.

dividio, *see* **dimidietas.**

dividuo, to deprive c 550.

divinculatus, fettered c 1410.

divin/us, religious c 740; ecclesiastical 858; (*subst.*) bishop 956. 12c.; **veteres -i**, (?) the Ancient Fathers 1144; **-a** (*n. pl.*) 12c., 1684, **res d.** 1551, divine service; theology c 1250, 1438; **-ator** c 1190, c 1514, †**-itor** 1406, **-atrix** (*f.*) 14c., diviner; **-atorius** c 1160, **-ativus** 1344, divinatory.

divis/io, division (math.) 1145, 1444; distribution (log.) c 850. 13c., c 1344; section (of a book) c 1362; separation by death c 793; tract of land, fief 1086, a 1120; form of divination c 700. 12c.; **-a** *c 1115, 1549, **devisa** 15c., boundary; court *or* court-day (leg.) c 1115, c 1200; a 1125, c 1192, **devisum** 1588, devise, bequest; 1415, **devisa** 1440, **devisamentum** 1436, device, badge, livery; **d. civitatis**, quarter of a city c 1160; **d. libera**, freeboard c 1250; **devisatio**, devising, bequeathing 1587; **-abilis** 1408, 1431, **-ibilis** a 1564, **devisibilis** 1588, able to be devised or bequeathed; **-ibile**, divisible matter 1267; **murus -ibilis**, party wall c 1324; **-ibilitas**, divisibility a 1250, c 1360; ***-im**, separately, severally c 1115, 1485; **-ive**, distributively p 1300, c 1360; **-ivus**, able to separate c 865; (?) solvent (med.) a 1250; (?) divisible p 1380; 12c., 1524, **-orius** c 850, distributive, classificatory; **-or**, apportioner c 1000. c 1340; **devisor**, surveyor, architect 1540; **deviso**, to delimit 1197; to aver 1554; to plan a 1564, 1588; to devise, bequeath 1588; *see also* DIVID

divolvo, *see* DEVOL

divorium, *see* **deverium.**

divort/ium, out-of-the-way place c 1150, 15c.; **-io**, separation c 1260; **-iatorius**, of divorce 1460; **-io** 1370, 1684, **devortio** 1526, **-ium celebro** 1340, to divorce.

divulg/atio, publication: †**dimulgatio** c 1343; **devulgo** a 1180, 1435, †**demulgo** c 1306, †**dimulgo** c 1343, *for* **-o**, to divulge, promulgate.

divulsus, erased (her.) 1595.

div/us, blessed, saint (eccl.) c 1500, 1586; **-issimus Paulus** c 1270.

diwerca, *see* **daywerca.**

dixionarius, *see* **dicentia.**

dizena, *see* **decenna.**

do, *see* **2 data.**

doageria, doarium, *see* **dos.**

dob-, *see also* DEALB

doblettum 1298, **doublettum** 1296, 1301, a due paid by Cornish tinners.

docibilitas, ability to teach 7c.

docillus, *see* DORS

docinna, *see* **decenna.**

docma, *see* DOGM

docmen, *see* **documentum.**

docti/logus, learned in the Word c 1370; **-loquus**, speaking learnedly c 950.

doctor/, religious teacher c 730. c 1130, 13c.; adviser 957, c 1038; learned man, scholar, c 1160, 1461; ***doctor** (ac.) 1293, 1583; **d. celestis**, St. Jerome c 1457; **d. communis**, St. Thomas Aquinas c 1320; **d. evangelicus**, John Wycliffe 1395, 15c.; **d. gentium**, St. Paul a 1290, 1466; **d. profundus**, Thomas Bradwardine c 1390; **d. subtilis**, Duns Scotus a 1347, c 1443; **d. utriusque juris**, doctor of civil and canon law c 1305, 15c.; ***-alis** 1271, 1527, **-ilis** 1389, doctoral (ac.); ***-atus**, doctorate (ac.) 1311, 1586; **-eus**, learned c 550; **-or**, to take a doctor's degree 1311, c 1458.

doctrin/atio 1346, c 1470, **-amentum** a 1135, teaching; **-abilitas**, teachability c 1365; **-ale**, name of a textbook of grammar 1271, c 1447; **-alia** (*pl.*), theoretical sciences 1267; **-alis**, doctrinal c 900. 1307, 1427; demonstrative (log.) a 1249, c 1344; theoretical 1267; **-aliter**, systematically, scientifically 1385, c 1409; **-o**, to teach a 1304, 1461.

‡**doctulus**, not wholly ignorant 1520.

doc/umentum, instruction c 750, c 950; document, documentary proof, 1252, 1559; **-men**, doctrine c 950.

dodarium, *see* **dos.**

dodd/a 1222, †**dedda** c 1290, **-ocus** 1299, measure of grain.

dodeca/edrum, dodecahedron c 1267; **-temorius**, twelvefold (of the zodiac) 1564.

dodr/ans, tidal wave (? ninth wave) c 550; **-a**, period of nine years c 1194.

doela, *see* **douella.**

doetus, *see* **ductio.**

doga, "wainscot" (*cf.* It. *doga*, barrel-stave) 1472.

doggera, dogger (boat) 1417.

doggetum, docket, summary 1457, 1647.

***dogm/a** (eccl.), **docma** 8c. 1274, dogma; **-atizatio** (-atisatio), dogmatizing c 1343, 1440; **-atista** 11c. 14c., 1427, **-atistes** 12c., specialist in dogma; **-atizo** (-atiso), to dogmatize 793. 1080, 1420.

†**dogm/atorium**, (?) *for* **dormitorium** c 1200; †**-itatio**, (?) *for* **dormitatio** c 1200.

doignus c 1312, †**donus** 1313, (?) dun (of a horse); **badius doynus** 1313, 1316, **d. badius** 1317; (?) *cf.* **dosinus.**

doitus, *see* **ductio.**

‡**dola**, "dorsal", curtain 15c.; *see also* **dalus.**

dol/abrum c 1178, 1471, **-arium** c 1200, **-um** 1502, broad-axe; **-abilis** c 1270, **-atilis** c 1170, easily hewn; **-abilitas**, susceptibility to hewing c 1270; **-atio** c 1412, 1533, **-ebratio** 1387, **-obratio** 1466, **-atura** c 1212, hewing, trimming with axe; **-atura**, chip, shaving a 1100; **-ator**, hewer c 700; **cnipulus** †**-eratus**, sort of knife 1242; **-o**, to hew (coal) 1460.

doli/um (**dole-**), *tun, cask 1173, c 1533; wooden casing round mill-stone 1282; 'Tun', name of a prison 1347, a 1422; **-ata** 1449, **-atum** c 1290, 1444, tunful, 'tun-tight' (*cf.* **pondus**); **-ator**, cooper 1561; **-o**, to pack in a tun 1440, 1449.

*dolor/osus 9c. a 1250, c 1470, **-iferus** (? **-ifer**) 1291, grievous; **-ose**, grievously c 1300.

*dolositas, guile 1041. c 1110, c 1430.

dolphin-, *see* DELPHI; DELPHIN

dol/um, -o, *see* dolabrum.

dolus, *see* dalus.

domalia, *see* domus.

dom/anium, -enium, *see* DOMIN

domatio, dressing (of leather) 1460.

domesca, understanding c 550.

domestic/itas, meekness c 1380; **-us**, tame, domesticated c 1180, 1461; meek c 1380; (*subst.*) inmate of religious house c 1220; **d. fidei**, member of the Faith c 1090; **-a**, maid-servant c 1197, 1480; **-alia** (*pl.*), household goods a 1452; **-atio**, familiarity c 1430; **-o**, to tame, domesticate c 1200, a 1446; to adopt into household 1427.

domic-, *see also* DOMIN, domus.

*dom/icella 1199, 1588, †donicella 1315, **-isella** 1265, **-icilla** c 1217, 1461, **-cilla** 1259, damicella 15c., damisella (G.) 1220, damsel, young lady, lady-in-waiting; (as title) 1235; damisella, harlot 1284; *-icellus a 1135, 1500, **-isellus** 1418, 'donzel', young gentleman, page *or* squire; catulus -icellus, *see* domus.

domiger/ium (†doungerium) 1241, 1444, **dongerium** 1234, **dangerium** 1235, 1267, **daungerium** 1143, c 1350 'danger', dominion, (area of) jurisdiction, power; cost, hardship c 1350, c 1380; danger c 1395, a 1422; **in -io sto**, to be in debt 1408; **dangerium**, insolence c 1340; **dangerium** 1175, c 1350, **dangerum** 1245, **dongerium** 1285, c 1350, payment by tenants of denn for right to cut trees (Kent); ‡**-osus**, dangerous c 1440.

Dominic/anus 1536, 1589, **-alis** 1567, Dominican (friar).

domin/us *705, 11c. c 1172, 1565, *domnus 7c., 930. a 1100, 1461, dompnus c 1190, 1461, lord, sir (title); c 1305, 1498, dompnus c 1190, 1518, dan (monastic title); bishop 1219, 1255; feudal lord 1074, 1559; lord of a hundred c 1040; reeve c 1150; husband 1142, 14c.; guardian 13c.; principal (of attorney) a 1245, 1684; lord of the ascendant (astr.) 1387; **d. anni** (astr.) c 1227; **d. (domnus) apostolicus**, Pope 7c., 9c.; **d. Aschone**, name of a comet c 1270; ***d. capitalis** 1194, c 1448, **d. in capite** c 1115, lord in chief (feudal); **D. Exercituum**, Lord of Hosts c 1250; ‡**d. legum**, man of law 15c.; **d. marchians**, lord marcher 1421; **d. naturalis** (feudal) a 1142, c 1250; **d. navis**, ship-owner 1328; ***d. rex** (title) a 1160, 1694; **d. superior**, overlord 1292; **d. Venetorum**, doge 1434; **d. ville** 1086; **-i** (*pl.*) **regni** 1387, **-i spirituales et temporales** 1408, 1419, Peers; **-a**, feudal lady, dowager 1185, 1344; lady-in-waiting 1242, 1268; *lady (title) 1235, 1566; (title of) nun a 1160, 1488; female principal (of proxy) 1684; c 1296, c 1335, **D. Nostra** 1461, 1515, Our Lady; *see also* frater; **domna**, mistress, lady; c 793, 825; **-a Capillorum**, name of a comet c 1270; **d. de nocte**, witch 13c.; **d.**

Pauper, Poor Clare c 1250; **d. regina** (title) 1347, 1694; **d. religiosa**, nun 1392; **-abile**, something over which lordship may be exercised 1374, c 1376; **-abilis**, (capable of) exercising lordship c 1258, 1295; 1282, **-alis** 1298, belonging to a lord; **-anter**, despotically 1378, 1380; **-atio**, *lordship (title) 1217, 1620; dominion, territory c 1188, 1461; (?) demesne 1086; **-ationes** (*pl.*) a 1125, 1344, †**-ati** a 1408, order of angels; **-ative**, by way of domination 1346, a 1400; **-ativus**, despotic c 1340, 1649; **paternitas -ativa** (title) c 1327; **-ella**, lady, damsel c 1200, ‡1483; ‡**-ellus**, squire 1483; **-ica**, Lord's prayer 980 (*cf.* oratio); **-ica** 8c., 9c. a 1090, 1556, *dies d. 1086, a 1564, Sunday;

***-icum** c 1120, 1502, **-ica** 1196, c 1293, **-ia** c 1130, **-icale** 1526, **-icatus** c 1080, c 1200, **-ium** 1086, c 1200, **domenium** 12c., a 1200, **demania** (Sc.) 1435, **demenium** c 1150, a 1337, **demenia** c 1140, c 1150, **diminium** c 1220, demesne, land held by feudal tenant to his own use (*cf.* meneum); **-icum antiquum** (regis, corone), ancient demesne 1241, 1588; ***-ium** a 1185, 1583, **domanium** 1189, 14c., **demanium** c 1192, c 1230, **-io** c 1250, 1573, **damnum** c 1290, 14c., lordship, domain, territory; **-ium**, royalty, royal dues (Fr.) 1287; **per -ium**, predominantly a 1446; **super -ium**, charged on the demesne (of knight service additional to that levied on fees) 1166; **-ium -icum**, (?) demesne lordship 1328; **d. Venetorum**, signory 1507, 1527;

-icalia (*pl.*) 1501, **Evangelia -icalia** 1396, Gospels; **-icalis** 980. a 1100, 1387, **-icus** 8c. a 1100, 1549, †**domicus** c 938, of the Lord, divine; c 1200, 1476, **-icatus** c 1160, of or for Sunday; c 1170, 1330, **-icus** 1086, a 1190, belonging to a lord, seigneurial; 1375, 1583, **-icatus** c 1140, ***-icus** 1080, 15c., **-ius** 1086, **-eus** 1189, 1290, **deminius** 1337, **demainius** 13c., belonging to a demesne or household; **-icatus**, landed, wealthy 5c.; **-icaliter**, despotically a 1250; **homo -icus**, divine man c 730, c 1380; **-icus** (*subst.*), young nobleman (Fr.) c 1190; demesne tenant 1392; *see also* ager, annus, ascensio, cena, corpus, curia, incarnatio, littera, mensa, missa, natale, nativitas, nummus, oratio, panis, passio, resurrectio, sanguis, simenellus; **-o**, to rule over c 1290, c 1298.

domisell/a, -us, *see* domicella.

domitialis, *see* mensa; tabulatus.

domn-, dompn-, *see* DOMIN

domum, *see* DON

dom/us, *room, outhouse, workshop 1241, 1573; **d. artificialis**, workshop 1450; †**d. belli**, (?) camp a 1150; **d. bibitoria**, "guildhouse" c 1190; **d. braciatricia** 1303, **d. bracinea** 1370, **d. brasinea** 1554, 1576, **d. brasinii** c 1500, **d. brasii** 14c., **d. pandoxatoria** c 1430, 1575, brew-house, malthouse; ***d. capitularis**, chapter-house a 1230, 1570; **d. carbonum**, coal-house 1421, 1533; **d. carceris**, prison 12c.; **d. carectarum** 1309, 1350, **d. carectiva** c 1300, cart-house; **d. cerea**, wax-house 1404; **d. cervisiana**, ale-house c 1542; **d. communis**, common room, public hall c 1350, 1430; (meeting-place of) House of Commons 1433; **d. compoti**, counting-house 1403, 1459; **d. consilii**, council chamber 1388; **d. custume**, custom-house 1359; **d. byer'**, byre 1286; **d. estatis** 15c., **d. estivalis** a 1090, summer-house; **d. fabricationis**, smithy 1279; **d. fenalis** 1623, **d. feni** 1514, **d. pro feno** 1350, barn; **d. flatica** 1618, **d. sufflatica** 1508, 'blow-ing-house' (for tin-smelting); **d. focalis** 1300, **d. focaria** 1216, dwelling-house; **d. forinseca**, outhouse 1221, 1235; **d. fortis**, fortified house, fortalice (G.) 1314; **d. in-firmorum**, infirmary c 980. c 1090; **d. jocalium**, jewel-house c 1472; **d. laboris**, plough-shed 1388; **d. lane** 1271, **d. lanaria** 1385, wool-shed; **d. molendini**, mill-house 1232, 1383; **d. necessaria** c 1220, c 1400, **d. necessariorum** c 1330, 14c., **d. evacuationis** c 1150, **d. privata** 1141, **d. purgatoria** c 1293, c 1400, privy; **d. occupationum**, work-house 1553; **d. piscalis**, fish-house 1270; **d. placiti** 1297, **d. placitorum** 1414, court-house; **d. ponder'**, weigh-house (for wool) 1338; **d. potationis**, ale-house c 1198; **d. providentie**, purveyance department of household c 1472; **d. regis** c 1115, **d. regia** c 1178, royal household; **d. sacramenti**, receptacle for consecrated host 16c.; **d. salina**, salt works 1362; **d. scholarum**, school-house c 1330, 1447; **d. stauri**, store-house 1529; **d. tegularis** 1547, **d. tegulat'** 1376, tile-kiln; **d. Parliamenti** c 1450; **d. inferior**, House of Commons c 1460, 1588; lower house of Convocation (eccl.) 1439; **d. Superior**, House of Lords c 1460; upper house of Convocation 1439; **d. gallinacea** c 1160, **d. gallinaria** 1546, **d. gallinarum** 1278, c 1321, **d. pro gallis et gallinis** 1350, **d. poletrie** 1301, hen-house; **d. ovilis**, sheep-fold 1553; **d. porcorum**, pig-sty c 1190, 1321; **d. vaccarum**, cow shed 1341; **-us**, religious house 12c., 1537; **d. religionis** 1217, 14c., **d. religiosa** c 1188, 1589; **d. Dei**, church or monastery 749; hospital or hospice 1176, 1421; **d. Domini** c 1250; **d. filia** c 1240, **d. filialis** 1319, daughter house; **d. matrix**, mother house c 1308; **d. monalis**, nunnery 1587; **-us**, college, hall (ac.) c 1290, c 1550; planetary house (astr.) c 1150, c 1620; **d. accidentalis**, ruling house (astr.) 1387; **-i** c 1290, c 1360, **-orsum** 1424, home-wards; **-alia** (*n. pl.*), household goods 1415; **-icellum** c 1150, **-icellulum** c 1210, **-icula** 1205, ***-uncula** a 1100, 1584, **-unculum** (? **-unculus**) 8c. c 1250, a 1446, small house, shed; **-uncula**, cell (mon.) 7c., 10c.; bird-cage a 1200; **-unculum**, room 747; **-icilium**, household, suite or department c 1395, 1479; planetary house (astr.) a 1200; **catulus -icellus**, house-dog a 1408; **-ifex** 15c., **-ificator** 1267, c 1365, carpenter, builder; ‡**-ifico**, to build a house c 1440, 1483.

Domus Dei, (?) Doomsday (name of a register at Salisbury) 1306.
dona, *see* **duna**.
don/atio, *etc.*, *see* **donum**.
Donat/us, primer (not necessarily of Donatus) 1362, 1400; **liber -icus** c 1000; **-ista**, ‡beginner in Latin 1483; Donatist heretic 12c., c 1546.
donerettum, *see* DOVER
dongerium, *see* **domigerium**.
donicella, *see* **domicella**.
donjo, donjona, *see* **dunjo**.
don/um, bridal gift, wedding 12c.; **d. anni**, New Year's gift c 1432; **d. hiemale** 1356; **d. S. Antonii**, gift of runt lamb, 'tantony' 1397; **d. arrentatum**, a royal due 1332; **d. comitatus** 1160, 1167, **d. civitatis** 1160, tallage; **d. Sancti Martini**, payment to sheriff (Dorset) 1258; **d. militum**, scutage 1130, 1160; **d. vicecomitis**, sheriff's aid 1234; **de -o**, as a gift 1221, c 1336; ‡**domum**, *for* donum, 966; **-abilis**, able to be given 793. c 1290, 1374; **-abilitas**, capacity of being given c 1290, 1374; **-amen**, presenting, presentation 7c.; **-antia**, giving 1374; ***-arium** 760. 1136, 1461, **-are** 810, **-ativum** 680. 12c., c 1250, **-atum** 11c., gift, offering; ‡**-arium**, horse-dung 1483; **-arius** 1374, c 1376, **-atarius** c 1212, 1560, **-aterius** (G.) 1315, **-atorius** 1235, 1516, donee, recipient of gift; **-atio**, presentation to benefice (eccl.) a 1160, 1426; giving in marriage (of ward by guardian) 1185, 1218; **d. inter vivos** (Fr.) 1280, 1316; ‡**danatio**, gift c 889; *see also* **forma**; **-atiuncula**, little gift 11c.; **-ativa**, right of presentation (eccl.) 1588; **-ativus**, disposed to give a 1100, 1374; **ars -ativa**, art of bribing c 1220; **-ator**, one who presents to a benefice 1426; **-eia**, feudal due (Fr.) 1190; **-atus**, layman surrendered to monastery 1338; 'donate', patron or associate of Hospitallers 1375; **-o**, to give in marriage 1198.
donus, *see* **doignus**.
dor/acus, -ea, -eta, *see* DEAUR
dorcerium, *see* DORS
doriferus, *see* **doryphorus**.
dormentilla, *see* TORMENT
dorm/itatio 12c., a 1564, **-itus** c 1180, sleep; **-itio in Christo**, death c 1250; ‡**d. membri**, numbness 14c.; **-itatorius**, for sleeping c 1000; ***-itorium** 10c., c 1000. a 1090, 1526, ‡**-entarium** c 1405, **dortoria** 1349, dormitory, dorter (mon.); **dortarius** c 1162, **dortorarius** c 1250, obedientiary in charge of the dorter; **-antus**, (?) dormer 1313; **-itior**, sleepier 1415; **liber -iens**, coucher c 1296; **mensa -iens** a 1220, **tabula -iens** 1254, 1343, table dormant; **-io** c 1076, **d. cum patribus** 12c., 1461, **d. in Domino** 12c., **d. in suos** 12c., to die, be dead; **-io** c 1364, 1549, **-ito** 1306, c 1326, to be dormant; **-iturio**, to be sleepy 8c. 1537.
dornedies, *see* **dirnum**.
doronicum, leopard's bane (bot.) 1634; *cf.* **deronicum**.
dors/um, fur of back 1374 (*cf.* **tergum**, **venter**); 'dorse', back (of document) 1198, 1332; **ad d.**, at the back 1427; **do d.**, to take to flight 1461; **fassus -alis**, back-load

1327, 1330; **-amentum,** endorsement 1389, a 1452; c 1396, **-ale** a 1090, 1513, **-alis** 1374, **-alium** a 1275, **-ellus** 13c., **dossale** c 1255, 1303, **dossellum** c 1220, 13c., ‡**docillus, ducellus** 15c., **-are** c 1365, **-arium** 1329, 1460, **-erium** c 1330, **-erum** 1395, ***-orium** 1369, c 1510, **dosserium** 1328, 1405, 'dossal', curtain; **-ale** c 1150, 1316, **-arium** c 1315, back of a cope; **-arium** 1242, **dossarium** 1213, **dosserium, dosserum** 1265, 1300, ‡**-ilollum,** **-olollum** 15c., ‡**-uale** 1570, cart-saddle; **-erium** 1419, 15c., **dosserium** c 1115, 1419, **dorcerium** 1316, 1390, **dossorium** 1419, 'dorser', basket slung on back; **dossarius,** sumpter beast 1252; **-ata,** blow on back a 1135; **-atim,** back to back c 1310; **-ilis,** reversed c 1180; **dosso,** to endorse c 1285; to cover on the back 1368; to plaster, pug (arch.) 1285, 1290; to pound 13c.

dort-, *see* DORM

dorwardus, door-ward, porter 14c.

doryphorus (doriferus), spearman, body-guard c 1434.

dos, endowment (eccl.) c 1000. c 1070, 1441; ***widow's dower 1086, 1419; d. adventicia** c 1258, **d. adventiva** c 1290, dowry given by other than bride's parent; **d. profecti-cia** c 1258, c 1290, **d.** †**perfectiva** c 1290, dowry given by bride's parent (or grand-parent); **d. nominata,** portion of bride-groom's estate set aside as dower c 1185; **dosclum,** dowry, marriage-portion 1278; **dot/abilis,** entitled to widow's dower 1441, a 1564; **-alicium** 12c., 1525, †**datalicium** 13c., †**-alium** 1461, dowry; (?) widow's dower 13c.; c 1070, c 1170, **-atio** c 1255, c 1483, endowment (eccl.); c 1192, †**-alitas** 1229, gift; **-alicius,** of a dowry c 1188, c 1338; of an endowment (eccl.) p 1330; **-atio,** bestowal of dower or dowry 1203, c 1554; **-arium** c 1192, c 1298, **dodarium** (Sicily) 1177, **doarium** 1176, 1518, †**doua-rium** (? **donarium**) 1525, **dowarium** a 1166, **duarium** c 1180, c 1250, **duaria** c 1200, 1332, dowry *or* widow's dower; **-ator** a 1400, c 1458, **-atrix** (*f.*) 1243, en-dower, benefactor (eccl.); **-atrix** 1536, **-issa** 1544, 1681, **-aria** 1559, **doageria** 1518, **dowaressa** 1520, dowager; **-o,** to endow (eccl.) c 1284, c 1520; to endow widow with her third 1249, 1294; **d. ad ostium ecclesie** c 1185, 1259.

dosca, *see* doxa.

dos/inus c 1300, 1447, **-ius (-eus)** c 1428, 1445, ashen grey.

dosis, dose 1252, 1620.

doss-, *see also* DORS

dossa allii, clove of garlic (O.F. *dousse*) a 1250.

dossena, *see* dozena.

dot-, *see also* dos.

dot/arius, -io, *see* 2 data.

douarium, *see* dos.

doub-, *see also* DEALB

doublett-, *see* doblettum; DUPL

douell/a, -um 1300, 1327, **duella** 1290, stave of barrel; **doela** 1309, **duella** 1299, 1312, **dula** 1297, dowel, wooden peg; **dewlegga, dewillegga,** 'duledge', dowel connecting

felloes 1351; **dulo,** to fit (nave) with dowels 1305.

doukera, diver (bird) 1544.

douna, *see* duna.

doungerium, *see* domigerium.

dova, *see* duva.

dover/antes, satellites, forest officers (Salop) c 1205; **-ettum** (†**donerettum**), payment levied by the same (W. *dofraeth*) 1227, 1232.

dowar/essa, -ium, *see* dos.

doxa 940, 960. c 1130, c 1390, **dosca** 12c., glory; adornment c 1200.

doynus, *see* doignus.

doytelettus, doytellus, *see* ductio.

dozena 1446, **dossena** 1299, 1509, **dussen/a, -um** 1467, 1504, **duzenna** 1226, **ducena** 1265, dozen.

draba, a cruciferous plant 1641.

dracena, rudder c 1250, c 1420.

drach-, *see* drasca.

drac/o, dragon-banner (carried in Rogation processions) c 1250, c 1400; kite (toy) *or* serpentine curve 1622; fire-drake, comet c 1250, 1343; mercury (alch.) c 1320, ‡1652; **d. herba** (bot.) 1632; *see also* sanguis; **d. lune,** lunar eccentric a 1250; **D. Rubeus,** Rouge Dragon (her.) 13c.; **-oneus,** dragon-like c 550; **-ontinus,** of a dragon c 1315; ‡**drag/o,** dragon 15c.; **-anita** 13c., ‡c 1440, ‡**-ontea, -untea** 14c., **draguntia** a 1250, snakeweed (bot.).

dracoma, *see* TRACH

dracus, water-sprite (in Rhône) c 1212.

draenerum, drain 1575.

draga, drag, draw-net 1275; drag, sledge 1248; *cf.* **draya, tragum.**

drag/agantum 13c., ‡**-antum** 14c., 1652, ‡**tragacanthum** 14c., vitriol; **d. rubeum** 13c.; *see also* **tragacantha.**

1* **drag/etum, -etta** 1234, 1402, **-ium** **(-eum)** 1227, 1316, **-ia** 1257, 1270, (?) **drenca** 1297, 'dredge' (mixture of barley and oats); *see also* **drasca.**

2 **drag/etum** 1317, c 1375, **-ea** 13c., **-ium** 1342, *dragée,* sweetmeat.

dragma, drachma 1144, c 1580; ‡bezant 13c., c 1440; ornament (? in form of gold coin) c 1200, 1465; *see also* **drama.**

drag/o, -untia, etc., *see* draco.

drailla 1361, **drayla** 1283, **dreyla** 1280, **dragla** 1284, 'drail', iron bow of plough.

draituria, *see* DIRECT

dram/a, action c 685; **dragma,** drama 13c., ‡1483; **-aticos,** dramatic c 700.

drana, *see* drava.

drangagium, *see* DRENG

drap/a 1337, †**-is** 1402, cloth; **-aria** 1302, c 1400, **-eria** 1257, 1302, **-erium** 1284, drapery, cloth (*coll.*); **-eria,** draper's shop or quarter, cloth market c 1220, 1424; **-arius,** standard-bearer a 1260; 1191, p 1330, **-erius** a 1200, 1435, **-erus** 1440, draper; **d. lineus,** linen-draper 1192, 1267; **-eletus,** little cloth (for straining) c 1258.

drasc/a 12c., 1322, **-um, -us** 1194, 1265, **-hia** c 1290, 1325, **drachia** 1276, **dra-cheum** 1272, 1314, †**dacheum** 1296, ‡**dra-gium** 15c., draff, malt dregs; dregs of dye 1200.

draul-, *see* TRAUL

drava (†**drana**) c 1170, 1442, **drawa** 1316, **drova** 1312, 1319, **drowa** 1260, drove, drove-road; **dravedenna** 12c., **drove-denna** c 1353, **drofdenna** 1356, drove-denn (Kent); **drofmannus**, drover (Sussex) c 1285; **drovio**, to drive beasts 1234.

draya 1250, 1312, **dreia** 1370, dray, sled; *cf.* **draga.**

dregemundus, *see* **dromo.**

dreitura, *see* DIRECT

drenca, *see* 1 **dragetum.**

dreng/us c 1117, 1271, **-nus** 1201, **dreinus** 1130, **threngus** 12c., **dreng** (class of tenant); †**-a** 13c., **-acium** 1205, **-agium** 1179, 1292, **drennagium** c 1210, **dranga-gium** c 1209, 1517, **dringagium** 1183, c 1380, drengage-tenure.

dress/or 1360, 1456, **-orium** 1289, 1416, †**drestrarium** 1307, **-ura** 1287, 1338, dresser, serving-board, cupboard; **domus dreszure** 1306; **-o,** to 'dress' (a plough-share) 1388; **dresceo,** to fit (boards) 1269.

dreyebarellus, 'dryfat', cask for dry goods a 1465.

dreyla, *see* **drailla.**

drigabulum, a burgage rent, (?) 'dry-gavel' (Oxford) 1535.

drimus, (?) field, plain (? δρυμός) c 550.

Drocensis, coin of Dreux (Fr.) a 1142.

drom/o c 1192, p 1348, **-ondus** c 1400, **-undus** c 1188, 15c., **-unda** 1223, ‡**-edus** 15c., **-edarius** p 1340, †**dregemundus** c 1457, dromond, galley; **-edarius** c 1327, **-edus** a 1250, ‡1483, dromedary; drome-dary driver a 1250.

drop/ax, †**-anum,** pitch-plaster (med.) (δρῶ-παξ) a 1250.

drov-, drof-, drow-, *see* **drava.**

drugemannus 1392, **turchemannus** 1292, dragoman.

dry/lyngus, dried ling c 1493; **-millewellus,** dried cod c 1493.

dual/itas, duality c 793. 1237, c 1470; two-thirds 1546; ‡**-is,** "doubler" (large dish) 1483; **-es** (*pl.*), two c 700.

duar-, *see* **dos.**

dubb/ator, dubber (beater) of leather 1288; (?) dubber of cloth c 1290; **-arius,** (?) dub-ber *or* dauber c 1200; **-o,** to dub (beat) leather 1300; to dub cloth 1288.

dub/itatio, argument that a proposition is doubtful (log.) p 1347; *-ietas 760. a 1090, c 1400, †**-itas** 1400, doubt; **-iosus** c 1470, **-italis** c 1178, **-itatus** a 1408, doubtful, questionable; **-itabundus** 1610, **-itativus** c 1430, doubting, hesitant, **-itativus** (gram.), expressing doubt or hesitation c 800. 1524; **-itative** a 1100, c 1343, **-itive** 1428, doubt-fully; **-ito,** to suspect 1209, c 1362; *1169, 1461, **d. me** 1411, to fear; **d. quod,** to doubt that c 793.

dubl-, dubelarium, *see* DUPL

duc-, *see also* **dux.**

‡**duc/a,** form, mould 15c., 1483; ‡**-amen,** moulding c 1440; *see also* **dux.**

ducellus, *see* DORS

ducena, *see* **dozena.**

ducent/ena, two hundredweight 1222; †**decenti** c 1293, **-eni** c 1250, 1461, two hundred; **-uplus,** two-hundredfold 13c.

duc/iclus 8c., **-iculus** c 1325, **-illus** c 1204, ‡c 1440, tap, spigot.

ducius, *see* **dusius.**

duc/tio, leading in (of harvest) (Sc.) 1433, 1539; **-tamen,** leadership 1006; **-ifer** 8c., **-tivus** c 1270, c 1344, leading, conducive; **-ibilis** 14c., 1379, **-tibilis** c 1290, capable of being led; **-tibilis,** ductile c 1250, c 1320; **-tibilitas,** ductility c 1270; **-tivus,** intro-ductory 1344; **-tator** c 1190, **-trix** (*f.*) 9c. c 1362, guide, leader; **-tor,** bearer, porter 9c. 1336, 1461; **d. generalis,** brigadier-general 1714; **d. navis,** pilot 1224, 1471; †**-ta** c 1150, **-tus** 1227, 1290, **duitus** a 1190, c 1220, **doitus** 1235, 1347, **doetus** a 1220, c 1290, **-tulus** 1226, **-tilus** a 1187, **-tellus** c 1270, **duitellus** (†**dintellus**) c 1200, 1282, **doytellus** 1248, **doytelettus** 1292, conduit, channel, watercourse; †**-tus,** game, quarry 1215 (*cf.* **deductus**); **-ito,** to bring 1013; **-o,** to lead in (hay) a 1128; to draw (criminals) 1378; to conduct (an affair) (G.) c 1285, c 1300; *(with *inf.*) c 1180, c 1448, *(with *gerundive*) c 1145, c 1542, to think fit to, cause to; **d. dignum,** to think fit, approve 1031. 12c.; **d. hundre-dum,** to convene a hundred court 1225; **d. in,** to multiply by a 1150, c 1150; **d. in se,** to square (math.) a 1150; *d. in uxorem, to take to wife 1217, c 1370; **d. in conjugium** c 1250, **d. virum** 1130, to take as husband; **d. navem,** to captain a ship 1217; **d. vitam per,** to live by 1290; **d. ad** 1430, 1524, **d. apud** 1369, **d. me** c 1300, 1349, **-or** 1430, to lead (of a road).

dudde (*pl.*), 'duds', clothes 1307, c 1335.

duella, *see* **douella.**

*duell/um a 1100, 1461, **-ium** c 1125, c 1324, **duillus** c 1160, duel, judicial combat; **d. ad ventum,** battledore-and-shuttlecock 1622; **-ium** c 740, **-io** 9c., war, strife; **-aris** 1314, 1508, **-icus** c 1325, concerned with a duel; **-is,** warrior c 550; **-o,** a challenge 1609; **-o** c 1408, 1609, **-or** 1508, to fight a duel.

duit-, *see* **ductio.**

dukettus, *see* **dux.**

dul/a, -o, *see* **douella.**

dulcarnon, Pythagoras' theorem (Ar.) c 1200, c 1300.

‡**dulc/edo Saturni,** white lead 1652; **-e fluo,** to flow with fresh water c 1460; **pratum -e,** fresh-water meadow 1296; ‡**herba -is,** liquorice 14c.; **-amara,** bittersweet (bot.) 1632; ‡**-emula,** polypody (bot.) 15c.; **-arius,** provider of sweetmeats c 1160; ‡**panis -iarius,** "marchpane" 1570; **-ibilis,** pleasant c 1000; **-icanus,** sweet-singing c 1200; **-ificatio,** sweetening, washing out of soluble salts a 1235; **-ifluus,** sweet-flowing c 1090, a 1350; **-iloquium,** sweet speech c 1198, c 1380; **-imodo,** melodiously 13c.; **-isapus,** honeyed (fig.) c 1200; **-isonus,** sweet-sounding 810, c 930. c 1130, a 1350; **-orarius,** flatterer c 1160, a 1205; **-oratio,** sweetening a 1250; **-orosus,** pleasant c 1177; †**-ero,** *for* **-oro,** to sweeten c 1204.

dul/ia, worship, service, reverence c 730. c 1200, a 1530; **-us,** slave (δοῦλος) c 865. ‡1483.

dum (with *indicative, present* or *future perfect*) when, as soon as 8c.; (with *indicative, perfect*) since, seeing that 8c.; **dum . . . dum** (with *ppl.*) whether . . . or, both . . . and c 793.

dumus, down (of chicks) (*cf.* O.F. *dumet*) a 1150.

dun/a 1086, c 1283, **-um** 1249, **douna** 1306, **dona** c 1230, down, hill; **-na, denna,** (?) dune (Sussex) 1194; *cf.* **denna, duva.**

dungia c 1267, **dingia** c 1115, dung.

†**dunio**, small coin, (?) *for* **Divionensis,** c 1218.

dun/jo 1223, 1348, **-geo** 12c., **-go** 1238, **dangio** c 1137, **donjo** 1320, 1348, **donjona** 1269, donjon, keep.

duodec/ima, tax of one-twelfth 1296, 1419; **-imhindus, -imhindenus,** (man) having weregeld of 1,200 *solidi* c 1115; **-imo,** twelfthly 1282, c 1343; **-aedron** 1344, **-edron** c 1267, dodecahedron; **-uplo;** twelve-fold c 1110.

***duoden/a** a 1155, 1562, **-um** c 1335, c 1502, **-arius** a 1180, c 1465, dozen, set of twelve; **-a magna, d. parva,** long and short dozen 1462; **-a** 1276, c 1450, **-um** 15c., jury of twelve; **-arius,** foreman of jury c 1290; (*adj.*) twelfth c 1310; **-um,** duodenum (med.) c 1210, a 1250; **-us,** twelfth c 1470; **numerus -us,** number twelve c 1325, c 1330.

duodenn/ium, period of twelve years c 1170, c 1250; ***-is** c 730. c 1125, c 1395, †**duodenus** c 1220, twelve years old.

duodigitalis, two fingers in breadth c 1115.

dupl/atio, doubling (math.) a 1150, 1344; **-aris,** in two parts 9c.; **-arium** 1242, c 1245, **dublarium** c 1245, 13c., **dublerum** 1212, **-ettum** 1300, **dublettum** 1300, (?) 1332, 'doubler', measure of wine; **dublarium** c 1195, 1231, **dublerum** 1191, 1223, **dubelarium** 1204, **mappa dublera** 1218, table-cloth; **-etum** 1442, **dubletta** 1336, 1421, ‡**-iteca** 15c., **dubliteca** 1454, **doubletta (de defenso)** 1406, doublet (garment); **doublettum,** (?) sort of print or stencil 1355; **dublettus (lapis d.),** kind of precious stone 1245, 1300; ‡**-atura,** lining (of gown) a 1519; ‡**-atus,** lined a 1519; **-ator fili,** thread-twister 1561; **-eitas,** doubleness c 1300, c 1340; **-e** c 1448, **in -o** c 1340, doubly; **-us,** two c 865; **in -um,** (?) in unison (mus.) c 1330; *see also* **per, crux; -ifacio,** to double c 1197; **-o,** to copy, duplicate c 1347, c 1384.

duplex, lined (of garments) 1220, a 1446; ***double,** solemn (of church festivals) c 1072, 1552; *see also* **2 bera, cervisia; duplic/us,** double c 790; **-amentum,** duplicate (of documents) 13c.; **-atio,** making of a duplicate c 1440; c 1290, c 1390, **-atum** 1549, 'duply', rejoinder (leg.); 1378, 1391, **-atura** 1408, 1458, lining; **d. redditūs** a 1300, **redditus -atus** c 1290, 1292, two years' rent; ‡**-arius,** double-dealer 1483; ***-itas,** duplicity, double-dealing c 730. 1124, c 1670; **-ium,** doublet (garment) 1419, 1457; **-atus,** double (of flowers) 13c.; *lined (of garments) c 1315, 1516; (*subst.*) one of two scribes presenting the same statement 1352; **-o,** to copy or

prepare in duplicate 1275, 1483; to make a rejoinder (leg.) 1392, 1559; to square (math.) 1686; **d. arma** (her.), to bear two coats of arms on one shield p 1394; to bear a plain colour showing a lining of another colour a 1446.

duplo/is, -ida, -mmis, *see* **diplois.**

duploma, *see* **diploma.**

duplus, *see* **duplatio.**

1 dur/atio 1267, 1686, **-amen** c 1250, continuance, duration; **-abilitas,** durability a 1250, c 1327; **-ativus,** concerned with duration p 1300, 1378; **-ative,** lastingly 1344; **-o,** to extend, stretch 1187, 1461.

2 dur/atio, hardening (of steel) 1397; **-us,** disagreeable (of smell) c 740; *see also* **caseus, mater, piscis; -e audio,** to be hard of hearing c 1255; **-iter,** with difficulty 1557; **-itas,** difficulty 1421; **-itia,** harshness (of weather) 1225, 1255; *1275, 1453, †**dirritio** c 1300, duress; ‡**-ibuccus,** block-headed 1440, 1483; **-icors,** hard-hearted c 700. 1166, 1427; **-ilis,** hard c 550; ‡**-ifico,** to harden 1483.

‡**durdales** (*pl.*), tree spirits 1652.

durnellum, *see* **dirnum.**

duscio, *see* DISCUSS.

dus/ius c 730, †**diusius** c 1212, ‡**ducius** 1440, 1483, Gallic demon or sprite; †**-mus,** devil c 550.

dussen/a, -um, *see* **dozena.**

dussinator, *see* **decenna.**

dutior, *see* **diu.**

duumvir, sheriff (of London) 1508.

duva (†**duna,** †**divia,** †**diva**) 1227, 1291, **dova** 1215, **duwa** 1241, *douve,* bank of ditch or moat; *cf.* **duna.**

dux, ealdorman 8c., 9c.; ***duke** 943, c 1000. a 1100, 1586; doge (of Venice) 1393; **D. Verbi,** Speaker of Parliament 1538; **dukettus,** dukeling a 1424; **duxissa** c 1320, c 1500, ***duc/issa** c 1190, c 1540, **-ata** c 1302, ‡**-ella** 1483, duchess; **-atrix,** guide (*f.*) c 1000; **-alis,** ducal c 1125, 1486; **-amen,** guidance c 1070 (*see also* **duca**); c 1170, ***-atus** c 1070, 1480, **ducheria** 1504, duchy; **-atus,** governorship 7c.; ducal status c 1190; escorting, arrest 1244, 1472; military expedition or service 812; vehicle or medium (fluid conveying a solid) c 1115; 1419, 1608, **-atum** 1392, **-ata** 1426, ducat (coin); **d. de Camera,** papal ducat 1432.

duzenna, *see* **dozena.**

dyas (dias), number two c 950.

dycenum, *see* **decenna.**

dyna/mis, power c 950; **-mida,** potency 13c.; †**dimi** (*pl.*), powers, means c 1437; †**dinaldis,** potentiality (log.) c 1200; **-stia** dynasty c 1212.

dyota, *see* **diota.**

dyrrhachium, cleavage c 950.

dyscol/us, (discol-) *c 1125, c 1546, **-icus** 1378, ill-tempered, spiteful; ‡"truant" 1483; ‡**-atus,** "truancy" c 1440; **-ia,** ill temper 1378; **-o** (? **-or**), to be ill-tempered 1378.

dyscrasi/a, distemper, disease c 1197, 1427; **-or,** to be distempered c 1320, 1378.

dyscritus, having a dangerous crisis (med.) a 1250.

dysenteria 1200, **dissenter/ia** a 1250, c 1540,

dissinteria c 1280, discenteria a 1250, 13c., dysentery; -icus c 1200, c 1330, dissintericus c 1200, c 1250, dysenteric.
dysenum, see decenna.
dysis (disis), west (δύσις) c 1180.

dysphonia, cacophony 1620.
dyspnia a 1250, 13c., disnoia, ‡disma, ‡dimpnia 14c., asthma (δύσπνοια); disnoicus, a̓sthmatic 1200.
dzifta, see sifta.

E

E, musical note 1351; see also ex.
ealdormannus, see aldermannus.
ea/propter, thereby 13c.; -tinus 939, eotenus 990, for -tenus.
eas-, see aisia.
ebalatio, see AVAL
ebanus, see HEB
ebba, ebb, ebb-tide c 1258; hebbyngwera, ebbing-weir 1547.
ebd-, see HEBDOM
ebes, see abietinus.
Ebionita, Ebionite heretic 12c.
ebiscus, see hibiscus.
Eboracensis, Yorkist 1586.
eboralis, see borealis.
ebraia, ibraia, (?) malt (Norm.) 1203; cf. brasium.
†ebri/catio (? -atio), tippling 1434.
ebulia, see eubulia.
ebull/atio c 1470, †-io c 1130, for -itio, boiling, bubbling up; -itus, invected (her.) c 1595.
eburneus, see ALB
eburninus a 1275, eborneus 1245, yburneus c 1250, of ivory; ivorium 1298, (?) ivo 1332, ivory.
eburso, to disburse c 1365, 1515.
ecario, see EXCARI
ecceco, see EXCEC
eccentric/itas 1267, excentricitas a 1250, 1686, eccentricity (astr.); -us (adj.) 1267, c 1612, encentricus c 1267, excentricus c 1160, a 1250, eccentric (astr.); (subst.) c 1233, c 1608, excentricus 1267, ecentris c 1184, eccentric orbit.
eccheudrum, see caldaria.
ecclesi/a, *a church, the Church (bibl.); diocese 8c.; the clergy (coll.) 1517; e. Anglorum 1169, e. Anglicana 12c., c 1600; e. Hibernicana 1216, 1404; e. Scoticana c 1250, 1545; e. antiqua a 1120, e. mater 1086, c 1250, *e. matrix c 1150, 1534, a mother church; *e. mater, the Church, Mother Church c 900, 1017. 12c., 1461; e. campestris, chapel c 1115; e. capitalis c 1115; e. episcopalis c 1080, 1317, e. major c 1178, 1235, e. principalis c 1133, cathedral church; e. catholica c 1090, 1381, e. universalis 1274, 1414; e. communis, church whose free revenue goes to common fund of a chapter, etc. 13c.; e. militans c 1284, c 1444, e. militaris 1479, church militant; e. triumphans c 1343, 15c.; e. primitiva 12c.; e. parochie, parish church c 1130; e. ville 1086, a 1128; *e.-ola, little church, chapel 1086, 1586; -archus, archbishop 1017; -asticus *c 1090, 1566, -alis c 1180, ecclesi-astical; spiritual c 1254, c 1273; (subst.) ecclesiastic, cleric, church official 705. c 1125, c 1546; -astice, according to ecclesiastical law c 1125, c 1334; -atim, church by church 12c.
echinus, for echeneis, remora 1150; ‡"tench" 15c.
echonizo, to echo c 1422.
ecio, to 'eche' (clean out) a ditch 1508.
ecligma, electuary (med.): eligma a 1250, ‡14c.
eclip/sis 12c., 1414, ‡clipsis 15c., eclipse; (fig.) failure, extinction, intermission c 1170, a 1408; -salis, of an eclipse 1344; -tica, the ecliptic 1267, 1326; -so c 1186, 1508, †-simo a 1186, -tico 13c., c 1400, to eclipse; -so, to suffer eclipse c 1436; (fig.) -so 1256, c 1450, -tico c 1184, to obscure; †-tito, to fail a 1250; see also ELLIP
economus a 615. c 1125, 1537, iconom/us (yco-) 1239, 1573, †conconomus c 1310, icopeta c 1437, steward; e. Domini, servant of the Lord c 950; e. (i.) ecclesie, patron or churchwarden c 1190, 1684; e. navis, purser 1560; -ia, husbandry c 1365, 1578; -ice, prudently, thriftily 1378; -icus, of a household 1429; -io 1436, ‡-ico c 1440, to husband, manage.
econtrario, to oppose 1449.
ecoquo, see excoquo.
ecsta/sis (exsta-, exta-) c 700, c 950. a 1100, 1620, -sia 1461, ‡extecis, extisis 15c., ecstasy, trance; -ticus, ecstatic c 870. 1345, 15c.
ecthesis, putting out, exposing 7c.
eculeus, see 2 acus.
ecumenicus 1437, icumenicus 1438, ecumenical.
ecurio, see EXCARI
edelingus, see adelingus.
‡edelphus, one who prognosticates by the nature of the elements 1652.
edema (oed-), swelling 1634.
edena, ear c 550.
‡edentator, "tooth-drawer" 15c.
edes c 1504, c 1590, e. sancta c 1130, religious house; edicula, tomb 1090; small religious house 1586; ediculum, chapel 1502; edeficium, building c 1255, 1583; edific/ium pontis, -amen p., -atio p., brigbote 12c.; -amen arcis, -atio a., burhbote 12c.; -abilis 1549, -arius 15c., -ativus a 1205, c 1400, -atorius 1235, 1378, edifying; *-atio, edification 1124, 1586; -ator 14c., -atrix (f.) c 1100, edifier; -ans, builder 1463; †edico, for -o, to build c 1204; -o, to build over, upon 1252, 1430; to domicile, establish c 1312; *to edify c 1125, c 1400; see also edituus, ethees.

ed/ia, sufficiency of food, health c 1340, c 1360; welfare, "ease" c 1336, ‡1483; ‡-iosus, "easy" 1483; -ibilis c 1362, ‡1483, -ilis c 1362, edible; *-ulium c 1000. a 1100, c 1362, -ilium 1307, food; -ulitas, famine 1192; cf. esura.

edic/o, to utter 1299; see also edes; †editum, for -tum, edict 12c.

edilis, (?) sacristan c 1000; see also edia; cf. edituus.

edit/io, declaration of the form of an action (canon law) 1236, 1242; declaration as to costs (leg.) c 1258; (?) presentation to a living (Sc.) 1236; tradition 12c.; -iuncula, short treatise c 1268; -iusculus, somewhat elevated 1528; -or, author c 1225, 1378; -rix, caterer, stewardess c 550; -um, see EDIC; edo pondus, to fix a weight by statute 1422.

edituus, sacristan 980. c 1115, 1414; church-warden 1533; e. regius, palace-keeper c 1178.

edoc/tio, teaching c 740; -te, learnedly c 710; see also educamen.

edomadarius, see HEBDOM

edom/atio, conquest c 1283; -itor, conqueror c 1250.

edormio in Domino, to die c 1450.

‡edorso, "to gall" (? a horse) c 1440.

edubito, to state as a subject of doubt c 1115.

‡educ/amen, -amentum, "team", brood 15c.; edocatus, for -atus, c 793.

educ/tio, expulsion 760; carrying away, export c 1170, 1338; actualization (phil.) 1267, c 1270; e. carruce, Plough Monday (first after Epiphany) 1378; -ibilis, potential, able to be actualized c 1290, c 1365; -tivus, 'eductive' (med.), tending to drain off a 1250; 'eductive' (log.), tending to actualize c 1270; -tus (4th decl.), leading forth c 1180; -o, to tear out c 1115; to knock out (pegs) 1350; to bail out (of prison) c 1115; to deduct c 1250, 13c.; to pervert (from) 1299; to bring into being, actualize 1267.

edulium, see edia.

eduma, see I iduma.

effeco, to drain to the dregs c 1193; ‡to cleanse 1483.

effect/io, production of an effect c 1365, c 1390; -ibilis, capable of being an effect c 1300, p 1300; -ivitas, power of producing an effect c 1270, c 1362; -ive, effectively, in effect 1267, c 1444; -ivus, effective c 1170, 1406; †effected c 1220; -ualis, effectual a 1100, 1687; *-ualiter c 850. a 1100, c 1582, -uose a 1100, 1378, effec-tually; -um capio 15c., c 1478, e. habeo c 1328, c 1516, e. sortior c 1325, 1522, to take effect; -ui mancipo c 1125, 15c., in -u pono c 1473, to put into effect; in -u, in effect, virtually 1482; see also ad; -us secundarius a 1250; -um, effect a 1250; efficiens a 1233, c 1444, causa e. c 1200, a 1233, efficient cause (log.); -o c 1360, -uo 1344, c 1376, to effect; -o (? for effeto), to destroy a 1250; see also AFFECT

†effer/beo, for -vo, to boil up c 1450.

effero calcaneum, to rebel c 1160, 1174; cf. elatus, elevo.

effeta, opening (bibl. ἐφφαθά) c 1220.

†effevus, (?) f.l. for efferus, c 950.

effibulo, to untie c 1200.

†effici/aliter (? offici-), effectively (? or officially) 15c.; †-atus, an official 1516; -o, see EFFECT, AFFECT

effictio, fiction, formation c 1500.

effigi/atio, making of images c 1200, c 1250; -alis, represented by a figure 1432; -atim, in the form of an image 12c., 14c.

effiguratus, fashioned as represented c 870.

‡effilatum, hem 1570.

effimer-, see ephemerida.

effitior, to speak 5c.

efflagratio, blazing up c 865.

efflat/or, one who breathes out c 1125, c 1315; †-us, f.l. for efferatus, c 1400.

efflor/escentia, excrescence 1622; -atus, adorned c 950.

efflux/io c 1160, c 1350, -us p 1300, effluen-tia c 1290, c 1350, flowing out, flood; lapse (of time) 1393; effluenter, abundantly 1307, c 1310; -us, elapsed, past (of time) c 1250, 1474.

effocale, fuel, firewood 1304.

efform/atio, formation, shaping c 1608; -o, to form, shape c 1200, 1620.

effort/iamentum (efforc-), fortification, strengthening 1175, 1254; e. judicii, afforcement of court (leg.) 1212, a 1246; -ium, force (of troops) 1372; -ialiter 1213, 1254, -iate 1208, c 1235, in force, so as to reinforce; -iatus, reinforced, stiffened (of cloth) 1225, 1245; -io (esforcio), to fortify, strengthen 1142, c 1293; to compel, distrain 1198, 13c.; to violate, rape c 1190, 1231; e. assisam, to afforce an assize 1240; e. curiam, to afforce a court (leg.) 1217, 1251; cf. AFFORT

effoss/io, tearing out, wound c 1100, c 1430; effoditio, digging up, excavating c 1440; -or, engineer, sapper c 1192; ‡-o, to dig up 15c., 1483.

effract/io, breaking 1277, 1385; e. carceris 1426; e. domorum c 1255; -or a 1142, 1258, -arius c 1255, house-breaker, burglar; e. carceris 1426; e. ecclesiarum 1377; e. treugarum 1451; effringo, to weaken c 1200; e. pacem 1226; e. pretium, to lower the price c 1125.

†effrago, to be diffused (of fragrance) c 1362.

effrai-, see AFFRAI

effrendeo, to rage c 1150.

effren/is, unbridled c 1125, c 1290; -e, with-out restraint 1378; -esco, to become un-restrained c 1362.

effrigesco, to grow cool c 1125.

effringo, see EFFRACT

effron/s, shameless c 1190, c 1357; -ter, shamelessly 1344.

†effrunitus, (?) for efferatus or effrons, c 1172; cf. also INFRUNIT

effug/atio, putting to flight, banishment c 1250, c 1457; driving out (of deer) 1336; *-o, to put to flight, banish c 730. c 1090, c 1470; to drive off (cattle) 1250, 1587.

effulgoro, to flash forth c 865.

effulminatus, struck by lightning c 1090.

effundo (1st conj.), to make (a road) foundrous 1383; see also EFFUS

effunerarius, undertaker c 1204.

effus/io, casting, melting down (of metal) 1387, c 1533; loss through leakage 1300; ***e. sanguinis** c 1160, 1382, **-us sanguis** 1275, 1281, bloodshed; **-or sanguinis**, shedder of blood 7c. c 1177, a 1408; †**-iva**, (?) abundance 13c.; **effundo**, to cast (metal) c 1440, 1447.

eg/entia, indigence c 1366; **-ene**, sparingly c 1125; **-ellus**, poor c 1250; **-eo** (with *inf.*), to need 9c.; **e. de** c 1324.

egersimon, rousing: †**engerimion** a 1180.

†**eges**, distilling vessel 13c.

egestura, *see* 1 **agistamentum**.

eglutio, to gulp down, swallow whole c 870.

ego: *acc.* **meme** 781; *gen.* **mis** 6c.; *dat.* **mihhi** 867, ***michi** 948, 993. 12c., c 1515; **meater**, in my manner 8c.

egocer/on, *for* **-os**, capricorn 11c.; **egloceron**, kind of rhinoceros a 1250.

egress/io, invasion, attack c 793; flooding (of Nile) 1267; **ekressus**, egress 1292; **-ibilis**, capable of proceeding or issuing c 1270; permitting egress 1345; **-or**, gadabout monk c 1470; **egredior**, to issue (of descendants) c 1250; (with *acc.*) to leave 1292; **e. viam universe carnis**, to die c 1326.

egr/itudo regis, king's evil 1278; †**agritudo**, sickness 12c.; **-e atque -e**, hardly c 1460; **-iuscule**, with a little reluctance c 1500; **-otativitas**, sickliness 13c.; **-otativus**, sickly c 1160, c 1250; **-ifero**, to be displeased with 15c.; **-oto**, to make ill c 1250, 1305.

egtendalum, 'eight-deal' (half quarter) 1199.

Egyptiacus, *see* **dies**.

ehtemannus, serf (A.S. *æhteman*) c 1115.

eicio, *see* EJECT

ein-, **eignecius**, *see* **esnecia**.

eirenarcha, justice of the peace 1579, 1609.

eir/ians, **-o**, *see* **eyrum**.

eis-, *see* **aisia**; **issaccum**.

ejaculatio, shooting 16c.; emission 1620.

eject/io, discharge, shooting 1426; 1277, 1419, **e. maris** 1285, **-us maris** c 1066, c 1300, jettison; (?) challenge c 1290; **e. firme**, ejectment from farm 15c., 1573; **-ivus**, ejective (med.) a 1250; **-or**, dispossessor c 1258; **eicio**, to jettison 1285.

ejulatorius, lamenting c 1325.

ejuro (†**eviro**) **forestam**, (?) to clear oneself by oath of offence against forest laws 1201.

ekressus, *see* EGRESS

ela, *see* **ala**.

elaale, gnomon (Ar.) a 1150.

elabor/atio, elaboration, extraction (alch.) c 1360, ‡1652; working out 1380; **-ator**, worker 15c.; **e. terre** 1559; **-atum**, (?) tilled land, estate c 1060; **-o**, (?) to go abroad 1439; (with *inf.*) to strive 1157.

elact-, *see also* **elasticus**.

elacto, to suckle, nourish (fig.) c 1115; ‡to wean 1483.

elanceatus, accurate 12c.

elango, *see* ELONG

elangueo, to be faint 12c., 1622.

elapido, to deprive by stoning c 1150.

elapsus, (*subst.*) lapse, expiry 1239; (*ppl.*) ***past**, elapsed c 1090, 1684.

*elarg/atio a 1250, 1546, **-itio** c 1376, c 1488, enlargement; **-itio**, expenditure 1312; **-iatio**, release from captivity 1440; **-imentum**, release on parole 1402; **-io** (**-eo**) c 1321, 1350, **eslargio** 1240, **-o** 1237, 1476, to enlarge; **-o**, to release 1440, 1453.

elasticus, elastic (*adj.*) 1686; **elater**, spring (mechanical) 1686; **elact/eris**, †**lacteris**, wild cucumber a 1250, ‡14c.; **-arium** a 1250, ‡**-erium** 14c., *for* **elaterium**, aperient juice of the same; **unguentum -ariatum** a 1250.

elatio, annealing (of tiles) 1373; **eleo** 1355, 1374, **elevo** 1371, to anneal; to calcine (iron ore) 1330.

elatus, high, arched (of nose) c 1200; *cf.* **effero**.

‡**elbidus**, "russet" (? *cf.* **helvus**) 1483.

†**eldefader**, ancestor 1263.

elect/io, deliberate choice (προαίρεσις) 1344; 'election', favourable conjunction (astr.) 1267; affinity (alch.) 1267; *see also* ELIC, **vas**; **-atio**, *for* **-io**, election c 1200; **-ive**, by election c 1194, c 1218; **-ivus**, selective, optional, concerned with choice c 793. 12c., c 1270; chosen 1450; elective 1293, 1459; expressive of choice (gram.) 1524; **-or**, chooser, decider c 1190; elector 1200, a 1564; **e. operariorum** 1354; **e. Imperii** c 1400, 16c.; **-oratus**, status of (imperial) elector 1414; **-orium**, principle of choice c 1360; **-a**, **-um**, sort of cloth 1171; **-i** (*pl.*) c 730. c 1123, c 1400, **e. Dei** c 1130, 1461, the elect (theol.); **-a**, abbess elect c 1220; ***-us**, abbot or bishop elect c 804, 824. c 1310, c 1470; **elig/ibilis**, desirable c 1290, c 1443; eligible c 1343; **-ibilitas**, desirability c 1344; **elegit**, name of a writ 1338, 15c.; **-o**, to seize under writ of *elegit* 15c.; (with *inf.*) to choose 8c., 9c. 1203, 1417; (with **quam**) to prefer c 1310; **elio** 933, **elego** 11c., **eliguo** (G.) 1315, *for* **-o**, to elect, choose; *see also* **compromissum**, **inspiratio**, **scrutinium**, **Spiritus Sanctus**.

1 **electr/um**, amber: ‡jet 1570; lightning c 730; **-icus**, of amber, amber-like 1267, 1622; electrical 1620, 1686.

2 **electr/um**, latten *or* pewter c 1270, 1509; **-arius**, pewterer 1492, 1508; **-eus** (**-ius**) 1492, a 1564, **-inus** 1387, 1535, made of pewter.

3 **electr/um** (†**-im**), (?) figwort (bot.) a 1150, ‡15c.

*electuarium 1171, 1417, **lectuarium** 1348, **letuarium** c 1250, electuary, cordial; *cf.* **ecligma**.

*eleemosyn/a (**elemosin-**) c 691, c 834. 1086, 1549, **elemoxsina** 847, **elimosina** c 730, 8c. 1456, 1500, **elemonia** a 1200, †**elemosia** c 1220, **-aria** c 1130, alms, almoign; **e. aratri** c 1102, **e. pro aratris** a 1100, **e. carrucarum** c 1115, a 1120, plough-alms; **e. ecclesiastica** 12c., **e. ecclesie** 1086, **e. franca** 1212, 13c., ***e. libera** c 1130, c 1492, **e. pura et perpetua** 11c. c 1140, c 1492, **feodum -ale** 12c., frank-almoign; **e. constituta** a 1128, 1284, **e. statuta** 1259, fixed alms; **e. (Sancti) Petri**, Westminster abbey estates c 1125, c 1362; **-a** c 1185, ***-aria** c 1150, 1488,

-arium 1206, 1345, **elimosinariatus** 1327, **elemosaria** c 1310, **elmoneria** 1213, **almaria** 1261, **almonera** 1225, **almoneria** 1213, almonry, office of almoner; -aria 1201, c 1515, -arium 1251, **elimosinaria** c 1400, **domus** -aria 1201, 1535, almshouse; *see also* **episcopus**; **amenerium**, (?) alms-bag 1247; **aumonera**, wallet 1261; -arie c 1362, c 1363, -anter 1412, by way of alms; -arius, charitable, concerned with alms c 1090, 1622; **discus e.**, alms-dish 1431; **-arius 6c. 1086, 1535, **elimosinarius** 9c. 1539, **elimozinarius** 1583, -ator c 1090, 1456, almoner; -arius, (?) recipient of alms c 1376; -atio, almsgiving c 1378; **-o, to grant in almoign c 1190, 1413; -o (-or), to give alms c 1378, 1427; *cf.* ARMARI

elefant-, *see* **elephas**.
elefuga 1267, 1345, **eleufuga** c 1200, fifth proposition of Euclid.
elegatio, (?) disherison 12c.
elegiace, in elegiacs a 1452.
eleg/it, -o, *see* ELECT
eleg/us, wretch, wretched c 1000. c 1100, 1345.
element/a (*pl.*), waves, sea, weather c 730. 12c., c 1400; **elimentum**, *for* -um, 930; -alis c 1227, c 1470, -aris c 1109, 1620, -arius c 1109, c 1605, elemental; -aris, elementary c 1177, a 1180; -aritas, elemental composition c 1270; -ariter, elementally c 1115; -arius, elementary treatise p 1300, 15c.; -atio, elemental formation c 1375; -ativus, characteristic of an element c 1270; -atus, composed of elements a 1166, 1564; -icus, specialist in the elements c 1300.
elemo-, *see* ELEEMOSYN
elempnium, *see* **helenium**.
elench/us, refutation c 1160, 1344; title of book by Aristotle c 1180, c 1549; -ice, by way of refutation 1344; -icus, concerned with refutation 14c., a 1361.
elec, *see* **elatio**.
ele/pannus, (?) plank or panel of elm-wood 1341; -postis, (?) elm-post 1341.
elephas, (?) elephant-house (at the Tower) 1277; ‡**olefans**, elephant 15c.; **elephant/-iosus** (**elefant-**) c 1200, a 1250, -uosus c 1180, -inus c 1325, -ius 1468, afflicted with elephantiasis; **lepra** -ia c 1200, **morbus** -iosus a 1135; -inus, huge c 793.
eleufuga, *see* **elefuga**.
eleus, (?) object of charity (ἔλεος) c 950; *cf.* **elegus**.
elev/atio, swelling (med.) a 1250; augmentation (of compensation) 13c.; removal c 1300; elevation to office, promotion c 1340, c 1370; levying (of dues) c 1292, 15c.; higher key (mus.) 1194, c 1296; pillar c 1255; ‡sublimation (alch.) 1652; c 1370, **e. corporis Christi** 1289, c 1447, **e. hostie** c 1223, c 1500, **e. sacramenti** 1394, elevation of the Host (eccl.); **e. arietum**, sort of quintain 1236; **e. feni**, hay-making 1394; **e. mercati**, instituting a market c 1290; -abilis, able to be lifted a 1346; **pons e.**, drawbridge 15c.; -ativus, physically uplifting a 1250; spiritually uplifting c 1367;

-atior, more exalted, puffed up c 1470; -atius, at a greater height 1267; -o, to disinter 10c.; to emboss 1232, 1303; to elevate morally, uplift c 793; to elevate in rank c 1340; to raise, levy (dues) 1324, 15c.; to exalt, puff up c 1180, c 1343; **e. me**, to exalt oneself c 730; **e. calcaneum**, to kick up the heels (fig.) 13c.; **e. cantum**, raise the pitch c 1266, c 1330; **e. de fonte**, to baptize c 900; **e. hostiam**, to elevate the Host c 1220, c 1238; **e. pratum**, to make hay c 1312, 1394; *see also* **elatio**.
eleyson, *Christe eleyson* 1271, c 1346; *cf.* KYRI
elfimerus, *see* **ephemerida**.
†**elia**, (?) *f.l.* for **elementa** *or* **animalia** 1267.
elic/itio p 1300, **electio** p 1300, c 1362, eliciting, actualization (phil.); -ibilis, able to be actualized p 1300, c 1375; able to be inferred 1423; -itivus, apt to elicit, actualize 1290, a 1361; -io, to actualize c 1300; to infer a 1233, c 1442; ‡to tease wool 1483; ‡to destroy 1483.
†**elicus**, (?) *f.l.* for **celicus**, celestial c 1150.
elido, *see* **elisio**.
elig-, *see* **ecligma**; ELECT
‡**elilifagus** 14c., **lilifagus** a 1250, wild sage (bot.) (ἐλελίσφακος).
elimate, clearly, precisely c 1180.
elimentum, *see* ELEMENT
elimino, to banish, get rid of (a thing) c 1197, 14c.
elimito, to banish c 870.
elimo-, *see* ELEEMOSYN
elio, *see* ELECT
Elion, Most High (Heb.) c 550.
eliqu/atio, draining off c 1395; -o, to liquefy, dissolve c 1115, c 1317.
eli/sio, parrying, countering (leg.) c 1258; -do, to quash 1200, c 1343.
eli/tropium, *see* HELI
Eliudianus, *see* **Helvidianus**.
elix/atio a 1250, 15c., †-is 1267, boiling, melting; -atura, water in which something is boiled a 1250, 15c.; -abilis, (?) soluble by boiling c 1270; -o, to wash with hot water c 550; to melt 1267.
elix/ir 1144, 1620, -er 1418, ‡15c., -erium 1337, ‡**alexir**, **yxir** 1652, (?) †**vexir** 1144, elixir (alch.).
ellip/ticus, elliptical (math.) 1686; **eclipticus**, *for* -ticus, elliptical (gram.) c 1180, 13c.; **eclipticōs**, elliptically 988; **eclipsis**, ellipsis (gram.) c 1125, 13c.
ello, *see* **helluo**.
elm-, *see also* **opus** (**elmatum**); ULM
elmoneria, *see* ELEEMOSYN
elmuhahin, rhombus (Ar.) a 1150; **helmunharifa**, trapezium (Ar.) a 1150.
elocericus, *see* HOLO
eloco, to give in marriage 1559, 1654
elocutio, *see* ELOQU
†**eloftina**, (?) *f.l.* for **clostura**, fencing material 13c.
elogi/um, statement c 950, c 1000; plea in defence c 1115; reproach, accusation c 1180, c 1325; -o, to utter c 1375; *cf.* EULOG
elong/atio, prolongation c 1115, c 1386; protraction, delay 9c. c 1302; enlargement c 1386; elongation (astr.) a 1233, 1686; 'eloignment', carrying off (leg.) 1254, 1314;

removal, departure c 1204, 1336; remoteness 1262, c 1366; estrangement 1253; **-abilis**, removable a 1250; **-atior**, remoter. 1378; **-ator**, one who 'eloigns', entices away 1362; **-o**, to prolong, extend (in space) 1188, a 1408; to protract (in time) 1218, c 1458; to postpone c 1200, a 1250; *to remove c 1102, c 1470; c 1285, c 1540, **elango** 1234, to 'eloign', take away, drive off; to estrange 12c., p 1377; to oust, dispossess 1184, c 1293; c 1180, ***-o me** c 1125, 1461, to withdraw; **-or** (*dep.*), to remove, separate c 870.

elopo, to elope 1538; *cf.* ALLOP

eloqu/ium, speech, language 12c., 15c.; c 730, **e. divinum** c 1080, **e. dominicum** c 1125, c 1414, **e. sacrum** c 1300, c 1381, scripture; **e. vulgare**, vernacular tongue 1417, c 1470; **elocutio**, parley, agreement c 1115.

elthedivir, epicycle (Ar. *falak al-tadwir*) a 1200.

elucesc/entia, manifestation 1620; **-o**, to shine forth c 1180, c 1415; *c 1125, 1518, **eluscesco** 1428, to become manifest.

elucid/atio explanation c 1150, c 1444; **-arium**, name of a book c 1300, c 1500; **-ate**, clearly 1344; **-ius**, more clearly c 1192; **-o**, to cause to shine c 730; to brighten, clarify a 1446; *to elucidate, explain c 1125, c 1470; *cf.* illucido.

elucr/atio, gain, profit c 1470; **-or**, to gain c 1430, a 1452.

eluctatorius, contradictory, refutatory c 1180.

elucubrat/io, labour, care 930; **-iuncula**, short treatise 14c.; **-im**, laboriously (?) 12c.

eluculenter, copiously a 1186.

elu/dium, trick c 950. c 1170, c 1494; joke c 1193; ***-sio**, mockery, contempt 1241, 1324; **†-sor**, (?) mocker c 793.

elumb/io c 1180, **-o** c 1620, to enervate.

elumin-, *see* ILLUMIN

eluvio, drain, sewer c 1190; *cf.* illuvio.

†elympsis, brightness c 870.

†ema, hawthorn 15c.

emaceratio, thinning, impoverishment c 1453.

emach, emath, *see* **hemagogum**.

emaciatio, emaciation c 1620.

emadeo, to drip, ooze 1252.

emagnus, very great 1451.

emal-, *see also* **esmallum**.

emalo, to prefer 14c.

eman/atio, flowing c 1080, 1345; emanation c 1250, c 1286; **e. brevis**, issue of a writ a 1564; ***-o**, to emanate (of a document) 1200, 1573; to send out, issue (a document) c 1283, 1686.

emancip/atio, emancipation of son (G.) 1313; exemption, release from obedience (mon.) c 1188; **-o**, to exempt (mon.) c 1250.

emando executioni, to put into execution 15c.

emanuale, *see* **manus**.

emarc/idus c 1407, 1620, **-uatus** 10c., withered; **-eo**, to wither away 1252, c 1400; **-esco**, to become obsolete c 570.

embadum, square measure (ἐμβαδόν) a 1180.

embass-, *see* AMBASS

embiginatio, *see* ERUBIGIN

emblem/a, (?) tile *or* pane c 950; emblem, device, allegory c 1595, 1620; **-aticus**, checky (her.) 1595.

emblicus, emblic (bot.) a 1250, 13c.

embol/a, recruitment, population 1296; **-us**, peg, stopper, ramrod 1620; **-ismus**, intercalary day or month 8c., 815; prayer inserted in canon of the mass c 1197; 7c., 8c., **annus -ismalis** 1079, 1344, **a. endibolismalis**, **a. endibolismus** 8c., leap-year; **-im**, by the way c 793.

embossatus, *see* **imbossatus**.

embotum a 1250, ‡14c., ‡**embula** 1652, funnel (Fr. *embut*).

embraciator, *see* IMBRAC

embraud/atio (enb-) 1441, inbroudatio 1432, embroidery; **-atus** 1415, **embroudatus** c 1412, 1421, **embrowdatus** 15c., **embrowdeatus** 1415, †**enbrordatus** c 1370, **enbroditus** 1430, **imbraudatus** 1415, 1489, **inbrudatus** c 1500, **imbroidatus** 1399, embroidered.

embroch/a, wet poultice a 1250, ‡14c.; **-atio**, embrocation a 1250, 1634; **-o**, to poultice a 1250.

embryo, embryo c 1200, c 1620.

embula, *see* **embotum**.

emedullate, without pith c 1200.

‡emembris, limbless 1483.

ememoro, to call to mind, remember 11c.

*emend/a 1086, p 1475, **amenda** a 1200, 1509, ***-atio** 1086, 1461, **-atis** 1267, amends, fine, compensation; **-a altaris** c 1102, **-atio altaris** c 1110, c 1115, fine for injury to priest; ***-atio** c 1080, c 1550, **amendatio** c 1195, improvement, reform; ***c 1228, 1532, **-amentum** 1306, mending, repair; **e. civitatis**, burhbote c 1110; **e. dominationis**, manbote c 1115; **e. domorum**, housebote 1086; **e. pontis**, brigbote c 1110; **e. regni**, acknowledgement of royal dignity c 1115; **-abilis**, subject to fine or compensation 1080, c 1125; **-ator treuge**, supervisor of truce 1215, 1254; **-o** 853. 1086, c 1420, **amendo** c 1258, to pay a fine, compensate, make amends (for); to improve, correct 1086, c 1343; to mend, repair c 1250, 1375; **e. me**, to benefit 1188; *see also* MEND

emensio, lapse (of time) c 1170.

ementior, to break an oath c 1115.

ementorium, *see* EMPT

ement/ulatio a 1250, **-elatio** 1252, castration; **-ulo**, to castrate c 1160, c 1255.

emeraldus, *see* **smaragdo**.

emeraudes, *see* HEM

emerciamentum, *see* AMERCI

emer/gentia (*n. pl.*) c 1298, 1495, **-gentie** (*f. pl.*) a 1452, **-genda** 1548, issues, arisings, accruals; **-gentia** (*f. s.*), emergence 1686; **-sio**, outflow c 1200; occurrence, emergency c 1306; **-sus**, having arisen 1269, c 1455; **-go**, to flood, inundate (*cf.* IMMER) 1289, 1433; *to arise, occur 1164, 1461; to accrue (of interest) 1253; *see also* **annus**; **-so**, to flow out c 1400.

†emeriatio, (?) polishing with emery 1397.

‡emerit/io, thanks 1483; **-e**, duly c 1150; **-orius**, meritorious 1325.

emerlio, *see* **mereella**.

emeroidus, *see* **smaragdo**.

emi-, *see also* HEMI

emibilis, *see* EMPT

‡emico, to crumble c 1220.

emigratio, going out into the world (mon.) c 1470; party of emigrants c 700.

Emilianus, type of gladiator c 1160.

emin/entia, eminence (title) 9c. c 1188, c 1338; 'eminence', quality transcending definition (log.) c 1300; -ens, eminent (log.) c 1300; -enter, in an eminent degree (log.) p 1300.

emingo, to urinate c 1172.

emin/or, to threaten c 1433; ‡-o, to drive out c 1220.

emiperus, *see* ephemerida.

emiss/io, rescue (from prison or pound) c 1075, c 1115; utterance c 1090, c 1204; offshoot c 793; -arius a 1120, c 1414, equus e. c 730. c 1180, c 1400, stallion; fama -aria, rumour put about 1620; -ivus, tending to emit c 1270; ‡-orium, sluice 1570.

emo, *see* EMPT

emol/itus 1251, c 1290, -utus (G.) 1283, edged (of weapons); -o c 1180, 1234, esmolo 1187, to grind, whet.

emollesco, to become soft c 1250.

emolog-, *see* HOMOLOG

emolumentum: emulumentum, benefit 12c.

emordeo, to bite away c 1470.

emoreissa, *see* hemagogum.

emortuus boscus, dead wood 1306.

empar/antia, -atio 1289, amparantia 1313, amparentia 14c., imparentia 1437, protection, possession, seisin (G.); -ator, occupier, possessor (G.) 1289; -o 1242, amparo 1279, to seize, take possession of (G.).

emp/ema, -ima, *see* empyma.

empericus, *see* empiricus.

empha/sis, stress c 1080, c 1210; -tice, especially c 730; with emphasis c 1200, c 1620; -ticus, denoting emphasis c 1277, c 1670; ineffable 1220.

‡emphraxis 14c., enfraxis (enfrasis) a 1250, obstruction (med.); ‡emphracticus 15c., †eufracticus a 1250, obstructive (med.).

emphyt/eosis (emphit-) c 1194, 1549, -iosis 1287, a 1446, -esis 1281, enfitheosis 1283, emphyteusis; -eota, lessee, tenant, in emphyteusis 1277, 1533; -eutarius 1549, -eotecarius 1285, -eoticus 1546, 1591, -ioticus a 1446, emphioteticus c 1220, emphyteutic.

empir-, *see also* EMPYR

emp/iricus c 1270, 1620, -ericus a 1250, c 1366, empirical.

emplast/ria 1277, implastrum 1312, plaster (for walls); emplaustrum c 1280, implastrum 1322, amplastrum 12c., ‡-icum 1570, *for* -rum, plaster (med.); -ratio 1266, implastratio 1534, plastering (walls); plastering (med.) c 1470; implastrator, plasterer c 1280, 1354; -rus, made of plaster, cement c 1500; -ro, to plaster (walls) 1240; to smear 14c.; a 1250, amplastro c 1300, to plaster (med.).

†templatin, (cited as) a term of civil law c 1200.

emploio, to employ, use 1452.

emponenth (†emponemb, amponenth),

good omen, passing from left to right (? *en ponant*) a 1235.

empori/um, business, deal c 1433; †impurium, market-town 12c.; -olum, small market-town 1586.

empriza, *see* imprisa.

empromtum 1199, 13c., emprumptum 1223, empruntum 1195, c 1214, loan (Fr. *emprunt*).

emprosthotonos, drawn forward (med.): emprotostonos (protostonos) a 1250.

empruo, *see* impruiamentum.

empt/io 1385, 1397, -oria 1502, 1529, acatry, office of caterer, purchasing department; e. viduarum, (?) widow's payment for right to remarry 1204; emibilis, purchasable, for sale c 1376, 1380; terra -ica, *tyrpryn*, land held by payment of *twnc* (W.) 1334; -icius, apprentice (Sc.) 15c.; -or, caterer 1264, 1336; -orium 12c., ‡1483, †ementorium 1272, place of sale, stall; -orius, acquired by purchase c 1444; -um, purchase 1200, 1213; emtus, *for* -us, c 973; †emtus (†enitus, †evitus), old, worn out *or* (?) bought (of horses) 1299, 1424; *cf.* envisus; -o, to buy 1230; emo sanguinem, to pay merchet 13c., 1279.

emp/yma (-ima) a 1250, ‡14c., -ema 16c., empyema, infected saliva; -icus, *for* -yicus, a 1250.

empyr/eum (empir-), the empyrean (astr.) c 1200, a 1350; -eus c 850. c 1182, c 1270 -icus 12c., empyrean, celestial.

emtus, *see* EMPT

emulamentum, mulled drink c 550.

emulumentum, *see* emolumentum.

emul/us, enemy 6c. c 1125, c 1470; e. pacis, disturber of the peace 1295, 1347; -abilis, zealous c 1250; -atorie, enviously, spitefully c 1430; -or, (with *acc.*) to envy c 1400.

emunct/io, emptying, squeezing out (of purse or money) c 1170, 15c.; -ivus, extortionate c 1250; -or, one who blows his nose c 1180; one who snuffs lights (in temple) c 1182; reviser c 770; -orium, handkerchief 1345; candle-snuffer (bibl.) c 1180, ‡1483; grating c 1478, c 1507; network of pores a 1250; boil, exudation 14c., ‡1652; locus -orius (med.) a 1250; emungo, to extort c 1188, 14c.

emund/atio, purification (of ale) c 760; purging (leg.) c 1115; e. cinerum, recovering of lead from lead ash 1420; -ator, cleanser c 1115, a 1275; esmundura (*coll.*), trimmings of wood 1223; -o, to purge (leg.) c 1115.

emunitas, *see* immunitas.

emurmuro, to mutter, complain 15c., 1520.

emutesco, to become dumb c 730.

emutilatio, mutilation 1311.

emutuo, to lend 1278.

enactus, *see* inactitatio.

enam/ulatura, enamelling 1447; -elo 1397, c 1500, -elio 1402, anam/ello 1409, c 1464, -elio 1426, -illo †1338, 1426, anem/ello c 1370, c 1488, -alo 1429, inamelo 1416, to enamel; *cf.* esmallum.

enarmonic/a 1252, -e c 1200, enharmonic scale or melody; -us, enharmonic c 1000. a 1200, 1267.

enas, *see* henas.
enato, to sail over 14c.
enavigatio, disembarkation c 1188.
enb-, *see* emb-; imb-
enbannum, *see* ambanum.
encaust/um 12c., 16c., enchastum 1552, *incaustum c 1000. 12c., a 1408, incaustrum 1299, incastum (in castum) 1201, 1456, incoustra c 1220, ink; ‡-rum, enamel 1570; incausterium, ink-horn c 1452, ‡ 1483; †-o, -ro, to varnish, enamel 1570.
encenium, (festival of) dedication (eccl.) c 1250, 1271; *see also* xenium.
encentricus, *see* eccentricus.
ench/ia, inch 1335; †-us 13c., -elondus 1299, (?) 'inch-land', small holding; *cf.* 2 uncea; *see also* euexia.
enchiridion, thing held in hand c 870; 1271, 1518, encheridion c 1334, 15c., handbook.
enchymatizo, to anoint: ‡jusquiamatizo 15c.
enclesis (*for* enclisis), declension c 1200; throwing back of the accent 1267; encletic/us a 1100, encliticus c 1400, bedridden; inclining downwards 1220; -o 1220, ‡15c., enclitico c 1200, to incline, bow down.
encomiasticus, laudatory 1537.
encre, *see* VIRID
encrochio, *see* INCROCH
encusa, *see* anchusa.
encycl/opedia, encyclopedia 1588; -ium (†enkidium) philosophema, popular philosophy 1344.
endecas, *see* HEN
endel/echia, -ichia, *see* entelechia.
†endemotum, (service at) Border court (Cumberland) 12c.
endentura, *see* 1 indentatus.
endibol-, *see* EMBOL
endict-, endit-, *see* indictamentum.
endivia, *see* intubus.
endrom/ada, *for* -is, fur cloak 13c.
enecto, to elucidate c 1000.
enector, murderer c 1200.
†enedos, a form of verse (? *for* epodos) c 1200.
eneor/ema (†-mia, †euerroima) a 1250, †-atium a 1252, scum in urine (ἐναιώρημα).
energ/ia, actuality c 1200, 1526; efficacy 12c., 1440; minister inergie, Devil 8c.; -umenus a 1100, c 1400, -umena (*f.*) c 1197, -omenos a 1250, (one) possessed by devil, demoniac; inergumino, to rave c 1115.
*enerv/atio, weakening, impairment c 1125, 1454; -ativus, apt to weaken c 1283, a 1292; -iter, weakly c 1000; -esco, to lose vigour a 1250; innervo, *for* -o, 13c.
enescia, enesius, eneyus, *see* esnecia.
eneus, *see* AEN
enfortunium, *see* EUFORTUN
enfraxis, enfrasis, *see* emphraxis.
engaignum, engania, engenium, enginator, *see* INGEN
engarano, *see* inwarenno.
engerimion, *see* egersimon.
engia (*pl.*), mortgage (ἔγγυα) a 1200, 1311.
Engl-, *see* ANGL
engreilatus, engrailed (her.) 1402.
enharmonic-, *see* ENARMONIC
†enichmus, a precious stone 1245.

enici/a, -us, *see* esnecia.
enicopo, *see* SYNCOP
enidium, *see* enopola.
enigm/a, obscurity 1241; -atice, in obscure language c 1194, 1552; -aticus, obscure c 804. c 1125, 1378; -atizo, to speak in riddles c 1250, ‡1483.
enisus, travail c 1115.
enitus, *see* EMPT
enk/a, -um, *see* inka.
enkidius, *see* ENCYCL
enkumbr-, *see* incumbramentum.
ennea, nine c 950.
ennos, (said to be Greek for) inhabitant (? ἐνναίων) c 1160.
ennullio, *see* 3 inoleo.
eno/pola (oeno-), wine-seller, taverner 1564, ‡1570; inopos, wine-coloured (of urine) a 1250, ‡14c.; enidium, wine-vessel c 1400; honophorum, barrel 1479.
*enorm/itas, wickedness, outrage c 950. c 1130, c 1540; disorderly house 1485; -ia (*n. pl.*), enormities, outrages c 1196, 1419; inhormis, inormis, *for* -is, c 550, a 710; -is c 1250, 1414, †-us 1296, 1300, -italis 12c., outrageous; -iter, prodigiously, outrageously c 1000. c 1190, 1414; -atus, irregular, disordered 1344, a 1452; -o, to defile 1241.
enpanello, *see* impanello.
ens, *see* entitas.
ens/is, shoulder-blade c 1190, a 1250; placita de -e, equivalent to *p. corone* (C.I.) 1289.
enta, root, plant, sapling 1233, p 1300.
ental/e a 1250, ‡-i 1652, finely divided alum; *see also* entitas.
entalli/ator, stone-carver 1313; -o, entellio 1318, intallio 1216, 1253, to hew, carve, engrave.
entarticus, *see* antarcticus.
entelechia, entelechy, actuality (phil.): endel/echia p 1300, 1427, -ichia a 1250, a 1275.
†entenasmon, form of derangement or hallucination (med.) a 1250.
‡entera (*pl.*), entrails (ἔντερα) c 1200, 15c.
enterliniarium, *see* INTERLIN
entheca, reliquary c 950. c 1100; coffin c 1212.
enthronizo, *see* INTHRONIZ
enthymematic/e, by way of enthymeme (log.) 1344; -us, enthymematic, rhetorical (log.) c 1360.
Enticon, *see* henas.
*ent/itas, entity, existence a 1233, 1378; e. positiva, concrete existence a 1304; *ens, being c 1160, 1686; e. rationis c 1300, a 1345; -alis, having a particular kind of being p 1300.
entole, command (ἐντολή) c 950.
entractum, *see* INTRACT
entremarta 1477, 1480, entraymarta 1480, entramarta 1496, kind of mart, fatted beast (Sc.).
entubus, *see* intubus.
enucho, *see* EUNUCH
enucl/eatio, elucidation a 1300, c 1490; -eatim, clearly a 1100, 1427; -eatius, more clearly 1432; -eator, elucidator c 1200; -io, to weaken c 1390.

enula, *see* inula.
enum, *see* AEN
enumer/atio simplex (log.) 1620; -ativus, concerned with enumeration 1620.
enund-, *see* INUND
enunti/abilis, utterable 12c., c 1290; -ativus a 1250, -atorius 1552, declaratory.
enutrico, to suckle 1620.
†envisus, (?) worn out with age (O.F. *enviesi*) 1213.
envius, *see* INVID
eo (*verb*), *see* ire.
eo/ quia, *for* eo quod, because 1421; -circa, thereabouts 1218, 1617; -tenus, *see* EA
eolagium, *see* oleagium.
eolus, the east 1578.
eona (*n. pl.*), aeons 12c.
eosus, *for* eous, eastern c 550.
*epacta, epact 1074, 1326.
epar, *see* hepar.
epaugmasticus, supervening on the crisis (ἐπακμαστικός) (med.) a 1200, a 1250.
epdomada, *see* HEBDOM
Epefania, *see* Epiphania.
epetogium, *see* epitogium.
ephebus, youth c 950. 1252; ‡"fair child" c 1440; ‡"clear" 1483.
ephecticus, suspending judgement, sceptical 1620.
‡ephemerida (epimeridia), notch on tally 1483; ephimera (effimera) a 1250, ‡epimera, epimora, emiperus 15c., †espimara 1407, fish (? sprat); effimeron, a fly c 1200; †elfimerus, ephemeral (med.) a 1252.
ephestris, surcoat (ἐφεστρίς) c 1595.
ephi-, *see also* epi-
ephialtes (epi-) c 1160, 15c., †ophialtes a 1250, nightmare, incubus.
ephipp/iarius, saddler 1563; equus e., caparisoned horse (?) 14c.; ‡epifia c 1440, ‡epiphium 1220, a 1520, pephia, piphia 16c., *for* -ium, saddle, caparison, *or* horse-collar; ‡epefio, epyphio, to put on a "hambargh" (horse-collar) 15c.
epial/a, -us, hot ague (ἠπίαλος) a 1250, ‡14c.
epibata, (?) trader c 950.
epicaust/erium, chafer, charcoal stove c 1200; ‡15c., ‡-orium 15c., ‡epicasterium 1483, -olium c 1200, flue; ‡-orium, "writing chair" 1483.
epicedion, song c 1000.
epicen/us 1267, -omenos c 793, epicene, common (gram.).
epicharis, endowed with grace c 1200, c 1350.
epicrius, (?) yard-arm (ἐπίκριον) 1271.
epicrocus, threadbare a 615.
Epicurus, Epicurean, epicure c 1170, c 1240.
epicycl/icus, epicyclic (astr.) 1267; -ois, epicycloid (astr.) 1686.
epidem/ia a 1250, 16c., epidimia c 1362, hypidemia 1406, ipidimia c 1360, ypedemica, ypidimia 1407, epidemic (*subst.*); -icus c 1607, c 1620, -ius c 1540, epidemic (*adj.*).
epieik/eia 1344, epikeia c 1340, 1374, equity; -es, equitable *or* respectable 1344, 1378.
‡epifemur, loin-cloth 15c.
epiglotum, epiglottis c 1210, ‡15c.

‡epilacium, hollow of hand 15c.
‡epilatum, a laxative (ὑπήλατον) 15c.
epilecticus, expressive of choice (gram.) 1524.
epi/lempsis a 1200, -lempsia a 1250, -lensia (? -leusia) c 1180, c 1250, †-lensis c 1250, -lentia 12c., 13c., epilepsy, frenzy; -lempticus 993. 12c., c 1200, -lenticus c 900. c 1180, c 1250, epileptic, maniac.
epilog/us, epitaph c 1140; epitome c 1165; sequel c 1300; -ium, summary account c 1250; -atio, summing up 12c.; -izo a 1100, -o c 1290, 1427, to sum up.
†epiltasia, swelling (? ἐπανάστασις) (med.) c 1190.
†epimenia (*pl.*) vite, bread of life (fig.) c 950; *v.l.* ermenia (*cf.* HERM).
epi/mer-, -mora, *see* ephemerida.
†epinasis, trichiasis, pilimiction (med.) a 1250.
epinicion, song of victory 12c.
†epinta, kind of herb a 1150.
epiousios, *see* epiusius.
*Epiphan/ia (eccl.), *E. Domini c 1125, 1466, festum -ie 1279, c 1493, dies -ie 1219, 1537, Epefania 1333, Piphania 1185, Epiphany (6 Jan.); manifestation (of star) c 1612; plane surface (geom.) c 1110; (?) surface of transparent body a 1250; ‡-es, "god showing" 15c.
epiphium, *see* ephippiarius.
‡epi/redium c 1440, -ridium c 1312, ‡-rodium c 1200, hand-barrow.
epirus, mainland (ἤπειρος) c 865.
episcop/us, *bishop (eccl.); e. cardinalis c 1220; e. cornutus, bishop in chess c 1280; e. elemosinarie 1356, 1435, e. innocentium 1321, c 1445, e. juvenum c 1327, c 1533, e. puer 1402, 1526, e. puerilis 1441, c 1500, e. puerorum 1295, 1555, e. Sancti Nicholai 1388, boy bishop (in feast of Holy Innocents); e. Judeorum, (meaning doubtful) 1178, 1242; -alia (*n. pl.*), episcopal dues 1114, c 1300; episcopal robes 1311; -alis, *episcopal (eccl.); (*subst.*) adherent of bishop c 1200, c 1346; -aliter, like a bishop c 1090, 1200; *-atus c 760, 10c. 1086, 1559, -ia 1386, -ium c 1000, 1060. c 1088, c 1414, bishopric, diocese; -ium, bishop's palace c 730, c 760. c 1130, c 1200; -o, to make a bishop of 1122, p 1348; to be bishop c 1362.
‡epispaticus, epispastic (med.) 15c.
epistasis, (?) superstitious veneration c 950.
epistites, *see* hephestitis.
epistol/a (epistul-), Epistle (of New Testament) c 1250, 1549; epistle of the day (liturgical) c 1090, 14c.; e. decretalis, decretal c 1125, 1461; epistile, (?) letter c 950; †epistiuncula, brief letter c 793; -aris c 793. c 1125, a 1452, -arius c 1204, c 1370, epistolary; full of letters or epistles c 793; -are c 1300, 15c., -aris 11c., 15c., -arius 1245, 1432, service-book containing the Epistles; -arius, letter-book 1344; letter-writer (mon.) 1535.
epitaphium (ephi-), epitaph 12c., 16c herse, framework over a tomb (Sc.) 1478, 1484.
epitasis, middle of a drama 1520.

epitegium, *see* epitogium.

epithalamicum, bridal song 12c.

1 epithema 12c., epithim/a a 1250, ‡15c., poultice; (fig.) solace c 950; -o, to poultice a 1250, ‡15c.

2 epi/thema, *for* epithymis, dodder parasitic on thyme 13c.; -thima, (?) ointment made of thyme flowers c 1200; -timium, (?) thymy hillside c 1140.

epi/togium c 1160, 1442, epetogium 1415, -tegium 1330, 1388, overcoat, gown; -togeus toralis, (?) bed-gown 1404.

epitomator, epitomizer 1595.

epitostonos, *see* opisthotonos.

epiusius, accessory (log.) 1620; panis epiousios c 1080, p. ephiusius p 1381, 'supersubstantial bread' (theol.).

epogdo/os, containing a width and an eighth: †-lus, †-nus a 1250.

eporizo, to hear c 550.

epotator, imbiber c 1125.

eptica, *see* hectica.

‡epudoratus, shameless 1483.

epul/a, meal c 760, c 1000; -atorius, as good as a feast 1153; -enta (*n. pl.*), food c 1190; -osus, gluttonous c 1470; -o, to have a meal c 793. 1236.

equipo, *see* skippagium.

equor, field (her.) c 1595.

1 equ/us, horse-shaped wedge 1326; ad -os, on horseback c 1360; -us ad arma 1297, 1300, e. armaturus c 1288, e. de guerra 1364, war-horse; e. carette 1531, 1533, e. caretti 1313, cart-horse (*see also* CARETT); e. carrucator 13c.; e. facticius, stalking-horse, decoy 1544; e. ad molendinum 1303, e. molendinarius 1264, 1279, gin-horse; e. pro sella, riding horse 1343; e. usualis, horse broken for riding c 1178; -a portans, brood mare c 1230, 1251; e. silvatica 1086, e. silvestris 1086, 1456, forest mare; -aria 1134, 1156, ‡-aricia 1483, stud; -arius 1086, 1182, -iductor 1526, groom;

-es, knight (feudal) 1122, c 1250; knight (chess) a 1150; e. auratus (esp. Sc.) 1537, 1685; e vexillarius, banneret 1586; serviens, mounted serjeant 1239, 1315; cuculla -estralis, riding-hood 1476; via e., bridle-path c 1390; conflictus -estrinus, cavalry battle c 1350; ‡-ifera, wild mare 15c.; -iferus, mount, (?) hack a 1200, 1340; ‡"hackney-man" 15c.; †-illus, "hackney" 15c.; -initas, equine nature p 1300, 1427; -inocephalus, horse-headed c 1212; -inus, -itius, *see* molendinum, panis, pondus, sella, sera, sericum; -ipes, horse-shoe 1260; -isequelus, henchman c 1472; ‡-istatium, stable 1483; -itans, forest rider 1255, 1461; courier a 1446; -itarius c 1306, 1342, *-itator a 1220, 1486, rider; -itator foreste 1270, 1572; -itarius 13c., -itatorius c 1220, horse-drawn; -itatorius, like a rider c 1188; vestis -itatoria, riding-habit c 1412; capa -itativa, riding-cape 1422; -itatrix, skilled in horsemanship (*f.*) 1252; †-itantia 1199, -itatio c 1115, 1416, -itatura c 1250, 1402, -itatus c 1160, 15c., cavalry service or expedition; *-itatura, horse, mount, mounted man or company

c 1125, 15c.; horse given as heriot 1405, 1407; riding 1219, 1437; e. foreste, forest-riding, perambulation c 1300; -itatus (*coll.*), knights at chess a 1619; -itiarius a 1250, ‡1483, ‡-inarius 15c., horse-herd, stud-keeper; -ito, to do escort duty c 1175, c 1182; to ride, bestride (a horse) 1200, c 1390; (?) to mount, provide with a horse 1333; to beat (or include within) bounds by riding round 1374.

2 equ/us: manus -a 1234, 1335, m. -alis 1200, 1299, *owel mein*, trustee (leg.); -e, so as to be quit, clear of debt 1274, 1476; -e inter, midway between c 1400; -e sicut, equally as c 1334; -alis, impartial 1218, 1263; -alitas, a level (of altitude) c 1180; -animiter, *with equanimity c 730, 804. c 1125, c 1430; equally 1261; -ans, equant circle (astr.) c 1233, 1326; -atio, equation, balance (in account) 1409; equation (math.) 1145, 1686; -ator, equator (astr.) 1265, 1686; -iangulus, equiangular 1267, 1686; -ibonus, equal in goodness 1497; -icolus, having two equal clauses a 1180; -idies c 1185, ‡-idium 1483, equinox; -idialis c 1160, -idius 1252, equinoctial;

-idistans a 1200, p 1394, -edistans c 1250, a 1446, equidistant; -idistans, (*subst.*) equidistant (astr.) 1267; -idistanter a 1250, 1326, -edistanter a 1350, at an equal distance; -idistantia, equidistance c 1267, a 1446; -idisto, to be equidistant c 1233, a 1350;

-ifaciliter, with equal ease 1326; -iformis, symmetrical 870; -iformiter, in equal measure 1427; -ilaterus, equilateral a 1150, c 1300; -ilibra, balance 1344, c 1427; -ilibris, equally balanced 1267, 1345; -ilibriter, in balance c 1178; -ilibro a 1205, a 1233, -elibro 1452, to weigh, apportion;

-ilocus, on even terms c 1130; -imanus, ambidextrous 870. ‡1483; -imembris, having two equal clauses a 1180; -imodus, just, regular a 1180; -inoctialis, (*subst.*) equinoctial circle (astr.) 1267, c 1360; (*adj.*) a 1350, -inoxialis c 1115, c 1360, equinoctial; -inoxium autumpnale 1340; -inomus, one of equal rank 7c.; -iparantia, equivalence, correspondence c 1290, c 1370; -iparativus, equalizing c 1360; -iparabilis 1509, -ipollens c 1125, a 1446, equivalent; -ipollenter, with equal significance 8c. c 1080, c 1343; equally 9c. 12c.; -ipollentia, equivalence c 1080, 1610; *-ipolleo, to be equivalent c 1160, c 1470;

-isapiens, equal in wisdom 1497; -itas, just claim c 1155; equity (leg.) 1586; †-ius, *for* -evus, a contemporary c 550; *-ivalens, equivalent c 1204, c 1450; in -ivalenti c 1357, -ivalenter c 1290, 1436, equally, at an equal rate; *-ivalentia, equivalence, equal value c 1190, 1549; *-ivaleo, to be equivalent 1205, 1458;

-ivelox, of equal speed 1686; -evelociter, with equal speed c 1340; *-ivocatio, equivocation, ambiguity c 1125, c 1445; *-ivoce, ambiguously c 1080, c 1445; -ivoca (*n. pl.*), ambiguous utterances 13c., 1523; -ivocus, bearing the same name 7c. c 1070, c 1400; c 1160, 1378, -ivocabilis c 1300, -ivocalis

c 1360, equivocal, ambiguous; **-ivoco,** to equivocate, express ambiguously 1267, 15c.
er, *see* **aer.**
era, payment (Aragon) 1290.
eradicator, uprooter 15c.; **eredico,** to uproot 1340.
er/amentarium, -arius, -ea, *see* **es.**
†erasticus, (?) *f.l.* for **ecclesiasticus,** 12c.
erb-, *see* **herb-**
erchiepiscopus, *see* **archiepiscopus.**
†erchimotum (†thermotum), (?) *for* **merchimotum,** march-moot c 1115.
erdescota, 'plough-scot' 1267.
Ereb/us, Christian Hell c 950. c 1068; **-eus** c 740, **-icus** 12c., 13c., infernal.
erect/io, uplifting, setting up c 730. c 1170, 1537; elevation, promotion c 1410; **e. in religionem,** conversion into a house of regular religious 1382; **-ivus,** uplifting 13c., 1344; **-or** c 1190, **-rix** (*f.*) 1620, uplifter, exalter; **-us,** rampant *or* displayed (her.) c 1595; **erigo,** to lift, remove 1354; to elevate, promote c 1170; to raise (a church) in status c 1395, c 1470; to rise c 1300, 1327; **e. calcaneum** 1317, (?) **e.** (**†exigo**) **caput** 1461, to rebel; **e. caudam,** to grow uppish 1421; **e. legem** c 1102, c 1115, **e. unlagam** c 1115, to establish law (or evil law); **e. placitum,** to disturb a moot c 1110; **e. vigilias,** to keep vigil c 1400; *see also* **eretto.**
eredico, *see* **eradicator.**
ereductile, *see* **es.**
erem/ina, -iticus, *see* **ermina.**
erem/us (herem-) 793. c 1125, 1461, **-is** a 1408, **-ius** c 1396, **herimus** c 1480, desert, hermitage, monastery; **-odicium,** abandonment of suit (leg.) c 1257, 1262; *****-ita** 793, c 870. a 1142, 1536, **hermita** 1220, c 1395, **-icola** 1171, 1521, eremite, hermit; **frater -itarum ordinis S. Augustini,** Austin friar 1255; **f. -ita S. Johannis** 1264; **-itagium** c 1160, 1445, *****hermitagium** 1130, 1588, **†thermitogium** c 1450, **-itorium** 1189, 14c., **hermitorium** 1152, 1292, hermitage; **-italis** c 700. 12c., **-itanus** 1284, 1535, **-itarius** 14c., **-itorius** 15c., *****-iticus** c 1235, 15c., **†-iticius** c 1172, eremitic; **-itice,** as a hermit 1370; **-ito,** to live as a hermit c 1300.
ereos, *see* **eros.**
erept/io, rescue, deliverance c 730. a 1250, 15c.; **-ibilis,** susceptible of deliverance c 1240; **-or** c 730. c 1325, **-rix** (*f.*) a 1275, c 1325, deliverer.
eresgieva, *see* **yeresiva.**
eretto (erecto), to accuse c 1290; *cf.* **RETT**
erga, *****against** (of persons) c 1198, c 1452; over against, opposite (of place) c 1185, 1552; 1415, 1547, **arga** 1535, against (of time).
†ergalum, rye 15c.
ergast/erium, monastery c 930 (*cf.* **arcisterium**); **argisterium,** market a 1085; **-ulum,** prison-house, dungeon c 730, c 770. c 1130, 1447; bird-cage a 1446; tomb c 1182; a 615, c 1000, **e. carnis** c 1080, 1438, the body; **-ularis,** of a prison c 1125; **-ulator,** gaoler c 1430.
ergla (*n. pl.*), legs c 550.

eri/a, -us, *see* **aeria.**
eric/a 1544, 1609, **†erix** 1570, heath, heather; **-etum,** heath, moor 1586, 1654.
ericius, *see* **hericius.**
erifilum, *see* **es.**
erigo, *see* **ERECT.**
erinaceus, fuller's comb, teasel a 1450.
eririum, *see* **error.**
ermin/a (hermin-) c 1200, 1331, **heremina** c 1200, **hereminium** c 1450, **hereminum** 1303, **irmina** 1302, ermine (fur); **-a** 1275, **armelinus** c 1595, ermine, stoat; **hereminus** 12c., 1303, **-alis** a 1446, **ermeticus** p 1394, **eremiticus** a 1446, **hermoniacus** 1654, **armelinus** c 1595, of ermine; **†armilium,** "miniver" 1570.
erna, erne, sea eagle 1544.
Ernaldensis, *see* **Arnaldensis.**
†ernator, †wernator, (?) salt-dealer 14c.
ernesium 1321, **†ernes** 1221, **†hernas** 14c., **†terrestum** 1279, earnest money.
ero, *see* **es.**
‡erodinium, presage recognized after the event 1652; *cf.* **essodinum.**
erodius (herodius), gerfalcon c 1060. 12c., a 1446.
erog/atio, alms-giving c 1192, 1467; **-acitas,** liberality a 1205; **-ator** c 1090, 13c., **-atrix** (*f.*) a 1155, bestower.
eros, passionate or wanton love: **(amor) hereos** a 1250, 1424; **†hereosus,** (?) erotic a 1250.
erra, *see* **arrha.**
erra-, *see also* **error.**
erramenta (*pl.*) (C.I.) 1270, **arramenta** (G.) 1312, legal proceedings or records, *errements.*
errarius, *see* **aeria.**
†errebellis, (?) rebellious 1379.
errhinum, sternutative medicine 1620.
err/or, miscarriage of justice c 1250, 1419; planet a 1553; **†eririum,** error 1363; **-abilis,** fallible 1344, 1378; **-aneus,** (?) *for* **-oneus,** straying 685, c 980; **-aticus,** vagrant c 1190; sinful 1532; unreliable, quack (med.) c 730. 14c.; **febris -atica** (med.) a 1250; **‡-atiuncula,** little fault 1520; **-atus,** sin, fault c 730. c 1150, c 1190; **-atice** 1373, **-onee** 1267, c 1400, *****-onice** 1244, 1434, **-anter** 1378, erroneously; *****-oneus** (*adj.*) 8c. c 1155, 1559, **†-icus** 13c., erroneous, heretical; **-oneus** (*subst.*) 9c. c 1125, c 1362, **-ans** 12c., 1552, one in error, heretic, sinner; **†-andus,** stray 1307; **-ans,** a vagrant 1212; **justitia (justitiarius) -ans** c 1178, 1219, **baro -ans** a 1200, justice in eyre; **ballivus -ans,** bailiff errant 1307; **fabrica -ans** 1230, **forgia -ans** 1282, 'going' (working) forge; *cf.* **eyrum, iter.**
erscha (herscha), 'earsh', 'arrish', stubble-field (Dorset) 1376.
eruatus, *see* **eruitio.**
*****erub/escentia,** blushing for shame c 1160, a 1450; **-eo,** to blush c 1125, c 1180; **-esco** (with *gen.*), to be ashamed of c 793. c 1460.
erubigin/atio (†embiginatio), burnishing 1462, 1501; **‡-o,** "to furbish" 1483; *cf.* **ERUGIN**
‡eru/ca, "charlock", "skirret" *or* "white pepper" 15c.; **†-tago** (bot.) a 1250.

G

eruct/atio, outpouring, utterance c 1430, a 1452; -uatio, belching a 1250, c 1257; -us, outburst 12c.; -uativus, provocative of belching a 1250; -atorium, drug to cause belching a 1250; -uo, to gush forth 1149, c 1227; to emit 8c.; c 1090, c 1362, -o c 550. 1136, 1461, to utter, proclaim.

eruder/atio, clearance a 1250; -o, to clear, dig out c 1250, 1345; ‡to "manure" 1483.

erud/itorium, school c 900; -itivus, educative 1344; -io, to learn c 1362.

erugin/amentum, burnishing c 1376; ‡-ator, "furbisher" 15c., 1483; -eus, tarnished 1662; -osus, corrupted by money c 1165; -o, to polish c 1266, ‡1483; cf. ERUBIGIN

eru/itio 1385, -tio 1355, tearing out; rescue c 1240; -atus, plucked (of hides) 1444.

‡erula, apple core 15c., 1483.

erumn/osus (erumpn-) c 550, 1024. 12c., a 1350, †-us c 1140, distressful; -o, to distress 1559.

eruptio, spring (of water) 1375.

erutago, see eruca.

‡erv/us, for -um, vetch c 1200, 1483.

erynge (bot.): yringus a 1250, ‡14c.

erysimum, (?) kind of cress (bot.) a 1250, ‡14c.

erysipelatus (herisipilatus), affected with erysipelas a 1250.

‡es ustum, calx cupri 15c., 1652; in ere tuo sum, I am indebted to you 1527, 1568; eramentarium, salt-pan 1633; erarius, moneyer 14c., ‡c 1440; ‡brazier 15c.; erea 1200, (?) hera a 1183, copper pan; ‡ereductile 1483, erifilum 15c., brass wire; ‡ero, to tip 1570.

esartico, see EXSART

esb-, see also exb-

‡esbrium, marjoram (bot.) 14c.

esc-, see also exc-, sc-

escafata, escaufatium, see scaffaldus.

escaldus (†escabinus), see alcaldus.

esc/ale, food-bowl 1428, ‡1483 (cf. 2 scala, skela); ‡-aria, dresser, sideboard 15c.; ‡-arinus, meat-dish 15c.; ‡-arium, manger 1483; ‡-arius, carver c 1440; -ifer, nourishing c 550; †-alenta (pl.) 16c., *-ulenta (pl.) c 1250, 1583, exculenta (pl.) 1294, 1334, -ulentia (pl.) 1412, -ulentia (f. s.) c 1200, food; ‡-o, to eat 1483.

escalleta, see SCARL

escampa, evasion (O.F. eschampe) 1141, c 1414.

escantio, butler (Fr. échanson) c 1135, 1266.

*escap/ium 1224, 1486, exchapium 1224, 1270, eschepium 1227, -iamentum 1458, scapagium 1278, (fine for) escape (of prisoner); per -ium, by straying (of animals into pasture) 1223, 1263; 1185, 1545, -agium 1178, -ura a 1205, 1298, ascapura 1226, fine for animals straying; -io, to stray 1279, 1293; 1315, 14c., -eo 1475, exchapio 1274, to escape.

escarl-, see SCARL

escarta, see quarta.

escartum, see EXSART

escaud- (eschaud-), see SCALD

escav-, escewinga, see SCAW

escawardus, see calewarus.

esch-, see also esc-, exc-, sc-, sk-

eschauberca, see scabergia.

eschaugwayta 1200, escheweita 1230, guard-service (Fr.) (O.F. eschauguette).

eschek, see SCACC

escheppa, see skeppa.

eschin/a 1235, 1321, skina 1322, chine (of pork or beef); e. dorsi 1301, †estinia 1278, chine, backbone (human); -um bracchii a 1186, esckingnum 1234, arm-bone.

eschi/va 1180, -vum 1242, -wa 1192, 1212, -wum 1209, guard-house (compartment partitioned off) (Fr. échiffe).

esc/ifer, -o, see escale.

esclata, see SCLAT

esclavus, see sclavus.

escomarius, see scumarium.

escorg/eria, (?) stripping of bark a 1250; -io, to flay 1236.

escoriatio, see EXCORI

escoto, see scotum.

escrenum, escrinium, see screna.

escrutor, for exscr-, to search out 1585.

escuagium, see scutum.

escuillio, to castrate 1198.

esculenta, see escale.

escur/atio c 1390, 1546, exscuratio 1471, *scuratio 1395, 1476, scuriatio c 1390, scouring, cleaning out (of channel); syuratio, scouring (of armour) 1377; scurator, 'scourer', scout (Calais) 1387, 1413; -o 1372, 1540, -io 1509, excuro 1504, †exeuro a 1295, †escuo 1398, †curo 1248, *scuro 1254, 1412, scurio c 1335, p 1394, scowro 1384, to scour, clean out.

escurellum, see curallum.

escur/ellus, -eus, see scurellus.

esemum, see SESAM

esertum, see exsartum.

esforcio, see EFFORT

esgar/ato 1221, -eto 1238, -gato 1198, to hamstring (O.F. esjareter); cf. agarecto.

esgard-, esguard-, see AWARD

esi/a, -amentum, see aisia.

esibilis, see esura.

esicius p 1290, c 1450, isicius c 730. c 1200, isicus a 1200, esor c 1180, (?) for esox, fish, esp. salmon; isicia, fish juice a 1200.

esiliquus, see exsiliquus.

esinon, see esophagus.

esk-, see also sk-

†eskeccum, (?) 'check', contention 1240.

eskeppa, eskippa, see SKEPP

eskermio, see skirmia.

eskettor, reiver (W.) 1292.

eskipp-, see skippagium.

eskiprus, see skippagium.

esklenka 1252, schlencha (†schleucha) c 1250, (?) shoulder or leg (of beef) (Fr. éclanche).

eslaium, see allaia.

eslargio, see ELARG

esleda, (?) sled or slide (Norm.) 1198.

eslingator, see SLING

esmallum, (?) badge 1241; 1205, c 1250, esmale c 1220, esmael'um 1290, esmalta 1620, asmal c 1270, a mallum, admallum c 1250, emalur ı c 1300, aimallum 1240, 1303, aim illum 1303, 1338, amalum c 1322, c 13 0, amalium 1315, ameilum 1332, en mel; aumellatio, enamelling 1286; es nelo 1326, emalo

c 1400, aimallo 1295, 1313, **aimello**
(†annello) c 1150, 1397, †anealo 1315,
†anelo 1370, amallo 1317, c 1336, **ammaylo** 1386, amello 1332, c 1503, hamelo
1403, **amulo** 1315, †aumollo 1345,
†amilaso 1448, to enamel; *cf.* ENAM
esmerald/us,-a, esmaraldus, *see* smaragdo.
esmerillunus, *see* mereella.
esmina, *see* hemina.
esmolo, *see* emolitus.
esmundura, *see* EMUND
esnacca, *see* 1 snecka.
esnamio, *see* exnamio.
esn/ecia 1199, 1293, -eseya 1200, aesnecia
1225, aesnescia c 1185, c 1258, aisnecia
1198, 1204, asnecia 1200, adnecia 1229,
aenecia 1253, aenescia 1218, enescia
c 1187, 1223, einecia 1265, 1309, einescia
1201, c 1265, hainescia 1195, etnesceia
1204, enicia 15c., †eylnescia 1240,
†inechia 1280, 'esnecy', privilege of
eldest co-heir; †-ecus 1198, enesius 1358,
einecius 1315, 1327, einescius 1268,
eignecius 1364, ennicius 1497, eldest;
einecius 1348, †eneyus c 1315, anecius
c 1420, enicius 15c., pertaining to the
eldest, concerned with esnecy; *cf.* ANTENAT
esnecka, *see* 1 snecka.
esomenon, predestined future (ἐσόμενον) 1344.
esophagus, gullet: isophagus c 1210, ysofagus a 1200, ‡14c.; †esinon 14c., †ysmon
a 1250, passage between oesophagus and
trachea.
esor, *see* esicius.
esp-, *see also* exp-, sp-
espaalto, espaltamentum, *see* expeditatio.
espan/ellus, -iellus, *see* HISPAN
esparvarius, *see* spervarius.
espau/dlera, -lera, *see* SPATH
espaulum, enclosure (Poitou) c 1190.
especialiter, *see* species.
espedor 1284, expedor 1284, c 1370, tenant
of Hospitallers, *yspydwyr* (W.).
espel/catio, spelkeria, curing fish (C.I.)
1248; -cator, -kiator, fish-curer (C.I.)
1248; speluco, to cleanse (flour) (Fr.
éplucher) 1335; *cf.* expercaria.
espelt-, espet-, *see* expeditatio.
esperiolus, *see* scurellus.
espernium, *see* sparnum.
esper/varius, -vicus, espreverus, *see* spervarius.
espicurnaucia, *see* spigurnellus.
espimara, *see* ephemerida.
espineta, *see* spina.
esporlum, *see* sporta.
esporonum, *see* spurrum.
esporum, espoerum, espurrum, *see* 1 spera.
esquarletum, *see* SCARL
esquarta, *see* quarta.
esqui-, *see* scutella; scutum.
essaia, *see* sagum.
essaiamentum, *see* aisia.
essai/ator, -o, -um, *see* exagium.
essaim-, *see* ASSEM
essart-, *see* EXSART
essata, (?) dish, *assiette* (G.) 1289.
‡essatum, essentiale, inherent virtue (alch.)
1652; ‡e. vinum, wine distilled and
rectified with herbs 1652.

ess/e (*subst.*), being, existence, essence c 870.
a 1109, 1432; e. debitum, rightful condition a 1250; e. specificum a 1250; e. quod
quid erat, τὸ τί ἦν εἶναι a 1304; *(gerund)
-endum c 1160, 1567; *(gerundive)* †-endus
12c., 1419; **fore, *for* esse *or* fuisse, c 1180,
c 1446; sum, (auxiliary verb with *present
ppl.*) 1218, 1414; (with in and *gerund*) 1214,
c 1448; to appear (leg.) 1217, c 1290;
omnes qui sunt et mori possunt 1269;
sum a, to be derived from c 1340; s. ad, to
belong to 1378; (with *gerundive*) to be
occupied with c 1283; s. ad pacem, to keep
the peace 1202; s. ad rectum, to stand to
right, stand trial c 1115; s. contra, to oppose
1216, 1362; idem est de, it is the same with
1254; quicquid fuerit de, however it may
be with c 1341; s. pro, to support c 1343;
est quod, it is possible that c 1341; sit
verum, discussion of hypothesis p 1347.
essecambium, *see* excambium.
essedum, Plough (constellation) 7c.
esselda, *see* selda.
essennum, *see* sagena.
essenti/a, **essence (theol. and log.) c 850.
c 1080, c 1470; actuality 12c.; fact of being
(in a place) 1415; existing thing, entity
c 1227, c 1250; e. quinta, quintessence
(alch.) a 1200, c 1345; -alia (*n. pl.*), essential
qualities 1537; **-alis, essential c 850.
a 1150, 1686; -alitas, essentiality c 870.
c 1270; **-aliter, essentially c 1080, c 1445;
-ficatio, making real 1344; -o c 865, -fico
1344, to make real, endow with essence.
essertum, *see* EXSART
essew-, essequia, *see* exaquia.
esseymo, *see* ASSEM
essicis, *see* EXCIS
‡essila, sun-burn 1652.
‡essodinum, certain prognostication 1652;
cf. erodinium.
**essoni/um (essoin-) c 1185, c 1470, -a 1194,
1259, exonium 1180, c 1220, -atus 1280,
assonia c 1320, sonium 1211, sonius
(soinus) c 1115, 1211, essoin, excuse for
non-appearance (leg.); -abilis, entitled to
essoin 1201, c 1320; -ator 1188, c 1320,
assoniator 1233, 1274, essoiner; **-o 1194,
1470, assonio 1233, 1419, assunio 1224,
sonio 1211, to essoin.
est-, *see also* exst-, ext-, st-
estach-, *see* 1 staca.
estagium, *see* stagium; 1 lastum.
estall-, *see* STALL
estampeta, *see* stampus.
estanum, *see* 2 stagnum.
estapula, *see* stapella.
est/as magna, cyclic extremity of drought
a 1553; -eus, summer 6c.; -ivalia (*pl.*)
c 1200, 1344, stivalia 1213, c 1330, -ivalla
1225, -ivella 1213, 1303, summer shoes;
-ivalis (†-ualis), of or for summer c 1125,
c 1396; *see also* carruca, caseus, domus;
-ivus, (?) stormy c 550.
‡estaurinus, gurnard 15c.
est/caput, east end a 1200; -gata 1147,
-porta 1315, east gate; -pars, east part
c 1197, c 1240.
esteinum, *see* 2 stagnum.
estencello, *see* stincillatus.

esteneatus, see stainiatus.

†esterium, measure of grain (? cf. sextarium or hostorium) 1294; see also estoverium.

esthi/omenus (esti-), devouring herpes (med.) a 1250, ‡14c.

estim/antia c 1365, -ativa c 1250, 1620, consideration, judgement, perception; -abilis, discernible by judgement c 1366; -ative, by estimation a 1350, 1415; -ativus, concerned with judgement 1267, 1620; extimatio, valuation 1255, 1454; extimo, for -o, to value c 1235, 1373.

estinia, see eschina.

estiro, measure of land (G.) 1276.

estiv- see estas; estoverium.

Est/landburda, -onius, see Estresius.

estop-, see stupatio.

est/overium c 1217, 15c., -uverium 1202, stuverium 1212, stuveria c 1300, -averium 1276, -iverium, stiverium 1205, †-orium 1155, †-ovium 14c., †-onium 15c., astovarium 1312, allowance, provision, maintenance; *-overium c 1212, 1588, -ovaria c 1240, -owarium c 1300, -averium 1389, -uvarium 1275, -uverium 1234, stuverium 13c., 'estover', allowance of wood.

est/pars, -porta, see estcaput.

estra-, see also straia.

estracus, estreca, estricha, see strica.

estrava, see thrava.

estre/cio (†-ycio) 1198, 1202, -scio 1201, extrecio 1274, extrico 1418, to narrow (a road or watercourse); 1202, -scio 1203, to overstretch (cloth); cf. STRICT

estremarius, see stramerius.

estrep-, estrip-, see STREPP

Est/resius 1176, 1188, -onius 1267, Eastlander, Easterling, Esthonian; borda -rensis c 1266, 1325, b. -rensia c 1325, -regebordia 1377, -richborda 1352, 1355, -landburda 1466, Eastland (Esthonian) board.

estrivus, see strepa.

estron-, see EXTRON

estruc/ta (pl.) 1130, -a 1316, ornaments (O.F. estruits).

estrumelaria (pl.), greaves (O.F. trumelieres) 1275.

estualis, see estas.

estu/atio, tide c 1212; disturbance, upheaval c 1130, 13c.; melting c 1178; esterium c 1288, 15c., sterium 15c., estuary (G.); -anter, passionately c 1470; -o c 730. c 1125, c 1362, e. ad c 1090, 1290, to desire passionately; e. ad, to be greatly perturbed by c 730.

estubula, see STIMUL

estuctia, see astutia.

estuff-, see STUFF

esturus, see AUSTUR

estuv-, see estoverium.

esul/a, spurge (bot.) a 1250, 1634; -atus, treated with spurge a 1250.

esumo, see EXHUM

es/ura, eating c 550; -us, food c 550; -ibilis, edible c 1375; cf. edia.

et etiam, and also 1086, 16c.; †etiam et (?) even also c 800; eque et (with abl.), equally with c 1102; etnon, for nec, c 790;

non . . . et, for non . . . nec, c 597; etenim (not first word), indeed, moreover 6c., 9c. c 1365.

eta/s, age (under 60) for legal duel 1198, c 1258; full age, legal majority 1198, c 1430; see also peto; e. completa 1468, e. legitima c 1178, 1535, e. major 1220, e. perfecta 1416, 1559, e. plena c 1185, c 1475; e. plenaria (of animals) c 1283; *e. minor c 1185, c 1482; e. rationabilis c 1228, 1413; e. trium hominum, term of three lives 1086; e. lune (astr.) a 1250; -tis sum, to be of (full) age 1199, 1258; -tulum, infancy 7c.

etern/alitas, eternal nature, timelessness 7c. c 1270; -alis, eternal (eccl.); -aliter, in an eternal sense c 870. 1344, 1378; *c 730, 1041. c 1070, 1461, -abiliter 1472, for ever; -ativus, immortalizing c 1185; -izo 1622, -o c 1220, 14c., to immortalize.

etexo, to unfold, expound c 1415.

ethees 1144, ‡edes 1652, gold (alch.).

ethem-, ethim-, see etymum.

eth/eralis 546, -ralis 590, 8c. c 1096, ethereal, celestial; †etra, (?) for aethra, c 550; -er, (?) roof 1306; -ereo, to search the heavens 1432; see also HETERO

ethic/a (n. pl.), Aristotle's Ethics c 1300, c 1440; -e, in a moral strain 15c.; -us, the moralist (Horace) c 1160, c 1258; see also hectica.

†ethleta, "noble" c 1130 (? cf. athleta or adelingus).

ethnic/us, heathen, gentile (bibl.); -ismus heathenism c 1620.

ethomologisatio, see etymum.

ethro-, see HETERO

etiam, see et.

etiatus, caused (αἰτιατός) p 1300.

etnesceia, see esnecia.

‡Etnici (pl.), fiery spirits 1652.

etra, see etheralis.

etsnus, see aesnus.

etymum, word 1537; etymolog/ia (ethem-, ethim-), etymology 1041. a 1275, c 1553; -ice, etymologically p 1330, c 1395; -ista, etymologist c 1620; -izatio 1419, ethomologisatio c 1430, tracing etymologies; -izo c 1250, c 1397, †-io c 1450, †-o c 1365, to trace etymologies.

eu-, see also ev-

eubulia (†ebulia), good counsel c 1300.

eucatalepsia, right understanding 1620.

eucharis/, gracious c 950. c 1200; *-tia (eccl.), eukaristia c 1266, 1427, ewkaristia 13c., eucharist, host; -tiale, pyx 1493; -tialis c 870. c 1102, -ticus 1552, c 1620, eucharistic; -tizo, to use in the eucharist c 1620.

euchymius, tasty 13c.

eucra/sia c 1260, ‡15c., ycracia c 1360, good temperament; -siatus c 1260, ‡-ticus 15c., well tempered.

eucritus, with a favourable crisis (med.) a 1250.

†eudica, (?) nitre (alch.) 1144.

eudoxus, glorious c 950.

euergetes, beneficent 1622.

eueria, see EW

euerroima, see eneorema.

euexia 1345, euechia 13c., c 1300, †enechia, †enchia 1341, good health.

eufamia, good repute c 1365.

eufortun/ium (†enfortun-), good fortune c 1250, 1344; ‡-atus, fortunate 15c.

eufra-, see emphraxis; euphrasia.

eufurbeus, see euphorbiatus.

‡eugenes, noble, "witty" 15c.

eulog/ia, -ium, fine language 540; blessing c 740. c 1130, 1191; commemoration or praise c 1200, 1424; good news c 1250, c 1370; (?) language a 1275; saying, utterance, grant 961. 12c., c 1457; gift c 793; food 8c., 9c.; consecrated bread, host a 615. c 1182; ‡-io 15c., †elogizo 1483, to praise.

euneus, see AEN

eunuch/izo c 1080, 1200, -o c 1204, c 1220, †enucho c 1370, to castrate.

euouae, sequence of vowels showing cadence (mus.) 1488.

euphon/ia, euphony c 793. 1125, 1620 †-istus, sweetened c 1200.

euphorbiatus, compounded with euphorbia a 1250; pulvis eufurbeus (†furbeus) 1307.

euphrasia a 1250, ‡eufragia 15c., eyebright (bot.).

euprep/ia, virtue c 950; †-ius, seemly c 1370.

euripus, strong current a 615, c 740.

euritides, see uritides.

euro/auster, south-east wind 10c. c 1125, ‡1483; south-west wind c 1400; †-clustus, (?) for -auster, south-east c 1300; -borus, north-eastern 6c.

euseb/ia, piety 1232; -ius, pious c 950. c 1250, ‡15c.

eustomaticus, palatable a 1250.

euthrogeneus, see HETERO

euthymia, cheerfulness 1620.

†eutrophoya, ready wit (εὐτραπελία) 13c.

eutyches, fortunate c 950.

evacu/atio, emptying 1399; purgation (med.) c 1150, a 1292; removal 1267, c 1367; weakening, annulment c 1105, 1588; e. aquarum, drainage a 1430, 1472; domus -ationis, privy c 1150; -abilis, removable c 1360; -ativus, purgative a 1250; -atrix, dispeller (f.) c 1180; *-o, to empty c 1250, c 1540; to exhaust c 1090; to vacate, clear out of c 1070, c 1362; to clear away, remove c 1400; to sweep away 1378; to drive out, get rid of 1202, 1373; to obviate a 1250; *to weaken, annul 9c. c 1080, c 1530; to exhaust (log.) 13c., c 1300; e. de, to depart from 1461; e. debitum, to discharge a debt c 1255.

evadio, to stand surety for 14c.; see also EVAS

evagatio mentis, wandering of the wits a 1350.

evan/eo, for -esco, c 793. ‡15c.

*evangel/ium (euangel-, ewangel-) (bibl.), †ewanglia 1335, gospel; -arium 1401, -iarium 1245, 1518, -istarium 1295, a 1380, 'gospeller', book containing the gospels; -icum, saying in the gospels 1136, c 1250; -icus, *evangelical, pertaining to the Gospel (bibl.); (subst.) a Christian 8c.; see also doctor; *-ista (bibl.), evaungelista 1261, euaggelistes c 870, evangelist; -izans c 1546, -izator c 1240, 1425,

preacher; ‡-izatio, preaching 1483; *-izo (bibl.), -ico c 1137, c 1434, to preach.

evapor/atorium, medicament causing evaporation a 1250; -abilis, capable of evaporation a 1250, c 1270; -o, to exhale an odour c 740; to pour out, utter c 1125.

evardum, see AWARD

evas/io, *escape c 730. a 1100, 1461; 1055. 1269, 1313, -ura 1236, fine for escape or straying; solution of a problem 1267; evasion, excuse c 1334, 1461; -or, escaper c 1365; -us, having escaped c 1190, c 1436; evadior, to escape 1249.

evatio, see evum.

evectio, ascent c 700, c 865; exalted station c 990; transport c 700. c 1125, 1415; *means of transport, conveyance, mount, retinue or travel permit 1177, 1461; cleaning out 1434, c 1527; evex/io (gurgitum), tossing (on the sea) c 1325; -a (pl.), promontories c 1188.

‡evectrum, astral body 1652; ‡evestrum, prophetic spirit 1652.

evedlonda, see HEV

evellero, to pluck (wool) 1324.

evendico, see evindico.

evenio, see eventio.

event/atio, ventilation, respiration a 1250, c 1375; -o, to fan 12c.

eventil/atio, discussion c 1125; -ator, dissipator 1427; -o, to dissipate, banish c 1102, c 1400; to discuss 8c., 10c. c 1125.

even/tio c 1362, -tus c 1193, c 1362, arrival; c 1200, a 1212, -tus 1214, casual profit or obvention; -tus (ad Parliamentum), attendance c 1320; -tu 1427, *in -tu 1294, c 1520, in -tum c 1326, c 1340, in the event; in -tu quo c 1472; in -tu si 1317, c 1325; -iendus, liable to happen c 1493; -tus, having arrived c 1362; -io ad, to belong to c 1270; -io de, to become of c 1268.

evero, see 2 averium.

ever/sus (aque), interference (with course of stream) 1419; -ticulum, destroyer 1518; -to, to turn inside out c 1448; see also ex, in.

evex-, see evectio.

evicero, see EVISCER

evict/io, eviction (leg.) c 1185, 1347; (?) entitlement (G.) 1313; -or, dispossessor c 1185; conqueror c 1190; *evinco, to acquire or take away by legal action c 1185, 1559.

*evident/ia, evidence, proof c 1125, 1535; ad -iam, as a guide 1258; -ialis, affording proof c 1414; in -i, in plain view c 1250; evidet, it is evident c 1343, 1513.

evigil/antia, wakefulness c 865; -antissime, most vigilantly 7c.; -ativus, rousing c 865; -o (trans.), to waken, arouse c 1080, p 1377.

evillo, to leave town, be absent p 1341, 1345; to drive out of town c 1320.

evinco, see evictio.

evinculo, to set free 1494.

evindico, to claim: evendico c 1000.

eviresco, to grow green, flourish c 1378, 1516.

eviro, see ejuro.

eviscer/atio, disembowelling c 1115, c 1430; -atus, heart-felt 1433; evicero, for -o, to disembowel 1245, 1461.

eviscus, *see* hibiscus.
†evispila, (?) shroud (or (?) *f.l.* for sine vespillone) c 1190.
evitabiliter, avoidably p 1300.
evit/aneus, -ernus, *see* evum.
evitus, *see* EMPT
evocat/io, death c 793; evocation (gram.) 13c.; -oria, summons 6c.
evolatio, flight 7c.
evolutio, clearing up c 1070; lapse (of time) c 1298, 1649.
evulgatio, publication 1520.
evum c 1250, p 1300, evatio 13c., evitern/itas c 1270, αἰών, duration prolonged throughout time but not timeless; -us, lasting throughout time 1267, c 1340; ‡evitaneus, "without end" 15c.
ew/agium, ferry due 1200, 1230; -aria 1477, -eria 1401, -eraria 1478, office of ewerer; -era 1440, -erum 1390, eueria 1268, ewer.
ewangel-, *see* EVANGEL
ewkaris-, *see* EUCHARIS
ex, e, made of (material) 1483, 1516; by (agent) c 1362; by, with (instrument) c 1330, a 1408;
(various phrases) *ex conventione, by agreement 1285, 1375; ex concessione 1445, ex curialitate 1368, ex dono 1404; ex gratia 1271, 1445; ex jure 1339; ex jussu 12c., ex mandato 1421, ex precepto 1336; ex nomine c 1200; ex officio c 1178, 1366; ex vi statuti c 1412;
(with *pronoun*) ex quo, since, inasmuch as c 1170, 1468; ex eo quod, because 1309, 1461; ex utraque, on both sides c 1250; ex se c 1330, ex sese c 1250, ex se ipso c 1290, spontaneously, inherently; ex hujusmodi, of this sort, from such sources c 1172, 15c.;
(with *adj.* or *ppl.*) ex abrupto c 1330, 15c., ex arrupto 1297, 1461, suddenly; *ex abundanti c 1220, 15c., ex habundantia 1390, moreover, beyond what is required; exhabundanti ad cautelam 1272; ex accidenti, by chance c 1210; ex antiquo, from of old 1359, 1434; ex complacito c 865, ex condicto a 1180, c 1204, by common consent; ex concesso, admittedly 1252; ex conjuncto, jointly 1222; ex consequenti, in consequence c 1341; e converso, conversely 11c. 1522; ex debito, duly 1086, 1301; e directo, directly 1470; ex everso, wrong way round 1461; ex incidenti, incidentally 13c.; ex integro, entirely 1070, 15c.; ex longo, far off 14c.; ex minimo, in the least degree (?) c 940; ex novo, anew 1508; *ex opposito, opposite 1203, 1477; ex ordinario, in due course c 1307; ex possibili, intentionally, ex impossibili, unintentionally c 1115; ex post facto, subsequently, retrospectively c 1250, c 1370; ex proposito, purposely c 1340; ex superabundanti, superabundantly 1414; ex toto, wholly c 1266; ex transverso, collaterally (of relationship) 1461; extransversum c 1266, c 1330, ex traversum 1527, ex traverso 1271, transversely;
(with *adv.* or *prep.*) e contra, on the other hand c 730; ex amodo 1321, ex deinde 1467, ex inantea 1419, *ex nunc

p 1147, 1546, henceforth, hereafter; ex nunc prout extunc c 1326, 1543, ex n. ut ex t. 1298, 1318; ex diu, for long c 1458; ex hinc, *see* exhinc; ex post c 1365, 1470, *ex tunc c 1170, 15c., ex tunc in antea c 1250, thereafter, thenceforward; ex tunc, forthwith, then c 1246, 1459;
ex gravi querela, name of a writ 1419.
ex-, *see also* es-, exs-, s-
exa, *see* 1 axella.
exabbas, ex-abbot 15c.
exacedrum, *see* HEXA
exacerb/ativus, irritant c 1190, ‡15c.; -o in, to rail against c 1430.
exact/io, charge, accusation (leg.) c 1115; *e. secularis, civil due or tax 1178, c 1324; causa -ionalis, action to exact a due c 1115; -or, judge c 793; reeve 1553; -orie, by compulsion c 1080, a 1452; -orius 14c., a 1452, -ivus c 1350, 1378, extortionate; *see also* rotulus; -rix, driver (f.) 8c.; -iono, to plunder 1432; -o, to exact 1148; *see also* EXIG
exacuatio, sharpening 1532.
exadmiror, to wonder 1431.
exag/ellia, bequest 5c.; -ilarius, by heredity 7c.
exaggeratio, extortionate demand c 1115.
exagit/atio, chase, hunting c 1190; instigation 13c.; -o, to bait (bulls) 1349.
exagium, weight a 1250, 13c.; assagium 1291, 1325, *assai/a 1236, 1587, -um 1229, 1534, asseium c 1266, essaium c 1178, -amentum p 1280, 1330, -mentum 1300, -atio 1387, †asseisina 1539, assay, testing (of metals); -a, testing (of ale) 1366; -atio, inspection (of arms) 1399; assagiator a 1307, -ator 1217, 1486, essaiator 1182, 1253, essaetor c 1221, esseiator 1253, assayer; assiator mensurarum 14c.; -o a 1275, 1369, essaio 1253, to assay; to test (weigh-beams) 1352; (fish) 1364; (obley irons) 1389; (arms) 1399.
exalacrito, to urge on 12c.
exalbatio, wearing white c 1330.
exalieno, to cause to migrate c 865.
exalligo, to release, revoke 1261.
exalt/atio, raising, erection c 1197, 1443; raising (of price or tax) 1362, 1419; *exaltation, glorification c 1090, 1559; exaltation, highness (title) 1274; exaltation (astr.) a 1233, 1620; evaporation (alch.) 1267, ‡1652; *E. Sancte Crucis c 760, c 1006. a 1142, a 1564, *festum (dies) -ationis S. Crucis 12c., c 1493, dies -ationis Vivifice Crucis c 1250, Holy Cross Day (14 Sept.); -abilis, worthy to be exalted 14c., c 1420; -ator, exalter c 1125; -o, to erect, build 1200, 15c.; to raise (rents, *etc.*) 1185, 1419.
exambium, *see* excambium.
exam/en, (specimen for) assay c 1178, 1236; c 1115, c 1362, -inatio c 1115, c 1180, judicial ordeal; c 1250, 1562, *-inatio c 1172, 1549, examination, investigation, test; examination (ac.) 1549; -inatio, torture c 1125; -en districtum c 1178, e. extremum 1157, 1426, -inatio districta 12c., e. ultima 1267, a 1349, dies -inationis c 760. 12c., 13c., Last Judgement; -inabilis, passing the assay a 1252; officium -inarium,

judicial office (eccl.) c 1397; **-inator,** assayer 1207, 1366; examiner (ac.) c 1477, 1560; judicial examiner (eccl.) 1295, 1469; Chancery official 1389; **e. generalis** (eccl.) 1299, a 1452, crucible 12c.; **-inatorium,** crucible 12c.; **-inatorius,** probative c 1376; **sermo -inatorius** (ac.) 1312, c 1516; **-inatrix,** weighing (f.) a 1275; **-ino,** to put to the ordeal c 1135; to examine judicially 1233, 1365; to examine (ac.) c 1350, 15c.

examens, lifeless 9c.

exam/itus, -etus, *see* **samitus.**

examplifico, to make prosperous 1149.

exangulo, to draw out 7c.; ‡to search out 1483.

exannalis, rotulus, Exannual Roll (of Exchequer) 1333, 15c.

exansatus, without handles c 1620.

exan/thema, eruption (med.): **-tima** a 1250.

exaquia 1322, 1323, **exsequia (essequia)** 1227, **essew/a** 1258, **-ioia** 1250, 1251, **sewicium** c 1200, **-era** 1269, *****sewera** 1260, 1547, **seweria** 1260, 14c., **sewara** 1316, **sewaria** 1439, **sewerum** 1535, **seuera, seuwera** 1375, **suera** 1375, 1468, **suerum** 1526, sewer, drain, drainage; **sewera** 1387, 1507, **suera** 1552, weir; **assewagium,** drainage dues 13c., 1297; **sewagium,** haulage (of casks) out of water 1337; **seweator,** drainer 1445; **exaquo** 1272, c 1293, **exequio** 1231, **-io** 1231, 1284, **-o** 13c., **assevio** 1327, **assewio** c 1306, 1337, **asseuo** c 1405, **assueo** 1271, **assuo** 13c., 1373, **seweo** 1374, 1382, **sewo** 1359, 1375, **sewero** 1315, **suewero** 1375, to drain, cleanse.

exarator, writer a 1183.

exarchus, exarch, Byzantine governor a 1142; exarch, metropolitan bishop 1274.

exar/dentia, fervour 1437; **-tio,** *for* **-sio,** conflagration c 1306; **-desco,** to set ablaze 1255; to sally out c 793; **-dessit,** *for* **-descit,** 1308.

exaridatio, *see* EXHERED

exarmatio, disarming c 1160; **exermis,** unarmed c 1160, ‡1483.

exart-, *see also* **exardentia;** EXSART

exartatus, constrained, enthralled 14c.

‡**texar/thema (†-chima),** dislocation 15c.

exasper/atio, sharpening 1460, 1533; exasperation, irritation 1300, 1620; **-us,** irritating 1283, 1409; **-esco,** to be irritated a 1250.

‡**texauctio,** sale 1570.

exauctor/izatio, deposition, dismissal c 1180; **-ito** 12c., **-izo** 1260, to depose, degrade.

exaud/itio, favourable hearing, grant (bibl.); **-ibilis,** worthy of a hearing c 690. c 1238; ready to hearken c 790; **-itor,** one who hearkens (bibl.).

†**exauferat,** *f.l.* for **exhauserat,** c 1293.

exbann/io c 1320, a 1452, †**-o** 15c., to banish.

exbraccatus, unbreeched 1166.

exbranc/atura 1229, 1270, **-hiatura** 1260, c 1290, **esbrancatura** c 1192, outer branches (of tree); **-atus,** stripped of branches 1282.

exca-, *see also* EXCID

*****excamb/ium** 1086, 1608, **-ia** c 1155, 1225, †**exambium** 1274, **exscambium** 12c.,

1217, *****escambium (escanbium)** 1086, c 1414, **escambia** c 1160, 1203, †**escambrium** 1186, †**ecambium** c 1280, **essecambium** 1221, **ascambium** (Sc.) c 1230, **scambium** 1086, 1385, **excangium** 1086, c 1140, **exchangia** c 1140, c 1200, **escangium** 1086, **scangium** 1086, **-itio** c 1170, 13c., **-iatio** a 1241, **escambitio** 1080, **escambiatio** c 1200, exchange, land given in exchange; **-ium,** substitute (food) c 1296; bill of exchange 1526; **e. regis** 1215, a 1347, **e. regale** 1686, (place of) royal exchange (of money); **-itor** 1199, **eschambitor** 1205, exchanger; **-iator** c 1190, **escambiator** c 1250, c 1350, **scambiator** c 1255, money-changer; **-io** 1086, 1583, †**-ito** 13c., **-eo** c 1103, **exscambio** c 1216, *****escambio** c 1185, c 1400, **excampio** a 1200, **escangio** 1163, to exchange.

excandens, burning with anger c 1250, 1461; †**exscando,** to be angry 1291.

excanonico, to degrade from office of canon a 1205.

excapito, to behead c 1155, 15c.

excardino, to perturb c 1400.

excari/atio 1366, **-agium** 1446, carting away; **-o** 1265, **ecario (†ecurio)** 1199, to carry off.

†**excasus** (? *for* **excessus**), trance a 1500.

excatur/izatio (exscatur-), scaturizatio, scalding c 1380; **-izo** c 1200, 15c., **-io** 1252, **excaterizo** 1348, ‡**excatariso** c 1440, **scaturizo** c 1200, 1322, **scaterizo** 1378, **scatalizo, scatulizo** 1243, ‡**scatigarizo** 1483, to scald (esp. hogs or poultry).

excec/atio, blinding, blindness 8c. c 1240, c 1363, **-o** a 1250, c 1390, **ecceco** 15c., to dazzle, confuse, disable.

excedo, *see* EXCESS

excelebro, to celebrate (? abnormally) 14c.

*****excell/entia,** excellency (title) 7c., 8c. c 1090, c 1455; **-endus,** excellent c 1340; **-entissimus,** most excellent 8c., 9c. 1254, c 1544; **-o** (*trans.*), to surpass c 793. c 1363.

†**excello,** (?) to cut down *or* uproot a 1300.

excel/sa (*pl.*), high places (of pagan worship) c 1546, 1562; **-sia,** elevation, dignity a 1205; **-situdo,** height c 685; highness (title) c 1192; **-cissime,** *for* **-sissime,** exceedingly 1599.

excennus, *see* XENO

excentric-, *see* ECCENTRIC

exceptatio, *see* ACCEPT

except/io, reception 6c. c 1125; (?) omission c 1200; liberty (eccl.), (?) *for* **exemptio,** c 1254; extract, (?) *for* **excerptio,** c 1188, 1444; **e. fori,** (?) exception of right (leg.) 13c.; **e. in factum,** plea of error (leg.) 1276, 1289; †**expectaculum,** *for* **-aculum,** receptacle 9c.; **-iva,** exception c 1332; **-ive,** by way of exception 13c.; **-ivus,** exceptive, exclusive (log.) 13c., c 1360; 1684, **-orius** 1446, exceptionable (leg.); **-or,** objector c 1290; ‡**excip/ium,** "frithed field", intake 1483; **-io,** to neglect, omit c 1000. c 1115; **e. contra,** to take exception (leg.) 1336, 1684; **e. me,** to betake oneself c 1400.

excerc-, *see* EXERC

excerebro, to brain 14c.

*excess/us, excess, outrage, transgression c 950. c 1115, 1536; **e. mentis,** trance, ecstasy (bibl.); ***-ive,** excessively c 1245, 1518; ***-ivus,** excessive c 1254, 1684; **excedo hominem,** to die a 1142.

exchapi-, *see* ESCAP

exchippo, *see* **skippagium.**

excidamentum 1141, ***excaeta** 1181, c 1350, **exscaeta** 1253, **excheta** 1250, ***escaet/a** c 1178, 1553, †**escheata** 1227, c 1407, **eschata** 1285, **acheta** c 1250, **ascaeta** 1239, 1335, **ascheita** c 1300, **askayeta** c 1300, escheat; **-a** 1231, 1369, **kaeta** c 1175, loppings, offal (of wood); offal (of venison) 1242; (?) sweepings (of grain) 1297; †**e. nubis,** (?) something fallen from the clouds c 1290; **-abilis,** liable to escheat 1389; **-aria** 1250, 1296, **-eria** 1248, 1330, **-ria** 1265, 1419, escheatorship, escheatry; **-arius** 1239, 14c., †**-orius** 14c., ***-or** 1214, c 1452, **-ator** 1212, **excaetor** 1217, 1296, **exscaetor** 1253, **excaetator** 1243, **exchator** 1271, escheator; **-us** 1160, 1329, **excaetus** 1174, **excaatus** 1141, escheated; **excido** 1141, 1242, **-o** 13c., **escato** 1202, **escaeo** 1229, a 1452, **escaio** 1205, **excaeo** c 1250, to escheat; **-o,** to take as escheat, confiscate (Sc.) 1429, c 1540.

excillo, to cohabit with one's wife c 1370.

excindo, *for* **exscindo,** to destroy 1241.

excinero, to burn to ashes c 1450.

excip-, *see* EXCEPT

excisa 1620, **exsisa** 1490, excise (foreign).

excis/or, hewer c 700; **petra -a** 1234, **essicis** (*abl. pl.*) 1253, squared stone; *cf.* **assisa, azeisa.**

excit/atio, awakening c 1245; appeal c 1380, 1423; ***1271,** 1489, **exitatio** 13c., a 1564, **-amentum** 1237, 1485, incitement, stimulus; **-ativus** a 1205, 15c., **-atorius** c 1343, 1537, arousing, stimulating; **-atoria,** letter urging action c 1300; **horologium -atorium,** alarm-clock 1537; **-ator** c 1210, c 1255, **-atrix** (*f.*) c 1450, inciter; **excitus,** wakened, **excitus,** alarmed c 1219; **-o,** to derive 1620; **exito,** *for* **-o,** to rouse c 1330.

exclam/atio, hue and cry c 1102; **-atorie,** in a loud voice c 1470.

exclaro, to decide 1205.

*exclus/a 1086, 1587, **-um** 1461, 1477, **esclusa** 1136, 1200, **sclusa** 1295, 1312, **clusa** c 1220, 1608, **clausa** c 1400, **-io** 1337, **exclotura** (C.I.) 1331, sluice, dam; **-orium,** sluice-gate 1240; **-agium** c 1070, 1304, **slusagium** 1189, 1606, (payment for having) sluice; **-im,** decisively 1325; **-io,** hatching out c 1200; **-io, -iva,** exclusion (log.) 1620; **-iva,** limitation c 1332; exclusive adverb (gram.) 1552; **-ive,** exclusively 1267, c 1450; **-ivus,** exclusive 13c., 1620; **excludo,** to hatch out c 1200, ‡1570; **e. diem ultimum,** to die c 1400.

exclus/or, -orius, *see* **excusor.**

excocio, *see* STOCK

excogitabilis, conceivable 1267.

excol/a c 950. 1319, **-us** c 1620, foreigner; **-icus,** alien (*adj.*) c 950.

excol/atio, filtering a 1250; **-o,** to ooze out 13c.

excomedo, to consume 6c.

*excommuni/catio (excommoni-) (eccl.),

-camen c 1200, †**-o** c 806, excommunication; **e. major** c 1300, 1560; **-cativus,** tending to excommunication c 1376; **-cator,** excommunicator 13c., c 1378; **bulla -catoria,** bull of excommunication c 1414; **-catus** 6c. 1247, 1684, †**-cius** a 1250, †**excommonis** c 806, excommunicated person; ***-co** (eccl.), †**exconvinco** 957, to excommunicate; **e. in genere** c 793. 1229, c 1520; **e. in specie** c 730. c 1250, c 1520; **e. nominatim** c 1250, c 1298.

excomptus, elegant c 1365.

excomputo, to deduct c 1450.

exconstabularius, former constable c 1140.

exconvinco, *see* EXCOMMUNI

excoquo: ecoquo, to brew 8c.

excori/atio, flaying c 1315, 1322; abrasion (med.) c 1200, a 1250; spoliation 1268; wear and tear 1425; 1185, 1370, **escoriatio** 1198, stripping of bark; *cf.* **escorgeria; -ativus,** abrasive, caustic c 1270; **-ator,** flayer, skinner 1238, 1285; despoiler 12c., a 1250; **e. (animalium, bidentium),** (unlawful) flayer 1198; **-o *a** 1100, c 1540, **scorio** 1275, to flay; (?) to scalp c 1115, 12c.; to peel 13c., c 1362; to strip (turf) 1261, 1430; ***c** 1204, 15c., **escorio** 1274, **exscorio** c 1260, to despoil; to separate (log.) c 1367; to lose skin (*intr.*) 1271; †**-iso,** to strip of bark 1365.

excortico, to strip of bark a 1150, 1424; to flay a 1250.

excossio, to clack (wool) (*cf.* **cottum**) 1442.

‡**excosto,** to rib (flax) 1483.

excoto, *see* **scotum.**

excrement/um, increase, excess c 1190, c 1288; ‡**excrement** 1652; **e. auri,** (?) gold filings 1255; **e. maris,** flooding a 1450; **-icius,** excrementitious 1622.

excretio, growth c 1250; **excresc/entia,** (*f. s.*) increase, excess p 1203, 1482; c 1336, 1587, (*n. pl.*) c 1550, casual profit or offering (eccl.); **dies -ens,** intercalary day c 1258; **-o,** to accrue 1218, 1469; to be in excess, exceed 1236, 1419; **e. assisam,** to exceed the fixed price c 1356.

excrispo, to curl 1267.

excrust/atio, stripping, spoliation 13c.; **-o,** to strip, despoil c 1125, c 1250.

excub/a, -ator c 1200, **-us** c 1160, ‡15c., *for* **-itor,** watchman; **-itor,** supervisor c 760; **-anter,** vigilantly c 1325; **-ialis,** vigilant c 1160.

‡**excudi/a (†studia)** 15c., 1483, ‡**-atorium** 15c., swingle-stock; ‡**-o,** to swingle (hemp) 15c., 1483; *cf.* EXCUSS

excudo, *see* **excusor.**

exculenta, *see* **escale.**

exculpo, (?) *for* **exsculpo,** to get rid of c 793.

excult/io, worship c 1500; **-abilis** c 1180, **-ibilis** 1141, cultivable.

excurator, guardian 1285; *see also* ESCUR

excursus, lapse (of time) c 1188, 14c.; spread c 1174; scope c 1178; (*ppl.*) having elapsed c 1172, 1414.

excurto, to shorten 1292; 12c., **escurto** 1214, **scurtio** 1236, 1247, to dock (a horse).

excus/amen (conscientie), relief 1508; **-abilis,** guiltless, excusable c 730, 10c. c 1188, 1474; **-abiliter,** excusably c 1196;

-abilitas, excusability c 1376; ***-ator,**
bearer of excuses c 1178, c 1472; **-ative,**
by way of excuse 1427; **-ativus** c 1115,
*-atorius a 1000. a 1142, 15c., excusatory;
-atorie (*pl.*), letters excusatory c 1250,
c 1430; **-o** (*intr.* with *dat.*), to excuse oneself
from 9c.
excusor, printer 1573; †**exclusor ferri,**
iron-founder c 1125; **ars** †**exclusoria,**
metalwork c 1255; **excudo,** to print 1516,
1552.
excuss/io, emission, knocking out c 1270,
14c.; forcible seizure c 1115; threshing
c 1250; investigation, discussion c 1255,
1267; **-or,** thresher c 1250; **-orium,** threshing-floor c 704; (?) flail 1560; ‡swingle-
stock 15c. (*cf.* EXCUDI); **-us,** collision c 1125;
(?) residue after threshing 1248; (*ppl.*)
violent, loud 7c.; **-e,** vigorously c 1237;
-io, to knock off c 1408; **excutio,** *to thresh
a 1166, 1251; to free, keep clear (of) 1284;
e. namium, to 'rescue' distrained chattels
(*cf.* RESCUSS) c 1115, 1169.
exdux, ex-duke a 1186.
execr/atorius (exsecr-), confirmed by a
curse 1646; **-andus,** accursed 7c. 1342;
-andissimus 8c.; **-o,** to curse, abhor 8c.;
to profane c 793. c 1236.
execut/io (exsecut-, exequt-) *1217, 1538,
execuscio c 1303, execution, performing;
execution of sentence, punishment 1418,
1516; writ or letter of execution 13c., 1545;
enforcement (of contract) (G.) 1304, 1316;
1231, 1432, **-oria** 1559, executorship (of
will); **e. judicii** 1229, 1383; **e. justitie**
c 1250, c 1410; **e. verbalis** 1684; **e. testamenti** 1227, c 1452; **-ionarius communis,** common executioner 1686; **-ive,**
in action, effectively c 1360, 1378, **-ivus,**
executive, effective 12c., c 1430; **-or,** *performer, administrator 1124, c 1520; papal
judge delegate 1200, c 1255; *1230, 1577,
e. testamenti c 1185, 1540, executor (of
will); **e. dativus,** executor dative (leg.)
1608; **e. officii,** celebrant of mass (eccl.)
c 1230, 1483; **-oria** (*f. s.*) sigilli, keepership
of seal (G.) 1312; **-oria** (**judicialia**),
executive duties 1330; **-orium officii,**
ordinal (eccl.) 1446; **-orie** (*pl.*) c 1308,
littere -orie 1221, 1441, **l. -oriales** 1456,
1608, letters of execution; **bulle -orie** 15c.,
1461; **nomine -orio,** in the capacity of
executor (of will) c 1310, 15c.; **potestas
-orialis,** executive power c 1450; **-rix,**
performer (*f.*) c 1190; a 1255, c 1400, ***e.
testamenti** 1287, 1586, **e. ultime voluntatis** 1549, executrix; **exequ/ax,** follower
15c.; **-ia** (*n. pl.*), obsequies c 793; **-ie** (*f. pl.*)
c 1336, c 1505, **-ies** 1478, office of the dead,
year's mind; **-ialiter,** with funeral cere-
monies 1503; **-or** (*passive*), to be executed
1219, c 1530.
exedr/a, (?) ante-room *or* chapel c 700;
‡lattice 1483; **-iola,** small ante-room, apse
c 704.
exege/ma 1588, **-sis** 1537, exegesis, exposition; **-ticos,** exegetic c 700.
†**exeleogeneus,** heterogeneous a 1200.
‡**exelerarius,** (?) *for* **cellerarius,** wine-
drawer, "birler" 15c.

†**exemphracticus,** disobstructive 15c.
‡**exemplasticus,** (?) adhesive 15c.
exempl/um, paradigm (log.) 13c., 1610;
sample (of goods) 1344; **-abilis,** able to be
formed after a pattern a 1360; **-ar(e),**
pattern, ornamental design 1381, 1433;
*-aris, exemplary, serving as a pattern 12c.,
16c.; (with *gen.*) modelled on c 865; **forma
-aris,** formal cause c 1200; **-ariter,** by way
of example or archetype 1252, c 1500; by
force of example c 1135; **-aritas,** archetypal
quality c 1270, c 1290; **-arius** 13c., **-ator**
1246, copyist; **-atim,** by way of example
12c.; **-atio,** serving as an example p 1300,
1378; **-ativus,** typical c 870. 1344; **-atum,**
copy 1219, c 1240; object typified c 1357;
-ificatio, citing an example 13c.; exemplification, copy (leg.) 1354, 1583; **littere
-ificatorie,** letters of exemplification 1504;
-ifico c 1125, 1427, **-o** 12c., c 1400, to
exemplify, adduce *or* serve as example;
-ifico 1284, 1583, †**-ico** 1427, **-o** 1306, 1465,
to exemplify, copy; **-o,** to form after a
pattern c 793. c 1265, c 1377.
exempt/io, *exemption, immunity c 1188,
c 1450; exemption from episcopal jurisdiction (mon.) c 1218, 1549; **-icius,** bought
c 1130; **-or,** one who claims exemption
(mon.) c 1220; **-us,** (*subst.*) exempt monk
1256, 1549; (*adj.*) exempt (mon.) c 1250,
1549; 980, **e. rebus humanis** 1317, dead;
eximo, to exempt (mon.) c 1220.
exen-, *see also* XEN
exensis, *see* exsensis.
exent/eratio, -erizatio, †**-ricatio** c 1422,
‡**-atio** c 1440, disembowelling; **-ero** c 1200,
1528, †**exentero** c 1400, *for* **exintero,** to
disembowel (*cf.* ἔντερα).
exeo, *see* exitus.
exepiscopus, ex-bishop 747. c 1218.
exeq-, *see* exaquia; EXECUT
exerc/itus (excerc-), military service 1086,
1329; **e. anterior,** vanguard 1349; **-itum,**
for **-itus,** force, muster (G.) 1248; **-itulus,**
small army c 1200; **-itualia** (*pl.*), heriot
c 1102; †**-itas** c 1193, †**-itia** 1549, **-isium**
1573, †**-ium** 1487, †**exertio** a 1547, *for*
-itium, exercise; **-itium,** business, duty,
administration c 1197, c 1597; model,
example c 1370; **e. spirituale,** spiritual
exercise, church service 1549; **e. scholasti-
cum** c 1250; **-itamentum,** exercise (ac.)
1520, c 1542; **-itatiuncula,** light (physical)
exercise 1520; **-itativus,** active c 865; in-
structional, affording practice 1132; **-itator,**
stirrer c 865; **e. officii,** practitioner of a
trade c 1324; **-itor tabernarum,** frequenter
of taverns 1397; **e. terre,** tiller of the
earth c 1200; **-eo cervisie,** to indulge in
ale 1452; **e. curiam,** to practise the law
1432; **e. histrionem,** to play the actor
c 1160; **e. nundinas,** to frequent or attend
a fair 1287; **e. scholas** c 1250, 1472; **e.
tabernas** c 1335, c 1448; **e. viam,** to
exercise a right of way 1368; **e. vices,** to
take the place, exercise the authority 12c.
exermis, *see* **exarmatio.**
exertero, *see* EXENT
exestuatio, storm a 1142.
exforesto, to remove from forest status c 1228.

exfredio, see AFFRAI
exfumigo, for effumigo, to smoke out c 1138.
exguo, see EXTINCT
exhalesco, to burst out c 1115.
exhau/stio, emptying c 1125; -rio pugionem, to draw a dagger 1577.
*exhered/atio c 1193, 1414, -itatio 1199, a 1564, -itio 1234, 1292, exaridatio 1363, †-itas 12c., disinheriting, disherison; -ator, disinheritor 1200, p 1377; -atus, disinherited person 12c., 1273; -ito c 1188, 1461, †-eo c 1332, to disinherit.
exhib/itio *8c., 1041. a 1100, 1457, -itus 12c., showing forth, display; *1155, 1544, -utio 1432, c 1434, maintenance, sustenance; -itio in scholis c 1452, e. scholarium c 1406, c 1485; e. juris c 1226, e. justitie c 1250, 1438, doing justice; e. operis, performance of good works c 1160, 1324; e. presentie, personal appearance c 1188; -itor, giver, performer c 1250, 1439; e. presentium, the bearer of these (letters) 1267, a 1452; e. litterarum 1265; e. scholaris c 1375; -itorius c 1188, -ilis c 1286, demonstrative; -itorius, munificent c 1415; -itum, exhibit (leg.) 1400, 1684; *-eo, to maintain, support, provide for a 1160, c 1450; e. ad scholas 1419, e. in scholis 1295, c 1400; e. justitiam c 1163, c 1290, e. rectitudinem c 1250, to do justice; e. presentiam (meam), to appear in person c 1072, c 1330.
exhil/ero, for -aro, to cheer c 1350, a 1519.
exhinc, hereupon, thereafter 1093, 1461.
exhomico (exomico), to display oneself c 550, c 1000.
exhomino, to dehumanize c 1200.
exhorren/tia, abhorrence 1620; -dissimus, horrific c 1250.
exhort/amentum 8c. ‡1570, -atorium 1432, -atus 1406, exhortation; -atorie (pl.), letters of exhortation 1430; *-atorius, exhortatory 793, 1006. c 1125, 1428; -atum, request 1282; †-or, exhorter c 793; -o, for -or, to exhort 5c., c 793. 1461, 1494.
exhum/atio, exhumation 1305, c 1440; -o 1290, 15c., hesumo 1317, to exhume.
exhumecto, to bedew with tears c 1070.
*exig/entia, exigency, necessity, demand c 1185, 1549; e. juris 1281, 1559; e. meritorum c 1195, c 1395; e. rationis c 1305, 1339; e. status 1294, 1446; e. temporis 13c., 1512; -itio, exaction c 1150; -itivus, obligatory a 1228; -ende (pl.) c 1290, 15c., -enda (s.) 1439, exigent, first steps in outlawry (leg.); pono in -endis 1275, 15c.; breve -endi, breve de -endo 1419, -i facias 15c., writ of exigent; -entarius, exigenter (leg.) 1439; -ens, necessary 12c.; (subst.) demandant (leg.) 1269; exiens, demanding c 1040; -o (with acc.), to ask c 550. 1353; to summon 1220, 1452; to exact, demand appearance in court (leg.) c 1220, 1364; †e. caput, see ERECT; e. curiam, to claim right of trial 1229, 1236; -uo, for -o, (G.) 1315; see also EXACT
†exigeo, (?) for exhibeo, a 1184.
exignio, to ignite c 1180.
exigu/itas mea (nostra), my humble self c 1000. c 1250, c 1343; -us, humble c 740; see also EXIG

exil/itas, scarcity, poverty 1302, 1441; e. mea, my humble self c 1250; -issimus 1264, -imus c 1410, c 1450, very slight.
*exil/ium (exsil-), waste, ruin, destruction 1199, 15c.; e. lingue, abscess causing protrusion of tongue a 1250; -is 1086, exul (exsul) c 1110, c 1115, outlaw; -iatio c 1420, exulium c 1408, exile; -io c 685. c 1115, c 1450, *exulo 1086, 1461, to exile or outlaw; exulo, to waste, destroy 1205.
eximi/etas, excellency (title) 1231; -a (pl.), finery c 1450.
eximo, see EXEMPT
eximperatrix, ex-empress c 1140, c 1200.
exinan/itio, diminution 12c.; impoverishment 1280, 1371; self-emptying, κένωσις (theol.) c 730. 12c., 1378; -io, to free or exempt from, empty of 944, 948; -isco, to empty 9c.
exinde, thereof 9c.; thereby 1062.
exire, see exitus.
exist/entia a 1109, 1559, -ere (subst.) a 1200, c 1363, existence; -enter, really a 1252; *-o, to be (auxiliary) c 1070, 1687; cf. exsto; -o ultra, to supervise 1280.
existimatrix, judge, critic (f.) 1555.
exit-, see also EXCIT
†exitero, (?) f.l. for exerceo, 1324.
exit/us, offal, entrails 1257, 1446; issue, offspring (of animals) c 1300, 1449; issue, heirs (human) 1293, 1560; *1086, 1540, exsitus 1255, exutus 1225, issue, produce, revenue, profits; derivation, origination 1267; (question at) issue (leg.) 1505, 1630; e. (primus) carrucarum, first going out to plough 1280, 1300; e. mensis 1315, m. exiens 1263, latter half (16th to 31st) of month, in which dates are reckoned back from last day (Fr.); e. mentis, ecstasy 14c.; e. patrie, verdict of jury 1433; e. placiti, issue of the plea (leg.) c 1443; e. sigilli regis, issue (profit) of royal seal 1259, 15c.; -icius, exile 1421; -ura, abscess, impostume 1267, ‡1652; exire, (subst.) egress 1155, 1215; exiens, see EXIG; exeo, *to leave, quit (trans.) a 1142, 1537; to die 1220; to issue from (of heirs) 1251, c 1434; *to issue, be derived, from (of revenue) 1086, 1533; e. extra juncturam, to be put out of joint 1268; e. in actum c 1332, e. in esse 1267, to become actual; e. in judicium, to submit to judgement c 463; see also exuitio.
†exjudic/aliter, extrajudicially 1515; -o, to oust by legal action p 1377.
exkippo, see SKIPP
exlex, outlaw 1086, 1557; terra e., outlawed land c 1115; exleg/alitas, illegal conduct c 1135; -o, to outlaw c 1125, c 1540.
exmonach/us, unfrocked monk a 1142, c 1220; -o, to unfrock a monk c 1220.
exnamio 1158, esnamio c 1111, c 1160, to distrain upon.
exnunc, see ex.
exo, see I axella.
exobto, for exopto, c 1140.
exoccupo, to put out of employment c 1160, c 1330.
exoculatio, blinding c 1190, c 1220.
exogallia, pattern c 463.

exoletus, destitute of, remote from c 1115.

exomico, *see* exhomico.

exoner/atio, unloading (of ship) 1258; discharge (of gun) 1573; relief, release 1236, a 1452; discharge, quittance (of debt) 1312, 1524; -atorium curatorum, title of book c 1528; -o, to discharge (gun) 1573, 1577; to discharge, acquit (of debt) 1236, 1524; †*for* superonero, to overstock 1388.

exonium, *see* essonium.

exoperor, to cause, produce c 1500.

exoppilo, to unblock a 1250.

exor/atio 1372, -atus c 1125, effectual entreaty; -ator, intercessor 760; -o, to beseech 9c. 12c., c 1330; *e. pro, to pray for 12c., 1461; ‡-or, to wed 1483.

exorbitas, blindness c 870.

exorbit/atio, missing the mark c 1200; c 1242, 1452, -antia 1422, transgression; -o, *to deviate, go astray c 685. c 1090, c 1478; to lead astray 1180; to eject 15c.

*exorc/ismus a 950. c 1160, 1400, -isma a 1250, exorcism; e. salis et aque c 1330; -ista c 1080, 1400, exorzista a 1452, exorcist; -ismo 13c., -izo c 760, a 950. c 1190, a 1452, to exorcize, conjure.

exordiarius, precentor c 1000.

exordin/atio, irregularity, breach of order (mon.) a 1110, c 1500; -o, to disorder c 1160; to degrade (priest or monk) c 1115, 13c.

†exorior, (?) *f.l.* for exordior, to begin (to speak) c 1150.

exornamentum, adornment, equipment c 870.

exor/o, -or, *see* exoratio.

exortus, source (of river) c 1115; origin c 1125.

exossator, remover of bones from body 1238.

exot/erus, exotic c 1160; -icus, strange, unfamiliar c 950, c 1000.

exp-, *see also* esp-

expaalto, *see* expeditatio.

expalio, to winnow c 1405.

expan/sa, measure of length, span c 1178; -sive, by way of expansion 1620; -sivus, expansive 1620; -sus, (?) at full length p 1327; displayed (her.) c 1595; *see also* annus; †-do sanguinem, (?) *f.l.* for expendo, c 1290.

expassio, spreading out c 1192.

expect/antia (exspect-), expectancy 1376; -abilis, promising *or* (?) *for* spectabilis, impressive 1041. c 1250; -aculum, *for* spectaculum, 6c.; *see also* EXCEPT; gratia -ativa, reversionary grace (eccl.) 1389, 1462; -ator, one who waits c 730; -o, *for* specto, c 800; to remain, stay 1416, 1446; (with *inf.*) to delay c 1340.

*exped/itatio c 1115, 1406, †-iatio 1278, †-itio c 1246, espeltatio 1209, -itamentum 1232, expeltamentum 1236, espeltamentum 1205, 1230, espaltamentum 1227, -itura 1207, hambling of dogs, *or* fine for not hambling ('dog-silver'); -o 1166, *-ito 1198, 1406, expelto 1171, 1336, expaalto 1328, espelto 1205, 1230, espaalto 1227, espeto 1204, espaeto 1199, espeato 1200, to hamble (dogs); to maim (man) by loss of foot 1168, 1177.

exped/itio, expeditionary force c 550; *c 800,

1021. 1086, 14c., expetitio 1086, military service; sending, dispatch a 1200, c 1467; 1319, 1420, -itus c 1545, ‡-imentum 1570, expediting, speed; execution, completion 1200, 1461; success, profit c 1270, c 1455; ‡"utterance of sale" 1570; -imentum, baggage 1167; -ibilis, profitable, *or* (?) *for* expetibilis, c 1180; -ibilius, more effectually c 1145; -itionalis, concerned with military service 739, 933. 12c.; -itrix, disengaging, extricating (*f.*) 1649; *-iens a 1205, c 1470, -itivus 1295, expedient; -ientior 1407; -ienter c 1250, 1254, -iter 1253, speedily; in -ito, in train 1220; †-itus, (?) *for* expertus, skilled, learned c 1250; -io iter, to hasten c 1250; exspedio, *for* -io, c 1162.

expedor, *see* espedor.

expello, *see* EXPULS

expelt-, *see* expeditatio.

expen/sa, 'spence', store-room c 1136, c 1212; c 1160, c 1395, -dium c 1190, expense; a 1200, -se (*pl.*) 7c. c 1250, c 1370, provisions, victuals; ad -sas c 1332, c 1400, in -sis c 1400, 15c., super -sas 12c., 1410, at the cost (of); -se contingentes, casual expenses 1532; -se forinsece, expenses outside the manor, *etc.* 1257, 1364; -sabilis c 1135, c 1400, -sibilis 1184, -dibilis 1325, ‡1483, kept in stock, ordinary (of wine or candles); -sarius c 1200, -sor c 1150, 1389, -ditor c 1290, c 1355, spender, dispenser; -ditus, *for* -sus, spent 1219, c 1533; -do, to use, consume 1227, 1514; to spend (time) c 1458, c 1478; *cf.* SPEN

exper/caria 1364, -queria 13c., esper/caria 1270, 1365, -keria 1274, 1366, -queria 1240, 1331, sperkeria 1274, esperqueria, royal pre-emption of congers, *etc.* (C.I.); *cf.* espelcatio.

experductum c 1300, exsperdutum 1313, esper/ductum 1173, 1183, -ducta c 1350, -duita c 1160, -dutum 1228, -dutium c 1262, perduca 1281, sperduta 1270, sperdux 1276, (iron) rod.

†exper/getio, awakening c 1365; -tus, awakened 5c.

experientia, situation, plight c 1204; e. conclusionis, conclusive or demonstrative experience (opposed to e. naturalis) 1267.

experiment/um, experiment (scientific) a 1200, a 1233; (?) amulet c 1390; e. crucis, crucial test 1672; -alis, experimental 1267, 1686; -aliter, by experience c 1325, 1485; -atio, experimenting c 1283, c 1362; -ator, experimenter a 1250, 1622; the Experimenter (*i.e.* Rhazes) c 1390; -o, to learn or know by experience p 1300, 1344; to experiment 1620; -or (*dep.*), to test c 1250.

experiolus, *see* scurellus.

expervarius, *see* spervarius.

expetitio, *see* expeditio.

‡expi/amen "cleansing" 1483; -abilis, expiatory c 1220, ‡"cleansable" 1483.

‡expignero, to take out of pawn 1483.

expir/atio (exspir-), exhalation c 1200; expiry, end 1450, 1558; -abilis, evaporable 1620; -abilitas, ability to be exhaled c 1260; -o, to come to an end c 1250, 1587.

explacit/atio, pleading 12c.; -o, to gain by

pleading c 1080, 1292; **e. me,** to clear oneself by pleading c 1115, c 1125.

explan/atio, planing (of timber) 1514; **-atiuncula,** short explanation c 730; **-ativus,** explanatory c 1375; **-atus,** displayed (her.) p 1394; **-o,** to display (a banner) c 1405; to clear (woodland) c 1250; to eradicate 15c.

explanto, to eradicate c 1115, a 1408.

explect/atio, distress, seizure (Norm.) 12c., 1422; **-um** 1279, 1289, **espleitum** 1255, exploitation, use (G.); ***exple/ta** (pl.) 1195, 1297, ***-tia** (pl.) 1218, 1315, **-icia** (pl.) 1265, **explicia** (pl.) 1330, **-te** a 1300, c 1340, ***-tie** 1219, 15c., **esplete** 1274, **espletie** 1198, **explicie** 1334, †**esplata** (pl.) c 1200, **espleta** (pl.) 1196, 'esplees', profits, rents; **explecto,** to exploit, use (Fr.) 1273, 1373.

explegio, to free from obligation to stand surety 1225.

†**explegitor,** f.l. for **explorator,** 1263.

explet/io, completion 760, 1006. 12c., 1267; **-ivus,** limitative (gram.) c 790; see also EXPLECT

explic/atio (jurisdictionis), functioning c 1352; **-atrix,** expounder (f.) 1564; **-atus syllogismus,** syllogism of first or second figure 1610; **-ite,** explicitly c 1290, 1541; **-itus,** uncrippled c 1180; explicit 1300, c 1367; ***-it,** here ends c 1090, c 1470; **-iunt,** here end c 1150, c 1470; see also EXPLECT

explor/atio, diagnosis (med.) 8c.; **e. (claustri),** office of subordinate prior c 1330; **-ator claustri,** third or fourth prior (mon.) c 1330; **e. vini** 1242; **-atrix,** investigator, spy (f.) 1006. 1213; **-ative,** upon close investigation c 700; **-o,** to know c 550.

explumo, to pluck c 1150.

expompo, to flaunt 12c.

expon-, see also EXPOSIT

exponsalia, see **sponsatio.**

expontifex, ex-pope c 1160.

exporrectio, extension c 1615, 1622.

exporto, to snatch away c 1327; to empty, rid c 1400.

exposco, to require c 1330, 1426.

exposit/io, putting up for sale c 1380; exposition of the Host (eccl.) 14c.; 1236, c 1460, **-orium** 1245, commentary; **e. capitis,** risk of death c 1250; ***-or** c 730. c 1073, c 1460, ‡**-rix** (f.) 1483, interpreter, expounder; **-orie,** by expository syllogism c 1365, 15c.; **-orius,** expository (log.) a 1304, c 1380; **expon/ibilis,** capable of exposition 13c., c 1360; **-ens,** exponent (log.) c 1360; **-o,** *to expend, lay out c 1250, c 1545; to dispose of, sell c 1100; to make available, put at the disposal of 1165, 1243; to deploy 1461; **e. de,** to deal with 1263; **e. in eventum,** to risk 15c.; **-or** (with inf.), to be ready, disposed 1235.

expost, see **ex.**

exprecor, to complete prayers 1409.

express/io, *express mention, statement c 1190, 1588; emphasis c 1180; **e. peccatorum,** confession c 1357; **e. verborum,** utterance c 1330; **-ibilis,** expressible c 1300; **-ivus,** squeezing out a 1250, c 1270; expressive, significant c 1195, c 1290; **per**

-um, expressly c 1403; **-issime,** most expressly c 1340; **-issimus,** most express c 1200; **-or,** expressor c 1250, a 1446; ***-o** 1254, 1588, **expremo** 1473, 1487, to state expressly; **exprim/o signum crucis,** to make the sign of the cross 670, 697. 15c.; **-or** (dep.), to express c 1000.

expretus, despised 1409; **exsperno,** to despise utterly 8c.

expromissor, vicarious promiser (G.) 1254.

expropri/atio c 1334, c 1376, **-etas** 1427, renunciation or deprivation of property; **-etarie,** without property c 1363, 1380; **-etarius,** propertyless c 1376, 1427; **-o,** to deprive of property c 1334, c 1450.

expugn/aculum (expungn-), siege-engine p 1348; **-ator** c 1130, **-atrix** (f.) 1451, assailant.

expuls/atio 1461, a 1564, **-us** 1500, expulsion; **-iva,** expulsive force (med.) a 1250; **-ivus** c 1160, 1622, **-orius** 1344, expulsive; **-io,** outlawry c 1110; **-us,** outlaw c 1110; **expello,** to outlaw c 1110; to subtract (math.) 815.

expungo, (?) to expel c 950.

expurg/atorius, excretory c 1210; **index e.** (eccl.) 1588; **-o,** to clear of a charge (leg.) c 1130, 1337.

†**exputio,** careful consideration c 865.

exquirius, see **scurellus.**

exquisit/io, search c 1250, c 1300; right of search c 1040; **-ive,** searchingly 13c., 1308; **-or,** searcher, seeker out 6c. c 1236, c 1360; **-a** (pl.) **nature,** natural needs c 1220, c 1250; †**exquietissimus,** for **-issimus,** most select 1242; **exquirentius,** more searchingly c 1343; **exquiro,** to acquire c 1185.

exregina, ex-queen c 1140, c 1200.

exromanus, ex-Roman c 1160.

exs-, see also **ex-**

‡**exsacco,** "to unsack" 15c.

exsacello, to dismiss from chaplaincy 1609.

exsacerdos, ex-priest c 1190.

exsagino, to slim a 1150.

***exsart/um (exart-)** 1086, 1324, **essartum** c 1092, c 1450, **essertum** 1203, c 1458, †**escartum** 1130, *assartum** a 1200, 1468, †**assaitum** 1588, **assertum** 1230, c 1458, **acertum** 1539, assart, land cleared of trees, etc.; **essartulum,** small assart 1226; **essartatio** c 1200, 1221, **assartatio** 1304, 1392, assarting, clearing; **-arius,** assarter (G.) c 1150; **assartarius,** tenant of assart 1299; **assartus,** assarted c 1311; **-o** a 1224, 1289, **essarto** c 1102, c 1324, **esartico** c 1115, *assarto** 1200, 15c., **asserto** 1222, 15c., to assart, clear (land); **assarto,** to pull up (saplings) c 1300; cf. SART

exsc-, see also **exc-, esc-, sc-**

exsci/o (? **-sco**), to learn c 1362.

exscreatus, phlegm 1267.

exscriptio, copying out 1620.

exseco, to cut out: †**exsicco** 12c.

exsecr-, see EXECR

exsemino, to engender c 870.

exsensis 1200, ‡1483, **exensis** c 1090, insensible.

exseq-, see **exaquia;** EXECUT

exser/tus, ready 1214; **-o,** to declare 8c.

exsiaimio, see ASSEM

exsicc/atio, drying c 1260, c 1470; -atio (†exsucator), drain 1227; -ativus, siccative a 1250; -o, to dry out (peats) c 1200, 13c.; (timber) 1355; to strand (a ship) c 1436; *see also* exseco.

‡exsiliquus 1483, esiliquus c 1200, shelled (of peas, *etc.*).

exsisa, *see* excisa.

exsolutio (exol-), morbid discharge (med.) 1622; e. judicii, content of a decision 10c.

exsortium, levy (of troops) 1267.

exsperno, *see* expretus.

exspero, to hope 1421.

exspir-, *see* EXPIR

exspoliatio (expol-), riddance c 793.

exst-, *see also* ext-

exstamen, *see* 2 stagnum.

exsto, to be (*auxiliary*) c 1250, 1423; *cf.* EXIST

exstopo, *see* exstupo.

exstrayus, *see* straia.

†exstrictus, (?) extended 1389.

exstudiosus, unenthusiastic c 1160.

1 exstup/o 1362, extupo 1336, exstopo 1275, to stop up, block; *cf.* stupatio.

2 ‡exstupo, to dress (flax) 1483.

exsucator, *see* EXSICC

exsuctio, suction c 1615, 1620.

exsuffl/atio, blowing away c 793; blowing out c 1608; -o, to blow, puff out c 730. c 1190, 1620; to banish or extinguish c 793. c 1250, 15c.; *to despise, reject 8c., 9c. c 1125, c 1400; e. animam, to give up the ghost c 1250.

exsul, *see* exilium.

exsult-, *see* EXULT

exsupero, to seize c 1115.

exsurgo, to emerge, result 1292; to issue (of rents) c 1178, 1378.

ext/a (*pl.*), entrails (in wide sense) c 550; -ima, entrails 1248.

exta/sis, -ticus, *see* ECSTA

extempor/aneus, sudden 1620; -arius, extemporary 1620; extimplo, *for* extemplo, c 956.

extencellatus, *see* stincillatus.

extenebro, to bring to light c 1180.

exten/sio, stretching out, prolongation c 1150, c 1363; extension (as property of space) 1267, c 1380; extension (log.) c 1260, 1593; *c 793. 1202, 1287, †extincio 16c., *-ta 1219, 1504, estenta 1292, astenta 1388, -tus c 1300, 1555, -sum 1162, 'extent', survey, valuation; -tio, extension, enlargement 1346; -ditor 1268, 1308, -sor 1220, 1413, -tor 1246, 1270, -tator 15c., 'extender', valuer; -sibilis, boastful c 870; capable of extension (log.) 13c., c 1363; -sivus, extensive, ampliative (log.) c 1270, c 1345; causing extension (med.) a 1250; humor -sivus, phlegm c 1270; -sive c 1290, 1593, -se c 1380, by way of extension (log.); -se, in a wide sense c 1332; stentus, 'extended', valued 1242; -do, (*intr.*) to extend, stretch 1257, 1460; to extend, be valid c 1240; to amount, suffice c 1377, 1531; (*trans.*) to apply (rules) in a wide sense c 1457; e. arcum 1370, e. ballistam 1378; e. manum gravem ad, to punish severely 1314; -dit se ad, amounts to 1332, 1559.

extenuativus, thinning a 1250.

exter/, foreigner 12c.; -nus, different a 1235.

extermin/atio c 1130, -ium c 1250, c 1600, expulsion, banishment; c 1150, a 1446, *-ium c 1125, c 1450, destruction; -ium, pestilence c 730; e. mentis, driving out of mind a 1250; -ator c 1125, c 1430, -atrix (*f.*) c 1160, destroyer; -o, to disguise c 1395.

externeatio, *see* EXTRAN

exterpo, *see* EXTIRP

exterr/or, undismayed c 1296; -ito, to terrify c 1125, c 1210.

extersivus, detergent a 1250.

extesticulo, to castrate c 1125.

†exthacius (†eustacius), (?) envoy or hostage 1188.

extim-, *see also* ESTIM

extima, *see* exta.

extimplo, *see* EXTEMPOR

extincio, *see* extensio.

extinct/io (exstinct-), extinction c 790; slaking (of lime) 1476; quenching (of red-hot minerals) 1622; discharge (of debt) a 1564; -ivus, tending to extinguish a 1250; -orium, extinguishing matter c 1250; extinguo 1239, 1388, †exguo 1316, to slake (lime).

extirp/atio (exstirp-), waste, damage 1205, 1467; uprooting (*literal*) 1333; extirpation, uprooting (*fig.*) 1376, 1549; -o 12c., c 1205, estirpo (G.) 1304, to clear (land); -o, to waste 1470; exterpo, to uproot 1203, 1291; *cf.* STREPP

extoco (†extoto), *see* STOCK

extollentia, *pride c 1100, c 1414; extolment 1452; superiority c 1376.

extolneo, to pay toll c 1115.

extopo (†extorpo), to scalp or shave c 1115.

extorris c 1125, 14c., †extors c 793, deprived, devoid.

*extor/sio 12c., c 1455, *-tio c 730. 1267, c 1475, extortion; -sive 1304, a 1564, -tive c 1448, -tiose a 1564, -tuose 1275, extortionately; -tativus c 1365, -tus 1570, extortionate; -sor c 1290, 1324, -tor c 1250, 1528, extortionate official; -te, in a distorted sense p 1381; -queo 1276, c 1402, -so 1275, to oppress by extortions.

extra, away from here, missing 10c.; (*prep.*) except c 900; e. finem, hors d'un fin, (founded) upon a fine (leg.) 1385; e. se c 1197, e. sensum 1226, beside oneself.

extracaptus, (?) withdrawn c 1235.

extract/io 1419, c 1556, *-a 1218, 1466, -um 1236, -us 1304, 1468, extrata 14c., estreat, copy; (?) clearance, bringing into cultivation (G.) 1289; removal 13c., 1534; c 1345, -ura c 1380, extrahura c 1300, taking animals from stock (*cf.* straia); extraction (alch.) 13c.; eliciting into actuality (phil.) p 1300; amount subtracted 1308; e. radicis (math.) c 1300, 15c.; e. sanguinis, bloodshed 15c.; e. straminis, (?) 'yelming' 1514; -a 1283, 1315, astracta 1313, (?) a toll (G.); -ivus, extractive (med.) a 1250; (alch.) c 1270; -or, miner c 1250; e. dentium 1416; extraho, to copy 1289, 1517; to extract (fluid) 14c.; to subtract (math.) 1145; to delete 1429; (?) to clear or weed (G.) 1289; e. (navem), to haul ashore c 1115; e. radicem (math.) a 1150; e.

sanguinem, to shed blood 1281, c 1290; -o vinum, to draw wine c 1320.

extradono, to alienate (Sc.) 13c., 1575.

‡extraduco, to lead out 15c.

extrah-, see EXTRACT; straia.

extrajudici/alis, extrajudicial 1314, 1555; -aliter c 1335, 1684, -abiliter 1347, extrajudicially; cf. EXJUDIC

extraliberatio, outgoing payment 1329.

extramanens, burgess not living in burgh (Sc.) 1359, 1479.

extramarinus, oversea (Sc.) 1480, 1484.

extra/missio, emission of sense (optics) a 1233, 1344; -mitto, to emit (optics) a 1233, 1267; to send out, release from store a 1130, c 1330.

extramontanus, Highland (Sc.) 1398.

extran/eitas, strangeness 1284, p 1300; -ietas, estrangement 1284; -eus, *stranger, outsider c 1080, 1609; third party (leg.) c 1185; external, foreign, extrinsic c 1080, 1360; strange, peculiar 1267, 1345; e. a dolore, exempt from pain 15c.; e. a veritate c 1343; e. adventus, arrival from outside 1306; -eatio c 1367, 1378, †externeatio c 1380, divergence, aberration; -atus, (?) strange, disguised 14c.; -eo, to reject 680; to diverge, deviate, warp p 1300, c 1380; to alienate (property) c 1376, c 1470; to estrange, banish c 1465.

extranominatus, named on the outside 1526.

extranotatus, noted on the outside 1526.

extransvers/o, -um, see ex.

extraordinarius, extraordinary (ac.) c 1333.

extrapendeo, to be appended (of seal) c 1175.

extrapercutio, to knock out 1303.

extraporto, to carry out 1425; to export 1429.

extrapo/sitio, extrusion (log.) c 1300, a 1323; -no, to put outside a 1116, 14c.

†extraria, f.l. for exemplaria, c 1250; see also straia.

extraten/tio, exclusion 1515; -eo, to exclude 1571.

extravag/us, vagrant a 1452; -ans, stray 1564; supplementary 12c., 1415; absurd 1461; (subst.) c 1196, c 1450, Constitutio E. 1298, 15c., Extravagant, papal constitution not embodied in Decretals; wandering friar 1384.

extravenditum (de foresta), sale (? of timber) outside the bounds 1185.

extravers/um, -o, see ex.

extravisio, external vision c 1367.

extrem/itas, lowest place c 793; stremitas, for -itas, 1299; -alis, at the extremity, outlying a 1350, c 1470; -aliter, as extremes 1427; -italia (pl.), ends c 1200; in -is, at the point of death c 1188, c 1400; †-a mollia, (?) slippers 7c.

extrenneum, see strena.

extrep-, see STREPP

1 extrico, extrecio, see estrecio.

2 extrico, to remove, banish c 550; to evolve, shape out of c 1115.

extrinsec/um (extrincec-), foreign parts 1347; ab -o, from without c 1325; -e, externally a 1150, p 1381; -us, external, exterior 1216, 1466; external, foreign (to a district or community) c 1105, 1473; outward, extrinsic (esp. phil.) c 1204, 15c.; see also 1 baillium, hundredum, servitium, teloneum; cf. forinsecus, intrinsecus.

extrippatio, see STREPP

extron/atura (coll.), estronicium, trimmings, loppings 1330; -o 1282, 1302, estrono 1241, to lop, cut back, pollard.

extrunco, to cut short c 1302.

extrus/io, expulsion c 1115, c 1197; -or, vendor c 1180.

‡extuber/arius, -ator, -atrix (f.), burler 1483; ‡-o, to burl (cloth) 1483.

extumul/atio, disinterment c 1180; -o, to disinter c 1180, 15c.

extunc, see ex.

extunico, to strip c 1200, a 1205.

extupo, see 1 exstupo.

exturbatio, disturbance c 1250.

exuber/antia, superfluity c 700. c 1250, c 1430; †-atio, (?) for extuberatio, swelling c 1200; -anter, abundantly 1339, 1541; -atus c 1350, exuber c 1302, abounding; ‡-is, giving no more milk c 1440; ‡weaned 1483; ‡-o, to wean 1843.

exudatio (exsud-), exudation 1620.

†exugia, (?) the fat round the kidneys 6c.

exu/itio, for -tio, stripping 1427; †exivit, for exuit, c 1170, c 1200.

exul-, see also exilium.

exulo, see 1 axella.

exult/abilis (exsult-), joyful, delightful 1200, 1457; -ans, rampant (her.) 1595; -anter, joyfully 9c.; -ativus, causing exultation 8c.; -o, (?) for exalto, to cheer, uplift c 1327.

†exumbratio, embracery (leg.) a 1564; cf. imbraciaria.

exundatio, overflowing c 1060.

exungo, to anoint especially 12c.

exungulo, to deprive of finger-nails a 1186.

exus, exungia, see 1 axella.

exusiarchia, beginning or source of power c 870.

exutus, see exitus.

exzenium, see XEN

eya, (?) island in marsh (A.S. ēg) (Sussex) c 1230.

eylnescia, see esnecia.

eyr/a, -ia, -erius, eyero, see aeria.

eyrum, eyre (leg.) 1285; justitiarius eir/ians p 1330; -o, to soar or hover (falc.) 1333; cf. aeria, ERR, iter.

eys-, see aisia.

F

(*See also* PH)

fa, musical note c 1330.

fab/a, ‡one-third of a scruple 1652; ‡**f. agrestis** 1652, **f. Egyptiaca** 14c., lupin; ‡**f.**, ‡**-aria, aquatica**, 14c., ‡**favida** 13c., brooklime; **f. inversa**, shrub growing on Vesuvius c 1212; orpine ‡14c., 1634; **f. lupina**, (?) henbane 14c.; *see also* **rex**; ‡**-icius** 15c., **-inus** 1381, made of bean flour; **favacium** 1296, ‡**-iola** 1652, bean flour; **-ula**, small bean 1372; ‡**febula**, bean-pod 15c.; **-ulus**, measure of water 826; **faverelli**, broad beans *or* (?) onions 12c.

‡**fabarius**, precentor 1483.

fab/er calcarium, spurrier 1351; **f. lignarius**, joiner 1188, 1588; **f. scriniarius**, cabinet-maker 1563; ‡**f. secarius**, "bladesmith" c 1520; **faveria**, smith's service 1219; **-rile** (Sc.) 1326, 1559, **-rina** (Sc.) 1336, 1382, smithy; **-rina**, iron-mill 1499; **-rilis** 1309, 1611, **-rinus** 1279, of or for a smith; ‡**-rissa**, "smith-wife" 15c., 1483; **-rifacio**, to fashion 1388; **-rifico**, to coin money c 1350.

fabric/a, forge: **faverca** a 1182; **-a** 704. 1313, c 1422, **-ium** c 1293, working, construction; fabric fund (esp. eccl.) c 1223, 1537; "frame" 1553; **-abilis**, malleable a 1252; **ars -alis**, smith's craft 1449; **-ativus**, manufacturing 9c.; **-ium, domus -ationis**, smithy 1279; **-atio**, false invention a 1564; **-ator**, inventor (of falsehood) 14c., a 1564; †workshop 1415; **-atura**, (manner of) making c 1300, c 1397; object made 1427; **-atus**, "framed" 1553; **-o**, to smite c 1253; to plot 1461; *1167, a 1564, **f. falsum** c 1102, to forge, counterfeit.

fabul/amentum, fable, tale c 550. a 1517; **-atio**, gossip, rumour c 1160, a 1452; ‡**-o**, "tale-maker" 1483; **-osus**, addicted to fables c 1220.

facca, *see* **vacca**.

fac/ellus, -illa, *see* **falcatio**.

fac/esso (*1st conj.*) 675, 760, **-esco** 939. 14c., to pass away, come to an end; *cf.* **fatisco**.

fac/etia c 1190, **-escia** a 1260, **-esia** 1374, c 1450, courtesy; **fascesia**, moral rule 13c.; **-etus**, eloquent c 1000; **-iditas**, elegance, refinement (of language) c 700.

faci/es, *presence 793. 12c., c 1362; front (of building) 1537; *part of a sign of the zodiac (astr.) c 1143, 1387; **-e ad -em**, face to face (bibl.); **a -e**, in the presence (of) a 1250; **de -e**, by sight 1537; **in -e ecclesie**, in the face (presence) of the church 12c., 1684; **-em do**, to confront c 1300; **-ale**, face-cloth c 1325, c 1362; *-alis, facial 1267, c 1400; **-aliter**, in front, facially 1267, c 1366; ‡**-ecula**, little face 15c.; **-tergium**, facetowel ‡c 1200, 1408.

facili/tatio, help p 1300, 1378; **-tativus**, helpful c 1375; **-o** a 1361, **-to** a 1350, 15c., to facilitate, help.

fac/imia, -uminaria, -inatrix, *see* **fascinatio**.

facina, *see* **fasciculus**.

†**facinens**, *f.l.* for **faciens**, 1308.

‡**facinum**, copper (alch.) 1652.

facnus, deception (A.S. *facn*) c 1115.

†**faco**, (?) lentil (φακός) a 1250.

fact/io, herd c 550; fine or penalty c 1115, c 1252; deed, action c 853. 14c., c 1400; feud c 1115; **f. pontis**, brigbote 14c.; **-iosus**, criminal c 1115; *-ibilis, makeable, feasible a 1233, 1427; *-ibilitas, quality of being made, feasibility c 1290, c 1365; **feticius**, 'featous', skilfully wrought 1281; **equus -icius**, stalking-horse 1544; **pulvis -icius**, gunpowder 1575; *-ivus, creative a 1233, p 1380; practical c 1443; actual c 870; (?) *for* **tactivus**, tactual 9c.; **-ivitas**, creativity c 1301, c 1365; **-ive** 12c., **-o** 1343, **de -o** 1279, 1470, **in -o** 1530, in fact; **ipso -o**, thereby c 1341, c 1520; **super -um**, in the act (leg.) 1499; **-or**, *factor, agent 1380, 1595; (?) *for* **fautor**, helper c 550; **f. bonus**, doer of good a 700; **-rix** (*f.*), dealing with 1522; creatress c 1270; **f. lecti**, bed-maker 1332; **-uarius**, factor, agent 1402; **-um**, deed, crime 1202, 1369; deed, document 1285, c 1580; dispute (G.) 1282; estate, territory (Fr.) 1265, 1289; *see also* **via**; **f. armorum**, feat of arms, armed conflict 1314, c 1437; **f. guerre**, act of war 1521; **f. in patria**, deed in pais (leg.) 1369; **f. speciale**, specialty (leg.) 1307, 1369; **-ura**, workmanship, style c 1321, 1446; working up, treatment (of material) 1379, 1464; inception (ac.) 1499; **f. feni** 1350, 1525, **f. prati** 1350, hay-making; **f. prima ferri**, calcining 1409; **-uragium**, factorage, commission 1599; **-us** (*sc.* **numerus**), product (math.) 1686; **faci/entia**, activity c 1362; ‡**-ens viduas**, poisonous plant, (?) spurge 14c.; *fiendus (*gerundive*) 1267, 1684; **fieri** (*subst.*), becoming c 1270, c 1470; **in f.**, in process (of) 14c.; **f. facias**, name of a writ (leg.) 1328, 1419; **facio**, to make up, amount to 1086, 1533; to repair 1284, 1378; to pay (fealty, homage) c 1100, 1489; to pay (money) 1287, 1298; to spend (time) c 730. c 1130; 1199, 1224, **f. fieri** c 1258, 1327, to levy (money); *(with *inf.*) to cause 740. c 1125, 1521; **f. ad**, to cause 1267; to indicate c 1204; to help towards c 1188, 1684; to help against a 1250, 14c.; **f. ad rem**, to be relevant 1393; **f. adversus** c 730, **f. contra** 1230, 1684, to tell against; **f. ante et retro**, to bow forward and backward c 1072, c 1330; **f. auxilium**, to give aid 1217, 1219, **f. bonum**, to make good 13c., 1342; **f. circa**, to work at 1341; **f. cum**, to support c 1125; to do with, behave towards 13c., 15c.; **f. de**, to do with, dispose of 1086, 1253; **f. multa de**, to make much use of c 1285; **f. falsum**, to forge, counterfeit c 1110, c 1115; **f. fenum** 1086, 1370, **f. pratum** 1388, to make hay; **f. lectum**, to make (tidy) a bed 1226, 1324; **f. nuntium**, to fulfil an errand 1322, 1416; **f. partem**, to take part with 1319, 1344; **f. pileum**, to take off one's hat c 1160; **f. plenum**, to make full payment 1252; **f. pro**, to tell in favour of c 1218, 1684; to use for the benefit of 1415; **f. sanguinem**, to draw blood, commit bloodshed 1086, 1249; **f. tantum . . . quod**, to urge so strongly that c 1160, 1269; **f. verba**, to make a speech, preach 12c., 1562; **f. versus**, to influence 1235; *see also* **1 habitus.**

factus, *see* **vatta.**

factuus, *see* **fatuus.**

facul/a, splinter 15c.; ‡-**o,** "to make faggot" 15c.

‡**faculent/ia,** "clearness", ‡-**us,** "clear", 1483.

facult/as, authority, sanction 1218, c 1556; constitutional practice p 1330; *branch of study (ac.) c 1184, a 1564; *see also* **curia;** -**o,** to stock 1241.

facundia, language c 1000.

fad/a, -us, *see* **fatalitas.**

fadmus, fathom 1397.

faedicius, *see* **FAID**

fag/etum, beechwood (grove) 12c.; c 1289, -**ina** 1227, beechwood (material); -**ina,** -**inum,** beech-mast 1183, c 1258; **focus** (*cf.* O.F. *fou*), beech 1293.

fagolidorus, *see* **PHAG**

*fag/ottus 1260, 1409, -**atus** 1278, 1397, -**ettus** 1297, 1573, -**ota** c 1400, 1406, faggot; 1294, **fangottus** 1440, measure of cloth; -**ator,** collector of faggots c 1532; -**attorius,** faggot-maker 1361; -**oto** 1296, (?) 14c., -**ato** 1400, to make into faggots.

faid/a (Sc.) 1608, **feida** (G.) 1283, -**ia** (†**faulia**) c 1115, feud; -**itus** (G.) 1228, **feiditus** (G.) 1253, **feditus** (G.) 1253, (Sc.) 1292, **faedicius** (Norm.) 1202, (person) exiled (for rebellion).

fairia, *see* **1 feria.**

faisantia c 1286, **fesantia** 1260, 1270 feasance, feudal service (C.I.).

faissus, *see* **fasciculus.**

1 †**fala,** (?) barb of arrow 1336.

2 ‡**fala,** faggot 15c.; *cf.* **facula.**

falanga, *see* **faldinga.**

falaric/a, gun 15c.; -**ator,** gunner 15c.

‡**falcanos,** arsenic, orpiment 1652.

*falc/atio a 1200, c 1530, **valcatio** c 1370, mowing; -**atura** c 1230, 1325, -**ura** c 1300, day's work at mowing; *-**abilis,** fit to mow 1222, 1388; -**agium,** (payment for) right of mowing 1536; -**ata,** measure of meadow 1410; -**atum,** swathe 1234; -**arius** 12c., -**ator** 1136, c 1390, mower; **opus -atorium** 1297, **falx** c 1185, mowing service (man.); **falx,** ‡jaw-bone 1570; **f. preliaris,** "halberd" 1553; **molendinum -atum** 1489, (?) **m. ad** †**falsam** 1204, blade-mill; -**a** 1199, -**us** c 1300, **fals** 15c., **falsa** 1281, †**fassis** 1564, **faux** 1283, *for* **falx,** scythe; **faucella** 1325, **faucilla** 1392, **facellus** 1196, **facilla** 1236, **falxiculus** 1276, sickle; -**astrum** a 1300, 1573, **faulcastrum** 1554, bill-hook; ‡-**o,** "woodknife" 1570; -**io** 1266,

fauchio (†**fanchio**) 1309, **faucho** 1319, c 1325, falchion; -**o,** *to mow 1086, 15c.: to mow down, massacre 1252.

falce, *see* **FALS**

Falcidia, portion secured to heir by *Lex Falcidia* 1308.

1 *falco/ 844. a 1100, 1528, **fauco** 1291, **faulco** 1334, falcon (bird); **faulco,** 'falcon' (small cannon) 1496; **f. Britannicus, f. montanus** a 1446, **f. peregrinus** c 1200, a 1446, peregrine falcon; *f. gentilis** 1200, 1334, **f. generosus** a 1200, falcon gentle; -**naria** 1199, 1243, -**neria** 1228, service of supplying falcons; ‡-**narium** 1483, ‡-**nerium** 15c., mew; *-**narius** a 1100, 1479, **fauconarius** 1398, **fauconerius** 15c., falconer; *cf.* **accipiter.**

2 **falco/,** 'hawk', horizontal axle of windlass 1317; mason's 'hawk', hod 1264, 1286; **f. ad mortarium** 1281; -**narius** 1282, 1316, **fauconarius** c 1300, hawk-boy, hod-bearer; *cf.* **hauka.**

3 **falco,** *see* **flato.**

falcula, sand-martin 1544.

*fald/a 1086, 1587, -**um** a 1214, 1277, **fauda** (†**fanda**) 1204, **faulda** 1086, (?) **felda** 1204, **folda** 1316, 1587, **valda** c 1250, a 1300, -**itium** c 1200, c 1366, fold (for animals); 1391, †**fulda** 15c., -**atum** 13c., 1275, -**itium** 1152, 1234, dung; -**e cursus,** foldcourse, sheep-walk 1325, 1573; -**a libera** 1508, -**e libertas** 1317, 1325, *-**agium** c 1140, 1587, **foldagium** 1587, -**atio** 1234, 1388, -**ura** c 1270, -**raria** (†-**rana**) c 1100, 'foldage', right to set up a fold; -**arius,** folder 1317, 1538; -**gata,** fold-gate 1308; -**soca** c 1130, 14c., -**sokya** 1306, -**sogna** c 1200, -**e soca** 1086, -**e secta** c 1200, suit of fold; -**io** 1189, -**o** c 1254, 1357, to fold (animals); -**o,** to dung, manure c 1160, 1400.

fald/estolium 1626, -**istolium** 13c., -**istorium** c 1550, **faudestol/a** c 1255, -**ius** a 1380, faldstool, *fauteuil.*

falding/a, -um 1285, 1372, **faling/a, -us** 1274, 1475, -**ua** 1507, (?) -**eria** 1310, **falanga** (**phalanga**) c 1200, c 1450, frieze cloak, *falaing* (Ir.).

fal/esa 1309, -**esia** a 1100, 1274, -**esium** 1271, 1348, -**eisa** 1257, -**eisia** 1221, -**isa** 1275, -**iscum** 1395, 1396, -**lacia** 1337, †**folisia** 1331, cliff (Fr. *falaise*); -**izatus,** *v.l.* for **infalisiatus,** *q.v.*

falia, *see* **felea.**

*fall/a, -um** 1211, 1318, †**filla** a 1275, 'fall', measure of land (? perch).

fall/acia, mistake c 1250; fallacy (log.) 1267, 1332; **f. consequentis** 130., c 1334, **f. secundum consequens** a 1200, fallacy of the consequent; *see also* **falesa;** †-**ians,** infertile 1185; -**ibilis,** deceitful 13c., 1461; fallible c 1344; -**ibilitas,** deceitfulness 1277; fallibility p 1300; -**ibiliter,** deceitfully 15c.; ‡-**onia,** "forfeiture" 1570; **absque -o** 1432, c 1470, **sine -o** 1399, c 1470, without fail.

‡**fallax,** madder (bot.) 15c.

falmotum, *see* **folkesmotum.**

fals, falsa, *see* **falcatio.**

fals/atio 1261, 1361, -**ificatio** 1205, c 1451, -**aria** c 1115, 1345, *-**ina** 1199, c 1300,

-onaria 1168, 1226, -oneria c 1192, -oria 1194, -um c 1187, c 1258, fauseria 1196, forgery, counterfeiting; -ina in pondere, coinage underweight 1204; f. in stagno, coinage of base metal 1200, 1204; -arius, liar, deceiver 793. c 1172, 1267; *c 1096, 1460, -ator c 793. c 1110, c 1362, †-ionarius c 1293, -enarius 1166, *-onarius c 1100, c 1320, -atrix (f.) 1336, forger, counterfeiter; -ator, false witness 793; falce, for -e, falsely 1588; camera fausa, (?) compartment 1323; fausardus, 'false-brace' (for saddle) 1316; faucecorda, false cord (of springald) 1348; -etum 1267, fausetum c 1148, falsetto (mus.); fausettum, faucet, spigot 1359; -ificatio, proving false c 1377; -igraphia, false or incorrect writing c 1200, 1344; -igraphicus, false, incorrect 1267, 1344; *-igraphus, false or incorrect writer 1344, c 1365; drawer of false diagram c 1300; -iloquium, lie, slander 793. c 1218, 1220; -iloquus, lying c 950; -itas, forging, counterfeiting c 1100, 1508; fallacy c 1357; note out of tune or incorrect (mus.) c 1200; -iter, falsely 14c.; -itia, falsehood, deceit 14c.; -ito, to deceive c 1400; -ifico, to pervert 1267; to maintain falsely 1378; 12c., 1463, -o c 1115, c 1370, to forge, counterfeit; *c 1102, a 1361, -o c 1115, c 1344, to prove false, disprove, nullify; f. curiam c 1192, 1199, -o curiam c 1185, c 1275, to appeal against court on ground of false judgement.

falta, default 1237.

falv/us c 1150, 1214, -osus 1303, *fav/us 1205, 1316, -ellus c 1200, 1311, -ius c 1311, c 1320, fallow, dun.

falx, see FALC

famatus, see famen.

†fambulo (? bambulo), (?) stammerer 709.

fam/elicus, scarce c 1160; see also familia; -eus, hungry c 550.

famella, see femella; fano.

fam/en, speech, language, report, utterance c 550, 993. c 1180, c 1470; -iger, conferring renown 793; -ose, reputedly c 1090; -ositas, fair fame 1344, c 1540; -atus, much talked of c 1300, c 1376; -o, to defame 1401, ‡1483.

famfaluca, bubble (πομφόλυξ) 709.

fam/ilia, religious community 765, c 980. 1260, 1537; bishop's household 811. 1259, c 1335; garrison, military force c 1140, 13c.; ship's company 1378; *c 1280, 1353, -ulia 1329, set of chessmen; f. regis, royal household c 1115, 1335; f. secreta regis 1353; -ulia, household, retinue 1432; -iliaris, (subst.) military follower 13c.; familiar (mon.) c 1220; student c 1200; familiar spirit c 1400; see also miles, missa, psalmus; -ularis 1265, -uliaris a 1423, 1441, -ulans 765. 15c., servant; -iliaratus, membership of a community c 1376; -iliaritas, position in household 13c.; ‡belonging to a household 1570; c 1125, c 1414, -elicus 1263, member of household, confidant; -ulariter, submissively c 1330; -ulamen c 970. 12c., -ulatio c 1343, *-ulatus 8c., 950. 1150, 1414, -ulitium c 950. c 1125, 1528, †-ulitus

c 900, servanthood, service; -ulativus, due from a servant c 1250; -ulus, priest 805; serf c 1185; -ilio, to serve 1253; -ulor (dep.), to be able c 550.

†fana, (?) rag or cloth 463; cf. fano.

fanaterius, serf (Savoy) 1533.

fanaticus, see fanum.

fanchio, see falcatio.

fanda, see falda; fatalitas.

fan/ella, -iculus, see fano.

fangottus, see fagottus.

‡fania, baulk, beam 15c.

fann-, see FEON; VANN

fan/o, banner 1207; c 790. *1200, c 1503, -entus (?) 1403, †-omus 15c., -onus 1320, 1415, -ona c 1360, -unus 1186, -ula, -ulus 1221, 1303, -um 1240, c 1300, -iculus 1252, -ella 1445, †famella 15c., maniple (eccl.).

fantas-, see PHANTAS

fantul/a, -us, see infans.

fan/um, church, monastery 15c., c 1553; -unculum, chapel c 1000; -aticus, (adj.) heathen 11c.; (subst.) madman c 1194; ‡sacristan 1483; ‡-istes, priest 1483; see also fano, VANN

fanus, see favillus.

fao, see FEON

fapesmo, a logical mood c 1250.

fara nova, new arrival c 1115.

faragium, see foragium.

far/cimentum, stopper 1620; 1463, -samentum 15c., bolster, pad; -tum 1378, 15c., fertum 15c., -ctura c 1180, -satura 1262, 1422, sausage, pudding; epistula -cita, 'farced' (expanded) epistle of New Testament 1295; -sura (psalmorum), 'gagging' a 1204; -ceo, for -cio, 810, ‡-to 1483, to stuff.

far/cinum, 'farcy', disease of horses 1284; -sum, eruption on mouth (med.) a 1250.

farcost/a 1375, 1433, fercosta (?) c 1240, †foriscota 15c., 'farcost', small boat (esp. Sc.); -arius 1380, farecostarius 1313, boatman; -ata 1380, farecostata 1313 boat-load.

farculum, see FERCUL

*fardell/um, -us c 1219, 1495, -a c 1390, ferdella 1407, fardel, bundle; see also ferdella.

farella, see paratella.

‡farfara, coltsfoot (bot.) 14c.

faria, see 1 feria.

farin/agium, flour due (claimed by millers) 1324; ferina, for -a, flour 1242, 1534; -ola, for -ula, c 725; -o panem, to make bread 1275.

farisea, gazelle (name of a horse) a 1142.

farlevium 1297, 1583, ferlevium 1525, 1583, 'farleu', payment to lessor on termination of lease (Devon & Cornwall).

farlingus, see 1 ferdingus.

farlota, see firlota.

farmerius, see 2 firma.

farr-, see also FERR

farr/eosus, -iosus, made of meal c 550; ‡-icapsa c 1440, 1483, ‡ferricapsa 15c., mill-hopper; -ifer, corn-bringing c 1206.

fars-, see farcimentum; farcinum.

fartagum, see sarracum.

‡**fartellus,** (?) spurrey (bot.) 14c.; *cf.* **paratella.**

farundellus, *see* **ferdella.**

farus, *see* **pharus.**

fascesia, *see* **facetia.**

fasci/a, fessa, fesse *or* bend (her.) c 1595; **feisa** 1180, **fessia** 1186, **fessa** 1189, 1242, row, measure of furs; **-amentum,** gravecloth 793; **-ola,** riband *or* pendent (of label) (her.) c 1595; **-olus,** bandage a 1250; **-olatus,** bandaged c 1072.

fasc/iculus 1086, 1575, **-icula** a 1452, **-iculum** 1252, **fassiculus** c 1370, 1542, ‡**fastaculus** 1276, **fesciculus** 1252, **fessiculus** 1296, ‡**fossiculus** 13c., ‡**vesticulus** 1299, **fescellus** 1253, **fesseletus** 1225, c 1320, **fessula** 1279, **faissus** c 1250, **fessus** 1279, 1309, **facina** 1276, bundle, faggot; **fassus dorsalis,** back-load 1327, 1330; **-iculus,** fascine 1413, ‡**-eninnea,** bastion c 1440; ‡**-is Gallicus,** a fragrant herb 14c.

fasc/inatio, witchcraft (bibl.); **-inatrix** 1574, 1588, **facinatrix** 1588, ‡**-ennina,** ‡**facimia,** ‡**facuminaria** 15c., witch; **-inula,** beguiling (*f.*) 6c.

fas/culum, -sulum, *see* **vas.**

†**fashum,** fringe 1509.

fasma, *see* **phasma.**

‡**fassio,** confession 1483.

fassis, *see* **falcatio.**

fasti (*pl.*), books c 550.

fastidi/atrix, disdainful (*f.*) p 1327; **-osulus,** somewhat disagreeable 1527; **-o,** to disgust 793; †(?) to feast c 1150.

fastigi/um, chevron (her.) c 1595; **-a** (*pl.*), endeavours c 1414; **-alis,** honourable 1307; **-atus,** exalted, high c 1200, 1518; chevroned (her.) c 1595; **-ose,** sumptuously c 1250; **-osus,** sumptuous c 1250, 1508.

fastuosus, haughty c 1150, 1421.

fat/alitas, fairy nature c 1190; **-atus,** haunted c 1212; **-ata, fada** (†**fanda**), fairy c 1212; **fadus,** warlock c 1212; **-a** (*pl.*), *see* 1 **cessus,** CONCESS, **decessus, discessus,** SECESS; **-or,** to be fated 14c., c 1450.

fatesco, *see* **fatisco.**

fatig/a, fatigue 1438, c 1440; **-ium,** trouble, pains 793; **-atio,** vexation c 1115, 1388; **-abilis** 793. c 1397, **-ativus** a 1250, wearisome; **-iosus,** servant, drudge 12c.

fatim, abundantly 8c.

fatimen, word 7c. 12c.

fat/isco, to be voided (her.) c 1595; **-esco,** *for* **-isco,** to droop, faint away a 710. c 1347, ‡15c.; *cf.* **facesso.**

fat/or, -um, *see* **fatalitas.**

fat/tum, -ula, *see* **vatta.**

fatu/us, fool, jester c 1250, 1461; (*adj.*) erroneous (leg.) c 1258, c 1290; **factuus** 1344, **-osus** 14c., foolish.

fau-, *see also* **fal–**

fauctor, *see* **fautoria.**

faufel, *see* **fulful.**

faulia, *see* **faida.**

faunus, demon, evil spirit c 1172; *see also* FEON

faus-, fauce-, *see* FALS

faut/oria, favour, consent, support 1340, 1414; **fauctor,** accomplice 1298; 641, **-urus** 12c., a favourite.

fav-, *see also* **faba;** FALV

faventer, *see* **favor.**

faverca, *see* **fabrica.**

faveria, *see* **faber.**

favill/a nivea, snowflake c 1470; **-ula,** ember c 1250; **favellosus,** of or for ashes c 550; **-o,** to reduce to ashes c 930. c 1180, c 1304; to burn, blaze c 780. c 1450.

‡**fav/illus,** small honey-comb 1483; **-ifluus,** flowing with honey c 1184; **-us** (†**fanus**), skin-disease marked by pustules a 1250, 14c.; *see also* FALV

‡**favoni/um,** capricious dislike 1483; **-ialis,** temperate a 1250.

fav/or, favourite c 1160; *-orabilis** c 1125, 1461, **-oralis** c 1488, **-eus** c 1000, **-orosus** 1440, favourable; **-orabilis,** specially requested c 1197; *-orabiliter** 1200, a 1564, **-orose** 1440, **-enter** c 1266, favourably; †**-isor,** partisan c 870; *-oro** 1457, c 1540, **-ouro** a 1564, to favour; to improve c 1290.

feagium, tenure in fee (C.I.) 1309.

feber, *see* **fiber.**

febeus, *see* PHEB

‡**febrimatio,** "stirring of land" 15c.

febr/is synocha, hectic fever 13c.; **f. tertiaria** 13c., **f. triduana** 1508, tertian malaria; *see also* **hectica, quintana; -e** (*pl.*), fever 1461; **-icitas,** feverishness 793; **-ilis,** feverish 12c., 1235.

febula, *see* **faba.**

fec-, *see also* FEON; **fex.**

fecund/itas, offspring 1296; **-ulus,** fruitful c 1184; **-o,** to supply lavishly 1241.

fed/ejusseo, -ifragium, *see* **fides.**

feder/atio, treaty, alliance c 1070, 1227; **-ator,** establisher c 1250; **-o,** to join in alliance 1227.

feditas, filthy object, nuisance 1298.

feditus, *see* FAID

fedoa, godwit (bird) 1544.

†**Fedro,** Plato's *Phaedo* or *Phaedrus* c 1267.

1 **fed/um, -ium, -firma,** *see* FEOD

2 ‡**fedum, fideum,** saffron 1652.

fef-, *see* FEOFF

fegadri, fegundri (*pl.*), gatherers of danegeld 1086.

feid-, *see* FAID

feinarium, *see* **fenum.**

feir/a, -ia, *see* 1 **feria.**

feisa, *see* **fascia.**

‡**fel/ draconis,** quicksilver 1652; **-era,** jaundice a 1150; **-leitas,** excess of gall a 1250; **-leus** c 1192, c 1385, **-losus** 1267, poisonous; †**-lechinum,** a purgative a 1250; **-livomus,** spitting out poison c 790; **-lifico, -lio,** to embitter c 1185.

felagus, fellow, sworn brother a 1160.

felapton, a logical mood 13c.

‡**felda,** elixir 1652; *see also* **falda.**

feldefarus, fieldfare (bird) 1430.

fel/ea c 1340, **-ia** 1322, **falia** 1318, **velia** 1276, 1347, **velga** 1281, 1347, **welgha** 1319, felloe (of wheel); **velgo** 1280, 1321, **welgo** 1280, **welghio** 1272, to fit (cart-wheels) with felloes.

felekelberug, zodiac (Ar.) a 1200.

felenga, *see* **felinga.**

felfetum, *see* **velvetum.**

felgeldum 1199, †**fengeldum** (? **feugeldum**)

c 1155, 1331, (?) a forest payment (*cf.* A.S. *feld*).
felger/a, -ia, felicetum, felix, *see* **filix.**
felica, *see* **fulica.**
felicit/atio, beatification a 1361, c 1365; **-abilis,** capable of beatitude 1344, 1361; **-abilitas,** capability of beatitude c 1365; **-o,** to make happy c 1250, a 1564.
fel/inga (-enga), 'felling', abatement, deduction (Norwich) 14c.
fell-, *see* **fel.**
1 ***felo/*** c 1258, 1583, ***-nus*** 1241, 1416, **-nius** c 1400, **-nicus** c 1390, **-na** (*f.*) 1276, felon; **f. de se** c 1258, 1583, **-nissa de se** (*f.*) 1309, a suicide; ***-nia** c 1115, 1583, **feolonia** 1274, 1275, felony; **f. de se,** suicide 1243; ***-nice** 1248, 1583, **-niter** 13c., 1309, **-nestiter** 1301, feloniously; **-nicus** 1354, 1583, **-nius** 1347, felonious.
2 felo, 'felon', abscess c 1116.
fel/paria, -iparius, *see* PELL
feltr-, *see* FILTR
fel/vetum, -uctum, -wetum, *see* velvetum.
femell/a 13c., 1620, **famella** 14c., 1461, a female; ***-ellus,** female (*adj.*) c 1234, 1506.
fem/erellum, -orale, -urale, *see* FUM
femin/a, wife 1086, c 1208; **f. sola,** *femme sole* (leg.) 1396; **-alis,** of a woman 6c.; c 1090, **-icus** c 1283, womanish; **-atio,** making into a woman 1427; **-eitas** p 1300, **-initas** c 1300, femininity; **‡-ella, -ula,** woman 1483; **-ine,** in the feminine (gram.) c 700; **-iter,** as a woman a 1520; **-o,** to make into a woman 13c.
fem/inalia 7c., c 790, ***-oralia** 826. a 1090, 1461, breeches, drawers; **-oralia,** (?) genitals 6c.
fem/itium, -o, *see* FIM
fen, section of a book (in Avicenna) 13c.
fen/agium, etc., *see* **fenum.**
fen/dicum, -dichum, fen-dike 13c.; **-nicola,** fen-dweller 1553.
fendidit, *see* **findes.**
feneratrix, usurer (*f.*) 12c., 1170.
†fenerinus, (?) groom (G.) 1243.
fenes, *see* FIM
fenestr/a, (?) lamp 1388; **f. bordea integra,** shutter in one piece 1245; **f. coquine,** serving-hatch c 1296, c 1330; **f. culicia** 1238, 1251, **f. culiciata** 1251, sliding window; **f. astantiva, estantiva, stantiva,** *see* STANT; **f. lapidea,** window with stone framework 1282, 1404; **f. lignea,** shutter 1236, 1464; **f. plumbea** 1244; **f. rotunda** 1296, 1360; **f. turibuli,** aperture in censer 1405, 1500; **f. vitrea** a 1200, 1478; **f. volans,** movable window or shutter 1267, 1272; **fenistra,** window c 1266, 1498; **-ale** 1313, c 1450, **-allus** 1236, **-alla** 1388, **-ella** c 1200, 1439, **-eola** c 1430, little window, pane; **-alla,** (?) port-hole (naut.) 1392; **†planus** (? **pannus**) **-ius,** "window-cloth" 1553; **-atio,** glazing 1498; ripply appearance (of urine) a 1250; **-atus,** ripply (of urine) a 1250; **-o,** to pierce a 1275.
†fenestrarius, (?) *f.l.* for **feretrarius,** c 1250.
fengeldum, *see* **felgeldum.**
fenic-, *see also* PHENIC
fenicul/um Grecum, fenugreek (bot.) 13c.; **‡f. porcinum, -aris,** hog's fennel 14c.; **‡f. Sancte Marie,** "toad fennel" 14c.

fenix, *see* **filix.**
fenoveciorium, *see* **cenevectorium.**
fens/ium, enclosure 12c.; **-ura** a 1564, 1604, **-ata** 1589, fencing, fence; **‡-ilis,** "defensable" 1483; **-us,** fenced a 1564; *cf.* DEFEN
fent/etius, -itius, *see* **findes.**
fentro, *see* FILTR
fen/um, hay-market 1324; **-a,** for **-um,** hay a 1300, 1583; **-a** (*pl.*), hay-fields 1340; **-um salsum,** salt hay 1389; **f. Sancti Michaelis** 1230, **‡f. serotinum** c 1440, latter hay; **-i factura,** hay-making 1370, 1525; **-ugrecum,** fenugreek (bot.) a 1250; **-agium** 1261, 1390, **-edium** 1309, 1324, **-atio** c 1200, 1373, hay-harvest; **-arius,** hay-merchant 12c.; **‡-erium** 1483, **feinarium** 1221, **-ile** 1141, c 1220, **horreum -ale** 1503, 1532, **domus -alis** 1623, **d. -i** 1514, hay-barn; **mullio †femalis,** hay-stack 1314; **-ator** 1467, **-ifactor** 1402, **‡-issa** (*f.*) 15c., hay-maker; **-ifer** 1514, **-osus** c 550, hay-bearing; **-o fenum** 12c., **-o pratum** c 1115, to make hay; *see also* ad, ADUN, FACT, LEV, UNIT, VERT
fenus, feo, *see* FEON
*feod/um c 1109, 1583, **-us** c 1115, c 1236, **pheodum** a 1123, **fedium** c 1109, **fedum** 1215, ***feudum** 1086, 1608, **pheudum** 12c., **feudus** a 1142, c 1220, **feuum** 1086, **feuodum** a 1200, 1274, **feoudum** c 1123, c 1300, **fewodum** 1255, **fieudum** 1226, **fodum** 1309, **foedum** 1131, **foedus** (C.I.) 1331, **fueodum** c 1200, **fuodum** 1250, fee, fief; **f. baronie** 1375; **f. censuale,** (?) fee-farm 1166; **f. ecclesie** 1339; **f. ecclesiasticum** c 1185; **f. elemosinale,** frank-almoign 12c.; **f. laicale** 13c., c 1254, ***f. laicum** 1155, c 1436; **f. forinsecum** c 1290; **f. francum** 1227, 1284, **f. francale** (G.) 1283, **f. liberum** c 1220, 1313; **f. hereditarium** c 1120; **f. ligeum** a 1446; **f. hauberci** 1275, **f. hauberticum** (Sc.) c 1350, 1609, **f. lorice** 12c., c 1216, **f. loricatum** 1609, hauberk fee (held by a form of serjeanty); **f. militare** 1166, 1586, ***f. militis** c 1145, 1489, knight's fee; **f. parvum militis** c 1220; **f. nobile** (G.) 1283, 1312; **f. perpetuum** 1147, a 1200; **f. primum,** principal fief c 1115; **f. simplex,** fee simple 1327, 1583; **f. talliatum,** fee tail 1283, 1513; ***in -o,** in fee (of tenure) a 1142, 1558; **f. firmum** a 1108, c 1130, **f. ad firmam** c 1120, **-ifirma** 1155, 1565, **-a firma** 1313, c 1492, **-ofirma** a 1100, c 1327, **feuda firma** 1200, 1573, **feudofirma** 1201, **feudumfirma** 1220, **feouda firma** c 1150, c 1160, **feoudi firma** c 1160, **feudifirma** c 1178, 1573, **feudfirma, fedfirma** a 1150, **feofirma** 1271, **feufirma** 1132, **feoudiscyfirma** c 1135, **-alis firma** c 1180, 1361, **feudalis firma** c 1230, fee-farm; **-ifirmarius** c 1200, 1573, **feudifirmarius** c 1200, 1569, tenant in fee-farm (esp. Sc.);
*-um 1201, 1576, **feudum** 1475, **feuum** 1417, fee, payment; **f. capelle,** fee of Chancery (Sc.) 1292; **f. coquine,** kitchen-fee, dripping c 1343, 1464; **-um,** office 1218, 1223; right or easement 1230, 1266; feudal service 1285;

-alis a 1087, 15c., **feudalis** 1221, 1608, feudal; 1461, **feudalis** p 1330, vassal, feudal tenant; concerned with fees (payments) 1413; **-alia** 1239, c 1400, †**-otalia** 1330, (*pl.*) feudal rights; **-alitas** c 1280, **-elitas** 1293, 1327, **-itas** 1303, c 1397, **feuditas** c 1283, feudal service, fealty (*cf.* **fidelitas**); **-aliter** 1125, 1315, **-otaliter** (G.) 1289, feudally; **-agium**, **-atarium**, feudal tenure (G.) 1289; **-amentum**, feoffment 1166; **-arium**, feudary, book of feudal services 1398, 1537; **-arius** a 1235, 1492, **foedarius** c 1250, **feudarius** 13c., **-atarius** 1213, 1565, **feudatarius** 1220, 1566, **fewdatarius** 1572, **feudatorius** 1289, 1479, **-otarius** 1223, 1289, †**feudator** (G.) 1448, vassal, feudal tenant; **-arius**, feodary, official in charge of fees in king's hand 1379; official of Duchy of Lancaster 1399, 1460; official of Court of Wards 1574, 1586; **-arius**, **fodarius**, entrant to guild 1358; †**fodasia**, payment for entrance to guild 1358; **feudastrum**, pseudo-fee 1608; **-atarius** 1289, 1461, **-atorius** 1461, **-itarius** c 1320, 1579, feudatory (*adj.*); **-atio** (Sc.) c 1315, 1464, **-ofatio** 1260, feoffment; **-ista**, feudal lawyer (Sc.) a 1609; **verbum -isticum**, term of feudal law (Sc.) 1608; **-o** 1166, 1560, **feudo** c 1100, c 1293, to enfeoff.

feoff/atio c 1258, 1400, **-actio** 1289, **fefatio** c 1250, **-atum** 1274, 1284, ***-amentum** 1195, a 1566, **-ementum** 1195, **-eamentum** 1199, **feffamentum** c 1166, c 1320, **feffementum** 1187, 1212, **feofeffamentum** 1279, **feufamentum** 1243, 1284, **feufementum** 1228, feoffment; **feffamentum novum, f. vetus** 1168; †**foefum**, †**foesum**, fief 1131; **-ator** c 1258, 1588, **feffator** 1203, **-atrix** (*f.*) 1287, feoffor; ***-atus**, feoffee 1195, c 1455; ***-o** 1201, 1500, **feffo** 1166, 1292, **feofeffo** 1275, 1453, **feuofo** p 1290, **feufo** 1195, 1223, **foffo** 1227, to enfeoff.

feolonia, *see* 1 **felo**.

feon/us 1274, **feo** 1209, **fao** 1227, **faunus** c 1190, **fenus** 1272, **feto** (†**feco**) 1209, 1297, **foo** 1235, 1249, **founus** 1208, 1354, fawn; **-atio** 1217, c 1300, †**fannatio** 1367, **feoffanatio** 1337, **founatio** 1256, 1293, **fetūs tempus** 1244, fawning season; **founinus**, of a fawn 1229; **-o** 1298, 1309, **founino** c 1290, to fawn.

feoragium, *see* **foragium**.

feoud-, *see* FEOD

fer/a 1232, 1547, **f. fugabilis** 1384, beast of chase; **f. grossa**, big game 1260; **f. regis** 1373, **f. regalis** c 1185, beast royal; **f. foreste** c 1185, **f. silvatica** 1086; **-alis**, bestial 1241; ‡wild 1483; **-alitas**, savagery 12c.; **-ancus** (pun on **Francus**), savage c 1188, c 1315; †**-anter**, savagely c 1293; **-icida**, deer-killer, poacher c 1196, c 1436; **-inus**, isolated (astr.) c 1616, 1620; **-uscula**, small animal 641. c 1325; ‡**-o**, to make fierce 1483.

ferans, *see* FERR

feratra, *see* **pharetra**.

feratrum, *see* **feretrum**.

ferbota, 'fire-bote', fuel 13c.

ferce, *see* **ferzia**.

fercosta, *see* **farcosta**.

fercul/um, dish: **farculum** a 1400, 1573; ‡**-um**, "ståll in a church" 1483; **fercillum**, small dish 1200; **-arius**, serving-man 1281; **vasa -aria**, dishes c 1250.

ferdell/a, -um c 1190, 15c., **fardellus** 15c., **farundellus** 1508, **ferndelia** 13c., **ferendellus, fernedellus, ferndellum, foerndellum, voerndellus** 1301, **ferundellus** a 1300, **fordalis** c 1230, **fordellum** 1234, c 1240, **fordolum** 1250, **forndalum** 13c., **forndellum** 1318, **furendellus** 1282, **verendallis** c 1300, **ferthyndelus** c 1309, **furthendellus** 13c., 'fardel' (of land), quarter-virgate; **fordola prati** a 1240, **fornedellum prati** 1441; **-arius** 1302, 1485, **ferndellarius** 1326, **ferendellarius** 1299, **-us** 1330, **fardellus** 1324, tenant of fardel; **-arius dimidius** 1325, 1330; **ferdendela** c 1180, **ferndalis** 13c., measure of grain; **ferendellus** 1381, **ferondellus** 1421, measure of fish; **ferthedellus**, measure (20 bushels) of salt c 1300; *see also* **fardella**; *cf.* 1 **ferdingus**.

ferdi (*pl.*), class of persons coupled with clerks and Culdees (Sc.) c 1250.

1 **ferdin/gus** a 1135, (?) 1159, **-ga** 1086, c 1109, **-ka** c 1219, **-us** 1086, **ferthinga** 1215, **ferthingus** 13c., **fertingus** 1086, **fertinus** 1084, †**fordinka** 1219, ***ferlingus** 1086, 1449, **ferlinga** 1201, 1337, **ferlinus** 1086, **farlingus** 1453, **ferlingata** 1199, 1611, **firlingata** 1686, **furdlingus** 1234, **ferdilonda, ferlinglonda** 1245, 'ferling' (of land), quarter-virgate; **-gus** (†**perdingus**, †**pardingus**) c 1115, **ferlingatarius** 1300, 1390, **ferlingsetus** 1189, tenant of ferling; *cf.* **ferdella, furlongus**.

2 **fer/dingus, -tingus** 1086, **-lingus** c 1266, 1302, **-linga** 1369, farthing; **-lingus auri**, lesser florin 1414, 1425; **-thingmannus**, 'farthingman', guild treasurer 1284.

ferdwita, *see* FYRD

ferecia, *see* **ferocia**.

*feret/rum 1096, c 1520, **-ra** 1433, **feratrum** 1404, **pharetrum** 1430, reliquary or shrine; ***-rarius** 1301, 1532, **-arius** c 1420, 1476, feretrar, sacristan (eccl.); **-raria**, office of sacristan 1383; **-ralis**, of a shrine c 1255; used as a litter c 1090; **-raliter**, in a litter c 1540; **-ratus**, laid on a bier c 1400; **-rizo**, to bury ceremonially 12c.; *see also* **pharetra**.

ferett-, *see* **furettus**.

fergabulum, *see* **forisgabulum**.

fergie, *see* **firgie**.

1 **feri/a ***1086, 1573, **-um** 1279, ***fairia** c 1170, 1317, **faria** 1385, **feira** 1189, c 1293, **feiria** 1194, 1300, **fieria** 14c., †**fiberia** 1324, fair; market-place 1199, 1419; **-o**, (?) to go to market c 1143.

2 **feri/a**, festival c 730; holiday 793; **f. communis** c 1280, 1377; **f.** †**conjuncta**, (?) *f.l.* for **f. quincta**, 1447; **-abilis** 1222, **-alis** 1267, of or for a festival or holiday; **-atio**, observance of festivals or holidays c 1115, 1558; **dies -atus** 1086, 1251, (?) **d. -alis** c 1443, 15c., holiday; **-o**, to keep holiday, be idle, abstain from c 1110, c 1258.

3 **feri/a**, week-day c 700, c 730. c 1360, 1517;

f. prima, Sunday a 1200; **f. Lune** 12c.,
*f. secunda c 980. 1086, 1517, Monday;
f. tertia c 980. c 1100, c 1503, **f. quarta**
c 980. a 1090, 1558, **f. quinta (quincta)**
831, c 1006. a 1100, 15c., **f. sexta** c 980.
c 1090, 1558, days of the week; **-alis,** of or
for a week-day c 1006. c 1080, 1517; **dies**
-alis c 1250, 1543, (?) **d. -atus** c 1344,
a 1564, week-day; *see also* 1 **regula; -aliter,**
(?) in workaday attire 1388.
4 **feri/a** 1322, 1588, (?) **veria** (Kent) 1301,
ferry; **-agium,** ferry-toll 1405, 1583; **-atio,**
ferrying 1387; **-o,** to ferry 1337.
†**feriarius,** scout 15c.
fer/iatio duelli, judicial combat c 1275; *see*
also **feria** (**2** & **4**); ‡**-itorium,** swingle-
stock 15c.; ‡c 1440, 15c., ‡**-atorium** 15c.,
battledore.
feriatorius, *see* FERR
feri/cida, -nus, *see* **fera.**
ferina, *see* FARIN
feri/-son, logical moods 13c.; *see also* **feria**
(**1, 2** & **4**).
feritorium, *see* **feriatio.**
ferlevium, *see* **farlevium.**
ferling-, *see* **ferdingus** (**1** & **2**).
ferlot/a, -um, *see* **firlota.**
ferm-, *see also* **firm-**
ferment/um, leavened bread (in eucharist)
12c.; ‡batch (of bread), dough 1570; simulation c 1370; **f. album,** silver (alch.) a 1252,
‡1652; **f. rubeum,** gold a 1252; **-arius,**
advocate of use of leavened bread in
eucharist c 1100; **-atio,** fermentation 13c.;
'brewing' of gold (alch.) 1144, ‡1652;
-atus, heated c 1540.
fern/dalis, -edellus, *etc., see* **ferdella.**
fernifalcatio, *see* 1 **firma.**
†**ferno,** *f.l.* for **sterno,** c 1225.
fernova, *see* **fert.**
fernum, *see* **verna.**
‡**fer/ocia** 1483, ‡**-ecia** 15c., mattress, quilt.
ferondellus, *see* **ferdella.**
ferragium, *see* **foragium.**
ferrellus, *see* **forulus.**
ferrera, *see* **forera.**
ferricapsa, *see* FARR
†**ferrugiendo (stridore),** (?) *f.l.* for **fero**
rugiendi, 1093.
ferr/um, *ordeal-iron, judicial ordeal 1082,
c 1437 (*cf.* **judicium, lex**); obley-iron
13c., 1389; branding-iron 1333; iron
cooking-pot c 1080, c 1266; 1190, 1303,
farrum 1504, **-us** 1304, arrow-head; 1086,
c 1540, **-a** c 1362, **-us** 1212, 1314, **f. ad**
equos 1289, **f. pedale** 1297, horse-shoe;
-a (*pl.*), irons, fetters 1276, 1465; **-um**
album, tin-plated iron 1464, 1530; **f. an-**
danicum, *see* 2 **andena; f. carruce**
c 1300, 1378, **f. pedale** 1273, 1424, **f.**
pediale 1278, †**ferropes** 1329, **f. longum**
1248, a 1308, plough-iron (*cf.* **pedale**);
f. equinum, horse-shoe vetch (bot.) 1634;
f. hirsutum, (?) scrap iron 1345; **f. molle,**
soft iron c 1365; **f. pensile,** stirrup 1562;
f. Hispanicum 1344, 1534, **f. Spaneum**
1336; **f. Indaicum** a 1250, ‡**f. Indicum**
1652; **f. Osemondi** 1284, **f. de Osmund'**
1325 (*cf.* **osmondum**); **f. wafrorum, f.**
eucharistie, wafer-iron, obley-iron c 1300;

-agia, toll on wheeled traffic (G.) 1230;
-alis, of iron c 550. 1438; **-alia** (*pl.*) 1402,
-eamentum 1399, **-iamentum** (G.) 1315,
farramentum 1504, *for* **-amentum,** iron-
work; **-amentum,** ordeal-iron c 850; obley-
iron 1373; horse-shoe 1306, 1404; fetter
1196, 1230; enclosure within iron rails
a 1447; instrument (fig.) 7 c.; **f. artificiale,**
tool of trade (G.) 1315; **f. carruce** 1209,
1410; **f. molendini** 1209, 1533; **-andus**
c 1204, 1316, **-antus** 1177, 1287, **ferans**
(†**serans**) 1282, **-entus** 1296, iron-grey
(of horse); **-aria,** smithy, forge 1086, c 1150;
‡**-arium,** deposit left in water by
hot iron 14c.; **molendinum -arium** 1542,
1553, **m. -eum** 1553, iron-mill; **-atio** 1527,
16c., **farratio** 1526, fitting with iron-work;
***-ator** 1193, 1378, **-urator** 1397, **-atorius**
p 1284, †**feriatorius** c 1270, *for* **-arius,**
farrier, smith; **-uarius,** iron-worker 1086;
‡**-atorium,** trave for shoeing horses 1483;
-atura 1171, 1539, ***-ura** 1234, 1534,
farrura 1388, c 1483, farriery, horse-shoes
(*coll.*); 1188, **-ura** 1212, 1425, iron-work;
-ura, judicial ordeal c 1350;
‡**-etum,** "tag of a point", "chape" of a
scabbard, "tip of a staff", 1570; **-eum,** iron
band 12c.; horse-shoe 1190, 1471; trivet
1418; **f. hamatum,** andiron c 1534; **f.**
quadratum, f. rotundum, wafer-iron,
obley-iron c 1331; **-eus,** iron-shod (of
carts) 1419; **-icudium,** *see* CUSS; **-ifaber,**
iron-worker, smith 1450; **-ifer,** iron-
bearing c 690; ‡**-ifilum,** iron wire 15c.;
-ifodina c 1180, **-ifodinum** 1284, **-ifodium**
c 1385, iron mine; ‡**-ipodium,** "patten"
c 1440; **-o** c 1200, 1419, **-onus** 1305, 1370,
-onarius 1419, smith *or* ironmonger;
caretta -ata, cart with iron-hooped tires
1204, 1221; **strata -ata** c 1240, **via -ata**
13c., hard road (*chemin ferré*); **vinum**
-atum, iron-tinctured wine c 1200, 1242;
-o *c 1125, c 1370, **farro** 1388, to fit with
iron-work; *to shoe (horses) a 1090, c 1437;
to put in irons c 1298.
fer/t, omen, **-nova,** good omen, **-vetus,** bad
omen, a 1235; *cf.* **confert.**
ferth/edellus, -yndelus, *see* **ferdella.**
ferthelota, *see* **firlota.**
fer/thingus, -tinus, *see* **ferdingus** (**1** & **2**).
fertil/is, *see* **plumbum.**
ferto, *see* **fortia.**
fertum, *see* **farcimentum.**
‡**feruca,** "throstle-cock" 15c.
†**ferucoco,** (?) *f.l.* for **fervesco,** to attack
wildly c 1225.
ferula, ornament, part of a chasuble 1241;
†**f. furcata,** (?) forked bristle (of boar)
(C.I.) 1248; *cf.* 2 **pilus,** 1 **seta.**
ferundellus, *see* **ferdella.**
feruscula, *see* **fera.**
ferv/entia, boiling heat a 1252; †**-iter,** fer-
vently c 1374; ‡**-orium,** cauldron 1483.
fervetus, *see* **fert.**
†**fervus,** (?) *for* **furvus,** 709.
ferzia a 1150, **ferce, fierce** c 1280, 'fers',
chess-queen (Ar. *firz*).
fesant-, *see* **faisantia; phasianus.**
fesc-, fess-, *see also* **fascia; fasciculus;**
fiscella.

fesicus, *see* PHYS
fess/itudo, weariness a 1232; ‡**-o,** to weary 1483.
‡**fess/ura, -era,** white bryony (bot.) 14c.
fest/agium, -ellum, *see* 2 festum.
festin/antia, haste a 735. 1267, 1461; **-e,** hastily c 760. c 1227, c 1462; **-o** (with *inf.*), to urge, impel a 910; to strive earnestly c 700.
festino, a logical mood 13c.
festis, *see* fusta.
festuc/a, pin 1312; cotise (her.) c 1595; **-arius,** cotised c 1595; **-o,** to ratify c 1170; *see also* **fisticus.**
1 ***fest/um** 1086, 1564, ‡**-ulum** 1483, **-alia** (*pl.*) a 1350, **-ivalia** (*pl.*) c 1443, ***-ivitas** c 730, 826. 1086, 1437, festival (eccl.); **f. commune** c 1296; **f. duplex** c 1072, 1552; **f. d. altum** c 1330; **f. d. majus** c 1330; **f. duplicatum** c 1321; **f. mobile** 1252, 1387; **f. principale** c 1282, c 1330; **f. puerorum,** feast of boy bishop 13c.; **f. simplex** c 1315; **-ivitas magna** 13c., **f. major** c 1324; **f. secundaria** c 1521; *see also* **lectio;** **-ivalis** 12c., a 1540, †**-ualis** c 1385, ***-ivus** a 1090, 1543, **-us** 1086, 1549, of a festival (eccl.); **-ivatio,** feast, treat 1391, c 1430; **-ivo,** to keep as a festival (eccl.) c 1213, 1432; to entertain 1505; ‡**-o, -ivo,** to keep holiday 1483.
2 **fest/um,** roof-tree 1141, ‡1483; **-agium,** house-tax (G.) 1204, 1310; **-ellum,** ridge-tile (O.F. *festel*) 1305, 1306.
3 †**festum,** ulcer (med.) c 1280; *cf.* FISTUL, gutta.
4 **festum,** *see* fusta.
‡**fetans,** sheep 1483.
fetialis, herald, writer on heraldry c 1595.
feticius, *see* FACT
fet/o, -us, *see* FEON
fet/or, dung 1416; 1290, †**-imane** 1572, dung-hill; ‡**-onarus, -ontria, -ontrus, -untrus** 15c., fitchew, polecat; **-osus,** foul 1371; **-ulentia,** stench c 1150.
†**fetulum,** (?) pad (med.) a 1250.
feud-, feufirma, feuum, *see* FEOD
feuf-, feuof-, *see* FEOFF
feuger/a, -ia, *see* filix.
feurnus, *see* FURN
feut-, *see* FILTR
fewd-, fewodum, *see* FEOD
fex, lye used in fulling 1256; ‡**f. argenti, f. auri,** silver and gold litharge (alch.) 14c.; **feces** (*pl.*), excrement a 1250.
fi, particle, jot c 1430.
fial-, *see* phiala; 2 vidula.
fiancia, *see* fides.
fiber c 1200, **fimber** 1352, ‡**feber** 15c., otter.
fiberia, *see* 1 feria.
‡**fibra,** "tet", lock of hair 1570.
fibul/a, boll or knob (her.) p 1394; **-atus,** pommelly (her.) p 1394; **-arius,** buckle-maker 1520, 1563; ‡**-atorium,** "shred" 1483.
fic/ale, (?) jewel in its setting 14c.; **-o,** to fix 1108; *cf.* FIX
ficell-, *see* fiscella.
fichtwita, fictwita, *see* fihtwita.
ficicus, *see* PHYS
fico, shoe, clog 559, c 1000. a 1150, c 1325; *see also* **ficale.**

fict/icia, -icium, fiction, simulation c 1290, a 1446; **-ilis,** feigned, fictitious 1433; **-ivus,** imaginative 13c., a 1347; **-or,** liar 1344; **-ior,** more feigned c 1400; *see also* FIX; *cf.* FING
ficus fatua, barren fig, sycomore 1354, ‡14c.; **fig/us,** fig 1212, ‡15c.; **-ula,** little fig 1310.
fid/atio, betrothal 1543; ‡swearing 1483; ‡**-o,** to swear 1483; *cf.* 2 AFFID
†**fidelia,** "churn" 1570.
fid/es *1168, 1290, **-elitas** 1361, pledge, security; c 1115, c 1258, *-elitas c 1115, 1489, **fiancia** 1111, fealty (*cf.* **feodelitas);** **-elitas,** fidelity (title) 1253, c 1340; religious faith 1417; good character, repute 1219, 1221; **ad -em,** bound by fealty 1217, 1237; **pono per -em,** to put on oath 1200, 1201; **-es corporalis,** corporal oath c 1250; **f. lesa** 12c., 1247, **f. mentita** c 1115, 1461, breach of faith; *see also* 1 **lesura; f. manualis,** pledge given by hand-clasp 1294; **f. media** 1253, 1482, **f. medians** c 1300, **f. mediata** 1220, plighted faith; *f. oculata,** eye-witness c 1125, 1536; **-es,** creed (eccl.); **f. Athanasii** c 1308; **f. Nicena** 12c., **-edignus,** trustworthy (person) 1200, 1461; **-efragium** 15c., **fedifragium** c 1520, breach of faith; **-efragus** 13c., c 1500, **-ifragus** c 1293, ‡1483, faith-breaker; **-eijussor,** *for* **-ejussor,** one who gives surety c 1250, 1609; **-ejussorie,** by way of surety c 1430; **-elis,** law-worthy c 1110, c 1360; lawfully acquired 1295; Christian (*adj.*) c 1177, a 1180; *c 1090, c 1509, **f. Christi** 1222, 1345, a Christian; faithful subject, liegeman 803. c 1070, 1461; **-eliter,** accurately a 1200; **-ucialiter,** confidently (eccl.); **fedejusseo,** to give surety 1372.
fidul/a, -ista, *see* 2 vidula.
fiendus, fieri, *see* FACT
fientamentum, *see* FIM
fieria, *see* 1 feria.
fieudum, *see* FEOD
fiffegha, *see* fisfeum.
figator, *see* FUG
fightwita, *see* fihtwita.
figment/um, deceit 793. c 1115; **fingmentum,** fiction 1283; †**figma,** figment c 1283; **-alis,** fictitious c 1250; **-o,** to fabricate c 1155.
fig/o, -itivus, *see* FIX
fig/ula, -us, *see* ficus.
figulator, potter 1240, 1374.
figur/a, diagram 793. 1387; figure, cipher (math.) a 1150, 15c.; note (mus.) 1357, c 1470; form of words, formula 1274, c 1397; **-alia** (*pl.*), types, figures 12c.; **-alis,** typical, figurative 6c. c 1160, c 1443; diagrammatic c 1267; **-aliter,** diagrammatically c 1178, 1267; **-atio,** drawing c 700; diagram 1267; plan (arch.) 1511; **-ative** a 1250, 1552, **-ate** c 825. p 1380, figuratively; **-ativus,** figurative, significant c 1115, c 1363; **-ator,** one who interprets Real Presence figuratively (theol.) 1552; **-atrix,** symbolic (*f.*) c 1250; **discantus -atus** (mus.) 1606; **-o,** to draw c 700; to typify c 1115, c 1444; to represent by a figure c 1343, c 1470.

fiht/wita, -ewita, fightwita c 1115, ficht-wita 1189, 1199, fictwita c 1175, fine for fighting; *cf.* frithwita, fyrdwita.

fil/acium, -ettum, *etc.*, *see* filum.

filago, (?) cudweed (bot.) a 1250, ‡14c.

†filastale, 'filst-ale', scot-ale, compulsory feast c 1258.

fil/atorium, -iaterium, *see* PHYL

filia, filly 1313, 1320; *see also* filius.

filic-, *see* filix; fulica.

filiolum, *see* finis.

fili/us, element in surname, not referring to actual father 1243, 1293; 1414, f. in lege 1288, 1332, son-in-law; f. imitationis, adherent 1363, 1377; f. naturalis, bastard 1303, 1506; f. navis, member of crew (Dutch) 1442; f. spiritualis, penitent 1350; godchild 1417, 1421; ‡f. unius diei, philosophers' stone (alch.) 1652; -a, granddaughter 1378; daughter-house c 1400; f. penitentialis, f. spiritualis, penitent (*f.*) 1237; f. preceptoris, the cane (ac.) 1520; f. rubea (alch.) c 1320; -osus, (?) assimilated (alch.) c 1250; *-alis c 1160, c 1507, -abilis 1575, filial; -aliter, filially 1239, 1410; -aster, stepson c 1130, 1417; -astra, stepdaughter 1204, 1362; †-astinus, (?) *for* -astrinus, due to stepchildren 1109; -atio 793, 990. c 1200, a 1519, -etas 790, sonship; (title) c 1365, c 1410; -ola, goddaughter c 1115, 1410; -olus, godson c 1115, 1533; -o, to acknowledge as son c 1200; -olo, to christen, name after c 1184.

filix arborea a 1150, †felix arboratica 13c., polypody (bot.); ‡f. quercina, oak fern 14c.; ‡f. silvestris, royal fern, osmunda 14c.; fenix, "bracken" 1613; filic/atus, ferny ‡1570, (her.) c 1595; -etum ‡c 1440, 1586, felicetum 15c., ‡-arium c 1440, ‡filacerium 15c., felgera c 1160, felgeria 1275, feuger/a, -um p 1212, 1352, -ia, -ium 1316, 1419, fugera 1235, 1389, fernbrake, bracken.

filla, *see* falla.

fillium, *see* phyllon.

filo, to file (metal) 1325; fula, (?) file 1325.

filoxinia, *see* philoxenia.

filtr/um, filter a 1235, 1652; c 1100, a 1517, feltrum 1086, c 1530, feltrium 1225, feutrum 1203, 1303, fultrum c 1180, 1296, (piece of) felt, cover, cloak, horse-cloth; feltrum, "woollen hat" 1532; -arius 13c., feuterarius 1222, felter; feltreus c 1150, feutreus 1224, made of felt; -atio, filtering 1652; feltratio, lining with felt 1367; feltro 1367, fultro 1225, feutro (†fentro) c 1248, to line with felt.

fil/um, string (of beads, *etc.*) 1387, 1388; tow 1295; bow-string 1279; fillet (arch.) 1253; kind of locust 1266; ‡wire 1570; f. argenti, f. auri, f. aureum 1295; f. ferreum 1461; f. tractum, drawn wire 1245; f. viscatum, "lime-string" (for fowling) 1470; *see also* PACC; f. altum 1399, 1458, *f. aque 7c. 1157, 1446, f. fluminis 1288, mid-stream; f. aque saline 1367; f. maris, deep sea 1275, 1447; -us, *for* -um, nerve *or* sinew (med.) a 1250; ‡-um, -ium, arsenicale, philosophers' stone (alch.) 1652; -um c 1420, -acium 1279, 1591, -icium 1332,

1336, -atio 1516, file (for documents); -ium 1208, 1224, -acium 1267, 1620, -eicium 1213, -atum c 1217, 1257, -etum 1205, 1694, yarn, thread; -acium 1291, -etta, -ettum 1237, 1439, fillet (arch.); -etum, net 1315; strip of wood 1357; -etta de perulis, string of pearls 1391; -aciarius 1501, philizarius 1515, -ator 1439, 'filazer', file-keeper; -acius, in the form of yarn c 1324; -amen, hair c 1000; ‡-andria c 1440, ‡-andra, -andrum, -iandra 15c., gossamer; philarium, (?) reel or bag of yarn (*cf.* O.F. *filiere*) c 1200; -atio, spinning 1351, 1476; ‡-ator, "sewer", -acista "spinner", -atura, "sewing" 1483; -atrix p 1229, 1380, -iatrix (ad rotam) 1372, spinster; f. candelarum, wick-maker 13c.; -ipendula, dropwort (bot.) a 1250, 1634; -o, *to spin c 1190, 1493; to provide with a wick 1242; 1501, c 1538, -acio a 1564, to file (documents).

fim/arium, *etc.*, *see* fimus.

fimber, *see* fiber.

fimbri/a, border (of field) 1453; bordure (her.) p 1394; -atus, fimbriated (her.) p 1394, a 1446; ‡-ale, fringe, guard (of garment) 1570; -arius, textor, fringe-maker 1563; -ator, "silk-lace man" 1710; -atio, fringing 1424; ‡-um, hem 15c.; ‡-o, to hem 1570; *cf.* FRENG.

fim/us, clay c 1188; fumus, *for* -us, dung 1243, 1356; -arium 1280, 1434, -orarium a 1250, fumarium 1287, fumerium 1286, dung-heap; -atio 1280, 1370, -itium 1251, femitium 1152, 1251, manuring; †fientamenta (*pl.*) c 1200, †fenes (*pl.*) 13c., droppings (of sheep); furca -alis 1388, f. -aria 1365, dung-fork; pottum -are, dung-cart 1357; -idus, manured a 1300; -eus c 1350, †funoralis 1334, (?) dirty; -osus, mucky a 1446, ‡1570; -o 1172, 1370, femo c 1200, -igo 1245, to manure; to void excrement a 1446.

fina-, *see* finis.

finctio, *see* FIX

fin/des, wedge 1390; -titius 1230, fentitius 1231, fentetius 1205, fit for splitting; fendidit, (?) *for* fidit, split 1272.

†findula, (?) *f.l.* for s(c)indula, shingle 1400, c 1477.

Fineaticus, *see* Phineaticus.

fingekest, agnus castus (bot.) (Persian) 12c.

fing/ibilis, imaginable c 1366, 1378; -mentum, *see* figmentum; finxio, feigning 1397; *cf.* FICT.

fin/is, marchland 1086; end (of a building) c 1400, 1518; *'fine', final agreement, compromise (leg.) c 1086, 1583; f. mense, foot of table 13c.; f. curie, composition for amercement of doomsmen 1277; f. duelli, settlement by judicial combat 1167, c 1219; f. secte, fine in lieu of suit of court 1632; f. terre, fine for recovery of land 1167, 1232; f. wapentagii, fine in lieu of suit of wapentake 1194, 1327; -e, in the end 1390; ad -em, to the end (that) 1343, 1406; in bona -e, (?) all in good time 1220; -e tenus, entirely 980, 1060. c 1130, 1429; -em sortior, to take effect c 1443; -abilis, subject to fine 1485; †-agium, (?) territory c 1180; †-ale, -olum, filiolum, finial (arch.) 1355; -alis, *see* causa, concordia, lapis; -alitas, limitation c 1344; -aliter, purposefully c 1444; *c 1135, c 1540, -abiliter c 1131, 1324, finally; *-antia 1310, 1556, -atio 1292, 1382, fine, settlement, payment, ransom; -atio, wager 13c.; -ibilis, capable of having a final cause p 1300; potentially finite a 1233, c 1290; -ibilitas, potential finiteness c 1290; -ifestus, feast on last day of month 1518; -itia (*pl.*), (?) effects of deceased monk 1298; -itas, finiteness, limitation 860. a 1233, 1378; -ities, a finite number of times a 1233, c 1300; -itio, ending, determining 1378, 1558; -itivus, acting as a final cause c 1300, p 1300; final, definite c 1363; *f.l.* for -itimus, c 1293; -itus, finite 1267, c 1300; -io, to direct to an end c 1300; *c 1115, 1560, -o 1193, p 1330, to make fine, settle, pay; -io hominem, to die a 1100; -ito, to make definite 13c.; to make finite c 1300.

fin/itio, refining 1405; †-itura, *see* fundaria; -stallum (†fuistallum), stall or shed for refining salt 1328; -us 1245, c 1452, -issimus 1432, of fine quality; -io 1324, c 1409, -o 1290, 1453, to refine; *see also* finis.

†fircus, spike c 1573.

fird-, *see* FYRD

firet-, *see* FURETT

firgi/e 1196, 1221, -a c 1224, fergie 1314, 1344, firchie 1265, fetters (*pl.*); -atus, fettered 1316, 14c.

firlingata, *see* 1 ferdingus.

firlota 1209, 1565, firlata 1478, farlota 1468, ferlot/a, -um 1292, 1460, furlot/a, -um 1460, 1475, ferthelota 1264, firthelota 1266, 'firlot', dry measure (Sc.); for/leta 1279, -lota 1290, 'forthlot', payment connected with ploughing (Norfolk); *cf.* forlottus.

1 firma, banquet (A.S. *feorm*, but confused with Fr. *ferme*) c 1115, c 1154; land appropriated to supply of provisions (mon.) 1086, 1275; f. diei, f. noctis, f. septimane 1086, f. hebdomade 1181, a 1200, fermfoltum 1302, fermfultum (†ferurfultum) a 1182, fermfoltatio (†fernifoltatio) c 1282, 1299 (*cf.* A.S. *fultum*), food-rents.

2 firm/a *1001. 1086, 1567, ferma 1200, farm, rent, fixed payment (Fr. *ferme*); rented area in forest 1330; farm, landed estate c 1400, 1583; f. alba 1086, 1627, album -e c 1178, 1224, f. blanca c 1178, 'blanch-farm'; f. burgalis 1391, 1539, f. burgi 1086, c 1200, f. de burgo 1253; f. civitatis 1167; f. comitatus 1167, 1261; f. hundredi 1313; f. Cuthberti (Northumb.) 1386, 1390 (*cf.* pecunia); f. denaria, penny farm 1086; f. equitiarum, "*kilgh grewour*", f. forestarii, "*comorth forestour*", f. serjantie pacis, "*kilgh kays*" (W.) 1505; f. feodalis, *see* FEOD; f. franca (?) 13c., f. libera 1336, 1440; f. mortua, 'dead farm' (no longer paid) 1284; f. nova, f. vetus 1155, c 1173; f. numero, farm payable by tale c 1178, 1224; f. perpetua c 1115, 1239; f. ad terminum c 1400; -abilis, suitable for farming (renting) 1424, 1574;

-aliter, (?) at farm 825; -agia c 1170, -aria 1440, -atio 1378, farm (rent); -arius, (*adj.*) of or for a farm (rent) 1232, 1579; *(subst.)* 1086, 1543; -erius, fermarius, farmerius 1587, -aria (*f.*) 1293, -arissa (*f.*) 1447, farmer, renter; -o, to pay a fixed rent c 1080; to pay rent to (with personal *obj.*) 1086; to farm out (Sc.) 1380.

3 firm/a, cage for young hawks (Fr. *ferme*) a 1150; †"skirt" 1483; fermia, box 1234; -aculum, binding agreement 1282; *1201, 1442, -aculus c 1100, c 1340, -iculum 1460, fermaculum 1338, -ale 1185, clasp, brooch, buckle (*cf.* FORM); ‡-acularius, brooch-maker 15c.; -amentum, dam c 1210; -aria c 1480, -ina 1234, fermina 1198, prison; -atio, wager 14c.; 1240, 13c., -asio 1291, -isona 1290, fermeso 1285, fermesona 1279, 1443, fermiso 1280, fermisona 1234, 1362, fermisio c 1245, vermiso 1463, vermesona 1435, close season for hunting; c 1069, a 1564, -atura 1252, 1451, maintaining, confirming, fortifying; f. stagni, building a mill-dam 1183; -atorium 1385, c 1427, ‡-atura 1483, clasp, fastener; -atura, binding agreement (G.) 1276, 1315; *-itas, fortress c 1150, 1461; validity (of charters, *etc.*) 679. 1222, c 1449; -itus, firmly c 1250; -ura, enclosure *or* custody 1198; -us, fledged (falc.) a 1150; cantus f. (mus.) 1606; fermus, *for* -us, firm, stable 14c.; pro -o, certainly c 1250, c 1430; -o, to impress, mark 793; to maintain (accused persons) c 1115; to build (mill-dam) 1183, 1430; to fledge (falc.) a 1150; to wager 12c., 14c.; to affirm 815; to rehearse c 1220 (with *inf.*) 1283, 1406, f. mecum c 1218, f. in animo meo 13c., to undertake, resolve; f. duellum, to wager battle (G.) c 1250, 1281; fermo, *for* -o, to support 13c.

firm/aria *c 1220, 1507, †fymaria 15c., †-ana 15c., -arium, fermaria c 1447, fermerarium 1275, infirmary (mon.); -aria, infirmaress 1415; -arius, infirmarer c 1200; *see also* firma (2 & 3); *cf.* INFIRM

firsa, *see* 2 friscus.

†firstum, (?) joist 1365.

firthelota, *see* firlota.

firthwita, *see* FYRD

fis-, *see also* phasianus; PHYS

fisc/ella, bee-skep c 1139; a 1180, ‡1483, (?) -a 1380, (?) visca 1381, fish-trap; ficella 1220, 1306, ficellum 1267, fessella 1281, fissina 1285, basket (esp. for cheese); ‡-ina, "churn" 1483.

fiscum, *see* VISC

fisc/us, tax c 844, 933. 14c.; -alia (*pl.*), taxes c 1188, c 1540; -alis, concerned with taxation 948. c 1180, 1475; judex -alis, royal judge c 1115; *see also* procurator; -alinus, *see* colonus; -anus c 1200, -arius 1193, c 1437, treasurer, fiscal officer; ‡-arius, -ator, "escheator" 1483; -o, to confiscate *or* tax 709. c 1296, c 1408.

fisfe/um c 1182, -ha (†fiffegha) 1203, fish-toll; fyssh/egarum, 'fish-garth', weir c 1394; -usum, fish-house 1290.

fiss-, *see also* fiscella; fusillus.

fiss/ura, splitting (wood) 1355, 1449; bar, baton (her.) p 1394, c 1595; **fixura**, crack c 1227; -us, double-headed (her.) p 1394; see also 2 **friscus**.

fisticus a 1250, **fusticus** 1424, **festuc/a** 13c., fistic (nut); -ada, confection of fistic nuts 1303, 1307; cf. **pistacia**.

fistul/a, underground channel c 1227, c 1362; eucharistic reed c 1100, 12c.; spout of altar cruet 1388; gun-barrel 1499, 1584; ‡f. **bufonis**, fumitory (bot.) 14c.; f. **pastoralis**, water-plantain 1538; ‡-aria, bugle (bot.) 14c.; -atio, whistling c 1608; ‡-ista, piper 15c.; ‡**fistilatrix**, "piper wife" 15c.; -osus, ulcerated c 1190; ‡-o, to pipe 1483, 1570; -or, to fester, be ulcerated a 615. a 1250, 1267; see also **cassia**.

fithera (terre) 1352, †pythera 14c., vithra 13c., (?) baulk (Staffs., Glos.).

fith/erbordum 1267, 1287, -elbordum 1236, viderbordum 1223, (?) 'feather-board' (with one feathered edge); cf. **wetherbordo**.

†fithris, (?) part of intestines 6c.

fix/atio 1267, 1620, -io 1267, a 1564, -ura 1340, c 1533, fixing, setting up; a 1292, 1622, **fictio** a 1235, fixation (alch.); -io 1238, c 1360, -itas 13c., fixity, fixed position; †finctio, affixing (of seal) 1459; -orium, attachment, support c 1212; (?) knife 1408, 1464; -ura, setting (of gem) 1297; **figitivus**, fitchy (her.) a 1446; -us, fixed, solidified (alch.) 13c.; -o, to solidify c 1250; **figo ancoras**, to anchor 1415; f. **lanceam**, to set lance in rest a 1200; f. **tentoria**, to pitch camp 1136, 1461; cf. FIC; see also **fissura**.

flab/ellum, weather-vane 1247; 1214, 1346, **flagellum** 1359, ‡-rum 1483, fly-flap, whisk (esp. eccl., for protecting Host); -elle 1223, -ela (pl.) c 1500, **flavellum** 1291, bellows; **flavellum**, fan 13c.; -ellatio, fanning c 1115; -ilis, of or for the wind, air c 550; see also FLAGELL

flacca, see **flaga**.

‡flacc/entia, -or, languor 1483.

1 flaco c 1250, **flact/ira** c 730, -ra a 1142, pool (cf. Fr. flaque).

2 **flaco, flado, flaganus**, see **flato**.

flacta, see **flageta**; FLATT; FLECC

flaga 1286, 1306, **flaggus** 1336, **flacca** 1270, 1336, flag, reed; (?) reed-bed 1223.

‡flag/e (pl.), spirits possessing occult knowledge 1652.

flagell/um 1199, 1301, †-ina 1274, flail; scourge (fig.), divine correction 7c., c 793. 13c.; beater (of fulling-mill) 1237; c 1397, **fleylum** 1347, clapper (of bell) c 1200, 1373 **flabellum** 1355, **flaellus** 1275, 'flail', swing-bar (of gate); **flaellum**, (?) tiller (naut.) 1296; see also **furca**; **flagillatio**, beating (of flax) 1418; -ator 1212, 1456, ‡-arius 1483, thresher; 1271, -atrix (f.) 746. c 1125, c 1414, scourger; -atoria, threshing 1453; -ifer, bearing a scourge 1654; †flagio, for **flagrio**, whipping-boy c 1200; -o, to thresh 1194, 1220; see also FLAB

flageta 1275, ‡flacta 1483, flakata 1404, 1463, **flaketum** 1383, **flago** 1448, flask, flagon; cf. FLASC

flagitium, pain, torment 1298.

flagr/amen c 950, -or 1427, ardent desire; -ans, consumed with hunger c 550; -o, to enflame, inspire 793.

flagr/antia (for fragr-), fragrance c 730. c 1090, c 1115; -ans, fragrant c 1021. 1090, c 1500; -o, to burst forth (of smell) 793.

flaka 1287, 1475, ‡flecta c 1440, 'flake', hurdle.

flak/ata, -etum, see **flageta**.

flalba, see **slabba**.

1 flam/en, bishop c 1137, c 1210; priest c 1414; druid 1535; -ineus, priestly c 950.

2 flamen **almum** c 950, c 1000. 12c., f. **sacrum** c 1170, c 1258, f. **sanctum** c 1000. 12c., Holy Ghost.

flamicia, see **flato**.

Flam/ingus 1267, 1412, -engius 1445, **Flemingus** 15c., -mensis 1086, *Flandr/ensis 1086, 1508, **Flaundrensis** 1465, **Flendrensis** 1228, -icus 1315, -igena c 1200, -ita c 1000. a 1142, 15c., -us 1516, 1608, **Vlandrus** 1608, Fleming, Flemish; see also **petra**.

flamm/atio, conflagration c 1160; -abilis c 1227, -aticus c 590, -ativus c 1184, fiery; -ea 1482, -eola c 1360, *-eolum 1253, 1393, -iolum 1370, -olum a 1564, kerchief; -eolum, bandage c 1395; brazier 1433; -ifluus, -inosus 14c., -ivomus 6c., c 950. c 1125, a 1452, belching flame; -ula, spearwort (bot.) a 1250, ‡1570; ‡f. **juniperi**, kind of fungus 1652; -eo, to ignite c 1184; -esco, to be aflame 1252, c 1450.

flanc/a, -us, flank 1301, 14c.

Flandr-, see **Flamingus**.

flangosus, see **frangor**.

*flasc/o 793, 1060. 1189, 15c., -a c 750. a 1142, ‡15c., -ula c 1300, -ulum c 1325, -ulus 793, -us 1342, flask, bottle; cf. **flageta**.

flas/ketum 1219, 1327, -sattum 1300, -sadum 1290, 1313, 'flasket', wicker container.

fla/to 1173, c 1450, †-co 1249, c 1450, †falco 1214, -do 14c., -vo c 1220, †-no c 1375, -o 1283, 15c., -ganus a 1160, ‡-micia c 1440, ‡-ta 15c., flan, flawn (cake); -to 1183, 1188, **flodo** p 1280, flan, blank coin, die for minting.

flatt/a (flact-), -um c 1154, 1574, -eria 1211, flat (piece of land).

flat/us almus c 950, f. **sacer** 1245, Holy Ghost; f. **organorum** 1439, -io organorum 1446, 1491, organ-blowing; -icus, for smelting 1618; -or 1618, -uor 1632, 'blower', smelter; f. **anterior**, 'foreblower' 1333; -ulentus, windy 1620; -uosus, flatulent 14c.; inflative 1622.

flaura, coltsfoot (bot.) a 1250, ‡14c.

flav/edo 1610, -itas a 1250, yellowness, glitter; -us, golden-haired a 1193.

flavellum, see FLAB

flavo, see **flato**.

flavor, (?) wind c 550.

†flebilitas, (?) feebleness 793.

*flecc/a (flech-) 1190, 1318, -ia 1194, 1305, **flacta** 1342, **flisca** 1333, fletch, arrowshaft; -ia, shaft of pillar 1292; -aria, service of providing arrow-shafts 13c.; -arius

1175, 1286, -iarius 1227, 1575, fliccharius 1192, -iator 1227, 1238, fletcher; -erius, archer (Port.) 1386; -ericius, (?) fletched arrow 1213; flegittatus, fletched 13c.; -o, -io, to fletch 1205, 1227.

flect-, *see also* FLEX

flecta, *see* flaka.

‡flect/aria, (?) mullein (bot.) 14c.; ‡-idos, (?) dove's-foot crane's-bill (bot.) 14c.

fleg-, *see* PHLEBOTOM; PHLEGM

flem/anfremtha, -eniswita, -neswita, *see* flima.

Flemingus, Flendrensis, *see* Flamingus.

flem/o, *for* -ina, congestion of blood c 1180.

flenium, *see* flunea.

fleob-, *see* PHLEBOTOM

†flera mule, (?) *for* flore inule, elecampane (bot.) a 1150.

flesgabulum, 'flesh-gavel', due paid by butchers 1297, 1300.

flet/a, -um 1184, 1513, -us (*4th decl.*) 1290, flietum a 1367, flota 1431, flueta 1464, fluettus 1202, flodum (Norm.) 1198, fleet, water-channel; -a, Fleet prison c 1290, 15c.; treatise supposedly written therein (leg.) c 1290.

fleub-, fleugb-, *see* PHLEBOTOM

fleugma, fleum-, *see* phlegma.

flex/us, movement c 550; -ibilitas 7c. c 1125, 1378, †fleccibilitas (? flect-) 13c., elasticity, pliability; -ibiliter, flexibly c 1194; -ilis, capable of inflexion (gram.) 1524; -uositas, winding, twist 1267; -uosus, wavy (her.) c 1595; -osus, pliant c 550; flectuosus, winding c 1400; †flectenum 463, flectio genuum c 700, 9c., genuflexion; -o, to bend c 1365; flecto, to move c 550; f. super jenua, to kneel 13c.

fleylum, *see* flagellum.

fliccharius, *see* FLECC

flictwita, fine for escape 1199; *cf.* fihtwita.

flietum, *see* fleta.

‡fligo, to elude 1570.

flima, fugitive or outlaw (A.S.) c 1115; flymonfirma c 1115, †fremefeuda 1189, †flem/anfremtha 1199, -eniswita c 1188, -neswita c 1175, †flesmelencenwita a 1190, (fine for) harbouring or maintaining fugitives.

flisca, *see* FLECC

flocca, 'flock', gang (of workmen) c 1200.

flocc/us (flokk-) 1275, 1465, †floscus a 1250, -unus 1268, villus flosum 13c., flock, refuse wool; ‡snowflake 1483; culcitra -a 1553, c. -ea 1533, flock-bed; ‡-at, it snows 15c., 1483; -ipendo, to disregard, hold cheap c 950. 11c., 14c.; *see also* FROCC

flodo, *see* flato.

flod/us, flood-tide c 1250, c 1290; †-a, (?) pond c 1200; -eyatum c 1337, flotgata c 1200, flood-gate; *cf.* fleta.

‡flon, kind of pear 14c.

flonerium, *see* flunea.

flonis, bunch (25 heads) of garlic c 1290.

flor-, *see also* flos.

florenaylum, floor-nail c 1445.

florencius, florin 1335; ‡goldfinch 15c.

*flor/enus a 1308, 1558, -ena 1391, -anus 1345, -inus 1277, 1333, florin, (gold) coin (usua y = 3s.–4s.); English gold coin 1344,

1347; f. aureus 1277, 15c., f. auri 1300, 1426; f. camere, f. de camera, papal florin c 1375, 1475; f. Carolinus (Imperial) 1555; f. Coloniensis c 1397, f. Renensis 1408 (Cologne); f. de Florencia (It.) 1303, 1335; f. magnus 1344, f. grossus 1425, noble; f. medius 1344, f. mediocris 1425, half noble; f. minor 1344, 1425, f. parvus 1315, gold farthing; f. agni, f. ad agnum a 1308, f. de agnello 1324, f. ad scutum et multonem 1357, f. de multone 1360, f. de motone 1370, 'lambkin', *mouton d'or* (Fr.); f. de pavillon (Fr.) 1342; f. regalis 1332, f. realis 1333, 1337, rial; f. de scuto 1339, 1349, f. scutaneus c 1362, *écu* (Fr.).

flos 1205, 1352, flora 1335, 1361, flour; menstruation 13c.; "spirituous substance" (alch.) 1652; f. amoris, amaranth (bot.) 1538; f. de auro, (?) florin 1509; f. canelle, powdered cinnamon 1342, 1372; ‡f. celi, nostoc 1652; ‡f. cervisie, yeast 1570; ‡f. chalcis 14c., f. eris a 1250, ‡14c., ‡f. salis (?) 14c., 1652, copper oxide; ‡f. cheiri, "essence of gold" 1652; f. crete, powdered chalk 1388; f. deliciarum 1388, c 1443, f. de liz c 1321, f. lilii, f. Francorum 1449, *fleur de lis*; ‡f. lactis, cream 1620; f. militie, flower of chivalry c 1310, 1461; f. ostriarum, oyster-spat 1377; f. plastri, powdered plaster 1388; f. plumbi, lead oxide a 1250, 14c.; f. Saracenorum, gold-embroidered daisy c 1365, 1443; ‡f. sectarum croe, nutmeg flour 1652; ‡f. Syriacus, mallow 14c.; f. Trinitatis, heartsease 1641; flor/alis, flower-like c 1115; -arium, ‡"flower-hill" 1483; anthology c 1432, 1521; ‡-ator, "flourisher" 1483; -atus, scented (of wine) 1236, 1242; 1245, 1415, -ettatus 1303, -issatus 1450, -ulentus 709. 1537, 'flourished', ornamented with flowers; -ettus, floweret 1245; -etum, flower-garden a 1452, ‡1483; ‡posy 1570; -iditas, eloquence 1241; c 1210, 1437, -ulentia c 1150, flourishing condition; -idus, (?) frothy a 1250; flory (her.) p 1394, a 1446; *see also* Pascha; -itura, form of composition (mus.) 1326; -iger, flowery c 810. c 1125, a 1452; -igero, to ornament with flowers 1245, a 1408; -o, to produce like flowers c 1180.

flos/cus, -us, *see* floccus.

*flot/a 1213, 1461, -um 1214, fleet (of ships); raft (of timber) 1200, c 1395; float (of net) 1269, 1306; bowyers' float 1303; -agium, †-agum 1416, 1458, -iscum 1390, -imen a 1335, -ura 1294, skimmings of fat; -esum maris, flotsam a 1540; navicula -ans, "float-boat" 1324; -o, to float 1248, 1470; *see also* fleta.

flotgata, *see* FLOD

floundra, *see* flundera.

fluct/us aque, tide-way 1086, 1324; f. altissimus, f. infimus, high and low tide 1283; -ivagus, wave-tossed 6c., c 1000. c 1170, 1252; -ualiter, by mixture a 1252; -uatio, engrailing (her.) 1595; -ifico, to raise waves c 870; -o, to be storm-tossed a 1338; *cf.* FLUX

flueta, fluettus *see* fleta.

†**fluettum**, (?) flew-net c 1353.
†**fluetum**, (?) *for* **bluetum** *or* **felvetum**, c 1353.
fluma, *see* **phlegma**.
flu/men (maris), flood-tide c 1290, c 1440; **f. maritimum**, inlet 1338; **-minalis**, of a river c 700. 1475; **-ens** 939. 15c., **-entum** c 730, stream; **-iditas** 1662, **-or** 1620, fluidity; **-idus**, suffering from dysentery 1241; **-vide**, fleetingly 826; **-itatio**, fluctuation 1266; **-or**, fluor spar 1634, ‡1652; †**-strum**, ford 1483; ‡stream 1570; **-stra** (*pl.*), swell, rough sea c 550, c 790; **-ento**, to abound c 1180; **-o**, to move along a line (geom.) c 1300; †**-o**, (?) to flow with c 550.
flund/era 1415, **-ra** 13c., **-ria** 1266, c 1300, **floundra** 1339, 1415, flounder (fish); *cf.* **fundolus**.
flun/ea 1377, **-us** (†**fluvus**) 1341, 1399, **-is** (G.) 1254, **flenium** (G.) 1308, **flonerium** 1332, 'floine', sort of ship.
flustrum, *see* **flumen**.
fluvi/us, flood-tide c 1290; **-a**, flood 1351, 1380; 1588, **-um** 13c., *for* **-us**, river; **-olus**, rivulet 641, 757. c 1325; 1586; **molendinum -ale**, water-mill 1419; *see also* **signum**; ‡**-osus**, "floody" 1483; ‡**-o**, to overflow 1483; *see also* **flumen**; *cf.* FLUCT
flux/us c 1300, **-io** 1686, fluxion (geom.); **f. maris**, flood-tide, high water 1284, 1307; tide-way 1470; **f. ventris**, dysentery 1188, 15c.; ***-ibilis** a 1233, 1524, **-ivus** c 1327, fleeting, transitory; ***-ibilitas**, fluidity, flow 12c., 1378; **-itas**, flux a 1250; *cf.* FLUCT
flymonfirma, *see* **flima**.
foagium, **foallia**, *see* FOC
†**foala**, foal 1218; *cf.* **phola**.
‡**focace**, (?) *for* **phoca**, "stockfish or porpoise" 1483.
focagium, *see* **focus**; **foggum**.
foc/us, fire c 1000. 1461; arson 1361; beacon 1303; focus (optics) 1686; **f. jocunditatis**, bonfire 1461; **-agium** ***1219, c 1309, **foagium** a 1190, 1274, †**foiagium** 1323, †**folcagium** (G.) 1276, †**frocagium** 1247, †**fragium** 1194, **fuagium** c 1189, 1285, **fuuagium** 1247, focage, feuage, hearth-money (Fr. & C.I.); **-agium** 1222, 1343, ***-ale** c 1160, 1531, **-alium** 13c., **-ellium** 1209, **fugellum** c 1310, **foallia**, **foallium** 12c., 1232, **fuale** a 1195, **fualia** (*f. s.*) c 1185, 1234, **fuallium** 12c., 1202, **fuailla** 1197, **-arium** 1201, **fuarium** 1317, fuel; **fogaca**, *for* **-acea**, unleavened loaf (G.) 1289; **-alagium** c 1255, 1331, **fogalagium** 1282, (?) payment for right to gather fuel (Fr. & C.I.); **-alis**, of or for fuel 1320, 1454; **domus -alis** 1300, **d. -aria** 1216, dwelling-house; **-aria** 1437, **-arium** c 1175, c 1438, hearth; ***-aria**, housekeeper or concubine c 1188, 1553; **-arius**, (*adj.*) concubinary 12c.; (*subst.*) concubinary priest a 1383; ***1084, 1377, **-elarius** 1460, hearth-keeper, stoker or fuel-overseer; **-ile**, 'fusil', steel for striking sparks out of flint (*cf.* **fugillum**) c 550; ‡'focile', bone of forearm 14c.; **-ina**, forge c 1227; **-ulus**, "chafing-dish" 1553; *see also* **fagetum**.

fod/arius, **-asia**, *see* FEOD
foddrio, **foeragium**, *see* **foragium**.
foder-, **fodhera**, **fodoro**, *see* FURR
fod/era 1269, c 1456, **-ra** 1394, 1475, **foudra** 1443, **fudra** 1487, **-rum** 1475, 1504, **foldrum** 1269, **fother/a** 1315, **-um** 1228, **-ium** 1550, fother (of lead).
fod/iatio c 1293, 1383, **-itio** 1198, 1566, (right of) digging; **-eum**, ditch 1288; **terra -ibilis**, cultivable land 1296; **-iator** 1212, 1336, **-itor** 1198, digger; **-eo** 1334, 1587, ‡**-ito** 1483, **foo** 1276, *for* **-io**, to dig; **-eo dentes**, to pick the teeth c 1180; *cf.* FOSS
fodmarta, *see* **foggum**.
fodrum, *see* **fodera**; **foragium**.
fodum, **foedum**, *see* FEOD
foefum, **foesum**, **foffo**, *see* FEOFF
foga, *see* **voga**.
fogaca, **fogalagium**, **foiagium**, *see* FOC
fog/gum, 'fog', late hay (Derb.) 1236; **-agium** 1266, 1539, **focagium** 1352, 1536, 'foggage', payment for grazing on fog (Sc. & N. Eng.); **-lammus**, lamb fattened on fog (Sc.) 1475; **-marta** 1468, **fodmarta** 1463, beast fattened on fog (Sc.).
†**foillius (thesauri)**, (?) sack *or* cellar 1213.
folaricium, **foler-**, *see* FULL
folcagium, *see* FOC
fold/a, **-agium**, *see* **falda**.
foldrum, *see* **fodera**.
‡**folea**, (?) *for* **solea**, kind of fish 15c.
folg/arius, attached to a household c 1115; **-eris** c 1182, **-erus**, †**-essa** (? **-eressa**) (*f.*) 1299, member of household; **-o**, to follow c 1115.
‡**folio**, to cry like a leopard 1483; *see also* **folium**.
folisia, *see* **falesa**.
Folitanus, member of religious order, *Feuillan*, 1620.
foli/um, ***folio**, page c 1200, 1549; one side of double seal 1347, 1392; **teneo per f.**, form of tenure 1339, 1413; **vinum de primo (secundo**, *etc.*) **-o**, wine of first (second, *etc.*) 'foil', *i.e.* vintage year (reckoning backwards) 1335, 1373; (?) **-um** 1234, ‡**f. album**, **f. nigrum**, **f. Paradisi** 14c., **f. Indum** 1620, malabathrum, (?) kind of cinnamon; **f. argenteum** 1245, 1360, **f. aureum** 1360, **f. auri** 1245, 1354, **f. stanni** 1355, metal foil; **f. plastri** 1341; **f. (folia) fenestre** 1378, 15c., **f. fenistre** c 1400, **f. ostii** 1378, **f. porte** 1279, 1357, **f. tabule** 1389, **f. pontis** 1444, wooden leaf, board; **f. penne**, (?) blade of feather c 1180; **f. tallie**, foil of tally c 1290, 1508; **-agium**, foliage 1324; **-aceus**, leafy c 550; **-atum** c 1115, **fuillata** (Norm.) 1180, leafy shelter, arbour (Fr. *feuillée*); ‡**-atus**, "crooked" 1483; **-balsama**, gum from balsam leaves 13c.; **-cia deliciarum**, *fleurs de lis* c 1503; **foletura**, design of foliage 1303; **-etturatus**, decorated with foliage 1303; **-fico**, to burst into leaf a 1446; **-o**, to beat (metal) into foil c 1215, c 1345; *see also* FOLL
folkesmotum 1274, 1331, †**falmotum** 1164, folk-moot.
foll/ator, **-o**, *see* FULL
foll/es (*pl.*), organ-bellows c 1245; (**folia**) (*pl.*) c 1280, 1473, **-i** c 1340, *or* **-es**,

bellows; -iculus cerebri (med.) a 1200; f. pulmonis a 1250; -ico, to blow bellows 13c.

follum, pit, valley c 550.

foll/us, folus, fool c 1200, 13c.; untrained (falc.) 1204, 1206; rete -um, sort of net (Norm.) 1195; festum -orum, Feast of Fools 13c.; -etus, brownie, imp c 1212; ‡-eo, -esco, to be, become, foolish 1483.

†folso, (?) f.l. for fosso, to ditch c 1300.

folsura, see VOLU

†foma, (?) f.l. for fovia (i.e. fovea) 1279.

fomenta (pl.), remedies of justice c 1115.

fomes, heat c 550.

fon/a, -e, -um, see PHON

fond-, see funda.

fonellum, see funellum.

†fonnum, (?) for A.S. fen, 679.

fons, *well 1239, c 1362; font (eccl.) c 760, 980. c 1102, a 1564; corner of eye a 1250; source of humours (med.) 13c.; argent circle representing a spring (her.) a 1446; f. baptismalis 793. c 1100, 1461; f. portabilis, portable font 1462; ‡f. philosophorum, bain marie 1652; f. hauribilis 1295, f. tractabilis 1331, 1349, f. tracticius 1339, draw-well; *font/alis 9c. a 1250, c 1474, -anus 14c., relating to a source, original; -aliter, as from a source, originally 1267, 1452; -ana c 1260, -anum (?) 780, fountain; -aninus, living in spring water a 1250; -iculus, effluence (med.) c 1412; -ifer, well-watered c 1200; -inella (†frontinella), fontanelle, hollow of neck a 1250, ‡15c.; -inus, drawn from a well a 1250, 13c.

Fontanus, inhabitant of Wells (Somerset) c 1460.

font/aria, -or, see fundaria.

fontinell-, see fons; fotmellum.

foo, see FEON; fodiatio.

for/a, for -is, door 1204; a -is, outside a 1100, c 1400; de -is, see deforis; pro -ibus, at the outset c 1218; -as do, to alienate (land) 930; -as positio, putting out (to sea) 1452; -enria, 'foreignry' (W.) 1426; -anus 1133, -aneus 1244, c 1326, -ensis 1125, c 1241, -encis c 1330, -insis c 1200, *-insecus (†-nisecus) 735. c 1090, 1560, -incecus 1255, 1578, -ensecus 1212, -encecus c 1263, -inceus 16c., -incesus 1252, a 1577, -incescus 1301, -incicus 1480, -inciscus 1451, †-nicus 1390, foreign, external (to a district or community); (subst.) -aneus 1274, c 1448, -ensis 12c., 1377, -insis (G.) 1314, -insecus, etc. 1233, 15c., foreigner, outsider, non-burgess; -ensis, layman c 1178; -ensior, outer c 1200; -insecum c 1218, 1282, -ense 1203, foreign service (cf. servitium); land outside manor 1247, c 1290; payment or receipt outside regular scope of account c 1300; -ensiter, by change of venue 1288; -insecatio, straying away c 1326; -insecor (dep.), to stray away c 1326; -ino, to remove 1340; see also foris-, ı baillium, domus, expensa, hundredum, secta, terra; cf. EXTRINSEC

for/agium 12c., 1451, -ago c 1235, 1447, faragium 1313, feoragium 13c., foeragium 1288, †ferragium c 1200, fouragium c 1461, furagium c 1150, 1414,

furra 1107, fodrum c 1115, 'forage', fodder or straw; -ator c 1290, -iarius 15c., forager; -ago c 1290, foddrio 1376, to provide with fodder; -ro 1242, furro c 1200, to forage.

foralis, see forum.

for/amen, window-pane 1473; pit-shaft 1371; -atorium, punch, piercer a 700; orifice c 1200; furator, borer (of pit-shaft) 1299; furratus, bored 1208.

foran-, see fora.

forari/a, -um, see forera.

foras-, see fora; foris-

forator, see foragium.

foratorium, see foramen.

foratura, see FURR

forb-, see also FURB

forban-, see FORISBANN

forbarr/amentum, 'forbarring', obstructing (of sale) 1288, 1289; -o, to 'forbar', debar (from buying) (Norwich) 1289.

forbenda, fore-band (of cart-harness) 1285.

forc/a, -atura, -ecta, forchetum, see FURC

†forcaria, (piece of) felt 1215.

forceapum, 'forecheap', forestalling the market c 1115.

forcelettum, see fortalitia.

ı for/cerium 1278, 15c., -cerum 1220, 1300, -carium 1265, -czarium 1241, -sarium 1295, -serium 1323, -serum 1305, 1323, -zerum 1275, -cellus 1300, 1395, 'forcer' strong-box.

2 forcerium, jurisdiction, lowy (Sc.) 1299.

forci-, see also FORTI

for/cipes (pl.), tongs: ‡-cipula 1483; -cipes c 1125, a 1205, -tisipes 1391, †-cie 1243, 1248, scissors; -ceps, mouth, beak c 550; cf. forfices, forpices.

forclutum, 'fore-clout' (of plough) 14c.

forda 13c., furdus 1414, ford.

ford/alis, -ellum, -ola, -olum, see ferdella.

†fordarius, (?) for bordarius, cottar (Norm.) 1316.

fordinka, see ı ferdingus.

fordwardmannus, see forwardmannus.

fordwita, see FYRD

fore, see esse.

forebannio, see FORISBANN

forefac-, see FORISFAC

forelandum c 1250, forland/a, -um c 1200, 1345, 'foreland', outlying land (esp. newly reclaimed land leased to tenant).

forellus, see forulus.

†foremannus, captain (naut.) 1266.

foren-, see fora.

*for/era c 1200, 1549, -eria, -erium a 1200, 1348, -eris a 1200, -aria, -arium 12c., 1433, †ferrera 1230, furura 1366, ‡-eta 15c., †-etata c 1283, †-tyra (Sc.) c 1250, margin or 'headland' in open field (O.F. foriere; but cf. forerda).

for/erda c 1200, -herda, -eherda 1268, -hurtha 1260, †-uhtha 1234, †fururcha 1290, 'fore-earth' (in open field); -hurtha 1285, -urda 1275, (?) outlying area of land.

fores, see forum.

forescheta, see forscheta.

foresfac-, forestura, see FORISFAC

foresposmannus, class of tenant 1272.

forest/a, -um *1086, 1583, -e (Norm.) 1103, -ia c 1450, forista 1215, forest, land under forest laws; (fine for) forest offence c 1115, 1198; -agium, forest service or dues c 1150, 1385; *-aria 1186, 15c., -eria 1179, 1222, -ria 13c., 1412, office of forester, forestry service or jurisdiction; *-arius 1086, 1670, -erius 1215, 1316, †-ius 13c., foristarius 1215, forester; f. capitalis 1215, c 1290; f. de feodo 1279, 1333; f. eques, f. pedes 1279; f. itinerans 1438; -o, to afforest, bring under forest laws 1279.

forestal-, see forstall-

foret/a, -ata, see forera.

forewardmannus, see forwardmannus.

for/factum, -faitura, -fectura, -feto, see FORISFAC

for/fangium (†forisfangium, †forsfangium) c 1115, forfongium 1297, †forfingium 1442, reward for rescue of stolen cattle (A.S. forfeng).

forfic/es (pl.) a 1090, 1260, -ula (f. s.) c 1200, scissors; cf. forcipes, forpices.

*forgabulum, see forisgabulum.

forgeldum, see fotgeldum.

*forg/ia 1086, 1409, -ium 1308, 1409, forge; f. errans 1282, f. itinerans 1226, 1231, f. iens 1296, 1321, f. operans 1220, 'going', working forge; f. ferri, forge for iron-smelting 1331, 1409; -eo, to smelt 1409.

for/herda, -hurtha, see forerda.

foriarius, see foragium.

forifac-, see FORISFAC

forigo, see 1 furra.

forin-, see fora; FORM

forisaffid/atio, renunciation 1220, 1270; -o 1220, c 1373, forasaffido 1231, forisfido a 1190, a 1225, to renounce, disclaim.

forisaffirmatio, renunciation 1206.

forisbann/itio (Sc.) 1482, -istura 1200, 1201, forbannissamentum (G.) 1277, banish-ment; -itus (†forsbannitus) c 1115, for-banitus (†forbanicus) 1282, 1320, banished man; -io 1227, c 1250, -o 1207, forbannio 1258, 1438, forbano 1203, 13c., forebannio (G.) 1297, forbannizo (G.) 1305, 1315, to banish.

foriscapio me, to find bail 1249.

foriscota, see farcosta.

forisfac/tio a 1087, c 1470, *-tura 1086, 1686, forefactura c 1102, 1361, forefatura 1331, foresfactura c 1115, forfaitura 1189, forfectura p 1300, †forestura 1343, -tum *c 1115, c 1414, forefactum c 1130, 1185, foresfactum 1286, forfactum 1192, forifactum c 1160, forfaitum c 1160, for-feiture, penalty; -tum, wrong, injury 1100, 15c.; -tor, one who does wrong or incurs forfeiture c 1130, c 1225; -tus, one who has incurred forfeiture c 1150; -io *1086, 1564, f. me 1086, c 1115, forefacio 1086, 1236, forifacio c 1188, forfeto p 1339, to do wrong, forfeit, pay or incur forfeiture; to mulct, exact forfeiture from 1156, 1419.

†forisfactus, for A.S. forwyrhta, representa-tive c 1115.

forisfamilio, to free from dependence, endow (heir) with due portion (leg.) c 1185, c 1290; to disown c 1237.

forisfamulo, to run away from service c 1290.

forisfangium, see forfangium.

forisfido, see FORISAFFID

forisgabulum c 1250, c 1285, forgabulum c 1215, 1365, †fergabulum c 1270, a form of quit-rent (Kent & Sussex).

forishabeo, to recover, redeem 1274.

forishabitans, non-resident (of borough) 13c.

forisjudico 1201, 1449, forjudico 1330, to dispossess.

*forisjuro c 1115, c 1370, forasjuro 1166, forjuro a 1168, 1276, to abjure, forswear.

forismitto, to alienate, sell 1086, c 1115; foras mitto me, to withdraw oneself 1237.

foriso, see forum.

forispriso, see forprisa.

forist/a, -arius, see foresta.

foristal-, foristell-, see forstall-

foristraho, to abduct 1204, 1227.

forisvadio, to pledge, mortgage 1215.

foris/veia 1235, c 1315, -via 1235, forsveia c 1180, c 1230, trespasser (Sc.); -via, fine for trespass (Sc. & Cumberland) 13c., c 1315.

forjudico, see forisjudico.

forjuro, see forisjuro.

forland-, see forelandum.

forlang-, forlong-, see furlongus.

for/leta, -lota, see firlota.

forloda, 'fore-lode', channel in front of em-bankment (Sussex) c 1220.

forlottus, tenant of quarter virgate 1308.

form/a, (mason's mould for) tracery (arch.) a 1210, 1396; architect's plan 1250; printer's forme 1520, 1535; form, bench c 1200, 1555; form, class (ac.) 1268, c 1582; formality, dignity a 1408; *formula, terms (of document) c 1188, 1461; ideal, moral pattern 793. c 1115; *form, essence, first principle, eidos (phil.) c 850. c 1160, 1620; †occult power derived from heavenly bodies 1652; f. ad caseum, cheese-mould 1277; f. capelle, Chancery form (Sc.) 1291; f. communis, common form 1248; f. donationis 1285, 15c., f. doni 1223, 1397, formedon (leg.); f. exemplaris, formal cause c 1200; f. habitus, form em-bodied in matter c 1270; districtio in -a pacis (leg.) c 1455; f. publica, form of notarial instrument 1308, 1417; f. sub-stantialis, substantial form (phil.) c 1200, a 1347; (leg.) c 1327, 1469; f. prima et secunda, First and Second Bench in Chancery 1317; f. pecia, form-piece, stone tracery (arch.) 1333; f. vitri, complete glass for window 1337; -abilis, susceptible of form c 1205, p 1300; -ale 1296, c 1430, -ile 1336, †forinaculum c 1340, †forni-cale 14c., clasp, brooch, buckle (cf. 3 firma); -alis, *concerned with essence (phil.) a 1250, c 1460; regular 1539; elabo-rately constructed 1609; see also causa, contradictio; -alitas, essential character c 1300, 1564; -aliter, *formally, in respect of form 1153, c 1470; in due order c 1327; -alista, pedant 1499; -aticus c 1100, -agius 1269, furmagius 1277, 1284, cheese; -aginarius (†forinaginarius) c 1400, fur-magerus 1285, cheese-maker; -atilis, shaped c 1400; -atio, moulding, casting (of metal) 1300; being the essence 13c.; -ativus, constitutive of form a 1233, c 1360;

-elus 1280, 1315, **furmelus** 1234, 'for-mel', formed, trained (falc.); **-elia**, cheese-mould 1326; ‡cheese 1483; hare's form c 1160; 1405, **-icula** 1378, **-ula** c 1200, 1551, **-ulum** 1441, **-um** (†**forinum**) 1302, bench; **-ificus**, creative 9c.; ‡**-ipedia**, shoemaker's last 15c., 1483; **-ositas**, quality of imparting form (phil.) c 1370, 1378; **-osus**, form-giving c 1370; exemplary 15c.; **-osiusculus**, good-looking c 1620; **-ola**, (?) small cheese 1351; **-ula**, cheese-mould 1316, 1390; bullet-mould 1381; tracery of window 1337; papal bull 1241; shape, image c 700; pattern, ideal 793; **-ule** (*pl.*), print, type 1518; **-ularium**, technical-ity 1609; **-ifico**, to give shape to 9c.; **-ito**, to form habitually 1344; **-o**, to inform c 1350; to declare 1306; **f. appellum**, to draw up appeal 1291; **f. pacem** c 1228, c 1362; **f. pannum** c 1429; **-ulo**, to formu-late 1456.

formannus, tenant of quarter virgate 1281, 1336; *see also* **forwardmannus**.

form/entada, -itta, *see* FRUMENT

formic/e (*pl.*), formica, abscess (med.) a 1250, ‡1652; **-aleon**, ant-lion 12c., a 1250; **-arium**, ant-heap ‡c 1440, 1620; **-o**, to hoard 1180.

formid/amen, terror c 1250; **-abiliter**, for-midably c 1250; †**-alis**, formidable 1461; ‡**-inosus, -olus**, fearful 1483; **-olositas**, fear, timidity c 1102, 15c.

forn-, *see also* **furn-**

forn/dalum, -dellum, -edellum, *see* **fer-della**.

fornicale, *see* FORM

fornic/atoria, fornication 1227; **-arius** c 1197, 1518, **-osus** a 1200, of or for fornication; **-o**, to fornicate c 1325.

forni/cus, -secus, *see* **fora**.

forniforus, *see* **phernophorus**.

fornix, *see* **ornix**.

foro, *see* **forum**.

for/pices 793. c 1120, 1421, ‡**-peculae** 1483, 1570, shears, scissors (*pl.*); *cf.* **forcipes, forfices**.

for/prisa, exception 1285, a 1300; **-ispriso**, to except 1660.

forr-, *see* **foragium**; FURR

fors/arium, -erium, -erum, *see* 1 **for-cerium**.

forsbannitus, *see* FORISBANN

for/scheta, -escheta 1399, **terra -sutata** 13c., (?) projecting piece of land (M.E. 'forthshetere') (Oxf.).

fors/ementum, -io, *see* FORTI

forsetum, (?) stock of an arblast 1260.

forsfangium, *see* **forfangium**.

forso (**lanam**), to 'force', clip 1460.

forstallitium, *see* **fortalitia**.

1 *****forstall/um** 1256, 1375, **forestalium** 1308, **-agium** 1290, 1419, ***-amentum** 1306, 1419, **forestallamentum** 1419, **for-stellamentum** 1357, **-aria** 1330, c 1540, **forstellaria** 1357, **foristalria** 1419, †**for-staria** 1547, **-atio** c 1290, 1375, forestalling the market; **-arius** c 1290, 1333, **fore-stallarius** c 1400, 1448, **-ator** 1324, 1419, **foristallator** (?) 13c., 1426, †**fristallator** 1439, forestaller; ***-o** c 1300, 1426, **fore-**

stallo 1276, 1308, **forisstallo** 1426, to forestall the market.

2 **forstall/um** 1249, 1306, **forestallum** a 1185, c 1305, **foristeallum** c 1115, **fore-stellum, foristellum** 1086, **-atio** 1535, **transgressio foris-stallis** (?) 13c., 'fore-stall', waylaying (esp. to recover impounded cattle or prevent recovery of stolen cattle); **forestallum** 1275, **-atio** 1184, encroach-ment, obstruction; ***-o**, to waylay, assault 1288, 1391.

3 **forstallum** 1285, 1375, **foristallum** c 1250, 1287, 'forestall', 'fostal', piece of land in front of building (Kent).

forsula, *see* FORTI

forsutatus, *see* **forscheta**.

forsveia, *see* **forisveia**.

*****fort/alitia, -alitium** 1254, 1588, †**forstalli-tium** (G.) 1313, **-alacia** c 1255, **-alecium** 1254, **-alisium** 1341, **-elescum** 1234, **-eletium** 1285, **-elitia, -elitium** 1200, 1343, **-ilescia** 1202, **-ilitium** 1461, **-elet-tum** (? *or* **forcelettum**) 1234, 1348, **fosseletum** 1314, **-iletta, -ilettum** c 1366, c 1400, †**-iligatum** 1523, **-ilagium** 1556, **-ericia** c 1227, 1255, fortalice, forcelet, fortress (esp. Fr.); **-ellatus** 1448, **-allatus, furtellatus** 1459, protected by forts.

fortanimus, resolute c 1398.

forte, *see* **fortitudo**.

*****forti/a** (**forci-**), force, power, violence c 1115, a 1564; **frisca f.** 1276, a 1564, **freschya f.** 1284, **frecheforc(i)a** c 1284, (assize of) fresh force (leg.); **-iunculum** c 1360, **forsula** c 1336, small fort; **-amentum** (**plegiorum, curie**), afforcement (leg.) 1230, c 1285; 1203, 1298, **forsementum** c 1250, deforce-ment (leg.); **-atum** c 1411, **forzatum** c 1180, second part of *Digest* (*cf.* **infortia-tum**); **forsio** (**curiam**), to afforce (leg.) 1276; **-o**, to deforce (leg.) c 1250; **-o** (**castellum**), to fortify c 1293, c 1437; †**ferto**, to force, compel 1389.

fortific/atio, fortification (arch.) c 1310, 16c.; corroboration 1427; **f. missae**, celebration of mass c 1483; **-abilis**, strengthening c 1362; **-o**, to fortify (arch.) 1277, 1461; to corroborate 1267, 1467.

fortisipes, *see* **forcipes**.

fort/itudo, *****force, violence, an armed force 1136, c 1397; celestial power (astr.) c 730. a 1282, c 1470; strength (of liquor) 13c.; overweight 1282; validity 15c.; stronghold, fortress 15c.; **-is**, strong (of liquor) c 1180, 1495; above standard weight 1222, 1425; (*sc.* **moneta**) sound money 1268; (*subst.*) c 1343, **domus f.** (G.) 1314, fort, fortalice; **-e**, strongly 13c., c 1540; **-iter**, strongly, with a large quantity 13c.; **-ius** 1444, **a -iori** c 1337, a 1343, by stronger reasoning; **-ioratio**, reinforcement 1384; **-ioro**, to reinforce, strengthen 1384; *see also* **aqua, herba, manus**.

fort/uia c 1200, c 1260, **-ua** 13c., 1270, 'forty', furlong (*cf.* 2 **quadragena**).

fortun/a, casual profit 1185, 1281; treasure trove c 1290; **-ula**, small fortune 1517; **-ium**, fortune, blessing c 1000. 13c., 1480; tournament 1241; **-alis**, of fortune, casual c 1250, c 1253; †**-issimus**, most fortunate c 1434; **-osus,** fortunate 15c.; **-o,** to risk, hazard 14c., 1388.

for/uius, scabbard a 1200; c 1178, 14c., **-olus** 1230, **-ellus** 1084, 1300, **furulus** c 1220, **furellus** 1225, 1285, 'forel', case or box (esp. that kept by marshal in Exchequer); **-ellus** 1265, **furellus** 1316, part of harness; **ferrellus,** quiver 1221.

for/um, trading, bargain c 1202, 1213; market price 1203, a 1408; *law-court, jurisdiction c 1160, c 1443; **f. anime** c 1344, **f. conscientie** 1330, c 1470, **f. penitentie** a 1290, c 1357, **f. penitentiale** 1204, c 1443, penitential jurisdiction; **f. contentiosum,** contentious jurisdiction c 1339, c 1443; **f. ecclesiasticum** 1220, c 1430, **f. ecclesie** 1282, c 1343; **f. personale,** private correction 1264; **f. presidis, f. proconsulis,** county court c 1160; **f. regium** 1291, **f. soli** c 1180, royal jurisdiction; a 1150, 1313, **f. liberum** 1276, **f. mercatorium** 1303, public market; **f. Jovis,** Thursday market 1336; **jus -i,** secular law 12c., c 1334; **ad bonum f.** 1251, **bono -o** c 1470, 'good cheap', cheaply; **pro meliori -o** 1328; **ad rationabile f.** 13c.; **-alis,** of or for a market c 1300, 1608; *-i (*pl.*) 1252, 1348, †**-es** 1310, laws (esp. G.); **-o,** to buy 1419; **-iso,** to bargain c 1444.

for/urda, -uhtha, *see* **forerda.**

‡**forus,** wine-press 1483; *see also* **forum.**

forward/mannus 1280, 1330, **fordward-mannus** 1327, **fordwarmannus** 1328, **forewardmannus** 1262, 1479, **forewar-mannus** 1303, †**-inus** 1315, 1480, **for-mannus** 1284, 'forwardman', guild officer.

forzatum, *see* **fortia.**

forzerum, *see* **1 forcerium.**

foss/a 1166, c 1236, **f. juise** 1169, **f. juisii** 1168, ordeal-pit; dike, embankment c 1395; eye-socket c 1325; 1256, 1434, **-atum** 1243, 1256, coal-pit; **f. lapidum,** quarry 1086; **-agium** a 1180, 1687, **-atum** 1113, 1203, (dues paid for) service of digging; **-ale** c 1145, 1290, *-ata 1180, 15c., **-atum** 1086, c 1450, **-atus** c 1155, c 1452, **-eta** a 1268, **-etum** c 1184, c 1550, **foscetum** 1329, **-eium, -eum** c 1182, **-is** a 1290, 1461, **-us** c 1190, ditch, dike, moat, embankment; **-ata maris** 1359, **-atum maris** 1316, **-edum maris** c 1200, sea-wall; **-atum salvationis,** protective embankment 1380; **-ataria,** (?) system of dikes 1396; **-icula,** little ditch 1293; **-ula,** little hollow a 1150; ovary c 1210, a 1250; **-atio** 1327, 1513, **-atura** c 1397, **-ura** 1280, 1422, digging, trenching; **-ura,** mining 1227; **-arius** 1086, 1320, **-ator** 1086, 1336, **-eator** 1245, **-atorius** 1181, digger, trencher; **-orium** a 1135, c 1443, **ferramentum -orium** c 1090, spade; **-o,** to dig, trench c 1180, 1566; to surround with a moat c 1362, 1448; *cf.* **fodiatio.**

fosseletum, *see* **fortalitia.**

fossellum, *see* **vas.**

fossiculus, *see* **fasciculus.**

fotaver/agium c 1285, c 1300, **-ium** 1310, carrying-service on foot (Kent).

fotclutum, clout on plough-foot 1268.

fot/geldum (forgeldum) a 1070, 1549, **-egel-**

dum 1354, a forest fine (?) for not hambling dogs.

fother-, *see* **fodera;** FURR

fot/io, cherishing c 1500; **-or,** fomenter c 1190; **-rix,** nurse (fig.) c 1378, 1412; **foveo larem,** to keep house 1281, 1406.

*****fot/mellum** 1222, c 1409, **-mallus** 1303, c 1341, **-emallus** c 1341, †**fontinellum** a 1310, **votmellum** 1302, c 1335, 'fotmel', measure of lead.

foudra, *see* **fodera.**

foulericius, *see* FULL

foun-, *see* FEON

fouragium, *see* **foragium.**

fourra, *see* FURR

fousura, *see* VOLU

fove/a, dike, embankment 957; coal-pit 1288, 1293; moat c 1130, 1455; **f. judiciaria,** ordeal-pit c 1160, a 1185; **f. pro molendino** 1419; **f. secretaria,** privy c 1250; **-ator,** ditcher 1295; **-o,** to pierce 1573; *see also* **fotio.**

†**fovero,** (?) *f.l.* for **superonero,** to overstock c 1290.

foyneo, to grub, rout (of pigs) 1248.

fraccin-, *see* FRAXIN

†**frachifitatio,** (?) breaking up (of uncultivated land) 1208; *cf.* **fracticium, 2 friscus.**

fracmen, *see* **fragmen.**

‡**frac/tillum** c 1440, ‡**-ulus** 15c., ‡**fraxillus, fretellum** 1483, "pepper-quern".

‡**fractill/us,** "dag of a gown" c 1440, 1483; **-atus,** jagged, cut in points 1450; ‡**-osus,** raggy 1483.

fract/io, *breaking c 1194, c 1580; breaking out (of prison) 1203, p 1460; fraction (math.) a 1150, 1686; refraction (phys.) a 1233, 1267; loss of wine through breakage (of cask) 1300; (?) enervation a 1250; **f. arresti,** breach of arrest 1380; **f. assise,** breach of assize 1330, 15c.; **f. corporis Domini** c 1362, **f. hostie** c 1500, **f. panis** c 1380, c 1550; **f. crucis,** (?) sacrilege 1304; **f. domorum,** house-breaking, burglary 1199, 1583; **f. capelle** 1195; **f. ecclesie** c 1303; **f. jejunii,** breakfast 1480; **f. pacis,** breach of peace a 1135, c 1380; **f. quarere,** quarrying 1371; **f. physica** c 1444; **f. vulgaris** (math.) 1267; **dies fraxionis,** (?) day of breaking fences round meadow 1467; **-or,** wrong-doer, criminal 691; prison-breaker c 1290, 1306; **f. assise** 1246; **f. ecclesiarum,** robber who breaks into churches 1217; **f. quarrere,** quarry-man 1276; **f. sepium** c 1482; ‡**-icius,** brittle 1483; **-ivus,** cracking, crackling c 1115, 13c.; **-icium** c 1135, c 1260, **-ura** 12c., newly broken land; **-ura,** breaking down of spirit, despondency c 1190; refraction a 1233; **f. burgi** c 1115, **f. domorum** c 1115, 1201, house-breaking; **f. gaole,** breaking out of gaol a 1540; **f. legis,** fine, penalty c 1102; **f. monete,** right to coin c 1102; **f. navium,** right of wreck a 1188; **f. ordinis,** injury to one in holy orders c 1102; **f. ossium,** fracture (med.) 14c.; **f. pacis,** breach of peace c 1080, c 1414; **f. petre,** stone-breaking 1364, 1372; **f. plena,** fatal injury c 1115; **cum uno -u penne,** at the cost of a feather (C.I.) 1331; **-e,** by refraction 1267;

-a (*n. pl.*), broken objects 1383; **-um aque,** (?) *for* **fretum** *or* **frettum,** (?) ferry 1319; **-us,** fractional (math.) 1686; *see also* **cantus, lana;**

frang/ibilis, fragile c 1250, 1267; ‡**-ibulum,** kneading-trough 1570; **-itivus,** tending to break a 1250; **-o,** refract a 1233; to fail c 1115; to swear (oath) clause by clause or word by word c 1115, 13c.; **f. baculum,** to deprive of office c 1155, c 1258; **f. domum,** to break into a house 1200, 1583; **f. prisonam (carcerem, gaolam),** to break out of prison 1220, 1440; **f. quarreram,** to quarry stones 1371, 1375; **frego,** to break open c 1500; **fringo,** to break 805. c 1257; to quash c 1270.

fraell/a 1230, 1395, **-us** 1197, 1410, **-um** 1384, **fraiellus** 1228, 1420, **fraillus** c 1217, **freellus** 1218, 1227, **frellus** a 1204, **fragella, fregella** 1295, **fredlus** 1202, **frethlus** 1204, 'frail', basket; **fraill' de armur'** 1397; **-atus,** packed in frails 1419; **-o,** to pack (armour) 1325.

fraeria, *see* FRATER

frag/aria a 1250, 1634, (?) **-ula** a 1250, strawberry-plant; **-ifer,** bearing strawberries 1634; **frasum** 1265, **fresum** 1316, strawberry.

fragella, *see* **fraella.**

fragium, *see* FOC

frag/men juris regalis, breach of the peace (*grithbryce*) c 1140; **fracmen,** *for* **-men,** 8c.; **-mentillum** 1520, **-mentulum** c 1530, ‡**-illum** 1483, crumb, particle; ‡**-illus,** grater 15c.; **-iliter,** insecurely 1345; **-efacio,** to break up 1344; **-orico,** to be noisy, resound c 550.

fragr-, *see* **flagrantia.**

‡**fragus,** "wrist, knuckle" (*recte* knee-joint) 15c.

frai/atio 1343, c 1372, **fraura** 1297, **freura** 1190, 1250, **frixura** c 1320, burnishing; **fraerium** 1303, **fraorium** 1297, **fraura** 1289, burnisher; **-o** 1297, 1343, **freio** 1190, 1213, **frao** 1305, to burnish (O.F. *froier*); *cf.* FRIC

fraillus, fraiellus, *see* **fraella.**

fram/a 1159, 1448, **-ea** 1265, 1475, **-um** 1551, frame; **-atio,** hewing 1401, c 1550; framing 1446; **-atura,** framework 1181; **-iatus,** framed, timbered (arch.) a 1500; **-is,** measure of woad 13c.; **-paldum,** frame-pole 1277; **-o,** to frame 1393, 1465.

framen, knife c 550.

francinus, *see* FRAXIN

Franciscanus, Franciscan 1537, 1586.

†**francnatus,** (?) *f.l.* for **superannatus,** 1200.

francursina, *see* **branca ursina.**

franc/us 1086, 1313, **-o** 1086, **-alis** (G.) 1280, 1283, free; **f. bancus** 1217, 1419, **-bancus** 1248, free-bench, widow's dower (leg.); **franchia moltura** (Fr.) 1419; **-us plegius** 1234, 1300, **-um plegium** 1185, 1535, †**fraschumplegium** 1284, **-iplegius** 1300, 1437, **-plegia** 1274, **-plegium** 1179, 1203, **-plegum** 1191, **-plegius, frangplegius, franplegius** 1276, frankpledge (leg.); **-opleggiagium,** suit of frankpledge 1278; **-us tenens** 1176, c 1192, **-otenens** 1166, c 1250, **-alingus** 1167,

-elengus c 1160, **-alanus** 12c., a 1300, **-elanus** c 1188, c 1258, **-ilanus** c 1154, **-olanus** 1166, 1270, **-elenus** 12c., 1203, **-olinus** 1201, **-olensis** 1166, **-alis** (G.) 1222, free-holder, franklin; *see also* **eleemosyna, feodum, firma, incensum, lapis, maritagium, petra, plastrum, servitium, terra, warenna;** **-agium** c 1250, **-ale** 1289, payment for protection (G.); **-alia** (*pl.*), fields exempt from certain dues or under special protection (G.) 1190; **-bordum** 1318, 1393, **-bordium** c 1372, free-board, land outside fence; **-um,** (?) free range for poultry or pigs 1318, 1419; **-um censum,** frankincense 1573; **-halimotum,** (?) free hall-moot (Salop) 1255;

franch/afalda, free fold (man.) 1298; **-asia** c 1500, *-**esia** 1230, 1587, **-ezia** 1577, **-isia** 12c., 1587, **-icia** 1407, **-esa** 1475, **-eisa** c 1150, **-isa** c 1200, 1269, **fraunchesia** 1421, **franquesia** (G.) 1289, franchise, liberty; **-esia ecclesiastica,** sanctuary 1393; **acquitantia -iata,** free quittance 1269; **-esio** 1413, 1417, **-isio** 1413 **-eso** 1554, **-ifico** 1227, **-io** 1169, 1279, to enfranchise.

*****Franc/us** a 710, c 900. a 1070, c 1422, **-anus** c 1530, **-icus** 12c., *****-igena** c 1000, 1041. a 1084, c 1450, **-igenis** c 1400, **-igenus** 1086, 1414, **Fransigenus** 1467, **-iscus** 1233, 1258, French, Frenchman; 'Frank' (Greek name for any Westerner) c 1190; *see also* **flos;** **-us (auri)** 1375, 1461, **-icus** 1521, (gold) franc; **-ice,** in French 12c.; **-igena,** French language c 1308; **terra -igena,** black vitriol c 1215; **-igeno,** to be Frenchified c 1315.

frang-, *see also* FRACT; **frengia.**

frang/or, (?) *for* **fragor,** noise c 550; **-osus, flangosus,** (?) noisy c 550.

franquesia, *see* **francus.**

fra/o, -orium, *see* FRAI

frappa (*pl.*), frapping, rigging (naut.) 1436.

fraschumplegium, *see* **francus.**

fraseus, *for* **fresus,** shelled (of beans) 1242.

frass-, *see* 2 **friscus.**

frasum, *see* **fragaria.**

frater/, *****member of religious order c 730, c 1000. 1070, 1539; *****friar** 1225, c 1565; 1108, 1432, *****f. conversus** 12c., 1570, **f. laicus** c 1220, c 1296, lay brother; **f. adjuratus** 12c., **f. conjuratus** 12c., c 1210, **f. claustri** 1250, **f. de claustro** 1342, **f. conventualis** c 1250, fellow monk; **f. gilde** 1322, 1539, **f. guildehalle** 1604, guildbrother; **f. in armis,** brother in arms 1461; **f. in lege,** brother-in-law 1419, ‡15c.; **f. officialis,** obedientiary (mon.) a 1216; **f. regularis,** canon regular 1131; **f. griseus** c 1400, *****f. minor** 1225, 1557, **f. minorum** c 1225, c 1400, **f. minorita** 1559, 1593, Franciscan; **f. (minor) de Observantia** 1490, 1549; **f. niger** 1413, 1527, *****f. predicator** 1229, 1567, Dominican; **f. de Pica** c 1250, 1290, **f. Pye** a 1422, Pied Friar; **f. (ordinis) S. Trinitatis (et Captivorum),** Mathurine 1246, 1471; **f. ordinis B. Marie de Areno** 1316; **f. de Domina** 1290; *see also* **Augustinensis,** CARMEL, **crux,** EREM, MENDIC, PENIT, PERDON, SACC; **-culus** 1562, **fratricellus** c 1590, friar

(contemptuous); **-cule** (*vocative*) 815; **frae-ria**, guild 1318; **-ia** 1295, **fraria** a 1233 ('Ho-spitalis Hierusalem'), brotherhood; **fraeria** 1338, **fraria** 1338, 1540, contribution (for confraternity) paid to Hospitallers; **-nale lumen**, light used at funeral 1414; *-**nalis** c 1250, 1564, **-nicus** c 1415, fraternal; **-naliter** 1389, 1536, †-**nitaliter** 1517, fraternally; **-natio**, fraternity a 1452, c 1476; letter of fraternity a 1250; **-nitas**, brotherly love (eccl.); *fraternity (title) 597, 811. c 1080, 1440; *membership of community (esp. mon.) c 1080, c 1468; guild c 1353, 1583; guild-house 1426; **fratorium**, meeting of members of a brotherhood 1307; **fratralis**, brotherly, friarly 1523; ‡-**na** 15c., ‡**fratria** 1483, ‡**fratruela** 15c., niece; **fratruus** c 730. c 1118, **fratruelus** c 1250, ‡15c., nephew; **fratrisso**, to take after one's brother c 1250, c 1534.
fratto, *see* FRETT
fraud/enter c 1362, **-ilenter** c 1408, **-olenter** 1320, **-ulose** 1275, 1367, deceitfully; **-ulens** c 1430, **-ulosus** c 1390, deceitful; **-ulo** 968, **frudo** c 973, to deceive.
fraunchesia, *see* francus.
fraura, *see* FRAI
fraxillus, *see* fractillum.
fraxin/a c 1339, **fraccinus** c 1250, 1583, **fraxennus** 1280, **francinus** 1360, **frena** c 1240, **frenis** 1401, **frenus** 1284, c 1323, *for* **-us**, ash tree; ‡-**aria**, (?) chervil *or* goutweed (bot.) 14c.; **-etum** 1086, 1233, ‡**fraccinetum** 15c., ash-grove; ‡**fraccinum**, ash-key 15c.
freborga, *see* friborga.
frecheforcia, *see* fortia.
frecinga, *see* fressingus.
fredallus, *see* frethellus.
fred/um, **-wita**, *see* FRITH
freellus, **fredlus**, **fregella**, **frellus**, *see* fraella.
frego, *see* FRACT
freio, *see* FRAI
freitum, *see* 1 fretta.
fremefeuda, *see* flima.
fremesco, to shudder c 1390.
fren-, *see also* FRAXIN; PHREN
‡**frendis**, *for* nefrendus, boar 15c.
freng/ia 1303, 1402, **-a** 1283, **frangia** 1368, **fringa** 1553, fringe; *cf.* FIMBRI
fren/um aquaticum, bridle for watering horses c 1366; **-um monachale**, bridle (with crosses) for use by monks 1415; **-alis**, pertaining to a bridle a 1446; **ars -ifactiva**, art of bridle-making c 1343.
frequent/atio, frequentation c 1238; frequent repetition c 1290, 1424; ‡"soken" c 1440; **-abilis**, resorted to c 1343; **-ativus**, repeated c 930. 12c.; **-ela**, retinue, suite c 1070; **-ia**, frequency 7c. c 1239, 1424; suit, service 1327; **-or**, to frequent, haunt 790; to say repeatedly c 1437.
fres-, *see also* FRIS
fresc-, *see* fressingus; friscus (1 & 2).
fresellus, fringe (O.F. *fresel*) 1220, 1291.
‡**fresgunda** 14c., ‡**frisgo** 15c., butcher's broom (bot.).
fressingus c 1300, **fresceng/a** 12c., **-ia** 12c., 1202, **frecinga** 1089, 1240, **fresscencia**

porci 1353, porker, sucking-pig (Fr. *frésange*).
fresum, *see* fragaria.
fretellum, *see* fractillum.
frethellus 1283, 1373, **fredallus** 1380, tenant by form of serjeanty, *fritheil* (Sc.); **frithelagium**, serjeanty (Sc.) c 1250, 1272.
Fretherícalis, adherent of Frederick II c 1255.
frethio, *see* fraella.
frethlus, *see* fraella.
freth/um, **-erus**, *see* fritha.
fretin/a 1333, 1335, **-um** c 1223, silver coin, *frétin*.
fretisfragium, breakwater 1453.
1 *frett/a, **-um** 1204, 1419, †**freitum** 1303, *-**agium** 1292, 1443, **-amentum** 1404, **-atio** 1307, 1312, **-ura** 1301, freight, freighting; **carta -agii**, bill of lading 1333; *-**o**, to freight, load 1227, 1417.
2 **frett/a**, **-um** 1203, 15c., **-ura** 1295, c 1315 ornament, diaper, embroidery; **-a**, fret (her.) p 1394, a 1446, **-atus**, fretted (her.) p 1394, a 1446; **-us**, embroidered c 1315; fretted (arch.) 15c.; **-o** 1205, 15c., **frato** 1220, **fricto** c 550. 1530, to embroider, diaper.
3 *frett/a 1302, 1372, **frutta** 1297, 1364, 'fret', hoop fitted to hub of wheel; **-o** c 1275, 1372, **fratto** 1374, **fricto** 1342, **frutto** 1318, 1355, to bind (with hoops).
freura, *see* FRAI
freyturari/um, refectory (mon.) 1260; **-us**, refectorer 13c.
frib-, *see also* FRIV
friborga (†**frithborga**) a 1130, a 1135, **freborga** 1178, **frithburgus** c 1258, frankpledge.
fric/amen, grinding c 1191, c 1200; **-abilis**, friable 14c.; **-o**, to burnish 1321 (*cf.* FRAI); **frixo**, to rub down c 1182; *see also* FRIX
frich-, **frictus**, *see* 2 friscus.
fricto, *see* FRETT (2 & 3).
frid-, **frigesoca**, *see* FRITH
†**frigdata** (*pl.*), (?) nuts c 1180.
frig/efactio, chilling c 1267; **-efactibilis**, able to be chilled c 1300; ‡**herba -ida**, liverwort 14c.; **-iditas**, coldness c 1160, 1652; ‡-**or**, ague 1483; **-oriticus**, (?) sufferer from ague 13c.; ‡-**orosus**, cold c 1440, 1483; **-efacio** a 1233, 1625, to chill; **-efio**, to be chilled c 1267.
frigell-, *see* fringillarius, frugella.
frightum, **frihtum**, *see* 2 friscus.
frigo, *see* FRIX
frigula (*pl.*), crude earthenware pots c 940, 10c.
fringa, *see* frengia.
fringillarius, hobby (bird) 1544; ‡**frig/ella** c 1440, 1483, ‡-**illa** 15c., 1570, robin; ‡**frugella**, chaffinch 1570; **-ellus**, finch *or* robin 1267, ‡15c.; *see also* FRUG
fringo, *see* FRACT
†**frino**, (?) *f.l.* for *ferme*, 1498.
frio, *see* frium.
1 **friscus**, *fresh (not salt) 1225, 1573; raw, untanned 1298, 1383; recent, *see* fortia; **caseus f.** 1297; **butyrum -um** 1366; **fresca**, fresh water 13c.; **frescoura**, coolness 1622.

H

2 *frisc/us a 1220, 1549, fruscus 13c., frissus c 1283, frictus 1255, c 1283, fallow or newly broken (of land); *-um 1199, 1379, -a, -ia 1227, 1357, fresca 12c., frichea 1381, firsa 1274, 1431, (?) fursa a 1175, frixcum 1261, frichtum 1285, frightum 1274, frihtum 1335, frusheum 1235, frussatum 1196, *frussetum c 1185, 1333, fruissetum c 1185, frussitium 1175, 1222, frucisium 1222, frussura a 1200, 1345, frissura 1299, 1430, †fissura 1230, frassura 1271, 'frith', ley or newly broken land (cf. fritha); frussura domus, house-breaking c 1200; f. (frissura) lapidum, stone-breaking 1355; frusco 1241, 1334, frusso 1200, 1339, frussio 1228, 1252, fruissio 1220, 1232, frassio 15c., to break up (land), bring into cultivation; frusso, to crush (apples) 1272.

frisesomoron, a logical mood 13c., c 1380.

frisgo, see fresgunda.

‡frisgula, chavender (fish) 15c.; cf. strengula.

fris/ia 1388, -ium 1390, 1415, -io c 1296, -ius pannus 1421, fresa 1457, frieze; -sones (pl.), 'frisons', sort of woollen material 1324; -io 1402, -o 1404, to frieze or fringe.

Fris/ius 10c., -ensis 1347, -io c 1188, -o c 900. 12c., 1347, Frixo a 1130, Fres/ius, c 1298, -us 12c., c 1250, -o c 730. c 1118, c 1250, Freiso c 950, Frisian; -o 1313, equus -onus c 1320, 'frison'.

frisoca, see FRITH

friss-, see 2 friscus.

fristallator, see 1 forstallum.

fritha, 'frith', woodland pasture (W.) 1390, 1443; †freth/um, (?) hedge (Durh.) 1369; -erus, hedger, wattler 1498; vrydo, to 'frith', wattle (Somerset) 1438; cf. 2 friscus.

frith/borga, -burgus, see friborga.

frithelagium, see frethellus.

frith/gildum, 'frith-guild', guild for maintenance of peace c 1115; -mannus, man within the king's peace c 1115; -motum 1443, fridmotum 1278, fridmanesmotum 1250, 'frith-moot', forest court (Cheshire); fridesocna 1189, fridsocna 1198, frigesocna, frigsoca, frisoca 1086, 'frith-soken', asylum, sanctuary; -wita 1286, fridwita 1321, fredwita 1199, 1286, fine for breach of peace (cf. fihtwita, fyrdwita); †frugabulum, (?) 'frith-silver' 13c.; †fredum, (?) fine or composition c 1140; frethio, to pardon 1412.

fritilla, see FRIX

fri/um 12c., c 1320, -tum 1281, fry (of fish); -o, to spawn 1269.

friv/ophilus, trifler 1344, 1427; -olose c 1150, -olanter c 1362, foolishly; -ulus 1518, fribolus 10c., for -olus; fribolum, wretched or unworthy object 969; †fribulus, unstable c 550.

friw/a, -arius, see FRUG

frix/atio 1481, ‡-atura 15c., 1483, fricatura 1329, frying; -ina c 1220, -ura 13c., c 1450, ‡fritilla 1570, (?) frutellum 13c., pancake; -orius 1313, -irius 1388, ‡-atorius 1483, for frying; *-orium, frying-pan, griddle or grid-iron c 1200, 1551; -ura, burning,

enkindling 7c.; frigo, to enkindle 70.; see also FRAI, FRIC, 2 friscus.

frocagium, see FOC

*frocc/us c 1072, c 1500, -a 1506, c 1509, froggus 13c., 1300, floccus 1351, 1388, flocculus c 1250, frock (mon.).

frodwita, see FYRD

‡frond/etum, "bob of leaves" 1570; ‡-ator, "titmouse" 15c.; -icomus, -uosus, leafy c 550.

frons 1401, c 1511, *front/ale 1279, c 1450, -allum 1295, c 1507, -ellum 1269, 1460, -ella c 1500, -inellum 1432, -inella 1345, -atellum 1483, fruntale 1407, fruntellum 1241, frountelium 1445, -iarium 1521, -erium c 1266, c 1330, pannus -alis c 1250, 1295, altar frontal or frontlet (eccl.); -ilectum, altar frontlet, superfrontal 1388; -agium, (payment for) frontage 1252, 1462; -era, foreland, promontory 1427; 1374, frunterum p 1377, front (of embankment); frontier-post 1378; 1391, 1434, -eria, -erium a 1347, 1444, -oria c 1400, -orius c 1400, -ura 1378, 1447, frontier; -ispicium, front, façade, countenance c 730. c 1125, 1620; f. (libri), frontispiece 1609; -ose, shamelessly 12c., 1461; see also fons.

froto, to rub (Fr. frotter) 1291.

†froxhalmum, (?) reed-bed c 1227.

frucisium, see 2 friscus.

fructico, see FRUT

fruct/us 1307, frutuyra c 1350, fruit (coll.); -us primi (pl.) 1308, a 1347, f. primi anni 1318, first-fruits; f. salmonum, salmon-fry, spawn c 1394; -ificatio, bearing of fruit 12c., c 1362; -ificus 1252, †-iforus 1432, fruitful; -uarius c 1136, p 1340, frutarius a 1212, fruterius 1212, fruiterer; *-ifico 1086, 1427, -ificor (dep.) c 730. c 1414, -ifero 1435, to bear fruit.

frudo, see FRAUD

frugabulum, see FRITH

frug/ella 1361, ‡c 1440, ‡frigella 15c. (cf. fringillarius), -a 1282, fruis 1277, 1366, friwa 1235, 1257, rook (Fr. freux); friwarius, rook-scarer 1232, 1235.

frugi/lega, rook 1544; -fer, transporting grain c 1200; -vura, devouring of crops 1238.

fruis, see frugella.

fruiss-, see 2 friscus.

fru/itio, c 1569, -itus c 1376, †-ictium 13c., fruition, enjoyment; -ibilis, enjoyable, beatific a 1290, 1345; -ibilitas, enjoyability p 1300; -o, for -or, 5c.

*frument/um, wheat c 700. 1086, 15c.; f. Saracenicum, buckwheat 1634; see also granum; -alis, under wheat 1296; ‡-arium, granary 1570; -eus 14c., -iceus c 1363, 1537, wheaten; ‡-icium 1483, furmentum 1338, 'frumenty', 'furmety', wheat porridge; †formitta, wheaten cake c 1414; formentada, a wheat duty (G.) 1233; oleum -inum, oil of wheat a 1250.

frumgildum, first payment of weregeld (A.S.) c 1115.

frunciatus, 'frounced', flounced 1331.

fruncina, calf-skin, vellum (O.F. froncine) 1303.

frun/itor 1406, 1504, -itarius 1504, ‡-es 15c., tanner; ‡-itorium 15c., †frumitorium

1711, tan-house; ‡-ium, "bark, powder for leather" c 1440; -io 1389, 1414, ‡-ito 15c., †frutino 1581, to tan.

frunt-, *see* frons.

frusc-, frush-, fruss-, *see* 2 friscus.

frust/ramen, obstacle, thwarting c 950; -rabilis, subject to frustration c 950. 1344, 1374; -raneus, vain 16c.; -ratorie, deceitfully c 1190, c 1400; vainly c 1470; -ratorius, deceitful (eccl.); vain c 1361, c 1430; -o, *for* -ro, to frustrate c 1470.

frust/um, lump, piece: -rum a 1087, c 1404; -um, bundle 1214; f. coni, f. conicum (math.) 1686; f. terre 1086, f. prati c 1185, plot; -ratim c 1180, 1276, -im c 1293, *for* -atim, piecemeal; -ro, to break in pieces c 1180, 13c.

frut-, *see also* FRUCT

frutellum, *see* FRIX

frut/icetum, thorn-brake: fruitectum, briar-bush 1263; -esco (*for* -icesco) 1153, fructico (*for* -ico) c 1125, to put forth shoots.

frutino, *see* FRUN

frutt-, *see* 3 fretta.

fu, *see* pheu.

fua-, *see* FOC

fucatio, dyeing c 1340; deception c 1150.

fuc/ellus, -illus, *see* fusillus.

fucin/a, -ula, *see* fuscina.

fudra, *see* fodera.

fueodum, *see* FEOD

fug/a, pursuit c 1178; 1239, -acia c 1130, 1293, chase, place for hunting or right to hunt; drove-way, right to drive animals 1272, c 1321; f. demonum, St. John's wort (bot.) ‡14c., 1634; -abilis, movable c 1250; fit for the chase 1292, 1384; drivable 14c.; -atio, driving away, pursuit c 1115, c 1390; *(right of) hunting a 1130, 1419; *driving (of animals) 1390, 1535; driving in (of piles) 1333, 1388; -ator 1130, 1235, -atarius 1157, -atorius 1167, courser (horse); 1242, 1398, figator 1279, ‡-arius 15c., driver, drover; f. carruce c 1290, 1364; f. plaustri 1450; -ibilis, perishable c 1200; to be shunned 13c., 1378; -itio, flight c 1366; -itivus, belonging to a fugitive (Sc.) 1373; fleeting, transitory 956; † (?) slight 794; -itorius, fugitive 1269; -atus, exile 838; -o *a 1130, 1419, f. ad 1243, to hunt; to drive (cattle, *etc.*) 1221, a 1452; to drive in (piles) 1325, 1397; *f. carrucam 1248, c 1362; -o, *for* -io, to flee 1239, 1330.

fugellum, *see* FOC

fugera, *see* filix.

‡fugile, abscess in ear 1652.

‡fugill/um, flint or steel 1483; ‡-ator, "fire-striker" 1468, 1483; ‡-o, to strike fire c 1440, 1483; *cf.* FOC

fuillata, *see* FOLI

†fuistallum, (?) *for* finstallum, refinery (for salt) 1328.

fula, *see* filo.

ful/cimen, leg, foot c 550; -cimentum, book-rest c 1340; -crum, hoof c 550; bed 10c.; -citor, supporter 12c.; -tura, buttress p 1550; -sus, lofty c 1380.

fulda, *see* falda.

fulemarta, (payment of) mart, fatted beast (Sc.) 1468, 1496.

‡fulful, faufel, peppercorn (Ar.) *or* oak-gall 14c.

fulg/entia, brilliance c 1250; -oratio, lightning c 870; -oreus, bright c 550; -ureus, lightning-charged 9c.; -eo erga, to favour 1290; -esco 8c., 9c., ‡-ido 1483, to shine, be clear; -oro, to lighten c 870.

ful/ica, coot: ‡"mavis" c 1200; ‡-ica, -iga, -ceca, filica, "sea-mew" 15c.; felica, (?) a water-bird a 1275; ‡filicus, "teal-cock" 15c.

fulignosus, soot-black c 670.

full/a, -us, (?) full measure (of ale) 1389.

full/atio 1269, 1487, -atura 1465, 1587, -onia 1300, fulling; follator 1363, -atrix (*f.*) 1245, -onus 1276, *for* -o, fuller; ‡herba -onis, soapwort 14c.; terra arti -onum apta 1326; *-aticus 1368, 1577, -arius a 1221, folereus 13c., -araticus 1327, -areticus 1324, -ariticus c 1390, -ereticus 1294, -eriticus a 1270, 1468, -eracius a 1205, 1237, -ericius 1276, 1278, -ericus 1189, 1260, -erettus 1212, 1292, -oraticus 1255, foulericius 1288, folericius 1248, foleraticus 1307, fulredicus 1358, fulreticus 1263, 1388, -enarius 1282, -onarius c 1087 (Norm.), a 1221, ‡1520, -onicus 1274, 1580, -onaticus 1349, -inaticus 1295, -oneus 1240, of or for fulling; *see also* molendinum; -atorium c 1450, -eria 1327, (?) folaricium (Norm.) a 1160, fulling-mill; -onia, -onium, fulling-house c 1200; -ibilis, capable of being fulled 1264; -o c 1170, 1419, follo a 1195, -io 1419, -ono 1324, -onio 1286, to full (cloth).

fullo (fenum), (?) to tread down in stacking c 1300, 1310; f. (vinum), to crush, tread (Fr. *fouler*) c 1300.

‡fullus, filbert-tree 15c.; *see also* fulla.

‡fulm/en, purified silver, -inatio, stage in purification of metal (alch.) 1652; -inalis, explosive 1609; -inatrix (*f.*), having thunderbolt as emblem c 1595; fulminating 1609.

fulmerdus, 'foumart', polecat 1381.

ful/sus, -tura, *see* fulcimen.

fultr/um, -o, *see* FILTR

fultum, maintenance (A.S. *fultum*) 1274; *cf.* 1 firma.

fulv/ereus, glittering 793; -esco, to glow yellow a 1275, ‡1483.

fum-, *see also* FIM

fum/us, flatulence 1424; f. albus, mercury vapour generating silver (alch.) 1144, ‡1652; f. citrinus, sulphur 1144; f. rubeus, red orpiment, vapour generating gold 1144, ‡1652; -agium, reek-silver, hearth-money 1086; tax paid for use of current coin (C.I.) 1248, 1331; † (?) *for* summagium, 1504; denarius -alis, reek-penny 1356; ‡-aria 14c., 1570, -us terre a 1250, ‡14c., fumitory (bot.); -arium 1239, 1537, -arius c 1256, -erium 1244, 1251, -erarium 1292, -erale 1365, ‡1483, femorale 1339, femurale 1365, -erallum 1315, femerallum 1397, -erellum 1236, 1373, femerellum 1344, -erillum 1242, 1273, -ericium 1240, -ibrellum 1473, -atorium

1250, chimney or louver; †-atim, (?) like smoke 570; -atio, fume, vapour 13c.; ‡-axius, cook 1483; -idulus, rather smoky c 1184; -igatio, smoke-cloud 860; fumigátion c 1362, c 1511; clouding of the mind c 1327; ‡calcination by vapour (alch.) 1652; -ivomus, belching smoke c 1130; *-ositas, fume, vapour a 1200, a 1446; rumour c 1327; -osus, dark c 550; talking foolishly 1461; -igo, to emit smoke c 1400; to vaporize c 1460; to smoulder (fig.) c 1180, p 1330.

†funabulum, (?) fountainhead c 950.

fun/anum, -arius, see funiculus.

funct/iones divine (pl.), Christian rites 1315; ‡-orius, customary 1483.

funct/orium, -ura, see fundaria.

1 fund/a 1198, c 1370, f. baculina 1302, fonda c 1275, 1495, -abulum c 1362, ‡-ula 1483, -us 1320, 1461, (sling of) siege-engine, "gun"; fonda, purse 1277; -alis, for slinging 1461; -ator 1317, 1319, -ibalarius c 1193, c 1206, -ibularius 13c., †-ibalius c 1100, ‡-ibalista 1483, slinger.

2 fund/a 1326, 14c., fondus 1323, for -us, bottom, foundation; -us, fundamental number (πυθμήν) 1344; keel 1296; †f. navis, (?) keelage 1401, 1486; -otenus, to the foundations 950. c 1150, c 1325; -abilis, firmly grounded c 1360, 1427; -alis lapis, foundation stone c 1400; -amen sancte crucis, sign of the cross 12c.; -amentalis, fundamental c 1246, p 1380; -amentaliter, from the foundation (arch.) 1426; by virtue of foundation (eccl.) 1380; basically (log.) p 1300, 1427; -amentatus, based c 1250; -amentum, fundament, anus 1266, c 1290; firmament c 1500; tenement (W.) a 1300; source of revenue p 1394; fondamentum, foundation 1407; -atio *foundation, endowment (eccl.) 12c., 1537; foundation deed or regulation 1506; basis (log.) c 1375, c 1457; f. arcis, burhbote 12c., 13c.; f. pontis, brigbote 12c.; *-ator, founder (eccl.) 9c. a 1230, 1586; -atorius, of a foundation (eccl.) 1560; -atrix, foundress (eccl.) 1243, 1535; -osus, shallow c 1150; -o, to found (eccl.) 12c., 1380; to grant in mortmain 1481; to establish (facts) 1296.

fund/aria, -eria 1242, fontaria 1238, -itorium 1280, 1282, funtorium 1262, functorium 1237, 1304, funterium 1261, foundry, office of founder or fusour; -atio 1300, c 1318, -eratio c 1300, -atura c 1318, *funtura (†finitura) 1198, 1305, founding, smelting; functura, process of malting grain or quantity malted c 1304, 1378; malthouse 1378, 1381; -ator 1219, c 1290, -or 1198, 1203, fontor a 1275, metal-founder or fusour; -atus 1276, -itus c 1220, 1226, smelted; sanguis fusus, (fine for) bloodshed 1269, c 1290; -o *13c., 1424, -ro 1273, to malt; (?) to fuse (sand) in kiln 1378, 1381; to defray c 1365, c 1440; to lie prostrate c 1395; f. me, to approach c 550; cf. fusio.

fundecus, 'fonduk', Moslem market 1221.

funderatus, foundrous 1444, 1661.

fund/olus 1525, ‡-ulus 15c., plaice or loach; cf. flundera.

fundus, see funda (1 & 2).

funellum 1313, 1335, fonellum 1303, 1391, funnel.

fune/neum, -num, -rius, -tum, see funiculus.

fun/eralia c 1270, 1467, -erabilia 15c., funeral rites; burial fees c 1357; -eraria, funeral c 1406; -eralis 1322, a 1564, -eraticus 1318, -eratorius 1380, -erialis 1312, funereal; -estus, worthless, powerless c 1115; -ifer, mournful c 1192; ‡-usculum, corpse 1483.

fung/ia 1431, 1504, -a 1527, ‡fongia 15c., stockfish.

1 fung/us, lamp-black c 950. 1468; 'frounce' (disease of hawks) a 1150; -imen, fungous growth c 550.

2 †fungus, "finch" 15c.; "ostrich" 1483; cf. fringillarius.

fun/iculus, boundary-line, allotment 793. c 1170, c 1320; -icularis, -icularius, allotted c 1170; -arius 1563, ‡-erius, -ifex 15c., rope-maker; -anum 1204, -enum 1188, -eneum 1229, -etum 1190, cordage; -eus, made of rope c 1125; -ipendulus, suspended by a cord 1686; -atus, roped c 1450; -em traho, to dispute c 1218, c 1220.

funoralis, see FIM

funt-, see fundaria.

funusculum, see funeralia.

fuodum, see FEOD

fur/ infracaptus 1110, -is apprehensio 1189, infangenthief; -arius 1222, ‡-iculus 1483, thief; -atio, theft 1541, 1579; -icidium, killing of a thief c 1115; -igildum c 1115, -tum 1086, fine for theft; ‡-tulum, petty theft 1483; -tivalis, secret, hidden 13c.; -tive, by theft 1217, 1408; -tivus, unfree c 1115; fyrtum, theft 9c.; -esco, to thieve c 1450; -o, to steal 12c., c 1362; †-or me, to abscond c 1115.

†fura, prop (arch.) 1377.

furagium, see foragium.

furator, see foramen.

furb/atio c 1372, 1377, -itura, -ura 1292, furbishing, burnishing; -arius 12c., -ator c 1200, 1230, -or c 1180, forbator c 1115, 1130, forbisor 1300, furbisher; -o 1172, -io 1188, 1238, forbio 1292, to furbish.

furbeus, see euphorbiatus.

furc/a, fork: forca 1279, 1466, forcecta 1292, furchettus 1300, 1315, (?) †-inula c 1200, 1528 (cf. fuscina); *-a 1223, 1325, furchia 1221, cruck, arched timber (arch.); f. ad ignem, fire-fork c 1311; cf. FIM; -e (pl.) *1177, 1423, furchie 1199, 1234, -ille 1279, -e judiciales 1296, 1305, gallows; (?) cross-roads 1221, 1347; ad (per) -am et flagellum 1199, 1226, ad -am et facellum 1196, cum -is et flagellis 1268, (tenure or service) by fork and flail (or sickle); -agium, form of tenure 1226; -arius 1299, c 1307, -ator 1308, 1398, forker (at harvest); -atio, 'fourcher', double essoin (leg.) c 1275; f. feni 1466; -atorium, fork-load 1411; -atura a 1200, 1225, forcatura c 1170, 1316, forking, bifurcation, angle; crux -ata, cross fourché (her.) p 1394, a 1446; -us, -ium, furchia 1209, forchetum 1201, breast (of deer); -ula,

forked bone, esp. breast-bone c 1210,
a 1250; **-illa pectoris** a 1250; ‡**-illo,** to
hang (a criminal) c 1440, 1483; **-o,** to fork,
divide c 1204, c 1385; to load with a fork
1402, 1407; to 'fourch', make alternate
essoins (leg.) c 1275.
furdlingus, *see* 1 ferdingus.
furdus, *see* forda.
furellus, *see* forulus.
furendellus, *see* ferdella.
furett/us 1223, 1495, **ferettus** 1475, **feretta**
1541, **furo** 1541, ‡1570, ferret; ‡**furunculus,** stoat 1570; **-arius** 1284, 1473,
firettarius c 1335, **firetor** 1447, ferreter;
-o, to hunt with a ferret 1223, 1292.
furfur/a, bran c 1327, c 1417; **-isca** a 1250,
‡**-ita** 14c., scurf; **-eus,** scurvy c 1180, a 1250;
‡**-io,** finch c 1440; *see also* PERFOR
furino, *see* FURN
fur/iositas, fury, madness a 1250, 1398;
-iosulus, paltry madman 1523; **-ico** c 550,
-io c 1562, to rage.
fur/longus 1251, 1612, **-langus** c 1177,
-lingus c 1155, **-lungus** c 1230, **-longa**
1441, **-lunga** 13c., **-lungia** 1182, **forlonga**
c 1150, **forlongus** 1408, 1561, **forlangus**
1309, furlong, division of open field;
-lingus, furlong, measure of length a 1564;
cf. 1 ferdingus.
furlot-, *see* firlota.
furm-, *see also* FORM
furmentum, *see* FRUMENT
furn/asium c 1265, ***-esia, -esium** 1205,
c 1397, **fornasium** 1274, **fornesium** 1282,
fornassis 1380, **-a** 1388, **fornum** 1290,
feurnus a 1295, furnace, oven; **fornix**
(distinguished from **fornassis**) 1380;
-aceum, forge 1573; **fornaceus,** for a
furnace c 1335; **fornax laterica,** "tile-kiln"
1573; **-agium** 1209, 1390, **fornagium** 1192,
1254, oven-due; **-ellus** 1293, **fornellus**
1295, a 1307, **fornella** a 1307, smelting-
furnace; **fornellarius (fusor),** smelter
1300, 1325; **-arius** c 1140, 1383, **fornarius**
c 1266, **-iator** 1322, 1330, **-itor** 1383, **-iens**
1287, baker; **-ata** 13c., **fornata** 1194,
c 1250, **-iatum** 1322, **-atura** c 1185, c 1325,
-iatura c 1304, **-itura** 1290, **-icius** 1283,
a baking, batch of loaves; **-atio** 1324, 1353,
-iatio 1317, baking; **-ia** c 1310, **-ile** c 1180,
-ilium 1205, **-illum** 1228, bake-house; **-um
calcearium,** lime-kiln c 1250; **-us philosophorum, f. physicus** (alch.) c 1345; ‡**f.
apertus, tectus, ascensorius, descen-
sorius, calcinatorius, cementatorius,
reverberatorius** (alch.) 1652; **-o** c 1200,
c 1395, **-io** 1254, 1415, **forno** 1276, **fornio**
c 1324, to bake; **-io** (‡**furino**), to heat an
oven 1419.
furn/itio, providing (? *or* cooking) 1342,
c 1350; ‡**fornitus,** (?) furnished (of a
saddle) 1265 (but *cf.* FRUN); **-itus (cum);**
furnished, provided (with) 1298.
furo, *see* fur, furettus.
furr/a 1225, c 1445, **fourra** c 1322, **fodhera**
1405, **-ata** 1342, **-arium** c 1300, 1310, **-era**
1382, †**-arura** 1445, **-atura** 1187, c 1452,
foratura 1337, **foderatura** 1328, 1436,
-uratura 1361, ***-ura** c 1200, c 1450, **for-
rura** 1207, 1336, **-atio** 1391, **-uratio** 1349,

1453, **foderatio** 1423, fur, lining or edging
with fur; **-ura,** (?) lining (of roof) 1452;
f. linea, lining with linen c 1250; ‡**forigo,**
"listing" (of cloth) 15c.; ‡**-ator** 1483,
fotherator 1492, furrier; ***-o** 1199, 1432,
forro c 1148, 1215, **-uro** 1358, 1452, **fodero**
1382, 1436, **fodoro** 1504, to fur, line
or edge with fur; to line (with cloth)
1282; 1212, **-uro** 1350, to mount or line
with metal; *see also* foragium, foramen.
fursa, *see* 2 friscus.
furt-, *see also* fur.
furtellatus, *see* fortalitia.
furthendellus, *see* ferdella.
furthwita, *see* FYRD
furulus, *see* forulus.
furunculus, *see* furettus.
furura, *see* forera; FURR
fururcha, *see* forerda.
furv/us, sable (her.) 1654; ‡**-eo,** to grow
dark 1483.
fus/ator, -ibilis, *see* fusio.
fusc/atio, darkening c 1000. a 1250; **-inus,**
dark 1298; **-otinctus** (†**fustotinctus,**
†**-octus**), cloth dyed a dark colour c 1150,
1419; **sericum** †**fustatum** (? **-atum),**
(?) dark silk 1444; *see also* **fustaneum.**
fuscina, hook or hinge: **fusina** 1474,
fucin/a c 1300, †**-ula** 1345; *cf.* FURC
fus/illus, shaft of wine-press c 1274; (?) tooth
of harrow 1299, 1309; axle of weathercock
1374; **-illus, -illum *1255,** 1448, **-ellus**
a 1135, 1275, **fucillus** c 1300, 1332, **fucel-
lus** 1272, **phisillus** 1297, **-ula** 1312, **fissula**
1305, **-us** 1287, 1479, mill-spindle; **-illa**
1276, ‡**-o** 15c., spindle (for spinning);
-illa, spindle of church-bell 1475; **foucilla,**
shaft of siege-engine 1284; **fussella,** stick
of eels 1331; **fusselletus,** skewer 1235;
-illata 1286, **-ellata** 1250, spindleful (of
yarn); **-illatio** 1325, ‡**-ura** 15c., spinning; ‡**-arius,** spindle-maker 1483; **-enus,**
spindle-tree a 1150; **-orius** c 1595, **-ulatus**
p 1394, a 1446, fusilly (her.); **-ulus, ula**
p 1394, a 1446, **-us** c 1595, 1654, fusil (her.);
-illo, to spin 1325.
fus/io, smelting 13c., 1492; **-or** 1169, 1240,
-ator 1495, 'fusour', Exchequer officer; **f.
typorum,** type-founder 1568; **-oria,** office
of fusour 1240, 1271; **-orium,** foundry
1296; ‡ladle for casting metal 1483; **ars
-oria,** art of melting c 1178; **-ibilis,** fusible
c 1250; **-ura,** spillage (of wine) 1367; ‡**-o,**
to smelt 1483; *cf.* **fundaria.**
fust/a, timber 1229, c 1280; **-is,** tree-trunk
1222, 1297; bow-staff 1390; **-um,** tree,
log, staff p 1145, 15c.; cask 1270; *see also*
per; festis, festum, cudgel 1585; **-arius,**
'fuster' (joiner or saddletree-maker) c 1200,
1419; **-igatio,** whipping c 1160, c 1280; ***-igo**
c 1172, 1383, **-or** c 1180, to whip, cudgel.
fust/aneum (†**-ainum,** †**-amum**), **-anea**
a 1142, 1292, **-annum** 1208, **-enia** 1226,
-ianum, -iana 1300, 1515, **-inum, -ina**
(Sc.) 1458, 1539, **-amen** c 1250, ‡**fusca-
men** 15c., fustian; **-inus,** made of fustian
c 1285, 1298; *see also* FUSC
fusticus, *see* fisticus.
fut/e, in vain c 1400; **murus -ilis,** unplastered
wall c 950.

†**futuela,** kind of spider a 1150.
futula, *see* **vatta.**
***futur/itio** a 1233, 1427, †**-atio** 1412, futurity;
  -um, future tense (gram.) c 1173; *see also*
  verbum; -o, to postpone c 1184.
fuuagium, *see* **focus.**
fymaria, *see* **firmaria.**
fyrd/eringa, 'fyrd', military service c 1115;

-wita c 1115, c 1290, ***ferdwita** (†**serdwita**) c 1087, 1321, **ferdtwita** 1200, **fordwita** 1331, †**frodwita** 1199, **firthwita**
  c 1188, 1321, **furthwita** 1321, fine for not
  going with fyrd; *cf.* **fihtwita, frithwita.**
fyrtum, *see* **fur.**
fysinus, *see* PHYS
fyssh-, *see* **fisfeum.**

G

gabalacrum, *see* **calewarus.**
gabalum, *see* **2 gabella.**
gab/alus, gallows: **-ulus** 778; 12c., 14c., **g.
  sancte crucis** 12c., sign of the cross.
gabanium, *see* **cabanum.**
gabara, small ship (Fr. *gabare*) (G.) 1325.
‡**gabarus,** tasteless 1483.
1 gabella, *see* **cabula.**
2 gab/ella (esp. Fr.) 1418, c 1490, **-ellum**
  a 1250, a 1452, **gebella** (Sc.) 1503, **-alum**
  1360, ***-lum** 1086, 1227, **-lium** 1155,
  1175, **-ulum** c 1200, 1313, **-la** 12c., **-ula**
  1196, 1308, **-ellagium** 1250, **-ilagium**
  1327, **-lagium** a 1190, **-ulagium** 1275,
  1354, **-ulazium** c 1316, **gavelagium** 1390,
  gavilagium 1388, *gabelle,* gavel, rent;
  -lum animalium, horn-geld a 1135, 1210;
  -ulum assisum 1209, **cabulum assisum**
  1205, fixed rent; **g. ignis** 1282; **-ulum
  liberum intrinsecum** 1308; **-ula prati,**
  'mead-gavel' 1277; **-ilonum molendini**
  1388; **-ellator,** collector of *gabelle* 1471;
  -ulator 1086, a 1300, **-ularius** 1297, 1307,
  jabularius 1376, **-ellarius** (Ir., W.) 1288,
  1333, **gavellarius** (Ir.) 1307, 1370, **gavi-
  larius** (Ir.) 1427, **gavelmannus** (Kent &
  Sussex) c 1285, 14c., gavel-payer; **terra
  -ellaria,** gavel-land (W.) 1304; **gavel-
  gildus,** paying gavel c 1115; **gavelacra,**
  acre reaped in lieu of rent 1267; **gavelbor-
  dus,** board (plank) given as rent 14c.; *cf.*
  gavelettum, gavelikenda, gavella.
3 gab/ella 1329, c 1540, ***-ellum** c 1320,
  1558, **-ellus** 1250, **-la** 1333, **-lum** a 1216,
  1324, **-lus** 1253, **-ula** 1270, 1469, ***-ulum**
  1155, 1592, gable of house; †**-ettum,**
  gablet 15c.
gabia, *see* **cagia.**
gabio, parrot a 1200; *cf.* **papagabio.**
gableicum, gablicium, *see* **cablicium.**
Gabricus c 1320, ‡**Garbilius** 1652, source of
  gold, (?) sulphur (alch.); *cf.* **alkibric.**
Gabrielitas, essential quality of archangel
  Gabriel c 1310.
gabul-, *see* **cabula; gabalus; gabella**
  (2 & 3).
gacha, *see* **gata.**
***gadd/um,** 'gad', bar, measure of iron 1257,
  1442; **-a,** 'gad', swath, measure of meadow-
  land (Lincs.) 1552; *cf.* **godum.**
gadgium, gajura, *see* **vadium.**
gadum, *see* **waida.**
gadza, *see* **gaza.**
gafra, gafrarius, *see* **wafra.**
gag-, *see also* **vadium.**

gag/ates c 1150, c 1436, ‡**-as** 15c., 1652, jet;
  -atinus, of jet a 1100.
†**gagelis,** (?) badger c 1215.
gagga, *see* GAUG
gaggo, to gag c 1443.
†**gagno,** (?) *f.l.* for **gravo,** to molest c 1180.
gaida, *see* **waida.**
gaig/ina, -na, *see* VAGIN
gaign-, gain-, *see* WAIN
gaiol-, gaiel-, gail-, *see* GAOL
gaira, *see* **gora.**
gaiwita 1205, 1370, **gawita** 1194, 1199, a fine
  or payment, (?) ward-penny.
galanga, *see* **galenga.**
gal/atia c 1220, 1250, **-antia** 1239, 1292,
  -anticia 15c., **-entinum** 1271, 1338, jelly,
  galantine; ‡**-atyrium,** "flawn custard"
  1570; **gelatina,** gelatine 14c.
gal/axia 1267, c 1612, †**-actina** 13c., Milky
  Way (astr.); **-axicus,** of the Milky Way
  13c.; **gelactis,** (?) **gelacia,** *for* **-actitis,**
  milk-stone c 1200.
galbalacrum, *see* **calewarus.**
Galdiffa, *see* CALIPH
1 gale/a, helmet: **-um** 1519; **-a,** helmeted
  warrior, knight a 1347; **-atio,** wearing a
  helmet 13c.; **-ator,** helmet-maker 1377.
2 ***gal/ea** c 1190, 1573, **-ia** 1205, 1317, **-eia**
  1206, c 1422, **calea** 1274, **-ida** 13c., **-era**
  c 1400, galley (naut.); **-easia,** galliass, large
  galley 1478; **-io,** galleon, short galley c 1200,
  c 1250; **-iota,** galliot, small galley 1227,
  c 1400; **-earius** 1333, c 1422, **-eator** c 1200,
  c 1320, **-inellus** 1225, **-iota** 1210, c 1436,
  -iotus 1206, 1460, **-iotensis** 1266, oarsman,
  sailor.
3 gale/a c 1200, **-otus** c 870 (? *for* **-otes**),
  snake.
galefurca, 'gallows fork', chimney-gallows
  1511, 1517.
galega, goat's rue (bot.) 1641.
gal/egia, -eium *see* **galetum.**
galeglasius, *see* **galloglassus.**
gal/ena, -eo, *see* **galo.**
gal/enga c 1330, 14c., **-engum** c 1335, **-anga**
  1220, 1424, **-inga** 1324, ‡1483, **-onga**
  1310, **-ingala** 1205, 15c., **-ingallus** 1262,
  -ingalia (*pl.*) 1265, galingale (bot.).
Galensis, *see* **Wallensis.**
galera, *see* **2 galea.**
galeria, gallery 1508, 1620.
gal/ericulatus, hooded 1626; **-ira** 1594,
  gallera 1457, hat.
galetta, *galette,* wafer 1295.
gal/etum a 1104, 1207, **-eium, -eia, -egi**

c 1220, shingle, beach (? *cf.* Fr. *galet*); -esta, (?) flint a 1150.

galetus, *see* galo.

galeum, *see* 1 galea.

galfra, *see* wafra.

galga, pot a 1150; *cf.* GAUG

galgulus, green woodpecker 1544.

gali-, *see also* 2 galea.

galige, *see* caliga.

Galilea, Galilee, west end or porch of church c 1220, c 1450.

galinus, *see* galo.

galiofirum, *see* gariofilum.

galira, gallera, *see* galericulatus.

1 ‡galla, cock's comb 15c., 1483.

2 ‡gall/a, shoemaker's last 1483; ‡-arius, -itarius, shoemaker 1483.

Gall/awidensis, -owidensis, *see* Galwalensis.

gallecta, *see* galo.

†galliare, chaplet, mitre 15c.

Gallic-, *see* Gallus.

galli/cantus, -prelium, *see* gallus.

gallin/a, hen: gaullina 1284, gellina 1324; -a 1240, g. de lak' c 1305, g. rentalis 1450, rent of hens; 1371, g. silvestris 1316, 14c., g. silvestralis 1466, female woodcock or other game-bird; g. campestris, grouse c 1200; g. muralis, moor-hen 1511; g. nigra, coot 1544; g. pavonis, pea-hen 1278; g. pucinaria, Hen and Chickens, Pleiades (astr.) c 1267; -aceus, cockerel c 1200, 13c.; -ago, woodcock 1544; -ar 1335, -arium 1297, -aria 1155, 1202, henhouse; *see also* domus; -arius, capon c 1200; -us, of a fowl c 1385.

gallitricus, *see* callitrichos.

galloglassus 1556, galeglasius 1584, 1586, gallowglass (Ir.).

gall/us de bosco 1348, g. silvester 1306, 1389, g. paluster c 1200, woodcock or other game-bird; ‡-us marinus, "gurnard" c 1440; g. niger, black-cock 1325; -us Numidicus 1629, g. Turcicus 1622, turkey; *-icantus, cock-crow, daybreak c 1118, c 1414; -iprelium, cock-fight ‡15c., 1574; ‡-i centrum, clary (bot.) 14c.; ‡-ulus, -iculus, cockerel 1483; -ivolatus, cock-glade 1467.

Gall/us p 1327, 1518, *-icanus c 730. c 1125, c 1422, *-icus a 1240, 1517, a Frenchman, French; *-ice, in French 1274, c 1553; *-icum, French language c 1200, c 1444; -obelgicus, Gallo-Belgian c 1595.

galm/aria, -illa, *see* calewarus.

galmula, whey c 1000.

galnape, rug, blanket 7c.

galnetum, *see* jampnum.

*gal/o c 1135, 16c., -ona 1202, c 1356, -onus 1185, 1205, -onium 1622, -ena 1535, -unus 1197, -inus 1262, -eo 1321, (?) †-lecta 1234, -etus 1159, jalo c 1290, 1355, jalonata c 1290, gallon, gallon-measure; -onagium a 1172, a 1190, -inagium 1189, duty on wine (Norm.).

gal/ocha c 1328, -ochia 1297, -oga 1364, (?) calecha 1297, galosh, clog; *cf.* calopodium, caliga.

galofra, *see* gariofilum.

Galterium, *see* GART

galupa, *see* calupus.

*Gal/walensis c 1188, c 1385, -lawidensis 1153, -lowidensis c 1150, -widiensis 1456, Gallovidian.

gamandrea, *see* germandrea.

gama/rus, -lus, *see* cammarus.

gama/theus, -he, *see* camahutus.

gamb/a 6c. a 1150, c 1280, camba c 550, leg; -ee 1297, -rie a 1446, jambere 1300, 1303, greaves; -o, gammon, leg of pork 1207, 1299; jamba, jamb, side-post of window c 1468.

gamb/eso 1276, gaumbeso 1293, -esio 1340, -iso 1277, 1303, -esona 1297, -ezionum 1275, -isio 1264, wambiso 1254, wambasia (wanbasia) c 1192, 13c., 'gambeson', military tunic; wambasarius, maker of gambesons a 1161.

gammula, *see* GRAMM

gammum, game (beasts of chase) 1550.

gamnum, *see* jampnum.

ganata (†gavata), bowl, scoop a 1250, ‡1483.

1 †ganea (? gavea), sort of arrow c 1200; *cf.* GENDER

2 gane/a c 1090, ‡1483, genea c 1000, harlot; ‡-aria, tapster c 1440; -atus, richly cooked 1517.

ganetus, gannet (bird) 1275.

ganga, *see* jampnum.

gan/io, -erium, -nagium, *see* WAIN

gann/atura, derision 709. c 1125; -io, to applaud c 1125.

†gannoxatrix, 'gannoker', ale-wife 1526.

†gansia, moon (? Cynthia) c 550.

gant/a c 1090, 1486, -is (†gautis) c 1200, janta 1247, janyta 1232, wild goose (O.F. *jante*).

gantaculum, *see* jentaculum.

ganterium, *see* cantera.

gantus 1283, 1325, gentus 1312, janta 1269, 1277, felloe of wheel (Fr. *jante*); *cf.* canthus.

1 gaol/a *1194, c 1465, -um c 1350, gaiola 1156, a 1408, jaola 1275, jaiola 1199, giola 1293, gialum p 1330, jail; *see also* 1 DELIBER, 2 liber; -a, part of a galley 1294; -arius 1276, a 1564, gaielarius 1230, *gaiolarius 1157, p 1341, -ator c 1422, gailator 1219, jailer.

2 gaola, 'gale', office of gaveller (Glos.) 1485.

gara, *see* gora.

garaldus, *see* quarellus.

†garamantes (*pl.*), (?) savages, apaches c 1193.

garan-, *see* GARN; WARANT

garatum, *see* gargata.

garb/a *1086, 1684, gerba c 1275, 1608, carba c 1090, a 1300, sheaf of corn; sheaf of (24) arrows 1335, c 1474; measure of steel 1173, 1338; g. allee, bunch of garlic c 1250, c 1353; -agium (C.I.) 1324, -aria 1157, decima -alis 1320, 1549, tax or tithe of sheaves; -arius, granger 1257; -atio, sorting (of spears) into 'sheaves' 1377.

†garbatum, crab-apple 1466; *cf.* arbutus.

garbel/agium 1419, -atio 1442, 1480, 'garbelage' (sorting or cleansing of groceries before sale); -ator, garbler 1442, 1480; -o, to garble 1442, 1480.

Garbilius, *see* Gabricus.

*garc/io 1141, c 1533, garsio 1283, 1550, garso 1588, gaso 1528, grassio 1464,

gressio 1461, garsionarius 1434, -ifer
c 1190, 1461, garsifer, gressifer 1461,
boy, groom, servant; g. de corpore, groom
of the body 1284; -iolus, little boy or
menial 1219; -ia 1212, 1227, -etta 1203,
-ifera 1286, 1306, girl, maid-servant.

gard-, see also 2 carda; ward-

*gardin/um 1130, c 1540, -a 1185, 1362,
-us c 1150, c 1200, †-ium c 1135, 1419,
jardina 1539, †gardum 1372, †car-
dium 1228, garden, orchard; g. carbonum,
coal-garth (Northumb.) 1357; g. herbarum
1388; -aria 1212, c 1413, -eria 1219,
office or service of gardener; *-arius 1168,
c 1485, gardenarius c 1200, c 1300, car-
dinarius 1267, gardener; gardus, (?) fish-
garth (Southampton) 1290.

gardio, fish, kind of roach c 1200.

gardono, to guerdon, reward 1415.

garegium, see WARECT

garen-, see GARN; WARENN

garent-, see GRAN; WARANT

garet-, see garita; WARECT

†garfo, see grypho.

garga, a form of exaction (Ir.) c 1428.

gargaro, to brag a 1260.

garg/ata 1275, -eta c 1300, garatum 1219,
throat (OF. gargate); -ola, gargoyle, spout
1433; -ulare, (?) throat disease (of sheep)
1284; cf. gorgia, gurgulatio.

gargia, see gercia.

garillum 1241, 1244, garuillum 1202,
garoillium (Norm.) 1203, garoillus 1225,
gariollum 1254, geroillum, gerullum,
gerullium 1244, jar/ella, -ellum 1221,
1322, -illum, -oylum 1257, -ola 1255,
-ollum 1239, 1256, -ullus, -ullum 1225,
1249, -ullius, -ullium 1225, 1265, -uyllium
1234, barrier, palisade.

garimentum, warranty, assurance (O.F.
gariment) G.) (1291.

*gar/iofilum 1207, 1593, -iofolum 15c.,
-iaphilum c 1220, -apholium 1279, -ifilum
1417, galiofirum 1303, -iofira 1373,
galofra 1323, gilofera 1285, 1303, geroffra
1364, girofria 1252, giroflum 1205, for
caryophyllum, clove or gillyflower, (coll.)
cloves (cf. clavus); -iofilata, avens (bot.)
(?) a 1250, ‡14c.; -iofilatum, spiced wine
c 1197, 1482; -iofilatus c 1200, 14c., gilo-
fratus 1285, giroflatus 1212, spiced;
-iofilo, to spice (wine) 1233.

gar/iso c 1170, 1277, -isio 1196, 1224, -isona
1238, 1300, -izona 1300, guariso, gwari-
sio 1203, wariso 1204, warisona 1233,
provision, maintenance, corrody; cf. GARN

gar/ita, -itum 1219, 1395, -etta, -ettus 1308,
1402, caretta 1388, guarettus 1181,
'garret', watch-tower or sentry-box; -etta,
(?) silver model of 'garret' 1341; -itarius,
1460, 1463, -itor 1315, 1326, sentry; -itatio,
fortification with 'garrets' 1254; -ito, to fit
with 'garrets' 1241, 1253; -eto, (?) to fit with
closets 1238.

†garla, (?) liquid measure c 1330.

garland/a, -um 1213, 1419, gerlanda 1268,
carlanda 1263, garlenda, garlonda 1279,
-ea 1263, -eschia 1232, 1261, garlen-
dechia 1244, garland, circlet; garlaunda
feni 1292.

garmen/, -tum, see GARN

garnagia, (?) grenache (wine of E. Pyrenees)
1359.

garnaria, see GRAN

garnatus, see 1 malum; pomum.

*garn/estura 1214, 1258, *-istura c 1220,
c 1405, gernestura 1337, guarnestura
1217, guarnistura 1199, varnestura (G.)
1255, warnastura 1203, 1206, warnestura
1224, c 1400, warenstura 1232, 1265,
warestura 1224, *warnistura 1177, 1282,
warnitura 1190, ‡wernestura 1483, -itio
c 1200, -isio 1190, -isona 1255, guarnisio,
guarnisia 1185, guarniso 1171, warnisio
1172, 1223, warnisona 1177, 1239, warni-
sionisio 1213, stock, provisioning, manning; *-estura 1271, c 1325, -istura 1314,
garenestura 1274, -izio a 1327, -isio
c 1217, a 1347, -iso 1201, 1267, -isona
1233, 1263, -esia 1417, -asium, garana-
sium 13c., garrison; g. mortua, 'dead
stock', provisions a 1267, 1309; *-ia-
mentum (†garmamentum) 1288, 1441,
-amentum 1271, -ementum 1328, -imen-
tum 1415, garmentum 1539, garmen
1285, warniamentum (†warmamentum)
1308, 15c., warnementum a 1200, garment, livery; *-iator, burnisher 1377, 1389;
-atus 1368, gernattus 1374, -esiatus 1414,
gernesiatus 1361, -isatus 1450, -izatus
1399, -itus 1338, forming a 'garnish' or set;
-esio 1462, -eizo c 1486, -iso (-izo) 1378,
1448, -io 1332, 1406, gernio 1332, to
garnish, adorn; cf. gariso.

1 garnett/a, -um 1315, 1412, gernett/a, -um
1224, 1300, granata, granatus 1205,
c 1325, graneta a 1450, †guarrata 1300,
garnet (gem).

2 garnett/a, -um 1350, 1401, charnetta
1303, kernetta 1277, 1329, -ura 1355,
1375, garnet-hinge; -um, (?) hinge-shaped
(i.e. T-shaped) strip of land c 1240; -atus,
hinged c 1331.

garocium, see WARECT

garoill-, see garillum.

‡garre (pl.), choir or altar rails 1483.

garrot-, garroc-, see GART; waroccum.

garr/ula c 1250, 1334, -ulatio a 1240, 1481,
-itio c 1212, chatter; -ilitas, for -ulitas,
c 1292, c 1391; -ulator 1364, 1519, -ula-
trix (f.) 1397, 1519, chatterer, scold;
-ulosus, talkative 1299; -ulo c 1250, a 1564,
-ulizo c 1172, to chatter; see also GERR

gars-, see also GARC; gersuma; GRAS

gars/um, scarification c 1220; -o, to 'garse',
scarify c 1296.

†garta, (?) 'guard', trimming (of costume)
1425; cf. WARD

gart/erium, garter 1332, c 1378; *1352,
1586, -arium 1492, -era c 1390, 1508,
Jarterum 15c., Galterium 1479, Garrotea
Garrotera 1500, (Order of) the Garter; G.
rex armorum 1452, rex armorum de
-era 1451, Garter King of Arms (her.); ordo
-erius c 1562.

garth/a 1567, -o 1583, -ona 1554, -onum
1553, garth (Yorks., Lincs.).

garucha, (?) instrument of torture c 1620.

garuillum, see garillum.

garwentarius, see GRAN

gas/co c 1266, c 1330, -so c 1266, flagon.
gascomarcon, sort of tunic (eccl.) 1453.
Gascon-, see Vasco.
gasitha, see cuscuta.
gaso, see GARC
gast/aldus, -oldus, see CASTALD
gastell-, see WASTELL
gastrimarg/ia c 1115, c 1330, gastrimaria,
gastrimonia 11c., castrimargia c 1220,
1378, gluttony; -us 12c., 1528, castri-
margus c 1200, 13c., glutton; castri-
margus, woodcock 1430, 1535.
gastum, see VAST
*gata 1213, 1421, †gacha (†stacha) 1309,
bowl, jar, trough (Fr. *jatte*).
gatgium, see vadium.
gat/ta, gate-way, gap 1321; -eleia, toll, payment for passage 1328.
gaudech/otum, -on', article of male attire
1241.
‡gaudeo (*subst.*), gaudo, see WAID
gaud/ium, *'gaud' (bead of rosary) 1395,
a 1564; 1387, 1424, -imonium c 1456,
c 1478, gaudy, feast (ac.); quinque -ia
(B. Marie) 1389, 1415; -iolum, imperfect
joy c 1196, 1618; jewel 1188; gaudeatus
1552, -ettus 1446, set with gauds; -entia
1438, 1525, -imentum (G.) c 1250, -eatura
1463, enjoyment, possession, profit; *-enter
c 1090, c 1470, -iflue c 1370, -iose a 1275,
joyously; -ifluus c 550. c 1370, *-iosus
c 1220, a 1446, joyous, delightful; *-eo (de)
c 1217, c 1578, g. me de (G.) c 1297,
guaudeo (G.) 1369, to enjoy the use of,
possess; *cf.* GAVIS
gaug/ia, -ium 1348, 1458, -atum 1356,
*-ettum 1271, 1420, -eatio 1419, -eria
1281, c 1400, -ieria 1425, †gagga, †gua-
geria (Sc.) 14c., gauge, gauging (of wine),
office of gauger; -arius 1342; -eator,
-iator 1342, 1536, gauger; -eo, to gauge
1302, a 1420; *cf.* galga.
gaul/a 1364, 1492, -um 1363, (?) sweet-gale
(bot.); *see also* gula.
gaullina, see gallina.
‡gaulus, bee-eater (bird) c 1440.
gaumbeso, see gambeso.
†gaurizo, to exult (*cf.* γαῦρος) 11c.
gausepium, altar-cloth c 1396.
gautis, see ganta.
gavata, see ganata.
gavea, see 1 ganea.
gavel-, *see also* 2 gabella.
*gav/elettum 1279, 1343, -ellata 14c.,
-erletum c 1320, 'gavelet', tenure by, or
action for default of, rent.
gavel/ikenda c 1200, 1283, -ikendum 1275,
-ikinda 1199, 1205, -ikonda 1199, -icunda
1212, -kendum 13c., -kinda 1204, -kin-
dum 1348, gavilekinda 1188, gavylkenda
c 1393, †gravelikinda 1232, kavelykenda
1312, gavelkind, socage (Kent); -kyndensis,
of gavelkind 1343.
1 *gavell/a 1315, 1587, -um 1309, -us 1294,
family holding, *gafael*, subdivision of *gwely*
(W.).
2 gavell/a c 1290, 1350, gavilla c 1182, 'gavel'
(of corn), unbound sheaf; -o, to spread
(corn) in gavels a 1186.

gavelocus, 'gavelock', javelin c 1260, 1327;
crow-bar 1367.
gavingabilis, see WAIN
gavis/io, rejoicing 7c.; enjoyment, use (Sc.)
1450, 1569; -ivus, inclined to joy c 1185;
cf. GAUD
gawita, see gaiwita.
gaymaria, see WAIN
gayum, see caia.
gaz/a (*n. pl.*) 790, 959, gadza (*n. pl.*) 12c.,
treasure, wealth; -atus, wealthy c 1180;
-ifer, containing or conferring wealth 11c.;
-ophylacium, treasury 793. 12c., 1620.
gazel/, gazelle (Ar.) 13c.; -la, swift horse
a 1142; ‡gosel, horned animal 1652.
geba, see cepa.
gebella, see 2 gabella.
geburhscipa, district (A.S.) c 1115.
geburus (†jeburus, †tyeburus), tenant-
farmer (A.S. *gebur*) c 1115; *cf.* burus.
*gehenn/a (ecci.), jehenna 1276, 14c., Hell;
jehenna, (?) name of a building 1275;
*-alis 960. 11c., c 1540, jehennalis 14c.,
hellish.
geira, see gora.
gelac/ia, -tis, see galaxia.
gelamen, gathering, assembly c 550.
gelatina, see galatia.
‡gelbus, "wen" 15c.
*geld/um a 1070, 1526, -a 1086, 1257,
geltum 1086, cheldum a 1155, gilda
c 1117, 1311, *gildum c 1115, c 1346,
gilledum a 1464, guldum 1274, -agium
1302, gildagium 1328, guldagium c 1150,
1535, gildwita 1200, geld, tax; -um animalium 1130, g. vaccarum a 1130, horn-
geld, cornage; g. commune 1096, 1163; g.
militum, (?) scutage c 1096; g. monete,
g. regis de monedagio, (?) payment to
prevent change of coinage 1086; -abile
1291, 1364, gildabile c 1290, 1415, gilda-
bulum 1326, land subject to geld; *-abilis
1181, 1371, gildabilis c 1120, 1279,
gildebilis 13c., guldabilis 1257, 1292,
gueldabilis, godabilis 1275, guyldabilis,
geodabilis, guadabilis, gudabilis 1285,
geldable, subject to geld; -o 1086, 1268,
gelto c 1105, gildo c 1100, c 1392, gyllo
c 1228, 1383, guldo 1285, goldo, geudo,
goddo 1275, to pay geld; -o, to tax 13c.;
see also GILD
‡gelena, gourd 14c.
gel/iditas, coldness c 870. c 1194, ‡1483;
-o, to freeze c 1337.
gelima, sheaf c 1200, ‡1483.
‡gelion, leaf 1652.
gelius, ridiculous (γέλοιος) c 1434.
gellina, see gallina.
gello, see gildo.
‡gelopto, to gallop 15c.
gelositas, see ZEL
‡gelseminum, jasmine 1652.
gem/ella 1233, 1435, gimella 1316, †-ea
1396, jomellum 1344, 'gemew', hinge;
stripe 1245; †gimella (†gunella), wooden
object in cattle-shed 1308; -ellus, crotch,
forked branch 1330, 1337; anulus -ellus,
gimbal ring 1224, 1241; -ellatus 1245,
gimellettus 1304, arranged in pairs;
gimellatus, striped 1245; -inalis, clary

(bot.) 1538; **-inifluus**, twofold, occurring in pairs 10c.; **-inus**, ambidextrous c 1450.

gem/entia, groaning 1280; **-abilis** c 1000, **-ituosus** c 1193, mournful; **-ebunde**, with sighs c 1100.

gemil/aria, *see* **genu**.

‡**gemm/a tartarea**, pebble formed of tartar 1652; **-alis**, gem-like c 1250; **-atim**, in a sparkling style c 1000; **-iger**, productive of gems c 1385; **-ula**, scion 1508; *see also* **gumma, sal.**

gemotum, moot (A.S. *gemot*) c 1115; *cf.* 4 **mota**.

gen/a, cheek: **-ula** c 1200; **-a**, side-piece of fulling-stock 1374, 1384.

genatus, *see* 1 **geneta**.

†**gender/ata, -esa**, sagitta, sort of unbarbed arrow 1248; †**jondericia** (? jou-), a weapon of the chase 1308; *cf.* 1 **ganea**.

genea, *see* 2 **ganea**.

genealis, *see* **genialis**.

gen/ealogia, offspring, family 11c., 1395; ancestry, origin c 1000; **-ologia**, genealogy 1420; **-elogizo**, to record the genealogy of 1378.

genect/a, -um, *see* GENEST

genedea, *see* **gyneceum**.

genelliacus, *see* **genethliacus**.

gener-, *see* **genus**.

genesis, ancestry, origin c 1000, c 1500; generation (geom.) 1686.

genest/eia 1213, **-eium** 1222, **geneteium** 13c., broom-land; ‡**-eola, -ula, -um** 14c., **-alla** 1245, **genecta, genectum** 1269, c 1397, **jenecta** 1297, broom, furze; **genistella**, needle-whin 1629, 1634; *cf.* **jampnum**.

genet-, *see also* GENIT

1 **gen/eta** 1309, **-atus** 1463, jennet, foal; **ginetes** (*pl.*) 1362, **janitarii** c 1365, light horsemen (Sp.).

2 **genet/a** 1228, **-is** 1224, **-ra** 1200, (fur of) genet, civet-cat.

geneth/eum, -aria, -arius, *see* **gyneceum**.

gen/ethliacus, caster of horoscopes: **-elliacus** c 1160; †**-iculum**, horoscope a 1142.

gengiva, *see* **gingiva**.

gen/ialis, (?) inspired c 950; **-ealis**, natural, native a 1260; **lex g.**, natural law 1241, c 1430.

gen/ica 1234, †**-uca** 1240, **-icula** 1209, **jenicia** c 1258, 'genice', heifer.

genicul-, *see also* **genethliacus; genu.**

genificus, productive 860.

genit/ura, rank, degree (of weregeld) c 1115; offspring c 1191, a 1408; **-alis**, native 6c., 704. c 1125; **genetivus**, indigenous 5c.; **-ive**, in the genitive case 13c.; **-ricula**, mother 1220; **-rix (genetrix)** Dei 697, 933. 12c., 1300, **g. Domini** 11c.; ‡**-o**, to father 1483; *cf.* GIGNI

geno/bodum, -bardum, *see* **gernoboda**.

genologia, *see* **genealogia**.

gen/s (*coll.*), **-tes** (*pl.*), *people, followers c 1180, 1461; *the heathen c 730. c 1090, c 1430; **g. ad arma** c 1443, **g. armorum** c 1297, 1461, **g. armatus** 1199, **g. armigera** c 1422, men-at-arms; **-tilis**, of good birth c 1188, 1426; **'gentle' (falc.) 1200, 1334; **-tilitas** (eccl.), **-tilismus** 11c., heathenism.

gent/aculum, -o, *see* JENT

gentianella, gentian (bot.) 1629.

gentus, *see* **gantus**.

gen/u, knee: **jenu** 13c.; **-u** c 1102, c 1125, **-iculum** c 1115, degree of relationship (A.S. *cneow*); **-ualia** 1303, **-ularia** (†**gemilaria**) 1275, 1289, knee-pieces (armour); ‡**-icularius**, kneeler 1483; **-uclum**, (?) knee-cap 6c.; **-uflexio (-uflectio)**, genuflexion a 1090, c 1460; **-uflexus**, on bended knee 1295, a 1408; **-uflectorius**, uttered on bended knee 1433; **-uscissio**, hambling (of dogs) c 1185; **-uflecto** 1336, c 1540, **-uflexo** 1395, **-iculor** c 1090, ‡1483, †**-ulo** 1410, a 1564, to bend the knee, kneel.

genuca, *see* **genica**.

†**genu/is, -us**, sort of candle c 1245.

genus, kind, *etc.*: **ex gener/e** c 1343, *in -e* c 1278, c 1574, generally; *-abilis*, able to be engendered a 1233, a 1361; **-abilitas**, power of being engendered c 1365; **-alatus**, generalship 1586; **-ale** 11c., 15c., **ferculum -ale** c 1266, allowance of food (mon.); **in -ale** c 1340, **in -ali** c 1343, in general; **-alis**, minister general (of Franciscans) c 1250, 16c.; commissary general (of archbishop) c 1374; **dies -alis**, Judgement Day c 870; **-alior**, more general 1300; **-alissime**, in a completely general sense c 1340; **-alissimus**, most general a 870. 1267, 1610; **-alitas**, common weal 797; generality, general body 934. 1120, 15c.; general term, rule or right in general terms 12c., 1344; lack of precision 1242, 1684; universality c 1380; **-antia**, procreation c 1376; **-atio**, *race, kind, generation c 730, 793. c 1160, 1461; descent, family c 1115, 1539; daughter house (mon.) 1232; **-ativa**, generation, race 1240; **-ativitas**, progenitorship p 1300; **-ativus**, *generative, productive c 1115, 1622; genitive (gram.) c 1430; **-osa**, gentlewoman 12c., 1427; **-osissime**, most nobly c 730; **-ositas**, race c 1115; nobility (of birth) c 1204, 1414; lordship (title) 1295; **-osus**, 'gentle' (falc.) a 1200, 1382; *(subst.)* gentleman (as title) 1413, 1606; **g. ad arma**, gentleman-at-arms 1557, 1587, **-o**, (?) to perform 5c.

geo, *see* **jampnum**.

geodabilis, *see* GELD

geo/meter, geometer c 1180, c 1553; **-metralis** a 1233, 1395, **-metricalis** 1344, c 1361, geometric; **-metricalia** (*pl.*), geometry 1267, a 1350; **-centricus** (astr.) 1636; **-detes**, land-surveyor 1649; **-graphus**, geographer 1518; **-logia**, earthly science 1345; **-mantia**, geomancy, divination by earth 1159, 1499; **-manticus**, geomancer c 1250, c 1553; **georgica**, husbandry 1345; *cf.* **gi.**

Georgianus 1267, **Jurgianus** 1313, Georgian (of Caucasus).

Georgius nobilis, george noble (coin) c 1470.

geraf, giraffe (Ar.) 1392.

gerarchia, *see* HIERARCH

gerarchitis, (?) *for* **hieracitis**, gem used as love-charm c 1200.

gerba, *see* **garba**.

*****gercia** c 1160, c 1380, **jercia** c 1300, 1364, **jerca** 1417, ‡**gargia** 15c., gimmer, maiden ewe (O.F. *gerce*); †**jercus**, (?) young ram p 1290.

ger/efalcus, -falcus, -falco, see girfalco.
gerenoxa, see hiera.
gerentarius, see GRAN
geresguva, see yeresiva.
geresuma, see gersuma.
geretorium, joist, rafter 1471.
gergenna, fastening or bolt 704.
†gerio, (?) behaviour 1352.
gerlanda, see garlanda.
‡gerlinus, "sherlocked" (of horses) 15c.
germandrea c 1200, ‡14c., †gamandrea 1538, germander (bot.).
Germanice, in German c 1434.
germanitas, brotherly feeling a 615; fraternity (title) 793.
germinativus, seed-producing 1344.
‡germion, yeast 14c.
gern-, see also garn-; GRAN
gernoboda c 1194, ‡geno/bodum 15c., ‡-bardum c 1440, moustache; cf. grino.
ger/o, -olocista, see gestatio.
gerofalco, see girfalco.
geroffra, see gariofilum.
geroillum, see garillum.
geron/, elder c 950, c 1000; ‡-teus, "priest", -tocomium, "hospital" 1483.
ger/ona a 1250, -una a 1260, (?) triangular piece of land (cf. O.F. giron); cf. GYR
geronoxa, see hiera.
gerra, see GUERR
gerr/io, for -o, sorry knave c 1500; ‡-onus, -onaceus, garro, trifler 1483; -ule (pl.), quibbles 1427; cf. GARR
gersa, see CERUS
gers/acra, -tona, see GRAS
*ger/suma 1086, 1573, -sumia c 1166, c 1248, -sumium c 1186, -esuma 1220, -soma 1086, c 1255, †-sona 1227, garsuma c 1230, 1415, grassuma 1460, 1479, gressuma c 1250, 1545, girsuma 1454, grisuma 1375, grossoma 1561, kersumia a 1200, 'gersum', premium, fine, esp. merchet; -sumarius, tenant paying premium 1275, c 1280; -summatio 13c., garsumatio c 1395, exaction of premia; -sumo 1252, c 1395, ‡gressummo 1483, to pay premium (or merchet) for.
gerthum, see girthum.
gerull/ium, -um, see garillum.
gerulphus, werewolf c 1212.
ger/ulus, -undivum, see gestatio.
geruna, see gerona.
‡geru/sa 1440, 1483, ‡-sia, -la 15c., goad.
ges/sus, -cia, see jactatio.
gest-, see also gist-
gest/a, -um, yeast, leaven a 1190, 1356.
gest/atio, bearing of arms (her.) 1595; -amen, porterage c 950; 1595, -um c 1320, bearing, device (her.); -amentum, posture a 1250; -arium, -iarium 1200, -atorium c 1090, c 1412, litter; ‡-arium, -atorium, pack-saddle 1483; -atorium, stay, support c 1090; -atorius, portable a 1100, c 1414; fitchy (her.) 1595; -icularius, pantomimic c 1433; -ator, actor 1344; jester 1548; -or (negotiorum), factor, proxy 1417, 1491; *-ura 1297, a 1564, *-us c 1250, a 1564, -a 1300, bearing, behaviour; -us, funeral c 1308; ‡gerolocista, "henchman" c 1440; gerulus, porter (mon.) c 980; G. Sigilli

Privati, Keeper of Privy Seal c 1340; gerundivum, gerund (gram.) p 1300; *-a (n. pl.), (records of) feats 12c., 1461; -o, to bear arms (her.) 1595; to endure c 1302; gero, to deem c 1210; g. pacem, to keep the peace 1407, c 1437; see also lupus, vicem.
*gestrum, dagger 1441, 1500.
gestum, ghestum (Northants.) 1203, (Somerset) 1234, 1380, feast for labourers (man.); (?) cf. westwa; see also gesta, gestatio.
get/eya c 1287, -esium 1319, -icium 1419, 1424, gitata (G.) 1291, gitteum 1441, 'jetty', overhang (arch.); jettea, jetty, breakwater 1427; -to supra, to jut over 1405; cf. jactatio.
gethinctha (†gewinetta), thinctha, (area of) jurisdiction (A.S. geþyncðo) c 1115.
geudo, see GELD
geu/zahar 1345, -sahar 1326, 'dragon', nodes (astr.) (Ar.).
geyta, see WAIT
ghenseria, see CENS
‡gi, earth (γῆ) 1652; ‡gicenum, common earth 14c.; prosgen, to the earth (πρὸς γῆν) c 550; cf. GEO
gialum, see GAOL
gib/a 1294, c 1471, -ra 1310, 'gib', wrapper for wool, etc.
gibbos/itas (†gilbos-), gibbosity, tumour a 1250, c 1325; -us, hump-backed 1172, 15c.; swollen, protuberant, elliptical c 1190, 1267; gippus, camel's hump 709.
gibbus, 'gib', hook c 1370.
Gibellinus, Ghibelline 1281, 1347.
*gibettus, gibbet, gallows a 1175, p 1330.
gibonifer, ciboneus, fiery c 550.
gibr/a, human being (Aramaic geber) c 550,6 c.; -iosus, -osus, human c 550 see also giba.
gibsum, see GYPS
‡gibum, cheese 1652.
gida, see gita.
Giez/ita, disciple of Gehazi, Simoniac 1395; -eticus, Simoniacal c 1173.
giftum, see gista.
‡gig/a, "flute" c 1440; "gittern" 15c.; -ator, minstrel a 1150, 1301.
*gigant/eus, gigantic c 1090, 1345; -icida, giant-slayer, (?) David c 950; -ulus, little giant c 1250; ‡"freak" 1570.
gign-, see also GYMN
*gigni/tio (gingni-), generation, creation c 1290, c 1375; -tivus p 1300, 1378, -ficus 860, generative, creative; casus -endi, genitive (gram.) 1538; cf. GENIT
gigra, gugra, head c 550, 6c.
gihal/la, -da, see GILD
gilb-, see also GIBBOS; gilvus.
Gilbertinus, Gilbertine, canon of the order of Sempringham 1586.
gilbogus, infant liable to mortuary dues (Isle of Man) 1229.
gild/a *1086, 1541, gelda 1229, 1232, guilda 1520, 1587, gulda 1210, 1340, gylta 1234, guild, association; guild meeting a 1109, 1316; vacancy in guild 1262, 1279; guildhouse 1518; g. adulterina 1180, 1198; g. capitalis 1403; g. communis 1254; g. corporata a 1564; g. hanceria 1334, g. hansaria 1327, 1337; g. libera 1319, 1327; g. villana 1327; g. mercalis c 1200, g.

marcalis c 1500, g. mercanda (marcanda) 12c., 1254, g. mercandizans a 1300, g. mercaria 1200, *g. mercatoria (marcatoria) c 1120, 1563, g. mercatorialis 1226, *g. mercatorum c 1110, 1246, g. mercatrix 1214, 1549, g. mercimonialis c 1273, 1520, -emercatura 1257, gillemercatura 1226, guild merchant; g. mercatorum, guild-silver 1297, 1328; †-ales (pl.), assemblies 1240; *-anus 1254, 1522, -o c 1200, 14c., guildsman, member of guild;

*-halla 1192, 1321, -halda 1330, 1333, -halia, -alia 1274, -aula (-haula) 1325, 1419, -a aula 1321, 1454, -e aula 1331, 1386, -ehalla 1375, -eshalla 1382, gilhalda c 1300, c 1393, gilthalla c 1200, gihalla 1086, p 1336, gihalda 1315, 1419, girhalda 1485, guildhalda 1438, guildehalda 1603, guildallia 1274, guildaula 1304, 1319, guilhalla c 1324, guihalla 1278, c 1324, *guihalda c 1290, 1573, gwyhalda c 1290, gwehalda 1462, guyaula 1304, aula gillatoria c 1225, 1382, guild-hall; -ewita, a fine paid by burgesses 1275; -scipa (gilscipa, gilsipa), guildship, guild c 1115; -o, to form into a guild 1409; see also GELD

gildo, camp-follower 12c.; ‡gillo, gello, churl 1483.
gilfalcus, see girfalco.
Gillelminus, Guillelmite, member of eremitic order a 1270.
gillus, gill pot 1390.
gilof-, see gariofilum.
gil/vus, pale: -bus c 550, -vius c 1000.
gimell-, see gemelle.
gimingeria, see CUNI
gindagium, see WIND
ginetes, see 1 geneta.
ging-, see also zinziber.
‡gingelide, (?) angelica (bot.) 14c.
ging/iva, gum: gengiva 1250, (?) -a 6c.
gingnasium, ginnasium, see gymnasium.
gin/nator, -um, see INGEN
ginnisius, see gumphus.
giola, see GAOL
Giotus, see Jutus.
gipponus, see JUP
gippus, see GIBBOS
gir-, see also GYR
gira pigra, see hiera.
gird/alium, -ella (Sc.) (?) c 1270, gridillum (Ir., Northumb.) 1296, girdle, griddle.
*gir/falco 1155, c 1350, -efalco 1213, 1290, -efauco 1235, *-ofalco a 1200, c 1315, gerfalco 1205, 1382, gerofalco 1280, -falcus 1203, a 1446, -ofalcus 1237, 1290, gerefalcus 1275, gerfalcus (v.l. gilfalcus) c 1212, cirefalco 1204, gerfalcon; g. Islandensis 1169; -falconarius, keeper of gerfalcons 1213, 1284.
girhalda, see GILD
girlsa, grilse (fish) 1466.
girof-, see gariofilum.
†girophea (†cerophea), a garment (? for chirotheca) c 1200.
girotheca, see chirotheca.
girsuma, see gersuma.
girthum 1307, 1403, gurthwebbum 1438, saddle-girth; gerthum, 'garth', hoop 1333.

gisar/ma 1242, 1389, †-um c 1190, gisarme (sort of halberd).
gisina, child-birth, accouchement (Fr. gésine) 1256; g. Beate Marie 1330, jesina 1384, image of the Virgin (eccl.).
gist/a, (?) bed 1275; g. aque, bed of stream or pond a 1190, a 1210; -um (†giftum), (?) abode 1178; *-a 1199, 1359, -um 13c., -ia 1285, gesta 1512, cysta 1250, justa 1450, ‡15c., joist; -amentum 1305, -aria 1269, -atio 1238, 1291, gestura 1335, joisting; -arius, invalid needing a litter, inmate of infirmary c 1305, c 1430; (?) infirmarer (mon.) c 1465; -o 1215, 1241, -eo 1242, gesto 1225, to fit with joists.
gist/amentum 1275, -iamentum 1306, gestamentum 1275, gestatio a 1300, agistment; -o, to assess or exact c 1298; cf. 1 agistamentum.
gita 1385, gida 1380, 'gite', gown.
git/ata, -teum, see geteya.
giternarius, gittern-player 1367.
githago, corncockle (bot.) 1538.
githserus (guthsera), extortionate exactor of fines, etc. (A.S. gitsera) c 1115.
†gittorium, (item in inventory) c 1100.
†giva, (?) gyves (coll.), prison 1401.
‡glab/ella 15c., -ra 1288, ‡1483, bald patch, scab; ‡-ries 14c., ‡-rio 1483, nit or ringworm; -rio, hairless person c 1180, 1370; -rosus, mangy 1488.
†glabum, something appertinent to a mill (Kent) 1194.
glaci/ale anterius, -alis anterior, lens of eye 1267; -e (pl.), ice, cold 939, 940. 12c.; -ecula, a crystal 1620; -um, ice c 1218; -o, to glance off (O.F. glacer) 1293, 1367.
Glacialis, Icelander c 1130.
1 gladi/us, sword: g. Scoticus 1288; g. Colones' 1281, g. de Colonia 1291; g. pro listis 1401; g. bastardus 1410; g. comitatus, ducatus, symbol of authority of earl or duke c 1200; g. Cestrie, lordship of Chester 1216, 1537; g. materialis, temporal power c 1169, 15c.; g. spiritualis, ecclesiastical power c 1250, c 1341; g. uterque 1413; g. versatilis, two-edged sword c 1212, 1588; see also miles, per, PLACIT; -alis, of a sword c 1462, ‡1652; -atio, sword-cut 13c.; -ator, soldier c 1150; murderer 12c., 1241; -atoria (n. pl.), swordplay c 1433; -atus, armed with a sword a 1408; -o, to put to the sword 1252, ‡1483.
2 glad/ius 1402, -iolus 1245, p 1394, glageolus 1245, glegellus 1296, 1300, fleur-de-lis; -iolus 1538, glagellus 15c., †glasellus 13c., water-flag (bot.); glegellus, rush (plaited) 1303; -ioletum a 1275, glagioletum 1295, glajoletum 1232, bed of flags; -eolatus 1245, glegellatus 1295, ornamented with fleurs-de-lis.
†gladum, (?) f.l. for bladum, corn c 1250.
glaga, see clata.
glaiva (†glavia, †glania, glayva) 1167, c 1300, glavum 1549, glaive.
glan-, see also glena.
glans 1166, c 1450, gland/icula c 1190, tumour, scrofula; -atio c 1100, -ia c 1246, glanum c 1311, acorns (coll.), pannage;

-o, bullet 1624; **-ifluus**, bolt-slinging c 1180; **-osa**, kind of snake a 1200; **-ulosus**, tumorescent a 1250.

glar/a, 'glair', white of egg a 1250; **-ea**, juice a 1250.

glar/ia, **-ies**, *for* **-ea**, gravel, earth c 550, c 950; **-igerus**, gravelly 709.

glascum, *see* CLASS

glassa, a glass 1504, c 1530; ‡**glaze**, varnish 14c., 1652; **glasiarius**, glazier 1489.

glassanus, glossan (fish) (Ir.) c 1200.

‡**glatio**, to howl, mew (O.F. *glatir*) c 1440.

glauc/edo a 1250, 14c., **-itas** a 1250, c 1267, **-osis** 14c., greyness; ‡**-ea**, "widgeon" 1570; **-eus**, greyish 1388; **-ia**, *for* **-ion**, celandine a 1250; **-icomus**, **-icomans**, **claucicomans**, grey-haired c 550; **-oma**, (?) brilliance, sheen c 950; **-omia** c 1000, ‡**-ophthalma** 14c., glaucoma; ‡**glaumaticus**, blind without obvious defect 14c.; **-ividus**, seeing in the dark, penetrating 860; **-us**, "yellow" p 1394, 1545; **-esco**, to turn grey a 1250.

glava, *see* **glena**.

glav/ia, **-um**, *see* **glaiva**.

gleb/a, clod: **gleva** c 550; **-a**, field c 950; peat c 1220, 1631; sediment a 1250; *mortal clay, corpse c 1090, 1461; ‡spark 1483; c 1290, 1608, **terra -alis** 1542, 1583, glebe, glebe-land (eccl.); **-aria**, **-arium**, turbary 1198, 1294; ‡**-arius**, rail (bird) 1483; ‡**turf-cutter** 1483; **-atus**, covered with turf 1535; ‡**-ella**, turf 1483; †**-enus**, (?) of mortal clay, human c 550; ‡**-o**, clod-hopper 1483.

glecca, slag c 1296, 1302.

glechon, penny-royal (bot.): **glico** a 1250, ‡**glyconium** 14c.

glegell-, *see* 2 **gladius**.

glen/a 1201, **glana** (†**glava**), **glanea** 1326, **glaneta** 1257, 1271, **glanata** 1335, **claneta** 1238, sheaf of (24) arrows; **glaneta** (**asseri**), measure of steel c 1280; **glania** c 1182, **glaniatio** 1325, gleaning; **glanator** 1331, 1356, **glaniator** 1319, **-atrix** (*f.*) 1283, **glanatrix** (*f.*) c 1230, 1331, gleaner; **-io** 1234, 1376, **-o** 1288, 1315, **glanio** 1234, 1329, **glano** 1302, to glean.

glesco, *see* **glisco**.

†**glesus**, (?) *f.l.* for **gloriosus**, 1293.

gleva, *see* **gleba**.

glico, *see* **glechon**.

gliphus, *see* **griphus**.

1 **glis/**, fuller's earth 1255; c 1200, 13c., **-era** 1306, 1307, **-eria** 1175, 1272, clay, mud, marl; **-ceratio**, marling 1291; ‡**glitosus**, marly 1483.

2 **glis**, thistle, burr (*cf.* O.F. *gleton*) 709. 13c., ‡1483; ‡**glos**, dandelion 1483.

glisc/o, to desire 13c.; **glesco**, *for* **-o**, 709.

glisterum, *see* CLYSTER

‡**glixis**, (?) knotgrass (bot.) 14c.

glob/us, circle c 550; clique 1380; totality 14c., 1620; cannon-ball c 1567; 1576, 1620, **-a** 1573, **-ulus lusorius** 1622, ball for playing bowls; **-ulus**, bullet 1573, 1584; cocoon of silkworm 709; pellet or roundel (her.) c 1595; **-amen**, round, circuit c 550; **-ea**, globular piece c 1250; **-osus**, circular c 550; crowded 1580; **-ulatus**, rolled up into a ball c 1615; **-ulatio** 1543, **-ilatio**

1539, playing bowls; **-ulo** 1543, **-ilo** 1539, to play bowls.

gloccum, *see* 3 **cloca**.

glom/ellus c 1112, c 1213, **-icellus** c 1325, ball; **-icellus**, mass, tangle c 1200; **-eramen**, pile 6c.; **-eratio**, crowd c 1390; accumulation c 1608; ‡**-erium**, mantle 1483; **-erosus**, crowded, dense c 1450.

glomer/ia, grammar 1276, 1308; **-ellus**, schoolboy learning grammar c 1257, 1276.

glori/a c 1148, 1245, **g. in excelsis** 12c., verses said after the Psalms; c 1340, 1423, **-ficatio** c 1006. c 1400, glory (theol.); *see also* **vana**; **-abundus**, triumphant c 1125; **-anter**, boastfully, exultantly c 1180, c 1325; **-ficantius**, with more giving of glory 1378; **-ficator**, glorifier c 1180, c 1464; **-ficatorius**, glorificatory c 1344; **-fice**, splendidly p 1290, 1461; in glory c 1250; **-ficus**, glorious (eccl.); **-ola**, slight glory c 900; **-osulus**, paltry braggart 1533, 1588; **-osus**, glorified (theol.) p 1300, 1423; **-atior**, more splendid 10c.; †**-co**, to boast c 1000; **-o**, to glorify 793; **-or**, to be in glory 1200.

glos, sister in the Lord c 950; *see also* 2 **glis**.

gloss/a, language c 950; *8c. c 1188, c 1553, **-atura** c 1320, **-iola** c 700, **-ula** c 1150, 1537, **gloza** 1253, gloss, commentary; **-ator** 1267, c 1553, **-ematarius** 1655, commentator; *-o, to gloss, comment on, interpret 12c., 1457.

‡**glossum**, shrine 15c.; ‡**crystal** 1570.

glostura, *see* 2 **clausa**.

gluco, *see* **glutitrix**.

gludum, 'gloy', straw for thatching (Fr. *glui*) 14c.

glumula, (?) heap, bunch 685.

glustrum, *see* **ligustrum**.

‡**glut/a**, pitch-glue 1652; **-en**, ox-gall 13c., ‡1652; ‡**g. Romanum**, mastic 14c.; ‡**g.** †**alliotinum**, (?) *for* **abietinum**, terebinth 14c.; ‡**-inarium**, glue-pot, **-inarius**, gluer, 1483; **-inatio**, joint in masonry 463; †**-innies**, (?) glue c 1408; **-inositas**, stickiness a 1250; **gluo**, to glue 1301.

glut/itrix, gulper (*f.*) 1220; †**gluco**, *for* **-o**, glutton 7c.

glyconium, *see* **glechon**.

glycyrrhiza, liquorice: **liqu/iricia** a 1250, 1538, †**-irica** c 1100, †**-incia** 1424, **-oricia** 1265, 14c., **licoricia** 1329, 1464.

gnadir, *see* **nadir**.

‡**gnidisperma**, "nettle-seed" c 1440.

gnominiose, notoriously 1447.

gnomon, gnomon (geom.) a 1150, a 1400.

‡**gnomus**, gnome 1652.

gnos/is, knowledge c 950; **-ticus**, learned (? *or* notable) c 550, c 978; †**-cus**, wise man 12c.

gnunctus, *see* CUNCTI

goballus, mythical bird 9c.

gobelinus, goblin (Norm.) a 1142.

gobellum, *see* **cobella**.

goberistum, investiture fee (W. *gobr estin*) 1326.

gobio, gudgeon (fish): **gubio** (†**guvio**) c 1200.

gob/lettus 1451, 1515, †**-ettus** 1463, **-elettum** 1358, **goubbelettus** 1537, goblet.

gob/o 1295, **-ettus** 1318, 1327, 'gobbet', block (of stone); **-onatus**, gobony, 'composed' (her.) 1292, p 1394.

gocile, *see* gutta.

god-, *see also* GELD

godettus 1303, 1385, gotettus 1368, 'godet', cup, cruet; scoop of water-mill 1331.

god/um, 'goad' (measure of cloth) a 1564; -a, 'goad', measure of meadow-land (Warw.) 1553; *cf.* gaddum.

goduvitta, godwit (bird) 1544.

gog/a, -gus, *see* cogga (1 & 2).

gog/eretta c 1313, -redum 1309, 1310, -retum 1309, 'sieve', measure of grain (W. *gograid*).

gog/io 1306, -o 1289, gojo 1283, 1297, gugo 1322, gujo 1313, gojonus 1388, gojona 1245, gudgeon-pin; †-inus, iron cramp 1414.

goidus, *see* gurges.

gold/a, corn marigold (bot.) 1316; -finca, goldfinch 1544.

golena, *"polygonia"* (bot.) a 1250; ‡marjoram 14c. (? *cf.* κονίλη).

golettum, *see* GUL

goli/ardus c 1200, -ardensis c 1250, -ator 1527, 1531, 'goliard', reveller; guliardia, mummery, juggling a 1240.

†goluo, (?) to dig 'gools' (drains) (Lincs.) 1316, 1338; *cf.* gula.

gomerus, *see* cammarus.

gomor/ c 1190, a 1250, -um a 1090, dry measure (Heb. *'ōmer*).

gon-, *see* gouna; gumfus; gunna.

gopillus, *see* vulpes.

*gor/a 1143, 1332, gaira, geira 1314, gara 1123, 1403, garum a 1285, 'gore', strip of land; -edula, (?) 'gore-dole' (Lancs.) a 1262.

gorc-, gord-, gorettus, *see* gurges.

gorellum, 'gorel', horse-collar (Fr. *goreau*) 1276.

gorg/ia a 1150, 1277, -ium 1282, -a 1429, gurges 1319, 1375, throat, gullet; -era 1263, -eria 1275, -erium 1282, 1313, -erum 1289, 1297, -ura 1197, gorger, gorget; *cf.* gargata; *see also* gurges.

gormettus, bridle-ring, curb (Fr. *gourmette*) a 1446.

gornardus, *see* gurnardus.

gornetarius, *see* GRAN

gorra, *see* cammarus.

gorsta, gorse c 1280.

gorsus, *see* grossus.

gortus, *see* gurges.

gos/efettus, 'goosefoot', ornamental bar (arch.) c 1400; -hirda, 'goose-earth' (? ploughing service in return for keeping geese on common) c 1182.

gosel, *see* gazel.

gospelare, gospel-book c 1500.

got/a, -erum, -tile, *see* gutta.

gotettus, *see* godettus.

goubbelettus, *see* goblettus.

*goun/a (†gonna) 1297, c 1450, -um 1380, 1406, gonum 1416, gowna c 1322, gowneum 1377, guna 1365, gonella 1250, 1393, gonellum 1317, gown, robe.

gourla, *see* guria.

Graal Sanctum, Holy Grail c 1400.

graantum, *see* GRANT

graba, (?) stall 1271; *see also* greva.

grabans, bed-ridden person 1461.

‡grabatum, skirt 15c., 1483.

grabba, *see* gropa.

gracemannus, *see* gratia.

gracetum, *see* CRASS

gracil/iatio, thinning (med.) a 1250; -is, high-pitched c 1362; grecilis, narrow 1457; -io a 1250, -o c 1376, to thin.

graculus, "rook" 10c., 11c.; "jay" a 1408, ‡15c.

grado, *see* greamentum.

grad/us, *degree (ac.) 1311, 1517; office (eccl.) 1369; *degree (geom.) a 1150, c 1300; *degree (astr.) 1120, 15c.; degree (of latitude) 1578, 1624; platform, pulpit (eccl.) 1245; shelf (for books, *etc.*) c 1320, 1472; year c 1121; proportion a 1250; 'grade' of distemper (med.) c 1200; ‡'grade' (alch.) 1652; g. cantus, step (degree) in anthem c 1000; g. chori, step on which gradual is chanted 1509; g. hereditatis 1257, g. juris 1430, degree of inheritance; g. litterarius (ac.) 1509; g. magisterii a 1200, c 1583, g. magistralis c 1432 (ac.); g. motus c 1330, g. velocitatis 1335, rate of movement; g. Parliamenti c 1320; g. satisfactionum, church step at which penance was done c 1330; -ale c 1132, 1509, -alis c 1006, -uale c 980. -uale 1140, 1326, 'gradual', anthem (eccl.); *c 1093, c 1517, -uale c 1432, 1567, -ualis 15c., c 1488, -arium c 1200, -iarium 1362, -uarium c 1182, liber -aliticus 1345, l. -ualis 15c., l. -uum 15c., 'gradual', service-book (eccl.); -alis, ascending in steps 1245; *see also* canticum, psalmus; -arium staircase c 1445; -arius c 1180, c 1324, equus -arius c 1160, ambling horse; c 1595, -ilis 1654, passant (her.); -atim, on successive steps c 1296; in the manner of steps 1348, p 1394; -uatim, by degrees c 1362, 1427; ‡-atio, gradation of metals (alch.) 1652; -atus, (?) equilateral 13c.; -ualis, of or for ascents (bibl.); of degree c 1365, c 1375; -ualiter, by degrees 1427; -ualitas 1427, -uatio 1380, grade, degree; -uatio, grading 13c.; gradual approximation 1620; graduation (ac.) c 1412, 1423; *-uatus, graduate (ac.) 1378, 1518; -uor, to graduate, take a degree (ac.) 1378, c 1412; -ior, to lead, go (of roads) c 1170; -or, to walk 1290; -o, to grade 1200, c 1267.

graffio, *see* gravio.

†graftum, (?) *for* croftum, c 1200.

graga, grange (Ir.) 1316, 1333.

graicemannus, *see* gratia.

gram/en c 1530, -inatio c 1488, pasturage; ‡couch-grass (med.) 14c.; g. Parnassi, grass of Parnassus (bot.) 1641; ‡g. solis, *see* GRAN; -ineus, strawy c 1000.

gramm/a, word, writing c 950, c 1000. 12c., 1252; -aticalia (*pl.*) 1267, c 1589, -aria 1509, ars -aticalis 1321, grammar; *see also* schola; -aticaster 1564, c 1620, †-icella 1271, ignorant scholar; -aticulus, elementary pupil 1515, 1520; -aticus, grammar-school pupil 1321; †-ula (†gammula), letter, character 1014, 11c.; -atico, to write grammatically c 1194, c 1255; -atizo, to study or use grammar c 1180, c 1225.

gran/a 12c., 1290, -is a 1250, *for* -um, grain;

an electuary (? fennel seed) 1253 (*cf.* **g. feniculi** c 1305); 1196, 1393, **-ea** c 1200, *** -um** a 1250, 1440, **greinum** 1190, 1207, scarlet grain, kermes; **-um dimidium** 1587, **g. medium** c 1467, half-grain (of cloth); **pannus -o dimidiatus** a 1410; **-a** (*pl.*), grain, corn c 1400, 1555; **-um**, coin (It.) 1292; grain, weight of metal c 1280, 1438; **g. frumenti**, fraction (1/640) of ounce 14c.; **g. hordei**, 'barley-corn', one-third of inch 1382, 16c.; ‡**g. pacificum**, rice 14c.; ***g. paradisi** 1310, 1480, **g. Paris'** 14c., **g. de Paris'** 1329, **g. Parisiense** 1328, grain of paradise (spice); **g. piperis**, pepper-corn (as rent) a 1230, 1549; **g. rosarum**, (?) a special stitch in embroidery 1386; **g. smaragdinum**, (?) small emerald 1315; **g. solis** a 1250, ‡15c., ‡**gramen solis** 1483, gromwell (bot.); **-amellum** 1348, **-omellum** 1304, ‡1483, 'grout', grain (for brewing);
—**-ale** 1461, 1479, **horreum -ale** 1503, **domus -alis** 1464, **-are** c 1411, **-aria** 1332, 1419, **-erium** 1460, **-atorium** c 1310, ‡15c., **-orium** 1417, **-etum** c 1266, †**-ica** 13c., **garnaria** 1503, **gernarium** 1247, **gernerium** 1335, *for* **-arium**, granary, garner; **garnaria**, reservoir 1443; **-arium**, (payment for) storage in granary 1236, 1267; 'graner', bale (of woad) 1304, 14c.; **g. (salis)**, store-house 1460; **-arius** c 1290, 1326, ***-atarius** 1234, 1566, **-atorius** c 1296, 1513, **-etarius** 1086, 1467, **-itarius** (Sc.) 1425, 1538, **-tarius** 14c., **gernetarius** c 1130, 1293, †**gornetarius** 1293, **garentarius** 1423, **gerentarius** a 1290, 1324, †**garwentarius** 1376, †**-urius** 1411, **-ator** 1327, 1539, granger (esp. mon.); **-acius**, *for* (storing) grain 1576; **molendinum -aticum**, grain-mill 1418, 1583; **-atio**, formation of grain 1371; cloth dyed in grain 1465; **-atus**, dyed in grain 1565; in the form of grains 1213; *see also* 1 **garnetta, pomum**; **-ea**, porridge 1236; ‡**-ellulum**, little grain c 1458; ‡grain of paradise 1483; ‡**-ificium**, malting 1483; ‡**-ulatio**, granulation (alch.) 1652; **-ulosus**, granular a 1250; ‡**-ulum**, pearl c 1440; †**-eo**, **-esco**, **-o**, to take out the kernel 1483; †**-imo** (†**gravimo**), (?) to steep (malt) c 1320; *see also* **grangia, grava.**

gran/ata, -eta, *see* 1 **garnetta.**

gran/cia, -dia, -ica, *see* **grangia.**

Grandimont/anus, -anensis c 1220, **-ensis** c 1190, c 1400, Grammontine (mon. order).

grandin/osus, like hail 1267; **-escit**, it hails a 1275.

grandi/tas, large quantity 7c.; **-tudo**, size 1262; †**-osus** 1380, **-usculus** 1544, 1620, fair-sized; **-sonus**, loud-voiced 1544; **-fico**, to magnify 1288; **-pendo**, to esteem highly 7c.

***grang/ia** 1086, 1582, **-ium** c 1300, c 1411, **graungia** 1573, 1582, **grancia** 1155, 1419, †**granica** 13c., †**grandia** 1210, †**-ranum** 1380, grange; **g. decimalis**, tithe-barn 1363, 1430; **-iarius** c 1148, 1434, **-erius** 1193, 1294, **-iator** c 1350, 1449, granger (esp. mon.); *cf.* **GRAN**

gransulla, *see* **groundagium.**

grant/a c 1142, ***-um** c 1145, 1260, **graantum**

1195, grant, disposal, goodwill; **-o** c 1140, 1268, **craanto** c 1224, **cranto** 1200, **creanto** c 1217, to grant; *cf.* **credentia.**

granum, *see* **grana.**

‡**grapa**, hole for (scaffold) pole 15c.; *see also* **gropa.**

grapellus, grapnel 1254.

graph/ium, register, cartulary 947. c 1200; charter, document 14c.; ‡**-agia**, holy writ 14c.; **-icus**, scribe c 1200; **-arius**, registrar, *greffier* (Fr.) 1550; **greffariatus**, office of *greffier* (Fr.) 1496; **-iolum**, pen *or* (?) sword 12c.; †**griphia** (*pl.*) letters, writing 12c.

grapia, *see* **CRASP**

grap/io, -yo, (?) to fork, work with a graip 1302, 1346.

grarlellus, *see* **quarellus.**

gras/acra 1279, c 1283, **garsacra** 1222, c 1283, **gersacra** c 1283, **-hurtha** 1260, **garslonda** 1234, ploughing service in return for pasturage; **gres/canum**, grazing cain (Sc.) a 1200; ***-mannus** c 1150, 1352, **-semannus** 1300, c 1323, **cresmannus** 1238, 'grass-man', cottar; **garstona** 1349, **gerstona** 1209, 'garston', grassy enclosure.

grasgropa, sort of wheel-clamp 1372, 1412.

grasp-, *see* **CRASP**

grass-, *see also* **CRASP; CRASS; GARC; GRIS**

‡**grassa**, borax 1652.

grass/atio, oppression c 1150; **-abundus**, violent c 1325; **-atrix**, perpetrator (*f.*) c 950; **crassor**, *for* **-or**, to rage, be violent a 1186, 1385.

grassuma, *see* **gersuma.**

grat/ia, ***grace (theol.) c 1006. c 1090, 1549; charisma, God-given talent 12c., 15c.; charitable gift 1260; period of grace 1227; mercy, pardon 1259, 15c.; bonus, remission c 1303; indulgence, Papal bull of grace 1257, c 1444; favour in tournament 1347; 'grace', licence (ac.) 1253, c 1506; *see also* **de, ex, annus, dies, lex, scientia, status; -ie** (*pl.*) 1234, 1515, **-iarum actiones** c 1250, c 1420, grace before or after meat; **-ia Dei**, a medicament a 1250, 1322; ‡**g. D. major**, (?) devil's-bit scabious (bot.) 14c.; ‡**g. D. minor**, (?) crane's-bill (bot.) 14c.; **g. regis**, pension (eccl.) c 1321; **-iamannus, graicemannus** 1389, **gracemannus** 1363, 1389, 'graceman', chief officer of religious guild (Lincs.); **-ialiter**, as an act of grace 1312; **-ianus**, semi-free tenant p 1290, c 1400; **-ificabilis**, able to receive grace p 1300, c 1366; **-ificatio**, discretion (to act) c 1370; bestowal of grace a 1349; **-ifice**, agreeably c 1250, 15c.; gladly c 1060; **-ificus**, bestowing grace (theol.) c 1250; **-iose**, ***graciously, freely c 1090, c 1570; by God's grace c 1331, 15c.; **-iositas**, graciousness 9c. c 1070; **-iosus**, grateful c 1135, c 1180; **littera -iosa**, letter of indulgence 1352; ***-is** 1086, 15c., ***-anter** c 1125, c 1540, **-uanter** 1374 **-ulanter** c 760, c 1080, c 1170, **-ulenter** c 1000, **-ulabunde** c 980. c 1127, 1439, **-uiter** (G.) 1242, gladly, willingly, thankfully; ***-itudo**, goodwill, favour, *or* gratitude c 1182, 1610; grace (title) 1298; **-iuncula**, grace 15c.; **-uitas**, favour c 1273, c 1390; gift 1508; **-uite**, graciously c 1303, c 1380;

free of charge 1299; **-uitus,** agreeable, acceptable 1136, 1461; conferred by grace (theol.) 9c. p 1300, c 1382; **-um,** goodwill, consent, pleasure c 1180, p 1377; **-us,** in a state of grace c 1344; *see also* **male, rata;** **-ifico,** to gladden, flatter c 1090; to bestow grace upon (theol.) 12c., c 1444; **-io** c 1115, **-ior** c 1170. **-or** 793. 1241, to thank.

grat/ura 1292, **-uarium** 1286, ‡**-arium** 15c., grater; ‡**-o,** to scratch 15c.; *see also* **crata.**

graungia, *see* **grangia.**

1 ***grav/a** 1086, 1540, **-ia** 1233, **grawa** 1297, **grova** c 1250, 1573, (?) **crava** (†**crana**) 1438, grove; **-etta** 1210, c 1506, **grovetta** 1546, 1573, **grovettum** 1391, 1587, **grovatta** 1586, 1587, 'grovet', little grove.

2 **grav/a** (? **grana**) (Norf.) 1198, (G.) 1289, **greva** (? **grena**) (Norf., Lincs.) 1199, a 1240, **-era** (Kent or Sussex) 1264, shingle, beach; **-era, -arium** 1300, **-era** c 1290, (?) gravel-pit; **-ella** c 1218, 1313, **-ellum** 1209, a 1564, gravel; **-elo,** to cover with gravel 1401.

grava capitis, *see* **greva.**

grav/arengus 1180, **-erengus** 1203, **-aringus** c 1137, *prévôt* (Norm.).

grav/atio 1220, c 1358, ***-amen** c 1080, c 1570, **-edo** 709, 960. 11c. c 1130, c 1150, **-ido** 811, 847. 14c., **-itas** c 1150, 12c., **-itudo** 463. 12c., injury, oppression; **-atio,** aggravation c 1378; dispute 1440; **-amen** c 1204, 1541, **-itas** c 1308, grievance, accusation; **-amen Dei,** wrath of God c 1115; **-itas,** sobriety (of dress) 1549; gravity (phys.) c 1362, a 1670; **g. specifica** 1686; **-ativus,** making heavy a 1250, **-ator,** oppressor c 1070, c 1250; **-atorium** 1540, **-itorium** 1470, aggravation of sentence; **-ia** (*pl.*), grievances c 1328; **pro -iori,** to make matters more serious c 1390; **-iter,** with difficulty 7c.; **-itanter,** with dignity 1308; **-efacio,** to weigh down 1378; **-ito,** to gravitate (astr.) 1686; **-o,** to pronounce with barytone accent 1267; **-o,** to oppress c 1110, 1414; *see also* **CRAV**

grav/atura, engraving 1245; **-io** 1249, 1293, ***-o** 1232, 1415, to engrave; **-io turbas,** to dig peat a 1250.

gravelikinda, *see* **gavelikenda.**

grav/ella, -elo, -era, *see* 2 **grava.**

grav/ennarius, tax-collector (Norm.) 12c.; **-eria** c 1309, ***greveria** c 1160, 1331, **grevereia** 1331, a rent or tax, *grèverie* (C.I.).

gravimo, *see* **GRAN**

gravio c 1115, (?) **graffio** 821, **greva** c 1160, reeve, sheriff (A.S. *gerefa*).

‡**gravus,** kind of porphyry (alch.) 1652.

greamentum, agreement, compact (G.) 1255; **grado,** to agree (Norm.) 1103; *cf.* **AGRE**

greci/a, -us, *see* **GRESS; GRIS**

grecilis, *see* **GRACIL**

Grec/ismus 1281, c 1300, **-issimus** c 1337, name of a grammar-book; **-istes,** Hellenist 1515; **-olatinus,** Greco-Latin c 1534; ‡**-omagia,** magic operated by optical illusions 1652; **Gregum,** Greek wine 1362; **-izo,** to talk Greek c 1125; (?) to whisper 8c.; *see also* **gregarius, ignis, vinum, VIRID**

gred/elingus p 1290, 1329, **-lingus** 1306, 1329, ram in second year (Somerset, Glos.).

greetmannus, *grietman,* head of district (Friesland) 1401.

greffariatus, *see* **GRAPH**

‡**greg/arius,** sheep-dog c 1440, 15c.; **miles g.,** constable c 1178; **greculus,** little flock c 1430; **-o,** to compile c 950.

Gregoriane, Gregorian decretals c 1250; *see also* **aqua, cantus.**

Gregum, *see* **GREC**

greinum, *see* **GRAN**

grem/ium, nave of church a 1142, c 1433; **de -io,** from the heart, sincerely c 1300; **-ium** c 1200, **-iale** (†**-ale**) 1432, 1620, apron; **-ialis,** nursling, alumnus 1423, 1466; (*adj.*) enclosing (of boundary streams) 814; **-io,** to foster c 1180; *see also* **CREM**

gren/a, village green 1232, 1279; **-efinca,** greenfinch 1544; *see also* 2 **grava.**

Grenlandicus, of Greenland 1577.

gres-, *see also* **GRIS**

gres/canum, -mannus, *see* **GRAS**

gress/a, -ia, grescia, *see* **CRASS**

gressi/o, -fer, *see* **GARC**

gressius 1253, **grossor** 1289, gritstone, whetstone (Fr. *grès*); *cf.* **ingressura.**

gressum-, *see* **gersuma.**

gress/us 1237, p 1265, **grecius** 1303, step (at doorway); **grecia,** staircase 1282; **-ibilis,** able to walk 860. a 1180, a 1446; **-ualiter,** by bodily movement c 1100.

gresura, 'grozier', glazier's grozing-iron 1342.

greva 1263, 1271, **grava** 1308, 1313, ‡**graba** 1483, crown of head (O.F. *greve*); *see also* 2 **grava, gravio.**

greveria, *see* **gravennarius.**

grevus, count, *Graf* 13c.; *cf.* **gravio.**

†**gricea,** (?) *for* **aprica,** c 550.

gridbriga, *see* **GRITH**

gridillum, *see* **girdalium.**

griff-, *see* **GRAPH; GRYPH**

grino, moustache 12c.; *cf.* **gernoboda.**

gripa, 'grip', sewer 1280, 1313; *see also* **gropa, grypho.**

griphus, enigma: **gliphus** c 1000; *see also* **GRAPH, GRYPH**

gris/eum, -ium c 1180, c 1436, **-eiium** 1254, **-um** 1208, 1428, **-o** 1312, **opus -eum** 1234, 1298, 'gris', miniver; ***-eus, -ius** 1177, a 1452, **-us** 1130, a 1408, **greseus** 1462, 1465, **gresus** 1447, **grecius** 1431, **grosius** (Sc.) 1461, 1508, †**grassus** 1378, **-ellus** 1313, 1367, **-illus** 1453, grey; *see also* **frater, lapis, monachus, ordo,** ***petra; g. liardus,** grey lyard 1313; ***-engus** c 1150, 1254, **-eingus** 1208, **-angus** 1276, **-ancus** 1313, †**griengus** c 1200, **pannus -engus** c 1115, **p. -ancus** 1325, 'grising', grey cloth; **-etus,** made of grey cloth c 1190; **-ea,** frieze cloth 1588; (auca) †**-ia** (†**bisia,** †**trisia),** (?) grey goose c 1200; **canis de grecia,** greyhound c 1320; ‡**gressenus,** badger 15c.; **-mulettus,** grey mullet 1242.

grisillum, (?) griddle c 1224; *cf.* **GIRD**

grist/a, -um, grist 1234, c 1300; **-arius,** 'grister' bringing corn to mill 1234.

grisuma, *see* **gersuma.**

grith/bricha c 1185, **gridbriga** 1199, (jurisdiction in cases of) breach of the peace;

-mannus 1429, **gyrthmanius** 1468, 'grith-man', refugee in sanctuary (Yorks.); **-serviens**, serjeant of the peace (Lancs.) 1291.
groc-, *see* GROSS
grollo, to fit (a plough) with (?) shares 1313.
grom/us c 1410, 1537, **-ettus** 1513, 1583, groom.
gron-, *see also* **groundagium**.
†**gronagium**, (?) form of tenement (God-manchester) 1324.
gronn/a 463, 1002. a 1118, **grunna** 7c., **-ium** c 900, marsh; **-osus**, marshy c 900.
*****grop/a**, **-um** 1273, 1425, †**grospa** 1377, **grapa** 1248, 1325, **grabba** 1446, **grippa** 1270, 1371, iron clamp (esp. for mending cart-wheels); **-o**, to clamp (cart-wheels) 1267, 1308; *cf.* **2 crabba**.
grosius, *see* GRIS
grossoma, *see* **gersuma**.
grossor, *see* **gressius**.
gross/um 1449, 1509, **grocium** c 1423, **-atum** 1427, a gross (measure); *****-us** 1358, 1609, **-a** 1378, **grotus** 1368, groat (coin); 'stooter' (Dutch) 1442; **g. Ludowycus**, *louis* (Fr.) 1362; **-us Turonensis** 1282, c 1565, **g. Toronensis** 1277, *gros de Tours*; **-um** 1292, 1343, **-um per se** 1292, a 1539, indivisible (and independent) tenement; **-us** *****c** 730. a 1100, 1586, **-ius** c 1450, †**gorsus** 1374, **grocius** 1550, large, thick, fat, coarse; rough c 730; big with child 1237, 1356; dull, stupid 13c., c 1380; gross, insulting 1269; (?) grandiloquent c 1400; important 1201, c 1390; broad, general 1267; gross, inclusive (in accounts) c 1300, c 1400; **-o** c 1316, *****in -o** 1221, 1506, **in -um** 1279, **per -am** 1559, wholesale; **in -o**, collectively, inclusively 1275, c 1494; **-e**, roughly, in general terms c 1340, c 1444;
-aria, engrossership 1299, 1302; **groceria**, grocery, wholesale business 1439; **-arius** 1290, 1323, **-erius** 1398, **-orius** 1423, **-ator** 1290, engrosser, copyist; **-arius** 1310, 1419, **-erus** 1443, **grocerius** 1419, **grocerus** 1387, 1429, grocer, buyer in gross, wholesaler; †**-idior**, tumour c 1280; *****-ities** 1177, c 1370, *****-itudo** c 1125, c 1540, **crossitudo** c 1125, magnitude, thickness, coarseness; †**groossies** 1313, **-itudo cordis** c 1315, **-ura** a 1400, grievance, indignation; **-esco** c 1090, 12c., **-esso** c 1204, to grow, swell; **-o**, to thicken, enlarge 1372, 1408; to engross, copy 1261, 1404; to engross, buy up 1419; to consider in general 1378;*cf.* CRASS
grot-, *see* GROSS; **grutum**.
groundagium, 'groundage', payment for ships lying aground (*cf.* **terragium**) 1448, 1545; **grund/a**, part of plough 1269; ‡**-arium**, **-atorium**, foundation 1483; **-sellum** 1398, **grunsilla** 1388, **grunsulla** c 1390, **gronnesella** 1390, **gransulla** 1410, ground-sill; **-sullo** 1382, **grondsullo** 1398, **-cello** 1409, **-sillo** 1449, **groundcillo** 1389, **grounsello** 1504, to fit with a ground-sill; ‡**-o**, to lay a foundation 1483; **groundo carrucam** 1352.
1 grov/a, -atta, -etta, *see* **1 grava**.
2 grova, groove, mine-shaft 1225, 1323.
gru/a, -arius, *etc.*, *see* **grus**.
gru/dum, -ellum, *see* **grutum**.

grugnus, *see* **grunnus**.
grum/a a 1446, ‡**-us** 1570, badger.
grumia, kernel c 1200.
grumillus, gromwell (bot.) a 1150.
grun-, *see also* **groundagium**.
gruncus, *see* **bruncus**.
grunna, *see* **gronna**.
grunn/us ‡15c., 1528, **grugnus** c 1250, snout; **-itio**, grunting c 1000.
gru/s, crane: **-a** 1241, 1290; **-agium**, hawking for cranes 1315; **-arius** 1200, 1291, **-erius** 1215, 1284, for hunting cranes; ‡**-cula**, young crane 1483; **caro -ina**, crane's flesh c 1180, c 1200; **-inus**, crane-like 1544.
grustifico, *see* CRUST
gruta, grouse (bird) c 1200.
gru/tum c 1165, 1275, **-dum** 1202, a 1283, grout, mash; **-ellum**, gruel *or* flour c 1200, c 1450; **grota** (*pl.*), groats 1325, 1375.
‡**gryll/arium** (grill-), **-etum**, cricket-hole 1483; **-us**, (?) coney (*cf.* **cherogryllus**) a 1250.
gryph/o (griph-, griff-) 1282, c 1511, †**garfo** 1446, **-a** c 1325, c 1362, **gripa** c 1495, **-es** a 1408, **-us** a 1446, griffin; **breve de -one**, writ under the Griffon (Chamber) seal 1343; **-ones** (*pl.*), Byzantine Greeks c 1192, c 1370; **ova -onis** 1232, **o. -is** a 1170, **o. agryph'** 1374, **o. -ina** 1383, **o. gripina** 13c., (?) ostrich eggs.
‡**gryposis**, curvature of the nails 14c.
gu-, *see also* w-
guad-, guag-, *see also* **vadium**.
guadabilis, *see* GELD
guadagna, garment of goat's hair a 1350.
guageria, *see* GAUG
guagn-, guan-, *see* WAIN
guald/a, -um, (?) weld *or* woad 1458, 1554; "woad" 1532; **g. rubea**, madder 1555; *cf.* **waida, 2 walda**.
Gualensis, Guallus, *see* **Wallensis**.
guar-, *see also* **gar-**; **war-**
guarettus, *see* **garita**.
‡**guarinus**, "man living by influence of sky" 1652.
guarn-, *see* GARN
guarona, *see* WARENN
guarra, *see* GUERR
guarrata, *see* **1 garnetta**.
guast-, *see* VAST; WASTELL
guaudeo, *see* GAUD
gubern/amen 11c., 1566, **-antia** 1374, c 1415, **-aculo** c 944, **-ale** c 1298, †**-atilla** (*pl.*) 1281, **-atus** 14c., **-io** 1439, **-ium** (Sc.) 1517, 1545, governance, guidance, rule; **-acula** (*pl.*), tackle, gear (naut.) 1419; **-a** 1357, **-ale** 1336, **-ile** 1296, helm, rudder; **-ativus** 1521, **-atorius** 1517, concerned with government; **-ator**, governor of school 1550; Cardinal Governor of Franciscans c 1250; **-eta**, *for* **-ator**, 709; †**gurberno** 12c., **guverno** 798, *for* **-o**.
gubio, *see* **gobio**.
gud-, *see* GELD
Guelphus 1281, 1343, **Gwelphus** 1281, c 1450, a Guelph.
guerantia, guerento, *see* WARANT
guerpio, *see* **werpio**.
*****guerr/a** 1091, 1587, **gerra** 1229, 1294, **gwerra** c 1115, 1419 **guarra** 1442, 1492,

werra 1088, c 1395, **warra** c 1150, 1199, **verra** 12c., war; retaliation, feud 1301, c 1366; **g. communis** (W.) a 1285; **ad -am** 1297, **de -a** 1273, 1344, at war, outside the Pale (Ir.); *cf.* **terra**; **-ator**, warrior c 1366; **-anter** 1584, **-ine** 1255, 1319, by war; **-icus** c 1590, ***-inus** 12c., 1558, **-enus** 1414, **gwerrinus** 1215, 1242, **werrinus** 1227, 13c., warlike, hostile; ***-o** c 1142, c 1450, **gwerro** 1255, **-eo** c 1150, c 1325, **gwerreo** 1242, **warro** 1204, to make war (against); *see also* **2 wera**.

gugla, *see* **gula**.

gugo, *see* **gogio**.

gugra, *see* **gigra**.

guidas, *see* WIND

guid/o 1265, (?) **-us** 1300, a guide; **-agium**, escort 1290; ‡"toll or custom" c 1440; 1402 (Ir.), c 1250, 1325, **-anagium, -onagium** 1289, **-oatgium** 1418, **-arium** 1254 (G.), (payment for) protection, blackmail; **-agium girfalconum** 1290 (?); **-o**, to protect (G.) c 1254; ‡to take toll c 1440.

Gui/enea libra 1387, **-anesius** 1422, coin of Guienne.

guigetta, guinchetus, *see* **wicattus**.

guig/ia 1213, **-a** 1303, 'guige', shield-strap.

guild-, guihalda, *see* GILD

guind-, *see* WIND

guirentia, *see* WARANT

Guiribecci, *see* **Hilibecci**.

guirpeo, *see* **werpio**.

guis/a (**guys-**), guise, apparel c 1395; **-o**, to arm, accoutre 1283.

guit, *see* **gyrus**.

guiteus, *see* TUNIC

gujo, *see* **gogio**.

gul/a, fur from throat of animal 1176; c 1230, c 1400, (?) **gaula** (G.) 1308, **-eta** 1221, gulley, watercourse; **de manu in -am**, from hand to mouth c 1204; ***-a Augusti** c 1185, 1449, **gugla A.** c 1280, **-austus** 1252, **-a autumni** 1279, 1282, Lammas day (1 Aug.); ‡**-a canina**, canine hunger, bulimy 15c.; **-erum** 13c., **-etta** a 1225, **-io** 1257, 1269, **-lonium** 1275, †**-um** 1239, collar; **golettum**, mouth ('gullet') of fish-trap (G.) 1316; part of springald 1327; ‡**-o**, to swallow 1483.

guld-, *see* GELD; GILD

gulf/us, †**-rus**, *see* **colpus**.

guliardia, *see* **goliardus**.

gum/ma 1276, 1344, **gemma** 1214, 1309, gum; **-a**, ‡cupping-glass 1483; ‡quicksilver 1652; ‡**g. Arabica** 15c., **-mi Arabicum** a 1250, ‡14c., **g. de Araby** 1440, gum Arabic; ‡**g. Paradisi**, orpiment 1652; ‡**-icula**, valerian (bot.) 1652; **-mositas**, gumminess a 1250, 1622.

gumph/us (**gunf-**) *** c 1130, 1413, **gonfus** 1324, †**gonsus** 1277, **gunchus** 1316, **guncius** 1271, 1305, †**gumus** 1268, †**gunnus** 1308, †**ginnisius** 1392, **gunda** 1268, hook of hinge (*cf.* γόμφος); bond, link 1220; ‡mortice of tenon c 1440; privy c 1180, 14c.; crotchet (mus.) c 1200.

guna, *see* **gouna**.

gunella, *see* **gemelle**.

gunfanum, gonfalon 1212; **confalonerius**, gonfalonier 1555.

Gunilda, name of a siege-engine 1330.

gunn/a 1346, c 1422, **-um** 1346, 1470, **-us** 1346, **gonna** c 1400, **gonnum** 1427, gun; **-arius** 1347, 1421, **-ator** 1387, 1486, **gonnator** 1498, gunner.

gunyngera, *see* **cuniculus**.

gupill-, *see* VULP

gurberno, *see* GUBERN

gurd/a, gourd-shaped vessel (of silver) 1272; **-a, -us** (**gingebrati**) 1285, 1303, **curda** 1242, 1253, measure of ginger; **g. de corio**, (?) leather bottle 1341.

gurg/es ***1086, 1547, **gorges** 1279, **cores** (W.) 12c., **gorda, gordus** (†**goidus**) 1194, 14c., **gortus** 1199, a 1250, **grodus** 1205, ‡**gurtus** 15c., **gorgia** 1313, **gorcia, gorcius** 1275, **gorettus** (Ir.) 1375, 'gorce', weir; drain, sink 1319, 1491; sluice 1630; **gordarius**, weir-keeper 13c.; ‡**-itivus**, deep 1483; *see also* **gorgia**.

gurgitium, *see* **gurgustium**.

gurg/ulatio, rumbling (in belly) a 1250, 13c.; ‡**-ilio**, to gargle 1570.

gurgulio, (?) Adam's apple (in throat) 6c.; *see also* **curculio**.

†**gurgus**, (?) *for* **garrulus**, 709.

gurg/ustium, fish-trap, creel 12c., ‡1483; **-itium**, hovel 1125; pig-sty c 550; **-ustus**, a fish c 550.

guriaga, *see* **currago**.

gur/la 1206, 1228, **-lus** 1230, **-rula** 1228, **gourla** 1314, purse (O.F. *gorle*).

gurnardus 1299, 1337, **gornardus** 1535, gurnard (fish).

‡**gurrex**, (?) *for* **hyrax**, "watermouse" 14c.

gurthwebbum, *see* **girthum**.

‡**gusis**, galbanum 14c.

gus/settum 1322, **-cettum** 1306, gusset (armour).

gusta, gustata, *see* **2 justa**.

gust/atio 14c., **-amen** c 990. 14c., taste; **-abilis** 1267, c 1270, **-alis** c 1361, tastable; **-anter**, by way of taste 1427; **-ativus**, pertaining to taste c 1240, c 1270; **-ator**, taster 1338, 1688; ‡**-ito**, to taste 1483.

gustitiarius, *see* **justitia**.

gutfirma, feast (A.S. *gytfeorm*) c 1115.

guthsera, *see* **githserus**.

gutt/a, gout (or other ailment) c 1000. c 1090, c 1540; goutte (her.) c 1585; gum 1382, a 1408; ‡**g. bona**, storax 14c.; **g. artetica**, arthritis 1421; **g. cadiva** c 1220, **g. caduca** 1221, ‡14c., epilepsy; **g. festra** c 1213, **g. fetre** c 1280, ulcer; **g. in renibus**, stone c 1280; **g. rosacea** a 1250, c 1400, ‡**g. ruonia** 1652, a rash; **g. sciatica**, sciatica 1398; **-a** 1307, 1374, **gota** a 1250, 1327, **gottile** (†**gocile**) (G.) 1283, 1289, ‡**-amen** 1483, **-ar** a 1315, **-aria** 1233, **-arium** c 1390, ‡15c., **-era** 12c., 1492, **-eria** 1180, c 1438, **-erium** c 1218, c 1449, **-erum** 1281, 1424, ‡**-orium** 14c., **-atorium** 1375, 1521, **-ur** 1297, c 1310, **-ura** 1259, 1583, **gotera** 1382, **goterium** 1180, **goterum** c 1437, 'gote', gutter, channel; **gotera**, gutter-tile 1374; **-atio**, drainage c 870; dripping a 1250; ‡**-eo**, "sea gum" 1652; **-iculus**, droplet c 1200; **gotus**, drop (alch.) c 1345; **-ose**, tearfully c 1390; **-osus**, provocative of gout c 1296; c 1296, a 1446, **-atus** c 1280, afflicted with gout (or other ailment).

gutt/er, *for* -ur, throat 1382, c 1390; -uralis, form of articulation (mus.) 1326; -uranum, (?) spout a 1496; -urnium, ewer 1508, 1537; ‡-urna, "quinsy", goitre c 1440, 15c.; -urnosus, goitrous c 1172, c 1362; -orico, to swallow c 550.
‡guttulus, "gudgeon" (fish) 15c.
guverno, *see* GUBERN
guvia, *see* 1 vidula.
guvio, *see* gobio.
guympla, *see* wimpla.
guyrentum, *see* WARANT
gw-, *see* gu-, w-
gwalstouua, *see* qualstowa.
gychettus, *see* wicattus.
†gylefatta, vat for fermentation 1266.
gyllo, guyld-, *see* geldum.
gyita, *see* GILD
gymbra, 'gimmer', maiden ewe 1364.
gymn/asium (gign-, gingn-, ginn-), fyrd, military service 11c.; *school, discipline c 1000. 1136, 1553; g. studiorum, university 1344; ‡-asiarcha, head master 1483; -adius, athlete or disputant c 1160, a 1180; -icanus, gymnastic 1544.
gyneceum: ‡gene/dea, brothel 13c.; -theum, dairy c 1250, ‡1483; ‡-tharia, -tharius, dairy-servant 1483.

gypsa, gypsas, *see* dipsas.
gyps/um 12c., ‡1508, gyphus 13c., gibsum 1526, chalk, marl, plaster; -arius 1500, ‡-ator 1520, plasterer; -eus, chalky c 1200, a 1250; aqua gyptica, (?) alkaline water a 1250.
gyragium, *see* cera.
gyrgill/us, reel, "yarnwindle" 12c., ‡1483; ‡-io, to wind yarn, reel 15c., 1483.
gyrthmanius, *see* GRITH
gyr/us (gir-), ring, hoop a 1446; instrument for marking trees 1401; per -um, in turn 1200, 1326; c 1250, 1278, in -o c 1400, around; -aculum, whirligig (toy) c 1385, ‡1483; ‡spindle whorl 1483; -amen, wheeling c 1195; -atio, rotation 1649; curving ornament c 1180; twisting, evasion 12c.; ‡-a solis, sunflower 14c.; -ativus, rotatory c 1267; linea -ativa, spiral 1335, 1427; -ator a 1200, -ans 1448, turnspit; ‡-o (†guit), magnet 14c.; skirt, fold (of dress) 1144, 1234 (*cf.* gerona); -ovagatio, roving, vagabondage c 1204, 1281; -ovagus c 1150, c 1436, -ivagus c 1250, stroller, vagabond; strolling monk 7c., c 943. c 1160, c 1553; -ovago, -ovagor, to roam about a 1166, a 1408; -o, to turn, go round (bibl.).

H[1]

hab/ardasshator 15c., -edassarius 1561, haberdasher.
habena, sling c 1180; †halandatio, (?) slinging 1334.
haber-, *see* HAUBER
habil/imenta (abil-) 1417, 1481, -amenta 1416, 1436, -ementa 1471, -iamenta 1495, -itamenta 1436, habiliments, accoutrements (*pl.*); -itas, capacity, fitness a 1250, 1409; -lus, *for* -is, able, fit 1540; -itatio, enabling, authorization c 1290, a 1452; *-ito, to enable, make fit, qualify a 1250, 1499.
habita, *see* amita.
*habit/aculum a 1100, 1586, -amen 14c., dwelling, abode; -abilis (*subst.*) 1267, c 1380, †habilitabilis c 1378, the habitable world; -or, *for* -ator, inhabitant 1275, c 1300.
1 hab/itus c 1180, a 1446, -itio c 1290, c 1470, having, possession; -itio rati, ratification c 1258; -ibilis, possessible c 1375; -eo, to get, receive 1226, 1385; to produce someone in court (leg.) 1189, 1352; to have to wife 1198; to possess sexually c 1218; to beget 1219; to owe 1173; *(with *inf.*) to have, be bound, to c 1115, 1537; (with ut) to have the power to 1271; h. me, to behave, be disposed, incline 1086, 1347; h. corpus (leg.) 1200, 1465; h. etatem, to come of age 1201, c 1220; h. ad faciendum c 1115, h. facere cum 1267, a 1347, to have dealings with; h. (virum) ad filium, to have a son by 1382; h. rem, to have sexual intercourse 1257; *see also* rectum;

h. male, to be ill 9c.; h. melius c 1000. c 1090.
2 habit/us c 850. 1267, c 1270, -um 1344, -udo c 1270, c 1377, habit, condition, relation, ἕξις (log.) (*see also* forma); *habit, garb (mon.) c 1066, 1461; h. pro equitatione, riding-habit (Ir.) 1471; h. secularis a 1142, 1259; -ellus, worthless habit (mon.) c 1620; cuculla -ualis, cowl (mon.) 14c.; -uabilis, capable of forming habits p 1300; -ualis a 1250, c 1444, -udinalis a 1250, 1412, habitual, customary; -ualiter c 1270, 1620, -udinaliter c 1270, 1427, habitually; -atio, familiarity 1344; -uatio, habituation c 1290; -uo, to habituate c 1290, 1412.
habulus, *see* HAVEN
habund-, *see* abunda.
haccasinus, *see* assassinus.
*hach/ia 1201, 1327, -a 1195, 1255, hacca (hakka) 1274, 1368, †ata 1340, -ium 1194, 1300, 'hack', axe, mattock; h. ad picum (picam) 1220, 1285, h. cum pik' 1266, pick-axe; h. Dacen[sis] 1200, h. Danachia 1200, h. Danechia 1280, h. Danescha 1231, h. Denachia 1270, h. Deneschia 1266, h. Denescha 1274, Danish axe, pole-axe; h. Irechia 1263, h. Irisca 1269, Irish axe; h. Scotencis, h. Well[ensis] 1270; -etta 1205, 1324, -ettum 1218, 1375, hatchet; hackio, to hack, break up (earth) 1347; *cf.* ASCI, axa.
hachiamentum, hatchment (*her.*) 1352.
hachus 1282, heckum (Yorks.) 1270, 'hatch', 'heck', hay-rack; 1294, c 1300,

[1]Spellings with intrusive or omitted H are not normally noted.

hech/a 1234, -ia 1296, hatch (naut.);
hecka cadens (on battlements) 1313;
cf. HECC, HES
hacia, *see* 1 hercia.
hackeneius, *see* hakeneius.
hactinus (act-, att-), *for* hactenus, c 1362,
c 1435.
had/a, -agium, *see* 2 hida.
haddera, heather (Sc.) 1521.
hadd/ocus 1250, 1419, -oukus, -ukus 1309,
haddock.
haderunga, respect of persons (A.S.) c 1115.
hadgabulum, *see* haga.
haer/ettus (canis) 1276, -icius 1312, herettius 1230, herricius 1287, hairecius 1249,
hairettus 1291, heirettus 1300, hayericeus 1324, harerus 1346, hound, (?) harrier;
bernarius -icius, keeper of hounds 1312.
hafneator, *see* HAVEN
hag/a 1086, c 1414, hauga 1534, 'haw', house
or enclosure in city; -gabulum 1259, 15c.,
hadgabulum 13c., house-rent; -abile,
(?) rental 1446; *see also* haia.
*hagard/um, -a (Ir., W.) 1212, 1471,
hogardum (C.I.) 1300, 'haggard', barn.
Hagarenus, *see* Agarenus.
hagi/os (agi-), -us c 550, 11c. 12c., c 1414,
ageus c 550, aius c 700, holy (ἅγιος);
-ographia, Holy Writ 15c.; -ographus,
writer of the Hagiographa 12c.; writer on
sacred subjects c 1204, c 1246; (*adj.*) hagio-
graphic c 800.
1 *hai/a (hay-) 1086, 1504, -um c 1250,
1307, heia (heya) 1086, c 1258, haga
12c., 1256, hagia 1086, hagium c 1280,
hega 1086, (?) hawetum (Beds.) 1447,
hedge or 'hay' (enclosure in forest); -a
1086, 1473, -us 1495, netted enclosure for
catching game; (?) peat-hag c 1300, 1460;
1362, h. piscialis 1275, h. piscarie 1460,
heia maris 1086, stake-net, "fish-garth";
h. alta c 1283; h. bassa 1229, c 1283; h.
firma, (?) fixed hedge 1086; h. mortua
c 1410; h. viva, quickset hedge 1240,
c 1300; -agium, (?) brushwood 1321;
†heyagium 1312, (?) †hawysbederipium
1408, (?) service of (or payment for) hedging
(man.); -atio 1388, -atura 1296, hedging;
-ator, hedger 1375; -bota, -botum c 1156,
c 1280, heybota c 1170, 1223, heybotum
1276, heynebutum c 1230, hay-bote, right
to gather wood for hedging; -mecta 1276,
heymecta 1334, hay-net, rabbit-snare;
-wardus 1209, c 1330, heywardus 1242,
1247, hayward; -warderia 1227, 1331,
heywardria 1306, office or tenure of hayward; -o 1368, 1635, heio c 1250, to hedge,
enclose with a hedge; *cf.* hachus, haga,
HECC, HES
2 haia 1277, heya 1286, plough-beam (Fr.
haie).
haic-, *see* HES
haimfara, *see* hamfara.
Hainaucus, Han/aucensis (Hann-), -oensis
a 1142, -o c 1385, -onicus p 1377, 1386,
-oniensis c 1420, Haynonensis 1271,
Hainaulter.
hainescia, *see* esnecia.
hair/a 1184, 1275, -ia 1201, heir/a 1205,
1270, -ia 1226, 1234, hair-cloth.

hair/ecius, -ettus, *see* haerettus.
hairenum, *see* maeremium.
hairo, *see* hero.
hais-, *see* HES
haiward-, *see* 1 haia.
hak/a 1247, 1265, -us 1232, 1327, hake (fish).
hak/eneius c 1285, 1337, hackeneius 1292,
1373, -eneus 1300, -enus 1332, -neius
c 1375, -neus 1291, -enettus 1360, 1413,
-inettus 1455, hackney; -eneya, hackney
mare c 1300.
hakeresweda, *see* acra.
haket-, *see* AKET
halandatio, *see* habena.
hal/barda, -lebarda, -bertus, halberd 1521.
halber-, *see* HAUBER
hal/cha c 1350, -ha 12c., 13c., haugh, flat
land by river (Sc., Durham).
‡halcium, "hame", horse-collar 1570.
halcyon-, *see* Alcyonite.
hal/ec, -icula, *see* allec.
haliaëtus, sea-eagle: ali/etus, kind of eagle
or hawk c 1190, a 1446; ‡-citor, ‡aluctor,
"hobby" *or* "merlin" 15c.; ‡-etor, hawker
1483; *cf.* almachor.
hal/la, -a, hall 1086, 1575; (?) market-house,
halle (Fr.) 12c., 1283; -lagium, market-due
(Calais) 1372; -gardum, hall-garth 1122,
1390; *-imotum c 1115, c 1450, -imota
1219, c 1306, -emotum a 1160, c 1340,
-imoda c 1250, -motum c 1200, 1531, hall-
moot, court baron; guild meeting c 1324,
1419; h. legale 1330; -eswanus, (?) 'hall-
swain' 1322; *cf.* GILD
1 hallandum, strip of land (? held by suit
at hall-moot) 1325, 1327.
2 hallandum, partition-wall 1491.
hallec-, *see* allec.
halleluia, *see* alleluia.
hal/o, *for* -os, halo c 1260.
halsa, hawse (naut.) 1336, c 1435.
halsfangium, 'were', fine (A.S.) c 1115.
haltanus, falco 1211, 1225, f. hautenus
1212, falcon hautain, (?) hobby.
halv/a a 1260, helva a 1300, 1493, measure
of land, half-acre; helflingus (?) 13c.,
-emitta 1299, measure of salt; alfebordum,
(?) half-board 1267.
hama 1282, 1312, (?) ames 1353, 'hame' (of
harness); *see also* hamma.
hamartus (amartus), sinner (Gk.) c 550.
hamdonus, *see* hyndenus.
hamell/um, -a 1186, 1427, *hamelett/um,
-a, -us 1212, 1534, hamiletta 1417, c 1443,
hamlett/um, -a 1308, 1583, hambletta
1550, hamlota (Sc.) 1479, hemlota (Sc.)
1480, hamlet.
hamelo, *see* esmallum.
†hamer/us, sort of fur c 1350; capa pro
†-a, sort of cape 1493.
hamestall/um, homestead 1274; -arius,
tenant of homestead 14c.
ham/fara, (†-stara) 1279, haimfara 1330,
heimfara 1130, heinfara 1086, breach of
peace in house; -socna c 1115, c 1290,
-sokina 1238, -soca 1198, 1331, -esocha
1189, ampsoca 1288, handsoca 1086,
ham-soken, (fine for) house-breach; -pso-
knyo, to commit ham-soken 1361.
ham/ma, -mus 1200, 1549, hommus 1367,

-na 1212, -pnus 1274, -pnia 1406, 'ham', portion of meadow.

hamoverium, see amobragium.

ham/unculus, little hook c 1444; -osus, attached to a book c 1180; -o, to angle for, entrap c 1180, c 1220.

hanap/arium c 1166, 1301, *-erium 1278, c 1400, -eria 1335, haneparium c 1220, haneparius 1292, hamperium 1337, 1402, hamper; 1258, 1267, -erium c 1282, 1586, Annaperium 1682, Haneparium 1257, 1271, Hamperium 1553, Hanaper (financial department of Chancery); H. Banci 1375; H. Scaccarii 1359; †-atus, measure of wheat (C.I.) 1309.

hanasterius, hancia, hancerius, see HANS

Hanaucensis, see Hainaucus.

hanch/a 1180, c 1390, -ia c 1400, hancus 13c., 1319, haunch, thigh-bone; -ia 1214, 1255, hauncha 1296, haunch of venison; cf. anca.

hanckus 1213, hanekus 1212, 1214, 'hank', (?) reef-point or gasket (naut.)

hand/ayna (and-), -ana, -eina, -ena, -ena, hayndena, day's manual labour (Somerset) 1234; cf. 1 andena, dayna.

handerium, some wooden object, (?) support for andiron (cf. 3 andena) 1292.

handhabbenda, caught red-handed (A.S.) c 1115.

handlum, handle (of plough) 1280, 1286.

handsoca, see hamfara.

hang/a 13c., -ylondum 1368, hanger, wooded slope.

hangerellum, 'hangrell', bridle-rail 1341.

hangewitha 1086, heng/ewita 1086, c 1199, -awita 1199, -wita c 1290, 1321, -ene-witha 1197, heingwita c 1188, fine for wrongfully hanging (? or failing to seize) a thief.

Han/no, -oniensis, see Hainaucus.

hans/a (ans-) 1154, 1336, -um c 1180, hancia 1297, (privileges of) hanse, guild of merchants; 1305, 1508, Anza 1550, Haunsa a 1564, the Teutonic Hanse; c 1190, 15c., -um 1219, -agium (†-agtum) 1204, 1324, -eria 1294, guild payment; gilda -aria 1327, 1337, g. hanceria 1334; domus -oria 1327; -terus 1410, hanasterius 1459, 1519, guild member (Oxford); -eaticus, Hanseatic 1585.

†thansacus, (?) f.l. for anelacius, 1213.

hanteso, see haucera.

hapalus (appalus), soft (of eggs) (ἀπαλός) ‡c 1200, a 1250.

hapsa, see haspa.

har-, see also her-

‡thar/a juniper 1652; ‡-mer 14c., ‡-mat 1652, juniper berry.

1 haraci/um a 1140, 1307, -a 1330, herra-cium c 1140, stud (of horses).

2 hara/cium 1325, 1388, -scium 1388, 1419, haras pisa 1336, kind of pulse grown as provender.

†tharaidum, troop of men (Frankish) c 1115.

harald-, see HERALD

har/anga, formula c 1280; arenga, harangue, formal address 1255, c 1396; ‡-inga, "long range of words" c 1440.

harboragium, see herbergagium.

harc-, see also HARD; 1 hercia; HES

harcabusarius, harquebusier 1556; arcus busius, harquebus 1499.

harduica, see HERD

hard/um 1282, 1297, harta, hartum (†harc-) 1208, 1344, hartis 13c., 1300, hortum 1284, withy (O.F. hart); -illo, tongue of buckle 1205; -illo 1238, 1243, harlio 1380, to skewer or hang on a hook (O.F. hardillier).

hareagium, see 2 averium.

†tharebannum, (?) f.l. for place-name (Harberton, Devon) 1307.

harell/a 1247, 1309, -um 1304, harou, hue and cry (C.I.).

†thare/nam (? -nari, herrenam), bad omen a 1235.

harengus, herring (Norm.) 1180, 1198.

harepipa, 'hare-pipe', snare 1495, 1541.

harerus, see haerettus.

hari/etum, -otum, see herietum.

hari/galdus, -gotum, see herigaldum.

hario, see hauritorium.

harlio, see HARD

harlotus c 1200, c 1340, herelotus c 1220, vagabond, beggar, hedge-priest.

harmegerius, see herbergagium.

harm/ela a 1250, ‡-ala 14c., harmel, wild rue (bot.).

†tharmoni/tas, harmony, symmetry c 1377; †-atus a 1110, †-acus a 1250, for -cus, well-proportioned.

harn/asium (arn-) 1177, 1381, -esium 1170, 1483, -esius 1243, -ezum c 1290, -icium 15c., hernasium 1179, 1295, hernesium 1161, 1457, hernesia 1492, herenesium 1226, 1228, hernecium 1336, hernisium 1216, hernisio 1175, -asiamentum, -esia-mentum (G.) 1254, 'harness', armour, equipment; -asium 1189, 1457, -esium 1266, 1390, -esia 1278, c 1533, -isum 15c., hernagium 1363, hernasium 1479, hernescium c 1330, herenesium 1261, hernisium 1242, harness (for horses); -esio 1205, 1440, -echio 1244, arlecho c 1231, herneschio 1225, 1242, hernesio 1254, to equip, fit out; -asio 1441, -esio 1296, 1479, -isio 1408, 1498, -izo 1385, 1489, hernasio 1431, hernescio 1332, hernesio c 1322, 1442, hernicio 1332, hernizo 1433, to decorate, mount; her-nesio, to harness (horse) 1303.

harnettum, (?) herring-net c 1353.

haroldus, see heraldus.

harp/a (arp-) c 950, hearpa c 1000, harp; -ator, harper 1208, 1331.

harpex, harpic-, see hirpex.

1 harpo (arpo), harpoon 1291.

2 harpo, to card (wool) c 1300.

harriet-, see herietum.

1 harta, (?) wall-cupboard 1291.

2 hart/a, -um, -is, see HARD

haruncellus, see hero.

harund/o frumenti, corn-stalk 1427; -ineus, weak as a reed c 1460; -inarius 1388, ‡1552, -inator 1304, 1324, thatcher.

harzura, see 1 hercia.

hasard/us c 1350, 14c., -eria 1388, hazard, game of chance; hazardor, gambler 1401.

hascia, see ascia.

*hasp/a 1192, 1346, **-um** 1318, **hespa** 1305, **hapsa** 1277, 1334, hasp (of door); **hapsa**, hasp (of book) 1327; **-a, -us**, part of plough-harness 1310, 1387.

hassacinus, *see* ASSASSIN

hassocus, 'hassock', tussock (of grass) c 1150.

hast/a (ast-), staff (of banner) 1401; shaft (on tomb) 14c.; shaft, stem (of cross) 14c., c 1400; stem (of plant) 14c.; shaft, handle (of tool) 1251, 1471; c 1072, c 1266, **-ula** c 1245, c 1330, candle-stick (eccl.); 1219, **-ia** 1219, spit; †**-ata**, (?) measure of land (G.) 1316; **-a porci** 1288, 1339, **-ilettum porci** 1309, roast (spit-load) of pork; **-a regia** a 1250, ‡14c., ‡**-ula regia** 13c., 15c., woodruff (bot.) (*cf.* **albula**); **-alla** c 1180, **-ella** 1213, 1316, **-ellium** 1235, **-illa** 1285, shaft, pole; **-alaria** 1294, **-elaria** c 1136, 1296, **-elleria** 13c., **-illaria** 1219, spit-house, office or service of turnspit; **-ellarius** c 1136, 1219, **-illarius** 1250, **hostilarius** 1250, **-ellator** 1378, turnspit, keeper of the spits; **-ellarius,** class of free-holder 1322; **-ator,** spear-maker 1327; **-icus** 1521, ‡1580, **-ilis** c 1362, concerned with spears; **-iliter,** with spears c 1298; ***-iludium** c 1180, c 1540, **-iludia** c 1300, **-iledium** (play on *laedere*) a 1200, ‡**-e ludus** 1570, **-iludiatio** 1399, 1404, tournament, joust; **h. ad anulum,** tilting at the ring 1508; **-iludiator** c 1343, ‡**-ilusor** c 1440, jouster; **-iludio** 1393, 15c., **-ilidio** 1391, **-iludo** p 1341, 1468, to joust; *see also* **astula.**

hast/ellaria (ast-) 1252, 1320, **-allaria** 1315, **-eleria** 1278, **-ellerium** 1222, **-elria** 1325, **-ilarium** 1279, 1371, mason's workshop (? *cf.* Fr. *atelier*); *see also* **hasta.**

hast/ivellum c 1250, 1467, †**hativellum** 13c., **-iverum** 1257, **-iberum** 1259, 1316, **-iberium** 1338, 1346, †**-ium** 13c., early corn, (?) barley or 'bere'.

haterellus, 'hattrel', crown of head *or* nape 1267, 1272.

hatia, *see* **athia.**

hattus, hat 1381.

hauber/cus 1196, 1539, **albergus** 1212, (?) **aliwerus** 1313, **-gius** 1185, (?) **holoberus** c 1620, **-gellus** 1185, 1233, **-gella** 1266, **habergellus** 1248, c 1315, **(h)albergellus** 1186, 1204, **halberghillus** 1241, **-jellus** 1219, **halberjolus** 1165, **haubregellus** c 1290, **haubrigellus** 1274, **hobirgellus** c 1320, **-gettus** 1305, 1333, **-jettus** 1319, **habergettus** 1207, 1318, **-geo** 1367, **halbergo** 1224, **-jo** c 1227, 1336, **hauborjo** 1327, **-jonus** 1231, 1333, **-junus** 1234, 1294, hauberk, habergeon; **-geria,** office of haubergier 1444, 1461; **-erius,** haubergier 1304; †**halbergum** 1213, **halbergeum** 1193, **-gium** 1190, **-gettum** 1203, c 1300, **halbergettum** 1196, 1228, **haubegerium** c 1217, 'hauberget', sort of cloth; **feodum -ticum,** hauberk-fee (Sc.) c 1350, 1609.

haubinus, *see* **hobinus.**

†**haucepinus,** foot-winch for cross-bow (O.F. *hausse-pie*) 1326.

haucer/a, -um 1296, 1417, **-ium** c 1311, **auncerum** 1302, **ausor** 1294, hawser (naut.); **hausera,** rope of siege-engine

1303; †**hauteso** (†**hanteso**), (?) to hoist 13c.

hauga, *see* **haga.**

hauka, 'hawk', horizontal axle of windlass 1329; (?) mason's hawk 1280; *cf.* **2 falco.**

hauloho, to halloo 1271; *cf.* **holulo.**

haulum, *see* **naulum.**

haun-, *see* **hancha; hansa.**

hau/ritorium, flask c 700; 1323, ‡1483, ‡**-stellum** 1483, bucket; 1521, **-riolum** 1329, **-sorium** 1472, ‡1483, **-storium** 1401, ladle; scoop (of mill-wheel) c 1280; ‡**ship's pump** c 1440; **-stulus,** slight draught (of fluid) c 1458; **-riator aque,** drawer of water 1325; **-sor (-stor),** drinker 1461; **fons -ribilis,** draw-well 1295; **-rio,** to haul up (coal, *etc.*) 1374, 1537; **hario,** *for* **-rio,** to draw (water) 1237.

hausassisus, *see* **assassinus.**

hausera, hauteso, *see* **haucera.**

†**haust/rum,** (?) *for* **hasta,** spear 1553; *see also* **hauritorium.**

hautenus, *see* **haltanus.**

havagium, *see* **havota.**

haven/a 1199, 1238, **havra** 1419, **habulus** 1483, haven; †**-agium,** (?) havenage, port due a 1190 (*cf.* **ulnagium**); **-aria** 1401, 1463, **-atoria** 1432, office of havener; **-ator** 1386, 1552, **-eator** 1376, **hafneator** 1276, havener, port officer (Cornwall).

havermaltum, oat malt 1531.

hav/erocus, (av-) -rocus, 'haverok', fork-load of hay (hay-maker's perquisite) 1234.

havot/a, dairy-farm, shieling, *hafod* (W.) c 1370; **-aria** 1315, **-eria** 1331, c 1370, **-ria** 1316, 1443, **havetria** 1383, **havagium** c 1327, 1450, (agistment of) summer pasture (W. & Marches); **-arius,** agister (W.) 1315.

haw/a, -yo, *see* **howa.**

haw/etum, -ysbederipium, *see* HAI

hay-, *see also* HAI

haydagium, 2 hida.

hayericeus, *see* **haerettus.**

haymald/a terra, 'hamald' land, private property (Yorks.) c 1200, c 1230; **-atio,** proving ownership (Lancs.) 1324; **-o, haymheldo,** to prove ownership of (Sc.) a 1566.

Haynonensis, *see* **Hainaucus.**

hazardor, *see* **hasardus.**

heafodwarda, *see* HEV

hearpa, *see* **harpa.**

heb/anus (eb-) c 1250, 1310, **ibanus** c 1300, ebony.

hebbyngwera, *see* **ebba.**

*hebdom/ada (bibl.), -as 8c. c 1200, c 1290, **-eda** c 1593, **-ida** 1471, 1486, **-oda** 1230, 1354, **ebdomita** 1454, **epdomada** 1274, **abdomada** 1259, week; weekly course or rota of duty (eccl.) c 1150; **h. magna** 1474 **h. sancta** 13c., 1586, Holy Week; **-as annorum** c 1090; **-adana,** fever recurring weekly a 1250; **-adalis** 1200, c 1290, **-edalis** 1306, **-idalis** 1462, **-odalis** c 1335, **-adarius** c 1006. c 1220, 1537, **-edarius** 1330, c 1450, **-odarius** c 1185, c 1296, **edomadarius** c 1500, weekly, on duty for the week; **-adarius,** everyday, for weekday use 1257; **misse -edarie,** masses said by the priest on duty 1376; **-adarius** c 980.

c 1080, c 1450, †-arius 1409, -odarius 1275, **abdomidarius** 1504, canon or obedientiary appointed to weekly course of duty; **h. circuitorum** c 1280; **h. coquine** c 1080, c 1330; **h. defunctorum** 12c.; **h. invitatorii** 12c.; **h. misse** 12c., c 1450; **h. psalterii** 12c.; -adatim c 1342, c 1670, †-atim c 1384, -idatim 1490, -odatim 1283, weekly.

hebet/as, dullness c 1364; -ativus, tending to dull a 1250, c 1283.

hecc/a (heck-) 1250, 13c., **hechium** 1293, 1337, hedge, fence; **h. cadens** movable palisade 1313; -agium, (payment for) upkeep of palisade (at Pevensey castle) c 1200, 1253; **hechinga**, hedging c 1230; **hechio**, to fence, 1281; *cf.* hachus, HAI, HES

hecceitas, *see* hoc.

hectica, hectic fever: **ethic/a** a 1250, c 1390, **eptica** 13c., **febris** -a c 1470; -us, sufferer from hectic fever a 1250, a 1361.

hed/a, kid 1359; **caro** -ulina a 1250; **corium** -ulinum 1444; -io, to stink (bear an ill-name) c 1180; *see also* hitha.

hedagium, *see* 2 hida.

hedclutum, *see* HEVED

‡**heder/a nigra** 13c., 14c., **h. terrestris** ‡14c., 1634, ground-ivy (bot.); -ula **aquatica,** water-ivy 1634.

hega, *see* 1 haia.

hegningus a 1250, **heiningus** a 1195, 'haining', enclosure (Yorks.).

hei-, *see also* HAI; 2 hercia; hitha.

heidengrana, (?) buckwheat (*cf.* Germ. *Heidekorn*) c 1404.

†**heilandus,** (?) island, eyot (Ir.) c 1180.

heimarmene, fate (εἱμαρμένη) 1344.

heimfara, heinfara, *see* hamfara.

heingwita, *see* hangewitha.

heiningus, *see* hegningus.

heir-, *see also* HAER; hero.

heira, heiria, *see* haira.

heis/a, -ia, *see* HES

†**hekfora,** heifer 1407.

Helceph, name of a book (math.) (? Ar. *alqeyf*, research) c 1150.

‡**helc/inum,** sledge 1570; ‡-tica, power of attraction (*cf.* ἑλκτικός) 15c.

helebota, sort of boat 1417.

helenium (bot.): **elempnium** a 1250.

helflingus, *see* halva.

heli/acus ortus, heliacal rising (astr.) a 1233, 1252; -ocentricus, heliocentric 1686; -anthemum, rock-rose c 1630; elitropium, blood-stone 1215; ‡oliotropium, "marigold" a 1520.

†**hellgabulum,** form of rent c 1310.

helluo, glutton: **ello** c 865.

helmo, helmet 1303.

helmunharifa, *see* elmuhahin.

heltus 1172, **heutus** (†houcus, †honcus) 1206, sword-hilt (O.F. *helt, heut*).

helv/a, helve, handle 1396; -o, to helve (an axe) 1335; *see also* halva.

helvewecha, a customary payment 1086.

Helvidianus (†Eliudianus), Helvidian heretic 12c.

helya, *see* hyle.

helydrus, *see* chelydrus.

hem/agogum, medicament to draw off blood

a 1250; **emach** 1241, **emath** a 1250, blood (αἷμα); -optoys, *for* -optysis, spitting blood a 1250, ‡14c.; -optoicus, *for* -optyicus, c 1200, ‡14c.; †-orosagia, haemorrhage a 1250; -orrhoides a 1250, 1622, **emeraudes** c 1400, haemorrhoids; -orroidale, flow of blood 1424; **emoreissa,** *for* -orrhousa, woman with haemorrhage 1271.

hematus, hemmed, stitched 15c.

hem/era, day (ἡμέρα): **hymera** c 1000. c 1100, **imera** c 950; **ymera examinationis,** Doomsday 14c.; **ante himerinum diem,** (?) before daylight 1166; †-orathios, *for* -erobios, ephemeral c 1160.

hemi/cadium (emi-), liquid measure a 1250; -cranium, (?) brain c 730; side of skull 1620; -grania, migraine a 1250, 1407; -cranicus 1620, -granicus a 1250, -graneus a 1250, ‡1483, of migraine; ‡-cyclum, "farthingale" 1570; ‡-dolium, pipe (of wine) 1483; -onitis, ‡"hart's tongue" (bot.) 1570; "small moon fern" 1641; -spheria 7c., -sperium c 1250, c 1265, -spirium c 1360, **hiemispherium** 7c. 12c., *for* -spherium, hemisphere (astr.); -sphericus, hemispherical c 1115; -spherice, hemispherically p 1300; -spherois, hemispheroid 1686; -thea, demigoddess a 1517.

hemina, liquid measure: **esmina** 1255, **himina** 570; *cf.* 1 mina.

hemlota, *see* HAMELL

hemo-, *see* hemagogum; hemera.

hemum, sort of song (? *for* οἴμη, *from* **prohemium**) c 1200, ‡1483.

hen/as (en-), unity c 870; -decas, series of eleven c 815. 13c.; -dias, hendiadys (gram.) 1427; **Enticon,** Zeno's *Henoticon* 12c.

heng-, *see also* hangewitta.

heng/a 1314, -ula 1307, 1382, -ella 1311, hinge.

hengestmannus 1360, **henxmannus** 1361, **henxstmannus** 1377, **hextmannus** 1380, henchman, groom.

‡**Henricus piger,** sort of furnace (alch.) 1652; ‡**H. rubeus,** red vitriol 1652; *see also* bonus.

hepa, *see* hepum.

*****hep/ar** (ep-), liver a 1150, p 1330; -atica, liverwort (bot.) c 1212, 1634.

hepdomada, *see* HEBDOM

hephestitis, kind of gem: **epistites** c 1200.

heps/esis (eps-), boiling 13c.; digestion c 1200; ‡psionomus, (?) *for* -omenus, boiled 15c.

hept/agonum, heptagon 1267; -agonus, heptagonal 1267, ‡15c.; -apylus, seven-gated c 1173; -archa, heptarch a 1100; -archia, heptarchy 1586; -as, week c 1200; -aticus 793. a 1142, 15c., -athecum c 550, heptateuch.

hep/um, -a, heap, measure of grain 1107, c 1360; -o (†trepo), (?) to heap, stack 1498.

her-, *see also* har-

hera, *see* es.

Heracli/te (*pl.*), Heracleonite heretics 12c.; ‡-a, clary (bot.) 1570.

herald/us p 1330, 1606, **herauldus** 1474, **haraldus** 1290, c 1557, **haroldus** 1433, **herodius** c 1440, 1446, herald; **h. armorum** 1356, 1555, **h. rex armorum** 1456; -icus 1536, c 1595, **haraldicus** 1620, heraldic.

‡herb/a Aaron, arum 14c.; ‡h. acetosa, sorrel, sourdock 14c.; ‡h. auricularis, h. Herculis, houseleek 14c.; ‡h. benedicta, hemlock 13c., 1483; ‡h. calida, columbine 14c.; ‡h. cancri, cock's comb 15c.; ‡h. capillaris, Venus' hair 14c.; ‡h. catholica, spurge laurel 14c.; ‡h. cervi, hart's-tongue 14c.; ‡h. Christiana, "toad-fennel" 14c.; ‡h. Christophori, fern, (?) osmunda 14c.; ‡h. cruciata, crosswort 14c.; ‡h. dulcis, liquorice 14c.; ‡h. fortis, wormwood 14c.; ‡h. frigida, liverwort 14c.; ‡h. fullonis, h. saponaria, soapwort 14c.; h. Gerardi, goutweed 1634; h. Gorberti a 1250; h. hircina a 1250, ‡15c., h. Judaica 15c., (?) hemp-nettle; h. impatiens, touch-me-not (balsam) 1641; h. impia, cudweed 1634; h. (sancti) Johannis a 1250, ‡1483, h. perforata a 1250, 1538, St. John's wort; ‡h. leporina, savory 14c.; h. Lucii, a plant that cures blindness c 1212; ‡h. Martis, martagon c 1440; h. mercurialis, charlock c 1000; ‡h. meretricum 14c.; ‡h. muralis (†mirabilis), pellitory 15c.; ‡h. muscata, woodruff 14c.; h. paralysis a 1250, ‡14c., ‡h. (Sancti) Petri 14c., c 1440, cowslip; h. paris, herb Paris 1634; ‡h. Sancti Pauli, (?) spurrey 15c.; ‡h. pelerine, goosegrass 14c.; ‡h. petiginaria, greater celandine 15c.; ‡h. pigmentaria, balm 14c.; h. Roberti, herb Robert a 1250, ‡13c.; h. salsifera, saltwort c 1215; ‡h. sanguinaria, shepherd's purse 14c.; h. Saracenica, birthwort 1585; h. savina, herb sabine, savin 13c.; h. sardonica 1538, ‡h. scelerata 14c., celery-leaved crowfoot; h. sigillata, see SIGILL; h. Stephani, enchanter's nightshade (Circaea) 1634; h. Syriaca, mallow a 1250, ‡14c.; ‡h. terrestris, purslane 15c.; ‡h. tinctoris, woad 15c.; ‡h. trutannorum, thapsia 14c.; h. venti, pasque flower 1641; ‡h. Walteri 14c., h. Galteri a 1250, "muge des bois", (?) lily of the valley; ad -am, at grass (of horses, etc.) 1234, 1327;

*-agium 1086, a 1564, -agia 1086, c 1185, harbagium 1567, (right of or payment for) pasturage; hay, cut grass 1188, 1583; (?) river-weed 1373; -agiatio, pasture-land c 1450; †-agius, grazier 1380; lapis -alis 1267 (?); firma -alis, pasture-rent 1460; *-arium 1160, 1435, -arius 1219, 'arbour', garden; ‡-arius, "tedder", grass-spreader 15c., 1483; botanist 1538; res -aria, botany 1538, 1629; ‡vinum -atum, "nectar" 15c.; -eus, of grass 1518; -idans, grassy c 970; ‡-iseca, mower 15c.
*herb/ergagium a 1142, 1462, -erbagium 1236, -ergiagium 1403, -urgagium 1392, -igagium 1452, 1487, -ergamentum c 1090, 1199, hervergamentum a 1278, -eria c 1107, -ergaria 1199, -ergeria c 1136, -egata (G.) p 1230, -ergatum 1124, albergagia (G.) 1235, †abbergageria (G.) 1236, albergata (G.) c 1238, 1401, †abberguata (G.) 1332, albergades (pl.) (G.) 1313, harbourage, procuration (right or service of lodging or payment in lieu); storage (of wine-casks) 1270; harboragium, harbour-due 1606; -igarius 1479, -ergiator

1403, 1417, harbinger; miles harmegerius, (?) knight harbinger 1376; albergamentum, (?) dwelling-place, settlement (G.) 1315; -ergatio, settlement, occupation (of land) 1216, 1275; -ergio, to exact free lodging 1403; c 1200, 1335, -egio 1335, -ergo 1124, 1200, -argo a 1190, -erio c 1140, erburgo a 1200, to build (a dwelling-house), settle, build on (a site); -ergo, to store (grain) 1290; h. me, to lodge, take shelter 1222; albergo (vina), (?) to retail (G.) 1289.

1 *herci/a 1221, 1538, herchia c 1200, harcia 1223, 1255, hacia 1358, hertica 1392, harrow; h. duplex 1288; h. ferri 1311, h. de ferro 1347, iron-toothed harrow; -agium c 1350, -atio 1279, 1388, †-o 1240, c 1388, *-atura 1261, 1414, -etura c 1250, arsietura 1338, -tura 1316, hersura c 1283, harzura a 1200, harrowing; -ator c 1130, 1364, -arius 1234, harrower; 1193, c 1315, -or 1186, hercharius 12c., hercerius 1152, hercatorius a 1127, 1187, caballus hercerius, equus herzerius, e. herzorius 1185, beast used for harrowing; *-o 1086, 1366, †-o 1326, herzo c 1220, to harrow; cf. hirpex.
2 herci/a c 1245, 1449, -um 1386, hersium a 1447, herse, frame for candles; h. (†heia) ad tenebras 1287, 15c.; -a, hurdle (of sheep-fold) 1388; (?) hurdle or hatch (in mill-race) 1284.

herd/a 13c., -ia 1247, herd; -ewica c 1100, 1210, -ewicum c 1200, harduica 1086, hordewica 1210, 'herdwick', dairy-farm.
herd/lus, -ellus, -illus, see HURD
hered-, see also heres.
heredito, to make an eyrie c 1090; cf. aeria.
heregaldum, see herigaldum.
heregeld/a, -um, see herietum.
heregripa, hergripa, hair-pulling, assault (A.S.) c 1115.
herelotus, see harlotus.
herem-, see EREM; ERMIN
herenac/us 1397, c 1606, -ius c 1592, 'herenach', (lay) lord of religious house (Ir.); -ia, office of herenach (Ir.) 1397.
herenesium, see HARN
hereos, hereosus, see eros.
*heres apparens, heir apparent 1202, 1505; h. de carne 1264, 1289, h. corporis c 1400, h. de corpore 1218, c 1490, h. corporalis c 1362, h. de se 1307, heir of the body; h. a latere, collateral heir c 1290; h. propinquior, next heir 1195, 1505; h. rectus, direct heir 12c., 1430; h. quartus 1251; h. tertius 1086; h. universalis (?) 1316; hered/alis c 1180, ‡-italis 1483, heritable; -atio, disherison 1263, 1290; p 1351, ‡-itaculum 1483, -itagium 1200, 1488, heretagium 1370, heritagium 1203, c 1336, -itarium c 1290, inheritance, heritage; -ipeta (†-epeta, †-ipota), next heir c 1115; -itabilis, entitled 1564, 1583; *-itabiliter c 1102, 1236, *-itarie 1121, 1461, -itario c 1179, 13c., by inheritance; -itamentum, hereditament 1453, 1543; -itaria, (n. pl.) hereditary rights c 1142; (f. s.) heiress 1279; -itarius 821. c 1070, 1512, heretarius 1461, hereditary; terra

-itaria, t. -itatis, bocland c 1115; -itarius
a 1100, 1409, heritator 1366, heir; -itatus,
entitled a 1564; †-itatus ex, disinherited
1266; *-ito c 1080, 1496, -o 1342, herito
1516, to inherit; -ito, to leave an inheritance
793; to make heir 793. c 1070, a 1250; (with
abl.) c 1170, c 1458, h. de a 1090, c 1170,
h. in 1404, a 1564, to make heir to, enfeoff
with.
*here/sis (eccl.), -sia (G.) 1289, †-ticio 1389,
heresy; *-siarcha c 1192, 1586, -siarches
c 1250, c 1400, herisiarcha 1433, heresi-
arch; *-ticus (eccl.), -sista c 1366, heretic;
c 1090, 1543, -ticanus, -ticativus c 1422,
heretical; -ticabilis, able to be turned into
heresy 1378; -ticalis, leading to heresy
1324, 1378; -tice, heretically 1378; -ticatio,
denunciation as heretical c 1362, 1378;
*-tico, to make, or denounce as, heretical
c 1332, 1427; -tizo, to hold heretical
opinions 12c.
here/streta (†-strata), military road (A.S.)
c 1115; -teama, private warfare, brigan-
dage c 1115; †-temius 13c., -tochius
(†-tochus, hertoheus) 13c., military commander, duke.
heret/agium, -arius, see heres.
herettius, see haerettus.
hergripa, see heregripa.
Heriani, see Aeriani.
heri/cius c 1325, c 1400, -cia (f.) 13c., for
ericius, hedgehog; yricius, sea-urchin
a 1250; -cius 1167, 1286, -cio 1215, -so
1264, -conus 1198, stockade; cf. hirsona;
see also haerettus.
*her/ietum c 1120, 1583, -ieta 1324, 1348,
harietum (harr-) c 1320, 1588, harieta
1086, -iotum a 1185, 1577, -iota 1453,
hariotum 1609, †heyrethotum (W.) c 1295,
heriot, feudal death-duty of best chattel;
h. mortuum, h. vivum 13c.; -egelda
(-eyelda, -ezelda) 1450, 1566, -gelda
1415, -igelda 15c., -ielda 1431, 1539,
-yhelda 1440, 1552, Scottish equivalent of
heriot; †-egeldum, a tax (?) 1022 (15c.);
-ietabilis, liable to pay heriot 1347; -ieto
1303, harrietto 1537, to pay heriot (for).
her/igaldum 1275, 1340, -egaldum 1255,
harigaldus 1258, -igaudum 1257, -igau-
dium 1294, -igota 1250, harigotum 1255,
'herigaut', surcoat.
herim-, see EREM
herisipilatus, see erysipelatus.
heriso, see hericius.
herit-, see heres.
†herlebecheria, a building at Clarendon
(? cf. herbergagium) 1244, 1252.
herm-, see also EREM; ERMIN
Herm/ula, Herm, armless statue 685;
-aphrodita c 1290, -ofrodita 1370, -ofro-
ditus a 1250, 13c., †armifraudita 15c.,
hermaphrodite; -aphroditicus, epicene
c 1200; -aphrodito, to combine the sexes
in c 1200; -enia, interpretation 1620 (cf.
epimenia); -odactylus a 1250, 13c., -oda-
tilus c 1215, (?) colchicum (bot.); -odacty-
lata, (?) drug containing colchicum a 1250.
hern-, see ernesium; HARN
her/o 1287, heiro 1300, c 1324, †hiero 1224,
hairo 1284, -ona 1404, heironus 1274,

heron; -onagium, hawking for herons
1315; -ouncellus 1419, -uncellus 1264,
1282, heiruncellus 1249, haruncellus
1257, heronshaw, young heron; -onera,
heironera(†-nia)1231, -onia 1330, heronry;
falco -onarius 1330, f. -enarius 1346, f.
heironarius 1229, 1346, falcon trained to fly
at herons; canis -unerius, dog trained to
retrieve herons 1279, c 1285.
herodius, see erodius; heraldus.
hero/s, noble, magnate c 1170, 1535; -ice,
in hexameters c 1130, c 1436; -icus, writer
of hexameters c 1470; (?) honourable 957;
pious or wise 943, 11c. 12c., 1378; divine
12c.; (?) belonging to a lord (erus) c 550.
herp/es cingulus, -etestiomenus (ἐσθιό-
μενος), herpes (med.) a 1250.
herpex, herpic-, see hirpex.
herracium, see 1 haracium.
herrenam, see harenam.
herricius, see haerettus.
herro, lord (Germ.) 1245.
hers-, herz-, see erscha; hercia (1 & 2).
hertica, see 1 hercia.
hertlatha, lath of heartwood 1333.
hertoheus, see heretochius.
herun-, see hero.
hervergamentum, see herbergagium.
heryhelda, see herietum.
hes/a c 1210, c 1273, -ia 13c., †-ta 13c.
haesia 1190, heisa 1203, heisia c 1187,
haisa (haisia) 1280, 1366, *haicia 1222,
1450, †haica 1275, 1291, †harcia 1297,
haicium c 1200, c 1270, brushwood, thicket,
hay (enclosure in forest), or (?) hedge (A.S.
hǽs); -ia 13c., c 1400, -kia 1225, hurdle
or hatch (at gateway); cf. hachus, HAI,
HECC
hesiamentum, see AIS
hesit/ative, doubtfully 860; ‡-ativus, doubtful 1483; -o †vultum, to look perplexed
(or ? multum) c 1250.
hes/kia, -ta, see hesa.
hespa, see haspa.
hesperiolus, see scurellus.
hestern/um, the preceding day c 1296; -o,
on the preceding day c 1245.
hest/ha, loaf (? cf. 'hestcorn') 1086; †-rasfia
(†-erasda), fodder (?) 14c.
hestoria, see 2 historia.
hesumo, see EXHUM
heteriarcha, captain of imperial guard
c 1595.
hetero/clitus c 1612, 1620, ethroclitus a 1250,
c 1430, heteroclitic, irregular (gram.); abnormal 1610; -genia, heterogeneity c 1612,
1620; -geneus a 1200, 1620, -genus 870,
etherogeneus a 1250, ethrogeneus c 1360,
c 1370, ethereogeneus c 1200, euthrogeneus a 1250, -mogeneus 1344,
-mogenus c 1380, ethromogenus 1378,
heterogeneous; -nerges, acting differently
p 1300; -theles, willing differently p 1300.
hetha, see hitha.
heuka, see huca.
heura, see hura.
heusira 12c., hyusira c 1160, a customary
payment, 'hewechyre' (Ramsey & Reading).
heutus, see heltus.
hev/edclutum 1269, hedclutum 1308, metal

clout on plough-head; **-edlanda** 1224, **-et-londa** c 1200, **evedlonda** 1202, (?) †**-edreta** 1234, headland; **heafodwarda**, (service of) head-ward, bodyguard c 1115.

hexa/gonum, hexagon 13c., 1267; **-gonus**, hexagonal 1267, c 1270; **-gonaliter**, hexagonally a 1200; **-hedrum**, **exacedrum**, hexahedron 1267; **-meron** a 1250, c 1520, **-emeron** c 1395, title of a book; ‡**-mitus**, see **samitus**; ‡**-pedia** 1570, **-peda** 1686, fathom; **-pla**, polyglot text of Origen 1267; **-ptotus**, having all six cases (gram.) 8c.; **-stichon**, poem of six lines 1518.

hextmannus, see **hengestmannus**.

hey-, see **haia** (1 & 2).

heyrethotum, see **herietum**.

‡**hezerhassen**, white bryony (bot.) 14c.

hiatus, noise, cry c 1125, c 1350; voidance (her.) c 1595; **hiantia** (pl.), lacunae 985.

hibern/agium 1199, 1252, **hivernagium** 1174, c 1350, †**invernagium** 1271, **semen -iale** 1274, winter sowing, winter crop; ‡**-ium**, winter-house 1483.

Hibern/ensis 9c., c 1000. c 1150, c 1315, **-iensis** c 1188, c 1400, **-ialis** 1411, **-icanus** 1510, *****-icus** c 1135, 1537, **-igena** c 1135, **-igenus** 1149, **-is** c 1360, **-us** c 730. **-icus** c 1090, 1252, †**Hiberionacus** 5c., Irish, Irishman; **-icus merus** 1409, **H. purus** 1283, 15c., mere Irish; see also **accipiter, pannus**; **ecclesia -icana** 1216, 1404; **-ice**, in Irish 1584.

Hiber/nicum corpus, -us, Hibrius 1267, **lapis -us** 1267, a 1292, gold (alch.); cf. **Hispania**.

hibiscus, marsh mallow (bot.): **ebiscus** 1538, **eviscus** a 1250, ‡14c.

hichacum, see **issaccum**.

†**hicticus**, sort of ship (? Byzantine) c 1457..

1 **hid/a** (corii), hide 1661; **-gildum** (†**hyngildum**), payment in lieu of flogging c 1115.

2 *****hid/a** c 1070, 1535, **hada** 1618, **hilda** 15c., 1609, †**-ria** a 1155, **-ata** c 1193, 1364, hide, measure of land (usually from 80 to 120 acres); *****-agium** c 1070, 1535, **hadagium** 1526, **haydagium** 12c., **hedagium** 1330, **hudagium** 1234, 1324, †**hisdagium** c 1180, **hildragium** a 1130, (?) **-warium** a 1150, hidage, hide-geld; (?) 'fulstingpound', composition for amercements in hundred-court (Oxf.) 1276; **-arius**, tenant holding hide (or half-hide) 1222, c 1283; **-emannus** 1351, 1466, **-mannus** 1381, small-holder; **-emanlandum** 1466, **-landum** 1381, small holding; **-o**, to tax, assess for hidage 1086, 1276.

3 **hida, hieda**, see **hitha**.

hiemi-, see HEMI

hiem/s magna, great winter, cyclic extremity of cold a 1553; ‡**-aculum**, winter-house 1483; **donum -ale (yemale)**, a customary payment (Berks.) 1356.

hiera (yera) abbatis, h. Archigenis, h. rufa (rufina, Rufini) a 1250, **h. logadii** a 1205, **h. logodion** a 1250, 13c., **h. picra** a 1205, **h. p. Galeni** a 1250, 1414, **h. pigra** a 1250, c 1465, **gira pigra** 1380, **h. p. Constantini** a 1250, purgatives; ‡**gerenoxa, geronoxa** (for ἱερὰ νόσος), epilepsy 1483; nightmare c 1440.

‡**hieraculus**, hawk, lanneret 1570.

hierarch/a, dignitary, prelate (eccl.) c 1090, 1437; **-us celestis patrie**, Jesus 12c., 13c.; **-ia** 9c., 1006. c 1236, 1620, **gerarchia** 1253, ‡1483, **-icum** c 1343, hierarchy, clerical office; **-ice**, hierarchically, in sacred order 9c. 1281; **-icus**, hierarchical c 1238.

hiero, see **hero**.

‡**hiero/botanum**, vervain (bot.) 14c.; **-chronographus**, sacred chronicler 14c.; ‡**-comium**, leper hospital 1580; **-glyphice**, symbolically 1564; **-martyr**, holy martyr 1171; †**-philosophus**, holy philosopher 1345; †**ierithicus**, (?) for **-thytus**, sacrificed to a god 1271.

Hierosolymi/peta (Jerosolymi-) 12c., **-tanus** c 1140, pilgrim to Jerusalem.

biggaster, see **hoggus**.

higra, eagre, Severn bore c 1125.

hilar/esco, to gladden, cheer 793; to be or become happy 8c. c 1170, a 1446.

hild-, see 2 **hida**.

Hilibecci, Guiribecci (pl.) a 1142, **Hiri-belli** c 1185, Norman nickname for Angevins.

hillelondus, see **hulla**.

hiltra, part of mill, (?) mill-tail (Hants) 1272, 1379.

himerinus, see **hemera**.

himina, see **hemina**.

hinc inde, mutually, on either side 1262, 1419.

hindonus, see **hynderus**.

hinni/bile (subst.), neighing 1267; **tumultus -tivus**, noise of neighing 15c.

hinn/iculus c 1260, **-ulus** a 1250, 1400, fawn.

hinnula, see **inula**.

‡**hippia major**, (?) burnet (bot.) 14c.; ‡**h. minor** 14c., ‡**ipia** 15c., (?) **ypia** a 1250, chickweed.

hippo-, see also **hypo-**

Hippocraticus (Hypo-), physician a 1100.

hippo/dromus (hypo-), keeper or trainer of horses 12c.; †(?) portico c 1130; **-dromium**, racing stable c 1212, c 1250; **-tamus** c 1200, ‡15c., **-tarus** c 1370, **-taurus** c 1315, †**-phagus** c 1212, hippopotamus; **ippus**, horse c 700.

hirchetum, see **hirsona**.

1 **hirc/us emissarius**, scapegoat c 1193; ‡**-ina**, (?) horsetail (bot.) 14c.; see also **herba**; **-itallus**, for **hirquitallus**, 709; **-ocervus**, tragelaph (fabulous animal) a 805. c 1160, 1378.

2 ‡**hir/cus** a 1519, **-quus** c 1180, ‡c 1440, corner of the eye.

hirda, 'earth', ploughing service (A.S. yrð) c 1182.

hirdellus, see HURD

Hiribelli, see **Hilibecci**.

hirmannus, see **hyremannus**.

hirpex, harrow: **herpex** 1374, **harpex** 1419, **herpic/a** 1352, 1446, **harpica** 1397, 1494; ‡**-arius** 1483, ‡**harpicator** 15c., harrower; **-atio** 1339, **harpicatio** 1456, harrowing; **-o**, to harrow 1406, 1467; cf. 1 **hercia**.

hirs/ellis, -ula, 'hirsel', red deer hind in second year 1494.

hirsillum, 'hirsel', cattle-pound or sheep-pen (Durh.) 1366, 1383.

hir/sona 1255, 1326, †**-uco** 1231, **-chetum**

1286, fence, palisade (W. & March); *cf.*
hericius.
hirstis, *see* hurstum.
hirsutus, hairy: †ursutus 12c.; *see also*
ferrum.
hirubin, *see* cherubicus.
hiruco, *see* hirsona.
hirund/ela, swallow c 1350; -inaria 1538,
‡-inea 14c., celandine (bot.); -ineus, swal-
low-like, migratory 12c.
hisma, origin (ἴσμα) 1528.
Hispan/ia, high-grade gold (alch.) 1267
(*cf.* HIBER); ‡-icum viride, verdigris
1652; espan/ellus 1230, -iellus (? espainel-
lus) 1211, 1242, spainellus 1200, 1279,
spaniel *or* (?) Spanish hawk.
Hispericus, *for* Hespericus, Latin c 550.
hispid/itas, roughness c 1180, c 1218; -e,
roughly c 1200.
hissirus, *see* ostium.
1 historia (ist-), story (arch.) 13c., a 1490;
h. clara, clerestory 1482.
2 histori/a, history, story: hestoria c 1135,
storia c 1177; -a 12c., 1519, storia c 1511,
pictorial representation, picture; special
service at matins on saint's day c 1006.
c 1072, 1472; h. naturalis, natural history
1620; histor, knower c 550; -ola 1334,
1648, -uncula c 900, short narrative;
-acus, historical c 1380; c 1197, -agraphus
a 1250, c 1400, historian; -ale, (?) lectionary
c 1215; sensus (intelligentia) -alis, literal
sense c 1180, a 1200; -aliter, historically,
in history c 730, 1006. c 1080, c 1140; ‡-o,
to decorate with pictures 1483; -o, -or
(*dep.*) c 1150, c 1362, -zo 1378, to record.
historium, *see* hostorium.
histrio/ c 1135, 1454, instrio 1260, strio 7c.,
player, minstrel; -naliter, theatrically 15c.,
1461; -natus, dramatic entertainment 1286,
c 1340; theatrical profession 1385; celum
-nium, 'stage heaven' 1595.
‡histrix, buffoon 1483; (?) *cf.* hystrix.
hitha 1220, 1464, heittha a 1170, hetha
1221, heda 1086, hieda a 1130, hida
c 1120, hutha c 1115, 1221, huda 1401,
†huca 1209, hithe, landing-place.
hiul/cus, -us, open c 550.
hivernagium, *see* hibernagium.
hlafordsocna (†hlasocna), free man's right
to choose lord, *or* lord's resulting authority
(A.S.) c 1115.
hlammator (†klammator), eel-catcher (? *cf.*
Gothic *hlamma*, 'trap') 13c.
hlosa, 'looze', sheep-cote (A.S. *hlose*) c 1283.
Hlotharius, *see* LOTHAR
hlothbota, fine for joining illegal association
(A.S.) c 1115.
hluttres (*pl.*), measures of ale c 1115.
hoa, *see* HOW
hob/bia 1544, -elus, oberus c 1200, hobby
(bird).
hob/inus c 1275, 1521, haubinus c 1521,
hobby, nag; *-elarius 1296, 1560, -ilarius,
(†-erarius) 1364, -iliarius 1536, -olarius
1318, -larius 1347, 'hobeler', light horseman.
hobirgellus, *see* HAUBER
hoc aliquid, individual thing (τόδε τι) a 1304;
hecceitas, 'thisness' (log.) a 1304.

hoccus, *see* hoga.
hock/dies c 1270, -edies, hokdies 1330,
dies de la hok' 1303, hockday (second or
third Tuesday after Easter).
hocsirocrocium, *see* OXY
hodi/ernitas, the present time 1427; -ernus,
present 759.; -etenus, till today c 1090.
hodoporion (od-), itinerary c 1190.
hog/a c 1170, 1303, -um c 1180, 15c., houca
1330, 'how', mound; 1199, 1459, hoccus
1086, mound for drying salt (esp. Lincs.);
see also HOW
hogardum, *see* hagardum.
hog/gus 1231, 1357, -aster a 1128, c 1300,
hocgaster 1155, -ettus 1257, 1449, hog,
boar (usually in second year); -ettus
porc[inus] 1297, -aster c 1175, 1426,
-ester c 1265, 1504, (?) higgaster 1508,
-erellus 1295, 1388, -ettus 1345, 1377,
-atus 1241, -rus c 1345, 1420, hogg, ram
(usually in second year); -aster bidentalis
1298; h. femellus 1296.
hoia, hoy (naut.) c 1586; *see also* HOW
hokdies, *see* hockdies.
hoket/us 1326, c 1470, hoquetus 1326,
'hocket', break in voice-part (mus.); -us,
-um, hitch, quibble (leg.) (G.) 1286, 1312.
1 hokum, hook 1307, c 1397.
2 hokum, 'hook', strip of meadow 1222, a 1400.
hola, hold (naut.) 15c.
Holand/arius 1438, -icus c 1370, -rinus
1443, Hollander.
holer-, *see* holus.
holetta 1286, hullettus 1374, 'holet', hut.
1 holm/a (†holina) 1181, 1422, -um c 1400,
*-us c 1150, c 1400, hulmus 1107, 1465,
holm, river-meadow.
2 holm/a (olm-) c 1362, -us 1352, 1355,
(?) holly; holrisus, (?) holly hedge 1238;
cf. hussus, ULM
holoberus, *see* HAUBER
*holo/caustum (eccl.), -caustoma c 1180,
c 1250, holocaust; olalogia, vernacular
tongue c 1175; -cericus c 1340, -siricus
a 1150; †obsericatus 1609, -xericus 14c.,
elocericus 14c., †olasterius 1521, *for*
-sericus, silken; -sericum, silk mantle
9c.; silken hanging c 1250; -sericus 1573,
†-cernus 1587, "velvet"; -vitreus, entirely of glass c 1315; olon, all 1271; olla,
God c 550.
holrisus, *see* 2 holma.
holt/a c 1135, -us 1372, holt, thicket.
holulo, to cry out 1286; *cf.* hauloho.
hol/us (ol-), vegetable: -erum c 793, -era
1255; -us regium, mallow 12c.; -erosus,
of forage c 550; †allerectum, (?) *for*
-eretum, vegetable-bed 1436; ulusculum,
dish of pottage 1553.
homag-, *see* homo.
homeomer/eus c 1300, -us 1620, homogeneous.
hom/ilia c 1080, 1517, *-elia c 730, 793.
c 1150, c 1553, homily, sermon; -eliarium
c 1250, -eliarius c 1182, 15c., †-elium
1295, book of homilies; -eliaticus 793.
c 1320, -iliaris 793, of or for a homily;
-iliariter, by way of homily 860; -elizator,
composer of homilies 12c.; -ilizo, to preach
1427.

homillime, see HUMIL
hommus, see **hamma.**
hom/o, *'man', follower, retainer 969, 11c.
a 1123, 1403; *1086, 1461, **h. feodalis**
a 1100, feudal man; Saturn (astr.) c 1260;
h. ad arma c 1297, 1587, **h. armorum**
c 1340, man-at-arms; **h. ad lanceam** 1362;
h. ad pedes, footman 1371; **h. legis,**
lawman, doomster c 1115; p 1387, **h. de**
lege 1384, man of law, lawyer; **legis h.,**
liegeman (Sc.) (?) 1190; **h. patrie,** "land-
man" c 1115; **h. de soca,** sokeman 1086; **h.**
uterque, (?) outer and inner man c 1250;
    *-agium 1086, 1608, †-inagium (? -ma-
gium) c 1155, c 1188, **humagium (uma-**
gium, †vinagium) 1111, 1440, -inium
a 1142, 1608, -inatio 1086, homage (feudal);
c 1210, 1544, **humagium** c 1135, -inia
(f. s.) a 1125, homage, tenantry (of a manor);
sacramentum -agiale, oath of homage
1439; -agialis 1397, -agiarius c 1377,
c 1400, -agerius 1514, vassal, man owing
homage; -agiarius, homager, tenant (man.)
1429; †-icidia 13c., †-icidus 1275, for
-icida, homicide, manslayer; †-icidum, for
-icidium, homicide, manslaughter c 1280;
-inicedium (†-icedium), assault, battery
c 1115; -icidium, fine for homicide, man-
bote 1086; -iniplagium (-iplagium),
wounding c 1115; -ifactivus, man-creating
c 1370; -isedo, to kill 1569.
homogen/eitas c 1360, -ia 1622, homogeneity; -eus a 1200, 1620, -ealis 12c.,
homogeneous.
homolog/us, corresponding 1686; **emologa-**
tio, agreement c 1290, a 1452; -o 1279,
c 1452, **emologo** 1317, c 1465, to agree.
homonymus, namesake c 800; equivocal 13c.
homo/tonus a 1200, -tenus a 1250, equable
(applied to fever).
homoüsios, of same substance (theol.) 12c.,
c 1460.
†**homstrata,** (?) private road (Kent) 1277.
honcus, see **heltus.**
hondredum, see **hundredum.**
honestas, grace (of literary style) 9c.; decency
c 1210, 1415; adornment 1417.
***honor/** 1086, 1586, -ium 1548, -um 1583,
feudal honor, group of fiefs; -ator, honourer
1442; -ificabilis 14c., -ificens c 1192,
-osus 15c., honourable; -ificabiliter c 1390,
-ificenter 14c., -anter c 1150, c 1290,
honourably; -ificatio, doing honour c 1125,
a 1155; -ificentia c 1235, -fica c 1250, fee,
due (eccl.); honour, worship (title) c 790.
hoo, see HOW
1 hop/a, 'hope', piece of enclosed marshland
(Essex & Kent) c 1200, 1488; 'hope', upland pasture, blind valley (Northumb.)
1326, 1373; -ellum, little 'hope' (Essex)
1339, -etus (pasture) 1539, -eta (prati)
1463, paddock.
2 hop/a 1173, 1350, -ha 1275, -fa 1234, -um
1089, **upa** 1376, dry measure, basket; -um,
(?) use of basket for loading grain 1267.
3 hop/a, -um 1311, 1388, **hoopa** 1351,
hupum 1349, hoop; -atio, hooping (of
cask) c 1440.
hop/ilandum 1400, -landa 1418, 'houpland',
long-skirted tunic.

hoppa canis, dog-collar (A.S.) c 1115.
hoquetus, see **hoketus.**
hor-, see also **or-**
hor/a, hour: **h. de clok'** 1387; **h. plane-**
tarum (astr.) 1387; **hora qua boves jun-**
guntur 1281; ad -**am,** for an hour c 1125,
c 1177; 1214, c 1397, **ad h. et terminum**
1200, 1220, at the appointed time (leg.);
ad h. unius diei 1260, **in una -a diei** 1220,
before nightfall; *-**a,** canonical hour
(usually pl.) 10c. c 1125, c 1545; **h. magna,**
h. minor (eccl.) 1472; *-**e canonice**
c 1006. c 1080, 1517, **h. ecclesiastice**
c 1192, **h. regulares** 1234; -e de beata
Virgine 1269, c 1370, **h. beate Marie**
1534, **h. sancte Marie** 13c., **h. nostre do-**
mine 1461, Hours of the B.V.M.; -e sancte
Trinitatis 1415; see also PULS; -ula, brief
hour, moment 704. c 1185, 1520; -aneus,
temporary c 1308; -arius, lasting an hour
c 1150, 1686; marking the hour 1326; of
the canonical hours 1517, 1523; -atim,
hourly a 1520; †-ia, fine for irregular observance of hours (eccl.) (Sc.) 1530;
    -acudium 1442, -icudium (or-) 1445,
1449, (hammer of) striking clock; *-olo-
gium c 1110, 1537, -ologia 1393, -alo-
gium 1501, 1510, -elogium 1291, 1535,
†-ilagium 15c., -ilogium 1284, 1423,
-logium 1272, 1521, **orlagium** 1434,
-oscopium 13c., -iscopium 1439, -eso-
nium 1415, †-isonium c 1440, clock (before c 1300 probably water-clock); -logium,
clock-tower 1341; -oscopium, (?) sun-dial
1418; -ologium excitatorium, alarm clock
1537; **h. nocturnale** 1675; **h. ollarum**
c 1305, **h. vitreum** 1346, (?) hour-glass;
-ologiarius, clock-maker 1325, 1561; 1283,
1353, -oscopus c 1266, c 1330, †-uspex
c 1440, 1483, timekeeper (mon.); -ologicus,
of time c 730.
horanus, see **uranus.**
hord/aria, office of 'hoarder' (mon.) (Winchester) c 1330, c 1533; -arius (†-aria)
c 1115, c 1533, -era (†-ea) c 1115, -erius
1239, 'hoarder', store-keeper, treasurer
(esp. mon.); -arii (†-agii) gildum 1247,
-erisgildum c 1250, payment made at
hundred-court (Devon); **teloneum de**
-esoca, a toll levied by Peterborough abbey
a 1128.
hord/eum (ord-), barley: **orgeum** c 1250,
(?) **ortum** c 1135; **h. hiemale,** winter
barley (Kent) 1285, 1286; **h. palmale**
1245, 1441, **h. palmer'** 1271, **h. palmatum**
14c., 1357, **h. paumelum** 1197, 1318,
palm-barley (mainly Kent); †**h. quadra-**
tum, "bere" 1570; **h. murinum,** wild
barley 1538; -eum, stye (in eye) a 1250;
-eiceus c 1125, 1424, -iceus 6c., -escius
13c., -inacius c 1000, of barley; see also
granum.
hordewica, see HERD
hordicius, hordo, see HURD
horizon/, horizon c 1180, p 1300; artificial
horizon a 1350; -talis, horizontal 1686;
-taliter, horizontally 1686.
horminum, clary (bot.) (ὅρμινον) ‡15c., 1538.
hormiscus (orm-), ornament, (?) collar
(eccl.) c 950.

†**hornagium,** *f.l.* for **homagium,** 1279.
horn/egeldum c 1170, 1266, **-geldum** a 1180, 1331, horngeld, cornage (Northumb. & Cumb.); **-iyeldum** c 1300, **-yeldum** 1331, 1383, *commorth* (W. & Heref.).
hornotinus (†**ortinus**), yearling c 1115.
hor/oma 8c., c 1000, **orama** c 800, ‡**-ema** 1483, vision (ὅραμα); outlook, scope c 950.
horre/um (ore-, ori-), barn: **-a** 1214, 1540, **-us** 1199; **-um decimale,** tithe-barn 1446, 1583.
horr/ibilitas, horribleness c 1260; (?) feverishness a 1250; **-ibilatio,** *for* **-ipilatio,** dread c 1395; **-iditas,** uncouthness 1555; **-orificus,** horrific 12c., c 1362; **-eo,** to horrify 793. c 1370; **-esco,** to sound uncouth 1267.
hors/acra, acre held by carriage service with horse (Kent) c 1300; **-gabulum,** horsegavel, a customary payment (Sussex) c 1300; **-pakkum,** horse-pack 1415; **-warda,** horse-watching c 1115.
horso, (?) to 'hawse', hoist (timber) 1357, 1384.
hort/atiuncula, a word of advice 16c.; **-o,** *for* **-or,** to urge c 1192.
hortum, *see* **hardum.**
hort/us (ort-) **carpentarii,** carpenter's yard 1532; **h. curialis,** courtyard 1471; **h. porcorum,** pig-yard 1470; **-alicium** 1416, **-ilicium** 1481, †**-olagium** (? **curtelagium**) c 1220, garden; **-icola** 7c., ‡**-icula** 1483, *-olanus** a 1190, 1520, †**-alanus** 1244, **-elanus** 1460, *for* **-ulanus,** gardener; **-ulo,** to garden 1416.
hos/a 1158, a 1186, **husa** 1212, †**huga** c 1250, small cask *or* (?) leather bottle; **-arius,** officer of royal buttery c 1136.
hos/e (*pl.*) c 1160, 1225, **-ee** 1292, **hoese** 1213, **huse** 1175, c 1300, hose; **husella** (*pl.*), boots 1207; **-arius** 1180, 1278, **husarius** c 1300, (?) hosier.
hose/bondus, -bundria, *see* **husbandus.**
hosewyva, *see* **husewiva.**
hosoetum, *see* **hussus.**
hospes, villein, customary tenant 1122, 1185; settler (W. Marches) 1086, (Ir.) 1290; member of ship's company 1416; host assigned to alien merchants 1440, 1474; 'host', fish-dealer 1309, 1382 (*cf.* **hostellarius**); **h. generalis,** quartermaster general a 1415;
    hospit/a 1235, **-issa** 1223, 1390, **-atrix** 1275, hostess; ‡**-abilis** 1570, **-alicius** c 1620, hospitable; **-acula** (*pl.*), lodgings 7c.; *-ale** c 730, 993. 1155, 1586, **-alaria** a 1273, 1279, **-alitas** 1300, 1378, *-ium** c 980. 1185, 1518, †**-ulum** 1275, **domus -um** a 1273, hospice, guest-house or hospital; *1151, 1440, **-alarium** c 1190, **-alitas** 1256, 1569, †**-ium** 1287, hospital (commandery) of Knights Hospitallers; *-alitas** c 1188, 1431, †**-ilitas** 15c., hospitality, entertaining guests; inn-keeping 1324; 12c., *-ium** 1221, 1537, household; *-ium regis,** royal household 13c., c 1550; **-agium** c 1200, 1440, *-atio** 1086, 1457, **-atura** 1441, *-ium** 1086, c 1437, (right or service of) lodging, procuration, billeting; **-atio,** harbouring 1321, c 1466; storage 1339, 1419; **-amentum** 1163, **-atum**

c 1125, 13c., lodging, house; **-ium,** townhouse 1126, 1416; billet c 1415, 1417; hostel, house (ac.) 1214, c 1452; inn of court 1312, 1586; form of tenure (W. Marches) 1086, (Ir.) 1290; **-ium tenens,** householder 1450; **-iolum,** small lodging, guest-room c 1160, c 1478;
    -alarius, giver of hospitality 1519; c 1285, 1557, **-arius** 1518, inmate of hospital or almshouse; 1196, **-alaris** c 1300, **-elarius** 1313, **-arius** c 1125, c 1295, ⸗**iarius** c 1220, hosteler (mon.); *c 1188, 1586, †**-alaris** c 1192, c 1400, **-aliarius** 1228, **-elarius** 1227, c 1320, **-ilarius** c 1190, 14c., **-ularius** c 1180, 1418, **-alius** 1215, c 1436, **frater -alius** 1419, **-arius** c 1362, Knight Hospitaller; **-iarius,** steward 15c.; inn-keeper 1661; **-atim,** from house to house c 1212; **-ator,** one who entertains or harbours 1269, 15c.; harbinger, billeter 1419, 1457; **h. dextrariorum** 1328; **-o** 1264, 1419, **-o me** c 1070, c 1450, *for* **-or,** to sojourn, lodge; *-o, -or** a 1135, 1489, ‡**-uo** 1483, to entertain, harbour; to keep (dogs) 1324; to billet, quarter 1447; *to house, store (goods or grain) 1230, a 1596; to inhabit, occupy, build on 1086, 1274; *cf.* **1 hostagium.**

1 host/agium c 1115, 13c., **-allagium** c 1230, 1292, **-ellagium** a 1300, 1410, **-ilagium** 1215, 14c., (right or service of) lodging, procuration; *-ilagium** (Sc.) 1266, c 1540, **-illaria** (Sc.) 1473, **-eria** 1295, 1514, hostelry, inn; **-illaria** 1234, 1473, **-ellaria** 1155, **-eleria** c 1266, 1340, **-illarium** c 1266, 1524, **-iliaria** c 1266, **-iliarium** c 1300, **-ria** 1401, c 1488, **-ellum** 1352, hospice, guesthouse or hospital; **h. ecclesie,** *see* **ostium;** **-ellarius** 1167, 1278, *-illarius** 1235, 1531, hosteler (mon.); c 1350, 1419, **-illarius** 1384, 1514, inn-keeper; **-ellarius, -ilarius,** 'host', fish-dealer (Yarmouth) 1357; *cf.* **hospes.**

2 host/agium (ost-) 1177, 1461, **-aticum** (G.) 1254, **-adium** (G.) 1255, **obstagium** 1385, **-agiamentum** 1313, 1405, **-agaria** (G.) 1255, hostageship, bail; **-agiamentum** 1287, **-agiatio** 1298, release on bail; **-agius** a 1110, 1253, †**-acius** 1204, hostage; **-agio** 1207, 1299, **-igo** (Fr.) 1194, to release on bail; *cf.* **obses.**
hostellamenta, *see* **USTIL**
hosti-, *see also* **ostium.**
*hosti/a,** consecrated host (eccl.) c 730. c 1080, c 1500; ‡**-arium,** pyx 15c., 1483; †**osternum,** (?) purse for the host a 1100.
hostil-, *see* **1 hostagium; hostis; hasta;** **USTIL**
hosti/mentum, -o, *see* **hostorium.**
hostinatus, *see* **OBSTIN**
host/is a 1142, c 1250, **h. antiquus** a 1125, c 1520, **h. humani generis** c 1343, **h. perennis** c 1545, the Devil; **-ilis,** diabolic c 1436; **-iles** (*pl.*), the enemy c 1250, 1417; *-ilitas,** hostility c 1125, 1474; military service 14c.; ‡**-icida,** enemy-slayer 1483; **-icum** (†**-ium**), host, army, military service c 1115.
‡**host/orium** c 1440, 1483, †**historium** c 1200, ‡**-imentum** 1483, strickle; ‡**-io,** to strake (a bushel) c 1440, 1483.

hostric-, see AUSTUR

hott/a, -us 1286, 1350, **oda** 1334, 'hot', hod; **-arius** 1198, c 1300, **-erius** 1326, **-ator** 1295, **-or** 1227, 1295, **-aria** (f.) 1282, hod-bearer; **-ata,** hod-load 1295.

houca, see hoga.

houcium, see HUC

houcus, see heltus.

houredes, see HURD

hous-, see HUC; **hus-**

hov/ellus, niche, stone canopy 1313, 1441; **-ella** 1467, **ofuellus** 1460, hovel, hut; **-allus,** cowl, cover (for louver) 1315.

how/a 1194, c 1284, **houwa** c 1280, 1288, **hawa** 1267, **hoa, hoga** 1165, **hoia** 1186, 1212, **-otta** c 1274, hoe; **-o** 1236, 1293, **houwo** 1286, **hoo** c 1358, **-io** c 1258, **hawyo** c 1290, to hoe.

†**hozorus,** liquorice 14c.

†**hreaccroppum,** top of haystack (A.S. *hreaccopp*) c 1115.

hs-, for s: hsabaoth, hsatis, hsi 863.

huca 1415, **heuka** 1418, 'huke', cape with hood; see also **hitha.**

hucetus, see hussus.

huch/a, booth 1278; (Sc.) c 1270, **-ia** 1166, 1240, **uchia** (G.) 1312, hugia 1160, 1226, 'hutch', chest; **hugia ad aves** (falc.) 1174.

*****huc/ia** 1199, 1343, **hucheum** c 1333, **hulcia** 1175, 1303, **huscia** 1205, 1265, **houcium** 1284, **housia** 1390, **husia** 1253, c 1327, housing, saddle-cloth; †**hutya,** coverlet (G.) 1254.

huda, (?) barehide (cf. **barhudum**) 1204; see also **hitha.**

hudagium, see 2 hida.

huervum, see WHARV

huesium, see HUT

huga, see hosa.

hugia, see HUCH

Hugnotus, Huguenot 1565.

huholus, green woodpecker 1544.

*****hujus/modi** 12c., c 1400, **-cemodi** c 1433, c 1546, this sort of thing (*subst.*); **ex h.,** of this sort c 1172, 15c.; **in h.,** to this effect c 1115.

hulcia, see hucia.

1 hulc/us c 1115, 1432, **-a** 1387, c 1465, **-um** 1412, (?) **hullockus** 1215, hulk, ship.

2 hulcus, (?) 'hulk', hut 1306.

huldo, (?) to shore up (a weir) a 1300.

hul/io 1330, **-o** 14c., to hull, thresh (grain).

huila, hill, knoll c 1180, 1298; **hillelondus,** hill-land 1316.

hullettus, see holetta.

hullockus, see hulcus.

hulmus, see 1 holma; ULM

†**huls/genga, -gonges** (*pl.*), houseling folk, communicants (A.S. *huslgenga*) c 1115.

hulus, measure of grain 1224, 1325.

hulva, 'hulve', drain 1539.

humagium, see homo.

human/itas, human nature of Christ 1380, 1552; **-alis,** human (play on *humus*) a 1446; **-itus,** as man c 730; see also CONTING; humanely c 1330; **in -is,** see ago; **-o more,** by a natural death 1325; **-atio,** incarnation 9c.; **-o,** to incarnate, make man c 700. c 1100, c 1248.

humbra, (?) marsh (Hackney, Middx.) 1185.

Humbraria, see UMBR

humect-, humid-, see **humor.**

humer/ulus, part of axle to which wheel is fixed c 700; **-ale,** humeral veil 1245, a 1408.

humil/itas nostra, my humble self c 760; **homillime** *for* **-lime** 1517; **-iatio,** token of reverence or repentance, obeisance a 615, c 980. 12c., 1432; reverse of sublimation (alch.) a 1233; **-iator,** one who humbles c 1125; **-iati** (*pl.*), religious order 1459; **-iatissimus,** deeply abased 1438; **-io me,** to prostrate oneself a 615. c 1125; †**-ito,** *for* **-io,** to humble 1406.

hum/irepus, creeping on the ground 1518; **-o,** to earth up 1270, 1306.

hum/or (um-), humour (med.) c 1180, 1424; **h. albugineus,** aqueous humour of eye a 1250, 1267; **h. crystallinus,** lens of eye a 1250, 1267; **-oralis,** of humour or fluid a 1250, 1424; **-orositas** a 1200, 1267, **-iditas** 870. c 1180, 1620, moisture; **-idatio** 1300, **-efactio** a 1150, **-ectatio (panni)** 1465, moistening; **-idum,** moist element c 1270, 1424; marshy ground c 1209; **-ectativus,** moistening a 1250, 1340; †**vinectatus,** f.l. for **umectatus,** c 1400; **-ito,** *for* **-ido,** to moisten 13c.

‡**humul/us,** hop (bot.) 1570; ‡**-ina,** beer c 1440.

*****hundr/edum** c 1080, 1583, **h. terre** c 1090, **-eda** 14c., 1546, **-edus** 1100, c 1362, **-etum** 1086, a 1275, **-etus** 1084, c 1115, **hondredum** 1285, c 1338, **-um** (Sc.) 1333, 1336, hundred (division of county) or its tenantry; *****1086, 1574, **-eda** c 1160, c 1300, **-edus** a 1100, 1276, **-etum** 1086, 1305, **-um** c 1155, c 1175, hundred-court or suit threat (attendance or fine for non-attendance); 1283, **h. magnum** 1270, 1279, **h. generale** 1276, 1337, **h. legale** 1330, 1485, law-hundred, sheriff's tourn; **-etum,** fine of 100l. c 1115, c 1370; **-edum foreste,** court of attachments (Essex) 1239; **h. forinsecum** 1208, 14c., **h. extrinsecum** 1228, 'out-hundred' (hundredal jurisdiction over lands not held in demesne); **h. intrinsecum,** 'in-hundred' (confined to demesne lands) 1212, 14c.; **h. liberum** 1237; **-edarius** 1240, 1575, **-edmannus** c 1250, **-emannus** (†**-annus**) 1086, **hundermannus** 1238, hundredor, hundred-bailiff; **-edarius** 1221, 1277, **-etanus** a 1275, tenant within hundred or suitor at hundred-court; †**-edfethum** 1226, †**-edesicha** 1203, **-escotum** 1279, 'hundred-fee', 'hundred-scot' (customary payments).

Hung/arus c 1200, 1586, **-arius** c 1118, **-rus** 1200, 1267, **-rensis** c 1200, **Hunn/us** a 1142, 13c., Hungarian; **-iscus,** (?) Hungarian 796; **-us,** (?) Avar c 730.

hunigab/lum c 1115, **-ulum** c 1300, honey-rent.

huntagium (†**hurtagium**), dishonour (O.F. *hontage*) 1201, 1277; cf. **ultagium.**

‡**hunullum,** "linch-pin" 15c.

hupa, see upupa.

huppelanda, see uplanda.

hupulus, hop (bot.) 1442; cf. 2 lupus.

hupum, see 3 hopa.

hur/a 1226, c 1255, **heura** 1419, 'hure' rough cap; **-arius,** cap-maker 1398, 1419.

hurcinium, form of service (mon.), (?) fencing (Yorks.) 1298; *cf.* **hirsona.**

†**hurdesylva,** hearth-silver c 1509.

hurd/icium, -icius 1261, **-eicium** 1202, **-ricium** 1261, †**burdicium** 1312, 'hurdis', wooden gallery (on castle); palisade 1240, 1419; 1300, 1325, **-icea** 1296, **-isium** 1294, **houredes** (*pl.*) 1263, bulwark (of galley); c 1192, c 1436, **-eicia** 1319, **hordicius** c 1366, **-esium** c 1362, siege-tower; **hirdellus** 1344, c 1396, **hyrdillus** c 1445, **herdellus** 1316, c 1440, **herdillus** c 1478, **herdlus** 1280, hurdle; **-icio** 1309, **-io** 1215, 1267, **-o** 1242, 1272, **hordo** (Norm.) 1195, to fortify (castle) with palisade or gallery; **-isso,** to fortify (galley) with bulwarks 1295.

hurdmannus, class of tenant (Sc.) c 1150.

hurmannus, *see* **hyremannus.**

hurstum a 1235, **hirstis** 1268, hurst, wooded hill.

hurtagium, *see* **huntagium.**

*****hurt/ardus** c 1222, 1446, **-erdus** 1487, **-aldus** 1274, †**-adus** 1286, †**-us** 1420, ram; **-orum, -orium** 1342, 1389, **-urum, -urium** 1285, 1363, **-arium** 1331, **-erium** 1283, **-ellum** 1305, 1310, **-yrnum** 1296, iron plate to protect axle; **-o,** to jostle, knock about (Norm.) c 1300; **h. me super,** to run up against 1290.

hus/a, -arius, -e, -ella, *see* **hosa; hose.**

‡**husacium,** sal ammoniac 1652.

*****hus/bandus** 1272, c 1540, **-bonda** c 1115, **-bondus** a 1128, 1130, **-ebondus** 1181, 1244, **-ebundus** 1212, **hosbondus** c 1182, **hosebondus** 13c., **osebandus** 1283, householder, husbandman, crofter (esp. Sc. & N. Eng.); **housebondus,** *taeog* (W.) 1304; **-bandria** 1344, 1529, **-banderia** 1325, **-bonderia** 1339, **-bondria** 1449, 1527, **hosebundria** 1388, 1419, **housbandria** 1420, husbandry, agriculture; **-bondria,** economy, housekeeping 1476; **-bandria** 1374, 1575, **-bondria** 1553, **terra -bandi** c 1290, 1369, **t. -banda** 1374, 1512, *****t. -bandia** 1456, 1608, **t. -bandria** 1467, 1490, **t. husbondrie** 1430, **t. -bandalis** 1479, 1485, husband-land (Sc. & N. Eng.); **-bandalis,** concerned with husbandmen (Sc.) 1325, 1433.

husbot/a c 1170, 1222, **-um** 1276, **housbotum** 1262, housebote, right to take timber for building; **-o,** to pay for housebote 1236.

huscarl/a, -us, -is 1086, 13c., †**huthsecarla** c 1130, house-carl.

hus/cia, -ia, *see* **hucia.**

husegabulum 1300, 1314, **husegabellum** 1318, **husegavellum** 1200, **husgab/lum** 1275, 1354, **-ulum** 1293, 1536, **-lium** c 1225, **housgabulum** 1323, house-gavel, rent.

hus/ewiva 1183, c 1380, **-wiva** 1183, **hosewyva, housewyva** c 1380, housewife.

huss/arius, -eria, *see* **ostium.**

Hussita, Hussite 1429, 1523.

hus/sus 1189, 1486, ‡**-cus, usus** 15c., (?) **-ya** 1286, **housus** 1538, **-setus** 1374, (?) **hucetus** 1296, holly; **-setum** 1249, 1314, **-cetum** 1251, †**hosoetum** 1275, **-seium** 1241, holly-wood; *cf.* **2 holma.**

hust-, *see also* USTIL

†**husta,** (?) barrier 1200.

hust/ingum c 1120, 1586, **-ingia** c 1170, **-engum, -engus** a 1120, 1587, **-engium** c 1220, **-angum** c 1130, husting court (London); (King's Lynn) 1327; (Northampton) 1387; **locus -engalis** 1419.

husum, house 1242.

huswiva, *see* **husewiva.**

hutellus, *see* **hutta.**

huterella (*pl.*), rubbish, silt 1275.

hut/esium (ut-, uth-) 1130, 1593, **-esia** 1276, 1340, †**vicesium** 1253, **-esius** c 1220, 1225, **-asium** c 1220, 1277, **-asia** 1240, **-ehesium** 1242, **outesium** 1405, **huesium** (Sc.) c 1315, **-agium** c 1225, 1276, †**ultragium** 1220, **-egium** 1346, 1378, hue, clamour of pursuit; **-o,** to 'hue', bait (a bull) 1389.

hutha, *see* **hitha.**

huthsecarla, *see* **huscarla.**

hutibannum, *see* **utibannum.**

hutt/a, hut for smelting lead c 1295; **-emannus,** man in charge of smelting-hut c 1295; **hutelius,** wooden cowl or cover over louver 1399.

hutya, *see* **hucia.**

hwearfum, hwerv-, *see* WHARV

hya/cinthus, blue colour or cloth 1200; **-zinthus** c 1270, **jacintus (jacinctus)** 1166, a 1446, †**jaguntius** 1245, jacinth; **jacinctus,** hyacinth (bot.) c 1200, a 1250; **jacintaria,** (?) confection of jacinth *or* hyacinth 1307; **-cinthinus** a 615. c 1180, 1537, **-zintinus** a 1233, **jacinctinus** 1200, 1553, blue or violet.

hyal/inus c 950, ‡**-icus** 1483, glassy; ‡**yalos, yelion,** glass 1652; ‡**-urgus,** glazier 1570.

hydr/iola (idr-), holy-water stoup c 1125; **idor,** water c 550; **-agor** c 1215, **-agitos** a 1250, *for* **-argyrus,** mercury; ‡**-agira,** "*aqua alkali*" 1652; **-agogicus** (†**-omagogus**), for drawing off fluid (med.) a 1250; **-auiia** (*pl.*), (?) founts, reservoirs (fig.) c 950; **-ographicus,** hydrographic 1583; **-oleon,** *for* **-eleon,** mixture of oil and water a 1250, ‡14c.; **-omanticus,** diviner by water a 1446; **-omellum,** hydromel, mead c 1100, ‡15c.; wort 15c., ‡1483; **-oforbia, -oforbicus,** *for* **-ophobia, -ophobus,** a 1250; ‡**-opiper,** water pepper (bot.) 15c.; **-opiens,** dropsical a 1250; **-opisis, -ops, -opsis** a 1250, **malum -opsi** c 1280, dropsy; **-opico,** to make dropsical c 1200.

†**hydrophagus,** *for* ichthyophagus, c 1212.

‡**hydro/rhodina,** rose-water 1652; **-statica,** hydrostatics 1686; **-staticus,** hydrostatic 1686.

hygia (ygia), an electuary 1241, a 1250.

hyle c 1115, 1345, **helya** 1220, matter (ὕλη).

hyllum, *see* **ileon.**

‡**hymen,** caul 1483.

hymera, *see* **hemera.**

hymn/us (hympn-, ympn-, impn-) (eccl.), **-icum** 1200, hymn; **-iculus,** little hymn c 1000; **-ale** c 1432, ‡15c., **-are** c 1283, 1427, *****-arium** c 1006. c 1200, 1439, hymnbook; **-idicus,** hymn-singing 9c., c 1020. c 1100, c 1450; a 1350, ‡**-ista** 1483, hymnsinger; **-idice,** by singing hymns a 1350; **-odia** c 1180, **-odium** a 1100, hymnody;

-ologia, praise in song 9c. 1344; **-izo,** to sing hymns 8c., c 1000. a 1100, 15c.

hyndenus (†**hindonus,** †**hamdonus**), hundred, association of a hundred men (A.S.) c 1115; **homo h.,** hundred-man c 1115.

hyngildum, *see* **x hida.**

hyoscyamus, henbane (bot.): **jusquiamus** c 1200, 1538.

hypallage, inversion of relations (gram.) a 1270.

hyp/apanti c 1090, c 1320, **-apanton** 12c., **-ante** 12c., c 1182, Candlemas (2 Feb.).

hyparcticon, substantive: †**hypracticon** 13c.

hyperbat/on, mark of transposition (in MS.) c 1200; **-ice,** with transposition of words 86o.

hyperbol/a, hyperbola (math.) 1686; **-icus,** insolent a 615; hyperbolic 1686.

hyperdulia, special veneration 1345, a 1530.

hypericon, St. John's wort (bot.) a 1250, c 1270.

hyper/lydius (mus.): **-lodius, -ludius** a 1250.

hyperlyric/us, supremely sweet 12c., a 1350; ‡**-e,** sweetly 1483.

hyperperum, Byzantine gold coin: **per- per/um, -us** c 1192, 1292.

hyperpyrosis (†**hypyrosis**), universal conflagration 1344.

hyperusia, supreme being c 1165.

‡**hyperythros,** reddish 15c.

hyphen, hyphen 1271.

hypidemia, *see* **epidemia.**

hypo-, *see also* HIPPO

hypochondriaca, affection of the hypochondria a 1250.

hypo/cisthis (bot.): **-quistis** a 1250.

*****hypocri/sis,** hypocrisy a 1090, c 1536; **-ticus** c 1150, 1378, **-talis** c 1283, hypocritical; †**-ssimus** a 1130, †**-sinus** c 1200, (most) hypocritical; **-tor** (*dep.*) c 1250, **-zor** 1427, to play the hypocrite.

hypodecanus, subdean c 1182.

hypodiaconus, subdeacon a 1450.

hypodia/stile, *for* **-stole,** mark of separation (gram.) 1271.

hypodidasc/alus 1550, **-olus** 1541, **-ulus** 1551, 1579, assistant teacher, usher.

hypodoricus c 1370, †**podorius** a 1250, a musical mode; ‡"sweet" 1483.

‡**hypofungia,** stockfish c 1440.

hypoge/a 14c., **apogeum** c 1112, ‡**apageum** 1483, *for* **-um,** underground chamber.

hypo/gnosticum 1427, †**-nesticum** c 1396, book by St. Augustine.

hypopheticus, prophetic 870.

‡**hypopium,** black eye (ὑπώπιον) 15c.

hypo/pyrgium 1551, 1553, **-purgium** 1473, 1517, **popurgium** 1472, andiron, fire-dog.

hypoquistis, *see* **hypocisthis.**

hyposarca, kind of dropsy a 1250, ‡15c.

hyposta/sis, substance (log.) 12c., p 1380; sediment (med.) a 1250, a 1452; **-sivus,** sedimentary a 1250; **-tice,** by way of substance a 1304, c 1380; **-ticus,** concerned with substance p 1300, 1564; †**hypotesto,** to subsist (log.) c 1360.

hypotenusa, hypotenuse (geom.) a 1150, c 1200.

hypothec/a, pledge: **upotheca** 1290; **-atorie,** by way of pledge 1286; **-o,** to pledge 1285, c 1450; *see also* APOTHEC

hypothe/sis, hypothesis, supposition c 1160, 1620; **-tice,** hypothetically 13c.; **-tice** (*f. pl.*), two parts of an hypothesis 13c.; **-ticus,** hypothetical a 1250, 1610.

‡**hypothyron,** "groundsel", threshold 1570.

hypracticon, *see* **hyparcticon.**

hypyrosis, *see* **hyperpyrosis.**

hyrdillus, *see* HURD

hyremannus, hirmannus c 1115, (?) **hurmannus** 13c., servant, dependant (A.S. *hiereman*).

hyrnessa, *cf.* **overhyrnessa.**

hysoplexus, *see* ISO

*****hyssop/us** (**isopus**), holy water sprinkler c 1220, c 1510; **ros -icus** c 1000.

hystera, womb: **ster/a** c 1200, ‡15c., ‡**-ia** 15c.

hystrix, porcupine: **strix,** hedgehog 1271.

hyusira, *see* **heusira.**

I

iambus, metrical foot: **jamb/us,** (?) limp 13c.; **-ico,** to limp 13c.

iare (*pl.*), hair 6c.

iarus a 1250, ‡14c., **yarus** a 1250, arum (bot.); *cf.* **aron.**

ibanus, *see* **hebanus.**

ibi 1086, 1375, **-dem** c 1266, c 1335, thither.

‡**ibis,** "snipe" 1483, 1570.

ibraia, *see* **ebraia.**

icarisma, *see* **charisma.**

ichor (**ycor**), ichor, fluid a 1250, 1622; ‡**ycar,** medicine 1652.

icon/ 12c., c 1180, **-a** c 1200, *****-ia** c 1180, c 1435, **-ium** c 1300, 1345, **conisma** 7c., image, picture; **-oclastes, -omachus,** iconoclast 1610; **-olatres,** image-worshipper c 1620; **-oyfana,** vision 12c.

ico/nomus, -peta, *see* **economus.**

icos, general probability (εἰκός) a 1180, 1344.

ico/saedron 1344, **-cedrum** 1267, icosahedron (geom.).

icter/icia c 1220, 1345, †**-istia** c 1315, jaundice; ‡**i. nigra,** melanosis 15c.; ‡**i. rubea,** erysipelas 1652; **-icius,** of jaundice c 1190, c 1362.

ict/us cecus c 1115, **i. orbus** 1221, 1271, blow without swelling or blood; **i. horologii,** stroke of clock a 1400; *****i. oculi,** twinkling of an eye a 1180, 1461; **-uo,** to beat (of wings) c 1000.

icumenicus, *see* **ecumenicus.**

id quod est, (used to express oblique cases of indeclinables) a 1233.

ide/a (**yde-**), idea, form, archetype (phil.) c 950. c 1160, 1620; (?) shadow, illusory appearance c 1350; **-abilis,** conceivable in idea c 1301; **-alis**, ideal, existing in idea c 1270, c 1488; **-aliter**, ideally, in idea c 1270, c 1362; **-atum**, copy of archetype c 1250, c 1362; **-atus**, mentally conceived c 1270, c 1470; **-o**, to form an idea or conception 13c.

idem, such c 1000; **id i.**, that same c 1266; **de eadem**, of the same place (denoting surname) 1238; **ejusdem** 1444, **de eodem** c 1370, c 1520, of that ilk (Sc.); *****ident/itas** (idempt-) c 1080, 1610, †**idempnitas** c 1220, 1309, **ydimptitas** c 1237, identity, sameness; **-ice**, identically, by way of identity c 1300, 15c.; **-icus**, identical c 1300, 1552; **-ificus**, identifying 1427; **-ificatio**, identification c 1380, 1381; **-ifico**, to identify c 1300, a 1361.

ides (pl.), sheep 6c.

idio/ma (ideo-), *****language a 615. c 1170, c 1553; dialect c 1270, 1303; pronunciation 1278; condition, peculiarity, property 12c., 1552; **-tes**, monoglot c 730; **-ta** 1286, c 1456, **ydeotus** 1279, **-ta** (f.) 1309, idiot, half-wit; fool, jester c 1180; **-tia**, idiocy 1354, 1586; **-tice**, foolishly c 1190, p 1382; **-ticus**, foolish 1427.

idol/um, *****idol (eccl.); dummy, effigy c 1325; popular hero c 1395; mental image 13c., 1344; illusory idea 1620; **-olatra**, **-olatres** c 1080, c 1546, **-atra**, **-atres** a 1155, c 1414, †**-ater** 1271, idolater; **-olatria** c 1080, c 1546, *****-atria** c 1100, c 1470, **-latratio** 1236, idolatry; **-atrice**, idolatrously 1497; **-olatricus** 1562, 1657, †**-aticus** 1271, †**-atrus** 1380, **-iticus** c 1193, **-olatria** (f.) c 730, idolatrous; **-omania**, fanatical idolatry c 1620; **-eum**, idol temple c 1257; **-olatro** 1281, a 1452, **-atro** c 1343, 15c., †**-atto** a 1228, to worship idols.

*****idon/eitas** a 1180, 1549, **-ietas** 1315, 1418, fitness, suitability; **-eius**, more suitably 1241; **-eor** 1287, c 1383, **-ior** c 1327, c 1470, more suitable; **-eissimus**, most suitable c 1340; **-eo**, to make good, amend c 1115; **i. me**, to clear oneself of a charge c 1115, a 1446.

idor, see HYDR

1 iduma, **eduma**, hand (Heb. yadaim) c 550, 6c.

2 †iduma, (?) image 930.

†**ieros**, kind of serpent (? hydra) c 870.

ifus 1271, 1306, **ivus** 1305, **ivyus** 1298, (?) **yva** a 1250, yew-wood (Fr. if).

ignatus, see innativus.

ign/is (ingn-), fuel 1086, c 1150; ordeal by fire 1134, 14c.; blanching (of money) 1086, 1214; beacon 1324, 1371; **i. aereus** a 1120, c 1366, **i. silvaticus** a 1120, c 1436, "wildfire", (?) meteor; **i. fatuus**, will of the wisp 1620; **i. Grecus** 1136, c 1340, **i. Pelasgus** 1252, 15c., Greek fire; **i. jocunditatis** 1461, **i. jubili** c 1608, feu de joie, bonfire; **i. novus**, new fire (lit at Easter) c 1315; ‡**i. Sancti Antonii** 1652, ‡**i. execrabilis** 14c., **i. Persicus** a 1250, ‡14c., erysipelas; **i. philosophicus** (alch.) 1144; **-e tenus**, by fire c 990; ‡**-arius**, **-aria** (f.), "fueller" 15c.; *****-eitas**, fieriness c 1215, c 1370; **-ibilis**, inflammable c 1270; ‡**-icipium**, tinder 1483; (?) **-ifer** 1508, **ferrum -iferum** 10c., steel

for making fire; **lapis -ifer**, flint c 1000; **quercus -iligna**, "firewood oak" 1587; **-itabulum**, (?) tinder-box 1591; *****-itegium** c 1200, 1504, **-itagium** 13c., 1348, †**-itegnium** 1293, †**-itergium** 1330, curfew; **catus -ius** (†**igmus**), fireside cat c 1100, 1303; **Titan -ivomus**, sun 8c.; **-itio**, incandescence or calcination a 1250, 1445; **-itivus**, incendiary a 1250; **-itosus**, fiery c 700; **-io**, to ignite c 1090, c 1540.

ign/ominiositas, ignominy c 1096; †**-omimicus** 12c., **-uminiosus** c 1246, ignominious.

ignor/antia elenchi (log.) 13c., p 1300; **-abiliter**, infamously c 1000; *****-anter**, ignorantly (eccl.); **-ans malitie**, innocent of malice 1255.

†**ignoscibiliter**, unpardonably a 1520.

†**ignosticus**, (?) uncultured (?) 937.

ihara, see yara.

†**ilda**, (?) island (Norf.) 1291.

ile, see ilum.

‡**ilech**, **ileias**, **ileadus**, **iliaster**, element, first principle 1652; (?) cf. hyle.

ileon, intestine (cf. εἰλεός) c 1210; ‡**hyllum**, sausage c 1200.

iliceus, oaken c 1220.

ilider, see chelydrus.

ill-, see also inl-

illabilis, constant c 1196.

illafeos, coltsfoot or burdock a 1250, ‡14c.

Illandicus, see ISLAND

illapidatio (inl-), transformation into stone 1427.

illapsus, interpenetration, inspiration p 1300, 1378.

illaqueatio, ensnarement c 1306, 1378.

illascivus, serious c 1185.

illateo, to lurk in 1220.

illat/io, bringing in c 1150, c 1400; inference c 1080, c 1370; attack, impact c 1115, 1378; **i. actionis**, impact of action, effect c 1270; **-ive**, inferentially 1516; **-ivus**, implying c 1370; **-rix**, producer (f.), cause a 1155; cf. INFER

illaudabiliter, unpraiseworthily c 1200, 15c.

illectivus, alluring 1246, c 1266; **inlic/itate**, under temptation or (?) for **-ite**, 5c.; **-ito**, for **-io**, to incite 8c.

illegal/itas, illegality c 1290; **-is**, lawless 1269, c 1362; **-iter**, illegally c 1376.

illegiatus, see illex.

illegitim/itas, invalidity (of marriage) c 1258; 1291, 1533, **-atio** 1236, 1406, illegitimacy (of birth); **-e**, unlawfully c 1250, c 1450; **-us** 1236, 1336, **illigitimus** 1237, illegitimate (of birth); **-o**, to declare illegitimate 1385, 1413.

illetus, joyless 15c.

illev/abilis 1425, c 1477, **-iabilis** 1535, unlevyable.

ille/x, outlaw 1086; ‡traitor 15c.; **-giatus**, outlawed c 1115; see also INLAG

ill/i (pl.) **de**, the men of 1086, c 1405; **-inc**, thenceforward 14c.; **inter i. et . . .**, between then and . . . 1543; **-uc usque**, up to that point 1378; **-ut**, for **-ud**, 836.

illib/atio, integrity, unimpairment c 1362; **-ate**, without diminution 1130, 1232.

illibenter, unwillingly 1588, c 1620.

I

illiber/ 1344, **-alis** c 1185, unfree; **-e,** without freedom 1344, c 1360; **-abiliter,** beyond deliverance 1344; **-tas,** serfdom 1419; **-tatio,** restriction of free will c 1360; **-to,** to enslave c 1360, 1380.

illibratus, unbalanced c 1190.

***illic/entiatus,** unlicensed 1228, 1519; **-entiabilis,** impermissible c 1470; ***-ite,** unlawfully c 1163, c 1443; **possessor -itus** c 1210; *see also* **illectivus.**

illigabilis, (?) unrestrainable c 1115.

illigitimus, *see* ILLEGITIM

illimit/atio, boundlessness c 1300, p 1300; **-atus,** unbounded 13c., c 1343; **-o,** to free from limits c 1360.

illimo, to file down, diminish c 1200; to sharpen 15c.

illinguis (inl-), speechless c 1325.

illinitio, anointment a 1250.

illiterat/ura, illiteracy c 1197; **-us,** unwritable 8c.

illitigiosus, exempt from litigation 1322.

illoc/alis 1205, c 1400, **-atus** 1268, unlocalized; **-aliter,** without locomotion c 1205.

illoculo, to put into one's purse c 1185.

ill/uc, -ut, *see* **illi.**

illucid/ius, more clearly c 1433; **-o,** (?) *for* elucido, to explain c 1460, c 1470.

illugubris, cheerful c 1450.

illumin/atio (inlumin-) 1424, **alumpnatio** 1399, **eluminatio** 1393, illumination, limning; **-abilis,** able to be lighted 1344; **-are,** altar light c 1330; **-ativus** c 1270, c 1290, **-atorius** c 1500, enlightening; **-ator,** adorner c 1402; a 1142, 1419, **aluminator** 1135, **eluminator** 1413, limner; **i. cere,** candle-lighter 1371; **-atissimus,** most enlightened c 1346, 16c.; **-o,** to set alight c 1006. c 1268, c 1415; to colour, (?) transmute (alch.) c 1215; c 1135, c 1436, †**alimino** 1388, †**allomno** 1452, **elumino** 1413, to illuminate, limn (manuscripts); **inlumino,** to heal from blindness c 730; to give light 9c.

illus/io, apparition, hallucination c 1190, c 1250; sport c 1190; nocturnal emission c 1325, c 1330; **inlusio,** imagination, deception 7c., 9c.; **-ivus,** deceptive 1378; **-orie,** with intent to deceive 1438; **inlusorius,** illusory c 730; **-us,** visited by nocturnal emission c 1245; **inludo,** to deceive 7c.

***illustr/atio** c 1000. c 1125, c 1365, **-amen** 1497, c 1500, enlightenment; blazon (her.) c 1595; **-ator** c 1250, 1279, **-atrix** (*f.*) c 1160, enlightener.

†**illustratus (inl-),** (?) polluted a 700; *cf.* **infrustratus.**

illuvio, flood a 1155, 1620.

‡**ilum, ile** 15c., ‡**ylum** c 1200, pith of quill.

imagicus, *see* MAGIC

imago auri, gold coin 13c.; **i. signorum,** diagram of zodiac 1387; †**imagin/a,** image c 1246; **imaguncula** c 700, **-ula** a 1300, little image; **-abilis,** clearly conceived 9c. c 1250, p 1347; imaginable 1335, 15c.; imaginary 1267; **-abiliter** a 1250, 1344, **-aliter** 7c., 8c., **-arie** 655. c 1195, c 1500, by imagination, symbolically; **-arium,** receptacle for images (eccl.) c 1200, 1371;

-arius, (*adj.*) in the form of an image c 1213; symbolic 12c., a 1520; imaginative a 1228; ingeniously contrived c 1380; (*subst.*) magician employing images c 1160; idolater c 1320; substitute c 1157; 1226, c 1320, **-ator** 1291, 1293, image-maker, sculptor; **-ator,** contriver a 1564; **-atio,** imagery c 1212; fantasy, illusion a 1110, a 1350; 1379, 15c., (?) **maginatio** 1300 (*cf.* MACHIN), contrivance, machination; argument c 1188; c 1160, c 1270, **-ativa** c 1270, 1378, (faculty of) imagination; **-ativus,** imaginative a 1250, 1622; imaginary 1620; **-osus,** adorned with images 1432; suspicious c 1350; **-o,** to imagine a 1235, c 1370; 14c., c 1450, **-or** 1336, c 1390, to plot, contrive.

imbalsamo, to perfume c 1185, 15c.; to embalm, mummify 1622.

imbaptizatus (inb-), unbaptized 1378.

imbarello, to store in barrels 1395.

imbargio, to embark or load on a barge (Norm.) 1417.

imbasio, debasing (of coinage) 1550.

imbassatorius, *see* AMBASS

imbatell/atio, embattlement (of walls) 1547; **-atus,** embattled (her.) p 1394; **-o,** to embattle (a manor house) 1449, 1493; 1571, **enbatillo** 1495, to marshal in battle array.

imbecill/itates (*pl.*), infirmities, ailments c 780; **-ito** 1424, **-o** c 1150, ‡1483, to weaken.

imbeneficiatus (inb-), beneficiary c 1212.

imbe/sillatio, embezzlement, misappropriation 1508; 1509, **-sillamentum** 1417, embezzlement, mutilation (of documents); **-sillo** 1486, 1555, **-cello** 1454, **-selo** 1448, to embezzle, suppress, or deface; *cf.* BESIL

imbibitio, absorption c 1250, 1620; infusion c 1470, 1622.

imbillo (inb-), *see* **imbullo.**

imblad/amentum (inb-) 1219, 1246, **-iamentum** 1199, 1242, **-atio** 1224, c 1324, **-atura** a 1240, c 1282, **-iatura** 1204, 1242, **-itura** 1292, **-ura** 1214, 1246, **inblaura** p 1290, †**-um** 1242, bringing under (sowing with) corn, growing crops, 'emblements'; **-o** 1191, 15c., **-io** 1224, 1230, to sow with corn, bring under cultivation.

imbocardo, to put in Bocardo (prison) c 1434.

imboiatus, fettered c 1130.

imbossatus (inb-) c 1510, **embossatus (enb-)** 1388, 1448, embossed.

imbrac/iamentum 1393, **-iata** 1400, **-iaria** 1447, 1508, embracery, bribery of jurors; **-iator** 1370, c 1400, **embraciator** 1365, one guilty of embracery; **-io,** to bribe (a jury) a 1564; *cf.* **exumbratio.**

imbracio, to embrace, hold in arms 1279; *see also* **imbrasio.**

imbraello (inb-), to cover (cart) with a net 1242.

imbra/sio 15c., **-cio** 1389, to brew.

imbraud-, *see* EMBRAUD

imbrechio, *see* **imbrochio.**

imbrev/iamentum (inb-) 1201, 1208, **-iatio** c 1258, **-iatura** 1549, record, register; **-ator,** recorder 1184; **-io** 1086, 1578, **-ico** c 1300, to record, put in writing.

imbric/a c 1595, **-amentum** 1537, tile; **-atio,** embattling (her.) c 1595; **-atus,** embattled (her.) c 1595; **crux -ata,** cross engrailed (her.) c 1595; **-ator,** tiler 1537.

imbrig/atio (inb-), dispute, broil c 1350, c 1377; **-abilis,** disputable c 1360, 1427; **-o,** to embroil, involve in a dispute c 1298, 1336.

imbrochio 1255, 1268, †**imbrechio** 1285, to broach (a cask).

imbrosus, showery 1302.

imbroud-, imbroid-, imbrud-, *see* EMBRAUD

imbu/imen, draught c 990; **-tor,** teacher 10c. ‡15c.; **-tus,** drunk 1280.

imbull/o (inb-), to seal with a bull 13c., 15c.; to embody in a bull c 1397; c 1397, **inbillo** 1376, to implead by bill.

imbulto, to bolt (flour) into 1311.

imburs/ator (inb-), appropriator 1541; **-o,** to put in one's purse, appropriate c 1200, 1541.

imbuscatus, lying in ambush 1381.

imbut-, *see* **imbuimen.**

im/e, low (*adv.*) c 1392; **-ius,** lower c 1470.

imera, *see* **hemera.**

imit/atus, imitation c 1250; **-abilis,** worthy of imitation c 730; **-abilitas,** capacity of being imitated a 1290, c 1343; **-ativus** a 1250, **-atorius** c 1205, 1412, imitative, mimetic; **-o,** *for* **-or,** to imitate c 1250, c 1362; **-o optionem,** to carry out an intention 1290; **-or,** to seek after 1264.

immadido, to moisten c 810.

immanens, immanent (theol.) c 1300, 1412.

immanifest/us, obscure 1344; **-e,** obscurely 1344.

immarc/escibilis c 1125, c 1326, **-essibilis** 1041. a 1155, 1528, **-iscibilis** 1090, 1458, **-idus** c 1325, 1435, unfading, unwithering; **-essibiliter,** fadelessly c 1000.

immarsupio, to put in one's purse c 1180.

immasso (inm-), to chew c 1115.

immateri/alitas, immateriality c 1270, 1344; **-alis** 860. c 1200, 1380, **-atus** 1620, immaterial, non-material; **-abilis,** incapable of having a material cause p 1300.

immatriculo (inm-), to enrol 1378, a 1446.

immaturatio, unmatured condition a 1250.

immeabil/is (inm-), impassable c 1250, 1461; **-iter,** impassably c 1150.

immedi/atio (inmedi-), immediacy (log.) 1290, c 1362; **-etas,** continuity p 1394; **-ate,** *immediately, without intermediary c 865. 12c., c 1564; *(with word denoting sequence in time) 1236, 1545; forthwith c 1262, 15c.; till now c 1467; **-atissimus** c 1200, 1345; **-atus** c 1080, 1537, †**-us** c 1150, immediate; adjacent 1446; **hora -ata,** the present hour c 1447; **dominus -atus,** immediate lord (feudal) c 1280, 1570.

immedicabiliter, incurably 1440.

immelioro (inm-), to ameliorate 12c.

immemor/ mentis c 1290, **i. sui** 1354, bereft of reason; **-ans,** forgetful a 1452; **-ialis,** lacking memory 13c.; c 1612, 1620, **-atus** 1500, 1508, immemorial; **-iter,** unmindfully c 1304.

immens/itas, hugeness (of stature) c 1250; large quantity c 1250; greatness (title) c 1337; **-e** c 1340, **in -um** 1259, c 1344, immensely, immeasurably; **-ibilis** a 1250, **-is** c 1250, c 1390, *for* **-us,** measureless.

immensur/atio c 1367, **-abilitas** c 865, immeasurability; **-abiliter** c 865. c 1380, **-ate** c 865, immeasurably.

immercio, to amerce c 1185, c 1290; *cf.* AMERCI

immeri/bilis, incapable of deserving 1344; **-biliter,** without power to deserve 1344; **-te,** without cause 1546.

†**immer/sivus,** involving immersion 1652; †**-sus,** (?) *f.l.* for **inversus,** overthrown c 1150; **-go,** (?) to take possession c 1362; **i. super,** to overrun 13c.; *cf.* **emergentia.**

imministro, to administer c 730.

imminu/tio, attack c 960; †**immuno,** *for* **-o,** to diminish 697.

immiscibilis, unmixable 13c.

immiser/abiliter c 1220, **-anter** c 1150, **-icorditer** 826, c 1000. c 1200, 1461, unmercifully.

immissio, sending in among 7c. c 1250, c 1267; instigation, suggestion 748. c 1160, 1340; **immitto,** to inspire c 1250.

immixtio, mixture 860.

immobil/itas c 730, c 760. c 1115, a 1452, **-itatio** 13c., 1378, immobility, fixity; **-ia** (*pl.*), immovable goods c 1178, 1282; **furtum -e,** theft of immovables c 1115; **-iter,** immovably c 730, 812. a 1155, 1461; **-itativus,** naturally fixed 1344; **-ito,** to immobilize, fix c 1270, c 1360.

immoder/antia c 1195, 15c., **-amen** 1235, c 1270, excess, lawlessness; **-ans,** immoderate, excessive c 1218; **-anter,** immoderately 1219, a 1452.

immol/atio, gift 5c.; **i. fermenti,** sacrifice of leavened bread 12c.; **-aticius** c 1080, c 1200, †**-aticus** 5c., **-ativus** 1378, sacrificial; **-o,** to offer, present 5c., 893. a 1155, c 1400.

immolestus, not troublesome a 1155.

immonstrabilis, not demonstrable c 1200.

immor/alitas, immorality c 1270; **-igerus** 1338, 1609, **-igeratus** 1295, 1541, **-egeratus** c 1540, intractable, disobedient.

immor/atio, delay c 1125, c 1242; **-or,** to linger 12c., c 1343; to abide, continue 1315; to fail, run short 1424.

immorose, without delay 1291.

immotabilis, immovable 860.

immoverius, nay rather 14c., 1537.

immund/anus c 865. 1344, †**-arus, -ialis** a 1350, immanent in the world, worldly.

immund/itia (inmund-) c 1080, a 1446, †**intermunditia** c 1115, **-ositas** c 1250, impurity, guilt; **-atus,** not cleaned 1353; **-o,** shamefully c 1102; **-us,** guilty c 1115.

immunio, to confirm, corroborate c 1337.

immun/itas ecclesie, ecclesiastical privilege, inviolability c 1200, 1461; sanctuary 1316; **emunitas,** *for* **-itas,** immunity c 796. c 1200, 1411; **-ia** (*pl.*), liberties, privileged areas c 1150; **-itus,** immune, exempt a 1540.

immunitio, lack of warning c 1324.

immuno, *see* IMMINU

immuro, to immure, enclose c 1125, 15c.

immut/atio (inmut-), absence of change c 1250; **-abiliter,** immutably 815. c 1192, c 1450; **-atus,** immature (of fish) 1230.

immut/ativum, transformatory force a 1250;

-ativus, transformatory a 1250, a 1446; -ator seculi, the Saviour c 1250; -o, to introduce as a substitute c 600. c 1180.

immutil/andus (inm-), inviolable c 1125; -atius, more firmly, more entirely c 793.

immutuatio (inm-) debiti, incurring of debt 1219.

impac/atio, non-payment 1291; -abilis, not payable, not current 1278; 14c., 15c., -ificus 1362, 1365, turbulent; -ifice, turbulently c 1456.

impacc/ator, packer 1504; -o, to pack 1280, 1504.

impact/io (inp-), stumbling-block c 730; -ivus 1312, inpectivus 1328, aggressive; ‡-or, stumbler 1483; impingo, to stumble, blunder, hesitate c 1125, 1552; to abut 13c.; to impute c 1135, c 1362.

impagino, to record, put in writing c 1190.

impalo (inp-), to impale c 1115, 1190.

impalpabil/itas, impalpability c 1270; -is, impalpable c 730, c 793. c 1250, c 1436; not to be touched 9c.

impan/atio, transubstantiation 1381, 1552; -ator, believer in transubstantiation 1427; -o, to turn into bread 1552.

impan/ellatus (inp-), impanelled juror c 1443; *-ello 1315, 1573, †-alo 1447, enpanello 1432, to impanel.

impapiro (inp-), to set down on paper 1299.

impar/, umpire c 1257, 1505; (adj.) odd (math.) a 1250; -iter, unevenly (math.) a 1250; -itas, unevenness, inequality c 865. c 1170, 1620.

impar/abilis (inp-), unobtainable c 1620; -atus, unprepared, undressed (of skins) 1359.

imparc/amentum (imperc-) 1317, -atio 1466, c 1488, enclosure (of park); 1189, 15c., -atio 1233, a 1564, -atura 1226, (right of) impounding; †-um, pound, pinfold a 1330; -arius 1481, -ator 1563, 1572, pounder, pinder; -o, to empark, enclose 1276, 1587; *to impound (animals) 1187, c 1452; to imprison (malefactors) c 1258.

imparentia, see EMPAR

†imparlico, (?) to accuse (leg.) (Ir.) 1380.

†imparochio, (?) to impropriate (eccl.) 1300.

imparouiamentum, see impruiamentum.

impart/ibilitas (impert-) c 865. c 1270, -icipatio c 865, indivisibility; -ibile, indivisible entity 1267; -ibilis, indivisible c 1270, c 1540; -ibiliter c 865. 1344, 1552, -icipate c 865, indivisibly; -icipabilis, unable to be shared p 1300; -icipatus, unshared p 1300.

impart/itio 1070, †-io c 1500, †imperitio 941, imparting, communication; -icipo, to impart, give a share of c 1250.

impassibilitas, exemption from suffering c 730, c 860. 12c., 1344.

impast/ino, -o, to make into paste a 1235.

impastrono, to shackle 13c.

impatesco, to be revealed c 1410, c 1415.

impatien/dus, unbearable c 1125; herba -s, touch-me-not 1641.

impatrisso, to follow in father's footsteps 14c.

impaupero (inp-), to impoverish c 1200, 1275.

impecc/abilitas c 1376, 1380, -antia 1427, -atio c 1377, sinlessness; -abilis, sinless c 1344, c 1383.

impech/iamentum c 1273, 1421, -ementum 1428, hindrance, interference; i. vasti, impeachment of waste (leg.) 1427; -io, to impeach, proceed against (leg.) c 1366; cf. impeditus, impetitio.

impectivus, see IMPACT

impectoratus (inp-), taken to heart 1349.

imped/ia, upper leather (of boot) c 1266, ‡15c.; ‡-atura, footstep 1483.

imped/itus c 1290, -itum c 1340, 1343, -itivum c 1318, hindrance; -imentum vasti, impeachment of waste 1426 (cf. IMPECH); *-ibilis, liable to be impeded c 1290, c 1360; -ibiliter, with the possibility of impediment 1344; -iose, so as to impede c 1100; -iosus c 1290, *-itivus 1239, 1609, impeding; -itor 1259, c 1290, -iens 1223, 1315, defendant (leg.); i. pacis, disturber of the peace 1318; -io, to harass by legal action 1274, c 1337; to hamble (dogs) 1310.

impejor/amentum, damage 1187; -o, to damage a 1185, 1573.

†impellatio, appeal against judgement (leg.) 1300.

impello see IMPULS

impend-, see impensio.

impenetrabilitas, impenetrability 1648, 1686.

impenit/entia a 1200, -endum c 730, -udo c 1080, impenitence; -enter, impenitently 1344, 1378.

impenno (inp-), to fletch (arrows) 1202, 1300.

impen/sio, affixing 1443; 7c., 11c. 1198, 1380, -sa 1241, gift, bestowal, payment; -dens (ppl.), pendent (of seal) 1313, 1451; -do, to give, supply, spend 676. 1086, 1545; i. me ad, to devote oneself to 980.

imper-, see also impar-

imperagratus (inp-), untraversed 6c.

imperat-, see imperium.

imperceptibil/itas, imperceptibility a 1250; -is, imperceptible c 1267, 1620; -iter, imperceptibly c 1267, c 1540.

†imperculsus, "unabashed" 1570.

imperdibil/is, imperishable 1344; -iter, inalienably 1427.

imperfect/io *1146, c 1450, -us 1342, imperfection; imperfection of note (mus.) c 1470; -ibilis, imperfectible c 1205, a 1250; -ius, more imperfectly c 1444; -um, imperfect tense (gram.) c 793; -us, of or for the imperfect (gram.) 8c.; imperficio, to make imperfect 1344, 15c.; to imperfect a note (mus.) 1326, c 1470.

imperforabilis, unpierceable a 1350.

imper/ium merum et mixtum, high and low jurisdiction (Fr.) 1285, 1407; I. Sacrum (Romanum), Holy Roman Empire 1302, 1487; *-atrix, empress 1130, 1461; -ativus, imperial c 1450; -atoria, masterwort (bot.) 1634; -atorium c 1364, -iositas c 1344, imperial power; -iale 1245, 1295, pannus -ialis c 1200, 'imperial' (silken fabric); -ialis, royal c 955. c 1125, c 1434; -ialiter, imperially 1041. c 1250, 15c.; -ialius c 900.

impermanentia, impermanence a 1250.
impermittibilis, impermissible c 1470.
*impermixt/us, unmixed c 1197, a 1446;
-ior a 1250; -e, without admixture c 1220;
see also INTERMIXT
impermotus (inp-), unmoved c 1125.
impermutabil/itas, immutability 13c.; -is,
unchangeable 1144, 1344; -iter, unchangeably c 1270.
†impernecabilis, (?) unquenchable c 1250.
*imperpetu/um (inp-) 679, 11c. 12c.,
c 1516, -e c 1511, -o c 1080, p 1348, for
ever; -o, to make (a claim) perpetual (leg.)
c 1258.
imperscrutabilis, inscrutable c 1355.
impersecutus (inp-), not proceeded against
(leg.) p 1348.
imperseverantia, lack of perseverance 12c.
impersolutus, not redeemed by weregeld
c 1110, c 1258; not paid in full (of debt)
c 1258.
imperson/alitas, impersonality (gram.) 13c.;
-o, to make impersonal (gram.) 13c.
imperson/atio, induction, institution (eccl.)
13c.; -o, *to induct, institute (eccl.) a 1183,
1450; to aggrandize c 1200.
imperspect/io, inadvertence c 1250; -ior,
somewhat inadvertent c 1250.
imperspicuitas, opacity c 1270.
impersuasibilis, obstinate c 1100.
imperterrite, intrepidly c 1250, 1285.
impertin/entia(f. s.), irrelevancy 1303, c 1365;
(n. pl.), irrelevant matters c 1250, a 1361;
*-ens, irrelevant c 1250, 1477; -enter,
irrelevantly 1344, 15c.
impertransibilis, impermeable, impassable
a 1350, c 1385.
imperturbator, disturber 1308.
impervertibilis, not to be misled c 1343.
impervestigabilis, unsearchable 1623.
impet/itio, *(action to establish) claim, interference with title (leg.) a 1180, 1486;
*impeachment, accusation c 1115, 1620;
i. vasti, impeachment of waste a 1516,
1562; -ibilis, liable to be attacked c 1200;
-itor, claimant (G.) 1281; accuser a 1200;
-o, to vex with claims 1253, 1583; *c 1170,
15c., -io 1216, 1583, †-ro 1305, to impeach,
accuse; (?) to command, prescribe c 1290,
1346; cf. IMPECH, impeditus.
†impetitus, "unwooed" 1570.
impetr/atio, petition, suit (leg.) a 1245,
c 1362; i. brevis 1307, 1315; i. bille
a 1452; i. bulle 1403, c 1473; -ativus, concerned with obtaining by request c 1344,
c 1367; -ator, claimant c 1258, 1569; -o,
to acquire, purchase 1299, 1537; *1242,
c 1327, i. me 1235, to make suit, initiate
proceedings (leg.); i. breve, to sue out a
writ 1219, 1315; i. litteras 1201, 1237;
see also impetitio.
impet/us (fluminis), current 12c.; -uositas,
impetuosity a 1240, c 1470; -uose, im-
petuously c 1188, c 1470; *-uosus 1242,
c 1470, -uensis (in a word-play) c 1370,
impetuous.
impi/etas, act of impiety or cruelty c 793.
c 1250, c 1343; -us, cruel, pitiless c 1400,
c 1470; -issimus c 1250, c 1362; -issime
c 1470.

*impign/oratio (impingn-) 1253, a 1564,
-eratio (Sc.) 1424, 1456, mortgage, pledge;
*-oro 12c., 1575, -ero a 1180, c 1464, †-o
1393, to mortgage, pledge.
impingo (inp-), to paint, depict c 1362, 1595;
see also IMPACT
impingu/atio, fattening 14c.; fertilization
a 1446, 1620; i. cordis, satisfaction c 1173;
-o *1086, 1336, †-ino 1483, to fatten; to
anoint c 1080, a 1350; to enrich c 1180,
c 1455; to fertilize (soil) c 1176, 1329.
implacit/atio (inp-), pleading, impleading
(leg.) c 1115, a 1564; -abilis, capable of
pleading (? or of being impleaded) 1500;
-ator c 1115, -ans 1423, impleader, plaintiff;
*-o c 1115, 1583, implicito c 1290, c 1480,
to implead, sue.
implaco, implecatio, see IMPLIC
implastr-, see EMPLAST
implegiatus (inp-), forced to act as bail
c 1115.
imple/mentum, supplement 12c., 1414;
1170, 1548, implimentum 1573, plenish-
ing, (item of) stock; land newly brought
into cultivation c 1109; arrears 13c.; c 1080,
1406, -tio c 700. c 1343, 1573, fulfilment;
-tio, fulfilment with grace (theol.) c 1200;
filling 7c., c 730. a 1128, 1532; laying on
(of manure) c 1290, 1532 (cf. implicatio);
-tor, fulfiller, accomplisher 9c.; i. muri,
waller 1302; †-nnire, (?) f.l. for implentes,
c 1298.
implic/amentum, entanglement 12c., c 1400;
-atio, implication (log.) c 1290, c 1367;
†implitatio, "employment", (?) invest-
ment 1547; †implecatio, (?) employment,
exploitation 1419; †1390, -atio 1450,
spreading (of manure) (cf. impletio);
-ativus, implying a 1350; -ite, implicitly,
by implication c 1290, 1541; -itus, implicit
c 1260, 1610; -o, to line (a hood) c 1443;
*to imply c 1290, c 1432; to bestow c 760;
a 1215, 1556, implaco 1208, 1212, to employ, lay out (money).
implicito, see IMPLACIT
implor/ator, suppliant 12c.; -atorius, supplicatory a 1452.
implumatus, featherless c 1200.
implurific/abilitas, unanalysability p 1300;
-abilis, unanalysable p 1300.
implutus, spoilt by rain 1257.
impnus, see hymnus.
impo, to 'imp', plant (beans) 1340.
impoisuno, see IMPOTION
impolleo, to abound in 1346.
imponderabilis, imponderable c 793.
impondo, to impound (beasts) 1432.
impon/o, -ibilis, see impositio.
import/abilitas, insupportability c 1340;
*-abilis c 1080, 1461, †-alis c 1250, in-
supportable; -abiliter, insupportably c 1200,
1485.
importiono, to apportion 1331.
*importo, to imply, mean c 1270, c 1444.
*importun/itas, importunity, persistent soli-
citation c 1090, 1461; -o, to importune
1220, c 1367.
importuositas (inp-), harbourlessness c 700.
impo/sitio, placing, putting on 1433, 1506;
appointment 1458; imposition (of a rule,

etc.) c 1200, 1513; first bestowal of name, primary meaning (log.) 12c.; choice of a temporary symbol (log.) c 1370; impost, exaction 1252, 1573; imputation, accusation c 1204, 1274; **i. manus** a 1090, 15c., **i. manuum** c 1160, c 1508, laying on of hands (eccl.); **i. prima, i. secunda,** first and second intention (log.) c 1160, c 1360; **-sitor,** imposer (of rule or tax) c 1343; c 1445; accuser c 1343; c 1180, ***-stor** c 1090, 1528, **-strix** (*f.*) c 1150, impostor; ***-stura,** imposture a 1183, 1537; **nomen -nibile,** name that can be imposed a 1361; **-no,** to spend 1317; to announce, give out c 1290; to appoint c 1330; to lay an impost c 1307; ***to impute,** charge with (accusation or liability) c 1202, c 1446; **i. clameum,** to advance a claim 1305; **i. manum (manus) ad,** to lay hands on, seize 1184, c 1327.

impositus (inp-), not firmly planted, faltering 9c.

impossibil/itas, *impossibility c 865. c 1070, 1442; inability c 1255, c 1325; **-ia** (*pl.*), impossibilities c 850; **demonstratio ad -e,** reduction to the absurd 1344; **-ior** c 1380; **-issimus** 1378; **ex -i,** unintentionally c 1115; **-iter,** perforce c 1115; **-itatio,** prevention c 1375; **-ito,** to prevent 1344, 1378; **impossum,** to be unable c 1127.

†**imposteratus,** (?) perverse c 1250.

*impost/erum (*for* in **post-**) 798. 1094, 1559, **-modum** 8c., henceforward, thenceforward.

impostulabilis, ineligible for postulation (eccl.) 1317.

impotenti/a, (?) lack of cultivation (man.) 1351; **-alis,** not merely potential (*i.e.* actual) 1344.

impotion/atio, poisoning c 1400; **-o** c 1130, 15c., **impoisuno** 1225, to poison.

imprebendo, to make into a prebend 1236.

imprec/atorius, invoking a curse c 1200; appropriate to prayer a 1228; **-aciter** c 1430, **-ative** c 1380, **-atorie** a 1228, by way of prayer; **-o,** *for* **-or,** c 1200.

impredestinatus, unpredestined 1344.

impredeterminatus, not foreordained 1344.

impregn/atio, impregnation a 1250, a 1446; **-atus,** inset (of gem) 1267; **imprengno** c 1510, †**imprimio** (? **imprinno**) 1535, *for* **-o,** to impregnate; **-o bursam,** to stuff one's purse 1342.

impremeditat/us, unprepared, not expecting c 1150, c 1400; **-e,** recklessly c 1100, c 1180; unexpectedly c 1150; **-ivus,** impulsive a 1350.

impremunit/us (inp-), unforewarned c 1200; **-e,** without preparation 1461.

imprescriptibilis, not subject to prescription 1309, c 1343.

impresent/i (*for* in **pre-**) c 1308, **-ia** c 1437, ***-iarum** (in **presentiarum**) a 1100, 1522, **in presentiarum tempore** (G.) 1310, at present.

impresepio, to be stabled c 1180.

impresonatio, *see* **imprisonamentum.**

impress/abilis, -ibilis, unshakeable, constant c 1450.

impress/io, stamp (on coins) c 730. c 1400; stencil 1355; printing 1549, 16c.; influence

a 1250; **i. dominice crucis** 780, **i. sancte crucis** 993, sign of the cross; **i. chirographi** c 1000; **i. sigilli** 1136, c 1415, **i. signi** 1261; **-e,** implicitly 1293; **-atus,** imprinted 1464; **-ivus,** impressible c 1270, c 1362; **-or,** master moneyer 1359; printer 1496, 1577; **-orius,** of printing a 1564; **-ura,** engraving c 1212; **-o,** to impress, stamp 1502, 1508; **imprimo,** to press (cheese) 14c.; to print 1479, 1686; *see also* **imprisa.**

impresto (inp-), to advance as an imprest c 1290.

impresumptuose, without presumption c 1220.

impreteribilis (inp-), impassable 1435.

impretermisse, uninterruptedly 7c., c 1000. 1200, c 1450.

*impreti/abilis, priceless c 1223, c 1476; ‡**-osus,** cheap 1570.

imprevertibil/is, unpreventable 15c.; **-iter,** irresistibly c 1400.

imprim/e, at first c 1250; **-itus,** especially c 730. c 1242.

imprimio, *see* **impregnatio.**

imprimo, to prime (walls with lead) 1355; *see also* IMPRESS

imprincipiatus, lacking a first principle p 1300.

impris/a (inp-) c 1192, 1327, **-ia** 1213, 1254, **-io** 1203, 15c., **empriza** (G.) 1242, enterprise, attack, raid; ***-ius** 1215, p 1330, **-us** 1217, 15c., **impressus** 1223, adherent, partisan; **impressus,** (?) taken over 1350; **-us,** undertaken 1279; **-imus** (*perf.*), we have undertaken 1252.

imprisio, misprision 1587, 1588; *see also* **imprisa.**

*impris/onamentum 1194, 1583, **-ionamentum** 1234, **-oniamentum** 1405, **-onantia** 1313, **-onatio** 1199, 1452, **impresonatio** c 1198, **-onatus** 1199, imprisonment; **-onabilis,** meriting imprisonment 1223; **-onagium** (*coll.*), prison dues 1428; **-onator,** imprisoner c 1290; ***-ono** 1194, 15c., **-iono** 1313, **-onamento** 1545, to imprison.

imprivabilis, inseparable c 1362.

improb/abilitas, improbability 13c., c 1343; **-abilis,** hard to prove c 1204; improbable c 1188, 1378; **-abiliter,** improbably, unreasonably c 1080, 1344; **-atio,** disproof, refutation c 1290, c 1460; **-ative,** by way of refutation 1378; **-ativus,** tending to refute 1378; ‡**-atus,** untried 1570; **-o,** to disprove, refute a 1100, 1380,

improbitates (*pl.*), assaults c 730.

improbro, to impute, charge with c 1192.

improcessibilitas, inability to proceed or issue (theol.) c 1290.

improduc/tio, non-creation 1427; **-ibilis,** exempt from creation c 1367.

improhibit/us, unmolested 1516; **-e,** in no forbidden manner 860.

impromptitudo, unreadiness c 1620.

*improper/ium c 1125, 1438, **-atio** c 790. 1137, c 1470, reproach, taunt; †**-us** c 1204, **-atorius** 1378, **-iosus** 12c., 1378, reproachful; **-iose,** reproachfully c 1340; †**improprio,** *for* **-o,** to reproach c 1323.

impropitiabiliter, implacably c 1420.

improportio/ c 1270, c 1362, **-natio** c 1362, disproportion; **-nabilis** a 1252, c 1326, **-nalis** 1267, 1284, **-natus** c 1300, c 1457, disproportionate; **-nabiliter** p 1300, c 1362, **-naliter** 1344, c 1362, disproportionately.

impropri/atio, impropriation (eccl.) c 1553, 17c.; **rectoria -ata** 1545, 1587; *see also* IMPROPER

improprie, improperly c 700.

improtractim, without delay 1402.

1 **improvis/io**, improvidence c 1367; **-us**, not expecting, off one's guard c 1220, c 1470; ill-considered a 1564; unprovided 1312, c 1400.

2 **improvisio (inp-)**, provision, ordinance p 1348.

impruiamentum 1268, **†imparouiamentum** 1598, 'improvement', exploitation; **improwio** c 1170, **empruo** 1265, to 'improve', exploit; *cf.* **approvamentum.**

impub/ertas, youth c 1450; **‡-eo, -esco**, to be young 1483.

impud/icator, seducer c 1150; **-oratus** 12c., **‡-orosus** 1483, shameless.

impugilatoria, inaptitude for combat 13c.

impugnabilis, irrefragable c 730. 1374.

impugn/atio (impungn-), impugnment, hostile criticism 1251, 1463; ***-ator** c 1125, 1528, **-atrix** (*f.*) 1345, assailant.

impugno, to pound by hand c 1266, c 1330; to clasp in the hand c 1250.

impuls/ivus, impelling c 1115, 1620; **-o**, to attack 1461; **impello me in**, to enter, trespass upon 1198.

impulvero, to cover with dust 10c.

†impunctuatio (? punctuatio), agreement c 1420.

†impun/us, *for* **-is**, unpunished c 1290.

impurium, *see* **emporium.**

impurus, debased (of money) c 1115.

imputabil/is, imputable, attributable p 1300, 1378; **-iter**, by imputation 1344.

imputr/escibilis c 1212, **-ibilis** a 1250, incorruptible.

in, (with *acc.*) in (of place, *etc.*) a 1135, 1461; *****within, to the limit of (of time) 11c., c 1324; ***for**, as (of purpose) c 1190, c 1470;

*(with *abl.*) into, to c 1150, c 1400; for, as (of purpose) c 1150, c 1400; ***with**, by means of (bibl.) c 1190, c 1457, *****in the name of (bibl.) c 1090, c 1530; **in et pro**, in and for c 1400;

(with *pronoun*) **in se ipsum**, squared (math.) c 1300; **in eo quod**, inasmuch as a 1110, 1223;

(with *adj.*, *etc.*) **in absconso** c 1330, **in occulto** 12c., **in secretis** 1375, secretly; **in amplo**, in width, extent c 1393; **in brev/e** c 1473, ***in -i** c 730. c 1170, c 1438, in a short time, soon; **in commun/e**, together c 740. c 1250; 1086, ***in -i** c 1000. c 1115, 1537, in common; **in confuso**, confusedly, generally c 1343, c 1443; **in direct/um** c 1080, c 1306, **in -o** 1267, c 1470, direct, straight; **in eversum**, adversely c 1397; **in evidenti**, in plain view c 1250; **in expedito**, in train 1220; **in extremis**, on the point of death 1275, c 1362; **in hujusmodi**, to this effect c 1115; **in**

longinquo, at a distance 14c.; **in manifesto** 12c., a 1250, **in patulo** c 1343, **in propatulo** a 1100, 1557, publicly, openly; **in majori**, for the most part c 1430, c 1470; **in minus**, in lesser quantity a 1250; **in minim/o** 1316, c 1455, **†in -e** 1433, to the least extent; **in modico**, to some extent c 1188; **in multo**, to a great extent c 1470; **in nullo**, not at all c 1197, c 1400; **in pendenti** c 1258, c 1290, **in pendulo** c 1188, c 1230, **in suspenso** 1229, c 1470, pending, in suspense; **in perpetuum**, *see* **imperpetuum; in plus**, in greater quantity a 1250; **in posterum**, in postmodum, *see* IMPOST; **in presentiarum**, *see* IMPRESENT; **in sero**, late in the day c 1253, 1347; **in quant/um** a 1233, c 1520, **in -o** 1267, c 1362, **in -is** c 1408, inasmuch as, in so far as; **in tant/um (quod, ut)** a 1175, 1426, **in -o (quod, ut)** c 1410, 1414, to such an extent that; **in toto**, wholly 1291, c 1515; **in transvers/um** 13c., **in -o** 1288, 1354, cross-wise, athwart; **in ultimo**, finally 1428;

(with *adv.*) **in antea**, beforehand c 1115; henceforth c 1080, c 1520; 1308, c 1380, **in perantea** 1434, **in ante** c 1362, formerly; **in invicem**, by turns, mutually c 1150, c 1470; **in obviam**, to meet c 1250, 1415; **in palam**, openly c 1170, c 1260; **in prope**, near by a 700.

inabsolutus, unabsolved c 1150.

inabstractus, not withdrawn c 860.

inaccept/abilis c 1250, **-atus** 14c., unacceptable; **†-ibilis**, unattainable c 865.

inaccess/us c 1434, **-ibilitas** a 1142, 15c., inaccessibility; **-abilis**, *for* **-ibilis**, 15c.

inact/itatio, enactment 1406, a 1452; **-us** c 1470, **enactus** 1548, enacted; ***-ito** 1413, 1584, **†-ino (? -ivo)** 1431, **-uo** 1504, **-o** 1411, 1523, to enact, register.

inact/orium, pound, pinfold 1516; **‡-or (†mactor)**, pinder 1483.

inact/ualitas, non-actuality c 860; **-ivus**, ineffective 1620; **-uosus**, concerned with inactivity c 793; **-us**, having accomplished nothing c 1200, c 1400.

inadministratus, unadministered (of testators' goods) 1684.

inadnichilabilis, indestructible c 1367.

inadorandus, unworthy of worship 793.

inadver/tentia c 1340, 1511, **-tantia** 1380, inadvertency; **-tenter**, inadvertently 1395; **-sabilis**, irresistible 1344.

inadvocatus, unsolicited c 1437.

inaffectio, lovelessness 7c., 819. a 1250.

inalimentatus, unnourished 1620.

inalleviabiliter, without hope of relief 1344.

inallio, to take into alliance c 1150.

inalterabilis, unalterable a 1233, 1344.

inalto, to exalt 6c. c 1125.

inamelo, *see* ENAM

inamic-, *see* INIMIC

inamissibil/is, inalienable c 1357; **-iter**, inalienably, unfailingly 1344, c 1361.

inangul/atus, gyronny (her.) p 1394; **-o**, to corner c 1270, 1375.

inanim/atio, lifelessness 12c.; **-ans** c 1595, **-atus** a 1250, 15c., inanimate; **-o**, to discourage, deter 1427.

inanimo, to encourage c 1325, c 1362.

inan/itio, emptying a 1250; destitution, lack a 1155, 13c.; starvation diet c 1160, 1424; kenosis (theol.) 1378; **-is,** void of effect, invalid 1270, c 1340; **-esco,** to be empty c 730, 9c.; **-io,** to nullify c 1200.

inanulatus, not ringed (of pigs) 1355, 1666.

inapparenter, unconvincingly 1521.

inappeto, to strive after, be eager for 1044.

inapprehensibilis, weak of apprehension 13c.

inappretiabilis, inestimable 1219, c 1375.

inapt-, see INEPT

inaquatus, steeped in water 1395.

inarabilis, non-arable 1180, c 1205.

inarmo, to reinforce (shields, etc.) 1213, 1224.

inarrho, to pay earnest-money to 1205, ‡1483.

inartificios/us, unskilful c 1200, ‡1483; **-e,** unskilfully 1231.

inascensibilis, unscalable c 1212.

inasinatio, transformation into an ass 1427.

†inastutive, unwisely 1378.

inattemptatus, untried c 1250.

inattent/io, inattention, oversight 14c.; **-e,** recklessly c 1456.

inattingibilis, unattainable c 1212, 1345.

inattritus, untrodden c 710, 10c.

‡inaudaculus, "squeamish" 1570.

inaudesco, to grow bold a 1175.

inaudi/entia 10c., **-tus** c 1212, strangeness.

†inaugeo, to add to 1347.

inaugmentabilis, incapable of increase a 1233, c 1360.

inaugur/atio, coronation 1608; inception (ac.) c 1550; **-o,** to incept (ac.) c 1570, 1583.

inaur/atio, gilding c 1200; **-o,** to embellish (a song) c 1170.

†inaurina, (?) for **maurina,** fog 5c.

inaurities, wearing ear-rings 13c.

inauthentic/itas, unauthenticity 1684; **-us,** unauthentic 1684.

inb-, see also **imb-**

inbannum, see **ambanum.**

inbasciatrix-, see AMBASS

inborgum, pledge, security (A.S. *inborh*) c 1115.

incalcinatus, calcined in c 1215.

incalculatus, unnumbered c 550.

incalleo, to be callous 1308.

incalumniabilis, unchallengeable c 1332.

incancellabilis, not to be cancelled 1344.

incandeo, to glow a 1400.

incanonico, (?) to invest with canonical habit c 1444.

incant/amen, charm c 1400; **-atorius,** magical 1552; †**-or,** for **-ator,** enchanter 1406; **-atrix,** enchantress, witch c 1110, 1588.

incantus, auction (Fr. *encant*) 1524.

incap/acitas, incapacity, disqualification 1378, c 1444; **-abilis,** that cannot be taken in c 730; **-iabilis,** impregnable 15c.; **-tabilis,** uncatchable c 1090.

incapatus, wearing a cape c 1325.

incapitulo, to make a member of a chapter (eccl.) a 1250.

incapso 1530, **incasso** p 1290, to encase.

*incarcer/atio, incarceration c 1192, c 1461; **-ator,** imprisoner c 1246; **-atus,** prisoner c 1250, 1423; ***-o,** to incarcerate, imprison 9c., 10c. c 1080, 1642; see also **inceratio.**

incardino, to incorporate, appoint 9c.; to make a cardinal 1610.

incardium, pith, heartwood (ἐγκάρδιον) 7c.

incario, to carry in 1366.

incarior, see INCHER

incarnalis, non-carnal 13c.

*incarn/atio 7c., 10c. c 1080, 1552, **i. Christi** 12c., 1461, **i. Domini** 1177, c 1450, ***i. Dominica** 1068, 1565, the Incarnation; see also **annus;** ‡**-ativa** (*pl.*), medicaments used in healing wounds 1652; ***-or,** to be made flesh (eccl.).

incart/atio, grant by charter 1315; ***-o** c 1180, 1428, **-ulo** 1189, c 1250, to grant by or embody in a charter.

incassabilis, unquashable 13c.

incass/um, in vain: †**incastum** 1400; ‡**-o,** to nullify 1483; see also **incapso.**

incast-, see also ENCAUST; INCASS; INCEST

incastell/atio, fortification, castle-building c 1204; ***-o,** to fortify (with or in castles) a 1150, 1420.

incastigabil/is, uncontrollable, incorrigible c 1180, 1411; **-iter,** uncontrollably c 1180.

incastonatus, inlaid c 1250.

incastro, to imbed c 1172, c 1225; to defend by fortifications c 1327; to imprison in a castle 1412, c 1447.

incasualis, not liable to accidents c 865.

incaten/atio, enchainment 1225; **-o,** to chain (a book) 1414, c 1453.

incathedr/atio, enthronement (as bishop) c 1182, p 1290; **-o,** to enthrone (eccl.) c 1180, c 1400.

1 incaus/atio, causelessness p 1300; **-abilis,** causeless c 1300, c 1620; **-abiliter,** without cause 1344; **-alis,** with no causal influence 860; **-atus,** uncaused c 1250, a 1361.

2 incaus/atio, impleading unfairly a 1260, c 1300; **-alis,** illegal, illegitimate c 1290; **-o,** to charge, implead (unreasonably) c 1115, 1251.

incaust/um, -rum, -erium, see ENCAUST

†incaustus (*v.l.* **infaustus**), (?) for **injustus,** 12c.

incedo, see INCESS; INCID

†incelebris, for **celeber,** c 1000.

incelo, to engrave 1208, 14c.

incen/dium, arson c 1115, c 1275; fine for arson c 1115; branding (of horses) 1453; ‡**tinder** 1570; **-sio,** assaying 12c.; **-sor,** kindler c 550; 15c., **-sator** c 1540, ***-tor** c 1125, 1461, **-trix** (*f.*) c 1125, 1345, instigator; ***-tivum** 9c. c 1125, c 1412, **insensamentum** c 1330, instigation; **-sivus,** inflammatory, exciting a 1250, 1620; **-sa** c 1197, c 1400, **-sus** c 1118, for **-sum,** incense; **-sum Alexandrinum** c 1200, **i. francum** a 1200, **i. liberum** a 1205 frankincense; **-sarium** c 760. c 1135, 1317, **insensura** 1415, **vas -sorium** 13c., censer; **-so,** to cense, burn incense c 1080, 1469; *cf.* **censura.**

incenso, to farm out (G.) 1309.

inceppo, see **incippo.**

incept/io, inception, admission to teach (ac.) c 1250, 1471; **-ive,** by way of origination 14c.; in first stages 1408; **-ivus,** introductory 12c.; originative 1620; ***-or,** inceptor (ac.) c 1322, c 1594; ***incipio,** to incept (ac.) c 1250, 1426; **i. celebrare missas,** to celebrate first mass 1374.

incer/atio a 1252, a 1292, †**incarceratio** 1267, melting together like wax, inceration (alch.); **pannus -atus,** waxed cloth 1238; **-o,** to melt together (alch.) a 1252, a 1292.

inceratus, unmelted (*or* unwaxed) c 1215.

incerebro, to brain 1220.

incero, *see* INCER; INSER

incert/itudo, uncertainty, vagueness 9c. 1220, 1684; **-im,** without specific subject (gram.) 13c.; **-io,** to be uncertain 1218.

1 incess/us, path (of a light-ray) c 1260, c 1300; **-io,** walking, gait c 1115; entry c 1290; **-or,** walker c 1340; (*adj.*) aggressive 1526; **inced/ens,** passant (her.) 1245; **-o viam patrum,** to die c 855, 11c.

2 †incessus, a tax or due 734.

incest/us, defilement, debauchery c 1150; **incastus,** *for* **-us,** unchaste c 700; **-or,** lecher c 1150; **-uose,** incestuously, lewdly c 1340, 1435; **-uosus** c 1223, 1549, †**-uus** 1201, incestuous, lewd.

incher/imentum, price-raising (G.) 1292; **-eo,** to make dearer (G.) 1292; **incarior,** to become dearer 1317.

inchirographo, to record in a chirograph 1259.

incho-, *see also* INCOH

†**inchocho sagittam,** to fit arrow to bow-string 1203.

incibatus, unfed c 1180, c 1325.

incibus, *see* intubus.

incida, kingfisher a 1446.

incid/entia, (*f. s.*) incidence (of light-rays, etc.) c 1240, 1686; incident, occurrence c 1362, c 1464; appurtenance a 1452; (*n. pl.*) occurrences c 1343, c 1362; matters involved 1426; remarks, observations c 1190, c 1400; **-entalis,** incidental, secondary c 1334; *see also* **angulus; -entaliter** c 1258, 1521, **-enter** c 1160, 1684, **insidenter** p 1280, **ex -enti** 13c., incidentally; **-o,** to fall into 9c. c 1178, c 1437; 1263, 1277, **incedo** 1419, to incur a penalty; *see also* INCIS

incidi/atio, -o, *see* insidie.

inciner/atio, burning to ashes 12c., 1620; **-o,** to burn to ashes 9c. c 1180, 1620.

incipi-, *see* INCEPT; INSIP

incippo 1232, 1289, **inceppo** 1249, 1281, to put in the stocks.

*****incircumcisus,** uncircumcised (eccl.).

incircumfinite, infinitely c 865.

incircumscript/us c 1180, a 1350, **-ibilis** c 865, 12c., c 1225, illimitable; **-e,** illimitably c 1212.

incircumseptus, unbounded c 860.

incircumspect/io, heedlessness c 1258; **-us,** heedless a 1180, a 1408; *****-e,** heedlessly 10c. c 1125, 15c.

incircumvelat/us, unconcealed c 865; **-e,** without concealment c 865.

incircumventus, not cheated a 1408.

1 incis/io c 1090, 1377, **inscisio** 14c., incision, cutting; breach (of wall) c 1192; carving (of stones) 1226, 1438; engraving (of coins) 1247, c 1270; **-io** (†**inscitio**), modification of outline, notching (her.) c 1595; **i. capitis,** decapitation 1318;

vendo (**pannum**) **ad -ionem,** to retail (cloth) a 1155, 1419; ‡**-ium,** hotchpotch 1570; **-ivum,** incision, cut a 1361; **-ivus,** incisive 13c.; (?) pungent a 1250, c 1270; **dens -ivus, -or,** incisor tooth a 1250; **-or,** stone-cutter 1226, 14c.; die-cutter, engraver 1237; maker of incisions (med.) 1385; **i. bursarum,** cut-purse c 1200, c 1400; **i. lignorum** 14c.; **-orium,** carving-table, trencher c 1160; **incido,** to cut (cloth, for retailing) a 1155, c 1185; 1342, 1385, (?) **inscido** c 1224, to slash (cloth, for ornament); **i. monetam,** to coin c 1115; **inscido,** to cut, carve 1226, c 1250; to notch (her.) c 1595; to make an incision (med.) c 1280; *cf.* inscissio.

2 †incisio, (?) assize a 1335.

3 incisio, incita, *see* INSIT

incist/atio, putting in a chest c 1384; **-o,** to put in a chest c 1384, 1448; *see also* INSIST

incit/ativum c 1180, 1378, **-atorium** 1378, incentive; ‡**-abulum,** decoy 1552; **insitamentum,** incitement 1504.

incitatus, not summoned (leg.) a 1175, c 1190.

incivil/is, contrary to civil law c 1258; **-iter,** in contravention of civil law (G.) 1312.

inclamo, to implead, charge (Sc.) 14c.

inclau-, *see* inclavo; INCLU

inclavo, to nail on 1245, 1274; (?) to mark (standard measure) by means of nails 1197; c 1330, **incloo** 1275, **inclaudo** 13c., **includo** 1295, to 'accloy', lame (horse) by pricking with shoe-nail (Fr. *enclouer*).

inclerico, to ordain as clerk c 1444.

inclin/antia, inclination 1440; **-anter,** willingly 1440; **-abilis,** inflected (gram.) 1524; 1421, **-us** c 1125, gracious; **-us,** with bowed head c 1266; **-ativus,** inclined, tending c 1250; producing an inclination p 1300, c 1362; supplicatory 15c.; **-atus,** salient (her.) c 1595.

inclipeo, to shield 1220.

inclit/udo, renown 1439; **-e,** gloriously c 1000. c 1204; **-o,** to praise c 860.

inclu/sio 1440, c 1473, **-satio** 1583, **inclausura** 1509, enclosing (of land); 1399, **inclausura** 1573, **inclaustura** c 1342, **inclosimentum** 1550, **-sum** 1359, c 1373, **inclausa** 1289, 1359, **inclausum** 1426, c 1538, **inclausatum** 1548, enclosure, enclosed land, close; **inclaustrum,** fence 1277; cloister a 1100, 1238; harbour (naut.) 1214; *****-sive** c 1258, c 1612, **-denter** a 1447, inclusively; **-sivus,** inclusive a 1200, c 1290; ‡**-sarius,** hayward 15c.; ‡c 1440, 1483, ‡**-sor** c 1440, 1483, pinder; **-sor parci** 1352; ‡**-sorium,** pinfold 15c., 1483; 1264, (?) **-sivum** 1326, **-sum** (?) c 1200, 1274, sluice or dam; 1245, **-sarium** 1221, hermit's cell; **-sus** 1159, 1328, *****-sa** (*f.*) 1155, c 1340, hermit, recluse; **diem †inclausit,** *for* **clausit,** c 1400; **-do** c 1127, 1447, **includo** c 1160, **inclauso** c 1258, to enclose (land); to dam up (water) 1450; **-dor,** to become a recluse 1233, c 1414; *see also* inclavo.

incoagulabilis, immune from curdling a 1250.

incogitantia, thoughtlessness 1516, 1520.

incognoscibilis, unrecognizable c 1193.

incogo, to compel 1344.
*incoh/atio (incho-) 12c., c 1565, -amentum c 865, beginning; -ativus, marking the beginning 1344, 15c.; -ative, rudimentarily a 1347; breve -atum, writ on which part payment has been made 1257; inquoo, for -o, to begin c 1266.
incolito, to inhabit c 810.
incol/omis, for -umis, c 793.
incolorabilis, inexcusable c 1367.
incombust/ibilis, incombustible c 1180, a 1252; -us, unburnt 771, c 950. c 1090, c 1400.
incomestibilis, inedible 12c., c 1227.
incommemoratus, uncommemorated c 1250.
incommendabilis, unpraiseworthy a 1450.
incommensur/atio a 1250, -abilitas c 1267, incommensurability; -abilis, incommensurable c 1277, 1620.
incommixt/im, without mixture c 860; -us, not mixed together c 860.
incommunic/atio, lack of correspondence 1267; -abilitas, incommunicability c 1290, c 1365; -abilis, incommunicable, not to be imparted 12c., 1320; -ans, without inter-communication c 1365.
incommutabilitas, unchangeableness 793, c 860. c 1180, 1344.
incompactus, lacking solidity 12c.; ‡"un-trussed" 1570.
incompar/abilitas (inconpar-), incompara-bility p 1300, p 1340; *-abiliter, in-comparably 9c. c 1080, c 1470; -andus, incomparable c 1140.
incompass/ibilis, incompatible (phil.) 1427; c 1239, 1372, incompatibilis c 1444, 1684, incompatible (of eccl. benefices); ‡incom-patibilis, (?) formally invalid 1424; -ibiliter 1344, -ive c 1150, without compassion.
incompeditus, unfettered 1663.
incompensabilis, irretrievable c 1200; un-requitable c 1375.
incompet/entia, incompetence a 1609, 1622; -ens, unsuitable, insufficient a 1100, 15c.; -enter, inappropriately, improperly c 1194, 1347.
incomplet/io, incompleteness 13c., 1378; -e, incompletely a 1250, c 1343; -ibilis, needing nothing to achieve completeness c 1205; -us, incomplete 1267, c 1500; in-satiable c 1200.
incomplex/io, freedom from complexity or involvement c 1270, c 1365; defect in con-stitution 13c.; -ionalis 1351, -us c 1160, c 1363, simple, not involved; -e, simply 1344, c 1363; -um, a simple term (log.) a 1323, c 1362.
incomplexus, embraced, involved 1552.
incomplutus, not rained upon 12c., a 1275.
incompos sui, incapacitated 1247, c 1266.
incompositio, lack of artistry c 1180; sloven-liness 1300, 1367.
incompossibil/itas, incompatibility c 1300, p 1300; *-is, incompatible, not simul-taneously possible 1267, 1378.
incomprehens/ibilitas, incomprehensibility 12c., 1267; -ilis c 1180, -ivus 12c., incom-prehensible.
incompulsus, unconstrained 14c.
inconcedibilitas, inadmissibility c 1360.

inconceptibilis, inconceivable 1636.
inconcinnatus, unbound (of books) 1523.
inconcludentia, inconclusiveness 1684.
‡inconcoctus, undigested 1570.
inconcorditer, discordantly c 1266.
inconcorruptus, not sharing in corruption c 860.
inconcretio, lack of concreteness c 1290.
*inconcusse, undisturbedly (of tenure) 1131, 1555.
inconductibilis, unable to be let (of houses) c 1306.
‡inconfertus, "unstopped" 1570.
incon/fessus c 1125, 1461, -fitens c 1172, unshriven.
inconfinius, lying beyond the borders c 1325.
inconfuse, without intermixture 815, c 860.
inconfutabiliter, incontestably 1441.
incongruitas, unsuitability, inconsistency c 1258, 1440.
inconjugatus, unwed 12c.
inconjunctus, disunited 1461.
‡inconscensus, "unstridden" 1570.
inconsecratus, unconsecrated c 1188.
inconservabilis, not conservable c 1362.
inconsideratio, thoughtlessness c 1250, 1443.
*inconsol/abiliter, inconsolably 1041. c 1070, c 1450; -atus, unconsoled c 1150, 14c.
inconson/antia, harshness of sound (gram.) 9c.; inconsistency c 1360; -e, inappro-priately c 1407; -us, harsh-sounding (gram.) 9c.; inconsistent 1311, c 1443.
‡inconspectio, inspection c 1414.
inconspicuus, invisible c 860.
inconsuet/us, unwonted c 790. 12c., 1461; -e, unwontedly c 1250.
‡inconsul/us, (?) for -tus, unprovided for 1220.
inconsumm/abilis, impossible of completion c 1325; -atus, incomplete 1205, 1277.
*inconsut/ilis c 1125, 1414, -elis c 1450, seamless; -ibiliter, without a seam c 1200; -us, unmended c 1340.
incontestabiliter, incontestably 1344.
incontin/entia, fornication c 1180, c 1434; †-ens 1419, †-ente 1461, *-enti 6c. a 1164, c 1473, †-entim 1313, -enter c 1257, 1495, immediately; incontentus, unsatisfied 1484.
incontinu/itas, discontinuity 1524; -e, dis-continuously c 1220.
incontracte, without contraction c 1360.
incontradictus, undisputed a 1130.
†incontrarius, (?) perverse c 1290.
inconveni/entia, incompatibility, inconsis-tency a 1100, 1295; *c 1258, 1461, -ens (subst.) 1300, c 1380, anomaly, impro-priety; -ens, (adj.) improper, inconsistent a 1080, c 1444.
inconver/sibiliter, unchangeably 1200; -ti-biliter, inconvertibly 13c.
inconvincibil/itas, invincibility 1283; -is, irrefutable c 1321.
*inconvuls/us c 760, c 1000. c 1090, c 1414, inconwlsus c 1196, undisturbed, unshaken; -e, undisturbedly p 1070.
incoopertus, unroofed 1424.
incop/amentum, -o, see inculpatio.
incoppicio, to enclose in a coppice 1238, 1583.

incord/atio, fitting string (to cross-bow) 1236; **-o,** to string (cross-bow) 1221, 1236.
‡**incornis,** "unhorned" 1570.
incornium, ink-horn 1383.
incorpor/atio, incorporation, union 1295, 1587; assimilation of food a 1446; incorporation (ac.) c 1576; inclusion in a corpus c 1400; **-ate,** corporately c 1411; **-atus,** incorporated (ac.) c 1516; **-atissimus,** whole-heartedly incorporated 1433; **-o,** to incorporate, embody c 1070, a 1452; to assimilate (food), devour c 1197, 1413; to unite to oneself c 1223, c 1334; to incorporate, annex (eccl.) 1417, 1586; to incorporate, admit (ac.) 1425, c 1516; to include in a corpus c 1188, 15c.
incorpor/eitas, bodilessness a 1250, p 1300; **-eus,** bodiless, incorporeal c 850. c 1080, c 1430.
incorrectus, uncorrected c 1250, a 1350; unpunished, unreproved 12c., a 1350; inaccurate 1378; ‡untaught 1570; **incorrigibil/is,** incorrigible (of person) c 1115, 1461; (of fault) 1062. c 1377; **-iter,** incorrigibly 1087, c 1200; without need of correction 1374; **-itas,** incorrigibility c 1266, 1521.
incorreptus, unreproved c 1250, 1299.
incorruens, not falling down c 1188.
*****incorrupt/io** (eccl.), **-itas** c 1362, **-ibilitas** c 1080, 13c., ‡**incorrumptibil/itas** a 1290, incorruptibility; †**-is,** incorruptible a 1290.
‡**incorticator,** "dyer" 1520.
incortino, see **incurtino.**
incoustra, see ENCAUST
incrass/atio, -or, see **ingrassor.**
incrasso 1086, 1345, **ingrasso** 1242, 1244, to fatten (animals); to thicken (wine) 1288; a 1130, c 1340, **ingrasso** 13c., to make stubborn; a 1350, c 1455, **ingrasso** 1347, to enrich; **ingrasso,** to manure 1511.
incrastinum, morrow 1275, 1314.
*****increatus,** uncreated c 1180, c 1444.
incred/entia, unbelief c 1190; **-ulitas,** discredit a 1564; **-ens** c 1436, **-ulus** c 1250, c 1400, infidel; **-ibilis,** untrustworthy person c 1115.
incremabilis, incombustible c 1180, 15c.
incre/mentum, newly won land, intake 1266, 1450; interest on a loan 1293, 1415; **i. maris,** flood tide 1359; **-mentatio** c 1465, **-scentia** a 1452, increase; **-tus,** included in composition (phys.) c 1115; **-sco,** to increase (*trans.*) c 1380.
*****increp/atio,** rebuke 7c., c 1006. c 1080, c 1414; **-abilis,** blameworthy p 1300, 1344; **-ative** c 1090, **-atorie** 1225, reproachfully; **-atorius,** reproachful c 1180, 15c.
incriminor, to accuse a 1446.
incroch/iamentum 1533, 1663, **incroachiamentum** 1609, encroachment; **-o super** 1616, **-io super** 1663, **encrochio super** 1404, 1409, to encroach on.
incroc/iatio, appropriation to the crosier (Ir.) 1292; **terra -iata (-eata),** cross-land, land appropriated to the crosier (*i.e.* to a bishopric or religious house) (Ir.) 1293, 1302; **-io (-eo),** to appropriate (land or church) to the crosier (Ir.) 1288, 1292.
incrucio, to torment 1370.

incrud/esco, to rage p 1327; **-o,** to make crude or raw a 1250, ‡15c.
incrum, see **nicrum.**
‡**incrust/ator,** "tinker" 15c.; ‡**-o,** "to parch" 1570; (?) to assail 13c.
incub/a 1250, c 1362, *****-us** c 1160, 1528, **-o** 1200, nightmare, demon; see also **intubus.**
incud- see **incus.**
inculc/atio (†**incult-**), inculcation c 1080, 1439; **-ativus,** tending to inculcate 1427; **-atius,** more pressingly a 1380.
inculp/abilitas, blamelessness 1378; **-andus,** blameless 1345.
inculp/atio c 1115, c 1365, **incupamentum** 1287, **incopamentum** 1270, 1275, accusation, charge; **-ans,** accuser 1269; **-atus,** accused party 1269; *****-o** c 1195, c 1400, †**incupero** 1274, **incopo** 1270, 1275, to inculpate, accuse.
incumb/entia, incumbency (eccl.) 1444, 1684; **-ens,** (*subst.*) incumbent (eccl.) c 1473, 1686; **i. de facto,** unauthorized incumbent (C.I.) 1248; **-o,** to rest on, be incumbent on or due from c 1090, 1582; to pertain to 1415, 1559; *****(with *dat.*)** to occupy as incumbent (eccl.) 1221, 1421.
incumb/ramentum 1231, c 1258, **enkumbramentum** 12c., **-ratio** 1231, 1281, encumbrance (leg.); **i. maritagii,** widow's plea for restitution of property alienated by husband (C.I.) 1248; **-ratio,** obstruction 1375; **-ro** a 1184, 1347, **-ero** 1235, c 1258, **enkumbro** 12c., to encumber, burden (leg.); **-ro,** to obstruct, block 1275, 1391.
incumbratus, disencumbered (leg.) 1448.
incunctatio, delay c 1362.
incuneo, to stamp (metal) 1220.
incup-, see **inculpatio.**
*****incur/abilis,** incurable c 1125, c 1470; **-abiliter,** incurably 1461; **-atus,** without a cure of souls c 1325.
‡**incurial/is,** "uncourteous" c 1440; **-ius,** more discourteously c 1200.
incurius, diligent 12c., ‡1570.
incur/ramentum 1254, 1308, **-rementum** 1280, 1295, **-rimentum** 1281, 1295, †**-romentum** (G.) 1312, **-sio** (G.) 1261, **-sus** (G.) p 1250, 1339, incurment, forfeiture; **-siva,** attack c 1325; **-sor,** one who incurs c 1255; **-ro,** to reach (sanctuary) by running c 1115; to coincide 1276; *****to** incur, be liable to c 740, 759.- c 1115, c 1520; *****to forfeit,** incur forfeiture 1216, 1320.
incursoria, inaptitude for running 13c.
incurt/atio, shortening c 1267; **-o,** to shorten c 1267.
incurtino p 1330, **incortino** c 1259, 1274, to adorn with hangings.
incurvo (*intr.*), to bow c 1306, c 1330.
incus, die for coining c 1300; **incud/us** 1573, **inquis** 1391, 1395, *for* i., anvil; **-eus** c 1410, ‡**-ineus** 1483, pertaining to an anvil.
incus/amentum, accusation 1275, 1292; **-atorius,** accusatory 14c.
incuss/io timoris, intimidation 1309; **-ivus,** provocative c 1388; ‡**-orium,** "causer", hammer 15c.
incustodia, carelessness c 1115.

incustumatus, without paying customs 1337.

ind/a, -acus, *see* **indus.**

indag/o, park, enclosure c 1200, c 1250; **-arius** 1361, **-ator** ‡c 1440, 1503, parker; **indigator,** tracker c 793; **-abilis,** tracking 8c.; **-ax** a 1205, **-us** c 1190, inquiring, inquisitive.

indamn-, indampn-, *see* INDEMN

inde, therefrom (*abl.*) c 1115, c 1310; therewith (*instrumental*) c 1115, c 1335; *thereof 1086, c 1544; in respect thereof c 1115, c 1533; on that account 9c. c 1180, c 1205.

indebit/atio, indebtedness a 1452, c 1470; **-us,** due 1200; owed 1427; **-o,** to involve in debt c 1292, 1503.

***indebit/e,** unduly c 1125, 1461; **-us,** undue 12c., 1541; not liable c 1400; **-atus,** not indebted c 1480.

indeceptus, not deceived c 1250.

indecidentia, unfailingness 1344.

indecimatus, not decimated c 1250; untithed 1275.

indecisus, unmutilated (of words) c 1238; c 1218, 1501, **indescisus** 1494, **indicisus** 1461, undecided.

†indecitatus, *f.l.* for inde citatus, a 1164.

indeclin/atio, indeclinability 1267; **-abiliter,** inflexibly, unchangeably 947. c 1180, c 1546.

indecoctus, undigested c 1258; unassuaged c 1180.

indecrementum, decrease 1331.

indeductio ventris, indigestion 7c.

indefatigabiliter, indefatigably p 1330, a 1450.

indefect/ibilitas c 1270, c 1283, **indeficientia** c 1270, faultlessness; **-ibilis** c 1270, 1427, **-ivus** c 730, 1378, *indeficiens c 1080, 1536, faultless, unfailing; **-ibiliter** 1282, 1521, **indeficienter** c 1080, c 1270, faultlessly, unfailingly.

indefen/dibiliter, irresistibly 1344; **-sus,** unforbidden c 1190; undefended (leg.) 1269, c 1320.

indefin/itio 13c., **-eitas** c 1361, indefiniteness; **-ite** a 1186, c 1534, **indiffinite** c 1125, 1442, indefinitely, without specification or distinction; **-itus** c 950. c 1080, 1266, **indiffinitus** 1535, indefinite, undefined.

indeflex/e a 1175, **-ibiliter** c 1200, inflexibly.

indegitamenta, *see* INDIGIT

indel/ebilitas, indelibility c 1270; **-ibilis** c 1343, c 1421, **-abilis** 12c., **-endus** c 1310, indelible, imperishable; **-ebiliter** c 1200, 1401, **-ibiliter** c 1250, c 1457, indelibly.

indelectabiliter, without delight 1344.

indeliberate, without deliberation c 1318, c 1427.

indemn/itas (indempn-), *immunity from, or protection against, damage or loss 12c., 1545; indemnity, compensation 1257; *-is c 1125, c 1510, **indampnis** a 1230, **-us** 1306, 1461, immune from damage or loss; innocent c 1150, c 1200; **indamnabilis,** immune from damnation (theol.) 1368; **-iter,** without damage or loss c 1200, c 1294; **-ifico,** to ensure against harm c 1380.

1 indent/atus, bitten in, penetrating c 1608; indented, inlaid 1245; indented *or* embattled (her.) p 1394, a 1446; *1290, 1536, **-uratus** c 1400, *indented (of documents

prepared in duplicate, *etc.*); **-atio,** indentation *or* embattling (her.) a 1446; **-ura,** indentation, wavy line 1245; *1300, 1684, **-atura** 1316, **endentura** 1494, indenture, document in duplicate or multiplicate; **-uratio,** indentation (of document) c 1400; **-o,** to make into an indenture c 1292; to embody in an indenture 1432; to draw up an indenture 1430, 1488.

2 indent/atus 1533, ‡**-osus, -ulus** 1483, toothless.

indepastus, starved c 1184.

independ/entia, independence c 1270; **-ens (ab),** independent (of) c 730. c 1270, c 1378; **-enter,** independently 1344, 1378.

indescriptibilis, indescribable 12c.

indesignat/us, indefinite p 1300; **-e,** indefinitely p 1300.

indesin/ens, incessant c 1180, 1461; **-enter,** incessantly c 760. c 1070, c 1546.

indestructus, undestroyed 1145, c 1440.

indetermin/atio, indeterminacy, indecision a 1250, 15c.; **-abiliter** 11c., **-ate** 1200, 15c., indefinitely; **-atus,** undecided c 1125, 1515; indefinite, unspecified p 1330, a 1446; indeterminate (log.) 1267, c 1361; aorist (gram.) 15c.

†indetestatus, intestate 1258.

indetritus, untrodden c 1170.

indeus, *see* **indus.**

indevexus, not curved c 860.

indevincibilis, unconquerable a 1230.

indevitabilis, inevitable 1274.

indevot/io, irreverence, impiety 1226, a 1452; **-e,** impiously a 1408, 1552; *-us, impious c 760. c 1180, 1461.

index, (?) bell (mon.) c 820; index (math.) 1686; **i. expurgatorius** 1588; *see also* **digitus; indic/ulus,** letter 8c., 893; **-atio,** meaning, relevance 1524; **pecunia -ationis,** payment to informer (A.S. *meldfeoh*) c 1115; **-ative,** indicatively 1292; **-ativus** c 1250, c 1470, **-atorius** 1552, **-atrix** (*f.*) 1315, c 1440, indicative, pointing out; **vis †-iaria,** (?) power of transmitting (sensation) *or* *f.l.* for judiciaria a 1520; **-avit,** name of a writ 1233, 15c.; **-o me,** to submit, give oneself up c 1115.

indextre, unbecomingly c 1280.

indic-, *see also* **index.**

***indicibil/is** c 700, 1041. c 1100, c 1450, **indiscibilis** c 1200, unspeakable, indescribable; **-iter,** unutterably c 1265, 15c.

indicisus, *see* **indecisus.**

***indict/amentum (indit-)** 1219, 1451, **-atio** 1324, 1461, indictment (leg.); **-ator,** one who indicts, grand juror 1309, c 1422; **-o *1219, c 1475, **endito** 13c., to indict (leg.); to command 1269; to dictate, proclaim c 1467; c 1390, **endicto** c 1450, to indite, set down in words.

***indict/io,** indiction, 15-year cycle a 1100, 1608; **cyclus -ionalis** c 1118; **-um,** edict c 760; (*for* nundine **-e**) fair (Norm.) 1162.

indicus, *see* **indus.**

indiffer/entia, indifference, equivalence 12c., 15c.; disregard of minor distinctions c 1160, a 1304; impartiality a 1452, c 147c; **-ens,** indifferent, without distinction c 1200, 14c.; impartial c 1292, 1684; **-enter,** indifferently 1200, 1461; impartially c 1428, c 1545.

indiffin-, *see* INDEFIN

indigator, *see* INDAG

indig/entia (*n. pl.*) 1369, **-entia** 15c., necessaries; **-ens,** necessary, requisite 1378, 1384; **-eo,** to be in need of knowledge, ignorant c 793; (with *acc.*) to need c 1330, 1382; (with *inf.*) to have need to c 1170, c 1362.

indigen/us 1417, **indigina** 1583, **indigines** 1407, *for* **-a,** denizen; **-atio** 1544, **-atus** c 1438, denization; **-o,** to make a denizen c 1450.

indigeries, surfeit c 1125, c 1370; **indigest/io,** indigestion a 1250; **-ibilitas,** indigestibility a 1250; **-abilis,** *for* **-ibilis,** indigestible 10c. 15c.

indigit/amenta, books of ritual: **indegitamenta** c 685; **-o,** to call, name 1620.

indign/itas (**indingn-**), imperfection, defect p 1300; **-iter,** to take amiss 1438; **-us,** humble 676, 860; **-atio curie,** contempt of court 1200; **-ifico,** to render unworthy 1380, 1381; **-or me,** to deign 1352.

indilat/io, promptitude c 1283; ***-e,** promptly, without delay 9c. c 1130, c 1540; **-us,** prompt c 1283, 1378.

indimension/abiliter, non-dimensionally 1344; **-atus,** unmeasured 1267.

indimissibilis, inalienable a 1384.

indimovendus, not to be moved away 10c.

indirect/us, indirect c 1258, 15c.; **-e,** indirectly a 1228, 1549; **-um,** (?) underside 1286.

indirupt/us, inviolate 798; **indisruptus,** unbroken c 793, 10c. c 1150; **-e,** without violation 6c.; uninterruptedly 1427.

indiscibilis, *see* **indicibilis.**

indisciplin/atio, indiscipline c 1160, c 1200; **-abilis,** intractable 13c., c 1344; **-ate,** in disorder c 1072, c 1330; **-atus,** undisciplined c 1125, a 1452.

indiscret/io, indiscretion a 1110, c 1250; ***-e,** carelessly, indiscreetly c 730, 9c. c 1080, 1552; **-us,** careless, indiscreet a 1110, 15c.; undiscriminating c 1080; undifferenced (her.) c 1595.

indiscuss/ibilis, that cannot be dispersed a 1519; ***-us** c 1080, 1537, **-atus** 1450, undiscussed, undecided; **-e,** indisputably 1287.

indisparsus, undispersed c 1457.

indispens/abilis c 1341, 1609, **-ibilis** c 1341, not subject to dispensation; **-abiliter** c 1341, 1472, **-ative** 1273, c 1340, without dispensation.

indispertitus, undivided c 793.

indispo/sitio, unfavourable condition, unfitness c 1270, c 1608; disinclination 1378; **-situs,** undisposed of c 1290; unfit c 1290, c 1444; **-no,** to make unfit c 1344, c 1470.

indisrupt-, *see* INDIRUPT

indissimilis, absolutely equal 8c.

indissimulat/io, candour 1620; **-us,** undisguisable 1382, 1415.

†**indissolute,** dissolutely 1293.

indissolu/tio 13c., **-bilitas** 1344, indissolubility; ***-biliter,** indissolubly c 1080, 1441; **-tus,** intact, unbroken c 730. 14c.

indissuasibilis, inexorable 1610.

indist/antia, nearness, contiguity c 1264, a 1323; **-abilis,** inseparable 1344; **-ans,** contiguous a 1323, 1516; uninterrupted c 1250; **-anter,** immediately, without delay c 1250, c 1308.

indistin/ctio, disorder 13c.; absence of distinction c 1250, c 1366; **-ctus,** undifferenced (her.) c 1595; **-guibilis,** indistinguishable c 1300, p 1300; **-guibilitas,** indistinguishability p 1300.

indistringibilis, not distrainable 1330, 1454.

indit-, *see also* **indictamentum.**

inditio, version c 1250; introduction 1620.

indito, to enrich 1294.

indivers/itas, absence of difference 1267; **-e,** not differently 870.

individu/alitas c 1270, c 1290, **-itas** c 1145, 1267, individuality; **-aliter** c 1115, c 1415, **-e** c 1180, 1345, inseparably; **-um,** an individual c 1125, 1524; **-us** c 1070, 1378, **-alis** c 1115, 1620, individual; *see also* **1 brevis; Trinitas -a** c 1090, c 1462; **-atio,** embodiment of universal in individual 1267, c 1361; **-o,** to individualize a 1250, 1378.

indivis/io, atom c 730; 1267, c 1361, **-ibilitas** c 1267, c 1360, unity, indivisibility; **-ibile,** an individual 1267; **murus -ibilis,** outside wall c 1324; **-im** 1289, 15c., ***pro -o** 1237, 1329, jointly, collectively, in common; **Trinitas -a** c 1300, c 1440; **-um,** property in which owner has undivided rights 13c.

indoct/ulus, somewhat uncultured 1520; †**-ualis,** (?) based on ignorance c 1361.

indoleo, to lament c 1434, 1535.

indoles, offspring c 550.

indolus, guileless 1461.

indomabil/is, unsubduable c 1000; **-iter,** invincibly 9c.

indomesticus, wild a 1250.

†**indomigeratus,** endangered c 1440.

indorm/itus, paralysed 1220; **-isco,** to doze c 1608.

indor/samentum c 1275, 1583, **-siamentum** 1352, **-ciamentum** 1434, **-satio** c 1395, endorsement; ***-so** c 1258, 1559, **indosso** 1286, c 1322, to endorse.

indosso, to knead 13c.; *cf.* DORS

indubi/tans, unhesitating c 790. c 1090; **-tanter,** unhesitatingly 8c., 815. c 1250, c 1400; ***8c.** c 1130, c 1493, **-tabiliter** 815, **-o** c 1400, indubitably; **-us,** undoubting c 730. c 1180, c 1440.

induc/tio, bringing in (of crops) (Sc.) 1355, 1538; bringing in (of rent, *etc.*) 1476, c 1550; right of bringing in goods to market c 1170; induction (log.) c 1200, 1620; c 1335, c 1450, **i. in possessionem** 1289, c 1444, induction (eccl.); 1262, c 1317, **-entia** c 1367, **-tivum** 1425, inducement; **-ibilis,** able to be introduced c 1300; demonstrable by induction c 1361; fit to be inducted (eccl.) 1556; open to inducement 1285; **-tive,** inductively (log.) 1267, 1377; **-tivus** c 1248, 1437, **-ticius** c 1344, inducing, leading to; **-tor,** importer 13c.; inductor (eccl.) c 1520; persuader, instigator 13c., c 1270; **littere -torie,** letters of induction 1393; **-o,** to induce belief by induction (log.) c 1300; 1340, c 1462, ***i. in (corporalem) possessionem** c 1217, 1565, to induct; **i. acum,** to thread a needle c 1200; *see also* **indutio.**

indulco, to sweeten (bibl.).

indul/gentia, indulgence (eccl.) a 1100, 1562; i. papalis c 1400, 15c.; littera -gentie 1420, 1509, l. -gentialis c 1250, c 1410, letter of indulgence; -gentiarius c 1553, †-gentarius 1562, seller of indulgences; -tor, bestower 7c.; forgiver c 1000; *-tum 1252, 1571, -ta 1273, indult (eccl.); -geo, to forgive c 950; to grant indulgence a 1165, 1454; (?) to condescend to particulars c 1200.

indu/mentum, -itio, -o, see 1 indutio.

indurat/io, hardening c 1470, 1620; *hardening of heart, stubbornness 7c., 8c. c 1080, 1425; -ivus, causing hardness a 1250; -us, armoured 1041.

ind/us 12c., 1345, -a 1257, -eus (†nidius) 1219, c 1340, -icus c 1220, c 1400, †-acus a 1250, indigo, dark blue (cloth).

indusi/um, shirt 16c.; -a, underclothing c 860.

industr/is, for -ius, 956. c 1343, c 1465.

1 indu/tio c 1343, -ctio 13c., -itio c 1332, c 1362, wearing clothes; -mentum, pall 8c.; binding, structure 11c.; i. altaris, altar cloth c 1330; -menta ecclesiastica c 1223; i. pontificalia c 1330, 1525; i. sacerdotalia c 1080, 1525; -o, to clothe in the habit of religion c 1250; i. monachum c 1250.

2 induti/o c 1266, c 1330, -e (pl.) c 760, delay; -e, stay in proceedings (leg.) c 1102, c 1283; fedus -ale, truce c 1200; littere -e, induciary letters c 1305; -o, to grant a stay (leg.) c 1102, c 1125.

induvie ferree, armour 1041.

induvo, to provide (a moat) with a douve 1241.

inebri/atio, irrigation c 1255; -o, to inspire c 730. c 1080; †-or (dep.), to inebriate c 1197.

inechia, see esnecia.

inedia (n. pl.), fasts, austerities 1461.

inedicibil/is, unspeakable c 1000. c 1096, c 1180; -iter, unspeakably c 1000. c 1100.

inedificatio, structure c 1612.

inedificat/orius, unedifying 1378; -us, not built upon c 1220, a 1564.

ineffabil/itas, ineffable greatness 1408; *-is, ineffable, unutterably great 7c., 9c. 1070, c 1430; *-iter, ineffably c 900. c 1080, 1437.

ineffect/ibilis, incapable of having an efficient cause c 1300, p 1300; -ualis, ineffectual a 1452; -us, unfulfilled a 1142.

ineffrenat/us, unbridled c 1433, c 1450; -e, unrestrainedly 1461.

inegressibilis, with no way out 1407.

ine/lectivus, incapable of choice 1344; -ligibilis, ineligible 1216.

1 ineleemosyno (inelemosino), to grant in frank-almoign a 1273, 1279.

2 ineleemosyno, to divert a gift in alms to secular use c 1255.

†inelementalis, not elemental 1267.

inelimatus, unpolished, inelegant 12c., c 1170.

ineloquentia, lack of eloquence c 790.

inemend/abilis, not expiable by fine c 1115; -abiliter 1506, -ate 12c., incorrigibly; -atus, unreformed, unpunished c 1250 1286.

inemo, to buy a 1220.

inenarr/andus c 700, c 790, †inenerrabilis 12c., for -abilis, indescribable; -abiliter, indescribably 680, 8c. a 1155, c 1200.

inentia, see inesse.

inenumerabilis, incalculable 1420.

ineo ad guerram, to go to war 1293.

inepiscopaliter, not as befits a bishop c 1196.

inept/io a 1250, c 1443, -itudo a 1250, 1570, unfitness; -ulus, rather silly 1662; inaptus, unfit c 1400; inapto, -ifico, to make unfit a 1250.

inequ/alitas, infirmity c 1125, c 1190; crux -alis, cross formy (her.) a 1446; -atio, disparity c 1365; -iparantia, disquiparancy 13c.; -iparabilis, peerless 6c.

inequitatio, cavalry raid c 1125.

inergumino, see ENERG

inermiter, defencelessly c 1370.

inerr/abiliter c 1540, -anter c 1250, unerringly; -atus, unerring c 1250; -oneus, faultless, accurate 13c.

inertia, inertia (phys.) 1687.

inescatorium, bait, allurement c 1160.

inescuratus, unscoured 1442.

inesse c 1160, 1378, inentia 12c., indwelling, inherence (phil.); propositio de i., simple proposition (log.) a 1304; insum, to give countenance to 1419.

inessential/itas, lack of essence c 865; -is, lacking essence (phil.) c 865 c 1367.

inestim/abiliter, inestimably, incalculably c 740. c 1125, 1461; -atus, not valued c 1290; a 1155, c 1400, -alis c 1250, incalculable; inextimatus, unransomed c 1434.

inestivatus, pastured in summer 1214.

ineulio, see 3 inoleo.

inevacuabilis, indestructible c 950.

inevid/entia, lack of evidence c 1366; -ens, unevident c 1343, 1378.

inevincibilis, invincible 12c., c 1200.

inevitabili/tas, inevitability c 1277, 1451; -tatio, making inevitable c 1367; -to, to make inevitable c 1367, 1374.

inewardus, see inwardus.

inexauditus, unheard, unheeded a 1175, 1235.

inexcogitabiliter, inconceivably a 1350.

inexcusabiliter, inexcusably 1256, 1271; without making an excuse 14c.; assuredly, without evasion c 730. 1460.

inexecrabil/is, not to be desecrated c 1127; unappeasable c 1362; -iter, without cursing 15c.

inexecutus, unfulfilled 1269, c 1433.

inexemplificatus, not illustrated by an example c 1434.

inexhau/ste, without exhaustion 1060; -riendus, inexhaustible c 1170.

inexhonoratio, dishonour c 793.

inexist/entia, inherence (phil.) p 1300, 1610; -o, to inhere, exist in c 1300, 1648.

inexoptabilis, undesirable a 1250.

inexorabiliter, inexorably c 1293.

inexpediens, inexpedient a 1293, c 1470.

inexpeditatus, not hambled 1234.

inexpir/abilis (inexspir-), undying c 1200; -atus, not yet expired, uncompleted 1587.

inexple/biliter, insatiably 7c., 793. c 1080; -tus, incomplete c 1400, 1583.

inexplicabil/is, inexpressible, ineffable 1081, 1437; **-iter,** inexpressibly c 1250.

inexpressus, inexpressible 1245; not clearly expressed 1267.

inexpugn/abilis, inviolable c 1150; **-abiliter,** irrefutably a 1100, 1332; **-andus,** impregnable 6c.; **-ate,** impregnably c 1150; **-atus,** invincible c 1437.

inexpulsus, not evicted 1450.

inexquisit/us, unsearchable 1441; **-e,** unfathomably 12c.

inexsatiabilis, never-cloying 1497.

inexscrutabilis, unexplored c 1200.

inexsiccabilis, inexhaustible 13c.

inexspir-, see INEXPIR

inextens/ibiliter, without extension 1344; **-us,** not extended (in space) c 1290, c 1360.

inextinguibili/tas, unquenchability c 1283; **-ter,** unquenchably 7c., c 793. 12c., 1461.

infacio, to form within c 1300.

infact/ibilis, unmakable p 1300, 1344; **-us,** *for* **infectus,** not done 1403; *cf.* **2 infectio.**

infaidio, to be at feud with c 1115.

infaldo, to fold (animals) 1375.

†**infalisio,** to execute by hurling over cliff c 1270; *cf.* **affaleisio.**

infall/ibilitas, infallibility 1267, 1610; ***-ibilis** c 1190, 1610, **-abilis** 1258, infallible; ***-ibiliter,** infallibly c 1236, c 1546; **-enter,** without fail c 1477.

infalso, to forge, interpret deceitfully 10c.

infam/atio, accusation, defamation c 1115, c 1470; **-ator** c 1414, **-atrix** (*f.*) c 1325, accuser, defamer; **-atorius,** accusatory 1520; **-ia,** evil rumour 893; **-osus,** infamous, of ill repute 12c., 1684.

infans, *infante* (Sp. & Port.) 1242, 1348; minor in wardship c 1443; **infant/atica portio,** ward's share 12c.; **-ia,** minority (leg.) c 1443; **-ibiliter,** like a child c 1200; **-ilitas,** childishness c 865; infancy 12c.; **-ula,** little girl c 1100, c 1400; ‡**fantula,** kitchen-maid 15c.; ***-ulus** 9c. c 1090, 1567, ‡**fantulus** 15c., little boy; (*adj.*) of infancy 14c.; **i. chori,** choir-boy 1461.

‡**infasciatus,** wrapped 1570.

infascino, to bewitch 1178, 1267.

infastidiosus, unwearying c 730.

infatig/abiliter c 1090, c 1540, **-anter** c 1190, c 1218, indefatigably.

infatu/atus, reduced to idiocy 1461; **-o,** to stultify, nullify c 1125, c 1200.

infaust/e, unpropitiously c 798. 1307; ‡**-or,** evil counsellor 1483.

infeco, to pollute c 930, c 980.

1 infect/io, adulteration 8c.; imbuing a 1250; ***infection,** poisoning 1245, 1522; **-ive,** by infection, poisonously c 1400, c 1457; **-ivus** c 1283, a 1540, **inficiens** a 1250, c 1290, infective, poisonous; **-uosus,** infected a 1564; ‡**inficiatus,** (?) poisoned c 1293; **inficio,** to give rise to c 865.

2 infectio (†**insectio,** †**insecutio**), undoing, dissolution 1331; **infici/enter,** without creative activity c 1360; **-o,** to undo a 1408; to leave undone 1220; *cf.* INFACT

infemino, to unman, weaken c 1190.

infendo, to attack 1442.

infenso curiam, to inform the court (leg.) 14c.

*infeod/atio 1274, 1555, †**infoedatio** 14c.,

infeudatio 1198, 1549, enfeoffment; **i. conjuncta,** conjoint feoffment (Sc.) 1395, 1460; **-ator,** feoffor (Sc.) 1309, c 1320; ***-o** 1189, 1478, **infeudo** 1281, c 1350, to enfeoff; to acquire in fee (G.) 1293.

infeof/amentum, enfeoffment (Sc.) 14c., 1587; **-o,** to enfeoff 1401.

inferabilis, immovable, impregnable 930.

infer/entia, inference (log.) 12c., 1166; **-ibilis,** inferable (log.) c 1360; able to be inflicted 1374; **-o,** to reply, interject, interpose 8c.; c 1150, c 1453; to imply p 1300, c 1363; **i. billas,** to introduce bills (into Parliament) c 1453; *cf.* ILLAT

inferetro, to enshrine c 1400.

inferi/or, lower (mus.) c 1266; **-us** 1266, 1537, in **-oribus** a 1347, below, in the sequel; in Hell c 1362; *cf.* **2 data;** **-oratus** 10c., **-oritas** c 1260, c 1380, lowliness, inferiority; **-oro,** to lower 1344; to subordinate c 1376; **i. velum,** to lower sail c 1200.

†**infermentaceus,** unleavened 1570.

*infern/us (bibl.), **-alia** (*pl.*) 12c., Hell; ***-alis,** hellish, of Hell c 590, c 1040. c 1070, c 1470; **-aliter,** hellishly 1271.

inferratus, iron-tipped 1385.

infertil/itas, barrenness c 1225; **-is,** barren 1608.

inferv/eo, to rage 1415; **-esco,** to bring to the boil c 1123.

infessatus, unwearied c 1390.

*infest/atio 6c., 10c. a 1100, c 1450, **-inatio** c 1250, molestation, persecution; **-ator** c 1302, **-atrix** (*f.*) a 1200, c 1250, enemy, disturber; **-im** c 1250, **-inanter** 14c., violently; **-ino,** to harass c 1362; **-o,** to inflict upon c 550.

infestro, see INFISTULAT

infeud-, see INFEOD

infici/o, -atus, see infectio (1 & 2).

†**infictio,** influence 1378.

infict/us, unfeigned 9c. 1421; **-e,** unfeignedly c 1452.

infidel/itas, disloyalty, treason c 1115, 14c.; fine for treason c 1115; branding as a traitor 1419; paganism, religious unbelief 7c. c 1090, c 1536; **-is,** untrustworthy (person) (leg.) c 1102, c 1258; traitor c 1250, c 1437; ***infidel** c 1090, 1505.

infil/atio, file (of documents) 1555; **-o,** to file c 1450.

infilialis, unfilial c 1196.

infin/alitas, infinity c 865; **-alis,** (?) unending or non-final (not desirable as an end) 1344; **-ibilis,** everlasting 13c.; incapable of having a final cause p 1300; **-itanter,** without limitation a 1360; **-itas** c 1188, c 1324, **-itudo** 1649, immense number or amount; **-itatio,** making infinite, removing limitation a 1250, 1374; ***-ities** c 1200, 1537, **-itupliciter** c 1360, an infinite number of times; †**-itum** (? *for* in **-itum**), infinitely 1378, 1380; **-ito,** to make infinite or indefinite 13c., c 1360.

†**infines** (*pl.*), boundaries c 1350.

infirgiatus, fettered 1214, 1221.

*infirm/aria, -arium 12c., 1545, **-atorium** 12c., c 1400, **-itarium** 1293, **-itoria** c 1266, ***-itorium** c 1185, c 1430, **domus -aria** c 1200, **d. -orum** c 980. c 1090, infirmary (mon.); **-aria,** infirmaress (mon.) 1422;

-arius c 1080, c 1450, **-itarius** 1293, infirmarer (mon.); **-atio,** becoming weak c 1500; **-atorius,** invalidatory (leg.) 1543; **-itates** (*pl.*), infirmities, ailments 7c. a 1135, 1519; **-us,** unfledged (falc.) a 1150; ***-or** c 730, c 1000. a 1100, 1518, **-itor** 1401, to be ill; *see also* **firmaria.**

infirmo, to secure, make fast 1195, 1245.

*infisco, to confiscate c 1178, c 1400.

infistulat/io, dysury (med.) a 1250; **-us,** lodged in urinary tract c 1325; **infestro,** to fester 13c.

infix/io c 1188, c 1250, **-itio** c 1540, fixing, implanting; blockage or sluggishness (of blood) a 1250; **-ivus,** causing blockage (med.) a 1250; **-us,** set (with a gem) 1415.

inflamm/abilitas, inflammability c 1360; **-abilis,** inflammable c 1227, 1620; **-ativus,** inflammatory a 1250, 14c.; **-ator,** kindler c 550; **-o,** to fire, touch off (gun) 1388.

inflat/io, pride c 730. a 1240, ‡1483; **-ivus,** causing flatulence a 1250; promoting pride 12c., c 1325; **instrumentum -ivum,** wind instrument (mus.) 1267; **-ura,** tumour, swelling (med.) c 1172, c 1280; **-us (venti),** blowing a 700.

inflech/etus, fletched (of arrows) 1319; **-io** 1224, 1240, **-o** 1252, **inflegio** 1241, 1243, to fletch.

inflexi/bilitas, constancy c 865; stiffening (of neck) c 1115; **-biliter,** inflexibly a 1100, 1461; **-lis,** uninflected (gram.) 1524.

inflexus, inflected (gram.) 1524.

inflictor, inflictor c 1180; **infligo,** to afflict, punish a 1250, 1435.

infloror, to bloom in c 1090.

influctuatio, surge 1468.

influ/entia, influx c 1270, 15c.; ***influence** (astr.) 1241, 1620; **i. divina** c 1250, a 1292; **-entialis,** influential (astr.) 1564; **-us,** flowing in c 1125, c 1173; **-o,** to pour, shed a 1205, c 1343; to exercise influence (astr.) c 1267, c 1362; to influence, inspire c 1444.

influxibilis, invariable a 1290.

influx/io, flood tide a 1135; 1426, **-us** 1426, influence; **influccio,** influx 1427.

infoedatio, *see* INFEOD

infolio, to enfold in petals 1220.

inforesto, to afforest, put in forest status c 1125, 1279.

inform/atio, instruction c 1250, 1620; moulding, influence c 1283, c 1325; establishing c 1115; c 1115, c 1365, **-antia** a 1361, infusion with form (phil.); **-abilis,** capable of receiving form c 1286, c 1360; **-ative,** by way of infusion a 1323; **-ativus,** informative, instructive 1620; formative, imparting form a 1250, c 1360; **-ator,** informer 15c.; ***c** 1190, 1554, **-arius** 1450, instructor, teacher; **i. primarius** 1541; **i. puerorum** 1530; **-atorie,** by way of instruction c 1334; **-atorius,** instructive 1401, a 1450; **-o,** to inform, give to understand c 1290, c 1540; to establish, fortify c 1115; to infuse with form (phil.) c 1115, a 1361.

inform/itas, formlessness (phil.) 860. c 1270, c 1365; **-ositas,** ugliness c 730; **-is,** formless (phil.) 1620; **-iter,** formlessly c 860; untidily c 1125; rudely, harshly a 1380; **-atus,** unformed c 1090.

inforo, to invest (capital) c 1415.

infor/tiamentum, fortification 1218; ***-tiatum** a 1275, c 1500, **-siatum** 1385, **Digestum -tiatum** c 1350, 1414, second part of *Digest* (*cf.* **fortiatum**); **-tio** 1141, c 1310, **-so** c 1305, to fortify (buildings); to accoutre 1313; to support 1375; **i. discrimen,** to reinforce judgement (leg.) c 1115.

infortu/na 15c., **-nia** 1427, 1429, **-num** c 1180, 1431, †**-nitum** 1577, **-nitas** c 1295, 15c., *for* **-nium,** misfortune; **-nus** c 1000, **-nius** c 1415, **-itus** c 1190, 1302, unfortunate; **-nate,** unfortunately a 1450, 1461; **-no,** to bring misfortune upon 1267.

infoss/atio, sunken appearance (of eyes) a 1250; **-o,** to enclose with a ditch 1152, 1433; to draw (water) into a ditch 1288; to dig in, bury 1461; to pierce 1461.

infra, ***within** (place) 1086, c 1590; ***within** (time) c 1200, c 1500; **i. aquas,** between Tyne and Tees 1334, 1363; **i. assisam,** within (the time limit for) the assize c 1185, 1201; **i. compotum,** within (period of) account 1460, 1469; **i. bordam navis,** on board ship 14c.; **i. breve,** in a short time 1334, 1461; **i. etatem,** under age 1198, c 1430; **i. sacros (ordines),** in holy orders c 1220, 1314.

infraannatus, under a year old c 1230.

infracaptus fur, infangenthief 1110.

infraclausus, enclosed 1310, c 1390.

infracomputo, to include in an account 1329.

infracontentus, within-contained 1369, 1505.

infract/io c 1115, c 1412, **infrictio** (Sc.) 1316, 1347, breach; **-io Christianitatis** c 1115, **i. ordinis** c 1115, **-ura ordinis** c 1115, c 1420, violence to clerk in holy orders; **i. pacis** 1086, 1202, **-ura pacis** c 1102, 1278, breach of the peace; **i. jejunii,** breakfast 1480; **i. plena,** wounding to death c 1115; **i. plegii** c 1115, **-ura plegii** c 1115, breach of pledge; **-ura ecclesie,** church-breaking c 1115; **-or** c 1086, 1487, **infrictor** 16c., violator; **infrictus,** infringed c 1320; **infringo,** to break into 13c., c 1305; to infringe, violate 1086, c 1520; to refute c 1300, c 1343; **i. jejunium,** to break a fast (unlawfully) c 1102, c 1115; **i. pacem.** to break the peace 1097, c 1362; **i. testimonium,** to bear false witness c 1115.

infractus, unbroken 12c.; undismayed 1537; **infrangibilitas,** unbreakableness c 1270; **infringibil/itas,** inviolability c 1367; **-is** c 1180, 1427, **infrangibilis** c 1362, 1452, inviolable; **-iter,** inviolably 1378, c 1450.

infraduco, to lead in, pilot c 1125.

infranch/io 1373, a 1452, **-esio** 1417, to enfranchise.

infranominatus, within-named c 1303, c 1515.

infrao, to burnish (armour) in 1313; *cf.* **fraiatio.**

infraobligatus, named in the bond c 1477.

infraordinarius, ordinary 1404.

infrapono, to put in 1300, 1335.

infrasalsio, to put (meat) in for salting 1405.

infrascript/io, writing below 1433; ***-us,** written below (or within) 1086, 1505; **infrascribo,** to write below c 1360, 1418.

infraspecificatus, specified below or within 1419, 1593.

infrasubscriptus, written below c 1500.

infratrusso, to pack in 1313, 1338.

†**infraudelentus,** guileless (?) 888 (c 1250).

†**infraudo,** (?) *f.l.* for **in fraude,** 1435.

infrectus, fretted, embroidered c 1335.

infrenabilis, unbridled 15c.

infrendeo, to resound c 1200.

infrict-, *see* **infractio.**

infrig/ibilis, coolable c 1270; **-idativus,** cooling a 1250, c 1290; **-ero** c 1300, **-do,** *for* **-ido,** c 1180, to cool, chill; **-or,** to become cool 13c.

infring-, *see* **infractio; infractus.**

infrocatus, not wearing a frock c 1330.

†**infrontarius (prepositus),** (?) on the frontier (Sp.) 1325.

†**infructico,** *for* **infrutico;** to sprout, 14c.

‡**infrug/i,** unthrifty 1570; **-ifer,** unfruitful c 1620.

infrunit/e, foolishly, rashly a 1142, c 1365; **-issimus,** very rash 1283; †**infronitus,** *for* **-us,** c 1250.

infrustrabil/itas, irresistibility c 1367; **-is,** not to be thwarted, irresistible 1344, c 1367.

infrustr/ans, foolish 993; †**-atus,** (?) polluted a 700; *cf.* **illustratus.**

infucatus, unfeigned c 1440.

infug/atus, fugitive, outlaw c 1115; **-o,** to pursue into c 1115; to drive (cattle) in 1274.

infugibil/is, ineluctable 1427; **-iter,** ineluctably 1427.

inful/a, *chasuble 1006. c 1135, 1466; ‡"tag of a mitre" 1570; **i. episcopalis** c 1194, 1274, **i. pontificalis** c 1090, c 1336, **i. pontificatus** c 760, emblem of episcopacy; **i. regalis** 15c., **i. regni** c 730. 12c., c 1400, emblem of royalty; **-atus,** wearing a chasuble c 1090, a 1250; vested with episcopal insignia c 900. c 1090, 14c.; ‡"tagged, labelled" 1570; **-o,** to vest with episcopal insignia c 1250, a 1452; to adorn (? with halo) c 1250; **i. me,** to put on vestments 14c.

infulcimentum, prop c 1320.

infulgeo, to shine down c 793; to shine c 1100, c 1362.

infum/ibulum, chimney flue ‡a 1520, 1574; **-igo,** to smoke c 1138.

infund/abilis c 1363, 1427, **-atus** 1378, unwarrantable, unfounded; **-abiliter** c 1380, 1427, **-amentaliter** 1380, unwarrantably.

infund/eratus c 1394, 1550, **-ratus** 1358, foundrous; **-ero,** to make (a road) foundrous 1402.

infundo, *see* INFUS

infuner/atio, interment 1325; **-o,** to inter 1424.

infurcatus, forked c 1210.

‡**infurno,** to put in an oven 1483.

infus/io, melting c 1313, 1337; an ailment of horses 13c.; **i. aquarum,** flood c 760; **i. gratie,** imbuing with grace (theol.) c 1357; **i. lacrimarum,** flood of tears c 760; **i. sanguinis,** bloodshed 1380; **-ibilis,** absorbable c 1270; susceptible of imbuing (with grace) c 1240; **-ivus,** liquefactory a 1250; ‡**-orium,** funnel 1483; **-o, infundo,** to malt 1307; **infundo,** to mould (bullets) 1380; to stain c 1250; to imbue, inspire 8c. c 1250, c 1343.

‡**infuso,** to wind a spindle 1483.

ingaleo, to cover with a helmet 1220.

ingarbelatus, ungarbled (of groceries) 1442.

ingelatus, frozen over c 1250.

ingello, *see* NIGELL

ingem/esco, *for* **-isco,** c 793.

ingenealogiatus, without pedigree c 1375.

ingener/atio, birthlessness p 1300; *-abilis,** birthless, not producible by natural generation a 1233, c 1365; **-abiliter,** as though birthless 1344; **-osus,** ignoble c 1470; **ingenitus,** not yet born c 1115; unbegotten (theol.) 11c. 12c., c 1250; not having happened (ἀγένητος) c 1300, c 1363; 6c. c 1267, **-atus** 1344, birthless, not naturally engendered.

ingeniculatio, kneeling c 700.

ingen/ium, *artifice, trick c 1110, 1461; *1232, 1583, **gynnum** 1392, contrivance, machine; *c 1140, 1456, **engenium** 1289, **ingaignum** 1167, **engaignum** 1191, **ingania** 1173, **engania** 1173, c 1180, **ginum** 13c., military engine; **i. malum** 1152, c 1225, **i. pravum** 1183, trickery; **-iculum,** *for* **-iolum,** feeble spirit c 550; **-iositas,** ingenuity c 1270, 1344; **-ialis,** intellectual c 1115; **-iatio,** contrivance c 1612, 1620; *-iator** 1086, c 1608, **-itor** 1179, **inginiator** 1212, **enginator** 1388, **ginnator** c 1295, engineer; **-io** c 1125, c 1470, **-ior** (*dep.*) a 1250, c 1360, to contrive.

ingenu/itas, manumission c 1115; noble birth c 1115; the nobility (*coll.*) c 1125; **-us,** nobly born c 1150, c 1200.

ingermino, to sprout 1223.

ingestio manuum, assault 1293; **ingero,** to ingest, swallow c 1188; (?) to incur (G.) 1315.

ingistiamentum 1297, **ingest/iamentum** 1306, agistment; **-o,** to agist c 1300; *cf.* AGIST

inglacio, to chill, freeze c 1177, c 1188.

inglossabiliter, so as not to be glossed or explained away 1344.

inglutio, to swallow c 1125, c 1380.

ingluvies, glue (for cross-bows) 1269.

ingn-, *see* **ignis.**

ingracilio, to make thin a 1250.

ingrad/atio, engrailing (her.) a 1446; **-o,** to engrail p 1394, a 1446.

ingran/atura 1323, a 1450, **-ura** 1415, 1417, storage (? *or* grinding) of grain; **-giatio,** garnering c 1470; **-gio,** to garner 1307, c 1470; **-o,** (?) to store (grain) *or* send to mill 1347; †**-o,** (?) to mature, turn into grain 15c.

ingranat/us, dyed in grain 1395, c 1450; **rosa -a,** red rose c 1250.

ingrassor (*dep.*) 9c. c 1250, c 1540, **incrass/or** a 1230, to rage; **-atio,** violence 1228; *see also* **incrasso.**

*ingrat/itudo** c 1125, c 1540, **-uitas** a 1275, c 1380, ingratitude; **-anter,** ungratefully 12c., 1461.

ingrav/atura, engraving 1280; **-ator,** engraver p 1280; **-o,** to engrave c 1150, 1338.

ingravo, to charge, accuse c 1115.

ingredi-, *see* INGRESS

ingremio, to embosom c 1250.

ingressura, gritstone, whetstone 1279, 1289; *cf.* **gressius.**

ingress/us, entry into a religious order 14c.; c 1178, c 1516, **-um** c 1218, 1219, (right of) entry into property or rights; dues paid for entry into possession 1247, c 1320; (?) treatise *or* polemic c 1363; **i. fortis,** forced entry 1419; **-ivus,** initial c 1250; †**ingredi/o me,** to enter c 1380; **-or** 13c., 1414, †**-o** c 1270, 1338, to enter into possession; **i. viam patrum** 1412, **i. v. universe carnis** c 1222, c 1465, to die.

ingross/atio, coarsening a 1250; 1480, 1536, **-amentum** 1366, engrossment, copying; **-ativus,** thickening a 1250; **-ator,** engrosser, copyist 1325, 1588; engrosser, wholesale dealer 1419; **-o,** to thicken, coarsen a 1250, 1267; to condense c 1250, a 1446; to engross, copy 1325, 1562; to engross, buy wholesale 1352; **-o me,** to batten, grow fat 14c.; *cf.* **incrasso.**

ingruentia, onset c 1190, c 1220.

inguadio, *see* INVAD

inguard-, *see* **inwardus.**

inguinaria pestis c 1188, 1362, **i. plaga** c 1362, bubonic plague.

ingul/abilis, (?) palatable 1351; **-o,** to swallow c 1197.

ingurgitatio, guzzling c 1160, 1523.

inhabil/itas, disability, disqualification c 1270, 1620; **-itudo,** infirmity 1424; ***-is,** disqualified c 1270, c 1575; **-itatio,** disqualifying 1318, c 1444; **-ito,** to disqualify, incapacitate 1274, c 1470.

inhabit/abilis, habitable c 1362; **-atrix,** indwelling (*f.*) 10c.; **-o,** (*intr.*) to dwell c 730. c 1362, c 1564; (with *dat.*) to inhabit c 793; **i. cum,** to cohabit c 1362; **inhibito,** to inhabit c 1400.

inhabitatus, uninhabited c 1150, 1379.

inhalatio, inhaling c 1170, 1497.

inheredatio, disherison 1294.

inhered/atus de, vested with by inheritance 1258, 1315; **-ito,** to appoint as heir a 1200.

inher/entia, inherence (log.) 12c., c 1365; †**-entie,** (?) inherently c 1267; **inhesio,** flocking in c 1000; persistence 1344; **-eo,** to inhere, be predicated 12c., a 1250.

inhi/atio, appetite, greed c 1125, 1388; **-ator,** rapacious seeker c 1100; **-o,** (with *inf.*) to long to 9c.; **i. post,** to hunger after c 1430.

inhib/itio, *prohibition 723. c 1193, c 1550; *1212, 1684, †**-utio** 1450, inhibition (eccl.); **-itivus,** restraining 1422; **-itorie** 1336, littere **-itorie** c 1250, 1684, l. †**-itatorie** c 1400, l. **-itoriales** 1549, letters inhibitory; **-eo,** to inhibit (eccl.) c 1190, c 1450.

inhibito, *see* INHABIT

inhibitus, not held or possessed c 793.

inhok/a, -us (innoc-), 'inhook', piece of fallow temporarily enclosed for cultivation 1235, c 1300; **-o,** to enclose from fallow 1235, 1301; *cf.* **inunco.**

inhominior, more inhuman 12c.

inhon/estas, awkwardness (of literary style) c 860; **-estatio,** shameful act c 1150; **-or,** dishonour (?) c 1150, c 1255; **-orifice,** dishonourably a 1250; **-orifico,** to dishonour c 1377.

inhormis, *see* ENORM

inhorre/atio (inorri-), garnering 1417, 1525; **-o,** to garner 1349, 1559.

inhorr/ibilis, terrible c 1390; **-eo** (? **-esco**), to be rife c 1115.

inhospit/atio, lodging, storage 1397, c 1400; **-o,** to lodge c 1225, a 1452.

inhospitatus, not built upon, uninhabited 1086, 1471.

inhumanatus, incarnate (theol.) 793.

inhumanit/er c 1305, 1461, **-us** c 1180, c 1385, inhumanly.

1 inhum/atio, burial 1543; **-o,** to bury c 1115, 1461.

2 inhum/atio, non-burial 1326; **-atus,** unburied 12c., 1326.

†**inhumilito,** (?) to utter with humility c 1365.

inhundredum, 'in-hundred' 1180, 1256; *cf.* **hundredum intrinsecum.**

inibi, thence 10c.

inicio, *see* INJECT

inidone/itas, unfitness c 1375, 1570; **-us,** unfit, unsuitable a 1250, 1552.

inignio, to illumine c 1200; to kindle 1252.

inimic/us, one liable to blood-feud c 1115; c 1123, 13c., **i. antiquus** c 1400, **i. humani generis** c 1440, c 1520, the Devil; **-ans** c 1200, **inamicus** 1415, enemy; **-ulus,** contemptible enemy 13c.; **-itia,** blood-feud c 1115; **inamicabilitas,** hostility a 1250; **-abilis** c 1000. 1344, ‡1570, ‡**inamicabilis** 1570, **-alis** c 1253, **-osus** c 550, hostile; **-aliter** 838. 1344, **inamicabiliter** 1344, hostilely; **-o, -or,** to be hostile to, at variance with c 1080, c 1430.

†**inimitandus,** inimitable c 1070.

inimpedibilis, irresistible p 1300.

ininherens, not inherent (log.) c 1360.

inintellig/ibilitas, unintelligibility 1427; **-ens,** mentally defective a 1100.

ininvicem, *see* **in invicem.**

iniqu/itas, wickedness, crime 6c., 957. c 1125, 16c.; the Fall (theol.) c 1332; **-iter,** wickedly 1231; **percursor -us,** uneven stepper (of horse) c 1200.

iniquito, *see* INQUIET

initi/a (*pl.*), corners c 730. c 1180; **i. frugum,** first-fruits c 1332; **-abilis,** having a beginning in time a 1250, c 1345; **-alia** (*pl.*), initial proceedings or stages c 1204, c 1220; **-aliter,** initially, originally c 1178, a 1452; **-atio** 15c., c 1450, **-o** c 1218, 1295, beginning; **-ative,** by virtue of origination a 1360; **-ativus,** originative 1620; **-atorius,** ushering in c 1193.

inject/io manuum, assault c 1250, 1684; **-or manuum,** assailant 1277; ‡**-orium,** instrument for probing nose 14c.; **-ura,** heaping on 15c.; **inicio manus ad,** to seize c 1115; **i. m. in,** to assault 1293, 1397.

***injun/ctio** 1237, a 1564, **-xio** 1293, **-ctum** c 1320, c 1340, injunction, command; littera **-ctoria** 1305; **-go,** to impute c 793; (with *inf.*) 596. c 1283, 1308, **i. (aliquem) ad** 1304, to enjoin, command; **i. cantus,** to pretone c 1230, 13c.

injur/ia (*n. pl.*) c 1362, 1493, **-a** c 1323, wrongs; **-iam habeo,** to be guilty of injury, in the wrong 1220, 1279; **actio -ialis,** action for redress of wrongs c 1290; **-iatio,** injury, damage 1234, c 1376; **-iativus,** injurious c 1375; ***-iator,** injurer, wrongdoer c 1125, 15c.; ***-io,** *for* **-ior,** to injure, wrong a 615. c 1115, 1558; (?) c 1436, **-ior** 1267, 1300, to insult, revile.

ink/a 1209, **-um (ynkum)** 1245, 1287, **enka** 1302, **enkum** 1287, 'ink', mill-rind.

inl-, *see also* **ill-**

inlacum, shortage, lack (Sc.) 1538.

inlag/aria c 1258, **-atio** 1234, c 1258, inlawing, reversal of outlawry; **-o** c 1157, c 1290, **inlego** c 1102, **inlegio** c 1115, to free from outlawry; *see also* **illex.**

inland/a, -um, 'inland', demesne land 1086, 1313; (?) land not fronting on a road a 1230; **-iscus,** native c 1115.

inm-, *see also* **imm-**

inmannus, dweller on manor c 1250.

innam/ia -ium (†juvamin') 1279, 14c., **innoma** (?) 13c., 'innam', intake, enclosure; **-um,** distraint, goods distrained 1226; **-io,** to seize in distraint 1199.

innascibil/itas c 1200, p 1300, **innassibilitas** a 1290, birthlessness; **-is,** birthless c 1200, 1276.

innativus c 1115, a 1200, **ignatus** c 1250, innate.

innatural/itas, supernatural occurrence c 1300; conflict with nature 1344; lack of natural feeling c 1370; ‡"unkindness" 15c.; ***-is,** unnatural 12c., c 1470; **-iter,** unnaturally c 1190, 1519.

innaufragus, unwrecked c 1184.

innavigo, to import c 1404.

innebulatus, nebuly (her.) p 1394, a 1446.

innerv/atus, unmanned c 1180; **-o,** to enfeeble 13c.; *cf.* ENERV

innexio, connexion, tie 1344.

innisus, reliance 1345; **innix/us,** effort, urge 1374; **-e,** zealously c 1180; **-orius,** supporting 1344; **innitor,** (with *inf.*) to strive c 1200.

innobilis, *for* ignobilis, c 1250, 1308.

innoc-, *see also* INHOK

innoc/entes c 1520, **innoscentes** c 1450, infants; the Holy Innocents c 1334; c 1006, c 1245, **dies -entium** c 1266, c 1533, **festivitas i.** c 1006, **festum i.** 1532, Holy Innocents' day (28 Dec.); *see also* **episcopus;** **-entialis,** of innocence c 1250, 1344; **†-issibilis,** (?) harmless c 1450.

innod/atio, binding, bond 1461; imposition, fastening on (of excommunication) 1167; **i. anathematis** c 1170, c 1375; **-o,** to oblige (by bond) 1218; ***to** 'bind' by apostolic authority (excommunicate or anathematize) c 1150, 1560; **i. debitis,** to involve in debts c 1255.

innoma, *see* innamia.

innomina/bilitas, namelessness c 860; **-tus,** unnamed, unspecified c 1115, c 1332; **contractus i.,** unclassified contract (leg.) c 1258.

innormo, to regulate, bring into conformity c 1170, 15c.; *see also* ENORM

innoscens, *see* INNOC

innotatio, inventory 1549.

innotesco, (with *dat.*) ***to** become known to 9c. c 1140, c 1450; ***to** make known, notify 7c., 957. c 1090, a 1595.

innov/ator, innovator c 1546; **littere -atorie,** letters of renewal 1498; **-o cartam,** to renew (confirm) a charter c 1250, 1306; **i. donationem** c 1150; **i. talliam** 1286.

innoxio, to clear of guilt c 1115.

†innuba, (?) married woman 12c.

innubialis, cloudless a 700.

innu/itio, hint, implication c 1375; **-tio,** beckoning c 1500; **-itative** c 1362, **-itive** c 1375, 1378, tacitly, implicitly; **-itivus,** hinted at, implied c 1197, 1380; ***-o,** to intimate c 1080, c 1450.

innumeratio, reckoning in or along with 10c.

innumeros/itas, countless multitude 1430, a 1450; **-e,** innumerably 1344.

*inobedi/entia, disobedience (eccl.); **-ens** 1231, 1558, **-entiarius** c 1378, disobedient person.

inobliquabilis, not to be diverted c 1343.

inobliv/iosus, unforgetting c 1400; **-iscens,** not unmindful c 1096.

inobserv/atio, lack of observation 1620; **-abilis,** unable to be observed or practised c 1332.

inobsessus, not besieged c 1200, 1440.

inob/strusus 1262, **-trusus** 1276, not blocked up.

inoccupatus, unoccupied, untenanted 1418.

†inocultus, *for* incultus, untilled 1388.

1 inofficiatus, provided with a special service (eccl.) c 1182.

2 inoffici/atus 1283, 1684, **-osus** 1421, unserved (eccl.); **-atio,** failure to provide services (eccl.) 1482, 1528; **-ose,** undutifully c 1534.

1 inoleo, to be on the increase 14c.

2 inoleo, to anoint c 950.

3 inoleo 1224, 1241, **inoilio** 1202, **ineulio** 1244, **ennullio** 1200, to make good evaporation from wine-casks; *cf.* **oleagium.**

inolibilis, insipid c 1190.

1 inoperatio, internal activity, inworking 12c.

2 inoper/atio legis, vacation c 1115; **-atus,** unworked, untreated a 1250, 1661; (?) uncultivated *or* unenclosed (? *for* **-tus)** c 1115; **non -ose,** not without labour c 1125; **non -osus,** not unhelpful c 1125.

inopin/io, non-expectation c 1250; **-e,** unexpectedly c 1125.

†inopi/um, *for* **-a,** destitution 15c.

inopos, *see* ENO

inopportunit/as, unsuitability c 860. c 1200; **-ates** (*pl.*), injuries c 1192.

inordin/atio, disorder a 1250, 1380; **-abilitas,** incorrigibility c 1290; **-abilis,** incorrigible c 1270; unable to be ordained (phil.) c 1376; **-abiliter** c 1195, **-anter** a 1400, ***-ate** c 1080, 15c., inordinately, irregularly; **-atus,** inordinate, excessive c 1260, a 1564; unordained, not in orders (eccl.) 14c.

inorganicus, inorganic, unorganized 1620.

inorm-, *see* ENORM

inoro, to pray 14c.

inorrio, *see* INHORRE

inossatus, embedded in bone 1237, a 1250.

inoysilo, to train (falc.) (O.F. *enoiseler*) 1290.

inp-, *see* imp-

inquam (with dependent clause), to say that c 1115, 1252.

inquerelatus, sued, impleaded 1309.

inquest-, *see* INQUIS

inquiet/as 1324, 1441, ***-atio** c 1188, 1450, ***-udo** c 1070, 1461, turbulence, disturbance; **-ativus** c 1258, **-ivus** c 1290, disquieting; **-atrix,** disturber (*f.*) c 1150; †**iniquito,** *for* **-o,** to disturb 1317.

inquin/amentum, defilement, sin c 730. c 1244, c 1414; †**-itas,** (?) impurity (or *f.l.* for **iniquitas**) c 1283.

†**inquiri, oleum,** (?) *for* **o. cheiri,** wallflower oil 13c.

inquis, *see* **incus.**

inquis/itio *1122, 1684, **inquestio** 1483, **-ita** (G.) 1279, **inquesta** a 1275, 1415, inquest, judicial inquiry, *or* record thereof; coroner's inquest 1212, 1583; body of jurors serving on inquest c 1290, 1419; (?) public sale 1190; (?) exaction, imposition c 1250; **i. confessionis,** inquiry by confessional priest 1415; **i. ex officio,** inquest of office (leg.) 1321; **i. liberorum,** inquest of freemen 1324; **i. patrie,** inquest of neighbourhood 1292, 1391; **-ibilis,** ascertainable by inquest a 1564; **-itius,** more precisely c 1343; **-itive,** interrogatively p 1300, 1427; **-itivus,** searching, inquisitive c 1277, 1647; **-itor,** juror on inquest 1204, 1570; official appointed to hold inquest 1254, 1385; local official (G.) 1313; inquisitor, investigator of heresy 1324, c 1400; sidesman (eccl.) 1584; spaniel 16c.; **-itorius,** of inquiry or summons 1293, 1684; **-itum,** question c 1343; **inquir/o,** to question, interrogate (a person) 1086, c 1400; to examine for heresy 1252; *c 1086, 1338, †**-or** (*dep.*) 1271, to ascertain by inquest.

inquoo, *see* **INCOH**

inr-, *see* **irr-**

insacco, to pack up 1241, 1253.

insacratus, unconsecrated a 1186.

insais-, *see* **insaysonatus; inseisio.**

insalso, to salt (meat) in 1374.

insanguino, to draw blood from 1194.

†**insanies,** diseased blood a 975; ‡weal 15c.

insan/us, unwholesome c 1290, 1419; ‡**-atus,** uncured 1570; †**-ibiliter,** *for* **-abiliter,** incurably c 1250; †**-is,** *see* **Parliamentum.**

insapidus, *see* **INSIP**

insartatus, not assarted 1243.

insatianter, insatiably c 1197.

insaucius, invulnerable c 1184.

insaysonatus, in season (of game animals) 1200.

inscal/atio, escalade 1444, 1448; **-o,** to take (town) by escalade c 1370.

inscelestus, innocent c 1192.

insci-, *see also* **INCIS**

insci/etas, ignorance a 1205; **-bilis,** unknowable 13c., a 1350; **-olus,** ignorant ⸌05. a 1530; †**-tior,** to be ignorant (? or *f.l.* for **infitior**) 1372.

insciss/ibilis c 1270, †**-ilis** c 1150, unsplittable; **-us,** undivided c 1160.

insciss/io, -ura, incision (med.) a 1250; **inscindo,** to cut into, cut away 9c. c 1220; *cf.* **INCIS**

inscript/io, inscribing (geom.) 1267; accusation c 1160; **-iones** (*pl.*), title-deeds 798. a 1446; **-ibilis,** inscribable (geom.) 1267, 1326; **-or,** author c 1362; **inscribo,** to accuse c 1343; ‡to expropriate 1483.

inscrut/abilis a 1155, c 1535, †**inscrustabilis** a 1166, inscrutable; **-atus,** unexplored c 1212, c 1362.

insculptor (cuniorum), engraver a 1200.

insecatus, uncut c 1290.

insectator, follower, partisan c 1306, 1545.

insectio, cutting 13c.; *see also* **2 infectio.**

inseculariter, according to an unworldly rule 1378.

insecurus, unsafe a 1350; insecure (of tenure) 1564.

insecut/io, pursuit, onslaught 9c. c 1250, a 1564; *see also* **2 infectio; -rix,** pursuer, harrier (*f.*) a 1446; **-us,** (*pass.*) pursued c 1258, c 1450; **insequor,** to follow, adhere to c 1362, 1426.

insedatus, unappeased c 1250.

insedeo, *for* **insideo,** to sit on (a horse) 1269, 1415.

insegniter, vigorously 1440.

inseisio (Sc.) c 1250, 1309, **insais/io** 1248, **-o** 1147, to seise, enfeoff.

inseisonabilis, insesionabilis, unsound, unwholesome 1438, 1444.

1 insellatus, seated in the saddle c 1250.

2 insellatus, unsaddled c 1115, (?) 1173.

insen-, *see also* **INCEN**

insens/atus, *frenzied, mad c 760. c 1190, 1440; irrational (of animals) c 1257, c 1358; lifeless (of objects) c 793. 13c., c 1271; **-ibilior,** more senseless c 730. c 1250; **-ibiliter,** without feeling 12c.; imperceptibly 1267, p 1381; **-itivus,** senseless c 1270.

insepar/atio, non-separation c 1250; **-anter,** inseparably 1344; **-atus,** unseparated c 1457.

insequentia, inconsequence (log.) 1610.

insequor, *see* **INSECUT**

inser/tio, inclusion c 1237; mention, entry (in document) c 12c., c 1400; **-tum,** *for* **insitum,** graft c 1250, 1282; **inser,** seedling tree 1265; **-tus** 1446, 1464, **-atus** 1245, embroidered, ornamented; **incero,** *for* **-o,** to mention c 1330.

inservio, to enslave c 1115; **i. fenum,** to carry in hay 1334.

insesionabilis, *see* **inseisonabilis.**

†**insetena,** 'inset', ditch (Romney Marsh) 13c.

insiccabilis, not to be dried up c 1250.

insidenter, *see* **INCID**

insidi/e (*pl.*), guard, sentinels c 1290; **-arius,** plotter 893; **-um** 1390, **-atio** 1415, 1513, **incidiatio** 1389, waylaying, ambush; **-ator viarum,** highwayman 1402; **-atrix,** insidious (*f.*) 1620; **-anter,** by craft c 1450; **-o,** to watch, spy on c 1258, c 1290; 1231, **incidio** 1381, 1382, to lie in wait for, waylay.

insigill/atio, sealing a 1564; **-o,** to seal up c 1115.

insign/e (insingn-), battle-cry c 1180, c 1250; ‡15c., ‡**-um** 1483, coat of arms; **-ia** (*pl.*, *2nd decl.*), emblems, badges c 1135, 1481; **-itas,** excellence 1268; **-itio,** distinguishing mark c 1500; **-io,** to honour 1308, 1461; to assign c 1115; **-o,** to mark 12c., 1557.

insileo, to keep silence c 1410.

insil/ium, evil counsel (= A.S. *unrǣd*; play on **consilium**) c 1118, c 1140, **-iarius,** evil counsellor c 1118.

†**insimiliter,** likewise 1339, 1533.

***insimul/,** together (of place) 1086, 1476;

-or (†**simulor**), to agree c 1115; **-to,** to unite c 1465.

insinu/atio (†**insum-**), notification, information, report 1162, 1461; record (G.) 1313; entering a will 1281, 1684; **-amen,** instruction c 990; **-ative,** insinuatingly 1622; **-ativus,** presumed 1380; **-o,** to intimate, make known c 730, 9c. c 1090, 1549; to enter, register (a will) 1322, 1587.

insip/iditas 10c. c 1260, †**-itudo** c 1260, insipidity; **-ide,** foolishly 15c.; **-idus,** dull c 730; **insapidus,** unseasoned 1569; **incipientia,** folly 14c., 1441; **-iens,** unwitting c 1177.

insist/o circa, to dwell upon, emphasize c 1343; **incisto,** *for* **-o,** to insist 1300; **-or,** to pursue c 800. a 1384.

insit/a, -um 1239, 1296, **incita** c 1300, seedling tree or graft; **-ivus,** for planting or cultivation c 1160; **incisio,** grafting c 1170; **-o,** to graft 1266.

insitamentum, *see* INCIT

insitiens, not thirsty 9c.

insociabiliter, incompatibly a 1100.

insocna, brawl between occupants of house c 1115.

insolesco, (?) to become accustomed to 1345.

insolidum, *see* 1 **solidus.**

insolito, contrary to custom 1284.

insoller/tia, clumsiness c 1250, a 1446; ‡**-s,** "uncrafty" 1483; **-ter,** clumsily c 1250.

insol/ubilitas, irrefutability, certainty c 1377; **-ubile,** insoluble proposition c 1360; **-ubilis** insoluble *or* irrefutable (log.) c 1080, 1457; not redeemable by weregeld c 1102, c 1115; **-ubiliter,** indissolubly c 1090, a 1452; irrefutably c 1343, 1409; **-utus,** unsolved, unrefuted c 1267, c 1343; *unpaid 1165, 1564; unredeemed by weregeld c 1115.

insop/ibilis, unappeasable a 1142; **-itus,** unsleeping 1417.

insopior (*dep.*), to be sleepy *or* stupid 10c.

insorb/eo, to imbibe 1378; **-esco,** to swallow, accept c 1125.

insorbibilis, unacceptable c 1193.

insord/escentia, state of being unabsolved (eccl.) 1552; **-esco** (Sc.) 1478, 1552, **-eo** 1475, to be unabsolved, under censure.

insor/s, involved c 1350; **-tiatus** (†**-ticatus**), bewitched c 1115.

inspecialiter, not specially c 1362.

inspectatus, unexpected 1537.

inspect/io, matter for looking into c 1160; **-or supernus,** God 1006; †**inspicio,** inspection, observation 13c.; **inspeximus,** exemplification of record c 1420.

inspico, to sharpen c 950.

†**inspillum,** (?) weapon c 550.

1 inspirabilitas, inability to emanate as a spirit (theol.) c 1290, p 1300.

2 inspir/abilitas, inhalability c 1260; **-amen** 1286, 15c., *-atio** c 1133, c 1445, inspiration; **-atio** (*sc.* **Spiritus Sancti**), inspiration (unanimous) as mode of election (eccl.) 1336, c 1485; inhaling 86o. 1267; ingestion (of food) c 1460; **-ator,** inspirer c 1180, 14c.

inspiss/atio, thickening a 1250, 1622; **-ativus,** tending to thicken a 1250; **-o,** to thicken, condense c 1210, 14c.

insplendeo, to illuminate c 1185, c 1250.

inspoliabiliter, safe from plunder c 1376.

insponsatus, unespoused c 1100.

instabilitas, constant motion, restlessness c 730.

1 install/atio 1294, **-amentum** 1298, (payment of debt by) instalment; **-o,** to pay by instalments 1293.

2 *install/atio, instalment in office (eccl.) 1240, 1684; **-ator,** installer (eccl.) 1317; *-o 12c., 1587, **instaulo**⌐ 15c., to install; to provide (choir) with stalls a 1385.

instan/tia, practice 1200; instance, example c 1070, 1620; negative instance, exception, objection (ἔνστασις) c 1240, 1620; instance, process (leg.) c 1250, c 1593; c 1250, 1500, **instatio** c 1390, urgent need, entreaty; *ad -tiam,** at the request c 1200, 1608; **-tiam capio,** to admit an exception c 1343, c 1430; **-tia crucis,** crucial instance 1620; **-s,** instant, moment of time a 1150, 1686; present incumbent (eccl.) c 1575; **in primo -ti,** in the first instance (log.) p 1300; **-ter,** instantly, immediately 1217, 1560; **-tanee,** instantaneously p 1300, 1344; *-taneus,** instantaneous 1236, c 1363; **-tive,** by way of exception a 1250, 1344; **insto,** to object, allege an exception c 1300, c 1343.

instatu/atus c 1190, †**-tus** 12c., turned into a statue.

***instaur/um** 1198, 1446, *-amentum** 1152, 1373, **-amentatio** 1225, **-atio** a 1125, 1470, **-alia** (*pl.*) 1261, stock, stocking (of manor, etc.); **-arius** 1270, 1388, **-ator** 1296, 1541, stockman; *-o 1113, 1471, **instaro** 1230, to stock.

instello, to ornament with stars c 1200.

instigativus, instigating 1385.

instimulatio, instigation c 1000. c 1270, 1424.

instinct/io, instigation, impulse c 1000. 1344, 1461; **-us nature,** instinct 13c., c 1270; **notitia -a,** (?) intuition c 1362.

instirpo, to implant a 1155.

instita, fess (her.) 1654.

institu/tio, institution, foundation c 1185, c 1362; *institution to a benefice (eccl.) c 1125, 16c.; ordinance c 1115; choice of temporary symbol (log.) p 1347; **i. placitorum,** general assembly for pleas c 1180; **i. prima,** first intention (log.) c 1160; **-tiones** c 1258, c 1340, **-ta** c 1258, c 1330, Justinian's *Institutes*; **-ta apostolica** (*pl.*), canon law a 1125; **-tivus,** designed to promote 1620; **-tor,** institutor (eccl.) 1159, 1414; *-o, to institute to a benefice (eccl.) c 1200, 1565; *see also* **natura.**

insto, *see* INSTAN

instr/atus, worked, embroidered c 1250; ‡**-o,** *for* **insterno,** 1570.

†**instrictus,** strict a 1166.

instringibilis, not distrainable 1456.

instrio, *see* histrio.

instruct/io ***c 1197, 1549, **-us c 1257, c 1430, instruction, guidance; **i. (fidei),** edification c 1343; **i. (negotii),** performance 1417; **i. arcis,** burhbote c 800, 947. 12c.; **i. pontis,** brigbote c 800, 947. 12c.; **-ivus,** guiding a 1250; **-or,** *instructor, teacher c 1250, 1529; one who draws up an instrument (leg.) 1293, 1414; **-rix,** instructress 1447, c 1470; **-orie,** by way of instruction c 1334; **-orius**, instructive, indicative a 1155, 12c.; **-issime**, in very good order c 1250.

instrument/um, instrument (mus.) c 1192, 1461; **i. musicale** 1267, 1413; **i. inflativum**, wind instrument 1267; **i. obligatorium**, bond 1301; **i. novum**, **i. vetus**, New and Old Testament c 1180, c 1536; **strumentum**, *for* **-um**, c 700; **-alis**, instrumental (phil.) c 1115, c 1670; 1496; 1503, **-arius** 1684, documentary; **musica -alis** 1252, 1267; **-aliter**, acting as instrument 1344, c 1620; **-atus**, equipped with instruments or organs c 1360.

nstudeo, to devote oneself 1252; (with *inf.*) to desire 1295.

instuffo, to stock, furnish p 1327, c 1370.

insuadibilis, unpersuadable c 700.

†**insuasio**, persuasion 1394.

insuaviter, disagreeably c 1191.

insubstantialis, unsubstantial a 1361.

insuccessibil/is, not admitting of succession (in time) 1344; **-iter**, without succession 1344.

insudo (with *abl.*) 8c. c 1150, 1504, **i. ad** 14c., **i. circa** c 1220, **i. in** 7c. c 1200, 15c., to toil at.

*****insufficien/tia**, insufficiency, incompetence c 1188, 1569; **-s**, *insufficient, incompetent c 1192, 1549; in poor condition 1342, 15c.; unable 1262, 1327; of insufficient means, poor 1420; **-tior**, too weak 1378; **-ter**, insufficiently, inadequately 1267, 1347.

insufflatio, breathing upon, blast 7c. 1424, c 1534.

insul/a, aisle of church c 1125, 1558; wing (of castle keep) 1370; **I. Sanctorum**, Ireland 1324; **-etta**, islet 1259, 1539; **-anus**, insular c 700, c 730. a 1275, 1392; c 1227, 1461, **-arius** c 1188, 1309, **-icola** c 1210, 13c., islander.

insulphuro, to taint with sulphur c 1180.

insulsus, fresh (of water) c 760.

*****insult/us** c 1190, 1622, **-a** c 1400, 1480, **-atio** 13c., 1461, assault, attack; **i. premeditatus** 1206, 1271; **-uosus**, insulting 1333; **-o**, to assault, attack c 1130, 1461.

insum, *see* **inesse**.

insumo, to obtain a wish c 730; *see also* INSINU

insumpt/uosus, inexpensive c 1200; **-ibilius**, at less cost 1378.

insuper, as mentioned above c 1190.

insuperabilitas, invincibility 1344.

insuro, to insure (a cargo) 1723.

*****insurrect/io**, insurrection 1380, 1568; **-or**, insurgent 1382, c 1450; **insurgo**, to arise a 1135, a 1446; to follow (log.) 1309; to raise (troops) c 1192.

insus/pectus 1385, 1438, **-picabilis** 1241, 1295, unsuspected, beyond suspicion.

†**insutilis**, unsewn 1570.

intabul/atio, registration 1411, a 1452; **-ator**, registrar 1411; *****-o**, to register, record a 1316, 1475.

†**intachgeira**, (?) 'intake-gore', piece of enclosed land (Lincs.) c 1315.

†**intactilis**, ticklish 1570.

intallio, *see* ENTALLI

1 intamino, to contaminate c 965.

2 intamino (assisam), to begin (Fr. *entamer*) 1221.

intangibilis, intangible c 1260.

intass/atio, stacking c 1303; **-o** c 1100, 15c., **intaxo** c 1125, to stack, garner.

intaxatus, untaxed c 1296; *see also* INTASS

integer, integer (math.) a 1150, 15c.; **intiger**, entire (Sc.) 1473, 1478; *see also* **ad, de, ex, per, panis, 2 pannus, villa**; **integr/a** 1378, **-alitas** 1620, **-itas** 12c., 1461, entirety, totality; **-itas**, immunity, privilege 1235, 1313; **-alia** (*pl.*), general constitution c 1612; **-alis**, *integral, essential to the whole 1163, 1620; 1461, **-italis** 1313, whole, entire; *****-aliter** c 1142, a 1539, **-iter** 1415, entirely, in full; **-atio**, completing a whole c 1360, 1406; **-o**, to integrate, constitute as a whole c 1270, 1610.

†**integumentum**, (?) allegory 13c.

intellect/io, understanding a 1235, 1662; **-us agens**, active mind 1267, p 1300; **i. possibilis**, potential mind 1267, p 1300; **i. speculativus** c 1260, 1267; **-ibilis**, apprehended by mind alone 12c., c 1360; **-ivitas**, ability to understand p 1300, c 1360; **-ive**, mentally c 1277; *****-ivus**, intellective, capable of understanding a 1250, 1427; **-or**, one who understands c 1125, 1427; **-ualis**, spiritual, mental 6c., 860. 12c., c 1437; **-ualista**, intellectualist, introspective philosopher 1620; **-ualitas**, faculty of understanding c 1270, a 1384; **-ualiter**, in meaning 6c.; intellectually 13c.

intellig/entia (intelleg-), meaning, sense 9c. c 1340; league, *entente* 1496; incorporeal being, angel c 1205, 1620; **i. moralis**, ethics c 850; **-ibilia** (*pl.*), spiritual realities 1006; **-ibilis**, trustworthy c 1115, c 1200; intellective 13c.; **-ibiliter**, intelligibly c 700. c 1125, a 1452; **-ibilitas**, intelligibility c 1290, 1378; **-ere** (*subst.*), understanding c 1300; **-i facio** 1276, **-o** c 1190, c 1350, to mean, give to understand; *see also* **2 data**; **-o**, to agree, believe 1220; **-o melius**, to incline to believe 1255.

intemno, to scorn, refuse c 1250.

intemp/estuosus c 1293, **-oraneus** c 1360, unseasonable; **-eries**, storm 1372; **-oralis**, timeless, a 1233; **-oraliter**, timelessly 8c., 9c.

intend/entia, intention c 1362; attention 16c., 1577; submission 1287; writ directing submission 1448; **-imentum**, equivocation, mental reservation 1278; **i. bonum et rectum**, true meaning or intention 1291; **i. illicitum**, unlawful compact c 1288; **-enter**, intentionally 1344; *****-ens**, attentive, submissive c 1195, 15c.; **littere de -endo**, letter enjoining submission 1334; **-o**, *to be attentive or submissive 6c., 8c. c 1115, 15c.; to observe, attend to (*trans.*) 1263, c 1514; to bring an action (leg.) 1231, 1549; to remember, consider 8c. c 1130, 1388; (?) to hear 14c.; to intensify 1335, c 1365; **i. circa**, to attend to 1264, 1429; **i. quod**, to intend that c 1297; to consider that 1315.

intener/atio, softening 1622; **-o**, to soften 1620.

intens/io c 1250, 1593, **intentio** a 1446 intensity, 'intension' (log.); **-ibilis**, intensifiable 13c., 1427; (?) capable of meaning (log.) a 1347; **-ive**, in relation to intensity or intension (log.) 1267, 1593; **-ivus**, intensive intensifying c790, 9c. c1300, 1620; **-e,** intensely 1267, c1466; **-us,** intense (log.) 1267, c1360; dark, rich (of colour) c1180, 1464; **-ior,** keener (of senses) 14c.; **-issimus,** most zealous c1090; *cf.* INTEND; *see also* **intentio.**

intent/ator (intempt-), informant c1140; **-or,** accuser (eccl.) c1160; **male -atus,** ill-conditioned c1290; **-o,** to accuse, bring an action (leg.) c1115, c1430; **i. contra,** to attempt against 1254, 1333.

†**intentia** (? *for* intendentia *or* **nitentia**), effort c1362.

intent/io, 'intention' (log.), concept c1200, c1365; **i. prima, i. secunda** (log.) 13c., c1360; **de -ione,** attentively c1343; **-ionis mee est** (existit), I intend c1347, c1380; **-or,** director c1180; **-um** 1267, c1433, **-us** c1363, 1419, **intensus** c1430, **intensio** (*for* -io) 1402, 1588, intention, purpose; **ab -o,** on purpose c1422; **-us** (salutis eterne), endangering c1290; **-ionalis,** intentional c1270, 1622; conveying a meaning a1304; **-ionaliter,** intentionally c1290, 1620; **-a,** earnestness c730; *see also* **intensio.**

intepidus, not lukewarm 961.

inter, approximately 1185; (with *gerund*) in the course of c1090, c1450; **i. . . . et,** both . . . and 1086, c1250; **i. canem et lupum,** *entre chien et loup,* at twilight 1265, 1295; **i. ecclesiam,** within the church 1086; **i. furcas,** on the gallows c1390; **i. totum,** in all 1086, c1362.

interadjicio, to interject 12c.

interambulatio, boundary walk c1300.

interaperio, to open between c1172.

interaudio, to hear incidentally 12c.

interbajulus, go-between c1250.

interbibitio, drinking together 1385.

intercadens, intermittent (med.) a1250.

intercal/ariter, by way of insertion p1300; **-o,** to interpose, insert c1172, c1225; (?) to distract c1500; †**interscalo,** to intercalate c1265; *cf.* INTERSCALAR.

intercap/edo, interspace 991; **-ido,** *for* -edo, 6c., 8c.

intercept/io, breach of truce 1221, 1274; blocking 1620; **-us,** intervening (of time) 1424; **intercipio,** to commit a breach of truce 1227, 1242; to get the better of 1260; **i. super,** to seize at the expense of 1086; **i. versus,** to offend against 1220,

*****intercess/io,** intercession 8c. c1090, 1549; littere **-orie,** letters intercessory c1218.

inter/cilium c1400, ‡1483, †**-culium** c1436, space between eyebrows.

intercino, to sing in between c1160.

intercipio, *see* INTERCEPT

‡**interciput,** "mid part of head" 15c., 1483.

intercis/io, intersection p1300; interruption c1400; **-us,** intervening (of time) c1400.

interclau/sio, shutting in c1460; 1373, **-sura** c1250, 1278, **-sum, -sa** 1239, c1412, **interclu/sa** 1374, **-sum** 1252, 1299, partition, parclose (arch.); **-sum,** (?) partition between casks 1313; ‡**-sorium,** pinfold 15c.; **-sorius,** partitioned off 1244; shutting off a1447; *****-do,** to enclose (in a letter) 1235, c1465.

†**intercolorati,** (?) *f.l.* for **vitri colorati,** a1250.

intercommunic/atio, intercourse 1382, 1440; **-o,** to have intercourse 1372, 1401; to intercommon, share common pasture 14c., a1564.

intercontinuo, to run between (of a wall) c1173.

interculium, *see* **intercilium.**

intercur/sus mercium, commercial intercourse 1496, 1513; **-sor,** courier, go-between 1297, 15c.; **-rentia** (*n. pl.*), incidents c1185; **-ro,** to interfere 1234, a1285; to pass to and fro c1188, c1390.

intercut/aneus, intercutaneous (med.) c1180, a1446; ‡**-ium,** welt of a shoe c1440, 1483: ‡**-io,** to welt 1483.

interdi/anus, lasting all day 7c.; **-u,** from day to day c1200.

interdic/tio, (?) second best throw at dice c1200; 697. 12c., 1169, **-tus** 1274, *****-tum** 1164, 1549, interdict (eccl.); **excommunicatio -tiva** c1440; **-tum Christianitatis** 1165, c1180; **-tum,** (explained as) "outlawry" 1213; *****-o,** to lay under interdict (eccl.) 1169, 1535; **i. Christianitatem** a1130; †**introdico,** to forbid c1250.

interea temporis, meanwhile c1550.

inter/emptio, *****slaughter, destruction c760. 1188, 1440; *****demolition of argument, ἀναίρεσις (log.) a1233, 1336; **-imo, to** demolish (log.) 13c., c1270.

interess/e, interest (leg.), concern c1250, 1684; *****(compensation for) damages *or* interest on loan c1200, 1559; **-entia,** active interest, presence c1260, 1418; *****-ens** (*ppl.*) 1328, 1555, †**interens** c1330; *****-endum** (*gerund*) 1309, 1546.

interfectibilis, mortal 1344.

interfercul/um 1296, 15c., **-are** c1493, c1515, *entremets;* **scutella -aris** 1267.

interfinium, boundary, march c1150; partition, stall 1335; pocket (in bag) 1341; ‡bridge of nose 15c., a1520.

interfixus (lapidibus), paved c1320.

interfrettus, embroidered between 1388.

interfugium, subterfuge (G.) 1254.

interfusio, influx, admixture c700.

interhabeo, to hold (land) between 1210.

interhumerale, space between shoulders 1245.

interimo, *see* **interemptio.**

interimus, *see* INTIM

interject/io, interruption 1062; placing between 1267; **-us,** interposed (of appeal) c1332.

interlabor, to elapse in the meanwhile c1192, 14c.

interlaqueatus, interlaced 1245, 1432; combined, joint c1258.

interlig/atio, league, conspiracy 1386; **-or** 1354, 1417, **-o me** 1397, to conspire.

interlin/eatio (-iatio) 1428, 1684, **-atio** 1420, **-iatura** 1283, 1294, **-eare** c1200, 1434, **enterliniarium** 1388, interlineation; *****-earis,** interlinear c1197, c1553; **-ealiter,** between the lines 1395; **-eatus,** interlined (of a doublet) 1445; **-eo,** to write between the lines 1376, 1684.

interlocut/io (interloquut-), parley c1362, 1461; conspiracy c1450; **-oria,** interlocutory sentence (log.) 1208, 1311; 1200, c1400

-orium 1293, c 1470, †**-urum** p 1341,
interloquium 1393, 15c., conversation,
discussion; **-orium**, parlour 1373; **-orie**, by
interlocutory sentence 1336; **-orius**, inter-
locutor (leg.) 1549; c 1196, 1522, **inter-
loquitorius** c 1298, interlocutory (leg.);
conversational c 1325; **interloquor**, *to
pronounce interlocutory sentence c 1155,
c 1442; to impart, discuss 1289, c 1470; to
be agreed (*passive*) 1282, c 1400.
interlu/dium 1296, a 1446, **-dum** 1519,
-sum 1542, interlude, play, episode; **-sor**,
player, entertainer 1519, 1542.
interme/atus, intercourse, coming and going
1195, c 1250; **-o**, to go between, mediate
c 1200, 15c.
intermed/ium, interval 14c., 1537; **-ia** (*pl.*)
a 1452, c 1470, **-iatio** 13c., 1350, good
offices, mediation; **-iator**, mediator c 1470;
-iatus, intermediate 1267; **-io**, to form a
boundary 1414; to intervene (of time) 15c.;
to interfere c 1265; to mediate 1461, c 1470.
1 **intermin/atio**, commination, anathema
(eccl.) a 1100, c 1540; **i. anathematis** 1174,
15c.; **littere -atorie**, letters comminatory
15c.; **-o**, to threaten c 1190.
2 **intermin/atio** 12c., 13c., **-abilitas** a 1250,
c 1300, endlessness, eternity; *-abilis*,
endless, eternal 1122, 1461; **-abiliter** a 1100,
-aliter a 1250, endlessly; **-atus**, indeterminate c 1270, 1686; unfinished c 1488.
intermitto, to abandon 5c.; *see also* INTROMISS
intermixt/io, intermixture 1279, 15c.; **-im**,
interspersedly c 1488; †**impermixtus**, (?)*for*
-us, 13c.
intermunditia, *see* immunditia.
intermundium, interval (in time) between
successive worlds 1649.
intermut/abiliter, reciprocally 1433; **-o
vestimenta**, to change dress (at night) a 615.
internamentum, *see* INTERR
internasum, nasal septum 6c.
inter/nicies c 1125, **-niscio** 1260, *for* -necio;
-niciosus, deadly c 1090.
†**interno**, (?) to enter into 8c.
internodatus, intertwined 1245.
internumeratus, counted in a 1155.
internunti/a (*pl.*), interchanged messages
c 1190; **-o**, to act as go-between c 860.
interoperatus, worked (embroidered) between 1416.
interpell/atio, interposition, intercession 9c.
a 1120, c 1340; **-ate** 1455, **-atim** c 1344,
at intervals; **-o**, to accuse c 1072, c 1285; to
demand 1318, c 1400; to intercede with
c 730. 1160, 15c.; c 1130, 1432, **-or** (*dep.*)
1157, to appeal to, call upon; *cf.* INTERPOL
interpercutio, to exchange blows 1276.
interplacit/atio, interpleading (leg.) 16c.;
-o, to interplead a 1564.
interplango, to utter intermittent laments 12c.
interpol/atio, insertion, interval, intermission
a 1155, c 1470; **-ate** c 1182, c 1385, **-atim**
c 1253, 1523, at intervals; **-o**, to interrupt,
interpose 7c. c 1125, c 1556; *cf.* INTERPELL
interpo/sitio, interposition (of decree, *etc.*)
c 1340, 1428; **i. fidei** c 1250, c 1400;
-no de, to interfere with c 1336, c 1478.
interpressura, breach (of truce) 1268.
interpret/abilis, explicable, explicit c 1080,

c 1250; **-ative**, by interpretation c 1250,
c 1414; **-ativus**, implicit, implied c 1212,
1609; **-o**, to expound 1286.
interprisa, enterprise, attack 1230, 1499.
interpugna, mutual conflict c 1440.
interpun/ctum, dividing line in a pattern
(her.) c 1595; **-go**, to divide a pattern (her.)
c 1595.
interr/agium c 1223, **-atio** 1420, interment
fee; **-amentum** 1441, †**internamentum**
c 1421, funeral feast; **-o**, to inter (esp.
without Christian rites) a 1135, 1398.
interrog/atio, exaction, demand a 1108,
c 1160; exaction, summons (leg.) 1221;
-ative, interrogatively c 700; **-ata** (*pl.*)
c 1290, *-atoria* 1293, 1684, interrogatories
(leg.), **-o**, to demand, claim c 1000. a 1100,
1265; to exact, summon, esp. under threat
of outlawry (leg.) 1203, 1271.
interruptivus, interrupting a 1292.
intersagitto, to exchange shots 1227.
interscalar/is, (†**interstalar-**), arranged like
rungs 1378; **-iter**, alternately c 1443; *see also*
INTERCAL
interscribo, to stripe, pencil (of plumage)
a 1446.
intersec/tio, intersection (geom.) c 1260,
1686; **-o** a 1200, 1686, †**intrinseco** 1267,
to intersect.
intersequor, to be involved c 1228.
intersertio, planting 1457.
†**intersessim**, incessantly c 1470.
intersign/ium c 1212, 1429, *-um* 1164,
c 1450, **introsignum** c 1266, token, countersign.
†**intersimonium**, wedge 15c.
interstellaris, interstellar c 1612, 1620.
interstinctus, checky (her.) 1586.
interstitium, partition *or* space between
partitions 1250, 1327; interference c 1302.
intersum, *see* INTERESS
intersumo, to adjourn c 1400.
interten/ementum 1510, **-tio** 1534, maintenance (of rebels) (Sc.); **-eo**, to maintain,
uphold (Sc.) 1567.
‡**intertextus**, tinsel 1570.
interti/are (*subst.*), arrest, seizure c 1115;
-o, to seize, lay claim to (leg.) c 1115.
intertin/ctus, veined with colour 7c., c 730.
c 1125, a 1250; **-guo**, to variegate, checker
819.
interturbo, to disturb, interrupt c 1536.
*interula**, undergarment, shirt, c 950, 1006.
1124, 1588; **inturala**, "smock" 1550.
interunitus, respective, corresponding c 1370.
interuter, each in turn a 1408.
interven/tio c 793, c 1006. 1124, 1440, **-tus**
a 615, c 980. c 1130, 1461, intervention,
intercession, mediation; **-tor** c 980, 1006.
c 1220, c 1464, **-trix** (*f.*) c 1090, c 1325,
intercessor, mediator; **-io**, to enter c 1308;
to act as go-between c 1295, c 1410; c 1130,
1461, **introvenio** 1254, to intervene,
mediate.
interversio, reversal c 1198.
intervideo, to see each other c 1188.
intervigilium, nap a 1180.
interviscinus, (?) exchanged between neighbours c 1390.
intervolo, to intervene c 1330.

intervolvor, to elapse in the meanwhile 14c.
intesilio, to gag 1201; *cf.* teseillum.
intestate, without a will 1377.
intesticulo, to castrate 1293.
intestine (*pl.*), intestines p 1327.
intesto, to club on the head 1274.
intext/io, weaving 819; -or, (?) embroiderer 1547.
*inthroniz/atio, enthroning (eccl.) c 1115, 1684; -ator, enthroner 1317; -o, to enthrone (lay ruler) 1006, 1041. c 1150, c 1540; *9c. c 1100, c 1414, enthronizo 12c., to enthrone (eccl.).
intiger, *see* integer.
intim/itas, intimacy, affection c 1370; -um, inmost depth 1304; balliva -a, inner bailey 1313; -ius, more earnestly or affectionately 1296, c 1448; interimus, *for* -us, innermost c 550; -atio, intimation, communication c 1180, c 1590; littere -atorie, letters intimatory 1416, 1417; -o, to enjoin, exhort c 730. c 1250.
intinct/io, dipping 1172; dyeing 1441; -us, infusion c 1125; intinguo, to baptize 1006.
intitul/atio, name, title c 1172, c 1450; entry (on register, *etc.*) 1323, c 1505; *-o, to entitle, name c 1125, c 1500; *to enter, record c 1265, 1555; to glorify c 1170, c 1250; to address, dedicate c 1335, c 1450; to grant (land, *etc.*) 1294, p 1341; to grant, appropriate (eccl.) c 1188, c 1430; to assign, devote c 1197; to assign (to benefice, *etc.*) 1237, 1439; to ordain (eccl.) c 1444, 1526; to entitle (leg.) c 1389, 1566; †to accuse, impeach 13c.
intollum, 'in-toll', due paid on taking possession of burghal land (Sc.) 1464.
inton/atio, booming c 1200, 1570; c 1230, -izatio 1409, intonation, chanting; -o, *to intone, chant c 1080, 1588; to tune (an organ) 1512.
intonno 1279, intonelo 1214, intunelo 1213, to put in casks.
intorticeum, sort of taper 1494.
intor/tio, rolling (of eyes) c 1125; crux -ta, wreathed cross (her.) c 1595; -queo, to distort 7c.
intoxic/atio, poisoning 1309, 1587; -ativus, poisonous c 1255, 1489; -ator, poisoner c 1457; *-o, to poison 1216, 1608.
intraclausus, enclosed 1441.
intract/atio, entreaty c 1470; -um 1281, entractum 1357, salve (O.F. *entrait*); -o, to entreat c 1458, c 1470; to treat, deal with c 1470; to treat, make terms c 1470; to harass c 1320; intraho, to bring in (hay, *etc.*) 1323, 1338; to transfer (to) 1537.
intragium, *see* intratio.
intraillatus, 'entrailed', interlaced 1409.
intrajaceo, to lie between 1430.
intra/le, inner room, "parlour" 1550; -lia (*pl.*) 1247, c 1485, -nea (*pl.*) c 1125, 12c., entrails; -neitas (†-vietas), essence 13c., c 1300.
intramanens, inmate, resident (Sc.) 1475.
intramuralis, within the walls 1236.
intranominatus, named within c 1475.
intranquillus, unquiet 15c.
intransferibilis, untransferable c 1375.
intransgressibil/itas, inability to pass through

9c.; -is, impermeable c 1212; unsurpassable 12c.
intransi/tio, intransitiveness 13c., 1378; -bilitas, permanence 1344; -bilis, impassable a 1155.
intransmeabilis, impassable c 950. c 1257.
intransmutabil/itas, immutability 1267, c 1270; -is, immutable 860. c 1520, 1360.
intransvadabilis, impenetrable c 1100.
†intra/rius, (?) *for* -neus, domestic 15c.
intrasum, to be within a 1233.
intr/atio, entry (into building) 1583; entry (into possession of land) 1496; entry (into office) 1389; entry (on register, *etc.*) 1417, a 1564; i. placitorum (leg.) 1498; -agium, entrance fee (G.) 1283; -ans, trader lacking municipal freedom 1430; -atus, having entered c 1440; -o, to begin (of periods) c 1188, c 1415; c 1258, c 1300, i. in 13c., to enter into possession of (leg.); to enter (papal) office (i. canonice c 1300, 1414, i. catholice 1213, c 1275); c 1250, i. monasterium c 1110, i. religionem c 1343, c 1400, to enter a religious order; to take into 893; to get in (crops) 1254, 1449; to put in (beasts to graze) c 1280, 1356; to reclaim (waste land) 1281, 1411; to enclose, appropriate (common land) 1274; 1196, c 1290, i. ad 1198, i. in 1203, 1232, to become answerable for; (with *inf.*) to undertake 1230; to enter (on a register, *etc.*), record 1295, 1539; i. in, to be put in (to graze) 13c., c 1280; i. ecclesiam, to take sanctuary 1221; i. libertatem, to enter (intrude upon) a liberty 1267, 1374; i. defaltam, to incur default (leg.) c 1275; i. defensionem, to enter a (plea of) defence (leg.) c 1290; i. essonium (leg.) 1280; i. placitum 12c., 1194, a causam c 1163, to enter a plea (leg.); i. plegium, to put in a pledge 1391; i. in responsum, to undertake to answer (leg.) 1219; i. Sententias, to incept in divinity (ac.) c 1445; *cf.* introitus.
intravenio, to interfere a 1452.
intravietas, *see* intrale.
intric/atio, winding c 1302; *entanglement, perplexity c 1160, 1437; -atura, knot, plait 1245, ‡1483; -abilis a 1452, -atorius 1427, -atus c 1334, 1345, perplexing; †-us, (?) crooked 13c.; -o, to plait c 1250.
intriffuratus, ornamented with trefoils 1338.
intrinsec/a (intrincec-) (*pl.*), inward parts 1296, c 1410; -e 1344, p 1380, intrinsice 1461, internally, intimately; -us, (*subst.*) citizen, resident 1303, 15c.; (*adj.*) internal, interior c 1115, 1414; *internal, domestic, concerned with a particular district or community 1233, 1473; inward, intrinsic (phil.) 1267, c 1444; esoteric c 1343; intimate 1421; *see also* I baillium, hundredum, servitium, teloneum; *cf.* extrinsecus, forinsecus.
intrinseco, *see* intersectio.
intritum, plaster 1518; *cf.* intractum.
intro, *see* intratio.
intro-, *see also* inter-
introactus, internal, domestic c 1250.
intro/ceptio, taking in 1622; -cipio, to take in, admit 1622.

introduct/io, innovation 1310; 1537, **-orium** 1267, c 1553, introduction (to book, *etc.*); **-ibilis,** maintainable 1395; **-ivus,** introductory, leading on towards, c 730. a 1250, c 1283; **-or,** introducer c 1250, a 1410; **-orie,** by way of introduction a 1150.

introicio, to introduce 7c.; to throw in 1345.

intro/itus, appearance in court (leg.) c 1320; (right of) ingress 1265, 1450; entry into possession (leg.) 1176, c 1280; entrance fee 1198, 1485; entry into religion 1420; 'entry', hostel (ac.) 1395, 1408; reclamation (of land) c 1295, c 1410; entry (on register, *etc.*) 1455, 1566; 12c., c 1197, **i. ad missam** c 1188, **i.* **misse** c 1125, c 1450, introit of the mass (eccl.); **i. Biblie** c 1456, 1463, **i. Sententiarum** 1421, 1463, inception as bachelor (ac.); **i. mensis,** earlier half (1st to 15th) of month (G.) 1255, 1369; *cf.* **exitus mensis; -itio,** entry, bringing in 1559; **-eo,** to enter (on register) 1409; *cf.* **intratio.**

intromisceo, to intermix, interpolate 1526.

intromiss/io, admission (eccl.) c 1070, 13c.; 1419, **intermissio** 1041, intervention; **-or* 1420, 1559, **-ator** 1608, **intermissor** 1549, 'intromitter', administrator of property, (Sc.); **potestas -atrix,** authority to administer 1522; **intromitto cum** 1463, 1473, **i. de** 1469, **intermitto** 1549, to 'intromit', administer (Sc.); **intromitto cum** 1497, 1577, **i. de** 1205, 1533, **i. in** 1533, **i. inter** c 1390, **i. super** c 1327, **i. me** (with *dat.*) 12c., c 1450, **i. me circa** p 1377, **i. me cum** 1405, c 1484, **i.* **me de** 1085, c 1452, **i. me in** c 1343, 15c., **i. me super** 1227, 14c., to intermeddle, concern oneself with.

introniz-, *see* INTHRONIZ.

intropono, to put in c 1362.

introsusceptio, absorption 1427; *cf.* **intussusceptio.**

intrunc/atio, penning (of horses) 1452; †**-atus (nervus),** (?) *for* **intricatus,** a 1250; **-o,** to put in a coffin 12c.; to put in the stocks 1275.

*****intru/sio** 12c., 1461, **-cio** 1583, **-soria** 1313, intrusion, trespass, usurpation; **-sor*, intruder, trespasser, usurper c 1180, 1494; **-do,* to thrust in 1206, c 1504; 1206, 1414, **i. me** 1199, 1562, to intrude.

intrusso, to pack, tie up 1286, 1423.

†**intua,** *for* **intra** *or* **intus,** within 839.

intub/us 1428, 1438, **entubus** 1453, †**incibus** 1434, (?) straw, litter (for floor); †**incuba** c 1200, **endivia** a 1250, 1622, *for* **-us,** endive, chicory.

intu/itio, contemplation 1153; intuition a 1350, 1363; **-ibilis,** apprehensible by intuition p 1300, a 1361; c 1285, **-itivus* c 1300, c 1400, intuitive; **-itive,** intuitively p 1300, 1609; **-itu Dei,** in the sight of God, for God's sake 1201, 1330; **-itu* **caritatis** 1200, c 1440; **-eor,** (with *acc.* and *inf.*) to observe c 730; (*pass.*) to be seen c 1330, p 1350.

intumbo, to entomb c 1190.

intumeo, to rise, swell c 1250, 1252.

*****intumulo,** to bury 1238, c 1362.

intunelo, *see* **intonno.**

inturala, *see* **interula.**

inturbate, without disturbance 1284.

intus (*prep.* with *acc.*), within 1086, c 1450; **i. et extra,** *see* **ad.**

intus/susceptio, taking in, admission c 1270; **-suscipio,** to take in a 1233; *cf.* **introsusceptio.**

‡**inula (hinnula),** "scallion" c 1200, 1483; **enula** 13c., 1622, **e. campana** a 1250, 1538, *for* **i.,** elecampane; ‡**i. campana,** houseleek 14c.; "spearwort" 15c.

inultus, not redeemed by weregeld c 1115.

†**inunco** (? **innuco),** to enclose (land) 1689; *cf.* INHOK.

inun/ctio, ointment c 1250; anointing (eccl.) c 1125, 1423; **-ctuositas,** oiliness a 1250; **-go (-guo),** to wipe 1241; to anoint (eccl.) c 1080, c 1470; **i. in regem** 12c., c 1400.

inund/antia c 793, **-atio** 1380, inflowing; c 730. c 1150, 15c., **enundatio** 1573, *for* **-atio,** overflowing, flood; **-atio maris,** flood tide 1277; **enundo,** *for* **-o,** to inundate 1353.

inuniform/itas, lack of uniformity c 1267; **-is,** not uniform 13c.; **-iter,** not uniformly c 1267.

inunis, not one (suggested derivation of **inanis)** a 1180.

inurbanitas, rusticity, discourtesy 12c., c 1470.

inust/atio, branding 1585; **-o,** to brand 1585.

inus/us, (?) discontinuance c 1380; **-itatum,** the unusual c 1200; **inutilis,** *see* **dies.**

inuxoratus, bachelor 1561, ‡1570.

invadabilis, unfordable c 1125.

invad/iamentum 1198, 1226, **-iatio** 1198, 1254, †**-iamium** 1365, pledging, mortgage; **-iator,** pledger, mortgagor 1205, c 1218; **-io* 1086, 1608, **-o** 1086, c 1362, **inwadio** 1086, **inwagio** (Ir.) 13c., **-emonio** (C.I.) c 1140, **-imonio** (Norm.) a 1125, to pledge, mortgage; ‡**inguadio,** "to custom" 1483; **-io duellum,** to wage judicial combat 1198, 1226; **i. juramentum** 1227; **i. legem,** to wage one's law 1198, 1258.

invado, *see* INVAD; **invasio.**

invagino, to sheathe c 1138.

invagitus, crying of infants c 550.

inval/escentia, growing strength or power c 1265, 1433; **-esco** 14c., 1420, **-ido** 1461, to grow in strength.

inval/iditas 1455, **-idatio** 1438, a 1452, invalidity, invalidating; **-idus,** invalid, void c 1290, 1549; **-itudo,** *for* **-etudo,** infirmity c 980. c 1266, 1461; **-etudinarium,** infirmary a 1275; **-etudinarius** 1300, **-itudinarius** 1426, invalid, sick person; **-eo,** to be invalid, incompetent 12c.; **-esco,** to grow weak c 1250, c 1380; **-ido,** to invalidate, annul 1449.

invallo, to wall in, encompass 13c., 1461.

invari/abilitas, invariability p 1300, 1344; **-abilis,** **invariable* 10c. c 1153, c 1620; unalloyed 9c., 10c.; **-abiliter,** invariably c 1265, a 1452; ‡**-atus,** unvaried 1570.

inva/sio, **invasion,* attack c 1080, 1545; **encroachment,* trespass 1086, c 1343; **i. domi (domus),** (fine for) hamsoken c 1102, c 1160; **-siva** (*pl.*) 1417, **arma -siva** c 1340, 1571, weapons of offence; **-sive,** aggressively a 1452; **-do (terram) super,** to annex, appropriate, from 1086.

*invect/io c730. c1080, 1450, **-iva** (*f. s.*) c1540, invective, scolding; **-ive**, reproachfully c1220, c1155; **-or**, reprover c790; **i. manuum**, one who lays (violent) hands on 1373; **-us**, invected, vairy (her.) p1394, c1595; **-o**, to impose 1234; to invect (her.) p1394.

invectissime, (?) *f.l.* for **invictissime**, 1344.

‡**invegeto**, to animate 1483.

inveneno, to poison a1186.

inveni/abilis, unrelenting 655; **-alis**, unpardonable c1500.

inven/tio, finding c1172, 15c.; thing found c790. 1191, 1302; provision 13c., 1523; maintenance, keep 1407, 1459; invention of relics (eccl.) c1090, c1300; *i. Sancte Crucis (3 May) 1199, c1545; see also* **thesaurus**; **-ibilis**, discoverable c1362; *-tarium 1220, c1555, -tarius c1365, -torium c1290, p1348, -tura c1344, inventory; -ticius (†-tius), foundling c1115, c1325; (*adj.*) fictitious c1212; **-tivus**, inventive c1270, ‡1570; **-tor** c1130, 1332, **-trix** (*f.*) 1301, finder; **-io**, *to provide 1086, 1510; to 'find', provide for, maintain c1353, 1509; to find, pronounce (of a jury) c1115, c1458; to befall c1200, c1470.

†**inverbis**, speechless, or (?) *f.l.* for **imberbis**, 5c.

inveridicus, untruthful c1432.

inveritio, to prove (leg.) c1115.

invernagium, *see* **hibernagium**.

inver/satio, turning out, evacuation (med.) a1250; **-se**, wrong way round 1528; conversely 1610; **-sivus**, imprinted in reverse c1170; **-sor**, perverter c1080; (**pannus**) **de duplici -so** 1235, **de duobus -sis** 1239, reversible (Fr. *à deux envers*); **crux -sa**, cross moliné (her.) p1394, a1446; **-so**, (?) to turn inside out, reverse 1250; to pervert c1115; ‡**-to**, "to warp" 1570.

invertibil/is, unswerving c1270; **-iter**, unswervingly c1270.

investigabilis, inscrutable a615. c1180, 15c.

invest/itio 1111, 1289, †**-io** a1186, †**-itutio** a1118, *-itura a1110, c1444, -ura c1255, c1482, investiture (eccl.); **-itura**, investiture (feudal) c1115, c1540; 'vesture', crop c1170, c1258; **-itor**, one who grants by investiture (eccl.) c1125; **-io**, to occupy, annex c1302; to grant (land or office) by investiture a1120, c1300; *to invest (person with land or office) c1100, 1560; **i. cum** 1583, *i. de 12c., c1500, **i. in** c1257, 1571, to invest with or in; *see also* **per.**

inveterat/io, becoming old p1300; **-us dierum**, ancient of days, old-established c1186, c1250.

invicem, simultaneously 1423; ‡"together" 15c.; **i. pro i.**, mutually c1180; *see also* **ab, ad, contra, in, per, pro.**

invict/oriosus, defeated 10c.; **-e**, invincibly 1530; *see also* **invitatio.**

invid/ia, censure c1000; **-ulus**, full of petty envy 1517; **invis/io**, envy c720; **-orius**, envious c1000; †**envius**, hater 1302.

†**inviduus**, (?) *for* **individuus**, inseparable c1190.

invigil/antia, vigilance c1250; **-anter**, vigi-

lantly c1180; **-o erga**, to bestow pains upon c730.

invin/atio, 'invination', incorporation of blood in eucharistic wine (theol.) c1380; **-o**, to incorporate (blood) in wine (theol.) 1552.

invincibil/is, *invincible c1125, 1461; irrefutable c1125, 1380; **ignorantia i.** 12c., c1343; **-iter**, invincibly, irresistibly c793. p1381, 1461.

†**invinctus**, unfettered (? or *f.l.* for **injunctus**) 1252.

invinculatus, enchained c1450.

inviolo, to lay violent hands on c1400.

invisc/atio, entanglement a1250; *-o, to entrap, beguile c1125, c1430.

inviscer/atus, heartfelt 1433, 1437; **-o**, to inspire, lodge in, fill heart of c1180, 1433.

invis/io, -orius, *see* **INVID**

invitabilis, unavoidable c1200.

invit/atio placitandi, summons (leg.) a1155; *-atorium c1006. c1080, 1440, †**invictatorium** c1295, invitatory, antiphon (eccl.); **-atorius**, antiphonal 9c. c1266; inviting c1125, c1375; **littere -atorie** c1326; **-o ad placita regis**, to summon (leg.) 13c.

invitiatus, unsullied, pure 7c. c1434.

‡**invitrio**, to glaze 1570.

invit/us: ab -o, unwillingly 1298.

invivificabilis, that cannot be restored to life irredeemable 1497.

invoc/ator, invoker c1125, 1610; **-avit (me)**, (anthem for) first Sunday in Lent c1300; **-o ad warentum**, to vouch to warranty 1297.

1 **invol/ubilis**, that cannot be willed 1344; **-untarie**, involuntarily a1250, 14c.

2 **invol/ubilis**, revolving 13c.; **-ubiliter**, with a rolling motion 14c.; **-utio**, envelopment, involvement c790. c1250, c1362; complication 1267, 1345; concealment c1115; **-utorium**, muffler c1362, 15c.; **-utum**, (?) fold, crease c1280; **-utus**, involute (geom.) 1326; involved (in debt) c1375; **-utissimus**, deeply involved c1204; **sub -ucro**, in a murmur 1362; **-ucro**, to wrap up c1180; **-vo**, to vault, roof c1213; **i. animo**, to think over c1280.

‡**invotivus**, "unvowed" 1570.

invultuatio, *envoutement*, witchcraft by injury to images c1115.

inwadio, inwagio, *see* **INVAD**

inwar/a c1160, **-e** a1190, military service within the country.

inwardus, inewardus, inguard/us, watchman 1086; **-a**, (service of) watch and ward 1086.

inwarenno 1259, 1279, **engarano** 1279, to put (land) in status of warren.

inwisa, *see* **juisa.**

iota, jot 7c. c1125, c1536.

‡**ipa**, sop in water 15c., 1483; *cf.* **vipa.**

ipia, *see* **hippia.**

ipidimia, *see* **epidemia.**

ipo- *see* **HYPO**

ippus, *see* **HIPPO**

ips/e, the same 1086, c1400; **-i de**, the people of 1204; **-ima**, *for* **-issima**, a1100; **-o facto**, *see* **FACT**

iraghtus, under-chieftain, *urraigh* (Ir.) 1299.

irascitivus, provocative of anger 1344.

ire (*subst.*), right of way, free movement 1199, 1215; **liberum i. et venire** a 1190; **eo**, to walk c 1370; to work, operate (of a forge) 1296; (of a plough) 1415; (with *inf.*) to set out to 1239; **eo ad**, to resort to (court, mill, *etc.*) 13c., 14c.; **eo ad dominum (cum terra)**, eo quo volo, to resort to (*i.e.* choose) a feudal lord 1086; **eo ad bellum** c 1110, **eo ad guerram** 1293; **eo ad carettam**, to drive a cart 1323; **eo ad carrucam** 1280, 1357, **eo in carruca** c 1220, 1325, to plough; **eo ad judicium** (leg.) 1185, 1313; **eo in manus**, to surrender c 1115; **eo in pastura**, to graze a 1250, 1276; **eo in solutionem**, to accept liability 1203, 1239; **eo iter meum**, to go one's way 1239; **eo pedibus et manibus**, to go on all fours 1211; **eo super pedibus** 1350; **eo post**, to depend on, be subject to c 1330; **eo pro** c 1125, c 1310, **eo propter** c 1245, to fetch; **eo sine die**, to be discharged (leg.) 1196, c 1290; **eo super**, to proceed against, attack c 1150, 1265.

Ir/echius, -ensis, -iscus, see **Irus.**
irenarcha, see **eirenarcha.**
irenmangaria, ironmongery 1490.
†iria, hyssop 15c.
irmina, see **ermina.**
iron/icus 1197, 1380, **-eus** 1254, ironical; **-ice,** ironically c 1198, 1570.
irradi/atio a 1200, 1620, **†-catio** c 1360, irradiation.
irradicabilis, ineradicable 1088.
irradico, to eradicate 1274, 1375.
irrado, to erase *or* indent (her.) p 1394, a 1446.
irras/ibilis, indelible 1344; **-us,** unshaven c 980.
irratio/ unlawful act 1194; a 1408, **-nabilitas** 1268, 15c., **-nalitas** c 1500, unreason, irrationality; **-nalis,** irrational (math.) p 1300.
irreatus, absolution c 1378.
irrecessibiliter, without means to withdraw 1344.
irrecitabilis, unrepeatable c 1250.
irreconcili/abilis, irreconcilable 1610; **-abiliter,** irreconcilably a 1450; **-atus,** unshriven c 1150.
irreconvincibilis, irrefutable 1255.
irrecordatus, forgetful c 1470.
irrect/itudo, injustice c 1306; **-ificabilis,** incorrigible a 1250; **-us,** unjust c 1100; *see also* IRRETT
*irrecuperabil/is, irreparable c 1125, 1519; ***-iter,** irreparably, irretrievably c 800, 9c. c 1070, 1587.
irredi/bilitas, irrevocability c 1283; **-bilis,** past beyond recall c 1283; **-turus,** never to return 1220, p 1330.
irreducibilis, irreducible (math.) 1686.
irreferibiliter, without reference to anything beyond itself p 1300.
irreflex/ibilis, unswerving 9c., 10c.; **-us,** not bent, rigid 1345, 14c.
irreformatus, uncorrected 1501.
irrefracte, without refraction c 1366.
*irrefrag/abilis c 1125, 1570, **-ibilis** c 985, indisputable; ***-abiliter** c 1160, c 1362, **-ibiliter,** **†irrefrangibiliter** 15c., indisputably.
irrefren/abilis, unrestrainable c 1457;

-abiliter, unrestrainably c 1306; **-atus** (?) 9c. c 1290, 15c., **†irrefranatus, irrefrainatus** (**†irreframatus**) 1331, unbridled, inordinate.
†irrefugium, "unhelp" 1483.
irregimen (**†irrigimen**), indiscipline 1472.
irregistratus, unrecorded c 1457.
irregressibilis, not about to return c 1196.
irregul/aritas, irregularity, oddity 1620; ***breach** of canon law, irregular status c 1200, 1531; **-aris,** irregular (phys.) c 1250, 1620; irregular (gram.) 1620; disorderly c 1125, 13c.; secular, not subject to rule (mon.) c 1310, 14c.; disobedient to rule (mon.) 12c., a 1452; irregular, canonically disqualified (eccl.) c 1250, 1537; (*subst.*) disqualified person (eccl.) c 1223, 1456; **-ariter,** contrary to rule (mon.) c 1193, c 1250; irregularly, unlawfully (eccl.) c 1343, c 1430; **-arius,** more irregularly (phys.) 1267; **-atus,** unregulated, disorderly 1327, 1554.
irreiterabilis, non-repeatable 1287.
irrelevantia, irrelevance a 1609.
irreligiositas, irreligion 1062. c 1125, 15c.
irremeaturus, never to return 1347.
irremedi/abilitas, incurability p 1300; ***-abiliter,** incurably c 1190, 15c.; **-atus,** uncured c 1190.
irremiss/ibilis c 1240, c 1250, **-us** c 1240, c 1250, unremitting; 1529, **irremiscibilis** a 1452, unpardonable; **-ibilior,** more unpardonable 8c., 9c.; **-ibiliter,** unpardonably, irrevocably 1200, 1552; **-e,** unremittingly 9c.
irremot/us, unremoved (from office) c 1290; **-e,** closely 7c., 9c. 1200.
irremuner/abilis 1149, **-atus** c 1125, c 1434, unrewarded; **-ans,** leaving unrewarded c 1340.
irrento (inr-), to record as rent 1276.
irrepar/atio 1336, **†irrepatio** 1528, disrepair; **-abilitas,** irreparability c 1290; **-abiliter,** irreparably 12c., c 1327; **-atus,** unrepaired 1324, 1417.
irrepleg/iabilis 1285, 15c., **-ibilis** 1588, not bailable, not subject to replevin; **-iabiliter,** without replevin c 1285, c 1290; **-iandus,** not to be replevied (Sc) 1276; **-iatus,** not replevied (Sc.) 1289.
irreprehensibil/itas, blamelessness c 1283; ***-iter,** blamelessly c 1000, c 1040. c 1100, 15c.
irrepressibilis, irrepressible c 1250.
irrep/ticius, surreptitious 1609; **†-io,** creeping in c 1200.
irrepugn/antia, consistency, absence of contradiction 1344; **-anter,** without contradiction 1344.
irrequiete, restlessly 1620.
irrequisitus, ***unsought** 1223, 15c.; ***unconsulted** c 1195, 1437; unconsidered c 1257.
irresist/ibilis, irresistible c 1595; **-abiliter,** irresistibly 1344.
*irrestaurabil/is, irreparable 1097, 15c.; ***-iter,** irreparably c 1250, 15c.
irresuscibiliter, beyond reviving 1344.
irretit/io 10c. 1284, 1439, **-us** c 1109, entanglement; *cf.* IRRETT
irretornabilis, non-returnable (of writs) 1301, 1327.

*irrett/itus (irrect-) 1255, c 1440, **-atus** p 1330, **irrit/itus** 1266, 1497, **-atus** 1507, charged, accused; *cf.* IRRECT, IRRETIT

irrevelatus, unrevealed c 1190.

irreverberat/us, direct, not reflected c 1125, a 1350; **-is oculis**, with unaverted gaze c 1150, 14c.; **-o fronte** c 1302; **-e**, by direct vision c 1240.

irrever/enter, irreverently c 790; ‡**-eor**, "to unworship" 15c.

irrevers/ibiliter, irreversibly c 860, 1344; **-urus**, never to return 1264.

irrevocatus, unrevoked (leg.) c 1335.

irrigesco, to become rigid c 1200, 1525.

irrigimen, *see* **irregimen**.

irrig/uum c 1125, 1421, †**-ium** c 1435, **-uitas** 1608, irrigation (esp. fig.).

†**irrio**, (?) *for* **irruo**, to rush into c 550.

irrisori/um, gibe c 1255; **-e**, mockingly c 700. c 1200, c 1218.

‡**irristiticus**, "martinet" (? hammer-pond) 1483.

irrit-, *see also* IRRETT

irrit/atio, invalidation 1341, 1451; ***-o** c 1185, 1559, †**irruo** c 1290, to invalidate, make void (leg.).

irritatorius, provocative 1378.

irrog/atum, question c 1115; **-o**, to impute 14c.

irroratio, bewewing, sprinkling 1136, 1622.

*irrotul/atio (inr-) 1215, 1421, ***-amentum** c 1270, 1583, enrolment, entering on a roll; **-arius**, enroller, registrar 1338; ***-o** 1182, 1595, **irrollo** c 1220, c 1350, to enrol, enter on a roll or register.

irruo, *see* **irrio; irritatio**.

irrupatio, breaking c 1358.

Ir/us c 1130, **-ensis** a 1142, **-echius** 1263, **-iscus** 1269, Irish.

isagog/e a 805. c 1160, 1528, **-icum** c 1443, **-ium** c 1500, introduction.

ischia (*pl.*), hips: **sci/a** (*f. s.*) hip c 1200, a 1250; **-asis** c 1200, ‡c 1440, **ciasis** (†**tiasis**) c 1200, **-atica** a 1250, ‡ 1483, **gutta s.** 1398, sciatica; **-aticus**, sciatic c 1210, 1267.

ischuria, stoppage of urine (med.): **suria** a 1250.

isculus, (?) *for* σκώληξ, earth-worm a 1250, ‡14c.

isic-, *see* **esicius**.

Islandensis 1169, **Illandicus** a 1265, Icelandic.

Ismaelit/a a 1142, **-icus** 1184, Saracen.

iso/cheles, isosceles (geom.) 13c., c 1360; **-chronus**, of equal duration 1686; **-perimeter**, of equal perimeter 1233, c 1360; **-pleurum**, equilateral triangle a 1150; †**hysoplexus**, (?) cuboid a 1250.

isophagus, *see* **esophagus**.

isopus, *see* **hyssopus**.

Israel/, lapis c 1411, **l. de I.** 1388, **l. -itarum** 15c., **l. -iticus** 1383, engraved gem, cameo; **-iticus**, made in the form of a cameo 1383.

†**issa** (*pl.*), rising (of tide) 815.

issaccum 1255, 1308, **eisacum** 1359, **yssaquum** 1289, **hichacum** 1313, petty custom on export of wine (G.).

isserellum, (?) hissing, whistling (*cf.* O.F. *hisser*) c 1310.

istoria, *see* **historia**.

*ita quod, on condition that c 1214, c 1520; **ita . . . sicut**, as . . . as c 1332, c 1400; **ita tenus**, thus far c 1400; **itaque**, *for* **ita**, 1303.

iter, right of way 1279; waterway 1157; **i. altum** 1271, **i. regale** 1276, c 1300, king's highway; **itiner**, *for* **i.**, 810; **iter** 1198, c 1455, **itiner/antia** 1276, ***-atio** 1218, c 1400, eyre, circuit of judges; **i. Camerarie** (Sc.) 1390, 1479; **i. foreste** 1255, 1334; **i. justitiarie** (Sc.) 1361, 1449; **expense -ales**, travelling expenses 1470; **-arium**, journey, route 1274, c 1362; **-arius**, traveller c 1200; **-atio exercitus**, service of fyrd c 1102; **-ans**, (*subst.*) vagrant, tramp 1201, 1236; **justitiarius -ans**, justice in eyre 1196, c 1414; **-o**, *for* **-or**, to travel c 1000. c 1172, c 1540; to go on eyre c 1205, c 1414; 1237, **-or** 1226, to work, function (of machinery); *cf.* **eyrum**, ERR; *see also* **baillivus, forestarius, forgia**.

iter/ate 815, ***-o** c 1180, 1461, again, repeatedly.

†**itnum**, (?) sea c 550.

†**itura**, rampart walk, alure 1250.

iturio, to wish to travel c 1520.

ivern-, *see* HIBERN

iv/orium, -o, *see* **eburninus**.

ivus, ivyus, *see* **ifus**.

J

(See also HI-, HY-, I)

‡**jab/ora** 1652, ‡**-rot** 14c., mandrake (bot.).

jabularius, *see* 2 **gabella**.

jacea, knapweed *or* heart's-ease (bot.) a 1250, 1634; **j. nigra**, "matfellon", black knapweed a 1250, ‡14c.

jac/ens, couchant (her.) p 1394; **res j.**, inanimate object c 1110; **-eo**, to lie (in), lodge (at) 1221, c 1362; to lie off (of a ship) 1413; ***to lie in**, appertain to (of land) 1082, 1560; to lie, be valid (of appeal, assise or essoin) 1201, 1337; to risk (*trans.*) 1274; **j. ad firmam**, to be farmed 1086; **j. pro, to** be assessed as c 1235, 1326; **j. pro warecta** 1411, **j. ad warectam** 1365, to lie fallow.

jacia, *see* 1 **chacea**.

jacint-, *see* **hyacinthus**.

jacobea, ragwort (bot.) 1632.

Jacob/ita, Jacobite (heretic) c 1343; c 1250, 1413, **-inus** c 1250, p 1330, **-itanus** 1252, Jacobite (friar); **-eus**, Jacobite (supporter of Stuarts) c 1700; **-io**, play the role of Jacob, deceive c 1218.

jact/atio, casting (of metals) 1329, 1410; puddling (of clay in tile-making) 1370, 1385;

-abilis, throwable c 1000. 1336; **-amen,** collapse 1351; †**-amen fundi,** (?) foundation 12c.; **-antia arene** c 1436, **-io maris** 1275, **-us maris** 1315, silting; **-io de recto,** procedure on writ of right c 1290; **-ura,** 'jetty', overhang (arch.) 1335 (*cf.* **geteya**); **j. maris,** jetsam c 1085, c 1170; **-urale,** counter (for reckoning) 1494;

-us a 1150, 1214, **jectus** 1235, **gessus** 1290, **gescia** 1346, jess (falc.); **j. sagitte,** bowshot (measure of distance) 1488; **-ator murorum,** pargeter 1390; **-itor,** tosser (of grain) 1335; **-o,** to cast (falc.) 1250, 1333; to cast lots for 1204; to cast (metal) 1222, c 1376; to puddle (clay) 1370; **j. fundamentum,** to lay foundation 13c.; **j. summam** 1235, a 1410, **j. valorem** 1242, 1262, to cast an account.

jact/itatio matrimonii, jactitation of marriage (leg.) 1684; **-abunde,** boastfully c 1220; **-atrix,** boaster (*f.*) c 1180, 1252; **-ito** c 1190, 1684, **-or** (*dep.*) c 1440, to boast.

1 †**jaculum,** (?) ferry (W.) 12c.

2 **jacul/um,** cross-bow bolt 1274; **-us,** *for* **-um,** dart c 1408; **-o,** to ejaculate, utter c 730.

jagg/a, jag, slash (in clothes) a 1446; **-o** (**tunicam**), to slash a 1446.

jaguntius, *see* **hyacinthus.**

jahunum, *see* **jampnum.**

jaia, jay (bird) 1544.

jaiola, *see* GAOL

jakkum, 'jack', sleeveless tunic 1451, 1466.

jalnetum, *see* **jampnum.**

jalo/, -nata, *see* **galo.**

jamb-, *see* **gamba; iambus.**

jam/dictus, already mentioned c 1080, 1339; **-tarde,** of late 1404, 15c.

jampn/um, -a, -us 1268, 1612, (?) †**gamnum** 1302, **jao** 1251, 1298, **javo** (Cornwall) 1345, **jawo** (Cornwall) 1290, **geo** c 1250, **javunum** 1389, **jahunum** a 1245, **jaunum** (? **jannum**) 1207, 1333, (?) **jauncum** 1291, (?) **jancium** 1305, (?) **jancum** 1349, (?) **ganga** 13c., gorse, furze; **jaonetum** 1210, **jaoneum** 1086, **jaunetum** (†**jannetum**) c 1180, **jalnetum** 1230, 1242, **galnetum** 1204, 1334, **calnetum** 1334, **janettum** 1365, furze-brake; *cf.* GENEST

‡**jancia,** colt's-foot *or* burdock (bot.) 14c.

janettarius, *see* **jonetum.**

janitarius, *see* 1 **geneta.**

jan/itor supernus, St. Peter c 1090; **-itator** 1242, **-uarius** c 1180, 15c., *for* **-itor,** door-keeper; **in -uis,** on the point of arrival c 1200, 1586.

jant-, *see also* **jentaculum.**

jan/ta, -yta, *see* **ganta; gantus;** WANT

Januinus, Genoese coin 1292.

jaola, *see* GAOL

jar-, *see also* GARDIN; **garillum; garterium.**

jarr/a, -um 1245, 1421, **jarda** c 1305, jar.

†**jasconius,** (?) whale c 1325.

jasp/is, *for* **iaspis,** jasper c 1200, 1451; **-erinus** 1415, **-ertinus** 1432, jasper-like.

‡**jassa,** persicaria (bot.) 1652.

jaun-, jav-, jawo, *see* **jampnum.**

jaunus, yellow 1286.

jeburus, *see* **geburus.**

jectus, *see* **jactatio.**

jehenn/a, -alis, *see* GEHENN

jejun/ium 1301, **j. quadragesimale** 11c., 1517, Lent; **j. quatuor temporum,** ember day a 1142, 12c.; **j. triduanum** c 1125, 1537; **caput -ii,** Ash Wednesday c 1150, c 1565; *see also* FRACT, INFRACT, SOLU; **-abilis,** observable as a fast c 1464; **-ialis,** Lenten c 1220; **-um** (†**-ium**), lower intestine c 1210, a 1250; ***-o** 10c. c 1080, c 1535, †**-io** 14c., †**jeuno** 1250, to fast; **-o,** to observe as a fast-day c 1125, 1428.

jenecta, *see* GENEST

jenicia, *see* **genica.**

jent/aculum, collation provided by new member of guild 1360, 15c.; **jantaculum** c 1283, 1393, **janctaculum** 1427, **gantaculum** c 1283, c 1300, **gentaculum** 1249, 1474, *for* **-aculum,** breakfast; **-or** 1311, 1336, **janto** 1467, **gento** c 1112, 1335, *for* **-o,** to breakfast.

jenu, *see* **genu.**

jer-, *see also* **hier-**

jerc/a, -ia, -us, *see* **gercia.**

jesina, *see* **gisina.**

Jess/e 1245, c 1320, **radix J.** 1236, **historia -ea** c 1400, tree of Jesse.

Jesu, St. Patrick's staff c 1193; (?) *cf.* **gaesum.**

Jesuit/a, follower of Jesus c 1500; Jesuit 1621, 1660; **-icus,** Jesuitical 1646; **-ismus,** Jesuitry 1646.

jettea, *see* **geteya.**

jeuno, *see* JEJUN

jeutum, *see* 2 **jus.**

Jewdaismus, *see* **Judaismus.**

jingeber, *see* **zinziber.**

Joannes, *see* JOHANN

jocale, *see* **jocus.**

Jocapatita, *see* **Jotapatita.**

*****jocund/itas** (*for* **jucund-**) c 1090, 1461, **joconditas** c 1200, **-um** 14c., delight; **focus -itatis,** *feu de joie,* bonfire 1461; **-iolum,** jewel 1185, 1188; ***-us** c 1090, 1461, **-abilis** a 1145, delightful, gay; **-o,** to delight, please c 1204; 5c. 1313, **-or** c 1070, a 1350, to be delighted, rejoice; to jest c 1220.

joc/us, play, dramatic scene 1441; **j. partitus** c 1258, †**locus p.** c 1290, *jeu parti,* jeopardy (leg.); **j. scaccorum,** set of chessmen 12c.; ***-ale** 1204, 1552, **joellum** 1223, **-osum** c 1436; **-ulum** 1480, **-ulare** c 1180, 15c., jewel, precious object; plaything c 1350; **-amen,** game, diversion c 1130; ‡1483, **-ulare** 1620, juggling, conjuring trick; **-ularia** (*f. s.*) 1168, **-ulatio** 1350, 1534, jesting, entertainment; **-ositas,** humour c 1620; **-osus,** gorgeous 13c.; **-ulabundus** c 1488, **-ulatorius** c 1080, 1330, sportive, entertaining; **-ista** c 685. ‡1483, ***-ulator** c 1000, 1086, 1461, **jugulator** 1310, 1540, **-ulatrix** (*f.*) 1086, 1385, †**jugulatrix** (*f.*) 15c., jester, entertainer, *jongleur;* **-ulator organorum,** organist 1530; **-o** c 1330, a 1408, **-ulor** 1448, ‡1483, to play, provide entertainment; **-or,** to rejoice 14c., c 1402; to move convulsively c 1125; to joust c 1140, c 1250; to narrate c 1160.

jod 1564, **joz** c 1200, Hebrew letter *yod.*

joellum, *see* JOC

Johann/ita, adherent of John XXII c 1343; **-itius**, Honein's *Isagoge* (med.) c 1180;
Joannes, coin, *écu d'or* 1359.
jolivo, to sport, wanton (O.F. *joliver*) 1223.
jomella, *see* **gemelle**.
joncaria, *see* 2 **juncaria**.
jondericia, *see* GENDER
jonetum 1316, **pirum janettarium** 1252, 'jenneting', early pear.
‡**jopp/us**, "fool" c 1440; ‡**-eria**, "foolery" c 1440.
jorn-, *see* DIURN
josum, *see* **jusum**.
jota, 'joute', pot-herb a 1250.
Jotapatita (†**Jocapatita**), follower of Josephus at Jotapata 12c.
Jov/ialis, jovial, under the influence of Jupiter (astr.) a 1200, c 1433; **-is**, *see* **dies**; *cf.* **Juppiter**.
Jovinianus, follower of the heretic Jovinian c 1250.
joynatio, *see* JUNCT
joz, *see* **jod**.
jub/ileus c 1080, c 1400, **-eleus** c 1070, **-leus** 1451, **annus -ileus** c 793. c 1190, c 1476, a. **-eleus** c 1397, jubilee year; **-eleus** 1474, 1535, **-ileum** 1562, special indulgence (eccl.); **-ilatus**, having attained a jubilee 1586; **-ilenarius**, "stager" (eccl.) 1519.
jubil/um 12c., c 1325, **-us** 9c. c 1070, a 1186, **-amen** 13c., †**-eum** 1274, song of joy, hymn of praise; **-um** c 1150, c 1470, **-us** 1382, c 1450, joy; **ignis -i**, bonfire c 1608; **-atio**, rejoicing c 1090, c 1450; **-o** c 1185, c 1445, **jubelo** 1427, to rejoice, praise.
‡**jubosus**, crested 1483.
juchio, *see* JUNC
jucund-, *see* JOCUND
Jud/aismus, Judaism c 1080, c 1250; 1232, 1266, **-eismus** 1268, 1283, Jewish community; 1236, c 1400, **Jewdaismus** 1279, indebtedness to Jews; *c 1183, 1449, **-aismum** 1274, **-aissimus** c 1350, **-aeria** 1221, Jewry, Jewish quarter; **-aismus Parvus** (Oxford) 1330, c 1450; **J. Vetus** (London) 1475, a 1564; **-aice**, like a Jew c 1430; **-aicus**, *see* **herba, lapis**; **-eus legalis**, recognized member of Jewish community 1201, 1274; **liber -eorum**, (?) Pentateuch 1201; **-aizatio**, observance of Jewish rites 12c.; **-aizo** (bibl.) c 1080, a 1452, **-eizo** c 1263, **-izo** 12c., c 1340, to Judaize, observe Jewish rites; to practise usury 1275.
Judas/ 1377, 1452, **-ium** 1310, 'Judas', paschal taper.
judex, doomsman, law-man 1086, 1216; doomster (Sc.) c 1198, c 1370, (I. of Man) 1418; **j. a quo**, judge appealed from 1684; **j. ad quem** 1684, **j. appellationis** c 1325, 1684, judge appealed to; **j. civitatis** 1086; **j. corone**, coroner c 1397; **j. fiscalis**, king's judge c 1115, 12c.; **j. errans, deambulatorius, perambulans, perlustrans**, justice in eyre c 1178; *see also* **delegatus, minutus, ordinarius; J. Summus**, God 1559; **dies Judic/is**, Doomsday 1252; **-es** (*pl.*), Book of Judges (bibl.) 1267, c 1396;
  judic/ium, jurisdiction, mode of trial

1086, c 1250; law, statute c 1110, c 1115; body of doomsmen c 1115; **j. habeo**, to undergo judgement 1221, 1269; *see also* **stare**; *ad j. de, judgement to be given against 1202, 1313; **super j.**, without judgement being given 1217; **j. parium**, judgement by equals 1215, c 1250; **j. sanguinis**, (right of delivering) death-sentence 12c., c 1390; **-ium** 1086, c 1185, **j. legis** c 1115, **j. aque** c 1110, 1221, **j. ferri** 1080, c 1436, **j. ignis** c 1200, 1219, **j. Dei** 1086, c 1185, **j. divinum** c 1102, **j. triplex** c 1102, c 1185, judicial ordeal; ordeal iron c 1103, c 1115; 8c. 1252, **j. extremum** c 1340, 1461, **j. finale** c 1400, c 1443, **j. generale** c 1334, c 1400, **j. districtum** c 1340, 1419, **j. novissimum** c 1245, **j. supremum** c 1220, **j. tremendum** 1232, **j. ultimum, j. universale** c 1343, Last Judgement; *dies -ii, Doomsday 671. c 1090, 1549; **-ium**, picture of Last Judgement 1250; prognostication (astr.) a 1150, a 1292; **j. astrorum** c 1440, **j. stellarum** c 1400.
  †**-alis** (*for* **-ialis**) c 1340, †**-arius** (*for* **-iarius**) c 1272, c 1340, judicial; **-amentum** 1086, 1383, **-atura** 1289, 1426, judgement, verdict; **-ativus**, exercising faculty of judgement a 1347, c 1375; decisive, critical 13c.; 1267, **-iarius** c 1345, c 1553, judicial (astr.); **-ator**, doomsman, law-man 1130, 1295; (Cheshire) 1289, a 1564; (C.I.) 1309; **-atoria**, law-court 1517; **-atorium** c 1275, c 1360, **-iale** a 1408, faculty or principle of judgement; **-iale**, right or means of enforcing judgement c 1290, 1388; **-ialis**, concerned with judgement c 730; concerned with ordeal c 1102, c 1115; subject to judicial punishment a 1290; **dies -ialis**, law-day (G.) 1305; *see also* **breve**; *-ialiter judicially, by judgement 1221, 1686; †**-iarius**, judge c 1300; *see also* **fovea, liber**; **-atum secundum**, (?) judgement on appeal (G.) 1315; **-ans**, judge c 1343, c 1444; †**-io**, *for* **-o**, to judge c 1285, 1331; **-o**, to adjudge, award c 1123; to prognosticate (astr.) 1267, a 1292; (with *inf.*) to decide 7c., 9c. c 1265; **j. ad**, to condemn to 1086, c 1272; **j. duellum**, to adjudge a duel 13c.; *cf.* JUIS
jug/alis, -ata, -er, *see* 1 **jugum**.
†**jugeria**, jurisdiction (G.) 1199; *cf.* **vigeria** (*s.v.* **vicaria**).
jug/itatio, (?) continuance c 1536; †**jungiter**, *for* **-iter**, perpetually c 1283.
jugul/a c 550, **-iettum** 1242, neck; ‡**-amen, -amentum**, strangling 1483; **-ator**, murderer c 1180, c 1422; **-atrix**, murderous (*f.*) 1648; **-o**, to 'yoke' (pigs) 1523; *see also* JOC
1 **jug/um**, measure of land, quarter of 'sulung' (Kent) 1086, 1425; tenth of 'wend' (Suss.) c 1283; **-ata, -atum** 1193, 13c., **-er** c 1178, **-era** 839, measure of land; **-alis**, wife c 1257; **-o**, (?) to 'yoke' (in some sense connected with ploughing) 13c.; **-o** (**collum**), to bow, submit (fig.) c 1562.
2 **jugum**, letter *yogh* (ȝ) 1413.
juis/a 1166, 1185, **-ium** 1168, ordeal; right of punishment 1285; 1296, **juwis/a** (†**inwis-**)

1279, **-um** 1275, pillory (O.F. *juise*); *cf.*
JUDIC
jujub/a, jujube (fruit) a 1250, 1622; **syrupus**
-inus a 1250.
jul/ap, -ab, (?) **-em,** julep a 1250.
†**juliafera,** "young hind" 15c.
***jument/um** 1221, 1364, **-a** 1221, c 1300,
mare; prostitute 1241; †**-us,** (?) *for* juven-
cus, c 1170; **-aria** (*pl.*), plough-teams c 1308;
-arius, groom 1171; **caro -ina,** mare's
flesh 1245, a 1446; **lac -inum** a 1250;
-o, to chair, carry in triumph a 1165.
jumnisum, *see* zyma.
1 **juncaria,** deceit (Fr. *joncherie*) 1370.
2 **junc/aria** (junct-) c 1180, 1580, **joncaria**
1200, **junchera** 1243, 1282, **juncherium**
1211, **junkeria** 1327, **jungeria** 1284,
junchetum 1210, **jungetum** c 1130, †**-tium**
1315, bed or field of rushes; **-ellus,**
dwarf rush 1634; ‡**-ata,** junket, "curd made
in rushes" 15c.; **-o,** reed-bunting (σχοινίλος),
1544; **-osus,** rushy 1325; **junchura,** strewing with rushes c 1250; **-o** c 1325, **junchio**
1222, †**juchio** 1245, to strew with rushes.
junct/ura c 1188, 1383, **-a** 1199, joint (of body);
joint, fastening (carpentry or metal-work)
c 1170, 1519; combined contract (leg.)
c 1258, 1312; joint tenancy 1438; wife's
jointure 1544, 1629; **-alis,** pertaining to
joints (med.) a 1250; **-e** 11c., **-im** 1558,
jointly; **-or** 1253 1553, **-arius** 1482, joiner;
j. talliarum, Exchequer official 1586;
joynatio, joinery 1419; **-us,** *for* adjunctus,
brought forward from lower age-group
1283; **carruca -a,** plough with team 1251,
1325; **ferrum -um,** welded iron 1352;
jung/o, to make by joinery 1313, 1551;
to enjoin c 1180; **j. duellum,** to fight a
duel a 1285; **j. tallias,** to match stocks
with foils 1355, 1526; **-or,** to be possessed
of plough teams 1275.
jungiber, *see* zinziber.
jungiter, *see* jugitatio.
junior, son or descendant 9c., 11c.; subordinate c 1115; **aldremannus j.** c 1115;
cf. JUVEN
juniperinum oleum, oil of juniper a 1250.
Juno, lower air c 1200.
*****jup/a** c 1180, 1420, †**nipa** 1400, **-ellium**
1332, **-ellum** c 1320, 1340, **-o** 1398, 1454,
gipponus 1382, tunic, gown, or skirt (Fr.
jupon); (?) bag 1418.
Juppiter, upper air c 1200; tin (alch.) c 1215,
‡1652; **dies Jovis,** *see* dies.
jura, conspiracy (G.) 1298.
*****jur/amentum** c 1080, c 1540, **-amen** c 950.
c 1562, *****-atio** c 943, 1080, c 1414, oath,
swearing; *****j. corporale,** corporal oath 1218,
1684; *****-ata** 1166, c 1443, **-ea** (Norm.) 1180,
-atio 1203, jury, body of jurors; **j. patrie,**
jury of the neighbourhood c 1185, 1394; **j.
de sociis in curia** 1291; **j. de utrum** 1309,
1324; **-andus,** person admitted to swear
c 1440; *****-ator** 1130, 1599, **-atus** c 1185,
1495, **-ans** c 1185, juror, juryman; **-atio,**
body of jurats (C.I.) c 1226; **-ator** (G.) 1281,
-atus 1206, 1565, jurat, municipal officer;
j. marisci (Romney) 1298; **-atus,** vassal,
liege-man a 1140, 1427; betrothed c 1298;
j. ad arma, one sworn to bear arms 1242,

1261; **-atissimus,** most solemnly sworn
c 1250; **-atorie,** by oath 1344, c 1430; **-o,** to
put to the oath 1284; **j. ad,** to swear to uphold c 1490, c 1516; **j. ad** (with *gerundive*)
c 1400, c 1420; *****j. ad Evangelia** 1273,
c 1530, **j. Evangeliis** c 1420, **j. super
Evangelia** 1254, c 1470; **j. ad. assisam,**
to swear in frankpledge c 1466; **j. assisam**
1167; **j. corporaliter,** to swear a corporal
oath c 1320, c 1407; **j. fidelitatem** 1247,
j. pro fidelitate c 1250, to swear fealty;
*****j. in animam cujusdam** 1175, c 1453.
jurdanus, 'jordan', pot, esp. chamber-pot
1385, ‡15c.
Jurgianus, *see* Georgianus.
juri-, *see also* jus (1 & 2).
jurinale, *see* DIURN
jurisdic/tio, area of jurisdiction c 1306, 1549;
juredictio, *for* **-tio,** jurisdiction p 1275,
1282; *see also* de; **-tio alta et bassa** (G.)
1313; **j. ordinaria** (eccl.) 1259, 1420;
j. peculiaris (eccl.) 1535, 1684; **-tionalia**
(*pl.*), matters belonging to a particular
jurisdiction 1333; **-tionalis,** jurisdictional
c 1376, c 1620; **-tionaliter,** with respect to
jurisdiction 1427; **-iarius,** judicial c 1343;
juridic/e c 1130, 1610, **juritice** c 1390, by
rights, lawfully; **-us,** lawful c 1470; **dies j.,**
lawful day for business c 1290, c 1593; **-ens,**
(?) judge 1466.
jurn-, *see* DIURN
juro, *see* juramentum.
1 **jus,** *****right, due, privilege 692, 11c. 1070,
1461; *****property to which one has a right
c 1185, c 1492; *****de jure** c 1180, c 1493,
ex jure 1339, **ipso jure** 13c., 1299, by rights,
lawfully; *****jus et clamium** 1227, 1471;
habeo j. ad, to have a right to 1246, a 1347;
see also stare; **j. armorum,** military law
1347; *****j. canonicum** c 1195, c 1534, **j.
canon** 1241, **j. canonum** c 1195, **j. poli**
c 1180, 1378, **j. papale** 1252, c 1430, **j.
pontificium** 1508, 1549, canon law,
ecclesiastical law; **j. ecclesiasticum,** frank-
almoign 8c.; 13c., **jura** (*pl.*) ecclesiastica
1267, 1313, **jura ecclesie** 1298, last rites,
absolution; **j. Cesareum,** civil law 1508;
j. utrumque, canon and civil law c 1343,
c 1490; **j. coli,** distaff right 13c.; *****j. commune,** common law (of realm or church)
1237, 1586; **j. consuetudinarium** c 1204,
1549; **j. fori,** secular law 2c., c 1334;
j. nativitatis 1200, **j. sanguinis** 1293,
birth-right; **j. naturale** c 1258, **j. nature**
c 1340, natural law; **j. parochiale** c 1200,
1287; **j. positivum** c 1200, a 1520; **j.
publicum** c 1115; **j. regni** c 1185, c 1514,
j. terrenum c 1380; **j. scriptum,** Roman
law 1238; **j. vidue,** widow-right 1366;
†**jur/igenius,** (?) derived from law or right
(phil.) 1427; **-isclamium,** claim of right
1543; **-is?** discretus c 1200, **-isperitus** 1445,
c 1452, **-ista** 1267, c 1595, jurist; **-ipareo,**
to obey the law 1218, 1362.
2 **jus/,** juice, fluid c 1110, ‡14c.; ‡**j. viride** 15c.,
(?) **jeutum** 1296, verjuice; **-cellatus,** made
into broth a 1250; †**jurilentum,** (?) pottage
c 1300.
jusanus, *see* jusum.
jusquiam- *see* enchymatizo; hyoscyamus.

juss/itio, *for* **-io,** command 13c.; **-or,** commander c 1000.

1 justa, *see* **gista.**

2 *just/a (†**vista**) a 1090, c 1450, **gusta** 13c., **-ia** 1255, **-itia** a 1090, 1260, **-ata** c 1180, c 1266, **gustata** 1233, 1358, 'just', flagon, just (lawful) allowance of ale (mon.).

3 just/a, joust, tourney a 1142, 1419; **-o,** to joust 1249, 1319; *see also* **juxta.**

justific/atio, judgement, doing justice, punishment c 1115, p 1382; correction, setting right 1451; establishing a claim c 1306, 1334; **-abilis,** lawful, qualified (G.) 1254; law-abiding 1408; justiciable, cognizable 1361; **-ator,** judge a 1100, c 1178; advocate c 1400; **-atorius,** justificatory c 1390, 1684; **-o,** *to justify (theol.) a 1090, c 1534; to justify (an act, *etc.*) a 1253, c 1470; to justify, vindicate (a person) a 1430, 15c.; to bring to justice, punish 1221, 1489; to compel judicially c 1165, 1209; to correct (measures) c 1115; **j. ad mortem,** to condemn 1461; **j. jus,** to establish a right c 1453; **j. me,** to justify, clear, oneself 1206, 1340.

justinum, sort of electuary 1241, a 1250.

1 justiti/a, right or jurisdiction c 1072, 1461; justice, sentence, punishment 1130, 1461; *c 1072, c 1190, †**-us** 1253, justice, judge; **j. capitalis** 1141, 15c., **j. prima** c 1200, chief justice; **j. errans,** justice in eyre c 1178, c 1212; **j. alta** 1279, 1309, **j. magna** 1283, **j. bassa** 1279, 1309, **j. parva** 1285, forms of jurisdiction (G.); **j. canonica** (eccl.) c 1156; **j. comitatus** 1156, 1167; **j. communis** 1276, 1304; **j. corporalis, j. de corpore,** corporal punishment 1086; **j. major** c 1115; **j. mortis et membrorum** a 1180, 1189; **j. sanguinis** (G.) 1242, 1254; **j. tota,** full court (Norm.) c 1130; **-abilis** c 1115, 15c., **justiziabilis** (C.I.) 1274, **-alis** c 1192, 1209, justiciable, subject to jurisdiction; **-alis,** (*subst.*) vassal 1152; **-aliter,** judicially, as a court 1341; **-aria,** court of law 13c., c 1283; (?) trial *or* writ 1278; *office of judge or justiciar c 1192, **j. prima,** office of chief justice (Sc.) 1358; *see also* **clericus;** **-arius,** (*adj.*) judicial c 1188; righteous 1461; (*subst.*) head of a frankpledge c 1115; *1100, 1583, **gustitiarius** 1199, **-archa** c 1193, justiciar, justice, judge; ***j. Anglie** c 1192, 1324; **j. Hibernie** 1199, 1558; ***j. capitalis** a 1120, 1586; **j. ad assisas** c 1258, 1586; ***j. de banco** 1201, c 1500, **j. in banco** 1210, c 1250; **j. foreste** 1232, 1285; ***j. itinerans** 1196, c 1414 **j. itineris** c 1320, **j. errans** c 1178, c 1220, **j.**

deambulatorius c 1178, justice in eyre; **j. Judeorum** 1220, c 1250, **j. Judeismi** c 1283; **j. major** c 1135; **j. minor,** puisne judge 1263; **j. laboratorum** 1391, **j. operariorum** 1355, **j. de operariis** 1350, 1352, **j. super operarios** 1351; **j. pacis** 1387, 1586, **j. ad pacem** c 1430, c 1448; **j. pavilonis** (at St. Giles' Fair, Winchester) 1327; **j. ad placita communia** 1252; **j. ad p. corone** c 1290; **j. ad p. omnia** 1225; **j. sewerarum** c 1448; **-atio** 1293, **-atus** (G.) 1277, 1501, jurisdiction; **-atus altus et bassus** (G.) 1313; †**-um,** (?) fine a 1100; **-es,** name of a writ 1255, 1287; **-o,** to bring to justice, punish 1200, 1460; to compel judicially, distrain 1164, 15c.; to justify (an act) c 1397; **j. me,** to submit to justice 1419.

2 justitia, *see* **2 justa.**

justo, *see* **3 justa.**

‡**justorium,** clapper of mill 15c.

just/us: -i (*pl.*), the just (theol.) c 1300, c 1536.

jus/um c 1134, c 1188, **josum** c 1000, *for* **deorsum,** down; **-anus,** lower 15c.; *cf.* **susanus.**

‡**jutto,** to jut, project 15c.

Jut/us, -a c 730. c 1125, c 1250, **Giotus** a 1100, Jute.

***juv/amen** a 1100, 1440, **-amentum** a 1250, c 1470, help; **j. arcis,** burhbote 956; **j. expeditionis,** service of fyrd 956; **j. pontis,** brigbote 956; **-antia,** helpfulness a 1376; **-ativus,** helpful, encouraging c 1246, 1622; **-o,** to repair 1336.

juvamin', *see* **INNAM**

juven/cellus, young man c 1220; bull calf 1230; **-cula,** *girl c 1070, c 1415; *heifer 1265, 1419; **juvincus,** *for* **-cus,** bullock 1201; **-culus,** fallow deer fawn 1494; **vene -iles,** veins behind ears a 1250; **-ta,** (?) council of warriors 1150; **-tus** (*coll.*), first-fruits of young animals c 1102; ‡**-eo** 1483, **-esco** 7c. c 1160, c 1180, to be young; **-esco** 1241, **-or** 12c., to act childishly; *cf.* **junior.**

†**juvera,** (?) mazer a 1564.

juwis/a, -um, *see* **juisa.**

juxta, *according to 7c., 8c. c 1080, c 1545; **j. aliquid,** to some extent c 1180; **j. quod** 7c., 10c. 12c., 1281, **j. id quod** 1389, according as; **j. posse** 1414, **j. possibilitatem** c 1178, 15c., as far as possible; **j. ratam,** in proportion 1340, 1567; **j. valorem** 1430; **j. vim** c 1502, **j. vires** 1377; **justa,** *for* **j.,** near c 1110.

juxtapo/sitio, juxtaposition p 1300, 1648; **-no,** to juxtapose c 1360, c 1380.

K

(*See also* C, Ch)

kaabulus, *see* **cabula.**

‡**kachimia, kakimia,** imperfect metal (alch.) 1652.

kadellus, *see* **kidellus.**

kaernia, *see* **KERN**

kaeta, *see* **excidamentum.**

kaira, *see* **1 carra.**

kakia, *see* **cacodemon.**

kaladrius, *see* **charadrius.**

kalandra, *see* **calendris; chalendra.**

kaldellum, *see* **CALD**

kalend/a (calend-) (*s.*) c 1330, †**kalon** 1252 calend; **-e** (*pl.*), fraternity 1440; **-are** c 1380, 1419, **-arium** 1267, 1519, **-inarium**

K

c 1430, calendar; **mensis -aris,** calendar month c 1411, 1457; **-arium,** rental c 1220; table of contents c 1258; **-o,** to 'calendar', list c 1295.

kalendarius, calender, cloth-presser p 1318, 1349.

kali, glasswort or saltwort (bot.) 1634; *cf.* **alkali.**

kam-, *see also* **camaca; camahutus.**

Kambr/ice (Cambr-), in Welsh c 1190, c 1315; **-icus** c 1150, **-ensis** c 1200, **-igena** c 1315, c 1400, **-ius** 1586, Welsh, Welshman; **-obritannus** 1586.

kanevillus, *see* **2 cavilla.**

kanna, *see* CANNAB

karabe, *see* **cacabre.**

karav/anna, -enna, *see* **carvanna.**

kardaga, sector of circle containing 15 degrees (math.) c 1300.

†**karella,** (?) chest (or *f.l.* for **barella**) c 1520; *cf.* **carola, quarellus.**

karexo, *see* **charaxo.**

kariagium, *see* **1 carra; 2 carruca.**

karkella, *see* **scarkella.**

karkia, *see* **carca.**

karmellus, *see* **carmellus.**

karnall-, karnell-, *see* **carnellus.**

karnus, *see* **kernus.**

karopos, *see* **charopos.**

kaskettum, *see* **caskettum.**

†**katacapta,** (?) arbitrarily 956.

Kataius, *see* **Cathaius.**

Katalonicus, pannus, *see* **chalo.**

katapos, *see* **charopos.**

‡**katariacum,** "shaving of hart's-horn" 15c.

katheran/us, -atus, *see* CATERAN

kathmatha, *see* **camahutus.**

katia, *see* **1 chacea.**

kavelykenda, *see* **gavelikenda.**

kay-, *see* CAI

kebb/a 1372, c 1470, **-ata** 1410, 1449, **kubba** c 1345, 'keb', ewe whose lambs are stillborn or have died.

kebuli (*pl.*), species of behen-nut a 1250, ‡14c.

kedellus, *see* **kidellus.**

keira, *see* **2 carra.**

keiri, wallflower ‡14c., 1634.

‡**keisim,** lovage (bot.) 14c.

kela, 'keel', barge 1340, 1351; **cyula, cyulus** 6c., 9c., **ceola** c 1125, **ciula** c 1210, sort of ship; **killagium** 1271, 1409, **culagium** 1271, 1446, **culiagium** 1291, (?) **quilhagium** (G.) 1312, keelage, moorage due.

Keledeus, *see* **Colideus.**

kella, 'kell', caul, hair-net 1327.

kem-, *see also* **2 caminus;** KIM

kemmotum, *see* **commotum.**

kempus, 'kemp', measure of fish c 1325, 1335.

kencha, 'kench', (?) strip of land (Kent) 1396.

kenchia, *see* **2 pannus.**

ken/illum, -elina, -ettus, *see* **canis.**

kermes, kermes, vermilion 1622.

kernell-, kernill-, *see* **carnellus.**

kernetta, *see* **2 garnetta.**

kern/us 1331, **karnus** 1584, 1586, **homo de -e** 1315, **-arius** c 1390, **-iator** (†**kerinator**) 1306, kerne (Ir.); **-ia** 1297, 1300, **kaernia** 1295, 1297, band of kernes.

kerra, *see* **2 carra.**

‡**kerse,** cinnamon 14c.

kers/enaria, -unera, *see* **cresso.**

kersetum, 'kirset', settlement in burgh with respite of building (Sc.) 1221.

kersumia, *see* **gersuma.**

kertellum, *see* KIRTELL

kervellum, *see* **carvella.**

ketha, stall, booth (Northumb.) 1365.

ketheran-, kethran-, *see* CATERAN

ketyllus, kettle 1537.

kev/ellus, -illus, -illus, -ildus, *see* **2 cavilla.**

keveragium, *see* **coopertio.**

keverchevium, *see* **covrechiefum.**

kevero, *see* **capro.**

kevesci/a, -um, *see* **1 caputium.**

key/a, -um, *see* CAI

key/setria 1360, 1383, **-cetria** 1392, **-cestria** 1425, serjeanty of the peace, office of *cais* (W.).

kianos, *see* **cyanus.**

kidda (kydda), 'kid', faggot 1553.

*****kidell/us** 1196, 1440, **-um** 1506, **kadellus** c 1300, **kedellus** 1313, p 1391, kiddle, stake-net, fishing-weir; **kedellus,** (?) floating kiddle or raft of similar design c 1390.

kietillum, *see* CARETT

kikelota, *see* **rikelota.**

kil/i, is-, *vena cava* (κοίλη) c 1210, ‡14c.

killagium, *see* **kela.**

Killedeus, *see* **Colideus.**

†**kimbilis,** close-fisted a 1350.

kimelingus, *see* **cumelingus.**

kim/enellus c 1277, 1306, **-elina** 1324, **kembelina** 1275, **kemelinus** (†**kemelmus**) 1338, **kemelyngus** 1390, **kymilinus** 1336, **cumelin/a** 1310, 1325, **-us** 1299, 1325, ‡**cumula, cumila** c 1440, 'kimnel', vat.

kimotha, *see* **commotum.**

kini, *see* **cebar.**

kip/clutum, -lynea, *see* CHIPP

kipp/um (kypp-), 'kip', bundle (of hides) 1347; measure of furs 1393; 'kip', hide of young animal 1340; **-o,** (?) to sort (hides) into kips *or* to treat them by some process 1409, 1449.

kipr/us, -a, 'kipper', breeding salmon 1333.

kirnell/us, -o, *see* **1 carnellus.**

kirrius, *see* **cherogryllus.**

kirtell/a 1476, 1532, **-um** 1420, **kertellum** 1457, **curtella** 1393, kirtle.

kirva, corf or cruive of turf c 1170, c 1300.

‡**kist,** a weight or liquid measure (Ar.) 14c., 1652.

‡**kitran** 14c., ‡**alchitram** 14c., 1652, cedar gum (Ar.).

kittum, 'kit', pail (for grease) 1306.

kivellus, kivill-, *see* **cavilla (1 & 2).**

klammator, *see* **hlammator.**

kn-, *see also* **cn-**

knollum, knoll (Derb.) c 1230.

knoppum, knob, boss c 1410, 1413.

kockus, *see* **1 cogga.**

koloyus, jackdaw (κολοιός) 1344.

kondesium, *see* **condorsum.**

kota, *see* **2 cota.**

kubba, *see* **kebba.**

‡**kufordasin,** cinnamon 15c.

kunda, kinship c 1311.

kuvulia, *see* **cavella.**

ky-, *see also* **ki-**

‡kycec, tragacanth 14c.
kyntallus, *see* quintallus.
kyri/us, -os, king, ruler (κύριος) c 860. 12c.,
c 1200; *see also* cherogryllus; -eleison
c 1006. c 1090, c 1296, kurie eleeson 12c.,

cirileison c 1400, kyrie 1245, invocation
at mass, "Lord have mercy" (κύριε ἐλέησον);
-adoxa, chief doctrine c 1160; -alis, royal
10c.; -archia, chief lordship c 860; chiriinomus, law of the Lord c 550.

L

la, musical note 1351.
lab/arum Christi, sign of the cross 12c.;
-rum, banner c 760.
lab/efactio, weakening c 1250; -esco, *for*
-asco, to totter, fall c 1340, p 1348.
lab/ella, -ellum, label (her.) a 1350, a 1446;
-ella, -ellum 1388, c 1450, -ellulum
c 1443, tippet, string (of mitre); -ellulum,
lip c 1200; -ium, language c 1160, c 1362;
-io, to mouth 1345.
*lab/ilitas, instability, fluidity c 1160, c 1437;
-ilia (*pl.*)., transitory things c 950; -ina,
quagmire, fen 1447, ‡1483; lavor, *for* -or,
to pass away 11c.; -or, to run (of colours)
c 1324; *cf.* LAPS
labor/, travel c 1180; domus -is, plough-shed
1388; l. communis 940. 12c., 15c., l.
triplex 12c., *trimoda necessitas*; -ans 1373,
1559, *-arius 1351, 1630, †-ius c 1533,
-ator c 1213, 1630, -atrix (*f.*) c 1250, 1380,
labourer, workman, l. terrarum 1559;
-atio, ploughing 1413; -atorius, held
by villeins (G.) p 1250; -itium, labour
c 1376, 1427; -o, to travel 1258, 1398; to
harass c 1350; l. ad, to work at 1262, 1409;
l. de partu 1200; l. in extremis c 1226,
1461; l. in terra, l. terram 1086.
laborintus, *for* labyrinthus, c 1325, c 1450.
†labrator, "brinker" (resident by roadside)
1618.
labrescura, *see* LAMB
labrum, *see* labarum.
labrusc/ula, *for* -a, wild vine a 1250.
1 lac (? lacis) 12c., lacca a 1250, ‡14c.,
gum-lac.
2 lac virginis, *aqua mercurialis* c 1345, ‡1652;
‡l. lune, agaric 1652; ‡l. papaveris, opium
14c., 1652; vacca ad l. 1457, v. lact/abilis
13c., v. -rix c 1290, 1353, milch-cow;
*-agium 1299, 1535, lectagium 1308,
*-icinium c 1255, 1550, †-unium 1347,
(profits of) dairy produce; -atio, milking
1316; nourishment (fig.) 14c.; -ativus
c 1184, -atrix (*f.*) 1220, nourishing; -atrix,
milk-maid 1277; pannus -eus, cloth for
straining milk 1277; -ifluus, flowing with
milk c 1175, c 1397; †-iphagus, milksop
1570; -ualia (*pl.*), tithes (eccl.) of dairy
produce (W.) 1535, 1588; -ucella a 1250,
lectuca c 1190, letusa 1414, *for* -uca,
lettuce; -ans, suckling c 1280; -o, to milk
1275, 1376.
laca, *see* lacus.
lacc/a, -um, lack, defect, loss (in weight or
material) c 1115, c 1420; -agium 16c.,
lecagium 1444, ullage; -us, lacking,
defective 1205; -o, to lack, be defective or
underweight 1205, 1229; *see also* 1 lac.

lacchea, door-latch 1297, 1299; lachettum,
latchet (on dress) 1290; (?) tie-beam 1303,
1313; strip *or* loop (of iron) 1420, 1446; *cf.*
LAQUE
‡laccia, chub (fish) 1570.
laccus, *see* lacca; locca.
lacena, *see* LACINI
lacer/atio 1533, lasceratio 1499, lasseratio
1506, 1533, carving (of wood); -us, cruel,
rending c 950.
‡lacerta rubra, colcothar (alch.) 1652.
lacertus, muscle a 1250; arm *or* strut of
timber 1233; *cf.* laqueus.
lacesc-, *see* lassus; lycisca.
laci-, lace-, *see also* LAQUE
‡ lacina, goldfinch 1483.
‡lacinatorium, "sleekstone" 15c.; *cf.* lamina.
lacini/ola, -olus, cotise (her.) 1654; -atus,
gobony (her.) c 1595; lacena, (?) *for* -a,
"lace" 1472; *cf.* LAQUE
lacis, *see* 1 lac.
lacisca, *see* lycisca.
laco, soldier's servant c 1160.
lacrim/a, measure of lead 1305; l. oculi, *lac
Virginis* (alch.) c 1345; -abiliter, tearfully
c 1090, 1461; -alis c 1180, †-ulus c 1000,
tearful.
lact-, *see also* 2 lac.
lacteris, *see* elasticus.
†lactrum, (?) *for* vitrum *or* electrum, piece
of glass c 1462.
lac/us a 1220, 1367, -a a 1212, c 1220, leach,
drainage channel; laka, stretch of river
a 1200; -ualis, living in lakes c 1385; laguna, *for* -una, pool (G.) 1289.
1 lad/a, (oath of) purgation (leg.) c 1115;
l. plena, l. simplex, l. triplex c 1115; -io
(†laido) me, to purge oneself (leg.) c 1115.
2 lada 1192, 1342, lata 1270, leda 1337,
c 1450, leta 1389, loda 1279, lade, leat,
watercourse.
3 lad/a c 1165, 1169, -um 1303, loda 1296,
1559, lodum 1473, load; 1297, 1366, -us
1243, loda 1323, 1409, measure of ore
(commonly 9 dishes); 1183, c 1380, (?) loda
1279, service of carrying loads; lodarius,
(?) pack-horse 1378, 1381; (?) groom (mon.)
13c., 1330; lodecorda, cord for securing
cart-load 1324; lodwara, (?) load-ware
1296.
ladanum (bot.): -onum c 1250, (?) lap-
dan/um a 1250; oleum -inum a 1250; *cf.*
laudanum.
lad/elus 1323, c 1337, -yllus c 1481, -lus
1302, 1344, ladle; -ellus, measure of salt
1299.
ladhieta, *see* lidiata.
laenerius, *see* lanarius.

laëro (†lareo), fur-bearing animal, (?) marten *or* dormouse 13c., ‡c 1440.

lag/a (lagh-), (privilege or status guaranteed by) law 1100, 1511; l. Anglorum c 1115; l. populi c 1115; l. regis Edwardi 1100, c 1436; lahcopum (†lahceopum), payment for protection of law c 1115; -edagha 1260, -edaius, -edaium 1275, 1319, -edeium 1313, lawedaium 1255, 1313, -dies a 1275, -edies c 1245, law-day; -ehundredum 1222, 1248, lauhundredum c 1258, lawehundredum 13c., law-hundred, sheriff's tourn; -helmotus, law-hallmoot 1419; -emannus (†lakemannus), lawman, magnate 1086, 1419; lahslita (†lashlita), fine for breach of law c 1115; *see also* lex.

laganarium, griddle 1537.

laganum maris, 'lagan', jetsam or goods lying on sea bottom c 1115, 1448.

lagardus, *see* legardus.

*lag/ena 1221, 1461, -ona 1290, -ina 1460, 1535, legena 1324, gallon, gallon vessel; "pint-pot" 1553; -enalis 1448, -enarius, 1441, containing a gallon; -uncula, dry measure, peck p 1348, 1532; †langungula, small bottle 1461.

†lagmundus, *f.l.* for languidus, 1258.

lagonus, *see* logos.

laguna, *see* lacus.

lah/copum, -slita, *see* laga.

1 laia, wild sow (Fr. *laie*) 1213, 1292.

2 laia (laya), pathway cut through woodland (Fr. *laie*) 1466.

†laiagium, (?) *for* sejagium, 1587; *cf.* sedes.

laic/us, *layman 803, c 1005. c 1125, c 1520; (*adj.*) *12c., 1516, *-alis a 1090, a 1519, -anus c 1333, lay; frater -us, lay brother c 1220, c 1296; -aliter, in lay fashion 1267, c 1330; -atus, laity c 1450, a 1452.

laido, *see* 1 lada.

laissa, *see* laxa.

laka, *see* lacus.

lakemannus, *see* laga.

lallo, to suck c 950.

lama, *see* lamia; lamina.

lambas, *see* lampa.

lambda, Greek letter: lauta 7c.

lambell/a, rake 1654; label, lambeau (her.) 1654; -a, -us, collar (of ·alb) 1238, 1253.

lambo, to sup a 615.

lambota, *see* LAND

lambr/a, -um, *see* 2 ambra.

lamb/ruscura 1237, 1243, -reschura 1233, labrescura c 1255, -rechura 1236, -richura 1276, †-uscura 1266, -ruscatura 1260, -ruschatio 1239, panel, wainscoting; -rusco 1228, 1265, -ruzco 1245, -risso 1275, to panel, wainscot (Fr. *lambrisser*).

lamen, *see* lamina.

lament/atio manuum, gesture of grief 9c.; *-abiliter, lamentably, dolefully 826. c 1250, c 1450; -ativus a 1295, -uosus c 1397, doleful; -ator, mourner c 1250.

lamgabulum, lamgravius, *see* LAND

lamia, witch or demon: †lama c 1212.

lam/ina, strip or layer of leather 1279, 1328; instrument of conjuration 1510; lamina (geom.) 1686; ‡orpiment 1652; ‡1483, ‡-a 15c., "sleekstone" (*cf.* lacinatorium); -a 1275, 1516, -ia 1237, -en c 1315, 1510,

for -ina, metal plate; -a, weaver's sley 14c.; -inosus, in layers a 1250; -inatus, plated 1388, c 1400.

lamp/a 1280, -ada c 1180, c 1295, -is 1505, lambas 1242, *for* -as, lamp; -abilis, gleaming c 950; -adarium, chandelier 1242, 1243; oleum -adium, lamp oil a 1540.

*lamp/reda 1180, 1422, laumpreda 1345, -rea 1207, 1401, -redus 1290, -rida 1226, 1290, -ridus 15c., -ada 1242, ‡15c. -ras 1290, -res 1298, c 1396, †-rus 1290, lempeta 1312, lamprey; lanpreo 1265, -ro 1234, 15c., -ronna 1321, -renus 1338, -redula 1274, -redulus 1257, -ridula 1086, -rilla c 1266, small lamprey, lampern; -redarius, lamprey-keeper 1282, 1291.

lan/a, wool-tax 1347, 1352; l. †boli, (?) thrown wool c 1324; l. grossa 1196, 1364, l. grossior 1194, coarse wool or wool of full-grown sheep; l. media 1242, l. mediana 1291, 1296; l. fracta, 'locks' 1264, 1425; l. pellicia, wool in the fleece 1280; l. refuse 1425, l. de refuso 1314, 1377, scrap wool; l. regine, queen's wool (a customary rent) 1086, 1238; collectio -e, collecta -e, wool gathered from the fields 1276; -aria 1279, c 1400, ‡-arium 1483, 1570, ‡-ifisium 15c., domus -e 1271, d. -aria 1385, woolshed; -arius 1258, 1452, -erius 1230, -ista 1294, †leinator 1275, wool-merchant; -ifex, clothier ‡1483, 1563; -eficium, *for* -ificium, working in wool 13c; -eum, woollen cloth 1694; -ifer a 1446, -igerosus c 550, wool-bearing; -gellum 1218, c 1450, -geolum c 1135, longellus 1311, 1416, -ugellum (? laungellum) 1325, 1363, -ugea c 1335, -ugium 1341, -ugo 1343, †-aquum 1380, blanket *or* woollen under-garment; *pellis -uta 1270, 1573, p. -ata 1277, 1483, p. -ita 1275, 1463, p. -osa 1303, p. †-igena (? -igera) 1276, wool-fell; *see also* 2 pannus.

lan/arius 1291, a 1446, -erius c 1200, 1284, -iarius c 1315, laynerius 1279, 1296, falco -arius 1205, 1340, f. -erius 1214, 1315, f. -orius 1287, f. laenerius c 1285, lanner (falc.); -erettus, lanneret 1367, 1382; *see also* lana.

lanc/ea, shaft of pillar 1293; l. suffulta, man-at-arms with retinue 1509; l. tincta, (?) lance with pennon 12c., 1243; -ia 1322, 1461, launcia 1385, -eola 1041, *for* -ea, lance; homo ad -eam 1362, -earius p 1377, -eator 1557, lancer; -earium, loop-hole c 1219; -eola, shuttle 1191; lancet (med.) a 1235, ‡1483; -eola (-eolata) aquatica, spearwort (bot.) a 1250, ‡14c.; ‡-eolata, 13c., 15c., plantago l. c 1200, a 1250, ribwort plantain (bot.); -eatus, lance-shaped 12c.; -eo (-io), to wield a lance a 1142, c 1194; *to pierce with a lance c 1182, 14c.; to arm with a lance a 1270, 1508; to throw a javelin a 1142; to launch, hurl 1146, 1257; to abut, project c 1240, 1373.

†lanceicea coria, *distinguished from* c. salata (? *for* lauteicea, cleaned) 1230.

lancett-, lanceagium, *see* LAND

lancia, lancella, *see* lancea; lanx.

*land/a 1086, 1588, -ea 13c., 1334, launda

1353, **laundea** 1435, **londa** a 1242, 1352, 'lawn', forest glade, untilled land; *lande* (G.) 1220, 1294; **-ella**, little lawn c 1200; **-arius** 1363, 1440, **-erus** 1661, **laundarius** 1606, 'lander', lawn-keeper; **-aria**, office of 'lander' 1399; †**-ebota** 1328, **lambota** 13c., **laundebota** 1504, land-bote, enclosure of waste (Devon); **-copum (-ceapum),** payment for land c 1115; **-gablum** c 1115, 1159, **-gabulum** 1188, 14c., **-gavelum** c 1130, **langablum** a 1140, **langabulum** (†**lamgabulum**) c 1155, 1453, **londgabulum** c 1225, **longabulum** c 1157, 1455, land-gavel; **-gravia** c 1250, c 1255, **lantegravissa** 1382, landgravine (German); **-gravius** c 1250, c 1256, **-egravius** c 1192, c 1250, **andegravius** c 1250, **langravius** c 1300, 1370, †**lamgravius** c 1400, **langravus** c 1362, **lantgravius** 1562, **lantgrafius** 1505, landgrave (German); **-homo,** **-mannus, -esmannus,** native c 1115; **-imera,** 'landmere', boundary c 1310; **-irectum,** charge on land c 1115; **-esricus,** land-owner, lord c 1115; **-serviens** 1203, **-sergantus** 1298, **-sergens, -serjans** 12c., 'land-serjeant', keeper of the peace (Cumberland, Lincs.); **-settagium** 12c., 13c., lancettagium (†**lanceagium**) 1239, 14c., form of tenure (Norfolk); **-esettus** c 1160, **lansetis** a 1128, **lancetta** 13c., **lancettus** c 1100, 1240, **lancettagius** 1239, 'land-sete', customary tenant, cottar.
landiocum, (?) *llan daeog,* villein land (Cornwall) 1297, 1355.
landonium 1303, **laundonum** 1286, **lann/a** 1273, 1335, **-ia** 1299, wooden bar or halter in plough-harness (*cf.* O.F. *landon*).
laner/ius, -ettus, *see* **lanarius.**
lanfranc/us 13c., c 1285, **mensura -i** c 1300, measure of ale (Canterbury).
lang-, *see also* **lana;** LAND; **lingua.**
Langobardus, *see* **Lombardus.**
‡**langra,** crab apple 14c.
langungula, *see* **lagena.**
lang/uor, illness (bibl.); c 1185, c 1258, **-or** 12c., illness as ground for essoin (leg.); **-uidus,** suffering from such illness 1200, 1269; **-uidule,** weakly 1520; **-uosus,** ill c 1118; **-uens in extremis,** sick to death 1370.
lan/iarius, -orius, *see* **lanarius.**
laniena, massacre 1610.
lanista, *see* **lana.**
lann/a, -ia, *see* **landonium.**
lannera 1228, **leynera** 1444, 'lainer', strap.
lansalis, *see* 2 **pannus.**
†**lantala,** (?) assessment for geld 1269.
lant/egravissa, -grafius, -gravius, *see* LAND
lantern/a pyxalis, box-lantern c 1255; **laterna,** *for* **-a,** c 980; ‡**-ula,** "sconce" c 1440.
lanug-, lanut-, *see* **lana.**
lanx vite, term of life 12c.; **lancia,** dish 1388; **lancella,** auncel 1363 (*cf.* **auncella**); *see also* **leux.**
lap/acium, *for* **-athium,** sorrel, dock *or confused with* **lappa** a 1250, ‡14c.; **-aciolum,** (?) sheep's sorrel a 1250.
lapdan-, *see* **ladanum.**
lap/is, ordeal stone c 1115, c 1150; stone (weight) c 1204, 1359; stone (med.) c 1200,

a 1446; testicle c 1370; cannon-ball 1418; lode-stone, compass 1516; 1144, 13c., **l. noster** c 1320, **l. occultus** c 1345, ‡1652, **l. philosophorum** c 1345, philosophers' stone (alch.); ‡**l. animalis,** human blood 1652; ‡**l. Arabicus, l. lune,** talc 1652; **l. ardens,** (?) coal 1313; **l. Armenicus,** blue vitriol a 1250, ‡14c.; ‡**l. calcis,** *scoria aeris* 1652; **l. calculatorius,** reckoning slate 15c; **l. cerasi,** cherry-stone c 1400; ‡**l. famosus, l. pretiosus,** *sal de urina* 1652; **l. ferri,** iron ore c 1275; **l. finalis,** boundary-stone 1236; **l. francus** 1258, **l. liber** c 1200, c 1324, **l. parius** c 1191, free-stone; **l. grisius,** (?) Kentish rag 1241; ‡**l. Hephaestionis,** pyrites 1652; ‡**l. Heracleus,** diamond 14c.; **l. Hiberus,** gold (alch.) 1267, a 1292; **l. (de) Israel** 1388, c 1411, **l. de Jerosalem** 1414, ‡**l. Judaicus** 14c., 1652, (engraved) agate, cameo; ‡**l. latus** 14c., ‡**l. Phrygius** 14c., 1652, pyrites; ‡**l. lazuli** a 1250, ‡14c., **l. lazuri** a 1250; **l. melior,** gold (alch.) c 1320; **l. pacis,** pax (eccl.) c 1148; **l. pavimentalis,** paving-stone 1473; **l. pregnans,** eagle-stone 1215; **l. purus,** ashlar 1398; **l. Tagi** (?), a 1292; **l. tegulatus,** roofing-slate 1535; **l. veritatis,** sapphire 1380;
-idarium, lapidary (book of gems) a 1250, a 1446; **-idarius** c 1362, **-idicesor** a 1250, **-icida** c 1250, 1520, **-iscida** 1431, **-icidarius** 1438, stone-cutter, quarryman; **-icidarium** 1438, *-icidium 1459, 1564, **-iscidium** 1466, **-iscedina** c 1170, **-icinum** 1268, **-idicina** (†**-idiana**), **-idicinum** 1189, c 1400, **-idicinia, -idicinium** 1189, 1431, **-ifodina** c 1230, c 1280, **-ifodium** c 1250, 1425, †**-istratum** 1316, quarry; **-idator,** *for* **dilapidator,** squanderer 1336; **-ideum,** stone erection c 1400; **-idicinus,** made of stone c 1340; **-idicus,** knowing about stones c 1300; **-idificativus,** petrifactive c 1270; **-idior,** stonier c 1290; **-iditas** c 1270, **-ideitas** a 1250, c 1270, stoniness; **-idista** c 1180, **-ister** 1560, (?) stone jar; ‡**-ista,** mortar 1483; **piscis -idosus,** fish living in pebbly streams, (?) trout 13c.; **-illulus,** small gem 1220, 13c.; **-illus,** fruit-stone 1144, c 1180; cannon-ball 1413; **-idatus,** seated on a stone c 1313; **-ido, -ideo,** to petrify a 1250.
lappa, weed, tare (fig.) c 950; **l. inversa,** burdock (bot.) a 1250, ‡14c.; *cf.* **lapacium.**
laps/us (*4th decl.*), lapse (of time) 1222, c 1400 (*see also* **pro**); the Fall (theol.) c 1195, c 1362; (*2nd decl.*), sinner 12c., c 1512; (*adj.*) fallen (from grace) c 1343; **-ura,** fall from grace, sin 1225; **-asco,** to stumble, err 1427; *cf.* **labilitas.**
lapwinga, lapwing 1544,
laqua, bay of barn c 1350.
laque/us 1235, 1439, **laceus** 1313, **lacius** 1267, **lacia (latia)** 1231, 1233, †**laquinus** 1297, tie-beam (*cf.* **lacertus**); cord for attaching seal 1182, c 1300; 1213, c 1340, **lacius** 1220, **-atura** 1245, **laciatura** 1245, lace; ‡**laciatorium,** web-beam 15c.; **-atus** c 1200, 1444, **laceatus** 1188, laced, trimmed with lace; **-amen,** snare c 1170; **-are,** 'postband', beam (arch.) 15c.; **-ator,** setter of

snares c 1430; **-olus**, little snare c 1188; **-osus**, ensnaring c 1430; **-o**, to skewer or hook on 1263; to lace, buckle on (armour) 1461; **lascio**, to ensnare 1199; *cf.* **lacchea.**

lar/, fire c 550; **-es** (*pl.*) **ecclesie**, bosom of the Church 13c.; **-es** (*acc.*) **foventes**, householders 1439; **-arium**, closet 1591; **-icomus**, fiery c 550.

lard/aria 1336, 1534, ***-arium** c 1136, 1535, **-earium** c 1220, **-eria** 1198, 1390, **-erium** 1221, c 1243, **-ria** 1429, **-enarium** 1380, 1460, **-eneria** 1212, **-inaria** 1462, 1490, **-naria** c 1540, **-ura** 1405, **-atorium** 1327, larder, store (of meat); **-arium**, preserved meat 1297, 1325; larder-rent (mon.) c 1150, 1300; **-arius** c 1125, 1322, **-enarius** a 1190, c 1300, **-inarius** 1164, 1509, †**laudennarius** 1200, ***-erarius** a 1097, c 1290, **-irarius** a 1180, larderer; **-enaremarta** 1460, **-enermarta** 1471, **-inermarta** 1476, 1496, **-naremarta** 1480, beast assigned to larderer (Sc.); **-eicius** 1214, **-icius** 1242, **-ec(i)us** 1239, **-icia** 1296, chine (of venison); **oleum -inum**, lard-oil c 1190; **porcus** †**lurdenus**, (?) fat hog 1239; **-o**, lardon (inserted in wound) a 1250; **-um**, butter c 950; **-o**, to lard, baste c 1180, 15c.

lareo, *see* **laëro.**

larg/itas, width c 1290, 1419; distension a 1250; **-us**, wide 1263, c 1520 (*see also* **pannus**); **-um**, opportunity 1433; **ad -um** 1338, 1575, **ad -a** 1331, at large, astray; **-a**, a large (mus.) c 1470; (?) measure of land 1476; **-e**, in a wide sense c 1332, c 1341; **-ibilis**, to be freely given c 1340; **-iflue**, liberally 1293, 15c.; ***-ifluus** 855, c 956. c 1090, c 1500, **-ipotens** 12c., lavish, bounteous; **-itatio**, bestowal c 1100; **-itiuncula**, small gift 11c.; **-itrix** (*f.*), bestower c 1150, 1345; **-eo** 1515, **-itor** 12c., to bestow; **-o**, to enlarge 1299; to diffuse 1252.

larrocinium, *see* LATR

larv/a 1169, 1284, ‡**-ale** 1570, mask or visor; "skein" (of silk) 1532; ‡scarecrow c 1200, c 1440; evil spirit, devil c 950. ‡15c.; **-alis** c 1170, **-aricus** 10c. 11c., **-osus** c 1180, diabolical; **-atus** c 1200, 1412, **-eolatus** c 1180, masked; **-o**, to mask a 1408; *cf.* **lerna.**

lasceratio, lasseratio, *see* **laceratio.**

lascivia (**cutis**), swelling c 1125.

lashlita, *see* **laga.**

lassus, worn out (of teeth) 7c.; **laces/cibilis**, soon tired a 1452; **-co** c 1197, c 1430, **-so** c 1254, *for* **lassesco**, to grow weary.

1 last/um, -a, -us c 1100, 1564, **lestum, lesta** (†**lesca**), **lestus** c 1166, c 1290, **-agium, -adium** (Dutch) 1443, last, load (of hides, wool, herrings, *etc.*); ***-agium** c 1130, 1544, **lestagium** 1130, 1419, †**estagium** 1185, **leystagium** c 1267, **listagium** 1336, 1341, lastage, export duty; bilge-water *or* ballast 1283, 1436; **-agio**, to take on ballast 1347.

2 last/um, -us c 1150, 1346, **lestus** 1086, c 1275, **latha** 1558, lathe, division of county (Kent); c 1300, 1315, **lestus** 1189, 1297, lathe court (Kent); **l. hundredorum** c 1260, 1279, **lestus hundredorum** c 1175, a 1185; **leidgreveus**, lathe-reeve 13c.

*lat/a (**latt-, lath-**) 1130, 1449, **-ea** 1253, c 1409, **-us** 1288, 1297, lath; **-ula** 1311, **-ila** 1366, small lath; **-atio**, covering with laths 1377; **-enaylum** c 1445, **-nayllum** 1449, lath-nail; **-erius**, lath-layer 1344; **-ura**, lath-work 1280, 1325; **-icium** 1240, 1353, **-eicium** c 1243, 1244, **-icia** 1291, lattice, wattlework; ***-o**, to cover with laths 1223, 1446; *see also* **2 lada, latitudo.**

latage, splash of wine drops (λάταξ) 1620.

latam-, *see* **latomus.**

latena, *see* **lato.**

latenia, *see* **litania.**

lat/entia, concealment 13c., a 1292; obscuration c 1270; **-itantia**, escaping observation 1620; **-ebrosus**, hidden c 550; **-ibulum**, act of hiding c 730; **-itanter**, secretly c 1180, a 1408; **-ito**, (?) to conceal (the entrance to) 1289.

latenus, *see* **lato.**

‡**later/ lictro**, quicksilver 1652; **-atus**, made of brick c 1239, 15c.; ‡**strator -icius**, "brick-layer" 1520; **fornax -ica**, "tile-kiln" 1573.

later-, *see also* **latus.**

Lateranensis, of or for the Lateran council c 1290.

laterna, *see* **lanterna.**

lath-, *see* **2 lastum; lata; latomus.**

latia, *see* **laqueus.**

Lati/aliter, -ariter, -atim, *see* **Latina.**

latibulum, *see* **latentia.**

laticium, *see* **lata.**

latifico, *see* **latitudo.**

latimus, *see* **latomus.**

Latin/a (*n. pl.*), Latin language 1419, 1467; **-alis**, Latin c 1460; **Latialiter** c 1000, **Latiariter** c 1125, in Latin; c 1188, **Latiatim** c 950, in the Roman manner; **-arius** 1086, 1212, **latimarius** 1086, 1212, **latimerius** 1292, **latimerus** 1167, 1292, interpreter; **-ismus**, Latin idiom 1241; **-ista**, Latinist 1345, †15c.; **-itas**, Latin Christendom 11c., c 1200; **nihil -ius** 8c.; **-obarbarus**, dog Latin 1520; **-o**, to translate into Latin a 1200.

†**latinus**, (?) *f.l.* for **lacivus** (*i.e.* **lascivus**), c 1250; *see also* **lato.**

lat/io, carrying c 1410; locomotion c 1250, p 1300; **l. armorum** c 1432, c 1457; **pons -ivus**, drawbridge 15c.; ***-or** c 1080, 1564, ***-rix** (*f.*) c 950. c 1160, 1472, bearer (esp. of letters); taker, stealer 1395; vehicle, medium (med.) a 1250.

latit/antia, -anter, -o, *see* **latentia.**

lat/itudo, latitude (astr.) 1267, c 1612; **l. pannorum**, standard width of broadcloth 1215, 1230 (*see also* **pannus**); **l. motus** a 1350, **l. velocitatis** 1335, variation or range of velocity; **-itudinalis**, of latitude (astr.) c 1361; **filus** (**nervus**) **l.** (med.) a 1250; **-itudinaliter**, breadthways 1378; **-ivius**, wide-wayed c 1000; **-a**, broad arrow 1455; **-um**, width a 1190, 1516; **l. gladii**, flat of sword c 1192, c 1436; **-ifico**, to widen 1383.

*lat/o 1144, c 1452, **-onia** 1382, **-unus** 1291, **-ena** 1472, latten (metal); **-inus** 1434, **-enus, -ineus** 1553, of latten; **ars -onaria** c 1452.

*lat/omus (lath-) c 1172, c 1553, **-omius** a 1564, ***-amus** 1306, 1541, (?) **talamus** (†**calamus**) 1500, **-imus** 1457, 1541, **lauthamus** 1415, *for* **lautumus**, stonecutter, mason; l. **positor**, stone-layer 1380; **-omia**, stone-cutting 1439; **opus -omicum**, masonry c 1456; ‡**-oma** 15c., ‡**-omega** 15c., 1483, mason's axe.

lator, *see* **latio**.

latratio (canum), barking c 1000.

*latria, service, worship c 950. c 1200, 1426.

latricubitum, *see* **latus**.

latrin/arius, scavenger 1520; **thalamus -alis**, latrine c 1180.

latrinus, *see* **luter**.

latrix, *see* **latio**.

latr/o *1086, 1461, **-onus** 1199, **-ocinator** c 1434, thief; right to take thieves or levy fines for theft c 1070, c 1170; l. **in terra captus**, infangenthief a 1107, 1189; **-ones homicide** (*pl.*), secret murderers c 1102; **-ona** 1287, **-onissa** 1176, 1281, **-uncula** 1345, thief (*f.*); ***-ocinium** 967. c 1077, 1313, **-onicinium** 11c., **larrocinium** 1605, theft, (fine for) larceny; stolen goods 1254, 1340; l. **commune** 1398; l. **magnum**, grand larceny 1276; l. **probatum** c 1130; **-ociniter** 1276, c 1315, **-unculose** c 1362, thievishly; **-onalis** c 1250, **-onicus** c 1410, thievish; **-unculorius**, chequered c 1595; **-ocino**, to be a robber c 1362.

latum, *see* **latitudo**.

latunus, *see* **lato**.

latus, party, faction c 1200, p 1330; friend, associate c 1178; l. **ad l.**, side by side p 1305; **a later/e**, by a third party c 1258; *see also* **heres**, **legatus**; **-alis**, companion, confidant c 1160, 14c.; (*adj.*) collateral 1267, p 1300; concerned with side-issues 1344, c 1357; ‡**-ale**, "corset" 15c.; ***-aliter** a 1142, c 1608, **-atim** c 1200, 13c., laterally, at or from the side, sideways; **-anea regis**, queen consort 13c.; **-culum**, small side c 1100; period of time, series of years 11c.; field of a shield (her.) 1654; **latricubitum**, solid with cubit-long sides 13c.; †**laturitorius**, (?) neighbour (Sc.) 1483; **-o**, cotice (her.) c 1595; **-o** c 1204, 1275, **-o ad** 1248, c 1397, **-o inter** c 1354, to skirt, adjoin.

laubus, *see* **lembus**.

laud-, *see also* **laus**.

†**laudanum**, opiate 1652; *cf.* **ladanum**.

laudennarius, *see* LARD

lauhundredum, *see* **laga**.

laumpreda, *see* **lampreda**.

launcia, *see* **lancea**.

laund-, *see* LAND; **landonium**.

laur/ea magisterii 1549, l. **magistralis** 1599, **-eatus titulus** c 1460, master's degree (ac.); **-eola**, spurge laurel a 1250, 1538; **-eatio**, crowning with laurels c 1200; **-eator**, giver of crowns c 1250, ‡1483; **-eo** (**-io**), to crown with laurels c 1250, c 1450.

†**laurum**, (?) ship's cordage 1216.

laus, advice 13c.; l. **tibi**, narcissus (Norfolk) 1538; **laud/is causa**, by courtesy 1343; ***-es** (*pl.*), lauds (eccl.) c 1125, c 1422; l. **matutinales** 12c., l. **matutine** 15c.; l. **nocturnales** c 1090, l. **nocturne** c 980. c 1130; **-a** c 1465, **-um** 1280, 1505, finding,

award (leg.); **-amen**, praise c 990; **-ativum**, **-emium**, heriot (Sc.) a 1566; **lausa**, payment to lord for licence to alienate (G.) 1255; **-ator**, arbiter c 1300, 1455; **-atorie**, eulogistically c 1334; **-atorium**, psaltery 1079; **-edignus** 1423, **-ibilis**, *for* **-abilis** c 1125, 1441, praiseworthy; **-ifluus** c 1150, 1424, **-isonus** c 1090, c 1414, laudatory; **-isone**, with voices raised in praise c 1090; **-o**, to advise, recommend 1041. 1136, c 1362; to pronounce an award, ordain, promulgate (leg.) c 1280, c 1465.

lauta, *see* **lambda**.

lauthamus, *see* **latomus**.

†**lauticius**, (?) honorific c1437; *cf.* **lanceicea**.

lav/acrum, laver, ewer 1306, 1454; c 1170, c 1546, l. **regenerationis** c 1080, c 1450, l. **salutare** c 1160, l. **salutis** 1124, l. **vite** c 1400, font, baptism; 12c., 1490, **-amentum** c 730. a 1446, washing, purification; **-acrum pendens** 1442; l. **ad tenendum vinum** 1405; **-andaria** 1241, c 1450, **-endaria** 12c., **-andria** c 1417, a 1452, **-endria** 13c., c 1483, **-enderina** c 1220, **-endrina** 13c., laundry (mon.); **-enderia**, **-endria**, laundering 1265; **-anderia**, laundress 1268; **-andarius** 1252, **-endarius** 1376, c 1418, **-endrius** c 1418, **-ator** 1086, c 1266, launderer (mon.); **-ator**, bather a 615; **-atio pedum** (eccl.) c 1060; **-atorium** *c 1200, 1454, **-orium** 1289, c 1296, laver, ewer; *c 1080, 1417, **-arium** c 1300, laver, 'lavatory', place for washing (esp. mon.); piscina (eccl.) 1417, 1503; (office of) ewery 1508; l. **pendens** 1395; **-atorius** 1214, c 1393, **-ativus** 13c., for washing; **-atura**, washing water, slops c 1125, c 1330; **-andula** 1538, **-endula** a 1250, 1634, ‡**-andria** 15c., lavender; **-o oves (bidentes)**, to dip sheep 1247, 1466; *cf.* LOT

lavor, *see* **labilitas**.

law-, *see* **laga**.

lax/a c 1190, 1297, **lessa** 1209, 1328, **lessia** 1281, 1293, **lescia** 1248, **lecia** 1291, **laissa** 1203, **lissis** 1286, leash; **-atio**, loosening (of bowels) a 1250; l. **seminis** (med.) a 1250; **-ativus**, laxative (med.) c 1250, 1267; **-o**, to allow c 1125; ‡**lesco**, to leash 15c.

laya, *see* **laia**.

laynerius, *see* **lanarius**.

layo, to lay (baulks of timber) 1400.

lazar/us a 1128, c 1467, **-ius** 1415, leper; **-icus**, leprous c 1130.

lazul/us 1267, **-um** 12c., ‡15c., **lazurium** a 1250, azure (*subst.*); **-eus**, azure (*adj.*) 1267; *see also* **lapis**; *cf.* AZUR

lea, *see* **leta**.

†**leafgabulum**, (?) payment for leave to plough 14c.

leaga, *see* **leuca**.

†**learefones**, a creature deadly to lions (λεοντοφόνος) a 1446.

leazura, *see* 2 **lesura**.

lebardus, *see* **leopardus**.

lebitina, *see* **libitina**.

lec/acitas (†**locacitas**), wantonness, obscenity a 1142 c 1220; **-ator**, lecher c 1125, 1267.

lecagium, *see* **lacca**.

lecebre (*pl.*), *for* **illecebre**, 8c.

lecentia, *see* **licentia**.

lechefrium, dripping-pan 1252.
lechia, see lescha.
lechin/a, -us, see lychnus.
lechitus, see lecythus.
lecia, see laxa.
lecisca, see lycisca.
lectagium, see 2 lac.
lect/alia, -ica, see lectus.
lect/io, *lesson, reading c 1160, 1556; lesson,
training a 1200; lecture (ac.) 1235, 1620;
lectorship (ac.) c 1456, c 1567; festum
(festivitas, vigilia) duodecim -ionum
(eccl.) c 1266, c 1330; f. novem -ionum
c 1220, c 1445; f. trium -ionum a 1245,
1335; l. divina, Holy Scripture c 740. 12c.;
l. Evangelica 1289; l. cursoria 1350,
l. ordinaria c 1350, 1455 (ac.); -ionale
c 1315, -ionarius 12c., 15c., liber -ionarius
c 1250, lectionary (eccl.); mensa -ionaria,
reading-table 14c.; auditio -aria (ac.)
c 1410; -aria, payment by teacher for pupils
1424; -or, teacher, reader, lecturer (ac.)
c 1000. c 1250, 1636; l. curie, Papal official
15c.; l. mense, monk who reads during
meals 1330, c 1451; -oratus, order or office
of reader (eccl.) (Sc.) 1200, 1245; ars -orea,
art of reading c 990; exercitus -alis, band
of students c 1000; -orale 1149, *-orium
c 1188, c 1500, -urium 1384, -urum c 1266,
-ernum 1303, 1484, -arnum c 1510, -rina,
-rinum c 1180, c 1437, -erinium 1414,
-rinium 1243, c 1458, -ricinium 1514,
-ricium 13c., -ricum 1222, 1268, -rium
c 1521, -ro 1300, -rum 1241, 1405, lectern,
desk (cf. -uarium, s.v. lectus); -riceus,
spent in reading c 550; -ricea c 550, -rix
c 1190, reader (f.), instructress; -ura 1345,
a 1564, †lettrura 1383 (but cf. litteratura),
reading; lecture, lectureship (ac.) 1302,
c 1504; l. aularis, lecture in hall (ac.) 1424;
-urio, to aspire to lecture (ac.) a 1260; cf.
legenda.
lecton, dictum (λεκτόν) 12c.
lectuarium, see electuarium; lectus.
lectuca, see 2 lac.
lect/us, set of bed-clothes or bed-hangings
1248, 1454; (?) saddle 1241, 1285; contemplative life 12c; hospital bed 1242, 1293;
river-bed c 1227; (?) garden bed, plot 1334;
bed of stone (in quarry) 1431; bed, socket
(of mill-stone) 1283, 1383; *c 1272, 1355,
-um 1334, gwely, family group of land-
holders (W.); -um facio, to make (tidy) a
bed 1226, 1324; -o deduco, to marry
c 1362; malum -i, 'bed-sickness', ground
for essoin (leg.) 1194, c 1290; -us anguillarum, eel-bed c 1180; l. campester,
camp-bed 1610; l. duplex, double bed
1421; l. egritudinis c 1255, 1435, l.
infirmitatis 1293, l. languoris a 1164,
-ulus egrotorum 1426, sick-bed; l. egritudinis ultime 13c., l. mortalis 1199,
1256, death-bed; l. plumalis c 1270, 1516,
l. plumialis 1298, l. plumeus 1463,
l. de plumis 1403, feather-bed; l. principalis, (?) full-sized bed 1457, 1459;
l. rotalis, truckle-bed 1459, 1479; -um, for
-us, bed 1269, 1497; -ulus, coffin 10c.;
-arium 1329, letera 1325, litera 1221,
c 1395, litura 1350, a litter; -erium 1319,

1342, -irium 1322, leterium (Sc.) 1290,
1434, *litera 1202, 1358, literum 1243,
1374, *literia, literium c 1180, 1300,
literagium 1281, littora 1300, litura 1487,
1523, litra 1415, -ica 1183, 1234, -icium
1583, -icinium 1487, 1574, litter, bedding,
straw; -ura straminis 1420; *-isternium
c 1000. a 1100, 1516, -alia 1435, *-ualia
c 1300, 1458, -uarium c 1220, bed-furni-
ture; -uarium, (?) altar-cloth or lectern-
cover 1423, 1518 (cf. lectio); vestimenta
-ualia, bed-clothes c 1266.
lecythus (eccl.), lechitus c 1430, ‡15c.,
lichitus c 1450, oil-flask.
leda, see 2 lada; leta; leuda.
ledda, ledga, see 2 lega.
ledibilis, see 1 lesura.
†ledina, (?) leaden vat 1471.
ledo(n), neap tide 655, 720. a 1130; tidal
bore c 1125, 15c.; flood-tide c 1270, ‡1483;
‡ebb-tide c 1440; cf. malina.
ledori/a c 1115, c 1324, lidoria c 1200,
abuse (λοιδορία); -ce, abusively 12c.
ledza, see leuda.
‡leffas, emanation from earth that vivifies
plants 1652.
1 lega c 1184, 1531, leya 1257, lea, ley, grass-
land.
2 leg/a 1279, 1316, -gum 1279, ledga 1413,
ledge, cross-bar (of door); (?) ledda 1276,
legga 1273, lestlegga 1270, †leyerlegga
1344, lurlegga 1316, 1394, lerlegga 1402,
'ledge', strip or band (of iron, etc., for cart-
wheels); leggo, to fit (wheels) with 'ledges'
1399 (cf. liga).
3 lega 1438, lex c 1178, 1253, alloy; cf. allaia.
4 lega, see leuca.
legabilis, see 1 legatio.
legal/itas, law-worthiness, legal status
c 1102, 1362; loyalty 1116, 1546; -ia (pl.),
laws, customs 12c., 1378; -is, (subst.) law-
worthy man c 1220, c 1289; (adj.) *law-
worthy, of legal status a 1100, 1586; c 1320,
legualis (G.) 1369, loyal; normal, of standard quality 12c., c 1257; standard, current
(of money) 1198, 1583; l. corpore, sound
in body 1211; see also curia, dies, hundredum, pater; -iter, *lawfully 1041. c 1125,
a 1564; by process of law c 1452; loyally
c 1160; l. expertus, skilled in law c 1290;
cf. lex.
legamen, see liga.
legantia, see 1 legatio.
legardus 1390, 1421, lagardus 1396, servant
(Durham).
1 *leg/atio c 1303, c 1518, -antia 1227,
legacy; -abilis, bequeathable 1280, a 1564;
-atarie, in accordance with a bequest 1290;
-atorius, for -atarius, legatee 1348; -atum
1242, l. altaris 12c., l. primum 1311,
l. secundum 13c., mortuary (eccl.); -o in
manus, to bequeath 1415.
2 *legat/io c 1125, 1552, -ia 1167, 1518, office
or jurisdiction of papal legate; mission,
request c 1266; -arius, emissary c 730, 1041.
c 1170, 1549; c 1397, -inus (†-ivus) 1426,
1526, legatine; -orie, as a papal legate 1274;
*-us, papal legate c 1125, 1461; l. a latere
c 1191, 1467, l. de latere 1412, c 1556,
plenipotentiary legate; l. natus, archbishop

or bishop with local legatine authority c 1300, 1536; **l. regis,** royal commissioner 1086.

lege/amentum, -itas, *see* **ligeus.**

legena, *see* **lagena.**

leg/enda, legend, saint's life c 1190, 1609; c 1250, c 1452, **-endarius, -endarium** c 1182, c 1510, legendary, book of legends; **l. sanctorum** 14c., 1430; *see also* **temporalis; -atura,** (?) reading c 1320; **dies -ibilis,** lecture-day (ac.) c 1350, c 1593; **-itorium,** lectern 1432; ***-o,** to lecture, teach (ac.) 9c. c 1140, 17c.; **l. ab,** to attend lectures given by c 1100; **l. super (librum)** c 1266, 1409; *cf.* **lectio.**

†**legergildum,** (?) *f.l.* for **weregildum,** c 1115.

legerwita, leghirwita, *see* **leirwita.**

leg/eus, -ius, -entia, *see* **ligeus.**

legg-, *see* 2 **lega.**

legi-, *see also* **lex; ligeus.**

legi/a, *for* **-o,** legion 8c.; **-onarius,** soldier c 1150; *see also* **leuca.**

legitim/atio, legitimation (of persons) 1232, 1608; 1220, 1406, **-itas** c 1220, 1418, legitimacy (of persons); **-us,** law-worthy c 1115, 1258; liege 1100; (*subst.*) legitimate heir a 1250; **-a** c 1269, **etas -a** c 1178, 1535, majority; **annus -us,** Jewish year c 1212; **viduitas -a,** independent widowhood 1232; **-o,** to legitimize (persons) 1220, 1608; *cf.* **lex.**

lego, *see* 1 **legatio; legenda.**

legu-, *see* LEGAL; **ligula.**

leida, *see* **leuda.**

leidgreveus, *see* 2 **lastum.**

leinator, *see* **lana.**

leira, fish trap 1419.

leir/wita 1185, 1360, **-witum** 1252, 1334, **-ewita** 1194, 1324, †**-wyadum** (*f.l.* for **leyrwyta domini**) 1295, **leerwita** 1286, **leerwitum** 1297, **legerwita** c 1115, c 1240, **legrewita** 1086, **leghirwita** 1325, **lejerwita** c 1115, **lerewita** 1504, **letherwita** c 1283, **letherwitum** 1384, **leytherwita** 1297, 'lairwite', payment for incontinence (man.).

leisura, *see* 2 **lesura.**

lembus, pinnace, yacht: **limb/us** c 1365, 15c., †**laubus** c 1150; **-aria,** (?) boat-yard c 1437.

†**lemiculus,** (?) pendant 14c.

lemma, theme: **limma,** thought, idea c 950.

lemnisc/us, (point of) label (her.) c 1595; **-atus,** decorated with labels c 1595.

lemo, *see* 1 **limo.**

Lemovi/cinus, -ticus, *see* **opus.**

lempeta, *see* **lampreda.**

lend/es, -ines, *see* **lens.**

lenepina, *see* **linca.**

leneus, *see* 1 **linea.**

leng-, *see* **linga; slinga.**

lenisticum, *see* **levisticum.**

leni/tivus a 1250, 1427, **linitivus** 1375, **-ficativus** a 1250, soothing; **-fico,** to soften a 1250, c 1376; **linio,** *for* **-o,** to soothe c 1070, c 1260; *cf.* **leviatio, leviga.**

lens palustris 1538, **lent/icula aquatica** a 1250, **l. fontis** a 1150, duckweed (bot.); **-es** (*pl.*), 1439, 1553, (?) **-icule** 1296, groats; **-illa,** lentil (Norm.) 1203; **hordeum -iculatum** 1291; **-icularis,** lenticular 1267,

c 1361; **-igines, lendines, lendes,** spots (med.) a 1250.

lenta, loin c 1370.

lentefirma, Lent farm 12c.

lenterna, jar *or* cask 12c.

lentiscus, kind of small tree 1374; a timber tree 1386, 1427; "‡beech" *or* "birch" 15c.

†**lentrix,** (?) a prickly shrub c 1200.

leo 1299, 1432, **leon/ina** c 1350, 'leonine', base coin; ‡gold (alch.) 1652; **l. heraldus** 1377, 1380, **l. rex armorum** 1413, 1464, **l. rex haraldorum** 1388, Lyon herald of Scotland; **teneo de -e,** to hold of the crown of Scotland 1336; ‡**l. citrinus foliatus,** orpiment 1652; **l. viridis,** (?) green vitriol (alch.) 1144; ‡**l. formicarum,** ant-lion 14c.; ‡**l. terre,** spurge (bot.) 14c.; **lio,** *for* **l.,** lion 1445; **-a** 1483, **-issa** c 1340, 1453, lioness; **-alis** 9c., **-icus** a 1450, leonine; **-inus,** in leonine verse 1241; **lepra -ina,** leonine leprosy c 1180, 1468; †**-ior,** *for* **-inior,** more lion-like c 1190; **leuncellus,** lion-cub 1215, 1245.

†**leofa** (†**liofa**), boar (? *cf.* A.S. *eofor*) c 1200.

leopardus, (?) lion passant gardant (her.) 1208, 1449; **lepardus** 1402, **lipardus** 1292, **leobardus, lebardus** 1440, **libardus** 1371, **libertus** c 1500, *for* **l.,** leopard; **lipard/arius, -erius,** leopard-keeper 1292.

lep/a 13c., 14c., **-us** 1224, 1557, 'leap' (dry measure).

lep/ido, grace c 990; **-oriter,** (?) gracefully 14c.

*lepor/arius c 1136, 1620, **leperarius** 1310, **leparius** 1469, **-alius** 1372, 'levrier', greyhound; **l. aquaticus** 1284; **l. gruarius** 1287, 1300; **l. herricius** 1287; **-aria** greyhound bitch c 1197, c 1350; ‡**herba -ina,** savory 14c.; ‡**-ium,** hare warren 1205; **leprus,** *for* **lepus,** hare 1243; **-o,** to hunt hares 1189.

lepros/us *c 1125, 1477, **liprosus** 1205, **-arius** 1417, **-a** (*f.*) 1128, 1321, leper; unsound (of food) c 1200, 1461; **-aria** 1257, 1279, **-ia** 1279, 1338, **-oria** 1230, **domus -ia** c 1298, lazar-house; **leprum,** *for* **lepra,** leprosy c 1197; **-or,** to be leprous a 1250.

lerca, lark (bird) 1544.

leri/pipium, -popeum, *see* **liripipium.**

lerlegga, *see* 2 **lega.**

†**lerna,** (?) *for* **larva,** ghost, evil genius 1523, c 1562.

lesa majestas, *see* 1 **lesura.**

lesca, slice (of bread, cheese *etc.*) (Fr. *lèche*) c 1180, ‡1483; *see also* 1 **lastum.**

lesch/a 1323, **-ia** 1316, 1422, **lesha** 1243, **lechia** 1234, sedge (Fr. *laîche*).

lesc/ia, -o, *see* **laxa.**

lesciva, *see* **lixivia.**

‡**leseoli morbus,** jaundice 1652.

les/io, -ivus, -or, *see* 1 **lesura.**

lesna, lesuna, market-due (G.) 1255; *cf.* **leuda.**

lessa, lease (?) 1177; *see also* **laxa.**

lest-, *see also* LAST (1 & 2).

lestlegga, *see* 2 **lega.**

1 ***les/ura,** injury, loss c 1273, c 1466; **l. fidei** c 1130, ***-io fidei** 12c., 1442, **-a fides** 12c., 1247, breach of faith; **l. majestatis** 1461, **-io majestatis** c 1192, ***-a**

majestas c 1160, 1687, **-a magistas** 1573, *lèse-majesté*; **-io**, malice, hate c 1115; **-io corone**, offence against the Crown 1351; **l. pacis**, breach of the peace 1252, 1336; **-ivus** p 1327, c 1470, **ledibilis** 1539, injurious; **-or**, injurer c 1250, p 1330; **-us** 1245, c 1272, **pars -a** 15c., injured party (leg.).

2 lesura 1547, 1587, **lezura** 1541, 1583, **leazura** 1552, **leisura** 1547, leasow, rough pasture.

*****leta** 1086, 1649, **leita** 1086, **letis** 1404, **leda** 13c., †**lea** 1198, **curia leta** c 1393, c 1544, leet, division of hundred (E. Anglia) *or* court leet; **l. burgi** 1306; **l. dimidia** 1195; **l. forinseca** 1275; *see also* **2 lada**.

let/abilis, -are, *see* **letitia.**

letania, *see* **litania.**

letegiosus, *see* LITIG

leter- (letter-), *see* **lectus; littera.**

letharg/ia 1267, 1288, **litargia** a 1250, c 1430, lethargy; **-us** c 950, **litargus** 1509, **-icus** 12c., **litargicus** a 1250, 1427, †**litergicus** 15c., lethargic.

lethea, lithia, water c 550.

leticia, 'lettice', fur of (?) snow-weasel 1220, 1230.

letifere, fatally c 1430, a 1450; **loetum,** *for* letum, 6c., 890.

let/itia, feast (Ir.) 9c.; **l. Galeni,** a stimulant (med.) 13c., **-ificatio,** rejoicing c 760; *****-anter** 8c. c 1090, 1440, **-abiliter** c 1125, joyfully; **-abilis,** capable of joy 1344; **-are** (Jerusalem), (introit for) Mid-Lent 1193, c 1300; payment to archdeacon at Mid-Lent 1222, 1321; **-ator,** rejoicer c 1000. c 1200.

letuarium, *see* **electuarium.**

letusa, *see* **2 lac.**

leu/ca *****815. 1086, 1443, **-ga** 1086, c 1283, **-gia** 13c., **leuuga** 1086, **liuga** 1086, †**leaga** 1319, **lewa** 1086, **lewedis** 1086, **ligua** 12c., **luca** 1282, a 1564, **lega** 1086, **legia** c 1090, **-cata** c 1200, c 1422, **-gata** 1086, 1286, measure of land, league *or* mile; **l. Anglica** c 1200, **l. Anglie** 1342; **-ca,** measure of time, hour 1276; c 1140, 1274, **-ga** 1086, 1418, **-a** 1086, **lewa** 1086, **-cata** 1080, c 1437, **-gata** c 1178, lowy, (area of) jurisdiction; *see also* **banleuca.**

†**leuc/asia,** quick-lime 1652; †**-oma,** albugo 14c.; **-oflegmantia,** *for* **-ophlegmasia** (med.), a 1250; **-ophlegmaticus** a 1250, **-oflecmaticus** c 1210, sufferer from leucophlegmasia; **-opiper,** white pepper a 1250, ‡14c.

†**Leucovius** (? Leutovius), Lithuanian 1267.

leuda 1190, 1289, **leda** 1283, 1315, **leida** 1283, **ledza,** 1255, market-due (O.F. *leude, leide*) (G.); *cf.* **lesna.**

leuicia, *see* **lueicia.**

leuncellus, *see* **leo.**

leura, *see* **lurcesca.**

‡**leux, lanx,** almond 1652.

lev/atio, *****raising, building, setting up 1198, a 1564; *****raising, levying (of dues) c 1260, c 1550; rising, revolt 1382, 15c.; rising of the court (leg.) c 1290; 1195, **l. de fonte** 1287, baptism; 1518, **l. corporis Christi** 15c., elevation of the host; **l. feni** 1325, 1439, **l. prati** 1282, 1317, hay-making;

l. finis, levying a fine c 1290, 1384; **l. tallie,** levying a tally c 1450; **l. shoppe,** setting up shop 1417, c 1424; **l. mercati** c 1258; **l. querele,** instituting a suit (leg.) 1523, a 1564; *****-abilis,** able to be levied 1327, 1545; **-abilis, -adicius, -aticius,** *see* **pons; -agium,** toll (on goods landed or transshipped) 1199, 1434; **-amen,** levying c 1427; *see also* **1 capella; -amentum** 15c., **-anum** c 1290, leaven; **-ata,** levy, impost (G.) c 1292; **-ator,** one who erects 1195; one who levies 1457; 1224, 1313, **-atorium** 1328, 1491, **-arium** 1185, **-orium** c 1275, 1289, **-orius** 1223, lever; **-atura,** embossed work c 1255;

breve de -erio, licence (to essoinee) to rise and appear in court (leg.) 1202; **-ans et cubans** 1207, a 1564, **l. et cumbens** 1275, levant and couchant (domiciled, of tenants or cattle); **-o,** to raise, build, set up 1198, 15c.; *****to raise, levy (dues) 1202, 1559; to emboss 1245, 1313; 1006. c 1188, c 1400, **l. in** 13c., c 1362, to raise, promote; (*intr.*) to rise (of a court) 1291; to rise in revolt 1381; 1279, **l. me** 1389, to be levied (of a fine); **l. fonte** 1234, **l. de fonte** c 1220, 1227, to act as godparent to; **l. a sacramento,** to charge with perjury c 1188; **l. de lege,** to charge with unfitness to take oath 1221; **l. billam,** to levy a bill c 1450; *****l. clamorem** 1194, c 1320, *****l. hutesium** 1202, 1413, to raise hue and cry; **l. crucem,** to preach a crusade 1377; *****l. fenum** c 1185, c 1400, **l. pratum** c 1185, 1343, to make hay; **l. feriam** c 1242, c 1272, **l. mercatum** c 1220, p 1250, to set up a fair or market; *****l. finem** c 1270, 15c., **l. chirographum** c 1267, c 1308, to levy a fine; **l. gildam** 1264; **l. juratam,** to empanel a jury 1630; **l. mineram,** to open a mine c 1250; **l. panem,** to leaven bread 1293, 1419; **l. placita** 1419, **l. querelas** 1419, 1462, to institute a suit (leg.); **l. shoppam,** to set up shop 1417; **l. talliam,** to levy a tally 1327, 1404; **l. turnum,** to institute a tourn 1258; **l. warennam** 1324; *see also* **pons.**

Levi/athan, the Devil 12c., c 1240; †**-annigena,** (?) Devil's spawn c 1193.

levi/atio, alleviation a 1250; **-ficabilis** c 1300, **-gabilis** 1276, that can be lightened; **-ficativus,** apt to lighten c 1300; **-ter** c 1250, c 1362, *****de levi** 1217, 1461, easily; **-usculus,** slight, trifling 1414, 1648; **-facio** 1497, **-fico** c 1300, to lighten (in weight); **-go** c 900. a 1090, c 1440, **-o** c 1000. a 1100, c 1400, to relieve, lighten, alleviate; **-pendo** to make light of c 1190, c 1400; **-to,** to levitate 1686; *cf.* LENI.

levi/ga, carpenter's plane c 1389, ‡1483; **-tersus,** rubbed smooth c 1300; **-tivus** (? **lenitivus**), apt to smooth c 1300; ‡**-torium,** "sleek-stone" c 1440.

levinarius, *see* LIG

levistic/um (†**lenistic-**), *for* **ligusticum,** lovage (bot.) a 1250, a 1446; **-us,** of lovage c 1198.

*****Le vit/a,** deacon c 760, c 985. a 1090, 1428; **L. Celestis** 9c.; **-ice,** like a true deacon 826; **-icus,** diaconal c 1000. c 1070, 1414; (*subst.*) book of Leviticus c 1223, c 1534.

lex, Mosaic law, Old Testament (bibl.); 'liberty', privilege c 1070, 14c.; legal status c 1115, 1372; fine (G.) 1280; 'law', division of England 1324; *'law', compurgation, body of compurgators c 1108, 1419; c 1115, **l. apparens** c 1185, **l. examinationis** c 1115, ordeal; **l. aque,** ordeal by water c 1178, p 1350; **l. ferri candentis,** ordeal by fire c 1178; **l. Anglescherie,** Englishry (in Welsh Marches) 1205; **l. Anglicana,** English common law c 1185, 1370; **l. Anglie,** curtesy 1251, 1321; **l. Britolli (Bretolli, Bristolli, Bretonica, Britannie),** law (privileges) of Bréteuil 1194, 1364; **l. Christiana** 1277, **l. Christianorum** c 1200, c 1343, **l. Dei** c 1115, Christian religion; **l. communis,** common law (of realm or church) c 1178, c 1456; **l. consuetudinaria** 15c.; **l. Danorum** c 1102, c 1150; **l. equitandi,** military service 11c.; **l. genialis** 1241, **l. genealis** c 1430, law of nature; **l. gratie** (theol.) c 1340, 1396; **l. legalis** c 1130; **l. libertatis** (theol.) c 1343; **l. magna,** 'law' requiring oath of 36 compurgators (London) 1274, p 1330; **l. media,** like 'law' in which half the compurgators are drawn from either side of Walbrook 1321; **l. Maumeti** c 1190, **l. Mahumetica** c 1200; **l. Marchie** 1215, c 1315; **l. marescalcialis** 1559, **l. mariscalcialis** 1584, **l. martialis** 1559, 1584, martial law; **l. marina** 1287, 1383, **l. maritima** 1361, 1399; **l. mercatoria,** 'law merchant' 1268, 1419; **l. Moysi (Moysis)** c 1115, 1277, **l. Mosaica (Moysaica)** c 730. c 1227, 1518; **l. Vetus (Vetusta),** Old Testament 1175, c 1536; **l. Nova,** New Testament a 1175, c 1536; **l. positiva** 1344, a 1408; **l. regni** 1215; **l. sacramenti,** wager of law c 1260; **l. terre** c 1115, c 1450; **l. Walensis** 1086, **l. Walenseca** 1345, **l. Wallie** 1215; **de leg/e,** according to law 1274; **facio -em (meam),** to wage law 1194, 1365; *see also* **homo, pater, pono, serviens, stare, tempus;** **-ifer,** law-abiding 14c.; (*subst.*) Moses c 760; a local official (Norway) 1393; †**-irupes** 12c., *-irups c 950, **-isrumpus** c 1200, *for* **-irupa;** **-islatio,** book of laws c 1238; **-islativus, -umlativus** 1659, **-islatorius** 1622, legislative; *-ista, lawyer, law student (ac.) 12c., 1690; **-istarius,** registrar 1297; *see also* **3 lega;** *cf.* **laga,** LEGAL, LEGITIM

lexipyretos, febrifuge (med.); ‡**lixaperiton** 14c.

lex/is, logic 1241; **-icon,** dictionary c 1610.

lexiv/a, -ia, *see* **lixivia.**

leya, *see* **1 lega.**

leyerlegga, *see* **2 lega.**

leynera, *see* **lannera.**

lezura, *see* **2 lesura.**

li, article introducing word to be considered simply as such, not as object denoted c 1250, 1378.

*liard/us** c 1180, a 1446, **-ius** c 1314, 'lyard', dapple-grey; liard, small coin (Sc.) 1521.

liatia, liacium, *see* LIG

lib/a, libation 890; **-amen baptismatis** c 950; **-o,** to utter c 1150.

libanus, frankincense: **olibanus** a 1250, 1622.

libardus, *see* **leopardus.**

libedo, libeo, *see* **libitum.**

libella, *see* **libellus; libra.**

‡**libellum,** wastel 13c., 1483.

libell/us *798, 1044. 12c., 14c., -a 11c.,** charter, deed; writ *or* 'libel' (leg.) c 1195, a 1564; episcopal profession c 804, c 816; **-ulus,** book c 980; small charter, deed 12c.; **-osus,** libellous 1686; **-o,** to sue, bring a 'libel' against 1336, 1684; to specify in a 'libel' 1548, 17c.; to reduce to writing a 1452.

1 lib/er, charter, deed 1001. 12c.; (?) Bible 7c.; 1199, 1526, **l. de Jure** 1398, book on which oaths were taken; **l. Geneseos, l. Levitici, l. Judicum** 1267, **l. Regum** 1219, 1267, **l. Dierum** c 1180, c 1546, **l. Paralipomenon** c 1180, c 1258, books of Old Testament; **l. dierum meorum** (fig.) c 1346; **l. dormiens,** coucher c 1296; **l. episcopalis,** service-book 15c.; **l. Judeorum,** (?) Pentateuch 1201; **l. judiciarius** c 1178, **l. regius** c 1100, **l. censualis** 1586, Domesday Book; **l. mortuorum,** book of service for the dead 1424; **l. Paschalis,** Easter Book 1535, 1576; **l. ratiocinii,** bill of lading 1535; **l. usuum,** book of uses (eccl.) 1526; **-raria,** library 13c., 1476; **-rariuncula,** little library 1501; **-ricola,** book-lover a 1260.

2 liber/ 1086, 1544, **homo l.** 1086, 1308, freeman; **femina (mulier, puella) -a** 1086; **l. tenens** 1291, 1386, *-e tenens** 1103, 1524, freeholder; **-us** 12c., **-ius** c 885, **-tus** 12c., **liver** 859, c 1000. 12c., *for* **l.,** free; *see also* **arma, bancus, clamo, consuetudo, divisa, eleemosyna, feodum, incensum, lapis, maritagium, 2 mortarium, petra, potestas, redditus, servitium, tenementum, terra, tus, viduitas, wara, warenna;** **-alis,** freeman a 1135, 1419; a 1135, **homo l.** a 1135, c 1185, thane; **-ales** (*pl.*), liberal arts c 1250; **-alitas,** thanehood c 1110; priesthood c 1110; liberty, franchise a 1130, c 1150; **-aliter** 796, 984. 1086, c 1258, **-ate** 1086, freely; **-atarius,** person receiving allowance 1343; **-ata** 1168, c 1458, **librata** c 1443, **-atum** c 1450, a 1452, *-atio** 1130, 16c., †**-tatio** 1539, **-atura** c 1290, 1583, (?) **-tas** c 1218, 1438, 'livery', allowance; *-ata** 1399, 1545, **-atura** 1509, livery, allowance of clothing, badge; **-atio assisa** 1201, 1234, **l. constituta** 1167, 1202, fixed allowance; **-atio ***1257, 1555, **liveratio** c 1353, livery, delivery, handing over; feoffment 1086; equipment 1156, 1174; (?) deliberation 15c.; c 1150, **l. hospitiorum** 1258, **l. marescalli** 1155, 1419, billeting; **l. gaole,** jail-delivery 1296; **-ate** 1230, 15c., †**-atum** c 1252, name of a writ; **littera de -ate** 1242, 1289; **-ator,** deliverer, hander over c 1280, 1315; feoffor 1086; **-atrix,** deliverer, releaser (*f.*) 1125, 13c.; **l. latrocinii,** disposer of stolen goods (*f.*) 1291; **-tas ***770, 1024. 1088, c 1500, **livertas** c 853, (grant of) privilege, franchise, liberty; *privileged area, franchise, liberty 1196, 1686; (?) payment for freedom 1294; **-tates** (*pl.*), debts arising within liberties 1230; **-tas Anglie,** curtesy (leg.) 1325; **l. chemini,** right of way 1215; **l. donationis,** grant of

privileges c 796, 875; **l. gladii**, palatine
privilege (Chester) 1242; **l. regia**, regality
1134; **l. Romana** 13c., **l. solida** 1086,
entire freedom; **-tatinus**, fighter for freedom
1344; **-tatio**, exemption (eccl.) a 1452,
c 1470; **-o** *1086, a 1564, **libro** 14c., **livero**
858, to deliver up, hand over; (?) to hold by
feoffment 1086; to pay (money) 1204, 1540;
to warrant c 1115; to deliberate 15c.; **l.
gaolam** 13c., 14c., **l. carcerem** c 1321,
to deliver jail (by trying prisoners); **-to**, to
liberate a 1450, c 1470; to exempt (eccl.)
a 1452; *see also* **libra**.
libertus, *see* **leopardus**.
libitin/a, -um c 1188, 1504, **lebitina** 1441, bier.
*lib/itum c 1180, 1559, **-itus** (*4th decl.*) c 730.
a 1100, 1569, will, pleasure; ***ad l.** 1086,
1559, **pro -ito** c 1125, 1569, **pro -ito
voluntatis** 1267, c 1440, **pro -itu v.** 1277,
1392, **per -itum v.** c 1250; **livens, liven-
ter**, willingly 858; **-edo**, *for* **-ido**, 1510;
-idinicola, voluptuary 12c.; **-eo**, to desire
12c.; to please c 1204.
liblacum, sorcery (A.S. *lybblac*) c 1115.
libo, *see* **liba**.
libosus, (?) yellow c 550.
libr-, *see also* **liber** 1 & 2.
libr/a, pound (weight): **libera** 1259; **-a
Londoniensis** 1303; **l. mercatoria** c 1300,
(?) **l. marcalis** c 1404, pound avoirdupois;
l. magna c 1300, c 1390, **l. grossa** c 1330;
l. parva c 1300, c 1390, **l. subtilis** c 1330; **l.
usualis** c 1330; **l. Troe**, pound Troy (Sc.)
1434; **-ata ponderis**, pound weight c 1450;
libella, half-pound 15c.; **livellum**, *for*
libella, a level 1238, 1306;
 ***-a**, pound (money) 1086, 1564; **l. ad
arsuram** 1086, **l. arsa** 1086, 1275, **l. alba**
1086, 1225, **l. blanca** 1086, 1230, **l.
candida**, **l. ad combustionem**, **l. ad
ignem** 1086, pound blanched (tested by
assay); **l. ad numerum**, **l. numerata**
1086, **l. numero** c 1094, 1257, **l. ad
compotum** c 1130, 1194, pound by tale
(*i.e.* counting of pence); **l. ad pensum** 1086,
c 1178, **l. pensata**, **l. ad pondus** 1086, **l.
ponderata** 1212, 1275, **l. ponderalis** (Sc.)
c 1400, pound by weight; **l. denariorum**
1086; **l. scaccarii** 1177; **l. sterlingica**
1528, ***l. sterlingorum** c 1166, 15c.; *see
also* **Andegavensis, Arnaldensis, Burdegalensis, Cennomanensis, Chipotensis,
Guienea, Parisiensis, Rothomagensis,
Tolosanus, Turonensis;** †**l. terre**, pound's
worth of land c 1220, c 1293; ***-ata (terre,
redditus,** *etc.*) c 1100, 1586, **liberata** 1225,
pound's worth;
 -atio, wielding 1380, c 1470; pondering
(*cf.* **liberatio**) 1437; libration (astr.) 1686;
‡**-atorium**, "counting-place" 1483; **-ator
celi**, God 1245; **-o**, to lift up c 1170; to
direct c 1197; to measure 14c.
libr/ella 1471, **-illa** 1413, c 1480, gun; *cf.*
vibrellum.
lica, kind of stone c 1396.
licent/ia *704, 853. 1086, c 1502, **lecentia**
1481, **lisentia** 1527, permission, authorization; leave, formal farewell 1266, 1461;
l. concordandi (leg.) 1202, 1285; **l.
incipiendi et legendi** (ac.) 1312; **l. vie,**

way-leave 1420; **-er** 1086, c 1125, **-ialiter**
1292, 1419, by permission; **-iabilis**, permissible 1374; **-ialis** 1350, 15c., **-iatorius**
c 1272, c 1464, permissive; **-iatio**, authorization c 1376, c 1448; licensing (ac.) 1312,
1431; **-iatus**, licentiate (ac.) 1350, 1560;
-io, *to permit, authorize c 1187, 1522;
to license (ac.) c 1253, c 1514; ***c** 1102,
c 1470, **l. ad propria** c 1293, c 1450, to
give leave to depart, to dismiss; **licet**, despite
(*prep.*) 1383; *for* **scilicet**, c 1236; **clausula
(de) l.** (leg.) 1413, 1419; **liceo**, to permit
c 1184; to be permitted c 1357.
†**licesterium**, (?) bedding 15c.; *cf.* **lectus**.
lich-, *see* **lecythus; lychnus**.
lici/atorium, weaver's beam c 1170, ‡c 1440;
‡treadle 15c.; **-tarium**, spindle c 1595; *cf.*
ligeum.
licie (**litie**) (*pl.*), lists, barriers, places fenced
in (Fr. *lices*) 1215, c 1250; *cf.* **lista**.
licin-, *see* **limatio; lychnus**.
licisca, licissa, *see* **lycisca**.
licius, *see* **luceus**.
lic/or, -umen, *see* LIQU
licoricia, see **glycyrrhiza**.
lictor, warrior *or* executioner c 760.
lidiata (**lyd-**) 1293, **lithieta**, †**ladhieta**
c 1160, 'lidgate', fence-gate.
lido, to slip 1302.
lidoria, *see* **ledoria**.
lieg-, *see* **ligeus**.
liem-, lien-, *see* LIG
lienter/ia, lientery, diarrhoea c 1185, 15c.;
-icus, lienteric a 1250.
lifus ‡15c., c 1495, **liphus** 1543, (?) *for*
libum, loaf.
lig/a 1317, c 1540, **-ia** c 1320, c 1350, **-ua**
1608, league, confederacy; 1229, 1461,
-amen 1296, 1526, **legamen** 1368, tie,
band, chain; **-amen** 1243, **liemum** 1286,
lienum 1251, 1287, **limerium** 1279, leash;
1305, c 1440, **-amentum** 1294, †**liemum**
1320, tie-beam; binding (for wattle and
daub wall) 1532; file (for documents)
1201, 1283; straw for binding sheaf c 1280;
boot-lace 1453; bend (her.) c 1450; oath of
allegiance c 1400; **l. ferreum** (for windows)
1409, 1472; **l. ligneum**, brace (for door)
1374; **-abilis**, combinable 1326, c 1470;
nota l., tied note (mus.) 1326; **-acia**, sheaf
(of arrows) 1213; **liatia** 1225, 1297,
liacium 1286, bundle; **-aculum**, cable
1564, 1568; ‡**-acularius**, dealer in points
(for hose) 1520; **-amentum**, cord, tether
c 1210, 1461; **l. conjugale** c 1265; **-ami-
narius** (fig.) c 1100, **liemarius** c 1135,
liemerius 1244, ***limarius** 1195, 1332,
limerius 1198, 1203, **limerus** 1202, ‡**levinarius** 1570, lyam-hound; **-aris**, obligatory
1292; **-ata**, note in a ligature (mus.) 1326;
-atio, binding, imprisonment 9c. 10c.
1253; binding (of sheaves) a 1295, 1449;
hooping (of casks) 1480; hoop (round a
beam) 1312; 'binding' (game played on
Hockday) 1450; **l. et solutio** (eccl.) c 1000;
l. federis 1302; **l. hanaperii** 1278; ***l. librorum** 1302, 1524; **l. planetarum,** (?) conjunction (astr.) c 1260; **l. rotarum** 1399;
-ator, -atrix (*f.*), reconciler 1245; binder of
sheaves 13c., 1279; (?) hooper 1225; **l.**

librorum, book-binder 1255, c 1510;
-atorie, by attachment c 1360; ‡-atorium,
"tether" 15c.; -atoria (*pl.*), rigging (naut.)
1382; -atura 720. 1202, 1452, -ituria 6c.,
(act of) binding; fastening, bond, band,
strap 790. 1207, 1458; 1292, 1381, liura
1190, binding for cloth, *etc.*; (?) boot-lace
1287; hoop or hooping 1306, 1446; metal
tire of wheel 1257, 1380; ligature (mus.)
1326, c 1470; binding principle (alch.)
c 1320; bond, compact a 1452; l. ad
fenestras, (?) window-frame 1344; l.
(domorum), (?) fixing of tie-beams 1254,
a 1452; l. hanaperie 1335; l. librorum,
etc., 1362, 1528; ‡-ium, mortise 1483;
-atus, confederate c 1160; *-o, to bind
(sheaves) c 1283, c 1345; to bind (cloth, *etc.*)
1295, 1343; to hoop (vessels, *etc.*) 1203,
1375; to hoop (wooden hafts) with metal
1338, 1388; 1211, 1454, †luo (*f.l.*) 1344,
*to fit (wheels) with metal tires (*cf.* 2 lega);
*to bind (books) c 1205, 16c.; to set (jewels)
1387; to bind, solidify, hold in combination
(alch.) a 1252, c 1470; *to be binding,
obligatory 1275, c 1534; -o tanquam
apprenticium 1371; see also potestas.
ligana, tongue 6c.
ligeum, (?) for licium, thrum 1275, 1280.
lige/us (ligi-) *c 1115, 1583, legeus, legius
c 1115, c 1443, liegus 1569, (*subst.*) liege,
liege subject; *1093, 1583, *legeus, legius
1391, c 1540, liugius c 1270, litgius (G.)
1309, (*adj.*) liege, bound by allegiance;
dominus l., liege lord c 1164; 1401; homo
l., liege man 1093, 1461; homagium -um
(G.) 1309; l. vassallus c 1250; -a potestas
1198, 1332; -a proprietas, lawful ownership
1205; -a viduitas, independent widowhood
(leg.) 1231, c 1307; ligie, as liege subjects
c 1140; -um a 1446, legium 1461, *-antia
c 1173, 1584, liegantia c 1330, *ligantia
1166, c 1400, lijantia 12c., ligentia c 1160,
c 1420, legentia 15c., 1468, legiantia
c 1400, c 1450, -amentum 1370, 15c.,
legeamentum p 1327, ligeitas 1285,
1456, legeitas a 1446, allegiance.
lightenaria, lighter (boat) 1475.
lign/um (lingn-), *trunk, beam, post 1086,
1505; tree 1251, 1383; (?) wood, forest
c 1325; stocks c 1290; wooden foundation for
cart-saddle 1315, 1377; c 1180, 1537, l.
Domini c 1125, c 1315, l. Dominicum
c 1220, 1403, the Cross; l. Paschale, Easter
cross 1421; ‡l. Alexandrinum, brasil wood
c 1440; ‡l. amarum, aloes 14c.; l. mortuum, dead wood a 1128; l. undulatum,
linen panelling 16c.; l. viride (Norm.) 1113;
see also per; -agium c 1115, 1203, linagium
c 1310, right to take timber; -amen c 1196,
1234, -arium c 866. c 1400, timber; -arium,
timber-yard 1300; -arius, fueller (mon.)
c 1356, c 1440; -eitas, woodenness c 1270;
-icisor (†-icifer) a 1300, -iscissor 1535,
wood-cutter; †-icismus, bill-hook a 1300;
-iculum c 1380, 1544, -ulum 13c., piece
of wood, stick; -iola sacra, fragment of
the Cross 1383; -ifaber c 1362, linifaber
1499, faber -arius 1188, 1588, carpenter;
-ifabrilis, of carpentry c 1440; -ifer 6c.,
-inus 1421, wooden; -ipes, wooden-legged

c 1180; 1294, ‡1483, †-ipedium 15c.,
-ipodium 1288, staff, stilt, *or* patten;
-ipeta, wood-pecker (bird) 1544; *see also*
1 linea.
1 ligo, (?) colour *or* darkness c 550.
2 ligo/ molendini, mattock (part of spindle
by which it is attached to mill-stone) 1344;
l. igneus, "fire shovel" 1553; -nizo, to
work with a pick ‡1483, 1525; *see also* liga.
†ligorius, unicorn (Fr. *licorne*) 12c.
ligua, *see* leuca; liga.
†liguans, (?) *for* linguatus, fringed (*or for*
lineatus, lined) 1242.
ligul/a c 1315, 1461, ligola 1344, legula
1394, strap, thong, 'point'; *file (for
documents) 1202, 1418; -atus, tongue-
shaped 1418; *cf.* lingula.
ligur/, glutton c 1370; -itor, flatterer, parasite
c 1115.
‡ligustr/um, ‡glustrum, primrose or cowslip 15c.; -o, to whiten c 1185.
lijantia, *see* ligeus.
lilifagus, *see* elilifagus.
lili/um, white outer margin of manuscript
1345; ‡mercury (alch.) 1652; ‡l. aquaticum, water-lily 14c.; l. celeste a 1250,
‡14c., ‡l. silvaticum 14c., iris; *see also*
flos; †-olum, (?) necklace c 1250; -aris
c 1250, -osus 1200, †-olus c 1000, lily-white;
-astrum, bindweed 1538; -ger c 1595,
-atus c 1595, adorned with fleurs-de-lis;
-o, to make lily-white c 1170, 1432.
lima, *see* luva.
lim/acia, *for* -ax, snail a 1250.
limarius, *see* LIG
lim/as, apron ‡c 1440, c 1499; ‡-us, "farthingale" 1570.
lim/atio, filing, polishing 1351, 1381; -aris,
see opus; -ator, filer 1295; ‡-atorium
(†licinitorium), "sleek-stone" 15c., 1483
(*cf.* litatorium); -atura, (*coll.*) filings
a 1150, 1424; polishing, correction 1267;
see also linitio.
lim/bernarius (lym-), lime-burner a 1215;
-kilna, lime-kiln 1255.
limb/us, bordure (her.) c 1595; c 1362, 1610,
lumbus c 1290, Limbo, region bordering
on Hell; -o, to border, fringe 1245; *see also*
lembus.
lim/en apostolorum 9c. 1422, c 1475, l.
Petri c 1139, 12c., Papal Curia; -inare,
threshold, lintel c 1160, 1309.
lim/erium, -erius, -erus, *see* LIG
limes, baulk (in open field) c 1280, 1315;
position in decimal notation (math.) c 1150;
division of province of Austin friars (17c.);
l. sagittarum, shooting-range, butt 1587;
limit/es (*pl.*), lists (for fighting) c 1290;
shrine (? *for* limen) 1366; -as, boundary
c 1285; -anus, *for* -aneus, bordering
c 1260; -ate, in a limited sense c 1360, 1374;
-atio, limitation, restriction 1267, 1570;
limitation of time (leg.) c 1258, 1279;
direction, command c 1380, c 1516; -ativus,
restrictive c 1300, c 1375; -ative, by way
of restriction 1530; -ator, surveyor c 1289;
'limiter' (friar licensed to beg within bounds)
1447, 15c.; †-us, *for* -atus, fixed 1356, 1559;
-o, to limit in time c 1258, c 1306; to assign,
appoint 1417, c 1470.

limin-, limio, *see* limen; 1 limo; lumen.
limma, *see* lemma.
1 *lim/o c 1200, 1385, †-eus 1385, lemo
1304, cart-shaft; -onarius 1213, 1316,
-inaris c 1350, for a shaft.
2 limo, lemon *or* lime a 1250, 1622.
3 limo, *see* 1 linea; linitio.
Limocenus, *see* opus.
limositas, muddiness, filth c 1191, 1620.
limpa, *see* LYMPH
limpid/itas, clarity 1435; -us, smooth c 1200,
1345; -issima majestas (title) 1404; -ius,
more clearly c 730. c 1317, 1414; -issime
c 990. 1415.
†limpus, (?) *for* limbus *or* limus, apron
1214; *cf.* limas.
linagium, *see* LIGN; 2 linea.
linca 1296, 1414, lynsum 1347, linch-pin *or*
axle; linepinna 1325, lenepina 1289, 1312,
linpinna 1309.
lincell/um, -us, *see* LINT
linchus, *see* 2 linkum.
lincia, 'linch', measure of tin 1404.
†linco, (?) to bind (rushes) 1567; *cf.* 1 linkum.
1 lin/ea (-ia), linen cloth or garment 1245,
15c.; 1279, lignum a 1300, *for* -um, flax;
-amentum, candle 7c.; -aria, wild flax *or*
toadflax a 1250, ‡14c.; -aria, -getta, -ota
1544, ‡-osa 1483, linnet; -aria c 1160, 1400,
-arium a 1190, 1238, -iarium c 1275, flax-
ground; -aria (*pl.*), (?) hangings 1485;
‡-arium 1483, ‡-erium 15c., -ea (*pl.*) 1224,
-i (*pl.*) 1266, -i semen 1472, linseed;
‡-atorium, flax-house 1483; ‡-atorium,
-itorium, bundle of flax 1483; -ecorda,
flaxen rope 1352; ‡-elion 14c., -i oleum
1338, -geti oleum 1466, linseed oil; -ensis
c 1250, -etus 1276, leneus 1461, 1534,
lingeus 1292, *for* -eus, of linen; -eus
armurarius, linen-armourer 1452, 1461; 1.
draparius 1260, 1. draperus 1192, -idra-
parius a 1227, lyndraperius 14c., linen-
draper; ‡-ifex, -ificator, -ificatrix (*f.*),
flax-worker 1483; ‡-ificium, flax-work 1483;
‡-ipedium, linen sock or hose c 1440, c 1483;
‡-ipulus c 1440, 1483, ‡-ipolus 15c., strike
of flax; ‡-istema, "tartarin" 15c.; ‡"linsey-
woolsey" 1483; ‡-odium, flax-boll 15c., 1483;
-onum, linen 1383; ‡-osina, curtain 15c.;
-ula, thread c 1200, c 1380; ‡-ifico, to work
flax 1483; -io (†limo), (?) to beat flax 1226.
2 lin/ea (-ia), 'line', twelfth part of inch 1686;
1. fiducie, part of turquet (astr.) a 1350;
1. meridiana 1326, 1. meridionalis 1267,
1326, meridian (astr.); 1. muliebris, female
line of descent 12c.; 1. recta, direct line of
descent c 1185; -agium, lineage 1299;
-ealis, lineal (of descent) 1402, c 1470;
numerus 1., number in general (whether
prime or divisible) a 1250; -ealiter *c 1143,
c 1438, -ionaliter 16c., in a straight line;
*c 1190, c 1470, -eatim c 1125, lineally;
-eamentaliter, by lineaments c 1315;
-eamentaris, concerned with lineaments
c 1150; -earis, lineal c 1250; interlinear
a 1384; umbrated (her.) c 1595; -earitas,
property of being linear c 1270; -eariter,
in lines a 1250, c 1270; -eatim, line by line
1345; -eatio, linear dimension a 1233;
figure, diagram 1267; measuring (Sc.)

c 1270, 1469; 1. (manus), pattern of lines
(in palmistry) 1378; -eator, 'liner',
measurer, surveyor (Sc.) c 1270, 1469; -eo
to delineate 1378; to measure c 1270, 1469;
see also linitio.
lin/eatura 1220, c 1452, -atura 1343, -iitura
1240, -ura 1323, 1472, -iatio c 1452, lining
(of clothes); -atus 1232, 1433, -etus p 1341,
lined; -eo 1208, -io 1250, 1403 to line.
†linellarius (? liv-), (?) *for* libellarius (liv-),
granted by charter a 1446.
line/pinna, *see* linca.
linga 1275, c 1493, lenga 1265, 1352, ling
(fish); *see also* lingua.
lingator, *see* SLING
ling/etta, -etum, -eus, *see* 1 linea.
lingn-, linifaber, *see* LIGN
lingu/a, slander c 1200, 1276; nation 1295,
1388; (?) retort (alch.) c 1345; linga,
(?) tongue or pin of brooch 1393; -a
gutturis, epiglottis a 1250; -e medietas,
jury composed half of Jews or aliens (?) 13c.,
‡1567; -a materna 1246, 1503, 1. mater-
nalis 1453, mother tongue; †1. agni, 1.
arietis, waybread, plantain (bot.) 14c.;
‡1. avis, stitchwort (bot.) 14c., 15c.; 1. bovis,
bugloss (bot.) c 1200, ‡c 1440; ‡1. cervi
c 1350, 15c., 1. cervina c 1200, 1634, hart's
tongue (fern); ‡1. hircina, ‡1. passerina,
(?) swine's cress 14c.; ‡1. serpentina 1570,
1. vulneraria 1634, adder's tongue (fern);
1. serpentina 1297, 1454, 1. serpentis 1310,
serpent-tongue, jeweller's ornament; -agium
c 1444, ‡15c., languagium 1395, 1428,
langagium a 1450, language; langetta 1303,
languetta 1300, metal tongue; 1238, languetta 14c., tongue of land; miles -aris,
knight of the tongue a 1446; -ositas, talkative-
ness c 1090; -or, to speak c 1180.
lingul/a, string, strap (on clothes) 1245;
(on bell) 1533; handle 1388; label (her.)
a 1446; strip (of land) 1237; 1. justitie,
scales of justice 1232; *cf.* ligula; *see also*
SLING
†linio, (?) filth 14c.; *see also* LENI; linea;
lineatura; linitio.
lin/itio 1225, c 1250, -iamentum 13c.,
anointing; 1403, -uratio 1239, -eamentum
c 1250, daubing, plastering; litura, plaster
1508; ‡-itor 1483, -eator 1507, (?) -iator
(†limator) 1245, ‡litor 15c., 1520,
"dauber", plasterer; -eo c 1200, 1242, -io
1301, to daub, caulk; -io (†limo), to anoint,
grease c 1170, 1385; *cf.* lenitivus.
1 linkum, link (of chain) 1351, 1486; *cf.*
linco.
2 lin/kum, 'link', plot of land (Sussex)
c 1285; -chus, linch, unploughed strip
(Dorset) 1337.
lino/sa, -ta, *see* 1 linea.
linpinna, *see* linca.
linquo (with *inf.*), to cease a 1408.
lintellum, lintel 1284, 1290.
*lint/eum (linth-) a 1090, 1423, -ea c 1520,
*-eamen c 760. a 1090, 1558, -eamentum
1375, 1385, -eomentum 1574, -eolus
c 1180, -iolare 1588, lincellum 1207,
lincellus 1201, 1255, linen sheet, napkin *or*
altar cloth; 1. picatum, tarpaulin 1675;
-eamen corporale, communion cloth 12c.;

l. de canabo 1380; †-eameus, flaxen 1583; -earius, linen-draper 1661, 1710.

lintrizo, (?) to wash 8c.

lin/um, -ula, *see* 1 linea.

linura, *see* lineatura.

lio, *see* leo.

liofa, *see* leofa.

lipard-, *see* leopardus.

lipar/ia, suppurated choler (med.) a 1250; -is, butterwort (bot.) 1634.

liphus, *see* lifus.

‡lipo/thymia 14c., -thomia a 1250, †-tosmia a 1142, fainting.

lippidositas, inflammation of eyes a 1250.

liprosus, *see* leprosus.

lipsan/a (*pl.*) 1200, c 1400, -ia c 1180, remains, relics (λείψανα).

liptodemon, *see* LITH

liptoriatus, *see* littera.

liqu/atio, melting, melting-point 1267, 1427; -amen, ‡"dripping", "suet" 1570; measure of tallow 1594; **licumen**, a liquid 6c.; -ebilis 1250, -efactibilis p 1300, liquefiable; -efactio, moistening 6c.; liquefaction a 1250, 1508; -efactivus, liquefying a 1250, a 1252; -ens, liquid (gram.) 8c.; **licor de brasio**, malt liquor 1437; -idatio, making clear, explaining 1478; declaration (of judicial sentence) 1684; -iditas a 1250, 1424, -orositas a 1250, liquidity; ‡-idum resolutum, l. de resoluto, substance naturally liquid 1652; -idus, liquid, clear (of debts) 1237, 1239; -ido, to declare, reveal 1599, 1622; to liquidate, turn into cash 1684.

liqu/iricia, -oricia, *see* glycyrrhiza.

1 †lira,] thread c 1464.

2 lira (lyra), baulk, selion 1455, 1683; drainage channel 1361.

liripipi/um c 1362, 1499, ‡leripipium 15c., †leripopeum 1505, liripipe, elongated point of hood or cap; ‡"pike of a shoe" c 1440; **sotulares -ati**, shoes with pointed toes c 1350.

lischa, sleek-stone, polishing-stone (*cf.* Fr. *lisse*) c 1297; *cf.* litatorium.

lis/era, -eria, *see* lista.

lisisca, *see* lycisca.

lissis, *see* laxa.

lis/ta 1215, 1587, -eria c 1200, -ura 1197, 1276, 'list', border (of cloth); stripe, band a 1273, c 1320; sort of plank (naut.) 1294, 1313; (?) sort of moulding (arch.) 1277; -era, border of cornice (arch.) 1355; -ta superior, (?) upper streak (naut.) 1296; -te (*pl.*), lists (for tournament) 1290, 1442 (*cf.* licie); l. nundinarum 1287; ‡-tia, "castle ditch" 15c.; -to, to border, edge (cloth, *etc.*) 1237, 1331; 1252, -tio 1286, to paint in stripes; to dye 1434.

listagium, *see* 1 lastum.

*litania 747. c 1080, 16c., *letania c 850, c 1000. a 1100, 1461, latenia 1489, litany (eccl.); l. major (25 April) c 1595.

litarg-, *see* lethargia; LITH

lita/tio, mass for the dead 1537; -tor, sacrificer 10c.

‡litatorium, "sleek-stone" 15c.; *cf.* limatorium, lischa, LUCIBRIC

liter-, *see* lectus; littera.

liteus, *see* lituus.

litgius, *see* ligeus.

lith/anthrax (lit-), mineral coal 1622, 1634; -argium c 1200, -argycum 13c., *for* -argyrus, litharge; -argyreus, made of litharge 13c.; -iasis, the stone (med.) a 1250; -odemon (†liptodemon), agate a 1250, ‡14c.; -osperma, "saxifrage" a 1250; -ontripon, lithontriptic (med.) a 1250; -otomus, quarryman 1390.

lithia, *see* lethea.

lithieta, *see* lidiata.

litie, *see* licie.

litig/atrix, scold c 1125, 1537; -atorius c 1250, -ialis c 1470, -osus c 550, letegiosus 1444, contentious, contested; **litispendium**, case before the court a 1452.

litor, *see* linitio.

litor-, *see* lectus; litus.

litter/a a 1300, c 1450, **par -arum** 1200, 1329, letter, epistle; verse of Scripture c 1130, 1344; word p 1347, c 1370; charter, deed 12c., 1295; learning, Latinity c 1250, c 1365; lettera, letter 1296, 1481; de bona -a, in a fair hand 1311; -e albe, blank letters 1318; -a Bononie, formal script used in Bologna (leg.) 1342; l. capitalis c 1178, c 1362, l. capitularis c 1250, capital letter; l. curialis, court hand 1419, 1560; l. dominicalis, Sunday letter c 1200, 1476; l. legum, the letter of the law c 1343; l. pacis, pardon 1262; l. patens 1255, c 1400, *-e patentes a 1165, 1687, -a pendens c 1290, -e pendentes c 1220, -a in pendenti sigillata 1309, -e aperte c 1285, 1436, letters patent; l. clausa c 1253, 1416, -e clause 1203, 1247, letters close; l. de capella, (?) letter under great seal (Sc.) 1348; -e divine c 1090, 1549, l. sacre 12c., divinity, scripture; l. liberales c 1226, 1345, l. humaniores 1620, liberal studies; l. in quatuor formis (Sc.) 1566; l. seculares, profane learning c 1090, 14c.; l. de soluto, letters of payment c 1270; -a textualis, text hand 1378, 1464; l. verior, better reading (in MS.) a 1350; *see also* ad; -e cambii, *see* cambium (*and so with other like phrases*); -alis, literal a 1185, 1620; -aliter, literally 8c., 10c. 1267; c 1259, 1461, -atorie 1200, 1558, by letter, in writing; -alius, more literally 1378; -atio, grammar 8c.; -ator, literalist c 730. a 1200; -atoria, epistle 1255; -atorius, literary, scholarly 948. c 1160; *expressed in writing 12c., 1460; -atura, *literacy, learning c 820. c 1188, 1549; script 1433; context, passage c 1080; (*coll.*) documents c 1040; **pono ad -aturam**, to educate 1325, 1330; -atus, embroidered with letters 1204, 1295 (*see also* miles); †liptoriatus, learned 13c.; *see also* lectus.

litura, *see* lectus; linitio.

liturg/ia, (?) expense a 1452; -us, messenger c 1434.

lit/us, shingle c 1290; side (of castle) 1588; -orium, shore 1309; -orius, maritime 890. 13c.

lit/uus, trumpet: (?) †-eus c 1200; -uo, to blow a trumpet c 1180.

liugius, *see* ligeus.

liura, *see* liga.

liv-, *see also* lib-

livellum, see **libra.**

liv/entia 1258, **-iditas** a 1250, lividness, bluish colour; **-orosus,** black and blue 690.

lix/a, water 6c., c 1000. ‡14c.; **-o,** to boil, seethe c 1150, ‡c 1440.

lixaperiton, see **lexipyretos.**

lixivia, lye: ‡**lexiv/ia** 14c., **-ium** a 1250, **-a** c 1267, c 1390, **lesciva** c 1080, ‡**luxivium** 15c.

lixo, "hedging-bill" 1557.

loadesmanagium, see **lodmannus.**

lobus, lobe 1544.

loca, see **logea.**

locacitas, see **lecacitas.**

loc/atio, -abilis, etc., see **locus.**

locc/a (lock-), -us 1232, 1299, **laccus** 1242, **lokettus** 1275, 1322, lock (of wool).

loccum 1281, **loktum** 1230, **lokkum** 1590, 1547, **loketta** 1310, **loculus** 1547, lock, weir; **lokettum,** lock (of door) 1292; **lokum,** compartment in sheep-fold, (?) milking-pen 1267; **loc/clata** 1311, **-clatis** 1333, **-claia** 1396, hurdle for pen.

loc/ellus, -illus, see **locus.**

loch/a 1337, 1358, **-ia** c 1200, loach (fish).

locmanagium, see **lodmannus.**

loculent/us a 1379, **-er** 1461, vv.ll. for **luculent/us, -er.**

locupl/ebilitas c 1470, †**-ecitas** (? **-etitas**) 1457, wealth; **-etatim,** abundantly 893, 903; **-etius,** more abundantly 13c.; **-etus** 13c., c 1396, **-ex** c 1190, c 1362, for **-es,** wealthy; **-etatio,** enrichment c 1470; †**-o** (? **-eto**), to enrich c 1423.

loc/us, religious house c 1086, c 1547; district, territory (G.) 1308, 1339; 'stead', part of manor (Sc.) 1460, 1484; group of documents on one topic 15c.; rank 1203; splendour, state 15c.; **-um habeo,** to take place, happen c 1300; 1274, 15c., **l. obtineo** 1342, **l. teneo** c 1220, 1413, to take effect, be applicable; **l. teneo,** to take the place, act as deputy c 1272, c 1380; ***-um tenens** c 1255, 1686, **l. gerens** 1414, lieutenant, deputy; (lord) lieutenant (of county) 1556, 1585; **l. generalis** 1461; **-umtenentia,** lieutenancy 1393, 1434; **-o meo pono,** to attorn (leg.) 1194, 1265; **de -o ad -um** c 1250, c 1340; **-us a conjugatis** (log.) a 1233; **l. a majori,** argument a fortiori a 1180; **l. a minori** (log.) c 1334; **L. Capitalis, L. Communis,** King's Bench and Common Pleas (Ir.) 1488 (cf. **placea); l. combustionis,** focus a 1233; **l. medius,** middle (Fr. milieu) 1320; **l. musculorum,** mussel-bed 1299; †**l. partitus,** see **jocus; l. positionis,** consecrated burial-place, burial rights c 1115; **l. pius** 1549; **l. religiosus** 13c.; **l. sanctus** 1316; **l. sancti** c 1280; **l. quo prius** 1270; **l. verus, l. apparens** (astr.) a 1233;

-abilis, capable of being localized c 1225, c 1290; for hire 1334, 1537; **-abilitas,** potential locality c 1270; **-alia** (pl.), passages in a book 1271; medicaments applied locally a 1250; **motus -alis,** locomotion c 1330; **-alitas,** locality (abstract) 1267, c 1270; **-aliter,** in (relation to) space 890, c 980. c 1205, 1378; **-anus,** (?) zone (astr.) c 1380; **-arium,** rule applicable to particular

places c 1283; **-atio,** location a 1361; wages 1318, 1436; 1086, 1357, ***-agium** 1213, 1560, **louagium** 1372, **lowagium** 1326, hire, lease; **-atim,** in places c 550; **-ative,** in regard to place 1378; **-ativus,** localizing c 1362; **-atorius,** lessee c 1376; **-atrix,** disposer (f.), 1220; **-ellus,** shrine, reliquary c 1000. c 1250, a 1447; treasure c 980; **-illus,** small compartment 1636; **-ulatus,** stored (in money-bags) c 1180; **-ulum,** for **-ulus,** coffin c 730 (see also **loccum); -ans,** determinant of space c 1250, 1267; **-atum,** thing localized c 1267; **-o,** to take on lease, hire 1086, 1369; for **alloco,** to allow (in account) 1228, c 1270.

‡**locusta,** "honeysuckle" 15c., 1570.

locut/io, pleading or impleading (leg.) c 1115; **-or** 15c., **loquutor** 1555, speaker (of Parliament); **-rix,** speaker (f.) 15c.; **-orius, -orius,** interlocutory (eccl.) c 1298; ***-orium** a 1090, c 1450, **loquitorium** 1300, **loqutorium** c 1296, parlour (mon.); **loquela,** suit, action (leg.) c 1160, 1497; request 1397; **l. matutinalis,** morn-speech, guild-meeting 1389; **loquelaris, loquelosus,** vocal c 550; **loquor,** to be mentioned, named 9c. 1298; to plead, implead (leg.) c 1115, c 1455; to discuss, confer (leg.) 1021, 1452; **l. cum,** to ask permission of 1100; **l. super,** to lay claim to c 1115; **l. versus,** to complain against, accuse 1208, c 1455.

lod-, see also **lada** (2 & 3).

lod/ex 1383, ‡15c., **-ica** c 1200, **-icius** 1326, **-icus** 1558, 1579, for **-ix,** blanket or sheet.

lodisingus, see **2 lozenga.**

lodium c 1200, 1434, **allodium** 1306, **aulodium** 1447, 1472, louver (arch.); cf. **lovarium.**

lod/mannus 1282, 1300, **-emannus, -ismannus** 15c., **-esmannus** 1394, 'lodesman', pilot; **-mannagium** 1282, 1442, **-emanagium** 1290, **-esmanagium** 1537, **-emonagium** 1335, **loadesmanagium** 1297, **loudmanagium** 1339, **lomanagium** 1298, †**locmanagium** (? **lot-**) c 1297, 'lode-manage', pilotage.

lodus, see **ludus.**

loerenium, see **lorengum.**

loetum, see **letifere.**

lof/a, -irna, see **1 lova.**

loft/a 1496, **-ium** 1299, loft.

*log/ea, -ia c 1180, 1575, **-eus, -ius** 1327, 1575, **-a** 1163, 1377, (?) **loca** 1275, **loja** 1225, **lugea** 1350, lodge, hut, shed; **l. cementariorum** c 1280, 1373; **-iagium,** (payment for) right to build lodges 1318, 1319; **-iarius,** lodge-dweller 1308; **-io,** to lodge, dwell 1380.

logg/um, log 1306; **-io,** to make logs 1205.

log/os, word, the Word (theol.) 6c. 12c., 1252; †**lagonus,** (?) reason c 950; **-arithmus,** logarithm 1614, 1686; **-ica** (f. s.) c 1125, 1458, **loyca** 1245, 1380, logic; logical treatise 1281, 15c.; **l. docens,** pure logic a 1304; **l. utens** a 1304; **l. formalis** a 1350; **l. nova,** syllogistic logic (based on Analytics and Topics) a 1304; **l. vetus,** logic of terms and propositions (based on Categories, etc.) a 1304; **-icalia** (pl.), logicals, logical treatises 1267, c 1590; **-icabilis** c 1365, **-icalis**

c 1250, 1609, **-icus** c 1080, a 1428, **loyicus** 13c., logical; **-icaliter** c 1444, **-ice** 1252, a 1428, **loyice** 13c., logically; **-icus**, logician c 1180, c 1434; **-ista**, accountant 1564; **-isticus**, intelligent (of animals) 1267; **cellula -istica** (of brain) a 1200; **-ium**, High Priest's breast-plate (λογεῖον) 1517; **-ostilios**, treatise attributed to Hermes Trismegistus 1345; **-otheta**, logothete (Byzantine official) c 1192, c 1310; **-otropus**, form of syllogism 1620; **-ico** c 1180, 1241, **-iso** c 1365, to reason, meditate.
logus, troop, company (? λόχος) c 550.
Loheringus, see **Lotharingus**.
‡**lohoc**, linctus (med.) 14c.
loignia 1213, 1242, **loin/a** 1288, **-ia** 1239, †**lonnia** 1220, **luigna** 1220, loin; see also **longia**.
loja, see **logea**.
†**loketus**, (?) lackey, groom c 1620; see also **locca, loccum**.
loli/atus, for **-aceus**, made of darnel a 1205.
‡**lolidodium**, "cart-saddle" 15c., 1483; †**lolla**, part of cart-harness 1384, 1466; cf. DORS
loligo, flying fish: **luligo** 690.
Lollard/us p 1382, a 1564, **-a** (f.) c 1446, Lollard; **-ia** 1401, a 1547, **-ria** 1417, a 1564, Lollardy; **-icus** c 1412, **-inus** c 1392, Lollardish; **-iter**, like a Lollard 15c.
1 loma, loom 1494, 1517.
2 loma cervisialis, 'ale-loom', vat 1512.
lomanagium, see **lodmannus**.
Lombardus a 1142, 13c., **Lumbardus** a 1142, 1379, **Longobardus** 9c. c 1100, **Langobardus** a 1142, Lombard; see also **pulvis**.
lombesina, see **bombyx**.
lona, lane 1353; see also **lova**.
lond-, see also **landa**.
Londrensis, Lundrensis, farthing 1280.
longa, see **longia; longitudo**.
longabulum, see LAND
longellus, see **lana**.
long/ia, lungia, 'lunge' (of horse's harness) 1215, 1320; **-ia** 1201, **-a** 1150, **loignia** 1235, 'loyn', 'lune' (falc.).
long/itudo, longitude (terrestrial) 1267, 1586; (astr.) 1344; **l. longior, l. †proprior** (astr.) a 1233; **diameter -itudinalis** (geom.) a 1233, c 1360; **filus (nervus) l.** (med.) a 1250; **-itudinaliter**, lengthwise c 1360, 1378; **-ale**, cart-pole 13c.; ‡**-ulus**, rail of fence 1570; *****-animis** c 1090, c 1470, †**-animus** c 1283, 1461, patient, long-suffering; **-animior** c 1250; *****-animitas**, patience c 1080, 1430; †**l. vite**, length of life c 1362; **-animiter**, patiently c 1250, 15c.; **-eve** 960. c 1378, 1461, **in -evum** c 1338, through a long life; **-ibarbus**, long-bearded 13c.; **-ilaterus**, long-sided (geom.) c 1145; **in -inquo**, at a distance 14c.; **-ior**, further removed 1278; **-iuscule**, rather far 990. c 1070, 1528; **a -e**, circuitously, indirectly c 1223, 1237; *c 1130, c 1457, **de -e** c 1090, 1461, **ex -o** 14c., afar off, from afar; **-um**, length c 1250; **ad -um** c 1444, 1461, **in -um** c 1135, c 1400, **in -o** a 1300, **-o ad -um** (?) 13c., **de -o in -um** 1230, 1255, **per -um** 957. c 1200, lengthwise, along; **secundum -um**, per pale (her.) p 1394; **-a**, long note (mus.) 1326, c 1470; **l. altera** (mus.)

c 1470; **l. duplex, l. erecta, l. imperfecta, l. perfecta, l. plicata** (mus.) 1326, c 1470; **l. triplex** (mus.) 1326; **-evo**, to bless with long life 1426, 1461; **-o**, to lengthen 1241, a 1408.
Longobardus, see **Lombardus**.
lonnia, see **loignia**.
†**lontellum**, (?) some object made of iron 1289.
lopp/a (pl.), lop (of trees) 1334, 1545; **-o**, to lop (trees) 1400, 1574.
loqu-, see LOCUT
lora, (?) narrow strip 1282.
lor/engum 1189, 1234, †**-ensum** 1242, **-anum** 1204, †**-ema** c 1324, **-einum** 1179, 1221, **-enum**, 1171, c 1335, **-ennium** 1213, **loerenium** 1232, **-imum** 1167, **-arium** 1208, **-ale** c 1225, ‡1483, †**-ax** 15c., bridle-rein; **-arius**, lyam-hound 1570; **-imaria**, trade of a lorimer c 1324; **-emarius** 1086, a 1190, *****-imarius** 1086, 1435, **-imerus** c 1185, **-inarius** c 1393, lorimer, harness-maker; **-ipes**, cripple 1086, c 1180; ‡**-ipedatio**, limping c 1440.
loric/a c 1200, c 1520, **lourica** 1391, hauberk; robe of penitent 1292; knight's service or equipment 1100, 12c.; **feodum -e** 12c., **f. -atum** 1609, hauberk fee; **-arius**, hauberk-maker 1303; a 1140, 1213, **-atus** 1086, c 1385, man-at-arms; **-ella** 1211, 1235, **-ula** 1195, p 1200, **-ulus** 1261, small hauberk; **lurica**, shield 6c.; **luricula**, small shield 890; **-atio**, wearing a hauberk 13c.; **-o**, to serve as a hauberk 1220.
loridium, (?) tithe-sheaf 1103.
los/inga, -anga, -enga, -onga, see **lozenga** (1 & 2).
loter, loter-, lotr-, see also **luter**.
Lothar/ingus c 1118, c 1370, **Loheringus** c 1187, **-ingensis** a 1142, **Hlotharius** a 1108, **-iensis** c 1118, Lorrainer.
lot/io, washing 1345, 1524; 1390, 1506, **-ura** 1550, sheep-dipping; **l. cinerum**, recovery of lead from ashes c 1372; **-io** a 1250, **-ium** c 1000, **-ura** c 1180, 15c., water used for washing; **-ura**, 'sweating' of coinage 1452, 1503; washing or washing-place of ore a 1307, 1323; **l. aque**, (?) water-meadow 1298, 1415; **-arius** 14c., **-or** 13c., 1438, launderer; **-or**, 'sweater' of coinage 1417, 1450; **-or, -rix** (f.), ore-washer 1300, 1325; **-or** 1420, **-orium** 1312, c 1400, laver, ewer; **-orium**, laver, 'lavatory', washing-place, 1235, 1384; piscina (eccl.) 14c.; **l. pendulum** 1351; *****-rix**, laundress 1175, c 1540; **-ricarius**, concerned with laundering 1620; **-o**, (?) to dip sheep 1251; cf. LAV
lotofagus, see **lutum**.
*****lott/um** 1159, 1440, **-a** 1405, **-us** 1275, †**-amum** 1346, lot, share (of taxation, coupled with scot); **-a**, lot, share (of task) 1518; king's share of lead (Derbyshire) 1322; **-abilis**, assignable by lot 1540; **-antus**, paying lot 1360; **-o** 1201, c 1353, **-io** 1275, to pay lot (with scot); to assess for lot 1292; to allot 1405.
lotus 1290, **lutus** 1282, measure of wine, lot (G.).
louagium, see **locus**.
loudmanagium, see **lodmannus**.
louna, loon, diver (bird) 1544.
loupa, see **lupa**.

lourica, *see* **lorica.**

1 **lov/a** 1214, 1378, **-um** c 1180, 1188, **lof/a** c 1296, c 1350, luff, (?) tacking boom (naut.); **-irna,** (?) loof-hook (G.) 1311.

2 **lov/a** (†**lona**) 1306, 1311, **-ebonda** 1279, **-ebona** 1252, 1279, 'love-boon' (man.); *cf.* **luva.**

lov/arium 1240, c 1314, **-are** c 1313, **-era** 1233, 1250, **-eria** 1245, 1371, **-erium** 1245, 1299, **luvarium** 1194, 1335, louver, smoke-vent (arch.); **-erborda,** louver-board c 1438; *cf.* **lodium.**

lowagium, *see* **locus.**

loy/ca, -ice, -icus, *see* **logos.**

1 **lozenga** 1384, **losinga** c 1437, flatterer.

2 **loz/enga** c 1320, **-inga** 1385, **losanga** 1326, **losenga** c 1315, c 1470, **losinga** 1385, **losonga** 1351, **lodisingus** p 1394, lozenge (esp. her.).

lubric/atio, lubrication, smoothing c 1260; **-ativus,** lubricative 13c.; **-itas,** lubricity, lewdness 1283, a 1452; **-um,** lewd desire, weakness c 1125, a 1205; **-us,** transitory 1241; *13c., c 1400, **-ulus** 1208, lewd; **-ans,** slimy a 1250; **-o,** to collapse 12c.; to wanton 10c.; **lubrifico,** to wear smooth a 1250.

luca, *see* **leuca.**

luc/arius, woodward, forester 13c., c 1300; ‡**-ar,** "wood-wale" (bird) c 1440; ‡**-etum,** "warren" 15c.

lucellus 1225, 1304, **lussellus** 1275, 1294, **lusshellus** c 1300, hank, skein, measure of yarn or hemp (O.F. *luissel*).

luc/entia c 1250, **-eitas** c 1270, **-iditas** c 1250, a 1446, brightness, luminosity; **-anar** a 1150, ‡15c., ‡**-ar** 1483, louver; **-anum** c 1193, **-idum** c 1115, dawn; **-enter,** brightly c 1340, 1342; **-eus,** bright (play on **luteus**) 1413; **-idissimus,** very clear 799; **-idum intervallum,** sane interval 1318, 1523; **-iducatus,** safe leading 858; **-iducus,** leading safely 858; **-iflue,** lucidly 858; **-ifluus,** shining c 1000; **-iformis,** light-giving 860; **-iola,** fire-fly 1620; †**-ivagus,** (?) *for* **-ifugus,** shunning light 13c.; **-ipotens,** tolerant of light c 1500; **-ubra,** lamp, lamplight c 1197, c 1200; **-ubratio,** shedding light 860; **lugubratio,** *for* **-ubratio,** lucubration 1433; **-ubratorium, lugubratorium,** (?) place of study c 1500; **-esco,** to be plainly visible c 1470; **-ido,** to elucidate c 1343, 1406; **-ubro,** to shed light 860.

lucern/aria, skylight c 1212; **hora -alis,** dusk c 1385.

*****luc/eus, -ius** c 1170, 1460, **luscius** 1237, 1240, **licius** 1254, ‡**-inus** 15c., 'luce', pike (fish); ‡**l. marinus,** ling c 1440; **-ia** 1250, **-ina** c 1404, female pike; **-ellus** 1303, ‡15c., **-eolus** a 1275, **-iculus** (†**luaculus,** †**luticulus**) 1274, ‡15c., ‡**-illus** 15c., **-ettus** 1250, 1260, young luce, pickerel; *cf.* 1 **lupus.**

‡**lucibric/unculum** 15c., **-iunculum** c 1440, **-iniculum** 1483 (? *for* **lubric-**), "sleek-stone"; *cf.* **litatorium.**

Lucifer/, Satan c 1180, 1377; **-ianus** c 1160, **-inus** 1377, 1440, †**-nus** 1427, Satanic; a 1233, **-anus** c 1250; Luciferian heretic.

lucinium, *see* **lychnus.**

lucr/um, interest on money 1182, 1488; **ad l.** et dampnum placiti (leg.) 1275; **l. terre,** (?) money-rent from land 1086; **terra-abilis,** profit-yielding (? arable) land 1130, a 1260; **-atio,** procuring, 'winning', getting in 1378, 1532; **l. feni** 1380, 1539, **l. prati** 1449, 1495, hay-making; **l. lapidum** 1425, 1449, **l. petre** 1409, 1434, quarrying; **-ative,** with an eye to profit c 1220; **-ifer** c 1255, **-iger** c 1180, profitable; **-ifactio** c 1250, 1414, **-itas** 13c., profit; **-efacio** c 1376, **-ifero** c 1400, **-ifico** 790. 1308, c 1536, ***-o, -or** 1086, 1415, *to gain, make a profit (of); *to 'win', get in c 1266, 1578; (attorney appointed) **ad -andum vel perdendum** c 1185, 1412; *see also* **luter.**

luct/amentum, struggle, effort 14c.; **-atrix,** fond of wrestling (*f.*) 1252; **-ura,** wrestling match 14c.

lucterinus, *see* **luter.**

luct/uositas, mournfulness a 1292; **-abilis,** mournful 970; **-uatio (oculorum),** watering a 1250.

lucubr-, *see* **lucentia.**

luculent-, *see* **LUCULENT**

†**ludricus,** (?) beast of burden 13c.

1 **lud/us,** sword-play 1320; stage-play or pageant 1389, 1584; (?) right to hunt game (Isle of Wight) 1349; holiday from routine life (mon.) 1391, 1464; **l. pasche, l. prioris, l. specialis** (mon.) 1534; **l. partitus,** choosing game, jeopardy (*cf.* **jocus**) c 1218; **l. de rege et regina** 1240; **l. ad tabulas** 1213; **l. tauri** 1365; **-i** (*pl.*) **Natalis,** Christmas games 14c.; **l. saltatorii,** dancing school 1553; **-ulus** c 1200, ‡**-iolus** 1483, **lodus** 1246, game; **-arius,** plaything 10c.; **-ator,** player (mus.) 1540; **-ibriosus** c 730. c 1400, **-ibricus** 12c., mocking; **-ibrius,** wanton 794; **-icola,** devotee of sport 14c.; **-icrum nature,** a sport 1586; **-ificatio,** delusion c 1290; **l. sensuum** a 1290; **-ificus,** playful 815; festal c 1180; **-ifluus** a 1349, **-ivagus** 747, playful, mocking; **-imagistra,** school-mistress 17c.; **scaccarium lusile,** chess-board c 1178; **lusor** 1389, 1533, **lusiator** 1558, player, entertainer; **l. ad talos,** dice-player 1375; **l. in organis** 1515; ‡**lusorium,** pageant 1483; **-ico,** to play c 550; **-ifico sensum,** to delude the senses a 1290; **-o,** to play, act (in drama) 1389; to take a holiday (mon.) 1327, c 1412; **l. ad,** to play at (a game) c 1192, 1472.

2 ‡**ludus,** stone in bladder, tartar formed from urine 1652.

lueicia (†**leuicia**) c 1160, **luitia** c 1180, **terra,** (?) land held by sokeman (Norfolk).

lugea, *see* **logea.**

lugereschia, *see* **bugerescha.**

lugubr/atio, mourning 14c.; **-iter,** mournfully c 760; ‡**-o,** to mourn 1483; *see also* **lucentia.**

luigna, *see* **loignia.**

luligo, *see* **loligo.**

*****lumb/are** c 1080, c 1362, **-ale** c 1250, ‡**-atorium** c 1200, loin-cloth, breech-girdle; **-aris,** of the loins a 1275; ‡**-ifractus,** broken-loined 1483; ‡**-osus,** "great-buttocked" 1570; *see also* **limbus.**

lumbric/us, worm: **semen -orum,** worm-seed 1480.

lumen nature, light of nature 1461; **l. sanctorum,** shrine 1444; **lumin/are, -ar** *a 1090, 1439, **-aria** 1268, **-arium** 797. 1200, 1552, light, lamp; harbour light 1261; shining light, example c 1125, c 1298; light (arch.), window 1424, 1438; **l. fenestre,** window-pane c 1365, 1416; ‡**herba -aria,** mullein (bot.) 14c.; **-arius** 13c., c 1356, **-ator** 1260, c 1290, limner; **-atio,** lighting c 1340; 1346, **-atura** c 1452, illumination, limning; **-ositas,** luminosity c 1188, c 1290; **-osius,** more resplendently 12c.; **-o** 1290, **-io** 1300, **-onum** 1265, **lumio** 1314, **limio** 1322, c 1330, **limino** c 1345, wick; **-o** 1303, 1450, **limino** 1432, c 1445, to illuminate, limn.

lumentum, washing a 615.

†**lumnarca,** (?) *for* **liminarcha,** officer, commander 15c.

lumpa, fish, (?) lump-fish c 1200.

lun/a a 615, **-atio** c 1110, 1344, lunation, lunar cycle; **-a,** silver (alch.) a 1235, c 1345; ‡**l. compacta,** *argentum fixum* 1652; **-e sputum,** mercury c 1320; *see also* **dies, 3 feria, lapis, saltus; -a currente per** (followed by golden number) 15c.; **-aria Greca,** honesty (bot.) 1634; **-aris,** of silver (alch.) c 1320; (?) lasting only a month c 1180; menstrual c 1200; *see also* **regula; -arius,** lunar 1234; **nox -aria,** Monday night 1249; **-ariter,** changeably 1427; **-acia,** lunacy 1585; **-aticus** c 1190, 1509, **lynaticus** 6c., lunatic; **-e dies** 1299, **-dinarium** c 1284, 'Monday-land' (subject to Monday work only); **homo -e, -aris** c 1182, **-denarius** 1284, **-dinarius** 13c., 1306, 'Monday-man', tenant of Monday-land; **-ella** a 1250, **-etta** 1245, **-ula** (her.) c 1595, crescent; **-ificum,** silver-making elixir c 1300.

lunda, *see* **binda.**

Lundrensis, *see* **Londrensis.**

lundum, (?) grove (Norse *lundr*) (Lincs.) 13c.

lungia, *see* **longia.**

luo, *see* **liga.**

lup/a 1289, **loupa** 1377, 1461, loop-hole, embrasure; **-um,** (?) loop of iron 1317; *see also* **1 lupus.**

lupan/is, domus -aria, stew, brothel 1541; †**lupnar,** (?) 'stew', fish-pond 1598; **-arius,** whoremonger c 1230; **-atrix,** harlot 1310; **-o,** to frequent brothels a 1142.

lupardus, kind of fur c 1250, 1303.

1 lup/us, skin disease a 1250, ‡1483; **l. belli** 1304, **l. guerre** 1306, (?) **-a** 1279, 'louvel', siege-engine; ‡**-i pecten,** teasel (bot.) 14c.; *-us aquaticus** c 1200, 1537, **l. fluvialis** 1570, 'luce', pike (*cf.* **luceus**); **-iculus** 1358, ‡**-ellus** 1570, ‡**-illus** 1519, pickerel; **-arius,** wolf-hunter c 1136, 1159; **(canis) -arius** 1250, 1275, **-orarius** 1250, **luverettus** 13c., **luvereticus** 1206, wolf-hound; **-atum,** toothed bit or curb c 1200; **-inum caput gerens,** outlaw 1202, c 1290; **-ulus,** wolf-cub a 1100, c 1177; **-ino** c 1180, **-io** c 1200, to be wolfish.

2 lup/us herba 1499, **l. salictarius** 1538, **-ulus** a 1250, 1670, (?) **-inus** 1565, hop (bot.); **-ulatus** 1612, 1661, ‡**-inatus** 1570, **-inaris** 1608, **-ulinus** 1574, treated with hops;

‡**-ularium,** ‡**-uletum,** hopyard 1570; **-ulentum,** beer 1554; *cf.* **hupulus.**

3 ‡**lupus,** antimony 1652.

lurc/esca c 1200, **-isca** (†**lurtisca**) c 1180, ‡15c., **leura** 1333, lure (falc.); ‡**-isco,** to lure 15c.

†**lurc/us** (*v.l.* **larva**), *for* **-o,** predator c 950.

lurdenus, *see* **LARD**

luric/a, -ula, *see* **LORIC**

lurlegga, *see* **2 lega.**

luscius, *see* **luceus.**

luscor, to look with half an eye c 1180.

lus/or, -orium, -iator, -ilis, *see* **LUD**

lussellus, lusshellus, *see* **lucellus.**

lussus, (?) lewis (for lifting stones) 1284.

‡**lustum,** cream 1652.

lut/a, lute (mus.) a 1452; **-stringus,** lute-string 1471.

lut/arius, -atio, -eosus, *see* **lutum.**

lut/eola, *see* **luteus.**

lut/er 1212, c 1218, **-rus** 655, 797, **-ra** 1232, **-rea** c 1325, **loter** c 1289, **lotrix** 1495, **-ricius** 13c., 1422, **lotricius** 1464, ‡**-ericius, -rissius, lucterinus** 15c., otter; **-er,** otter-skin 1220, 1291; **-erarius** 1235, 1333, **loterarius** 1276, *-rarius** (†**luccrarius**) 1179, 1334, otter-hunter; **(canis) -erarius** 1333, **-rarius** 1160, 1212, **-arius, -orius** 1286, **-ericius** 13c., **-oricius** 1291, otter-hound; **-raria** c 1221, **-ratio** 1179, office of otter-hunter; **-inus** (†**butineus,** †**lucrinus**) a 1200, 1303, **lotrinus** (†**latrinus**) 1333, of an otter.

lut/erium, rug, coverlet (? *cf.* Fr. *lodier*) a 1142; **-or,** sheet 1588.

lut/eus, yellow-hammer 1544; **-eola,** siskin (bird) 1544; dyer's rocket, weld (bot.) 1634.

Luther/anus 1523, 1588, **-ianus** 1521, 1523, **-ista** 1523, Lutheran; **-ismus,** Lutheranism 1534; **-issime,** in true Lutheran style 1523.

luticulus, *see* **luceus.**

lutstringus, *see* **luta.**

lut/um philosophorum, 'lute', (?) bitumen (alch.) 1144; **l. sapientie,** sealing material (alch.) c 1345, 1620; ‡**l. stelle,** gypsum 1652; **-i appositor** 1212, **-arius** 1417, (?) 1477, dauber, plasterer; **-eosus,** muddy c 1400; **-ositas,** muddiness 1421; †**lotofagus** (?) *for* **-ophagus,** filth-eater 1243; **-atio,** coating with lute (alch.) 1622; **-o,** to coat (a vessel) with lute (alch.) c 1345,; 1316, **-eo** 1359, to daub, plaster.

lutus, *see* **lotus.**

luv/a, love, peace; **in -a** (†**lima**) **et laga** a 1180, 1235; *cf.* **2 lova.**

luvarium, *see* **lovarium.**

luver/ettus, -eticus, *see* **1 lupus.**

luxivium, *see* **lixivia.**

luxur/atio, lechery a 1408; **-iator,** lecher 1419.

lychnus, wick: **lichinus** 790, c 1000. a 1142, 1534, **lichenus** 1497, **lechinus** c 1450, **lechina** 1426, **licinius** c 1200, **licinium** (**lucinium**) c 1180, a 1250.

lyc/isca (**lic-**) 1392, 1532, **licissa** a 1250, **lisisca** 1373, 1380, **lecisca** 1476, 1541, **lacisca** c 1325, ‡**lacesca** 15c., (grey-hound) bitch; **-octonum,** poison (fig.) c 1620; **-opodium,** club-moss (bot.) 1634.

‡**lycium,** *succus caprifolii* (bot.) 14c.

1 **lyda**, "dray", dung-cart 1279.
2 **lyda**, 'lith', slope (A.S. *hlid*) 13c.
lydiata, *see* **lidiata**.
†**lymber**, (?) sort of ornament 13c.
lymkilna, *see* **limbernarius**.
lymph/a, water: **limpa** 6c.; **-alis** c 1250,
-aticus 655. c 1422, ‡1483, **-atus** 655,
containing water; **-aticus**, dropsical 14c.;
‡**-arium** 1483, **-atorium** 1434, 1448, ewer,
holy water stoup; **-ans**, raving c 950; **-o**,
to provide water c 1180; to dilute with
water a 1250, 1417; to water (cloth) 1358.

lyna, 'line', sort of ship c 1394.
lynaticus, *see* LUN
†**lynia**, (?) main upright of door-frame 1373.
lynsum, *see* **linca**.
1 **lyra**, *see* 2 **lira**.
2 **lyra** c 1452, **pannus de -a** 1391, 1450, cloth
of Lire (France).
3 **Lyra**, the postils of Nicholas of Lyra 1384.
4 **lyr/a Judaica**, Jew's harp c 1608; **-o**, to
play the harp 1570.
lysuria, fever in which heat is mainly internal
a 1250.

M

maam-, *see* MAHEM
mabathemati/con a 1250, ‡**-cum** 14c., wild
cabbage juice.
macarius, blessed (μακάριος) 950.
mac/ecraria 1264, 1275, †**-eacaria** c 1190,
-ecaria c 1200, c 1280, **-ecria** 13c.,
mazacaria a 1200, meat-market, shambles;
-ecrarius c 1067, 1275, †**mascetrarius**
13c., **-erarius** c 1130, c 1225, butcher.
macedo, *see* **marcedo**.
‡**macedon/ia** c 1440, **-icum** a 1250, ‡14c.,
alexanders (bot.).
macell/a 1260, 1439, **mascellum** c 1200,
-aria 1416, *for* **-um**, meat-market, shambles;
-arius 1247, 1506, **macillarius** c 1436,
‡**-io** 1483, butcher.
mac/enerus (†**-everus**), **-erinus**, *see* **mazer**.
macenoria, *see* **mazo**.
macer, pomegranate ‡14c., (?) c 1615; *see
also* 2 **macia**, **mazer**.
macer/atio, castigation, mortification c 730.
c 1125, c 1390; **-ativus**, ascetic c 1283.
macer/ius 12c., ‡**-io** 1483, mason; **-iola**,
little wall c 700.
macero, to cleave (? *cf.* μάχαιρα) c 550.
macerus, *see* 1 **macia**.
macetum, malt 1223, 1475.
maceum, *see* 2 **macia**.
‡**macha**, flying worm 1652.
mach/ecollum 1387, **mascalcio** 1547,
machicolation (arch.); **-ecollo** 1433, 1460,
-icollo 1449, 1491, to machicolate.
†**machidis**, (?) battlefield *or* precipice 6c.
machin/a, missile 1461, 1622; **m. penalis**,
gibbet c 1250; **m. rotalis**, windlass c 1170;
-amentum, device, plot 760. c 1100, 1516;
-anter, craftily 1337; ‡**-ar**, pottery glaze
1652; **-aria**, mechanics 1620; **virga -aria**,
beam of siege-engine 1270; **-ator**, engineer
1274; **-osus**, crafty 1296, c 1318; ‡**-us**,
buttress c 1440; **-o**, to invent, devise c 730.
c 1250, 1573; **-or** (with *inf.*) to contrive to
7c. 1295, 1415.
macholum (†**mancholum**), rick, stack (O.F.
machau) c 1115.
machomaria, **Machymetanus**, *see* **mahomaria**.
1 **mac/ia** (**-ea**) 1239, 1308, **-ium** 1266,
mascea 1201, **masa** 1421, **massa** (G.)
1312, **maxuca** a 1142, **-uellus** 1419, **mas-**

suellus 1319, 1419, **mazuellus** 1327, mace,
club; **-erus** 14c., **massarius** 1380, **mas-
suerius** c 1335, mace-bearer.
2 **mac/ia** 1285, ‡1483, **-eum** c 1335, 15c.,
maseum 15c., **-is** 1205, 1593, **-ir** 1538,
1555, **-er** 1538, ‡1570, mace (spice).
macian-, *see* MATIAN
†**macidus**, (?) *for* **marcidus** *or* **matidus** (*i.e.*
madidus), a 1250.
macilentia, slimming a 1250.
macillarius, *see* MACELL
†**macino**, (?) to powder c 1227.
mac/io, -o, -ieno, -oneria, *see* **mazo**.
‡**maclonis**, wormwood (bot.) 14c.
macomatum, *see* **mahomaria**.
‡**macra**, "*terra rubea*" 1652.
macro/cosmus, macrocosm, external universe a 1250, c 1450; ‡**-logus**, "great
speaker" 1483; ‡**-nosia** 14c., **-noxia** a 1250,
prolonged illness; **-piper**, long pepper
a 1250, ‡14c.
macrum (**piscis**), lean (of a fish) a 1087.
mact/atio, slaughter 12c., 1419; **-abilis**, fit
for slaughter 15c.; **-o ruscam**, to break up a
hive 1336; *see also* **inactorium**.
mactus, blest c 950.
macuellus, *see* 1 **macia**.
macul/a p 1394, c 1595, **mascula** p 1394,
mascle (her.); ‡15c., 1483, **maillia** 1243,
ring of mail armour; **mascula** 1274,
mascra 1292, **maskera** 1375, **mallium**
1344, 16c., †**meta** c 1358, mesh (of net);
maela, link (of chain) 1236; **-atus** c 1595,
masculatus 1291, 1445, mascally (her.);
masculatus, reticulated 1243; **-osus**, full
of holes c 730.
macul/abilis, liable to defilement 1378;
-ativus, apt to defile c 1283.
Macuta, name of a comet c 1270.
mad/efactio, moistening, moisture c 1180,
15c.; **medefactus**, moistened c 1330;
matidatio, damping (of cloth) 1360; **-idum**,
bog a 1250; *see also* PREC; **-itudo**, bogginess
1334; ‡**-ulus** 1483, **matidus** (†**motidus**)
1296, 1334, *for* **-idus**, moist; **-eo**, to moisten
c 1188, a 1408.
mad/era 1393, 1439, **-ra** 1421, madder (bot.);
-reselva, clary (bot.) 1622.
mad/iada, -iana, *see* **mediada**.
Madi/us, -alis, *see* **Maius**.

madlardus, *see* **mallardus.**

†**madrya** c 1357, †**mandria** 1329, 'madrean', (?) kind of ginger.

maegbota (**magbota,** †**mesbota**), fine, weregeld (A.S.) c 1115.

maela, *see* **macula.**

maem-, *see* MAHEM

maerdredum, demesne vill, *maerdref* (W.) 1284; **mairareus,** keeper of a vaccary (W.) 1372; **maronia,** dairy-due (*cf.* W. *maeroni*) 1294.

*****maer/emium** (**mer-**) 1181, 1583, **maheremium** 1233, 1364, **-emum** 1200, **-emies** c 1270, **-esmium, maresmium** 1275, **-imium** 1241, 1464, **mearemium** 1324, 1535, **meer/emium** 1299, 1315, **-empnium** 1295, *****maremium** a 1230, 1391, **marrimum** 1242, **mair/ema** 1240, **-emia** c 1170, *****-emium** 1199, c 1255, **-emum** c 1170, **-enum** 1173, †**hairenum** 1227, **-ebium** 13c., †**-onia** c 1192, **maisr/emium** 1179, c 1185, **-emum** 1178, 1194, **-enum** 1177, 1190, **meir/emium** 1198, 1229, **-emum** 1242, **-enum** 1222, **-imium** 1222, 1241, **miremium** 1382, **mur/emium** 14c., **-ennium** 1460, 1468, **-inium** 1467, **marramentum** 1107, timber (Fr. *merrain*); **mer/imarius** 1275, †**-enemius** 1253, timber-dealer; **-emiatio,** timbering a 1307; **-emio,** to timber a 1307; *cf.* **materia.**

mafor/a a 1142, c 1198, **-te** 690, veil, head-dress (Heb.).

Magalus 1275, **Moal/** 1267, **-lus** c 1326, Mongol.

†**maganum,** dagger c 1188.

magbota, *see* **maegbota.**

magdalio, 'magdaleon', cylindrical plaster (med.) a 1250, c 1257.

magenellus, *see* **mangonellus.**

magest-, *see* **majestas.**

magic/a c 1170, 1267, **ars ymagica** 1331, magic; **-e,** magically 1267; **-us,** sorcerer 1406.

maginatio, *see* **imago.**

magior, *see* **major.**

magis, but (Fr. *mais*) 9c.; (with *adj.*) most 1316, 1470; **ad m.,** at most c 1362; **m. volo,** *for* **malo,** 738; *cf.* MAJOR

magist/er, the Master (theol.) a 1166; captain (of troops) 1193; master or captain (naut.) 1205, 1547; master workman c 1150, 1417; master of apprentices c 1115, 1410; guild official 1451, 1577; eldest son of lord (Sc.) 1478; Rabbi 1240, 1261; head of ecclesiastical order, house or department 1215, 1549; head of college (ac.) c 1285, 1537; *****master (ac.) c 1120, 1577; **m. actu regens** 1231, c 1415, **m. actualiter regens** c 1278, **m. regens** 1238, c 1578, **m. nonregens** c 1280, c 1515 (ac.); **m. burse,** purser (naut.) 1385, 1412; **m. Cancellarie,** Chancery master 1375, 1684; **m. cementarius,** master builder 1259, 1367; **m. coquinarius** 1315, **m. coquus** a 1128, 1408, **m. coquorum** c 1290, chef; **m. dispensator,** household official c 1136; **m. forestarius** 13c., 1400, **m. regardator, m. pasnagator** c 1160, forest officials; **m. generalis** c 1332, 1498; **M. Historiarum,** Peter Comestor 1267, c 1443; **M.**

Sententiarum, Peter Lombard c 1343, 1549; **m. magnus,** Grand Master (of Hospitallers) 1335, 1347; *****m. militie Templi** c 1200, 1308; **m. marinarius** 1336, **m. marinellus** (G.) 1242, **m. nauta** 1221, 1419, master mariner; **m. monialium** c 1155, 1275; **m. noviciorum** c 1330, c 1400, **m. operum** c 1200, **m. operis** 1402, **m. operarie** a 1452; **m. palatii** 14c.; **m. postarum,** postmaster 1516, 1698; **m. Requestarum,** (Sc.) 1389, 1515, (Engl.) 1586, **m. Requisitionum** 1573, Master of Requests; **m. Rotulorum,** Master of the Rolls 1485, 1686; **m. schole** (**scholarum**) 950. a 1128, c 1380; **m. serviens,** chief serjeant (W.) 1348; **m. summus,** head of Gilbertine order 1366; **m. de virga** (eccl.) 1494; **verba -a,** words spoken (to servant) by master c 1177; **-ellus,** pedant 1520; **-ra,** prioress (mon.) 1145; **-eria,** mastership (of hospital) 1311; **-erialis,** of a teacher 770; (?) used in alchemy 1267; **-erialiter,** expertly c 1212; **-erium** c 1155, 1620, **-ratio** a 615, skill, artifice; art of alchemy 1144, ‡1652; 1311, 1549, **-ralitas** 1523, **-ratus** c 1317, 1517, degree of master, licence to teach (ac.); **-ralia** (*pl.*), qualifications of master (ac.) c 1340; **-ralis,** of a master (ac.) 1296, c 1332; scholastic c 1290, c 1367; masterly a 1384, 1620; (*subst.*) magnate 1200, 1530; **m. clericus** 1419, 1427; **m. corda,** tiller-rope 1287; *see also* **breve; -raliter,** like a master, didactically c 1370, 1620; **-ratus,** mastership of college c 1340, 1456; term of office (of abbot) 1537; **-rea,** title of a play performed in Venice c 1433; **-ro,** to rule c 1170, c 1550; to confer master's degree on (ac.) 1311, 15c.

*****magiziarius,** class of craftsman 1275.

‡**magmentum,** "tripe" c 1440.

magn/es, compass 1516; **manes,** *for* **-es,** magnet a 1250; **-esia,** philosophers' stone, mercury, vitriol, *etc.* 13c., c 1345; **-eticus,** magnetic c 1608, 1686; ‡**-etinus tartarus,** "*lapis in homine durissimus*" 1652; **-etismus,** magnetism 1662.

magn/itas, amplitude 9c.; **-itudo,** magnitude (astr.) 1267, 1686; 1188, 1362, **-ificentia** 1155, 1441, magnificence (title); **-alia** (*pl.*), miracles (bibl.); **-aliter,** greatly c 1380, a 1564; **-anime** 1267, **-animiter** 7c., 10c. c 1125, 1414, magnanimously, with spirit; **-animitates** (*pl.*), heroic acts c 1150; **-animus,** arrogant c 1000; *****-as** c 1040. c 1125, 1586, **-atus** a 1100, c 1400, †**-itas** 1512, magnate; **scandalum -atum,** offence to the authorities 1539; **-atior,** greater magnate c 1362; **-atium,** greatness 14c.; **-ificat,** magnificat c 1080, 1245; **-ilogus,** eloquent a 1142; **-iloquens,** boastful c 1180; †**-ipendissimus,** most highly esteemed 1402; **-ipotens,** mighty 790; **-ivocus,** loud-voiced 860; **-us,** senior, the elder 1220; **mangnus,** *for* **-us,** c 1255, c 1507; *see also* **altare, annus, lex, mensa, missa, rotulus;** *cf.* **major,** MAXIM

magonalius, *see* **mangonellus.**

magono, *see* **mango.**

magor, *see* **major.**

magual, diameter a 1233.

magul, unknown quantity (math.) (Ar. *maqul*) 1145.

magunellus, *see* **mangonellus.**

*****mahem/ium (maem-)** c 1185, 1487, **mahamium (maam-)** 1201, 1331, **mahaimium** c 1290, mayhem, maiming; **-iator,** maimer c 1290; **-io** (†**mahenno**) 1199, 15c., **-o** c 1216, c 1266, **mahamio** 1201, 1274, **mahamo** c 1290, †**mahino** 1214, **maimo** 1199, 1263, **maymeo** c 1350, **mamo** 13c., **mahaingno** (Norm.) 1198, **meishaimo** (Norm.) 1180, to maim.

maher-, *see* **maeremium.**

mahom/aria c 1250, **machomaria** a 1142, **mahumeria** c 1150, c 1200, **mahumera** c 1220, **macomatum** c 1190, †**malmaria** 1221, mosque *or* Moslem quarter; **-etanus** 1517, 1586, **Mahumetanus** 1502, **Machymetanus** 1635, **Maumeticola** 1200, Mahometan; **lex Mahumetica** c 1200.

mai/a, -o, *see* **MEI**

maignagium, *see* **MANS**

maill/ia, 'mail', halfpenny (Fr. *maille*); **m. de muz,** gold halfpenny 1243; *see also* **macula,** **MALL**

mail/marta, -emarta, *see* **2 mala.**

maim-, *see* **MAHEM**

main-, *see also* **MANS; manu-**

mainardus (may-), weight of wool 1221, 1226; large cheese 1235, 14c.

mair-, *see also* **maeremium.**

mairareus, *see* **maerdredum.**

mairus, *see* **major.**

mais-, *see* **MAER; MANS; MEIS**

Maius, May: **Madi/us** c 1212, c 1320; **-alis** (**Majalis**), of May c 1212.

majest/as, *****majesty** (title) c 1170, 1684; authority, sanction c 1130; divine thing 12c.; picture of Christ as judge c 1160, 1412; *lèse-majesté* c 1185; *see also* **1 lesura; magestas,** *for* **m.,** 901. 1278, 1461; **-ativus** 10c. c 1184, c 1193, **magestativus** 14c., majestic.

major/, (*adj.***)** of full age 1225, c 1258; (*subst.*) adult 1559; magnate 1079, 1461; *****mayor** (of town) 1193, c 1540; major premiss a 1250, c 1400; **magior** 822, **magor** 1267, *for* **m.,** greater; *see also* **altare, etas, in, locus, missa; m. domus** 777, 1062. c 1100, c 1400, **m. in domo** c 1362, major-domo; **m. familie,** steward a 1275; **m. feodi** 1391, **marifeodus** 1488, mair-in-fee (Sc.); **m. gilde** 1397; **m. mercatorum** 1318; **m. palatii** 12c.; **m. primarius** c 1462; **m. societatis,** head of trading company 1438; **m. stapule,** mayor of the staple 1341, 1587; **mairus** 1450, **marus** c 1200, 1539, mair (Sc.); **majus** *for* **magis** c 1370, c 1449; **-abilis,** susceptible of increase a 1361; **-amentum,** c 1370, **-atio** a 1250, 1620, increase, enlargement; **-atus** 1274, c 1540, **-ia** 1254, 1312, **-itas** 1217, c 1390, mayoralty; **-atus domus** c 1320; **-atus stapule** 1341, 1499; *****-itas,** greater size, quality of being greater a 1100, 1620; higher rank, precedence c 1188, c 1536; majority, greater number c 1310; **-issa,** mayoress (of queen's household) 1251, 1258; (of Canterbury) 1472; **-ita,** play on minorita, 1593; **-o,** to increase, enlarge c 1115, c 1608; to lengthen (mus.) 1326, c 1470.

majorana a 1250, 1622, **marjorana** 1620, marjoram (bot.)

makau, cameo 1243.

makementum, match, proposal c 1290; bargain, collusion 1306.

*****makerellus** 1262, 1419, **mackarellus** 1535, **maquerellus** 13c., 1409, mackerel; *cf.* **megarus.**

1 mal/a 1180, 1480, **-ia** 1164, **-etta, -ettum** 1299, 1480, †**-is** 1335, **-o** 1480, mail, bag, case; **-emannus,** (?) bagman 1360; **-sella,** pack-saddle 1388.

2 mal/a, mail, rent a 1115, 15c.; **mollondum,** land on which rent is paid 1336; **-mannus** c 1183, c 1380, **-emannus** 1317, **mollmannus** 1297, 1336, **molemennus** 1300, 1402, **molmennus** 1302, rent-paying tenant; **-emarta** 1459, 1480, **mailmarta** 1549, **mailemarta** 1479, 'mailmart', cow paid as rent (Sc.); **molagium,** (?) form of tenure 1402 (*cf.* **mola**).

3 mala, *see* **malus.**

malache, mallow (bot.): **molochia** a 1250.

mal/acissatio, softening 1620, 1622; **-agma,** an emollient (fig.) c 900.

malad/ia, malady, disease 15c.; **-aria** 1200, 1204, **-eria** 1268, **-ria** c 1220, 1275, **malederia** c 1200, lazar-house.

malancol/ia, -icus, *see* **MELAN**

mal/andrinus c 1422, **-endrinus** c 1450, brigand (It.).

‡**malaribio,** opium 1652.

malarium, *see* **1 malum.**

mal/atolta (tolta mala) 1202, 1310, **-a torta** 13c., **-atosta** 1205, **-atouta** 1255, 1315, **-etolta** c 1300, **-etota** c 1290, c 1353, **-etotum** 1444, **-itota** c 1353, **-tollia** 1303, †**maustosta** 1199, maltolt, unjust or illegal tax or exaction; *cf.* **tolta.**

male/ sum de, to be out of favour with c 1180; **-contentus,** malcontent, rebel 1587; **-credo,** to suspect, hold in ill repute 1199, 1419; **-factio,** stolen property 1195; **malfactio,** illness, suffering a 1250; **-factrix** (*f.*) 1206, **malificator** c 1000, wrong-doer; **-ficiosus,** necromantic c 1130; **malificiosus,** malicious, wicked c 1370; **-ficio,** to harm 1232; to bewitch c 1260, 1620; **-fidus,** faithless c 950; **-gestura,** misbehaviour a 1564, 1661; **-grate** 1262, **malo grato** 1253, c 1259, with an ill grace, 'maugre'; **-gratis dentibus** despite oneself 1278; **-mitto,** to insult, dishonour c 1115; **-morigeratus,** of bad character c 1000; **-sanus,** unsound c 1125, 1267; **-suasus,** ill-advised c 1204; **-tractatio, -tractio,** maltreatment a 1564; **-tracto,** to maltreat 1224, 1661; **veniendo,** *see* **2 malum;** **-versor,** to act dishonestly 1348.

malederia, *see* **MALAD**

malemarta, *see* **2 mala.**

malencolia, *see* **MELAN**

malendrinus, *see* **malandrinus.**

male/tolta, -tota, *see* **malatolta.**

malett/a, -um, *see* **1 mala.**

maleuta, *see* **manuleuta.**

malevesinum, *see* **MALV**

malholmus, *see* **MALL**

malibolus, *see* **MALIVOL**

malific-, *see* **MALE**

malign/antia c 1170, -atio c 1000. a 1452, -um c 1400, malice, reviling; -anter, maliciously 1334; -issime, most maliciously 710; -osus c 1180, malinus c 1260, *for* -us, malicious; -o, to injure c 1115.

mali/loquium, fine for slander c 1115; -pendo, to object to c 1370.

malina, high *or* spring tide c 550, 860. a 1130; *cf.* ledo; † (?) measure of length 6c.

malis, *see* 1 mala.

maliti/a preconcepta c 1300, 15c., m. precogitata 1304, 1391, m. excogitata c 1323, malice aforethought; -es, malice c 1190.

malivol/entia regis, king's ill will 1130, 1168; malibolus, ill-intentioned 738; -o, to intend ill 1378.

mallardus *c 1220, c 1397, mallertus 1523, madlardus 1198, 1297, mathlardus 13c., maulardus 1292, 1391, mallard, wild drake; domestic drake 1285.

malleria, *see* MARL

mall/eus campane, clapper of bell c 1180; -eum 1399, 1573, -ia 1462, 1481, maillia 1233, maillus 1276, *for* -eus, hammer, mall; -iolus, small hammer c 1200, 1400; ‡-eolus a 1520, -eola 1550, ankle; ‡-us 15c., †malholmus c 1280, plough-beetle; -eabilis, malleable 1267, a 1275; -earis, of a hammer a 1275; -eatio, hammering 1195, 1620; -eator, hammerer c 1180, c 1385; -eatoria, art of hammering 12c.; aurum -iatum, gold leaf 1472; -eo, to hammer 1267, a 1275; 1291, -io 1293, 1306, -o 1299, to break (clods) with a hammer; -ico, to beat, kill 6c.

malleuta, *see* manuleuta.

mallium, *see* macula.

mallum, moot (Frankish; *cf.* A.S. *mǣđl*) c 1115.

malluvium, wash-basin: mallouvium 1550.

malmannus, *see* 2 mala.

malmaria, *see* MAHOM

malm/ator, -o, *see* MARL

malo, *see* 1 mala.

malo grato, *see* MALE

‡malonomus, shepherd (μηλονόμος) c 1440.

malpiger/noun 1219, -gum 1377, sort of pottage.

malsella, *see* 1 mala.

malt/halla, malt-hall, brewery (?) 15c.; -mannus, maltster 15c.; -mulna, maltmill 15c.

maltollia, *see* malatolta.

maltura, *see* mola.

1 māl/um, apple: m. aureum 1555, m. Medicum 1538, m. Punicum 1480, orange (*or* lemon); m. garnatum, pomegranate 1307; m. storacis a 1250, ‡m. styracis 14c., birthwort; m. terre, cyclamen a 1250, ‡14c.; -arium, orchard c 1250; melarius, apple-tree 7c.

2 mālum, evil: m. lecti 1194, c 1290, m. veniendi 1196, c 1290, male veniendo 1419, m. ville 1199, c 1258, various grounds for essoin (leg.); m. mortuum, a skin disease a 1250; *cf.* MALE, PEJOR, pessimo.

mal/us, mast: -a 1269, -um c 1296; *cf.* retro.

‡malva alta, m. silvestris, m. viscus, holly-hock 14c.; ‡m. crispa, musk-mallow 14c.

malv/esia 1390, -eisyn 1361, -asetum 1448,

1531, -esinum 1480, 1482, malevesinum 1482, vinum -aticum 1531, 1622, malmsey, wine of Monemvasia.

Mamaluchus 1517, Menelo c 1200, Mame-luke.

mammaza, metal tag 9c.

mammola, *see* manumola.

‡mammonetus, marmoset 15c.

mam/mula, teat-shaped body c 1115; †-ia, *for* -ma, 1392; -mella, *for* -illa, 463; -illatus, with teat-shaped protuberances 14c.

mamo, *see* MAHEM

mampa, *see* mappa.

mamura, *see* mangerium.

managium, *see* MANS

man/ale, ewer: -ile a 1090, a 1400, ‡-ilium a 1520.

manant/ia, -isa, *see* manentia.

†manapium, (?) napkin 1373; *cf.* maniphora, mappa.

manaria, *see* 2 mina.

manbota, 'man-bote', weregeld c 1115.

manbra, *see* 1 ambra.

1 man/ca 1220, 1226, -chia 1280, 1282, -cum 1234, -icus c 1188, handle; -cio (mantio), to fit with a handle 1205.

2 manc/a (?) 867, a 975. c 1115, c 1130, monca a 1123, -ola 841, -una 948, -osa 811, -usa 799, a 910. c 1125, c 1250, -usus 11c., mancus (coin); -a auri c 1115, c 1414, -usa auri 785, 987, -usus auri 10c.; -usa argenti c 1397; -usus nummorum c 960.

†mancagium, (?) *f.l.* for avantagium, 1284.

mancholum, *see* macholum.

mancio, *see* 1 manca; MANS

*mancip/ium, manciple (ac.) 1339, 1535; -ius, servant (G.) 1316; -ator, emancipator, liberator 6c.; m. carceri, one who commits to prison 1377; -atus, assigned, appointed 947. 12c.; mansipo, *for* -o, c 1330; -o, (?) to receive 5c.; *m. carceri, to commit to prison c 1220, 1494; m. effectui, to carry into effect c 1125, 15c.

mancor/num 12c., 1333, †-dia a 1128, 'mancorn', (?) 'mongcorn' (maslin) *or* grain for human consumption.

manc/umentum, lack, shortage 1458; -o, to maim 1276; -or, to fail, fall short of 1423.

mancus/a, -us, *see* 2 manca.

mand/a 1382, maunda 1465, 1533, 'maund', hamper; -ula, little hamper 1478.

mand/amen, message or command c 1070; -atum, message 1242; habeo in -atis c 1411, c 1456, recipio in m. c 1180, to receive a command; -atum a 1090, 1482, dies cene ad m. c 1300, festum -abile c 1397, maundy (eccl.); maundy chamber c 1312, 1397; †1263, *-atarius 1295, 1686, -ator a 1245, 1587, -atorius 1506, -atus a 1253, 1271, mandatary, agent; -aticius, conveying commands 1395; -ativus, dona-tive (gram.) 790; -amus, name of a writ 1261, 1573; -o, *to send for, send word to, command c 1130, 1456; to report, return 1214, 1419; to send, send out, issue c 1310, 1424; m. pro, to send for 1254, 1310.

‡mandella, black hellebore seed 1652.

mandicatio, *see* MANDUC

mandra, fold 7c.; monastery 790, 980.

mandragor/a, *for* **-as**, mandrake (bot.) 1271, 1622; **-icus**, of or for mandrake c 730, 10c.; **oleum -atum** a 1250.

mandria, *see* **madrya**.

manduc/atio c 1380, **mandicatio** 13c., eating; **-abilis**, eatable c 1188, c 1250; **-atorius**, concerned with eating c 1337; ***-o**, to eat c 730, c 1006. a 1090, 1461.

mandula, *see* **manda**.

mane/ facto c 730, c 1000. c 1150, 1346, **de m.** c 600. 1415, 1545, **in m.** c 1470, in the morning, at day-break; **summo m.**, early in the morning c 1150, 1423; **-loquela** 1679, **-loquium** 1389, 1585, morn-speech, guild-meeting; **manico**, to visit early (bibl.).

†**maneia**, (?) *f.l.* for **manus**, c 1397.

mane/lata, -leta (Sc.) 13c., ‡**menelaca** 14c., c 1440, weed, corn marigold.

man/entia, duration c 1360; **-antia**, abode 1220; **-antisa**, right of residence (O.F. *manantise*) 1245; **-ens**, serf 1327, c 1332; measure of land 676, 825. 12c.; **terra -entis** c 692, 812. c 1112, c 1414; **-eo**, to rest with, be in one's power 1559; **m. de**, to be part of 1219; *cf.* MANS

maneria, *see* **manerium**; **mangerium**; **2 mina**.

maner/ies c 1160, 1395, **-ium** 1241, manner, mode, kind.

*maner/ium c 1070, 1586, **-ia** 1200, 1292, **-ies** 13c., 1637, **-ius** 1082, 1086, manor, manor-house; **m. capitale** 1086, 1306; **m. dominicum** 1086, 1324, **m. dominium** 1086, demesne manor; **m. forinsecum** c 1250; **m. laudis causa vocatum**, manor by courtesy 1343; **m. liberum** 1086; **m. partibile** 1241; **-ettum** 1296, **-iolum** 1086, c 1470, small manor; **villa -ialis**, village appurtenant to manor 1322.

manerus, 'manned', trained (falc.) 1201, 1202.

manes, *see* **magnes**.

manfares (*pl.*), (?) small boats 1326.

man/gerium 1276, c 1382, **-gerum** c 1300, **-jeria** 1214, 1311, †**-eria** 1214, 1320, **-gorium** 1373, **-gor** 1301, **-jor** 1287, **-gura** 1272, **-jura** (†**mamura**) 1214, 1276, **maungerium** (†**manugerium**) 1388, 1454, **maunjorium** 1427, manger *or* nose-bag; 1393, **-geria** (C.I.) 1274, meal, banquet.

‡**manglisa**, "chop-church" 15c.

mangn-, *see* **magnitas**.

mango/, monger, dealer 11c., 1380; **-no** (†**magono**), to deal c 1115.

mang/onellus 1207, 15c., **-onellum** c 1250, **-enellus** 1254, 1338, **magenellus** 1245, 1275, **-unellus** 1173, c 1253, **magunellus** 1198, ‡**-onale** 15c., mangonel, siege-engine; **m. Turkesius** 1214; ‡**magonalius**, "gunner" c 1440.

‡**mangoraria**, art of lifting weights by pulleys 1652.

mani-, *see also* **manu-**

maniac/us, maniac, madman c 1250, a 1484; **-e**, madly 1378.

manic/a, maunch (her.) c 1450, c 1595; **-ia** 1261, **-ium** 1415, **manuca** 1252, 15c., *for* **-a**, sleeve; **manucatus**, sleeved, 1217, 1289; **-ularia** (*pl.*), cuffs 1295; **-ulum**, manacle 13c., 1389; **-ule** (*pl.*) c 1290, **-le** 1287, manacles; **-ule ferree**, gauntlets 1303;

manuce f., "Almain rivets" 1553; **manucale**, maniple 1385; ‡**-ulo**, to manacle 15c.

manico, *see* **mane**.

manicus, *see* **1 manca**.

manifest/abilis, to be made manifest 13c.; **-ative**, by way of manifestation 1344; **-ativum**, manifestation 13c.; **-ativus** a 1250, c 1290, **-ivus** a 1361, **-atorius** 870, expressive, revelatory; **-im** c 1267, **in -o** 12c., manifestly; **-or**, to appear for judgement c 600.

†**mani/ficus**, *f.l.* for **-festus**, c 1290.

manil/e, -ium, *see* **manale**.

manimola, *see* **manumola**.

man/iphora c 1450, ‡15c., ‡**-ifra** 1483, napkin.

*manip/ulus a 1090, c 1520, **-lus** c 1192, 1282, **-ula** c 1216, 1407, **-la** 1245, **-ulum** 1180, c 1255, **manupulus** c 1411, **manuplus** 13c., **manupulum** c 1330, maniple, vestment (eccl.); **-ulata**, handful 1281; **-ularis**, concerned with mere handfuls 1620.

man/jeria, -jor, -jura, *see* **mangerium**.

manleuta, *see* **manuleuta**.

mann/a, miraculous fluid or dust from saints' tombs 12c., 1383; flour 1461; **-ifluus**, like manna, ambrosial c 730; **-is**, grain of frankincense a 1250, ‡14c.

Mannensis, Manx c 1298, 1324.

mann/inga (†**manunga**), **-itio**, (area of) jurisdiction (Frankish) c 1115; **-io**, to summon c 1115.

manreda, homage (A.S.) a 1086, c 1105.

mans/a 939, c 1000. c 1066, 1336, **-ia** 1185, **-ium** 790, **-us** 1001, 11c., **massa** (?) 745 (c 1125), **terra -us** c 1255, **-io** (?) 867, **terra -ionis** 11c., 12c., **-io terre** 1086, measure of land; ***-eolum** (? *or for* **mausoleum**), hospital or almshouse c 1200, c 1325; **-io**, 'house' (astr.) a 1200, 1267; ***790**, c 1000. 1070, 1559, **-o** 13c., **mancio** c 1000. 1359, 1500, **masio** c 1190, †**mensio** c 1290, ***-um** 12c., 1558, **-ua** (? **-na**) c 1185, 1206, **-uagium** (? **-nagium**) c 1185, p 1230, ***managium** a 1140, 1330, **mainagium** 1261, 1264, **maignagium** c 1130, **menagium** 1296, c 1320, **maisagium** c 1200, **masagium** c 1160, 1311, ***masuagium** (? **masnagium**) c 1180, 1332, **mesagium** c 1174, 1259, ***mesuagium** (? **mesnagium**) 1190, 1580, **meswagium** a 1242, **mainamentum** (G.) 1312, **-ionarium** a 1100, **maisera** (C.I.) 1248, **maiseria** (C.I.) 1247, (?) **masera** 1472, ‡**-orium** c 1400, 1483, ***-ura** 779. 1086, c 1397, **maisura** c 1120, 1276, **masura** 1086, 1377, **mesura** 1201, dwelling-house, tenement, manor, messuage, household; ***mesuagium capitale** c 1185, 1573;

-ia, life 6c.; **-iuncula** 805. a 1100, a 1446, ‡**-ula** 1483, **mainilla** (Norm.) c 1185, **mesnillum** (Norm.) 1200, small dwelling or building; **maisneda**, meinie, household c 1192; **domus -ionalis** 1583, 1635, **d. -ionaria** 13c., mansion-house, dwelling-house; **mesonagium**, housing, storage 1387; **-ionarius**, one in charge of lodgings 804; a resident (G.) 1286, 1292; **locus -ionarius** c 1257; **-ive**, permanently c 1250; **-ivitas**, permanence, durability c 1270; **-ivus** a 1250, c 1360, †**-ius** 1336, **-orius**

c 1154, permanent, abiding; **-orius,** sojourner 6c.; **-iono,** to dwell c 1290; *cf.* **manentia.**

mansetum, manchet flour 1540.

mansipo, *see* MANCIP

mantargium, *see* **manutergium.**

mant/ellum *1195, 1495, **-ella** 1291, 1532, **-ellus** 13c., c 1472, **-ale** c 1425, **-allum** c 1335, c 1370, **-ea** c 1192, **-um** c 1160, c 1450, mantle, cloak; **m. ad portandum panem** 1216; **m. ferreum** 1322; ***-ellum,** mantel (over fire) 1237, 1398; 1348, **mauntela** 1337, **-elettum** 1378, 1399, ring-wall; **-ilettum,** mantelet, movable shelter 1374; **-ellettum,** 'mantelet', caparison 1316; **-ile,** altar-cloth c 1190, c 1330; **-iliolum** 1520, †**-iolum** 1553, napkin; **pannus -elinus,** mantle-cloth 1394; **-ello,** to make into a mantle 13c.

manti/a c 1260, **-ce** 1267, 1393, divination (μαντεία).

mant/ica, cloak-bag: †**-issa** 1540, †**-ua** 1587; **-ica ad carrucam** 1276; **-icularium super rotular' pendens,** roller-towel 1553; **-icellum,** (?) bellows a 1235; **-icalis** c 1382, c 1430, **-icatus** c 1180, c 1250, panniered; **-ico,** to stow, truss 1279, ‡1483; **-iculo,** to deceive 950.

mantineo, *see* MANUTEN

mantio, *see* 1 **manca.**

manu-, *see also* **manica; manus.**

†**manubie** (*pl.*), (?) guards c 1150.

manub/ium c 1200, c 1296, **-rium** 1344, sleeve; **-rium,** "javelin" 1553; **-riator,** (?) haft-maker *or* sleeve-maker 13c.; **-eatus** c 1200, **-riatus** 15c., sleeved.

***manucap/tio,** mainprise, bail (leg.) 1260, 1583; ***-tor** a 1183, 1583, **-iens** 1238, mainpernor; keeper, maintainer 1389; **-tabilis** c 1395, **-tibilis** 1346, entitled to bail; **-io,** *to go bail (for) 1216, 1402; *(with *inf.* or **quod**) to undertake c 1126, a 1452; **m. habendi** 1219, c 1290.

manuduc/tio, guidance 870. 1165, 1378; **-tor,** leader 870; **-o,** to lead, guide c 1257, 1686.

manugerium, *see* **mangerium.**

manu/leuta 1294, **manleuta** 1285, **malleuta** 1293, 1314, **-levatio** c 1260, mainprise, bail (G.); **-levator,** mainpernor, surety (G.) c 1252; **-levo,** to go bail for (G.) 1242, 1259; to raise, levy (military stores) 1242.

manu/mola 1171, c 1330, **manusmola** 1171, **-mula** 1221, **manimola** (†**mammola**) 12c. c 1308, **-molendinum** a 1183, hand-mill.

manunga, *see* **manninga.**

manuop/us 1256, a 1564, **manum opus** 1218, 'mainour', stolen goods; (product of) handiwork 1319; 1210, 1660, **-eratio** 1286, 1387, work, handiwork; **officium -erale,** handicraft a 1330, 1419; **-erarius,** handicraftsman 1321, 1329; **-ero** 1263, 1366, **-eror** 1210, 1352, to labour, till; *cf.* **manura, menura.**

manup-, *see also* MANIP

***manupast/us** (*4th decl.*) c 1115, 1334, **-um** c 1115, †**mainpastus** (? **manipastus**) c 1220, 'mainpast', household; **-us** (*2nd decl.*) 1271, a 1539, **-a** (*f.*) 1279, **-or** 1292, member of household.

manupes, measure of length, (?) *pied de main*

(two fists joined by outstretched thumbs) 1189, 1229; *cf.* **pes palme.**

manuprisa 1295, **meinprisa** c 1463, mainprise, bail (leg.).

manur/a 1483, **-atio** 1376, 1548, tillage; **-o,** to 'manure', till 1504, 1584.

manu/s, person c 1115; ***possession** (of feudal suzerain) 1086, c 1431; *hand raised in oath of compurgation, compurgator (leg.) c 1115, c 1446; *see also* **ad, ante, capio, 2 data, de, gula, pono, pre; m. alta,** high hand, violence c 1430; **m. altior** c 1400, **m. superior** c 1327, upper hand, advantage; **m. Christi,** a cordial 1514; **m. correctionis,** punishment c 1265; **m. equa** 1234, 1335, **m. equalis** c 1200, 1299, *owel mein,* trustee (leg.); ***m. fortis (-fortis)** c 1188, c 1520, **fortitudo manus** c 1250, main force; **m. inferior,** lower class c 1188; **m. media,** middle class c 1180, c 1220; **m. media,** (payment to) middle-man 1304; ***m. mortua** 1276, 1587, **manumortua** 1535, mortmain; **m. publica,** public authority c 1185; notarial attestation 1304, c 1476; **manu in manum,** hand to hand 1347; **in manu prima (secunda),** at first (second) hand 1490; **cum manu rubea,** red-handed (Sc.) 14c.; **-us portum,** 'mainport', payment in lieu of tithe (eccl.) 14c.; †**-abilis,** (?) able-bodied c 1423; **-agor,** to get a living 1406;

-ale, handle 1299; stipend (eccl.) 1346, 1389; sign manual, signature 1441; *1200, c 1447, **emanuale** 1439, **liber -alis** c 1250, 1429, manual, service book (eccl.); **ars -alis,** handicraft 1554; **sacramentum -ale** c 1400; *see also* **mola, 2 pila, signum, spectaculum; -aliter** c 1330, 1461, **-atim** c 1380, 1445, by hand, hand to hand; **-artifex,** handicraftsman a 1235, 1267; **-factura** 1617, **-fictile** c 1115, manufactured article; **-factus,** manufactured c 1260, 1344; **-firmatio,** promise c 1102; **-lus,** *see* **mappa; -positio,** assault 1485; **mensura -rasa,** measure razed by hand 1419; **-scriptus,** (*adj.*) manuscript 1514, c 1620; **-theca,** glove 13c. (*cf.* **chirotheca**); **-vectum,** (?) hod c 1450.

manuten/ementum c 1140, 1234, (?) **mentenementum** c 1275, **-entia** p 1300, 1460, †**-entio** 1452, 1552, **-tio** 1220, 1587, **-sio** 1511, maintenance, support; c 1290, 1293, **mayntenementum** c 1290, **-entia** 1293, 1508, ***-entio** 15c., **-tio** 1313, c 1419, maintenance of suit (leg.); **-ibilis,** maintainable c 1390, a 1564; **-tor,** supporter c 1115, 1435; maintainer of suit c 1320, 1419; ***-eo** c 1115, 1471, **mantineo** 1232, to maintain, support; **m. juramentum,** to take an oath a 1408; **m. partem,** to maintain suit 1293, 1313.

***manuterg/ium** 760, c 1000. 1130, 1564, **-a** c 1550, **manitergium** 1306, 1509, **mantargium** 1419, towel.

manzerinus, bastard, mongrel (Heb.) a 1142; *see also* **mazer.**

mapp/a a 1090, 1564, **m. mensalis** c 1330, 1496, **m. mensula** 1574, **m. commensalis** 1390, table-cloth; canopy 1436; c 1204, c 1553, **m. mundi** c 1212, 1347, map; **m.**

manula, hand-towel 1574; -ale, cloth,
altar-cloth c 1200, 1494; opus -ale, (?) linen
damask 1295; -aria 1294, 1374, -arium
a 1380, -eria c 1400, napery, linen; -arius,
naperer, keeper of the napery 12c., 1356;
-ula, maniple (eccl.) 790, 9c. 1168; table-
cloth c 1148, 1574; -um 1509, †mampa
1225, for -a, napkin; cf. NAP

mara, see mare.

mar/abotinus 1177, -bodinus 1295, -botinus
c 1250, 1314, -betinus 1311, morabotinus
c 1436, -avidus, -vidus, -vedus 1523,
maravedi (coin).

maragdo, see smaragdo.

maragium, see mariscus.

mar/anatha c 1100, -enatha (?) 867, form of
anathema (bibl.).

mararius, see mare.

marasc-, see marescallus; mariscus.

mar/asmus 1622, -agmon a 1250, wasting
away (μαρασμός).

maravidus, marbetinus, marbo/dinus,
-tinus, see marabotinus.

marbr-, see MARMOR

marc-, see also merc-

*marc/a (march-) c 1115, c 1545, -ia c 1354,
-ula c 1220, -us a 1142, c 1449, merca (Sc.)
c 1180, 1564, mark, weight (1 oz.) or sum
of money (13s. 4d.); *m. argenti 1086,
1259; m. auri 1086, 1413; m. Coloniensis
c 1185; m. Scotica 1537; *m. sterlingorum 1237, c 1440; -a c 1253, *-ata c 1150,
1461, -atum c 1160, -atus c 1160, c 1400,
mark's worth; -um, weight, standard 1347
(cf. 1 marqua); see also MARCH, marqua
(1 & 2), musca.

marcalis, see gilda; libra.

marcas/ita a 1250, 1620, -ida, margassita
a 1235, marcasite, (?) pyrites.

marc/edo p 1300, †macedo a 1250, decay;
-escibilis 12c., -essibilis c 1160, -issibilis
934; perishable; -ido, to wither (trans.)
a 1184, ‡1483; -isco, for -esco, to wither
(intr.) c 1290.

mar/cella, -cilia, see marsilium.

marcellus, (?) limit (G.) 1285.

marces, see merces.

march-, see also MARESCAL; MERCHET

1 march/a 10c. 1086, *-ia 1168, 1545,
merchia a 1564, -ium c 1362, margia
1223, †marrhea 1377, †-esia 1593, march,
borderland; dies -ie, 'march-day', law-
day 1291, 1423; marca c 1115, c 1225,
merca c 1115, 13c., mark, boundary; -io
c 950, 991. c 1194, 1403, -ianus 1260, 15c.,
-iensis c 1256, 1347, marcensis c 1157,
-esis 1281, -isius c 1250, 1265, -isus 1168,
c 1265, †-ius 13c., marcher, borderer; *-io
1041, 11c. c 1125, 1608, -isius 12c., c 1250,
-isus a 1142, c 1200, markisus 1257,
†-iatus c 1370, margrave, marquis (foreign
title); 1397, 1619, markisius 1398, marquisus 1461, marquis, marquess (Engl. or
Sc. title); -io Dublin' 1386; -ionatus,
marquisate 1386, 1619; -isia c 1200, -isa
c 1125, 14c., -ionissa 1159, margravine,
marquise (foreign); -io 1235, 1558, m. me
(G.) 1311, to march with, border on; to be
a marcher, hold bordering lands 1204, 1421;
see also erchimotum, 2 marqua.

2 marcha, (?) import duty (G.) 1314.

marchio, to march, walk 1569; see also
1 marcha.

marcho, marc/o, -uo, see marqua (1 & 2).

marciat/on a 1250, -um 1414, sort of ointment (μαρκίατον).

marcipium, see MARSUPI

†marcudium, (?) part of clock 1400.

marc/ula, -us, see marca.

mar/e c 1150, 1583, *-a 1086, 1564, -ia
c 1180, mere, lake; -a c 1160, 1288, -um
c 1160, moor, marsh (cf. 1 mora); -e,
estuary (G.) c 1253, 1401; m. altum, high
sea 1325, 1606; m. plenum, high-water
mark c 1240, 1283; -arius a 1196, c 1200,
-erius a 1240, (?) water-bailiff; merewardus, 'mere-ward' (Cambs.) 1316; -eta
(C.I.) 1309, -eia 1253, -ina 1357, tide; -ea,
fish caught during one tide (G.) 1289; -ina,
limpet 6c.; †marma, (?) sea-animal 6c.;
-ina *1167, c 1300, *-itima c 1218, c 1362,
sea-shore, coast; -inaria, seamanship 1357;
-inallus 1248, *-inellus 1203, 1431,
*-inarius 1188, 1554, -enarius 1235,
-inerius (G.) 1293, -inator 1204, †-itima
c 1150, mariner, sailor; -itanus, maritime
1228, 1305; see also carbo, curia, lex,
molendinum, murus; -ino, to marinate,
pickle 1223; -io, to sail (G.) 1315.

mareccum, see marochum.

maremium, see maeremium.

†marena, (?) stepmother (or f.l. for mater)
1200.

marenatha, see maranatha.

marescal/lus, *farrier, horse-leech 1247,
1419; *12c., c 1450, -cus 1086, c 1212,
-dus c 1180, c 1220, marascallus c 1192,
1314, mariscallus c 1218, c 1443, mari-
scalcus c 1080, mariscaldus 1199, marreshallus c 1422, marscallus c 1136, 1461,
marshal; m. Anglie 1260, 15c.; m. aule
c 1250, c 1330; m. austurcorum 1250;
m. exercitus 1346; m. magnus c 1233;
m. mercati 1296; m. scaccarii 1236; m.
Scotie 14c., 1461; -a, marshal's wife 1315,
c 1325;

*-cia 1198, 1534, marescacia 1309,
marescaucia 1198, 1286, merescaucia
1219, mariscalcia c 1530, mariscacia
1212, marchalcia 1314, marchaucia
1314, marscalcia 1251, 1284, marscaucia
1212, 1285, -cio 1307, marshalria 1387,
merchelatio 1300, stable, stabling, farriery,
treatment of horses, etc.; *-cia 1166, 15c.,
-lia 1377, †-a 1306, -lecia 1307, mare-
schaucia c 1136, mariscalcia 1559,
-chacia 1307, marchesia c 1488, marscalcia 1307, office of marshal; -cia 15c.,
marascalcia a 1452, mariscallia c 1380,
marchalcia 15c., marchalsia c 1336,
marchesia c 1412, Marshalsea (court or
prison); m. prioris (Durham) c 1375;
marescaucia accipitrum 15c.; lex-cialis,
see lex; -cio 1205, 1284, -iso 1318, -lizo
c 1335, -lo c 1254, c 1320, mariscallo 1309,
marscallo 1232, 1311, marchalo 1232,
marchello 1336, to shoe or doctor (a horse).

mare/scus, -sium, -tum, see mariscus.

maresmium, see maeremium.

mareta, see mare.

marfaca, murfaca, rough cloth (Sp. *márfaga*, rug) 1470.

margalerius, *see* MATRICUL

margar/ita, pearl: -eta 13c.; -ita, silver (alch.) 1267; weight of plumb-line a 1350; -etula, little pearl c 1100; -itaria, (?) solution of pearls (med.) 1307; -itifer, pearl-bearing 1652.

margassita, *see* marcasita.

margeria, border 6c.

margia, *see* 1 marcha.

margin/alis, marginal c 1265, c 1553; -osus, of the shore c 550.

Margites, type of a simpleton 1523.

maria, *see* mare.

mariagium, *see* MARIT

Mari/ale, book in praise of the Virgin 1329, 14c.; -ola c 1200, c 1400, -olum 1265, 1380, image of the Virgin; (auca) -ola 1282, 1398, -iolis c 1230, unmated goose.

maricius, *see* mariscus.

marifeodus, *see* major.

marin-, *see* mare.

mario, *see* mare; MARIT

marisc-, *see also* MARESCAL

*mar/iscus 692, 858. c 1125, 1588, -isca 798, -iscis 778. 12c., -iscum c 1250, 1485, -ascus 832. 13c., -escus 1086, c 1448, †-oscus 1361, meriscus 679, 692, mer-scum c 1250, 1338, -icius 1190, c 1205, -isius c 1300, -isus c 1230, -issa a 1275, -agium 1451, 1511, -assum 1320, -esium c 1140, 1591, meresium (Sc.) 1476, 1605, merrasium 1400, morisium c 1300, morressa c 1200, -etum c 1170, 1284, marsh, morass; -iscus durus 12c.; m. friscus 1369, 1531; m. salsus 1198, 1583; -iscus 1230, -escus 1329, -iscalis 1540, 1587, -iscosus 1329, marshy.

marit-, *see also* mare.

marit/agium c 1224, c 1450, -atio c 1125, c 1500, marriage, giving in marriage; *1220, 1487, -atio 1217, 1608, feudal right of giving in marriage; *c 1080, c 1400, mari-agium c 1140, 1295, -atio 1100, c 1436, marriage-portion, dowry; m. francum 1166, *m. liberum c 1111, 1419, m. liberale a 1200, frank-marriage; m. ratio-nabile, marriage without disparagement 1235; ‡-olus, -ellus, husband 1483; m. maritaceus (? play on gallinaceus), husband *par excellence* c 1500; -o, to bind, unite c 1180, 1524; -o me, to marry 1188, 1309; mario, to give in marriage 1295.

marjorana, *see* majorana.

marketta, *see* merchetum.

markis/us, -ius, *see* 1 marcha.

*marl/a c 1170, c 1362, -ia 1234, 15c., -era 1315, -atura c 1303, marl, clay soil; -aria, -arium c 1160, 1298, -eria, -erium c 1200, 1301, malleria 1284, *-era 1217, 1345, -erum 1314, merlera c 1284, -etum 13c., -eputtus 1234, puteus -ere 1374, fossa -eria 1316, marl-pit; -atio c 1300, -ura 1234, 1317, marling (of land); -ator 1223, c 1304, malmator 1235, 1245, marler; -osus, marly c 1290; -eo 1223, -io 1280, c 1284, *-o c 1160, 1336, malmo 1235, 1245, to marl, apply marl.

marl/angus, -utus, *see* merlengus.

marma, *see* mare.

marmor/, marble; mormor 6c.; -arius 1183, 15c., (?) marbrarius 1106, vir -eus c 1470, marble-worker; -eus, marbled, variegated (of cloth) 1295, 1430; -ifodina, marble-quarry 1608; marbro, (?) to paint like marble 1256; *see also* MURMUR

Maro, type of a guide a 1142.

mar/ochum 1283, -ekkum 1303, -eccum 1338, 1410, 'marrock', pasturage (Lincs.).

marocum, maroquin, Morocco hide 1372.

maronia, *see* maerdredum.

Maronide (*pl.*), Maronites c 1250.

maroscus, *see* mariscus.

marpillus, louse (*cf.* Fr. *morpion*) a 1250.

1 marqua 1417, merc/a 1220, 1356, -um c 1220, mark, stamp, sign; merca, mark, target 1272; -amentum, (?) indication c 1180; marco c 1115, 1360, merko 1263, to mark, stamp; *cf.* marca.

2 marqu/a 1293, 1422, mercha 1295, marca (G.) 1313, †marta a 1446, marchia (G.) 1318, marque, reprisals; -o 1293, marco 1295, 1313, to seize under letters of marque; marcho 1254, marcuo 1289, to seize as pledge (G.).

marquisus, *see* 1 marcha.

marr/amentum, -imum, *see* maeremium.

marreshallus *see* MARESCAL

marrhea, *see* 1 marcha.

marro, (?) to acquire (G.) 1243; to appropriate (eccl.) (*cf.* O.F. *marance*) c 1375.

Mars, iron (alch.) c 1215, c 1345; *see also* dies, herba; gules (her.) 1595; Marti/a (*pl.*), warfare c 1200, c 1250; -alis, occurring in March c 1210; *see also* lex; -aliter, in a martial spirit c 1255.

marsc-, marshal-, *see* MARESCAL

†marses, (?) scrotum 6c.

mar/silium a 1250, ‡14c., (?) -cella a 1250, ‡-cilia 14c., (?) kind of hellebore (bot.).

mars/uinus c 1100, †-um (? -uin) 1086, 'marswine', porpoise.

marsupi/um c 1000. 12c., c 1540, marsy-pium 1271, marcipium c 1340, 1486, mercipium ‡15c., 1510, -olum a 1200, pouch, purse; -alis, money-grubbing c 1180; -ator, one who puts in his purse c 1180.

mart/a 1308, 1539, -us 1306, 1557, merta 1525, 'mart', (rent of) fatted beast (Ir., Sc., N. Engl.); m. fodella 1468, -foddala 1459, -fodella 1463, 1469, kind of 'mart' (Sc.); *see also* 2 marqua.

martagon, (?) martagon-lily *or* moonwort 1267.

*mart/ellus 6c. c 1125, c 1400, -ellum 1253, 1356, -iolus c 1160, -ulus c 1204, hammer.

marter-, martin-, martir-, *see* martrina.

Martha, type of the active life 1241.

marther, martil-, *see* MARTYR

marthinus, late, recent 6c.

marti/a, -alis, *see* Mars.

martineta, bird (water ouzel *or* kingfisher) c 1188.

mart/iolus, -ulus, *see* martellus.

mart/rina a 1185, c 1200, -urina c 1150, -ina c 1242, -ynia 1243, -rinus 1284, 1303, -inus c 1250, †-rius 1303, -rix c 1188, c 1200, -rixus 1436, -ira c 1125, a 1180, -erellus 1528, ‡-es 1570, -ur 1431, †morder

13c., marten, marten-fur; -rinus 1086, 1451, -erinus 1138, c 1200, -renus c 1452, of marten-fur.

martus, see marta.

martyr/ (martir) (eccl.), marther 1517, martyr; -ialis, of a martyr c 1125; -ialiter, in martyrdom c 1100; -ium (eccl.), -ia 7c., -iatio c 1300, -izatio a 1100, c 1367, martyrdom; *-ologium c 730, c 1000. c 1066, c 1553, *martilogium c 1150, c 1473, martilagium 1368, martilegium 1438, 1504, mortilegium 1513, calendar of saints and benefactors, book of obits; mortilegiatus, enrolled in book of obits 1432; *-izo, to martyr 704, 1041. c 1100, c 1414; to suffer martyrdom 7c.

marus, see major.

†marutia, (?) some construction of stone 1231.

marv/edus, -idus, see marabotinus.

mas (indecl.), male 1307.

mas-, see also MANS

masa, see 1 macia.

masarus, see mazer.

masc-, see also macecraria; macella; macia.

masc/a, mask 704; nightmare c 1210; -us 1545, 1560, -ulus 1551, masque.

mascalcio, see machecollum.

masco, see mazo.

masc/ra, -ula, -ulatus, see macula.

mascul/initas, masculinity c 1300, c 1500; -ine, in the masculine gender c 700, 790; -inior, more masculine c 1500; -arius, (?) pervert c 1193; ‡-us, mercury (alch.) 1652; -o, to turn into a man 13c.; for emasculo, to geld or spay 1271.

maser-, see MANS; mazer.

maseum, see 2 macia.

masio, masn-, see MANS

masius, see muscum.

maskera, see macula.

maso, see mazo.

mass/a, mass (mechanical) 1686; mass of metal, bullion 1381, 1465; m. ferri 1086; -atus c 1197, c 1213, -icus, -icius 1245, massy; -o, to amass p 1330; see also 1 macia, MANS, muscum, sal.

Massamutinus, obolus, a Spanish coin 1282; cf. musca.

mass/arius, -uellus, -uerius, see 1 macia.

masso, to eat c 1115, 1252; see also massa.

masta, see mastus.

masti/catio, chewing-gum a 1250; c 1430, c 1444, †-gatio c 1422, rumination, meditation; -co, to ruminate, think over c 1300, c 1470; to mock at c 1193.

mastig/abilis, fit for whipping 1497; -ophorus, bearing a scourge c 1120.

mastillio, see MIXT

*masti/nus (? -vus) c 1140, c 1400, canis m. c 1240, c 1362, -o c 1185, mastiff (Fr. mâtin).

mast/ix, gum mastic a 1250; -iceleon, mastic oil a 1250.

*mast/us 1205, 1421, -a 1308, -um 1338, 1509, mast (naut.); m. magnus, main-mast 1411.

masu-, see also MANS

‡masuclum, "orange" 15c.

1 mat/a 14c., -um a 1159, mat c 1190, checkmate; -o, to check-mate 12c.

2 †mata, measure of ale c 1300; (?) cf. 3 muta.

matax/a, -o, see METAX

mateo/logica, idle talk 1541; -technia, vain technicality 1610.

mater/, source c 1250; lees of wine 1233, 1241; part of the Albion (astr.) 1326; m. aqua, matrix a., main stream 12c.; m. ecclesia, matrix e., see ecclesia; m. dura, m. pia, outer and inner membranes of brain c 1210, 1267; ‡m. herbarum, matricaria, wormwood (bot.) 14c.; ‡m. silvarum, honeysuckle (bot.) 13c., 14c.; ‡m. metallorum, mercury (alch.) 1652; m. spiritualis c 1170, c 1250, ‡-na 15c., matrina ‡c 1440, c 1559, ‡matricia 1483, godmother; -nitas, maternity p 1300; (title) c 1380; -nalis, maternal c 1380, c 1480; -nus, in the mother tongue (cf. lingua) 1293; matartara, for -tera, aunt 1265; matr/inomius, named after the mother 8c.; -isylva, honeysuckle 1538; -ius, maternal c 1360; ovis -ialis 12c., o. -ix 1185, 1464, o. -ica 1195, ewe; -isso, to take after the mother c 1196, 1623.

matera-, see matracium.

*mater/ia 13c., 1539, -a 1510, matter, affair; occasion, pretext c 1315, 1382; potential candidate (for office) 9c.; material cause (log.) c 850; m. contingens, m. naturalis, m. remota c 1160; m. prima (alch.) a 1252, ‡1652; m. subjecta, subject-matter 1461; -ies 1130, 1316, matrinum c 1300, timber (cf. maeremium); -iabilis, capable of having a material cause p 1300; -iale, material object, thing, 1267 1620; -iali impositum, word used to denote the word itself c 1108; -ialis, *material, physical c 1125, c 1466; concerned with matter (phil.) 1240, c 1362; consisting of raw material c 1370; material, relevant 1477; see also causa, gladius, suppositio; -ialitas 860. 1267, 1344, -iatum c 1180, a 1250, material quality or embodiment; -ialiter, as (in the way of) materials c 730; materially, in relation to matter 10c. c 1160, 1346; in substance (not verbatim) 1294, c 1395; -ialius, more materially 15c.; -iatus, embodied in matter a 1233, 1622; -io, to make material or actual c 1180, c 1360.

mathematic/a (pl.) c 700. 13c., c 1550, -alia (pl.) 1267, c 1457, mathematics; -alis, mathematical 13c., c 1361; -e, mathematically 1267; -itas, mathematical property or character c 1270; -us, abstract, theoretical 1385, 1521; magical c 1212, c 1250; (subst.) magician c 1190; math/ĕsis, mathematics, science a 1150, 1686; -ēsis, matēsis, divination, magic (? associated with μάτην) c 1125, c 1260; -ites c 950, -ita 981, disciple.

mathlardus, see mallardus.

matian/um (macian-) a 1250, ‡14c., ‡malum m. 14c., 15c., crab-apple; ‡-us, crab-tree 15c., 1483.

matid-, see madefactio.

matin-, matitunellum, see MATUTIN

mato, see 1 mata.

matokk/us 1275, mattaccus 1338, mettoccus 1283, mattock or bill (of mill); -o, to break (earth) with mattock 1338.

mat/racium 1208, c 1450, -racia 1496, *-eracium 1248, c 1340, -eracia c 1330, -erasium 1405, †-ra c 1330, *-rax 1327, -ricia 1454, -ericia 1473, mattress.

matri-, *see also* mater.

‡matria, pantry 15c.

matricul/a, list, register c 1160, 15c.; roll of students (ac.) c 1231, c 1307; alms-house of hospital 1200; registrum -are 1402; rotulus -aris, list of patrons 1238; -aris c 875, 11c., -arius c 875, 11c. 1300, 1414, one named in a list of beneficiaries; -arius 1086, c 1296, margalerius c 1250, mergularius 1367, sacristan, sub-sacristan, churchwarden; -atio, matriculation (ac.) c 1564; -o, to enrol, matriculate 1402, c 1564.

‡matricuria, "*custurere*" (sempstress) c 1180.

matrimoni/um, marriage-portion, dowry 1086, c 1350; -aliter, *by, in, marriage c 1195, c 1540; by right of wife c 1450.

matrinum, *see* materia.

matron/a, ewe p 1290; ‡thistle 14c.; -o, to make matron-like c 1184; to behave like a matron 13c.

*matt/a, mat c 1050. c 1080, 1521; -ula, little mat c 1197, c 1330; *cf.* natta.

mattaccus, *see* matokkus.

matum, *see* 1 mata.

matur/atio, haste c 1191, 1266; c 1191, 14c., -itio 794, †-itium 1267, ripening; -abilis, able to ripen 12c.; -aliter, early c 1460; -ativus, promoting ripeness a 1250, ‡1652; -itas (*coll.*), those of riper years c 1456.

*matutin/e (*pl.*) c 1080, c 1520, -i (*pl.*) c 730, 1050. c 1125, c 1250, †matine c 1204, matins (eccl.); -alis c 730, 1006. c 1400, †maturalis c 730, of or for matins; *see also* altare, missa; -ale a 1452, liber -alis 1342, 1489, service-book of matins; vigilia -aria c 1330; colloquium -ale 1476, 1543, loquela -alis 1389, morn-speech, guild meeting; -um, canonical hour of matins 1201, 1419; matinellum c 1185, 1234, matitunellum 13c., lunch; -o, (?) to say matins c 1400.

maulardus, *see* mallardus.

Maumeticola, *see* MAHOM

maunda, *see* manda.

maundrellus, mandrel (for gun) 1385, a 1396.

maungerium, maunjorium, *see* mangerium.

mauntela, *see* mantellum.

maurella, *see* 3 morus.

maus/oleum c 700. 1200, 1432, †-eolum 14c., tomb, shrine; coffin c 1397, c 1436; -oleo, to bury a 1100; *see also* MANS

maustosta, *see* malatolta.

mavelle, *for* malle, 7c.

maviscus, mavis, thrush, 1422, ‡1483.

maxil/la, cheek c 1250, c 1450; †-ia, jaw 1325.

*maxim/a, maxim c 1180, 1620; -ates (*pl.*), magnates 1433.

maxuca, *see* 1 macia.

may-, *see also* mai-, mei-

mayntenementum, *see* MANUTEN

mazacaria, *see* macecraria.

*maz/er, -erus 1245, 1419, -arus a 1273, -era 1453, -erius 1293, 1358, -eria 1330, 1361, -orius 1361, macer c 1300, *mas/er, -erus 1385, 1437, -arus 1434, *-era c 1341,

1453, -erius 1275, 1406, mazer, (bowl of) maple-wood; mazerinus (†manzerinus) c 1188, macerinus c 1255, of maple-wood; mazenarius c 1136, mazelinarius c 1196, †macenerus c 1340, (?) mazer-keeper (Fr. *madrinier*).

maz/o 1166, 1256, macio a 1142, maco 1225. maso 1276, 1333, masco 1222, -unus 1221, mason; -onaria 1212, maconeria c 1227, 1277, maconnereia 1198, †macenoria 1225, masonry; macieno, to work in masonry 1274.

mazuellus, *see* 1 macia.

meand/er (? -rus), roundabout way, trick 1345, 1527.

†meandri (*pl.*), (?) lower orders, menials (*v.l.* calones) c 950.

meanialis, *seee* menialis.

mearemium, *see* maeremium.

meater, *see* ego.

mechalis, adulterous, lewd c 1000. c 1090.

mechanic/a, workmanship 1432; -um, device, system c 1115; -e, mechanically 1267; by handicraft c 1340.

mecio, *see* messio.

mecon, poppy: micon a 1250.

Mecubalis, Mecubalist, expert in Hebrew lore 1564.

med/a 1130, 1407, *-o c 1135, c 1436, -us c 1200, c 1255, mead (drink); -arius, obedientiary in charge of mead (mon.) 1202, 1535; -aria 1284, -eria 1191, c 1400, office of *medarius*.

mede-, *see* madefactio; MEDIC

medgabulum, (?) 'mead-gavel', meadow-rent (Berks.) 1205.

media-, *see also* medium.

mediada, madi/ada c 550, -ana 6c., (?) loins, flanks.

mediannus, spurge (*Euphorbia lathyris*) (Ar. *mâhûdâna*) 12c.

medic/ina, elixir, philosophers' stone (alch.) c 1227, c 1345; remedy (leg.) c 1115; medecina c 1384, 1573, -atio 13c., -atura c 1115, medicine or medical treatment; -inatio, healing 1445, 1456; -ator, healer 760; medeliferus c 730, -abilis 7c., -alis c 600. c 1180, 1293, *-inalis c 730, c 800. c 1185, c 1362, -amentarius 1499, -ativus 1344, healing, medicinal; *see also* anulus; *-inale, medicament a 1250, c 1400; -inaliter, medicinally, by way of cure a 1100, 15c.; -inus, physician 14c.; digitus -us, leech-finger, third finger 1266, 1488; -inatus, treated with the philosophers' stone (alch.) c 1435; medeor (*pass.*), to be healed c 730, 826; medificor, to heal a 1519; -ino, to dose, treat, cure 12c., 1350.

med/icon a 1200, -us c 1200, the gem Medea.

mediolus, *see* modius.

medit/abundus, thoughtful c 1562; -ator, planner 760; -ativus, desiderative (gram.) 790; -o, to plan c 1325.

medi/um, *means 13c., c 1466; medium (phys.) a 1446; middle term (log.) c 1250, c 1380; breve de -o, writ of mesne (leg.) 1259, 15c.; -um arithmeticum 1686; m. celi (astr.) 14c.; -ana, mid-Lent (eccl.) c 1164; midius, *for* -us, 12c.; *-us, mesne tenant (leg.) 1228, 1458; dominus -us, mesne lord c 1208; **-us**, intermediate in age (of three persons bearing the same name) 1463; *see also* **fides, lex, locus, quadragesima; m. color**, secondary colour a 1200; azure, gules, *or* or p 1394, a 1446; **m. proportionalis** (math.) 1686; **-um tempus** 1586, **-a tempora** 1620, Middle Ages; ***-o tempore**, meanwhile 1240, 1404; **lana -a** 1242, **l. -ana** 1291, 1296, wool of middling quality; **-alis**, median, midway c 1200; **-amen**, intermediary c 1376; **-amna** c 1200, **-amnis** 1310, c 1320, **-ampnis** c 1400, island in a river; **-amnus**, lying in a river c 1190; **-ana**, median vein (med.) a 1250; **-anata**, middle-born daughter 1290;

*-atio 12c., c 1458, **-anetum** (Sp.) 1177, mediation; mediate position or status 1266, c 1366; halving (math.) a 1150, 15c.; **-ate** 12c., c 1425, †**-etate** 1281, mediately (log.); **-atius**, more mediately c 1270; **-atus**, mediate, separated by a mesne (leg. & log.) 1279, 1461; **terra -ata** (G.) c 1283; ***-ator** a 1090, c 1536, **-atrix** (*f.*) c 730. 1137, c 1470, mediator, intermediary; **-ator caprarum**, goatherd 1086; **-atorius**, of a mediator c 1670; **-atrix**, sighting-line (of turquet) a 1350; **-clinium**, alidade (of astrolabe) c 1233;

-etas *c 1000, 1041. 1086, c 1540, †**-es** 1419, (?) **moeta** 1557, moiety, half; middle term (math.) c 1150, c 1160; 1233, **-etaria** 1199, *métayage*; **m. hominis**, half a man's services 1086; **m. hore prime**, half-hour before prime 1325; **m. lingue**, *see* **lingua**; **-etatio**, halving (math.) 1145; **-ocris** (**homo**), (one who is) free but not noble c 730. c 1110, c 1185; **-ocris**, one lower than an archbishop c 730; **m. foreste**, lesser forest officer c 1185; **-oxissimus**, *for* **-oximus**, midmost c 1433; †**-tanei** (? **-terranei**), Mercians c 1400; **-terraneus**, at the centre of the earth (of Jerusalem) c 700; ***-tullium**, midst c 1000. c 1125, 1537; **-tullinum**, (?) pith a 1250; **hora -ante**, in the middle of an hour 980; (?) at mid-day (?) 932; *see also* **fides**; ***-o**, to be between, in the middle c 1125, c 1457; to mediate (log.) c 1300; to take a middle course c 1300; to distinguish between c 1115; ***to mediate**, be the means 890, c 1000. c 1125, c 1556.

medle/a, -ta, -tum, *see* MELL
medo, *see* **meda**.
medua, meadow c 1157.
medula, *see* **merulus**.
medull/a, nerve a 1180; **-are**, essence 1267; **-aris**, marrowy a 1250; essential 1267; **-atus**, 'meaty', rich (fig.) 770; **-iter**, heartily c 800; with might and main 1303.
medus, *see* **meda; medicon**.
meduse (*pl.*), bodily organs 13c.
meerem-, *see* **maeremium**.
meeta, *see* 3 **mota**.
mega/lus, great 6c.; **-cosmus**, macrocosm a 1200; **-tegni** (τέχνη), a medical work a 1250.
megar/us c 1200, c 1370, **-is** c 1200, †**mega** 1289, mackerel; *cf.* **makerellus**.
meggildo (†**neggildo**), to pay weregeld (A.S. *mæggieldan*) c 1115.
meguc/arius 1419, **-erus** c 1320, whittawyer.

*mei/a (**mey-**) c 1160, c 1350, **maia** c 1150, c 1250, 'mow', stack; **-ator**, stacker 1276, 1312; **-o** 1279, 1402, **mayo** c 1320, 1374, **moyo** 1350, to stack.
meida, (?) 'meith', land-mark 1180.
meinburgensis, lesser burgess 1086.
meinellus, *see* 2 **monialis**.
meinprisa, *see* **manuprisa**.
meiosis, *see* **mionexia**.
meir-, *see* **maeremium**.
meis/a 1205, 1421, **-ia** 1243, **maisa** 1339, **maysa** (Sc.) 1327, 1329, **mesia** 1283, 1294, **misa** c 1185, 'mease', measure of herrings.
meishaimo, *see* MAHEM
mekotes, summa, Providence c 950.
mel/a, -us (Sc.) 12c., a 1160, (?) **-ia** (Ir.) 1212, measure of cheese or corn; (?) **-la**, 'mele', large bowl 1345, 1513.
melagium, *mélage*, grain rent (C.I.) c 1090, 1309.
melago, *see* **melissa**.
melagogum, purge for melancholy (med.) a 1250; †**melan/chiros**, (?) †**-chiton** a 1250, ‡**-chiron** 15c., black jaundice (med.); **-cholia** c 1125, 1424, **melencolia**, †**-conia** a 1250, **malencolia** a 1150, **malancolia** 1491, melancholy, black bile; spite, grudge 1336; **-cholicus** a 1200, a 1250, **malancolicus** a 1200, melancholic; **-opiper** (†**menalopiper**), black pepper a 1250, ‡14c.; ‡**-teria**, ink prepared from iron filings 14c., 1652.
melarius, *see* 1 **malum**.
melasses, molasses 1570.
melchilentus, *see* MELLI
Melchisedinus, of Melchisedech c 1430.
melda, announcing *or* announcer (A.S.) c 1115.
melewellus, *see* 1 **morus**.
‡**melga**, salamander (*cf.* German *Molch*) 1652.
meliaritio, *see* MELIOR
melic/a, melic poetry 1252; **-e**, (?) in song c 1194, c 1204; **-us**, **meliger**, tuneful c 950; *cf.* **mellicus**.
meli/cratum a 1150, 13c., **-gratum** c 1000, hydromel, mead.
melidioma, *see* MELOD
‡**melina**, cornet, pipe 1570.
melinus, yellow: **milin/us, -icus** 8c.
melior/, higher in rank or standing c 1086, c 1140; **m. preter unum** 1293, **secundus m.** 1234, 1417, second-best; **tertius m.** 1234, a 1250; **pro -i**, to improve matters 1347; **ad melius**, on the best terms 1227, c 1324; **melius meum facio**, to do one's best 1297; **-amentum** (G.) c 1283, ***-atio** a 1100, 1500, †**meliaritio** c 1176, **-itas** a 1100, a 1252, improvement; **-o**, ***to** improve, repair c 1000, 1041. a 1090, 1558; to cure c 730. 12c.; to enrich c 1115; to make safer c 1115.
‡**melisodium**, lead oxide 1652.
mel/issa a 1250, 1622, **-ago** a 1250, ‡c 1440, balm (bot.),
mella, *see* **mela; melleta**.
mellen-, *see* MILLE
mell/eta 12c., c 1320, **-ata** 1282, †**-a** 1267, **-ea** 1194, 1209, **medleta** 1234, c 1275, **medlea** c 1185, 1232, **metletum** 1293, **mesleta** 1170, 1221, **meslea** 1222, 1232, **mislata** (Norm.) 1091, mellay, affray;

-etum 1328, c 1337, **medletum** 1318, mixed cloth, motley; *cf.* MIXT

rnelli/cus c 1260, 1461, **-tatus** 8c., **melchilentus** c 550, ***-fluus** c 1000. c 1090, c 1410, honeyed, sweet (*cf.* **melica**); **-flue**, sweetly c 1380; **-phonus** a 1349, **-sonus** c 660. a 1275, ‡1483, sweet-sounding; **-tarius**, bee-keeper 1086; **-tas**, sweetness 7c.; **-fico** 1307, **-o** c 1177, c 1250, to sweeten.

mellon, contingent future (μέλλον) 1344.

‡**mellosus**, earth-worm 1652.

mel/o a 1250, ‡14c., **-onus** 1427, melon; **m. Palestinus** a 1250.

melod/ema 860, **-iama**, **melidioma** c 1200, melody, song; **-ifico**, to make melody c 1100.

melongenia, egg-plant, aubergine a 1250.

†**melonites**, gem emitting honeyed juice (*cf.* μελιτίτης) a 1250.

melot/a (bibl.), **-es** c 1000, **-ina** a 1142, sheep-skin; a 1200, 1241, **-us** c 1190, **-is** 14c., **melus** a 1250, badger; badger-skin a 1250; **moleta**, 'pelt' 1597; **-is**, byssus, filament (on oyster) a 1250.

meltarius, smelter 1370, 1371.

‡**Melusina**, malign spirit, Peri 1652.

membran/arius 1317, ‡1483, **-ator** 1355, parchment-maker; **-ulum**, phylactery 7c.; †**-us**, of parchment 1397.

membr/um (**menbr-**), member (of manor) 1086, c 1500; **m. Christi** c 1320, 1526; **m. Diaboli** c 1250, c 1340, **m. diabolicum** 1461, limb of Satan; **m. ecclesie** c 1150, c 1388; **m. servitutis**, class of villein status c 1115; **-alis**, of the limbs, physical c 1180; **-iculum**, small member (of manor) 1212; **-ificatio**, formation of limbs 1620; **-ifico**, to form limbs 1620.

meme, *see* ego.

mem/ento, 'remembrance' (part of the mass) c 1340, c 1502; **-inens**, mindful, thinking a 1408, a 1564; **-iniscor**, to remember 1684.

memitha, celandine (bot.) a 1250, ‡14c.

memor/, remembered a 1408; **-ale facio**, to make mention c 1160; **-alis** c 730. c 1204, **-ialis** c 1220, c 1450, memorable; reminiscent c 1170, c 1250; **-aliter** 704, c 800, **-ialiter** 704, 793. p 1300, from memory, by heart; **-amen**, remembrance, record 1422; **-anda**, sort of tally c 1178; **-andum**, memorandum, note c 1178, 1442; **-anda** (*pl.*), Exchequer Memoranda Rolls 1199, 16c.; **-andorium**, inventory a 1447; **-antius** 1237, **-ator** 1254, 15c., remembrancer (of Exchequer); **-atio**, recollection 1245, c 1375; **-atius**, more mindfully 1378; **-ativus**, concerned with memory 803, 10c. c 1210, 15c.;

-ia, commemoration service (eccl.) a 1100, 1489; memorial 7c., 8c.; c 700. c 1090, 1236, **-iale** a 1142, tomb, shrine; 1237, **-iale** 948. 1163, c 1643, **-ialis** 1452, memorial, note, certificate; **-iam facio**, to mention c 1000; **-ia artificialis**, mnemonics c 1450; **-iale**, memorable event 12c., 1320; **cellula -ialis** (of brain) a 1200; **-o**, to remember c 1170, c 1290.

‡**memp/erium** 1483, ‡**-irium** 15c., "wisp" wiper.

menagium, *see* MANS

menalopiper, *see* MELAN

menbrum, *see* **membrum**.

mendaciolum, little lie 1516.

mend/atio, *for* emendatio, 1384, 1458; **-ositas**, false reading c 730; **-ula**, blemish 1427.

mendic/ans c 1250, 1517, **-ulus** 690, beggar; **frater m.** 1364, 1424, f. **-ator** 1361, mendicant friar; **ordo -antium** c 1317, c 1478; ***religio -ans** 1333, 1549; **-anter** 1427, **-itus** 1440, like a beggar; **-atrix**, begging (*f.*) a 1275; **-ativus** 1345, **-atorius** 1427, concerned with begging.

‡**mendium**, "dressing-board" 15c.

mene (*n.*), moon (μήνη) c 550.

men/eia 1237, 1349, **-ya** 1293, **-etum** (Sc.) 13c., blast of a horn (O.F. *menee*).

menelaca, *see* **manelata**.

Menelo, *see* **Mamaluchus**.

menestr-, **menistr-**, *see* MINIST

menetum, *see* **meneia**.

meneum, demesne c 1160; *cf.* DOMIN

meneverum, *see* MINU

menialis 1438, **meanialis** 1460, menial (*adj.*).

menica c 870, **miringa** c 1180, c 1360, membrane of brain (μῆνιγξ).

menie (*pl.*), *for* moenia, walls 1260.

†**menio**, (?) to perform carriage service 1234.

menitus, little bell c 1245.

mens, purport 1166, c 1430; **in ment/e existo**, to be minded, intend 1573; ***-alis** 1200, c 1470, **-aneus** 1302, mental, of the mind; unspoken c 1286, c 1444; *see also* **reservatio**; (?) intentional, deliberate 1518; **-aliter**, mentally, mindfully c 1225, a 1408; **-alius**, more mindfully c 1456.

*mens/a, food, board, table-money, revenue 805. c 1204, 1536; board-land, land providing food 1086; demesne (G.) 1310, 1315; table, panel, list 1472; **m. alta** 1336, 1464, **m. capitalis** c 1330, **m. magna** 13c., **m. magistrorum** c 1440. **m. superior** 1532, high table; **m. canonica**, common table (of canons) 12c.; **m. Domini** 13c., **m. Dominica** c 1080, c 1643, Lord's table, altar; **m. altaris** 760; **m. dormiens** a 1220, (?) **m.** †**domitialis** 1290 (but *cf.* **tabulatus**), **m. stationaria** 1373, table dormant, fixed table (not on trestles); **m. orbicularis** c 1595, **m. rotunda** c 1212, 1347, (Arthurian) Round Table, *or* form of tournament; **m. plicata** 1275, **m. applectata** 1553, folding table; **m. Pythagore**, multiplication table c 1200; **m. solis**, meridian (astr.) 1267; ‡**m. structuaria**, dresser 1570;

‡**-acula**, "dressing-knife" c 1440, 15c.; ***-ale** c 1200, 1511, **-uale** c 1296, **-ile** 1261, table-cloth; **-alis**, (?) table, board 1374; supertunic, dinner-jacket 1342; **-alitas**, food, board 1504; ‡**-ifium**, "cupboard" 15c.; **-ula** 1432, 1531, **-illa** 1519, small board; **-ulus**, *see* **mappa**; **-o**, to lay on the table c 1180.

mensio, *see* MANS; MENTION

mens/is exiens 1268, **-is exitus** 1315, latter half of month, in which days are reckoned retrogressively (Fr.); **-is introitus**, earlier half of month 1255, 1315; **m. kalendaris**, calendar month c 1411, 1457; ‡**m. philosophicus**, period of 'digestion' (alch.), 30 or 40 days 1652; **m. venationis** (fortnight before and after June 24) 1366; **m. vetitus** 1238, 1387, **m. prohibitus** 13c., close season; **dies -is** 1417, 1420, **d. m. obitus** 1412, month's mind (eccl.) (cf. MENTION);

-**ivus**, of a month 1267; **cursus -trualis** (of moon) 815; -**truatim**, monthly 1609; -**truatus**, dimmed 1620; -**truosus**, menstruous (med.) a 1292; -**truum**, ‡key substance (alch.) 1652; germ, elementary form 1620.

menstrallus, see MINIST

mensur/a, measure: **mesura** 1371, c 1500, **misura** 1252; -**a**, gauge 1228; right to test measures c 1280, 1336; 12c., 1267, **candela de -a, c. -ata** c 1280, wax taper of the height of the donor; "broadcloth" 1583; moderation c 1170, c 1436; purpose 1380; measured song (mus.) 1326, c 1470; **m. burgi, m. ville** 1086; **m. cumulata** 1275, 14c., **m. cumula** (†**annula**) 13c., heaped measure; **m. magna** 1270, **m. major** 1086; **m. parva** 1496; **m. rasa** 1206, 1449, **m. baleata** 1335, razed or straiked measure; **m. regis** 1086, c 1300;

-**abilis**, measurable 1315; moderate, reasonable c 1228, 1276; measured (mus.) 1351, c 1470; **pollex m.**, inch 1447; **virga m.** c 1150, **v. -alis** c 1115, **v. mensoria** c 1200, measuring-rod; -**abilitas**, measurability 1649; -**abiliter**, proportionally c 800. 1175, c 1300; moderately 1231; -**agium** 1276, 1420, **mesuragium** 1275, 1451, measurage, tonnage-due; **vas -ale**, measuring-vessel c 1521; -**amentum**, admeasurement 1275; -**arius** 1275, 1419, -**ator** 1275, 1419, -**atrix** (f.) 13c., a 1452, measurer, meter; *-**ate**, moderately, in due measure 725, 890. c 1266, c 1362; *-**atio**, measurement c 1218, 1481; measuring against relic c 1280; -**ative**, by way of measurement c 1362; -**atus**, of medium size 890; *-**o**, to measure 1086, c 1470; **m. (me)**, to measure against or touch relic (as means of cure) c 1257, 1319; **m. me**, to act moderately 1231.

ment-, see also mens.

menta Romana, m. Saracenica, (?) wormwood or birthwort (bot.) a 1250, ‡14c.

mentagra, eruption (med.) c 670; toe 6c.

ment/amentum, lie, fabrication 1429; -**itor**, liar c 1306, 1378; -**ior**, to give the lie 1364, 15c.

mentan-, see mens; **mento**.

mentenementum, see MANUTEN

mention/arius dies, month's mind (eccl.) c 1452 (cf. mensis); **mensio, for mentio**, 1279, 1378; -**o**, to mention 1401, 1630.

ment/o 12c., -**ona** 1266, 1313, for -**um**, chin; -**anea**, tuft on chin 1163; -**onalis** (†**-ionalis**, †**-olanis**), chin-high c 1115.

†**men/torium** (vv.ll. emp-, ten-), merchant's stall 12c. (14c.).

mentula episcopi, pilewort, crowfoot (bot.) a 1250, ‡14c.

menura, 'mainour' 1361; cf. **manuopus**.

menu/sa, -sia, -cia, see MINU

menya, see **meneia**.

menyanthes, see **minyanthes**.

meo (trans.), to traverse c 550.

meota, see 3 **mota**.

meprisio, see **misprisio**.

1 **mer/a** c 1220, 1399, -**us** 1272, 'mere', boundary; 'mere', claim (in lead mine) (Derb.) (?) a 1250, 1287.

2 **mer/a**, unpressed wine 1225, 1229; (?) -**arium** 1294, ‡-**otheca** 1483, tavern; ‡-**ulentus**, intoxicating 690; -**osus**, pure, unmixed c 730; -**um**, inheritance 1487; in -**o**, in gross a 1300; -**us**, see debitum, Hibernicus, imperium, motus (s.v. motatio).

†**meratorius panis**, (?) light bread 1419.

merc-, see also MARC; MARCH; MARESCAL; MARQU

*****merc/atum** a 1086, 1419, **marcatum** 1088, 1443, **marcheium** 1198, 1330, -**atio** c 1102, 13c., market; right of purchase at special price, bargain 1214, 1221; c 1150, 1253, -**andia** (f. s.) c 1160, 1483, (n. pl.) 1461, †-**a** 1188, *-**andisa** 1214, c 1443, **merchaundisa** 1312, -**andiza** 1331, 1583, *****marcandisa** 1195, 1395, †**marchidisa** 1221, **merchangisa** 1199, -**andisia** c 1217, 1290, -**andicia** c 1530, -**antia** 1274, 1496, -**ansia** 1460, 1496, **marcansia** 1279, 1433, **marchansea** 1456, **marchasia** 1340, -**atio** c 1170, 1268, -**atus** c 1280, -**aturius** 799, -**ecies** 12c., merchandise, goods, wares; -**atum** a 1050. c 1110, c 1150, -**andia** (f. s.) 1274, c 1400, -**andisa** a 1190, 1478, -**andiza** 1308, 1686, **marcandisa** 1254, -**andisia** 1279, c 1404, -**andisatio** 1411, 1417, trade, buying; -**andizabilis**, marketable 1315, 1502; -**andizius** 1577, -**atorius** a 1086, a 1564, -**ionalis** c 1240, mercantile; see also **curia, gilda, lex, signum, villa;**

-**antaliter** 1412, -**atorie** 1353, a 1564, by way of trade; **marcator**, for -**ator**, merchant 1205, 1456; -**ator adventurarius** 1597, **m. venturarius** c 1550, **m. venterarius** 1550, merchant adventurer; **m. navis**, supercargo 1425; -**atrix**, market-woman 1284, 1395; -**andio** 1294, -**andiso** 1306, 1425, -**andizo** c 1275, 1523, **marcandiso** 1260, to trade.

merc/enarium, merchandise c 1240, c 1390; -**eria**, mercery 1324, 1455; **selda -eria**, mercer's stall 1455; -**enarius**, (adj.) rent-paying p 1245; (subst.) 1437, 1511, -**arius** 1170, -**iarius** 1155, 1188, -**erius** c 1170, 1419, -**er**, -**erus** c 1175, 1582, **marcerus** 1551, mercer.

†**mercere**, f.l. for **vincere**, 1233.

merc/es, reward: **marces** 1490; -**icula**, small reward c 1220, ‡1483.

mercha, see 2 **marqua**.

Merchenelaga, see **Mercius**.

*****merchet/um** 1086, 1500, -**a** 1212, c 1308, **mergettum** 1279, **marchettum** 1088, 1503, **marchetta** 1196, **marketta** 1527, 'merchet', payment by unfree tenant for daughter's marriage.

merc/ia 1178, 1423, -**iamentum** 1198, 1290, †-**is** 1279, amercement; -**io**, to amerce a 1186, 1199.

mercicula, see **merces**.

mercimoni/a, a reward c 1180; 1250, 1311, **mersimonium** c 1283, merchandise; -**um**, trade c 1115, c 1362; -**alis** c 1200, c 1220, †-**us** c 1325, mercantile; **gilda -alis** c 1273, 1520; **navis -alis** c 1218; **mercemonarius**, tradesman 1332; -**atus**, regulation of commerce c 1370; -**o**, to trade (G.) c 1285, 1409.

mercipium, *see* MARSUPI

Merc/ius (Myrcius) c 710, a 1000. c 1100, 1528, **-ensis** c 1100, c 1250, **-inensis** c 730, **Mircenus** c 1115, Mercian; **Merchenelaga,** Mercian law c 1315.

mercur/ius, mercury, quicksilver (alch.) 12c., 1620; *see also* **dies**; **-ialia** (*pl.*), (?) name of a book c 1436; **-ialis,** (*adj.*) of quicksilver a 1250, 1686; (*subst.*) disciple of Mercury, student 1167; 13c., ‡14c., **-ella** a 1250, dog's mercury (bot.); **herba m.,** charlock c 1000.

‡merdasengi, litharge 14c., 1652.

merd/osus, filthy a 1250, 1412; **-us,** sea-bird (play on **mergus**) 1200; ‡**-o,** to befoul 1483.

mer/eella c 1180, **-illio** c 1280, a 1446, **-lio** c 1380, **-lina** 1544, **-ulus** c 1188, ‡1483, **-lenio, -lio** 1336, **emerlio** c 1333, **esmerill/unus** (†**-imus**) 1213, merlin (falc.).

merellus c 1350, **mirellum** 1368, 'merel', counter.

merem-, meren-, meresm-, *see also* **maeremium.**

merementum, (?) merit 1497, c 1500.

merescaucia, *see* MARESCAL

meresium, *see* **mariscus.**

mereta, *see* **myrica.**

meretric/alis, meretricious c 1170, 1378; **-aliter** c 1430, **-ialiter** 1236, in whoredom; **radix -alis** a 1250, ‡**-aria, herba -um** 14c. (bot.); **meritricatio,** fornication 1497; **-or,** to fornicate c 860. c 1160, 1497.

merewardus, *see* **mare.**

merg/a 1377, **-us** ‡15c., 1608, bucket; **-a** a 1275, ‡**-es, -iacio** c 1200, **mers/ilis avis** c 1315, sea-bird; **-io,** immersion 12c., c 1250; drowning p 1341; **-or,** diver c 1140, 1250; **mirgus,** water-dog c 1250.

mergettum, *see* MERCHET

†mergo, (?) *f.l.* for **jungo,** c 1285.

mergularius, *see* MATRICUL

mer/i, -y a 1250, ‡14c., **-in** a 1250, oesophagus (Ar.).

meribilis, *see* MERITOR

merica, *see* **myrica.**

meridi/es, meridian (astr.) 1267, 1326; **merities,** south 859, 863; **-anum,** (?) culmination a 1385; **-onalis,** southern c 1200, c 1410; *see also* **circulus, 2 linea; -ana,** siesta c 1072, c 1330; **-o,** to be at zenith, to be full 890; to halt at noon c 1000; ‡**-or,** to take a siesta 1483.

merillio, *see* **mereella.**

meri/lus, -nula, *see* **merulus.**

merim-, *see* **maeremium.**

merin, *see* **meri.**

meriscus, *see* **mariscus.**

*meritor/ius, deserving well, earning merit 1177, 1480; **-ior,** more deserving c 1380; ***-ie,** deservedly c 1340, 1445; **meribilis,** capable of earning merit 1344.

merko, *see* 1 **marqua.**

merl/engus 1241, c 1283, **-ingus** 1236, 1419, **marlangus** a 1350, **-ucius** (G.) 1292, **marlutus** 1288, fish, (esp.) whiting; *cf.* 1 **morus.**

merlera, *see* **marla.**

merl/ina, -io, *see* **mereella.**

mer/osus, -otheca, *see* 2 **mera.**

mer/rasium, -scum, *see* **mariscus.**

mers/a, gloom, night c 550; **-eus,** nocturnal c 550.

mers/ilis, -io, -or, *see* MERG

mersimonium, *see* MERCIMONI

merta, *see* **marta.**

mertatio, *see* **mortasius.**

mer/ulentus, *see* 2 **mera.**

mer/ulus p 1394, a 1446, **-inula** c 1450, martlet (her.); **-ilus** 1462, **medula** a 1446, blackbird; **-ulinus,** of a blackbird c 1250, a 1380; *see also* **mereella.**

merus, *see* **mera** (1 & 2).

meruta, *see* **myrica.**

mery, *see* **meri.**

mes-, *see also* MANS; **mis-**

mesbota, *see* **maegbota.**

‡mescara, sausage 14c.

mes/chenninga, -kenninga, *see* **miskenninga.**

meschinus, servant (Fr. *mesquin*) c 1414.

mescinga, *see* **metebederepa.**

mesellus, *see* MISELL

mes/embria, south c 1180; ‡**-imbria,** midday c 1440.

mesengis, tit (bird) (Fr. *mésange*) c 1213.

mes/enterium 1622, ‡**-enterion** 14c., mesentery (med.); **-eraicus** c 1210, a 1250, **miseraicus** c 1375, (?) **meteoricus** c 1200, mesenteric.

mesestantia, grievance (O.F. *mesestance*) 13c.

mesg/a c 1150, **-uium** c 1115, **†mestha** (? **mescha**) c 1185, whey.

mesia, *see* **meisa.**

mesl-, *see* MELL

mesn-, meson-, *see* MANS

mespr-, *see* **misprisio.**

mess-, *see also* **missa; missio.**

mess/io 1199, 1326, **mecio** c 1200, **-ia** 1230, **-ura** a 1190, 1276, **†-urcium** a 1240, harvest-service (man.); **-io extrema, -oria Christi,** Last Judgement 1212; **-agaria, -ageria** 1289, **†-agneria** 1285, **-egaria** 1317, **-egeria** 1313, authority to appoint overseers of harvest (G.); **-arius** 1226, 1329, **†-erius** 1380, **-erus** 1275, ***-or** 1233, 1402, **-egarius** (G.) 1284, **-egenarius** (G.) 1289, overseer of harvest, reap-reeve, hayward; **-or Celestis** 1252; **-oria,** office of reap-reeve 1295; **mestrix,** reaper (*f.*) 1355; ‡**-ibilis,** "reapable" 1570; **-ilis,** of harvest c 1180; **†mestiva,** harvest (Fr.) 1177.

messuagium, *see* MANS

mester/a, -um, *see* MINIST

mestha, *see* **mesga.**

mestil-, mestulum, *see* MIXT

mest/uosus, sad 1282, 1307; **-o,** to sadden 1497.

mesur-, *see* MANS; MENSUR

meswagium, *see* MANS

met/a, *mete, boundary 1086, 15c.; **-e et bunde** 1278, c 1395, **-e et divise** 1300, **-e et fines** 1276; **-a,** 'meer', claim (in lead mine) 1288; mark, target (in archery) 1280, c 1551; mark, brand (on horses) 1358; merchant's mark 1367; (stamp used for marking) measure 1366; purpose 1200; **-atio,** stage of a journey 1200; *see also* **macula.**

‡metacataphoras, an epileptic during seizure 14c.

L

metacentesis, tapping, drawing off (med.) (*cf.* παρακέντησις) a 1250.

meta/lepsis (gram.): **-lemsis** 795, **-lipsis** 1427.

metall/um, hard wood 760; **m. nobile** (alch.) 1267; **-us,** *for* **-um,** 6c.; **-inus,** made of metal 1041. 1295, c 1400.

metamorphosicus, metamorphosed a 1100.

metanomia, *see* **metonymia.**

metaphor/ica 13c., **-um** 1293, metaphor; **-icus** c 1270, 1552, **-us** 13c., metaphorical; **-ice,** metaphorically c 1080, p 1381.

metaphysic/a (*f. s.*) c 1250, 1620, **-e** 1537, **methephisica** c 1390, c 1510, metaphysics; **-e,** metaphysically 1267, 1344; **-alis** 1267, 1344, **-us** 1267, c 1363, metaphysical; **-us,** metaphysician c 1250, 15c.

metaschematismus, rearrangement 1620.

met/atio, reaping 1279; **‡-ellus** 15c., **‡-illus** 1483, reap-reeve; **-or,** reaper 1297; *cf.* MESS; *see also* **meta.**

metax/a, raw silk: **mataxa** a 1200; **-arius,** mercer 1710; **‡setter** of a price c 1440; **‡-o,** to set a price c 1440; **‡mataxo,** to higgle c 1440; **‡to** "rib" (flax, *etc.*) c 1440.

mete/bederepa, boon-reaping with food supplied 1242; **-gablum,** 'meat-gavel', food rent c 1115; **mescinga,** a food-rent (A.S. *metsung*)(Essex) 1222; **†methamus,** a form of estate (? paying food-rent) (Essex) 1300.

mete/eria, †-reius, farm, *métairie* (Norm.) c 1160.

meteor/a (*n. pl.*), meteorics (title of work by Aristotle) c 1233, c 1443; **-um,** meteor 1686.

meteoricus, *see* **mesenterium.**

methis, vine (*cf.* μέθυ) 1150.

method/us, road 1500; **-ium,** jest c 950; **-ice,** methodically 1564; **-icus,** methodical (log.) 1610, 1620.

methologia, *see* **mythologia.**

meticul/ositas, timidity c 1204, 15c.; **-ose,** timidly c 1400, 1421; **-osus** c 950. c 1218, **†-us** c 1220, terrible, perilous; **metuendissimus,** most dread (royal title) c 1388, 1543; **metifico,** to frighten a 1450.

metletum, *see* MELL

met/onymia c 700. c 1125, c 1200, **-onomia** c 1125, c 1258, **†-onomina** c 1380, **-anomia, methaomia** 1344, metonymy (gram.); **-onomice,** by metonymy a 1250; **-onomasticus,** metonymic 13c.

metor, *see* **metatio.**

‡metorium, ladle 15c.

metra, *see* **mitra.**

metr/anus, measure c 600; **-icum,** verse a 1350; ***-ice,** in verse c 1194, c 1500; **-icus,** metrical, versified c 1125, p 1377; 1370, c 1470, **-ista** c 1440, c 1540, versifier; **-ificatio,** versification c 1470; **-ifico,** to versify 1271, c 1370.

Metridat-, *see* **Mithridatium.**

*metropol/is c 700, 798. c 1090, c 1445, **civitas m.** 1124, **sedes m.** c 1125, metropolitan city, see or church; **-itanatus,** archbishopric c 1382; ***-itanus** c 600, c 1000. c 1125, 1536, **-iticus** 1169, 1543, **-icus** 1229, c 1355, **†metrolicus** 11c., metropolitan (eccl.); **-ita** c 1200, c 1310, **-itanus** c 1050. 1136, 1582, **metripolitanus** 1582,

archbishop; **-itice,** by archiepiscopal authority 1286.

metta, *see* 1 **mitta.**

mettoccus, *see* **matokkus.**

metuendissimus, *see* METICUL

meuta, *see* 3 **mota.**

mey-, *see also* MEI

meylo, *see* 2 **mullo.**

mi, musical note c 1330.

mic/a c 600. 1237, c 1370, **michea (michia)** 1268, 16c., small loaf; **-ella** 1377, **-ulum** 990, crumb; **-atorium** c 1200, 1390, **myoura** 1329, grater; **‡-o,** to crumble 1570.

michi, *see* **ego.**

michina, nostril 6c.

‡micippa, blackbird 1483, 1570.

†micleta, (?) kind of herb a 1250.

mic/o, (?) to bustle about 1241; **migo,** *for* **-o,** 8c.; *see also* **mica.**

micon, *see* **mecon.**

micrus, migrus, small 6c.; **micro/cosmus,** microcosm c 1110, c 1470; **-logus,** small 7c.; title of book (med.) 1210; **-metrum,** micrometer 1686; **-scopium,** microscope 1662.

mictos, composite (μικτός) c 700.

mictura 1259, **minctura, minctus** a 1250, urination; **‡mins/atorium, -orium,** urinal, drain c 1440, 1483; **‡-o, -ito,** to urinate 1483.

midd/a, -um, *see* 1 **mitta.**

midius, *see* MEDI

miffa, *see* **muffla.**

‡mifros, asphalt 1652.

‡migma, "provender for horses" c 1440; **‡soap** 1483; *cf.* **smigma.**

migo, *see* **mico.**

migr/atio, death 8c., c 1000. 1136, 1440; **-atus,** dead c 1310; **-o** c 1072, **m. a corpore** c 1336, **m. e corpore** c 1090, **m. ab hac luce** 1347, 1438, **m. e seculo** c 1188, c 1400, **m. ad Christum** c 1330, **m. ad Dominum** c 1188, 1537, **m. Domino** c 1362, to die.

migrus, *see* **micrus.**

mihhi, *see* **ego.**

mila, *see* **mille.**

milda, a mild tonic (falc.) a 1150.

miles, *knight c 1072, 1686; knight's fee or service c 1130, c 1430; knight (in chess) a 1200, 15c.; name of a comet c 1270; a 1200, **m. armatus** c 1212, fish, (?) swordfish; **m. agrarius,** holder of knight's fee c 1188; **m. argentarius,** pesour (Exchequer official) c 1178; **m. bachelarius** c 1380, **m. bachilarius** 1360, 1388, knight bachelor; **m. Balnei,** knight of the Bath 1586; **m. banericius** 1260, **m. banericus** 1283, knight banneret; **m. comitatus** c 1320, 1440, **m. de comitatu** 13c., **m. de shira, m. de pago** 15c., **m. Parliamenti** c 1400, **m. Parliamentalis** 1421, knight of the shire (in Parliament); **m. pro corpore,** knight of the royal body-guard 1474, 1506; **m. crucifer,** crusader 1608; **m. equitans,** (?) radknight 1166; **m. familiaris,** knight of the (royal) household 1235; **m. de fraternitate garteriorum** 1416, **m. ordinis gartarii (gartarii)** 1492, 1558; **m. gladio cinctus,** belted knight 1275, 1281; **m. gregarius,** (?) knight on active service c 1178; **m. literatus**, knight with legal training c 1260; **m. simplex** 1298; **m. sacramentalis**, knight of crusading order c 1200; **m. Templi** c 1140, c 1320, **m. de Templo** c 1142, p 1340, Knight Templar; **m. vexillifer**, (?) banneret a 1350, c 1362; *see also* **curia, feodum, servitium**; **milit/es faciendi**, name of a writ (leg.) 1240, 1419; **-aria** (*n. pl.*), knighthood c 1188, c 1434; **-aris**, (*subst.*) water-soldier (bot.) 1641; (*adj.*) knightly c 1170, 1461; *see also* **arma, ecclesia, cingulum, ordo, panis**.

-ia, army 1041; band of knights 12c., 1461; *a 1142, 1401, **-ies** a 1408, **-atura** c 1400, knighthood; c 1185, c 1290, **-atio** 1200, knight's fee or service; **m. celestis** (*coll.*), the religious orders c 1337; **m. Templi**, order of Knights Templar 1137, 1419; ‡**-issa**, dame 1483; **-o**, soldier c 550; **-ulus**, petty knight c 1200; **-anter**, as a soldier c 1390; **-o**, to serve as a knight c 1306; *to serve in a religious order a 1090, c 1444; **-o in nocte**, to be delirious 13c.
mili-, *see also* MILLE.
milin/us, -icus, *see* **melinus**.
militus, *see* **mola**.
mili/um solis, gromwell (bot.) a 1250, ‡c 1440; **-aria**, linnet 1544; **-aceus (-atius)**, millet bread 1239.
mille/na 1325, 1419, **mellena** c 1283, **-nare** 1407, **-arium**, **-arius** c 1086, 1289, **-narius** c 1178, 1284, **mellenarius** 1283, **-naritas** c 1270, **-rium** 1205, c 1310, **miliare** 12c., 1573, **miliarium** c 1200, c 1324, **miliarius** 1303 (set of a thousand; **-narius**, millennium 1381, c 1450; commander of a thousand men 1319, 1336; millenarian heretic 1546; **-narium** (? **-narius**), measure of herring 1086, 1419; **miliare**, measure of tin 1198; *12c., 1684, **miliarium** 1090, c 1450, **mila** (Fr.) 1409, mile; **m. Anglie**, **m. Gallicum** c 1400; **miliarium dimidium**, half-wheel (in bell-ringing) c 1350; **milio**, million c 1365, 1514; **-cuplus**, thousandfold p 1300; **-formis**, of a thousand shapes 670; **-grana**, rupturewort (bot.) 1634; **-nus**, thousandth c 1190, c 1470; **-podia**, millepede 890; **-sies**, a thousand times a 1240, c 1470.
millioli, bishop's robe c 730.
‡**millo**, to sew 1483; *see also* **2 mullo**.
millus, *see* **1 mullo**.
milnum, mill a 1300; *cf.* **mola**.
mil/vellus, -wellus, *see* **1 morus**.
mimeticos, mimetic c 700.
1 min/a, dry measure c 1165, c 1586; **-agium**, toll on corn (Fr.) c 1170, 1214; *cf.* **hemina**.
2 *min/a 1293, 1461, **-ea** 1384, **-aria**, **-arium** 1086, c 1270, **-eiria** 1130, **-eria** c 1180, c 1400, *-era 1144, 1620, **-erum** 1577, **manaria** 1130, **maneria** 1243, **-iteria, -iterium, -oria** c 1190, **-ura** 1517, mine, mining rights; **-a** 1196, 1317, **-eria** 1086, c 1177, **-era** 12c., c 1365, **-erum** 1361, *-erale c 1250, c 1470, mineral, ore; **-a alba**, carbonate of lead, 'wheatstone' 1297, 1300; **-a nigra** 1297, 1323, **-era nigra** 1246, sulphide of lead, galena; **-era** (fig.), source, origin a 1250, 13c.; **-eralis**,

mineral (*adj.*) a 1233, 1620; **-erarius**, rich in mines 1586; **-erarius** 1264, 1310, **-earius** 1191, **-iarius** 1355, **-etarius** 1163, 1283, **-itarius** 1207, **-ator** 1205, 1299, **-eator** 1214, 1371, **-iator** 1218, **-erator** 1287, **-eritor** 1287, 1290, **-itor** 1221, c 1282, †**-utor** 1221, miner, sapper; **-eatio**, mining, sapping 1224, 1356; **-eo** 1224, 1384, **-eto** 1397, to mine, undermine.
min/acitas, threatening aspect c 1218; **-abunde** 1521, **-atorie** c 1414, threateningly; **-ativus** c 1376, **-atorius** c 1250, a 1564, threatening; **-o**, *for* **-or**, to threaten 1378, 1381.
min/atio, driving (of beasts or carts) 1364, 1537; **m. feni**, leading hay c 1530; **-ator**, driver (? threatener) 1193, p 1348; **-o** c 780. c 1100, 1534, **-or** 690. c 1100, to drive (beasts or carts); **-o in prisonem** 1275; **-o aratrum**, to plough 1494, 1534; **-o vestigium**, to follow track (of stolen cattle) c 1115.
minct-, *see* **mictura**.
mine-, *see* **2 mina**.
mineta, *minet*, measuring-vessel for grain (C.I.) 1331; *see also* **moneta**.
†**mingo**, to mix 1395.
mini/ator, -atus, *see* **2 mina**; **minium**.
minim/a, minim (mus.) 1326, c 1470; **-itas**, minim length (mus.) 1351; *see also* **ex, in**.
minist/er, thane 863, 1044. 12c., 13c., (?) tenant by serjeanty 1086; minor official, reeve, bailiff, or serjeant 11c., 1482; 1166, c 1553, **m. ecclesie** c 1090, 1461, **m. ecclesiasticus** c 1400, priest or bishop (esp. Sc.); 1225, 15c., **m. generalis** c 1250, 1549, **m. provincialis** c 1250, 16c., Franciscan official; **m. episcopi** a 1135, 1397; **m. evangelicus** c 1298; **m. de feodo** c 1285; **m. foreste** 1287, 1299; **m. portus maris** a 1130; **m. verbi**, (Lutheran) pastor 1561; **-erialis**, (*subst.*) 893. c 1180, c 1318, **-ralis** a 910. a 1135, p 1348, officer, official; obedientiary (mon.) 7c. p 1290, c 1330; (*adj.*) ministerial, acting on another's behalf 1423; **liber m.**, service-book, pontifical (eccl.) 816; **-erialiter**, by virtue of (priestly) office c 1357, c 1367;
-erium, administrative district, bailiwick (Norm., C.I.) 1180, 1200; c 1250, **-eriatia** 1445, **-eriatus** c 1518, 16c., **-ratus** c 1332, office in Franciscan order; a 1090, 1552, **misterium** 1557, **-ratus** 1347, ministry, priesthood; 1130, p 1341, **misterium** c 1108, 1687, **misteria** 1327, 1427, **mistera** 1321, 1577, **mestera** 1344, 1362, **mesterum** 1319, 1331, 'mistery', craft, craft-guild; sacred vessels, *etc.* (*coll.*) 8c.; **m. divinum**, divine service c 1266; **m. maris**, functioning of the sea, (?) ebb and flow 7c., a 700; **m. regis**, serjeanty 1086; **-ura** c 1210, **misterium** 1086, c 1180, *for* **-erium**, service, office; **mistarium** (†**miscarium**), loom (Fr. *métier*) (C.I.) 1309; **-rabilis**, helpful 14c.; **-ralcia** 1377, 1391, **menestralcia** 1300, 1332, minstrelsy; **-rallus** c 1266, 1534, **-rellus** 1469, 1499, **menestrallus** a 1227, c 1340, †**monestrallus** c 1335, **menestrellus** c 1320, **menistrallus** 14c., **menstrallus** 1392

minstrel; **m. ad organa** 1418; **m. tacitus** 1466; **-ralis** c 1280, **-rallus** 1348, 1439, servant, officer; **menestrallus,** craftsman 1275;

-ratio, service, exercise of office c 1090, c 1520; office (mon.) c 1266; sphere of office, province (Franciscan) c 1250; **m. de bonis** (of deceased), administration 1420; **m. capelle** 1198; **m. divinorum** 1409; **m. ecclesie** c 1188; **m. ad altare** 1371, p 1400; **m. sacramentorum** c 1500; **-rative,** by virtue of office 1346; **-rativus,** serviceable a 1250, 1374; exercised as an office 1346; **-rator,** official (eccl.) 1268; **m. bonorum** 1423, c 1448; **m. sacramentorum** c 1385; **-ratorie,** by way of service 1377, 15c.; ***-ro,** to minister as a priest c 1115, 1549; to serve as minister (Franciscan) 15c.; **m. in,** to provide with c 1300, c 1390; **m. bona,** to administer estate (of deceased) 1423; **m. sacramenta** (eccl.) 14c., c 1520.

minit-, *see also* **2 mina.**

minitatim, *see* MINU

mini/um, gules (her.) c 1595; **-atus,** gules (her.) (*adj.*) c 1595; **‡-ator, -iographus,** limner, miniaturist 1483.

mino, *see* **minacitas; minatio;** MINU

minor/, minor premiss of syllogism a 1253, c 1400; minor semibreve (mus.) 1326, c 1470; *see also* **ad, annus, etas, locus; -es** (*pl.*), minor orders (eccl.) 1245; 1230, c 1458, **fratres -es** 1225, 1557, (**fratres**) **-ite** 1559, 1609, Franciscan friars; **soror m.** (G.) 1289, (s.) **-issa** 1289, 1419, Minoress, Poor Clare; **-abilis,** capable of decrease a 1361; **-ata,** double minim (mus.) 1326; **-amentum** c 1370, ***-atio** c 1120, 1412, **-izatio** 1438, decrease, diminution; **-ativus,** humiliating 890; **-itas,** minority, nonage 1339, 1586; lesser amount or size, inferiority c 1236, c 1612; depreciation (of currency) 1308, a 1400; **-asco,** to be deficient 15c.; ***-o** 1086, 1443, **minŏror** c 800, to lessen.

min/oria, -ura, *see* **2 mina.**

mins-, *see also* **mictura.**

minsterium, *see* **monasterium.**

minta, *see* **moneta.**

minturnio, *for* **minurrio,** to twitter c 1200.

†min/ulus, *for* **-usculus,** small letter (?) 937 (12c.).

minumentum, *see* **2 munimen.**

minu/tio 12c., c 1488, **m. sanguinis** c 1080, blood-letting, bleeding (esp. mon.); **-tor** c 1150, c 1400, **†munitorius** c 1270, blood-letter (*see also* **2 mina**); **‡-torium,** trencher 1483; **-atim** 730. 1328, **†minitatim** c 1270, *for* **-tatim,** minutely, in detail; **-tatim,** by retail 1303; **†-atus,** lessened (in value), damaged 1213; **abbas -taris,** lesser abbot a 1186; **-tellus** 1241, **-tulus** 1609, very small, petty; **-te,** shrilly c 1400; **‡-tal,** "cantle" c 1440, 1483; **‡-tarius,** "haberdasher" 1570; **-tum** (*coll.*), small goods, spices 1307;

-ta, minute, note 1387, 1539; 1086, c 1362, **-tum** 14c., coin (farthing *or* mite); **‡**1483, 1622, **-tum** c 1265, c 1608, **-tia** c 1260, **-tum primum** 1686, minute ($\frac{1}{80}$th of hour); **-tum,** tenth of hour c 1265; **m. diei,**

24 minutes 1344; **m. secundum,** second (of time) a 1670, 1686; **m. tertium,** $\frac{1}{80}$th of second 1686; **-tia** 1120, **-tum** a 1150, 1326, minute, $\frac{1}{80}$th of degree (astr. & math.); **-tia,** fraction (math.) a 1150, 15c.; **-ettum** 1220, **-tum varium** 1204, 1640, **m. verrum** 1275, c 1335, **meneverum** c 1443, minever (fur);

-tus c 1150, c 1450, **-ta** (*f.*) c 1150, one who has been bled; **liber -torum,** book for the bled (mon.) c 1330; **homo -tus,** lesser tenant, villein 1130, c 1185; **homo m.,** judex m., doomsman of minor court a 1130; **-ti** (*pl.*) 1337, **-sia** a 1150, **menusia** 1267, c 1514, **menucia** c 1493, **menusa** 1219, 1248 (*coll.*), 'menise', small fry; **mino,** *for* **-o,** to diminish, impair 11c.; **-o,** to subtract (math.) 1145; c 1100, c 1436, **m. sanguinem** c 1080, c 1400, to bleed, let blood.

minyanthes (bot.): **menyanthes,** buckbean 1634.

mionexia, defect 890; **meiosis,** understatement c 1620.

mira, mire, bog 1179.

mirabolanum, *see* **myrobalanum.**

‡mirac (**†mirath**), abdomen (Ar.) 14c.

mir/aculum, miracle-play c 1244, 14c.; **‡m. hortulanum,** sunflower 14c.; ***-aculose** 1177, 1461, **-aculabiliter** c 1400, miraculously; **-aculosus,** miraculous c 1180, 1487; **-anter** 1324, **-ative** c 1380, wonderingly; **-ative** 1201, **de -o** c 1390, wonderfully; **-ificandus,** to be magnified 10c.; **-ificatio,** bewilderment, wonder 10c. c 1150; **-ificentior,** more marvellous 1041; **-ifico,** to magnify, make wonderful c 1000. a 1100, c 1458.

Mircenus, *see* **Mercius.**

mircetum, *see* MYRT

mirellum, *see* **merellus.**

miremium, *see* **maeremium.**

mirgus, *see* MERG

mirica, *see* **myrica.**

miringa, *see* **menica.**

mirra, *see* **murra.**

mis, *see* **ego.**

mis/a *****c 1180, c 1515, **-ia** 1295, 1337, outlay, expense; proposition, statement 1378; award, agreement 1262, 1293; **positor -arum,** "geld-layer" (Lancs.) 1537; **-or,** awarder 1259; *see also* **meisa;** *cf.* **missio.**

misca, *see* **muscum; nusca.**

miscarium, *see* MINIST

misc/ibilis, -ito, -uo, *see* MIXT

miscravatio, mistake in pleading c 1115.

misdoceo, to misinform c 1115.

†misefurra, sort of fur 1421.

misell/us 1254, **‡**1483, **mesellus** c 1300, **-a** (*f.*) 1254, **‡**1483, leper; **-ulus,** poor wretch 690. c 1090.

miseraicus, *see* **mesenterium.**

miser/amen, pity c 950; **-ia,** complaint 9c.; **-atio** c 1220, ***-icordia** 1100, c 1400, amercement; **-icordia, ***'mercy', discretion to amerce 1086, c 1540; allowance of food (mon.) c 1245, 15c.; misericord, seat in church c 1148, c 1452; 1222, 1434, **-ia** 1416, **domus -icordie** c 1266, **d. -icordiarum** c 1280, parlour (mon.); **m. Domini,** second Sunday after Easter 13c.; **septem opera**

-icordie 1415; **psalmus** m., 51st psalm c 1212; **-icordialiter**, mercifully a 1564; **-icorditer**, pitiably, cruelly p 1330, c 1400; by way of amercement a 1200, c 1258; **-icordiosus**, merciful 1378; **-icordissimus**, most merciful 799. 15c.; **-icors** 1299, 1310, **-icordum** 1325, dagger; **-abilitas**, pitiableness 1344; **-issime**, for **-rime**, 5c.; **-tus** 720, **-atrix** (*f.*) c 1090, c 1325, merciful, compassionate; **-ere**, penitential (51st) psalm (eccl.) c 980. c 1293; **-eor** (with *dat.*), to pity c 730, 790. c 1090, c 1400.

misevenio, to miscarry, fail, c 1115.

misfacio c 1115, **mesfacio** 1217, 1221, to injure, wrong.

misia, *see* **misa**.

miskenninga c 1130, 1419, **meschenninga** 1136, 1419, **meskenninka** 1292, miskenning, mistake in pleading (leg.).

mislata, *see* **melleta**.

mislocutio, miskenning (leg.) c 1115.

mispris/io 1203, **-ia** a 1347, ***mesprisio** c 1190, 1573, **meprisio** 1513, misprision, concealment (leg.); **m. proditionis** 1569, 1687, **mespricio** p 1573, misprision of treason; **mespriso**, to transgress, commit misprision 1397.

1 ***miss/a**, mass (eccl.) 597, 870. 1086, 1537; ***m. alta** a 1200, c 1530, ***m. magna** 1290, c 1530, ***m. major** c 1130, 1418, **m. solemnis** c 1336, 1549, **m. summa** c 1426, 1552, high mass; **m. bassa**, low mass 1429; **m. anniversaria** 1357; **m. cantata** 690. c 1125, 1549; **m. capitalis** a 1215, c 1330; **m. capitularis**, chapter mass 1503, 1509; **m. communis** c 1190, c 1395; **m. de die** c 1335; **m. de Domina** 1246, c 1449, **m. de Beata Virgine** c 1282, 1434, **m. B. Virginis** 1504; **m. dominica** 1556, **m. dominicalis** c 1447; **m. familiaris** c 1125, 13c., **m. peculiaris** c 1447, **m. privata** c 1400, 1415, private mass; **m. de Jesu** 1536; **m. judicii**, ordeal mass a 975; **m. matutinalis**, morrow-mass c 980. a 1090, c 1556; ***m. cum nota** c 1320, 1478, **m. de nota** 1489, choral mass; **m. nova**, priest's first mass c 1280; **m. obituum** 1472; **m. parochialis**, public (parishioners') mass 13c., 1388; **m. de requie** c 1400, c 1517, **m. de requiem** c 1340, c 1503, requiem mass; **m. specialis** c 1190; **m. de Spiritu Sancto** c 1200, 1414; **m. Sancte Trinitatis** 1289, **m. de Trinitate** a 1100, 1417; *see also* **tabula**;

*-ale 796, 801. a 1090, 1537, **messale** 1369, 1469, **-alis** c 1300, 1336, **liber -alis** c 1130, c 1494, missal, mass-book; **denarius -alis**, mass-penny c 1218, 1433; **officium -ale** a 1090, 1430; **oratio -alis** c 1325; **presbyter -alis** 824, **p. misse** c 1115, **sacerdos -alis** 1296, mass-priest; **-ans**, mass-sayer c 1380, 1427; **apparatus -aticus**, furniture of the mass 1609; **-ator**, expert on the mass 1523; **-ifico**, to celebrate mass 1609.

2 **missa**, 'miss', default 15c.

miss/io, instigation, incitement 1194, c 1218; commission (leg.) c 1390; loss, expense 1260, 1317; **m. (S. Spiritus)**, emanation (theol.) a 1260; **m. in possessionem**, putting in possession 1296; **-aticum** 826. c 1115, c 1120, **-iaticum** c 1110, message,

errand; **-aticus** 1086 (*see also* 1 **missa**), **messegerius** (*see also* **messio**) 1337, **-us** a 1125, 1450, messenger, envoy; **messageria**, 'messagery', (office concerned with) dispatch of messengers 1393; **‡-arius**, steward 1483; **-atio**, calling, vocation (Sc.) c 1230; **-ibilia** (*pl.*), missiles c 1260; **-ibilis**, missile (*adj.*) c 1212; ***littere -ive**, letters missive c 1364, a 1558; **-urium**, *for* **-orium**, dish 605. c 1397, c 1414; **‡-o**, to send 1483; **mitto**, to contribute, pay 1086, c 1178; **m. crimen**, to impute a crime a 1446; **m. falcem in messem** c 1341, c 1432; **m. foro**, to bring into fashion 1241; **m. manum in verum, m. in manum, m. in verum**, to swear c 1115; **m. per plegium**, to pledge c 1115, c 1135; **m. sortem**, to cast lots (bibl.); **m. ad** 1144, ***m. post** 1274, 1431, ***m. pro** c 1100, c 1450, ***m. propter** c 1150, c 1400, to send for, fetch, summon; **m. pro**, to send a substitute for 1230; **m. super**, to lay upon 1086, c 1362; to send (agents) to attack 1215; *cf.* **misa**.

mist-, *see also* **MIXT**

mister-, mistarium, *see* MINIST; MYST

‡mistrum, hatred (*cf.* μῖσος) c 1440, 1483.

misura, *see* MENSUR

mit/anna, -ena, *see* 2 **mitta**.

mitella, *see* **mitra**.

Mithridat/ium, antidote: **Mitridatum, Metridatum** a 1250, **Metridatos** 13c.; **Metridaticus**, *for* **-icus**, c 1100.

mit/itas c 1340, 15c., **-itia** 1368, 1413, mildness; **-is**, malleable p 1394; **-igabilis**, mitigable c 1250; **-igativum**, anodyne a 1250, ‡14c.; **-igatrix**, tranquillizer (*f.*) c 1248; **-igium**, relief (med.) a 1250.

mitr/a *c 1188, 1537, **-um** 1361, 1388, **metra** c 1390, mitre (eccl.); nightcap c 1148; **mitella**, bend (her.) c 1595; **-um**, mitreblock 1377; **-arium**, (?) mitre-case (eccl.) 14c.; **-atus**, mitred (eccl.) c 1180, 1421; **-o**, to cover c 1180; to honour with a mitre c 1200.

1 ***mitta** 1086, c 1500, **metta** c 1186, 1252, **†muta** 1252, **midd/a** a 1200, 1316, **-um** 1298, 1399, measure of salt, malt, *etc.* (? 6 or 8 bushels).

2 **mit/ta** c 1296, **‡c** 1440, **-anna** c 1150, **‡**1483, **-ena** 1298, mitten.

mitto, *see* **missio**.

mitu/o, -us, *see* MUTU

mixt/io, false syllogism c 1360; 1276, 1286, **-um** 1306, ***-ura** 1297, 1364, ***-ilio** 1205, 1437, **-ilo** 1275, **-illum** 1248, **mistilio** 1271, **mestilio** 1225, **mestillo** 1205, 1251, **mestilona** 1243, **mestilium** 1233, **mestillum** 1225, **†mestulum** c 1162, **mastilio** 1284, 'maslin', mixed corn (esp. rye and wheat); **-itio**, mixture 1526; **mixibilis** c 1250, **miscibilis** c 1250, c 1360, miscible; **-arabs**, *see* **Muceravius**; **-im**, mixedly c 600. c 1136, 15c.; **-or poculorum**, meadbrewer (W.) a 1300; **pannus -letus** 1301, **p. -us** 1310, c 1419, **-ura** 1347, **-um** 1285, 1382, mixed cloth, motley (*cf.* **melleta**); ***-um** c 980. c 1148, c 1330, **mistum** c 1080, c 1182, special allowance of food, breakfast (mon.); **-o**, to take breakfast (mon.) c 1148; c 1380, **miscito** c 790, **miscuo** 1419, 1461, to mix, dilute.

mna (†**mua**), mina (weight or coin) c 1100, a 1452; bezant (her.) p 1394.

Moal, *see* **Magalus**.

mobil/e (*coll.*), movable goods c 1178, c 1276; **m. primum** c 1250, 1620; **-ia** (*pl.*), burdens 9c.; **-ia se moventia**, livestock 1268; **-is**, removable, dismissable 1441; **redditus m.**, a poultry rent 1535, 1583; **-itatio**, universalization 1378; **-ito**, to universalize c 1361; **-io**, to move c 1361.

modal-, *see* **modus**.

†**modellus**, (?) support 6c.; (?) cheese-mould 1327.

***moder/amen** c 730. 12c., 1415, **-antia** c 1192, p 1300, moderation; 1247, c 1446, **-atio** c 1294, c 1344, adjustment, modification; intervention 760; **m. regni**, statecraft 1041; **-atio** 1274, **-atus** (*4th decl.*) c 1470, authority; **-ativus**, regulative p 1300; **-atorium**, (?) mode (mus.) c 1470; **-atorius**, governmental c 1670; **-anter**, moderately c 1180; 1347, **-ate** 1324, in good order; **-o**, to fix, regulate 1426, 1559; to govern c 1250; **-or**, to moderate (ac.) c 1565.

modern/itas, modern times c 1178, c 1190; **-us**, *present, of the present day c 730, 799. 1074, 1554; (?) the late c 1395; ***-i** (*pl.*), men of today, moderns (esp. nominalists) 1144, c 1470; **-ior**, more recent c 1200, 1378; ***modo**, now 6c., 957. 1086, c 1365.

†**modestinus**, moderate a 1564.

modiatio, *see* **modius**.

***modic/itas**, smallness 7c. c 1190, c 1452; **m. mea**, my humble self 5c.; **-um**, small amount c 1080, 1363; ***a** little (adv.) c 1290, c 1452; in or for a short time c 1250, c 1400; *see also* **ad**, **post**; **-issimus**, very little 1426, c 1470.

***modific/atio**, modification, qualification, specification c 1225, c 1629; **-ativus**, regulative c 1283; **-atrix**, moderator (*f.*) a 1233.

modi/us 1086, 1399, **-um** 1086, 1241, **moyus** 1300, liquid or dry measure (? 8 gallons); "bushel" 1478; **muiolus**, measure of salt (G.) 1418; **moela**, deep bowl a 1250; **-us**, measure of land a 1100, 1136; c 1200, 1398, **-olum** 1365, **modulus** 1270, 1291, **medio-lus** 1310, **moellus** 1267, 1309, **muella** 1273, 1280, **muellus** 1316, nave of wheel; **-atio**, prisage c 1135, 1201; *cf.* **3 muta**.

modo, *see* MODERN; **modus**.

modul/us, custom, manner c 1115, c 1210; scanty measure c 1185; mould, model 1620; *see also* **modius**; *cf.* **modellus, molda**; **pro -o**, duly, according to capacity *c 1000. 1166, c 1430; **-us**, (*adj.*) tuneful c 810; **-abiliter** c 700, **-anter** c 1000. a 1452, **-enter** a 1446, tunefully; **-ose**, with care, accurately 860.

mod/us, modality, mood (log.) c 1160, a 1250; **sub -o**, with modification 1295; **omni -o** c 1360, **-is omnibus** 1314, by all possible means; **-us acutus** (mus.) 1351; **m. adverbialis**, **m. nominalis** (log.) a 1250; **m. crucis**, sign of the cross 949. 12c.; **m. manerii**, **m. ville**, local custom a 1128; **m. vivendi**, settlement 1357; **-um digiti teneo**, to measure one inch c 780; **m. vite facio**, to die c 1006; **-alia** (*pl.*), modals (log.) 1284; **-alis**, modal, qualified (log.)

c 1160, 1610; **-aliter** c 1164, 1344, **-o** c 1363, modally (log.); *see also* **hujusmodi**.

moel/a, **-lus**, *see* **modius**.

moeta, *see* 3 **mota**; MEDI

mogatus, *see* **nux**.

mol/a, mill or millstone: part of distaff 7c.; jaw c 1200; grindstone, whetstone c 1180, 15c.; (?) multure 1310; (?) rent of millstone 1300; **m. ad manum** 1301, ***m. manualis** c 1200, 1325, **-us manualis** 1316, hand-mill; **m. pro mustardo** 1314; ‡**m. piperis** 15c., **molda piperialis** 1390, pepper-quern; **m. pomorum** 1275, **m. torcularia** 1287, cider-press;

-aria, right to grind 1421; 1086, **-era** 1298, millstone quarry (*cf.* **-iarium**, *infra*); **-erum** 1368, **-atura** 1282, millstone; **-aris**, pivotal 1326; **crux -aris**, cross moliné (her.) c 1595; **-aris jacens**, (?) stationary millstone 1372; **-ariter**, pivotally 1326; **-arius** a 1204, 1421, **-aticus** 1375, for grinding; **-atio**, *etc.*, *see* **-itio** (*infra*); **-ator**, grinder, mill-hand 1355, 1455; **-itorium**, hand-mill 1471;

***-endinum** 1080, 1580, **-endinus** 1086, c 1327, **-endina** c 1226, 1415, **-andinum** 1234, 1307, (?) **-endinarium** 1588, **-ina** c 1120, c 1414, **-inum**, **-inus** 1086, c 1485, **mulina** 1086, **mulinum** 1212, **-etrina** 1608, **-etrinum** 1537, mill; **m. domini**, suit at lord's mill 1352; **m. ad aquam** c 1250, **m. aquarium** 1265, ***m. aquati-cum** 1196, 1542, **m. aquatiquum** 1378, **m. †aquatum** 1284, **m. fluviale** 1419, water-mill; **m. ad bladum** 1224, 1542, **m. ad blada** 13c., **m. de blado** c 1185, **m. bladi** 1336, 1465, **m. multicium** 1255, **m. ad segetem** a 1195, corn-mill (*see also* BLAD, GRAN); **m. ad braesium**, malt-mill 1251 (*see also* BRAS); **m. ad conteren-dos cortices**, bark-mill 1289; ***m. ad equos** c 1224, 1335, ***m. equinum** a 1185, 1588, **m. equitium** c 1198, c 1440, **m. equorum** 1183, 1193, horse-mill, gin; **m. ad †falsam**, (?) blade-mill 1204; **m. fal-catum**, "scythe-mill" (Derb.) 1489; **m. ferri** 1346, **m. ferrarium** 1542, 1553, **m. ferreum** 1553, iron-mill; **m. ad fullandum** 12c., 1419, **m. fullonum** 1206, 1275, **m. fullonis** 1303, fulling-mill (*see also* FULL); **m. manuale**, hand-mill 1242, 1388; **m. maris** 1226, **m. marinum** 1419, **m. maritimum** 15c., tide-mill; **m. pomorum**, cider-press 1245, 1302; **m. pulsatile**, stamping-mill 1511; **m. ad secures acuendas**, blade-mill 1212; **m. tanerez** 1206, **m. tannarium** 1288, 1349, tanning-mill, bark-mill; **m. ad turnum**, quern 1289; ***m. ad ventum** (? a 1180), a 1200, c 1400, **m. adventri'** 1279, **m. de vento** 1198, a 1250, **m. venti** 1200, 1332, wind-mill (*see also* VENT); **-inum estivum**, **m. hiemale** 1086; **-endinare** c 1278, **-endinarium** 1289, 1315, (?) **-iarium** 1312, mill-site (G.); **crux -endinaris** (**-endinaria**), cross moliné (her.) p 1394, a 1446; **-endinaria**, mill-wife a 1300; ***-endinarius** a 1128, 1573; **-endarius** c 1200, c 1283, **-endinator** 1276, 1292, †**-endenator** 1393, **-inarius** 1086, miller; **equus -endinarius**, mill-horse 1264, 1279;

-itio, grinding, milling (of ore) 13c.; sharpening 1397; grinding (of colours) 1472; 1226, 16c., -atio c 1150, 1422, -inagium 13c., (?) -agium 1247 (but *cf.* **2 mala**), -enditium c 1250, -entura 1302, -atura c 1160, -itura 7c. 1086, 1245, *-tura 1197, 1351, -ctura c 1150, †maltura c 1226, motura a 1190, 1274, *multura 1167, c 1540, mulctura 1583, mutura c 1236, -ta c 1090, 1199, (payment for) grinding, multure; -tura (multura) sicca a 1230, 1371, -tura †suta (?) c 1300, 1402, multure paid in cash; -ura, milling (of cloth) 1397;

arma -uta, ground, edged, arms 1243, c 1290; ensis -utus 1299; †militus, *for* -itus, ground 1241; -endino a 1190, 1419, †-ino c 1184, -io c 1240, 1435, -o (*1st conj.*) 1253, c 1468, multo 1300, to grind (corn); -o, to grind, sharpen (knives) 1213, 1350; to grind (paint) 1253; 1291, multuro c 1200, 1331, to pay multure.

molanus, *see* **1 mullo**.

mol/aris, of mass or volume c 1360 (*see also* **mola**); -osus, massive, heavy c 1250, 1461; †-estus, (?) powerful, momentous c 1115.

mold/a 1279, 1333, moula 1244, †muldicia 1372, mold' pecia 1333, mason's mould, template; m. falsa 1333, -us falsus 1324, (?) converse of mould; -a 1319, 1399, mulda 1387, mould (for casting lead); m. piperi-alis, *see* **mola**; *cf.* MODUL

moldbredclutum, mouldboard-clout (on plough) 1318, 1326.

molemennus, *see* **2 mala**.

‡molena, mullein (bot.) 14c.

molend-, moler-, *see* **mola**.

moleschus, *see* **molossus**.

*molest/atio 1201, c 1452, -amen c 1250, trouble, annoyance; -ia, mishap c 1000; -ator, troubler 1200, a 1450; *see also* **molaris**.

moleta, *see* MELOT

molettum, *see* **motlettum**.

molit/arius corii, leather-worker 1444; -o, to work (leather) 1444; *see also* **mola**.

1 molle, (?) bundle c 1150; *cf.* **1 mala**.

2 moll/e, soft land c 1200; -iceps, grey shrike (bird) 1544; -icors, soft-hearted 1166; †-ifer, (?) gentle 6c.; -ificabilis, able to be softened c 1270; -ificatio, softness c 1200; mollification a 1452; -ificativus a 1250, c 1260, -itivus a 1250, softening; -iformis, smooth in form 6c.; -ifico a 1250, 1501, -ior (*dep.*) p 1381, c 1433, to soften; -io 1291, mullio 1304, to moisten (Fr. *mouiller*); *see also* **1 mullo**.

mol/londum, -mannus, -mennus, *see* **2 mala**.

molochia, *see* **malache**.

mol/ossus, hound, "ban-dog" c 1190, ‡15c.; (?) †-eschus 1212.

molosus, *see* **molaris**.

molt-, molura, molutus, molo, *etc.*, *see* **mola**.

molula calcarium, mullet, rowel (her.) 1654.

mol/umentum 1313, 1315, ‡-imentum 1483, emolument.

moment/um, $\frac{1}{40}$th of hour a 1150, c 1265; per m., for an instant c 1250; -iolum 690, -ulum c 1000, brief moment; -alis, momen-

tary 12c.; -ana, sort of balance 7c.; -anee, momentarily c 1125, 15c.; from moment to moment 1296.

†monachia, *f.l.* for monomachia, c 1293.

*monach/us (eccl.), monahus 873, monk; piscis m., 'monk', sea monster c 1200, c 1212; m. albus c 1180, 1537, m. grisius 1154, c 1300, m. grisus 1167, 1324, Cistercian; m. niger, Benedictine c 1220, 1537; m. claustralis c 1125, 1526, m. conventualis 14c., 1441; m. de episco-patu, (?) canon 1086, c 1100; m. laicus 1537; m. officialis 1229, 1515, m. officia-rius 1450, 1500, obedientiary; m. predicator c 1125; m. regularis 1407; m. secularis c 1130;

-a, nun 1080, 1544; -alia (*pl.*), monk's habit 14c., c 1450; *-alis c 1090, 1472, †moniarchalis c 1370, -ilis c 1000, 11c. a 1100, c 1436, -icus c 730, c 1000. c 1090, c 1450, monkish, monastic; *see also* **panis**; -aliter c 1430, a 1452, -iliter 12c., as a monk; *-atus 7c., c 1006. c 1100, c 1467, -ia c 1190, -ismus 1608, monastic status or life; -atus (*coll.*), body of monks 1282; -ellus, little monk c 1125; -izo, to become like a monk c 1260; c 1100, 12c., *-o c 1125, c 1450, to make a monk, admit as a monk; -o, to admit as a nun c 1220, c 1362.

mon/acornus, -adicus, *see* **monos**.

monalis, *see* **1 monialis**.

*monarch/a c 1090, 1538, -es c 1000. 12c., -us 6c., 950. 12c., c 1450, monarch, sole ruler; -us, a dice game c 1160; -alis 1370, -icus c 1376, 1380, monarchic; -atus 1260, *-ia c 1000, 1062. c 1090, 1570, monarchy; -ia, single (united) kingdom 12c.; unity c 960.

monas, *see* **monos**.

monast/erium, *monastery (eccl.); cathedral chapter c 1082; 1086, 1519, minsterium c 1365, minster, parish church; in -erio, within the territory of a minster 1086; -erium cathedrale 13c.; m. conventuale 12c., 13c.; *-eriolum, small monastery (eccl.); *-erialis (eccl.), †-eralis c 730, †-eriolus 12c., *-icus c 730, 826. c 1125, 1517, monastic; -erialiter 1427, -ice 11c., 1526, in a monastery, monastically; -eri-archa, abbot or prior c 1100, c 1553.

monat-, *see* MONET

monca, *see* **2 manca**.

moncellus, *see* **mons**.

mond-, *see* **mundus** (**1 & 2**).

mon/edinum, -dinum 1305, mundaylon-dus 1316, 'Monday-land' (E. Angl.); *cf.* LUN

monestrallus, *see* MINIST

1 monet/a, purity standard of coins c 1100, 1230; moneia 1086, monta c 1102, mineta 1433, 1472, minta 1413, 1495, *for* -a, coin, mint; -a debilis a 1222, c 1250, m. levior 1468; m. fortis, m. grossa 1205; m. episcopi, money coined by Stephen bishop of Waterford (Ir.) c 1285; m. S. Elene, gold coinage (? bezants) 1261; m. legalis 1198, 1583; m. nigra 1468, 1487; m. reprobata c 1258, c 1294; m. usualis c 1323, 1543; -agium 1100, 1296, mone-dagium 1086, monoiagium 1386, †-icum

(? **-aticum**) (Sp.) 1282, (payment for) coinage, mintage; **-agium** 1331, **moneagium** 1309, 'reek-silver' (C.I.); ***-aria** 1205, 1248, **-arium** 14c., mint, office of moneyer; **-atio**, minting 1248, p 1280; **-alis** 1279, **-arius** 1306, for coining; ***-arius** 1086, 1419, **monatarius** 1219, **monatorius** 1282, **monitarius** 1465, **monearius** c 1253, 1260, moneyer; **domus -aria**, mint (Norm.) 1091; **-o**, to coin, mint c 1115, 1465.
2 †**moneta**, part of womb (med.) a 1250.
1 ***mon/ialis** 893, 955. 1086, 1588, **-alis** c 1000. c 1195, 1586, **munialis** 1200, nun; **m. alba**, Cistercian nun 1257, 1299; Austin Canoness 1537; **m. nigra**, Benedictine nun 1537; **m. consecrata**, abbess 1222; **-ialis** (*adj.*), of or for a nun 1286, 1546; 13c., **-ilis** a 1408, monastic; **-iale**, 'soul-silver', payment for food (mon.) (Durham) 1364, 1397.
2 **monialis** 1357, 1359, **meinellus** 1339, monial, mullion (arch.).
moniarchalis, *see* MONACH
monimen/ 9c., **-tum** c 950, counsel, warning; **monit/io**, muster, (calling up of) local population (A.S. *manung*) c 1115; 13c., 1559, **-oria** 1488, **-orialis** 1549, **-orium** 1543, **littere -orie** 1220, l. **-oriales** 1522, 1545, monition (eccl.); **-orialis** 1609, **-ivus** c 1376, monitory; **-or**, monitor (scholastic) 1560; summoner (leg.) 1277; *cf.* 2 **munimen**.
mono-, *see also* **monos**.
***monocul/us**, one-eyed (man) c 1125, c 1450; robbed of half livelihood c 1218; **-o**, to rob of one eye 1253, c 1450.
monoiagium, *see* MONET
†**monopilla**, (?) sort of pill (med.) a 1250.
mon/os, one 13c., c 1450; **-as**, unit c 950. a 1250, c 1500; **-adicus**, of units 1564; **-odicus**, unique c 1616, 1620; **-acornus**, unicorn c 1393; **mono/chordium**, monochord 1499; ‡**-cosmus**, one-horse cart c 1440; **-cubitus** a 1233, **-cubitalis** c 1500, of a cubit's length; **-genus**, homogeneous 860; **-gramma**, single letter c 950; **-logion** c 1070, 1510, **-loquium** c 1070, book by Anselm; **-machicum certamen**, single combat c 1210; †**-pagia**, †**-pogia**, (?) *for* **-plegia**, localized headache a 1250; **-peda-lis**, one foot long c 1265; **-phrontistes**, man of one idea 1620; **monoptalmus** 670, **monotalmus** c 1000. c 1450, ‡1483, one-eyed (man); **-phyllon**, maianthemum (bot.) 1641; **-pola**, monopolist 1585; **-ptotus**, having only one case (of nouns) 790; **-scemus**, of one form c 1125; **-syllaba** 1267, **-syllabica** 1267, monosyllable; **-syl-labicus**, monosyllabic 1267; **-thelita** c 1118, **-thelista**, **-scelita**, **-scelitus** 12c., Mono-thelete (theol.).
mons molendini, mill-mound 1299, 1372; **m. talpe** 1323, 1466, **mont/icula t.** 1383, molehill; **M. Jovis** a 1200, **-isgaudium** c 1250, Monjoie (French war-cry); **m. pietatis**, *mont de piété*, pawn-shop 1585; **-ana** (*f. s.*), mountain c 1150, c 1345; **-anarius**, mountaineer 1253; **-anus** c 1188, 1400, **-aneus** 1324, **-anius** 1525, mountainous; **falco -anus**, peregrine falcon

a 1446; **-arius**, **-or**, **muntorius** 1255, †**-aris** 1279, **muntor** 1282, †**munitor** c 1250, **muntator** 1166, mounted soldier, usually holding ½ knight's fee (W. March); **mountura**, 'mounter' (horse and harness) 1403, 1451; **-ea** 1248, **munteia** 1247, flood-tide (C.I.); **-icellus** c 700, ***-iculus** c 700. 1090, c 1540, **-ulus** c 1202, hill, hillock; **-iculus** 1185, **moncellus** 1275, 1354, **mouncellus** 1325, 1388, **muncellus** 1234, 1357, **monsellus** 1289, **mussellus** 1294, 14c., **musshella** 1399, heap, stack (esp. of plaster); †**-ifodina**, mine 1414; **-ifringilla** 1544, ‡**-ifrugella** 1570, brambling (bird); **-igena**, mountain-born 1220.
***monstr/atio** 1404, 1560, ***-um** (†**mou-strum**) 1384, 1587, **-a** (G.) c 1289, muster (of soldiers); **-um**, visit or view c 1115; sample c 1160, 1374; c 1460, c 1500, **monsterum** 1544, **-antia** (?) 15c., monstrance (eccl.); **-abilis**, demonstrable 1103, c 1115; **-amen**, indication 1245; **-atrix**, indicator (*f.*) c 700. c 1180; **-avit**, name of a writ 1315, 15c.; **-o**, to muster (soldiers) 1253, 1339; **mostro**, to show 1225, 1313.
monstr/uositas, monstrosity c 1200, c 1267; **-iparus**, monster-bearing c 1180, c 1440.
mont-, *see also* **mons**.
monta, *see* **moneta**; **munda**.
montura, *see* MORTU
monumentum, *see* 2 **munimen**; *cf.* **moni-men**.
moota, gull (Fr. *mouette*) c 1200.
1 **mor/a** a 1085, 1650, **-us** c 1150, 1527, moor, marsh (*cf.* **mare**); turf, peat c 1290. c 1400; **carbo -e**, peat charcoal a 1307; **-ehaia** 1513, **-haya** 1332, peat-hag (Somerset); **-estarius**, tenant of moorland 1299; **-gabulum**, moor-gavel 1234; c 1310; †**-mitta**, (?) tenant service in moor 1234; **-osus** c 1090, 1334, **murosus** 1400, marshy; **morhenna** 1544, **gallina muralis** 1511, moor-hen; **-tettera**, 'moor-tether', stonechat (bird) 1544; **-wardus**, 'moor-ward' (Somerset) 1302.
2 **mor/a**, stay, residence 1275, 1416; **-am facio** 1208, 1335, **m. contraho** 1262, **m. contracto** 1314, ***m. traho** c 1250, 1559, to remain, abide; ***-ula**, brief delay or stay 1041. c 1090, 1470; **-antia**, interruption 1200; **-iatio**, storage c 1442; **-ose**, gradually, protractedly c 1180, 1526; **-ositas**, delay, hesitation c 1220, c 1395; ***-osus**, lingering, protracted c 1180, c 1470 (*see also* **mos**); **-ari**, (*subst.*) sojourn 1215; **-io** 1428, **-o** 797, *for* **-or**, to remain; **-or in lege**, to demur (leg.) 1555; **-ulo**, to stay for a short time c 1170.
morabotinus, *see* **marabotinus**.
mor/agium, moorage (due) 1285, 1341; 1386, **-arium** 1390, (?) a moorland rent (Northumb.).
Moralensis, *see* **Morlanus**.
moral/itas, character, virtue, moral significance c 1170, c 1670; c 1250, c 1378, **-e** 1610, moral (of story); **-ia** (*pl.*), ethical writings a 1100, c 1550; **-is**, moral philosopher 1267, c 1470; ***-iter**, morally, ethically 1267, 1380; allegorically c 730. c 1217, c 1470; **-izatio**, moralizing c 1432,

1515; **-izator**, moralizer c 1320; **-izo**
(**-iso**), to moralize 1344, 1427; *cf.* **mos.**

morat-, *see* **3 morus; mos.**

morbosium, *mortbois*, dead wood c 1200,
1234; *cf.* **2 bosca.**

morb/us Gallicus, pox 1583, 1634; **m. mortuus** 13c.; **m. regius**, king's evil, (?) jaundice
1278, 1344; **m. rubius**, a disease of sheep
1398, 1449; **m. sudarius** 1508, c 1517, **m.
sudificus** 1508, sweating sickness, plague;
m. superbus 13c.; **-idus**, depraved c 1343;
-igenus, disease-born c 730; **-illus**, pustule
a 1250, c 1365; **-ose**, so as to corrupt c 950;
-ositas, sickness c 1220, c 1268; **-esco**, to
sicken c 1205; **-ido**, to infect 13c.

morcellus, *see* **morsellus.**

morder, *see* **martrina.**

mord/icitas, bite, pang 12c.; **dolor -ica-
tivus**, griping pain a 1250; **-aculus**,
rather harsh 1520; ‡**-aculum**, bit, curb
1483; **-ans, -ens**, tongue of buckle 1215;
-ice, with the teeth 1518; **-ico**, to gripe
a 1250, a 1446; *cf.* MORS

mordifico, *see* **mors.**

mord/ra, -rum, -uratio, *see* MURDR

‡**morecla**, osmunda (bot.) 14c.

mor/ehaia, -estarius, *see* **1 mora.**

Morelensis, *see* **Morlanus.**

morell/us, -a, *see* **3 morus.**

morenatus, *see* **morina.**

moresca, morris dance 1508.

morespechium, *see* **morgangifa.**

moretum, *see* **3 morus.**

morgabulum, *see* **1 mora.**

morg/agium c 1365, 1608, **mortgagium**
a 1564, **mortuum vadium** c 1185, 1245,
mortgage; **-agio** 1575, †**-anizo** a 1564, to
mortgage.

mor/gangifa (†**-hangifa**), morning-gift to
bride c 1115; **-ganaticus**, morganatic 1608;
-espechium, morn-speech, guild meeting
1255.

morgellina, *see* MORS

mor/haya, -henna, *see* **1 mora.**

mori/atio, -o, *see* **2 mora.**

mor/icus, foolish (play on surname More)
1520; **-oteros**, more foolish 1520; **-osophus**
wise fool 1518.

morig-, *see* **mos.**

*****mor/ina** 1257, 1464, **murina** 1418, **muri-
num** 1420, **murena** 1329, c 1336, **muren-
num** 15c., murrain, plague, accidental
death (of animals); **-enatus**, diseased c 1445.

morisium, *see* **mariscus.**

morius, *see* **1 morus.**

Mor/lanus p 1250, 1311, **-lanensis** 1251,
1253, **-lacensis** p 1250, **-alensis**, †**-alen-
silis**, **-elensis**, **-olensis** 1242, **-lingus**
1276, **Murlensis** 1242, coin of Morlaix.

mormitta, *see* **1 mora.**

mormor/, -eus, *see* MARMOR; MURMUR

mor/o, -or, -osus, *see* **mora (1 & 2); mos.**

moro/sophus, -teros, *see* **moricus.**

morphe/a, morphew, skin-disease c 1180,
c 1270; **m. rubra** a 1250; **-atus**, affected
with morphew a 1250.

morph/eia, form (log.) (μορφή) a 1360; **-osis**,
metamorphosis c 1148, c 1200.

morressa, *see* **mariscus.**

mors antecessoris, assize of mort d'ancestor

(leg.) 1184, 1419; **m. hominis**, homicide
(leg.) 1134, 1269; **m. propria** 1210, **m.
recta** 1221, 1276, natural death; **morti/-
cinium**, plague, murrain c 1250, 1377;
carcass 1041. 12c., 1322; **-kinus**, mortekinus 1199, †**-tivus** (? **-cinus**) a 1150, dead
(of animals); †**-cina** (*pl.*), (?) dead *or* transitory things 7c.; **-cida**, slayer of death c 1190;
-ferus, dead 6c.; **-ficatio**, *****mortification,
repression c 600, c 790. c 1195, 1622;
mortification (med.) a 1250; mortification of
metals (alch.) 1267; *****1312, 1505, **-zatio**
c 1300, alienation in mortmain; **-ficativus**,
destructive a 1250, c 1270; a 1250, †**mordi-
ficativus**, **-ficatorius** a 1250, mortifying
(med.); **-ficator**, slayer c 730. c 1102, 14c.;
tenant in mortmain 15c.; **-ficatura**, murder
c 1102; **-ficia** (*pl.*), spells, witchcraft c 1115;
-fico, *****to kill 9c. c 1080, 1454; *****to mortify (eccl.); a 1250, †**mordifico** a 1250,
to mortify (med.); to mortify (alch.) 13c.,
a 1292; to deaden (sound) c 1227; to
terminate (law-suit) c 1330, 1331; to extinguish (rent) c 1283, 1297; *****1316, 1487, **-zo**
(**-so**) c 1415, 1434, to alienate in mortmain;
cf. MORG, MORTAL, MORTU

mors/ellus a 1150, a 1350, †**moysellus** 1245,
morcellus a 1205, ‡1483, morsel, bit;
-ellatim, piece-meal a 1452; **-io** 13c.,
a 1270, **-ura** c 1218, 14c., bite; **-ivus**, biting
c 1362; causing remorse 1380; **-us**, *****'morse',
buckle, clasp for cope 1207, c 1510; **m.
diaboli**, devil's-bit scabious ‡14c., 1629;
m. galline ‡14c., 1538, ‡**morgellina** 14c.,
'margeline', chickweed *or* pimpernel; **m.
rane**, frog-bit (bot.) 1634; *cf.* MORD

*****mortal/itas**, plague 680, c 730. c 1320,
c 1500; **-e** (*sc.* peccatum), mortal sin
c 1197, 1380; **-is**, fatal, deadly c 1190,
a 1564; **-iter**, fatally c 1250, c 1360; *****-iter,
-issime (pecco) c 1240, c 1444.

†**mortaria**, sort of ship 13c.

1 mort/arium, a mortar: **-erium** 1265, 1506,
-irium c 1500, **-orium** c 1534; **-arium**,
mortar (carried by scold) 1423; **-ariola** c 1500,
-ariolus c 1520, little mortar; **-arium**
c 1175, 1419, **-erium** c 1350, **-ariolum** 1296,
c 1443, **-eriale** c 1510, small lamp, cresset;
(?) mortar (of gun) 1550.

2 mort/arium 1284, 1336, **-erium** 1244,
c 1400, **-era** c 1300, mortar (building
material); **m. vetus, m. novum**, (?) mortar
made in old and new fashion 1289; **m.
liberum**, rough-cast 1251.

mortasius, mortise (arch.) 1285; †**mertatio**,
(?) mortising c 1352.

mortekinus, *see* **mors.**

mort/erellus c 1266, 1305, **-rellus** c 1300,
c 1514, **-rellum** 13c., 'mortrel', milk pudding; ‡**-icium**, "culice", broth 15c., 1483.

mortettera, *see* **1 mora.**

mortgagium, *see* **morgagium.**

morth-, *see* MURDR

morti-, *see also* **mors.**

mortileg-, *see* MARTYR

mort/irium, -orium, *see* **1 mortarium**; MORTU

mortrellus, *see* **morterellus.**

mortu/arium *****1229, 1569, **mortorium**
c 1220, †**montura** 1403, †**munetura** 14c.,
mortuary payment (eccl.); service for the

dead 1567; 1352, 1519, **liber -orum** 1424, book containing service for the dead; **m. -um**, mortuary chattel 14c., 1381; **m. vivum** 14c., 1383; **bos -arius, vacca -aria** 1345; **ad -os**, at the burial service a 1340; †**-inus** (? **morticinus**), dead (of animal) 12c.; **-um** (*sc.* **boscum**), dead wood a 1190; *see also* **manus, morgagium, opus.**

morul/a, -o, *see* 2 **mora.**

1 **mor/us** c 1200, c 1472, **-ius** c 1180, ***-uca*** 1256, 1337, †**-utus** 1290, **muruca** 1325, **-ua** c 1472, **-vellus** 1373, **murvellus** 1288, ***mul/vellus*** c 1190, 1419, †**muvellus** 1268, **-vellus** c 1200, 1306, **-ewellus** 1232, 1311, **-uwellus** 1234, 1243, **melewellus** c 1375, **milvellus** c 1320, **milwellus** 1419, fish, (esp.) cod; *cf.* **merlengus, 1 mullo.**

2 **morus,** *see* 1 **mora.**

3 **mor/us, -um,** mulberry: c 1182, 14c., **m. vaticana** 1538, ‡**murum** 13c., blackberry; ‡1652, **-um** a 1250, ulcer resembling mulberry; **-atum** a 1155, c 1436, **-etum** c 1220, **muretum** 1237, 'morat', wine flavoured with mulberry juice; **-etum** 1249, 1258, **amoretum** 1243, **murrata** 1303, **murretus** 1236, 1303, murrey, dark cloth; **murreus,** murrey-coloured 1362, 1388; **-ellus,** 'morel', dark brown (of horses) a 1220, 1338; **-ella** a 1250, ‡c 1440, **maurella** c 1200, morel, black nightshade (bot.).

mos lascivus, m. longus, m. mediocris, musical forms 1326; **mor/atior,** better behaved 1516; †**-igenus** c 1000, **-iger** c 1160, **-igeratus** 1272, †**-iginatus** a 1250, **-igerosus** c 1400, *for* **-igerus,** obliging, compliant; **-iger** (? **-igerus**) a 1408, ***-igeratus*** c 1180, c 1465, **-osus** c 1340, 1409, of good character, virtuous, sober (*cf.* 2 **mora**); **-ose,** virtuously c 1180, c 1470; *cf.* MORAL

Mosaicus, *see* **lex.**

mosca, moss-, *see* **muscum.**

moscus, moschocaryon, *see* **muscus.**

mostro, *see* **monstratio.**

†**moszhacumia,** "*fex vitri*" (? *nitri*) (? Ar.) 1144.

1 **mota,** motte, castle-mound 1141, 1527; heap, measure of plaster (*cf.* **moncellus**) (Norm.) 1325; moat *or* fishpond 1472, 1509.

2 **mot/a** 1294, **-um** 1328, cheese-moat.

3 **mot/a** c 1180, 1333, **-us** 1307, **meota** 1350, **meuta** 13c., **moeta** 1235, 1350, **meeta** 1284, **mueta** c 1136, 1236, **muta** 1275, 1446, 'mute', pack of hounds.

4 **mot/a (domus de -a),** (?) moot 1165; *cf.* **gemotum.**

5 †**mota,** (?) *f.l.* for **meta,** 1246.

mot/atio, buffeting (?) 8c.; c 1202, 1223, **-eamentum** a 1200, application to court; **-abilis,** active, mobile 14c.; **primum -abile** c 1362 (*cf.* MOBIL); **-abilitas,** affectibility, emotion 9c.; **-amentum,** instigation 1275; ‡**-arium, -orium,** "pot-stick" 15c.; **-atus,** moved 930; **-ibilis,** removable c 1290; **-ibilitas,** removability c 1290;
-io, expedition c 1217, c 1436; riot c 1424; ‡mew, cage 1570 (*cf.* 5 **muta**); motion, suggestion 1417, c 1472; 1378, a 1408, **-iva** 1279, ***-ivum*** c 1305, 1559, †**-um** 1461,

motive, impulse, reason; **-ivum,** consideration, matter put forward 1433; **m. primum,** prime mover a 1233; **-ive,** persuasively c 1250; **-ivitas,** motive power c 1270; **-ivus,** setting in motion 1237, a 1250; *inducive, persuasive c 1250, 1414; emotive c 1270; (?) well-founded 1461; **-or** c 1248, **m. primus** 1252, 1518, Prime Mover; **-rix,** mover (*f.*) c 1250, 1686; **-us,** movement (in bell-ringing) c 1245; journey, pilgrimage 1194, c 1217; impulse c 1350; **m. merus,** free impulse, volition c 1350, c 1544; **m. proprius** 1327, 1461; *cf.* MOV

motatorium, *see* **mutamen.**

motetus, motet (mus.) 1326, c 1470.

motidus, *see* **madefactio.**

motlettum, modlettum 1337, **molettum** 1297, 1301, 'motlet', a customary payment (Cornwall).

mot/o, -ulus, -ulinus, *see* **multo.**

mot/um, -us, *see* **mota (2 & 3); motatio.**

motura, *see* **mola.**

moula, *see* **molda.**

moulus, *see* **mulettus.**

moun/cellus, -tura, *see* **mons.**

moustrum, *see* **monstratio.**

mov/entia 1344, c 1362, ‡**-ementum** 1483, movement; **-eatio (bladorum),** carrying in 1424; **primus motus** c 1250; **primum -ens** a 1292; ‡**-eo,** to mew (hawks) 1570; to start (game) 1276, 1293; **m. a** 1190, 1315, **m. de** c 1220, c 1290, to be held of (feudally); **m. calumniam,** to advance a claim 12c., c 1225; **m. causam** c 1290, c 1465, **m. placitum** c 1226, 1360, to institute a plea (leg.); **m. difficultates,** to raise objections (ac.) c 1407, c 1555; **m. questionem,** to institute an inquiry c 730. c 1255, c 1325; **m. guerram** 1279; **m. (in Parliamento),** to make a motion 15c.; **m. seditionem,** to brawl! c 1102; **nullum lapidem non m.,** to leave no stone unturned 1570; *cf.* **motatio.**

mox, recently 1200; **m. atque** 1438, **m. ut** c 1300, 1420, as soon as; **m. tunc,** immediately 1276.

moyo, *see* **meia.**

moysa, *see* 2 **musa.**

Moysaicus, *see* **lex.**

moysellus, *see* **morsellus.**

moyus, *see* **modius.**

mua, muarius, *see* **mna; 5 muta.**

muca, muce, *see* **musca.**

mucc/aria, (?) peat-moss 1199, 1544; **-osus,** wet or miry 12c.; *cf.* **muscum.**

mucceror, *see* **mucilago.**

Muceravius a 1142, **Mixtarabs** a 1200, Mosarabe, Christian under Moslem rule (Sp.).

mucetta, hole, hidden entrance (O.F. *mucete*) 1293.

muchettus, *see* **musketus.**

muc/ilago c 1200, 1267, **muscillago** c 1200, a 1250, mucus; †**-ilaginosus** c 730, **muscilaginosus** a 1250, mouldy; 13c., **muscilentus** a 1250, viscous; **muscidus,** *for* **-idus,** musty 12c., 1345; **-ceror,** to become musty 13c.

mucronatus, fitchy (her.) 1654.

mucrum, *see* **murra.**

muell/a, -us, *see* **modius.**

muerius, muerus, *see* 5 muta.
mueta, *see* 3 mota.
muff/la c 1115, -a 1322, miffa 1310, glove.
mug/a, -atus, *see* nux.
mugettum, (?) nut-shell made into cup (*cf.* nux) 1296.
mugibilis, lowing 13c.
muia, *see* 5 muta.
muillo, *see* 2 mullo.
muiolus, *see* modius.
‡mula, chilblain 14c., 1652.
mul/cator, despoiler 6c.; ‡-tator, murderer 1200; ‡executioner 1483; *see also* mulctura.
mul/cedo, charm, alleviation c 550, c 1000. c 1204; -cebris, mild, agreeable c 1115, 1414; -sura, melting 1372; -sum 13c., -sa a 1250, ‡14c., mixture of honey and water, mead; ‡-sum, whey 1483; *see also* muscum.
mul/ctrale 1580, ‡-trale 15c., -tra c 1200, -gar(e) 1329, -garium a 1250, ‡1483, milk-pail; -gatus, moistened with milk 1383; vacca -seria, milch cow 1438; -sor, milker 15c.; -trix, milk-maid c 1175; -tura, milking c 1175; mungo, to milk 1267.
mulct/ura (mult-), mulct, amercement 1446, 1559; ‡-abilis, "finable" 1570; -atrix, punisher (*f.*) c 950; -ito, to mulct c 1313; *see also* mola, mulcator.
†mulctus, *f.l.* for merciatus, a 1186.
muld/a, -icia, *see* molda.
muldr-, *see* MURDR
mul/ettus, young mule 1515; moulus, *for* -us, mule 1292; *see also* 1 mullo.
mulewellus, *see* 1 morus.
mulg-, *see* mulctrale.
mulier/, wife c 1280, 1304; m. publica, prostitute 1317; m. subintroducta, woman living in priest's house 8c. a 1400, -atus, born in wedlock c 1185, 13c.; -ositas, effeminacy 1555; -osus, effeminate 1528; -o, to play the woman c 1500.
mulin/a, -um, *see* mola.
mullio, *see* 2 molle; mullo (1 & 2).
1 mull/o c 1200, 1429, -io c 1200, fish, (?) mullet; m. aridus, stockfish (Sc.) 1457, 1464; -us c 1200, †millus c 1370, ‡molanus 15c., -ettus 1265, 1535, -ecius c 1234, mullet; *cf.* 1 morus.
2 *mull/o c 1140, 1547, -io 1236, 1467, muillo a 1250, (?) meylo 12c., millo 1296, mollio 1273, c 1380, hay-cock (Fr. *meulon*); -ionatio, stacking 1430; -o 1315, 1325, -iono 1398, to gather (hay) into cocks.
muls-, *see* mulcedo; mulctrale; muscum.
mult-, *see also* mulcator, mulctura.
multi/angulus c 1267, -angularis c 1270, polygonal; -ceps, many-headed 12c.; -cidium, (?) repeated homicide 1194; ‡-cuba, prostitute 1483; -dicus, prolix 7c.; -facio, to multiply c 1197; *-farius c 1188, c 1470, -fer 8c., manifold; -farie, in many ways 7c., c 1000. 1432; -foratilis, fretted (arch.) 12c.; -formitas, multiformity 860. c 1250, c 1362; ‡-gamus, concubinary 1483; -genus, of many nations 1041; -gonus, polygonal 860; -laterus, multilateral 1267; -locus, talkative c 1330; ‡-loquor, "to blab" 1570; -mode, in many ways c 1090, c 1375; -nomicus, -nomius, many-named 1344; -petax, greedy c 950. 12c.

multici/us, *see* molendinum -um, *s.v.* mola.
multilinus, *see* multo.
multiplex, (*subst.*) multiple (math.) a 1250, 13c.; (*adj.*) double-minded 1497, c 1500; having many meanings, ambiguous c 1343; c 730, †multiplius 1480, abundant; multiplic/abilis, able to be multiplied 13c., a 1360; -andus, multiplicand (math.) a 1150, c 1150; -ans a 1150, c 1150, -ator a 1150, multiplier; -ator cunagii, coiner, counterfeiter 1437; -atio, transmutation (alch.) 1456, 1550; -ativus, apt to multiply a 1250, c 1283; pars -ativa, aliquot part a 1200; -atus, number multiplied a 1150; -ior, more varied 12c., c 1250; †-is, in many ways a 1100; -itas *c 1070, c 1400, -itudo c 1365, multiplicity, multitude; ambiguity c 1332, c 1334; †-itus, manifold 1303; -ius, more manifold c 730, 860; -o (metalla), to transmute (alch.) 1418, 1456.
multitoties, *see* multoties.
multi/varius, manifold c 1090; -vidus, seeing much c 950; -vocus, having many names 890. c 1160, 13c.; -volus, variable c 730.
†multivus, multiplex c 1184.
*mult/o 1086, 1566, moto 1370, muto 13c., 1566, mutilo 1277, motulus 1342, mutton, wether, sheep; m. matrix, ewe c 1300; m. silvestris, wild sheep 1250; -o, battering-ram 1244, 1300; head of pile-driver 1292; -o auri a 1327, muto auri 1461, florenus de -one 1360, 1370, *mouton d'or* (coin); -onarius 1307, (?) †-ardus 14c., shepherd; -oninus c 1384, -ilinus 1333, 1347, mutulinus c 1340, c 1392, motulinus 1392, of mutton; mutono, mutumo, to ram 1237; *see also* mola.
multolucens, shining on many 890.
*multoti/es (-ens) 790, 826. c 1100, 1467, multitoties c 1125, c 1451, many times, often.
mul/tra, -trale, -trix, *see* mulctrale.
multrum, *see* MURDR
multur-, *see* mola, mulctrale, mulctura.
mul/vellus, -wellus, -uwellus, *see* 1 morus.
†mum/a, †-ata, measure of soap (Sc.) 12c.
mummia, mummy, gum prepared from mummies (med.) a 1250, ‡14c.
mummo, to act as a mummer 1337.
munamen, *see* 1 munimen.
muncellus, *see* mons.
mun/ctor, swindler c 1180; -go, to defraud, rob c 1200; ‡to snuff a candle 1483.
mund/a c 1110, a 1275, monta c 1102, 'mund', fine, compensation; -iburdium, "commandment of a king" (*cf.* A.S. *mundbyrd*) c 970. ‡c 1440.
mundaylondus, *see* monedinum.
mundro, *see* MURDR
1 mund/us, clear of guilt, purged c 1115; in -um, neatly 15c.; in -um redigo, to make a fair copy of 1439; -atio plumbi, recovering lead from ashes c 1350; -ativus 860. 1276, -ificativus c 1197, 1267, cleansing, purifying; -ator c 760. 14c., -atrix (*f.*) c 1200, cleanser; -ificatio a 1250, c 1503, -ifactura 1512, cleansing, purification; (alch.) 1144, a 1252; -itia, moral purity a 1090, c 1340; -ura, puning 1299; mundifico a 1250, mondo 1324, *for* -o, to purify,

cleanse; **-ifico** c 1115, **-o** c 1192, to purge, clear of an accusation; **-ifico (plumbum)**, to refine a 1292.

2 **mund/us**, world: **mondus** c 1250; **-us minor** a 1150, a 1250, **m. inferior** a 1150, microcosm; **m. totus**, *tout le monde*, everyone 1461; **aliqui in -o** 1219, **a. mundi** 1460, any at all; **dies -i,** (?) weekday 1461; **-ane**, in worldly fashion c 1334; ***-anus** c 730, 842. a 1090, 1461, **-ianus** 6c., **-alis** a 700. 1304, ***-ialis** c 730, 957. c 1090, c 1450, **-inalis** a 1270, worldly, secular; *see also* **annus**; (*subst.*) **-anus** c 1332, c 1450, **-ialis** 1377, secular person, layman; **-ialitas**, worldliness c 1377.

muneda, mountainous land (W. *mynydd*) c 1250, 1307.

munegunga, *see* **mynegunga**.

muner-, *see* **munus**.

munetura, *see* MORTU

mungo, *see* **mulctrale; munctor.**

munialis, *see* 1 **monialis**.

municeps, castellan, constable a 1142, c 1250; ‡"franklin" 1570; **municip/atus,** (?) earldom c 1140; **-ialis**, burgess c 1250; **-iolum**, little town c 1194; **-ium**, *castle, fortress c 1140, 1461; (?) protection c 1125.

munific/entia c 1396, **-ientia** c 1341, munificence (title); **munivicentia**, *for* **-entia**, 873; **-ens**, generous c 1410; **-enter**, generously c 1125; **-o**, to present with a 1100, c 1362.

1 **mun/imen**, enclosure 6c.; ***723. 1083, 1461, †-amen** c 1400, protection, corroboration; **m. arcis** c 1020. 12c., **-imentum arcis** c 793, **-itio arcis** 842, 858, burhbote; **m. pontis**, brigbote c 1020, 12c.; **m. ecclesie**, sanctuary 14c.; **m. carte** 12c., c 1298; **m. scripti** c 1268; ***m. sigilli** c 1192, 1380; **-itatus**, fortification 1341; **-itio**, fortress 9c. c 1153, 1461; garrison 1231, 1461; provisioning 1180, 1416; **m. mortua**, dead stock 1295; **-itiuncula**, small fortress c 1100, c 1320; **-io**, to equip, provision c 1200, 1511; **m. sigillo** 1266, 1461.

2 **mun/imen** 1146, ‡**monimen** 1483, ***-imentum** c 1130, 1536, †**minumentum** 15c., **monumentum** 1390, 1415, **-itio** 1157, muniment, deed, charter; **-imentum**, remembrance c 1325; **-itio**, monition c 1325, a 1564; **-itivus**, admonitory 14c.; **-io**, to admonish, warn c 1250, 1294; *cf.* **monimen.**

†**munio**, castellan a 1142; *see also* **munimen** (1 & 2); *cf.* **municeps.**

munitas, immunity 6c., 7c. 1199.

munitor, *see* **mons.**

munitorius, *see* MINU

†**munium,** (?) function *or* defence 12c.; religious function c 1000.

munivicentia, *see* MUNIFIC

munt-, *see* **mons.**

mun/us, grace (theol.) c 1160; **m. spirituale** c 1337, c 1504; **m. benedictionis**, episcopal blessing 1261, 1296; **m. ecclesiasticum** 15c., **m. rogificum** 15c., ecclesiastical due; **-eratio**, reward c 550; gift c 1218; †**-erative,** (?) by way of reward 1421; **-erator** c 1400, **-uscularius** c 1160, donor; **-usculum**, signet-ring 1457.

muo, *see* 5 **muta.**

mur/a p 1185, c 1190, **-um** a 1200, (?) toft (in salt-marsh); *cf.* 1 **mora.**

mura-, *see also* **murus.**

†**muracidum ferrum**, low-grade iron (? *f.l.* for **mucidum**) c 1227.

muralis, *see* 1 **mora; murus.**

murca, *see* **amurca.**

Murcia, *see* **musca.**

***murdr/um** c 1080, 1587, **-a** c 1115, 1313, **-ia** p 1330, **-edum** 1156, 1566, **murderium** c 1300, **murthra, murthrum, murthium**, **mordrum** 12c., **morthrum** c 1110, **murtrum** (G.) 1289, 1315, **muldrum** 1220, **muldra** c 1130, **multrum** 1322, **-erum** c 1187, **murderatio** a 1540, **morduratio** c 1470, **-igildum** 13c., murder, murderfine; **mordra anime**, destruction of soul c 1340; **m. forinsecum**, murder-fine arising from alien fee 1233; **-aria**, murderess c 1340; **-arius** c 1255, c 1280, **murtrarius** 1215, 1312, **-ator** 1166, c 1370, **murdator** 1530, **-itor** c 1115, c 1258, murderer; **-atus** c 1130, **-itus** c 1115, murdered person; **-o** c 1130, 1629, **-io** c 1115, 1309, **murdo** 1587, **murdero** 1520, 1629, **murthuro** 1392, **mundro** 1204, to murder; **-io appellum**, to quash an appeal (leg.) c 1290.

mure/legus, -lagus, -ligus, *see* **muriceps.**

mur/emium, -ennium, *see* **maeremium.**

1 **mur/ena, -ennum**, *see* **morina.**

2 **murena**, marsh 1559; *cf.* 1 **mora.**

mur/enula, ear-ring c 1095, c 1200; **-inula**, lampern 1430.

muretum, *see* 3 **morus.**

murfaca, *see* **marfaca.**

†**murica,** (?) *f.l.* for **matrix** (*sc.* **ovis**), 1420.

muricatus, purpure (her.) 1654.

mur/iceps 670. c 1200, ***-ilegus** a 1142, a 1446, **-ilega** (*f.*) c 1432, **-ilegius** c 1400, **-elegus** c 1190, a 1408, **-eligus** c 1435, 15c., **-elagus** 1322, †**-legus** 1279, **musio** a 1250, ‡1483, mouse-catcher, cat; **pellis -elegina**, cat-skin 1277; ‡**-icida** 1483, ‡**-icidus** 1538, mouse-killer; ‡**-ion**, mouse-ear (bot.) 14c.; *cf.* **myosuros.**

murin-, *see* **maeremium; morina; murenula; murus.**

†**murisculus,** (?) little stream 13c.; *cf.* **mariscus.**

Murlensis, *see* **Morlanus.**

‡**murmentum**, marmot 1652.

mur/moreus, -murius, -num, *see* **murra.**

murmur/ium 7c. c 1180, c 1330, **marmor** 6c., murmur; ‡**-abilis**, "grudgeable" 1570; **-anter**, querulously c 1470; **-atio**, rumour 1136, 1379; **-osus**, buzzing a 1205; **mar-moreus, mormoreus**, murmuring, roaring 6c.

murosus, *see* 1 **mora.**

murr/a ***1276, 1416, **-um** c 1315, 1371, **murnum** 1341, maple-wood; ***1304, 1497, **-um** 1356, c 1400, †**mucrum** 1292, 1299, **mirra** 1472, †**nirra** 15c., maple-wood bowl, mazer; **m. stans**, standing bowl 15c., 1489; **-eus** c 1266, a 1452, **-inus** c 1250, 14c., **murmoreus** 1416, **murmurius** c 1450, made of maple-wood.

murr/ata, -etus, -eus, *see* 3 **morus.**

murt-, *see* MURDR

muruca, *see* 1 **morus.**

murum, see 3 **morus; mura.**
mur/us defensorius, mill-dam 1450; **m. divisibilis,** party-wall c 1324; **m. indivisibilis,** outside-wall c 1324; **m. maritimus,** sea-wall 1567; **m. siccus,** dry-stone dike 1286, 1501; **reparatio -i,** burhbote 1086; ***-agium,** murage, toll for repair of walls 1128, 1526; **-agiarius,** murager, collector of murage c 1320; **-ale,** wall a 1155, 1392; **-alis,** embattled (her.) c 1595; see also **herba, tegula; ruta -aria,** wall-rue (bot.) 1627; **-arius** 1423, 1432, **-ator** 1420, ‡15c., ‡**-inator** 15c., **-atorius** 1315, 1352, wall-builder, waller; **-atio,** building a wall c 1330, 1532; †fortification c 1436; **-o,** to build a wall c 1140, c 1250; to wall round 1278, 1453; to hem in 15c.
‡**murusculum,** gun c 1440.
murvellus, see 1 **morus.**
mus/ peregrinus, ermine, stoat a 1142; **-ca,** mouse 1478; ‡**-cula,** squirrel 1652; cf. **muriceps.**
1 musa, kind of medicament a 1250; ‡fruit (said to be Adam's apple) 14c.
2 mus/a, muse: **moysa** c 870; **-aicus** c 1325, **-ius** c 1188, **-ivus** c 1212, mosaic; cf. MUSIC
musardus, dullard c 1200, 1291.
musc/a, obolus de, 1239, 1396, **o. de -ia** 1211, c 1310, **o. -e** 1193, 1258, **o. -ii** 1192, 1241, **o. de -ze** 1190, **o. de muca, o. de muce** 1234, 1245, **o. de muz** 1243, **o. murc'** 1262, **o. de Murcia** 1264, 1270, **o. de Murtz** 1300, small gold coin (? of Murcia); **maillia de muz** 1243; **denarius de -e** 1240, 1244, **d. de Murcia** 1270; **marca auri de -ia** 1211; cf. **Massamutinus;** see also **mus, muscum, 2 pannus.**
muscat-, see also **muscus.**
musc/atorium 1295, 1345, **-atoria** c 1296, ‡**-arium, -alarium** 1483, **-ifugium** 1429, fly-flap (esp. eccl. for protecting the host); ‡**-ella,** midge 1570; ‡**-etum, -eletum, -arium, -alarium,** place infested with flies 1483; †**-ivus,** (?) worm-eaten or moss-grown (or f.l. for **mucidus**) c 1125.
musc/hettus, -etus, see **musketus.**
musc/idus, -illago, -ilentus, see **mucilago.**
muscipul/a 9c. a 1142, c 1412, **-us** c 950, trap (fig.); **-o,** to entrap c 1250, c 1308.
musc/ulus 1278, 1486, **-ula** c 1150, 1382, **-lus** 1401, **muskelus** 1358, 1378, mussel; **-ladum,** (?) mess of mussels 1474; see also **mus.**
musc/um c 1300, 1383, **-ida** c 1325, **mussum** 1237, 1292, †**mulsa** 1297, **mossa** 1265, †**masius** 1536, for **-us,** moss; **-a** c 1150, 1318, †**misca** c 1180, **mussa** c 1180, 1386, **mussum** a 1150, c 1200, (?) **mulsum** 13c., **mosca** c 1300, **mossa** c 1210, 1565, †**massa** 1228, **mussetum** 1388, **mossetum** 1357, 1587, †**massetum** 1355, peat-moss, bog; **supervisor mosse** 1401, **s. mosseti** 1536, "moss-reeve" (Lancs.); **mossicus,** boggy c 1450; cf. **muccaria.**
musc/us 13c., ‡14c., **moscus** 1267, musk, etc. (bot.); ‡**m. de campo,** (?) galingale 14c.; ‡**acus -ata,** musk crane's-bill 14c., ‡**herba -ata,** woodruff 14c.; **-ata** 1220, **moschocaryon, moschocaridion** 1538, nutmeg (see also **nux**); **rosa -atella,** musk rose 1620,

1622; **-atum** c 1260, 15c., **-us** 1212, 1218, muscadine wine; **-eleon** a 1250, ‡14c., **-ellinum** a 1250, oil of musk.
musella, tribute levied from pilgrims to Holy Land a 1135.
musellum, see **musum.**
Muselmannus, Mussulman 1586.
music/alis, musician (?) 12c.; 1267, 1537, **musaicus** c 1440, c 1458, musical; **-aliter,** musically 1267; **-um,** faculty of music 13c.; **-o,** to praise c 1362; cf. **2 musa.**
musio, see **muriceps.**
musivus, see **2 musa.**
muskelus, see **musculus.**
mus/ketus 1256, **-chettus** 1234, 1286, **muscetus** a 1446, **muchettus** 1271, 'musket', male sparrow-hawk (falc.).
musona, (?) standard measure (of ale) (cf. O.F. *moison*) 1305.
muss/a, -um, see **muscum;** VETER
mussellus, musshella, see **mons.**
‡**mussetum,** mushroom (cf. μύκης) 15c.; see also **muscum.**
mussit/atio, grumbling, murmuring c 730, 790. c 1125, c 1362; **-o,** to muse c 1197, 1378.
***mustard/um,** mustard c 1250, 1314; **-arius,** mustard-server 1523.
must/elerie (pl.) 1253, **-elaria** 1277, **-ileres** 1290, knee-caps (armour).
must/us, for **-um,** grape-juice 8c.
mus/um c 1250, **-ellum** 1300, 1313, muzzle, snout; **-ellum,** muzzle (for bear) 1252.
1 muta, see **3 mota.**
2 muta, see **1 mitta.**
3 muta, measure of wine 1198, 1273; cf. **2 mata, modius.**
4 mut/a, name of a small (? muted) bell c 1255; mute (letter) 1220, ‡1570; **-itas,** dumbness 1380; **-eo,** to be dumb 1378, 1426.
5 *mut/a a 1150, 1333, **muia** 1171, **mua** 1198, **-atorium** a 1250, **-atoria domus** a 1446, mew (falc.); **accipiter de duabus -is,** twice-mewed hawk 1179; **-arius** 1201, 1281, **muarius** 1237, 1275, **muerius** 1255, **muerus** 1242, **-atorius** 1331, **-orius** 1235, **-uarius** 1199, mewed; **-atio,** mewing a 1150, a 1446; **-o** a 1108, 1425, **muo** 1255, 1535, to mew, moult.
mutakefia, mutual equality (Ar.) 12c.
mut/amen c 1470, **-amentum** 1325, change; **-abunda,** (?) reed c 1000; **-abundus,** changeable c 1300; **-atio,** exchange c 1150, 1254; **m. vite,** entering religion a 1200; **-atorium** (bibl.), **motatorium** 6c., ‡**-arium** 15c., change of raiment; **-atorius,** for changing (of clothes) 7c. a 1250, 15c.; **-ativus,** causing change c 1360; **-atrix,** changer (f.) c 1250; **-o faciem,** (?) to cover the face c 1250; ***-o vitam,** to enter religion c 1120, c 1270; **-or,** to break (of a child's voice) c 1335.
mutatim, see MUTU
mutil/atio *a 1142, 1562, **mutulatio** 1423, ‡**-amen** 15c., mutilation, maiming; curtailment 7c.; **-ator** 12c., 1266, **mutulator** c 1333, mutilator; **m. pecunie,** coin-clipper 1278; **-o,** to castrate c 1115; to deprive 1219, 15c.; **mutulo,** for **-o,** to mutilate 1189, 15c.
‡**mutilus,** garfish a 1520.

mut/o, -ilo, -ono, -uno, *see* multo.

mutu/itas, reciprocity c 1290, p 1300; -atim 1271, **mutatim** c 1266, c 1330, †mituo 1421, mutually; †mituus, *for* -us, mutual 1421; -ator, borrower 1204; -icapio, to borrow 1324; -o, *to lend c 1163, 15c.; (?) to obtain on credit 1260; to purchase p 1330; to exchange, transpose c 1265, c 1400.

mutul-, *see* multo; MUTIL

mutura, *see* mola.

muvellus, *see* 1 morus.

‡mya, blind man's buff (μυῖα) 1570.

Mylerensis, (?) *for* Miliarensis, coin (Sp.) a 1275.

‡mylphe (*pl.*), eye-salves 1652.

mynecena, nun (A.S.) 1009.

myn/egunga (†-igunga, †munegunga), monition (A.S.) c 1115.

myosuros, mouse-tail (bot.) 1634.

myoura, *see* mica.

myra, conserve 1622.

Myrcius, *see* Mercius.

myri/as, myriad, ten-thousand 1562, c 1620; -adalis, ten-thousand-fold 1344; -ophyl-lum, (milfoil bot.) 7c.

myric/a (miric-) a 1250, 1397, **merica** 1402, 1553, †mereta 1287, †meruta 1378, shrub (esp. broom); -etum, thicket of broom c 1150, ‡1652.

myristica a 1250, **nux m.** a 1250, ‡1570, nutmeg.

myrm/icaleo, ant-lion 7c.; -icina, *for* -ecium, kind of wart a 1250.

myrobalanum, myrobalan (bot.): **mirabo-lanum** a 1250, ‡14c.

myrt/igerus, myrtle-bearing c 1180; ‡-acantha, wild myrtle 14c.; †mirce-tum, *for* -etum, 1344; -illus, myrtle-berry a 1250, ‡14c.; †virotus, (?) *for* -us, c 1257.

‡mysis, stoppage of pores (μύσις) 1652.

myst/a (mist-), devotee (of a game) 1516; -es, (?) priest 1562; -agogia, revelation 1564; -erialis, mysterious, supernatural c 1150, c 1470; ‡-erialiter, privily 1483; -eriarcha, celebrant of eucharist 990; *-erium c 1090, 1552, **m. divinum** c 1000. c 1187, c 1296, eucharist; *see also* MINIST; -ice, mystically 7c. c 1180, 1461; -ico, to symbolize 1245, 1252.

mystron, liquid measure (6 *cochlearia*) c 1100; *cf.* cignus.

mythologia, mythology: **methologia** c 1500.

N

nabil/itas, buoyancy c 1260; -is, buoyant, sea-worthy c 1160.

nabl/a, *for* -um, musical instrument a 1100; ‡-arius, "nakerer" c 1440.

nabulum, *see* naulum.

nacaria (*pl.*) 1303, **nacharia** a 1347, naker, kettledrum; **nakerarius**, drummer 1338.

nacella, *see* navis.

1 ‡nacta, pectoral abscess 1652.

2 nacta (nakta), a rich fabric (O.F. *nac*) a 1390.

nacticus, *see* sal.

nadir c 1233, c 1380, **gnadir** a 1400, nadir (astr.); **nader**, orrery (astr.) 14c.

nagia, *see* natis.

†nagilie, (?) *f.l.* for **Vergilie** (astr.), c 1270.

nahamo, *see* namium.

†nahuna, (?) *f.l.* for **pastura**, c 1200.

nailforgium, nail-smithy 1357.

naio (nayo) 1219, c 1277, **neo** 1276, to drown (Fr. *noyer*).

naivitas, namitas, *see* NATIV

nak-, *see* nac-

nallum, *see* naulum.

nam, *for* sed, but c 600.

*nam/ium a 1100, 1419, -um, -us 1090, 1400, -a c 1130, 1273, -ea 1292, (?) †nauvia c 1308, †naumeum 1275, -num 1080, 1096, -pnum c 1130, 12c., -nium c 1197, †nantum 1248, nemia 15c., (goods seized in) distress, distraint; n. excussum, forcible rescue of distress 1166; *n. vetitum 1198, 1481, n. wetitum 1275, *vee de naam*, pre-vention of distress (leg.); -atio (Sc.) c 1300, 1473, -iatio 1223, 1258, distraining; -iator, distrainer 1204; *-io c 1115, 1375, -o 1204, 1509, †-tio 1177, nahamo 1290, to distrain, distrain upon.

nampa, a disease of hawks (falc.) a 1446.

nanio, to dwarf c 1180.

*nap/a (napp-) c 1160, 1288, table-cloth *or* napkin; -ero, -erona 1215, 1285, -rona c 1410, small table-cloth *or* apron; 1315, -ro 1313, apron (worn by falconers); -aria 1405, 1433, -eria 1346, 1430, -iria 1395, napery, table-linen; 13c., c 1290, -eria 1208, 1300, -ria 1390, -reum 1415, napery (service or office); -arius, naperer, keeper of the napery c 1110, 1230; *cf.* MAPP

napellus, monkshood (bot.) a 1250, 1632.

narc/os, cramp-fish, torpedo a 1200; -oticus, narcotic a 1200, 1620.

nard/us rustica, asarabacca (bot.) 1538; -ileon, oil of spikenard a 1250, ‡14c.; -ifluus, fragrant c 1100, c 1414.

nar/is (*s.*), nostril c 1200; ‡-icus, snivelling 1483; ‡-ico, to snivel 1483; ‡-io, to scoff 1483.

*narr/atio c 1115, a 1564, -atus 1243, count, statement of claim in pleading (leg.); (?) cry-ing for sale 1339; n. pecunie, counting out of money 1311; -amentum c 1450, -atus a 1100, 1239, narrative; -ative, by counting c 1470; in narration c 1470; -ator, tale-bearer 1279; teller (Exchequer official) 1357, 1447; 'counter', pleader, advocate (leg.) 1220, 1377; n. Banci c 1250, n. de Banco 1268, serjeant-at-law; n. com-munis, common serjeant (London) 1373, c 1490; ‡-ito, to narrate 1483; -o, to tell, count (money) 1250, 1329; *to 'count', plead, make a claim (leg.) 1220, 1419; (?) to cry for sale 1339.

nasale, *see* nascale; nasus.

‡nas/cale (-ale, -care, -caplere) 14c. †-tare a 1250 'nascal' pessary (med.).

‡nascativion, an Indian tree (νάσκαφθον) 14c.
nascella, see navis.
nasci/tura, birth 1372; -o, see natio.
‡nasda, natta, "gibbus" 1652.
nasellum, see nasus; vas.
Nasidienita, devotee of Nasidienus, nouveau riche c 1160.
nassa, weir, fishery (G.) 1280, 1309.
nast-, see nascale; nostla.
nas/us, spout, nozzle 1417, c 1500; -ale 1136, -ellum c 1190, 'nasal', nose-piece of helmet; tube for nasal injection a 1250 (cf. nascale); -atus, big-nosed c 1400.
nata, see natis.
nat/abundus, swimming a 1186; ‡-or, swimmer 1483; -ito, to swim 1461; -o (trans.), to drown c 1362 (cf. naio).
natal/e (†-ium), -icium, natus, birth, status (for assessment of weregeld) c 1115; c 730. 12c., c 1400, -is c 1303, -icium 7c., 980. 12c., c 1362, birthday, saint's day; *1185, 1532, -is 1234, 1508, -icium c 1250, 1336, -e Domini 1086, c 1514, dies -is Domini 11c., -e Dominicum c 1170, c 1324, -icium Dominicum c 1460, 1476, Christmas; firma -is, Christmas farm c 1115; panis -icius, (?) Christmas loaf c 1200.
nathineus, one of the Nethinim (Heb.), sub-deacon c 1182, ‡c 1440.
naticus, see sal.
natio, territory, habitation c 1400; 'nation', group of students (ac.) c 1350, 1453; nascio, nation 1252.
nat/is, buttock: -a c 1330, ‡-ica, -icula 1483, nagia 1227.
nativ/itas, birth, status (for assessment of weregeld) c 1115; nativity, horoscope (astr.) 1344, 1620; birth-place c 1218; 1198, 15c., naivitas (†namitas, nayvitas) 1250, 1328; naevitas 1443, †navietas 1304, navitas c 1400, neyvitas 1354, neovitas 1414, noevitas 1528, neifty, villein status; *birth-day, saint's day 12c., 15c.; 1086, c 1340, n. Christi c 1400, n. Domini c 1250, c 1400, festum -itatis Dominice c 1250, 1501, Christmas; *n. beate (Virginis) Marie (8 Sept.) 1086, c 1450; *-us 1155, 1583, homo -us a 1188, 1315, -a (f.) 1185, 1583, mulier -a c 1362, neif, villein; (?) soke-man 1290; taeog (W.) 1334, 1355; native (subst.) 1461; *terra -a, land held by villein tenure 1277, 1611; -us conventionarius 1297, 1355, -a conventionaria (f.) 1355, conventionary tenant (Cornwall) -us de stipite (Cornwall) 1355, n. de sanguine 1399, c 1418; -um, birthright c 1400; -e teneo, to hold in villeinage 1396, c 1442.
nat/ron, -aron, see NITR
*nat/ta c 1125, 1376, -ula c 1220, reed mat; -taria, mat-dealer (f.) 1326; cf. matta; see also nasda.
natur/a cunabilis, infancy c 1290; n. instituta, n. destituta, nature before and after the Fall (theol.) c 1334; n. -ans, creative nature c 1250, 1620; n. -ata, created nature 13c.; n. quinta, quintessence a 1200; in rerum n., in existence c 1290, c 1343; facio -am c 1305, f. -alia c 1250, to relieve nature (cf. NECESS, SECRET); -alia, works on natural philosophy 1267, 15c.; -alis (adj.), con-

cerned with natural philosophy 12c., a 1446; native-born 1204, c 1250; see also dies, dominus, filius, historia, scientia; (subst.) neif, villein c 1124, c 1200; natural philosopher, naturalist 1267, c 1470; native c 1250, c 1450; -alizatio, naturalization 1608; bene -atus, naturally good 1344; -o, to produce naturally 1344.
natus, see natale.
naucella, see navis.
naucipendo, to set at naught c 900. c 1190, ‡1483.
†naucupletio, ship-load 12c.
naufrag/ium, wreckage, right of wreck c 1115, c 1500; -or, to be shipwrecked c 1125, c 1450.
*naul/um 9c. a 1100, c 1530, †haulum 1289, nallum c 1530, ‡nabulum c 1440, -agium (G.) 1289, passage-money, freight; -icus, paid for freight 12c.; -ificator 1528, -isator 1523, pilot.
naumachia, sea-fight 12c., ‡c 1440.
naumeum, see namium.
nausa, swampy pasture-land (Fr. noue) (G.) 1291.
naus/ea, object of loathing c 1190; usque ad -eam a 1142; -eatio, vomiting a 1250; -eo, to loathe c 1125, c 1170; -ito, to disgust, bore a 1100.
†naut/arius, (?) head boatman 1352; -iceus c 550, naviticus c 1350, for -icus, nautical; †-o, (?) to carry by boat 1279.
nautegildum, see noutegeldum.
nauvia, see NAM
nav/ietas, -itas, see nativitas.
nav/is, *nave (of church) c 1125, 1586; (?) ounce (weight) c 1250; *1303, c 1510, *-icula c 1160, c 1500, -icella 1518, nacella c 1220, 1272, -etta c 1321, -ettum c 1400, incense-boat; -ella c 1325, †-etula 1321, naucella c 1125, c 1200, nacella 1274, nascella 1225, 1229, small boat (cf. vas); -icula, weaver's shuttle a 1200, ‡c 1483; house-top 9c.; n. ecclesie, (?) crypt 13c.; n. de Venetiis, astr. instrument, zaouraq a 1400; †-a 1252, *-ata c 1160, 1419, -iculata 1277, -iagium 1285, ship-load; -alis (sc. scientia), navigation c 1457; -iductor, skipper (Dutch) 1442; -ifactiva c 1300, -igatoria 1267, art of ship-building; -atim, by ship 1322; -eria, fishing-weir (G.) 1293; -igalis, concerned with sailing c 1362; -igatio, freight 1500, 1505; -iger, sailor 1547; -igium 1086, 1382, -agium 1192, 1262, -iagium 1391, carriage by water, shipping service (or toll); *a 1100, 1461, -agium 1296, -egium 1263, fleet; voyage c 1220, c 1250; (?) sailor p 1377; -igo, to transport by water 1376.
naviticus, see NAUT
nayo, see naio.
nayvitas, see nativitas.
Nazareatus, status of Nazirite 1610.
ne, for ut non (consecutive), c 1135, 1520; for ne...quidem, c 1180,14c.; for nec, a 1250; ne proinde, for nedum, 13c.; nedum, not only c 1396, 1447.
neatus, see netus.
‡nebrid/a, "ribbing-skin" 15c., c 1483; ‡-o, to "rib", scrape (flax) 1483.

*neb/ula c 1170, 15c., -la 1310, neula (? nevla) 1295, -ulo c 1335, obley, wafer; -ularius c 1136, -ulator 15c., obley-maker.
nebul/ator a 1205, 1286, -o 1291, fool, jester; -atrix, harlot 1221; -onice, impudently 1523; -onicus, impudent 1518.
nebul/atus a 1450, -osus c 1595, nebuly (her.); -ose, obscurely c 1350; ‡-gea, salt formed from atmospheric moisture 1652; -esco, to become cloudy c 1184.
nec/, not even 1341; nec . . . aut c 1250, 1385, nec ... vel c 1330, neither . . . nor; -ne, for -non, 10c., c 1000. c 1125, c 1140; for nondum, c 1000; nec omitted in first of successive negative clauses 1384.
nec/atio c 1300, c 1335, -atura c 1380, slaughtering; †nex, (?) death by drowning c 600; -abilis c 1250, -atrix (f.) 9c., -ifer a 1275, deadly, murderous; -o, to flood 1086; cf. naio.
necess/e, need, necessity c 1115; n. habeo, to be bound c 900. 1279, 1384; -aria c 1195, 15c., -arium 1356, 1395, cellula -ariorum c 1185, -itatis secrete locus c 1450, privy (see also camera, domus); -aria (n. pl.) nature c 1185, c 1245; -ario, by all means c 1087; -ario-serviens, slave (A.S. nydþeowan) c 1115; -arius, useful c 1270, 1271; suitable, qualified 13c.; -etissimus, most cogent c 1340; -itabilis, potentially necessary 1344, a 1361; subject to compulsion a 1350; -itas, strain, suffering c 1000; emergency 1499; necessary object 12c.; n. ecclesie, ecclesiastical payment, due 1017, 11c.; n. expeditionis, military service, fyrd c 799; n. trimoda, fyrd, burhbote, and brigbote †680 (c 1000); de -itate c 1341, c 1474, de -e 1460, necessarily; -itatio, necessitation, compulsion 1344; -itativus, compulsive 1344, c 1367; *-ito, to compel, constrain c 1277, 1440.
necglig-, neclig-, see negligentia.
necio, see nescio.
necka, see 1 snecka.
neco, see necatio; NEG
necotiana, see nicotiana.
‡necro/comica (pl.), portents by objects falling from air 1652; ‡-lium, prophylactic against death 1652; -logium, necrology 16c.; -mantica, sorceress 1528; nicromantia c 1250, nigrimantia 1432, *nigromantia c 1125, c 1446, for -mantia, necromancy; -manticus 1419, 15c., negromanticus c 1380, nigromanticus c 1212, c 1447, necromancer, sorcerer; nigromanticus, necromantic 12c., 16c.
nect/ar, spiced wine c 1200, ‡1652; -arinus a 1275, -orius c 550, nectar-sweet; -areo, to sweeten, perfume c 1250.
ned/acra, 'need-acre', boon-acre, acre subject to ploughing service c 1283; -erepium, -ripum, reaping service 1408.
nedelum, 'needle', temporary wooden prop 1434.
nedulus, white c 550.
nedum, see ne.
neelo, see nigellus.
nefflatum, see rieflacum.
neflum, medlar (Fr. nèfle) 1300, 1315.
nefre-, see NEPHRE

neg/amen, veto c 1470; -atio, purgation (leg.) c 1115; n. singularis c 1115, n. simplex 13c.; n. triplex 13c.; -ativa, a negative c 1332, c 1357; -ative, *in the negative c 1125, c 1470; by way of denial (leg.) 1306, 1684; *-ativus, negative c 1250, 1686; -atorie, by way of refusal c 1430; neco, to deny 1278; -o, to abjure Christianity c 1190; (with inf.), to refuse 8c. 1369, c 1400; n. ab, to distinguish from a 1323; to withhold from, deny to c 1343.
neggildo, see meggildo.
negligentia, act of negligence c 730; necglig/ens 1293, -entia 1289, c 1470, neclig/enter c 1466, -entia 1282, c 1511, -o 1340, c 1514, for neglig-; nexglexit, for neglexit, 1417.
negot/ia (pl.), goods purchased a 1220, 1457; n. secularia, worldly affairs c 1125, 1414; †-io (? -iatio), commerce 1290; -iatio, activity p 1300; -iativus, active, busy p 1300; -iositas, devotion to business c 1220; ‡-ius, hobgoblin 15c.
negromanticus, see NECRO
nemes/es (pl.), retributions 1620; -o, to be indignant 1344.
nemia, see NAM
nemirum, see nimirum.
nemo, (adj.) none c 1102.
nempe, indeed: nemphe, nimphe c 1000.
Nemphroteus, disciple of Nimrod 1344.
nem/usculum, underwood, scrub 1086; nimus, wood (material) 1444; wooden tablet a 1520; -orista, woodlander c 1325; ‡-orarius, forester 1570.
‡nenior, to babble 1483.
†nenora, kind of speckled fish c 1200.
nenuphar/ (-far) a 1250, 1538; newfar, ninufer 1414, water-lily; -inus, made of water-lily a 1250; ‡-eni (pl.) aerial spirits 1652.
neo, see naio.
neo/apostolus, new or first apostle 13c.; -martyr, recent martyr c 1180, 1200; neumenia 13c., -nides c 1212, new moon; -phyta c 730, -phytus 980. 1096, c 1540, -bitus 760, neophyte, novice (eccl.); neutericus, for -tericus, new, modern c 685, 950; scriptura -terica a 615.
‡neopellum, spindle-whorl 1483.
neovitas, see nativitas.
nep/eta, calaminth (bot.): -ita a 1250, ‡14c., ‡-ta 13c.
nepeus, scorpion 9c.
nephilis, cloudy part of urine (νεφέλιον) a 1250.
nephre/sis (nefre-), nephritis a 1250, ‡1470; -ticus, nephritic c 1200, ‡14c.; neufrocatharum, purge of kidneys a 1250.
nep/os, nephew c 1090, 1461; kinsman 1253; ‡"stagnum aëneum" (alch.) 1652; -otulus, young nephew c 1458; -otatio, prodigality a 1142; -ta, for -tis, niece 1139, c 1307.
nepta, (?) for naphtha, tinder c 550; see also nepeta, nepos.
neptunus, brownie c 1212.
nequando, never 9c.
nequi/tiosus 1345, 1523, -osus 15c., wicked.
nera, see NIGR
nerenus, see ninerus.

‡**neriges,** nightmare, incubus 15c.

Neronizo, to play the Nero c 1200.

nerv/us sensibilis c 1200, c 1270, **n. sensarius** 1649, sensory nerve; **-a,** *for* **-us,** sinew c 1362; **-alis** 1267, **-icus** c 1320, **-inus** c 1410, belonging to a sinew, sinewy; **unguentum -ale** 1414; **-itia,** strength 1269; **-o,** (?) *for* enervo, c 1180.

nescio, to be ignorant: **necio** 1212, 1293, **nessio** 1212, c 1310.

nessum, ness, headland (Sc.) c 1180, c 1265.

netarius, *see* NOT

netrix, spinster 1355.

net/us 13c., 1348, **-is** 1234, **neatus** 13c., **nietus** 1189, class of villein (A.S. *geneat*).

neufrocatharum, *see* NEPHRE

neula, *see* nebula.

neu/ma, -pma, *see* pneuma.

neumenia, *see* NEO

Neustr/ensis 1150, c 1385, **-icus** 1252, Norman.

‡**neuta,** caul 1652.

neutegeldum, *see* noutegeldum.

neuter, indifferent, impartial 1378; **neutr/alitas,** neutrality c 1160, 1521; **-aliter,** neutrally c 1255, c 1430; in the neuter (gram.) c 700; without reference to gender 1374; **-atus,** (*adj.*) (?) of neutral tint c 1180; (*subst.*) eunuch c 1213; **-opassivus,** semideponent (gram.) 8c. 1524; **-o,** to make neuter (gram.) c 1225.

neutericus, *see* NEO

nev/us, blemish c 1125, c 1362; **sine -o,** without prejudice c 950.

newfar, *see* nenuphar.

nex, *see* necatio.

nex/us curie, imposition, obligation 12c., c 1227; **-atus,** knitted 1555.

ney/landa, island (in Thames) 1450, 1463; **-ta,** ait, eyot (in Thames) 1450, 1463.

neyvitas, *see* nativitas.

nichil, nichil-, *see* NIHIL

nichon, 'louvel', siege-engine (νικῶν) c 1306.

Nico/laita 12c., c 1430, **†-alita** 1267, Nicolaitan heretic (bibl.).

nicotiana 1634, 1701, **necotiana** 1634, tobacco.

nicromantia, *see* NECRO

nicrum (? **incrum**), sort of cloth 1215.

nidius, *see* indus.

nid/us, home of villein 1308; 'nest', set (of boxes, *etc.*) 1472, 1474; **n. avis,** bird's-nest (bot.) 1634; **†-ifer,** (?) nesting c 793; **-ificatio,** nest-building c 1190, c 1325.

nietus, *see* netus.

nigell/a a 1250, ‡1570, **-astrum** 1634, corn-cockle (bot.).

nigell/us, black c 1000; (*subst.*) black-haired man 8c.; **-o** (†ingello) c 1180, 15c., **neelo** 1245, to inlay in niello.

†Nigra (? **Virga**), name of a comet c 1270.

nigr/edo, stain c 730; black dye 1287; **-edulus,** Negro c 1200; **-ifer,** black 8c.; **-ogemmeus** c 730, c 1150, c 1315, **niger-gemmeus** c 730, of a black gem, jet; **nera,** black cherry (?) a 1250, ‡14c.; **-um,** black cloth 1393; **niger badius,** dark bay (of a horse) 1317; **n. liardus** 1316; *see also* **canonicus, corium, frater, 2 mina, monachus, moneta, monialis, opus,**

ordo, panis, pars, sal, spina, 2 stagnum, Turonensis.

nigromant-, nigrimant-, *see* NECRO

nihil/itas, nothingness p 1381; **-ior,** less than nothing a 1205; ***nichil, nichilum** 1021. 1086, c 1533; **nichilominus** c 1217, c 1516, **nilhominus** 704, **-hominum** 868, *for* **-ominus; episcopatus nichilensis** c 1382; **-o,** to destroy, annihilate c 1180, a 1408.

nimirum, assuredly: **nemirum** 1440.

nimph-, ninfea, *see* nempe; NYMPH

nimus, *see* NEM

†nina, (?) trick, means (or (?) *f.l.* for **mina**) a 1385.

nin/erus a 1446, ‡15c., **‡-arius** 15c., **‡-irus** 1483, **†nerenus** 15c., cuckold.

ninufer, *see* nenuphar.

nipa, *see* jupa.

nipulus, *see* cnipulus.

nirra, *see* murra.

nisi *a 1142, 1585, **n. tantum** c 1300, a 1446, *for* **non n.,** only; than 1321; 1475, **n. prius** c 1290, 1444, *nisi prius* (leg.).

nis/us c 1180, 1547, **-a** (*f.*) c 1200, hawk, (?) sparrow-hawk (falc.); **n. rubeus,** sore hawk 1274, 14c.

nithingus, nithing, dastard c 1115.

nitid/us, fresh (of bread) c 730; **-ius,** more brightly c 1000.

nitr/um, natron, lye, potash c 550. c 1215, c 1350; **†-a rosa** (?) 13c.; **-ositas,** nitrosity a 1250; **‡nat/ron, -aron** 1652, **anatron** 1144, ‡1652, nitre, saltpetre.

niv/ealis, *for* **-alis,** formed from snow c 1362; **‡-enodium,** snowball 1483.

niveo, to wink c 1340.

†nixutorius, strenuous a 1250.

noa c 1150, **nova** 1313, 'sound', swimming bladder, *etc.* (of fish) (Fr. *noue*).

*nobil/e c 1365, 1509, **-is** a 1347, 1535, **-us** 1532, **-ia** 1406, **-e Anglicanum** 1422, **-e aureum** 1401, a 1564, noble (coin); **Georgius -is,** George noble c 1470; **-ata,** noble's worth 1385; **-is,** thane c 1115; nobleman c 1250, c 1590; **falco -is,** falcon gentle a 1280; **novilissimus,** *for* **-issimus,** c 730; ***-itas,** nobility (title) c 1170, 1452; **-itatio,** ennoblement 1361, 1620; **-ito,** to ennoble 12c., 1608; to act in a lordly way c 1180.

noc/a (**nocta, nocka, noka**) 1231, 1347, **-ata** 1301, 1552, nook (measure of land); *see also* **nux.**

noc/entia 13c., c 1376, **-itura** c 1138, ***-umentum** c 1125, 1461, **-imentum** c 1317, 1394, **-ivitas** c 1270, c 1375, harm, injury, nuisance; **-ibilis** c 1260, **-ifer** 12c., **-itivus** a 1250, **-umentivus** 1394, harmful; **-ivior,** more harmful c 1343, c 1444; **-uum** 1463, **-umentum** 1483, weed.

nochia, *see* nusca.

nocium *see* nux.

noct-, *see also* nox; NYCT

†nocta, button of glove 1385; *cf.* **nodulus;** *see also* **noca.**

nocuplus, *see* NOVEM

nod/ula c 1410, c 1540, **-olus** c 1550, (?) *for* **monedula,** jackdaw *or* chough; **‡-osa,** "ouzel" 15c.

nod/us, knob, boss 1245, c 1503; boss (at

intersection of ribs in fan-vaulting) 1432, 1471; (?) blockage in gallery of mine 1302; multiple of ten (math.) 1145; **n. ascendens**, ascending node (astr.) 1686; **n. capitis**, (?) crown of head 1411; ‡**n. rose**, rose-gall, bedeguar 14c.; **-atus**, embossed 1295; **-ifex**, girdler 1561; **-ositas (lingue)**, vigour c 970; **-ulum**, knot, joint c 1362; **-ulus** 1344, 1419, (?) **-ile** 1403, button; 1448, (?) **nuwellus** 1241, boss; **-ulatio**, knotting (of cloth) 1465, 1587; **-ulatus**, knotted c 1340; *see also* **crux**; **-ulo**, to button 1299.

noeletta, *see* **nola**.

‡**noera**, cover of alembic (alch.) 1652.

noevitas, *see* **nativitas**.

noffus, coffin (Frankish) c 1115.

***nol/a** c 1102, c 1520, **-ea** 1245, **-ula** c 1182, **noeletta** (falc.) 1215, 1235, little bell.

nol/itio p 1300, **-utio** 1344, c 1365, **-untas** 1304, c 1620, unwillingness; **-ubilis**, undesirable 1344; **-us**, one who is unwilling c 600; **-ens volens**, willy-nilly 1684; **-i me tangere**, ulcer c 1200, ‡14c.; balsam (bot.) 1641; **-o pro mille marcis** (expression of unwillingness) 13c.

nomannia (‡**nomaimia**) (*pl.*), no man's land (N.E. of London) 1366.

nomen proprium, baptismal name 1390; **per n.**, under the description 1507; **ex nomin/e**, by name c 1200, c 1410; **-etenus**, so-called, nominal c 793, c 800; **-abilis**, nameable c 865. c 1115, c 1365; **-ale**, roll of names 1433; **-alis**, (*adj.*) of a noun 13c., p 1381; nominal, in name only 1413; (*subst.*) nominalist c 1160, 1168; **-aliter**, as a noun c 850. 1267, c 1370; by name 1312, 1438; **-anter**, specifically a 1252; **-atim**, by name (of pleas) c 1115; **-atio**, naming, mentioning 8c. c 1115, c 1470; **-ative** c 793. 12c., 1219, **-ativo** c 1148, (?) c 1193, by name; in the nominative (gram.) 13c., c 1300; **-ativitas**, occurrence in the nominative 13c.; **-ativus**, renowned c 1370; **-ator**, nominator (at election) 1264, c 1350; **-atior**, more renowned 10c.; **naminatus**, named 867; *see also* **dos, pecunia**; **-o**, to denote (log.) c 1160; to name (of pleas) c 1115; to assign 1418.

nomisma, coin, coinage: ***numisma (nummisma)** 8c. c 1185, 1486.

nommus, *see* NUMM

non (**dico**, *etc.*, **quod non**), no c 1290, c 1320; *for* **ne** (with *imp.*, *etc.*) 8c. a 1170, c 1450; **nundum**, *for* **nondum**, c 1227, c 1285.

non/a, noon 1086, 1500; nones (eccl.) c 1125, c 1344; subsidy of a ninth 1297, c 1400; ninth, second tithe (eccl.) 1341, 1355; **n. alta**, high noon 1248; **-agesies**, *for* **-agies**, 1267; **-ogesimus**, *for* **-agesimus**, c 1295; **-aginti**, nine hundred c 1310; **-eus**, of or for noon 11c.; **nonodecimalis** (‡**novo-**), of or for 19 years 13c.

non/-accidens, what is not an accident (log.) 13c.; **-admissio**, non-admission (eccl.) 1307; **-adventus** 1212, 1494, **-apparentia** 1422, non-appearance (leg.); **-agia**, nonage, minority c 1480; **-attendentia**, non-attendance 1627; **-causa ut causa**, a logical fallacy p 1300; **-celebrans**, non-celebrant priest 1496: **-celestia** (*pl.*), earthly

objects c 1220; **-clameum**, non-claim 1331; **-comparentia** 1475, **-comparitio** c 1373, 1389, non-appearance (leg.); **-compassio**, incompatibility c 1270; **-confiteri**, non-confession p 1381; **-corpus**, incorporeal stuff 1267; **-custodia**, non-observance c 1520; **-ens**, a non-existent c 1270, 1620; **-entitas** 13c., **-esse** a 1233, 1267, non-existence; **-eternus**, non-eternal c 1270; **-executio**, non-execution 1439; **-exhibitio**, non-payment a 1447; **-existentia**, non-existence a 1233, 1378; **-finibilitas**, illimitability a 1233; **-inceptio**, existence from eternity 1378; **-intelligens**, non-intelligent c 1270; **-introitus**, non-entry (Sc.) 1539, 1566; **-jurare** (*subst.*), non-swearing 1324; **-movens**, non-moving 13c.; **-motor**, non-mover a 1233.

nondinor, *see* NUNDIN

noneus, *see* **nona**.

nonn/a c 1000, 11c. 1086, 1155, **nunna** c 1115, c 1425, nun, anchoress; blue-tit 1544; **-o**, monk 747; **-us**, senior monk 981; title applied to Pope a 615; dan (mon. title) c 1245, c 1330.

non/nullies, several times c 1350; **-numeralis**, non-numerical a 1233; **-observatio**, non-observance 1274; **-obstante**, notwithstanding 1226, 1587; **-obstantia**, clause of reservation c 1352, 1407; **-omittas**, name of a writ 1335; **-ordinatio**, non-ordination (eccl.) 1302.

nono/decimalis, -gesimus, *see* **nona**.

nonotrochalus, *see* **onocrotulus**.

non/-paritio, non-appearance, default (leg.) 1516, 1520; **-perpetuus**, non-perpetual c 1270; **-plevina**, default of surety 13c.; **-prestatio**, non-payment 1341; **-prosecutio**, default of prosecution c 1290; **-quantus**, devoid of quantity c 1380; **-ratio**, illegality 1194, 13c.; **-recuperabilia** (*pl.*), irrecoverable debts 1479; **-reditus**, failure to return c 1364; **-regens**, non-regent (ac.) c 1306, c 1503; **-religiosus**, someone not under monastic vow c 1245; **-reparatio**, disrepair 1384; **-residentia**, non-residence (eccl.) 1300, a 1564; **-sacerdos**, one who is not a priest c 1450.

nonschenchum 1410, **nouncheynchum** 1375, nuncheon, midday meal.

non/-secta, non-suit (leg.) c 1290, 1412; **-separalis**, not held in severalty 1411; **-servatio**, non-observance c 1423; **-socius**, one who is not a fellow (ac.) c 1292; **-solutio**, non-payment c 1400, 1543; **-solvendo**, insolvent 1310; **-subjectum**, what is not a subject (log.) c 1270; **-substantia**, non-substance (log.) 13c., c 1270; **-tempus**, timelessness 13c.; **-tenura**, non-tenure 1227, c 1285; **-titulus**, non-title (leg.) 1298; **-usus**, non-user, disuse 1367, 1428; **-vivus, -vivens**, lifeless c 1270.

nord-, *see* NORMANN; NORTH

Nor/ensis a 1180, p 1340, **-icus** a 1142, 1269, **-dicus** a 1142, **-iscus** 1130, 1159, **-us** (?) 11c., **-thigena** a 1100, **-thwigena**, **-dguigena** a 1142, **-reganus (-raganus, -riganus)** a 1100, c 1370, **-wagenus (-vagenus)** 12c., c 1315, **-wegius** 1252, **-wingus** c 1170, **-wegensis (-wagensis)**

1150, c 1360, **-guigensis** c 1385, Norse, Norwegian.

‡**norga**, "wreck of the sea" c 1440.

norm/a, monastic rule c 1090, c 1325; **-ula**, rule 760, c 1060. c 1125, c 1470; **-alis**, regular (mon.) c 950. a 1275; perpendicular (geom.) 1686; **-aliter**, according to rule (mon.) c 980; perpendicularly 1686; **-atrix**, abbess c 950.

*****Normann/us** a 910. 1087, c 1450, **North-mannus** a 1000. 1324, 1620, **Nordman-nus** a 910, **-icus** c 1130, c 1595, **-igena** c 1170, 14c., Norseman, Norman; **-anglus**, **Normanglus**, Anglo-Norman 12c.

North/anhymbrus, **-anhumbrus** a 1000. c 1100, c 1250, **Nordanhymbrus** c 730, a 910, **-umbranus**, **-umbrianus** c 1100, c 1315, **-umbrensis** c 1350, **-umbrus** 1528, Northumbrian.

north/us 12c., **nordus** a 1200, c 1225, north; **-molendinum**, north mill c 1190; **-mora**, north moor 1260; **-pars**, **norpars** c 1225, **nordpars** a 1190, p 1200, **nortpars** 1200, c 1200, north part; see also **Norensis**.

Norv-, Norw-, see **Norensis**.

nosc/ibilitas, knowableness p 1300, c 1362; **-ivus**, cognitive c 1367; **-o**, (with acc. and inf.) to know 8c., 9c.; (with inf.) to know how to, be able 9c. 1356; to know carnally c 1125.

nostla, 'nostel', band (of harness) 1265, 1316; **nast/ilus** c 1180, **-ulus** c 1218, latchet; ‡**-ula**, string of nets c 1440.

‡**nostoch**, 'nostoc', stellar emanation 1652.

not/a *c 1255, 1556, **-arium** 15c., note, notation (mus.); **n. ligabilis**, tied note (mus.) 1326; **n. quadrata**, square note (mus.) 1326, c 1470; **n. trium perfectionum** (mus.) 1326; **-ā non indignus**, noteworthy c 1204; †**-ia** c 1185, **-abile** c 1260, c 1430, note, comment, gloss; **-abiliores** (pl.), notables 1432; **-abilitas**, distinction, distinguished appearance c 1125; noteworthy point c 1396; **-amen**, designating 9c.; name 1080; **n. crucis**, sign of the cross 11c.; **-anter**, (?) emphatically p 1381; precisely 1427; **-aria** 1281, c 1434, **-ariatus** c 1418, 1684, †**-aritatus** 1336, office of notary; **-arius**, (adj.) secretarial c 793; literary 12c.; see also **notificatio**; (subst.) *c 1125, 1549, **-orius** 1392, †**netarius** 1374, †**-atorius** 1296, notary; **n. publicus**, notary public 1291, 1686; **-atio**, scoring (mus.) 1462, 1485; **-atiuncula**, brief note, comment 1649; **-ative**, specifically c 1376; **-ator**, clerk c 1180; notary c 1433; author, narrator c 1450; **ars -atoria** a 1292, **a. -oria (-aria)** c 1212, 'art notary', form of magic; **-ariacus**, magical 1564;

-ula, mark a 1180, a 1452; short note, memorandum 1202, 1684; gloss c 1260, c 1450; note, notation (mus.) c 1160, c 1396; 'difference', mark of cadency (her.) c 1595; **n. chirographi**, note of fine 1250; *****-o**, to score (mus.) a 1100, 1489.

notalgicus, see **otalgicus**.

note/geldum, -gildum, see **noutegeldum**.

†**noti seliton** c 1160, †**nothis elithos** c 1200, for γνῶθι σεαυτόν.

*****not/ificatio** c 1150, 1489, **-escentia** c 1367

notification; **-ificativus**, designative 1276; **-io**, fame 13c.; **-ionalis**, conceptual, subjective c 1290, 1649; **-ionaliter**, conceptually, in relation to thought c 1290, c 1362; **-ior**, more intelligible 13c., 1620; **-ioritas**, greater intelligibility c 1365; **-itia** *1160, 15c., **-etia** 1450, **-issia** 1383, **-itio** 1346, knowledge, cognizance; foreknowledge c 1040; note, copy c 1266, 1414; see also DEDUC; *****-orie** 1265, 1582, **-orio** 1299, 1586, notoriously, publicly; **-orietas**, notoriety 1280, 1554; **-orium**, notorious offence c 1188, 1300; knowledge 1424, 1454; **-orius** c 1192, 1591, **notarius** 1423, 1461, notorious (see also **nota**); **-eo** c 793, *****-ifico** c 1080, 1559, to notify; **-ifacio**, (?) to denote c 1270; **-ifico**, to score (mus.) c 1570.

notivagus, see **nox**.

not/o, -ula, see **nota**.

nou/chea, -schia, see **nusca**.

nouncheynchum, see **nonschenchum**.

nounpar, umpire 1384.

nous, see **nus**.

noutegeldum 1177, 1203, **noudtegeldum** 1193, **nouthtegeldum** 1188, **nowtegeldum** a 1180, **noutegildum** 1159, **note/-geldum** 1169, 1198, **-gildum** 1157, 1177, **nautegildum** a 1180, **neutegeldum** 1179, 1200, 'neat-geld', cattle-rent (esp. Cumberland).

1 **nova**, see **noa**.

2 *****nov/a** (pl.) 1274, 1468, **-ella** (pl.) c 1400, **-elle** (pl.) c 1200, **-ellula** (pl.) a 1452, news; **-alia** (pl.), (?) tithes of newly tilled land c 1380 (cf. **terra**); (?) **-alitas**, fruit, profit 13c.; **-aneus**, newly settled, immigrant c 1362; **-ates** (pl.), Moderns c 1620; **-atio**, innovation 1324; newly tilled land 1369; **-ator**, innovator 1562; **-ella**, shoot, scion 12c., c 1450; Novel (Roman law) c 1357, c 1450; **-iluna**, new moon c 1298; ‡**-ellus** 15c., *****-icius** c 1080, 1586, **-iscius** c 1480, novice (mon.); **-icius**, convert 9c.; **-icialis**, of a novice 1291, c 1430; **-iciatus** c 1330, 1537, (?) **-icium** c 1380, **-itas** c 1296, c 1330, noviciate; **-itas**, innovation c 1090, 1559; (?) youth c 1256; recent assumption of office 1274, a 1347; usurpation 1402; (?) **-itas** 1041, **-itates** (pl.) c 1325, 1403, news; **-issima** (pl.), the latter end c 1170, 1266; **-iter** c 730. 1296, 1371, *****de -o** 1209, 1484, **ex -o** 1508, anew, as a novelty or innovation; *****c** 793. c 1125, 1558, **de -o** 1233, c 1362, recently; **-ello**, to renew, refresh 1399; **-ito**, to originate, innovate c 1115; **-o**, to be new or renewed a 1408.

novacul/a, razor: **n. lune**, crescent moon 1267; ‡**-um chirurgie**, spearwort (bot.) 14c.; ‡**-arius**, razor-maker 1520.

Novembr/is 676, **-ius** c 1452, of or for November.

novem/denarius, the number nineteen 13c.; **-plex** 1497, **nocuplus** 1267, ninefold; **noven/dium**, space of nine days c 1550; **-nium**, space of nine years c 1125, c 1414; **-a** (sc. **pars**), a ninth a 1150; **febris -a**, nine-day ague a 1250; **-arium**, set of nine c 1182; *****-us**, ninth c 1443, 1512.

noverc/arius, stepfather 1219; **-aliter**, like a stepmother c 1212, a 1452; ‡**-atus**, maternal

half-brother c 1440; having (? oppressed by) a stepmother c 1150; **-o** c 1390, ***-or** c 1190, c 1470, to behave like a stepmother.
novilissimus, see NOBIL
nov/o, etc., see nova.
novodecimalis, see nona.
nowtegeldum, see noutegeldum.
nox, nightfall c 1283; **n. Dominica,** Sunday night c 1188, c 1362; **n. de firma,** night's farm or provision 1086; **n. mellis,** night's provision of honey 1086; **n. sacra,** (?) Christmas night c 1245; ***noct/anter** 1278, 1583, **-uatim** 1503, **-urnaliter** a 1160, **de -u** c 1160, by night; **-icula,** for **-icola,** (?) owl c 1160; ‡**-icula** 15c., **-iluca** a 1200, 1344, glow-worm or fire-fly; **-ivagus** 1375, 1467, **-ivaga** (f.) c 1193, **-ivagax** 1371, **-ivagans** 1395, **-ifigus** 1445, **notivagus** 1391, **ambulator -urnus** 1389, 'night-walker', prowler; **-ualis,** nocturnal 15c.; **-urna** c 1080, c 1182, **-urnum** c 1072, 1351, **-urni** (pl.) 1236, c 1245, officium **-urnale** c 980, c 1000, nocturn, night office (eccl.); **-urnum psalterii** c 1320, 1537, **-urni psalterii** 1475; **-urnalia** (pl.) c 1080, c 1330, **-urnales** c 1072, **calcei -urnales** 980, slippers; **-esco,** to grow dark c 1184, c 1250; **-ivago,** to prowl by night 1419, c 1452; **-o** c 1180, **-urno** c 1310, c 1362, to spend the night; **-urno,** to say nocturns 14c.
‡**noxa,** witch 1483.
noys, see nus.
nub/es, cloud: **-s** 7c., 9c., **-ula** c 1326, ‡15c.; **-ulum,** fog, confusion 1284; **-eculosus** 1166, **-ileus** c 1190, **-ulosus** 1338, cloudy, dark; **-ilosus,** doubtful, confused c 730; **-iger,** cloud-borne c 1190.
nubo, see nuptorium.
nuch/a, medulla oblongata (med.) c 1210, a 1250; ‡"hole of the poll" 15c.; **-us,** nape 1198.
nuch/eum, -ia, see nusca.
nuci-, see nux.
‡**nucl/eus pini,** pine-cone 14c.; ‡**-earius,** nut-tree 15c., 1483; ‡**-iarium,** nut-grove 15c.; ‡**-eatio,** cracking of nuts 1483; ‡**-eo,** to crack nuts 1483.
nud/itas, emptiness c 730; naked truth 1421; **n. verborum,** empty words c 1125, c 1250; **-icollum,** bare part of neck c 1180; **-ulus,** (?) half naked 1200; **-e,** barely, simply 1260, 1380; **in -um,** on the naked flesh c 1115; **-us,** with unshod wheels 1388, 1486; **rota -a** 1297, 1325; see also **pactum, possessio; -ito,** to strip naked, bare c 550.
nudius tertius, three years ago c 1140.
nug/e (pl.), poor, helpless people 1200; **-acitas,** folly c 800. c 1236, c 1250; **-atio,** trifling, vain repetition a 1250, 1461; **-igerolus,** dealer in female finery 8c.; **-iger** 14c., **-egerulus** c 1430, **-igerulus** c 790. c 1160, c 1380, †**-erulus** 9c., **-idicus** (subst.) c 1200, **-ivendus** 13c., trifler; **-idicus** (adj.) a 1180, **-iloquus** 1167, trifling, babbling.
†**nugigerulus,** (?) for **novigerulus,** messenger c 800.
null/itas, nothingness, non-existence a 1292, 1620; nullity, invalidity c 1332, 1686; ***-atenus** c 1090, c 1540, **-atinus** c 1265, c 1458, **in -o** c 1197, c 1400, by no means;

-atensis (episcopus), of nowhere c 1620; **-atio,** ruin c 1400; **-ibi** 1308, 1518, **-ic** 14c., **-icubi** c 1315, 1453, **-ubi** ‡1570, 1662, **-ucubi** ´1346, nowhere; **-ifidius,** infidel c 1620; **-imodus,** of no sort c 1234, 1532; **-ipotens,** powerless c 1300, 1344; **-issimus,** unimportant c 1193; **-iter,** invalidly, illegally 1389, 1550; **-otiens,** never c 1430; ***-us,** null, invalid, illegal c 1219, 1684; **-o,** to annul, invalidate 1430.
num/ c 1340, a 1408, **nunquid** c 1340, for **nonne; -quidnam, nunquidnam,** for **num** (intensified) c 730, c 793.
numell/e (pl.), stocks 1649; ‡**-o,** to shackle c 1440, 1483.
numen, dominion, property 944.
Numer/us 14c., c 1396, **-i** (pl.) 1267, c 1334, Book of Numbers (bibl.); **ad -um** 1086, 1130, **-o** 1086, 1257, by tale (in unblanched coin); **idem -o,** precisely the same a 1290; **-us aureus** 1231, 1499, **n. terminarius** c 1265, golden number (in calendar); cf. **luna; n. circularis,** square number 1344; **n. sphericus,** cube a 1250, 1344; **-a** (n. pl.) **dierum,** days, lifetime 11c.; **-abilis** 12c., **-alis** c 950. c 1178, c 1574, **-icus** c 1670, numerical; **-ale,** calendar c 998. c 1396, 1470; **identitas -alis,** unqualified identity 1286; **-aliter,** numerically a 1150, 1427; **-alitas** c 1270, **-atio** 13c., numerical quality; **-atio,** numbering c 730. c 1290, c 1549; **-ator,** teller (Exchequer official) 1226, 1526; numerator (math.) **-ositas,** abundance c 865; plurality a 1250, 1267; **-o,** to assign number (to a verb) 13c.; to specify c 1170; see also **pecunia; numbrio,** to enrol, register 1360.
numisma, nummisma, see nomisma.
numm/us 1086, 1334, **nommus** 1086, penny; counter 12c., 1465; roundel (her.) 1654; **n. albus,** penny blanched 1086; **n. Dominicalis,** Sunday penny, mass-penny 13c.; ‡**-acius,** "penny-toller" 15c.; **-ata** c 1180, 1309, **-us** c 1200, 1222, pennyworth; **summa -atica,** sum of money c 1377; **-icola** a 1200, 1345, **-ipeta** c 1160, 1345, money-lover; **-osus,** moneyed, wealthy c 1180, 1336; **-ularia,** money-wort (bot.) 1634; **-ulatria,** worship of money c 1200; **-ulum,** for **-ulus,** coin 8c.
***nunc,** (used as adj.) the present c 1280, 1686.
nunci-, see NUNTI
nuncupat/ive, literally, in virtue of the meaning of the word c 1204; nominally, merely as a name c 730. 12c., a 1452; **-ivus,** named 793; nominal c 1250, 14c.; **testamentum -ivum** 1351, a 1564, **t. -ive factum** 1355, oral testament; **-orius,** naming, calling by name c 793.
nundin/e (pl.), ***fair c 1110, c 1550; tournament 12c., c 1235; **n. Clementine,** sale of dispensations etc. by Clement VI 1347; **-ale,** site of fair c 1080; **-alis,** for sale 1287; **-aria** (pl.), market-tolls 1334; **nondinor,** for **-or,** to purchase, earn 8c.
nundum, see non.
nunna, see nonna.
nunquid/, -nam, see num.
nunti/us (nunci-), angel 5c., 6c.; groom 1289; **n. Apostolice Sedis** 1275, c 1360, **n.**

Apostolicus 1461, **n. Camere** c 1400, **n. Pape** c 1250, 15c., papal nuncio; ***n. solempnis** 1234, c 1370; **n. specialis** c 1439; **dies -a**, critical day (med.) a 1250; **-atio**, Annunciation 1204; denunciation 1259; office of nuncio c 1332; **-ativus**, reporting c 1390; **-atorius**, inviting c 1338; **-um**, mission, errand c 1090, c 1470; **-o**, (?) to denounce 1301; †**nuncito**, *for* **-o**, to announce c 1343.

nuo, to intimate 760.

nuper, (used as *adj.*) the late 1419, 1588.

‡**nuptorium**, bridal house c 1440, 1483; **nubo**, to give in marriage 13c., 1461; to take to wife 1006. c 1400, 1408; **n. me**, to wed 1232.

nus c 960, **nous** 1344, **noys** c 1115, c 1200, mind (*νοῦς*).

nusc/a (†**misca**) c 1170, 1249, **-hia** 1238, 1260, **nouschia** 1296, **nuchia** 1303, **nucheum** 1332, **nochia** 1398, **nouchea** 1300, †**oficha** 1432, †**uncia** a 1250, **uchium** 1436, 'ouch', ornament.

nutr/itio 1267, c 1458, ***-itura** c 1125, a 1564, **-icatura** c 1115, **-amentum** 1313, **-itus** 1240, nutrition, nurture; **-imentum** c 1150, c 1400, **-ivum** 1252, increase, young of animals; **-ibilis**, nourished c 865; c 1267, c 1270, **-itibilis** 13c., **-imentalis** a 1235, c 1270, **-imentativus** a 1250, ***-itivus** c 1170, 1424, nutritive; **-icia**, food, fodder 1310; ‡1483, **-iciaria** 1318, **-itorium** c 1440, nursery; **-icius**, pupil or foster-son a 1142, c 1412; **porcus n.**, sucking pig 1239; **-itiva** (*pl.*), digestive organs c 1210, ‡14c.; **-itor**, foster-father c 700; **-ix sicca**, dry

nurse 1445; **-iens** (*subst.*), food a 1250; **-itus**, monk reared from childhood in monastery 12c.; foster-son c 1215, 13c.

nuwellus, *see* **nodus**.

nux, ***nut** (of siege engine, *etc.*) 1222, 1337; ***1295**, c 1506, **poculum nuceum** c 1508, coconut shell made into a cup; **n. Gallica**, (?) gall-nut 14c., 1511; **n. Indica** a 1250, ‡14c., ‡**n. vomica** 14c., *nux vomica*; 1424, ‡**n. I. magna** 14c., **n. I. major** 1627, coconut; **n. Maroquitana** a 1250; **n. minuta** 1265, ‡14c., **n. Pontica** c 1200, ‡14c., hazel or filbert; **n. muc'** 1256, **n. muga** 1325, **n. de muga** 1314, **n. musci** c 1357, **n. mogata** 1377, **n. mugata** 1328, 1372, **n. musgata** 1207, **n. muscata** c 1200, 1622, **n. myristica** a 1250, ‡1570, (?) **n. amistica** 1607, nutmeg; **n. pini**, (?) pine-cone c 1315; **n. regalis** 1186, **n. regia** 1538, 1634, **n. Persica** 1538, walnut; **noca**, nut 1309; **nocium carnis**, morsel of meat 1340; **nuci/fraga**, nutcracker (bird) 1544; ‡**-fragus** 15c., **-peta** 1544, nuthatch (bird); ‡**-frangium**, "nutcracker" 1570; **oleum -num** a 1250; **-o**, **nuceo**, to gather nuts 1226, 1249.

nyct/hemera, period of 24 hours 1564; **-icorax**, night-owl 7c. c 1190, c 1540; **noctilopa**, *for* **-alopia** (med.), a 1250, ‡14c.

nymph/ula, maid-servant c 1200; 'maiden', 'dolly', made of last corn-sheaves (Sc.) c 1384; ‡**-idica** (*pl.*), spirits of solvent waters (alch.) 1652; **ninfea**, *for* **-ea**, water-lily a 1250; **nimphus**, servant, attendant c 550.

O

o c 1330, 14c., **o sapientia** c 1250, c 1330, Advent antiphon; **o** 13c., 1494, **o et olla** 1323, allowance of food at Advent (mon.).

ob (with *abl.*), on account of c 1400, c 1471.

obaccepto, to accept, submit to 13c.

obalata, *see* OBOL

oballo, *see* **obvallo**.

obambio, to walk round c 1200; to envelop 14c.

obambulatio, walking about 1517.

obat/er, dark 1622; **-resco**, to grow black c 1115.

obaud/itio c 1040. c 1070, c 1180, **-itus** c 1070, obedience; **-itor**, obeyer 6c.; **-ibilis**, able to be listened to 1344; **-io**, to hear p 1377; ***to obey** (eccl.); (?) to disobey, disregard 1245, c 1453; †**abaudio**, to obey c 1125; *cf.* OBEDI

obb/a, jug, joust 13c., 1460; **-ata**, jugful 1278, c 1310.

obbucco, to chide c 1150, 1200.

obburgo, to burgle 1275.

obc-, *see also* **occ-**

obcedeo, *see* **obses**.

obcetrix, *see* **obstetricatio**.

obditus, (?) vassal (G.) 1254.

obdorm/itio c 1185, **-itatio** 13c., falling asleep; **-itus**, fallen asleep 12c.

obedi/entia, (oath of) allegiance or fealty 1325, 15c.; vow of obedience (mon.) c 1125, 1509; dependency (mon.) c 1150, 1199; (papal) jurisdiction 1346; subject territory 1509, 1514; ***c 1070**, c 1410, **-entiaria** 1256, c 1300, (revenues of) monastic office; **o. canonica** c 1250, c 1408; **o. exterior**, external office (mon.) 1234; **o. manualis**, obedience signified by taking or kissing hand c 1265, c 1520; **-bilis**, obedient 10c. 1378; **-ens** 15c., **-entialis** c 1166, 1256, †**-entalis** c 1220, ***-entiarius** c 1115, 1549, †**-entarius** c 1300, †**-onarius** 1239, obedientiary, office-bearer (mon.); ***-entialis**, concerned with obedience c 1250, c 1380; **-entialiter**, obediently 1425; as an obedientiary (mon.) 1279; **-entiarius**, one owing obedience c 1377, c 1450; **-tivus**, capable of obeying 1374; **-entio** c 1143, **obidio** 1559, *for* **-o**, to obey; *cf.* OBAUD

‡**obel/chera, -kara, oubelcora**, gourd 1652.

†**obellum**, conflict, battle c 550.

obel/us, critical mark in book: **-is** 1267; *cf.* OBOL

oberratio, travel c 1240.

oberus, *see* **hobbia**.

obex, spigot c 1138.

obf-, *see* off-
obgrunnio, *see* oggannio.
obicio, *see* OBJECT
†obiciter, (?) *for* obiter, c 1325.
obidio, *see* OBEDI
obinde, on that account c 1302.
obit/us, obit, service on anniversary of death
(eccl.) c 1150, 1583; mortuary payment 1279,
1396; -arius, reporter of obits 1421; dies
-arius, anniversary of death c 1470; liber
-arius, book of obits c 1476; obiit (*subst.*),
death c 1258.
*object/io (eccl.), †obicio c 1290, -um c 1125,
c 1343, -us c 1250, 1380, objection, charge;
objectivation a 1361; -iuncula, trifling objection 1610, 1649; -alis c 1360, -ivus c 1360,
c 1363, objective; -ive, objectively, as immediate object of thought c 1270, c 1444;
-or, objector 1304; -um, object (phil.)
c 1286, c 1444.
objur/atio, -o, *see* ABJUR
objurg/atrix, shrew, scold 1436, 1563; -anter,
reprovingly c 1370.
oblargo, to widen 1344.
oblat/io *c 1080, 1559, -um 1177, c 1310,
oblation, payment; Sacrament of Lord's
Supper c 600, c 1000. c 1090, c 1362; 10c.
1343, -a c 1130, 15c., -um 1345, 1413, obley,
wafer, 1262, c 1470, -um c 1218, c 1310,
offer, proposal; festum -ionis B. Marie
(21 Nov.) c 1354; -iuncula, humble offering
a 1150; altare -orium, altar of offering
c 1197; oblia (*pl.*) 1283, oblie 1310, 1321,
'obleys' rendered to lord by vassal (G.);
-a nova (*n. pl.*), section of Pipe Roll containing items of revenue not shown in previous
years 1199, 1284; de -is, reference to items
new in last account 1199; oblo, to offer
1386; *cf.* OBTUL, OFFER
oblat/ratio 1220, c 1250, -ratus c 1250, railing, reviling; -rator, railer 15c.; -ero, *for*
-ro, to rail 12c.
oblectatrix, entertainer (*f.*) 1620.
oblia, *see* oblatio.
oblig/atio *1219, 1482, oblegantia 1513,
-atorium c 1308, c 1400, scriptum -arium
1310, s. -atorium 1274, p 1464, instrumentum -atorium 1301, bond; 'obligation' (a
dialectical exercise) 1344, c 1370; -antia,
alliance 1393; ‡-ar, garter 15c.; -ate, duti-
fully c 1236; -atissime, very strictly c 1250,
c 1530; -atior, more binding c 730; -ativus
c 1375, 1647, -atorius p 1348, binding,
obligatory; -atorius, serving as a bond
c 1250, c 1470; -atorius c 1344, c 1361,
-isticus c 1360, concerned with 'obligation'
(dialectic); -ator, warrantor (leg.) c 1290;
-atus, person bound by agreement c 1435;
-o, to bind by special condition (dialectic)
1344, c 1370; oblixo, *for* -o, to bind 1314.
obligia, intestinal organ, (?) navel 6c.
obliqu/atio, deviation 1267, c 1470; -ax, cast
askance c 1318; -ilineus, curvilinear c 1361;
-itas, obliquity (gram.) 13c.; oblique note
(mus.) 1326, c 1470; circulus -us, zodiac
c 1233; -o, to slope away, diverge 1155; to
glance off 1280; to disagree c 1376; to warp
1168, c 1340.
obliv/iositas, forgetfulness c 1285; -isco, *for*
-iscor, to forget 9c.

oblixo, *see* obligo.
oblo, *see* oblatio.
oblo/cutio *c 1150, 1443, -quamentum
c 1357, *-quium c 1125, 1486, obloquy.
oblong/itudo, disproportionate length a 1250;
-inquitas, elliptical shape c 1270; -um, long
distance 8c.; in -um, lengthwise c 1400.
obluceo, to flash against 1252.
oblus, *see* OBOL
obministr/atio, administration 1341; -o, to
minister to 14c.
obmissio, failure c 1235; obmitto, *for*
omitto, c 793. c 1235, p 1377.
obmut/entia, silence 1378; -eo, to be silent
c 1306.
obmutio, to murmur against c 1160.
obnebulo, to overcloud 1518.
obnixius c 730. 1200, 1428, †obnoxius c 1250,
most urgently.
obnox/ietas 12c., a 1228, -itas 1293, liability;
-ius, owing obedience c 1115; prejudicial
c 1125; (?) crippled c 1150; (with in and
abl.) guilty of, answerable for 9c.; *see also*
obnixius.
obnub/ilatio, darkening c 1070, 1413; -ulo,
for -ilo, to darken, befog 12c., 1426.
obo, *see* ovamen.
*obol/us 1086, 1534, -a 1086, 1242, -um 1218,
oblus 1488, obulus 1195, 1587, halfpenny;
o. albus c 1300, 1341, o. argenti 15c.; o.
aureus 12c., 1401; *see also* auca, musca;
o. ponderis, half-pennyweight 1425; *-ata
c 1102, 1426, †obalata 1326, obulata 1208,
14c., -atus 1264, 1377, obulatus c 1400,
‡-itas c 1440, halfpennyworth; panis -atus
c 1290, p. obulatus c 1419, halfpenny loaf.
oborsus, *see* aborsus.
obp-, *see* opp-
obpacitas, *see* OPAC
obrepticie, by stealth 1389.
obri-, *see also* OBRYZ
obripo, *for* obrepo, 1461.
obrixor, to struggle against 1220.
obrosio, back-biting a 1205.
obrotundus, roundish 14c.
obrufus, reddish 14c.
obru/itio, overwhelming, immersion c 1500;
-o, to roof 1292; *cf.* abrutio.
obrumpo, to break off 1461.
obryz/um (bibl.), obrisum c 1200, 15c.,
†obrigon c 1215, pure gold; -eus, golden
8c.; -us c 1213, 1345, obrisus 1171, c 1340,
obridzus 958, obrixus 972, pure (of gold).
obscenitas, cacophony (gram.) c 800.
obscur/abilis, able to be darkened 1344;
-rimus, very dark c 600.
obscur/atio, scouring 1378, 1458; -o, to scour
1374, 1379.
obsecr/abilis, execrable 1293; -or (*dep.*), *for*
-o, c 730.
obsecund/atio, compliance c 1180, 15c.;
-arius, assistant priest 15c.; †absecundus,
(?) pleasant 1327; -o, to subjugate 13c.; -or
(*dep.*), to show obedience 12c.
obsed-, *see* obses.
†obsensum mentis, sanity 11c.
obsequ/ium c 1080, c 1443, -ie (*pl.*) c 1000,
divine service; -ium, office p 1377; obsequies 1441; -ia conjugalia, conjugal rights
1684; o. pedum, gait c 1350; -ium regis,

king's service 1266, 1325; **o. trium rerum,** *trimoda necessitas* 12c.; **-ialia** (*pl.*), obsequies 1467; **-ialis** 1343, **-alis** 1303, 1378, assistant; c 1250, 1416, **-iosus** 1431, 1440, obedient, compliant; **-ialiter** c 1317, c 1470, **-aliter** c 1456, obediently; **-iolum,** obedience, deference 12c.

obseratio, barring c 1185.

obsericatus, *see* HOLO

observ/antia *c 1080, 1559, **-atio** c 1296, 1517, observance, rule (mon.); observance (by strict Franciscans) c 1450, 1549; **o. verborum,** oath sworn clause by clause *or* word by word c 1115; **-atio,** note, comment 1537; **-abilis,** able to be observed 1343, c 1382; **-atinus** 1496, **-ans** c 1562, Observantine (of strict Franciscans); **-atorium,** observatory (astr.) 1686; **-atrix,** attendant (*f.*) c 1000; **-andissimus,** worthy of deference 1531; **observo,** *for* **-o,** c 730, 873; **-o,** to swear clause by clause *or* word by word c 1115; to seize, arrest c 1115; to remark, state c 1258; **o. me (ab),** to keep oneself from c 793. c 1102.

observio, to serve 1537.

obses, guarantor of covenant 1142; **abses,** *for* **o.,** hostage c 1000; **castellum obsessorium,** siege tower c 1150; **obsid/atio** c 1540, **obsisio** 1404, **obsicio** c 1470, siege, blockade; **-io,** hostageship 1249; **obsederica,** service as hostage (G.) 1255; **-iatus,** held as a hostage c 1370; *cf.* **2 hostagium;** **-eo,** to possess (of evil spirits) c 730. c 1080, c 1250; **-eo bellum,** to wage war 13c.; **obsedeo** 1461, **obcedeo** 1282, *for* **-eo,** to besiege.

obsigillo, to seal up 1598.

obsio, *see* optatus.

obsistentia, resistance c 1370, 1415; obstruction c 1250, c 1362.

obson/ium, offering of food 1041; lodging, procuration 12c.; **-ator,** manciple (ac.) 1535, c 1578; **-ior** (*dep.*), to feast c 1125.

obsonor (*dep.*), to dispute c 1220.

†**obsons,** hurtful c 1177.

obsordesco, to be defiled c 1250; †**obsurdo,** (?) to fester a 1250.

obsorveo, *for* **obsorbeo,** c 730.

obsqualeo, to be in a state of neglect 9c.

obstagium, *see* **2 hostagium.**

obstetr/icatio, bringing to birth c 865. c 1250; **obcetrix,** *for* **-ix,** 1326.

*****obstin/acia,** obstinacy 1173, 1494; **-aciter** c 1250, 1305, †**-ater** c 1362, obstinately, persistently; **-ax,** obstinate c 1150, 1438; **-ativus,** retentive 1344; **-atus,** stunned 1212; **hostinatus,** obstinate 1303; **-or** (*dep.*), to refuse obstinately 1450.

obstip-, *see* **obstupatio; obstupescibilis.**

obst/itus, fine for assault c 1102; **-o,** *see* **non obstante.**

obstomachor, to be angry 14c.

obstricamen, covering a 975.

†**obstringilis,** under constraint c 1370.

obstruct/io, organ stop 1512; **obstruxio** 1223, **abstructio** c 1320, **-ura** c 1100, 1427, obstruction; ‡**-orium,** stopper 1570; **abstruo,** to block c 1320, 1321.

obstru/sio 1291, **obtrusio** 1452, stoppage;

-sior, more baffling or abstruse 1344; **-do** 1198, a 1273, **obtrudo** 1408, to stop up.

obstup/atio 1313, 1446, **obstipatio** 1375, stopping up; stuffing (of fowl) 1376; stoppage (of payments) 1456, c 1467; **o. sanguinis** a 1564; *****-o** 1192, 1428, **opstupo** 1333, **ostupo** c 1256, **obstipuo** 1362, †**obsturpo** 1275, **absturpo** 1293, to stop up, block (road, watercourse, *etc.*); to caulk (naut.) 1295; to stop, withhold (payments) 1456; **o. dentem** 1612; **o. sanguinem** a 1564; **o. visum,** to block a view a 1250; ‡**obstipo,** to sprinkle 1483; *cf.* ASTUPP

obstupescibilis, amazing 12c.; **obstipuo,** to be amazed c 1390.

obsumo, to consume c 1125.

obsurdo, *see* **obsordesco.**

obtabe, *see* **octave.**

obtalgicus, *see* **otalgicus.**

obtalm-, *see* **ophthalmus.**

obtarmicum, *see* **ptarmicum.**

obtect/io, covering c 730; **-us,** overshadowing c 730.

obtemperantia, obedience c 793, c 805.

obtend/entia, -iculum, allegation, pretext c 1250.

obtent/us (optent-), protection, patronage c 760; acquisition c 1270, c 1450; hindrance 7c.; occupation (of space) c 1115; (?) expenditure 1399; *****-u,** by means, on account (of) c 1130, c 1462; **-u gratie** c 1220, **sub -u g.** c 1362, as you value the favour (of); **in salutari -u,** in a good cause c 1250; **-us,** (*adj.*) established 1237; **-or,** maintainer c 1200; acquirer c 1430; **obtineo,** to conquer c 950; to win a case (leg.) c 1194, c 1593; †**abtineo,** *for* **o.,** 1221; *see also* **locus.**

obtero, *see* OBTUR

†**obtestaculum,** that which obscures c 550.

obticus, *see* OPTIC

obtimas, *see* OPTIM

obtingo, to colour c 1200.

obtitulo, to nominate c 990.

obto, *see* **optatus.**

obtrectatrix, traducer (*f.*) 1537.

obtrepido, to tremble a 975. c 1123.

obtritus, contrite c 800.

obtruncatio capitis, decapitation a 1142.

obtru/sio, -do, *see* **obstrusio.**

obtuitus c 1270, c 1467, **optutus** 793. c 1250, c 1400, gaze, eye.

obtul/atio (optul-), appearance in court (leg.) 1269; **-o,** to offer 1317, 1555; *cf.* OBLAT, OFFER

obtunc, thereupon c 1127.

obtur/atio (optur-) 1246, 1459, **-itio** c 1430, **-amentum** 1291, stopping up; **-ator,** obstructor c 1430; ‡**-atorium,** stopper 1483; †**obtero** c 1218, **opturor** (*dep.*) 1295, *for* **-o,** to stop up.

obtus/io, bludgeoning (fig.) 12c.; **-itas,** (?) passivity a 1200; **-ivus,** tending to make dull 12c.

obul-, *see* OBOL

obumbr/atio, shade, covering c 1060; c 1302, **-aculum** p 1290, c 1500, shelter; **abumbro,** (?) *for* **-o,** to shadow c 550.

obunc/o, to bend c 793; to beckon to c 1125.

‡**obvadio,** to lay a wager 15c.

obvallo, to surround, fortify: **obvello, oballo** c 550.

obvel/atio, veiling, shrouding 1552; **-o**, to veil c 1125, 1318.

***obven/tio** c 1140, 1550, **oventio** 12c., c 1230, **-tus** 1304, **-ientia** (*pl.*) 1304, obvention, income (eccl.); **o. Terre Sancte** 1287, 1308; **-io**, to oppose c 1220; †**obvio**, *for* **-io**, to fall by inheritance 1357.

obversio, opposition 15c.

obvestio, to clothe, embody c 1520.

obvi/atio, meeting, encounter c 1115, 1460; hostile encounter c 1150, c 1458; rejoinder, counter-argument c 1160, c 1343; **o. hostilis** c 1115; **in -am**, so as to meet c 1250, 1415; **-am habere**, to be faced by c 1000; (processio) **-alis**, passing along the road c 1266, c 1330; **-anter**, in the way c 1298; **-us contravenio**, to come to meet 7c.; **o. me** (with *dat.*), to meet 1248; c 790, **ovio** c 1250, 1300, *for* **-o**, to oppose; **ovio**, to meet 1199, 1255; to collide 1275; **ovior** (*dep.*), to meet, fall upon 9c.; *see also* OBVEN

obvol/ucrum, disguise, deception 1412; **-vo** (pedes), to embrace 12c., c 1325.

†**obvolutorium**, cockshoot c 1440.

occ/a, harrow: ‡1468, ‡**-atorium** 1483, mallet to crush clods; ‡**-arium**, clod 1483; **-asio**, payment for right to make essarts 1227; **-atio**, essart, forest clearing c 1178; equus **-arius**, e. **-ator**, horse used for harrowing c 1200; **-o**, to break (stones) 1472; to cut (thread) c 1190, a 1408; to quench (fire) a 1142; ‡to kill 13c., 1483.

occasio/ *c 1125, c 1520, **occatio** 1686, **occasivum** 1252, *cause, reason, account; *c 1115, 1486, **-namentum** 1324, **-natio** 1275, molestation, interference; dispute, prosecution c 1290, p 1330; exaction c 1170, 1274; *see also* **occa; per -nem**, as it happened 1537; **-nalis**, occasional, timely c 1220, c 1360; *-**naliter**, as occasion arises c 1190, 1461; **-nativus**, providing occasion or opportunity c 1283, 1646; **-natus**, subject to qualification a 1446; **-no**, to cause, occasion p 1300, c 1400; *1213, 1583, **-nor** (*dep.*) c 1307, to molest, interfere with; *to prosecute (leg.) 1220, 1571.

occecatio (obc-), blindness, obscuration 1062. c 1265, c 1470.

occidental/is, westerner c 1365; **oxidentalis**, *for* **-is**, western c 1270, c 1390; **-ior**, more westerly 1260; **-iter**, on the west 1423, 1587; **occiduus**, nether c 1250.

occino, to sing against c 1160.

occipio, to come upon, lay hold of c 1433.

occis/or, man-slayer 1203, a 1446; **-us**, victim of manslaughter 1221, c 1290.

occlamo, to cry out 12c., 1562.

occlaustrum (obc-), block c 700.

occo, *see* **occa**.

occolitatus, *see* ACOLYT

occubitus, coition c 1000.

occult/atio, occultation (astr.) 13c.; **-or** c 1400, 1403, **-rix** (*f.*) c 730, concealer; **-us**, occult, latent 1620; **in -o**, secretly 12c.

occumbens, on death-bed c 1200.

occup/atio, occupying of another's time c 1000; land wrongfully occupied 1086; care, vigilance c 1125, 12c.; **domus -ationum**, workhouse 1553; **-ativitas**, power of occupying (space) 1344; *-**ator**

c 1185, 1559, **-atrix** (*f.*) 1462, 1479, (unlawful) occupier; **o. artis**, one who plies a trade 1472; **-atum**, encroachment, purpresture c 1178; **-atus latrocinio**, caught with stolen goods c 1140; **-o**, to be in office 1408; **o. artem**, to ply a trade 1551; **o. super**, to encroach on 1086, 1319.

occurs/io, encounter c 1150; **-or**, (?) sensory nerve 9c.

ocean/us, ocean girdling earth latitudinally at equator a 1233; **-alis anguis**, sea-serpent c 1212.

ocellus, *see* OISEL

ocimum, basil (bot.): **ozimum** a 1250, ‡14c.

Ockanicus, Ockhamist 1427.

ocr/eatio, covering with ochre 1358, 1376; **-io**, to ochre 1388.

***ocre/e** (*pl.*), thigh-boots *or* leggings c 1090, 1570; leather piping (of harness) 1307, 1325; **ferrum -ale**, greave c 1190; **-atus**, wearing thigh-boots *or* leggings c 1072, 1420; **-o** 1309, 1364, **cocreo** 1373, **cokrio** 1382, to pipe (traces) with leather.

oct/aedrum, **-ocedron**, octahedron 1267, 1344; **-agonum**, octagon 1267; **-ogonus**, octagonal c 1255.

***oct/ave** (*pl.*) c 760, c 980. c 1072, 1552, *-**abe** c 1070, c 1450, **obtabe** 12c., **-ava** c 1320, c 1407, **-avus** c 1210, octave, eighth (seventh) day after feast; **-abus**, *for* **-avus**, eighth 805; **-ava**, tax of one eighth 1297, c 1400; **-avo**, in the eighth place 1279, c 1332; **numerus -avarius** 1503; **-ans**, octant (math.) 1686; **-ember**, October c 1015; **-enalis**, eightfold, with eight branches c 700; **-eni**, *for* **-oni**, 8c.; **-iplex**, eightfold 1378; **-upliciter**, in eight ways 1380; **numerus -odenarius**, eighteen c 1400; **-aginta** 1219, **-ogenti** 1269, *for* **-oginta**; **-oagesimus** c 1386, c 1400, **-uagesimus** c 1482, 1492, eightieth; **-ogecuplus**, eighty-fold c 1613; **-ogenarius**, of eighty 9c.; **-uagenarius**, eighty years old 1461; **-ogenti**, eight hundred c 1254; **-omestris**, lasting eight months 1524; **-onaria** 1531, **-onarium** 1427, group of eight verses; **-onarium**, period of eight hours 14c.; **denarius -onarius**, tax of one eighth c 1310, 14c.; **-onatio**, ogdoad 16c.; **-oplicitus**, sort of textile 13c.; ‡**-opondium**, stone (weight) 1570.

oculagium, *see* **oleagium**.

oculamari/um 1507, 1519, **-a** 1509, **oculomarium** 1518, **oclomarium** 1515, (?) *for* **calamarium**, pen-case.

ocul/us, hole in mill-stone 1285; eyelet hole 1368; **-i mei**, (anthem for) third Sunday in Lent c 1000. c 1300; **-o ad -um video**, to know by visual testimony c 1245; **-us auri**, (?) nugget 1269, 1271; **o. bovis**, a begemmed reliquary of St. Pancras a 1135, 13c.; ‡14c., ‡**o. consulis** 14c., ox-eye (bot.); **o. Christi**, clary (bot.) ‡14c., 1634; ‡chickweed c 1440; ‡**o. licii**, ‡**o. lucidus**, honeysuckle 14c.; **o. spatule** (med.) a 1250; **-amen**, sight 950; **-are**, (?) eye-salve 1384; ‡eye-glass 1483 (*cf.* BERYLL); **-arium**, eye-hole (in helmet) c 1250; **-ate**, visibly c 1296; **-atus**, *see* **fides**; **-osus**, full of eyes 9c.; **-o**, to bud on, graft c 1200; to pierce with holes 1350; c 1180, **-or** (*dep.*) 9c., to eye, look at.

oda, ode, ode, song c 700, c 1000. c 1070, a 1452; singing 14 c.; *see also* HOTT
oder-, *see* ODOR
od/ibilis, hateful (eccl.); **-ibiliter,** hatefully c 1250, p 1300; **-itus,** hated p 1300; **-io,** to hate (bibl.).
‡**odicus,** danewort (bot.) 14c.
odoporion, *see* **hodoporion.**
odor/, repute 1279; **-abilis,** perceptible by smell a 1250, 1267; fragrant 14c.; c 1210, a 1250, **-ativus** c 1270, olfactory; **-amen,** perfume c 1125; **-ator,** diffuser of fragrance c 1500; **-iferus** (with *abl.*), smelling of c 1227; **-ificus** 14c., 1432, **-ifluus** c 990, **-osus, oderosus** c 550, fragrant; **-isequus,** follower of fragrance c 1500; c 1125, 1528, **-insecus** c 1180, 1364, **-encicus** 1460, **-encecus** c 1500, 1505, ‡**oderinsicus** 15c., (dog) hunting by scent; **-o** 8c. c 1180, †**adoro** 1285, to smell, use sense of smell; to smell sweet c 1410, c 1435.
oe-, *see also under* **e-**
oelagium, *see* **oleagium.**
oëst/er, *for* **oestrus,** gadfly c 1140, a 1408; **-rus,** incentive c 950.
ofasium, *see* **ovum.**
off/a judicialis, holy wafer used in ordeal c 1102; **-ula,** bit, mouthful c 1000.
offecina, *see* OFFIC
offen/sio, breach (of statute) c 1347; **-siones** (*pl.*), weapons of offence 1415; **-cio** c 1330, **-sum** a 1100, 1606, offence; **-sior,** more hostile 1378; **-sivus,** causing offence c 1357, c 1470; impinging c 1115; offensive (of arms) c 1217, 1569; **-sor,** offender c 1255, c 1430; **-sus** (a), displeased (by or with) c 730; offended party c 1343; **-dens,** offending party c 1343; **-do,** to find (of a jury) 1570; (*trans.*) to offend against (a statute) 1357; **o. mortem,** to die c 1125.
offertissimus, crammed full c 1433.
offer/torium *c 790, c 980. a 1125, 1517, **-enda** c 1072, c 1230, offertory chant (in the mass); c 1220, c 1396, **-etorium** 1241, **offretorium** 1357, **pannus -torius** 1303, offertory-cloth or chalice-veil; **-enda** c 1150, c 1250, **offrenda** c 1095, oblation (eccl.); **-endarius,** service-book 15c.; **offrum,** offer, proposal 1276; **-o,** to make an oblation (eccl.) a 975. a 1125, 1473; c 600, 10c. c 1330, **o. missam** c 1245, **o. mysteria** 7c., to offer mass; *(with *inf.*),* to offer, undertake c 1190, c 1470; *o. me,* to appear in court (leg.) c 1218, 1402; *cf.* OBLAT, OBTUL
offex, dissuader, deterrent c 950.
offic/ium, *office, rite, divine service c 1000. c 1125, 1537; department of household c 1335, c 1477; trade, calling c 1175, 1419; workshop or outbuilding a 1180, c 1475; power, capability of acting c 1115, 1382; inquisition, verdict 16c.; **ex -io** c 1178, 1366, **virtute -ii** 1365, 1518, by virtue of office; **o. merum, o. mixtum,** mere and mixed office of judge (canon law) c 1408, 1595; *see also* PROMOT; **-iabilis,** implying mental action (log.) c 1370; *-iabilis,* **-iabilis** *(log.)* c 1370; *-iabilis,* ***-ialatus,** municipal office (Sc.) 1450, 1522; **-iale,** organ, functional part of body (med.) a 1250; **-ialis,** (*adj.*) instrumental, functional c 1115, 1424; subordinate p 1300; official 1274, c 1352; ethical

c 793. c 1360; (*subst.*) *9c., 1041. c 1130, c 1480, *-iarius* c 1090, 1686, †**-iatus** 1371, p 1377, official, officer; *c 1185, 1684, **-iarius** c 1238, 1516, official appointed by bishop or archdeacon; **-ialis generalis** (eccl.) 1257, 1536; **-iarius,** officiating priest c 1266; *-ialitas* 1200, 1524, **-iatus** 1447, 16c., officiality (eccl.); **-ialiter,** ethically c 1360; **-iaria,** official of nunnery 1441, 1520; (?) office 1584; **-iarium,** business 1504; **-iatio,** officiation, celebration (eccl.) 1518;
†**-ina,** function 14c.; *-ina* 7c. c 1125, 1481, **-inum** 12c., c 1400, **-inus** 1250, **offecina** c 1507, outbuilding, shed, domestic office; **-ine** (*pl.*), apothecaries 1538; **-inium,** office (mon.) 1224; **-iose,** duly c 1185; **-iositas,** obligingness c 1070, c 1160; **-iosus,** useful 1385; **-io,** to serve c 1220, c 1400; 1217, 1416, **-ior** 1252, to serve a church, celebrate divine service.
offnama 1157, 1310, **avenama** 1189, **ovenama** c 1180, intake, enclosure.
offr-, *see* AURI; OFFER
offula, *see* **offa.**
offuscatiuncula (obf-), tinge c 1500.
oficha, *see* **nusca.**
ofuellus, *see* **hovellus.**
oga, *see* **auca.**
ogetharius, lesser lord, *ochiern* (Sc.) 13c.
oggannio, to growl, snarl at: †**oggarrio** (obg-) 12c., 1344, **obgrunnio** c 1250, 1421.
ogiva, rib of vaulting (arch.) 1289, 1325.
oilettus, eyelet hole (Fr. *oeillet*) 1388; *cf.* OCUL
oill-, *see* **oleagium.**
oinonetta, shallot 1388; **oynonus** 1346, **oygnunus** (†**cygminus**)1254, onion.
ois-, *see also* OSER; **2 ostrium.**
oisel/etta 1345, **ocellus** a 1150, little bird; **-arius** c 1200, **-ator** 1213, fowler; **-eria,** place where birds are kept or sold 1200.
ola/logia, -sterius, *see* HOLO
oleagin/itas, oiliness a 1292; **-us,** oily c 1125, a 1250.
ole/agium (oli-) 1233, 1372, **olagium** 1290, **aolagium, auloagium, oculagium** 1242, **oelagium** 1264, **eolagium** 1226, **oillagium** 1214, c 1345, **oilliagium** 1261, **ullia-gium** 1313, **ullagium** 1315, 1381, †**ulna-gium,** †**ulnatio** 1336, ullage; **-o** 1238, 1272, **oillio** 1335, **oillo** c 1327, **ulio** 1329, **ulo** 1377, to make good evaporation from wine-casks.
†**ol/edus,** (?) *for* **-idus,** stinking c 550; **-eo,** to have the sense of smell 12c.
olefans, *see* **elephas.**
oler-, *see* **holus.**
ole/um, holy oil 12c., 1537; axle grease 1410; lamp oil 1338; fish oil 1365; **o. allecis** 1278; **o. album,** (?) magistery of sulphur (alch.) a 1235; ‡**o. anethinum,** oil of anise 15c.; ‡**o. ardens,** oil of tartar (alch.) 1652; **o. benedictum,** (?) oil from holy sepulchre *or* a confection 1307; **o. b. a lateribus** 13c.; **o. lini,** linseed oil 1338; **o. de nucibus** 1256; ‡**o. de petra,** petroleum 14c.; **o. regum** 13c.; **molendinum -arium,** oil mill 1705; ‡**-itas** 1652, **-ositas** 1620, 1622, oiliness; **-atus,** anointed c 950; **-o,** to give extreme unction to 1097.

olf/atus, sense of smell a 1250; **-abilis, -atibilis,** perceptible by smell a 1250.

oli-, *see also* **oleagium.**

oliba, *see* OLIV

olibanus, *see* **libanus.**

olig/archia, oligarchy c 1343, c 1434; **-archice,** oligarchically c 1343; **-archicus,** oligarchic c 1343; **-opolium,** right of sale restricted to few 1516.

ol/im (*adj.*), former c 793; *see also* **ab; -itanus,** ancient, primitive c 793. c 1188.

oliotropium, *see* HELI

oliv/are oleum, olive oil 1337; **oliba,** *for* **-a,** c 730; **-ero currente,** in full tide of fortune (*cf.* O.F. *olivier courant*) c 1200; **-o,** (?) to moisten *or* darken c 550.

oll/a, measure of ale 1290; crater of volcano 1252; chimney-pot 1363; fish-trap 1508; gun-barrel 1400; **o. correa,** leather bottle 1428; †**o. crucea,** "gyngyll" 1430; **o. galear',** (?) skull-piece of helmet 1172; **o. pistrina,** baking-pot 1200; **-um,** *for* **-a** 1274; **-eola, -iola,** small pot 1317, 1388; **-ula,** "posnet" 1553; **-aria,** pottery 1086; **-arius** 1288, 1399, **-ator** 1311, potter; **metallum -earium,** "pot metal" 1551; **-ata,** potful 1266; *see also* HOLO

olmus, *see* **2 holma.**

olo-, *see also* HOLO

oloflamma, *see* **auriflamba.**

†**olto,** to fit or tune strings c 1160.

Olym/phus (Olim-), *for* **-pus,** heaven c 550; **-phius, -peus, -brianus** c 550, **-piacus** c 950, Olympian, celestial; **-phas,** Olympiad 1271; **-pias,** quadrennium a 615, c 950.

‡**oma,** mace (spice) 13c.; ‡**stench** 13c.

omasia (*n. pl.*), tripe 1422.

†**omasus,** (?) intermediary a 1142.

omellus, *see* ULM

om/en, authority, status (esp. contrasted with **nomen**) c 1197, c 1430; **-inalis,** ominous c 1160.

omentum: aumentum, (?) gut 1430; ‡**"haggis"** 15c.

omn/is, any c 1200; **per -ia,** in all respects c 1200, c 1340; **-i via,** always c 1115; *see also* **anima, sanctus; -ibonus,** all-good c 1357; **-icreans** (?) c 1000. 12c., 14c., **-icreator** 12c., all-creator; **-icremus,** all-consuming c 1184; **-ifarie,** in every way 1345, c 1457; **-ifarius** c 1125, c 1453, **-igenus** c 1000, of all sorts; **-ificus,** versatile, changeable c 1180; busy about everything c 1200; **-ifidius,** accepting any faith (theol.) c 1620; **-imode** 8c. c 1180, 1345, **-imodis** 1041, †**-imodum** 13c., **-ino** 8c., in every way; entirely 8c.; ***-imodus,** of all sorts c 1090, 1547; **-ipatrans,** all-accomplishing, God 931, 11c. 12c., 14c.; **-ipatro,** to accomplish all 933; **-ipotentatus** c 1250, 1315, **-ipotentia** c 1190, 1461, omnipotence; **-ipresens,** omnipresent 1344; **-iquaque,** in every way 1344, 1427; **-isapiens,** all-wise c 1357; **-isciens,** omniscient 1378, 1686; **-iscientia,** omniscience c 1343, c 1380; **-itenens,** all-sustaining c 810, c 1000; **-ivolens,** all-willing c 1290.

†**omonisia,** a compound drug a 1250.

omo/plata a 1250, ‡15c., ‡**-spalta** 14c., shoulder-blade (ὠμοπλάτη).

omphax, sour grape: **onfacus** (†**onifacus**) a 1250.

on/ager, (?). aurochs c 1222; **anager,** *for* **o.,** 1281; **-ocephalus,** ass-headed 1662; **-ocrotulus** 1353, **anacrotulus** 14c., *for* **-ocrotalus,** (?) bittern; **-ocratulus** c 1000, †**nonotrochalus** c 1260, (?) pelican.

‡**oncus,** tumour 15c.

onoma c 605, 1031. c 1125, a 1275, †**ononoma** 965, name.

onus, load (measure of coal) 1415; burthen (naut.) 1296; c 1300, 1541, **oner/atio** c 1335, 1544, 'charge', debit side of account; **o. armorum,** war-scot c 1185; **o. hominis,** man-load 1296; **o. naturale,** excrement 1401; **o. juris,** force of law a 1408; **o. redditus,** rent-charge c 1470; **in -e,** in the charge (of) 1575; **-atio,** loading, burden 12c.; 1420; charge, commission 1348; charging a jury c 1395; **-abilis,** chargeable c 1456, a 1539; **-agium,** cargo due, (?) lastage (Lymington) 1271; **-ator (navis),** merchant providing cargo 1560; **navis -ifera,** cargo ship c 1190; **animal -iferum** a 1200; **-osus,** hostile 1041; **onusta,** pregnant c 1190; **-o,** to load (gun) 1573, 1622; to stock (woodland) 1086; to charge (a jury, etc.), adjure a 1250, 1533; *to charge, debit 1236, 1538; **o. super compotum,** to debit (accountant) with disallowed item of expenditure 1356, 1449; **onoro (honoro),** *for* **-o,** a 1230, 1487, **onusto** (eccl.), **onustro** 1454, to load.

onych/a (onic-) c 1250, **-ulus** 1215, **-leum** 1267, onyx.

opac/itas, opacity c 1360; obscurity c 1150; **obpacitas,** darkness c 1266; ‡**-um,** flawn, pancake 15c., 1483.

opal/ius 1620, **optalius** a 1250, *for* **-us,** opal.

‡**opanachum,** a medicinal gum (? *or* opopanax) c 1200.

opelandensis, *see* UPLAND

***opella,** shop, workshop 1431, 1580.

oper-, *see also* **opus.**

oper/tio, closing of eyes 8c.; ‡**-itio ignis,** curfew 1570; **-iculum,** hiding-place 9c.; **-imentum,** altar-cloth 1434; roofing c 1185; **-itor,** thatcher 1185; **-torium,** (?) garment or coverlet (of fur) 1184; **-tum,** covert 1214; **-tura,** lid 1432; **oportura,** covering c 1500; **-tus,** oppressive c 1000; **-atus,** *for* **-tus,** covered a 1150; **-io,** to roof 1188.

ophialtes, *see* **ephialtes.**

‡**ophiasis,** disease causing baldness 14c.

ophthalm/us, eye: ‡**talmus** 14c., 1483; **-ia** 1345, **obtalmia** a 1250, ophthalmia; ‡**optalma alba** 15c.; **obtalm/icus (-us),** ophthalmic c 550. a 1250.

opiat/um, opiate a 1250, 1622; **-us,** soporific 1620.

†**opicizum,** (?) roof *or* window-frame c 950.

opi/cula, help, contribution c 1000; **-ficus,** helpful 1276.

opifer, *see* OPIPAR

†**opigaidum,** (?) *for* **abrotonum,** southern-wood (bot.) 12c.

opi/men, -minium, rich food c 550.

opin/abilis c 1343, **-iabilis** c 1361, 1426, tenable, resting on opinion; **-ans,** maintainer

(of opinion) c 1343; **-anter** 12c., **-ative**
c 1343, a 1452, **-iative** c 1361, as an opinion;
-atissimus (bibl.), **-iatissimus** c 990, most
renowned; †**-iatiuncula**, whimsy c 1500;
†**-io**, to opine a 1361.
†**opi/nus**, (?) *for* **-imus**, c 950.
opipar/atus 12c., †**opifer** (? *for* **-us**) 1281,
sumptuous; ‡**-o**, to ennoble 1483.
opirus (panis), made without bran (?αὐτόπυρος)
a 1250, ‡14c.
opisthotonos, drawn backwards (med.): **epitostonos** a 1250.
opitul/atio (bibl.), **-amen** 13c., 1529, help;
‡**-ativa** (*pl.*), drugs for curing flux 1652; *see
also* **opulentia**.
oplondina, *see* UPLAND
‡**opo/meconium**, poppy juice 15c.; **-pyra**,
"*succus ignitus*" a 1250, ‡15c.
oport/ativus, right, fitting 13c.; **-et**, it is
inevitable 1267.
oportura, *see* OPER
oppallio (**obp-**), to clothe c 1200.
opparo, to prepare against a 1142.
oppid/um, castle a 1142, 1419; **-ani**, townsmen, non-members of university (ac.)
c 1550, 1578.
oppilat/io, obstruction (med.) a 1250, 1424;
-ivus, obstructive a 1250, ‡15c.
opploratio, complaint 1518.
opposit/io, opposition, objection c 1080,
p 1381; setting against (in equation) (math.)
1145; disputation (ac.) c 1410, c 1590;
apposal, examination 1357; opposition
(astr.) 1120, 1686; **-as**, opposite property
(mus.) c 1470; **-ivus**, resistant, conflicting
a 1250, 1327; **-or**, opponent, objector 1292,
1684; 1332, 1406, **o. forinsecus** 1399, 1593,
†**opponitor** 1338, foreign apposer (Exchequer official); *cf.* **appositor**; **-um**, the
opposite, contradictory (log.) c 850. 1241,
c 1382; **-us**, inversely proportional (math.)
1145; **-um augis**, perigee (astr.) 1267; *see
also* **ad, ex, per**; **-us**, opposite (astr.) 13c.;
oppon/ens, disputant (ac.) a 1345, c 1583;
-o, *to dispute (ac.) c 1282, c 1592; to appose
examine a 1410; to lay to the charge of, urge
against (leg.) c 1290, c 1343; **o. contra**, to
object 1416, 1417.
oppress/ura, tribulation c 730. c 1332; **-ivus**,
oppressive c 1250, 1303; **-or**, oppressor
c 1250, 1381; **-o**, to burden c 1470.
opprobr/iose, opprobriously c 1250, c 1400;
-ius, *for* **-osus**, opprobrious 1419.
ops-, *see* **obs-**
opt-, *see also* **obt-**
optalius, *see* OPAL
optalma, *see* **ophthalmus**.
opt/atus 1612, **obsio** c 1397, *for* **-io**, desire;
-abiliter, desirably c 1000; **-ative**, opta-
tively, as a wish c 1080, c 1197; **-ator**,
desirer c 1180; **obto**, *for* **-o**, to desire 875.
c 1115; **-o** (with *acc.* and *ut*), to beseech 6c.
opte/sis, roasting c 1270; **-ticus**, of or for
roasting c 1270.
optic/itas, magnifying power 1267; **-a** (*n. pl.*)
1267, (*f. s.*) 1686, optics; **-us** c 1115, 1686,
obticus a 1250, optic.
optim/as 1070, c 1370, **-atus** 779, **obtimas**
957, c 1040. 12c., magnate; **-us Maximus**,
divine epithet 1537, 1552.

optomera, sort of pill (med.) a 1250.
optutus, *see* **obtuitus**.
opulentia, abundance: **opitulentia** c 760.
opus, *customary service, esp. day-work
(man.) 739, 11c. 1100, 1536; workmanship
c 1220; peltry 1325; embroidery 1445; **in
oper/e**, in practice c 1265; *see also* **ad**; **o.
-atum**, objective action of sacrament (theol.)
c 1175; product of handicraft (G.) 1295;
o. album, silver-making, **o. rubeum**, gold-
making (alch.) c 1320; **o. nigrum**, black ore,
(?) galena 1300, 1323 (*cf.* **2 mina**); **o.
mortuum**, (?) rock containing no ore 1323;
o. aquaticum, drainage works 1587; **o.
custumale** 1293, **o. custumarium** 1390,
1573, **o. manuale** a 1300, 1336, **o. rusticum**
1086, **o. servile** c 1258, **o. grossum**,
o. parvum 1296, types of villein service;
o. dierum 1573, **o. diurnale** c 1115, day-
work; **o. precarium**, boon-work 1398,
1449; **o. regis**, *trimoda necessitas* 1086;
o. carreti, carrying service 1097; **o. castelli**,
burhbote 1097, c 1176; **o. pontis**, brigbote
1097, c 1280; **o. conjugale**, conjugal rights
c 1220, 1397; **o. Dei** the mass c 1185; **o.
ecclesie**, (upkeep of) church fabric 1190,
1377; **o. expulsi**, maintenance of an outlaw
c 1110; **oper/a** (*pl.*) **caritatis** 12c., 1361,
-a pietatis c 1200, c 1220, **-a pia** c 1528,
1559, good works;
(kinds of peltry, esp. squirrel) **o. bissum**
1303; **o. grossum** 1303; **o. griseum** 1234,
1298; **o. nigrum** c 1324; **o. rubeum** 1397,
15c.;
(styles of embroidery, *etc.*) **opus acus**,
needlework c 1509; **o.** †**araeni**, (?) arras
c 1395; **o. circulare** c 1315; **o. fili** 1300;
o. Flandrense 1465; **o. mappale** 1295;
o. Northfolchie, (?) worsted 1388; **o.
orbiculare**, **o. orbum** 1245; **o. Parisiense**
1388, 1393; **o. plumarium**, feather-stitch
c 793. c 1295; **o. pectineum** 1295; **o.
pulvinarium**, cushion-work 1295; **o.
Romanum** 1388; **o. scabellinum** c 1550;
o. tapistre 1521;
(styles of metal-work, *etc.*) **o. Dunel-
mense** 1208, 1295; **o. elevatum** 1303,
o. †**elmatum** (? **elivatum**) 1445, **o.
levatum** 1245, 1313, **o. propulsatum**
c 1255, embossed work, chasing in relief;
o. †**liniare** (? **limare**, filing) 1326; **o.
nigellatum**, niello work 1295; **o. Parisiense** 1232, c 1452; **o. pinonatum** 1295;
o. Salamonis 12c.; **o. trifarium**, tri-
forium, **trifuriale, trifuriatum**, trefoil
work 1245; **o. Lemoviticum** 1229, **o.
Lemovicinum** 1240, **o. Limocenum** 1298,
Limoges enamel; **o. Saracenicum**, **Sara-
cenum** 1295, **o.** †**Sartacinitum** 1245, **o.
Saresinum** c 1503, arabesque design;
oper/abilia (*pl.*), handicrafts 1419; matters of conduct or practice 1345, 1380;
-abilis, able to be produced (or affected) by
action c 1250, p 1300; **dies -abilis** 1226,
1449, **d. -alis** 1352, **d. -ativus** 1467, work-
ing-day; **-abilis** 1222, **-arius** 1181, 1306,
subject to labour-service; **-agium**, coining
1282, 1289; **-alis**, expressed in action c 1376,
c 1377; **-amentum** c 550, **-amen** 1280,
work; **-ans** 1195, 1439, *-ator** 1207, 1566,

worker; **-ans,** casual worker (distinguished from **-arius**) 1371; **-aria,** forge c 1315; †**-arium** 15c., **-atorium** c 1182, 1329, workshop; **-arius** (with *gen.*) worker, maker, of 6c., 7c. 1321, 1474; **-arius** 1222, 14c., †**-ariator** a 1300, customary tenant; **statutum de -ariis** 1353, **s. pro -ariis** 1364, Statute of Labourers; *see also* **justitiarius;** **-aticus,** capable of working a 1361;

-atio, *labour-service, day-work 1142, 1430; *effectual power, effect c 1080, 1414; *working up, treatment (of material) 1242, c 1534; manufacture, construction (of product) 1193, 1456; work, product 1358, 1416; operation, experiment (alch.) a 1235, 1419; *construction, building-work 1203, c 1458; literary work, book c 1397; **o. castelli** a 1100, 1190, **o. castri** 1415, burhbote; **o. pontis,** brigbote 1189; **o. ecclesie,** (upkeep of) church fabric c 1125, 1221; **o. stanni,** tin-works 1398; **-ativa,** practical experiment 1620; **-ativus,** practical a 1250, 1620; **-atrix,** worker (*f.*) c 1000. c 1160, c 1423; **-ata** (*pl.*), operations 1267; **-osissime,** most carefully c 730; **-o,** to work, perform c 730. c 1258, c 1362; to perform labour-services a 1125, 1450; to work up (raw material) c 1400, 1456; to embroider 1269, 1432; to engrave, chase (metal) 1208, 1423; to operate, predict (astr.) a 1292; to till the earth 1231; **-or** (*dep.*), to perform good works c 1275.

1 ora, class or order 793.

2 ora 1086, 13c., **ores** c 1200, 'ore', ounce of silver.

oracul/um, demonstration of divine will c 600; 5c., 8c., **oramen** 9c., c 950, prayer; church 645; sanctuary 955; shrine, oratory c 1250; **-a** (*pl.*) 1472, 1532, **-e** (*pl.*) 1509, c 1534, beads; **-um celeste,** Scripture 8c.; **o. vive vocis,** authoritative utterance 1259, c 1520.

orama, *see* **horoma.**

‡**oranum,** treasury 15c.

orapondina, *see* **crapaudinus.**

orarium, vestment, stole (eccl.) c 760, 9c. 12c., 1537; bordure (her.) c 1595.

*orat/io** (eccl.), **-us** c 950, orison, prayer; **o. de die, o. diei,** prayer of the day c 1395; **o. dominica** 11c. c 1102, 1549, **o. dominicalis** 1298, Lord's Prayer; **Liber de -ione Communi** 1551; *see also* **pars;** **-ionalis,** of or for prayer c 1125; **-ionaliter,** in the form of a sentence 13c.; **-iuncula,** short prayer 1516; **-or,** one who prays, petitioner, bedesman a 1142, 1477; spokesman, ambassador 1324, 1570; **o. populi,** Speaker of House of Commons c 1532, a 1536; **o. publicus** (ac.) 1522, 1636; **-oricus,** rhetorical 1271; **-oriolum,** little oratory 6c., c 1000. 14c.; **-orium,** church c 900; *oratory, bedehouse c 1090, 1586; rosary 1533; **-rix,** bedeswoman 1408, 1518; **oro me,** to pray c 1280.

orb/a, 'orb', blank panel (arch.) a 1490; **-um** (†**orobum**), part of intestine a 1250; **ictus -us, -is,** blow without swelling or blood 1221, 1271; **placitum -i,** (?) plea arising from such a blow 1171; **-o,** to desert, leave empty c 550.

†**orbanibulus,** false prophet (Sc.) 1282.

orbateria, *see* **AURI**

orb/is, natal planet (astr.) c 1390; roundel (her.) c 1595; **-s, for -is,** world 1413; **-icularis,** rounded, spherical c 1220, 1415; orbital, cyclic a 1250, 1252; *see also* **opus; -iculariter,** in a circle c 1115, p 1394; **-iculatus,** with round spots a 1250, 13c.; rounded off 1326; **-iculus,** eye-ball 12c., c 1400; bead 1583; **-i** (*pl.*), game, marbles c 1160; *see also* **orba.**

orbit/a, (?) round pillow c 1180; ‡wheel-rim c 1200; ‡swathe 1483; **-alis,** cyclic c 1325; **-o,** to diverge 793. c 1357.

orb/us, -o, *see* **orba.**

orceolus, *see* **urceolus.**

‡**orchestra,** "chair" 13c., 1483; **orcistra,** pulpit a 1142.

orcigenus, hell-born 9c.

ord-, *see also* **hordeum.**

ord/alium c 1115, 1586, **-ela, -elum** c 1125, 1200, **-olaium** 1419, (trial by) ordeal (leg.); **o. simplex, o. triplex** c 1115; **lex -alia,** law of ordeal 1608.

ordium, measure of land (G.) 1289; (?) *cf.* **hordeum.**

ordo, bookshelf c 1296; position in decimal notation (math.) c 1150;

clergy, status or person of priest c 1102, c 1115; ordination 760, 10c. 1220, 1523; **o. acolytatus** 1220, 1552; **o. clericalis** c 1090, 1270, **o. clericatus** c 1115, 1194; **o. ecclesiasticus,** (?) ordained clergy c 1000; **o. diaconatus** c 1250, 1279; **o. episcopalis** c 1080; **o. presbyteratus** a 1100, c 1480; **o. psalmistatus** 1345; **o. sacer** c 1444, **o. sacerdotalis** c 1464, **o. sacerdotis** 1234, c 1250; **o. subdiaconalis** c 1331, **o. subdiaconatus** c 1250, 1279;

*religious order c 1125, 1565; **o. albus** 1370, **o. dealbatus** c 1188, Cistercian; **o. griseus,** Franciscan c 1250; **o. niger,** Benedictine 1242, 1530; **o. regularis,** order of Canons Regular 12c.; **o. Cartusie** c 1180; **o. Castri** 1275; **o. Cistercii** 1147; **o. Fontis Ebroudi** 1260; **o. Grandis Montis** 1242; **o. de Grosmund** c 1217; **o. mendicantium** c 1317, c 1478; **o. minorum** 1230, c 1458; **o. m. de Observantia** 1549; **o. Prati Monstrati** c 1230, **o. de Pratomonstrato** c 1220; **o. predicatorum** c 1250, 16c.; **o. S. Clare** 1294; **o. S. Augustini** 1306; **o. S. Benedicti** 1306, 1499; **o. S. Salvatoris** 1432; **o. de Semplingham** 1233, **o. de Simplingham** 1194, 1203; **o. tertius,** Tertiary Order (Franciscan) 15c., 1453;

o. militaris, order of knighthood 1347, 1429; **o. Christi** (Port.) 1454; **o. Garterii (Gartarii)** 1492, 1558;

*ordin/es** (*pl.*), holy orders c 1110, 1552; **o. sacri** c 1090, 1551; **o. majores** a 1245, c 1408; **o. minores** 1244, 1573; **littere -um,** letters of ordination 14c., 1686;

*-abilis,** orderly, able to be placed in order 13c., c 1367; able to be directed 1659; **-abilitas,** orderliness c 1283, c 1367; *-abiliter** c 820, 9c. c 1088, c 1400, **-aliter** 815. c 1250, 1347, in good order, in orderly fashion; *-ale** c 1200, 1555, **-arium** c 1080, c 1450, **liber -alis** c 1437, **l. -arius** c 1350,

ordinal, directory (eccl.); **-alis**, disciplinary c 1283; **-amentum**, regulation, moderation a 1250; 1344, **-antia** c 1367, 1591, ordinance; **-antia**, ordering, arrangement c 1362; p 1439, 1490, **o. ad bellum** 1460, ordnance, military equipment; **-arie**, as a regent master (ac.) c 1250, c 1350; **-arium**, lecture of a regent master (ac.) 1424, c 1453; *see also* **lectio**; (*subst.*) ordinary (eccl.) c 1160, 1549; (*adj.*) of or for an ordinary (eccl.) 1200, a 1558; **judex o.** (eccl.) 1200, 1418; **ex -ario**, in due course c 1307;

-atio, *ordination (eccl.) c 1070, c 1450; ordnance (military) 1404, 1583; 1325, **-atum** 1347, allowance (mon.); **o. pro communitate ville**, by-law 1369; **-atissime**, most methodically c 1250, 1440; **-ative**, in respect of order or succession c 1250, 1378; **-ativus**, ordering p 1300, c 1362; **-ator**, corrector, punisher c 730; one who ordains c 1000; arbiter 1231, 1354; ordainer (eccl.) c 1100, 1307; **-atores** (*pl.*), Lords Ordainers 1311, c 1400; **-ium**, posterity, succession (G.) 1254, 1339; **-andus**, candidate for holy orders c 1220; **-atum**, ordinance 13c., 1549; **-atus** (*4th decl.*), equipment c 1193; **-atus** (*2nd decl.*), ordained priest c 1102, c 1420; **-ata** (*sc.* **linea**), ordinate (geom.) 1686; **potentia -ata**, ordinate power c 1334, c 1361; **-o** (with *abl.*), to furnish 9c.; *to ordain (eccl.); to supply with an incumbent (eccl.) 1194, c 1250; **o. me**, to take holy orders 1418; **o. regem**, to consecrate a king 893, c 1050. 12c., c 1197.
ordolaium, *see* **ordalium**.
ord/ura, ordure, rubbish 1248, 1313; **-us**, filthy 1275.
oreginale, *see* ORIGIN
oregm/os a 1250, **-on** 13c., c 1255, death-rattle.
ores, *see* 2 **ora**.
orf-, *see* AURI
organ/um, instrumentality, agency c 1397, 1448; instrument, document 1419; part of psalter c 1090, a 1205; form of harmony (mus.) 1326, c 1470; organ of body c 1200, c 1270; tongue, organ, or power of speech c 1070, 1449; **o. vocis**, mouthpiece 1424; **o. Spiritus Sancti**, mouthpiece of Holy Ghost c 1414, c 1444; **-icus** c 950. c 1267, 1620, **-ius** a 1360, organic; accompanied by organ c 1000; **liber -icus**, book of organ music 1390; **vena -ica**, jugular vein a 1250; *see also* **cantus**; **-arius** 1364, **-ista** c 1200, 1537, **-izator** 1496, **lusor in -is** 1515, **ministrallus ad -a** 1418, organ-player; composer of harmonies 1326; †**-istrum**, a musical instrument 1149, c 1325; **-izatio**, organization a 1250, c 1362; **-izo**, to contrive, arrange c 1190; to provide (body) with sense organs c 1270, 1620; to sing, croon (of birds) 1149, c 1325; to play organ 1307, 1530; to accompany on organ c 1090, c 1248.
orgeum, *see* **hordeum**.
orgi/um, duty, work c 550; **o. bellicosum**, warfare c 1000; **-a** (*pl.*), religious mysteries c 1000.
orgya, fathom (ὄργυια) 1622; **oria**, yard c 700.
orichalceus 13c., **auricalc/us** c 1200, **-atus** 1431, brazen.

oriellum, *see* **oriolum**.
orien/s, eastern c 1250, c 1266; ‡*sal urinae* 1652; **-taliter**, on the east 1423, 1587.
orifalus, *see* **oxybaphus**.
oriflamma, *see* **auriflamba**.
Origen/ica (*pl.*), writings of Origen 1529; **-sis**, follower of Origen c 730.
origin/atio p 1300, a 1350, **-antia** c 1375, origination (log.); origin c 1470; **-ale** *1202, 1447, **-alis** c 1476, **oreginale** 1480, original (? or authentic) document, as distinct from copy; complete (esp. patristic) work, as distinct from excerpts c 1270, 15c.; 1270, 1337, **o. Cancellarie** 1405, Exchequer copy of Chancery enrolment, item on Originalia Rolls; c 1258, 15c., **breve -ale** 1200, 1595, original (i.e. originating) writ; c 1225, **peccatum -ale** c 1080, c 1510, **p. -is** 1562, original sin; **-alis**, of or from our origin 9c. c 1170; belonging to the principal (of a debt) c 1400; **linea o.**, line of descent c 1325; **mundus o.**, antediluvian world 12c., 1345; **-aliter**, by origin, originally 655, 8c. 1267, 1461; **-arius** c 1212, 13c., **-alius** 1327, neif, villein; (*adj.*) native 1486, 1489; originating, creative c 1160, a 1350; **-ativus**, originative (phil.) p 1300; **-o**, to originate, give rise to c 1290, 15c.; †**origo**, to rise 1519.
orilogium, *see* **hora**.
oriol/um *1233, c 1450, **-a** 1236, **-dum** 1186, **oriellum** 1236, **auriolum** 1268, oriel, gallery, upper room; porch 1234, a 1452; *see also* AURE
ori/on, rising c 550; **-or**, to issue (of a rent) 1237.
‡**oristrigium**, muzzle c 1440.
orium, *see* **horreum**.
orlagium, *see* **hora**.
orlo, *see* **urla**.
ormesta (mundi), title of a book, (?) *Or[osii] m[undi] ist[ori]a* a 1142, c 1443.
orminum, *see* **horminum**.
ormiscus, *see* **hormiscus**.
orn/amentatio a 1564, **-atio** 1330, 1424, **-atura** c 1118, **-aculum** c 950, ornamentation, adornment; **-anter**, finely c 1450; **-aticius**, ornamental 1041.
ornix, pheasant 1419, 1422; ‡**orna, fornix,** woodcock 15c.; **ornith/ius ventus**, Etesian wind 1622; **-opodium**, birdsfoot (bot.) 1629.
ornotinus, *see* **hornotinus**.
orobum, *see* **orba**.
oroma, *see* **horoma**.
‡**oroyda**, whey (ὀρρώδης) 15c.
orphan/us, orphan (bibl.); (*adj.*) orphaned, destitute 13c., c 1362; c 1200, **-atus** 1435, bereft; **-a**, orphan girl 1419; **-inus**, like an orphan 1293; **-itas**, destitution 1136; ‡**-atorium**, "alms-house" c 1440.
orphar-, orphr-, orpimentum, *see* AURI
‡**orpina**, orpine (bot.) 15c.
orriale, *see* AURICUL
orstonum, ore-stone 1353.
orte (*pl.*), 'orts', scraps of fodder 1376.
ort/ellus 1310, **-illus** 1217, 13c., claw, dog's toe (Fr. *orteil*).
***orthodox/us**, orthodox Christian c 1080, 1467; **-e**, according to ecclesiastical procedure c 1250; according to true doctrine c 1400, 1534.

orthogon/us (†**ortoganus**), right-angled a 1250, 1326; **-alis**, drawn at right angles c 1109, 1326; **-aliter**, at right angles c 1109, c 1595; ‡**-ium**, square 15c.

orthonoismus, straightforwardness 12c.

orthopnea (med.): **orthomi/a** a 1250; **-acus**, orthopnoic a 1250.

orticumetra, *for* **ortygometra** (bird), c 550.

ortillus, *see* **ortellus**.

ortiphinium, *see* **arcifinium**.

1 ort/o, -or, to procreate c 597, c 730.

2 †orto, (?) to trim (wood for fuel) 1401.

ortum, *see* **hordeum**.

orvala, 'orval', clary (bot.) 1538.

orynale, *see* URIN.

oryza, rice: **ris/a** 1205, 15c., **-ia** 1358, **-um**, **-us** 1258, 1538, **rizum** a 1250, **-i** (*indecl.*) a 1250, ‡1483, **rizi** a 1250, ‡14c.

1 os, board, personal expenses 1300; **os regis**, royal table, 'bouche of court' (leg.) 1237, 1461; ***os gladii**, edge of the sword c 1100, 1461; **os stomachi** (med.) a 1250; **ore ad os**, by word of mouth a 1142, c 1240; **ex ore**, in the name (of) c 1250; **per os**, (?) dictated by c 1250; **uno ore**, unanimously 1432.

2 os cerebri, brain-pan 1323; **o. unicorni**, (?) narwhal's tusk 1431; **oss/a Ade** (alch.) a 1292; †**-a** c 1362, **-um** 1221, **-u** c 730, *for* **os**; **-amenta** (*pl.*), collection of bones 1209, 1419; **-aria**, *for* **-arium**, charnel-house 1465; †**-aceus** 1605, **-ilis** c 550, bony; **-atio**, ossification 1427; **-iculum** c 970, **oscillum** 1200, little bone; **-uositas**, boniness a 1250.

osceum, scrotum (ὄσχεον) c 1248, ‡14c.

oscill/atorius, oscillatory 1686; *see also* **2 os**.

oscitantia, negligence, sloth 1537, 1590.

oscul/um 12c., 13c., ***o. pacis** 9c., c 1000. 1169, 1435, **o. sanctum** 771, kiss of peace; bridal gift (G.) 1255, 1292; **-amentum**, kiss 1282; **-are** 1281, **-atorium** 1248, 1532, **tabula -atoria** 1388, **tabella o.** c 1524, pax (eccl.).

osebandus, *see* **husbandus**.

oser/a c 1140, 1297, **-ia** 1296, **osiera** 1344, osier, willow; †**osorium**, (?) osier-bed 1515; **oisereum**, wicker basket (Norm.) 1198.

osmondum 1397, 1504, **ose/mondum** 1284, c 1300, **-mundum** 1438, 'osmond', Swedish iron.

osmunda, royal fern (bot.) a 1250, 1632.

oss-, *see* **2 os**.

ost-, *see also* HOST

ostadum, sort of cloth 1521.

osten/sio, demonstration, proof 8c. a 1185, 1236; ostentation c 1250; 'shewage', scavage a 1100, 1419; c 1257, 1339, **-tatus** c 1173, muster (of troops); 8c. **o. terre**, view of land 1205; **-cio**, *for* **-sio**, manifestation 1461; **-sibilis**, ostensible c 1300; ***-sive**, by way of showing 1292, 1378; ***-sivus**, demonstrative 1274, 1416; **-sor presentium**, bearer 1328; **-sum**, exhibit (leg.) 1400; **-tamen**, show, display a 1100; **-tatrix**, ostentatious (*f.*) a 1200; **-tatum**, small division of time 8c.; a minute c 730. c 1265.

osterius, *see* **austurcus**.

osternum, *see* **hostia**.

†**ostigeloricon**, form of syllogism c 1200.

osti/um (**hosti-**), door: **ad o. ecclesie** c 1185, 1259, **ad hostillariam e.** 1294, at marriage;

o. pincerne, ushership of the Buttery 1199; **-olum**, little door c 1197, 1518; †**-anus**, (?) sought from door to door a 1250; **-aria**, portress 12c., 1250; *1198, 1357, **-eria** a 1190, **-aratus** 1200, **-ariatus** 1245, 1258, **-aritas** 1212, office of porter or usher; **-aria** (*n. pl.*), (?) usher's fees 1236; **-arium** 1250, **husseria, usseria** 1274, 1286, door-frame; **ussera** 1212, **uscerium** 1336, **vicerius** c 1220, **hissirus** c 1460, barge for horses (Fr. *huissier*); **-arius**, 'ostiary', member of minor clerical order (eccl.) c 1123, 1423; usher (school-teacher *or* pupil door-keeper) 1242, c 1432; **ussarius**, usher, door-keeper 1219; **-arius Cambii** a 1275; **o. Camere** c 1390, 1468; **o. Garderobe** 1258; **o. Parliamenti** c 1300, **o. de Recepta** 1226, 1291, **o. de Scaccario** 1220, 1332, **o. Thesauri** c 1178; **usherpageus**, page acting as usher c 1358.

Ostmann/us 12c., 1317, **-icus** 13c., Osmannus 1201, 1215, **Hostimannus** 1234, **Ostomannus** 1584, **Estmannus** 1290, **Oustmannus** (†**Custmannus**, †**Eustmannus**) 1213, c 1312, †**Custumannus** 1283, Ostman, Scandinavian settler (Ir.).

ostorius, ostur-, *see* **austurcus**.

ostri/ca, -cium, -gius, -us, *see* **struthio**.

1 ostrium, (?) *for* **astrum** *or* **atrium**, hearth 1251.

2 ostr/ium c 1200, 1337, **-eus** 655, **oistra** 1338, 1454, *for* **-ea**, oyster; ‡**-a**, oyster-shell 15c.; purple colour c 550; **-eus**, purple c 550; **-iger**, purple-bearing c 685; †**osturinum**, (?) purple cloth a 1100.

ostupo, *see* OBSTUP

otalgicus, afflicted with ear-ache: **notalgicus**, deaf c 550; **nervus obtalgicus**, auditory nerve c 1210.

otios/itas, idleness (bibl.); **animal -um**, ox not used for draught *etc.* a 1128; **-us homo**, 'idleman', retainer (Ir.) 1297, 1339.

oto/mega, omega (ὦ τὸ μέγα) c 1200, 15c.; **-micron**, omicron c 1200.

otrix, otter 1428; *cf.* **luter**.

oubelcora, *see* **obelchera**.

ouncia, *see* **2 uncea**.

ousias, *see* **usia**.

Oustmannus, *see* **Ostmannus**.

outesium, *see* **hutesium**.

outlag-, *see* UTLAG

outorius, *see* **austurcus**.

outtollum, 'out-toll', due paid on giving up possession of burghal land (Sc.) 1464.

ov/agium, -aceum, -alis, -atio, *see* **ovum**.

ov/amen, triumph 1413; **-anter**, exultantly c 1000. c 1125, c 1470; **obo**, to exult c 550.

†**ovecarius**, (?) shepherd c 1140.

ovenama, *see* **offnama**.

oventio, *see* **obventio**.

†**overepa**, part of cart harness, (?) 'over-rope' 1307.

over/hyrnessa (†**-seunessa**, *etc.*), fine for disobedience (A.S. *oferhiernes*) c 1115.

overinstura, *see* WARECT

overlondum, 'overland', excess land 1302, 1355.

over/restclutum 1278, 1279, **-risclutum** 1308, 'over-reest clout' (of plough); *cf.* **2 resta**.

ovio, *see* **obvio.**

ov/is 1252, 1559, **-icula** 8c. 12c., c 1400, sheep of Christ's flock; **o. mater** c 1175, **o. matrialis** 12c., ***o. matrix** 1185, 1464, ewe; **-ianus,** shepherd c 1200; **-iale** a 1260, **-ilium** 1152, **domus -ilis** 1553, *for* **-ile,** sheepfold; **-ile,** the Church c 1090, 1559; monastery 12c.; **-illa,** 'flock' (eccl.) c 950; **-inus,** *of sheep c 1178, 16c.; woollen 1241; **-ilio,** to fold (sheep) c 1180.

ovisborda, eaves-board c 1438; †**owa,** (?) eave 1280.

ov/um griphonis (grifis), *see* **grypho; o. philosophicum** a 1292, **o. physicum** c 1345 (alch.); **-ulum,** little egg a 1200; **-agium,** (?) egg-rent (C.I.) 1182; **-alis,** oval 1267, 1686; relating to eggs 13c.; ‡**-aceum** 1570, ‡**ofasium** c 1440, egg-caudle; **-aria,** hen-wife 13c.; **-atio,** egg-laying c 1265; **-o,** to lay eggs a 1250, a 1446.

ox/boum 1368, **-ebowum** 1316, ox-bow; **-gabulum,** ox-gavel 1307.

oxidentalis, *see* OCCIDENTAL

oxy/acantha, hawthorn ‡14c., 1634; 1538, ‡**oxochanta** 1570, barberry; **-baphus** (†**-falus,** †**orifalus**), measure of 1½ *cyathi* c 1100, a 1250; **-croceum, oxirocroceum** a 1250, †**oxerocrosin** 1322, **hocsirocrocium** (†**hoc sirocrotium**) 1307, electuary containing saffron; **-gallum,** sour milk c 1200; **-phenix,** tamarind a 1250, ‡14c.; ‡**-phyllon,** geranium 14c.; **-reuma** (**-remia**) a 1250, ‡**-reum** 14c., strong vinegar; **-rodinum (-redinum),** vinegar and oil of roses a 1250; **-zacara,** vinegar and sugar a 1250, 13c.; **-zacia,** crab-apple cider a 1250; ‡**oxillo,** "to wax sour" 15c.

oy-, *see also* **oi-**

oysteria, *see* **sitarchia.**

†**ozima,** *for* **ozena,** nasal ulcer a 1250.

ozimum, *see* **ocimum.**

‡**ozo,** arsenic 1652.

‡**ozon,** henna 15c.

†**ozyanius,** (?) *for* **uranius,** heavenly c 865.

P

paag/ium, -ator, pacagium, *see* **pedagium.**

pac/amentum a 1200, c 1310, **pagamentum** 1293, 1437, **-a** 1254, **pacha** 1256, **paga** 1254, 1295, **-atio** 1196, c 1335, satisfaction, payment; **-abilis,** placable c 1250, 1307; payable 1225, c 1350; *1194, 1375, **pagabilis** 1217, marketable; **-ator,** payer, paymaster 1232, 1297; **-o** 12c., 1232, **pago** (G.) 1254, to appease; *-**o** **(de)** c 1178, c 1290, **pago** 1268, 1270, to pay (a person); *-**o** 1221, 1446, **-io** 1267, 1359, **pago** 13c., c 1275, **paio** 1284, c 1508, to pay (money, *etc.*); **-o alapam,** to deal a blow c 1190.

pacatium, *see* PACT

pacc/a (†**pact-, pack-, pak-**) 1286, 1463, *-**um** -**us** c 1300, 1506, pack, bale; **-agium** 1299, c 1335, **-atio** 1303, 1503, **-atura** 1419, 1478, **-ura** 1365, †**-aerum** c 1300, packing (esp. of wool); **-arius** 1462, 1478, **-ator** 1275, 1419, packer; **-ator,** surveyor of packing (at port) 1399; **-ettum,** packet 1304; **-filum** 1374, 1509, **pakkefilum, packum filum** 1401, pack-thread; **-o,** to pack (wool, *etc.*) 1290, 1440.

paci/ferum 1452, **tabula -fera** 1303, pax (eccl.); **-ficus,** peace-maker c 1180; **-fica** (*n. pl.*), peace offerings 1339; ‡**granum -ficum,** rice 14c.; *-**fice** c 1125, 1559, **-fico** c 1325, peaceably; **-ficentius,** more peaceably 1461; **-ficarius** 1233, **-arius, -ficator** c 1250, keeper of the peace (G.); **-fluus,** peaceful 9c.; **-fico,** to pacify c 1115; *cf.* **pax.**

pac/o, -io, pacha, *see* **pacamentum.**

Pactolus, gold (alch.) 1267.

pact/um 1401, **-icium** 1401, **paticia, paticium** 1396, 1421, **patissium** 1440, form of tribute (O.F. *pactis*) (G. & Norm.); **p. nudum, p. vestitum** (leg.) c 1290; †**pacatium,** (?) *f.l.* for **-icium,** pact 1197; **-ilis,** concocted, agreed 1518; **-ionalis,** subject to a compact c 1218; **-ionaliter,** by way of a compact c 1220; **-ionarius,** one paying tribute for licence to trade (Wallingford) 1227, 1439; collector of tribute 1471; *see also* PACC

padagium, *see* **pedagium.**

pad/ela 1380, **-ula** 1307, 'paddle' (for freeing plough from adhesive soil).

padnagium, *see* PANNAG

pad/oentum, -oentium 1289, †**paodentum** 1320, **-uentum** 1255, 1312, **-uentia** 1236, **locus -uensalis** 1289, pasture, common (O.F. *padouent*) (G.); **-erius,** overseer of pastures (G.) 1289; **-oio,** to pasture (G.) 1289.

paeletta, *see* 1 **palettus.**

paella, *see* **patella.**

paga, paga-, *see also* **pacamentum; pagius; pagus.**

pagagium, *see* **pedagium.**

pagan/ismus c 1102, c 1436, **-ia** 1397, ‡15c., the pagan world, heathenesse; c 1115, 15c., †**-issimus** c 1102, **-itas** c 1192, c 1450, paganism; **-icus,** heathenish 760; **-issimus,** most heathenish 8c., 1041. 12c., c 1430; **-izo,** to become pagan p 1380, c 1500.

pagen-, pagett-, *see* 1 **pagina; pagius; pagus.**

1 **pag/ina,** side, 'pane' (arch.) 1424, 1535 (*cf.* 1 **pannus**); 1376, 1472, **-enda** 1411, stage, pageant; **-entes** (*pl.*), pageants 1390, 1540; **-etta,** window pane 1478.

2 **pagin/a,** deed, document c 740. c 1125, 1418; Testament (bibl.) 13c.; **p. celestis** c 1180, **p. divina** c 1266, **p. sacra** c 1160, c 1553, Holy Writ; **-aliter,** in writing 9c.; **-pagines** (*pl.*), sheets (of cloth) 1445.

pagium, *see* **pedagium.**

pag/ius 1292, 1508, †**-a** 1294, **-eta** 1415, 15c., *-**ettus** 1296, 1485, **-itus** 1380, **paigettus** 1380, **pajettus** 1327, 1416, page, servant; **-ettus** 1427, 1501, **-ettarius** 1427, ship's boy.

pagnagium, *see* PANNAG

pago, *see* **pacamentum.**

pagula, bar, rail 1464, 1641; bar (leg.) 1412.

pag/us c 1250, 15c., **-a** 893, county; *cantref* (W.) a 1250; **-a,** district (Fr.) 1191; **-eni** (*pl.*) 1203, **-enses** c 1136, c 1450, **-ences** c 1350, **paisanti** 1204, countrymen, peasants.

paiagium, *see* **pedagium.**

paiella, paila, *see* **patella.**

paigettus, *see* **pagius.**

paio, *see* **pacamentum.**

pairol/ius, -us, copper pot (Provençal *pairol*) (G.) 1289.

paisa, *see* **pensa.**

paisantus, *see* **pagus.**

paiss/o, -io, *see* 1 **pesso.**

Paitevinus, *see* PICTAV

pajettus, *see* **pagius.**

pak-, *see* PACC

pal/a, spade: **-ea** 1280; *see also* 1 **palus,** 1 **pola.**

palafred-, palafrid-, *see* **palefridus.**

pal/am, in, into the open, openly c 1170, c 1260; **-o,** to reveal, declare c 550, a 700.

1 **palat/ium, -im, -or, -us,** palar/ia, -is, *see* 1 **palus.**

2 ****palat/ium,** palace (royal or episcopal) c 1125, 1526; **-inus,** courtier c 1000. a 1100, 1536; (*adj.*) 948. a 1100, c 1170, †**palentinus** a 1408, Palatine, imperial; *see also* **comes, comitatus, consul.**

pale/a 1253, **palleola** 1254, **palliola** 1245, **paylola** 1237, **aurum -ale** c 1200, a. de **palliolo** 1272, gold-flake, gold-dust; **-rium,** *for* **-arium,** chaff-house 1428; †**-stria,** (?) straw, litter (for horses) 1275; *see also* **pala.**

palearia (*pl.*), wattles of cock c 1200.

paleat/io, -us, *see* 1 **palus.**

****pal/efridus** 1086, 1452, **-efredus** 1164, c 1245, **-afridus** c 1400, 1421, **-afredus** c 1250, **-efretus** c 1290, **-fridus** 1237, c 1370, **-fredus** c 1330, 1390, **pelefridus** 1223, 1234, †**parafrithus** (?) 823, palfrey; **p. vicecomitis** 1234, 1275, **p. de Beauvyr** (Leics.) 1327, 'palfrey silver' (a form of sheriff's aid); **-efridarius** 1214, 1420, **-efridiarius** 1359, **-afridarius** 1377, **-fridarius** 1328, 1460, **-efrenarius** c 1400, **parafrenarius** c 1494, **-fraypageus** c 1358, palfreyman, groom.

pal/erium, -estria, *see* **palea.**

palest/arius, -rarius, *see* 1 **palus.**

‡**palestr/ator, -iticus,** wrestler 1483; **-o** c 1060. ‡1483, ‡**-izo** c 1440, 1483, **palustro** 1324, to wrestle.

paletta 1410, (?) **patellus** 1360, pallet (of clock).

1 **palett/us** 1213, 1417, **-a** 1273, **paeletta** 1224, 1237, 'palette', piece of plate armour.

2 **palettus,** pallet bed 1423.

palfrid-, palfray-, *see* **palefridus.**

pali-, *see also* 1 **palus.**

paliandrium, *see* **polyandrium.**

palinodia, recantation: **polinodia** c 1200.

pall/a c 790. 1150, c 1414, **-adium** c 1240, **-iolum** 1274, ****-ium** c 900, c 1000. c 1090, c 1520, **-eo** 1245, archbishop's pall; ****-a** c 790. c 1080, 1481, **-ium** c 760. 1096, 1443, **-ea** c 1240, c 1330, **-ia** c 1350, **-um** 12c.,

altar-cloth, frontal; **-a,** chalice-cover, corporal 760. 1200; crozier-cover c 1395; 1200, c 1250, **-iolum** c 1325, **-ium** c 1000. 12c., a 1273, funeral pall, shroud; c 1256, **-ium** a 1100, 15c., **-ium aureum** 12c., **-um** c 1308, **pauleum** 12c., pall, rich material; **-a marina,** species of tree a 1250, ‡15c. (but *cf.* **perla**); **-eum,** *for* **-ium,** cloak c 793. 1130, c 1434; **-ium** (fig.), cloak, pretence c 1265, c 1343; **-icatio,** wearing a cloak 13c.; **-iatio,** cloaking, disguising 12c., 1620; **-iative,** under a cloak, covertly c 1375; **-ionatus,** ornamented like archbishop's pall 1245, c 1315; **-io (-eo),** to cover, wrap c 1180, 1243; to invest (archbishop) with pall 1294, 1295; ***to cloak, disguise, palliate 9c. c 1125, 1494.

pallaius, ancient (παλαιός) c 1070.

pallamentum, *see* 1 **parliamentum.**

palleda, *see* 2 **palus.**

pall/edo c 1430, **-iditas** 1267, ‡15c., pallor.

†**pall/io,** (?) *f.l.* for passio, 12c.; *see also* **palla, papilio.**

pall/iolum, -ium, -um, *see* **palea; palla.**

†**palludum,** (?) cart-cover 1292; *cf.* **barhudum.**

1 **palm/a,** tennis (*jeu de paume*) 1393, 1461 (*see also* 2 **pila**); hand'sbreadth 1203, 1395; **p. plena,** handful 1254; **pes -e,** *see* **pes; -a ancore,** fluke of anchor 1452; **-alis** c 1190, c 1435, ‡**-aris** 1520, of a hand'sbreadth; ‡**-aria,** broideress 15c.; **-ata,** handful 1204; bargain made by handclasp 1258; slap (as penance) 8c. c 1160; **-atoria** c 1180, ‡**-atorium** 1483, 'palmer', schoolmaster's ferule; **cervus -atus,** stag with palmed antlers 1262; **-atio,** stunning blow 1270; ‡**-ito,** to bargain 15c.; **-o,** to stun 1270; to grasp 1308, ‡1570.

2 **palm/a,** 'palm', willow twig (in Palm Sunday celebrations) 1538; **p. Christi,** ‡castor-oil plant *or* (?) gromwell (bot.) 14c.; species of orchis 1634; **p.** †**mutalis,** Thebaic palm a 1250; **p. Domini** 1383; **-e** (*pl.*) c 1188, c 1330, ****dies -arum** c 1060. 1086, c 1397, **Dominica -arum** c 1080, c 1460, **(dies) D. in -is** 1124, 1533, Palm Sunday (*see also* **ramus**); **hebdomada -arum** c 1393; **frater de -is,** member of a Spanish military order (eccl.) c 1130; **-aria** (†**-acia**), palmgrove 1188; **-inus,** bearing a palm a 1275; **-arius** a 1123, 1457, **-erius** 1198, 1319, **-erus** 1212, 1242, **-ifer** c 1200, 13c., palmer, pilgrim.

palm/alis, -atus, *see* **hordeum.**

palna, *see* 1 **pannus.**

†**palnagium,** a form of toll c 1180.

palo, *see* **palam;** 1 **palus.**

palp/atio, touching, handling c 1270, 1419; **-abiliter,** palpably 1344; **-abilius,** more palpably c 1470; **-amentum** c 1000, **-atus** c 1000. c 1230, caress; **-ativus,** tactile c 1260; **-atorius,** tentative 1620; flattering 1279; **-ito,** *for* **-o,** to grope c 1230, c 1250; **-o,** *for* **-ito,** to throb 1223; to touch, handle 1306, 1371; to examine c 1458, 1465; to be conscious of 1302, 1308; c 1178, 1252, **p. iter** a 1408, to grope, feel one's way; **p. tenebras,** to grope in darkness c 1125; **p. manum,** to bribe c 1436.

‡**palpita, paupita,** "psaltery" (mus.) 15c.; (?) *cf.* **barbita.**

‡**palpo,** to cry like a vulture 1483.

paltenerius, rogue, sturdy beggar, (O.F. *pautonnier*) c 1220; **paut/oneria** (†**pant-**), beggar's wallet c 1290; **-enera** (†**pant-**), 'partner', socket for mast or supporting framework (naut.) 1296.

paltokkus, 'paltock', sleeved doublet c 1362.

palud-, *see also* **2 palus.**

palud/amentum, "jack" 1553; **-andus,** fit to be clad as soldier c 1200.

palumbarius (**accipiter**), φασσοφόνος, sparrowhawk 1544.

1* pal/us 1086, 1457, **-a** 1237, 1526, pale, stake; **-ices** 1286, **-udes** 1252, 1335, stakes (*pl.*); **-a,** stripe 1388; **-us,** pale (her.) c 1595; *1226, c 1302, **-atium** 1236, c 1460, †**-atum** 1251, ***-itium** 1091, 1573, **-itia** 1257, 1296, **-izium** 1172, **-etia** 1305, **-eatio** 1571, **-istrum** 1271, **-ura** 1276, 1502, palisade; **-atiator** 1485, 1606, **-itiator** 1435, 1606, **-ator** 1504, **-estarius** 1487, **-estrarius** 16c., **-icerus** 1368, **-itiarius** 1366, 1464, **-isarius** 1388, 'paliser', fence-keeper; **-aria,** office of paliser 1475; **-atim,** palewise (her.) p 1394; **-aris** c 1595, **-atus** 1295, a 1446, paly (her.); **-atus** c 1200, 1428, **-eatus** c 1330, c 1395, **-iatus** c 1315, 1464, **pauliatus** 1400, (?) **-idus** 1416, striped; **-eatus,** fenced 1528; **-o,** to fence, enclose with paling 1224; *cf.* **2 pela.**

2 pal/us, marsh: **palleda** 1334; **-udapium,** marsh celery 1632; ‡**-ustris,** "reed sparrow" 15c.; **-ustralis, -ustrosus,** marshy c 1362.

palustro, *see* PALESTR

palustrum, *see* **1 plaustrum.**

pama, *see* **prama.**

pamentum, *see* **pavagium.**

pamfilius 1415, **panfletus** 1345, **paunflettus** 1388, pamphlet.

pampa (**cerebri**), cortex 8c.

pampilio, a fur (? from Pampeluna) 1462; *see also* **papilio.**

pamplicium, folding screen 1509, 1512.

pan/, everything (πᾶν) 1271, ‡15c.; **-tes** (*pl.*) 6c., **-tus** 901, 11c., **pontus** 11c., all; **-anglium,** Parliament 1586; **-tegni,** *for* **-techne,** title of book (med.) c 1180, 13c.; **pant/eros** c 1200, **-eron** 13c., a precious stone; **-ocrator** 8c. 14c., **-acrator** 930, the Almighty; †**-onomasivus,** (?) taken in a universal sense c 1360.

pan/a, -ator, *see* **1 pannus.**

panagericus, *see* **panegyris.**

panagia, consecrated host (παναγία) 1424.

pan/aria, -atria, *see* **panis.**

pan/arium, pannier, basket: **-erium, -erius** 1194, 1419, †**-eorium** 1307, **-erus** 1300; *see also* **panis.**

panatus, *see* **pavagium.**

pancrati/atus, outplayed, overwhelmed c 1370; ‡**-or,** to juggle 1483.

pand/agium, -nagium, *see* **pannagium.**

pan/dectes, library c 1000; **-dochium,** universal receptacle c 1595.

pandox/atio 1229, 1471, **-atorium** c 1255, brewing, alehouse-keeping; **-atorium** 1442, 1533, **-atoria** 1466, **-eterium** 1497, **-atria** 1380, 1471, **-atrium** 15c., **-ina** 1352, 1450,

domus -atoria c 1430, 1575, **mesuagium -atorium** 1549, brewhouse, alehouse; **vasa -atoria** (*pl.*) 1442; **-ator** 1229, 1532, **pandaxator** 13c., 1383, **pandexator** a 1295, 1375, brewer, alehouse-keeper; **-atrix,** alewife 1223, c 1440; ***-o** c 1180, 1462, **pandocino** c 1325, to brew.

pandum, pawn, pledge (Sc.) 12c.

pand/us, (?) curved c 700; **-ulus,** (?) revelatory c 950.

pan/egyris, fair: **-igeria** c 1188; **-agericus,** panegyrical, complimentary c 1112, c 1125.

panell/us, strip (of cloth) 1213; pane (of glass) 1284, 1388; saddle-pad 1130, a 1408; panel (of wood) 1237, 15c.; c 1295, c 1400, **-a** c 1382, a 1490, **-um** c 1340, 'pane', side (arch.); weir 1440; section of an account 1318, 1325; *1238, 1513, **-a** 1294, 1379, **-um** c 1290, 1461, panel, list (esp. of jurors); **-o,** to empanel c 1365, 1419.

paner-, *see* **panarium.**

panfletus, *see* **pamfilius.**

panga, pang, pain 1541.

pangnagium, *see* **pannagium.**

pan/icula, tumour (med.): **-ocula, -ucola** c 790.

†**paniculum,** (?) panic, millet 1318.

panigeria, *see* **panegyris.**

pan/is, pasty 1225, 1306; cake (of wax or tallow) 1300, 1437; **p. (salis),** loaf of salt 13c.; **p. (zucri, de sucre,** *etc.*), sugar-loaf 1256, 1390; **p. albus,** white bread a 1128, 1482; **p. bissus,** brown bread a 1128, 1419; **p. niger** 1283, 1338; ‡**p. avenacius** 15c., **p. avenosus** 1269, **p. latus** 1537, oatcake; **p. braciatus,** (?) malted bread 1294; ‡**p. fabicius,** bean-bread 15c.; **p. hordei** 14c., **p. ordeaceus** a 1125, **p. ordeicius** c 1125, c 1400, **p. ordescius** 13c., barley-bread; ‡**p. pisacius,** pease-bread 15c.; ‡**p. sigalinus, p. siliginis,** rye-bread 15c.; **p. de blado toto** a 1190, **p. de b. integro** 14c., **p. integer** 1293, 1326, wholemeal bread, (?) 'toutsain';

p. ad denarium 1256, 1260; **p. obolatus** c 1290, **p. obulatus** c 1419, halfpenny loaf; **p. de quadrante** 1266, **p. quadrans** 1436, **p. quadrantalis** 1267, c 1290, farthing loaf; **p. dimidii quadrantis** 1371;

p. armigerorum, p. garcionum 1314, **p. militaris** 1250, 1369, **p. ad militem** 1233, **p. militum** c 1266, **p. canonicalis** 1430, **p. carpentarii** c 1248, 1338, **p. conventus** c 1190, **p. conventualis** c 1300, c 1370, **p. monachalis** 1214, 1325, **p. monachi** 12c., 14c., **p. ad monachum** 1233, different sizes of loaf or allowances of bread;

‡**p. Alexinus,** biscuit 15c.; **p. artocopi,** simnel bread 1293, c 1324; **p. ciragii,** *see* **cera; p. cribrarius** c 1197, c 1400, **p. cribratus** 14c., 1453, cribble-bread; **p. dispensabilis,** bread for everyday use 13c., 1363; **p. dominicus** 1205, 1529, **p. de dominico** a 1088, ‡**p. vigoris** c 1440, 'pain demaine'; ‡**p. dulciarius,** "marchpane" 1570; **p. equinus** c 1355, 1535, **p. equorum** 1367, **p. pro equis** 1310, **p. caballinus** 1326, horse-bread; **p. Gallicus** 1345; **p. levatus** 1293, 1419, **p. levis** 1419, leavened bread *or* puff-bread; **p. natalicius,**

M

(?) eaten at Christmas c 1200; **p. perditus,** scrap-bread 13c.; **p. piperatus,** spiced bread c 1200; **p. propositionis,** 'shew-bread' (bibl.); **p. secundus,** bread of second quality c 1185; **p. rengatus (ringatus),** 'ranged' (sifted) bread, 'clermatin' a 1380, c 1400; **p. de trait** c 1267, a 1380, **p. de treyt** c 1290, 1326, 'treat', bran bread; **p. tostus,** toast 1620;

‡**p. cuculi,** wood-sorrel (bot.) 14c.; ‡**p. porcinus,** sow-bread (bot.) 14c.;

p. benedictus, bread blessed for distribution c 1000. 1324, 1484; c 1110, **p. conjuratus** c 1115, ordeal of consecrated bread; 1244, 1397, **p. Dei** c 1090, consecrated host; -**aria** 1552, -**arium** 1542, -**atria** c 1400, -**etaria** a 1190, 1419, -**eteria** 1260, 1350, -**etera** 1288, *-**etria** 1235, 1588, -**etrium** 1295, -**etorium** 1366, -**itria** 1314, 1490, -**taria** c 1225, 1508, -**teria** 1336, 1423, -**tleria** 1450, pantry; *-**etarius** 1163, 1357, -**eterius** 1309, -**itarius** 1299, c 1540, -**tarius** c 1300, **penetarius** 1224, ‡-**itor** 15c. pantler, steward; -**esculus** c 1397, ‡-**iculus** 1483, small loaf; -**ifex** 1086, -**ificus** c 1130, c 1160, baker; **ars** -**ifica,** baker's art c 1325; ‡-**ificina,** bake-house 15c.; -**ita,** one who holds that substance of bread remains in Eucharist 1427; -**ifico** c 1125, c 1325, -**ifigo** 1340, to bake; -**ito,** to hold doctrine of *panitae* 1427.

panna, "dripping-pan" 1551; part of mill, (?) socket 1293, 1301; *cf.* **patella;** *see also* **pannus** (1 & 2).

***pannag/ium** (†**paunagium**) 1086, 1583, **pastinagium** c 1115, ***pasnagium** 1086, c 1324, **pesnagium** (†**pesuagium**) c 1290, **pathnagium** a 1160, c 1250, **padnagium** c 1200, 1426, **pagnagium, pangnagium,** †**pannangium** 1199, **pandnagium** 1212, **pandagium** 1281, **pawnagium** 1573, **ponagium** 1274, 1358, (?) **pounagium** 1279, †**pannum** 1171, pannage, (payment for right of) pasturage of pigs; **p. ultimum,** 'rere-pannage' 1255 (*cf.* **retropannagium**); **pasnagator,** collector of pannage dues c 1160; -**io** (**porcos**), to pay pannage for 1198, 1296.

pannicul/us, rag c 1188, c 1540; shred, morsel c 1220; membrane a 1250, c 1375; linen book-cover c 1266; -**atim,** in tatters c 1190; -**osus,** ragged c 1180, a 1205; membranous a 1250.

panno, *see* PENN

1 **pann/us** 1286, -**a** (? **pauna**) a 1200, 1419, †-**ia** 1295, **paudna** 1235, **palna** 1223, 13c., wallplate, squared timber; (?) roof, roof-timber, story 1335; 15c., -**a** (**pana**) 1373, 15c., 'pane', side of building; **pan/a,** pane of glass 1473; -**ator,** (?) maker of wall-plates 1469; *cf.* 1 **pagina, panna.**

2 **pann/us** *1086, 17c., -**a** 1445, -**um** c 1511, cloth; -**us,** *measure of cloth, web 1249, 1420; (?) garment 1420; skirt c 1194; (?) maniple (eccl.) 1437; book-cover c 1330; film over eye (med.) a 1250, ‡14c.; ‡birthmark 1652; -**i** (*pl.*), clothes c 1125, c 1450; bed-clothes c 1245; religious habit c 1125; -**i probationis** (mon.) c 1250; -**i ferrati,** armour 1370; -**us de armis,** cloth bearing

coat of arms 1404; **p. argenteus** 1445, **p. argenti** 1461, cloth of silver; **p. aureus** 1402, 1449, **p. auri** 1303, 1461, ***p. ad aurum** 1240, 1521, **p. de auro** 1288, 1318, **p. adauratus** 1406, 1415, **p. adaureus,** †**p. adauro** 1406, **p. deauratus** 1404, cloth of gold; **p. de assisa,** cloth of standard size and quality 1393, 1408; **p. Attaby,** tabby, striped cloth 1406; **p. Calicutianus,** calico 1701; **p. ceratus** 1230, 1414, **p. inceratus** 1238, cere-cloth; **p. clericalis** 1470; **p. coloris** 1337, 1415, **p. de colore** 1300, 1408, cloth of one colour; **p. curtus** 1410, 1504; **p. de Cypro,** Cyprus lawn 1388, 1406; **p. dalmaticus,** "damask" 1605 (*cf.* DAMASC); **p. de le hardyn,** 'harden cloth', coarse linen 1487; **p. Hibernie** 1291, 1393, **p. Hibernicalis** 1475, Irish frieze; **p. imperialis,** 'cloth imperial' c 1200; **p. integer,** web of cloth, broad-cloth 1289, 1506; **p. Islandie** 1443; **p. de kenchia,** a rich (?) oriental fabric 1285; **p. lacteus,** cloth for straining milk 1277; **p. lanetus** 1276, **p. lanosus** 1309, **p. lanutus** 1344, woollen cloth; **p.** †**lansalis,** (?) lawn 1358; **p. largus** 1322, 1556, **p. latus** 1285, 1454, broad-cloth; **p. longus** 1350; **p. de Luca** (Lucca, It.) 1388; **p. monachalis** 15c.; **p. de Musc'** 1167, 1241, **p. de Murceo** 1171, (? Murcia, Sp.; *cf.* **musca**); **p. pauperum** c 1300; **p. pedalis,** foot-cloth, towel 1378; **p. pictus** 1440; **p. planus** 1438; **p. quadragesimalis,** lenten veil 13c.; **p. rasus,** satin 1499; **p. saccinus** 1338, **p. saccorum** 1441, **p. sacci** 1531, sack-cloth; **p. status, p. statuum,** cloth of state 1508; **p. strictus** 1330, 1472; **p. de Turky** 1301, 1345; **p. ad vela** 1305, **p. ad velum** 1303, **p. pro velis** 1338, sail-cloth; **P. Viridis,** Green Cloth, Lord Steward's Department c 1472; **p. de Wadmale,** coarse woollen cloth 1404; **p. Wallie,** 1421; *see also* **aresta, Atrebaticus, carsea, chalo,** 2 **lyra,** TARS, 2 **tartara, tirretena, toteneisum, worsetum;**

-**ulus,** patch 1516; **p. (ad faldestolium),** frontal c 1220; **p. (casule),** (?) skirt 1514; †-**acorium,** (?) cloth reinforced with leather 1310; ‡-**arium,** draper's shop 1483; *-**arius** 1258, 1583, -**erius** 1419, -**ator** 1299, 1494, (?) -**icarius** 1548, clothier, draper; ‡**textor** -**arius,** cloth-weaver 1520; -**eus,** of cloth 1559, ‡1570; -**ifactura,** cloth-making 1587; -**ifex,** cloth-maker 1561; -**ificus,** of a cloth-maker a 1408; -**iger,** attendant of prior (Canterbury) c 1214, a 1227; ‡-**iplicium,** clothes-press c 1440, 1483; -**itonsor,** shearman 1561; -**osus,** "coarse" 1553; -**ifico,** to make cloth a 1410.

panocula, *see* **panicula.**

Panormia, title of book (by Ivo of Chartres) c 1395.

†**pansa,** (?) paunch-pot 1419; **poncherium,** 'pauncher', waist-band 1399.

pan/selenos a 1233, 13c., -**silenos** a 1200, c 1212, full moon.

†**pansio,** (?) *for* **pensio,** taxation 12c.

panso, to stretch c 1225.

panspermia, mixture of (generative) seeds c 1200.

pant-, *see also* **pan.**

pant/aria, -arius, -eria, *see* panis.
pant/enera, -oneria, *see* paltenerius.
panthe/on, heathen temple c 1190; -ologus c 1440, pantilogius 1329, title of book.
panucola, *see* panicula.
paodentum, *see* padoentum.
*pap/a, Pope c 597, 830. c 1080, 1536; -abilis, qualified to be elected Pope 1610; *-alis, papal c 1138, 1558; -atia c 1118, *-atus c 1125, 1562, papacy; -ismus, popery c 1550, 1647; -ista, papal partisan 1413, 15c.; 1523, p 1650, -ianus c 1620, -icola c 1600, 1647, Papist; -isticus, popish 15c., c 1670; -o, to be Pope 15c.
pap/agabio c 1180, c 1200, -agabius c 1200, †-egallus 1204, -aga 1421, -agaus 1328, -egeus c 1334, popingaius 1421, popinjay, parrot.
pap/alardus 12c., -elardus c 1250, 'papelard', hypocrite.
pap/arius, -erus, *see* PAPYR
‡papatum, pap 15c., 1483,
paphinus, *see* puffo.
paphus (†baphus), heaven c 550.
*papil/io a 1142, 1443, -lo 1250, 1307, †-um 1159, -ionium 1248, pampilio 1242, 1245, papirio 1204, pallio 1234, pavilio c 1333, 1548, pavillo 1205, 1333, paveillo 1171, pavillionia 1377, pavilonus 1292, pavilion, tent; -ionarius 1233, 1300, -lonarius 1290, 1336, pavillonarius 1305, 1496, pavilioner, tent-maker; pavillonia, office of pavilioner 1358.
papul/um salis, pinch of salt c 1250; popela, *for* -a, pimple c 1180.
papyr/us (papir-), rush 1302, ‡15c.; 1352, 1533, paperus 1292, 1541, paperium c 1000, paupirus c 1470, c 1553, paper; *1291, 1477, -a 1319, 1424, paparius c 1300, -ius 1324, p 1330, paupirus 1304, 1412, paupirius 1407, paper document (roll or book); -us regalis 1355, 1445, p. realis 1366, paper royal; p. spendabilis, (?) wrapping paper 1384, 1467; -aceus 1575, -eus (-ius) c 1387, 1486, -icus 1517, of paper.
par/, even (math.) a 1250; *an equal in legal status c 1102, c 1422; burgess or municipal officer (esp. G.) 1242, 1484; *peer, noble 1136, 1461; -es (*pl.*) parliamenti c 1320, *p. regni 1339, 1568; *par (*n.*) 1167, 1480, -ia 1130, 1480, pir 1269, pair, set, suit; (followed by noun in apposition) 1339, 1460; p. armorum 1461, 1471; p. decretorum 1303, p. decretalium 1434, p. institutionum 1430; *p. litterarum, letter 1200, 1329; p. organorum 1427, 1537, p. de orgues c 1350, organ (mus.); p. precum 1399, 1414, p. precularum (†precularium) c 1423, 1519, p. de paternosters 1402, 1431, rosary; p. sufflettorum 1356, p. sufflonum 1462, pair of bellows; p. tractuum, pair of traces (harness) 1285, 1399; p. vestimentorum 1432, 1489; de -i, on equal terms c 1204; -iter, evenly (math.) a 1250; in common 1086;
-agium, tenure in common 1086; 1299, 1439, †-agenium 1437, community of burgess-right (G.); -iagium 1285, 1315, -itas 1285, admission of overlord to share

in tenants' rights or revenues in return for protection (G.); -itas, status as a peer, peerage 1264, c 1450; *c 1130, 1518, -ietas c 1190, equality; p. rationis 1301; -alitas, *for* -ilitas, similarity 1266, 1309; -ierius, co-tenant, parcener (G.) 1289; -iformis, similar 1427; -iformiter, in like manner 1427, 1558; -iformitas, comparable instance c 1325; -ificabilis, able to be equated c 1360; -ificatio, equating, equalization c 1250, c 1283; *-ifico, to equate, equalize 5c. 1136, a 1452.
par-, *see also* per-
*parabol/a (eccl.), parobola c 1340, parable; parabola (geom.) 1686; -e (*pl.*), the Book of Proverbs c 1197, 15c.; -atim, in parables c 730; -icus, figurative p 1300, 1344; parabolic (geom.) 1686; -ois, paraboloid (geom.) 1686; -izo, to speak in parables 1344.
paracenium, side-dish c 1160.
paracev-, *see* parasceve.
parach-, *see also* PAROCH
para/charaximum, false coin: -carissimum, -caximum c 600.
para/cletus, -clitus (eccl.), -clytus c 793, paraclete; -clesis c 730, ‡-clisis 1483, consolation.
par/adella, -adilla, *see* paratella.
*paradis/us, paradise (bibl.); *see also* avis, granum, gumma; -us 12c., 1375, parvisus (per-) c 1312, c 1443, parvisius a 1260, c 1457, parvis, precinct (eccl.); parvisa, chamber 1449; -iacus 1090, a 1186, -icus 15c., -igenus c 730, celestial; -icola, dweller in paradise 990. c 1375.
para/frithus, -frenarius, *see* palefridus.
parag/ium, -enium, *see* par.
paragoricus, *see* paregoricus.
paragraph/um, -us c 1070, 1620, -a p 1394, pergraffum 1304, ‡paraphus 1483, paragraph.
†paragroma, (?) epistle c 1190.
‡paragus, bird of ill omen 15c.
Paralipomen/a (bibl.), -on (Gk. *gen.*) c 796. a 1142, c 1396, the Book of Chronicles.
paralitas, *see* par.
paralla, *see* paratella.
parallaxis, parallax (math.) c 1612, 1686.
parallel/us, zodiac (astr.) 1241; an equal a 1270; pro -ois c 700; ‡-i (*pl.*), "frets of a lute" 1570; -ismus, analogy 1620, 1649; -ogrammum, parallelogram a 1150, 1686.
paralog/us a 1200, 1609, -icus 13c., fallacious; -ismus c 1200, 1610, peraloysmus c 1380, perlogismus 1271, fallacy; -ista a 1180, perlogista 1418, false reasoner; -izo c 1190, 1427, -izor c 1173, 1427, to reason falsely.
paraly/sis, herba, cowslip ‡14c., 1634; -tice, as if paralysed c 1200; -tico, to paralyse a 1250, 1344.
par/amentum (per-) 12c., c 1550, -ella c 1450, -olla c 1467, -atura c 760. 1164, 1514, -ura 1225, c 1450, ‡peruria 15c., -mentaria 1186, 1239, -menteria 1214, apparel, parure (eccl.), adornment; 'parrel', rigging (naut.) 1442; -eta, set of vestments (eccl.) 1251; -ura, (?) paring, shaping (of wood) 1304; parer (kitchen implement) c 1335, 1390; p. unguium, paring of nails c 1298;

-amentor 1377, †peramenator 1263, -mentarius 1086, c 1280, parmenter, robe-trimmer or furrier; -arius, (?) cloth-comber, 'rower' 1180; -atrix, author (*f.*) c 1180; -uratus, trimmed c 1396; -o*, to trim, adorn c 1160, c 1315; ‡to "pare" (bread) 1483.

†parandrus, fabulous beast with power of changing its form (? *for* tarandrus) 12c.

parapcis, *see* paropsis.

parapetasma, hanging, curtain c 1620.

paraphern/alia (*pl.*) c 1270, 14c., para-pharna c 1258, res -ales c 1200, c 1290, res paraphonales a 1564, married woman's property.

paraphonista, chorister c 1375, ‡15c.

para/phrastice, paraphrastically 1564; -frasticus, paraphrastic 9c., c 950.

paraphrenesis, false frenzy (due to humours other than choler and blood) a 1250.

paraphus, *see* PARAGRAPH

parapilio, *see* pavelio.

parapligia, partial paralysis (παραπληγία) a 1250.

parari/um, -us; *see* PERR; paramentum.

*parascev/e c 1006. c 1080, 1441, p. Pasche 1267, dies -e c 1192, c 1396, d. Veneris -e c 1293, c 1300, d. -a 1461, *d. -es c 1200, 1586, d. -is c 1250, d. paraceves c 1283, d. parasseue 1391, 1522, d. parasseuhes 1406, d. parasciphe 1494, d. parasiphes 1541, d. parassaphes 1519, d. paraceven-sis 1208, Good Friday.

†Parasis, Great Bear (astr.) c 1200.

parasivus, *see* pirasmus.

parasol, sunshade 1292.

paraster, *see* patraster.

‡parastes, cable, stay c 1200, 15c.

par/atella c 1200, -adella c 1422, -alla a 1150, -ella c 1290, †-adilla, farella 1483, ‡perdilla 15c., dock (bot.); *cf.* fartellus.

paratitlus, secondary title 1609.

parat/rix, -ura, *see* paramentum.

parca-, *see also* parcus.

parcam-, *see* PERGAM

parce, *see* parcitudo.

parcell/a (percell-), *part c 1367, a 1564; *c 1212, 1686, -ula c 1470, parcel (of land); *detail, item c 1300, c 1533; per -am, in detail c 1335; per -as, retail 1272, 1379; -atim, in equal parts 1403, 1430; in parcels (of land) 1372, 1405; in detail, item by item 1418, 1471; p. deauratus, parcel-gilt 1431; -o, to set out in detail 1526; *cf.* particula.

parcellum, *see* petrocilium.

parcen-, parcin-, parcon-, *see* partitio.

parchia, *see* pertica.

†parchus, (?) *for* pardus, 1274.

parci-, *see also* parti-

parc/itudo, scarcity, lack 1461; -e, scarcely (Sc.) 1456, 1461; -ibilis, merciful c 1102; ‡-ipollex, shoe-horn c 1440.

*parc/us (park-, perc-) c 820. 1086, 1573, -a 12c., 1521, -um 1189, a 1525, (?) -aria 1204, park, enclosure; *1221, c 1600, -amentum 1232, 1295, pound, pinfold; par-gulus, paddock c 1200; -agium, (?) payment for exemption from impounding 1157, 1307; pargagium, (?) payment for

infringement of park rights 1367; -aria, office of parker 1334, 1475; †parcheria, (?) parker's house 1345; *-arius 1084, a 1564, perquerius 1268, -ator 1202, 1305, parker, park-keeper *or* (?) pinder; -atura 1451, (?) percatio 1567, imparking; -atio, impounding 1243; -mannus, a class of tenant (Chilcombe, Hants) 1287; -o, to impark, enclose c 1200, 1367; to impound 1243, 1397; *cf.* PARROC

pardingus, *see* 1 ferdingus.

paregina, pound, pinfold (G.) 1289; *cf.* parcus.

paregoricus (med.): paragoricus a 1250; peragorizo, to soothe (med.) a 1250.

parella, *see* paramentum; paratella.

†parellus, (?) flat dish (Sc.) 1343.

parent/es primi, Adam and Eve c 1343; †paurentes, *for* -es, 1330; -aliter, as a kinsman 12c.; -atim, from father to son c 1190; -ela *c 1125, c 1450, (?) -ula c 1090, kinship; *8c. a 1100, 1461, †-elum c 1400, -alia 1380, family, kin; p. mona-chorum, (?) household or dependants (mon.) c 1213; †-elis, *for* -alis, c 1410; -elus, kinsman 1446; -o, to engender c 1190, c 1200.

parenthe/sis, parenthesis 9c. c 1080; -ticus, for use on special occasions c 1160.

pareo, *see* paritio.

parergon, irrelevance 1610.

pareta, *see* paramentum.

parex, (?) *for* parus, tit 15c.

parexelenchus, refutation on a side issue (log.): peralenchus 13c.

parg-, *see also* parcus.

pargam-, pargomentum, *see* PERGAM

parget-, pargo, *see* PERJACT

pari-, *see also* par.

pari/es, (?) faction 13c.; side or branch of family c 1200; p. medius, partition 1374; infra quatuor -etes 1277; -taria a 1250, peretrum 15c., ‡peritoria 15c., *for* -etaria, pellitory (bot.); -etatus, walled c 1250; *see also* PERJACT

pario, *see* 1 paro.

Paris/iensis 1267, 1427, -iacensis c 1193; c 1298, coin of Paris; *see also* candela, granum, opus, plastrum.

parissibilis (ignis), (?) issuing spontaneously (*cf.* O.F. *parissir*) c 1227.

par/itio, obedience 1374; -eo (*trans.*), to obey 6c. c 1192; p. recto, to stand to right (leg.) 1201.

paritotus, *see* PERIDOT

Parius, lapis, free-stone c 1191.

parjet- (pariet-), *see* PERJACT

parla, *see* perla.

1 parl/iamentum (-eamentum, -amentum) c 1210, 1290, -antia 1313, discussion, conference, parley (esp. between adver-saries); *colloquy (mon.) c 1200, c 1330; unlawful assembly (London) a 1274, 1299; a 1220, 1438, dies -iamenti 1248, 1291, conference or court held by Marcher lords (W.); *1236, 1588, pallamentum (Fr.) 1308, 1313, court or council summoned by king, Parliament; p. commune, borough-moot (Winchester) 1467; p. generale c 1250, 1275, p. generalissimum c 1250,

p. magnum c 1250, c 1450, **p. regium** c 1412, **p. regni** 1549; **p. plenum** 1323, 1461; **P. Bonum** c 1440; **P. †Insane** (? **insigne**) 1274; **P. Mirabile** c 1390, **P. Operans Mira** a 1500; **P. Nigrum** 1461; **P. Sine Misericordia** a 1500; **P. (regis) Francie** 1263, c 1422; **P. (Imperii)** 1294; **P. Hibernie** (**P. in Hibernia**) 1264, 1485; *P. (regis) Scotie** 1258, 1564; **p. tenentes,** holders of *parlement* (Fr.) 1308; **-iamentalis,** belonging to a colloquy c 1412; c 1400, 1588, **-amentalis** 1540, **-iamentarius** 1346, 1620, **-amentarius** c 1550, 1586, parliamentary; (*subst.*) Member of Parliament 15c.; **-iamentaliter,** in council 1536; **-iamento** 1310, 1350, **-amento** c 1250, to confer, parley; to hold a Parliament c 1308.

2 parl/iamentum (**perl-**) 1382, a 1452, **-atorium** 1200, c 1412, **-itorium** 1298, c 1340, **†-etum** 1465, **-ara** 1472, **-arium** 1440, 1473, **-eyria** 1467, **-ora** 1396, 1500, **-oria** 1452, 1494, **-orium** 1301, 1500, **-ura** c 1423, 1539, parlour (esp. mon.); **-ura patens,** (?) open-air parlour 1425; **-arius** c 1140, **-uraria** (*f.*) 1530, obedientiary in charge of parlour.

parmenus, see **pirum.**
parment-, see **paramentum.**
parna, see **perna.**
1 par/o c 1118, **†-io** a 1130, war ship (of Vikings).
2 par/o (**per-**) 1209, 1297, **-onus** 1209, 1248, **-onellus** 1209, 1309, swingle-tree.
3 paro, see **paramentum.**
parobola, see **parabola.**
paroch/ia 7c., c 1000. c 1072, c 1436, **parachia** 1236, **paruchia** 5c., diocese or province; *8c. c 1075, 1559, **parohhia** c 900, **†porrehia** 12c., **†-iala** 1646, parish; parish church c 1250; (*coll.*) men of parish c 1180, c 1250; **p. peculiaris** 1684; **-ialia** (*n. pl.*), dues paid to parish clergy c 1140, 1253; **-ialis** *c 1125, 1684, **-ianus** c 1125, 1404, **-itanus** 1297, **-itianus** (C.I.) 1205, **-ionalis** c 1266, **paroeciensis** 1610, **-ius** c 1115, parochial; of a parish church 1415; **clericus -ialis** 1549; **altare -iale,** altar for parish priest in monastic or cathedral church 1336; *see also* **prebenda; -ialitas,** parochial status 1309; **-ialis** c 1250, *-ianus* c 1075, 1547, **parachianus** 1295, **-iana** (*f.*) 1173, c 1357, **†-us** c 1363, parishioner; **-anus,** diocesan 1236; **-ianus,** member of a diocese 8c., c 793. c 1125, 1269; 1259, **-us** 1301, 1559, **-us sacerdos** 1555, parish priest.
parodicus, accompanying, incidental c 1160.
parolla, see **paramentum.**
paropsis (bibl.), **parapcis** 1553, **perapsis** 1200, 1460, **†peradapsis** 1460, **†pereympa** 1342, dish, platter.
†parostheta, (?) platter c 1430.
parotis (**vena**), parotid vein a 1250.
parox/ysmus, paroxysm, fit (med.) 1200, c 1620; **‡-iticus,** exacerbating 15c.
parroc/us (**peroc-**) 1223, 1547, **-a** 1612, **parricus** (**†particus**) c 1115, 'parrock', enclosure, paddock, park; **†-us,** (?) local court or moot (Kent) 1337; *cf.* **parcus.**
pars, heretical sect c 600; one-fifteenth of an hour c 1265; *party to a suit (leg.) 1187,

c 1580; counsel, advocate (leg.) 1296; *see also* **cantus, capio,** MANUTEN; **p. actrix** 1269, 1684, **p. conquerens** 14c., plaintiff; **p. defendens** 14c.; **p. appellans, p. appellata** 1684; **p. lesa,** injured party 15c.; **p. alba, p. nigra,** front and dorse of membrane 1372, 15c.; **p. decani, p. thesaurarii,** two sides of choir (York) c 1400, 1472; **p. deterior,** worse course of action c 1250; **p. essentialis, p. integralis** (log.) c 1300; **p. orationis,** part of speech (gram.) 1267, c 1370; **p. satisfactionis,** part satisfaction 1270, 1332; *p. solutionis,** part payment 1224, c 1472; **‡p. cum part/e,** equal mixture of gold and silver (alch.) 1652; **a -e** partly c 1240, c 1470; **a -e ante,** from before 1267; **a -e post,** from behind 13c., 1267; **ex -e** c 1200, c 1324, **de -e** 14c., **per -em** c 1340, c 1370, **pro -e** 1373, 1471, **pro et ex -e** 1411, **pro -e a** c 1000, on behalf (of); *in hac -e,** in this regard 1227, 1365; **in-em,** by way (of) c 1250; c 1180, c 1324, **ad -em** c 1320, c 1470, apart, aside; **pro magna -e,** to a great extent c 1234; **pro majori -e,** for the most part 1291, 1446; **pro -ibus,** in proportion c 1364; **pars sum,** to take sides c 1412; **-em capio cum** c 1435, **-es fero** c 1562, **-ibus sto** 1327, to take the part of, side with; *-es** (*pl.*), district, region 8c. c 1090, 1475; **per -es,** in detail 1297; **-es appono** c 1250, *p. interpono** 1226, 1430, to use influence or good offices.

parsagium, see **pensa.**
parsiuncula, see **partiuncula.**
parson-, *see* PERSON
†parterra, (?) piece of land 1252.
parthenalis, of or for the Virgin 990. 12c.
partia, division, distribution (Norm.) 1200.
partial/itas, condition of being a part p 1300; partiality, partnership 1342, c 1502; **-ia** (*pl.*), partly paid debts 1228, 1466; *see also* **rotulus; -is,** partial, incomplete 12c., 1461; partial, biased c 1332, 1648; **p. deauratio,** parcel gilding c 1335; **-iter,** partially, in part c 1220, 1426; in the interest of one party 1309; partially, by favour 1346.
partiarius, see **partitio.**
partibil/itas, divisibility 1267, 1344; **-is,** divisible, separable 870. 1200, a 1564; **-iter,** by division 1344, 1380.
particip/atio *c 1115, 1487, **†partipatio** 1264, **†parcipatio** 14c., *-ium** a 1100, 1441, participation, sharing; association, fellowship c 1080, 1545; distribution of food 1300, 1331; participation (log.) c 1200; **p. facienda,** name of a writ (leg.) 1419; **-abilis,** able to be shared c 1270, p 1300; **-aliter,** in portions 9c.; 1344, 1427, **-ative** p 1300, 1427, by way of participation (log.); **-ativus,** participative (log.) 12c., c 1360; **-ator,** one who shares out or allots 1270; partner (part of style of Sultan of Egypt) 1291; **-ium,** link between species (log.) 1620; **†-io,** (?) *for* percipio, to receive 1279, 1313; **-o,** to share out, distribute, allot 1264, 1372; to hold as parceners 1279; (with *dat.*) c 730, (with *abl.*) c 1178, c 1434, **-o in** c 1343, c 1444, **-or in** 1289, to share, partake of.

particul/a 1169, 1540, **-are** c 1382, c 1542,

detail, item; **per -as,** in parcels, retail 1280, 1331; **-aritas,** particularity c 1270, 1620; **-aris,** *particular (not general) a 1090, 1549; separate, individual c 1197, 1459; detailed 1242, c 1564; **eclipsis p.,** partial eclipse c 1200; **emptio p.,** retail purchase 1271; **venditio p.,** retail sale 1234, 1271; **rectoria p.,** peculiar rectory 1549; **solutio p.,** part payment c 1258, 1438; **in -ari,** in particular c 1340; **-arior,** more particular 1378; **-arius,** more particularly 1380; **-ariter,** partly c 793. c 1115, c 1190; particularly, especially p 1382; in a particular (not general) sense c 850. 1267, c 1332; in separate parts, singly 1253, c 1450; 1318, 1416, **-atim** 1086, dispersedly (of land in open field); c 1125, c 1564, **-aratim** (Sc.) 1329, 1375, *for* **-atim,** in detail; 1335, 1419, **-atim** c 1300, 1321, retail; **-ariter deauratus,** parcel-gilt 1446; **-atim,** one and all c 1000; **-atio,** particularizing c 1300; **-ariso** a 1360, **-o** 1267, c 1290, to particularize (log.); **-o,** to share, apportion c 1204, a 1408; to specify c 1170, c 1365; *cf.* **parcella.**

particus, *see* **parrocus.**

parti/tio, divorce c 1258; 1536, **-tium** 1351, partition, screen; division of a shield (her.) a 1446, c 1595; **p. Parliamenti,** dissolution of Parliament c 1320; **portitio** a 1350, **-sona** 1290, **-zona** 1300, *for* **-tio,** distribution; †**-o** c 730. 1198 (? *for* **portio**), **-men,** **-monium** c 550, portion, division; **-arius** 1251, **-onarius** 1200, c 1400, †**parconarius** 1220, c 1242, *parcenarius* 1199, 1489, **parcinarius** 1319, **personarius** 1411, parcener, joint tenant (*cf.* **portio**); **parcenaria** 1287, 1342, †**parcenuria** 1334, parcenary, joint tenancy; **-tativus** c 1360, **-tivus** 13c., c 1670, partitive (log.); **-tum principale,** (?) party per pale (her.) 1449; **-tus,** party (her.), particoloured 1245, c 1595; *see also* 1 **carta, jocus, ludus; -o** 815. c 1225, †**-tior** 1204, to divide; **-o,** to divorce 1222, c 1258; **-or,** to depart 1274, 1419; **p. terram,** to divide arable land for cropping 1241.

partiuncul/a c 1115, c 1204, **parsiuncula** 13c., small piece or parcel; **-ariter,** one by one, separately 12c., *cf.* **portio.**

par/trix, -tricarius, *see* **perdix.**

partura, *see* **pastura.**

†**parturiter,** (?) with birth-pangs c 1410.

paruchia, *see* PAROCH

parum et parum, bit by bit 1340; **p. plus** 12c., **p. ultra** 15c., a little more; **p. terre,** plot of land 1086.

parur/a, -atus, *see* **paramentum.**

parvis-, *see* **paradisus.**

parv/itas mea (perv-), my humble self c 790, c 1060. 12c., 14c.; **-itudo,** meanness c 1453; **-ulitas,** smallness p 1380; **-us,** deficient in weight or strength 13c., 1270; **cervisia -a,** small ale 1275; **-iculus** c 1300, ‡**-unculus** c 1440, **-ulinus** 1345, very small; **-issimus,** smallest 980; **-iloquium,** speaking little c 1400; **-ificatio,** diminution c 1360; **-ificentia,** miserlinesss c 1472; **-ipensio,** belittling, underrating 1345, 1461; **-ipontanus,** scholastic (of Petit-Pont, Paris) a 1200; **-ifico,** to diminish c 1360;

1220, 1381, **-ihabeo** c 1125, *-ipendo* (†**perinpendo**) 7c., 8c. c 1070, c 1540, **-ipenso** 12c., **-ipondero** c 1080, **-ipretio** 12c., **-ulo** c 1180, to make light of, belittle, underrate; *see also* **minor,** MINIM

parypatheticus, *see* **Peripateticus.**

parypostasis, subordinate existence 1344.

pascatio, *see* PISC

*Pasch/a** (*f. & n.*) 7c., 10c. 1086, 1559, **Phasca** 12c., 1272, *dies -e** 1086, 1393, **d. -alis** c 1006. a 1100, c 1334, **P. annuum** c 1212, Easter Sunday; **P. annotinum,** Easter full-moon not being a Sunday c 1212; **P. Album,** Low Sunday c 1200; **P. Florum** c 1130, *P. Floridum** (Florida) 1191, c 1436, **P. Minus** c 1182, Palm Sunday; *see also* CLAUS; **-alitia** (*pl.*), Easter week 1201; **-alia** (*pl.*), Eastertide, Easter festival 1167, 1295; *-alis,** paschal, of Easter 8c., c 1006. a 1090, 1559; **dies Lune -alis,** Easter Monday c 1200, 1461; **Phas/a, -e,** (ceremony of) Paschal lamb, Passover c 1180, 1378; *see also* AGN

pascio, *see* **passio; pastio.**

*pasc/ua,** (*f. s.*) *for* **-uum,** "feeding", pasture, pasture-land 1086, 1587; (*n. pl.*) pastures of heaven c 1100; **-uum,** service of providing pasture 11c.; **-uarium,** pasture-land 1208; **pascherium** (dues paid for) grazing-rights (G.) 1199, 1285; **-uagium,** pasturage 1292, 1421; **-ualis,** affording pasture 704, 10c. 1086, c 1362; **bos p.,** pasture-fed ox c 1178; **arbores -uales** a 1150; **-ibilis** a 1250, **-itivus** a 1250, c 1270, alimentary; **passet,** *for* **-et,** c 1310; **-ito,** to feed c 1000. 12c.; *cf.* **pastio.**

pasnag-, *see* PANNAG

pas/pucellum, pirum -epucellum, kind of pear 1293.

passag-, *see* **passus.**

passer/ harundinarius, reed-bunting 1544; **p. troglodytes, p. sepiarius,** hedge-sparrow 1544; **-ulus,** *for* **-culus,** a 1446; ‡**-ella,** ‡**-ina,** cowslip (bot.) 15c.

passeria, *see* **paxeria.**

pass/io, passion, *martyrdom (of saints) c 730, c 1006. c 1115, c 1450; *the Passion, Passion week 8c. c 1080, c 1536; **P. Christi** c 1236, 1559, **P. Domini** 1185, c 1514, **P. Dominica** c 1188, c 1493, **-us Dominicus** c 1320; **-io,** reading of the Passion c 1266, c 1296; c 1270, c 1430, **-us** c 1267, sufferance, state or power of being acted upon (log.); quality, attribute c 1200, c 1380; passion, affection (astr. & alch.) 1267; punctuation-mark 1271; **pascio,** *for* **-io,** suffering 1313; **-ialis,** patient, tolerant 1347; **qualitas -ibilis,** perceptible quality a 1233, 13c.; **-ibilitas,** capacity to suffer a 1120, c 1250; **virtus pascibilis** a 1250; **-ibilior,** more sensitive a 1250; **-ionabilis,** passionate 1456; **-ionaliter,** with reference to quality or property (log.) c 1366; **-ionale** 970. 1245, **-ionalis** c 1400, **-ionarium** 1245, 1439, **-ionarius** c 1182, 15c., passional, martyrology; **-ionarium,** medical book by Galen c 1210, a 1250; **-ionatus,** affected c 1360, 1374; **-ionista,** celebrant of the Passion c 1330;

-ive, passively, by being acted on 1305,

c 1444; in a passive sense (log.) a 1250; passively (gram.) 1285; **-ivus,** passive, being acted on a 1250, a 1446; **-um** a 1323, 1374, **pati/ens** a 1250, c 1470, subject of action (log.); **-ens,** patient (med.) c 730. c 1160, c 1463; **-entia,** patience-dock (bot.) ‡14c., 1538; **-or,** to suffer martyrdom c 730, c 1006. c 1195, 1461; to bear the expense 1086; to be suffered or allowed 1378, 15c.; **p. de,** to suffer loss of c 1115; *cf.* **passus.**

passonum, *see* 1 **pesso.**

passula (*pl.*), (?) dried fruits, raisins a 1250, 1424.

pass/us, *pass (through mountains or woods) c 1190, c 1450; passage (in document) 1271, 1543; 'gang', set (of mill-spindles) 1453; cross-bar 1295; **p. assise,** standard pace (linear measure) 1462; **pari -u,** simultaneously 1417; *see also* **passio;**
-agium, passage-way, path c 1260, 1558; *1086, 1499, **-uagium** a 1230, ferry, means of transport over water; (?) mill-lade 12c.; *ferry-toll, transport due a 1110, 16c.; transport of goods 1178, 1346; *crossing, expedition overseas 1160, c 1450; payment in lieu of service overseas 1203; **p. aque** 1086, 1477; **p. commune** 1364, 1399, **p. liberum** 1223, 1555, right of way; **p. navis,** fairway 1362; **p. Sancte Crucis** c 1250, **p. sanctum** c 1350, crusade; **-eria** 1464, **-ingera** c 1404, 1606, **navis -agiaria** 1295, **n. -agaria** 1315, 1326, **n. -agiatrix** c 1250, **n. -iagiatrix** c 1303, **n. -eretta** 1223, 1225, ferry-boat, transport vessel; **-agiarius** 1251, 1440, **-iagiarius** c 1397, **-ajor** 1301, **-ator** 1190, 1327, **-iator** 1276, **-or** a 1237, c 1262, ferryman, boatman; **-eportus,** passport 1670; **-evelutum,** 'passevelours', amaranth (bot.) 1538; **-ans,** moving about, 'levant' (of animals) 1306; **-o** c 1348, **-agio** c 1303, to cross, pass (*intr.*); **-o,** to ferry, carry over 1206, 1492.

past/a 1190, 1521, **-um** c 1197, a 1540, **-us** 1327, c 1392, **-ea** c 1192, dough; material, (?) gold 1395; **-ellum,** 'pastel', woad 1567; *-ellus (-ella, -ellum) c 1185, 1523, *-illus (-illa, -illum) c 1180, 15c., **patillus** 1212, **-icius** 1288, **-elleria, -eria** 1390, (?) **basto** c 1338, pastry, pasty, loaf containing meat or fish; **-ellarius** 1390, **-illarius** c 1353, ‡1483, **-illator** 1446, †**pistillator** 1490, **-iciarius** 1288, **-icerius** 1539, pastrycook; **-illatus,** cooked in pastry c 1180.

†**past/aforium,** (?) *for* **-ophorium,** portable shrine 9c.

†**pastin/a,** (?) *for* **-aca,** parsnip 1285.

pastinagium, *see* **pannagium.**

past/io 781, **-icium** 1086, food-service; **-io** (†**pascio**), pannage 1086, 13c.; (punishment for) feeding or maintenance of criminals c 1115, 14c.; shepherding c 730; spiritual sustenance c 730. c 1250, c 1380; **-inatio** 788. 12c., 15c., **-icium** c 1140, 1198, pasture; **animalia -eciata,** grazing animals 1325; **silva -ilis,** woodland for grazing 1086; **-ino,** to feed (fig.) c 1000; *cf.* **PASC**

‡**pastomis,** muzzle (? ἐπιστομίς) 1570.

pastor/, *pastor (bibl.); visitor, inspector (eccl.) 1537; *Pastoureau,* anticlerical insurgent (Fr.) c 1250; **P. Summus** 1438, **P.**

Supremus c 1457; *see also* **bursa; -agium,** pasturage 1222; **-ale, -alis** c 1180, c 1400, **-alia** (*pl.*) 1434, c 1500, Gregory's *Pastoral Care*; **-alis,** the *Shepherd* of Hermas 12c.; **-alis,** *pastoral (eccl.) 8c., 9c. a 1090, 1543; *see also* **canis; -aliter,** like a shepherd or pastor 1427, c 1488; **-alitas,** shepherding 9c.; c 1125, **-atus** c 1343, 1593, office of pastor; **-ella,** pastoral or bucolic song 12c.; **-ius** 1252, **-icus** 1537, belonging to a shepherd; **-ia** c 1248, **past/rix** c 1362, shepherdess; **-rix,** abbess 1414; **-rico,** to control c 550.

pastr/o c 1250, 1313, **-onus** 1329, 1339, pastern (hobble for cattle or horses).

pastum, *see* **pasta.**

pastur/a *1086, c 1543, †**partura** 1086, pasture, right of pasturage; †**-a,** (?) *for* **pultura,** sustenance 1471; **p. communis** (**communa, communia**) 1086, 1671; **p. hiemalis** 1411; **p. indivisa** c 1150; **p. separalis** a 1272, 1449; **p. silve** 1086; **-agium** c 1300, 1590, **-agia** c 1100, **-ata** 1550, **-atio** a 1564, 1588, (right of) pasturage; **terra -alis,** pasture-land c 1368, 1587; **-o,** to depasture, graze 1230, 1533.

pastus, drink c 550; service of providing food, entertainment 831, 845. 11c., 1334; †*for* **pastor** (eccl.) 1204; *see also* **pasta.**

Patarinus (Paterinus), Patarin, heretic c 1190, c 1250.

pat/ella, bowl, pan: †**platella** 1291, **paella** 1205, 1295, **paiella** 1403, **paila** (**payla**) 1302, 1305, **-ula** c 1456, pan, pail, vessel; **-illa,** ‡"pan" a 1520; (?) spoon or scoop 1460; **-eliula,** little pan c 1380, c 1500; **-ella,** lamp 1372; 1272, 1327, **paella** 1268, part of mill, (?) socket (*cf.* **panna**); c 1180, c 1250, **p. ad sal faciendum** c 1220, c 1270, **p. salina, p. salis** 1374, 1460, **p. saline** c 1180, salt-pan; **p. ad califaciendum,** warming-pan 1551; **p. ad carbonem,** charcoal-pan c 1350.

patellus, *see* **paletta.**

*pat/ena** 760, c 1006. c 1090, c 1500, **-ina** 1234, paten (eccl.); **-ina,** axle-plate (of mill) 1290; **p. salina, p. salis,** salt-pan 1460; **-enarius,** patener (eccl.) c 1320, 1439; ‡**-inarius,** "pan-maker" 1483; **-ino,** to cook c 1150.

paten/tia, patency, obviousness c 1366; **-s** 1367, 1435, **littera -s** 1255, c 1400, **-tes** (*pl.*) 1224, c 1397, **littere -tes** a 1165, 1467, letters patent; *see also* **1 brevis, crux, sigillum; -ter,** publicly, openly, clearly 770. 1165, 14c.; in patent form, by means of letters patent 1257, 1328; **-tissime,** most plainly c 1340, c 1445; **-tarius** 1449, **-tator** c 1350, **-tor** 1432, patentee, holder of letters patent; ‡**-to,** to gape *or* straddle c 1440.

pater/, *title (eccl.) c 1090, c 1470; title (royal) 1166; father of the Church 705, 11c. c 1090, c 1580; godfather a 700; ‡sulphur (alch.) 1652; 1245, c 1365, *p. noster c 1006, a 1050. c 1115, 1549, Lord's Prayer; **p. noster,** rosary, chaplet 1267, 1517; **p. beatissimus** 12c., **p. patrum** 1347, papal titles; **p. confessionum,** father confessor c 1118; **p. familias,** divine title c 1000; "franklin" c 1460; **p. legalis** c 1320, **p. in**

lege c 1225, 1390, father-in-law; **P. Lumi-num** c 1257, 1345, **P. Misericordiarum** 1345; **p. monasterii**, chief cellarer (Canterbury) 1298; **p. Veteris Testamenti**, patriarch c 1334, c 1340; **-culus**, unworthy father 1252.

Paterinus, *see* **Patarinus.**

patern/itas, *title (eccl.) 798, c 990. c 1125, 1686; right of abbey over daughter-houses c 1381; *-alis, paternal c 1250, c 1440; *-aliter c 1000. c 1192, c 1470, -e c 1180, 1456, as a father; *see also* PATRIN

patha, (?) forehead 6c.

pathema, passion 1620; †**patisus**, trance c 1180.

pathnagium, *see* **pannagium.**

patibulum, gibbet, gallows c 1138, 1480; cross, rood 11c. 1240, p 1340; ‡"pillory" 1570.

pat/icium, -issium, *see* PACT

pati/ens, -entia, -or, *see* **passio.**

patilla, *see* **patella.**

patillus, *see* **pasta.**

patin-, *see* **patena.**

patisus, *see* **pathema.**

patmum, *see* **bathmus.**

patraster 1195, **paraster** 1184, c 1258, stepfather.

patrat/io, performance (of miracles) c 793; **-or mirabilium** 985, **-rix** (*f.*) **miraculorum** c 1396, miracle-worker.

patrellum, *see* **pectusculum.**

patri/a, *country as a whole (not necessarily native) 6c., 7c. 1086, 1502; *country, district, neighbourhood c 1150, 1575; local populace 6c., c 1362; *local body of suitors, jury (leg.) c 1185, 1499; sheriffdom (Sc.) 1393, 1398; Welshry (W.) 1306; country (as opposed to town) c 1170, 1320; *see also* decanus, factum; **-a** c 1180, 1421, **p. celestis** c 1125, **p. summa** 1245, **p. vite** c 1250, Heaven; **p. alta**, district, *haut pays* (G.) 1385; **-alis**, of the country, popular c 1432; **-alis** 15c., **-ensis** 1041, native, inhabitant; **-o**, to travel c 1115.

patriarch/a *8c., a 1050. 12c., c 1450, †**-us** 1267, patriarch (bibl.); patriarch (eccl.) *8c. c 1090, c 1534; ‡**-us**, stepfather 15c.; **-alis**, patriarchal (eccl.) c 1220, c 1620; **-aliter**, like the patriarchs (bibl.) c 1100; *-atus 1006. c 1090, 1420, **-ia** c 1220, patriarchate, archbishopric; **-ium**, papal palace c 1125, c 1450.

patricida, slayer of (another's) father c 1190.

patricinium, *see* PATROCIN

patrici/us, nobleman 686, 11c. a 1110, 15c.

patrimoni/um, endowment (eccl.) 1549; **p. Crucifixi**, the Church's temporalities c 1380; **-olum**, revenue 6c.; **-alis** c 1170, c 1450, **-us** c 1410, hereditary; **-aliter**, by way of patrimony c 1204.

patrinomius, *see* **patronymicum.**

patrin/us c 1115, 1559, †**paternus** c 1219, godfather; **-alis**, relating to a godfather 1223.

patriota, *native, inhabitant c 1100, 1461; jurat (C.I.) 1332.

***patr/isso** 1090, 1393, **-izo** a 1100, to take after father.

patrocin/atio c 1090, **-iatio** 1380, **-atus** c 1255,

patricinium 13c., *for* **-ium**, patronage, protection; **-ia** (*pl.*), relics of saints a 1125, 14c.; **-ator**, patron saint a 1100; patron c 1414; **-atorius**, giving countenace c 1180.

1 **patron/us**, patron saint c 950. c 1127, c 1507; *c 1185, 1551, **patro** 1386, patron of benefice, owner of advowson (eccl.); owner (? *or* master) of ship 1338, 1560; **-a** c 1262, 1429, **-issa** ‡1483, a 1564, patroness of benefice; **-agium** c 1308, 1583, **-atus** c 1170, 1549, advowson (eccl.); **-alis**, of a patron (eccl.) c 1170, a 1564; **-ico**, to own (a ship) 1394; ‡**-izo** (**-iso**), to protect 15c., 1483; **-o**, to be patron of (eccl.) 1309, 1549.

2 **patron/us** 1355, 1445, ‡**-a** 1483, pattern, mould, stamp; **-o**, to stamp, mark 1315, 1356.

patr/onymicum, patronymic c 1125; **-inomius**, named after father 6c.

patru/us magnus, great-uncle 1461; **-elis**, maternal uncle c 953.

patula, *see* **patella.**

patul/e 1375, 1441, **-o** 990, **in -o** c 1343, openly, publicly; **-us**, open, manifest c 1000. c 1380.

‡**pauc/edo**, scarcity 1483; **-e**, sparingly, in brief a 1408; **-iloquus**, speaking little c 1340, 1629; **-ioritas**, lesser number 1335; **-ula**, small piece 1504.

paudna, *see* 1 **pannus.**

paul/ative a 1250, 1378, †**-atine** a 1270, gradually; **-ativus** (†**-atinus**), gradual a 1250; **-umper**, for a little while c 1150; **-us**, little one (title) c 793; **-isculus**, trifling 14c.

pauleum, *see* **palla.**

Paul/ianus, Paulianist heretic 12c.; ‡**betonica -i**, "woodpenny" (bot.) 1570; **-inum**, a laxative drug a 1250, (*cf.* **potio**); **-izo**, to imitate St. Paul 14c.

pauliatus, *see* 1 **palus.**

paumelus, *see* **hordeum.**

pauna, *see* 1 **pannus.**

paunagium, *see* **pannagium.**

paunfletus, *see* **pamfilius.**

paunum, *see* **pomum.**

pauper/, servile c 1115; **-taculus**, poor little c 1180; **-atio**, impoverishment 1370; **-itas**, *for* **-tas**, 1264, 1577; **-tas mea**, my poor self c 1250; **-inus**, 1006, **-tinus** 990, fit for a poor man, shabby; **-asco**, to look shabby c 1090; **-izo**, to act the pauper 13c.

paupirus, *see* **papyrus.**

paupita, *see* **palpita.**

paurentes, *see* **parentes.**

paus/a c 1397, 1414, **-atio** c 1100, resting-place, sepulchre; 1326, c 1470, **-atio** c 1296, c 1470, rest (mus.); **-atio**, rest, pause a 1100, 1483; suspense, trance c 1000; interval (gram.) 1267, 1278; **-atorium**, bed c 1266, c 1330; **-atim**, with pauses or rests (mus.) 1515, 1526; **-o**, to rest, sleep 8c., c 1006. c 1090, c 1540; to die c 1450; to rest, repose (*trans.*) c 1225, a 1452; **p. contencionem** (leg.) 1325; **p. ad terram**, to set down 1461.

paut/enera, -oneria, *see* **paltenerius.**

pauxille, a little a 1100.

pav/a -enna, -iculus, *see* 1 **pavo.**

***pav/agium**, pavage, toll for paving streets 1223, 1419; c 1340, **-iagium** c 1350, 1430, **-imentum** 12c., 16c., **-ementum** c 1266,

1469, -iamentum c 1380, †-ientum c 1390, †pamentum 1468, pevimentum 1505, -imentatio 1410, c 1470, -atio 1388, -itura, 1461, paving, pavement; -ator c 1378, 1480, -iator 1442, -itor 1457, ‡-imentor 1483, -or 1289, pavior; lapis -imentalis, paving-stone 1473; tegula p., paving-tile c 1255; via -iamentata, paved road 1291; †panatus, (?) for -atus, paved 1229; -eo 1238, 1346, -io 1244, 15c., -o 1303, 1419, to pave.

pavelio 1322, †parapilio 1343, part of helmet (? cf. papilio).

pav/idulus 1520, -estus c 1405, fearful.

pavil-, see PAPIL

pavis/ium pavis, large shield 1374, 1418; -arius c 1365, -or c 1400, paviser, man armed with pavis.

1 pav/o, peacock: p. gallus 1278, -us 1321, povo c 1200, pocokus c 1472; p. Indicus, "cock of Ind", turkey 1544; -onis gallina 1278, -a 1271, 1299, -enna 1350, 1375, peahen; -iculus, young peacock 1271, 1350; -icula, young peahen 1273; -o 1232, poenacium 1208, 1225, †pennacium 1225, ponacium 1239, 1252, pounacium 1236, 1285, powenacius 1236, pounettum 1298, a brightly coloured cloth.

2 †pavo, (?) wheelbarrow 1378.

3 pavo, see pavagium.

pawnagium, see pannagium.

pax, *pax (eccl.), kiss of peace or pax-board a 615, c 1006. c 1148 1605; benediction c 980; silence 14c.; consent, agreement c 1125, 1230; exemption c 1220, 1259; release from outlawry (leg.) 1276; (fine for) breach of peace 1086, c 1258; area of jurisdiction c 1115; 'peace' (leg.), agreed period of peace, protection (p. abbatis 1287, p. communis 1219, p. crucesignatorum 1219, p. Dei 1080, 1583, p. ecclesie c 1115, c 1290, p. nundinarum (Sc.) c 1270, p. regia 1260, 14c., *p. regis a 1087, 1461, p. r. corone 1251, p. r. curie, p. r. manus c 1115, p. vicecomitis 1202, 1221); ad pacem 1202, 1297, de pace 1323, within the peace; pro bono pacis 1220, c 1317; salva pace, with all respect a 1200; see also asser, clericus, constabularius, curia, custos, dies, forma, fractio, gero, infractio, justitiarius, lapis, 1 lesura, littera, osculum, recipio, secta, serjantia, serviens, sessio, stare, tabella, tabula, teneo, terra, via, vigilator; cf. PACI

paxatorium, pax (eccl.) c 1478.

pax/ema (-ima, †-ma), -imatum, (†-matium) c 600, †-matus panis 7c., -imatio panis 6c., toast or biscuit.

paxeria 1279, 1309, passeria 1290, paysseria 1283, pazeria 1283, dam, weir, sluice (O.F. passiere) (G.).

paxillus, boundary mark 1286; pivot 1326.

payla, see patella.

paylola, see palea.

paytrellum, see pectusculum.

peagium, peadgin-, see pedagium.

peautrum, see peutrum.

peblum, see peplum.

Peca, see 1 Pica.

pecc/a -um c 1283, 1460, †pica c 1496, †peciata 1364, peck (dry measure); vessel, peck measure 1338; measure of wool 1225.

pecc/amen, sin (eccl.); -atum actuale, sin in act 1219; p. carnis, sin of the flesh c 1450; *p. mortale c 1220, 1549; *p. originale c 1080, c 1510, p. originis 1562; p. veniale c 1258, p 1330; -atulum, -adillum, peccadillo c 1620; -abilis 1344, c 1670, -abundus 1497, sinful; -abilitas, sinfulness c 1343; -atissimus, overloaded with sin 12c.; -o mortaliter, to sin mortally c 1240, 1444.

pecha, tallage (Sp.) 1282.

pec/ia (pet-) *1205, 1442, -ium 1419, 1460, -ies 1313, piece; *1205, 1470, -ium 1292, -ies 1292, 1483, measure of cloth; piece (of ordnance) 1360; number of parchment leaves, (?) gathering p 1250; head (of cattle, etc.) 1366, 1579; 1202, 1505, -ies c 1412, -ium 1361, -is 1364, 1386, p. argentea 1417, c 1450, p. argenti 1269, 1464, piece of plate, vessel; p. aurea 1475, p. auri 13c., 1539, gold piece (coin); p. ferrea a 1300, p. ferri c 1290, 1323, -ium ferri 1320, measure of iron; p. plumbi, pig of lead 1267, 1322; p. prati 13c., 1587; *p. (piecia, peza) terre 1200, 1559, -iata terre 1299, -iuncula terre 1247, 1434, †-tura terre c 1135, -torale terre 1256; armo ad omnes -ias, to arm cap-a-pie 1380; -iola, small piece a 1250; -ius, (?) moulding, template (arch.) 1300 (cf. forma pecia); -iatus, patched c 1250.

peconus, see pego.

pec/orinus c 1180, 1427, -ualis c 1090, c 1197, †-ulialis c 1400, brutish, animal; caro -orina, beef 15c.; sepum -orinum a 1250; see also cauda; -orans, indulging in unnatural vice c 1290; -oreus, fleecy c 550; -uleus, monstrous c 1212; -udalitas, form of cattle 9c.; -uscula (pl.), sheep and cattle c 704; cf. PECUN

pect/en, comb (eccl.) 1245, 16c.; teeth (coll.) of portcullis c 1180; (teeth of) harrow (?) 14c., ‡15c.; ‡"battledore" 15c.; a 1200, ‡a 1520, ‡-unculus 1570, plaice, flounder; -enarius 13c., -inarius ‡15c., 1563, comb-maker; -inatio, combing a 1250, c 1330; ‡-inatrix 1483, -rix c 1180, 13c., "kempster", carder (f.); casa -inea, "comb-case" 1553; dens -ineus, tooth of comb a 1100; opus -ineum, style of embroidery 1295; -us, for -itus, combed c 1330; -ino, to comb 826. c 1080, c 1330; (?) to preen (feathers) c 550.

pect/usculum, breast c 793, c 1000. c 1090, 1537; (?) breast-bone 6c.; -orale, pectoral (vestment) 1295, c 1520; a 1200, 1416, peterellum 1238, peiterellum 1320, peytrellum a 1430, patrellum, paytrellum 1316, poitrel, horse's breast-plate; amicus -oralis, bosom friend c 1090; arteria p. (med.) 1345; -oreus, of or for the breast c 550; -orius c 1180; -oriosus, broad-chested c 1362; see also pecia.

peculanter, fraudulently c 1400.

peculialis, see pecorinus; pecunia.

pecul/ium, private property (mon.) c 1470; -iaritas, possession of private property (mon). c 1125, 1472; ‡"meekness" 1483; -iarius, ‡"meek" 1483; 'peculiar', exempt from diocesan authority 1535, 1684; see also curia, missa; -io, to appropriate a 1142, c 1212.

pecun/ia *1086, 1307, p. viva c 1100, c 1300, livestock; c 1400, 1539, *p. numerata 1296, 1583, p. †nominata c 1280, cash; p. crucis, tithe in aid of crusades 1255; p. deaurata 1445; p. fracta, broken coins 1420; p. mundata, (?) refined coinage 1395; p. ponderalis, money by weight c 1325; p. Romana 11c., p. Sancti Petri c 1110, Rome-scot, Peter's pence; p. S. Cuthberti, a rent (Durham) 12c. (cf. 2 firma); p. sicca, hard cash 1331, c 1450; -ium, for -ia, 11c.; -iola, a little money 1518, 1591; -ialis c 1343, 15c., †peculialis 14c., pecuniary; -ialiter 1258, a 1347, -iariter c 1178, -iarie 1229, financially.

pecunus, see pego.
pecuscula, see pecorinus.
ped-, see also pes.
†pedacia, (?) vagabond 12c.
*ped/agium c 1180, 1498, †predagium c 1373, -aticum 12c., padagium 1329, peagium 1203, 1409, paagium c 1185, 1415, paiagium 1290, 1321, pacagium 1220, 1269, pagagium a 1160, pagium (?) c 1120, toll paid by travellers; peadgina, toll district (G.) 1283; -agiarius (G.) 1289, peadginus, piagerius (G.) 1283, paagator (Savoy) a 1260, collector of toll; -agio, to pay toll on (G.) 1283.
pedagog/ia, school 1550; petagogus 1364, petegogus 1407, ‡ 15c., for -us, schoolmaster; -icus, educative a 1100; scholastic 1620.
pedal/e, footpath c 1250; measure of length, foot a 1350, c 1365; awning, curtain 14c.; 1286, 1352, -e ferreum 1352, 1389, ferrum -e 1273, 1424, f. pediale 1278, 'plough-iron' (?) plate protecting underside of share-beam; -is, foot-soldier 13c.; pilla -is 1409, 1567, p. pedaria 1588, football; see also ballista, carruca, plata, pons, via; -itas, possession of feet c 1300; cf. pes.
pedamentum, pediment a 1452.
pedan/eum, stool c 1000; -eus, low, base 12c.; hired man 1398.
pedantius, pedant 1620.
pedarium, boy (παιδάριον) c 1435.
pedarius, see PEDAL; pedum.
pedaticum, see pedagium.
pedda, 'ped', pannier 1390.
pedellus, see bedellus; pes.
pederos, a gem (παιδέρως) c 1400; cf. PERIDOT
pedi-, see also PEDAL; pes.
‡pediculus elephantis, cashew nut 14c.
pedic/um c 1115, pega, peja 1250, 1285, (?) pegia (Norm.) 1203, for -a, trap (Fr. piège); -ator, trapper 1168.
pedo, part of mill 1271; see also pes.
pedonomus, teacher (παιδονόμος) 1528.
pedor, deafening 6c.
pedul-, peducilis, see pes.
ped/um, crozier 1245, 1537; ‡-arius, crozier-bearer c 1440.
peerlia, see perla.
pega, see PEDIC

peganon, rue (bot.): pig/anum (†-amum) a 1250.
peggatio, pegging (of a pig) 1445.
peghtella, see pitellum.
pego c 1126, 1300, pec/unus c 1245, 'pricket', candlestick; -onus, crampon (holding stone in ring) c 1258, 15c.
peirarius, see pirum.
peis-, see pensa.
peiso, see 1 pesso.
peit/erellum, -rellum, see pectusculum.
Peitevinus, see PICTAV
peja, see PEDIC
pejor/amentum 1198, 1207, -atio 1195, 1550, injury, deterioration; -abilis, capable of deterioration c 1367; -itas, inferiority c 1250; *-o, to injure 1200, c 1465.
1 pel/a 1335, -um 1341, baker's peel.
2 pel/a 1237, -um 1241, 1272, paling, stake; -a 1300, 1405, -um 1299, 1355, pila 1435, pilium 1312, palisade or peel-tower; cf. 1 palus.
Pelagian/us 9c. 12c., -ista c 730. 1427, Pelagian (heretic).
pelagus, sea: pilagus c 730.
Pelasgus, Greek, Byzantine a 1142,
pelcheria, see PISC
pelefridus, see palefridus.
‡pelerine herba, goosegrass 14c.
pelet-, see pellis; pelota.
pelf/ra, -rum 1203, 1275, -a 1243, 'pelf', stolen goods; forfeited goods 1260, 1499; -o 1211, 1218, -ro 1218, to pilfer, rob.
†pelia (salis), (?) shovelful c 1175.
pel/icanus, pelican c 1070, 1489; ‡-ecanus, retort (alch.) 1652.
pelitria, see peutrum.
pella, heron 1544; see also perla.
pell/ax, bogus 1041; -aciter, alluringly, deceitfully c 1200.
pell/is 1258, 1586, p. ovina a 1142, 'pell', membrane of parchment (esp. in Exchequer); p. grossa 1258, p. pilosa a 1185, woolfell; p. lanuta, see lana; p. nuda 1258, 1449, p. pelletta 1303, p. pelluta 1258, *-etta (-ecta) 1270, c 1380, -ettula c 1300, 1449, †pelta 1425, 'pellet', pelt, (shorn or plucked) sheep-skin; p. viridis, untanned hide 1294; -ita, (?) skin c 1000; -icula, membrane (med.) c 1200, ‡14c.; surface film 1620; -iculosus, membranous (med.) c 1210; -eus, made of hide 1220, 14c.; †-iagium, (?) duty on hides (Sc.) 1370;
*-icia, -icium 9c., c 1000. c 1135, c 1450, -icies c 1180, †-ix 1256, a 1408, -ina c 1300, pilchia 1419, pelisse, pilch, leather garment; lana -icia, wool on the pelt 1254; -icia 1303, -ectria (-etria) 1266, 1410, -etaria (G.) 1253, -eteria 1307, piletteria 1318, -ipatorium 1242, felparia 1376, 1492, peltry, skins (coll.); -etria, trade of pelterer c 1324; -iparia 1260, pheliperia 1308, peltry, pelterers' quarter; -ator 1603, -etarius 1349, 1419, -itarius a 1609, peltarius 1260, peltenarius c 1270, -iciarius c 1170, -ifex c 1125, c 1325, -eficus a 1170, †-inarius c 1266, -iparia (f.) 1290, *-iparius 1176, 1497, phelliparius (feliparius) 1290, 1419, philipparius 1324, -aparius c 1260, -eparius 13c., c 1400,

pelterer, skinner; ‡-**icudia**, muff 1483; **ars
-iparia**, skinner's craft c 1172, c 1325;
*-**ura** 1248, 1435, -**oura** 1364, -**uria** 1254,
fur; -**itus** 1553, †-**ulatus** (? *for* **penulatus**)
1423, furred; -**iparo**, to dress (skins) c 1258.
pelo, to peel (a rush) 1287, 1297; to pluck
(skins) 1284; *cf*. **2 pilatio**.
peloca, 'pellock' (porpoise *or* large fish) (Sc.)
1331.
pelora, song-bird, thrush c 1315.
pelot/a, (?) ball 1268; 1221, 1327, -**is** 1319,
pellet (discharged from cross-bow); 1342,
1387, **peleta** 1339, cannon-ball; 1217, 1225,
†**poleta** 13c., ball of dog's foot (Fr. *pelote*);
cf. **pilettus**.
pelt-, *see also* **pellis**; **peta**.
pelta, (?) shield-play, jousting c 1325.
peltrum, *see* **peutrum**.
pelum, *see* **pela** (**1** & **2**).
pelv/is, font c 1414; basin-shaped lamp c 1266,
1412; -**a** 1286, 1288, -**ea** 1365, -**eus** 15c.,
-**inus** 1586, *for* -**is**, basin; -**ata**, basinful 1279.
pen/a dura et fortis 1368, **p. mutorum**
c 1370, *peine forte et dure* (leg.); **p. perdita**,
damages (leg.) 1515; -**e Gehennales**, pains
of Hell c 1105, 14c.; -**e purgatorie** 12c.,
c 1310; -**alitas**, punishment, penalty c 1182,
1588; prohibition c 1250; *-**aliter**, by way
of punishment c 1070, c 1470; -**alis** a 1275,
c 1340, -**osus** 1345, 1423, painful; **septi-
mana -osa**, Passion Week 1265; *see also*
penula.
penarium, cupboard c 1500.
pencellus, *see* **penno**.
pencio, *see* **pensio**.
pend/itio 1370, 1390, -**atio** 1517, hanging up,
suspension; -**ale** c 1494, -**ile** c 1495, c 1511,
-**ilium** c 1465, hanging, curtain; -**alis**,
hanging (*adj.*) 1388; -**iculum** 1250, 1411,
-**eculium** c 1450, tassel; padlock c 1336;
parchment strip (to which seal is affixed)
1391; *'**pendicle**', appurtenance (Sc.) 1481,
1573; -**agium**, payment, tax c 1375;
-**eica** (*pl.*), weights (used with scales) 1578;
-**entale** (†-**entrale**), (?) hanging chain 1473;
-**ibilis**, hanging (*adj.*) 1443; *see also* **2 scopa**;
-**icia** (*pl.*), appendages, pendent strips (on
vestments) a 1315; out-lands, appurtenances
1109; *see also* **penticium**; †-**iculus**,
dependent (*adj.*) 1267; -**ule**, in the balance,
doubtfully c 1258, c 1452; -**ula**, pendant
(her.) p. 1394; -**ulum**, pendant (ornament)
1300, ‡c 1483; tail of mitre 1295, c 1500;
pendent scroll 14c.; balance (*v.l.* -**ibulum**)
1327; **in -ulo** c 1210, c 1250, **in -enti**
c 1258, c 1290, pending; *see also* **porta**.
-**entia** (*f. s.*), schedule (of arrears),
amount pending (Sc.) 1391, 1479; **p. litis**,
period during which a suit is pending (leg.)
c 1440, 1684; -**entia** (*n. pl.*), vaults (arch.)
1253, 1279; male genitals c 1180, 1221; -**ens**,
hanging, curtain 1434, 1516; pendant (ornament) 1573; hanger, hillside 13c., 1369;
rotulus -ens, schedule 1263; *see also* **littera,
pons, sera, sigillum**; -**eo** to be pending 1272, 1535; to be the balance (of
accounts) 1327, 1471; **p. ad,** to be appended
(of seal) 1274; to depend on 7c. c 1250; **p.
super,** to be due from (Sc.) 1460, 1469; **p.
extra sigillum,** to be sealed without closing

1166, c 1180; **p. versus,** (?) to slope towards
1252; -**o**, to hang (a criminal) 1220, c 1362;
p. allec, to hang herring (to dry) 1357;
p. lectum, to string a bed 1464; *cf*. **PENS**
pen/e, barely c 1365; **p. quasi**, almost 8c.;
-**ultimus**, recent, late 1285.
pene/cella, -cellus, -sellus, *see* **penno**.
‡**penelope**, gannet (bird) 1570.
pen/es, *towards, as regards (persons) c 1193,
1461; in respect of, as regards (things) 1278,
1549; towards (places) 1334, c 1410; in
(a register) 1430; near to (W.) 1225, 14c.;
-**eitas**, (?) relativity c 1360.
penetarius, *see* **panis**.
penetentiarius, *see* **PENIT**
penetr/atio, compenetration (phil.) c 1360;
p. putei, boring, sinking a pit 1532, 1537;
-**abilitas**, power of penetration c 1115;
-**ale** 1295, 1462, -**abile** c 1325, **penitrale**
c 1448, ‡15c., gimlet; -**anter**, searchingly
12c.; -**ativus**, penetrating c 1170, 1622; -**o**, to
see through c 1320; to bore (in mining) 1404.
penicellus, *see* **penno**.
penicillus, pencil (geom.) 1686; **pin/cellus**
c 1125, 1355, -**cillus** c 1400, paint-brush.
penicula, *see* **PENUL**
penid/ii (*pl.*) a 1250, 13c., -**i** 1253, ‡-**ie** 15c.,
†-**re** c 1357, 'penide', 'pennet', barley-sugar.
pen/igeldum a 1070, 1330, -**ingeldum** a 1180,
1199, a customary payment; -**yhenna**,
penny-hen (food-rent) 1338.
penit/entia, *peine forte et dure* (leg.) 1315,
1326; *a 1100, 1551, -**emen** 964, -**udo**
a 1200, 1344, penance (eccl.); sacrament of
penance c 1238; **ago -entiam,** to do
penance c 600. c 1160, c 1444; **Frater
-entie (de -entia)**, Sacked Friar 1256, 1419;
-**ens** (*subst.*) 12c., c 1520, -**entialis** c 1172,
c 1464, -**entiaria** (*f.*) 13c., a penitent;
-**entiale** c 1197, c 1520, -**entialis** 9c.,
-**entionalis** 970, **liber -entialis** c 1110,
1414, a penitential; -**entialis**, (*adj.*) penitential (eccl.) 9c. 12c., 1415; *see also*
forum, psalmus; (*subst.*) 1200, c 1220,
-**entiarius** c 1170, 1573, **penetentiarius**
13c., penitentiary, confessor (eccl.); -**entiali-
ter**, penitently, by penance c 1100, 1427;
-**entiaria**, office of confessor c 1232, 1460;
court of papal penitentiary c 1290, 1518;
littere -entiarie c 1217; -**eo**, to do penance
c 1115, c 1443.
1 †**peniteo**, (?) *f.l.* for **eniteo**, c 900.
2 †**peniteo**, a medicinal herb c 1200.
penit/imus, uttermost, inmost c 1190, 1204;
-**ior**, inmost part c 1197; -**issime**, utterly
1537.
penitrale, *see* **PENETR**
†**penitus**, (?) troublesome 8c.
1 ***penn/a** c 1311, c 1470, -**ula** c 1170, pen,
quill; -**ula**, lobe (of lung) (*cf*. πτέρυξ) a 1250;
-**are** c 1452, ‡15c., -**arium** 1295, 1517,
penner, pen-case; -**inus**, winged 939, 946.
12c.; -**ositas**, featheriness a 1250; -**osus**,
densely feathered a 1446; -**ata**, arrow
c 1370; †-**ator**, (?) archer c 1370; -**atio**,
fledging (of arrows) 1295, 1387; (?) bevelling
(of edged tools) 1327; -**atus**, fledged (of
arrows) 1307; -**ifico**, to wing, lend wings to
c 1180; *-**o** 1225, 1335, **panno** 1225, to
fledge (arrows).

2 penn/a, -elatio, -ellatus, see PENUL
pennacium, see 1 pavo.
pennaethium, lordship, *pennaeth* (W.) 1309.
pen/no c 1422, 1461, -ona c 1400, 1421,
pennon; -uncellus c 1200, 1375, ‡-ucella
15c., -ocella, -ocellus 1275, 1371, -ecella,
-ecellus 1236, 1320, -esellus 1250, 1276,
-icellus 1388, c 1422, -cellus 1290, c 1422,
pensellus 1347, 1390, †ponecellus 1322,
pincellus 1355, 15c., pensell, small banner;
see also 1 penna.
pens/a 832, c 1030. 1086, 14c., *peisa 1130,
1573, peisia 1171, 1242, pesia c 1293,
paisa 1419, pisa 1214, 1535, pisum 1182,
1319, wey, unit of weight (of cheese, wool,
glass, *etc.*); peisa, weighing scale c 1150;
-um, allowance c 980; ad -am, -um
c 1067, c 1178, ad peisam 1086, c 1150,
by weight; ad -um magnum, ad. p.
parvum c 1166; pesagium 1200, 1526,
pisagium 1278, †parsagium 1506, †poia-
gium 1315, pesage, toll; pesagaria 1370,
pesageria 1379, collectorship of pesage;
peisagium 1312, peisatio 1486, weighing;
peisator, pesour, weigher 1486; -ate
c 1437, -iculatim 1521, with consideration;
ferrum -ile, stirrup 1562; -ilitas, hanging
loose 1620; sera -ula, padlock c 1200; -ata
(*pl.*), expenses 1301; -is, tax (fig.), expenses
c 793; -o (with *inf.*), to decide c 1200.
pensellus, see penno.
pensi/o *c 1185, 1565, pencio c 1200, 1560, -tio
(Sc.) 1331, 1410, pension (eccl.); 1549,
ecclesia -onalis 1169, 1243, e. -aria 1204,
a 1452, church burdened with pension;
-onaliter teneo, to hold as a pension 1200;
-onarius, (*adj.*) c 1258, c 1540, pencio-
narius 1557, receiving a pension; (*subst.*)
pensioner, recipient of pension 1336, 1591;
payer of pension c 1204, 1535; *see also*
VICAR; littere -onarie, letters granting
pension a 1280, c 1340; generosus pencio-
narius, gentleman pensioner 1573; -ono, to
burden (church) with pension c 1467.
penta/, five 1200; ‡-culum, pentacle, amulet
1652; -gonalis, pentagonal c 1267; -gonum,
pentagon 1267; pentalpha, pentalpha (her.)
c 1595; ‡-meron, oil of horehound 15c.;
-nomius, five-named c 1160; -scemus, *for*
-semus, having five divisions (gram.)
c 685; having five forms c 1125; -sona,
harmony of five voices or notes c 1200;
-stichos, verse of five lines 1610.
‡pentalon, (?) *for* eupetalon, laurel (bot.) 14c.
pentaria, see SERPEN
pent/econtarchus c 730, †-ecomarchus 12c.,
-ecosiarchus c 1182, †-icotharchus c 685,
captain of fifty.
*Pentecost/e (eccl.), -a 1086, Penticoste
12c., Pentecost; -alis, Pentecostal 1248,
c 1520; -alia (*pl.*), Whitsun dues 1560.
*penti/cium 1291, a 1452, -cia 1285, 1330,
-cius 1300, -sium c 1430, c 1515, pendi-
cium 1325, pentice, projection, lean-to;
1282, 1289, Pendicia c 1500, Pentice court
(Chester); *cf.* APPEN
penticonus, five-pointed star, mullet (her.)
c 1595.
penucella, see penno.
penul/a 1181, c 1495, -aria 13c., penicula

1208, hood; 1180, 1298, penna (pena)
c 1150, c 1180, †perrula 1305, fur edging
or lining; fur 1236, 1242; ‡-arius 15c.,
-ator ‡1483, 1518, furrier; -atio 1517, 1520,
pennelatio 1482, edging or lining with fur;
‡-atum, pad, saddle 1570; *-atus c 1200,
a 1564, pennellatus 1429, furred; ‡-o, to
fur c 1440.
penultimus, see pene.
penuncellus, see penno.
penuri/a recti, default of justice 1088, a 1190;
-um, *for* -a, poverty 6c.; -osus, needy 14c.
c 1465.
penyhenna, see penigeldum.
peonia, peony *or* peony-seed: pionia a 1200,
c 1357, piauna 1291.
pepan/sis, ripening c 1270; germination
a 1250; †-um, (?) pulp a 1250; ‡-us, lungwort (bot.) 15c.
†peparium, (?) handspike (naut.) 1294.
peper, see piper.
pephia, see ephippiarius.
pepilion, see populeon.
‡pepinum, "umbles of a deer" 1483.
pepl/um, wimple or veil c 1125, 1470; banner
c 1180; peblum, robe c 550; -alis, acting as
a veil c 1180; -atus, wearing a cloak c 1190;
-o, to veil, mask (med.) a 1250; to veil
(widows) (eccl.) a 1490, 1516.
‡pepsis, digestion 15c.
pepulus, bullace tree c 1393, ‡15c.
per, by (of agent) 1086, 1508; on (a particular
day of the week) c 1190, 1220; by (an
interval of time) 1218, 1430; by (a distance
in space) c 1188, c 1452; by, past (in space)
c 1296; on payment of 1216, c 1400;
     (forms of tenure) p. anulum et baculum
12c.; p. baculum c 1120, 1430; p. folium
1339, 1413; p. furcam et flagellum 1220;
p. fustem (fustum) et baculum p 1147,
1496; p. f. et bastonem 1201, 1227; p.
lignum et baculum 12c.; p. virgam
1335, 1413;
     (modes of investiture) p. anulum c 1193,
c 1300; p. librum c 1300; p. pileum 1262,
15c.; p. birreti traditionem 1415; p.
cincturam gladii 1557;
     (other phrases) p. ancoram, at anchor
1438; p. austrum, southwards 957; p.
cancellum, crosswise 1241; p. certitu-
dinem, certainly c 1341, c 1343; p.
gyrum, in turn 1200, 1526; c 1250, 1278,
p. circuitum c 1190, 1415, round, around;
p. hoc, on this account c 1090, c 1290; p.
momentum, for an instant c 1250; p.
omnia, in all respects c 1200, c 1340;
p. quantum, in so far as 1265, 1374; p.
tantum, to that extent c 1160; p. quos,
record of customs payments (Sc.) 1342; *p.
se, separately 1677, 1404; p. vitam, on
pain of death c 1115;
     (with *adj.* or *ppl.*) p. accidens,
accidentally (log.) c 1200, 1345; *p. consequens 1232, c 1470, p. sequens 14c., in
consequence; p. duplum, in duplicate 1214;
p. integrum c 1450, p. plenam (G.) 1253,
in full; p. longum (with *gen.*) along 957.
c 1280; p. oppositum, in opposition (astr.)
a 1270; p. perpetuum, in perpetuity
c 1262; p. totum, throughout a 1240

c 1525; in general 1230; **p. transversum**, across c 1210, 1430; **p. traversum**, inverted (as sign of dishonour) (her.) p 1394; (with *adv.*) **p. aliter**, otherwise c 1357; **p. ante**, in front 1392; c 1172, c 1450, *****p. antea** 1377, 1508, **p. prius** 1318, 1529, formerly; **p. prius**, above all 1330; **p. demum**, for long 1402; **p. extra**, outside a 1408; **p. intus**, inside c 1370; **p. ibi** 1375, **p. ibidem** 1379, 1433, by that way; **p. invicem**, mutually c 1090; **p. seorsim**, separately c 1240; *****p. sic quod** 1196, 1287, **p. sic ut** 1199, 1204, on condition that.

per-, *see also* **par-**

pera, pier (of bridge) c 1120, 1340; pier (in harbour) 1390; stone 550; *cf.* PERR

peraccipio, to receive in full 1419.

peracerbe, with grave displeasure 16c.

peracquieto, to pay in full 1213.

†**peracta**, (?) *f.l.* for **per astra**, 1150.

peradapsis, *see* **paropsis**.

peradota, *see* **peridotus**.

peradversor, to oppose bitterly c 1434.

peraffin/atio, refining (of ore) 1338; **-o**, to refine thoroughly 1300, 1338.

peragro, to plough through c 1115.

peragrum, *see* PERR

peralenchus, *see* **parexelenchus**.

peralloco, to allow in full (in account) 1275.

peraloysmus, *see* PARALOG

†**peraltatus**, *f.l.* for **paraliticus**, 1223.

peraltus, lofty c 1180.

peram/atio, persevering love 1344; **-abilis** c 793. 1309, c 1363, **-andus** c 1415, much beloved; **-o**, to persevere in love 1344, c 1400.

*****perambul/atio** 1183, 1620, **-ata** c 1190, 1220, perambulation, survey, walking of bounds; marginal zone round forest 1344, 1370; **-us**, spreading abroad (or (?) *for* **preambulus**) a 1408; **-ator**, surveyor 1201, 1300; explorer 1622; **-atorium**, walk, path 1408; **-atorius**, for travelling on c 1400; **judex -ans** c 1178; **-o** a 1130, 1430, **perambilo** 12c., to survey, walk the bounds; (?) to rehearse 1194.

peramenator, *see* **paramentum**.

perampl/ius, more abundantly c 1333, c 1415; **-io**, to increase c 1192.

perangari/a, additional service or imposition a 1200, 1453; **-o**, to burden with additional services 14c.

perannatus, over a year old 13c.

perante/, **-a**, *see* **per**; *cf.* **preantea**.

peraperte, quite openly 9c.

perappositus, placed c 1078.

perapsis, *see* **paropsis**.

peraria, *see* **perraria**.

perastutus, very crafty c 1210.

peraudio, to hear to the end c 1190; to audit completely 1268.

peravidus, desirous, greedy c 1000.

perbarbarus, very uncultivated 9c.

perc-, *see also* **parcus**.

perca, perch (fish): **perch/a** a 1200, ‡15c., **-ia** c 1190, c 1290, **-ius** c 1200, **percida** a 1275, **pertica** 1250, 1417; *see also* PERTIC

percalco, to tread on 13c.

percallide, very skilfully c 1400.

percam-, *see* PERGAM

percant/atio, singing through 15c.; *****-o** c 1125, 1555, **percino** 1537, to sing through.

percaptura, purpresture 12c.

percario 1279, 1390, †**precario** 1321, to carry in full, complete carrying.

†**percassus**, completely null 1303.

percata, *see* PERTIC

†**percaveo**, to be very careful 1257.

perceleb/er (? **-ris**), very famous c 1170, 1537; **-ro**, to celebrate (divine service) in full c 980. c 1125, 15c.

percell-, *see also* PARCELL

percell/o (? *for* **pre-**), to triumph 760; **p. fedus**, to strike an agreement c 1125, 1497; **perculo**, **percullo**, *for* **-o**, c 550.

percelsus (? *for* **pre-**), exalted c 1354.

percenettarius, *see* BERS

perceno, to finish supper c 1266.

percept/io c 1320, 1327, **-um** c 1393, levy, payment; receiving sacrament (eccl.) c 790, c 1000. c 1192, 1504; **-ibilis**, perceptible a 1230, c 1444; a 1180, c 1200, **-ivus** a 1250, c 1360, perceptive; **-ibilitas**, perceptibility c 1270, c 1344; **-ivitas**, perception 1344; **-ivus**, perceptive 1344; **-or**, receiver, levier c 1403, 1543; **percipio in manu regis**, to take into king's possession 1086, 1349; **p. sacramentum** (eccl.) 13 c.; *see also* PRECEPT

percetum, *see* **2 persicum**.

perch-, **percida**, *see* **perca**; **pertica**.

perchetus, *see* PROJECT

percino, *see* PERCANT

percissor, incisor tooth a 1250.

perclar/eo, *for* **-esco**, to become very clear c 730.

perclino, to instigate, induce 1379.

percludo, to enclose completely 1250.

perclusorium, *see* PRECLU

percogito, to consider carefully 956, c 970. 1267.

percognitio, examination, inquiry 1176.

percolligo, to collect in full 1299.

percomburo, to burn up, consume completely c 793.

percomenum, *see* PERGAM

percompleo, to fulfil completely 1235.

percomputo, to account in full 1298, 1381.

perconsulo, to consult c 1180.

percrebrius, much oftener c 1356.

percul/lo, **-o**, *see* **percello**.

*****percur/sus** (**parcur-**) 1109, p 1290, **procursus** 1255, 1276, right to pursue game into forest, runway; **-sor**, pacer c 1200; **-ribilis**, current (of money) 1254.

percus, *see* **parcus**; **pertica**.

percuss/io, disciplinary stripe (mon.) c 600. c 1330; stroke, shock (med.) a 1250; stroke (of clock) 1405, 1416; a 1235, **-a** a 1235, puncture; **p. serpentina**, snake-bite c 1313; **-ivus**, causing shock (med.) a 1250; **-or**, striker (in game of quintain) c 1324; **castigatio -oria**, corporal punishment 1344; **-ura**, striking (of coinage) 9c. c 1196, c 1320; **-us auro**, (?) adorned with beaten gold 1401; **percut/ientia**, striking 1344; **-io**, to strike (of clock) 1387, 1416; to give signal for c 1330; **p. mensam**, to rap on table (as signal) c 1330; **p. duellum**, to fight judicial combat 1218, c 1400; †**p. in sarculum**, (?) *f.l.* p 1348; **p. pacem**, to

conclude a peace 1508; **p. super,** to abut on c 1230; **-o,** *for* **-io,** to strike 1464.
perdebitus, thoroughly deserved 1494.
perdelectabilis, very agreeable 14c.
‡**perdetta,** small yellow turnip 1652.
perdibilitas, *see* **perditio.**
perdica, *see* **pertica.**
perdic/arius, -inarius, *see* **perdix.**
†**perdicialis (succus),** (?) of pellitory (bot.) a 1250; *cf.* **paries.**
perdico, to recite in full c 1125, c 1330.
perdilectus, *see* **predilectus.**
perdilla, *see* **paratella.**
perdingus, *see* 1 **ferdingus.**
perdissuadeo, to forbid expressly c 1260.
perd/itio, perdition (theol.) 1235, 1427; 'perdition', 'sconce' (ac.) 1636; *c 1192, c 1470, †-a c 1300, loss, injury; **-ibilitas,** potential perdition (theol.) 1427; **-ens,** loser 12c., 1265; **-ita** (*pl.*), losses 1168; **-itus,** damned c 1250, 1314; **-o,** to let escape (leg.) c 1115; *see also* LUCR, **panis, pena.**
per/dix, partridge: **-drix** 1242, 1395, **-dricia** 1271, **-dricies** 1275, †**-dricium** 1285, **-dricus** 1242, **partrix** 1392; **-dicarius** 1300, **-dicinarius** 1232, **-dricarius** 1303, **-driarius** 1310, **-tricarius, -triciarius** 1290, **partricarius** 1287, 1291, partridge-catcher; **-driarius,** dog used in partridge-hunting c 1280; **-drico** 1303, **-trico** 1291, **-tricio** 1290, to catch partridges.
perdominor, *see* PREDOMIN
*perdon/a (pardon-),** **-um** 1130, 1252, **-antia** 1441, †**-entia** 15c., *-atio** 1202, 1501, pardon, remission; **-arius (frater)** 1362, **-ista** 15c., pardoner; *-o,** to pardon, remit a 1100, 1583.
‡**perdonium,** herb wine 1652.
perduca, *see* **experductum.**
perducti/o, bringing c 1470; **-or,** accomplisher a 1220.
perduellio, enemy c 590.
perdur/abilis, lasting a 1142; *-o,** to remain, continue to be c 730. 1086, 1461.
peredeta, *see* **peridotus.**
perefficax, highly efficacious c 1250.
pereffluo, to overflow a 1200.
peregenus, very needy c 1180.
peregr/inus, (*adj.*) wandering, unsettled c 1115, 12c.; (*subst.*) pilgrim, crusader a 1142, 1586; **habitus -inus,** pilgrim's dress c 1250; ‡**-inus** 15c., **falco p.** c 1200, a 1446, peregrine falcon; **mus p.,** ermine a 1142; **-e** c 1135, 1461, **perigre** 1461, **-ine** c 1193, **-inaliter** c 1255, **-inatim** 1478, on pilgrimage; **-inalis,** of pilgrimage c 1255; *-inatio** 9c., c 1120, 1461, †**-atio** 15c., **perigrina-gium** 1424, **-e** 1411, pilgrimage, crusade; foreign land 8c.; earthly sojourn c 760, c 1000. 12c., c 1266; clerical career c 760; **-inatus,** travel c 1180; exchange of hospitality between foreigners 8c.; **-ine,** metaphorically c 1200; **-inor** c 1115, c 1462, **-ino** c 1468, to go on pilgrimage; to sojourn on earth c 1080, c 1460; **perigrinor,** to sojourn c 1130.
perempt/io, murder c 1000; destruction c 1343; **-icius,** apprentice 1535 (*cf.* **prenti-cius**); **-ivus** destructive c 1250; *-orie** c 1170, 1686, **-orio** c 1220, peremptorily;

-orium, peremptory summons (leg.) 1208, a 1245; **-o,** to kill c 1445.
perendin/atio (perhendin-), postponement 15c.; *sojourning, visiting c 1125, c 1470; 1205, 1414, **prehendinatio** c 1250, 1316, board, maintenance; **locus -alis,** dwelling place 15c.; **-arius** 1318, **-ator** 1292, ‡1483, **-atrix** (*f.*) c 1363, boarder, sojourner; *-o** c 870. c 1125, a 1564, **perundino** 1220 **prehendino** c 1070, 1338, to sojourn, visit; to tend 1263, 1293; **p. diem,** to spend the day c 1290.
perenn/alis (perhenn-), eternal c 1250, c 1340; *-iter** (eccl.), **-itus** 725, eternally.
pereo, *see* **peritus.**
perera, *see* PERR
peressenti/a, -alis, (?) *for* **paressentia,** equal essence, *or* **par essentia,** *etc.,* a 1360.
peretrum, *see* **paries.**
perexcutio, to cut through c 1115.
perexigo, to demand c 1300.
perexiliter, very slightly 15c.
pereximius, admirable c 1270, c 1460.
perexplico, to explain fully 1153.
perexstruo, to build up completely c 1190.
pereympa, *see* **paropsis.**
perfalcatio, complete mowing c 1230.
perfastus, overweening pride 1427.
perfectialis, *see* PREFECT
perfect/io, completion (of something bad) 6c.; completion (of sum) 1219; a measure of time (mus.) 1326, c 1470; **numerus -ionis** a 1030, **n. -us** a 1200, a 1250, number equal to the sum of its aliquot parts; **-ibilitas,** perfectibility c 1283; **-ibiliter,** perfectly c 1283; **-ibilis** a 1233, c 1445, **-ionabilis** c 1300, perfectible; **-ionalis,** concerned with perfection c 1290, c 1445; **-ivus** 9c. c 1238, 1524, **-orius** c 1500, making perfect; *see also* **dos; -o** c 1180, **ad -um** c 1250, c 1430, **in -um** c 1298, to perfection; †**perfitior,** more perfect a 1520; **-ioro,** to perfect c 1375; *perficio,** to make up, complete (a sum) 1196, 1266.
per/fectus, -ficuum, *see also* PROFECT
perfelix, very happy 9c.
‡**perfidus,** very faithful 1483.
perfiguro (? *for* **pre-),** to symbolize c 1006.
perfindo, to gash c 1180.
perfingo signum crucis, to make sign of cross 12c.
perfinio, to complete c 1140, c 1488.
perfitior, *see* PERFECT
perflag/o, *for* **-ro,** to blaze fiercely 6c.
perflo, to inspire c 1250.
perfloreo, to flourish a 1412.
perflu/idus, wallowing c 1190; †**-enter,** transitorily 968; **-osus,** abundant a 1150.
perfoliata, thoroughwax (bot.) 1629.
perfor, to recount in full c 1400.
perfor/atio, piercing, hole 1240, 1620; **-abilis,** vulnerable c 1197; ‡**furfuraculum** (*for* **-aculum**) 15c., ‡**-ale** 15c., 1483, **-ator** 1297, auger or gimlet; **-amen,** hole c 1000. c 1250; **-ativus,** penetrative a 1250, c 1320; **-ator,** piercer c 1404, 1528; **-ata (herba)** St. John's wort (bot.) a 1250, ‡c 1440; **-atus,** stippled (of urine) a 1250; **-o,** to transfix, kill c 550; to broach (wine) 1276; to void (her.) a 1446; *see also* **crux.**

perform/atio, performance c 1455, 1549; **-o,** to perform 1291, c 1538.
perfosso, to stab 1461.
perfoveo, to cherish 9c.; to favour (? *for* **perfaveo**) c 1150.
perfragilis, very slight c 1250.
perfricte, impudently 1610.
perfru/o, *for* **-or,** to enjoy thoroughly 814.
perfugo, to hunt (C.I.) 1309.
perful-, *see* PREFUL
perfunctor, one who attains c 1204.
perfuratus, furred 1463.
perfurnio, to furnish or perform in full (Fr. *parfournir*) 1166.
per/fusio unguenti, anointment c 760; **-fundo,** to found (metal) a 1400.
***pergam/enum (pargam-), -ena** c 1000. c 1125, 1532, **-inum** 1393, 1497, †**pergani- mum** 1475, **-entum** 12c., **pargomentum** 12c., **-en** 1299, ***percamenum** (par-) 1218, 1452, **percaminum** 1291, **percomenum** 1416, **parcamen** 1298, †**caminum** c 1511, parchment, document; **p. virgineum,** virgin parchment (from young lamb) 1510; **p. vituli** 1249, **p. vitulinum** 1342, vellum; **-enarius** c 1290, 1453, **-inarius** 15c., **-entarius** 1355, †**percamnius** 1359, **parcamenarius** c 1150, 1252, **perca- menator** a 1295, parchment-maker; **-enius** 1441, **-ineus** 12c., of parchment.
pergamum, citadel, court c 950.
pergata, *see* **pertica.**
per/gestus, concluded, enacted 1449; **-gero,** to perform c 1000.
pergetus, *see* PROJECT
perg/o (ad hundredum), to pay suit 1086; **porrigo,** *for* **-o,** to proceed 1200, c 1400.
pergraffum, *see* **paragraphum.**
pergravo, to oppress c 980. c 1175, c 1480.
pergulum, platform or pulpit 1395; ‡"pin- fold" 15c.; *cf.* **parcus.**
pergusto, to taste a 1350, c 1410.
pergyro, to go round c 980, 1041. c 1150, c 1408.
perhabeo, to hold, possess c 1115.
perhen-, *see* **peren-**
perhercio, to harrow thoroughly c 1350.
perhorr/endus, very horrible c 1310, c 1433; **-eo** (with *inf.*) c 1400, **-esco** (with *inf.* or *acc.* and *inf.*) 6c., 933. c 1130, to be very loath, shrink (from).
perhospitalis, most hospitable 1517.
perhumectatio, soaking a 1250.
perhumilis, very humble c 1380, 1431.
peria, *see* PERR
peri/bolus, voided escutcheon c 1595; ‡**-bolum,** "alley of a garden" c 1440; **-buia** (*pl.*), precincts c 960.
periclit/atio, peril 13c., 15c.; shipwreck 1342; **-ator,** adventurer 1624; **-o,** to be in peril 1225, a 1292; c 1250, 1427, **-or** 1186, 1337, to suffer shipwreck; **-or,** to fail in ordeal 1195; to adventure 1624.
pericul/ositas, peril, perilousness a 1250, c 1375; **-or,** to be in peril 1373.
peridot/us 1245, 15c., **lapis p.** 1245, **-os** c 1450, **-a** 1265, †**perido** 1204, **peradota** 1272, †**peredeta** 1300, **paritotus** c 1411, peridot (gem); *cf.* **pederos.**
periergia, extreme care, diligence c 960.

perigeum, perigee (astr.) 1620, 1686; base (her.) c 1595.
perignitus, full of fire 1411.
perigr-, *see* PEREGR
perihelion, perihelion (astr.) 1686.
Perihermenias, Aristotle's *De Interpretatione* c 793, 11c. 12c., 15c.
perilla, *see* **perla.**
perillustro, to glorify c 1412.
perimetrum, perimeter ‡15c., 1686.
perimpedio, to hinder a 1175.
perimpendo, to expend, lavish c 1421.
perimple/mentum, supplementary portion 1314; 1413, **-tio** 1449, 1573, fulfilment; **-tio,** filling 1537; **-mentum hundredi** (Derb.) 1373, **curia -toria** (Cornwall) 1575, special hundred court; **-o,** to fill 1300, 1379; to make up, complete 1192, 1435; *to fulfil c 1300, 1620.
perin/a, -um, -us, *see* PERR
perinchelis, *see* **periscelis.**
perinclytus, celebrated c 1300.
perinde, by that route a 1215; thereby c 1258.
perindustriosus, most diligent c 1426.
†**perinformiter,** (?) very inaccurately a 1323.
perinhumanus, very brutal c 1433.
perinpendo, *see* PARV
†**perio,** (?) district 1150.
periocha, section c 790; head of discourse c 850.
period/us, recurring portion 9c.; period, cycle a 1252, c 1488; period (punctuation mark) 1267; **-icus,** periodic 1686.
Peripatetic/us Palatinus, title given to Abelard a 1150; **parypatheticus,** *for* **-us,** 1292.
peri/pheria, circumference c 1160, a 1670; ‡**-perium,** "surface of a wall" 15c.
periphrasticus, periphrastic c 700, c 990.
peri/pleuronicus, (?) *for* **-pneumonicus** *or* **-pleuriticus,** a 1250.
peripneumonia, pulmonary consumption (med.): **peripleumon/ia, -icus** a 1250.
peripsema (bibl.), **peripsim/a** c 1170, ‡15c., off-scouring, refuse; **-o,** to peel off c 1180, ‡ c 1440.
peripsius, odd (math.) (περισσός) 13c.
periscelis, the Garter c 1458, c 1595; †**perinchelis,** bracelet c 1200.
peristasis, environment 1620.
peritiuncula, small skill 10c.
per/itus, ruined 1315; **-eo,** to fail in ordeal 1166, 1214; to be found guilty by jury 1218; **p. vite eterne,** to lose eternal life 7c.
perizorium, *see* **perzorium.**
perjact/atio, pargeting c 1326; **perjectator** 1401, **pargettator** 1314, **pargettor** 1417, pargeter; **-o** 1237, 1323, **perjecto** 1251, **perjaceo** 1290, ‡**perjacio** 15c., **parjetto** (parieto) 1390, 1416, **pargetto** 1372, †**pargo** c 1365, **projacto** 1312, **progetto** 1452, **purjetto** 1313, to parget, rough-cast; †**parjetio,** (?) to caulk (naut.) 1575; *cf.* **paries.**
perjectum, *see* PROJECT
perjur/ator c 1460, †**-ius** c 1340, perjurer; **dies Lune -ata,** (?) Hock Monday (second after Easter) c 1185; **-o,** to swear 1074, 1370; **-o me** 1221, c 1470, **-or** c 1290, to commit perjury.

perjuvenis, too young c 1437.

per/la 1204, 1622, parla c 1365, -lus 1439, pella c 1250, -lia 1225, 1332, †peerlia 15c., -illa c 1315, 1404, -ula 1240, 1432, pearl; mother of pearl 13c.; bead c 1322; p. (parla) marina a 1250 (cf. palla); -leatus, pearl-coloured or ornamented with pearls 1207.

perlatio, range, extension 1620; see also PROLAT

perlatus, very wide 7c.; cf. 2 prelatus.

perlaudo, to commend greatly c 1300.

perlect/or, reader 1267, c 1390; -ito, to read through 1525; perlego, to lecture (ac.) c 1380, c 1565.

perlimo, to file down 1326.

perlingo, to skim through 1345.

perlio, purlin, horizontal beam (arch.) 1448.

perlog-, see PARALOG

perlonge, for a very long time p 1330.

perloquor, to discuss thoroughly 1102, 1274; to speak in vain c 1102.

perloria, see 2 parliamentum.

perlucror, to earn c 1415.

perlucto, to struggle violently a 1525.

perludus, see preludium.

perlustr/atio, radiance 14c.; travel 7c.; circumnavigation 1620; -ator, irradiator 14c.; surveyor 1399; judex -ans, justice itinerant c 1178; -o, to irradiate c 1320, c 1477; -or, to traverse c 1265.

permagnifice, see PREMAGN

permando, to charge, enjoin 793, 9c.

perman/entia, permanence 9c. a 1233, a 1452; -enter, permanently c 1250, p 1300; -ens c 1250, c 1444, -sibilis c 730, -sorius 9c., permanent, continual; †premaneo, for -eo, to remain 13c.

per/manus, -menus, see pirum.

permaturo, to improve c 1296; cf. PREMATUR

permaximus, see PREMAGN

permedito, to meditate deeply or purpose strongly 8c.; cf. PREMEDIT

perment-, see paramentum.

permerdo, to befoul a 1252.

permeto, to complete reaping 1345, 1347.

permico, to sparkle 1433.

permiss/iones (pl.), permission 9c.; ‡-arius, swordsman 1483; -ibilis c 1290, permittibilis c 1300, c 1470, -ivus c 1400, permissible; -ivus, permissive c 1344, 1649; *-ive, by permission 1284, 1430; permitto, to let be, neglect 1374, c 1540; (?) for pretermitto, to set aside 1326.

permixtura, confusion c 1115.

permodicitas mea, my humble self c 1250.

permollio, to soften c 1410.

permortuus, completely dead 12c.

permund/atio, thorough cleansing c 730. 12c.; -o, to cleanse thoroughly 810. 1414.

permut/atio, transposition (log.) p 1300; exchange of benefices (eccl.) 1414; -abilis, mutable a 1233; -atim 1267, 1344, -ative 1267, 1310, by way of variation; conversely a 1350; -o, to transpose (log.) p 1300.

perna, limb 6c.; parna baconis, ham 15c.

pernecabil/is, fatal c 1250, 1253; -iter, fatally c 1240.

pernego, to deny on oath (leg.) c 1115.

pernesciens (†prenesciens), wholly ignorant c 1250.

per/niciositas, perniciousness c 1283; ‡-nix, pernicious c 1220, 1483.

pernitidus (? for pre-), bright, clear 6c.

perniveus, snowy white c 685.

pernoct/anter, by night c 1390; -esco, to grow dark c 1250; -o, to put (sheep) for night 1372; to spend night in vigil (eccl.) c 1280; -or (dep.) 1236, c 1434, †provocitor c 1370, to spend night.

pernoscito, see PROGNOSTIC

pernotatus, marked 760; notorious 1461; see also PRENOT

‡perobliquus, crooked 1483.

perobtentus, see preobtentus.

perocus, see PARROC

peronellus, see 2 paro.

‡peronizo, "to purchase" 15c.

peropacus, very dark c 1302.

†perope, (?) f.l. for pompe, a 1452.

peropt/abilis, very desirable c 1250; *-o, to desire ardently 12c., c 1470; cf. PREOPT

*peroptim/us, excellent a 1100, c 1520; *-e, excellently 1120, c 1470.

peropus, urgent need 1062.

peror/ator, advocate (leg.) c 1115; spokesman 15c.; -atorius, humbly supplicatory c 1172; -o, to entreat, pray 1244, c 1470; to receive answer to prayer 1241; cf. prooro.

perorior, to rise completely (astr.) c 1233.

perornat/io, fine adornment c 1400, c 1470; -us, finely adorned c 1248; cf. preornatus.

*perpac/atio (parpac-) 1226, c 1340, perpagatio 1297, 1299, payment in full, completion of payment; -o 1202, c 1320, perpago 1297, to pay in full, complete payment.

per/panus 1290, -pent' achillar' c 1400, parpeyn ashlar (arch.)

perpars, see PROPAR

perparvissimus 12c., †preparvissimus a 1100, extremely small.

perpassio, see PERPESS

perpatul-, see PROPATUL

perpavidus, sore afraid c 810.

perpavo, to pave completely 1242.

perpedio, see PREPED

perpendicular/itas, perpendicularity 1267; -is, (subst.) perpendicular line a 1233, 1326; -ior, nearer to perpendicular c 1260; -iter, perpendicularly a 1233, 1686.

perpen/sio, consideration c 1534, 1552; -sior, (?) more deliberate (or for propensior) c 1250; -sius, more deliberately 1299; -do, to pay in full 1415; prependo, for -do, to infer, consider c 1225, c 1415; -so, to plan, propose 7c.

perperus, misleading c 815; see also hyperperum.

perpess/us (p.p.), suffered c 1204, c 1403; ‡-ivus, suffering 1483; perpassio, enjoyment a 1180.

‡perpetra, rowel of spur 1483.

perpetr/atio confessionis, making confession c 1000; †petratio, (?) for p., purchase 1357; †-ator, (?) for appropriator, a 1350; -o, to purchase, acquire 1373.

perpet/uatio a 1290, 1620, †-io c 1443, perpetuation, continuation; c 1285, 1380, -uitas c 1400, 1535, (grant in) perpetuity, perpetual benefice (eccl.); -im c 760. c 1077, c 1250, (?) -e c 950, -ue c 1170, c 1362, **-ualiter** 793, c 1000. c 1125, c 1503, perpetually, for ever; **-ualis,** perpetual, everlasting 8c., 10c. a 1100; **meo (suo) -uo** 1265, 1313, **pro meo (suo) -uo** 1311, c 1400, all my (his) life long; **decedo a meo -uo,** to die c 1400; **-o,** to appoint *or* acquire in perpetuity 1377; *see also* **imperpetuum, per, pro, cantaria, capellanus, vicarius.**

perpingo, to paint (chamber) throughout 1239; *cf.* **prepingo.**

perplacit/um, plea 15c.; **-o,** to complete pleadings (leg.) 1269, 1330.

perplano, to explain 9c.

perplector (*dep.*), to apprehend, discern a 1408.

perpletus, completed c 1000.

perplex/io 9c., **-itas** c 1125, c 1535, perplexity, obscurity; **-us,** (*subst.*) writhing c 1250; (*ppl.*) involved, entangled 1229, c 1340; c 1357, 1419, **-ionatus** a 1452, perplexed, puzzled.

‡**perplicar,** garter 15c.

perplur/es (*pl.*), more c 1285; c 730. 1414, **-imi** c 730, c 1000. c 1191, c 1250, ‡**preplurimi** c 1170, very many; **-imum,** exceedingly c 1433.

per/pointus, -pontus, *see* **purpunctus.**

perport-, *see* **proportum.**

perprest/ura, -um, *see* **purprestura.**

perpret/iosus, very precious 14c.; **-io,** to appraise 1222.

perprius, *see* **per prius.**

perpropere, in haste c 1300.

perpro/stratus, completely laid low 1417; **-sterno,** to raze 1176.

per/providus c 1200, **-prudens** c 1000, very prudent.

perpulch/er, very beautiful c 1365; **-re,** very beautifully c 1362.

perpulsatio, *see* **PROPULS**

per/punctus, -puntus, *see* **purpunctus.**

perpur/us, very clear 1282; **-e,** quite clearly 9c.

perquaquam, anywhere and everywhere 6c.

perquerius, *see* **parcus.**

perquisit/io c 1185, 1224, **-um** 1221, 1222, request, instance; c 1185, c 1450, **-a** 1242, **-um** 1219, 1344, **-us** c 1300, purchase, acquisition, thing acquired; 1168, 1583, **-a** 1249, **-um** 1205, 1537, **perquirendum** 1253, perquisite, profit; **-um curie** (man.) 1257, 1540; **-or** p 1285, 15c., **-rix** (*f.*) 1304, purchaser, acquirer; **perquero,** to seek for 1461; **perquiro,** to restore c 1115; to request c 1185; *c 1115, c 1450, ‡**proquiro** 12c., to purchase, acquire; **p. cum,** (?) to purchase from p 1411; **p. breve,** to purchase writ (leg.) 1431; **p. malum,** to contrive mischief 1164; **p. mineram,** (?) to assay ore 13c.; **p. me** 1200, 1219, **p. mihi** 1198, 1229, to take action, fend for oneself; *cf.* **purcacium.**

perradio, to shine upon, illumine 8c.

perrado, to shave completely c 1266.

perr/aria c 1192, c 1436, **-arium** 1290, **-eria** c 1192, 1231, **pararium** c 1436, 'perrier', 'petrary', siege-engine; **-era** 1383, **-eia** 1425, **peria** 1253, 'perrie', jewellery; **-edum,** (?) gravel-pit *or* shingly beach (Fr. *perroy*)

1185; **-eium,** beach (Norm.) a 1170; **-einum** 1220, **-inum** 1223, 13c., **-ina** 1253, (?) ‡**peragrum** 1466, stone building; ‡**-inus,** gem-like 12c.; **pera,** stone c 550; *cf.* **PETR**

perrasmus, *see* **pirasmus.**

perreddo, to render in full 1258, c 1266.

perrim/o, -or, to scrutinize c 1100, c 1415.

perroca, *see* **pertica.**

perrula, *see* **penula.**

persalto, to run over (in reading) c 1444.

persalvo, to preserve 9c.

persapidus, very tasty c 1415.

pers/atum, -ecum, *see* 2 **persicum.**

perscissio (narium), slitting 1585.

perscitor, an expert 14c.

perscriptibilis, *see* **PRESCRIPT**

perscrut/ator, searcher, examiner c 793. c 1090, 1416; **-or mare** to scour the sea 1338.

persecut/oria actio, action for recovery (leg.) c 1258; **-rix,** persecuting (*f.*) 7c., c 730; **-us** (*pass.*), persecuted 1274; **persequibilis,** to be pursued 1344; ‡**prosequor,** (?) *for* **persequor,** c 1362; *see also* **PROSECUT**

persedulus, painstaking c 700.

perse/itas, 'perseity', self-subsistence (phil.) c 1300, c 1367; **-icus,** self-subsistent, existing *per se* 1427.

persemino, to sow completely c 1290, 1326.

persepius, very often c 1285, c 1415.

perseptimano, to stay a week c 1070.

persequestro, *see* **prosequestro.**

pers/etum, -eum, *see* 2 **persicum.**

persever/abilitas, perseverance 11c.; **-abilis** c 760. 1078, 15c., **-atrix** (*f.*) 12c., persevering; **-ans,** lasting, abiding 798; **-ator,** one who continues c 1260; **-atim,** perseveringly c 1250.

1 **persic/um,** peach: **pessicum, pessicus** c 1184, 1252; **-aria,** peachwort, water-pepper (bot.) a 1250, 1635; *see also* **ignis.**

2 **pers/icum** 1233, 1329, **-ecum** 1200, **-atum** 1200, **-etum** 1296, **parsetum** 1327, **percetum** c 1300, **-eum** 1315, **-um** 1265, 1328, 'perse', dark-blue cloth; **-icus** 1432, **-eus** 1301, 1309, **-us** 1259, ‡**perticem** (? **percicem**) (*acc.*) 1312, perse-coloured (of cloth).

persilium, *see* **petrocilium.**

persist/entia, persistence, continuance 12c., 1649; **-o,** to be, exist 941, 1031. c 1080, c 1400.

perso, *see* **PERSON**

persolidus, strengthened, repaired 11c.

persol/utio, payment in full 1086, 1413; c 1115, **prosoluta** c 1102, compensation; **-ta, prosolta,** perquisite c 1178; **-utor,** payer 1254; **-vo,** to pay twice, pay again c 1102, c 1250; to pay (a person) 1254, c 1444; to pay for, buy c 1123; *to perform, celebrate (religious offices) c 1090, c 1500.

person/a (parson-) 867, 11c. 12c., c 1395, **-is** 825, 986. 12c., character, recognized position; person of Trinity (theol.) 9c. c 1170, c 1362; *c 1125, 1469, **perso** 1218, parson, beneficed priest (eccl.); parsonage 1552; **-a ad -am,** man to man 1415; **p. media,** arbiter 1461, 1497; **p. prima** c 1262, **p. secunda, p. tertia** 1225 (gram.); **p. privata** c 1258, c 1409; **p. regni** 1164, **p. grossa** (Ponthieu) 1311, magnate; **p.**

standi, status, right to be heard 13c.;
*in propria -a, in person 1214, c 1350; pro
p. p. c 1343;
-agia c 1140, -agium 1144, 1583, -alitas
c 1200, -atus c 1150, a 1540, parsonage,
benefice (eccl.); -alitas, personality, character 12c., c 1670; personality (gram.) 13c.;
-alis, dignified c 1191, c 1220; *c 1188,
1587, -abilis a 1290, personal; forum
-ale, private correction 1264; -aliter, by
appearance c 730; *c 1125, 1684, -abiliter
c 1250, personally; -atio, possession of
person (gram.) 13c.; personification (theol.)
c 1367; -atus, minor dignity (eccl.) c 1204,
c 1436; character or representation (in
pageant) 1508; -o, to honour a 1100, 1416;
to institute as parson (eccl.) c 1160, c 1330;
to personalize (gram.) 13c.; to personify
(theol.) c 1367.
‡personacia, burdock (bot.) 15c.
person/antior, more resounding or renowned
1441; -avit, for -uit, c 1000.
personarius, see PARTI
perspeciosus, showy c 1180.
*perspect/iva, optics a 1233, 1620; -ivus,
optical 1267, p 1380; (subst.) optician a 1233,
1564; -ius, with fuller insight c 1270.
*perspic/acia, insight c 1125, 1620; †-entia
(? for prospicientia), foresight 12c.; -ator,
investigator c 1270, c 1345; -illum, optic
glass (telescope or microscope) c 1608,
1686; -uum (†-ium), transparent medium
a 1223, a 1446; lens a 1292; -uitas, perci-
pience c 730; -uus, clear-sighted 9c. c 1250;
expert 1144; (? for propitius) favourable
1136; -or (dep.), to see clearly c 1350.
perspiratio, perspiration c 1605.
persplendo, to gleam very brightly c 685.
perstricte, very briefly c 1125; perstringo,
to restrict 9c.; p. signo crucis, to mark
with sign of cross 774. 11c., 12c.
persua/sio, popular discourse 1267; -siones
(pl.), incentives c 730. c 1320; -sorie,
persuasively c 1190, c 1220; *-sorius 8c.
c 1115, c 1470, -dibilis c 760, persuasive;
-dibilitas, susceptibility to persuasion
a 700; -sus, persuaded c 1125; -deo, to
strive to convince c 1000. c 1250.
persulco, to plough through 1440.
persultatio, 'leap' of an interval (mus.) c 1200.
pers/um, -us, see 2 persicum.
persuperfluus, utterly superfluous c 600.
†pert/a, -um, (?) pail (? or for perca, rod)
c 1395.
pertasso, to stack in full 1299.
pertener, tender 13c.
pertero, to harry c 1400.
perterrifico, to terrify utterly c 790.
pertic/a (partic-) c 1150, a 1446, perroca
1227, perch (for bird); 1232, 1389, parchia
1337, cross-bar used as candle-stick;
clothes-rail c 1330, 1402; fuller's perch (bar
or frame supporting cloth during nap-
raising) 1337; rod supporting canopy 1292;
ale-stake, tavern-pole 1419; name of a
comet c 1270; ‡"start" (stalk) of an apple
15c.; 1209, a 1250, perchia 1220, c 1325,
beam of antler; *-a 969, 1044. 1086, 1573,
perdica 1229, perca (percha) 1086, 1370,
percus c 1200, perchia c 1230, c 1242,

*-ata c 1150, 1567, †peticata 1275, percata
(parcata) c 1180, 1338, perchiata 13c.,
c 1300, pergata c 1310, perch, linear
measure (16 to 25½ feet) or measure of land;
-a regis 1203, c 1280, p. communis
c 1290; p. de foresta 1315; p. feni,
"soylon", (?) selion 1234; -us (ligneus),
pole c 1188; -o, to measure (land) in perches
(G.) 1289; see also perca.
perticem, see 2 persicum.
perticul-, see PARTICUL
†pertilligo, f.l. for colligo, 1253.
pertin/acitas, obstinacy c 1343, c 1444;
-acia, dependent area, 'lowy' c 1130;
-entia (f. s.) coherence, relevance c 1342,
c 1361; appurtenance 679. c 1072, c 1185;
(n. pl.) c 1070, c 1400, *-entie (f. pl.) 1156,
1539, appurtenances; -ens, kinsman c 1115;
-entior, more appropriate 1378; -eo, to
refer to c 730; to be akin to c 1115; p. ad,
to be assessed with 1086; †protineo, for
-eo, to pertain 1293.
pertisicus, see phthisis.
†pertract/io, for -atio, handling, treatment
c 1115, 1267; -o linealiter, (?) to mark in
lines 1251; †pertraho moram (? for pro-)
to delay c 1250; p. ad consequentiam, to
make a precedent of 1299; cf. PROTRACT
pertrans/itio p 1300, 1620, -itus 1267, 1620,
transit, passage; -itive, (?) continuously,
throughout the period 1278; -itor, one who
passes through 12c.; -eo, *to pass through,
traverse 12c., 1504; *to pass by c 1090,
c 1470; to pass away c 1115, c 1362; to over-
pass, transcend c 1250; to pass over (from
one thing to another) c 1195; to pass over,
ignore c 1200, 1376; to pass (unnoticed or
unpunished) c 1170, c 1266; to escape, elude
1301, 1335.
pertransvector, reciprocal 7c.
pertric-, see perdix.
perturb/amen, disturbance c 1250; -atio,
interference, prevention 1312; p. pacis,
disturbance of the peace c 1358, c 1516;
-ativus c 1258, 15c., -atorius 1431, causing
disturbance; -ator, disturber (eccl.); *p.
pacis c 1180, c 1586; -o, to prevent 1310,
1357; p. pacem c 1444.
pertus/agium, due paid on broached casks
(G.) 1215; -atus, insatiable a 615.
peruber, plentiful c 1446.
peruca, perruque 1729.
perula, see perla.
perunct/io, anointing (eccl.) p 1381; †-us,
anointing, bedewing p 1381; perungo
manum, to bribe c 1197.
perundino, see PERENDIN
perundo, to abound c 1180; to overflow
c 1293.
peruria, see paramentum.
perusit/atio, using up 1427; -o 1364, 1427,
perutor 1317, ‡1570, to use up, wear out.
perv-, see also parv-
pervado, see pervasio.
pervag/atio, roaming about 9c. 15c.; -o, to
roam through c 1250.
pervaleo, to continue in good health 9c.
†per/vantum, -ventum, part of cart (cf. O.F.
parvineau, bar to which traces are attached)
1285.

perva/sio, wrongful occupation or misappropriation c 1086, c 1250; **-sor**, invader 1041. a 1100, 1414; misappropriator c 1125, 13c.; **-sorie**, wrongfully a 1100; **-do**, to trespass on or misappropriate c 1086, 14c.

pervenenatus, envenomed 11c.

perven/tio, hostile report, defamation (G.) 1313; **-tus** (*p.p.*), having arrived c 1265, c 1426; **-io** (*trans.*) to reach 7c.; to defame (G.) 1313; **p. ad**, to come by, acquire 1278, 1279.

perver/sitas, perverting 9c.; **-sor** 5c., 760. c 1080, 1421, **-trix** (*f.*) p 1200, perverter, destroyer; **-tibilis**, subject to perversion c 1343.

pervestigabilis, traceable c 1160.

pervicacitas, obstinacy c 1200.

pervictor, conqueror c 793.

†**per/videntia**, insight (? or *f.l.* for **pro-**) 1555.

perviolentus, very violent c 1250.

pervolo, to persist in willing c 1070.

per/zorium 1226, **-izorium** 1224, piercer, punch.

pes, *base (of cup, bowl, *etc.*) 1224, c 1315; pedestal (of font) 1390, 1451; plough-foot c 1280; *foot, lower half (of document) 1200, 1537; (?) foot-step (of fulling-mill) 1374, 1384; (?) foot-soldier c 1298; unit of time c 1150; measure of lead 1289, 1322; measure of glass 1296, 1539; (measures of length): **p. Algari** (London) 12c., c 1182, **p. assise** 1400, 1441, **p. de assisa** 1431, c 1443, **p. foreste** (?) 14c., **p. hominis** 1342, 1381, **p. manualis** (*cf.* **manupes**) c 1100, **p. palme** 1218, 1243, **p. (Sancti) Pauli** 13c., 1459, **p. regalis** 1382, **p. de standardo** 1459; **p. squarrus**, square foot 1377; **p. ante**, forefoot 1234; **p. eneus** 1472, **p. ereus** 1226, part of mill; **p. finis**, foot of fine (leg.) 1200, 1384; **p. ligneus**, last 1344; **p. originationis**, pedigree c 1470; **p. pontis** 1461; **p. pulveris** 1452, 1458, **p. pulverizatus** a 1337, 1573, **pedepulvericatus** 1306, **pedepulverosus** (Sc.) 14c., 'pie-powder', wayfarer (leg.); **p. sigilli**, half seal 1283, c 1560; **p. tabule**, corbel (arch.) 1342;

(bot.): ‡**p. accipitris, p. galli**, (?) columbine 14c.; **p. anserinus**, goosefoot 1634; **p. asini**, garlic mustard 1634; **p. cati**, cudweed 1641; **p. columbinus**, dove's-foot crane's-bill a 1250, 1634; **p. corvi**, crowfoot ‡14c., 1538; **p. leonis**, lady's mantle c 1000. ‡14c., 1634; ‡**p. leporis**, avens 14c.; ‡**p. milvi**, ceterach 15c.; ‡**p. nisi**, (?) watercress 15c.; ‡**p. pulli**, purslane 14c.; **p. vituli**, cuckoo-pint ‡14c., 1538;

ped/em porto, to stir a foot c 1290; **serviens ad -em** (G.) 1313, **s. -es** 1310, 1340, foot-serjeant; **in -ibus**, fit to stand (of invalid) 1218; **-e tenus**, down to the feet a 1100; *see also* **eo, homo, sub**;

-ata, foot (measure) 1305, 1487; **-atus**, having pendants or points (her.) 1654; **-efossa**, (?) bed of ditch 1309; **-ellus**, small foot c 1200; **-epulverosus**, *see* **pes pulverizatus**; †**-es** (*pl.*), for **-ites**, c 1200; **-es** a 1150, 15c., **-ester** a 1150, **-inus** c 1280, pawn (chess); **via -estralis**, footpath c 1390; **-ifer**, royal foot-holder, *troydyauc*

(W.) a 1250; 1593, **-inus** a 1446, **-itarius** 1466, footman; **-ilis**, *see* **2 averium**; ‡**-ipiludium**, camp-ball, football c 1440; ‡**-ipomita**, "sock", "pinson" c 1440, 1483; **-isseca**, waiting woman 13c., 1388; ‡**canis -isequus**, bloodhound 1570; **-esecus** 858, **-essessor** 811, follower, attendant; (?) **-itaneus** 1276, **-o** c 1100, 12c., foot-soldier; **-itatio**, fitting with a foot 1354; **-itatus** (*coll.*), pawns (chess) a 1619; ‡**-ium**, "vamp" 15c.; **canis -ucilis**, spaniel 1534; **-ule, -ulis** c 1200, 1324, **-ile** c 1418, **-ulus** c 1250, 1301, slipper; **-itans**, passant (her.) p 1394, 1449; *-ito, to walk c 1200, c 1488; to descend c 810; to tread (stacked corn) 1547; **-o** 1284, 1350, **-ulo** 1316, to fit (plough or pot) with foot; *cf.* **pedagium**, PEDAL.

pes/a, -sa, (?) road c 550.

pesaceus, *see* **pisa**.

pesag-, pesia, *see* **pensa**.

pesc/agium, -aria, pesqueria, *see* PISC.

pesco, to restrain a 1408.

pessagium, *see* **pisa**.

pessarizo, to use a pessary (med.) c 1210, a 1250.

pessic/um, -us, *see* **1 persicum**.

pess/imo c 950, **-imissime** c 1432, **-issime** 1336, very badly indeed.

1 pess/o p 1198, 1285, *-ona 1205, 1504, -ana 13c., -onium 1222, passonum a 1185, †-um c 1100, -io 1241, paissio 12c., paisso 1086, 13c., peiso 1196, †pestio c 1300, †poosum c 1350, mast (as food for swine); **-onaria**, feeding-place for swine 1208.

2 pess/o, peg 1218, 1233; boundary-mark 1230; **-ula** c 1200, 1490, **-ulum** 1060, *for* **-ulus**, bolt; **-ulum**, spigot, tap c 1140; **-ularia**, stockade 1267; **-ulo**, to bolt 14c.

pess/onsera, -unarius, *see* PISC

pessum: **in p. do**, to destroy 8c., c 1000.

pest-, *see also* **1 pesso**; **pistatio**; **pistellum**.

pesti/lentia 1349, 1360, **-latio** 1352, the Plague; **-lentialis** a 1252, 1622, †**-bulus** a 1200, ‡**-cus, -lenticus** 1483, pestilential.

pesuagium, *see* **pannagium**.

†**pesulens**, (? *f.l.* for **petulcus**) savage 1257.

*peta 1159, 1545, †pelta, †petra 1521, peat; **-amora**, peat-moor (Sc.) c 1240; *-aria, -arium c 1180, 1608, -eria c 1180, 1337, -era (Sc.) 1174, c 1220, -ria 1354, -ura 1170, c 1270, peat-bog, turbary.

petagius, *see* **betagius**.

petagogus, *see* PEDAGOG

petalli/a 1236, 1287, **-um** 1235, infantry, service as foot-soldier (O.F. *pietaille*).

petal/um, wheat-husk a 1250, ‡14c.; †paving-stone c 1140; **-oides**, husk-like a 1250.

petan/tia, -saria, *see* PIET

petas/arius, capper 1563; **-ites**, butter-bur (bot.) 1634; **-ita**, ermine (her.) 1654; **crux -ata**, pointed cross (her.) c 1595.

pete-, *see also* **petitio**.

petecanonicus, *see* **peticanonicus**.

petegogus, *see* PEDAGOG

petellus, *see* **potellus**.

peter/a, -ia, *see* **peta**.

peterellum, *see* **pectusculum**.

peti/a, -ta, measure of land, 'tathe' (Ir.) c 1606; *see also* pecia.

pet/icanonicus 1558, -ecanonicus 1535, minor canon; -yta (*pl.*), petty subjects (ac.) 1477.

peticata, *see* pertica.

‡petiginaria (herba), (?) *for* impetiginaria, greater celandine 15c.

pet/ilium, -ilius 1320, 1420, -ilio 1383, -illa 1474, -ulium 1313, 1376, -ibulum 1317, †putilium c 1430, bird-bolt; -illarius 1474, -iliarius 1436, 1472, -ularius ‡1440, 1516, bolt-maker, fletcher.

pet/itio, postulate (geom. & log.) a 1180, p 1347; p. principii, begging the question (log.) c 1160, p 1300; -itiuncula, slight request c 1250, c 1290; -itionarius, petitioner 15c.; -etionarius, collector of alms (mon.) 1528; -eredium, seeking inheritance 8c.; -itoria c 1250, -itorium c 1180, 1304, petition, claim (leg.); *-ens, demandant (leg.) c 1185, 15c.; -o (with *inf.*) to ask c 730. 1219, 1461; (with double *acc.*) to ask something of someone c 600; (?) to challenge 1442; p. curiam, to claim (cognizance by) court (leg.) 1200, 1221; p. etatem, to claim acknowledgement of minority 1218, 1220; p. principium, to beg the question (log.) a 1233, p 1300.

petr/a, *stone (as building material) 1086, 15c.; tomb-stone 13c., 1423; touch-stone c 1350, 1425; precious stone 1300, c 1500; the stone (med.) a 1150, 15c.; weight for weighing 1276, 1404; *stone, unit of weight (7–20 lb.) 864. 1199, 1539; 1388, p. canonum 1426, p. pro canonibus 1400, p. gonnorum 1427, p. rotunda 1388, 1403, p. sagittabilis 1498, p. ferrea 1553, "gun-stone", cannon-ball; p. apostolica, the Church 1156; p. blevia (? blue stone) 1279, 1284, p. de Cadomo (Caen) 1287, 1427, p. dura 1279, 1287, p. Flandrensis (? brick *or* clinker) 1450, p. grisa, p. grisea 1223, 1289, p. grossa c 1283, p. veluta 1258, c 1320, p. velosa 1314, building materials; *p. franca 1173, 1351, *p. libera 1261, c 1452, freestone; p. lavatoria, washing-stone 1383; p. molaris a 1230, 1333, p. molendini 1285, millstone; p. pro pictoribus, stone to be ground for paint 1404; p. rubea, red ochre (for marking sheep) c 1356, 1398; p. rubylla, rubble 1367; p. Sancti Sepulchri (med.) a 1250; ‡p. sanguinaria, haematite 1652; p. Scotie, the Coronation Stone 1300; p. vertibilis, part of windlass (naut.) 1363; ‡p. vini, tartar 14c.;

‡-ella 1483, ‡-illa 15c., small stone; murus -alis, stone wall 1297; vasa -ea, stone jars 1328; -aria, 'perrie', jewellery 1300, 1338; quarry *or* (?) *f.l.* for petaria 12c., c 1180; (?) stone (weight) 1446; *c 1125, 15c., -arium 1194, 1236, p. Turkesia 1212, 'perrier', 'petrary', siege-engine; -arius, (?) stone-cutter or quarryman 1214, 1215; officer in charge of petrary, 1210; ‡"gunner" c 1440; -atio 1427, -ificatio a 1250, petrifaction; -ificus, petrifactive c 1270; -ifodina, quarry c 1220; ‡-iluda, "quoit" c 1440; ‡-ima, "gun" 15c.; -ina 1196, 1407, -inum 1303, stone house; *-inus, of stone

c 1180, c 1475; ‡-o, "a chip of stone" 15c.; -oleon a 1250, -oleum 1198, 1622, -eleum 1620, mineral oil; -ositas, stoniness a 1250; -ifico, to petrify a 1250; *cf.* PERR; *see also* peta, sal.

petratio, *see* perpetratio.

petro/cilium 13c., ‡a 1520, -cillum 13c., a 1564, -cellum a 1250, -silinum (†-filinum) c 1200, a 1250 -silium ‡c 1200, 1392, -sillum 1265, 1375, persilium a 1205, 1538, parcellum 1413, parsley.

pettum, breaking wind c 1227, 1331.

petul-, *see also* petilium; putacius.

petulcus, aggressive 9c.; sensus p. 810; *cf.* pesulens.

petura, *see* peta.

petyta, *see* peticanonicus.

peut/rum 1342, 1356, -erum 1364, -reum 1382, 1417, pewtreum 1392, peautrum 1388, peltrum c 1227, piltrum 1464, pelitria 1294, pewter.

peverarius, *see* piper.

pevimentum, *see* pavagium.

peza, *see* pecia.

ph-, *see also* f-

Phaethoneus, solar: Phetoneus c 550.

phag/iphania, manifestation of Christ's divinity in feeding of multitude c 1182; -oloedorus a 1530, fagolidorus c 900. 1215, foul-mouthed.

phala, *see* fala.

phalanga, *see* faldinga.

phal/angium, venomous spider: -aggium 9c., spalangio, †spalana a 1250, spalangia 1315, spalangus c 1362.

phalanx, company (not military) c 1000; phaulanx, *for* p., c 1190.

phaler/a (faler-) (*n. pl.*) 1275, 1312, -arie 1519, -etica 1293, (?) †phamiles c 1350, *for* -e, trappings for horses; -atura equorum c 1422; -amentum, adornment 704; ‡-arius, "sumpter-horse" 15c.; ‡-ator, "sumpter-man" 15c.; *-atus c 950, c 1000. 1136, c 1450, -iatus 1350, adorned (with showy harness); -o, to harness (ornately) a 1100, 1252.

phalterium, *see* psalterium.

phantas/ia (fantas-) 570, c 850. c 1150, c 1500, -ma c 1080, 1497, *fancy, mental image, imagination; *c 1115, 14c., -ma c 1170, c 1340, phantasm, figment, illusion; pomp, display 6c.; figure of speech 793; -ma, whim c 1308; -iabilis, imaginable c 1300; -iasta, a visionary c 1165; -iatio p 1300, a 1361, -matio c 1300, formation of mental image; -ialiter a 1350, -matice 1374, -tice c 730, 9c. c 1334, fancifully, in fancy; -malis c 1250, *-ticus 9c., 1006. c 1090, 15c., imaginary, visionary; *-ticus, fantastic, absurd c 1070, 1378; imaginative, concerned with imagination c 1210, p 1300; -ticatus, stimulated by fancy c 1257; -io a 1346, c 1367, -ior (*dep.*) a 1304, 1374, to fancy, imagine.

Pharaonicus, of Pharaoh c 820.

phararius, *see* pharus.

pharetra, quiver: feretra 1237, feratra 1461, ‡pharatra 15c.

pharetrum, *see* feretrum.

Phari/saice c 1412, -zaice 1378. Pharisaically; -seo, (?) to separate c 1180.

pharmac/um 1267, 1518, -ia 13c., drug, medicine; -opeus, apothecary 1622, 1634.
pharro, Irish war-cry 1584.
phar/us, lighthouse c 730. c 1150; branched candlestick or chandelier 793, 9c.; -os, tower c 950; -arius, lighthouse-keeper (at Dover) 1201; -ius, see dies.
Phas/ca, -e, see Pascha.
phasianus 1059. 12c., c 1315, Phasidos gallus a 1200, phasis avis 12c., phes/ianus (fes-) 1392, 1577, -anta, -antus 12c., 1324, -auntus 1251, -antia, -antius 1200, 1480, -andus c 1112, fisantus 1232, pheasant.
phasis, phase (astr.) 1686.
phaslterium, see PSALT.
phasma (fasma), speech c 950.
phaulanx, see phalanx.
1 pheb/us, day 8c.; -eus, -eos, 650, -iger c 1185, solar; ‡-ella, solstice or sunrise c 1440; -ifico, to shed sunlight on c 1185.
2 ‡phebus, "puer virgo" (? for ephebus) 1652.
phegopyron (feg-), buckwheat (bot.) 1634.
phellandrion, dropwort (bot.) 1538.
phelli/parius, -peria, see pellis.
phengus, see thanus.
phenic/ium (fenic-), scarlet c 793. 1427; ‡"teasel" 1483; ‡-arius, "teaseler" 15c.
1 phenix, palm or wild barley (bot.) 1538.
2 ‡Phenix, philosophers' stone, quintessence (alch.) 1652.
phenomenon, phenomenon 1620.
phernophorus, bearer of dowry: forniforus 10c.
phes-, see phasianus.
Phetoneus, see Phaethoneus.
‡pheu valeriana 1570, ‡fu 14c., valerian (bot.).
pheudomnus, see pseudonymus.
pheudum, see FEOD
*phiala (f-) c 1070, 1415, viala 1253, 1586, *phiola c 1200, c 1540, viola 1430, c 1506, †violarium 1526, †phicta 1550, phial, vial, cruet (eccl.).
phil-, see also FIL
phil/anthropus, (?) goose-grass (bot.) a 1250, ‡14c.; -ontrophus, philanthropic c 1200.
philarg/yria (eccl.), -uria 13c., †-ia 1378, ‡1483, love of money; -yrus, covetous c 730.
philarium, see filum.
phil/aterium, -atorium, -etrum, see phylacterium.
philautia, self-love 15c., 1620.
philipparius, see pellis.
Philipp/us, -eus, French coin a 1142.
Philistinus, secular 1570.
philizarius, see filum.
philo/biblon, title of book by Richard of Bury 1345, c 1500; -captus, infatuated c 1380; ‡jealous man 1483; -christus, lover of Christ, Christian 1006. a 1142; -compus, boaster c 950. ‡c 1440; -cosmia, worldliness a 1110; -cosmus, worldly, lover of the world c 1363, 1378; -falsus, lover of falsehood 1378; -geus, lover of the earth c 1200; ‡philogisticus, deceitful 1483; -logice, academically 1608; -logicus, literary 1620; -mena, nightingale 1180, c 1470; (?) swallow c 1190; -meno, to sing like a nightingale c 1150, c 1248; -mythus, fond of stories 1344.
philonium, a cough-cure a 1250.

philontrophus, see philanthropus.
phil/os c 1277, -us, pilus c 550, friend.
philosoph/us, teacher c 900; Aristotle c 1160, c 1457; -icus, Aristotelean p 1394; -ice, philosophically a 1200, c 1444; -atio, philosophizing 1516; -ema, demonstrative syllogism c 1160, 1344; -antes novi c 1270; -or, to teach c 1000; see also lapis, ovum.
philo/symbolus, (?) believer in the creed a 1205; -volus, loving indulgence 1344; filoxinia, for -xenia, hospitality c 550.
philtonissa, see pythonissa.
Phineaticus (F-), worthy of Phinehas (bibl.) c 1000.
phiola, see phiala.
‡phionitides (pl.), naturally hostile creatures 1652.
phipon, see TYPH
†phisilega, (?) f.l. for philologus, c 950.
phisillus, see fusillus.
phit-, see psittacus; pythonissa.
phlebotom/ia (f-) c 730. 1200, 1378, fleobotomia a 1300, 1461, fleobotumia 1299, fleubotomia c 1180, c 1330, fleugbotomia 13c., fleubotimia 1397, blood-letting (esp. mon.); fleubotomus, 'fleam', lancet c 1210; fleubotomarius c 1150, -ator c 1266, fleobotomator c 1266, c 1298, blood-letter; -o c 730. a 1100, 14c., fleobotomo 1284, 1382, fleobotamo 1278, fleubotomo c 1180, c 1400, flubotomo c 1330, flegbotomo 1390, flegbotaomo 1279, to let blood, bleed.
Phlegethon (Flegeton), hell-fire c 950.
phlegm/a, watery fluid 1620; fleugma c 1315, fleuma c 1180, 15c., fluma c 1400, for -a, phlegm; fleuma marinum, tide c 1362; -agogum a 1250, ‡flemnagogum 15c., ‡flamgogon 14c., drug to purge phlegm; fleumania, for -asia, inflammation under skin a 1250; -aticitas, phlegmatic quality a 1250; -aticus a 1142, c 1362, fleumaticus a 1250, a 1446, phlegmatic; ‡fleumatico, fleumatizo, to snuffle, spit 1483.
†phola, (?) image of foal 1267; cf. foala.
†phon/astrus, (?) for -ascus, tuning-fork c 1164; fon/a 12c., 14c., -e c 550, -um 8c., c 1000, voice, word.
Photinianus, Photinian (heretic) c 1160.
photis/ma, baptism 9c.; -ticus, baptismal 9c.
phren/eticus (f-) c 730. a 1100, 1287, -seticus 1283, mad, madman; -onphysicus, title of book on soul (περὶ φρενῶν φύσεως) 12c.
phron/esis, prudence c 1200, 1345; ‡-icus 1483, -ymus c 950, prudent; -yme, prudently c 950.
phrut, see ptrut.
phryg/ium (frig-), mitre c 1160, ‡1483; -io, embroiderer ‡c 1440, 15c.; -io, ‡to put on a mitre 1483; to embroider ‡c 1440, 1567.
phthisis (ptisis), consumption (med.): tis/is (tys-) c 1190, 1467, †tylys c 1280; -icus c 1200, c 1505, †pertisicus a 1150, consumptive; †portisus, "full of heats" 15c.; †tesga, a disease of hawks a 1150.
phyl/acterium (fil-), phylactery (bibl.); *c 730. 1080, c 1400, -acteria c 1180, c 1330, *-aterium c 1175, c 1330, -iaterium 13c., -atrium a 1250, -atorium c 1200, 1345, -iterium 1223, -itorium c 1200, -etrum 1295, reliquary; ‡-axo, to safeguard 1483.

phyll/on (bot.): (?) **fillium** a 1250; **-itis**, "hind's-tongue" (bot.) 1538; ‡**-ophanes**, (?) horehound (bot.) 14c.

‡**physalidos** 14c., (?) **fiseleum** a 1250, bladderwort (bot.) (φυσαλλίς).

physanimum, see SESAM

phys/is (fis-), nature c 1190, 1252; **-ica** (*f. s.*) 1125, 14c., **-icalia** (*pl.*) c 1210, natural science, medicine; 1537, (*n. pl.*) 1267, 15c., Aristotle's *Physics*; **-icalis**, physical a 1100, c 1362; **-ice**, physically c 1270, 1583; **-icus**, (*adj.*) medical c 1362, a 1564; **fractio -ica** (math.) 15c.; ***-icus** (*subst.*) c 1190, 1537, **ficicus** 1236, 15c., **fesicus** 1498, (?) †**fysinus** 1421, **-icianus** 1391, **-iciarius** c 1320, physician, leech; **-iculatus**, carnal *or* (?) induced by witchcraft c 950; ‡**-iognomia** 1652, **-iognomonica** 1610, **-onomia** c 1260, (art of) physiognomy; **-ionomia** 15c., **-onomia** 1440, appearance; **-onomia Aristotelis** 14c.; **-iologus**, chemist 9c.; **-ologicus**, consonant with natural philosophy a 1361; **-ologice**, in natural philosophy a 1361.

pia, piatus, see **mater; 2 pica;** PIENT

piacul/aris, needing atonement, sinful c 1160, 1200; **-osus**, nefarious 1298.

piagerius, see **pedagium.**

piauna, see **peonia.**

1 Pica 1497, 1555, **Peca** c 1511, name of a directory (eccl.).

2 pica c 1310, 1419, **pia** 1230, 1317, pie, pasty.

3 pica, (?) pike (fish) 1446, 1480; **pikerellus,** pickerel, young pike 1257, 1881.

4 pic/a (pick-, pik-), (?) pike (weapon) c 1250; **-a, -ula,** bird's beak c 550; **frater de -a** c 1250, f. **-atus** a 1270, Pied Friar; **-us,** part of mill 1325; 1278, 1368, ***-oisa** 1167, 1328, **-oisia** 1172, 1326, **-osa, -osum** 1215, 1415, ***-osia, -osium** 1157, 1318, pick-axe; **-us hachie,** spike of pick-axe 1220; *see also* **hachia; -osus,** magpie-like c 1180; ***-agium** 1156, 1526, †**pigagium** 1526, †**piscagium** 1436, 'pickage', (payment for) right to break ground for erecting stall; **-ator,** pick-man 1214; **ferrum -atum,** (?) cut *or* pointed iron 1338, 1352; **-o,** to prick 14c.; **-o super,** to peck at 12c.; †**-to** (? **-co**), to dig with a pick 14c.; *see also* **picco.**

5 pica, piece of land, (?) 'pitch' (slope) *or* pightle (Berks.) 1325.

6 pica, see **pecca.**

Picard/us a 1142, 1372, **-icus** 1271, Picard; **-a,** sort of ship 1417; *see also* **picarius.**

picaria 1398, **pigatio** 1475, larceny.

picarius p 1290, 1305, ***pich/erius (pitch-), -eria, -erium** 1213, c 1335, †**picius** (*f.l.*) c 1290, †**picteria** 1313, ***-erus, -era** 1236, 1340, †**pichorum** c 1270, †**picardum** c 1150, †**pigium** 1323, pitcher, jug; *cf.* **bika.**

picch/ator (pitch-) 1446, **-iator** 1375, **-erius** 1318, 1324, **-erus** 1319, pitcher, tosser (of hay); **-io,** to pitch (hay) 1330; **piceo,** to pitch, fling (rubbish) a 1250; **-o,** to pitch, set up (a sheep-fold) 1334; to pitch (boundaries), delimit 1613; to 'pitch', pave (with cobble-stones) 1454.

picco, to pick (beans) 1323.

pich-, see **picarius.**

picis, see **1 pisa;** *cf.* **pix.**

pic/o, -oisa, -osus, *etc., see* **4 pica.**

picria, rancour, anger c 950; **pigra Galeni,** a purgative 13c.; *see also* **hiera.**

pict-, *see also* **4 pica; picarius;** PITTACI; **Pythagoreus.**

pict/atio 1354, c 1452, **-io** c 1510, 1516, **-atura** 1519, **-uratio** c 1200, c 1496, **-aria** 1355, **-oria** c 1395, 1620, **pinctura** c 1413, painting; **-aria,** office of painter (mon.) 1240; **-arius,** overseer of painting (mon.) 1239; **opus -arium,** paint-work 1289; **-ator** 1521, ‡**-o** 1483, **pinctor** 1247, 1369, *for* **-or, -rix** (*f.*) c 1420, 1559, painter; **-ura,** writing c 550; drawing c 700; paint, painting material 1466; **-uraliter,** picturesquely c 1115; **-uratio,** portrayal (in rhetoric) 12c.; **-uratus,** florid (of literary style) a 1205; **-o** 1295, c 1533, †**puto** 1380, ‡**-ito, -uo** 1483, **-uro** 12c., c 1436, to paint; **pingo crucem,** to cross oneself c 1400.

Pictav/ensis 1086, c 1370, **-us** c 1125, a 1300, **-inus** a 1142, 1266, **Paitevinus** 12c., Poitevin; 1255, **-us** 1205, †**-a** 1305, **-ina** 14c., **Peitevinus** 1219, coin of Poitou.

pictillum, see **pitellum.**

picus, peak 1620; *see also* **4 pica.**

piecia, see **pecia.**

pient/ior, more pious c 1546; **-issimus** c 1500, **pissimus** c 730, most pious; **piatus,** pious 1150; **pia mater,** see **mater.**

piet/as, religion 1537, 1549; (title) 9c. c 1180, 1256; charitable gift 11c., 1424; *mercy (of God) 686, c 1006. 12c., 1296; **p. superna,** God in his mercy c 730. c 1090; **opera** (*pl.*) **-atis** c 1200, c 1220, **o. pia** c 1528, 1559, good works; ***-antia** c 1235, 16c., ***pitantia** c 1135, 1507, **pitantium** 12c., 1188, **petantia** c 1296, 1444, pittance, allowance (mon.); **panis pitantialis** c 1264; **-antiarius** 1279, **-entiarius** 1277, ***pitantiarius** 1234, 1450, **pitansarius** 1535, **pitentiarius** 13c., pittancer (mon.); **pitantiaria** 1206, c 1450, **pitantieria** 15c., **pitanceria** c 1220, c 1450, **petansaria** 1485, pittancer's office or store; **-osus,** merciful a 1408.

pigagium, see **4 pica.**

piga/num, -mum, see **peganon.**

pigatio, see **picaria.**

pigeo, to disdain c 793.

pightell/a, -um, see **pitellum.**

pigium, see **picarius.**

pig/la a 1250, ‡**-ula** 15c., 'pigle', (?) stitchwort (bot.).

pigment/um, a spice c 1180, a 1408; a 1155, c 1436, **pingmentum** 1243, **pimentum** a 1200, 1252, spiced wine; **-aria** (*n. pl.*), fragrance 1414; **-arius,** (*subst.*) spicer c 1165, c 1265; (*adj.*) spiced, containing spices c 1200, 1345; **-aria cella,** drug-store (fig.) c 793; ‡**herba -aria,** balm 14c.

pign/aculum, -etum, -o, see **1 pinna.**

pignonada, see **pinus.**

pignus, sacred relic c 1170, c 1200; **pignor/agium (pingnor-)** 1284, **-antia** 1341, **-atio** p 1229, 1496, **cautio -aticia** 12c., 15c., **c. -atoria** c 1290, 1684, pledge, pledging; **-atrix,** serving as pledge (*f.*) c 1170.

pigra, see **picria.**

pigr/itas, repose a 1450; **-itudo,** sloth c 1325;

-anter, slowly c 1150; **-ito** 12c., p 1330, ***-itor** a 1100, 1345, **-or** 1041, to be slow or slothful.

pigula, *see* **pigla.**

pik-, *see* **pica** (3 & 4).

1 pila, 'pill', channel in tidal river 1242, 1509.

2 pil/a, ball: 1552, **-ia** 14c., **-um** 1375, **-a plumbea** 1389, cannon-ball; roundel (her.) p 1394, c 1595 (*see also* **1 pilus**); **p. aurea,** bezant (her.) c 1595; **p. calefactoria,** pome 1388; **p. bacularis,** 'staff-ball', hurley 1363, 1447; **p. clavaria** (Sc.), (?) golf 17c.; **p. manualis** 1363, 1452, **-um manuale** 1472, hand-ball; **p. nivis** 1289, **p. de nive** c 1256, snowball; **p. palmaria,** tennis a 1580; **p. pedalis** 1409, 1567, **p. pedaria** 1588, **-um pedale** 1472, football; **ludo ad -am** c 1277, **l. ad -um** 1280; **-iludus,** "ball-play" ‡c 1440, 1519; **-ula blanca, p. reg[ine] Cecilie, p. Romoaldi,** sorts of pill (med.) a 1250; **-atus,** charged with roundels (her.) a 1446.

3 pil/a 1293, **-us** 1317, 1320, pile, under-iron (of mint); *cf.* **trussellus.**

4 pila, pile, set of weights 1491.

5 pil/a, pier of bridge 1285, ‡1483.

6 ‡pila, tavern p 1394, 15c.

7 pila 1354, (?) **-us** (*or* **-um**) c 1290, bale or wrapping; *see also* **pilum, 1 pilus.**

8 pila, *see* **2 pela.**

pil/agium (pill-) 1361, **-aria** 1431, **-eria** 1385, 1389, pillage, robbery; **-ardus** c 1365, ‡**-ator** c 1440, pillager, robber; **-ax,** cat 7c. ‡15c., 1483.

pilagus, *see* **pelagus.**

pilar/e 1097, **-ius** c 1185, 1289, pillar; **pilerius butericius,** buttress 1249.

Pilat/alis, imitator of Pilate 15c.; **-iso, -o,** to behave like Pilate c 1198.

1 pilatio, (?) piling, stacking (of dried meat and fish) 1387.

2 pil/atio, (?) plucking (of wool) 1381; **-o,** (?) to pluck (wool) 1245, 1322; to pluck (hides) 1258; (?) to pick (apples) 1224, 1275; to peel (rushes) 1336, 1357; *cf.* **pelo.**

pilatium, *see* **1 pilus.**

pil/ator, -ax, *see* **pilagium.**

pilatus, *see* **2 pila; pilettus; 1 pilus; piolus; pirata.**

pilchardus, pilchard (fish) 1565.

pilchia, piletteria, *see* **pellis.**

pilesco, *see* **2 pilus.**

pilettum, *see* **2 pilum.**

pil/ettus 1194, 1363, **-atus** 1252, 1282, **-otus** 1255, pellet (discharged from cross-bow); *cf.* **pelota.**

pili (*pl.*), piles (med.) c 1260.

pili/a, -ludus, *see* **2 pila.**

pilio, pillion 1418.

pilium, *see* **2 pela.**

†pilivertentia, (?) versatility c 990.

pilizenii, *see* **2 pilus.**

pill-, *see also* **pilagium.**

pill/eus (pilius) 1289, 1453, **p. quadratus** c 1565, doctoral cap (ac.); ducal cap of honour 1386; **p. de Parys** 1450; *see also* **facio, per; pilium** 1404, **-iolus, -iolum** c 1180, 1338, *for* **-eus,** cap; **-eolatus,** wearing a cap c 1180.

*pillor/ia, -ium a 1190, 1686, **-ius** 1236, **pillor** c 1370, **-ella** 1350, **-icum** 1186, 1262, **spilloria** (G.) 1289, †**pissoria** 1334, pillory; **pena -alis** 1231, c 1258; **judicium -ale** c 1290, **j. -are** c 1295.

pilo, *see* **2 pilatio; pilus** (1 & 2).

pilo-, *see* **2 pilus.**

†pilotria (*pl.*), (?) guard-houses (πυλώρια) c 950.

pilot/us 1404, 1486, **-a** 1537, 1547, pilot; *see also* **pilettus.**

piltrum, *see* **PEUT**

1 pilum, spear: bolt (of cross-bow) a 1320 (*cf.* **pilettus**); (?) tooth, tine (of harrow) 1311, 1316; *see also* **2 pila.**

2 pil/um, a mortar: ‡**-us** c 1200, 1483, **-ettum** 1310; ‡**-umen,** "draff", dregs c 1440.

1 *pil/us 12c., 1419, **-a** 1383, 1422, †**-o** c 1188, pile, stake; **-a,** pile (her.) p 1394, a 1446; †**-atium,** palisade 1279 (*cf.* **1 palus**); **-atus,** bearing piles (her.) p 1394 (*see also* **2 pila**); **-o,** to drive in piles, support with stakes 1379, 1419.

2 pil/us, hair: **p. furcatus,** forked bristle (C.I.) 1331; *cf.* **ferula, 1 seta; -ositas,** hairiness c 1190, a 1250; **-osella,** mouse-ear (bot.) a 1250, 1634; **pellis -osa,** wool-fell a 1185; ‡**-izenii** (*pl.*), hairs surrounding hare's tail 1652; **-esco,** to grow hair a 1250; **-o,** to scalp c 1102.

3 pilus, *see* **philos;** *see also* **pila, pili, pilum.**

pilwarecto, to fallow after pulse crop 1324.

pimentum, *see* **pigmentum.**

pimpernell/a, -us, 'pimpernol', small eel 1256, ‡15c.

pimpinella (bot.) a 1250; **p. (major),** burnet or burnet saxifrage, **p. (minor),** pimpernel or chickweed ‡14c., 1632.

pina, *see* **pinus.**

pinacia (G.) 1289, **pinassa** (G.) 1311, †**pynnea** 1546, **spinaci/a, -um** 1295, 1495, **spinea** 1353, pinnace (naut.).

pinax celica, (?) heavenly register c 950.

pinca, *see* **pinta.**

pin/cellus, -cillus, *see* **penicillus; penno.**

pincenia (pyn-) (*pl.*), slippers, *pinsons* 1311.

†pinceoli, (?) tweezers a 1250.

†pincera, piece of land, pightle 1445.

*pincern/a (bibl.), **-us** c 740, **pinscerna** 1331, **pinserna** 1336, c 1517, †**piscerna** c 1180, **-arius** c 1110, c 1487, butler; **-a** (*f.*), housekeeper 1519; ‡**-aculum** c 1440, 1483, ***-aria** 1164, c 1450, **-ia** 1198, buttery, office or service of butler.

pinct-, *see also* **PICT; pinta; pinus.**

pinctura, (?) pinking (of hose) c 1565; *see also* **PICT**

pindo, *see* **PINS**

pine/us, -atus, *see* **pinus.**

pin/faldus, -foldus, *see* **punda.**

pingn-, *see* **pignus.**

pingo, *see* **PICT**

pingu/atio, fattening 1389; **-edo,** abundance c 730. 12c.; ***1241, 1298, p. ferina** 1362, **seisona -edinis** 1312, **pingwedo** 1298, season of grease (for venison); game in grease 1312; **-ido,** *for* **-edo,** lard 1280, 1423; ‡**-edinosus,** fat 1652; **-entum,** hair oil 14c.; **-etudo,** fatness 1370; unction c 1322; **-icula,** butterwort (bot.) 1634; **-e lactis,**

cream 1572; **jus -ius,** stronger claim 1339; **-esco** 14c., **-o** 1276, c 1400, to fatten.

1 **pinn/a** c 1087, c 1185, **-aculum** c 1185, c 1595, **-iculum** 1367, spire, steeple; ‡**-a** c 1200, 1570, **-atura** 15c., c 1480, battlement; **-acula,** stronghold 15c.; **-acula** (*pl.*), extremities (of silver cross) 1388; **-aculum,** weather-vane 1622; stalactite c 1480; (?) ventpipe 1388; (?) **pignaculum** 1280, †**-o** (? **punio**) 1238, 1456, **-io** 1359, **pigno** 1330, **pugnio** 1315, †**pugnum** 1393, **pignetum** 1396, gable-end (arch.); **-atio,** embattling (her.) c 1595; **-atus** 1595, **-ulatus** 1654, embattled (her.); battlemented c 1562, 1608; **pignono,** to pinion (swans) 1285.

2 **pinn/a,** peg (of mus. instrument) 1622; 'peg' (in drinking vessel) 1102; 1329, 1536, **-us** 1380, pin, peg; tile-pin 1316, c 1478; **-arius,** pinner, pin-maker 1439; **-ula,** sight-vane (of astr. instrument) 1326, a 1350; **-agium** 1304, **-atio** 1376, pinning, pegging (of boards); **-atio,** underpinning (arch.) 1388; **-o,** to pin 1380; 1343, 1449, **-io** c 1438, to strengthen (wall, (?) by pointing *or* laying bond-stones); **-io subtus** c 1398, **-o subter** 1373, to underpin.

pinnagium, *see* 2 **pinna; punda.**

pinn/icula, small (quill) pen c 1000; **-atus,** finny a 1446.

pinonada, *see* **pinus.**

‡**pins/a,** kneading trough or board c 1440, 1483; †**-inochium,** kneading room c 1255; **-o** 1384, c 1464, **pindo** c 1463, ‡15c., to knead; ‡**-o,** "to bake" 1570.

pin/scerna, -serna, *see* **pincerna.**

pinsis, (?) derisive gesture with fist (*cf.* It. *pizzo*) c 1250.

pinsus, hard c 550.

pint/a (pinc-, pinct-) c 1254, 1622, **-um** 1389, pint, liquid measure; pint-pot 1282, 1326.

pin/us, pine-seed 1314; **-a,** *for* **-us,** pine-tree c 1362; †**pinctiolus,** (?) figure of pine-cone 1388; *cf.* **pomum; -eus** c 1270, **-eatus** c 1227, c 1367, conical, pointed; **-eatus,** (?) decorated with cones 1295; **opus -onatum,** sort of metal-work 1295; **-onada** 1303, 1307, **-ionata** 1329, (?) **pignonada** 1286, (?) **pyonada** 1327, sort of electuary (? flavoured with pine-seed); **-osus,** pineclad c 700.

pinwithum, sort of withe (for fastening plough-harness) 1282.

piol/us 1314, **-atus** 1311, 1313, **-itus** 1317, **pilatus** 1312, piebald (O.F. *piole*).

pionia, *see* **peonia.**

pip/a, pipe, tube, conduit 1239, 1443; *pipe (of wine *etc.*), cask 1212, 1469; piping (tube encircling traces of harness) 1314, 1418; (?) piping for bell-ropes 1396; *1320, 1586, **rotulus magnus -e** 1259, Pipe-roll (of Exchequer); summons of the Pipe 1342; **-arius,** piper, pipe-player 1362, c 1377; **-ata,** pipeful (of wine) 1444; **-o,** to store (wine) in pipes 1440, 1449; to cover (traces) with piping 1390, 1458; to pipe (mus.) 1287.

piper/ album, white pepper a 1250, ‡15c.; **p. longum,** long pepper a 1250, 1480; **p. integrum** 1292, **p.** †**to[tum]** a 1250; ‡**p. nigrum,** black pepper 14c., 15c.; **p. rotundum** 1300, 1454, **granum -is** 1230,

1549, **semen -is** c 1300, pepper-corn; **peper** c 1282, **-um** c 1375, *for* **p.; mola -alis** 1200, **molda- -ialis** 1390, pepper-mill; *-**arius** 1180, 1419, **peverarius** 1339, pepperer, spicer; **-ata,** pepper-sauce c 1180, a 1250; **panis -atus,** spiced bread c 1200.

Piphania, *see* **Epiphania.**

piphia, *see* **ephippiarius.**

pipina, pippin 1499.

pipinnus, (?) *for* **bipennis,** adze c 1000.

pipio 1417, 1480, ‡**pugio** 15c., squab, young pigeon.

†**pipunculus,** falcon 15c.

pir, *see* **par.**

pir-, *see also* **pyr-**

pir/a, -arium, -atum, *see* **pirum.**

‡**pir/asmus** c 1440, ‡**-amus** 1483, ‡**parasivus, perrasmus, spirasmus** 15c., tang of knife.

pirat/a c 894, c 1215, c 1313, **pirotans** 1188, sailor; **-us** 1297, 1554, †**-ator** 1414, **-icus** c 1250, **pireta** 1489, **pilatus** 1380, *for* **-a,** pirate; **-ia** 1419, 1606, **-io** 1559, piracy; **-ice,** piratically 1606.

pir/ettum, -ottum, *see* **birretum; pirum.**

piritrum, *see* **pyrethrum.**

pirolus, *see* **scurellus.**

pirrus, *see* **pyrgus.**

pirula (†**purula),** tip of nose c 1250, ‡c 1440.

pir/um, pear: **-a** 1297, 1327; **-um,** pearshaped receptacle 1420; **p. de Cailloel'** 1252, **p. de Cailhou, p. de Caylowel** 1262, **p. Calwell'** 13c., calewey pear; **p. magnum** a 1250, **-omagnus** 1212, 1316, **permanus** 1166, 1430, **parmenus** 1109, **-um de** †**permenis** (? **permeins**) 1315, **p. parmennorum** 1285, pearmain; **p. Martini** 1316; **pirum Sancti Reguli** a 1200, **p. Regul'** 1293; **p. sorell'** 1293, **p. de sorellis** 13c., 1252; *see also* **jonetum, paspucellum; -arium,** pear-tree 1220, 1355; 1294, ‡**-etum** 15c., pear-orchard; **planta peiraria,** sapling pear 1240; **-atum** 1175, ‡**-etum** c 1200, 1483, **-otaria** 1398, perry.

1 ‡**pis/a agrestis,** wild pea 14c.; **p. alba** 1328, 1375; **p. virida** 1325, 1535, **p. viridis** c 1357, 1440; **picis** 1208, **pisibus** c 1250, *for* **-is; -aria** 1309, 1314, (?) **pessagium** 1291, pease (*coll.*); ‡**-acius** 15c., †**-atus** 1622, **pesaceus** 1306, (?) **-agius** a 1300, of pease.

2 **pis/a, -agium,** *see* **pensa.**

pisan/a, -um, 'pisane', cuirass 1303, 1345.

Pisanus, coin of Pisa 1292.

pisc-, *see* 4 **pica; pincerna.**

Piscillianista, *see* **Priscillianista.**

pisc/is, fish (*coll.*) 1086, 1425; **pissis,** *for* **-is,** a 1250, 1415; **p. albus,** (?) whiting 1266, 1333; **p. caninus,** (?) dog-fish 1351, 1373; **p. crassus, p. grassus,** *see* **craspesius;** *p. durus** c 1285, 1402, **p. siccus** 1357, dried fish; **p. lapidosus,** (?) trout 13c.; **p. marinus,** sea-fish 1257, 1482; **p. aque dulcis** 1307, 1482; **p. recens** 1390, 1490, **p. viridis** 1425, 1439, fresh fish; **p. salitus** 1357; **p. regalis** 1331, 1386, **p. regius** c 1178, fish royal (whale, *etc.*); **-ellus,** little fish c 550; **stagnum -abile,** fish-pond c 1358; **navigium -ale** 1461, **navis -aretta** 1224, **n. -aricia** 1223, 1230, **n. -arucia** 1224, **n. -atrix** 1294, 1379, **batellus -arius**

1242, **pessonsera** 1341, fishing-boat; *see also* **dies, domus, haia;** *-aria 679, 736. 1086, 1566, **-arium** 1236, 15c., **-ara** 679, 967, **-eria** (G.) 1283, **pescaria** 1086, **pescheria** c 1090, 1236, (?) †**pelcheria** c 1182, **pesquaria, pesqueria** (C.I.) 1240, **-uaria** 11c., 12c., **-amen** 1262, 1307, †**pascatio** (?) *for* **-atio** 13c., **-atoria, -atorium** 1086, c 1300, **-atura** 1086, 1388, **-ura** 1460, **-ina** 1086, 1290, **-inia** 1317, **-io** 1199, **pescagium** 1189, fishery, fishing; *p. **separalis** 1272, 1428; **-aria,** (?) toll on sale of fish (Oxford) 1294; **ars -arie,** art of fishing 1459; **-aria** 1203, 1462, **-enaria** c 1210, 1419, **-onaria** c 1235, 1275, fish-market; **-atio** (Sc.) 1387, 1537, **-atura** 1194, 1388, fish-trap; **-ator marinus,** sea-fisher 1395; **p. aque dulcis** 1395; **-enarius,** (*adj.*) for fishing 1409; *(*subst.*)* a 1123, 1575, **pissenarius** 1443, **-inarius** c 1400, 1420, **-ionarius** 1403, 1417, †**-onarius** 1275, **pessunarius** a 1200, fishmonger; **-eus** c 1191, **pissius** a 1446, **-inus** c 1362, of fish; **-ina,** piscina (eccl.) c 1266; **-inula,** little pond a 1150; **-ositas** c 1200, ‡**-olentia** 1483, abundance of fish; **-uosus,** abounding in fish 811; **-ulentus,** ‘fishy’, rank 1610; **-o,** *for* **-or,** to fish 5c. 12c., 1419; **p. pro,** to fish for 1427.

pissimus, *see* PIENT
pissoria, *see* **pilloria.**
pist/acia a 1250, 1424, **-aqium** 1392, *for* **-acium,** pistachio; *cf.* **fisticus.**
pistariolum, *see* PITTACI
pist/atio 1321, **-ratio** (G.) 1293, **-rinura** 1392, **-ura** 1450, 1490, baking; **-ura,** batch 1337; **-oria,** bakery service 1212; **-orium** c 1258, **-rina** 1262, 1446, †**-ernum** 1252, **pristinum** c 1485, **pestrinum** 1206, *for* **-rinum,** bakehouse; **officina -rina** c 980; **-rinarium,** baker’s peel 1553; †**-icator,** (?) baker c 1253; **ars -atoria,** art of baking a 1250; **mensa -oralis,** kneading-board c 1239; **-o** c 1275, 1484, **-oro** 1299, **-ro** (G.) 1293, **-rino** 1415, to bake; *cf.* PINS
pist/ellum a 1250, 14c., **pestellum** 1294, c 1450, **pestella** c 1520, **pestollum** 1360, (?) **pesta** c 1398, **pustellum** 1311, *for* **-illum,** pestle; **pestellum porci,** ‘pestle’ (leg) of pork 1307, 15c.; **-rilla,** pounding mill c 793; **-illo** 1345, **pestello** 13c., to pound.
pisticus (πιστικός), believing, devout c 950; genuine 1078, 13c.
pistillator, *see* **pasta.**
pistoleta, *pistole* (Sp. coin) 1608.
pistrix, shark (fig.) c 950.
pisum, *see* **pensa.**
pit-, *see also* PIET
pitcherius, *see* **picarius.**
pitcho, *see* PICCH
pit/ellum (pict-, pyth-) c 1250, 1549, **-ella** 1358, **-illum** c 1250, 1498, **pightell/a, -um** 1378, 1588, **peghtella** 1553, (?) **putellum** 1275, **puddellum** c 1300, ‘pightle’, small piece of land.
pitheus, *see* **pythonissa.**
pitois, *see* **putacius.**
pitt/a, -um, *see* **puteus.**
pittaci/um (pictaci-), label, tag 1293; **-um,**

-a 1362, 1378, †**putacia** c 1360, appendage to proposition, modifying clause (log.); **-a,** (?) playing card 1427; ‡**putacia,** “scantling” 15c.; **-olum** 8c. c 1000, †**pistariolum** 7c., parchment strip, amulet; ‡**-uncula,** “clout of leather” 1483; **-arius** 1411, ‡15c., ‡**-ator** 1483, cobbler; †**-o** (? *for* **-atio**), cobbling 1476; **-o,** to patch, cobble 1417, ‡15c.
pitura, *see* **pultura.**
‡**pityriasis** (med.) 15c.
pius, *see* PIENT
‡**pix alba,** resin 14c.; **p. Greca,** colophony a 1250, ‡15c.; ‡**p. liquida,** turpentine 14c., 1652; **p. navalis** a 1250.
pix-, *see* PYX
plac/amen, gratuity, *douceur* 1353; **-abilis** (bibl.), **-avilis** 853, appeasing, pleasing; **-atus,** gratified 1461.
placatum, ‘placket’, piece of plate armour 1322.
plac/ea (plat-), **-ia** *c 1080, 1512, **plecea** 1284, open space, site, plot or square; 1440, **p. edificata** (?) a 1295, c 1450, residence, building; fortified place, *lieu fort* (G.) 1409 (*cf.* **locus**); place of judicial combat 1229, 14c.; (?) tennis court 15c.; court (leg.) 1315, 1583; **-eum commune,** ‘Common Place’, Common Pleas 1561; †**-eam teneo,** (?) *f.l.* for **-itum teneo,** 1365; **-ea nundinationis,** market-place 12c.; **p. pasture** 1338; **p. prati** 1289, c 1380; **p. subbosci** 1333; *p. **terre** 1286, 1583; **p. vacua** 1303, 1368, **p. vasta** 1296; **p. viridis,** green c 1290, a 1452; **plateola,** open space, broad way c 704; †**plateatim,** “street by street” 1520.
plac/enta 1309, 15c., **-ens** c 1266, **-ida** c 1200, **-ius** c 1250, c 1324, **plecta** c 1200, **plaicius** 1257, **plais** c 1188, 1220, **plaga** 1265, **plagma** 15c., plaice (fish); **-entula,** bun 1523; 1654, **-entum** c 1595, roundel (her.).
plac/entia, pleasure c 1200, 1437; **-enter,** pleasantly c 1340, c 1430; **-entius,** with more approval 1299; **-entior,** pleasanter 1378, c 1470; **-ibilis,** gratifying, plausible c 1410, 1431; **-idissime,** very calmly c 760; **-idus,** *for* **-itus,** pleasing, welcome 1365, 1436; **-ite,** graciously c 1450; lawfully c 1115; **-itus,** agreed c 1200, p 1348; *for* **-idus,** calm c 1242; *-ebo,** office for the dead (eccl.) c 1220, c 1503.
plachia, *see* 1 **planca.**
placit/um, appointment, tryst c 550; pleasure, will 1255; **ad -um** c 1090, 1461, **pro -o** c 1125, at pleasure; **-um,** fee, payment c 1150, c 1204; assembly, moot, court c 1100, 1286; **p. civile,** burgh-moot c 1110; **p. fori,** market-court (Boston) 1275; **p. generale,** witenagemot a 1275; **p. populare** c 1110, **p. populi** c 1110, c 1115, **-atio vulgi** c 1102, folk-moot; *-um c 1075, 16c., **-a** c 1325, c 1400, **placidum** 1182, 1311, †**-agium** c 1330, **-amentum** a 1609, plea (leg.); *pono in -um** c 1115, 1354, **traho in -um** c 1185, 1588, to implead; **sum in -o,** to be impleaded 1215; **p. capitale,** capital (chief) plea 1194, 1360; **-a** (*pl.*) **aule** (Calais) 1372; **p. communia,** common pleas (between private persons) (?) c 1130, *1215, 1586 (*cf.* **placea**); **p. corone,** (criminal) pleas of the crown 1130, 1586; **p. de**

ense 1289, **p. gladii** 1190, **p. de spatha**
1199, **p. spade** 1300, criminal pleas (C.I. &
Norm.); ***p. foreste** 1167, 1277; **p. regis**,
(criminal or civil) pleas concerning the king
c 1115, 1299; *see also* **custos, justitiarius**;
    -abilis, pleadable c 1150, 1464; **dies p.**,
lawful day for business (leg.) c 1443; **-atio**,
pleading, holding of pleas (leg.) a 1100,
c 1440; **-ator**, judge, doomster c 1100,
c 1200; 1240, 1609, **-or** 1431, 1461, pleader,
advocate; **p. ad pagulam**, hired pleader,
'man of straw' 1412; **p. regis** 14c.; **-osus**,
litigious c 1456; ***-o** 1086, 1583, **-or** (*dep.*)
c 1115, c 1200, to plead (leg.); to sue, implead c 1130, 1431; to hold pleas c 1130,
c 1400; *see also* **placentia**, PULCHR
†**placius**, (?) *for* **planus** (of land) c 1290; *see
also* **placenta**.
placoreus, pleasing c 550, c 1000.
plact/eris, -ilus, louse a 1250.
1 **plag/a**, plague (bibl.); fine for wounding
1134, 1243; **-um,** *for* **-a**, wound 1198; **-alis**,
penal 7c.; ‡**-ius**, wounder *or* surgeon
1483; **-atio**, wounding a 1250; **-io** (†**plegio**),
to wound c 1115.
2 **plag/a**, mode (mus.) a 1100; **modus -alis**
(mus.) 1351.
3 **plag/a**, county 13c.; **p. ecclesie**, aisle
c 1395.
4 **plag/a, -ma, plaicius, plais**, *see* **placenta**.
plagella, pledget, compress (med.) a 1250.
plaissetum, *see* **plessetum**.
plaistr-, *see* PLAST
plaka, plack (coin) 1486.
plana, (?) timber of plane-tree 1275.
planarius, *see* PLEN
plan/atio, -atorium, *see* **planum**.
1 ***plan/ca** 1172, 1472, **plauncha** 1266, **-cus**
1288, 1340, **-chia** 1186, c 1400, †**plachia**
1246, **planga** 1327, **-chera** 1257, plank;
1342, **-cus** 1561, gangway (naut.); **-cagium**,
plankage, payment for use of gangway 1341,
1387; office of collector of plankage 1409;
-catio 1304, **plaunchuratio** 1377, planking, covering with planks; **-catura** 1250,
-chiatura 1260, †**-iatura** 1250, **-chura**
1250, 1326, **plaunchura** 1297, 1354, **-chera**
1335, **-cherium** 1193, **-cheicium** 1243,
1257, **-chicium** 1223, 1259, planking,
flooring; **-cherum**, sty *or* trough c 1220;
-co 1195, p 1275, **-chio** (**-cheo**) 1188, 1285,
-gio 1188, **-gchio** 1286, to plank, floor.
2 **plan/ca** 1210, 1281, **-chia** 1210, **-ga** 1232,
1261, 'planch', small horse-shoe.
planct/a (**plant-**), plaint (Fr.) 1313; †**-ura**,
plaint, *or* (?) assault or battery (leg.) 1207;
-uosus, lamentable 1277, c 1325; **plan-
gentia**, lamentation c 1250; **-o**, to complain
c 1334, c 1550.
plan/e, -esco, -etum, *see* **planum**.
1 ***plan/eta**, planet (astr.) 1120, c 1470;
†**-eacus** (? **-eticus**), wandering c 1200;
febris -etica, erratic fever a 1250; **-icus**,
deceptive 1518.
2 ***planeta**, 'planet', chasuble (eccl.) c 760.
c 1110, 1512.
plang-, *see* **planca** (1 & 2); PLANCT
plani-, *see* 1 **planeta; planum**.
†**plant/a Christi**, (?) castor-oil plant 14c. (*cf.*
    palma Christi); ‡**p. leonis**, mallow 14c.;

-us, *for* **-a**, sole of foot 13c.; †**-icuila** 15c.,
-ula c 1250, 1276, **-etta** 1296, little plant;
***-ula**, shoot, scion (fig.) c 1200, c 1450;
-ago aquatica, water plantain (bot.) 1538,
1634; **p. feminina** a 1250; **p. lanceolata**
c 1200, a 1250, **p. minor** c 1200, ‡14c., ribwort; **p. major**, waybread c 1200, ‡14c.;
-amen, plant, germ (fig.) 1430; **-atio**,
planting 1232, 1520; foundation, establishment 12c., c 1450; plantation, colony 1624;
plantation, nursery c 793. c 1180, 1433;
-ativus, fit for planting c 1362; vegetative
1344; able to implant or establish a 1265,
a 1270; **-ator**, planter c 1212; implanter,
establisher c 1220, 1517; planter, colonist
1624; **-icium**, brushwood 1236, 1271;
-icus, skilled in botany c 1300; **-ista**,
botanist c 1300; **-o**, ***to plant 1239, 1583;
to set up (a sheep-fold) 1325; to implant,
settle 12c., 1624; to found c 1200, 1471; to
settle, colonize (a district with cities) c 1362;
see also PLANCT
***plan/um** c 1070, c 1317, **-etum** c 550, **-ura**
c 1227, plain, level or open country; **-um
gladii** (? **-us gladius**), flat of the sword
c 1180; **de -o**, summarily c 1155, 1558;
secundum -um, literally, according to the
plain sense c 1250; **-us**, level or open (of
land) 1086, 1227; plain, unadorned 12c.,
c 1510; honest (G.) 1254; couped (her.)
p 1394; **cantus -us**, plain-song 1434, 1502;
dictamen -um c 1370, **oratio -a** c 1437,
prose; **sacramentum -um**, complete oath
(sworn as a whole, not in sections) c 1115;
-e, by a complete oath c 1115; **-atio**, shearing (of cloth) 1277; levelling (of ground)
1490; planing (of wood) 1419, 1499;
‡**-atorium** 1483, **-ula** c 1180, 1570, carpenter's plane; **-imetria**, surveying 12c., 1345;
-ispherium, planisphere (astr.) 1326,
c 1615; **-istra**, patch of open ground 1436;
-ities, plainness, clarity 1267, 1378; †**-itus**,
plainly 1337; **-esco**, to grow smooth a 1250;
-ifico a 1250, 14c., ***-o** c 1177, 1430, to plane,
level, smooth.
plasm/a (eccl.), **-amen** c 550, creature; **-atio**
c 1180, 1362, **-atura** c 550, **-atus** c 960,
creation, forming, fashion; ***-ator**, fashioner,
creator a 1142, c 1470; **-atorius**, of a creator
12c.; **plasticus**, creative c 950; ***-o** (bibl.),
†**plasno** c 550, †**psalmo** 12c., to form,
create.
plassagia, (?) *plaçage*, assignment of market-
stalls (G.) 1445.
plasscho, *see* PLESS
plassetum c 1290, **plassheta** (Sussex) 1323,
(?) plashet, shallow pool; *cf.* PLESS
‡**plastograph/ia**, "false writing" c 1440;
‡**-us**, "false writer" c 1440.
plastrona, plastron, breastplate 1290.
plast/rum 1243, c 1390, (?) **blastrum** 1323,
plaustrum 1246, 1504, **-erium** c 1533, **-ria**
1300, **plaustria** 1244, **-ricium** 1237, **-ura**
1253, 1423, †**plystrura** 1294, plaster (for
building, *etc.*); **p. Anglicanum, p. de
Purbik**' 1388; **p. francum**, gypsum 1251,
1296; **p. combustum** 1415; **p. de Paris**'
1323, 1335, **p. Parisiense** 1252, 1338, plaster
of Paris; **-rarius** c 1275, 1422, **-erarius**
c 1395, 1422, **-rator** 1292, 1305, **-reator** 1388,

plaistrator 1361, **plaustrator** c 1450, **-ratorius** 1323, plasterer; **-ratio** 1314, **-riatio** 1324, **-ratura** 1303, **-rura** 1292, 1324, plastering; **-ro** 1198, 1464, **-rio** c 1212, **playstro** 1294, 1353, **plaustro** 1302, 1437, to plaster; *cf.* EMPLAST; *see also* PLAUST

plat/a *1196, 1472, (?) **-ena** 1276, plate, bullion, piece of precious metal; piece of iron 1280, 1306; *1297, 1404, **-ea** 1289, plate (of armour); 1355, **p. pedalis** 1279, plate of plough; flat of sword 1277; piece of wood, board 1279, 1385; 1310, c 1450, **-eum** 1296, **-ella, -ellus** 1242, 1338, **-era** 1342, **-erellus** 1373, **-ula** 1461, plate, platter; **-ea**, flat block (of sugar) c 1335; **-ee Flandrenses**, materials used in forging silver coins 1394; †**-ipera**, game, (?) 'duck on a rock' 1301; **-oma**, tablet, slab a 1130, a 1140; ‡**-um**, "shoulder-bone" 15c.; **-us**, (?) flat 1334; **argentum -um**, silver plate 1300; **-us argento** 1280, **p. argenteus** p 1290, silver-plated; **-us ad aurum** 1257; **-o**, to plate (with metal) 1283, 1386; *see also* **patella, placea.**

plat/era c 1218, 1308, **-eria** (G.) 1291, water-meadow or swamp; **-eum aque**, plash, pool 1255; *cf.* **plassetum**; *see also* **plata.**

Platon/itas, quality of being Plato (log.) 13c.; ‡**-ismus**, Platonism 1570.

plaudo, *see* PLAUS

plaunch-, *see* 1 **planca.**

1 **plaust/rum** c 833, c 1218, c 1562, **-ra** 1468, *-rata, -ratum** 1086, 1588, **plastrata** 1433, 1528, **-ratus** (*4th decl.*) 1284, 1485, **-ura** 1583, wagon-load; †**palustrum**, *for* **-rum**, wagon a 1250; **-rum nudum**, wagon without iron tyres 14c.; **p. longum** 1439, 1446; **-ellum**, small wagon c 1250, c 1298; **-rarius** 1322, 1537, **-rator** 1374, wagoner; *see also* PLAST

2 †**plaustrum**, (?) item of bed furniture 1388.

plaus/us, cry (of animal) 1200; **-ificus**, provoking applause c 1346; **plaudo**, to be pleasing a 1408.

playstro, *see* PLAST

pleb/s, parish 12c., c 1197; people of diocese 1416; **pleps**, *for* p., 9c.; **-es** (*pl.*), a people 8c.; **-anatus** 1298, **-ania** 1333, c 1527, prebend (eccl.); **-anus** c 1443, **-eicus** 1435, **-ialis** c 793, **-ilis** 12c., of the populace or laity; **ecclesia -ana** c 1220, e. **-analis** 1423, mother church; *-anus 1292, 1524, **decanus -anus** c 1213, rural dean; rector, *pievano* (It.) 1441; **-ani** (*pl.*) 1136, 15c., **-ici** (*pl.*) 1213, **-icula** a 1100, common folk; **-eius sacerdos**, secular priest c 1115; **-eii** (*pl.*), the Commons 15c.; **-ilis**, (?) layman 8c.; **-iscitum**, by-law ‡1483, 1511; (?) court leet *or* parish meeting (Yorks.) 1472, 1481; **-iscitor** 1539, 1543, **custos -isciti** 1478, c. †**-icitatis** 1563, 1573, 'burleyman' (Yorks.); **-esco**, to become notorious c 1173; to associate with the common folk c 1180, c 1200.

†**pleca**, 'pleck' of land (*or* (?) *for* **placea**) 1280.

plecea, *see* **placea.**

plect/a, plait 7c., c 730. c 1250, c 1325; c 1190, c 1325, †**prolecta** c 1190, halter; ‡hurdle c 1440; **-o** (**parietem**), to wattle 1383; *cf.* PLESS; *see also* **placenta.**

plector-, *see* PLETHOR

1 **plect/rum**, whip 1419; **p. lingue**, tip of tongue c 1325, ‡1483; ‡**-ellum**, "harp-wrest" 1483; **-ibilis**, culpable 1188, c 1343; **-ibiliter**, culpably c 1218, c 1220; **plico**, to pluck, strike (stringed instrument) c 1250.

2 †**plectrum**, pewter (*or* (?) *for* **electrum**) 1463.

plectura (Norm.) 1134, **pledura, pleidura** (G.) 1254, vacant plot, building-site (O.F. *pledure*).

*****pleg/ium** c 1115, 1441, **pligium** c 1310, †**-ia** 1293, **-agium** 1210, c 1320, **-ajum** 1204, *-iagium** p 1147, 1458, **plejagium** 1256, **-iamentum** 1274, **-iatio** c 1115, 14c., pledge, bail, surety (leg.); pledge, promise c 1195; tithing c 1110, c 1115; **p. liberale** c 1115, **-iagium liberum** 1269, frank-pledge; *see also* **francus; p. Dei, p. divinorum**, oath (A.S. *godborg*) c 1115; **p. regis**, king's peace c 1115; **p. sacrum** (Sc.) 1359; *-ius** c 1095, c 1540, **pligius** 1259, **-ia** (*f.*) 1301, one who acts as pledge, goes bail; **p. capitalis**, headborough 15c., ‡c 1440; **pono ad -ium** 1210, **p. in -ium** 1218, to pawn; **p. per -ios**, to put to bail c 1095, c 1414; **-abilis**, pledgeable, entitled to bail c 1255, c 1290; **-io**, *to pledge, go bail for c 1115, 1274; to give as surety 1194; to find surety 1302; **p. de prisona**, to bail out c 1290; *cf.* PLEV; *see also* 1 **plaga.**

†**pleicia**, (?) balance 1274.

pleidura, *see* **plectura.**

pleis-, *see* PLESS

†**plenagium**, (?) *f.l.* for **pannagium**, c 1180.

plen/itudo (ecclesie), plenarty c 1285, c 1290; **p. aque**, high tide 1591; **-um**, complete sum 1254; **-us**, *open, in full session (of a law-court) 1203, c 1400; filled, occupied (of a benefice) c 1298, c 1341; **p. de** c 1310, 1374, **p. ex** c 793, full; **p. de** 1474, **p. per** 1450, occupied by; **p. dierum** (bibl.), full of days c 1190, c 1400; *sede -a**, when the see is occupied c 1323, 1418; **in -a processione** c 1280; **allec -um**, herring with roe 1550; **-um facio**, to pay in full 1252; **-um posse**, full authority 1282, 1496; **-o**, in full c 1218; *see also* **ad, de, per, terra; -e**, 'full', very c 1220; **-iter** c 793, c 1006. a 1090, 1331, *-arie** 8c., c 980. c 1140, 1684, **-ariter** 1359, **-itudinarie** c 1414, fully; **-arius**, more fully 1362; *-arius** 8c., 9c. a 1128, 1549, †**planarius** 1222, full, complete, plenary; **-ipotens** c 1407, **-ipotentiarius** c 1375, plenipotentiary; **-o**, to lavish c 1180.

pleo, (?) pin or 'brooch' for thatching (*cf.* O.F. *ploion*) c 1440.

pleonexia, advantage c 550.

pleps, *see* PLEB

plerophoria, assurance, certainty c 1595.

plerumquitas, ordinary course, normal occurrence c 1610.

plessa (de apris), (?) 'bag', number entrapped (*cf.* O.F. *plaisse*, enclosure) 1246.

pless/etum 1219, **-eitium** (Norm.) a 1142, **plaissetum** 1228, **pleissa** (Norm.) 1203, 'plash', pleached hedge; **-o** 1280, 1324, **pleisso** 1244, **pleisio** 1223, **plasscho** 1336, to pleach; *cf.* **plassetum, plecta.**

plethor/ea (plector-), -icitas, plethoric habit (med.) a 1250; -icus, plethoric a 1250, c 1250.

pleu/monia, -rimonia, see PNEUM

pleur/esis a 1250, 1508, ‡-is c 1255, for -isis, pleurisy; -eticus, pleuritic c 1180, a 1250; -ida (pl.), flaunches (her.) c 1595.

*plev/ina 1177, c 1320, -inum 1285, pluvina 1196, pledge, security (leg.); p. stulta, faulty security 1198; -io, to pledge 1293; cf. PLEG

plex/io capitis, nod 1006; ‡-uosus, "fro-ward" 1483.

pliades (pl.), stars c 550.

plic/a (†plit-), fold, ply 1177, 1620; twist (for binding thatch) 1427; shred, particle (of danger, deceit, etc.) 1197, 15c.; grace-note (mus.) 1326; -abilis, susceptible of orna-mentation (mus.) 1326; 1345, 1455, -atus 1275, c 1396, folding, pliable; -atio, rump-ling a 1150; payment 15c.; -atrix, woman who folds or wraps (wool) 1334; -atura, folding (of letter) c 1280; fold (of charter) 1347; fold (in shirt) c 1565; -o, to turn (a horse) 1241; to ornament (mus.) 1326, c 1470; to give as oblation (eccl.) c 1180, 1291 (see also cultellus, denarius); to supplicate 1220; p. brevia, to fold writs (for sealing) 1389, c 1420; see also 1 plectrum.

pligi/um, -us, see PLEG

pliris, an electuary 1241, 1335.

ploidum, fold (measure of cloth) 1438.

‡ploma, mullein (bot.) 1652.

plomarius, see PLUMB

plongeo, to plunge 1539.

plonkettum, see plunkettum.

ploratorium, weeping-place (play on ora-torium) c 1130.

plou/clutum 1393, -cloutum 1307, 1351, ploweclutum 1386, plowclutum 1391, plough-clout; †plowshum, plough-shoe 1406; ploxlanda, plough-land (Lincs.) c 1150.

plovarius 1250, ‡1483, plouverius 1338, pluv/iarius 1525, 1528, -erius, -erus 1255, 1389, †plumerius c 1324, ‡plumacius 15c., plover (bird).

pluidus, see pluviale.

plum/a, quill, pen c 1220; (coll.), feathers (for sale) 1265, 1376; see also alumen; -aceolus, feather-pad (med.) a 1250; -ago, plumage 1620; -acium 1553, -ale 14c., 1520, -alis 1341, -are 13c., 1404, ‡-arium c 1440, -atiuncula 8c., feather-bed or pillow (see also culcitra, lectus, pluviale); acus -arius c 1255, opus -arium c 793. 1295, feather-stitch; -ata, 'casting', meal of feathers (falc.) a 1150; -atio, fledging (of arrows) 1542; -ator, flock-puller 1281; †-axis, (?) pad for beating metal on a 1180; -eus, light as a feather c 1340; -osus, covered with fluff c 1180; ‡-itor, "moulter" c 1440; ‡-eo, "to moult" c 1440; †"to be feathered" 1483; -esco, to become fledged c 730; -o, to 'plume', pluck (falc.) a 1150; to fledge (arrows) 1456; see also plovarius.

plumba ferri, see bloma.

plumb/um, leaden seal, bulla c 1397, 1522; lead weight (of clock) 1371; plumpum 1221, blumbum 1243, 1254, for -um, lead; -um album 1277, 1472, alba -i 1301, white lead, ceruse; ‡p. arsenicum, litharge 15c.; p. arsum, (?) smelted lead 1198; p. azure, (?) 'blue lead', galena 1301; ‡p. candidum, white lead ("improperly tin") 1652; p. cinereum, bismuth c 1615, ‡1652; p. fer-tile, lead admixed with silver 1300, 1323 (opposed to p. sterile 1300, c 1350); ‡p. philosophorum, a derivative of antimony 1652; p. rubeum, red (oxide of) lead, minium 1277, 1472; *-um 1086, 1521, -eum 1387, -ium c 1430, leaden vessel (vat, cistern, or salt-pan); p. manuale, (?) port-able vat 1388; -us 1295, ‡-etum 1570, plummet; -acia (pl.), leads (arch.) 1297; -aria, lead-mine 1086; salt-pan 1437, 1544; c 1300, 1461, -arium 1419, plum-meria 1259, plumbery, plumber's shop or office; *-arius c 1112, c 1540, -erius 1428, -iarius c 1423, plummarius 1320, 1380, plummerius 1435, plomarius 1307 -ilarius 1523, -ator 1228, 1474, (?) pluma-tor 1230, blumbator 1291, -inator 1313, plumber; -atio a 1250, c 1470, -ria 1360, opus -arium 1433, plumbing, soldering; -eitas, leaden colour a 1250; -eus a 1250, p 1394, -inus a 1250, leaden-coloured; -icidium, lead-mine c 1385; -icinium, -icinum, lead-work, plumbing 1250; ‡-ila-mina, "plate of lead" 15c.; cineres -ini, lead ash 1299 (cf. cinis); -osus, leaden 1300; -ata, leaded scourge c 1170, c 1340; -atus c 1365, 1546, (?) -eatus c 1325, sealed with a leaden seal; -eatus, weighted with lead 1377; *-o 1199, c 1433, plummo 1238, plunco 1285, to plumb, roof with lead.

plunkettum c 1378, 1414, plonkettum 1399, 'plunket', coarse woollen cloth.

plur/alitas c 600, 9c. c 1160, 15c., -itas c 1376, plurality, number, multitude; majority c 1343, c 1450; 9c. c 1197, 1559, -itas c 1444, plurality (eccl.); -ale, plural (gram.) 1218, 13c.; -alis, pluralist (eccl.) 1318, 1347; -ales (pl.), several 1270; -aliter, several times or in several places 1267, 1411; in the plural 815. c 1120; -ies, *often c 1200, 1461; more often 1521; name of a writ a 1452, 1469; -iores (pl.), more 826. c 1204; -ifici (pl.), numerous c 550; -ificabilis, capable of 'plurification' (log.) c 1290, 1344; -ificatio, 'plurification', differentiation into many instances (log.) c 1270, 1427; -ifico, to 'plurify', multiply 1267, 1427; -ipendo, to value more highly c 1188.

plus/ (with comp. adj.), more c 1362; any longer c 1218, c 1433; ad p., at a higher rate 1227, c 1283; p. ab aliis, more than others 7c.; p. minus, more or less 1546; -agium, surplus (of expenditure over re-ceipts) 1289, c 1480; -culum, increase c 1115; -petitio, excessive claim 1227, c 1290; -quamperfectio, being pluperfect (gram.) 8c.; -quamperfectum, pluperfect (gram.) 8c. c 1332.

pluscul/a (plustul-), -um c 1310, 1512; ‡puscula c 1200, ‡pustula 15c., buckle; ‡-arius c 1440, ‡-ator 1483, buckle-maker; ‡-o, to buckle 1483.

pluv/erius, -erus, -iarius, see plovarius.

plu/viale (†plumale), cope for wet weather

c 1397, 1473 (*see also* **capa**); **-viositas,** raininess c 1200; **-idus,** rainy 1508; ‡**-tina,** drizzle c 1440; ‡**-tinat,** it is drizzling c 1440; **-viebat,** it was raining 1324.

pluvin-, *see* **plevina; pulvinar.**

pneum/a 9c. c 1112, c 1346, **neuma** c 1170, **neupma** c 1250, spirit; **p. almum** 1245, **p. divinum** c 1200, **p. sacratissimum** c 1246, **p. sacrum** c 1170, **p. sanctum** c 960, 11c. c 1100, 1252, Holy Ghost; **-a** c 1200, a 1452, **neuma** a 1100, 1444, **neupma** c 1296, 1326, 'neum' (*mus.* phrase or note); **-aticus,** gaseous 1620; ‡**-atosis** 15c., **neumatosis** a 1250, windiness (*med.*); ‡**pleumonia** 14c., **pleurimonia** c 1412, pneumonia (*cf.* PULMON); **-atizo,** to prolong a neum c 1182, 1349.

†**poalum, pol/eum, -iadum,** bellows 7c.

poc/a (pok-), -um 1275, 1463, **puka** 1242, **-etta, -ettus** 1314, c 1530, **pochetta** 1280, **pukettus** 1287, 'poke', bale, measure of wool, *etc.*; **-a, -um** c 1300, 1328, **pocha** 1294, **pochia** 1265, 1341, **powchia** c 1397, **pucha** 1276, **puchea** 1262, 1319, **puchica** 1385, **pugica** 1390, **-etta, -ettus** 1307, 1344, **pochettus** 1300, poke, bag, pouch; **pokellum,** measure of grain 1313; **pulvis pokettatus,** (?) spice in bags 1387.

†**pocarius,** *f.l.* for **pottarius,** 1222.

poc/enettus, -enetta 1286, 1329, †**-eneitus** 1327, **-inettus** 1208, c 1335, **poscenetus** 1303, **posnetus** 1410, 1449, **possenettus** 1311, **possinetus** 1251, 1327, **postnetta** 1398, posnet, metal pot.

pocharda, pochard (duck) 1544.

pocibilis, *see* POSS

pocillator, cup-bearer 1640; *****pocul/enta** (*pl.*), drinkables c 1250, 1583; **-o,** to drink c 1198; ‡to give to drink 1483.

pocokus, *see* 1 **pavo.**

pod/agra, gout: **-raga** 13c., ‡**potagra** c 1440; **-agra lini,** dodder (bot.) 1538; **-agrice,** goutily c 1200; **-agriso,** to suffer from gout a 1250.

poderis, alb (eccl.) 9c., c 1000. c 1137, a 1408; ‡"rochet", "chasuble" 15c.

1 **pod/ium,** staff, support a 1142, 14c.; part of choir-stall serving as support during psalms c 1250; ‡**-iarius,** crosier 15c.; **-ismus,** step c 1370.

2 **pod/ium, -um,** district *or* estate (W.; (?) *cf.* Breton *pou*) c 1150.

podorius, *see* **hypodoricus.**

poenacium, *see* 1 **pavo.**

poe/sia c 1380, **-tria** c 1180, c 1500, poetry; **-ta familie,** household bard (W.) a 1300; **p. laureatus** 1486, 1553; **-tissa,** poetess c 550.

poff/o, -onus, *see* **puffo.**

pogeta, farthing, *pougeoise* (G.) 1253.

poiagium, *see* PENS

poign-, poingn-, *see* 2 **pugna.**

point-, *see* PUNCT

pok-, *see* **poca.**

pol/a a 1185, 1369, **-us** c 1180, 1290, **pulla** c 1180, 1307, **pulia** (Norm.) a 1160, pool, fish-pond; 1166, 1268, **-us** 1285, **poula** 1274, **pala** 1268, ordeal-pit; *see also* 2 **polus.**

polagium, *see* 2 **pulla.**

polanus, *see* 1 **pullanus.**

polaris, *see* 1 **polus.**

‡**polata,** fig 15c.

pol/axis 1450, **pollexa** 1414, **-haxa** 1336, **-hachettum** 1319, pole-axe.

polaynnia, *see* 2 **pullanus.**

poldrum, polder, land reclaimed from marsh (Sussex) 1418.

pol/ea, pulia 1284, **-ia** 1212, **-eium** 1348, **puelea** 1279, **-iva** (†**-ina**) 1295, 1346, **puliva** 1293, 1318, (?) †**pullum** 1285, †**pulica** 1367, †**pulytum** 1296, pulley; *cf.* 2 **pullanus.**

poledrus, *see* 1 **pullanus.**

polemicus, controversialist c 1363.

polemita, *see* **polymita.**

pol/entarium (**poll-**) , brewery 1668; **-entarius,** maltster (?) 14c.; **-entra,** *for* **-enta,** gruel 1367; **-entrudium** c 1200, **-entridinum** 1368, ‡**-entridium,** ‡**-entriticum** 15c., ‡**-entriduum** 1483, **-itrudium** 1343, **-itridium** 1485, **-utriduum** 1325, bolting-cloth, sieve; ‡**-entradinator,** "bolter" 15c.; ‡**-entriduo** 1483, ‡**-entritico** 15c., **-entrudio, -itrudio** c 1220, to bolt, sift.

polenus, *see* 2 **pullanus.**

poles, *see* **poples.**

poleta, 'pollet', epaulette 1348; *see also* **pelota,** 2 **pulla.**

polet/ia, -ica, *see* 1 **polis.**

poletria, poletarius, *see* 2 **pulla.**

pol/eum, -iadum, *see* **poalum.**

pol/hachettum, -haxa, *see* **polaxis.**

poli-, *see also* **poly-**

poli/a, -na, *see* **polea.**

poli/arches, -cus, -nus, -tas, -tronum, *see* 1 **polus.**

poli/bilitas, susceptibility to polish c 1270; **-bilis,** polishable c 1191; **-so** 1325, **-ceo** 1325, 1327, *for* **-o,** to polish.

policaria, *see* **pulicaria.**

polifex, *see* 2 **polus.**

polinodia, *see* **palinodia.**

1 **pol/is,** city c 1193, 15c. (*ablative pl.* in **polisi** 1169); *****-itia (-icia)** 1345, 1624, **-issia** 1461, state, (orderly) government; strict rule c 1472; improvement of estate (Sc.) 1521; **-itia** (*pl.*) 1538, **-etia** (*pl.*) 1567, 'policies', improvements, grounds (Sc.); **-ita,** citizen c 1434; **-itanus,** urban c 700; **-itica** (*f. s.*), (?) urbanity 1220; 1267, 1537, (*n. pl.*) 1329, 1345, **-etica** (*n. pl.*) c 1350, Aristotle's *Politics*; (*n. pl.*) public affairs c 1488; †**-iticuma,** commonwealth c 1341; **-itice,** politically, in public affairs c 1343, c 1443; prudently c 1422, c 1470; **-iticus,** politic, prudent c 1470; layman, man of the world c 1160; statesman c 1370; **-itizo,** to have a constitution, practise statecraft 1344, 1521.

2 **polis,** much, many (πολύς) 1271; *cf.* **poly-**

poliso, *see* **polibilitas.**

poli/tridium, -trudium, *see* **polentarium.**

polium coconidium, p. montanum, 'poly', 'poly-mountain' (bot.) a 1250.

poliva, *see* **polea.**

pollandum, *see* **polyandrium.**

1 **pollardus,** 'pollard', bran 1284.

2 **pollardus,** 'pollard', base coin 1299, c 1422.

pollenus, *see* 1 **pullanus.**

poll/esco, *for* **-eo,** to be strong c 685.

poll/ex 1211, c 1550, ‡-icium 15c., measure of
length, inch; **p. assise** 1585; **p. mensurabilis** 1447; **p. ulne** 1347; -icium, thimble
c 1200, ‡1483.
pollexa, *see* **polaxis.**
polliceo, *see* **polibilitas.**
pollis, *see* **2 pulla.**
pollutor, defiler c 1520.
polomit-, *see* POLYMIT
Polon/ia, fine gold (alch.) 1267; -us, Pole
1241, 1267.
polo/pus, -podium, *see* **polypus.**
pols, *see* PULMENT
polt-, *see* **2 pulla.**
†**polua,** item of glazier's stock 1404.
polulamen, *see* **3 pulla.**
1 pol/us, Heaven c 550. 1345, 1413; *see also*
jus; -aris, polar 1620; a 1275, c 1325,
-icus c 550. ‡1483, -inus c 950, heavenly;
-iarches, Lord of Heaven 1020; -itas,
polarity, direction of axis c 1612, 1620;
-itronum, celestial throne c 550.
2 pol/us 1200, 1487, -a 1242, 1286, pole, stake;
1469, 1588, (?) -a 14c., -ata 1540, pole,
measure of land; -ifex, (?) pole-maker 1630;
cf. **1 palus;** *see also* **pola.**
*****polyandr/ium, -um** c 760, 9c. a 1142,
a 1530, **paliandrium** 10c., †**polianesum**
a 1100, †**pollandum** 13c., cemetery,
charnel-house, tomb.
†**polycernia,** (?) rule of many (πολυκοιρανίη)
c 1343.
polychrestus, of general utility 1620.
Polychron/ica (*f. s.*), title of book by Higden
c 1350, c 1450; -itudo, longevity 1345; title
of a chronicle a 1530.
polycrates (virtutum), strong in, master of
11c.
polygam/ia, polygamy c 1250; -us, poly-
gamous c 1250; ‡"leman" 1483.
polygon/us, *for* -ius, many-angled 9c.; -ia,
(?) knot-grass (bot.) a 1250.
polyjugium, polygamy 1427.
‡**polyloquus,** "chattering" 1483.
polymit/us (bibl.), **pollimidus** (†**pollinudus**)
c 1400, **polemita** 1478, **polomitus** 1440,
polomitatus 1448, damask; ‡"motley"
a 1520; variously inlaid c 1135; -arius, of
damask c 1456, 1537; (*subst.*) embroiderer
1345; ‡"painter" 1483.
poly/onymus c 790, 9c., -nomius c 1160,
many-named.
polyphem/us, blind man c 1200; -o, to blind
c 1212.
‡**polypola,** "grocer" 1570.
polypragmosyne, officiousness 1620.
polyptycha (poliptica), charter, deed 12c.
‡**poly/pus** 15c., 1483, **polopus** 1445, -pes
1521, "lobster", crayfish; -pus, *for* -posus,
afflicted with a polyp (med) a 1200; **polo-
podium,** *for* -podium (bot.), a 1250.
polysyllaba, polysyllable 1267.
polythe/ismus, polytheism 1609; -us, poly-
theist 1609.
pom-, *see also* **pum-**
pomac-, pomar-, pomell-, *etc., see* **pomum.**
pomerium, space next to wall: **promerium,**
space c 550; *see also* **pomum.**
pompla, 'pomple', kind of fodder 1349.
pomp/ositas, pomp, display c 1150, c 1470;

-asticus, bombastic 1378; -ifer c 793,
-ulentus c 1125, pompous, proud; -isonus,
with resounding pomp c 950; -atice (bibl.),
-ose c 950. c 1250, 15c., †-ociter c 1293,
pompously, grandly; -ator, boaster 1375.
pom/um, apple: **mola** -orum 1275, **molendinum** -orum 1245, 1302, cider-press;
-um, ball, orb 1245, 1482; pome, hand-
warmer c 1220, 1345; **p. de ambr',** poman-
der 1213; **p. bosci,** crab-apple 1296; **p.
durum** 1337; **p. cedrinum** 1290, ‡**p.
citrangulum, p. citrinum** 14c., **p. de
orenge** 1290, **p. dorenge** 1409, -erangium
1470, lemon *or* orange; **p. granatum** 1252,
1309, **p. garnatum** 1265, †**paunum
granatum** 1223, pomegranate; **p. pinei,**
-ulum **pinale,** pine-cone 1245; ‡**p. quer-
cinum,** oak-apple 14c.; ‡**p. S. Johannis,**
jujube 14c.; *see also* **costardum;** -acium
c 1250, 1316, -agium 1256, **vinum** -orum
13c., ‡**v. de pomis** 14c., cider; -alis, of an
apple 1267; -arium, -arius 1229, 1355,
-erium, -erius 1220, 15c., apple-tree;
*****erium** 1086, 1570, †-erhaneum 12c., *for*
-arium, orchard; -arius **bosci** 1250,
-erium **silvestre** 1268, 1304, crab-tree;
‡-elio, gardener *or* fruiterer 15c.; *****ellum,
-ellus c 1150, 1457, **pumellum** 1279,
†**punulum** a 1273, ball, knob, boss; -ellum
gladii, pommel 1213, 1251; -ellatus 1310,
pumulatus a 1273, embossed; c 1311,
c 1320, -ellus 1311, dappled.
ponacium, *see* **1 pavo.**
ponagium, *see* **pannagium.**
ponc-, *see also* PUNCT
poncherium, *see* **pansa.**
pond-, *see also* **punda.**
pondicitas, *see* **ponticitas.**
pond/us 1209, c 1375, -a 1286, -o 1276,
*****wey,** measure of weight (of wool, cheese,
flour, *etc.*); (?) payment for right to inspect
weights 1192; **ad** -us, by weight (in reckoning money) 1086, 1258; **aurum de** -ere
1242; -us **aureum,** ornament 1414; **p.
denarii,** pennyweight 1159, 1269; **p. diei,**
burthen of the day (bibl.) 1234, c 1335;
p. dolii, 'ton-tight', ton's burthen (naut.)
1326, 1369; **p. equi** 1289, 1293, **p. equorum**
1360, **p. roncini** (G.) 1315, horse-load;
p. hominis, man's load (G.) 1315; **p. Lan-
franci** (Canterbury) c 1330; **p. magnum**
1280, 1298, **poundus majus** 1431; **p.
parvum** c 1280; **p. pretii** 1272; **p. regis**
c 1330; **p. Troie** 1416, 1460, **p. Troge** 1417,
p. de Troye 1408, **p. Trojanum** c 1445,
Troy weight; **p. Trajectense,** (?) weight of
Utrecht 1487; *see also* **1 averium, falsina,
libra, pundum;** -a, *for* -us, weight for
weighing 1274;
-agium 1404, 1503, -eragium 1274,
1303, -eratio 1419, poundage, pesage, toll;
-agium, poundage levied for repair of walls
(Winchester) 1304, 1420; **plaustrum**
†-atum, loaded wain c 1305; ‡-erale 15c.,
(?) †**poudrellum** c 1280, avoirdupois;
-eralis, *see* **libra, pecunia;** -erantia,
weight, importance 1378; -erator (Scaccarii), pesour 1207, 1260; -eraria 1287,
1298, -eria 1262, 1266, office of pesour;
-eratrix, weighing (*f.*) 6c.; -anter, weightily

1344; **-erose,** heavily, oppressively c 1196, 15c.; **-erositas,** *weight, heaviness 9c. c 1115, a 1540; drowsiness a 1250, c 1340; **-ium,** measure of weight, (?) pound c 1115; **-ero,** to have weight c 1265, 1622; to weigh, have (a specified) weight c 1296, 1517; to carry weight, be important c 1185, c 1363; to weight, make heavy 1326; **-or** (*dep.*), to weigh (an object) 1274.

1 pone, beside 1150.

2 pon/e, -ibilis, -o, *see* POSIT

poneceilus, *see* penno.

ponfalda, ponefalda, *see* punda.

pons, 'bridge-tree' (of mill) 1314; *1189, 1390, **pont/us** 1338, gangway; **-us,** bridge c 1165; **-is claustura** 1331, **coedificatio** 940. 12c., 15c., **confectio** 12c., 14c., **constructio** 858, 943, **cooperatio** 14c., **edificium** *etc.* 12c., **emendatio** c 1110, **factio** 14c., **fundatio** 12c., **instructio** c 800, 957. 12c., **juvamen** a 1100, 1440, **munimen** c 1020. 12c., **operatio** 1189, **opus** 1097, c 1280, **recuperatio** 1024. 12c., **reedificatio** 1198, **refectio** c 1102, c 1115, **restauratio** 1017, 11c. 12c., 13c., **restructio** (?) 1066, 1331, **structio** c 1414, **structura** c 796, 858, brigbote; *see also* **punda;**

pons argenteus, bribery c 1160; **p. pedalis,** foot-bridge 1375, 1438; **p. pendens** c 1160; **p. colehicius (colehisius)** 1239, **p. elevabilis** 15c., **p. lativus** 15c., **p. levabilis** 1395, c 1450, **p. levadicius** (G.) c 1280, **p. levaticius** (G.) c 1290, **p. ad levandum** 1263, **p. tornalis** 1212, **p. turnarius** 1219, **p. tornatilis** 1196, c 1250, **p. turnatilis** 1239, **p. torneicius** 1213, 1274, **p. turneicius** 1221, 1265, **p. tornicius** 1242, 1313, **p. turnicius** 1220, 1304, **p. turnisius** 1313, **p. torneiz** (Norm.) 1198, ***p. tractabilis** 1233, 1385, **p. tractivus** 1256, **p. tracticius** 1328, ‡1483, **p. trahiceus** 1297, **p. vergens** 1252, **p. versatilis** 1261, 1333, **p. vertens** 1238, c 1250, **p. vertibilis** 1250, 1388, drawbridge *or* swing-bridge;

***pont/agium** a 1130, 1526, **puntagium** a 1175, **-enagium** (G.) 1305, **-onagium** (G.) 1314, **-inegium** (Austrian) 1483, pontage, toll levied for repair of bridges; **p. equorum** 1244, **pountagium** 1390, payment for transport (? *or* embarkation) of horses; **-agiarius,** tenant paying pontage 1362; **-arius** a 1220, 1234, **-erius** (G.) 1284, **-enarius** 1170, 1568, bridge-keeper *or* bridge-wright; **-ellum** 1296, **-ellus** 1286, little bridge; **-io,** pontoon 1287; **-ifico,** (?) to serve as a bridge 1220; **-o,** to bridge (a river) 1296.

pons-, *see* PUNCT

pont/icitas 12c., c 1270, **pondicitas** c 1250, †**punctuositas** c 1215, brininess; **-icus,** briny, bitter, tart 12c., c 1270; †(?) fat 13c.; *see also* **reu; -ia,** water c 685; **nubes -ie,** sea mists c 550; **ventus -ianus,** sea-breeze c 1212; **fervor -ificus,** ocean swell a 1100.

pontifex, *bishop 7c., 944. a 1090, 1461; archbishop 8c., 805. c 1125, c 1260; 12c., 1381, **p. generalis** 1293, **p. Maximus** c 1500, **p. Romane ecclesie** c 730, **p. R. sedis** c 1250, **p. Romanus** c 1080, 15c., ***p. summus** c 1090, 1537, the Pope; 1438;

p. eternus 9c., Christ; Jewish high priest c 1345; **p. Judeorum,** official of English Jewry (*cf.* **presbyter**) c 1255; **p. parvus,** boy bishop 1388;

***pontific/alia** (*pl.*), episcopal vestments c 1130, 1537; **-alis,** *episcopal c 760, c 900. c 1070, c 1520; papal 8c. c 1125, c 1450; **-ale** c 1296, c 1488, **liber -alis** 1291, 1416, pontifical, service-book; ***-aliter,** as befits a bishop 1006. a 1100, c 1450; **-atus** c 770, c 900. c 1090, c 1414, **-ium** c 900, 1006. c 1090, c 1413, bishopric, episcopate; 8c. c 1072, 1465, **-ium** c 1160, 1588, papacy; **-ius,** papal 1254, 1620; Papist 1545, 1609; **-ulus,** paltry bishop 1513; **-o,** to consecrate as bishop 12c., 1330; to be a bishop 1241, c 1400; to be Pope c 690, c 730. a 1155, c 1414; to raise (a city) to an episcopal see a 1155, 1414; *see also* **pons, ponticitas.**

pontor, *see* punda.

pontus, *see* pan.

ponzonatus, *see* PUNCT

poosum, *see* 1 pesso.

pop/a c 1180, ‡c 1440, **-isma** 13c., grease; **-o,** to make greasy c 1180.

popela, *see* PAPUL

pop/ellus 1327, **-lus** 1301, summer fur of squirrel; *see also* POPUL

pop/ileon, *see* populeon.

popina, kitchen c 1190, ‡15c.

popingaius, *see* papagabio.

pop/les, back of knee or thigh: **-lex** c 1180, ‡15c., (?) †**poles** 6c.; ‡**-liliga,** "garter" 15c.

†**popl/us** (? **-or**), 'popeler', spoonbill (Norfolk) 1300.

pop/uleon a 1250, **-ileon** 1200, (?) **pepilion** 1414, unguent made of poplar-buds.

popul/us, multitude c 730. c 1090, 1274; laity 12c., c 1330; **p. communis** c 1370, **p. inferior,** p. minor 1314, **p. minutus** 1274, **p. simplex** a 1142, 13c., common people; **p. mediocris,** middle class 1336; ***-i** (*pl.*), people, citizens c 1125, c 1470; **popellus,** people c 950; **-aris,** secular c 1110; (*subst.*) commoner c 1197; **-ares** (*pl.*), populace c 790. c 1365, 1461; **-atio,** peopling c 1249, 1283; c 1267, **-ositas** 13c., 1468, populousness; **-atrix,** murderess c 1000; **-ivorus,** anthropophagous 1518; **-o,** to increase (*trans. & intr.*) c 550; to people, populate c 1249, 1296.

popurgium, *see* hypopyrgium.

por-, *see also* pur-

porallum, *see* puralea.

porcasium, *see* purcacium.

porcellana, cowrie shell a 1250; porcelain 1622, 1626.

porcentus, *see* precinctus.

porch-, porcius, *see* porcus; porticus.

porcio, porcionarius, *see* portio.

porc/us 1198, 1258, **p. silvester** c 1188, 1256, wild boar; **p. campester** a 1300, 1325, **p. campestralis** 1466, pig feeding in fields; **p. herbagii,** pig paid for grazing rights c 1115; **p. ad plancherum,** trough-fed pig c 1220; **p. marinus** 1433, **p. maris** c 1324, **p. piscis** 1265, ‡**-a** 15c., porpoise (*cf.* PORP); **p. marinus,** "seal" 1512; **caput -i,** hogshead, cask 1407, 1417; †**-upina,** (?) porcupine 1432;

*-aria c 1080, c 1411, **porcheria** c 1120, c 1350, †**porchoria** 1262, ‡**-atorium** 15c., ‡**-icetum** 1488, **-iscetum** 1389, ‡**-ile** 1570, **-ina** 1385, **porsenarium** 1398, **domus -orum** 1321, piggery or pig-sty; ***-arius** 1086, c 1400, **-ator** 1300, swineherd; **canis porkaricius** 1214, **c. porkerecius** 1213, boar-hound; **-aster** 8c., **purcellus** (*for* **-ellus**) 1185, 1306, **-ellulus** 12c., 14c., **-ellilus** 1388, **-iculus** c 1335, **-iolus** 1358, †**-inuncula** c 1280, piglet; **-ellus de sude**, stall-fed piglet c 1115; **-ellus lactans** (opposed to **-ellus separatus**) 1336; ***-ello**, to farrow 1233, 1311.

pordmannimotus, *see* **portegravius**.

porellia, *see* **puralea**.

poretum, *see* **porretum**.

porism/a (?) supply c 950; acquisition a 1142; corollary (log.) a 1350, 1380; **-atice**, by way of corollary 1344.

porium, *see* **porrus**.

pork-, *see* PORC

poroffra, *see* **profrum**.

poros/itas, porosity a 1250, 1620; **-us**, porous a 1200, 1620.

porp/asius 1248, 1275, **-eisius** c 1353, **-ecia** 1588, **-esia** 15c., ***-esius** 1232, 1309, †**-etus** 1547, **-iscis** 1293, **-iscus** 1309, 1332, **purpasius** 1342, porpoise; *cf.* PORC

porphyr/icus 12c., c 1400, **-iticus** c 1225, c 1310, *for* **-eticus**, purple; **-ogenitus**, born in the purple c 1188.

por/prestura, -pristura, -prisa, *see* PURPRES

porrect/io, delivery (of letters) 1330, c 1470; **-ura**, extent, elevation a ː142; **-or**, deliverer (of letters) c 1290, c 1390; **porrigo**, to deliver (letters) 1218, c 1275; *see also* **pergo**.

porrehia, *see* PAROCH

*porr/etum c 1227, 1369, †**-iolum** 1483, *for* **-um**, 'porret', leek; ‡**-arium**, **-etarium**, leek-bed 15c.; ‡**-ata**, **-eta**, leek pottage 15c., c 1483; **-um** (**de ferro**), poker 1379, 1454.

porro/, but c 730; **-dicium**, suggested etymology of **prodigium** a 1100; **-videntia**, far-sightedness, prudence 7c.

porrus a 1150, ‡**porium** c 1440, wart.

porsenarium, *see* PORC

‡**porsitigon**, iron filing 1652.

port/a aque 1223, **p. aquatica** 1294, 1395, **p. fluvialis** 1465, **-ifluvium** 1411, watergate, flood-gate; **p. cadens** 1461, **p. culeicia** 1212, **p. culicia** 1284, **p. coleicea** (Norm.) 1203, **p. colicea** 1261, **p. collusea** c 1316, **p. currens** 1344, **p. pendula** 15c., portcullis; **p. tornesia** 1274, **p. turneicia** 1279, **p. turnicia** 1278, **p. volubilis** 1456, revolving door or gate; **festum S. Johannis ante -am Latinam** (6 May) c 1220, 1340; **-ula**, doorway, wicket c 700. 1397, 1432; **-ale** c 1212, 1315, **-allum** 1180, †**-alicium** 1313, portal, gateway; **-aria**, gatehouse, porter's lodge c 1266; p 1290, 1441, **-erium** 1297, (?) **-agium** (G.) 1356, office of porter; ***-arius** a 615. 1086, 1430, **-atorius** c 1000, **-itor** 1086, ‡1483, porter, door-keeper; **-itor Magne Garderobe** 1573.

port/agium, *****(payment for) transport, porterage 1090, 1583; (?) collectorship of porterage (G.) 1356 (*see also* **porta**); 1327, 1497,

-itura 1496, capacity, burthen (naut.); **-abilia** (*pl.*), portable goods c 1340, 1365; **-abilis** c 1194, 15c., †**-ivius** 1388, portable; wearable (of clothes) 1259; endurable 1246, c 1343; **-amentum** c 1250, **-atus** 1324, deportment, behaviour; **-atilis**, portable c 1190, 1518; *see also* **altare, castellum, crux**; **-atio**, carrying 1283, 1531; **p. armorum**, bearing arms c 1115, c 1465; **-ativus**, capable of carrying c 1360; **-ator** c 1135, 1537, ***-itor** a 615. c 1080, 1451, **-or** 1325, c 1353, porter, bearer; **-ator armorum** c 1516, **-itor armorum** c 1322; **-ator presentium** 15c., **-itor** (†**postitor**) **presentium** 1214, 1450, bearer of this letter; **-itor Privati Sigilli**, keeper of the Privy Seal c 1380; *see also* **porta**; **-atorius** 1341, **-itivus** 1432, portable; **liber -atorius**, breviary 1369 (*cf. also* **portiforium**); **-ehachius**, axe-bearer, tool-boy (arch.) c 1280; **-esium**, (?) bale (of cloth) 1275; †**-itorium**, part of harness *or* (?) barrow (O.F. *portoir*) 1352; **-agio**, to perform transport service 1299;

-o, to endure, tolerate c 597. c 1115, c 1400; to bear young c 1230, 1251; to bear fruit 1086, a 1250; to wear (clothes or crown) 1274, 1549; to bear as arms (her.) c 1400, a 1446; to bear a charge of, be debited with 1227, 1242; to have the burthen of (naut.) 1328; **p. bene** c 1264, **p. dure** c 1325 (of horses); **p. male**, to take amiss c 1343; **p. me**, to behave oneself a 1185, 1269; **p. florem** 14c.; **p. folium** 1267; **p. breve**, to take out a writ (leg.) 1269, c 1308; **p. datam**, to bear date 1419, 1432; **p. ferrum** 1202, 1203, **p. judicium** 1086, c 1258, to undergo ordeal (leg.); **p. fidem**, to keep faith c 1258, 1274; **p. recordum**, to keep a record 1272; **p. testimonium**, to bear witness 1086, c 1185.

port/egravius, -gravius 1419, **-grefius** a 1300, **-grevius** 1314, 1586, port-reeve, mayor (of London); **-revus, -reva** (*f.*), port-reeve (Sussex) 1577; **-mannus** a 1327, 1446, **-mennus** 1200, port-man, member of borough council (Ipswich); **-imotus** 1156, c 1335, **-emotus** 1307, 14c., **-motus** a 1186, 1467, **-esmotus** 1290, **-imannimotus** 1324, **pordmannimotus** c 1200, **curia -is** (Newport Pagnell) 1544, port-moot, borough court; **-soka** c 1160, 1419, †**-locha** c 1170, **-esoka** 1419, **-sokna** 1275, c 1324, portsoken, (extramural) civic liberty.

portella, basket 1356; *cf.* **sporta**.

Portenses, *see* 2 **portus**.

portento, *see* PROTEN

port/erium, -ifluvium, *see* **porta**.

portic/us (*2nd decl.*) c 730. c 1300, **-a** 1243, c 1478, **-ius** 1242, **porcius** 1367, **porcha** 1364, **porchia** 1232, 1402, porch; **-us**, chapel for minor altar 12c., 1358; **porchia**, borough court (Lewes) 1268; *see also* 2 **portus**.

*port/iforium c 1282, 1555, **-iferium** 1465, **-iferum** 1313, **-oforium** 1388, 1423, †**-etorium** 1242, 'portas', portable breviary (eccl.); **p. notatum** (mus.) 1368, 1489; **p. sine nota** 1317; **p. stabile** (made to lie on a desk) 1385; **-ifolium**, (?) volume (Ir.) 1477.

porti/o (porci-), portion of divided benefice (eccl.) 1144, 1260; symmetrical figure (math.) c 1300; **-onem habeo cum,** to share the lot of c 1445; **placitum -onis,** plea of apportionment (leg.) 1196, 1219; **-onaliter,** proportionately 1344; **-onarius,** joint tenant, parcener (*cf.* **partitio**) 1286, 1456; joint holder of benefice or recipient of stipend (eccl.) 1276, c 1520; **ecclesia -onaria,** church subject to charge on part of revenue a 1322, c 1444; **-onista,** 'post-master' (Merton College) 1380, 1498; **portciuncula,** *for* **-uncula** 12c. (*cf.* **partiuncula**); **-ono,** to apportion 1367, c 1470.

portisus, *see* phthisis.

portitio, *see* partitio.

portitor, *see* porta; portagium.

port/locha, -mannus, -mennus, -motus, -revus, -soka, *see* portegravius.

porto, *see* portagium.

portratura, *see* PROTRACT

Port/ugalensis c 1190, **-igalensis** 1200, c 1250, **-ingalensis** c 1192, c 1420, Portuguese.

portul-, *see* porta, 2 portus.

portunus, elf, brownie c 1212.

1 **port/us,** apport, impost 1464; **-um manus,** 'mainport', payment in lieu of tithe (eccl.) 14c.

2 **port/us salutis,** port of refuge 1440, 1449; **-icus,** *for* **-us,** 1397; **-ūs quinque** c 1155, 1586, **p. maris** 1217, c 1250, **-ui quinque** c 1236, Cinque Ports; **-enses** c 1298, **-uenses** c 1270, c 1400, **Quinque -enses** c 1293, **Q. -uenses** c 1227, 1257, men of Cinque Ports; **-ulus** a 1275, **-ulettus** 1407, little port, cove.

posca, dilute vinegar: **pusca** a 1250.

poscenetus, *see* pocenettus.

posit/io, setting (of plants) 1378; burial c 1115; laying (of edged tools) 1366; (?) fitting together (of ploughs) 1302; exposure (for sale) (G.) 1315; impost 1330; appointment 1230, 1440; local existence (phil.) c 1380; thesis, proposition a 1180, 1549; charge, accusation 1441; **p. crucis,** making the sign of the cross 11c.; **p. casus,** putting a case (leg.) c 1556; **-ive,** in a positive sense a 1250, c 1270; **-ivus,** productive 1241; egg-laying 1441; *positive (log.) c 1160, 1620; **jus -ivum** c 1200, a 1520, **lex -iva** 1344, a 1408, man-made law; **-or,** *stone-layer, brick-layer (arch.) 1316, 1500; one who posits (log.) c 1270; **-ura,** punctuation a 1180; buttress c 1447; **ponibilis,** supposable c 1277, 1378; **-um,** statement, charge (leg.) c 1115; **per -um,** hypothetically c 1343; **-o quod,** on the assumption that c 1282, c 1444; **pon/e,** writ removing action from other court c 1185, 15c.;

-o, to appoint, fix 1086, c 1422; to lay (stones) 1327, 1456; to 'lay' (tools with steel cutting edge) c 1357, 1382; to set (with gems) 1425; to remove (legal proceedings) 1205, 1324; to produce or bring up in court (leg.) 1269, 1686; (?) to depose, testify (Fr.) 1263; to lay out, spend (money) 1199, c 1400; to pawn c 1218; to impose (taxation) 1217, 1218; **p. ad arma,** to arm 1265; *p. ad firmam,** to farm out 1086, c 1300;

p. ad frenum to break in (colt) 1344; **p. ad largum,** to set free 1384; **p. ad legem,** to compel resort to legal proof 1215; **p. ad litteraturam** 1325, 1330, **p. in literam** 1348, **p. ad scholas** 1344, **p. ad studium** c 1330; **p. ad manum,** to take into possession 1275, c 1332; *p. ad m. mortuam** c 1310, c 1492; **p. ad mortem,** to put to death 1219; **p. ad opera,** to subject to labour service c 1115, c 1283; *p. ad rationem,** to interrogate, call to account c 1190, c 1343; **p. ad redemptionem,** to put to ransom 1217, 1451; **p. calumpniam** c 1220, **p. clamium** 1217, 1268, to enter a claim (leg.); **p. faciem,** to set one's face c 1343; **p. foris,** to alienate 1086; **p. in** (with *acc.*) to accuse 1276; **p. in** (with *abl.*) to put on (a jury, *etc.*) 1202, 1267; **p. in defens/am** 1247, *-um 1219, 1288, -o 1234, 1419, to put in defence, forbid entry into; **p. manum super** c 1200, **p. manus in** c 1380, to lay (violent) hands on; **p. per ballium,** to put on bail 1271; **p. per fidem,** to put on oath 1200, 1201; **p. sigillum** (*for* appono) 1240; **p. silentium** c 1340; **p. super,** to charge with 1203, 1236; **p. me,** to appear in court (leg.) 1265, 1402; **p. me extra,** to obtain exemption from 1241; *p. me in** c 1190, 1421, *p. me super** 1196, 1499, **p. super** 1196, 1424, to put oneself on, submit (an issue) to (leg.); **p. me in fugam,** to take flight c 1319.

posnetus, possinetus, *see* pocenettus.

poss/e (*subst.*), *power, ability c 1115, 1592; dominion 1224, 1343; a force, body of men c 1252, 1405; **ad p.** c 1250, *pro posse (meo) c 1070, c 1507, **p. tenus** 1453, as much as possible; **p. civitatis** 1324, *p. comitatus** 1234, 15c., effective force of city or county; **-ibilitas,** intention c 1115; possibility 1200, a 1564; potentiality (log.) c 1286, c 1363; means (financial) 1296; *power, ability a 1100, c 1492; **pro -ibilitate** 1234, c 1520; **-ibile,** potential matter c 850; **p. logicum** (opposed to **p. reale**) p 1300; **-ibilis** *c 1258, 1464, **pocibilis** (G.) 1369, possible; potential 1267, c 1286; **ex -ibili,** intentionally c 1115; **-ibilior,** more possible 1378; **-ibiliter,** possibly c 1470; (?) as well as possible c 1404; **-ibilito,** to be conducive to c 1376.

possess/io corporalis, physical possession 1217, c 1500; **p. realis** 1456, 1565; **p. nuda,** unsupported possession c 1258, c 1367; **p. pacifica,** uninterrupted possession 13c.; **sum in -ione quod,** to be apprised that c 1300; **-ionaliter,** by way of possession 1170; **-ionate,** with possession of property (mon.) 1380; **-ionarius** 15c., c 1522, *-ionatus (*adj.* or *subst.*) 1345, 1438, owning property (mon.); *-ionatus (de),** possessed of c 1380, 1583; **-or,** owner (naut.) 1426, 1460; **postsessor** 11c., (?) **possor** c 550, *for* **-or;** **-orium,** possessory claim or action (leg.) 1219, c 1304; **breve -orium,** possessory writ 1308; **-iono** 1516, **possedeo** 1461, *for* **possideo,** to possess; **possideor,** to be possessed (by demon) c 1090, a 1100.

possia, wisdom c 550.

post, in search of c 793, c 1000. 1238, a 1446

N

(*see also* **eo, mitto**); according to c 1115; **p. atque**, after (*conj.*) 1442; **p. breve** c 1400, **p. modicum** c 1090, c 1400, soon after; **ex p. facto**, subsequently, retrospectively c 1250, c 1370.

1 posta, roll (of cloth) 1362.

2 post/a c 790, c 980. 1236, 1381, **-us** 1294, **-ella** 1180, a 1450, **-icula** 1292, **-ilis** 1416, *for* **-is**, (wooden) post; **-is**, post of mill 1259, 1282; (?) quarry site 1419; **-atio**, shaping into posts 1419; **-o**, to 'post', square, shape (wood) into posts 1336, 1419; †**-ulo**, to fit (wall) with posts 1294.

postcommunio, 'postcommon', prayer after mass (eccl.) a 1210, 1434.

postdictus, hereinafter-named a 1100.

postdisseisina, disseisin after recovery (leg.) 1340, 15c.

post/ella c 1200, c 1460, **-ena** c 1255, crupper; *see also* **2 posta**.

postema, *see* **apostema**.

posterg/um, behind 7c.; **-o**, to leave behind 1252; to postpone 1414, 1441; to turn one's back on 1528.

poster/itas, sonship, inheritance c 793; c 1258, 1414, **-ioritas** a 1233, c 1362, coming after; **-ioritas**, posterity, descendants p 1300; **a -iori**, inductively (log.) c 1300, c 1380; **-iora** (*pl.*), buttocks c 1250, 1338; **liber -iorum**, Aristotle's *Posterior Analytics* 13c. (hence **-ista**, expert in the same, **propositio -istica**, **cano -isticus** 1523); **-ius**, in the rear 1440; **-im**, afterwards c 1280; **in -is**, for the future, hereafter 1017; *cf.* **imposterum**; **-ioro**, to outstrip c 1267; to put after, subordinate 1344; †**-io**, to despise 1404 (*cf.* **postergo**); **-o**, (?) to follow c 1177.

*****post/erna** c 1100, 1461, **-ernum** 1278, c 1300, **-erula** a 1100, c 1430, **-icium** 1188, 15c., **-icus** 1246, 1439, postern gate.

postessentia, changed state 9c.

postestas, *see* **potestas**.

‡**postfenium**, "fog", aftermath 1570.

postgenitus, younger 1198, c 1290; posthumous 1234, 1242.

posthinc, henceforward c 1000.

postic-, *see* **posterna**.

postill/a, postil, note, commentary 1271, 1515; **-atio**, commenting 1374; **-ator**, commentator c 1343, c 1363; *****-o**, to annotate, comment on 1235, c 1470; *cf.* APOSTILL

post/is, **-ilis**, *see* **2 posta**.

postitor, *see* **portagium**.

postliminium, delay in return c 760.

postlocutio, subsequent action (leg.) c 1115.

‡**post/meridies**, **-mesimbria**, afternoon c 1440.

postmitto, to add subsequently a 1245.

postnatus, puisne, younger 1218, c 1437.

postnetta, *see* **pocenettus**.

posto, (?) to 'post', 'poss', beat (hemp) 1315; *see also* **2 posta**.

postor, (?) impostor c 1170.

postpondero, to give less heed to c 1170.

postpo/sitio, postponement 13c.; setting aside, allaying c 1458; **articulus -sitivus**, relative pronoun (gram.) 1524; **-sitis oculis**, (?) with averted gaze c 1400; **-no**, to postpone, delay c 1220, c 1432; to set aside c 1250, c 1400; to write below c 1300.

postprandius, postprandial 1345.

postpuncto, to mark after c 1265.

postscriptio, postscript c 1300; (?) *for* **proscriptio**, 1418.

‡**postsellium**, hind bow of saddle 15c.

postsessor, *see* POSSESS

postsummonitio, subsequent summons (leg.) c 1290.

postul/ata c 1180, **-atus** c 760, demand; **-atum**, axiom (math.) 1620; **-ator**, intercessor 7c.; **-atio**, choice by chapter of ineligible person (*e.g.* bishop of another see) 1231, 1559; **-atus**, 'postulate', person so chosen c 1250, 1559; **-o**, to choose such a person c 1125, 1499; to nominate as prior 1261; **p. orationem**, to offer a prayer c 600; *see also* **2 posta**.

postum generale, general post 1731.

postuma, *see* **apostema**.

potado, potato (*or* sweet potato) 1622.

1 pot/agium 1330, 1352, **-atio** 13c., 1428, drink-money; **domus -ationis**, ale-house c 1198; **aqua -abilis**, drinking water c 760; **-abilitas**, fitness for drinking c 1260; **-amentum** 655, **-atiuncula** 1573, drink; **dolium -arium**, cask of liquor c 1220; **-ator** (bibl.), **-ista** 1523, **-atrix** (*f.*) 1252, drunkard; **-us** (*coll.*), dregs 1370; **p. caritatis**, loving-cup c 1266, c 1445; **-o**, to give to drink c 1000. c 1160, c 1243; *cf.* **potio**.

2 *potagi/um 1206, 1587, †**protagium** 1337, pottage (broth *or* porridge); **-arius** c 1266, c 1335, **-aria** (*f.*) c 1312, pottage-maker (mon.).

potagra, *see* **podagra**.

pot/arius, **-ata**, *see* POTT

pot/ecarius, **-icarius**, *see* **apotheca**.

potell/us, **-a**, **-um** *****1279, 1534, †**petellus** 1448, pottle, liquid measure (2 quarts); 1321, 1417, **-are** 1405, pottle-pot; *cf.* POTT

poten/s, (*subst.*) potentate 1345, c 1362; (*adj.*) 1278, **p. in bonis** 1422, rich; 1315, **p. ad arma** 1265, 1303, fit to bear arms; (with *acc.*) worth 14c.; (with *inf.*) able 1313, c 1343; **p. in corpore**, able-bodied c 1350, 1422; †**-tas**, strength (?) 869; potentate c 1341; **potentgarnetta**, cross-garnet (sort of hinge) 1388;

-tia, support, crutch c 1172, 1245; Power (order of angels) c 1200; *****force, body of men 1217, 1461; a 1200, 1344, *****-tialitas** c 1270, c 1360, **-tiality** (log.); **-tia activa** c 1260, c 1300; **p. factiva** c 1300; **p. logica** c 1300; **p. objectiva** (opposed to **p. subjectiva**) c 1300; **p. passiva** c 1260; **p. absoluta** (opposed to **p. ordinata**) c 1314, c 1334;

-tiabilis c 1270, **-tialis** c 1190, 1620, **-tionalis** a 1250, potential; **-tialis**, (?) actual 793; **-tialiter**, powerfully 12c., 1461; as much as possible c 1193; *****potentially 12c., c 1443; in the potential mood (gram.) 1524; †**potientialiter**, effectively 8c.; **-tificus**, imparting power 9c.; ‡**-tilla**, valerian (bot.) 14c.; **-tor** (*dep.*, with *gen.*) to have power over 9c.

potest/as, one in authority, official 1297, c 1390; *****podestà** (It.) 1220, c 1320; majesty (title) c 1362; *****Power (order of angels) a 975. c 1186, c 1444; power, virtue (astr.) a 1200, a 1233; power (math.) 1686; force, body of men 1228, 1381; *dominion, area of authority 9c., 948. a 1150, 1419; document conferring authority 1289, 1413; property, wealth 943; potentiality a 1233; **p. ligia** 1198, c 1317, **p. legia** c 1285, 1332, **p. libera** 1220, full power of disposition (leg.); **p. ligandi et solvendi** (eccl.) c 1225, c 1400; **p. plena** c 1290, ***p. plenaria** c 1298, 1564; **p. sana**, sound mind 1219; **p. secularis** c 1250, c 1280; **postestas**, power 12c.; -alis, productive of power c 1500; -arius, (?) permitted by one's power c 1275; -ative, *by authority c 1188, p 1475; vigorously, powerfully 12c., 13c.; within one's power c 1360; potentially c 1290; -ativus, having power or authority 1086, c 1343; conferring authority 1238, 1378; subject to will (leg.) c 1258; †-atus, power, act of power (?) c 975. 12c., c 1375.

potevolo, to prefer c 1500.

potio/ S. Pauli (med.) a 1250; -natio, poisoning 15c.; -nator, poisoner c 1255; -no, to physick (mon.) 13c.; *to poison 12c., c 1540.

pot/ista, -o, -us, *see* 1 **potagium**.

potitum, power c 550.

pott/um, -us, *pot 1213, 1474; fish-trap 1271; (?) barrel (of gun) 1375; part of metal-work of plough 1262; **p. fimare**, 'dung-pot', dung-cart 1357; -ata, cart-load (of dung) 1278; -a, (?) pot-hole c 1240 (*cf*. **puteus**); -aria, pottery 1086; -arius (†**pocarius**) 1086, 1419, -erius c 1285, potter; **potfalda** 1235, 1401, **putfalda** 1235, foldage; -ulum, little pot 1479; *cf*. POTELL

potura, *see* **pultura**.

poud-, *see* **pulvis**.

poudrellum, *see* 1 **pondus**.

poukewaynum, 'poke-wain', (?) hay-cart 1327.

poula, *see* **pola**.

poun/acium, -ettum, *see* 1 **pavo**.

pounagium, *see* **pannagium**.

pounce-, pouns-, *see* PUNCT

poundagium, *see* PUND

poundus, *see* 1 **pondus**.

pountagium, *see* **pons**.

pout/ura, -o, *see* **pultura**.

povo, powenacius, *see* 1 **pavo**.

powchia, *see* **poca**.

powzonatus, *see* PUNCT

poyada, a due or toll (G.) 1255.

poynt-, *see* PUNCT

†**pracionabilis (porcus)**, (?) running at large 1477.

pract/ica *12c., c 1470, -ice 6c., practice; stratagem c 1540; -icabilis 1444, -izabilis c 1377, practicable; -isatio, observance c 1377; -ice, in practice p 1300, 1552; -icus c 1170, 1474, -icalis 1385, practical, actual; -ica vita, life of action c 1000. c 1170; -icus c 1180, -izator c 1350, -icans c 1212, -izans c 1180, c 1400, practitioner (med.); -ico, to construct, contrive 1432, 1517; to experiment 1620; p 1300, 1486, -izo (-iso) 1377, 15c., to practise; -izo in arte chirurgie c 1462; -izo in medicina c 1350, 1536; *cf*. **praxis**.

prae-, *see also* **pre-**

prae- *for* **pre-**: *see* PREC; PRETI

praeri/a, -um, *see* 1 **pratum**.

pragmatica, office, function: **prammatica** 1161.

praia, 'pray', thatching-pin 1237.

pram/a, *for* -nion, precious stone c 1270, c 1328; †**pama**, toad-stone 15c.

pramo, master of 'pram' (naut.) 1392.

prandiolum, lunch 1535; **prans/um**, food, meal 1280; -ilis hora, meal-time c 1115; ‡-orium, "eating-place" c 1440, 1483; ‡-o, to eat 1483.

pranga, *see* **pronga**.

prasin/a 1261, 1268, †**prasma** 1267, †**presme** (? **presine**) 1245, **prasius** a 1250, **pranchius** 1267, a green gem; -us, vert (her.) 1654; **pressinius**, *for* -us, green c 1400.

1 ***prat/um**, meadow-land, grass-land 1086, 16c.; **p. aquosum** 1374, **p. stagni** 1350, water-meadow; **p. debile**, (?) meadow gone to waste c 1254, 1329; **p. dulce** 1296, **p. friscum** 1338, fresh-water meadow; **p. salsum** 1296, 1390, **p. sulsum** 1256, salt meadow; **p. falcabile** 1222, 1388; **P. Monstratum**, *see* **ordo**; *see also* **facio, levo, sublevo, verto**; -a c 834. 12c., -eum c 755, -is 812, *for* -um; -eila c 1362, *-ellum c 1190, a 1446, -iculum c 1150, c 1250, -unculum 1182, small meadow; ‡-ellus, bunting (bird) 15c., 1483; -erium, cloister garth (mon.) c 1266; **praeri/a**, meadow-land (G.) 1243; heath 1306; -um, lawn 1289; †**pressura**, (?) hay-growing 1234.

2 †**pratum**, coverlet c 550.

pravates, apostate 8c.

prav/itas, wicked deed c 730. c 1364; -icola, pursuing evil courses *or* worshipping evil c 950; -ilegium, wicked privilege (play on **privilegium**) c 1125, c 1370; -o, to misrule a 1530.

praxis, *practice, action c 1250, 1684; handiwork 1345; practice (med.) c 1450, c 1580; model, exemplification 1610; *cf*. PRACT

*pre (prae) manibus, in advance, cash down c 1200, 1531.

preabundo, to predominate c 1200, a 1446.

preaccendo, to kindle before c 1310, c 1325; **preascendo**, to enflame (with zeal) 1436.

preaccept/us, admitted in advance (log.) c 1270, c 1343; -o, to accept in preference c 1430; **preaccipio**, to accept in advance a 1250, c 1400.

preact/io, previous action 1344; -ivus, acting before 1344; **preago** c 1220, 1344, **proago** (G.) 1283, to act, execute, previously.

preaddo, to add to a group c 730.

preadductus, previously adduced c 1343.

preadjacens, adjacent in front 1431.

preadvisatus, forewarned, primed 1474.

preaffecto, to desire in advance c 1456.

preag/nitio, foreknowledge 1344; -nosco, to recognize previously 1433.

preago, *see* **preactio**.

*preallego, to mention, allege, before a 1245, 1461.

*pream/abilis 1339, 1440, -atus c 1302, most lovable; -o, to prefer 12c., c 1160.

preambio, to encompass beforehand 9c. 1344.

preambul/um c 1194, 1684, -a 1378, preamble, preface; -us, over-hasty c 1188; preliminary c 1260, c 1343; previous c 1404; (*subst*.)

1167, 15c., **-a** (*f.*) c 1250, 14c., forerunner; **-o**, to arrange or send beforehand 1194, 14c.
preamplexor, to embrace beforehand 1237.
pre/amplus (? *for* **per-**), very large c 1200.
pre/angustus (? *for* **per-**), very narrow c 1190.
preannecto, to bind previously c 1310.
preantea, previously c 1390, 1583; *cf.* **per.**
preanticipo, to anticipate c 990.
preapus, *see* **priapus.**
pre/arduus (? *for* **per-**), very steep c 1225; very difficult c 1160.
preargutus, previously argued c 1340.
prearmatus, fore-armed c 1325; **p. aculeo** (fig.) 1662.
preascendo, *see* **preaccendo.**
preascensor, the first to mount 1461.
preassero, to assert previously 1456, c 1465.
preassignatus, previously appointed 1214, 1461.
preassuetus, previously accustomed c 1440.
preassumo, to choose beforehand 1345, c 1452; to assume previously (log.) c 1343; to prefer c 1345.
preattendo, to consider in advance 1424.
preattexo, to compose as preface 1662.
prebend/a *c 1125, 1540, **probenda** 1242, **provandum** 1294, **provendum** 1356, provender, fodder; corrody, allowance of food c 1190, c 1325; *1086, 1567, **-aria** 1533, prebend (eccl.); **p. bursalis**, prebend carrying a stipend (Exeter) 1334, 1523; **p. parochialis**, prebend conferring a vicarage (Exeter) 1321, 1395; **p. simplex**, prebend of canon who is not a dignitary 13c.; **-ula** c 1197, 1332, **-iola** 1586, little prebend; †**-a** c 1125, ***-arius** 1130, 1686, **provendarius** 1194, **-atus** c 1197, 1549, prebendary (eccl.); **-arius de choro** c 1162; **-ales** (*pl.*), prebendal churches c 1250; **-alis**, connected with a prebend 1248, c 1280; ***ecclesia -alis** a 1228, 1453, **e. -abilis** 1285, **e. -aria** c 1223, **e. -ata** 1200, 1239, prebendal church; **-aria**, almswoman (?) 1086, 1218; **-arium** 1124, c 1220, **provenderium** c 1283, measure of corn; **-arius**, purveyor of fodder, *etc.* (?) 1086, 1226; pensioner c 1115, 14c.; **capellanus -arius**, presbyter **-arius** 1192; **clericus -arius** c 1400; **-atio**, constituting a prebend 13c., c 1258; **-o**, to supply with fodder c 1290; to endow with a prebend 1200, 15c.; to constitute a prebend c 1365.
prebitorius, ready to supply 1622.
prebravio, to reward most richly a 1452.
prec/amen 7c. c 1170, c 1450, **-atus** c 770. c 1125, 1334, prayer; **-amina** 1440, **-alia** 1433, **-arie** 1364, **-aria** 1415, **-es** 1399, **-e** 1434, **-atoria** 1415, **-lee** 1457, **-ule** c 1410, 1519, beads (*cf.* **par**); **-ulare**, beaded wreath (in stained-glass window) 1471; **-anter**, supplicatingly c 1177; **-aria, -arium** c 1160, 1548, **opus -arium** 1548, **-atio** a 1128, 1183, **prex** c 1115, 14c., boon-work, boon-service (man.); **prex**, forced service, *corvée* (G.) 1243; **p. regis**, royal favour 1198; **prex amoris** (**de amore**), love-boon (man.) 1303, 1327; **p. autumpnalis** 1209, 1308; **p. hiemalis** 1242; **p. quadragesimalis, p. vernalis** 1242; **p. carruce** c 1185, 14c.; **p. cervisie** 1185, 1222, **p. madida** 1222, boon-

work with ale supplied; **p. sicca**, boon-work without free ale 1222, 1402; **p. libera**, boon-work due from freehold 1356; ***p. magna** 1185, 1398; **-arius**, concerned with boon-work 1277, 1449; (*subst.*) beadsman 1455; 1242, 1352, **-ariarius** c 1280, boon-worker; †**-atio**, (?) bargain 12c.; **-atorium**, petition 1295; **-arius** 590, c 1000, **-atorius** 1041. c 1220, c 1242, **praecatorius** 9c., supplicatory; **-atrix**, suppliant (*f.*) c 1190; **carruca -ata**, boon-plough 1278; **-o stipulam**, to cut stubble as boon-work 1294; **-o**, *for* **-or**, 8c.; *see also* **percario.**
precant-, *see* **PRECENT.**
precapto, to forestall c 1356, c 1450.
precar/us c 1350, 1529, ***-issimus** c 1280, 1585, very dear.
precastro, to castrate before c 1190.
precatus, *see* **precamen; pricka.**
precauso, to precede as cause 1344.
pre/cautio 1236, **-cavitio** c 1375, 1378, warning.
preced-, *see* **PRECESS; preses.**
pre/celeber (? *for* **per-**), celebrated 1440.
precellent/ia, pre-eminence c 1188, 1537; **-er**, pre-eminently c 1246, 1427; **-issimus**, most eminent c 730. c 1077, 1433; **precelsius**, more exaltedly c 1090.
precenseo, to forewarn 1252.
***precent/or** c 1090, 1549, **presentor** 1202, 1497, **precintor** c 1160, precentor (eccl.); **-rix**, precentress (of nunnery) c 1250, 1519; announcer, herald (*f.*) c 1200; **-oria** 12c., 1549, **-aria** 1213, 13c., **-eria** 1207, precentorship; ‡**-ura**, "chantry" 1483; ‡**-us**, "treble" 1483; **precant/atio**, preliminary chant (in burial service) c 1182; **-o**, to sing before c 1182, 15c.; **precino**, to lead the singing c 1445.
precept/or, preceptor (of Templars or Hospitallers) 1196, 1558; writ-master (leg.) 1389; **p. civitatis**, governor c 1150; **-oria** 1328, 1583, **-ura** c 1470, preceptory (Hospitallers, *etc.*); **-orie** (*adv.*), by way of precept c 1268, c 1365; **-orie** (*pl.*), letters of instruction 1166; ***-orius**, giving instructions c 730. c 1204, 1448; **-iuncula**, trifling rule 1515, 1520; **-um**, incitement to crime 13c., 1297; †**perceptum**, *for* **-um**, command c 1290; ***precipe** 1200, 1309, **p. in capite** 1299, 1535, **p. quod reddat** c 1185, 1309, writs (leg.)
precerno, to foresee c 1455.
preces, *see* **precamen.**
precess/io, going before a 1100; procession 1517; preceding in time a 1350; **p. (equinoctiorum)**, precession (astr.) c 1267, 1686; **-ivus** c 1200, **precedaneus** 1647, introductory, antecedent; **-or**, *predecessor c 1188, c 1450; one who has precedence c 1257, c 1430; **preced/ens**, a precedent c 1523; **-o**, to be of advanced age c 1212.
precibo, to give a foretaste a 1275.
precido, *see* **PRECIS**
***precin/ctus** 12c., 1686, **presinctus** 1550, **procinctus** a 1200, 1583, **porcentus** 1334, **purcinctus** 1371, **purcingtus** 1279, precinct, surrounding area; boundary 1481; **in -ctu**, in haste c 800; **-go**, to invest with a dignity 1461; *cf.* **PROCINCT**

precin/o, -tor, *see* PRECENT
†precipatio, (?) cutting off 1378.
precipe, *see* PRECEPT
precip/itium (†-ium), headlong fall, plunge
c 1115, c 1400; annoyance, obstacle c 1125;
-itatoria, -itaria, siege-engine a 1260;
-itarius, (?) tall c 1250; ‡**-itatio,** precipita-
tion (alch.) 1652; **p. matricis** (med.) a 1250.
precipuitas, outstanding excellence c 1115.
precircino, to circulate (news) in advance
a 1255.
precis/io, excommunication (eccl.) c 1204;
precision, exactitude 13c., c 1360; **(dens)
-or,** incisor c 1115, c 1258; **-ura,** vertical
section of triangle a 1150; ***-e** 1221, c 1440,
prescise, presise 1333, precisely,
exactly; ***-us,** excommunicated 1295, 1298;
precise, exact c 1250, c 1360; **prescido,** *for*
precido, c 1160, c 1270; **precido pedes,**
to expeditate c 1130.
precitatus, previously cited c 1277.
precitus, *see* **prescientia.**
preclamatio, *see* PROCLAM
preclaritas, illustriousness c 1320, 15c.
preclaudo, to enclose (land) 1275.
preclea, *see* **precamen.**
preclu/sio, prevention 1437; bar (leg.) 1523,
a 1564; **p. vocis,** aphasia 15c.; **-sibilis,**
subject to bar (leg.) 1423; **-sivus,** debarring
(leg.) 1308; **-sorium** (†**perclusorium**),
screen 15c.; **-do,** to bar (an action) 1423.
preclu/us c 900. c 1125, †**preclivis** c 1400,
for-**is,** renowned; **-enter,** with renown c 990.
preco, appraiser c 1298; watchman (Sc.) 1434;
crier (Sc.) 1435, 1461; crier (ac.) c 1427,
c 1550; ‡"beadle" 15c.; mayor (G.) 1254,
1276; preacher 8c. c 1250, 1565; "beadsman" 1425 (*cf.* **precamen**); **p. mortuorum** 1502, **p. pro mortuis exorandis**
1424; **precon/ator,** eulogist c 1485; **-atrix,**
announcer (*f.*) c 1163; ‡**-izator,** "crier in
the market" 1483; **vox -aria** 1041. c 1200,
15c., **v. -ialis** c 1236, voice of crier or herald;
-ialis, laudatory 12c., c 1204; laudable
c 1218, c 1250; **-atus** c 1190, 13c., ***-izatio**
c 1275, 1684, proclamation, announcement;
-ium, praise, worship (eccl.); **-io,** to
prophesy 13c.; ***-izo (-iso)** a 1275, c 1540,
-o (*for* **-or**) c 670, c 730. c 1192, to proclaim; **-or insignia (ambitionis),** to blow
one's own trumpet c 1160; *see also* **precamen.**
precollatus, previously conferred 1345.
precollaudo, to praise previously c 1225.
precollectus, previously collected c 1360.
precomes, premier earl 1444.
precomminatus, previously threatened
c 1280.
precomptus, adorned 810.
precomputo, to account for in advance 1267,
1351.
precon/cessio, previous grant 1245; **-cedo,**
to grant beforehand c 1178, 1566.
preconcipio, to preconceive, foreordain
c 1200, c 1470; *see also* **malitia.**
preconfessus, previously confessed c 1357.
preconfundo, to spread confusion c 1200.
preconi-, *see* **preco.**
preconsecratus, previously consecrated
1610.

preconsidero, to consider beforehand c 1200,
1461.
preconsilior, to deliberate beforehand p 1300.
preconspicio, to see before one 13c.
preconstan/s 1451, **-tissimus** c 1410, very
constant.
preconsul/aris, wise in counsel c 1393; **-o,** to
consult beforehand c 1250; to premeditate
1345.
precontestis, previous fellow-witness 1443,
1510.
precon/tractus, precontract (of marriage)
1397, 1598; **-traho,** to make such a precontract 15c.
precopul/atio, previous copula (log.) a 1360;
-o, to predicate or couple previously (log.)
a 1360.
precord/ialis, cardiac (med.) c 1250, c 1325;
*heartfelt, sincere 940. c 1172, 1442; beloved
12c., 1329; **amicus -ialissimus** 1298, 1377;
***-ialiter,** heartily, sincerely c 1164, c 1423;
-ialius c 1250, c 1298, †**-alius** 1262;
-ialissime 1208.
precorrectus, previously corrected 1314.
precrucio, to torment beforehand a 1275.
precul/a, -are, *see* **precamen.**
preculdubio, *see* **procul.**
†precupio, to bestow c 1115.
precursus (dies), preceding a 1275.
pred/a, share (of food) c 1000; **-abundus,**
rampant (her.) 1654; **avis -alis** c 1177,
a. -aria c 1235, bird of prey; **-anter,** as
plunderers p 1348; **-o anime,** the Devil
1241; **-o,** *for* **-or,** to plunder 1041. c 1195,
c 1400; *see also* **predialia, prida.**
predagium, *see* **pedagium.**
predapifer, steward who lays table c 1180.
predebitus, due in advance c 1310.
***pre/decessor** 1070, 1537, **prodecessor** 6c.,
8c., **-dicessor** 1460, **-desestrix** (*f.*) 1277,
-decedens 1380, predecessor; **p. im-
mediatus** 1293, 1546.
prededuco, to deduct previously c 1258,
1362; to enumerate previously c 1357.
predefinio, prediffin/io, to fix beforehand
9c.; **-itio,** prearrangement c 760.
predefunctus, previously defunct 1415.
predelibero, to consult beforehand 12c.
predenuntio, to foretell c 1298.
predescriptus, already described 12c., 1440.
predesestrix, *see* **predecessor.**
predesideratus, desired as aforesaid c 1448.
predestin/atio (eccl.), **-antia** c 1365, pre-
destination; **-ator** a 1233, **-atrix** (*f.*) 1220,
predestinator; **-atus,** predestined to salvation, elect (theol.) c 1080, 1432; **-o** (with *inf.*),
to determine 9c.
predetermin/atio, prearrangement c 1367;
-o, to predetermine, prearrange c 1185, 1331.
predevotus, deeply devoted 1426, c 1431.
pred/ialia (*pl.*), landed estates c 1220; ***-ialis**
c 1225, 1684, †**-alis** 1367, **-iosus** c 1450,
predial.
predic/a, bead 1554; **-o,** to pray a 1408; *cf.*
precamen.
predic/atio *1124, 1549, **-amen** 9c., **-amen-
tum** c 1000. ‡1483, preaching, sermon;
(?) preaching fee, collection at sermon 13c.;
predication, assertion (log.) c 1160, c 1380;
p. identica, assertion of identity c 1380;

-**abile,** a predicable (log.) 12c., a 1250; epithet c 1436; -**abilia** (*pl.*), Porphyry's *Isagoge* 1537; *-**abilis,** predicable (log.) 1267, c 1444; commendable c 1100, 15c.; **dies** -**abilis,** preaching-day c 1340; -**abilitas,** predicability (log.) c 1270, c 1365; -**amentum,** sign, earnest 8c.; predicament (log.) a 805. c 1160, c 1445; -**amenta** (*pl.*), Aristotle's *Categories* a 1150, c 1620; -**amentalis,** concerned with predicaments (log.) c 1160, 1427; -**ator** *c 1080, 1549, †**prediator** c 1293, preacher; *1227, 1549, **frater** p. c 1225, 1567, Dominican friar; **p. verbi Dei** 1504, 1583, **p. v. Divini** 1588; -**atissa,** Dominican sister 1384; **ars** -**atoria,** art of preaching 1508; **ordo** -**atorius,** Dominican order c 1500; -**atum,** predicate (log.) c 1080, a 1452; *-**o** c 1080, 1549, †**prettico** 1418, to preach; to convert by preaching c 1400; to predicate (log.) 1267, a 1347.

predicessor, *see* **predecessor.**

predict/io, proclaiming p 1341; -**o** a 1155 (†**predico** c 1436) **sacramentum,** to administer oath.

prediffin-, *see* **predefinio.**

predign/atio, reverence 12c.; -**e,** right worthily c 1250; -**us,** right worthy (?) 8c. c 1250.

*-**predilect/us** c 1000. c 1170, 1559, **perdilectus** c 1257, c 1404, well-beloved; -**issimus** c 1300; **prediligo,** to prefer c 1177.

predimissus, previously demised or leased 1573.

prediscors, formerly at variance c 1265.

predispo/sitio, predisposition 1620; -**no,** to predispose, arrange beforehand 12c., 1620.

predistinguo, to distinguish, or make distinct, before a 1186, c 1230.

predito, to enrich c 1255, c 1410.

predivido, to specify previously c 1205.

predo, *see* **preda.**

predomin/ium 13c., p 1300, -**antia** c 1277, 1622, predominance, supremacy; *-**or** c 1180, 1620, †**perdominor** a 1250, to predominate, be supreme.

predono, to give beforehand c 1302, 1374.

predoto, to endow beforehand (eccl.) c 1250, c 1488.

pre/dux, leader, guide c 730, c 1000. 1137, c 1400; -**duco,** to marry (a wife) previously a 1164.

preefficientia, previous efficiency (log.) 1344.

preegregius, very distinguished 1450.

preejectus, previously ejected c 1265.

preelapsus, already past (of time) c 1365, c 1436.

preelect/io, choice, preference c 1160; previous election c 1190; -**us,** choicest, picked c 1200, c 1488; **preelig/enter,** preferably 1344; -**o** 9c., c 1100. c 1160, †**proeligo** c 1192, to choose, prefer; *(with *inf.*) c 1125, 1456; to elect previously c 1258, c 1365.

preemin/entia, *pre-eminence c 1250, c 1580; (title) c 1241, 1382; "preferment" 1605; -**ens,** pre-eminent c 1325, c 1340; -**entissimus** 1297; -**enter,** pre-eminently c 1335; -**eo** 12c., c 1407, †**proemineo** 12c., to excel; *cf.* PREMIN

preem/ptio, previous purchase 1337; -**o,** to buy beforehand c 1160, 1275.

†**preeo,** (?) *for* **predor,** to prey 1331.

preequit/ator, outrider 1290, 1315; -**o,** to ride before 15c.

†**preerera,** (?) boon-ploughing (Lincs.) 1316.

preerigo, to lift up beforehand 1344.

preeripio, to snatch away 10c.

preevitatio, avoidance in advance 15c.

preexamino, to pre-examine 1445.

preexcellen/s, outstanding 12c.; -**tissimus** c 730. 1433; -**ter,** most especially 12c.; **preexcelsus,** highly exalted 793. c 1340.

preexceptus, previously excepted c 1433, a 1564.

preexcogito, to premeditate c 1268, 1415.

preexercitamen, preparatory exercise a 1180.

preexhaustus, previously spent c 1305.

preexhibitus, previously applied c 1185, c 1250.

preexig/entia, presupposition p 1300; -**o,** to presuppose c 1267, 1380.

preexist/entia, pre-existence 13c., 1380; *-**ens,** pre-existent c 1225, p 1381; -**o,** to be previously c 1343, c 1427.

preexpectatio, pre-expectation 1620.

preexpertus, previously experienced 1346, c 1421.

preexpositus, previously expounded c 1300, c 1370.

preexpressus, previously expressed c 1432.

preexulto, to rejoice beforehand 7c.

prefactus, *see* PREFECT

prefalco, to fit (spears) with curved points 1252.

prefat/io (**misse**), preface of the mass (eccl.) c 760, a 975. 1124, 14c.; -**iuncula,** brief preface c 690; *-**us,** aforesaid c 1090, c 1540.

prefect/io, appointment c 1225, a 1564; superior status c 1365; -**orius,** mayor of the palace c 1180; -**oria dignitas,** official status c 1137, 1307; †**perfectialis,** official c 1137; -**ura,** office of reeve c 1115, 1205; -**us** (*4th decl.*), advancing, growth (? *for* **profectus**) 943; (*2nd decl.*), (?) reeve or steward (man.) 1086; reeve or provost (of borough) c 1115, 1586; provost (ac.) 1550, c 1565; **p. Anglie,** justiciar c 1200; **p. aule, p. palatii,** mayor of the palace 12c.; †**profectus,** *for* -**us,** chief c 793; **prefactus,** previously made c 1255; **preficio,** (?) to make previously 1263.

prefer/entia, precedence c 1266, c 1330; -**ramentum** 1413, 1459, -**rementum** 1478, 'preferment', prerogative, privilege; -**o,** to exalt 8c.; (with *acc.* and *dat.*) to put in command of 7c., 8c. c 1250; to prefer to a benefice (eccl.) c 1140, 1434; to pronounce, promulgate (? *for* **profero**) 1279, c 1325; *to mention previously c 1330, c 1563; *cf.* PRELAT

prefestinatio, outstripping 1620.

prefic-, *see* PREFECT; PROFECT

prefigur/abilis c 1250, -**atrix** (*f.*) c 1160, prefiguring; -**ative,** so as to prefigure 9c.

*-**prefix/io** c 1281, 15c., -**itio** c 1333, -**tio** 1276, pre-arrangement, fixing (esp. of date); appointment (of official) p 1322, c 1470; **prefigo,** *to prearrange, fix (date, etc.) c 1170, 1545; to appoint (an official) c 1465.

preflo, to blow upon c 1258.
preflor/ens, flourishing c 1180; **-eo,** to blossom forth (fig.) c 760.
prefragilis, very delicate 793.
prefucatus (†profucatus), outwardly feigned c 1200.
†prefuditia, (?) profusion c 1220.
prefugitivus, fleeing before 1220.
preful/sio, brilliance 9c.; **-gidus** 7c., c 960. c 1180, **perfulgidus** 16c., **perfulgens** c 1217, **profulgentissimus** c 1185, brilliant, illustrious; **perfulgeo,** to gleam c 760.
prefundamentum, preliminary foundation a 1250.
prefurcatus, pointed (of spears) c 1180.
pregarrulus, chattering prophetically 1252.
pregaudeo, to rejoice first c 1160.
pregest/o (**virgam**) to carry in advance 1450; **†-io,** to bear (her.) 1654.
pregidicium, see PREJUDIC
pregn/ans, (?) loaded (with booty) 1150; productive, profitable 1267; **lapis p.,** eagle stone 1215; **-atus** c 1380, 1424, **-ativus** c 1184, pregnant; **-o,** to fertilize, impregnate c 1204, ‡1483; to generate 1399; to be swollen a 1408; to signify 1378; **prenascor,** to be first-born c 1180.
†pregratus, (?) *for* **pergratus,** very welcome c 1470.
pregust/atio c 1185, c 1500, **-amentum** c 1500, foretaste; **-atus,** previously tasted (bibl.).
prehab/itus, *previously held c 1170, 1543; obtained in advance c 1345, 1543; 1267, 15c., **prehibitus** 1267, c 1410, aforesaid; **-eo,** to possess previously c 1290, c 1380; 1300, **prehibeo** 1295, (?) to hold in readiness.
prehendin-, *see* PERENDIN
***prehonor/abilis** c 1310, c 1475, **-andus** 1426, c 1475, **-atus** c 1310, c 1475, right honourable; **-ifico** 9c., **-o** 1292, 1345, to prefer in honour.
prehumecto, to moisten previously a 1250.
preimpensus, previously rendered 1385, 1451.
preincantatus, previously bewitched 1200.
preinexistens, previously immanent 1620, 1622.
preinquisitus, previously inquired into 1283.
prein/sertus 1426, 1454, **-certus** c 1475, previously inserted, aforementioned.
preinsisto, to insist vehemently 1207.
preinstructus, previously advised a 1250.
preintelligo, to understand beforehand c 1270, a 1452.
preintrusus, intruded beforehand 1219.
preinvitatus, previously invited 12c.
prejacens, pre-existent c 1115, c 1270; prior to modification (log.) a 1250, c 1360.
prejaculator, expert dicer 1241.
prejecto, to vaunt 13c.
prejectum, see PROJECT
prejudic/ium, injustice c 1125; **pregidicium** 1380, **-iale** 1338, 1419, *for* **-ium,** prejudice, injury; **-ialis** *1266, 1450, **-ativus** 1295, 1396, prejudicial, injurious; prejudiced (in favour) 1336; **-ialiter,** with prejudice, injuriously 1279, c 1475; **-io** 1304, **-ior** c 1324, 15c., *-o c 1080, a 1540, †**projudico** 1242, †**brejudico** c 1280, to count against, be prejudicial to; **-o,** to judge badly 793;

to choose a 950; to surpass (in discernment) 9c. c 1160, c 1436; to be preferable a 1250; to create a precedent, legislate in advance 1072, c 1190.
prejur/amentum (†projur-) c 1102, c 1115, **-atio** c 1115, preliminary oath (leg.); **p. simplex, p. triplex** c 1102, c 1115; **-o,** to swear preliminary oath c 1110, c 1115; to swear previously c 1250, c 1365.
prejussus, previously commanded c 1330.
prekatus, see **prikettus.**
prelaboro, to labour before 1412.
prelacto, to give preliminary nurture a 1180.
prelargi/o 9c., **-or** c 1160, to give first.
†pre/latibilis (? *for* **pro-**), utterable a 1228.
1 prelat/us, ruler (in general) a 1155, c 1343; secular official (reeve, *etc.*) or feudal lord c 800, c 1000. c 1115; *prelate, dignitary (eccl.) a 1115, 1562; **-a,** head of nunnery c 1250; **-us** (*4th decl.*), precedence 799; †**prelate** c 1458; 15c., *-ia c 1178, 1543, †-ina 1302, *-io c 1060. c 1070, 1472, **-ura** c 1200, c 1545, prelacy (eccl.); *-io 7c., c 1000. c 1080, c 1545, **-ura** c 1255, a 1275, preferment, authority; title (eccl.) c 1250; **-icus,** of a prelate (eccl.) 13c.; *cf.* PREFER
2 prelatus, very wide 1241; *cf.* **perlatus.**
prelector 1529, c 1595, **prolector** c 1535, c 1565, reader (ac.).
prelib/amen, foretaste 9c.; †**-ium,** form of impost (Ir.) c 1390; *-atus, aforementioned c 960, 1041. c 1125, 1567; **-o** 798, c 1000. c 1250, †**-ero** 12c., to mention before.
prelimito, to define beforehand c 1448, 1550.
preli/um campestre, pitched battle 1136, 1406; **-alis,** of battle 7c.; **-osus** (**annus**), troubled by wars c 1250.
prelocut/io, prediction 1231; speech *or* preamble c 1290; stipulation, bargain c 1115, 15c.; **preloquium,** previous report c 1250, 1314; **-or,** spokesman c 1125, 1425; borough official 1416; speaker (of Parliament) 1406, 1471 (*cf.* **prolocutor**); **-orius,** introductory 12c.; **-us,** aforesaid c 1000. c 1250, c 1445; *preloquor, to arrange or agree beforehand c 1115, 1502.
prelotus, previously washed 14c.
prelucid/us, brilliant 9c.; **-e,** brilliantly c 1000.
***preludium** c 1177, 1517, **perludus** c 815, prelude, preliminary.
prelum, printing press 1507, 1620.
premachinor, to plan beforehand 9c.
premagn/ifice a 1275, **permagnifice** c 1310, right nobly; **-us,** very great c 1240, 1437; **premaxim/e,** very much 1285; **-us** c 1150, 15c., **permaximus** c 730, the very greatest.
premaneo, see PERMAN
premanibus, see **pre.**
‡premanic/a c 1440, 1483, **-are** 1562, cuff.
premanifestus, very obvious a 1450.
‡premantia, "divining before" (?προμαντεία) 1483.
premarcidus, gaunt 1200.
premastico c 1200, **p. ad** 1168, to enjoy a foretaste of.
prematialis, see PRIM
prematur/us, very prudent c 1475; **-o,** to hasten c 1200.

premaxim-, *see* PREMAGN
premedit/ate, with premeditation 1552; **-o,** *for* **-or,** to premeditate c 1192, c 1362.
premellio, to sweeten c 1184.
***prememor/atus,** aforementioned 798, 11c. c 1130, a 1564; **-or,** to mention before c 910.
†premens, (?) preening (falc.) 1202, 1242.
premensuro, to measure beforehand a 1270.
prementionatus, aforementioned a 1564.
prementitus, fabled of old c 1190.
premer/eo c 1160, c 1250, **-eor** c 1290, 1423, to deserve particularly.
premetior, to measure beforehand c 1180; to consider beforehand c 1180, c 1304.
premi/atio, rewarding c 1240, 1378; **-abilis,** worthy of reward p 1300, c 1430; **munus -ale,** reward a 1275; **-ator,** rewarder 1308, 1449; **opera -atoria,** works that earn a reward 1344; ***-o,** to reward c 1204, c 1444.
***premin/entia** 12c., c 1458, **†prominentia** 1235, pre-eminence; **-enter,** pre-eminently a 1275; **-eo,** to excel c 730. c 1125, 1290; *cf.* PREEMIN
†premineo, †promineo, *f.l.* for **minor,** to threaten 1339.
premir/us c 810, **-ificus** a 1350, very marvellous; **-ifice,** very marvellously a 1350.
premiss/io, prearrangement p 1377; (?) mission c 1325; **-a,** **-um,** premiss (log.) c 1080, c 1400; ***-a** (*pl.*), premises, things mentioned before 1219, 1575; **premitto,** to premise, mention before 8c. c 1115, 1461.
premit/ie, -us, *see* PRIM
premitis, very sweet 810.
pre/modicus (? *for* **per-),** very small 793.
Premonstratensis, Premonstratensian (canon) c 1145, 1537; *see also* **ordo.**
premonstr/atio, preliminary indication c 1266; **-ativus,** premonitory 1461; **-o,** to show forth c 730.
premorior, to be near dying 9c., c 1060; to predecease 1173, 1461.
premotio, previous motion 1344.
pre/mulceo (? *for* **per-),** to soothe c 1160.
premunero, to bribe c 1172.
***premun/itio,** premonition, warning, notice 1204, c 1475; **-itivus** 1304, **-itorius** c 1295, 1428, premonitory; **-ire facias** 1383, c 1448, **-iri facias** 1434, 1490, name of a writ (leg.); **-iri,** offence against statute of *premuniri* (16 Ric. II) 16c.; **lex de -iri** 1535; **-io** *c 1150, c 1450, **†prominuo** c 1318, to premonish, forewarn; to cite (leg.) c 1290, c 1530.
premutilo, to mutilate c 1180.
prenarratus, aforesaid c 1542.
prenascor, *see* PREGN
prencio, prendo, *see* **prensio.**
preneglectus, hitherto neglected 1345.
prenesciens, *see* **pernesciens.**
prenit/idus, illustrious 1220; **-esco,** to shine forth a 1275.
prenitor, to lean on c 1090.
prenobilis, right honourable c 1188, 1583.
prenomen, ancestor c 1000; **pronomen,** *for* **p.,** forename c 793; **prenomin/atio,** preliminary nomination for office c 1160; ***-atus,** aforenamed 804, 11c. 1086, 1583; **-o,** to name before 12c.
prenostic-, *see* PROGNOSTIC

prenot/atio, preliminary observation 12c.; heading c 1178; **-arius,** protonotary, chief clerk c 1200, c 1290; ***-atus** c 1150, c 1470, **†pernotatus** c 1290, **†pronotatus** 1303, previously noted; **-o,** to note before c 978. c 1283, c 1540.
prenotio, prenotion (log.) 1620.
pren/sio, taking: **-cio** 1548; **-do,** to take (in chess) a 1150; **p. juramentum,** to take an oath 13c.
prent/a, -um, *see* PRINT
prenticius, *see* **apprenticius.**
prenum, 'preen', pin 1346.
prenumer/atus, previously enumerated 12c.; **-o,** to count or pay before c 1218.
prenunti/us, scout 12c.; **-atio,** announcement c 1115, 1441; **-atrix,** prophetic (*f.*) a 1200; *cf.* **pronuntiatio.**
preobeo, to predecease 1256.
preobjectum, previous objection (log.) a 1228.
***preob/tentus (preop-)** c 1258, 1382, **†perobtentus** c 1400, previously obtained.
preoccup/atio, being overtaken or taken by surprise 7c.; **-o,** to antedate (an event) c 730; **p. super,** to encroach upon 1086, 1248.
preoccurro, to meet 1370.
preodarius, *see* PROPRI
preoffero, to offer before c 1236, 1433.
preoper/atio, causation c 1367; **-ative,** previously 9c.; **-atrix,** working beforehand (*f.*) 9c.; **-or,** to work before, cause c 1188, 1344.
preoperio, to cover before c 1250.
preopt/atio c 1290, **-io** c 1608, preference; **-abilis,** very desirable c 1450; *cf.* PEROPT
preordin/atio, prearrangement c 1192, c 1340; **-ativus,** preordaining c 1325; **-o,** to array in front 12c., 1461; *c 1000, 1041. 1124, 1583, **proordino** c 730, to foreordain.
preornatus, conspicuously adorned 1377; *cf.* PERORNAT
preostensio, foreshowing c 1218.
‡prepalmito, to bargain c 1440.
prepalo, to publish 12c.; *cf.* PROPAL
prepar, superior c 1212.
prepar/amentum, preparation 1274, c 1500; **-atio,** Parasceve, preparation for Passover c 1006; prophylactic (med.) c 1280, c 1330; dressing (of wool) 1291; **p. cordis** (theol.) c 1343; **-abilitas,** preparation of food c 1283; **-aticia** (*n. pl.*), rudiments a 1180; **-ativus,** preparatory 1327, 1620; **-ator,** dresser (of wool) 1291; **-atorium,** preparation, preliminary c 1188, 1684; **-atorie,** by way of preparation 1377; **-atorius,** preparatory (leg.) c 1195, c 1258; prefatory c 1343; **-atrix,** preparer (*f.*) 1200; **-o lanam,** to dress wool 1281, 1291.
preparvissimus, *see* **perparvissimus.**
prepateo, to appear obvious c 1370; *cf.* **propatulus.**
prepectus, cuirass c 1250; *cf.* **purpunctus.**
preped/itio, hindrance c 820. 1235, 1504; **perpedio** 1306, 1456, **propedio** c 1270, c 1394, (?) *for* **-io,** to hinder.
prepindo, *see* **perpensio.**
preperditus, formerly lost 1461.
prepertior, to bestow 1284; *cf.* **propars.**
prepingo, to ornament c 1000; to sketch, design (?) 985. c 1090, c 1325; *cf.* **perpingo.**

preplaceo, to be preferred c 1160.

preplurimus, *see* PERPLUR

pre/politus (? *for* **per-**), highly polished c 1403.

prepollenter, pre-eminently c 1250.

preponder/atio, heavy weight 1377; **-antia,** preponderance c 1378; **-anter,** chiefly 1344, 1380.

preposit/io, relation of superiority (log.) 13c.; **-ura,** primacy c 1546; *office of provost (eccl.) c 1188, 1549; *c 1115, 1471, †**prepustura** 12c., **-atus** 1283, 1346, **-iva** c 1180, †**provosta** 1297, **provostria** 1588, **provosteria** 1212, office of provost or reeve (local official); **p. burgi** 1200, 1375; **p. wapentagii** c 1200; ‡**-or,** "sewer", steward 15c., 1483; **p. ecclesie,** churchwarden 1427;

    -us 7c., c 1000. a 1100, 1325, **propositus** c 730. c 1100, prior or abbot; provost (of collegiate church, *etc.*) c 1188, 1536; head of Dominican convent c 1239; ***-us** (†**preposterus**) 1084, 1396, **propositus** 665. 1086, †**propositor** c 1500, **-arius** 1550, reeve (of manor, hundred, *etc.*); c 1200, 1608, **propositus** c 1280, provost or reeve (of borough); *prévôt* (Fr.) c 1140, 1516; **p. aule** c 1364, c 1450, **p. collegii** c 1412, c 1550, **propositus** c. c 1547, **provester** c. 1535, provost (ac.); **p. fossate** 1396, **p. fossati** 1439, dike-reeve; **p. martialis,** provost marshal 1696; **p. regis,** royal official c 1040. c 1075, 1298; †**preponitus,** *for* **-us,** placed at the head 11c.; **prepono,** *for* **propono,** to set before, suggest 9c.

prepossessus, seized beforehand 1307.

prepostulatus, previously elected (from one office to another) (eccl.) c 1365.

prepotenter, very powerfully c 1250, 1307.

preproperatus, hastened, premature a 1100.

preprudens, very prudent 1267.

prepsallo, to sing in front c 1180.

prepugnis, very warlike c 550.

prepulcher, very beautiful 810.

prepunctuatus, previously specified 15c.

prepungo, to mark with a cross 14c.

prepustura, *see* PREPOSIT

preput/atio, circumcision a 1205; **-ialis,** concerned with circumcision 1378; **-o,** to cut off (in circumcision) 12c.

prerecitatus, previously recited c 1350, 1587.

prerectus, prorectus, very right 8c.

prereligiose, very devoutly 1526.

prereptio, seizing beforehand c 1380.

prerequiro, to imply as prerequisite (log.) c 1360.

preresero, to reveal in front c 1180.

prerog/ativa *c 1115, c 1546, †**prorogativa** 12c., 1356, **-antia** c 1290, **-atio** c 1260, prerogative, special claim, precedence; preponderance (log.) 1620; **-ativus,** outstanding, exceptional 793. c 1250, 1330; **jurisdictio p.** c 1344; *see also* **curia;** **-o,** to grant, give c 1090, c 1362.

preruinosus, very ruinous c 1540.

prerumo, *see* PRESUM

preruptio, attack 12c.

prerutilo, to shine resplendently 1426.

presagmen, presage c 590, 685.

presbyter/ (**presbiter/**), elder, old man

c 1270; *6c., 848. 1086, 1559, **prespeter, prespiter** c 550, priest; (?) coarb (Ir.) c 1300; head of house of Austin canons c 1296; ***p. cardinalis** c 1142, 1545; **p. curatus, p. non curatus** 1413, 1545; **p. Johannes,** Prester John a 1193, c 1420; **p. Judeus,** official representative of (English) Jewry 1199, 1230; **p. laicus** a 1408; **p. misse** c 1115, **p. missalis** 824; **p. parochialis** 1274, 1495, **p. parochianus** c 1275; **p. religiosus** 1419; **p. secularis** 12c., 1419, **p. vulgaris** c 1102; **p. simplex** (non beneficiatus) 15c.; **p. stipendiarius** 1406, 1588;

    -a c 1100, 1517, **-issa** c 1370, ‡15c., priest's wife or concubine; **-alis** 1282, 1445, **-ialis** 1402, priestly; **-aliter,** like a priest 1424; **-atus,** priesthood c 770, 1006. a 1100, 1552; **p. Judeorum,** office or function of Jewish representative 1199, 1281; **-ianus,** Presbyterian 17c.; **-icida,** priest-slayer 1511; **-icidium,** murder of priest (Sc.) 1463, c 1540; **-ium,** office of elder c 730; priesthood 6c. c 1130, c 1310; gold coin given to cardinals by Pope at coronation c 1127; *c 1080, 1537, **-arium** 1427, presbytery, choir, sanctuary (of church); ***-o,** to ordain as priest 12c., 1500.

presci/do, -se, *see* PRECIS

***presci/entia,** foreknowledge (eccl.); ***-tus** c 1200, 1427, **precitus** a 1300, foreknown, predestined (to damnation).

prescissio, abstraction (log.) c 1310; **prescind/ibilis,** separable by abstraction (log.) 1560; **-o,** to split up 655; **p. (principium),** to abstract (log.) c 1300.

prescript/io 1197, 1586, **p. temporis** 1219, 1285, prescription, right created by lapse of time (leg.); **-ibilis,** prescriptible c 1305, 1521; **tempus** †**perscriptibile,** time sufficient to create a prescription c 1397; **prescribo,** to prescribe, claim by lapse of time (log.) c 1240, 1431.

presecmen, *for* **presegmen,** paring c 1432.

‡**presellum,** saddle-bow 15c.

presenior, older 1414.

presens, (*adj.*) *present, actual 12c., 1461; †**presented** 1564; (*subst.*) bearer 8c.; 1558, **present/atus** 1269, c 1350, presentee to benefice (eccl.); **-es** (*pl.*), the present letter or document 8c. c 1125, 1564; *see also* **de, pro, verbum; -um** c 1086, c 1366, **-ia** c 1192, 1285, present, gift; **-abilia** (*pl.*), matters to be presented (leg.) 1315, 1408; **-abilis,** to be presented a 1564; **-amentum** 1295, a 1564, ***-atio** a 1185, 1690, **-atum** 1449, presentment (leg.); **-atio,** presentation, delivery 1086, 1345; *(right of) presentation to benefice (eccl.) 1160, 1549; presentation (ac.) c 1350, c 1580; **p. Beate Marie** (21 Nov.) 16c.; **p. falsa** (leg.) 1198, 1230; **p. ultima,** (assize of) darrein presentment (leg.) c 1185, 15c.; **-ator,** one who presents 1202, c 1320; one who presents to holy orders c 1220; one who presents to benefice (eccl.) 1230, c 1290; **littere -atorie,** letters of presentment (eccl.) 1232, c 1308;

    -er 1267, ***-ialiter** 6c., 9c. c 1070, 1516, **-aliter** 1275, 15c., in actual presence, face

to face; 1563, **-ialiter** 8c. 12c., 1440, at present, 'presently', immediately; **in -iarum,** *see* IMPRESENT; **-ialis,** present in person a 1100, c 1344; **-ialitas,** presence, presentness c 1267, c 1380; **-ifico,** to make present 1344; **-o,** to bring forward to 6c., 793; to give, show, present for approval 1086 1577; to present to benefice (eccl.) c 1185, 1549; to make presentment, present (leg.) 1170, c 1540; to present for degree (ac.) c 1526, c 1582; **p. cum,** to present with 1426; **presum,** to pre-exist c 1300, p 1380.
presentor, *see* **precentor.**
‡**preseratum,** tip of bolt 1483.
preserv/atio, preservation c 1365, 1545; **-ativum,** a preservative (med.) a 1452, ‡1652; **-ativus,** preservative c 1329, c 1510; *-o, to preserve c 1329, 1559.
preses, alderman c 1102; (?) sheriff 12c., c 1160; president (ac.) c 1525, c 1555; **presessio,** precedence c 1165; **presid/atus,** (?) shrievalty 12c.; **-ens,** president (eccl.) c 1090, 1549; president (ac.) c 1350, c 1590; **presitens,** presiding c 800; **-entia,** rule, government c 1343, 1548; presidency (eccl.) 1309, c 1620; (title) 1328; **-entialiter,** as president a 1452; **-ium,** service of watch and ward 1412; **-eo,** to appoint as president 1357; **precedeo,** *for* **-eo,** to preside c 1340.
presign/aculum, preliminary rite (eccl.) c 1325; **-atus,** aforementioned c 655, c 1000. c 1218, 15c.; **-o,** to administer preliminary rites c 1325; to foretell, portend c 1125, c 1400; **-io,** to ennoble, make famous c 1200, 1241.
presinctus, *see* **precinctus.**
presise, *see* PRECIS
†**presistarchia,** (?) *for* **sitarchia,** scrip, wallet c 1150.
presitens, *see* **preses.**
pres/me, -sinius, *see* **prasina.**
‡**presmucum,** *cerussa* (alch.) 1652.
presolido, to make very firm 1001.
presolutus, paid in advance c 1365, 1421.
prespecificatus, previously specified 1432.
presp/eter, -iter, *see* **presbyter.**
presplendeo, to outshine c 1250.
press/a 1393, **-orium** 1237, 1409, **-ura** 1395, 1410, clothes-press; **-orium,** ‡"pile of cloth" c 1440; *1248, 1313, **-oria** 1295, (?) **-or** 1227, **-ura** 1272, 1418, cider-press; c 1258, 1305, (?)**-ura** c 1300, cheese-press; **-ura,** press (as instrument of torture) 1388; (?) printing-press 1501; *see also* PRAT, **presura; -im,** shortly, neatly 9c.; †**-ure,** oppressively 1346; **-uro,** to press 1241; **-o caseum** 1275; **-o vinum** 1278; **-us,** printed 1520; **primo,** *for* **premo,** to oppress 1418.
prest/antia, excellency (title) 1520; **-atio,** *payment, levy, exaction c 1162, 1420; 1241, 1374, *-**itum** 1086, 1441, **-itus** 1221, 1230, **-um** c 1150, 1419. imprest, advance payment or loan; **-atio juramenti** 1248, 1421, **p. sacramenti** 1220, taking an oath; **p. homagii et fidelitatis** (G.) 1279; **-um,** (?) lease 1086; **-abilis,** able to be lent 1374; performable 1620; **-aria,** lease of church land c 1030; **-arius,** borrower 1374, c 1376; **-imonium,** annuity to priest 1294, 1352; **-itor,** provider c 793; **-o,** to lend 732.

1086, 1458; (with *inf.*) to cause a 1408; **p. fidelitatem** 13c., **p. fidem** c 1178, c 1490; ***p. juramentum** 1183, 1419, ***p. sacramentum** c 1178, c 1412; *see also* **prestituo.**
prestatutus, previously fixed 1416.
prestig/ium, wonderful work c 730; pretext c 1070; trick c 1255; *c 1090, c 1450, **-iatura** c 1115, magic, illusion; **-ialiter,** by illusion c 1196; **-iatrix** 1513, 1528, †**prestitigatrix** 13c., witch; **-io,** to bewitch c 1190, c 1306; **-ior,** to practise magic c 1362.
prestimulo, to sting a 1408.
prestinus, *see* **pristinus.**
prest/itutio, authority 1344, **-ituo** c 1188, c 1220, †**-o** c 1220, to set in authority.
prestrenuus, very active c 1437.
pre/stulatio, *for* **-stolatio,** granting 14c.
prestum, *see* **prestantia.**
presuavis, very gracious a 1275.
presubstituo, to establish beforehand 870.
pre/subtilis (? *for* per-), very ingenious c 1109.
presul/, *bishop c 730, c 990. 1066, 1508; abbot c 950; **p. comitatus,** *"scire biscop"* c 1115; **p. Romanus,** Pope 7c.; **-aris** c 1130, c 1470, **-eus** 1089, 1156, episcopal; **-atus,** bishopric c 730, c 1060. c 1100, c 1540; **-o,** to appoint as bishop 12c., 1274; **-or,** to be bishop 14c.
presum, *see* **presens.**
presummus, highest 12c.
presum/ptio, premature action c 1115; usurpation c 1115; **-psio** c 1040, **-tio** 8c. 1219, *for* **-ptio,** presumption; **-ptibilis** 14c., **-ptivus** c 1212, c 1258, presumptive; **-ptivus** c 1150, 1545, **-ptuosus** c 1080, 1461, **-ptrix** (*f.*) (eccl.), presumptuous; **-ptior,** over-rash c 1090; **-ptive,** presumptively 793. c 1258, c 1405; c 1150, **-ptuose** 12c., 1461, presumptuously; **-ptuose,** presumably c 1340; **-ptuositas,** presumptuousness c 1395, 1461; **-ptor,** usurper c 1306, 1332; perpetrator c 1250; **-o** 597, 10c. 1070, c 1520, †**prerumo** c 730, to presume, venture, undertake; **p. de,** to presume on c 1160, c 1400; ‡**-ptuo,** "to mistake" 15c.
presuper/ior, a superior 1684; **-o,** to surpass c 1450.
presuppo/sitio, presupposition 13c., c 1365; *-**no,** to presuppose 1267, c 1540.
presura (pressura) 1223, 1345, **bresura** 1223, **prisura** 1233, rennet (Fr. *présure*); *cf.* PRESS
presusurro, to whisper softly c 1190.
***pretactus** 12c., 1540, †**pretictus** (? *for* predictus) 822, aforementioned; **pretango,** to mention before 15c.
pretax/atio, previous agreement c 1193; **-atus,** *appointed, agreed beforehand c 1130, 1419; *aforementioned c 950. 1145, c 1534; **-o,** to mention previously 1145, c 1225.
pretelo, *see* PROTEL
preteneo, to hold previously 1360, 1440; **pretineo,** to hold in readiness 1295.
preten/sio 1588, **-tio** c 1250, pretence; **-se,** in pretence 1378; c 1325, **-sive** c 1432, allegedly; *-**sus,** pretended, alleged 1347, 1588; **-do,** to indicate a 1250.
preter, (?) in accordance with 1433; **p.**

assensum, without agreement 1228, 1333; **p. propter,** approximately 1686.
pretergeneratio, abnormality c 1612, 1620.
pretergredior, to transgress c 1080, c 1375; to overlook, let pass 1438.
preterit/io, the past 13c., 1378; **-e,** in the past 1344; **-um,** preterite (gram.) c 1173.
preternatural/is, preternatural c 1360, 1622; **-iter,** preternaturally c 1360, 1620.
preternecessarius, superfluous c 1375, 1378.
preterrendus, awe-inspiring 1433.
pretersacramentalis, non-sacramental 1378.
pretersorium, stray animal c 700.
pretervolatio, flying past 1620.
pretestificatus, previously testified c 1265.
pretextus, reason or authority for act c 1273, 1542.
pretia-, *see* pretium.
pretictus, *see* pretactus.
pre/timeo, to fear more c 1160; **-timesco** (? *for* per-), to fear c 1410.
pretineo, *see* preteneo.
pretitul/atio, title, heading c 730. c 1096; **-atus,** aforementioned c 1090, 15c.; **-o,** to sign 1065; to foreordain 1006; to remark by way of preface c 1090; to assign c 1125, c 1410; to entitle c 1130, c 1250; to have a title to 12c.
preti/um (preci-) c 1110, c 1185, **p. natalis, p. nativitatis** c 1115, weregeld; **de -o,** valuable 1226, 1230; **aurum de -o** 1242; **praecium,** *for* **-um,** 1086; **-olum,** little gift 955. c 1200; **-amentum** c 1530, priseia 1260, appraisal; **-arius,** pecuniary c 1220; **-ator,** appraiser 1516; **-osa (est in conspectu Domini),** an antiphon 1505; **-atus,** valuable a 1408, **-or,** to be worth 1086; to make valuable c 1070; to prize 1378.
pretollo, to remove beforehand 1344.
pretor/, reeve, provost c 1155, 14c.; archbishop c 1218; mayor 1508,¹ 1588; **p. maximus,** God 810; **-ium,** moot-hall, council-chamber 1269, 1552; **sedes -ia,** office of bailiff 1203.
pretracto, to treat of, discuss, beforehand 12c., c 1365; (?) to discuss as prior (log.) c 1160.
pre/tristis (? *for* per-), very sad, very bitter 8c.
prettico, *see* predicatio.
preululo, to presage by howling c 1190.
pre/urgens (? *for* per-), very urgent c 1250.
pre/utilis (? *for* per-), very useful a 1100; **-utor,** to use beforehand c 600.
preval/entia, predominance a 1250, c 1258; **-enter,** predominantly 1344; **-eo** (with *inf.*), to be able to 8c., 948. c 1205, c 1440.
prevari/cantia 1378, 1427, **privaricatio** c 1296, a 1519, *for* **-catio,** error, transgression; **†-tor,** *for* **-cator,** opponent 12c.; **privaricatrix,** wrongful (*f.*) 1277.
prevasto, to waste, destroy, in advance 15c.
prevaticinor, to foretell 12c.
prevecto, to carry in front c 1200.
prevendo, to sell prematurely c 1223.
prevenor, to detect in advance 15c.
preventilo, to air, discuss c 1250.
preven/tio, rescue of stolen goods, *forfang* c 1115; anticipation 1255; helpful intervention, aid c 1185; unfavourable intervention,

impediment c 1265, c 1343; **-tor,** forerunner c 1345; **gratia -trix,** prevenient grace (theol.) c 1190, c 1340; **-tus (mortis),** intervention a 1186; **-ire facias,** name of a writ c 1458; **-io,** to occupy in advance c 1450; to anticipate, prepare for (a feast) 14c.; to prepare for, help forward, guide, impel c 600, 9c. c 1100, 1461; to forestall, be beforehand with 8c.; to forestall the market c 1150, 1258; to win over, court favour of 12c., 1356; **-to,** to prevent 1409; *see also* PROVEN
†prevetustatio (†privetustatus), old, timeworn 1267.
previ/a, -e, *see* previus.
previam, in the way c 1185, c 1200.
previd/entia c 1325, 1418, **previsio** 12c., 1595, prevision, foresight; **previsor,** superintendent, overseer 9c., c 1000. 12c.; **-eo,** to go beforehand 8c.; to intend 8c.; to take care of, provide for 9c. c 1125, 1564; *cf.* PROVIS
previgilia, day before the eve c 1400, 1452.
prevignus, *see* privignus.
previleg-, *see* PRIVILEG
previnco, to conquer beforehand c 1160.
previridans, of forward growth c 1125.
previs-, *see* PREVID
previ/us, (*subst.*) leader 6c., 8c. 12c., c 1200; (*adj.*) outdistancing 7c.; (?) primal c 1346; *previous, former c 1240, 1549, **-e,** previously 1378, 1433; **-a Phoebi,** dawn c 1180; **-o,** to go before 1125, 1244.
previvo, to live before 1235.
prevocatus, previously summoned 1297.
prevol/entia, -untas, -utio, antecedent will, predetermination 1344; **-o,** to will beforehand 12c., 1344.
prevolvor, to prostrate oneself before c 1317.
prewnum, *see* PRUN
prex, *see* precamen.
prey/a, (?) capture, round-up 1340; **-o,** to round up 1340.
preyntum, *see* PRINT
priapus 1424, ‡15c., **preapus** 1209, genital organ.
prichpottus, four-gallon vessel 15c.
pricka, pin 1330; spur c 1335; **cantus precatus,** prick-song 1504.
prid/a 1361, 1464, **preda** 1233, form of mortgage or conditional sale (W.); **-o,** to mortgage (W. *prydau*) 1416, 15c.
prid/ie, (?) *for* **-em,** long ago 1274; 1253, **†-ium** 15c., previously.
prigg/um 1288, c 1395, **-ius** 1225, 'prig', brad, flat nail.
prikettus 1300, 1352, **prekatus** 1466, 'pricket', (candle stuck on) spike; 1353, 1369, **p. cervi (de cervo)** 1285, 1334, **p. dami, p. dame** 1287, 1334, 'pricket', hart or buck of second year.
prim/a, first day after c 730; (?) first day of month 1252; *(canonical hour or office of) prime (mon.) c 950, c 1006. c 1080, 1556; **dimidia p.,** half-prime 1385, 1419; **p. secundaria** (mon.) c 1290; ‡**p. rosa,** ‡**p. veris** 15c., ‡**-arosa** 1483, **-ula** c 1250, 1634, **-ula veris** a 1250, 1538, daisy *or* primrose; **ad -am,** *f.l. for* **ad firmam,** 1389; **-agium** 1297, 1537, **†brimmagium** 1300, 'primage', allowance for loading or

unloading; **-alis,** of the first rank c 1180; ‡**-ales** (*pl.*), hallucinatory bodies 1652; **-ariola,** primipara (med.) a 1250; **-arie** c 1363, **-ario** c 1267, primarily; **-arium,** **-arius** 1323, a 1564, **-erum** 1323, primer (eccl.); **-arius,** first, primary p c 1250, c 1470; **lapis p.,** foundation-stone p 1330, c 1400; **-arius,** (*subst.*) chief man c 730. c 1194; leader in psalmody a 615; c 1185, **-as forestarum** 13c., head forester; **-as,** (*adj.*) chief 9c.; **ecclesia -as** c 1188, **sedes -as** 1072, c 1080 (eccl.); **-as,** (*subst.*) magnate, noble c 730. 1124, 1586; 6c. c 1090, 1586, **-atus** c 793, primate (eccl.); **p. basilice** 961, 1031; ***p. totius Anglie** c 1125, 1535, **p. t. Britannie** c 1072, c 1250, archbishop of Canterbury; ***p. Anglie,** archbishop of York 1267, 1333; **p. Hibernie,** archbishop of Dublin c 1265; **p. totius regni Scotie,** archbishop of St. Andrews 1536; ***-atia** c 1180, 15c., **-atialitas** 1531, ***-atus** 749, 10c. 1119, c 1580, primacy, office of primate; **-atus,** ruling class c 1000; **-aticus** 1262, **-atialis** c 1204, c 1520, **prematialis** 1496, of or for a primate (eccl.); **-atio,** first appearance of new moon 13c., 1267; priming (arch.) 1355; **-ator,** stevedore 1449; **-eintentionaliter,** as of first intention (log.) 1516; **-evus,** primeval, original c 1150, 1511; oldest c 1200; ~-**ecerius** 953, **-ichaerius** 955, †**-icerus** c 1400, *for* **-icerius,** chief; **-icerius,** dean (eccl.) 1278, c 1444; **p. pape** 1277, **p. sedis apostolice** 640, 802, papal chancellor or protonotary; **p. martyrum,** protomartyr c 1090; **-icola,** first inhabitant c 950; **-ifestus,** feast on first day of month 1518; **-igeni** (*pl.*), Adam and Eve c 1160; **-ipilarius** 14c., **-ipilaria** (*f.*) a 1205, 14c., chief; **-ipotens,** the Almighty 14c.; **-itas,** priority, primacy (log.) 1267, a 1361; final cause c 1300; primacy (eccl.) c 1343, 1427; (title) c 1350; **-itius,** young c 1115, c 1362; **premitie,** *for* **-itie,** c 1285, **-itiva** (*n. pl.*) 7c., first-fruits; **-itiva,** enforced new-year gifts c 1250; **-itivus,** original a 1250; **-itive,** originally a 1250; ***-itus** c 1077, 1549, **premitus** 1529, †**-ito** 14c., first (*adv.*), in the first place; ~-**odictus,** first-mentioned 1215; ***-ogenitura,** (right of) primogeniture 1169, 1461; ***-ogenitus,** (*subst.*) first-born c 1170, 16c.; **-onatus,** (*adj.*) first-born 1296; **-ordialis,** original (eccl.); **-oregenitus,** first-regenerated c 1500; **-ule,** at first c 700; **-um mobile** c 1250, 1620, **p. motabile** c 1362, **-us motus** c 1250 (phil.); **-um movens** a 1292, **-us motor** 1252, 1518; **-i** (*pl.*), the Ancients 7c.; **-us,** (*subst.*) magnate 1150, 15c. **p. de assisa,** foreman of jury 13c.; **-itio,** to initiate c 1160, 15c.; **-o,** to fix first day of new moon c 1265; to prime (arch.) 1383; *see also* PRESS

primnum, *see* **prymnum.**

prin/ceps, alderman 7c., 1040. c 1115; bishop 12c.; **p. militie,** *pennteulu* (W.) a 1300; †**p. regis,** (?) atheling 967, 1018; **-cipissa** c 1400, 1543, **-cissa** 1321, 1467, princess; **p. civitatum,** capital city 1266; **-cipativus,** princely 9c.; **-cipatus,** kingliness

948; lordship (*astr.*) c 1150; **-cipor** (with *gen.*), to rule over 9c.; **-cipo** 1424, 1461, †**-cipior** 12c. c 1380, *for* **-cipor,** to rule.

principal/itas, *headship (ac.) c 1250, c 1450; governance 1547; seat of governance c 790; **-e,** principal (of debt) 1271, 1338; principal action (leg.) 1279, 1324; essence (phil.) c 1270; principal point in argument (log.) c 1343, 1347; original document c 1444, 1549; principal feast (eccl.) 1363; mortuary payment (eccl.) 1292, 1426; **-ior,** superior 893. 1321; **-is,** emperor c 800; principal person, chief, 7c. c 1125, 1549; principal (ac.) c 1282, c 1580; **judex p.** (eccl.) 1043; color p., argent *or* sable (her.) p 1394, a 1446; **dominus p.** (feudal) 1230; **homagium -e** 1461; **littere -es,** originals 1437; **nomine -i** 1232, 1408, **n. -ii** c 1300, (?) *for* **n. -is,** by way of mortuary; *see also* DEB, I **festum, lectus, sors;** †**principibilis,** *for* **-is,** c 1250; **-iter,** as a principal (not an accessory) c 1265, 1289; **-itivus,** of a principal (ac.) c 1432.

princip/ium (**regni**), capital city 12c.; selected passage c 1197; inception, admission to teach (ac.) 13c., 1420; **p. (efficiens et) materiale** 1267, **p. motionis** 1334, efficient cause; *see also* **petitio; p. nasi,** base of nose a 1250; **-ificus,** original 9c.; **-iabilis,** deducible from a first principle p 1300; **-iatio** a 1233, c 1365, †**-atio** c 1362, origination, acting as first principle (phil.); **-iantive** 1344, **-iative** p 1300, a 1361, so as to originate; **-iativus,** originative, causative c 1300, c 1362; **-iator,** originator c 1290; **-iata** (*pl.*), derivatives of first principles c 1300; **-io,** to initiate a 1275, c 1488; to deduce or derive from first principles c 1250, 1374.

print/a 1485, **-um** 1401, **prentum, preyntum** 1355, print, stamp; **prenta,** die (for coinage) 1404; **-um** 1463, **prentum** 1391, print, boss (on mazer).

priodarius, *see* PROPRI

prior/, *prior (mon.) 825. c 1090, 1536; **p. capitalis** c 1478, **p. major** c 1266, chief prior (under abbot); **p. claustralis** 1353, c 1530, **p. claustri** 1072, c 1330, sub-prior; **p. tertius** (mon.) c 1266, 1532; **p. quartus** (mon.) c 1266, c 1336; **p. generalis** 1237, 1312, **p. provincialis** 1235, 1511, officials of mendicant orders; **p. juratorum,** foreman of jury 1288; **-ulus,** petty prior (mon.) c 1430, a 1452; **a -i,** deductively (log.) c 1300; **-a** (*pl.*), Aristotle's *Prior Analytics* 13c., 1301; **-alis,** of a prior (mon.) c 1260, c 1465; ***-issa** 1179, 1543, **-essa** 1287, c 1403, prioress; **p. tertia** 1520; **-issalis,** of a prioress 1524; ~***-atus** c 980, 993. c 1125, 1526, **-itas** 1272, 1497, office of prior (mon.); **p. claustralis** c 1400; **p. provincialis** a 1328; ***-atus** c 1140, 1543, **-ia** 1212, 1415, priory; **-issatus,** prioress's house 1543; **-atus** c 705. c 1130, c 1400; **-itas** 1225, c 1444, priority, precedence; **-itas** (*coll.*), forbears, ancestry 1282, 15c.; capital, *caput* (of estate) 1312; **gradus -isticus,** scale of priority c 1365.

pris/a *1100, c 1448, **priza** 1254, **-ia** 1421, **proisa** 1330, prise (wine, *etc.*, taken by way

of custom); **p. antiqua** 1255, 1369; **p. recta**
1252, 1300; **p. averiorum** (W.) 1304; **-a**,
prize, booty 1459; **-agium**, prisage, wine-
custom 1503, 1519; **-alie** (*pl.*) reprisals
1421; **-ia** 1313, **-io** 1281, 1313, seizure,
imprisonment; **-e** (*pl.*) **navium** (Norm.)
1198; **-ius**, prisoner 1242; **-us**, seized as
prise 1307, 1327.
Priscillianista c 1250, †**Piscillianista** 12c.,
Priscillianist (heretic).
priscus, (?) old, worn out a 750.
priseia, *see* PRETI
prisma, prism 1620.
pris/o c 1210, c 1370, *-**ona** 1198, c 1448,
-onaria (G.) 1310, prison; *see also* **sueta**;
-ona arta 1399; **p. bona**, (?) alleviation of
prison 1277; **p. fortis et dura** 1368; **p.
libera** 1269, 1331; **-o** *1130, c 1470, **-ona**,
-onus c 1290, 1419, **prizonus** 1313,
*-**arius** c 1185, c 1458, **-onaria** (*f.*) 1422,
a 1446, prisoner; **-onarius**, **-onator**, jailer
c 1290; **-onabilis**, liable to imprisonment
1292; **-onagium**, imprisonment *or* prison-
due (G.) 1289, 1315; **-ono**, to imprison
1196, 1245.
pristinum, *see* **pistatio**.
pristinus, former: **prestinus** c 1250, 1510.
prisura, *see* **presura**.
prius, at first c 1330; (*prep.*) before c 1220,
c 1343; *see also* **per prius**.
privari-, *see* PREVARI
priv/atio, deprivation of office (esp. eccl.)
1265, c 1520; c 850. c 1258, 1267, **-atus**
p 1394, privation, lack; **-abilis**, capable of
privation (log.) c 1367; liable to deprivation
(eccl.) 1425; **-ans**, depriver c 1332; **-antia**,
(*pl.*) privative opposites (log.) 1610; (*f. s.*)
definition in negative terms (log.) 790;
-ate 1041. c 1194, c 1362, **-atim** c 1266,
1559, **-iter** c 1305, 15c., privately, in private;
-icarnium, *see* **carniprivium** (*s.v.* caro);
-itas, private capacity 1333; **-ata** a 1200, 13c.,
-eta c 1450, privy (*see also* **camera, domus,
sella**); **-ata** (*pl.*) 1221, 1241, **-itates** 1241,
schedule of suspects secretly indicted at
eyre (*cf.* **secreta diei**); **-atum** 1459, 1479,
sigillum -atum 1204, 1586, privy seal;
consilium p., Privy Council 1324, 1555;
-atus, close friend, confidant c 1300, p 1348;
dies -atus, week-day 1072, c 1325; **-o**, to
be deprived c 1270; **p. de**, to deprive of
(office) c 1290, c 1400.
privetustatus, *see* **prevetustatus**.
privignus, step-son: **prevignus** (**previn-
gnus**) c 1325, c 1430.
privileg/ium, charter or bull 897. a 1070,
c 1450; area of jurisdiction c 1102, 1567;
liberty to print 1518; **p. apostolicum**,
papal exemption from episcopal jurisdiction
(mon.) c 1160; **p. clericale** 1259, 1424, **p.
clericatus** 1273, p 1340, **p. ecclesie** 1368,
privilege (benefit) of clergy; **p. universitatis** (ac.) c 1275; **privelegium** 1258,
priveligium 1231, **previlegium** (Sc.)
1420, 1461, *for* **-um**; **-ius**, intimate, special
c 1000; **-ialis**, privileged c 1196; **-ialiter**,
by way of privilege c 1250, 1429; **-iatio**, grant
of privilege c 1255, 1378; **-iatus**, privileged
.tenant (G.) 1267; **-io** 11c., a 1564, **previlegio**
c 1540, to privilege, grant a privilege.

priz-, *see* **pris-**
pro, *because of 597, c 960. 1086, c 1330;
concerning, as regards 7c. c 1220, c 1450;
for (with verbs of going or sending) c 1100,
1537; for (with *gerundive*) 1086, 1549; for
(with *inf.*) c 1185, 15c.; during c 1370,
c 1450; (in attributive phrase) **canis pro
cervis** 1393; **c. pro ripa** 1332; **equus
pro sella** 1343; **miles pro corpore** 1474,
1484; **mola pro mustardo** 1314; **obba pro
vino** (wine-jar) c 1450; **sagitta pro bosco**
1391; **sella pro carecta** 1338; **serura pro
equis** 1316, 1388;
(various phrases) **p. amore**, gratis c 1330;
p. causa, for the purpose (of) c 1332, 1454;
p. Deo, in God's name c 1219; **p. die illo**,
for that day c 1390; **p. eo quod** 1086, 1580,
p. eo quia c 1285, because; **p. eodem
modo**, in the same way a 1446; **p. escangio
de**, in exchange for 1086; **p. et contra**, for
and against c 1390; **p. expensis**, at the
expense of 1352; **p. foribus**, at the outset
c 1218; **p. lapsu casuum**, before the opportunity passes c 1390; **p. medietate**, as to half
13c., 1253; †**p. sic quod** 1276, †**p. sic ut**
c 1265, on condition that (*cf.* per); **p. quali**,
in what capacity 1275; **p. tali** c 1340, **p. tanto**
c 1332, on that account; **p. tanto quod**,
for as much as c 1410, c 1470; **p. vita**, on
pain of death c 1115; *see also* **beneplacitum; libitum; pars; placitum; posse;
volitio; votum**;
(with *adj.* or *ppl.*) **p. certo** 11c., 1239, **p.
constanti** c 1300, c 1430, **p. constantissimo**
c 1365, **p. firmo** c 1250, c 1430, certainly;
p. futuro 1345; **p. perpetuo** c 1364, c 1470
(*see also* PERPET), **p. †perpetuito** 1465, **p.
sempiterno** c 1470; **p. presenti** c 1380,
c 1446; **p. graviori**, to make matters more
serious c 1390; **p. meliori**, to improve
matters 1347; **p. indifferenti**, indifferently
1330; *p. indiviso, collectively, in common
1237, 1329; **pro malo**, amiss c 1390; **p. toto**,
wholly c 1362; **p. vero**, truly c 1250;
(with *adv.*) **pro frustra**, (deemed) as of no
effect c 1390; **p. invicem**, mutually c 1080,
1359; **p. nunc**, for the present c 1292, 1450;
*p. tunc, then, for that time 12c., 1545;
p. semper, for ever c 1343, 1346.
proago, *see* PREACT
proalo, *see* **puralea**.
proaro, *see* **prooro**.
proastium, suburb (προάστειον) c 1302.
proaula, porch c 1130, ‡15c.
proava, great-grandmother 1266, 15c.
prob/a 1198, **-um** 1205, 1378, **-amen** c 1450,
-amentum 1200, a 1250, (certificate of)
proof, evidence; **-a**, (?) sample (of grain)
taken for testing 1274; **-abilis**, demonstrable, conclusive c 1115, 1451; c 1077,
1200, **provabilis** 740, worthy of approval;
-abilissimus c 990; **-abilitas**, qualification
for approval c 1297; **-atio**, probate of will
1274, 1684; noviitate (eccl.) 1223, c 1450; pro-
bation of fellow (ac.) c 1390; wager of battle
c 1178; **p. eucaristialis**, ordeal by holy
wafer (A.S. *corsnæde*) c 1102; **p. simpla,
p. tripla**, forms of ordeal by boiling water
c 1150; **-ationarius**, probationer (ac.)
c 1565; *-**ator** 1155, a 1452, **-atrix** (*f.*) 1155,

'approver', accuser of accomplice (leg.);
-atorium, novices' quarters (mon.) 1221,
c 1325; **terminus -atorius,** term allowed
for proof (leg.) 1684; **testis p.** (leg.) 1684;
-ilio, free tenant c 1140;

    -itas, competence *or* wealth c 1180,
c 1400; prowess, doughty deed a 1142,
a 1408; **p. regia** (title) 15c.; **-i** (*pl.*), free
men, warriors 13c., c 1400; **-us,** *preu,*
doughty a 1142, c 1470; **p. homo,** good
man (leg.) c 1105, 1573;

    -o, to prove (a will) c 1303, 1535; to
prove ownership of (impounded beasts)
1372; to prove (oneself to be) c 1185; to
prove by judicial combat or ordeal 1086,
1201; **p. per corpus** 1201, 1221; **p.
duellum,** to wage battle c 1400.

probat/us, sheep (πρόβατον) c 1220; **-icus,** of
sheep c 1200, a 1452.

probenda, *see* prebenda.

problema, problem: **probleuma** 1267,
c 1520, **proplema** c 1443.

prob/ose, *for* **-rose,** p 1330, c 1400.

proc/acitas, shameless deed c 1190; **-ator,**
seducer a 1350.

procancellar/ius, vice-chancellor (ac.) c 1549,
c 1551; **-iatus,** vice-chancellorship c 1549.

procassium, *see* purcacium.

‡**procatarricus,** procatarctic (med.) 15c.

procedo, *see* PROCESS

1 **procello** (*1st conj.*) to rave, storm c 1180,
c 1435; to sweep along c 1180.

2 **pro/cello** (*3rd conj.*), to overwhelm, reprove
12c., c 1360; (? *for* pre-) to exalt c 1325.

proceneticus, *see* proxeneta.

procer/, (*adj.*) chief c 1190; (*subst.*) thane
c 1102; **-us,** lofty, noble c 810; *preu,*
doughty 13c.

procerno, to survey, direct c 810.

process/io, act of proceeding 9c.; continuing
proceedings (leg.) c 1400; progression,
progressive realization (phil.) c 850. p 1300;
*procession (eccl.) c 1006. c 1070, c 1565;
right to hold procession (eccl.) 12c., c 1248;
***p. Spiritus Sancti** (theol.) c 1118, c 1443;
-ibilis, capable of proceeding (theol.) p 1300;
-ionabilis 1345, **-ionalis** c 1125, 1423,
-ionarius c 1220, 1360, used or taking part
in processions (eccl.); ***-ionale** c 1200,
c 1432, **liber -ionalis** 1417, 15c., **libellus
p.** 1317, **-ionarium, -ionarius** c 1306, 1472,
a processional, procession-book (eccl.);
-ionabiliter 1435, ***-ionaliter** c 1172,
1461, **-ive** c 1266, p 1340, in procession;
-ive, in due order c 1255; progressively
1344, 1427; **-ivus,** favourable to advance
(astr.) a 1233; **motus p.,** progressive
movement c 1250, 1344;

    -us, procession, emanation (theol.) 12c.;
process, procedure 1286, c 1460; *action,
process, proceedings (leg.) c 1130, 1684;
record of proceedings (leg.) 1268, 1385;
p. dicendi, argument 1344; **p. in infinitum**
infinite regress (log.) a 1233; ***p. temporis**
c 1188, c 1503; **-us** (*pl.*) **bellici,** warlike
proceedings (G.) 1296; **-um do,** to make
request, pray c 793; **-iono,** to go in procession (eccl.) 1389, c 1432; **procedo,** to
proceed (leg.) c 1115, 1684; to behave
c 1250, 1461; to be valid p 1330, c 1343; to

proceed, emanate (theol.) c 1250; (with *inf.*)
to proceed, go on to c 1310, c 1470; †to
declare, display (? *for* prodo) a 1250, c 1250;
p. contra, to take proceedings against (leg.)
c 1250, c 1462; **proscido,** (?) *for* **p. c** 1195.

proch (†**proth**), *for* pro (*interj.*), 13c., 1485.

Prochristus, opponent of Antichrist 1344.

procidens, preying (her.) c 1495.

procinct/us, military service, fyrd 11c. 12c.;
equipment, array c 1150, 1200; attack,
onset 12c., 1276; **in -u,** on the point of
c 1204, c 1320; **-oria** (*pl.*), fortifications 1204;
procingo, to prepare c 1160, 1218; **p. me,**
to dress in preparation c 1250; *see also*
precinctus.

proclam/atio, claim, plea (leg.) c 1115;
denunciation (mon.) c 1266; *1199, 1608,
-a 1608, †**preclamatio** c 1102, proclamation; **-ator** 1300, 1506, **p. curie** 1516, crier;
-atorie, by way of proclamation 1264;
litere -atorie, letters declaratory 1309,
1336; **-ito** a 1100, **-o** c 1290, 1562, to
proclaim, announce; **-o,** to protest c 1150;
to denounce in chapter (mon.) c 1080,
c 1362; to summon by proclamation 1283;
p. (caput), to set a price on 1283.

proclivium, descent c 700.

†**pro/cognosco** (? *for* pre-), to foreknow 11c.

†**pro/compleo** (? *for* pre-), to complete 1316.

proconsul/, sheriff 12c.; municipal official
(Sc.) 1526, (Baltic) c 1404, 1498; **forum -is,**
county court a 1160.

procre/amen, offspring c 1470; **-atio,** appointment (G.) 1254; **-ativus,** generative a 1200,
c 1200; **-o,** to appoint (G.) 1254.

procrucio, to crucify, afflict 1308.

procul/, far (in time) c 1400; †**preculdubio,**
for **p. dubio,** c 1200; ‡**-ius,** born during
father's absence 15c.

procur/atio *c 1250, 1461, **-amentum** 1275,
15c., procurement, instigation, agency;
p. juratorum, suborning of jurors 15c.;
-atio, stewardship 737. a 1142, 1410;
harvest 1305; c 1102, 1397, **-ata** a 1250,
sustenance; corrody (mon.) c 1133, c 1155;
*12c., 1684, **-atia** c 1250, 1338, **-antia**
c 1255, **-agium** 1535, maintenance, entertainment, esp. of visiting officials (eccl.), *or*
payment in lieu; c 1250, 1425, **-atia** 1348,
annual payment to papal nuncio, legate or
collector; 1219, 1318, **-atia** 1342, ***-atorium**
1259, 1684 proxy; **littere de -atia** 1220,
1342, l. **-atorie** c 1235, 15c., **-atorie** 1284,
letters of proxy; **-ativus,** productive, tending
to promote a 1250;

    -ator, -atrix (*f.*), provoker of suits in
ecclesiastical courts 1390; **-ator,** *proctor in
ecclesiastical courts 12c., 1684; *proctor
(ac.) 1248, 1550; official (steward) of guild
or chantry 1284, 1491; head of lay brothers
in Carthusian house 1200, 1570; Franciscan
friar charged with begging for the house
c 1250; layman holding property, *etc.,* on
behalf of Franciscan house 1232, 1282; **p.
cleri (de clero),** proctor in convocation
1413, 15c.; **p. ecclesie,** churchwarden
1349, 1527; **p. fiscalis** (Sc.) 1434, 1552;
p. f. Camere Apostolice 1427; **-atoria**
1499, **-atorium** 1399, office of proctor
(mon.); **-atorius,** of proxy c 1235, 15c.;

of maintenance c 1423; proctorial (ac.)
c 1593; **-atrix**, agent, proctor (*f.*) c 1340,
c 1430;
-o, *to procure, provide, bring about
c 730. c 1090, 1549; (with *inf.*) to endeavour
8c., 11c. c 1188, c 1340; c 1102, 14c., **p. in**
c 1321, c 1370, to entertain, provide with
maintenance; to act as proctor (ac.) c 1460;
to procure, suborn (jurors or electors) 1285,
1400; (?) to accuse 1526; **p. paginam**, to
produce a pageant 1420; **p. placitum**, to
provoke a suit (leg.) c 1290, 1300.
procursus, course, progress c 1196, c 1250;
see also **percursus.**
procurvus, (?) bowing low c 950.
prodecanus, vice-dean (ac.) 1560.
prodecessor, *see* **predecessor.**
prodeo, to come to be c 1212.
prodessentia, use, advantage c 1367.
*prodigal/itas**, prodigality c 1160, 15c.; **-is**,
prodigal, lavish c 1540; **-iter**, prodigally
c 1250, 1478.
prodigi/um, proof (τεκμήριον) 1344; **prode-
gium**, *for* -um, 1510; **-aster**, miracle-
monger, trickster 1620.
prodit/io alta, high treason 1399, 1583;
†**productio**, *for* -io, treason 1280; *-iona-
liter 1283, 15c., †-ialiter 1282, -iose c 1192,
1461, *-orie c 1192, 1569, treasonably;
-iosus c 1250, c 1470, *-orius c 1250, 1609,
treasonable, traitorous; **-rix**, traitress a 1142.
produc/tio 9c. 1267, c 1470, **-entia** c 1370,
production, bringing forth; production of
witnesses (leg.) c 1200, 13c.; production
(math.) c 1250; *see also* **proditio; -ibilis**,
producible, able to be brought into existence
c 1290, c 1362; **-ibilitas**, producibility
c 1360, c 1362; **-tivitas, -itas**, creative
power c 1360; **-tive**, by creation 1610;
-tivus, productive, creative a 1250, c 1444;
-torius, for production (of witnesses) a 1452;
-o, to produce by multiplication (math.)
c 1150; **p. ad actum**, to actualize (phil.)
a 1250; **p. sectam**, to bring suit, supporting
evidence (leg.) 1200, 1419.
proeg/umenus, antecedent: †**propigmenus**
15c.; **proheceticus**, *for* -eticus, (?) governing (gram.) 13c.
proeligo, *see* PREELECT
proemi/alis, prefatory 1344, 1427; *prohemium**, *for* -um, c 980. c 1125, c 1450;
cf. **hemum, prophemium.**
proemineo, *see* PREEMIN
profa/men, utterance *or* prediction c 1450;
-tus, prophecy c 950.
profan/atio (prophan-), profanation c 1200,
c 1325; **-ator**, profaner, contemner 1174,
c 1250; **-o**, to be false to 704.
profect/io, advancement 9c. c 1250, c 1545;
-ibilis, (?) originating c 1290; †**provecticius**,
for -icius (leg.), c 1446; *see also* **dos; -ivus**,
causing growth p 1263; ‡**-um**, gut, "giblet"
1483; **-ualiter**, profitably c 1306; *-us
c 1170, 1518, †**perfectus** 1252, *proficuum
1086, 1549, **profecuum** 12c., **profiquum**
1282, †**proficium** 1333, 1419, †**perficuum**
1467, †**preficuum** 1409, †**profiscuum** 15c.,
proficuus 1286, c 1545, profit; **-us privatus**
private employment c 1110; **proficuus**
a 1100, 1549, **profitabilis** (via) 1263,

†**proficubilis** 1359, profitable, serviceable;
proficuarius, beneficiary c 1250; **proficio**,
to progress in study (ac.) 1417; to set out
(*for* **proficiscor**) 1274; *see also* PREFECT
profer-, *see* **profrum.**
profess/io, profession of canonical obedience
by bishop, *etc.*, c 1072, c 1444 (*see also* **capa**);
profession of vows (mon.) c 1100, 1440;
record of profession (mon.) 1401; rule or
order (mon.) c 1160, c 1460; admission to
teach *or* subject taught (ac.) 1302, 1577;
-or, one who professes a faith c 1195, 17c.;
one who takes the vows (mon.) c 1170,
c 1400; one who makes a business of 12c.,
1345; *professor (ac.) 1265, 1583; **-orius**,
professional 1620; **-us**, (one who has)
professed (mon.) 1179, 1537; **profiteor**, to
confess (eccl.) c 1115, c 1434; to profess
canonical obedience 1121, c 1190; to make
profession (mon.) c 1250, c 1483; c 1330,
c 1467, †**profiteo** 13c., to receive professions
(mon.); to profess, lecture (ac.) c 1135, c 1550.
profest/um c 1197, 1481, **dies -us** c 1220,
c 1370, eve of a festival (eccl.).
profic-, *see* PREFECT
profilo, *see* PURFIL
†**profinellus**, (?) *f.l.* for **prope nullus**, c 1180.
profitabilis, *see* PROFECT
profiteor, *see* PROFESS
profligo, to dispel c 1087.
proflo, to blow (a mus. instrument) c 550.
profluxus, flow (fig.) c 730; flux (med.)
c 1362; **venter profluvius**, diarrhoea 8c.
profodio, to dig up (a road) 1354.
*prof/rum 1256, 1495, **-erum** 1271, **poroffra**
c 1285, **puroffrus** 1279, 1287, **purofrium**
1255, proffer (provisional payment) at
Exchequer; **-erum**, proffer (leg.), offer to
convict criminal 13c., c 1290; **-ero**, to
lengthen (in pronunciation) 1267; to proffer,
produce in court (leg.) 1201, 1322; **p. legem**
to offer to wage law (leg.) 1322; *cf.* **prolatio.**
profucatus, *see* **prefucatus.**
profug/a, exile 5c.; fugitive c 1150, c 1295;
-io, driving out c 1115; **-o**, to put to flight,
banish c 1212, 1461.
profulgentissimus, *see* PREFUL
profund/itas, *depth c 1190, c 1443; bottom
(of ditch) 1378; foundation (arch.) 12c.;
hollow c 1290; depth (fig.), profundity c 730.
c 1080,c1377; **-alis**, possessing depth, extending downwards c 1380; **-aliter**, downwards,
in depth 1378; **-atio**, deep penetration c 1237,
a 1250; **-e**, gravely (of offence) a 1120; deeply
(of sleep) 12c.; **p. literatus** 14c.; **-issime**,
most deeply c 730; **-ius**, lower down (on the
page) 12c.; **-a** (*pl.*), entrails, vitals a 1100;
-um, hold (naut.) 1354; **-us**, deep (of colour)
1438; bogged, foundrous a 1215, 1424;
-o, to deepen 1253, c 1400; (?) to enhance,
intensify a 1250; to plunge, engulf c 1250,
1427.
†**profusor** *or* †**protrusor** (*dep.*), to pierce deep
c 600.
progeniculo, to fall on one's knees c 800.
progen/ies, stock of descent, *wyrion* (W.) 1334;
clan, sept (Ir.) 1350; **-ia** c 730, **projenies**
c 1218, *for* -ies; **linea -ialis**, pedigree 1412;
-itura, primogeniture 1461; **-itus**, first-born
c 1239.

progetto, see PERJACT

prognos/co, to foreknow c 730; †-**se,** sign c 730.

prognostic/on (pronostic-), verse read at bishop's consecration, regarded as augury c 1125, c 1250; -**um** c 950. c 1130, c 1370, **prenosticum** c 1160, c 1450, -**atio** a 1233, 1252, **prenosticatio** c 1302, 1461, **prognostria** 1610, prognostication, prognostic, presage, prediction; -**um** 13c., -**atio** c 1320, prognosis (med.); **prenosticum,** motto c 1250; -**alis,** auspicious 1200; **prenostice,** prophetically 1380; -**us** 9c. c 1165, c 1345, **prenosticus** c 1185, c 1395, -**ativus** 15c., prognostic, prophetic; -**o** a 1100, 1521, **prenostico** 1250, c 1436, †**pernoscito** 1290, to prognosticate, presage, foretell.

programmatizo, to proclaim publicly 1396.

progress/io, expedition p 1377; progression (astr.) a 1233; **p. arithmetica, p. geometrica, p. musica** 1686; -**ionarius** a 1200, -**ivus** p 1300, 1622, progressive (astr.); -**ivus,** moving forwards c 1300, 1686; **voluntas -iva,** (?) active will a 1228; -**or,** (?) sensory nerve 9c.; -**us,** 'progress', tour, round of visits 1447, 1547.

progymnasma, essay 1518.

proheceticus, see PROEG

prohemium, see PROEMI

proheres, one in place of heir c 760.

proheresis, choice, election (phil.) (προαίρεσις) c 1300, 1380.

prohibit/io regia, writ of prohibition c 1357, 15c.; -**ive,** by way of prohibition c 1357; -**ivus,** prohibitive, obstructive 13c., c 1370; -**orius,** prohibitory 1462; **littere -orie** 1222, c 1400; -**um,** prohibition c 1180, c 1192; **prohib/eo,** to refuse 8c.; -**eor** (dep.), to prevent c 1000.

proicio, see PROJECT

proinvicem, see pro invicem.

proisa, see prisa.

projactatus, tossed by sea c 1250; see also PERJACT

project/io, projection, transmutation (alch.) 1267, ‡1652; planning c 1450; -**ile,** a projectile 1686; -**or,** thrower c 1340; one who throws down 1464; -**um** c 1200, 1283, **prejectum** 1289, **perjectum** 1276, 1315, **pergetus, perchetus** 1293 (G.), projecting roof; -**us maris,** jetsam, wreck a 1100; -**us,** cast up, washed ashore 1343, 1395; **terra -a (de silva),** land reclaimed 1086; **proicio,** to project (alch.) c 1320; to frame, draw up (leg.) 1280; to subtract (math.) c 815; **p. sortem,** to cast lots 1136, 1312; **p. turbas,** to 'cast' peats 1435.

projudex, deputy judge 13c.

projudico, see PREJUDIC

projuramentum, see PREJUR

prolapsus temporis, lapse of time 1345.

prolat/io, bearing 6c.; offer c 1365; production of document (leg.) c 1290; **p. major, p. minor,** extension of semibreve to equal three or two minims (mus.) 1351; **p. sententie** c 1328, 1684, †**perlatio s.** 1428, pronouncement of sentence, -**or,** utterer, spokesman c 1210, 13c.; **prolo,** to bring forth or forward c 550; cf. **profrum.**

prolecta, see plecta.

‡**prolect/atio,** extraction 1652; ‡-**o,** to extract by rarefaction (alch.) 1652.

prolector, see prelector.

‡**prolego,** to outlaw 15c.

prolegomena (pl.), preface 1610.

prolemp/sis, prolepsis, anticipation c 1200, 13c.; -**ticus,** proleptic 13c.

prol/es, genealogy c 1218; the Son (theol.) 11c., 12c.; **P. Virginea** 1252; -**is** 8c., -**es** (pl.) 1301, c 1400, offspring; -**etarius** c 1188, c 1300, -**ificus** 1620, prolific; -**ificatio,** procreation c 1375, c 1500; -**ifico,** to procreate c 1370.

prolix/ia, extension c 1300; -**itas,** procrastination 1254; †**proluxus,** lengthy 1324; -**o,** to prolong (time) 14c., 1415.

prolocut/io c 1115, 15c., **prolucutio** 1309, agreement, negotiation; utterance, statement c 1258; -**or,** *spokesman c 1170, 1431; advocate (leg.) 1200, 1398; sponsor at baptism 12c.; speaker (of Parliament) 1421, 1535 (cf. **prelocutor**); -**orium** 1497, **locus -orialis** 1506, parlour (mon.); -**us,** agreed, arranged 1201, c 1333.

prolog/us, preface, introduction to book 12c., c 1510; -**ismus,** preliminary statement 1344; ‡-**izo,** to speak a prologue 1483.

prolong/atio a 1120, 1620, **prolungatio** (G.) 1279, extension (in time), postponement; -**abilis,** able to be prolonged c 1270; -**us,** (?) oblong c 1362; lengthy, tedious c 1150; -**o** (bibl.), **prolungo** 1274, to extend (in time); to postpone c 1125, 1461; to put off, keep (someone) waiting c 1250, c 1362; 5c. a 1100, 1305, **prolungo** 1511, to extend (in space); to remove 5c.; to dispossess 1215 (cf. **elongo**); to purloin 1384, c 1404.

proludium, (?) by-play c 1125.

prolumen, (?) wick 1310.

proluxus, see PROLIX

promachus, champion 1654.

promagister, Dominican official 1296.

proman/atio c 1500, -**antia** 13c., emanation, effluence; -**o,** to emanate, flow forth c 1500, 1518.

promeo in, to turn towards (of talk) c 1125.

promercalis dies, market-day 1608.

promeritor/, deserver 1344; -**ie,** by merit 1344; -**ius,** well deserved 1207.

promerium, see pomerium.

prominentia, see preminentia.

promineo, see premineo.

prominuo, see PREMUN

promiss/arius c 1160, -**or** c 1160, c 1360, promiser; -**iuncula,** promise c 704; -**ive,** in the sense of a promise 1516; -**orius,** promissory c 1290, 1609; **promitio,** for -**io,** (C.I.) 1321; -**um,** offering 1199, 1221; **promitto,** to contain, offer (of a document) 1387; **p. sacramentum,** to take an oath (W.) 13c.

promitorium, see PROMPT

promontori/um c 730. 1415, **promuntorium** c 1320, ridge, hill; hill-fort 1136; **promunctoria** (pl.) **turrium,** towering turrets c 1315; -**olum,** little promontory 1586; -**us,** mountainous 1385.

promot/io, advance c 1400; *preferment (eccl.) c 1125, 1559; advancement to a degree (ac.) c 1473; *furtherance 1201,

1427; advancement, advantage 1215, 1274; **ad -ionem,** at the instance (of) c 1340; **-ivus,** tending to promote, favourable 1296, 15c.; **epistole -ive,** letters recommending promotion (ac.) c 1400; **-or** 1239, 1448, **-rix** (*f.*) 1337, c 1400, promoter, furtherer; grantor of preferment (eccl.) 1378, 1686; promoter, prosecutor (eccl. law) 1283, 1684; **p. jurum (ducis)** (G.) 1316; **-orius,** concerning a promoter (eccl. law) 1426; **-us,** beneficed clerk c 1410, c 1452; **promoveo,** *to promote, prefer (esp. eccl.) 1124, 1461; to help (someone) 1220, 1222; to induce c 1125, c 1450; **p. ad gradum** (ac.) c 1516; **p. bellum,** to wage war 1461; **p. officium,** to institute criminal proceedings by information in ecclesiastical court c 1408, 1595.

prompt/io c 1283, *-**itudo** 1191, c 1470, promptitude; *-**uarium** c 900. c 1125, 1546, **prontuarium** c 1210, store-room; **p. memorie** (fig.) c 985; **promitorium,** "brewhouse" c 1365; **prompator,** prompter c 1400; **-e confectus,** ready made 1428; **in -o,** *for* **-u,** in readiness 1461; **pecunia in -u** 1282, **pecunia -a** 1259, 1459, **denarii -i** 1275, 1538, ready money; **-us** (with *inf.*), about to c 730; **-ulus** c 950, **prumptulus** 9c., **prumptus** c 793, prompt, ready.

‡**promulada,** "gravy" 15c.

promulg/eo, *for* **-o,** c 1340; †**provulgatio,** (?) *for* **-atio,** c 1343.

promun/torium, -ctorium, *see* **promontorium.**

‡**promurale,** counterscarp 15c., 1570.

pronascor, to originate c 730.

pronefas (*for* **pro nefas!**), crime 8c.

proneptis, great-niece c 1362.

pronga 1288, **pranga** 1394, **branga** 1407, prong, pointed tool.

***pron/itas,** propensity c 1260, a 1520; **-ifico,** to incline, make prone c 1375.

pronomen, *see* **prenomen.**

pronostic-, *see* **PROGNOSTIC**

pronotatus, *see* **PRENOT**

prontuarium, *see* **PROMPT**

pro/nuba c 1150, c 1443, **-noba** 1419, bawd, procuress; 1519, **-nobus** 1419, procurer; **-nubacia,** bawdry c 1443, c 1502.

pronuntiat/io, pronunciation, utterance c 1160, c 1553; reading c 790; **-ivus,** dogmatic 1622; **-or,** utterer (leg.) a 1564; *cf.* **PRENUNTI**

proordino, *see* **PREORDIN**

prooro, to plead convincingly c 1220; †**proaro,** to pray for c 1200; *cf.* **PEROR**

propag/ative, by propagation, dissemination 1270; **-inaliter** c 1220, †**-aliter** a 1452, lineally; **-atus,** well-built, vigorous c 1250, c 1437.

†**propagato,** *f.l.* for **pro pagato,** 1294.

†**propagulum (defensionis),** (?) support 1298.

propal/atio, disclosure, publication 8c. 1165, a 1450, **-o,** to display c 730. c 1125, c 1380; *to publish c 1060. a 1100, c 1540.

***propar/s (proper-)** 1218, 1542, †**perpars** 1290, ***purpars** c 1258, 1583, **-tia** 13c., a 1564, **purpartia** 1310, a 1564, **proportia** 1364, purparty, share (leg.); **purpartia,** apportionment 1431; *cf.* **proportio.**

propassio/, propassion, first impulse to sin c 730. 12c., c 1375; **p. humana,** anthropopathy (rhetorical figure) c 1220; **-nalis,** concerned with propassion 12c.; †**propatior,** (?) to endure for another 6c.

propatul/us, open: †**perpatulus** ‡1483, 1488; **in -o** a 1100, 1557, **perpatulo** c 1000, openly.

propedio, *see* **PREPED**

propen/cius, *for* **-sius,** more readily 1242; **-satus,** (?) *for* **prepen-,** aforethought c 1320; **-deo,** to depend on 1537; *cf.* **perpensio.**

properatio, anticipation, advance (of payment) 1620.

propertia, *see* **propars.**

prophan-, *see* **PROFAN**

prophemium, (?) *for* **proemium,** preface 1423.

***prophet/a,** prophet (eccl.); prophetic book c 730; *-**ia** (eccl.), **-icum** 11c., c 1450, prophecy; **-alis,** *-**icus** (eccl.), **-ialis** c 1370, prophetic; **-aliter** c 1090, **-ice** (eccl.), prophetically; **-issa,** prophetess (eccl.); **-izatio,** prophesying c 704; **-izo** c 1180, a 1452, *-**o** (eccl.), to prophesy.

‡**prophylacticum** (†**prosilaticum**), a prophylactic 15c.

†**prop/iamen,** (?) nearness, narrow extent c 550; †**-rior,** *for* **-ior,** nearer c 550; *cf. also* **PROXIM**

propifer, *see* **PROPRI**

propigmenus, *see* **PROEG**

propin/ator, drinker 1153; "butler" 8c. ‡1483; c 1458, **-atrix** (*f.*) 1220, supplier, giver; **-atus,** drink, draught c 1250.

propincernarius, cup-bearer, steward 13c.

propinqu/atio, approach a 1250; **-abilis,** approachable a 1275; **-alis** 5c., **-alia** c 1125, kinsman; **-itas,** kinsfolk (*coll.*) c 1343; **-ior,** next of kin (in hereditary succession) 1247, 1430; **amici** (*pl.*) **-i** 1507; *see also* **heres; de -ioribus,** from the neighbourhood (*or* neighbours) c 1290; **-issime,** very near a 1233.

propit/iatio, mercy, kindness c 1070, c 1470; clemency (title) a 1165; **-iabiliter,** by way of propitiation c 1268; as an act of grace 1424; **-iativus,** propitiatory c 1378; **-iatius,** more earnestly c 1115; †**prospitius,** *for* **-ius,** propitious c 1180; *-**ior,** to be propitious 8c. c 1156, c 1406.

proplasticum, mould (for casting) 1620.

proplema, *see* **problema.**

propon-, *see* **PROPOSIT**

proporti/o, purparty 1200, 1203 (*see also* **PROPAR**); *-**onabilis** a 1250, 1406, *-**onalis** a 1200, c 1380, **-onatus** c 1250, 1457, proportionate, corresponding; *-**onabiliter** c 1334, 1477, *-**onaliter** 1125, c 1470, †-**onate** a 1233, proportionately, correspondingly, in fair shares; **-onabilitas** c 1270, c 1375, **-onalitas** a 1200, 1686, just proportion; *-**ono,** to proportion, share out, adjust c 1150, c 1470.

proport/um, charge, accusation (leg.) 1275; c 1218, **-amentum** c 1208, 1238, **-atio** (†-**itas**) (Sc.) 14c., **purportum** c 1218, 13c., verdict of assize; *1230, 1330, **perportum** 1236, **purportum** 1232, 1587, purport (of dŏcument); **-o**, to accuse 1275; to extend or define (of boundaries) c 1165, c 1452; to claim 1331; c 1200, 1365, **perporto** 1219, 1433, **porporto** 1205, to purport (of charters, *etc.*).

proposit/io, *see* **panis**; **-iuncula**, tiny proposition a 1180; **-ionalis**, in the form of propositions (log.) a 1360; **-ionaliter** c 1365, c 1375, **-ive** c 1367, as in a proposition (log.); **ad -um**, to the point, *à propos* a 1200, c 1343; **a -o** 1336, **ex -o** c 1340, purposely; **in -o sum** 1375, **in -o habeo** c 1390, to have in mind, intend; **†-ura,** (?) putting off a 1270; **propon/ibilis**, able to be propounded c 1290; **-o** (**verbum Dei**), to preach 1414; *see also* PREPOSIT

proposse, *see* **posse.**

propreses, sub-warden (of stannaries) 1586.

proprest-, *see* **purprestura.**

propri/etas, *(owning of) property (mon.) c 1204, 1526; propriety, correctness c 1363; (?) monograph, treatise c 1400; a 'proper', service proper to a saint (eccl.) 1416; chief note of a ligature (mus.) 1326; **p. opposita,** semibreve in ligature 1326; **p. substantialis** (phil.) a 1200; **onus -etatis,** personal responsibility 1478; **-etaria,** proprietress c 1470; **-etarie,** in possession of property (eccl.) c 1363; acquisitively 1454; **-etarius,** owning property (mon.) c 1220, c 1450; (*subst.*) property owner (mon.) 1234, c 1450; owner (naut.) 1454, 1552; 1391, **priodarius, preodarius** 1334, free tenant, *priodawr* (W.); 1439, 1551, **-ator** a 1452, appropriator of benefice (eccl.); **-cida,** suicide 1427; **-fer (propifer),** one's own c 550; **-etorie,** specifically a 1360; **†-onabilis,** (?) *for* **proportionabilis,** proportionate c 1270; **-issime,** in the strictest sense c 1332, 1378;

-e (*pl.*), property, possessions 1340; **-um,** property (log.) a 1304; **ad -a,** at home 1130, 1432; **in -a,** homewards c 1362; **in -o,** in demesne 11c.; **in -o sto,** to be consistent 1350; **de -o,** spontaneously 1265; **de -is,** at the expense 1460; **-atio,** claim or proof of ownership c 1115; **-o,** to claim or prove ownership c 1115; to appropriate (a church) a 1452.

proprior, *see* **propiamen.**

proprisum, *see* **purprestura.**

propter (?) towards (of feeling) c 730; in exchange for c 1200; (with *gerundive*) 1086, c 1350, (with *inf.*) c 1180, c 1444, for the purpose of; *see also* **ire, missio; p. quid,** the wherefore (τὸ διότι) p 1300, 1344); *see also* **scientia.**

propugnaculatus, fortified with bulwarks or battlements c 1255.

propuls/a, repulse c 1298; **-atio, -io** c 1266, **perpulsatio** 13c., ringing (of bells); **-io,** urging on c 1236; onslaught c 1200; **opus -atum,** embossed work c 1255; **-o,** to ring (bell) 1352; to urge 1294.

propunctus, *see* **purpunctus.**

proquestor, under-treasurer a 1536.

proquiro, *see* **perquiro.**

pror/a cerebri, front part of brain a 1250; **-eta,** mate (naut.) a 615, c 770. c 1192; pilot (fig.) 6c.; **‡-eto,** to steer 15c.

†proradio (? *for* pre-), to be illustrious c 1315.

prorectus, (?) *f.l.* for **projectus,** 1312; *see also* **prerectus.**

prorex, viceroy c 1190, 1654.

prorog/atio, extension, adjournment 1219, 1559; **p. temporis,** lapse of time 1419; **-atior,** more prolonged c 1250; **-o,** to do good c 793; (?) *for* **subrogo,** to substitute c 1404; *see also* PREROG

prorsus, thoroughly: **prossus** 1284, 15c.

prorumpo, to begin, burst forth with 7c.; **p. in verba,** to break (rudely) into speech 1361.

pros/a, prose c 1200, c 1470; rhymed (not quantitative) verse 13c.; sequence (eccl.) 1200, 1508; **-aice,** in prose 8c. 1267, c 1470; **-aicus** 1200, c 1470, **-alis** 8c., in prose; **vox -aica,** speaking voice c 1213.

proscenium, tent, house c 950.

proscido, *see* PROCESS

prosecut/io, verbal explanation c 793; *carrying out 1223, 1440; *prosecution, initiation of action (leg.) c 1115, 1595; **†persequssio litis** 1333; **-io sanguinis,** bloodshed 13c; **-or,** one who carries out c 1400; prosecutor (leg.) 1199, 15c.; pursuivant (her.) 1426, 1446 (*cf.* **pursevandus**); **-orius,** concerned with following up a theme c 1375; **-um** (**nutrimenti**), pursuit 13c.; **-us** (*pass.*), pursued c 1362, 1378; **prosequ/ens,** uniform 1317; **-o,** *for* **-or,** c 740; **-or,** to prosecute, bring or proceed with a suit (leg.) c 1115, 1558; to raise a question c 1320; ‡"to purchase" 15c.; **p. breve,** to procure a writ 1369, 1444; **p. debitum,** to proceed for recovery of a debt 1271; **p. gildam,** to attend a guild meeting c 1260; **p. versus,** to proceed, bring a suit, against 1268, 1419; *see also* PERSECUT.

proselytus, proselyte (eccl.) c 1080, 1378.

proseneta, *see* **proxeneta.**

prosequestro, (**†persequestro**), to banish, avert c 1350.

pros/eucha, oratory: ‡"alms-house" c 1440; **†-ueca,** 'bedern' (Ripon) 1454.

prosgen, *see* **gi.**

prosilaticum, *see* **prophylacticum.**

pros/logium a 1100, a 1186, **-ologium** 14c., c 1500, title of book by Anselm.

prosol-, *see* PERSOL

prosopon, person (of Trinity) c 1160, c 1200.

prospect/io, foresight c 1250; **-ius,** more providently c 1250; **-us** (*pl.*), scouting parties 1413; (*p.p.,* with *gen.*), having an eye to c 1000; **prospicio,** to provide for c 1190, 1548.

prosper/atio, prosperity 1438; making prosperous c 1465; **-ator,** one who makes prosperous c 1170; **-itas,** beatitude (theol.) c 1270; **-osus,** prosperous, successful 1432; **-or,** to prosper 7c. c 1090, c 1414.

prospertura, *see* PURPRES

prospitius, *see* PROPIT

prossus, *see* **prorsus.**

prostern-, *see* PROSTR

prosthapheresis lune, equation of moon's centre 1686.

prostibularius, of a brothel c 1200.

†prostituo, to throw down 1230.

prosto, to stand by, stand ready 1295.

prostr/atio *c 1180, 1531, **prosternatio** a 1155, c 1230, prostration; *1199, 1509,

prosternatio c 1192, 1483, throwing down, overthrow; cutting down (from gallows) 1248; **-ator**, overthrower, feller 1250, 1319; **psalmus prosternalis** c 1305, **p. -alis** c 1266, 1343, **p. -atus** c 1255, c 1266, psalm repeated by congregation when prostrate; ***-o** 12c., c 1402, **prostarno** 1529, *for* **prosterno**; 1214, **prosterno** 1231, c 1290, to quash; **prostern/o me** 12c., **-or** 14c., c 1520, to prostrate oneself; **p. fossatum**, to level a dyke 1274, 1430; †**p. hominium**, (?) to pay homage by prostration (play on **presto**) c 1125.

†**prostruo**, to throw down 1242.

prosueca, *see* **proseucha**.

prosultus, assault c 1225.

prosumo, to direct, make provision 1431.

prosyllogismus, syllogism whose conclusion forms first premiss of another c 730. p 1300.

protagium, *see* **2 potagium**.

protagollum, *see* **protocollum**.

Prote/amen, -atus, -o, *see* **Proteus**.

protecdicus, Byzantine official: **prothedicus** 1274.

protect/io, feudal patronage or suzerainty 1086, c 1160; **littere -ionis** c 1192, **l. de -ione** 1200, c 1242, **l. de p. simplici** 1258, **l. -orie** 15c.; **-or**, warrantor 1086; regent c 1422, c 1549; Cardinal Protector (Franciscan) c 1250, 15c.; **-rix**, protectress 797. a 1155, 1424; ‡**-orium**, swingletree of harrow 1483 (*cf.* PROJECT); **protego**, to cover, submerge c 700.

protel/atio, delay, postponement 8c. c 1166, 1610; **-o**, to bring forward 9c., c 1000; to extract 1241; to postpone c 760; †**protolo** 15c., †**pretelo** c 1160, *for* **-o**, to protract.

proten/sio, extension a 1233, 1267; **-tus**, extent 14c.; **-sior**, more protracted c 1250; **-sus**, long (of hair) c 1225, c 1520; **-do** c 1244, p 1260, **portonio** 1306, **protineo me** 14c., to extend; to exhibit, show c 1255, 1413; to favour, prefer 1310; to portend c 1250, c 1362.

protermino, to postpone c 1204, c 1218.

protero, *see* **protritor**.

*proterv/ia, impudence, wantonness a 1180, 1441; **-iter**, wantonly c 1385; **-io**, to be wanton c 1160, p 1380; to assert impudently 1344; **-o**, to rage c 1190.

protest/atio, protestation in pleading (leg.) 1224, 15c.; **-ans**, Protestant 1545, 17c.; ***-or**, c 700. c 1125, 15c., **-o** 1226, to declare.

‡**Prote/us**, mercury 1652; (*adj.*) fickle 14c.; **-amen**, versatility a 1452; **-atus**, Protean a 1452; **-o**, to transform c 1200, 1252.

proth, *see* **proch**.

prothedicus, *see* **protecdicus**.

prothema, (?) proposal c 950; exordium, invocation 1267.

protho-, *see* **proto**.

prothrophium, *see* **ptochotropheum**.

protimesis, preference 1608.

protineo, *see* PERTIN; PROTEN

protinus, formerly c 1275.

proto, firstly c 550; **protus**, first c 700, c 1125; ***proto/collum (protho-)** 1166, 1684, **-gollum** (Sc.) 1502, 1549, **protagollum** (Sc.) 1464, 1503, **papirus -galis** (Fr.) 15c.,

protocol, original document; **-collo**, to embody in protocols (G.) 1316; **-doctor**, first teacher (St. Augustine of Canterbury) c 1090, 1414; **-dux**, first leader 1414; **-forestarius**, chief forester c 1250, 1586; **-genes**, (*adj.*) first of its kind, original 957; (*subst.*) first-formed man, Adam 15c.; **-gonus**, founder of family c 1595: **-graphum**, original document 1654; **-justitiarius**, chief justice c 1250; ***-martyr**, first martyr (St. Stephen *or* St. Alban) 8c., 826. c 1125, c 1470; **-minister**, first attendant 6c.; **-monarcha**, first king (Alfred) c 1293; ***-notarius** c 1194, 1609, **-notator** 1419, prothonotary; **-notariatus**, office of prothonotary 1492; **-parens**, first parent (Adam) c 760. c 1100, a 1452; **-pater**, primate c 1100; **-pirus**, pioneer 1620; ***-plastus** (eccl.), **-plaustus** a 615. a 1275, c 1450, **-plausta** 1461, first-created man (Adam); **-pola**, privileged seller 1585; **-sevastus** c 1192, **-salvastos** c 1188, **-salvator** c 1190, Byzantine mayor of the palace (πρωτοσέβαστος); **-singellus**, chief official of patriarch (πρωτοσύγκελλος) 1437; **-spatharius** a 1142, **-spartarius** 12c., Byzantine commander-in-chief; **-syllogismus**, basic syllogism 1427; **-symbolus**, title assumed by Mahomet (? *al-Furken*) c 1250; **-trophium**, *see* **ptochotropheum**; **-typum**, prototype 1345; **-vates Anglie**, title assumed by Robert Whittinton as laureate 1521; **-vestiarius**, official of Greek church, sacristan 1437.

protolo, *see* **protelo**.

protostonos, *see* **emprosthotonos**.

protract/io, protraction, extension c 1260, 15c.; drawing (of criminals) p 1348, 15c.; 1204, 14c., **-atio, -atura** 1355, **portratura** 1449, 1457, drawing, diagram, portrayal, portrait; **purtrator**, worker in drawn thread 1441; **-e** c 1160, **-im** a 1452, **-ive** c 1423, protractedly; **-us**, prolongation c 1362; sum, amount 1245; **-o**, to transact 1283, c 1405; 1267, 1355, **protraho** c 1200, c 1325, to draw, portray; *cf.* PERTRACT

†**protrajicio**, to pierce c 1400.

protribunal, judgement seat c 1240.

protritor (tramitum), treader c 1315; **protero vitam**, to sustain life c 1400.

protrus/io, forward thrust 1620; **-or**, *see* **profusor**.

protumeo, to swell c 1324.

protus, *see* **proto**.

prout (*prep.*), with respect to 1252, 1314; **p. quod**, because c 1290.

provabilis, *see* **proba**.

provandum, *see* PREBEND

provecticius, *see* PROFECT

provect/io, promotion 1219, a 1255; progress c 1178, 15c.; **p. etatis**, advanced age c 1250; **-ior**, more advanced (not of time) c 730; **-rix**, benefactress 1337.

provencialis, *see* PROVINC

provend-, *see* PREBEND

proven/tio c 1200, ***-tus** 1215, c 1545, †**preventus** 1484, **-tualia** (*pl.*) 1227, **-ientia** (*pl.*) c 1298, 1361, income, proceeds; **-tus** (*p.p.*), produced, issuing c 1437; **-io**, (*impers.*) to happen, turn out 8c.; 1230, c 1545, †**prevenio** 1315, 1329, to issue from (of revenue or profits); **p. contra**, to take action against, resist 1294; *see also* PREVEN

proverbi/a (*pl.*), Book of Proverbs c 1343, c 1534; **-alis**, proverbial c 1500; **-aliter**, metaphorically c 730.

Provesinus, coin of Provins (Fr.) 1292.

provester, *see* PREPOSIT

provic-, provid-, *see* PROVIS

provignio, to layer (vines) (Fr. *provigner*) c 1235.

provinc/ia, shire, county 10c., c 1040. c 1115, 1461; cantred (W.) a 1250; *province or see (eccl.) 8c., 9c. c 1115, 1549; province (of friars) 1511; **p. Dacorum, p. Danorum**, Danelaw c 1115; **-iola**, small province or district c 700. 1586; **-ialatus** 1518, **-ialitas** 1311, office of provincial (of friars); **-ialis**, (*adj.*) of a county c 1185; 798. a 1218, 1549, **provencialis** 1573, of a province (eccl.); (*subst.*) person belonging to a province (eccl.) 1472; provincial (official of an order of friars) 1488, 1564; *see also* **prior; -ialiter**, with reference to provinces (eccl.) 1398.

Provincialis, Provençal (language) 1267.

*****provis/io** 1234, 1530, **-e** (*pl.*) 1330, *****providentia** 1243, a 1564, provision, purveyance, supply; *****1228, c 1470, **provicio** 1587, **providentia** c 1250, c 1440, **-um** p 1330, provision, stipulation, ordinance; papal provision, appointment to benefice c 1188, 1565; **providentia**, supervision c 1000; **-ionalis**, conditional 1608; **-ionaliter** c 1420, **-orie** c 1365, by papal provision; **-ivus**, provident c 1250, c 1270;

-or, guardian c 730; steward, administrator, overseer 826. c 1130, c 1434; purveyor of food or lodging 1197, 1524; *****person appointed by papal provision c 1250, c 1440; supervisor of will 1435; provost (of Eton) 1468 (*cf.* **prepositus**); **-orius**, concerned with papal provision a 1300, 1309; **-e**, expectedly c 995; **-o** c 1457, *****p. quod** c 1266, 1549, **p. ut** 13c., provided that; **provideo**, to appoint by papal provision c 1240, a 1533; (with *inf.*) to undertake c 1270, c 1395; *****p. de** 1242, c 1442, **p. in** c 1218, c 1284, to provide with; **p. gaudium**, to afford joy p 1330; **provideor**, to be ready 1378; *cf.* PREVID

provoc/abilis, stimulating c 1350; **-o**, to claim 1321, (?) 1416.

provocitor, *see* PERNOCT

provost-, *see* PREPOSIT

provulgatio, *see* PROMULG

proxeneta, agent, broker: **proseneta** 1347, **prozenetarius** 1421; **proxinetum**, procuration (eccl.) 1560; †**proceneticus**, (?) concerned with procuration c 1200.

proxim/itas (*coll.*), the neighbours c 1180; **-e**, near by c 730; **-ius**, more closely (?) 13c.; *****-ior**, nearer 6c., c 900. 12c., c 1540; **-o**, next c 1225, c 1452; **in -o** c 1090, 1438, **de -o** c 1188, c 1470, soon; **in -o est ut**, it is on the point of happening c 730.

proxinetum, prozenetarius, *see* **proxeneta**.

pru/ceum 1435, **-cia** 1388, 1454, **-sia** 1435, 1454, spruce (wood).

Pru/cianus 1390, **-scenus** 1267, †**-ctenus** c 1250, **-cinus** 1456, Prussian.

prudent/ia, costume, finery c 1298, 1327; (title) a 1090, 1136; **-ie** (*pl.*), learned authorities- 1327; **-er**, purposely, wittingly 1229, c 1258; **prudens de**, with knowledge of 1684; **-es** (*pl.*), the Witan c 1414; **-ialis**, prudential 1646; **-o**, to deck c 1298.

†**pruina**, *for* pruna, live coal 1345.

pruin/ula, snow-flake c 1184; **-o**, to be chilly, disagreeable c 1180.

prumpt-, *see* PROMPT

prun/a 1501, **prewnum** 1565, *for* **-um**, plum; 15c., **-arius** c 1290, plum-tree; ‡**-um Damascenum** 15c., **p. Damascenorum** a 1250, damson; **-ella silvatica** a 1150, ‡**-ellum** 1570, sloe; **-ella**, burnet (bot.) 1570; ‡**-eolus**, bullace (bot.) 1570; **spina -ellifera**, blackthorn a 1150; **-ifera**, plum-seller (*f.*) 1378; ‡**-etum**, plum-orchard 1483.

prurio, to rub or scratch c 1290.

prus-, *see* **pruceum; Prucianus.**

prymnum (**primnum**), stern (naut.) 10c.

psal-, *see also* **saliares; salicia.**

psall/itium, singing c 1170; **-omenos** (*ppl.*), hymned c 970; **-o** (with *acc.*) to hymn 9c.; *****-o** (eccl.), **spallo** 800, **spalleo** 801, **sallo** 1290, 1409, to make music, hymn, chant.

psalmo, *see* PLASM

psalm/us commendationis, psalm of commendation (on All Souls) c 1296; **p. familiaris**, psalm in honour of patrons, *etc.* (mon.) c 1072, c 1296; **p. ferialis**, week-day psalm c 1006. c 1080, 14c.; **p. graduum** c 980. c 1125, c 1330; **p. gradualis** c 1354, psalm of degrees; **p. misericordie**, 50th (51st) psalm c 1212; **p. penitentialis**, penitential psalm c 1006. c 1080, 1474; *see also* PROSTR; **spalmus**, *for* **-us**, c 1220, c 1511; ‡**-atus** 15c.; "**citole**" 15c.; **-icen** c 1000. c 1125, **-icanus** c 1100, **-icinus** c 1280, psalm-singer, choir monk; **-icus**, in the form of a psalm 9c.; **-igraphicum**, saying of David 1284; **-ographus**, a psalm-writer c 1553; a 1100, 15c., **-igraphus** 8c., c 1000. a 1135, c 1420, **-igrapha** c 1000, **-idicus** 10c., *****-ista** c 1080, 1534, the Psalmist, David; **-ista**, a psalmist (clerical order) 10c. c 1310; **-istatus**, order of psalmist 1345, a 1433; **-isticus**, of David 1245; *****-odia** a 615, c 1050. c 1070, a 1452, **spalmodia** 800, psalmody, psalm-singing; **p. principalis, p. secundaria** c 1296; **-ocinor** c 1180, **-odio** a 1100, c 1330, *****-odizo** (**-odiso**) c 1266, 1509, **-onizo** 1466, to sing psalms.

*****psalt/erium** 8c., c 1006. 1086, c 1540, **-arium** 1376, **-erum** 1402, **phsalterium** 1416, †**phaslterium** 1291, **phalterium** c 1510, **spalterium** a 1150, c 1511, **salterium** c 1220, 1520, psalter (eccl.); **p. beate Marie**, rosary of 150 Ave Marias 1430; **p. Daviticum** 1535; **p. glosatum** c 1300, 1416; **-es** (bibl.), **-a** c 790, minstrel; **saltarius**, psalmist 1477; *see also* **saltus.**

psalvus, *see* **salvatio.**

pseud/us c 1192, (?) a 1452, **-olus** c 1390, false; **-o**, falsely c 1080, c 1450; **pseudo/-abbas**, false abbot c 1135, c 1400; **-adversarius**, lying adversary 1378; **-anachorita** c 1190, **-anchorita** 14c.; **-apostolus** c 1192, c 1380; **-archiepiscopus** c 1325; **-bunias**, winter-cress (bot.) 1632; **-cardinalis** c 1380,

15c.; -christianus a 1142, 1570; -christus
c 1343, 1406; -clericus c 1250, c 1400;
-clerus 1412; -color 15c.; -comes,
pretended earl a 1186; -discipulus 1378,
c 1380; -doctor 1381; -ecclesia c 790;
-episcopus c 790. a 1205, c 1553; -evange-
lista c 730; pseudevangelium 1523;
-frater c 1190, p 1382, speudofrater 1201,
false monk or friar; -glossarius, false
commentator 1378; †-graium, (?) for
-graphum, forged document c 710;
-logicus c 1200, a 1452, -logus 1378, 1609,
false reasoner; -lollardus c 1395; -melan-
thium, corncockle (bot.) 1634; -monachus
c 1250, 1535; -nuntius 1323; (?) pseudonymus (†pheudomnus), someone mis-
named c 1390; -ordines (pl.) p 1382 (eccl.);
*-papa c 1300, 15c.; -pastor 1380; -poeta
1344; -predicator 1080, c 1553; -prelatus
1380; -presbyter c 1343, 15c.; -professor
(religionis) c 1250; *-propheta c 1180,
1413; -rector 1380; -rex c 1310; -sacerdos
1378; speudosanctus 1201; -scholaris
c 1275; -subactor, usurper c 1350; -sug-
gestor, suggester of falsehood c 1200;
-theologus c 1400; -theosebia, false piety
c 950; -versificus, plagiarist 1345; -vica-
rius, false pope 1378; pseustis, cheat c 1325,
1427.
psiath/um, rush mat: -icum 14c.
psidia, pomegranate bark a 1250, c 1250.
psimmythium, white lead: ‡psincus, simmitium 1652.
psionomus, see HEPS
psittacus, parrot: ‡psitagus 15c., citacus
1245, 1295, phitacus c 1400.
psychomachia, spiritual conflict: sycomachia c 1200, sychomagia 11c.
psyll/ium, flea-bane (bot.): -iticum a 1250.
ptarmicum, drug to cause sneezing: obtarmicum a 1250.
ptis/ana, barley-water: -ina a 1250, 1531,
tipsana c 1260, 1271, ‡tapsaria 1652;
-inaria, massa -anaria, digested food
a 1250.
ptochotropheum 1414, 1646, prothrophium
a 1186, prototrophium c 1182, tochium
c 1160, poor-house.
ptrut c 1200, phrut c 1212, exclamation of
scorn.
pub/erculus, stripling c 1365; -etini (pl.),
young people c 1000; -eo, to have reached
puberty 1347.
Publicanus, Paulician heretic (?) c 1118,
a 1142, c 1520.
*public/atio c 1080, c 1555, puplicatio 1274,
publication, proclamation; p. (evangelii),
preaching 1378; -amentum, ill fame,
notoriety 1166; -ator, proclaimer, preacher
c 1250, 1449; littere -atorie, letters
declaratory 1416; puplice, for -e, 1219,
c 1355; puplicus c 799, c 1000. c 1102,
c 1420, -alis 790, public; -atus, notorious
1166; publigo c 1248, puplico 1201, c 1355,
for -o.
pucell/a, girl, maid 1418; -agium, virginity
c 1258.
puch/a, -ea, -ica, see poca.
pucin-, see 2 pulla.
puct-, see 2 pugna; PUNCT

puddellum, see pitellum.
pudingum, pudding (of entrails) 1246.
pud/or, (amends for) affront 1208, 1334;
-ibunda (pl.), pudenda c 1180, c 1200;
-ibunde 13c., putibunde c 1335, 15c.,
-oriter c 1290, shamefully; putibundus,
shameful c 1340; -efio c 760, -eo c 1362, to
be ashamed; -oro c 1400, ‡15c., -orifico
14c., to shame, affront.
pud/ratus, -urlumbartus, see pulvis.
pudreo, see PUTR
puelea, see polea.
puell/a, virgin c 600; the Virgin c 1370; nun
7c., 802; -agium 1345, -aritas 13c., a 1300,
maidenhood; -itas, girlhood 1461; -us, lad
1503.
puer/ 1285, 1334, p. femineus p 1330, female
child; p. chorista, choir boy 1402; p.
stabuli, stable-boy 1531; see also episcopus,
1 festum; -culus 12c., -ilus c 1388, small
boy; -ula, little girl c 1255; -ilia (pl.),
rudiments (of grammar) 1549; -pera,
woman (other than virgin), mother c 1000.
c 1200; -perium, pregnancy 1200.
puffo 1297, 1303, poff/o 1336, 1367, -onus
1336, paphinus 1237, puffin (Cornwall).
pugica, see poca.
pugil/, (adj.) disputing 1241; (subst.) soldier
or champion c 1137, 1461; p. fidei 1345, p.
pro fide c 1450; -latice, truculently 1520;
-atoria, bellicosity 13c.; see also 2 pugna.
pug/io, point c 1400, 15c.; ‡"tang" 15c.;
‡"punch" 1570; -o, a sharp instrument
1496; p. molendini (?), 1388; see also pipio.
1 pugn/a (pugn-), retinue (G.) 1253; p. in
domo facta, hamsoken c 1160, 1189; p.
Dardana, 'game of Troy' c 1160; p.
gallorum cock-fight a 1190, 1363; -atio,
fighting c 700. p 1348; -ator, champion (in
judicial combat) 1231.
2 pugn/a (pugn-), for -us, fist c 550; -alis
1238, -ellus 1240, 1256, poingnellus 1252,
(?) puctus 1241, cuff; -alis (salmo), as
thick as a fist 1234; -ata c 1180, c 1258,
-eta 1234, pugillata 1222, fistful; liquid
measure (of blood) 1230; poignator 1213,
poingnator 1243, 'hawk of the fist' (falc.).
†pugnalea, (?) some beast of prey c 1350.
pugn/io, -um, see 1 pinna.
pugo, see pugio.
puk/a, -ettus, see poca.
‡pula, mixture of water and wine 15c.
pulbitum, see pulpitum.
pulchr/a placitatio 1416, -um placitare
1275, -um placitandi 1279, *-e placitan-
dum 1250, 1466, beaupleader, amendment
of faulty plea (leg.); -um loqui, fair words
1201; -aliter, beautifully (?) 844; -ificus,
beautifying 9c. 1344; -ificatio, embellish-
ment c 1236, 1374; *-ifico, to beautify
c 1236, 1427.
pulcinus, see 2 pulla.
puleginum oleum, oil of pennyroyal a 1250.
puli/a, -ca, -va, see pola; polea.
pulicaria, policaria, (?) fleabane (bot.)
a 1250, ‡14c.
pulinus, see 2 pullanus.
1 pull/a, -us, see pola.
2 pull/a (f.) c 1380, 1404, -inus c 1330,
*pulcinus 1249, 1411, pucinus 1277,

pulvinus 1603, pulo 1308, ‡-iculus 1483,
-iolus 1277, -etus c 1284, 1583, (?) pultra
1477, pultria 1266, 1567, poletta 1337,
pollis 1297, pullet, chicken; pulcinus auce,
gosling 1321; gallina pucinaria, Hen and
Chickens, Pleiades c 1267; -agium 1265,
1331, polagium (C.I.) 1270, 1274, fowl
rent; -ale 1409, -ina 1473, -etaria 1271,
-eteria 1392, -etria 1365, 1462, poletria
c 1290, 1419, pultaria 1389, pulteria 1252,
1390, polteria 1326, pultria 1337, 1419,
pulturia 1475, poultry; -eteria 1255,
domus -etrie 1301, hen-house; *-etarius
1241, 1419, -itarius, politarius 1337,
pultarius 1308, c 1390, pulterius 1330,
-atterius 1302, (?) poltarius 1159, poletarius c 1290, 1419, -entarius 1288,
‡-arius 1520, ‡-iferus 15c., poulterer;
caro -ina, chicken flesh a 1150; -ificatio,
hatching a 1250, ‡15c.; ovum -ificativum
a 1250; -ifico, to hatch, produce chicks
c 1200, a 1446.

3 pull/a c 1125, -ulamen, polulamen c 550,
shoot, sprout; -ulatio, sprouting, growth
c 1258, 1451; pupulo, to sprout 1200.

4 pulla, see PULMON

1 *pull/anus 1214, 1425, -einus c 1123,
pollenus 1276, pulnus 1226, -us 1086,
1512, poledrus a 1250, colt, foal; 12c.,
polanus c 1200, half-caste (Palestine); p.
femellus 1273, -ana c 1440, pultra 1270,
1338, pultrella 1326, 1333, filly (cf. O.F.
poltre); -us 1219, 1282, rotulus -orum
c 1241, 1295, small roll (esp. one annexed to
Pipe Roll, containing desperate debts);
-enatio, foaling c 1300; -ano 1235, -eno
1196, c 1275, -ono c 1258, -o 1234, 1281,
-ulo 1315, to foal.

2 pullanus 1241, pulinus 1236, (?) polaynnia
1238, polenus 1198, 'puleyn', slide for
lowering casks; cf. polea.

pullatus, blackened, defiled a 615; sable (her.)
1654.

pullum, see polea.

pulment/um a 1128, 1417, -arium 12c., 15c.,
(dish of) pottage; caseus -atus c 1266;
-ificus, alimentary 9c.; pols, for puls,
pottage 13c.

pulmon/aria, lungwort (bot.) ‡14c., 1629;
†pulla, (?) for pulmo, lung a 1250; ‡-ia,
phthisis 1570; ‡-icus, phthisical 1570; cf.
PNEUM

pulnus, see 1 pullanus.

pulo, see 2 pulla.

*pulp/itum c 1200, 1562, -etum 1426, 1583,
-utum 1258, pulbitum 1369, ‡-etorium
15c., pulpit, ambo (eccl.); -itum, (?) seat
c 550; -itium, platform p 1341; -itulum,
small ambo, lectern c 1255.

puls/atio, impulse, influence 12c., 1486;
*1194, 1589, -io 14c., ringing (of bells); p.
hore c 1350, c 1450; p. horilogii 1399;
p. ignitegii c 1275, c 1407; p. organorum
1399, 1526; campana -atilis, bell for
ringing c 1520; molendinum -atile, stamping mill 1511; vena -atilis c 1375, ‡1652,
v. -ativa, v. -ilis a 1250, artery; -atilla,
pasque-flower (ḅot.) 1641; -ativus, causing
pulsation (med.) a 1250; -ator, attacker
c 1125; plaintiff (leg.) c 1115; suppliant

(for divine grace) c 1180; *c 1245, 1535,
-atorius 1320, bell-ringer; ‡-atorium,
clapper 15c.; examination room (mon.)
c 1000; -atus (4th decl.), throb c 950;
-atus (2nd decl.), defendant (leg.) c 1196;
-ans organa, organist 1535; -ito, to knock
repeatedly c 1432; -o, *to urge, entreat
c 1090, 1438; to din c 1000; to call for c 600.
c 1125, c 1320; -ari facio, to ring or toll
(bell) c 1370; -andi hora, time for ringing
(bell) c 1190; hora -at, the hour sounds
c 1296; -atur ad vesperas c 1218; -o (intr.),
to ring (of a bell) a 1230, c 1375; (trans.) to
announce by ringing c 1245, 1526; p.
campanam c 980. 1159, c 1520, p. classi-
cum c 1080, 15c., p. signum c 980. a 1142,
p. tabulam, p. tintinnabulum c 980; p.
horam 1293, 1403; p. obitum 1421; p.
organa 1468; p. humum, to fall dead
c 1125, c 1150; p. pro, to intercede for 5c.;
p. super, to border on a 1200, a 1235.

puls/io (pectoris), pursiness (falc.) a 1150;
-ius, pursy (falc.) a 1150.

pult-, see also 2 pulla; 1 pullanus.

pultura a 1200, p 1265, *putura 1204, 1499,
potura 1204, 1360, poutura 1209, 1293,
†pitura c 1400, (allowance of) food, maintenance; p. satellitum 1283, 1445, p.
servientum 1300, 1304, p. serjantie 1357,
p. stalonum 1315, c 1330, customary payments (W. & Cheshire); putor, keeper, feeder
(falc.) 1275; pouto, to fowl, hawk 1290.

pulver-, see pulvis.

pulv/inar, -inarium c 1170, 1573, pluvinar
a 1250, -inus 1496, cushion, pillow; -illus
c 980. c 1200, 1605, -illa c 1396, -illulus
a 1100, small cushion; -inar, part of siege-
engine c 1275, 1279 (cf. bolstrum); -inum,
(?) roller c 1180; opus -inarium, cushion-
work 1295; see also 2 pulla.

pulvis, *spice 1286, 1480; *1337, 1550, p.
bellicus 1584, p. bombardica 1624, p.
bombardiaricus 1567, p. facticius 1575,
p. gunnorum (gonnorum) 1382, 1427,
p. pyrius 1622, p. tormentalis 1573, p.
tormentarius 1577, 1686, p. vibrellinus
1495, p. librillarum 1448, gunpowder;
‡p. ad oculos, kohl 14c.; p. albus, a confection of (?) sugar and ginger 1265, 1311;
p. clareti 1313, p. †furbeus 1307, p.
Lombardus, pudurlumbartus 1372, sorts
of spice; pulviculus, a little dust 12c.;
poudragium, toll on foot-passengers (Norm.)
c 1180; proditio pulver/aria, gunpowder
plot 1609; -ilingus, dust-licker 1610;
†-inabilis, crumbly c 1270; -osus, dusty
c 1400; -ulentia, dustiness 9c.; -isatio
c 1212, †-ilatio 1207, sprinkling with dust
or sand; -izatio, reducing to dust 1267;
'powdering' (her.) p 1394, a 1446; *-izatus
(-isatus) 1328, 1488, poudratus 1295, 1403,
pouderatus 1426, powderatus 1430,
'powdered', spangled, parsemé; poudratus
c 1324, pouderatus 1409, powderatus
1440, pudratus 1247, 1252, poudrus 1390,
salted or spiced; -izo a 1250, c 1330,
powdero 1449, to pulverize, powder; -izo,
to spangle 1245, a 1446; to salt or spice
c 1443; -ico, to cover with dust c 1340, 1375;
see also pes.

pulytum, *see* polea.
pum/ellum, -ulatus, *see* POM
pumex, pumice: **pomex** c 1222, 1332; **punex,** reef c 550; *see also* PUNIC
pumilio, dwarf: **pomilio** c 1200, c 1393.
puncardus, pynardus (cervisie), (?) stoup 14c.
punct/atio (punt-) 1267, **-uatio** 1344, 1351, punctuation (gram.); marking of points a 1250; 1238, 1301, **-uatio** 1469, 1533, **poyntatio** 1308, **-ura** 1356, 1386, pointing (of masonry); **-io,** piercing (fig.) c 730; 8c., 9c. 1284, **-ura** c 1390, 15c., compunction; **-uatio,** sharpening 1403; appointment, agreement c 1420; **-ura,** quilting 1303; **-orium** c 1180, 1267, **ponsor** 1291, **punso** 1320, **punzonus** 1301, **ponconius** 1275, **poncona** 1350, punch, pricker; **ponsarius** 1495, **punchona** 1358, punch, stamp, graving tool; **punsonus** 1313, **punzunus** 1236, **ponso** 1291, puncheon, short timber; **poyntellum,** 'pointel', (?) pricker 1435; **pointellum,** measure of woad 1347; **-ale** 1378, **-uale** c 1362, point (geom.); **-ualitas,** precision c 1620; **-alis** a 1250, c 1360, **-ualis** c 1205, c 1270, relating to a point (geom.); **-aliter** p 1300, **-ualiter** c 1362, at a point (geom.); **-ualiter,** punctually 1521; **-atim,** punctiliously 1378; **-uatim,** with attention to punctuation (gram.) 1352;
-um, -us, point (of sword, *etc.*) 1172, c 1470; 'point', tag, lace 1387, 1507; passage of arms (in tournament) 1409, 1442; point, detail, item c 1218, 1439; punctilio 1620; station, situation c 1200, a 1408; square (on chess-board) c 1280; note (mus.) c 1330, c 1470; quarter hour a 1150; fifth of an hour 12c., c 1263; minute (astr.) 1120; 3⅓ seconds 1344; **ad -um,** punctually 1425; **de -o in -um,** punctiliously 1446; **in -o** 1375, **in -u** c 1340, c 1390, on the point (of); **in -o blanco,** point blank 1620; **in -u temporis,** in the nick of time c 1390; **in -o ad -um,** in detail 1305; **per -um carte,** by the letter of a charter (Fr.) a 1350;
-atus, pointed c 1270; **-us,** quilted 1257; **-atus** 1265, **poncionatus** 1385, **ponsonatus** 1417, **ponsonetus** 1415, **ponzonatus** (†powzonatus) 1338, **ponciatus** 1420, **pounceatus** 1409, **ponsatus** 1475, **pounsatus** 1454, 'pounced', chased, embossed; **-o** (†pucto, †pucco), to quilt c 1200, 1496; (?) to tattoo 12c.; c 1150, c 1296, **-uo** c 1330, 1472, to punctuate; 1243, **-uo** a 1400, to mark with a point; 1275, 1466, **-uo** 1238, 1376, to point (masonry); 1363, 1384, **-uo** 1352, 1620, **pungto** 1292, to sharpen, tip (with steel); **-uo,** to appoint, fix, agree to c 1350, 15c.; *cf.* PUNG
punctuositas, *see* ponticitas.
pund/a, -us 1274, 1560, **pondus** 1419, 1432, **pons** 1364, **-falda** 1294, 1506, **puntfalda** 1250, 1302, **puntfauda** 1223, **punfalda,** ͵unfaldum 1234, 1410, **punfauda** 1257, 1260, **pondfalda, pondfolda** 1276, **ponfalda** 1282, 1326, **ponefalda** 1351, **pinfalda, pinfaldus** 1272, 1535, **pinfoldus** 1275, pound, pinfold; **-agium** 1424, **pondagium** 1369, 1436, **poundagium** 15c., **pinnagium** 1558, 1598, fine for impounded

animals; **-erus** (Durham) 1183, 1418, **ponderus** (Durham) 1365, †**pontor** 1253, pinder.
pund/um, -us 11c., **-is** c 1200, pound (weight); *cf.* pondus.
punex, *see* pumex.
pung/entia, piercing, penetration c 1250; **-ens** c 1374, **-ibilis** c 1252, *-itivus c 1190, c 1296, pungent, poignant, prickly; ‡**-ito,** "to prick" 1483; **-o** (*perf.* punxi), to punctuate c 1200; to quilt 1303; *cf.* PUNCT
pugn-, *see* PUGN
punic/eus, gules (her.) 1654; †**-o,** to rouge, or (?) *for* pumico, c 1250.
punicus, *see* 1 malum.
pun/itio, fine or forfeiture p 1341, 1419; **-issio,** *for* -itio, c 1393; **-ibilis,** punishable c 1325, c 1444; **-itivus,** punitive c 1290, c 1343; **-itorie** (*pl.*), letters of castigation 1166.
puns-, punt-, punz-, *see* PUNCT
puntagium, *see* pons.
punt/falda, -fauda, *see* punda.
punulum, *see* POM
pupilla, the pip (disease of falcons) a 1446.
pupillus, pupil (ac.) c 1550, 17c.
puplic-, *see* PUBLIC
puppis (cerebri), rear part of brain a 1250.
pupulo, *see* 3 pulla.
pur/alea 1202, **-ialea** 12c., **-ale** 1421, **porale** 1301, **porallum** 1448, 1493, **-aleamentum** a 1250, perambulation, beating the bounds; **-lea** 1462, **porellia** 1413, purlieu, boundary (of forest); **via porall',** 'purrilly way', boundary path 1493; **proalo,** to perambulate 1192.
pur/amentum, liquidation (of debts) 1270, 1276; **-us,** net, clear (of debts) c 1220, 1256; mere a 1205, c 1390; **lapis p.,** ashlar 1398; **p. Hibernicus,** mere Irish 1283, 15c.; **-i claustrales,** monks holding no office c 1282; **ad -um,** completely, thoroughly c 600, 8c. c 1160, c 1343; **de puro,** net 1397; **-e,** merely, unconditionally 12c., 1686; **-atus,** (of fur) trimmed (so as to leave only pure white) 1365, 1382; made of trimmed fur 1314, 1329; **-itanus,** Puritan 1609; **-itanismus,** Puritanism c 1620; **-ificatio,** churching (eccl.) c 1223, 1539; 12c., c 1550, *p. B. Marie* 1216, c 1545, **p. S. Marie** c 980. 1086, c 1350, **-ificans** (*met. grat.*) 1413, Purification, Candlemas (2 Feb.); **-efacio,** to cleanse, perfect c 1390; **-ifico,** to church (eccl.) 1240, c 1250; **-o,** to refine (ore) 1296; to liquidate (debt) 1276, 1419; to grant in pure almoign 1273, 14c.
*pur/cacium (-cachium) 1185, c 1350, **-cattum** 1185, **-kasium** 1207, 1210, *-chacium 1166, c 1250, **-chasium** 12c., **-gacium** 1195, **procassium** 1313, purchase, acquisition, thing acquired; **-chacium,** procurement, instigation 1194, 1221; **-chasium** 1209, 1237, **porcasium** (Norm.) 1180, perquisite (of court); **-chacio, -chacio me de,** to purchase, acquire 1230; **p. me erga,** to proceed against (leg.) 1232; *cf.* PERQUISIT
purcellus, *see* PORC
pur/cinctus, -cingtus, *see* precinctus.
purcivandus, *see* pursevandus.
pure, *see* puramentum.

purfil/atio 1397, **-atura** 1443, purfling; **-o**
1303, 1313, **purfelo** 1512, (?) **profilo** c 1218,
to purfle, trim with border.

purgacium, *see* **purcacium.**

purg/amen c 1160, ***-atio** a 975. c 1102, 1684,
clearance by compurgation or ordeal (leg.);
p. triplex c 1102, **-atio triplex** c 1110; **p.
virile,** weregeld c 1102; **p. spirituale**
c 980; **-amentum** 1262, **-atio** 1271,
liquidation (of debt); expiation c 1450; **-atio,**
refining (of ore) 1338, 1422; expiation in
purgatory (theol.) c 1400, c 1466; **p. canonica** 1262, c 1330; **-abilis,** expiable c 1125,
c 1400; **-ativus,** cleansing 9c.; **-ativum,**
-atorium c 1269, **-atoria** a 1564, purgative
(med.); **-ator,** compurgator (leg.) c 1320,
1684; **-atorianus,** believer in purgatory
(theol.) c 1620; **-atorie,** by way of expiation
12c.; **-atorium,** sewer c 1507; purification,
expiation c 1180, 1562; ***purgatory** (theol.)
c 1150, 1549; **p. Sancti Patricii** (in Lough
Derg) c 1188, c 1400; **-atorius,** purgatorial
(theol.) c 1220, a 1350; **ignis p.** (theol.)
c 1080, c 1465; (for refining metal) c 1178;
domus -atoria, privy c 1293, c 1400;
-atura, filth c 1125; **-o,** to refine (ore) 13c.,
1338; to clear by compurgation or ordeal
(leg.) c 1102, 1684; to liquidate (debts)
1271; to cleanse (soul) in purgatory c 1343;
1613, **‡-ulo** c 1440, to "garble".

purialea, purlea, *see* **puralea.**

purific-, Puritanus, puro, *see* **puramentum.**

Purim, Jewish festival (Heb.) 1277.

purjetto, *see* PERJACT

puroffr/us, -ium, *see* **profrum.**

purpar/s, -tia, *see* **propars.**

purpasius, *see* **porpasius.**

pur/pointus, -po, *see* **purpunctus.**

purportum, *see* **proportum.**

***purpres/tura** 1086, 1539, **†burprestora**
c 1218, **†perprestura** c 1280, **proprestura**
1167, 1235, **porprestura** 1321, **porpristura**
c 1123, **prospertura** 1225, **-io** 1459, **-tum**
c 1130, **†perprestum** 1086, **purprisa,**
purprisum c 1120, a 1564, **purprisium**
a 1190, c 1250, **proprisum** 1336, **porprisa**
1290, **porprisum** (Norm.) 1180, 'purpresture', encroachment; **purpriso** 13c., **-to**
1255, 1407, **-turo** c 1400, **-si** (*perfect*) 1292,
to encroach (on).

pur/punctus 1231, 1266, **†-puctus** 1230,
-pinctus 1224, **-puntus** 1225, 1236, **-puin-
tus** 1198, 1236, **-pointus** 1242, 1336, **†-po**
1447, **propunctus** 1195, 1220, **per/punctus,**
-punctum c 1200, 1304, **-pointus** 1279,
-pontus (G.) 1283, **parpuntus** 1247,
parpuintus 1214, doublet (Fr. *pourpoint*);
cf. **prepectus.**

purpur/amentum, elaborate adornment
c 1200; **purpretura,** (?) purple fabric 1251;
-esco, to grow red a 1275; **-o,** to brighten
c 1204.

purritus, *see* PUTR

pursa, *see* **bursa.**

pur/sevandus 1492, 1526, **-sivandus** 1550,
-civandus ad arma 1570, **p. armorum**
1555, pursuivant; *cf.* PROSECUT

purtrator, *see* PROTRACT

purula, *see* **pirula.**

purus, *see* **puramentum.**

‡pus, custody 1483.

pusca, *see* **posca.**

pus/cula, -tula, *see* **pluscula.**

pusill/itas, feebleness (mental) c 730; **p. mea,**
my humble self c 985, c 1060; **†-anus,** *for*
-animis, 1461; **-ulum,** (*adv.*) a little c 1457.

pusiol/us, little boy c 1125, 1421; **-a,** little
girl 15c.

pustellum, *see* **pistellum.**

putacia, *see* **pittacium.**

put/acius c 1200, **-esia** a 1275, **-osius** 1284,
(?) **pitois** 1295, **petulio** 1285, polecat.

putagium, fornication c 1185, c 1365; tax on
prostitutes 1354.

put/atio, idea, thought c 655; **‡-amen,** belief
1483; **-o** (with *inf.*), to intend c 1180, 1266;
to expect 1219, c 1340; **p. ut,** to suppose
that c 797.

putatorium, pruning-hook c 1190.

Puteal (fig.), business c 1190.

putellum, *see* **pitellum.**

pute/us, grave 11c.; pit (for rain-water) 1361;
cess-pit 1479; brine-pit 1087, c 1250;
***1307, 1587, putuus** 1593, coal-pit, mine-
shaft; **p. aquaticus** 1262; **p. arene** 1392,
p. arenosus 1552, sand-pit; **p. calcis** 1280,
1514, **p. †torreduli** a 1250, lime-kiln; **p.
minere ferri** 1294; **-olus,** well c 1370;
putta 1217, p 1220, **pitt/a, -um** a 1200,
1349, pit.

putfalda, *see* POTT

putibund/us, -e, *see* PUD

putilium, *see* **petilium.**

put/itus, *for* **-idus,** witless c 1314.

puto, *see* **putatio;** PICT

putor, *see* **pultura.**

putr/edo, sheep-rot 1319, c 1400; **-ido,** *for*
-edo, 1385; **-edus,** *for* **-idus,** 6c.; **febris
-edinalis** a 1250; **-efactibilis,** capable of
putrefaction a 1250, c 1360; **-efactio,** putrefaction a 1250, 15c.; **-efactivus** a 1250,
‡1570, -efactorius a 1250, putrefactive;
-escio, putrescence 1288; **-idie** (*pl.*), filth
c 1390; **-ilis,** rotting c 1100; **purritus,** rotted
1313; **pudreo,** *for* **-eo,** to moulder c 1450;
-ido 1408, **-ifico** c 1414, to rot (*trans.*).

putta, *see* **puteus.**

putura, beam, wooden upright (of ambo)
1267; beam of clock 1371 (*cf.* Fr. *poutre*);
see also **pultura.**

puwa, pew (eccl.) 1423.

puzona, (?) filthy rag p 1330.

py-, *see also* **pi-**

pyn-, *see* **pinacia; puncardus.**

pyonada, *see* **pinus.**

pyr/ (pir), fire c 950. c 1200, 1413; **-a,**
bonfire c 550. c 1225; **-alia** (*pl.*), torches
c 1180; **‡-icudium,** steel for striking fire
1483; **-icus,** fiery c 550; **-itegium** a 1195,
1275, **-etegium** c 1250, curfew; **pulvis
-ius,** gunpowder 1622; **-omantia** c 1160,
c 1260, **‡-onomia** 1652, **ars -onomica**
1564, divination by fire; **†-on,** (?) sulphur
(alch.) c 1215; **-opulverea proditio,** Gunpowder Plot c 1620; **-opus,** 'pyrope' (ruby
or carbuncle) 1518; **‡-othechnia,** "preparation of natural things by aid of fire" 1652.

pyracanthos, kind of tree 14c.

pyram/is, (?) canopy c 700; (?) coffin lid
c 1180; (?) roof *or* gable 1519; **‡**"hearse"

c 1440; ‡funnel-shaped vessel (alch.) 1652;
p. rotunda, cone (geom.) a 1233, 1267;
opus †-iticum, (?) lime-burning a 975;
-idalis, pyramidal *or* conical 12c., 1648;
-idalitas, conical shape c 1270; **-idaliter**,
in the form of a cone a 1233, 1267; **-or**, to
taper to a point 12c.
pyrena, barberry (bot.) 1538.
pyrethr/um (bot.): **piritrum** a 1200; **-oleum**,
oil of pyrethrum a 1250.
pyrgus, tower c 1225, c 1370; tower on dice-
board c 815; ‡c 1440, 1483, ‡**pirrus** 15c.,
square of chess-board; **p. specularis**,
look-out tower c 1180.
pyrola, wintergreen (bot.) 1641.
pyrrhocorax, chough (bird) 1536.
Pythagoreus: **Pictagoricus** 1344.
pyth-, *see also* **fithera**; **pitellum**.

pythonissa (bibl.), **phit/onissa** c 1150, 1348,
philtonissa c 1193, sorceress, witch; **-o**,
spirit of divination c 1160; 1406, **-onicus**
11c. c 1160, 14c., **-ius** c 1160, diviner; **-ius**,
pitheus, snaky, venomous c 550.
pyx/is (pix-) *1171, c 1540, **pix** c 1503, pyx,
casket for the host (eccl.); money-box *or*
deed-box c 1200; *offertory box, revenue
from oblations (eccl.) c 1180, c 1530; pyx
containing sample coins for trial 1280, 1534;
(?) case or matrix of seal 1243; (?) ointment
1324; **p. mercati** 1301, 1327, **tolnetum**
-idis 1547, revenue from market-tolls; **p.
nautica**, mariner's compass 1622, 1675;
p. pro pulvere, spice-box c 1410, 1430;
-idis, *for* **-is**, 1279, 15c.; **lanterna-alis**, box-
lantern c 1255; **-o**, (?) to keep locked up 1442;
to fit (wheels) with axle-boxes 1343; *cf.* BUX

Q

quabba, quagmire 1185.
†quaceolus, (?) little swamp c 1130; *cf.*
whasshum.
quachetus, *see* 2 **coketus**.
quactum, *see* 1 **coactio**.
quadam, *see* **quondam**.
quadr/a, quarter of moon 13c.; **q. argentea**,
silver tablet 1550; **q. -abilis**, able to be
squared c 1360; **-aticus**, quadratic, of a
square (math.) 1686; **radix -atica**, square
root (math.) p 1650; **-ato-cubus**, fifth power
(math.) 1686; **-ato-quadratum**, raised to
fourth power (math.) 1686; **-atrix** (*sc.* **linea**)
(math.) 1686; **-aria** 1086, c 1400, **-arium**
c 1180, 1230, **-atura** c 1180, quarry (*cf.*
quarraria); **lapis -atilis**, squared stone
c 1170; **-atio**, squaring (of stone or timber)
1417, 1454; **-ator**, quarry-man, stone-
cutter c 1300; **-atura**, fourfoldness (of
cardinal virtues) c 730; quarter, 1200;
aspect (astr.) 1267; quadrature (math.)
1686; quartering (her.) c 1595; **-atim**,
quarterly (her.) 1654; **-ium**, square (in city)
1236; **†-um**, (?) gadroon, moulding 1517;
(?) quartz c 1270; **-i** (*pl.*), four each c 1362;
-us 1241, **-atus** 9c. c 1130, fourfold (of
cardinal virtues); **-atum**, quadrangle (arch.)
c 1437; **-atus**, natural (mus.) 1326; *see also*
nota; **q. solidus**, cubed c 730; **velum
†-atum**, *see* 1 **quadragena**; **-o**, to form as
a cross 1241; to multiply by four c 1470;
to square (math.) 15c., 1686; to 'square',
accord c 1562.
quadradans, *see* **quadrans**.
quadraga, *see* **quadriga**.
quadrag/ecuplus c 1615, **-intuplus** 1267,
forty-fold.
1 quadrage/na c 1190, c 1450, **quadrantena**
1207, **quarantena** 1163, **quarentena** 1227,
a 1564, **quarentina** 1419, **-num dierum**
c 1260, **-sima** 1430, period of forty days;
quarantena c 1395, ***quarentena** 1236,
c 1290, **carentena** c 1236, forty days during
which widow is entitled to dower, free-
bench (leg.); forty days of military service
1190, 1292; **-na** 1252, ***-sima** a 615, c 730;

c 1115, 1559, forty-day fast, Lent; **-sima**
9c., **Dominica -sime** c 1250, first Sunday
in Lent; **q. media** 12c., c 1320, **quatrage-
sima m.** c 1220, **†quateragia m.** c 1310,
mid-Lent; **q. intermedia** c 1450; **q. major**,
Great Lent (as distinct from other fasts)
c 1250; **jejunium -narium** 12c., c 1362,
j. -simarium 1537, forty-day (Lenten) fast;
***-simalis** c 760, 11c. c 1115, 1498, **quadri-
gesimalis** c 1300, **quadringesimalis** 1418,
Lenten; **pannus -simalis** 13c., **velum
-simale** 1263, 1519, (?) **v. †-atum** 1290,
Lenten veil (for altar); **semen -simale**,
Lenten sowing c 1283, a 1540; **quatra-
gesimus**, *for* **-esimus**, fortieth 1271;
quatraginta, *for* **quadraginta**, a 1140,
c 1255; **-simo**, to observe Lent c 1385; to
exact one-fortieth from 1235.
2 quadr/agena 1086, a 1190, **-agenaria**,
-ans 1086, **-antena** 1145, **quar/antena**
a 1200, 1292, **-entana** a 1187, c 1200,
***-entena** c 1080, 1535, **-entena** c 1180,
-entina 1325, 1381, **-entela** a 1250, 1466,
carentela 14c., **†-etarium** 1316, furlong
(linear measure *or* strip of land).
quadrangul/us c 700. p 1300, c 1470, **†qua-
dragulatus** c 700, **quadrungulum** c 730,
quadrangle or square; **-um carnis**, human
body (composed of four elements) c 1250;
-us c 700. c 1190, c 1400, **-aris** c 1250,
c 1612, quadrangular; **-ariter**, at the four
corners c 1172.
quadr/ans, quarter circle c 1500, 1537;
quadrant (instrument) c 1227, a 1350; *1086,
1564, **†-adans** 1185, **-anta** 1310, **†-ata**
c 1440, farthing; **q. aureus** 14c., **q. auri**
1379, **q. de auro** 1393, quarter of gold florin
or noble; **q. ponderis**, quarter pennyweight
1425; **q. terre** "farthing-land" (Cornwall)
1500; **-anta terre** 14c., **-antata terre** 1359,
measure of land (Sc.); **-antata** 1259, 15c.,
-antatus c 1400, **-entata** 1259, **-entale** 13c.,
farthing's worth (of land or rent); **-antalis**,
costing a farthing 1267, 14c.; quadrantal, of
90° (math.) 1686; *see also* **quadragena**.
quadrar-, **quadrat-**, *see* **quadra**.

quadravus, great-great-grandfather c 1395.

quadrellus, *see* **quarellus.**

quadr/ennium 1261, 1272, **quatriennium** c 1434, period of four years; †**-ennius,** aged four c 1280; **-iennalis,** four-yearly c 1330, c 1340.

quadrent-, *see* **quadrans.**

quadricata, *see* **quadriga.**

quadri/ceps, four-headed c 1545; **-cerii,** four lights (of the church) 1531; **-color,** four-coloured a 1450; **-duanus (mortuus)** c 1190, c 1414, **quatriduanus** 1345, (one) dead for four days (of Lazarus); **quatri-duanus,** occurring on the fourth day c 800; **dies -duanus,** fourth day c 1150; **-farie,** in four parts c 800. a 1100, a 1446; **-fidi** (*pl.*), all four c 1000; **-fidus,** cruciform (of church) c 700; **-folio,** quatrefoil 1345; ‡**-folium,** "four-leaved grass" (bot.) 15c.; **-formis,** made of the four elements c 730, 993; **-furcatus,** four-pronged c 1362; **-gama,** four times married (*f.*) a 1186; **-laterum** 1326, 1686, **-latria** a 1250, a quadrilateral (geom.); **-membris,** fourfold a 1200; **-mil-lesimus,** four-thousandth c 1250; **-modus** 7c., **quatrimodus** c 800, of four kinds; **quadrepartura (meremii),** (?) squaring 1532; **-partitus,** title of a collection of laws c 1150; *Tetrabiblon* (attributed to Ptolemy) 1267; **-patens,** (?) extending in four directions c 950; **-varius, -vidus,** fourfold c 800; **quatri/fido,** to quarter c 1307; **-pertio,** to quarter (felons) 15c., c 1450.

quadrig/a c 1160, 1461, **quadraga** 1316, wagon; **q. ferrata,** iron-tired wagon (Norm.) 1180; **-aria** 13c., **via -aria** c 1180, 1199, wagon-road; **latitudo -aria** (20 feet) c 1315; **pons -arius** c 1315; **-arius,** wagoner 1277; **-ata** c 1130, 1559, **quadri-cata** 1201, wagon-load (*see also* **carrucata**); **-o,** to carry in a wagon c 1120, c 1450; *cf.* **1 carra.**

quadr/igesimalis, -ingesimalis, *see* **1 qua-dragena.**

quadripl-, *see* QUADRUPLIC

quadrivi/um, group of four c 815; c 850. c 1080, 1421, **quadruvium** 1089, **quatru-vium** 12c., **-ales** (*pl.*) c 1283, c 1435, the four liberal arts; **scientie -ales** 1344, c 1450; **orbis -us,** the four quarters of the world c 1362; **quadruvium,** road of life c 800; four c 550.

quadr/o, -ium, -um, -us, *see* **quadra.**

quadrug/a, -ata, *see* **2 carruca.**

quadrungulum, *see* **quadrangulus.**

quadrupes, four-legged trivet 1328; **quadru-pedal/is,** four-footed c 800; four feet long c 1125; **-itas,** four-footedness 9c.

quadruplic/atio c 1258, **quadriplicatio** c 1390, rebutter (leg.); **-iter** 9c. 13c., c 1343, **quatripliciter** c 1470, in four ways; **quatriplicatus,** quadruplicate a 1446; **dentes quadrupli,** (?) molars a 1250; **-atus,** of the fourth power (math.) 1686; **-o** c 1258, 1559, **quadriplico** c 1390, to rebut (leg.); **-o arma,** to bear four arms in one shield (her.) p 1394; **quadriplo,** to multiply by four c 1410.

quadrupunctalis, of four points c 1360.

quadruvium, *see* **quadrivium.**

quaila 1384, ‡**qual/ia, -ena** 15c., quail (bird); *cf.* **quiscula.**

qualific/atio, qualification, condition 1389, 1552; **-atus,** qualified, adapted (of things) c 1612, 1620; qualified (of persons) 1526, 1549; **-o,** to qualify, modify c 1270, 1684.

qual/itas, rank c 1390, c 1565; **q. substan-tialis,** quality inherent in substance (phil.) c 1270; **-is,** which (*relative*) c 1260; ***-isqualis,** of whatever kind c 1188, c 1258; **-iter,** by what right c 1204, 1415; (with *subj.*) in such a way that c 600, c 1000; **-itercumque,** by whatever right 1224, 15c.; **in -i** c 1200, **-itative** 1335, as regards quality, qualitatively; ***-itativus,** qualitative, dependent on quality c 1115, c 1380; **-itatus,** endowed with qualities c 1362.

qualstowa (†**gwalstouua**), place of execution (A.S. *cwalstow*) c 1115.

quam/, *for* **tam . . . q.,** as well as c 1318; rather than (after *positive adj.*) 1166; **non . . . q.,** not otherwise than c 1285; **nullus . . . q.,** no other than 1537; (**ad aliud**) **q.** (pertinet), *for* **q. quod,** c 1290; **q. honorifice,** very honourably c 1450; **q. brevius poterit** c 1389; **q. quietius possit** c 1330; ***-citius** c 1100, 1450, ***-cito** c 1204, 1583, as soon as; **-dignus,** right worthy 1454; **-diu,** until c 1090, c 1266; c 1250, **-diu est** c 1300, for a long time; **-pluries** c 1130, 15c., **-sepius** c 1335, often; **-que,** *for* **quam** (*correlative*) c 1450.

quamtoci/us, -ens, *see* QUANT

quand/eitas p 1347, **-alitas** a 1361, c 1370, **-olitas** 1427, 'whenness', temporality (*see also* QUANT); **-olificanter,** so as to produce temporal distinction 1427; **-oque,** at length c 780; **-oquando,** whenever c 1437.

quandros, magical gem (found in vulture's head) a 1250, ‡1652.

quant/itas, size c 1200, c 1540; 1272, **quan-ditas** 1280, gravity (of an offence); **-us,** a certain 13c.; having quantity c 1380; **-um,** quantity a 1233, c 1520; (*conjunction*) in so far as 1205, c 1340; **q. ad** 1252, **q. de** 1293, with regard to; **q. minus potest,** as little as possible c 1340; *see also* **de, in, per;** **-umcum** p 1250, **-umcumque** 1289, although; **-o,** *for* **quo magis,** a 1100; ***quamtocius** c 1170, 1507, **quamtociens** c 1393, *for* **-ocius,** as soon as possible; **in -o** c 1200, **-itative** 1335, a 1384, as regards quantity, quantitatively; **-itativus** c 1250, c 1380, **-itivus** 1267, quantitative, relating to quantity; **-ificatio,** quantification, measurement c 1362; **-ifico,** to quantify, measure c 1360, c 1380.

***quaquaversum,** in every direction 7c. c 1125, 1537; c 730, c 950, **quaqueversum** c 730, wheresoever, whithersoever.

quaquina, *see* COQU

quarant-, *see* **quadragena** (**1 & 2**).

quarc-, *see* QUERC

quare, because c 1343, 14c.; (with verb of perceiving) that 836; **non sine q.,** not without reason 13c.; **q. non,** *for* **quominus,** c 1327; **q. ejecit** 1419, **q. impedit** 1198, 1368, **q. vi et armis** 1309, names of writs.

quare-, *see also* **quadragena** (**1 & 2**).

***quarell/us** 1160, 1405, **-a** 1296, 1315,

†**grarlellus** 1190, **quadrellus** 1246, **carellus** (G.) a 1325, **cayrellus** (G.) 1304, **querellus** 1266, †**garaldus** 1540, quarrel, bolt for cross-bow or gun; **q. ad duos pedes, q. ad unum pedem** 1293, **q. unius pedis** 1305 (cf. ballista); c 1296, a 1316, **carrelis** 1398 (?) square cushion; (?) 1279, **-a** 1287, squared stone or brick; **-a, -um**, quarry c 1280, 1327; **-o**, to diaper (walls) 1241, 1256; cf. **quadra, quarraria.**

quarena, (?) stone-carving, moulding 1333.
quarent-, quaret-, see **quadragena** (1 & 2).
quareria, see 1 **carra.**
quarnellus, see 1 **carnellus.**
quarr/aria, -arium 1163, c 1310, **-eria, -erium** a 1200, 1373, ***-era** 1229, 1587, **-iria** 1222, **querrera** 1407, 1516, †**querra** 1314, **-ea, -ia** 1312, 1583, **-ium** c 1170, **-ina** 1535, **-ura** 1302, 1430, **querrura** 1409, 1463, **-elia** (Norm.) 1198, quarry; **-etereia,** quarrying (Norm.) 1198; **-arius** 1280, 1420, **-earius, -iarius** 1222, 1319, **-erarius** 1319, 1434, **querrerarius** 1339, **querrurarius** 1450, †**querurius** 1416, **-ator** 1287, 1371, **-eator** 1198, 1337, **-ior** (Sc.) c 1330, quarryman, stone-cutter; **-io**, to quarry 1287; cf. **quadra, quarellus,** QUEST
quarrucata, see 2 **carruca.**
quart/a 1241, a 1564, **-us** 1287, c 1478, **carta** 1303, **squarta** (G.) 1254, **esquarta** (G.) 1283, **scarta** (G.) 1289, 1312, **escarta** (G.) 1289, **swarta** (G.) 1242, **carto** (G.) 1254, measure of volume, quart; quart pot 1440; ‡peck (quarter bushel) 1483; quarter (of moon) c 1265; quarter (of year) 1194; farthing 1282 (cf. **quadrans**); unit of 240 acres, 'cartron', ceathramhadh (Ir.) c 1606 (cf. **quartarium**); quartering (her.) a 1446, c 1595; **q. diminuta,** canton (her.) c 1595; **-ale**, measure of sturgeon c 1404; **-allum**, measure of timber (Dutch) 1474; ‡**-atio**, separation of gold and silver (alch.) 1652; **-um**, 1/3,600 of a second a 1150, 1344; **-o**, fourthly 1279, c 1332; **-ogenitus,** fourthborn 1406; **-us,** quarter, aspect (astr.) 13c.; fourth (to distinguish bearers of same name) 1390; **feria -a,** Wednesday c 980. a 1090, 1558; **heres -us,** heir to one-fourth a 1251.
Quart/adecimani (pl.) c 1125, **Quatuordecimani** 10c., sect celebrating Easter on fourteenth day (of Nisan); **-odecimo,** fourteenthly 1282, c 1343.
quart/anarius, -enarius, sufferer from quartan malaria a 1250.
quart/arium 1422, 1460, ***-erium** 1086, 1460, **-eria** 1200, **-erius** c 1212, 1344, **-erus** 1221, 1468, **-eris** c 1200, **-ero** c 1295, **-eronus** 1285, 1307, **-ronus** 1267, 1298, **-rona** 1310, quarter, fourth part (in general); ***-erium** 13c., 1569, **-eria** c 1420, **-ernum** 1344, quarter (of human body); ***1227,** 1475, **-erius** 1205, c 1483, **-ura** c 1530, quarter (of year); †**-erium,** (?) fourth day after 1297; **-arium** 1450, ***-erium** 1271, 1531, **-rona** 1275, 1354, quarter of city; **-erium** 1244, 1315, **-era** 1287, **-ero** 1279, **-rona** 1314, 1468, **quatrona** 1452, plot of land, (?) fardel, quarter-virgate; **-erium,** ceathramhadh (Ir.) 1501 (cf. **quarta**); **-rona** commune c 1318; **q. prati** 1446; **-erium,** quartering (her.)

p 1394, a 1446; **-eria** 1289, **carteria** c 1255, measure of wine (G.); **-arius,** measure of ale 1504; **-arium** c 1250, 1364, **-aria** 1291, **-arius** (C.I.) c 1150, ***-erium** a 1155, c 1450, **-eria** 1255, c 1400, **-erius** 1206, 1535, **carterium** (C.I.) 15c., **squarterium** (G.) 1289, **-ernus** c 1220, †**-inarium** a 1190, **-erium Londoniense** 1215, 1303, quarter, measure of grain, (usually 8 bushels); **-ionarius,** quarter of caboteau (of grain), quarchonnier (C.I.) 1309; **-eronus** 1233, 1324, **-ro** 1224, 1335, **-rona, -ronus** 1297, 1340, **-o** 1375, **-onus** 1324, **quatronus** 1342, unit of weight, quarter of pound or hundredweight; **-ro subbosci** 1322; **-ronarius,** tenant of quarter-virgate (W.) 1349; **-eragium** 1274, 1477, †**-erlegium** 1414, quarterly payment; **-erinus,** quarterly c 1365; **sessio -erialis,** quarter session 1661; **-ernatim,** every quarter (of year) 1562; **-eriatim,** quarterly (her.) p 1394, a 1446; **-ellatus** 1374, **-ilatus** p 1340, 1383, quartered (her.); **-erizatio,** quartering (of felon) p 1382, 15c.; **-erio,** to quarter (her.) p 1394, a 1446; 15c., **-ero** c 1340, **-erno** 1344, **-erizo** c 1330, 1468, **-irizo** c 1400, to quarter (felons) 1286; **-ero,** to quarter, divide into four 1275.
quartelettus 1413, **cartellus** 1439, 1474, measure of wine; cf. **quarta, quarteria.**
quart/enarius 1424, **-imagister** 1461, **-ermagister** 1502, **quatronus magister** 1444, quartermaster (naut.); cf. **contramagister;** see also **quartanarius.**
quarter-, quart/ilatus, -inarium, -ionarius, see **quartarium;** QUATERN
†**quartina,** (?) sort of weapon c 1180.
quarto, see **quarta; quartarium.**
quartodecimo, see **Quartadecimani.**
quartr-, quartura, see **quartarium.**
quart/um, -us, see **quarta.**
quasi/ si c 1090, **q. et si** 1432, as if; **vel q.** 1279, c 1330, **seu q.** 1555 (at end of clause), or virtually so; **q. compositio,** virtual composition a 1304; **q. possessio,** virtual possession 1279, c 1325; **possessio corporalis et quasi** 1313; ***-modo geniti,** Low Sunday c 1125, c 1450; **-modo,** (?) payment due on Low Sunday (eccl.) 1286.
quasillum, basket: ‡**quaxill/um** c 1200, 15c.; ‡**-arius,** basket-maker c 1440.
quass/atio, affliction (bibl.); **cassatura,** shock (med.) a 1250; **cassabundus,** apt to be broken in pieces 685; **casso,** for **-o,** to break down 13c.; see also CASS
quatenus (quatinus), ***that** (in indirect command or request) 8c. c 1125, 1583; ***in** order that 7c., 8c. c 1072, c 1450; with the condition that 7c.; in so far as c 1250.
quateragia, see 1 **quadragena.**
quater/angulatus, quadrangular 1445; **-deni,** forty 1200; **-geminus** c 1250, **-partitus** 1404, 1435, quadripartite; **-viginti** 1086, c 1400, **quatuorviginti** (G.) 1254, 1281, eighty.
*quatern/a, -um, -us c 1165, 1535, †**quatrinus** c 1250, **quarternus** 1390, c 1423, **-io** c 800, 873. c 1125, 1516, **quarternio** a 1300, 1445, **quinterna** 1538, quire, gathering, booklet; **-ulus,** small quire 1427; **-io,**

quarter (her.) c 1595; **-atim**, quire by quire c 1438; **-alis** (*pl.*), four c 700; **-arium**, number four c 815; **-itas**, 'quaternity', group of four c 1250, 1427; **-o (Trinitatem)**, to turn into a quaternity (theol.) a 1275; *see also* **quartarium**.

quatinus, *see* **quatenus**.

quatrag/inta, -esimus, *see* I **quadragena**.

quatri-, *see* **quadrennium**; QUADRI; QUADRU- PLIC; QUATERN

quatron-, *see* **quartarium**; **quartenarius**.

quatruvium, *see* **quadrivium**.

quattum, *see* I COACT

Quatuordecimani, *see* **Quartadecimani**.

quatuortempor/a (*pl.*), Ember days (eccl.) 980. 1072, c 1520; **jejunium -ale**, Ember- day fast c 1115.

quatuorviginti, *see* QUATER

quaxill-, *see* **quasillum**.

queint/isa (queynt-, †quenit-) 1251, 1290, **quentesia** 1303, **quoyntisa** 1251, **coin- teisia** 1247, **cointisa** 1260, 'cointise', ornate dress; **-esio**, to decorate 1306.

‡quelanea, henbane (bot.) 15c.

quererarium, *see* **quiriacum**.

queratio, fetching 1466; *cf.* QUEST

querc/ulus, 1233, a 1564, **-ula** 1257, **querulus** 1309, 1389, **-ina** 1460, oak sapling; **quarcus**, *for* **-us**, oak 1420, 1528; ***-inus** a 1200, a 1540, **-ineus** 1313, **-ulinus** 1356, made of oak, oaken; **‡pomum -inum**, oak-apple 14c.; **vipera -ina** (quarcina), kind of snake 13c.; **-ula**, germander (bot.) a 1250, 1538.

●quer/ela c 1070, 1684, **-entia** c 1358, **-imonia (-emonia)** 1274, c 1515, **-ula** 1272, c 1380, plaint, plea, suit, esp. one instituted without writ (leg.); **q. bona**, just cause 1461; **ex gravi -ela**, name of a writ 1419; *see also* **stultus**; **causa -ebunda**, cause for complaint 1518; **-ula** c 1362, **-elatio** c 1397, c 1458, **-ulatio** 1426, c 1450, complaint; **-elositas**, plaintiveness c 760; **-elosus** 1241, 1417, **-imonialis** c 1250, 14c., **-imoniosus** 14c., complaining, querulous; **‡-itabundus**, "a busy complainer" 1520; **-ulus** c 1220, **-elator** 1219, **-elans** 1289, c 1455, ***-ens** 1199, c 1450, complainant, plaintiff (leg.); **-elatus**, defendant (leg.) 1295; **-elo**, *for* **-elor**, to complain 1304, a 1452; 1220, c 1465, **-ulor** 1437, **-or** 1378, c 1390, to bring an action, implead (leg.); **-elo loquelam**, to plead a plea (leg.) 1294.

querellus, *see* **quarellus**.

queresta, beast c 550.

quer/estarius, -ista, *see* I **chorus**.

querna, quern, hand-mill 1358.

quer/o, -io, -ibilis, *see* QUEST

querr-, querio, quererurius, *see* **quarraria**.

querreus, *see* **scurio**.

querulus, *see* QUERC; **querela**.

quest/a, inquest 1431, c 1450; 1461, **-us** c 1367, quest; 1199, 1313, **-us** 1241, 1400, tax (on domicile), *quête* (G.); **-us**, collection of alms (eccl.) 1308, 1352; acquisition, pro- perty acquired c 1170, 1343; **queribilis**, open to question (log.) c 1365; **-abilis** 1400, **-alis** 1276, 1436, **-ialis** 1366, subject to *quête* (G.); **-abiliter**, by payment of *quête* (G.) 1289; **†quisita**, question c 1070;

quesitus, questioning c 730; **quesitio lapidum** 1458, **quisitio** l. 1402, getting stone;
-io, *question, disputed point (phil.) 838. a 1200, c 1590; begging (Sc.) 13c.; exaction (Sc.) 1550, 1564; section of canon law 14c., c 1444; form of jurisdiction, soke c 1115; relation to a dispute, involvement (G.) 1281; **-ionarius** c 800. c 1180, 14c., ***-or** 1207, 1562, **-uarius** 1288, c 1350, collector of alms, 'limiter' or pardoner (eccl.); **modi -uarii**, procedure of alms-collecting 1317; **-ionatio**, questioning c 1470; **-ionative**, by questioning c 1508; **-ionista**, questionist (ac.) c 1250, 1552; **quisitus**, sought for 1228, 1452; **-iono**, to question 1444, c 1470; to torture 1309, 1315; **-o**, to beg 1308; **quero**, to question 1202, 1388; **querio**, to get, dig up (marl) (? *cf.* **quarrio**) 1276.

questuosus, plaintive c 1195; *cf.* **querela**.

queynt-, *see* QUEINT

quia, that (*indirect statement*) (bibl.); on con- dition that 1234; as being 1086, c 1450; **adeo q.**, so that c 1250; *see also* **scientia**.

quib/iba, -ebatus, *see* **cubeba**.

†quibinus, (?) reliquary 1383.

quicinus, *see* **quissinus**.

quicquid sit de hoc, however that may be' c 1343.

quicumquemodus, whatever kind 8c.

quid juris clamat, name of a writ (leg.) 1419; **in quid**, in the category of substance c 1160; **cujus gratia**, final clause (οὗ ἕνεκα) 1344; ***quiddit/as**, quiddity, essence (phil.) a 1233, 1620; **-ative**, with reference to quiddity c 1300, 1427; **-ativus**, essential c 1300, 1518.

quidam . . . quidam, one . . . another 8c.

quideles, intestate (A.S. *cwydeleas*) c 1115.

qui/es, immobility 1335, a 1350; **-es, locus -etionis**, tomb c 1325; **-escio**, *for* **-etio**, coming to rest c 1345; **-etio** c 1090, **-etudo** c 1190, 15c., quietude, peace; **-eta**, (?) bed c 810; **-etativus** c 1270, c 1365, **-etivus** c 1270, bringing to rest; **-escibilis**, capable of rest c 1250; **-esco**, to die c 1250, 13c.; to acquiesce c 1413; to restrain a 1408; **q. a**, to desist from c 1115, 13c.; **q. ad anchoram**, to ride at anchor 1427; **-esso**, to sleep c 1266.

*quiet/antia c 1096, 1499, ***quittantia** 1156, 1545, ***-atio** c 1102, 1461, **quitatio** 1255, 1361, **-udo** 1100, 1248, quittance, dis- charge, immunity; **littere quitatorie** 1426, l. **†quittancie** (*adj.*) 1442, letters of quittance; ***-e**, freely, with immunity 1086, 1267; net 1388; **-us** c 1070, 1461, **quitus (quittus)** c 1180, 1461, quit, immune; ***-us redditus**, quit-rent a 1200, c 1564;
*-a-clamantia c 1150, 1419, ***-a-cla- matio** 1140, 1564, **quitaclamatio** 1235, **-clamatio** 1296, **-e-clamatio** c 1200, 1450, **-a acclamatio** c 1470, **-um-clamatio** 1530, **-e-clamium** 1342, **-um-clamium** 1196, 1419, quit-claim, release of claim (leg.); ***-um clamo** c 1070, 1451, **-e clamo** c 1180, c 1495, **quite clamo** 1410, 1496, **quitclamo** c 1500, **-um acclamo** c 1470, **-um concedo** a 1100, **-um voco** c 1330, to quitclaim; ***-o** 1086, 1461, **quitto** 1216, 1461, to quit, discharge.

quietudo, *see* quies, QUIET
quilhagium, *see* kela.
quilibet, anyone at all c 800; *each, every 1199, c 1565; quilicet, any 1264, a 1450; *cf.* quis.
quil/os, (said to be Greek for) moist (*cf.* χυλός) 1326; -isma, note sung lightly (mus.) 1326.
quilt-, quilc-, *see* culcitra.
quin/ancia, -ciacus, *see* cynanche.
quin/arius, number five c 815. 1267; -cunx, lozenge c 1595.
quinba, *see* cubeba.
quindalla, *see* quintallus.
quin/decima 1204, c 1353, -dena 1205, c 1375, -ta decima 1219, 1575, tax of a fifteenth; *-dena 1201, 1482, -zena c 1200, quinzaine, period of fifteen days; -decennalis, lasting for fifteen years c 1293; -decimo, to pay a fifteenth c 1225.
quinminus, *for* quominus, that not c 800.
quinquag/ena, period of fifty years c 1255; 1299, 1426, -enarius c 1115, set of fifty psalms; -enarius, person fifty years old 14c.; -enti, five hundred 1327; -esima 7c., 8c., Q. Paschalis, -enales dies c 730, -esimi dies c 1160, fifty days between Easter and Pentecost; Shrove Tuesday 9c.; c 980. c 1125, c 1493, -issima c 1266, Quinquagesima, Shrove Sunday; -esies, fifty times 1267, c 1330; jejunium -esimale fifty-day fast c 1535.
Quinqu/e Portus, *see* portus; -efolium, cinquefoil (in design) 1245; -enarius numerus, number five 1237; -enervia a 1250, ‡14c., -inervia a 1200, plantain (bot.); -epartite, in five parts c 1340; -ifarius, five-fold c 1250.
quinquennale, (?) payment for quinquennial mass (eccl.) 1426; *cf.* triennale.
quint/a (quinct-) (*sc.* leuca), banlieu (Norm.) 1215; -a essentia a 1200, c 1345, -essentia 1620, -a natura a 1200, quintessence; -a feria, Thursday 831, c 1006. a 1100, 15c.; -ana c 1204, (?) 1362, -ena c 1255, -ina c 1293, quintain; febris -ana, f. -ena (med.) a 1250; -ifolium, cinquefoil (her.) a 1450; -ipartitus, in five parts 1338, 1427 (*cf.* quinque); -o, fifthly 1279, c 1332; -odecimo, fifteenthly 1282, c 1343 (*cf.* quindecima); -um, ¹/₆₀ of a *quartum* 1344; -upliciter, in five ways 1380, 1466; -uplus, five-fold c 1267, c 1615; -uplo, to multiply by five c 1300.
quintall/us, -a, -um c 1100, c 1436, quintale c 1328, quindalla 1253, kyntallus 1523, unit of weight, quintal.
quinterna, *see* QUATERN
quinzena, *see* quindecima.
quiper/um, -ium, *see* cubeba.
quirculus, *see* circulus.
quir/ea, -eta, *see* corium.
‡quiri/acum (malum) 15c., ‡-anum, -arium c 1440, ‡querarium 1483, “costard” (apple).
quirin, gem found in hoopoes’ nests a 1250.
‡quirinarium, quintain c 1440.
‡Quirini plaga, form of gout 1652.
Quirites, mounted warrior a 1260.
quir/ius, -reus, *see* scurio.
quis/, who (*relative*) c 800. c 1270; whoever

(*for* quisquis) 1108, c 1250; -libet, *for* quilibet, c 600, c 800. c 1170; -que 7c., -piam 9c., *for* -quam; -que *for* quis, c 730, (?) c 985; 8c., *-cunque c 1340, 1441, *for* quicunque; -quis (*interrog.*) c 800.
quiscinus, *see* quissinus.
quis/cula 15c., ‡-quila 1483, ‡-tiola c 1440, quail (bird); *cf.* qualia.
quisinarius, *see* coquina.
quisit-, *see* QUEST
quisqu/alie, *for* -ilie, loppings 1496; ciscilia (*pl.*), rubbish c 550; -ilarium, rubbish bowl a 1250.
quiss/a, thigh (*Fr.* cuisse) 1209; stub (of oak) c 1330; -ellus 1215, 1272, -ettus 1277, 1297, -ottus c 1282, 1289, -o 1275, 1300, -era 1213, 1224, cuissaria 1303, cuisse, thigh-armour; *cf.* coxa.
quissin/us, -a, -um 1232, 1445, †quissius 1300, -ettus 1292, quicinus 1290, quiscinus 1445, cucina 1493, cussin/us, -a, -um 1215, 1516, cosinus 13c., cushion.
quit-, *see* QUIET
quo/ warranto, name of a writ (leg.) 1287, 1555; ostensurus (ad respondendum) q. w. 1196, c 1258; -modolibet c 1250, 1535, -vismodo 1344, c 1448, in any way; -vismodus, of any sort 1485.
quoadjuvo, *see* COADJU
quoad/tenus as far as c 1408; -usque, in order that c 1000; coad, *for* quoad, 1235, c 1337.
quod, *that (ind. statement)* (bibl.); *(ind. command or request)* c 1100, c 1450; *(final)* 1216, a 1408; *(consecutive)* p 1150, c 1450; q. ad aliquid, to a certain extent c 1160; q. ad universitatem, generally c 1160; q. permittat, name of a writ (leg.) 1227, c 1290; q. quid erat esse, essence (τὸ τί ἦν εἶναι) 1344.
quodamtenus, to a certain extent a 1100.
quodlibet/ 1329, 14c., *-um a 1300, c 1450, quolibetum c 1500, quotlibetum 1521, ‘quodlibet’, disputation (ac.); -alis c 1410, c 1520, -icus c 1500, concerning disputations.
quoequo, *see* coequatio.
quoexecutor, *see* COEXECUT
quolibertus, *see* colibertus.
quomodolibet, *see* quo.
quonamen, *see* 1 conatus.
quondam, formerly: condam c 1247, 1382, quadam 6c.
quoniam, *that (ind. statement)* 1140, c 1362; *(ind. command)* c 1194; qwoniam, *for* q., c 1300.
quonius, *see* cuneus.
quonubialis, *see* connubialis.
quoopero, quopertura, *see* coopertio.
quoqu-, *see* COQU
quorsumcumque, whithersoever 9c. c 1240.
quorulus, *see* corylus.
quoscetus, *see* 2 cota.
quosciens/, *for* quotiens, 1234; -cumque a 1300.
quot/a 1289, 1549, cota c 1344, 1539, quota, share; -ula, small share c 1470; -us, quotient (math.) 1686; -atio c 1380, 1414, cotatio c 1432, numeration, reckoning; -ator annalium, annalist c 1470; -uplus, as many fold 1520; -uslibet, as many as

you please c 1197; -o c 1315, a 1452, **coto** c 1295, c 1420, to quote by number.
quotarius, *see* **2 cota.**
quotenus, as long as c 1170.
quotidi-, *see* COTIDI
quotlibetum, *see* **quodlibet.**

quousque, as far as c 731; *until c 1188, c 1485.
quovismod/o, -us, *see* quo.
quoyntisa, *see* queintisa.
quum, *for* **cum**, since c 1130.
qwarva, *see* WHARV

R

rabb/i c 1227, 1345, **-inus** 1552, 1620, rabbi.
rabeo, *see* REHAB
rabettus 1407, **robettus** 1473, young rabbit.
rabiola, 'rafiol', 'raviol', meat-ball 1243.
rab/iosus, rampant (her.) c 1595; **-ula,** slanderer c 950; **-ulus**, slanderous, brawling c 1000. c 1160; **-ulatus**, brawl, wrangle c 965; **-io**, to be rabid, behave wildly 870. c 1307.
rabota, (?) gaff (*cf.* O.F. *rabette*) 1275.
rabri, *bolus Armenicus* a 1250.
racatum, *see* RECHAT
raccheristus, *see* RAD
raccus, *see* RACK
rac/emus 1230, 1533, **-enus** 1300, c 1335, **-imus** a 1310, **rascemus** 1223, **rasinus** 15c., **resinus** 1308, **reisinus** 1282, 1267, **reysingus** 1302, raisin or cluster of raisins; **r. Corinth[ius]** c 1305, **r. de Corenc'** (**Coryns, Curansz**) c 1335, 1531, currant; **r. de Maleque (Maleg', Mallek')**, Malaga raisin 1285, 1307; **r. zinziberis**, *see* **radix**; **-enus** (of garlic) 1290, c 1300 (*cf.* **rasus**); †**-einus (querculorum)**, (?) spray *or* root 1402; *see also* **radix.**
racha, *see* ragadia.
rachan/atus 1136, **recanatus** c 1250, **rechinnatus** c 1362, hissing or roaring; ‡**-o** 1483, ‡**recano** 15c., to roar like a tiger.
rach/ementum, -imentum, -iamentum, ratchment, flying buttress (arch.) 1397.
racheta, raschete, (?) membrane between fingers a 1250; *see also* RECHAT
rachinburgius, criminal judge (Frankish) c 1115.
racimus, *see* racemus.
racin/a, -us, *see* radix.
rack/a (rakk-) 1279, 1398, **raccus** 1338, **rekka** 1346, rack (for feeding animals); **-a,** rack (used with pulley) (naut.) 1295; 1391, **rekka** 1322, 1419, rack, tenter (for cloth); **-o,** to fit (sheep-fold) with racks 1392.
racum, *see* reccum.
rad/a, riding-service, escort duty (Durham) 1183, c 1380; **-chenister** 1086, †**raccheristus** c 1120, †**ratenihctis** 1138, **-mannus** 1086, 12c., **rudmannus** 1285, 'radknight', 'radman', tenant liable to escort duty; †**redingel[andum]**, (?) land held by radknight 1212; *cf.* **ridemannus**; *see also* I **roda.**
radagia, *see* ragadia.
radeventia, *see* redhibentia.
radi/us, furrow c 1240, c 1290; arm of cross c 1595; 'ray', striped cloth 1265; ‡baker's strickle 1585; 1235, c 1315, **raya** c 1450, row, stripe; **r. cruoris,** spirt of blood c 1436;

r. oculi, glance a 1165; **r. visualis,** visual ray 1326, 1345; **-olus,** (?) projection on spine (med.) c 1180; baton (her.) c 1595; **-alis,** radial 1267; radiant a 1275; **-atim** a 1520, **-ose** p 1300, c 1430, radiantly, as by rays; **-etas solis,** solar radiance, halo a 1142; **-ositas,** radiance, radiation a 1233, 1267; **-osus,** radiant 1252, c 1360; radial c 1260; *-atus 1235, c 1400, **raiatus (ray-)** 1377, **reatus** a 1175, 1486, **reiatus** 1215, †**retatus** 1248, (?) **ridatus** 1251, rayed, striped; **-o,** to furrow c 1290; *cf.* **reo;** *see also* **ragadia.**
radix 1145, c 1445, **r. quadratica** p 1650, square root (math.); unknown first power (math.) 1145; radix, starting-point (astr.) a 1350; **r. cordis** (med.) c 1200; **r. nervi** (med.) a 1250; **r. Jesse,** tree of Jesse 1236; **r. rosea,** rose-root (bot.) 1641; **r. zinziberis (gingiberis)** 1270, 1295, **racina z.** 1275, **racinus z.** 1279, **racemus z.** 1431, 'race', root, of ginger; **membrum radic/abile,** primary organ of animal a 1250; **-alis,** radical, fundamental a 1250, 1620; **-aliter** a 1233, 1461, **-abiliter** 13c., radically, fundamentally; **-iter,** *for* **-itus,** by the roots 1333; **-atio,** rooting, establishing 1267, 1427; **-ator,** (?) *for* **eradicator,** one who stubs up roots 1489; **-o,** to uproot, stub up roots (?) 1200, 1489; to establish, ground c 1258, 1502.
rado, *see* rasura.
raff/urnum, lime-kiln (O.F. *rafour*) 1286; **-orarius,** lime-burner 1286.
raftera, rafter 1351.
ragadia c 1200, c 1408, **regadia** 1430, †**regardia** 1290, ‡**radagia** a 1520, †**rogaterea** 15c., **ragana** 1252, a 1300, †**tracha** c 1130, **radius** c 1180, 1294, **rayus** 1419, **reia** 1309, **retia** 1280, (?) **riggus** 1589, ray, skate (fish); *see also* RHAGAD
†**rag/ema, -ma,** vestment 1415.
rag/emannus, document with many seals on tags, return to *quo warranto* inquiry 1280, 1331; **indenture** (*pl.*) **-mannice,** ragman rolls (Sc.) a 1385.
rag/lottus 1315, c 1400, **reglatus** 1315, **-lator, -larius** 1485, 'ragler', chief officer of commote (W. *rhaglaw*); **-lauthia** 1318, **-lotia** c 1341, 1404, **-oltia** 1335, **-elotia** c 1370, †**-elotta** 1320, †**-olotia** 1331, **rogelotia** c 1370, **-eloia, -lawria, reglawria** 1386, **-loria** 1334, 1437, **-laria** 1390, 1505, office of ragler (W.).
raiatus, *see* radius.
rail/a (rayla) 1318, 1535, **reyla** 1318, **rellia** c 1155, rail, paling; **rela** 1308, **relia** 1303,

rilia 1301, **ryela** 1355, framework of mill-sail; **releatio**, railing 1571; **-o** 1379, **rilo** 1266, to fit with rails; *cf.* **1 regula**.

raimatus (raym-), 'raimed', put to ransom (Sc.) 1318; **reimatus**, despoiled 1276.

raingia, *see* RANG

raka, rake 1329.

rakk-, *see* RACK

‡**ralla**, 'rail', shaving-cloth c 1440, 1483; ‡**rella**, "ray", cloth, 15c.

rallum, plough-staff: **rulla** 1560.

ram/agius, 'ramage', snared after leaving nest (falc.) 1237, 1333; **columba -ata** 1255, **c. -era** 1249, wood-pigeon; *cf.* **ramus**.

ramio assisam, to 'arraign' (hold) an assize 1205, 1222; **r. sectam**, to produce suit (leg.) 1280, 1281; *cf.* ARRAM

ramm/a, ram, pile-driver 1329, 1332; **-ellum**, rammer (for packing flour) 1348; **-atio** 1348, **-atura** 1304, **-ura** 1278, ramming, packing; ***-o** 1267, 1465, **-eo** 1272, 1363, **-io** 1275, 1295, to ram, pack.

ramn- (rampn-), *see* **ramum; rhamnos**.

rampans, rampant (her.) 1245, 1384.

rampesia, rampart 1606.

ram/um c 1227, **-num** c 1188, bronze (O.F. *rame*).

ram/us, (?) toe 6c.; branch of road 1345; **-a**, *for* **-us**, branch 1488; **-us magister**, (?) main branch (of oak) 1256; ***-i** (*pl.*) **Palmarum** c 1135, 1526, **-ispalme** (*pl.*) 1114, 1538, Palm Sunday; **-iculus** c 1280, **-illus** 1271, **-ellus** 1372, 1394, **-uncula** c 1212, **-unculus** c 700. 1234, 1445, **remunculus** 1297, **-usculus** 7c. c 1135, c 1520, small branch, offshoot; **-ailia** (*pl.*) 1396, **-aillum** (*coll.*) 1285, **-allum** 1374, **-iclum** 13c., **-ilia** 1169, 15c., **-illa**, **-illum** c 1175, 1398, **-ella**, **-ellum** 1242, 1267, **remale** 1166, 1378, **remellum** 1430, (?) **romeseum** 1213, **-ea** c 1140, **-ia** c 1315, branches, loppings; **-ellus**, rubble 1434; **remelus** 1279, 1305, **remulus** 1306, **reomellis** c 1300, **rimulus** 1485, bunch (of flax); **-atus** 1303, **-osus** 1310, branched; **-osus**, (?) reaching out, grasping c 1180; **-ificatim** branchwise 1432; **-esco** 1275, **-ificor** a 1250, 1421, to branch out.

‡**ramuscium**, ramson, wild garlic c 1000.

rana, 'rain', 'rean', furrow or ditch (Lancs.) a 1235, a 1250.

†**ranabdus**, (?) *f.l.* for **invalidus**, 1288.

†**franci/a (†rautya)** 1208, **-anum** 1221, sort of cloth.

rancinus, *see* **runcinus**.

rancio, to 'rancel', ransack (Sc.) 1364.

*ranc/or 7c., 8c. c 1080, c 1470, †**-ordia** c 1200, rancour, grudge; **-idulus**, putrefying c 950; †**-osus**, malicious 1378.

rang/a c 1365, c 1436, **-ea** 1261, 1460, **raingia** 1300, **rengia** 1235, c 1400, **rengus** c 1185, 1321, **ryngea** 1352, **rengata** c 1285, range, row; **rengia**, (?) range, fire-grate c 1335; a 1230, 1235, **rengata** 1194, 1199, **rengiata** 1276, strip of land of fixed length (Norfolk); **renca**, (?) strip of land 1401; **-eator** 1319, 1711, **raungeator** 1437, 1443, **rengiarius** 1339, ranger, forest officer; **-ose**, in order 1378.

ranson/a, ransom 1326; **raunsiator (†renu-**

siator), kidnapper, one who puts to ransom 1354; **-o**, **raunsono** 15c., **raunciono** 1377, to ransom; *cf.* **raimatus**, REDEMPT

rapa, *see* **rapum (1 & 2)**.

rap/acitas, rapidity c 1200, c 1324; **-ax** 1365, c 1595, **-idus** c 1595, rampant (her.); **-ina aperta**, A.S. *rán* c 1115; ‡**-inosus**, thievish 1483; †**-inus**, ravening 15c.; **-tor itinerum**, highwayman, *routier* (G.) 1312; **-tura**, poaching 749; ‡**rape** 1570; **-tus**, swift movement c 1250, c 1620; rapture, ecstasy c 1250, c 1343; (*p.p.*) rapt in an ecstasy a 1142, 15c.; **-iens vitam**, poisonous plant, (?) spurge 14c.; **-io**, to scurry 14c.

rapatorium, receptacle for turnips a 1250.

rappum, (?) tide-race (Brittany) 1267.

1 rap/um c 1080, c 1495, **-a** 1213, a 1540, **-us** 1227, 1586, **ropa** 1423, †**raspum** 1214, rape, division of county (Sussex).

2 rap/um 1180, 1278, **-a** c 1411, rape, violence.

3 rapum geniste, broomrape (bot.) 1634.

rapun/culus, harebell 1634; **-tium**, rampion (bot.) 1634.

rar/efactio a 1233, 1686, **-escentia** c 1620, rarefaction; **-efactibilis**, able to be rarefied a 1233, c 1267; **-efactibilitas**, susceptibility to rarefaction c 1270; **-efactivus**, **-ificativus**, rarefying a 1250; **-iberbis**, thin-bearded 1163; **-iloquus**, seldom speaking c 1340; **-itas (dentium)**, gap a 1250; **-issimus**, most precious c 1270; **de -o**, seldom c 1470; **-efacio** a 1233, c 1361, **-ifico** a 1250, a 1446, to rarefy, refine; ‡**-eo**, "to be few" 1483.

ras/a, -arium, *see* **rasura**.

rascalilia (*pl.*), canaille 14c.

rascatio, coughing up phlegm a 1250, ‡14c.

ras/cemus, -inus, *see* **racemus**.

raschete, *see* **racheta**.

ras/era, -etum, *see* **rasura**.

‡**rasga**, arum (bot.) 14c.

rasp/atum 1195, **vinum r.** 1210, **v. -eys** 1290, *vin râpé*, wine freshened after it has gone stale.

raspum, *see* **1 rapum**.

‡**rasta**, dodder (bot.) 14c; *see also* **rasura**.

‡**rastella**, thrush 15c.; *cf.* **rostellus**.

rast/ellus 1235, 1331, **-allus** 1299, **r. standardus** 1374, rack (for fodder); 1221, 1279, **-ella** 1279, rake or hoe; **-ratio** 1466, **-elatio** a 1250, raking; **-rator**, raker 1419; **-elo** a 1250, **-illo** 1234, **-lo** 1275, **-lico** 1269, **-o** 1276, **resto** 1466, **rostro** 1405, to rake, rake up.

ras/ura a 1140, 13c., **-tura** 1309, **-arium**, **-era** 12c., **-eria** 1314, **-a** 1282, 1376, †**-ta** 1234, **-us** 1270, c 1356, razed measure of grain; c 1178, 1450, **-tura** 1220, 1331, erasure; ***c** 980. c 1080, 1549, ***-tura** 1255, 1458, shaving of tonsure (eccl.); clipping (of coin) c 1310; c 1218, †**-or** 13c., ***-orium** c 1080, c 1330, **-urium** c 1000, **-oriolum** 1244, razor; **-tura**, shaving-room (mon.) c 1400; **-urus**, cutting tool, file 1220; **-or**, barber, shaver 1130, ‡15c.; (?) **-etum** 1388, **pannus -us** 1499, satin; **-tus**, *for* **-us**, erased 1331; **-o** 1228, 1250, **-eo** 14c., to raze, level (building or ditch); 14c., **rado** a 1166, 1449, to raze or straik (a measure of grain); 1275,

rado 1179, 1200, to erase (writ); **rado,** to shave tonsure (eccl.) a 1221, 1537; to pare down, reduce gradually 1430.

rasus c 1290, (?) **rathis** 1303, measure (500 heads) of garlic; *cf.* **racemus, radix;** *see also* **rasura.**

1 **rat/a, -um,** share, proportion 1278, 1543; **littere de -a** 1204, **l. de -o** c 1204, c 1250, letters of authorization; **-e,** duly c 1155, c 1427; as a thing 1344; **-itudo** c 1300, p 1300, **-itas** 1344, status as a thing (*res rata*); **-us,** right, desirable c 790; **r. et gratus,** approved 1217, 1512; **-o,** to rate, assess a 1564.

2 **rat/a,** (?) *for* **-is,** raft 1340.

ratabusta, funeral pile c 700.

ratenihctis, *see* RAD

rathel/atio, 'raddling', wattling (of cow-shed) 1341; **-o,** to wattle 1341.

rathis, *see* **rasus.**

rati/ficatio 1228, 1566, ***-habitio** 1167, 1557, **habitio rati** c 1258, **-habitatio** c 1193, c 1293, **ratahabitio** c 1235, approval, ratification; **littere -ficatorie,** letters of ratification 1464; **-fico** c 1224, 1566, **-hibeo** 1287, to ratify.

ratio/, motto 1416, 1437; definition (λόγος) 13c.; underlying principle c 1380; ratio, proportionate sum (math.) 1324; **r. geometrica** 1686; **r. communis, r. naturalis,** common sense 1380; **r. seminalis,** generative principle (λόγος σπερματικός) c 1300; ***-ne** 1217, 1509, **in -ne** c 1380, on account, by reason (of); **ex -ne,** by rights 14c.; **-nis est,** it is right (G.) 1289; **-ne prima,** in the first instance 13c.; **-cinatio,** reckoning, account c 1182, c 1395; **-cinabilius,** more correctly 9c.; **-cinalis** a 1280, **-cinarius** c 1595, concerned with reckoning; c 1408, **-nativus** a 1228, reasonable; **-cinator,** reasoner c 1340, 1552; **liber -cinii,** bill of lading 1525;

*-nabilis c 1170, 1569, **resonabilis** 1617, moderate, fair; 1124, c 1322, **-nalis** a 1200, **†-nibilis** c 1293, regular, formal; **r. etas,** years of discretion c 1228, 1413; **-nabilior,** more moderate 1238; **-nabilitas** c 1080, c 1360, **-nalitas** c 1110, c 1367, reasonableness, rationality; **-nabiliter,** regularly, in due form 10c. 1162, c 1370; according to ratio (math.) c 815; **resonabiliter,** reasonably c 1313; **-nabilius,** more reasonably 8c.; **-nale,** breast-plate (eccl.) c 790. c 1180, 1517; **-nale Divinorum,** title of a book 1425, 1488; **-nalitas,** proportion 1267; **‡-narius,** auditor 1570; **-natio,** reasoning 12c., c 1390; **-cino,** to persuade by reasoning c 1130; to discuss, converse 13c.; **-no,** to claim, prove title to (leg.) 1086, 1227; to arraign, call to account 1270, 1274; **-nor,** to reason c 1300.

1 **rat/o, -itas, -itudo,** *see* 1 **rata.**

2 ***rat/o** c 1250, c 1435, **-us** c 1190, a 1347, rat; **-onarius** c 1357, **rattinarius** 1347, **‡-onicida** 15c., rat-catcher.

ratraho, *see* RETRACT

rattorneo, *for* **reattorno,** to acknowledge as new overlord 1425.

rattus, *see* 2 **rato; rottus.**

†ratula, bird, (?) rail, corncrake c 1200.

ratus, *see* 1 **rata;** 2 **rato.**

raubum, *see* **roba.**

rauc/edo a 1250, a 1330, **-itudo** c 1250, c 1395, hoarseness; **-idus,** hoarse 12c., ‡1483; **-atus,** grown hoarse a 1446; **-io,** to be hoarse c 800.

rauma, *see* **rheuma.**

raun/siator, -sono, -ciono, *see* RANSON

rautya, *see* **rancia.**

ravellum, coarse cloth for straining milk 1276, 1407.

raviosus, timorous 9c.

raxas, skilled c 550.

ray/a, -atus, *see* **radius.**

rayus, *see* **ragadia.**

re, musical note c 1330, 1351.

reaccedo, to return 12c., c 1400.

reaccen/sio, rekindling c 1185; **-do,** to rekindle c 1180, c 1328.

reaccept/io, recovery c 1400; **-o** c 1395, c 1400, **reaccipio** c 1170, c 1470, to recover, take back.

reaccuso, to accuse again c 1250.

reachatum, *see* RECHAT

reacquiro (readquiro), to get back c 1250, c 1400.

reactio, reaction c 1345, 1686; **reago,** to react p 1300.

readduco, to bring back c 1470.

readeptio 1470, 1472, **†readoptio** 15c., recovery.

readjorno, to readjourn 1290.

readjungo, to reúnite c 1365.

read/missio, readmission a 1452, c 1470; **-mitto,** to readmit c 1290, c 1470.

readoptio, *see* **readeptio.**

readquiro, *see* **reacquiro.**

reafforesto, to restore to forest status 1258, 1397.

reaggrav/atio, reaggravation, making still more severe c 1520; **-o,** to reaggravate 1428, c 1520.

reago, *see* **reactio.**

realgar a 1250, ‡14c., **resalger** 1418, **†reisalgum** 1421, realgar, red arsenic, orpiment.

real/itas, reality c 1300, 1620; **-is, *real,** actual c 1218, 1565; concerned with things, as opposed to names c 1310, 1610; real, as opposed to personal (of property) 1226, c 1502; binding (of agreements) 1237, c 1450; (*subst.*) realist (phil.) 12c., 1620; **-ior,** nearer to actuality 1298, 1378; **-iter, *really,** in fact c 1050, 1557; with regard to real property (leg.) c 1258; **-ius,** more really c 1380; *cf.* **res;** *see also* REGAL

reamen, *see* **reatus.**

reamo, *see* REDAM

reamplexor, to embrace in return (fig.) 1237.

reannexus, annexed, attached c 1365.

reappello, to recall from banishment (G.) 1315; to 'appeal' (accuse) again (leg.) c 1290; **r. ad,** to appeal to again 12c.

rearceo, to keep back, repel c 1250.

rearmo, to rearm 1413.

rearo, to plough again 1222.

rearripio iter, to resume a journey a 1452.

reascendo, to remount, climb again 12c., c 1400.

reassido, to set up again 1322.

reassigno, to restore, return 9c.; to reassign c 1266, 1345.

reassum/ptio, resumption, taking back c 1300, c 1400; ***-o,** to reassume, take back a 1142, 1684.
reator, lime-burner (Norm.) 1198; *cf.* **rogus.**
reattach/iamentum, reattachment (leg.) 15 c.; **-io** to reattach (leg.) 1204, 15 c.; to re-fasten 1374.
reat/us (bibl.), **-itudo** c 730. c 1325, a 1414, guilt; **reamen,** guilt *or* impeachment c 550; **reus,** liable to (penalty of) c 1102, c 1115; **r. sui ipsius,** liable to death penalty c 1115; *see also* **radius.**
reaudio, to reaudit 1291.
reaufero, to take away again a 1142.
rebaptizatio, rebaptism c 1620.
1 rebato, to rebate, deduct, a 1564.
2 rebato, to batter (tools) 1318; to repair (barrels) 1377.
rebbussa, *see* **rubisum.**
rebell/ium c 1150, c 1330, **-itas** 1365, **revellio** 1407, rebellion; **-io,** counter-attack c 1218; **-io** 1250, 1305, **-anus** 1336, **-ator** 5 c. 1569, 1573, **-us** 1267, 1467, **repellis** c 1382, **revellis** 1560, rebel; **-ice** 1382, 1396, **-iose** 1569, **-iter** 1378, 1545, rebel-liously; **-io** 1419, **-or** c 1150, c 1362, to rebel.
rebendatio, fitting (vestment) with new bands 1534.
rebeneficio, to repay a benefit 1344.
rebibo, to take one drink after another 1241; to drink up again c 1457.
rebin/a c 1250, **-ium** 1272, **-atio** 1273, 1351, **-ura** c 1290, third ploughing; **-um,** crop from fallow land after third ploughing 1208; ***-o** 1152, 1540, **†rubino** 1400, **†revivo** a 1564, to plough (fallow land) a third time.
rebis, "*lapis ex spiritu albo vel rubeo*" (alch.) a 1252, ‡1652.
reblangio, to furbish up (coins) like new 1205.
reboatio, resounding, re-echoing 15 c.
‡rebona, mummy 1652.
‡rebroccator, cobbler c 1440.
recac-, *see* **RECHAC**
recalcio, to put shoes on again c 980. c 1266, c 1330.
recalcitr/atio, resistance a 1452; **-osus,** re-calcitrant a 1200; **-or,** *for* **-o,** to kick against, resist c 1450.
recalefactor, heater up (of victuals) 1390.
recalumpnio super, to bring a further charge against (leg.) a 1087.
recamb/ium, changing back (of money) 1503; **-io,** to change back (money) a 1250, 1507.
recamera, withdrawing room c 1620.
recan/atus, -o, *see* **RACHAN**
recapit/atio, refitting (plough) with ‘head’ 1358; **-o carrucam** 1373.
recapitul/atio, recapitulation a 1142, c 1414; **-arium,** list c 1250; **-o,** to recapitulate, enumerate c 1115, 1461.
recap/tio, taking back, recapture 1298, c 1400; withholding, deduction 1420; **r. averiorum,** rescue of cattle seized in dis-traint 1284, 15 c.; **-io,** to recapture 1354, 1461; to readmit 15 c.; to take back (into king's hand) 1267, 1331; to take (informa-tion) again c 1405.
recarco, to reload 1267, 1472.
recard-, *see* **REWARD**

recari/agium, carriage back 1316, 1471; **-o,** to carry back 1221, 1542.
recarpent/aria 1272, **-atio** 1293, repair of wood-work; **-o,** to repair (wood-work) 1272.
recascio, *see* **RECHAC**
recasus, falling back c 1500; *cf.* **RECID**
recatum, *see* **rechatum.**
recauso, to cause in return c 1367, 1374; *for* **recuso,** a 710.
recautum, counter-tally, foil c 1178.
recc/um (rect-, rett-): **vinum de -o** 1225, 1312, **v. reckum** 1232, **v. de raco** 1250, **v. de reek'** 1341, racked wine (drawn off from lees); **seisona -i** (G.) 1316; **-o,** to rack (wine) 1236, 1265.
reced/ens, -it, *see* **residentia.**
reced/entia, -o, *see* **RECESS**
recedivus, *see* **RECID**
recella, *see* **res.**
recelo, to conceal 1337.
recen/sor, reciter, narrator c 1500; **-ceo** c 1457, **-seor** c 1250, **-sio** c 1212, *for* **-seo.**
recen/tia, recency, freshness 1231, 14 c.; **-tatio,** freshening c 1197; **-s,** fresh, not salted 1201, 1531; **aqua r.** 1290, 1546, **a. rescens** 1289, fresh water; **corium r.,** untanned hide 1221, 1407; **‡-situs,** "new ripe" c 1220, 15 c.; **-tio,** to renew 1233.
†receo, (?) *f.l.* for **cecutio,** 12 c.
recept/atio, refuge c 1250; admission to citizenship 1274; c 1192, a 1553, **-io** c 1115, **-amen** 1285, ***-amentum** 1203, c 1400, **recettamentum** 1197, 1214, (?) **recita-mentum** 1198, **-um** 1218, 'resetting', har-bouring of criminals (leg.); **-amentum,** lair 1336; **r. latrocinii,** receipt of stolen goods 1254; **-io** 1336, c 1414, **-amentum** 1315, 1337, (right of) entertainment; a 1250, 15 c., **-a** 1271, 14 c., recipe (med.); ***1226, c 1423, *-a, -um** c 1178, 1569, **-us** c 1285, c 1485, receipt, money received; **r. grossa,** gross receipt c 1300; ***-a** (Scaccarii), department for receipt of cash, Lower Exchequer c 1178, 1586; **rotulus -e,** Receipt Roll 1227, 1366; **-io,** 'reception' into planetary house (astr.) c 1260; c 1343, **-us** c 1545, approval, acknowledgement; **-io assise** (leg.) 1242; **r. sacramenti** (eccl.) 1461; **r. testium** (leg.) 1510; **-acu-lum,** pocket 7 c.; guest-chamber (mon.) 1274, 1304; **-ator,** harbourer (of exiles) c 1250; harbourer (of heretics) c 1343, 15 c.; ***1201, 1419, recettator** 1270, **-or** 1169, c 1320, **-arius** 1288, **-atrix** (*f.*) 1288, 1332, **recettiatrix** 1275, **-rix** 1275, 'resetter', har-bourer of criminals or receiver of stolen goods; **-atorium,** fine for 'resetting' (leg.) 1276;
-ibilis, capable of being received, admis-sible c 1125, 1295; capable of receiving, receptive c 793. a 1233, c 1345; **-ibilitas** a 1233, c 1365, **-abilitas** a 1250, capacity to receive; **†-ior** (? *for* **-ivior**), more recep-tive c 1270; **-ive,** by way of reception c 1270; **-ivitas,** receptivity c 1270; **-ivum,** recep-tacle a 1250; **-ivus, *receptive** a 1233, a 1361; giving entrance c 1308;
-or, welcomer c 760; ***c 1192, c 1542, -ator** 1569, receiver (of money, rents, *etc.*); lessee c 1350; receiver of candidates (to

order of Templars) c 1309; receiver (attached to garrison) 1289; c 1296, **r. hospitum** c 1266, receiver of guests (mon.); *****r. generalis** 1476, 1583; *see also* **-ator** (*above*); **-oria,** receivership 1469; **-orium,** place of receipt (of money, *etc.*) 1274, 1342; socket c 1500; 1200, **-us** 1562, refuge, shelter; harbour c 1195; **-ura,** receiving 13c.; **recettum,** place of harbourage (of criminal) 1255; *****-o** c 1192, 1450, **recetto** 1203, 1313, **resetto** 1327, to 'reset', harbour (criminals); **recito,** to receive, entertain (guests) 1340; **recipi/ens,** recipient, devisee c 1270; **-o,** to include as ingredients (med.) a 1250; to learn, be informed 1326; to approve, authenticate (leg.) (G.) 1316; to acknowledge as canonical (eccl.) c 1343; (with *inf.*) to undertake 1324; **r. habendi,** to undertake to produce 1209; **r. in,** to provide with 1218, 1415; **r. ad pacem regis,** to free from outlawry c 1260; **r. crucem,** to become a crusader a 1200; **r. sacramentum** (eccl.) c 1468, 1559.

†**recesco,** (?) *for* requiesco, to rest 1326.

recess/io c 730, 1041. c 1090, a 1564, **recedentia** c 1620, withdrawal, decline; **-a,** receding c 550; **-um,** ebb c 815; **-us,** return 1373; recompense 1224; **-or,** retirer c 1180; **resecit,** *for* **-it,** 1301; **reced/ere,** departure (*subst.*) 1200; **-o,** to return, revert c 1088, a 1347; to dismiss 1272, 1446; to withdraw homage 1086; **r. a brevi,** to resile, withdraw from a writ (leg.) 1272; *see also* RESID

recett-, *see* RECEPT

rechac/ea (recac-), -ia, (right of) driving back cattle c 1200, c 1400; *****-io** a 1160, 1405, **recascio** 13c., to drive back; to prop up 1236.

rechat/um (recat-) 1191, 1447, **-a** 1317, †**reachatum** 1214, **racatum** c 1125, 1205, **rachetum** 1279, c 1315, **racheta** 13c., †**rocatum** 1191, repurchase, redemption, relief; **-o,** to give the right to repurchase c 1320.

ɿ**echinnatus,** *see* RACHAN

‡**recia,** (?) vervain (bot.) 14c.

reciantia, *see* residentia.

reciatus, *see* RETT

recid/ivatio a 1250, 1620, **residivatio** c 1367, *****-iva, -ivum** c 1180, c 1470, **-ivia** 1314, recurrence, relapse; recurrent fever *or* (?) epilepsy a 1250; **recedivus** 1263, **-uus** c 550, **residivus** c 1402, *for* **-ivus,** recurring; **-atus,** having relapsed c 1250, 1508; **-ivo** c 1197, 1609, **residivo** c 1340, 1419, to relapse; to renew, revive c 1310, 14c.

‡**recilla/tor, -trix** (*f.*), nurse 1483.

recincer/atio c 1197, **rinsura** 1301, c 1330, rinsing; **-o, resincero** 16c., †**recingo** 1229, to rinse.

recipio, *see* RECEPT

reciproc/atio, repetition, recurrence c 730; reflexive action (gram.) c 800; **-abilis,** capable of reciprocation c 1115; **-atim,** interchangeably 9c.; **-e,** reciprocally c 700. 1318, 1380; (geom.) 1686; **via -ativa,** reverse course c 1325; **-o,** to sing antiphonally c 1325.

recirculor, to revolve 1344.

recis/ura, piece cut off, shaving c 730. 14c., c 1400; **rescisio,** cutting off 14c.; **-us** c 1595, **rescissus** p 1394, couped (her.).

recit-, *see also* RECEPT

recit/atio, written description c 1227; recital (leg.) 1566; **-abilis,** fit to be told c 1250; recited, read out c 1414; †**-abulum,** (?) reading-desk *or* sort of megaphone 8c.; **-ative,** by way of declaration a 1346, p 1381; in quotation 1380, c 1620; **-ativus,** reciting, quoting 1378, 1391; **-atorie,** like a public reader c 1210; **-o** c 1115, c 1503, **resito** 1587, to relate, repeat; to summon or resummon (leg.) 1269, c 1324; **r. male,** to misquote c 1334; *see also* RECEPT

reckus, *see* RECC

reclam/atio c 1077, c 1450, **-antia** 1274, **-ium** c 1255, 1276, claim, counter-claim; **-atorium,** 'recall' (falc.) a 1446; **-atorius,** denying, objecting a 1452; **-o,** to claim, counter-claim, claim back 1081, 1461; to confess, declare 1274.

reclavo, to nail on again 1378.

reclin/atio c 730, *****-atorium** a 1100, 15c., resting-place; **-atorius,** supporting a 1350.

reclu/sio, shutting up c 1340, c 1343; seclusion (mon.) 1321, 15c.; **-sa,** sluice 1367 (*cf.* **exclusa**); **-sagium** 1219, 1321, **-sorium** 1234, 1392, cell of a recluse (mon.); ‡**-sorium,** "pinfold" 15c.; **religio -soria** 1385; **-sus,** cloistered 1234, 15c.; (*subst.*) c 1100, 1457, **-sa** (*f.*) a 1100, c 1553, recluse, anchorite; **-do,** to bar, block c 1130, c 1258; to seclude as an anchorite 1265, 1321; **reclaudo,** to shut up again c 1412.

recluto, to refix, patch up c 1220, 1245.

recogn/itio (recongn-), acknowledgement (in general) 1191, 1527; acknowledgement of debt, recognizance 1268, 1507; acknowledgement of lordship (feudal or man.) or payment therefor 1086, 1449; *****examination, inquest by jury, judgement or explanatory statement (leg.) c 1150, 15c.; **-itor,** *****juror (leg.) a 1200, a 1452; editor 1529; **-izo** 1284, 1315, *****-osco** 1094, 1419, to investigate by jury (leg.); to find guilty c 1305; **-osco,** to acknowledge 1086, 1507; to 'recognosce', resume possession of (Sc.) 1266, 1461; to pay in acknowledgement of lordship 1279.

recola, *see* res.

recoldellus, kind of horse 1254.

‡**recol/entia,** recollection 1483; **-endus,** memorable c 1300, c 1458; **-endissimus** 1439; **-o,** to record 9c. c 1204, c 1362; to honour, commemorate 1461; c 800, (with *gen.*) c 730. p 1177, to reflect.

recoll/ectio, gathering in, harvesting 1308; additional collection 1282; regress from particular to general (log.) c 850; mystical concentration c 1283; **-igo,** to recollect, remember a 1200, 1393; to welcome, entertain c 1250, c 1342; to agree to 1263, 1268; **r. me,** to withdraw a 1240; to accommodate oneself c 1287; **r. summonitionem,** to accept or acknowledge summons (leg.) 1235.

recolloco, to gather again c 1150.

recommasso, to intermingle, interfuse 1427.

recommemor/atio, remembrance 1299; **-o,** to remind again 1490.

recommend/atio *1218, 1438, **-a** c 1430, a 1452, recommendation, greeting; commendation, praise 1382, 1461; committing, entrusting 9c.; commending (in prayer) c 1400; **-abilis,** commendable a 1400; **-aticia** c 1250, **littere -aticie** 1336, 1492, **-atoria** c 1303, letter of recommendation; **-atior,** more highly commended c 1250; **verbum -ativum,** word of recommendation 1421; **-o,** *to recommend c 1080, 1461; to commend, praise 1225; to commend in prayer 1340, 1432.

recommercium, goods for sale 1258.

recommitto, to recommend 1282, c 1450; to send back 1587.

recompagino, to reunite c 1125, 14c.

*recompen/satio (reconpen-) c 685, c 800. c 1080, 1573, **-sio** c 1272, 1524, **-sa** a 1253, 1521, recompense; **-sabilis,** requitable c 1402; **-sator,** rewarder c 1380, 1443; **-so,** to weigh in mind c 1000; *c 730, 8c. c 1090, c 1540, **-do** c 1150, c 1362, to recompense, compensate for.

recomprehensio, recompense c 1150.

recompromissarius, (?) person elected to appoint collectors (eccl.) 1339.

reconcedo, to grant back, restore 1232, 1573.

reconcili/atio (reconsili-), 'reconciliation', reconsecration (of a church) c 1110, 1397; readmission (of an excommunicate) c 1340, 1461; **-ator** c 1250, **-atrix** (f.) a 1200, reconciler; **reconsultus,** reconsecrated 1371; **-o,** to reconsecrate c 1130, c 1514; to readmit after excommunication c 1115, c 1408; **r. Deo** c 1006; **r. treugam,** to renew a truce 1461.

reconcinnator, refurbisher 1552.

recondit/io, reception, containing 13c.; **-orium,** receptacle, storehouse c 1125.

reconfero, to bestow again c 1311.

reconfirm/atio, renewed confirmation c 1470; **-o,** to reconfirm, renew a 1250, 1461; to confirm a second time (eccl.) 1385.

reconfiteor, to confess again (eccl.) c 1225.

reconfort/atio, reinforcement 1461; **-o,** to encourage 15c., 1461.

recongn-, *see* RECOGN

reconjungo, to reunite, reattach c 1250, 1348.

reconpen-, *see* RECOMPEN

recon/questo 1309, **-quiro** c 1250, to reconquer.

reconsecro, to reconsecrate 1298.

reconsign/atio, readdressing of documents c 1250; **-o,** *to resign, give back 12c., c 1400; to seal up again c 1400.

reconsili-, reconsultus, *see* RECONCILI

reconstruo, to rebuild c 1400.

recontinu/atio, recontinuance, resumption 1344, 1588; **-o,** to resume (tenure of) 1453.

recontristo, to sadden c 1240.

reconvalesc/entia, recovery (of health) 1302, a 1452; **-o,** to recover health 1450, 1461.

reconven/tio, resummons or counter-petition (leg.) c 1258, 1684; **-io,** to resummon (leg.) 1231, 1684.

reconverto, to transform c 1420; to recommend c 1458.

reconvicior, to return reproaches 12c.

recooper/io c 1192, c 1446, **-o** 1308, to cover again, re-roof.

recopulo, to link up again, recapitulate c 800; to uncouple, detach a 1250.

*record/um 1167, 1591, **-a** c 1330, 1365, **-ia** 15c., a 1452, record, report; **-a** (*pl.*), section of Exchequer Memoranda Rolls 1309, 16c.; **de -o,** of record (leg.) 1337, 1591; *see also* **curia, custos; -atio,** recording c 1115, 14c.; **-ativus,** reminiscent a 1250; p 1347, 1399, **-atrix** (f.) c 1400, recording, commemorative; **-ator,** recorder (civic official) 1321, a 1564; **-atorium,** book of records p 1419; *-o c 1180, c 1420, **-or** (*dep.*) 1198, 15c., to record; **-or,** to intend c 800.

recorono, to recrown 15c.

recrastinatio, procrastination 673. c 1414.

recrean/tia c 1258, *-**tisa** 1157, c 1258, 'recreancy', acknowledgement of (*or* fine for) defeat in judicial combat; **-s** 1198, **-tus** c 1258, 1368, a recreant, craven (leg.); *cf.* RECRED

recre/atio c 1182, **-atura** c 1500, creating afresh; *recreation, refreshment c 1194, c 1530; **-ator,** one who creates afresh c 800, c 1000. c 1125, 1267; reliever c 1250, c 1335; **-atorium,** pastime c 1553; **-o,** to create anew (in Christ) 1385; **r. visum,** to refresh the sight c 1250; *see also* recrutus.

recrebresco, to grow frequent c 1190.

recred/entia, bail, security (G.) 1279, 1314; **-o,** to pledge, give security for delivery of (G.) c 1250, 1315; **r. de duello,** to play the recreant 1170; *cf.* RECREAN

recresto, to reaffix ridge-pieces (arch.) 1237.

recron[atus] 1339, †**retron'** 1398, old animal weeded out of flock; *cf.* **cronardus.**

recrutus 1290, 1300, **recreatus** 1290, c 1290, worn out (of horses) (O.F. *recreü*).

rect-, *see also* RECC; RETT

rectangul-, recti-, *see* **rectum.**

rectific/atio, rectification, setting right 13c., 1620; **-abilis,** able to be set right p 1300, c 1360; **-ativus,** corrective a 1250, 13c.; **-o,** to steer 1252; *to rectify, set right, reform a 1233, 1620; to observe correctly 1326; to rectify, purify (alch.) c 1215, 1620.

rector/, corrector c 1260; regent 1216, c 1250; *rector (eccl.) c 1157, 1565; *rector (ac.) c 1250, 1549; **r. chori** c 1230, 1555; **r. misterii,** master of guild 1419; **r. navis,** master c 1193; **r. ordinis** (mon.) 13c.; **r. rerum,** man of affairs c 1000; **r. scholarum** c 1100, 1388; *-**ia** 1239, 1686, **-atus** 1431, office or benefice of rector (eccl.); rectory, rector's house 1296, 1545; **rectrix,** (queen) regent 1513; female rector (eccl.) c 1290, 15c.; **-o,** to govern (G.) 1220; *cf.* **regentia.**

*rect/um, right, justice 1086, 1458; **facio r.** 1086, 1419, f. **-itudinem** 1106, 12c., **teneo r.** c 1096, 1419, to do justice or conform to law; **sto ad -um** c 1185, 1274, **s. in -o** 1269, *s. **-o** 1194, 1419, s. **†-e** 1583, s. **†-us** 1573, **sum ad -um** c 1115, **venio ad r.** c 1188, **pareo recto** 1201, to 'stand to right', take one's trial; **habeo ad -um** c 1115, 1419, **h. -o** 1196, 1272, **h. ad -itudinem** c 1130, c 1200, **represento ad -um** c 1115, **teneo -itudini** c 1140, to 'have to right', produce for trial (leg.); **-ius,** more nearly vertically a 1233; **-itudo,** straightness, upright position c 1100, c 1470; *righteousness c 1080,

1438; correctness c 1070, c 1325; *customary right *or* service 1086, c 1436; **r. Dei**, ecclesiastical due c 1115; **r. patrie** c 1115; **r. testamenti**, *bocriht* c 1115;

-**angulum**, a rectangle c 1596; **-angulus**, name of an astr. instrument 1326; (*adj.*) 1267, **-iangulus** a 1150, rectangular; **-igradus**, walking in the right way 7c.; **-ilineus** a 1200, 1686, **-ilinearis** 1620, rectilinear; **-ilocus**, in the right place c 800; **-ilogus**, right-thinking c 1365; **-iloquium**, correct speech c 800; **-iloquax**, correct speaker c 1363; **-io**, perpendicularity 1499; government (gram.) 1610; †**-io**, to do justice 1221; *cf.* **regentia**; *see also* **breve**, **heres**, RETT

recub/us, recumbent c 730, c 800; **-itor**, one who reclines 9c.; **-o**, to re-lay 1285, 1357.

recudo, to hammer out again, recast (fig.) c 1100, c 1260.

reculco, to retrace c 1125; to drive back a 1250.

reculo, to recoil, rear (of a horse) c 1200.

reculpo, to object to, reject c 1115.

recuper/atio, restoration to office 8c.; c 1185, 1684, *-are (subst.) c 1185, 1395, -amen a 1452, -antia 1435, recovery, regaining (esp. leg.); -atio arcis, burhbote 1024. 12c.; r. pontis, brigbote 1024. 12c.; -abilis, recoverable 11c., a 1100; -abiliter, recoverably c 1070, c 1360; -ator, restorer c 760; -o, to restate, re-enact c 760; to compensate for a 1446; r. ad loquelam, to revoke a plea (leg.) c 1200, 1203; r. super c 1204, 1253, r. versus 1219, c 1415, to recover (land *etc.*) from.

1 **recurs/us**, recourse a 1200, 1452; resort 1385, 1440; **versus -antes**, verses with a refrain c 1200.

2 **recursus, recuss-, recutio**, *see* **rescussio**.

recurvitas, a bending back a 1446.

recus/antia, recusancy (eccl.) 1593; **-ans**, refuser c 1367; recusant 1589, 1593; **-ativus** a 1100, 14c., **-atorius** 1336, 1684, concerned with denial or refusal; *see also* **recauso**.

‡**recussorium**, hammer 15c.

† **reda**, (?) ploughing and sowing service 13c.

redactio, reduction c 1258, c 1367; **redigo**, to record, register (Sc.) 1461, 1549; **r. in**, to reduce to, convert into 1086, 1369; **r. in scriptis** 1309.

redalbo 1302, **redaubo** 1272, to re-daub, replaster.

redam/atio 1344, 1497, **-or** 12c., 1497, reciprocal love; **reamo**, to love in return 12c., c 1500.

redargu/tor, reprover c 1253; *-o c 1090, c 1400, -or (dep.) 1274, to reprove, rebuke.

redbana, adviser, abettor (A.S.) c 1115.

redd/itio, *giving up, surrender c 800. c 1115, 15c.; render, payment 1086, c 1488; *r. compoti 1302, 1419, -itus c. 1392, rendering of account; r. judicii, giving sentence 1419, 15c.; r. soche 1086; -ibilis, payable 1233; -itivus, restorative a 1250; -itor, repayer, requiter c 730. c 1150, 1401; -itarius 1236, 1333, -ituarius 1271, 1478, rentpayer, renter; -ituarius, rent-collector 1338, 1471; -itale 1310, c 1460, *-ituale 1261,

1417, †**-unale** c 1438, **rotulus -italis** 1301, **r. -itualis** c 1280, 1340, rental, rent-book, rent-roll; **-itualis**, of or for rent 1242, 1376;

*-**itus** 1070, 1565, **-ita** 1086, **-ere** (*subst.*) 1382, rent, revenue; render in kind (at Exchequer) 1322, 1327; tenement yielding rent 6c. 1086, 1431; **r. albus**, blanch-farm c 1283; *r. assisus 1185, 1540, r. assessus 1222, c 1265, r. asseisus 1321, r. assise c 1300, 1412, 'rent of assise', fixed rent; r. averiorum (W.) 1306; r. capitalis, (?) rent payable to overlord 1416, 1540; r. certus, 'cert', fixed rent 1462, 1535; r. cervisie, scot-ale, drinking-bout 1195; r. duplicatus c 1290, 1292, -itūs duplicatio a 1300, two years' rent; r. extente, rent specified in extent 1304; r. liber, rent of freehold c 1268, 1450; r. mobilis, a poultry rent 1525, 1583; r. mutabilis, variable rent 14c.; r. quietus, quit-rent a 1200, c 1564; r. reservatus, rent reserved 1542, 1553; r. resolutus, rent resolute (paid out by landlord) 1311, 1588; r. siccus, 'rent-seck' (without power of distress) a 1539, 1540; r. vitalis, life-rent 1504, 1560; -itūs onus, rent-charge c 1470; -ituatus, possessed of (a rent of) 1423; -ituo, to let at a rent a 1275;

-**o**, *to pay 1086, 16c.; *to recite (eccl.) 1234, c 1350; to make up, amount to a 1250; r. animam, to give up the ghost 1537; *r. compotum 1086, c 1585, r. computationem 1234, 1526, *r. ratiocinium c 1220, c 1450, to render account; r. judicium, to give sentence (leg.) 1238, c 1290; r. loquelam (leg.) c 1285; r. me (alicui), to become the (feudal) man of 1201; r. me in religionem 1221, r. me religioni c 1220, 1269, to take vows (mon.); r. prelium, to yield the day c 1250; r. promissum, to fulfil a promise 1219; r. sursum, to surrender c 1220, 1288 (*cf.* SURSUMREDD).

redecim/a 1113, 1201, **-atio** c 1130, 1296, second tithe (eccl.); **-o**, to tithe again (eccl.) 1240, 1586.

rededico, to re-dedicate (eccl.) c 1450.

rededuco, to put back (in reversal of postponement) c 1290.

redelector, to be delighted again 7c.

redelibero, to deliver back, restore c 1350, 1527.

redell/us, -a, *see* RIDELL

redempt/io (redemt-), *redemption (eccl.); *(price of) ransom 948. c 1194, 1461; weregeld c 1102, c 1150; *fine or relief c 1185, 1324; due paid for appointment (eccl.) 1356, c 1365; r. curie (leg.) 1237; r. furti 1293, r. latrocinii 1291, compounding larceny; r. monetariorum, fine paid by moneyers on receiving office or on a change of the coinage 1159, c 1178; r. pro operationibus, commutation of labour-services 1281; r. sanguinis, merchet a 1185, c 1320; -ivus, subject to ransom c 1315; *-or, Redeemer (eccl.); -i (pl.), the redeemed (theol.) c 1250; redim/ibilis, redeemable (theol.) 1378; -o, to hold to ransom, exact a fine from 1155, 1293; to bribe 1329; r. filios, to pay fine for children (leaving manor) 1240;

r. sanguinem, to pay merchet 1279; *cf.* **raimatus,** RANSON, REEM

redeo, *see* **redibilitas.**

redestino, to send back 1461.

red/hibentia 1309, 1313, **-evantia** 1309, **-eventia** 1279, 1360, **radeventia** (G.) 1314, due, payment, *redevance* (Fr. & C.I.).

red/ibilitas, revocability c 1283; **-ibilis,** revocable 1344; **-itivus,** regressive (from retroactive particular to general) c 850; (?) c 1270; **-itus,** having returned 1226, c 1436; ‡**-i domum,** an umbelliferous plant 14c.; **-ire** (*subst.*), right of return c 1198; **-eo,** to revert (leg.) 1086, c 1400; to have recourse (G.) 1283; **r. ad cor,** to return to one's senses c 1180, c 1430.

†**redico,** (?) to answer c 1296.

rediffero, to re-postpone c 1190.

redigo, *see* REDACT

†**redigularis,** rule, order 8c.

redi/lectio, requited love 1441; **-ligo,** to love in return c 1250.

redilla, *see* RIDELL

‡**redimentum,** "ornament" 15c.

redim/ibilis, -o, *see* REDEMPT

redimitto, to re-demise (leg.) c 1400.

redimpendo, to redeem c 1375.

redingel[andum], *see* **rada.**

redin/tegro, to restore: **-degro** p 1290, *reintegro 9c. c 1250, c 1607.

redipisc/o, *for* **-or,** to regain 1200.

redisseis/ina, redisseisin (leg.) 1236, 15c.; **-itor** 1259, c 1265, **-or** c 1290, redisseisor (leg.); **-io,** to redisseise 1387.

redistillo, to distill again 14c.

redit-, *see* **redibilitas.**

redobator, *see* **redubbator.**

redol/entia, fragrance c 1185, c 1362; **-esco,** to be fragrant c 1425, 1435.

redon/atio, giving in return, requital 14c., c 1365; giving back a 1564; **-o,** to re-endow c 1100.

redorsatus, lying on its back a 1200; endorsed c 1315.

redresso, to redress, set right 1405.

redshanca, redshank (bird) 1544.

redubbator, redobator, 'redubber', refurbisher 1284.

reduc/tio, haling (of thieves) to judgement c 1115, 1340; reduction, analysis (log.) 13c., 1610; reduction (math.) 15c.; **-ibilis,** reducible a 1233, c 1365; **-tive,** in a restricted sense 1610; †**-ivus,** restored 1327; **-tivus,** reductive (from particular to general), analytical (log.) c 850. a 1250, c 1300; inferential c 1620; **-o,** to reduce (log.) a 1250.

redund/antia, flowing back 7c; **-atio,** rebound c 1306; **r. aque,** flood-water 12c; **-o ad** 1283, 1337, **r. in** c 1170, 1433, to redound to, tend to.

reduplic/ativus, reduplicative, repeated c 1360, c 1363; **-ative,** by way of reduplication c 1360, c 1380; **-o,** to redouble, repeat p 1300, c 1360.

*reedific/atio, rebuilding c 960. c 1170, 1554; **r. pontium,** brigbote 1198; rebuilder c 700; *-o, to rebuild (eccl.).

reeffluo, to overflow c 1420.

†**reeicio,** to eject in turn (leg.) c 1258.

reeligo, to re-elect c 1250, c 1470.

reemend/atio, repair, restoration 1573; **-o,** to repair 1086, 1281.

reem/ptio, buying back c 800. a 1228; **-o,** to buy back 1309; *cf.* REDEMPT

reentro, *see* REINTR

reequito, to ride back c 1430, a 1564.

reerigo, to re-erect c 1125, c 1470.

reeskipp/atio 1434, **-amentum** 1398, **reskippamentum** 1432, shipping back; **-o,** to reship 1417, 1434.

reexamino, to re-examine 1283, 1587.

reexcommunico, to re-excommunicate c 1308.

reexcussio, *see* RESCUSS

reexpando, to rehoist (sail) c 1540.

reexpello, to re-expel c 1290.

reextendo, re-extend, revalue 1290, 1304.

refabrico, to reforge (iron-work) 1304; to rebuild (fig.) 1440.

refamulor, to serve in return 1344.

refarcio, to provide or establish c 1150, 1549.

refect/io, maintenance 798, 903. 12c., 1324; *c 730, c 1006. c 1135, 1560, **-ura** 1386, refection, food, repast; **r. burgi** c 1115, **r. urbis** c 1102, c 1115, burhbote; **r. pontis,** brigbote c 1102, c 1115; ‡**-iuncula,** light meal, "pittance" 1520, 1570; **-ivus,** (?) assimilative (of food) c 1250; **-oria,** refrain (mus.) c 1197 (*cf.* REFRACT); *-orium 7c., c 1000. 11c., 1586, **-uarium** c 1273, c 1293, refectory (mon.); **-arius** a 1128, c 1440, **-orarius** c 1080, 1532, **-oriarius** c 1320, †**-orius** c 1254, **-uarius** 1526, **-oraria** (*f.*) 1415, 1530, refectorer (mon.); **-oraria,** office of refectorer a 1273, c 1320; **-oralis,** from the refectory 1351, 15c.; **-ualis,** of refreshment c 1293; **reficio,** to do in return 1344; to 'refresh', bribe c 1160; to take a meal, eat 7c., c 1000. c 1170, c 1400; **refio,** to be rebuilt 1289.

refeoff/amentum, re-enfeoffment 1307, 1425; **-o** 1294, 1497, **refeffo** c 1350, to re-enfeoff.

*refer/endarius, referendary, master of requests (?) 605. c 1250, 1620; **-endariatus,** office of referendary c 1426; **-ibilis,** referable (to something other than itself) p 1300, c 1365; †**-ero,** to refer to 14c.; †**-io,** to recover possession of 13c.; *-o, to relate, report c 1090, 1684; **r. ad,** to refer to 1482, 1549; *cf.* RELAT

referro, to re-shoe (horses) 1319.

refersus, *see* REVERS

refert, it makes a difference c 1193.

†**refertismus,** passage, text 1427.

reficio, refio, *see* REFECT

refiguro, to recall in imagination c 1115; to refashion c 1450.

refinio, to refine (ore) c 1295.

refirmo, to refortify, re-establish 1086, 1280; (?) to treat, heal 1341.

reflammasco, to flame up again c 1218.

refletum, reflectum, *see* **riffletum.**

reflex/io, reflexion (of light) a 1250, 1414; reflexion, self-knowledge 13c., p 1300; **r. voluntatis super se** c 1270; **-ibilitas (super se),** power of turning back c 1270; **-e** 1267, **-ive** 1267, a 1304, by way of reflexion (of light); **-ivus,** caused by reflexion (of light) 1267; 1267, c 1300, **-us** c 1300,

1620, reflexive, recoiling or directed upon itself; **-us**, reflex movement c 1325; **reflecto**, to reflect (of a mirror) c 1240.

***refloreo**, to flourish again c 1250, 1549.

reflura, *see* **rifflura**.

reflux/io 14c., **r. maris** a 1135, 1359, **-us** 12c., 15c., **-us aque** 1296, 1347, **-us maris** c 1190, 1620, ebb-tide, low water; **-io aque** 13c., **-us aque** a 1190, c 1283, **refluum** 1279, overflow (from mill-pond); *cf.* REFULL; **refluamen (lingue)**, outpouring c 790.

refo, *see* **rieflacum**.

***refocill/atio** c 655. c 1192, 1622, **-amen** 12c., **-antia** c 1350, revival, refreshment; ‡**-ium**, "kindling" c 1440; **-ativus** 1345, **-atrix** (*f.*) c 685, refreshing; ***-o** (bibl.), **refoculo** c 550, **refossilo** c 1540, to revive, refresh.

refol-, *see* **refullum**.

refor, to reply 13c., a 1408.

reform/atio ***c 1080, 1549, **-atorium 1421, reformation, amendment; restoration, repayment c 1258, c 1395; ***r. pacis**, re-establishment of peace 1218,†15c.; **-abilis**, reshapable a 675; **-ativus**, reformative 1344; **-ator**, reformer, regenerator c 760, c 770; "visitor" (eccl.) ‡1483, c 1490; **r. pacis**, restorer of peace c 1310; **-ata religio** 17c.; **-o**, to reflect (an image) c 1115; to make amends for 1415; to restore, give back 13c.; to settle 1405, 15c.; to make terms with (G.) 1289; ‡to visit (eccl.) 1483; ***r. pacem**, to re-establish peace c 1150, 1461; **r. responsum**, to return an answer 1403.

†**reform/o**, (?) *for* **-ido**, 1166.

reforti/uncula, small fort c 1422; **-ficatio**, refortification 1461.

refossilo, see REFOCILL

refract/io, refraction (of light)1267, 1686; **-oria**, refrain (mus.) c 1197 (*cf.* REFECT); **refrangibilitas**, refrangibility (of light) 1686; **-us**, refracted (of light) c 1365, 1620.

refrag/atio, opposition c 1125, c 1414; **-aneus** (play on **suffraganeus**), refractory 1166, 1283; **-ator (precepti)**, breaker 1509; **-o**, to oppose c 1115; to be repugnant 1346.

refrenaculum, curb a 1446.

refreto, to recross, sail back 1136.

refricatio, renewal, re-excitement c 1160, 1552.

refrig/idatio (†refredatio), cooling a 1155; **-erium**, refreshment, mitigation (bibl.); **-escentia**, cooling off, weakening 1377, 1378; **-erativus**, cooling a 1250; **-eratorium**, fan, punkah 1622; **-eo**, to grow cold 1309; **-ido** a 1155, **-do** (*met. grat.*) c 1180, to cool.

refrisco, to refresh, comfort 1428; to polish (leather) 1316.

refug/ium, (right of) sanctuary (W.) 12c.; (right of) protection (W. *nawd*) a 1250; **-atio**, driving back (of cattle) 1364; escape c 1400; relief (of besieged castle) c 1400; **-iarius**, protective 14c.; **-us**, shunned 1241; **-o**, to drive (cattle) back c 1302, a 1564; to put to flight 1292, 1461; to relieve (besieged town) p 1377, 1400.

refulg/entia, refulgence, reflexion 1268, c 1290; **-uro**, to shine c 1125.

refullo, to re-full (cloth) c 1250.

refull/um (†resull-) 12c., c 1290, **refollum** 1176, **-atio** a 1240, 1412, **refollatio** c 1315,

refulsum a 1265, 1272, **refulsus** 1287, overflow from (*or* inflow into) mill-pond (O.F. *refol*); **-o** .1204, **refolo** 1371, to overflow.

refultus, supported, sustained 1241.

refus/io, back-flow c 1125; remelting 1329; ***refunding 1221, 1427; **-a**, **-um**, *see* **lana**; **refundo**, to refer, impute c 1125, c 1375; ***to refund 1217, c 1542; to refute 1204; to refuse c 1450; **r. gratias** 1451, **r. gratiarum actiones** 1220, to return thanks.

refut/atio 1220 c 1390, **-antia** c 1390, quittance; rejection, refusal a 1186, c 1293; ***-o**, to reject, refuse 8c., 1041. c 1125, 1461.

regadia, *see* **ragadia**.

regainum, *see* **rewaynum**.

regal/bordum, -tum, *see* **righoltum**.

regal/e, ornament used at coronation 1166, p 1341; service to the crown 1243; c 1200, 1217, ***-ia** (*n. pl.*) c 1125, 1583, ***-ia** (*f. s.*) 1279, 1494, **-itas** c 1115, 1461, royal power, dignity, right, prerogative; ***-ia** (*n. pl.*), regalities, temporalities (eccl.) c 1188, c 1300; **-ia** (*f. s.*) c 1395, 1499, **-ium** 13c., ***-itas** 1327, 1621, regality, district or jurisdiction (esp. Sc.); c 1450, **-ium** c 1400, allegiance; 1415, **-itas** 1219, royal highness (title); **-is**, king's minister or partisan c 1213, c 1422; **-e** c 1500, **-is** 1292, 1608, **realis** 1292, rial (coin); *see also* **avis, consilium, fera, florenus, papyrus, pes, piscis, sanguis, servitium, via**.

regard-, regargium, *see* **ragadia**; REWARD

regen/eratio, reproduction 13c.; **r. carnis** (med.) a 1250; **-erativus** c 730. c 1188, **-eratrix** (*f.*) c 730, regenerative; **-erativa** (*pl.*), medicaments to regenerate flesh a 1250; **-itor**, regenerator c 1500; **-itus**, regenerate c 1670; **-ero**, to regenerate (bibl.).

reg/entia, regency (in state) 1521; regency (ac.) c 1380, 1528; **-emen**, *for* **-imen**, guidance 12c.; **-imen**, course of study (ac.) c 1350, c 1450; a 1252, 1424, **-imentum** a 1250, 13c., treatment, *régime* (med.); **-imen animarum**, canon law c 1075; **r. chori** (*coll.*), rulers of the choir c 1330, 1425; **r. scholarum**, schoolmastership c 1350; **r. regale**, royal stock 7c.; **-imina** (*pl.*), governing position 7c.; **-imonia** 676, (?) **-men** 8c., 10c., government; **-itivus**, governmental c 1246, c 1443; **-ens**, regent, ruler c 1343, 1567; ***regent, lecturer (ac.) c 1246, 1577 (*see also* **magister**); **r. chorum** c 1330; **-mino** c 550, **-ito** 9c., to govern; **-o**, to govern (gram.) 1610; c 1255, 1412, **r. de** p 1341, **r. in** c 1250, c 1590, to lecture (in) (ac.); **r. schol/am, -as**, studium 12c.; *cf.* **rector, rectum**.

regero, to regurgitate c 1620.

regest-, *see* REGISTR

regetum, *see* **rochetum**.

regin/a, king's mistress 1236; queen (at chess) a 1150, 15c.; *see also* **aurum, lana**; **r. autumpnalis**, harvest queen 1476; **R. Celorum**, Blessed Virgin c 1250; **r. consors**, queen consort 1280; **r. mater**, queen mother 1347; ‡**-a** 13c., **r. prati** ‡14c., 1634, meadowsweet (bot.); **-ula**, princess (of Wales) c 1200; ‡**regilla**, "queen's cloth" 15c.; **-alis** c 1100, 1573, **-eus** 1550, 1634, queenly, of a queen; **-aliter**, as befits a queen 1252.

regi/o, realm 1086, c 1150; (?) royal demesne 1086; **e -one**, face to face a 1164; **-uncula**, earldom, county 1528, c 1595.

***registr/um** c 1188, 1620, **-a** 1459, **regestrum** 1281, 1312, **regesterum** 15c., **-arium** 1408, register, record; **r. finio**, to make up the register c 1334; **-um** c 1200, c 1432, **registerium** c 1503, book-marker; **domus -alis**, register-house a 1525; **-arium**, registry c 1416; **-arius** c 1307, 1687, †**-us** c 1400, **-ator** 1379, c 1450, **regestor** c 1540, registrar; **-arius universitatis** (ac.) c 1470, 1590; **-atio** 1381, 1620, **-atura** c 1520, registration; **-o**, to register, enrol c 1268, 1562.

regit-, regm-, see **regentia**.

regius, royal: see **avis, hasta, nux, piscis, strata, via; reyus,** for **r.**, (G.) 1267.

reg/latus, -lawria, see **raglottus**.

reglutio, to swallow again c 1457.

regn/atio (rengn-) 1219, 1461, **-atus** 1267, reign, rule; **-iculum** c 1385, 1461, †**-aculum** c 1400, petty kingdom; **-alis**, royal 1409; **-ativus**, of government c 1365; **-ator Olympi**, God c 950; ***-icola**, subject c 1258, 1545; **-um**, regulation, control (med.) a 1250; **-ans**, ruler c 1360; **-or**, to rule 1225.

rego, see **regentia**.

regrad/e, in reverse c 1170; see also REGRAT

regrat/aria c 1200, 1547, **-eria** 1258, c 1293, **regraderia** c 1422, **-ia** 1406, **-atio** 1511, **-iatio** 1235, **-um** c 1270, 1279, regrating, resale with (unfair) profit; **-aria** 1258, ***-erissa** 1241, 1419, †**-issa** 1300, **-atrix** 1381, **-iatrix** 1443, **-rix** 1357, regrater (f.); ***-arius** 1221, c 1450, **-erarius** c 1300, **regradarius** 1357, **-ator** 1368, 1496, **-iator** 1223, 1446, **regradiator** 1328, **-or** 1279, 1428, **-orius** 1439, regrater; **-o**, to regrate 1719, 15c.

regrati/atorium 1298, **-atoria** 1303, c 1458, **epistola r.** c 1470, **littera r.** c 1335, 1451, **-atorie** (pl.) 1440, a 1452, **littere r.** c 1390, a 1452, letter of thanks; **-ator**, thanksgiver 1345; **-o** (? for **-atio**), thanksgiving 1285, c 1435; **-o** 1259, a 1450, ***-or** (dep.) c 1150, c 1450, to return thanks.

regressio, recourse c 1318.

regrunnio, to murmur against 14c.

reguard-, see REWARD

1 regul/a, rail, row 1091 (Norm.), 1374 (cf. **raila**); *monastic or religious rule 803. c 1102, 1526; **r. juris**, legal maxim c 1290, c 1443; **r. sancta**, divine commandment c 1006; ‡**-are**, "ruler" 15c.; **-aris**, regular, according to rule c 1160, 1457; *related to rule (mon.) 8c., 11c. a 1100, 1549 (**-arior, -arissimus** 9c.); see also **canonicus**; (subst.) member of mon. or religious order 1169, 1465; **r. ferialis**, fixed number used for calculating the day of the week of any date c 1263; **r. lunaris**, the like for calculating lunar phases c 1263; **-aritas**, regularity c 1608; ***-ariter** 8c., c 1000. c 1080, 1472, **-anter** c 1000, according to rule (mon.); **-atio**, regulation c 1266, 15c.; **-ativus**, regulative, normative p 1300, 1378; **-ator** c 1375, 1552, **-atrix** (f.) a 1250, 1447, regulator; **male -atus**, misbehaved 1416; **-o**, to rule (lines) c 1178, 1444; (?) to mark out or fit with rails (arch.) 1323; *to regulate, direct 1267, 1494; **r. disputationem** (ac.) c 1470; **r. scholas** c 1380.

2 ‡regul/a, duchess 15c.; **-us**, duke c 1562; wren (Fr. roitelet) c 1160, a 1270; see also **pirum**; **-osus**, serpentine, venomous c 550.

regurgito, to overflow c 1212.

regwannum, see **rewaynum**.

regwardum, see **rewardum**.

regyro (regiro), to round, circumnavigate c 1100; *to turn back or round a 1142, 15c.; **r. me**, to turn over or round 7c. 1327.

rehab/itio, recovery 1331, 1340; **-eo** *c 1115, c 1475, **rabeo** 12c., to regain, recover; to get instead 1277; **-ilito**, to re-establish c 1400, 1517.

rehospito, to rehouse 1221.

rehs see **resh**.

rehumilio, to humble again 14c.

reia, (?) stripe a 1135; row (of land) c 1150, c 1190; cf. **radius**; see also **ragadia**.

reicio, see REJECT

reimatus, see **raimatus**.

reimpetro, to ask and receive back, regain c 800. c 1293.

reimpositio, reimposition c 1185; replacing 1472.

rein/a (reyn-) 1318, 1350, **-um** 1320, **renna** 1219, c 1335, **royna** c 1335, rein or bridle-bit; strap (for galley) 1214.

rein/ceptio, recommencement c 1200; *-cipio**, to recommence c 1125, c 1500.

reinchoo, to recommence a 1250, c 1375.

reincid/entia, reservation 1543; **-itio**, incurring again 1380; **-o**, to relapse 1219, c 1298; to incur again 1461.

reincido, to cut (quill) again c 1185.

reinclin/atio c 1250, 1378, **-antia** c 1365, turning back or away; **-o**, to turn back again a 1233, 1267.

reincludo, to shut up again 1450.

reincorporo, to reincorporate (eccl.) 1417, a 1452.

reinduco, to readmit c 1400, c 1463; to re-induct (eccl.) 1296.

reinduo, to put on again c 1200; to reclothe c 1130, p 1400; to reinvest (eccl.) c 1293.

†**reingardus**, (?) 'renger' (baker's sieve) or strap (O.F. rengere) 1232.

reingredior, to re-enter a 1135, a 1540.

reinsero, to reinstate 1437.

reintegro, see REDIN

reintr/atio, re-entry 1341, a 1564; *-o** c 655. 1107, 1521, **reentro** 1379, to re-enter.

reintroduco, to readmit c 1197.

reintroitus, re-entry c 1400.

reintrusio, placing again 1413.

reinvado, to invade again 1327.

reinvenio, to rediscover 9c. a 1100, c 1470.

reinvestio, to reinvest, repossess c 1400.

reinvigoratus, refreshed a 1452.

reinvito, to invite back (bibl.).

reis/a, military expedition (German Reise) 1391; **-terus**, 'reister', Reiter, trooper 1577.

reisalgum, see **realgar**.

reiseisio, see RESEIS

reisin-, see **racemus; resina**.

reitatus, see RETT

reiter/atio, repetition 13c.; **-o**, to repeat c 1100, c 1290; to resume, continue c 1125.

reivera, *see* RIP

rejaceo, to be deposited c 1196.

reject/io, ejectment (of disseisor) c 1258; **-iuncula**, trivial refutation 1610; **-us**, exclusion c 1390; **-ictus**, outcast a 1520; **-ivus** (play on **adjectivus**), to be rejected c 1620; **reicio me**, to exculpate oneself (leg.) c 1115.

rejunctio, reunion 1331; rejoinder (leg.) c 1420, 1507; **rejungo**, to re-yoke c 1470; to reunite c 1180, c 1458; to rejoin (leg.) c 1420, 1492.

†**rejuno**, *f.l.* for **jejuno**, 1250.

rejuro, to swear again 1461, c 1470.

rejuvenesco, to renew youth a 1250.

rekka, *see* RACK

rela, *see* **raila**.

relaps/us, relapse (into heresy) 1324, 1419; **-us** 1324, a 1428, **-a** (*f.*) 1324, relapsed heretic.

relat/io, naming 940. 12c.; relation (phil.) 11c., c 1534; kinship c 1250; reputation 1461; **-iuncula**, short account c 700. a 1200; **-e** 1267, **-ive** 793. a 1250, 1461, relatively; **-ivus**, relative (eccl.); **-or**, reciter, story-teller c 730, c 1000. a 1142, 15c.; **-rix**, restorer (*f.*) c 1298; **-orius**, binding over (*adj.*) c 1350; **-a** (*n. pl.*), relative terms 13c., 1610; *cf.* REFER

relav-, *see* RELEV

*****relax/atio** c 700. a 1175, c 1520, †**-io** c 1267, **-atia** 1319, **-amentum** 1188, 1204, **relessum** c 1225, release, remittance, discharge; **-ativa** (*n. pl.*), laxatives (med.) a 1250; **-ius**, less strictly c 790; **-o**, to set free c 1125, 1461; to exempt c 1250, c 1283; to forgive c 730. 14c., 1583; *****to release, remit (leg.) 1211, c 1536; to dispense with c 1188; to redeem (a pledge) 1415; **r. sententiam**, to reverse a sentence c 1250, c 1310.

rel/eatio, **-ia**, *see* **raila**.

releg-, *see also* **religio**.

relego, to banish: **religo** c 1350, 1461.

relessum, *see* RELAX

relev/atio, rehoisting 14c.; *****a 1100, c 1470, *****-amen** 1296, 1587, **-ium** 1587, relief, succour, alleviation; *****1086, c 1258, **-agium** c 1145, 1282, *****-amen** 1086, c 1170, **relavamen** 1587, **-amentum** 1086, c 1350, **-ata** c 1180, 16c., **-atum** 1166, **-atus** c 1160, **-eium** (C.I.) 1284, 1331, *****-ium** c 1150, 1583, **-ia** 1276, **relavia** 16c., **-um** c 1186, **relivium** 1224, 1492, feudal relief (payment to overlord by heir on succession); **-atio**, churching (eccl.) 1316; **-atura prati**, lifting hay 15c.; **-ium**, remnant of meal (given as alms) c 1296, a 1316; afternoon (Fr. *relevée*) 1297; **-ator** 1414, **-atrix** (*f.*) c 1100, 14c., reliever, helper; **-ans**, relevant 1549; **-o**, *****to rebuild 1204, c 1400; to rise again c 1400, 1461; *****1086, c 1292, **-io** c 1185, c 1350, to redeem by (feudal) relief; **-o breve**, to revalidate a writ (leg.) c 1285; **r. carrucam**, to restock a plough-team 1245; **r. pecuniam**, to levy money 15c.

reliber/atio, restitution 1414; *****-o**, to hand back, restore 1309, 1487; **r. prisone** 1327.

relibo, to nibble at 1241.

relict-, *see* RELIQU

*****religio/**, cult (of saint) 8c.; *****c 1066, 1536, **-sitas** 1277, 1518, religious or monastic life,

order or house; **relegio**, *for* **r.**, religion 705. 11c.; **fides -nis**, pledge of an oath c 1185; **r. Alba**, Carmelite order 1461; **r. privata**, a special (authorized) religious order 1416; **r. reformata** 17c.; **r. universa**, Christendom, the Church 1173; **tua (vestra) r.** 1104, 1231, **-sitas** c 1125, 1526, your worship (title); **-se**, monastically c 1100, 1255; **-sus**, (*adj.*) *****monastic c 1125, 1588; (*subst.*) *****1030. 12c., 1570, **-sa** (*f.*) c 1090, 1420, member of religious or monastic order; *****r. mendicans** 1333, 1549; *****r. possessionatus** c 1350, 15c.; **relegiosus**, *for* **-sus**, religious 948.

religo, to gather (men, like sheaves) c 1192; 1286, **relio** 1198, to hoop; *see also* **relego**.

*****reliqu/ie** (*pl.*), sacred relics c 730, a 1050. c 1080, 1461; **-ia**, a relic 1351; **dies -iarum** c 1397, **festum -iarum** 1514, Thursday in Easter week; **d. Dominica -iarum**, Relic Sunday (first after 7 July) a 1564; **-iare**, reliquary c 1250; **-imentum**, relinquishment (G.) 1289; **de -o**, henceforth 14c.; **relicta**, *****relict, widow 6c. c 1125, 1539; divorced wife c 1199, c 1450; †**-o** (? **relinquo**) **ad firmam**, to farm out 1200; **relicto**, to abandon c 1435.

relivium, *see* RELEV

rella, *see* **ralla**.

rellia, *see* **raila**.

‡**relolleum**, virtue derived from composition (alch.) 1652.

relucr/atio, regaining c 1400; **-um**, (?) backrent 1286; aftermath, 'fog' 1307, 1366; **caseus de -o** 1277, 1345 (*cf.* **rewaynum**); to regain c 1400; to mow aftermath from 1376.

reluct/atio c 760. 1304, c 1620, **-amen** 14c., **-amentum** 13c., resistance; **syllogismus -atorius**, 'elenchus', refutation (log.) c 1160.

†**rema**, kind of fish 1452; *see also* **rhema**.

remagium, *see* **rumagium**.

remale, *see* **ramus**.

remaledico, to curse back 12c.

remando, to send back c 990. 1347; *****to send back word 1166, 1461; to send word cancelling previous order 1262; **r. loquelam**, to remit plea (to court of origin) 1497; **r. breve**, to withdraw writ p 1330.

reman/entia, remaining c 1124, c 1450; 1275, 1533, **-ens** 1167, 1226, **-erium** 1318, **-et** c 1270, remainder (on account); 1358, 1457, **-entum** 1509, **remenantum** 1309, **-sio** c 1285, **-ens** 1086, 1509, remnant; **r. panni** 1388; **-ere** c 1416, 1583, **-erium** 1569, 1614, remainder (leg.); **remasilia** (*pl.*) (vaccarum), droppings 12c0. **-ens**, surviving heir (leg.) 1437; **ad -ens**, for the future 1164, c 1250; **-eo**, *****to stand over, be stayed (leg.) c 1106, 1324; to default (leg.) 1086, c 1450; to remain over (in accounts) 1086, 1338; **-eor**, *for* **-eo**, to remain 1086, 1324; **-eo de**, to be quit of c 1115; **r. in** c 1110, c 1430, **r. pro** 1230, to rest with, be the responsibility of; **r. intus**, to remain in seisin 1221.

rematisma, *see* RHEUM

remedi/um, salvation (theol.) 7c., 9c. c 1130, c 1190; concession, relaxation (mon.) c 1305, 15c.; 'remedy', margin of impurity (in coinage) 1408; **-arium [conversorum]**, title of

a book c 1396; **-abiliter**, not incurably c 1306; **-aliter**, as a remedy 12c.

remel-, *see* ramus.

remem/oratio c 1160, c 1470, †**remorantia** 1405, **-brantia** 1431, remembrance, recollection; anamnesis (phil.) c 1270; c 1300, **-oratorium** 1381, record; **-oranda** (*pl.*), memoranda c 1265; **-orativus**, commemorative 13c.; **-orissarius** 1430, **-orantiarius** c 1345, **-orator** (G.) 1437, remembrancer, recorder; **-orator** 1263, 1587, **-orantiarius**, **-brancarius** 1290, remembrancer (of Exchequer); **r. regis** 1248, 1526, **-brator regis** 1452; **r. (ex parte) thesaurarii** 1299, 1526; **r. capitalis** (Ir.) 1446; **-oro,** *for* **-oror**, to remember c 730, 793. c 1115, c 1340; to bring to mind, mention c 1340, c 1458.

remendo, to repair 1291.

remensuro, to measure out 1323.

remeo, to revert (leg.) c 1235; to have recourse 14c.

‡**remigabilis**, "rowable" 1570.

†**remig/o**, (?) *f.l.* for **-ro**, to return p 1341, c 1400.

*****reminisc/entia**, remembrance c 1250, c 1580; **-itivus**, concerned with memory a 1250, p 1300; **-ere**, second Sunday in Lent c 1300.

remino, to drive back (cattle) c 1400, a 1564.

remiss/io, diminution of intensity 1335, c 1340; thaw 1339; remission, written grant 1435; **-ibilis**, able to be made less intense 1344, c 1360; remissible (theol.) c 1368, 15c.; **-ibilitas**, remissibility (of sin) c 1375; **-ivus**, remissive (gram.) c 790; c 1197, c 1345 **-orius** 1344, 1684, of remission or absolution; **annus -ivus**, jubilee year 1276, c 1520; **littera -iva** c 1300, **-oria** 1546, **epistola -oria** c 1260, reply; **-us**, lessened, lacking intensity 1296, c 1340; light (of colour) 1446, 1464; †**remitt/a**, abatement c 1270; **-o**, to thaw 1343; to adjourn 1268, (?) 1294; to reply (?) c 1200, c 1255; **r. post**, to send after c 1000.

remittabilis, remobilis, *see* remotio.

remollit/io, softening a 1250; **-ivus**, making soft a 1250.

remor/a, 'stayship', sucking-fish 1535, 1620; **-atio**, delay c 1200; **-o,** *for* **-or**, to detain c 1435.

remorantia, *see* REMEM

remorsus, remorse 1276, c 1443.

remortuus, dead a second time c 1306.

remo/tio, remoteness, distance 9c. c 1125, 1377; **-bilis** a 1540, **-vibilis** 1385, 1535, **remutabilis (*remittabilis*)** 1309, **-tivus** a 1250, 15c., removable; **a -to, a -tis**, from afar a 1250, c 1343; **in -tis**, in distant parts 1336, 1345; **-tus**, privative (log.) c 1160, a 1250.

‡**remulco**, to tow 1483.

rem/ulus, -unculus, *see* ramus.

remuner/abilis, worthy of reward c 1197, 1344; **-ativus**, rewarding 1344.

remurmur/, repining 1374; **-o**, to protest a 1200.

remuro, to re-wall, refortify 1461.

remutabilis, *see* remotio.

remuto, to change back 1344.

remutuo, to repay a 1186.

ren/ a 1452, ‡15c., **-iculus** 6c., kidney, loin; ‡**-ale**, "gardecorse", "pauncher" c 1200, 1483.

renanciscor, to recover c 1562.

rena/scentia 1437, **-scitura** 1497, rebirth; **-tivus**, regenerative 1220; **-tus**, born again (theol.) c 1182, c 1508.

renca, *see* RANG

rend-, *see* RENT

renegatus, renegade, apostate 1166, 1421.

Ren/ensis, -isetus, *see* florenus; vinum.

renettum, *see* rennettum; revettum.

reng-, *see also* ranga; ringa; runga.

rengat/us 1380, **ringatus** a 1380, c 1400, **-orius** 1365, 'ranged', sifted (of bread).

regn-, *see* REGN

reniculus, *see* ren.

reni/tentia c 1242, c 1362, **-xus** 1649, opposition, resistance.

renna, *see* reina.

rennettum, rennet 1276, 1352.

reno, pelisse a 1142, ‡13c.; *see also* ARRAIN

renod/ura, loose knitting together of bones c 1258; **-atrix**, restorer (*f.*) c 1248; **-o**, to release 1200; to reunite, restore c 1200, 1245.

renominatio, renown 1281.

renormo, to remodel a 1205.

renov/atio arcis, burhbote 12c.; **r. plegiorum**, view of frankpledge, *borhnewing* (Suffolk) c 1186, c 1258; **-ativus**, renewing 9c. a 1250; **-ator**, Redeemer c 780; **-o plegios**, to view frankpledges (Suffolk) a 1130, 1206.

rent/a 1182, c 1315, **-ale** (Sc.) 1528, 1566, rent; *****-ale**, rental, rent-book c 1283, 1540; **-aria**, rented tenement 1461, 1553; **-alis** 1335, 1460, **rendalis** (G.), **rendualis** (G.) 1289, 1313, rentable, of rent; **gallina -alis**, rent-hen 1450; **-arius**, rent-collector 1270, 1455; rent-payer 1338; **-allarius**, 'rentaller' (Sc.) 1608; **-alizo** 1510, 1560, **-alo** 1555, to admit as a 'kindly tenant' (Sc.); **rend/o, -eo**, to pay rent (? or *f.l.* for **respondeo**) 1233, 1294; *cf.* REDD

†**renumero**, (?) *f.l.* for **remunero**, to award 1355.

renunti/atio, renunciation c 800. c 1090, 1563; **littera -atoria** c 1300; **-o**, to renounce c 1125, 1559.

renusiator, *see* RANSON

renverso, *see* REVER

reo/, spoke (Fr. *rayon*) 1269; furrow (O.F. *roion*) c 1225, 1271; **-no**, to furrow 1281, 1284; *cf.* radius.

reobjicio, to object again a 1452.

reobligo, to oblige in return or mutually c 1258, 1378.

reobsideo, to besiege again a 1118.

reobstupo, to block again 1354, 1375.

reobtineo, to recover c 1345.

reoctabe, octave of octave, quinzaine 1243, 1254.

reomellis, *see* ramus.

reonero, to recharge (on account) 1329.

reono, *see* reo.

reoperio, to re-cover c 1170.

reordino, to reordain (eccl.) c 1095, c 1188; to order differently c 1400.

repacc/atio, repacking 1503; **-o**, to repack 1338.

repacifico me cum, to become reconciled with c 1100.

repagul/a, -um, bar, barrier c 1180, a 1564; **-atus,** barred c 1250.

repar-, *see also* REPER

repar/atio (reper-) 7c. 1157, 1583 **-atura** 1286, repairing, repair; healing 1300; redemption (theol.) c 1457, c 1510; **r. ad infra, r. extrinseca,** internal and external repair 1457; **r. ferri hirsuti,** working up scrap iron 1345; **r. lane,** dressing wool c 1300; **r. manerii,** a customary payment (W. *treth lles*) 1505; **r. muri,** burhbote 1086; **r. Terre Sancte,** recovery of the Holy Land c 1250; **-alia** (*pl.*), apparel 1513; **-amentum,** suit of vestments (eccl.) 1493; ‡**-arius,** 'rache', hound c 1440; **-ativa** (*pl.*), restoratives, tonics (med.) c 1160; **-ativus,** restorative 1344, a 1446; **-ator,** repairer c 1178, 1528; **-atrix,** restorer (*f.*) c 1170; **-alio,** to 'reparel', repair 1363; ***-o** 1086, 1570, -io c 1218, 1322, to repair; **r. cibum,** to cook up food 1465; **r. fenum** 1350; **r. lanam,** to dress wool 1279.

repari/um (reperi-) c 1260, 15c., **repairium** (G.) 1313, (place of) repair, resort, haunt; **-o,** to repair, resort 1276.

reparturio, to bring forth again c 1500.

reparvipendo, to retaliate a slight c 1292.

*repass/agium, recrossing, passage back 1302, 1464; **-o,** to ferry back (*trans.*) 1367.

*repast/us, -a, -um, repast, meal c 1283, 1580.

repatior, to suffer in turn c 1380.

repatri/atio, returning home 1274, c 1300; **-atus,** having returned home 1274; ***-o,** to return home c 1020. c 1070, c 1540.

repaus/atio, repose c 1125, a 1350; **-o,** to give rest or lodging to 771; ***c 1150, c 1450, reposo** c 1000. c 1100, to repose.

‡**repeci/um,** "clout" 1483; ‡**-arius,** "clouter" 15c.; **-o,** to clout, patch c 1250, ‡1483.

reped/io 1510, **-ito** 12c., *for* **-o,** to go back; **-o** (with *acc.*), to go back to c 800. c 1125, c 1200; **r. iter** c 1000.

repellis, *see* REBELL

†**repello,** (?) *for* refello, to refute c 1343; *see also* REPULS

repens, *see* reptio.

repen/satio 8c. c 1414, **-samen** 12c., **-siva** 1288, 1350, **-sum** c 1300, **-dium** c 1325, c 1380, recompense; **-sator,** requiter 12c.; **-sivus,** compensatory c 1320.

reper-, *see also* repar-

reperculsus, struck c 1125.

repercuss/io, second signal (in church) c 1330; reflexion (of light) c 1320; friction p 1394; throbbing c 1327; hitting back (in self-defence) a 1564; **-ivus,** reflective (of light) p 1394, a 1446; corrective of fluxion (med.) a 1250, ‡1652; **-or,** riveter 1296; †**repurcussus,** reflected c 1194; **repercutio,** to abut p 1182; to rivet 1296, ‡1483; to hit back c 1218, a 1564; to strike (with wonder), impress c 1188.

repereva, *see* riperevus.

reperquiro, to regain 1276, 1293.

reper/tio, discovery c 1400; ***-torium** c 1330, c 1500, **reportorium** 1303, c 1430, (?) **reportorius** 1420, inventory, summary; **-trix,**

discoverer (*f.*) a 1200; **-ibilis,** to be found c 1345, 1454; **thesaurus -tus,** treasure trove a 1088.

repet/itio, 'repetition', discourse (ac.) c 1340, a 1350; †**reputatio,** repetition c 1450; **-itor,** repeater c 1180, 1345; (?) a functionary in choir 1479; **-ens,** demandant (leg.) c 1115; **-o,** to deliver a repetition (ac.) c 1340.

‡**repignoratio,** "replevin" (leg.) 1570.

replacito, to plead again (leg.) 1293, a 1564.

replano, to smoothe, stroke (falc.) a 1250.

replanto, to reinstate c 1402.

repleg/iatio c 1185, 1404, **-iamentum** 1221, 15c., **replevina** 1198, 1432, †**replevia** a 1452, **repleviatio** 1274, **replivatio** 1275, replevin, release on bail (leg.); **-iare** 1285, 1419, **-iari** 1309, 1445, writ of replevin; **-iabilis,** repleviable 1220, 1405; **-iator,** one who goes bail (Sc.) 1389; ***-io,** to replevy, redeem or release on bail c 1150, 1451.

reple/tio, filling up, fullness a 1250, 1526; †**-tie** (*pl.*), (?) *for* expletie, esplees, profits 1467; **-bilitas,** capacity of being filled c 1290; **-tivitas,** capacity of filling 1344; **-tive,** by filling 1621; **-tivus,** capable of filling or satisfying 9c. a 1275, 1344.

replic/atio *c 1258, 1549, **-atum** 1549, †**-um** c 1343; replication (leg.); repetition (mus.) c 1160; replication (ac.) c 1407, c 1542; reconstitution (phys.) 1620; **-ator,** one who takes part in replications (ac.) c 1550; **-atorie,** by way of replication (leg.) c 1470; **atorius,** concerned with replication (leg.) c 1375, 1446; **-o,** *to repeat, recount c 730, c 970. c 1080, 15c.; c 730. c 1190, c 1420, †**repleo** 13c., to reply; c 1185, 1539, †**replio** c 1487, to make replication (leg.); (ac.) c 1400; 1288, †**ripplico** 1289, (?) to replough (*cf.* REBIN).

replivatio, *see* REPLEG

repono, *see* REPOS

report/atio 1244, 1485, **-agium** 1300, 1379, carrying back; p 1300, c 1500, **-amen** c 1458, **-um** 1505, report; **-ator,** reporter, tale-bearer c 1343, a 1385; **-o,** to suffer, incur 1236, c 1320; **r. dampnum,** to inflict damage 15c.; ***r. fiduciam,** to repose confidence 1242, 1336.

reportiono, to reapportion 1316.

reportori/um, -us, *see* repertio; REPOS

repos/itio, placing, arranging c 1080, a 1564; c 1190, c 1218, **-itorium** c 760. 12c., 1588, **-torium** 12c., repository, storage place; **-itorium** 1287, 1342, (?) †**reportorium** 1406, 'burse', receptacle for corporal cloth (eccl.); **archa -itoria,** storage chest c 1178; **vas -torium** a 1142; **-taculum,** hiding-place c 1102; **-tallum,** (?) recess (O.F. *repostaille*) 1357; **repono ad manum,** to restore to possession 1310; **r. in legem,** to free from outlawry c 1258.

reposo, *see* REPAUS

repostulo, to demand afresh a 1452.

†**reppomis,** (?) *f.l. for* respouns, 'responds' half-pillars (arch.) 1341.

repredo, to plunder 1347.

reprehen/sibilitas, reprehensibility c 1250; ***-sibilis** c 1080, a 1452, **-dibilis** a 1350, reprehensible; **-sibiliter,** reprehensibly c 860. c 1343; **-sive,** by reprehension c 1250;

-sivus, condemnatory c 1204, 1298; **-sus,** accused party, defendant a 1150.

represalie, *see* REPRIS

represent/atio, right of presentation, advowson (eccl.) c 1414; **-antia,** representation (phil.) c 1367; **-abilis,** representable to the intellect (phil.) c 1270, p 1300; **-ative,** by way of representation (phil.) c 1270; **;-ativus,** representative (phil.) c 1270, 15c.; **-atrix,** representative, type (*f.*) a 1200; **-o,** to present c 1192, c 1450; to present in return c 1415; to present again 1253, 1419; to present again to a benefice 1216, 1238; to represent, act as representative of c 1290, 1559; **r. me,** to present oneself, appear c 1060, c 1200, 1341; (?) to devote oneself c 1170; **r. ad rectum,** to produce in court (leg.) c 1115.

*repress/io c 1160, 1461, **-orium** 1472, repression, restraint; **-ivus,** repressive a 1250.

repreva, *see* **riperevus.**

*repris/a, 'reprise', deduction from profits 1276, 1505; **-alia** (*n. pl.*) c 1405, a 1446, (*f. s.*) 1384, 15c., **-alie** (*pl.*) c 1390, 1505, **-elia** (*f. s.*) c 1450, **represalie** (*pl.*) 1288, c 1450, reprisals; **littere -aliarum** 1496, l. **-oriales** 1627, letters of reprisal.

reprivo, to remand (leg.) 1575, 1587.

reprob/atio, reproof (eccl.); refutation, counter-argument c 1332, c 1343; **-abilia** (*n. pl.*), blameworthy things c 1260; **-abilis,** meriting rejection or condemnation 680, c 730. c 1160, c 1400; **-abiliter,** disgracefully 15c.; **-ativus,** disapprobatory 1344, 15c.; **-e,** with disapproval c 1280; ***-us,** (*adj. or subst.*) reprobate (bibl.); **r. sacer-dotio,** disqualified for priesthood c 1197; **moneta -a,** false coin c 1258, c 1294; **in -um sensum** c 1080, **-o sensu** 1425, heretically; **-o,** ***to** disapprove, reject, condemn (bibl.); †to prove c 1290; **r. testamentum,** to refuse probate of will 1415.

reprob/osus, (?) *for* **-rosus,** opprobrious 1379, 1389.

reproduco, to produce again (leg.) a 1452.

repromissi/o, promise of return c 730. c 1185; fresh promise c 800; (?) fulfilment of promise c 1185; **Terra -onis** (bibl.), **Patria -onis** 12c., the Promised Land.

repropiti/atio 1517, **-atorium** c 760, atonement; **-atus,** reconciled 12c.; **-or** (*dep.*), to repropitiate 8c.

repsallo, to sing again c 1000.

repticus, *see* **rhypticus.**

rep/tio, crawling c 1360; **-tile** c 1100, c 1362, **-tilis** 8c., 9c., **-ens** 9c., reptile; **-titatrix,** creeper (*f.*) 1544.

†**trepturio,** (?) *f.l. for* **repatrio,** to return 13c.

republico, to publish 1412.

repugn/aculum, opposition c 1273; **-ator,** opponent c 730. c 1250.

repullulamen, rebirth c 1325.

repuls/io, ejection (from monastery) c 600; banishment, cure (med.) a 1250; **-us maris,** ebb or backwash 1315; **-ivum,** ground for rejection 1426; **-ivus,** repellent 9c. c 1258, c 1270; **repello,** to subtract c 815.

repumicator, polisher c 1620.

repunio, to take vengeance on c 1240.

repurcussus, *see* REPERCUSS

repurg/atio, purging away 9c.; clearance (after eclipse) 1344; **-o,** to expurgate, correct (books) 1520, 1529.

reput/atio, ***reputation,** credit p 1330, c 1434; order, condition 1291; **-abilis,** reputable c 1250; **-ative,** reputedly c 1375, 1427; **-o,** to assign as due c 800; ***to** repute, deem c 1115, 1549; *cf.* RETT; *see also* REPET

requantifico, to requantify (log.) c 1360.

request-, *see* REQUISIT

requi/es, tomb c 1090, c 1325; **-em,** requiem mass c 1195, c 1330 (*see also* **missa**); **-etio,** rest (bibl.); day or period of rest 7c., 8c. 12c.; 14c., **-escio** c 1398, resting-place; **locus -etionis,** grave c 1000.

requisit/io, suit (of court) c 1077; seeking of sanctuary c 1110; investigation a 1175, a 1361; requisition 1437, 1552; **requesta,** payment or oblation (eccl.) 1268, 1276; **-io *a** 1125, 1583, **-um** 13c., **requesta** 1279, 1461, **requestus** 1385, 1471, request; **clericus consilii -ionum** (leg.) 1483; **magister -ionum** 1573, m. **Requestarum** (Engl.) 1586, (Sc.) 1389, 1515, master of requests; **Curia Requestarum** 1586, C. **Requestuum** 1550, Court of Requests; **-or,** inquisitor (eccl.) 1385; **littere -orie,** letters of request 1393, a 1446; **-e,** adequately 1549; **requiro,** ***to** interrogate 597. c 1090, c 1400; to render (walls) with cement 1244; to render suit at (court) c 1105; **r. faldam,** to do suit to a fold 1086.

reragium 1165, c 1335, **rieragium** 1187, **riragium** 1205 (*coll.*), arrears; *cf.* **arreragium.**

reregardia, *see* **retrowarda.**

res/, reality, essence (phil.) a 1100, c 1160; unknown first power (math.) 1145; **ad rem facio,** to be relevant 1393; **r. bellica,** warfare 1415; **r. Christiana,** Christendom c 1500; **r. divina** 1551, **r. sacra** 1537, 1552, divine service; **r. expeditionalis,** fyrd 739. 12c.; **r. medica,** medical science 1520; **r. rationis,** ideal essence c 1300; **r. vicecomitis,** service due to sheriff 1086; **r.** (*pl.*) **assise,** items of farm of county 1269; **-cella** c 1125, 1421, **recella** c 1250, **recola** c 970, small matter, trifle; *cf.* REAL

†**tresa,** poleaxe c 1450.

resais-, *see* RESEIS

resalger, *see* **realgar.**

†**tresarcino,** to unpack 1570.

resaro, *see* **reseratio.**

resar/tio c 1503, 1539, **-tura** c 1507, repair; reparation, recompense 9c. a 1400, 1521; **-cio,** to reinvest with office (eccl.) 1105; 1254, **resercio** 1502, to make good (a deficit).

resaucio, to wound again 790.

rescarifico, to cut again c 1180.

resceisio, *see* RFSEIS

rescella, *see* **res.**

rescens, *see* **recentia.**

rescio, to know 5c.; to find out c 1178.

rescis-, *see* RECIS

resconsitus sol, sunset (*cf.* O.F. *resconser*) 1247.

rescript/io, written answer 1433; c 1200, ***-um** a 1175, c 1487, papal rescript; **-um,** order by Court of Arches c 1342; copy a 1165, 1414; written account 1173, 1432.

rescuss/io 1268, 1305, ***-us** 1177, 1432, **-a** 1189, 1275, **rescursus** 1287, 1341, **recussus** 1278, 1337, **recussa** (Fr.) 1293, **recursus** 1274, 1449, 'rescue', illegal recovery of cattle, *etc.*, taken in distraint; 1219, **-ura** 1175, **rescousa** (Fr.) 1282, rescue (of a prisoner); 1260, 1340, **reexcussio** 1253, **-us** 1233, 1419, **rescursus** 1413, 1461, relief (of besieged castle); **-us**, shaking down (of grain before measurement) (C. I.) 1247; ‡**-or**, 'rescuer' (leg.) 17c.; **rescutio** *1210, a 1564, **recutio** 1175, 1202, to 'rescue' distrained chattels; to rescue, recover (at sea) 1265, 1419; 1231, 1300, **rescuo** 1274, 1412, to rescue (prisoners); to deprive (of prisoners) by rescue 1313; *1184, 1495, **-io** 1314, to relieve (a castle); *cf.* EXCUSS

reseant-, *see* **residentia.**

resec/atio, cutting up, dividing 13c.; reaping 1261; clipping (of coins) 1361; **-o,** to divide c 1350; to clip (coins) 1361; ‡"to carve" *or* "to lance" 1570; **reseo,** to cut 1354.

resecit, *see* RECESS

resecundo, to repeat (action) c 1170.

reseis/ina, reseisin (leg.) 1220, 15c.; **-io** 1242, 1415, **-o** p 1139, ***resaisio** 1086, 1243, **resceisio** 1370, **reseicio** 1484, to reseise, reinstate in possession; (?) to restore (recovered pledge) to custody (G.) 1315; **-io** 1291, 1518, **-eo** c 1130, **resaisio** 1077, 1459, †**reiseisio** 1225, to resume possession of; **resaisio tenementum de catallis** c 1185.

resemino, to resow 1369, a 1564.

reseo, *see* RESEC

reser/atio, opening c 730, 790. c 1430, a 1452; unlocking, unfolding 870; solving 9c. c 1370; **-o,** to release from solidity (alch.) c 1320; to lock c 1290, 1442; **resaro,** *for* **-o,** to disclose 1379.

resercio, *see* RESAR

reserv/atio, reservation, keeping back 1258, 1549; *(papal) reservation of benefice 1252, 1444; 1646, **r. mentalis** 1380, c 1620, mental reservation; **-abilis,** to be kept in reserve 1398; **-ator,** reserver of benefice c 1444; **littere -atorie,** (papal) letters of reservation c 1313; **-o Corpus Domini** c 1220, **r. hostiam** 13c., to reserve the sacrament (eccl.); **r. terminum,** to keep a term (in repaying debt) c 1300; *see also* **casus, redditus.**

resessio, sitting down again 860; *cf.* RESID

resetto, *see* RECEPT

resh, rehs, Hebrew letter c 1200.

resid/entia c 1120, 1229, **-ensia** 1199, **reseantia** 1319, **reseantisa** 1212, 1405, **reciantia** 15c., residence, settled place of abode; sediment a 1250; right of residence (in realm) 1208; *c 1130, 1494, **resethantisa** c 1130, residence, obligation to reside (eccl.); residence (ac.) c 1400, c 1556; **r. personalis** (eccl.) 1247, c 1520; **r. anime in Deo** c 1190; **r. in Concilio** c 1450; **reseantisa,** detention at home (by illness, *etc.*) as ground for essoin c 1185, 1400; **r. militis,** residence of knight (in fee) 1255; **resians** 1507, 1555, **recedens** 1392, resident; **-ens,** resident tenant c 1115, c 1450; 1586, **-entialis** 1475, **-entiarius** 1317, 1517, **canonicus r.** 1356, 1536, resi-

dentiary canon (eccl.); **r. magni consilii** 1440; **-entiaria,** office of resident fellow (ac.) c⁻1452; **-eo,** to be situated c 1362, c 1366; to stay, be kept (of things) c 1250, 1437; to reside (of persons) c 1115, 1507; (eccl.) c 1350, 1380; (ac.) c 1407, c 1550; to sit (of judges) c 1115, 1263; to rest a judgement 1472; to be decided c 1200, c 1272; to subside (of anger) c 1204; **r. in dubiis,** to remain in doubt 1295; **recedit,** *for* **resedit,** c 1272.

residiv-, *see* RECID

resid/uitas, residue 1378, 1424; †**-ius,** *for* **-uus,** 15c.; **-ua placitorum** (*n. pl.*), 'remanets', adjourned pleas (leg.) 1212; **-uo,** to leave over c 1115.

resigillo, to seal up again 1290, 1292.

resign/atio (resingn-), *giving up, surrender 1268, c 1540; *resignation (of office, benefice, *etc.*) c 1180, 1537; **r. homagii,** repudiation of homage c 1320; **-ator thesaurorum,** treasurer c 1150; **littere -atorie** c 1308, **scriptum -atorium** 1409, letters of resignation; **-o,** to give up, surrender c 1185, c 1450; (*intr.*) to resign from office c 1300, c 1470; to report under seal 1200; **-or cruce,** to become a crusader c 1250.

‡**resil/itio (ossis),** dislocation 15c.; *-**io (ab),** to 'resile', go back on, repudiate c 1170, c 1470.

resina (bibl.), **reisina** 1234, 1467, ***ros/ina** 1325, 1531, **-inum** 1296, **-enum** a 1564, **-etum** (Sc.) 1449, 1466, **-ilium** 1295, resin, rosin; **-inatio (navium),** treating with rosin 1371.

resincero, *see* RECINCER

resinus, *see* **racemus.**

resipisc/entia, change of mind, repentance 8c. c 1375, 1537; **-o ad,** to relapse into 12c.; †**r. sacramentum,** (?) to bethink oneself of an oath c 1204.

resis, *see* RHE

***resist/entia** a 1250, 1686, **-antia** 1293, **-atio** 1232, resistance; **-ivus** c 1270, c 1412, **-entivus** c 1340, resistant.

resito, *see* RECIT

†**resius,** (?) *for* **cesius,** blue-grey c 1550.

reskippamentum, *see* REESKIPP

resna, 'reson', beam (arch.) (A.S. *ræsn*) 1272.

***resocio,** to reunite c 1250, c 1422.

resolid/atio, reunion c 1075; **-o,** to rebuild, reunite 8c. a 1100, c 1325.

resol/utio c 1283, 1531, **resulutio** 1377, repayment, money paid out; solution (alch.) a 1250; dissolution a 1250, 15c.; (?) condensation c 1270; death c 760. c 1125, 1438; analysis (log.) c 850. p 1300; changing c 730; **r. dubitationis,** resolving of doubt 1552; **r. redditus,** payment of 'rent resolute' 1338; **-ubilis** p 1300, c 1360, **-vabilis** 13c., susceptible of analysis; **-utivus,** relaxing c 1283; resolutive (med.) a 1250, 1276; c 850, **-utorius** a 1180, solvent, analytic; **-utor,** a solvent c 1250; **-utorie,** analytically c 1360; **-utus,** (?) undisputed a 1270; resolute, steadfast 1461; c 1313, c 1411, **r. in mortem** c 1475, deceased; **-vo,** to pay out 1332, 1388; *see also* **redditus; r. debitum,** to remit debt c 1343; **r. vadium,** to redeem pledge 1415.

resommoneo, see RESUMMON

resonabil/is, -iter, see ratio.

***resort/um** 1279, c 1450, **-us** 1305, 1308, **resors** c 1365, 'resort', authority, appellate jurisdiction (not Engl.); resort, attendance 1447; **-ium,** reversion (leg.) 1315; **-itus,** rebound, glancing off 1278; **-io,** to re-emerge c 1188; 1294, a 1564, ***-ior** 1292, 1454, **-o** 1385, **-or** 1372, to revert (leg.); **-io, -ior (ad, in),** to resort, have recourse 1281, 1507; **r. ab,** to go back on, repudiate c 1290.

respect/io, regard 7c. c 1310, 15c.; **-us *** 1086, 15c., **-uatio** c 1350, c 1540, **-atio** c 1115, **respicium** 1194, 1204, respite, postponement; **in -u,** respited c 1120, 1275; **-us,** aspect (astr.) c 1150, a 1233; grace c 550; **r. supernus,** Providence c 1317; ***-u** c 1188, 1525, **in -u** c 1220, 1461, in respect (of); **in -u,** relatively a 1250; **habito -u ad** 1336, **habendo -um ad** 1384, c 1470, having regard to; **-u diverso,** from a different point of view c 1115; **-u libero,** freely a 1150; **-ive,** respectively, relatively c 1260, 1686; ***-ivus,** respective 1267, 1684; **-or,** considerer c 1150; ***-o** 1108, 1345, ***-uo** 1235, 1581, to respite, adjourn; **respice quesumus,** Good Friday collect 1556; **respicio,** to reward, compensate 1216, 1309; (with *acc.*) to concern 1216, c 1473; to have an aspect (astr.) a 1200.

resper/sus inopia, oppressed by want 1416; **respargo,** *for* **-go,** 795.

respir/aculum, breathing-passage, outlet a 1250; **-amentum,** respiration c 1260; **-atio anni,** (?) seasonal rhythm c 1367; **-ativus,** respiratory c 1210; **-atus,** exhausted c 1290.

resplendentia, reflexion (of light) a 1233.

respon/dentia, correspondence c 1267; **-cio,** *for* **-sio,** c 1425, 1583; **-sio,** 'responsion', disputation (ac.) c 1380, 1462; annual payment to treasury of Hospitallers from revenue of preceptories 1313, 1501; yield (of grain) 1347; accountability 1215, 1559; **r. plena** 1267, **r. mala** 1248, 1267, adequate or inadequate statement of account; **r. stulta,** miskenning (leg.) a 1135, 13c.; **-siuncula** 1344, †**-siunculum** c 1200, **-soriolum** c 1250, c 1283, short or paltry response (eccl.); **-sorium,** response (eccl.) 680, c 1006. c 1080, 1556; **-salis,** (*subst.*) respondent (in debate) 1344; deputy, representative 1175, 1475; answer 1301; (*adj.*) answerable c 1190, 1461; ***1239,** c 1444, **-sorius** c 950, 1006. c 1200, 1433, responsive, written in answer; **-sor,** chorister making responses (eccl.) c 1250; c 1546, c 1549, **-dens** c 1425, c 1583, student making responsions; ‡a **-sis,** "lawyer", "pleader" 15c., 1483; **petitio -sa,** answered petition 1425; **-deo,** to make responses (eccl.) a 1250; to make responsions (ac.) c 1264, c 1564; to yield (of grain) a 1300, 1398; 1583, **r. de** c 1080, 1338, **r. pro** c 1225, 1559, to be answerable for; *see also* **reppomis.**

respublica litteraria, republic of letters 1564.

1 rest/a, *for* **-is,** rope 1484; **-iculum,** thin cord 793.

2 rest/a 1287, 1362, **-is** 1294, 1402, **riesta**

1364, 'plough-reest', (?) mould-board; **-clutum** 'reest-clout' (of plough) 1269, 1328; **-raka,** plate for strengthening reest 1277; **roestirum** 1358, **rustirum** 1308, 1433, (?) reest-iron; **-o** 1307, 1374, **risto** 1323, **rusto** 1318, 1345, **rustio** 1373, to fit (plough) with reest; **-ringo,** to fasten to reest with rings 1323.

3 rest/a, -um 1215, c 1550, **-antia** (Sc.) p 1358, 1491, rest, residue.

4 rest/a bovis, see **restum.**

restaur/atio, *restoration, reparation, renewal c 730. 1204, c 1470; **r. arcis,** burhbote 1017, 11c.; **r. pontis,** brigbote 1017, 11c. 12c., 13c.; **-atio** 1130, 1168, **-amentum** c 1150, 1204, restocking; a 1090, **-amentum** 1204, 13c., compensation; 1314, ***-um** 1277, 1339, compensation for loss of horse; **-um bidentium,** compensation for sheep (killed by hounds) 1290; **-atio numeri,** balancing of equation (math.) 1145; **-abilis,** reparable c 1250; **-ativus,** restorative (med.) a 1250; **-ator** c 1130, 15c., **-atrix** (*f.*) c 1180, restorer; surgeon a 1250; **-atorius,** renewing c 1620; **-o** 1086, 1263, **restoro** c 1217, to restock (manor, fish-pond, *etc.*); to give back 13c., 1390; *to make good, compensate (loss) 1086, c 1352; to recompense (sufferer) a 1205; to transfer in order to balance equation (math.) 1145.

rest/clutum, -is, -raka, see **2 resta.**

resticulum, see **1 resta.**

restitu/tio, (?) return to starting-point (astr.) 1620; **-tivus** 9c. 1344, c 1620, **-torius** 870, restorative.

resto, see RAST; **2 resta; restum.**

restrepo, to make a noise again c 1190.

restrict/io, restrictive proposition (log.) 1292, 1518; c 1325, c 1545, **-us** c 1448, restraint; **r. castri,** (?) keeping a castle 1342; **-ive,** by way of restraint c 1530; **-iva** (*pl.*), (?) bandages (med.) a 1250; ‡**-orium,** "tether" 1483; **restring/ibilis** (? *for* **distringibilis**), liable to distraint 1454; **-o,** to restrict extension of a term (log.) a 1250; **r. castrum,** (?) to keep a castle 1342; *see also* **2 resta.**

restruct/io, 12c., 1365, **-ura** 1335, rebuilding; **-io castrorum,** burhbote (?) 1066, c 1160; **r. pontium,** brigbote (?) 1066, 1331.

rest/um, judgement, *arrête* (Fr.) c 1322; **-a bovis,** rest-harrow (bot.) a 1250, ‡14c.; **-o,** to arrest, seize 1208, c 1250; *cf.* ARREST; *see also* **3 resta.**

resu/atio, restitching 1477; **-o,** to restitch, patch up c 1250, c 1470.

resullum, see REFULL.

result/atio, repercussion, rebounding 850. a 1200; effectuation c 1370; **-atorius,** resisting, refusing 8c.; **-o,** to be reflected a 1200; to resist c 730. c 1125, c 1400; to exult, jump for joy c 1177, c 1402; *to result c 1197, 1473.

resulutio, see **resolutio.**

resummon/itio 1221, 15c., **-itum** 1284, fresh summons (leg.); **-eo** 1195, 1419, **resommoneo** 15c., to summon afresh (leg.).

resum/ptio, resumption, taking again c 1258, a 1540; resumption, taking back (of grant) c 1450, c 1492; repeated consumption c 1115; recommencement of studies (ac.) c 1292, c 1360; †-ptivum, a drug for restoring humidity a 1250, 1265; -o, to regain consciousness c 1125; to recommence studies (ac.) c 1265, c 1407; r. in manum, to take back into possession 1086, 1338.

resuo, *see* resuatio.

resupine, upside down 1345.

resurr/ectio (-exio) 826, r. Domini c 1250, c 1450, *r. Dominica 12c., c 1507, Easter; -exi, introit for Easter c 1212.

resuscipio, to readmit 7c.

*resuscit/atio, resurrection (eccl.); -ator, reviver c 730, c 800.

resuspendo, to hang up again c 1395.

retactus, signal to stop bell-ringing (mon.) c 1266, a 1330.

retall/ia, retail 1320, 1559; vendo ad -iam 1320, 1419, ad -am 1320, ad -ium 1311, c 1350, ad -um 1419, per -am c 1425, per -ationem 1493; emo ad -ium c 1340, in -ia 1451; solvo per -iam, to pay by instalments 1445; -ium victualium, food sold retail 1421; -ium, (?) loppings (coll.) 1284; -iator, retailer 1577; -o, to retail 1492, 1494.

retardativus, hampering, delaying c 1270, 1378.

retatus, *see* radius.

retax/atio, reassessment 1256, c 1300; -o, to reassess 1256, a 1452.

ret/e, fishery 13c., 1336; r. aquaticum, fishing-net 1388; r. cuniculorum 1270; r. cerebri (med.) a 1250; r. vicecomitis, a fishing due (Cumb.) 1461; -a 1530, -ia 1275, 1305, -ium 1419, -tum 1234, (?) †rita 1378, ryte 1323, *for* -e, net; -iolum, little net (eccl.); -iaculum c 1250, c 1470, instrumentum -iale a 1446, snare; nervus -ilis, sensory nerve c 1360; -ilia a 1250, -ina a 1250, 1267, tela -ina a 1250, retina (of eye).

retegulo, to retile 1297.

reten/tio 1421, retinatio 1234, -tus c 1150, *-ementum 1088, 1458, retinementum p 1147, 1494, retinentia a 1250, 1332, withholding, reservation; p 1377, 1461, retinentia 1331, 1465, maintenance, support (of dependants); 1296, 1493, -ementum c 1380, 15c., -entia 1322, retinentia 1335, a 1452, †retinecia c 1450, retinue, body of retainers; -amentum 1305, -tamentum 1241, -tatio c 1300, 'resetting', harbouring (leg.); -tatio, retention of soul in body 640; -tibilis, retainable c 1286; -tivus a 1250, 1620, -trix (f.) 1344, retentive; -tura, detinue (leg.) c 1300; retinabula (pl.), traces (of harness) c 1200; retinaculum, embankment c 1320; -taculum, fork supporting roof-tree a 1300; -tor, employer 1371;
   -tius, more thoroughly 1277, c 1380; -tus in, caught in the act of c 1115; retinens, retainer 1378; ‡r. boves, rest-harrow (bot.) 14c.; -eo, to restrain 790; -o, to retain c 1334; to 'reset' (leg.) 1269; †-to, (?) *for* recenseo, to rehearse c 1340; retineo, to contain 1317; to retain (followers) c 1178, c 1400; to retain (as advocate or attorney) 1309, a 1564.

reti/a, -um, *see* ragadia; rete.

retin-, *see also* rete; RETEN

retinctor, rebaptizer, Anabaptist c 1546.

retinga, *see* tethinga.

reton/sio 1221, 14c., -sura 1180, c 1300, -tura 1243, retuntura 1247, retundura c 1283, †rotuntura 1217, clipping (of coins); 1276, -sura 1245, c 1290, -tura 1200, retundura 1241, metal clipped from coins; c 1285, 1320, -cio 1300, -sura c 1285, shearing (of cloth); -sor 1205, c 1320, retuntor 1196, 1242, †retoritor 1206, -darius 1419, clipper of coins; -sor (panni), shearman 1278, 1320; -deo, to shear (sheep) a 1300; 1204, 1419, retundeo 1247, 13c., to clip (coins); r. robas 1285.

retorn/um 15c., returnum 1226, c 1315, return, restoration *or* recompense; 1230, 1308, returnum 1230, 1419, -atio 1322, c 1440, returnatio c 1400, -atus c 1315, 1322, return, reply, report; *r. brevis (brevium) 1229, 1583, -a b. 1340, 1416, *returnum b. 1198, c 1500, -atio b. 1334, turnum b. 1267, return of writs; -aculum (ferreum), part of plough 1388; -abile 1583, breve -abile 1293, 1454, b. retournabile 1396, b. returnabile 1315, 1332, returnable writ; littera †-a, reply c 1360; -atio, livery of seisin 1448, 1449; returnatio prisone, sending back to prison (Norm.) 1203;
   -o 1253, returno 1270, to return, go back; 1200, 1300, returno c 1285, 15c., to return, give or send back; c 1258, returno c 1280, to turn or bend back; 1276, 1492, returno c 1290, a 1452, returnio 1313, to return, reply (to); report; r. breve 1278, 1482, retourno b. 1419, returno b. 1199, c 1443, returnio b. 1293, to return a writ; -o heredem, to return (report) as heir (Sc.) 1482.

retor/ta, withe 12c., ‡15c.; retort (alch.) 1622, ‡1652; -queo, to retort, turn upon c 730.

retourn-, *see* RETORN

retract/atio, reconsideration c 1322; c 1160, 1494, -io c 1115, 1494, retraction, withdrawal; -io, 'relation' (leg.), identification of distinct times 1620; absque -ione, without gainsaying 8c.; -io gladii, drawing a sword c 1442; -io aque c 1400, -a 1248, -us maris 1247, 1309, ebb-tide; -io maris, land from which sea has withdrawn 1307, c 1318; -a, -um, (right of) redemption (of rent or land) (cf. Fr. *retraite*) 1309, 1369; 1359, -um c 1178, deduction, drawback; -ivus, causing withdrawal c 1377, 1426; retraxator servientium, one who tempts away servants 1392; ritracto 1494, †ratraho 13c., to withdraw; retraho, to draw (sword) a 1442; to draw backwards and forwards c 790; r. me, to withdraw from suit 1169, c 1320.

retrad/itio, redelivery c 1314, 1361; *-o, to hand back 1200, c 1447.

retransfero, to reconvey (possessions) (G.) 1313.

retransfreto, to return from overseas 1214.

retrans/itio, crossing back c 1200; -eo, to cross back 1447.

retransmitto, to send back again c 730. c 1440.

retrior, past 1647.

retro, (adv.) in arrears c 1115, c 1185; *(prep. with acc.) 12c., 1430, (with abl.) 1417, (with gen.) c 1408, c 1450, behind; r. communitatem, against the community a 1295; r. malum 1274, 1419, r. malo 1260, r. mastum 1327, abaft the mast; r. manum, at the back 1306; r. emo, to buy back c 1165; see also a retro, facio ante et r.

retroact/a (n. pl.), past proceedings (leg.) a 1267, c 1400; *-us, past (of time) c 1080, 1457.

retroambulo, to walk backwards a 1446.

retroassumo, to take back, resume 13c.

retrobannum, arrière-ban (Norm.) 1200.

retrocado, to fall backwards a 1408.

retrocess/io, retreat 1370; decline 1378; -ivus, retrograde c 1270; -us, having retired 15c.

retrochorus, 'rere-choir' (arch.) a 1273, c 1296.

retro/comitatus 1285, 1380, -vicecomitatus 1322, 'rere-county' (minor court held on day following county court).

retrocorda 1316, rirecorda 1347, 'rerecord' (of harness).

retrocurro, to run backwards 796.

retrodors/um 1436, -orium 1374, 1376, reredos.

retroductus, past (of time) 1222.

retro/duva (†-duna), rear 'douve', embankment 1240, 1275.

retro/feodum 1276, 1428, -feudum 1286, arierefeodum 1281, arrière-fief, tenure under mesne lord (Fr.).

retrofero (gradus), to retrace 1252.

retrofluxus, past, bygone 1342, 1428.

retro/garda, -guarda, see retrowarda.

retrograd/atio, (apparent) backward movement (astr.) 1233, 1267; -e, backwards c 1125, c 1444; -or (dep.), to go backwards 12c.

retrohab/itus, previously transacted c 1311; -eo, to regain c 1130, c 1290.

retrohundredum, rere-hundred court (Wilts.) 1262.

retrojicio, to throw back 1345.

retrolapsus, past, elapsed 1390.

retromitto, to send back c 1128.

retromordeo, to back-bite, slander a 1100.

retronatus, see recronatus.

retronominatus, (?) named further back 1686.

retro/pannagium 1255, 1491, -pagnagium 1255, -pasnagium 1179, 1188, retrum pannagium c 1300, 'rere-pannage' (after Martinmas).

retropastura, pasturage in meadow after mowing 1276.

retropello, to push to the back 1241.

retropono, to lay aside 9c. c 1125, 15c.

retroscript/um, papal rescript a 1452; littere -e, written reply c 1446, 1686; -us, written further back 1555; retroscribo, to date back c 1265.

retrossum, for retrorsum, backwards c 1467.

retrosurgo, to rise in the rear 12c.

retrosynodus, meeting after synod c 1210.

retrotemporibus, in time past 1236, 1274.

retro/tractus, apostate 9c.; -traho, to refer back c 1258.

retrotrudo, to thrust back 680.

†retroturnus, (?) court held after tourn a 1200.

retrovaco, to have been void for some time back 1279.

retrovenda, due paid on alienation of land (G.) 1423.

retrovertor, to return 1508.

retrovicecomitatus, see retrocomitatus.

retro/warda c 1212, -uuarda (Norm.) 1200, -guarda 1212, -garda 1239, 1274, reregardia 1461, rearguard.

retru/sio, thrusting back c 1197, 1324; ‡-do, "to retrieve" 1570.

rett/um (rect-) 1202, 1265, -atio c 1200, 13c., indictment, accusation, suspicion (O.F. ret); -um bonum, good repute 1204; r. malum, ill repute 1198, 1238; -a foreste, charge of a forest offence 1166, 1168; male -atus, of ill repute 1219; †reitatus c 1241, †reciatus 1195, accused; *-o, to 'ret', indict, accuse 1164, 1583; cf. ARRETT, REPUT

retun-, see RETON

return-, see RETORN

retusio, checking, restraining 1620.

reu/, rhubarb: r. Ponticum a 1250, 1538, r. Indie. r. Senith 13c.; -barbarum a 1250, 13c., -barbum 13c., 1253, rhabarb/arum 1620, 1634, ‡-um 1570, rhubarbarum 1622, rubarbera 1480, rybarba 1305, (?) †ruber 13c.; reubarbaratus, compounded with rhubarb a 1250.

reum-, see also RHEUM.

reumex, see rumex.

reunio, reunion a 1350; (v.) to reunite c 1320 c 1500.

reus, see reatus.

revadeo, to wager in return 15c.

reval/itudo, restoration to health 1442; revelo, (?) for -eo, to revalue 15c.

revanesco, to vanish again 1150.

revardum, see REWARD

revelatrix, revealer (f.) c 1325.

reveli (pl.), revels 1545, 1560.

revell-, see REBELL.

revelo, to sail back 1438; see also REVAL

revendo, to resell c 1192, 1661.

reven/tio 1378, -tus 1432, a 1564, return, reappearance; *-tiones 1380, 1560, -tus (pl.) c 1400, revenues; -tus, having returned 1340; -io, to grow again (of a wasted wood) 13c.; -ior, to be repayed 1255.

reverber/atio, reflexion (of light), dazzle a 1100, 1570; reflexion (of heat) 1620; ‡1652, flooding, backwash c 1400; r. lapidum, volley of stones a 1450; -atorium 1620, ‡1652, fornax -atorius 1622, reverberatory furnace; -o, to reflect c 1160, c 1250; to dazzle 11c., c 1362; to flood 1577, reveren/tia, *reverence (title of bishop or abbot) c 730, 797. c 1125, 1476; -tie (pl.), tokens of respect c 1296, c 1467; -tialia (pl.), bells rung in welcome c 1430; -tialis, respectful c 1250, c 1470; -tialiter, respectfully 1408, a 1452; -dus c 1300, 1536, *-dissimus c 730. c 1130, 1684, *-tissimus c 1125, 1355, title (eccl.).

rever/sio, recovery, return to life c 1000; *1285 c 1502, -tio 1307, 1583, -tere (subst.) 1429, -sus 1319, reversion of property or title (leg.); (?) repayment (Sc.) 1543; c 1310,

r. processus c 1290, 1310, **-satio** a 1564, reversal of judgement (leg.); **r. aque,** backflow from mill-dam 1275; **r. foliorum,** turning over leaves (of book) c 1296; **-satio armorum,** reversal of arms (her.) 1419; **-sus** 1252, **-timen** (Sc.) 1330, return; **-tibilis,** revertible (leg.) 1309, 1331; **-satus,** lined (of sleeves) 1342; **-sus,** rolled back (of eyes) a 1446; †**refersus,** having returned c 730; **-so,** to turn over c 1170, 1270; 1430, a 1564, **-to** c 1290, to reverse (leg.); **-so** (†**renverso**) **arma,** to reverse arms c 1370, 15c.; **-to,** to fold back c 1180; to avert c 1200; to root up (earth) 1353; (*intr.*) to overturn 1386; 1285, c 1353, *-tor c 1130, c 1400, to revert (leg.); **r. cursum aque** 1204, 1278; **-tor ad me, r. in me,** to think over c 1250; **r. super,** to turn upon, attack 1235.

revest/itura, reinvestiture (eccl.) c 1100, c 1130; reversion of property (G.) 1199; †**-io,** (?) *for* **-itio,** reclothing 796; **-iarium** 12c, 1414, **-arium** 1403, **-erium** c 1365, **-itorium** 1341, vestry (eccl.); **-arius,** vesturer (mon.) 1234, c 1470; **-io,** *to robe (eccl.) a 1100, c 1450; to reinvest (eccl.) a 1110, c 1350.

revettum (†**renettum**), fur collar or edging (*cf.* O.F. *riveter*) 1380.

‡**revictica,** "graving iron" 15c.

revig/esco, to revive (*intr.*) c 1250, 15c.; **-ilo,** to rouse c 1363.

revirgin/atio, restoration of virginity 1344; **-o,** to restore to virginity 1344.

revi/sus, review, retrial (leg.) 1620; **-deo** c 1414, c 1556, †**-so** c 1549, to review.

reviv/ificatio, revival (of a use) (leg.) 1567; **-ificativus,** restorative 9c.; **-us,** restored c 1400; **-ifico,** to revive, resuscitate 9c.; 1567, **-isco** 1253, c 1290, to revive (leg.).

revivo, *see* REBIN

revoc/atio *1230, a 1500, **-amentum** 1392, revocation, repeal; recovery, resumption c 1190, 1298; **r. pyxidis** (eccl.) 1409; **-ativus,** tending to bring back (med.) a 1250; **potestas -ativa,** power of revocation (leg.) c 1377; **constitutio -atoria** c 1357, c 1430; *littere -atorie c 1192, c 1470; **-ator, -atrix,** parties to divorce suit 1305; **-o,** to vow again c 730; to depose (G.) 1302; to vouch, appeal to (leg.) 1086; **r. warant** c 1102, **r. in warrantiam** c 1400, to vouch to warranty; **r. in irritum,** to repeal c 1343.

revol/utio (†**revoculo**), curved part of crosier 1245; revolution (astr.) 1086, a 1250; prostration c 1220; turning over of pages c 1125, c 1370; turning over in mind c 1200, c 1287; **r. temporum,** lapse of time 12c., 1267; **r. anni (annorum)** 12c., p 1348, **r. annua** 12c.; **-ubilitas,** ability to turn round 870; **-umen,** revolution c 860; **motus -utionalis,** rotatory movement c 1267; **-utor,** solicitor (leg.) 14c.; **-utus,** lined (of sleeves) 1342; turned (in carpentry) 1444; **-vo ad mentem,** to recall c 1396; **r. folium,** to turn over a page c 1125.

revoveo, to vow again, rededicate 14c.; (?) *for* **refoveo,** to comfort c 730.

reward/um 1347, 1412, **-a** 1419, *regardum

1248, 1583, †**regargium** c 1502, **rigardum** 1492, reward, payment; arbitrator's award 1365; *1185, 1457, **-a** 1204, **revardum** 1205, **reguardum** c 1160, 1369, **reguarda** 1175, 1188, **regwardum** 1199, 1330, *regardum 1199, 1331, **recardum** 1215, 'regard', (jurisdiction or fine of) forest inspection or court; **-ator** 1275, **reguardator** 1221, 1229, *regardator c 1160, 1369, **recardator** 1215, **-or** 1275, **reguardor** 1217, 1369, **regardor** 1199, c 1300, 'regarder', forest officer; **regardo,** to 'regard', inspect (forests) 1200; to regard, concern, 1573.

rewaynum 1257, a 1345, **reweynum** 1288, **regainum** 1230, **rewann/um, -ium** 1258, 1337, **regwannum** 1232, 1271, **ruannum** 1398, **ruwannium** 1297, 'rowen', aftermath of hay; **lac de -o** 1288; **butirum de -o** 1283, 1286; **caseus de -o,** rowen cheese 1232, 1310; **rowannium vaccarum** 1277.

rew/mannus 1442, 1525, **-ymannus** 1414, **-mennus** 1516, suitor to hundred court, (?) 'reeve-man' (Wilts., Somerset).

rex a 1150, 15c., **r. scaccorum** a 1200, c 1346, king (at chess); **r. armorum,** king of arms (her.) 1415, 1606; **r. haraldorum** 1290, p 1394; **r.** †**attumnalis,** (?) *for* **autumnalis,** 'harvest king' 1488; **r. coronatus** (alch.) c 1320; **r. fabe,** 'king of the bean' (at feast) 1334; **r. junior,** heir to throne c 1300; **r. ministrallorum** 1387; **r. piscis coronatus,** kind of fish c 1212; **r. ribaldorum,** *see* RIBALD; **r. de Viridi Bosco,** champion at tournament p 1340; *cf.* REGAL, regius.

reyla, *see* raila.

reyna, *see* reina; rina.

reysingus, *see* racemus.

reyus, *see* regius.

rhabarb- *see* reu.

rhagad/ie, *for* **-es,** sores (med) a 1250.

rhamnos, buckthorn: **ramnus (rampnus),** thorn-bush c 1150, a 1408.

rhe/ma (re-), word 10c.; **-sis,** rhetoric c 1160, 1247; **-torizo,** to play the orator 790. 1515.

rheum/a (reum-), flood, current, tide a 615, c 1060. a 1118, c 1413; ship c 1150; †**trauma,** rheum (falc.) a 1150; **-aticus,** watery 13c.; **rematisma dentium** a 1250; **-atizo,** to suffer from rheum (falc.) a 1150, (med.) a 1250.

rhexis, blood-letting (med.): **rixis** a 1250, ‡15c.

rhinoceros, unicorn c 1200, ‡c 1440; †**cinoroceros,** *for* **r.,** c 1362.

rhizotomus, herb-gathering 1632.

rhodo/stagma ‡1652, **-stoma** a 1250, ‡14c., †**-maste** a 1250, rose-water; ‡**rodolium,** oil of roses 1483.

rhombul/us, lozenge (her.) 1586, c 1595; **-atus,** lozengy (her.) c 1595; **rumbus,** turbot *or* sturgeon c 1100, 1531; **rhombus** (math.) 1145; **ad rumbum,** to the point, relevant c 1388.

rhomphea (romphea) c 730, 795, **rumphea** a 1142, c 1346, sword.

rhonchus, snoring, sneer: †**rouchus,** runcatio c 1125.

rhubarbarum, *see* reu.

‡**rhypticus** (†**repticus**), purgative (med.) 15c.
rhystes (**ristes**), Saviour c 950.
rhythm/us (**ritm-**) c 730, 797. c 1173, 1549, **rismus** 1324, **rima** 1392, verse (esp. accentual, rhymed verse); harmony, a harmonious part c 550, 860; **-ica**, accentual (? rhyming) poetry 1252; **-ice**, in verse or rhyme c 1125, 15c.; **-icus** c 1140, c 1470, **-iticus** a 1240, **rimiatus** 1382, composed in verse or rhyme; **-ificator**, rhymer 1521; **-ico** c 1000, **ridmifico** c 1248, to compose (in rhyming verse).
riagium, tax for carting (Ponthieu) 1281.
1 †**riba**, (?) branch c 550.
2 **riba**, (?) 'rib', cross-timber, purlin (arch.) 1297, 1365.
*****ribald/us**, 'ribald', menial, rascal 12c., c 1540; groom 1293; **rex -orum**, official with criminal jurisdiction (G.) 1314; **-us** 1345, 15c., **ribardus** 1346, *ribaudequin*, small cannon; **-icus**, rascally c 1218; *see also* **righoltum**.
riban/um 1371, **rubanum** 1369, 1390, **-dum** 1508, ribbon.
‡**ribes**, sorrel (bot.) (Ar. *rībās*) 14c.
ribicilla, *see* **rubicilla**.
ribulus, *see* RIV
ric/a 1550, 1579, **-ula** 1550, 1605, "kerchief".
ricamum, embroidery (It. *ricamo*) 1494.
ricardinus, 'richardine', kind of rosy appple 1220.
ricklo, to 'rickle', stack (peats) (Durham) c 1337.
rict/us, grinning head of beast turned full-face (her.) c 1595; **-uosus**, open-jawed c 1191.
†**riculus**, *f.l.* for **mulus**, c 1436.
ricus, (?) knock-kneed c 1200.
rida 'ride', band or strap of hinge 1306, 1478; *see also* **ridia**.
rid/atio 1433, 1460, **rudatio** 1372, riddance, clearing; **-inga** c 1220, **rudinga** 12c., 1314, 'ridding', cleared land; **-o** 1350, 1434, *****rudo** 1325, c 1437, **rudio** 1383, to rid, clear away, clear out; **-o**, to weed out 1389.
ridatus *see* **radius**.
1 *****ridell/us**, **-a**, **-um** c 1266, 1446, **redellus** 1375, c 1410, **redella** 1401, †**redilla** 1380, curtain (Fr. *rideau*).
2 **rid/ellus** 1301, 1449, **-lus** 1302, riddle, sieve.
ridemannus, riding bailiff (making a round of manors) 1258, 1294; *cf.* **rada**.
rid/ia (Beds.) a 1230, (?) **-a** (Lincs.) a 1327, 'rithe', (dry bed of) watercourse.
ridiculose, ridiculously 1220, 15c.
ridigus, *see* **rigiditas**.
riding/a, **-um**, *see* **ridatio**; **trithingum**.
ridmifico, *see* RHYTHM
rieflacum (†**nefflatum**), robbery (A.S. *reaflac*) c 1115; **refo**, to reave, rob c 1115.
riesta, *see* 2 **resta**.
*****riffl/etum** 12c., 1292, **-atum** 1249, **-eium** 1227, **-eum** 1190, **reflet/um** (**reflect-**) 1244, c 1290, **-a** 1285, **ruffleium** 1329, thicket, undergrowth (*cf.* O.F. *rifle*, 'rod').
riffl/ura 1249, c 1258, **rufflura** c 1290, **reflura** c 1218, scratch; **-erius** p 1341, **-iator** 1328, robber.
rifta (†**trisca**), (?) rift (topographic feature, Lincs.) 1202, c 1235.
rig/a (**rygg-**) 1477, (?) **-eteza** 13c., ridge,

row, 'selion'; **rugweia**, ridge-way 1315; **-wythum**, 'rigwiddy', back-band for cart-horse 1420; **-atio**, ridging (of roof) 1443; **-io** 1380, **-o** 1450, 1459, to ridge (a roof).
rig/amen, watering c 1200; **-olus**, channel, groove (arch.) 1292, 1386.
rigardum, *see* REWARD
riggus, *see* **ragadia**.
rig/holtum 1352, **ringoltum** 1354, **-aldum** 1345, (?) **ribaldum** 1310, **regaltum** 1357, Riga wood, deal timber from Baltic; **-holtbordum** 1356, **-olbordum** 1401, **regalbordum** 1369, Riga board.
rig/iditas, severity a 1100, a 1400; *****ridigus**, *for* **-idus**, stiff 6c.; **-ide**, harshly, brutally c 1300; **-idissime**, most austerely 10c.; **de -ore**, by strict rule c 1470; **-orosus**, severe 1350, c 1433; *****-orose**, severely, sternly 1337, 1521.
†**rigna** (*pl.*), (?) plaits *or* curls 1483.
rigolagia, 'recolage', roistering (O.F. *rigolage*) 1298.
rigolus, *see* **rigamen**.
†**rikelota** (*or* (?) **kikelota**), magpie c 1340.
rilia, *see* **raila**.
rilla, rill, stream (Norm.) a 1190.
‡**rillus**, goldsmiths' mould 1652.
rilo, *see* **raila**.
rim-, *see also* RHYTHM
†**rim/a**, (?) eruption, rash (med.) a 1250; **-ula**, disease of eyes a 1250; *see also* **rinus**.
rimagium, *see* **ripa**.
rim/atio, scrutiny c 1343; ‡**-atorium**, "searcher" 15c.
rimulus, *see* **ramus**.
rin/a 1288, 1325, **-us** 1277, 1342, **ryinus** 1276, **rynia**, **reyna** 1308, mill-rind.
‡**rinca**, rye 1570.
Rinensis, *see* **vinum**.
ring/a, sword-belt c 1258; *****a** 1140, 1435, **renga** 1279, 'ring', (?) hoop, measure of corn or lime; vessel, (?) ring measure 13c.; *cf.* **rengatus**; **-la**, 'ringle', harness ring 1312; curtain ring 1467; **-talus**, 'ringtail' (female of hen-harrier) 1544; **-o**, to ring (pigs) 1302; 1347, 1377, **-lo** 1276, 1336, **-ulo** 1330, **rengulo** 1275, to ring or hoop (hubs, harness, *etc.*).
ring/ildus 1315, 1518, **-illus** 1262, **-eldus** 1351, **-oldus** 1485, 1505, 'ringild', underbailiff, beadle (W. *rhingyll*); *****-ildia** 1311, 1414, **-eldia** 1343, 1501, **-aldia** 1335, **-ilderia** 1360, **-ildria** 1335, 1392, †**-ildiva** 1505, office of ringild (W.).
ringoltum, *see* **righoltum**.
rin/marta (**ryn-**), 'ryn-mart', ox or cow paid as part of rent in kind (Sc.) 1458, 1496; **-muto**, 'ryn-mutton' (Sc.) 1460, 1480.
rinsura, *see* **recinceratio**.
†**rinus** 1326, (?) **runa** (†**rima**) 1479, 1497, 'rine', ditch (Somerset & Glos.); *cf.* 1 **rivus**; *see also* **rina**.
riolus, *see* RIV
*****riot/a** 1388, 1513, **-us** 14c., 1489, riot; **-or**, rioter 1516; **-osus**, riotous 1451, 1460; **-ose**, riotously 1481, 1541.
rip/a, brim of cup 1417, ‡1570; †**-us**, slope 1468; **-a**, hithe, wharf, landing-stage 1219, 1470; 13c., 1547, **-aria** 1215, 1509, **-arius** 1362, **-eria** 1289, 1300, **-era** 1347, a 1500,

-erarium 1234, -arina 1268, riva 1448, rivarium 1247, 1274, riveria, riverium a 1180, c 1400, rivera c 1250, 1573,†reivera c 1293, river; -a alta 1442, r. communis c 1240, r. regia 1288, public water-way; r. currens 13c.; -agium (G.) 1282, 1288, rivagium a 1190, 1482, †rimagium 1447, river-toll; rivagium, moorage, mooring place 1297, 1316; rivagium (Norm.) 1083, c 1180, rivaria 1167, rivera c 1296, river-bank; -aria 1234, c 1320, (?) †rivaria 13c., riveria c 1120, 1238, rivera 1241, 1305, place for fowling (on river-bank); volucres de rivera 1305; canis -erarius, c. -araris 1337, c. pro -a 1332, dog trained for hawking; -ariatio 1259, riveatio 1313, fowling, hawking; -aritor c 1192, -ator c 1233, hawker (falc.); -ario 1259, 1271, -erio 1249, -o 1287, 1306, riveo 1234, 1333, to fowl, hawk; cf. RIV

riperev/us 1267, c 1345, -a 1316, 1345, repereva 1303, repreva 1316, 'reap-reeve' (appointed to supervise reaping).

ripilio, stickleback c 1160.

ripplico, see replico.

riragium, see reragium.

rirecorda, see retrocorda.

ris-, see also oryza.

riscus, part of plough 1309; ‡"cranny", "rift" c 1440; see also rifta.

ris/ibilitas, risibility, laughter c 1267; -ibilis, capable of laughter c 1188, c 1410; ludicrous 12c.; mocking 1461, c 1540; -orie, mockingly 12c.

‡risidus, "sling-stone" 15c.

rismus, see RHYTHM

rispalia (pl.), (?) thorns, brushwood 1086.

rist-, see 2 resta; rhystes.

rita, see rete.

rithm-, see RHYTHM

†rithmachia, game, (?) spillikins or skittles 1168.

rito, to perform according to custom c 1112; ‡"to custom or make a custom" 1483.

ritracto, see RETRACT

riv- see also RIP

rivett/us, rivet 1234, c 1300; -o, to rivet 1311, 1325.

1 riv/us, river bank 1274; r. regius, public waterway 1485; -olus 1313, 1583, ribulus c 793, riolus 5c., 7c., -ellus (C.I.) 1309, -unculus 1296, -uleta 13c., for -ulus, rivulet, stream.

2 rivus, reeve 1485, 1486; cf. REW

rix/atrix, scold (f.) 1498; -atorius c 1250, -osus a 1100, 1556, contentious; -ose, contentiously 1497.

rixicum, risk 1458.

rixis, see rhexis.

riz/i, -um, see oryza.

†roancle, form of ephemeral fever a 1250.

roatus, see rota.

‡rob, "succus inspissatus" (Ar.) 14c., 1652.

rob/a *1157, 1461, raubum 1328, robe, garment, or suit of clothes; *livery 1202, 1583; ad -as c 1250, c 1422, de -is 1324, 1337, wearing livery (of); r. integra, complete suit 1257, 1266; *-arium, (?) robing room 1327; -eria, (allowance for) clothing 1204, 1282.

rob/aria (†-arium, †-orarium) c 1115, 1326, *-eria 1180, 1593, rubberia 1415, -erium 1306, *-oria 1231, 1513, (?) -oratio a 1540, robbery; c 1115, -eria 13c., fine for robbery; -eria (coll.), stolen goods 1199, c 1300; -ator a 1130, 1317, -iator 1297, -erator 1166, -orator 1352, robber; -ero c 1218, 1284, -oro 1285, 1344, -io 1254, 1309, -o c 1115, 1408, to rob.

‡robelia, green pea 15c.

robettus, see rabettus.

robinettus, name of a siege-engine 1300.

roboreus, see rubedo.

rob/ousa, -usum, -usium, -ulla, see rubisum.

1 rob/ur 1236, 1292, rubbur 1463, -ra 1335, rodrus 1297, roffrus 1307, (?) pollard or dead tree; -orarium 1573, -oretum 14c., terra -usta 1587, oak-grove.

2 *rob/ur 7c. c 1194, c 1556, -oramen c 1395, -oratio 1307, 1516, validity, confirmation; rubus, strength c 550; -oratio, strengthening 1344, 1620; r. fidei a 1300, 1428; -orative, with authority or validity 1442; -ustitas, robust health 1497; *-oro, to validate, confirm c 1130, 1461.

rocatum, see rechatum.

rocea, roche alum 1476; cf. alumen; see also rochia.

rochea, see roka.

rochet/um 1207, 1558, -a c 1296, 1524, rochatum 12c., rogettum 13c., †regetum c 1344, †rosetum 1411, rochet (eccl.); -um, -us, woman's gown 1208, 1317.

roch/ia c 1200, 1267, rocea a 1275, roscia 1220, -a, -us c 1180, 1415, roach (fish).

roctus, see rottus.

rocus (rochus), rook (in chess) a 1150, 15c.

1 roda 1357, 1363, rooda 1321, rada 1310, 1482, roadstead.

2 roda, 'rood' measure of (Rhenish) wine (Dutch roede) 1371.

3 rod/a, rood, cross 1395; *a 1128, 1586, ruda (Sc.) (?) c 1150, 1558, rood, square measure (¼ acre); rod, linear measure c 1265, 1535; -alis, square measure (Westmld.) 1298.

rodda, rod, wand 1320, 1440.

rodefall/a, rudefalla c 1400, -us 1324, 'rod-fall', measure of land; cf. casus virge.

rodevallum, perambulation, purlieu (W. rhodiawl) (Pembr.) 1320, 1323.

rodio, see rotatio.

rodrus, see 1 robur.

roella, roetum, see rota.

roestirum, see 2 resta.

roffrus, see 1 robur.

rog/a, dole, alms ‡c 1440, 1493; -us, question c 1112; *-amen 1281, 15c., -ata 1355, *-atus 1303, 1476, -itamen c 900, -itatus a 1452, request; -atio, surrogation, procuring a substitute 1508; c 760, *-ationes (pl.) c 1080, 1534, dies -ationis 1327, Rogation Day(s); ‡-atorium, almonry c 1440, 1483; ‡-atorius, almoner c 1440; -atoria 1380, littera r. 1312, c 1363, littere -atorie c 790, letter of request; munus -ificum, a customary payment (eccl.) 15c.; -o, to surrogate, entrust to a substitute 1503; to initiate (of precentor) c 1330; (with inf.) to ask leave c 780; *to request, invite c 1090, c 1620; **r. pro,** to ask for 1309.

rogaterea, *see* **ragadia.**

rogelotia, *see* **raglottus.**

rogettum, *see* **rochetum.**

rogettus, 'rochet', red gurnard c 1514.

rog/us, pile of wood, beacon c 550. 1136, c 1325; fire 8c.; †**rotum,** (?) bonfire c 550; **-us,** potter's oven 1255; 1193, c 1400, **r. calcis (de calce)** c 1180, 1328, lime-kiln; **-arius,** lime-burner 1227; *see also* **roga.**

roillatus, rusty (Fr. *rouillé*) 1323.

roill/um, (?) stockade (*cf.* O.F. *roillis*) 1226; **-o,** (?) to protect with a stockade (Norm.) 1203.

rok/a, -era (C.I.) 1324, **rochea** 1291, rock; **-arius,** rock-dealer 1333.

roll-, *see* **rota;** ROTUL

roma, 'room' (space between piles of weir) 1362.

rom/ancia 1390, ‡**-agia, -agium** 1483, romance, story.

Rom/escotum c 1260, **-scotum** 1207, **-ascot** 1103, **pecunia -ana** 11c., Rome-scot, Peter's pence; *-ipeta c 1160, 15c., †-ipeda c 1260, pilgrim to Rome; **-anicensis** c 1362, **-eus** 1492, Byzantine Greek; **-anizatus,** Romanized c 1385; 1357, **-anus** 13c., 1337, (written in) French; **-ana** (*n. pl.*) 14c., **-anum** c 1180, French language; **-ane,** in French c 1192; **-ani** (*pl.*), Frenchmen c 1192; **-ano-Catholicus, -anus Catholicus** a 1700; **-uleus,** Latin 7c.; Roman c 900, c 1000.

romeseum, *see* **ramus.**

†**rommum,** (?) form of rent (Durham) 1364.

romphea, *see* **rhomphea.**

ronche (*pl.*), form of rash (med.) 1588.

ron/cinus, -sinus, *see* **runcinus.**

rondell/a a 1450, **rundellus** 1300, 1328, roundel, disc, medallion; (?) bundle (of fur) 1431; **r. de pewtervessell'** 1440; **-us,** round, catch (mus.) 1326; 'rundle' (of cart) 1285; **rundellus,** 'rundle' (of mill) 1308; **rundeltus,** part of springald, (?) metal washer 1311; **rundella, rundellus** 1290, 1436, **-ettum** 1312, 1351, **roundelettum** 1301, 1337, **roundilettum** 1402, **rundilettum** 1358, runlet, cask; *cf.* ROTUND

ronga, *see* **runga.**

rooda, *see* **1 roda.**

rop/a, rope 1292, 14c.; **-eria,** ropery, rope-works 1333, 1410; **r. ferrea** 1403; **-arius,** roper, rope-maker 1319, 1333; *see also* **1 rapum.**

1 ros celi, (?) nostoc 14c.; **r. Madii,** *aqua mercurialis* (alch.) c 1345; **r. Syriacus,** "*flos querci*" a 1250; ‡ "*flos orni*" 14c. (? confused with *rhus*); **r. solis** 1620, 1629, **ror/ella** 1634, sundew (bot.); ‡**-astrum,** (?) bryony (bot.) 15c.; **-atio,** shower a 1233; **-itas** a 1235, **roscidatio** 1620, dewiness; **-eus** 6c., **-ificus** c 1180, **-iger** c 950, dewy; **-ifluus** c 685, c 810. 12c., †**rurifluus** c 1450, flowing like or with dew; **-ifico** 13c., **roscido** c 550, to bedew.

2 ros/, head (Heb.) c 550; **-ana,** Jewish New Year (*rosh-ha-shana*) 1277.

ros/a, name of a comet c 1370; c 1308, **-arius** 1297, c 1422, 'rosary', base coin; **corona de**

duplici -a, crown of the rose (English coin) 1532; *see also* **grana; -a canina,** dog rose, brier a 1250, ‡15c.; ‡**r. marina** 15c., 1570, **-emaria** a 1564, *for* ros marinus, rosemary; **gutta -acea,** rash (med.) c 1400, ‡1652; **-aria,** rose-garden c 1365; **-arium,** (?) wreath of roses 1295; pattern of roses 1388, a 1447; rosary (book) 1417, c 1620; rosary (of beads) 1605; *see also* RUSC; **-ata** a 1250, 1252, **aqua -ata** c 1190, a 1270, **a. -ata de Damasc'** 1307, **a. -alia** 1421, ‡**a. -acea, a. -arum** 14c., rose-water; **vinum -atum** 1236, 1242, **v. -etum** c 1200, *vin rosé*; **-atus,** rose-coloured 795; *see also* **auca, sucrum; -eatus,** roseate a 1275; **-eus,** red-hot c 550; virtuous c 1180; blissful c 1180; **equus -eus** 1338; **-inus,** abounding in roses c 1191; **-ula alba, r. rubea,** silver and gold (alch.) a 1252; **-ans,** rose-bearing a 1408; **-eo** 1220, c 1250, **-ulo** 1220, to redden; **-esco,** to grow red a 1275; **-o,** to decorate with rose-patterns 1238; to embellish c 1180.

rosana, *see* **2 ros.**

rosari/a, -us, *see* **auca; rosa; 2 rusca.**

roscia, *see* **rochia.**

roscid-, *see* **1 ros.**

ros/cus, -eium, -ellus, -era, -eria, *see* **auca; 2 rusca.**

rosella, *see* **2 rusca, 2 russellus.**

roserell/a (†**roscrell-**), **-um,** weasel fur 1179, c 1200.

rosetum, *see* **resina; rochetum; rosa; 2 rusca.**

‡**rosia,** aristolochia (bot.) 14c.

rosin/a, -um, -atio, rosilium, *see* **resina.**

ros/inus, -eus, -o, *see* **rosa.**

rossa, *see* **2 rusca.**

rossetum, *see* **rusca, 2 russetum.**

rosta, dam, embankment (*cf.* It. *rosta*) 1248.

‡**rostellus,** "spink", chaffinch 15c.; *cf.* **rastella.**

rostina, file 7c.

rostio, to roast c 1450.

rostr/um, spike for fastening scaffold-poles 1285, 1293; 'pike' of pointed shoes 1388, 15c.; **r. longum,** long bill (weapon) 1451; **r. porcinum,** sow-thistle *or* dandelion ‡14c., 1629; **rustrum,** ‡"neb" 15c.; †(?) altar c 600; ‡**rustiferum,** "hornkeck", gar-fish 15c.; **-atus,** with pointed toes c 1220, c 1470; **-o,** to stick out one's beak (fig.) c 1340; *see also* RAST

rosul/a, -o, *see* **rosa.**

rosus, rostus, *see* **2 rusca.**

rot/a, windlass 1237, 1384; 1372, **r. manualis** 1390, **r. filabilis** 1390, (reel of) spinning-wheel; ringing-wheel (of bell) 1427, 1535; wheel set with bells (eccl.) c 1189, 1484; rowel-light 1448; part of quintain 1236; †(?) shovel 1336; round loaf c 550; iris of eye 6c.; papal rota 1414, 1541; **r. ad carrucam** 1291, 1301, **r. carrucalis** 1350; **r. ad herciam** c 1290; **r. aëria,** (?) sail of wind-mill 1528; **r. aquatica,** water-wheel (of mill) 1297, 1409; **r. exterior** 1297, 1446, **r. interior** c 1435 (of mill); **r. fortune,** design of fortune's wheel 1417; **r. magna,** tread-wheel 1488; **r. molendini** c 1180, 1448; **r. nuda** 1297, 1325, **r. simplex** 1295, untired wheel; **r. pendens** (of water-driven forge) 1409; **-abilis** c 1172, 1388, **-alis** c 1170, 1479, **-arius** 1257, 1264, **-atus** c 1445, wheeled, on wheels; **-alis** c 815, **-iger** 930, 14c., rotatory, revolving; **fortuna -alis**, fickle fortune c 1140; **-arius**, wheelwright 1167, c 1335; *see also* 1 **ruta**; **-atio fortune** c 1170; **r. molendini** c 1170; **-atus**, turning round, revolution 8c.; **-atus** 1245, 1265, **roatus** 1262, **-ulatus** 15c., adorned with roundels;

    -icula (annorum), cycle c 1000; **-ella** 1245, 1295, **roella** 1240, **ruella** 1257, a 1293, roundel, disk; c 1250, 1275, **-ula** c 1245, c 1330, **ruellus** c 1330, rowel-light; **r. cartule**, *see* **rotulus**; **-ulus ad arma** 1270, **rollus** 1305, roll (for burnishing arms); **roella** 1309, **ruella** 1327, 1398, **rolla** 1397, 1480, **rollus** 1313, 1338, roll (of cloth); **roella** 1303, **ruella** 1224, **ruillium** 1195, pulley; **ruella** 1293, 1315, **ruellus** 1295, **roetum** (C.I.) 1331, cogged wheel of mill; **ruella calcaris**, spur-rowel 1293; **ruellus**, ringing-wheel c 1436; **-ellus** 1324, **-ula** 1248, 1267, **-ulus** c 1345, plough-wheel; **-ula**, little wheel 8c.; 'trundle', castor (of bed) 1426, ‡1570; **-ularium**, roller (for towel) 1553; **roula**, roller (for launching ship) 1296; **-ulus maeremii**, timber roller 1461;

    rollagium 1306, 1390, **roulagium** 1282, **rollatio** 1331, (payment for) rolling (of casks); **roulura**, burnishing 1283; **-o**, to surround 12c., 14c.; (?) to bandy about 1378, 1380; 1197, c 1200, **rollo** 1213, 1282, **rollo** 1218, 1344, **rollio** 1311, to burnish, furbish; **-ulo** c 1160, **rollo** 1337, to roll; *see also* ROTUL

rotabulum, *see* **rutabulum**.

†**rotalle**, *f.l.* for **jocale**, 1415.

rotarius, *see* **rota**; 1 **ruta**.

rot/atio c 1200, **-io** 1529, **roura** 1210, retting (of flax); **rodio**, to ret 1253; *see also* **rota**.

rotherum, rudder 1295.

Rothomagensis 1086, 1131, **Rod/mensis, -mesinus** 1086, **-omensis** a 1142, coin of Rouen.

rotiger, *see* **rota**.

rottus (roctus) 1211, 1411, **rattus** 1245, **ruttus** 1284, rotted (sheep).

rotula, measure of juice, 'rotl' (Ar. *ratl*) a 1250, c 1260.

*****rotul/us** a 1142, 1569, -a c 1180, 1445, **rollus** 1162, **rolla** c 1220, (register or record in form of) roll; rotulet, single membrane of roll 1203, 14c.; **rotella cartule** c 1000; **-us contra**, counter-roll 1225; **r. annalis** c 1178, 1296, **r. magnus** c 1178, 16c., **r. m. pipe** 1259, Exchequer Pipe Roll; **r. de corporibus comitatuum** 1295, **r. partialium** 1295, **r. exannalis** 15c., offshoots of Pipe Roll (*see also* 1 **pullanus**); **r. curie**, court roll (man.) c 1300, 1483; **r. Exactorius**, roll of farms to be accounted for at Exchequer c 1178; **r. Judeorum**, Pentateuch 1194, 1236; **r. maeremii**, *see* **rota**; **Custos -orum** 1269, 1507, **Magister R.** 1485, 1586, Master of the Rolls; **-amentum** 1290, c 1320, **-atio** 1219, 1301, enrolment, entry on a roll; **-arius**, chronicle 1361;

-aria 1488, **-ataria** 1489, comptrollership (Sc.); *****-ator compotorum**, comptroller (Sc.)ʹ 1426, 1573; **-o** 1271, a 1410, **rollo** c 1220, to enrol; *see also* **rota**.

rotum, *see* **rogus**.

†**rotumba**, (?) alembic (alch.) 13c.

rotund/itas, circuit, environs 1136, c 1400; c 1257, **-icium** 1345, disk, roundel; **-o**, around a 1408; **in -o**, in circuit 1279; **-us**, flat (mus.) 1326; **numerus -us**, round number 1686; *see also* **tabula**; **-e**, roundly, clearly c 1225, 1295; **-atio**, rounding (of stones into cannon-balls) 1387; **-ator verbi**, one who speaks roundly c 1160; **-ellum**, riding-cape 1351; **-iformis**, round c 860; **-uinus**, Roundhead c 1643; **-ula**, runlet, cask (Sc.) 1329; *cf.* RONDELL; **-o festa**, to hold a feast in the style of the Round Table c 1370.

rotuntura, *see* RETON

rouagium, due paid on carts (Norm.) c 1167.

roubeus, *see* **rubedo**.

rouchus, *see* **rhonchus**.

roul/a, -agium, -ura, *see* **rota**.

roumagium, *see* **rumagium**.

rouncinus, *see* **runcinus**.

round/elettum, -ilettum, *see* RONDELL

roura, *see* **rotatio**.

rout-, *see* 1 **ruta**.

†**rova**, (?) lane or strip of land 1316; †**rowa (fimi)**, row 1268.

rowannium, *see* **rewaynum**.

royanum, a custom originally levied at Royan (G.) 1312.

royna, *see* **reina**.

ru/a, street (G.) 1289; **-ella**, alley (G.) 1288.

ruannum, *see* **rewaynum**.

rubanum, *see* **ribanum**.

rubarbera, *see* **reu**.

rubbatus, (?) mangy 1343.

rubberia, *see* **robaria**.

†**rubboura**, measure of wine (? 'rove') 1463; *cf.* **arrova**.

rubbur, *see* 1 **robur**.

*****rub/edo** 1245, c 1430, **-icunditas** c 1325, c 1340, redness; ‡**-ella**, **rugella**, red mullet (fish) 15c.; **-efactio**, reddening a 1250; **-etus** 1225, 1303, **-itus** 1241, **-eus** 1203, c 1500, **-inus** 1328, 1620, †**-ua** c 1500, ruby; **r. baleis**, balass ruby 1232, c 1328; ‡**-eum**, false gold, *cuprum tinctum* 1652; 1398, **r. grisium** 1231, fur, (?) red squirrel; *****-eus (-ius)** 1172, c 1550, **roubeus** 1292, **-reus**, †**roboreus** c 550, †**-igdus** 13c., red; gules (her.) p 1394, c 1450; sore (falc.) 14c.; chestnut (of horses) 1321, 1377; **r. liardus** 1316 (*cf.* **rughliardus**); *see also* **allec, corium, fumus, manus, opus, rubus, vinum**; ‡**-iaria**, 'wine of grapes' 15c.; †**-idagius**, (?) reddish 1370; **-icundius**, more redly c 1000; **-ificatio**, reddening 13c.; making gold (alch.) c 1320; **-ifico** c 1260, c 1375, **-ico** 13c., a 1446, **-icundo** c 1340, to redden; to turn into gold (alch.) a 1252, 1267; *cf.* RUBRIC

ruber, *see* **reu**.

‡**ruberca**, iris (bot.) 15c.

rubet/ra, -arius, *see* **rubus**.

rubia 1547, ‡**r. major** 14c., 15c., madder (bot.); ‡**r. media**, (?) spurrey 15c.; ‡**r. minor**, goosegrass, cleavers 14c., 1570.

rub/icilla 1544, ‡**ribicilla** 1570, bullfinch; **-isca** c 1190, **-esca** 1510, (?) robin.

‡**rubicula**, pot-stick, stirrer 1570.

‡**rubidus**, "cracknel", biscuit c 1440.

rubig/o, glow c 550; **-inatio** (*for* **erubiginatio**), burnishing 1448; ‡**-inator**, "furbisher" 15c.; ‡**-ino**, "to furbish" 1483.

rubino, *see* REBIN

rub/inus, -itus, *see* rubedo.

rub/isum 1430, 1446, **-usa** 1397, **rebbussa** 1260, **robousa** 1325, 1364, **robusium** 1292, **robusum** 1373, **-ylla** 1367, 1425, **robulla** 1427, rubbish, rubble.

*****rubric/a**, rubric, chapter heading c 1200, c 1460; **-ella**, small rubric c 1200, c 1534; **-o**, to adorn, enliven c 950; to authenticate (by reddening with blood) 13c.; ‡to provide with rubrics 1483.

rubua, *see* rubedo.

rub/us, (?) bush 12c.; ‡**r. agrestis**, broom (bot.) 15c.; ‡**r. caninus**, dog-rose 14c.; ‡**r. Ideus**, raspberry 1570; **-etra**, unidentified bird (βατίς) 1544; **-etarius**, hen-harrier 1544; **-eus**, (?) briery 1276; *see also* **2 robur**.

rub/usa, -ylla, *see* rubisum.

rucha, *see* **1 ruta**.

ruchia, *see* **1 rusca**.

ruchliardus, *see* rughliardus.

†**rucillaria**, a form of serjeanty (? strewing rushes) in king's chamber c 1212; *cf.* **2 rusca**.

ructarius, *see* **1 ruta**.

ruct/uatio, *for* **-atio**, belching a 1250, c 1280; **-atorium**, drug causing belching a 1250.

ruda, measure of tiles (Sc.) 1469; *see also* **3 roda**.

rud/atio, -inga, -io, -o, *see* ridatio.

rudefalla, *see* rodefalla.

rudellum, ruddle 1371.

rud/er (? **-us**), sink ‡c 1200, c 1475; ‡"muck" 1483; ‡**-or**, gutter 15c.; ‡**-ero**, to manure c 1440.

†**rudis**, (?) mast (or *f.l.* for **rudens**) c 1325.

rud/itas, lack of skill or polish c 1190, c 1466; **-e** c 1362, **-iter** c 1283, 1552, unskilfully; **-ifico**, to barbarize c 1150.

rud/itio c 1000, **-itus** c 1190, **-ibile** 1267, braying; **-ibilis**, inclined to bray, asinine 13c., 1427; **-ibiliter**, asininely 1427.

rudmannus, *see* RAD

ruell/a, -us, *see* rota; **rua**.

ruf/edo, redness (of hair) a 1250; **-inus**, imaginary saint representing gold 12c.; **-um**, red gold a 1408; **allec -um**, red herring 1250; **nisus -us**, sore hawk a 1190.

ruffa, ruff, frill c 1565.

ruffianus, ruffian 1553.

ruffleium, *see* riffletum.

rufflura, *see* rifflura.

rufus, fish, (?) ruff c 1200; *see also* rufedo.

rugella, *see* rubedo.

ruggus, measure of grain, *rugghio* (It.) c 1362.

rughliardus (equus) 1303, 1313, **ruchliardus** 1313, red lyard; *cf.* liardus, rubeus.

rug/ifactio, 'rowing' (of cloth) 1611; **-atus**, pleated 13c.

rugine, 'rugine', rasp (med.) a 1250.

rug/itus, chewing the cud c 1290; **-io**, to chew the cud c 1290.

Rugus, *see* Russus.

---

rugweia, *see* riga.

ruillium, *see* rota.

ruin/a (**imbrium**), downpour a 732; **-e** (*pl.*), ruinous charges c 950; **-ositas**, state of ruin 1425, 1546; †**-us**, *for* **-osus**, ruined 13c.; **-o**, to ruin 12c., 13c.

ruisia, *see* **2 rusca**.

ruit/or, one who falls 1378; **-o**, to collapse c 810, c 860; **ruo**, to throw c 1340.

ruja, *see* **1 rusca**.

rulla, *see* rallum.

rum/agium 1290, 1337, **remagium** 1335, **roumagium** 1313, †**runagium** 1390, stowage, packing material (naut.); **-o**, to stow 1337.

rumbus, *see* rhombulus.

rum/en, first stomach of ruminant 690; rumination, consideration c 1218; **-inum**, gullet c 1204; **-ino**, to mutter c 1090, c 1343.

rumex spinosa, (?) bramble *or* thistle c 550; **reumex**, (?) *for* **r.**, sorrel a 1250.

rum/iger, talkative *or* talked about c 590, c 790; **-igerulus**, spreading rumours (eccl.); **-oreus** c 1000, **-orosus** c 550, †**-erosus** 1378, noised abroad, celebrated; **-usculus**, report c 950. 1200, 1283; **-orizo** c 1080, ‡**-osito** 1483, to noise abroad.

rumo, *see* rumagium.

rumphea, *see* rhomphea.

runa, *see* rinus.

runagium, *see* rumagium.

runc/a, bramble, brier (Fr. *ronce*) 1283, c 1485; **-aria** c 1282, 1303, **-etum** 1086, bramble-patch, thicket; **vimina -ina**, bramble sprays 14c.

†**runcata**, (?) *for* **reduncata, crux**, cross moline (her.) c 1595.

runcatio, *see* rhonchus.

*****runc/inus** 1086, 1327, †**-us** (W.) a 1250, †**rancinus** c 1102, **roncinus** 1086, 1289, **ronsinus** 1281, **rouncinus** c 1322, 'rouncey', nag; **-inettus**, little rouncey 1308.

rundel-, rundil-, *see* RONDELL

rung/a 1385, **ronga** 1440, **renga** 1313, rung of ladder; 1209, 1326, **ronga** 1235, rung of mill-wheel (*cf.* wranga); **ronga**, (?) cross-bar of windlass 1414; **renga ferrea**, part of a barge 1284 (*cf.* **ranga**); **-o**, to fit (ladder) with rungs 1401.

ruo, *see* RUIT

rupell/a (Sc.) 1461, **-is** (C.I.) 1309, rock.

‡**rupeste**, 'ripple', flax-comb 15c.

rupt/io a 1250, 1267, **-ura** 1267, 1461, breaking, eruption; 1498, **-ura** 1437, 1473, breach of agreement; **-ura**, assart (Norm.) a 1142; 15c., **-a** 1433, breach (in dike); rupture (med.) a 1150, c 1320; **-ibilis**, breakable c 1190; **-orium**, medicine causing eruption (of ulcers, *etc.*) (med.) a 1250; **-orius, -ivus**, causing eruption (med.) a 1250; **-us**, ruptured (med.) a 1250; *cf.* **1 ruta**.

rur/iculum 779, 811, †**-isculum** 12c., **-usculum** 11c., **rusculum** 1529, estate, piece of land; **decanus -alis**, rural dean c 1220, 1559; **-ensis** 790, **-icalis** c 1350, **-icolus** c 800, 940. 12c., **-icula** 12c., rustic (*adj.* or *subst.*); **-o**, to live in the country c 1315.

rurifluus, *see* **1 ros**.

‡**rur/iscus** c 1440, 1483, ‡**-uscus** 15c., fieldfare (bird).

1 **rus/ca** *1086, 1388, **-chia** 1275, **-sa** 1488, †**ruja** 1307, bee-hive (Fr. *ruche*); firkin (of butter) 1086; 1295, **ruchia** 1290, measure of rosin.

2 **rusc/a** 1326, **-us** 1287, 1523, *****roscus** (†**rostus**) 1243, c 1400, **rossa** 1271, **rosus** a 1185, **rosella**, **rosellus** 1198, c 1530, †**ruscubardus** c 1350, rush, rushes (*coll.*); **-aria** 1353, 15c., **rosaria** 1199, 1300, **roseria** 1180, 1286, **rosera** c 1200, **roseium** c 1256, **roseum** 1306, **rosetum** 1347, †**ruisia** 1256, bed of rushes; †**rosarius**, worker in bakehouse, (?) sweeper 13c.; ‡**-ator**, "tile-kilner" 15c.; *cf.* 1 **russellus**.

rusculum, *see* **ruriculum**.

rusc/us, (?) *for* **-um**, butcher's broom c 550; *see also* 2 **rusca**, **Russus**.

1 **russellus**, brook (Fr. *ruisseau*) *or* (?) rush-bed 1198, 1236; *cf.* 2 **rusca**.

2 **russ/ellus** 1281, 1376, **rosella** c 1285, rissole.

*****russ/etum** 1215, c 1460, **-eta** 1219, **rossetum** 1260, 1317, **pannus de -eto** 1259, 1327, *****p. -etus** 1218, p 1475, russet (cloth); **r. nigrum** 1397; **-eticus**, made of russet c 1450; **-etus**, russet-coloured 1368; (**equus**) **-us liardus**, herd lyard 1311 (*cf.* **rughliardus**); **-um grisium** 1232, **-um bissum** 1255, (?) red squirrel fur; *cf.* **roserella**, **rubedo**.

Rus/sus c 1180, **-cus** c 1324, **-cenus** 1267, **Ruthenus** c 1250, **Rugus** 12c., Russian.

rustic/us, (*subst.*) *****serf, villein 1086, c 1422; (term of abuse) 1440; **r. plenarius**, holder of complete villein tenement 12c.; **-a**, serf-woman 12c., 1290; **-us** (*adj.*) 1086, 1243, **-alis** 1361, **-anus** c 1115, 12c., servile, or for a villein; **-issimus**, most rustic 5c., 7c.; **-alis** c 1362, 15c., **-arius** c 1258, rustic

(*adj.*); **villa -ana**, *taeog-tref* (W.) a 1300; **-atio**, rusticity, lack of education 5c.; **-atus**, (?) rural (C.I.) 1248; **-itas**, villeinage c 1200, a 1446; **-itatem facio**, to misbehave, commit a nuisance 1252, 14c.; **-o**, to debase c 1180.

rust/irum, **-io**, **-o**, *see* 2 **resta**.

rust/rum, **-iferum**, *see* ROSTR

1 **rut/a** (**rutt-**), route, road (Ir.) 13c.; c 1190, c 1250, †**trucha** c 1436, rout, band of routiers; **routa** 1385, 1569, **routeria** 1463, rout, unlawful assembly; (?) enclosure (for catching fish) 1416; **routose**, in a rout 1716; **-arius** 1200, c 1328, **rotaria** 1214, **ructarius** c 1296, 1385, **ruptarius** 1215, c 1280, routier, mercenary soldier.

2 **rut/a capraria**, goat's-rue (bot.) 1641; **r. muraria**, wall-rue 1578, 1629; **r. pratensis**, meadow-rue 1597, 1634; **-eleon**, oil of rue c 1250.

rutabulum, baker's pele: ‡**rotabulum**, "fire-fork" a 1520; "moulding-board" 1483.

rutesio, *see* **rutum**.

Ruthenus, *see* **Russus**.

ruticilla, redstart (bird) 1544, ‡1570.

rut/ilus, **-ulus** c 550, **-ilantia** c 1325, **-ilatio** c 1612, beam, ruddy glow; **-ilis** a 1408, **-ulus** 1550, ‡**-eus** a 1520, red; **-eus**, gules (her.) c 1595; **-ilans**, flowing c 1000.

ruttus, *see* **rottus**.

rut/um 1241, **-esio** 1265, rut, rutting (of stags).

ruvulia, *see* **cavella**.

ruwannium, *see* **rewaynum**.

ry-, *see also* **ri-**

rybarba, *see* **reu**.

ryela, *see* **raila**.

ryngea, *see* **ranga**.

ryte, *see* **rete**.

S

saban/um, cloth (σάβανον) c 730, c 860; **-a**, napkin 7c.

†**sabatarium**, (?) *for* **salarium**, payment (to tenants) c 1300.

sabat/um 1425, (?) **-erium** 1303, shoe (Fr. *sabot*); **-agium**, due paid by cobblers (G.) 1254; **-arius**, **-erius** (G.) 1254, 1285, **-or** c 1353, cobbler.

*****sabbat/um** (eccl.), *****dies -i** 954. 1086, 1491, **d. Saboti** c 1280, **d. -inus** c 1370, 1434, Saturday; week 690, 8c.; (?) Sunday or feast-day a 1240, 15c.; (?) peace and quiet 1086; Saturday's labour (man.) 1245; **s. anni**, summer solstice c 1465; **s. Dominicale** c 1006; **s. Palmarum**, eve of Palm Sunday c 1266; **s. Pasche** 1245, **s. Sanctum** c 1070, c 1450, Holy Saturday; **-a quatuor temporum**, Ember Saturdays c 1266, c 1448; **-izatio**, Sabbath observance a 1292, 1383; **-izo**, to keep the Sabbath, rest 690. c 1188, c 1430.

Sabellieni (*pl.*), Sabellian heretics 7c., 8c. 12c.

sabel/us c 1200, **zabellus** c 1595, **zebellinus** 1499, sable; **-ina**, **-inum** 12c., c 1436,

sablinum 1303, †**cabelum** 1308, **pellis -ina** 12c., 1608, **p. zebellina** c 1595, sable fur.

sabina ‡14c., c 1620, (**herba**) **savina** c 1200, 13c., savin (bot.).

sab/lo c 550, a 710. c 1125, 1336, **-ilo** 1228, 1313, **zabilo** c 1335, **-olo** 1236, **-ula** 1558, **zabula** 1463, **zablum** c 1336, **-olum** 1394, 1469, **zabulum** 1230, 1534, **-ulona** c 1270, *for* **-ulo**, **-ulum**, sand, gravel; **-ulum**, grain of sand a 990; **s. vivum**, quicksand c 1180, c 1300; **-olum** 1264, **-lunum** a 1185, **-loneria** 1201, **-lanarium** 1329, **-lunarium** c 1190, **-ulonarium** 1334, **zabulonarium** 1491, **-lunatorium** c 1190, sand-pit; **-lonarius**, sand-digger 1282; **-ulositas**, sandiness c 1270; **-lonosus** 1297, **-ulonosus** 1461, **-ulosus** 14c., **zabulosus** 1538, **-ulonatus** a 1262, sandy; **-lono** 1286, 1316, **-ulono** 1323, **zabulono** 1356 **zabulo** 1475, to spread (soil) with sand.

sabonus, *see* **sapo**.

sabor, *see* **sapor**.

‡**sabracia**, 'sabras', decoction c 1440.

sabu/cum, **-tum**, *see* 1 **sambuca**.

sabus, *see* 1 sappus.

*sac/a c 1070, 15c., -um a 1152, a 1400, 'sake', jurisdiction.

sacc/a (sack-, sakk-) 1330, 16c., -ula 1391, *for* -us, -ulus, sack; -us 14c., -ulus a 1280, bag for chessmen; -um, dry measure, 12 sextarii (Heb.) a 1250; -us 12c., c 1360, pannus -i, p. -orum 1441, 1531, p. -inus 1338, sack-cloth; *s. lane 1228, 1478, -um l. c 1290, wool-pack; frater de -a 1292, f. de -o 1275, 1327, f. de -is 1271, 1402, f. -atus c 1260, f. -inus a 1270, c 1422, f. Saxinus 1370, Sacked Friar; -ulus, pocket 1543; -atio, packing (of wool) 1306, 1338; -ello, -illo, to use as poultice (med.) a 1250; -o, *to pack (wool) 1211, c 1345; to pack (victuals) c 1300.

sacchar/um, sugar 1528, 1620; -arius, sugar-baker 1561; *cf.* sucrum.

sacell/ulum, little chapel p 1550; -anus 1531, 1555, -arius 1560, †-us 1575, chaplain; -arius, treasurer, bursar 12c., c 1266.

sac/er, saker (falc.) 1237, 1382; -rettus, sakeret 1382; *see also* sacra.

sacerdos c 730. 1086, 1586, saserdos 1536, *Christian priest; (?) nun c 1433, c 1562; head of Jewish community in England 1257; s. cantarialis, chantry priest 1498; s. choralis, choir priest 1498; s. confessionis confessor c 1150; s. familie (W.) a 1300; s. magnus 12c., s. summus 12c., Jewish High Priest; s. summus, bishop or arch-bishop 7c. c 1090; Christ a 1142; s. minor, priest (as distinct from bishop) c 1225; s. missalis, mass priest 1296; s. monacho-rum (distinguished from chaplain) 11c.; s. parochialis 1287, c 1370; s. secularis 1326, c 1553; s. vulgaris, priest living like a layman c 1115;
  sacerdot/alia (*pl.*) priestly robes c 1185, c 1311; *-alis, priestly (eccl.) c 730. c 1070, 1560 (*see also* sal); -aliter, like a priest (eccl.) c 1070, 1427; -alitas c 870, -ium c 730. c 1125, c 1500, priesthood (eccl.); -ium, Jewish priesthood 12c.; headship of Jewish community in England 1257; prelacy, episcopal see (Sc.) 1537, 1565; s. summum, episcopate c 1090; -issa, nun c 1219; priest's concubine 1180, ‡15c.; -ilus, paltry priest c 1500; ‡-ulus, priest's son 15c.; ‡-ula, priest's daughter 15c.; -ificans, priest-making c 1500.

†sacio, (?) *f.l. for* saucio, 1291; *see also* seisina.

sacr/a (*f. s.*), imperial letter 1610; (*n. pl.*), vestments 1336; res -a, divine service 1537, 1552; -um, rite, sacrament of the mass 1245, 1552; oath 1258, 1333; s. corporale, corporal oath 1336, 1347; -e, holily 870; -alia (*pl.*), sacraments 1451; confessio -alis 1314; ‡color -anus, purple 1652; -arium cemetery c 730; sacristy c 980; piscina (eccl.) c 1080, c 1360; -atio, consecration c 1080, 13c.; -ator, consecrator c 1250; -atorium judicum, judicial court (eccl.) a 1245; -atorius, holy, sacramental 801; -atius, in a holier way c 730; -atum, halidom (touched in taking corporal oath) c 1102; -o, to consecrate c 1080, 1461.

sacra/bar, -barrus 1234, 1279, -ber 1216, -bor' 1285, -bord 1207, †sakabor c 1258, public prosecutor in local court (Norse *sakar-áberi*); -barrum, (?) action instituted by the same 1293, 14c.

sacrament/um, corporal oath 1086, 1406; inquiry on oath (leg.) 1201, 1285; *sacra-ment (eccl.) c 730, c 1006. c 1090, 1552; s. altaris 12c., c 1400, s. eucharistie 1236, 1461; *-ale c 1190, a 1564, -arium 8c. 1361, sacramental, observance analogous to sacrament; -alis, sacramental (*adj.*) 12c., c 1470; bound or confirmed by corporal oath 12c., c 1293; confessio s., confession sealed by oath c 1325, c 1357; *see also* miles; -aliter, by or under oath c 1218, 1609; by means or in the form of a sacrament c 1182, c 1620; -arium, piscina 1287, 15c.; -arius, Sacra-mentarian, denier of Real Presence (theol.) 1549, c 1620; -atio, ministration of sacra-ment 1427; verba -ifica, words constitutive of sacrament c 1500; -o, to minister a sacra-ment p 1380, 1427.

sacr/at-, -arium, -e, *see* sacra.

sacrettus, *see* sacer.

sacrifex c 1180, c 1358, sacrific/us 1537, priest (eccl.); -ulus, paltry priest 1562, 1586; -ium *c 600, 11c. c 1090, 1535, s. misse 1549, (sacrifice of) mass; -o, to celebrate mass 1508.

sacrist/a *c 1125, 1537, -es 1145, 12c., se-crista 1224, ‡15c., -anus 12c., 1283, secre-stanus 12c., segrestanus a 1128, sextanus 1299, -arius 1216, 1425, sacrist, sacristan (eccl.); -a (*f.*) c 1400, 1520, -ana 14c., sacrist of nunnery; -a 1388, *-aria 1160, c 1537, -arium 13c., ‡1483, -erium c 1195, secrestaria 1206, -ria c 1450, *-ia c 1209, 1468, *-ina c 1250, -atus 1279, sacristy, office of sacrist.

sacritecta, *see* sartaria.

sacr/o, -um, *see* sacra.

sacro/duodenarius, holy twelve c 1000; *-sancta (*n. pl.*), halidom (touched in taking corporal oath) c 1180, 1425; -scriptus, holy-written 870.

sacrofagus, *see* sarcographia.

sacum, *see* saca.

sadda, *see* sagda.

sadelepa, *see* sedlopum.

sadelo, to saddle (a roof with overlapping boards) 1401.

sado, *see* saticulum; sedes.

saesina, *see* seisina.

saffaria, (?) sea-faring (Ponthieu) 1289.

saffr/anum 1217, -onum 1218, 1281, seffrana 1303, ‡zafran, zauhiron 1652, saffron.

safna, *see* sagena.

sag/a, -ellum, *see* sagum.

sagaci/a 15c., -tia 8c., wisdom.

‡sagani (*pl.*), spirits of the four elements (alch.) 1652.

sagda, kind of gem: sadda c 1200.

sagemannus, accuser, prosecutor c 1115.

sag/ena (bibl.), -enula 12c., -ina 7c. 1335, †safna c 1230, saina 1319, seina c 1230, †essennum 12c., seine, fishing-net; †-ino, (?) to sweep into a net (fig.) 13c.

sagh/ator, -iator, *see* sawyator.

sagibaro, member of the Witan c 1115.

*sag/imen c 1080, 1531, †**segamen** c 1130, **segimen** 14c., **-men** 1337, 1392, **sangmen** 1318, **secchimen** 1265, **sigimen** 1531, **-iminium** 1531, **-imentum** 1229, 'seam', fat, lard, suet; **-eno,** *for* **-ino,** to fatten 12c.

sagin-, *see* **sagena;** SAGM

sagisterium, *see* **seges.**

†**sagitides** (*pl.*), veins under tongue a 1250.

sagitt/a, arrow-head 1252; (?) barrel-stave 1392; sagitta (geom.) 1686; **s. ampla** (Sc.) 1456, 1475, **s. larga** 1383, **s. lata** 1358, 1491, broad arrow; **s. pro bosco** 1391; **S. Walisca,** **S. Wallensis,** Welsh (? barbed) arrow 1246; **-ella,** lancet (med.) a 1250; **signum -abile,** target for arrows c 1250; **petra -abilis,** cannon-ball 1496; **imber -alis,** shower of arrows a 1350; **-amen** (*coll.*), arrows a 1400; **-aria,** fast ship c 1188; 1464, **-eria** 1298, ***-atio** c 1238, 1620, archery; **-atio,** shooting (of guns) 1427, 1573; **s. arcus,** bowshot (distance) 1478; **-arius ad equum,** mounted archer 1333; **s. de corona** 1389; **s. vigiliarum,** archer of the watch 1399; ‡**-ator** 1483, **-atrix** (*f.*) 1220, **-ans** c 1150, *for* **-arius,** archer; **-ipotens,** skilled at archery 1535; **-o,** to shoot (with bow) c 1150, c 1540; to shoot (with gun) 1337, 1471; to enter Sagittarius (astr.) a 1370; **s. ad** 12c., 1494, **s. contra** 15c., **s. in** c 1180, to shoot at; **s. ignem** 1372.

sagm/a (†**sagin-**), saddle (for riding) 1200; **salme** (*pl.*), baggage (It.) 1483; **summa,** *for* **-a,** pack-saddle a 1385; **-a** 1086, **salma** 1190, (?) †**silina** c 1193, **sauma** (†**savina**) 1195, **sema** 1270, 1512, ***summa** 1086, 1415, **summagium** 1201, 1419, **simagium** 1573, **summarium** 1215, c 1303, †**sumnile** 1268, **salmata** (G.) 1283, **saumata** (G.) 1254, **summata** (G.) 1305, 'seam', horse-load; **summa equestris** 13c.; **summa vini** 12c., **summarium vini** (G.) 1254; **sum-magium *1086,** 1428, **sulmagium** c 1145, (service of *or* payment for) carriage by pack-animals; team of pack-animals 1157, 1499 (*see also* **semen**); **summagialis,** **sum-maricius, summarius,** *see* **sella;** (equus) **-arius** c 1190, c 1204, (?) **salmerius** (G.) 1312, **saumarius** (G.) 1281, ***summarius** 1086, 15c., **sumerius** c 1200, 1332, **sumeri-cius** 1228, **sumeriticus** 1234, **summalis** 1303, pack-horse; **-arius** 1084, **sum-marius** 1172, **summerarius** 1130, **some-rarius** 1303, **sumetarius** 1190, 14c., **sumitarius** 1281, **sumptarius** 1313, 1329, **sumptuarius** 1514, **sumularius** c 1136, packman, groom of pack-horse; **sum-marius, sumerus,** transport vessel 13c.; **somerius (somerus, somera),** 'breast-summer', horizontal bar (arch.) 1296, 1462; **sumerus pressoris,** beam of press 1227; **summagio** 1189, c 1350, **summo** c 1290, to carry, transport (by pack-animal).

sago, *see* **sawyator.**

sag/um, bolting-cloth 1341, 1408; c 1330, 1532, **-a** c 1397, **-ium** c 1200, **saium** 1180, 1346, **saia (saya)** 1171, c 1300, **saiea** 1553, (?) **essaia** 1170, 1307, **assaia** 1272, 1278, †**saxum** c 1150, 'say', woollen material; **-ellum,** blanket 7c.; *cf.* 1 **seta;** *see also* **segga.**

†**sahaffa,** "*rubor faciei*" 14c.

sah/etor, -eo, *see* **sawyator.**

sai/a, -ea, -um, *see* **sagum.**

saiatus, *see* **seisina.**

sail/clathum (sayl-), sail-cloth 1352; **-evan-dum** 1296, **-wandum** 1343, wand for mill-sails; *cf.* SIGL

saillio, *see* **saliares.**

sail/o, -ona, *see* 1 **selio.**

saina, *see* **sagena.**

sainctarius c 1195, **sainterius** a 1212, **seintarius** 1212, **sanctuarius** 1209, bell-founder (O.F. *saintier*).

sais-, *see* **seisina; seiso.**

saitum, *see* 1 **seta.**

sakabor, *see* **sacrabarrum.**

sakemannus, *see* **soca.**

sakeo, a material used in alchemy 1418.

sal/, a salt (alch.) c 1215, c 1345; salt-cellar 1600; **s. acrum** a 1235, **s. agrum** c 1215; **s. Africanum** (med.) a 1250; **s. album,** refined salt 1280, 1460; ‡**borax** 1652; **s. ammoniacum** c 1227, **s. armoniacum** c 1215, c 1345, sal ammoniac; **s. atramenti,** copperas 13c.; **s. del Bay** 1369, **s. de Bayon'** 1374, bay salt; **s. gemma** a 1250, c 1270, ‡**s. gemme** 14c., 'sal-gem', rock-salt; **s. gracile** 1342, **s. minutum** 1278, 1325, fine salt; ***s. grossum** 1302, 1532, **s. magnum** 1328, coarse salt; **s. Indicum, s. rubeum,** c 1215 (?); ‡"mercury" 1652; **s. Marcelli, s. sacerdotale,** remedies for phlegm a 1250; **s. masse,** (?) rock salt c 1215; **s. nacticum** a 1235, **s. naticum** c 1215 (alch.); **s.** †**nigrum,** (?) *for* nitrum, 12c., 1620; ‡**s. panis,** common salt 1652 (*cf.* panis); **s. petre** c 1215, 1346, **s. petri** 1375, **-petra, -petrum** 1346, 1444, **-spetra** 1384, **-tepe-trum** 1346, †**-vistrum** (? *for* **-nitrum**) 1380, saltpetre; *see also* **alembrottus, alkali;**

-agium, (?) profit of salt-making (Kent) 1570; **-arga,** salt-pan, measure of salt (G.) 1276, 1346; **-are** c 1180, c 1390, ***-arium** 1207, c 1440, **-aria** c 1165, c 1330, **-erium** 1295, c 1443, **-era** 1214, **-inare** 1588, **-inum** c 1330, 1491, **-ina** 1468, **vas -arium** c 1160, salt-cellar; **-arium,** larder 1423; 1429, ***-ina** 1086, 1583, **-inum** 1199, c 1350, †**-ismus** 1461, **-inaria** 1086, c 1150, **-inarium** 1167, 1201, (?) **-inagium** (Sc.) 15c., salt-works, salt-house or salt-pan; **-is,** hot salt spring c 700; **-ifodina,** salt-pit 1574; **-atio** (C.I.) 1274, **-itio** 1244, 1622, **-atura** 1251, salting; **-ator** 1213, **-iator** 1225, ‡**-inator** 1483, salter; ‡**-inaria,** "saltster" 15c.; **-inarius,** salt-boiler 1086, 1237; *see also* **area, domus, patella, patena; aqua** †**-inatica,** salt water c 1260; **a. -macina** (†**-inacina**), *for* **-macida,** a 1250; †**-atus,** salt-loaf c 1136; **-atus** 1173, 1251, **-iatus** 1290, **-itus** 1231, 1357, salted; *cf.* SALS, **salterius.**

sala 'sale', hall 1086, 1283.

1 **salacia,** sea c 950.

2 **sal/acia,** lust 15c.; **radix -ax,** (?) *eruca* (bot.) a 1250.

‡**salamand/er, saldinus,** spirit inhabiting fire 1652; ‡**-ra,** "cricket" 1483, 1570; **-re pellis,** asbestos a 1200.

salamo, *see* **salmo.**

salari/um *12c., 1583, selarium a 1452, celarium 13c., 1426, salary; (?) Danegeld c 1400; -o, to fee, pay a salary to c 1507, 1684; see also sal.

salaunca, see saliunca.

sal/cea, -cedo, -cistrum, see SALS

sal/cetum, -ectum, -etunia, see salicia.

sald-, see saldanus; 2 solidus.

saleber, rugged c 1190.

saler/a, -ium, see sal.

salerarius, see cellarium.

saletta 1451, 1489, selleta 1471, 'sallet', steel cap.

salexotemo, see salmo.

salg-, see salvia.

sali/ares, -i (pl.), tumblers, dancers c 1160; -ens, salient (her.) p 1394, c 1595; psalio, for -o, to leap c 1296, a 1446; saillio, to mount, mate (of stallion) 1319.

sal/icia 1275, selix 1377, -sus 1275, †psalc' 1283, for -ix, willow; †-iculus, little willow 12c.; -icetum 1218, c 1400, -cetum 1227, 1305, -setum 1305, -ectum 1584, †-ectuna, -etunia c 1130, osier-bed; virga †ciliciva, willow-rod 1425; fossatum -icinum, ditch with willows growing c 1320; oleum s., oil of willow (med.) a 1250; carbo -isinus, willow charcoal c 1385.

salicornia, glasswort (bot.) 1634.

salifico, see salvatio.

saligia, acrostic of seven deadly sins c 1370; see also salvia.

saligo, see siligo.

salin-, see sal; SALIV; salvia.

salisamentum, see SALS

sal/iunca 13c., ‡15c., †-aunca 1493, seliunca 1563, whin; "foxglove" 13c.

saliv/a, (?) for salina, sea c 950; savour (fig.) 5c.; -are c 1200, -aris 12c., -arium c 700, bit (for horse); -alis (†salinalis) a 1250, 1267, -abilis c 1270, salivary; -o, to dribble on c 1180.

†sallanis, (?) sand-pit (Ir.) 1264; cf. sablo.

sallio, see 1 selio.

sallo, see PSALL

salm-, see also sagma.

salm/atinus, -antinus, see aqua.

*salm/o 1086, 1537, salamo 1333, †salexotemo c 1130, samo 1467, salmon; -unculus (†-iniculus, †-uniculus), young salmon 1256, 1438; -onarius, salmon-fisher a 1250, 1661.

Salomonicus, of Solomon 1252; cf. sigillum.

salp/ix c 700, 933, -inx c 1000, trumpet; ‡-o, "horn-pipe" 15c.

sals/a, salt water c 1180, 1252; salt-pan or salt-works c 1200, 1252; salt (sold direct from salt-pan) 1236; c 1180, 1530, -ea 1301, 1358, salcea 1335, -amentum c 1200, 1560, salisamentum 1375, -iamentum 1307, 1393, sauce, condiment (see also VIRID); -amentarius, dealer in condiments 1561; -ago 1245, -icia 14c., -ucia c 1200, ‡1483, †-inia c 1266, -istrum 1302, -isterium 1340, salcistrum 1268, sausistrum, saucistrum 1292, sausage; -ago 1329, -atio 1343, 1387, salting; -aria 1242, 1313, *-arium c 1188, 1514, -arius 1295, 1460, -eria 1291, -era 1511, sausaria 1405, sauserium 1391, †saserium 1326, sau-

cerium 1266, 1382, -orium 1414, c 1470, sosorium 1519, -ettum 1403, 'saucer', salt-cellar; -arium triplicatum 1329; -aria, measuring vessel (? for salt) 1419; 1214, 1393, -eria 1327, 1390, †salteria 1327, sauceria c 1315, 1366, saucery (room or office of 'saucer'); *-arius 1201, c 1335, sausarius 1415, -ator 1415, 'saucer' (royal officer or mon. obedientiary); sauce-maker 1415;

-e, with salt water c 1460; -edo a 1250, 14c., salcedo a 1250, saltiness; ‡-ulus, saltish 1570; -ochymus, having excessive salt in bodily fluids a 1250; mortarium -orium, salt mortar c 1212; -ugo 738. 13c., a 1347, -ilago 12c., salt-marsh or salt-pan; -ugenus c 550, -ugineus c 1115, -uginosus c 1212, ‡1483, briny; -uginatus, salted c 1250; mariscus -us, salt-marsh 1198, 1583; pratum -um 1296, p. sulsum 1256, salt meadow; fenum -um, salt hay 1389; -esco, to grow briny a 1250; -ifico a 1250, *-o 1214, 1490, to salt; cf. sal; see also salicia.

salsotes, vene, varicose veins c 1210.

salt-, see also PSALT; salsa; stalo.

salt/erius, salter 1351; -kottum, salt-pan c 1350; -o, to salt 1380; cf. sal, SALS

saltim, forthwith p 1330.

salt/osus, growing in upland woods c 550; -arius, 'lander', lawn-keeper 1385.

salt/us, assault 1199; 1322, -atio 1318, mating (of stallion); cf. asaldus); omission of a degree in ordination (eccl.) 1237, c 1400; s. aquarum, spring 1433; s. lune, subtraction of a day from a lunation at the end of a cycle c 790. c 1265; *-atorium 1190, 1363, -atarium 1334, -arium 1190, a 1446, †-anarium 1190, -uarium 1320, -orium 1189, 1285, sautorium 1331, sauturum 1223, deer-leap; 1291, c 1595, psalterium p 1394, saltire (her.); ludi -atorii, dancing school 1553; -iger, springing c 800; -ans, salient (her.) p 1394; (subst.) tumbler, dancer 1381; dies -atus, leap-day 1307; -o, to assault (a fortress) 1275; to break into (a park) 1269.

salubro, to make healthy c 1212.

1 salus, "heath-cock" 1573.

2 *salus, salut/are, -arium, salvation (eccl.); see also annus; *s. anime 838, 993. 1070, c 1520; s. populi, (introit for) 18th Sunday after Trinity or 4th Thursday in Lent 12c., c 1340; -a, -ius 1452, -ia 1430, saluceum 1451, 'salute', gold coin; -aris, ‡rosemary (bot.) 1483; 12c., c 1504, *-ifer c 1070, 1505, †-ivus (? for salvativus) c 1250, bringing salvation (theol.); -ifer c 750. c 1090, c 1343, -ificus 1308, salutary; †-issimus, most salutary c 1260; -ariter, healthfully 870; -amen, greeting 1041; -atio, antiphon Salve Regina 1272; *S. Angelica c 1300, 1549, S. B. Virginis c 1340, S. B. Marie c 1220, the Ave Maria; -arium, treatise on hand-writing c 1380; -atorium, audience-chamber a 1142, c 1283; -atorius, of greeting 961. c 1070, p 1377; -atrix, welcomer (f.) a 1200.

salv/a a 1150, -ia 1355, salve, ointment; -o, to salve, anoint 1302, 1438.

salvag/ina, -ius, *see* SILV

salv/atio *c 1090, 1493, **-itas** 1209, preservation; protection against flooding 1269, 1535; salvage (naut.) 1293, 1455; saving clause (leg.) 1563; *salvation (eccl.); **s. anime** c 1197, c 1220; **-abilis,** preservable c 1270; **-amen,** protection 1369; **-amappa** 1314, 1338, **sauvenapa** 1300, 1313, **savenappa** 1385, **savenappus** 1328, **saunapa** 1325, 1350, **sanape** 1353, **sanappa** c 1450, **sanepa** 1410, 'sanap', cloth to protect table-cloth; **-atella** a 1250, **‡vena s.** 14c., vein of hand or foot; **-ator,** salvager (naut.) 1330; **-ativus** 870. a 1250, c 1290, **-aticus** 870, **-ifer** c 1000, **-ificus** c 950. 12c., c 1470, **-atrix** (*f.*) c 800, saving, preservative, salutary; ***-ator** (eccl.), **-ificator** c 800, Saviour; **-ifluus,** flowing with salvation c 850; **-e** 1295, c 1467, **-e Regina** 1417, 1526, an antiphon; **-o** c 1196, c 1514, **†-ato** c 1275, safely; **in -o suo,** in his protection (G.) 1255; **-a pace** c 1193, c 1290, **s. reverentia** c 1193, c 1444, with all respect; **-o quod** c 1257, c 1465, **s. eo quod** c 1090, 1243, **hoc s. quod** 1261, save that, except that; **psalvus,** *for* **-us,** excepted c 1280; **per -os plegios,** by reliable pledges (leg.) 1199, c 1265; **-um venire et stare (et recedere),** right to come and stay (and go) 1200, 1224; **-us et (atque) sanus,** safe and sound 1252, 15c.; *see also* **conductus, custodia, warda;** **-ifico** c 1400, **†salifico** 1427, to save; **-ifio,** to be saved c 1270; **-o,** *to save, preserve c 1170, c 1540; to protect (from flooding) 1266, c 1460; to salve, salvage (naut.) 1330, 1455; *to save (theol.) 1c 1080, c 1444; to save, except c 1285, c 1343; to make good, compensate 1249; **s. defaltam** 1230, c 1290, **†-eo defaltam** 1203, **s. diem** 1169, c 1320, **s. essonium** c 1267, to remedy default, make essoin (leg.); *cf.* **sano; s. indem(p)nem,** to guarantee against loss c 1337, c 1448; **s. jus,** to save or reserve a right (leg.) 1222, 1279; **s. sacramentum,** to keep an oath c 1204; **s. me,** to escape 1461; *see also* **salva.**

salvi/a, sage (bot.): **†salina** 14c., **salgea** c 1200, 14c., **saligia** 13c., (?)**†sarretum** (**†savigeum**) c 1180; **‡-a agrestis, s. sylvatica, s. domestica** 14c.; **vinum -atum** (**†salinatum**) a 1250, 14c., **v. salgeatum** 1300, sage-flavoured wine; *see also* **salva.**

salvistrum, *see* **sal.**

1 **sambu/ca** c 1000. a 1142, 1316, **†-ia** 1243, **-a** 1295, **sabucum** (**†sabutum**) 1251, saddle-cloth; **sambulla,** (?) side-saddle c 1000.

2 **sambuc/a,** musical instrument: **zambuca** c 1393; **-us,** *sambuca*-player c 1000; **-arius,** "sackbutteer" 1636; **simbice** (*pl.*), "virginals" 1553.

3 **sambuca,** *see* **cambuca.**

‡sambuc/etum, elder-grove 1488; **†-eleon** a 1250, **oleum -inum** a 1250, 13c. (?) oil of elder.

samellum, *see* **scamellum.**

***sam/itus, -ictus** 1130, c 1400, **-ita** 1313, 1396, **-etus** 1245, 15c., **-itellus** c 1315, c 1370, **-itrus** 1243, **examitus (hexamitus)** c 1180, c 1255, **exametus** 14c., **xamittus**

c 1450, (piece of) samite, rich fabric; **-iteus** p 1330, **-itricus** 1310, of samite.

samo, *see* **salmo.**

sampsuch/um, marjoram (bot.): **sansucum** a 1250.

†samum, (?) sky *or* summit c 550.

sana-, *see also* **sanitas.**

sanap/e, -pa, *see* SALV

sanct/us, *saint c 693, c 1006. c 1067, 1545; *(as title) c 730. 1067, 1558; *(with proper name) feast of a saint 1200, 1245; sanctus (liturgy) 1006. c 1000, 1245; **sancitus,** *for* **-us,** c 800; **-i omnes (festum, festivitas, omnium -orum),** All Saints' day (1 Nov.) c 1130, 1517; **-ulus,** 'plaster saint' 1520, c 1620; **-a** (*n. pl.*), halidom (touched in swearing of corporal oath) c 1115; **-ificator,** sanctifier (eccl.); ***-ificatio** (eccl.), **-ificium** 1537, conservation; ordination (eccl.) c 1180; **-ificium,** holy place 12c.; **-imonia** c 1250, c 1430, ***-itas** 705. c 1080, c 1520, **-itudo** c 1170, holiness (title); ***-imonialis** (eccl.), **-emonialis** 1201, 1483, nun; **s. laica,** lay sister 12c.; **-io canonica,** rule of canon law c 1330, c 1530; **sanxio,** *for* **-io,** c 1330, 1505; **-isacer,** holy c 800; **hymnus ter -isonus,** sanctus c 1100; **-uarium** a 1115, c 1330, **-uaria** c 1248, **†scuarium** 1288, **†scumarium** 13c., holy object, relic or reliquary; 7c. c 1125, c 1534, **-iarium** c 1330, **santuaria** 1257, **saunctuarium** c 1470, **sayntuarium** a 1540, shrine, (right of) sanctuary; (?) secret counsel c 1320; consecrated ground, cemetery 1292, 1324; 1169, 1583, **terra -uaria** 1249, 'santry', glebe-land (esp. Devon & Cornw.); *see also* **sainctarius;** **-itum** a 1408, **sancitum** c 1450, decree; **-ifico,** to ordain c 1180; **-io** 12c., c 1298, **sanxio** c 1220, *for* **sancio,** to affirm.

1 **sand/alum,** sandal 12c.; **-ala** (*pl.*) 1245, 1425, **-alia** (bibl.), **-alie** c 790, **-aria** c 1190, **-arie** c 1220, p 1400, **scendalia** 1251, sandals, slippers.

2 **sand/alum, -alus, -us** a 1250, **‡**14c., **santalum** c 1615, 1622, **-rium** 1377, **saundrium** 1372, **zandria** 1453, sandal-wood, 'sanders'.

3 **‡sandal/um, -ium,** horse-cloth 1483.

4 **sand/alum, -allium, -elum, -atum,** *see* **cendallum.**

sandela, sand-eel 1307.

sand/ix, (?) madder 1328; **‡**"madder", "woad" *or* "weld" 13c., 15c.; **-icinatus,** "maddered" 1465, 1587; **†-rinus,** (?) scarlet c 1550.

sanepa, *see* SALV

sangmen, *see* **sagimen.**

sangreda, 'sangrede', service for the dead (Suffolk) 1572.

sangu/is 1134, 1263, **s. effusus** 1275, 1281, **s. fusus** 1269, c 1290, **-inis effusio** c 1160, 1382, **s. tractus** 1272, (fine for) bloodshed; sanguine temperament 1424; orpiment (alch.) 1144; **s. et fides** (as pledge of prosecution) 1293; **-inem facio,** to cause bloodshed 1086, 1249; **s. emo** 13c., 1279, **s. redimo** 1279, to pay merchet; **-inis redemptio,** merchet a 1185, 1320; **-inis causa,** action involving bloodshed (leg.) 13c., c 1343; **-inis defectus,** want of an

heir 1333; **-inis particeps,** blood relation
c 1250; **consanguineus de integro -ine**
1405; **-is Domini** c 1220, c 1266, **s. Dominicus** 13c, consecrated wine; **s. draconis,**
dragon's blood (bot.) 1220, ‡14c.; **s. Israe-
lite** (med.) a 1250; **s. martis,** asara bacca
(bot.) 1538; **s. naturalis et innaturalis,**
arterial and venous blood a 1250; **s. regalis,**
sangrael 1357;
  -initas, bloodiness a 1408; kinship c 1180,
p 1330; **-ensis,** blood-red 1478; **-ibundus**
c 1150, **-ilentus** 5c., c 700, **-inolens** 1220,
1370, bloody; **-idus** 1424, **-ineus** a 1200,
c 1362, sanguine (med.); **-ineus,** kinsman
13c.; **-inea,** kinswoman c 1180; **-ificatio,**
formation of blood 1620; **‡-ifuca,** filtre
1652; **‡-inacium,** blood-pudding 15c.;
canis -inarius c 1190, **‡(c.) -isecus** 15c.,
1570, blood-hound; **-isorba** c 1620, **-isuga**
(bibl.), leech, blood-sucker; **-ifico,** to form
blood 1622; **-ilento,** to bespatter with blood
c 700; **-ino,** to let blood c 1266, c 1450.
sani/atio, -ositas, purulence a 1250; **-esco,
-o,** to grow purulent a 1250.
san/itas, miraculous healing (eccl.) c 1188,
1414; **-um,** soundly, well c 730, 799;
-abilitas, curability c 1300; **-atio,** (?) medicament a 1250; **-ativitas,** healthfulness 13c.;
-ativus, health-giving, healing a 1255,
c 1380; healthy c 1160; **-ator,** healer
c 1090, c 1125; **-amunda,** avens (bot.)
a 1250, ‡c 1440; **-icla** a 1250, ‡**-icula** 13c.,
14c., sanicle or other umbellifer (bot.); **fons
-ifluus,** fountain of health 12c.; **-o defaltam**
1256, 1294, **s. diem** 1194, 1199, to remedy
default (leg.); *cf.* **salvo.**
sansucum, *see* **sampsuchum.**
sant-, *see also* SANCT; **2 sandalum.**
‡santonicum 14c., centonica a 1250, san-
tonica, wormwood (bot.).
sanxio, *see* SANCT
sap/a, -inus, -ineus, *see* **1 sappus.**
saphea, 'saphey' (type of astrolabe) 1326.
saphene, vene, c 1210, **sophene** a 1250,
‡1483, inner and outer veins of foot (Ar.).
saphrophilus, *see* **saprophilus.**
sapidus, sapifur, *see* **sapor.**
Sapien/s, Solomon 600. a 1155, c 1340; **S.
mundi,** Aristotle c 1334; **-tes** (*pl.*), doomsmen (leg.) c 1115; 831, 861. c 1115, **S.
Anglie** c 1115, **S. Gentis** 720, **S. Regis**
c 1115, **-tia** (*coll.*) c 1102, c 1115, the Witan;
-tia c 1296, **liber-tie** c 1396, *Book of Wisdom*
(bibl) **-talis,** esoteric 1378, 1344; ***-tialis,**
concerned with wisdom c 1237, c 1375;
-tificatio, precept 870; **-tificus,** instructive
870; **‡sapissimus,** (?) rabbi c 550; **sapio,**
to smack of, give an impression of c 1270,
1346.
sap/o c 1000. a 1250, 1404, **sabonus** 1392,
-una c 1000, **savo** 1267, 1342, **‡asabon** 1652,
soap; **‡s. durus** 14c.; **s. Gallicus** a 1250,
‡14c., ‡‡**s. Judaicus, s. mollis** 14c., soft
soap; **‡s. muscatus** 14c.; **s. Saracenicus,**
mixture of soap-lye and olive-oil a 1250,
‡14c.; **s. spatarenticus,** "soap that cuts like
a sword" a 1250, ‡14c.; **-onaria,** soapwort
(bot.) a 1250, ‡15c.; **-onarius** c 1193,
‡1483, **savonarius** c 1165, soap-maker,
soaper.

sapor/, sauce, condiment c 1200, 1252; **sabor,**
savour 6c.; **-abilis,** tastable 1267, 1344;
‡sapifur, "sleuth-hound" 1483; **-ifer,**
piquant c 1220; 14c., **-us** c 800, **sapidus**
c 860. c 1204, delightful; **sapidus,** prudent
c 1470; **-ose,** with relish c 1300; **-ositas,**
tastiness a 1250; **-itus,** flavoured a 1250,
13c.; arrived at years of discretion 7c.; **-o,**
to sweeten, flavour c 800. a 1250, a 1408;
to be pleasant, seem good 5c.; to taste c 1180.
sapphir/us aquaticus 1200, c 1360, **s.
aquosus** c 1315, iolite or diochrite; **s.
citrinus (citerinus),** topaz 1241, 1267;
s. niger c 1315; **zaphirus,** *for* **-us,** sapphire c 1250, 1303; **-icus,** sapphire-blue
c 1414.
1 sapp/us (sap-) 1186, 1325, **-a** 1213, **sabus**
1232, **-ius** 1224, 1260, **-inus** 1279, 1326, fir,
deal (Fr. *sapin*); **-ineus,** of fir or deal 1230,
1326.
2 sappus, sap, moisture c 1290.
sapro/philus (saphro-), false philosopher
870.
sara, *see* **shara.**
Sarabaita, Sarabaite, vagrant monk c 1160,
c 1470.
sarabara, trousers: **serabara** c 1306, **‡sar-
buissinum** c 1190.
Saracen/us c 730, c 800. c 1118, 14c., **Sara-
zenus** c 1270, **Sarasinus** 1371, c 1503,
-atus 1272, **-icus** c 1250, c 1380, Saracen,
Moslem; heathen c 1250, 13c.; **caput -i**
(used for divination) 1371; **-ismus,** Islam
c 1400; *see also* **flos, frumentum, herba,
opus, sapo.**
saracra, *see* **seracra.**
sarax, *see* **sarcographia.**
sarbuissinum, *see* **sarabara.**
sarcella, *see* **cercella.**
sarcellus, *see* CIRCUL
sarcin/a, load, pack: **sarsina** 1488, **‡saroma**
1588, **‡sarcuta** 1275, **cercina** 1493, 1505,
cersina 1465, 1540, ‡**-ale** a 1520; **sercinola**
1496, **‡-ucula** 1484, **‡circunicula** 1495,
small load; **-arius,** driver of pack-animal
a 1142; ‡"driver of cloth" a 1520; ‡**-ator,**
"charger" 1483; **-o,** to load, pack c 1437,
‡1570.
sarcl-, *see* **sarculatio.**
sarc/ocolla, Persian gum: **-acolla** 1267,
-otalla c 1200.
sarc/ographia, †-ofegia (? *for* **-opegia),**
prosopopoeia, description in corporeal
terms c 1160; **-ofagum** 5c., c 800. 12c.,
1220, **sacrofagus** c 1474, **sargifagium**
6c., **‡sargosagus** 15c., *for* **-ophagus,** coffin
or tomb; **-oma,** excessive growth of flesh
1652; **sarx** 8c., **sarax** c 550, flesh.
*sarc/ulatio (†sart-) 1222, 1388, **-latio** 1251,
1410, **serculatio** 1315, **-ulatura** c 1325,
-latura 1239, 1316, **-lura** 1279, **serclatura**
1284, hoeing, weeding; **-larium,** weeding
service 1282; **-lator** 1230, **serclator** 1234,
-ulatrix (*f.*) 1388, weeder; **-ulo,** to weed
out 8c. c 1115; ***1199,** 1425, **-lo** c 1120,
c 1350, **sarkalo** 1279, **-lio** 1326, **serculo**
c 1300, a 1540, **serclo** c 1185, 1294, **†seglio**
c 1300, **serchelo** 13c, **carculo** c 1300,
cerculo 1284, 1324, **cerclo** 1227, 1243,
circulo 1281, 1286, to hoe, weed.

sardonicus, *see* herba.
sardura, (?) *f.l.* for sarclura, 1302.
sard/us, kind of fish c 1324; ‡-allus, "sperling" 15c.; ‡-ellus, "swordfish" 15c.
sarfa, *see* sarpa.
sar/gens, -giens, -jantia, *etc.*, *see* SERJ
sarg/ifagium, -osagus, *see* sarcographia.
sarg/ium c 1135, 1327, -ia (-ea) 1230, 1432, -a 1279, 15c., serge, woollen cloth; -io, to sift (? through serge) 1329.
sarkalo, *see* sarculatio.
sarkella, *see* scarkella.
sarment/um, (?) pruning-hook 1149, a 1452; -atio, "shredding" 1478; *cf.* sertamina.
sarp/a 1289, c 1385, -e c 1330, (?) sarfa 1301, hoe; -o, to prune 1289; serplo, (?) to hoe 1279; *cf.* sarculatio.
*sarp/ellarium, -ellaria, -ellarius 1171, 1413, -illarium 1207, c 1300, -illerium, -illeria 1177, 1292, -larius 1211, 1365, -lare, -laris c 1333, 1463, -lera 1322, 15c., -lerium 1278, 1478, sherplerium 1503, scarpellarium 1295, serpalarius 1208, serpelleria 1506, serpleria 1499, serplarium (Sc.) 1483, 1495, †serperale a 1564, -ellum 1407, -illum 1277, -lea 1301, 'sarplier', wrapper for wool, bale; -ellatio, making into sarpliers 1303; -lator, sarplier-maker 1303; -ello, to make into sarpliers 1303.
sarr-, *see also* sera; serra.
sarracum, wagon: †fartagum 13c.
sarretum, *see* salvia.
sarsaparilla (bot.) 1622.
sarsina, saroma, *see* SARCIN
sarsinettum, sarsenet, silk fabric 1397.
sartago, frying-pan: sertago 1390, ‡15c., certago 1501, cartago 1400.
sart/aria c 1330, c 1418, -arium 12c., c 1330, -oria 1279, c 1330, -ria 1280, c 1412, -rina 13c., c 1450, -rinum a 1128, c 1296, (?) satrinum 1273, -erina c 1220, -arinum c 1266, †-inum c 1296, -rinarium c 1135, domus -aria c 1308, sartry, tailor's shop or workroom (esp. mon.); -atecta (†sacritecta) (*pl.*), roofing, fabric c 1190, c 1377; -itector, thatcher 1354, ‡c 1440; -rator a 1118, sertor 1474, *for* -or, tailor; sertrix, repairer (*f.*) 790; sertura, tailoring, patching c 1522.
sart/um c 1120, 1433, -a c 1185, c 1200, -ium c 1185, assart, clearing of woodland, *etc.*; -atio, assarting c 1180, 1430; -o c 1130, 1430, serto 1197, to assart; *cf.* EXSART
sarura, *see* sera.
sarx, *see* sarcographia.
saserdos, *see* sacerdos.
saserium, *see* SALS
sas/ina, -io, *see* SEIS
†sasinata, (?) *f.l.* for scismata, 1281.
sassafras (bot.) 1622.
satag/entia, bustle, ado c 1608; *-o (with *inf.*), to endeavour (?) 939. c 1125, 1537.
Satan/ista 1523, †-ita 1166, Satanist; -icus, Satanic 1281, 1609.
sat/elles 1283, r305, -alles 1255, -illes 1445, -illes pacis 1334, serjeant of the peace, *cais* (W.); galloglass or 'idleman' (Ir.) 1333, 1392; bishop (in chess) a 1620; satellite

(astr.) 1686; s. Sathane 1444; -alles, follower, gangster 1446.
sati/culum, seed-basket c 1200, 1298; sado, measure of land (? c. 1,000 sq. yards) (G.) 1289, 1315; -onalia (*n. pl.*), arable fields c 1160; -onalis 704, 10c. 1173, c 1414, -onarius c 1175, c 1267, arable; *cf.* seiso, serendum.
sati/etas, riches 601; -abilis, satiable c 1360, ‡1570; 9c., -ativus 1344, satisfying; -atum, object causing satiety c 1360.
†satifi/catorius (†fatifi-), (?) *f.l.* for ratificatorius, 1502; -o, (?) *f.l.* for ratifico, 1273.
satinum 1401, ‡c 1440, sathana 15c., satin.
satio, *see* seisina.
satior, better c 1220.
satirice, satirically c 1250, a 1452.
satisfac/tio, fulfilment of penance c 600. 12c., c 1357 (*cf.* gradus); -sio, *for* -tio, satisfaction, amends c 805; -torius, atoning (theol.) c 1225, 1385; -io, to accept as satisfactory 1419; s. pro, give a verdict for 1414.
satispassio, atonement by suffering (theol.) c 1378.
satis/ratio, (?) *for* -datio, satisfaction, amends 839.
satrap/a c 1191, 1463, -s 12c., military official; count a 1142; -us archiepiscopi 1370.
satrin-, *see* sartaria; satureia.
satularis, *see* subtal.
satum, dry measure (bibl.).
satur/atio, satiety 1245, 13c.; -ativus, satiating 1427.
satur/eia, savory (bot.): ‡-gia a 1520, (?) -ien 1424, (?) satrina a 1170.
Saturn/us, lead (alch.) c 1215, c 1345; ‡-i crocus, red lead 1652; -alis 1220, -ius 1686, of Saturn (astr.); -inus, Saturnine (astr.) a 1200; *see also* dies.
sau-, *see also* sal-
saum-, *see* SAGM
saun-, *see* san-
saunapa, sauvenapa, savenapp/a, -us, *see* salvatio.
saura 8c. a 1250, †suara 12c., lizard.
saurus, *see* sorus.
sauvagina, savagina, savagius, *see* SILV
savaldor, *see* schavaldus.
savigeum, *see* salvia.
savina, *see* sabina; sagma.
sav/o, -onarius, *see* sapo.
sawyator 1302, saghiator 1333, saghator 1307, sah/etor 1303, sawyer; -eo 1303, sago 1296, to saw; *cf.* scegga, seca.
sax/agonus, -ogonus, *see* sexagonus.
Saxinus, *see* SACC
Sax/o 6c., 10c. 12c., 14c., -onicus c 730. c 1130, 1419, Saxon; -ones Antiqui, Old (Continental) Saxons c 730; S. Australes c 710, c 730; S. Occidentales c 710, a 910; S. Orientales c 730, a 910; -onice, in Anglo-Saxon 796, 836. 1136. c 1220.
saxum, saya, *see* sagum.
sax/us, *for* -um, stone 1255; -ifragia, (?) burnet saxifrage (bot.) a 1446; -ivomum, siege-machine 15c.
sayl-, *see* SAIL
sayntuarium, *see* SANCT
saz/ina, -io, *see* seisina.

sc-, *see also* **esc-**

scab/a, -ea, *see* **scabies.**

scabell/um *c 1080, 1530, **-a** c 1423, c 1524, **scabillum** 1462, stool or bench; **s. clausum**, "close stool" 1553; **-um** (†**stabellum**), *market-stall, shambles 1279, 1493; c 1325, **-ulum** a 1100, c 1400, crutch; **-arius**, walking with a crutch c 1172; **opus -inum**, style of embroidery c 1550; *cf.* **scamellum.**

scabergia 1223, **scaubergum** 1251, **scarbergium** 1205, **eschauberca** 1204, scabbard.

scab/ies mendacii, foul slander c 1000; †**-a** 1271, **-rigo** c 800, scab, itch; **-ia affrorum** 1322; **-ea**, scab (in wool) 1303; **-iosa**, scabious (or other plant) a 1250, c 1300; **-redo**, rough surface a 1142.

scabinga, *see* **scawagium.**

scabin/us *1213, 1419, **skivannus** 1332, municipal official, *échevin, Schöffe* (Flanders, *etc.*); 1287, 1448, **skyvenus** 1389, **skivinus** (†**skyminus**) 1378, 1389, 'skevin', steward of guild (esp. Norfolk); **skivinus**, official of London commune 1193; **skivinagium** 1378, 1391, †**skuvinagium** 1431, **scunagium** (†**scuvagium**) 1413, 1486, 'skevinage', 'scunage', office or jurisdiction of *échevin* or perquisites thereof (Calais); **littere -ales**, letter from *échevins* (Brabant) 15c.

scablicium, *see* **cablicium.**

scabro, *see* **scarabo.**

scabul-, *see* **cabula; scapulatio.**

***scacc/i** (*pl.*), chess-men, chess c 1125, c 1444; (?) counters 1237; **-um** a 1150, **scak'** 15c., **eschek** c 1280, check!; **scacha mattum** a 1150, **chekmat** c 1410, check-mate!; ***-arium** c 1190, 15c., **s. lusile** c 1178, chess-board, game of chess; chequer (her.) p 1394; *reckoning board or cloth 1168, 1378; c 1277, 1499, **-aria** c 1250, 1373, exchequer, accounting department (mon.); ***a** 1120, 1586, **scheccarium** 1185, 1274, **scaquerium** 1313, 1416, exchequer (royal); meeting of Exchequer court c 1178, 1362; **s. Cadomi (Normannie)** 1176, 1203; **s; Cestrie** 1246, 1301; **s. comitis** a 1183; **s. Garderobe** 1324; **s. Judeorum** 1220, 1261, **s. Judaismi** 1255; **S. Hibernie** (**S. in Hibernia, S. Dublin'**) 1200, 1415; **s. magnum**, **s. parvum** (Dublin) 1292; **s. inferius** c 1178, **s. recepte** 1235, **s. de recepta** 1234, 1265 (*cf.* RECEPT); **s. superius**, Exchequer of account c 1178; **S. Scotie** c 1305, 1559; **-ariasticus**, exchequer official 1272; **-ariatim**, chequer-wise p 1394; **-atus** c 1325, 1402, **-iatus** 1235, **-arizatus** 1507, **chekeratus** 1295, **chekerellus** c 1318, checked, chequered; **-atus** p 1394, c 1595, **-iatus** p 1394, **-ariatus** p 1394, **-arisatus** p 1394, **scachificatus** c 1595, **schekeratus** 1285, checky (her.); **-o**, to blazon checky (her.) a 1446.

scacia 1224, **scachia** 1239, 1285, **chacia** 1296, stock of tally (Fr. *échasse*); *see also* **1 chacea.**

scadda, shad (fish) 1535.

scafa, *see* SCAPH

scaff/aldus, -aldum 1258, 1336, **-olda, -oldum** 1322, c 1533, **-olta** 1320, *-ota,

-otum 1249, 1333, **scavota** 1289, **scoffoldum** 1230, **scalcofaga** (*n. pl.*) 1252, **calfacium** 1251, **escafata** 1271, **escaufatium** 1248, **-atura** 1276, **-otura** 1292, scaffold, scaffolding (arch.); **-alda**, scaffold (for execution) 1468; **-ator** 1317, 1332, **-otor** 1333, **-aldarius**, **-oldarius** 1355, scaffold-builder (arch.).

‡**scajole** (*pl.*), "spiritual powers of the mind" (alch.) 1652.

1 scal/a (carecte), cart-rail, 'ladder' (for extending loading capacity of cart) 1245, 1486; platform 1539; **s. plicata**, folding ladder c 1396; **s. verne**, part of windlass 1333; **S. Celi**, chapel or altar associated with special indulgence (eccl.) 1504; **-e** (*pl.*), (?) design of ladders 13c.; **ad -am**, *see* **2 scala**; **-amentum** 1444, **-ata** 1372, escalade; ‡**-are**, rung 1483; **puteus -aris**, well approached by steps 1378; ***-aria, -arium** 1239, 1453, **-aris** 1372, **-era** 12c., 1503, **-oria** 1275, stile; (?) footbridge 13c.; **-etta** 1278, 1299, **scaretta** 1171, 1274, vineprop; **-acio** 1297, **-etto** c 1235, 1278, to prop (vines); **-o** 1372, **escalo** 1410, 1413, to scale, take by escalade.

2 scal/a, shell (of oyster) 1290, 1338; **-e** (*pl.*), scales (for weighing) 1172, 1485; **ad -am**, (?) according to the scale c 1130, c 1178; *cf.* **skela.**

3 scal/a c 1290, 1307, **schela** 1478, **scialis** a 1291, ***-inga, -ingum** a 1165, 1538, (?)†**stalungia** 12c., **-engium** a 1225, **eschalinga** c 1160, **shelinga** 1403, **-ingeria** 1377, shieling (N. Eng. & Sc.); **shela**, miner's hut (Cumberland) 1356.

scalanga, *see* **scalonia.**

scalap/us, -ius, *see* **scalopus.**

scalciatus, *see* **discalceo.**

scalcofaga, *see* SCAFF

scald/arius, scalder (of pigs) 1212; **schalderia** c 1275, **eschauderia** 1227, (service of) scalding; **-o** c 1277, 1454, **scaldo** c 1277, **-io** 1363, **escaldo** 13c., **ascaldo** 1248, **escaudo** 1220, to scald (pigs).

1 Scaldingus, Dane (?) 11c.

2 scaldingus, 'scalding', carcase of sheep 1302.

3 scaldingus, 'scalding', base coin (of Brabant) a 1350.

scalenos, scalene (geom.) a 1200.

scal/era, -etta, *see* **1 scala**; **scutella.**

scal/inga, -engium, *see* **3 scala.**

scalm/a, *for* **-us**, thole-pin 1296.

scal/onia 1324, **-anga** (†**stalanga**) 1424, scallion.

scal/opus, -opa 1245, 15c., **-upus** 1303, **-apus** 1328, 1430, **-apius**, †**scapolus** 1295, scallop-shell; †**scapolatus**, scalloped 1295.

scaloria, *see* **1 scala.**

scalpa, *see* **shelpa.**

scalp/atio a 1250, **-tus** 1518, scratching; **-ellum**, (?) sculptor's chisel 14c.; **scarpellum**, scalpel (med.) a 1250; *cf.* SCULP

scalpo, *see* **scapulatio.**

†**scalta**, (?) clover (? *cf.* **caltha**) c 550.

scam/a, -osus, *see* **squama.**

scamara, brigand c 550.

scamb-, *see* EXCAMB

scam/ellum 1269, **-ella** 1276, †**-nium** 1267, **scannum** (†**scamium**, †**stannum**) c 1210,

1553, †scannilium (? -ulium) a 1396, *for*
-num, stool or bench; inter iiij -na gild-
halle (Totnes) 1387, 1409 (*cf.* bancus);
-ellum 1278, 1471, -ella 1321, †-ulium
1288, shamellum c 1320, 1629, shamella
1290, shambles, market-stall; -ellum (*f.l.*
samellum), (?) tumbrel or cucking-stool
1278; 1281, 1316, shamellum 1282, 1345,
part of wheel (of cart or plough); s. ad
caseum pressandum 1275; scannum,
(?) embankment c 1115, 1349; pew c 1502;
-nale (? scannale) 1080, scannile 1440,
‡-narium c 1440, bench-cover, "banker";
-no (ecclesiam), to provide with pews
1405; *cf.* SCABELL
scamma, arena (σκάμμα) c 800, c 950.
†scamo, (?) *f.l.* for strucio, ostrich c 1400.
scamoneatus, compounded with scammony
(bot.) a 1250.
scan/cile, -do, *see* scansio.
scandal/um, *stumbling, offence(bibl.); scandal, ill repute, slander c 1180, 1419; s.
magnatum, offence to the authorities 1539;
-osus *c 1332, 1587, -izosus (G.) 1314,
scandalous, shameful; slanderous 1419,
1549; spurned, shamefully treated 1497;
-ose, to the public scandal c 1334, c 1378;
slanderously 1539; c 1343, c 1444, -izabili-
ter c 1390, shamefully; -izatio, causing
offence c 1378, c 1470; s. titulorum, slander
of title (leg.) a 1564; -ista, offender 12c.;
-izator (?) 14c., -izatrix (*f.*) a 1640, slanderer; -izo, *to cause to stumble, offend,
shock (bibl.); c 1250, a 1564, †scandilo
c 1526, to slander.
scandulo, *see* scindula.
scangium, *see* excambium.
scann-, *see* SCAM
†scansilium, (?) *for* stansilium, stencil
(arch.) 1488; *cf.* stincillatus.
scan/sio, scansion (of verse) a 735. c 1125,
1267; -sile a 1180, 1521, -cile 1461, ‡-dile
1483, -sillum 1243, stirrup; c 1270, 1402,
-cile 1388, 1474, -dile 1501, -sillum 1493,
-sum 1451, stile; -sus, having climbed
a 1408; -do tumberellum, to mount the
tumbrel (penalty for women) 1340.
scapa-, *see also* scapus.
scapagium, *see* ESCAP
scapel-, scapil-, *see also* SCAPUL
†scapellus, vomitus †scarpelle, an emetic
a 1250.
scapero, *see* caparo.
scaph/a (scaf-) *c 1390, c 1467, -ula 1472,
bowl; instrument of torture 1591; -ila, *for*
-ula, boat c 1250; ‡-arius, "sculler" 1570.
scapol-, *see* scalopus.
scapsa, *see* capsa.
†scapton, (?) cup *or* rod (?) a 1100, c 1397.
scapul/a c 1196, 1366, -us c 1180, p 1460,
(?) chapula 1300, shoulder; -as do, to turn
tail c 1188; per -as capio, to arrest 1567;
-are, -arium c 1220, -us c 1250, scapelo-
rium 1236, (?) shoulder-strap, sword-belt;
c 1296, 1524, -arium 1218, capulare 1198,
scapelarium 1198, scapeloria, scape-
lorium 1249, c 1298, scapular, shoulder-
cloak (mon.); ‡-aris, "crook-backed"
a 1520; ‡-agito, to shrug one's shoulders
c 1440.

scapul/atio (†stapul-) 1298, 1519, scarpelatio 1272, scrapulatio 1526, scopula-
tio 1241, escapeltura 1234, 'scappling',
trimming (of timber); scopella (*pl.*), loppings 1251; *-o 1237, c 1533, escapulo
1232, †scipulo 1333, scapello 1238,
scapelio 1240, 1322, escaplo 1198,
escapelio 1262, scapillo 1238, escapilio
1261, scaplio 1385, scabulo 1411, scalpo
1389, scrapulo 1282, 1288, chapulo 1278,
to 'scapple', trim, dress (timber or stone);
cf. capulatio.
scap/us, arm of a cross 1654; -a, beak c 1000.
scarabo 12c., c 1212, scabro 870. 1208,
scrabo 12c., c 1362, †strabo 1208, beetle;
cf. crabro.
scarbergium, *see* scabergia.
scarbo, *see* carbo.
scarcementum, 'scarcement', off-set (arch.)
1398.
scareletum, *see* SCARL
scaretta, *see* 1 scala.
scaria, *see* SQUARR
†scaries ligni, remedy against lice a 1250.
scarif/icatio, scarification c 1260; ‡-icator,
-actor, -actrix (*f.*), "grater" 15c.; ‡-acio
15c., ‡-ico 1483, to "grate", scarify.
‡scarioball/um c 1440, 1483, ‡scorioballum
15c., cog (of wheel); ‡-o, "to cog (a mill)"
c 1440.
scariola a 1250, c 1260, escariola 1322,
endive (Fr. *escarole*).
scarkella (? starkella) 1247, 1287, strirkelda
(†stirkelda) 1269, strakella, karkella
c 1290, scorcella 1289, sarkella 1254,
1324, fish-trap (? *cf.* O.F. *escarcelle*, 'pouch');
cf. cartallum.
*scarl/etum, -eta c 1190, 1552, -atum, -ata
c 1155, 1449, scareletum 1207, 1448,
escarletum, escarleta c 1192, 1436, escalleta (C.I.) 1289, escarlata 1171, 1188,
exscarletum 1167, 1182, esquarletum
1421, ascarletum c 1228, 'scarlet' cloth or
robe (not necessarily red); s. rubeum
1250, 1449; escarlata nigra 1178; pannus
-etus 1285, 1421; pallium -eticum c 1540.
scarno, to strip of flesh (O.F. *escharner*)
a 1250.
scarpelatio, *see* scapulatio.
scarpella, *see* scapellus.
scarpellarium, *see* sarpellarium.
scarpellum, *see* SCALP
scarta, *see* quarta.
scassar (scimasar, scismasar) nova, good
omen a 1235; s. vetus, bad omen a 1235.
scat/alizo, -erizo, *see* EXCATUR
scat/avena, -braseum, -farina, 'scot-rent',
paid in oats, malt, or flour (Durham) 1307,
c 1380; -cheldra, 'scot-chalder' (Durham)
1183; *cf.* scotum.
scatebra, fountain (fig.), source c 900.
†scatesum (*v.l.* †stantillum), place of refuge
c 1200; (?) *cf.* stagium.
scatians (piscis), (?) stinking 1395.
‡scatuncellus, navelwort (bot.) 14c.
scatur/igo, spring, source c 1190, 1620;
swarm c 1185; powdering (her.) c 1595; -izo,
for -io, to gush forth c 1260, c 1362; *see also*
EXCATUR
‡scatus, skate (fish) 1483.

scaubergum, see **scabergia.**

scavota, see **scaffaldum.**

scaw/agium 1267, 14c., **scavagium** 1458, 1504, **scauvagium** 1274, **-angia, -ynga** 1419, **scabinga** 1408, **schewinga** 1235, **escewinga** c 1155, 1298, 'scavage', import duty on goods of non-burgesses; **-agerius** 1307, **escavingor** 1205, scavager, collector of scavage or officer of the ward; **scavingeri filia,** 'scavenger's daughter', instrument of torture 1580; **-ator (marisci),** (?) 'shower', inspector (Sussex) 1341, 1342.

sce-, see also **ce-; sche-; se-**

sceattum, sceatt, coin (A.S.) c 1115.

scedula, see **scheda; scindula.**

scegga, saw 1294; cf. **sawyator, seca.**

sceidmannus, sailor (A.S. sceiðman) c 1115.

sceld-, see CALD; SELD

scell-, see **sella.**

scel/us, felony 1100; **celus,** crime 1268; **-erata** a 1200, ‡**herba s.** 14c., celery-leaved crowfoot (bot.); **-eratio** 7c., **-eritas** c 1258, 1262, **-erositas** c 1173, wickedness; **-eriter** c 1436, **-erose** c 1191, wickedly; **-estis,** wicked 1446; see also **celer.**

scendal-, see **cendallum; 1 sandalum.**

scendula, see **scindula.**

scene/factorium, -vectorium, see **cenevectorium.**

scen/oma, tabernacle c 730; **-ophegia** 1271, **-ophagia** 1378, for **-opegia,** Jewish feast of Tabernacles.

sceolanda, see **scolanda.**

sceorpum, equipment (naut.) (A.S.) c 1115.

scepetere (pl.), carcasses of sheep (A.S. sceapætere) c 1115.

scepp/a, -um, see **skeppa.**

sceptr/um c 550, **sciptra** (pl.) 870, kingdom; tribe (of Israel) c 730; **s.** Elisei, aspalathus (bot.) a 1250; **ceptrum** 14c., c 1433, **septrum** 1242, p 1350, **septra** 1331, for **-um,** sceptre, authority; **septrum,** bar, rod 1420; **-alis** a 1275, c 1422, **-inus** 8c., **-iger** c 1000. 12c., c 1450, sceptral, royal; **-igeratus, -igerium,** rule, sway a 1100; **-igero,** to rule a 1100; **-o,** to furnish with a sceptre a 1275.

sceptum, see **sepes.**

scepum, see **sebum.**

scetha, see **theca.**

sceuda, see **selda.**

sceutum, see **scutum.**

scevenesie, see **stemphri.**

sch-, see also **sh-**

schafum, see **shava.**

schal-, see also **scala; SCALD; skela.**

schalo, see **chalo.**

schandria, see CANDEL

schasea, see **1 chacea.**

schav/aldus 1323, c 1350, **-aldor** c 1327, **shavaldor** 1322, 1336, **savaldor** c 1330, **-eldarius** a 1347, robber, reiver (Sc.); **shavaldria,** reiving 1324.

scheccarium, schekeratus, see SCACC

sched/a, sheet of paper: **sceda** 9c., **ceda** a 1275; **-ula (scedula)** *682, 1045. 1179, 1583, *cedula c 1160, 1610, **cedela** 1437, **scidula** 704, **sedula** c 1255, a 1452, **sedulum** 1224, schedule, document (esp. one attached to roll, etc.); literary trifle c 1190;

proclamation 1518; **cedulariter,** in writing c 1430.

schela, see **3 scala; skela.**

scheldrestclutum, scheltrum, see **schildebredum.**

schem/a, contrivance c 1306, 15c.; **s. crucis,** sign of the cross c 1000; **-a,** costume c 1170, c 1190; **s. monachile** c 1125, c 1170, **s. sancte religionis** 14c.; **s. seculare** a 1142; **cema,** form, fashion c 1436; **-atice,** pictorially c 1430; **-atismus,** pattern, constitution 1620; cf. **stema.**

schen/anthus, lemon-grass: **squinantus** 13c.; ‡**-efactor** (scen-), rope-maker c 1440, 1483; ‡**-ofacio,** to make ropes 1483.

Schenchensis moneta, coinage of Sancho of Navarre 1290.

†**scheppa,** (?) shippon, shed 14c.; cf. **shopa;** see also **skeppa.**

†**scher/a,** (?) shearing 1211; **-lingus** 1303, **sorlingus** 1303, 1311, 'shearling', 'shorling', skin of newly shorn sheep; **-mannus,** shearman 1411.

scherda (skerda), shard, splinter (of bone) c 1258, c 1290.

scherumbinus, see **cherubicus.**

schesellus, see **cisellus.**

scheta 1304, **chetum** 1337, **shedum** 1313, **shettum** 1340, sheet (naut.).

schewinga, see **scawagium.**

schewlarda, see SHOVEL

schildebredum, shield-board (of plough) 1326; **scheldrestclutum,** 'reest-clout' 1340 (cf. **2 resta**); **scheltrum,** sheltron, square of pike-men (Sc.) 1346; **scild/wyrhta** (-wircta, †-wica), shield-wright c 1115.

schilla, schiletta, see **scutella.**

schinus (bot.): **cin/us (cyn-),** (?) hawthorn c 1112, 1232; ‡**-um,** "haw" c 1440, 1483.

schip/a a 1142, 1196, **sciprus** 1157, 1161, **eskiprus** 1171, oarsman; **-wrichtus** 1295, **-whritus** 1297, **-wirhictus** 1304, **shipwrightus** 1295, c 1300, shipwright; **sipessocna** c 1115, **sipesocha** 1170, **sibsocha** 1177, **sibbesocha** 1179, (?) 'ship-soke', district liable to furnish a ship; see also SKIPP

schippo, schirpio, see CHIPP

schipus, see **scyphus.**

schir/a (scir-) *1086, 1436, **-ia** 12c., **shira** 1156, 15c., **sira** c 1190, **siria** c 1192, shire, county; 1178, 1369, **sira** 1305, parish or district (Sc.); diocese c 1115; ward, division of city (York) 1086; *c 1070, c 1400, **shira** c 1130, 1324, **shirus** c 1300, **sira** 1086, 1321, **-um** c 1105, **-us** a 1293, **chira** 1203, **cyra** 1285, shire-moot, county court, suit thereat (attendance or fine for non-attendance), body of county jurors; **-mannus, -ehomo,** 'shire-man', county court officer c 1115; **-emotus (siremotus),** shire-moot c 1115; **schirifus** 1508, **shyrevus** 1533, 1588, **shryvus** 1535, sheriff.

*****schism/a (scism-)** (eccl.), **cisma** 1241, c 1400, schism; quarrel c 950. 12c, p 1341; dilemma c 1443; **-atice,** schismatically p 1341; *-aticus a 615, 9c. c 1080, 1543, **cismaticus** c 1258, c 1330, **sismaticus** c 1450, ‡15c., schismatic (adj. & subst.); **-atico,** to split c 1194; **-atizo,** to cause a schism c 1250, 1427.

schitta, *see* **scitta.**
schlencha (schleucha), *see* **esklenka.**
schok-, *see* **shockum; 2 soccus.**
schol/a (scol-), retinue (of archbishop) 7c.;
choir c 760, c 980; ***-e** (*pl.*), school a 1150,
1548; **-a (-e) de cantu** c 1147, 12c., **-a
cantus** 12c., **-e cantuales** 1385, **-e musice**
12c., c 1316, song-school; **-a (-e) gram-
matice** 12c., 1498, **-a grammaticalis** 15c.,
1549, **-e grammaticales** 13c., 1446, **-e
gramadicales** 1384, grammar-school; **-e
liberales** 1424; **-e publice** c 1125, 1446,
(ac.) c 1584, 1636; **-e universitatis** c 1511;
-a ville 12c.; **s. Judeorum,** synagogue
1244, 1297;
   -agium, (payment for) schooling 1301,
1482; †**-agius,** (?) tenant of 'scholar-lands'
(Sc.) 1387; **-archa** 1586, **-aster** c 1182,
school-master; **-aria,** school 1255; scholarship 1417, 1421; **-aris** 8c., c 1000. a 1100,
1538, **-arius** c 1300, 1576, **scoloccus** (Sc.)
c 1260, scholar, student; **-astice,** like a
scholar 799; according to scholastic logic
c 1363, c 1444; **-asticus,** (*adj.*) scholastic
7c., 8c. c 1125, c 1365; of the schoolmen
a 1470, 1620; (*subst.*) schoolman c 1283,
1620; **magister s.,** chancellor (ac.) 1309;
-atim, in each school (ac.) 1432, c 1448;
-arizo 1305, **-atizo** c 1380, 1438, **-o** 1281,
1354, to study, be a student.
scholettus, *see* **cauleria.**
schopa, *see* **shopa.**
schopina, *see* **chopinum.**
schorum, 'shore', prop 1389.
schoutum, schuta, *see* **scuta.**
schovelum, *see* **shovelum.**
schrempus, scrympus, shrimp 1415.
schricus, shrike (bird) 1544.
schultetus (scu-) (Holland) 1289, 1442,
scoutettus (Antwerp) 1318, municipal
official, *schout.*
schura 1455, **shira** 1393, 1494, shed (Gloucester) (? *cf.* Germ. *Scheuer*).
schyngula, *see* **scindula.**
schyva, *see* **shava.**
sci-, *see also* **ci-; schi-; si-**
1 sci/a, -asis, -aticus, *see* **ischia.**
2 sci/a, -ator, *see* **seca.**
scialis, *see* **3 scala.**
sciamachia, sham fight 1610.
scibil/is, -itas, *see* **scientia.**
scicat/io, -or, *see* **seca.**
scicia, *see* **sicyos.**
scicidon, *see* **cecidos.**
scidula, *see* SCHED
scient/ia altior a 1150; **s. civilis** 1583; **s.
experimentalis** 1267, c 1382; **s. litteralis**
c 1250, 1383; **s. naturalis** c 850; **s. physi-
calis** c 1362; **s. practica** c 1250, 13c.; **s.
secularis** a 1200; **s. speculativa** c 1250,
1458; **s. quia,** knowledge of fact (ἐπιστήμη
τοῦ ὅτι) c 1300; **s. propter quod,** knowledge of cause (ἐ. τοῦ διότι) c 1300; ***-er,**
wittingly c 1090, c 1482; **-ialia** (*pl.*),
scientific or philosophic matters 1267, c 1357;
***-ialis,** concerned with knowledge, scho-
larly c 1250, 1439; **-ialiter** 1271, **-ifice**
a 1233, c 1457, scientifically; **-ificus,** scientific a 1280, 1610; learned c 1400, 1503;
-ivitas, capacity for knowledge 1344;

sci/bilis, knowable c 1080, 1344; **-bilitas,**
knowableness c 1330, 1344; **-olus,** *instructed, aware a 615, c 1000. c 1090, 1684;
uninstructed, pretender to knowledge c 1250,
1518; **-tote,** (?) with full knowledge c 1150;
***-tus,** knowledge, awareness 1272, c 1450;
-vus, *for* **-us,** wise 6c.; **-re** (*subst.*), knowledge c 1142, c 1415; **s. facias,** a writ (leg.)
1318, c 1465; **s. facio,** to make known, inform
1202, 1315; **-o grates** c 1125, c 1324, **s.
gratias** c 1125, to thank.
sciffus, *see* SCYPH
scignus, *see* **cygnus.**
scildwyrhta, *etc.,* *see* **schildebredum.**
scilenter, *see* **silentiarius.**
scilicet, namely: *silicet 1269, 1488, **siliset**
c 1330.
scilla, squill: **squilliticum,** (?) vinegar
flavoured with squills a 1250.
†**scillingum,** (?) *f.l.* for **ferlingum** (Devon)
12c. (1329).
scimasar, *see* **scassar.**
scimilinus, *see* **simila.**
sciminum, *see* **cyminum.**
scinchia, *see* **cincia.**
scincus (†**stincus**), kind of fish, (?) stickleback c 1188, 1451; ‡**stingus,** prawn or
shrimp c 1440.
scind-, *see also* SCISS
scind/allum, -ellum, *see* **cendallum.**
scind/ella, -illosus, *see* SCINTILL
scinderesis, *see* **synteresis.**
scindicus, *see* SYNDIC
*scind/ula, -ulum** 8c. c 1125, a 1447, **-la**
12c., **cindula** 1207, 1427, **cidula** c 1200,
sindula 1179, 1467, **scendula** 1162, 1316,
scedula 1130, **cendula** (†**tendula**) 1227,
1335, **sendula** 1221, **cenla** 1296, **shingula**
1357, 1403, **shingilla** 1434, **schyngula**
c 1412, **cingula** c 1324, **cingulum** 1254,
1286, **singula** 1323, 1339, shingle, (wooden)
tile; **cindula,** lath (of loom) c 1200;
†**cedularia** (*pl.*), laths 1272; **sendulatio,**
shingling 1376; **-ulator, sindulator** 1388,
sendulator 1376, shingler; ‡**-ularius,**
"blade-smith" 15c.; **cenlatus,** shingled
c 1265; **-ulo** 1235, 1260, **cindulo** 1277,
sindulo 1355, **shingulo** 1356, **singulo**
1323, ‡**scandulo** 1570, to shingle (a building).
scingulum, *see* **cingulum.**
sciniphes, *see* **cinyphes.**
scinterna, *see* **cinterna.**
scintill/atio 1267, **sintillatio** c 1458, twinkling (of stars); **-arium,** anthology c 1300;
sintilla c 1400, c 1430, **scindella** 7c., spark;
-osus (scindillosus), sparkling c 550; **-izo,**
to sparkle c 1200; *see also* **stincillatus.**
scio 1220, 1269, **cio** 1220, scion, shoot or
sapling; *see also* SCIENT; **seca.**
sciperalis, *see* SEPAR
scippa, *see* **skeppa.**
sciprus, *see* **schipa.**
sciptra, *see* SCEPTR
scipulo, *see* **scapulatio.**
scir-, *see also* SCHIR
scire, *see* **scientia.**
scir/mentum, -mengium, *see* **cirmanagium.**
scirotega, *see* **chirotheca.**

scirpus, rush, rushes (*coll.*): *cirp/us (cyrp-) c 1160, 1513, -a 1533, **sirpus** 1382, 1445, **serpus** 1435; **sirpus**, wick for rush-light 1415; -etum, rush-bed c 1280, ‡1483; -eus, rushen, made of rushes 1220, 1296; -osus, rushy 1326; **scirpo** (†stirpo), to strew with rushes c 1290.

scirra, *see* **scurellus**.

‡**scirtum**, "scallion" 1570.

scisellus, *see* **cisellus**.

scisimus, *see* **cisimus**.

scismasar, *see* **scassar**.

sciss/io (ciss-), rent, rending, cutting c 800. c 1125, c 1414; snippet 14c.; 1257, -ura 1444, 'cut', watercourse; 1266, -ura 1295, 1505, sawing; c 1250, c 1343, -ura c 1165, 1440, schism (eccl.); -ura, rupture, dissension a 1142; reaping 1199; (*coll.*) loppings 1297; 1295, c 1430, †ciceserum c 1350, 'cut', tailoring; 'slashing' (of clothes) c 1565; **s. bursarum**, purse-cutting 1255, 1330; **s. panni**, shearing cloth 1303, 1386; **sissio viarum** (to impede enemy) 1372;

-ibilis c 1270, **scindibilis** 1252, fissile; -ibilitas, divisibility c 1360; *-or 1219, 1533, **sissor** 1266, 1520, (?) **scinditor** c 1220, -or **vestiarius** 1549, cutter (of cloth), tailor; (?) carver (of meat) c 1270; **s. albus** 1253, **s. lapidum** 1224, stone-cutter; **s. bursarum** 1275, c 1290, **s. loculorum** c 1324, 15c., **sindor loculorum** 1352, cutpurse; **cinditor lignorum** 1302; -oria, -orium c 1390, 1517, **scinditorium** c 1330, trencher; **ars -oria**, sartorial art c 1250, c 1490; **pannus -uratus**, shorn cloth 14c.; **vestes -e (cisse)**, (ornamentally) 'slashed' clothes 1299, 1389;

scindo (cindo, sindo), *to fell or lop (trees)* c 1218, c 1340; to prune (vines) c 1270, 1312; to carve (at table) c 1330, 1377; to mark (animals) 1307; to retail (cloth or meat) 1280, c 1353; **s. per particulas** 1341; **s. pannos**, to tailor (? or shear) cloth c 1218, 1378; **s. robas** 1259, c 1350; **s. bursas** 1220, 1419, **s. loculos** 1352; **s. guttur** a 1525.

scistis, *see* **cystis**.

scit-, *see* **CIT**; **SCIENT**; **sitis**; **situs**.

scitta (schitta), dysentery (A.S.) c 1118.

sciurellus, *see* **scurellus**.

scivus, *see* **scientia**.

sclabba, *see* **slabba**.

*sclat/a (sklat-), -um 1223, 1533, **esclata** 1245, 1286, **slatta** 1478, 1535, **clatum** 1265, **lapis clateus** 1329, slate, roofing-stone; -arius 1306, 1367, -erus 1424, **slattarius** 1478, -ator 1265, 1372, -or 1245, 1428, **slattor** 1517, slater; -o, to slate 1297, 1401.

sclav/ina c 1190, c 1370, -inium (clavinium) 1149, 'slavin', long woollen cloak, (esp.) pilgrim's robe; -onium, caparison c 1310.

1 **Sclav/us**, Slav a 1142, 13c.; -onicus, Slavonic 1267.

2 **sclav/us** c 1220, 1252, -a (*f.*) c 1250, **esclavus** 1240, 1252, **esclava** (*f.*) 1195, slave.

sclerotica 1267, **sclir/otica, tela s.** a 1250, sclerotic membrane of eye; -osis, sclerosis, callosity c 1180, ‡14c.; ‡seclirotenta, "*viscera indurata*" 15c.

sclop/us 1499, c 1595, -etus 16c., 1620,

harquebus, carbine; -etarius, harquebusier 1573, 1587.

sclusa, *see* **exclusa**.

scob-, *see* **scopa** (1 & 2).

‡**scofa**, body not passed through filter 14c.

scoffoldum, *see* **scaffaldus**.

scogilatus, sheathed (of a sword) (Frankish) c 1115.

scoka, *see* **SHOCK**

scol-, *see* **also** **SCHOL**

scolanda (scholanda), (?) 'shoe-land' (granted to cover cost of footwear) 1177 (*cf.* **terra calciatoria**); 1181, 1279, †scotlanda 1181, **sceolanda** 1104, **solanda** 1183, 1222, prebendal land (of St. Paul's, London).

scold/a 1519, -atrix 1564, a scold; -o, to scold 1519.

scomerium, *see* **scumarium**.

scomm/a, taunt, jest c 1160, c 1173; -atice, scoffingly 12c.; ‡-or (*dep.*), to scoff 1570.

scons/a, -orum, *see* **ABSCON**

1 **scop/a**, birch (tree) a 1250; 1412, 1588, **scoba** 1504, 1528, -arium c 1266, broom, besom; ‡**s. regia**, St. John's wort (bot.) 14c.; -arius, concerned with sweeping 1620; **scobator**, (papal) sweeper (It. *scopatore*) 1494; -atio, sweeping 1401; -ature (*pl.*), sweepings of goldsmith's shop c 1100; ‡-ilia, "sweeping of a house" c 1440; *-o c 650, c 1000. c 1080, 1542, **scobo** 1374, to sweep.

2 **scop/a** 1267, 1460, **scoba** 1291, **scupa** 1507, scoop or shovel; **s. manualis** 1333; **s. pendibilis** 1333; -atio, cleaning (of fish) 1329; -ula, shovel c 1440; †-iola 15c., **scuposa** 1159, (?) mill-scoop; -o 1326, 1333, ‡**scobo** 1483, to scoop; to clean (fish) 1329; *cf.* **stoppa**.

3 **scopa**, *see* **shopa**.

scop/ella, -ulatio, *see* **scapulatio**.

scopus, intention (σκοπός) a 700.

scorcella, *see* **scarkella**.

scorella, *see* **scurellus**.

scoria (*n. pl.*), slag, dross 13c.

scorio, *see* **EXCORI**

scorp/icho, (?) stickleback 1317; -iacea cauda, scorpion's tail c 1125, a 1142; -ionarius, crossbowman 1654.

1 **scort/a**, *for* -um, 6c. c 1400, -atrix c 1620, whore; -atio, fornication c 1160, 1562; ‡-orium, brothel 15c.

2 **scort/a** 1317, 1320, -um 1332, -ex 1355, 1388, tie for scaffold poles, (?) strip of bark; -ex 1241, -ium 1234, *for* **cortex**, bark.

3 **scort/a** c 1365, 1410, -um a 1452, escort.

scort/ia, *for* -ea, leather oil-flask a 1250.

scorum, white pustule a 1250.

scota, *see* 1 **cota**.

scotagium, *see* **scutum**.

scotal-, scotamum, *see* **scotum**.

scotella, *see* **scutella**.

†**scoterellus**, (?) *f.l.* for **coterellus**, peasant c 1200.

scotlanda, *see* **scolanda**.

scot/oma 1267, -omia a 1250, ‡14c., †-otomia 1622, dim sight, dizziness (σκότωμα); -omaticus 685, c 900. a 1250, -omiosus a 1250, dim-sighted.

*scot/um (scott-) a 1070, 1526, -us c 1105, 1275, -a 1405, †-amum (W.) 1346, -agium

P

1172, 1331, scot, shot, payment; **s. de capite**, poll-tax (E. Anglia) 1086; **-ale** 1199, c 1436, **-alis** 1237, 1364, **-alia** c 1156, 1206, ***-alla, -allum, -allus** 1156, 1324, **-eala** 1475, **escothala** 1234, scot-ale, compulsory feast; **-enus** (Ir.) a 1210, **-or** 1275, scot-payer; †**escotantus**, paying scot c 1360; **-o** 1086, c 1353, **-io** 1275, **escoto** 1086, c 1350, **excoto** 1263, to pay scot; *cf.* SCAT

Scot/us (Scott-) 5c., 9c., **Scytha** 9c., Scot (of Ireland); ***c** 710, c 1000. c 1000, 16c., **-icus** c 730. 12c., 16c., **-to** 826, **-ensis** p 1377, **-icanus** 1256, c 1305, **-enus** (*met.grat.*) 1327, Scot, Scottish; **ecclesia -icana** c 1250, 1545; **-ice**, in Irish 9c.; in Gaelic (Sc.) 1256; **-ista**, disciple of Duns Scotus 1517.

scouda, *see* selda.

scouriolus, *see* scurellus.

scouta, *see* scuta.

scoutettus, *see* schultetus.

scowro, *see* ESCUR

scrabo, *see* 1 crabba; crabro; scarabo.

scrappa, *see* 2 crappa.

scrapul-, *see* scapulatio.

scre/a c 1100, ‡15c., **-amen** c 1200, spittle; **-atio**, spitting, hawking c 1180, c 1325.

scren/a 1313, **-us** 1283, **escrenum** 1250, **scrineum** 1553, ‡**scrinium** 1570, **escrinium** 1251, screen; *see also* SCRINI

scrib-, *see also* SCRIP

scribro, *see* CRIB

scriddo, *see* SHRUD

scrini/um *c 1000. a 1100, 1535, **-olum** 1528, shrine, reliquary; 14c., **-olum** (†**strincolum**) c 1524, compartment in muniment-chest; record, roll 1516, 1570; **screnium** 1466, **scrunium** 1313, (?) **scrutinium** c 1170, †**-ulum** 1225, *for* **-um** *or* **-olum**, chest or wallet for muniments; **-alis** c 960. c 1125, **-arius** 802. c 1125, 1230, papal notary; **-arius**, (?) drudge c 730; archivist, custodian of books 735, c 804; **faber s.**, cabinet-maker 1563; **-fer**, secretary c 1200; *see also* screna, strepa.

scrip/titatio, scribbling 1165, c 1610; **-sio**, *for* **-tio**, writing c 1400; **-siunculum**, small document 11c.; **-tor**, engraver 1461; **s. littere curialis** 1425, 1560; **-torarius**, chief copyist (mon.) c 1395; **-toria**, penner 1234; scriptorium (mon.) c 1266, c 1330; **-torium regis**, scribal department c 1178, 1200; †**-tura**, membrane (in bird's mouth) c 1250; ***-tura** (eccl.), **s. canonica** c 1160, c 1396, **s. divina** c 850, 939. c 1090, c 1410, **s. sacra** c 1080, c 1580, **s. sancta** c 1125, 1438, Holy Scripture; **-turalis**, mentioned in Holy Scripture a 1250; **evidentia s.**, written evidence 1389;

    scriba communis, town clerk c 1457, 1471; **s. curie** a 1123; **s. scaccarii** 1537; **s. universitatis** c 1470, c 1506; †**scrina** (? **scriva**), (?) *for* scriba, 1525; **-tura** 1298, **scribania** 1281, 1438, **scrivania** 1304, scrivenership (G.); **scribatus**, clerical office 12c.; **scrivarius**, Byzantine official 1274; **paperus scrivabilis**, writing paper 1380;

    -tum, deed, bond 1187, 1461; **s. authenticum** 12c., 1415; **s. chirographatum** 1304, 1430, **s. indentatum** 1536; **s. con-** ventionale 1260, 15c., ***s. obligatorium** 1274, p 1464; **-ta** (*pl.*) **pacis**, articles concerning the peace (A.S. *friðgewritu*) c 1115; **in -tis**, in writing c 1250, 1684; **scribens**, scribe a 1347, 1417; **scribo**, to brand c 1125; **s. ad coronam** (sigillum) to be clerk of the crown (*or* seal) 1389.

scrip/tula, -ulus, scroplum, *see* SCRUPUL

‡**scrobs**, "grit for scouring" 1570.

scrofa, 'sow', siege-engine c 1250; **scrophus**, boar 1199.

scrofule (med.): **scrofe** c 1200, **scroph/ile** 13c., †**scurole** c 1250, **-ula** 1535; **-ularia**, figwort (or other plant) a 1250, 1634.

scropes, *for* **scrupus**, rock c 550; ‡**scroph/us**, "a little gravel" 15c.; **-eus**, rocky c 550; *see* **scroph/us, -icus**, *see* scrofa; STROPH

†**scrotagia**, (?) form of tenement (C.I.) 1309.

scrotulus 1230, **scrowett/us** c 1290, 1301, **-a** 1371, **scruettus** 1597, scroll, escrow.

scrudlanda (**scrutlanda**, †**scrublanda**), 'shroudland' (granted to cover cost of apparel) 1177.

scrudo, *see* SHRUD

scrugga (*pl.*), 'scrogs', brushwood 1449.

scrunium, *see* scrinium.

scrupul/us, trifle, jot c 1160; minute of arc (geom.) 1686; **scripulus** 790. a 1250, **scriptula** 5c., *for* **-us**, small measure; ‡"little stone" 15c.; a 1452, **-a** c 1390, ‡1483, scruple (of conscience); †**scroplum**, **scropulum**, (?) shyness c 550; **-ositas**, knobbiness c 1200; hesitation c 1110; **-o**, to trouble 14c.

scrut/atio, vetting 1277; **-amen**, scrutiny c 1204, 1413; **-inium**, study c 780; search in records, *etc.* a 1155, 1430; ***mode of election** (by ballot) (mon.) 1284, c 1550; **s. gaole**, jail inspection 1440; **s. nature**, experimental research 1620; **s. naturale** 1344; *see also* **scrinium**; ‡**-abilis**, "searchable" c 1483, 1570; **-abiliter**, searchingly c 1250, 1378; **-abundus**, searching a 1155, c 1200; **-arius** (**carnium**, *etc.*), inspector 1541; **-ator**, searcher (customs officer) 1299, 15c.; scrutineer (of votes) c 1290, c 1575; 12c., c 1330, **-atorius** 1318, **-atrix** (*f.*) 12c., 1284, visitor, inspector (mon.); **s. nature**, 12c.; **s. rotulorum** 1242; **-o**, to search (esp. records) 1274, 1331.

scrutlanda, *see* scrudlanda.

scrutum, paunch, tripe c 1430, ‡1483.

scrympus, *see* schrempus.

scua-, scuch-, *see* scutum.

scuagium, *see* scutum; SYNOD

scuarium, *see* sanctuarium.

sculpa, *see* stulpa.

sculp/atio, carving (of wood) 1323; **-ator**, engraver (of coinage) 1486; **-tor lapidum liberorum**, free mason 1212; ‡**-atorium**, "shaping-board" 1483; **-rum**, *for* scalprum, chisel (fig.) c 1200; **-tile**, graven image (bibl.); **celtis -torius**, graving tool a 1180; **-tura**, cutting, cut (of clothes) a 1370, 1424; **-o**, to cut (clothes) c 1390; to trim (timber) 1357, 1374 (*cf.* scapulo); **s. retia** 1509; **-to**, to cut out, shape (a sail) 1295; (a purse) 1345.

scultell-, *see* scutella.

scultetus, *see* schultetus.

scumarium 1310, scomerium 1357, scummer, skimmer; escomarius, barge (O.F.
escumeur); skumeria, piracy c 1360; *see
also* sanctuarium.
scunagium, *see* scabinus.
scup/a, -osa, *see* 2 scopa; shopa.
scur-, *see also* ESCUR
scurallum, *see* curallum.
*scur/ellus c 1100, 1355, -ulus a 1200, ‡15c.,
sciurellus (G.) 1254, *squirellus 1255,
1410, scouriolus 1292, †turilus 1295,
scorella (Sc.) 1329, escurellus 1250,
escureus 13c., scirra 8c., squirrius c 1325,
exquirius 8c., experiolus c 1200, 1251,
(h)esperiolus c 1200, asperiolus c 1212,
asperialus 1434, pirolus a 1446, squirrel,
squirrel-fur.
scurgia, (?) scourge c 1325; *cf.* escorgeria.
scurio 1229, querreus 1573, quirreus 1573,
1583, quirius 1579, equerry.
scurole, *see* scrofule.
scurr/a, mercenary c 1218, 1345; -ilis,
unchaste 6c.; -ilitas, coarse jest 7c., 8c.
scurtio, *see* excurto.
scussellus, *see* scutum.
scuta 1204, 1275, scouta 1295, 1465, schuta
c 1320, schoutum c 1365, shut/a, -us 1279,
1383, shouta 1321, 1403, (?) shota 1329,
'scout', barge (naut.); -agium, carriage by
barge 1367; -arius, barge-man 1355.
*scut/ella c 1080, c 1502, -ellum a 1128,
1330, -ellus 1214, 1419, scotella 1425,
scultella c 1296, squdellus 1335, schilla
15c., skylla c 1266, squilla 1263, dish or
bowl; ‡-ellula, "voider" 1520; -ellulum,
"saucer" c 1500; -ella c 1125, 1198, -ellus
1232, squela a 1200, -ellata 1234, scul-
tellata 1222, bowlful (measure of corn,
etc.); schilla (skilla), bell (at high table in
refectory) (mon.) c 1072, c 1520; schiletta
1376, skeletta, scaletta 1308, skillet;
skeletta, small peal of bells 14c.;
 -ellaria 1242, 1390, -elria c 1290,
-illaria 1325, squillaria 1366, 1403,
squileria 1317, 1403, scullery (household
office); 1255, squieleria 1237, swileria
1310, scullery (room or building); squy-
lerya 1317, esquillaria 1332, pots and pans
(*coll.*); ‡-ellarium, "dish-bench" 1483;
*-ellarius c 1136, 1378, -illarius 1340,
-ularius 1086, c 1270, squelarius c 1300,
squillarius 1377, squylourius c 1472,
-ilator a 1300, 'squiller', scullion; squillarius, (?) bellringer (mon.) 1398.
scutico, to lash 1252.
scut/um 1243, c 1488, -us c 1320, -ulum
1415, 1654, ‡-ellum c 1440, -icum 1285,
scucheo a 1210, 1338, scucho 1338,
scuchettum 1367, 1377, coat of arms,
scutcheon; unit of scutage, knight's fee
c 1220, c 1395; (?) metal plate 1301, 1543;
skew ashlar (arch.) 1253, 1318; 1334, 1338,
sceutum 1309, -ella 1338, shield of brawn;
c 1160, 1608, -us 1362, -um auri 1341,
1461, -us aureus 1359, florenus -aneus
c 1362, f. de scuto 1339, 1349, scussellus
(G.) 1339, coin, *écu*; s. carruce, plough-
shield 1316; s. liberalitatis, (symbol of)
noble rank c 1185;
 *-agium 1100, 1586, scuagium a 1165,

a 1230, escuagium 1284, scuachium
1310, scotagium c 1200, scutage, commutation of knight service; squieria, (?) service
as squire 13c.; -arius, shield-wright 1166,
‡15c.; a 1100, c 1400, (?) †sucarius c 1280,
squierius c 1208, esquierus 1216, esqui-
erius 1301, esquirius (Norm.) 1200,
*-ifer 1226, 1508, -iferus 1361, -iger
a 1123, 1213, shield-bearer, squire; -ifer,
esquire (title, esp. Sc.) 1412, 1478; (*adj.*)
shield-bearing 1252; c 1595, -iger c 1595,
armigerous; -ile, shoulder-blade c 550;
-ulatus, dappled c 1300, ‡c 1440; -atus,
decorated with scutcheons 1388.
scuvagium, *see* scabinus.
scuyra, *see* SQUARR
scybalon (σκύβαλον), dung: squibalum a 1250,
‡c 1440.
scyldwyrhta, *see* schildebredum.
Scylla: (?) silla (cilla), slanderous critic
c 1180.
scynifes, *see* cinyphes.
†scynthenium, mark, blemish a 615.
scyphus (sciphus), bowl, goblet, cup: scipus
(schipus) 1386, 1432, *cyph/us (ciph-, cif-,
chiph-) 1136, c 1450, cipus c 1000. 15c.,
cephus 1435, cepus 15c., siphus (siffus),
siphum 1200, 1449, ciffa 13c., cippa 1251;
-us cum pede 1224, 1371, s. stans 1448,
a 1525, standing cup; *cf.* cuppa, sippa;
sciffus, communion cup c 1000; -ulus,
small cup a 1150, 1202; -a 1419, -us (C.I.)
1309, dry measure; cipha allecium
c 1472; -ata c 1208, 1232, -atus 1241,
c 1340, -iata c 1250, cupful; -arium 1440,
-orium c 1443, siphorium c 1456, cupboard or cup-band; -arius 1439, 1462, -ifer
c 1487, ‡-igerulus 1483, cup-bearer; ‡"cup-
maker" 15c., 1483; squivatus (†squinatus),
gold coin, *scyphatus* (It.) 1245.
‡scytal/a, "ermine", "mouse" 1570; -is, kind
of snake 8c.
scytheaticum, molendinum, "blade-mill"
1577.
Scyth/ia, liquorice: ‡squicia 14c.; *see also*
Scotus.
se, *him (not reflexive)* 12c., 15c.; *per se,
separately 1167, 1404; se altero, with one
other 1215, 1270; pro se a., for himself and
one other 1324; se tertio, with two others
1215, c 1410; se quarto (ad equum) 1367;
se quinto c 1220, 1466; se decimo c 1260,
1367; se duodecimo c 1135; se solo, by
himself c 1340; sibe c 730, sivi (?) 824, *for
sibi; *cf.* suus.
seas/enabilis, -onabilis, *see* seiso.
seasio, *see* seisina.
seatium, *see* SECAL
‡sebel, inflammation of the eye 14c., 1652.
sebesten, Assyrian plum a 1250, 1424.
‡sebibo, to drink alone 1483.
seb/um, tallow: cebum c 1250, 1531,
*cepum c 1130, c 1550, cepa 1419, sepum
c 1130, 1329, scepum 1286, 1301, sepe
1307, sepium 1185, c 1200, sepo 1224,
seubum 1276, sevum 1528; s. ad cande-
las 1284, 1301; candela cepi 1461, c. de
cepo 1288, c 1550; secutum 1182, suetum
1318, secta 1548, suet; ‡-ator, chandler
1570; †-o, (?) to grease c 1177.

sec/a, sica c 1330, (?) **sechia** 1214, saw; **s. ad trussandum**, trussing-saw c 1330; sia (sya) 1219, 1299, scia 1373, sickle *or* reaping service; ‡-arium, trencher 1483; ‡faber -arius, "blade-smith" c 1520; -atio 1304, a 1540, scicatio 1294, siatura 1279, cutting, sawing; -atura c 1186, p 1200, siatura 1278, reaping; -ator, cutter 1294; -tator 1307, scicator 1295, cicator 1289, sciator 1279, siator 1260, c 1280, sior 1283, sawyer; syator, reaper 1276; -ans, secant (geom.) 1686; -o, to dissect (med.) 1552; **s. pannum** c 1270, 1294; **s. prata, s. in pratis**, to mow 1086; ceco 1405, sico 1279, sicco 1461, ciko 1280, cyco, scio 1296, sio 1283, 1298, to saw; *cf.* sawyator, scegga, sectio.

secal/e, rye: sigalum 1212, 1518, sigulum 15c., ‡seatium c 1250; -icius c 1620, ‡sigaliceus 1483, sigulaceus, (?) selaceus 1500, -inus 1634, ‡sigalinus 15c., made of rye; *cf.* siligo.

seccheria, *see* SICC

secchimen, *see* sagimen.

seceliones, secallones, *see* seckeliones.

sec/ennium, *see* sexannalis; -enti, *see* SEXCENT

‡secerniculum, "portcullis" c 1440; *cf.* SECRET

secess/io, rising of court (leg.) c 1178; -us, defecation *or* anus (med.) c 1210, a 1446; death c 1470; -or, seceder 6c.; secedo, to withdraw homage 1086; **s. in fata**, to die c 1470.

sechet/a, -um, *see* 1 sica.

sechia, *see* seca.

secida, *see* cecidos.

seck/eliones 1246, seceliones 1261, secallones 1255, -iliones 1251, -illones 1234, 1253, sequilones 13c., seculones 1251, loppings (*pl.*).

secla, *see* sigla.

seclino, to ward off 1427.

seclirotenta, *see* sclerotica.

seclus/io, setting aside c 1470; -im, privately c 1500.

secondarius, *see* SECUND

secors, *for* socors, c 1434, ‡1483.

secrest-, secrist-, *see* SACRIST

secret/a a 975. c 1182, c 1500, -um 1195, 1502, 'secret' (liturgical); **in** -is, secretly 1375; -um, privy seal (Sc.) 1382, 1426; private room c 1000; 1223, 1401, **fovea** -aria c 1250, **thalamus** -us c 1285, privy; -a nature, privy parts (?) 14c.; relieving nature c 1330, 14c.; -a 1281, **s. diei** 1304, secret presentments at court leet (*cf.* privata); **clericus ad** -a **regis** 1420; -a (*pl.*) **ecclesie** 14c., -aria c 1072, -arium c 760, c 1006. c 1125, c 1414, sacristy *or* sanctuary (eccl.); -aria, secretariat p 1337; **clericus** -arie (Sc.) 1479, 1496; -arium, bishop's room c 730; hidden place 7c.; **meditationis** c 1250; **s. refectionis** (mon.) 1549; **s. sapientie** (fig.) a 1175; -alis, confidential c 1325;

-arius, *confidential adviser or representative, secretary 794. c 1190, c 1540; (?) spy 1322; sacristan (eccl.) a 1090, c 1414 (*cf.* SACRIST); **s. astrorum**, confidant of the stars c 1160; **s. Dei** c 1340; **s. regis**, *king's clerk or counsellor c 1190, 1364; 1395, 1535, **s. regius** c 1550, keeper of signet, secretary of state; -im, secretly 826; -issime, most secretly 826; *-us, intimate, confidential, a confidant c 1300, 1461; -o, to deal with confidentially c 1470; *see also* **a secretis**, consilium, sella, sigillum; *cf.* secerniculum.

1 sect/a, *pursuit (of hue and cry) 1195, 1394; *suite, following, faction 1166, a 1450; crew (naut.) 1223; family or household (of serf) a 1190, c 1350; c 1190, c 1400, -um c 1200, offspring (of animals); *1260, 1533, **s. unica** 1393, *suit (of clothes), livery, fashion; *set (of vessels, *etc.*), standard shape or size 1320, 1490; 1202, c 1502, seuta, sieuta 1313, *suit, prosecution (leg.); suit, petition 1587; *'suit', body of witnesses produced in court (leg.) 1196, 1419; **s. de sanguine**, suit produced from among kindred 1282; *-a c 1150, 1543, secuta c 1170, suita 1181, -antia 1178, sectatio 1276, suit of court (leg.) or service, attendance or fulfilment of customary obligation (or payment in lieu); **s. cerevisie**, attendance at 'fust-ale' 1299; **s. comitatus** 1247, 1258, **s. scirarum** 1227; **s. communis** (leg.) 13c., 1366; **s. curie** a 1230, 1531, **a. ad curiam** c 1150, 1430, suit of court; **s. hundredi** 1156, c 1284, **s. ad hundredum** 1222, 1289; **s. falde**, 'fald-soken' c 1200; **s. forinseca**, (?) 'outsoken' (payment by outsiders for use of mill) c 1267; **s. molendini** c 1170, 1276, **s. ad molendinum** 1222, 1352, **s. multure** 1418, 'mill-soken'; **s. pacis (regis)**, liability to prosecution for breach of peace 1241, 1583; **s. regis** 1357, 1361; **s. ad Parliamentum** c 1320; **s. prisone**, *see* sueta; **s. ad scutagium** c 1397; **s. ad tinctoriam** 1327; **s. ad wapentachium** 1258; *cf.* soca; *see also* sebum;

terra -abilis, t. cectabilis, land subject to suit 1255; -arius 12c., 1234, *-ator 1230, 17c., cectator 1462, sutator 1470, sutor 1292, suitor, tenant owing suit of court (*see also* seca); *-ator curie 1269, 1595; **s. hundredi** 1275, c 1340; **s. capelle**, member of chapel congregation 1261; **s. chori**, chorister 1506; **s. Parliamenti**, member of Parliament c 1320; **s. regalitatis** (Sc.) 1509; -atrix, follower, practiser (*f.*) c 800, c 980. a 1200, 15c.; -atus, pursuit c 1160; -o, to sue, prosecute (leg.) 1586, 1588; -or curiam 1255, **s. ad c.** 1496, to pay suit of court; *cf.* SECUT

2 sect/a (eccl.), -atio c 730, sect; -alis, sectarian (*adj.*) 1412; -arius, adherent, partisan c 1250, c 1318; sectary, schismatic 1552, 1609.

†sectagium, *f.l.* for **scutagium**, c 1362.

secties, *see* sexies.

sect/io, portion, fragment c 1362; portion of benefice (eccl.) 1284; section of book c 1080, 12c.; dividing line (her.) c 1595; a 1200, 1267, **s. communis** a 1150, intersection (geom.); **s. crucea**, optic commissure 1267; **s. pannorum** c 1130; -ator burci, cut-purse 1304; -ivus, cutting c 1300; *cf.* seca.

seculones, *see* seckeliones.
secul/um, *this world, this life 815, 939.
c 1070, c 1400; *the created universe c 1125,
c 1546; *temporal affairs, worldly cares or
temptations c 1080, 1467; s. futurum, the
next world a 1142; -are, secular benefice
(eccl.) 1459; -aris, (*adj.*) *worldly, transitory 732, 869. c 1075, c 1400; pagan c 1100,
1448; *765. c 1075, c 1553, †-arus 1287,
secular, lay (as opposed to ecclesiastical);
*secular (as opposed to regular) (eccl.)
c 1180, 1461; (*subst.*) layman c 1006. c 1125,
c 1520; member of the secular clergy c 1150,
c 1520; *see also* bracchium, canonicus,
capellanus, exactio, habitus, littera,
monachus, negotium, presbyter, sacerdos, servitium; -arior, more secular 1378;
-aritas, worldliness, worldly life c 1130,
c 1610; -ariter, in worldly fashion c 1115,
15c.; -arizo, to live a worldly life 1378.
secund/um, second (of time) a 1150, 1344;
second (geom.), fraction of degree c 1233,
1326; -e (*pl.*) stellarum, falling stars, mete-
ors 1267; -eintentionaliter, as of second
intention (log.) 1516; *cf.* intentio; *feria
-a, Monday c 980. 1086, 1517; panis -us,
second-rate bread c 1185; -us melior 1234,
1417, -o melior 1279, second-best; -ogeni-
tus, second-born 1347, 1499; -oprimus,
second c 730; -alitas, quality of being
second (log.) c 1290; *cf.* intentio; -arius
c 1250, 1483, -icerius c 793, eccl. official;
c 1275, 1526, secondarius 1431, second-
grade clerk or other secular official; an accessory (leg.) c 1258, c 1290; effectus -arius
a 1250; -aria (*pl.*) c 1524, festa -aria
c 1266, minor feasts (eccl.); -arie 1220,
c 1466, -ario c 1218, 1610, in the second
place; -ina a 1250, 1267, tela s. a 1250,
choroid coat of eye; -o, to repeat c 1100;
to place second, subordinate c 1200; to put
in second place (math.) a 1150.
secundum quid, in a certain respect, κατά τι
(log.) 13c., c 1357.
secuplex, *see* SEXT
secur/is carecte, (?) axle 1218; s. Danica,
pole-axe c 1118; s. guerrina, battle-axe
1451; -icula, little axe 1440; "brick-axe"
1490; -a, (?) *for* -is, axe 1297, 1533.
secur/itas, -atio, preservation, safeguarding
c 1470; -e, surely, certainly c 1330, c 1370;
correctly 1512; -o, safely a 1408; -us, trustworthy a 1408; c 1330, c 1370, (with *gen.*)
1166, 1221, s. de a 1142, 1416, sure (of);
see also conductus; -um facio, to give
surety to (leg.) 1218, 1266; -ato quod, provided that a 1250; -o, to preserve, safeguard
c 1443, c 1470.
secursus, *see* SUCCURS
secus (*prep.*), against c 730; *beside, near
(bibl.) c 760, c 900. c 1090, c 1400; *see also*
CEC
secut/a, -icen, *see* 1 secta; CICUT
secut/io, following 13c., a 1292; -a (*n. pl.*),
consequences 1419;
    sequ/ax, follower, disciple, successor
a 615, c 980. c 1135, c 1470; -aces (*pl.*)
a 1190, c 1330, -acia (*coll.*) 12c., young (of
animals); -acitas, willingness to follow
a 615; -ela, act of following 1318, 16c.;

pursuit 13c., 1297; *suite, following, retinue
c 1175, 1558; *family or household (of serf)
c 1180, 1583; offspring (of animals) 12c.,
1512; appurtenance 1259, (?) 1301; 'suit',
body of witnesses produced in court (leg.)
c 1190, 1263; suit of court (leg.) c 1185,
1553; suit of service c 1150, c 1370; s.
foreste, suit of forest court 1189; s. molendini, 'mill-soken' c 1197, 1559; s. tabernarum, frequenting of taverns 1274;
    -entia, *sequence, hymn (eccl.) c 980,
c 1006. c 1080, c 1480; sequence-book
(eccl.) c 1450, 1521; -ipeda 794. c 1160,
1200, †-ipedus 1200, follower; -ens, successor 1308; suitor to a court 1324; (*adj.*)
uniform in quality 1312; per -ens, in consequence 14c.; secor, *for* -or, 1232, 1263;
-or (*pass.*), to be followed 893. 1251, 1321;
s. carectam, to drive a cart 1278; s. con-
ventum, (?) to follow conventual routine
1324; s. scottum, to share scot and lot
1229; -or c 1200, 1327, s. curiam c 1180,
c 1397, s. placitum c 1110, 1183, to pay
suit of court; s. faldam 1086; s. molendinum 1197, 1430; s. huthesium, to
follow the hue and cry 1271, 14c.; -or, to
sue for, claim 1201; to sue, prosecute (*absolutely*) 1199, c 1334; s. homicidium 1167,
s. mortem c 1220, to prosecute for homicide; s. appellum, to pursue an 'appeal'
(leg.) 1260; s. billam, to prosecute a bill
1334; s. breve, to prosecute a writ a 1218,
c 1290; s. petitionem 1327; s. placitum,
to prosecute a plea c 1236, 1376; s. contra
1274, s. versus c 1218, c 1320, to proceed
against, to prosecute (leg.); *cf.* 1 secta.
secutum, *see* sebum.
sed, unless, except c 1320; *set, *for* sed,
1086, 1319.
sed/agium, -alis, *see* sedes.
sedeo, *see* SESS
sed/es, site (of building) 1086, c 1400; siege
1199, 1465; *episcopal see 725, c 900. c 1070,
1549; abbatial see c 1100; office (of bailiff)
1203; judgement-seat or meeting-place of
court (leg.) 1202; session (of guild or council)
1227, 1335; place, membership (in guild)
1198, 1260; (?) measurement of width (of
cloth) 1272, 1278; s. apostolica 803. c 1070,
1565, s. Romana 1074, 1345, papal see;
s. campane 1427; s. in Parliamento
c 1412; s. piscarie, fishing-place 1086,
1311; s. navis 1267, 1304, (?) †seyya 1190,
-agium 1318, 1341, segeagium 1317, 1451,
seggagium 12c., 1376, sejagium 1330,
1348, harbour-due; seges, seat a 1300;
ecclesia -alis, episcopal church a 1250;
sado, (?) *f.l.* for -o, to set in place 1328;
cedo, *for* -o, to assuage c 1290, 1506; *see
also* cedes.
sedil/e, Exchequer bench c 1290, 1454; s.
altum 1391; s. longum 1446, 1481; s.
sub pedibus, foot-stool 1382; -ia 1518,
-ium c 1320, sidile, cidile 1499, *for* -e;
sedula, stool c 1311.
sedimen, *see* SESS
seditio, dissension: cediti/o 1461; -osus,
seditious 1279; sedutiose, seditiously 1485;
cf. seductio.
sedlopum 1235, sadelepa a 1211, sellopum

c 1230, (?) †sellus (Norfolk) 1127, a 1145, (?) solopium 1317, 1338, 'seed-lepe', seed-basket, measure of corn.

seduala, see zedoaria.

seduc/tio (bibl.) c 1115, p 1380, -tus 1425, c 1434, seduction, misleading; (?) for seditio, treason 1280, 1292; -ibilis c 1250, c 1343, -tibilis c 1196, gullible, easily misled; c 1190, -tivus c 1250, c 1380, seductive; -tive c 1290, -torie c 1196, 1347, seductively, deceitfully; *-tor (bibl.) 6c., c 730. c 1090, c 1450, -trix (f.) c 600. 12c., 1302, seducer, deceiver, traitor; *-o (bibl.), to mislead, deceive, bring to harm c 1080, 1461; s. curiam (leg.) 1199, 1226; s. ad mortem, to condemn to death c 1115.

sedul/us, chronic (med.) c 730; sidule, for -e, 9c.; see also SCHED; SEDIL

seduus, see ceduus.

seellus, bucket (Fr. seau) (Norm.) 1198.

seferus, see ZEPHYR

seffrana, see saffranum.

seg/amen, -imen, see sagimen.

seg/eagium, -gagium, see sedes.

segeara, see sicera.

seg/es, field (Ir.) 1501; -etella, little harvest 1252; -esterium 1537, -isterium ‡c 1440, 1532, ‡sagisterium, sigesterium 15c., sigisterium c 1470, -estrum 1364, -istrum a 1408, draff, hog's wash; -isilium, (?) fodder-rack (for pigs) 1282; see also sedes.

segga 1272, (?) sagum a 1200, (?) segera 1424, (?) †setum (Ir.) 1343, sedge.

segla, see sigla.

seglio, see sarculatio.

segment/atio, gobbony blazoning (her.) c 1595; -atus, gobbony (her.) c 1595.

segnor-, seignur-, seinur-, see senior.

segreg/atio, separation c 1250, c 1325; -atim, separately 1136, c 1390; -ativus, separative c 860. 1610.

segrestanus, see SACRIST

seia, see 1 seta.

seil-, see also 1 selio.

seilam, darnel (bot.) (Ar. shailam) 12c.

seina, see 1 sagena.

seintarius, see sainctarius.

*seis/ina c 1157, 1583, *saisina 1159, 1512, sasina (Sc.) 1366, 1564, sazina (Sc.) 1537, sesina 1305, c 1370, saesina (C.I.) 1321, †-na c 1385, saisio 1086, saisitio 1086, 1130, seisin, sasine (Sc.), possession (leg.); s. plena 1196, 1390, s. plenaria c 1195, 15c., plenary seisin; s. prima, primer seisin 1245, 1282; s. simplex 1229, 1333; s. de catallis 1241; -iatio c 1196, saisiatio a 1200, seising, putting in possession; (G.) 1283, -itio c 1400, (?) saisina (G.) 1315, seizing, taking possession; -itio in manus c 1396;

saisitor 1086, -itor c 1290, seisor, one who gives seisin; -itor 1186, 1265, -iator 1265, one who seizes (into king's hand); -iatus de furto c 1115; saiatus ad opus regis 1086; †-ino 1291, *-io (de) 1086, 1583, *saisio (de) 1086, 1575, sasio (de) 1086, (Sc.) c 1540, sesio (de) 13c., -o (de) c 1170, -io in 1194, c 1300, to seise, put in possession (of) (leg.); *-io 1185, 1583, seizio 1313, saisio c 1115, 1461, saisisco

(Norm.) 1080, sasio (G.) 1279, 1283, sazio (G.) 1283, 1304, †seasio 13c., -o 1361, sacio (satio) 1269, 14c., to seize, take possession of; *s. in manum 1185, 1513, s. in manu 1209, 1419.

seis/o 1214, -ona 1221, 1367, †-ina 1280, sesona 1272, 1341, season; 1279, -ona (terre) 1262, 1364, -io seminabilis 1222, sowing of grain, course of cropping, land sown in a particular course; season of heat (for mares) 1359; -ona, saisona 1219, sesona 1272, s. asturcorum 1297, season (falc.); 1400, s. pinguedinis 1272, 1298, hunting season; s. fermesonis 1272, s. mortua 1290, 1300, close season (for game); s. piscationis 1321, 1357; s. vindemie, vintage season 1312; s. estivalis 1309, 1340, s. estatis 1315, summer; s. hiemalis (yemalis), winter 1297, 1340; winter sowing 1299, 1398; s. quadragesimalis c 1340, s. quadragesime 1364, spring sowing; saisione (saisuna) mutationis (falc.) 1204; sesena 1303, (?) sesinitas 1393, well seasoned condition (of wool-fells); -onabilis 1487, -ionabilis 1400, seasenabilis 1504, seasonabilis a 1564, sesionabilis 1483, cesionalis 1477, seasonable; -onabiliter, seasonably 1388, 1439; male -inatus, ill-seasoned (of bread) 1412; -ono, to sow (land) 1275, 1323; to impregnate (mares) 1359; cf. saticulum; see also sessio.

sejagium, see sedes.

sejagium, see sedes.

sekeria, see SICC

sel-, see also cel-

selaceus, see SECAL

selare, see 2 celum.

selarium, see cellarium; salarium; sol.

†selauma, (?) a garment c 1370.

*seld/a a 1155, 1419, †selida 1401, scelda 1160, celda 1250, 1549, seolda a 1549, c 1220, †soelda a 1205, *seuda c 1185, 1342, sceuda 15c., scouda 1198, †seunta 14c., solda c 1220, 1395, shelda 1287, 1588, esselda c 1135, 'seld', stall, shop; -agium c 1170, 1257, seudagium 1245, toll on stalls; see also sella.

seldra, see CALD

selen/ographia, map of the moon c 1612, 1620; silenites, for -ites, selenite c 1200, a 1250.

selfod/us 1282, 1317, -is 1282, 1378, 'selfoder', class of tenant (Cumb. & Northumb.); sulfodis, villein householder (Glos.) 1209.

sel/ichus, seal, 'selch' (Sc.) c 1150; pellis -ina, corium -inum, seal-skin 1295.

1 *sel/io a 1190, 1588, †-vus a 1182, -o c 1220, 1222, †-lennia a 1224, seilio c 1185, 13c., seillo c 1182, 1276, †seillum c 1250, †seilinium (? seilunum) c 1185, †seullenia a 1225, sailo c 1240, c 1265, sailona c 1182, sallio a 1250, c 1270, †seygnus, †seyglus c 1182, silio 1282, 1302, sullo 1234, 1421, -iunca a 1182, a 1190, -iuncula a 1190, 'selion', strip of ploughland (Fr. sillon); s. capitalis, strip lying in headland c 1182, 1430; s. curtus c 1240; s. magnus a 1200.

2 selio, (?) faggot 1342.

selithe, see theriaca.

seliunca, see saliunca; 1 selio.

selix, *see* salicia.

sell/a, saddle: *cella c 1282, 1539, scella 1242, c 1322, zella c 1533, selda 1217, †acella c 1397; -a, 'stool', purging (med.) a 1250; s. canonicorum 1281, s. monachalis 1454; s. ad carectam 1282, 1312, s. pro carecta 1338, s. carecte c 1300, 1350, s. carectaria 1309, 1449, s. carectiva 1294, 1486; s. cariagii 1356, 1398; s. equestris c 1170, s. equina 1381; s. Francigena 1510; s. lignea, saddle-base 1309, 1325; s. privata 1214, s. secreta 1213, (?) seat for privy; s. somalis 1313, s. summagialis 1377, s. summaria (somaria) 1225, c 1335, s. summaricia 1238, s. ad summarium (someram) 1242, c 1232, sumpter-saddle; -aria, saddlers' quarter 1288; ‡-arium, saddler's shop 1483; *see also* cellarium, salarium; *-arius a 1123, 1588, cellarius c 1350, *-ator 1175, 1500, cellator 1472, (?) -eator 1185, saddler; -io, saddle-horse 1275; -atus, saddled c 1370, 1461.

sell/atura, sel/um, -o, -ura, *see* 2 celum.

sellennia, *see* 1 selio.

selleta, *see* saletta.

sellum, *see* sillum.

sellus, *see* sedlopum.

sema, *see* sagma.

semel atque simul c 1090, simul et s. c 1250, 1309, at one and the same time.

semela, *see* simila.

semella, sole (of shoe) 1245, c 1330; somellatus, (?) soled 1392; *see also* semita.

sem/en, sowing 1271, c 1345; s. hiemale 1330, c 1397; s. quadragesimale c 1283, a 1540, s. vernale 1358, 1364; s. Canariense, "canary seed" 1634; s. lini, linseed 1472; s. lumbricorum, worm-seed 1480; †-entina (? -entiva) traductio, procreation a 1200; -entinum 1349, -ellio 1297, -elo 1329, -ilio 1269, 1485, -ilo 1245, 1538, †servilo 1297, -ulo 1309, 1315, semin/ale 1375, -arium 1251, 1321, -atorium 1274, 1325, (?) semiculum 1270, 'seed-lepe', seed-basket; seisio -abilis, sowing season 1222; terra -abilis 1086, 1348, t. -alis 1394, land ready for seed; -agium, (?) seed-plot 15c.; †summagium, (?) seed-time 1199; -alis (bibl.), -arius a 1235, 13c., -ativus a 1235, c 1362, seminal, germinal; -aliter, like a seed 1153; -arium, brood c 550; sacerdos -arius, seminary priest 1660; -ium cultus, monastery c 950; -atio 1222, c 1458, -atura c 1175, c 1236, †sementia 1274, †sementus c 1313, sowing; s. discordie 1284; s. Verbi, preaching 1549; -ator, sower c 730. c 1300; s. discordiarum c 1250; s. Verbi 1549, -iverbius c 900. c 1090, 1345, preacher; -atrix, disseminator (f.) c 1157, 1526; †semo 1204, zemno (†gemno) 1275, *for* semino, to sow.

semens/is, (?) lasting six months c 1310; -tre 1241, -truum p 1394, *for* semestre, half-year; *see also* semimenstruus.

sement-, *see* CEMENT

semetra (pl.), out-of-the-way places, devious ways c 980. c 1090, c 1125.

semevectorium, *see* cenevectorium.

semia, *see* simia.

semi/albus, half-white c 730. c 1217, 15c.; -annus, half-year 9c.; -antrum, half-cave c 700; -argenteus, party-argent (her.) 1654; -aureus 1235; -bene, half-well c 1432: -berengarius, inclining to the doctrine of Berengarius 1427; -bos, half the time or labour of an ox 1086; half bovine in form 13c.; -brevis, semibreve (mus.) 1326, c 1470; s. major, s. minor 1326; s. minorata, s. obliqua c 1470; -bulla, half-bubble c 1615; ‡-cadium, "kilderkin" 1570; ‡-cadus, "runlet" 1570; -calciatus, half-shod c 1000; -cancellarius, titular chancellor c 1250; -canus, grizzled c 1190; -carcatus, half-laden 1290; -cardinalis, midway between cardinal points 1622; ‡-cecus, half-blind 15c.; -chalceus, half of copper 1235; ‡-cinctorium, apron 15c.; -cingo, to half-encircle c 1212.

semicircul/us, semicircle 1267, c 1470; -aris a 1233, 1267, -atus c 1200, semicircular; -ariter, in a semicircle c 1270; -atio, semicircular course 13c.

semi/circumferentia, semi-circumference a 1233, 1686; -clausio, half-shutting a 1250; -claudo, to half-close 794. 1267; simicommune, half-rations (ac.) c 1546; -conversus, half-transformed c 1217; -corrosus, half-elided, clipped c 1180; -cotlandum, half cot-land 1364; ‡-cupium, bath-tub 15c.; -cyclium c 860, -cyclus c 1250, semicircle; -cyclois, hemicycloid 1686; -demon, half-devil a 1408; *-diameter, radius a 1233, 1686; -diametralis, radial c 1270; -diametraliter, radially c 1270; -ditonus, a minor third 1351; -dormito, to be half asleep 6c.; -equus, half-horse (of a centaur) c 1217; -eternitas, semi-immortality 870; -evaginatus, half-unsheathed 14c.; -excitatus, half-awake a 1200; -facio, to perform imperfectly (A.S. samwyrcan) 1102; -femina, half-woman (of a mermaid) 13c.; -ferdellarius, tenant of half-fardel 1485; -foramen, notch a 1350; -fractus, half-broken c 730; -frater, half-brother c 1300, c 1400; †-gilatus, half-covered c 550; -gradus, half-degree (ac.) 1435; -gratia, partial favour c 1330; -homunculus, incomplete man a 1205; -horula, brief half-hour c 1620. -insula, peninsula c 1325; -laicus, partly layman a 1186; -lancea, half a lance a 1525; -longa, imperfect long note (mus.) 1326; -lotum, half-ounce 15c.; -marca, half-mark 8c.; -mas, unmanly man 1136; -masculus, half-man 794; -menstruus, lasting a fortnight c 1616; recurring fortnightly 1620; ‡semensis, fortnight 1570; -miles, half-knight's fee or service a 1200; -milliare 1622, -milliarium c 1470, half-mile; -minor, half-minor note (mus.) c 1470; -minutum secundum, half-second 1686; -mutilatus, half-mutilated c 1125, c 1362; -niger, half-black c 1200, c 1217; party-sable (her.) 1654; -nox, half-night c 1370; -opus, half-task (man.) c 1230.

semin-, semil-, semiculum, *see also* semen.

seminellus, *see* simila.

seminum, *see* cyminum.

semio, *see* ASSEM

semi/panis, half-loaf 634; **-pannus**, half-garment 14c.; **-paralyticus**, half-paralysed c 1090, a 1135; **-pars**, half 14c.; **-passagium**, one-way ferry-due 1606; **-pauper**, almost destitute 1574; **-pedale**, distance of ½ foot a 1350; **-penitentia**, half-penance c 600; **-perimetrum**, **-peripheria** (geom.) 1686; **-pilarius**, 'respond' (arch.) c 1190; **-pisa**, half a split pea 1427; **-piscis**, half-fish (of a mermaid) 13c.; **-puratus**, half-prepared (of fur) 1327; **-putridus**, half-decayed c 1185; ‡**-quarta**, "pint" 15c.; **-quarterium**, measure of land (Ir. *leathcheathramhath*) 1501; **-receptus**, half-restored (of health) c 1172; **-rex**, half-king c 1000. c 1170, c 1434; **-rubeus**, half-red 15c.; **-ruptus**, half-broken c 1192; **-sanus**, half-sane c 1200; half-restored to health c 1325; **-Scotus**, half Scot 1461; **-secularis**, half-secular c 1255, c 1257; **-sedeo**, to adopt a half-sitting position c 1350; **-sericus**, half-silken 1537; **-sextula**, half a sixth fragment c 1620; **-sonus**, semi-vocalic (gram.) 7c.; **-sphera**, hemisphere a 1233; **-structus**, half-built c 1100; **-summa**, half-sum (math.) 1686; **-suspirium**, half-sigh c 1250.

semishida, half a hide (of land) c 1450.

1 **semita**, bar (her.) c 1595; s. **pedalis**, footpath 1449; s. **regia** c 1225; **semella**, narrow path 15c.

2 †**semita**, (?) *f.l.* for **scutica**, 1300.

semi/terium, **-torium**, *see* **cemeterium**.

semi/tonus, semitone (mus.) c 1248; **-tracto**, to discuss in part 14c.; **-truncatus**, half-mutilated c 1192; **-Turchicus**, half-Turkish 1555.

semitus, *see* **semen**.

semi/ulcus, *for* **-hiulcus**, half-open c 1115; **-uncia**, *for* **semuncia**, half of one-twelfth 12c.; (fig.) scanty dress 13c.; ‡**-urna**, "gallon" 1570.

semivectoria, *see* **cenevectorium**.

semi/verbium, half-word 1200; **-vestitus**, half-clothed 15c.; **-videns**, half-seeing 1302; **-villa**, half-townland (Ir. *leathbhaile*) 1501; **-villanus**, villein holding half the usual tenement a 1128; **-virgata**, half-yardland 1390, 1466; **-virgatarius**, tenant of half-yardland 1253, 1485; **-vivens**, half-alive c 1250; **-voltatus**, half-vaulted c 1488.

semo, *see* **semen**.

semotim, separately c 1190, a 1250.

sempecta, *see* **senpecta**.

semp/er secundo anno, every second year 1299; **ad s.** c 1343, **pro s.** c 1343, 1346, for ever; **-ermobile**, (*subst.*) constant changing 870; **-iternitas**, eternity c 760; **-iternaliter** 680, 790. c 1090, c 1270, **pro -iterno** c 1470, eternally, **-erternus**, for **-iternus**, c 1284.

Sempinghamensis, Gilbertine (mon.) 12c., c 1260.

†**semulentum**, sediment c 1360.

†**semus**, (?) bastard c 1250.

Semy mare, (? sea of Shem) Mediterranean (Ar.) c 1270.

sen/a 1480, 1538, **-e** a 1250, 13c., senna (bot.); *see also* **cena**.

senagium, *see* **SYNOD**

senapium, *see* **SINAP**

sen/arius, space of six days c 1450; sixth place (play on **denarius**) a 1166; **denarius -arius**, (tax of) sixth penny c 1310; **-us**, six 870, 944; (in rhyming verse) sixth c 1190.

senat/or, member of Witan (?) 10c. c 1115, 13c.; *jurat* (C.I.) 1565; †**-orium**, senatorial rank c 1362; **-ulus**, petty senate 1555; **-us**, senate (ac.) 1610; s. **domesticus**, s. **regius**, Privy Council 1535; s. **Parliamentarius** c 1548, s. **Parliamenti** 1709.

send/allum, **-ale**, **-ellum**, **-illum**, **-atum**, *see* **cendallum**.

sendul-, *see* **scindula**.

sene, *see* **sena**.

sen/ea, **-ectudo**, *see* **senior**.

senecia, jaw (of pike) a 1200; ‡gill (of fish) c 1440, 15c.

sen/ecio (bot.): **-acio**, **-ecium**, **-ectio** a 1250.

senedale, *see* **SYNOD**

senefectorium, *see* **cenevectorium**.

senellio, *see* **sevellio**.

*****senescal/lus** 1066, 1606, **-dus** c 1167, c 1270, **senscallus** 1396, ‡**sinescallus**, **siniscallus** 15c., seneschal, steward; s. **foreste** 1256; s. **hospitii regis** 1263, 1419, s. **regis** 12c., 1419; s. **Anglie** c 1220, 15c.; s. **Vasconie** 1259, 15c.; **sinscalus**, waiter 790; *****-cia** 1191, 1509, **senescacia** 1253, **senechacia** 1269, **-sia** 1260, c 1370, **senescaucia** 1200, 1276, **-dia** c 1220, **-ea** c 1397, **-lia** c 1191, 1452, **-laria** 1279, 1388, †**senescaria** c 1370, *****-latus** c 1370, 1538, **-liatus** 1461, seneschalry, stewardship; **-latus**, seneschartry (area) (Sc.) 1456, 1558; **-cia**, seneschalry (area) (W.) 1306; s. **foreste** 1253, 1452; s. **hospitii** 1212, 1221; s. **Anglie** 1265, 1377; s. **Vasconie** 1217, c 1250.

seneucia, *see* **soinantagium**.

senevectorium, **senne-**, *see* **cenevectorium**.

seng/ulus, **-larius**, *see* **SINGUL**

sengum, *see* **SYNOD**

senheria, *see* **SICC**

senialiter, *see* **sententialiter**.

senio, dice c 1160; ‡"hazard" 15c.

sen/ior, (*adj.*) the elder 786. 1199, c 1574; principal, most respected 1086, c 1115; (*subst.*) prior or abbot c 600; bishop 720; magnate or official a 1075, c 1115; lord, superior 8c., 893. c 1100; s. **populi**, alderman c 1150; **S. de Musse**, Old Man (*Sheikh*) of the Mountain a 1200; **-ioria**, signory (Venice) 1507; **-ioritas**, seniority 1415, c 1565; 1538, **-ioratus** c 1000, **segnoria** 1563, **seygnuria** 1243, **segnoragium** 1200, **seignuragium** 1189, 1316, **seingnuragium** c 1190, **seinuragium** 12c., 1203, seigneury, lordship; **-iuragius** 1205, **-noragius** c 1225, overlord; **-issimus**, eldest 1391; **-ea** (*for* **-ium**) 6c., **-ectudo** 800, old age.

senn/a, tooth (Heb. *shen*) 6c.; **-osus**, dental c 550.

senodochium, *see* **XENO**

senodoxia, *see* **CENODOX**

senodus, *see* **SYNOD**

senpecta (**senipecta**) 7c. c 1266, c 1330, **sempecta** c 1130, 14c., senior monk (of 50 years' standing).

sens-, *see also* **censura; census.**
senscallus, *see* **senescallus.**
sens/us, feeling expressed in writing, sentiment 802; **s. animalis,** (?) physical sense 14c.; **s. compositus, s. divisus,** proposition modified respectively by qualification of one of its terms and adverbially a 1308; **s. communis,** common source of all senses c 1240, a 1346; **s. grammaticalis** p 1380, c 1590; **census,** *for* **-us,** c 1125; **-arius,** *see* **nervus; -atio,** sensation, perception c 1300, 1378; **-atum,** object of perception a 1250, c 1340; **-ate,** sensibly, prudently c 1090, c 1470; **-atus,** *(adj.)* perceptible to the senses c 1240, c 1360; intelligent (bibl.); *(subst.)* intelligent person c 600, c 1087, c 1258; **-ibilia** *(pl.)* **propria, s. communia,** αἰσθητὰ ἴδια, αἱ. κοινά (log.) c 1300; **-ibilis,** (?) believing on evidence of senses c 1270; **-ibiliter,** perceptibly, on evidence of senses c 1190, 15c.; **-ibilius,** more clearly c 1204; **-ibilitas,** sensitiveness, sensation c 725. c 1090, 13c.; perceptibility 1267, c 1362; **-ificatim,** according to the sense of the word 12c.; **-ificatio,** endowment with sensation c 1240, c 1270;

-ilis c 1115, 1610, **-ualis** a 1233, 1267, perceptible, affecting senses; **-itivus** a 1233, a 1361, **-ativus** a 1230, **-ivus** c 860, **-ualis** a 1110, c 1334, concerned with sensation, sensory; c 1270, a 1446, **-ativus** 1552, capable of sensation, sentient; **concupiscentia -itiva,** sensual lust c 1344; **vita sensualis,** opposed to **v. spiritualis,** c 1250; **-ualiter,** by sense-perception c 1090, c 1430; **-ualitas,** responsiveness to senses, dependence on senses a 1090, 14c.; subservience to senses, sensuality c 1172, c 1456; **-um,** sense, meaning 1555; **sentire** *(subst.),* opinion c 1382; **sentio** (with *inf.*), to think fit 7c.; **-io** 12c., c 1280, **censio** 1433, **sentisco** c 950, *for* **sentio;** *see also* **seusus.**
sententi/a, judicial sentence, condemnation 7c., 8c. c 1125, 1686; **-e** *(pl.),* Peter Lombard's *Sentences* c 1250, 1461; **-aliter** 720. 1196, c 1450, **†senialiter** 1231, in the form of a judicial sentence; implicitly c 1340, c 1365; **petitio -aria,** petition for sentence (leg.) a 1452; **-arius,** student reading the *Sentences* c 1380, 1478; **-atio,** pronouncing sentence c 1376, c 1412; **-ativus,** sententious 1344; **-o,** to decree, pronounce sentence 1177, 1569; to opine, maintain 1267, c 1380.
†senteria, measure of fish (Ponthieu) 1289.
sentinarius, foul 1284.
sent/io, -ire, -isco, *see* **SENS**
sent/is, brooch 7c.; **‡-ix,** *for* **-is,** thorn 14c.; **-icosus,** briery, thorny 8c., c 750. ‡1483.
senus, *see* **senarius.**
senvectorium, *see* **cenevectorium.**
seolda, *see* **selda.**
seorsum *(prep.),* along 1411.
sepa, *see* **cepa.**
***separ/atio (seper-),** weaning 1211, c 1400; 'separation' (astr.) 1184; **-abilitas,** separability c 1270, 1620; 1303, a 1452, **-abile** 1233, 1427, ***-alitas** 1303, a 1452, ***-ale** c 1205, 15c., **ceparale** 1368, **†-ia** 1299, **severallum** 1284, severalty, private hold-

ing; ***-abilis** 1276, c 1395, ***-alis** a 1272, a 1564, **sciperalis** 1567, **severalis** 1255, 1367, **-atus** c 1340, 'several', held in severalty; **-alis** 1271, 1671, **severalis** 1533, several, separate, individual; **-abiliter,** separably c 1070; c 730. 1237, ***-aliter** 1335, 1583, **†-ariter** (?) 11c., **-atim** 1329, 1583, severally, separately; **‡-atorium,** vessel used for separating fluids (alch.) 1652; **-atus,** (?) immaterial, spiritual c 1300; **-ativus,** divisible 790; tending to separate a 1250; **-o,** to place in solitary confinement c 600; to part (tenant) from land 1086; to wean c 1345; **ceparo,** *for* **-o,** 1375; **s. de brevi,** to depart from writ in pleading (leg.) c 1219, 1220.
sep/e, -o, -arius, -atio, *see* **sebum; sepes.**
sepe/ et sepius, time and again 1274; ***-dictus** c 730, c 1000. c 1125, c 1470, ***-fatus** 8c. 11c., c 1542, **†-factus** c 1365, **-memoratus** 798, **-nominatus** 798. 12c., c 1415, **-prefatus** 798, **-tactus** c 1407, oft-mentioned; **sep/ies,** often 1275; **-iuscule,** fairly often 1537; **-issimus,** very frequent p 1330, 14c.
sepel-, *see* **SEPUL**
seper-, *see* **SEPAR**
sep/es captatoria piscium, fish-garth 12c.; **s. venatoria** 12c.; **s. vitis,** vineyard c 1250; **-e** a 1250, 1392, **cepes** 1478, 1491, *for* **-es; -iscula,** little fence 720; **-atio** a 1190, **-issio** 1478, **-ura** 1567, hedging; **-imentum,** trace, tressure (her.) c 1595; **-arius,** hayward 1388; **-ator** 1388, **‡-or** 15c., **-itor** 1407, **-iens** 1508, hedger, "hay-maker"; **-ta** *(pl.),* folds (of wraps) c 1000; **-tum,** "screen" a 1600; ***ceptum** c 1260, c 1520, **sceptum** c 1296, 1494, *for* **-tum,** enclosure; **-trico,** to hedge about c 550.
†sepetella enea, sort of utensil 1440.
sepha, *see* **shopa.**
sepherus, *see* **ZEPHYR**
‡sephirus, hard, dry imposthume (med.) 1652.
sephunculus, (?) *for* **scyphulus** *or* **siphunculus,** "goblet" 1537.
sepillum, *see* **serpyllum.**
seppito, *see* **CESP**
seppus, *see* **cippus.**
sepria, *see* 1 **seta.**
sept-, *see also* **sepes.**
Sept/em Fratrum, festum, (10 July) 1230; **ceptam,** *for* **-em,** 1248; **-emteriones** c 1200, 1333, **tiriones** c 550, *for* **(septem) triones; ‡-entrio,** *aqua fortis* (alch.) 1652; **-emvir,** Imperial Elector 1586; **-ena,** measure of grain 13c.; **febris -ena** (med.) a 1250; **-endialis,** celebrated on the seventh day 1517; **†-emium,** *for* **-ennium,** 1424; **-ennalis** c 1191, 1428, **-ennis** 781. c 1090, c 1475, **†-ennius** c 1290, septennial; **-erni** *(pl.),* groups of seven pages 1267; **-iceps,** seven-peaked 1609; **-ifarie (-ipharie)** c 1436, **-iformiter** 12c., in seven divisions; **-iformitas,** sevenfoldness 7c.; **†-iformus,** *for* **-iformis,** c 1230, **-igenus** 790, **-imembris** p 1300, sevenfold; *see also* **septiplex,** *etc.*
***septiman/a,** week (eccl.); **S. Penosa,** Passion Week 1265; **-alis** c 1115, **‡septimalis** 1378, **-ius** 700, weekly, for the week; **-arius,**

official appointed to weekly course of duty (mon.) c 1125, c 1330; **-atim**, week by week 1333, a 1564.

septim/o, for the seventh time, seventhly 12c., c 1332; **-o decimo**, seventeenthly 1282.

septin/centissimus, for **-gentesimus** 736; **-ginti**, for **-genti**, 1262.

septiped/alitas, seven-foot length 1380; **-alis**, seven feet long 1374, 1380; ‡**-ia**, "gagrylle" (some insect or reptile) 15c.

septipharie, see **septifarie**.

sept/iplex c 800, **-uplus** c 1110, sevenfold; **-empliciter** (bibl.) c 815, **-ipliciter** c 1340, a 1452, **-uplum** 1345, 1414, **in s.** c 1250, sevenfold, seven times over, **-uplo**, to increase sevenfold c 1363.

septr-, see SCEPTR; **sepes**.

Septua/gesima, Septuagesima Sunday 9c., c 1006. c 1080, 1559; **-ginta**, Septuagint 1267.

septus, sept, clan (Ir.) 1566.

sepul-, see also **cepa**.

sepul/crum, tomb-shrine c 1280; the Holy Sepulchre 1461; 13c., 1421, **s. Dominicum** 1421, 1436, (?) **-tura** 1423, Paschal model of Sepulchre; **s. philosophorum**, sort of vessel (alch.) c 1345; **-cretum** 17c., **-tura** c 1450, tomb, burial-place; **-tio** c 700, †**-tera** (for **-tura**) 1310, burial; **-tura** *c 1077, c 1324, **sepelitio** 1083, 1419, burial right or fee; **sepeliarius**, official in charge of burials 14c.; **-crarius**, Knight of the Sepulchre 1276; **-tuarius**, book of obits (eccl.) 1383; **-ta** (pl.), funeral rites a 1408.

sepum, see **cepa**; **sebum**.

sepura, see **sepes**.

sequ-, see also SECUT

*****sequest/rum** 1220, 1684, **-ra** 1279, 1283, sequestration, property sequestrated; **-rarius** 1276, ‡**-arius** 15c., **-rator** 1255, 1684, sequestrator, diocesan collector of spiritual revenues; **-ratim**, in sequestration 1427; **-ratio**, separation c 1000; sequestration (eccl.) 1236, a 1564; **-ro**, to cut off, excommunicate 8c. 12c., c 1478; *to sequestrate (property) (esp. eccl.) c 1188, c 1520; to constrain (person) by sequestration c 1258; to secrete, excrete (med.) a 1250; **s. me**, to abstain c 1400; **s. mente**, to go mad c 1470.

sequilones, see **seckeliones**.

*****ser/a** (cer-) c 833. c 1125, 1510, **-atura** 1254, 1308, **sarratura** (G.) 1312, *****-ura** 1209, 1573, **sarura** 1289, †**-uca** 1332, bolt, lock; key c 1102; **s. equina** 1397, 1510, **-ura equina** 1388, **-ura pro equis** 1316, 1385, fetter-lock; **s. pendens** 1449, 1490, **-ura pendens** 1296, 1389, **-ura pendula** 1306, 1354, hanging-lock, padlock; **s. truncata**, stock-lock 1490; **-ula** c 1000. 1280, ‡15c., ‡**-icula** 15c., small lock, "clicket"; **-ura**, (?) fish-trap 1345; ‡**-arius**, "lockyer" 15c.; **-atio**, locking 1505; **-uratus** 1337, 1417, †**-utus** (f.l.) 1203, locked; **-o**, *to lock c 1125, 1524; to confine (a substance) within its own nature (alch.) a 1252; see also **cera**, **seroitas**.

serabara, see **sarabara**.

seracra (†**sexacra**), **saracra**, (?) acre held

by service of carting dung (A.S. scearn) (Essex) 1222.

seralupinus, see **serapinum**.

serans, see FERR

serapellina, see **xeropellina**.

seraph/, seraph (Heb.) 12c.; *****-in** (bibl.), **ceraphin** 13c. (pl.); **-icus** 1345, 1506, **-inus** a 1205, seraphic.

serapillum, see **serpyllum**.

sera/pinum a 1250, 1322, (?) **-lupinum balsamum** a 1250, serapine (bot.).

†**seratus**, (?) reins c 550.

sercellarius, see CERCELL

serch-, **serciero**, see **cerchia**.

serchancya, see SERJ

sercinola, see SARCIN

sercl-, **sercul-**, **serchel-**, see **sarculatio**; CIRCUL

serdwita, see FYRD

Serena, see SIREN

†**serendum**, measure of land, (?) sowing 1553; cf. **saticulum**.

seren/itas, serenity, serene highness (title) 790, 11c. c 1188, c 1500; **-issimus**, most serene (title) 8c. c 1188, 1558; **serrinus**, (?) for **-us**, a 1250; **-iter**, cheerfully 1508; **-ius** c 1400, **-issime** c 1250; **-atio**, clearing, soothing c 1344, 1437; *****s. conscientie** 1281, c 1397.

serentia 1289, 1290, **cerentia** 1283, (?) churn (cf. O.F. seraine) (Suffolk).

seresum, see **cerasum**.

sercus, see **cera**.

serevisia, see **cervisia**.

serg-, see **cera**; SERJ

sericula, see **sera**.

1 seric/um, silk: *****cericum** 1298, 1521, **cerecum** 1521, **zericum** 1451, **siricum** c 1437, **ciricum** 1509, (?) **ciliquum** 1491; **-a**, choir cope c 1197, 1234; **siricum**, robe 8c.; **-um apertum** 1421; **s. crudum**, raw silk 1384; **s. de Damasco**, damask 1462; †**s. equinum**, horse-hair 1246 (cf. 1 **seta**); ‡**s. villosum**, "velvet" 1570; **-eus**, **seritius** c 1180, c 1400, **cericeus** c 1330, c 1400, **cericus** c 1315, c 1476, **siricus** 1289, silken; **-arius**, **-aria** (f.) 1561, **cericator** 1437, ‡**sereatrix** (f.) 15c., silk-worker; **-atus**, (?) lined with silk 1347.

2 seric/um, **siricum** a 1250, ‡**-on** 1652, red pigment, minium; ‡**zericum**, arsenic 1652.

seri/es, relation c 900, 985; purport, contents (of document) c 1125, 1545; religious order c 1125; **s. convergens** (math.) 1686; **-e** (pl.) 11c., (?) **-a** (pl.) 1136, for **-es**; **-alis**, continuous 1200; **-aliter** a 1452, †**-ater** 1397, *****-atim** c 1090, 1620, in due order, successively; **-atus**, arranged in order 1235, 1252; **-o**, to arrange, settle 1242, ‡1483; cf. **seriosus**.

†**serior**, (?) for **selio**, strip of land (Lincs.) 1331.

serios/us, serious c 1255, 1506; **-e**, seriously, earnestly 1296, a 1452; duly, effectually c 1343; minutely, in due order or detail, c 1300, 1443; *****-ius**, in fuller detail c 1300, 1467; cf. **series**.

seriteca, see **chirotheca**.

serius, see **cera**.

*****serj/antia** 1194, 1472, **-auntia** 1286, 1322,

†-eantia 1234, †-iantia 1364, †-ansia 14c., **sarjantia** 1212, **cerjantia** 1279, **sergantia** 1166, 1295, **serchancya** 1279, **-andia** (Sc.) 14c., 1397, **-antaria** 1193, 1226, **-anteria** 1180, 1236, **-aunteria** 1219, **sargentaria** a 1128, 1234, **sergantaria** 1191, **serganteria** 1196, 1226, **sergaunteria** 1230, **sergentaria** c 1300, **sergenteria** 1198, c 1265, †-**andria** (Sc.) 14c., (tenure, or land held, by) serjeanty; **s. arrentata**, arrented serjeanty 1257, 1333; **s. magna**, grand serjeanty c 1258, 1324; **s. parva**, petty serjeanty 1215, 1364; **s. forinseca** (*cf.* **servitium**) 1212; **sergantia**, office of (borough) serjeant (Leicester) 1271; **-anteria** (Norm.) c 1160, **-antaria**, **-anteria** (G.) 1289, **-auntaria** (G.) 1315, office of *sergent*; **-antia generalis** (G.) 1316; **-antia** 1327, 1360, **-andia** 1331, office of, or rent paid to, *cais* (W. & Marches); **s. hundredi** 1357, **s. magisterialis** c 1220, **magistralis** 1242 (Cheshire); **s. principalis** (W.) 1383; **s. pacis** (Cheshire) 1295, (W.) 1334;

-ans 1311, 1334, **sergens** c 1298, c 1300, **sargens** (papal) 1294, **sergiens** 1460, **-antus** 1212, 1422, **-auntus** 1275, **sergantus** 1198, a 1408, **-antius** 1212, †-**anceus** 1238, **sergentius** 1276, **sergiantus** (Sc.) 1435, *-andus (Sc.) 1333, 1539, †-**iandus** (Sc.) 1457, **sergeandus** (Sc.) 1449, 1532, **sergendus** (Ir.) a 1216, **-anus** (Ir.) 1205, (?) **sergenterius** c 1250, serjeant (esp. royal servant or officer); Sc. esp. municipal officer); **-antus**, attendant (mon.) 1311, 1422; **s. ad legem** c 1370; **s. communis** (of borough) 1311, 1460; **s. pacis**, 'grith-serjeant' 1276 (Salop), 1334 (W.); **sargiens ville** (W.) 1487; **assergeanticus ad arma** (London) 1444; **-anto**, to act as *sergent* (G.) 1316; *cf.* **serviens**.

sermo/, word 7c., 11c.; *sermon c 1125, 1537; **s. examinatorius** (ac.) 1312, c 1516; **S. Patris**, Logos (theol.) a 1233; *-cinalis 12c., 1378, **-cinosus** c 550, **-nialis** c 1250, locutional, vocal; **-cinatio**, chattering c 730; preaching 11c. c 1343; **-cinator**, preacher c 1125, c 1553; **-ciunculus** 12c., **sermunculus** c 700. 12c., little speech; **-cino**, *for* -cinor, c 1000; **-cinor**, to say, declare 893; c 1430, 1549, **-nizo** 1378, to preach.

†**sermologus**, (?) *for* **spermologus**, book of discourses c 1182.

sero, (?) to overspread, occupy c 550; *see also* **sera**, **seroitas**.

sero-, *see also* **chiro-**

ser/oitas, lateness c 1360, 1374; **-o**, (?) in time 1233; 1265, c 1325, **cero** 1264, c 1430, **ad -am** c 1006, **ad -o** 1194, a 1254, **de -o** 1450, 1461, **in -o** a 1250, 1347, **-o facto** c 1190, in the evening, at a late hour; **-o primo**, early in the evening c 1190; **-o quodam**, one evening c 1362; **a -o usque mane** 1220; **in -o vite** c 1340; **in -tinis**, in the evenings c 1173; ‡-**otino**, "to make late" 1483.

seropellinus, *see* **xeropellina**.

seros/itas, serous quality (med.) a 1250; **-us**, serous, whey-like a 1250.

serp-, *see also* **SARP**

serp/edo, mange (of cattle) p 1282; ‡"tetter", ‡"measles" 15c., 1483; **-igo**, ringworm c 1180, a 1250.

serpell-, *see* **serpyllum**.

serpen/s 12c, **s. antiquus** c 1180, c 1440, the Devil; **s. ignitus**, a firework (used in war) c 1192; **-tarius**, (stone engraved with) figure of snake 13c.; **-taria** a 1250, ‡**pentaria** 14c., **-tina** c 1200, dragonwort (bot.); **-taria minor**, cuckoo-pint (bot.) 1538; **herba -tina**, (?) cinquefoil a 1150; **-tina** 1416, **-tinum** c 1530, serpentine (mottled stone); **-tinum**, serpentine, cannon 1483; **-tine**, like a snake (secretly) 12c.; **-tinus**, diabolic 1044. 12c.; **-tosus**, infested with snakes c 1170; **-tulus**, small snake a 1250.

serpus, *see* **scirpus**.

serp/yllum, thyme: **serapillum** a 1250, †**sepillum** a 1564; **-ellum**, **-ella**, (?) herb *or* grass c 550.

serr/a, saw: *sarra 1311, 1458; **-a**, *sierra*, ridge (G.) 1308; **-arius** 1319, **-ator** 1324, c 1478, *sarrator 1296, 1526, sawyer; **-atio** 1416, *sarratio 1317, c 1533, **-atura** c 1478, **sarratura** 1375, c 1413, sawing; **-o** (bibl.), *sarro 1296, 1436, **sarrio** 1412, to saw.

serraculum, bung, spigot c 800. c 1325.

†**serranus**, (?) *for* **Syrianus** *or* **Tyrianus**, c 950.

serrinus, *see* **SEREN**

sert-, *see also* **CERT**; **SART**

sertamina (*pl.*), (?) *for* **sarmenta**, "lops" 1573.

sert/ulum, chaplet 1216; **-im**, in union c 1500.

ser/ula, **-ura**, †-**utus**, *see* **sera**.

serusum, *see* **cerasum**.

serv-, *see also* **cerv-**

serv/atio, preservation a 1361, a 1564; **-abilis**, observable c 1375; **-arium** 1229, 1255, **-orium** 1176, **cervorium** 1256, **-urum** 1204, **-atorium** 1250, 1260, stew, fish-pond; **-atorium**, repository a 1100, c 1250; **-ator**, Saviour 1537, 1562; **-antior**, more observant c 1562; **-o**, to contain (fluid) c 1450; to observe, view (of coroner) 1269; to have custody of (land) 1086; **s. diem**, to appear on appointed day (leg.) 1205, c 1290; **s. finem**, to observe (terms of) a fine 1180; **s. ostium**, to act as usher 12c.; **s. indemnem**, to keep immune 1293, c 1510.

servilo, *see* **semen**.

Serviolus, (?) abridged copy of Servius 12c.

serv/itium, employ c 1250, c 1500; c 1250, 1458, **cervisium** 1382, work done; service at table, meal served 1336; voluntary service, benefit c 1080, c 1192; 7c. c 1080, 1467, **s. commune** 1467, **s. Dei** 12c., 1377, **s. divinum** c 1090, 1617, **s. ecclesiasticum**, 1234, divine service, worship; (?) chantry (eccl.) 1573; (?) 1322, **-agium** 1209, 1320, villeinage; *805, 955. c 1070, 1545, **-isium** c 1300, 1338, tenant service (feudal or man.); commuted service, money-rent 1202, c 1290; body of tenants owing service, armed force 1222, c 1325; **in -itio** 1220, c 1311, **in -ientia** 1198, opposed to **in dominico** (referring to lord's tenure of land held of him in fee); **-itium commune**, **s. triplum**, *trimoda necessitas* 12c.; **-itia consueta quinque**, petty services paid by prelates confirmed or collated by Pope 1327; **-itium corporale**, (feudal) service in person 1333; **s. corporis**, suit of court c 1120; **s. equitis** 1122, **s. militis** 1086, 1269, **s. militare** c 1130, 1587, knight-service; **s. ad faldam**, fold-service 1086; **s. foraneum** a 1190, c 1200, **s. forense** c 1160, 1320, ***s. forinsecum** a 1162, 1384, **s. extrinsecum** (Sc.) c 1230, c 1240, foreign service (not due to immediate overlord); **s. intrinsecum** c 1230, c 1320; ***s. liberum** c 1185, 1280, **s. francum** c 1150, p 1348 (due from freeholder); **s. maris** 1086, **s. ad mare, s. in mare** 12c.; **s. mortuorum**, mortuary service (eccl.) c 1335; **s. regale** 860. 1086, 1234, (?) **s. reale** 1359, 1389, **s. regis** 1086 (due to crown); **s. regis**, as ground for essoin 1278, a 1311; **s. rusticorum** c 1160, **s. servile** 14c.; **s. seculare** 1199, c 1250, **s. terrenum** c 1400;

-ientia c 1375, **-itio** 11c., submission, subservience; **-ilitas** c 1332, ‡1570, **-imen** c 1170, servitude; **-itus**, tenant service c 853, 948; serfdom, villeinage c 1115, 1528; impost (G.) 1311; monastic life c 980; office, function 1543; **s. coactitia, s. exactoria**, forced service c 1130; **s. rusticana** 12c.; **s. tributorum** 1017; **s. divina**, divine service 947, c 1006. 12c.; ***-ilis**, involving villein service or status c 1115, 1388; **-iliter**, in villeinage c 1340; **-itialis** 1292, **homo s.** 1293, servant (G.); ‡**-itiosus** 1483, **-itivus** c 1380, 1427, serviceable;

-itor *a 1100, 1545, **-itrix** (*f.*) 1476, **-us** 15c., c 1550, servant; workman's mate 1410, 1513; 1307, 1473, **-ulus** c 600, c 990. c 1090, 1523, **-unculus** 700. a 1135, 14c., (your) humble servant; (?) c 1266, c 1296, **s. cultelli, s. manutergii (abbatis)** c 1330, attendant at table (mon.); one who performs divine service c 1080, 1331; (Sc.) 1373, ***-us** 1086, 1540, **-a** (*f.*) 1290, serf, villein; **s. communis** 1326, **-us communis** c 1292, common crier; **s. armorum** 1435, **s. ad arma** 1496, serjeant-at-arms; **s. religionis regis** 1335; **-us Beate Marie**, Servite (eccl.) 1267; **s. fugitivus**, mercury (alch.) 1292, ‡1652; **s. -orum Dei** (papal title) 1156, 1347; **s. testamentalis**, slave c 1115;

-iens *1086, 1430, **-ans** 1336, servant; workman's mate c 1533; tenant under rank of knight holding land by military service 12c., c 1437; serjeant (soldier inferior to knight) c 1198, c 1296; 1156, 1278, **s. hundredi** 1186, 1221, serjeant (official subordinate to sheriff); 1324, 14c., **s. de curia** 1326, **s. narrator** 1297, a 1340, **s. placitor** c 1340, serjeant (leg.); **s. ad. legem** 1310, 1686, **s. ad leges** c 1410, 1560, **s. de lege** 1380, **s. legis** 1419, serjeant-at-law; ***s. ad arma** 1225, 1587, **s. de armis** c 1422, serjeant-at-arms; **s. autumpnalis**, harvest labourer 1259; **s. capelle** a 1123; **s. ecclesie** 1470; **s. carcarum** (naut.), supercargo 1486; **s. ad clavam** 1419, 1575, **s. clave** 1404, **s. pro clava** 1392, serjeant-at-mace (borough official); **s. cum massa**

(G.) 1312; **s. communis** (of borough) 1446; **s. eques**, mounted serjeant 1239, 1315; **s. ad haubergun** 1236; **s. hospitator** serjeant harbinger 1419; **s. liber** 1233, 1338; **s. manerii** 1297; **s. pacis** c 1250, 1393, **s. ad custodiendam pacem** 1295, 'grith-serjeant' (W. & Chester); **s. ad conservationem pacis** (Yorks.) 1238; **s. pedes** 1310, 1340, **s. ad pedem** (G.) 1313, foot-serjeant; **s. regis**, king's serjeant 1086, 1332; **s. rotulorum Cancellarie** 1257, 1261; **s. universitatis** (ac.) c 1288; **s. virgam deferens** 1263;

-io, to serve at meals c 1135, 1377; c 1190, 1432; **s. altari** c 1220, **s. ad missam** c 1072, to officiate, celebrate (eccl.); to stand surety (?) 1222, 1245; to perform feudal service 1085, 1102; to pay papal *servitia* 1262; (*trans.*) to serve 7c.; **s. breve**, to serve a writ 1505; **s. de officio**, to hold office 1251; ‡**-o**, *for* **-io**, 1458; **-itio**, to engage the services of 1266.

serv/o, -orium, -urum, *see* **servatio**.

sesam/um, sesame: **sisamum** a 1250; **-aceus**, resembling sesame 1641; **sisamileon**, oil of sesame a 1250; †**esemum** a 1150, †**physanimum** c 1375, (?) *for* **-eum**, sesamoid bone.

sescuplicatus, *see* SEXT

†**sesebram**, (?) wild thyme 12c.

seselis (bot.): **sisolis** a 1250.

ses/ena, -initas, -ionabilis, -ona, *see* **seiso**.

sesi/na, -o, *see* **seisina**.

sesperale, *see* SUSPIR

sespes, *see* **cespes**.

sesqui/alter, one and a half: **sesqualter** 870, **sexqualter** c 1193, 13c., **sexquialter** c 1360; one tone and a half (mus.) c 1200; **-annus**, a year and a half 1570; **-cubitum**, 1½ cubits 1537; **-furiosus**, a lunatic and a half 1523; **-millesimus**, fifteen-hundredth 1528, 1570; **-pedanter**, to a length of 1½ feet 1521; **-plicatus**, sesquiplicate (math.) 1686; **sexquaternarius**, one and a quarter 13c.; **sexquiquarta**, of one and a quarter 13c.; **sexquiternarius**, one and a third 13c.; **-tertius** c 1361, **sexquitertius** a 1200, 13c., of one and a third; **sexquartano, sexquinterno**, to increase by a quarter or a fifth a 1250.

sess/io, setting in place 1402; assessment 1480 (*cf.* ASSESS); *1252, 1549, **cessio** 1293, 1508, **seissona** c 1335, session, sitting (of court or other body); Court of Session (Sc.) 1608; (?) record of proceedings 1433; **-iones** (*pl.*) 1345, **s. magne et parve** 1388 (W.), 1573; **-io pacis**, session of the peace c 1470, 1661; **s. quarterialis**, quarter session 1661; **-ivus**, able to sit 870; **-or**, dean 7c.; member of court (Exchequer) c 1178; **-um**, seat c 550; **-us (cessus) ad arma**, assessed for arms 1299;

sed/imen, weight, erudition c 1130; **-ens**, sejant (her.) p 1394; **austurcus bene -ens**, (falc.) 1201; **-eo**, to ride upon 1200, c 1400; to rest on the foreshore (of a ship) 1419; to sit, be held (of market) 1086, 1259; to suit, be convenient c 990. c 1170, c 1330; *to occupy a see (eccl.) c 1125, 1535; to establish (a see) (eccl.) 12c.; to assess 1280;

s. ad bancum (leg.) 1252; s. ad calculum (account-table) c 1160; s. ad mensam 13c., s. in mensa 1347; s. ad placita c 1290; s. ad scaccarium 1198, c 1250, s. super scaccarium 1359; s. in 1086, s. super 12c., to be situated in; s. in aere, to sit alone c 1150; s. in prejudicium, to be prejudicial 1304; s. super, to sit in judgement on c 1120, 1352; see also ASSESS, CESS
sest-, see also SEXT
sestertius, shilling c 1380.
set, see sed.
1 set/a, (?) bristle used as taper 1344; seya equorum, horse-hair 1276; pannus de -a a 1155, 1303, ceda 1292, seia 1254, c 1300, silk; sita, bristle c 1120; sia furcata 1248, †sepria furcata 1247, forked bristle (of boar) (C.I.); cf. ferula, 2 pilus; saitum 1305, ‡-acium 1483, ‡-arium c 1440, 1483, (?) citerium 1262, hair-cloth, sieve; -o, seton (med.) a 1250; cf. sagum.
2 seta, (?) spiny tree c 500; sethim, shittim, acacia (Heb.) c 730. a 1250, 1275.
setto, to set, lay (stones) 1433.
setula, see situla.
setum, see segga.
seu 796, 862, sive 8c., and; nor 1377; seu si, or if 1341; siv/e . . . vel, whether . . . or 1238, 1279; -i, for -e, c 834, 863; see also ceu.
seubum, see sebum.
seuda, seudagium, seunta, see selda.
seudra, see CALD
seuera, seuwer-, see exaquia.
seullenia, see selio.
seura, sowing-service (man.) c 1210, 13c.
seusus (†sensus), hound hunting by scent (O.F. seüs) 1205, 1206.
seuta, see 1 secta.
†sevellio (†senellio), (?) f.l. for scurellorum, c 1290.
sever/a, -ia, see civera.
several/is, -lum, see SEPAR
sever/unda c 1160, 1419, ceverunda 1281, -o c 1203, 'severon', eaves or cornice (arch.); cf. suggrundium.
sevocatio, withdrawal into self 1620.
sevum, see sebum.
sewellum, 'shewel', decoy 1286.
sew/era, -icium, -o, etc., see exaquia.
sewettum, see sueta.
sex/a, 'sax', slater's chopper c 1485; -atus, rebated (arch.) 1418.
sexacra, see seracra.
sexag/esima, Sexagesima (eccl.) 9c., c 980. ‡1483, c 1493; -ecuplus, sixtyfold a 980, 1620; -enus, sixtieth c 1250, c 1450; sexsaginta, sixty 1226.
sexa/gonus (†saxagonus, saxogonus), hexagonal a 1385, c 1437; -ptotus, sexta-ptotus, with six cases (gram.) 790; cf. HEXA
sex/annalis (decima) c 1330, 1335, -ennalis c 1370, 15c., -cennalis c 1356, -ennualis 1335, recurring every six years (of a tax); secennium, for -ennium, c 1125.
sexatus, see sexa.
sexcent/enus, having weregeld of 600 shillings c 1115; -uplum, sixhundredfold 1267; secent/i 1204, cecenti 1205, six hundred; -esimus, six hundredth c 1185.

sexcuplicatus, see SEXT
sexdec/ennis, sixteen years old c 1434; -ies, sixteen times 13c.; -uplus, sixteenfold a 1250.
sexhindus, see sixhindus.
sexhorarius, lasting six hours c 1616, 1620.
sexies, six times: sexcies (†sexties) 1227, 1269, seccies (†secties) 1226.
†sexonicum, (?) coarse towel c 1000.
sexpertitus, sixfold c 860.
sexqu-, see SESQUI
*sext/a, sext, a canonical hour (eccl.) c 980. c 1130, 1556; feria s., Friday c 980. c 1090, 1558; -adecima, subsidy of a sixteenth 1226, 1317; (febris) -ana, recurring every six days a 1250; *-arium, -arius 1086, 1499, *-erium a 1200, 1430, -ertium, -ertius c 1190, c 1290, -era (G.) 1254, sestera c 1100, cestarium 1282, 1447, cestrus 1309, c 1427, sixterium 1307, sixtera 1295, sistarium a 1155, sistra (Sc.) 1436, 1457, cisterium c 1400, stara (It.) 1392, sester, dry or liquid measure; -ionarius, sixtonnier (one-sixth of caboteau) (C.I.) 1309; -arius p 1250, *-ernus p 1250, 1418, book or gathering of six leaves; -erium, sixth part c 1434; †-efotha, (?) six-foot length (of stone) 1337; -ies, see sexies; -ilis, sextile (astr.) c 1150, 1610; -iplicitas, sixth house (astr.) c 1260; -iplex 1427, -uplex 1610, secuplex a 1520, -uplus c 1200, 1267, six-fold; †sexcuplicatus (? sext-), †sescuplicatus, multiplied by six c 730; -o, sixthly 1279, c 1332; -o decimo, sixteenthly 1282; -um, product of multiplying unit (or degree) by 60 six times (math.) a 1150; -us (sc. liber decre-talium), section of canon law a 1300, c 1450.
sextanus, see sacrista; sexta.
†sextulatio (granorum), (?) for serculatio, 1529.
sexus, class 814. a 1408; planetary quality (astr.) 1387; s. fragilis, weaker sex c 1455; s. melior, male sex a 1200.
sey-, see also sei-
seya, see 1 seta.
seyg/lus, -nus, see selio.
seyya, see sedes.
sh-, see also sch-
shaculum 1315, shakelum 1365, shackle (for horse).
shaft/a, mine-shaft 1453; schafta, strip of meadow (Lincs.) 1331; -ela (†shastela), shaft-eel 1257.
shamell/a, -um, see scamellum.
shara c 1353, 15c., sara a 1190, share of proceeds (naut.).
shar/rum, (?) plough-share 1404; -cloutum, share-clout 1377.
shastela, see SHAFT
shava, sheaf (of garlic) 1291, 1397; 1336, schafum c 1320, sheaf (of arrows); schyva (Dutch schijf) cardonum, bunch of teasels 1474, 1480.
shavald/or, -ria, see schavaldus.
shawa 1397, schawa 1310, shaw, thicket (S.E. Eng.).
shedum, see scheta.
shel/a, -inga, see 3 scala.
shelda, see selda.

shelpa 1486, **sholpa** 1540, **scalpa** 1507, **shelfa** 1544, 'shelf', shellfish-bed; (?) shoal 1366; **scalpa**, shell-fish (*coll.*) a 1672.

Shepeweia, Shipway court (Cinque Ports) 1447.

sheppus, *see* CHIPP

sherplerium, *see* **sarpellarium.**

shettum, *see* **scheta.**

shilo, to shell (hemp) 1425.

shing/illa, -ula, ulo, *see* **scindula.**

Shipotensis, *see* **Chipotensis.**

shipwrightus, *see* **schipa.**

shir-, *see* CHERCH; SCHIR; **schura.**

shock/um, -us 1315, 1366, **schokkum** 1325, **schoca** 1223, **socca** 1181, **soka** 1282, **scoka** 1201, 'shock', stook (of corn); **-o** 1336, **socco** c 1350, to stook.

sholda, *see* SHOVEL

sholpa, *see* **shelpa.**

*****shop/a** 1189, 1549, **-um** 1422, *****schopa** 1257, c 1430, **scopa** c 1195, c 1460, **scupa** c 1384, **choppa** 1349, **sopa** c 1100, 1295, **sopha** (†**sepha**) 1305, shop; **schopparius** c 1200, **soparius** 1130, 1255, shop-keeper.

shota, shot of cable (naut.) 1460; *see also* **scuta.**

shotbordum, shot-board (planed board *or* wainscot) 1354.

shottum, (?) 'shoot', cross-bar 1376.

shouta, *see* **scuta.**

shovel/um 1333, **schovelum** 1480, (?) **sholda** 1388, shovel; **-arda** 1544, **schewlarda** 1499, shoveller duck.

shrud/atio 1469, **-eratio** 1539, 'shredding', lopping; **sroudura**, trimming (of mill-wheel) 1325; **shredo** 1397, 1589, **shrido** 1381, **scrudo** (†**strudo**) 1364, to shred, lop (trees); a 1378, **sredo** a 1378, **-o** 1401, 1451, **scriddo** 1374, to strip, trim (mill-wheel or plough).

shryvus, shyrevus, shyra, *see* SCHIR

shuddum, (?) shed 1442.

shut/a, -agium, -arius, -us, *see* **scuta.**

si, whether (*in indirect question*) 1223, 1456; **si non omnes**, name of a writ 1508.

si-, *see also* **ci-; cy-; sci-; scy-; sy-**

sia, siator, siatura, *see* **seca**; I **seta.**

sibbesocha, sibsocha, *see* SCHIP

sibe, *see* **se.**

sibettum, *see* I **sica.**

sibil/a 1235, **siflus** 1212, **siffletus** (†**suffletus**) c 1227, a whistle, whistling noise; **-ator**, whisperer, tale-bearer c 1255; piper (Sc.) 1521; **scibilo**, to whistle 12c.; **-o**, to insinuate c 1115; **-o**, (?) *for* sibyllo, to speak words of wisdom c 1160.

sic/, *for* tam 790. 14c.; (**dico, respondeo**) **quod sic**, to answer "yes" 1281, 1461; **sic quod**, so that, on condition that c 1290, c 1456; *see also* **per, pro; sic sic** 870, **sic sicque** c 1250, just so; *****-ud**, *for* -ut, c 1287, c 1357; **-ut**, *for* si, if c 1000.

I *****sica** a 1160, 16c., *****sicus** c 1160, 1259, **siccum** 1284, syke, stream, ditch (Sc. & N. Engl.); **siculus** c 1250, **sichetum** c 1130, 1305, *****siket/a, -um, -us** 1201, 1479, †**sibettum** 1257, **secheta** c 1300, **sechetum** 1262, **sigettum** 1290, small syke; **-a matrix**, main syke c 1250; **s. herbagii** 1297; **sychetta pasture** 1299; †**siccetta prati**, (?) water-meadow 1380.

2 sic/a, dagger: **cica** ‡15c., (?) 1466; **-aria**, assassin (*f.*) 14c.; **-ariatus** 9c., †**-arium** c 1310, assassination; ‡**cicario**, to assassinate c 1440.

3 sica, *see* **seca.**

4 †**sica**, *f.l.* for **cicuta**, c 1362.

‡**sicassis**, clover or medick (bot.) 15c.

sicca, cuttle-fish (Fr. *seiche*) (?) 1130, c 1200.

siccida, *see* **cecidos.**

sicc/itas, drought 1221, 1410; 1325, **-atio** 1330, 1531, **-aria** (C.I.) 1324, **sekeria** (C.I.) 1320, **seccheria** (†**senheria**) (Brittany) 1382, 1396, drying (of fish, hides, malt, *etc.*) or place therefor; **-atio brasii** 1289; **s. feni** 1368; **s. petarum** a 1300, **s. turbarum** 1303; **s. retium** 1283; **-abilis**, dryable c 1270; **-ator**, drainer 1619; **s. brasii**, malt-dryer a 1250; **-atrix (brasii)**, "dryster" 1344, 15c.; **-um**, dry wood c 1090, 1381; **-us**, dried (of fish) c 1086, 1357; (?) water-tight (of shoes) 1512; hard (of cash) 1269, c 1450; *see also* CEC, PREC, **moltura, murus, redditus, seca**, I **sica; -o allecia** 1357, **s. carnem** 1302.

*****sicera** (eccl.), *****cicera** 1234, c 1390, **scicera** c 1200, **cizera** 1295, 1333, **cizer** 1241, **ciser** 1388, *****cisera** 1267, 15c., **cisara** 1298, 1420, **cisarum** c 1300, **cisar** 1412, **cesera** 1297, 1303, **cesar** 1436, ‡**sisera** 1483, **sissera** 1276, †**segeara** 1398, cider; **dolium cisorium** c 1317, **d. cysaricum** 1281, cider-cask.

sichetum, *see* I **sica.**

sicia, *see* **sicyos.**

sicladon, siclas, *see* CYCL

siclo, *see* **siculus.**

siclus (bibl.), **ciclus** a 1250, 1378, shekel.

sico, *see* **seca.**

sicora, *see* **sucrum.**

†**sicsewarda**, pasture for sixty cattle (Lancs.) 1298.

sic/ulus, sickle 1564; **-lo**, to reap 14c.; *see also* I **sica.**

sicus, *see* I **sica.**

sic/ut, -ud, *see* **sic.**

sic/yos, squirting cucumber (bot.): (?) **-ia** a 1250, ‡**-ida** 14c.; *cf.* cecidos; ‡**scicia**, gourd-shaped cupping-glass 14c.

sid/clutum, 'side-clout' (of plough) 1269, 1308; **-ropa, -eropa**, 'side-rope' (of plough) 1316.

sidile, *see* **sedile.**

sidule, *see* **sedulus.**

sid/us, eye 12c., c 1325; **rex -ereus**, heavenly king c 1090.

sieuta, *see* I **secta.**

siffus, *see* **scyphus.**

siflus, siffletus, *see* **sibila.**

sifta, †**dzifta**, measure of land, (?) virgate (? 'shift' = share) (Suffolk) c 1186.

sigal-, *see* SECAL

sig/ellus, -illus, hobble for horses c 550.

sigesterium, *see* **seges.**

sigettum, *see* I **sica.**

sigia, storax c 1200, ‡14c.

sigill/um 796, 1001. 1086, 1684, **sigullum** c 550, seal; **s. armorum** 1415, **s. ad arma** 1431, 1499, armorial seal; *****s. authenticum** c 1192, 1684; **s. ad causas**, seal used for lawsuits c 1240, c 1465; **s. clausum** (G.)

1276; **s. communale** 1191, ***s. commune**
1201, 1566; **s. confessionis** (fig., eccl.)
1234; **s. contractuum** c 1290, **s. ad contractus** 1304 (G.); **s. conventuale** (mon.)
13c., 1584; **s. crucis** 933, c 975, **singillum
c.** 966, sign of the cross; **s. dependens**
1228, **s. pendens** c 1290, 1293, **s. impen-
dens** 1313, pendant seal; ‡**S. Hermetis**,
"orificium vitri" (alch.) 1652; **s. magnum
(Anglie, regis,** *etc.*), Great Seal 1206,
1684; **s. parvum** c 1200, 1254, **s. privatum**
1208, 1586, Privy Seal; **s. patens**, open or
common seal 1279, 1324; **s. patulum**,
broad seal 1343; **s. secretum**, Privy Seal
or Signet 1234, 15c.; ‡**s. Salamonis** 14c.,
s. Solomonis 1634, (?) **herba -ata** a 1250,
Solomon's seal (bot.); **s. Beate Marie** 1634,
s. Sancte Marie a 1250, ‡14c., black
bryony (bot.); **-um**, baker's stamp on bread
1203, c 1324; *see also* SCRIP;
    -agium, (payment for) sealing (of wine-
casks) 1230; **-arius** c 1180, 1419, **-ator**
c 1190, **-ifer** c 1188, 1380, keeper of a seal;
-ator, seal-maker 1292; affixer of seal, spigurnel 1471, 1586; **-atim**, under seal 1312;
-atio, *sealing, stamping with a seal c 1115,
a 1564; marking, stamping a 1250, c 1270;
anulus -atorius, signet-ring c 1465; **terra
-ata**, Lemnian earth a 1250, 14c.; **-o** *c 1070,
1559, **-or** (*dep.*) 1266, *to seal (documents);
to seal up (chest, building, *etc.*) c 1125, 15c.;
to seal (standard measures) 1366, 1419; to
mark, stamp c 1180, c 1260; to seal (fig.),
confirm 1252, 1345; **s. mente**, to keep
secret c 1180; *see also* **pes, sigellus**,
SINGUL, SUGILL.
sigilo, *see* **siligo**.
sigimen, *see* **sagimen**.
sigisterium, *see* **seges**.
sigl/a c 1100, **secla** 1309, sail; 1294, 1357,
segla 1352, sail of wind-mill; **-atura**, sailing c 1200; **-o**, to sail 1301, 1319; *cf.* SAIL.
sign-, *see also* CYGN
signatio, *etc.*, *see* **signum**.
signetagium, *see* **soinantagium**.
signific/abilitas, potential significance c 1360;
-abilis, potentially significant c 1270, c 1365;
-ative, with a typical purpose c 830; by
way of significance 1267, c 1444; ***-ativus**
790, 870. a 1110, 1332, **-ator** 13c., 1267,
-atrix (*f.*) 13c., 1344, indicative, significant
(of); *see also* **suppositio**; **littere -atorie**
(G.) 1312; **-atum**, thing signified, meaning
a 1200, c 1488; **-avit**, name of a writ 15c.,
c 1470; **-o**, to connote (log.) a 1110, c 1365;
to portray 1427.
sign/um (singn-), miracle (eccl.); *c 760,
c 1006. c 1095, c 1520, **cyngnum** 1297,
bell; boundary-mark c 1150, 1349; buoy
(naut.) 1297, 15c.; beacon 1258, 1335;
target c 1343, 14c.; pattern, sample (of
cloth) 1259, 1264; tradesman's sign (outside
shop) 1373, 1406; brand on cattle 1274;
swan-mark 1357, 1472; baker's mark on
loaf 1289; mark on document (equivalent
to signature) (?) 1087, 1136; notarial mark
c 1418, 1684; badge 1285, 1542; p 1394,
c 1450, **s. armorum** 1398, 1419, armorial
bearing (her.); **s. capitale**, chevron (her.)
p 1394, a 1446; **s. criminis**, branding of

criminal c 1110; **s. crucis**, sign of the cross
c 600, 1001. 1107, 1461; **s. ferreum**, branding iron c 1330; **s. fluviale**, "water-mark"
(boundary-mark in river) (Sc.) 1632, 1637;
s. manuale c 1204, 1487, **s. manus**
676, 738, sign manual; **s. mercatorium**
1443, 1539, **s. (mercatoris)** c 1245, 1404,
merchant's mark; **s. mortuum, s. vivens**,
inanimate or animate object as charge (her.)
p 1394; **s. Salomonis**, Solomon's seal
(? bot.) a 1236; **-a** 836, **cignum** c 1420, *for*
-um, sign;
    -abilis, expressible, picturable c 1270,
1378; ‡"sealable" 1570; **-abilitas**, expressi-
bility c 1290; **-aculum** 720. c 1090, c 1266,
***s. crucis** 8c., 867. c 1125, 1482, sign of the
cross; signal (naut.) 1357; 1345, c 1500,
-iculum 1519, tag or clasp of book; small
device (her.) c 1595; **s. plumbi**, "Easter
token" 1574; **-aliter** c 1363, **-ative** 1378,
figuratively; **-anter** 7c., 8c. 13c., **-ate** 13c.,
significantly; *expressly 12c., 1521; **-antia**,
signification c 1362, 1378; **-arius**, standard-
bearer 13c.; **-atio**, marking 1274, 1546;
sealing c 1250, 1447; designation, indication
c 1204, c 1370; assignment (of money)
c 1323 (*cf.* ASSIGN); **s. crucis**, taking
of the cross 1220, c 1250; **-ativus** a 1250,
p 1381, **-atrix** (*f.*) 13c., significant; **-ator**,
standard-bearer 1344; characteristic (astr.)
1344; **s. (temporis)**, indicator a 1233;
-atum, thing signified c 1250, 1378; imprint 13c.; c 1200, c 1430, **-etum** 1281,
1536, †-**itum** a 1553, signet; **-etum**, the
royal signet 1354, 1472; **s. Unicornis** (Sc.)
1459, 1462; **anulus -etus**, signet-ring 1472;
-atura, marking 1485, 1495; mark, stamp
1417, 1508; *signature, sign manual
a 1452, 1565; 'signature', impress (phil.)
c 1608, 1620; **-ifer**, (*adj.*) significant c 1250;
(*subst.*) armorial bearing c 1400; pursuivant (Sc.) 1434, 1476; **-iferosus** c 1090,
-ipotens c 1230, miracle-working;
    -o, to mark with the sign of the cross a 615,
c 1000. c 1148, 15c.; to mark or brand
(animals) 1270, 1399; to brand (criminals)
c 1115, c 1283; to mark with a boundary
mark 13c., 1349; to mark (stones) with
mason's mark 1442; to inform, notify 1219,
c 1430; to assign c 1180, c 1465; to desig-
nate (log.) a 1300, c 1330; ‡"to clasp" 1483.
sigonia, *see* **ciconia**.
sigrillus, *see* **cherogryllus**.
sigullum, *see* **sigillum**.
sigul/um, -aceus, *see* SECAL
siket-, *see* ι **sica**.
silaginarius, *see* SILIG
sil/ba, -fa, *see* **silva**.
silempsis, *see* **syllepsis**.
silenites, *see* SELEN
sil/entiarius, *gostegwr* (W.) a 1300; **s. Pape**,
papal secretary c 1188; **-enter** (bibl.),
scilenter c 1330, silently; **-eo ab**, to
refrain from c 1185, c 1197; **-io**, *for* **-eo**,
1200.
silex, flint; **cil/ex** c 1340; **murus -icinus**,
flint wall 1448.
siliba, *see* SYLLAB
silicernius, old man c 950.
sili/cet, -set, *see* **scilicet**.

silicium, *see* CILIC

*silig/o 1086, 1537, ciligo a 1295, ‡1483, †saligo a 1250, 1475, sigilo 1583, -nus a 1525, rye; †silaginarius, (?) corn-controller 1549; panis -inea, rye bread c 1125; terra -inosa, land used for growing rye 1296, 1307; *cf.* SECAL

silina, *see* sagma.

silinga, *see* SULLIN

silio, *see* selio; silentiarius.

‡siliqu/arium, "hog's trough" c 1440; ‡-osus, "husky" 1570; ‡fabe -e, unshelled beans c 1200.

silla, *see* Scylla.

sillum (molendini) 1324, 1326, sellum 1322, sill, horizontal beam; sullo, to furnish with a sill 1331, 1372; *cf.* solea, soliva.

silluratio, *see* 2 celum.

silobalsamum, *see* XYLO

silv/a (sylv-), timber c 1178, c 1200; silba c 740, 873, silfa 839, *for* -a; s. cedua (sedua) 1287, 1425, -icedium 1237, 1479, †-iadium 14c., s. minuta, s. vilis 1086, coppice-wood; -acedus, wood-cutter 1344; -anus, forest officer (Durham) 12c.; ‡"wodewose", satyr c 1440, 15c.; (*adj.*) sylvan 13c.; †-agius c 1220, salvagius c 1100, 1263, savagius c 1250, *for* -aticus, wild; salvagina c 1180, 1336, sauvagina 1340, savagina 1398, 1442, wild game (*coll.*), beasts of chase; pelles -atice, skins of wild beasts c 1330; *see also* ignis; †-atinus, belonging to woodland †672 (15c.); cilvella 1086, -iuncula 11c., small wood; homo -ester, wild man, merman c 1227; -ositas, wooded region c 1200, c 1220; -esco, to revert to woodland c 1125; (fig.) 1153, a 1205, -estresco 12c., to run wild.

sim-, *see also* sym-

sima (syma), (?) 'sime', straw-rope (Suffolk) 1268; *see also* cyma, simitas.

simagium, *see* SAGM

simallus, *see* thymallus.

simba, *see* cymba.

simbalum, *see* cymbalum; symbolum.

simbice, *see* 2 sambuca.

simenellus, *see* simila.

simentum, *see* CEMENT

sim/eterium, -iterium, *see* cemeterium.

simi/a, ape: cimea c 1500, 1533, semia 1427; -ola, baby monkey a 1200; caricature 1620; -alis, ape-like c 1255, 1378.

simiacus, *see* simonia.

simicommune, *see* SEMI

sim/ila, fine wheaten flour: -ula 1252, 1342, semela c 1500; panis -ilago, (?) a 1088 (1312), (?) scimilinus (†scumluns) 13c., (p.) -enellus c 1135, c 1436, -inellus 12c., c 1450, -nellus c 1175, c 1400, seminellus 1282, (loaf of) simnel bread; -enellus dominicus c 1135, c 1293 (*cf.* panis d.).

simil/itudo, wax image (as *ex voto*) 1290; -aris, homogeneous 1686; a -i, likewise c 1197, 1393; in -i, in like terms c 1343; -iter, at one time 7c.; -itudinaliter, as a likeness c 1325; -itudinarie, figuratively c 1200, c 1380; -itudinarius, figurative a 1250, c 1500; *see also* simulatio

siminum, *see* cyminum.

simirnis, *see* smyrnion.

sim/itas, flatness (of noses) c 1260, 1344; -a, hollow of liver (τὰ σιμά) a 1250, ‡14c.

simmitium, *see* psimmythium.

*simon/ia c 1115, 1567, †-iaca 12c., c 1308, simony, sale of things spiritual (eccl.); *-iace 1136, 1537, -ice c 1341, simoniacally; -iacus *c 1188, c 1534, -icus 1341, †-achus 12c., -ianus c 1465, -ida c 1352, simoniac; (*adj.*) *a 615, 8c. c 1100, 1549, -ialis c 1130, 13c., -icus c 1125, †simiacus c 1340, simoniacal.

simpl/icitas, simplicity (title) 8c.; Trinity 957; half-wittedness 1275, c 1400; -ex, simple (in rank), low-born c 1300, 15c.; unembroidered 1345, 1420; 1318, 1434, †-icus 1402, unlined; (*subst.*) a half-wit 1521; 1252, 1634, s. medicamentum 1544, a simple (uncompounded drug); Dominica s., Sunday that is not a feast-day c 1245; *see also* cantus, feodum, festum; -iciter, entirely, completely c 1400; -us, simple 790, c 860. c 1218, 1416.

simul/ tempore, at the same time c 1343; -taneitas 13c., c 1360, *-tas c 1267, c 1362, simultaneity; -taneus, simultaneous c 1360; -tatio, dispute, clash c 1362; riot c 1415; *see also* semel, simulatio.

simula, *see* simila.

sim/ulatio, pretence: -ilatio c 1511; -ulatorius c 1200, 1620, †-ilatorius c 1200, †-ultatorius c 1197, fictitious; -ulatorie a 1205, 1437, †-ilate 1461, fictitiously; -ulatrix, deceptive (*f.*), 720, 9c. c 1180, c 1190; -ultas, illusion c 1190; concurrence 1344; -ilor, *for* -ulor, to resemble 1267, 1461; *see also* INSIMUL

simus, *see* thymus.

sin, letter of Hebrew alphabet (*shin*) a 1200.

sin alias, *for* s. aliter, 8c.

sin-, *see also* syn-

sinalimpha, *see* synalepha.

sinan/cia, -tis, -ticus, *see* cynanche.

sinap/ium 1265, c 1493, -um 1271, cinapium 1368, 1463, senapium 1313, 1415, cenape 1390, cenapium 1290, c 1500, mustard; ‡-inus 14c., -ius c 1200, of mustard; -isma, mustard plaster a 1250; -izatus, compounded with mustard a 1250.

sinc/atio 1374, †-tatio 1377, sinking a shaft; sinko, to sink (a shaft) c 1358.

*sincer/itas (vestra) c 1220, 1479, scinceritas 1235, sincerity (title); -iter 720, 9c. c 1125, c 1525, cinceriter c 1330, sincerely; cincerus c 1338, scincerus c 1200, c 1410, *for* -us; -o, to purify, cleanse c 1180, 1283.

sin/chia, -cio, *see* cincia.

Sinchialis, *see* Cynthia.

sincubo, *see* SYNCOP

sindatum, *see* cendallum.

*sindo/(bibl.) c 980. c 1200, 1432, cindo 1288, c 1370, muslin *or* fine linen; -nicus, of muslin c 1392; *cf.* cendallum; *see also* SCISS

sind/regabulum 1234, †-egabulum 13c., (?) (gavel payable for) lease (Devon); (?) *cf.* sundernota.

sine, minus (math.) 1145; (with *inf.*) c 1227, (with *gerundive*) 1315, without; s. hoc quod . . . esset, without being 1220.

sinedoche, *see* synecdoche.

sinefecturum, *see* cenevectorium.

sin/escallus, -iscallus, *see* senescallus.
singillum, *see* SIGILL
singn-, *see* CYGN; SIGN
singul-, *see also* cingulum; scindula.
singul/aritas, singleness, being alone 790.
a 1250, a 1347; peculiarity, outstanding
character 720. c 1070, c 1450; individual
ownership c 1190, c 1266; -aris 893. ‡14c.,
singlaris c 1346, senglarius a 1185,
c 1200, wild boar (Fr. *sanglier*); colloquium
-are, *tête-à-tête* c 1200; -arior 1207,
-arissimus c 1343, 1526, most remarkable;
-ariter, in relation to one object (log.)
c 1200; in singleness of heart c 1600;
sigillatim 1215, 14c., †-tatim 1408, one by
one; -us, every 1365; 13c., 1482, sengulus
a 1220, unlined (of cloth, gloves, *etc.*); ‡-o,
to make single 1483.
singult/atio, sob 15c.; -atim, in sobs a 1250;
-ivus c 1150, -uosus a 1110, 1423, sobbing.
sinimum, *see* cyminum.
sinist/er, evil, treacherous c 1197, 1560;
-erior c 980; -imus (†finistimus), left-
most c 1150; -ralis, northern 7c., 893;
ecclesia s., church built north and south
c 500; -raliter c 1430, -ranter c 1397,
evilly; -re, on the left a 1235; -ro, to be
or pass on the left c 1194, c 1250; to thwart,
be adverse c 1180, 15c.; to do wrong a 1408.
sinko, *see* sincatio.
†sinnilatio, (?) trimming (of stones) 1371.
sino/dochium, -dogium, *see* xenodochium.
sinoglossitorium, *see* cinglocetorium.
sinollus, *see* cepa.
sinomomum, *see* cinnamomum.
sinonum (syn-), (?) wild parsley a 1250,
‡14c.
sinopis c 1200, ‡c 1440, cinoprum 1337,
1342, 'sinople' (red or green dye); *cf.* cinnabrium.
sinothus, *see* SYNOD
sinscalus, *see* senescallus.
sinthom-, *see* symptoma.
sin/us, sine (math.) c 1300, 1686; flaunch
(her.) c 1595; -uatus, -uosus, wavy (her.)
c 1595; -uositas c 860, †-ositas c 1436,
sinuosity.
sio, sior, *see* seca.
siosbole, Διὸς βουλή (as etymology of *Sibylla*)
c 1160.
sipes, *see* stipes.
sipe/socha, -ssocna, *see* SCHIP
siphac, peritoneum (Ar.) c 1210, a 1250.
siph/us, -um, -orium, *see* scyphus.
sippa, measure of salt (5 quarters) c 1320;
cf. scyphus, siva, skeppa; *see also* cippus.
sipula, *see* cepa.
siquidem, but 957; *without doubt, certainly, indeed c 1000. a 1170, 1421.
sir/a, -ia, -emotus, *see* SCHIR
siragium, *see* cera.
Siren/ c 1212, ‡15c., Serena 1285, Cerena
1445, mermaid; -ici cantus c 1177.
siric-, *see* sericum (1 & 2).
siringia, *see* syringia.
siro, *see* ciro.
siro-, *see also* chiro-; ciromelum.
sirogrillus, *see* cherogryllus.
sirpus, *see* scirpus.
sir/upus, -opus, *see* syrupus.

sirurg-, *see* CHIRURG
sisa, *see* ASSESS
sisamum, *see* sesamum.
sismaticus, *see* SCHISM
sisolis, *see* seselis.
sison, *see* soter.
†sissa, fountain c 550; flood c 800.
sissera, *see* sicera.
siss/io, -or, *see* SCISS
sista, "counter" (Sc.) 1466; *see also* cista.
sistarchium, *see* sitarchia.
sist/arium, -ra, *see* SEXT
sist/entia, rest a 1520; ‡"chase" (of tennis)
c 1440; -ens, being 13c.; -o (with *inf.*), to
cease, forbear c 1180.
sistrum, *see* thistrum.
sit-, *see also* CIT
sita, *see* 1 seta; situs.
sit/archia (bibl.), sitharcha 790, sitharsia
a 1250, sistarchium c 1255, cistarcia
c 1293, 1336, (?) cysteria (†oysteria) 1256,
(?) cistarida 1247, scrip, wallet; -onomus,
distributor of food 1609.
sitella, *see* situla.
sithcundus, noble (A.S. *gesiðcund*) c 1115.
sit/is, thirst: -ies 1424; *-ibundus c 1130,
1546, †-abundus c 1410, -ibilis c 1470,
thirsty; -ibunde, thirstily, eagerly c 1180,
c 1196; -ula, dipsas (serpent) c 1212;
-ientes (*pl.*) c 1227, 1342, scitientes 1419,
(introit for) Saturday preceding Passion
Week.
situl/a, bucket (or other vessel): citula 1378,
16c., scitula 1425, setula 1423, cetula
1461, 1471; -a, holy water stoup c 1080,
c 1443; cupping-glass c 1200; ‡sitella,
"cheese-vat" 1483; -aris, contained in a
bucket c 1250; -atio, sluicing with buckets
1634; *see also* citola, sitis.
sit/us molendini 1460, -um molendinum
1267, (payment for) mill-site; -us (*pl.*)
patrie 1241, s. terre (*cf.* A.S. *landsidu*)
c 1115, local customs; -um c 1200, c 1460,
-a 14c., *scitus c 1380, 1583, citum
c 1383, *for* -us, site; -us (*adj.*), assessed
1289; -ualis, local, localized c 1205, c 1360;
-ualiter, by situation c 1250, c 1365; -itas
a 1250, -ualitas c 1270, -uatio c 1270,
c 1360, localization (phil.); -uatio, situation,
site c 1325, 1450; laying, putting in position 1313, 1534; *-uatus 1198, c 1595,
scituatus c 1322, 1671, cituatus 1389,
c 1503, situated; *-uor 12c., 15c., scituor
c 1392, 1550, cituor 1274, c 1460, scitor
1430, to be situated; -uo, to put in place,
set up 1267, 1505; to set (a gem) 1303,
c 1315; s. ad firmam, to farm out 1421;
s. leges, to establish laws a 1408; s. summam pecunie, to fix (impose) a payment
1461.
siva, 'sieve', measure of grain c 1186, a 1200;
1281, 1300, syvis 1300, measure of salt;
cf. cribrum, scyphus, sippa.
sive, *see* seu.
sivera, *see* civera.
sivi, *see* se; seu.
six/hindus (†-hundus, -ihindus, sexhindus), (one) having a weregeld of 600 shillings
c 1115.
sixt-, *see* SEXT

sizannia, *see* zizania.

sk-, *see also* sc-

skamberlengeria, *see* CAMER

skarcasium, *see* carcasium.

skebettum, *see* skipettum.

skela 1306, 1388, schela 1271, schala 1270, 'skeel', wooden bucket; *cf.* 2 scala.

skeletta, *see* scutella.

skepp/a 1183, 1412, sceppa 1109, 1261, sceppum c 1250, scheppa 1371, skippa 1299, scippa 13c., escheppa 1142, 1237, *eskeppa 1173, 1354, eskippa c 1320, chepa 1200, 'skep', basket, dry measure; skipo, (?) box or barrel 1291; -arius, basket-maker 1311.

skerda, *see* scherda.

skermia, *see* SKIRM

†sketevata, (?) sort of vat 1421.

skevephilax, treasurer, σκευοφύλαξ (Byzantium) c 1310.

skilingum, 'sheeling', husks (Yorks.) 1319.

skilla, *see* scutella.

skina, *see* eschina.

skipettum 1358, skebettum c 1500, 'skippet' (containing charters, *etc.*).

skippa, skipo, *see* skeppa.

skipp/agium 1332, 1390, schippagium 1334, freight; 15c., -amentum 1315, -iamentum 1302, 1315, eskippamentum 1334, 1360, exkipiamentum 1319, schippatio 1225, eskippatio 1259, -esona 1300, eskippisona 1322, 1329, equipment or manning of ship; s. duplex, manning with double crew 1316, 1329; eskippamentum 1338, 1430, eskippatio 1434, 1508, shipping, shipment; eskippo 1206, 1262, exkippo 1242, exchippo, equipo (G.) 1242, to equip or man (naut.); -o a 1190, eskippo 1233, 1549, exkippo 1233, to ship; eskippo, to sail (*intr.*) c 1150 (C.I.) 1434; *cf.* SCHIP

skir/ewhittus 1338, -wythus 1336, skirret (vegetable).

skirm/ia 1419, skermia 1220, sword-play, fencing (Fr. *éscrime*); -agium, skirmish 1387; -issarius 12c., -isor a 1170, fencer; eskermio, to fence 1207.

skiv-, skuv-, skym-, *see* SCABIN

skumeria, *see* scumarium.

slabba (†flalba) 1270, 1353, sclabba 1301, 1400, 'slab', measure of iron.

slaccum, 'slack', valley (Chesh.) 13c.

sladum, 'slade', stream (Glos.) 1584.

slatt-, *see also* SCLAT

slatta, 'slate', bastard incense 1346.

sledd/um, sledge (Sc.) c 1400; -atio, drawing on a sledge (Yorks.) 1433, 1442; -o, to draw on a sledge (Yorks.) 1434, 1537.

slegium, sledge-hammer 1362.

slepa, measure of linen yarn, (?) slipe 1316.

sletta (†slecta), 'sleet', level field (Norse *slétta*) (Lincs.) c 1160, 1216.

sling/a 1364, -eropa 1325, loop, sling-rope; lenga, sling 1257; (of siege-engine) 1300; eslingator 1193, lingator 1316, lengator 1257, 1318, slinger; ‡lingulo, to sling 15c.; *cf.* lingula.

sloppum, 'slop', loose gown 1378, 1416.

slusagium, *see* EXCLUS

slycatura, (?) liming *or* manuring 1304.

smale/mannus, 'small-man', minor free-

holder 1130; -molmennus, minor rent-payer (Middx.) 1272.

*smaragdo c 1200, 1315, †maragdo 1261, esmaraldus c 1200, esmerald/us, -a c 1200, 1225, emeraldus 1332, amerald/us -a 1234, 1338, ameraud/us, -a 1216, 1300, amarauda 1300, aymeraldus 1303, amarillus 1303, †esmesrada 1234, emeroidus 1345, emerald.

smaragmus, (?) convulsion (σπαραγμός) a 1250.

smelt/atio, -ura, smelting 1433; *cf.* meltarius.

smelt/us 1267, 1324, -is 1296, 1313, smyltus c 1324, smelt (fish).

smeremangestra, dealer in butter and cheese (*f.*) c 1115.

smigm/a (†sungina), *for* smegma, soap c 1200, 1529; s. album 1395; s. nigrum 1395, 1462; -arius c 1340, ‡-ator 15c., soaper.

‡smirtus, (?) betony (bot.) 14c.

smoltus, smolt, young salmon (Sc.) c 1320.

smyrnion (bot.): (?) simirnis a 1250.

snappa, 'snap', morsel (of land) (Sussex) c 1200.

1 snecka 1156, 1303, esnecka 1156, 1203, esnacca 1173, necka c 1200, fast warship.

2 snecka, 'sneck', latch 1317, 1396.

snitelingus, late-born lamb 1288.

snocum, 'snook', point of land (Berwick) c 1230.

†soalagium, (?) *f.l.* for stallagium, 1189.

soc/a (sok-), -um *1086, 1448, -na c 1070, c 1414, sokena c 1087, soke, suit of court, (profits derived from) jurisdiction; *1086, 1588, -na a 1100, c 1320, -agium 1088, 1511, †sochogia 1147, soke, area of special jurisdiction; -na, recourse, refuge c 1115; s. de falda, s. falde, fald-soken 1086; s. molendini, mill-soken c 1130, 1312; s. placitorum c 1115; *cf.* 1 secta;

-agium 1173, a 1443, soggagium 1190, socage, form of free tenure involving suit; a 1125, c 1220, sokemannia 1166, 1392, sokemanria 1275, 1392, -omoneria 1302, land held in socage; service or rent due from a socage c 1128, p 1370; s. divisum, partible socage, gavelkind c 1185; s. forinsecum, foreign (outlying) soke 1203; s. altum c 1186, s. francum 1279, *s. liberum 1185, 1587; s. villanum c 1258; s. quadragesimale, a rent payable to the king at mid-Lent in aid of the farm of the city (London) 1317;

-amannus 1086, c 1300, -omannus c 1140, 13c., sokemannus, sochemannus c 1080, 1392, -mannus 1324, 1374, sakemannus 1201, †-agius c 1300, soke-man, tenant in socage; s. regis 1086, 1276; s. liber c 1130, 1324; s. villanus c 1258, 1307; s. gersumarius c 1280; s. parvus 1307; sochemanna femina 1086; sokemannus c 1320, -arius 1244, sokereva c 1320, sokerevus 1273, 1419, soknerevus 1312, soke-reeve; sokemotus, soke-moot (Lincs.) 1300, 1421.

socagium, bridge-toll paid on passing barrier (? *cf.* Sp. *soga* = rope) (G.) 1314; *see also* soca.

socc/a, -o, *see* SHOCK

1 soccus (sokkus), (woollen) sock 1363.

2 soccus, 'sock', plough-share 1086, c 1258; (?) core (of bell-mould) 1340; **schokus,** (?) socket (of mill-spindle) 1316; **sokettus,** 'socket', spear-head c 1325; **s. de ferro,** (?) spike 1334.

soci/us, servant, (?) reeve c 1115; †(?) opponent c 1150; *****fellow** (ac.) c 1290, 1555; **s. senior** (ac.) 17c.; **sossius,** *for* **-us,** 1279; **-alis,** sociable c 1250; **-ialiter,** sociably 1200; gregariously a 1446; **-ative,** unitedly 870; **-etas,** fraternity (eccl.) 692, 957. c 1130, c 1148; complicity, confederacy (leg.) c 1115, 1291; company (of soldiers) c 1415; **s. Fortune** 1370, **s. Magna** c 1365, the 'Great Company' of mercenaries; **s. Garteriorum,** knighthood of the Garter c 1378; **s. adventuraria,** society of merchant adventurers 1597; **s. Stapule,** society of merchants of the Staple 1463.

Socrat/itas, quiddity of Socrates 13c.; **avis -is,** hoopoe 13c.; †**Sor, Sortes,** for Socrates, as type of the individual (log.) c 1200, c 1380.

socrugenes, sort of medicament a 1250.

soda, head-ache, migraine (Ar.) a 1235, ‡14c.

sodal/is Garterii, knight of the Garter 1416; †**-es,** (?) *for* **-is,** c 550; **-es** (*pl.*) **regis,** magnates 720.

sodom/ia p 1330, 1660, †**-idicum** c 1450, sodomy; *****-ita,** sodomite 1105, a 1446; **-itanus** 1136, c 1250, **-itarius** c 1362, *****-iticus** 6c. 1102, c 1450, **-itus** 6c.; sodomitic; **-ito,** to practise sodomy 1310.

sodularis, *see* SUBTAL

sodurum, *see* **1 solidus.**

soela, *see* **solea.**

soelda, *see* **selda.**

soffrantia, *see* **2 sufferentia.**

soggagium, *see* SOC

soinantagium 1227, **soynentagium** 1260, **suinantagium,** †**sunetagium** 1227, **suignetagium, signetagium** 1221, **suinetagium** 1225, **sunytagium** 1242, **sonentia** (†**seneucia**) 1343, concubinage (Fr. *soignantage*); **sunianta,** concubine 1199.

soinus, *see* ESSONI

sojorn/atio, sojourn, stay c 1474; **-o** 1320, 1466, **sojurno** 1411, **sujurno** c 1250, †**surgerno** c 1456, to sojourn; **subjurno,** to keep, feed a 1216.

sok-, *see* SHOCK; SOC; **soccus.**

sol/, badge of sun 1388; *****gold** (alch.) c 1215, c 1345; or (her.) c 1595; **corona de -e,** *écu au soleil* (Fr. coin) 1532; **in -e,** 'in glory', haloed 1537; **versus -em** 1222, c 1300, **ex opposito solis** 1306, **ex parte -is** c 1282, 1306, **ex p. -ari** a 1190, **proximior -i** 1340, towards the south; **remotior a -e, medius a -e** 1275; *see also* **aqua, granum; -aris,** Southerner c 1470; (*adj.*) heavenly c 970; **natura -aris,** substance of gold (alch.) c 1320; **-anus** c 825, **-arius** 1274, solar; *****-arium** c 1125, 1537, **-aria** (G.) 1291, **-erium** 1264, 1291, (?)†**-ium** 1195, 1555, †**selarium** 1286, solar, upper room or story; **s. caritatis** 1403, **s. caritativum** 1336, (?) misericord loft (eccl.); **s. navis,** upper cabin c 1200; **shopa -erata,** shop on upper floor 1378; **-emstitialis,**

solstitial (astr.) c 730; **-icidium,** sunset c 1360; **-ifer,** sunny 8c.; **-ificum,** gold-making elixir c 1320; **-ifluus,** emanating from the sun c 550; **-isequium,** following the sun c 1612; **-issequa** 7c., **-sequium** c 1200, ‡14c., heliotrope or marigold (bot.); **-cequinus,** of the colour of (?) heliotrope 1355.

sola, *see* **solea.**

sol/acium, -acia, help, helper 7c., 10c.; (time of) relaxation, recreation (mon.) 1293, 1439; **-acius** 1242, c 1350, **-acia** (*f.*) c 1250, relief, deputy (mon.); **-amen,** food c 550; **s. cibi** 10c.; **-atio,** consolation c 1562; **-aciosus** c 1325, **-ativus** c 1183, 15c., consoling, comforting; **-atrix,** consoler (*f.*) a 1100; **-acio** c 730, **-acior** (*dep.*) 596. c 1125, c 1470, to console, solace; **-or,** to console oneself a 1408.

solagium, *see* **solum.**

solanda, *see* **scolanda.**

solanus, young salmon c 1320; *see also* **sol.**

solar-, *see* **sol.**

solatrum, nightshade (bot.) a 1205, 1634.

sold-, *see also* **solidus (1 & 2).**

solda, *see* **selda.**

sol/danus c 1118, 1508, **saldanus** 1228, **-idanus** 12c., 1339, **-idompnus** c 1190, **-tanus** c 1320, **sultanus** c 1188, 1535, **soudanus** 1274, soldan, sultan; ‡**-dana,** sultana 1483; **-danatus,** sultanate c 1250; **-danella,** sea-bindweed (bot.) 1632; *see also* **subdominus.**

solduri (*pl.*), sworn companies of troops 1413.

sol/ea, sole of shoe: **-a** c 1150, **-earium** c 1197; **-a,** sole (fish) 1257, c 1266; **-a molendini** 1325, **soela m.** c 1315, 'sole', sill; 1297, 1306, **soella** 1316, 'sole' (lower frame) of plough; **-ecartum,** sort of cart 1486; *cf.* **sillum, soliva.**

solecismus, solecism, fault: **solocism/us** 13c., 15c.; **-aticus,** faulty (gram.) 13c.

solemn/e (solempn-, solenn-, sollemn-, *etc.*) 1324, **-ium** c 1250, 1269, *****-ia** (*pl., decl. 3 or 2*) c 1188, c 1470, *****-itas** 601, 826. c 1090, 15c., solemn service (eccl.), esp. mass; **-ia** (*pl.*) **missarum** c 1070, c 1545; **-itas,** formality (leg.) c 1285, 1684; **s. juris** c 1452, c 1516; **s. major** (eccl.) c 1223; **s. Pasche** c 1200, **s. Paschalis** c 1006. c 1125, 1559; **-is,** eminent, illustrious 1215, c 1343; †**-us,** *for* **-is,** solemn 1234; **-issimus,** most eminent c 1357; **-issime,** most solemnly c 1220; **-izatio,** rite (of coronation) 1308, c 1341; (of benediction) c 1400; formality (leg.) 1684; *****s. matrimonii** 1236, 1564, **s. nuptiarum** 15c.; **-izo,** *****to solemnize, celebrate a 1100, c 1444; c 1200, 1274, ‡**-io** 1483, to keep holiday; (?) to canonize 1427; to distinguish, dignify 14c.; *****s. matrimonium** c 1290, c 1540, **-o matrimonium** 1309.

sol/emstitialis, -eratus, -erium, -icidium, *see* **sol.**

solesco, *see* **solite.**

soliata, terra, 1401, 1572, **t. solidata** 1400, (?) 'soiled' land, former freehold land purchased by bondman (Norf. & Suff.).

solicit-, *see* SOLLICIT

soli/cola, -colus, -cula, *see* **solum.**

1 solid/us, undisturbed (of tenure) a 1121, c 1150; settled (of weather) c 1200; staunch, reliable 1347, c 1470; **numerus -us,** product of three or more factors a 1250; **-e,** undisturbedly (of tenure) c 1180; **-itas,** firmness (of character) 1166, 14c.; **-iusculus,** fairly solid c 1115; **-um,** undivided property 15c.; **ex -o** c 1125, **in -o** 1267, c 1532, ***in -um** 1200, 1502, collectively, jointly, in entirety, wholesale; **-amen,** defence, mainstay 720. c 1450; **-amentum,** confirmation c 730; **-atim,** firmly 1001; **-ator,** strengthener c 1184; **-atio,** strengthening 12c.; c 1437, **souldatio** 1430, **-atura** 1326, 1580, **soldatura** 1297, ‡15c., **soldura** c 1290, 1370, **soudura** 1268, 1376, **soudara** 1408, **soudyra** 1423, **soldarium** c 1460, **solderium, soulderium** 1533, **sodurum** c 1450, soldering, solder; **-atura,** "ground-selling" 1580; **-ativus,** consolidating a 1250; **sowdelis** 1338, **soudeletta** 1388, 1466, **solderetta** 1277, saddle-bar (arch.); **-o,** to combine c 1180; to drain (marsh) 15c.; 1295, **soldo** 1333, ***soudo** 1274, 1386, **soldero** 1277, **souduro** 1284, to solder; *see also* **soliata.**

2 solid/us, **shilling, sou* 6c., 955. 1086, 1564; unit of weight (12 dwt.) c 1100, 1419; 1209, 1294, **-i** (*pl.*) 1230, 1243, **solda** c 1362, **-atio** 1130, c 1180, **-ata** 1086, 1422, **soldata** 1234, c 1250, **soldea** 1212, **soldeia** c 1300, wages, pay; **secundum -um et libram,** in money paid by weight (G.) 1289; **-us argenti** 11c., 12c.; **s. auri** 955. 12c.; **s. Cennomanensis** c 1140; **s. Parisiensis** 1337; **s. Scoticus** 1537; ***s. sterlingorum** c 1185, 15c.; **s. Toronensis** 1274, **s. Turonensis** 1158, 1418; **-arius** c 1125, 1162, **-atorius** 1405, hired; hireling c 1115; 1086, 1468, ***soldarius** 1086, 1583, **souldarius** 1495, **sowdarius** 1471, **soldiarius** a 1564, **souldiarius** 1548, **soldatarius** 1234, **solditiarius** 1315, **solitarius** 12c., **saldator** 1488, **soudatus** c 1450, (mercenary) soldier; **soldarius ad arma** 1316; **s. ad lanceam** c 1415; ***-ata** 1086, 1555, **-atus** c 1185, c 1460, shilling's worth; **-o,** to pay c 1123, 1241.

soli/ficum, -fer, -fluus, -ssequa, *see* **sol.**

†soli/fugum, *for* **-puga,** venomous animal c 1212.

soliloquus, speaking for or to oneself c 600.

solinus, *see* **sullinga.**

†solitana, (?) jar 9c.

sol/itarius, hermit 7c., 826. c 1182, 14c.; **-itarie,** in solitude, singly 1265, c 1443; **-itivus,** solitary c 1150; **-ivagium,** solitary roaming c 1250; **-ivagans,** straying alone c 1360; ***-omodo,** *for* **-ummodo,** only 1292, c 1450; *see also* **2 solidus.**

sol/ite c 1440, **-ito** 12c., 14c., customarily; **-esco,** to become accustomed 8c.

solium, *see* **sol.**

soliva 1223, 1321, ***sulliv/a** 1231, 1327, **-um** 1289, sill (arch.), horizontal beam (Fr. *solive*); *cf.* **sillum, solea, subsulliva.**

solivag-, *see* **solitarius.**

sollagium, *see* **solum.**

soll/emnis, -empnis, -ennis, *etc., see* **solemne.**

sollenda, solan goose, gannet (Sc.) 1521.

sollicit/as (solicit-), *for* **-udo,** care, toil a 1408; **-arius** 1452, 1540, **-ator** c 1444, 1546, **-or** 1480, 1620, solicitor (leg.); **-ator generalis** 1566, 1588; **-or regis** 1533; **-er,** *for* **-e,** carefully 1414; **†sollicior,** *for* **-ior,** c 1250; **†sollicius,** *for* **-ius,** c 1250, 1262; **-o,** to be anxious 7c.; 1381, **s. negotia** 1447, to transact business.

sollinga, *see* **sullinga.**

solocism/us, -aticus, *see* **solecismus.**

solomodo, *see* **solitarius.**

solopium, *see* **sedlopum.**

solor, *see* **solacium.**

solotenus, *see* **solum.**

solsequium, *see* **sol.**

solt/a, -um, *see* **solutio.**

soltanus, *see* **soldanus.**

sol/um, field (her.) 1654; ***-otenus,** down to the ground c 950. c 1090, 1461; **-us,** site (G.) 1315; **-agium** 1182, 1325, **sullagium** a 1200, 1302, 'solage', ground-rent; **-icola** 931, c 1021, **-icolus** 11c., **-icula** 11c., 12c., **†colicola** 12c., cultivator, inhabitant.

solutare, *see* SUBTAL

solu/tio, dissolution, destruction 870; absolution c 1160; refutation (log.) c 1343, c 1357; solution (alch.) a 1235, ‡1652; **s. matrimonii** c 1200; **s. termini,** end of term 1569; **eo in -tionem,** to accept liability 1203, 1239; **-scio** 1226, *for* **-ta** 1205, **-tum** 1283, ***solta** 1130, 1230, **soltum** c 1000, payment; *see also* **pars;** **†-tatio,** (?) payment (or *f.l.* for **solicitatio**) 14c.; **-bilis,** destructible c 860; payable 1535, 1583; **-tivum** 13c., **‡-torium** 15c., a laxative (med.); **-tivus,** laxative a 1250; **potestas -tiva,** power of loosening 1609; **littere -torie,** magic characters with power to set free c 730; **-tor,** payer, paymaster c 1236, c 1394; **-te,** freely, without disturbance (of tenure) a 1100, a 1135; **-tus,** free, undisturbed 1086, a 1123; c 1220, 1684, **s. conjugio** 13c., unmarried (person); divorced 1234; **†-tus,** concerned (? *f.l.* for **solicitus**) c 1360; **solvo,** to pay (with personal *obj.*) 1297, c 1450; to pay off (a fleet) 1416; to relax sentence, absolve (eccl.) 1195, c 1332; to refute (log.) c 1343; to act as a laxative c 1180; **s. debitum (nature),** to die c 1230, c 1362; **s. in lacrimas,** to burst into tears 1415; **s. jejunium,** to violate a fast 1410; **s. silentium,** to break silence c 1245; **s. extra,** to pay out a 1300; **s. pro,** to pay for 1309, c 1434; **s. sursum,** to pay up, surrender 1293, 1294.

som-, *see also* SAGM; SUMMON

soma c 550, c 1000. a 1142, **suma** c 550, **zoma** c 1220, body (σῶμα).

somalis, *see* **sella.**

somellatus, *see* **semella.**

somn/iatio (sompn-), dreaming c 1450; **-iatim,** in a dream c 860; **-iator,** sleeper c 1090; **-iculus,** light sleep a 1100; **-iculosus,** fanciful 1521; **-ositas,** drowsiness a 1250; **-osus,** afforded by sleep c 550; **-iger,** soporific c 800; **-ilocutio,** talking in sleep c 1260; **-olenter,** sleepily (eccl.); **-olentia,** sleepiness c 800. c 1125, 15c.

somon-, *see* SUMMON

sona, *see* **zona.**

son/atio, making a sound p 1300, c 1375; **-abilis,** audible, utterable c 730; **-alia** (*pl.*), bells a 1530; **tabula -atilis,** clapper (mon.) c 1266, c 1330; **-ativum,** source of sound a 1233; **musca -ipes,** buzzing fly 1414; **-itus,** ringing (of bells) c 1250, 1326; (*adj.*) deep-voiced, full-voiced c 1000; **-orabilis,** high-sounding a 1205; **-oreus,** sonorous, sounding c 550; **-ore** c 980, **-oriter** c 950, c 1006. c 1266, c 1330, noisily; **-oritas** c 1190, **-itas** 14c., (sweet) sound; (vocal) euphony or clarity 790, c 1000. c 1125, c 1520; ring (of metal) 1282; **-um,** *for* **-us,** sound 12c.; **in -um dishonerationis,** in insulting tones 1468; **-o,** to ring, reject (coins) c 1115, c 1192; **s. ad** 1380, **s. in** c 1337, 1419, to have a ring of, point towards; **-oro,** to snore c 1266; to tune (an organ) 1512.

sonentia, *see* **soinantagium.**

1 †sonium, (?) fishing-place 1350.

2 soni/um, -us, -o, *see* ESSONI

sopa, soparius, *see* **shopa.**

soperum, *see* **suppa.**

sophene, *see* **saphene.**

sophi (*pl.*), **sufis,** contemplatives (Ar.) 1221.

1 sophia, sophy, shah 1508.

2 soph/ia c 550, c 990. c 1125, 1345, **-isma** c 760, 11c., wisdom; **-isma accidentis,** fallacy of the accident (log.) p 1300; **-icus,** concerned with wisdom c 550, c 790; **-us,** wise 8c., c 860. c 1200 (*see also* **sophi**); **-ista,** learned man 781. a 1142; student who has passed his first examination (ac.) 1292, c 1550; **s. antiquus,** the Devil c 1250; **-isticator,** sophist, quibbler c 1283; **-isticalis,** sophistical 1377; **-isticatio,** tampering, adulteration a 1250, 1385; c 1267, 1523, **-istica** c 1300, **-istria** 1428, ‡1483, **-estria** c 1500, sophistry, trickery; **-istria,** passing first examination (ac.) c 1384, 1424; **-istice,** sophistically, deceitfully c 1190, 1594; **-isticus,** forged (of document) c 1250; bogus (of gold) c 1227, 15c.; adulterated 13c., c 1356; **disputatio -istica,** first examination (ac.) c 1550; **-istico,** to tamper with, adulterate, disguise c 1212, 14c.; to quibble, trick with words c 1267, 1461.

sopi/tivus, soporific a 1250; **†-talis,** (?) occurring in sleep (or *f.l.* for **sospitalis,** salutary) c 1000; **-o** (*intr.*), to sleep, be quieted c 1170, 14c.

sopo, *see* **suppa.**

sopor/atio, sleep c 850; **-ativus,** soporific a 1250; **-eus,** (?) **†sorporeus,** of or for sleep c 550.

sopositus, *see* SUPPOSIT

Sor, *see* SOCRAT

soragium, *see* **sorus.**

sorb/a, *for* **-um** (bot.), a 1235, ‡15c.

sorb/itiuncula, little draught (eccl.); **‡-illum,** "sop" 1570; **-ello,** to gobble up c 550; **-eo,** to overwhelm c 730.

sorc-, *see* **sors.**

sord/itas 13c., **-ia** (*pl.*) 1313, **-iuscula** c 1195, **sors** 790, filth; **-idatio,** defilement 720; **-idatrix,** defiler (*f.*) c 1100; **-ido,** to defile (eccl.); to find guilty (leg.) c 1115.

sorellus, *see* **sorus.**

sor/ex, shrew: **-ix** c 650, **surex** a 1446; **‡-ex,** "dormouse", "rat" 15c.; "water rat" 1552; **-icidium,** "rat's bane" 1555; **†-dilegus,** cat 1220.

sorgh/um 1641, **gramen -inum** 1634, sorghum (bot.).

†soria, (?) *for* **storia** *or* **sophia,** c 550.

sorlingus, *see* SCHER

sormulettus, *see* **sorus.**

†sornagium, 'sorning', enforced hospitality (Sc.) or (?) *f.l.* for **servagium** a 1400.

sornecc/a, -um, sort of ship 1204, 1225.

soroga, *see* **wroga.**

soror/, nun c 730, c 1125, c 1480; lay sister a 1106, 1432; **s. minor** (G.) 1289, **s. minorissa** 1294, 1321, minoress (mon.); **-a,** *for* **s.,** sister 785; **-itas,** sisterhood (mon.) c 1422, c 1458; **‡-ia,** sister's daughter 15c.; **-ius,** *sister's husband c 1080, 1456; wife's brother 1239, 1295; (?) sister's son c 1160.

sorporeus, *see* SOPOR

sors 893. c 1275, c 1362, **sort/a** 1387, portion, lot (of land); *c 1340, 1587, **-a** 1395, **-um** 1433, sort, kind, set; 1467, **-a** 1463, 1471, 'sort', measure of fruit; divination c 1115, c 1160; **s. Dei,** the religious life 1087; **s. Domini,** clergy c 1534, c 1546; **s. regni,** upper class c 1000; **s. principalis,** principal of debt 1267, 1684; **sorceria** 1169, 1432, **-ilegia** c 1220, *-ilegium c 1225, c 1446, sorcery, divination; **-iaria** 12c., c 1225, **sorcera** 1275, **-ilega** a 1142, p 1330, **†-iloga** c 1470, sorceress; **-iarius** c 1225, **-ilegus** c 1115, 1406, **†-ilegius** c 1290, sorcerer, diviner; **-io,** to elect c 1000; **-ior,** to be allotted c 1260; (?) to contain c 1200; (with *dat.*) to sort with, befit 14c.; to issue, come to pass 13c., 1378; **s. effectum** c 1325, 1522, **s. finem** c 1443, to take effect; *see also* SORD

sor/us *1179, 15c., **†sozus** 1413, **saurus** a 1147, *'sore', unmewed (falc.); **accipiter de -agio,** sore sparrowhawk c 1200; **-us,** brown (of hounds) 1213; 1235, 1314, *-ellus 1277, 1452, sorrel (of horses); **s. badius,** sorrel bay 1300, 1312; **-bauzanus** a 1181, **s. bauszanus** 1326; **s. brunus** 1313; **s. liardus** 1316; **allec -um,** red herring 1297, 1534; **-mulettus,** red mullet (fish) 1299; *see also* **pirum; surus,** brown (of bread) c 1234; **sourus** 1286, 1356, **coerus** 1255, **zoerus** 1271, **szoherus** 1256, **zourus** 1255, 1300, **zhourus** 1282, buck or hart of fourth year; **s. cervi** 1323; **cervus saurus** c 1350; **sourellus** 1354, **sowrellus** 1494, (?) buck of third year; **sourellus cervi** 1334.

†soscallus, (?) stag-hound c 1250.

sosorium, *see* SALS

***sospit/as** (eccl.), **-atio** 1313, health; *see also* SOPI

†sossile, (?) *for* **fossile,** some chemical substance c 1215.

sossius, *see* SOCI

sot/er, Saviour 10c.; **-ira,** an anodyne (σώτειρα) a 1250; **sison,** save (σῶσον) c 550.

sottus, sot c 1125.

sotular-, sotilar-, *see* **subtal.**

soucio, *see* **succinium.**

soud-, sould-, *see also* solidus (1 & 2).

soudanus, *see* soldanus.

†sounda, 'sound', bladder (of fish) 1324, 1418.

soursa, 'source', corbel or bracket (arch.) 1333; sursa, source, fount c 1160, 1322.

sour/us, -ellus, sowrellus, *see* sorus.

southpars, *see* SUTH

sowd-, *see* solidus (1 & 2).

soynentagium, *see* soinantagium.

†sozor, (wooden) part of windlass 1333; (?) *cf.* soursa.

sozus, *see* sorus.

spad-, *see also* SPATH

spadon/atus (equus), gelded 1326; ‡caro -ia, "capon flesh" 15c.

spagyr/icus, disciple of Paracelsus (alch.) 1620, ‡1652.

spainellus, *see* HISPAN

spalan-, *see* phalangium.

spald/a, -era, spall/a, -eria, *see* SPATH

spalm-, spall-, spalt-, *see* psal-; SPASM

spaloreus, *see* SQUAL

spalto, to spay (sows) 1336.

spameus, *see* SQUAM

spanga, spangle 1415.

span/shakelum, part of plough-harness 1361; -natus, yoked 1340.

‡spara, spar (mineral) 1652; *see also* SPARR

sparagus, *see* asparagus.

‡sparallium, *clyster uterinus* 1652.

sparg-, *see also* sparsio.

spargan/um, swaddling band c 950; -a (*pl.*), seeds 10c.

spargula, *see* spergula.

sparhauca, sparrow-hawk 1544.

sparnum 1199, 1205, espernium (†esperinum) c 1330, (department dealing with) reserve in store (mon.) (Fr. *épargne*).

*sparr/a (sperr-), -um, spar (esp. of roof) 1302, 1464.

sparrus, *see* spervarius.

spar/sio (sper-) c 1283, 1390, -cio 1357, -gatio 1390, -gitio 1430, spreading (of hay, *etc.*); s. seminis, scattering of seed a 1186, c 1290; s. sanguinis, bloodshed 1415; -go, sprinkling c 1000; -gibilis, easily dissipated a 1275; ostentatious c 1325; -gitor 1397, ‡-gillum 1570, sprinkler (for holy water); -se, sparsely c 1290, c 1517; -sim, more or less 8c.; -sor, scatterer a 1408; -go c 1283, 1430, -so 1352, to spread, ted (hay); to calumniate c 1402; *cf.* aspersio.

spart/a (spert-) c 1250, spretta 1398, 'spart', rush (for thatching); (?) mat 1436; 1214, spreta 1308, (?) fender *or* sprit (naut.); (*pl.*) sort of garment c 1200.

spartha, 'sparth', battle-axe 1294, 1381; s. manualis 1340.

sparv/arius, -erius, *see* spervarius.

spasm/a 1461, c 1540, -us a 1250, (?) spalmus c 1260, spasm, convulsion (med.); -aticus a 1250, c 1462, -osus c 1210, a 1250, spasmodic, convulsive; -osis, "*scabies vesice*" a 1250; -o, to convulse a 1250, a 1408.

spath/a (spat-) 13c., 15c., spada c 1298, sword; spade c 1200; placita de -a 1199, p. ad -am pertinentia 1200, p. spade 1300, pleas of the sword, equivalent to pleas of the crown (Norm. & C.I.); -amen

(-umen), trepan a 1250; -arius c 1170, c 1362, spadarius 1198, swordsman; -arenticus, *see* sapo; -ula, flat spoon, ladle 1524, 1622; flag, gladiolus (bot.) ‡14c., 1402; c 1170, 1480, -ulum 1507, spada 1455, spadula 1308, spalda 1240, 1360, spalla 1290, spaulla 1253, 1291, shoulder-blade, shoulder; spaula 1384, -ularia 1295, spaldera 1223, spalleria 1310, spaulerium (†spanlerium), espaudlera 1215, espaulera 1224, shoulder-strap, *épaulette*.

spati/um 11c., 12c., -olum c 1125, lifetime, span; measure of length, (?) span c 1456, 1410, c 1460, -a 1380, 1386, bay (arch.); s. arcus, bow-shot 1478; -atim, at intervals, dispersedly c 1266; -atio, dimension c 1620; -ator (per noctem), prowler 1380; -atus, a walk or ride c 1140, c 1200; -ose, for a space of time 1344; -ositas, spaciousness, size c 1070, a 1250; -o me, to roam 1227; -o 1336, -or c 1250, 1375, to walk abroad (mon.); -or, (?) to expatiate (on) *or* investigate 1289, 1303.

specca, 'speck', patch of leather 1532.

speci/es, form, εἶδος (phil.) c 850. a 1100, c 1360; specific effect 1267; class of numerals (math.) a 1150, 15c.; *species, kind (of the elements of the eucharist) a 1240, 1523; (*pl.*) *a 615. a 1142, 1602, -e (*pl.*) 1290, 1304, †spicis (*abl. pl.*) p 1330, 1364, -ata (*n. pl.*) c 1180, spices (including groceries, drugs, *etc.*); s. immaterialis, form as distinct from matter c 1200; s. informans, form as source of representation a 1304; s. intelligibilis, s. sensibilis a 1304; s. singularis, s. universalis, mental impression of individual and of universal c 1267; -es confecte, comfits c 1335; in -e, in its own shape 13c.; *specifically, in particular c 1327, 1545; -etenus, in appearance (only) c 1110, c 1200; face to face 13c.;

-ale, particular case or quality c 1170, 1457; in -ali, in particular 1241, c 1343; -alis, confidential c 1195, a 1408; *(subst.) special friend, intimate c 1250, a 1408; -alior, more intimate 1227, c 1250; -alissimus, most intimate c 1250, 16c.; relating to *infima species* (log.) c 850; -es -alissima c 1270, 1610; *-aliter c 1080, 1582, especialiter 1419, -atim c 800. 15c., c 1546, especially, specifically; -alius, more especially 12c., c 1378; -alissime, most especially a 1250, 1327; -alitas, special quality, peculiarity c 1191; special degree c 1450; a characteristic of a species 1374, 1420; special food (mon.) c 1266, c 1293; special friendship 1224, 15c.; special spiritual benefit 1225; special mention 1276; trusted self (title) c 1250; 1205, a 1564, factum -ale 1307, 1369, specialty, special deed or bond (leg.); -amen, embodiment of a species 1421;

-aria (*n. pl.*) 1259, (*f. s.*) 1265, 1332, -eria 1305, speceria 1236, 1307, spiceria 1270, grocery, spices, *etc.* (*coll.*); -aria 1315, 1390, spicieria c 1279, spiceria 1397, c 1472, spisaria 1454, spicery (office, store-room, or market); -arius 1176, c 1438, spesarius c 1205, spiciarius 1257, c 1283, spicerius

1251, **-etarius** c 1330, **-enarius** c 1270, **-narius** c 1477, spicer, grocer; **-ficatio**, specification, detailed statement 870. c 1258, 1684; working up of materials c 1258; **-ficative** c 1300, c 1363, **-fice** a 1233, 1686, specifically; **-ficativus**, specifying a 1250, p 1300; **-ficitas**, specific quality 13 c.; **-ficus**, specified, specific 870. c 1238, 1620; **-fico**, *to specify, classify c 790, 870. c 1180, 1684; to cause to appear 790.

specill/a, mirror 870; **s. ocularia** (*pl.*), spectacles 1620; **-um opticum**, telescope c 1622.

speci/men 781, *-ositas c 860. c 1125, 1528, beauty; spice a 1200; **s. crucis**, sign of the cross 12c.

spect/us, aspect 6c.; **-abilitas generis**, nobility of race c 1090; **-abiliter**, illustriously c 1250; **-aculum**, ‡beacon 1570; lens c 1200, 1383; **s. manuale**, gazing crystal c 1410; **-acula** (*pl.*), spectacles, eyeglasses 1416, 1518; **-amen**, phenomenon c 1200; **-atio**, expectation 1413; **-o**, to look after, have charge of c 1270; *(with *dat.*) c 1244, 1533, *s. ad 1185, 1540, to pertain, belong to.

specul/um comburens, burning-glass 1267, 1620; **s. perspicuum**, lens a 1292; **-a**, *for* **-um**, mirror 8c., 1090; **-e** (*pl.*), spectacles 1514; **-a**, position of overseer 7c.; *-abilis, able to be an object of speculation c 1290, 1380; **-amen**, thing observed 870; **-ar**, mirror (fig.), model c 1125; **-aris**, brilliant p 1341; seen as in a glass 1378; **-ariter** 12c., 1374, †-**anter** 12c., as in a glass; **-arius**, crystal-gazer c 1160, c 1320; **-atio**, outlook, prospect c 730, c 790; supervision 7c., 723. c 1250, c 1296; contemplation 948. c 1080, 1382; speculation, theory 12c., c 1430; **-atius**, with closer observation c 1212; **-ative**, theoretically c 1300; **-ativa**, speculative philosophy 1252; **-ativum** a 1408, **-ativa** (*pl.*) 1406, c 1440, theoretical knowledge; **-ativus**, vigilant 1414; *speculative, theoretical c 1160, 1549; **-ator**, overseer, bishop a 615, 956. c 1072; theologian c 1343; author of *Speculum Judiciale* (Guillaume Durand) p 1394, a 1446; (*adj.*) rampant (her.) c 1595; **forma -atoris**, a form of compromise (leg.) 1490, 1492; †-**ator** (*v.*), to observe c 550; **-or** (*pass.*), to be observed 1062.

*specumina, (?) *f.l.* for speciaria, 1220.

speka, *see* 2 spica.

spel/keria, -uco, *see* espelcatio.

spelta, tin or copper ore 7c. a 1250.

spelunca, (?) covered passage 1232; kilntower 1351; tomb c 1343, c 1400.

spen/dimentum, treasury (mon.) 1360; **-sa**, ‘spense’, store-room (Sc.) 1299, a 1566; **(papyrus) -dabilis** 1467, **(candela) -sabilis** c 1330, for everyday use; *cf.* DISPENS, EXPEN

sper-, *see also* **spar-**; SPHER

1*sper/a 1285, c 1444, **-um** 1238, **espera** c 1300, **spora** 1250, **espoerum** 1268, **esporum** 1251, **spura** 1287, 1233, **espurrum** 1261, ‘speer’, screen, partition; (?) sideboard, dresser 1405, 1415.

2 **spera**, spire (of church) 15c.

3 †**sper/a** (*n. pl.*), hopes 1165; **-atio**, hopefulness 1344; **-ativus**, **-atorius**, hopeful 1344; †**-atum**, (?) estimate a 1564; **-o** (with *inf.*), to hope, intend c 1200, c 1307; **s. in**, to rest hope in c 1180, c 1504; **s. super**, to hope for 12c.

sper/dux, -duta, *see* **experductum**.

spergula, spargula, spurrey (bot.) a 1250; *cf.* **aspergula**.

sperkeria, *see* **expercaria**.

sperlingus 1342, ‡1483, **spirlingus** 1342, ‘sparling’, sprat (fish).

sperm/a, sperm 12c., c 1362; **s. divinum, s. salutis** c 950; **s. cete** 1267,‡ **s. ceti** 14c., spermaceti; **s. piscium**, spawn 1377; **-aticus**, relating to sperm a 1250, 1252; †**sperniolum**, *sperma ranarum* 1652; **-ologus**, word-sower c 950 (*cf.* **sermologus**); **-atizo**, to emit sperm c 1210, a 1250.

sper/varius (spar-) 1214, c 1400, **-verius** c 1180, 1333, -**ivarius** 1197, **sprevarius** 1086, 1185, **spirvarius** 1230, **sprivarius** 1198, 1203, *esper/varius (espar-)* 1210, 1336, **-verius** 1316, 15c., **-everius** 1286, †**-verus** c 1200, **expervarius** 1320, **espreverus** c 1160, ‡**aspervarius** 1483, †**sparrus** 1464, **espervicus, supravicus** a 1446, sparrowhawk (falc.).

speta, a spit 1422.

speudo-, *see* PSEUD

sphalma, error 1687.

spher/a (sper-), sphere (fig.), rank c 1396; **s. obliqua, s. recta** (astr.) c 1233; **-alis** c 1267, *-icus c 1125, c 1450, spherical; **numerus -icus**, cube number a 1250, 1344; **opus -icum** (in carving) a 1150; **-aliter** c 1270, **-ice** a 1200, 1267, spherically; **-icitas**, spherical shape 1267, c 1360; **-isterium**, “tennis play”, “tennis court” 1550, 1593; **-ois**, spheroid (astr.) 1686; **-ula** little ball, knob 1149, c 1250; (?) gazing crystal a 1400; **spirule** (*pl.*), “bowls” (game) 1541; **spurula**, ball-game 1481; 1313, 1368, (?) †**spicula** 1547, incense-boat; †**-ulatum**, (?) object ornamented with knobs 14c.

sphingius (spingius), sphinx-like c 1470.

spia, spy, look-out (*f.*) 1292.

spic-, *see also* **species**.

1 **spic/a Celtica** 13c., ‡14c., **s. Selteca** 1414, **s. Indica** c 1260, **s. nardi** a 1250, 1480, spikenard; ‡**-amentum**, straw 1483; **-ator**, gleaner 1401; **-o** 1234, 1401, ‡**-iligo** 1570, to glean; to sort (seed) 1328.

2 **spica** 1276, 1278, †**splica** 1460, **speka** 1480, (wooden) thatch-pin; **spik/a** 1282, 1320, (iron) spike; **-ingus** 1261, 1324, **clavus -ingus** 1302, c. **-us** 1336, **-naylum** c 1445, spike-nail.

spicul/a, *for* **-um**, (?) dart 14c.; **-um**, thatchpin 1297; **-ator**, (?) dart-thrower c 1197; *executioner c 900. c 1250, 1570; assassin a 1142; **-atus**, ruthless c 1250; ‡**-or**, “to cast a dart” 1483; *see also* SPHER

†**spidecia**, a skin-disease a 1250.

spig/urnellus 1193, 1586, **-ornellus** 1258, 1294, **espigurnellus** 1213, †**sprigonellus** 1260, ‘spigurnel’, hereditary sealer of writs; **-urnalcia** 1286, **-urnaucia** c 1328, **espicurnaucia** 1279, **-ornelia** c 1283,

-urnelria 1284, -ornaleria 1286, office of spigurnel.
spik-, *see* 2 spica.
‡spilamenes, "slut" 1570.
spillo, *see* 1 vispilio.
spilloria, *see* pilloria.
†spillum, (?) rock c 550.
spin/a, goad, spur 13c.; spigot c 1140; s. alba 12c., 1268, arbor -alis 1573, hawthorn; s. nigra a 1250, 13c., s. prunellifera a 1150, blackthorn; ‡s. sancta, buckthorn 14c.; s. viva, quickset thorn 1310; -ale, spine, back-bone a 1235; -alis, -ealis, of thorns a 1275; -ata, ridge-pole, roof-tree a 1050; -aticus, fish, (?) stickleback c 1160; ‡-eolum, sloe 1570; *-etum, -eta 1086, 1353, -ata 1282, spinney *or* thorn tree; -etum, thicket (fig.), tribulation a 1200; thorny nature c 730; haia -eta, thorn-hedge c 1362; espineta, spinet (mus.) c 1608, 1620; -etum, aspinetum 1368, pannus diaspinet' 1358, 'spinet' (cloth made at Spinney, Cambs.); -ivorus, thistle-eating (ἀκανθοφάγος) 1544; -us, bird, (?) greenfinch (ἀκανθίς) 1544; -eum 1338, -ula (?) 12c., skewer, pin; -osulus, objector 794; -ula, thorny point, objection 794; ‡-ulentus, thorny 1483; -ulosus, captious a 1090; -eo a 1275, -o c 1180, ‡1483, to prick, pierce; -o, to crown with thorns 1431; (?) to make a thorn hedge c 1285.
spinachi/a 13c., 1622, -um 1270, †spinarchia a 1250, spinach.
spin/acia, -acium, -ea, *see* pinacia.
spinct/er (spint-) c 1200, ‡1483, -rum 1444, c 1510, †spinetrum p 1500, †sprinctum 1532, pin, brooch; pin, spike (arch.) 1470, 1490; s. rhombulatus, lozenge (her.) c 1595.
spindul/a, pall-pin c 1188; -atus, fastened with a pin c 1188.
spinella, sort of ship 1438; *cf.* pinacia.
spingius, *see* sphingius.
spin/ula, -us, *etc.*, *see* spina.
‡spinx, "spink", chaffinch 1483; ‡glow-worm 15c.
†spipatus, (?) *for* stipatus, c 550.
spir/aculum venti, blast of air c 1308; -abilitas, inspirability c 1290; -amen, aspirate (gram.) 7c.; 760. c 1436, -amentum c 1250, -antia, -atio c 1362, inspiration, afflatus (theol.); S. Divinum c 1250, 1416, S. Sanctum c 670, Holy Ghost; -atio, breathing, breath 870. c 1170; -ativus, acting by inspiration c 1290, p 1300; -ator, inspirer c 1290, p 1300; aspirant c 1218; -o (with *inf.*) c 1170, a 1408, s. ad 12c., c 1218, to aspire; s. federa (in), to conspire a 1408.
spir/alitas, spiral shape c 1620; -alis, spiral 1620, 1686; -ula, coil 12c.; ‡ferrule 1483; *see also* SPIRIT
spirasmus, *see* pirasmus.
spirit/us, spirit, vapour (alch.) c 1215, 1620; (with *gen.*) spirit, mood, disposition (bibl.) c 1155, c 1534; soul (theol.) c 1266, c 1343; spirit, supernatural being, apparition (bibl.) c 1090, 1546; 12c., c 1400, s. almus c 1180, c 1420, S. Dei c 1250, c 1370, s. sacer 1252, *s. sanctus c 1080, 1545, Holy Ghost; -u

c 1390, *in -u 12c., c 1450, in the spirit (bibl.); via -us sancti, mode of election by unanimous 'inspiration' (eccl.) 1417, 1426; -um habeo, to have a mind to c 1192; ‡s. fetens, sulphur 1652; s. salium, spirits of salts 1686; s. vini, spirits of wine c 1620, 1686; s. animalis a 1250, 1620, s. corporeus a 1233, -ūs (*pl.*) motivi a 1233, s. vitalis c 1270, vital principle or substance; s. visibilis, visual medium c 1115, a 1250; -alis (-ualis) 8c., c 1006. c 1090, 15c., -eus c 1160, spiritual; ecclesiastical 1252, 1686; spiritual (of relationships) c 1125, c 1414; -ualissimus, most spiritual c 1250; -alia (-ualia), respiratory organs (med.) a 1250; spiritual things, spiritual benefits 939. c 1125, 1686; spiritualities (eccl.) c 1125, 1580; -aliter (-ualiter) 597, 8c. c 1080, 1468, †spiraliter c 1500, spiritually; in respect of spiritual things 12c., c 1450; -ualitas, spiritual intercourse c 1520; 1267, c 1444, spiralitas 870, spiritual nature; spirituality, ecclesiastical possession 1219, 1575; -uosus, spirituous 1622; containing animal spirit 1620; -ificatio, spiritualizing c 1500; -ifico, to spiritualize, transform into spirit, c 1500.
spirlingus, *see* sperlingus.
spiro, *see* spiraculum.
spirula, *see* sphera; spiralitas.
spirvarius, *see* spervarius.
spisaria, *see* species.
spiss/itudo 1248, 1323, -um 1251, thicket; -ificatio, thickness 1335; -im, densely, frequently c 1100, c 1412; -ius, more frequently 1421.
spiteclutum, iron 'clout' on some part of plough (Essex, Suffolk) 1208, 1362.
spitella, spade 1335.
spitham/a, span 1620; -eus, span-long 1641.
splatto, to 'splat', split (fish) 1335.
splendi/ficus 690, c 860. a 1300, -fer (? -ferus) c 1125, 1433, brilliant; -ficativus, illuminating c 1260; -fluus, bright-flowing 8c.; -fico, to glorify c 860. a 1155.
splen/dilidion (*-dilidino), spleenwort a 1250, ‡14c.; ‡-etica, hart's tongue (bot.) 14c.
‡splendona, "sword" (? *for* σφενδόνη) c 1440, 1483.
splent/a (†splouta) 1283, 1375, -ea 1357, splinta 1277, 1305, splint, lath; 1328, splinta c 1334, metal plate; -ea (ossis), splinter 1223; -atio, fitting with laths 1524; -o, to fit with laths 1272, 1336.
splica, *see* 2 spica.
splot/tum, plot of land (Dorset) 1280; spotellum, (?) small plot (Som.) c 1230; -gabulum, a pasture rent (Hants) 13c.
spoka, spoke 1279, 1346.
spola, spool, bobbin a 1200, ‡1483.
spoli/ativus, extortionate 1380; ‡-atorium, den of thieves 1483; spulum, spoil 772; -o (domum), to unroof c 1300.
†spolio, a fur-bearing animal 1220.
spon/da, barrier c 1250; s. cordis constricta, "trussing bedstead" 1553; -dea rotans, "trundle bedstead" 1553; -dale c 1450, -tale 1272, altar frontal.
spond/aicus, -eus, slow-moving c 1180.

spondyl/ia c 1180, -is, -e a 1250, *for* -us, vertebra; ‡"rib-bone" 15c.; ‡-us, spindle-whorl 1570.

spongi/ositas, sponginess a 1250; -alis, spongy c 1250; spungia, puff-ball c 550.

sponsagium a 1160, 1205, †apponsagium 1381, 1447, quay due.

spon/satio, wedlock c 1375; -sio, responsibility c 730; -sale, betrothal 1423; -salia (*pl.*), marriage banns 1225, 1228; 1199, 1539, -salicia (*pl.*) 1402, marriage dues; -salicia 12c., 1200, exponsalia 14c., espousal; -sor, promiser c 730; -sa c 1115, c 1425, †-sata c 1250, wife; s. episcopi, church 1292; s. solis, sunflower, marigold, *etc.* a 1200, 1538; -sus celestis c 1370, s. ecclesie c 1488, prelate; sposus 1389, -datus 8c., *for* -sus, betrothed; -do, *for* -deo, c 860; (*perf.*) spospondit 13c.; -so, to marry c 1000.

spontale, *see* sponda.

*spontane/us, voluntary (eccl.); *-e (eccl.), -o 1361, voluntarily.

sponto, spontoon, halberd 1298.

spora, sporum, *see* 1 spera; spurrum.

spor/ta, (?) litter, stretcher a 1100, c 1280; asporta, *for* -ta, basket c 1460; spurta 1252, spurtica c 1282, †spurtis 1329, fish-trap; -tarius c 1236, 1561, -tularius 1561, basket-maker; -tula (G.) 1275, -tla (G.) 1254, -la (G.) 1255, c 1420, -lia (G.) 1445, †-lanum (*f.l.*) 1289, ‡-ticula 15c., esporlum 1219, 'sporle', relief (feudal); -lo, to pay sporle (G.) 1289, c 1420.

sportum, *see* DISPORT

sposus, *see* sponsatio.

spotellum, *see* SPLOT

spowta, spout (outlet from gutter) 1392.

sprendla, 'sprendle', (?) split rod for thatching (Essex) 1361.

spret-, *see also* SPART; sprittum.

spretus curie, contempt of court 1195.

sprevarius, *see* spervarius.

sprigetum, kind of grain 1333.

sprigonellus, *see* spigurnellus.

sprinctum, *see* SPINCT

*springal/dus, -dum 1296, 1386, -a 1293, 1305, -e 1297, 1313, -lus 1295, 1320, espringaldus 1337, espringalda 1322, springald, siege-engine.

sprittum 1424, spretum 1286, 'sprit', pole; *cf.* SPART

sprivarius, *see* spervarius.

sprottus, sprat (fish) 1292, 1419.

spu/itio 1308, p 1330, -tio 1324, spitting.

spulum, *see* SPOLI

spum/a cervisie, ale-froth 1521; -aticus c 550, -alius a 1250, foamy, frothy; -itorium 1440, 1447, ‡-atorium 15c., 1483, skimmer; -ositas, frothiness c 1115, c 1270.

spungia, *see* SPONGI

spura, *see* 1 spera.

spurarium, *see* spurrum.

spur/calia (*pl.*), pollutions 690; †-ia, (?) *for* -citia, filth 1322.

spureccatum, spirket (naut.) 1295.

spurg/ea, -ia, spurge (bot.) 14c., ‡15c.; -ellum, waste-pipe or purification tank 1275, c 1400; *cf.* EXPURG

spuri/osus, bastard, illegitimate c 1470; -atus, bastardized c 1456; *see also* spurcalia.

spur/rum 1514, -arium 1292, esporonum 1190, spur; sporum, 'spur', cog (of mill-wheel) 1338; -ningus, 'spur', projecting strip (of land) c 1180; -no, to project, abut c 1180.

spurt-, *see* sporta.

spurula, *see* SPHER

sputio, *see* spuitio.

squal/iditas, atrophy (med.) a 1250; -idus, gloomy, stern c 600; -orosus, -erosus, wretched c 1390; †spaloreus, dirty c 550; -ens, dimmed (of eyes) c 1325; -esco, to lie in ruins 1136.

squam/a, 'scale', tartar (on teeth) 1620; †-ma, sea-monster a 615; scama, *for* -a, scale a 1250; scamosus a 1250, spameus c 550, scaly; tunica †-atata, "brigander", coat of mail 1471; -ositas, scaliness a 1250; filth 1276.

squarr/atio, squaring (of timber) 1419; lapides -osi, (?) squared stones c 1200; pes -us, square foot 1377; squirra (?) 14c., scuyra 1325, mason's square; scaria, squadron 1249; -o, to square (timber) 1350, 1465; *cf.* quadra.

squart/a, -erium, *see* quarta; quartarium.

squdellus, squel/la, -arius, squieleria, squileria, squill/aria, -arius, *see* scutella.

squibalum, *see* scybalon.

squicia, *see* Scythia.

squieri/a, -us, *see* scutum.

‡squilla, hake (fish) c 1440, 15c.; *see also* scutella.

squilliticum, *see* scilla.

squinan-, squacia, *see* cynanche.

squinantus, *see* SCHEN

squir/ellus, -rius, *see* scurellus.

squirra, *see* SQUARR

squirrallum, *see* curallum.

squivatus (†squinatus), *see* scyphus.

sredo, sroudura, *see* SHRUD

stabell-, *see* SCABELL

stabil-, *see also* STABUL

1*stab/ilia 1146, 1447, -elia 1290, -lia 1222, 1255, establia 1284, c 1370, -ilium 1379, -ula 1290, -ulum 1310, -ilio a 1128, -ularia 1337, stapularia 1355, -ilitas (-ilita) c 1105, c 1115, -ilitio, -ilitura 1086, estabulatio 1290, -ilata, -ilita (*pl.*) 1243, -ulata (*pl.*) c 1125, buck-stall, besetting the woods (for game).

2 stab/ilia 1246, -ellia, estabelia 1260, -lia 1257, 1275, kitchen dresser, serving-board.

stabiliceum, *see* cablicium.

stabil/imentum 11c. 12c., c 1362, establiamentum 1305, -itio 1453, 1539, establishment, confirmation; ordinance 1399; s. regni 1378, c 1540, -itio regni 1378, -itas regni 1159; -is, irremovable c 1220; valid 1275; -itas, standing-place, station 7c.; s. fidejussionis, security c 1290; -ita, garrison, post 1348; -io, to ordain c 1212, 1548; s. me sub securitate c 1150; -ito, to stand firm 6c.; p 1330, stabulo 1492, to establish; *see also* STABUL

stablementum, *see* TABUL

stablus, *see* stapellus.

stabul/a 1257, c 1440, estabulum 1278, *for* -um, stable; -aria, stable-woman c 1325; hostess c 1362; -arius c 1270, c 1540,

-ator 1378, stable-man, hostler; 1105, 1169,
-ator a 1066, 'staller' (constable or marshal);
-atio c 1188, 1378, **-agium** 1277, **stabila-
gium** 1292, stabling; **stabilio**, *for* -o, to
stable c 1204; *see also* STABIL
1 **stac/a (stach-)** a 1115, 1277, **estacha** 1198,
-ia, -ium 1234, 1430, **estachia, estachium**
1352, 1362, **-erium** 1191, stake, post;
-eam appono 1378, **-iam figo** 1290, 1352,
-iam prosequor 1299, **per -am conquiro**
1352, to proceed for recovery of burgage
tenement; **-inga, stakinga**, (?) fish-preserve
1282, 1288.
2 **staca (staka)** 1189, 1290, **stagga** 1234,
dry measure (? 1/9 quarter).
stacc/us, stack 1282, 1352; **-o**, to stack 1302.
stacha, *see* gata.
stachia, *see* 1 staca; tachia.
stacnaria, *see* 2 stagnum.
staddellus, 'staddle' (pole used for base of
stack) c 1182; 'staddle' (sapling left standing
in cleared woodland) 1575.
stadi/um, measure of length (esp. furlong)
c 1190, 1415; *1403, 1567, (?) **stagium**
(Cheshire) a 1250, furlong, strip (in open
field); course of time 6c.; **s. vite** c 730; **s.
hominis**, man's height c 1188; **s. prati**,
stretch of meadow c 1000; **-o**, to measure
(land) c 1300; *see also* stagium.
staer/a 1282, 1331, **-ia** 1285, 1290, **stera** 1354,
stayera 1324, **stayra** 1323, **steira** 1355,
stairus 1436, **stairura** 1256, (?) **steyringa**
1323, stair, stair-way.
staffa (stapha), stirrup or stirrup-leather
c 1188, 1499; *cf.* stapeda, strepa.
stafizacra, *see* staphis agria.
stagg/a, *see* 2 staca.
stagg/us 1353, **-ardus** 1487, young stag or
hart; 1321, **-ettus** 1322, 1388, 'stag', colt,
young stallion; c 1345, **-ettus** 1422, **-ardus**
c 1345, 1388, 'stag', male swan; **s. bisse** 13c.,
s. cervi 14c., 1368, stag (hart or buck of
fifth year).
stagherum, staggers (disease of pigs) 1302.
stag/ium 1229, 1419, **-ia** 1241, **estagium**
1244, 1289, **astagium** 1246, **stadium**
1245, 1249, (upper) story; c 1250, 1411,
-ia c 1300, 1315, (?) **stadium** (G.) 1289,
house with upper story; shelf or tray (in
chest) 1343; stage, platform 1508; **-ia**, deck
(naut.) 1303; **stadium**, sort of quintain
1253; stage (for fishing nets) 1411; c 1350,
stageria 1311, canon's term of residence
(eccl.); **-iarius** 1304, 1399, **stadiarius**
(canonicus) 1329, 1331, stagiary, canon
bound to keep terms of residence (St.
Paul's); **-iarius** c 1266, c 1330, **-erius** 1462,
monk residing permanently in infirmary;
cf. stadium, statio.
stagmen, *see* stamen; 2 stagnum.
1 **stagn/um (stangn-)** *1086, 1509, **stamnum**
c 1212, †**stragnum** 1354, †**stancum** c 1472,
†**-arium** 1535, 'stank', pond; 1167, 1275,
-amentum c 1400, dam; **s. molendini**
1088, 1539; **s. piscium** 1363; **s. carbonum**,
s. metallorum, (?) pit 1553; **insula
-ensis**, island in the Fens c 1125; **-eus**,
slow-flowing (?) a 1100.
2 *stagn/um (stangn-)** 801. 1157, c 1465,
*stannum** 1203, 1549, **estanum** a 1235,

esteinum 1290, **stamnum** 1196, 1503,
staminum 1196, 1253, **stagmen (stang-
men)** 1255, 1315, **stamen** c 1135, 1268,
exstamen 1296, tin or pewter; **s. album**
1305, 1508; **s. nigrum** 1195, 1508; **s.
fabricatum** 1393;
-aria, -arium 1203, 1298, **-eria** 1199,
1419, **stacnaria** 1217, **stannaria, stanna-
rium** 1202, 1587, **stanneria, stannerium**
1497, 1594, †**stanna** 1410, **staminaria**
1185, 1230, **stamnarium** 1242, †**stainaria**
1178, †**stamarria** 1198, †**stameria** 1201,
stangminaria 1291, **-ifodina** 1253, **stanni-
fodium** 1507, stannary, tin-mine; **-arius**
1222, **stannarius** 1305, 1563, **-ator** 1198,
1324, **stannator** 1202, 1508, **stagminator**
1301, 1304, **staminator** 1253, tin-miner,
tinner; **s. albus, s. niger** 1296; ‡**fusor
stannarius**, "pewterer" 1520; **opera** (*pl.*)
stannaria, tin-works 1586; **-eus** c 1180,
1534, **stanneus** 1240, 1537, **stampneus**
1287, †**stranguineus** 1418, made of tin or
pewter; **-atum**, tinned vessel a 1250; **-atus**
a 1250, 1354, **stannatus** 1295, 1366, **stag-
minatus** 1275, tinned, covered with tin;
stagmino, to cover with tin 1284.
3 **stagnum**, *see* stanga.
stainiatus (†stannatus) a 1447, **staynatus**
1436, **steynatus** 1392, 1393, **steygnatus**
1384, **steniatus** 1368, **esteneatus** 1403,
stained, decorated in colour; *cf.* distainiatus.
stainrasius, cairn (Norse *steinnhreysi*)
(Lancs.) a 1236.
stair-, *see* STAER
stak-, *see* staca (1 & 2).
stalanga, *see* scalonia.
stalanus, *see* stalo.
stall/um, -a, -us 1275, 1298, **stellum** 1150,
1308, stake (for stake-net); *1200, 1573,
estallum c 1140, c 1240, stall (in market);
* c 1150, 1583, **estallum** a 1155, stall (eccl.);
-us, (?) stable or cow-shed 1215; stall for
horses (on ship) 1335; **staulum librarie**,
book-stall, book-case 1473; **-agium** *a 1088,
1587, **estallagium** a 1125, 1253, †**estalia-
gium** 1306, **astallagium** 1383, stallage,
site or payment for market-stall; timber-
stalling for water-course (Winchester) 1366,
1386; staithe (Yorks.) 1415, 1471; payment
for stalls (for barrels in ship) 1303, 1337;
-agarius a 1200, 1397, **-agerius** 1306,
-angiator (?) 13c., **-igiator** 1348, **-aris**
1323, stall-holder in market (esp. Sc.);
mercator -arius c 1290; **-agiator**, collector of stallage 1291; **-arius** c 1100, **stalrus**
1086, 'staller' (constable or marshal); stall-
holder (eccl.) c 1323, 1539; **-eia**, buckstall
1336;
-atio, installation (eccl.) a 1273, 1419;
c 1250, **estallatio** 1573, **-amentum** 1276,
1573, **-iamentum** 1295, **estallamentum**
1415, 1447, **astallamentum** 1339, instalment (of debt); **-o**, to fit (casks on ship) with
stalls 1337; to fix stalling or planks 1346,
1501; to have a market-stall 1297; to expose
for sale 1445; 1274, 1378, **stelio** c 1258, to
assign a market-stall to; to install (eccl.)
c 1255, 1467; to stall (cattle) 1376; 1232,
1283, **estallo** 1423, 1573, **astallo** 13c., to
assign terms for payment.

stal/o 1130, 1341, (?) **salto** 1315, **-onus** 1165, a 1205, **-anus** 1315, stallion.

‡**staltic/us, -ativus,** 'staltic', causing contraction (med.) 15c.

stalungia, see **3 scala.**

stam/en c 1135, 1511, **-ina, -inum** c 1200, c 1330, *-**inea, -inia, -inium** 7c. c 1080, 15c., (shirt of) linsey-woolsey; **-inius,** made of linsey-woolsey c 1135, 1511; **-en,** thread (fig.), framework c 760; jot c 1255; **stagmen,** for **-en,** warp 1254; see also **stagnum** (1 & 2).

stampus, stamp, die 1546; **estampeta,** form of composition (mus.) 1326.

stan/cillum, -cio, see STANT

†**stancium,** (?) f.l. for **scannum,** bench c 1190.

stancum, see **1 stagnum.**

standagium, (?) stallage (Dunstable) 1340.

standard/um, -us *12c., 1526, **-ium** 12c., **standarium** a 1135, **stantarum** a 1142, standard, banner; quintain c 1257; boundary mark 1442; 1296, 1317, **stanstardus** 1289, **stontardus** 1304, 'standard', upright timber; scaffold-pole 1332; post of postmill 1248, 1275; upright of windlass 1372; tall candle-stick 1313; upright water-pipe 1443, 1451; pack, case 1300, 1484; *1274, 1419, **staundardum** 1322, **stondardum** c 1400, standard weight or measure; **s. monete** p 1280, 1534; **coffrum -um,** (?) standing chest 1313, 1406; **-ius** c 1150, **-arius** 1327, standard-bearer.

standizo, see STANT

stan/egeldum 1252, **-geldum** 1330, a customary payment.

***stang/a** c 1220, c 1400, **estanga** 1282, 1333, **-um** c 1200, 1268, **-num (stagnum)** c 1280, c 1400, **stonga** 1700, 'stang', rood, measure of land (Ir., Sc., N. Eng.).

stann-, see SCAM; **2 stagnum; stainiatus.**

stans, see **stare.**

stansilium, see **scansilium.**

stan/stardus, -tarum, see STANDARD

stant/icium 1271, **s. ferreum** 1307, **-io** 1335, **stanso** c 1300, **stancillum** 1280, stanchion, 'stanchel', upright prop; **-ivus,** upright, standing on end 1265, 1276; **auribus -ivis,** with ears pricked up 1251; **rete -ivum,** 'standing net' c 1225; **fenestra -iva** 1231, 1252, f. **estantiva** 1233, 1244, f. **astantiva** 1241, gabled window projecting above level of wall; **-iono** 1224, **stonchono** 1376, (?) **standizo** 1389, to prop up.

stantillum, see **scatesum.**

stantraba, (?) stake, paling 1191.

stap/eda 14c., 1610, **-es** ‡1570, 1620, **-is** 1584, stirrup; cf. **staffa, strepa.**

stap/ella c 1356, **-la** 1573, *-**ula** 1339, 1587, **estapula** 1314, **-ulum** 1382, 1573, staple, regulated market; **-ularius,** stapler, merchant of the staple 1516; **Aula -ulina,** Staple Hall (Oxford) c 1409; **-lus** (adj.), of standard size 1509; **-ulo,** to market (wool) through a staple 1617.

***stap/ellus, -ellum** c 1185, 1417, **-lus** c 1115, 1307, **-olus** 1294, *-**ulus, -ula** 1306, 1461, **stepellus** 1276, **stopla** 1367, **stoupla** 1365, **stablus** 1371, **-elbarrum, -olbarrum** 1336, staple, stake, bar; **-elcloutum,**

staple-clout (of plough) 1354; **-ulo,** to fit with staples 1275, 1362.

stapha, see **staffa.**

staphis agria, stavesacre (bot.): **stafizacra** 1480.

stapul-, see **scapulatio; 1 stabilia.**

stara, see **sexta.**

staratio, see STAUR

stare (subst.), stay, sojourn 1200, 1224; **stans,** 'standing', standard, fitted with a base (of cups) 1448; **sto,** *to be, remain c 1115, c 1514; to stand idle (of mill) 1384; to be valid c 1220, 1308; *(with dat.) 1214, 1558, **s. ad** 1218, 1383, **s. juxta** c 1336, to stand by, observe, keep; **s. ad,** to cost (Sc.) 1358; **s. cum,** to be in the service of 1299, 1348; to take part with a 1230; to be compatible with c 1334, c 1343; to be charged with 1446; **s. judicio** 1164, 1413, **s. ad judicium** 13c., **s. in judicio** 1174, c 1343, **s. juri** 1194, 1504, **s. ad rectum, (in) recto** c 1185, 1419, to 'stand to right', stand trial (leg.); **s. legi** a 1295, **s. in lege** a 1245, to plead (leg.); **s. in l.,** to be free from outlawry 1378; **s. paci** 1293, 1382, **s. ad pacem** 1202, to keep the peace; **s. de pari,** to stand on equal footing c 1204; **s. pro,** to count for, be reckoned as c 1450; **s. in scholis** 1323, **s. in studio** 1306, 1432, to be at school; **s. in testimonio,** to bear witness c 1115.

starkella, see **scarkella.**

starlingus, see **sterlingus.**

starnus, see **sturnus.**

1 starr/um 1208, c 1300, **estarrum** 1234, 1235, **-ius** 1274, 'starr', Jew's deed or bond (Heb.); indenture (apparently not Jewish) 1283, 1305; **s. chirographum** 1272.

2 starrum, 'star', bent-grass (Lincs., Yorks.) 1308, 1338.

†**stasus,** fish, (?) for isicus or scarus, 16c.

stater/, balance of judgement p 1377; **stetera,** for **-a,** balance 1431; **-um,** wey, measure of cheese 859, 863; **-alis,** of or for a balance 870; **-o,** to weigh, balance c 850.

statha 1391, 1462, **staya** c 1312, 'staithe', wharf.

stathmus, standing post, door-post c 850; balance 870.

†**statia,** a customary payment (? for scacia, i.e. chacea) a 1309.

statica (pl.), statics 1686.

stat/im, instantly: **ad s.** 1418, 1686, **-issime** a 1380, c 1458.

statio/, standing idle (of a mill) 1384, 1532; (?) boundary c 1115; station (astr.) a 1233, p 1300; quarter (of wind) 1365; story (arch.) c 1250; (?) gallery of wooden bridge 1469; session (leg.) 1265; station or stall in market 1341, 1573; station (of mistery play) a 1490; *station in ritual (eccl.) c 1080, 1517; **s. crucis,** station of the cross 1411; **s. lanarum,** (payment for) storage of wool (Boston) 1397, 1462; ‡**-naria,** "stale", decoy c 1440; **-nariatus,** office of stationer (ac.) c 1380; **-narius,** *stationer, bookseller (esp. ac.) 1262, c 1530; canon in permanent residence c 1192; monk residing permanently in infirmary 1234, c 1505; (adj.) stationary 8c. c 1160, c 1324; 'statant' (her.) c 1595; **symbolum -narium,** an 'ordinary' (her.) c 1595; **mensa -naria,** table dormant 1373; ‡**statiuncula,** "booth" 1483; *see also* 1 **chacea;** *cf.* **stare.**

statissime *see* **statim.**

stat/orius, *for* **-or,** attendant 1461; **vis -oria,** force that keeps objects at rest 1649.

†**stattara,** *for* **statura,** 1383.

†**stattuitas,** *f.l.* for **nativitas,** 1373.

statuifex, sculptor a 1233.

staturum, *see* **staurum.**

stat/us, standstill, equilibrium c 1200, p 1300; (?) calm weather 1340; boundary c 1115; station, post (in hunting) a 1142; (?) stage, level (in a multiple phial) 1432; aspect, point of view c 1160; period of study c 1204; *state of account, inventory 1307, c 1530; tenantry (man.) 1343; constitution (mon.) c 1400; *estate, title or interest in property (leg.) 1256, 1540; **s. gratie** (theol.) c 1356, 1461; **s. magnus,** high estate 1395; **s. quo alias** 1203, **s. quo nunc** 1320, **status in quo prius** 1315; **s. regis** 1256, c 1400, **s. regni** c 1115, a 1142, state of the realm; **s. trinus** (Sc.) 1461, **-ūs** (*pl.*) c 1422, 1521, ***s. regni** 1391, 1537, estates of the realm; **-ūs** 1592, **S. Generales** 1587, States General (of Netherlands); **pannus -ūs, p. -uum,** cloth of state 1508; **-uliber, -uservus,** freeman or serf *de facto* only c 1258; **-utio,** fixed allowance (mon.) c 1255; 11c., ***-utum** 12c., c 1520, †**-uta** 1324, statute, regulation; **-utum autumpnale,** harvest regulation 1289, 1331; **s. de le belawe, s. villate,** village 'by-law' 1288; **s. curie,** (?) standing order (leg.) 1269; **s. decretum,** legislative act c 1145; **s. Parliamentale** c 1430; **s. mercatorium** 14c., 1432, **s. stapule** 1419, a 1564, statute merchant, statute staple (forms of bond); **-utarius** 1223, 15c., **-utuarius** c 1520, promulgator of statutes; **-uo,** to still (a wind) c 1210.

staulum *see* **STALL**

staundardum, *see* **STANDARD**

***staur/um** 1196, 1487, **stawrum** 1544, †**staturum** 1448, **estaurum** 1268, **-amentum** 1188, 1204, **estauramentum** 1385, **estoramentum** c 1250, **-atum** 1194, store, stock (esp. man.), store-room; **s. mortuum, s. vivum** 1364, 1501; **s. castrorum, s. principis,** customary rents, *dawn bwyd* (W.) 1284; †**staratio,** (?) stocking (of land) 1202; **-arius,** stock-man 1405; **-ator,** victualler (naut.) 1424; **-o,** to store, stock a 1128, 1425.

1 **staurus,** cross (σταυρός) 10c. c 1100, c 1200.

2 †**staurus,** (?) steer (or *f.l.* for **taurus**) c 1440.

staya, *see* **statha.**

stay/era, -ra, *see* **STAER**

staynatus, *see* **stainiatus.**

stechas (stoechas), French lavender (bot.); **sticados** a 1250, ‡14c.

stecus, *see* **studa.**

steia, stay (naut.) 1226; **steycorda,** stay-cord 1397.

steilingus (stey-), ` kind of fish (Cambs.) c 1200, 1268.

steira, *see* **STAER**

steka, 'steak', stitch, piece of cloth (Sc.) 1466.

stell-, *see also* **STALL**

stell/a c 1290, 1316, **-ula** 1234, 'star', white mark (on animal); light representing star at Epiphany 1404, a 1450; **festum -e** c 1250; **s. comata** 1267, 1468, **s. cometa** c 1400, **s. cometis** c 1132, c 1188, comet; **-a Maris,** the Virgin c 1200, 1267; **s. nautica,** pole-star 1267; **-aris,** bittern (ἀστερίας) 1544; **-icus,** astral 1344; **-atus,** *see* **camera; -esco,** to become starry c 1602, 1620; **-ifico,** to endow with a starry nature 13c., 1267.

stellicidium, *see* **STILL**

stellingus, *see* **sterlingus.**

stellio, felloe of wheel c 1200, ‡1483; *see also* **stilo.**

‡**stello,** to send (στέλλω) 1483.

stema, sign 6c.; *cf.* **schema;** *see also* 1 **stemma.**

†**stemic/a, -amen** c 550, **-atio** c 1000, (?) adornment, ordering; **-o** (†**sternico**), (?) to prepare, adorn c 550.

1 **stemma** c 950. a 1142, c 1400, **stema** (*f.*) c 1000, crown.

2 †**stemma,** (?) branch, lopping 1265.

†**stemphri** c 1320, †**stempnevre** 1402 †**scevenesie** 1319, 'stem-free' or 'steven-free' (enjoying priority at mill).

sten-, *see also* **EXTEN; stainiatus.**

stentorophonicus tubus, megaphone 1686.

stepedes, *see* **stipes.**

stepellus, *see* **stapellus.**

stepula, *see* **STIPUL**

stera, *see* **hystera; staera.**

sterc/orarium, privy c 1315; ‡dung-hill 1570; **-olum,** dung 1351; **-oralis** c 700, **-orinus** 790, excremental; **-oro,** to void excrement 1416.

sterelingus, *see* **sterlingus.**

steremannus, *see* **stermannus.**

stergeo, *see* **tersorium.**

stergio, *see* 1 **sturio.**

steril/is: plumbum -e, lead unmixed with silver 1300, c 1350; *see also* **sterlingus.**

sterion, solid (στερεόν) (geom.) c 1200.

sterium, *see* **ESTU**

ster/lingus *a 1160, 1583, **-elingus** a 1200, 1430, **-ilensis** (?) 1081, a 1142, **-lengus** (C.I.) 1309, **stellingus** a 1250, 1331, **starlingus** 1587, **-linguus** c 1255, **-linus** 1282, ***esterlingus** c 1192, c 1365, **estellingus** p 1186, **exterlingus** 12c., 'sterling', silver penny (Engl. *or* Sc.); (*adj.*) 1202, 1214, **stirlingus** 1461, 1486, **-lingicus** (?) 15c., sterling; **s. Aquitanie** 1400; **s. blancus,** blanched penny 1199, 1324; **s. grossus** (groat), **s. minor** 1280; *see also* **COMPUT**

stermannus c 1076, 1204, **steremannus** 1266, **estermannus** 1173, **stiremannus, stirmannus** 1086, **sturemannus** 1198, 1208, **sturmannus** 1173, 1190, **esturmannus** 1266, **esturmannius** 1293, steersman.

stern-, *see also* **STEMIC; STRAT**

sterna, tern (bird) 1544.

stern/utatio, braying a 1408; **-itatio,** *for* **-utatio,** sneeze c 1280; **-utatorium,** sneezing powder 15c., 1517; **-uto,** to bray a 1408.

stetera, *see* **stater.**

steycorda, *see* **steia.**

steylingus, *see* **steilingus.**

steynatus, steygnatus, *see* stainiatus.
steyringa, *see* STAER
stibarius, *see* stivarius.
stibes, *see* stips.
†stibium, (?) stab *or* dagger c 1200.
stibulor, *see* STIPUL
stica 1086, 1430, stichis 1086, estika 1307, 1328, stiqua c 1180, stiga 1220, stikus c 1324, 1430, 'stick', measure of eels (? 25).
sticados, *see* stechas.
†sticax, (?) *for* silex, 15c.
stichia 1344, estichia 1354, †stihchis 1234, stugcha c 1222, 'stitch', measure of land.
stich/us (stic-), line of poetry 12c.; -iologus, inverted form of speech (liable to misconstruction) 12c.
sticio, *see* 1 titio.
sticus, (?) stick, prop (naut.) 1296.
stiferus, stiver (coin of Netherlands) 1555.
‡stig/a, goad, spike c 1440, 1483; -o, ‡to goad 1483; to provoke, instigate c 550; *see also* stica.
stigium, *see* strigium.
stigm/a, (?) soldier a 547; (?) oath c 990; badge 15c.; **s. Christi** 7c., c 950, **s. clavi** c 950, **s. Passionis** 1233, **s. sacrum** c 1170, c 1400, **s. sacramentorum** a 1350 (eccl.); -aticus, bearing the mark (of) 1610; -atizo, to tattoo c 1315.
stik-, *see* stica.
stileum vitreum, 'steel-glass', mirror 1553.
still/agium, (allowance for) leakage of barrels 1282, 1333; -atio, urination c 1220; -atorium, still, alembic 1356, 1622; -icidium 1186, 1436, stellicidium 1289, gutter, spout; drop (of "nectar") c 1000; stellicidium, drop or shower c 1540; †-idia (*pl.*), (?) *for* -icidia, c 550; -ula, little drop c 700. c 1166, c 1414; -o, to urinate, stale c 1190, ‡1483; to distill 1469, ‡1483.
Stilliard/us 1561, Stillierda 1683, the Steelyard (London Hanse); -anus 1585, -ensis 1587, of the Steelyard.
stilo, (?) *for* stellio, lizard 12c.
stil/us (styl-), style, title 12c., 1610; heading (in accounts) c 1337, 1470; (?) item in letter 1286; process (leg.) 1489, 1549; **s. curie (Romane)** c 1444; -isonus, eloquent, cultured 791.
stimul/us, goad: stumblus(†strublus)c 1115, estubula c 1258, -atorium 1440; stumulus, sting 1461; -ator, goad-boy c 1194, c 1258.
stincill/atus (scintill-) 1239, c 1266, estencellatus 1233, 1241, extencellatus 1240, 1241, tencellatus 1276, c 1412, tensellatus, tensalatus c 1320, spangled; -o 1252, estencello 1244, extencello 1256, to spangle.
stin/cus, -gus, *see* scincus.
†stingnum, a regular solid (geom.), (?) prism 13c.
stipa, *see* stipes.
‡stipadium, "exchequer table" c 1440.
stip/amen, throng c 1322; -atim, in throngs 12c.; -o, to get with child a 1300.
stipatus, *see* stipum.
stipend/ium, stipend (eccl.) 12c., c 1520; hire (of thing) 1328, 1337; stupendium, *for* -ium, hire, pay 1276; -ialiter 1419,

-iarie 1121, by way of payment; -iaria, recipient (*f.*) c 1090; prostitute 1201; -arius, (?) recipient of alms c 1100; mercenary soldier c 1250, 1511; hired labourer 1250; a stipendiary (eccl.) 1336, 1585; (*adj.*) 1305, 1429, †-arius 1524, hired, mercenary; c 1345, 1588, †-arius 1348, stipendiary (eccl.); -io c 1212, 1588, †-o c 1200, to pay.
stip/es, stem (of candle-stick) c 1180, c 1500; executioner's block c 1450; money-box, fund (*cf.* truncus) 1466, 1519; stock (of tally) 1286, a 1410; stock (of descent), ancestry 1198, c 1550; heir c 1350; †s. elationis, (?) spirit of arrogance p 1348; -a, *for* -es, stake, post c 1310, †1483; sipites (*pl.*) 1381, stepedes (*pl.*) 1462, stocks, fetters; -ido, to stub up 1494.
stipo, *see* stipamen; stupatio.
stips, payment: stibes 6c.
*stipul/a a 1230, 1411, stipla 1344, stepula 1449, stupula 1276, stubula c 1290, stubla c 1350, stubble, straw (esp. for thatching); -atio, thatch, thatching 1420, 1509; -ator, thatcher 1350, 1435; -inus, of straw 1497; -osus, strong c 1385; auca †stubulata, stubble goose 1408; -o 1277, 1279, stupulo 1276, to gather stubble; to thatch 1430; stibulor, *for* -or, to stipulate 6c.
stip/um, stud c 1411; -atus 1342, 1424, stupatus 1372, 1473, studded.
stiqua, *see* stica.
stirc/us 1185, 1462, stirkettus 1297, 1388 'stirk', bullock; -a, -ata, heifer 1225; corium -inum, hide of a stirk 1345.
stir/emannus, -mannus, *see* stermannus.
‡stirillum, goat's beard c 1440, 15c.
stirkelda, *see* scarkella.
stirp/es, 'staddle' (sapling left standing in cleared woodland) 1602; stryps, *for* stirps, stock c 1400; -ator, extirpator c 1170, 1385; *see also* scirpus.
stirrop/um, stirrup 1341, 1510; (of bell) 1537; -lethirrum, stirrup-leather 1510.
†stithum, stithy 1379.
stiv/ale, -ellum, *see* estas.
stivarius 700. c 1190, stibarius 700, ploughman.
stivera, *see* strepa.
stiverium, *see* estoverium.
stivitor, an occupational surname 1189.
sto, *see* stare.
stob/s, -um, *see* STUBB
stocgabulum, form of market-due 1297, 1300.
stock/us, 'stock', part of cart, (?) wooden upright 1276; -ingum, 'stocking', clearing in woodland 1230; extoco (†extoto, †excocio), to stub up, clear (woodland) 1199.
stod/ardus, 'stud-herd', stud-groom (Durham) 1341.
stod/um, -io, -o, -falda, *see* studa.
stoff-, *see* STUFF
*stola, stole, vestment (eccl.) c 760, c 1006. c 1070, 1586; **s. anime** 12c., c 1343, **s. innocentie** 1586 (fig.); **s. archiepiscopatus** c 1125; **s. imperialis** 12c.; **s. Levitica**, deacon's stole c 1070; **s. sacerdotalis** 12c.
stolidosus, foolish c 1400.

stolpa, see **stulpa.**

stol/us (στόλος) c 1125, a 1186, **-ium** (Sicily) 1177, **storium** (Port.) c 1192, fleet.

stom/a, mouth 14c.; **-aticum** (†**-acicum**), **-aticon,** medicine for mouth 1228, 1253.

stomach/atio, anger a c 1453; **-anter,** angrily a 1452, c 1455; †**stomaticus,** for **-icus,** with stomach trouble c 900.

stompa, whipping-post a 1540.

stonchattera, stone-chat (bird) 1544.

stonchono, see **STANT**

ston/dardum, -tardus, see **STANDARD**

stonga, see **stanga.**

stop-, see also **stapellus; stupatio.**

stopp/a 1309, 1362, **-um** 1285, 1295, **stuppa** (**stupa**) 1288, 1531, stoup, vessel; measure of wine or honey a 1250, 1391; cf. **2 scopa.**

stor/ax c 1200, ‡14c., **-ace** 797, for **styrax,** gum, gum-tree; **-acius,** dipped in gum 802.

storia, see **2 historia.**

storio, see **1 sturio.**

stor/ium, for **-ea,** rush mat 1443, ‡1483; **-earius** 1620, ‡**-iator** 15c., mat-maker; **-io,** to spread bedding 7c.; ‡to make mats 1483; see also **stolus.**

stornellus, see **sturnus.**

stot-, see also **studa.**

stott/us, *‘stot’,* steer or (?) horse c 1160, c 1450; **-a,** heifer 1371; **-arius** 1271, **-erius** 1245, stot-keeper; **-ropum,** stot-rope 1407.

stowagium 1313, 1427, **stouagium** 1300, 1348, **stouvagium** 1337, stowage; **-o,** to stow 1313.

†**stoyla,** (?) ‘stool’, stump 1346.

strabo, see **scarabo.**

strabus, cunning 700.

1 *strac/a (**strak-**), **-us** 1267, 1425, **stric/a** (**strik-**), **-us** 1301, 1419, **stroka** 1316, ‘strake’ (iron plate on outer rim of wheel); **strakeclutum,** ‘strake-clout’ 1269; cf. **strica.**

2 straca, (?) streak, stripe c 1510; **stricatus,** (?) streaked (of candle or wax) c 1245, c 1330.

†**strada,** stripe (in cloth) 1228.

stradlingum, see **stranlingum.**

strad/ulum, (?) end of axle 1344; **-clutum** 1288, **-eclutum** 1361, **-cloutum** 1402, **-elclutum** 1276, 1337, **-ulcloutum** 1351, **stredelclutum** 1294, **stratelclutum** 1316, ‘straddle-clout’ (iron plate protecting end of axle); **-elo,** to fit (plough) with ‘straddles’ 1352.

strag/es, (?) rabble c 950; **-icus,** slaughterous c 730.

stragmen, see **stramen.**

stragnum, see **1 stagnum.**

stragul/a, ‘strail’, bed-cover c 725, c 1000. c 1250, c 1330; c 1373, 1409, **-um** 1310, 1398, (strip of) striped or panelled cloth; ‡**textor -arius** 1520; **-ator,** “arras-maker” 1535, 1660; ***-atus** c 1200, 1489, †**strangulatus** c 1315, **striagulatus** 1310, striped or panelled.

stra/ia (?) 1115, a 1564, **streya** 1330, †**streysa** 1399, †**strangum** 1349, stray (*subst.*), stray animal; **de -io,** astray 1375; **estraius** 1331, **exstrayus** 1275, **estraatus** 1251, **estraetus** a 1250, **estratus** 1276, 1277, stray (*adj.*), strayed; **-ura** 1330, 1408, **astraura** 1274, 1281, **estraura** 1275, 1322, **extrahura** 1331,

1424, †**dextraura** 1548, †**extraria** 1576, ‘stray’, right to impound strays; **extrahura,** (?) goods escheated for intestacy, etc. 1451, 1555; see also **EXTRACT; -iatus** 1526, **extrahuratus** 1530, (?) escheated.

†**strainarium,** strainer 1553.

straitura, see **STRICT**

strak-, see also **STRAC**

strakella, see **scarkella.**

strako, to ‘strake’, run ahead (of greyhounds) 13c.; cf. **astraco.**

stram/en, for **-entum,** saddle-cloth c 730; a straw c 1475; straw for thatching 1333, 1384; **stragmen** 1572, **-enta** 14c., **-entalia** (*pl.*) c 1350, **-ura** c 1330, straw for strewing; **-inatio,** (?) strewing straw a 1452, 1475; **-ineus,** woven of straw 1344; **-ento** c 1350, 1415, **-ino** c 1290, 1323, **-o** 1232, 1325, to strew with straw.

stramerus 1302, **estremarius** 1337, streamer, flag.

strand/a 1238, 1436, **stronda** 1244, 1482, strand, beach; **-agium** 1317, 1419, **strondagium** 1341, ‘strandage’, due for right to beach boat.

strang-, see also **2 stagnum; STRAGUL; straia.**

strang/uiria 1125, **-ulia** 1508, †**-alis** c 1190, for **-uria** (med.).

strangul/atio, asphyxia c 1200; **-o** 1198, 1296, †**transgulo** 13c., to strangle; **stringulo,** to block, obstruct 1313, 1318.

stran/lingum c 1266, c 1298, **-glinum** c 1324, **stradlingum** 1310, 1327, **strenlingum** 1252, **strelingum** 1303, ‘strandling’, (?) squirrel fur at Michaelmas.

strapha, see **strepa.**

*strat/a alta, highway c 730, 798. 1253, 1429; **s. communis** 1276, c 1400; ***s. publica** 839, 857. c 1125, 1497; ***s. regia** c 1160, 1452, **s. regis** 1198; **sepes -alis,** wayside hedge 1378; **-ilectile,** coverlet c 1250; **-io lecti,** making a bed c 1470; **sternatio,** felling 1379; **sternitio,** strewing (cf. **struatio**) 1485; **-or,** oppressor 1252, c 1295; groom c 1100, c 1477; marshal (Byzantine) a 1142; **s. Pape,** papal stirrup-holder c 1220, 1324; ‡**s. latericius,** “brick-layer” 1520; **-ura,** horse-cloth c 770; bedding c 1180, 1330; 1253, **sternatus** 1379, equipment; ***-us,** bed c 730, 801. a 1090, 15c.; cf. **STRET**

strat/agema, for **-egema,** 1345, 1535; **-ilates,** soldier (στρατηλάτης) c 1160, 1325; 14c., **-illites** 13c., c 1295, foot-pad.

†**strate,** (?) *f.l.* for **stricte,** 1316.

stratelclutum, see **STRAD**

strauberia, strawberry 1329.

straura, stray-, see **straia.**

strecium 1292, †**stregura** 1350, (?) strap.

stredelclutum, see **STRAD**

stredwarda, see **stretwarda.**

streillus, see **2 strigilis.**

streitura, see **STRICT**

streka, see **strica.**

strelingum, strenlingum, see **stranlingum.**

†**strem/a,** stream 1199; †**-um** (†**stromum**), (?) drifting ice c 1360.

stremitas, see **EXTREM**

stren/a, earnest money c 1410, 1457; **extrenneum,** (?) New Year’s gift 1376; †**-o,** to “hansel” c 1440, 1483.

strendstavum, *see* trendstavum.
‡strengula, "chub" (fish) 15c.; *cf.* frisgula.
strenu/itas, *effort, vigour a 1100, 1461;
violence c 730; -iter, vigorously c 1200,
c 1400; -ior c 1300, c 1362; -osissimus
c 1250; -issime c 730.
*strep/a c 1190, 1610, -e 1284, -um a 1185,
†strapha c 1180, †stupa c 1250 (16c.),
striva 1220, strivium (†scrinium) 1227,
strivile c 1125, strivarium 1170, 1213,
striverium 1208, strivera (†stivera) 1221,
stirrup or stirrup-leather (Fr. *étrier*);
strivium (†strumum) 1215, stritum,
estrivus 1213, stripodium 1284, stirrup
for cross-bow; -arius, (?) stirrup-maker
c 1393; *cf.* staffa, stapeda, teripes.
strep/itus 1289, *s. judicialis 1238, 15c.,
s. judiciarius 1289, c 1332, s. judicii
1280, 1577, s. juris 1289, c 1430, judicial
clamour or formality; -idus, *for* -itus,
13c.; -erus, noisy 1620; *see also* STREPP
*strepp/um 1274, 1534, strippum 1408,
extreppa 1316, -ementum c 1275, c 1322,
-iamentum c 1344, estrepementum
c 1350, 15c., estreppamentum 1396,
1412, †estrepinamentum 1399, strippa-
mentum 1347, estrippamentum 1448,
-itus 1353, stripitus 1540, stripping,
estrepement, (right of) waste; extrippatio,
pruning of trees 1455; -o 1266, c 1397,
estrepo 1205, a 1564, extrepio 1290,
astrepo 1261, to strip, waste, devastate; *cf.*
EXTIRP
stret/warda 1203, 1271, -ewarda 1255,
stredwarda (†scredwarda) 1199, 'street-
ward", (service of *or* payment for) guarding
streets; *cf.* strata.
strey/a, -sa, *see* straia.
stria, *see* 1 strigilis.
striagulatus, *see* STRAGUL
striatus, engrailed (her.) 1654.
stribula, *see* tribula.
stric/a, -um 1185, 1475, estricha (estrika)
1294, 1305, streka 1306, estreca 1307,
estracus c 1280, strugum 14c., 'strike',
dry measure, (?) levelled bushel; -agium,
(?) payment for use of straiked measure
1446; strucella, (?) strickle 1276; -atus,
'straiked', levelled with strickle c 1250; *see
also* straca (1 & 2).
strict/itas c 1290, c 1356, -itudo 12c., c 1400,
-ura 1401, 1415, narrowness, tightness; 1421,
1427, -itudo 1456, stringency, strictness;
-itudo, parsimony c 1453; -o, closely 1388;
-orium, bandage c 1412; -ura, distraint
c 1202; 1444, (?) streitura, straitura 1285,
wire; 1447, -us 1460, strait (of Morocco);
-us (*sc.* pannus), narrow cloth 1450; -us,
(*adj.*) *strait, narrow 1200, 1461; fine-
meshed c 1335; close, near 1324; close,
intimate 1496; necessary 1241; scarce
c 1330; strict, exact c 1292, c 1343;
stringo, to strain, sift 1375; to distrain
1275; to constrain, compel a 1403, c 1432;
s. manus, to wring hands c 1200, c 1400.
stridingum, *see* trithingum.
stridor carceralis (*coll.*), fetters 14c.
striggum, 'strig', (?) withy 1276.
1 strig/ilis c 1190, stria c 1212, *for* -a, witch.
2 strig/ilis 1220, ‡-il 1570, "truss" for horse;

‡"stirrup" 1483; c 1200, 1421, ‡-il 1570,
-ula c 1317, -ulus 1285, 1311, strilla 1225,
1229, streillus 1292, curry-comb; -ilator,
curry-comber c 1180; ‡-ilo 1483, strilio
c 1290, to curry (cattle).
‡strigi/um, tight-fitting garment c 1440;
‡stigium, "jack" (armour) 1570; ‡-o, to
"stride" c 1440.
strignus, *see* strychnus.
‡strigo, "bumpkin" 1570.
strik-, *see* 1 straca.
stril/la, -io, *see* 2 strigilis.
strincolum, *see* SCRINI
stringo, *see* STRICT
stringulo, *see* STRANGUL
strio, *see* histrio.
strip-, *see* strepa; STREPP
strirkelda, *see* scarkella.
stristegum, *see* TRISTEG
stritum, striv-, *see* strepa.
strix, *see* hystrix.
stroda, 'strood', marshy thicket (S. Engl.)
12c., 1453.
strofilus, *see* trochilus.
stroka, *see* 1 straca.
stromum, *see* strema.
strond-, *see* STRAND
stroph/a (strof-), (?) roll or twisted packet
1303; †scrophus, morbus †scrophicus,
for -us, colic (med.) a 1250; -ium, fess
(her.) c 1595; trophium, woman's girdle
c 1182, 13c.; man's girdle c 1194; ‡-ina
c 1440, -nia c 1450, grooping-iron, cooper's
gouge; -osus, versifier, dramatist c 800;
(*adj.*) crafty or malicious a 710, c 1000.
stropp/agium, strapping (of casks) 1331, 1337;
-o, to strap (casks) 1333, 1335.
†strua, (?) post (of paling) 1297; *cf.* studa.
†struatio, strewing (? *f.l.* for sternatio *or*
straminatio) 1417.
strublus, *see* stimulus.
struceila, *see* strica.
struc/io, -ona, *see* struthio.
struct/io, edification c 730; s. arcis c 1414,
-ura a. 9c., burhbote; s. pontis c 1414,
-ura p. c 796, 858, brigbote; ‡culter -orius,
"voiding-knife" 1520; ‡mensa -uaria,
tabula -oria, "dresser" 1570; -uarius,
builder c 1200; -us vestium, suit of
clothes a 1142.
strudo, *see* SHRUD
stru/ella c 1150, ‡-ecula 1483, small wood
pile.
strugum, *see* strica.
struio, *see* 1 sturio.
struma (*n. pl.*), red-hot cinders 6c.
strumentum, *see* instrumentum.
strum/o, hump c 1250; -ellus, glandular
swelling in neck c 1197; -osus, swelling,
pompous c 1190.
strumum, *see* strepa.
struthio (strucio) 1150, 1443, ostrica a 1250,
ostrigius 1400, ostrius 1384, ostrich;
sparrow 1620; †strucona, puffin p 1327;
ostricium, (?) *for* struthion, soapwort
c 1200.
strychnos, nightshade (bot.): (?) strignus
a 1250.
stryps, *see* STIRP
stubb/um a 1190, 1358, stobum a 1270,

stobs 1334, stub, stump; **-atio,** stubbing 1389; **-o,** to stub up 1315, 1344; to clear by stubbing 1307.

stub/la, -ula, -ulatus, *see* STIPUL

stud/a 1285, c 1478, **stodum** 1269, 1420, **stothum** 1373, 1504, 'stud', upright timber (in wattle wall); **-dum,** metal stud 1536; **stodfalda,** (?) shingle (used in roofing) (Sc.) 1558; **stottarius, stottator (scindularum),** fastener, (?) studder 1316; **clavus stotus (†stecus),** stud-nail 1296; **-o** 1282, c 1478, **stodo** 1372, 1398, **stodio** 1374, to fit (a wall) with 'studs'.

studia, *see* excudia.

stud/ium, treatment (med.) c 730; opinion (leg.) c 1115; *a study (room) 1258, 1476; *school or university 12c., c 1470; **s. commune** 12c., *s. generale 13c., 1528, s. universale 1253, 1346, university; -ia liberalia, the liberal arts c 1172, c 1250; liber -ialis, book of study c 1350; -iose, purposely c 1466; -iositas, studiousness, earnestness c 1125, 1345; *-ens, student 1231, 1586; -eo in, to study (a subject) 1291, c 1358; -eor (*dep.*), to be sure to 797.

stuell/um, -us, pad (med.) (*cf.* O.F. *estuele*) a 1250.

stuff/um 1364, 1460, **-a** 1360, **stoffa** (Sc.) 1340, 1380, **-agium** 1311, **estuffamentum** 1376, 1434, *-ura 1390, 1543, **estuffura** 1507, stock, store; material (metal) 1460; s. mortuum, s. vivum 1446; -atus, stocked, equipped c 1320, c 1370; -o, to stuff (with moss) 1386; to load (gun) 1388; *see also* STUPH

stugcha, *see* stichia.

stuk/marta 1460, 1488, **-emarta** 1469, 1496, (?) beast with its throat cut (Sc.).

stulp/a (†sculpa) 1324, 1405, **-is** 1374, **-um** 1463, **stolpa** 1289, 'stoop', post, stake.

stult/us, untrained (falc.) 1204; professional fool 1260, c 1530; **festum -orum** 1236, 13c.; **baculus -orum,** 'bishop's' staff at Feast of Fools 1245; **-a plevina,** inept pledging (leg.) 1199; **-a presentatio** 1243, 1260, s. querela 1231, s. responsio a 1135, 13c., -um dict'm 1185, 1199, *-iloquium 1195, 1257, faulty or frivolous pleading *etc.*, miskenning (leg.); -um attachiamentum (leg.) 1245; -a saisina 1198, -a summonitio 1203, -um warantum 1180 (Norm.); -icen, frivolous rhymester c 1160; -icinia (*pl.*), frivolous songs c 1160; -ifex, infatuator 1523; -ilogus (play on theologus), expert in folly p 1381; -itia, folly (as name of building) a 1236; -ivagus, foolishly gadding 1427; -izo, to play the fool 1267, ‡1483.

stum/ulus, -blus, *see* stimulus.

stupa, (?) room 1418; *see also* **stoppa, strepa, stupha.**

stupacium, sort of cloth 6c.

stup/atio (stupp-), stopping (of payment) 1456; **-es** (*pl.*), wads 1274; **-o** 1451, 1460, **stipo** 1449, to stop payment; 1279, **estupo** 1185, 1324, **estopo** 1252, **estopio** 1274, to stop, block (roads; *etc.*); **stoppo,** to stop up (cracks, *etc.*) 1341, 1355; **estoppo,** to estop (leg.) 1473; **†sthopio,** (?) to stop (flow of blood) 1244; *cf.* ASTUPP, EXSTUP

stupatus, *see* stipum.

stup/efactio, stupefaction 1622; **-efactivus** a 1250, 1622 **-orifer** a 1200, stupefying; **-idus,** numb 1461; **-ido,** to be astonished at c 860.

stupendium, *see* STIPEND

stuph/a (stuff-) c 1191, c 1550, **stupa** 1353, **stuva** (G.) 1282, stove, hypocaust, hot bath; **s. herbarum** (med.) 1307; **-o,** to bathe in hot water a 1250, c 1330.

‡stupo, to call a hawk 1483; *see also* **stupatio.**

stupul-, *see* STIPUL

sturco, *see* asturco; x sturio.

stur/emannus, -mannus, *see* stermannus.

x *stur/io (-jo) c 1125, 1535, **-ionus** 1265, *-gio 12c., 1588, -go 1205, 1325, -genus 1292, †sturco 1508, storio 1305, 1314, stureus 1474, †stergio 1293, †struio c 1350, sturgeon, fish royal.

2 †sturio, (?) to reconstruct (a causey) 1324.

sturnus, starling: **starnus, stornellus** a 1250.

stuum, stew, fish-pond 1251.

stuva, *see* stupha.

stuveri/a, -um, *see* estoverium.

Styg/ius 11c, **-ialis** a 1100, **-neus** 15c., Hellish (theol.).

styl-, *see* STIL

stypticitas, astringency a 1250, 1622.

styrax, *see* storax.

sua/dibilis 12c., c 1250, **-debilis** 796, **-sibilis** c 1204, 15c., **-srix** (*f.*) c 790, persuasive; c 1170, **-sibilis** c 790. c 1290, persuadable; **-sibilis,** commendable, to be encouraged c 1334; **swadeo,** *for* **-deo,** 1305.

suaga, suagia, *see* SWAG

suanimotum, *see* SWANIMOT

suara, *see* saura.

suarium, *see* sudarium; sus.

suas, suat-, *see* suus.

suas-, *see* suadibilis.

suatio, *see* sutor.

suav/itas (title) c 1250; 1319, 1351, s. prisone 1299, 1324, *suete de prison* (*cf.* sueta); **-esco,** to grow sweet 795; **-ifico,** to sweeten 870.

Suavus, Suanus, *see* Suethedus.

sub (*adv.*) **et super** c 1470, **s. et supra** 1343, c 1455, below and above;

(*prep.*, with *abl.*), subsumed under (log.) c 1343; less than 1362; in, with (of attendant circumstances) c 1155, c 1450; (?) in addition to c 1000; on condition of c 1180, 1361; on pain of 1262, c 1384; in, on (of time) **s. anno** c 1188, c 1563; **s. curriculo temporis** c 1250; **s. data** 1337, 1545; **s. die** 1200, c 1422.

(of various relations) **s. brevitate** 946. c 1188, c 1362, **s. breviloquio** 1282, c 1453, **s. compendio** c 1250, c 1470, briefly; **s. celeritate** c 1204, c 1340, **s. festinatione,** 1217, 1265, **s. maturitate** c 1250, 1264, speedily; **s. certitudine,** certainly 1272; **s. confidentia,** in trust c 1301, 1337; **s. expectatione,** in expectation 1398; *s. forma** c 1210, c 1490; **s. Latino,** in Latin c 1427; **s. litteris,** by letter c 1308; **s. pede,** (lurking) close at hand 1293; (?) under the spade 1285; **s. periculo,** on peril (of) c 1285, c 1534; **s. presentia,** in the presence (of) c 730. c 1128, 1200; **s. protestatione,** under protest c 1270, c 1433; **s. silentio,** in silence c 1180, c 1415; **s. spe,** in hope c 1375, c 1470; **s. verbis,** in words c 1340; (with *adj.* or *ppl.*) **s. abscondito** c 1408; **s. absconso** c 1190, in secret; **s. salvo,** in safety c 1230, c 1404.

subaccas/atus, under-tenant (G.) 1289; **-o,** to subinfeudate (G.) 1291.

subact/io, constraint c 1170, 1620; subjugation c 1190, c 1200; **-ivus,** acting as a subordinate 1344; **-or,** deputy, vicar 768; conqueror c 1178; plunderer c 1362; **subago,** to act under orders 1344; †**subigo,** (?) *for* subeo, to undergo c 1362.

subaddo, to add 1343, c 1450.

subadjutorium, additional (payment in) aid 1296.

subadmirallus, under-admiral 1364, 1406.

subadoro, to accost covertly c 1562.

subaffectatus, somewhat affected a 1164.

subago, see SUBACT

subagrius, boorish 9c.

subalbedo, slight pallor a 1250.

suballoquor, to address a 1452.

subaltare, fixed part of altar 1368.

subaltern/atio, hypallage (gram.) 870; c 1250, c 1300, **-itas** c 1300, subordination (log.); substitution of a lower authority (eccl.) c 1308; **-atim,** in subordination (log.) c 1200, a 1323; †alternatively c 1340; **-atus,** a subordinate, a lower authority 1345; c 1250, *-us c 1160, 1610, subaltern (log.); -us, subordinate 1419, c 1470; substituted a 1452; with divisions of alternating colours (her.) c 1595; **a -is,** at opposite corners c 1173; *-o, to subordinate (esp. log.) c 1200, c 1432.

subambulus, successor †c 1210, c 1213.

subanathematizo, to anathematize 1264.

subangustus, rather narrow c 1434.

subannoto, to subscribe, write below c 1020. c 1180.

subappar/ator, sub-apparitor (eccl.) 1327; **-eo,** to appear below c 1500.

subapto, to arrange below c 1170.

subaquila, species of eagle (ὑπάετος) 1544.

subarmo, to arm secretly 1316.

subaro, to plough up 1288, 1499; to subscribe, inscribe below 893, 1065. 12c., c 1436.

subarraiator, sub-arrayer (Sc.) 1327, 1336.

subarrendo, to sublet (Sc.) 1485.

subarrh/atio, (payment of) earnest c 1250, 1283; espousal 13c.; **-o,** to pay earnest money (to *or* for) 1153, 1466; to undertake, pledge oneself c 1250, c 1275; to espouse, betrothe c 1100, 1335; (fig., of abbacy or diocese) 12c., c 1444.

†**subarro,** to subjugate c 1437.

subascendens, subdescendens, kinds of meteor (apparently rising or falling) 13c.

subaspicio, to peer at c 1090.

subas/sessor, sub-assessor 1304; **-sedo,** to sublet (Sc.) 1531.

subasto, to come to assist c 1436.

subauctorit/as, subordination c 1290, p 1300; **-ative,** as a subordinate agent p 1300; **-ativus,** subordinate p 1300.

subaud/itio, disobedience c 1115; implication a 1109; *-io, to 'understand', take as implied c 1072, c 1390; *see also* **subjanitor.**

subaul/a, undercroft, crypt c 1250; ‡**-eum,** curtain c 1440; **-icus,** courtier 11c.

subauthentic/us, delegated c 1378; **-e,** vicariously c 1367.

subazurius, bluish c 1215.

*subballivus,** under-bailiff 1260, 1472.

subbedel/lus 1258, 1415, **subbudellus** 1274, under-beadle; **-ria,** under-bedelry 1309.

subbercarius, under-shepherd 1276, 1278.

subbordarius, subtenant in bordage (C.I.) 1309, 1331.

*sub/boscus** c 1185, 1583, **-buscus** 1272, **-poscus** 1229, underwood.

subbracchialis, under the arm c 1250.

subbrevitas, abbreviation c 1200, 1271.

subbuteo, hen-harrier (ὑποτριόρχης) 1544.

subc-, *see also* **succ-**

subcacherellus, under-cacherel 1275.

*subcamerarius,** under-chamberlain c 1266, 1437.

subcancellarius, under-chancellor (eccl.) 1371.

subcant-, *see* SUCCENT

subcapellanus, under-chaplain c 1334, 16c.

subcapitaneus, under-captain 1294, 1587.

subcarectarius, under-carter 1281, 1297.

subcator, under-caterer 1531.

subcaudatus (equus), goaded under the tail c 1115.

subcelatus, hidden 14c.

subcelest/is, earthly 1344, 1416; (?) near to heaven 15c.; **hierarchia s.** c 1257, **h. -ium** c 1443.

*subcellerari/us** c 1150, c 1470, ‡**succellerarius** 15c., under-cellarer (mon.); **-a,** under-cellaress 1441; c 1320, †**subselaria** 1318, under-cellarership.

subcellium, *see* **subsellium.**

subcementarius, under-mason 1343.

subceppo, to undercut (trees) 1270.

subchorarius, under-choirmaster 1434.

subcido, (?) *for* **subsido** *or* **succido,** to collapse c 1275.

subcinctor, *see* SUCCENT

subcissor, *see* **subscissor.**

subcitrinus, yellowish a 1250, a 1252.

subclamator, under-crier (of Parliament) c 1320.

subclaudico, to limp slightly 1535.

subclavis, duplicate key 1371, 1372.

subclericus, under-clerk 1337, 1526.

subcocus, *see* **subcoquus.**

subcogito, to think covertly 12c.

subcollector, sub-collector (eccl.) 1299, a 1564; **succollectoria,** sub-collectorship 1389.

subcommend/atio, sub-commendation (feudal) 1086; **-o,** to sub-commend 1086.

subcommissarius, assistant commissary (eccl.) 1301.

subcongrego, to form into a subordinate collection c 1450.

subconserv/ator, sub-conservator (of judge delegate) 1384; (of privileges) c 1400; **-atia,** sub-conservatorship 1416.

subcon/stabularius *1264, 1348, **-estabulus** 1273, under-constable (of castle); petty constable (of town) 1320; **s. Anglie** 1445.

subconstituo, to appoint in succession c 1160.

Q

subcontinu/ativus, introducing a clause that implies a fact (gram.) 1524; -o, to continue c 1477.

subcontraho, to withdraw, subtract c 1290.

subcontrari/etas, subcontrary opposition (log.) 1610; -us, subcontrary (log.) a 1250, 1610; somewhat adverse a 1452.

subcoqu/us 1535, subcocus 1301, 1535, †succoques 14c., under-cook; -inarius, under-kitchener (mon.) c 1266.

subcoronator, under-coroner (London) 1324, p 1330.

subcroceus, yellowish a 1250.

‡subcubicularius, "groom" 1570.

subcurvo, to wind, be tortuous 8c.; to subdue c 810.

subcust/os, sub-warden, under-keeper c 1320, a 1564; -odia, sub-wardenship c 1335, 1491.

subcutaneus, subcutaneous 700. 13c.

*subdecan/us, sub-dean (eccl.) 1160, 1549; -atus, sub-deanery 1167, 1472.

subdecenna, under-tithing (contrasted with decenna capitalis) 1227.

subdeleg/atio, sub-delegation, delegation by a delegate 1251, 1415; *-atus, a sub-delegate 1200, 1560; -o, to sub-delegate 1247, 1469.

subdeput/atus, sub-deputy c 1448; -o, to sub-depute c 1448.

subdescendens, see subascendens.

*subdiacon/us, sub-deacon (eccl.); -alis, sub-diaconal c 1330, 1423; *-atus, sub-deaconry c 1070, 1549.

subdisjunct/io, reduced disjunction a 1304; -ive, with weakened disjunctive force (i.e. not exclusively) c 1178.

subdistin/ctio, punctuation other than full-stop 799; secondary distinction (log.) a 1245, c 1334; -guo, to punctuate c 700; to draw a secondary distinction a 1245, 1344.

subdistributio, secondary distribution a 1360.

subdit/io, subjection c 1325; -a, inferior (in nunnery) c 1250; -us *a 1090, 1471, †subitus c 1197, a subject, one under authority; *member of flock (eccl.) c 1115, 1586; obedientiary (mon.) 1281; subdo, to sub-join c 1197, c 1470; s. me 7c., s. meam intentionem c 1115, to apply myself.

subdivi/sio, subdivision c 1188, c 1363; -do, to subdivide c 1188, c 1540.

subdominus, under-lord c 1380; soldanus, 'sous-dame' (G.) 1312, 1450.

subduc/tio, removal, withdrawal c 700. 1340, c 1550; subtraction (math.) 1686; -ticius, subtracted (math.) 1686; -tura, trimming or lining 1419; -o, to cut back (stones) (arch.) 1409; (?) for seduco, to mislead c 1250, c 1362.

subduo, to subject, subdue 1439.

*subdupl/us a 1110, 1521, -ex 13c., half; -icatus, pertaining to square root 1686; -ico a 1233, -o c 1360, to halve.

subeleemosyn/aria (subelemosin-), sub-almonry 1357, 1458; *-arius 1234, 16c., subelimozinarius 1504, sub-almoner.

subenervo, to enervate c 1210; cf. subnervo.

subequester (collegii), (?) groom 1535.

subera (cerebri), cortex c 1180.

suberigo, to suggest c 730.

suberro, to stray 7c.

*subescaet/or 1262, 15c., subscaetor 1292, sub-escheator; -ria, sub-escheatry 1333.

subessentia, substance c 860; subsum, to belong to (as an attribute) c 730; *to be inferior, subordinate 1257, 15c.

subestimo, to estimate at 12c.

‡subeth, lethargy (Ar. subāt) 14c.

*subex/ecutor, subordinate agent c 1332, 1488; -ecutive, as an agent 1344; -ecutivus acting as subordinate 1344; -equor, to carry out as a subordinate 1344, c 1375.

subexpansus, half-open (of book) 1345.

subf-, see also suff-

subfeud/atio, sub-feuing (Sc.) 1608; -o, to sub-feu (Sc.) 1608.

subforestarius, under-forester 1275, c 1348.

subfrontale, under-frontal (of altar) 1423, 1441.

subfullo, see SUBSULL

subg-, see also sugg-

subgaolerius, under-jailer 1330.

subgardianus, sub-warden (ac.) 1455, 1508.

subgrav/is, very low (mus.) c 1160; -atus, heavily burdened 795.

subhast/atio, auction sale 1328, 1608; -o, to subdue by the spear c 1200; to sell by auction c 1220, 1554.

subhebdomadarius, assistant to obedientiary on duty (mon.) c 1266.

subhiemalis, wintering, northern c 860.

subhortor, to urge covertly c 1185.

subhostillarius, sub-hostiller (mon.) c 1266.

subhumerale, space between shoulders (in chasuble) c 1245.

subic-, see SUBJECT

subietas, see SUBIT

subigo, see SUBACT

subindico, to mark an inferior division 720; to hint 1649.

subinduco, to bring in secretly c 1080, c 1188; to insert, fit in c 1250; to bring on, cause c 1412.

subinequalitas, lesser inequality c 1612.

subinfero, *to subjoin (bibl.); to supply (mentally) c 655, c 730; to imply 1006; to reply a 1100, c 1197.

subinfeud/atio, sub-feuing (Sc.) 1608; -o, to sub-feu (Sc.) 1608.

subinfirmarius, sub-infirmarer (mon.) c 1470.

subin/gressus, contraction, shrinking c 1615; -gredior, to enter in (additionally or instead) c 790. c 1360, 1620.

subinsequor, to follow up c 1562.

subinstaurarius, assistant stockman 1322.

subinstitor, subordinate agent 1461.

subinstituo, to appoint as substitute c 1470.

subinsutus, stitched on c 1200.

subintell/ectio, tacit understanding c 1200, 1378; -igo, to imply, take as implied c 730, 793. c 1080, c 1430.

subinterpolo, to apply intermittently c 1212.

subintono, to mutter 13c.

subintr/atio, covert entrance a 1250, c 1030; *-o, to enter (esp. by stealth) 8c., 1041. c 1090, c 1470; -o penam, to incur penalty c 1402.

subintroduc/tio, bringing in c 1115; mulier -ta, woman living in priest's house 8c. a 1400; -o, to bring in stealthily 8c., 9c. c 1125, c 1414.

subinvicem, mutually, in turn c 730. 15c.

subirrepo (†subinepo), to creep in c 1170.

subit/atio (bibl.), †subietas 1461, suddenness, sudden event; taking by surprise c 1220; -io, arrival c 1320; -alis, sudden c 1180; *see also* SUBDIT.

subjaceo, *to be liable, subject, to 814. 1070, c 1480; to succumb, perish p 1330; (*trans.*) to undergo 1274; †s. me, to submit c 1223.

subjanitor 1300, 1397, (?) †subauditor a 1564, under-porter.

subject/io *c 730, 956. c 1115, 1461, subjectio c 850, subicientia c 1365, submission, subordination, obedience; jurisdiction c 1100, c 1337; (?) payment in token of obedience c 1308; -atio, (?) assignment to a subject (log.) a 1360; forma -alis, (?) form inherent in subject c 1375; -ive, subjectively (log.) c 1300, 1378; -ivus, submissive 1262, c 1435; subjective (log.) c 1270, c 1363; pars -iva, part predicated of whole as subject 13c.; -or, subduer c 1362; -ibilis 13c., c 1270, subicibilis c 1270, c 1367, capable of being a subject (log.); subicibilitas, capacity for being a subject (log.) c 1300; *-um c 850. c 1080, 1444, †-a 1267, subject (log.); field (her.) p 1394, a 1446; materia -a, subject matter 1461; -o, to subject, subordinate c 1382, p 1394; *to provide with a subject c 1360, 1427.

subjud/ex, subordinate judge c 1430; -icium, subordinate judgement c 1430.

subjug/atio c 1250, c 1414, †-um 14c., subjugation; -alis, beast of burden (bibl.); -alium, lower part of a phrase (mus.) c 1200.

subjunct/ive, in the subjunctive (gram.) 1524; -ativus, *for* -ivus, subjunctive (gram.) c 790.

subjurno, *see* SOJORN

subjuvenis, youngish a 1100.

†subladataria, *f.l.* for inbladatura, c 1235.

†sublarium, (?) *for* subula, awl 1175.

sublarvo, to mask a 1452.

sublateo, to lurk under 14c., c 1470.

sublectilia, *see* supellex.

sublego, to read c 1188.

sublev/amen (sullev-), lifting power c 1265; 1300, c 1400, -atio c 1250, c 1325, relief, mitigation; -atio, underpinning (arch.) 1360; lifting up, exaltation c 1125, a 1564; -ator c 1125, 12c., -atrix (*f.*) c 1627, uplifter, helper; attendant a 1142; -o pratum, to make hay 1279; -io, to relieve a 1250.

sublevis, smoothish 14c.

sublevita, subdeacon 1245.

subliberalis, villein c 1110.

sublic/a, pile (her.) c 1595; -es (*pl.*), piles, stakes 1516.

sublig/ar, bandage 14c.; 13c., ‡a 1520, -a 1575, -aculum c 1565, 1588, garter.

sublim/atio (sullim-), elevation, exaltation c 1185,. a 1520; elevation (astr.) a 1200; sublimation, vaporization (alch.) 1144, c 1360; s. magistralis, conferment of master's degree 1333; -ator, vaporizer (alch.) a 1235; -ipeta, soaring 1552; *-itas, high rank, highness (title) c 1000. c 1075, c 1534; -o, to raise (bibl.); to rise c 1000; *to sublimate, vaporize (alch.) 1144, c 1615.

†sublingua, (?) sinew under tongue 6c.

‡sublitio, "greasing of cloths" 1570.

sublocumtenens, sublieutenant 1587.

*sublunaris, sublunary c 1160, c 1605.

sublustris, dim, gloomy c 790. a 1100.

subm-, *see also* summ-

submagister, under-master 1289; (ac.) 1418; (naut.) 1497.

submajor, assistant mayor (G.) 1289, 1295.

†submando, to summon (leg.) 1268.

submansio, stopping-place c 990.

submarc/idus, slightly shrunken 1200; -eo, to droop p 1377.

submarescallus, under-marshal 1309.

submarinus, submarine c 1136.

submarsus, *see* SUMMER

submedius (color), formed of mixture of primary colours (her.) p 1394.

submercator, commercial agent 14c.

submolendinarius, miller's man 1251.

submuralis, under the walls 1288.

subnectio, anchoring c 730.

subnecto, *see* SUBVECT

subnemus, underwood c 550.

subnervo (fig.), to enervate, weaken c 1185, 14c.; *cf.* subenervo.

subnix/us, humble c 1125; -e, humbly c 950, c 960. c 1270, c 1430; subnitor, to confirm, support c 1150.

subnominatus, undernamed 13c.

subnoto, to subscribe 948. 1274.

subnutrio, to brood over, foster c 1180, a 1250.

subobedientiarius, sub-obedientiary (mon.) c 1266.

subobscuro, to overshadow 12c.

suboccup/atio, immediate succession a 1250; (febris) -aris, following without intermission a 1250; -o, to follow 13c.; to occupy below c 1470.

subodoror, to have an inkling 1526.

suboleo, to get wind of c 1562.

suboneratus, charged (to accountant) below 13c.

suboperarius, assistant c 1115.

subopto, to long for c 1150.

suborbium, *see* SUBURB

subordin/arius, deputy to bishop's ordinary (eccl.) 15c.; -atus, subordinate c 1300, 1620; -o, to subordinate c 1343, c 1444.

suborior, to rise, be stirred up c 1160, 1336.

suborn/atio, supply, provision 1307, c 1383; subornation, instigation, c 1443, 1684; -atus, disguised 1169.

subostendo, to show indirectly 790.

subostiarius, under-doorkeeper 1290, c 1330.

subp-, *see also* supp-

subpannus, lower wall-plate (arch.) 1335.

subparcarius, under-parker 1389, 1446.

subpedagogus, assistant teacher 1550, 1587.

subpena, *sub poena* (leg.) 1503, 1663.

subpenitentiarius, sub-penitentiary (eccl.) 1415, 1443.

subpincerna, assistant butler 1319, 1541.

subpinno, to underpin (arch.) 1364.

subplaudo, *see* SUPPLO

subportarius (supp-), under-doorkeeper 1322, a 1350.

subposcus, *see* subboscus.

subprecent/or 1420, -rix (*f.*) 1520, succentor (eccl.).

subpreposit/us, *sous-prévôt* (G.) 1289; **-a**, sub-prioress (Gilbertine) c 1250.

subprim/arius (**supp-**), sub-principal (ac.) 1549; **-us** (**suppremus**), next below the first 7c. 1383.

subprinceps, subordinate ruler c 1470.

*subprior/ (**supp-**), sub-prior (mon.) c 1125, 1549; s. **claustralis** 1458, 1526; **-atus**, office of sub-prior 12c., 1456; **-issa**, sub-prioress c 1200, 1530.

sub/quadruplus, quarter 1335; **-quintuplus** fifth (fractional) 1335.

subr-, *see also* **surr-**

subreceptor, assistant receiver (eccl.) c 1448, 1475.

subrefectorarius, sub-refectorer (mon.) c 1266, c 1470.

subregulus, petty prince or vassal 714, c 1000. c 1100, c 1450; ealdorman 720, 934.

subrelinquo, to omit 7c.

subrepetitio, demanding back c 900.

subroscidus, moistish 1622.

subrub/eitas (**surrub-**), reddishness c 1270; ***-eus** a 1250, 1465, **-easter** 15c., reddish.

†**subruptius**, (?) more completely c 1436.

subsacrista (**sups-**), sub-sacrist (eccl.) c 1175, 1541; (*f.*) sub-sacress 1530.

subsalutatio, greeting at end of letter c 1435.

†**subsann/a**, grimace c 1225; ***-atio** (bibl.), **-atus** c 1350, mockery; ***-o**, to mock (bibl.).

subscaetor, *see* **subescaetor**.

subschisma, subdivision of schism (eccl.) 1418.

subscissor (**subcissor**), assistant tailor 1295.

subscript/io, assent 1562; s. **manualis**, sign manual 1463, 1566; **-o**, to underwrite (a bill of exchange) 1599; **subscribo**, to underwrite (a cargo) 1723.

subsecut/io, following a 1100, c 1250; **-ivus**, subsequent c 1212, c 1220, **-or** 720, 12c., **-rix** (*f.*) c 1190, follower; **subsequ/ax**, successor a 1147, 1324; **-entia** (*f. s.*), consequence c 1275; **-entes** (*pl.*), followers, descendants 12c.; **-ens**, the following 1086, c 1365; posterior (log.) a 1233; **-enter**, in succession c 1194, 1424; ***subsequently**, afterwards 1281, c 1467; **-itur**, it follows (log.) 1308; **-or** (**emendam**), to obtain c 1267.

subsedeo, to besiege p 1377; *see also* **subsido**.

subsedo, to allay 1150; *see also* **subsido**.

subselaria, *see* **subcellerarius**.

subsell/ium c 1148, 1206, **subcellium** c 1200, **-a** 1416, saddle-pad, equipment for saddle.

subsenescall/us, under-steward 1279, 1583; sub-seneschal (G.) 1283; **-ia**, sub-seneschalry (G.) 1289.

subsequ-, *see also* SUBSECUT

subsequestrator, deputy sequestrator (eccl.) 1295, 1377.

subsericarius, assistant silk-worker 1561.

subserv/itor 1374, **-iens** c 1360, under-servant; **-ienter**, as a servant 1344; **-io**, to perform divine service c 1365.

subsesonator, (?) assistant 'seasoner' (*i.e.* temperer of metal) 1370.

subsesqui/alter (**subsexqui-**) 870. 13c., c 1360, **-plicatus** 1686, contained 1½ times (in another number); **-quartus**, contained

1¼ times 13c.; **-tertius**, contained 1⅓ times 13c., c 1360.

subsessor, (?) under-tenant (London) a 1125.

subsid/ium, maintenance, sustenance c 1220, c 1464; subsidy, grant in aid 1225, 1539; feudal aid c 1240, 1284; subsidy granted to crown, tax 1333, 1467; **-es** (*pl.*), auxiliaries 10c.; **-ialis** 1308, **-iarius** 1283, in the form of a subsidy; **-io**, to aid c 1177.

†**subsido**,ˈto neglect c 1290; **subsed/o** (? **-eo**), to die down, rest undisturbed c 1250.

subsignifico, to imply 1497.

subsileo, to keep silent c 1180.

subsilia, "kirtle" 1588.

subsimulo, to bear some resemblance to 15c.

subsist/entia, subsistence (phil.) 680, c 860. c 1250, c 1362; existence c 1390, a 1452; **-entivus**, subsistent (phil.) 1427; **-o**, to hold good (leg.) c 1337, c 1444; to subsist (phil.) c 1160, a 1323; to subsist, maintain oneself c 1337, c 1432; to be c 1470; **substito**, *for* **-o**, c 600.

subsol/ana (*n. pl.*) a 1180, **-aria** c 1160, earthly things; **-aris**, earthly 12c.; *for* **-anus**, east wind c 1200.

subsolarium, room under 'solar' 1286, p 1327.

subsp-, *see also* **susp-**

subspecies, subspecies (bot.) 1533.

subst-, *see also* **sust-**

†**substantatio**, (?) attenuation 13c.

substant/ia, ***property**, wealth (bibl.); (?) building 1409; quantity *or* square (math.) (Ar. *mal*) 1145; substance, *οὐσία* (phil.) 6c., 11c. c 1250, c 1400; s. **prima**, primary substance a 1100, a 1180; ultimate subject (log.) 1350; s. **secunda** a 1110, a 1345; s. **universalis** a 1110; **-ialia** (*n. pl.*), essentials (esp. leg.) c 1275, 1549; ***essential vows** (mon.) c 1296, c 1390; **-ialis**, ***substantial** (log. &ˈtheol.) c 850. c 1080, c 1444; essential, important, of substance 1431, 1684; **causa s.** (phil.) c 1250; **forma s.** (phil.) c 1200, a 1347; (leg.) c 1327, 1469; ***-ialiter**, in substance or essence (phil.) 6c., c 860. 1144, c 1444; **-ialitas**, substantiality (phil.) a 1340; **-iatus**, endowed with substance (phil.) c 1270; **-iola**, meagre substance, scanty wealth c 550, 8c. c 1220, c 1250; **-ificus**, creative 870; **-ive**, in essence c 1115, c 1160; as a substantive (gram.) p 1300; **-ivus**, essential c 1115; 1267, 1292, c 1360, to give essence or substance to (phil.); to use as a substantive (gram.) c 1225, p 1300; **substo**, to uphold c 1280; to underlie as substance (phil.) c 1267, c 1363.

sustantivus c 1210, substantive (gram.); **-ifico** 870. c 1340, **-io** a 1250, **-ivo** c 1290, c 1360, to give essence or substance to (phil.);

substatuo, *see* SUBSTITU

substern-, *see* SUBSTRAT

substes, in the rank behind 1610.

substimulo, to spur on (fig.) c 870.

substito, *see* SUBSIST

substitu/tio, substitution (theol.) 7c., 9c.; alteration c 730; **-tor**, **-trix** (*f.*), creator of substance 870. 1344; **-tor**, appointer of substitute c 1300; ***-tus**, substitute c 1285, 1684; **substatuo** 1485, †**substo** 1367, *for* **-o**, to substitute.

substo, *see* SUBSTANT; SUBSTITU

substomachor, to be rather angry c 1125, c 1300.

subs/tractio, -traho, *see* SUBTRACT

substrat/io, treatment as a subject (log.) c 1300; **-orium,** bier c 760; carpet c 1182; corporal cloth (eccl.) c 1283, a 1450; mattress c 1340; **substern/ium,** litter (for animals) c 1212; **-o,** to subject, devote c 1100, 1200; to treat as subject (log.) c 1270, p 1300.

subsubjungo, to subjoin c 730.

subsull/iva, under-sill (arch.) 1283, 1300; (?) **-o** (†subfullo), to support by means of under-sill 1238.

subsultori/us, fitful 1620, 1646; **-e,** fitfully c 1626.

subsum, *see* subessentia.

subsum/ptio, subsumption (log.) a 1360; **-o,** to subsume a 1360.

subsuper/particularis, contained (in another number) together with an aliquot part of itself (math.) 13c.; **-partiens** 13c., †**subsuppartiens** a 1250, contained with two or more aliquot parts; **-bipartiens, -tripartiens, -quadripartiens,** contained with two, three, *or* four aliquot parts 13c.

subsuspicor, to mistrust 1570.

subtaceo, *see* subticeo.

‡**subtal/,** *for* subtel, "sole of foot" a 1520; **-aris** 7c., c 1000. a 1300, c 1324, **subtolaris** a 1142, **subtularis** a 1300, **sotularis** *c 1172, 1450, **sodularis** 1256, †**satularis** 1206, **sotilaris** 1318, **sutularis** c 1250, **sutularius** 1292, †**solutare** 13c., 1297, shoe; **sotularis,** socket c 1400.

subtango, to mention below c 1407.

subtax/ator 1327, 15c., †**sustaxuarius** 1398, sub-assessor; **-atus,** described below 1432.

subtegmen (propheticum), mantle 12c.

‡**subtela,** crupper, "tail-band" c 1440, 1483.

†**subtellarium,** fume, vapour a 1235.

subtempero, to be moderate c 1370.

subten/ens, under-tenant a 1250, 1611; "inmate" 1661; **-eo,** to hold as subtenant c 1350.

subten/sa, subtense (geom.) 1686; **-do,** to subtend 1264, 1611.

subter/, under: **supter** 808, c 1000; **-ior,** lower a 1250, c 1250.

subterfugium, hiding-place, refuge c 1200, 15c.; subterfuge, evasion c 1178, c 1470.

subterjaceo, to be under c 1362.

subtermitto, to prostrate oneself 768.

subterpositus, placed beneath 1136, c 1503.

subterr/atio, interment 1427; ‡**-arium** 15c., ‡**-atorium** 1483, dibble; **-anee,** underground c 1400; **carbo -enus,** pit-coal 1499; **-o,** to inter 1238, 1438.

subterscriptus, written below 1086.

subthesaurarius, under-treasurer (eccl.) 1424, 1481; **s. Anglie** 1468, 1526; **s. Hibernie** 1583.

subthronizo, to enthrone c 700, c 1000. c 1125, 12c.

*****subticeo** c 1188, c 1465, **subtaceo** 13c., 15c., to be silent (about), leave unspoken.

subtil/itas, subtlety, guile c 790. 1290; **-imembris,** of immaterial limbs 870; **-iatio,** rarefaction a 1250, 1446; hair-splitting c 1360; **-iativus,** rarefying, refining a 1250, 13c.; **-io,** *to rarefy, refine c 1200, 1686; to refine (fig.) a 1252; to beat out thin c 1200; c 1240, 1380, **-izo** 1389, to draw subtle distinctions (about).

subtimidus, somewhat fearful c 1434.

subtitulo, to name below 13c., c 1266.

subtolaris, *see* SUBTAL

subtollo, *see* sustollo.

subtract/io 12c., c 1470, **substractio** 1307, 1364, **subtraxio** 1281, **subtramentum** a 1250, removal, withdrawal; c 1190, 1272, **substractio** 1370, departure, absconding; subtraction (math.) c 1178, 15c.; detraction c 1316; **-or,** remover, embezzler 1336, 1425; **-o,** to treat of next c 1115; 1243, c 1290, **substraho** 1253, 1583, *for* subtraho, to remove, withdraw; c 1288, **subtraho** 1145, 1275, **substraho** 1276, to subtract; **subtrahor a luce** 1432, **s. de medio** c 1330, to die.

†**subtragmen,** (?) tunic 1189.

subtrappura, under-trapping (of horse) 1360.

subtripl/us a 1200, 1335, **-ex** 13c., one-third the size.

subtularis, *see* SUBTAL

subtum/idus, slightly swollen a 1250; **-esco,** to swell slightly a 1250.

subtunic/a 1347, **-ula** 1457, under-tunic.

subturibularius, assistant censer-bearer 1535.

subtus *(prep.* with *acc.*), beneath c 730, 785. c 1080, 1478; (with *abl.*) 1270; **suptus** 790. 1252.

subtuspinno, to underpin 1366.

‡**subucula,** "wig", simnel cake 1570; **subuncula,** *for* s., shirt c 1180, 13c.

subulcanus, of a swine-herd c 1150.

†**subumbr/ale,** (?) canopy 14c.; **-o,** to overshadow c 1298, c 1390.

subundo, to overwhelm c 1180.

*****suburb/ium** 1070, 1540, †**burbium** 1086, †**-um** 1293, †**suburgium, suborbium** c 1338, **-anum** 7c. c 1173, 1517, suburb; **-anitas,** rusticity c 1200; **-anus,** dependent on a town 812; *(subst.)* (?) minor free tenant (Norm.) c 1185.

†**sub/vavaser** (?) 1296, †**-vasor** (?) 13c., subvavassor (Sc.).

subvect/io, (?) aid, support c 1125, 1188; **-o** 1136, **auxilium s.** (†subnecto) c 1362, to aid.

subveneror, to respect c 1610.

subven/tio *c 1090, 1543, **-tus** 720. 1109, aid, assistance; subvention, financial aid 700. c 1188, 15c.; (?) attack 1338; **-tor** c 1250, **-trix** (*f.*) a 1100, helper; **-torius,** helpful 1171; **-io,** to come to mind 1276; **suvenio,** *for* **-io,** 1378.

*****subvers/io** (bibl.), **-atio** c 1192, overthrow, rebellion c 1368; **-ivus,** subversive 1437; **-or,** overthrower c 990. c 1180, 1451.

subvetus, oldish 1622.

*****subvicecomes,** under-sheriff c 1130, 1419.

subvigilia, day before the eve (of a festival) 1330.

†**subvinctus,** (?) *f.l.* for **subjunctus,** subdued c 1450.

†**subvivo,** *for* **supervivo,** to survive 1489.

†**subvocatus** (?) *f.l.* for **subnotatus,** under-mentioned 1252.

sucara, *see* sucrum.

sucarius, *see* **scutum.**

succ-, *see also* **subc-**

†**succades**(*pl.*),'succades', candied fruits 1570.

succed-, *see* **succendines**; SUCCESS; SUCCIS

succematus, *see* **superseminatus.**

succendines (*pl.*) c 1200, ‡**succedines** 1483, bays, compartments (of ceiling) (arch.).

***succent/or** a 1090, 1537, **subcentor** 1242, **subcinctor** 1220, **subcantor** 1414, c 1470, succentor (eccl.); **-rix** 1520, **subcantarista** 1530, succentress; **-oria** 1255, c 1266, **subcantoria** c 1230, succentorship.

succenturiatim, by way of reinforcement a 1275.

success/io, successiveness p 1300; progeny c 1204, c 1450; **-ibilis,** subject to succession 1344; **-iones** (*pl.*), successive ages or generations c 1160; ***-ive** a 1183, 1686, **succedenter** 1136, p 1475, successively; ***-ivus** 1125, 1649, †**succidius** c730, **succiduus** c 1125, successive, succeeding; **sussessor,** *for* **-or,** 1213, **succestrix** (*f.*) c 1414, successor; **succed/entia,** succession c 1200; **-o,** to devolve by succession or inheritance p 1250, c 1447.

succid-, *see* SUCCESS; **succinium**; SUCCIS

succin/ctorium, apron (eccl.): girdle c 1325; ‡**-gula,** "surcingle" 1483; **-ctim** 1041, **-te** c 1070, 1263, *for* **-cte,** succinctly; *see also* SUCCENT

succiner/icius (subciner-), baked in ashes (bibl.) a 1166, c 1400; greyish a 1200, a 1250; **-o,** to bank up (fire) c 1325.

succi/nium 1213, **-num** 1214, **-um** 1215, **-duum** 1250, 1282, **sucsiduum** 1296; **-divum** 13c., **-dium** 1302, 1325, souse, pickled pork; **-tus** 1241, 1247, **-duatus** c 1200, **suliciatus** 1214, soused; **-dio** 1257, **suscio** 1240, **soucio** 1198, to souse, pickle.

succinus, amber necklace 6c.

succis/io, felling *or* pruning c 560. c 1160, 1575; **-ura,** hamstringing c 1125; **-or (arborum),** feller 1464; **succedo** 1353, **succindo** 13c., c 1308, *for* **succido,** to fell.

succit, *see* **sugo.**

succito, *see* SUSCIT

suc/clusus, half-closed a 1250; **-claudo,** to half-close a 1250.

succollatio, propping (of vines) c 1390.

succollectoria, succoques, *see* **subc-**

succoraria, chicory (bot.): **zuccoraria** a 1250.

†**succoria,** (?) *f.l.* for **victoria,** c 1258.

succub/a, concubine c 1160, 1202; 1528, **-us** c 1190, p 1300, demon causing nocturnal emission.

succumb/entia, succumbing 1620; **-o,** to undertake 800; **s. ad,** to be subject to c 1362.

***succurs/us** 1136, 1461, **subcursus** (Sc.) 1315, 1337, **secursus** 1216, †**-ivum** 15c., succour; **ad succurrendum,** as a means to salvation (of those donning monastic habit at point of death) c 1148, c 1296; **succurro** (*trans.*), to support, corroborate c 1470; *see also* SUCCUSS

succ/us Celei, a medicament a 1250; **suxus,** juice c 550; *see also* VIRID; **-ulentus,** appetizing a 615.

succuss/atio, shaking c 1212; **-atura,** trotting 1587; **-arius** 1499, 1535, **succursorius**

c 1200, ‡**succursarius** c 1440, †**succursa** (? **succursarius**) 1444, trotter; **-o** a 1200, 1378, ‡**succurso** c 1440, ‡**succutio** a 1520, to trot; **succutio,** to heave c 1125.

sucgillatio, *see* SUGILL

such/a, -eus, *see* ZUCH

sucronensis, name of a wind 8c.

suc/rum 1303, 1531, **-urum** 1380, **-ra** c 1303, 15c., **-ara** 1305, **-ura** 1358, 1440, **-uris** 1340, **sicora** 1267, **sugr/a, -um** 1392, 1421, †**surgera** c 1335, **szucra** 1292, ***zuc/ara** 1176, c 1390, **-arium** c 1290, **-arum** c 1200, 1480, **zukera** 1301, **zuccerum** 1480, **-ra** 1256, 1323, **-rum** 1335, **-ura** 1292, 1456, **-urium** 1393, **xukeris** 1305, sugar; s. (z.) **album** c 1260, 1407; s. **nigrum** 1407; s. **Alexandrinum** 1226; s. **candi** 1390, s. **candidum** 1380, sugar candy; s. de Cipre 1316; s. **rosarum** 1285, c 1390, s. **rosatum** 1226, 1303, s. **rosaceum** c 1260, s. **rosetum** 1393, **sucurossetum** 1307; s. **violarum** 1285, s. **violatum** 1226, 1252, s. **violetum** 1301; **aqua sugurata** 1392; *see also* **alumen;** *cf.* SACCHAR

sucsiduum, *see* **succinium.**

sucur-, *see also* **sucrum.**

***sud/arium** c 1080, c 1450, **-orium** c 1450, **-ariolum** c 1180, c 1330, napkin, kerchief; 1130, c 1200, **suarium** 1180, c 1200, saddle-cloth; cloth used in handling paten or reliquary (eccl.) 1383, 1401; shroud 1461; **-or** 1508, 1528, **morbus -arius** c 1508, 1517, m. **-ificus,** lues **-ifica** 1508, 'sweating sickness', plague; **-orosus,** sweaty c 1340; **-esco,** to toil c 1125; **-o,** to be ill of the plague 1508.

sud/es c 1400, **-ex** 1452, beam, stake; ‡"misericord" 15c.; *see also* **porcellus.**

sud/pars, -tridinga, *see* SUTH

sudus, cloud, shadow c 550.

†**suelis,** (?) *f.l.* for **sulcus,** 1307.

suella, sues, suettis, *see* **sus.**

sueo, *see* **sutor.**

suer/a, -um, *see* **exaquia.**

suet/a, -um 1322, 1383, s. **prisone (prisonum)** 1323, 1414, s. **carceris** 1421, **secta prisone** 1351, **sewettum prisone** a 1564, *suete de prison,* (payment for) relaxation of prison conditions or freedom from detention before trial; *cf.* **suavitas.**

Suethedus c 1385, †**Sueticus** (? **Suecicus**) 1613, **Swevus** c 1125, **Suavus** (†**Suanus**) a 1142, c 1250, Swede, Swedish.

suetio, custom c 1375.

†**suetta,** (?) some form of payment 1263.

suetum, *see* **sebum; sueta.**

suff-, *see also* **subf-**

suffalc/um (subfalc-) 1270, 1282, **-atio** 1286, 'fog', aftermath.

suffarcin/atio, cramming 1421; ‡**-ator,** "briber", (?) thief 15c.; **-o,** to stuff (with wool) 1406.

suffasciatus (†suffaciatus), wrapped up a 1142.

†**suffator,** (?) *f.l.* for **suffossor,** c 1250.

suffect/us a 1142, c 1250, **persona -a** c 1412, agent; **-ivus** c 1100, ***suffici/ens** c 1090, c 1559, sufficient, reliable; **-entior,** more reliable 1316, 1509; ***-enter,** sufficiently c 1070, 1663; **-entissime** a 1090, c 1444;

*-entia a 1090, 1461, **suffisientia** 1279, sufficiency.

‡**suffercio**, to "snuff", "foist" 1570.

1 **suffer/entia, -antia, dimidia,** half sovereign 1558.

2 **suffer/entia,** carrying 1378; sufferance (eccl.); (G.) 1293, **soffrantia** 1224, respite; *1295, 1440, **s. guerre** 1298, **sufrentia** 1420, armistice; **-o,** to hold up c 1115; (with *acc.* & *inf.*) to permit 1242, c 1250.

sufflagrantia, fragrance c 860.

suffl/atio p 1300, **-amen** c 1180, c 1362, breath; **s. organorum,** organ-playing 1389; **domus -atica,** blowing-house (for tin-smelting) 1508; **-ator,** smelter, ore-blower 1300, 1508; **-atoria** (*pl.*) 1386, **-etta, -etti** 1293, 1356, **-ete** 1363, **-ones** 1462, **-a** 1352, bellows; *see also* SIBIL; **-orium,** (?) furnace c 1188; **-o,** to mock by blowing (on bagpipes) 1486; to smelt 1508; **s. folles** 1409.

sufflexio, bow 870.

suffoc/atio, suppression, destruction 1324, c 1450; **-alia** (*pl.*), bellows c 1346; **-ativus,** choking c 1620; **-o (mucrone, sagittis),** to kill 1136, c 1450; to drown 12c.; to dim, outshine c 550; to stifle, suppress 7c. c 1180, c 1450.

suffoltarium, *see* SUFFUL

†**suffonio,** (?) black hellebore (bot.) a 1250.

suffoss/or, sapper, underminer c 1236, 15c.; **-orium,** (?) spade c 560. 12c.; **suffodio,** to prick (with compunction) 13c.

suffrag/ium, *aid, support 7c., 981. c 1110, 1549; prayer, intercession 1171, 1516; **s. vite,** life-time c 1000; means of life c 1220; **-aneus** c 1150, †**-is** c 1220, supporter; *9c. c 1100, c 1507, †**-ancius** c 1325, **episcopus -aneus** a 1120, 1536, **e.** †**-anus** 1274, suffragan bishop; **ecclesia -anea** c 1200, 1280; **-ator** c 1090, c 1255, **-atrix** (*f.*) 700, intercessor; †**-io,** ballot 1429; **-or** 676, **-o** c 1225, c 1475, to grant.

suffrag/o, leg c 950; ‡**-inatio,** kneeling 1483; ‡**-inor,** to kneel 1483.

sufful/tio (subful-) 1381, **-tus** 590, 810. c 1370, support, aid; **-torium** (†**suffol-tarium**), (?) buttress or undercroft (arch.) c 1412; **-to,** to bear, support c 500; *-**cio,** to support (*fig.*), aid c 1160, 16c.; *see also* **lancea.**

suffumig/ium, fumigation a 1250, 1344; **-o,** (?) to choke c 1250.

suffuratio ventorum, stealing the wind (from sails) 1622.

suffusco, to obscure, darken 7c. a 1250, 1281.

sufrentia, *see* 2 **sufferentia.**

sugg-, *see also* **subg-**

*sugges/tio 597, 8c. a 1090, 15c., **-sio** c 900, **-tus** c 1125, c 1458, instigation, prompting, temptation; accusation (leg.) 1281, c 1470; *ad **-tionem** 12c., 15c., **ex -tione** c 1192, **super -tione** 1291; **-tio falsa** 1236, 1461, **s. falsi** a 1250, **s. falsitatis** c 1195; **-tor,** prompter, adviser 12c., 1281; accuser 1442; **s. falsus** c 1265; **-tum** 1552, 1647, **-tus** c 1587, pulpit; **sugger/ens,** plaintiff, accuser 1342; **-o** (with *inf.*), to prompt 1136, c 1400.

suggrundium c 950, †**subgrudium** a 1240, eaves; *cf.* **severunda.**

sugill/atio, scoffing, insulting: **sucgillatio** 825; **-ator,** scoffer 1620; **sigillo,** *for* **-o,** to scoff at 12c.; *see also* **sugo.**

†**sugmentum,** (?) insinuation 8c.

sug/o (suggo), to suck: **succit,** *for* **suxit,** suckled a 1408; **-illo,** to suck down c 550.

sugr-, sugur-, *see* **sucrum.**

suign-, suin-, *see* **soinantagium.**

suil-, suist-, *see* **sus.**

suissio, *see* **sutor.**

suit-, *see* 1 **secta; sutor; suus.**

sujurno, *see* SOJORN

1 †**sulcus,** (?) *f.l.* for **fuscus,** dark 1415.

2 **sulc/us** 1278, 1340, **-a** a 1260, **-o** 14c., furlong or baulk; (?) plough a 1408; 1399, **s. aquaticus** 1308, channel, watercourse; **-atio,** furrowing, "balking" ‡15c., 1459; **-o ad -um,** in adjoining strips (?) 12c.; undulation 1622; **-atrix,** furrower (*f.*) 1220; **-o (carrucas),** to fit with plough-shares 1314, 1323.

sulfodis, *see* **selfodus.**

sulghbemum, share-beam (of plough) 1306.

suliciatus, *see* **succinium.**

sull-, *see also* **subl-**

sullagium, *see* **solum.**

*sullin/ga, **-gus** 1204, 1340, **-a, -us** c 1150, c 1300, †**suligium** 1329, **sollinga** 1196, **solinus** 1086, c 1397, **silinga** 1293, 1313, **swullinga** c 1200, **swollinga, swolingus** c 1300, c 1397, **swillinga** 12c., 1441, **-gata** c 1300, c 1397, **-ghida** c 1160, 'suling', measure of land comparable to hide (Kent); **-arius** 1290, **sullimannus** c 1300, †**sull-mannus** 13c., **swillingmannus** 1441, tenant of a suling; *cf.* **scillingum.**

sulliv/a, -um, *see* **soliva.**

sullo (sulo), *see* 1 **selio; sillum.**

sulmagium, *see* SAGM

sulphur/ album c 1215, c 1320, **s. canellatum** (*see* **canale**) c 1215, ‡15c., **s. croceum** c 1215, **s. citrinum** c 1270, **s. flavum** c 1215, **s. nigrum** c 1270, **s. rubeum** c 1215, c 1320, **s. philosophorum** c 1345, **s. vulgi** a 1252, **s. simplex** 1334, **s. vivum** a 1252, 1335, ‡**s. extinctum** 14c., varieties or compounds of sulphur (alch.); **-aca,** (?) galingale (bot.) a 1250, ‡14c.; ‡**-ata,** "match" a 1520.

sulsus, *see* SALS

sultanus, *see* **soldanus.**

sum, *see* **esse.**

suma, *see* **soma.**

sumach a 1250, 1634, **cymachum** 1216, sumach (bot.).

sumer-, sum/etarius, -itarius, *see* SAGM

summ-, *see also* SAGM; **subm-**

summ/a, *compendium, treatise a 1245, 1620; **s. compoti** 1298, **s. vicecomitis** 1225, 1279, 'sheriff's summ'; **s. -arum** 13c., *s. **totalis** 1218, c 1564, sum total; **-aliter** c 1270, 1455, **-arie** 1278, 1684, summarily; **-arius,** summary, concise c 1250, 1620; summary (of legal procedure) 1327, 1547; **-as** c 1150, **-us** 1153, magnate; **-ipotens** c 950. 1462, **-itonans** (?) c 955, **-us** c 1370, titles of the deity; **-ista,** writer of compendia c 1444, c 1494; *-**itas,** summit, top (eccl.); end, extremity 720, c 980. a 1180, c 1540; **-ula,** short compendium, epitome 1292,

1515; **-ulista,** student of *Summule* of Petrus Hispanus 1516; **-um scuti,** 'chief' (her.) 1449; **-us,** *see* **altare, missa;** ***-o mane,** early in the morning c 1150, 1423; **-o,** to add, reckon up 1168, c 1540; *see also* SAGM

†**summanuteneo** (? **sub manu t.**), to maintain, uphold c 1130.

*summer/sio (subm-), submersion, immersion, drowning 790, 870. c 1250, c 1470; **submarsus,** *for* **-sus,** c 1280; **-go,** to be drowned c 1218, 1362.

summinist/ratio (subm-), supply c 1125, 15c.; administration 12c.; **-er** c 1266, c 1290, **-ralis, -rans** c 1220, subordinate officer; **-ro,** to serve (eccl.) 12c., c 1230.

summiss/io (subm-), submission 1277, c 1542; acceptance of arbitration c 1280, 1358; **summitto,** to leave behind 768; to subjugate, make submissive c 1090, c 1250; to propose 1357; *(intr.)* to submit 1234, c 1534; **s. me clerimonie,** to claim benefit of clergy p 1330; †**susmito,** to submit c 1130.

summon/itio (subm-) ***c** 1115, 16c., **-atio** 1467, **somonitio** 1233, **-itia** 1286, **-sa** 1194, †**summensa** c 1200, summons (leg.); threat of excommunication 9c.; **s. communis** 1194, 1268, **s. generalis** 1255, 1412; **s. itineris,** summons of the eyre c 1218, c 1240; **s. libera,** summons due to a free man 1258; **s. Scaccarii** 1227, 1332; **-itor** *****1170, c 1480, **somonitor** 1414, summoner (leg.); Exchequer official 1226, 1371; **submonitor,** usher (in school) 1321; **-itorie** *(pl.)* c 1188, **littere s.** 1264, letters of summons; ***-eo** c 1072, 1461, ***-io** 1191, a 1564, **-o** c 1300, **sommoneo (somonio)** c 1283, 1414, **somono** 1275, **-ito** (†**-ico**) 1269, to summon; to allot (a debt) for collection by Exchequer summons c 1178, c 1370; **s. iter,** to issue summons of the eyre 1269; **s. recognitionem,** to summon a jury 1203; **s. veniendi,** to summon to appear 1381.

summonstro (subm-), to go on to show a 1110.

summotio (subm-), removal c 1620; suppression 1414.

summulti/plex, fractional (math.) a 1150, a 1250; **-plicitas,** fractionality 13c.; **-pliciter,** fractionally a 1250.

summurmur/atio (subm-), grumbling 15c.; ***-o,** to murmur secretly, mutter, grumble 8c. c 1125, 15c.

summus, *see* **summa.**

summussito (subm-), to murmur 1662.

sumnile, sumpt/arius, -uarius, sumularius, *see* SAGM

sumpt/io, taking (of food) 13c., 1461; c 1223, c 1380, **sumpsio** 13c., receiving the elements (eccl.); **-ibilis,** consumable (of food) a 1250; **-or,** collector of tithes 1229; **-uositas,** costliness c 1190, c 1415; **-ura,** wealth, property c 760; **-us** *(pl.)* **agri,** fruits of the earth (W.) 14c.; **-a Maria** *(met. grat.),* the Assumption 1413; **-um,** transumpt, copy 1302, 1306; **sumo,** to take, understand (in a particular sense) c 1332, c 1530; **s. pro,** to use in the sense of 14c.; **s. dilationem,** to undergo delay c 1325; **s. exordium**

c 1400, **s. initium** 12c., to originate; **s. experientiam de,** to put (a person) to the test c 1250; **s. in notam,** to take note of 1542; **s. iter,** to take one's way c 1250; **s. judicium,** to submit to punishment c 1266.

suncula, *see* **sus.**

sundernota, special task or service (A.S.) c 1115.

sundra (†**cindra**), 'sounder', herd of swine (Sc.) 14c.

sungina, *see* **smigma.**

sun/ianta, -etagium, *see* **soinantagium.**

supedifico, *see* SUPEREDIFIC

supel/lex, *membrum virile* c 1180; **-lectile** p 1377, **-lectilia** *(pl.)* 1328, 1477, **superlect/ile** c 1300, c 1400, **-ilia** *(pl.)* c 1223, 1457, **-ulus** 1382, 1455, **-us** 1461, **superpellect/ile** 1457, bedding; **-ula** *(pl.)* 1518, **sublectilia** *(pl.)* 768, furnishings; *see also* **superpelliceum.**

super *(prep.* with *acc.),* on, at, against (of place) 7c., 948. 12c., 1537; against, about (of time) c 1218, c 1335; on (a day of the week) 1340; (imposed) on (of taxation, *etc.*) 1218, 1559; against (of adversaries) 1103, 1353; (debited) against 1086, 1524; in defiance of, in breach of c 1080, c 1516; against, in exchange for a 1123, 1359; on, in the possession of (= *penes*) c 1115, 1412; on (security of) 1217, 1260; on pain of, at risk of c 1075, 1238; on, by (of oaths) c 1115, 1228; ***about,** concerning 12c., c 1470;

(with *abl.*) on (a charge of) 1257, 15c.; (spent) on 1415, 1480; (?) without c 1318; (with *abl.* & *gerundive*) for the purpose of 1230, 15c.;

s. caput 1368, **s. capita** 1372, per head; **s. compotum,** on or at the account 1223, 1479 *(see also* **onus,** VEND); **s. equum,** more than reasonable 1377; ***s. forisfacturam,** on pain of forfeiture c 1110, c 1448; **s. judicium,** without judgement being given (leg.) 1217; **s. librum** (of oaths) 1201, c 1444; **s. sacramentum,** on oath 1219, 1412; **s. Scaccarium,** at the Exchequer 1235, 1375; **s. suam,** at his own expense c 1311;

s. eo quod 1285, c 1310, **s. hoc quod** 1488, because; **s. quibus,** whereupon c 1340; **s. inde,** *see* **superinde;** *see also* **abutto, attendo, capio, eo, occupo, pono, recupero.**

*superabund/antia (bibl.), †**-ia** c 1180, excess; **-atio maris,** inundation 1225; **-anter** (bibl.), **-e** 12c., **-antissime** 1344, **ex -anti** 1304, c 1460, **de -anti** c 1414, superabundantly; **-o,** to inundate, overflow 1225, 1375; *(trans.)* to exceed c 1245.

superaccen/sio, feverish heat a 1250; **-do,** to heat a 1250.

superaccido (with *dat.*), to befall 870.

superaccresco, to increase 8c., c 1115.

superaccumul/atio, excess c 1250; **-o,** to heap up 1253, c 1255.

superacuo, to sharpen on 1325, 1355.

superaddit/io, further addition a 1250, 13c.; **-amentum,** supernumerary 8c.; **-amenta** *(pl.),* epacts c 730.

superad/jectio, further addition c 730; **-jicio** (**-icio**), to superadd c 1115, c 1180.

superaduno, to unite in addition 870.

superadventus, coming in addition 870; coming against, onset c 1250.

superaffectualis, transcending the affections c 1250.

superafflu/enter, excessively c 1250; **-o,** to overflow 790.

superaffundo, to pour over 1634.

superag/enda (*pl.*), tasks noted above c 1266; **-o,** to drive over 14c.

superalloco, to allow in addition (on account) 1224.

*****superaltar/e** 1217, 1519, **-ium** 1236, portable altar, altar-slab; **pannus -is,** altar-cloth c 1220.

superaltus, transcendent 6c.

superamabilis, supremely lovable c 1250, 1344.

superann/uatio, expiry of a year's time-limit (leg.) c 1338, 1432; **-uatus,** having outrun a year's time-limit, time-expired (leg.) c 1338, c 1511; more than a year old (of dried meat) c 1324; a 1198, *****-atus** a 1150, 1364, **-alis** c 1300, between one and two years old, yearling (of animals); **-o** 1325, **-uor** 1244, to pass one year in age (of animals).

superanxius, very anxious c 1236, c 1250.

superappar/itio, super-appearance 870; **-ens,** appearing above, haughty c 730.

superappendo, to hang up above c 1275.

superarcanus, hidden farthest away 6c., 870.

superargentatus, silver-plated 1605.

superaro, to plough over 1275, p 1348.

superascendo, to rise above c 1250, c 1325.

superaspersio, sprinkling over a 1250.

superassisa, *see* SUPERSED

superasto, to stand above c 1260.

superatrox, very violent c 1250.

superattentio, superintendence 1593.

super/atrix, victory c 1265; **-atrix,** victorious (*f.*) a 1350; **-o,** to overwhelm, bury c 700; to convict (G.) 1289; to precede c 1595.

superaud/itio, (fine for) disobedience (A.S. *oferhiernes*) c 1115; **-itor,** chief auditor (of accounts) (Sc.) 1326, 1368; **-io,** to hear, overhear c 1115.

superaug/mentum, surplus increase (of livestock) c 1115; **-eo** 8c., c 1000. 1250, **-mento** c 730, 804. 1267, to increase.

superauratus, gilt 1255, 1605.

superbeatus, supremely blest 1344.

superben/edictus, supremely blest c 1100, c 1250; **-evolus, -ignus,** supremely benevolent c 1250.

superb/iose, arrogantly a 1564; **-ificus,** making proud c 1293; **morbus -us** (?), 13c.; **-uit,** *for* **-iit** or **-ivit,** p 1330, c 1452; **-io,** to make proud (?) c 1362, a 1408.

superbipartiens, containing a number plus two aliquot parts a 1150, 13c.

superbonus, transcendently good 870. c 1270.

superbrudatus, embroidered over c 1400.

supercado, to fall on 1371.

supercarco, *see* **superchargium.**

supercastrum, siege-tower (G.) 1293.

supercausalis, transcending causation, unconditional 870.

super/cedeo, -cessio, *see* SUPERSED

supercelestis, supercelestial 870. 12c., c 1405; *cf.* **supracelestis.**

super/cellium, -cilicium, *see* **superpelliceum.**

supercengula, *see* **supercinctorium.**

superchargium, surcharge 1266, 1267; (?) **surcarc/a** c 1220, **-amentum** c 1265, overstocking (of pasture); **supercarco,** to overstock (pasture) 1244.

supercil/ium, projecting moulding (arch.) 1346, 1465; **S. Veneris,** yarrow (bot.) ‡14c., 1538; **in -io,** in the twinkling of an eye 7c.; **-is,** disdainful 943; **-iositas** c 1302, **-iosum** c 600, disdain; **-iose,** disdainfully 15c.; ‡**-io,** "to gloom" 1483.

supercinctorium, covering 795; **supercing/ulum, -ula** 1214, c 1395, **supercengula** 1239, **supersingulum** 1324, c 1417, **supracingulum** 1290, c 1414, **surcinglum** 1332, **sursingulum** 1308, 1323, **surzenglum** 1307, surcingle (of horse); **-o,** to gird 1342.

supercipio, to obtain in excess c 1260.

superclarus, supremely bright c 1250.

†**super/clasura,** head of door or window (arch.) 1349; **-cludo,** to cover over 700.

superclemens, supremely merciful c 1250.

supercognosco, to have full knowledge of 870.

supercol/loco, to place above 870. 1344; †**-latus,** *for* **-locatus,** 870.

supercompassus, taking compassion c 1290.

superconfido (†**superfido**), to be over-confident c 1115.

superconsummativus, supremely consummate 870.

supercooper/torium, outer garment 1280; **-io,** to cover over 14c.

supercota c 1200, **surcotus** 1199, 1206, surcoat.

supercresco, to grow to excessive size 804. (?) 1336; to overgrow, overhang c 1482, 1533; to exceed c 1306.

supercucullus, outer hood 1351.

‡**superculum,** "covercle" 15c.

superdeauratus, gilt 1363.

superdecorus, supremely beautiful c 1250.

*****superdemand/a** 1168, 1307, †**superdimanda** 1189 (1227), excessive claim; **-atus,** claimed in excess 1226.

superdeus, above God 870.

superdic/tus, above-mentioned c 1340, 14c. (*cf.* SUPRADIC); (?) *for* **superductus,** covered over a 1446; **-o,** to accuse c 1115.

superdignissimus, supremely worthy c 1250.

superdiversus, very varied 1421.

superdivin/itas, highest divine being 870; **-us,** beyond the divine 870.

superdominor, to rule over 1374.

superdors/aria, -orium, -ura 1214, **superdoss/aria** 1213, **-erium** 1265, back-band (of harness).

superdubito, to doubt about a 1250.

‡**superduc/tio,** smearing 1483; **-o,** to mark with c 730; to cover c 1072, 1345; to introduce in addition c 1362; a 1164, c 1448, †**supraduco** 15c., to marry a second wife.

superebullitio, boiling over a 1250.

superedific/atum c 1246, c 1345, **supraedificium** 1329, c 1340, superstructure; *****-o** (bibl.), †**supedifico** 1295, †**supraedifico** c 1300, to build over.

supereffectualis, supremely efficacious c 1250.

supereffu/entia, exuberance c 1239; **-entissime,** abundantly 1344; ***-o,** to overflow (eccl.).

supereffundo, to overflow 795.

superemin/entia, pre-eminence (eccl.); **-enter,** pre-eminently 1307, 1457; **-eo,** to be left as remainder (math.) a 1150; **supermineo,** *for* **-eo,** c 860.

superemptio, *see* **supraemptio.**

superempyreus, above the empyrean c 1212.

superens, *see* SUPERESSENTIAL

superequito, to override c 730.

supererigo, to build on c 1246.

supererog/atio, supererogation (theol.) c 1340, 1610; **-ativus** c 1343, **-atorius** c 1340, 1346, supererogatory; **-anter,** by way of supererogation c 1363, c 1367; **-o,** to give or perform in addition (bibl.).

superessential/itas, transcendence (theol.) c 870; **-is** 6c., c 870. 12c., 1344, **superens** 1374, transcendent; **-iter,** transcendently 6c., c 870. c 1250, 1344; **supersum,** to surpass 870. a 1408.

superestainatus, coated with tin 1198.

supereternus, transcending eternity 870.

superexalto, to exalt above others (bibl.); to rise above c 1197.

superexced/entia, excess c 1250; **superexcessivus,** excessive c 1375; **-o,** to surpass 6c., 9c. c 1150, c 1250.

superexcel/lentia superexcellence 870. c 1100, a 1350; **-lens,** superexcellent 12c., c 1340, **-lenter** 1137, **-lentissime** 1344, superexcellently; **-sus,** exalted above others (bibl.); **-lo,** to excel c 1170, c 1343.

superexceptus, neglected, unfulfilled c 1115.

superexcresc/entia, excess, increment c 1220, 1505; **annus -ens,** leap year c 1212, 1267; **-o,** to be redundant c 1265; to be overgrown, grow above a 1250, c 1450; to outgrow, exceed c 1185, 1477.

superexistentia, transcendent existence c 1377.

superexoneratio, *see* SUPERONER

superexpansus, excessively spread out 870.

superexpen/se (*pl.*), expenses in excess of receipt (esp. Sc.) 1266, 1480; **-do,** to overspend (Sc.) 1266, 1451.

superexpo/sitio, outlay in excess of receipt (Sc.) 1451; **-no** 1435, 1479, **supraexpono** 1459, to overspend (Sc.).

superexten/tus, overstretched 870; **-do,** to overstretch (bibl.).

superexuberans, supremely abundant c 1250.

super/factum, encroachment 1086, 1225; transgression 1214; **-fectum,** (?) frontage c 1206; action in excess of what is required 1230; **-factuosus,** excessive 1262; **-ficienter,** excessively 13c.

superfelix, supremely happy c 1250.

superfervidus, very fervent 870. c 1236, a 1350.

superfici/um, *for* **-es,** building above the surface c 1180, c 1450; **-etenus** c 1172, 1570, ***-aliter** a 1250, c 1426, superficially; **-alis,** superficial c 1195, c 1458; **numerus s.,** product of two prime numbers a 1250; *see also* **superfactum.**

superfido, *see* **superconfido.**

‡superfilo 15c., **surfulo** 1399, to 'surfle', embroider.

superfinalis, transcending finality 1344.

superfirmatus, superfixed 870.

superfixus, barbed c 1285.

superflu/ctio 1555, **-itio** 13c., **-entia** 1542, **-itas** 1302, overflowing; **-itas,** *superfluity, excess, extravagance 6c., 850. c 1090, 1610; waste matter (med.) c 1210; **s. digestionis** 14c.; **-e,** superfluously 791, c 815; **-um,** surplus a 1250, 1251; **numerus -us,** number exceeded by the sum of its aliquot parts a 1200, a 1250.

superformis, transcending form 870. 1344.

‡superfossorium, draw-bridge 15c.

superfrontal/e 1303, a 1452, **pannus -is** 1295, superfrontal (eccl.).

supergabulum, 'over-gavel' (a customary payment) (Somerset) 1234.

†supergenitivus, (?) developed after birth 870.

superglori/osus, supremely glorious 6c., 790. c 1360; **-fico,** to glorify beyond all 870.

supergratiosus, supremely gracious c 1100, c 1250.

supergress/io, transgression a 1100; **-or,** transgressor a 1100.

superhab/eo, to have authority over c 1115; to neglect, leave unfulfilled c 1115; **-ito,** to reside on a 1075.

superhidagium, excess hidage 1155, 1160.

superhonoratus, highly honoured c 1310; *see also* SUPERONER

superhorrendus, extremely horrific c 1250.

superhumerale, vestment, pall c 700, c 800. a 1100, a 1400.

superidem, transcending identity 1344.

superilluceo, to shine over 870.

superillustr/issimus, supremely noble c 1422; **-o,** to shine on 1267, 1410.

superimpleo, to overfill 1413.

superimpono, to substitute (?) 12c., 13c.

superimprimo, to stamp on c 1000.

superinaccessibilis, more than unapproachable 6c.

superincido, to occur additionally c 1434.

superincognitissimus, utterly unknown 870.

superincommunicabilis, utterly incommunicable 6c.

superincommutabilis, beyond all change 6c.

superincomprehensibilis, beyond all comprehension 6c.

superinconversibilis, beyond all change 870.

*superinde, on that account 1393, 1494.

superindivisibilis, transcending indivisibility 1344.

superinduc/tio, introduction of extraneous matter or persons c 1200, c 1454; keeping a concubine 1397; **-o,** to bring in from without 1222, c 1400; to take as a concubine or bigamously 1397, 1684.

superindu/itio, enduing in addition (theol.) c 1375; **-mentum,** ephod, vestment c 1287, c 1486.

superineffabilis, beyond all description 870.

superinenarrabilis, beyond all description 6c.

superinfero, to heap up 1301.

superinfluo, to overflow a 1250.

superinfractus, broken, unfulfilled c 1115.
superinfundo, to impart in addition c 1457.
superinscrutabilis, defying all scrutiny 6c.
superinsero, to insert above c 1188.
superinspector, overseer c 730, c 760.
superinstantane/us, transcending instantaneity 1344; -e, less than instantaneously 1344.
superinstituo, to replace c 1180.
superinsuccessibilis, transcending timelessness 1344.
superintellectual/itas, transcendent power of mind 870; -is, supremely intelligent c 1250; superintellig/entia, supreme understanding 870; -ibilitas, transcendence of comprehension 6c.; -ibiliter, with transcendent intelligence 6c.
superinten/tio, superintendence c 1250; -dens, superintendent, overseer 7c. c 1237, 1569; -sus, supremely intense c 1239; -do, to superintend (eccl.); -to (superintempto), to superinduce c 1115.
superinterculum, "shirt-band" 1574.
superintroductus, additional, excessive c 860.
superintrudo, to thrust upon, over 12c., c 1218.
superinund/atio, inundation, overflowing 12c., c 1460; -o, to inundate 1300, 1378.
superinveni/o, to devise in addition c 730; -or, to be left as surplus 1267.
superinvergo, to pour down upon c 1180.
superinvisibilis, utterly invisible 870.
superior/, above-mentioned 1086; (subst.) a superior, higher authority c 1250, 1461; a superior (mon.) 1275, c 1470; suzerain (feudal) p 1330, 1577; royal official in town c 1228; chief officer of borough 1206, 1552; foreman of jury 1225, 1235; *-itas 1292, 1566, †-atas 1356, -atus 1400, suzerainty; -itas 1504, -atus 1490, office of municipal 'superior' (Ir.); -itas, supremacy (eccl.) 1351; precedence 15c.; superiority c 1260, p 1300; -o, to raise c 1200.
superium, see suppa.
superjucundus, supremely agreeable c 1250.
superjur/amentum, oath c 1115; -o, to swear c 1115; to overswear c 1115; to make to swear c 1115.
superlabrum, upper lip c 1115.
superlat/io, elevation c 1470; -ive, to a superlative degree 1153; -issimus, advancing beyond all bounds 870.
superlaud/abilis (bibl.), -andus 870, beyond all praise.
superlect-, see supellex.
superlig/atio, bandaging a 1250; -o, to fasten over a 1250, a 1446.
superliminare, lintel (bibl.).
super/linitus, for -litus, smeared c 1250.
superlocalis, transcending spatial limitations 870.
superloquor, to accuse c 1115.
superlucr/um 1260, 1334, -atio a 1452, additional gain, profit; -or, to gain in addition (bibl.).
superlunaris, superlunary (astr.) c 1190, 1620.
supermachin/atio, additional creation 870; -or, to create in addition 870.
supermaneo, to be left over c 1330.

supermanifest/issimus, far transcending revelation 870; -o, to reveal further 870.
supermano, to flow on top of 870.
super/mappa 1285, 1314, -napero 1222, surnap/a 1397, -ium c 1423, 'surnap', over-tablecloth.
supermaterialis, transcending matter 870.
supermemoratus, see supramemoratus.
supermineo, see SUPEREMIN
supermirabilis, transcending admiration 6c. c 1402, 1418.
supermitto, to add 1086; to 'surmise', impute 1275, 1426.
supermund/anus 870. 12c., 1344, -anis, -ialis 870, supermundane; -ane, supermundanely 870.
supernalis, supernal 13c., c 1465.
supernapero, see supermappa.
supernatural/itas, supernaturalness 870. c 1360; -is, supernatural 870. c 1301, c 1444; -iter, supernaturally 9c. 1253, 1461.
supernavigo, to outsail c 1400.
supernominatus, see supranominatus.
supernuntiativus, emphatic (for ὑπεραποφαντικός, f.l. for ὑπεραποφατικός) 1610.
supero, see superatus.
superobscuratus, profoundly dark 870.
superobumbrans, overshadowing 870.
superoffero, to offer in addition c 1193.
superoner/atio, overloading (naut.) 1243; overburdening, overcharging (fig.) 1269, 1291; 1227, 1415, †superexoneratio c 1285, overstocking (of pasture); 1302, 1622, superonus 1327, 1463, surcharge (on account); -osus, burdensome (fig.) 1322; -o, to load (with fetters) c 1254; 1315, 1620, superhonoro 1242, to overburden (fig.); *to overstock (pasture) c 1185, 1533; to surcharge (on account) 1271, c 1367.
superoperatus, worked over, embroidered c 1420, 1438.
superoptimus, surpassing the best 870. c 1434.
superorior, to rise up c 1253.
superorno, to arrange perfectly 870.
superoro, to pray over 870.
superpart/icularitas, superparticularity (math.) a 1150, 13c.; -iens, superparticular, containing whole number plus aliquot part a 1250.
superpellect-, see supellex.
*superpell/iceum c 1125, 1588, -icius (G.) 1254, -ex 15c., -ix 1419, suppelliceum 1207, c 1500, †superpocilium 1376, supercellium 1605, supercilicium 1506, surplicia 1380, surplice (eccl.); cover (for parchment) 1393.
†superpendio, hanging, suspension (of door on hinges) 1407.
superperfectus, supremely perfect 870.
superpius, supremely pious c 1250.
superplen/itudo, perfect fullness 870; -us, replete 9c.
superpluo, to rain upon 700.
superplus/ 1086, c 1235, sureplus 1452, -um 1217, 1237, -ium 1211, 1243, -agium 1167, 1341, surplusagium 1199, 1300, surplus, excess, remainder, balance due; 1130, 1190, *-agium 1224, c 1533, †supplus/ 1205, †-agium c 1290, c 1505, surplus c 1250,

surplusagium 13c., excess of expenditure over receipt, balance in favour of accountant.

superpocilium, *see* **superpelliceum**.

†**superpolio**, to polish highly c 1184.

‡**superpondero**, "to overweigh" 1570.

superpo/sitio, placing on or above 1388, 1467; higher position 750. 1239; relation of attribute to subject (log.) p 1300; strict discipline, fasting or flogging (mon.) c 550. c 1160; **-situs**, placed higher 870; **-no**, to fast 7c.; *cf.* **suprapositio**.

superpresentanee, so as to transcend immediacy 1344.

superprincipalis, transcending the first principle 870. 1344.

superprisa, excess prise 1161; **surpris/ia**, exaction (G.) 1275, 1279; **-us**, exacted, usurped (G.) 1279, 1289; **superpressus**, overcome (by emotion) c 1370; **surprisus**, taken by surprise (G.) 1312; *cf.* SUPPRIS

superpropino, to pledge c 1150.

superquadripartiens, **supraquadruplex**, containing a number plus four-fifths 13c.

superquero, to expect too much of 796; to ask in addition c 1100.

superrationalis, transcending reason 6c.

superreddo, to pay c 1115; to renounce c 1400.

superremotus, supremely remote 870.

superrepletus, filled to repletion 870. a 1250.

superrollo, to roll (casks) over 1348.

superroro, to moisten c 1290.

supersaisitus, seised in chief c 1200.

supersanctus, supremely holy c 1250.

superscateo, to bubble out over 870.

superscript/io, superscription (bibl.); additional writing c 1250, 1553; marking on garments (mon.) c 1266, c 1330; **-ura**, (?) writing on cover 1422; **superscribo**, to write on (parchment) 1501; *see also* SUPRASCRIPT

supersculpo, to carve over 1424.

supersecularite, more than everlastingly c 1250.

supersed/ementum (Sc.) 1416, **-entia** 1473, **supersessio** 1240, 1446, surcease, stay in proceedings (esp. leg.); **supersessio** (†**supercessio**) c 1115, 1194, *****supersisa** c 1185, 1275, **superassisa** 1187, 1275, *****sursisa** 1168, 1384, 'sursise', (fine for) default (leg.); **-eas**, name of a writ (leg.) c 1344, 1419; **-eo**(†**supercedeo**), to neglect, default (leg.) c 1115; *****to stay proceedings (leg.) 1222, 1545; **s. a** 1231, c 1448, **s. de** c 1400, 1478, to refrain from; **-eo**, to seat on 1291; **supersideo**, to press upon 826.

super/sellium, shabrack, saddle-cover 1237; **-silium**, "carpet" 1588.

supersemin/atus (†**supersennatus**) 1288, 1365, **suscematus** c 1290, †**succematus** 1350, spotted, measly; **-o**, to sow on or after (eccl.).

supersignanter, most signally a 1452.

supersilium, *see* **supersellium**.

supersim/plex, transcending simplicity c 1250, 1344; **-pliciter** 1344; **-plicio**, to unify completely 870.

supersimul, transcending simultaneity 1344.

supersingulum, *see* **supercinctorium**.

supersisa, *see* SUPERSED

supersobrius, exceedingly sober c 1220.

superspargo, to sprinkle over a 1150.

superspeciosus, supremely beautiful c 1100.

superspec/tio, supervision c 1250; **-ulator**, overseer, bishop 760, 870; **-ulor**, to superintend 870; to speculate about 870.

supersplend/ens, supremely bright 870. c 1250, c 1275; **-eo**, to shine from above c 1270.

superstan/tia, form (phil.) 14c.; **-s**, formally existent, οὐσιῶν c 1362.

superstit/io, (?) frivolity, gaud a 700; wrongheadedness 1200, a 1275; monastic order c 1553; **-iosus**, heathen c 780; c 1150, c 1452, **-ialis** c 1444, superfluous.

superstudeo, to be excessively devoted c 1434.

superstupendus, supremely horrific c 1250.

supersuavis, supremely sweet c 1250.

supersublimis, supremely sublime c 1250.

supersubsellia (*pl.*), upper seats c 1296.

supersubstan/tia 1374, **-tialitas** 870. c 1290, transcendence of substance; **-s** 1374, **-tialis** c 1080, 1421, transcending substance (ἐπιούσιος *or* ὑπερούσιος); **-tialiter**, so as to transcend substance p 1300, 1344.

supersufficiens, supremely satisfying c 1250.

supersum, *see* SUPERESSENTIAL

supersu/tura, stitching over c 1180; **-o**, to stitch over c 1180.

supertactus, *see* **supratactus**.

supertallio, to tallage in excess (Norm.) 1195.

supertemporal/is, transcending time 870; **-iter** 1344.

superten/ura, undue detention 1200; holding (a market) beyond allotted time 1230; **-eo** (**suprateneo**), to withhold c 1115; to omit (A.S. *oferhealdan*) c 1115.

superterranus, on the earth 1420.

supertexo, to weave over c 1182, c 1488.

supertimidus, over-timid 870.

supertracto, to draw (a load) on 1325; to draw (sketches) on 1325.

supertranscendo, to survive 11c.

†**supertranscriptus**, transcribed above 1332.

supertripartiens, containing a number plus three-quarters 13c.

*****supertunic/a** 1198, 1419, **-ale** c 1192, 1330, **-ula** 1306, 1329, surcoat.

superturbo, to disturb 1573.

superturno, to turn over 1343.

superubero, to overflow c 1250.

superund/atio, overflowing c 1280, 1323; **-o**, to overflow c 1390, 15c.

superun/icus, transcendently unique c 1250, 1344; **-ice** 1344; †**-itus**, completely united 870; †**-ite**, in complete unity 870.

superutilis, supremely useful c 1402.

supervacue, superfluously (bibl.).

superval/entia, excess value 1225; **-eo**, to prevail 12c.

supervend/itio, selling above the assize 1207, 1274; **survenditio**, additional sale 1269; **-o**, to sell above the assize 1180, 1331.

superveniens, impending c 1150; incomer, visitor, (person) coming in from outside 1273, 1412.

supervere, with supreme truth 870.

supervestio, to endue a 1200.

supervideo, *see* SUPERVIS

supervigilia, day before the eve (of saint's day) 1292, 1318.

supervinco, to outvote c 1115.

supervindico, to exact excessive penalty c 1115.

*__supervis/io__ 1338, 1583, †-itio a 1564, *-us c 1322, 1540, survey, supervision; 1500, -us 1397, surveyorship; -or *1295, c 1599, **supravisor** 1439, surveyor, supervisor; *supervisor (of will) 1381, 1517; **s. armature, s. domorum,** "harness-looker", "houselooker" (Lancs.) 1536; **s. generalis** 1547, 1583; **s. mosse** 1401, **s. mosseti** 1536, "moss-reeve" (Lancs.); **s. nocumentorum,** surveyor of nuisances (municipal official, Oxford) 1433; **s. operationum,** surveyor of works 1333; **s. testamenti** 1399; *__supervideo,__ to survey, supervise 9c. 1199, 1533; **s. oculis,** to be an eye-witness c 1115.

supervitalitas, supreme vitality 870.

*__supervivo__ (*trans.*), to survive c 1115, 1533.

supervolo, to overcome (fig.) 7c.

supin/itas, indolence c 1460; **-um,** past participle passive 1517; **-o,** to conjugate (verbs) 1241; to enervate c 1135.

supjectio, *see* SUBJECT

†**suplus,** simple (? *f.l.* for *simplus*) c 1200.

supp-, *see also* **subp-**

‡**sup/pa,** "a sop" 15c.; **-erium** 1233, **soperum** 1257, supper; **-o, -po** 1220, ‡15c., **sopo** 1232, to sup.

suppallio (**subp-**), to cloak 1252, 15c.

1 **supped/itatio** (**subped-**), subjection a 1450, 1512; **-aneum** c 1160, c 1330, †**subpetaneum** c 1150, **scabellum -aneum** c 1072, (?) **-ium** c 1257, foot-stool; **-aneus,** underfoot c 1400; **-estris,** prosaic 870; ‡**-ium,** "treadle" 15c.; *-ito c 1180, a 1540, **suspedito** 1218, to trample on, subdue.

2 **suppeditatio,** supplying, maintaining 11c.

suppellect-, *see* **supellex.**

suppelliceum, *see* **superpelliceum.**

suppendo, *see* SUSPEN

suppet/entia, opportunity 893; capacity 15c.; †**-icium,** (?) gift 745.

supplant/atio, supplanting, deceit (bibl.); **-ator,** supplanter (bibl.); **-atorie,** by supplanting c 1400.

suppl/etio c 1115, 1453, **-itio** 1398, completion, fulfilment; supply 1290; supplementary payment c 1484; supplementary document c 1327; **s. defectuum** c 1236, a 1245; **-etive,** additionally 1378; **-etorius,** supplementary 1684; **-emento,** to supplement c 1270; **-e** (*imp.*), supply (missing words), 'understand' c 1434, 1438; **-eo,** to fulfil, carry out c 1180; **s. me,** to refresh oneself c 1000; **s. officium,** to perform function 1227, 1279.

supplex, well broken (of horses) 1238.

*__supplic/atio__ c 1090, 1559, **-atus** a 1155, c 1266, entreaty; **-abilis** 1093, **-ativus** 1421, **-ator** c 1300, **-atorius** c 1450, supplicatory; **-atorie** (*pl.*) c 1250, c 1423, *__littere s.__ 1224, 1559, letters supplicatory; **-atorie** (*adv.*), beseechingly 13c.; **-ator** 1440, **-ans** c 1408, 1437, suppliant, petitioner; †**-o,** to yield to entreaty c 1177; **-ui,** *for* **-avi,** c 1177.

supplo/sio (**manuum**), clapping c 1437; **-do,** to drive out, dispel c 1115; **subplaudo,** to applaud c 520.

supplus-, *see* SUPERPLUS

suppluvialis, somewhat rainy c 1160.

suppo, *see* **suppa.**

suppodi/atio, propping (of mine gallery) a 1307; **-amentum** 1294, 1310, **-mentum** 1301, prop (arch.); ‡**-um,** treadle of loom 1483; *-o, to prop c 1200, a 1350.

suppollio, to prop 1301, 1306.

suppono, *see* SUPPOSIT

supportarius, *see* **subportarius.**

support/atio (**subport-**), supporting, holding up c 1260, c 1436; *c 1125, a 1564, **-amen** c 1325, **-us** 1407, support, help, defence; 1236, 1498, **-amen** 1433, support (financial), bearing of charges; **-ator,** support, prop 1486; supporter, defender 15c.; **-itor onerum,** bearer of charges c 1239; **-o** c 1197, c 1400, **susporto** 13c., to hold up; *to help, encourage c 1223, c 1540; to endure c 1080, c 1297; to bear the cost of 1487; (with *inf.*) to bear c 790; *__s. onus__ 1236, c 1478.

supposit/io, support, underpinning 1319, 1395; submission 1279, c 1283; (?) pledge 1180; subsumption (log.) a 1228, 1276; 13c., p 1347, **-atio** 1344, 1427, hypostasis (log. & theol.); *supposition, hypothesis (log.) 13c., 1518; **s. materialis,** reference to a word as such c 1360; **s. significativa,** reference to the object signified by a word c 1360; †**supposibilis,** capable of being hypostatized (theol.) c 1377; **-aliter,** with reference to hypostasis a 1360; †**-er,** supposedly 1430; **-alis** c 1362, 1427, **-ivus** p 1300, hypostatic; **-ivus,** substituted c 1212; (?) contributory c 1360; in a diminished positive sense (gram.) 1610; c 1344, **-orius** c 1344, hypothetical; **-or,** supposer 13c.; **-orium,** prop, buttress 1291, 1357; suppository (med.) a 1250, 1537;

-um, subordinate part c 1470; subject, hypostasis (log. & theol.) c 1290, c 1380; hypothesis 1271, c 1300; **-us,** (*subst.*) a subordinate c 1072, 1593; **sopositus,** subordinate 1374; **-o quod,** on the assumption that c 1340, c 1343; **-o,** to hypostatize 1344, c 1367; **suppono,** to lay (stones) 1434; *to prop up 1241, 1386; to know carnally c 1370, c 1450; to compel 1381; to suppress 1318; to dismiss c 1390; to subsume (log.) a 1250, 1523; *to suppose, assume, imply c 1244, a 1564; **s. me,** to submit (to jurisdiction) 1263, 1275; to represent oneself 1274; **s. pro,** to do duty for, take the place of a 1228, c 1370.

suppr-, *see also* **subpr-**

suppress/io, (?) lowering of voice c 600; cancellation c 1400; suppression, oppression c 1287, 1473; suppression (of religious house) 1586; **s. veri** 1269, c 1400, **s. veritatis** c 1195; **-or,** suppressor, repressor 799. 15c.; **supprimo,** to oppress c 1325; to suppress (religious house) c 1538.

suppris/a (**subpris-**) 1289, 1340, **-ia** 1277, 1334, exaction (Fr.); **-or,** exactor 1441, 1442; **-us,** exacted (Fr.) 1340; *cf.* **superprisa.**

suppsalma, (?) refrain of psalm 1427.

suppullulo, to spring up secretly 1523.

suppungo (**subp-**), to stimulate 870.

suppurgo, to purge (med.) a 1250.

suppurpureus (subp-), purplish 14c.

supputatio, computation (eccl.); catalogue 893.

supra (*prep.* with *acc.*), against, about (of time) c 1115; beyond, after 1388; on (= *penes*) a 1450; in breach of 1257; about, concerning c 1343, c 1533; (with *abl.*), above 15c.; **s. mare**, on (the shore of) the sea 1265, 1305.

supra-, *see also* **super-**

supracelestis, supercelestial a 1200, 1351; *cf.* **supercelestis.**

supracitus, *for* **suprasitus**, situated above c 1383.

supracontentus, contained above 1330, 1422.

*supradic/tus, above-mentioned 7c., 9c. c 1080, c 1540; **†-o**, to mention above 12c., c 1200; *cf.* SUPERDIC

supra/effatus 14c., **-fatus** 991. c 1125, above-mentioned.

supraemptio 1276, 1326, **superemptio** 1313, **suremptio** 1269, additional purchase (to make up stock).

suprafero, to place (in authority) above 1267.

suprahorizontaliter, above the horizon c 1360.

suprainfusio, pouring in on top c 1330.

suprajaceo, to lie on 1420.

suprajacto, to cast (accounts) on 1303.

supralimitatus, defined above 1434.

*supra/memoratus 1086, 1520, **super-memoratus** c 1200, **-mentionatus** 1686, **-narratus** 1408, ***-nominatus** 736, c 950. 1082, 15c., **supernominatus** 771. 1086, 1250, **-notatus** 1223, 1294, above-mentioned.

supraobligatus, above-bound (in a bond) 1447, 1504.

suprapo/sitio, relation of superiority (log.) 13c.; **-situs**, placed above c 1180, c 1283; **-no**, to place above 1267, c 1470; *cf.* **superpositio.**

suprarecitatus, recited above 1583.

suprascript/io, superscription c 1250, 1433; ***-us** 1086, c 1493, **superscriptus** 1422, c 1450, above-written; **suprascribo**, to write above c 1313, c 1503; *cf.* SUPERSCRIPT

suprasculptus, carved over c 1447.

suprasolaris, above the sun 12c., c 1160.

supraspecificatus, specified above c 1530.

suprasuasus, argued above c 1357.

suprasumo, to posit as including (log.) c 1360.

supra/tactus c 1304, **supertactus** c 1344, **-taxatus** 12c., above-mentioned.

supraterminatus, completed above 14c.

supratractus, produced above 1312.

supratuale, cover of altar-cloth 1389.

supravendit/io, selling off (of balance of stock) *or* (?) sale as noted above 1257, 1297; **-us**, sold off 1209.

supravenio, to come in from outside c 1390.

supravicus, *see* **spervarius.**

suprem/as (supprem-) c 1200, **-atia** 1537, **-atus** c 1530, 1610, supremacy; **-atista**, asserter of papal supremacy c 1620; **-e**, supremely c 1180, c 1340; **-us**, divine epithet 1245.

sups-, supt-, *see* **subs-; subt-**

sura, (?) tree-stump 1293, 1330; ‡"ridge of land" 1570.

surcarc-, *see* **superchargium.**

surcinglum, *see* **supercinctorium.**

surcotus, *see* **supercota.**

surcul/us, branch (? of nerve) (med.) c 1270; **-amen**, small shoot c 550; **-eus**, of a twig c 1000; **‡-o**, to graft 1483.

surdo, *see* **surrectio.**

surd/us, surd (math.) c 1300, c 1615; **-esco**, to grow deaf 6c. 1526.

suremptio, *see* **supraemptio.**

sureplus, *see* **superplus.**

surex, *see* **sorex.**

surfulo, *see* **superfilo.**

surg-, *see also* **surrectio.**

surgera, *see* **sucrum.**

surg/eria, -icus, surigicus, *see* CHIRURG

surgerno, *see* SOJORN

suria, *see* **ischuria.**

surnap/a, -ium, *see* **supermappa.**

surpl-, *see* **superpelliceum; superplus.**

surpris/ia, -us, *see* **superprisa.**

surr-, *see also* **subr-**

surrect/io, raising up 8c. c 1160; rising up a 1180, 1566; leave to rise after essoin of bed-sickness (leg.) c 1258, c 1290; **-or**, insurgent 1382; **surgitorius**, gushing forth c 1227; **surgo**, to rise and go 771; to rise from the dead c 1080, c 1362; to rise from bedsickness (leg.) 1200, 1219; to rise in rebellion 798. 1461; c 1180, c 1186, **†surdo** 1451, to arise, accrue.

surrejunctio, surrejoinder (leg.) 1531.

surrept/io (subrept-), theft, robbery 770. c 1218, p 1377; ***deceit**, trickery 8c. c 1142, 1533; **de -ione** c 730. c 1130, ***per -ionem** 7c. 1119, p 1300, **per †-itionem** 1249, **-icie** c 1323, 1462, **-ive** 1331, a 1564, by stealth, surreptitiously; **moneta -icia**, coinage secretly imported c 1400; **littere -icie**, secret letters c 1196, 1462; **†-icus, *for* -icius**, 1331; **surripio somnum**, to snatch a nap 14c.

surrep/to, to creep in stealthily a 1250; **surripere**, (?) *for* **-ere**, 1200.

surrigicus, *see* CHIRURG

surr/ipus, -upus, *see* **syrupus.**

surri/sio (subri-) 1378, **-sus** c 1370, smile; **-denter**, smilingly a 1452; **-deo** (*trans.*), to smile at c 1090.

surrog/atio (subrog-), substitution c 1150, 1425; **-atus**, surrogate (leg.) 1537, 1684; **-o**, to substitute, depute 12c., c 1360; to beseech a 1100, c 1430.

surrogus, *see* CHIRURG

sursa, *see* **soursa.**

sursingulum, *see* **supercinctorium.**

sursisa, *see* SUPERSED

sursum/ (susum) capio, to take back a 1525; **s. coreddo** 15c., **s. libero** 1385, to deliver up; **s. solvo**, to pay up 1350; **-itas**, upwardness p 1300; *cf.* **susanus.**

sursumpo/sitio, shoring up 1461; **-no**, to support 1388.

*sursumredd/itio, surrender 1365, 1612; ***-o**, to surrender, give up 1254, 1540 (*cf.* **reddo sursum**).

sursum/tractatio, hauling up 1433; **-traho**, to haul up 1291, 1464.

sursumtrado, to surrender a 1216, 1408.

surugicus, sururg-, *see* CHIRURG

surus, *see* **sorus.**
survenditio, *see* SUPERVEND
surzenglum, *see* **supercinctorium.**
su/s, 'sow', siege engine c 1125, 1402; 'swine', measure of land (Sussex) 1558, 1595; **-es,** *for* **sus,** sow c 1290; **-arium,** pig-pasture 1317, ‡1483; **-atim,** swinishly 690; **-ella** 1282, 1511, **-illa** c 1191, ‡15c., †**suncula** 1350, young sow; †**-ettis** c 1230, **-ista** c 550, ‡**-istacium** 15c., **hara -ilis** c 1150, pigsty; ‡**-illinus,** swinish 1483.
Susannicus, of Susanna 1427.
sus/anus, upper 15c.; ***terra -ana** 1206, c 1397, **t. (pastura) -enna** 1222, 1309, **t.** †**suserna** c 1230, upland (S.E. Engl.); **curia -ana,** upland court (Kent) 1350; *cf.* **jusum, sursum.**
suscematus, *see* **superseminatus.**
suscept/io, *taking, receiving, receipt 597, c 1000. a 1090, c 1360; entertainment, maintenance c 1006. 1200, c 1300; standing godparent 1385; **s. baptismatis** c 1343; **s. eucharistie** c 1340, c 1357; **s. gradus** (ac.) c 1410, c 1546; **s. habitus** (*sc.* **religionis**) a 1205, c 1296; **s. latronum,** resetting thieves 1313, c 1414; **s. ordinum** (eccl.) 1559; **s plena,** gestation 1274; **-ibilis,** receivable, acceptable c 790. a 1110; 6c., 8c. a 1100, 1620, **-ivus** 12c., 1620, **-orius** 870, **-rix** (*f.*) c 1109, receptive, admitting of; **-ibilitas,** receptivity a 1233, a 1250; **-or,** guardian (bibl.); godfather c 1182; **s. confessionum** (eccl.) c 1090; **s. hospitum** (mon.) c 1072; **s. processionalis,** participant in procession c 1125; **-rix,** foster-mother 8c., 9c.; **-orium,** receptacle c 1090;
-o, to undertake c 950; **suscipio** c 1150, †**suspicio** c 1204, to catch, take up (a remark); 13c., **s. ad fontem** c 1102, **s. de lavacro** a 1155, to stand god-parent to; **s. ad pacem** 1265; **s. fidem** c 1178, **s. juramentum** c 1390; **s. gradum** (ac.) 1405; **s. habitum** (mon.) 1219, c 1450; **s. in religionem** 1221; **s. homagium** c 1200, c 1330; **s. ordinationem** (eccl.) c 1072; **s. in me** 1236, **s. super me** 1426, to undertake.
suscio, *see* **succinium.**
suscit/atio, raising from the dead 13c., c 1546; stirring up (fig.) 13c.; begetting c 1290; suscitation, promotion of a cause (ac.) c 1400, c 1410; **-abilis,** able to be roused c 1239; **-ator** c 1188, 1423, **-atrix**(*f.*) c 1298, c 1434, rouser, instigator; **-o,** to raise from the dead 1221, c 1362; to set up c 1285, 1419; to exalt, promote c 1204, c 1343; to beget 1226, 1272; **s. breve,** to sue out a writ (leg.) c 1285, c 1290; **succito,** *for* **-o,** 1177.
susennus, susernus, *see* **susanus.**
susmito, *see* SUMMISS
suspect/io c 1188, a 1564, †**-atio** c 1125, **suspicatio** 12c., c 1363, **-us** 1198, suspicion; **-e,** under suspicion c 1463; **-ive** a 1564, **-uose** 1502, suspiciously; **-uosus** c 1370, 1541, **suspesionarius** 1360, suspicious, arousing suspicion; **-us** (*p.p.*), anxious, taking thought 601, c 730. c 1087, 14c.

suspedito, *see* SUPPED
suspen/sio *9c. 1199, 15c., **-dium** 1199, 1428, (right of) hanging (criminals); *suspension from office c 1125, 1545; *c 1188, 15c., **-cio** 1336, 15c., suspension from sacraments (eccl.); checking, withholding, refusal to sanction c 1238, a 1564; **-dium,** imprisonment (A.S. *hengenne*) c 1102, c 1115; **funis -diculus,** rope for hanging 1461; **-dulus** c 1115, **-sibilis** 1245, hanging, pendent; **-sive,** in a suspensive construction (gram.) c 1080; **-sivus,** (?) tending to lift a 1250; suspensive, involving an unfinished sentence (gram.) 1267, 1524; **-sorium,** stalk (of grapes) 1267; **armilla -soria,** ring for hanging up 1326; **in -sa** c 1410, **in -so** 1229, c 1470, in suspense or abeyance; **in -sum pono** (leg.) c 1393; **-sius,** more remotely c 1090;
-do *1169, 15c., **-deo** c 1219, to hang (criminals); **-do** (*sc.* **naso**), to sneer at c 1125; *to suspend from office 12c., 1545; *to suspend from sacraments (eccl.) 679. c 1104, 1456; to postpone c 1090, 1231; (?) to leave c 1300; to suspend from action or operation 1292, 15c.; **s. ad,** to attach to 7c.; †**suppendo,** to hang up 1385.
suspic-, suspes-, *see* SUSCEPT; SUSPECT
suspir/ale 1443, 1451, **sesperale** (†**sesperabile**) 1433, 1440, 'suspiral', wind-vent (of conduit); **-iose,** with sighs 1281, c 1397; **-iosus,** sorrowful c 1204, **-o** (with *acc.*) c 790. c 1090, (with *abl.*) c 734, **s. ad** c 1170, c 1250, to long for.
susporto, *see* SUPPORT
sussessor, *see* SUCCESS
sustamen/, -tum, *see* SUSTENT
sustantivus, *see* SUBSTANT
sustaxuarius, *see* SUBTAX
sustent/aculum 790. 15c. †**sustamen** 14c., **-amentum,** †**sustamentum, -atio** c 1280, **baculum -ale** c 1100, stay, crutch; 8c. 1274, 1414, **-amen** 11c. c 1440, †**sustamen** 14c., *-amentum a 1130, 15c., *-atio 790. c 1070, 1549, **-ificatio** 1427, **sustinementum** c 1150, **sustinentia** 6c. a 1564, support, maintenance; **sustinentia,** endurance (bibl.); **-ativus** c 1250, **-ivus** c 1365, **-atorius** 12c., giving support or maintenance; **-ator** c 1200, 15c., **-atrix** (*f.*) c 1090, 15c., supporter, maintainer; **-ibilis,** endurable c 1102, **-orium,** trestle c 1500; **-ifico,** to cause to be sustained c 1300, p 1300; **sustendo,** *for* **-o,** 1182; **susteneo,** *for* **sustineo,** 1266, 1461; **sustineo,** to maintain a thesis c 1343; (*intr.*) to wait 1187, 1261; **s. dextram,** to be placed at the right 12c.; **sustinuo** to keep up c 1250.
sustollo, to extol 9c.; **subtollo,** *for* **s.,** to lift a 1250.
†**sustulio,** (service of providing) maintenance 11c.
susum, *see* **sursum.**
susurr/atio (bibl.), **-ium** 12c., 1423, whisper; **-anter** c 1470, **-atorie** 1405, in whispers; **-ator, -o,** tale-bearer (bibl.).
†**suta,** *f.l.* for **sicca;** *see* **moltura** (*s.v.* **mola**).
sutaneus, (?) petty officer (Port.) 1386.
sutator, *see* I **secta.**
suth/campus, south field 1234; **-mora,** south

moor 1260; **sud/pars** a 1190, a 1220, **sut-pars** a 1250, **southpars** c 1255, south part; **-tridinga,** south riding (Lincs.) a 1200.

sut/or caligarum 1577, ‡**s. caligarius** c 1520, hosier; ‡**s. chirothecarius,** glover c 1520; **s. vestiarius,** tailor 1550; *see also* **1 secta;** **-oria,** cobbler's craft c 1290, 1355; a 1195, 1367, **-arium** 1341, **-eria** 1406, **-rinum** 14c., cobbler's shop or quarter; **-rix,** sempstress 1380, ‡1483; **suitio** 1301, 1519, **suatio** 1413, sewing; **-o** 1320, 1364, **suissio** 1381, **sueo** 1492, to sew, stitch.

sutular-, *see* SUBTAL

suus, one's own (feudal) man c 1115; **suum** c 1115, c 1220, **suatia** 1220, one's own property; **super suam,** at his own expense c 1311; **suas,** fellow countryman or townsman 6c.; **suatim** c 760, c 1000, **suater** 8c., in his own manner; on his own initiative 898; **suitas,** selfishness 1620; *cf.* **se.**

suvenio, *see* SUBVEN

suxus, *see* **succus.**

swad-, *see* **suadibilis; swatha.**

swag/a 1415, **suaga** 1417, **suagia** 1245, 'swage', ornamented border or groove; **-atus,** ornamented with a swage 1432.

swanimot/a (†**swainmot-**), **-um** 1199, 1450, **suanimotum** 1217, 1306, **swanemot/a, -um** 1271, 1489, **swanomotum** c 1308, **swonymotum** 1240, **swaynimotum** 1321, 'swanimote', forest court.

swarmum (apum), swarm 15c.

swarta, *see* **quarta.**

swatha 1202, 1503, **swada** 1358, 'swathe', measure of meadow-land.

Swevus, *see* **Suethedus.**

swileria, *see* **scutella.**

swilling-, swolling-, swuling-, *see* SULLIN

swinlondus, 'swine-land' (held by rent of a pig) 1299.

swivelum, swivel 1294, 1323.

swonymotum, *see* SWANIMOT

swopa, 'sweep', mill-sail 1282.

sy-, *see also* **si-**

1 sya, 'sye', milk-strainer 1281.

2 sy/a, -ator, -atura, *see* **seca.**

sycomachia, sychomagia, *see* **psychomachia.**

sycophant/a: sichophanta c 900; **-icus,** slanderous 1552; †**-isissimus** 1520.

syc/os, fig (σῦκον) c 1212; ‡**-osis,** ulcer (med.) 1570.

sylarium, *see* **2 celum.**

†**sylen,** (?) hypsilon c 1200.

syllab/a, letter, epistle c 790; section (geom.) a 1233; **siliba,** *for* **-a,** syllable c 1365; **-icatio,** forming of syllables, spelling 1271, 1489; **-icus,** syllabic 790. c 1218, c 1370; **-ico,** to articulate in syllables, spell c 1218, 1521; **-izo,** to quibble c 1160.

syllepsis, conclusion or concept (log.) 1620; **silempsis,** *for* **s.** (gram.), c 1218.

syllog/ismus practicus, syllogism leading to practical conclusion p 1300; **s. perfectus, s. imperfectus** a 1250; **sylloysmus,** *for* **s.,** c 1380; **-istice,** in the form of a syllogism a 1413; **-isticus,** syllogistic c 800. c 1080, c 1365; **-izatio,** reasoning in syllogisms p 1300, c 1430; **-izo,** to reason in syllogisms c 1160, 1620.

sylo, *see* **synolon.**

sylor, *see* **2 celum.**

‡**sylphes,** pygmies 1652.

sym-, *see also* **cymba; sima.**

symballoton, garment of goat's hair 1499.

symbol/um c 1006. c 1087, 1609, **simbalum** 1432, **cymbolum** 1314, 1428, the creed (eccl.); **s. apostolicum** 1442, **s. apostolorum** c 1266, 1414, **s. minus** c 1182, c 1238, Apostles' creed; **s. majus** c 1238; **s. catholicum** c 1362; **-um,** 'shot', contribution c 1362, 1378; **s. luminis** c 1115, **s. lucis** 13c., 'wax-scot' (eccl.); **-a anime,** 'soul-scot' c 1102; **-um,** affinity, combination a 1250, c 1620; device, badge (her.) c 1595; **s. mutum,** inanimate object as device (her.) c 1595; **s. stationarium,** 'ordinary' (her.) c 1595; **-icus,** symbolic, possessing or derived from affinity c 1270, 1610; relating to devices (her.) c 1595; **-us,** concordant, tallying c 1370; **-izatio,** concordance, correspondence c 1620, 1622; **-izo,** to accord, correspond 1250, 1620.

symmachus, ally 870.

symmatita, fellow pupil (συμμαθητής) a 1142.

symmetrus, commensurable c 1250.

symmyst/a, -es, companion, colleague 790, 11c. c 1125, c 1160.

symphon/icus, harmonious c 1194, c 1393; **-ista** c 1090, c 1250, ‡**-izator** 15c., harmonist; **-izo,** to set forth c 860; ‡to sing or make music 1483.

symplasis, fashioning together a 1180.

symptoma a 1250, 1620, **sinthom/a** c 1180, 14c., symptom; **-aticus,** symptomatic a 1250.

*****synagog/a,** synagogue (bibl.); **-icus,** of synagogues 1282.

synalepha, contraction (gram.): **sinalimpha** c 1125, 12c.

synanchia, *see* **cynanche.**

synax/is c 600, c 1000. a 1100, 14c., **-us** c 1400, meeting for prayer; eucharist c 1500, 1610; **s. matutin/arum** a 1100, **s. -a** c 1125, **s. -alis** 1302, matins; **s. nocturna,** nocturns c 1148, c 1308; **s. vespertin/a** c 1180, 13c., **s. -alis** c 1130, c 1132, vespers.

syncategor/ema 12c., 15c., **cincathegorema** c 1340, **-ementum** c 1362, consignificative word (unable to be subject by itself); **-ematice** c 1250, 1427, **sincathegoreumatice** c 1290, c 1343, **-ice** c 1360, consignificatively; **-ematicus** c 1200, **-eumaticus** a 1250, c 1290, **-icus** p 1300, consignificative.

syncellus (sin-), domestic chaplain 7c. c 1125.

†**synchasis,** confused word order (σύγχυσις) (gram.) 13c.

syncop/a, syncope (gram.), elision a 1178, 1414; pause, gap 7c. c 1200; diminution, whittling down c 1430, a 1452; **cincopa** c 1200, **-i** (? **-is**) c 1170, 1520, **-ica (-ia) passio** c 1193, c 1220, syncope (med.), swooning; **-atio cantus** (mus.) 1508; **-atus,** elided, clipped (gram.) c 1182, c 1200; **-o** *****c 1170, 1526, **cincopo** (†**enicopo**) c 1250, 1398, to elide syllable, slur; *****c 1170, c 1430, **sincubo** 1238, to cut short, dock; c 1270, **cincopo** c 1200, **-izo** c 1310, to swoon.

synctor, *see* **cintra.**

synder/esis, -isis, *see* **synteresis.**

***syndic/us** c 1182, 1634, **scindicus** (G.) 1291, **cyndicus** 1298, †**-atus** 1374, †**-tus** 1499, **-a** (*f.*) 1432, syndic (proctor, agent or advocate); **-atus,** office or status of syndic 1281, 1588.

syn/ecdoche (gram.): **-edoche** 12c., **-odoche** c 1200, 1276; **-ecdochice,** by synecdoche 798; **-odochice,** in succession c 1250; **-ecdochicus** 790, c 800, **-odochicus** c 1360, synecdochic.

synergus, fellow-worker, colleague c 950.

synettus, *see* CYGN

syngramma, writing 786.

syngraph/a (-us) crucis, sign of the cross 12c., 14c.; **-ia,** signature, superscription 12c.; **-is,** document c 950; †**-um,** "bill of hand" 1570.

synjugus, yoked together c 1200, ‡1483.

synoch/us a 1250, 13c., **-a** a 1250, ‡15c., unintermittent fever; **causon -ides,** fever due to excess of blood a 1250.

synodoch-, *see* **synecdoche; synodus; xenodochium.**

***synod/us** (eccl.), †**-um** 1336, †**-ochium** c 1385, **senodus** 1338, **cinodus** 1319, **sinothus** 13c., synod; book of synodal acts or constitutions c 730. 1330, 1342; conjunction (astr.) 1586; 1157, †**-um** c 1400, ***-ale** c 1155, 1560, **senedale** 1567, **cinodale** 1535, ***-aticum** 1258, 1535, †**-othicum,** **-ochicum** 1269, 1276, ***senagium** 1184, 1535, †**scuagium** 1285, †**sengum** 1365, **cenagium** 1338, 1555, synodal due (eccl.); **-alia** (*pl.*), synodal decrees 1458; ***-alis** (eccl.), **-aticus** 1258, c 1558, **-icus** c 730, c 794. a 1100, c 1414, synodal; **-icus,** synodic (astr.) 1686; **-aliter,** in a synod a 1100, p 1440.

synolon, compound of matter and form c 1300; ‡**sylo,** "*totus mundus*" 1652.

synonym/us, synonymous 790. a 1250; **-os,** having more than one signification 870; **-ice,** synonymously 1374.

syn/tagma, document, charter, book c 790, 11c. 12c.; synod c 950; **-taxis,** syntax, grammar-book 1271, 1537.

synteresis, perception of moral values, conscience (συντήρησις): ***synder/esis** a 1228, c 1375, **-isis** 1440, **scinderesis** a 1200.

syn/texis, consumption (med.): **-thesis** a 1250; **-theticus,** consumptive a 1250.

synthe/ma, veil (fig.), symbolism c 950; **-sis,** apposition (gram.) c 1200, 13c.; **-sina,** finery 12c.; **-ticus,** synthetic 1713; *see also* **syntexis.**

synziberum, *see* **zinziber·**

synzygia, synzugia, *see* **syzygia.**

‡**syphita prava,** St. Vitus' dance 1652; ‡**s. stricta,** somnambulism 1652.

‡**Syr/iaca herba, flos -iacus,** mallow 14c. (*cf.* ros); **-iso,** to act like a Syrian c 1620.

syringia, buttermilk (A.S.) c 1115.

syrin/x ‡c 1443, 1622, **-ga** a 1250, syringe.

syrma, robe (eccl.); prolonged note (mus.) a 975.

†**syrtum,** (?) *for* **sistrum** (mus.), c 1180.

syr/upus (sir-) a 1250, 1622, **-opus** a 1250, **surrupus** 1252, **surripus** 1303, **ciripis** 1414, syrup; **-upo,** to make into a syrup a 1250.

syst/ema, (?) harmony c 950. c 1200; **-aticus,** constitutive 1620.

systichia, parallel series (συστοιχία) 1344.

systole, systole, contraction (med.) a 1250, 1622.

syuratio, *see* ESCUR

syvis, *see* **siva.**

syzygia 1686, **synzygia** 7c., **synzugia** a 1200, syzygy, conjunction.

szoherus, *see* **sorus.**

szucra, *see* **sucrum.**

T

t, symbol of zero c 1150; *cf.* **teca.**

***tabard/um, -us** 1253, c 1450, **-a** c 1445, **tabarum** 1257, **taberdum** c 1350, **taberda** c 1390, **tabertum** 1274, †**talbartum** c 1310, tabard, sleeveless tunic or surcoat; **-atus,** wide-sleeved 1311; **-arius, -us** 1691, **taberd/us** 1566, **-ius** 1569, tabardar (ac.).

tabel/iamentum, -lamentum, *see* **tabula.**

tabell/a, sideboard c 1300; tablet displaying arms (her.) 1391; diagram, tabulation a 1250; sight on astronomical instrument 1326; **t. osculatoria** c 1524, **t. pacis** c 1521, pax (eccl.); **-ula,** small board 12c.; drawbridge 15c.; 'tableman', gaming-piece 1235; **-arium,** tabler, gaming-board 1235; **-ata,** tablet, picture 1418; **-atum** 15c., **-atus** 1421, 15c., partition *or* flooring; **-arius** (publicus), *for* **-io,** notary 1608; **-ionalis,** notarial 1547; ***-ionatus,** office of notary 1284, 1549; **-iono,** to act as notary 1389.

taberculum, *see* **tabor.**

tabern/a ***1182, 1518, **domus -arie** 1549, tavern, inn; allowance for lodging 1278, 1342; brew of ale 1269, 1400; sale of wine or ale by retail 1185, 1372; **t. cervisiaria,** ale-house 1516, ‡1520; **t. vinaria** 1516, c 1542, **t. ad vinum** c 1219, **t. de vino** 1192, **t. vini** 13c., c 1360, wine-shop; ‡**-aria,** "strumpet" 15c.; **-arius,** tavern-haunter 1293; ***1236, 1419, ‡**-a** (*f.*) 15c., **-aria** (*f.*) c 1320, 1385, **-ator** 1259, 1430, **-atrix** (*f.*) 1266, ‡**-io** 1483, taverner, inn-keeper; **-atio,** subletting 1324, 1376; **-o,** to sublet c 1340, 1578; to buy or sell retail, 'tipple' 13c., 1466; *see also* **zaberna.**

tabernacul/um, body as dwelling-place of soul c 730. c 1325; lodging c 1220; ***canopy,** covered shrine, niche 1242, 1520; coping 1424; reliquary 1404, 1509; receptacle for Host (eccl.) 1424, 1518; **t. federis,** Tabernacle of the Covenant (bibl.); **-arius,** pavilioner a 1204; **-atus,** canopied 15c.

tabertum, *see* **tabardum.**

tab/es, relaxation (in good sense) c 550;

-iditas, consumption, wasting (med.) a 1250;
-esco, to grow quiet or mild c 550; to afflict
1293.
tabetum, *see* **tapes.**
tabl-, tabil-, *see* TABUL
tab/or c 1227, 1303, **-ur** c 1192, **-ura, -urus**
1183, 1300, **-erculum** c 1250, **-urcum**
c 1154, **-urdum** 1296, **-urella aquatica**
1287, **-urna** 1180, tabor, drum (esp. falc., for
starting game); **-urarius,** drummer 1213;
-oro, to beat a drum 1269.
tabul/a, plank, board: scaffold-plank 1412,
1413; sluice 1315; shutter 1466; wooden
scale-pan 1460, 1476; *c 980, 1006. c 1080,
c 1330, **t. manualis** c 1266, 1355, **t.
sonatilis** c 1266, c 1330, clapper (mon.);
board for book-binding 1389, 1415; chess-
board or square a 1150, 15c.; Jew's badge
1218, 1281; flat reliquary 1383, 1419; 1388,
t. osculatoria 1388, **t. pacifera** 1303,
t. pacis 1305, c 1443, **t. pro pace** c 1340,
c 1360, pax (eccl.); sheet (of lead) 1086,
c 1210; board painted with device (her.)
1392; panel of box-bed 1373; panel, screen
or frontal (eccl.) 893. 1231, 1432; **in -a,** 'in
table' (of a gem) 1387; **t. vitri,** pane of glass
1479, 1510; **t. lapidea** 1447, **tabla** 1342,
coping, cornice (arch.);
*-**a** c 1080, 1537, †**tebula** 1371, table,
table-top; board, maintenance 1360, 1496;
money-changer's counter or office 1331;
t. altaris c 1093, **t. are** 1537, altar-table;
t. comensalis 1390, **t. mensalis** 1221,
1464, trestle table; **t. dormiens** 1252, 1344,
tabila dormitaria 1388, 'table dormant',
fixed table; **t. marmorea,** Marble Table
(in Chancery) 1359; **t. movens,** movable
table 1313; **t. plicabilis** 1388, **t. plicata**
1341, 1388, folding table; **t. rotunda,**
table ronde, form of tournament 1232, 1461;
t. ad sectam, (?) table belonging to a set
1458; ‡**t. structoria,** dresser 1570; **t.
volvens,** revolving table 1473;
-a a 1190, 1303, **t. computi** 1464, reckon-
ing-board, abacus; astronomical table
c 1227, 1686; table of Mosaic law 15c.; **t.
ludend',** gaming-board 1553; notice-board,
roster (mon.) 1237, 1451; **t. misse,** roster
for attendance at mass c 1335, c 1515;
-amentum 1234, **tablamentum** 1222,
tablementum 1289, **tabellamentum** 1252,
1286, **tabeliamentum** 1507, **tabliamen-
tum** 1291, 1325, entablement, coping,
slabbing, string-course (arch.); 1364, 1368,
tablementum 1415, wooden altar-frontal;
(?) **stablementum,** hoarding 1223; **-aneum,**
Jew's badge c 1220; **-aris,** of a writing tablet
c 1250; of a table (astr.) 1267; of a coping
1403; **-arium,** document c 980; c 1178,
1376, **tablerium** 1392, tabler, gaming-
board; **-arius,** tabellar, chorister noting
attendance at mass c 1395, c 1490; courier
1532; **-ata,** (dining) table c 1470; **-atio,**
panelling 16c.; roster (mon.) 1475, 1524;
table of contents 1345; account-book
c 1530; **-atum,** fabric, structure c 550;
stockade 1535; **-atus** (*subst.*), tablet a 1100;
floor, story a 1100, 15c.; platform c 1220;
bracket 1252; †**t. domitialis,** (?) wall-plate
c 1255 (*cf.* **mensa**); **t. lapideus,** stone

floor c 1191, c 1400; **t. marmoreus** c 1188;
-etta 1396, 1448, **tablettum** 1403, (golden)
tablet; **-osus,** made of planks, boarded
c 550; **-atus** (*adj.*), flat, 7c.; chequered
1245; (?) with plane surfaces 1326; **-o,** to
board up 1323, 1465; to fit with a coping
1291.
tabur-, *see* **tabor.**
tacamentum, *see* **tachia.**
tacco, *see* 1 **taccum;** 2 **tactus.**
1 **tacc/um** (tack-, takk-), iron 'tack' on axle
of cart 1248, 1486; **tachettum** 1306, 1358,
takettum 1307, 1346, tacket, needle; **-o,**
to fit (cart) with 'tacks' 1280; to tack (carpet)
1323; to tack together (cloths) 1447, 1564;
cf. **taco.**
2 **taccum** 1257, **takcum** c 1290, 'tack', due
paid for feeding swine in forests; **takman-
nus,** 'tacksman', farmer (Lincs.) 1390, 1420;
thacio, to pay 'tack' a 1350.
tacea, *see* 1 **tassa**
tacellus, *see* **tassellus.**
tacentia, keeping silence 1378; **tacit/e,** in a
low voice 1150; **-er,** silently 5c.; **-urnalis,**
silent a 1100; **ticesco,** to pass over in
silence c 1000.
tacere, *see* **tessella.**
tach/ia (thach-) 1214, 1366, **stachia** (C.I.)
1254, 1289, fastening, clasp; **-amentum**
a 1190, **tacamentum** c 1155, 1163, attachment (of mill-pond); **-iamentum,** attachment, arrest (leg.) 1258; **-eo,** to make as an
abutment (of mill-pond) 1354, 1356; *-**io,**
to attach, fasten 1303, c 1354; *cf.* ATTACH;
see also 1 **taccum,** 3 **taxa.**
tack-, *see* 1 **taccum.**
taco, tag (of leather) 1150, 1293; *cf.* 1 **taccum.**
tacris, *see* **dacra.**
Tacrus, *see* **Turcus.**
1 **tact/us,** 'touch', stamp (on metal) 1323, 1361;
time (mus.) 1200; (?) heat c 550; **-ivus,**
of or for touching c 1257, a 1361; **tang/ibilis,**
tangible a 1250, 1457; **-ibilitas,** tangibility
1648; **-ens,** tangent (math.) 1686; **-o**
c 1250, c 1597, **t. ad.** c 1362, to concern;
to amount to 1315; **t. affinitate** 1219, **t.
consanguinitate** c 1290, to be akin to; **t.
de,** to touch upon, allude to c 1180, 1408;
t. super, to abut on 12c.
2 **tact/us armorum,** wapentake c 1150; **-o**
c 1290, **tacco** c 1150, to confirm (cited as
alleged etymology of wapentake).
‡**tacumo,** danewort (bot.) 14c.
†**tafaro, spica,** kind of herb a 1250.
taf/fata 1331, 1591, **-eta** 1423, taffeta, silk
material.
tagnus, tahinus, tainus, *see* **thanus.**
tail-, *see* TALL
taissellus, *see* **tassellus.**
taium, (?) mud (O.F. *tai*) 1300.
tak-, *see* **taccum** (1 & 2).
tala, *see* 2 **tallia.**
talamus, *see* **latomus; thalamus.**
talar/is, ankle-length robe 13c., 1425; **-iter,**
down to the ankles 1331; **-o,** to vest in a
long robe c 1500.
talasus, *see* **thalassa.**
talbartum, *see* **tabardum.**
talc/ 1267, a 1292, **-um** c 1215, ‡1652, talc.
†**talcstona,** (?) table-stone (arch.) 1415.

tale/a, -ator, -o, -ola, *see* TALL
talendiola, *see* CALEND
talent/um, a sum of money c 1180, c 1436;
t. auri, *maravedi* 1253; t. Saracenicum,
dinar c 1200; -um, talent, opportunity,
thing entrusted 8c. 1236, c 1536; bezant
(her.) 1388, a 1446; -atim, -atus, bezanty
(her.) a 1446; -o, to make bezanty p 1394.
‡taleteca, (?) *for* galatia, "blancmange" 15c.
talevati/um 1198, -a 1200, 'talevace', wooden
shield.
talh/a, -ia, *see* 2 tallia.
†talie (*pl.*), (?) loins 6c.
†talimpulum, small measure 6c.
taliorchus, a game c 1160.
talisicus, *see* thalassa.
tal/itas, 'suchness', possession of a quality
c 1300, p 1300; -is *c 1267, 1552, t. et t.
1684, so-and-so; pro -i, on that account
c 1340; -es (*pl.*), the following c 1219;
(applied to jurors) c 1250, 1433; -em
qualem, name of a writ c 1268; *-iter, thus
8c. 1080, c 1540.
1 *tall/ia 1107, 1586, -ium 1236, 1534, -a
(*metri gratia*) a 1410, talea c 1115, c 1380,
taillia c 1130, 1240, tally; t. alba, blank
tally 1275; t. corulina, hazelwood tally
c 1370; t. dividenda, tally covering a
number of payments 1284; t. memoranda,
memoranda tally c 1178; t. tripartita
c 1290; talee (*pl.*), the Exchequer c 1178;
taleator, tally-cutter 1130; taleola, little
tally c 1178; taleo, to cut a tally c 1178;
-io 1237, c 1321, t. contra 1199, 1297, to
check (by tally); to count 1461, 1608.
2 *tall/ia 1180, 1451, -ium 1279, -a (tala)
1287, 1352, tailla, tailgia 1086, taillia
c 1196, taillium 1226, talha, talhia (G.)
1313, -agia 1157, 1320, *-agium 1151,
c 1539, -iagium 1201, c 1414, taillagium
a 1165, p 1330, tailliagium 1202, c 1397,
teylagium 1255, -atio 1275, -iatio c 1210,
a 1309, -iamentum 1455, -iata c 1155,
tailliata 1203, c 1222, *taille*, tallage, tax;
-iabilis 1257, 1419, -agabilis 1275,
taillabilis 1308, liable to tallage, taxable;
-iator c 1122, 1274, tailliator 1237, assessor
of taxes; *-io 1199, 1462, -o 1227, c 1250,
taillio 1194, 1274, taillo c 1308, to tallage,
tax; -o, to pay tallage 1200; -io ad 1241,
1256, -io in 1253, to assess at.
3 *tall/ia c 1370, 1608, -ium 14c., -iatio
c 1430, -iatum 14c., entail, estate tail;
feodum -iatum, fee tail 1283, 1513; -io,
to entail 1308, 1608.
4 tall/ia 1251, 1287, -ium 1230, a 1242,
talea c 1160, cutting (of cloth), retailing;
-ia, piece of metal sliced from ingot, un-
stamped coin p 1280; -atio, pruning 1493;
taillatio, modelling 1275; -iatio 1322,
-iatura 1346, 1445, tailloria 1355, cutting
(of cloth), tailoring; tailleria, tailoring
department 1265; -iarius 13c., taylator
1317, stone-cutter; -iator, carver 1359;
(?) coin-slicer 1354; 1230, 1243, -ator
c 1136, taillator 1212, tailliator c 1320,
taillor c 1240, tailor; lana tailler', sort of
wool 1291; †teilluus, carved 1204; tailliata,
(?) strip (of leather) 1390; -iatus ex transverso, cut on the cross (of costume) 1326;

-eo, to prune (vines) c 1182; -io, to cut
(cloth) 1212, 1435; 1237, 1342, taillio
c 1300, taillo 1198, to hew (stone); to carve
(metal) 1290, 1320; to slice from ingot
p 1280; c 1115, -o 1261, taillo 1185, to cut
(corn); -o, to quarry (sand) 1295.
†tallignum, (?) clog almanac 1267.
Talmamud (Th-), Talmud (Heb.) 1286.
talmus, *see* ophthalmus.
talneum, *see* telo.
1 talo, keel (naut.) 1296.
2 talo, tallow 13c.
3 talo, *vinum coctum* 1652.
talp/anarius c 1335, -ator 1336, mole-catcher;
-onarius, sapper 1193; ‡-efodium 15c.,
‡-etum 1483, mole-hill; *see also* mons.
talwoda, 'talwood', firewood c 1304, 1375.
tamarind/us a 1250, 13c., -a c 1357, tamarind
(bot.).
tamariscinus, of tamarisk wood a 1250.
tamaxo, *see* thaumatopeetica.
tam/isium, 'temse', sieve 1294; †-mezca,
hopper c 1180; temeso, to sieve, sift 1331;
cf. trimodius.
tamnus, *see* thanus.
tamp/o 1388, -onus 1399, tampion, wad.
tan/acetum, -esetum, *see* athanasia.
tanaliter c 550, 934. c 1125, tonaliter c 550,
mortally.
*tancardus (tank-) c 1266, c 1423, tangardus
1392, 'tankard', hooped bowl.
tandem, at the latest 1584.
tandundem, *see* TANT
tanell/e, -o, *see* tenacula.
tang-; *see also* 1 TACT; tancardus; TANN
tang/o, -nus, wrack, sea-weed (Jersey Fr.
tangon) (C.I.) 1324.
*tann/um a 1135, 1573, -a c 1200, tan, oak-
bark; *-aria c 1200, 1486, -arium 1356,
-eria c 1265, 1427, -atorium 1376, tannery;
molendinum -arium, tan-mill 1288;
-arius a 1188, a 1564, -erus c 1190, *-ator
1168, 1446, tanner; -ator albus, whittawyer
1239; -atio 1323, 1534, †-inatio 1325,
tanning; tangabulum, 'tan-gavel', due
paid by tanners 1297, 1300; -etum, tan-
coloured (? tawny) cloth c 1325, c 1337;
-atus (†taunatus), tan-coloured, tawny
13c.; -ettus, tanned 1332; -itus, *see* 1 turba;
*-o, to tan (leather) c 1100, a 1564; to tan
(nets) 1286.
tansetum, *see* athanasia.
tantariso, *see* taratantarum.
tant/e, so much 1256, 15c.; *see also* de, in, per,
pro; -illitas, slightness c 1458; -illulus, ever
so little c 1210, a 1452; ex -illulo, slightly
c 1458; -iplex, so many fold 1427; -ivalen-
tia, an equivalent c 1300, -ummodus,
tantamount 1344; tandundem, *for* -un-
dem, 825; -ipendo, to value so highly
c 1115.
‡tantellus, "cousin" 15c.
‡tantula, "antelope" 15c.
tanus, *see* thanus.
‡tap/acitas, "michery", -ax, "micher", -io,
"to mich", c 1440; *cf.* tapinagium.
tapenarius 1275, tapinarius 1202, 'tapener',
cloth-worker.
taper/a 1539, -is 1389, taper.
tap/es c 550. c 1330, c 1386, *-eta (†capeta)

793. 1080, 1459, -ete c 1000, *-etum
c 1080, c 1520, tabetum c 1510, -etus
c 1290, 1390, tepeta c 1300, tepetum
c 1400, -ita 1341, -itum 1205, 1401,
-isetum c 1000, -esium 13c., c 1365,
-esteum 1460, -etium c 1255, 1564,
-eceria 1432, 1440, -eceries 1377, -eseria
1415, -iceria 1390, 1398, -icerium 1419,
-issaria 1466, -isseria 15c., -seria 1388,
-estria c 1315, a 1452, -istria 1433, -etoria
1431, tapet, tapestry, carpet, hanging,
valance, figured cloth; -eta pro mensa,
"table carpet" 1553; -eterius 1395, †-istus
a 1429, of or for tapets, etc.; -etiarius,
upholsterer 1710; -iciarius 1367, -icerius
1419, 1539, -icerus (-iterus) 1378, 1462,
-isarius 1436, -itarius 14c., -setrix (f.)
c 1452, ‡textor -etarius 1520, tapisser.
taphus, tomb (τάφος) 870.
tap/inagium c 1220, **-enagium** 1227,
'tapinage', secrecy.
tapinarius, see **tapenarius**.
tapinosis, depreciation (gram.) c 1210.
tapp/ator, tapster 1430; **vendo (vinum) ad
-am** c 1250, **-o (cervisiam)** 1442, to sell
retail.
tapsaria, see **ptisana**.
†**tapsia**, kind of animal 1252; cf. **taxus**.
tapsus, see **thapsus**.
taragium, see **terragium**.
tarambium, see **teratio**.
tar/anta 1250, **-ens, -entus** c 1200, tarantula.
tarascus, fabulous monster, tarasque (Fr.)
c 1212.
taratantar/um c 1177, 1474, **-a** 1328, **teratan-
tera** 1390, **tiratantrum** 15c., flour-sieve,
bolting-cloth; sieve for plaster 1313; **t. ad
lac** 1297; ‡**-izator, -izatrix** (f.), bolter
c 1440; **terratantarizatio**, bolting, sifting
1463; **-yatio**, bolting (of wood with a bolt)
1483; **-izo** c 1177, ‡1483, †**tantariso** 1144,
to bolt, sift.
‡**taraxacon, altaraxacon**, gromwell (or
other herb) 14c.
tarcha, tarcia, see **targia**.
tarcinus, see **thanus**.
tarcosium, 'tarcays', quiver (for arrows)
1212, 1235.
‡**tard/arius** c 1440, 15c., ‡**-earius** c 1200,
lanneret (falc.); cf. **ardearius**.
tard/atio 793. 1231, a 1564, **-antia** c 1376,
delay; **-ativus**, delaying, hindering c 1375;
-e, lately, recently 1397; **ad -ius**, at latest
1325; **-eo**, to be late c 1263; **-o** (with inf.),
to delay, put off c 790. c 1180, c 1440.
taren/s, -tus, see **taranta**.
tarentinillum, sort of cloth 1265; cf. **tirretena**.
*targ/ia** 1173, 1461, **-a** 1165, 1266, **tergia**
c 1540, ‡**terga** 15c., **tarcha** 1173, **tarcia**
c 1190, **-etta** 1298, targe, shield; screen to
cover embrasure 1298; 14c., **-a** 1296, escutcheon; boss, stud 1300; Privy Seal c 1320.
‡**tarin/ca** c 1440, ‡**-ga** 1483, spike.
tarinus 1292, **terinus** (†**terrim**) 1190, 1292,
coin (It.); see also **tarmus**.
tar/ita (†**carrica**) 1354, 1387, **-eta** c 1385,
'tarette' (ship); cf. **carraca**.
‡**tarm/us** (†**tarinus**), for **-es**, maggot c 1440,
1483; ‡**-osus**, maggoty 1483.

‡**taro**, lentisk 1652.
tar/pica 1350, **-pix** 1324, 1345, **-pissum** 1323,
tar-pitch.
tarqua, see **dacra**.
tarquinasis, see TRICH
tarr/a 1329, 1467, **-um** 1281, c 1300, **terra**
1390, 1485, **terrum** 1301, tar; **-o**, to tar
(rope) 1281.
tarragium, see **terragium**.
tarrer/a (†**carrera**) c 1218, 1266, **-ia** 1214,
auger (Fr. tarière); cf. **teratio**.
Tars/ensis 1303, 1327, **-icus** 1295, **-inus**
1303, pannus **-ensis**, p. de **-e** 1300, 1329,
'cloth of Tars', rich oriental fabric.
tars/us, -ator, see 2 **tassa**.
tarta, tart, pie 1265, 1310; cf. 1 **torta**.
1 **Tartar/a** (n. pl.), Christian Hell 6c., 11c.
a 1236; **-eus** 12c., c 1440, **Tertareus** c 1180,
hellish; **-ismus**, infernal disorder c 1620.
2 **tartar/a** 1493, **-anum** c 1432, **-inum** 1388,
1449, **-o** c 1451, pannus **-eus** 1289, **p.
-inus** c 1412, (?) p. tartenus 1324, **linura
de Tartron'** 1472, tartarin, rich silk fabric;
cf. **tirretena**.
tartaro, Byzantine coin (τεταρτηρόν) a 1142.
tartar/um, tartar (made from wine lees)
c 1200, 1622; ‡**-us**, stone (med.) 1652.
Tartar/us c 1250, 1586, **Tattawa** 1243,
-eus 1252, **-icus** 1267, **-escus** 1292, Tartar,
Tatar, Mongol.
tasc-, tasch-, see 2 **tassa**; **taxa** (2 & 3).
tasellum, see **teselum**.
1 **tass/a** 1312, 1450, *-ea** 1434, 1549, **tacea**
1434, 1498, **tazza** c 1345, 'tass', goblet,
cup.
2 **tass/a** 1200, 1435, *-us, -um** c 1160, 15c.,
-is 1344, ‡15c., **-ius** 1407, **tarsus** 1282,
†**tussa** (f.l.) 1359, **-atus** 1388, 'tass', rick or
haycock; **-iculus**, hay-cock c 1218, 1297;
-agium, service of stacking (C.I.) 1274,
1309, **-atio** 1289, 1449, †**tussio** 1574,
stacking; *-ator** 1275, 1398, **-or** 1286,
tarsator 1289, stacker; *-o** 1206, 1577,
tasco 1222, **taxo** 12c., 1270, to stack.
tass/ellus, -ellum c 1150, 1383, **-allus**
a 1100, 1245, **tacellus** c 1330, **taissellus**
c 1080, tassel, fringe; **-ilatus**, tasselled,
fringed 1383; **-ello**, to fit (pavilions) with
tassels 1303.
‡**tassus**, worm 1652; see also 2 **tassa**, **taxus**.
tast/um, taste, test, choice (of ale or wine)
1293, 16c.; **-a**, probe (med.) a 1250, ‡c 1440;
-ura (cervisie), tasting c 1250; **-or**, 'taster',
shallow cup 1374; *-ator (cervisie)** 1267,
1460, **tassator** 1297, **-or** 1279, **testator**
1486, **testor** 1461, ale-taster; **-ator corei**,
inspector of leather 1453; **t. gurgitum**
1325; *-o**, to taste (ale) 1247, c 1370; to
inspect (weirs) 1289, 1325; see also 2 **taxa**.
tata, 'tathe', 60 acres (Ir.) c 1606.
Tattarus, see **Tartarus**.
tau/, thave, Hebrew letter c 1200; **tau** (Gk.)
agie crucis 961, 1021. 12c., **-maticum
sigillum** c 974, sign of the cross; **-malis**,
tau-shaped, 'patent' (her.) c 1595.
taulagium, see **telo**.
taunatus, see TANN
taur/us liber 1252, 1368, **-i libertas** 1307,
1325, liberty of bull (man.); **-ellus** 1275,
1388, **torellus** 1205, **-illus** 1310, **-iculus**

1312, steer, bull-calf; ‡-ocolla, bull's gall 14c.; -o, to cover (a cow) 1296.

tauto, eyelash or eyebrow 6c.

tautolog/us, one who repeats himself c 1620; ‡-ia, "fatuus sermo" 13c.

tawagium, see towagium.

taw/yator, tawyer 1365; -o, to taw, dress white leather 1334, 1366.

1 taxa, blame 1408.

2 *tax/a a 1300, 1543, -um 1338, c 1400, -is c 1322, tascha c 1115, tax or assessed payment; tasca (†tasta), taxable tenement (G.) 1242; -abilis, liable to tax c 1356; *-atio, taxing or assessing for payment 844, 933. a 1160, 1608; *-ator c 1223, c 1549, tascator 1284, 1330, assessor of taxes; taxor (ac.) c 1590; -o, *to tax or assess for taxation (?) 685 (c 975). c 1130, 1543; to fix, assign 786. c 1178, c 1514; to mention, touch upon 786, 939. c 1170, 1424; *t. ad, to assess at c 1250, c 1452; -or (dep.), to regulate 1344; see also 2 tassa.

3 taxa 1314, 1425, tachia 1292, 1296, *tasc/a 1166, c 1438, -um 1251, 1373, task, piece-work; -ator task-worker 1286.

taxill/us, cube 1267; i- (pl.) c 1247, 1461, -e (pl.) 1531, dice; ‡-ator, dice-player 1483.

tax/is, sign, badge 870; -iarcha, root or beginning of order 870.

*tax/us a 1200, a 1446, tassus c 1215, -o 655. a 1250, c 1325, -is a 1430, *tesso 1255, 1343, tisso c 1310, badger (cf. German Dachs); ‡-eus c 1200, ‡-inus 1483, of a badger; see also thapsus.

tay/cia, -sa, see tensa.

Tays, see Thais.

tazza, see 1 tassa.

tebia, see tibia.

tebula, see tabula.

teca, (?) for theta, symbol of zero (math.) c 1230; see also t, theca.

techellatus, tetchellatus, brindled, spotted (cf. O.F. teche) 1248.

techna, trick c 950; tegn/a, art 1041. c 1200; -i, Galen's Techne c 1180, c 1500.

tecno (†tecto), to produce, exhibit (A.S. tæcnan) c 1115.

tect/um, *roof, roofing c 1090, 1557; roofed building 1540; coverlet 1588; -im, allegorically c 1182; -or, roofer, thatcher 1296, 1459; -um, loft 10c.; teg/es, shed, hut c 1190, ‡c 1440; ‡-ilectum, coverlet 15c.; -men, straw for thatching 1222, 1300; -umentator, concealer c 1432; -o, to roof or thatch 1314, 1510; t. stramen super 1374; see also tecno.

tecul-, see TEGUL

teddo, to ted (hay) 1277, 1333.

tedero, see tera.

tedinga, see tethinga.

Tedis, see Tethys.

ted/ium, injury 1276; habeo t. de, to be weary of c 790; -ialis, wearisome 865; -iosus, ill at ease c 800; *c 1125, c 1412; -iatus c 1400, c 1436, disgusted, weary; -eo, to be weary (bibl.).

†tega, (?) box, stall 1491; cf. theca.

tegater, see thygater.

teges, see TECT

tegg/a (†-us), 'teg', fallow doe in second year 1494.

teg/illarius, -lator, see TEGUL

tegillum, see tigillum.

tegn/a, -i, see techna; TIG

tegn/io, -us, teglanda, see THAN

teg/o, -men, -umentator, see TECT

tegor-, tegur-, see tugurium.

1 tegul/a, tile: -um 1461, tecula 1292, 1329, tigula c 1440, 1460; -a 1259, 1354, -um 1280, tiling (coll.); -a, cake (of soap) 1380; t. canill', drainage tile 1388; t. cavata 1253, 1388, t. concava 1223, 1245, hollow tile; t. cornar', corner tile 1253; t. crocea 1274; t. Flandrensis (t. de Flandria) 1320, 1388; ‡t. fornicata, cover for crucible (alch.) 1652; t. lignea, shingle 1302; t. muralis, 'wall-tile', brick 1335, 1389; t. ad pavimentum, paving tile c 1275; t. plana, flat tile 1365, 1388; t. subtilis, (?) ornamental tile 1289; t. aria 1334, 1360, -ria 1360, tiling, tile-work; -aria, -arium, tilery (Yorks.) 1287, 1370; domus -aris 1547, d. -at' 1376, tile-kiln; petra -aris c 1325, lapis -atus 1535, stone tile, slate; -arius c 1180, 1684, tigularius 1461, tegillarius 1371, *-ator 1223, 1520, teglator 1371, teculator 1292, 1329, tigulator 1348, 1541, -atrix (f.) 1327, tiler; -atio, tiling 1371, 1504; *-o c 1190, 1540, teculo 1580, to tile.

2 †tegula, "blanket" 1588.

teholneum, see telo.

teia, see theca.

teign-, tein-, see THAN

teilluus, see 4 tallia.

teint-, see TINCT

teis/a, -ia, -o, -um, see tensa.

teissilo, see teseillum.

teitinga, see tethinga.

1 tela, see tilia.

2 tela, teal (bird) 1544.

3 tel/a c 1185, c 1451, -um 1467, 1509, cloth; membrane of brain c 1210; t. aranee, part of inner coat of eye a 1250, 1267; t. conjunctiva, t. cornea, t. retina, t. sclirotica, t. secundina, t. uvea (med.) a 1250; t. in oculo, spot in eye a 1250, 14c.; t. auri, cloth of gold 1509; t. lata, broad-cloth 1460, 1466; t. stricta, narrow cloth 1466; t. de muro, 'pane', stretch of wall 1221; t. plumbi, sheet of lead 1326, 1430; -arium, loom 1229, ‡c 1440; -arius c 1150, 1419, -aris 7c., of or for weaving; (subst.) 1130, 1457, -onarius 1310, †tolo 1251, weaver; -o, to weave 1424.

telari/a 1228, c 1335, -um 1205, 1337, -us 1225, telera c 1272, telerum 1313, tiller of crossbow; tiller of gun 1346; see also 3 tela.

teld/um 1171, 1421, (?) †toldum 1314, teuda 1292, telta (†celta) 1226, tilda c 1311, tilt, awning for ships; -o, to cover with awning 1209.

telescopium, telescope 1686.

†telgis, (?) for thelygonon (bot.), a 1250.

telifer, see telum.

telligraph/ium 798. 12c., 13c., -us 821, 951. 12c., c 1250, land-book, charter, deed.

tell/us, land, kingdom 7c., 8c.; (gen.) -i c 590;

-urium, land, district 823; †**-atus** c 550, **-eus** 8c., terrestrial.

telo/ (thelo-) c 1100, 12c., ***-neum, -nium** c 790, 893. 1086, 1608, **-num** c 1160, ***theoloneum** 1086, 1583, **theolonum** 1344, **teholneum** 13c., **tiolonium** 1309, **tolleneum** c 1215, 1330, †**toloneum, tolonium** c 1150, 1444, **tolneum** c 1115, 15c., **tolneium** c 1200, 1267, †**talneum** c 1217, **tollenetum** c 1189, c 1255, ***tolnetum** c 1145, 1566, **tolnetta** 1498, 1586, **toulnetum** 13c., **tolonetum** c 1255, 1311, †**tonnutum** c 1280, 1295, †**tomicata** (G.) 1199, **tollum** c 1220, 1444, **-nagium** c 1400, †**taulagium** (G.) 1283, †**tollagium** (? **tall-**) 12c., 1562, **tollenagium** 1428, **tolnagium** 1281, 1321, †**tonnagium** (? **toun-**) 1255, 1275, **tolliamentum** 1424, **-neatio** c 1157, toll, levy; **tolnetum baronie,** 'baron-toll' (Tutbury) 1262; **t. intrinsecum et extrinsecum,** (?) tolls payable by citizens and by others (Carlisle) 1292; **theolonium de ripa,** bank toll 1253; **t. transversum** 1330, **tolnagium transversum** 1281, **tolnetum transeuntium** 1336, 'toll traverse'; **-neum** (bibl.), **domus -nei** c 1200, **theolonium** 1288, 14c. **toloneum** 1316, 1368, †**tholeonora** 1261, **tolneta** 1553, toll-house, tolbooth, jail; **-narius** c 1086, 1654, **-nearius** c 730, 11c. c 1100, c 1250, **-nicus** 11c., **theolonarius, theolonearius** 1441, 1483, †**tolnearius** c 800, ‡**tolonarius** 15c., 1483, **theolenarius** c 1250, toll-gatherer; **theolono** 1373, **teolonizo** c 1230, to pay toll; **tolneo,** to levy toll 1312; *cf.* **tolbotha, tolfatum, tolselda, tolsextarium.**

‡**telon,** fire (alch.) 1652.

telonarius, *see* 3 **tela; telo.**

telta, *see* **teldum.**

tel/um, shaft: **-a** (*pl.*), tools c 1115; **-ifer,** archer c 1185; *see also* 3 **tela.**

tem/a (them-) c 1160, **-um** c 1220, 'team', vouching to warranty (in action for recovery), jurisdiction involving such action.

temanatala, *see* **tenemannetala.**

†**temanentia,** (?) *f.l.* for **remanentia,** c 1194.

tembria, *see* **timber.**

temens, *see* TIMID

temer/arie c 600. c 1188, 1461, **timerarie** 1461, rashly, audaciously; **-atrix,** violator (*f.*) c 1381; †**-ucus,** (?) *for* **-atus,** vile 1418.

temeso, *see* **tamisium.**

teminus, grove (τέμενος) c 550.

tem/o a 1200, 1375, **-us** 1316, **timo** 1288, main-beam *or* draught-pole of plough; **timo,** rudder 1171.

Tempellarius, *see* TEMPL

temper/amen, (?) a mixed drink 1325; **-amentum,** compromise c 800; consonance (mus.) a 1250; **-antia,** temperateness (of climate) c 1200; **-atio,** balance-wheel (of clock) c 1519; **-ativus,** moderative a 1250; **temporo,** *for* **-o,** to mix, temper 1300, 1399.

tempest/arius, weather-maker 8c.; **-ative,** at the proper time, on occasion c 1290; **nimis -ive,** too early 1409; **-ivus** c 550, **-uosus** c 1000. c 1180. c 1421, stormy; **-o,** to torment 1252.

1 **templum,** church 1086, 1586; **frater Templ/i (Salomonis)** c 1140, 1233, **f. de -o** a 1145, **miles -i (de -o)** c 1140, p 1340, **-aris** 12c., ***-arius** 1166, 1586, **-ator** 1276, Knight Templar; **-arius** 1450, 1531, **Tempellarius** 1441, of or for a Knight Templar; **-um** 1230, 1252, **militia -i** 1137, 1419, order of Knights Templar; church or commandery of Knights Templar 1349, 1433; Temple (London district) 1419; 1161, **T. Dominicum** a 1161, **T. Vetus** 1167, 1586, Old Temple (in Holborn); **T. Novum,** New Temple 1213, 1586; **T. Interius,** Inner Temple 1399, 1586; **T. Medium,** Middle Temple 1687; **t. misericordie,** sanctuary 1586; **-alis,** of or for a church c 1397.

2 **templum,** templet (arch.) 1422.

tempor-, *see* TEMPER; **tempus.**

tempt-, temt-, *see* **tentatio.**

tempus, period of office 1267, 1327; time value of breve (mus.) 1326, c 1470; season of year 1258; weather c 1190, c 1435; fashion, style c 1250; **a tempor/e,** betimes 1374; **a -ibus,** for some time (past) 1432; **ad -a,** for some time (to come) c 1400; **post multa -a,** after a long time 685; **a -e in t.** c 1470, **de -e in t.** 13c., c 1503, from time to time; ***a -e (a) quo memoria (hominum) non extat (existit)** 1276, c 1451, . . . **in contrarium** c 1451, c 1493, **a -e cujus contrarii (de cujus contrario) memoria (hominum) non existit** 1289, 1462, **a -e unde nemo recolit** 1255, **de tam antiquo -e quod non occurrit alicujus memorie qui nunc vivit** 1276, time out of mind; **t. apertum** 1269, 1430, **t. exclusum** 1270, open season for pasturing cattle; **t. compoti,** period covered by account 1340, 1469; **t. legis,** period during which oath could not be taken (leg.) 1220, 1259; *see also* **quatuortempora; timpus,** time 930; temple of head c 550. 1136, 1250;

***-ale** 12c., 1558, ***-alitas** c 730. 1252, 1504, temporality, temporal right, business, or possession; c 1230, c 1450, **legenda -alis** 1417, 15c., **l. -alium** 1430, temporal, part of breviary dealing with seasons and movable feasts; **-alis,** ***temporal** (not eternal) a 1100, 1461; ***lay, secular** c 1090, 1565; **-aliter,** with regard to temporal things c 800. c 1125, p 1377; **-aneus,** temporal, short-lived c 790, c 1170, c 1362; worldly 8c.; contemporary c 1252; **-eus,** of or for time c 550; **-o,** to time 1640.

temus, *see* **temo.**

***ten/a** c 180, c 1448, **tina** 1291, coif, clerical head-dress; **t. ferrea,** head-piece 1303; **-ator,** (?) coif-maker 1389; **-atus,** wearing coif c 1180; *see also* **tina;** *cf.* **tenia.**

tenacia, grasping or keeping 7c., 8c., obstinacy c 1250; *see also* **tenentia.**

ten/acula (*pl.*) c 1090, 1337, **-abule** (*pl.*) 1345, ‡**-alia** 1483, **-aila** c 1280, **-elle** (*pl.*) 1323, c 1409, **tanelle** 1269, **-icule** 1339, pincers, tongs; **-aculum,** crampon 15c.; ‡**-ello, tanello,** to make loop-holes in walls 1628.

Tenaculum (†**conaculum),** name of a comet c 1270.

tenagium, *see* THAN

tenan-, *see* **tenen-**

tenasmon, tenesmus (med.) a 1250, ‡14c.

ten/atio, -ator, -atorium, *see* **tentio.**

tenatura, *see* tenetura.
tencellatus, *see* stincillatus.
tenceria, *see* tenseria.
ten/cha c 1191, 1418, -chia 1249, c 1290, -ga 1246, ‡-giagio, -ia 15c., tench (fish).
tend-, *see also* tenta (1 & 2).
tend/entia 1290, 1649, -ere (*subst.*) a 1200, tendency, direction.
tendicul/um, *for* -a, snare c 1090, 1296.
tend/itor 1350, 1378, -ator 1389, tender, keeper; -o, to attend to, keep in repair 1278; *cf.* ATTEND
tendlus, 'tandle', fish-basket 1307.
tendo, tendon 1634, 1686.
tendro, *see* tener.
tendula, *see* scindula.
teneatura, *see* tenetura.
tenebr/a 1267, -ositas 9c., 870. a 1100, c 1450, darkness; -ositas, opacity c 1270; -e (*pl.*), three days before Easter 1201, 15c.; *see also* crata, 2 hercia; -ativus, apt to obscure c 1283; -ifer, bringer of darkness 1169, c 1500; -osus, blind 12c., c 1250; spiritually blind 1431; -esco, to make dark a 1408; -o, to blind 11c.; -or, to be in darkness c 730.
†teneicius, (?) with tined antlers 1263.
tenelle, *see* tenacula.
ten/ellus, banqueting-hall (O.F. *tinel*) 1384; †-erella, refectory (mon.) c 1394; *see also* tonna.
tenemannetala 1189, tienmannatala c 1150, temanatala 1160, themannetala 1201, 'ten-man-tale', form of geld (Yorks. & Lincs.) confused with frankpledge.
tenement/um, content, ingredient p 1280; *c 1096, 1516, tenamentum a 1189, teneamentum a 1176, 13c., tenimentum 1157, 1258, tenement, feudal holding; house 1275, 1539; t. laicum c 1300; *t. liberum, freehold 1185, 1575; terra -alis, land held by servile tenure 1664.
ten/entia, content (of metal) p 1280; tinentia, contents, tenor (G.) 1289; -entia 1209, 1275, -antia 1230, 1283, †-acia 1234, (tenure as) gage, pledge; *c 1280, 15c., -antia 1304, 1333, -endia (Sc.) 1448, -andia (Sc.) 1328, 1465, -endria (Sc.) 1451, 1510, -andria (Sc.) 1395, 1480, †-enta c 1108, (mode of) tenure, tenancy; †-entio, *see* tentio;
-ens, holder-up (in ship-building) 1296; defendant in real action 1191, 15c.; *1120, 1569, -endus (Sc.) 1460, -andus (Sc.) 1497, c 1520, -entiarius (G.) 1283, 1433, tenant, feudal land-holder (*see also* terra); t. ad terminum annorum c 1400; t. ad. terminum vite c 1306; t. ad voluntatem (*sc.* domini), tenant at will c 1400, 1446; t. conventionarius, 'conventioner' (Cornw.) 1534; t. custumarius, customary tenant 1544, 1690; t. francus 1176, c 1192, t. liber 1291, 1386, libere t. 1103, 1524, freeholder; t. inferior, under-tenant 1392; t. parvus, small-holder 1279;
-eo, *to hold (land, *etc.*) c 1067, 1572; t. a 12c., 1244, *t. de c 1080, 1440, t. sub 1086, to hold (land) of *or* from (lord); *t. ad 1086, 1453, *t. in 1086, 1572, *t. per 1155, 1483, t. pro 1219, c 1540, to hold (land) in *or* by (tenure); t. ij hidas pro j manerio 1086;

see also per; t. ad voluntatem (domini) 1086, 15c.; t. libere 1086, 1342;
-eo, to bind, oblige c 1163, 1549; t. ad grates, to bind in gratitude 1258, c 1310; t. de 1286, t. debitum 13c., *teneor in c 1188, c 1400, to be indebted;
-eo, to maintain, harbour c 1115, 1397; to maintain, provide (troops) 1230; t. ad robas, to keep as liveried retainer 1336;
-eo, to hold (session, market, festival, *etc.*) *c 1086, 1552; to keep, fulfil (agreement, appointed day, *etc.*) c 1196, 1379; to hold, consider c 1203, c 1458; to maintain a thesis (ac.) c 1343, c 1461; to concern a 1408; (*intr.*) c 1185, c 1357, -eor (*passive*) c 1258, 1338, to hold good, be valid; (? *for* tendo) to bend (bow) 1261; to extend (G.) 1289;
t. me ad, to have recourse to 1212, c 1290; t. contra, to oppose c 1077, c 1343; t. cum, to hold with, favour 1253, c 1362; t. campum, to take the field for war 1391, 1405; t. carrucam, to perform ploughing service a 1300; t. humum meam, to hold one's ground 15c.; t. justitiam, to do justice a 1087, c 1243; t. missas, to celebrate mass 7c., c 730; t. modum, to measure c 730, c 780; t. ordinem, to take one's turn a 1090, c 1265; t. pacem, to keep the peace 1100, c 1265; t. placitum, to hold a plea (leg.) c 1075, c 1290; t. rectum, to do right, c 1096, 1419; t. shopam, to keep shop c 1280; t. silentium, to keep silence c 1180.
tener/, unsubstantial, uncertain 1227, c 1268; -ior, more juvenile c 1204; -inus, sapling 1463; tendro, young shoot 1385; -itas, youthfulness c 1220, 1461; uncertainty c 1265, c 1268; -itudo, tenderness of heart c 730; -iusculus, somewhat youthful 1537.
tenerella, *see* tenellus.
†tenesa, (?) maintenance *or* livery 1418.
tenesie, *see* tennisii.
ten/etura 1086, c 1135, -atura a 1128, 1315, -eatura 1200, -tura c 1160, -endura 1141, -edura 1136, 1447, -eura c 1150, 1377, -uaria c 1465, -uera 1407, 1537, *-ura 1101, 1547, -uria 12c., c 1160, tinura 1276, -uta (G.) 1289, feudal holding, tenure or tenement; extra -uram, untenanted 1388; -ura antiqua c 1150, a 1300; t. bassa, base tenure c 1300, 1495; t. libera 14c.; t. magna, t. parva (Norf.) 1281; t. Walensica 1309, t. Wallensis 1389; -etura, state, condition 1214; -ura, handle 1300.
teng-, tenia, *see* tencha.
ten/ia, lace 1611; bar (her.) 1654; †-ua, fringe c 1200; *cf.* tena.
tenicule, *see* tenacula.
ten/nisii (*pl.*) 1525, -isie (*pl.*) 15c., -isia (*s.*) 15c., -esie (*pl.*) c 1450, ‡-iludus c 1440, tennis; ‡-iludius, tennis-player c 1440; pila vocata -es 1375.
tenor/, *tenor, wording or effect of document 7c. c 1090, 1565; condition, stipulation c 790, 955. c 1100, 1324; period of time 1136, 13c.; style, character, manner c 550. 12c., c 1200; *motif* (mus.) 1326, c 1470; campana -is, tenor bell 1536; *see also* tentio.
‡tenorcula, tiller of cross-bow 15c.; *cf.* 2 tenta.
tensa 1351, ‡15c., teis/a 1200, 1377, -ia 1212,

1302, **-um** 1325, **-o** 1287, **tesa** 1224, **tesia** 1198, 1269, **tesio** 1296, **taysa** 1332, **taycia** 1350, **theya** (G.) 1253, **toycis** 1298, 'toise', fathom; *see also* CENS

tens/ellatus, -alatus, *see* stincillatus.

tens/eria 1141, c 1250, **-aria** 1175, c 1250, **tenceria** c 1255, 'tenserie', payment for protection, blackmail, exaction; **-arius,** non-burgess paying for trading rights 1283, 1301 (*cf.* **censarius**); **-abilis,** fenced (?) 13c.; **-o,** to enclose, fence round a 1214, c 1258; to protect a 1150, 1216; to tallage, exact payment for protection 1202, 1265.

tens/itudo, stretching, extending 1146; **-ilis** 1267, 1622, **-ibilis** c 1615, tensile.

1 **tent/a** 1253, c 1362, **tenda** a 1142, tent, pavilion; **-orium,** sleeve c 1298; scaffold 1533; (?) canopy c 1093; **tendura,** material for awnings (naut.) 1225, 1234.

2 **tent/a** 1295, **-ura** 1384, 1495, tenting-frame; **-orium** a 1251, 1539, (?) **-ura** 1407, tenter-yard, rack-yard; device for bending cross-bow 1246, 1322; **-urhukum,** tenter-hook (or similar hook) 1501; **-ura** 1358, **-uratio** 1358, 1465, tentering, racking (of cloth); **-urator,** racker 1358; **-uro** 1358, **tendo** 1290, to rack (cloth); **-o,** *for* **tendo,** to bend (a bow) 1306.

3 **tenta (salmonum),** (?) stew, fish-pond c 1160.

4 ‡**tenta,** "brush" 1652.

5 **tenta,** 'tent', probe, pledget (med.) c 1180, c 1280.

tent/atio (tempt-) *c 790. c 1125, 1461, **temtatio** 697, **-amen** c 1170, c 1325, **-amentum** a 975. c 1180, a 1408, temptation; testing, examining 1248, 1350; attempt, effort, struggle 9c. 1345; **-amentum,** tentative beginning 1620; **-abilis,** liable to temptation c 1380; **-ative,** tentatively a 1204, c 1363; **-ativus,** tentative (log.) a 1200, c 1363; tempting 1378; **-ator,** tempter, the Devil c 1090, c 1450; one who argues tentatively 13c.; assayer (G.) 1253; **t. cervisie,** ale-taster 1221, 1381; **-o,** to test 1311; **temto,** *for* **-o,** to attempt c 730; **-or,** *for* **-o,** c 760.

†**tentilium,** (?) household (W.; *cf.* W. *teulu*) 1282.

ten/tio, holding 1430; possession c 1270; harbouring c 1110; obligation c 1290; holding (a court) 1402, 1441; †**-entio Parliamenti** a 1564; **-atio,** tenure 1255; **-atorium** 1309, **-torium** 1289, 1298, tail, handle (of plough); **-tivus,** obligatory (?) c 1376; **-tor,** holder (of opinion) 1409, c 1412; 1515, **-or** c 1300, 1429, tenant, occupant; 1325, 1425, **tinctor** 1234, 1267, **-torius** 1350, **-or** 1297, **-ator** 1297, 1325, **-tor carruce** 1298, 1364, **-ator** c. 1316, plough-holder.

tento, *see* 2 **tenta; tentatio.**

tentorium, tentur-, *see* **tenta** (1 & 2); **tentio.**

tenua, *see* **tenia.**

‡**tenuale,** barbican 15c.

tenu/atio, thinness c 1377, c 1470; **-ifolius,** narrow-leaved 1634; **-cla,** whey 6c.; **cervisia -a,** small ale 1511; **-is,** thinly attended 1258; **-itas (curie),** thin attendance 1258, 1302; **-isso,** to weaken 13c.

tenu/ra, -ria, -aria, -era, -ta, *see* **tenetura.**

tenus (with *abl.*), before c 600; *see also* **calcaneum, cor, corpus, finis, 2 funda,** HODI, **ignis, ita, nomen,** NULL, **pes, posse, quatenus, quoad, quodam, quotenus, solum, species, superficies, terra,** ULL, **usque, verbum.**

teodum, *see* **theodum.**

teol-, *see* **telo.**

Teotonicus, *see* **Teutonicus.**

tep/efactio, warming 1620; **-iditas** c 700, 787. a 1250, 1327, †**-iditos** 1358, **-editas** 1415, 1421, **-itudo** a 1250, lukewarmness; **-efacio,** to cool a 1175.

tepet/a, -um, *see* **tapes.**

ter/a 1264, 1381, **tira** 1337, **tirum** 1352, tether; **-o** 1380, **tedero** 1535, to tether.

teramabin, *see* **tereniabin.**

†**teramasium,** (?) locality (G.) 1312.

†**teranum,** (?) *for* **teramon** (bot.), a 1250.

teraphim (ther-), images (Heb.) 12c.

ter/atio, drilling, boring 1443; **-ebratio,** piercing (her.) c 1595; **-ebellum** 1310, 1373, **terribellum** 1413, †**tarambium** c 1160, gimlet; *cf.* **tarrera.**

***terc/ellus** c 1200, 1389, **-ellius** c 1260, **-iolus** a 1446, **-elettus** 1287, 1382, tercel (falc.); (*adj.*) 1234, **tersello** (G.) 1313, tercel, male (of hawks); *cf.* TERTI

tercennale, *see* TRIG

terc/eria, -ius, *etc.,* *see* TERTI; **torcha.**

terdecas (*met. grat.*), thirty 1413.

ter/decimus, thirteenth c 1263; **-deni,** *for* **-ni deni,** thirteen each 1200; *cf.* **trideni.**

‡**terdi/na, -ne, -ola,** valerian (bot.) 1652.

tereb-, *see also* **teratio.**

tere/benthina (†**-bantina,** †**therebitina**), *sc.* **resina** a 1250, **-bintinum** 1307, **turbentinum** 1314, **termentinum** 1453, turpentine.

‡**tereniabin** 1652, (?) **teramabin** a 1250, "manna", nostoc.

tereticus, observant (τηρητικός) 870.

teret/ifolius, smooth-leaved 1632; ‡**-rum,** roundel 1570.

terg/ia, -a, *see* **targia.**

terg/um, fur of back 1225 (*cf.* **dorsum, venter**); **t. cathedre,** chair-back 1553; **-iversatorie,** evasively 7c.

teribilis, friable 13c.

terinus, *see* **tarinus.**

teriones (*pl.*), *see* **septem.**

teripes, stirrup a 1142; *cf.* **strepa.**

Termaximus, Trismegistus (title of Hermes) 1564.

termentinum, *see* **terebenthina.**

termin/us, *term, fixed period of time 1086, 1450; portion of Zodiac (astr.) c 1150, 1387; *term, term-day, fixed date or point (leg.) 1194, 1564; stage of legal action 1549; *term (ac.) c 1275, 1569; *term, expression, word a 1228, 1461; **t. a quo, t. ad quem** 1267, 1328; **t. communis,** middle term (log.) a 1110; **t. crucesignatorum (crucitorum,** *etc.*), period of immunity granted to crusaders (leg.) 1195, 1253; **t. regis,** king's term of felon's land 1221; **t. vite,** term of life c 1258, c 1516; life estate or interest 1327; **ad -um,** name of a writ 1259;

-abilis, *able to be limited a 1250, c 1361;

able to be brought to an end 15c.; able to be tried (leg.) c 1432, c 1452; **-abilitas**, susceptibility of limitation a 1250, c 1290; **-amentum**, settlement (of debts) 15c.; **-arius**, *'termor'*, lessee (leg.) 1281, 1419; **numerus t.**, golden number (in calendar) c 1265; **-atim**, term by term 1279, c 1545; **-atio**, ending c 1090, 1559; termination (gram.) c 790; limitation c 1290; determination (ac.) c 1350; **-ative**, by way of limit p 1300, c 1362; **-ativus**, limiting a 1250, c 1361; **-ator**, surveyor c 1397; that which limits c 1233, c 1408:

-o, to determine, decide cases (leg.) c 1108, 1587 (*see also* **audio**); to come to an end c 1250; to determine (ac.) c 1340, c 1350; (?) *for* **attermino**, to adjourn 1219; to attermine, furnish with terms for payment 1239.

termo, "leash" (falc.) 1554.
termodius, *see* **trimodius**.
termopile, *see* THERM
terna, tarn (Cumb.) 1262.
tern/arius, number three c 815. 1160, c 1450; (*adj.*) threefold c 1090; **-ario**, in three ways c 1250, 13c.; **-ales** (*pl.*), three c 700; †**-itas**, (?) *f.l.* for **trinitas**, Trinity c 1200, c 1270; **-us**, third 12c., c 1562.
†**ternis**, (?) *f.l.* for **cervis[ia]**, 1325.
ternistrator, principality (evil angel) c 730.
tero, *see* **tera**.
terpolus, *see* **tribulus**.
terr/a, country, kingdom c 790. c 1115, 14c.; piece of land, feudal holding, tenement 604, c 831. c 1067, 1532; *arable land 1086, 1583; courtyard c 1110; t. alba, (?) gypsum 1297, 1377; t. alta, high ground (above marsh) 13c.; t. aratri c 1397, c 1414, t. carruce 1086, a 1235, t. ad. carrucam 1086, carrucate; t. argentea, *see* t. sigillata; ‡t. argenti, silver litharge, ‡t. auri, golden litharge 1652; t. bipartita, t. tripartita, land worked on the two-field (three-field) system c 1290; t. bovis, t. ad bovem, bovate 1086; t. campestris c 1215, t. campestralis 1378, open (unenclosed) land; t. censaria c 1115, t. censualis 12c., 1222, gafol-land; t. certa, firm land a 1271; *t. communis (communia), common land 1086, 1613; t. ecclesiastica, church land 1086, 1253; t. familie, 'hide' c 730; t. firma, mainland 1502; t. fetida, sulphur 1144, ‡1652; ‡t. fidelis, silver 1652; ‡t. figula 1652, ‡t. figuli 14c., potter's clay; t. arti fullonum apta, fuller's earth 1326; ‡t. foliata, mercury 1652; t. forinseca, land outside manor or borough c 1150, 1288; t. franca 1095, t. libera 1086, 1378, freehold land; t. guerre, land outside the Pale (Ir.) a 1272; t. hereditaria, t. hereditatis, t. testamentalis, bocland c 1115; ‡t. Hispanica, vitriol 1652; t. laboratoria, land held by villeins (G.) p 1250; t. limosa, brick earth 1362; t. nova, newly cleared land 1292, 1375; t. operaria, 'work-land' (held by labour service) 1306, 14c.; t. pacis, land within the Pale (Ir.) c 1230, 1297; t. plena, (?) virgate (E. Angl.) 13c.; t. sicca, dry land 13c., 1275; t. sigillata a 1250, 14c., t. argentea, t. Saracenica a 1250, Lemnian

earth; *see also* **camera**, **carbo**, **finis**, **lex**, **villa**; **-e** (*pl.*) date, (allowance for) crown lands granted out 1130, a 1284; **-am tenens** 13c., 1319, **-etenens** 1334, 1418, tenant, *terretenant*; **-atenus**, on the ground c 1334;

-agium *c 1172, 1526, **tarragium** 1422, land-tax, charge for occupying ground at fair or market; tenure of land 1364; 1552, **tarragium** 1553, plot of land; 1416, 1448, **taragium** 15c., 'tarage', field, ground (of picture); **-agitor**, assessor of land-tax 1215; ‡**-aneola**, bunting (bird) 1570; **-aneus**, earthen c 1353, 1412; **-aria**, territory 1336; **-arium**, 'terrier', land-book 1316, 1326; **-arius**, (*adj.*) land-owning c 1115; (*subst.*) land-holder c 1157, c 1540; *'terrar', mon. obedientiary c 1268, c 1530; terrier (dog) 1210; **-atio**, layer of earth 1305; **-efodina**, turbary 1273; **-ella**, 'little earth', spherical magnet 1600, 1620;

-enis, *for* **-enus**, earthly c 1000. 1330; **-enus**, land-owning 1461; **-enitas** 8c. a 1250, **-estritas** 1378, earthliness; *-estreitas a 1232, a 1446, **-estrietas** a 1250, c 1270, **-estritas** a 1250, a 1270, **-eitas** c 1270, c 1345, earthiness; **-estreus**, **-estrius**, earthly c 550; ‡**herba -estris**, purslane 15c.; **murus -ester**, earthen wall 1258; **-eus**, earth-coloured p 1394, a 1446; †**-evastentius**, destroying the earth 1267;

*-icidium, **-icidia** 1277, 1555 **-escidium** 1466, †**tresidium** 12c., **turicidium** 1338, peat, turbary; **-icula** c 1250, *-ula c 700. c 1130, 1512, little estate; **-igena**, native c 1365; mainlander c 1385; c 1090, c 1325, **-igenus** 870, 935, earth-born, worldling; **-itorie** (*pl.*), territories, districts 814; **-itorium** 1489, 1553, **-ura** 1513, 'terrier', land-book; t. terre, division, district 744; **-itorius**, of or for a territory, district 1045, 12c.; **-itura** 1240, **-ura** c 1177, a 1349 territory, district;

-agio, to assess for land-tax 1402; **-ifico**, to reclaim (land) from sea 1577; **-o** 1185, 1419, **-eo** 1250, **-estro** 1419, to cover with earth, earth up or (?) daub; *see also* TARR
terratantarizatio, *see* **taratantarum**.
†**terretrum**, (?) restrictive clause 1609.
†**terretta**, prise of ale (W.) 1541; (?) *cf.* **tina**.
terribellum, *see* **teratio**.
terri/bilitas, terrifying appearance 9c. a 1142; terrible character c 1450; **ultimum -bilium** death 1408; **-bilius**, more awfully 1301; **-fice**, terribly c 1250.
terribulum, *see* **tus**.
terr/ifico, **-o**, *etc.*, *see* TERR
terrim, *see* **tarinus**.
tersegus, *see* **carsea**.
tersello, *see* **tercellus**.
tersionarius, *see* TERTI
tersorium, drying cloth, towel (esp. for feet) a 1090, 1396; place where feet are washed a 1090; *see also* **trituratio**; †**stergeo**, *for* **tergeo**, to wipe c 1290.
Tertareus, *see* 1 **Tartara**.
terti/a c 1352, 1460, **-ana** 1505, **terceria** 1282, third, third part; vessel containing ⅓ quart c 1380, c 1400; tierce (canonical hour) c 950, 1006. c 1148, 1556; **t. episcopalis**,

bishop's third (Ir.) c 1606; **feria -a,** Tuesday c 980. c 1100, c 1503; **-um,** $\frac{1}{60}$ second a 1150, 1344; **-um decimum,** a thirteenth 1419; **t. melior,** third best 1234, 1309; **-ana,** unit of land (Manx) 1527; **t. duplex,** double tertian malaria 1262; **-arius,** sufferer from tertian malaria a 1250 (*cf.* **febris**); number three c 1470; **-lis,** trine 13c.; **-odecimo,** thirteenthly 1202; **-ogenitus,** third-born 1406, c 1422; **-onarius, tersionarius** 1308, **tierchionarius** 1331, measure of grain, *tierchonnier* (C.I.); **tresellus,** measure of wine (*cf.* O.F. *tiercel*) 1240; *cf.* **tercellus.**

tertrum, (?) ridge (Lincs.) 1274.

terugena, basil (bot.) (Ar. *turungán*) 12c.

tes/a, -ia, -io, *see* **tensa.**

teseillum, wooden gag (O.F. *tesillon*) c 1172; **teissilo,** to gag 1228.

tes/elum 1434, **-ella** 1440, **tasellum fullonicum** 1334, teasel (for carding); **-o,** to tease, maul, tear to pieces 1209, 1248.

tesga, *see* **phthisis.**

tessarescedecas, set of fourteen c 730.

tessaur-, *see* THESAUR

tess/ella lignea, tile, shingle 1537; **-ellatus,** checky (her.) c 1595; **-era,** coat of arms 1654; ‡"bushel" 1483; **tacere** (*pl.*), *for* **-ere,** dice 1519; **-ara precaria,** praying bead 1605; **-erarius,** heraldic 1654; ‡**t. ludus,** "chess" 1570; *see also* **testa.**

tesso, *see* **taxus.**

tessu-, *see* TEX

test/a capitis c 1175, 15c., **-ula** c. c 1200, skull *or* crown of head; **t. ovi** a 1250, **-ula o.** c 1212, egg-shell; **t. lecti** 1420, **-erium** 1338, **-erum** 1438, **-orium** 1415, **-rum** 1386, ***-ura** 1371, c 1443, 'tester', canopy (for bed); **tessera,** canopy c 1550; **-aria** 1213, **-arium** 1303, 1322, **-era** 1214, 1301, 'tester', head-piece, head-stall (for horses); **-agium,** poll-tax (Ir.) c 1284; †**-ua,** earthenware pot c 1100.

testament/um, charter c 1115; proof 1570; heriot c 1250; **rectitudo -i,** *bocriht* c 1115; **servus -alis,** slave c 1115; **terra -alis,** *bocland* c 1115; **-arie,** by testament *or* bequest (leg.) 1291, 15c.; **-arium,** treatise ɔn testaments c 1300; **-arius,** executor (leg.) 1257; ‡**-or,** to make a testament 1483.

test/atio, bequest c 1170; **-ator,** witness 1332; **-antius,** with clearer evidence 1378; **-antissimus,** most convincing c 1090; **-idictio,** witnessing c 1432; **-ifer,** witness c 1430; **-ificatio,** Testimony (theol.) c 730, 1062; **-ificatorius,** bearing witness c 1374; **-imoniale** 1298, ***littere -imoniales** 1202, 1559, testimonial, letters of attestation; **-imonium,** text, extract, passage 893; compurgation (leg.) c 1067; knowledge, foreknowledge c 1115; character, repute 1166, 1558; bequest, last testament c 1290, 15c.; celestial power (astr.) 1230; **-is,** compurgator (leg.) c 1115; **-ifico** c 780, c 1040. 1198, 1331, **-o** 1293, to give evidence concerning, bear witness to; **-imonio,** to witness a document c 1077, a 1100; **-o,** to bequeath c 1290, a 1446; to attest 1199, c 1370; *see also* TAST

testicul/us, orchis (bot.) 1634; 'ballock',

leaden weight (of draw-bridge) 1366; **-ata** (*f.*), mannish, domineering c 1180.

testo, testooñ (coin) 1608; *see also* **testatio.**

test/udo, protection c 790; body of men in close formation 893; c 1177, 14c., **-itudo** a 1446, snail; **t. sancte crucis** 947, 993, **-itudo s. crucis** 12c., protective sign or shield of the cross; **-itudo,** *for* **-udo,** vaulted roof c 1220, c 1468; **-udinalis,** vaulted a 1100; ‡**-udino,** to vault c 1440.

test/ula, -ua, -ura, *see* **testa.**

teta, dove, c 700.

tetanus, spasm: **thetinos/itas,** straining, stretching a 1250, 13c.; **-us,** tetanic a 1250.

tetchellatus, *see* **techellatus.**

tet/er, obscure c 1370; ‡**-ritudo,** darkness 1483; **-rico,** (? *f.l.* in *Ecclesiasticus* 32. 15) to be cross, ill-tempered c 1200, c 1325.

***tething/a** c 1125, c 1300, **-us** 1281, 1287, **tedinga** (thed-) c 1160, 1280, **thedginga** (Sc.) c 1265, **theghinga** 1281, **teitinga** 1189, **theothinga** c 1219, **teothunga** c 1200, **tewinga** 1269, **thuinga** 13c., **thuthinga** c 1258, (?) **tutina** 1376, **tithinga** c 1250, a 1600, **tyddinga** 1169, 1215, †**trithinga** 1276, c 1436, †**retinga** 1215, tithing, frankpledge group *or* division of hundred, suit at view of frankpledge; **visus -arum,** view of frankpledge 1189, 1287; **-mannus** 1234, 1264, **thedigmannus** 1201, **thegingmannus** 1275, **thuingmannus** 13c., **thuthingmannus, tuthinmannus** 1275, **tuthemannus** c 1250, **caput thethinge** 1221, tithingman, headborough; *cf.* **decenna, trithingum.**

Tethys (? *or* **Thetis**), ocean: **Tedis** 14c., **Tith/is, -on, Titon** c 550; **-icus, Titicus,** of the ocean c 550.

tetr/a, (*adj., n. pl.*) four 685; (*subst.*) tetrad 13c.; **-acubitus,** four cubits long a 1232; **-agonalitas, respectus -agonus,** quadrature, quartile aspect (astr.) c 1150; **-agonaliter,** in the form of a quadrangle a 1200; **-agonus,** tetragonal, four-angled *or* four-sided 870, 930. 13c., 1253; (*subst.*) quadrangle c 1362, c 1457; **t. longus,** oblong rectangle a 1150; **-agrammaton,** tetragram, four-lettered name of God c 730. c 1190, c 1452; **-ahedrum,** tetrahedron 1267, 1564; **-angulum,** quadrangle c 790; **-ans,** quarter (her.) 1654; **-apolis,** group of four towns c 1090; **-ardus,** interval of four notes, fourth mode in plain-song (mus.) a 1100, c 1200; **-aspurius,** fourfold bastard c 1434; **-astichum** 1518, **-asticon** c 900, quatrain; **-asyllabicum** 1267, **-as** a 1400, word of four syllables; **-archizo** a 1100, ‡**-arco** 15c., to rule.

‡**tetra/hit, -hicus,** hemp-nettle (bot.) 14c.

†**tetrex,** (?) *for* **tetrao,** large bird, (?) goose c 550.

tetrico, *see* **teter.**

teuda, *see* **teldum.**

Teutonic/us (Teotonic-, Theotonic-), German c 1118, 1502; Teutonic knight 1235, 1389; 1307, 1419, **Tutannicus** 1456, Hanse merchant; (?) dull-witted 12c.; **-e,** in German 1243; in German fashion c 1290; in Anglo-Saxon *or* Norse 1041.

tewinga, *see* **tethinga.**

tex/tator a 1449, tixtor 1225, 1338, tissutor 1285, *for* -tor, weaver; -tor, (?) *for* tector, thatcher c 1195, 1316; ‡t. stragularius, coverlet-weaver 1520; -toria 1422, -torium c 1200, loom; -trilis, of or for weaving c 1125, c 1400; opus -trine, weaving c 1090; tixtura, weaving, web 1297; tissutum 1284, 1300, tissuum 1433, tessutum c 1520, tissue, fabric; tessua, (?) piece of webbing 1286; -tualia (*pl.*), textual matters 1431; littera -tualis, text hand 1378, 1464; -tualiter, textually c 1317; -tuarius, gospel-book c 1432; -tus, text, content, terms c 730, 798; *text, passage, treatise c 1100, c 1540; written document, charter 12c.; 801. c 1080, 1479, t. Evangelici c 1363, t. Evangelicus c 1334, 1383, t. Evangelii c 1100, 1404, book of the gospels, gospel book; -entes, Weavers (Albigensian sect) c 1308; †-o, (?) to upholster with tapestry 1251; -o, (?) *for* tego, to cover c 1390; -to 1419, ‡1483, tixo 1264, *for* -o, to weave.
teylagium, *see* 2 tallia.
th-, *see also* t-
Thaan, *see* Chanus.
thac/bordum, bordus -kus, b. -gus, thack-board (arch.) 1355.
thach-, *see* TACH
thacio, *see* 2 taccum.
thain-, *see* THAN
Thai/s (Tays), harlot c 1195, ‡1483; -do, -o, to play the harlot c 1180.
thalam/us, treasury c 1190; council 1378; crop, gizzard c 1200; chamber of heart c 1200; t. secretus, privy 1306; ‡-ista, chamberlain 1483.
thalass/a, sea: talasus c 550; talesicus, talisicus, of the sea c 550; -iarcha, high admiral 1586.
thaler, German dollar 1608, 1671.
*than/us 1086, 1586, tanus c 1160, c 1225, thainus c 1115, 1200, tainus a 1086, 1130, tahinus 13c., †tarcinus a 1087, tagnus 1086, tamnus c 1414, tegnio 12c., tegnus 1086, c 1117, teignus 1086, theignus 1203, theingus 1196, teinus 1086, 1178, *theinus c 1139, 1229, thenus c 1200, -aus 1528, thainetus (Sc.) c 1130, 15c., †the-ningus 1199, thingus 1336, dingus 1086, phengus 1335, thane, thegn; -agium 1137, 1460, thainagium 1212, 1359, teinagium 1177, theinagium 1183, c 1211, thena-gium 1200, 1212, tenagium 1309, thanage; -landa 1086, teglanda 1086, theinlanda 1080, teinlanda a 1100, thaneland.
thapsus, mullein (bot.) 13c., 1634; t. bar-batus a 1250, taxus b. 1538.
thaumatopeetica 1564, ‡thamatica 1652, hydraulics; tamaxo, to marvel (θαυμάζω) c 550.
thearchi/a, divinity 870; divine rule 870. 1344; -cus, beginning from God 870; †theartichus (? *for* -cus), of the kingdom of God c 1200.
theatr/um, spectacle c 1199; platform c 1450; -ica, stagecraft 13c.
Thebet, Tibetans 1267.
theca (teca), *money-box 12c., 1524; letter-bag c 960; coffin c 810. c 1087, 14c.; tomb c 1000; corporas case 1448; ‡thimble c 1200,

1483; 1502, 1517, t. linea c 1266, c 1330, ‡t. culcitaria 1570, teia 1208, 'tay', pillow-case *or* bed-ticking; *cf.* tiketum; t. cochlea, nut (of screw) 1686; †cetha, †scetha, *for* t., book-case 10c.
thed/inga, theghinga, etc., *see* tethinga.
thein-, theign-, then-, *see* THAN
theleton, thing willed (θελητόν) 1344.
thelhindus, *see* twelfhindus.
them/a, text of sermon c 1250, 15c.; -atice, by way of text c 1470; *see also* tema.
themannetala, *see* tenemannetala.
themesis, *see* tmesis.
thenecium, *see* 1 caputium.
theo/dochus, receptive of God 870; -doctus, God-taught 12c.
Theodor/icum (-itum), a purgative a 1250.
theodum (teodum) c 1200, 1283, thoytum 1252, tudum 13c., twedum 1199, 13c., *tuath*, district (Ir.).
†theoficus, kind of lizard 13c.
theogenesia, divine birth 870.
*theolog/ia 12c., c 1502, -ica 13c., theology; -ice, theologically 1267, c 1363; -icus, *theological 12c., 1518; c 1362, *-us c 1190, 1559, ‡-ista 1483, theologian; -aster, paltry theologian 1552, c 1670; -izatio, theo-logical quibble a 1361; -izo c 1270, 1427, ‡-ico, -or 1483, to argue theologically.
theolon-, *see* telo.
theomach/us, adversary of God c 1400, 1620; -a, witch 12c., c 1325; -ia, war against God 1620.
theophan/ia, manifesting of God 870. 12c.; Epiphany (6 Jan.) c 730. a 1100, c 1325; -icus, declaring God c 1200.
theophilus, God-lover c 1000.
theor/ia, vision, contemplation a 615, 9c. a 1100, c 1270; *c 990. c 1140, 1484, *-ica 12c., c 1565, speculation, theory; -euma 1326, †-emna 1378, *for* -ema, theorem, maxim; -etice, theoretically c 1470; -ice, by contemplation a 1275; -icus, *specula-tive a 1180, c 1375; c 1000. c 1170, 14c., -asticus c 790, contemplative; vita -ica, contemplative life c 1000, 1024. 12c.; -izo, to engage in speculation, contemplate 870; -o, to look at c 1258.
the/os c 1112, c 1370, -us 8c., 11c. 12c., God; -osis, deification 870; -osebia 12c., -usebia a 1142, worship.
theosoph/ia, knowledge of God 12c., c 1270; -icus c 1270, -us c 950. 15c., divinely in-spired; -us, (*subst.*) theologian 870. 12c., c 1270; -o, to teach divine wisdom c 1270.
theothinga, *see* tethinga.
theotoc/os c 974. 1345, 1413, -hus 870, thotocos c 1125, mother of God.
Theotonicus, *see* Teutonicus.
thepa, *see* cepa.
Therapeute (*pl.*), members of an ascetic order 1238, 1427.
theraphim, *see* teraphim.
theriac/a 1345, ‡1652, -um c 1420, tiriac/a (tyriac-) c 550. c 1200, 1480, -is c 1000, -um c 1190, theriac, antidote, electuary, 'treacle'; t. selithe a 1250; t. magna a 1250; tiria c 1200, tirus a 1250, ‡15c., a venomous snake; theriotrophium, game park c 1595.
therm/ealis, thermal 1385; -ometrum,

thermometer 1686; **-opile** (*pl.*), (?) defence-work, stronghold c 550.

†**thernebedellus**, beadle summoning suitors to county and hundred courts (Somerset) 1189; (?) *cf.* **tornus** *or* **tremura**.

thesaur/us, Court of Exchequer c 1110; 1130, c 1290, ***t. inventus** c 1115; c 1448, **t. repertus** a 1088, **-i inventio** c 1106, 1169, treasure-trove; **-um**, *for* **-us**, treasure a 805. 1276, c 1400; **-aria**, treasuress (mon.) 1422; ***c 1090, 1457, **thezauraria** c 1370, **-arium** c 1250, 1419, **-ia** 1224, 1419, **tresoria** c 1308, treasury *or* sacristy; a 1142, 15c., **-ariatus** c 1336, 1428, **-iatus** 1418, office of treasurer *or* sacrist; ***-arius** 1086, 1583, **teszaurarius** a 1278, **thesorarius** 1322, **treserarius** 1283, **-ator** (*met. grat.*) a 1410, **-izarius** c 1200, 1395, **tessaurius** 13c., treasurer *or* sacrist; *see also* **pars**; **t. Anglie** c 1290, c 1443; ***t. regis** 1192, 1431; **t. summus** 1415, c 1459; **-abiliter**, as a treasure c 1370; **-izatio** laying up treasure c 1334; ***-izo**, to lay up treasure a 1100, c 1430.

theshindus, *see* **twelfhindus**.

thesis, placing 1177, †14c.; thesis, scientific question *or* proposition c 1160, c 1549.

thestrum, *see* **thistrum**.

theta, (as initial of θάνατος) death a 1100, 13c.

thetinos-, *see* **tetanus**.

Thetis, *see* **Tethys**.

theus, theusebia, *see* **theos**.

theya, *see* **tensa**.

‡**thia, tia**, maternal aunt (θεία) c 1440.

thifhindus, thithindus, *see* **twihindus**.

thillum, 'thill', cart-shaft 1324.

thinctha, *see* **gethinctha**.

thing/emannus, Danish soldier, house-carl c 1115.

thingus, *see* **thanus**.

thinus, *see* **thyinus**.

‡**thisma**, vein or gallery of mine 1652.

thistrum 1303, 1379, **thestrum, sistrum** 1325, part of plough-harness (iron).

tholl/um 1321, 1419, **-ium** 1419, thole-pin (naut.).

tholus, dome: **tolum** c 550, †**trullus** c 1188, †**tuleus** c 1400.

Thom/ipeta, pilgrim to St. Thomas c 1180; **-isonans**, calling on St. Thomas c 1180; **-ista**, Thomist (phil.) 1517, 1523; **-istice**, Thomistically 1523; **-isticus**, Thomistic 1523, 1555.

thomus, *see* **tomus**.

thor-, *see also* **tor-**

†**thoracicl/a, -us** c 700, †**torricula** c 550, (?) bust, torso; **toracus**, cuirass 12c.

thornacra, acre of spinney 1353.

thorpus, thorpe 12c.

Thoth, September c 1015; **Thoz**, Hermes a 1200.

thotocos, *see* **theotocos**.

thoytum, *see* **theodum**.

thraa, *see* **traha**.

‡**thrapneus**, purified medicine 1652.

thrascias, north-west wind: **threscias** 870.

Thras/o (Tras-), type of a braggart c 1200; **-onior**, more boastful than Thraso c 1200.

thrav/a (trav-) 1098, p 1478, **-is** 12c., 1249, **-us** 1343, **traba** 1249, 1338, **trabs** 1086, **treva**

1242, (?) **estrava** c 1280, thrave, measure of corn; **t. turbarum** 1282, 1361; *see also* TRAB

thren/a, dirge, throe c 1346, c 1414; ***-i** (*pl.*), *Book of Lamentations* 12c., c 1452; ‡**-osus**, lamentable 1483.

threngus, *see* **drengus**.

threscias, *see* **thrascias**.

thrimsum, coin (A.S. *þrimsa*) c 1115.

thriplus, *see* **tripes**.

throcc/um (trok-), 'throck', plough-head, 'chep' *or* share-beam 1303; **-atio**, fitting (plough) with throck 1365, 1367; **-o** (†**chroko**), to fit with a throck 1351, 1364.

thromb/us, globe ‡14c.; **trumbus**, clot (med.) a 1250; ‡**-osus**, globular, 14c.; **trumbosus**, clotted a 1250.

thron/us (tron-), episcopal throne c 1100, c 1125; **t. gracie**, (apostolic) throne of grace c 1317; **-i** (*pl.*), 'Thrones' (angelic powers) a 975. c 1123, c 1250; **-eus**, of the 'Thrones' 1497; **-izatio**, enthronement 1331, 1505; **-izo**, to enthrone 1331, 1433.

throsnum, *see* TRON

throtebolla, Adam's apple, larynx (A.S. *þrotbolla*) c 1115.

thrucha 1337, **trosca** c 1315, thrush (bird).

thrya, *see* **tia**.

thuing-, *see* **tethinga**.

thuista, *see* **twista**.

thumelum, thumb, measure of thickness (of fat) (A.S. *þymele*) c 1115.

thupetum, *see* **tuppetum**.

thur-, *see also* **tus**.

†**thurlio**, (?) to drill *or* dig up c 1300.

thuthing/a, -mannus, *see* **tethinga**.

thuuf, *see* **tufa**.

thyelfindus, *see* **twelfhindus**.

thygater (tigater, tegater), daughter (θυγάτηρ) c 550.

thyinus, of juniper wood: **thinus** c 730.

thymallus, fish, (?) grayling c 1191, c 1200; ‡**simallus**, "sparling" 15c.

thymiam/a, incense (bibl.); **-aterium**, censer (bibl.).

thymus, thyme: **timus**, (?) **simus** c 1200.

tia, 'tye', water-conduit (in stannary) 1389; †**thrya pro aqua bullente** 1478; **tya**, (?) trough or box (Salop.) 1259; *see also* **thia**.

tiara, mitre (eccl.) 1150, 1562.

tiasis, *see* **ischia**.

tibi/a, fur from (lambs') shanks 1361, 1433; twig, shoot 1282; part of astr. instrument 1326; 1332, 1384, **tebia** 1374, shank of fulling-mill; **t. cultri** (of plough) 1285, 1304; **t. pneumatica**, organ-pipe 1565; **arbalista ad -am**, sort of crossbow 1418; **tubia**, *for* **-a**, shin 1381, 1478; **-alia** (*pl.*), shin armour 1325, 1374; **-ola**, little pipe c 1620; ‡**-osus**, "great-legged" 1570; **-o** (= **citharizo**) 8c.

tibracus c 730, **trib/ucus** 1342, stocking, legging; ‡**-racca**, "breech girdle" 15c., 1483.

ticesco, *see* **tacentia**.

ticnum, *see* TIG

tid/a 1315, 15c., **-us** 1253, tide (of sea); **t. fluvialis** 1430; **-a**, turn, spell 1326.

tienmannatala, *see* **tenemannetala**.

tierchionarius, *see* TERTI

tigater, *see* **thygater**.

tig/illum, label (her.) 1654; **tegillum**, beam

c 550; "rail" 1627; **-na, tegna** c 550, **ticnum** 13c., *for* **-num**; **-nus, tingus,** pail-yoke 1308.
tigrus, striped 13c.
tigul-, *see* TEGUL
tihindus, *see* **twihindus.**
tihtla (tihla), charge, accusation (leg.) (A.S.) c 1115.
tiketum, bed-ticking 1515; *cf.* **theca.**
tilda, *see* **teldum.**
tilia, lime-tree: **tela** 1287.
tillagium, tillage 1532.
tilliator, *see* ATTILL
†**tilo,** (?) to pluck (τίλλω) 1271.
timarr/ia, land-holding, **-iota, -us,** land-holder (Turkish) 1608.
timb/er 1086, **-ra** 1242, 1373, **-ria, -rium** c 1150, 1444, **tembria** 1244, **-rum** 1275, 1303, **tymerium** 1444, 'timber' of fur (bundle of 40 skins).
timbr/a (tymbr-), 'timbre', timbrel c 1200; **-ea** 1335, (?) 1342, **-ia** 1339, 'timbre', crest (her.).
timerarie, *see* **temerarie.**
timid/us, terrifying c 1436; **-ulus,** rather timid 1497; **temens,** fearing 1382; **timo-r/ate,** reverently c 1197, 1250; **-atus,** frightened 685, c 900. p 1340; *God-fearing a 1130, c 1450; **-ifer,** frightening c 1115; **-ose,** timorously a 1452; **-osus,** timorous 13c., c 1457; formidable a 1250; **-o,** to be timorous c 1200; to frighten c 1316.
timo, *see* **temo.**
timocratia, timocracy c 1343.
†**timodos,** fever without much heat (? θερμώ-δης) a 1250.
timpus, *see* **tempus.**
timus, *see* **thymus.**
*tin/a a 1135, 1419, **-ea** 1245, **tena** c 1360, 1403, 'tine', cask, tub; 1188, 1330, **t. cervisie** 1256, 1327, **t. castri** 1323, 1403, prise of ale paid by townsmen to constable (Gloucester & Bristol); ‡**-arium** 15c., 1483, **-ellus** c 1218, 1275, **-ulus** 1303, cowl-staff (for carrying buckets, *etc.*) (O.F. *tinier, tinel*); **-ata,** tubful 1185, 1299; **-etta** 1326, 1398, **-ellum** c 1182, small tub (O.F. *tinette, tinel*); *cf.* **tenellus, tonna;** *see also* **tena.**
tinaculus, *see* TUNIC
tin/car 1144, ‡**-kaar** 1652, **atincar** c 1215, ‡1652, tincal, borax.
tinct/io, baptism 8c. 14c.; dipping 8c. c 1196; coloration a 1250; staining c 1266, c 1330; 1455, 1520, *-ura** 1279, 1523, **-uratio** 1337, dyeing; **-ura,** dye-stuff 1278; coloration 1252; *transmutation (alch.) 1144, 1470; **-us,** (?) neutral colour paint 1275; *-or a 1123, 1524, **tingtor** 1286, **teintor** 1196, **teintarius** 1185, 1214, **-uarius** 1175, c 1250, **-urarius** 1201, **teinturarius** c 1200, dyer; ‡**herba -oris,** woad 15c.; **-oria** 1261, 1441, **-orium** c 1200, 1306, †**tuntorium** c 1302, **tyngtorium** 1357, **tingtaria** 1271, dye-works; ‡**-ars -oria,** "dyer's craft" 1520; ‡**-o** 1483, **-uro** 1337, to dye; **tingo,** *to transmute (alch.) 1144, c 1320; to baptize (eccl.); *see also* **lancea, tentio.**
tind/a, tine, tooth (of harrow) 1297, 1406; **-o** 1318, 1406, **tineo** 1387, to fit (harrows) with teeth.

tine/a c 1060. a 1250, ‡14c. (?) †**tiria, tirra** 13c., ring-worm (med.); **-osus,** one infested with worms or ringworm 12c., a 1250.
tin/ellum, -ellus, -etta, *see* **tina.**
tinentia, *see* **tenentia.**
tineo, *see* TIND
tin/ettum 1450, **-sellum** (?) 14c., **-sillum** 1374, 'tinnet', 'tinsel', brushwood.
tineus, *see also* Titan; **tinneum.**
ting-, *see* **tigillum; tinct-**
tin/neum, tin 1486; **boxa -ea,** tin box 1549.
tinnipo, to crow c 1315.
tinnitum, *see* **tintinnum.**
tin/olus, -ulus, shrill c 550.
tin/sellum, -sillum, *see* **tinettum.**
†**tinsurus,** (?) *for* **tonitruosus,** thundering c 550.
tintachus, *see* TURK
tintin/num c 1115, **-nus** 8c., †**tinnitum** 13c., **-abile** 15c., **-abilum** ‡15c., 1472, *for* **-nabulum,** bell; **-arius,** "tinker" 1486; **tintillatio,** ringing c 1302.
tinulus, *see* **tina; tinolus.**
tinura, *see* **tenetura.**
tiolonium, *see* **telo.**
tipet/um, tippet (of hood) 1342, c 1565; **-atus,** having a tippet c 1365.
†**tiprum,** sort of vessel or utensil 6c.
tipsana, *see* **ptisina.**
tip/ulator 1391, 1553, **-lator** 1539, **-pilator** 1603, 'tippler', retailer of ale and wine; †**tirpillatrix,** ale-wife 1547; **domus -ula-toria,** ale-house 1661; **-lo** 1371, **-ulo** 1507, to 'tipple', keep an ale-house.
tir/a, tier, row (of furs) 1301, 1397; **-um,** row (of pig-lead) 1228; *see also* **tera.**
tiratantrum, *see* **taratantarum.**
Tiresio, to change sex c 1200.
tiria/, -ca, -cum, *see* THERIAC; **tinea.**
tiriones, *see* **septem.**
1 tir/o (tyr-), squire, aspirant to knighthood 1252, 1461; 6c., **-uncula** 685, soldier, champion; **-ocinium,** (conferment of) knighthood a 1260; tournament c 1180, c 1400; ‡**-onia,** knighthood c 1440.
2 tiro (†ciro), (?) to tug, wrench (Fr. *tirer*) (G.) 1283.
tirpillatrix, *see* TIP
tirra, *see* **tinea.**
tirretena 1285, **pannus tyrtenus** 1305, **p. tirtannus** 1331, cloth of wool mixed with cotton or linen (Fr. *tiretaine*); *cf.* **2 tartara, tarentinillum.**
tirum, *see* **tera, tira.**
tis/is, -icus, *see* **phthisis.**
†**tispecialis,** (?) *f.l.* for **trispecialis,** of three species 1283.
tisso, *see* **taxus.**
tissu-, *see* TEX
Titan/, sun 6c., 8c. 1136, 15c.; **-eus,** (?) †**ti-neus,** solar c 550; ‡**-ia,** moon 1483.
tithinga, *see* **tethinga.**
tith/ingarius, -ringum, *see* **trithingum.**
Tith/is, -on, -icus, *see* **Tethys.**
titillares vene, veins under arm-pits c 1210, a 1250.
1 titi/o, fire-wood 10c.; fire-brand (fig.) c 1170; "coal-pit" 15c.; †**sticiones,** (?) incendiary masses c 1227; ‡**-onarium,** hearth 1483.

2 titio, to twitter c 1200.
Titivillus, a tale-bearing demon a 1408, c 1430.
titlinga, titling, warbler 1544.
Titon, *see* **Tethys.**
titul/us, title (eccl.) 787. 1125, 1686; *title, claim, right (leg.) c 1170, 1560; headship c 760; heading, section c 1125, c 1350; chief (her.) c 1595; **t. sancte crucis,** sign of the cross 956, c 1065; **-aris,** titular 1610; **-ate,** under headings c 815; **-atim,** name by name 964; **-atio,** inscribing, entering a title 9c.; letter c 990; **-o,** to inscribe, make an entry c 980, 1031. 12c., 1419; to head, serve as preface to c 815; to divide into sections c 1115, c 1300; to indicate as chief c 1115; to ascribe 12c., c 1400; 1006, c 1160, 1426, †**tutelo** c 760, to nominate to a benefice (eccl.).
Titus, type of a generous giver 1241.
tityrus, offspring of sheep and goat a 1446; ‡bell-wether 15c.
tix-, *see* TEX
tlefhindus, *see* **twelfhindus.**
tmesis (gram.): **themesis** c 1200.
toagium, *see* TOW
toall-, toaill-, tobal-, *see* TUALL
tobaccum, tobacco 1612.
tobba, *see* **tubba.**
‡**tobir,** rosemary (bot.) 14c.
tochium, *see* **ptochotropheum.**
tockagium, *see* TOW
todda, 'tod' (of wool) 1516, 1599.
†**todina gracilitas,** (?) extreme thinness c 1180.
toft/a 1086, c 1395, *-um c 1150, 1573, **tophtum** c 1180, **-us** 1199, c 1400, **touftum** c 1160, **tufta** a 1200, **tuftum** 13c., †**tuptum** c 1200, toft, house-site; **-arius** 1279, **-mannus** 13c., **-londus** 1316, tenant of toft; **-landa,** toft-land 1222.
tog/a, *outer garment, gown c 1386, 1504; cassock (eccl.) 1425, 1686; assembly 1511; **t. longa,** gown (ac.) c 1452, c 1565; **t. pro nocte,** dressing gown 1525; **-atus,** civil, in civil life c 1125, c 1450.
togale, togell/a, -us, *see* TUALL
togwithum, *see* **tuggum.**
tol/botha 1229, 1336, **-butha** 1378, tolbooth, jail.
tolcester, *see* **tolsextarium.**
toldum, *see* **teldum.**
toler/antia, continuance, long-suffering c 730; toleration c 1343, c 1444; relaxation (of statute) 1400; **-o,** to persevere c 730.
tol/es, -is, limb c 550.
toletum, (?) grate, fire-iron 13c., 1324.
tol/fatum 1222, 1297, **-vatis** 13c., 1298, 'toll-vat', 'tovet', measure of grain (? half-bushel) paid as multure; **-hopa, -opum,** 'toll-hoop', measure of grain c 1258, 1267.
†**tol/ia, -ea** (?) throat 6c.
toll-, *see also* **telo.**
†**tollatus,** (?) *f.l.* for **collatus,** c 1290.
tollus, full stream, cataract c 550, c 700.
toln-, tolon-, *see* **telo.**
tolo, *see* **3 tela.**
tolopum, *see* **tolfatum.**
Tolosanus, coin of Toulouse 1315.
tolpacius, *see* **topazius.**

tol/selda 1352, **-setum** 1349, **-sonetum** 1600, **-situm** 1517, 'tolsey', court-house; **curia Tolseti** 1518, 1523, **c. Tolsedie** 1438, Tolsey Court (Bristol); *cf.* **telo.**
tol/sextarium c 1160, **-sexterium** c 1250, 1308, **-sester** 1232, 14c., **-cester** 1275, 1312, **-syster** 1398, toll of one sester (on ale).
tolta, writ removing plea into county court 1294, 15c.; *illegal exaction 1201, c 1320; *see also* **malatolta.**
tolum, *see* **tholus.**
tolvatis, *see* **tolfatum.**
Toma, the Lord c 550.
tomb/erellum, -orella, -rellum, *see* **tumberellum.**
tomentum, stuffing for cushion: ‡**tumentum,** "nap", "burl" 15c.; ‡**tormentum,** mattress a 1520.
tomicata, *see* **telo.**
tom/us (thom-), tome, book *or* letter c 1362; (?) literary flourish c 1359.
†**tona,** (?) township, vill 1221; *see also* **zona.**
ton/ale, -arius, *see* **tonus.**
tonaliter, *see* **tanaliter.**
Tonans, *see* **tonitru.**
tond-, *see* TONS
tonegalla, *see* **cogallus.**
tonell-, tonerium, *see* **tonna.**
tonic/a, -ula, *see* TUNIC
tonitr/u 870, **-uus** c 1188, 1502, thunder; **-ualis** 685, c 1000, **-uosus** c 550. 15c., thundery, thundrous; **-um,** peal c 600; ‡rattle 1570; **Tonans,** God c 780, 957. c 1170, 1252; ‡**tonito,** to rattle 1570.
tonizatio, *see* **tonus.**
ton/na a 1142, 1577, **tunna** 790. c 1404, c 1490, **-nula** 1473, **-ella** 1390, *-ellus, **-ellum** c 1115, c 1494, **tunella** c 1160, **tunellus** 1198, 1327, †**tenellus** 1277, tun, cask; *cf.* **2 tina; -ellus,** Tun, London prison 1296; bird-trap 1328; *-agium,** tonnage, wine duty 1404, 1606 (*see also* **telo**); **t. cervisie** 1270; **-ellata,** caskful 1195; **-erium,** 'tunner', funnel 1290; **tunno,** to 'tun', put into tuns (?) 14c.
tonnutum, *see* **telo.**
tonsa, oar: **tunsa** c 550.
†**tonsilla,** (?) for **Scylla,** the bird *ciris* c 700.
tons/io c 1200, 1534, **toncio** a 1300, 1506, shearing (of sheep); shearing (of cloth) 1326, a 1564; cutting, mowing 826. a 1180, 1434; chastening c 730; clipping (of coins) c 1298; **toyso,** fleece (Fr. *toison*) 1265;
-ura, shearing (of cloth) 1188, 1391; mowing 1450, 1550; clipping of trees 1573; *clipping (of coins), clippings (*coll.*) from coins 1221, 15c.; *c 730, c 1000. c 1100, c 1450, †**-a** 1252, clerical tonsure; **accipio -uram,** to profess (as monk) c 730; **-or,** cloth-shearer, shearman 1314, 1416; c 1250, 1437, **-ator** 1375, coin-clipper; **-orator,** (?) barber 1086; **-oria** 1286, ‡**-orium** 1483, barber's shop; **-oratio** a 1100, 1328, **-uratio** 1425, bestowal of tonsure; **-a,** shorn sheep c 1197;
-o 1327, 1385, **-oro** c 1298, **tondeo** 1280, 1340, to clip (coins); c 1330, *-oro c 826, c 1000 c 1125, c 1436, **-uro** 1235, 1456, **tondeo** 9c. 1202, to tonsure (eccl.); **tondeo,** to shear (nap off cloth) 1352, 1506; to trim

(timber) 1232; **t. digitos,** to pare nails c 1330; **tondo,** to cut (hair) c 1340; **tundeo,** *for* **tondeo,** to shear 1277; *see also* **tunsio.**

†**tonstrum, mestum,** (?) pang of grief c 550.

†**tonsus,** (?) a shade of blue 1463.

ton/us, tone, interval (mus.) 870. c 1182, c 1470; **-ale** c 1350, 1368, **-arius** c 1400, 'tonal', book or table of musical rules (eccl.); **-izatio,** intonation (mus.) c 1400.

top/azius 1245, a 1275, **-acius** c 1135, c 1315, **tolpacius** 1294, **-asius** 1528, **-azium** c 826, **-azion** c 1196, 1451, **-asion** c 1476, **-ax** 1215, topaz; (*adj.*) **-azius** c 1125, c 1325, **-asius** c 1325, of topaz.

topcastellum, topcastle (naut.) 1353.

tophtum, *see* TOFT

top/icus c 1366, 1622, **-icalis** c 1343, 'topical', based on general considerations (log.); **-ice,** on a basis of probability (log.) 1380; aptly c 1200; **-ographia,** topography c 1188, c 1400; **-ographicus,** topographic c 1553.

topp/a (*pl.*), toppings (of trees) 1535, 1545; **-o,** to top (trees) 1574.

toracus, *see* **thoracicla.**

toral (thoral) c 1182, **Thorah** a 1205, the Law (Heb. *torah*).

***toral/e** (thoral-) a 1183, 1460, **-is** c 1265, **-lia** 1335, **-lium** a 1250, 1275, **-lus** a 1183, c 1360, **torellum** 1283, 1325, **turaillia** c 1198, **turallia** c 1210, a 1250, **turallium** c 1220, **turella** 1305, 1330, **turellum** 1232, 1327, **turriolum** 1255, 1342, malt-kiln (Fr. *touraille*); **-e** 1326, c 1380, **turrellum** 1325, **turriolum calcis** 1336, lime-kiln; **-e,** tile-kiln 1439; **torellio** 1315, **torello** 1300, to dry in a kiln; *cf.* **torredula;** *see also* **torus.**

torb-, *see* 1 **turba.**

†**torca,** quantity of hides c 1423.

torch/a 1290, 1385, ***-ea, -ia** 1220, 1441, **-eus, -ius** c 1350, c 1450, †**tercius** 1284, **-eta** 1420, c 1464, **-isius** 1399, (?) **torcia** c 1115, **torg/a** 1404, **-ia** 1352, 1399, **tort/a** 12c., 1430, **-era** 1415, **-essa** 1454, ***-ex** 1292, 1474, **-ica** 1275, 1447, **turtica** 1274, **-icus** c 1327, c 1472, ***-icius, -icium** c 1290, c 1522, **-isius** 1287, 1397, **-iculus** 1331, **-ura** 1290, **-us** 15c., torch, 'tortis', large candle; **-ia de candela** 1220.

torch/aria 1289, **-iaria** 1318, **-eria** 1360, **-ura** 1301, plastering; **-arius** 1287, **-iator** 1212, c 1432, **torgator** 1286, **torgetor** 1274, dauber, plasterer; **-io** c 1219, c 1324, **-o** 1362, to daub, plaster; **torco,** to wipe down (cattle) c 1290.

tor/cia c 1320, **-sia** a 1186, embankment (on Loire); *see also* **torcha.**

torc/ula c 1235, **-lear** 1129, *for* **-ular,** wine-press; **-ular(e),** cider-press 1185, 1412; torture 1290, c 1443; **-ulatus,** "writhen" (of silver-work) 1468.

torell-, *see* **taurus; torale; torus;** TURR

tor/ettus, -illus, *see* **turettus.**

torg/a, -ia, *see* **torcha.**

torg/ator, -etor, *see* **torcharia.**

torkeyno, to rack *or* (?) 'turken' (cloth) 1375.

torment/um 1535, 1694, **turmentum** 1572, gun, fire-arm; ‡species of plant 14c.; †**-iolum,** pistol 1570; **pulvis -alis** 1573, **p. -arius** 1577, 1686, gunpowder; **-arius,** (?) gunner 1623; **-ularius,** gunsmith

1561; **-illa** a 1250, ‡1483, ‡**dormen-tilla** 13c., tormentil (bot.); **-o,** to torment 1136, c 1450; to hurl from an engine c 1310; *see also* **tomentum, tornamentum.**

†**tormovela,** gate, bar 7c.

torn/amentum, (?) windlass a 1200; c 1197, 1380, ***-eamentum** c 1192, 1586, ***-iamen-tum** c 1125, 1508, **-eimentum** c 1196, **-ementum** c 1219, **tournamentum** a 1347, **turnamentum** 1342, **turneamentum** 1220, 1508, **turniamentum** a 1135, 1347, **turneiamentum** 1198, **tormentum** c 1180, 1387, **-agium** c 1250, tournament, joust; **tormentum,** skirmish 1387; **-eator** 1220, 1254, **-iator** c 1188, 1225, jouster; **-eo** c 1218, c 1370, **-io** c 1188, c 1370, **tourneo** 1419, **turneo** 1270, 1341, **turnio** 1152, 1194, to joust, hold a tourney.

torn/us molarius a 1204, **turnus molarum** 1250, 1330, mill-stone; **molendinum ad turnum,** quern 1289; **turna,** turn, bend 1251; (?) **-um** (†**cornum**), varvel (falc.) a 1150; **turnus,** *for* **-us,** lathe c 550; alidade (astr.) a 1350; *1213, 1300, **-us** 1307, **turna** 1213, winch (for cross-bow); turn, order, recurrence in succesion c 1186, 1549 (**atturnum** *for* **ad turnum,** 1248); trip, voyage 1248; **-us carruce,** space to turn plough; **-us** 1226, c 1300, ***turnus** a 1184, 1587, **turnum** c 1270, 1540, **turna-tus** 1276, 'tourn', periodical court or visita-tion (of sheriff, *etc.*), suit thereat or payment in lieu; **t. monete,** payment by moneyers a 1128;

-atilis, twisted 13c.; revolving c 1180; c 550, c 730. c 1160, c 1330, **-us** c 550, round *or* smooth; **-ator** 1308, 1337, **-bro-chus** 1492, turn-spit; *1183, 15c., **turnator** 1227, 1297, **-arius** c 1220, 1563, **turnarius** 1316, 1419, turner (of woodwork); **-erius,** (?) successor (G.) 1293; **-era** 1250, **turnera** 1235, (?) **turnarica** 13c., headland in field (Fr. *tournière*); **ingenium turneicium,** crane 1263; **turnysollium,** 'turnsole' (blue dye) 1377; **-o** 1155, c 1325, **turno** 1246, to turn, direct; (*intr.*) to turn a plough-team c 1270; **turno me,** to turn (of a bridge) 1313; *see also* **pons, porta,** ATTORN, RETORN

toroillus, *see* **turettus.**

torpedula, *see* **torredula.**

torpescit (*impers.*), a weariness arises c 1266.

torqu/es, 'twist' (for binding scaffolds) 1368; **-amen,** gripe, spasm a 1250; **-atio,** wearing a torque 13c.; **-atus,** interlaced (of wattle) c 1135, c 1400; (*subst.*) knight of the Garter 1505; †**-eola,** item in stock of castle, (?) cable c 1180; ‡**-inus,** hangman's rope c 1250.

†**torr/a,** (?) clod 1283; †**-o,** (?) to break clods 1283.

torr/agium, -ella, *see* TURR

torredul/a (†**torpedula**) 1221, **puteus -i** a 1250, (?) lime-kiln; *cf.* **torale.**

torricula, *see* **thoracicla.**

torr/idus, violent c 1390; †**-estrinus,** (?) parched (of flour) 14c.; ‡**-undo,** cake 15c.; **-esco,** to dry up c 1125; *cf.* TOST

torsia, *see* **torcia.**

torsus, *see* **tortitudo.**

tort-, *see also* **torcha.**

1 tort/a c 1200, 1534, **turta** c 1250, 1322, **-ata** 1338, **-ellus** a 1142, c 1257, **turtellus** c 1250, 1279, †**tratellus** 1353, 'torte', 'tourte' (sort of cake or loaf); **turtarius**, baker of 'tortes' c 1324, 1419; **-us**, of or for 'tortes' 1382, 1419; *cf.* **tarta.**

2 tort/a (C.I.) 1331, **-illus** 1608, (upper) mill-stone (O.F. *torte*); ‡**-illus**, "shackle" 15c.

3 torta, mala, *see* **malatolta.**

tort/ella a 1446, **-illa** p 1394, roundel (her.); **-ello** a 1446, **-illo** p 1394, to compose of roundels.

tort/itudo 7c., c 1060. c 1100, 1344, **-ura** 1078, c 1219, crookedness, wrong, injustice; **-ulosus** c 1190, **-ilosus** a 1250, **torsus** 1214, twisted, gnarled; **-uose,** crookedly, wrongfully 1267, c 1390; **-uositas,** twistiness 1267; crooked dealing 14c., 1461; **-uosus acutus,** zigzag, dancetty (her.) p 1394; **-ator,** torturer 1411; *see also* TROTT

tortu/ca 12c., a 1250, **-a** c 1200, tortoise; **t. marina, t. silvestris** a 1250; ‡**-ga,** "whelk" 15c.

tortus, *see* **1 torta.**

tor/us (thor-), **-ulus,** flower-bed 1620; **t. legitimus,** wedlock 1302, 1503; **-ale** 1144, ‡15c., **-ellum** 1386, *for* **-al,** coverlet.

tost/a 1466, ‡**-um** 15c., ‡**-ura** 1570, **panis -us** 1620, toast; ‡**-ilis,** "toastable" 1570; **-io,** to grill 9c.; *cf.* **torridus.**

†**tota,** (?) *f.l.* for **cota** (= **quota**) 1356.

tot/alitas, totality 12c., c 1361; **-ale,** a total 1238, c 1320; ***-alis,** total, entire c 1170, 1620; ***-aliter** c 1115, c 1540; **-o** 1461, totally, entirely; **-a bona,** *toute-bonne,* clary (bot.) 1538; **-i** (*pl.*) all 5c.; **-issimus,** quite complete c 1430; ‡**-um simul,** "sweepstake" 1570; **-us** quite c 1315; *see also* **a, de, ex, in, inter, per, pro.**

†**totalum,** an insect a 1200.

toteneisum 1230, **pannus de Totenays** 1334, cloth of Totnes (Devon).

tot/farius 1440, **-iplex** 1509, so manifold; **-upliciter,** so many times c 1361; **-iens quotiens,** name of a writ 1445; †**-olibet,** as much as you please c 1370.

totillans, tottering 931, 933.

1 toto (totto), to tot, mark with *T* 1311, 1374.

2 toto, this (τοῦτο) c 550.

3 tot/o, -us *see* **totalitas.**

touagium, *see* **towagium.**

touchum, touch-stone 1369; 'touch', match (for gun) 1388, 1399.

touftum, *see* TOFT

toulnetum, *see* **telo.**

tourn-, *see* **tornamentum.**

touta, mala, *see* **malatolta.**

tov/ale, -ella, *see* TUALL

tow/agium 1286, 1417, **touwagium** 1297, **touagium, tauuagium** 1328, **tawagium** 1308, 1313, **toagium** 1294, **tockagium, tuckagium** 1318, (dues for) towage; **-atio,** towing 1437; **-o,** to tow 1333, 1437.

towallo, to boil separately (A.S.) c 1115.

towella, towailla, *see* TUALL

toxi/ca, poison 1378; **-catio,** poisoning 1405; **-cativus** a 1252, 1378, **-cus** c 550, c 790. c 1177, 1378, **-fer** c 1212, poisonous; ***-co** c 790, c 1000. c 1125, c 1450, **-igo** 1414, to poison.

‡**toxilla,** nipple 14c.

toycis, *see* **tensa.**

toyso, *see* **tonsio.**

trab/ea, -ia, robe c 550.

trabiculus, *see* **trebuchettum.**

trab/s (-es), beam in the eye 1241; beam of light c 1106; driving-shaft of wind-mill 1285, 1302; c 1200, 1364, **-a** 1289, 1358, plough-beam; projecting moulding (arch.) 1465; rood-beam 1244, 1477; weaver's beam 1260; weigh-beam 1396, 1549; (?) wooden building 1285; **-a** 1296, c 1300, **-ula** 1325, *for* **-s,** beam; **-ale,** axle-beam 13c.; **-ealis,** of or for a beam a 1275; ‡**-ula,** transom of bed 1570; **-o,** roof-tree c 1595; **-eatura** 1179, **-etura** 1187, timber-work; **trav/a** 1278, ‡1483, **-is** 1275, **-um** 1407, 'trave', shackle for shoeing horses; *see also* **thrava.**

tracea, *see* **1 tracia.**

tracera, *see* **trasura.**

tracessantia, *see* **tresantia.**

trach/ea c 1200, a 1250, **arteria t.** a 1250, 1528, windpipe; ‡**dracoma,** *for* **-oma** (med.) 14c.

trachelium, bellflower (bot.), 1634.

trachia, *see* **craccha.**

trachicium, *see* **trahicium.**

tracho 12c., c 1255, †**tractio** c 1293, underground channel.

1 trac/ia, -ea, trace, (following) trail (of stolen cattle) 1203, c 1258; **-io** 1209, 1210, **-o** 1236, **trasso** 13c., to trace, track.

2 tracia 1289, **trassia** 1283, measure of garlic (?) string (Salop.).

†**tracis,** twitching, tic (med.) c 1280.

tracta, measure of volume ‡14c., 1514; *see also* **dacra.**

tract/atio, hauling, dragging 1336, 1433; plucking, pulling out 1483; drawing (of criminals) c 1330; delivery, handing over 1344; **t. sanguinis,** drawing blood c 1232; **-abilis,** movable c 1330; **fons t.,** draw-well 1331; **pons t.** drawbridge 1233, 1385; **-agium,** (payment for) haulage 1281, 1392; **-amen,** handling, dealing a 1452; **-atim,** slowly c 1330; **-ativus,** capable of hauling 1340;

-ator, drawer (of liquor) 1283, c 1335; salt-drawer, 'tiesman' 14c.; **t. vitri** c 1190; **-itor,** haulier 1335; **-ator,** handler c 1343, 1462; ***writer,** commentator c 730. a 1090, p 1380; negotiator, treaty-maker 1285, c 1470; **-atulus,** drawer, shelf c 1550; short treatise c 1343, 1523; **-atus,** draught (of fish) 1425; trace (of harness) 1388; ***conference,** discussion c 1188, 1549; treaty, agreement c 1229, c 1540; treatise, discourse c 1300, 1432; (?) *for* **-us,** antiphon 1257; **t. vite,** course of life c 1218;

-o, to raise (shutters) 1434; to 'yelm', pluck (straw) 1323, 1384; to draw (criminals) 14c., 15c.; 1322, c 1362, **t. ad** 1248, 1280, to shoot at; to drag (pond *etc.*) 1315, 1336; to draw (water) 1378; to draw (ale) c 1266; to milk 1270, 1376; to draw, sketch, trace 1330, 1445; to carve (stone, according to design) 1324; to decide c 600; to try, deal with (person) according to law a 1238, 1243; **t. causam (placitum, loquelam)** c 1115, 1221; **-or** (*dep.*), to treat, handle 1274; *cf.* TRAX

tract/io, hauling, dragging 1364, c 1400;
plucking, pulling out 1457; drawing (of
criminals) c 1422, 1447; drawing (of water)
1534; trace (of harness) 1374; attraction
13c., 1344; drawing, delineation 1581;
t. veli, hoisting sail 1398; see also tracho;
-a, -icia, see tractus (below); -icius,
outstretched c 1160; drawn (of a face)
c 1530; fons t., draw-well 1339; pons t.
1328, ‡1483, p. -ivus 1256, drawbridge; -or,
drawer (of liquor) 1283, 1322; (?) worker
in drawn thread 1441; (?) for -ator, critic
13c.; negotiator 1347; ‡-orium, windlass
15c., 1570; -ura, hauling, dragging 1391;
drawing (of criminals) c 1415; 1388, trai-
tura 1314, trace (of harness); milking 1185;
‡a plaster 1483;
    -us, (?) step c 950; drawing up (of nourish-
ment by plant) c 1115; haulage 1275, 1329;
load (Sc.) c 1230; 1213, 1486, -a 1308, -um
1177, -icia 1388, *trace (of harness); drawing (of criminals) c 1402; draught, drawing (of
liquor) c 1220, 13c.; draught (of fish), place
for fishing c 1150, 1460; drag-net 1086,
1231; swinging (of balance) 1274; stroke
(of bell) 1403; device for bending cross-bow
1462; bow-shot (distance) 1274, c 1397;
movement of straking a measure 1419;
1267, c 1470, -ulus c 1182, c 1470, written
stroke, tail of a letter; voided scutcheon,
orle, or tressure (her.) p 1394, a 1446;
*antiphon sung after epistle esp. in Lent
c 790, c 1006. a 1090, 1517; due form 1511;
salve (med.) a 1250 (cf. intractum); (?) for
-atus, treatise 11c., c 1540; treaty 1426;
conference 1461; opinion c 1160; t. communis, discussion, consideration 944, 947;
t. boum, payment for driving cattle
(Hereford) 1331; t. bracchiorum, fathom
1377; t. navium, portage 1338; t. sanguinis, (fine for) bloodshed 1272; -ior,
more protracted c 1250; -ius, more slowly
or restrainedly 1472; -um filum, drawn
wire 1245;
    trahebaculum, (commission of) trail-
baston c 1320 (cf. trailbasto); trahibilis,
able to be wrested 1374; trahura, training
(falc.) 1251; traho, to draw (a sword etc.)
c 1315, 1472; to hoist (anchor) 1322; to
trawl c 1150, 1445; to 'yelm', pluck (straw)
c 1450; to draw (criminals) c 1300, c 1470;
to draw (liquor) 1296, 1324; to drain c 1200,
1306; to milk 1185, 1234; to suck at the
breast 1289; to swing (of balance) 1274; to
disturb 1419; to wrest, twist c 1334, c 1343;
to drag (in singing) 1351; to draw, delineate
1221; to train (hawks or horses) a 1150,
c 1440; (a teacher) 1552; (?) for trado 811;
    t. ad, to shoot at 1214, 1440; to apply,
make applicable, to c 1357; to tend towards
1239, 1267; t. me ad, to withdraw to 1369; t.
in causam c 1342, c 1400 (in †cam[eram]
1218, 1255), t. ad curiam 1397, t. in
placitum c 1185, 1588, to sue, implead;
t. causam, to bring a suit c 1435; t. con-
nubium c 1170, t. matrimonium c 1170, to
contract marriage; *t. ad (in) consequentiam c 1188, 1419, t. ad sequentiam c 1523,
t. in consuetudinem c 1166, c 1266, t. in
exemplum 15c., to make a precedent of;

t. curiam, to incur adverse verdict 1293;
t. folles, to work bellows c 1245; t. funem
(inter se), to dispute c 1218, c 1220; t.
ignem, to shoot fire 1372; t. in dominicum (dominium), to take into demesne
1209, c 1345; t. lac, to milk 1306; *t.
moram, to tarry, sojourn c 1250, 1559; t. m.
pro, to lie in wait for 1573; t. organa, to
blow the organ c 1245, 1322; t. originem,
to emanate c 1188, a 1491; t. pisces 13c.,
t. rete 13c., 1445, t. cum retibus c 1150,
1268, to fish; t. sagittam, to shoot 1214,
1255; t. s. ad aures 15c.; t. sanguinem, to
draw blood 1288, 15c.; t. velum, to set sail
1300; t. ad (in) warantum, to vouch to
warranty 1169, 1275.
tracto, see tractatio.
tracula, see traha.
trada, haven 1331.
‡tradarius, palfrey 15c.
tradbenda, part of cart, (?) 'tread-band' 1328.
trad/itio, handing down, inheritance c 790;
c 1125, 1461, treasona c 1500, treason;
    t. ad firmam, letting to farm c 1370;
-itiuncula, worthless tradition a 1200;
-itiva, tradition 1620; -itivus, hereditary
a 1446; -itator (for -itor) 1566, traiturarius
(pun on thesaurarius) c 1313, traitor;
-itorie c 1325, 15c., -itiose, 1305, trai-
torously; -itorius, traitorous c 1325, 1461;
-itor, lessor c 1350; -o c 1270, c 1285, *-o
ad firmam 1185, 1419, to farm, demise; t.
ad feodifirmam 1260, c 1303; t. in feudum c 1350; t. ad bullam, to seal (papal
letters) 1263; t. per ballium, to deliver on
bail 1255, 1257.
tradux, heredity, inheritance c 730. c 1178;
(adj.) hereditary, derivative c 1170, 1535;
traduc/tio, marriage c 1270, 1282; translation c 1470; export 1503; transductio,
removing, transferring 863. 1389; -tivus,
conductive c 1290; -o, to export 1375, 1506;
c 1293, t. in uxorem 12c., to marry; to
translate c 1439, c 1470.
traer, trawler c 1150.
trafico, to traffic 1554.
trafretatio, see TRANSFRET
traga, see traha.
tragacanth/a, gum tragacanth: dragagantum a 1250, ‡14c.; see also dragagantum.
traged/ia, rigmarole, rumpus a 1517; -icus,
tragic 1252; -igraphus, tragedian c 700;
trajedus, tragic actor 1267.
†trag/os, -us, (?) sprat 11c.; ‡-us, sponge
14c.
tragum, drag-net c 1170, 1334; cf. draga.
traha c 1180, 15c., thraa 14c., traga 1147,
tracula 6c., drag, sledge; see also treia.
trah/ebaculum, -ibilis, -o, -ura, see tractio.
*trah/icium c 1250, 1343, -icia (traicia)
1269, 1335, traycius 1279, trachicium
1349, †-itum 1294, ‡-iculum 15c., trace (of
harness); pons -iceus, drawbridge 1297.
trahino, see TRAIN
trail/basto (trayl-) 1319, 15c., -ebasto a 1347,
c 1395, treilbasto 1319, †-bastunria 1306,
(commission of) trailbaston; cf. trahebacu-
lum (s.v. tractio).
trail/ia, -lo, see tricleia.
train/a (trayn-), lure (falc.) 1222; -ellum,

-ellus 1284, 1339, **tranellum** 1360, **trey-nellum** 1359, rein (*cf.* **tramale**); (?) **-o** (†**tramo**), to drag 1309 (C.I.); **-o** 1324, **trahino** 1309, to draw (criminals) (C.I.); **-o** 1290, 1315, **traigno** 1291, to train (falcons).
trai/o, -tor, *see* **triatio.**
traitur-, *see* **tractio; traditio.**
Trajectensis, *see* **pondus.**
trajectoria, trajectory (geom.) 1686.
trajedus, *see* TRAGED
tralio, *see* **tricleia.**
trama, tram, cart-shaft 1349; *see also* **trames.**
tram/agium, -asium, -esium, -isium, etc., *see* TRIMENS
tram/ale 1459, **-allum** 1269, ‡**-ellum** 15c., trammel-net; *cf.* TRAIN
tram/ellum, -ildum, *see* **trimodius.**
tram/es, fess (her.) c 1595; **t. vite,** lifetime 957. 12c., 15c.; †**-a,** *for* **-es,** path c 1240.
†**tramo,** (?) *for* **trameo** or **trano,** to cross c 550; *see also* TRAIN
tramontana, *see* **transmontanus.**
tranagium, *see* **trona.**
tran/atorium, creek, inlet, estuary c 1100; **transnatatio,** swimming across c 1400; **-o,** to pass through or over, to cross c 550; to fly through 7c.
tranch-, *see* TRENCH
trand/allus, -lus, *see* **trendella.**
trandstevum, *see* **trendstavum.**
tranellum, *see* TRAIN
tranetarius, *see* **traventarius.**
trano, *see* **tranatorium.**
tranquill/itas, serenity (title) c 1188; **-imus,** *for* **-issimus,** 14c.; **-atio,** calming c 1470; **-o,** to be calm c 1436.
trans, in excess of c 1204, c 1320.
transaccid/entatio, 'transaccidentation', transformation of accidental attributes c 1300, 1427; **-entatus,** transformed in respect of accidents 1610; **-ens,** (?) transcending accidental attributes c 1380.
transact/io **c 1160, 1549, †**tranxactio** c 1220, agreement, compromise; transition 1622; ****-us,** past (of time) a 1100, c 1452; **-o,** to transact 1146.
****transalpin/atio,** crossing Alps c 1257; **-us,** resident south of Alps, Italian c 1250; **-o,** to cross Alps (or other mountains) a 1205, c 1370.
transcedo, to transcend 930.
transcen/sio, climbing over 14c.; **-sus,** crossing (bibl.); excess 12c.; transcendency (log.) c 1360; **-dens** c 1270, 1620, **-dentivus** c 1366, transcendent (log.), transcending the Aristotelian categories; **-do,** to outlast c 720; to transcend the categories (log.) c 1270.
transcheia, *see* TRENCH
transcopi/atio, recopying c 1470; **-o,** to recopy c 1470.
transcorporo, to transfer to the body c 1190.
transcript/io 1345, ****-um** 1200, c 1476, transcribing, transcript, copy; **-or,** copyist 1345; plagiarist 1622; **transcribo,** to convey (land) by a written deed or charter c 693.
transcur/sio, climbing over 15c.; middle years of a century or period c 800; **-sus,** passage (of time) 15c.; **-sorie,** cursorily c 1317; **-renter,** in passing ⊂ 1270.

‡**transdelatus,** epileptic during fit 14c.
transdono, to transfer 811.
transductio, *see* **tradux.**
transelement/atio, change of elements 1552; **-o,** to change the elements of 1562.
‡**transenno,** to mew (hawks) 1570.
transeo, *see* **transitio.**
transeptum, *see* **transseptum.**
transequito, to ride across p 1327.
transfero to translate (bishop) 1242, 16c.; to translate (saint's relics) 8c. 13c., c 1370; to convey, alienate (possessions) (G.) 1313; (*intr.*) to cross the sea c 1340; to change one's university or course 1291, c 1407; **transtulo,** to transfer 1461; *cf.* TRANSLAT
transfigo, *see* **transfixura.**
transfigur/atio a 1090, c 1546, **t. Domini** c 1250, c 1514, (feast of) Transfiguration (6 Aug.); **-ate,** in disguise c 1450; **-o,** to transfigure (theol.) 12c., c 1546; to transmute (alch.) c 1215.
transfinctio, transfiguration 5c.
†**transfio,** to be transferred 1350.
trans/fixura, piercing 14c.; **-figo,** to cancel, delete 1520.
transflammo, to change into flame a 1275.
transform/atio, transformation 13c., 1362; **-ative,** by way of transformation c 1270; **-ator,** paraphraser 1345.
transfrancio, to cross France 13c.
****transfret/atio** 1127, 1447, **trafretatio** 13c., **-a** 1332, **-um** c 1325, **-orium** 14c., crossing the sea; **-abilis,** suitable for crossing the sea 1190.
transfugo, to chase c 1213, 1461.
transfundo, to translate (in language) c 730. 1267; to transmit c 1188, c 1362.
transgluti/o c 1125, c 1330, †**-no** c 1290, to swallow.
****transgress/io** c 1115, 1516, ****-us** 1200, c 1470, transgression, offence, trespass; **t. fidei,** breach of faith 1220; **t. legis,** fine (A.S. *lahslit*) c 1102; **t. super casum,** trespass on the case (leg.) 1538, a 1564; **-or,** ****transgressor,** offender c 1125, c 1540; surpasser (in iniquity) c 1250; **-ibilis** c 1265, **-ivus** c 1258, **-orius** c 1200, wrongful, culpable; **transgredi/o** 7c., 8c. 1267, **transgradio** 790, *for* **-or,** to cross, pass; 1274, c 1337, ****-or** a 1090, c 1534, to transgress, offend against.
transgulo, *see* STRANGUL
transhumanus, superhuman 1427.
Transhumbranus, Northumbrian c 1118, a 1166.
transinferioratio, change for the worse c 1380.
trans/itio, crossing-place (in river) 1324; change of status c 1115; transport 1242; transitiveness (gram.) 13c., 1524; **-itive,** transitively 13c., p 1300; **-itivus,** transitive 1267, c 1290; 1120, p 1380, ****-itorius** a 1090, 1570, transitory; **-itorius,** cursory 1267; **navis -itoria,** ferry-boat 1233; **-itorie,** transitorily c 1180; **-itus,** passing away, death 604, 1041. c 1125, 15c.; noon c 1250; toll traverse 1327, 14c.; governing of a case (gram.) 1524; **-ibilis** transient 944; changeable c 1360; **-iens,** operating beyond itself c 1300; passant (her.) c 1320, c 1595;

-eo c 1090, c 1265, **t. ex hoc mundo** c 1331, to die; to be translated (of bishop) 1242; to be transmuted (alch.) c 1200; to pass, take place (of legal proceedings) c 1115, 1335; to pass (of bill in Parliament) c 1453; to pass, be conveyed (of property) 16c.; to be let pass c 1220, c 1397; (with *dat.*) to be granted c 1350; to hand on c 1436; to be transitive (gram.) 13c., 1524; to run over (of vehicle) 1276; to run loose (of dogs) 1380; **t. ad leges,** to study law 1421; **t. ad scholas,** to go to school c 1452; **t. in exemplum,** to serve as a warning 1281, 1426; **t. sub sigillo,** to pass under seal 1376; **t. super assisa,** (?) to traverse an assize 1398.

translanceatus, pierced c 1540.

translat/io, transcript 870; 10c., c 1000. c 1090, c 1514, †**transplatio** 1293, (festival celebrating) translation of saint's relics; translation of bishop c 1188, 1558; transfer of nun to another house c 1350; remaking (of costume) 1527; **-e** 1267, **-ive** 793, c 850, metaphorically; **-o,** to offer a 1235; to transfer 1274; **translo,** to translate (bishop) c 1300; *cf.* **transfero.**

transloco, to transfer c 1250.

translucentia, translucency a 1250.

transmar/inus ultramarine (colour) 1253; **-itanus** 1136, 12c., **-itimus** c 1210, †**transmirinus** c 730, *for* **-inus,** beyond the sea; **de -e,** from overseas c 1200, c 1400; **in -inis,** overseas 1236, 1454; **-ito,** to cross the sea 9c.

transmea/tio 1440, **-tus** c 1310, crossing; **-bilis,** passable c 730. c 1191, 14c.

trans/mensus (*pass.*), traversed 970; **-metior,** to traverse, pass through c 1000. c 1218.

†**trans/meto,** (?) *for* **-muto** *or* **-moto,** to translate 10c.

transmigr/atio, passing away, death c 730, c 900. 1274; passing under new control c 1000; **-abilis,** passing easily from one thing to another 1649; **-o,** to remove 790; to die c 1450.

transmirinus, *see* TRANSMAR

trans/missio, sending c 1185; message c 1470; **tromitto,** *for* **-mitto,** (G.) 1220; **-mitto,** (with *inf.*) to entrust 7c.; **t. me de,** to take part in c 1266; **t. pro,** to send for 1287; **t. venum,** to sell 1150.

transmisum, *see* TRIMENS

transmontanus, south of Alps 1240; **tramontana septentrionalis, t. austri,** north and south pole c 1227.

transmot/atio, removing c 700, 870; **-o,** to remove 811, 870; to change c 700.

transmundialis limes, world's end a 615.

transmut/atio, removal c 1150, c 1250; exchange c 1280, 1315; change, transformation 870. a 1090, 14c.; transmutation (alch.) a 1233, 1620; counterchanging (her.) c 1595; *-abilis,** changeable a 1228, c 1430; **-abilitas,** changeability c 1270, a 1349; **-ativus,** causing change 1267; **-atorius,** concerned with transmutation 13c.; **-o,** to translate (in language) c 1170, c 1362; *to transmute (alch.) c 1215, c 1470; to counterchange (her.) a 1446, c 1595; to divert (watercourse) 1376; *see also* TRANSUMPT

transnatatio, *see* **tranatorium.**

transnavigabilis, navigable c 1191.

transpar/entia, transparency a 1250, 1267; **-ens,** transparent a 1233, 1267; **-eo,** to shine through a 1252.

transpenetr/abilis, piercing through a 1275; **-o,** to pierce through c 1190, c 1362.

transpervius, permeable a 1275.

transplantatio, transplanting 13c., 1620.

transplatio, *see* **translatio.**

transpono, *see* **transpositio.**

transpontanus, living across the bridge c 1200.

transport/us, conveyance, cession (leg.) 1428; **-o,** to convey, cede 1448.

transpo/sitio, transporting 13c., a 1304; **-sitor,** ferryman c 1180; **-no,** to invert (her.) p 1394.

transremigo, to row across 15c.

transseptum (transeptum), transept (eccl.) 1586.

transsolaris, eclipsing the sun a 1275.

transsorbeo, to engulf 1220.

transsu-, *see* **transu-**

trans/tavum, -tevum, *see* **trendstavum.**

Trans/tinanus, north of Tyne 12c.; **-tuedanus,** north of Tweed 1535.

transtulo, *see* **transfero.**

transturn/um 1227, **tresturneia** 1199, **trestornatio** c 1200, diversion, turning aside; **-o** 1215, 1275, **trestorno** c 1185, c 1290, **tresturno** 1200, 1221, **treturno** 1287, to divert, turn aside; **trestorno,** to put to flight (Norm.) 1195.

transubjectio, change of subject (log.) c 1381.

***transubstanti/atio,** transubstantiation (theol.) c 1182, 1608; **-alis,** changed by transubstantiation 1427; **-aliter,** by transubstantiation 1427; **-arius** c 1620, **-ator** 1552, believer in transubstantiation; ***-o** c 1182, 1622, **-vo** 1427, to transubstantiate.

‡**transud/atio,** dripping (into still) (alch.) 1652; ‡**-o,** to drip 1652.

transulco, to sail across 1437.

†**transumalis,** transverse 1530.

transumpt/io, use of one word for another a 1090, c 1386; copying c 1343, c 1413; ***-um,** 'transumpt', copy c 1291, 1536; **-e** 1344, ***-ive** c 1263, a 1446, †**transmutive** 1344, with a transferred meaning; **-ivus,** having a transferred meaning 12c., a 1446; **transumo,** to transfer c 1180; to use one word for another 1177, 14c.; *to transcribe, copy 1344, 1551.

transundo, to overflow 655.

***transvado,** to cross over, ford c 1125, 15c.

transvect/or, one who conveys overseas, seaman c 790. c 1190, 1200; conductor c 1430; **-ivus** 870, **-orius** c 1200, 15c., carrying over, transporting; **-us,** crossing the sea p 1330; **-o,** to convey overseas c 1200, c 1362.

transvelificor, to sail across c 1365.

transverberatio, breaking through c 730. 15c.

transvers/io, width 8c.; **transvercio** 1228, ***-um** c 1115, c 1437, **traversum** 1024. 1180, 1449, †**traverisum** 1345, (toll for) crossing, traverse, pontage; *see also* **ad, ex, in, per, telo; traversum,** traverse, denial, (leg.) a 1564; **-alis** a 1250, 15c., **-anus** c 1250, **-atilis** c 1361, transverse, oblique; set fesswise (her.) a 1446; **-aliter,** transversely 1378, 1414; fesswise (her.) a 1446; **-aria,** transverse stripe (her.) c 1595; **-orius,** set crosswise 1245, a 1250; **-orium** p 1330, **traversorium** 1275, 1314, **-um** 15c., cross-piece, cross-beam; **traversinum,** staybar (for window) 1288; bolster (Fr. *traversin*) 1418; **-us** (*prep.*), across 1340; **-o,** to cross over a 1250, c 1400; to traverse (leg.) 1295, 1405; **transverto,** to divert, turn aside c 1185, 1305; to thwart 12c.; to misappropriate c 1250; **t. me in,** to transform oneself into c 1150, c 1362.

transvolo, to transfer oneself (to another religious order) c 1325, c 1343.

trantator, *see* **traventarius.**

tranxactio, *see* **transactio.**

trap/ezium, trapezium (geom.) 1686; **-ezeta** c 1100, c 1200, **-azeta** 800. 13c., *for* **-ezita,** banker, money-changer.

‡**trapha,** case, box 1652.

1 **trapp/a,** trap, snare 1250, 15c.; 1242, 1305, **-um** 1301, **treppa** c 1284, trap-door.

2 **trapp/a** 1289, c 1468, **treppa** 1277, 1303, **-atura** c 1422, **-ura** 1416, c 1421, trapping, 'trapper', harness.

‡ **trarames** (*pl.*), noises made by poltergeists 1652.

†**trasa** (*pl.*), (?) *for* **strata,** beds c 1258.

†**trasse** (*pl.*), (?) stocks (G.) 1354.

trass/ia, -o, *see* **tracia** (1 & 2).

trasura, chasing (of silver) 1238; 1324, 1373, **tracera** 1453, tracing *or* tracing-house (arch.).

tratellus, *see* 1 **torta.**

traul/us 1370, ‡1483, **draulus** a 1250, stutterer (τραυλός); **draulizatio,** stuttering a 1250; ‡**-o** to stutter 1483.

trav-, *see also* THRAV; TRAB

trav/entarius (†**tran-**) 1300, 1360, ***-etarius** 1215, 1282, **-entor** 1447, **trantator** 1557, **-entrix** (*f.*) 1404, tranter, itinerant vendor *or* tapster; **-entria,** 'trantery', custom levied from tranters 1301; retail sale of ale 1448, 1485; **-entura,** ale-house 1339, 1505; **-ento,** to retail (ale) 1373, 1384.

traver-, *see* TRANSVERS

trax/atio, drawing (of criminals) c 1400; **-es** (*pl.*) 1325, **-illa** 1298, traces (of harness); *cf.* **tractatio, tractio, trahicium.**

traya, *see* **treia.**

traycius, *see* **trahicium.**

trayl-, *see* TRAIL

trayn-, *see* TRAIN

trea, *see* **treia.**

treagium, *see* **creagium.**

treasona, *see* **traditio.**

treba, *see* **treuga.**

†**trebida,** (?) *for* **turbida** *or* **trepida,** violent c 1310.

trebuchettum 1241, 1325, **tribechettum** 1228, **tribegettum** 1388, **tribigettum** 1375, **tribuchettum** 1224, 1244, **trubechettum** 1224, 1244, **trubuchettum** 1315, **trebuculus, tribuculus,** †**tribunculus** c 1250, **trabiculus** a 1385, trebuchet (siege-engine); 1206, 1388, **tribuchettum** 1278, ‡**tripotheum** 1483, ‡**terbichetum** 1500, trebu-

chet (cucking-stool); **trubechetarius,** maker of siege-engines 1228.

trecenarium, *see* TRIG

trecent/um c 1302, p 1348, **trescentum** c 1219, c 1267, **trescenti** 1226, 1523, **tricenti** 1310, *for* **-i,** three hundred; **-anus** c 1197, **tricentenarius** 6c., of three hundred; **tricentesimus** c 1320, 1327, **tricentenus** 1327, *for* **-esimus; tricenteni,** *for* **-eni,** c 793.

trechea, *see* TRENCH

tredecim/a, tax of one-thirteenth 1207; **tresdecem** c 1430, **tresdecim** c 1206, c 1400, **tridecim** 1475, thirteen; **-o,** thirteenthly c 1343; **-us,** thirteenth 13c., c 1343; **-o,** to tax one-thirteenth 1207.

tredellus, *see* **trendellus.**

tredingum, *see* **trithingum.**

tredo, to tread (clay) 1355, 1370.

treforium, *see* **trifolium.**

trege, *see* **treuga.**

treginta, *see* TRIG

tre/hengum, -hingum, *see* **trithingum.**

treia (**treya**) 1317, 1333, **traha** 1317, tray (for carrying mortar); c 1080, 1395, **trea** 1343, **traya** 1359, 'tray', dry measure, (⅛ of a quarter).

treilbasto, *see* **trailbasto.**

†**treinga,** (?) *for* **tethinga** *or* **treminga** (*cf.* **tremura**), a 1130.

treing/um, -reveus, *see* **trithingum.**

trellicium 1240, **treylicium** 1257, trellis; *cf.* **tricleia.**

trem/bla, -eo, *see* **tremulus.**

trem/eia, -ula, -ulta, -uta, *etc., see* **trimodius.**

tremes-, tremis-, *see* TRIMENS

trem/ulus a 1250, **-bla** a 1201, aspen; ‡**wagtail** 15c.; **-ebundus** c 1190, c 1390, **-ibundus** 704, 10c., formidable; **-ulositas,** tremor, quiver a 1250; **-ulosus,** palsied, quaking a 1250; **-eo** a 1155, c 1400, **-ulo** 870, to tremble, fear; *see also* **trimodius.**

trem/ura, 'trimming', view of frankpledge (Devon and Somerset) 1240, 1543; **-o,** to hold a view of frankpledge 1240; *cf.* **bortreminga** (*s.v.* **borga**).

trench/um c 1160, 1270, **-us** 1163, **-a** 1242, 1419, **-ea** a 1204, 1434, †**trechea** 1331, **-eia** 1192, 1232, **-era** 1330, **-etum** 1312, **-iata** 1219, **trencata, trencatum** c 1160, 1331, **tranchea** c 1200, 1272, **transcheia** 1285, **tranchetum** 1232, **truncata** 1199, trench, ditch, moat; ***-ea** 1207, 1316, **-eia** 1231, 1252, **-iata** 1282, **-era** 1282, clearing or path cut through woodland; **-a** c 1170, 13c., **-ea** 13c., 1338, strip, length (of cloth); **-ata** (†**treneata**), griping pain (Fr. *tranchée*) c 1212; **-ans,** cutting edge (of sword) 1277; **-eator** 1439, 1553, **tranchiator** 1497, carver; **-orium** 14c., c 1450, **-ura** c 1330, trencher; **panis -erius,** bread used as trencher c 1300.

trenda, measure of wax, (?) 'trindle' 1393.

***trend/ella, -ellus** 1273, c 1400, **-illus** 1472, **-la** 1306, **-lus** 1333, **-ulus, trandallus** 1287, **trandlus** 1267, **trindellus** 1343, 1391, †**tredellus** 1287, trundle-wheel (of mill, windlass, *etc.*).

trend/stavum 1302, 1305, **strendstavum**

1294, **-stevum** 1274, **trandstevum** 1285, **transtavum** 1293, **transtevum** 1288, (?) stave or cross-bar of lantern-wheel (in mill).

treneata, *see* TRENCH

trent-, *see also* TRIG

trenta, (?) sort of tracery (arch.) 1366.

trepanum, trepan (med.) a 1250.

trep/arium, -erium, *see* triparium.

trepha, meat unacceptable to Jews (Heb. *trephah*) 1289.

trepid/atio, oscillation 1620; **-itas**, nervousness c 1315.

trepo, *see* hepum.

trepos, *see* tripes.

treppa, *see* **trappa** (1 & 2).

trepudium, *see* tripudium.

tres/antia c 1160, 1388, ***-entia** 1239, a 1452, **-centa** 1261, ‡**tracessantia** c 1440, **trisant/a** 1141, **-ia** 1279, 'tresance', passage.

trescent- *see* TRECENT

tresdec/im, -em, *see* TREDECIM

tresellus, *see* TERTI

tres/erarius, -oria, -orium, *see* THESAUR; trituratio.

tresferdellarius, *see* triferdellarius.

tresidium, *see* TERR

trespass/agium 1199, **-us** 1322, trespass.

tressoria, *see* trica.

***trest/ellum, -ellus** 1274, 1450, **tressellum** c 1224, **-allum** c 1300, 1408, **-illus** 1291, c 1449, **-lum** c 1160, **-ula** c 1300, 1416, †**-um** 1475, **tristallum** 1392, ***tristellus** 1282, 1480, ‡**tristula** 1483, trestle.

trestorn-, tresturn-, treturn-, *see* TRANSTURN

trestrega, *see* tristega.

trething-, *see* trithingum.

treuffatorius, *see* TRUF

treug/a c 1204, c 1450, ***-e** (*pl.*) c 1196, 16c., **trebe** (*pl.*) c 1250, 1297, **trege** (*pl.*) c 1192, **treuva** 1086, **trevia** a 1142, c 1196, **trevie** (*pl.*) c 1100, 1265, **trewge** (*pl.*) 1237, 1388, **trewie** (*pl.*) c 1188, **trigue** (*pl.*) a 1186, **truge** (*pl.*) 1395, 1463, truce; **-a**, (?) tribute 1245; **-arius**, arbiter, "truce-taker" c 1293, ‡1483; **-o** 15c., ‡**trevulgo** 15c., to make a truce.

treumia, *see* trimodius.

treutino, *see* TRUTIN

treva, *see* thrava.

trev/ia, -ulgo, *see* treuga.

treylicium, *see* trellicium.

treynellum, *see* TRAIN

treyta, form of market toll (G.) 1254; *see also* panis.

triabilis, *see* triatio.

trialis, one holding three benefices 1577.

Tri/alogus 1394, **-ologius** 1397, book by Wycliffe.

triamita, *see* tritamita.

triangul/atio, triangulation 1267; **-aris** 1267, **-atus** a 1250, c 1315, triangular; **-atim**, triangularly p 1394; **-um**, cope-chest 13c., c 1396.

triasandali, electuary of red, white, and yellow sandal-wood a 1250, 1265.

triateris, *see* trieteris.

tri/atio, trial of action (leg.) 1330, 1437; trial of jurors (leg.) 1462, 1478; inspection (of soldiers) 1334; **-abilis**, subject to trial (leg.) c 1451, 1573; **-ator**, one who tries jurors

(leg.) 1332, a 1564; inspector (of soldiers) 1334, 1536; money-tester, assayer 1292; **t. petitionum** 1425; **traitor**, inspector (of customs) 1488; **-o**, *to try (an action) c 1290, 1630; *to try (jurors) 1292, 1686; 1333, 1511, **traio** 1325, 1342, to inspect (soldiers); 1248, c 1397, **-co** 1250 to test, assay (money); **t. piscem** 1357.

triav-, *see* tritamita.

trib/echettum, -igettum, -uchettum, -uculus, *etc., see* trebuchettum.

tribolarius, *see* triobolarius.

trib/racca, -ucus, *see* tibracus.

tribul/a, -um, -us** 1200, 1551, **trobulus** 1287, **trubla** 1190, c 1300, **trubula** 1229, 1284, †**turbula** c 1331, ‡**stribula** 15c., a tool (esp. shovel); scoop of mill-wheel 1305; **trubla**, measure of flour (Ir.) 1313; **-agium** 1362, 1537, **trublagium** 1297, 1298, **trubilagium, trubulagium** 1301, 'shovel money', due paid by tinners (Cornwall); ‡**-arius**, "shoveller" c 1440; ‡**-ator**, "thresher" 1483; **-atio**, tribulation c 844. a 1090, c 1540; †**-entus**, (?) *f.l.* for **turbulentus**, troublesome c 1293; ***-o**, to afflict c 1070, 1461; to dig, quarry 1396.

†**tribulum**, (?) *for* **turibulum**; *see* tus.

tribul/us, -um 1285, ‡c 1440, **trivolus** 1299, ‡**tripolus** 15c., †**terpolus** 1285, **trillabus** 1286, 1300, bird-bolt.

tribunculus, *see* trebuchettum.

tribun/us, (?) thane a 1066; **-al**, sanctuary c 1160; criterion 1610; **-aliter** c 1266, †**tribualiter** c 1255, judicially, officially.

tribus (*coll.*), kinsfolk c 1115.

tribut/arium c 793, c 1000, **-arius** 14c., **terra -arii** 770. 11c., 14c., measure of land; **-alis**, of or for tribute or fiscal dues 11c.; **-arie**, as a tributary c 1400; **-arius**, tributary, vassal 725. p 1330; tax-collector 1384; **-or**, giver c 1180; **tribuo**, to pay taxes 1290, 1369.

tric/a c 1180, c 1450, **-atura** (*coll.*) c 1200, 13c., **tressoria** (*pl.*) c 1290, tress, hair; **-a**, comet a 1250; ‡**-atorium**, "tressure" 15c.; **-atura**, interlacing c 1190, 13c.; ‡c 1440, 1483, ‡**-a** 1483, ward of lock; **-o**, to plait c 1112; *see also* TRICH

‡**tricalilba**, sea-foam 1652.

tric/atio, perplexity, hesitation c 760; **-abilis**, vexatious 15c.; **-ator**, impostor c 1190; **-o**, to cheat, entice c 1125; c 810, **-or** c 950, to delay.

tricenal-, tricenar-, *see* TRIG

tricent-, *see* TRECENT

tricephalus, three-headed 1609.

Tricerberus, Cerberus c 1400, ‡1570.

trices-, *see* TRIG

trich/es (**tric-**), **-aria** (*pl.*), hair c 550; †**tarquinasis**, trichiasis, pilimiction (med.) a 1250.

trichotom/ia, tripartition 1610; **-os (luna)**, reduced to ⅓ of full size a 1200.

tricleia, *for* **trichila**, bower c 1320; **trailia**, 'trail', trellis c 1300; **traillo** 1401, **tralio** 1297, to pleach, wattle; *cf.* trellicium.

trico, *see* triatio, trica, tricatio.

trico/cino a 1250, **-nizo**, a 1250, ‡14c., †**-trino** 15c., to sift.

†**tricolus**, a game c 1160.

Tricopleri/us, -atus, *see* TURC

†tricorium, (?) *for* triclinium, refectory a 1142.

tricoronis, triple-crowned c 1620.

tricubit/alis c 1300, 1654, -us c 1300, three cubits long.

tridecim, *see* TREDECIM

†triden/i, (?) for ter deni, thirty c 1218; numerus -arius, number thirty c 1250; *cf.* terdeni.

tridictionalitas, composition of three words 13c.

tridigitalis, three fingers thick (of fat) c 1115.

triding-, *see* trithingum.

tridu/ana, three days' fast c 1160; -ane (*pl.*), space of three days 7c. 14c.; -anus, occurring on third day 8c.; *see also* febris; -alis c 1300, c 1370, -us c 1200, 1452, lasting three days.

tridumma, *see* trimodius.

triellum, combat of three (play on *duellum*) c 1250.

trienn/ale, (payment for) triennial mass *or* (?) *for* tricennale, trental (eccl.) 1232, 1287; -alis a 1564, *-is c 1090, c 1450, -ius 1461, †-us c 1436, three years old; c 1125, c 1436, -is c 1250, lasting three years; recurring every three years 1310, c 1400.

triens, ⅓ penny c 1115; canton (her.) 1654.

trieteris, triennium: triateris c 1200.

trif/a, -o, *see* TRUF; trypheron.

trifacio, to treble c 1197.

trifari/e, in three parts c 1258, c 1362; -us, *see* trifolium.

trif/era, -ea, *see* trypheron.

triferdellarius 1485, †tres/ferdellarius (? tref-) 1330, tenant of ¾ virgate (Somerset).

‡trifertes (*pl.*), spirits inhabiting fire 1652.

trifilis, vessel supported by three legs a 1250.

tri/folium 1245, -foria c 1295, -forium 1295, treforium c 1215, -fura 1310, 1388, -furata 1388, -furium 1245, ornament, (?) trefoil; -forium, gallery or arcade (at Canterbury) a 1210; -foriatus 1245, 1295, †triporiatus 1295, -forius, -farius, -furialis, -furiatus 1245, -furatus 1388, ornamented (?) with trefoils; -furiatim, with (?) trefoil ornaments 1245.

triform/iter, in three parts c 1172; -us, *for* -is, threefold, triple 12c.

trifurca, three-pronged fork 1424.

*trig/intale a 1115, 1530, -entale 13c., 1458, *trentale c 1216, 1473, trentalium 1423, trentellum 1406, trintennale c 1240, *tricenale a 1195, c 1454, tercennale 1235, 1245, trentenarium 1250, tricenarium (officium) a 1090, 1378, trecenarium 1229, 1467, (payment for) trental, service of thirty masses (eccl.); *cf.* triennale; dies -intalis 1425, c 1451, d. tricennalis 1425, d. tricennarius 1420, d. tricesima 1424, month's mind, mass celebrated thirty days after death; -enarius, lasting thirty years 1270; -intenarius 1400, tricenalis c 730, thirty years old; tricenarius, thirtieth c 1310; -esies 1267, tricesies c 1362, c 1422, thirty times; tricesima, tax of one-thirtieth 1236, c 1370; †-intas 1213, treginta 1086, *for* -inta, thirty; -intuplum, thirty times as much 1267.

‡trigla, mullet (τρίγλα) 1570.

trigon/alitas, triangularity (astr.) c 1150; -aliter, triangularly a 1200; -ometricus, trigonometrical 1686; ‡-um, cyclic transformation of elemental spirits 1652; -us, triangular c 815.

trigue, *see* treuga.

tri/hengum, -hingum, *see* trithingum.

triling/a, -um, 'thirdling' (name applied to Thredling hundred, Suffolk) 1223, 1328.

trilitteralitas, composition of three letters 13c.

trilix, three-pronged c 950.

trillabus, *see* tribulus.

trilucus, three-lighted 870.

trilustralis, lasting fifteen years c 1180.

trimatertera, *see* tritamita.

‡trimembr/ale, wooden collar for cattle c 1440; -is, threefold a 1250, 1380.

trimens/truum, period of three months c 1160; -e, trimesium c 1182, trem/ese c 1345, -esium 1174, 1254, -esum 1252, -eysium 1229, 1257, -isium 1232, 1234, -iscum 1234, *tram/esium, -esia 1199, 1325, -ecium 1276, -eysium 1243, -isium 1255, -asium c 1220, 1256, -agium 1324, tromesium 1223, †transmisum 1299, summer corn, summer sowing (Fr. *trémois*).

trimodius, termodius c 1150, †tridumma c 1220, trimoia, trem/uta 12c., †-na (? -ua) c 1208, †treumia (? -uia) 1203, -eia 1210, -ea a 1230, -ium 1271, -ulta 1268, -ultura 1272, -ula, -ulum 1235, 1358, tramellum 13c., tramildum 1303, hopper of mill (Fr. *trémie*); *cf.* tamisium.

trimod/us, triple 10c. c 1170; *see also* necessitas.

†trimordis, (?) with triple bite c 1180.

trindellus, *see* trendella.

trindingum, tringa, *see* trithingum.

trin/itas, a triad c 1180, c 1470; *the Trinity a 1090, 1537; Trinity Sunday 1200, c 1330; flos -itatis, heartsease 1641; frater (ordinis) S. Trinitatis, Mathurine friar 1246, 1471; -arius, ternary c 1267, c 1300; *-us, threefold 767, 957. c 1170, c 1564; t. unus c 550, t. et unus c 1090, c 1464, triune (theol.); aspectus -us, trine (astr.) a 1233; -o, (?) to redouble c 1180; *cf.* TERN

trinomi/us 12c., c 1362, -nis c 1330, three-named.

trintennale, *see* TRIG

trinthingum, *see* trithingum.

trinubus, thrice-wed 12c.

trio, *see* triatio.

tri/obolarius 1654, †-bolarius 1564, 'two-penny-halfpenny', worthless.

Triologius, *see* Trialogus.

‡trip/a, tripe 15c.; -eria, tripe-sellers' quarter (G.) 1289; -olarius, tripe-seller 1333.

trip/arium 1207, 1374, -erum 1326, trep/arium 1180, -erium 1205, trivet, tripod.

tripart/ite, in three parts c 1258; †-us, *for* -itus, c 1000; tallia -ita c 1290; -io c 1266, 1421, -ior 1427, c 1546, to divide into three; to work on three-field system c 1290, 1334.

tripatruus, *see* tritamita.

tri/pes 1387, 1461, -pedium 1300 -pedale ferrum c 1524, -podium 1303, -pudium

1388, **-pus (-pos)** 1157, 1504, (?) **thriplus** 1286, **trepos** 1294, tripod, trivet; **-pus**, "trestle" 1553.

tripido, *see* TRIPUDI

tripl/icitas, threefoldness 13c., 1427; (position in) third house (astr.) a 1233, 1387; ‡**-ex**, treble (mus.) 1570; **in -um, in -is,** in treble (mus.) 1266; **in -o** 1347, c 1470, **in -um** c 1365, trebly; **-us**, *see* **tripes; -arius**, three-fold a 1452; †**-asequeseptima**, three and one-seventh c 1267; **-icatio**, surrejoinder (leg.) 1258, c 1390; **-atorius**, concerned with a surrejoinder 1446; **pecia -icata**, (?) triptych 1415; **-ico** 1258, 1559, **-o** 1487, to make a surrejoinder (leg.); to make three copies of 1204, c 1400; c 1170, 1461, **-o** c 1190, c 1410, to multiply by three; to cube (math.) 1686; **-ico arma**, to wear three scutcheons on one shield (her.) p 1394.

tripolarius, *see* **tripa.**

tripolus, *see* **tribulus.**

tri/pondium (†**-podium**, †**-pos**), triple weight c 1115, a 1275.

triporiatus, *see* **trifolium.**

tripotheum, *see* **trebuchettum.**

*****tripudi/um** a 615, 1019. c 1070, c 1450, **trepudium** 1274, jubilation; **-alis**, jubilant 1237; **-aliter**, jubilantly 1272; **camera -antium**, dancing chamber (Eltham) 1388; **-o** to set dancing c 550; to rejoice, exult c 1135, c 1400; **tripido** 1508, **triputo** c 1450, *for* **-o**, to dance; *see also* **tripes.**

tripunct/alis, three pointed a 1250; **-ualis**, composed of three points c 1361.

tripus, *see* **tripes.**

triquadr/us, triangular *or* tripartite c 550, c 790. 12c., c 1315; **-um,** the earth 9c.

triroda, plot of three roods (Northants.) c 1250, c 1340.

Tris/agion c 1457, **-hagium** 1276, the anthem 'Holy, Holy, Holy'.

trisant/a, -ia, *see* **tresantia.**

‡**triscalamus**, St. John's wort (bot.) 14c.

trisia, *see* GRIS

trist/a c 1150, 1336, **-ra** 1244, c 1385, **-rum** 1282, **-ria** c 1175, 'trist' (appointed station in hunting) *or* service of keeping trist.

trist/abilitas, grievousness c 1270; **-abilis,** a 1250, 1344, **-ibilis** 1267, c 1350, grievous, mournful, sad; **-ifico** c 793. c 1192, 13c., **-o** c 1362, to sadden; *****-or**, to be sad a 1100, 15c.

trist/allum, -ellus, -ula, *see* **trestellum.**

tristate (*pl.*), magnates (τριστάται) c 950.

tristeg/a (*f. s.*) c 720. c 1250, ‡**stristegum** 1570, *for* **-um**, story (of the ark), upper room; ‡privy 13c.; c 1400, †**trestrega** 1244, trestle; **-um**, cabin (naut.) c 1250.

trisulc/us, triple-tongued a 615; **-atus**, three-forked c 1325.

trisyllab/a, trisyllable 1267; **-alitas**, composition of three syllables 13c.; **-icus**, trisyllabic 1267.

trit/amita c 1290, **triamita** c 1258, **trimatertera** c 1258, sister of a *tritavia;* **-avunculus**, **triavunculus**, **tripatruus**, brother of a *tritavus* c 1258; **triavus**, *for* **-avus**, 1331, a 1546; ‡**triava**, "the third from the mother" 15c.

trit/atus, -orium, *see* **trituratio.**

trithingum (**thrithingum**) c 1290, 1393, †**tithringum** c 1290, **tridinga** a 1200, **tredingum** 1268, **trehinga** (†**trehigga**, †**trihengum**, †**trihingum**, †**tringa**) c 1135, **trehingum** 1238, **ridingum** a 1564, trithing, riding, third part of shire (Yorks. or Lincs.); 1114, 15c., **tridingum** a 1170, 1353, **trething/a, -um** 1226, 1330, **tredingum** 1202, **trehengum** 1204, **trehingus** 1292, **treing/a, -um** 1222, 1228, **triyng/ia** 1298, **-um** 1275, †**trindingum** 1200, 1299, †**trinthingum** 1200, †**stridingum** 1204, court of the trithing *or* suit thereat; **secta trithing/i** 1201, 1276, **s. ad -um** 1279, 1353; **-arius** (†**tithingarius**) 1275, **treingreveus** 13c., bailiff or reeve of a trithing; *see also* **tethinga;** *cf.* **treinga.**

triti/ceus, sown with wheat c 1191, c 1220; **molendinum** †**-scium**, (?) flour-mill (or *f.l.* for **ventriticum**) 12c.; †**-co**, (?) *f.l.* for **trituro**, to thresh 1239.

tritul/o, to chirrup c 1315; *see also* **trituratio**, **truta.**

*****trit/uratio**, threshing 1222, 1534; *****-urator** 1227, 1534, **-ulator** 1315, thresher; **-uratorium** a 1300, 1325, (?) **-orium** (W.) a 1250, threshing-floor; ‡**-orium** 15c., **tersorium** 1417, pestle (*cf.* **tunsorium**); ‡grater 1570; ‡funnel 1652; ‡**tresorium**, "scummer" 15c.; **-atus**, worn down (of money) c 1285; *****-uro**, to thresh a 1090, c 1430.

triumph/us, sign of victory 957; **-um sancte crucis**, sign of the cross 12c.; **-abilis**, triumphant 685; **-aliter** c 760, 1006. 12c., c 1350, **-ose** c 1150, c 1436, in triumph, triumphantly; **-atrix**, triumphant (*f.*) c 1160, 1252; **-or** (*dep.*), to triumph over c 1150.

triundialis, three waves high a 615.

*****trivi/um**, trivium, course of liberal arts (ac.) 1089, 1421; **-alis**, relating to the trivium c 1225, c 1344; **-atim**, far and wide, everywhere c 1000, 1031. 12c.; (?) in rows c 950.

†**trivius**, *f.l.* for **trimus**, c 1362.

trivolus, *see* **tribulus.**

troa, *see* **libra.**

trobulus, *see* **tribula.**

trochilus, kind of bird: **strofilus** a 1200.

trochisc/us quatuor magistrorum, sort of pill (med.) a 1250; **-atus**, made up into a pill a 1250.

trochl/ea, halter c 1180; ‡cylinder of loom c 1200, 1483; ‡1483, **trolium** (G.) a 1278, wine-press; ‡spiral staircase 1483; 1369, **trokellus** 1274, 1289, (?) 'truckle', roller; **-eum** 1274, **troculum** 1293, **troilia** 1222, 1328, winch for cross-bow (*cf.* **ballista**).

trochoides (*sc.* **linea**), trochoid (geom.) 1686.

trogulus, sack-cloth *or* monk's frock 10c. 1253, c 1325.

†**troina**, buzzing wind-instrument, (?) drone c 1200.

†**troinapium**, tournament c 1200.

Trojanus, British, Welsh c 1212, c 1500; *see also* **pondus.**

trok-, trolium, *see* THROCC; TROCHL

trollius, globe-flower (bot.) 1641.

tromesium, *see* TRIMENS

tromitto, *see* transmissio.

tromp/a, -ator, *see* trumpa.

*tron/a 1267, 1467, -um, -us 1195, 1489, trosnum 1194, throsnum 1191, -ium 1274, -arium 1686, 'tron', weigh-beam; -ettus, small tron 1352; *-agium 1200, 1506, -achium 1275, †tranagium 1269, †truagium 15c., tronage, toll for weighing; -arius (Sc.) 1365, 1366, -ator 1292, 1489, officer in charge of tron; -atio, weighing on tron 1346; -izo 1274, 1411, -o 1265, 1686, to weigh on tron; *see also* THRON; *cf.* TRUTIN

tronc/us, -atus, *see* TRUNC

‡tron/us, -ossa, nostoc 1652.

trop/eum, -ium, trophy c 550; troph/eum (-eus) agie crucis 933, 943, t. sancte crucis 933, 961, (sign of) cross; -icus, victorious 11c.; *see also* STROPH

trop/us, trope (mus.) a 1100, c 1470; t. orationis, manner, style c 1160; -arium, -arius a 1142, c 1450, -erium 1295, 14c., ‡-orium 1483, trophonarius c 1182, liber -arius c 1250, 'troper', book of tropes (eccl.); -ologia, figurative language c 793, c 1180, 1427; ethical application c 730, c 1160; -ice c 1180, 1381, -ologice c 1343, figuratively; -icum 1267, -icus 1326, c 1616, signum -icum a 1200, circulus -icus 1267, tropic (astr.); '-icus, changeable c 1200; figurative c 720. 1180, p 1380; -ico c 1381, 1427, -o c 1381, to treat figuratively.

trosca, *see* thrucha.

trosnum, *see* trona.

tross-, *see also* TRUSS

‡tross/a 1552, ‡-ula 1570, trull, trollop.

trott/ans c 1180, equus t. 1194, 1472, e. -arius 1423, -erius, tortor 1330, trotting horse.

trouss-, *see* TRUSS

trowa, (?) trough (Suffolk) 1268.

trow/ella, -lia, *see* 1 trulla.

troya, Troy weight, pound Troy (Sc.) 1434, 1460; *cf.* libra, pondus.

troyta, *see* truta.

trua, *see* truia.

truagium, *see* TRON

trubechettum, *etc.*, *see* trebuchettum.

trub/la, -ula, -ulagium, *see* tribula.

†truciparcus, (?) relentless c 1112.

truc/ta, -eta, -ula, *see* truta.

truella, *see* 1 trulla.

*truf/a c 1220, 1461, -um 1435, trifa c 1218, trifle, quibble, trick; *-ator c 1180, 1461, trifo c 1350, trifler, trickster; -atorius c 1308, 15c., treuffatorius c 1340, -aticus 1427, trifling, frivolous; -o c 1270, c 1362, (?) †trusso 1270, -or (*dep.*) 1427, 1461, to trick, trifle (with).

truga, 'trug', dry measure (⅔ bushel) (W. Marches) 1257, 1420.

truge, *see* TREUG

trugon, *see* trygon.

truia 1181, trua a 1151, 1195, sow (Fr. *truie*).

1 trull/a c 1200, 1519, truella 1295, trowella 1344, (?) trowlia 1350, (mason's) trowel; t. leporis, hare's form a 1142; -isso, to plaster c 950.

2 trulla, abdominal rumbling c 1370, ‡1483.

trullus, *see* tholus.

trumb-, *see* THROMB; tumberellum.

trump/a c 1200, 1303, trompa c 1200, trumpet; -arius 1274, -ator 1202, 1303, trompator 1292, -ettor c 1472, trumpeter.

truncata, *see* TRENCH

trunc/us, block of wood (as market-stall) c 1324; block (impeding traffic, *etc.*) c 1250, 1419; 1276, 1374, †truttus 1384, fuller's block; headsman's block c 1395, 1398; stocks c 1006. c 1325; trunk, chest, box 13c., 1465; c 1188, a 1450, troncus c 1335, offertory box (Fr. *tronc*); (?) 'trunk' over salt-pan (Chesh.) 1274, 1276; cooling-trough (in forge) 14c.; part of wolf-trap (? compartment *or* tree-trunk) 1303; fish-trunk, submerged box 1269, 1286 (*cf.* tryinkus); c 1245, c 1330, trunso c 1330, candle-stub; 1384, 1406, -a 1399, gun-stand; t. ad Natale, Yule log c 1220; t. campane, bell-stock 1427; t. lancee, lance-shaft 15c.; t. mellis, (?) bee-tree c 1200; -ulus, stool c 1266; -unus (porci), (?) 'truncheon', portion lopped off 1269; -agium, service of carting logs (Bamborough) 1224, 1327; rent of fish-trunks (Cambs.) 1285; -atio, felling, lopping 1334, 1453; chopping off, maiming 1174, 1461; mutilation (of text) 1267; (?) carrying a club 13c.; fitting (guns) with stands 1399; -ate, in a mutilated form c 1343; troncatus, fitted with stand 1399; crux -ata, tau cross (her.) p 1394, a 1446; sera -ata, stock-lock 1490; -o, to expediate (dogs) 1190; to geld (horses) 1331; to mutilate (a text) c 1339, c 1343; -ulo, to cut off, maim 12c.

†trusorium, sort of weapon (*cf.* tritorium, tunsorium) 1316.

truss/a, truss (naut.) 1337; *c 1165, c 1440, -um 1509, trossum 1250, troussa a 1135, -ata 1279, troseta 1284, -ellus 1086, 1573, trossellus 1267, 1303, troussellus 1204, 1267, truscellus 1267, truss, bundle, bale, pack; -ellus equinus, horse-load 1362, 1373; trossulus, wallet 990; -ellus, (?) market stall c 1154; upper-iron (of mint) 1317, 1484 (*cf.* 3 pila); t. ad equum c 1300, t. ad quadrigam 14c., -ula c 1200, pack-saddle; -erellus, costrel 1239; -abilis 1397, 1406, -atilis 1311, -ibilis 1358, 1445, for packing; -agium 1290, 1343, -atio 1335, 1399, -ura 1290, 1390, trussing, packing; -io 1535, -ura 1532, 'trussing' (of bell); *-o 1220, 1390, -io 1238, to pack; *see also* TRUF

*trut/a c 1000. c 1200, 1654, tructa c 1125, truceta a 1250, troyta 1200, turtra c 1191, trout; -ula (†trucula, *tritula), salmon-trout c 1200.

trutann/us, 'truant', vagabond c 1172, c 1350; herba -orum, *thapsia* 14c.; -icus c 1194, c 1380, -us 1204, beggarly, rascally; -ice, like a truant c 1218, c 1220; -ia c 1220, -izatio c 1340, ‡-itas 1483, truancy, trickery; ‡-izo, to play truant 1483.

trutin/atio, weighing, examining 12c.; *-o c 1170, 1586, treutino 14c., to weigh, examine; *cf.* trona.

truttus, *see* truncus.

truveria (*coll.*), 'trover', objects found 1313.

trygon, sting-ray: trugon 870.

tryinkus, 'trunk', sort of net 1419; *cf.* **truncus**.

trymerum, trimmer (arch.) 1389.

trynga, moor-hen (τρύγγας) 1544.

‡**trypheron** 14c., **trifera** 13c., (?) **trifea** c 1200, mild purgative (med.); **trifera Sarracenica** a 1250, **trifa Sarazenica** 1414.

***tuall/ia**, **-ium** 1157, 1416, ***-a** 1225, 1347, **tuale** 1330, 1431, **tueale, tueallium** c 1360, ***tuella** 1179, c 1500, **tuellus** 1305, 1433, **tuellia** 1243, **toalla** 1242, **toallia** 1220, **toaillia** 1236, **tobale** 1521, **tobalia** c 1350, 1417, **tovale** ‡15c., 1521, **tovella** 1533, **togale** 1372, **togella** c 1266, c 1450, **togellus** 1388, **towailla** 1426, **towella** 13c., c 1510, **twalla** 1225, **twallium** 1325, **twella** c 1423, towel or altar-cloth; **tuella**, piece of cloth for towel 1352.

tuat/er, in thy manner 8c.; ‡**-io**, **-us**, addressing as "thou" c 1440; ‡**tuo**, to address as "thou" (*cf.* Fr. *tutoyer*) c 1440, 15c.

tub/a, tube, pipe p 1327; **t. ductilis**, (?) sackbut 14c.; **-us opticus**, telescope 1686; **-arius** c 1340, **-ator** c 1340, 1421, **-icinarius** 1397, trumpeter; **-icino** 1324, a 1446, ‡**-o** 1483, to blow the trumpet.

***tubba** (†**tulba**) 1296, 1531, **tobba** 1304, tub.

tuber/iculum, *for* **-culum** (med.), a 1250; **-culatus**, nebuly (her.) c 1595; **-ositas**, swelling a 1250; **-osus**, hunchbacked c 1283.

tubia, *see* **tibia**.

tubicin-, **tubus**, *see* **tuba**.

‡**tucet/arius** 1483, **-rix** (*f.*) 1469, "haggismaker".

tuchia, *see* **tutia**.

tuckagium, *see* TOW

tudum, *see* **theodum**.

tuell/us, drain, pipe, spout (Fr. *tuyau*) 1240, 1328; 1317, 1364, **t. camini** 1238, 1432, **-um** (†**cuellum**) **chemini** 1243, flue; *see also* TUALL

tueor, *see* TUIT

tufa (†**thuuf**), sort of pennant c 730. c 1150, c 1400.

tuft-, *see* TOFT

tuggum, 'tug' (harness) c 1250, 1350; **togwithum**, 'tug-withe' (for fastening swingletree) 1360, 1386.

tug/urium, hut: **-orium** c 550, **tegurium, tegorium** c 550, c 1000, **teguriolum, tegoriolum** c 460, 685, **-uriunculum** c 790; **-uriarius**, cottager c 1130.

tuit/io, protection: **tuiso**, (?) close season (for game) 1294; **littere -ionis** a 1250, **-orie** (*pl.*) 1342, letters of protection; **-orie** (*adv.*), protectively c 1308, 1336; in quest of protection 1342, 1494; **-orius**, tutelary 1433; seeking protection 1282, c 1408; **tueor** (*pass.*), to be observed c 760; *cf.* TUT

tul-, *see also* **tholus**; **tubba**.

tul/ipa 1634, **-upa** c 1612, tulip.

tulkesius, *see* TURK

tulo, *for* **fero**, 1282, 1378.

***tumb/a** 8c., c 1000. c 1090, c 1540, **-us** c 1250, c 1300, tomb, tomb-shrine; **-ula**, little tomb c 700; **-arius**, tomb-keeper 13c., 1314.

tumbatio, *see* 2 **cumba**.

tumb/erellum, **-erellus** 1279, 1333, **-rellum** 1311, 1486, tumbrel, dung-cart (used for transport); *1200, 1406, **tumerellum** 1300, ***-rellum** 1247, 1539, **-orale** c 1290, **tomberellum, tomborella** 1275, **tombrellum** a 1540, **twimberellum** 1234, **trumbellum** 1326, tumbrel (as punishment); weighing-machine 1290; 1230, **-rellum** 1323, **trumbellum** 1325, (?) windlass for bending siege-engine; part of drawbridge 1325; **pena -eralis**, p. **tumpilloralis** 1229, **p. tymboralis** c 1258, punishment by tumbrel.

tumbo, to tumble, perform acrobatics c 1287.

tumel-, **tumil-**, *see* **tumulus**.

tumentum, *see* **tomentum**.

tum/or aque, high tide p 1300; **-orositas**, swelling c 1257; **-ex**, tumour (med.) c 1620.

†**tumulentus**, (?) *for* **temulentus**, drunken 5c.

tumul/tuositas, turbulence c 800; **-ans**, (?) *for* **-tuans**, heaving c 1436; **-tuo** (with *acc.* and *inf.*), to announce noisily c 1087.

tumul/us c 1280, 1490, **tumolus**, tomb or tomb-shrine; (?) pier (arch.) c 700; **-atio** c 1170, c 1470, **tumelatio** 1439, **tumilatio** 1334, **-atus** a 1452, c 1470, interment; **-o**, to be interred c 1000.

***tunc temporis**, at that time c 1090, 1471.

tundeo, **tunsa**, *see* TONS

tun/dredum 1442, **-dera** 14c., 'Toundrye', local court (Bristol).

tundulum, bell-clapper 14c.

tunell-, **tunn/a**, **-o**, *see* **tonna**.

tunga, tongue of land, gore c 1200, 1262.

tungravi/o, **-us**, **tungrevius**, town-reeve c 1115.

tunic/a, *tunic, coat, tabard 12c., c 1451; livery c 1358; *a 1090, 1366, **tonica** 1305, **-ella** c 1300, 1523, ***-ula** 1225, c 1470, **tonicula** 1415, **tinaculus** (?) 1550, 1553, tunicle (eccl.); **t. armanda** 1224, **t. armaria** 1208, **t. armorica** 1461, **t. armorum** 1384, 1466, coat of arms; **t. arteriorum** (med.) a 1250; **t. conjunctiva**, membrane of eye a 1250; *see also* **uva**; **t. de estate** c 1324, **t. estivalis** 1261, c 1330, summer coat; **t. ferrea**, coat of mail c 1250, 1551; **t. nocturnalis**, night gown 1523; **-ula**, †**guitea**, membrane of brain a 1250; **-ella**, petticoat or jacket 1535, 1583; **-atio**, wearing a tunic 13c.; clothing (fig.) c 1456.

tunina, *see* **covina**.

†**tunnus census**, a customary rent (Suffolk) a 1350.

tun/sio c 1160, 1420, **-tio** 1438, 1513, **tonsio** a 1275, c 1340, beating, bruising; **-sorium** c 1524, **tonsorium, tusorium** c 1500, pestle.

tuntorium, *see* TINCT

tuo, *see* **tuater**.

†**tupa**, (?) pinnacle 1355.

tupina, a form of tournament 1329.

tuppetum 1239, **thupetum** 1238, (?) chimney-pot.

tupp/us, rammer 1365; **-o**, to ram 1365, 1374.

tuptum, *see* TOFT

tur/aillia, **-allia**, **-allium**, *see* **torale**.

1 ***turb/a** a 1128, 1545, **turva** 1159, a 1564, turf, peat; **t. tannita**, tan-turf (refuse

block of oak-bark from tannery) 1294;
-agium, payment for right to cut peat
c 1230, 1449; ***-aria, -arium** c 1180, 1555,
-ara 1227, 1230, **-era** (†**virbera**) 12c., 1282,
-eria 1188, 1275 **torbaria** 1315, turbary;
(?) peat-stack c 1400; heap of tan-turves
1395; **-atio,** covering with turf 1291; **-o,**
to turf 1168, 1301.

2 turb/a, striking of bell c 1150; **-aldus** (play
on **Theobaldus**) 1397, **-ativus** 1273, 1425,
-atorius c 1125, turbulent, disturbing;
-amen, disturbance c 1250; **-atior,** more
disturbing 1378; **-arius,** kern (Ir.) 1535,
1557; **-iditas,** muddiness a 1250; **-ido,**
for **-o,** whirlwind 14c., a 1452; **-inaceus,**
conical c 1595; **-ineus** c 1470, **-inosus**
1442, disturbed; **-o,** intestinal wind c 1180;
-ulentum, whirlpool 14c.; †**-undus,**
alarmed 1413; **-us,** *for* **-o,** top 13c., ‡1483.

3 turb/a 1303, ‡15c., **-o** c 1324, ‡15c., **-otus**
1334, 1535, **-ultus** 1248, **-utus** 1267, turbot;
‡**-o,** "whelk" 1570.

turbentinum, *see* **terebenthina.**

turb/ith 13c., 1480, (?) **-ia** a 1250, turpeth,
jalap (bot.); ‡**t. minerale,** a form of
mercury 1652; ‡**turpethum,** a mineral
residue 1652.

turbula, *see* **tribula.**

turcatus, turchesi/a -us, *see* **turkesius.**

turchemannus, *see* **drugemannus.**

Turc/us c 1118, 1508, **Tacrus** 1488, Turk;
-anus a 1142, **-icus** 1523, **Turkesius** 1212,
Turkasius c 1217, **Turkeisius** 1220,
Turkish; **caro -ina,** Turk's flesh a 1142;
-omannus c 1190, **Turkemannus** 1188,
Turcoman (*see also* **drugemannus**);
-opolus, Turcopole, light-armed soldier
c 1118, c 1224; **-oplarius** 1408, **-oplerius**
1444, 1480, **-ipelerius** 1480, †**Tricoplerius**
1441, Turcopolier (second English knight
of order of St. John); †**Tricopleriatus,**
office of Turcopolier 1440, 1441.

turd/ula, little thrush c 1184; ‡**-inus,** *for*
coturnix, quail 15c.

turell-, *see* **torale; turettus; turris.**

Turenensis, *see* **Turonensis.**

turett/us 1235, c 1322, **-eus** 1377, **torettus**
1267, 1304, **turellus** 1283, 1304, (?) **torillus**
1275, **toroillus** 1198, (?) **turricula** c 1160,
terret, torret, ring; (?) wreath, loop 1403;
see also **turris.**

turg/escentia, exuberance 1622; **-or,** swelling
c 950; **-ide,** in an inflated style 15c.

turib-, turif-, *see* **tus.**

turicidium, *see* TERR

turilus, *see* **scurellus.**

turk/esius 1205, 1295, **-esus** a 1222, 13c.,
-eisus 1205, †**-eus** p 1290, c 1400, **turche-
s/ius** 1245, 13c., **-ia** c 1620, **tulkesius** 1204,
turcatus 1149, (?) **turgotis, turrois** a 1250,
(?) †**tintachus** c 1325, turquoise; *see also*
TURC

turketus, 'turquet' (astr. instrument) 1326,
a 1350.

turmentum, *see* **tormentum.**

turm/ula, troop 1252, c 1310; **-osus,** commoner c 1370.

turn-, *see* **torn-;** ATTORÑ; RETORN

Tur/onensis, libra T. 1242, 1427, **-enensis**
1461, **-onica** 13c., **-onus** 1521, pound

Tournois (usually ¼ of sterling); **solidus T.**
1158, 1418; **T. albus** 1295, 1311; **T. niger,
denarius T.** 1277, 1316; **T. (Toronensis)
grossus** 1282, c 1565; **T. parvus** 1285,
c 1370.

turp/itudo, nakedness 597; dirtiness, filth
13c., 1553; **-is,** filthy, muddy 1390, 1433;
-idus, shameful c 1340; **-iloquium,** slander
1299, 1336; **-ilocus,** foul-mouthed c 1330;
-ilucrium, filthy lucre 1610; **-ifico,** to defile
1499, 1517; †**-ifo,** to maltreat 1201.

turriolum, *see* **torale.**

turr/is *1171, 1476, **-a** 1307, keep (arch.);
Tower of London 1130, 1461; pillar, prop
(fig.) 1421; tower-shaped vessel c 1220, 1383;
pyx (eccl.) 8c.; a zodiacal sign a 1200;
-agium 1309, 1417, **torragium** 1289, 1315,
payment to castle-warden or jailer (G.);
-atus, towered c 1219; **-ella** 1162, 1349,
*-ellus c 1220, 1353, **torella** 1260, 1386,
-illa 15c., **-iolus** 1260, **-ettus** 1275, turret
(*see also* **torale, turettus**); **-ensis,** castellan,
warder of keep c 1156, 13c.; **turulus,** knoll,
hillock 1249; **-ello** 1329, 1460, **-illo** 1422,
to fit with turrets.

turrois, *see* TURK

turt/a, -arius, -ellus, *see* 1 **torta.**

turtica, *see* **torcha.**

turtra, *see* **truta.**

†**turtur,** turbot c 1200, 1483.

turtur/eus c 1250, **-inus** c 1250, a 1275, of
a turtle-dove.

turulus, *see* **turris.**

turva, *see* 1 **turba.**

tus liberum, frankincense 1307; **tur/ibile**
(**thur-**) 1402, 1407, **-ibilum** 1438, c 1467,
-iblium 1345, c 1400, **-ebulum** 1423,
-ibularium 1442, 15c., **terribulum** 1371,
c 1499, †**tribulum** 1461, *for* **-ibulum,**
censer; **-ibularius,** censer-bearing 1294,
c 1350; *1200, 1556, **-iferarius** c 1296,
‡**-ifex** 1483, thurifer, censer-bearer; **-ifica-
tio,** censing 1314, c 1414; *-**ifico,** to cense,
burn incense, sacrifice (?) 980. a 1100, 1483.

†**tuscho,** to fit (plough-share) with (?) point
1326.

tusorium, *see* **tunsio.**

tuss/a, -io, *see* 2 **tassa.**

†**tustatus,** (?) tousled (? *cf.* O.F. *tuster,* to
buffet) 1449.

†**tustea,** (?) tuft (of silk) (Sc.) 1471.

Tutannicus, *see* **Teutonicus.**

tut/atio c 1102, c 1500, **-io** c 1343, protection,
maintenance; **-abilis,** defensible c 1090;
-amen, warranty 1086; **-ator** 790. c 1188,
1528, **-atrix** (*f.*) c 1258, **-rix** (*f.*) 8c. 1289,
guardian; **-or,** warrantor 1086; tutor (ac.)
1560, 1564; **-orium,** guardianship 1517;
-o, *for* **-or,** 7c.; **-or** (*dep.*), to 'defend', be
responsible for geld of (land) c 1102; *cf.*
TUIT

tutelo, *see* TITUL

tuth/emannus, -inmannus, tutina, *see*
TETHING

tuti/a (†**tuchia**) a 1235, c 1267, **tuthea**
a 1250, tutty (zinc oxide); **-ana,** compound
of tutty c 1267.

twall-, *see* **tuallia.**

twedum, *see* **theodum.**

twelfhindus (†**thelhindus,** †**theshindus,**

†**thyelfindus,** †**tlefhindus,** †**tyehindus),** (one) having weregeld of 1,200 shillings c 1115.

twella, *see* **tuallia.**

twihindus (†**thifhindus,** †**thithindus,** †**tihindus,** †**wifhindus),** (one) having weregeld of 200 shillings c 1115.

twillum, twill, ribbed cloth 1346.

twimberellum, *see* **tumberellum.**

twinplix, St. Mildred's measure, 2½ bushels (Canterbury) c 1300.

twista 1294, c 1438, **thuista** 1265, eyed part of hinge.

tya, *see* **tia.**

tyddinga, *see* **tethinga.**

tyeburus, *see* **geburus.**

tylato, *see* **dilatatio.**

tylys, *see* **phthisis.**

tymboralis, *see* **tumberellum.**

tymbra, *see* **timbra.**

tymerium, *see* **timber.**

tympan/um, bell-wether c 1115; nave of wheel c 1200, ‡15c.; **-arium,** belfry c 1115; **-izatio,** melody c 1200; **-izo,** to make music, ring out a 675. c 1200, c 1380; to beat one's breast a 1200.

typh/us (eccl.), **typus** 7c., 934. c 1125, c 1352, elation, pride; **phipon,** *for* **-on,** whirlwind c 1200.

typ/us a 1100, a 1250, **typhus** c 1193, 'type' of intermittent fever; type (for printing) 1518, 1596; **-orum fusor,** type-founder 1568; †**-arium,** seal c 1192, 1296; **-ice,** figuratively, as a type or portent c 793, 10c. a 1090, c 1620; 'typically' (of fever) a 1250; **-icus** 7c., c 990. c 1197, a 1452, **-icalis** 14c. figurative, allegorical; **-ocosmia,** 'typocosmy', method of learning 1620; **-ographia** 1564, 1595, **-ographica** 1620, printing; **-ographicus,** of printing 1550, 1564; **-ographus,** printer, 1518, c 1603; **-ico,** to conform to a 'type' (of fever) a 1250.

tyragra, *see* **chiragra.**

tyrann/ia c 730. c 1458, 1464, **-ium** 15c., tyranny; **-ilis,** tyrannical 1345; **-ior,** more tyrannical c 1250, c 1255; **-iter,** tyrannically 1275, c 1460; **-us,** shrike (bird) 1544; **-izo,* to tyrannize c 1177, 1461.

tyr/iaca, -us, *see* **theriaca.**

tyr/o, -ocinium, -uncula, *see* 1 **tiro.**

tyrtenus, *see* **tirretena.**

tysis, *see* **phthisis.**

U

uber/ nasi, fleshy part of nose a 1250; **-atio maris,** (?) increase in tidal force a 1250.

ubi/ (*subst.*) 1267, c 1270, **-etas** c 1250, c 1270, **ubeitas** p 1347, **-catio** a 1361, 'whereness', position; (*adv.*) whither c 730. 1086, 1366; whereupon c 1305; **u. et u.,** wherever 8c.; **-cumque,** whithersoever c 1283; **-libet,** anywhither c 1304; **-quitas,** ubiquity 1610; **-quetarius,** ubiquitous 1622; **-co,** to situate c 1360.

ucha, cry c 550.

uchia, *see* **hucha.**

uchium, *see* **nusca.**

ud/lago, -ago, *see* UTLAG

ulio, ullagium, *etc., see* **oleagium.**

ulla, (?) 'tug' (of harness) 1277, 1297.

*ull/atenus, in any respect whatever c 1090, 1439; **-ibi** 1445, **-icubi** c 1370, **-ubi** 1649, anywhere.

ulmaria, meadowsweet (bot.) 1634; ‡**valmaria,** "penny-grass" 14c.

ulm/ellus c 1191, 1220, **urmellus** c 1275, 1279, **omellus** 1278, 1306, **hulmus** 1241, 1333, **elmus** 1284, 1434, *for* **-us,** elm; **-etum,** elm-grove 1213, 1250; **-ineus,** of elm c 700; *cf.* 2 **holma.**

uln/a **a* 1128, 1587, **u. regia** 1329, 1430, **-us** c 1396, **alna** a 1180, 1536, †**ala** 1382, **-ata** 1289, c 1460, measure of length, ell; 1269, 1419, **u. ferrea** 12c., 1319, **alna** c 1300, ell-measure; ‡**-alis, -arius,** ell-long 1483; **-etum,** ell length 1302; **-agium** 1304, 1587, †**avenagium** (? **aulnagium**) 1398, **-atio** 1300, 1587, 'aulnage' (duty on cloth) *or* measuring in ells; **-ator** 1287, 1587, **-eator** 1291, 1419, **-erator** 1330, **-arius** 1327, 'aulnager'; **-o** 1259, 1587, **-eo** 1291, **-ero**

1330, **alno** c 1290, to measure by the ell; *see also* **oleagium.**

ulositas, woolliness 13c.

†**ultagium,** (?) *for* **ultragium** *or* **huntagium,** outrage *or* disgrace 15c.

ulteri/or, further, additional 1248, 1427; **-us,** for the future c 1000. a 1236.

ultim/itas, ultimate limit a 1250, p 1300; lowest position or status (mon.) c 1303; highest generality 1620; **-ate* c 1334, 1461, ‡**-atim** 1483, finally; **-atim,** extremely a 1250; **-atus,** completed 1267, c 1343; **final* c 1290, c 1470; placed at bottom, degraded c 1395; **-o,* lately, recently c 1204, c 1452; **-ogenitus,** last-born 1255, 1347; **-um terribilium,** death 1408; **ad-um** c 730. c 1066, c 1250, **in -o** 1428, at last, at latest; **in -o,** at the hour of death 12c.; *see also* **presentatio; -o,** to oppose as extremes a 1250.

ulti/o, punishment 13c., c 1362; †**-matio,** *for* **-o,** vengeance p 1377.

ultra (*prep.*), above (of place) c 1266, c 1450; (in authority) over 1242, 1280; **u. mare,** absence overseas as ground for essoin (leg.) 1194, c 1290; *cf.* **de ultra.**

ultraequinoctialis, inhabitant of opposite temperate zone 1516.

ultragium, *see* **hutesium; ultagium.**

Ultrahumbrensis, Northumbrian c 710.

ultramarinus, **oversea,* of or from overseas c 790, c 1000. c 1192, 1549; person dwelling overseas c 1172, 13c.

ultramontanus (*adj.*), beyond mountains 1330; north of Alps c 1125, 1460; south of Alps 1240, 1301; (*subst.*), person dwelling beyond mountains c 1277.

ultroicio, to cast off 1317.

ultr/onee, voluntarily c 1150, 1470; **-oneus** c 1190, a 1236, **-aneus** c 1000, wilful, perverse; **-aneus,** *for* **-oneus,** spontaneous c 1365.

ulusculum, *see* holus.

umagium, *see* homo.

umbell/a, sunshade c 1217; **-atus,** umbellate (bot.) 1641.

umb/ilicus, clock-hand 1499; focus (of ellipse) 1686; ‡**u. marinus** 14c., ‡**u. Veneris** 1652, kinds of gem; **-iculus** c 1250, a 1408, **-elicus** 1322, 1583, *for* **-ilicus,** navel, centre.

umbr/a, north 1209, c 1300; outline, 'ghost' (her.) 1415, a 1446; **-aculum,** shrine 14c.; pretence c 1194, 1461; c 550, c 730, **-amen** 870, 993, **-ositas** c 1115, 1267, darkness; **-amen,** shadow c 1325; protection c 1180; ‡**-ago,** pygmy 1652; **-alis,** shady (Sc.) 1527, 1585; Umbraria, *Ombrière,* (provostry of) extramural district (Bordeaux) 1222, 1405; viserium **-arium,** (?) visor overshadowing face 1322; **-atice,** covertly c 1305, c 1370; c 730. c 1283, 1427, **-aliter** a 1090, **-atiliter** c 1500, **-ositer** c 1500, symbolically; c 1125, c 1400, **-atiliter** 14c., in outward show; **-aticus,** covert c 1125; ‡1440, **-atilis** c 1340, shy (of horse); **-atilis,** symbolic c 730. a 1204; insubstantial, delusive a 1100, 1620; ‡spectral 1652; **-atio,** representation in outline (her.) a 1446; **-atus,** 'umbrated', represented in outline (her.) p 1394, a 1446.

‡**umbrina,** halibut 1570.

umer-, *see* HUMER

umid-, umor-, *see* humor.

un/a, -arius, *see* unus.

unatim, *see* unitio.

unbod/mota, 'unbidden moot' of borough court (Newport Pagnell) 1544; **-hundredum** (Reading) 1548.

1 uncea, ounce, wild cat c 1250, 1290.

2 unc/ea 1329, 1587, **ouncia** 1341, **-eata, -eus** 1587, **-ius** 1363, **-tia** 1221, 1222, **unx** 1377, *for* **-ia,** ounce (weight); **-ia de Troy** 1434; **-ia,** inch c 1115, c 1250; **-ialiter,** in letters an inch long 15c.; *cf.* enchia; *see also* nusca.

†**unciatus** (?) *f.l.* for initiatus, 12c.

unc/inus, hook (bibl.); **-us pro olla,** pot-hook 1440; **-ifer,** claw-footed 1220; **-osus,** crooked c 1180; *cf.* unga.

uncosta (*pl.*), 'uncosts', 'oncosts', extra expenses (Sc.) 1466.

unct/io, anointing (of king, *etc.*) 12c., 1570; papal title 1339; 1382, 1506, **ungtio** 1377, greasing, lubrication; **u. calciamentorum,** polishing shoes 980; **u. extrema,** extreme unction (eccl.) c 1220, 1549; **u. ovium,** sheep-salve 1506, 1534; **uncxio olei** c 760; **-uositas,** greasiness 12c., 1622; ‡**-uosa,** self-heal (bot.) 14c.; **-uosus,** greasy a 1250, 1452; **-ura,** anointing (with salve) c 1266, 1357; 1254, 1327, *****-um** c 1115, 1419, grease, fat; **-uralis,** (?) requiring anointment (med.) a 1250; **-us Domini,** the Lord's anointed a 1155, c 1340.

†**uncula terre,** small piece of land 859.

und/a sacra, holy water 8c.; ‡**-a, -ena,** water sprite 1652; **-atio,** flood, deluge c 1320, 1465; **-anter,** in waves c 1213; **-anus,** on the waves c 780; **-atus** 1295, a 1446, **-osus** p 1394, a 1446, **-ulatus** c 1595, 'undy', wavy (her.); *see also* ungosa; **-ipotens,** ruling the waves c 1608; **-isonus,** rippling, lapping c 1000. a 1142; **-ivagus,** sailing c 780; **-ivomus,** spouting water c 1125; **-ositas,** flood 14c.; **-ula,** wavelet c 700, c 790; **-ulatio,** undulation 1620, 1622; invecting (her.) c 1595; **-ulatus,** invected (her.) c 1595; *see also* lignum.

und/e, *****whereof (*partitive*) 1220, 1516; whereof (*possessive*) 1323, c 1427; wherewith, whereby (*instrumental*) c 1115, c 1441; *****concerning which 1072, c 1400; *****wherefore, whereupon 955. 12c., c 1451; inasmuch as 1231, c 1301; whereas 14c.; **habeo u.,** to have the wherewithal 1220, 1226; **u. vivere,** the means of livelihood c 1349; **u. nihil habet,** name of a writ 1260, 1419; †**-equandoque,** whencesoever (G.) 1255; *****-equaque** c 1250, c 1470, **-iquaque** 1380, on every side; **-iquever-sum** c 730, **-iqueverso** c 1115, in every direction.

und/ecima, tax of one-eleventh 1295, c 1400; **-ecimo,** eleventhly 1279, c 1343; **-enarius,** group of eleven a 1180, c 1188; (?) cycle of eleven days 1424; **-ennis,** eleven years old c 1212; lasting eleven years c 1470.

under/clutum, 'under-clout' (of plough) c 1315; **-mannus** c 1300, **-setis** a 1128, **-setlus** c 1250, under-tenant.

unfrithmannus, one not included in the peace c 1115.

†**unga,** item in stock of castle, (?) *for* unca, hook, c 1180.

†**ungebend/eus** (†**-rus**), (?) unbidden, unsummoned (leg.) c 1115.

‡**ungosa, undosa** (*pl.*), excrement 1652.

ungtio, *see* unctio.

unguentum, grease 1242, 1422; **u. album,** a horse-salve 1334; **u. argenti,** lead ointment 13c.; **u. Aragonium** 1414, **u. Cesarinum** a 1270, sorts of ointment; ‡**u. croceum** (alch.), elixir 1652.

ungu/is, fish-hook c 1000; nail's breadth 11c.; **-ilinum,** ring with gem inset c 1362; **-illa,** translucent substance, onyx c 1250.

ungul/a, finger-nail c 780; thumb-nail c 1110, 1274; **u. (oculi),** tumour in eye a 1250, ‡1652; **u. caballina,** coltsfoot (bot.) a 1250, 1634; ‡**u. c. aquatica,** water-lily 14c.; **u.** †**Saracenica** (bot.) a 1250; **-o,** to ride, prance 14c.; **-or** (*dep.*), to paw 14c.

unialis, single, only one c 480.

unianim/itas, *for* unanimitas, unanimity 838; **-iter,** unanimously 705, 770; **-is,** unanimous c 630, 11c.; **-us,** harmonious c 730; †(?) intimate c 790.

unibil/itas, capacity for union c 1270, p 1300; *****-is,** capable of being united c 1225, c 1367.

unicola, monotheistic c 950.

unicorn/us a 1446, 1489, **-is** 12c., 1340, unicorn; (?) narwhal 1431; Scots coin 1487; (*adj.*) one-horned 1271; ‡**-u solare, u. minerale,** potable gold (alch.) 1652.

unicor/s, unanimous 1283, c 1402; **-diter,** of one accord 1438.

unic/us, (adj.) entire c 1190; (subst.) un-married man c 1197, c 1250; -a, only daughter c 800.

unific/us, unifying 870; -o, to unify 870.

unifolium, maianthemum (bot.) 1641.

*uniform/itas, uniformity 1224, c 1451; -is, conformable, concordant c 1225, c 1306; -iter c 1160, c 1332, †univerformiter 1427, uniformly; in agreement c 1194, 1459; in conformity (with) 1220, 1461.

unigen/eitas, homogeneity c 1270, c 1290; -eus c 1250, c 1320, -ius, -us c 1250, homogeneous; *-itus, only-begotten son 793, 948. a 1090, c 1504.

unimode, unitedly 870.

unio, union, *joining 793, 984. c 1125, 1549; †corn (on foot) c 1160; see also unitio.

uni/parus, producing one at a birth 1622; -pedes (pl.), (fabulous) one-footed men c 1212; -sonus, in unison (mus.) 1351, 1686.

unissimus, see unus.

unit/as, unity (title) c 600. 1231; community c 1410; unit a 1150, 1218; total c 1470; -ates (pl.) 815, 870.

unit/io, uniting, union c 1205, 1493; -e a 1290, c 1411, -im 870, unatim c 790, -ative c 1300, -ive 13c., c 1367, unitedly, in union; -atorius c 1381, *-ivus 870. a 1275, c 1460, uniting, unitive; -or, unifier c 1180, 1343; -ior, more united 1378; -um, unit 870; -us, one c 550; -o, to unite 870. 12c., 1378; unio fenum, to make hay c 1250, 1260; cf. unus.

universal/itas, universality, generality a 1233, 1603; *-e, universal (log.) c 1115, c 1500; in -i, in general c 1470; heres -is, sole heir (G.) 1316; morbus -is, disease attack-ing all members a 1250; via -is, public highway c 1150; -iter, *universally, with-out exception 793, 870. c 1125, 1549; in a universal sense (log.) c 850. c 1160, a 1280; -isatio, universalization a 1360; -ista, believer in universals (log.) a 1360; supporter of papal claim to universal supremacy c 1620.

univers/itas, universality, generalization 1160, c 1220; *the whole (body), community c 730. c 1160, 1419; commonalty (of town) c 1221, 1438; *university (ac.) 1231, 1586; u. Anglie, all England 1199, 1274; *noverit u. vestra 1148, c 1452; see also via; in -um c 1200, in -a 1258, in -o 1308, c 1400, in general; per -um, wholesale 1299; -o me, to abandon oneself wholly (to) c 1115.

univoc/atio, calling by the same name 870. c 1270; use of the name in the same sense a 1250, c 1362; *-us, having one meaning c 1160, c 1362; *-e, in a single sense a 1180, c 1470; *-o, to name in the same sense a 1232, 1378.

unlaga, wrong, illegality (A.S.) c 1115.

unlandiscus, foreign 12c.

†uno, (?) f.l. for vero, 1086; see also unus.

un/us, *a, an (article) 967, c 1000. 1086, 1416; u. .... alius 1086, c 1340; u. .... alter 1228; u. et idem, one and the same 1378; -i (pl.), one pair c 1155, p 1205; in -um, in unity c 1343; de -o in -um, one by one 1245; -a, first day c 730; -o dierum c 1137, -a dierum c 1250, one day; -o modo vel

alio 1220; -arius, unit c 815; -opere, unanimously c 790; -issimus, unique 1344; -o, to bring together, collect c 1370, c 1450; u. bladum, to gather corn into sheaves 1388; cf. unitio.

unx, see 2 uncea.

upa, see 2 hopa.

upland/a 14c., huppelanda 1168, 1170, oplondina (n. pl.) a 1190, upland; -ensis (opelandensis), uplander, countryman (Sc.) 13c.

upotheca, see hypotheca.

upte/ia 1226, -ium 1234, -um 1417, -sium (†urtesium) 1253, up-tie (naut.).

upupa, "lapwing" ‡1440, 1544; hupa, hoopoe 1284.

ura, furrow c 550.

uran/us c 550, c 1433, horanus c 550, the heavens; -eus c 965, -icus c 1000. c 1100, 1418, heavenly.

Urbanista, adherent of Pope Urban VI 1385.

urb/s (m.) 738; -is refectio, burhbote c 1102, c 1115; -ecula, little town c 1000; -anitas, eloquence c 1000; kindness, service 1319; u. Anglie, curtesy (leg.) 1398.

*urce/olus a 1090, 1432, -ola c 1411, 1524, -olum 1288, c 1534, orceolus 1276, urseolus 1388, c 1455, -a 12c., -us c 1200, 1519, urseus c 1445, cruet, ewer for holy water (eccl.); -lus 1312, urcielus 1373, urscellus 1379, ursiolum 1388, for -olus, pot, pitcher; -us, (adj.) with a water-pot 11c.

urgen/tia, urgency c 1188, c 1250; *-s, urgent a 1164, 1564; -ter, urgently c 1188, c 1293; -tius c 1250; -tissime c 1236, c 1255.

uricomus, see uritivus.

†urin/a puerorum, mercury (alch.) 1652; ‡u. vini, vinegar 1652; *-ale 1209, 1476, (?) orynale 1392, urinal, chamber-pot; vessel used in alchemy c 1345; -atrix, diver (bird) 1544; -o, to urinate c 1180, 1508.

†urio, the game of Troy c 1160.

uritides, pori, c 1210, p. euritides a 1250, ureters (med.).

ur/itivus, caustic a 1200, a 1250; †-icomus (†viricomus), fiery-haired c 550; -o, to be burnt c 800. a 1250, c 1336; cf. ustio.

url/a 1157, 1200, -ura 1216, c 1323, edging, border; -o 1205, 1295, orlo 1204, to border, ornament at the edge.

urmellus, see ulmellus.

urna, bushel 11c.

Uronica, image of the Saviour (distinct from Veronica) c 1220.

urs/eolus, -cellus, -eus, etc., see urceolus.

urs/us albus a 1200, 1252, u. marinus a 1200, -a alba 1290, polar bear; -anus, bearish 13c.; -arius c 1125, c 1325, -enarius 1484, -uarius 1542, -urarius 1472, -iator 16c., bear-ward; -igerulus, bear-carrier c 1620; †-ula, (?) bear-cub 1334; see also branca.

ursutus, see hirsutus.

urtesium, see upteia.

urtic/a, nettle-cloth 1371; u. mortua, dead-nettle ‡14c., 1538; -atio, stinging with nettles 1622; -o, to sting c 1180, c 1376.

†urtinercha, (?) furlong (in open field) c 1217.

†uruscus, (?) for bruscus (bot.), 1267.

us/agium, -ito, *etc.*, *see* usus.
uscerium, usherpageus, *see* ostium.
usi/a c 800, 11c. 12c., 14c., ousias 9c., -on·
c 1370, -osis c 1200, c 1370, substance
(οὐσία); ‡-alis, substantial 1483.
†usiformis, (?) *f.l.* for versiformis, changeable c 1200.
usque/ (*conjunction*), *until c 1127, c 1459;
(*prep.*), up to, as many as c 800. c 1400; as
far as concerns 1086; u. ad, with a margin
of, falling short by 1270; for the duration of
1285; u. ad annum, for a year 1281; u. ad
in (with *acc.*) 1230; u. alias, till another
time c 1390; u. ante, until (*prep.*) c 1343;
-hac 7c., u. hodie c 1362, u. modo 1086,
c 1444, till now; -nunc (*subst.*), the present
c 800; u. post, till after 1263, c 1343; *-quo,
until (*conjunction*) c 700, c 1006. c 1080,
1420; -tenus, always 797.
uss/arius, -era, -eria, *see* ostium.
ussim, *see* ustio.
ustil/menta (hustil-) 1435, 1503, -amenta
1453, -imenta c 1443, 1539, hustelementa
1426, hustelmenta 1452, hostellamenta
1411, 1420, hostilamenta 1402, hostil-
menta 1541, usticia 1319, hustensilia
1313, household goods, utensils (*pl.*);
-amentum 1321, 1324, -ementum 1324,
weaver's loom; *cf.* utensile, vas.
ust/io c 1400, †-ala 1370, scorch, mark of
burning; -ibilis, combustible a 1250,
a 1446; -ivus, incendiary a 1250, c 1270;
speculum -orium, burning-glass c 1595;
-ulatio 12c., ‡-illatio a 1440, burning;
-ura, burn (med.) c 1200; ‡ussim, "burn-
ingly" 15c.; -rina, -rinum, *maltkiln
1388, 1567; 1539, u. calcis 1416, 1420,
u. calcina 1443, lime-kiln; ‡-rinator,
-rinatrix (*f.*), maltster 1483; ‡-rino, to
make malt 1483; *cf.* uritivus.
usu/alis, -fructus, *etc.*, *see* usus.
†usula, fish found in Danube, (?) *for* alausa,
c 1190.
usur/ia, *for* -a, interest, usury 12c., c 1272;
-atio, exaction of usury c 1375; -arius,
usurious 1290, 1457; *c 793. c 1125, 1684,
-aius (C.I.) 1274, -aria (*f.*) 1185, 1275, -ator
1269, 1508, -atrix (*f.*) 1397, usurer; -o,
to bear interest c 1192, c 1267; to practise
usury, exact as interest c 1310, 1419.
usurp/atio, usurpation a 1090, 1461; -aticius,
prescriptive (leg.) 1537; -ative, by usurpation 12c., c 1414; -o super, to encroach
upon (privileges of) 1365.
us/us, use, right of possession (leg.) 1574,
1588; 'use', rite (eccl.) c 1220, 1526; easement 812; (G.) 1253, -agium (Fr.) 1280,
customary payment; -agium c 1157, 1416,
-aticum (Fr.) 1388, *-uagium 1219, 1273,
-uaria 1199, -uarium 1154, -itatio c 1370,
c 1456, -itatum 1509, use, usage, right to
use; -antia, usance, period allowed for
payment a 1564; -atus, used, worn (of
cloth) c 1135; -ibilis, usable c 1361, 1378;
-or, one who uses a 1300; -ualia (*pl.*),
necessaries a 1400; -ualis *c 1000, c 1178,
16c., -uarius 1433, -itabilis 1344, ordinary,
in current use; *usual, customary c 1191,
c 1340; (of horses) broken in c 1178;
*-ualiter a 1100, c 1460, -itate 1555,

usually; -itatissimus, most familiar 1006;
-uarius a 1220, c 1400, -ufructuarius
c 1258, 1559, one who has use without
ownership; -ufructuarium 1088, c 1170,
-ufructus 1313, 1575, usufruct (leg.);
-ufructuo, to hold in usufruct 1546; -ito,
to use p 1147, c 1450; *cf.* utensile; *see also*
hussus.
1 ut, musical note 1351.
2 ut (*final* or *consecutive* with *indicative*)
c 1000. 12c., 1537; (with *inf.* after sic) c 1000;
ut communius 1346, ut in pluribus
c 1300, ut multum 14c., for the most part;
utico, in order that c 550; utique, namely
796; utpote si, as if for instance 1252;
†utpoti, inasmuch as 1451; utquid, to
what end? why? (bibl.).
ut/ensile 13c., c 1256, -ensilium 1321, 1400,
weaver's loom; a 738, c 1021. 12c., -ilitas
778, 860, appurtenance, easement (of land);
-ensilis, of the nature of an easement 674;
-encilia 1266, -enselia 1340 (*pl.*), res
-ensiles c 1000, necessaries; *cf.* USTIL; -en-
tia c 1367, -ilitas 1288, a 1347, use, usage,
right to use; -ilitatem facio, to relieve
nature 1409; -ilis (annus *or* dies), available
(leg.) c 1185, c 1303; -illimus, most useful
1169; -or, to dwell c 1000; (with *inf.*) to
be accustomed to c 1290, c 1451; (*passive*)
to be used, employed (?) a 700. a 1340, 1519;
cf. usus.
1 ut/er, *for* uterque, each of two c 550.
c 1177, c 1380; -ralis, both 812; -rum,
name of a writ c 1290, c 1324; u. et ... et,
both ... and 793.
2 ut/er, (glass) bottle 1480; bucket of well
1209; -rus, bag or bottle 1411; -res (*pl.*),
bellows 1391; -rinus, *for* -erinus, c 1527.
utesium, *see* hutesium.
utewara, *see* utwara.
†utflatta, (?) (fine for) escape of felon 1330; *cf.*
utleipa.
uthundredum, 'out-hundred' (*cf.* hundredum forinsecum) 1180, 1238.
utibann/um (hut-) c 1150, c 1170, -a a 1279,
'foreign service' (due to crown) (S.W. Eng.).
uti/co, -que, *see* 2 ut.
uti/nam ut! would that! 800; -natio, expression of wish, vain regret c 1430, a 1452; -no
c 1435, a 1452, -nizo a 1640, to express
a wish.
utlag/a 1086, 1221, -us 1130, 1608, -ius
c 1115, 1230, -arius, utlegarius c 1275,
*-atus c 1115, c 1436, utlaatus c 1298,
utlegatus c 1570, 1684, outlaw; *-aria
1086, 1687, outlagaria 1274, 1333, -eria
1255, c 1436, utlaria c 1115, c 1370,
utlegaria c 1150, c 1470, †utlugaria 1348,
-ia 1166, *-atio c 1130, c 1370, utlegatio
c 1470, 1684, outlawry; *-o 1086, 1687, -io
c 1227, 1275, outlago 1274, 15c., utlawyo
1269, utlego 1293, 1304, udlago 1166,
†udago c 1200, to outlaw; -o, udlago, to
be outlawed 1086; u. me 1086.
utlanda, 'out-land' (outside common field)
1160.
utleipa, payment by serf for flight (A.S.
uthleap) c 1115.
utor, *see* utensile.
utpote, utpoti, utquid, *see* 2 ut.

utr-, *see* uter (1 & 2).

utsoka, 'out-soke' 1086.

utter/atio, offering for sale 1612, 1617; -o, to offer for sale c 1400, 1490; 1551, 1588, uttro 1575, to utter, issue (false coin); to utter (words) 1716; -o falsam commissionem 1361.

utwara c 1115, c 1157, utewara c 1150, 'foreign service' (due to crown) (esp. Lincs.).

1 †uva, (?) tuft of grass *or* cluster of seeds c 550.

2 uv/a, grape: u. canina (bot.) a 1250; u. Corinthiana, currant 1600; ‡u. crispa, "gooseberry" 1570; ‡u. lupina, black nightshade 14c.; -a c 1200, -ula c 1200, a 1250, uvula (med.); -ea a 1250, 1267, tela -ea, tunica -ea a 1250, retinal coat of eye; -ularia, Canterbury bell (bot.) 1634; apostema -atum (med.) a 1250.

†uvaria, (?) *for* ovaria, belly (of bird) a 1150.

uxor/, (as title) goodwife, Mrs., 1547; -atio, marriage c 1377; -ialis, conjugal 14c.; -ata, married woman 1279, c 1448; -atus, married man c 793. c 1115, c 1400, born in wedlock 1227; *-o c 1150, 15c., -or (*dep.*) c 1115, 12c., to marry a wife; to give in marriage 1194, 1284.

uzifur, cinnabar a 1250, ‡15c.

V

vacabundus, *see* VAG

vac/atio *1219, 1549, -atura c 1230, 1417, -antia 1399, vacancy of see or benefice, or appointment thereto (eccl.); vacancy of tenement c 1545; voiding, annulment 1285; leisure, holiday c 1430, 1461; vacation (leg.) 1295, c 1503; *vacation (ac.) c 1250, c 1549; v. deliberandi, time spent in deliberation c 1218; -atura, cessation a 1142; -atius, with more leisure 1422; -o, *to be vacant (eccl.) c 1185, 15c.; to be null and void 1257, 1378; to be available (of money) 1259; to disregard 14c.; *cf.* VACU

vacc/a cervina, fabulous animal, half cow, half deer c 1190; facca, cow a 1300; *-aria 1086, c 1300, -arium c 1160, 1199, vacheria c 1184, 1375, †vachivia c 1100, wacheria 1380, 'vachery', cow-pasture, grazing-farm; 1200, a 1452, -asterium c 1255, domus -arum 1341, cow-shed; *-arius, cowherd 1086, 1399; -ineus, of a cow c 1362; -inus, made of cow-skin 1213, 1265; -ipotens, lord of cows c 790.

vaccini/ensis, (?) of whortlebury c 550; ‡vaxinum, "violet" 15c.; vacietum, grape-hyacinth (Fr. *vaciet*) 1538; -o, (?) to make fruitful c 1148.

vacellum, *see* vas.

vacerra, pile (her.) 1654.

vach-, *see* VACC

vacillant/er, falteringly 13c.; -ior, more wavering c 1546.

vaco, *see* vacatio.

vacor, *see* VAG

vacu/itas, leisure 1345; -us, empty-handed, with nothing accomplished 13c., 15c.; null and void 1226, c 1451; vain, useless c 1310; allec -um, herring without roe 1463, 1550; in -um, in vain c 1080, 14c.; -atio, emptying 1226, c 1437; voiding, annulment c 1298; v. fumi, smoke-vent 1252; -ativum, a purgative c 1324; -o, to annul c 1125, c 1400; to release c 1370, c 1400; v. terram, to leave the country 1221; *cf.* vacatio.

vad/a, -abilis, -arium, *see* vadum.

vaddum, *see* waida.

vad/ium *1086, p 1478, wadium 1184, -um 1166, guadium 1608, vagium 1174, c 1192, wagium a 1185, 1275, gagium (G.) 1279, 1313, guagium 1289, c 1397, -emonium 1200, -iamentum 1200, 1279, gageria 1260, gagieria (G.) 1305, 1310, pledge, bail, security; *1168, 1583, wagium 14c., gagium 1265, 1434, gagea 1473, gadgium 1283, gatgium (G.) 1314, pay, wages; v. mortuum, *see* morgagium; pono ad -ia, to put on pay-roll, engage 1272; p. in -ium, to pawn c 1185, 1201; ‡guadia, "custom" 1483; -ius, surety, bail c 1275, 1561; -iatio c 1115, c 1220, -atio c 1125, c 1400, -itio c 1225, giving, or being held to, bail or pledge; gagiatio, reprisal (G.) 1293; -ium duelli 13c., 1290, gagium duelli (G.) 1290, -iatio duelli c 1185, 1383, wager of battle (leg.); -iatio legis, wager of law c 1290, 1588; wagerum 1464, gajura (G.) 1243, wager, bet;

-io 1084, 1350, wagio 1206, 1399, gagio (C.I.) 1270, (G.) 1313, †gagino 1272, to give security for; 1199, 1424, †vidio 1250, guadio 1608, to give as security; to pay wages to 1376; to wager 14c., ‡1483; gagio, to seize in reprisal 1293; ‡guadio, "to ordain" 1483; -io bellum c 1115, c 1437, *v. duellum c 1185, 15c., wagio duellum 1202, 1212, to wage (give surety for) battle (leg.); v. judicium, to wage ordeal (leg.) c 1115; v. legem (meam), to wager law c 1115, 1425; v. l. magnam 1274, c 1320; v. misericordiam, to put oneself at mercy (leg.) 1236, 1293; v. pacem, to pledge peace 1275; v. probationem, to pledge proof (leg.) c 1258; *see also* vadum.

vadlettus, *see* valettus.

vado, to go, run (of an argument) c 1300; v. et venio, to go to and fro 1251; v. ad, to pay suit of court at c 1100; v. ad aratrum 1189, v. ad carrucam 1370, to plough; v. ad mentem, to go according to intention c 1332, c 1343.

vad/um, water 1241; -a 1252, p 1377, -ium c 1200, *for* -um, ford; -arium, (?) causeway 1269; -abilis, fordable c 1160, c 1370; *see also* vadum.

vaeta, *see* waita.

vafra, *see* wafra.

vafrities, cunning 1518, 1608.

vag/a c 1300, **-um** 1297, 1462, waif; **-abundus** 1255, 1461, *****vacabundus** 1300, c 1480, **-ipalans** c 1115, vagabond (*subst.*); **-ibundus**, tottering c 1115; **-acitas**, love of wandering 7c.; **-atio**, (?) mental derangement c 1160; **-ativus**, mobile a 1250; **-itus**, wandering 1319; **-ans**, planet 1184; **vacor**, *for* **-or** 1406; *see also* **waga**.

vagin/a, plough-sheath 1340, 1344; **vagena** 1332, **gaigna** 1326, †**gaigina** 1314, *for* **-a**, scabbard or bow-case; **-arius** 1248, 1419, **-ator** 13c., c 1393, scabbard-maker; **-atus**, sheathed 1312, 1462; **-ella**, pod (bot.) 14c.

vagito, to wail 6c.

vagium, *see* **vadium**.

vaifio, vaivus, *see* WAIV

vainio, *see* WAIN

vaisda, *see* **waida**.

vaissella, *see* **vas**.

‡**vala/torium**, ‡**-trum**, "churn" 15c.

valcatio, *see* **falcatio**.

valda, *see* **falda**.

Valdesius, *see* **Waldensis**.

val/e c 800, 1041. 1423, **-efactio** 13c., c 1325, leave-taking; **-efacio**, to say farewell to c 730. c 1180, 1508; **v. seculo** 1200, 1443, **v. vite** (**huic, presenti**) c 1115, c 1320, to die.

1 **val/entia**, power 1060; asset 1086; weight c 1370; *****c 1115, 1588, **-lantia** c 1180, **walentia** 1229, **-ens** c 1115, **-ere** 1292, **-itudo** c 1180, c 1400, *****-or** c 1102, c 1587, value; *see also* **ad**; **-iditas**, strength, force, c 700; **-itas**, profit 1242, c 1318; **-itudo**, valour 1461; **v. regis**, king's evil, scrofula c 1125; **-itudinarius**, infirm 1461; weakling 1427, 15c.; 1461, **-iosus** 13c., valiant; **-itura**, health c 1325, c 1455; **-itor** c 1226, p 1377, **-ettor** 1295, supporter; **-or**, time-value (mus.) c 1470; validity 1428; **-imentum**, validating a 1235 (*cf.* **valla**); **-idus** c 1290, c 1433, **-ibilis** a 1564, 1566, **-abilis** 1567, valid; **-idiusculus**, powerful c 1115; **-iabiliter**, valuably a 1564; **-ens**, magnate c 1358; vaillant, penny 1125, c 1190, **-eo**, to be alive 12c.; to be valid 13c., c 1380; **-ido**, to be able c 1400.

2 **valentia**, bed valance 1553.

valeriana, valerian (bot.) a 1250, ‡14c.

Val/esheria, -icus, *see* **Wallensis**.

valesium, *see* **valisium**.

valesona, *see* **vallis**.

*****valett/us** (**valect-**) 1184, 1588, **vallattus** 1293, **vadlettus** 1197, 1286, **vaslettus** a 1142, 1237, **vatlettus** 1205, 1257, **varlettus** 1461, **verlettus** (Sc.) c 1450, c 1540, **walettus** c 1298, **wadletus** c 1243, **watlettus** 1213, 'varlet', young man, esquire, yeoman, groom or servant; journeyman 1302, 1419; **v. ad arma** (G.) 1315; **v. Camere**, yeoman of the Chamber 1333, 1583; **v. Corone** c 1472, **v. de Corona** 1526; **v. itinerans**, vagabond 1230; †**-rius**, (?) acting as a groom 1300.

valgi/um c 1257, ‡**-a** c 1440, grimace; ‡**-ator**, "mower", grimacer c 1440; **-o**, to puff out (cheeks) 12c.

val/isium 1428, 1441, **-esium** 1298, 1413, valise.

valis/o, -ona, *see* **vallis**.

valit-, valid-, vallantia, *see* **valentia**.

vall/a 1227, 1331, **-ia** 1351, *for* **-um**, embankment; **v. dura in capite** (med.) c 1280; **-um**, boundary-wall (mon.) c 600; castle bailey a 1200, 1220; **-atio**, walling, fortification c 1200, c 1315; protection, confirmation 1439, 1465; **-atum**, ditch, moat, mill-lade (G.) 1284, 1289; **-ata** (*pl.*), earthworks c 1212; **-ettum**, (?) mound 1379; **-o** c 1258, c 1514, **-io** c 1422, to confirm, validate; to beset, besiege 12c., 1274; to beset (fig.) c 1230; **-eo**, to wall (a house) 1525; *cf.* **walla**.

vall/ettus, -attus, *see* **valettus**.

vall/is, pit, hole a 700; **contra -em aque**, upstream 1268; **-eia, -eium**, valley 1290, c 1350; **-osus** c 1260, **-iculosus** 1461, lying in a valley; **-agium**, toll on wine going downstream (G.) 1200; **valis/o** 1327, **-ona** (†**vasilona**) 1330, **valesona** 1337, catching of eels on way downstream; *cf.* AVAL

valmaria, *see* **ulmaria**.

valor, *see* **valentia**.

valt/a, -um, *see* VOLU

valt/rus 1213, **vealtris** 1204, kind of greyhound (Fr. *vautre*); ‡**veltria** c 1440, (?) **veltrum** 1471, leash of greyhounds; **-eria**, **veautria** 1212, **veltraria** 1130, **veauteria** 1225, office of 'fewterer' (greyhound-keeper); **-rarius** 1169, 1213, **waltrarius** 1192, **vautarius** (†**vantarius**) 1308, **vautrarius** 1317, **veltrarius** a 1100, 1208, **vealtrarius** 1202, 1206, **veauterarius** 1287, **veutrarius** (†**ventrarius**) 1219, 1393, **weutrereus** 1301, **vetrarius** 1250, **veautrator** 1219, **veutror** 1277, **venator veutrarius** 1301, fewterer; **veutrarius daemericius, v. haericius** 1312.

valutia, *see* **velvetum**.

valv/a, door, opening c 550; c 1400, †**vulva** 1292, flood-gate; **v. vitrea**, window-pane c 700; **walva**, leaf of door 1260; **-arius** 1376, **custos -aris** c 1180, door-keeper; **-ifragus**, door-shattering c 1160; **-ipatus**, door-opening c 1160; **-ula**, mouth (of bag) c 1000; **-ulus**, field (her.) 1654.

valvassor, *see* **vavassor**.

van/a gloria, vainglory 1399, 1461; **-iglorius**, vainglorious c 1200, 1421; **-iloquia** (*pl.*), vain-speaking c 600 c 793. 15c.; **-e** (eccl.), **-iter** c 1305, **in -um** c 1188, c 1370, in vain; *see also* VANN

Vandaliensis, Andalusian, light horseman 1362.

vandela, *see* **wandaila**.

vandor, *see* **viandator**.

vang/a 1276, 1464, **-ia** c 1317, **wangia** 1149, spade, shovel or (?) mattock; **v. ad secandum fenum** 1448; **-alis**, of a spade 1454; *cf.* **voga**.

van/guardia c 1383, **-gardia** 1461, 1540, **wangardia** 1461, vanguard (Sc.).

vannagium, *see* WAIN

vann/us, winnowing-fan: **fanna** c 1310, **-atorium** 1388; **vana** 1365, **fanum** 1313, vane; **-arius** 13c., 1251, *****-ator** a 1128, c 1335, winnower; **-atarius**, overseer of winnowing 1234; **wannatio**, winnowing 1336; **-ellus,**

lapwing (bird) 1255, 1544; **-o** c 1230, 1324, **fanno** c 1200, to winnow.
vantagium, *see* avantagium.
vantarius, *see* valtrus.
vanum, *see* vana.
vapentagium, *see* wapentacum.
vapor/, (?) light, gleam c 550; **-abilis,** transitory 9c.; capable of evaporation c 870. c 1257; c 1212, 1344, **-alis** 12c., **-arius** 1622, **-eus** c 870, **-osus** a 1250, 1424, vaporous; **-aliter** c 730. c 1236, **-ose** a 1450, as vapour; **-ativus,** evaporative c 1270.
vappasco, to turn flat (of wine) 1520.
vapul/atio, flogging 11c.; threshing 1266; 1397, 1440, **-atura** 1445, stamping (with a design); **-ator,** flogger c 1310; **wapulator,** thresher c 1225; **-o,** to thresh 1200, 1279; to stamp 1416, 1445.
varand-, varant-, varent-, *see* WARANT
vard-, *see* warda.
varect-, *see* WARECT
varellus, *see* barellus.
varenn-, *see* WARENN
†**vargariaton,** (?) *for* arachnida (bot.), 12c.
vari/atio c 1365, c 1380, **-amen** c 1257, **-antia** 1313, variation, variance; dispute c 1452, 1507; discrepancy in pleading (leg.) 1275, c 1380; **v. cutis,** scar or discoloration c 1115; **-abilis,** changeable c 1170, c 1295; interchanging c 798; **-abilitas,** changeability c 1290, p 1300; **-abiliter,** changeably a 1452; **-ator,** waverer c 1180; *see also* vitrum; **-atus,** various c 1380; **-egatio,** variegation 1620; **-opus,** variegated work c 1405; **-ose** c 1457, **-pliciter** 1437, variously; **-fico,** to work in divers ways 870; **-o,** to divert, alienate (property) 1461; **to** dispute c 1457, c 1458; **v. in narratione,** to vary in pleading (leg.) 1218, 13c.; *see also* varietas.
varicatio, transgression, straying a 1520.
varida, *see* warda.
vari/etas 1432, c 1488, ***-um** c 1180, c 1436, **bayrum** 1382, **verium** c 1192, 'vair', squirrel fur; **-um grossum,** 'grover' 1256, 1374; **v. minutum** 1198, c 1432, **verium minutum** 1280, **verrerum minutum** c 1308, **werellum** 1204, miniver; **-us,** of vair a 1154, a 1273; **-us, -atus, -egatus,** vairy (her.) c 1595; 1277, **verrus** 1242, **veyronus** 1390, 1317, brindled or dappled; **verrum,** (?) coloured marking c 1275; **veragium,** payment of pied or blemished animals to marshal c 1275, 14c.; *see also* variatio; *cf.* virgeus.
variol/a a 1250, c 1310, **-us** 13c., **verola** 1297, **veroles** (*pl.*) 1306, (?) †**barras** 13c., pustule, pox.
varlettus, *see* valettus.
varn-, *see* GARN; **vernantia.**
varr-, *see* WARECT
vas/, holy water stoup 1248, 1493; ***1209,** 1430, **-culum** 1086, 1511, †**fossellum** 1227, measure of flour; 1280, 1281, **-um** 1563, 1587, measure of ore; ***c 1130,** 1617, **-um** 1242, 1554, **-ellum** (†**nasellum**) 1324, vessel, ship (*cf.* **navis**); **v. apium,** **-culum** 1086, (?) †**basia** 1351, bee-hive; **v. electionis,** chosen vessel (St. Paul) 11c. c 1125; **-a** 1323, 1388, †**vosum** 1446, vessel,

pot; **-um,** vessel (of body) (med.) a 1250; **-ella** 1160, 1205, **-sallum** 1417, **vaissella** 1130, 1189, **veisella** 1204, 1206, **vessella** 1206, 1303, **vescella** 1296, plate (*coll.*); **-sallum** c 1322, **vaisellum** 1214, **veisellum** 1216, **vessellum** 1300, 1325, **-salamentum** 1338, ***vessellamentum** c 1150, 1415, **vessalamentum** 1400, piece of plate; **vessellamenta** (*pl.*), shipping, craft 1427; †**vestillamenta** (*pl.*), equipment, gear (naut.) 15c.; *cf.* USTIL; **-cellum** c 1160, 1254, **vacellum** c 1190, c 1240, **wacellum** c 1202, **wascellum** c 1190, 1251, **wascella** 1218, stream-bed (Sc. & Yorks.); **-culum,** coffin 771, 790; **-sulum** 1485, **fasculum** a 1150, **fassulum** c 1325, a 1400, *for* **-culum,** small vessel; *cf.* **basculus; -arius,** scullion c 1136.
vasa 1280, 1305, **wasa** 1293, **basa** 1277, 1308, mud-flat, beach (Fr. *vase*) (G.); *cf.* **wosa.**
Vasc/o 1252, 1347, **Wasco** a 1142, c 1420, **Guasco** a 1142, **Gasconensis** c 1420, **-onicus** c 1310, c 1350, **-oniensis** 1278, **Wasconiensis** 1231, c 1420, **Gasconius** 1400, Gascon; *cf.* **Basculus.**
vasilona, *see* vallis.
vaslettus, *see* valettus.
vass/allus 967. c 1185, 1608, **-alis** 1446, **-allulus** 13c., **-ellus** (G.) 1289, **-arius** 1608, **-us** c 800. a 1142, 1608, vassal; **-allagium** c 1250, a 1446, **-allargium** (G.) 1313, **-alegium** 1608, vassalage.
vassum, *see* bacia.
vastagium, *see* WAFT
vastell-, *see* wastellus.
vastracium, *see* batrachium.
vast/um *c 1130, 1563, **-a** a 1300, **wastum** 1275, 1291, **guastum** a 1195, †**wastina** (? **wastiva**) 1160, 1275, **guastiva** 1185, †**-ura** a 1300 (? *or for* vestura, crop), waste land; ***1155,** 1523, **-us** 1213, c 1296, **-a** c 1270, 1455, **wastum** 1155, c 1322, **wastus** 1212, **gastum** c 1320, waste, damage, destruction (to land, *etc.*); ***c 1154,** 1453, **wastum** 1155, c 1298, **guastum** 1199, 1324, **gastum** 1199, 1214, waste, (fine for) forest offence; ***'waste'** (leg.), king's or lord's right to felon's land c 1290, 1419 (*see also* **annus**); **-atrix,** ravaging (*f.*) 6c.; **wastus** 1086, c 1400, **guastus** 1086, *for* **-us,** lying waste, desolate: **wasto,** *for* **-o,** to lay waste 1086, 1219.
vasum, *see* vas.
vat/es, Christian priest or prophet c 550. c 1100; **-icinalis** c 1190, p 1377, **-idicus** c 730, c 950. c 1090, c 1450, prophetic; **-icus,** poetical 1241; **-ifer,** prophet c 790; **-ivomus,** that throws up a prophet 870; **-icino,** to prophesy 6c., 9c. 1330, c 1362.
vatlettus, *see* valettus.
vatta 1290, **fattum** 1327, c 1400, **factus** a 1283, **fatula** 1460, vat; ‡**futula,** "stand" (open tub) c 1440.
vau, letter of Hebrew alphabet c 1200.
vauga, *see* 2 waga.
vaulta, vauta, vausura, *see* VOLU
vautrarius, *see* valtrus.
vavass/or 1086, 1586, **valvassor** c 1450, 1586, **-orius** 1086, vavasour, undertenant;

-aria 1220, p 1380, **wavassaria** c 1300,
15c., **-eria** 12c., c 1200, **-oria** c 1115,
c 1258, **-ura** 1199, estate of vavasour.
vavnagium, *see* WAIN
vawta, *see* VOLU
vaxinium, *see* VACCINI
ve (*subst.*) cry of woe, prophetic denunciation
a 1205, a 1408; woe, grief c 730. 1166, c 1365.
-ve (enclitic), *for* **-que,** c 730.
veagium, *see* **viagium.**
vealt-, veaut- *see* **valtrus.**
vechrus, vecrus, defect, fault a 550.
vecia, *see* 1 **vicia.**
*vecordi/ter c 1300, c 1462, **-aliter** 1380,
foolishly, madly.
vect/io, carrying c 1185, 1528; (?) vehicle
1238; **Petri -igal,** (?) Peter's pence c 950;
-igatio (corporis), exercise a 1250; **-ura,**
*mount *or* baggage-wagon c 1188, c 1340;
baggage c 1190; load c 1522; "entunning"
(of ale) 1462; **-ito,** to carry c 1125, c 1450;
cf. VEH
veeria, *see* **via.**
veges, butt of wine (Port.) 1443; *see also* VEGET
veget/atio c 1145, 1620, **-abilitas** 12c.,
c 1360, power of growth; ***-abilia** (*pl.*),
vegetables, plants a 1250, 1686; **-abilis**
c 1200, 1620, **-alis** c 1361, ***-ativus** a 1250,
1344, vegetative, capable of growth; **-ativus**
c 1280, **veges** 1283, vigorous, lusty; **-atrix,**
invigorating (*f.*) 12c.; **-eto,** to grow 1241,
c 1277; to corroborate c 1002; **vegito,** to
invigorate 7c.
vehagium, *see* **via.**
vehementer, very c 730. 14c.
veh/iculum, vehicle, medium c 1270, 1424;
‡fluid in which drugs are administered 1652;
-icula equorum, horse-drawn carriage
1243; **-iculatorium,** wheelbarrow c 1440;
-ia, wagon-load 1541; **†-imen,** (?) uplifting 870; **-itio** 12c., 1448, **-itura** 1233,
carrying, transport; **-o,** to sail (*intr.*) 1347;
to "entun" (ale) 1462; *cf.* VECT
veiagium, *see* **viagium.**
veicium, *see* 2 **vicia.**
veirium, *see* **vitrum.**
veisell/a, -um, *see* **vas.**
veivo, *see* WAIV
vel, nor c 797; and c 1115; if not, otherwise
(Fr. *autrement*) 1224, 1276; **v. non,** *for*
necne, c 1224, c 1290; **v. plus v. minus,**
more or less 1221.
vel/a, -amen, -ivolo, *etc., see* **velum.**
†veletus, (?) *for* **veles,** light-armed soldier
1267.
velfedum, *see* **velvetum.**
velg/a, -o, velia, *see* **felea.**
velle, *see* **volitio.**
vellicator, subverter c 1125; **villic/atio,**
robbery 1194; **-o** to rob c 1385.
vellifico, to pluck, fleece c 1125.
vellus, cloak, disguise (fig.) c 1250; ‡**v.**
aureum, a preparation of May-dew (alch.)
1652.
velosus, *see* **villositas.**
vel/ox, quickly approaching c 730; **volox,**
quick 15c.; **-ocito,** to accelerate 1335,
c 1430.
velt/a, welt of shoe c 1335; **†-arius,** (?) welter
or felter (*cf.* FILTR) 1299.

veltr-, *see* **valtrus.**
vel/um *1223, 1395, **-a** 1308, **-amen** 1282,
1376, sail of windmill; part of clock c 1425;
v. professionis 1291, **-amen sacrum**
760. c 1090, 1415, nun's veil; **v. ecclesie**
1325, **v. quadragesimale** 1263, 1519,
(?) **v. †quadratum** 1290, **v. sanctum**
c 1115, Lenten veil; **-amen altaris** 8c.;
-o extenso, under full sail 1331; **-um**
depono, -amentum prosterno, to strike
sail (in surrender) 1378; **v. traho,** to set
sail 1300; **v. suscipio,** to become a nun
a 1142; **-a** c 1362, **-amen** 14c., 1372, *for*
-um, sail (naut.); **-amentum,** guise,
pretext c 1220, 1503; **-atio,** sailing 1437;
"ceiling" 1519; blindfolding c 1340; veiling,
concealing 1239; taking the veil (mon.)
1249, 1314; **-atura oculi,** blindfolding
a 1275; **-ator,** disguiser 1378; **-ifer,** veiled
(mon.) 1220; **-ificata,** *for* **-ificatio,** sailing
c 1000; **†-ipulum,** (?) maniple (eccl.) 1501;
†-ivox, cited as word containing *-ǐv-* 1267;
-ate, as through a veil 1344; **-ata,** veiled
nun c 1180; **navis -ata,** ship with sails
hoisted 14c.; **-o,** to veil or receive as nun
c 1090, c 1436; to veil a widow (eccl.) c 1110,
c 1514; 1318, 1591, **-ivolo** c 1125, to sail;
to sail over (*trans.*) c 900. 14c.; to furnish
(windmill) with sails 1287; *see also* **vitulus.**
velu/sus, -tus, *see* **villositas.**
vel/uti, *for* **qualis** (*after* **talis**) c 793; **-ud,** *for*
-ut, 931, 944. 12c., c 1480.
*vel/vetum 1285, a 1564, **-veta** c 1534,
-wetum 1383, **-fedum** c 1433, **-utum**
c 1321, 1441, **-vellum** 1393, **†valutia**
1493, **felfetum** a 1347, **felvetum** (**†fe-
luctum**) 1342, c 1467, **felwetum** c 1443,
wellvetum 15c., velvet; **-utus** 1432,
villutus 1499, of velvet; **-uto,** to make with
velvet 1421, a 1452; *see also* **villositas.**
ven/a minere, vein of ore 1474; ‡**v. Veneris,**
vervain (bot.) 1652; **-atim,** through the
veins 1210; in veins or streaks a 1250.
venal/is, -lum, *see* **venella; venia.**
venal/itas, sale c 1170, 1423; venality,
corruption c 1125, c 1450; **-iter,** expensively
c 1220; venally, corruptly c 1125, c 1325;
-itium, market a 1180.
ven/atio, (place for or right of) hunting 765,
853. 1086, 1499; (fine for) illegal hunting
1091, 1453; c 1080, 1368, **-eso** 1268,
-isona 1357, venison, game; **-abulum,** trap
or buckstall 11c., c 1150; **-aria** c 1115,
a 1564, **-eria** 1212, **†-us** c 1185, venery,
hunting; **-ativus,** pursuing, ambitious
c 1184, a 1200; **-atricius,** used for hunting
c 700; **bestia -etica,** beast of the chase
c 1362; **canis †-aneticus,** hunting dog
c 1334; **-ator ad lupos,** wolf-hunter 1234;
v. communis, common poacher 1427; **-o**
c 1272, c 1362, **-or ad** 1300, *for* **-or,** to
hunt; **-or,** to woo c 1090.
vend/a c 1156, 1254, **venta** c 1200, toll on
goods for sale (G.); 1289, a 1422, **-itio** 1316,
payment to lord on sale of lands, *etc.* (G.);
-agium, (?) right of sale (G.) 1254; **†-entio,**
f.l. for **-itio,** a 1272; **-itio** a 1168, 1253,
†-atio 1284, sale (of wood); rate of selling,
market price 1379, 1419; **v. operum,**
commutation of labour services a 1300,

1504; **v. particularis**, retail sale 1234, 1271; **v. super compotum**, debiting to accountant 1273, 1449; **-iticius** a 1186, †**-icabilis** c 1300, for sale; **homo -itus**, (?) one allowed to compound for offence (Sc.) (?) 13c.; **-it se**, is on sale c 1325; **-o super compotum**, to debit to accountant during audit 1273, 1449; †**veneto**, (?) to display for sale 1279.

vend/agium, -emia, vene/a, -arium, *see* **venda; vinum.**

vendic-, *see* **venda**; VINDIC

***ven/ella** 1252, 1588, **-ellis** 1586, **-ellum** p 1147, 1513, **-ala** a 1300, **-alis** c 1217, **-allum** 1240, **vinella** (Sc.) 1487, 1578, **-ula** a 1200, 1242, 'vennel', lane; **v. pasture** 1502.

venen/ator, poisoner c 1357; **-ose**, poisonously c 937. 13c., 15c.; **-ositas**, poisonousness c 1220, c 1362; **-osus** c 550. c 1090, 1461, **-ifer** c 1000, poisonous, deadly; **venificatio**, witchcraft 1660; **venefico**, to envenom c 1250.

vener/atio 1231, **-abilitas** 12c., c 1400, reverence (title); ecclesiastical due 1228; **-amen**, object of veneration c 950; ***-abilis** 803. 12c., 1560, **-andus** c 1090, 1343, venerable (title); **-abillimus**, most venerable c 950.

ven/eria, -eticus, *see* **venatio; Venus.**

veneto, *see* **venda.**

venet/us, azure (her.) 1654; †**-alitas**, blue colour 12c.

veni/a, privilege, dignity c 1115; property c 1115; prostration, genuflexion c 1160, c 1200; **v. longa** c 1266, c 1442; **v. major** c 1330; **v. curta** c 1245, 1351; **v. minor** c 1330; **v. parva** c 1412, **veni parvum** a 1316; **-alia** (*pl.*), venial offences c 1197, c 1343; **-alis**, privileged c 1115; *see also* **dies, peccatum;** †**venalis**, *for* **-alis**, venial c 1188, 1324; **-alitas**, pardonability c 1375, c 1376; **-aliter** a 1228, 1378, **-abiliter** c 600, venially.

veniatus, *see* WAIV

venificatio, *see* VENEN

venigrum, *see* **vinum.**

venisona, *see* **venatio.**

ven/itare 1287, **-itarium** 1298, 1342, **liber -itarius** c 1350, music-book for invitatories (eccl.); **-ura ad curiam**, suit of court 1303; **malum -iendi** 1196, c 1290, **male -iendo** 1419, a ground for essoin (leg.); **-ire** (*subst.*), arrival 1155, 1324; **v. facias** 1444, 1543, **breve de v. faciendo** 1327, 1334, writ of summons; **-itus** 7c., **-tus** c 1362, having come (*p.p.*); **-io**, (with *inf.*) to come to 8c. a 1142, 1346; **v. ad**, to come by, get 1086, 1232; **v. ad pacem** 1276, 1297, **v. in rectum** c 1192, to submit to trial; ***v. contra**, to contravene c 1170, c 1499; c 1325, **v. super** 1260, to proceed against (leg.); **v. cum lege**, to come with compurgators (leg.) 1221, 1419; **v. de**, to go free (from a charge) c 1115; to become of, happen to c 1250; **v. palam**, to become known c 1434.

†**venta**, (?) jest c 1204; *see also* **venda.**

vent/aculum, -agium, *etc.*, *see* **ventus.**

ventenarius, *see* **vintena.**

vent/er, fur of belly 1235, 1416 (*cf.* **tergum**);

part of cross-bow 1306; **v. ecclesie** (arch.) 1389; ‡**v. apis**, milfoil (bot.) 14c.; **v. rotuli**, front of membrane 1264, 1580; **-rale**, ‡"gardecors" c 1200; "apron" 1573; **-riculus cerebri** (med.) a 1250; **-ricosus** c 1218, **-rosus** 1252, pot-bellied; **-rilocus**, ventriloquist 8c.; **-ripotens** greedy c 1180, ‡1483.

ventrarius, *see* **valtrus.**

ventum, omen a 1235.

vent/uras quero, to seek one's fortune 1532; **-urarius, -erarius**, *see* **mercator.**

‡**vent/us**, spirit, vapour (alch.) 1652; ‡**v. albus**, mercury, **v. citrinus**, sulphur, **v. rubeus**, orpiment 1652; **herba -i**, pasqueflower 1641; **-aculum** c 1190, **-ale** 1380, 1387, **-ellum** 1414, ventail, visor (*cf.* **aventallum**); **-ailla** 1233, **-ilagium** 1331, (?) **-inula** c 730, window or louver; **-atorium** 1306, **-orium** 12c., 14c., **-ellum** 1306, **-ilamen** 1433, **-ulamen** 1406, **-ilarium** 1155, **-osum** 1308, winnowing-fan; **-agium** 1266, ***-ilatio** 7c., 8c. 1242, 1412, **-ulatio** 1527, 1534, winnowing; **-ilatio** c 1125, c 1400, **-ulatio** 1370, airing, discussion; **-ilatio**, airing (of a sail) 1387; **-ilator**, examiner a 1100; **-ilatrix** 1351, 1456, **-rix** c 1290, 1297, winnower (*f.*); †**-ifuga** c 1440, ‡**-ifica** 15c., screen; ***-ilogium** c 1200, 1425, **-ilegium** 1620, weather-cock; **-iloquus**, windy talker, windbag c 1160; **-osa**, 'ventose', cupping-glass c 1200, 1620; air-hole in conduit (Fr. *ventouse*) 1443; **-ositas** 13c., **-osatio** a 1250, cupping; storminess 1461; **-uosus**, of or for wind 800; inflated, long-winded 13c.;

***-icius** 1196, c 1400, **-icus** 1279, c 1440, ***-riticus** 1280, 1562, **-ricius** 1252, c 1400, **-ericius** c 1260, 1275, †**-ricus** c 1321, †**-rificus** 1514, **-ricalis** 1330, **-ilagius** 1279, **-alis** 1303, **-ualis** 1268, **-ilis** 1202, **-orius** 1265, **-osus** 1307, worked by wind: *see also* **molendinum; -rimola**, wind-mill 1557; **pannus** †**-riticus**, winnowing-cloth 1345;

-ilo, to cause to veer (in opinion) c 1250; ***-o** a 1128, 1349, **-ulo** c 1358, a 1564, to winnow; **-ulo cornibus**, to toss 12c.; **-oso** c 1220, c 1245, **-uso** 1296, to cup (med.).

venula, *see* **venella.**

venum deduco, to bring for sale a 1142; **v. loco**, to hire out c 1125.

venura, *see* **venitare.**

Ven/us, copper (alch.) c 1215, c 1345; ‡**filius -eris**, "*aurichalcum*" 1652; **-us** c 1102, **-eria** c 1115, lust, venery; **-erinus**, bastard c 1370; **-usto**, to beautify (eccl.); *see also* **dies, umbilicus, vena, venatio.**

veprosus, thorny c 1190.

veractum, *see* WARECT

veragium, *see* **varietas.**

verantizo, *see* WARANT

verbascum, mullein (bot.): ‡**barbascus** c 1440.

verbena, vervain (bot.): **vervena** a 1446, **berbena** 790; *cf.* **vena.**

‡**verber/**, yard measure 1570; **-amen** 1429, **-antia** c 730, ***-atura** 1250, 1333, beating, battery; **-atura**, pounding (of spices) 1286; **-ator**, one who beats, assaults c 700. 1290, 1377; **-o**, to thresh (grain) a 1128, c 1300;

to beat (hemp) 1305; to beat (gold) 1243; to stamp (with design) 1303, 1415; to thrash out (argument) c 1470.

verbica, *see* **verveculus**.

verb/um, right of speech (in manor court) 1541; c 1115, c 1268, v. **veritatis** c 1206, c 1365, promise; c 730, c 793. c 1125, 1549, v. **Dei** 12c., c 1470, v. **salutare** c 1330, v. **Vite** c 1250, gospel; c 1090, c 1470, V. **Incarnatum** 1071, c 1188, V.**Patris** c 1080, Word, Logos (theol.); **-a facio**, to make a speech, preach 12c., 1562; **-a curie**, formal allegations of court (leg.) 1269, 1408; v. **sacerdotii** (eccl.) 1514; v. **de futuro** c 1229, 1397, v. **de presenti** c 1201, 1397, words used in forms of marriage service; ***in hec v.***, in these words c 1204, c 1478; **-o ad -um** c 1216, 1290, **de -o ad -um** 1245, 1549, **-o in -um** 1196, **de -o in -um** 1198, 1219, **-atim** a 1400, 1502, word for word; ***-otenus** 980. a 1100, 1418, †-atenus 1475, *-aliter a 1258, 1684, -ialiter 10c. c 1125, -abiliter c 1343, in words, orally; c 800, -aliter 1344, 15c., in word only; -aliter, by means of verbs 870; -alis, expressed in words c 1444; literal p 1380; *existing in word only c 1265, 15c.; -aculum 14c., -eculum 1201, -iolum c 1432, -ulum c 970. c 1160, 1622, little word, mere word; -atio, being a word p 1300; -igena c 1100, 1413, -igenus c 1308, begotten of the Word (theol.); -ipotens, eloquent c 790; *-ositas, verbosity a 700. c 1125, c 1470; ‡-escor, "to chide" 15c.; -osito a 1100, c 1191, -oso 9c., -osor 13c., ‡1483, to prattle.

verd-, *see* VEREDIC; VIRID; **warda**.

verecum, *see* **wreccum**.

verecund/ia, injury, insult, assault c 1100, c 1436; **-a** (*pl.*), privy parts 12c., 1236; **-us**, shameful c 1200, c 1325; **-ose**, timidly a 1236; **-o**, to put to shame 1231, c 1436; (with *inf.*) to be ashamed 7c.

vered/a, chariot c 1365; 1439, ‡15c., **-us** c 1200, ‡1483, **-arius** c 1000. c 1100, 1534, courier, carter; **-arius**, esquire, retainer a 1142; c 1200, **equus v.** c 1250, c 1255, cart-horse; *see also* VIRID

veredic/tio c 1310, p 1330, *-tum c 1185, 1461, **verdictum** c 1200, **veridictum** 1382, **verumdictum** 1168, 15c., sworn statement, verdict or presentment (leg.); **-us** c 796. c 1321, 15c., **vereticus** 15c., truthful; **veridicus**, juryman 1199.

†veredium, (?) green *or* horse-market (Glasgow) 1500.

verella, *see* **virolla**.

verendallis, *see* **ferdella**.

ver/enter, devotedly, devoutly c 780, c 950; **-itor**, to fear 1426.

verg-, *see also* VIRG

vergablum, (?) verge-board, barge-board (of gable) 1335.

verg/euta, -utum, *see* **verjutum**.

verg/ibilis, changeable, turning c 730. a 1142; Oceanus **-ivius**, Irish sea (or Atlantic) 1574; pons **-ens**, drawbridge 1252; **-o**, c 1340, v. **ad** c 1200, v. **in** c 1258, 1549, to tend to, redound to; v. **me ad**, to resort to c 1330; to abut on c 1210.

veria, *see* 4 **feria**; **verjutum**.

vericum, *see* **wreccum**.

veridic/tum, -us, *see* VEREDIC

veridis, *see* VIRID

verific/atio, verification, proof c 1250, 1620; v. **patrie**, averment by jury (leg.) c 1290, 1315; **-abilis**, verifiable a 1323, c 1363; **-us**, accurate 1326; *-o, to justify, prove, establish c 1250, c 1607.

verigropa, *see* **waregrapa**.

veriloqu/ium, truthfulness c 1255; **-us**, true prophet c 730.

verina, *see* **verna**; VITR

veriscum, *see* **wreccum**.

verisimilatio, likelihood 1297.

verit/as, truth, orthodox belief c 730. c 1080, c 1410; Christ c 780, 955. c 1296, c 1343; lapis **-atis**, sapphire 1380; **-o**, to verify c 1270.

veritor, *see* **verenter**.

verium, *see* **varietas**.

ver/jutum 1480, 1521, **-gutum** 1458, †-jo 1467, †-ia c 1420, verjuice; **-geuta zinziberis** 1380; *cf.* VIRID

verlettus, *see* **valettus**.

verm/esona, -iso, *see* 3 **firma**.

verm/is, the serpent, Satan 1252; term of reproach 1323; v. **lucens**, glow-worm a 1250; **-es** (*pl.*) 1334, **-einum** 1322, 1341, **-ina** 1324, **-inum** 1322, 1358, vermin (esp. foxes); **-erius**, 'verminer' (official of New Forest) 1635, 1666; (?) **-es** (*pl.*) 1421, **-iculus** c 1250, p 1290, †-icylum 1652, **-eillo** 1358, **-elio** 1418, **-ilio** 1254, 1346, **-ilo** 1314, vermilion (*subst.*); **-iculatus** c 1125, c 1212, **-eillius, -eillus** 1205, **-ilius** 1292, **-ilo** 1254, vermilion (*adj.*); **-iculus**, kermes c 1212; **-icularis** a 1250, ‡15c., **-icularia** a 1250, stonecrop (bot.); **frusta -ia**, scraps of worms c 550; **-ivorus**, worm-eating 1544; **-ultura**, dust from worm-holes in wood a 1150; **-esco**, to breed worms c 730. c 1197, c 1220; **-iculo** c 1000. c 1325, c 1595, **virmiculo** 1468, to inlay or paint in different colours, to enamel.

vern/a 1223, 1372, **-um** 1333, 1413, †verina 1286, **fernum** 1313, (?) 1388, 'fern', small crane or windlass.

vernacul/um (**vivendi**), custom, usage c 1115; **-a**, vernacular language 1546; **bernacula**, *for* v., 690; **-us** (*adj.*), conversant with, at home with c 793; (*subst.*) 798. c 1188, c 1220, **berna** c 800, slave or servant; **-us**, serf, villein c 1150, c 1450; **vernul/a**, faithful servant 990, 1041. c 1180, 13c.; **-itas**, service c 1000. c 1200; *see also* **veronica**.

vern/agium 1336, ‡c 1440, **vinum v.** c 1350, **vinum -ach'** 1313, 1367, **vinum -acium** 1328, 'vernage', wine of Vernaccia; *cf.* **garnagia**.

vern/antia c 1325, ‡**varnantia** c 1440, **-ia** c 550, springtide beauty or gladness; **semen -ale**, spring sowing 1358, 1364; **-ax**, vernal c 1400; **-ulus**, spring-like c 1393.

vern/ica 1298, **-icium** 1239, 1279, **-iculum** 1301, **-ix** 1296, 1622, ‡bernix 14c., varnish; **-itio** 1277; **-atio** 1358, 1397, varnishing; **-iso** 15c., **-izo** 1291, **-o** c 1180, 1301, to varnish.

vernicula, *see* Veronica.

vernul-, *see* VERNACUL; **vernantia.**

†**vernum**, cooking-dish a 1250; *see also* verna.

vero, minnow (Fr. *vairon*) c 1200.

verol/a, -es, *see* variola.

Veronica c 1192, 1464, **vern/aculum** 1444, 1527, **-icula** 1432, vernicle (eccl.); toadflax (bot.) 1632.

verr-, *see also* guerra; **varietas**; VITR

verr/es liber 1252, **-i libertas** 1325, liberty of boar (man.); **-us**, *for* **-es**, boar 1198, 1325; **-ificatio**, (hole made by) rooting of swine c 1190; **-o**, to grub up c 1190; to ring swine 1296.

verriculum crineum, hair-brush 1553.

verrucula/tio, blazoning in nebuly (her.) c 1595; **-tus**, nebuly c 1595.

1 **vers/us**, turning 1041; (*adj.*) reverse c 1300; †**-utilis**, *for* **-atilis**, turning every way c 550; †**-atibilis**, versatile 1497; **pons -atilis**, drawbridge 1261, 1333; *see also* **gladius**; **-ibilitas**, changeability c 700, c 790. c 1160, 1169; **-io**, turning, wheeling a 1446, c 1450; change, conversion c 1270, 1290; version, translation c 1580; **-orium**, (?) swinging sconce 1516; pivot 1620; compass needle c 1620; *cf.* VERT

2 **vers/us**, verse of Bible c 1148, c 1363; **-arius** p 1290, **-icularius** (?) 13c., responsory (eccl.); **-iculus**, versicle (eccl.) c 700. c 1148, 1516; **-iculatio**, antiphonal chanting 1409; **ars -ificatoria**, art of versification c 1200; **-ifice**, in verse 1125, c 1500; **-ificus**, versified 815, c 950. c 1090, c 1170; producing melody c 790; (*subst.*) c 1170, c 1414, ‡**-ista** 1483, versifier; **-iculo** 1442, **-ifico** 760, †**-ilio** 1292, to recite (psalter) antiphonally.

3 **versus**, to, towards 12c., 1415; (*pregnant*) going to, destined for 1303, 1413; next to, over against c 1188, 1443; *against c 1175, 1687; against (of time) 1549; for the benefit of a 1242, 1420; with a view to 1549, 1583; with regard to c 1325, c 1470; in the possession of 1324, c 1380; **concelo v.**, to hide from 1237.

vert/egrecum, -grisium, *see* VIRID

vertenarium, a toll or custom (Manx) 1505.

verthingalum, farthingale 1591.

vert/itio 1506, **virtitio** 1505, turning, diversion; ‡**-ebra**, “cobbard” 15c.; ‡**-ebrum**, spindle-whorl 15c.; ‡**-ebellum**, drilling tool 14c.; *vert/ivella (†-inella) 1250, c 1444, *-evella 1223, 1329, -ivollum 1334, 1336, -ewella 1223, -iwella 1298, hinge; 1346, -evella 1347, ‘varvel’, ring linking jess to leash (falc.); part of a springald 1313; **-ibilis**, able to be turned c 1239, 1276; a 1150, c 1376, **-ilis** c 1270, concerned with change, mutable; **pons v.** 1250, 1388, **p. -ens** 1238, c 1250, drawbridge; **-ibilitas**, mutability, pliability a 1232, 1427; **-ibulum**, coal-rake ‡1483, 1517; spinning-top 1622; **-iculum**, ring (of tether) 1325; **-icudium**, (?) sort of weapon 1440; **-icalis**, of a summit, topmost 1620, 1686; **-icatio** 1267, **-icitas** c 1616, 1622, (tendency in) vertical direction; **-iginosus**, *for* **-icosus**, full of eddies 15c.; **-ilis**, *for* **versilis**, winding 1411;

-o, to consider, ponder c 1473; **v. fenum** c 1283, 1365, **v. pratum** 1311, c 1418, to turn hay; **v. in questionem**, to call in question c 1343; **v. me ad**, to resort to (feudal lord) 1086; **v. super**, to abut on 13c.; **moneta -ente**, on a change of currency 1086; *-or, to be pending (of lawsuit) 1199, 16c.; *cf.* 1 **versus**.

‡**verto**, quarter pound 1652.

Veru, name of a comet c 1270.

†**verula**, (?) *for* **vitula**, calf 7c.

verumdictum, *see* VEREDIC

*verumptamen, *for* verum tamen, 948. 12c., c 1430.

†**verunca vis**, (?) a malign force c 1150.

verur-, *see* VITR

*verutum, spit c 1450, c 1524.

vervactum, fallow: *see* WARECT

verveculus, tup 12c.; **berb/ix** 1086, **-icius** a 1350, wether; ‡**-ica**, **verbica**, ewe 15c.; **-icio**, sheep-tick 1200; **-iagium** (Norm.) 1180, (Cornwall) 1297, 1357, †**-ragium** 1301, rent of sheep; *cf.* 1 **bercaria**.

vervena, *see* verbena.

†**vesagia (apostolica)**, (?) utterances (?) 955 (14c.).

vesan/ia, mad doctrine c 600; **-us**, untrained (falc.) 1306.

vesc-, *see also* 1 vicia.

vescella, *see* vas.

vesc/entia, eating c 1380; **-ibilis**, eatable c 1366.

vescio, *see* WISC

vesia, *see* 1 vicia.

vesic/a, urinal 1384; ‡copper pot for holding alembic (alch.) 1652; **v. gutturis** a 1446, **-ula** c 550, ‡1483, (?) **viscula** a 1250, ‡**vicecolla** 15c., bird’s crop; **-alia** a 1250, †**vessada** 1287, (?) *for* **-ula**, bladder; **viscago**, *for* **-ago**, bladderwort (bot.) a 1250; ‡14c.; **-atio**, formation of pustules a 1250, **-or**, to form pustules a 1250.

vesp/a, wasp: **-is** c 1180; ‡**-erium, -etum**, wasp’s nest 1483.

vesper/a (*s.*) c 980. c 1090, *-e (*pl.*) c 700. c 1182, c 1520, **-i** c 1188, c 1470, vespers (eccl.); **-e principales** 1466, **v. prime** c 1393, first vespers; **v. secunde** c 1393; **-ata**, evening 1194; **Vesper Siculus** Sicilian Vespers 1535; *-ie (*pl.*), ‘vesperies’, disputation preceding inception (ac.) c 1246, 1432; **-tinalis**, of or for evening c 700, c 1006. a 1100, c 1132; **-tinus** 14c., **-us** 1221, 1262, of or for vespers (eccl.).

vespil/io, -lo, *see* 1 vispilio.

vessa, *see* 1 vicia.

vessada, *see* VESIC

vessall-, vessell-, *see* vas.

vestalis, nun c 1434, c 1553.

†**vestatus**, (?) *f.l.* for **vastatus**, 1269.

vest/er, your (*s.*) 8c. a 1090, 1564; **-rior**, more truly yours a 1205, c 1370; **-rissimus**, most truly yours a 1205, c 1260; **-rates** 1333, 1518, **-rati** p 1396, men of your nation; *see also* **vos.**

vest/iarium, -ibulum, *see* vestis.

vesticulus, *see* fasciculus.

vestig/ium, (following) a trail c 1115, 13c.; projection (math.) 1686; **canis -abilis**, sleuth-hound (Sc.) 13c.; **-iatim**, step by step a 1519; **-ialis**, of the nature of an imprint p 1300; **-iatus**, imprinted p 1300; **-io**, to bear the imprint of c 1365.

vestillamenta, *see* **vas**.

vestio, *see* WISC

vest/is, cloth, material c 1212, 1415; c 1452, **-imentum** 1407, 16c., altar-cloth; c 1115, c 1180, **-imentum** c 1330, 1497, **-ura** 1329, coverlet; **-imen**, garment 8c.; 1245, *-imen- tum 11c., c 1508, **-amentum** 14c., **-ura** 15c., vestment, set of vestments; **-imentum** c 1258, **-itura** c 1383, 1461, **-ura** c 1293, c 1480, investiture, putting into possession; **v. pacti** (*leg.*) c 1290; **-itura** 1130, 1220, *-ura c 1266, 1501, **-itus** 1086, 13c., (providing with) clothes, livery; 1180, 1293, *-ura 1198, 1588, **-itus** 1199, crop (of corn, *etc.*); **-ura**, hangings (*coll.*) c 1400; clothing (windmill sails) with canvas c 1419; boarding (of plough) 1362, 1391; **-itus monachorum**, 'shroudland' 1086;

  *-iarium a 1090, 1537, **-iaria** 14c., **-imentarium** 1422, 1423, **-ibulum** c 1200, c 1503, **-ibilum** c 1455, **westibulum** 1447, **-ibularium** 1432, vestry (eccl.); **-ibulum regis**, revestry, wardrobe 1462; **-iarius**, keeper of a vestry (eccl.) 1301, c 1450; c 1125, 1272, **-imentarius** 15c., keeper of a wardrobe (mon.); tailor 1551 (*cf.* **scissor, sutor**); **†-igatio**, wearing clothes 13c.; **-ilis**, concerned with clothing c 550; **-imentaliter**, sartorially, in externals 12c.; **‡-iplicium**, clothes-press 15c., 1483;

  crux -ita, bound rood 1384; **pactum -itum** (*leg.*) c 1290; **-io** (**de, ex, in**), *to vest, invest, put into possession 1086, 1571; to clothe (land) with crops or trees 1086, 1222; to cover (plough, cart, mill or cupboard) with boards 1275, 1451; **v. tabulas**, (?) to occupy tables (at meals) c 1330.

yetatio, prohibition c 1361; *see also* **namium**.

veter/ (*2nd decl.*) 1274, 1349, **-anus** c 1188, c 1462, **-nosus** 1427, **vetustiosus** 1275, **wetus** 1263, old, ancient; **Vetus de Monte** 1195, c 1250, **V. de Montanis** 1274, **V. de Mussa** 1238, Old Man (*Sheikh*) of the Mountains; **-amentarius**, cobbler 1561; **-ascentia** c 1363, **-itas** 1470, growing old; **-esco**, *for* **-asco**, 7c.

vethelarius, *see* 2 **vidula**.

vethirus, *see* **wedderus**.

vetrarius, *see* **valtrus**.

‡vettonica 14c., **betonica** a 1200, 1622, (?) **brittanica** a 700, betony (bot.); **b. aquatica**, figwort 1629; **b. altilis, b. coronaria**, pink or carnation 1538; **‡b. Pauli**, "wood-penny" 1570.

veua, view, inspection (G.) 1289.

veusura, *see* VOLU

veutr/arius, -or, *see* **valtrus**.

vex/atio, plaguing by devils c 790; **-amen** c 1250, c 1450, **-ura** c 1250, burden, tribulation; **-ans**, defendant (leg.) 1234.

vexill/um, banner-fee (form of tenure) 1331; cross-cloth (eccl.) a 1340; **v. crucis** 805. 11c., c 1414, **v. triumphale** 12c., sign of cross; **v. mortuum**, sign of mourning 13c.; **-ator** a 1300, 1583, **-aris** c 1267, **-ifer** 11c., 1508, **-iger** c 1385, standard-bearer, banneret; **-aris** borne as a banner 12c.; **-ifer**,

(*adj.*) bearing the standard (fig.) a 1000; **v. justitie**, gonfalonier (It.) 1347, a 1452; **-atim**, in the form of a banner 1432; **-atus**, equipped with banners c 1150, c 1306.

vexir, *see* **elixir**.

†vex/o, (?) to travel 1357; *see also* **vexatio**.

veyfia, *see* WAIV

veyronus, *see* **varietas**.

veyrum, *see* **vitrum**.

via, gangway 1333; c 1260, 1344, **viatio** 1377, a 1452, earthly pilgrimage; **in via**, in a state 15c.; **per viam**, by means 1261, 1484; **licentia vie**, way-leave 1420; **viis omnibus** a 1347, **via omni** c 1115, by all means; **do viam**, to give way c 1434; **v. alta** 1248, 1547, **v. magistra** c 1115, highway; **v. aquatica**, waterway, drain 1351, c 1360; **v. bige** c 1230, **v. bigarum** 1230, **v. carecte** c 1350, **v. caretaria** 1269, **v. caretata** 1467, **v. quadrigaria** c 1180, 1199, carriage-way; **v. equestralis**, bridle-path c 1390; **v. ferrata**, hard road 13c.; **v. ad pedites** 1375, **v. pedalis** 1392, 1538, **v. pedestralis** c 1390, **v. pedestris** 1482, foot-path; **v. publica** 1086, c 1168, **v. communis** c 1250, 1547, **v. generalis** 1255, **v. universalis** c 1150, public way; **v. regalis** 7c. 1243, c 1308, **v. regia** c 1110, c 1452, **v. regis** 1086, 1202, king's highway; **v. viridis**, grassy track 12c., c 1250; **v. facti**, violence (*voie de fait*) 1521; **v. pacis**, path of peace c 1250, c 1338; **v. †patruum** 11c., **v. patrum** 1421, **v. totius mundi** c 790, *v. universe carnis 11c. c 1222, c 1465, **v. universe nationis** c 1000, **v. universitatis** c 910, 943. 12c., c 1400, death;

  *viagium 1279, 1583, **veagium** 1300, 1325, **vehagium** 1327, **veiagium** 1300, 1335, **voiagium** (G.) 1305, voyage, expedition; *viaticum, last sacrament (eccl.) 731, 1006. 1072, 1562; memorandum, instruction c 1115; medical handbook (of Constantinus) a 1250, ‡14c.; **v. populare**, fyrd, military service 12c.; **viatim**, by the way c 1130; **viando**, on the way 1276; **viaticus** c 1415, *viator a 1228, c 1457, **viatrix** (*f.*) c 1343, **vians** 1374, 1423, soul on earthly pilgrimage; **viator**, (*adj.*) travelling 6c.; **vians**, traveller c 730; **†veeria**, (?) *voirie*, surveillance of roads (G.) 1221; **viiculum**, path 1461; **vio**, to perform earthly pilgrimage c 1380.

vial-, *see* **phiala**; 2 **vidula**.

viandarius, (?) viander, provision dealer 1155.

viand/ator 1661, **-itor** 1705, **vandor** 1588, 'viander', borough official acting as returning officer (Newport, Cornwall).

†vianus, (?) a local official (Cornwall) 1461.

†viar/am (**-um**), **viviam**, kinds of omen a 1235.

viaria, *see* **vicaria**.

viat-, *see* **via**.

vibo, *see* VIV

vibra/men, shock c 1381; quivering c 1414; **-tio**, brandishing c 1195; **-tor**, brandisher c 1325.

vibrell/um, gun 1496, 1554; **-ia** (*pl.*), firearms 1587; **-arius** 1490, **-ator** 1486, 1583, gunner; **pulvis -inus**, gunpowder 1495; *cf.* **librella**.

viburnum (bot.): **viurna**, wayfaring-tree 1634; **viorna**, traveller's joy 1634; †**vipurnum**, bush or thicket 6c.

vicanus, *see* vicus.

vicar/ia *1184, 1549, **-agium** 1251, vicarage, office or benefice of vicar (eccl.); revenue of a vicarage c 1276, 1440; parish (G.) c 1250; **v. pensionaria** 1399, 1479; **v. perpetua** c 1180, 1449; **v. Sancti Petri** 1377, **-iatus** sedis apostolice 1462, papacy; **-agium**, vicarage (building) 1452; **vigeria** 1202, 1315, **viaria** a 1142, *viguerie, haute justice* (Norm. & G.); *cf.* jugeria; *-iatus, status of vicar or deputy c 1339, 1610; **v. generalis** 1558; **-iatim** 1427, **-ie** 1377, c 1383, vicariously, as a deputy; **-ius**, *(adj.)* mutual p 1130, 1200; (?) successive (or *f.l.* for **varius**) c 1212; **decima -ia**, vicarial tithe 1606; **-ius**, *(subst.)* sheriff (Engl.) 1096, (Sc.) 1384, 1416; governor of city (It.) 1281; subprior (Carthusian) 1570; (?) rural dean c 1182; *vicar (eccl.) a 1160, 1565; **v. choralis** c 1452, c 1643, **v. chorarius** 1470, **v. chori** 1465, **v. in choro** 1353, 1425, vicar choral; **v. perpetuus** a 1160, c 1468; **v. amotivus** 1519; **v. pensionarius** 13c., c 1540; **v. prebende** 1185; **v. curatus**, vicar having a cure of souls 1409; *v. generalis c 1307, 1686, **v. in generalibus** c 1370, vicar general (of bishop or religious order); **v. provincialis** c 1451; *v. Christi 980. c 1220, 1562, **v. Dei** 13c., **v. Sancti Petri** c 1414, Pope; **vigerius**, *viguier* (G.) 1242, 1243.

vice, *see* vicem.

vice/admirallus 1337, 1587, **-admiralius** 1586, vice-admiral; **-archidiaconus**, deputy archdeacon a 1138, a 1285; **-ballivus** (Calais) 1501; **-baro**, (?) sheriff a 1155; **-camerarius**, deputy chamberlain c 1430, 1573; **-cancellarius**, deputy chancellor 1189, 1517; vicechancellor (ac.) 15c., 1612; *v. sancte Romane ecclesie 1235, 1347; **-cancellariatus**, vicechancellorship (ac.) 1413, c 1584; **-capitaneus**, deputy captain 1382, 1583; **-collector**, deputy taxcollector 1513.

vicecolla, *see* VESIC

vicecom/es *c 1067, 1586, **wicecomes** 1230, 1237, sheriff; reeve or alderman c 1110; private (baronial) sheriff c 1100, 1266; viscount (Fr., *etc.*) a 1123, 1440, (Engl.) 1440, 1586; son of count or earl 16c.; **v. capitalis** (as opposed to undersheriff) 1243; **v. maritime** (G.) 1295; **-italis**, of or for a sheriff 1321, 15c.; **-itatus**, *shrievalty, office of sheriff 1086, 1434; *shire, district administered by sheriff c 1070, 1539; county court 1086; 1427, **-itia** (Norm.) a 1142, *vicomté*; **-itissa**, female sheriff c 1125, 1189; sheriff's wife c 1170; viscountess (Fr., *etc.*) 1157, 1254.

vice/commissarius, deputy commissary c 1556; **-constabularius**, deputy constable 1196; **-consul**, sheriff 1086, 13c.; **-custos**, vice-warden (ac.) 1276, 1535.

vicecuplus, *see* vicena.

vice/decanus, deputy dean (eccl.) 1257, 1541; **-deus**, Pope 1609, 1610; **-dominus**, *vidame*, deputy c 780. a 1110, c 1436;

-domina, *vidamesse* (Fr.) a 1142; **-dominatus**, office or jurisdiction of *vidame* c 1200, c 1223; **-gardianus**, vice-warden, deputy keeper 1491, 1529; **-gardianatus**, deputy keepership 1491.

vic/egerens 1274, a 1574, **-emgerens** 1414, c 1551, **-esgerens** 1276, 1456, deputy.

vic/em (*acc.*), *time, occasion 7c., 9c. 1086, 1549; **bina -e**, twice c 1290, 1461; **ad -es** c 1400, c 1470, **per -es** c 793. 12c., c 1450, **per -em** 12c., by turns; **per -es**, sometimes, on occasion c 798. 1217, 1310; **-e post -em** c 1320, **-e iterata** c 1333, **-ibus iteratis** c 1329, c 1407, repeatedly; **-e versa** 676, c 793. 1136, 1461, **-eversim** 1425, in turn, the position or role being reversed; **-em adimpleo** 1090, **-es ago** 12c., c 1250, *-em gero 1201, c 1551, *-es gero c 1250, c 1470, **-es reddo** c 600, **v. teneo** c 1343, to take the place (of).

vice/magister, vice-master (of Hospitallers) a 1260; **-monitor**, assistant teacher 1301, c 1322.

vice/na, vigena, period of twenty days 1174; 1335, 1372, **-nia** 1173, troop of twenty men; **-narius**, commander of twenty 1295; **-ni**, twenty c 700; **-cuplus**, twentyfold c 1615; **-sima**, tax of a twentieth c 1220, 1275; **v. quinta**, tax of a twenty-fifth 1310; **-sies** 1308, c 1400, **vigesies** c 1190, c 1293, twenty times; **vigenarius**, the number twenty c 1250; **vigenus**, twentieth 1347; **vigennis**, twenty years old c 1434; **vigenti** 1490, **vinginti** 1255, **wiginti** 1230, *for* viginti, twenty; *cf.* VINT

vicenetum, *see* VICIN

vice/papa, deputy Pope c 1125; **-plebanus**, deputy of rural dean 1413, a 1452; **-prepositus**, vice-provost (ac.) 1456; **-preses** 1516, **-presidens** 1535, vice-president (ac.); **-prior**, deputy prior (mon.) 1254; **-provincialis**, deputy provincial (mon.) 1256, 1275; **-thesaurarius**, deputy treasurer 1530, 1586.

vicer-, *see* VISCER

vicerius, *see* ostium.

vices/ies, -ima, *see* vicena.

vicesium, *see* hutesium.

vicetoxicum, *see* VINC

1 vicia, vetch: *vesc/a c 1270, 15c., **-ia** 1208, c 1327, **vecia** c 1283, **vesia, visea** c 1310, **vessa** a 1300, 1326, **vischia** 1258; **-osus**, mixed with vetch 1360.

2 vici/a 1282, 1309, **viscium** 1300, winch (of cross-bow); 1318, **-um** 1252, 1318, **veicium** 1244, spiral staircase.

vicin/etum a 1539, **vicenetum** 1608, **visenetum** 1343, **visinetum** c 1235, a 1564, †**visnietum** 1242, *visnetum c 1185, 1354, **vinetum** c 1196, 13c., **-a** c 700, **-agium** a 1564, **-alis** (G.) 1315, **-ium** a 1100, a 1408, **visinium** 1282, **visinia** 1341, 'visne', 'venue', neighbourhood; 13c., 1397, **visnetum** c 1185, 1274, †**vincnetum** 1196, **voisinetum** a 1609, **-ia** 1223, **-um** c 1115, men (jury) of visne (*coll.*); **-aliter**, locally c 1115; **-itas**, common *pur cause de vicinage* (leg.) 1198, 1378; neighbourliness 1251, 1461; **viscinus**, *for* **-us**, neighbour c 1250, c 1340; **visinus**, fellow-gildsman 1315; **-o** c 1370, †**-ior** a 1164, *for* **-or**, to be near.

vicis (*gen.*), *see* **vicem.**

vicissitud/o, exchange, requital 811, 11c. c 1125, 1686; **-inaliter** 1344, †**viscidudi-naliter** c 1260, by turns; **-inarius,** recurring c 1170, c 1293; †**vicitudinarius,** mutual c 1500.

Viclefensis, *see* **Wyclefensis.**

victim/atio, sacrificing c 730; **-alis,** sacrificial 1517.

Victorinus (canonicus), of the order of La Victoire (mon.) 1519.

victori/ola, petty victory c 1195; **-alis,** victorious c 700; **-aliter** c 1376, *-**ose** c 1200, c 1540, victoriously; **-osior** 1041; *-**osissimus,** most victorious c 730, c 800. a 1100, c 1494; **-ositas,** victoriousness c 1283.

victri/cus, *for* **vitricus,** stepfather c 1198, 1252; ‡**-ca,** stepmother 15c.; ‡**-gena,** stepsister 15c.; ‡**-genus,** stepbrother 15c.; **-cans,** acting the stepfather 1239.

†**victuarius,** (?) *f.l.* for **arcuarius,** c 1220.

vict/us canonicorum 1086, 1130, mensal lands; **-itus,** *for* **-us,** sustenance 12c.; *-**ualia** c 1125, c 1559, **-uabilia** c 1362, **vitualia** c 1465, **vitalia** 1060. c 1188, p 1341, victuals (*pl.*); **-uale** c 1320, ‡15c., **vittalia** (*f. s.*) 1275, foodstuff; **-ualis,** dietary c 1170, c 1448; **-ualiter,** by way of sustenance a 1100; **-uarius,** for provisions c 1150; **-ulatio** (†**-ualio**) 1492, 1587, **vitellatio** 1379, a 1564, **vitulatio** 1575, victualling; **-ualarius** 1428, 1661, **vitallarius** 1419, **vitellarius** 1384, 1448, **vitularius** 1421, victualler, provision-dealer; **vitellarius,** official victualler (of Calais) 1420, a 1564; 1444, 1474, **vitulator** 1450, victualler (naut.); **vitularius,** victualler (mon.) 1456, 1494; **vitelatorium,** victualling-place 1378; **vitellatus,** victualled 1402; **-ilo,** (?) *for* **-ito,** to make a living 1553; **-urio,** to desire to live 8c.

vic/us altus 1376, c 1515, **v. communis** 1548, **v. regis** 1167, 1340, **v. regalis** p 1202, **v. regius** 1185, 1499, **v. summus** 1320, high street, highway; **-ulus,** lane, alley 12c., 1671; **-anus,** fellow-countryman c 1190.

videl-, *see* 2 **vidula.**

viderbordum, *see* **fitherbordum.**

vid/ere 1406, **-eri** 1440, **-imus** 1428, c 1440, view, opinion (*subst.*); **-entissimus,** clear-sighted 1344; **viso quod,** seeing that c 1334, 1438; **-eo,** to view, inspect (leg.) c 1185, 1534; (*for* **-eor**) to seem c 1258; **v. mihi,** to beware a 1408; 9c., **-eor** 8c., to resolve (with *inf.*); **v. quod,** to see to it that c 1230, 1275; *cf.* **visio, visus.**

vidio, *see* **vadium.**

vidu/a, widow (as title) 1539, 1588; **v. Beate Marie,** widow in receipt of special allowance c 1299; ‡**faciens -as,** (?) spurge (bot.) 14c.; **-alis,** widowed c 730; of a widow c 1250, a 1452; **-aliter,** as a widow 1344, 1427; **-arius** 1257, 1356, **wydyarius** c 1280, widower; **weduagium,** widowhood c 1250; **-atio,** bereavement (of church by loss of pastor) c 1250, c 1470; **-etas,** *for* **-itas,** widowhood, bereavement 1300, 1504; **-itas,** celibacy 6c.; **v. legitima** 1232, **v. libera** c 1200, 1392, **v. ligia** 1231, c 1307, **v. legia**

1292, **v. pura** a 1300, 1327, **-alitas proba** 1267, **jus -e** 1366, widow-right, widow's power of disposition (leg.); **-o,** to bereave (church of pastor) c 1000. 1134, c 1444.

1 †**vidula** (*v.l.* **guvia**), (?) pruning-knife, twibill (*cf.* O.F. *vouge,* Gaulish *vidubium*) a 1142; *cf.* **voga.**

2 **vidul/a** c 1210, 1267, ‡**vitula** c 1440, ‡**vidella** 1483, **viella** c 1250, a 1452, **viala** c 1362, **viola** 8c. 1212, 1588, **fidula** c 1197, (?) †**fialus** c 1150, fiddle, viol; ‡**-arius** 15c., **vethelarius** c 1417, **viellarius** c 1130, 1329, *-**ator** 1213, 1332, ‡**vitulator** c 1440, **videlator** c 1200, **via-lator** a 1223, **viellator** 1130, 1299, **violator** 1290, (?) 1297, ‡**-ista, fidulista** 1483, fiddler, viol-player; ‡**-o** 15c., 1483, **viello** 14c., ‡1483, to play the fiddle.

†**viella,** (?) old woman 1220.

Viennensis 1285, **denarius V.** c 1250, coin of Vienne (= 1½d. sterling).

vigen-, viges-, *see* **vicena.**

vigent/ia, vigour, authority c 1390, ‡1483; **-er,** actively c 1250; **-ior,** more active c 1250.

vigeri/a, -us, *see* **vicaria.**

vigil/ia *c 1000. a 1090, 1556, **wigilia** c 1200, vigil, eve of festival (eccl.); vigil, night spent in prayer c 1090, c 1340; 'wake', holiday 1212, 1324; c 1150, 1458, **-atio** 760. 1326, 1534, watch and ward; **v. maris** 1294, 1338, **-ie marine** (*pl.*) 11c., coast-guard; **-ie** 1347, **v. pro defunctis** 980. 12c., c 1400, **v. defuncti** 1284, **v. mortuorum** c 1266, c 1461, **vigelia m.** 1504, watching the dead, lyke-wake, or payment therefor; **-ator,** watchman 1212, 15c.; night-walker, reveller 1408, 15c.; **v. ad ripam,** tidewaiter 1552; **v. pacis,** constable of the watch 1340; **-ifer,** gonfalonier (Florence) 1306; *cf.* VEXILL

vigimen, *see* **VIM**

vigneterrus, *see* **vinum.**

***vigor/,** validity, force (of document) 1244, 1549; **-atio,** invigoration 13c.; **v. curie,** afforcement of court (leg.) 1315; ‡**panis -is,** "pain demaine" c 1440; **-abilis** 12c., **-osus** 1212, 1622, vigorous, strong; **-ose,** strongly 1421, 1508; †**vigrico,** to agitate strongly c 550.

viiculum, *see* **via.**

vikettus, *see* **wicattus.**

‡**vilirum,** alembic or filter (alch.) 1652.

vil/itudo, cheapness 1427; **-is,** in bad condition (of road) 1423; **-ificatio,** debasement 1267; **-ipendiosus,** disparaging c 1564; **-ipendium** p 1330, 1537, **-ipensio** 1253, 1461, disparagement, contempt; **-ipensor,** despiser 15c.; **-ipendo,** to disparage, hold cheap a 1090, 1445; to debase (currency) 1311; **-esco** *c 800. a 1100, 1552, **-eo** c 1178, to lose value, be held cheap; c 1330, **-ifico** c 1204, 15c., to debase, abuse.

vill/a *805, 11c. 1070, 1545, **willa** 1086, 1481, *-**ata** a 1153, c 1465, **-atum** c 1456, **-atus** 1130, **-eta** c 1290, 'vill', town, township; town-house (?) 855 (12c.); **ballibo** (Ir.) c 1606; **constructio -e,** burhbote (?) 836; **malum -e,** a ground for essoin (leg.) 1199, c 1258; **v. campestris,** village c 1200, p 1330; **v. integra,** 'leet', division of hundred (Suffolk) c 1186; **v. marcanda**

1198, 1273, **v. marchandia** c 1290, **v. mercanda** 1225, 1273, **v. mercata** 1295, **v. mercatoria** 1265, 1419, **-ata marcatoria** 1275, market town; **v. terre** 1277, **-ata terre** 1268, 1333, **-ata, -iata** 1606, townland (Ir.); **-ata* (*coll.*) 1157, 1446, **willata** 1166, 1275, population of town or vill; †**-atus**, burgess 1433; **-agium**, village 1289 (G.), 1370, c 1540;

-anus, (*subst.*) inhabitant of a vill c 1125, a 1566; **1086, 1583, **willanus** c 1120, 1331, **-icanus** c 1192, **vilenagarius** 1196, villein, customary tenant; **v. dimidius** 1086, a 1128; **v. integer** 1086, **v. plenus** (**plenarius**) 1086, a 1128; (*adj.*) of a vill c 1306, c 1470; vulgar, ignorant c 795; **1086, 1315, †**-asius** 1225, **-enagius** (G.) 1243, of or for a villein; **-anagium** 1198, c 1230, **-enagium** c 1185, 1608,†**-encagium** 1205, **-inagium** 1320, c 1511, **vilnagium** c 1270, †**vilenagina** 15c., **wilenagium** 1234, **-enatio** 13c., villeinage, tenure, status or service of villein; 1176, 1205, **-agium** a 1250, **-enagium** c 1160, 1419, **-inagium** c 1250, c 1283, **vilnagium** 1393, **-anatus** c 1140, land held by villein tenure; **-ania** 12c., 14c., **-enia** 1373, 'villainy', discourtesy;

-icatio, parish (G.) c 1250; ‡**-icatura**, **-icatus**, bailiwick 1570; **-icus**, villager, townsman c 1470, ‡1570; (*adj.*) of a villein (W.) 1384; **-itim**, from house to house c 1180; **-ula** c 730, 1060. a 1100, 1452, **-icula** 1461, †**-ela** 15c., small town, hamlet.

villic/o, -atio, *see* **vellicator**.

villositas, shagginess c 1310, 15c.; **villosa** 747, (?) **vel/osa, -usa** 1212, rough cloth, towel; **petra -osa** 1314, **p. -uta** 1258, c 1320, (?) coarse-grained stone; **corium -utum**, (?) shaggy hide 1311; *see also* **floccus**, **velvetum**.

villum, weak wine 1241, ‡1483.

vim/icillum, hurdle 1550; **-ina** (*f. s.*) c 550, **vigimen** 15c., *for* **-en**, osier, withy; **-inaceus**, of wicker 1570; **-inarium**, osier-bed (G.) 1315.

vina, *see* **vinna**.

vinagium, *see* **homagium**; **vinum**.

vinc/ibilis, conquerable 1374; conquering 1520; **-etoxicum** (†**vicetoxicum**), (?) daisy (bot.) a 1250, ‡14c.; **-o**, to convict c 1185; to prevent 1313; **v. super**, to prevail against c 1250.

vincimentum, bond, tie c 1365.

vincnetum, *see* **VICIN**.

vincul/um, boundary 1334; ox-bow c 1280, ‡15c.; (?) measure of oats, thrave (W.) a 1300; copula (log.) 1610; **-a Sancti** (**Beati**) **Petri** c 1200, 1535, **festum** (**dies**) **S. (Beati) Petri ad Vincula** 1202, c 1514, **advincula** (*f. s.*) **S. Petri** 1244, c 1245, **avincula S. Petri** c 1300, St. Peter's Chains, Lammas day (1 Aug.); **-atio**, chaining c 1343, 1378; **-atus**, prisoner c 1090, p 1348; **-o**, to chain a 1090, 1461.

vind/agium, -emiatio, *see* **vinum**.

vindic/ta, payment, due c 802; weregeld c 1115; **-abilis**, punishable c 1382; **vendi--cabilis**, claimable c 1361; **vendicatio**, claim c 1250, 15c.; **-ator**, challenger (at

tournament) 1494; **vendicator**, claimant 15c.; **-amentum** 1313, †**-ium** c 1220, vengeance; **-ativus** c 1376, 1622, **vindeca-tivus** 1461, **-osus** c 1362, vengeful, vindictive; **-atrix**, avenging (*f.*) 1256; **-o in**, to punish c 793; **vendico**, *for* **-o**, to punish c 1335, 1419; to challenge a 1446; **to claim c 1140, 1509.

vinea, vinet-, vinit-, *etc., see* **vinum**.

vinectatus, *see* **humor**.

vinella, *see* **venella**.

vinetum, *see* **vicinetum**.

vingint/i, -inarius, *see* **vicena**; **vintena**.

vin/na, -a, fin (of fish) 1419.

vint/ena, space of twenty days 1206; **troop of twenty men 1318, 1434; **-enarius** c 1287, 1384, **-arius** 1355, **ventenarius** 1298, **vingintinarius** c 1280, commander of twenty soldiers; foreman over twenty labourers 1278, 1286; *cf.* **vicena**.

vin/um acerbum 1305, ‡**v. acidum** 14c., **v. acre** 1334, 1358, **v. acrum** 1265, 1415, **-acrum** 1534, **-egra** 1421, **venigrum** 1448, ‡**v. austerum** 15c., sour wine, vinegar; **v. adustum**, brandy 1674; **v. album** 1187, 1495; **v. de Alicante** 1474; **v. Andega-vie** (**Andegavense**), of Anjou 1176, 1242; **v. Anglicum** 1184, 1238; **v. assisum**, settled wine 1244; **v. Autisiodorense** 1186, 1212, **v. Aucerense** (**de Aucerna, Aucerr'**) 1200, 1242, of Auxerre (Burgundy); **v. avene**, ale made of oats 13c.; **v. bastardum** 'bastard', sweet wine 1265, 1443; **v. de Blanco** (**Oblenco, Oublenc, Ublinquo**), of Le Blanc (*dép.* Indre) 1202, 1244; **v. de Caprik'**, 'caprike' 1456; **v. color** 1337, **v. de teynt'** 1402, (?) dark red *or* artificially tinted wine; ‡**v. correctum**, distilled wine, "alcohol" 1652; **v. Cret'** (**de Creto**), Cretan 1337, 1342; **v. delicatum** 1242; **v. dis-pensabile** 1205, 1214, **v. expensabile** c 1135, a 1400, **v. expensibile** 1184, *vin ordinaire*; **v. dulce** 1264, 1482; **v. electum**, choice wine 1295; **v. franeboyse**, (?) rasp-berry-flavoured 1237; **v. Franciscum** (**de Francia**) 1175, 1547, **v. Gallicum** 1195, 1269; **v. Gasconicum** (**Wasco-nie**, *etc.*) 1207, 1606; **v. Grecum** (**Grek'**) 1313, 1387; **v. Hispanie, v. de Ispania** 1354, 1383; **v. Lotarengie**, of Lorraine 1177; **v. de Oseye** (**Osye**) 'osey', sweet wine, (?) originally of Alsace 1366, 1456; **v. de Mussac** (**Muissac**), of Moissac 1207, 1228; **v. Pictavense** (**Pictavie**), of Poitou 1157, 1402; **v. pomorum** 13c., ‡**v. de pomis** 14c., cider; **v. Portugalie** 1349, 1411; **v. Renense** 1461, 1474, **v. de Renesie** (†**Remes'**) 1275, 1419, **v. Reno-sum** 1296, **v. Renisetum** 1533, **v. Rinense** 1383, 1428, **v. Rini** (**de Rino, de Rina**) 1299, 1393, Rhenish wine; **v. de Saxonia** 1212, **v. de Romeney** (**Romney, Romo-ney**), 'rumney', Greek wine 1410, 1449; **v. rubeum** 1175, 1470; **v. vocatum sacke** 1552; **v. ultionis** (fig.) 1416; *see also* CLAR, essatum, FERR, **flos, gariofilum, garna-gia,** HERB, **malvesia, 3 morus, muscus, raspatum, reccum, rosa, salvia, ver-nagium**;

-agium, custom on wine or vineyards

(Fr.) 1138, 1344 (*see also* **homagium**); (?) wine in which relics have been dipped c 1248; **-ago**, kind of pigeon (οἰνάς) 1544; **-arium,** ‡wine-store 15c.; 1463, **vene-arium** 1245, vinery (*cf.*) **vivarium; taberna -aria,** wine-shop 1516, c 1542; **-arius** 1333, 1463, **-eator** 1130, 1369, **-itor** 1086, 1353, **-erator** 1278, 'viner', vine-dresser, man in charge of vinery; **-ator** c 1200, **-etor** c 1205, 1508, **-itor** c 1130, c 1250, **-aterus** c 1190, *-etarius c 1190, 1420, **-eterius** 1386, **-eterus** c 1195, **vigneterrus** 1380, **-itarius** 1179, 1493, **-iterus** c 1200, **-tarius** p 1330, 15c., **-tenarius** 1320, 1573, vintner (*see also* VINT); **-etaria** 1275, **-etrix** 1235, vintress; **-atus,** intoxicated a 1519; **aqua -ata,** wine and water c 1197;

-**dagium** 1483, **vendagium** 1372, 1419, **vendemia** 1254, **-demiatio** 1169, 1620, **-demiatus** 1163, vintage; **-dimiator,** *for* **-demiator,** vintager 1277; **venea,** *for* **-ea,** vineyard c 1250, c 1370; **-ealis,** of a vine 1245; **-ealiter,** in the manner of a vine 1245; **-eatus,** ornamented with vine-leaves 1245, 1295; **dolius -erettus,** wine-cask 1241; **-etria** 1221, c 1320, ‡**-itria** 15c., **-tria** c 1488, vintry, wine-market; **-iarium** 14c., **-egerium -agium** 1368, vessel for altar-wine; **-osus,** wine-coloured 1267; **-um -osum,** strong wine 13c.; **vendemio,** *for* **-demio,** 1253; **-esco,** to become wine a 1275.

vio, *see* **via.**
viol-, *see also* **phiala; 2 vidula.**
viola, kind of fish 1634.
viol/acium 15c., **-etum** 1188, **-etta** 1194, violet cloth; **oleum -aceum** 13c., **o. -atum** a 1250, oil of violets; **syrupus -aceus** a 1250; **-aticus** 15c., **-eticus** a 1273, 1415, violet-coloured; *see also* **sucrum; -etta,** violet (bot.) 15c.; **color -ettus** c 1325; **-aria,** wallflower a 1250, ‡14c.
viol/atio monete, (fine for) coining c 1110; **-amen** 1632, **-atus** 12c., **-entia** 1086, c 1115, violation; **-entie** (*pl.*), violent attacks c 730. 12c., 1422; **-ento** c 1300, 1374, **-or** (*dep.*) 12c., to violate.
viorna, vipurnum, *see* **viburnum.**
‡**vipa,** sop (in wine) 15c., 1483; *cf.* **ipa.**
vipere/alis, viperish c 1180; **-e,** viperishly 1170.
vir/ armorum, man-at-arms c 1340, 15c.; **v. Dei** c 1170, 1416, **v. Domini** c 1170, c 1250, man of God; **v. pacis,** man of peace c 1470; **v. religionis** 1303, *v. religiosus** c 1194, 1526, monk; **v. sanguinis** 1207, c 1220; **v. scelerum** c 1400; **-atio,** manliness c 730; **pro -ili,** *for* **pro v. parte,** 1439, 1558; **-ilitus,** in the male line a 1135; **-lupus** werewolf c 1102; **-osus,** manly, vigorous c 1115, c 1325.
vlrago, woman c 550, c 950; shrew c 1000. c 1205.
virbera, *see* **1 turba.**
vired-, *see* VIRID.
virella, *see* **virolla.**
virg/a *c 1200, 1378, **verga** c 1200, yard, yard-arm (naut.); sail-yard (of windmill) 1238, 1504; withy for harness 1243, 1386; 1086, 1398, **verga** 1270, withy, twig (for wattled fence); 1253, 1264, **vurga** 1253,

scaffold-pole; weaver's reed c 1200; shaft (of column) 1293; upright (of cross) 1291; shank (of anchor) 1452; 1245, 1327, **v. machinaria** 1270, **verga** 1275, beam (of siege-engine); blade (of shears) c 1325; *membrum virile* a 1150, ‡14c.; 1245, **v. episcopalis** c 1090, **v. pastoralis** 1200, crosier; wand of office, (symbol of) jurisdiction c 1000. c 1090, 1483; **v. aurea,** ducal emblem 1397; golden-rod (bot.) 1632; **v. pastoris** a 1250, 1632, **v. pastoralis** a 1250, teasel; **v. sanguinea,** dogwood 1634; **v. tippata,** tipped staff, tipstaff 1348; **per -am,** mode of tenure 1375, 1413; **sub -a,** under authority (of husband or lord) c 1218, 1300;

-**a** 1280, a 1452, **-ata** 1290, verge, area of jurisdiction; section of document 15c.; yard-stick 1380, c 1427; c 868, 956. 1225, 1507, **verga** 1392, 1421, **-ata** 1425, 1630, yard, linear measure of 3 feet; 13c., 1329, **-ata** c 1283, rod, linear measure of 20 feet; *868. 1086, c 1414, *-ata 1086, c 1539, **vergata** c 1165, **-ulata** 1138, ‡**-ulta** c 1153, **-eia** (C.I.) c 1150, **vergeia** (C.I.) c 1165, **-ea** c 1185, yardland, virgate, square-measure usually of 20 to 30 acres (¼ carrucate); **v. ferrea** 1295, 14c., **v. ferri** 1324, **v. regis** 1321, measure of length; **v. mensuralis** c 1115, **v. mensurabilis** c 1150, **v. mensoria** c 1200, measuring-rod;

-**arium,** osier-bed a 1222; **-arius** c 1283, 1327, *-atarius** 1234, 1449, 'yardling', tenant of virgate; **v. dimidius,** tenant of half virgate 1234, 1327; **-arius** 13c., 1503, **-ator** 1249, c 1290, **-ebajulans** 1527, **-ebajulus** 1423, 1471, **-ibajulus** 1483, **-ifer** 1541, **vergifer** 1463, **vergefer** 1529, **-iferarius** 1506, verger, wand-bearer; 1283, **-ator** 1253, erector of scaffold-poles; **-atio,** transformation into a rod 1427; **-eus,** brindled (of greyhound) 1191 (*cf.* **varietas**); **-ula,** withy c 1300, 1362; ‡weaver's temple 1483; blade (of shears) c 1325; *membrum virile* c 1172; accentual mark (of diphthong) c 1200; file or label (her.) c 1595; **v. fumi,** thread of smoke 1283; **-ildum,** *for* **-ultum,** shrub 1237; **-ulatus,** striped, ripply (of urine) a 1250; **-ulo,** to wattle 1487, 1507.
Virginianus, Virginian 1634.
*virgo** c 600, 9c. c 1090, c 1450, **virgin/eus** c 1090, 12c., chaste (of man); **-al,** maiden-head c 1125; service-book containing office of the Virgin 1415; **cera -ea,** virgin wax a 1250, 1331; **pergamenum -eum,** parchment from first-born calf 1510; **-itas,** chastity (of man) c 800. c 1090, c 1340; **virguncula,** young nun 790; **-o,** to remain virgin 1220, a 1275.
virgulariter, *see* **burgaria.**
viricomus, *see* **uritivus.**
*virid/e, -is** 1169, c 1455, **-um** 1288, 1333, greenwood, (right of) vert; (fine for) illegal assumption of right of vert 1091, 1453; **-e** 1175, c 1307, **-um** 1252, green cloth; green vitriol c 1215; **v. encre,** sort of green (? ink) 1213, 1244; **-e eris** a 1250, ‡14c., **-eraminum** c 1227, ‡**-e Hispanicum** 1652, **-e grecum** 1286, 1313, **vertegrecum** 1332, **vertgrisium** 1328, **-igresium** a 1300,

-igratum 1306, †-igranum 1306, verdigris; verdettum, 'verdet' (copper acetate) 1313; -e succum 1313, *-is succus 1265, 1388, -um succum 1297, ‡-isiccus 15c., verjuice; -e salsum 1305, ‡-e salsamentum c 1440, ‡-is salsa 1483, 'vertsauce'; -is, fresh, untanned (of leather) a 1242, 1294; fresh (of wine) 1288; see also allec, cera, 2 pannus, piscis, via; -us a 1200, 1588, veridis 1460, 1496, veredis 1462, -ens 1245, for -is, green; *-arius 1203, 15c., viredarius 1230, 1400, veredarius a 1275, verderer, forest officer; -aria, office of verderer 1218, 1263; ‡-arius c 1440, ‡virudiarius 15c., robin (bird); -a 1558, -e 1272, -ium 1411, viredetum 1461, -arium 1233, 1461, veredera 1316, green place, green or garden; viredo, freshness a 1275; -osus, evergreen c 1293; -o, to paint green 1289; to turf 1306.

virmiculo, see VERM

vir/o 1337, -onus 1286, oar; cf. aviro.

vir/olla 1283, 1388, -ella 1242, verella 1519, ‡-ula 1483, ferrule, boss.

virosus, (?) liquid c 1115; see also vir.

virotus, see MYRT

virrerium, see vitrum.

virro, thane c 1102, c 1130.

virtitio, see vertitio.

virtu/s, virtue, property (alch.) 1267, 14c.; *miracle, miraculous power 6c., 10c. 12c., c 1400; angel, heavenly power 6c., c 1000. c 1067, 13c.; force, body of men p 1348; *force or effect (of document) c 1258, c 1534; -tem facio de necessitate 1244; v. juratorum, charge to jury c 1290; v. sancte crucis, sign of cross 11c.; *-alis, virtual 1153, a 1446; -alitas, virtuality p 1300; *-aliter, virtually a 1252, c 1620; *-ose, virtuously, manfully c 1150, 1461; -ositas, virtue a 1250, c 1376; -osus, *virtuous, valiant c 1170, c 1470; possessing special (supernatural) potency c 1100, 1381; sound (of food) c 1290; -tiformis, miraculous 870.

virulent/ia 15c., 1537, †viruculentia 1284, virulence (of language); (n. pl.) stenches 7c.; -us, poisonous c 1090, c 1260; baleful c 1250, 1293; virulent (of language, etc.) c 1343, 1520.

vis, force, troop (of men) 1263, 1298; in vim, in spite (of) c 1450; 1426, in vi 13c., in virtue (of); in vi cum, as an accomplice of c 1218; vim alicui facio (with inf.), to give the chance to 8c.

visaria, see visera.

visatie, see bisaccia.

visca, see fiscella.

viscago, see vesicago.

viscer/a (vicer-) (pl.), bowels of compassion c 1125, 1549; -alia, entrails 1333, 1419; in -ibus (Jesu) Christi c 1195, 1549, in v. Salvatoris c 1459; -abiliter 1307, 1330, -aliter 8c., 1281, c 1470, -ose 1433, 1440, inwardly, sincerely; -alis c 1125, 1433, *-osus c 1280, 1450, inward, sincere; -alis, true-born, genuine 685; -ius, of or for flesh c 550; -atim, internally c 1115, a 1200.

vischia, viscium, see vicia (1 & 2).

visco, see WISC

visc/ositas, stickiness a 1250, c 1620; -osus, sticky a 1292, 1620; fiscum, for -um, glue 1266, 1298; ‡-alcus, gum from trees 1652; ‡-arium 1483, ‡-erium 15c., pot or brush for bird-lime; filum -atum, "lime-string" 1470; -o, to trap with bird-lime c 1180.

viscula, see VESIC

visea, see 1 vicia.

visenetum, visin-, viscin-, see VICIN

viser/a c 1218, 1366, vizera 1367, -ia, -ium 1239, 1378, visaria 1316, visura 1328, visor (of helmet); visorum, (?) mask 1440.

visi/o, appearance, aspect 7c., 8c. c 1362; view, inspection c 1106, 1404; spectacle, display 1483; v. mutua, interview 1310, 1325; -bilis *c 682, c 974. c 1090, c 1444, -lis c 1200, visible; a 1250, a 1446, -vus a 1250, 1620, visual; -bile, -bilitas, visibility 1267; *-biliter, visibly c 974, 1060. a 1090, 15c.; cf. visus.

Visisaxo, West-Saxon 1586.

visit/atio, visiting 7c. c 1090, c 1390; blessing 970; visitation (ac.) c 1549, c 1556; *c 1188, 1684, †-io c 1192, visitation, inspection (eccl.); paying visitation-dues or visiting with presents (eccl.) c 1160, 1327; division of Dominican province 1376, 1427; V. Beate Virginis Marie, (feast of) Visitation (2 July) 15c., c 1490; v. divina c 1250, 15c., v. Altissimi c 1540, heaven-sent affliction; v. epistolaris, letter c 1096; v. nemorum, 'regard' c 1178; -ativus c 1200, -atorius 1330, of or for visitation (eccl.); -ator, visitor (ac.) c 1352, c 1556; visitor (eccl.) 1189, 1549; v. generalis, official of Templars 1308; -atrix, visitor (f.) 6c., 8c.; -o, to punish, afflict c 1160, c 1340; to view (of coroner) 1276; to visit (ac.) c 1542; to visit (eccl.) c 1250, 1549; to pay visitation dues or visit with presents (eccl.) 1204, c 1395; v. litteris, to write to c 1115, c 1250.

visn/etum, -ietum, see VICIN

visor, viewer, inspector 1185, 15c.; v. ecclesie, (?) churchwarden 1359; v. et auditor de sacramento (G.) 1307.

visorum, see visera.

1 vispil/io c 1190, 15c., -lus c 1400, vespilio c 1204, c 1225, vespillo 1345, †spillo 14c., nocturnal robber, rogue.

2 vispilio, wisp of straw c 1290; 1288, c 1339, wispilio 1255, holy water sprinkler (Fr. goupillon).

vista, interview (Fr. & Sp.) 1279, 1286; see also 2 justa.

visura, see visera.

*visu/s, view, inspection 1140, 1459; 1279, 1315, v. franciplegii 1190, c 1539, view of frankpledge; v. certus, (?) a fixed due or perquisite (man.) 1289, 1349; v. compoti, (preliminary) view of account c 1178, c 1478; v. coronatoris 1221, 1368, v. corporis 1328, 1583, coroner's view; v. fenestre, access of light to window 1274; v. forestarii, regard 1203, c 1300; v. hundredi, hundred court c 1290; v. servientis 1184, 1212; v. tethingarum 1189, 1287; v. vicecomitis 1279; -alis, of or for sight 1267, c 1366; -alitas, visibility c 1300; -aliter, as regards sight 8c.; cf. veua, videre, visio, visor.

vit/a, eternal life c 730, c 800. c 1362, c 1430;

per -am, pro -a, on pain of death c 1115; *see also* **aqua; -alis,** (*subst.*) a living creature c 1365, a 1408; (*adj.*) spiritual c 730; life-long 1608; **redditus v.,** life-rent 1504, 1560; *see also* VICT

vitanter, reluctantly c 1190.

vitell-, *see also* VICT; **vitulus.**

vitell/inus a 1250, a 1252, **-inosus** 1564, yolky.

viterarius, *see* **vitrum.**

†**vitherum,** (?) part of ironwork of plough (Kent) c 1285.

vithra, *see* **fithera.**

viti/amen, fault c 950; **-abilis,** corruptible c 1000.

vit/is, mantlet c 1200; **v. Idea,** whortleberry 1634; **-icella,** black bryony (bot.) 13c.; ‡white bryony 14c.; ‡"wood-bine" c 1440.

vitreola, pellitory (bot.) a 1250, ‡14c.

vitr/eolum, -iolum c 1227, 1620, **-iallum** 1418, vitriol, copperas; **v. nigrum,** *"terra Francigena"* c 1215; **v. Romanum,** blue vitriol a 1235, ‡1652; **v. ustum** c 1250; ‡**v. viride** 14c.; **-iolatus,** impregnated with vitriol 1620, a 1700.

vitric-, *see* VICTRI

vitr/um, glass vessel (alch.) c 1320; **v. album,** uncoloured glass 1240, 1351; **v. coloratum** 1296, 1422; **v. flor',** 'flourished' glass 1388; ‡**v. nigrum,** smalt 1652; **v. calendare,** air-thermometer 1620; **v. objectivum,** object lens 1686; †**vuitrum,** *for* **-um,** 1291; **-arius** c 1130, c 1506, ***-earius (-iarius)** 1170, c 1533, **-erius** 1173, 1291, **viterarius** 1257, **verrarius** 1198, 1349, **-ator** 1361, 1509, **-iator** 1187, c 1533, †**variator** 1496, **verror** 1299, **-atorius** 1514, **-ifaber** 1517, **-ifactor** c 730, **-ifex** c 1400, glazier, glass-worker; **ars -iaria** c 1414; **opus -earium** 1417; **-iarium,** glazier's workshop 1399; **-iatria,** office of (royal) glazier 1443; **-agium,** (?) varnishing 1416;
     -atio c 1400, 1443, ***-eatio (-iatio)** 1354, c 1533, **-iatura** 1319, **-ifactio** 1466, glazing; ‡**-ificatio,** vitrification 1652; **-ea** a 1090, **-eola** 1240, **-ina** c 1250, 1260, **verrina (verina)** 1233, a 1273, **verrinum** 1236, 1284, **verrura** 1240, c 1400, **verrera** 1252, (?) †**virrerium** 1421, **veirium** 1243, **veyrum** 1279, pane of glass; **verrina alba** uncoloured pane 1238; **-eum stans,** "standing glass" 1553; **v. stileum,** "steel-glass", mirror 1553; ***-eo (-io)** 1251, c 1480, **-o** 1241, 1532, **veruro** 1384, to glaze.

vittal-, vitual-, vitul-, *see also* VICT; **2 vidula.**

vitul/amen, offering, sacrifice c 1115; †**-annam,** (?) *f.l. for* **-amina,** shoots 1328.

vitul/us, deer calf (hart under one year) 1341, 1355; **v. bisse** 14c., **v. cervi** 1341, 1354, **v. cervinus** 1307; **v. marinus,** 'sea-calf', seal c 1325; **vitellus,** calf a 1128; **-inium** 1322, **-ina** (*pl.*) c 1457, **pergamenum -i** 1249, **p. -inum** 1342, **velum** a 1180, vellum; **-atio** 1299, 1389, calving; ***-o,** to calve 1234, 1364.

●**vituper/ium,** insult, disparagement 9c., c 980, c 1160, 1549; **-abiliter,** culpably c 1250, c 1400.

viurna, *see* **viburnum.**

●**viv/a vox,** oral statement or evidence c 793.

c 1178, 1684; *see also* **oraculum; -us,** in full vigour (of feudal tenure) (G.) p 1250; **-e,** vigorously c 1150; **-aria** 1292, c 1393, **-arius** 1298, *for* **-arium,** fish-pond, stew; ‡**-arius,** warrener 1570; **-ifer** 870, **-ificativus** a 1250, 1552, **-ificator** c 730, **-ificatrix** (*f.*) 8c. 1552, ***-ificus** c 1090, c 1414, life-giving; **-ificatrix,** life-giver (*f.*) c 800. c 1112, c 1160; **-ificatio,** animation, quickening c 1180, 1344; ***-ifico** c 1070, c 1414, †**-ico** 14c., 15c., to quicken, restore to life; **vibo,** *for* **-o,** 867; **-o in,** to live on (a food) 1326; **v. per,** to live by (a trade) 1306.

viviam, *see* **viaram.**

vivole, disease of horses, glanders c 550.

vix (with *negative*): **nemo v.,** *for* **v. quisquam,** 1275.

vixo, *see* WISC

†**vixus,** (?) *for* **fixus,** c 730.

vizera, *see* **visera.**

vizier, vizier 1666.

Vlandrus, *see* **Flamingus.**

voc/alis, -iferatio, -ula, *see* **vox.**

voc/atio, naming 870. c 1380; description a 1100; invitation c 1330; invocation c 1125, c 1520; ***vocation** (eccl.) c 793. a 1090, c 1536; 'call', summons to death c 730, 1006. c 1090, c 1400; summons, citation (leg.) 12c., c 1540; 1290, **v. ad warantum** c 1275, **v. waranti** c 1285, **-are** (*subst.*) 1315, **-are ad warantiam** 1309, 1428, voucher to warranty (leg.); **-abilis,** nameable a 1361; **-abolum** 12c., **-amen** c 690, **-itamen** c 950. 12c., name; **-abularium, -abularius,** vocabulary 1523; **-abularius,** consisting of words c 1553; **-ativus,** called c 1370; vocative (gram.) c 700. 1430; **-ator,** one who vouches (to warranty) c 1275; **-atus** 1308, **v. ad warantum** 1269, vouchee to warranty; **-itatio,** summons c 1157; **-ito,** to call (by name) c 730; **-o,** to vouch, call as evidence or support (leg.) 1086, c 1324; **v. quietum,** to quit-claim c 1330; **v. ad warantiam** c 1200, c 1400, ***v. ad warantum (warentum)** c 1185, c 1400, **v. warantum** c 1115, c 1275, **v. warantem** c 1110, **vochio warantiam** 1293, **voucho warentum** 1278, **vucho warantum** 1166, to vouch to warranty.

voerndellus, *see* **ferdella.**

vog/a 13c., c 1320, **-um** 1267, **-ea** 1270, **foga** 1248, **wogium** c 1160, **vougia** 1274, **volgum** 1208, **volgonium** c 1175, pruning-knife, twibill (O.F. *vouge*); *cf.* **vanga,** 1 **vidula.**

voiagium, *see* VIA

voisinetum, *see* VICIN

vol/a, wing c 1150, ‡1483; **-abilis,** capable of flight c 1300; ***-ata** a 1163, 1320, **-atum** 1255, **-atus** c 1220, c 1280, **-eta** 1359, **-etus** 13c., **-ea** c 1282, **-eynum** c 1275, **-atile** 1229, decoy, fowling-glade; ***-atile** c 1195, c 1530, **-atus** 1266, c 1402, fowl; **-atus,** flight (falc.) 1272; **-atilitas,** winged-ness 870; **-ativus,** volatile (alch.) c 1215; **-ator,** fowler, bird-catcher 1380; ‡**-atorium** fowling-net 15c.; **-itatio,** flight c 1250; **-ucer S. Cuthberti,** eider-duck 1381; **-ux,** cited as example of *adj.* in *-ux,* 1267; **-ans,** (*subst.*) mercury (alch.) 1652; (*adj.*) soaring

(her.) c 1595; **fenestra v.**, movable
(? hinged) window 1267, 1272; **-o**, to
evaporate c 1215; **v. ad**, to fly (hawks) at
1284, 1291.
volaria, slap of the hand c 1180.
vole/mum c 1200, 1575, **-num** 1508, pearmain, warden pear; **-mus**, pearmain tree
c 1200, a 1564.
volentia, *see* **volitio**.
volg/um, -onium, *see* **voga**.
volitellum, *see* **bultellum**.
vol/itio c 1300, 15c., †**-itium** 13c., **-utio** 1344,
1380, **-entia** 1313, c 1344, **-le** c 1380, 1449,
***velle** 956, 11c. a 1100, c 1470, will,
volition; **ad velle** a 1100, c 1385, **pro velle**
c 950, a 1140, c 1250, at will; **-ibilis** c 1300,
p 1300, **-ubilis** c 1290, 1378, **-untabilis**
1344, able to be willed; **-ibilitas** p 1300,
-untabilitas 1344, capacity of being willed;
***-itivus** c 1270, c 1380, **-utivus** 1344, c 1365,
-untativus c 1344, 1374, **-untivus** c 1301,
volitional; **-untando**, at will 1225; **-un-
tarium**, (object of) desire c 1185, c 1390;
-untarius, arbitrary c 1096, c 1465; **-un-
tarie**, ***willingly** 8c. a 1090, 1454; wilfully
c 1200, 1299; arbitrarily c 1250, c 1546;
-umptas, *for* **-untas**, 1267, c 1340; **-untas**,
arbitrariness 1220, c 1290; **v. ultima**
c 1266, 1549, **v. suprema** c 1250, last will;
sum in -untate 1243, 1365, **existo in
-untate** 1447, **habeo in -untate** 1220, to
be minded; **dico -untatem meam**, to say
what one pleases 1201; **facio -untatem de**
c 1218, 1336; **ad -untatem**, *see* **tenentia**;
de -untate, arbitrarily 1232; **pro -untate**,
at will c 1250, 1326; **-itum**, object of will
c 1200, 1304; **-itus**, willed c 1240, c 1301;
velit, nolit, willy-nilly c 1170; **-o**, to prefer
9c.; (as *auxiliary* equivalent to *conditional*)
1293, 1385.
volo, partisan c 1170; *see also* **vola, volitio.**
volox, *see* **velox**.
volsura, volto, volu/men, -bilis, *see* **volutio.**
volucer, *see* **vola.**
volunt-, *see* **volitio.**
volup/por 1281, **volutor** 1335, wool-wrapper;
-o, to wrap (wool) 1271, 1306.
volupt/as, sport, game animal 1532; **-uositas**,
indulgence in pleasure 1287; **-uose**, volup-
tuously c 730. c 1194, c 1461; **-ualis**,
sensual c 1250; **-o** c 1283, **-or** (*dep.*) 14c., to
indulge in pleasure.
volu/tio, roller, billow c 1180; c 1115,
-tabilitas 12c., circular motion, revolution;
8c., ***-ta** c 1213, c 1553, **-tum** c 1100, c 1325,
avolta c 1250, **wolta** 1290, **vouta** 1212,
1382, **voutum** c 1304, **vota** c 1228, **vulta**
c 1250, **valta** 1467, c 1533, **valtum** 1403,
c 1533, **vaulta** c 1533, **vauta** c 1362, 1560,
vawta 1394, **-ticium** c 1245, 1276, vault
(arch.); **volticula**, little vault 1461; **volsura**
c 1200, a 1273, **vousura** 1284, 1397,
†**veusura** 1330, **vosura** 1279, 1284,
vausura 1348, **folsura** 1253, **fousura** 1347,
vaulting, groining, *voussoir* (arch.); **vousu-
ratus**, vaulted 1270;
   volu/men, charter, deed 12c., 15c.;
porta -bilis, revolving gate 1456; **-bilis**
a 1250, 1634, **-crum majus** 1538, bindweed (bot.); **-tarius** (*sc.* **equus**), ambler

a 1520; ‡**-to**, to amble a 1520; **volvo**, to
curve 870; 12c., **volto** 1244, c 1540, to
vault; *see also* **tabula, volitio, voluppor.**
volux, *see* **vola.**
vomer/ estivalis 1291, **v. estatis** 1278, **v.
pro estate** 1333, share for summer ploughing; **-ulus**, blunted spear-head 1252;
‡**-ellus**, sheath of knife 1483.
vom/itus, debauchery c 730; **-itivus**, emetic
13c., ‡1652; ‡**-ex**, vomiting 1483; *see also*
nux.
vora/citas, whirlpool c 1200; **-go**, down-
shaft, sink, drain, cess-pool c 550. 1314,
1419; **-tor** 9c., **-trix** (*f.*) c 1070, 1220,
gluttonous, devouring.
vor/atrum, -otrum, *see* **barathrum.**
vorset/um, -icus, *see* **worsteda.**
vos/, you (*s.*) 8c. c 1127, 1453; ‡**-o**, to address
as *vos* 1483; *cf.* **vester.**
vosum, *see* **vas.**
vosura, vota, *see* **volutio.**
†**votennarius**, (?) fodderer (man.) 1280.
votmellum, *see* **fotmellum.**
vot/um, vow (mon.) c 660. c 1250, c 1470;
curse 1461; ***vote** c 1200, 1537; **pro -o** 1350,
p. †**vota** 14c., at will; **-aliter**, as an offering
c 1172; **-ifragus**, vow-breaker 1590, 1609;
-ifrangium, vow-breaking c 1172; **-ivalis**
(**militia**), subject to a vow a 1446; **-ive**,
prayerfully c 1300, c 1365; **voveo**, (with *inf.*)
to vow 9c. c 1250, c 1430; 1242, **v. ordinem**
c 1272, **v. regulam** c 1341, to take vow
(mon.)
voucho, *see* VOC
vougia, *see* **voga.**
vou/sura, -ta, -tum, *see* **volutio.**
voveo, *see* VOT
†**vovet**, areca nut (Ar.) 12c.
vox, vowel 8c.; voice, vote, authority 12c.,
c 1470; **v. activa**, **v. passiva** (gram.)
c 1450; **v. appellandi**, right of appeal (leg.)
1221; **v. materna**, mother tongue c 1457;
v. prosaica, speaking voice c 1213; **v.
simplex** c 1217, 1308, **v. sola** 1269, mere
word (leg.); **v. viva**, *see* VIV; **voc/ule
quinque**, five categories (leg.) 12c.; **-alis**,
(merely) nominal, so-called c 850. c 1218,
c 1334; **-aliter**, orally 1292; nominally
c 1218, c 1400; **-alitas**, utterance c 1430;
-iferatio, hue, outcry c 1115; *cf.* VOC
vrydo, *see* **fritha.**
vucho, *see* VOC
vuitrum, *see* VITR
vulgago, asara bacca (bot.) a 1200, 1538.
vulg/aritas, inelegant Latin c 1290; ***-are**
c 1300, c 1470, **-aris** a 1227, **lingua -arica**
c 760, vernacular, vulgar tongue; passage
in the vernacular 1549; passage for translation a 1520, 1560; **-ares** (*pl.*), common
people 12c., c 1422; **-aris**, living like a layman c 1102, c 1115; couched in the vernacular 1417, 1549; **fractio v.** (math.) 1267;
-ariter 957. c 1191, 1494, **wlgariter** c 1302,
1461, **-arice** c 1000, in the vernacular;
-aliter 12c., a 1387, **wlgaliter** 1276, 1331,
for **-ariter**, commonly; **-ata**, exemplar
-atum 1267, **Wlgatum** 1292, Vulgate
version of Bible; **-o**, to wander c 550.
vuln/us, wound: **wlnus** 1200, c 1300; **-uscu-
lum**, slight wound 12c., c 1400; **-erator**,

wounder c 1290, c 1400; **v. sanctorum**, the Devil c 820; **-eratura** c 1290, **wulneratio** 1235, wounding; **-ereus** c 1250, **-erosus** a 1250, of a wound; **wulnero** 1288, c 1404, **wlnero** 1200, 1343, **wolnero** (G.) 1255, *for* **-o**, to wound.

vulp/es (*pl.*), 'foxes' (a game) c 1160; **wulpes** 1230, ***wlpes** a 1100, 1323, **gupillus** 1221, 1303, **gopillus** 1198, fox; **-ecularis** 1228, **canis v.** 1230, 1274, **c. wulpecularis** 1248, **c. wlpiclaris** 1230, **c. -ericius** 1234, 1300, **brachettus -ericius** 1213, **c. -erinus** 1290, **c. gupillerettus** 1211, 1215, fox-hound; **-ecularis** a 1155, 15c., †**-eculus** c 1362, **-is** (*f.*) 14c., foxy, crafty; **-eculariter**, foxily c 1430, 15c.; **-eculus**, little fox c 1325; sly rogue 1410; **-anser**, merganser (bird) 1544, ‡1570; **-eum**, fox fur 1365; **wulpinus** 1228, **wlpinus** c 1302, **wolpentinus** 1292, of a fox; **-eculo**, to creep like a fox c 1200.

†**vulphi**, kind of animal (Ar.) 1144.

vulta, *see* VOLU

vultur, (?) mercury (alch.) c 1320.

vulturn/us, south-east c 780; south-easterly c 700; **-alis**, easterly c 1400.

vult/us, purse c 1115; **v. de Luca** 12c., **v. Lucanus** c 1212, crucifix at Lucca; **-um bonum (hilarem) facio**, to be of good cheer, offer a welcome 1395, 1461; **-uosus**, haughty c 1125, c 1436; c 1320, †**-ivolus** c 1160, **-uaria** (*f.*) c 1193, necromancer, sorcerer using wax figures (*cf.* **invultuatio**); **-uositas**, facial expression c 1204; scornful frown 8c. a 1200, 13c.

vulva, womb: **wulwa** 1380; *see also* **valva**.

vurga, *see* **virga**.

†**vyratus**, (?) twisted 1294.

W

wab/entacum, -itaculum, *see* **wapentacum**.

waca, wake, watching the dead c 1086; **wakagium**, (?) payment for a 'wake' or feast 1337.

wacheria, *see* VACC

wacressa, *see* **wagessa**.

wad-, *see also* VAD

wadda, wadium, *see* WAID

wadl/a, -o, -ura, *see* **walla**; **wattillum**.

wadletus, *see* **valettus**.

waeri/a, -um, *see* **wayarium**.

*waf/ra 1236, c 1450, **vafra** 1267, ‡15c., **gafra** 1310, ‡c 1440, **gwafra** 1303, **galfra** c 1180, 15c., wafer, obley; **ferrum -rorum**, wafer-iron c 1300; **-ria**, wafery (of royal household) c 1472; **-rarius** 1210, 1303, **-erarius** 1290, 1449, ‡**gafrarius** c 1440, waferer.

waft/or, 'wafter', convoyer 1482, 1491; **-agium** (†**wastagium**, †**vastagium**), 'waftage', convoying 1572.

1 †**waga**, (?) wave (Fr. *vague*) (C.I.) 1309.

2 wag/a 1228, c 1530, **vaga** 1321, 1509, **-ia** c 1070, **vauga** 1351, **waya** 1241, 1550, †**wawa** 1489, **waysa** 1275, **wayza** 1303, **wedia** 1473, 1487, **weya** 1302, 1372, 'wey', measure of weight; weighing-machine 14c.; **-ator**, officer in charge of weighing-machine 14c.

wag/erum, -ium, -io, *see* **vadium**.

wagess/a (†**wacressa**), **-um**, swamp (Essex) (*cf.* O.F. *wachas*) 1390, 1409.

*waid/a 1204, 1392, **-ia** 1327, **-um** 1200, †**warda** 1298, ***weida** 1176, 1267, **weidia** c 1216, **waisda, waisdia** 1198, **vaisda** 1199, **wasdia** 1196, **wesda** 13c., **weisda** (**weysda**) 1177, 1309, **wisda** 1303, 1458, **wisida** 1274, **gaida** a 1250, **gadum** 1523, **vaddum** 1228, **wadda** 1380, 1504, **wadium** 1303, 1379, **waoda** 1504, **woda** 1304, 1504, **wodum** a 1564, ‡**gaudo** c 1440, ‡**gaudeo** 15c., woad; **-arius** 1221, (?) c 1300, **wesdarius, westdarius** 13c.,

wisdarius 1419, woad-dealer; **-o**, to dye with woad 1359; *cf.* **gualda, 2 walda**.

waif-, *see* WAIV

wain/agium *1203, c 1448, †**wannagium** (? **wainiagium**) a 1198, 1275, †**wanniagium** 1226, **waignagium** 1237, **gainagium** 1276, **gainiagium** 1284, **gaignagium** 1227, **guanagium** 12c., 1236, **guagnagium** c 1200, **gwainagium** 1214, †**vavnagium**, †**vannagium** (? **vainiagium**) 1214, 1314, cultivation; 1222, **wagnagium** 1325, land under cultivation; 1215, 15c., †**wannagium** 1229, c 1293, **waignagium** c 1217, †**gannagium** (? **gainiagium**) 1286, means of cultivation, farm-stock; **w. (waignagium) carruce**, plough-team 1185, 1198;
  -abilis 1216, 1293, **-iabilis** a 1200, **wanabilis** c 1250, 13c., **wanibilis** c 1200, **waignabilis** 1215, 15c., **gaingabilis** (†**gavingabilis**) 1290, †**gwaigabilis** 12c., cultivable; **-eria** 1199, 1222, †**wanneria** 1216, **waigneria** 1177, **gaineria** (**gainaria**) 1222, c 1412, †**gaymaria** (? **gayniaria**) 1348, **ganerium** 1572, 'gainery', (yield of) cultivation; †**wanita** (*pl.*), (?) profits 1587; **-o** c 1220, **-io** 13c., **wannio** 1226, **gaino** (**ganio**) 1243, 1431, **gaignio** a 1564, **vainio** 1181, to cultivate (profitably), exploit; to gain, acquire 1385.

†**wainares (wayn-) cineres**, an article of commerce 1284.

waino, measure of weight (Yorks.) 1275; *cf.* **2 waga**.

wainscot/um, wainscot, panelling 1375; **-bordum**, wainscot-board 1352.

wainum, wain, wagon 15c.; **wen/clutum**, 'wain-clout' 1348; **-sevis, -sewis**, (?) 'wain-sheaf' (wagoner's perquisite) 1234.

waisd-, *see* WAID

wait/a (wayt-) c 1268, **weyta** 13c., **geyta** 1271, watchman; c 1184, (?) **vaeta** 1219, **-efeodum** 1272, **-feodum** 1275, **-isfeodum** 1278, watchman's fee; **w. maris**, coastguard service 1203 (cf. **awaita**); **-agium,** (payment for) escort 1199, 1265; **weyta- gium,** payment for care-taker 1300; **terra †-iatoria,** (?) land held by service of watch and ward (Cornwall) 1201.

waitingum (Sc.) 1266, 1296, (?) **weintin- gum** (Northumb.) 1201, a food-rent.

waiv/ium c 1258, 1293, **-um** (**†wavium**) 1230, 1274, **waifum** 1275, 1399, **weiva** (**†wevia**) 1275, **weyvium** c 1290, **weyvum** 1278, 1330, **veyfia, †wayfrum** 1279, waif, (right to seize) abandoned property; **-us** (**†wavius**) 1168, **vaivus** 1166, vagrant, masterless; **†-iagium, -agium,** (?) profit from impounding stray animals (or *f.l.* for **wainiagium**) c 1300; **-iaria** 1358, 1573, **-aria** (**†waviaria**) a 1564, 1587, **-eria** 1419, 'waivery', outlawry of woman; **-io** 1234, 1278, **-o** c 1320, **weivo** (**†wevio**) p 1290, 1378, to waive, renounce (rights, land, *etc.*); **-io, -eo,** 1452, a 1564, **-o** (**wavio**) 1526, 1562, **waifo** 1284, **vaifio** 1381, **weyvio** c 1370, 1415, **weyveo** 1451, **weyvo** 1378, **weyfio** 1404, **weyfo** 1398, **veivo** 1467, to waive, abandon (chattels, esp. beasts); **-io** 1221, 1573, **-o** (**†wavio**) 1239, 1587, **†wawo** 1526, **weyfio** 1355, to 'waive', outlaw (a woman); **-io** (W.) 1245, **weyvio** (Ir.) 1264, **veivo** (**†venio**) (Ir.) 1276, to outlaw (a man).

wakagium, *see* **waca.**

wala, *see* **walla.**

walcum, 'walk', perambulation (Waltham forest) 1552, 1553.

1 ***wald/a** 1167, 1419, **-ia** c 1288, c 1308, **wilda** c 1200, 1535, weald, woodland.

2 **walda** 1327, 1443, **welda** 1328, **wolda** 1336, 1359, (?) **weda** 1350, weld, dyer's rocket (bot.); *cf.* **gaula, gualda, waida.**

3 **walda,** *see* **walla.**

waldana (**gwaldana**), rabble, band of raiders (It. *gualdana*) 1297.

wald/atura, -ura, -o, -uro, *see* **wattillum.**

waldelvum, *see* **walla.**

Waldensis 1252, **Valdesius** c 1190, Walden- sian (heretic).

walebrunum, coarse, dark cloth (O.F. *gale- brun*) 1198.

walentia, *see* 1 **valentia.**

†walerandus, (?) henchman, hanger-on c 1204; (?) *cf.* **wandelardus.**

walettus, *see* **valettus.**

***wall/a** (**wal-**) a 1190, c 1450, ***-ia** (**-ea**) c 1200, 1497, **-um** a 1135, c 1200, **waulla** 1247, **wadla** a 1237, **walda** a 1220, **-ata** c 1280, sea-wall, dike, embankment; **-atura maris** c 1300, **waldura maris** 1296; **wala,** gunwale 1277, c 1300; **-agium,** (?) murage, due for making embankment c 1352; **waldelvum,** 'wall-delf', ditch beside em- bankment (Sussex) c 1220, 1234; **wallanda,** land charged with maintenance of town- wall c 1165; **walplata,** wall-plate (hori- zontal beam) 1295, 1355; **-ator,** waller c 1350, 1388; **-o,** to build an embankment c 1180; *see also* **valla, wattillum.**

***Wall/ensis** 1086, c 1553, **-encis** c 1280, **Gualensis** a 1142, c 1553, **Galensis** 1149, **-anus** c 1118, c 1315, **-ensicus** 1218, 1284, **-ensecus** 1345, **-icanus** 1294, 1505, **-icus**

c 1315, 1553, (?) **Valicus** 1252, **-igena** 1413, **-igenus** a 1450, **-iscus** 1086, c 1115, **-us** p 1327, c 1553, **Guallus** a 1142, Welsh, Welshman; **-ensice** a 1250, **-ice** c 1315, c 1553, in Welsh; **-escaria** 1275, **-escheria** 1250, 1304, **Gwalescheria** 1279, **-echeria** 1268, 1292, **-ensheria, Valesheria** 1284, **-eschyria** c 1272, Welshry (land or tenure).

walnux, walnut 1373.

walplata, *see* **walla.**

walstottus, *gwalstawd,* officer in charge of Welshry (W.) 1386, 1410.

waltrarius, *see* **valtrus.**

walva, *see* **valva.**

wambas-, wanbas-, wambiso, *see* **gambeso.**

wambi curia, a local court (G.) 1314.

wan/daila 1160, c 1285, **-dala** a 1220, **vandela** c 1150, 'wandale', strip of land in open field (N. Eng.); *cf.* **wendus.**

wandelardus, 'wandelard', rogue 13c.; *cf.* **walerandus.**

wando, *see* **wattillum.**

wanga, 'wong', strip of land in open field (Lincs.) a 1200.

wangardia, *see* **vanguardia.**

wangia, *see* **vanga.**

wanlass/um, 'wanlace', (beasts put up by) beating the forest 1310; **-ator,** one who beats the forest, poacher 14c.; **wanlaceo,** to beat the forest 1287.

wann-, *see* **vann; wain**

want/us 7c., (?) **†janta** c 1355, glove; **-arius** 1180, 1214, **wauntarius** c 1193, **-erus** c 1200, glover.

waoda, *see* **waida.**

***wapenta/cum** c 1115, 1231, **-ca** c 1457, ***-cium** (**-chium, -kium**) c 1210, c 1470, ***-gium** 1178, 1573, **vapentagium** 1176, **wapintacium** 1243, 1275, **wapintagium** c 1400, 1516, **wepentagium** 1260, **wapel- takium** c 1210, **wapeltaca** 1224, **wapeta- cum, wabetacum, wabentacum** 1231, wapentake (division of county in Danelaw) or its tenantry; c 1115, 1324, **-ca** c 1192, 1267, **-cus** 1235, **-cium** a 1170, 1324, **-gium** c 1115, c 1400, **wapuntagium** 1282, **-culum** 1279, **wabitaculum** 1223, wapen- take-court or suit thereat (attendance **or** fine for non-attendance); *cf.* **finis; -charius,** suitor at wapentake court 1331; **w. capi- talis,** chief officer of wapentake 1292.

wapulator, *see* **vapul**

***war/a** 1086, 1277, **werra** 1224, measure of land (? virgate), unit of geld; **w. libera,** geld or rent (? on freehold land) a 1250, 15c.; **w. terre** 1293, 1301; (?) **-a terra** 1358, **-landa** c 1120, 13c., **werlanda** 1206, 'war-land', land liable for geld; **-lota, -lotata** c 1250, **-lotum** 1205, **-nadum** c 1160, **-netum** 1086, 13c., **-neta** 1277, **-notum** 1268, **-enotum** 1321, (?) 'war-land' or service due from it; *see also* **wera** (1 & 2).

waract-, *see* **warect**

waran-, *see also* **warenn**

warantia 1259, 1336, **warenti/a** 1326, 1358, madder (Fr. *garance*); **-o,** to dye in madder 1263.

***warant/um** (**warrant-**) 1086, 1511, **waran- dum** c 1150, 1292, **warentum** 1244, c 1470, **varantum** 1242, 1498, **varentum** 13c., garantum c 1178, 1282, garentum (G.) 1255, 1312, **guarantum** c 1155, 1329, **guarentum** (G.) 1255, guyrentum (G.) 1289, -ium 1180, *-ia 1185, 1531, ***waren- tia** c 1204, 1284, **garantia** 1255, **garentia** 1253, **guarantia** 1222, **guerantia** 14c., **guirentia** (G.) 1313, †-io c 1240, -iza 1317, -isio c 1200, 1253, **garantisio** 12c., †-izatio c 1180, 1460, -isazio 1223, **warentizatio** c 1200, 15c., **varantizatio** 1244, **guaran- tisatio** 1233, **gwarrantizatio** a 1540, **gwa- rantatio** 1233, warrant, warranty, guarantee; *see also* CLAM, **dicentia**, REVOC, **tractio**, VOC; **warentum** 1322, -us 1474, 'warrant', dam; -us c 1115, 1609, -a (*f.*) 1200, 1225, **warans** c 1110, c 1270, **warentus** c 1160, 1465, -atus c 1330, †-ius c 1258, -or 1240, warrantor; **garenticius**, concerned with warranty 1493; *-izo c 1130, 1564, †-azo 1402, **warentizo** c 1150, c 1400, **warendizo** c 1280, **varantizo** 1197, p 1330, **varan- dizo** 1340, **varentizo** 1260, 1282, **veran- tizo** c 1500, **garantizo** c 1234, 1281, **garandiso** 1370, **garentizo** 13c., **guaran- tizo** 1107, 1165, **guarentizo** 1189, **gwaran- tizo** 12c., **garentio** 1281, 1360, -o a 1160, 1419, **garanto** 1199, 1256, **guaranto** c 1195, **guarento** 1292, **guerento** 1313, to warrant, guarantee.

ward/a *c 1185, c 1495, -ia 1460, -um 1482, **varda** c 1220, 1533, **verda** (C.I.) 1536, **vardia** 1272, **garda** 1212, c 1255, **guarda** 1217, 1225, **gwarda** 1242, 1281, wardship, guardianship of person or estate of minor, estate in ward; 1239, 1296, **varda** 1274, safe-keeping (of impounded beasts); 13c., **varda** 1526, **vardia** 1331, **garda** 1291, **gardia** 1294, c 1330, **guardia** 1283, **gwardia** 1223, **gwardum** 1315, **garda- gium** (G.) 1289, **gardiagium** (G.) 1289, 1317, wardenship of land or castle; *1130, c 1376, -ia c 1185, †**varida** 1212, **garda** 1236, **w. castelli** c 1178, a 1273, **w. castri** c 1150, 15c., -**agium** a 1070, 1330, (payment for) service of watch and ward, castle-guard; ward or keep (arch.) c 1422, 1459; **garda**, bodyguard 1476, 1573; -**a**, organization similar to tithing or frank- pledge c 1102, 1221; *a 1123, c 1450, **varda** c 1397, 1539, **garda** 13c., 1419, ward, division of town (esp. London); administra- tive area (Canterbury estates) 1447; 'ward', division of county (N. Eng. & Sc.) 1278, 1428; area of jurisdiction in forest (N. Eng. & Sc.) 1312, 1479; 1204, **w.** (**varda**) **facta** 1225, 1247, -um **factum** 1287, c 1400, (fine for) watch set in forest pastures; **guardum foreste**, obligation to guard royal forests 1198, 1324; -**a**, judicial award 1286, 14c. (*cf.* AWARD); **w. gaole**, jail- guard 1200; **w. maris**, coastguard service c 1326, 1364; **w. prima**, vanguard 1247, c 1362; **w. ultima**, rearguard c 1362; -**am teneo**, to keep guard c 1300; **gardia salva**, safe-guard 1336, 1583; *cf.* **custodia**; -us ward, minor 1364, 1586; *see also* **curia**; -**ator** 1309, c 1324, **gardiator** 1293, a 1446, ***gardianus** 1241, 1549, **guar- dianus** 1263, 1684, **gardennius** 1368, **gardinus** 1240, 1554, ‡**gardicius** 15c.,

vardatarius 1608, warden; **gardianus**, under-master (in building works) 1438; **g. ecclesie**, churchwarden 1462, 1587; **garda- rius** 1291, **garderius** 1254, **gardius** c 1540, 1591, warder; -**eria**, office of warder (G.) 1254; **gardianatus** 1482, c 1552, **gardinatus** 1548, **gardiania** 1548, **gardianitas** 1471, 1486, wardenship; **gardura**, 'guard', border, trimming 1591; **gardecorsatum**, *garde-cors*, short gown 1285; -**emota**, -**mota** 1275, -**emotum** 1274, 1419, -**imotum** 13c., **garde- motum** 1419, wardmoot (London); -**acra**, (?) acre reaped in lieu of ward service 1222; -**panegus** 13c., †-**panis** 1274, **warpannus** 1279, -**penna** a 1100, **warpenna** 1086, 1186, **werpena** 1157, 'ward-penny', pay- ment in lieu of ward service; **gardo** 1283, **gardio** c 1305, to keep, protect (G.); *see also* WAID

wardegropa, *see* **waregrapa**.

***ward/eroba** 1176, 1339, **wardaroba** 1224, 1235, -**arobia**, -**aropia** 1230, -**roba** 1235, c 1412, -**ropia** 1471, **gardaroba** 1235, c 1290, ***garderoba** 1251, 1534, **gardiroba** 1490, **gardroba** 1334, c 1488, **garderopa** 1375, 1395, **gardropa** c 1488, **gardaroba** 1245, **gwarderoba** 1225, **gardroperium** 1313, wardrobe (room or household office); **garderoba**, privy 1313, 1377; **g. bassa** 1251; *w. (etc.)* **regis** 1176, 1513; w. **regine** 1242, 1450; **g. lectorum** 1471, 1504, (?) **g. parva** 1458, petty wardrobe; **g. magna**, 'great wardrobe', royal department dealing with bulky stores 1253, 1606; **g. privata** 1323, 15c., (?) **g. parva** 1295, **g. armorum** 1337, **g. secreta** 1346, 1353, privy wardrobe; **g. pro pannis** 1376; **g. robarum** 1323, c 1472; -**erobarius** c 1465, **garderobarius** 1165, 1452, **gardrobarius** 1285, 1292, **gar- deroparius** c 1385, ***gardroparius** (Sc.) 1330, 1435, **gardroperius** 1328, keeper of (royal) wardrobe.

wardo, warden pear c 1389.

wareccum, warekkum, *see* **wreccum**.

***warect/a** (**waret-**), -**um** c 1160, 1428, **waractum** 1223, c 1258, **warocia** 1332, **varectum** c 1260, 1281, **veractum** c 1200, †**varrita** 1302, ‡**varratum** 15c., **garetum** a 1128, **garegium** (*cf.* O.F. *garrigue*), **garocium** (G.) 1289, *for* vervactum, fallow, fallow-land; -**us** 1306, -**abilis** 1281, fallow (*adj.*); -**atio** 1355, 1399, ‡**varratio** 15c., (?) †**overinstura** 1293, fallowing; *-o 1152, c 1413, ‡**barecto** 1483, **waracto** 15c., **wareito** a 1128, **guareto**, **gwareto** c 1230, **warro** 1242, ‡**varro** 15c., to fallow.

wareddus, mixed fodder, pulse (O.F. *warat*) 1296, 1329.

waregrapa 1269, 1276, **wardegropa** 1302, **verigropa** 1316, sort of wheel-clamp; *cf.* **gropa**.

warenga, *see* **wranga**.

***warenn/a** 1086, 1582, -**um** 1275, c 1457, -**ia** c 1195, 1336, **waranna** 1238, 1422, **waran- nium** 1317, **varenna** 1275, 1331, **garenna** a 1273, 1346, **guarenda** c 1188, **guarenna** 1255, 1305, †**guarona** 1286, †**warancia** 1422, warren (place for, or right of, hunting small game); **g. cuniculorum**, rabbit warren (C.I. & G.) 13c., 1285; **w. franca**

1295, **w. libera** 1241, 1582, (right of) free
warren; ***-arius** 1155, 1587, **warannarius**
1320, **varennarius** 1331, **garennarius**
1329, **guarennarius** 1168, **warnarius**
1274, **warnerus** 1255, **-ator** 1271, warrener;
-o, to put (land, *etc.*) in status of warren
1331, c 1400.
warenotum, *see* wara.
war/enstura, -estura, *see* GARN
warent-, warend-, *see* warantia; warantum.
waret-, *see* WARECT
warf-, *see* WHARV
waris/o, -ona, *see* gariso.
war/landa, -lota, -nadum, *see* wara.
warl/o, -ura, *see* wattillum.
warn-, *see also* GARN
warnalium, *see* warvalium.
warn/arius, -erus, *see* WARENN
war/netum, -notum, *see* wara.
waroccum, (?) garotte, packing-stick 1247,
1280; wedge for tightening lashings of
scaffold-poles (*cf.* O.F. *waroqueau*) 1325,
1373; **garrocum** 1336, **garottus** (G.) 1293,
(?) bolt for springald, *or* (?) 'garrot', lever
for bending cross-bow.
warocia, *see* warecta.
war/pannus, -penna, *see* warda.
warra, *see* GUERR
warrant-, *see* WARANT
warrea, *see* 1 wera.
warro, *see* GUERR; WARECT
warrokum, *see* waroccum.
wartha 1296, 1372, **†wurthia** c 1300,
wordinus c 1182, 'worth', enclosure.
warv-, warw-, *see* WHARV
warvalium (**†warnalium**), (?) round hill,
barrow (A.S. *hwyrfel*) (Sc.) c 1250.
wasa, *see* vasa.
wascell/a, -um, *see* vas.
waschetum, 'watchet', blue cloth 1206.
Wasco, Wascon-, *see* Vasco.
wasdia, *see* WAID
wassh/um (**whassh-**) **maris**, wash, inlet
c 1370; **-ebayum piscium** (C.I.) 1332;
wascerum, mill-lade (Salop) 1320; *cf.*
wosa.
wast-, *see also* VAST
wastagium, *see* WAFT
*wastell/us c 1200, c 1450, **-um** 1493,
wastallus 14c., **vastellus** c 1192, c 1290,
gastell/us, -um 1190, p 1341, **guastellum**
c 1200, 13c., (loaf of) wastel-bread, *gâteau*,
cake; **†vastellarium**, (?) bake-house for
wastel-bread 1234.
wastwa, *see* westwa.
wasum, *see* wosa.
water/baillia, office of water-bailiff 1403;
-bederipa, boon-reaping without ale 1398;
-furgio, to drain furrows 1279; ***-ganga**
12c., 1324, **watreganga** 1258, **-gangia** 1258,
15c., **†-gagia** 1313, **†-gandum** c 1350,
watercourse, drain, sluice; **-leta** 1225,
-letum 1286, waterlade; **-tabula**, weather-
ing, string-course (arch.) 1417.
watlettus, *see* valettus.
wattill/um 1424, 1464, (?) **wadla** 1245,
wattle; **watelatio** 1307, **watlatura** 1344,
waldatura 1297, (?) **wallatura** 1281,
watlura 1235, 1306, **wadlura** c 1200, 1282,
waldura 1223, 1329, ***wallura** c 1200,

c 1300, **waulura** 1235, 1251, **warlura** 1310,
wattling; **wallerus**, wattler 1498; **-io** 1289,
-o 1438, **watelo** 1308, 1383, **watlio** 1326,
wattlo 1271, 1289, **wadlo** 1282, **watulo**
1307, **waldo** 1223, **waudo** (**†wando**) 1308,
(?) **wallo** 1237, **warlo** 1310, **walduro** 1309,
to wattle, fence with wattle; *see also* **walla**.
waulla, *see* walla.
waulura, *see* wattillum.
wauntarius, *see* WANT
wavassaria, *see* VAVASS
wavi-, wawo, *see* WAIV
way-, *see also* wai-
way/a, -sa, -za, wawa, *see* 2 waga.
way/arium c 1320, **-eria** c 1290, **-era** 1275,
-ria 1348, **-hura, -ura** 1268, 1282, **-oura**
1282, **waeria** c 1290, **waerium** 1303,
weyera c 1300, 'wayour', horse-pond.
weda, *see* 2 walda.
wedderus 1566, **vethirus** 1496, wether.
wed/dum, (?) weed c 1300; **-bedripa**,
(?) boon weeding service 1325.
wedia, *see* 2 waga.
weduagium, *see* vidua.
wegga 1368, 1378, **†wedga** 1537, wedge.
weid/a, -ia, weisda, *see* waida.
weintingum, *see* waitingum.
weiv-, *see* WAIV
wekum, candle-wick 1373.
welcomo, to welcome c 1320.
welda, *see* 2 walda.
welg-, *see* felea.
welkus 1337, 1419, **welekus** 1267, **wilkus**
c 1340, **wylcus** 1288, whelk.
wellatio, 'welling', melting 1413.
wellium, *gwely*, tribal stock (W.) 1419; *cf.*
lectus.
wellvetum, *see* velvetum.
wen/clutum, -sevis, -sewis, *see* wainum.
wendus, 'wand', measure of land (10 yokes)
(Sussex) 1283; (?) *cf.* **wandaila**.
wepentagium, *see* wapentacum.
1 wera 1289, 1509, **wara** 1129, 1472, **warrea**
1550, weir.
2 wer/a (**†wara**) c 1115, c 1420, **guerra** 1189,
'were', pecuniary valuation of status;
-alada, -elada, oath in accordance with
were c 1115; **-efactio**, manslaughter (A.S.
werfæhðe) c 1115; **-egildum**, weregeld
c 1115; **-egildus fur**, thief liable to pay
weregeld c 1115; **-eplegium**, security for
payment of were c 1115; **-eplegius**, one
who acts as surety for were c 1115; **-etihla**,
charge concerned with were c 1115 (*cf.*
withertihla).
wer/eccum, -cum, -egum, -equum,
-iscum, *see* WRECC
werellum, *see* varietas.
werk/acra, workacra, measure of land
(Sussex) c 1283; **-gabulum**, rent in lieu of
service (man.) (Kent) 13c.; **-mannus**
(**coquine**), workman (Durham) 1439.
werlanda, *see* wara.
wernator, *see* ernator.
werpena, *see* warda.
werphagium, *see* WHARV
werpio, to set aside 1088; **guerpio** (G.) 1289,
guirpeo (It.) 1157, to surrender (feudal
tenement).
werr-, *see* GUERR; **wara**.

werv-, *see* WHARV

weryo, to worry, maul 1398.

wesd/a, -arius, westdarius, *see* WAID

west/balliva, west bailiwick 1355; **-campus**, west field 1234; **-caput**, west end a 1200; **-pars**, west side c 1180, c 1240; **-porta**, west door a 1200; **-pratum**, west meadow 1305; **-redingum**, West Riding 1268.

westibulum, *see* VEST

west/wa 1275, 1331, **-ewa** c 1295, **-ua** 1316, wastwa 1356, *gwestfa*, food-rent (W.); (?) *cf.* gestum.

wetherbordo, to cover with weatherboard 1515; *cf.* fitherbordum.

wethirnamum, *see* withernamium.

wetus, *see* VETER

weudegeldum, *see* WOD

weutrereus, *see* valtrus.

wevi-, weyf-, *see* WAIV

wexo, wescio, *see* WISC

weya, *see* 2 waga.

weyera, *see* wayarium.

weysda, *see* waida.

weyt/a, -agium, *see* waita.

weyv-, *see* WAIV

wharv/a 1310, 1472, **-us** 1345, hwarva 1342, warvia 1192, warvum a 1250, 1432, warfa 1320, a 1564, warfus 13c., wharfus 1386, 1539, hwearfum a 1335, wherva 1154, 1438, hwervus 13c., huervum c 1220, wervum a 1128, 1257, qwarva c 1320, wharf; **-agium** 1295, 1419, hwarvagium 1283, 1360, hwervagium 1395, warvagium 1198, 1314, warwagium 1209, 1286, wharfagium 1285, 1587, warfagium c 1160, 1325, wervagium 1229, werphagium c 1395, wharfage, wharf-dues.

whasshum, *see* WASSH

whinnum, whin, gorse (Norf.) 1289; † winuardus, (?) whinward (Yorks.) 1267.

whittawy/arius 1284, **-ator** 1275, whittawyer.

wianum, *see* biannum.

1 wic/a, 'wick', dairy-farm 1086, c 1300; **-arius** 1220, 1234, wickmanus 1264, wikmannus 1230, tenant of a dairy-farm.

2 wic/a (wich-) 1086, **-us** 12c., 1275, 'wich', salt-working; **-ewerca** a 1167, 1456, **-worcum** 13c., measure of salt.

wicattus 1212, 1302, wichettus 1201, *wikett/us, -a 1235, c 1397, vikettus 1289, gychettus 1285, gwychettus 1284, guigetta 1278, guinchetus (Norm.) 1198, wicket.

Wiccleffista, *see* Wyclefensis.

wicecomes, *see* vicecomes.

wich-, *see* 2 wica; wicattus.

Wicingus c 1155, Wikinus (Manx) 1212, Wichinga 1086, Viking.

wifhindus, *see* twihindus.

wigilia, *see* vigilia.

wiginti, *see* vicena.

wig/io 1255, **-ona** 1337, **-ena** 1544, widgeon (bird).

wikenarius 1392, 1397, wigenarius 1493, 'wickner', collector of amercements, *etc.* (Suffolk).

wikerellum, (?) 'wicker', withe (Essex) 1269.

Wikinus, *see* Wicingus.

wilda, *see* 1 walda.

wilkus, *see* welkus.

will-, *see also* VILL

willum, 'weel', fish-trap (Glos.) 1325.

wimpl/a 1228, c 1250, guympla 1275, **-are** c 1160, wimple, head-band; **-arius**, wimple-maker c 1185, c 1200.

winbargia, 'wind-barge', projecting hood of gable 1238.

***wind/asius** c 1180, 1348, **-asa** 1348, †**-asmus** 1307, **-agius** 1296, †**guidas** (? gindas) 15c., windlass; ***-agium** 1266, 1337, gindagium 1329, 1333, guindagium 1296, 1384, gwindagium 1328, **-arium** 1327, 1392, **-atio** 1226, 1374, (payment for) hoisting; **-or**, hoister 1325; **-o** 1226, 1340, gindo 1333, guindo 1309, 1329, gwindo 1328, to hoist with windlass.

windbandum, nave-band, iron wheel-tire 1318, 1350.

windellus, *'windle', measure of meal 1252, 1325; 1271, 1306, wyndlus 1351, basket.

Winilus, Guinilus, Lombard a 1142.

wintringus, 'winterling', yearling beast (Cumb.) 1320.

winuardus, *see* whinnum.

wippa, whip c 1273; wisp, bundle (of rushes) 1286; wispa, measure of glass 1536.

wirsetum, *see* worsteda.

wirum, wire c 1322.

wisc/a, wattle c 1360; ***-o** c 1180, c 1360, visco 1223, 1274, wescio 1357, vescio (†vestio) 1337, wixo 1237, 1401, vixo c 1258, wexo 1401, 1408, to wattle (*cf.* 'wisket' = basket).

wis/da, -ida, -darius, *see* WAID

wispa, *see* wippa.

wispilio, *see* 2 vispilio.

wist/a a 1133, 1564, **-um** 1320, 'wist', measure of land, 1–4 virgates (Sussex).

wita/, 'wite', amercement c 1115; (?) feud c 1115; **-servus**, (one) enslaved as punishment c 1115.

Witclevist/a, -icus, *see* Wyclefensis.

witecocus, *see* WOD

withernam/ium 1281, 1462, wethirnamum c 1400, wydernamium 1244, 'withernam', counter-distraint (leg.); **-io**, to take withernam from 1388.

withertihla, charge, accusation (A.S.) c 1115.

Wittenbergensissime, in true Wittenberg style 1523.

wixo, *see* WISC

wl-, *see* vul-

wobodus 1304, 1307, †**wodebouus** 1306, chief falconer (? derived from proper name).

woch!, woe! c 1200.

wod/a, -um, *see* waida.

wod/arius, -iarius, wudiarius, woodyer 1234; **-cokkus** 1430, wode/cokus 1337, woodcoccus 1544, wydekokus 1244, witecocus 1219, 1290, woodcock; **-gabulum**, 'wood-gavel' (Pembr.) 1366; **-geldum** 1331, weudegeldum 1199, payment for taking wood in forest; **-husus**, (tenant of) 'wood-house' (Leics.) 1274; **-motum**, 'wood-moot', court of attachment 1298, 1565; ***-wardus** 1238, c 1376, wodwardus c 1280, 1449, wudewardus 1224, 1255, woodwardus 1547, 1666, wood'vard; **-wordia** 1331, 1404, **-wardia** c 1370, office of woodward; **-weya**, wood-way 1142; **woerova**, woodruff (bot.) a 1150.

wodebouus, *see* **wobodus.**
wogium, *see* **voga.**
wolda, *see* **2 walda.**
wolnero, *see* VULN
wolpentinus, *see* VULP
wolta, *see* VOLU
wombus, 'womb', hide from belly 1361.
wood-, *see* WOD
wordinus, *see* **wartha.**
workacra, *see* **werkacra.**
wor/steda 1398, **-setum** 1350, **wursetum (wirsetum)** c 1422, **vorsetum** 1444, pannus de Worstede 1303, 1390, p. de Worthstede 1296, p. de Wrthstede 1291, worsted; **vorseticus**, of worsted 1537.
wosa, ooze 1313, 1385; **wasum (maris)**, mud, silt (Kent) 1252; *cf.* **vasa, wasshum.**
wranga 1234, c 1435, **wronga** 1284, **warenga** 1229, floor-board (naut.); *cf.* **runga.**
*****wrecc/um** a 1107, 1587, **warekkum** 1195, 1275, †**wercum** 1331, **wereccum** c 1200, 1332, **werequum** 1254, **weregum** c 1155, **verecum** (C.I.) a 1272, 1331, **vericum** (C.I.) 1319, **weriscum, veriscum** (C.I.) 1300, 1309, wreck, (right to seize) objects cast on shore; **wereccum**, fine for illegal seizure of wreck 1089; **-um** 1299, 1300,

wareccum 1333, wrack, seaweed; **-atus** c 1120, 1490, **wraccatus** 1495, 1499, wrecked, washed up.
wroga (†**soroga**), 'wragh', part of timberwork of mill 1499.
wronga, *see* **wranga.**
wroto (super), to 'wroot', root (of pigs) 1398.
wud-, *see* WOD
wul-, *see* vul-
wursetum, *see* **worsteda.**
wurthia, *see* **wartha.**
wy-, *see also* **wi-**
Wyclef/ensis c 1422, **Viclefensis** 15c., **-ianus** 1523, **-icus** 1523, 1533, **Wyclev/icus** c 1553, **-ista** 1382, c 1553, **Wyclivianus** c 1395, c 1422, **Wiccleffista** 1610, **Witclev/ista** 1427, follower of Wyclif, Lollard; **-isticus**, of Wyclif 1427.
wydekokus, *see* WOD
wydernamium, *see* **withernamium.**
wydyarius, *see* **vidua.**
wykettus, *see* **wicattus.**
wylcus, *see* **welkus.**
wyndrawerius, wine-drawer 1301.
wytyngus, whiting (fish) 1535.
†**wyvra (wyura)**, (?) 'wiver', beam (in wardrobe) 1253.

X

xamittus, *see* **samitus.**
xanthos, yellow, orange (med.) a 1250, ‡14c.
‡**xenech/don**, **-tum**, **zenexton**, amulet against plague 1652.
*****xen/ium** (bibl.), *****exennium** 780, 1044. c 1150, 1534, **exzenium** 1313, **zenium** 1203, 1227, †**encenium** c 1300, present, gift; **-iolum** c 1125, c 1190, **exeniolum** c 1188, c 1298, little gift; **-io** a 1100, **exenio** c 1211, c 1350, to present, give; *cf.* **encenium.**
*****xeno/dochium** a 1142, 1570, **-dicium** c 550, **zenodochium** c 1325, ‡c 1440, **senodochium** c 1223, **cenodochium** c 1250, ‡1483, **sinodochium** c 1223, ‡c 1440, ‡**sinodogium** 15c., guest-house, almshouse, hospital; ‡**cenodochiarius**, "hospi-

taller" 1483; ‡**-trophium**, hospital 1483; †**zeno**, (?) inmate of hospital 1258; †**excennus**, (?) stranger, outsider 1519.
xenodoxia, *see* **cenodoxia.**
‡**xeropellin/a** 1483, **serapellina** c 1200, threadbare garment; ‡**-us** 1483, ‡**seropellinus** 15c., threadbare (ξηραμπέλινος).
xerophagus, ascetic a 1142.
‡**xilum** (? *for* ὀξέλαιον) 14c., ‡**xis/inum**, **-sium** 1652, vinegar.
‡**xirio**, poultice (ξηρίον) 14c.
xukeris, *see* **sucrum.**
xylo/aloes, aloe-wood 13c., ‡14c.; **-balsamum** a 1250, ‡14c., **silobalsamum** c 1212, †**colobalsamum** 13c., balsam-wood; **-caracta** a 1250, ‡**exilo cataracta** 15c., carob-wood.

Y

(*See also* I-, HY-)

yalos, yelion, *see* HYAL
yara 1307, 1398, **yera** 1275, **ihara** 1199, c 1220, 'yare', fish-lock (Sc. & Durham).
yarus, *see* **iarus.**
yaxo, *see* 1 **axella.**
yburneus, *see* **eburninus.**
yburthananseca, 'byrthynsak', 'back-bearing', theft (Sc.) a 1609.
ycar, *see* **ichor.**
yconomus, *see* **economus.**
ycracia, *see* **eucrasia.**

yemalis, *see* HIEM
yera, *see* **yara.**
yeresiva a 1250, **geresguva (eresgieva)** 1155, 'yeresyeve', gift to official at beginning of year of office.
yersa, confection of arum, *etc.*, a 1250; *cf.* **iarus.**
ygia, *see* **hygia.**
ymera, *see* **hemera.**
†**ymetta** (? **yujetta**), measure of marsh-land (Sussex) c 1300.

ynkum, *see* inka.
yochio, to yoke (pigs) 1433.
yomanus, yeoman c 1548.
ypedemica, ypidimia, *see* epidemia.
†ypepis, sort of building (? *for* hypaethrus) 13c.
ypia, *see* hippia.
yricius, *see* hericius.

yringus, *see* erynge.
†yrmos, a punctuation mark (? *cf.* εἱρμός) c 1200.
ysmon, ysofagus, *see* esophagus.
yssaquum, *see* issaccum.
yva, *see* ifus.
yxir, *see* elixir.

Z

zabellus, *see* sabelus.
zaberna c 1197, c 1340, taberna c 550, wallet, cloak-bag; ‡book-case 1483.
zabil-, zabl-, *see* sablo.
Zabius, Sabian 1344.
zabol-, zabul-, *see* diabolus; sablo.
Zacharizo, to speak like Zacharias a 1100.
zadu/aria, -ra, *see* zedoaria.
zafran, *see* saffranum.
†zakio, (?) to pull up c 1350.
zalapium, jalap (bot.) 1634.
zallus, yellow (It. *giallo*) c 1227.
zambanus focus, fire made with sulphur (alch.) c 1227.
zambuca, *see* 2 sambuca.
zandria, *see* 2 sandalum.
zaphirus, *see* sapphirus.
zarnec, orpiment 1144, ‡1652.
zauhiron, *see* saffranum.
zebellinus, *see* sabelus.
zed/oaria, -oarium a 1250, 1622, -uaria 13c., zeodoaria 1253, zaduaria, zadura 1538, zituala a 1200, citoaldum 1265, citovalens c 1290, 1328, cytowalla c 1242, 1301, cetewallum 1285, 15c., seduala 1421, zedoary; -eoriatus, spiced with zedoary 1244.
zel/atio, zeal 1505; -ans c 1000, *-ator c 1160, 1482, -atrix (*f.*) 1414, zealous supporter, zealot; -antissimus, most zealous c 1185, c 1401; -osus, zealous c 1552, 1559; gelositas, ardour, love 14c.; -o de 5c., z. pro c 1196, c 1450, to be zealous for.
zella, *see* sella.
zelotyp/ia, zeal 1586; cuckoldry c 1180; -us, zealot c 700; cuckold c 1180; zelotopatus, jealous c 1370; -o, to cuckold c 1180, p 1330.
zemech, *see* zimiech.
zemno, *see* semen.
zenefactorium, *see* cenevectorium.
zenexton, *see* xenechdon.
zenith a 1232, c 1380, cenith c 1200, c 1365, zenith (astr.).
zenium, *see* xenium.
zen/o, -odochium, *see* xenodochium.
zeodoaria, *see* zedoaria.
zephyr/icus, westerly c 870; seferus, *for* -us, wind c 550.
zeric-, *see* sericum (1 & 2).
‡zerna, acute impetigo 14c., 1652.
zeta, *see* dieta.
zeum/a, zeugma (gram.) c 1200, c 1210; -iticus, zeugmatic 13c.

zhourus, *see* sorus.
zib/ethus 1620, -etta 1626, civet.
‡zim/a 14c., -ia, -us a 1250, pustule cause by phlegm, (?) eczema.
zimiech c 1250, ‡zemech 1652, lapis lazuli.
ziminum, *see* cyminum.
‡zin/zer 14c., ‡-gar, zynser 1652, verdigris.
*zin/ziber c 1200, c 1400, zimziber c 1330, -zibra 1242, -ziberum c 1335, 1419, -zeber 1295, zhinciber 1265, -ciper, -ziper 1542, -zeper 1472, -siber 1310, -suberum 1392, cinciber 1303, cinziber c 1250, synziberum c 1450, gingeber 1309, *gingiber 1130, c 1350, gingibarum 1291, gingiver 1243, jingeber 1309, jungiber 1279, *for* zingiber, ginger; z. viride 1380, 1421; -ziberus, made with ginger 1307; ging/ebrada 1226, 1290, -ebratum 1258, 1303, -iberatum a 1250, 1258, -ebrasium, -ibrasium 1285, -ibrattum 1236, 1242, -ibretum 1242, ‡-ium 15c., cemzebrata 1244, preserved ginger.
zinzito, to chirp c 1315.
ziphera, *see* cifra.
zirbus, caul (med.) a 1250.
‡zitanus, badger 15c.
zituala, *see* zedoaria.
*zizan/ia (*f. s.*) c 660. c 1270, 1461, -ion (bot.) 1538, sizannia c 1390, zinzania c 1400, tare, weed (esp. fig.); -icus, of a tare c 1410.
zoas, animal c 1200; zod/aicus, *for* -iacus, zodiac c 1200; -iacius, of the zodiac 797.
zoerus, *see* sorus.
Zoïleus, censorious 1540.
zoma, *see* soma.
zon/a, belt: sona 1351, 1467, (?) †tona 957; -arius, girdler 1230, 1573; -o c 1177, c 1180, ‡-ico 15c., to gird.
‡zonnetti (*pl.*), "*gnomorum corpora phantastica*" 1652.
zoticus, life-giving (ζωτικός) c 1200.
zoundo, to sound (depth of water) 1391.
zourus, *see* sorus.
zucar-, zucr-, zucur-, *etc.*, *see* sucrum.
zuccoraria, *see* succoraria.
zuch/a 1220, 1266, -ia 1227, zuschia 1234, -eus 1330, 1348, sucha 1306, sucheus 1371, stump, base of tree-trunk (Fr. *souche*).
zym/a 1200, ‡1483, ‡-um, zomus 14c., ‡jumnisum 1652, leaven (ζύμη).
zythicoctor, brewer 1623.

SUPPLEMENT

This Supplement is designed to contain corrections of any major errors in the *Word-List* that have been noted, and a selection of new words and usages that have come to light. Both corrections and additions are naturally fullest for the letters A–D, which have been thoroughly revised during preparation of the *Dictionary of Medieval Latin from British Sources.*

Additions to the bibliography are not included here. A complete bibliography of the sources used will be found in the *Dictionary* (Fascicules I and II).

Two errors have been noted in the bibliography of the *Word-List* on p. xxiii: section G, for 'Thomas Rastell' read 'William Rastell'; section H, for 'William Thompson' read 'William Johnson'. For John Fortescue (p. xxii, section F) a more accurate date would be c 1470.

CORRIGENDA

These Corrigenda are normally confined to substantial errors of definition or of spelling (mainly due to misreading of the manuscript), without regard to errors of date.

They are given under the key-word of the entry in the *Word-List*, followed, where necessary, by a reference to the particular section of the entry. Thus under *aer* it is intended that readers should delete (*d.* = *dele*) the entire section beginning with *aria*, i.e. '*aria*, air, song c 1370'. Under *abstractio* the section to be deleted has been cited more fully, so as to distinguish it from the other sections covered by the verb *abstraho*.

Under *assubvolvo* readers are instructed to read (*l.* = *lege*) this as two separate words, the meaning of *assub* being that given in the *Word-List*. Under *anaroxia* they should see (*v.* = *vide*) the entry in the *Word-List* for *anorexia*, where they may assume that the variant '†*anaroxia* a 1250' can now be included. Under *antillium* the reference is to the Classical Latin *ancile* (shield); under *antipasis* it is to the entry for *antispasis* in the Addenda below.

A

abstractio: abstraho, to retire, *d.*
accapito: achesunor, *v.* achesuno Ad.
acreo, *d.* (*f.l.* for C.L. acervo).
adaliqualitas, *l.* adaliquitas.
admann/io: -io ad, *d.*
advenagium, *v.* ulnagium.
aer: aria, *d.*
affa/men: -tus, *d.*
aliwerus, †alner/ia, -ium, -um, *v.* alloverius.
allecho: †alensco, †allencella, *l.* aleuzco, alleucella (*cf.* O.F. *alleuchon*).
anaroxia, *v.* anorexia.
antabata, *v.* andabata Ad.
antecedentia: ancestor c 1200, *d.*
antillium, *v.* ancile C.L.
antipasis, *v.* antispasis Ad.
aorasia: aurata, *v.* aurata Ad.
apprehen/sio: †-tia, *v.* apparentia, appearance (in court).
†aproximeron, *v.* †approximantia Ad.
†apterium, *v.* arcisterium.
aquil/a: -ianus, *v.* Aquilianus C.L.
arcus: a. pravus, 'deceitful bow' (*Psalm* lxxviii 57).
aren, *l.* Aren (place-name).
argu/ella, -illa, *l.* 'argol' (tartar of wine); arzilium, *l.* fuller's earth (*cf.* argillum).
†artuuerum, *v.* arcenarium Ad.
asilus: azilus, *v.* asylum.
assatio: assugia, *v.* axungia.
assubvolvo, *l.* assub volvo.
†aurica, *v.* amicta.
aven/a: -alis, (?) *l.* vernalis.

B

babewinus: bobinus, *v.* bobinus Ad.
baculus: plough-beam, *l.* plough-staff.
2 baillium: ballivium, *d.*
bajulus: †badivola, *v.* bajonula Ad.
bala: balesium, *v.* valisium.
balteus: baltinus, *v.* blatteus C.L.
baro: baronicius, *l.* Baronicius (personal name).
barrarius, pall-bearer, *l.* railing.
barras, *v.* albaras Ad.
basto: bezel, *l.* stick on which rings are kept.
1 batellum: †batha, *d.* (*f.l.* for botha = booth); botagium a 1172, *l.* 1474.
bateria: batiro 1316, *l.* baturo.
beremannus: brimmanagium, brummanagium, *v.* brimmagium Ad.
bika: bickaria, *v.* bukina Ad.
2 billa: billus, billet, *d.*
bladum: blaeria, corn-market, *l.* corn-due.
blaserius: †blessagha, *l.* blesshaga (*d.* Norm.).
bobinus, *v.* bobinus Ad.
bokerellum, *v.* bikerellum Ad.
bolhagium, *l.* (?) 'bull-hay' (bull-paddock).
bos: b. arator, *d.*
2 bosc/a: -alium, *v.* boscalium Ad; †buscagium, *l.* bustagium; †boiscagium, *l.* boistagium (*cf.* O.F. *boiste* = box).
botur, *v.* buttorium Ad.
bousa, *d.*
brachinellum, *l.* (?) malted loaf.
bracteus: c 1188, *v.* blatteus C.L.

2 brao, *v.* **brao** Ad.

brigand/a, -ina, -inum, *l.* brigandine, body-armour.

1 broca: †**briucca,** *v.* **brincca** Ad.

burgus: burgaticum, *d.*

burricus: burrica 1221, *l.* burrock, fish-trap.

bursa, exchange, *bourse, d.*; weekly statement of expenses, *d.*; **b. braccalis,** *l.* purse worn on breech-belt.

buttorium, *v.* **buttorium** Ad.

C

cacabus, brain-pan, *d.*

callida, hedge, *d.*

camer/a: cambra, trap for deer, *d.* (**cambris** *f.l.* for **canibus**); **-o,** to round off, *l.* (?) to impart secretly.

camp/us: -ernolla, †**compernola,** *l.* little bell (*cf.* **campana**); **-io,** to fight as a champion, *d.*

candid/atio: -atrix, prostitute, *l.* laundress.

cantellus, *l.* cantle, portion of food c 1135, c 1335; corner (of land) 1567; (allowance for) difference between razed and heaped measure a 1140, c 1356.

capr/a: chevro 1209 *d.* (transfer to **capro,** rafter).

capsilide, *v.* **cassidile** Ad.

caput, cabbage, *d.*

1 cart/a: -a divisa, *d.* (*f.l.* for **certas divisas**); **-o,** to register, *d.* (*f.l.* for **carco**).

carvanna: karavannus *etc.,* baggage train, *l.* (?) stud.

cassator, mower, *d.* (*f.l.* for **tassator**).

cavile, *v.* **canibis,** Ad.

†**cerna,** †**charna,** (?) *l.* **cerva, charva** (*cf.* Eng. 'kerf').

chennetum, *l.* **chennotus.**

cherogryllus: cereum, *d.* (*f.l.* for **orreum,** *i.e.* **horreum**).

circumvectio, *l.* **circumventio.**

cise, scissors, *d.*

Cishumbranus, for 'south' *l.* 'north'.

civ/eta, chive, *l.* leek soup (O.F. *civete*); †**-us** c 1150, *l.* **cinus** (*v.* **schinus**).

claustr/um: -arius, *v.* **claustrarius** Ad.

clavus: cloera, cluarium, forge, *l.* nail-bag.

cliens, household monk, *l.* household servant.

clochbulgie, bagpipes, *l.* bags of stones.

collum: c. oculi, *d.* (*f.l.* for **collyrium**).

com/es: †**-itaneus,** *d.* (*f.l.* for **convicaneus**).

commun/a: -ium, banquet, *d.* (*f.l.* for **convivium**).

concess/io: †**-e** 1285, *d.*

concustumarius, fellow customary tenant, *l.* fellow collector of customs.

condictum: condetum, *d.* (**Condetum** = Condé, Norm.).

†**conea,** *l.* (?) **conca;** *cf.* **concha.**

confessio, homage, oath of fidelity, *d.* (*f.l.* for **consessio,** *i.e.* **concessio**).

confultus, *d.* (*f.l.* for **consultus**).

constellatio, constellation, *l.* (prognostication by) position of heavenly bodies.

†**contidalis: conicalis,** *l.* **conoidalis.**

†**corinphus,** (?) *f.l.* for **coipha.**

corpus: c. comitatus, territory of county, add 'excluding franchises 1391, 1416'.

corrig/ia: theca -ialis, (?) container for straps, *l.* (?) container hung on strap.

†**corvagium,** *v.* **2 cornagium** Ad.

costa, incommensurate part of diameter, *l.* side of square.

†**costrum,** keg, *d.* (*f.l.* for **cestrum;** *v.* **sextarium**).

2 cota: quotarius, *d.*; †**cotteldus,** *l.* **cotceldus;** *cf.* **cotsetlus.**

†**covaria,** (?) *l.* **coneria,** rabbit warren; *cf.* **conyera** *s.v.* **cuniculus.**

crakeria, *l.* (?) brawling.

1 crappa, *d.* (*f.l.* for **trappa** = trap-door).

creagium, *v.* **greachia** Ad.

creantia: †**crator,** *d.* (*f.l.* for **pantocrator**).

†**credus, panis,** *d.*

crista: †**crusta,** *d.* (*f.l.* for **crufta;** *v.* **crofta**).

2 crocus: †**crokellus,** crook, *l.* (?) prickly weed, cockle.

crucifix/io: prerogativa -a, *l.* **p. -i.**

†**cufmelum,** *l.* (?) **cufinellus** (*i.e.* **coffinellus,** little basket).

D

dapsilitas: †**-ito,** *d.*

1 deliber/atio: †**-ator,** counsellor, *d.* (*f.l.* for **deliberatorius**).

deobstup/atio: -o, to block up, *d.*

depossum, to prevail in, *l.* to fail.

†**deservo** 12c., *d.* (*f.l.* for **de serva**).

†**desuto,** *d.* (*f.l.* for **defuco**).

determino actu, *d.*

devalo, *v.* **devalo** Ad.

dia-: †**-disnia,** (?) *l.* **-clisma** (for **clysma**), lotion.

†**diaconios,** *v.* **diatomos** Ad.

diesis, *d.* astr.

dieta, day's output of coin, *l.* diet (allowance for living expenses).

†**digress/ive: -o,** *d.* (*f.l.* for **disgrego**).

discalc/eo: -io vineam, to clear roots, *l.* to clear of vine-stakes; *cf.* **scalacio** *s.v.* **1 scala.**

dispers/io: -abilior, *d.*

dispun/ctuo, to settle accounts, *l.* to discharge, dismiss; **-ctuor,** to disagree, *l.* to disappoint, deprive.

†**dividiatio:** *see* **dimidietas,** *l. see* **divadiatio.**

domestic/itas: -us fidei, *d.*

domicellus, catulus, *d.*

†**domigerium,** add '(?) *f.l.* for **doungerium**'.

dom/us: -icula 1205, *d.*

dorm/itatio: -antus, dormer, *l.* 'dormant tree' (horizontal beam).

1 drager/um: †**drenca,** *v.* **dreuca** Ad.

dragma, ornament, *d.*

drasca: dacheum, *v.* **dacheum** Ad.

dupl/atio: doublettum, sort of print or stencil 1355, *d.*; **dublettus (lapis d.),** kind of precious stone, *l.* 1245, 1300, **doublettus** 1355, 'doublet' (counterfeit stone); **-e** c 1448, *d.*; **-ifacio,** to double, *l.* to provide (mass) with double preface.

E

ecclesi/a: †-**archus,** *l.* -**arches.**
editio, declaration of the form of an action, *l.* statement of the ground of an action.
effluxio: effluentia, flowing out, flood, *d.*
ele/pannus, -postis: for 'elm-wood' *l.* 'ell' (lean-to).
1 **equ/us: conflictus -estrinus,** *d.* (*f.l.* for -**estrium**); †-**itantia,** *d.*
escapium: scapagium, fine for escape of prisoner, *l.* fine for animals straying.
exagium: essaio, (of obley irons), *l.* (of obleys, *i.e.* wafers).

F

familio, *d.* (*f.l.* for **famulor**).
†**fonnum,** *d.* (*f.l.* for **fontana**).
formannus, *v.* **formannus** Ad.

H

haubercus: aliwerus, *d.*; *v.* **alloveria.**

I

intemp/estuosus: -eries, *l.* -**esteries.**

K

kalendarius, *d.*
kil/i: is-, *l.* -**is.**
kimbilis, *l.* **kimbix.**

L

lectio: lettrura, reading, *l.* 'lettrure' (book learning).

M

marla: malm/ator, *l.* one who applies 'malm' (light loamy soil); -**o,** *l.* to treat (land) with 'malm'.
merg/a: -iacio, *d.* (*f.l.* for **mergi, alciones**).
2 **monialis:** †**meinellus,** *l.* **moinellus.**
mov/entia: -eatio, *d.* (*f.l.* for **inoreatio,** *i.e.* **inhorreatio**).

N

naucupletio, ship's load, *l.* district charged with service of manning a ship (*cf.* **sipes-socna** *s.v.* **schipa**).

P

nicrum, *v.* **incrum** Ad.
nundine: n. Clementine: for 'Clement VI' *l.* 'Clement V'.
nusca: †**oficha,** *v.* **afficha** Ad.

P

†**parostheta,** *l.* (?) posset (*f.l.* for **poschetum**).
perimplementum: p. hundredi, special hundred court, *l.* (court of) area annexed to hundred (Derb.) 1298, 1597.
2 **pila: p. reg[ine] Cecilie,** *l.* **p. reg[is] Cecilie** (*i.e.* **Sicilie**).
prima: brimmagium, *v.* **brimmagium** Ad.

Q

quotarius, *d.*

R

radius: ridatus, *v.* **riddio** Ad.
relucr/atio: -o, to mow aftermath from, *l.* to reclaim (flooded land).

S

†**selauma,** *d.* (*f.l.* for **sclavina**).
sext/a: -arius, -ernus, book or gathering of six leaves, *l.* of six sheets.
shrudatio: sroudura, trimming, *l.* 'shrouding'; **shredo, sredo** a 1378, **shrudo, scriddo,** to strip, trim, *l.* to 'shroud' (cover with planks).
spin/a: -etum, *etc.*, 'spinet', cloth, *l.* **pannus diaspinetus** 1358, **p. de aspinet'** 1368, diaper; *cf.* **diaspera.**
sylen, hypsilon, *l.* smooth breathing (ψιλήν).

T

temperamen, a mixed drink, *l.* pickle or souse 1325, 1344.
†**tracis,** add 'for **taraxis**'.

V

variola: barras, *v.* **albaras** Ad.
vesania: -us, untrained (falc.), *l.* pheasant (**phasianus**).
viride: v. encre, *v.* **incrum** Ad.

ADDENDA

These Addenda are confined to items thought likely to be helpful to most users of the *Word-List*: they do not normally include extensions of date or minor variations in spelling or words whose meaning is self-evident.

An entry of the form '**alluminatio** 1342, *v.* **illuminatio**' indicates a new variant of a word included in the *Word-List*, with the meaning there given.

A

abramutium, abramouncy (a fabric) 1574.
abrustura, browsing (Norm.) 1157.
acerto, to make certain, assure c 1185; **ascerto me** 1293.
acherium, rush-bed (Fr.) 1165.
achesuno, to molest (O.F. *achoisoner*) 1291.
afficha c 1160, †**oficha** 1432, buckle, clasp.
agulettus 1342, **aguyllettus** 1349, 'aglet', tag.
aisiamentum: domus -i, privy 1497.
albaras a 1350, †**barras** 14c., leprosy.
albatio, tawing (of hide) c 1300, 1323.
algarab, lachrymal abscess or fistula (med.) a 1350.
alkemia 1287, **alcumen** 1604, alloy resembling gold; *cf.* **alchimia.**
alluminatio 1342, *v.* **illuminatio.**
†**almerium**, (?) pouch c 1180; cf. **alloveria.**
almonera, ambria, *v.* **eleemosynaria**(*infra*).
amaisimentum, perpetual rent (Fr.) c 1160.
ambulator, horse-trainer 1290.
andabata, blindfold gladiator: **antabata** 1527.
anelatio, annealing (of metal) 1422.
antispasis, drawing off of humours (med.): †**antipasis** a 1250.
apechiamentum, hindrance, interference 1294.
apparco, to impound: **aparko** 1276.
appat/isatio, imposition of tribute a 1430; **-icio**, to levy tribute 1457.
appediamentum, 'foot', support (of dam) 1259; *cf.* **appodiamentum.**
†**approximantia**, sexual impotence a 1350; *cf.* †**aproximeron** (? *l.* **apraximeron**).
aquatorium, watering-place 1256.
arbagium 1535, *v.* **herbagium.**
arcenarium, arsonerium, (?) cover for saddle-bow 1349; *cf.* **2 arco,** †**artuuerum.**
archiantistes, archbishop 964.
†**areddatio** 1394, *v.* **arrendatio.**
aspectus (hundredi), view (leg.) 1211.
assisator, assize juror 1294; assessor 1350.
†**audatio**, encouragement 1344.
aunagium 1369, *v.* **ulnagium.**
aurata, sty (on eye) a 1250.
ausibilis, audacious 1188.
austratus, occupied by a hearth-site 1567; *cf.* **astrum.**
†**aventatio** c 1250, *v.* **arrendatio.**

1 aventura, casual profit 1267, 1332; risk (in trading) 1253, 1489; *cf.* **adventura.**
2 aventura, (?) winnowing fan 1211.
averalis, used as draught animal 1295.
azurettus, blue (cloth) 1313.

B

bac/ile (†**bat-**), lamp used for blinding 14c.; **-ino**, to blind a 1250.
bageta, little badge 1397.
bahurum 1290, *v.* **barhudum.**
baissa, maid-servant 1297.
bajonula a 1180, †**badivola** a 1142, ‡**bojenila** 14c., litter.
ballistrix, crossbowman's wife or (?) dancer 1288.
balnearius, bath-attendant 1376.
barbetta, breast-band 1290.
bar/etto, to pick a quarrel with 1305; **-rato**, to foment (a suit) 1622.
bassetum, (?) sort of coarse cloth 1290.
bastardus (equus), cross-bred 1397, 1411.
baticium, (?) beater or wicker hurdle 1321.
batile, *v.* **bacile** (*supra*).
batillatio (muri), fitting with battlements 1320.
bato, to reclaim (land) by 'beat-burning' 1339, 1347.
batura (auri), beating 1286.
baudera, bell-pull 1348.
bavenum, 'bavin' (bundle of brushwood) 1319, 1371.
becagium 1330, 1362, **begagium** 1352, payment for pasturage.
becco, to hack (with pick-axe) 1198 (Norm.).
bechasa a 1350, **bekasa** 1344, woodcock.
benda, measure of flax 1285; *cf.* **binda.**
bera, clearing (in woodland) 1181 (Fr.).
berbicarius, shepherd 1284.
bercella, (?) enclosure 1352; *cf.* **bersa.**
berewardus, bearward 1472.
bermayster, 'barmaster' (manager of mine) 1390.
bikerellum, bokerellum, beckerel (sort of derrick) 1325.
billerus 1352, **bilrus** 1339, (?) kind of shellfish.
binda, bandage a 1350.
birchettum, birch-grove 1321.
bisectus, 'bisset' (gold thread) 1332.

bistinguium, beestings c 1115.
bistucus, a disease of hawks (O.F. *bestik*) a 1150.
bobinus (? for **bovinus**), yokel 12c.
bodekynus, dagger 1345.
borderus clavus, board-nail 1211.
bordinarius, *v.* **burdinarius** (*infra*).
borgan/a, -is, (?) mound or ridge (Yorks.) 1170, a 1200.
bos marinus, seal a 1350.
boscalium 1421, **buscalia** 1397, brushwood (O.F. *boschel*).
bossatus, embossed 1340, 1390; *cf.* **bocium.**
botonatio, buttoning 1345; *cf.* **buto.**
boturum, *v.* **buttorium** (*infra*).
boura, (?) tenement attached to 'bower' (residence) 1567; but *v.* **neta** (*infra*).
bovicularius, bullock-keeper c 1310.
brao, to 'bray' (caulk) 1237, 1238; to brace (a cart) 1316.
bricca, breach 1461; *cf.* **brecca.**
brimmagium 1300, **brymmagium** 1284, **brimmiagium** 1288, (?) **brimmanagium,** **brummanagium** 1313, payment involved in transport of casks; (?) *cf.* **primagium.**
brincca (†**briucca**) c 1250, **brincha** a 1250, 'brink' (bluff of land).
broc/agium, toll or export duty (Southampton) 1342, 1439; **-arius** 1477, **-ator** 1445, toll-collector.
broch/ia, thatching peg 1297; **-io,** to stake (a length of paling) 1257; *cf.* **2 broca.**
buga 1346, *v.* **2 boga.**
bukina (†**bickaria**), goat-skin 1243.
buna, bound 1337; *cf.* **bunda.**
buncha 1440, **bunda** 1393, measure of garlic.
bungus, (?) faggot c 1276.
burdinarius 1343, **bordinarius** 1340, (?) castrated he-goat.
†**burg/agium** 1294, 1330, **-eseria** 1284, burglary; **-eria,** swag 1221; **-atrix,** burglar (f.) 1242.
burnissura, burnishing 1287.
burralis, (?) felty, matted a 1350.
butello, to bolt 1284; *cf.* **bultellum.**
buto, (?) pimple 1235.
buttor/ium 1247, a 1320, **boturum** 1255, device for fishing, (?) butt; **-ium** 1242, **butor** (†**bucor**) 1310, 'butteris' (for paring horse's hoof).

C

cado ab, to lose c1185, c 1350; **c. super,** to abut on c 1220.
caffatina, zucara, loaf sugar 1349.
calder/o, -onus, cauldron 1290.
calidile, *v.* **cassidile** (*infra*).
camacatus, (?) adorned with cameos 1340, 1349; *cf.* **camahutus.**
camba, brew-house (O.F. *cambe*) c 1185.
cameraria, hereditary chamberlain (f.) 1230; grant to pay for lodging (acad.) 1384, 1483.
cameshida, 'campshed', protective board 1573.
campigena (†**capigena**), champion c 1250.
campi/partitor 1305, 1321, **-partor** 1294, champertor (leg.); *cf.* **cambipars.**
canabus, hobby-horse a 1215.

candelabrum, 'chandelier' (for carrying artillery) 1435.
canibis (†**cavilis**), 'toil' (hunting-net) 1548, 1587; *cf.* **cannabis.**
canta/plora (†**-fora,** †**cataplora**), 'chante-pleure', vessel releasing drops of water a 1350.
capicopertura, kerchief 1251.
capigena, *v.* **campigena** (*supra*).
capist/erium a 709. a 1173, **-orium** a 1025, corn-trough (*cf.* σκαφιστήριον).
capistrarius, halter-maker 1211.
capitiarius, sacristan 1232; *cf.* **capicerius.**
capotum, hood or cape 1256.
capraria, (?) goat-pen 1474.
capsarius, book-carrier, colporteur a 1212.
capsilide, *v.* **cassidile** (*infra*).
Carcinus, Cancer (astr.) c 1200.
carettalis, belonging to a cart 1398, c 1400.
carriabilis (**cari-**), portable 1394.
carruco, (?) to plough 1331 (but *cf.* **carrico**).
cartekypum, (?) cart-pole 1323.
cassidile 14c., †**calidile** c 1000, †**capsilide** a 1200, wallet.
castellettum, (?) ornament in shape of castle 1340.
cataplora, *v.* **cantaplora** (*supra*).
cauda tremula, wagtail a 1350.
cedula, shingle 1211; *v.* **scindula.**
celero, to store in a cellar 1429.
cembelinus c 1312, *v.* **kimenellus.**
cer/atio 13c., **-eatio** 1345, †**teratio** 1368, waxing; **-o** c 1200, **-io** 1342, to coat with wax.
cervelura, skull-cap 1342.
chapelerium, hat-box 1209; *cf.* **3 capella.**
chemino, to make one's way 1295.
chova, (?) cove (Lundy Island) c 1225.
ciculus c 1308, *v.* **siculus.**
cifro, to set at nought 15c.
cillula, little bell c 1400; *cf.* **scutella.**
cinierus, (?) hawthorn-tree 1359; *cf.* **schinus.**
cipharia, office of cup-bearer 1387; *cf.* **scyphus.**
‡**cironomon** (*for* **creanomon**), carver 15c.
clamo, to start game 1289.
claustrarius, hedger 1287, c 1532.
clavinus (†**clamnus**), measure of grain (Sc.) 1164.
clepra, bell-clapper 1500; *cf.* **clapera.**
†**climacterra,** summit 864.
clotettum, curtained recess (O.F. *clotet*) 1342.
cocatrix, crocodile c 1323.
coctura, refining 1286.
coffringus, axle-box 1368.
cojudex 1175, *v.* **conjudex.**
colbertus, churl c 1115; *cf.* **colibertus.**
colirium, horse-collar 1323; *cf.* **collarium.**
2 color, colander 1289; *cf.* **colatorium.**
coloro, to disguise 1412, 1443.
columbinus (**pannus**), (?) dove-coloured 1251.
communicator, commoner, one having rights of common 1567.
compassum, circlet 1342, 1352.
conglobatim, in a mass a 1166, c 1250.
contrafacio, to make as a likeness 1395, 1396.
cordosus, spasmodic, jerky (med.) a 1350; **-o,** to string, fit with strings 1221, 1266.
2 corn/agium (†**corv-**), a custom, (?) on wine (Fr.) 1099, 1180.

corn/aila (†**corv-**), crow-bar 1278.

coronmotum 1492, **corounmotum** 1398, 'crown-moot' (Chester).

†**corrobucum** 1137, (?) *f.l.* for **corium bullitum**.

cortigatio, stripping of bark 1538.

cosinarius 1567, (?) *v.* **coquinarius**.

cosso, †**corso**, horse-coper (O.F. *cosson*) 1290.

costardius, costermonger 1300.

cotarmura, surcoat 1349; *cf.* **1 cota**.

cot/egardum, 'cot-garth' (Yorks.) c 1200; **-setlemannus**, cottar 1323; *cf.* **2 cota**.

cotellus mensalis, table knife 1397; *cf.* **cultellus**.

cotus, tree-stump c 1276.

covella 1344, *v.* **cuvella**.

crato, to scratch a 1235.

creber, quail a 1250.

crepatura, cracking, rupture (med.) a 1250, a 1350.

crido, to proclaim (G.) p 1250.

cromba, bent strip of metal 1304, 1323.

cron/eum, weeding out of old animals c 1308; **bos -icus**, worn out ox 1295; *cf.* **cronardus**, †**cromium**.

crosa, (?) pit (Fr.) a 1190.

croskinum, *v.* **cruskynnum** *s.v.* **crusum** (*infra*).

croupa 1298, *v.* **cropa**.

cruc/ea, olla, cruse, or (?) vessel marked with cross 1430; **-ea sectio**, (?) optic commissure c 1267.

crucka, 'crutch', tie-beam 1341.

crudator, 'crowder' (W.) 1290; *cf.* **crudarius**.

crus/um, cruse 1467; **-kynnum** 1390, **croskinum** 1340, 'cruskyn', little cruse.

curreum 1290, *v.* **corium**.

cursia, running a 1248.

curtenata, cart-load 1348.

cuverchetum 1293, *v.* **covrechiefum**.

D

dacheum, (?) straw (O.F. *dache*) 1296.

2 dampa, fire-damp (Notts.) 1390.

daunsa, dance c 1200.

decado, to decay 1392; *cf.* **decasus**.

decambium, exchange c 1152.

decana, senior nun (Fr.) 1161.

decanonizo, to deprive of the status of canon c 1250.

decarraxo, to write 958; *cf.* **charaxo**.

decastro, to castrate a 1025.

decontinuatio, discontinuity a 1248.

decooperio, to uncover a 1235.

deductus, sport, amusement 1341.

defecto, to weaken, impair a 1250.

deglomero, to unfurl c 1446.

deguttatus, spotted 1344.

delectus, delight a 1235.

delia, minera, sort of mine 1517.

demisceo, to 'unmix', separate a 1166.

demonicus, devilish c 730. c 1267.

demonstr/atio, display of wares 1444; **-o**, to muster (troops) 1373, 1404; *cf.* **monstratio**.

dencherus, form of day-work (Wilts.) 1315.

denn/a, -um, (use of) Denne (higher ground) at Yarmouth (Norf.) c 1157, 1238.

deosculatoria, pax, pax 1340; *cf.* **osculatorium**.

deplano, to trample flat p 1378.

depucelo, to deflower 1286.

deputro, to defile 1399.

derudio, to refine a 1180.

destauro, to unstock c 1905; *cf.* **deinstauro**.

destorno, to divert 1315; *cf.* **distorno**.

desutus, (?) dislodged c 1446; *cf.* **dissuo**.

devalo, to strike down, cut down 1247, 1305.

dextus c 1495, **dixtus** 1472, desk; *cf.* **1 discus**.

diamarte, confection of marciaton a 1350; *cf.* **marciaton**.

diatomos a 1212, †**diaconios** c 1212, half (moon).

dies amabilis, love-day 1410; *cf.* **dies amoris**.

digito, to count, reckon a 1260.

dimitto, to appoint as successor or representative 1236, 1451.

directura, ordinance or due (G.) 1219.

discata, dishful (measure of barley) 1328; *cf.* **2 discus**.

discommunico, to 'discommune', exclude from intercourse a 1380.

discorio, to strip of bark 1357.

discorporo, to dissolve (corporate body) 1550.

disjungatio, unyoking 1312.

†**dissictus** 14c., *f.l.* for **dissutus**.

dissuria, dysury (med.) a 1250, a 1350.

distinctoria, aqua, dye 1342.

disto, to quarrel 1361.

divido tallias, to divide sum specified in tally 1258, 1288.

dixtus, *v.* **dextus** (*supra*).

dom/a, house, home 10c. c 1067, c 1250; roof a 1143, 1406; **-esticus**, inward-facing a 1350; *cf.* **silvester** (*infra*); **-uitas**, essential quality of house 13c.

drappale, piece of cloth 1278.

draynetta, drag-net 1290.

dresso, to dress food c 1310.

dreuca (†**drenca**) 1297, **draueka** 1328, (?) kind of wheat (distinct from **dragetum**).

dubberia, dubbing (of cloth) c 1290.

ductile, iter, passable road a 1408.

duellio, duellist, champion a 1190, 1417.

duplifestarius, celebrant of double festival a 1450.

durnum, door-post c 1450.

E

ebulliaria, boiler (in kitchen) c 1518.

ebutiratum, lac, buttermilk a 1350.

edero, to 'edder', interlace with osiers c 1235.

eglentia, eglantine, brier-rose a 1350.

Egyptianus, gipsy 1577.

eleemosynar/ia c 1125, **-ium** a 1345, **almonera** 1223, alms-bag, wallet; **ambria almonry** 1511.

elfarius, elver 1290.

elingo, to lick up a 1166.

elongantia, prolongation 1361.

embatellatus, embattled (her.) 1390.

encathisma, sitting bath a 1350.

enchetourus 1439, *v.* escaetor.
epigastrum, abdomen 1532.
era, ivy 1277.
erios, iris (bot.) 1439.
escorchio, to strip of bark 1277.
escumator, scummer 1290; *cf.* scumarium.
espeium, sword 1210; *cf.* spatha.
2 espernium, *v.* sperna (*infra*).
estuchia 1229, *v.* stichia.
estuffo, to provision, stock 1443; *cf.* stuffum.
eswardum 1203, *v.* awardum.
exactio, demand to appear in court 1258.
exil/is, (?) outlying, detached 1316; -io, exulo, (?) to ruin 1392.

F

fabrura, smith's work c 1312.
farinalis arca, flour-chest 1320.
fausilla, sort of cutting tool 1288; *cf.* falx.
femerium 1290, *v.* fimarium.
fen/iso, hay-harvest 1199; -eso, hay-making service 1225.
fennum, fen (Essex) 1260.
ferthingatarius, tenant of ferling 1315; *cf.* 1 ferdingus.
fetherbordum 1340, *v.* fitherbordum.
figularius, potter 1295.
fil/um sutorum, cobbler's twine 1342; -o, (?) to provide (nut) with screw-thread 1325.
fixator, class of harvest-worker c 1400.
flabe (*pl.*), bellows 1343.
flachia, 'flage', covering 1290.
flodum, (profit of) flood-tide 1212; *cf.* flodus.
floretura, floral design 1342.
foliarium, foliage 1340.
forcelettum, (?) strong-box 1340; *cf.* fortalitia.
formannus, 'foreman', (?) man guiding plough-team (N. Eng.) 1281, 1326; tenant of quarter virgate (Essex) 1304, 1336.
forum guerre, arbitrament of war 1385.
founcerium, (?) malt-yard 1276; *cf.* fundaria.
fraeo 1284, freo 1288, to burnish; *cf.* fraio.
fraiamentum, alarm 1385.
franca, domus, (?) freestone building 1567.
frecira, (?) fringe 1209; *cf.* fresellus.
frimbria, fringe 1349; *cf.* fimbria C.L.
frio 1290, frisco c 1308, frixo 1349, to fry; *cf.* frixatio.
frounciare, to 'frounce', flounce 1345.
fugellus, mill-spindle 1284; *cf.* fusillus.
full/aria, fulling-house 1295; -aretius c 1240, -erarius 1243, of or for fulling.
fundratio, malting 1268.
furb/issura, furbishing 1284; -eo 1290, fourbio 1342, to furbish.
furnellum 1400, *v.* funellum.
furnio, to furnish (a bed) 1349.

G

ganga, gang (of cogs or spindles) 1320.
gargulla, gargoyle 1320.
garnis/sura 1342, -tura 1345, adornment.

gavelata, terra, gavel-land 1397; *cf.* 2 gabella.
ghita 1349, *v.* gita.
gila, guile, trick 1235.
gobettus, pill 1313.
golfa, pit or ditch (Essex) 1553.
gonnia, petra, stone thrown by cannon 1434.
gramfus a 1350, *v.* crampa.
grata, grating 1429.
greachia 1306, creagia 1300, a game of chance (*cf.* O.F. *griesche*).
gromillus 1290, *v.* grumillus.
grondcello c 1400, gruncello 1374, *v.* grundsullo.
grus, crane (for hoisting) 1429.
guido, guidon, pennon 1349.
gungus 1211, *v.* gumphus.
guttatus, spotted 1349.
gwarata, terra, 'war-land' 1211; *cf.* warlanda *s.v.* wara.

H

hachiatus, hatched (her.) 1342.
haia spinea, thorn hedge 1303.
hala, halling, arras 1290.
halituosus, respiratory 1532.
hardeum (caruce) 1308, *v.* hardum.
harp/arius, -iator 1290, *v.* harpator.
hengmannus 1349, *v.* hengestmannus.
herbig/atio, lodging, -o, to lodge, accommodate 1404; *cf.* herbergagium.
heric/iator, -io 1211, for herc-; *v.* 1 hercia.
†herkagium 1248, *v.* heccagium.
hilta 1314, 1342, hulta 1315, *v.* heltus.
hurt/ardiculus, young ram c 1400; -o to tup c 1312.

I

idiotria 1335, *v.* idiotia.
in preterea, moreover 1234.
inartificialiter, unskilfully 1398.
inburgagio, to include in burgage 1308.
incarnatio, flesh colour 1349.
inclavo, to stud 1349.
incluserium, lock-up 1456.
incrum (†nicrum), sort of cloth (? 'inky') 1215; viride encre, sort of green cloth 1209, 1244.
inculto, to till 1357.
inducta, inflow of water c 1245.
infilo, to embroider with thread 1345.
informo, to break in, train (horse) 1290.
infraelo, to pack in frails 1284; *cf.* fraella.
infra/frango, to break (metal) in 1449; -jacto, to cast (metal) in 1449; -lineo, to line (hats) within 1313; -porto, to carry (bricks) in 1452.
infrettatus 1340, *v.* infrectus.
ingeniarius, engineer 1348.
ingottum, mould (for casting metal) 1453.
innodatus, innuatus, embossed 1342.
inseisionabilis, unseasonable 1392.
insidiator, spy 1284.
installo, to put (cattle) in stalls 1287.
intamio, to broach (cask) 1290.
inter/affidatus, mutually pledged, -alligatus, mutually bound 1294.

interflecto, to intertwine 1342.
interludo, to perform in an interlude 1466.
introduco, to lead in (harvest) 1397.
introsso 1386, v. intrusso.
inventario, to make an inventory of 1626.
invitus, v. dens.
†izanium, (?) gift 1375; cf. xenium.

J

janua saltabilis, 'leap-gate' (for deer) 1525;
   cf. porta s. (infra).
jung/atio, yoking 1312; -o exitum, to join
   issue (leg.) 1505.

K

kalendarium, list of names (at gaol delivery)
   1365.
kalendratio, calendering (of cloth) 1342.
ketilhatum, 'kettle-hat', helmet 1386.

L

labellum, label (on hamper) 1496.
lamprunculus 1290, v. lampredulus.
landinarius 1335, v. landarius.
†latinus, latten 1287; v. lato.
lavator ovium, sheep-washer 1567.
lectaria 1209, v. lecterium, s.v. lectus.
lectrionarium, lectern-cloth 1397.
leissa 1209, v. laxa.
lenticulosum, hordeum, 1295; cf. lenti-
   culatus s.v. lens.
leyn/a, 'oyster-lane' (Essex) 1366; -agium,
   revenue therefrom 1345.
ligatio librorum, book-binding 1348.
locklana, lock-wool 1248.
longe ante, long before 1233.
lucro (terram), to reclaim, assart 1286.
lugga 'lug', measure of land (Wilts.) 1567.
lumilio c 1308, v. luminio s.v. lumen.
luparium 1211, v. lovarium.
lya, lye 1284.

M

maella, mesh 1278; cf. macula.
malmasia a 1530, v. malvesia.
marbrinus, pannus 1359, v. marmoreus.
marescallaria, farriery 1250; v. marescal-
   cia.
mastagium, payment for beech-mast, pannage (Devon) 1567.
mediastinum, diaphragm 1532.
meis/agium, (?) packing (of wax) in parcels
   (cf. meisa) 1342; -o, (?) to pack (wax) 1342.
meredies noctis, 'noon of night' 1538.
merga, pitchfork ‡1440, 1461.
messageria, requirements for messenger
   (coll.) 1290.
mierum 1308, v. micatorium.
molett/um, mullet (her.) 1422; -atus,
   decorated with mullets 1317.
mostardum 1290, v. mustardum.
muletta, young mule (f.) c 1308.

muntana, mountainous land 1288; cf.
   montanus.
muwerus, muherius 1226, v. mutarius s.v.
   5 muta.

N

nasale, candle-stick 1390.
nervo, to fit (cross-bow) with string 1266.
neta, terra, (Wilts.) 1567, distinguished
   from boura; (?) cf. A.S. geneat and gebur.
nodus (fili), hank 1312.
nonpar 1414, v. nounpar.

O

oblator, waferer 1290; cf. oblata.
Occitana, lingua, Languedoc 14c.
ollagium, pottage 1284.
1 os: in ore sto, to be a legitimate plea 1236.

P

palagium, (?) paling service (Chesh.) a 1340.
paletta, metal plate (man.) 1248.
panatrallum c 1312, v. penetrale.
pannus plumbi, sheet of lead 1320.
parabolo, to parley c 1080.
parchamentum 1211, v. pergamenum.
passaportus 1507, v. passeportus s.v. passus.
pastatio (carnium), baking in pastry 1521.
patellus, pasty 1495.
pavillonaria 1342, v. pavillonia s.v. papilio.
pediva, pila 1363, v. p. pedalis.
pell/icula pergameni 1290, v. pellis; -izo
   1200, v. pellicia.
pendulum, padlock 1284; cf. sera pendens.
pennator, fletcher 1325; cf. 1 penna.
per/fourniamentum (domus), putting in
   order, furnishing 1399; -furnatio, -furnitio,
   preparation (of fur) 1349; -fornio, to trim,
   (with fur) 1290.
persorium 1290, v. perzorium.
perverbocino, to recite in full 1275.
†pessungium 1221, (?) v. 1 pesso.
†pigwithum (? l. pingwithum) 1323, (?) v.
   pinwithum.
2 pila, orb (symbol of royalty) 1377.
†pilloria 1443, v. pilaria s.v. pilagium.
3 pilum, pile, heap 1299.
pimpernola 1344, v. pimpernella.
pincicariola, (?) pincers a 1340.
pinolada 1306, v. pinonada.
pinzo c 1312, v. punso s.v. punctatio.
piscaria, stalla, fish-stall 1292.
†piscula 1326, v. pluscula.
plana, (?) plane (tool) 1290.
plancula, little plank 1355.
plaustralis, domus, wagon-shed 1462.
plebiscetum (Yorks.) 1297, v. plebiscitum.
plecticius, lectus, folding bed 1209.
plumentatus, plumeté, adorned with feathery
   spots 1290.
pomum silvestre 1315, v. p. bosci.
poncellum, v. punchettum (infra).
poplerus, poplar c 1240.
porcellatio, farrowing c 1312.

porta saltabilis, 'leap-gate' (for deer) 1461; *cf.* **janua s.** (*supra*).
potellaria, olla, pottle-pot 1421.
†**predix** 1272, *v.* **perdix.**
prinsura 1290, *v.* **presura.**
propior, having preference, entitled to discount (as tenant) a 1250, c 1255.
protractator, (?) worker in drawn thread 1349.
pull/anatio, foaling 1335; **-eta,** filly 1278; **-iolus,** young colt 1397; **pulonus,** young male swan 1311.
punchettum 1316, **poncellum** 1307, object paid as fine (? *cf.* **punctorium**).
purfil/amentum 1341, **-iatio** 1345, *v.* **purfilatio.**

Q

quadrangularis, set in four corners 1342.
quartus melior, fourth best 1317.
quissaria c 1312, *v.* **quissera.**
quyntesia 1290, *v.* **queintisa.**

R

realitas, concern with real property 1288.
rebateria, repair (of barrels) 1288.
recaptio, (?) rent resolute 1270.
recrescentia, regrowth 1392.
recronium, weeding out (of animals) c 1312.
recubatio, re-laying 1321.
redemptio, merchet 1387 (*cf.* **merchetum**).
relevagium, (?) churching 1349; *v.* **relevatio.**
religatio, hooping 1290.
relinquo exitum, to leave issue (leg.) 1505.
rengerium, flour-sieve 1289.
repello ab, to debar from (leg.) 1384.
replico (bullam), to make a replica of 1285.
reprisa, support, bracket (for statue) 1286.
rescituo, for **resituo,** to replace 1344.
resortum, rebound 1236.
reto, to ret 1312; *cf.* **rotatio.**
retromoror, to stay behind 1290.
reve/galdum 1354, **-yeldum** 1384, 'reevegeld' (Chesh.).
rid/dio 1210, **-o** 1251, to gather (cloth) in tucks (*cf.* Fr. *rider*).
romagium 1361, *v.* **rumagium.**
roughliardus 1300, **rouliardus** 1340, *v.* **rughliardus.**
rubantum 1345, *v.* **ribanum.**
rugettus, red gurnard 1346.
runcia 1295, *v.* **runca.**

S

sabatina, 'sabatine', buskin 1342.
sabulones, sands, sandy beach 1321.
sagitto, (of land) to project 1567.
sakettus, little sack 1440; *cf.* **sacca.**
saliatio, mounting (of stallion) 1357; *cf.* **saillio** *s.v.* **saliares.**
salsarius, salt-dealer 1221.
salterna, saltern 1315.
saltor 1247, *v.* **saltatorium** *s.v.* **saltus.**

satrapa, (?) minstrel 1466, 1479.
scal/o 1211, **-io** 1323, *v.* **scalonia.**
scaloppa (molendini), (?) hopper 1313.
scapulator, 'scappler' 1388; *cf.* **scapulatio.**
scaubellum 1287, *v.* **scabergia.**
schraggo, to 'shrag', lop 1330.
scio, †**cicio,** (?) to 'sye', strain 1434; *cf.* **1 sya.**
scloppa 1393, *v.* **sloppum.**
scocho 1449, *v.* **scucho** *s.v.* **scutum.**
scrutagium, (?) search-due (for wine) 1361.
seignoragium, seignorage, duty on coinage 1425; *cf.* **senior.**
†**semella** 1211, *v.* **semellio** *s.v.* **semen.**
semicommunarius, recipient of half-commons (ac.) 1540.
sheldebredum 1295, *v.* **schildebredum.**
sigo, to saw c 1312; *cf.* **seca.**
silvester, outward-facing a 1350; *cf.* **domesticus** (*supra*).
sizellatus, chiselled 1340; *cf.* **cisellus.**
soc/enagium 1297, 1306, **-jonagium** 1307, (?) partnership or warranty granted to miller (Yorks.).
sola 1325, (?) *v.* **soliva.**
soldagium 1211, *v.* **seldagium.**
somerettus, *v.* **sumerettus** (*infra*).
sorcarkya 1283, *v.* **surcarca** *s.v.* **superchargium.**
sper/geatorium 1390, **-sorium** 1345, *v.* **spargitor** *s.v.* **sparsio.**
sperna 1211, †**espernium** c 1308, sort of hurdle.
spina, (?) carding-comb 1321.
spindelum, mill-spindle 1284.
spio, to spy out 1287.
splentea, splint (med.) 1356.
sprigetum 1333, (?) mixture of wheat and oats.
stabilia 1211, *v.* **stabula.**
staurator, stockman 1308, 1311.
sterkilda 1278, *v.* **scarkella.**
stillor, to leak 1339.
stiv/arius, -ator, piper (*cf.* O.F. *estive*) 1290.
stopella, stopper 1390.
strallingum 1290, *v.* **stranlingum.**
stricte, narrowly, scarcely 1332.
stuff/a, padding 1349; **-o,** to stuff (with down, etc.) 1341, 1342.
†**sturellum** 1323, *v.* **curallum.**
subboscolus, little underwood 1397.
subdomicella, assistant lady's maid 1341, 1344.
subnemus, underwood a 1250.
subpostis, supporting post 1323.
succanea, coat (*cf.* Fr. *souquenille*) 1210.
sufflat/a (pl.), bellows 1342; **cornu -ile,** horn (mus.) 1368.
sukeneia, 'suckeny', smock 1341.
sullio 1297, *v.* **1 selio.**
†**sulpellum,** (?) book-cover 1268.
sumerettus, somerettus, portable by pack-animal 1300; *cf.* **sagma.**
super/effluentia, overflow 1241; **-porto,** to carry (loads) on 1320; **-talliatura,** roof-carving 1343; **-tractio,** dragging (of weir) 1439.
supra/emptus, -venditus, bought or sold as noted above 1248.
sursum aro, to plough up 1328.

T

tabula plicans 1390, *v.* **t. plicata.**
tacca, cart-tack 1211; *cf.* **1 taccum.**
talshida, 'talshide', (billet of) firewood 1321, 1344.
tango, to test (gold) with touchstone 1400.
tark/aisium 1209, **-eisium** 1210, *v.* **tarco-sium.**
tassellarius, tassel-maker 1342.
tegul/a 1309, **tigula** 1299, (?) brick-dust; **petra -atoria,** roofing slate 1439.
tenditor (*sc.* **falconum**), falconer 1363.
tenellum, handle (of pot or spoon) 1390.
tent/atio cervisie, ale-tasting 1236; **-o cervisiam** 1221.
tent/or, tent 1290; **-orium,** tenting-frame 1357.
teratio, *v.* **ceratio** (*supra*).
testa, (?) sheath (of cistern) 1228.
textus, desk 1395; *cf.* **dextus** (*supra*).
tilla, lump (of lard) 1344.
tillarius 1339, *v.* **attilliator.**
tinelle c 1312, *v.* **tenacula.**
tonellator, cooper 1221.
topettum, lid (of cup) 1449; *cf.* **tuppetum.**
torquesia, tongs a 1350.
tortula, small candle 1520; *cf.* **torcha.**
tragades a 1350, ‡**tradus** 15c., wagtail.
traho, to pull up (flax) 1312; to drag (a pond) 1323.
transgressio solutionis, non-payment 1236.
traventura, due paid by fish merchants (Cornw.) 1339.
†**trebolla,** (?) sort of wine-skin (Sp.) 1288.
tremua 1202, *v.* **trimodius.**
tremulus, arrow of aspen-wood or (?) bird-bolt; *cf.* **tribulus.**
†**trenora,** customary service or due (Leics.); (?) *cf.* **tremura.**
tress/orium, -arium, 'tressure', hair-band 1290.
treyno, to train (falc.) 1290; *v.* **traino.**
trippo, to trample (G.) 1288.
trist/era, 'tristre', 'trist' (appointed station in hunting) 1357; **leporarius -atus,** (?) greyhound on leash 1248.

trosso, *v.* **trusso.**
truffaria, knick-knack 1343.
tunica hard', coat-hardy 1326.
tyia, (?) casket 1290; *cf.* **tia.**

U

ulnaria, office of aulnage 1349.
undimia, 'undimy', tumour a 1350.

V

vaccina, domus, cow-house 1507.
vadiator, wage-earner 1320.
†**vaginus,** stray 1275.
vapulatum, aurum, beaten gold 1340, 1390.
vastatorium, (?) dam 1357.
verbocino, to recite in set words 1275.
veriagium (Ir.) 1375, *v.* **feriagium** *s.v.* **4 feria.**
†**veronica,** disease of pigs 1323; *cf.* **variola.**
verr/atus 1355, **-onus** 1340, brindled; *cf.* **varius** etc. *s.v.* **varietas.**
veya 1297, *v.* **2 waga.**
vinegarium 1317, *v.* **viniarium** etc. *s.v.* **vinum.**
violarius, fiddler 1313; *cf.* **2 vidula.**
virgultura, grove 1567.
viridicira, 'green wax' 1292; *cf.* **cera viridis.**
visc/a, -us 1248, *v.* **1 vicia.**
volatio 1567, *v.* **volata.**
voluperium, kerchief or head-band 1340, 1345.

W

wanlacia, 'wanlace' 1277; **wenlator,** beater 1293; *cf.* **wanlassum.**
1 wica, sheep-farm c 1400.
wichardus, kind of fish 1344.
widia, withy-bed 1211.
wiscator (falde), wattler 1211.